Hoover's Handbook of

Private
Companies

2018

HOOVERS™

A D&B COMPANY

Austin, Texas

Hoover's Handbook of Private Companies 2018 is intended to provide readers with accurate and authoritative information about the enterprises covered in it. Hoover's researched all companies and organizations profiled, and in many cases contacted them directly so that companies represented could provide information. The information contained herein is as accurate as we could reasonably make it. In many cases we have relied on third-party material that we believe to be trustworthy, but were unable to independently verify. We do not warrant that the book is absolutely accurate or without error. Readers should not rely on any information contained herein in instances where such reliance might cause financial loss. The publisher, the editors, and their data suppliers specifically disclaim all warranties, including the implied warranties of merchantability and fitness for a specific purpose. This book is sold with the understanding that neither the publisher, the editors, nor any content contributors are engaged in providing investment, financial, accounting, legal, or other professional advice.

The financial data (Historical Financials sections) in this book are from a variety of sources. Mergent Inc., provided selected data for the Historical Financials sections of publicly traded companies. For private companies and for historical information on public companies prior to their becoming public, we obtained information directly from the companies or from trade sources deemed to be reliable. Hoover's, Inc., is solely responsible for the presentation of all data.

Many of the names of products and services mentioned in this book are the trademarks or service marks of the companies manufacturing or selling them and are subject to protection under US law. Space has not permitted us to indicate which names are subject to such protection, and readers are advised to consult with the owners of such marks regarding their use. Hoover's is a trademark of Hoover's, Inc.

A D&B COMPANY

10 9 8 7 6 5 4 3 2 1

Publishers Cataloging-in-Publication Data

Hoover's Handbook of Private Companies 2017

Includes indexes.

ISBN: 978-1-68200-727-3

ISSN 1073-6433

1. Business enterprises — Directories. 2. Corporations — Directories.

HF3010 338.7

U.S. AND WORLD BOOK SALES

Mergent Inc.

580 Kingsley Park Drive
Fort Mill, SC
29715
Phone: 800-342-5647
e-mail: orders@mergent.com
Web: www.mergentbusinesspress.com

Mergent Inc.

Executive Managing Director: John Pedernales

Managing Director of Print Products and Publisher: Thomas Wecera

Managing Director of Relationship Management: Chris Henry

Director of Print Products: Charlot Volny

Director of Data: Mohamed Hanif

Quality Assurance Editor: Wayne Arnold

Production Research Assistant: Davie Christna

Data Manager: Jason Horvat

MERGENT CUSTOMER SERVICE
Support & Fulfillment: Melanie Horvat

ABOUT MERGENT INC.

For over 100 years, Mergent, Inc. has been a leading provider of business and financial information on public and private companies globally. Mergent is known to be a trusted partner to corporate and financial institutions, as well as to academic and public libraries. Today we continue to build on a century of experience by transforming data into knowledge and combining our expertise with the latest technology to create new global data and analytical solutions for our clients. With advanced data collection services, cloud-based applications, desktop analytics and print products, Mergent and its subsidiaries provide solutions from top down economic and demographic information, to detailed equity and debt fundamental analysis. We incorporate value added tools such as quantitative Smart Beta equity research and tools for portfolio building and measurement. Based in the U.S., Mergent maintains a strong global presence, with offices in New York, Charlotte, San Diego, London, Tokyo, Kuching and Melbourne. Mergent, Inc. is a member of the London Stock Exchange plc group of companies. The Mergent business forms part of LSEG's Information Services Division, which includes FTSE Russell, a global leader in indexes.

MERGENT
BUSINESS PRESS
by FTSE Russell

Abbreviations

AFL-CIO – American Federation of Labor and Congress of Industrial Organizations

AMA – American Medical Association

AMEX – American Stock Exchange

ARM – adjustable-rate mortgage

ASP – application services provider

ATM – asynchronous transfer mode

ATM – automated teller machine

CAD/CAM – computer-aided design/computer-aided manufacturing

CD-ROM – compact disc – read-only memory

CD-R – CD-recordable

CEO – chief executive officer

CFO – chief financial officer

CMOS – complementary metal oxide silicon

COO – chief operating officer

DAT – digital audiotape

DOD – Department of Defense

DOE – Department of Energy

DOS – disk operating system

DOT – Department of Transportation

DRAM – dynamic random-access memory

DSL – digital subscriber line

DVD – digital versatile disc/digital video disc

DVD-R – DVD-recordable

EPA – Environmental Protection Agency

EPS – earnings per share

ESOP – employee stock ownership plan

EU – European Union

EVP – executive vice president

FCC – Federal Communications Commission

FDA – Food and Drug Administration

FDIC – Federal Deposit Insurance Corporation

FTC – Federal Trade Commission

GATT – General Agreement on Tariffs and Trade

GDP – gross domestic product

HMO – health maintenance organization

HR – human resources

HTML – hypertext markup language

ICC – Interstate Commerce Commission

IPO – initial public offering

IRS – Internal Revenue Service

ISP – Internet service provider

kWh – kilowatt-hour

LAN – local-area network

LBO – leveraged buyout

LCD – liquid crystal display

LNG – liquefied natural gas

LP – limited partnership

Ltd. – limited

mips – millions of instructions per second

MW – megawatt

NAFTA – North American Free Trade Agreement

NASA – National Aeronautics and Space Administration

NASDAQ – National Association of Securities Dealers Automated Quotations

NATO – North Atlantic Treaty Organization

NYSE – New York Stock Exchange

OCR – optical character recognition

OECD – Organization for Economic Cooperation and Development

OEM – original equipment manufacturer

OPEC – Organization of Petroleum Exporting Countries

OS – operating system

OSHA – Occupational Safety and Health Administration

OTC – over-the-counter

PBX – private branch exchange

PCMCIA – Personal Computer Memory Card International Association

P/E – price to earnings ratio

RAID – redundant array of independent disks

RAM – random-access memory

R&D – research and development

RBOC – regional Bell operating company

RISC – reduced instruction set computer

REIT – real estate investment trust

ROA – return on assets

ROE – return on equity

ROI – return on investment

ROM – read-only memory

S&L – savings and loan

SEC – Securities and Exchange Commission

SEVP – senior executive vice president

SIC – Standard Industrial Classification

SOC – system on a chip

SVP – senior vice president

USB – universal serial bus

VAR – value-added reseller

VAT – value-added tax

VC – venture capitalist

VoIP – Voice over Internet Protocol

VP – vice president

WAN – wide-area network

Contents

Companies Profiled

Companies Profiled (continued)

Companies Profiled (continued)

Companies Profiled (continued)

Companies Profiled (continued)

Companies Profiled (continued)

Companies Profiled (continued)

Companies Profiled (continued)

Companies Profiled (continued)

Companies Profiled (continued)

Companies Profiled (continued)

Companies Profiled (continued)

About Hoover's Handbook of Private Companies 2018

Finding current relevant information about non-public companies can be a challenge, as many of these organizations see secrecy as a competitive strategy. In this edition of *Hoover's Handbook of Private Companies*, we have done for you the tough work of compiling these hard-to-find facts.

We consider this volume to be one of the premier sources of business information on privately held enterprises in the US. It features the facts on 900 of the largest and most influencial of those enterprises. Entries feature overviews of company operations, up to five years of financial information, product information, and lists of company executives as found in Hoover's huge database of company information. Some larger and more visable companies will feature an additional History section.

HOOVER'S ONLINE FOR BUSINESS NEEDS

In addition to Hoover's widely used MasterList and Handbooks series, comprehensive coverage of more than 40,000 business enterprises is available in electronic format on our website at www.hoovers.com. Our goal is to provide our customers with the fastest path to business with insight and actionable information about companies, industries, and key decision makers, along with the powerful tools to find and connect to the right people to get business done. Hoover's has partnered with other presigious business information and service providers to bring you all the right business information, services, and links in one place.

We welcome the recognition we have received as a provider of high-quality company information — online, electronically, and in print — and continue to look for ways to make our products more available and more useful to you.

Hoover's Handbook of Private Companies is one of our four-title series of handbooks that covers, literally, the world of business. The series is available as an indexed set, and also includes *Hoover's Handbook of American Business, Hoover's Handbook of World Business,* and *Hoover's Handbook of Emerging Companies.* This series brings you information on the biggest, fast-growing, and most influential enterprises in the world.

We believe that anyone who buys from, sells to, invests in, lends to, competes with, interviews with, or works for a company should know all there is to know about that enterprise. Taken together, this book and the other Hoover's products and resources represent the most complete source of basic corporate information readily available to the general public.

HOW TO USE THIS BOOK

This book has four sections:

1. "Using Hoover's Handbooks" describes the contents of our profiles and explains the ways in which we gather and compile our data.

2. "A List-Lover's Compendium" contains lists of the largest and fastest-growing private companies. The lists are based on the information in our profiles, or compiled from well-known sources.

3. The company profiles section makes up the largest and most important part of the book — 900 profiles of major private enterprises, arranged alphabetically.

4. Three indexes complete the book. The first sorts companies by industry groups, the second by headquarters location. The third index is a list of all the executives found in the Executives section of each company profile.

Using Hoover's Handbooks

SELECTION OF THE COMPANIES PROFILED

The 900 enterprises profiled in this book include the largest and most influential companies in America. Among them are:

- private companies, from the giants (Cargill and Koch) to the colorful and prominent (Bad Boy Entertainment and L.L. Bean)
- mutuals and cooperative organizations owned by their customers (State Farm Insurance, Ace Hardware, Ocean Spray Cranberries)
- not-for-profits (Red Cross, Kaiser Permanente, Smithsonian Institution)
- joint ventures (Motiva Enterprises, Dow Corning)
- partnerships (PricewaterhouseCoopers, Baker & McKenzie)
- universities (Columbia, Harvard, University of California)
- government-owned corporations (US Postal Service and New York City's Metropolitan Transportation Authority)
- and a selection of other enterprises (National Basketball Association, AFL-CIO, Texas Lottery Commission).

ORGANIZATION

The profiles are presented in alphabetical order. You will find the commonly used name of the enterprise at the beginning of the profile; the full, legal name is found in the Locations section. If a company name is also a person's name, such as Henry Ford Health System or Mary Kay, it will be alphabetized under the first name; if the company name starts with initials, for example, L.L. Bean or S.C. Johnson, look for it under the combined initials (in the above examples, LL and SC, respectively).

Basic financial data are listed under the heading Historical Financials. The annual financial information contained in the profiles is current through fiscal year-ends occuring as late as October 2014. We have included certain nonfinancial developments , such as officer changes, through December 2014.

OVERVIEW

In the first section of the profile, we have tried to give a thumbnail description of the company and what it does. The description will usually include information on the company's strategy, reputation, and ownership. We rec-ommend that you read this section first.

HISTORY

This extended section, which is available for some of the larger and more well-known companies, reflects our belief that every enterprise is the sum of its history and that you have to know where you came from in order to know where you are going. While some companies have limited historical awareness, we think the vast majority of the enterprises in this book have colorful backgrounds. We have tried to focus on the people who made the enterprises what they are today. We have found these histories to be full of twists and ironies; they make fascinating reading.

EXECUTIVES

Here we list the names of the people who run the company, insofar as space allows. In the few cases where available, we have shown the ages and pay of key officers. In some instances the published data is for the previous year, although the company has announced promotions or retirements since year-end. The pay represents cash compensation, including bonuses, but excludes stock option programs.

Although companies are free to structure their management titles any way they please, most modern corporations follow standard practices. The ultimate power in any corporation lies with the shareholders, who elect a board of directors, usually including officers or "insiders" as well as individuals from outside the company. The chief officer, the person on whose desk the buck stops, is usually called the chief executive officer (CEO). Often, he or she is also the chairman of the board.

As corporate management has become more complex, it is common for the CEO to have a "right-hand person" who oversees the day-to-day operations of the company, allowing the CEO plenty of time to focus on strategy and long-term issues. This right-hand person is usually designated the chief operating officer (COO) and is often the president of the company. In other cases one person is both chairman and president.

A multitude of other titles exists, including chief financial officer (CFO), chief administrative officer, and vice chairman. We have always tried to include the CFO, the chief legal officer, and the chief human resources or personnel officer.

The people named in the Executives section are indexed at the back of the book.

The Executives section also includes the name of the company's auditing (accounting) firm, where available.

LOCATIONS

Here we include the company's full legal name and its headquarters, street address, telephone and fax numbers, and Web site, as available. The back of the book includes an index of companies by headquarters locations.

In some cases we have also included information on the geographic distribution of the company's business, including sales and profit data. Note that these profit numbers, like those in the Products/Operations section below, are usually operating or pretax profits rather than net profits. Operating profits are generally those before financing costs (interest income and payments) and before taxes, which are considered costs attributable to the whole company rather than to one division or part of the world. For this reason the net income figures (in the Historical Financials section) are usually much lower, since they are after interest and taxes. Pretax profits are after interest but before taxes.

Headquarters for companies that are incorporated in Bermuda, but whose operational headquarters are in the US, are listed under their US address.

PRODUCTS/OPERATIONS

This section contains selected lists of products, services, brand names, divisions, subsidiaries, and joint ventures. We have tried to include a company's major lines and most familiar brand names.

The nature of this section varies by company and the amount of information contained in Hoover's storehouse of business information. If the company publishes sales and profit information by type of business, we have included it.

COMPETITORS

In this section we have listed companies that compete with the profiled company. This feature is included as a quick way to locate similar companies and compare them. The universe of competitors includes all public companies and all private companies with sales in excess of $500 million. In a few instances we have identified smaller private companies as key competitors.

HISTORICAL FINANCIALS

Here we have tried to present as much data about each enterprise's financial performance as we could compile in the allocated space. The information varies somewhat from industry to industry and is less complete in the case of private companies that do not release data. (We have always tried to provide annual sales and employment, although in some instances those numbers are simply not available). There are a few industries, venture capital and investment banking, for example, for which revenue numbers are not reported as a rule. In the case of private companies that do not publicly disclose financial information, we have statistics when reliable sources are available.

The following information is generally present.

A five-year table, with relevant annualized compound growth rates, covers:

- Sales — fiscal year sales (year-end assets for most financial companies)
- Net income — fiscal year net income (before accounting changes)
- Net profit margin — fiscal year net income as a percent of sales (as a percent of assets for most financial firms)
- Employees — fiscal year-end or average number of employees

The information on the number of employees is intended to aid the reader interested in knowing whether a company has a long-term trend of increasing or decreasing employment. As far as we know, we are the only company that publishes this information in print format.

The numbers on the left in each row of the Historical Financials section give the month and the year in which the company's fiscal year actually ends. Thus, a company with a March 31, 2017, year-end is shown as 3/17. The last item in the Financials section is a graph, which for private companies shows net income, or, if that is unavailable, sales.

Key year-end statistics are included in this section for insurance companies and companies required to file reports with the SEC. They generally show the financial strength of the enterprise, including:

- Debt ratio (long-term debt as a percent of shareholders' equity)
- Return on equity (net income divided by the average of beginning and ending common shareholders' equity)
- Cash and cash equivalents
- Current ratio (ratio of current assets to current liabilities)
- Total long-term debt (including capital lease obligations)
- Fiscal year sales for financial institutions

Hoover's Handbook of

Private Companies

A List-Lover's Compendium

The 300 Largest Private Companies by Sales 2018

Rank	Company	Sales ($ mil.)	Rank	Company	Sales ($ mil.)	Rank	Company	Sales ($ mil.)
1	STATE OF CALIFORNIA	$249,923	61	HILL/AHERN FIRE PROTECTION, LLC	$5,669	121	CITY OF BOSTON	$3,278
2	STATE OF TEXAS	$107,351	62	CHALMETTE REFINING, L.L.C.	$5,648	122	VIRGINIA DEPARTMENT OF TRANSPORTA	$3,240
3	PUBLIX SUPER MARKETS, INC.	$34,274	63	AEROTEK, INC.	$5,492	123	THE UNIVERSITY OF CHICAGO	$3,238
4	ASCENSION HEALTH ALLIANCE	$21,898	64	THE CHARLOTTE-MECKLENBURG HOSPIT	$5,479	124	FAIRVIEW HEALTH SERVICES	$3,218
5	CANDID COLOR SYSTEMS, INC.	$21,742	65	ADVOCATE HEALTH CARE NETWORK	$5,393	125	KAISER FDN HEALTH PLAN OF COLORADO	$3,197
6	TELCO INTERCONTINENTAL CORP	$19,067	66	NEW YORK STATE CATHOLIC HEALTH PLA	$5,305	126	PROVIDENCE HEALTH & SERVICES-WAS	$3,178
7	STATE OF OKLAHOMA	$16,789	67	CH2M HILL COMPANIES, LTD.	$5,288	127	PUGET SOUND ENERGY, INC.	$3,165
8	KAISER FOUNDATION HOSPITALS INC	$14,795	68	HEALTHPARTNERS, INC.	$5,223	128	PUGET ENERGY, INC.	$3,164
9	DAIRY FARMERS OF AMERICA, INC.	$13,803	69	NEW YORK UNIVERSITY	$5,172	129	RALEY'S	$3,162
10	UNIVERSITY OF TEXAS SYSTEM	$13,282	70	ACE HARDWARE CORPORATION	$5,045	130	DUKE UNIVERSITY HEALTH SYSTEM, INC.	$3,160
11	UNIVERSITY OF TEXAS AT TYLER	$12,635	71	AMERICAN TIRE DISTRIBUTORS HOLDIN.	$5,031	131	HENSEL PHELPS CONSTRUCTION CO.	$3,142
12	WAKEFERN FOOD CORP.	$12,574	72	ST. JOSEPH HEALTH SYSTEM	$4,956	132	LOS ANGELES DEPARTMENT OF WATER	$3,126
13	STATOIL MARKETING & TRADING (US) INC.	$12,076	73	PLACID REFINING COMPANY LLC	$4,929	133	DYNCORP INTERNATIONAL LLC	$3,101
14	SUTTER HEALTH	$11,873	74	PLACID HOLDING COMPANY	$4,929	134	UNIVERSITY OF CHICAGO	$3,092
15	PARTNERS HEALTHCARE SYSTEM, INC.	$11,666	75	NCL CORPORATION LTD.	$4,874	135	BON SECOURS HEALTH SYSTEM, INC.	$3,085
16	ALLEGIS GROUP, INC.	$11,222	76	SENTARA HEALTHCARE	$4,834	136	BIG WEST OIL, LLC	$3,053
17	KIEWIT CORPORATION	$11,220	77	BATTELLE MEMORIAL INSTITUTE INC	$4,811	137	CLARK COUNTY SCHOOL DISTRICT	$3,048
18	PETER KIEWIT SONS', INC.	$11,220	78	JOHNS HOPKINS UNIVERSITY	$4,794	138	HOUCHENS INDUSTRIES, INC.	$2,987
19	ROBERT BOSCH LLC	$10,868	79	BATTELLE MEMORIAL INSTITUTE	$4,775	139	AXEL JOHNSON INC.	$2,982
20	THE TURNER CORPORATION	$10,524	80	LUKOIL PAN AMERICAS, LLC	$4,746	140	CORNELL UNIVERSITY	$2,957
21	TURNER CONSTRUCTION COMPANY INC	$10,485	81	THE SCOULAR COMPANY	$4,668	141	BVH, INC.	$2,955
22	TENASKA MARKETING VENTURES	$10,310	82	SPECTRUM HEALTH SYSTEMS, INC.	$4,625	142	SCRIPPS HEALTH	$2,944
23	LIMETREE BAY TERMINALS LLC	$10,048	83	BIOURJA TRADING, LLC	$4,622	143	COUNTY OF SUFFOLK	$2,938
24	CHEVRON PHILLIPS CHEMICAL COMPAN	$9,859	84	DUKE UNIVERSITY	$4,612	144	YALE UNIVERSITY	$2,937
25	HY-VEE, INC.	$9,842	85	LEVI STRAUSS & CO.	$4,553	145	THE SCHOOL DISTRICT OF PHILADELPHIA	$2,931
26	ALTICOR INC.	$9,460	86	NEW YORK PRESBYTERIAN HOSPITAL	$4,506	146	DO IT BEST CORP.	$2,926
27	DIGNITY HEALTH	$8,958	87	THE PRESIDENT AND FELLOWS OF HAR	$4,409	147	J.E. DUNN CONSTRUCTION GROUP, INC.	$2,911
28	ASSOCIATED WHOLESALE GROCERS, INC.	$8,936	88	MERCY HEALTH	$4,275	148	J.E. DUNN CONSTRUCTION COMPANY	$2,909
29	TRAMMO, INC.	$8,922	89	SANFORD HEALTH	$4,231	149	THE UNIVERSITY OF UTAH	$2,908
30	THE PRIDDY FOUNDATION	$8,792	90	MEDSTAR HEALTH, INC.	$4,217	150	THE WASHINGTON UNIVERSITY	$2,877
31	QVC, INC.	$8,682	91	CHRISTUS HEALTH INTERNATIONAL	$4,212	151	UNIVERSITY OF WISCONSIN HOSPITAL A	$2,861
32	METROPOLITAN TRANSPORTATION AUTH	$8,408	92	THE NEW YORK AND PRESBYTERIAN HO	$4,206	152	RICH PRODUCTS CORPORATION	$2,859
33	SOLSTICE HOLDINGS INC.	$8,235	93	MARYLAND DEPARTMENT OF TRANSPORT	$4,171	153	BATHXCESSORIES, INCORPORATED	$2,856
34	UPMC PRESBYTERIAN SHADYSIDE	$8,046	94	WINCO HOLDINGS, INC.	$4,104	154	IOWA HEALTH SYSTEM	$2,841
35	WEGMANS FOOD MARKETS, INC.	$8,006	95	CHS MCPHERSON REFINERY INC.	$4,081	155	MEMORIAL HERMANN HEALTHCARE SYS	$2,841
36	CHEVRON PHILLIPS CHEMICAL COMPANY	$7,990	96	AVAYA HOLDINGS CORP.	$4,081	156	MCCARTHY HOLDINGS, INC.	$2,838
37	CATHOLIC HEALTH INITIATIVES	$7,731	97	ADVOCATE HEALTH AND HOSPITALS CO	$4,072	157	SWINERTON INCORPORATED	$2,828
38	CFJ PROPERTIES LLC	$7,672	98	MEMORIAL HERMANN HEALTH SYSTEM	$4,026	158	SWINERTON BUILDERS	$2,826
39	R. DIRECTIONAL DRILLING & UNDERGROU	$7,668	99	NEW YORK UNIVERSITY	$4,017	159	WILBUR-ELLIS HOLDINGS II, INC	$2,812
40	RACETRAC PETROLEUM, INC.	$7,502	100	ONCOR ELECTRIC DELIVERY COMPANY	$3,920	160	NAVY EXCHANGE SERVICE COMMAND	$2,800
41	WORLD WIDE TECHNOLOGY HOLDING CO.	$7,438	101	UNIVERSITY OF SOUTHERN CALIFORNIA	$3,861	161	UNIVERSITY OF COLORADO	$2,775
42	FEDERAL-MOGUL HOLDINGS LLC	$7,434	102	GILBANE BUILDING COMPANY	$3,841	162	COUNTY OF CLARK	$2,768
43	SHI INTERNATIONAL CORP.	$7,269	103	THE TRUSTEES OF COLUMBIA UNIV. NYC	$3,739	163	CEDARS-SINAI MEDICAL CENTER	$2,761
44	GROWMARK, INC.	$7,031	104	KWIK TRIP, INC.	$3,640	164	MASSACHUSETTS INSTITUTE OF TECHNO	$2,727
45	BANNER HEALTH	$6,971	105	THE SCHOOL BOARD OF MIAMI-DADE CO	$3,632	165	UNIVERSITY OF MISSOURI SYSTEM	$2,702
46	STATE OF RHODE ISLAND AND PROVIDEN	$6,860	106	TEKSYSTEMS, INC.	$3,619	166	UNIVERSITY OF CALIFORNIA, DAVIS	$2,697
47	U.S. VENTURE, INC.	$6,413	107	ALLINA HEALTH SYSTEM	$3,604	167	ALERIS CORPORATION	$2,664
48	STATE OF RHODE ISLAND	$6,282	108	AURORA HEALTH CARE, INC.	$3,601	168	FRANCISCAN ALLIANCE, INC.	$2,661
49	REGENTS OF THE UNIVERSITY OF MICHI	$6,278	109	STANFORD HEALTH CARE	$3,571	169	TEMPLE UNIVERSITY-OF THE COMMONW	$2,635
50	NIELSEN HOLDINGS PLC	$6,172	110	UTI, (U.S.) HOLDINGS, INC.	$3,568	170	THE SCHOOL BOARD OF BROWARD COUN	$2,630
51	INTERMOUNTAIN HEALTH CARE INC	$6,059	111	UNIVERSITY OF WISCONSIN SYSTEM	$3,539	171	NEW YORK POWER AUTHORITY	$2,625
52	SUNY COLLEGE AT CORTLAND	$6,049	112	STATOIL NATURAL GAS LLC	$3,507	172	UMASS MEMORIAL HEALTH CARE INC	$2,614
53	STATE UNIVERSITY OF NEW YORK	$5,961	113	KIEWIT INDUSTRIAL GROUP INC	$3,474	173	SUFFOLK CONSTRUCTION COMPANY, INC.	$2,611
54	CGB ENTERPRISES, INC.	$5,935	114	THE WALSH GROUP LTD	$3,462	174	LEXA INTERNATIONAL CORPORATION	$2,598
55	WORLD WIDE TECHNOLOGY, INC.	$5,928	115	BEARINGPOINT, INC.	$3,456	175	CALIFORNIA INSTITUTE OF TECHNOLOGY	$2,562
56	THE PENNSYLVANIA STATE UNIVERSITY	$5,765	116	THE REGENTS OF THE UNIVERSITY OF C	$3,451	176	MONTEFIORE MEDICAL CENTER	$2,553
57	BOARD OF EDUCATION OF CITY OF CHIC	$5,760	117	THE GOLUB CORPORATION	$3,427	177	SCHOOL BOARD OF BROWARD COUNTY,	$2,549
58	CONSOLIDATED GRAIN & BARGE COMPA	$5,760	118	THE METHODIST HOSPITAL	$3,408	178	PEACEHEALTH	$2,544
59	THE WHITING-TURNER CONTRACTING	$5,730	119	SHARP HEALTHCARE	$3,397	179	CRESTWOOD MIDSTREAM PARTNERS LP	$2,521
60	ZEN-NOH GRAIN CORPORATION	$5,722	120	COUNTY OF RIVERSIDE	$3,390	180	KFHP OF THE MID-ATLANTIC STATES INC.	$2,512

SOURCE: HOOVER'S, INC., DATABASE, JANUARY 2018

The 300 Largest Private Companies by Sales 2018 (continued)

Rank	Company	Sales ($ mil.)
181	STANFORD HEALTH SERVICES	$2,511
182	MARTIN RESOURCE MANAGEMENT CORP	$2,494
183	THE CARLE FOUNDATION	$2,493
184	TRINITY HEALTH-MICHIGAN	$2,475
185	THE GENERAL HOSPITAL CORPORATION	$2,452
186	API GROUP INC.	$2,449
187	JOHNS HOPKINS HEALTH SYS CORP	$2,439
188	J M SMITH CORPORATION	$2,404
189	YALE NEW HAVEN HOSPITAL, INC.	$2,389
190	BOARD OF TRUSTEES OF STATE INSTIT	$2,383
191	COBANK ACB	$2,380
192	UMASS MEMORIAL HEALTH CARE, INC.	$2,373
193	ESTES EXPRESS LINES, INC.	$2,367
194	HOUSTON INDEPENDENT SCHOOL DISTR	$2,334
195	BAPTIST HEALTHCARE SYSTEM, INC.	$2,332
196	UNIVERSITY HOSPITALS HEALTH SYSTE	$2,326
197	ORLANDO HEALTH, INC.	$2,324
198	ARCTIC SLOPE REGIONAL CORPORATION	$2,297
199	CITY PUBLIC SERVICES OF SAN ANTONIO	$2,258
200	ALEX LEE, INC.	$2,229
201	MEMORIAL SLOAN-KETTERING CANCER	$2,220
202	TAUBER OIL COMPANY	$2,215
203	TRUSTEES INDIANA UNIVERSITY	$2,208
204	NORTHWEST DAIRY ASSOCIATION	$2,207
205	NORTHWESTERN UNIVERSITY	$2,201
206	SCHAUMBOND GROUP, INC.	$2,200
207	OCHSNER CLINIC FOUNDATION	$2,197
208	INDIANA UNIVERSITY	$2,195
209	NEW YORK CITY SCHOOL CONSTRUC	$2,190
210	OHIOHEALTH CORPORATION	$2,180
211	UNIVERSITY OF ARKANSAS SYSTEM	$2,172
212	OREGON HEALTH & SCIENCE UNIVERSITY	$2,170
213	CROWLEY HOLDINGS, INC.	$2,158
214	ATLANTIC HEALTH SYSTEM INC.	$2,156
215	INOVA HEALTH SYSTEM FOUNDATION	$2,141
216	INOVA HEALTH CARE SERVICES	$2,135
217	HDR, INC.	$2,132
218	KNIGHTS OF COLUMBUS	$2,116
219	UNIVERSITY OF PITTSBURGH	$2,107
220	SCHOOL BOARD OF PALM BEACH COUNTY	$2,093
221	CONTINUUM ENERGY SERVICES, L.L.C.	$2,093
222	COMMUNITY HEALTH NETWORK, INC	$2,077
223	DORMITORY AUTHORITY - STATE OF NY	$2,075
224	THE UNIVERSITY OF IOWA	$2,068
225	SMMH PRACTICE PLAN, INC.	$2,061
226	PROVIDENCE HEALTH & SERVICES - OREN	$2,058
227	DANFOSS POWER SOLUTIONS INC.	$2,057
228	UNIVERSITY OF MASSACHUSETTS	$2,056
229	HILLSBOROUGH COUNTY SCHOOL DISTR	$2,043
230	MEMORIAL HOSPITAL FOR CANCER AND A	$2,035
231	THE MOUNT SINAI HOSPITAL	$2,025
232	CHEMIUM INTERNATIONAL CORP.	$2,016
233	ASSOCIATED FOOD STORES, INC.	$2,011
234	VIZIO, INC.	$2,006
235	THE SCHOOL DISTRICT OF WEST PALM	$1,986
236	COMENITY BANK	$1,977
237	CROWLEY MARITIME CORPORATION	$1,956
238	ST. LUKE'S HEALTH SYSTEM, LTD.	$1,937
239	PRINCE GEORGE'S COUNTY PUBLIC SCH	$1,932
240	SPRINGLEAF FINANCE CORPORATION	$1,924
241	RECTOR & VISITORS OF THE UNIVERSITY	$1,910
242	SOUTH BROWARD HOSPITAL DISTRICT	$1,897
243	UNIVERSITY OF NEW MEXICO	$1,893
244	INDIANA UNIVERSITY HEALTH, INC.	$1,890
245	ALBERICI CORPORATION	$1,886
246	SUTTER HEALTH SACRAMENTO SIERRA	$1,885
247	JOHNS HOPKINS HOSPITAL	$1,880
248	SOUTH CAROLINA PUBLIC SERVICE AUTH	$1,880
249	PRAIRIE FARMS DAIRY, INC.	$1,879
250	FIDELITY INV CHARITABLE GIFT FUND	$1,875
251	SL GREEN OPERATING PARTNERSHIP, L.P.	$1,864
252	UNITED SPACE ALLIANCE, LLC	$1,860
253	THE FRESH MARKET INC	$1,857
254	TRIBOROUGH BRIDGE & TUNNEL AUTHO	$1,843
255	THE UNIVERSITY OF NORTH CAROLINA	$1,839
256	DPR CONSTRUCTION, INC.	$1,836
257	SCHOOL BOARD OF ORANGE COUNTY FL	$1,824
258	THE BRIGHAM AND WOMEN'S HOSPITAL I	$1,812
259	WHEATON FRANCISCAN SERVICES, INC.	$1,809
260	SOUTHWEST CATHOLIC HEALTH NETW	$1,809
261	INVACARE CORPORATION (TW)	$1,801
262	HUGHES SATELLITE SYSTEMS CORPORA	$1,800
263	GWINNETT COUNTY BOARD OF EDUCAT	$1,791
264	OREGON UNIVERSITY SYSTEM	$1,782
265	JACKSONVILLE ELECTRIC AUTHORITY	$1,782
266	BARTON MALOW COMPANY	$1,777
267	BARTON MALOW ENTERPRISES, INC.	$1,777
268	SPECTRUM HEALTH HOSPITALS	$1,765
269	SKANSKA USA CIVIL INC.	$1,754
270	ASI COMPUTER TECHNOLOGIES INC	$1,747
271	NEIGHBORHOOD HEALTH PLAN, INCOR	$1,744
272	CATHOLIC HEALTH INITIATIVES COLORA	$1,735
273	UNIVERSITY OF FLORIDA	$1,735
274	NORTHSIDE HOSPITAL, INC.	$1,733
275	ICAHN SCHOOL OF MEDICINE AT MOUNT SI	$1,728
276	BARNES-JEWISH HOSPITAL	$1,726
277	OCEAN SPRAY CRANBERRIES, INC.	$1,719
278	NORTON HOSPITALS, INC.	$1,712
279	UNIVERSITY OF NORTH CAROLINA AT CHAL	$1,705
280	THE TRUSTEES OF PRINCETON UNIV	$1,688
281	THE MOSES H CONE MEMORIAL HOSPITAL	$1,678
282	PETROLEUM TRADERS CORPORATION	$1,667
283	METHODIST HEALTHCARE MEMPHIS HOS	$1,666
284	LEGACY HEALTH	$1,659
285	RDO EQUIPMENT CO.	$1,652
286	CARY OIL CO., INC.	$1,647
287	ARIZONA STATE UNIVERSITY	$1,644
288	MISSION HEALTH SYSTEM, INC	$1,633
289	WALSH CONSTRUCTION COMPANY	$1,627
290	SUMMIT MATERIALS, LLC	$1,626
291	UMASS MEMORIAL MEDICAL CENTER, INC.	$1,622
292	LEHIGH VALLEY HEALTH NETWORK, INC.	$1,621
293	NORTH SHORE UNIVERSITY HOSPITAL	$1,618
294	NORDIC PCL CONSTRUCTION, INC.	$1,617
295	PCL CONSTRUCTION ENTERPRISES, INC.	$1,617
296	TRANSCONTINENTAL GAS PIPE LINE CO	$1,616
297	SUTTER BAY HOSPITALS	$1,616
298	THE UNIVERSITY OF CHICAGO MEDIC	$1,611
299	STEWART'S SHOPS CORP.	$1,611
300	GLOBAL HEALTH SOLUTIONS INC	$1,609

The 300 Largest Private Companies by Employees 2018

Rank	Company	Employees	Rank	Company	Employees	Rank	Company	Employees
1	STATE OF CALIFORNIA	208,580	61	PORTLAND ADVENTIST MEDICAL	12,000	121	THE UNIVERSITY OF AKRON	5,445
2	PUBLIX SUPER MARKETS, INC.	191,000	62	THE ROMAN CATHOLIC ARCH LA	12,000	122	UNION COUNTY BOARD OF EDUC	5,427
3	KAISER FOUNDATION HOSPITALS	175,668	63	VIA CHRISTI HEALTH, INC.	11,970	123	HAWAI I PACIFIC HEALTH	5,400
4	STATE OF TEXAS	144,175	64	AVAYA HOLDINGS CORP.	11,701	124	ADVANTECH CORPORATION	5,390
5	ASCENSION HEALTH ALLIANCE	111,489	65	THE PRES. AND FELLOWS HARVARD	11,500	125	SISTEMA UNIVERSITARIO ANA G.	5,387
6	ASCENSION HEALTH	109,000	66	METHODIST LE BONHEUR HEALTH	11,459	126	HARTFORD HEALTHCARE CORPOR	5,100
7	DAKOTA ELECTRIC ASSOCIATION	100,000	67	ST. MARYS DEAN VENTURES, INCO	11,000	127	LEON COUNTY SCHOOL BOARD	5,030
8	STATE UNIVERSITY OF NEW YORK	88,024	68	BEAUMONT UNIFIED SCHOOL DIST	11,000	128	PRIDE INDUSTRIES	5,003
9	ALLEGIS GROUP, INC.	85,000	69	KIEWIT CORPORATION	10,441	129	COASTAL INTERNATIONAL SECURITY.	5,003
10	HY-VEE, INC.	84,000	70	MCLAREN HEALTH CARE CORPORA	10,003	130	THE TURNER CORPORATION	5,000
11	UNIVERSITY OF TEXAS SYSTEM	81,260	71	TEMCO SERVICE INDUSTRIES, INC.	10,000	131	TURNER CONSTRUCTION COM	5,000
12	CATHOLIC HEALTH INITIATIVES	72,500	72	PDS TECH, INC.	10,000	132	CHEVRON PHILLIPS CHEMICAL COL	5,000
13	METROPOLITAN TRANSPORTATION	67,457	73	UMASS MEMORIAL COMMUNITY HOS	10,000	133	CHEVRON PHILLIPS CHEMICAL CO	5,000
14	PARTNERS HEALTHCARE SYSTEM,	67,000	74	DIVERSIFIED MAINTENANCE SYST	10,000	134	MARION COUNTY PUBLIC SCHOOLS	5,000
15	THE CHARLOTTE-MECKLENBURG	62,000	75	BAPTIST MEMORIAL HEALTH CARE	9,877	135	MOSAIC	5,000
16	FEDERAL-MOGUL HOLDINGS LLC	53,700	76	KENTUCKYONE HEALTH, INC.	9,809	136	YOUNG ADULT INSTITUTE, INC.	5,000
17	DIGNITY HEALTH	49,363	77	PROVIDENCE HEALTH & SERVICES	9,700	137	FJC SECURITY SERVICES, INC.	5,000
18	SUTTER HEALTH	48,000	78	CATHOLIC BISHOP OF CHICAGO	9,604	138	YMCA OF SAN DIEGO COUNTY	5,000
19	WEGMANS FOOD MARKETS, INC.	45,000	79	FROEDTERT HEALTH, INC.	9,000	139	COLUMBIA ST. MARY'S, INC.	5,000
20	THE PENNSYLVANIA STATE UNIVER	44,000	80	KENTUCKY COMMUNITY AND TECH	9,000	140	HOUSTON COMMUNITY COLLEGE, .	5,000
21	NIELSEN HOLDINGS PLC	43,061	81	FRANCISCAN MISSIONARIES OF OUR	9,000	141	ABACUS CORPORATION	5,000
22	BOARD OF EDUCATION OF CITY CHI	43,000	82	IVY TECH COMMUNITY COLLEGE INDI	8,553	142	PRESBYTERIAN HOMES AND SERVIC	4,750
23	STATE OF OKLAHOMA	37,613	83	PARSONS BRINCKERHOFF INTERN	8,500	143	KANSAS CITY PUBLIC SCHOOLS	4,700
24	INTERMOUNTAIN HEALTH CARE INC	36,000	84	LOS ANGELES COMMUNITY COLLE	8,500	144	THE INTE THE SOUTHERN BAPTIST	4,686
25	BANNER HEALTH	35,000	85	CATHOLIC HEALTH SYSTEM, INC.	8,400	145	SAINT THOMAS HEALTH SERVICES,	4,650
26	MERCY HEALTH	35,000	86	UPMC PRESBYTERIAN SHADYSIDE	8,200	146	ST. VINCENT'S HEALTH SYSTEM	4,620
27	REGENTS OF THE UNIVERSITY MICH	34,624	87	ACCENTCARE, INC.	8,060	147	TOURO COLLEGE	4,600
28	MEDSTAR HEALTH, INC.	33,000	88	LIFESPAN CORPORATION	8,000	148	CROWN BUILDING MAINTENANCE CO.	4,600
29	JOHNS HOPKINS UNIVERSITY	30,228	89	ALEXIAN BROTHERS HEALTH SYSTEM	8,000	149	ACE HARDWARE CORPORATION	4,500
30	SENTARA HEALTHCARE	28,000	90	BATTELLE MEMORIAL INSTITUTE INC	7,457	150	CHANDLER UNIFIED SCHOOL DIST	4,500
31	DUKE UNIVERSITY	26,000	91	SUMMA HEALTH	7,406	151	NORTH DAKOTA STATE UNIVERSITY	4,500
32	ROBINSON HEALTH SYSTEM, INC.	26,000	92	PARKVIEW HEALTH SYSTEM, INC.	7,107	152	GUTHRIE MEDICAL GROUP, P.C.	4,500
33	ADVOCATE HEALTH CARE NETWORK	25,000	93	HERSHEY ENTERTAINMENT & RES	7,100	153	THE UNIVERSITY OF SOUTHERN MIS	4,500
34	CHRISTUS HEALTH INTERNATIONAL	25,000	94	ALLIED SECURITY HOLDINGS LLC	7,010	154	WEBSTER UNIVERSITY	4,500
35	NCL CORPORATION LTD.	24,900	95	DAIRY FARMERS OF AMERICA, INC.	7,000	155	YOUNG MEN'S CHRISTIAN NYC	4,500
36	CH2M HILL COMPANIES, LTD.	22,000	96	UNITED STATES BEEF CORPORATION	7,000	156	GUNDERSEN CLINIC, LTD.	4,500
37	HEALTHPARTNERS, INC.	22,000	97	UNIVERSITY OF WYOMING	7,000	157	THE QUEEN'S HEALTH SYSTEMS	4,500
38	NEW YORK UNIVERSITY	21,000	98	YOUNG MEN'S CHRISTIAN ASSOCIAT	7,000	158	ST. LUKE'S EPISCOPAL HOSP	4,500
39	BATTELLE MEMORIAL INSTITUTE	20,000	99	LOS RIOS COMMUNITY CLLT	7,000	159	DEFENDER SERVICES, INC.	4,500
40	STAFF FORCE, INC.	20,000	100	UNIVERSITY OF ALASKA SYSTEM	6,629	160	COAST COMMUNITY COLLEGE DIS	4,409
41	ESSENTIA HEALTH	18,177	101	T & T STAFF MANAGEMENT, INC.	6,600	161	NEMOURS FOUNDATION	4,400
42	ST. JOHN PROVIDENCE	17,806	102	EDWARD-ELMHURST HEALTHCARE	6,500	162	NEW PARTNERS, INC.	4,400
43	QVC, INC.	17,700	103	BALL STATE UNIVERSITY	6,426	163	ADVANCED DISPOSAL SERVICES SO	4,380
44	SCOTTSDALE HEALTHCARE CORP.	17,000	104	CFJ PROPERTIES LLC	6,250	164	UNIVERSIDAD INTERAMERICANA DE	4,306
45	MINNETONKA INDEPE SCHOOL 276	16,000	105	ST. VINCENT HEALTH, INC.	6,243	165	NEWPORT NEWS PUBLIC SCHOOL	4,300
46	THE NEW YORK AND PRESBYTERIA	15,078	106	SIMPLIFIED BUSINESS SOLUTIONS	6,008	166	DIAKON LUTHERAN SOCIAL MINIST	4,300
47	LAWRENCE HOSPITAL CENTER	15,000	107	MUSCOGEE COUNTY SCHOOL DIST	6,000	167	ALACHUA COUNTY PUBLIC SCHOOLS	4,299
48	PETER KIEWIT SONS', INC.	14,700	108	DELI MANAGEMENT, INC.	6,000	168	THE CATHOLIC UNIVERSITY OF AME	4,239
49	ADVANCE SERVICES, INC.	14,200	109	ROSE INTERNATIONAL, INC.	6,000	169	AEROTEK, INC.	4,200
50	ALTICOR INC.	14,000	110	VERITY HEALTH SYSTEM OF CALIF	6,000	170	LAMAR CONSOLIDATED INDEPEN	4,200
51	SOLSTICE HOLDINGS INC.	14,000	111	MEMORIAL HEALTH SERVICES	6,000	171	RICHMOND SCHOOL, INC.	4,200
52	WINCO HOLDINGS, INC.	14,000	112	LIFEBRIDGE HEALTH, INC.	6,000	172	PAULDING COUNTY BOARD OF ED	4,200
53	MEMORIAL HERMANN HEALTH	14,000	113	ARCHDIOCESE OF CINCINNATI	6,000	173	AMERICAN HEALTH COMPANIES, INC.	4,200
54	MORTON HOSPITAL AND MEDICAL	14,000	114	CORPUS CHRISTI INDEPENDENT SCH	5,920	174	AUTOMATION PERSONNEL SERVICES	4,200
55	STATE OF RHODE ISLAND AND P	13,535	115	ASSOCIATED WHOLESALE GROCER	5,500	175	BELFLEX STAFFING NETWORK, LLC	4,200
56	LEVI STRAUSS & CO.	13,200	116	RICHMOND COUNTY BOARD OF ED	5,500	176	AUSTIN COMMUNITY COLLEGE	4,200
57	TRIHEALTH, INC.	13,000	117	EXCELITAS TECHNOLOGIES CORP.	5,500	177	BRONSON HEALTH CARE GROUP, INC.	4,180
58	WILLOW VALLEY COMMUNITIES	13,000	118	YONKERS CITY SCHOOL DISTRICT	5,500	178	FORSYTH COUNTY BOARD OF EDUCA	4,160
59	ROBERT BOSCH LLC	12,986	119	CENTRACARE CLINIC	5,468	179	SHAWNEE MISSION SCHOOL DIST	4,132
60	PULSE ELECTRONICS, INC.	12,000	120	YOUNG MEN'S CHRISTIAN ASSOCIATI	5,450	180	ADVOCATE HEALTH AND HOSPITALS	4,110

SOURCE: HOOVER'S, INC., DATABASE, JANUARY 2018

Rank	Company	Employees
181	CARROLLTON-FARMERS BRANCH I	4,020
182	OLATHE UNIFIED SCHOOL DIST 233	4,000
183	KENNEDY HEALTH SYSTEM, INC.	4,000
184	PORTLAND STATE UNIVERSITY	4,000
185	LITTLE ROCK SCHOOL DISTRICT	4,000
186	DELAWARE NORTH COMPANIES PARK	4,000
187	VISALIA UNIFIED SCHOOL DISTRICT	4,000
188	WORLD OF JEANS & TOPS	4,000
189	WILDLIFE CONSERVATION SOCIETY	4,000
190	MERCY HEALTH YOUNGSTOWN LLC	4,000
191	MONTEBELLO UNIFIED SCHOOL DIS	4,000
192	CENTERLIGHT HEALTHCARE, INC.	4,000
193	JOINT SCHOOL DISTRICT 2	4,000
194	BERKELEY COUNTY SCHOOL DISTRI	4,000
195	INTERTEK USA INC.	4,000
196	GLENDALE UNIFIED SCHOOL DISTRI	4,000
197	GRAND RAPIDS PUBLIC SCHOOLS	4,000
198	WHEATON FRANCISCAN HEALTHCARE	4,000
199	SHARI'S MANAGEMENT CORPORATIO	4,000
200	OSF HEALTHCARE SYSTEM	4,000
201	MORTON PLANT MEASE HEALTH CARE	3,950
202	DOUGLAS COUNTY BOARD OF ED.	3,947
203	AKRON PUBLIC SCHOOLS	3,937
204	IRVING INDEPENDENT SCHOOL DIST	3,934
205	AVALON HEALTH CARE, INC.	3,900
206	ECTOR COUNTY INDEPENDENT SCH	3,900
207	ERMC II, L.P.	3,900
208	PEORIA UNIFIED SCHOOL DIS NO.11	3,889
209	NORTHERN ARIZONA UNIVERSITY	3,863
210	HOUSTON COUNTY BOARD OF ED.	3,856
211	GASTON COUNTY SCHOOL DISTRICT	3,848
212	SHI INTERNATIONAL CORP.	3,800
213	MT. DIABLO UNIFIED SCHOOL DISTR	3,800
214	COMPTON UNIFIED SCHOOL DISTR	3,800
215	TUFTS MEDICAL CENTER PARENT,	3,800
216	EDINBURG CONSOLIDATED INDEP	3,779
217	CALVIN COLLEGE	3,774
218	UNIVERSITY OF TEXAS AT EL PASO	3,700
219	NEW HANOVER REGIONAL MEDICA	3,692
220	OHIO VALLEY HEALTH SERVICES ED	3,650
221	AMARILLO INDEPENDENT SCHOOL	3,600
222	PARADISE VALLEY UNIFIED SCHOOL	3,600
223	HALL COUNTY BOARD OF EDUCATION	3,600
224	THE NEW HANOVER COUNTY BLACK	3,600
225	NORTH CAROLINA AGRICULTURAL	3,600
226	MONTGOMERY COLLEGE	3,600
227	DALLAS AREA RAPID TRANSIT	3,600
228	MARTHA JEFFERSON HOSPITAL	3,569
229	LODI UNIFIED SCHOOL DISTRICT	3,516
230	KENT SCHOOL DISTRICT	3,505
231	WAKEFERN FOOD CORP.	3,500
232	NASSAU HEALTH CARE CORPORATION	3,500
233	PARKS XANTERRA & RESORTS INC	3,500
234	XANTERRA, INC.	3,500
235	PHARR SAN JUAN-ALAMO INDEPEND	3,500
236	DEER VALLEY SCHOOL DISTRICT 97	3,500
237	GRAND PRAIRIE INDEPENDENT SCH	3,500
238	ST. VRAIN VALLEY SCHOOL RE-1J	3,500
239	MCALLEN INDEPENDENT SCHOO	3,500
240	FREMONT UNIFIED SCHOOL DIST	3,500
241	JUDSON INDEPENDENT SCHOOL DIS	3,500
242	SCO FAMILY OF SERVICES	3,500
243	FAYETTE COUNTY BOARD OF EDUCA	3,500
244	NEW HANOVER COUNTY SCHOOLS	3,500
245	UNIVERSITY OF NORTHERN COLOR	3,500
246	NEW YORK CONVENTION CENTER	3,500
247	TRANSPERFECT TRANSLATIONS	3,500
248	NEXTSOURCE INC.	3,500
249	WEBER STATE UNIVERSITY	3,500
250	THE COLLEGE OF WILLIAM & MARY	3,500
251	THE BUDD GROUP INC	3,500
252	YASH TECHNOLOGIES, INC	3,500
253	MADISON AREA TECHNICAL COLLEGE	3,500
254	RACETRAC PETROLEUM, INC.	3,479
255	BOARD OF TRUSTEES OF ILLINOIS	3,441
256	EAST JEFFERSON GENERAL HOSPITAL	3,436
257	GRAND VALLEY STATE UNIVERSITY	3,428
258	LAFAYETTE PARISH SCHOOL BOARD	3,400
259	KELLER INDEPENDENT SCHOOL DIS	3,400
260	OKALOOSA COUNTY SCHOOL DIST	3,400
261	RAPIDES PARISH SCHOOL DISTRICT	3,400
262	ECUMEN	3,400
263	BRADFORD HOLDING COMPANY INC	3,400
264	GENERAL HEALTH SYSTEM	3,400
265	UNIQUE STAFF LEASING III, LTD	3,400
266	THE WICHITA STATE UNIVERSITY	3,395
267	GOODWILL INDUSTRIES OF SOUTHE	3,391
268	YUKON-KUSKOKWIM HEALTH CORP	3,365
269	SHELBY COUNTY BOARD OF ED	3,353
270	REGENTS OF THE UNIVERSITY DAHO	3,350
271	ROCKWOOD SCHOOL DISTRICT R-6	3,328
272	BROOKLYN HOSPITAL CENTER	3,300
273	DENTON INDEPENDENT SCHOOL DI	3,300
274	LUBBOCK INDEPENDENT SCHOOL DIS	3,300
275	ASCENSION PARISH SCHOOLS	3,300
276	SIOUX FALLS SCHOOL DIST 49-5	3,300
277	IREDELL-STATESVILLE SCHOOLS	3,300
278	COMMUNITY DEVUTE HEAD START	3,276
279	HARMONY PUBLIC SCHOOLS	3,262
280	THE METHODIST HOSPITALS INC	3,260
281	COLUMBIA COUNTY SCHOOL DIS	3,240
282	INDIANA UNIVERSITY HEALTH BLOO	3,200
283	SALT LAKE CITY SCHOOL DISTRICT	3,200
284	EVERGREEN PUBLIC SCHOOLS	3,200
285	SALT LAKE CITY CORPORATION	3,200
286	SOUTH WASHINGTON COUS ISD 833	3,200
287	HINES INTERESTS LIMITED PART	3,200
288	MESA COUNTY VALLEY SCHO 51	3,200
289	VICTORIA INDEPENDENT SCHOOL	3,200
290	YOUNG MEN'S CHRISTIAN TENN	3,200
291	SALT LAKE COMMUNITY COLLEGE	3,200
292	UPMC HAMOT	3,159
293	BOONE HOSPITAL CENTER	3,150
294	GEMOLOGICAL INSTITUTE OF AME	3,141
295	BIRDVILLE INDEPENDENT SCHOOL	3,109
296	BETHESDA LUTHERAN COMMUNIT	3,106
297	PLAINFIELD COMMUN. DISTRICT 202	3,100
298	YOUNG LIFE	3,100
299	LAKE WASHINGTON SCHOOL	3,100
300	NATIONAL SURGICAL HOSPITALS,	3,100

The 100 Largest Private Companies by Net Income 2018

Rank	Company Headquarters	Net Income ($bil)	Rank	Company Headquarters	Net Income ($bil)
1	STATE OF CALIFORNIA	$6,252	51	MEMORIAL HERMANN HEALTH SYSTEM	$379
2	AMERICAN BALANCED FUND, INC.	$4,903	52	STANFORD HEALTH CARE	$372
3	THE PRESIDENT AND FELLOWS OF HARVARD COLLEGE	$4,608	53	THE UNIVERSITY OF CHICAGO	$371
4	CHEVRON PHILLIPS CHEMICAL COMPANY LLC	$2,651	54	SCRIPPS HEALTH	$371
5	CANDID COLOR SYSTEMS, INC.	$2,535	55	METROPOLITAN TRANSPORTATION AUTHORITY	$370
6	ST. JOSEPH HEALTH SYSTEM	$2,083	56	IOWA HEALTH SYSTEM	$369
7	PUBLIX SUPER MARKETS, INC.	$2,026	57	WALTON FAMILY FOUNDATION INC	$369
8	CHEVRON PHILLIPS CHEMICAL COMPANY LP	$2,020	58	CEDARS-SINAI MEDICAL CENTER	$366
9	STATE OF TEXAS	$1,993	59	HEALTHPARTNERS, INC.	$366
10	YALE UNIVERSITY	$1,965	60	PILOT CORPORATION	$366
11	UNIVERSITY OF TEXAS SYSTEM	$1,589	61	CHALMETTE REFINING, L.L.C.	$364
12	TELCO INTERCONTINENTAL CORP	$1,372	62	UNIVERSITY OF CALIFORNIA, DAVIS	$360
13	THE TRUSTEES OF COLUMBIA UNIVERSITY IN NYC	$1,049	63	SHARP HEALTHCARE	$356
14	BATHXCESSORIES, INCORPORATED	$1,048	64	OHIOHEALTH CORPORATION	$354
15	COBANK ACB	$937	65	SPECTRUM HEALTH SYSTEMS, INC.	$353
16	RECTOR & VISITORS OF THE UNIVERSITY OF VIRGINIA	$909	66	DEKALB COUNTY BOARD OF EDUCATION	$351
17	CATHOLIC HEALTH INITIATIVES	$902	67	GWINNETT COUNTY BOARD OF EDUCATION	$350
18	THE JPB FOUNDATION	$827	68	TRUSTEES OF THE ESTATE OF BERNICE PAUAHI BISHOP	$334
19	THE BLOOMBERG FAMILY FOUNDATION INC	$737	69	SAN FRANCISCO BAY AREA RAPID TRANSIT DISTRICT	$332
20	CHS MCPHERSON REFINERY INC.	$687	70	GMTO CORPORATION	$331
21	SADDLE BUTTE PIPELINE LLC	$656	71	FOUNDATION FOR THE CAROLINAS	$330
22	NCL CORPORATION LTD.	$644	72	CLARK COUNTY SCHOOL DISTRICT	$328
23	QVC, INC.	$642	73	FEDERAL HOME LOAN BANK OF CHICAGO	$327
24	VANGUARD CHARITABLE ENDOWMENT PROGRAM	$608	74	PREMIER HEALTHCARE ALLIANCE, L.P.	$327
25	FIDELITY INV CHARITABLE GIFT FUND	$599	75	UNIVERSITY OF PITTSBURGH MEDICAL CENTER	$326
26	UNIVERSITY OF SOUTHERN CALIFORNIA	$588	76	BOARD OF EDUCATION OF CITY OF CHICAGO	$324
27	PRESIDIAN DESTINATIONS, LTD.	$583	77	OCEAN SPRAY CRANBERRIES, INC.	$317
28	NIELSEN HOLDINGS PLC	$575	78	THE METHODIST HOSPITAL	$316
29	NEW YORK UNIVERSITY	$564	79	BAINUM FAMILY FOUNDATION, INC.	$316
30	JOHNS HOPKINS UNIVERSITY	$526	80	PUGET ENERGY, INC.	$313
31	TRANSCONTINENTAL GAS PIPE LINE COMPANY, LLC	$523	81	MEDSTAR HEALTH, INC.	$311
32	PETER KIEWIT SONS', INC.	$515	82	JOHN D. AND CATHERINE T. MACARTHUR FOUNDATION	$311
33	FARM CREDIT SERVICES OF AMERICA, PCA	$514	83	UNIVERSITY OF COLORADO	$309
34	KIEWIT CORPORATION	$512	84	WASHINGTON METROPOLITAN AREA TRANSIT AUTHORITY	$306
35	UNIVERSITY OF WISCONSIN SYSTEM	$503	85	KILROY REALTY, L.P.	$304
36	AIMCO PROPERTIES, L.P.	$483	86	THE PEW CHARITABLE TRUSTS	$300
37	VIRGINIA DEPARTMENT OF TRANSPORTATION	$473	87	LEVI STRAUSS & CO.	$291
38	ROBERT BOSCH LLC	$457	88	BROWN UNIVERSITY IN PROVIDENCE IN THE RHODE ISLAND	$290
39	ESSEX PORTFOLIO, L.P.	$438	89	TEXAS HEALTH RESOURCES	$286
40	ONCOR ELECTRIC DELIVERY COMPANY LLC	$431	90	NATIONWIDE CHILDREN'S HOSPITAL	$286
41	KAISER FOUNDATION HOSPITALS INC	$429	91	SL GREEN OPERATING PARTNERSHIP, L.P.	$279
42	SUTTER HEALTH	$422	92	FEDERAL HOME LOAN BANK OF ATLANTA	$278
43	STANFORD HEALTH SERVICES	$416	93	UPMC PRESBYTERIAN SHADYSIDE	$277
44	THE DAVID AND LUCILE PACKARD FOUNDATION	$413	94	PRODUCERS RICE MILL, INC.	$275
45	EAST BATON ROUGE PARISH SCHOOL DISTRICT	$393	95	FRANCISCAN ALLIANCE, INC.	$274
46	ADVOCATE HEALTH AND HOSPITALS CORPORATION	$393	96	THE GEORGETOWN UNIVERSITY	$272
47	UNIVERSITY OF NORTH CAROLINA AT CHAPEL HILL	$391	97	NEW YORK STATE CATHOLIC HEALTH PLAN INC	$272
48	COMENITY BANK	$389	98	THE UNIVERSITY OF NORTH CAROLINA	$268
49	PUGET SOUND ENERGY, INC.	$381	99	HOUSTON INDEPENDENT SCHOOL DISTRICT	$267
50	BAYLOR UNIVERSITY MEDICAL CENTER	$379	100	NEW YORK PRESBYTERIAN HOSPITAL WEILL CORNELL	$266

SOURCE: MERGENT DATA , JANUARY 2018

The 100 Largest Private Companies by Total Assets 2018

Rank	Company Headquarters	Net Income ($bil)	Rank	Company Headquarters	Net Income ($bil)
1	STATE OF CALIFORNIA	$322,220	51	QVC, INC.	$11,545
2	STATE OF TEXAS	$279,111	52	CATHOLIC HEALTH INITIATIVES	$11,388
3	GOODWILL INDUSTRIES OF SOUTHEASTERN WISCONSIN	$175,984	53	PUGET SOUND ENERGY, INC.	$11,297
4	FEDERAL HOME LOAN BANK OF ATLANTA	$138,671	54	THE WASHINGTON UNIVERSITY	$11,081
5	COBANK ACB	$117,471	55	DIGNITY HEALTH	$11,076
6	AMERICAN BALANCED FUND, INC.	$87,395	56	CORNELL UNIVERSITY	$10,900
7	FEDERAL HOME LOAN BANK OF CHICAGO	$78,692	57	STATE OF RHODE ISLAND	$10,866
8	METROPOLITAN TRANSPORTATION AUTHORITY	$72,681	58	NEW YORK UNIVERSITY	$10,396
9	THE PRESIDENT AND FELLOWS OF HARVARD COLLEGE	$69,810	59	NORTHWEST FARM CREDIT SERVICES	$10,253
10	UNIVERSITY OF TEXAS SYSTEM	$66,887	60	NEW YORK CITY HOUSING DEVELOPMENT CORPORATION	$10,085
11	UNIVERSITY OF TEXAS AT TYLER	$63,142	61	BANNER HEALTH	$10,084
12	ALASKA PERMANENT FUND CORPORATION	$55,347	62	CHEVRON PHILLIPS CHEMICAL COMPANY LP	$9,983
13	DORMITORY AUTHORITY - STATE OF NEW YORK	$45,583	63	MILTON HERSHEY SCHOOL & SCHOOL TRUST	$9,942
14	STATE OF OKLAHOMA	$41,201	64	CITY OF LONG BEACH	$9,836
15	ASCENSION HEALTH ALLIANCE	$32,469	65	TRANSCONTINENTAL GAS PIPE LINE COMPANY, LLC	$9,831
16	YALE UNIVERSITY	$31,265	66	INTERMOUNTAIN HEALTH CARE INC	$9,763
17	THE TRUSTEES OF PRINCETON UNIVERSITY	$27,380	67	SPRINGLEAF FINANCE CORPORATION	$9,719
18	COUNTY OF CLARK	$25,996	68	UNIVERSITY OF CHICAGO	$9,704
19	FARM CREDIT SERVICES OF AMERICA, PCA	$24,773	69	ADVOCATE HEALTH CARE NETWORK	$9,634
20	KAISER FOUNDATION HOSPITALS INC	$22,753	70	CITY PUBLIC SERVICES OF SAN ANTONIO	$9,596
21	ONCOR ELECTRIC DELIVERY COMPANY LLC	$20,811	71	NEW YORK POWER AUTHORITY	$9,575
22	KNIGHTS OF COLUMBUS	$20,534	72	MUNICIPAL ELECTRIC AUTHORITY OF GEORGIA	$9,442
23	VIRGINIA DEPARTMENT OF TRANSPORTATION	$20,173	73	CITY CENTER HOLDINGS, LLC	$9,153
24	ONEAMERICA FINANCIAL PARTNERS, INC.	$19,921	74	COMENITY BANK	$9,149
25	MARYLAND DEPARTMENT OF TRANSPORTATION	$19,829	75	TRUSTEES OF THE ESTATE OF BERNICE PAUAHI BISHOP	$9,072
26	REGENTS OF THE UNIVERSITY OF MICHIGAN	$18,551	76	SAN FRANCISCO BAY AREA RAPID TRANSIT DISTRICT	$8,913
27	PUBLIX SUPER MARKETS, INC.	$17,464	77	JACKSONVILLE ELECTRIC AUTHORITY	$8,806
28	SUNY COLLEGE AT CORTLAND	$15,972	78	UNIVERSITY OF SOUTHERN CALIFORNIA	$8,790
29	SL GREEN OPERATING PARTNERSHIP, L.P.	$15,858	79	UNIVERSITY OF WISCONSIN SYSTEM	$8,556
30	SUTTER HEALTH	$15,674	80	ST. JOSEPH HEALTH SYSTEM	$8,551
31	NIELSEN HOLDINGS PLC	$15,303	81	COUNTY OF RIVERSIDE	$8,425
32	PARTNERS HEALTHCARE SYSTEM, INC.	$15,070	82	MODERN WOODMEN OF AMERICA	$8,318
33	STATE UNIVERSITY OF NEW YORK	$14,780	83	THE REGENTS OF THE UNIVERSITY OF COLORADO	$8,237
34	THE TRUSTEES OF COLUMBIA UNIVERSITY IN NYC	$14,729	84	JOHNS HOPKINS UNIVERSITY	$8,212
35	DUKE UNIVERSITY	$14,171	85	THE CHARLOTTE-MECKLENBURG HOSPITAL AUTHORITY	$8,087
36	WASHINGTON METROPOLITAN AREA TRANSIT AUTHORITY	$13,985	86	THE UNIVERSITY OF NORTH CAROLINA	$8,061
37	STATE OF RHODE ISLAND AND PROVIDENCE PLANTATIONS	$13,726	87	NEW YORK UNIVERSITY	$8,038
38	NORTHWESTERN UNIVERSITY	$13,660	88	VIRGINIA HOUSING DEVELOPMENT AUTHORITY	$8,025
39	CHEVRON PHILLIPS CHEMICAL COMPANY LLC	$13,597	89	RECTOR & VISITORS OF THE UNIVERSITY OF VIRGINIA	$8,001
40	MASSACHUSETTS INSTITUTE OF TECHNOLOGY	$13,371	90	UNIVERSITY OF MISSOURI SYSTEM	$7,996
41	PUGET ENERGY, INC.	$13,266	91	UPMC PRESBYTERIAN SHADYSIDE	$7,918
42	NCL CORPORATION LTD.	$12,951	92	THE METHODIST HOSPITAL	$7,778
43	THE PENNSYLVANIA STATE UNIVERSITY	$12,781	93	UNIVERSITY OF TEXAS AT AUSTIN	$7,707
44	THE UNIVERSITY OF CHICAGO	$12,525	94	ROBERT BOSCH LLC	$7,435
45	LOS ANGELES DEPARTMENT OF WATER AND POWER	$12,520	95	REGIONAL TRANSPORTATION DISTRICT	$7,429
46	THE FORD FOUNDATION	$12,400	96	ADVOCATE HEALTH AND HOSPITALS CORPORATION	$7,308
47	SOUTH CAROLINA PUBLIC SERVICE AUTHORITY (INC)	$12,251	97	TRUSTEES OF DARTMOUTH COLLEGE	$7,280
48	ESSEX PORTFOLIO, L.P.	$12,217	98	DARTMOUTH COLLEGE	$7,267
49	ATHENE ANNUITY & LIFE ASSURANCE COMPANY	$11,776	99	THE BLOOMBERG FAMILY FOUNDATION INC	$7,156
50	NEW YORK STATE ENVIRONMENTAL FACILITIES CORP	$11,649	100	BASIN ELECTRIC POWER COOPERATIVE	$7,132

SOURCE: MERGENT DATA JANUARY 2018

Hoover's Handbook of

Private Companies

The Companies

4 EARTH FARMS, INC.

EXECUTIVES

Chief Executive Officer, David Lake
Financial Executive, Olivia Sawran
Accountant, Marlene Lee
Director, Sheri Normandin

LOCATIONS

HQ: 4 EARTH FARMS, INC.
5555 E OLYMPIC BLVD, COMMERCE, CA 900225129
Phone: 323 201-5800

HISTORICAL FINANCIALS

Company Type: Private

Income Statement

FYE: December 31

	REVENUE ($ mil.)	NET INCOME ($ mil.)	NET PROFIT MARGIN	EMPLOYEES
12/15	209	7	3.6%	330
12/14	190	0	0.5%	—
12/13	174	1	1.1%	—
12/12	149	4	3.1%	—
Annual Growth	11.8%	16.9%	—	—

2015 Year-End Financials

Return on assets: 6.6%   Cash ($ mil.): 7
Return on equity: 3.6%
Current ratio: 1.30

A G EQUIPMENT COMPANY

EXECUTIVES

Chief Executive Officer, Henry Ash
Marketing Director, Michael Johnston
Auditors: CCK STRATEGIES PLLC TULSA O

LOCATIONS

HQ: A G EQUIPMENT COMPANY
3401 W ALBANY ST, BROKEN ARROW, OK 740121174
Phone: 918 250-7386
Web: WWW.AGEQUIPMENTCOMPANY.COM

HISTORICAL FINANCIALS

Company Type: Private

Income Statement

FYE: June 30

	REVENUE ($ mil.)	NET INCOME ($ mil.)	NET PROFIT MARGIN	EMPLOYEES
06/15	486	48	10.0%	370
06/14	402	29	7.4%	—
06/13	362	34	9.6%	—
06/12	315	17	5.6%	—
Annual Growth	15.6%	40.5%	—	—

2015 Year-End Financials

Return on assets: 4.5%   Cash ($ mil.): 46
Return on equity: 10.0%
Current ratio: 1.00

AAA COOPER TRANSPORTATION

They might not give you a map like that other AAA but AAA Cooper Transportation can freight your cargo from point A to point B. A non-union regional less-than-truckload (LTL) freight hauler AAA Cooper (ACT) operates in a dozen southeastern US states as well as Puerto Rico; it also maintains facilities in Chicago and a few other industrial crossroads. (LTL carriers combine freight from multiple shippers into a single truckload.) ACT operates a fleet of approximately 2400 tractors and 6000 trailers. ACT also offers freight brokerage services and dedicated contract carriage.

Operations

The company's five primary service offerings are LTL Services dedicated services international Services (including port services) managed services and fleet maintenance services.

Its port services provide services to the port the shipper and the customer. It transloads the goods from the container to its trailer or dock and returns the container to the port. Its fleet maintenance services provide maintenance services for all types of diesel engines including the CAT VOLVO International Detroit and Cummins brands.

The company's distribution operations offer assembly operations manufacturing plant transfers warehouse transfers wholesale distribution and retail distribution.

Geographic Reach

ACT operates more than 70 facilities in the Southeast Southwest Midwest and Puerto Rico. It has nearly 40 maintenance facilities nationwide and partners with carriers to extend its coverage into Canada and Mexico. The company's international partnerships allow it for operate across the Caribbean Latin America Europe Asia Africa and Australia.

Sales and Marketing

ATC serves a range of sectors including Automotive Manufacturing Automotive Parts Heavy Equipment Parts Building Materials Retail and HVAC. ACT customers include Schneider Logistics Volvo Logistics Mastio & Company Global-Tranz Technicolor John Deere and Nissan.

Strategy

As part of its growth strategy ACT seeks to offer new services and expand into new geographies. In 2014 the company launched a new Managed Services offering adding Truckload Brokerage and Parcel Audit to its services.

In 2013 the company opened a service center at Corpus Christi Texas.

Company Background

The ATC was founded in 1955.

EXECUTIVES

President CEO, Reid Dove
CFO, Steve Roy
Director Dedicated Services, Charles (Charlie) Prickett
VP Strategic Services, Lee McMillan
VP Information Services, Dan Christian
Senior Vice President Finance, Mark Griffis
National Account Manager, Bob Menas
Vice President of Safety and Maintenance, Steven Aronhalt
National Account Manager, David Hunt
National Account Manager and Business Development Manager, Andy McMillan
Executive Vice President and Chief Operating Officer, Charlie Prickett
National Account Manager, Joe Hanks

National Account Manager, Bob Mazzeffi
Vice President, CORY Bingham

LOCATIONS

HQ: AAA COOPER TRANSPORTATION
1751 KINSEY RD, DOTHAN, AL 363035877
Phone: 334 793-2284
Web: WWW.AAACOOPER.COM

PRODUCTS/OPERATIONS

Selected Services
Dedicated
  Company branding
  Specialized equipment
International LTL
LTL
Port
  Consolidation
  Drayage
  Transloading

COMPETITORS

ArcBest	Saia
Averitt Express	Southeastern Freight
Estes Express	Lines
FedEx Freight	UPS Freight
Old Dominion Freight	YRC Worldwide
R+L Carriers	

HISTORICAL FINANCIALS

Company Type: Private

Income Statement

FYE: January 3

	REVENUE ($ mil.)	NET INCOME ($ mil.)	NET PROFIT MARGIN	EMPLOYEES
01/16*	595	14	2.4%	4,933
12/14	576	20	3.5%	—
12/13	575	20	3.6%	—
12/12	553	20	3.8%	—
Annual Growth	2.5%	(12.1%)	—	—

*Fiscal year change

2016 Year-End Financials

Return on assets: 1.2%   Cash ($ mil.): —
Return on equity: 2.4%
Current ratio: 1.10

ABINGTON MEMORIAL HOSPITAL INC

Abington Memorial Hospital brings health care to residents of southeastern Pennsylvania. The not-for-profit community hospital has some 670 beds. In addition to general medical and surgical care the hospital offers specialized care centers for cancer and cardiovascular conditions operates high-tech orthopedic and neurological surgery units and serves as a regional trauma care facility. It also runs an inpatient pediatric unit in affiliation with The Children's Hospital of Philadelphia. Abington Memorial also known as Abington Health operates the neighboring 125-bed Lansdale Hospital and several area outpatient facilities.

Operations

The not-for-profit community hospital has some 670 beds and employs about 1400 physicians. Its specialty units include the Pilla Heart Center the Rosenfeld Cancer Center the Diamond Stroke Center as well as a level II trauma center and institutes for senior health and bariatric surgeries. Abington Memorial is affiliated with several medical schools including the Temple University School of Medicine

and offers residency programs and postgraduate medical education.

In addition to its hospitals Abington Memorial operates an extensive outpatient care facility named Abington Health Center-Warminster. The Warminster facility is located in Bucks County and features an inpatient hospice center. Other outpatient facilities include Abington Health Center-Schilling (in Willow Grove) Abington Health Center-Blue Bell and Abington Physicians at Montgomeryville.

Altogether the organization's facilities handle 677000 outpatient visits and 33000 inpatient admissions each year.

Additionally Abington Memorial operates a nursing school and a clinical research center.

Geographic Reach

Abington Memorial provides care to residents of southeastern Pennsylvania. The hospital serves Montgomery Bucks and Philadelphia counties.

Strategy

Abington Memorial began using the Abington Health moniker to reflect its larger network of facilities after it acquired Lansdale Hospital which was previously known as Central Montgomery Medical Center from Universal Health Services in 2008. Abington Memorial has since invested in a number of improvements at the acquired hospital. The main Abington Memorial facility has also been enhanced including a new hybrid operating room for cardiac procedures in 2013.

Mergers and Acquisitions

In 2013 Abington Memorial acquired a home health agency the North Penn Visiting Nurse Association (NPVNA). The purchase expanded the geographic reach of Abington Memorial's home health operations.

Company Background

Abington Memorial first opened its doors in 1914.

EXECUTIVES

President Abington Hospitals, Margaret M. (Meg) McGoldrick
Chief Medical Officer, John J. Kelly
Executive Vice President Of Information Technology, Jan Seip
Senior Vice President Professional Ser, Gary Candia
Medical Director Of Labor And Delivery, Amy Mackey
Senior Vice President Patient Services and Chief Nursing Officer, Barbara Wadsworth
Vice President, Christopher Pezzi
Executive Vice President and Administrator, Michelle Henrie
Vice President of Administration, Regina Harte

LOCATIONS

HQ: ABINGTON MEMORIAL HOSPITAL INC
1200 OLD YORK RD, ABINGTON, PA 190013788
Phone: 215 481-2000
Web: WWW.ABINGTONHEALTH.ORG

PRODUCTS/OPERATIONS

Selected Facilities
Abington Health Center ; Blue Bell Campus (Blue Bell PA)
Abington Health Center ; Schilling Campus (Willow Grove PA)
Abington Health Center ; Warminster Campus (Warminster PA)
Abington Memorial Hospital (Abington PA)
Abington Physicians at Montgomeryville (North Wales PA)
Lansdale Hospital (Lansdale PA)

COMPETITORS

Albert Einstein Healthcare Network
Aria Health
Crozer-Keystone Health System
Doylestown Hospital
Grand View
Main Line Health System
Memorial Hospital (PA)
Mercy Health System
Moses Taylor Hospital
North Philadelphia Health System
TUHS
Tenet Healthcare
University of Pennsylvania Health System
Virtua Memorial

HISTORICAL FINANCIALS
Company Type: Private

Income Statement
FYE: June 30

	REVENUE ($ mil.)	NET INCOME ($ mil.)	NET PROFIT MARGIN	EMPLOYEES
06/15	697	28	4.1%	4,018
06/14	697	0	0.1%	—
06/13	708	20	2.9%	—
06/10	783	16	2.1%	—
Annual Growth	(2.3%)	11.8%	—	—

2015 Year-End Financials
Return on assets: 6.2%   Cash ($ mil.): 132
Return on equity: 4.1%
Current ratio: 1.60

ACADEMY SCHOOL DISTRICT 20

EXECUTIVES

Superintendent, Dr Mark Hatchell
Manager, John Smith
Director, Marita Vogrin
Consultant, Jordan Voltz
Director, Carol Young
Auditors: CLIFTONLARSONALLEN LLP GREEN

LOCATIONS

HQ: ACADEMY SCHOOL DISTRICT 20
1110 CHAPEL HILLS DR, COLORADO SPRINGS, CO 809203923
Phone: 719 234-1200
Web: WWW.ASD20.ORG

HISTORICAL FINANCIALS
Company Type: Private

Income Statement
FYE: June 30

	REVENUE ($ mil.)	NET INCOME ($ mil.)	NET PROFIT MARGIN	EMPLOYEES
06/15	232	0	0.2%	3,000
06/14	215	1	0.9%	—
06/13	209	3	1.8%	—
06/12	203	3	1.8%	—
Annual Growth	4.6%	(54.2%)	—	—

ACCESS BUSINESS GROUP LLC

Somehow all those Amway products have to get from factories to the sales floor and that's where Access Business Group (ABG) comes in. The company manufactures and distributes cosmetics nutritional supplements home care and personal care products for its sister company Amway. (Both companies are units of Alticor.) It also offers contract manufacturing services for third-party consumer goods companies but to a lesser extent. Other offerings include product packaging services as well as catalog and direct mail printing services. In addition the company operates R&D labs that develop and test products for Amway.

Operations

A major function of ABG is the manufacturing and distribution of some 200 products in Amway's NUTRILITE line which includes nutritional food supplements in liquid powder food bar tablet and capsule form. Other key operations include manufacturing and distributing products in the ARTISTRY cosmetics and skin care line.

Geographic Reach

ABG owns and operates 10 manufacturing plants that comprise more than 1 million sq. ft. of space.

Sales and Marketing

The company offers its products through distributors and retailers both in North America and Internationally.

Strategy

Amway announced in 2012 it was investing nearly $180 million to expand manufacturing and processing capacity to meet growing global demand for its NUTRILITE brand of vitamin mineral and dietary supplements. The investment includes a new $81 million nutrition plant at the company's Spaulding Avenue site in Ada Michigan near Amway's headquarters. In support of this initiative the Michigan government has approved a $1.6 million incentive from a fund to support construction of this nutrition products manufacturing facility for ABG.

EXECUTIVES

Vice President, Jim Siewertsen

LOCATIONS

HQ: ACCESS BUSINESS GROUP LLC
7575 FULTON ST E, ADA, MI 493550001
Phone: 616 787-6000

PRODUCTS/OPERATIONS

Selected Services and Products
Beauty
  Blushes
  Eye shadows
  Lipsticks
  Mascara
  Skin care
Fulfillment
  A-Frame
  B2B & B2C
  Customized order picking at the store level
  High volume pick pack & ship
  Pick-to-light
  Tilt tray sorter
Home Care
  Household cleaners
  Plastic bottles
  Powder and liquid dish washing detergents
  Powder and liquid laundry detergents
Nutrition
  Antioxidants/supplements/herbals
  Food bars

Granulation
Multiminerals/multivitamins
OTC tableting
Powdered drinks
Personal Care
  Bar soaps
  Bath oils
  Body mist
  Conditioners
  Lotions
  Plastic bottles
  Shampoos
  Shower gels
  Styling products
Print
  Catalogs
  Corrugated cases
  Fine printing
  Labels
  L-Boards
  Paperboard packaging

COMPETITORS

AppTech	Pfizer
Berry Global	Procter & Gamble
Botanical Laboratories	Strathmore
Essential Nutrition	UPS Supply Chain
Johnson & Johnson	Solutions

HISTORICAL FINANCIALS
Company Type: Private

Income Statement
FYE: December 31

	REVENUE ($ mil.)	NET INCOME ($ mil.)	NET PROFIT MARGIN	EMPLOYEES
12/15	1,009	0	—	3,000
12/14	1,068	0	—	—
12/13	1,135	0	—	—
12/12	1,145	0	—	—
Annual Growth	(4.1%)	—	—	—

ACCESS GROUP, INC.

As if paying for Albert's undergraduate degree didn't set you back enough now your little Einstein wants to attend graduate school. It may be time to contact Access Group a not-for-profit organization that offers graduate and professional student lending. The company issues and services private student loans for continuing education part-time and international students and their parents. It specializes in financing educations in business dental law medical engineering and other professional courses of study. The company also issues specialized loans for bar and dental board exams and medical and dental residencies. Access Group was founded in 1983 to provide funding to law students.

Access Group's loan portfolio is valued at some $8 billion in outstanding principal. To focus on its financing activities the company outsourced the servicing of its portfolio to Xerox subsidiary Affiliated Computer Services (ACS) in early 2012. Prior to the conversion Access used ACS as a back-up loan servicer.

The company offered Federal Stafford and PLUS loans until 2010 when the Student Aid and Fiscal Responsibility Act put an end to federal subsidies for private school loans. Due to regulatory changes the company ceased funding for student loan consolidations in 2008. Also that year it embarked on its first national branding campaign.

Prior to the sweeping changes to the student lending industry Access Group originated more than 120000 new loans annually with an average loan size of about $12000. The company occa-

sionally raises funds for its lending by issuing securities that are backed by pools of loans that it has originated.

EXECUTIVES

Chief Executive Officer, Christopher P Chapman
Financial Executive, John Kolla
Assistant Controller, John Jackson
Manager, Mary E Gray
Vice-President, Eileen Santos-Perez
Manager, Melissa Layfield
Auditors: GRANT THORNTON LLP PHILADELPH

LOCATIONS

HQ: ACCESS GROUP, INC.
  10 N HIGH ST FL 4, WEST CHESTER, PA 193803014
Phone: 484 653-3300
Web: WWW.ACCESSGROUP.ORG

COMPETITORS

Bank of America	First Marblehead
College Loan	JPMorgan Chase
Corporation	Nelnet
Discover	Sallie Mae

HISTORICAL FINANCIALS
Company Type: Private

Income Statement
FYE: March 31

	ASSETS ($ mil.)	NET INCOME ($ mil.)	INCOME AS % OF ASSETS	EMPLOYEES
03/16	5,056	16	0.3%	60
03/11	8,767	58	0.7%	—
03/10	10,316	(0)	—	—
Annual Growth	(11.2%)	—	—	—

2016 Year-End Financials
Return on assets: —
Return on equity: 15.1%
Sales ($ mil): 110

ACCORD HEALTHCARE, INC.

EXECUTIVES

President, Gerald Price
Account Manager, Joan Mulford
Officer, Rakesh Barmy
Account Manager, Vipul Patel
Auditors: JANSEN VALK THOMPSON REAHM PC

LOCATIONS

HQ: ACCORD HEALTHCARE, INC.
  1009 SLATER RD STE 210B, DURHAM, NC 277038446
Phone: 919 941-7878
Web: WWW.ACCORD-HEALTHCARE.COM

HISTORICAL FINANCIALS
Company Type: Private

Income Statement
FYE: March 31

	REVENUE ($ mil.)	NET INCOME ($ mil.)	NET PROFIT MARGIN	EMPLOYEES
03/16*	223	8	3.7%	35
12/12	105	0	0.4%	—
12/11	64	2	4.6%	—
12/10	1,574	0	—	—
Annual Growth	—	1035.2%	—	—

*Fiscal year change

2016 Year-End Financials
Return on assets: 0.4%   Cash ($ mil.): 2
Return on equity: 3.7%
Current ratio: 0.70

ACE HARDWARE CORPORATION

In an age of big-box home improvement centers (Home Depot Lowes) wholesaler Ace makes the case for the local hardware store. By sales it is the #1 hardware cooperative in the US ahead of Do It Best. Ace dealer-owners operate more than 95% of the 4800 Ace Hardware-branded stores home centers and lumber and building materials locations selling more than 75000 products across all 50 US states and about 70 other countries. Stores range in size from small urban shops to large rural locations. From about 15 warehouses Ace distributes such products as electrical and plumbing supplies garden equipment hand tools housewares and power tools. Ace was founded in 1924 by a group of Chicago hardware store owners.

HISTORY

A group of Chicago-area hardware dealers — William Stauber Richard Hesse Gern Lindquist and Oscar Fisher — decided in 1924 to pool their hardware buying and promotional costs. In 1928 the group incorporated as Ace Stores named in honor of the superior WWI fliers dubbed aces. Hesse became president the following year retaining that position for the next 44 years. The company also opened its first warehouse in 1929 and by 1933 it had 38 dealers.

The organization had 133 dealers in seven states by 1949. In 1953 Ace began to allow dealers to buy stock in the company through the Ace Perpetuation Plan. During the 1960s Ace expanded into the South and West and by 1969 it had opened distribution centers in Georgia and California — its first such facilities outside Chicago. In 1968 it opened its first international store in Guam.

By the early 1970s the do-it-yourself market began to surge as inflation pushed up plumber and electrician fees. As the market grew large home center chains gobbled up market share from independent dealers such as those franchised through Ace. In response Ace and its dealers became a part of a growing trend in the hardware industry — cooperatives.

Hesse sold the company to its dealers in 1973 for $6 million (less than half its book value) and the following year Ace began operating as a cooperative. Hesse stepped down in 1973. In 1976 the dealers took full control when the company's first Board of Dealer-Directors was elected.

After signing up a number of dealers in the eastern US Ace had dealers in all 50 states by 1979. The co-op opened a plant to make paint in Matteson Illinois in 1984. By 1985 Ace had reached $1 billion in sales and had initiated its Store of the Future Program allowing dealers to borrow up to $200000 to upgrade their stores and conduct market analyses. Former head coach John Madden of the National Football League's Oakland Raiders signed on as Ace's mouthpiece in 1988.

A year later the co-op began to test ACENET a computer network that allowed Ace dealers to check inventory send and receive e-mail make special purchase requests and keep up with prices on commodity items such as lumber. In 1990 Ace es-

tablished an International Division to handle its overseas stores. (It had been exporting products since 1975.) EVP and COO David Hodnik became president in 1995. That year the co-op added a net of 67 stores including a three-store chain in Russia. Expanding further internationally Ace signed a five-year joint-supply agreement in 1996 with Canadian lumber and hardware retailer Beaver Lumber. Hodnik added CEO to his title in 1996.

Ace fell further behind its old rival True Value in 1997 when ServiStar Coast to Coast and True Value merged to form TruServ (renamed True Value in 2005) a hardware giant that operated more than 10000 outlets at the completion of the merger.

Late in 1997 Ace launched an expansion program in Canada. (The co-op already operated distribution centers in Ontario and Calgary.) In 1999 Ace merged its lumber and building materials division with Builder Marts of America to form a dealer-owned buying group to supply about 2700 retailers. Ace gained 208 member outlet stores in 2000 but saw 279 member outlets terminated. The next year it gained 220 but lost 255.

Sodisco-Howden bought all the shares of Ace Hardware Canada in February 2003. To better serve international members Ace opened its first international buying office in Hong Kong in April 2004.

In all the company added 131 new stores in 2005. That year after 33 years with the company David F. Hodnik retired as president and CEO of Ace Hardware. He was succeeded by COO Ray A. Griffith.

In 2007 Griffith sent a letter to Ace's retailers saying the company was considering changing from a cooperative to a traditional corporation to become more competitive and to better fuel growth. Shortly after the company announced an accounting shortfall of about $150 million or nearly half of its equity which was uncovered while Ace prepared to convert formats. The error turned out to be an accident by a mid-level employee.

In 2009 Ace launched Aisle411 a free product-location service that can be accessed via phone similar to dialing for information. The company launched the service after learning that shoppers who were unable to find a product either left (about 20% of the time) or asked store associates for assistance (about 60%) which created a high demand for staff attention. Dedicated to pleasing its shoppers Ace was ranked "Highest in Customer Satisfaction among Home Improvement Stores" by J.D. Power and Associates in 2007 2008 and 2009.

In mid-2010 the hardware store chain became the first retailer — outside of Sears and Kmart stores — to sell Craftsman brand tools.

In January 2011 the company reorganized its international division into a stand-alone entity: Ace Hardware International Holdings. Ace Hardware owns about 78% of the newly-created entity.

In December 2012 Ace exited the paint manufacturing business with the sale of its paint manufacturing division including two paint manufacturing plants near Chicago to Valspar Corp. for about $45 million. Under the terms of the sale Valspar will continue to make and supply Ace-branded paint under a long-term supply agreement. Also it will supply a comprehensive line of Valspar-branded paints to Ace retail stores.

EXECUTIVES

President and CEO, John S. Venhuizen, age 47
VP Information Technology and CIO, Karen Fedyszyn
EVP CFO and Chief Risk Officer, Bill Guzik

Vice President General Counsel and Secretary, Howard Japlon
Chairman, Jim Ackroyd

LOCATIONS

HQ: ACE HARDWARE CORPORATION
2200 KENSINGTON CT, OAK BROOK, IL 605232100
Phone: 866 681-1836
Web: WWW.ACEHARDWAREINTL.COM

PRODUCTS/OPERATIONS

2014 Sales

	$ mil.	% of total
Wholesale Revenues	4,466	95
Retail Revenues	233	5
Total	**4,700**	**100**

Selected Services

Assembly
Automotive chip key cutting
Blade sharpening
Glass & Acrylic sheet cutting
Glass Repair
Hunting/Fishing license
In-store lock servicing
Selected Brands
ACCO BRANDS
ACE
ACME
ADANAC
BIG BEN
BILCO
EUREKA
EVEREADY

COMPETITORS

84 Lumber	McCoy Corp.
Akzo Nobel	Menard
BMC Stock	Northern Tool
Costco Wholesale	Orgill
Do it Best	Sears
Fastenal	Sutherland Lumber
Grossman's	True Value
Home Depot	United Hardware
Kmart	Distributing
Lowe's	Wal-Mart

HISTORICAL FINANCIALS

Company Type: Private

Income Statement

FYE: January 2

	REVENUE ($ mil.)	NET INCOME ($ mil.)	NET PROFIT MARGIN	EMPLOYEES
01/16	5,045	156	3.1%	4,500
01/15*	4,700	141	3.0%	—
12/13	4,154	105	2.5%	—
12/12	3,840	82	2.1%	—
Annual Growth	9.5%	23.9%	—	—

*Fiscal year change

2016 Year-End Financials

Return on assets: 11.0%   Cash ($ mil.): 11
Return on equity: 3.1%
Current ratio: 0.50

ACT, INC.

A C and T... three little letters that can strike fear in the hearts of high school students across the US. ACT most notably develops and administers the ACT national college admission exam with about 2 million high school seniors taking the test each year. ACT also designs other educational assessment tests and programs as well as career planning and workforce development programs for people of all ages around the world. Other op-

erations provide assessment training and consulting to employers. The not-for-profit organization was founded in 1959 by E. F. Lindquist and Ted McCarrel who sought to create an exam to measure potential college students' capacity for critical thinking.

Operations

The organization's College and Career Readiness System culminates in the ACT test but it also includes the PLAN assessment test for 10th graders and the EXPLORE assessment test for eighth or ninth grade students. The ACT test has been taken by millions of people seeking to enter college and all four-year colleges and universities in the US accept ACT scores.

ACT maintains the ACT Center Network which delivers computer-based testing and training services to individuals employers and professional organizations. Located primarily at two- and four-year colleges ACT Center locations serve as a comprehensive resource for developing and serving a community's workforce and economy.

ACT has a strategic plan to invest in its product and service portfolios to ensure their effectiveness in meeting the challenges and opportunities of the rapidly changing world. ACT also plans to take a more pronounced position as a participant in national and international discussions regarding education and success in the workplace.

The company also engages in research and publishes reports aimed at policymakers researchers and educators. ACT's policy-related publications cover national topics that describe the implementation of education and workforce solutions or that focus on a single topic. Its research efforts are focused on test and test-item fairness test reliability and validity the meaning of test-score differences improving achievements of at-risk populations and the determinants of academic and career success. For educators ACT conducts free and fee-based research services to help postsecondary institutions recruit and better understand how to serve their students.

Geographic Reach

ACT operates globally from about a dozen US offices and international offices in Seoul Shanghai Singapore and Sydney. The company offers its services in all 50 states and in more than 130 countries worldwide.

On the global front ACT operates ACT International a for-profit subsidiary divided into two divisions: ACT Education Solutions which provides English-language instruction for international students hoping to attend English-speaking universities and ACT Business Solutions which focuses on employers. The latter includes a program English WorkKeys that analyzes key skill abilities and language proficiency of potential employees.

Mergers and Acquisitions

As part of its plan to use technology to improve its products ACT in 2016 acquired OpenEd a K-12 standards-aligned open educational resource provider. OpenEd offers half a million assessments homework assignments videos games and lesson plans to teachers schools and districts across the country.

EXECUTIVES

SVP and CFO, Thomas J. Goedken
COO, Janet E. Godwin
CEO, Marten Roorda
Chief Commercial Officer, Suzana Delanghe
CTO, Lucas Kuhlmann
Chief Officer Center for Equity in Learning, Jim Larimore
Chief Talent Officer, Jennifer Yi Boyer
Assistant Vice President Talent Strategy, Laura Seamans

Assistant Vice President Item Review Test Development, Kelli Ingalls
Vice President of Product Development and Management, David Zasada
Chairman, Robert M. (Bob) Berdahl, age 80
Vice Chairman, Chad P. Wick
Auditors: MCGLADREY LLP CEDAR RAPIDS I

LOCATIONS

HQ: ACT, INC.
500 ACT DR, IOWA CITY, IA 522439003
Phone: 319 337-1000
Web: WWW.ACT.ORG

Selected US Locations
Atlanta
Aurora Colorado
Austin Texas
Chattanooga Tennessee (KeyTrain)
Gahanna Ohio
Hunt Valley Maryland
Iowa City Iowa (headquarters)
Lansing Michigan
Lincolnshire Illinois
Rancho Cordova California
Southborough Massachusetts
Tallahassee Florida
Washington DC

PRODUCTS/OPERATIONS

Selected Programs
ACT Online Prep (practice tests with real ACT®; test questions)
The ACT®; Test (curriculum-based achievement exam that measures skills and knowledge deemed important for college success)
ACT Pro (customized testing services)
ASSET®; (course placement assessment for college and university students)
CAAP (Collegiate Assessment of Academic Proficiency is a standardized nationally normed assessment program)
COMPASS®; (postsecondary placement test)
COMPASS®;/ESL (postsecondary placement test with assessment of English language ability levels)
CoreWork®; Diagnostics (online research-based benchmarking program)
CPAt (career programs assessment test)
Engage; (academic behavior assessment)
Educational Opportunity Service (a tool to help colleges and universities build a pool of qualified prospective students)
EXPLORE®; (career investigation for 8th and 9th grade students)
Global Assessment Certificate; and English Language Programs (GAC - university preparation program for students who do not have English as their first language; ELP - a suite of general and academically oriented English language programs)
KeyTrain®; and Career Ready 101®; (interactive training system for career readiness skills; comprehensive career training course)
NCRC; - NCRC Plus - ICRC (career-readiness certificates)
PLAN®; (pre-ACT for 10th grade students)
QualityCore®; (high school instructional improvement component of ACT's College and Career Readiness System)
Research Services (survey services free and fee-based research services policy reports research and information services for educational institutions)
Scholarship and Recognition Services (consultation in scholarship and recognition program management for organizations)
State Services (Statewide adoption of one or more key ACT assessment products)
WorkKeys®; (workplace skills assessment)

Selected Operations
ACT Centers (training and testing sites)
ACT Education Solutions (English-language education)
National Center for Educational Accountability (public school data collection)

COMPETITORS

Bridges Transitions	Huntington Learning
College Board	Centers
College Coach	Kaplan

ETS	Questar Assessment
Edmentum	S&P Global
Educate	The Princeton Review

HISTORICAL FINANCIALS
Company Type: Private

Income Statement — FYE: August 31

	REVENUE ($ mil.)	NET INCOME ($ mil.)	NET PROFIT MARGIN	EMPLOYEES
08/16	350	17	5.1%	1,200
08/14	328	9	3.0%	—
08/05	179	208	116.2%	—
08/03	151	15	10.2%	—
Annual Growth	6.7%	1.2%	—	—

2016 Year-End Financials

Return on assets: 7.2% Cash ($ mil.): 21
Return on equity: 5.1%
Current ratio: 0.80

ACTION CAPITAL CORPORATION

EXECUTIVES

Chief Executive Officer, Becky J Cronister
Board of Directors, Cicero Garner
Board of Directors, Hugh Inman Jr
Executive Vice-President, Brendan Dete
Auditors: MCGREGOR & COMPANY LLP COLUMB

LOCATIONS

HQ: ACTION CAPITAL CORPORATION
230 PEACHTREE ST NW # 810, ATLANTA, GA 303031568
Phone: 404 524-3181
Web: WWW.ACTIONCAPITAL.COM

HISTORICAL FINANCIALS
Company Type: Private

Income Statement — FYE: December 31

	ASSETS ($ mil.)	NET INCOME ($ mil.)	INCOME AS % OF ASSETS	EMPLOYEES
12/15	140	6	4.3%	17
12/14	128	5	4.6%	—
12/13	125	6	4.9%	—
12/12	109	5	5.1%	—
Annual Growth	8.6%	3.3%	—	—

ACTION FOR BOSTON COMMUNITY DEVELOPMENT, INC.

Action For Boston Community Development (ABCD) strives to make helping others as easy as 1-2-3. The not-for-profit serves more than 100000 low-income people in New England in areas such as advocacy child care consumer services education health and housing. The group operates through a decentralized model that utilizes a city-wide network of Area Planning Action Councils Neighborhood Service Centers and Family Service Centers. It partners with more than a dozen programs like SUMMERWORKS (work experience for low-income teens) Foster Grandparents Urban College of Boston and another 10 or so government agencies. ABCD was established in 1962 as one of several national programs to combat poverty.
Geographic Reach
From its headquarters in Boston ABCD and its affiliates maintain a presence in every Boston neighborhood.
Operations
The organization offers a series of core services and unique programs to Boston neighborhoods and communities. It boasts a network of 14 neighborhood service sites consisting of Neighborhood Service Centers Family Service Centers and Area Planning Action Councils.
Strategy
As it works to cater to the specific needs of these neighborhoods and communities ABCD partners with a pair of affiliate organizations to extend the reach of its services. The John F. Kennedy Family Service Center provides services to the Charlestown area. Catering to the heart of Chinatown the Asian American Civic Association also assists ABCD to boost its capacity.
One initiative of the ABCD group is ensuring that people have heating assistance during the cold winter months. It supplements the funds provided by the federal fuel assistance funds.

EXECUTIVES

Vice President Supply Chain Management, Aja Robinson
Senior Vice President and Group Director, Ted Stocker
Auditors: KPMG LP BOSTON MA

LOCATIONS

HQ: ACTION FOR BOSTON COMMUNITY DEVELOPMENT, INC.
178 TREMONT ST, BOSTON, MA 021111006
Phone: 617 357-6000
Web: WWW.BOSTONABCD.ORG

PRODUCTS/OPERATIONS

Selected Services
Adult Education
Child care choices of Boston
Elder education
Energy and fuel services
Family services
Head start and early childhood education
Health
Housing
Immigration Services
Jobs and Job training
Money management
Nutrition and food
Youth programs

HISTORICAL FINANCIALS
Company Type: Private

Income Statement — FYE: August 31

	REVENUE ($ mil.)	NET INCOME ($ mil.)	NET PROFIT MARGIN	EMPLOYEES
08/15	175	0	0.1%	1,000
08/14	157	0	0.0%	—
08/10	151	(0)	—	—
08/09	143	0	0.2%	—
Annual Growth	3.5%	(2.0%)	—	—

2015 Year-End Financials

Return on assets: 6.7% Cash ($ mil.): 27
Return on equity: 0.1%
Current ratio: 2.20

ACTIONET, INC.

ActioNet provides information technology services such as custom software development computer security assessment network design consulting project management systems integration and design and training. Customers come from industries such as manufacturing retail transportation telecommunications financial services and the public sector. ActioNet was founded in 1998 by president and CEO Ashley Chen. Key customers have included Qwest the Department of Energy and the Department of Labor.

Geographic Reach

ActioNet is based in Vienna Virginia and has offices in the Washington D.C. where many of its federal agency clients are as well as more far flung locations such as New Orleans Honolulu and Guam. The company has employees in 35 states.

Strategy

Part of ActioNet's strategy is to be where the action in. When your client include federal agencies such as U.S. Department of Commerce Department of Defense Department of Energy Department of Transportation and several others that means being in and around the Beltway. The company has new offices in Washington D.C. and in Tysons Corner Virginia.

ActioNet partners with a range of technology companies to offer complementary and comprehensive IT services to clients. Its primary partners are BMC Microsoft Terremark Hewlett-Packard ServiceNow Amazon Symantec and Cisco Systems.

EXECUTIVES

President and CEO, Ashley W. Chen
EVP and CTO, Jeffrey D. (Jeff) Abish
VP and CFO, Steven A. Crespy
Senior Vice President 6 Chlnf Str Wgy Off Icer, Michael Genebach
Vice President and Chief Financial Officer, Kendra Leser
Vice President of Health Services, David Collignon
Vice President of Applied Innovation, Tom Boyce
Auditors: ARONSON LLC

LOCATIONS

HQ: ACTIONET, INC.
 2600 PARK TWR DR STE 1000, VIENNA, VA 22180
Phone: 703 204-0090
Web: WWW.ACTIONET.COM

COMPETITORS

Amadeus Consulting	Leidos
CACI International	Lockheed Martin
Computer Sciences	ManTech
Corp.	Northrop Grumman
HP Enterprise Services	Unisys
IBM Global Services	

HISTORICAL FINANCIALS
Company Type: Private

Income Statement — FYE: December 31

	REVENUE ($ mil.)	NET INCOME ($ mil.)	NET PROFIT MARGIN	EMPLOYEES
12/15	411	32	7.8%	1,352
12/14	352	25	7.2%	—
12/13	298	23	8.0%	—
12/08	23	3	13.4%	—
Annual Growth	50.6%	39.3%	—	—

2015 Year-End Financials

Return on assets: 4.2%   Cash ($ mil.): 48
Return on equity: 7.8%
Current ratio: 4.10

ACTS RETIREMENT-LIFE COMMUNITIES, INC.

No acting here! ACTS is serious about providing seniors with the opportunity to live independently but with a helping hand when needed. ACTS develops owns and operates continuing-care retirement communities (CCRSs) in nine US states along the Eastern Seaboard. The company's properties feature resort-style amenities in Christian environments (ACTS comes from a Biblical reference). One of the largest not-for-profit operators of CCRCs in the US ACTS serves about 8500 older adults at about 25 communities from Pennsylvania to Florida. The not-for-profit organization was founded as Open Door Estates by a group of Pennsylvania church members in 1971.

Operations

Though ACTS' communities are predominantly geared toward independent living (its residents must be able to live safely on their own) all of its community members also have access to skilled nursing and personal care.

ACTS affiliates include Azalea Trace in Florida Heron Point of Chestertown Maryland Lanier Village Estates in Georgia Magnolia Trace in Alabama Park Pointe Village in South Carolina and Peninsula United Methodist Homes in Delaware. ACTS also owns two subsidiaries: ACTS Acquisition Company LLC and Village Nursing Care.

Geographic Reach

Based in West Point Pennsylvania ACTS has retirement communities in Pennsylvania Delaware Maryland North and South Carolina Georgia Alabama New Jersey and Florida. Pennsylvania is home to eight of its communities.

Mergers and Acquisitions

In February 2018 ACTS entered the New Jersey market when it acquired CCRC The Evergreens. That facility was founded in 1919 and includes 200 residences and a 34-bed skilled nursing center.

EXECUTIVES

Board of Directors, Stewart J Stambaugh
Manager, Jo Homa
Vice-Chairman, George R Gunn Jr
Director, John L Esterhai Jr

LOCATIONS

HQ: ACTS RETIREMENT-LIFE COMMUNITIES, INC.
 375 MORRIS RD, WEST POINT, PA 19486
Phone: 215 699-3204
Web: WWW.ACTS-RETIREMENT.ORG

COMPETITORS

AV Homes	Five Star Senior
Brookdale Senior	Living
Living	Golden Horizons
Capital Senior Living	HCP
Diakon Lutheran Social	Life Care Centers
Ministries	PulteGroup
Enlivant	Sunrise Senior Living

HISTORICAL FINANCIALS
Company Type: Private

Income Statement — FYE: December 31

	REVENUE ($ mil.)	NET INCOME ($ mil.)	NET PROFIT MARGIN	EMPLOYEES
12/16	386	(6)	—	5,375
12/15	372	1	0.4%	—
12/14	362	8	2.5%	—
Annual Growth	3.1%	—	—	—

2016 Year-End Financials

Return on assets: 19.1%   Cash ($ mil.): 14
Return on equity: (-1.6%)
Current ratio: —

ADAMS 12 FIVE STAR SCHOOLS

EXECUTIVES

Superintendent, Christopher E Gdowski
Office Manager, Jeanne Morrison
Manager, Sandy Noon
Superintendent, Scharis Gdowski
Assistant Manager, Cathy Ortega
Auditors: CLIFTONLARSONALLEN LLP BROOMF

LOCATIONS

HQ: ADAMS 12 FIVE STAR SCHOOLS
 1500 E 128TH AVE, THORNTON, CO 802412601
Phone: 720 972-4000
Web: WWW.ADAMS12.ORG

HISTORICAL FINANCIALS
Company Type: Private

Income Statement — FYE: June 30

	REVENUE ($ mil.)	NET INCOME ($ mil.)	NET PROFIT MARGIN	EMPLOYEES
06/15	394	24	6.2%	5,040
06/14	379	9	2.4%	—
06/13	376	(5)	—	—
06/12	374	(7)	—	—
Annual Growth	1.8%	—	—	—

ADAMS COMMUNICATION & ENGINEERING TECHNOLOGY, INC.

EXECUTIVES

Chairman, Charles M Adams
Chief Financial Officer, Phuong T Truong
Vice-President, Larry Hunt
Vice-President, John Pellecchia
Vice-President, Michael Seldes
Financial Executive, Reli Suillioti
Auditors: ARONSON LLC ROCKVILLE MARYLA

LOCATIONS

HQ: ADAMS COMMUNICATION & ENGINEERING TECHNOLOGY, INC.
 11637 TERRACE DR STE 201, WALDORF, MD 206023708
Phone: 301 861-5000
Web: WWW.ADAMSCOMM.COM

HISTORICAL FINANCIALS
Company Type: Private

Income Statement
FYE: December 31

	REVENUE ($ mil.)	NET INCOME ($ mil.)	NET PROFIT MARGIN	EMPLOYEES
12/15	231	15	6.5%	400
12/11	15	1	11.8%	—
/ 0	0	—	—	—
Annual Growth	—	—	—	—

2015 Year-End Financials
Return on assets: 7.1% Cash ($ mil.): —
Return on equity: 6.5%
Current ratio: 1.30

ADELPHI UNIVERSITY

It may not house an oracle but Adelphi University hopes to provide answers to students' questions about their future. Founded in 1896 the university has about 7700 students enrolled at its four campuses located in New York (Garden City Hauppage Manhattan and the Hudson Valley). Adelphi University a private institution offers graduate undergraduate and continuing education programs in areas including business management education nursing and social work. Its Swirbul Library contains about 600000 books and documents and 33000 audiovisual materials. The school counts Nextel co-founder Brian McAuley US Chamber of Commerce CEO Thomas Donahue and author Alice Hoffman among its alumni.

Operations
Arts and Sciences and Nursing and the two most popular degree fields at Adelphi. Average annual tuition is about $32000 and the school has an impressive student to teacher ratio of 10 to 1.

Geographic Reach
Students from 43 states and 45 nations attend Adelphi.

Strategy
Given the popularity of its nursing programs and continued growth in the health care field Adelphi is expanding both it physical space for nursing with a new 100000-square-foot College of Nursing and Public Health building and its degrees by adding a Master of Science in Healthcare Informatics online degree in 2013.

Company Background
Adelphi University began in 1863 as the Adelphi Academy a private prep school in Brooklyn.

EXECUTIVES

Provost And Senior Vice President Academic Affairs, Gayle D Insler
Vice President of Administrati, Julianna Claase
Vice President of Internal Affairs, Kristen Weeks
Co Chairman, Andrew Lackmann
Auditors: GRANT THORNTON LLP MELVILLE

LOCATIONS

HQ: ADELPHI UNIVERSITY
1 S AVE LVH 310 310 LVH, GARDEN CITY, NY 11530
Phone: 516 877-3000
Web: WWW.ADELPHI.EDU

PRODUCTS/OPERATIONS

Schools & Colleges
College of Arts and Sciences
Gordon F. Derner Institute of Advanced Psychological Studies
Honors College
School of Business
School of Education
School of Nursing and Public Health
School of Social Work
University College

HISTORICAL FINANCIALS
Company Type: Private

Income Statement
FYE: August 31

	REVENUE ($ mil.)	NET INCOME ($ mil.)	NET PROFIT MARGIN	EMPLOYEES
08/16	199	2	1.3%	1,400
08/15	182	(8)	—	—
08/14	210	23	11.1%	—
08/13	195	13	7.0%	—
Annual Growth	0.6%	(43.3%)	—	—

ADENA HEALTH SYSTEM

Adena Health System serves the residents of some 10 counties in southern and central Ohio centered on the city of Chillicothe. Its main facility is the 261-bed Adena Regional Medical Center which provides general medical and surgical care as well as specialty care in a number of areas including cardiology women's health oncology and rehabilitation. The health system also features two smaller hospitals outpatient clinics surgery centers and a counseling center among other facilities. The history of the Adena Health System goes back to 1895 when a group of local women established an emergency hospital in the wake of a fatal train wreck.

Operations
Adena Health System facilities include three hospitals (located in Chillicothe Waverly and Greenfield) and five regional clinics with a total of 311 beds. Other facilities include Adena Cancer Center Adena Home Care and Hospice and Adena Rehabilitation and Wellness Center.

Geographic Reach
Adena Health caters to the Ohio communities of Chillicothe Circleville Greenfield Jackson Oak Hill Pike Piketon Washington Court House and Waverly.

Financial Performance
In 2013 the system increased its revenue by 6% to $1 billion (over $976 million in 2013) due to an increase in bills submitted to Medicare Medicaid individuals and insurance providers.

Strategy
Like most hospital systems Adena Health is always looking to expand the services it offers patients and add locations. In 2014 it opened a new occupational health facility and an inpatient palliative care unit at its Adena Regional Medical Center.

EXECUTIVES

Division Chair Women's and Children's, Sathish Jetty
VP Adena Regional Medical Center, Nick Alexander
COO, Eric Cecava
CFO, Lisa Carlson
Interim CIO, Ryan Mountjoy
Chief Nursing Officer, Kathleen Dye
Medical Director Adena Cancer Center, Alex Wilson
President and CEO, Jeffrey J. Graham
Operating Room Director, Jeff Collins
Director of Pharmacy, Fred Yingling
Director of Radiology Services, Dave Zanni
Clinic Manager, Tina Agnew
Vice President Payor Integration, James West
Operating Room Director, Heather Wright
Chairman, Steve Burkhardt
Vice Chairman, Virginia Wettersten

LOCATIONS

HQ: ADENA HEALTH SYSTEM
272 HOSPITAL RD, CHILLICOTHE, OH 456019031
Phone: 740 779-7360

PRODUCTS/OPERATIONS

Selected Services
Behavioral Health
Colon and Rectal Services
Endocrinology and Diabetes
Endoscopy Home Care
Hospitalist Laboratory
Occupational Health
Pain Management
Radiology
Rehabilitation Services
Sleep Urology
Surgery and Procedures
Wound Care

Selected Facilities
Adena Counseling Center (Chillicothe)
Adena Health Center - Jackson
Adena Health Center - Oak Hill
Adena Health Center - Waverly
Adena Health Center - Western Avenue (Chillicothe)
Adena Health Pavilion (Chillicothe)
Adena Home Care Services (Chillicothe)
Adena Pike Medical Center (Waverly)
Adena Medical Office Building (Chillicothe)
Adena Regional Medical Center (Chillicothe)
Adena Rehabilitation & Wellness Center (Chillicothe)
Adena Urgent Care Centers (Chillicothe and Waverly)
Greenfield Area Medical Center

COMPETITORS

Catholic Health Initiatives	Mercy Health (OH)
Fairfield Medical Center	Mount Carmel Health
	Nationwide Children's Hospital
Licking Memorial Health Systems	OhioHealth

HISTORICAL FINANCIALS
Company Type: Private

Income Statement
FYE: December 31

	REVENUE ($ mil.)	NET INCOME ($ mil.)	NET PROFIT MARGIN	EMPLOYEES
12/15	393	11	3.0%	2,500
12/14	394	14	3.7%	—
12/13	420	25	6.0%	—
12/09	315	15	5.0%	—
Annual Growth	3.8%	(4.9%)	—	—

2015 Year-End Financials
Return on assets: 7.9% Cash ($ mil.): 40
Return on equity: 3.0%
Current ratio: 0.50

ADVANCED HOME CARE INC.

EXECUTIVES

President, Joel C Mills
Director, Roy Bigler
Financial Executive, Christina Dunn
Manager, Joel Jordan
Manager, Judy Sparks
Manager, Angela Foxx

LOCATIONS

HQ: ADVANCED HOME CARE INC.
4001 PIEDMONT PKWY, HIGH POINT, NC 272659402
Phone: 336 878-8950
Web: WWW.ADVHOMECARE.ORG

HISTORICAL FINANCIALS
Company Type: Private

Income Statement
FYE: September 30

	REVENUE ($ mil.)	NET INCOME ($ mil.)	NET PROFIT MARGIN	EMPLOYEES
09/16	175	4	2.6%	1,700
09/15	173	8	5.2%	—
09/14	167	8	5.0%	—
09/13	162	5	3.7%	—
Annual Growth	2.5%	(9.0%)	—	—

2016 Year-End Financials
Return on assets: 2.1%   Cash ($ mil.): 26
Return on equity: 2.6%
Current ratio: 2.00

ADVANCED TECHNOLOGY INTERNATIONAL

EXECUTIVES

Director, Madelyn B McIntire
Assistant Controller, Diana Kokinda
Vice-President, Jack Corley
Program Manager, Michael Stiteler
Program Manager, John Tuite
Treasurer, Ashley Hannah
Director, Rick Self
Auditors: BDO USA LLP RALEIGH NC

LOCATIONS

HQ: ADVANCED TECHNOLOGY INTERNATIONAL
315 SIGMA DR, SUMMERVILLE, SC 294867790
Phone: 843 760-4500
Web: WWW.ATI.ORG

HISTORICAL FINANCIALS
Company Type: Private

Income Statement
FYE: June 30

	REVENUE ($ mil.)	NET INCOME ($ mil.)	NET PROFIT MARGIN	EMPLOYEES
06/16	423	(2)	—	117
06/15	385	1	0.4%	—
06/14	273	2	1.0%	—
06/13	224	1	0.9%	—
Annual Growth	23.6%	—	—	—

2016 Year-End Financials
Return on assets: 16.2%   Cash ($ mil.): 123
Return on equity: (-0.6%)
Current ratio: 1.00

ADVANTECH CORPORATION

EXECUTIVES

Chief Executive Officer, Ke-Cheng Liu
Manager, Charles Kang
Marketing Manager, Lynette Anderson
Chief Operating Officer, Yizhong Lin
Engineer, David Demint
Director, Mike Bolender

LOCATIONS

HQ: ADVANTECH CORPORATION
380 FAIRVIEW WAY, MILPITAS, CA 950353062
Phone: 408 519-3800
Web: WWW.ADVANTECH.COM.TW

HISTORICAL FINANCIALS
Company Type: Private

Income Statement
FYE: December 31

	REVENUE ($ mil.)	NET INCOME ($ mil.)	NET PROFIT MARGIN	EMPLOYEES
12/15	340	4	1.4%	5,390
12/11	247	5	2.4%	—
12/09	116	0	0.7%	—
12/08	1,158	0	—	—
Annual Growth	(16.1%)	796.4%	—	—

2015 Year-End Financials
Return on assets: 0.5%   Cash ($ mil.): 41
Return on equity: 1.4%
Current ratio: 1.80

ADVENTIST MIDWEST HEALTH

EXECUTIVES

Financial Executive, Randy Johnson
Account Manager, Macuen Tingzon
Supervisor, Cindy Dionne
President, Susan King

LOCATIONS

HQ: ADVENTIST MIDWEST HEALTH
120 N OAK ST, HINSDALE, IL 605213829
Phone: 630 856-9000
Web: WWW.KEEPINGYOUWELL.COM

HISTORICAL FINANCIALS
Company Type: Private

Income Statement
FYE: December 31

	REVENUE ($ mil.)	NET INCOME ($ mil.)	NET PROFIT MARGIN	EMPLOYEES
12/15	289	17	5.9%	2,470
12/14	287	0	0.3%	—
Annual Growth	0.7%	1690.6%	—	—

2015 Year-End Financials
Return on assets: 4.6%   Cash ($ mil.): 64
Return on equity: 5.9%
Current ratio: 1.60

ADVOCATE HEALTH AND HOSPITALS CORPORATION

Advocate Lutheran General Hospital also known simply as Lutheran General provides acute and long-term medical and surgical care to the residents of Park Ridge Illinois and the surrounding northern suburban Chicago area. As one of the largest hospitals in the region Lutheran General boasts nearly 640 beds and a Level I trauma center. Its operations also include a complete children's hospital and pediatric critical care center. Lutheran General serves as a teaching hospital and its specialized programs include oncology cardiology women's health emergency medicine and hospice care. Lutheran General is part of the Advocate Health Care network.

Operations

Lutheran General the sixth largest hospital in the Chicago area is a not-for-profit faith-based organization related to the Evangelical Lutheran Church in America and the United Church of Christ. With some 1150 physicians representing more than 50 specialties and subspecialties Advocate Lutheran General saw 62500 patients in its emergency department in 2012.

That year the company reported more than 29000 admissions 19000 surgeries and more than 4000 births.

Geographic Reach

The hospital system is the primary academic referral hospital for northwest Chicago and north Greater Chicago.

Strategy

Increase its services to meet specific demographics in 2012 Lutheran General opened a new South Asian Cardiovascular Center in the Midwest; it also launched Expressions a program aimed at helping seniors in the early stages of Alzheimer's disease.

That year thee hospital introduced a new Pet Therapy program to the Adult Oncology unit. It also launched of its neuroendovascular program to expand Lutheran General's acute stroke care to provide advanced acute stroke care to patients throughout the northern Chicago area.

Company Background

Lutheran General serves those who live in the northern suburban Chicago area specifically Park Ridge Illinois.

The hospital was founded in 1897.

EXECUTIVES

Director, Michael Wegel
Manager, Alice Sullivan
Manager, Jo Myeong
Manager, Rebecca Loret
Manager, Sharon Spak

LOCATIONS

HQ: ADVOCATE HEALTH AND HOSPITALS CORPORATION
1775 DEMPSTER ST, PARK RIDGE, IL 600681143
Phone: 847 723-6610

Selected Hospitals
Advocate BroMenn Medical Center
Advocate Children's Hospital - Oak Lawn
Advocate Children's Hospital - Park Ridge
Advocate Christ Center for Breast Care
Advocate Christ Medical Center
Advocate Christ Medical Center - Physical Rehabilitation Center Center for Hearing and Sleep Center
Advocate Christ Outpatient Center
Advocate C

Advocate Condell Medical Center
Advocate Eureka Hospital
Advocate Good Samaritan Hospital
Advocate Good Shepherd Hospital
Advocate Illinois Masonic Medical Center
Advocate Lutheran General Hospital
Advocate South Suburban Hospital
Advocate Trinity Hospital

PRODUCTS/OPERATIONS

Selected Services

Adult Day Hospital
Adult Down Syndrome Center
Anticoagulation Center
Behavioral Health
Caldwell Breast Center
Cancer Care
Center for Fetal Care
Children's Services
The Comprehensive Continence Center
Emergency Services
Heart and Vascular
Hyperbaric Treatment
Interventional Radiology
Joint Reconstruction & Replacement
Nutrition Services Opthamology
Outpatient Testing Prep Instructions
Pain Management Center
Rehabilitation
Senior Services
Sleep Disorders
Surgical Services
The Center for Robotic Surgery
Women's Services
Wound Care

COMPETITORS

Children's Hopsital of Chicago	Northwestern Lake Forest Hospital
Gottleib Memorial Hospital	Northwestern Memorial HealthCare
NorthShore University HealthSystem	Rush System for Health
Northwest Community Healthcare	University of Chicago Medical Center

HISTORICAL FINANCIALS

Company Type: Private

Income Statement   FYE: December 31

	REVENUE ($ mil.)	NET INCOME ($ mil.)	NET PROFIT MARGIN	EMPLOYEES
12/15	752	104	13.9%	4,818
12/14	741	107	14.5%	—
12/02	2,603	(6)	—	—
Annual Growth	(9.1%)	—	—	—

2015 Year-End Financials

Return on assets: 41.8%   Cash ($ mil.): 120
Return on equity: 13.9%
Current ratio: 0.50

ADVOCATE HEALTH CARE NETWORK

Advocating wellness in Chicagoland from Palos Heights to Palatine Advocate Health Care is a not-for-profit integrated health care network with more than 250 care sites serving the Chicago and surrounding areas. Advocate's operations include about a dozen acute and specialty care hospitals (including Christ Medical Center Hope Children's Hospital Advocate BroMenn Medical Center and Lutheran General Hospital) with more than 3550 beds as well as community health clinics and home health care and hospice services. The health system includes the largest physician network of primary care physicians specialists and sub-specialists in the state. Advocate Health plans to merge with Wisconsin-based Aurora Health Care.

Operations
Along with providing the full spectrum of health care services Advocate Health has a clinical laboratory joint venture ACL Laboratories with Aurora Health Care. ACL provides analytical and diagnostic testing services for both companies' facilities.

With more than 35000 associates the company is one of the largest employers in the Chicago area. Its staff includes 6300 affiliated physicians and more than 10000 nurses.

The system has teaching affiliations with area medical schools such as the University of Illinois at Chicago and the University of Chicago Pritzker School of Medicine. Its three major teaching hospitals — Christ Medical Center Illinois Masonic Medical Center and Lutheran General Hospital — train 600 residents and fellows per year and provide more than 1600 medical student rotations annually

Geographic Reach
Advocate Health operates more than 250 care sites serving Chicago and surrounding areas. Physician group Advocate Medical Group part of Advocate Health has more than 1200 physicians and specialists; it operates in more than 300 neighborhood-based practices that are located throughout Chicagoland and Bloomington and Normal Indiana.

Financial Performance
In 2014 Advocate Health's revenue increased 6% to $5.2 billion (over $4.9 billion in 2013); a 7% increase in patient service revenues and a 6% increase in capitation revenues primarily drove that growth but the increases were partially offset by declines in other operating revenues.

Strategy
Advocate Health has grown through a series of acquisitions; recent purchases have included central Illinois health network BroMenn Healthcare System the 280-bed Condell Medical Center the Midwest Physician Group (now part of the Advocate Medical Group division) and Sherman Health Systems.

The system also expands its presence through partnerships. In 2014 it launched a clinical affiliation with Silver Cross Hospital boosting its Advocate Physicians' Partners (APP) organization's clinical integration program. As part of the partnership Silver Cross Hospital was clinically integrated with APP and Advocate Health (but it stopped short of becoming part of the system itself).

In 2017 Advocate Health dropped its plans to merge with NorthShore University Health System another Illinois hospital operator. The combination would have created a 16-hospital market leader in Chicago's North Shore area. The merger was blocked by the FTC which claimed that it would harm consumers by raising prices and lowering health care quality.

Later that year Advocate Health and Wisconsin-based Aurora Health Care agreed to combined forces. The merged company to be named Advocate Aurora Health Care will operate 27 hospitals and more than 500 care sites; it will serve nearly 3 million patient annually. The two companies already have a working relationship through their ACL Laboratories joint venture.

Company Background
Advocate Health was formed in 1995 by the United Church of Christ and the Evangelical Lutheran Church in America.

EXECUTIVES

EVP and Chief Medical Officer; President Advocate Physician Partners, Lee B. Sacks
SVP CFO Treasurer, Dominic J. Nakis
President Advocate Condell Medical Center, Ann Errichetti
President Advocate Good Shepherd Hospital, Karen A. Lambert
President Advocate Home Health Services, Denise M. Keefe
President Advocate Physician Partners, Martin F. (Marty) Manning, age 62
President Advocate Medical Group, James R. Dan
President recognized associates, John Bruss
SVP and Chief Marketing Officer, Kelly Jo Golson
President Dreyer Clinic, Donna Copper
President ACL Laboratories, Barbara Bigler
COO, Dana Gilbert
Vice President Human Resources Operations, Robin Fell
Vice President Physician and Ambulatory Services, Lois Elia
Vice President Advocate Operating System, Alex Andrade
Vice President of Clinical Effectiveness, Debra Oconnor
Senior Vice President and General Counsel, Earl Barnes
Medical Director, Martin Doot
Medical Director, Alvia Siddiqui
Managing Director, Nimit Aggarwal
Vice President of Finance and Ambulatory Division, Neil Beck
Advocate Medical Group Interim Vice President Operations South Region, Amy Place
Director of Pharmacy, William Forslev
Medical Director Cardiology, Patrick Fenner
VP GLOBAL APPLICATIONS, Jennifer Steinman
Pharmacy Manager, Paul Miller
Vice President Research, William Summerfelt
Vice President Operations, Karen Moore
Vice President Cardiovascular Service Line, Dawn Imburgia
Vice President Professional Arrangements Professional Arrangements, Peg Stone
Medical Director of Women and Childrens Services, Julie Ms
Auditors: ERNST & YOUNG LLP CHICAGO IL

LOCATIONS

HQ: ADVOCATE HEALTH CARE NETWORK
3075 HIGHLAND PKWY FL 6, DOWNERS GROVE, IL 605155563
Phone: 630 572-9393
Web: WWW.ADVOCATEHEALTH.COM

PRODUCTS/OPERATIONS

Selected Locations

Advocate BroMenn Medical Center (Normal Illinois) - 221 beds
Advocate Christ Medical Center (Oak Lawn Illinois) - 695 beds
Advocate Condell Medical Center (Libertyville Illinois) - 281 beds
Advocate Good Samaritan Hospital (Downers Grove Illinois) -340 beds
Advocate Eureka Hospital (Eureka Illinois)- 25 beds
Advocate Good Shepherd Hospital (Barrington Illinois) - 183 beds
AdvoAdvocate Hope Children's Hospital (Oak Lawn Illinois)
Advocate Illinois Masonic Medical Center (Chicago Illinois) -408 beds
Advocate Lutheran General Hospital (Park Ridge Illinois) - 639 beds
Advocate Sherman Hospital (ElginIllinois)- 225 beds
Advocate South Suburban Hospital (Hazel Crest Illinois) - 284 beds
Advocate Trinity Hospital (Chicago Illinois) - 250 beds

COMPETITORS

Alexian Brothers Health System	Mercy Hospital and Medical Center
Central DuPage Hospital	NorthShore University HealthSystem
Children's Hospital of Chicago	Northwest Community Healthcare
Covenant Ministries	Northwestern Lake Forest Hospital
Elmhurst Memorial Healthcare	Northwestern Memorial HealthCare
Gottlieb Memorial Hospital	Pronger Smith
HCA	Rush System for Health
Hospital Sisters Health System	SSM Health Care
	Silver Cross Hospital
KishHealth	Sinai Health System
Loyola University Health System	University of Chicago Medical Center

HISTORICAL FINANCIALS

Company Type: Private

Income Statement

FYE: December 31

	REVENUE ($ mil.)	NET INCOME ($ mil.)	NET PROFIT MARGIN	EMPLOYEES
12/15	5,392	60	1.1%	25,000
12/06	3,268	286	8.8%	—
12/05	2,973	140	4.7%	—
Annual Growth	6.1%	(8.1%)	—	—

2015 Year-End Financials

Return on assets: 7.7%
Return on equity: 1.1%
Current ratio: 0.60

Cash ($ mil.): 203

AEROTEK, INC.

Aerotek a unit of staffing powerhouse Allegis Group offers commercial and technical staffing services throughout North America. Through several divisions Aerotek staffs workers such as engineers mechanics scientists and technical professionals as well as administrative staff members general laborers and tradespeople. The company also provides training and support services. Along with aerospace auto and engineering companies Aerotek's clients include companies from the construction energy manufacturing health care and finance industries.

Geographic Reach

Aerotek is headquartered in Hanover Maryland. The company has office locations in Asia Australia Europe and North America. Aerotek also operates a network of more than 250 non-franchised offices.

Sales and Marketing

Aerotek serves a wide variety of industries including the accounting construction engineering financial services government and public administration health care manufacturing and pharmaceutical industries among others. The company serves more than 18000 clients and 300000 contract employees every year.

Strategy

Aerotek has expanded its operations over the years through organic growth and acquisitions especially in niche markets such as the biotechnology health care clinical research chemical and plastics sectors. Despite the economic downturn demand within these industries has been consistent along with engineering giving Aerotek some continuity during the recession. Aerotek has also widened its client focus to include the niche market of minority and woman-owned companies.

EXECUTIVES

VP Technical and Professional Services, Mark Cooper
President, Todd M. Mohr
CFO, Thomas B. (Tom) Kelly
SVP Operations, John Flanigan
Regional VP Northeast, John Rudy
Regional VP Midwest, Marty Schager
Regional VP Central, Mike Hansen
Regional VP West, Tony Bartolucci
Regional VP Northwest, Brooks Wells
VP Canada, Bryan Toffey
Regional VP Southwest, Brad Kennedy
Regional VP Mid-Atlantic, Jeff Colvin
Regional VP Southeast, Greg Jones
Senior Vice President And Project Director, Lori Clanton
Auditors: PRICEWATERHOUSECOOPERS LLP B

LOCATIONS

HQ: AEROTEK, INC.
7301 PARKWAY DR, HANOVER, MD 210761159
Phone: 410 694-5100

PRODUCTS/OPERATIONS

INDUSTRIES SERVED

Accounting
Administrative & Support Services
Aerospace Aviation & Defense
Architecture & Design
Automotive
Construction
Customer Service
Energy & Utilities
Engineering
Environmental
Financial Services
Government & Public Administration
Healthcare
Manufacturing
Pharmaceutical
Sciences
Warehouse & Distribution

COMPETITORS

AMN Healthcare	MSX International
Adecco	ManpowerGroup
Bryant Bureau	On Assignment
CDI	Pinnacle Staffing
COMFORCE	Randstad Holding
Kelly Services	Robert Half
Kforce	

HISTORICAL FINANCIALS

Company Type: Private

Income Statement

FYE: December 31

	REVENUE ($ mil.)	NET INCOME ($ mil.)	NET PROFIT MARGIN	EMPLOYEES
12/15	5,492	0	—	4,200
12/14	5,353	0	—	—
12/13	5,268	0	—	—
12/12	5,119	307	6.0%	—
Annual Growth	2.4%	—	—	—

2015 Year-End Financials

Return on assets: 1.2%
Return on equity: —
Current ratio: 3.40

Cash ($ mil.): 14

AFFILIATED FOODS MIDWEST COOPERATIVE, INC.

Affiliated Foods Midwest Cooperative is a wholesale food distribution cooperative that supplies more than 800 independent grocers in some 15 states in the Midwest. From its handful of distribution centers in Kansas Nebraska and Wisconsin the co-op distributes fresh produce meats deli items baked goods dairy products and frozen foods as well as general merchandise and equipment. It distributes goods under the Shurfine brand (from Topco Associates) and IGA labels. Additionally Affiliated Foods Midwest provides marketing merchandising and warehousing support services for its members. The cooperative was formed in 1931 to make wholesale purchases for a group of retailers in Nebraska.

Geographic Reach

Norfolk Nebraska-based Affiliated Foods Midwest Cooperative has distribution centers in Norfolk Elwood Kansas and Kenosha Wisconsin. It serves customers in 15 states across the Midwest.

Financial Performance

Affiliated Foods Midwest rang up an estimated $1.6 billion in sales in fiscal 2013 (ended June).

EXECUTIVES

Vice President Of Information Technology, Linda Mattson
Auditors: BKD LLP LINCOLN NEBRASKA

LOCATIONS

HQ: AFFILIATED FOODS MIDWEST COOPERATIVE, INC.
1301 W OMAHA AVE, NORFOLK, NE 687015872
Phone: 402 371-0555
Web: WWW.AFMIDWEST.COM

PRODUCTS/OPERATIONS

Selected Private-Label Brands

CharKing
ChuckWagon (pet food)
Clear Value
Cow Belle Creamery (ice cream)
Domestix (household products)
Full Circle (organic natural products)
IGA
PAWS Premium (pet products)
Shurfine
TopCare (OTC drugs health and beauty)
Valu Time
Wide Awake Coffee Co. (coffee)
World Classics Trading Company

COMPETITORS

Associated Wholesale Grocers	Kroger
C&S Wholesale	McLane
Central Grocers	SUPERVALU
Certco	Wal-Mart
Dearborn Wholesale Grocers	

HISTORICAL FINANCIALS
Company Type: Private

Income Statement				FYE: June 26
	REVENUE ($ mil.)	NET INCOME ($ mil.)	NET PROFIT MARGIN	EMPLOYEES
06/15	1,527	1	0.1%	850
06/14	1,477	2	0.2%	—
06/13	1,391	2	0.2%	—
06/12	1,486	2	0.2%	—
Annual Growth	0.9%	(19.5%)	—	—

AGLAND CO-OP, INC.

EXECUTIVES

President, Jeffrey Osentoski
Assistant Treasurer, Robin Hanely
Chief Financial Officer, Ron Angelilli
Auditors: FOUR-FIFTEEN GROUP CANTON OH

LOCATIONS

HQ: AGLAND CO-OP, INC.
364 LISBON ST, CANFIELD, OH 444061422
Phone: 330 533-5551
Web: WWW.AGLAND.COOP

HISTORICAL FINANCIALS
Company Type: Private

Income Statement				FYE: August 31
	REVENUE ($ mil.)	NET INCOME ($ mil.)	NET PROFIT MARGIN	EMPLOYEES
08/15	269	4	1.8%	129
08/14	280	3	1.1%	—
08/13	0	0	—	—
08/12	0	0	—	—
Annual Growth	—	—	—	—

2015 Year-End Financials
Return on assets: 4.0%
Return on equity: 1.8%
Current ratio: 0.80
Cash ($ mil.): 1

AGMARK, LLC

EXECUTIVES

Board of Directors, Cloud County Co-Op
Board of Directors, Randall Co-Op
Board of Directors, Jeff Bechard
Board of Directors, Robert Johnson
Board of Directors, Arthur Thompson
Manager, Sharra Odle
Operations Manager, Derek Sandmann
Accountant, Teri Bell
Manager, Mark Hafliger
Auditors: LINDBURG VOGEL PIERCE FARIS H

LOCATIONS

HQ: AGMARK, LLC
118 W MAIN ST, BELOIT, KS 674202745
Phone: 785 738-9641
Web: WWW.AGMARKLLC.COM

HISTORICAL FINANCIALS
Company Type: Private

Income Statement				FYE: January 31
	REVENUE ($ mil.)	NET INCOME ($ mil.)	NET PROFIT MARGIN	EMPLOYEES
01/16	314	23	7.4%	27
01/15	334	18	5.6%	—
01/14	399	20	5.1%	—
01/13	442	18	4.1%	—
Annual Growth	(10.8%)	8.6%	—	—

2016 Year-End Financials
Return on assets: 0.4%
Return on equity: 7.4%
Current ratio: —
Cash ($ mil.): —

AGRI-AFC, LLC

EXECUTIVES

President, Mike Malone
Board of Directors, Bob Kincade
Board of Directors, Jodi Hanson
Board of Directors, Melodee Cannon
Board of Directors, Micki Mathiesen
Board of Directors, Robin Pachuta
Board of Directors, Susan Spaniol
Manager, Gary Wigley
Manager, Mitch Raby

LOCATIONS

HQ: AGRI-AFC, LLC
121 SOMERVILLE RD NE, DECATUR, AL 356012659
Phone: 256 560-2848
Web: WWW.AGRI-AFC.COM

HISTORICAL FINANCIALS
Company Type: Private

Income Statement				FYE: July 31
	REVENUE ($ mil.)	NET INCOME ($ mil.)	NET PROFIT MARGIN	EMPLOYEES
07/16	339	11	3.4%	165
07/15	344	8	2.5%	—
07/14	343	13	3.8%	—
07/13	328	10	3.1%	—
Annual Growth	1.1%	5.0%	—	—

2016 Year-End Financials
Return on assets: 10.6%
Return on equity: 3.4%
Current ratio: 0.80
Cash ($ mil.): —

AHMC GARFIELD MEDICAL CENTER LP

EXECUTIVES

General Partner, Philip Cohen
Partner, Steve Maekewa
Director, Martin Cheung
Director, Michael Liu
Director, Alethea Hsu
Auditor, Gloria Stiles
Engineer, Joe Quijada

LOCATIONS

HQ: AHMC GARFIELD MEDICAL CENTER LP
525 N GARFIELD AVE, MONTEREY PARK, CA 917541202
Phone: 626 573-2222

HISTORICAL FINANCIALS
Company Type: Private

Income Statement				FYE: June 30
	REVENUE ($ mil.)	NET INCOME ($ mil.)	NET PROFIT MARGIN	EMPLOYEES
06/15*	204	28	14.1%	150
05/05	0	0	30.3%	—
Annual Growth	178.0%	157.5%	—	—
*Fiscal year change				

2015 Year-End Financials
Return on assets: 3.1%
Return on equity: 14.1%
Current ratio: 1.10
Cash ($ mil.): 109

AIDS HEALTHCARE FOUNDATION

EXECUTIVES

Chief Executive Officer, Michael Arthur Weinstein
Director, Kenny Burns
Director, Marlene Lalota
Auditors: VASQUEZ & COMPANY LLP LOS ANG

LOCATIONS

HQ: AIDS HEALTHCARE FOUNDATION
6255 W SUNSET BLVD FL 21, LOS ANGELES, CA 900287422
Phone: 323 860-5200
Web: WWW.AIDSHEALTH.ORG

HISTORICAL FINANCIALS
Company Type: Private

Income Statement				FYE: December 31
	REVENUE ($ mil.)	NET INCOME ($ mil.)	NET PROFIT MARGIN	EMPLOYEES
12/15	1,039	56	5.4%	2,331
12/14	879	30	3.5%	—
12/13	772	16	2.1%	—
12/12	515	29	5.7%	—
Annual Growth	26.4%	24.1%	—	—

2015 Year-End Financials
Return on assets: 5.8%
Return on equity: 5.4%
Current ratio: 0.40
Cash ($ mil.): 31

AIKEN COUNTY SCHOOL DISTRICT

EXECUTIVES

Superintendent, Elizabeth Everitt
Personnel Manager, Grady Belger
Personnel Manager, John Heron

Superintendent, Rose Puckett
Superintendent, Vicky Durden
Plant & Facilities Manager, Kip Gunter
Superintendent, Sean Alford

LOCATIONS

HQ: AIKEN COUNTY SCHOOL DISTRICT
1000 BROOKHAVEN DR, AIKEN, SC 298032108
Phone: 803 641-2428
Web: WWW.AIKENCOUNTYSC.GOV

HISTORICAL FINANCIALS
Company Type: Private

Income Statement

	REVENUE ($ mil.)	NET INCOME ($ mil.)	NET PROFIT MARGIN	EMPLOYEES
				FYE: June 30
06/16	249	100	40.2%	3,050
06/10	203	11	5.6%	—
06/09	203	5	2.6%	—
06/04	0	0	—	—
Annual Growth	—	203.8%	—	—

2016 Year-End Financials

Return on assets: 2.2%   Cash ($ mil.): 117
Return on equity: 40.2%
Current ratio: 4.00

AIMCO PROPERTIES, L.P.

AIMCO Properties' aim is true. The company is the operating arm of multifamily real estate giant Apartment Investment and Management Company (AIMCO) which owns and/or manages some 500 apartment properties (with nearly 94000 individual units) throughout the US. AIMCO Properties holds most of AIMCO's assets and manages its day-to-day operations including property management and asset management. Its portfolio includes suburban apartment communities urban high-rise properties and government-subsidized affordable housing properties. Investment management operations include management of its own portfolio as well as services for affiliated partnerships. AIMCO controls more than 90% of AIMCO Properties.

EXECUTIVES

Board Member, Cara M Nelson
Auditors: ERNST & YOUNG LLP DENVER COL

LOCATIONS

HQ: AIMCO PROPERTIES, L.P.
4582 S ULSTER ST STE 1100, DENVER, CO 802372662
Phone: 303 757-8101

COMPETITORS

AMLI Residential	Home Properties
Alliance Residential	LEDIC
Berkshire Income Realty	Simpson Housing Trammell Crow Residential
Camden Property	
Education Realty	Transcontinental
Equity Residential	Realty

HISTORICAL FINANCIALS
Company Type: Private

Income Statement

	ASSETS ($ mil.)	NET INCOME ($ mil.)	INCOME AS % OF ASSETS	EMPLOYEES
				FYE: December 31
12/16	6,232	483	7.8%	15,301
12/15	6,144	271	4.4%	—
12/14	6,097	356	5.8%	—
12/13	6,079	237	3.9%	—
Annual Growth	0.8%	26.7%	—	—

2016 Year-End Financials

Return on assets: 3.7%   Sales ($ mil): 995
Return on equity: 48.5%

ALASKA NATIVE TRIBAL HEALTH CONSORTIUM

The Alaska Native Tribal Health Consortium (ANTHC) brings good health to Alaska Natives. The company is a not-for-profit statewide health care organization managed by regional tribal governments and their respective regional health organizations. The organization connects disparate medical providers by providing a range of health programs and services including community health care public health advocacy and education initiatives health research (including water and sanitation) and medical supply distribution. The 150-bed Alaska Native Medical Center (ANMC) a native-owned hospital is jointly managed by ANTHC and Southcentral Foundation a regional health corporation based in the Cook Inlet region.

Operations

ANMC's services are reserved primarily for Alaska Native Tribal groups with the exception of its Urgent Care centers and Emergency Room. (Emergency rooms are compelled to take patients of all types under US fair care guidelines.) The hospital handles about 8000 patient admissions each year as well as 300000 outpatient and 57000 emergency room visits. It also conducts some 11000 surgeries and 1600 births. ANMC has about 100 physicians.

The organization's primary mission is to improve the health of Alaska natives through health sanitation technology and advocacy services. It conducts a number of community outreach programs and it works to create a continuum of care for its members so they can move smoothly through the health care process (including initial specialist and follow-up care visits). The hospital is the regional hub of that health care continuum offering general and specialist care in a range of fields. ANTHC also operates outpatient care centers and it operates an extensive telemedicine network (allow providers to care for and consult with patients in outlying areas).

ANTHC provides administrative support to Alaska's Tribal health groups and it supports state legislative efforts such as the reauthorization of the Indian Health Care Improvement Act. The consortium formed in 1997 also works to improve the Alaskan health system by participating in strategic summit meetings and sponsoring electronic health record initiatives.

Geographic Reach

ANTHC and ANMC are located in Anchorage Alaska. The organization provides services throughout the state.

Financial Performance

The company's 2014 revenues stood at $643 million about 33% of which came from patient revenues. Other major operating segments include compact revenue (25% of sales) and grant and project income (17%).

Strategy

Infrastructure and service expansions are a key means of growth for ANTHC.

In 2015 ANTHC awarded Neeser Construction Inc. a contract to build the new ANMC patient housing facility on the Alaska Native Health Campus in Anchorage. The building will house patients and their families travelling to ANMC for medical care. The a new patient housing facility is expected to open in fall 2016. It will have 202 private rooms and six floors with a dedicated floor for new families.

In 2015 Alaska Governor Walker introduced legislation declaring his plan for Medicaid reform and expansion. ANTHC supports the Governor's efforts to expand Medicaid coverage to more than 41000 Alaskans.

Company Background

In 2012 ANMC expanded its maternal child health and neurosurgery departments due to increasing patient populations in the Anchorage area. In 2010 the medical center opened the only Level II trauma center in Alaska making it a referral hospital for major trauma cases.

The organization has also improved its health care technology resources; it expanded the use of electronic health records at ANMC in 2012 and it is expanding its telemedicine operations (as telemedicine is becoming an increasingly popular way for specialists to see patients without the expense of a personal visit). It has increased other community outreach efforts as well such as smoking cessation and behavioral health programs.

EXECUTIVES

VP Professional and Support Services Alaska Native Medical Center hospital, Vivian Echavarria
CFO, Garvin Federenko
CEO and Administrator, Roald Helgesen
CIO, Stewart Ferguson
Chief Medical Officer, Paul Franke
Chief Nursing Executive Alaska Native Medical Center hospital, Richard Hall
Chairman and President, Andy Teuber
Vice Chairman, Lincoln A. Bean
Auditors: BDO USA LP ANCHORAGE AK

LOCATIONS

HQ: ALASKA NATIVE TRIBAL HEALTH CONSORTIUM
4000 AMBASSADOR DR, ANCHORAGE, AK 995085909
Phone: 907 729-1900
Web: WWW.ANTHC.ORG

PRODUCTS/OPERATIONS

2014 Sales

	$ mil.	% of total
Patient revenue	213	33
Compact revenue	161	25
Grant & project revenue	109	17
Warehouse revenue	22	3
Investment income	4	1
Other	133	21
Total	**643**	**100**

Selected Services

Ear Nose Throat
Emergency and Trauma
Family Medicine
Imaging and Laboratory Services
Internal Medicine Clinic
Maternal Fetal Medicine
OB/GYN Services
Oncology
Orthopedics Clinic
Pediatric ICU

Pediatrics
Pharmacy Services
Pregnancy and Childbirth
Primary Care Services
Respiratory Care

COMPETITORS

HCA	South Peninsula
Immediate Care	Hospital
PeaceHealth	Tenet Healthcare
Providence St. Joseph	
Health	

HISTORICAL FINANCIALS

Company Type: Private

Income Statement

FYE: September 30

	REVENUE ($ mil.)	NET INCOME ($ mil.)	NET PROFIT MARGIN	EMPLOYEES
09/15	511	3	0.7%	1,850
09/14	618	154	24.9%	—
09/13	459	21	4.6%	—
09/12	447	21	4.9%	—
Annual Growth	4.6%	(46.4%)	—	—

2015 Year-End Financials

Return on assets: 15.1%   Cash ($ mil.): 127
Return on equity: 0.7%
Current ratio: 1.20

ALASKA PERMANENT FUND CORPORATION

EXECUTIVES

Chief Executive Officer, Angela Rodell
Financial Executive, John Seagren
Administration Director, Kathy Thatcher
Director, David Fallace
Principal, Chris Poag
Auditors: KPMG LLP ANCHORAGE AK

LOCATIONS

HQ: ALASKA PERMANENT FUND CORPORATION
801 W 10TH ST STE 302, JUNEAU, AK 998011878
Phone: 907 796-1500
Web: WWW.APFC.ORG

HISTORICAL FINANCIALS

Company Type: Private

Income Statement

FYE: June 30

	ASSETS ($ mil.)	NET INCOME ($ mil.)	INCOME AS % OF ASSETS	EMPLOYEES
06/16	55,346	(30)	—	50
06/15	55,900	1,586	2.8%	—
06/14	54,614	6,360	11.6%	—
06/13	49,797	4,520	9.1%	—
Annual Growth	3.6%	—	—	—

ALBANY MEDICAL CENTER

Albany Medical Center (AMC) provides medical care in upstate New York. Serving residents of northeastern New York and western New England the health system has at its heart the 730-bed Al-

bany Medical Center Hospital. The general medical-surgical facility also provides specialty care in such areas as oncology rehabilitation and organ transplantation. AMC also features a children's hospital an outpatient surgery center and a group medical practice. It employs some 400 full-time physicians. Its Albany Medical College is one of the nation's first private medical schools. It offers undergraduate and graduate medical degrees and residency programs as well as fellowships and continuing medical education.

Operations

AMC's assets includes a biomedical research enterprise and one of the region's largest physicians practices with more than 400 doctors. Its physicians have extensive training and experience in 34 subspecialties of pediatric medicine. The system's subsidiaries include the Albany Medical Center Kidskeller Corporation a not-for-profit day care facility and Madison Avenue Services Corporation a taxable corporation.

AMC is affiliated with several community physician groups including Albany Vascular Group Capital Cardiology Associates and Capital Region Orthopaedic Group.

In 2013 the system reported some 33000 admissions 581000 outpatient visits 28000 surgical cases and 68000 emergency department visits.

Geographic Reach

AMC offers services in 25 counties in northeastern New York and western New England. In addition to treating patients at the main site in Albany providers also treat patients at community-based locations throughout the region including Clifton Park Latham Malta North Greenbush Delmar and others.

Sales and Marketing

HMOs account for around a third of net patient revenue while Medicare and Medicaid represent about 20% and 15% respectively.

Financial Performance

The company's revenues grew by 3% to $752 million in 2013 (versus $728 million in 2012) due to an increase in net patient revenue; this was partially offset by declines in interest income dividends and other revenue. Net income grew 21% to $63 million in 2013 as net realized gains on sales of securities and impairment charges rose. Other gains were made in pension-related changes and net unrealized gains and losses in investments.

Cash flow from operations fell 55% that year to $37 million as more was used in receivables and other liabilities.

Strategy

AMC grows through organic expansion partnerships and product initiatives. The company is in the midst of a $360 million expansion including a new patient tower with more than 100 beds and increased intensive care resources. The project — expected to last several years — will also increase Albany Medical Center Hospital's bed count to more than 700.

In 2014 The Neurology Group and The Endocrine Group joined AMC's Albany Med Faculty Physician Group.

AMC and Union Graduate College joined forces in 2013 to offer a new joint degree combining medical school with an MBA.

That year AMC and Saratoga Hospital formed a joint venture and opened the $17.5 million Malta Med Emergent Care to provide area residents an alternative to hospital emergency rooms for all but the most serious medical circumstances.

On the product innovation side in 2013 AMC introduced advanced imaging technologies in a pair of its new Patient Pavilion operating rooms that provide for greater precision and patient safety during brain and spinal surgeries.

Also that year the company opened a Chronic Kidney Disease Clinic as the sole source for com-

prehensive care for 6000 people in its service area suffering from the slow loss of kidney function.

AMC also engages in research and development of new pharmaceuticals through partnerships with companies like Aegis Therapeutics with which it is developing an anti-obesity peptide to benefit patients with type 2 diabetes. The college's research department is also studying brain mapping techniques as well as Alzheimer's disease vascular disease and cancer and multiple sclerosis treatments.

Company Background

AMC which produced Nobel prize winners in both 2009 and 2011 annually awards its own $500000 prize the largest monetary award in medicine and biomedical research in the US. In 2010 combined federal-state entities awarded the center $10 million the center's largest grant since its founding which will be used to expand research labs at Albany Medical College.

AMC's status as the Capital Region's reigning health care giant was toppled by the 2011 merger of four locals hospitals to form St. Peter's Health Partners with nearly 12000 employees vs. 6000 at AMC. Post merger the newly-merged group has nearly 50% of the Capital Region market while AMC has 25%. While AMC is no longer the area's largest hospital as the region's trauma center and only medical school it continues to draw many patients from outside the four-county area.

Albany Medical College was formed in 1839; the hospital's predecessor was formed in 1849. The two combined under the AMC umbrella in 1982.

EXECUTIVES

President and CEO, James J. Barba
COO, Gary J. Kochem
EVP and CFO, William C. Hasselbarth
EVP and CIO, George T. Hickman
EVP IDS and Hospital Systems General Director, Steven M. Frisch
EVP Policy Planning and Communications, Kim Fine
SVP Hospital Business Services and COO Hospital, Bernadette Pedlow
Dean and EVP Health Affairs, Vincent Verdile
SVP and Chief Nursing Officer, Mary Ellen Plass
Senior Vice President and Chief Compliance Officer, Noel Hogan
Assistant Vice President Deve, Vicki Messick
Vice President Communications, Jeffrey Gordon
Vice President Information System, Dennis Delisle
Vice President, Michael Gruenthal
Chairman, Robert Cushing
Auditors: KPMG LLP ALBANY NY

LOCATIONS

HQ: ALBANY MEDICAL CENTER
43 NEW SCOTLAND AVE, ALBANY, NY 122083478
Phone: 518 262-3125
Web: WWW.AMC.EDU

PRODUCTS/OPERATIONS

2013 Sales

	% of total
Net patient service	96
Inter-institutional	1
Interest & dividends	.
Other	2
Net assets released from restrictions	1
Total	**100**

2013 Net Patient Service Revenue

	% of total
Health maintenance organizations	32
Medicare	19
Medicaid	15
Blue Cross and Blue Shield	14
Commercial carriers	9
No fault & worker's compensation	5
Private pay	2
Other third-party payors	4
Total	**100**

Selected Services

Cancer center
Children's Hospital
Center for Donation and Transplant
Diabetes service
Emergency medical services
Hearing center
HIV medicine
Pain management
Perinatal
Physical therapy
Radiology
Rheumatology
Surgical
Trauma center
Women's wellness center

COMPETITORS

Berkshire Health
  Systems
Ellis Hospital
SUNY Upstate Medical
  University
Southwestern Vermont
  Health Care

St. Joseph's Hospital
  Health Center
St. Peter's Health
  Partners
United Health Services
  Hospitals

HISTORICAL FINANCIALS

Company Type: Private

Income Statement

FYE: December 31

	REVENUE ($ mil.)	NET INCOME ($ mil.)	NET PROFIT MARGIN	EMPLOYEES
12/15	1,167	5	0.5%	7,000
12/13	980	115	11.7%	—
12/12	935	76	8.1%	—
Annual Growth	7.7%	(58.5%)	—	—

2015 Year-End Financials

Return on assets: 5.8%
Return on equity: 0.5%
Current ratio: 1.10

Cash ($ mil.): 123

ALBANY MEDICAL CENTER HOSPITAL

EXECUTIVES

President, James J Barba
Board of Directors, Sabine Needham
VP Finance, Fran Albert
Financial Executive, Patrick Kelly
Manager, Donna Harat
Director, Jennifer Cassin
Auditors: KPMG LLP ALBANY NY

LOCATIONS

HQ: ALBANY MEDICAL CENTER HOSPITAL
  43 NEW SCOTLAND AVE, ALBANY, NY 122083478
Phone: 518 262-3125
Web: WWW.AMC.EDU

HISTORICAL FINANCIALS

Company Type: Private

Income Statement

FYE: December 31

	REVENUE ($ mil.)	NET INCOME ($ mil.)	NET PROFIT MARGIN	EMPLOYEES
12/15	893	16	1.9%	1,568
12/14	812	51	6.3%	—
12/13	773	26	3.4%	—
12/09	604	15	2.5%	—
Annual Growth	6.7%	1.9%	—	—

2015 Year-End Financials

Return on assets: 6.0%
Return on equity: 1.9%
Current ratio: 1.20

Cash ($ mil.): 60

ALBERICI CONSTRUCTORS, INC.

EXECUTIVES

President, Gregory J Kozicz
Vice-President, Alan D Gough
General Manager, Daniel A Baima
General Manager, Jeff Tyers
VP Operations, Joseph E Turner
General Manager, Mark W Okroy
Vice-President, Ronald W Wiese

LOCATIONS

HQ: ALBERICI CONSTRUCTORS, INC.
  8800 PAGE AVE, SAINT LOUIS, MO 631146106
Phone: 314 733-2000

HISTORICAL FINANCIALS

Company Type: Private

Income Statement

FYE: December 31

	REVENUE ($ mil.)	NET INCOME ($ mil.)	NET PROFIT MARGIN	EMPLOYEES
12/15	1,028	0	—	2,000
12/14	729	0	—	—
12/13	578	0	—	—
12/12	489	0	—	—
Annual Growth	28.1%	—	—	—

2015 Year-End Financials

Return on assets: 14.1%
Return on equity: —
Current ratio: 0.90

Cash ($ mil.): 75

ALBERICI CORPORATION

Alberici helped shape the St. Louis skyline; it now sets its sights — or its construction sites — across North America. As the parent company of Alberici Constructors the company encompasses a group of enterprises with a presence in North America Central America South America and Europe. Operations include construction services building materials and steel fabrication and erection units. Alberici offers general contracting design/build construction management demolition and specialty contracting services while also offering facilities management. Founded in 1918 the Alberici family still holds the largest share of the employee-owned firm.

Operations

The company boasts more than a dozen operating companies in the US Canada and Mexico that serve the automotive energy health care industrial manufacturing and wastewater treatment markets. Its Gunther-Nash subsidiary provides construction services to the mining industry. Another division Vertegy specializes in construction consulting for green and sustainable projects.

Geographic Reach

Alberici is active throughout North America and has offices in St. Louis Missouri; Detroit Michigan; Atlanta Georgia; Topeka Kansas; Burlington and Cambridge Ontario; Saskatoon Saskatchewan; and L ©on Mexico.

Sales and Marketing

Alberici serves a range of different companies including those that are automotive building energy healthcare heavy industrial industrial process mining infrastructure or water-related.

Some of Alberici's completed projects include casinos for Ameristar modernization and new facilities for Anheuser-Busch and factories for Boeing. Nearly 80% of its revenue comes from repeat clients.

Financial Performance

While full financial information was not available for the privately held company Alberici reports that its annual revenue typically exceeds $1 billion. In 2013 the company took home $1.9 billion and was ranked the 46th largest contractor in the US by the Engineering News-Record .

In 2012 the company reported more than $530 million in industrial-related revenue thanks to a recovering economy supporting demand for major industrial projects in the US and Canada.

Strategy

In recent years the heavy construction firm has pursued acquisitions to better diversify its business both geographically and by entering new specialty markets. In 2013 for example Alberici purchased contractor Flintco LLC to broaden its reach into new markets in the southern and southwestern regions of the US. In early 2012 Alberici acquired a water treatment facility specialist to expand its service offerings in the water plant construction market.

Alberici has also become a recognized contractor in recent years which could help give the company a higher profile and thus more exposure to new potential clients. In 2013 the Associated General Contractors of St. Louis awarded Alberici with top prizes at its 16th Annual Keystone Awards for the company's work on the Seabrook Gates Complex and the Knights of Columbus Child Development Center. To date Alberici has won 14 Keystone Awards more than any other general contractor.

So far its high standing hasn't hurt business. In July 2014 Alberici was chosen to lead in the engineering procurement and construction of a major air quality improvement project — with the goal of installing environmental controls and reducing sulfur dioxide emissions by 90% — at one of the generating stations owned and operated by Alliant Energy's Wisconsin utility Wisconsin Power and Light Company.

Mergers and Acquisitions

Expanding it range of capabilities in January 2012 Alberici acquired water treatment facility specialist CAS Construction. The addition of CAS which has built facilities throughout the central and western US strengthens Alberici's capabilities in the water market. The company was renamed CAS Constructors.

In early 2013 Alberici closed on its acquisition of Flintco LLC a century-old Native American-owned contractor based in Tulsa Oklahoma. With offices in Oklahoma New Mexico Texas Arkansas and California Flintco presented an attractive geographic diversification opportunity for Alberici.

EXECUTIVES

President, Gregory J Kozicz
Manager, Sherry Morrow
Financial Executive, Deborah Sparrow
Vice-President, David Calcaterra
Vice-President, David M Kress
VP Operations, Joseph E Turner

Chief Operating Officer, Leroy J Stromberg
Director, Philip Freeze

LOCATIONS

HQ: ALBERICI CORPORATION
   8800 PAGE AVE, SAINT LOUIS, MO 631146106
Phone: 314 733-2000

PRODUCTS/OPERATIONS

Selected Markets
Automotive
Building
Energy
Green building
Health care
Industrial
Manufacturing/Food and Beverage
Mining infrastructure
Steel fabrication
Water and Wastewater Treatment

Selected Subsidiaries and Brands
Alberici Global Group GmbH
   Alberici Constructors Ltd. (Canada)
   Alberici Construcciones S.A. de C.V. (Mexico)
Alberici Group Inc.
   Alberici Constructors Inc.
   Alberici Global Automotive Constructors (automotive construction)
   Alberici Healthcare Constructors
   Alberici Industrial LLC
   CAS Construction LLC (water wastewater)
   Flintco LLC (Native American-owned contractor)
   Gunther-Nash Inc. (shaft slope and tunnel construction for mining industry)
   Hillsdale Fabricators (steel fabrication)
   Kienlen Constructors (structural concrete structural steel)
   Vertegy (green building consulting)

COMPETITORS

Barton Malow	Jacobs Engineering
Bechtel	McCarthy Building
Black & Veatch	Parsons Corporation
DPR Construction	Peter Kiewit Sons'
Fluor	TIC Holdings
Hensel Phelps	Tutor Perini
Construction	Walbridge Aldinger
Hoffman Corporation	Walsh Group
Hunt Construction	Zachry Inc.

HISTORICAL FINANCIALS
Company Type: Private

Income Statement
FYE: December 31

	REVENUE ($ mil.)	NET INCOME ($ mil.)	NET PROFIT MARGIN	EMPLOYEES
12/15	1,885	0	—	2,080
12/14	1,532	0	—	—
12/13	1,736	0	—	—
12/12	772	0	—	—
Annual Growth	34.7%	—	—	—

2015 Year-End Financials
Return on assets: 14.9%   Cash ($ mil.): 170
Return on equity: —
Current ratio: 1.00

ALBERICI GROUP, INC.

EXECUTIVES

Chief Executive Officer, Gregory J Kozicz
Manager, Sherry Morrow
Financial Executive, Deborah Sparrow
Manager, Dave Driemeier
Director, Frederick Biermann
Quality Control Manager, Jerry Grubbs

LOCATIONS

HQ: ALBERICI GROUP, INC.
   8800 PAGE AVE, SAINT LOUIS, MO 631146106
Phone: 314 733-2000
Web: WWW.ALBERICI.COM

HISTORICAL FINANCIALS
Company Type: Private

Income Statement
FYE: December 31

	REVENUE ($ mil.)	NET INCOME ($ mil.)	NET PROFIT MARGIN	EMPLOYEES
12/15	1,124	0	—	2,000
12/14	729	0	—	—
12/13	1,736	0	—	—
12/12	629	0	—	—
Annual Growth	21.3%	—	—	—

2015 Year-End Financials
Return on assets: 13.2%   Cash ($ mil.): 95
Return on equity: —
Current ratio: 0.80

ALBERT C. KOBAYASHI, INC

EXECUTIVES

Chief Executive Officer, Russell Young
Board of Directors, Colette Ruiz
Financial Executive, Shaun Shimizu
Engineer, Heather De La Garza
Project Manager, Brian Niitani
Auditors: N&K CPAS INC HONOLULU HAWA

LOCATIONS

HQ: ALBERT C. KOBAYASHI, INC
   94-535 UKEE ST STE 101, WAIPAHU, HI 967974275
Phone: 808 671-6460
Web: WWW.ACK-INC.COM

HISTORICAL FINANCIALS
Company Type: Private

Income Statement
FYE: July 31

	REVENUE ($ mil.)	NET INCOME ($ mil.)	NET PROFIT MARGIN	EMPLOYEES
07/16	383	5	1.4%	200
07/15	280	4	1.7%	—
07/14	180	9	5.5%	—
07/13	127	8	6.6%	—
Annual Growth	44.2%	(13.4%)	—	—

2016 Year-End Financials
Return on assets: 24.2%   Cash ($ mil.): 46
Return on equity: 1.4%
Current ratio: 1.20

ALBERT EINSTEIN MEDICAL CENTER

EXECUTIVES

President, Richard Greenberg
Director, Susan McCulley

Vice-President, Lynn Kornblatt
Director, Raymond Schwartz

LOCATIONS

HQ: ALBERT EINSTEIN MEDICAL CENTER
   5501 OLD YORK RD STE 1, PHILADELPHIA, PA 191413098
Phone: 215 456-7890
Web: WWW.ACCREDITEDUNIVERSITYCOURSES.COM

HISTORICAL FINANCIALS
Company Type: Private

Income Statement
FYE: June 30

	REVENUE ($ mil.)	NET INCOME ($ mil.)	NET PROFIT MARGIN	EMPLOYEES
06/15	679	38	5.7%	66
06/11	744	52	7.1%	—
06/10	713	(38)	—	—
06/09	635	23	3.7%	—
Annual Growth	1.1%	8.8%	—	—

2015 Year-End Financials
Return on assets: 6.7%   Cash ($ mil.): 32
Return on equity: 5.7%
Current ratio: 0.80

ALBUQUERQUE MUNICIPAL SCHOOL DISTRICT NUMBER 12

EXECUTIVES

Superintendent, Jason Martinez
Assistant Manager, Diane Kerschen
Plant & Facilities Manager, John Dufay
Plant & Facilities Manager, Karen Alarid
Purchasing Director, Tami Coleman
Auditors: MOSS ADAMS LLP ALBUQUERQUE N

LOCATIONS

HQ: ALBUQUERQUE MUNICIPAL SCHOOL DISTRICT NUMBER 12
   6400 UPTOWN BLVD NE, ALBUQUERQUE, NM 871104202
Phone: 505 880-3700
Web: WWW.APS.EDU

HISTORICAL FINANCIALS
Company Type: Private

Income Statement
FYE: June 30

	REVENUE ($ mil.)	NET INCOME ($ mil.)	NET PROFIT MARGIN	EMPLOYEES
06/16	998	11	1.2%	7
06/11	924	114	12.4%	—
Annual Growth	1.5%	(36.9%)	—	—

2016 Year-End Financials
Return on assets: 0.3%   Cash ($ mil.): 150
Return on equity: 1.2%
Current ratio: 0.90

ALDINE INDEPENDENT SCHOOL DISTRICT

EXECUTIVES

Superintendent, Wanda Bamberg
Principal, Ruth Dimmick
Principal, Jeannette Ross
Purchasing Agent, Carlota Nichols
Director, Hank Bauer
Plant & Facilities Manager, John Thames
Manager, Luis Pratts
Purchasing Agent, Nancy Willis
Bookkeeper, Darnesheia Turner
Auditors: WHITLEY PENN LLP HOUSTON TE

LOCATIONS

HQ: ALDINE INDEPENDENT SCHOOL DISTRICT
2520 WW THORNE BLVD, HOUSTON, TX 770733406
Phone: 281 449-1011
Web: WWW.ALDINE..K12.TX.US

HISTORICAL FINANCIALS
Company Type: Private

Income Statement
FYE: June 30

	REVENUE ($ mil.)	NET INCOME ($ mil.)	NET PROFIT MARGIN	EMPLOYEES
06/16	766	104	13.7%	7,000
06/13	625	26	4.2%	—
06/12	607	12	2.0%	—
Annual Growth	6.0%	70.8%	—	—

2016 Year-End Financials

Return on assets: 2.9%   Cash ($ mil.): 26
Return on equity: 13.7%
Current ratio: —

ALERIS CORPORATION

Aleris is a global leader in the manufacture of aluminum sheets and extruded aluminum products. The company's rolled and extruded products unit supplies product to manufacturers in most major industries but particularly the automotive building and construction transportation and consumer durables industries. It has manufacturing sites in North America Europe and Asia that turn out over 800000 tons of finished product each year. Facing a tough commodity market in 2016 Aleris agreed to be acquired by China's Zhongwang International in a $2.3 billion deal although the deal is making US regulators anxious and as of Q3 2017 is yet to be finalized.

Change in Company Type
In August 2016 Aleris agreed to its acquisition by Chinese firm Zhongwang for $2.3 billion. However a year later and the deal is yet to go through. The Committee on Foreign Investments in the US takes a tough stance on the acquisition of US companies by Chinese firms due to their often close links with the Chinese government. The upswing in protectionism following the election of Donald Trump in November 2016 has also played a role in the hold-up.

Operations
Aleris divides its operations between its three major geographies: North America Europe and Asia.

The North America segment consists of nine manufacturing facilities that produce rolled aluminum and coated products. It produces rolled products for a wide variety of applications including building and construction distribution transportation automotive and other uses in the consumer durables general industrial segments.

The Europe segment produces a range of rolled aluminum. Types include aerospace plate and sheet; brazing sheet (clad aluminum material used for among other applications vehicle radiators and HVAC systems); automotive sheet; and heat treated plate for engineering uses; as well as for other uses in the transportation construction and packaging industries.

The Asia-Pacific unit uses a state-of-the-art aluminum rolling mill in China to produce value-added plate products for the aerospace engineering distribution building and construction and other transportation industry segments worldwide.

Geographic Reach
Aleris has 13 production facilities in North America Europe (one in Belgium and one in Germany) and China. North America contributes 50% of total company revenue and Europe brings in most of the remainder. The Asia-Pacific region only accounts for about 5% but Aleris is intent on capitalizing on growing demand from China.

Sales and Marketing
Aleris' rolled and extruded products are sold to end-users as well as to distributors for use in the aerospace automotive transportation building and construction electrical mechanical engineering metal distribution and packaging industries throughout North America and Europe.

Sales of rolled products are made through each segment's own sales force which are strategically located to provide international coverage and through a broad network of sales offices and agents in North America major European countries as well as Asia and Australia. The majority of its customer sales agreements in these segments are for a term of one year or less.

Major customers in North America include American Construction Metals Ryerson Utility Trailer Cuprum Metals Laminados and D&W Fine Pack. European customers include Bombardier Renault and HallaVisteon; Asia-Pacific customers include Avic AMS and Hengtai.

Financial Performance
Aleris' revenue has been on a downward slant in recent years and despite an uptick in sales in fiscal 2015 fiscal 2016 saw another marked decline.

Sales fell 9% to $2.7 billion amid notable declines in North America and Europe offset slightly by a 5% increase in sales to the small Asia-Pacific region. Revenue was hit by lower aluminum prices a fall in North America truck trailer and distribution volumes and the negative impact of the strong US dollar.

Aleris made a net loss of $75.6 million due to an increase in provisions for income taxes.

Cash from operations was down sharply at $12.0 million versus $119.5 million the previous year. The change was down to an increase in net operating assets.

Strategy
In anticipation of an increase in demand for aluminum from the North American automotive industry Aleris is investing $400 million in adding auto-body sheet capabilities to its Lewisport Kentucky aluminum rolling mill. It is building a new wide cold mill two continuous annealing lines and an automotive innovation center. It is also improving existing functions at the site such as widening its hot mill.

Company Background
Aleris was formed in 2004 through the merger of Commonwealth Industries Inc. and IMCO Recycling Inc. It was acquired by Texas Pacific Group (now TPG Capital) in 2006 and taken private. Oak-tree took up a major stake in Aleris in 2010. The name Aleris combines alliance aluminum and era.

To meet fast-growing demand for technically advanced aluminum plate products for global aerospace and commercial plate customers in 2013 the company introduced a new $350 million hot rolling mill in Zhenjiang China.

EXECUTIVES

EVP General Counsel and Secretary, Christopher R. Clegg, age 59, $427,875 total compensation
Chairman and CEO, Sean M. Stack, age 50, $875,000 total compensation
EVP; President Europe and Global Markets, Jacobus A. J. (Jack) Govers, age 50, $262,635 total compensation
EVP CFO and Treasurer, Eric M. Rychel, age 43, $475,000 total compensation
EVP and Chief Human Resources Officer, Tamara S. (Tami) Polmanteer, age 52, $272,708 total compensation
Auditors: ERNST & YOUNG LLP CLEVELAND

LOCATIONS

HQ: ALERIS CORPORATION
25825 SCIENCE PARK DR # 400, CLEVELAND, OH 441227392
Phone: 216 910-3400
Web: WWW.ALERIS.COM

2016 Sales

	$ mil.	% of total
United States	1,324	50
International		
Asia	184	7
Other Europe	433	21
Germany	548	16
Mexico Canada and South America	148	5
Other	24	1
Total	**2,663**	**100**

PRODUCTS/OPERATIONS

2016 Sales

	$ mil.	% of total
North America	1,363	51
Europe	1,206	45
Asia-Pacific	94	4
Total	**2,663**	**100**

COMPETITORS

Arconic	Quanex Building
Arconic	Products
David J. Joseph	Reliance Steel
David J. Joseph	Reliance Steel
Kaiser Aluminum	Reserve Management
Kaiser Aluminum	Group
Novelis	Reserve Management
Novelis	Group
Quanex Building	Wise Metals Group
Products	Wise Metals Group

HISTORICAL FINANCIALS
Company Type: Private

Income Statement
FYE: December 31

	REVENUE ($ mil.)	NET INCOME ($ mil.)	NET PROFIT MARGIN	EMPLOYEES
12/16	2,663	(75)	—	5,100
12/15	2,917	48	1.7%	—
12/14	2,882	88	3.1%	—
12/13	4,332	(36)	—	—
Annual Growth	(15.0%)	—	—	—

2016 Year-End Financials

Return on assets: 9.3%   Cash ($ mil.): 55
Return on equity: (-2.8%)
Current ratio: 0.60

ALEX LEE, INC.

The business of wholesaling groceries is only part of the bigger picture for Alex Lee. The company is a leading distributor of food and other products to retailers and food service operators. Its Merchants Distributors Inc. (MDI) subsidiary supplies food and general merchandise to more than 600 retailers in nearly a dozen mostly southeastern states. MDI's own Consolidation Services business provides warehousing and logistics services. As part of its business Alex Lee also operates Lowe's Food Stores a chain of about 100 grocery stores located in the Carolinas and Virginia. Alex and Lee George started the company in 1931. The George family continues to control Alex Lee.

Operations

Alex Lee named after Lebanese immigrant founder Moses George's two sons Alex and Lee boasts two operating companies: Merchants Distributors Inc. and Lowe's Food Stores Inc. Run as a division of MDI Consolidation Services operates under the Alex Lee and MDI umbrellas.

Geographic Reach

The company's reach extends to about a dozen US states. Alex Lee operates its Merchants Distributors Inc. (MDI) retail distribution unit across the Carolinas Georgia Tennessee Virginia Alabama West Virginia Ohio Florida Pennsylvania and Kentucky. Regional supermarket chain Lowe's Food Stores serves customers in Virginia South Carolina and North Carolina.

Strategy

The company's retail arm has grown to account for half of its total sales increasing Alex Lee's exposure to the competitive low-margin retail grocery business. Alex Lee is keeping its Lowe's stores network lean to maintain its focus on key markets. In 2012 it sold 10 stores to rival Harris Teeter in exchange for half a dozen Harris Tweeter stores. The deal which gave Lowe's $26.5 million allows Lowe's to focus on core areas such as the Triad the Triangle and Hickory. However the chain closed two stores in the Triangle region in September 2013 ahead of Publix Supermarkets entry and as grocery giant Kroger prepares to take of Harris Teeter Supermarkets. With these two grocery giants encroaching on Lowe's Food's turf the chain can look forward to more intense competition.

EXECUTIVES

CEO, Boyd L. George, age 75
President Lowe's Food Stores, Steve Hall
President, Brian George
SVP and CFO, Joyce Reto
Vice President of Sales Development, Tim Markham
Vice President, Roger Henderson
Senior Vice President and Chief Financial Officer, Andrew Almquist
Auditors: MCGLADREY LLP CHARLOTTE NC

LOCATIONS

HQ: ALEX LEE, INC.
120 4TH ST SW, HICKORY, NC 286022947
Phone: 828 725-4424
Web: WWW.ALEXLEE.COM

PRODUCTS/OPERATIONS

Selected Operations
Lowe's Food Stores Inc.
Merchants Distributors Inc.
Consolidation Services Inc.

COMPETITORS

ALDI	Kroger
Associated Wholesale	MAINES
Grocers	McLane
Ben E. Keith	Meadowbrook Meat
C&S Wholesale	Company
Food Lion	SUPERVALU
H. T. Hackney	Southeastern Grocers
Harris Teeter	Sysco
Supermarkets	US Foods
Ingles Markets	Wal-Mart
K-VA-T Food Stores	Winn-Dixie

HISTORICAL FINANCIALS
Company Type: Private

Income Statement
FYE: October 1

	REVENUE ($ mil.)	NET INCOME ($ mil.)	NET PROFIT MARGIN	EMPLOYEES
10/16	2,229	8	0.4%	9,200
10/15*	2,287	25	1.1%	—
09/14	30	(1)	—	—
09/13	2,231	6	0.3%	—
Annual Growth	**(0.0%)**	**9.3%**	**—**	**—**

*Fiscal year change

2016 Year-End Financials
Return on assets: 8.8%   Cash ($ mil.): 4
Return on equity: 0.4%
Current ratio: 0.30

ALEXANDRIA INOVA HOSPITAL

Inova Alexandria Hospital provides medical surgical and therapeutic services in northeastern Virginia. The hospital was founded in 1872 and became part of the not-for-profit Inova Health System in 1997. Inova Alexandria Hospital has about 320 beds. The hospital offers specialty services such as heart and cancer treatment women's and children's health care emergency medicine vascular procedures interventional radiology and sleep disorder and heartburn treatment services. The Inova Health System provides health care services in northern Virginia through a network of hospitals clinics assisted living centers and other provider facilities.

EXECUTIVES

Managing Director Inova Strategic Investments, Peter Jobse

LOCATIONS

HQ: ALEXANDRIA INOVA HOSPITAL
4320 SEMINARY RD, ALEXANDRIA, VA 223041535
Phone: 703 504-3000
Web: WWW.ALEXANDRIARADIOLOGY.COM

COMPETITORS

Ascension Health	Johns Hopkins Health
Bon Secours Health	System
HCA	MedStar Health

HISTORICAL FINANCIALS
Company Type: Private

Income Statement
FYE: December 31

	REVENUE ($ mil.)	NET INCOME ($ mil.)	NET PROFIT MARGIN	EMPLOYEES
12/15	369	63	17.2%	1,750
12/14	361	56	15.6%	—
12/08	276	24	9.0%	—
12/06	247	22	9.2%	—
Annual Growth	**4.6%**	**12.1%**	**—**	**—**

2015 Year-End Financials
Return on assets: 2.8%   Cash ($ mil.): 6
Return on equity: 17.2%
Current ratio: 1.50

ALEXIAN BROTHERS MEDICAL CENTER INC

EXECUTIVES

President, John Werrbach
Financial Executive, Deborah Mau
Director, Mike Humphrey
Director, Jeffery Fein

LOCATIONS

HQ: ALEXIAN BROTHERS MEDICAL CENTER INC
800 BIESTERFIELD RD FL 1, ELK GROVE VILLAGE, IL 600073310
Phone: 847 437-5500

HISTORICAL FINANCIALS
Company Type: Private

Income Statement
FYE: June 30

	REVENUE ($ mil.)	NET INCOME ($ mil.)	NET PROFIT MARGIN	EMPLOYEES
06/15	449	47	10.6%	3,500
06/14	450	29	6.6%	—
06/13	439	28	6.6%	—
Annual Growth	**1.1%**	**28.4%**	**—**	**—**

2015 Year-End Financials
Return on assets: 0.4%   Cash ($ mil.): —
Return on equity: 10.6%
Current ratio: 0.70

ALFRED I.DUPONT HOSPITAL FOR CHILDREN

EXECUTIVES

Chief Executive Officer, Thomas Ferry
Manager, Jeanette Driscoll
Supervisor, Amy Gutowski
Manager, Kimberley Frantsi

HOOVER'S HANDBOOK OF PRIVATE COMPANIES 2018

LOCATIONS

HQ: ALFRED I.DUPONT HOSPITAL FOR CHILDREN
1600 ROCKLAND RD, WILMINGTON, DE 198033607
Phone: 302 651-4000
Web: WWW.NEMOURSDUPONTHOSPITAL.ORG

HISTORICAL FINANCIALS

Company Type: Private

Income Statement
FYE: December 31

	REVENUE ($ mil.)	NET INCOME ($ mil.)	NET PROFIT MARGIN	EMPLOYEES
12/15	450	28	6.4%	3,068
12/09	706	150	21.4%	—
12/08	420	12	3.0%	—
Annual Growth	1.0%	12.6%	—	—

2015 Year-End Financials

Return on assets: 3.8%   Cash ($ mil.): —
Return on equity: 6.4%
Current ratio: 2.80

ALHAMBRA UNIFIED SCHOOL DISTRICT

EXECUTIVES

Vice-President, Jane Canderson
Manager, Sue Moseley
Assistant Manager, Marsha Gilbert

LOCATIONS

HQ: ALHAMBRA UNIFIED SCHOOL DISTRICT
1515 W MISSION RD, ALHAMBRA, CA 918031618
Phone: 626 943-3000
Web: WWW.AUSD.US

HISTORICAL FINANCIALS

Company Type: Private

Income Statement
FYE: June 30

	REVENUE ($ mil.)	NET INCOME ($ mil.)	NET PROFIT MARGIN	EMPLOYEES
06/16	287	(1)	—	1,800
06/05	184	36	19.9%	—
06/04	201	41	20.8%	—
06/03	160	(5)	—	—
Annual Growth	4.6%	—	—	—

ALIEF INDEPENDENT SCHOOL DISTRICT

EXECUTIVES

Superintendent, H D Chambers
Superintendent, Sue Belsaas
Sales Manager, Bill Marshall
Administrative Assistant, Brian Pilgreen
Manager, Donna Senf
Board of Directors, John Hansen
Auditors: NULL-LAIRSON PC HOUSTON TX

LOCATIONS

HQ: ALIEF INDEPENDENT SCHOOL DISTRICT
4250 COOK RD, HOUSTON, TX 770721115
Phone: 281 498-8110
Web: WWW.ALIEFISD.NET

HISTORICAL FINANCIALS

Company Type: Private

Income Statement
FYE: August 31

	REVENUE ($ mil.)	NET INCOME ($ mil.)	NET PROFIT MARGIN	EMPLOYEES
08/16	514	38	7.5%	6,000
08/07	400	2	0.6%	—
08/06	402	23	6.0%	—
08/05	1,992	0	—	—
Annual Growth	—	178.7%	—	—

2016 Year-End Financials

Return on assets: 2.2%   Cash ($ mil.): 182
Return on equity: 7.5%
Current ratio: —

ALLEGHENY GENERAL HOSPITAL INC

If there is a critical trauma anywhere near Pittsburgh Allegheny General Hospital (AGH) is ready to take it on. The roughly 630-bed hospital is the Level I Shock Trauma Center for the five-state region surrounding Steel City. AGH offers traditional medical and surgical services as well as cardiology care and organ transplants. The hospital also is engaged in research in areas such as neuroscience oncology trauma and genetics. AGH which treats nearly 22000 patients each year has about 800 physicians on its staff. The hospital which is affiliated with Philadelphia's Drexel University College of Medicine is a subsidiary of Allegheny Health System which itself is owned by Highmark Inc.

Operations

AGH receives more than 50000 emergency visits each year as well as had 300000 outpatient visits and more than 21000 surgical procedures. In order to receive those emergencies in an expedient manner the hospital also operates a LifeFlight aero medical service.

The hospital's cancer center provides programs for a wide range of diseases such as lung breast colon prostate brain and liver cancer.

AGH also operates a smaller satellite facility in the northern Pittsburgh suburb of McCandless as well as an outpatient facility in suburban Pittsburgh.

Strategy

In 2014 AGH proposed investing part of $175 million from Highmark Inc. in renovations and technology upgrades at its AGH and West Penn hospitals anticipating that they will accommodate more patients when Highmark insurance subscribers lose in-network access to the University of Pittsburgh Medical Center in 2015.

Company Background

AGH first opened in 1885.

EXECUTIVES

Vice President, John Raves
President and CEO, Michael Harlovic
Vice President of Finance, Rick Fries
Chief Operating Officer, Ronald Andro
Director of Pharmacy, Edward Seidl
Director of Medical Records, Linda Bridgens
Director of Clinical Services, Russell Fuhrer
Vice President Finance, Dawn Javersack
Infection Control Director, Susan Kriznik
Nursing Director, Marge Hardt Dicuccio
Director of Nursing, Kathy Clouse
Division President, D S Parda

LOCATIONS

HQ: ALLEGHENY GENERAL HOSPITAL INC
320 E NORTH AVE, PITTSBURGH, PA 152124772
Phone: 412 359-3131
Web: WWW.WPAHS.ORG

COMPETITORS

Butler Health System
Excela Health
Heritage Valley Health
Jefferson Regional Medical Center of Pennsylvania
Ohio Valley General
St. Clair Health
The Western Pennsylvania Hospital
UPMC
UPMC Mercy
Weirton Medical Center

HISTORICAL FINANCIALS

Company Type: Private

Income Statement
FYE: June 30

	REVENUE ($ mil.)	NET INCOME ($ mil.)	NET PROFIT MARGIN	EMPLOYEES
06/15	700	107	15.4%	5,064
06/08	0	(0)	—	—
06/05	559	16	2.9%	—
06/04	637	0	—	—
Annual Growth	—	191.3%	—	—

2015 Year-End Financials

Return on assets: 4.5%   Cash ($ mil.): 2
Return on equity: 15.4%
Current ratio: 1.10

ALLEGIS GROUP, INC.

Allegis Group is one of the world's largest staffing and recruitment firms. Among its group of staffing companies are Aerotek (engineering automotive and scientific professionals) Stephen James Associates (recruitment for accounting financial and cash management positions) and TEKsystems (information technology staffing and consulting). Other Allegis Group units include sales support outsourcer MarketSource. Allegis Group operates through more than 500 offices worldwide. Chairman Jim Davis helped found the company (originally known as Aerotek) in 1983 to provide contract engineering personnel to two clients in the aerospace industry.

Operations

Allegis Group has more than 12000 internal employees including 3000 dedicated recruiters and 130000 contract employees working with customers around the world.

Geographic Reach

Allegis Group's corporate headquarters are located in Hanover Maryland. Outside of the US the company has operations in Canada Europe the Middle East the Pacific Rim Puerto Rico and the UK.

Financial Performance

Allegis Group averages about $11 billion in annual revenue.

Strategy

Allegis Group has expanded its geographical footprint and improved its position in specialist staffing markets through the use of acquisitions. The company's specialized staffing firms cater to various industries.

Mergers and Acquisitions

In 2016 Allegis Group acquired Switzerland-based staffing recruiting and services organization The Stamford Group. The deal increased Allegis Group's global footprint and strengthened its European presence.

EXECUTIVES

CFO, Paul J. Bowie
President, Andy Hilger
Chairman, James C. (Jim) Davis
Auditors: PRICEWATERHOUSECOOPERS LLP BA

LOCATIONS

HQ: ALLEGIS GROUP, INC.
7301 PARKWAY DR, HANOVER, MD 210761159
Phone: 410 579-3000
Web: WWW.AEROTEK.COM

PRODUCTS/OPERATIONS

Selected Subsidiaries
Aerotek
  Aerotek Automotive
  Aerotek Aviation LLC
  Aerotek Canada
  Aerotek CE
  Aerotek Commercial Staffing
  Aerotek E&E
  Aerotek Energy Services
  Aerotek Germany
  Aerotek Netherlands
  Aerotek Professional Services
  Aerotek Scientific LLC
  Aerotek United Kingdom
Allegis Group Canada
Allegis Group Europe
Allegis Group India
Allegis Group Services
InSearch Worldwide
Major Lindsey & Africa
MarketSource Inc
Stephen James Associates
TEKsystems
  TEKsystems Canada
  TEKsystems Germany
  TEKsystems Netherlands
  TEKsystems United Kingdom

COMPETITORS

ASG Renaissance	Kelly Services
Adecco	Korn/Ferry
CDI	ManpowerGroup
Curran Partners	RDL Corporation
ExecuNet	Randstad Holding
Heidrick & Struggles	Robert Half
Horton International	Snelling Staffing
Innovative Management	Volt Information
Solutions Group	

HISTORICAL FINANCIALS

Company Type: Private

Income Statement
FYE: December 31

	REVENUE ($ mil.)	NET INCOME ($ mil.)	NET PROFIT MARGIN	EMPLOYEES
12/15	11,222	0	—	85,000
12/14	10,827	0	—	—
12/13	10,440	0	—	—
12/12	9,544	0	—	—
Annual Growth	5.5%	—	—	—

2015 Year-End Financials
Return on assets: 1.7%   Cash ($ mil.): 390
Return on equity: —
Current ratio: 2.50

ALLEN LUND COMPANY, LLC

The Allen Lund Company (ALC) knows loads; it matches shippers' loads with a network of truckload and less-than-truckload (LTL) carriers. (LTL carriers collect consolidate and haul freight from multiple shippers.) The brokerage firm arranges the transport of dry refrigerated (predominantly produce) and flatbed cargo. It operates from 30 offices throughout more than 20 US states. ALC Logistics ALC Perishable Logistics and ALC International (an international division) assist shippers in managing transportation costs tracking and tracing shipments managing appointments and executing freight forward management services overseas. The company was founded in 1976 by Allen Lund and his wife Kathie Lund.

Operations

ALC has a Logistics & Software division ALC Logistics.

Geographic Reach

The company's international division provides transportation services worldwide along with transportation to and from the US including Puerto Rico Hawaii Alaska and ground transportation for Canada and Mexico.

Strategy

In an effort to expand its operation in 2012 the company opened a new office in Joplin Missouri and another in McAllen Texas which mainly focuses on handling heavy haul flatbed particularly in and out of Mexico. In addition the company opened four additional offices in 2012.

Mergers and Acquisitions

In an effort to grow its business in early 2014 ALC acquired Wisconsin based Northern Freight Service Inc. a company provides truckload LTL and intermodal services to the customers ranging from small shippers to FORTUNE 500 shippers.

EXECUTIVES

National Accounts Manager, Mark Betance

LOCATIONS

HQ: ALLEN LUND COMPANY, LLC
4529 ANGELES CREST HWY # 300, LA CANADA FLINTRIDGE, CA 910113247
Phone: 818 790-1110
Web: WWW.ALLENLUND.COM

PRODUCTS/OPERATIONS

Selected Services
Software and Logistics
  LTL Freight
  Scheduling
  Spot Pricing and Bid Management
  Truck Load
Transportation Services
  Dry Van
  Flatbed Trucking
  International Freight Shipping
  LTL Freight
  Refrigerated Transportation

COMPETITORS

C.H. Robinson	Ryder System
Worldwide	Universal Logistics
CEVA Logistics	

HISTORICAL FINANCIALS

Company Type: Private

Income Statement
FYE: December 31

	REVENUE ($ mil.)	NET INCOME ($ mil.)	NET PROFIT MARGIN	EMPLOYEES
12/15	457	13	2.9%	310
12/14	476	8	1.9%	—
12/13	421	1	0.3%	—
12/12	355	3	0.9%	—
Annual Growth	8.8%	62.1%	—	—

2015 Year-End Financials
Return on assets: 4.0%   Cash ($ mil.): 19
Return on equity: 2.9%
Current ratio: 2.30

ALLEN MEMORIAL HOSPITAL CORP

EXECUTIVES

President, Pamela K Delagardelle
Manager, Jim Henderson
Manager, Dan Norman

LOCATIONS

HQ: ALLEN MEMORIAL HOSPITAL CORP
1825 LOGAN AVE, WATERLOO, IA 507031999
Phone: 319 235-3941
Web: WWW.LEADERPHARMACIES.COM

HISTORICAL FINANCIALS

Company Type: Private

Income Statement
FYE: December 31

	REVENUE ($ mil.)	NET INCOME ($ mil.)	NET PROFIT MARGIN	EMPLOYEES
12/15	221	21	9.6%	1,800
12/14	219	26	12.1%	—
12/09	210	12	6.0%	—
12/08	184	12	6.5%	—
Annual Growth	2.6%	8.4%	—	—

2015 Year-End Financials
Return on assets: 6.1%   Cash ($ mil.): 10
Return on equity: 9.6%
Current ratio: 1.20

ALLIANCE FOR SUSTAINABLE ENERGY, LLC

EXECUTIVES

President, Martin Keller
Chief Financial Officer, Owen Barwell
Secretary, Karen Stiveson
Vice-President, Peter Green
Chief Operating Officer, Bobi Garrett
Manager, Jeanie Latz

Director, Bull Stan
Manager, Lalida Crawford
Auditors: ANTON COLLINS MITCHELL LLP GR

LOCATIONS

HQ: ALLIANCE FOR SUSTAINABLE ENERGY, LLC
15013 DENVER WEST PKWY, LAKEWOOD, CO
804013111
Phone: 303 275-3000
Web: WWW.NREL.GOV

HISTORICAL FINANCIALS
Company Type: Private

Income Statement
FYE: September 30

	REVENUE ($ mil.)	NET INCOME ($ mil.)	NET PROFIT MARGIN	EMPLOYEES
09/15	388	4	1.2%	1,678
09/14	378	5	1.5%	—
09/13	382	4	1.1%	—
09/11	532	6	1.2%	—
Annual Growth	(7.6%)	(8.2%)	—	—

2015 Year-End Financials
Return on assets: 15.6%   Cash ($ mil.): 4
Return on equity: 1.2%
Current ratio: 1.30

ALLIED BUILDING STORES, INC.

EXECUTIVES

President, Dale Mercer
Officer, Henry R Bockus III
Treasurer, Dennis Stine
Personnel Director, Sherry Lewis
Purchasing Agent, Michelle Garvan
Purchasing Agent, Todd Snuggs
Auditors: HEARD MCELROY & VESTAL LLC

LOCATIONS

HQ: ALLIED BUILDING STORES, INC.
850 KANSAS LN, MONROE, LA 712034776
Phone: 318 699-9100
Web: WWW.ABS-LINK.COM

HISTORICAL FINANCIALS
Company Type: Private

Income Statement
FYE: August 31

	REVENUE ($ mil.)	NET INCOME ($ mil.)	NET PROFIT MARGIN	EMPLOYEES
08/16	497	0	0.0%	125
08/15	485	0	0.0%	—
08/14	487	0	0.0%	—
08/13	503	0	0.0%	—
Annual Growth	(0.4%)	10.1%	—	—

2016 Year-End Financials
Return on assets: 7.1%   Cash ($ mil.): 3
Return on equity: —
Current ratio: 0.90

ALLIED SECURITY HOLDINGS LLC

Better than a blanket Allied Security Holdings gives customers a sense of security. One of the largest private contract security firms in the US it does business as AlliedBarton Security Services. It recruits and employs trained security guards to serve thousands of customers (some of which are large FORTUNE 500 companies) and their facilities. They include government facilities hospitals offices ports residential communities shopping centers and universities. The firm also provides employment and background screening services through its HR Plus subsidiary. In mid-2016 AlliedBarton merged with Universal Services of America to create Allied Universal North America's largest security services group.

Geographic Reach
Allied Security Holdings operates through more than 120 regional and district offices nationwide.

Strategy
In the last few years the company has made strides to further build out its service offerings both organically and through acquisitions expand its geographic footprint across the US and increase the number of industries and types of facilities that it serves.

EXECUTIVES

Chief Executive Officer, William C Whitmore Jr
Board of Directors, Kim Gorman
Vice-President, Paul Laconi
Office Manager, Nicola Serasin
Manager, Carlos Medina
VP Operations, Bud E Bradly
Manager, Allen Mansfield
Manager, Dave Wolstinholme

LOCATIONS

HQ: ALLIED SECURITY HOLDINGS LLC
161 WASHINGTON ST STE 600, CONSHOHOCKEN, PA 194282083
Phone: 484 351-1300
Web: WWW.ALLIEDBARTON.COM

COMPETITORS

AFI International	Kroll
Asset Protection & Security Services	Securitas
Command Security	TransNational Security
G4S Secure Solutions	Walden Security
Guardsmark	Whelan Security

HISTORICAL FINANCIALS
Company Type: Private

Income Statement
FYE: December 31

	REVENUE ($ mil.)	NET INCOME ($ mil.)	NET PROFIT MARGIN	EMPLOYEES
12/15	199	(0)	—	7,010
12/14	2,149	24	1.1%	—
12/13	2,042	51	2.5%	—
12/12	1,923	43	2.3%	—
Annual Growth	(53.0%)	—	—	—

2015 Year-End Financials
Return on assets: 42.0%   Cash ($ mil.): 4
Return on equity: (-0.2%)
Current ratio: 1.30

ALSCO INC.

Alsco has built a big business outfitting its customers in uniforms linens and related products. Operating from more than150 branches in about 10 countries worldwide the company (whose name stands for American linen supply company) rents and sells uniforms linens towels and clean room garments to more than 300000 customers in North America. It also manages janitorial services provides washroom supplies and launders and sterilizes garments. Alsco serves the automotive food processing restaurant medical and IT industries as well as the federal government. Founded in 1889 by George Steiner the company is owned and operated by the Steiner family.

Geographic Reach
Utah-based Alsco has locations in Australia Brazil Canada China Germany Italy New Zealand Singapore Switzerland Thailand and the US.

Strategy
Alsco heavily promotes its green cleaning solutions and the company has focused on international expansion in recent years. In 2014 the company expanded its uniform and linen services in Texas with a branch in San Antonio and service centers in Austin Houston and Waco.

In addition to uniforms and linens Alsco supplies promotional products for trade shows conventions golf outings sales meetings and other special events and occasions.

EXECUTIVES

Co Chief Executive Officer, Robert Stephens

LOCATIONS

HQ: ALSCO INC.
505 E SOUTH TEMPLE, SALT LAKE CITY, UT
841021004
Phone: 801 328-8831
Web: WWW.ALSCO.COM

PRODUCTS/OPERATIONS

Selected Products and Services
Clean room garments
Gown room management
Hospitality/restaurant apparel
Laundry services
Linens
Mats
Mops
Napkins
Restroom service
Towels
Uniform rental and sales
Vacuum filters
Washroom supplies

COMPETITORS

ARAMARK	ISS A/S
Angelica Corporation	Rentokil Initial
Berendsen	ServiceMaster
Cintas	Sodexo USA
Crothall Healthcare	Superior Uniform Group
Diversey	Swisher Hygiene
Ecolab	Tranzonic
G&K Services	UniFirst
Healthcare Services	

HISTORICAL FINANCIALS
Company Type: Private

Income Statement
FYE: December 31

	REVENUE ($ mil.)	NET INCOME ($ mil.)	NET PROFIT MARGIN	EMPLOYEES
12/15	683	30	4.5%	16,000
12/14	658	25	3.8%	—
12/13	633	33	5.2%	—
12/12	614	35	5.8%	—
Annual Growth	3.6%	(4.7%)	—	—

2015 Year-End Financials
Return on assets: 8.8%
Return on equity: 4.5%
Current ratio: 0.90
Cash ($ mil.): 3

ALSTON CONSTRUCTION COMPANY, INC.

Panattoni Construction Inc. (PCI) is in the business of building businesses. The design/build general contractor specializes in commercial and industrial construction projects which include manufacturing and distribution facilities master-planned business parks and office and retail buildings. The company provides construction management services for such clients as Clorox Amazon.com PetSmart and Whirlpool. The company's project portfolio ranges from smaller 2500 sq. ft offices to large warehouses spanning more than one million sq. ft. PCI operates from 20 offices in Arizona California Colorado Florida Georgia Illinois Indiana Missouri Nevada New Jersey Oregon Tennessee Texas and Washington.

EXECUTIVES

Vice President General Manager, Alecia Wilmeth
Vice President General Manager, Ed Gorton
Vice President General Manager, Deren Wilcox
Auditors: CAMPBELL TAYLOR & COMPANY ROS

LOCATIONS

HQ: ALSTON CONSTRUCTION COMPANY, INC.
8775 FOLSOM BLVD STE 201, SACRAMENTO, CA 958263725
Phone: 916 340-2400
Web: WWW.PANCONINC.COM

COMPETITORS

Alter Group	H and M Construction
Balfour Beatty Construction	KPRS Construction
Bechtel	Skanska USA Building
Fluor	Turner Corporation

HISTORICAL FINANCIALS
Company Type: Private

Income Statement
FYE: December 31

	REVENUE ($ mil.)	NET INCOME ($ mil.)	NET PROFIT MARGIN	EMPLOYEES
12/15	642	6	1.1%	200
12/14	470	3	0.8%	—
12/13	332	4	1.3%	—
Annual Growth	39.0%	26.4%	—	—

2015 Year-End Financials
Return on assets: 19.1%
Return on equity: 1.1%
Current ratio: 1.10
Cash ($ mil.): 15

ALTA CALIFORNIA REGIONAL CENTER, INC.

EXECUTIVES

President, James Huyck
General Manager, Nelly Stark
Chief Operating Officer, Peter Tiedemann
Personnel Director, Brianne Harris
Director, Lori Banales
Auditors: STROUB THOMPSON NOBLE CPAS SA

LOCATIONS

HQ: ALTA CALIFORNIA REGIONAL CENTER, INC.
2241 HARVARD ST STE 100, SACRAMENTO, CA 958153332
Phone: 916 978-6400
Web: WWW.ALTAREGIONAL.ORG

HISTORICAL FINANCIALS
Company Type: Private

Income Statement
FYE: June 30

	REVENUE ($ mil.)	NET INCOME ($ mil.)	NET PROFIT MARGIN	EMPLOYEES
06/15	322	0	0.0%	487
06/14	300	(0)	—	—
06/13	291	(0)	—	—
06/12	288	0	0.0%	—
Annual Growth	3.8%	46.2%	—	—

2015 Year-End Financials
Return on assets: 8.5%
Return on equity: —
Current ratio: 1.00
Cash ($ mil.): 4

ALTICOR INC.

At the core of Alticor there's Amway. Holding company Alticor operates direct-selling giant Amway International and North American Web sales affiliate Amway Corp. which does business as Amway Global. Its Access Business Group offers manufacturing and distribution services primarily catering to the Amway units but also to contract clients. Outside the direct-sales realm Alticor Corporate Enterprises operates resort management firm Amway Hotel and health diagnostics developer Interleukin Genetics. Formed in 2000 Alticor is owned by Amway's founders the DeVos and Van Andel families.

Operations

Alticor is the parent company to Amway Access Business Group LLC and Alticor Corporate Enterprises.

Collectively through its network of businesses Alticor serves more than 100 countries and territories worldwide. The company offers consumer products and business opportunities not available elsewhere. Its services include product development manufacturing and logistics. Besides Alticor's Amway Hotel and Interleukin Genetics businesses the company operates several other unique entities. Its Metagenics unit a global life sciences company focuses on reversing chronic illness and on improving health through nutrition. Fulton Innovation another subsidiary is a technology licensing company. Its KinDex Therapeutics unit concentrates on the discovery of molecules associated with chronic disease.

In 2016 Alticor sold upscale cosmetics maker Gurwitch Products (known for its Laura Mercier and ReVive brands) to cosmetics maker Shiseido Americas Corporation.

Geographic Reach

Based in Ada Michigan Alticor's headquarters spans more than 1 million sq. ft. The company owns or manages manufacturing and distribution facilities worldwide. It boasts manufacturing facilities in the US China Vietnam and India and oversees organically-certified farms in the US Mexico and Brazil for growing food supplements. Alticor's distribution facilities are located in North America Europe and the Far East.

Sales and Marketing

Amway boasts more than 3 million independent distributors worldwide. China has become its largest market. It's a well-known multi-level marketer and direct seller of household personal care nutrition and cleaning items. The company also peddles the products of other companies worldwide in more than 80 markets.

Financial Performance

While privately-owned Alticor doesn't report its results Amway reported global sales of $10.8 billion in 2014 down from $12 billion in 2013.

Strategy

The company's success depends on setting up Independent Business Owners (IBOs) to sell its name-brand products but more importantly build its network. The company has been accused of focusing on new IBO recruitment rather than on selling and developing new products or services. Although individuals are required to pay a membership fee Amway asserts that they can then buy its products and sell them at a 20% to 25% markup. IBOs that recruit get a cut from the sales made by those members.

The direct-selling business model is popular; Amway reaches across North America and Europe. Its focus however is increasingly on Asia's fertile market. Sales from its Amway China and India units are anticipated to jump by double-digits as consumers increase retail spending. The company deepens its presence by outsourcing its manufacturing operations to third parties in the Asia/Pacific region as well as by aligning its product design and branding around their cultures.

To this end Amway is investing $335 million in manufacturing and research and development expansion. The initiative involves upgrading four factories in the US building a new manufacturing facility in India and adding second sites in both China and Vietnam. In 2013 Amway broke ground on a new $95-million production plant in Tamil Nadu India set for completion in 2015. Its second plant in China will be located in Guangzhou; the $75-million facility is slated for completion by 2016.

Alticor continues to invest in its supply chain manufacturing and scientific resources to ensure distributors have access to products when and where they need them.

Mergers and Acquisitions

In 2015 Alticor purchased energy drink brand XS Energy which the company says has $150 million in sales in nearly 40 global markets. XS Energy creator David Vanderveen is a former Amway salesman.

EXECUTIVES

President, Doug DeVos
Vice President, Richard Holwill
Senior Vice President Internal, Michael Duong
Executive Vice President Sales, Glenn Armstrong
Vice President Logistics, Ken Davis
Chairman, Steve Van Andel

LOCATIONS

HQ: ALTICOR INC.
7575 FULTON ST E, ADA, MI 493550001
Phone: 616 787-1000
Web: WWW.ALTICOR.COM

PRODUCTS/OPERATIONS

Selected Operations
Access Business Group LLC
Alticor Corporate Enterprises
  Amway Hotel Corp.
  Fulton Innovation
  Interleukin Genetics
  KinDex Therapeutics
  Metagenics
Amway
  Amway International
  Amway Corp.

COMPETITORS

Avon	Kao
Bath & Body Works	L'Or ©al
BeautiControl	MacAndrews & Forbes
Bluestem Brands	Mary Kay
Brown-Forman	Melaleuca
CCL Industries	Newell Brands
Clorox	Nikken
Colgate-Palmolive	Nu Skin
Daiei	PFSweb
Est ©e Lauder	Procter & Gamble
Forever Living	S.C. Johnson
GNC	Shaklee
Henkel	Tupperware Brands
Johnson & Johnson	

HISTORICAL FINANCIALS
Company Type: Private

Income Statement
FYE: December 31

	REVENUE ($ mil.)	NET INCOME ($ mil.)	NET PROFIT MARGIN	EMPLOYEES
12/15	9,459	0	—	14,000
12/14	10,804	0	—	—
12/13	11,754	0	—	—
12/12	11,338	0	—	—
Annual Growth	(5.9%)	—	—	—

2015 Year-End Financials
Return on assets: 5.0%   Cash ($ mil.): 1,300
Return on equity: —
Current ratio: 0.70

ALTRU HEALTH SYSTEM

Altru Health System provides medical care throughout northeastern North Dakota and northwestern Minnesota. The integrated health care network administers everything from primary care to inpatient medical and surgical care through its Altru Hospital (with roughly 265 beds) and about a dozen primary care clinics. It also operates a cancer center a rehabilitation center dialysis facilities and home health providers. For area seniors Altru Health operates Parkwood Place a senior living facility that provides several levels of care to residents depending on need. The not-for-profit center was formed in 1997 by the integration of Grand Forks Clinic and United Health Services.

Operations

The system employs more than 200 physicians and serves over 200000 residents. Altru Hospital with a Level II Trauma designation has a 16-bed critical care unit a 10-bed surgical critical care unit pulmonary and sleep labs and cardio and pulmonary rehabilitation facilities.

In 2013 Altru Health System had 12603 inpatient discharges 275000 outpatient discharges 1600 births and some 29000 emergency visits.

Sales and Marketing

Medicare and Medicaid payments accounted for more than 50% of net patient revenue in 2013; Blue Cross accounted for more than 30%. Self-pay and other third-party accounts represented the rest of patient revenue.

In 2013 the system paid $901799 for advertising up from $892641 in 2012.

Financial Performance

Altru Health System's net revenue increased 1% to $457 million in 2013 due to increased patient services charges. Net income also rose 5% to $26 million due to gains on investments. Cash flow also held steady rising 3% to $40 million due to a decline in cash used in receivables plus an increase in cash generated from accounts payable and accrued expenses.

Strategy

The system looks for opportunities to expand both its locations and its services. To that end it is building a new hospital in Grand Forks to replace Altru. The replacement will be built in three stages and is expected to be complete by 2020. The replacement for its main clinic is expected to be operational by 2022.

Altru opened its newest hospital the 45-bed Altru Specialty Center in Grand Forks North Dakota in 2014. The center has four operating rooms and offers such services as elective orthopedic and podiatry surgeries joint replacement and inpatient rehabilitation.

In 2013 Altru opened clinics in Thief River Falls Minnesota and East Grand Fork; it also expanded a clinic in Devils Lake North Dakota.

Company Background

The system was created in 1997 when United Hospital merged with the Grand Forks Clinic.

EXECUTIVES

CEO, David Molmen
CFO, Dwight Thompson
President, Eric Lunn
Administrative Director Primary Care, Renee Axtman
Chief Nurse Executive, Margaret Reed
Administrative Director Information Services, Mark Waind
Administrative Director Medical Specialty Care, Kerry Carlson
COO, Brad Wehe
Executive Director Altru Health Foundation, Jon Green
Medical Director Primary Care, Colleen Swank
Administrative Director Cardiology and Musculoskeletal Services, Kelly Hagen
Administrative Director Surgical Services, Joseph Myers
Vice President For Finance Operations University of North Dakota, Liz Brekke
Chairman, John Snustad
Vice Chairman, Kris Compton
Treasurer Home Care Advisory Meadowbrook Township, Marie Rose

LOCATIONS

HQ: ALTRU HEALTH SYSTEM
1200 S COLUMBIA RD, GRAND FORKS, ND 582014044
Phone: 701 780-5000

PRODUCTS/OPERATIONS

2013 Sales

	% of total
Net patient service	93
Other operating revenue	7
Total	**100**

2013 Net Patient Revenue

	% of total
Medicare	41
Blue Cross	31
Medicaid	11
Other third party	14
Patients	3
Total	**100**

Selected Centers
Bariatric Center
Breast Center
Cancer Center
Diabetes Center
Family Birthing Center
Grief Center
Hand Therapy Center
Hearing Center
Heart and Vascular Center
Joint Replacement Center
Medical Fitness Center
Outpatient Procedure Center
Pre-Admission Center
Psychiatry Center
Truyu Aesthetic Center

COMPETITORS

Avera Health	St. Alexius Medical
Catholic Health	Center
Initiatives	St. Mary's Innovis
First Care	Health
Sanford	
Health-MeritCare	

HISTORICAL FINANCIALS
Company Type: Private

Income Statement
FYE: December 31

	REVENUE ($ mil.)	NET INCOME ($ mil.)	NET PROFIT MARGIN	EMPLOYEES
12/15	488	16	3.3%	3,800
12/14	456	19	4.3%	—
12/13	3	0	1.9%	—
12/08	1	0	—	—
Annual Growth	133.2%	—	—	—

2015 Year-End Financials
Return on assets: 3.4%   Cash ($ mil.): 48
Return on equity: 3.3%
Current ratio: 1.90

ALVAREZ LLC

EXECUTIVES

Chief Executive Officer, Everett Alvarez Jr
Board of Directors, Marc Alvarez
Financial Executive, Jennifer Kaiser
Auditors: KELLY & COMPANY LLC TYSONS CO

LOCATIONS

HQ: ALVAREZ LLC
8251 GREENSBORO DR # 230, TYSONS CORNER, VA 221024900
Phone: 703 635-7040
Web: WWW.ALVAREZASSOCIATES.COM

HISTORICAL FINANCIALS
Company Type: Private

Income Statement
FYE: December 31

	REVENUE ($ mil.)	NET INCOME ($ mil.)	NET PROFIT MARGIN	EMPLOYEES
12/15	241	0	0.0%	13
12/14	287	0	0.1%	—
12/13	189	0	0.1%	—
12/12	148	0	0.2%	—
Annual Growth	17.6%	(35.2%)	—	—

2015 Year-End Financials
Return on assets: 10.6% Cash ($ mil.): —
Return on equity: —
Current ratio: 1.00

AMARILLO INDEPENDENT SCHOOL DISTRICT

EXECUTIVES

Principal, David Bishop
Board of Directors, Kae Austin
Department Manager, Theresa Miller
Auditors: CONNOR MCMILLON MITCHELL SH

LOCATIONS

HQ: AMARILLO INDEPENDENT SCHOOL DISTRICT
7200 W INTERSTATE 40, AMARILLO, TX 791062528
Phone: 806 326-1000
Web: WWW.AMAISD.ORG

HISTORICAL FINANCIALS
Company Type: Private

Income Statement
FYE: June 30

	REVENUE ($ mil.)	NET INCOME ($ mil.)	NET PROFIT MARGIN	EMPLOYEES
06/16	317	(9)	—	3,600
06/15	312	(17)	—	—
06/14	300	53	18.0%	—
06/13	285	(8)	—	—
Annual Growth	3.7%	—	—	—

2016 Year-End Financials
Return on assets: 1.6% Cash ($ mil.): 117
Return on equity: (-2.9%)
Current ratio: —

AMERICA'S HOME PLACE, INC.

America's Home Place builds custom homes on its customers' land. The company builds single-family detached houses with more than 100 custom floor plans and designs. Its two- to five-bedroom cabin chalet ranch two-story and split-level houses range in price from about $80000 to more than $300000. Sizes start at about 900 sq. ft. and go up to to 4000 sq. ft. America's Home Place operates nearly 40 home building and model centers in the southeastern US. Buyers typically already own their land from a single lot to many acres. The company also assists buyers who are not landowners in locating available property. President Barry Conner owns the company he founded in 1972.

Customizable home options include choice of flooring lighting roofing siding cabinets and countertops. The company uses products with such brand names as Armstrong (flooring) Certain-Teed (roofing and siding) Sherwin-Williams (paint) and Whirlpool (appliances).

America's Home Place traditionally services its customers at retail outlets where buyers select their design carpet paint tile and window options. However the company added to its marketing strategy to begin providing model centers which feature full-sized model homes plus product and sales centers. The company builds its homes in Florida Georgia Louisiana Mississippi North Carolina South Carolina and Tennessee.

America's Home Place does not offer financing. However it does have relationships with several preferred lenders that are recommended to home-buyers.

EXECUTIVES

Division President, Russell Miskin
Vice President of Construction, Keith Brown
Auditors: BRADY WARE & SCHOENFELD ATLAN

LOCATIONS

HQ: AMERICA'S HOME PLACE, INC.
2144 HILTON DR, GAINESVILLE, GA 305016172
Phone: 770 532-1128
Web: WWW.AMERICASHOMEPLACE.COM

COMPETITORS

Beazer Homes	Lennar
CalAtlantic	M.D.C.
D.R. Horton	NVR
David Weekley Homes	PulteGroup
KB Home	

HISTORICAL FINANCIALS
Company Type: Private

Income Statement
FYE: December 31

	REVENUE ($ mil.)	NET INCOME ($ mil.)	NET PROFIT MARGIN	EMPLOYEES
12/15	175	5	3.0%	285
12/11	125	4	3.7%	—
12/07	173	8	4.9%	—
12/06	0	0	—	—
Annual Growth	—	—	—	—

2015 Year-End Financials
Return on assets: 6.8% Cash ($ mil.): 4
Return on equity: 3.0%
Current ratio: 0.20

EXECUTIVES (American Associated Pharmacies)

Account Manager, Carolyn Williams
Sales Manager, James Lovelady
Sales Manager, Richard Nastasi
Vice-President, Tracie Heyrman
Manager, Wendy Radicy
Auditors: GANT CROFT ASSOCIATES PC SC

LOCATIONS

HQ: AMERICAN ASSOCIATED PHARMACIES
201 LNNIE E CRAWFORD BLVD, SCOTTSBORO, AL 357697408
Phone: 256 574-7521
Web: WWW.RXAAP.COM

HISTORICAL FINANCIALS
Company Type: Private

Income Statement
FYE: December 31

	REVENUE ($ mil.)	NET INCOME ($ mil.)	NET PROFIT MARGIN	EMPLOYEES
12/15	642	(0)	—	75
12/14	513	0	0.0%	—
12/13	498	0	0.0%	—
12/12	476	0	0.1%	—
Annual Growth	10.5%	—	—	—

2015 Year-End Financials
Return on assets: 10.5% Cash ($ mil.): 34
Return on equity: —
Current ratio: 0.50

AMERICAN BALANCED FUND, INC.

EXECUTIVES

Board of Directors, Patrick F Quan
Auditors: DELOITTE & TOUCHE LLP

LOCATIONS

HQ: AMERICAN BALANCED FUND, INC.
1 MARKET, SAN FRANCISCO, CA 941051596
Phone: 707 864-3945

HISTORICAL FINANCIALS
Company Type: Private

Income Statement
FYE: December 31

	ASSETS ($ mil.)	NET INCOME ($ mil.)	INCOME AS % OF ASSETS	EMPLOYEES
12/15	87,394	4,903	5.6%	9
12/00	6,203	832	13.4%	—
12/99	5,996	218	3.6%	—
Annual Growth	18.2%	21.4%	—	—

AMERICAN ASSOCIATED PHARMACIES

EXECUTIVES

President, Jon Copeland
Secretary, Kevin Foshee
Quality Control Manager, Jim Giles

AMERICAN FURNITURE WAREHOUSE CO INC

Tony the Tiger hawking home furnishings might give some marketers pause but the combination seems to work for American Furniture Warehouse. American Furniture's television commercials often spotlight white-haired president and CEO Jake

Jabs (who has become a well-known personality in the state as well as in the home furnishings industry) accompanied by baby exotic animals mostly tigers. The company sells furniture electronics and decor at discounted prices. It boasts about a dozen retail locations in Colorado and Arizona and sells through its website which also features bridal and gift registries. The company has built a reputation as a home-spun local furniture retailer. Jabs bought the company in 1975.

Geographic Reach

American Furniture has locations in the Colorado cities of Aurora Englewood Centennial Lakewood Thornton Westminster Colorado Springs Firestone/Longmont Fort Collins Glenwood Springs Pueblo and Grand Junction. In Arizona it has locations in Phoenix Gilbert and Glendale. It serves customers in the neighboring states of Wyoming Utah Kansas Nevada and New Mexico.

Financial Performance

American Furniture's 2013 sales reached more than $390 million.

Strategy

In 2013 the company made its first move outside Colorado when it opened a 630000-sq.-ft. store in Gilbert Arizona (near Phoenix). It opens another store — in Glendale Arizona — in late 2014. American Furniture hopes to net $3.4 million in direct revenue from the Glendale store during its first year in operation. The furniture retailer also has an eye on expanding into north Scottsdale.

EXECUTIVES

Vice President, Jackie Brookshire
Auditors: BAUERLE AND COMPANY PC DEN

LOCATIONS

HQ: AMERICAN FURNITURE WAREHOUSE CO INC
8820 AMERICAN WAY, ENGLEWOOD, CO 801127056
Phone: 303 799-9044
Web: WWW.AFWONLINE.COM

PRODUCTS/OPERATIONS

Selected Products
Decorative accessories
Electronics
Furniture
    Bedroom
    Chairs
    Dining room
    Home office
    Indoor/outdoor
    Living room
    Occasional tables
    Sectionals
    Sofas
    Youth bedroom
Lighting
Mattresses
Rugs

COMPETITORS

Ashley Furniture	Pier 1 Imports
Big Lots	Rooms To Go
Costco Wholesale	Sears
J. C. Penney	Target Corporation
Kmart	Wal-Mart

HISTORICAL FINANCIALS

Company Type: Private

Income Statement

FYE: March 31

	REVENUE ($ mil.)	NET INCOME ($ mil.)	NET PROFIT MARGIN	EMPLOYEES
03/16	615	23	3.7%	1,900
03/15	530	20	3.8%	—
03/14	413	12	3.0%	—
03/13	353	11	3.2%	—
Annual Growth	20.3%	26.4%	—	—

Return on assets: 2.5%   Cash ($ mil.): 7
Return on equity: 3.7%
Current ratio: 0.20

AMERICAN INSTITUTE OF CERTIFIED PUBLIC ACCOUNTANTS

When you add it all up the American Institute of Certified Public Accountants (AICPA) makes perfect sense. One of the nation's leading nonprofit professional associations the AICPA has more than 400000 members from more than 145 countries who are involved in public accounting business education law and government. The group which generates just more than half of its revenues from membership dues promotes awareness of the accounting profession; identifies financial trends; sets certification licensing and professional standards; and provides information and advice to CPAs. The AICPA distributes its information through websites conferences and forums and publications.

Operations

The organization develops and grades the Uniform CPA Examination and offers specialty credentials for CPAs who focus on personal financial planning; forensic accounting; business valuation; and information management and technology assurance. Through a joint venture with the Chartered Institute of Management Accountants it has established the Chartered Global Management Accountant designation which sets a new standard for global recognition of management accounting.

The AICPA members represent many areas of practice including business and industry public practice government education and consulting.

Geographic Reach

The AICPA has offices in New Jersey New York North Carolina and Washington DC.

Financial Performance

The AICPA's 2014 revenues increased by 4% due to growth in membership dues revenues as a result of a higher membership base and an increase in revenues from professional development and member service conferences and contributions.

Net income decreased by 44% due to loss from pensions and postretirement benefits.

Operating cash flow increased by 151% as a result of higher cash received from members and customers.

Strategy

The institute's Chartered Global Management Accountant (CGMA) designation is designed to reverse a shortage of PhD accounting faculty at US colleges and universities.

To better serve the public in a time of rapid technological innovation increasing business complexity and regulatory scrutiny the AICPA has launched the Enhancing Audit Quality initiative.

The AICPA and its joint venture partner (the Chartered Institute of Management Accountants) have also launched a competency framework that raises the skills of CGMAs in the marketplace.

Company Background

Other initiatives in recent years have included private business financial reporting rebuilding investor confidence and the implementation of the Sarbanes-Oxley Act.

In 2012 the institute launched the CPA Examination internationally in six countries and administered more than 7000 sections in Bahrain Brazil Japan Kuwait Lebanon and the United Arab Emirates.

The AICPA was founded in 1887.

EXECUTIVES

VP Professional Standards and Services, Arleen R. Thomas
President and CEO, Barry C. Melancon
SVP and COO, Anthony J. Pugliese
SVP Public Practice & Global Alliances, Susan S. Coffey
SVP Congressional and Political Affairs, Mark G. Peterson
SVP Strategy People & Innovation, Lawson Carmichael
CFO, Tim LaSpaluto
Vice President Professional Development And Group Study Program, Paden Neeley
Vice President Information Technology, Hemchandra Nerkar
Vice President, Edward Karl
Director Media Relations, Jay Hyde
Vice Chair, Eric Hansen
Chairman, Kimberly N. Ellison-Taylor, age 47
Auditors: COHNREZNICK LLP ROSELAND NJ

LOCATIONS

HQ: AMERICAN INSTITUTE OF CERTIFIED PUBLIC ACCOUNTANTS
220 LEIGH FARM RD, DURHAM, NC 277078110
Phone: 919 402-0682
Web: WWW.STARTHEREGOPLACES.COM

PRODUCTS/OPERATIONS

2014 Revenue

	$ mil.	% of total
Dues	124	53
Professional development & membership service conference	43	18
Professional examinations	23	10
Publications	21	9
Investment & other income	19	9
Contributions	2	1
Total	**235**	**100**

HISTORICAL FINANCIALS

Company Type: Private

Income Statement

FYE: July 31

	REVENUE ($ mil.)	NET INCOME ($ mil.)	NET PROFIT MARGIN	EMPLOYEES
07/15	247	(7)	—	800
07/13	219	15	6.9%	—
07/09	199	(13)	—	—
07/08	0	0	—	—
Annual Growth	—	—	—	—

2015 Year-End Financials

Return on assets: 19.0%   Cash ($ mil.): 55
Return on equity: (-2.9%)
Current ratio: 0.50

AMERICAN INSTITUTES FOR RESEARCH IN THE BEHAVIORAL SCIENCES

The American Institutes for Research (AIR) lives and breathes to enhance human performance. The not-for-profit organization conducts behavioral and social science research on topics related to education and educational assessment health international development and work and training. Clients including several federal agencies use AIR's research in developing policies. As a major ongoing initiative the organization provides tools to improve education both in the US and internationally particularly in disadvantaged areas. John C. Flanagan who developed the Critical Incident Technique personnel-selection tool to identify human success indicators in the workplace founded the organization in 1946.

Operations

AIR has organized its group into six program areas: Analysis of Longitudinal Data in Education Research Assessment Education Healthand Social Development Workforce and International Development Evaluation and Research.

AIR's assessment program focuses on score reports and online reporting tools to translate large-scale testing data on student achievement into a benchmark for school performance. International human and social development programs aim to improve the quality of life and education in developing areas. It works to achieve this through teacher and school administrator training curriculum development and teaching materials coupled with mobilizing health communications HIV/AIDS education and raising awareness about such issues as child labor exploitation. Working with governments private health care providers and the general public AIR's health programs design implement and evaluate the impact of health care policies.

Geographic Reach

Begun as a small research group affiliated with the University of Pittsburgh AIR's corporate headquarters and business offices are located in Washington DC. The group maintains about a dozen offices in the US. Domestic offices are located in San Mateo and Sacramento California; Atlanta Georgia; Honolulu Hawaii; Chicago and Naperville Illinois; Indianapolis Indiana; Baltimore Frederick and Silver Spring Maryland; Portland Oregon; Columbus Ohio; Chapel Hill North Carolina; New York New York; and Waltham Massachusetts. AIR also operates nearly 10 international offices located in Egypt Honduras Kyrgyzstan Liberia Tajikistan Cote d'Ivoire and Zambia.

Strategy

The National Center for Education Statistics a key source for statistical data about education and AIR team up to develop large-scale databases for policymaking. Among various efforts AIR designs surveys and assessments develops questionnaires and tests items as well as informational materials. It also helps in producing The Condition of Education the agency's chief report. The organization's successes include campaigns that address public health emergencies such as the flu and H1N1 and the prevention of HIV/AIDS heart disease and birth defects.

Adding to its educational research capabilities AIR has pursued a number of strategic alliances and acquisitions. In 2015 SEDL joined forced with AIR. The combined organizations will have new and enhanced capabilities around for example disability research as well as an increased capacity to conduct large-scale randomized control trials and provide technical assistance to diverse populations across a broader geographic area.

In 2015 AIR awarded a $500000 grant to Impact Network a nonprofit seeking to make high-quality education in Zambia sustainable.

In 2014 AIR launched the Education Policy Center.

Company Background

In 2011 the National Center for Analysis of Longitudinal Data in Educational Research (CALDER) began operating as a joint project of AIR. CALDER examines how public policies and community conditions impact teacher-student results. A year earlier AIR acquired Learning Point Associates a Chicago-based firm that delivers research in the educational sector. Its clients include state education agencies single-school districts private foundations and for-profit organizations.

EXECUTIVES

Chairman, Patricia B Gurin
Board of Directors, Dona Kilpatrick
Financial Executive, Lisa Binner
Accountant, Lubna Bashir
Chief Operating Officer, Lydia Quijada
Project Director, Joyce Burrell
Financial Executive, Greg Derritt
Auditors: RUBINO & COMPANY CHARTERED BE

LOCATIONS

HQ: AMERICAN INSTITUTES FOR RESEARCH IN THE BEHAVIORAL SCIENCES
1000 THMAS JFFERSON ST NW, WASHINGTON, DC 200073835
Phone: 202 403-5000
Web: WWW.AIR.ORG

PRODUCTS/OPERATIONS

Selected Program Areas
Education
Education assessment
Health
Human development
International development
Work & training

HISTORICAL FINANCIALS
Company Type: Private

Income Statement
FYE: December 31

	REVENUE ($ mil.)	NET INCOME ($ mil.)	NET PROFIT MARGIN	EMPLOYEES
12/15	488	45	9.2%	1,700
12/14	396	24	6.2%	—
12/13	356	24	6.8%	—
12/12	326	22	6.9%	—
Annual Growth	14.4%	26.1%	—	—

2015 Year-End Financials
Return on assets: 8.6% Cash ($ mil.): 22
Return on equity: 9.2%
Current ratio: 1.50

AMERICAN KIDNEY FUND, INC.

EXECUTIVES

Executive Director, Lavarne Burton
Manager, Rae Kelley
Program Manager, Dennis Cooper
Vice-President, Carol Cohen
Director of Finance, Beverly Matlock
Director, Brock Field
Director, Fiona Lawless
Auditors: CLIFTONLARSONALLEN LLP TIMONI

LOCATIONS

HQ: AMERICAN KIDNEY FUND, INC.
11921 ROCKVILLE PIKE # 300, ROCKVILLE, MD 208522737
Phone: 301 881-3690
Web: WWW.KIDNEYFUND.ORG

HISTORICAL FINANCIALS
Company Type: Private

Income Statement
FYE: December 31

	REVENUE ($ mil.)	NET INCOME ($ mil.)	NET PROFIT MARGIN	EMPLOYEES
12/15	265	(0)	—	40
12/14	239	2	1.1%	—
12/13	219	1	0.9%	—
12/12	186	(9)	—	—
Annual Growth	12.4%	—	—	—

2015 Year-End Financials
Return on assets: 0.5% Cash ($ mil.): 4
Return on equity: (-0.3%)
Current ratio: 3.20

AMERICAN LEBANESE SYRIAN ASSOCIATED CHARITIES, INC.

EXECUTIVES

President, Rick Shadyac Jr
Chief Financial Officer, Jeffrey T Pearson
Officer, Sara Hall
Officer, Martin Hand
Officer, Melanee Hannock
Officer, Sue Harpole
Senior Vice-President, Wilfred Busby
Senior Vice-President, Steve Cox
Auditors: DELOITTE TAX LLP NASHVILLE T

LOCATIONS

HQ: AMERICAN LEBANESE SYRIAN ASSOCIATED CHARITIES, INC.
501 SAINT JUDE PL, MEMPHIS, TN 381051905
Phone: 901 578-2150

HISTORICAL FINANCIALS
Company Type: Private

Income Statement
FYE: June 30

	REVENUE ($ mil.)	NET INCOME ($ mil.)	NET PROFIT MARGIN	EMPLOYEES
06/15	1,182	251	21.2%	1,200
06/13	976	210	21.5%	—
06/12	780	72	9.3%	—
06/11	1,066	444	41.7%	—
Annual Growth	2.6%	(13.3%)	—	—

2015 Year-End Financials
Return on assets: 2.4% Cash ($ mil.): 115
Return on equity: 21.2%
Current ratio: 1.80

AMERICAN MEDIA, INC.

These publications cover some American obsessions: celebrity gossip and good health. American Media is the nation's top publisher of tabloid newspapers and magazines including National Enquirer and Star . The company also publishes women's health magazine Shape as well as a number of other magazines including Flex Men's Fitness and Natural Health . In addition to publishing its own titles American Media also distributes and markets other publishers' periodicals. The company is owned by a group of investment firms including Angelo Gordon & Co.

Geographic Reach

American Media sells its magazine worldwide although the US and Canada are its primary markets. The company offers distribution and marketing services to other publishers to get their periodicals in the racks at supermarkets throughout the US and Canada.

Financial Performance

The company reported revenue of $245 million in fiscal 2015. That was a decrease of almost $100 million (or 29%) in fiscal 2014 compared to the prior fiscal year. The drop in revenue resulted in American Media reporting a net loss of more than $27 million in fiscal 2014 although that was an improvement of about $27 million compared to the $54 million net loss the company suffered in fiscal 2013.

During fiscal 2015 the company's cash inflows increased by 30% to $12.71 million compared to $9.79 million in fiscal 2014.

Strategy

With the magazine and newspaper industries in decline the company's publications are struggling to remain viable in the era of Internet blogs and expanding choices on cable television. American Media transformed its core publications Star and National Enquirer into celebrity gossip papers but that niche is quickly being dominated by online and multimedia operators such as TMZ and Gawker Media.

HISTORY

Generoso Pope Jr. bought the weekly New York Evening Enquirer in 1952 changed it into a tabloid added unusual news items and gave it a more national focus. It was renamed National Enquirer in 1957. Pope died in 1988 and Macfadden Holdings (publisher of such magazines as True Confessions) and Boston Ventures bought the company the next year. In 1990 they formed American Media and acquired the Star; a year later American Media went public.

In 1994 Macfadden Holdings and Boston Ventures were rebuffed in a $315 million LBO that would have taken the company private again. Advertising cuts and increased coverage of celebrities on TV and by other magazines caused circulation to slide but the O. J. Simpson trial boosted sales by 15%-20% for both the Enquirer and the Star.

Soft circulation continued in 1996 but a price increase helped revenues. In 1997 many retailers limited the tabloid content they would sell following the death (allegedly caused by paparazzi) of Diana Princess of Wales. Echoing their concern new editor Steve Coz said the Enquirer would scale back its lurid content.

In the first half of 1998 circulation fell about 15% for both the Enquirer and the Star. American Media that year introduced its first newsletter HealthPlus in an effort to diversify.

In 1999 American Media ceased publication of Soap Opera News and Soap Opera Magazine both massive money pits and sold the magazines' trade-

marks to PRIMEDIA. Later that year Evercore Partners bought the company and David Pecker the former head of Hachette Filipacchi Magazines (now part of Lagardère Active Media) took over as CEO. Pecker initiated a makeover for the Enquirer to give it a more newsy look attracting large advertisers such as Procter & Gamble and Bristol-Myers Squibb. The company also launched National Enquirer TV (renamed National Enquirer's Uncovered in 2000) and bought rival Globe Communications for about $105 million.

American Media launched two new titles Spanish-language tabloid Mira! and AMI AutoWorld Weekly in 2000. Also that year it acquired Country Music Magazine giving the company the two best-selling titles in the country music category. The anthrax scare touched American Media in 2001 when spores were found in company headquarters and an employee died from anthrax. The local health department quarantined the company's headquarters for an additional 18 months in 2002. The company relocated to a building two blocks away and sold the contaminated building.

Facing a difficult newsstand market Pecker announced in fall 2003 plans to cut 7% of the staff about 70 positions mainly in the legal manufacturing and editorial departments. That same year American Media moved to expand its publishing operations by acquiring several health and fitness publications from Weider Publications including Muscle & Fitness Shape and Flex for $350 million. It also hired Us Weekly editor Bonnie Fuller to revamp Star and build credibility at its publications. (Due to declining sales she was bumped up to the corporate executive ranks as chief of editorial operations and relieved of her duties at the tabloid after just 16 months; she resigned in 2008.)

American Media formed a joint venture with Integrity Multimedia in 2008 to acquire the website Radar Online as part of an effort to boost its online publishing operations. The following year however the company was forced to restructure its mounting debt by selling a 95% stake to a group of bondholders including Angelo Gordon & Co. The move helped the company avoid bankruptcy. American Media eventually did file for Chapter 11 bankruptcy protection in 2010 before emerging at the end of the year after restructuring its debt through a revolving credit agreement.

EXECUTIVES

Publisher, Alan Stiles
Manager, Armando Montalvo
Vice-President, Bobbie Halfin
Advertising Director, Jeff Vogel
President, John Swider
Senior Vice-President, Michael Esposito
Executive Vice-President, Barbara Harris
Auditors: DELOITTE & TOUCHE LLP BOCA R

LOCATIONS

HQ: AMERICAN MEDIA, INC.
4 NEW YORK PLZ FL 2, NEW YORK, NY 100042466
Phone: 212 545-4800
Web: WWW.HEALTHDIRECTUSA.COM

2015 Sales

	$ mil.	% of total
US	234	96
Europe	10	4
Total	**245**	**100**

PRODUCTS/OPERATIONS

2015 Sales

	$ mil.	% of total
Circulation	166	99
Advertising	67	1
Other	11	1
Total	**245**	**100**

2015 Sales

	$ mil.	% of total
Celebrity Brands	179	74
Men's Active Lifestyle Group	59	24
Corporate and other	6	2
Total	**245**	**100**

COMPETITORS

Bauer Publishing USA	Northern and Shell
Cond © Nast	Rodale
Gawker Media	TMZ
Hearst Magazines	Time Inc.
Lagard ¨re Active	Wenner Media
Meredith Corporation	

HISTORICAL FINANCIALS

Company Type: Private

Income Statement

FYE: March 31

	REVENUE ($ mil.)	NET INCOME ($ mil.)	NET PROFIT MARGIN	EMPLOYEES
03/16	223	18	8.1%	2,475
03/15	245	(25)	—	
03/14	344	(53)	—	
Annual Growth (19.5%)				

2016 Year-End Financials

Return on assets: 4.8% Cash ($ mil.): 1
Return on equity: 8.1%
Current ratio: 0.40

AMERICAN MUNICIPAL POWER, INC.

Power to the Public is the motto of American Municipal Power (AMP). The non-profit membership organization supplies wholesale power to more than 80 community-owned distribution utilities in Ohio 30 in Pennsylvania 6 in Michigan 5 in Virginia 3 in Kentucky 2 in West Virginia 1 in Indiana and 1 in Delaware (a joint action agency). AMP and its members own and operate plants that generate more than 1500 MW of power. The company also handles projects on behalf of the Ohio Municipal Electric Generating Agency (OMEGA) Joint Ventures program (jointly owned generation and transmission projects). The power generation company is owned by its member municipalities. AMP member utilities serve some 635000 customers.

Operations

The company provides electric capacity and energy and furnishes other services to its members on a cooperative basis. As part of its joint venture responsibilities American Municipal Power also operates the Belleville Hydroelectric Plant a 42 MW plant located in Belleville West Virginia. AMP's wholly-owned subsidiary AMPO provides assistance in establishing electric and gas aggregation programs to benefit local consumers.

Geographic Reach

Ohio-based American Municipal Power serves 130 members - 129 member municipal electric communities in the states of Ohio Pennsylvania Michigan Indiana Virginia Kentucky and West Virginia as well as the Delaware Municipal Electric Corporation a joint action agency headquartered in Smyrna Delaware.

Financial Performance

American Municipal Power (AMP) reported $982.5 million in revenue in 2013 representing a 19% increase over 2012. Rising electric revenues

and service fees up 19% and 44% respectively drove growth in 2013. AMP's net margin expanded to $5.3 million from $1.9 million over the same period.

Strategy

Expanding into Indiana in 2014 AMP gained its newest member the city of Cannelton.

Implementing a strategy to reduce carbon emissions the company is building six hydroelectric projects on the Ohio River. The Meldahl plant (with 105 MW of capacity) will be the largest hydroelectric plant on the Ohio River. American Municipal Power also has a deal to develop up to 300 MW of solar power with solar panel company Standard Energy. It also has wind power and landfill gas operations. Indeed AMP members' projected energy resource mix will be approximately 21% renewable by 2015.

In 2013 American Municipal Power and the Vermont Energy Investment Corporation agreed to extend the operation of Efficiency Smart beyond the end of the year. The program provides a broad range of energy efficiency services for the power coop's member utilities. Some 49 member communities in Ohio Pennsylvania and Michigan participated in Efficiency Smart in 2013.

Company Background

To replace lost capacity in 2011 it acquired the Fremont Energy Center in Fremont Ohio from FirstEnergy for $500 million. The 707-MW natural gas combined-cycle facility commenced commercial operation in early 2012. In 2010 American Municipal Power also secured a 368-MW ownership stake in the Prairie State Energy Campus in Illinois.

Expanding geographically American Municipal Power moved into a seventh state in 2011 when it made Delaware Municipal Electric its 129th member.

American Municipal Power was founded in 1971.

EXECUTIVES

President, Marc Gerken
Assistant Vice-President, Ray Merrill
Director, Jerry Willman
Manager, David Fields
General Manager, Dan Moats
Auditors: PRICEWATERHOUSECOOPERS LLP CO

LOCATIONS

HQ: AMERICAN MUNICIPAL POWER, INC.
1111 SCHROCK RD STE 100, COLUMBUS, OH 432291155
Phone: 614 540-1111
Web: WWW.AMPPARTNERS.ORG

PRODUCTS/OPERATIONS

2013 Sales

	% of total
Electric revenues	97
Service fees	1
Programs & other	2
Total	**100**

Selected Services

Aggregation
Business Development
Clean Energy & Conservation
Community Outreach
Financial
Legislative Regulatory & Legal
Power Supply / AMP Energy Control Center
Safety Programs
Scholarship Programs
Technical Services

COMPETITORS

Dominion Energy   Ohio Valley Electric
Duke Energy Ohio

HISTORICAL FINANCIALS

Company Type: Private

Income Statement

FYE: December 31

	REVENUE ($ mil.)	NET INCOME ($ mil.)	NET PROFIT MARGIN	EMPLOYEES
12/15	1,127	5	0.5%	229
12/14	1,039	2	0.2%	—
12/13	982	5	0.5%	—
12/12	823	1	0.2%	—
Annual Growth	**11.0%**	**45.0%**	**—**	**—**

2015 Year-End Financials

Return on assets: 10.7%   Cash ($ mil.): 107
Return on equity: 0.5%
Current ratio: 0.50

AMERICAN SYSTEMS CORPORATION

American Systems provides government and commercial clients with IT management and consulting services including custom engineering and application development. Its consulting division advises clients on such issues as network access and identity management data security and process optimization. The company also provides managed technical support and staffing. American Systems works with government customers to develop systems related to command and control logistics and national security functions. Its commercial-focused operations serve the energy financial services retail and telecom industries among others.

Operations

American Systems' government unit serves every branch of the US military as well as government agencies ranging from the Federal Aviation Administration to the Department of Agriculture. Its commercial unit on the other hand has served such companies as AT&T The Coca-Cola Company and The Home Depot.

Geographic Reach

The company has 16 offices along the Eastern Seaboard and in Arizona and California.

Mergers and Acquisitions

The company's acquisition of Science Applications International Corporation's (SAIC's) Test & Evaluation (T&E) business unit strengthened American Systems' T&E capabilities and expanded the company's offerings to include testing scientific engineering logistic administrative and ancillary support.

EXECUTIVES

Vice President Executive Director, Peter Pflugrath
Vice President, John Manning
Vice President Operations, William Killham
Vice President and Director, Steve Bonwich
Vice President and Ed Navy Programs, Stephen Bonwich
Vice President General Manager, Jason Frye
Vice President C4I Director, Frank Muller
Vice President, Joseph Di Zinno
Vice President Capture Management, Helene Johnson
Vice President Director, Jeff Jancek
Auditors: BDO USA LLP MCLEAN VIRGINIA

LOCATIONS

HQ: AMERICAN SYSTEMS CORPORATION
14151 PK MADOW DR STE 500, CHANTILLY, VA 20151
Phone: 703 968-6300
Web: WWW.AMERICANSYSTEMS.COM

PRODUCTS/OPERATIONS

Selected Mergers and Acquisitions

FY2012
Science Applications International Corporation's (SAIC's) Test & Evaluation (T&E) business unit (undisclosed price; Raleigh NC; testing and evaluation services)

COMPETITORS

Alion
Allen Corporation of America
Booz Allen
CACI International
Computer Sciences Corp.
General Dynamics Information Technology
HP Enterprise Services
IBM Global Services
Jacobs Engineering
Kratos Defense & Security Solutions
Leidos
ManTech
Unisys
Ventera

HISTORICAL FINANCIALS

Company Type: Private

Income Statement

FYE: December 31

	REVENUE ($ mil.)	NET INCOME ($ mil.)	NET PROFIT MARGIN	EMPLOYEES
12/15	303	(3)	—	1,150
12/14	318	5	1.7%	—
12/13	324	5	1.6%	—
12/12	242	10	4.3%	—
Annual Growth	**7.8%**	**—**	**—**	**—**

AMERICAN TECHNOLOGIES INC.

EXECUTIVES

President, Gary Moore
Financial Executive, Steve Peace
Director, Norman Carmichael
Manager, Hernan Lopez
Manager, Hugo Viruete
Branch Manager, Tim Kassen
Director, Julie Marchus
Administrative Assistant, Francine Venditte
Auditors: MOSS ADAMS LLP IRVINE CALIF

LOCATIONS

HQ: AMERICAN TECHNOLOGIES INC.
210 W BAYWOOD AVE, ORANGE, CA 928652603
Phone: 714 283-9990
Web: WWW.ATIRESTORATION.COM

Income Statement				FYE: December 31
	REVENUE ($ mil.)	NET INCOME ($ mil.)	NET PROFIT MARGIN	EMPLOYEES
12/15	180	11	6.5%	500
12/14	138	7	5.3%	—
12/13	121	3	2.7%	—
12/10	98	4	4.4%	—
Annual Growth	12.9%	21.9%	—	—

2015 Year-End Financials

Return on assets: 2.8% Cash ($ mil.): —
Return on equity: 6.5%
Current ratio: 1.20

AMERICAN TIRE DISTRIBUTORS HOLDINGS, INC.

Business for American Tire Distributors Holdings starts where the rubber meets the road. The company through its American Tire Distributors (ATD) unit is one of the largest independent tire wholesalers in the North America. Its offerings include flagship brands Bridgestone Continental Goodyear Pirelli and Michelin as well as budget brands and private-label tires. ATD also markets custom wheels and tire service equipment. Its network of 140-plus distribution centers serve independent tire dealers retail chains and auto service centers in more than 40 US states and now Canada. The company is owned by private equity firm TPG Capital.

Operations

Beyond tires which account for about 98% of ATD's total sales the company also distributes wheels and other automotive products. Its brands include Cruiser Alloy Drifz O.E. Performance and Racing which are made a numerous manufacturers. The company also sells lower-priced tires under the brands Capitol and Negotiator.

Passenger & Light Truck Tire sales contributed about 83% to the company's total revenue in fiscal 2015 (ended January 3) with medium truck farm vehicles and specialty tire sales making up the remainder.

Geographic Reach

North Carolina-based American Tire Distributors Holdings rings up about 87% of its sales in the US. Canada accounts for the remainder. The company has nearly 120 distribution centers across some 43 US states and 24 distribution centers in Canada.

Sales and Marketing

ATD sells tires to local regional and national independent tire retailers which are located in the US primarily in the Southeastern Mid-Atlantic regions as well as the Midwest Northeast Southwest and West Coast. Other customers include mass merchandisers warehouse clubs tire-manufacturer-owned stores automotive dealerships and web-based markets.

The company's main suppliers for tires are Bridgestone Continental Goodyear and Michelin from whom it bought more than 55% of its tire products in 2014. Other top suppliers include Hankook Kumho Nexen Nitto and Pirelli.

Financial Performance

ATD's sales have been rising at a healthy clip over the past few years swelling from $3 billion in FY2011 to more than $5 billion in the latest fiscal year. The company's bottom line however has slipped into heavy losses in recent years due to thin operating margins and large (and growing) interest expenses stemming from its long-term debt.

The company's net sales jumped by 31% to $5 billion in fiscal 2015 (ended January 3) thanks to a combination of new distribution centers as well as from added business from slew of wholesale-retail distribution center acquisitions made in 2014 and 2013. Additionally comparable unit tire sales also grew thanks to stronger sales unit environment and because of the fiscal year period adjustment that added four selling days to the fiscal year.

Despite higher revenue in FY2015 ATD suffered a net loss of $94.6 million — its deepest loss in three years. The company's losses worsened considerably from the prior year's $6.4 billion loss mostly as its interest expenses ballooned by an additional $51.3 million compared to the prior year as it borrowed more for acquisitions and because its selling general and administrative costs increased after making those acquisitions. ATD's operating cash levels declined sharply to $31.7 million for the year mostly due to the large decline in cash earnings.

Strategy

ATD plans to grow steadily over the years by opening or selectively acquiring distribution outlets in new and under-served markets particularly in Canada. Before making a slew of acquisitions throughout 2014 to expand its presence in select US markets and Canada the company in 2013 opened distribution centers in Chattanooga Tennessee; Manchester New Hampshire; Missouri City Texas; Albany New York; and West Palm Beach Florida.

The tire wholesaler entered Canada in late 2012 and has been strengthening its presence there through acquisitions ever since.

Mergers and Acquisitions

During 2014 American Tire Distributors and its subsidiaries made several acquisitions to expand its market reach. That year the company acquired wholesale tire distributor Regional Tire Distributor operations in Langley Vernon Victoria Calgary and Edmonton in Canada. It also purchased Canada-based wholesalers Trail Tire Distributors and Extreme Wheel Distributors as well as Canadian wholesale and retail tire businesses Kirks Tire Ltd and Kipling Tire Co.

Also in 2014 the company purchased Hercules Tire Holdings including its Hercules Tire & Rubber Company subsidiary 15 distribution centers in the US six distribution centers in Canada and one warehouse in northern China. The acquisition strengthened ATD's presence in the major markets of California Texas Florida and Canada.

ATD's 2014 acquisition of wholesale-retail distributor Terry's Tire Town Holdings and subsidiaries added 10 US distribution centers spanning from Virginia to Maine and in Ohio expanding its market reach in those regions while aligning distribution centers nicely with ATD's recently opened centers in the Northeast and Ohio.

ATD in November 2012 acquired Triwest Trading (Canada) Ltd. (dba TriCan Tire Distributors or TriCan for short). TriCan is a wholesale distributor of tires tire parts tire accessories and related equipment in Canada with 15 distribution centers nationwide. The purchase marked ATD's entry into Canada.

EXECUTIVES

EVP General Counsel and Secretary, J. Michael (Mike) Gaither, age 64, $400,000 total compensation
EVP and CFO, Jason T. Yaudes, age 43, $400,000 total compensation
President and CEO, Stuart Schuette
EVP Product Strategy and Supply, Jason Shannon
Senior Vice President Proprietary Brands, Joshua Simpson
Regional Vice President, John Reid
Senior Vice President Supply Chain, Mark Chandler
Vice President Supply Chain, Randy Arthur
Assistant Treasurer, Chris Ravenberg
Auditors: PRICEWATERHOUSECOOPERS LLP CH

LOCATIONS

HQ: AMERICAN TIRE DISTRIBUTORS HOLDINGS, INC.
12200 HERBERT WAYNE CT # 150, HUNTERSVILLE, NC 280786335
Phone: 704 992-2000
Web: WWW.ATD-US.COM

2014 Sales

	% of total
US	87
Canada	13
Total	**100**

PRODUCTS/OPERATIONS

2014 Sales by Product

	% of total
Passenger & light truck tires	83
Medium trucks farm vehicles & other specialty tires	17
Total	**100**

2014 Sales

	% of total
Tires	98
Tire supplies tools custom wheels & accessories	2
Total	**100**

Brands

Brands
Capitol®; tires
Negotiator®; tires
Regul®; tires
Dynatrac®; tires
Cruiseralloy®; custom wheels
Drifz®; custom wheels
ICW®; custom wheels
Pacer®; custom wheels
O.E. Performance®; custom wheels

Selected Products

Equipment tools and supplies (valve stems auto lifts)
Tires
Wheel covers
Wheel Wizard (computer program allowing customers to virtually see wheel types on their vehicle)

COMPETITORS

Dealer Tire	Tire Distribution
TBC	Systems
TCI Tire Centers	Wal-Mart

HISTORICAL FINANCIALS
Company Type: Private

Income Statement				FYE: January 3
	REVENUE ($ mil.)	NET INCOME ($ mil.)	NET PROFIT MARGIN	EMPLOYEES
01/15*	5,030	(94)	—	500
12/13	3,839	(6)	—	—
12/12	3,455	(14)	—	—
12/11	3,050	0	0.0%	—
Annual Growth	18.1%	—	—	—

*Fiscal year change

Return on assets: 14.8%   Cash ($ mil.): 35
Return on equity: (-1.9%)
Current ratio: 0.50

AMERICAN TRANSMISSION COMPANY, LLC

American Transmission Company is an entrepreneur in the US power grid business — a for-profit multi-state transmission-only utility. Connecting electricity producers to distributors American Transmission owns operates monitors and maintains 9480 miles of high-voltage electric transmission lines and 529 substations in portions of Illinois Michigan Minnesota and Wisconsin. The company a member of the Midwest Independent Transmission System Operator (MISO) regional transmission organization operates the former transmission assets of some of its shareholders. About 30 utilities municipalities electric companies and cooperatives in its service area have an ownership stake in American Transmission.

Operations

Unlike most other power utilities American Transmission is not engaged in the generation distribution or marketing of electricity. Its duties include reliable operation of the transmission system growing the system to meet current and future needs and upgrading and maintain the transmission equipment as needed.

American Transmission is a member of the MISO regional transmission organization and provides nondiscriminatory service to all customers supporting effective competition in energy markets without favoring any market participant.

Geographic Reach

American Transmission meets the power needs of about 5 million people in 72 counties in Illinois Michigan Minnesota and Wisconsin. It operates North central Wisconsin Michigan's Upper Peninsula and Northern Wisconsin South Central/Southwest Wisconsin and North Central Illinois Northeast Wisconsin and Southeast Wisconsin.

Sales and Marketing

The company's customers include local electric distribution companies municipal utilities and cooperative utilities (that procure primary network transmission service and are interconnected or plan on interconnecting to its transmission system) local and national marketers generators and utilities (that procure primarily point-to-point transmission service generators and other transmission systems that want to interconnect with American Transmission's system).

Financial Performance

American Transmission reported revenues of about $603 million in 2012 a 6% increase over 2011 revenues.

Strategy

The company is trying to use its single focus on power transmission to win more customers. American Transmission has invested more than $2.8 billion on infrastructure upgrades (since 2001) including 2305 miles of power line. It has also built more 560 miles of new lines during this time period. By 2021 the company plans to spend a further $3.9-$4.8 billion on infrastructure improvement with a focus on adding new renewable sources to its expanded grid.

In 2014 American Transmission filed applications with the Public Service Commission of Wisconsin to rebuild a 12.5 mile 138000-volt transmission line in western Kenosha County at a cost $12.2 million and a 69000-volt transmission line between Dyckesville Wisconsin and Sturgeon Bay Wisconsin (for $23 million).

In 2013 American Transmission received authorizing to build two new 138-kilovolt transmission lines needed to improve electric system reliability in western Milwaukee County and began construction activities on a new 5.8-mile 345-kilovolt electric transmission line to strengthen the electric system in southeastern Wisconsin and northeastern Illinois. That year it energized the 32-mile 345-kilovolt Rockdale-West Middleton Transmission Line; and placed in service. In 2013 American Transmission

In 2012 it teamed up with ALLETE to study transmission options for transporting Midwestern wind energy as well as Canadian hydroelectric power into Minnesota Wisconsin and Michigan to help local utilities enhance reliability and meet renewable energy goals. To further enable movement of renewable energy that year the company and Minnesota Power agreed to develop a 50-mile double-circuit 345-kilovolt transmission line from the Mesabi Iron Range to the companies' jointly owned Arrowhead Substation in Duluth. The project is due to come into service in 2020.

Company Background

In 2010 it signed two agreements with the Department of Energy to access $12.7 million in investment grants for incorporating smart grid technologies into its transmission system.

In 2011 it announced a plan to build seven new transmission line projects (1800 miles of new line) aimed at filling gaps in the existing transmission grid improving grid reliability and enabling increased delivery of renewable power in Iowa Wisconsin Illinois Indiana and Ohio. The projects in total will cost about $4 billion. It also agreed to purchase of the Zephyr Power Transmission Project (950 miles of transmission line between Wyoming and southern Nevada) in another $4 billion deal.

Boosting its transmission assets in 2011 American Transmission formed a transmission utility joint venture with Duke Energy. Duke-American Transmission Co. builds owns and operates new power transmission infrastructure across North America.

American Transmission is one of the first for-profit transmission companies formed (in 2001) when the US market deregulated in the early 2000s. It is 88% owned by investor-owned utilities and 12% owned by municipalities municipal electric companies and electric cooperatives.

EXECUTIVES

NATIONAL SALES MANAGER, Jennifer Miller
Auditors: DELOITTE & TOUCHE LLP MILWAU

LOCATIONS

HQ: AMERICAN TRANSMISSION COMPANY, LLC
W234N2000 RDGVIEW PKY CT, WAUKESHA, WI 531881022
Phone: 262 506-6700
Web: WWW.ATCLLC.COM

PRODUCTS/OPERATIONS

Contributing Owners
Adams-Columbia Electric Cooperative
Alger Delta Cooperative Electric Association
Badger Power Marketing Authority
Central Wisconsin Electric Cooperative
City of Algoma
City of Columbus
City of Kaukauna
City of Menasha
City of Oconto Falls
City of Plymouth
City of Reedsburg
City of Sheboygan Falls
City of Sturgeon Bay
City of Sun Prairie
City of Wisconsin Rapids
Cloverland Electric Cooperative
Edison Sault Electric Company
Madison Gas & Electric Company
Manitowoc Public Utilities
Marshfield Electric and Water Department
Ontonagon County Rural Electrification Association
Rainy River Energy
Rock Energy Cooperative
Stoughton Utilities
Upper Peninsula Public Power Agency
Wisconsin Electric Power Company
Wisconsin Power & Light Company
Wisconsin Public Service Corporation
WPPI Energy

COMPETITORS

AES	Exelon
Ameren	FirstEnergy
Duke Energy	

HISTORICAL FINANCIALS

Company Type: Private

Income Statement   FYE: December 31

	REVENUE ($ mil.)	NET INCOME ($ mil.)	NET PROFIT MARGIN	EMPLOYEES
12/15	615	200	32.5%	547
12/14	635	238	37.6%	—
12/13	626	247	39.5%	—
12/12	603	237	39.4%	—
Annual Growth	0.7%	(5.5%)	—	—

AMERICAN UNIVERSITY OF BEIRUT INC

EXECUTIVES

President, Fablo R Khuri
Board of Directors, David Bickers
Board of Directors, Phillip Winder
Manager, M S Darwih
Director, Jem De Alwis
Editor, Fadi Lakkis
Auditors: DELOITTE & TOUCHE LLP NEW YOR

LOCATIONS

HQ: AMERICAN UNIVERSITY OF BEIRUT INC
3 DAG HAMMARSKJOLD PLZ # 8, NEW YORK, NY 100172324
Phone: 212 583-7600
Web: WWW.AUB.EDU.LB

HISTORICAL FINANCIALS

Company Type: Private

Income Statement   FYE: June 30

	REVENUE ($ mil.)	NET INCOME ($ mil.)	NET PROFIT MARGIN	EMPLOYEES
06/15	390	(2)	—	4,400
06/14*	508	53	10.5%	—
09/03	0	0	—	—
06/98	131	70	53.5%	—
Annual Growth	6.6%	—	—	—

2015 Year-End Financials

Return on assets: 21.5%   Cash ($ mil.): 94
Return on equity: (-0.7%)
Current ratio: —

AMERICARES FOUNDATION, INC.

AmeriCares Foundation provides emergency medical aid around the world. The not-for-profit charitable organization helps victims of natural disasters and supports long-term humanitarian programs by collecting medical supplies in the US and overseas and delivering them to places where they are needed. AmeriCares has provided aid in more than 90 countries worldwide. In the US the organization offers medical assistance runs a camp for kids with HIV/AIDS and conducts HomeFront a program that renovates housing for the needy in parts of Connecticut and New York. Robert C. Macauley founded AmeriCares in 1982.

Geographic Reach

The company has presence in US Latin America Caribbean Asia and Eurasia Africa and Middle East.

Financial Performance

AmeriCares' revenue decreased 9% to $572 million in 2014 due to a decline in public support and loss on investments.

EXECUTIVES

President, Michael Nyenhuis
Director, Brian Hoyer
Supervisor, Greg Loop
Director, Karl Erdmann
Administrative Assistant, Robin Bram
Manager, Jennifer Martins
Manager, Emanuela Chiaranda
Director, Randy Weiss
Auditors: GRANT THORNTON LLP NEW YORK

LOCATIONS

HQ: AMERICARES FOUNDATION, INC.
 88 HAMILTON AVE, STAMFORD, CT 069023100
Phone: 203 658-9500
Web: WWW.AMERICARES.ORG

HISTORICAL FINANCIALS

Company Type: Private

Income Statement

	REVENUE ($ mil.)	NET INCOME ($ mil.)	NET PROFIT MARGIN	EMPLOYEES
				FYE: June 30
06/15	742	101	13.7%	231
06/14	560	(4)	—	—
06/12	526	5	1.1%	—
06/11	671	(0)	—	—
Annual Growth	2.5%	—	—	—

2015 Year-End Financials

Return on assets: 0.6%   Cash ($ mil.): 10
Return on equity: 13.7%
Current ratio: —

AMERIGREEN ENERGY, INC.

EXECUTIVES

President, Jeffrey B Lyons
Board of Directors, Heather Woratyla
Marketing Manager, Dave Hessen
Administrative Assistant, Jen Peters
Consultant, Gena Kotarsky
VP Operations, Jason Lawrence
Director, Karen Shreiner
Consultant, Mark McGaha
Auditors: HOROVITZ RUDOY & ROTEMAN LLC

LOCATIONS

HQ: AMERIGREEN ENERGY, INC.
 1650 MANHEIM PIKE STE 201, LANCASTER, PA
 176013088
Phone: 717 945-1392
Web: WWW.AMERIGREEN.COM

HISTORICAL FINANCIALS

Company Type: Private

Income Statement

	REVENUE ($ mil.)	NET INCOME ($ mil.)	NET PROFIT MARGIN	EMPLOYEES
				FYE: September 30
09/15	212	0	0.4%	22
09/14	257	0	0.0%	—
09/13	181	1	0.7%	—
09/12	93	0	0.0%	—
Annual Growth	31.3%	226.8%	—	—

2015 Year-End Financials

Return on assets: 3.4%   Cash ($ mil.): —
Return on equity: 0.4%
Current ratio: 0.70

AMES CONSTRUCTION, INC.

Ames Construction aims right for the heart of heavy construction. The company is a general contractor providing heavy civil and industrial construction services to the transportation mining and power industries mainly in the West and Midwest. The family-owned company works on highways airports bridges rail lines mining facilities power plants and other infrastructure projects. Ames also performs flood control environmental remediation reclamation and landfill work. Additionally the firm builds golf courses and undertakes commercial and residential site development projects. Ames typically partners with other companies to perform the engineering and design portion of construction jobs.

Operations

Some of Ames Construction's project include the Arlington Power Plant Dry Fork Station Unit 1 Site Work and Substructure Construction Rentech ClearFuels Cortez Hills Mine and Mills Site and Airport Extension Projects such as its MSP International Airport work.

Geographic Reach

Ames Construction has offices in the US in Minnesota Arizona California Colorado Nevada and Utah as well as in Canada.

Strategy

Ames Construction is also known to take on subcontracting work. It contributed to the construction of the new Minnesota Twins ballpark. Ames also is serving as subcontractor and partner in a joint venture with Fluor and Balfour Beatty Rail that is undertaking the $1 billion design/build portion of a rail line project for the Denver Regional Transit District. The contract involves designing and constructing electrified commuter rail lines stations and a vehicle maintenance facility. The joint venture will also operate and maintain the system for a period of 40 years. All lines are expected to be in service by 2016.

Having earned the contract in 2013 Ames Construction is the construction manager general contractor (CMGC) contracting team for the Winona Bridge the first Minnesota Department of Transportation project to use the CMGC procurement method.

EXECUTIVES

Vice President Of Engineering, John Tripi
Vice President of Management Services, Roger L Mcbride
Vice President Structures, Jerry Volz
Vice President and General Counsel, Todd Goderstad
Regional Vice President of Engineering, Robert Gillis
Vice President Engineering, Jeff Williamson
Vice President of Engineering, Butch Trebesch
Vice President Design build, Richard Fahland
Auditors: CLIFTONLARSONALLEN LLP MINNEA

LOCATIONS

HQ: AMES CONSTRUCTION, INC.
 14420 COUNTY ROAD 5, BURNSVILLE, MN
 553066997
Phone: 952 435-7106
Web: WWW.AMESCONSTRUCTION.COM

Selected Locations
Arizona
California
Canada
Colorado
Minnesota
Nevada
Utah

PRODUCTS/OPERATIONS

Selected Markets
Commercial
  Commercial site development
  Environmental remediation/ landfills
  Residential site development
Mining
  Contract mining
  Leach pad construction
  Mine development
  Mine infrastructure
  Mine reclamation/remediation
  Mine tailings dam
Power
  Coal fired
  Combined-cycle/natural gas
  Nuclear
  Transmission
  Wind
Transportation
  Airports
  Bridges
  Highways
  Railroads
Water resources
  Dams reservoirs and flood control
  Wastewater/water treatment
  Water delivery
  Water retention structures

COMPETITORS

American Civil Constructors Holdings
Balfour Beatty Construction
Clyde Companies

Granite Construction
Meadow Valley
Peter Kiewit Sons'
SEMA Construction
Skanska USA Civil
Sterling Construction
Tutor-Saliba

HISTORICAL FINANCIALS
Company Type: Private

Income Statement
FYE: November 30

	REVENUE ($ mil.)	NET INCOME ($ mil.)	NET PROFIT MARGIN	EMPLOYEES
11/15	1,068	5	0.5%	2,200
11/14*	1,074	26	2.4%	—
12/12	582	5	1.0%	—
11/10	685	18	2.7%	—
Annual Growth	9.3%	(23.0%)	—	—

*Fiscal year change

2015 Year-End Financials
Return on assets: 7.9%   Cash ($ mil.): 55
Return on equity: 0.5%
Current ratio: 0.80

ANAHEIM UNION HIGH SCHOOL DIST

EXECUTIVES
Superintendent, Michael Matsuda
Account Manager, Karen Orr
Director, San Phan
Director, Susan Stocks
Purchasing Director, Brad Minami
Consultant, Leticia Gomez
Consultant, Linda Owen
Auditors: VAVRINEK TRINE DAY & CO LL

LOCATIONS
HQ: ANAHEIM UNION HIGH SCHOOL DIST
501 N CRESCENT WAY, ANAHEIM, CA 928015401
Phone: 714 999-3511
Web: WWW.AUHSD.US

HISTORICAL FINANCIALS
Company Type: Private

Income Statement
FYE: June 30

	REVENUE ($ mil.)	NET INCOME ($ mil.)	NET PROFIT MARGIN	EMPLOYEES
06/15	365	41	11.2%	2,300
06/14	343	7	2.1%	—
06/09	109	1	1.6%	—
06/05	321	0	—	—
Annual Growth	1.3%	—	—	—

ANDERSEN CONSTRUCTION COMPANY

Andersen Construction Company focuses on commercial and industrial construction in the Western US. The group which introduced concrete tilt-up construction to the Pacific Northwest builds everything from parking structures to medical facilities manufacturing plants and industrial complexes. It also works on institutional projects for the government and education markets. Other projects include tenant improvements seismic upgrades and remediation construction. The company provides construction management (which accounts for 80% of its work) as well as general contracting and design/build delivery. It also offers startup and commissioning services. Chairman and CEO Andy Andersen founded the company in 1950.

Andersen Construction has offices in Oregon and Idaho. It has built and renovated more than 35 Bank of America branches throughout the Pacific Northwest constructed a computer chip manufacturing facility for Hewlett-Packard and worked on the Cole M. Rivers Hatchery the largest fish hatchery on the West Coast. Projects under way include an expansion and renovation of the Shriners Hospitals For Children in Portland.

As a green builder Andersen Construction incorporates LEED standards into its design/build plans and is a founding member of the Oregon Natural Step Network an international network that follows a scientific framework that helps businesses individuals and organizations achieve sustainability.

EXECUTIVES
Executive Manager, Adele Rygg
Auditors: THOMPSON KESSLER WIEST & BORQU

LOCATIONS
HQ: ANDERSEN CONSTRUCTION COMPANY
6712 N CUTTER CIR, PORTLAND, OR 972173933
Phone: 503 283-6712
Web: WWW.ANDERSEN-CONST.COM

PRODUCTS/OPERATIONS

Selected Services
Commercial development (acquisition due diligence financing land entitlements leasing master planning and permitting)
Construction management
Design/build
Estimating
General contracting
Green building
Preconstruction
Startup and commissioning

COMPETITORS
Absher	PCL Construction
GLY Construction	Enterprises
Hoffman Corporation	Skanska USA Building
Howard S. Wright	Swinerton Builders
Construction	Turner Corporation
M. A. Mortenson	

HISTORICAL FINANCIALS
Company Type: Private

Income Statement
FYE: January 31

	REVENUE ($ mil.)	NET INCOME ($ mil.)	NET PROFIT MARGIN	EMPLOYEES
01/16	582	0	0.2%	150
01/15	392	0	0.1%	—
01/14	329	0	0.1%	—
01/11	278	1	0.4%	—
Annual Growth	15.9%	(1.4%)	—	—

2016 Year-End Financials
Return on assets: 10.2%   Cash ($ mil.): —
Return on equity: 0.2%
Current ratio: 0.90

ANDERSON AND DUBOSE, INC.

You might say this company keeps the Big Mac big and the Happy Meals happy. Anderson-DuBose Pittsburgh is a leading wholesale distributor that supplies food and non-food items to McDonald's and Chipotle fast-food restaurants in Ohio Pennsylvania New York and West Virginia. It serves about 500 Golden Arches locations with frozen meat and fish dairy products and paper goods and packaging as well as toys for Happy Meals. One of the largest black-owned companies in the US Anderson-DuBose was started in 1991 by Warren Anderson and Stephen DuBose who purchased control of a McDonald's distributorship from Martin-Brower. Anderson became sole owner in 1993 when he bought out his partner's stake in the business.

EXECUTIVES
President, Warren Anderson
Account Manager, Ray Bonner
Finance Manager, Tony Wiglusz

LOCATIONS
HQ: ANDERSON AND DUBOSE, INC.
5300 TOD AVE SW, WARREN, OH 444819767
Phone: 440 248-8800
Web: WWW.ANDERSON-DUBOSE.COM

COMPETITORS
Golden State Foods	Meadowbrook Meat
Gordon Food Service	Company
Keystone Foods	Reinhart FoodService
MAINES	Sysco
Martin-Brower	US Foods

HISTORICAL FINANCIALS
Company Type: Private

Income Statement
FYE: December 25

	REVENUE ($ mil.)	NET INCOME ($ mil.)	NET PROFIT MARGIN	EMPLOYEES
12/15	546	2	0.4%	100
12/14	550	2	0.5%	—
12/11	372	1	0.3%	—
12/10	341	1	0.5%	—
Annual Growth	9.9%	7.8%	—	—

2015 Year-End Financials
Return on assets: 2.0%   Cash ($ mil.): —
Return on equity: 0.4%
Current ratio: 0.40

ANDERSON REGIONAL MEDICAL CENTER

EXECUTIVES

Chief Executive Officer, W Jeff Anderson
Board of Directors, Larry Fortenberry
Director, Scottie Stokes
Vice-President, Ann Lundy

LOCATIONS

HQ: ANDERSON REGIONAL MEDICAL CENTER
2124 14TH ST, MERIDIAN, MS 393014040
Phone: 601 553-6000
Web: WWW.JARMC.ORG

HISTORICAL FINANCIALS

Company Type: Private

Income Statement

FYE: September 30

	REVENUE ($ mil.)	NET INCOME ($ mil.)	NET PROFIT MARGIN	EMPLOYEES
09/15	177	(14)	—	1,314
09/14	145	8	5.8%	—
09/13	0	12	—	—
09/12	141	(6)	—	—
Annual Growth	7.9%	—	—	—

2015 Year-End Financials

Return on assets: 5.7% Cash ($ mil.): 17
Return on equity: (-8.4%)
Current ratio: 1.30

ANMED HEALTH

EXECUTIVES

President, John A Miller Jr
Director, Dan Corrigan

LOCATIONS

HQ: ANMED HEALTH
800 N FANT ST, ANDERSON, SC 296215708
Phone: 864 261-1000
Web: WWW.ANMEDHEALTH.ORG

HISTORICAL FINANCIALS

Company Type: Private

Income Statement

FYE: December 31

	REVENUE ($ mil.)	NET INCOME ($ mil.)	NET PROFIT MARGIN	EMPLOYEES
12/15	590	(1)	—	2,600
12/14	570	37	6.6%	—
12/13*	463	93	20.1%	—
09/12	512	55	10.9%	—
Annual Growth	4.8%	—	—	—

*Fiscal year change

2015 Year-End Financials

Return on assets: 3.0% Cash ($ mil.): 54
Return on equity: (-0.2%)
Current ratio: 1.50

ANN & ROBERT H. LURIE CHILDREN'S HOSPITAL OF CHICAGO

When it comes to caring for kids Ann & Robert H. Lurie Children's Hospital of Chicago has the Windy City covered. Founded in 1882 the not-for-profit hospital provides a full range of pediatric services with acute and specialty care. Lurie Children's provides services through its main hospital campus with about 300 beds and outpatient centers in Chicago's Lincoln Park neighborhood and through more than a dozen suburban outpatient centers and outreach partner locations in the greater Chicago area. A leader in pediatric research the hospital operates the Children's Hospital of Chicago Research Center and is the pediatric teaching facility of Northwestern University's Feinberg School of Medicine.

Operations

Lurie Children's serves roughly 150000 patients each year and employs some 1350 pediatric specialists with expertise in 70 different specialties. The hospital is one of only about a dozen children's hospitals nationwide to perform more than 1000 liver transplants. The center performs on average 50 solid organ and 50 stem cell transplants annually.

A major research center Lurie Children's is one of nearly 30 interdisciplinary research centers and institutes belonging to the hospital's academic partner — Feinberg School of Medicine. Its research arm Stanley Manne Children's Research Institute employs some 200 physician-scientists and research investigators who in 2014 were awarded more than $40 million in external funding.

Geographic Reach

Based in Chicago Lurie Children's has cared for patients from throughout the US and about 50 countries around the globe.

Financial Performance

Lurie Children's saw revenues increase by 8% to $826 million in fiscal 2014 (ended August). That growth was attributed to a rise in patient care revenues and other earnings. Net income increased 198% to $128 million that year largely due to the higher revenue as well as strong investment returns.

Cash flow from operations rose 36% to $124.5 million in fiscal 2014.

Strategy

The hospital has all-private rooms even in the neonatal intensive care unit; private rooms are said to speed healing by reducing hospital-acquired infection and minimize noise. Lurie Children's is working to enhance its specialist services and has upgraded its information technology systems. In 2013 it implemented a Voalte system that allows nurses to communicate through rapid-response systems including text messages and high-definition voice calls. Also that year it opened the first pediatric gender identity clinic. In 2015 the hospital acquired the fourth-generation da Vinci Xi robotic system for use in minimally invasive surgery.

In 2014 Lurie Children's Health Partners (composed of Lurie Children's and two groups of pediatricians) launched the Clinically Integrated Network the first health care network in Chicago to focus exclusively on children and their families. Its areas of focus include care coordination obesity asthma immunizations and child development.

EXECUTIVES

Assistant Vice President Corporate Giving, Erin Coleman
Assistant Vice President Founders' Board and Affiliated Organizations, Katie Spieth
Executive Vice President and Chief Development Officer, Grant Stirling
Vice President Human Resources CHRO Chief Diversity Inclusion Officer, Winifred Williams
Medical Director, Gregory Gruener

LOCATIONS

HQ: ANN & ROBERT H. LURIE CHILDREN'S HOSPITAL OF CHICAGO
225 E CHICAGO AVE, CHICAGO, IL 606112991
Phone: 312 227-7132
Web: WWW.LURIECHILDRENS.ORG

Selected Illinois Locations

Lurie Children's at Cadence Health (Winfield)
Main Hospital (Chicago)
Outpatient Center in Arlington Heights (Arlington Heights)
Outpatient Center in Glenview (Glenview)
Outpatient Center in Lake Forest (Lake Forest)
Outpatient Center in Lincoln Park (Chicago)
Outpatient Center in New Lenox (New Lenox)
Outpatient Center in Westchester (Westchester)
Outpatient Services in Grayslake (Grayslake)
Outpatient Services in Gurnee (Gurnee)
Outpatient Services in Lincoln Square (Chicago)
Pediatrics - Uptown (Chicago)
Rehabilitation Services at Westbrook (Westchester)

PRODUCTS/OPERATIONS

2014 Sales

	% of total
Patient care revenues	85
Grants gifts & endowment income	8
Other revenues	7
Total	**100**

Selected Services

Adolescent Medicine
Allergy and Immunology
Anesthesiology
Audiology
Autonomic Medicine
Brain Tumor
Cancer and Blood Disorders
Cardiology (Heart Center)
Child Abuse Pediatrics
Child and Adolescent Psychiatry
Clinical Nutrition
Convenient Care
Critical Care
Cystic Fibrosis
Dentistry and Oral Surgery
Dermatology
Emergency Medicine
Endocrinology
Epilepsy
Fetal Health
Gastroenterology Hepatology and Nutrition (Digestive Disorders)
Gender and Sex Development
General Pediatric Surgery
General Pediatrics
Genetics Birth Defects and Metabolism
Heart Failure and Transplants
HIV/AIDS Prevention
Infectious Diseases
Intestinal Transplants
Kidney Diseases
Kidney Transplants
Liver Transplants
Medical Imaging (Radiology)
Neonatology
Neurology
Neurosurgery
Occupational Therapy
Ophthalmology
Orthopaedic Surgery
Orthotics/Prosthetics
Otolaryngology (ENT)
Palliative Care

Pathology and Laboratory Medicine
Physical Therapy
Plastic and Reconstructive Surgery
Pulmonary Medicine
Rehabilitative Services
Rheumatology
Speech-Language Pathology
Spina Bifida Center
Sports Medicine
Stem Cell Transplants
Transitioning to Adult Care
Transplantation
Urology

COMPETITORS

Advocate Health Care	NorthShore University
Advocate Lutheran	HealthSystem
General Hospital	Northwestern Lake
Alexian Brothers	Forest Hospital
Health System	Northwestern Memorial
Covenant Ministries	HealthCare
HCA	Rush System for Health
Loyola University	SSM Health Care
Health System	Sinai Health System
Mercy Hospital and	University of Chicago
Medical Center	Medical Center

HISTORICAL FINANCIALS
Company Type: Private

Income Statement
FYE: August 31

	REVENUE ($ mil.)	NET INCOME ($ mil.)	NET PROFIT MARGIN	EMPLOYEES
08/15	625	47	7.7%	2,800
08/13	694	28	4.2%	—
08/10	599	52	8.8%	—
08/09	533	(5)	—	—
Annual Growth	2.7%	—	—	—

2015 Year-End Financials
Return on assets: 13.2% Cash ($ mil.): 22
Return on equity: 7.7%
Current ratio: 0.90

ANNE ARUNDEL MEDICAL CENTER, INC.

The ill and infirm get the royal treatment at Anne Arundel Medical Center. The full-service acute-care hospital serves the residents of Anne Arundel Calvert Prince George's and Queen Anne counties in Maryland. With about 425 beds the hospital administers care for women's health oncology pediatrics (it has a level III neonatal intensive care unit) neurology orthopedics and cardiovascular care. The medical center also has weight loss sleep disorder and rehabilitation centers. Anne Arundel which opened its doors in 1902 and is part of the Anne Arundel Health System has expanded its service offerings through various affiliations with regional specialty and primary care clinics. It also has a partnership with Johns Hopkins Medicine.

Operations

With more than 1000 staff members Anne Arundel handles some 26000 inpatient visits and 102000 outpatient visits per year. It also manages more than 5000 births and 93000 emergency room visits.

Johns Hopkins and the not-for-profit Anne Arundel share some services faculty and patients through their collaboration. They also operate a joint outpatient urgent-care facility. Additionally the two organizations work together to perform

clinical research projects and conduct physician graduate medical education programs.

Geographic Reach

In addition to its 57-acre Annapolis campus Anne Arundel has outpatient centers in Bowie Kent Island Odenton Pasadena and Waugh Chapel.

Sales and Marketing

In 2014 Medicare payments accounted for about one-third of net patient revenues.

Financial Performance

In 2014 revenue grew 3% to $591 million as net patient services revenues increased. However net income fell 23% to $42 million due to a decline in non-operating income (investment earnings). Cash flow from operations spike 188% to $56 million as cash generated from patient receivables prepaid expenses and other sources rose.

Strategy

Anne Arundel has in recent years added new facilities to better keep up with a continued growth in demand for health care services throughout its service area. In 2015 it opened the second phase of its Pasadena Pavilion adding physical therapy orthopedics and sports medicine capabilities. It also opened a new FastCare walk-in clinic in a grocery store/pharmacy in Annapolis. In 2014 the system opened an outpatient mental health clinic in Annapolis which provides services for patients 13 years of age and older.

In 2013 Anne Arundel opened a training center — the James and Sylvia Earl Simulation to Advance Innovation and Learning (SAIL) Center — to enhance its medical education programs and improve the quality and safety of care in the region. It also opened the Hackerman-Patz House that year to provide an affordable and convenient housing option for families of patients.

Also in 2013 the organization was designated as a Medicare accountable care organization (ACO) by the US government. ACOs work to coordinate care for Medicare patients to improve quality and reduce expenses.

EXECUTIVES

Vice President Quality and Patient Safety, Shirley Knelly
R V Pres, Joseph Moser
Vice President Learning and Training, Michael Epstein
Vice President Finance, Marc Brassard
Medical Director Anne Arundel Medical CTR. Research Institute, Watkins Stanley
Ambulatory Services Director, Kathy Bieler
Vice President of Finance, Catherine Yurkon
Director of Pharmacy, James Caldwell
Secretary Treasurer, Robert Reilly
Auditors: SC&H TAX & ADVISORY SERVICES L

LOCATIONS

HQ: ANNE ARUNDEL MEDICAL CENTER, INC.
2001 MEDICAL PKWY, ANNAPOLIS, MD 214013773
Phone: 443 481-1000

PRODUCTS/OPERATIONS

Selected Centers and Services
Blood Donor Center
Breast Center
Cardiac Cath Lab
Chest Pain Center
DeCesaris Cancer Institute
Diabetes Wound and Hyperbaric Center
Diagnostic Imaging
Heart and Vascular Institute
Joint Center
Laboratory
Pediatrics
Rehabilitation
Research Institute
Sleep Disorder Center
Spine Center

Stroke Center
Surgery
Women's and Children's Center

COMPETITORS

Ascension Health	Johns Hopkins Medicine
Bon Secours Health	LifeBridge Health
Dimensions Healthcare	MedStar Health
Franklin Square	Sinai Hospital of
Hospital Center	Baltimore
GBMC	St. Agnes HealthCare
Harbor Hospital	University of Maryland
Johns Hopkins Health	Medical System
System	

HISTORICAL FINANCIALS
Company Type: Private

Income Statement
FYE: June 30

	REVENUE ($ mil.)	NET INCOME ($ mil.)	NET PROFIT MARGIN	EMPLOYEES
06/15	526	39	7.6%	1,890
06/14	492	20	4.1%	—
06/13	493	16	3.4%	—
06/11	445	24	5.4%	—
Annual Growth	4.2%	13.4%	—	—

2015 Year-End Financials
Return on assets: 16.6% Cash ($ mil.): 59
Return on equity: 7.6%
Current ratio: 0.30

ANNE ARUNDEL MEDICAL CENTER, INC.

EXECUTIVES

Chief Executive Officer, Victoria W Bayless
Officer, Caroline Rader

LOCATIONS

HQ: ANNE ARUNDEL MEDICAL CENTER, INC.
2001 MEDICAL PKWY, ANNAPOLIS, MD 214013773
Phone: 443 481-1000

HISTORICAL FINANCIALS
Company Type: Private

Income Statement
FYE: June 30

	REVENUE ($ mil.)	NET INCOME ($ mil.)	NET PROFIT MARGIN	EMPLOYEES
06/15	498	(16)	—	4,000
06/14	1	0	23.5%	—
06/13	1	0	16.2%	—
06/09	1	(0)	—	—
Annual Growth	181.2%	—	—	—

2015 Year-End Financials
Return on assets: 3.7% Cash ($ mil.): 93
Return on equity: (-3.2%)
Current ratio: 1.50

ANTELOPE VALLEY HOSPITAL AUXILIARY

EXECUTIVES

President, Michael Wall
Representative, Henry B Marvin

LOCATIONS

HQ: ANTELOPE VALLEY HOSPITAL AUXILIARY
1600 W AVENUE J, LANCASTER, CA 935342894
Phone: 661 949-5000

HISTORICAL FINANCIALS

Company Type: Private

Income Statement

FYE: June 30

	REVENUE ($ mil.)	NET INCOME ($ mil.)	NET PROFIT MARGIN	EMPLOYEES
06/15	380	6	1.8%	2,200
06/08	265	(1)	—	—
06/05	0	0	25.4%	—
06/04	2,143	0	0.0%	—
Annual Growth	(14.6%)	135.4%	—	—

2015 Year-End Financials

Return on assets: 3.8%   Cash ($ mil.): 8
Return on equity: 1.8%
Current ratio: 0.30

API GROUP INC.

Holding company APi Group has a piece of the action in two main sectors: fire protection systems and industrial and specialty construction services. APi boasts about 40 subsidiaries which operate as independent companies across the US (nearly half of them in Minnesota) the UK and Canada. Services provided by the company's construction subsidiaries include HVAC and plumbing system installation; electrical industrial and mechanical contracting; industrial insulation; and garage door installation. Safety-focused units install a host of fire sprinkler detection security and alarm systems. The family-owned company was founded in 1926 by Reuben Anderson father of chairman Lee Anderson.

Operations

Through its various companies APi Group is involved in engineering designing constructing and installing LEED green-building certification program projects. Its divisions include Architectural Roofing and Mechanical Classic Industrial Services APi Construction APi Distribution and Industrial Fabricators among others.

Geographic Reach

Minnesota-based APi Group operates companies throughout North America and the UK.

Sales and Marketing

APi Group serves several sectors such as security and defense education commercial industrial medical oil and gas and residential.

Strategy

Although APi Group companies are independent they often pool resources and work together to service clients.

Mergers and Acquisitions

The highly acquisitive APi Group regularly acquires new companies to strengthen its growing group.

In 2013 the company's Western States Fire Protection (WSFP) acquired Advanced Fire an Oklahoma City-based fire-suppression company that specializes in military work. Buying Advanced Fire extends the company's reach in the fire protection industry and boosts its market share within Oklahoma City and the surrounding area. APi Group's Delta Fire Systems acquired Idaho's 3-D Fire which provides full-fire-system design fabrication installation testing and certification capabilities for commercial and private projects.

APi Group previous purchases include Dynamic Fire Protection LLC (DFP) Omlid & Swinney Fire Protection and Security Canada-based Fire Stop Enterprises Ohio-based 3S and Kansas-based mainline pipeline contractor Jomax Construction.

EXECUTIVES

President, Russell Becker
Board of Directors, William M Beadie
General Manager, Shane Shipman
Plant Engineering Manager, Peter Kaz
Vice-President, Ronnie Davidson
Manager, Patrick Kolb
Assistant Controller, Michael Davis
Auditors: KPMG

LOCATIONS

HQ: API GROUP INC.
1100 OLD HIGHWAY 8 NW, SAINT PAUL, MN
551126447
Phone: 651 636-4320
Web: WWW.APIDISTRIBUTION.COM

PRODUCTS/OPERATIONS

Selected Subsidiaries

Fire Protection Systems
  Alliance Fire Protection Inc.
  APi National Service Group
  Davis-Ulmer Sprinkler Company
  Delta Fire Systems Inc.
  Grunau Company
  Halon Banking Systems
  International Fire Protection Inc.
  Island Fire Sprinkler Inc.
  Reliance Fire Protection
  Rich Fire Protection Co Inc.
  Security Fire Protection Company
  United States Fire Protection Company
  VFP Fire Systems Inc.
  Viking Automatic Sprinkler Company
  Vipond Fire Protection Inc. (Canada)
  Vipond Fire Protection Ltd. (UK)
  Western States Fire Protection Inc.
Industrial and Specialty Construction Services
  3S Incorporated
  Anco Products Inc.
  APi CAD Services
  APi Construction Company
  APi Distribution Inc.
  APi Electric
  APi Supply Inc.
  Classic Industrial Services Inc.
  Doody Mechanical Inc.
  Garage Door Store
  Grunau Company Inc.
  Industrial Contractors Inc.
  Industrial Fabricators Inc.
  Jamar Company
  Jomax Construction Co.
  LeJeune Steel Company
  NYCO Inc.
  Tessier's Inc.
  Twin City Garage Door Company
Low Voltage
  APi Systems Group Inc.
  APi Systems Integrators
  Vipond Systems Group

COMPETITORS

Comfort Systems USA	TDIndustries
EMCOR	Team
IES Holdings	Turner Industries

Irex   Tyco Fire & Security
John E. Green

HISTORICAL FINANCIALS

Company Type: Private

Income Statement

FYE: December 31

	REVENUE ($ mil.)	NET INCOME ($ mil.)	NET PROFIT MARGIN	EMPLOYEES
12/15	2,448	106	4.3%	4,237
12/14	2,419	103	4.3%	—
12/13	2,049	93	4.6%	—
12/12	1,731	62	3.6%	—
Annual Growth	12.2%	19.5%	—	—

2015 Year-End Financials

Return on assets: 3.9%   Cash ($ mil.): 58
Return on equity: 4.3%
Current ratio: 1.00

APPALACHIAN REGIONAL HEALTHCARE, INC.

Under-the-weather coal miners (and their daughters) can turn to Appalachian Regional Healthcare (ARH) for medical services. The not-for-profit health system serves residents of eastern Kentucky and southern West Virginia through 10 hospitals with more than 1000 beds as well as dozens of clinics home health care agencies Home-Care Stores and retail pharmacies. Its largest hospital in Hazard Kentucky has 310 beds and features an inpatient psychiatric unit that serves as the state mental health facility. Several of the system's hospitals are Critical Access Hospitals a federal government designation for rural community hospitals that operate in medically underserved areas.

Operations

ARH's HomeCare Stores provide home medical equipment and oxygen delivery as well as 24-hour support through eight respiratory therapists. Its HomeCare Stores are supported by the ARH Home Health Agencies which provide access to nursing care occupational and physical therapy and social services.

Among the system's hospitals are Beckley ARH Hospital a not-for-profit 173-bed acute-care facility; Harlan ARH Hospital a state-licensed 150-bed acute-care facility; and Mary Breckinridge ARH Hospital a critical access facility.

ARH is the largest provider of care and single largest employer in southeastern Kentucky and the third-largest private employer in southern West Virginia. It employs almost 5000 people and has a network of more than 600 medical staff members. In 2013 the system had 153000 emergency department visits 482000 outpatient visits some 1500 births and about 12000 outpatient surgeries.

Geographic Reach

ARH serves residents of eastern Kentucky and southern West Virginia. It has hospitals in Harlan Hazard Hyden McDowell Middlesboro Morgan County South Williamson and Whitesburg Kentucky; and in Beckley and Summers County West Virginia.

Strategy

As the primary provider of health care to medically underserved populations ARH doles out millions of dollars in uncompensated care each year to un- or underinsured residents of the Appalachian region.

Along with a larger population of uninsured patients and the resulting unpaid medical bills that come along with them rural health care providers face a number of hardships not encountered by their urban brethren. For example physician recruitment is more difficult at rural hospitals especially for some higher-risk specialties such as obstetrics. In order to attract and retain doctors ARH and other rural health care providers have to offer more competitive compensation packages pay for relocation and invest in technology and facility upgrades.

Also patients in rural areas are more likely to suffer from chronic health problems such as diabetes and obesity which can become a significant drain on a health system's resources. ARH is one of many health care providers looking to benefit from changes to the health care system outlined in Affordable Care Act especially the requirement that all US citizens carry health insurance.

To keep up with patient demand ARH also focuses on building and acquiring new facilities as well as investing in new technology and medical capacities.

In 2013 ARH teamed up with Appalachian Heart Center and UK HealthCare's Gill Heart Institute to create an extension of the Gill Heart Institute's services into eastern Kentucky. The collaboration will provide advanced treatment options not readily available in the area which is home to some of the highest heart disease- and stroke-related mortality rates in the country.

Beckley ARH Hospital is undergoing a nearly $7 million renovation project that will add 19 more private rooms decrease utility costs and improve patient flow processes. In 2014 ARH completed a $47 million expansion project at the Hazard ARH Regional Medical Center that added an additional 100000 sq. ft. to the medical center including a new patient tower a new 24-bed emergency department on the first floor a dedicated 16-bed cardiac critical care unit and 34 private rooms. Hazard ARH is now the largest hospital in southeastern Kentucky.

In 2014 ARH changed the name of its hospital in South Williamson Kentucky from Williamson ARH Hospital to Tug Valley ARH Regional Medical Center. The change reflects the facility's growth and its commitment to providing services across the Tug Valley region.

Company Background

Appalachian Regional Healthcare was formed in 1956 by the United Mine Workers of America but became an independent not-for-profit entity in the early 1960s.

EXECUTIVES

Vice President Sales and Marketing, Holly Harris
Vice President of Business Development, Bill Dixon
Director of Pharmacy, Pat Amburgey
Pharm.D, Tiffany Herald
Vice President Corporate Strategy, Hollie Harris
Clinic Manager, Stephanie Wooton
Auditors: MOUNTJOY CHILTON MEDLEY LLP L

LOCATIONS

HQ: APPALACHIAN REGIONAL HEALTHCARE, INC.
2260 EXECUTIVE DR, LEXINGTON, KY 405054808
Phone: 859 226-2440
Web: WWW.ARH.ORG

PRODUCTS/OPERATIONS

Selected Facilities

Beckley ARH Hospital (Beckley West Virginia)
Hazard ARH Regional Medical Center (Hazard Kentucky)
Harlan ARH Hospital (Harlan Kentucky)
McDowell ARH Hospital (McDowell Kentucky)
Middlesboro ARH Hospital (Middlesboro Kentucky)
Morgan County ARH Hospital (West Liberty Kentucky)
Summers County ARH Hospital (Hinton West Virginia)
Tug Valley ARH Regional Medical Center (South Williamson Kentucky)
Whitesburg ARH Hospital (Whitesburg Kentucky)

Selected Services

Bariatrics
Behavioral Health
Cancer Care
Clinics
Emergency
Heart Care
Home Health
HomeCare Stores
Imaging
Laboratory
Medical Spa
Nephrology
Obstetrics and Gynecology
Pediatrics
Pharmacy
Rehabilitation Therapy
Respiratory Therapy
Rheumatology
Senior Care
Skilled Nursing
Sleep Lab
Surgery
Swing Beds

COMPETITORS

Baptist Health
Bon Secours Health
Carilion Clinic
Catholic Health Initiatives
Community Health Systems
Highlands Health
Jewish Hospital & St. Mary's HealthCare
Kindred Healthcare
Mercy Medical Center (NY)
Montgomery Regional Hospital
Norton Healthcare
Pikeville Medical Center
University of Kentucky Chandler Hospital
University of Virginia Health System

HISTORICAL FINANCIALS

Company Type: Private

Income Statement				FYE: June 30
	REVENUE ($ mil.)	NET INCOME ($ mil.)	NET PROFIT MARGIN	EMPLOYEES
06/16	653	17	2.6%	4,520
06/15	620	48	7.8%	—
06/13	610	19	3.2%	—
Annual Growth	2.3%	(4.2%)	—	—

2016 Year-End Financials

Return on assets: 3.7%
Return on equity: 2.6%
Current ratio: 0.50
Cash ($ mil.): 50

APPLETON AREA SCHOOL DISTRICT

EXECUTIVES

Superintendent, Lee Allinger
Director, Julie Hoffman
Auditors: SCHENCK GREEN BAY WISCONSIN

LOCATIONS

HQ: APPLETON AREA SCHOOL DISTRICT
122 E COLLEGE AVE STE 1A, APPLETON, WI
549115741
Phone: 920 832-6161
Web: WWW.AASD.K12.WI.US

HISTORICAL FINANCIALS

Company Type: Private

Income Statement				FYE: June 30
	REVENUE ($ mil.)	NET INCOME ($ mil.)	NET PROFIT MARGIN	EMPLOYEES
06/16	193	7	3.7%	1,425
06/15	187	(16)	—	—
06/14	168	23	14.1%	—
06/13	164	(0)	—	—
Annual Growth	5.5%	—	—	—

ARCHBOLD MEDICAL CENTER, INC.

EXECUTIVES

Chief Executive Officer, J Perry Mustian
Financial Executive, Skip Hightower
Chief Financial Officer, Charles Hightower
Chief Operating Officer, Kevin Taylor
Personnel Director, Zach Wheeler
Accountant, Donna Johnson
Director, Robin Godwin
Auditors: DRAFFIN & TUCKER LLP ALBANY

LOCATIONS

HQ: ARCHBOLD MEDICAL CENTER, INC.
GORDON AVE AT MIMOSA DR, THOMASVILLE, GA
31792
Phone: 229 228-2739
Web: WWW.ARCHBOLD.ORG

HISTORICAL FINANCIALS

Company Type: Private

Income Statement				FYE: September 30
	REVENUE ($ mil.)	NET INCOME ($ mil.)	NET PROFIT MARGIN	EMPLOYEES
09/16	363	20	5.6%	2,700
09/14	24	0	—	—
09/13	23	0	—	—
Annual Growth	148.7%	—	—	—

2016 Year-End Financials

Return on assets: 3.0%
Return on equity: 5.6%
Current ratio: 2.10
Cash ($ mil.): 47

ARENA ENERGY, LP

EXECUTIVES

Board of Directors, Todd L Stone
Board of Directors, Bryan L Nelson
Marketing Manager, Bernice Norris
Engineer, Ben Frederick
Engineer, Brett Ozene

Marketing Manager, Mike McGinnis
Manager, Michael F. McCauley
Auditors: ERNST & YOUNG LLP

LOCATIONS

HQ: ARENA ENERGY, LP
4200 RES FREST DR STE 500, THE WOODLANDS,
TX 77381
Phone: 281 681-9500

HISTORICAL FINANCIALS

Company Type: Private

Income Statement

	REVENUE ($ mil.)	NET INCOME ($ mil.)	NET PROFIT MARGIN	EMPLOYEES
12/15	275	(347)	—	8
12/08	244	116	47.6%	—
12/07	188	64	34.0%	—
12/05	82	25	30.5%	—
Annual Growth	12.8%	—	—	—

2015 Year-End Financials

Return on assets: 19.7%   Cash ($ mil.): 26
Return on equity: (-125.8%)
Current ratio: 0.10

ARGO TURBOSERVE CORPORATION

EXECUTIVES

Chairman, John Calicchio
Director, Alberto Viti
Auditors: EISNER AMPER LLP ISELIN NEW

LOCATIONS

HQ: ARGO TURBOSERVE CORPORATION
160 CHUBB AVE STE 102, LYNDHURST, NJ
070713526
Phone: 201 804-6200

HISTORICAL FINANCIALS

Company Type: Private

Income Statement

	REVENUE ($ mil.)	NET INCOME ($ mil.)	NET PROFIT MARGIN	EMPLOYEES
12/15	320	4	1.3%	366
12/14	352	13	3.9%	—
12/13	0	13	—	—
12/12	178	10	5.7%	—
Annual Growth	21.6%	(26.4%)	—	—

2015 Year-End Financials

Return on assets: 13.5%   Cash ($ mil.): 1
Return on equity: 1.3%
Current ratio: 0.60

ARIA HEALTH

Aria Health wants to get you back to singing arias in no time flat. Aria Health provides medical care from two acute care hospitals in Philadelphia (Frankford Campus and Torresdale Campus) as well as the Bucks County Campus in Langhorne

Pennsylvania. Combined the three facilities boast about 480 beds and offer a full range of specialty care from anesthesiology and pain management to women's care and invasive oncology as well as cardiac and surgical procedures. Aria Health also operates primary care and specialty outpatient facilities throughout its service area. In 2016 Aria announced plans to rejoin forces with Thomas Jefferson University Hospitals eight years after the systems separated.

Operations

Aria Health has more than 4000 employees. It has a staff of more than 1000 medical professionals.

Geographic Reach

Aria Health has three hospital campuses (Bucks County Frankford and Torresdale) two outpatient centers and a network of physicians that serve the Northeast Philadelphia and Bucks County communities.

Strategy

In early 2016 the system announced a definitive agreement to merge with Thomas Jefferson University Hospitals which has been on a merger spree as of late. The transaction will allow for Aria Health to have equal representation on the combined organization's governing board.

The company is also looking to expand its facilities to meet growing demand.

Aria Health is planning a new hospital in the area to be named the Lower Makefield Campus but has met with some resistance from local citizens who say it will cause higher taxes and traffic congestion. Aria Health plans to relocate the services currently offered at its Bucks County Campus to the new $300 million 455000 sq.-ft. replacement hospital. Services would include maternity and birthing as well as advanced technology such as robotic-assisted surgery. In late 2013 the system was still waiting on approval from the town's board of supervisors before beginning construction on the 225-bed facility.

In 2013 the company broke ground on $37 million emergency department expansion at its Torresdale campus in Northeast Philadelphia. The project is expected to increase the facility's emergency admissions annual capacity by more than 25000 patient visits.

In 2013 Aria Health officials met with Lower Makefield officials and area residents to propose a healthcare village on the 41-acre tract of land at the corner of Stony Hill Road and the Newtown Bypass. The 180000 square foot village would include a medical office building an area to conduct clinical research an ambulatory care center as well as restaurants and a spa.

Company Background

To improve its information technology systems and comply with health reform incentive measures Aria Health joined an accountable care organization (ACO) in 2010. The ACO is a collaborative effort among regional care providers to improve quality and efficiency in the health care system.

The organization changed its name from Frankford Health Care System to Aria Health in early 2009 to reflect its independence and growing presence in the Philadelphia area. The health system was part of the larger Jefferson Health System until the end of 2008 when the two entities realigned their relationship after determining that they could better serve customers as independent entities.

Aria Health was formed in 1902 after a resident of the Frankford section of Philadelphia contracted typhoid fever.

EXECUTIVES

Medical Director of Cardiovascular and Vascular,
Nche Zama

Clinical Director, Mary Snyder
Director of Pharmacy, Kathy Punzo
Vice President Finance, Bill Degnan
Pharmacy Manager, Cassandra Cooper
Director of Admissions, Marie Leonard
Board Member, Ronald Thomas
Secretary Performance Improvement, Barbara
Lawrence

LOCATIONS

HQ: ARIA HEALTH
10800 KNIGHTS RD, PHILADELPHIA, PA 191144299
Phone: 215 612-4000
Web: WWW.ARIAHEALTH.ORG

PRODUCTS/OPERATIONS

Selected Medical Services

Allergy and Immunology
Anesthesiology
Bariatrics
Behavioral Health
Breast Health
Breast Surgery
Cancer
Colorectal Surgery
Cardiothoracic Surgery
Cardiovascular Disease/Cardiology
Clinical Trials & Research
Diabetes
Dermatology
Endocrine Surgery
Endocrinology
Emergency Medicine
Eye Care
Family Practice
Gastrointestinal Disease/Gastroenterology
General Surgery
General Practice
Gynecology & Women's Health
Heart Care
Hematology Medical Oncology
Home Health
Infectious Diseases
Internal Medicine
Joint Replacement Program
Medicine (Department of Medicine)
Medical Oncology
Mental Health
Minimally Invasive Surgery
Nephrology
Neurology
Neurosurgery
Occupational Health
Oncology
Ophthalmology
Oral Medicine
Orthopedic Surgery
Otolaryngology (Ear Nose & Throat)
Pain Management
Pathology
Physical Medicine & Rehabilitation
Plastic/Reconstructive Surgery
Podiatry
Primary Care
Psychiatry
Pulmonary Medicine
Radiation Oncology
Radiology
Radiosurgery
Respiratory Disease
Rheumatology
Robotic Surgery
Sleep Medicine
Smoking Cessation and Lung Screening Program
Sports Medicine
Stroke
Surgery
Surgical Oncology
Thoracic Surgery
Trauma
Urology
Vascular Surgery
Weight Loss
Wellness
Women's Health

COMPETITORS

Abington Memorial Hospital
Albert Einstein Healthcare Network
Children's Hospital of Philadelphia
Crozer-Keystone Health System
Doylestown Hospital
Fox Chase Cancer Center
Liberty Healthcare
Lourdes Health
Main Line Health System
Mercy Health System
North Philadelphia Health System
Our Lady of Lourdes Medical Center
TUHS
The Cooper Health System
Thomas Jefferson University
Universal Health Services
University of Pennsylvania Health System
Virtua Health

HISTORICAL FINANCIALS

Company Type: Private

Income Statement

	REVENUE ($ mil.)	NET INCOME ($ mil.)	NET PROFIT MARGIN	EMPLOYEES
06/15	432	31	7.3%	4,000
06/13	460	51	11.3%	—
Annual Growth	(3.1%)	(21.9%)		

FYE: June 30

2015 Year-End Financials

Return on assets: 5.1%   Cash ($ mil.): 12
Return on equity: 7.3%
Current ratio: 0.50

ARISTEO CONSTRUCTION COMPANY

EXECUTIVES

President, Joseph A Aristeo
Project Manager, Andrew Maness
Project Manager, Anthony Larosa
Financial Executive, Bill Dupuie
Chief Financial Officer, Bill Litz
Manager, Craig Kreza
Project Manager, Kevin Wolf
Auditors: YEO & YEO ANN ARBOR MI

LOCATIONS

HQ: ARISTEO CONSTRUCTION COMPANY
    12811 FARMINGTON RD, LIVONIA, MI 481501607
Phone: 734 427-9111
Web: WWW.ARISTEO.COM

HISTORICAL FINANCIALS

Company Type: Private

Income Statement

	REVENUE ($ mil.)	NET INCOME ($ mil.)	NET PROFIT MARGIN	EMPLOYEES
12/15	289	19	6.6%	1,025
12/14	259	10	4.1%	—
12/13	173	7	4.5%	—
12/12	137	3	2.9%	—
Annual Growth	28.2%	68.5%	—	—

FYE: December 31

2015 Year-End Financials

Return on assets: 12.8%   Cash ($ mil.): 17
Return on equity: 6.6%
Current ratio: 1.00

ARIZONA STATE UNIVERSITY

Sun lovers and knowledge seekers can turn to Arizona State University (ASU) for a well-rounded college education. The research university offers a wide variety of bachelor's master's and doctoral degree programs with more than 300 majors through some 18 schools teaching a range of disciplines including nursing journalism and engineering. It has an enrollment of more than 98100 undergraduate graduate and professional students on its six campuses in metropolitan Phoenix; most students attend the Tempe campus. The university has a student-teacher ratio of 23:1. ASU was founded in 1885 as a teachers college and has become widely known for its extensive research programs.

Operations

ASU offers more than 90 undergraduate and graduate degrees and certificates online through some of its colleges including the W. P. Carey School of Business Mary Lou Fulton Teachers College College of Nursing and Health Innovation and the Ira A. Fulton School of Engineering. ASU also partners with Pearson Digital Learning to administer online courses; Pearson also monitors and analyzes student performance trends.

The university's extensive research programs cover a variety of fields in life science medicine and physical science categories. In addition subsidiary Arizona Technology Enterprises (AzTE) manages technology ventures for ASU. AzTE manages the university's intellectual property (much of which is the result of its research programs) and facilitates startup businesses which have led to the formation of 80 companies and attracted $500 million in funding between 2002 and 2016.

Geographic Reach

ASU has an enrollment of students from more than 130 countries.

Financial Performance

The university's revenues increased by 11% (or $162 million) to $1.6 billion in fiscal 2016 primarily due a 10% increase in enrollment including a 23% growth in nonresident enrollment. Research grants and contracts revenue primarily funded by federal agencies rose by 7%.

Operating expenses grew by $143 million (or 7%) that year largely related to the increase in enrollment. Instruction and academic support expenses experienced the largest rise of $81 million.

Strategy

The university is working to become a top research university in interdisciplinary fields of science and technology. As part of that goal ASU is seeking to expand its AzTE entrepreneur business through additional technology discoveries and startup formations. It also seeks to help stimulate the Arizona economy by reaching out to local businesses and encouraging startups that will maintain a presence in the state.

ASU is also working to improve graduation rates increase graduate enrollment and enhance individual learning programs. The university intends to increase the quality of its academic programs and its student facilities.

In 2015 and 2016 the US News & World Report named ASU as the most innovative school in the US.

In 2016 the school opened the $130 million Arizona Center for Law and Society at its downtown campus. The center provides law students with greater access to Arizona's judicial political and economic centers. Other planned facilities include new educational and research centers near Phoenix's Mayo Clinic Hospital; they will deepen ASU's partnership with the Mayo Clinic and provide learning opportunities for ASU students.

In 2014 the university launched a partnership with Starbucks to provide tuition reimbursement to employees nationwide attending ASU online.

EXECUTIVES

EVP Treasurer and CFO, Morgan R. Olsen
President, Michael M. Crow, age 62
CIO and Professor of Parctice, Lev S. Gonick, age 57
SVP and President ASU Alumni Association, Christine K. Wilkinson
EVP and University Provost, Mark Searle
CIO, Gordon Wishon
EVP Knowledge Enterprise Development and Chief Research & Innovation Officer, Sethuraman (Panch) Panchanathan
SVP and Chief Marketing Officer, Daniel Dillon
Dean Educational Initiatives and CEO EdPlus, Philip Regier
CEO and Director General Thunderbird School of Global Management and Professor of Global Strategy and Leadership, Allen Morrison
Board Member, David Heineking
Auditors: DEBBIE K DAVENPORT CPA PHOE

LOCATIONS

HQ: ARIZONA STATE UNIVERSITY
    300 E UNIVERSITY DR # 410, TEMPE, AZ 852812061
Phone: 480 965-2100
Web: WWW.ASU.EDU

PRODUCTS/OPERATIONS

2014 Sales

	% of total
Tuition & fees	67
Research grants and contracts	18
Auxiliary enterprises	10
Other operating revenues	5
Total	100

Selected Colleges and Schools

Barrett Honors College
College of Health Solutions
College of Liberal Arts and Sciences
College of Nursing and Health Innovation
College of Public Programs
College of Technology and Innovation
Graduate College
Herberger Institute for Design and the Arts
Ira A. Fulton Schools of Engineering
Mary Lou Fulton Teachers College
New College of Interdisciplinary Arts and Sciences
Sandra Day O'Connor College of Law
School of Letters and Sciences
School of Sustainability
Thunderbird School of Global Management
University College
Walter Cronkite School of Journalism and Mass Communication
W.P. Carey School of Business

HISTORICAL FINANCIALS

Company Type: Private

Income Statement

FYE: June 30

	REVENUE ($ mil.)	NET INCOME ($ mil.)	NET PROFIT MARGIN	EMPLOYEES
06/16	1,644	108	6.6%	8,000
06/13	1,227	85	6.9%	—
06/12	1,155	121	10.5%	—
Annual Growth	9.2%	(2.7%)	—	—

2016 Year-End Financials

Return on assets: 8.0%
Return on equity: 6.6%
Current ratio: 0.50

Cash ($ mil.): 72

ARIZONA STATE UNIVERSITY

LOCATIONS

HQ: ARIZONA STATE UNIVERSITY
951 S PALM WALK, TEMPE, AZ 852870001
Phone: 480 965-4385
Web: WWW.ASU.EDU

HISTORICAL FINANCIALS

Company Type: Private

Income Statement

FYE: June 30

	REVENUE ($ mil.)	NET INCOME ($ mil.)	NET PROFIT MARGIN	EMPLOYEES
06/15	1,482	92	6.2%	26
06/14	1,348	103	7.7%	—
Annual Growth	9.9%	(10.7%)	—	—

2015 Year-End Financials

Return on assets: 6.4%
Return on equity: 6.2%
Current ratio: 0.60

Cash ($ mil.): 47

ARKANSAS CHILDREN'S HOSPITAL

As the only pediatric medical center in the state Arkansas Children's Hospital (ACH) serves the youngest Razorbacks from birth to age 21. The not-for-profit hospital with its 370 beds specializes in childhood cancer pediatric orthopedics and neonatology. Besides acute care services it operates more than 80 specialty clinics and outpatient centers. One of the US's largest pediatric hospitals ACH is also engaged in teaching and medical research through its affiliation with the University of Arkansas for Medical Sciences. Its Arkansas Children's Hospital Research Institute focuses on biological mechanisms underlying birth defects diabetes-related complications and childhood diseases.

Operations

ACH each year performs more than 14500 operations and boasts 55000-plus emergency department visits nearly 330000 outpatient visits and about 14800 inpatient admissions.

ACH's Circle of Friends clinic treats more than 20000 patients annually. The clinic which opened in 2008 provides primary care as well as a broad range of specialty care services related to endocrinology dermatological conditions hemophilia and tuberculosis.

The hospital also offers community outreach services that include help for children of domestic abuse and wellness programs as well as a number of clinics to support those with eating disorders and diabetes.

As a prime destination for treatment ACH also runs Angel One Transport an intensive care medical transportation system that brings critically ill and injured infants children and adolescents as well as adult burn patients from throughout Arkansas and the surrounding states to ACH. It also boasts a high risk obstetric transport program in partnership with the University of Arkansas for Medical Sciences.

ACH has a staff of 500 physicians including 95 residents in pediatrics and pediatric specialties. Its mobile clinics annually serve more than 6000 patients and provide more than $3 million in dental treatment.

Geographic Reach

Based in Little Rock Arkansas on a campus that extends nearly 30 city blocks ACH serves children nationwide as one of the largest pediatric hospitals in the US. It has several locations across Arkansas in Little Rock Jonesboro and Lowell.

Financial Performance

The hospital gets about 82% of its net sales from net patient service revenues.

Strategy

In 2015 ACH announced plans to build a $184 million hospital in Springdale. The 24-bed hospital will be located on 37 acres of land near Arvest Ballpark. The hospital is targeted to be completed in 2018.

In 2013 ACH inked a contract with Aetna health insurance under which patients with Aetna health insurance will be able to seek in-network care at ACH. The contract allows the company to reach more families throughout the region.

Company Background

The hospital opened a new $121 million south wing in mid-2012 that added more than 50 inpatient beds to the hospital's capacity. The nearly 260000-sq.-ft. four-story building features telemedicine technology (for remote patient care) new trauma rooms a dedicated orthopedics suite and a decontamination unit.

To its benefit ACH became the state's only pediatric Level I trauma center in 2010 after receiving a four-year designation from the Arkansas Department of Health. The designation means that the hospital is equipped for and capable of taking care of children with the most severe of traumas. Level I trauma centers serve as referral locations for hospitals that are unable to provide the same level of care.

EXECUTIVES

President CEO and Director, Jonathan R. (Jon) Bates
EVP, Scott R. Gordon
President Arkansas Childrens Hospital Research Institute, Richard F. Jacobs
SVP and CIO, Darrell T. Leonhardt
SVP and CFO, Gena G. Wingfield
SVP and COO, David T. Berry
President ACH Foundation, Fred Scarborough
Senior Vice President Chief Quality Officer, Jayant K. Deshpande
Senior Vice President Medical Director, W. Robert Morrow
Director Of Health Information, Marilyn Ambrose
Radiology Director, Karen Craig
Nursing Director, Terri Songer
Medical Director Pediatrician, Brian Hardin
Vice President finance, Cindy L Hill
Director of Nursing, Rebecca Kersten
Clinic Supervisor, Jennifer Mickle
Director of Nursing, Gail Wilson
Nursing Director, Carrie Lee
Director of Nursing, Leslie Bradley
Vice President of Information Technology Applications, Michael Hart
Senior Vice President, Katherine Friend
Nursing Director Of The Special Staffing Team, Jenny Janisko
Senior Vice President and General Counsel, Rhonda McKinnis
Senior Vice President Chief Nursing Officer, Lori Brown
Vice President Of Facilities, Larry Beckius
Physical Therapy Director Occupational Therapy Director Physical Rehab Services Director, Marilyn Randle
Vice President Business Development and Physician Alignment, Beth Petlak
Vice President, Curtis Summers
Medical Director, Stephen Schexnayder
Vice President and General Counsel, Rhonda Thornton
Vice President, Elizabeth Petlak
Vice President Finance, Cheryl Edward
Infection Control Director, Michelle Honeycutt
Director of Government Relations, Rosi Smith
Nursing Director, Tammy Diamond-wells
Secretary to Vice President Human Resources, Charlotte Johnson
Secretary III Manged Care, Susan Henson
Auditors: KPMG LLP MEMPHIS TN

LOCATIONS

HQ: ARKANSAS CHILDREN'S HOSPITAL
1 CHILDRENS WAY, LITTLE ROCK, AR 722023500
Phone: 501 364-1100

PRODUCTS/OPERATIONS

Selected Services

Ambulatory Surgery
Audiology
Center for Good Mourning
Cleft Clinic
Dennis Developmental Center
Dental Clinic
ECMO
Gastroenterology Clinic
Genetic and Metabolic Clinic
Infectious Diseases
Neuroscience Unit
Physical Medicine & Rehab Outreach Clinics
Sleep Disorders Center
Volunteer Services
WHAM (Wellness Health Action & Motivation) Clinic

COMPETITORS

Arkansas Heart Hospital
Baptist Health (Arkansas)
Children's Healthcare of Atlanta
Children's Medical Center of Dallas
Children's Mercy Hospital
Children's National Medical Center
Cook Children's Health Care System
Dell Children's Medical Center
East Tennessee Children's Hospital
Jefferson Regional Medical Center of Arkansas
Methodist Healthcare
Shriners Hospitals For Children
St. Joseph's Mercy Health Center
St. Jude Children's Research Hospital
St. Vincent Health System
Texas Children's Hospital
Universal Health Services
White County Medical Center

HISTORICAL FINANCIALS
Company Type: Private

Income Statement
FYE: June 30

	REVENUE ($ mil.)	NET INCOME ($ mil.)	NET PROFIT MARGIN	EMPLOYEES
06/16	585	70	12.1%	3,700
06/15	562	44	8.0%	—
06/14	562	47	8.5%	—
06/11	509	48	9.5%	—
Annual Growth	2.8%	7.9%		

2016 Year-End Financials

Return on assets: 7.1%   Cash ($ mil.): 107
Return on equity: 12.1%
Current ratio: 2.50

ARKANSAS ELECTRIC COOPERATIVE CORPORATION

Having access to power is the natural state in the Natural State thanks to Arkansas Electric Cooperative Corporation (AECC) the sole wholesale power provider for 17 Arkansas electric distribution cooperatives. The company operates power plants with 3418 MW of generating capacity owns transmission assets and buys wholesale power to meet its members' demands. Affiliate Arkansas Electric Cooperatives Inc. (AECI) provides administrative and maintenance services to the distribution companies. The distribution utilities serve about 500000 customers in more than 60% of Arkansas. AECC and AECI along with the state's 17 electric distribution cooperatives are known as the Electric Cooperatives of Arkansas.

Operations

AECC's diverse generation assets include three hydropower plants three natural gas/oil-based plants and three natural gas-based-only plants. It also co-owns portions of four low-cost coal-based plants and has a long-term power purchase agreement for 51 MW wind energy. The coop also has four transmission lines.

Sales and Marketing

In fiscal 2013 co-op members Mississippi County Electric Cooperative First Electric Cooperative Carroll Electric Cooperative and Arkansas Valley Electric Corporation together accounted for 59% of AECC's total revenues.

Financial Performance

Thanks to a rebounding economy and growing demand for power the company saw its revenues grow by 13% in fiscal 2013.

Net income declined by 37% in fiscal 2013 due to higher operations maintenance generation and transmission expenses as well as an increase in administration and general expenses.

Strategy

AECC is ramping up its renewable energy resources in order to meet state and federal clean energy power requirements.

In 2013 the company signed a long-term deal to buy 150 MW of wind energy from RES America Developments Inc. a subsidiary of Renewable Energy Systems Americas Inc.

In 2012 it reached a long-term purchase power agreement for 51 MW of wind energy from the Flat Ridge 2 South Wind Farm in Kansas. AECC's

51 MW of capacity is part of 470 MW of potential generation provided by the farm's 294 GE wind turbines. BP and Sempra U.S. Gas & Power are equal joint venture partners for the facility which has a combined investment of more than $800 million. A wholly-owned affiliate of BP Wind Energy will monitor and maintain the farm

Mergers and Acquisitions

In another move to cut back on the use of coal-fired power plants in 2012 AECC bought a 746-MW combined cycle natural gas-fired power plant near Magnet Cove for $240 million.

Company Background

The first electric cooperative in Arkansas was formed in Jacksonville in 1938 as part of the Roosevelt Administration's national rural electrification drive.

EXECUTIVES

Chief Executive Officer, Gary Voigt
VP Sales, Pat McClafferty
Vice-President, Carmie Henry
Supervisor, Kevin Riddle
Auditors: BKD LLP LITTLE ROCK ARKANSAS

LOCATIONS

HQ: ARKANSAS ELECTRIC COOPERATIVE CORPORATION
1 COOPERATIVE WAY, LITTLE ROCK, AR 722095493
Phone: 501 570-2200
Web: WWW.AECC.COM

HISTORICAL FINANCIALS
Company Type: Private

Income Statement
FYE: December 31

	REVENUE ($ mil.)	NET INCOME ($ mil.)	NET PROFIT MARGIN	EMPLOYEES
12/15	462	35	7.7%	220
12/14*	455	30	6.6%	—
10/11	657	35	5.4%	—
Annual Growth	(8.4%)	(0.2%)	—	—

*Fiscal year change

2015 Year-End Financials

Return on assets: 2.9%   Cash ($ mil.): 116
Return on equity: 7.7%
Current ratio: 2.00

ARKANSAS ELECTRIC COOPERATIVES, INC.

EXECUTIVES

President, Duane Highley
Vice-President, Doug White
Financial Executive, Samantha Lewis
Engineer, Pat Patterson
Auditing Manager, Ken Bland
Auditors: BKD LLP LITTLE ROCK ARKANSA

LOCATIONS

HQ: ARKANSAS ELECTRIC COOPERATIVES, INC.
1 COOPERATIVE WAY, LITTLE ROCK, AR 722095493
Phone: 501 570-2200
Web: WWW.AECC.COM

HISTORICAL FINANCIALS
Company Type: Private

Income Statement
FYE: December 31

	REVENUE ($ mil.)	NET INCOME ($ mil.)	NET PROFIT MARGIN	EMPLOYEES
12/15	462	35	7.7%	840
12/13	416	32	7.7%	—
12/12	438	35	8.0%	—
12/11	357	18	5.1%	—
Annual Growth	6.7%	18.3%		

2015 Year-End Financials

Return on assets: 2.9%   Cash ($ mil.): 116
Return on equity: 7.7%
Current ratio: 2.00

ARLINGTON INDEPENDENT SCHOOL DISTRICT

EXECUTIVES

Superintendent, Marcelo Bavazls
Principal, Michael Martin
Consultant, Cristina Hernandez
Manager, Patricia Bianchini
Plant & Facilities Manager, Javier Fernandez
Auditors: WHITLEY PENN LLP HOUSTON TEX

LOCATIONS

HQ: ARLINGTON INDEPENDENT SCHOOL DISTRICT
1203 W PIONEER PKWY, ARLINGTON, TX 760136246
Phone: 682 867-4611
Web: WWW.AISD.NET

HISTORICAL FINANCIALS
Company Type: Private

Income Statement
FYE: June 30

	REVENUE ($ mil.)	NET INCOME ($ mil.)	NET PROFIT MARGIN	EMPLOYEES
06/16	636	115	18.1%	8,000
06/15	613	143	23.4%	—
06/14	592	12	2.1%	—
06/13	543	(7)	—	—
Annual Growth	5.4%			

2016 Year-End Financials

Return on assets: 4.3%   Cash ($ mil.): 555
Return on equity: 18.1%
Current ratio: 5.20

ARNOLD MACHINERY COMPANY

Arnold Machinery helps keep construction on the move. Through its many divisions the company distributes construction mining industrial and material handling equipment as well as farm machinery throughout the US. Arnold Machinery also of-

fers used equipment and provides repair and maintenance rebuild exchange and rental services. The company's divisions include General Implement Distributors Mining Equipment Construction Equipment and Material Handling. Arnold Machinery operates about 20 branch facilities covering some 15 states in the Western US.

Strategy

Since its founding the company has expanded geographically and built its product offerings by acquiring complementary businesses. Arnold Machinery continues to acquire other distributors in its territory and to expand its facilities in many markets.

Company Background

L. E. "Doc" Arnold and Floyd Stannard founded predecessor company Stannard-Arnold Machinery Company in 1929. The company's name was changed to Arnold Machinery Company upon the resignation of Stannard later that year.

EXECUTIVES

President and CEO, Russ Fleming
President Material Handling Division, Rex Mecham
Co-President MH Division, Kirk Reese
Corporate VP; President GID Division, Wendell Nelson
VP Mining Division, John Ragsdale
Vice President Of Technical Services, Billy Greenlee
Chairman, Alvin Richer
Auditors: GRANT THORNTON LLP SALT LAKE

LOCATIONS

HQ: ARNOLD MACHINERY COMPANY
2975 W 2100 S, SALT LAKE CITY, UT 841191273
Phone: 801 972-4000

COMPETITORS

Cashman Equipment	NES Rentals
Cummins	Sunbelt Rentals
Empire Southwest	United Rentals

HISTORICAL FINANCIALS
Company Type: Private

Income Statement

FYE: September 30

	REVENUE ($ mil.)	NET INCOME ($ mil.)	NET PROFIT MARGIN	EMPLOYEES
09/16	298	5	1.9%	450
09/15	309	12	3.9%	—
09/14	319	13	4.1%	—
09/13	294	12	4.3%	—
Annual Growth	0.4%	(23.8%)	—	—

2016 Year-End Financials
Return on assets: 3.9%   Cash ($ mil.): 4
Return on equity: 1.9%
Current ratio: 0.70

ARROWHEAD REGIONAL MEDICAL CENTER

Find yourself dehydrated after searching the Inland Empire deserts for arrowheads? Arrowhead Regional Medical Center (ARMC) can fix you up. The San Bernardino County owned and operated hospital provides a range of health services from general medical and surgical care to emergency services rehabilitation inpatient psychiatric care pediatric and women's health services. It also serves as a Level II trauma center a regional burn center

and medical training facility. ARMC with some 460 beds (370 inpatient and 90 behavioral) opened in 1999 to replace the aging San Bernardino County Hospital. The hospital also offers outpatient services on its main campus and at area clinics.

Operations

Along with a full range of health care services ARMC offers about 10 residency programs including emergency and family medicine general surgery geriatrics orthopedics neurosurgery and gynecology. The hospital trains about 170 residents each year and also provides training programs for nurses pharmacists clinical laboratory scientists and radiologic technologists.

The ARMC emergency room handles about 140000 visits each year. The hospital's inpatient capacity handles about 25000 patients annually while its outpatient centers see some 250000 patients.

The Medical Center's Internal Medicine Primary Care Clinic offers services for individuals ranging in age from 18 to 100. Its Outpatient Care facility offers more than 60 different specialty services including pediatrics geriatrics orthopedics surgery internal medicine women's health and rehabilitation services.

ARMC's two Breath Mobiles provide pediatric asthma care management at sites throughout San Bernardino County.

Geographic Reach

The company serves patients in San Bernardino Riverside Inyo and Mono counties in California. ARMC's main facility campus in Colton includes an outpatient services complex. It also runs three primary care Family Health Centers in the nearby towns of Fontana Rialto and San Bernadino as well as wound care and elder care clinics.

Financial Performance

ARMC's revenues dropped by 1% to $385 million in 2012 due to a decline in net patient service revenues.

However net income decreased by 63% to $12 million in 2012 due to higher operating expenses (salaries benefits and purchased services) partially offset by a rise in non-operating revenues due to an increase in state funding.

Strategy

To better serve the needs of patients in its service territory ARMC looks to expand services in high-demand areas.

To enable doctors and technologists to provide a vastly expanded number of procedures for cardiac patients neurology patients and those requiring interventional radiology in 2013 ARMC opened its new Dual Purpose Interventional Lab (medical suite).

That year it also opened a new and larger Westside Family Health Center which was expanded from 12 to 21 exam rooms in a new co-location facility in Rialto. It also expanded its Breath Mobile service to the High Desert with service to sites including Adelanto Apple Valley Barstow Hesperia Phelan Victorville and Trona.

Company Background

An increase in cases of asthma (particularly among children) in the Central Valley led ARMC to expand its Breathmobile program an asthma clinic on wheels that travels to schools throughout San Bernadino County in 2010.

The hospital is also enhancing stationary outpatient care clinics. It added the ARMC Medical Office Building to its main campus in 2011; the center includes physician practices and an internal medicine clinic.

EXECUTIVES

Director of Pharmacy, Cliff Hiroshige

LOCATIONS

HQ: ARROWHEAD REGIONAL MEDICAL CENTER
400 N PEPPER AVE, COLTON, CA 923241819
Phone: 909 580-1000
Web: WWW.ARROWHEADNEUROSURGERY.ORG

PRODUCTS/OPERATIONS

Selected Services
Audiology
Breast Cancer Clinic
Cardiology
Child Health Disability Program
Dialysis Center
Emergency Medicine
Family and Elder Care
Internal Medicine
Level II Trauma Center
Oncology/Infusion Therapy
Ophthalmology
Orthopedics
Pediatric Clinic
Psychiatric Emergency Services
Radiation Oncology
Rehabilitation Clinic
Surgery
Women's Health

COMPETITORS

Anaheim Regional Medical Center	HCA
Cedars-Sinai Medical Center	Loma Linda University Medical Center
Children's Hospital of Orange County	Memorial Health Services
City of Hope	St. Jude Medical Center
Community Hospital of San Bernardino	Tenet Healthcare
Dignity Health	Trinity Health (Novi)

HISTORICAL FINANCIALS
Company Type: Private

Income Statement

FYE: June 30

	REVENUE ($ mil.)	NET INCOME ($ mil.)	NET PROFIT MARGIN	EMPLOYEES
06/15	468	74	15.8%	2,500
06/09	225	25	11.3%	—
06/04	439	3	0.8%	—
06/03	313	(1)	—	—
Annual Growth	3.4%	—	—	—

2015 Year-End Financials
Return on assets: 4.4%   Cash ($ mil.): 72
Return on equity: 15.8%
Current ratio: 1.00

ARYZTA LLC

EXECUTIVES

Chief Executive Officer, John Yamin
Manager, Anthony Garside
Manager, Allison Parker
Manager, Bob Merrill
Director, Dan O'Connor
Manager, Jeanne Mosgrove
Vice-President, Jim White

LOCATIONS

HQ: ARYZTA LLC
6080 CENTER DR STE 900, LOS ANGELES, CA 900459226
Phone: 310 417-4700
Web: WWW.ARYZTA.COM

HISTORICAL FINANCIALS

Company Type: Private

Income Statement

FYE: July 31

	REVENUE ($ mil.)	NET INCOME ($ mil.)	NET PROFIT MARGIN	EMPLOYEES
07/15	1,599	120	7.6%	5,000
07/14	1,595	132	8.3%	—
07/13	1,608	139	8.7%	—
07/12	1,228	110	9.0%	—
Annual Growth	9.2%	3.1%	—	—

ASCENSION HEALTH

Ascension Health has climbed to the pinnacle of not-for-profit health care. As the largest Catholic hospital system in the US and thus one of the top providers of charity care in the nation the organization's health care network consists of some 130 general hospitals along with a dozen long-term care acute care rehabilitation and psychiatric hospitals (combined about 22000 beds). Ascension Health also operates nursing homes community clinics and other health care providers. Its network of medical facilities spans more than 20 states and the District of Columbia. Ascension Health was created in 1999 from a union of the Daughters of Charity National Health System and the Sisters of St. Joseph Health System.

HISTORY

The Daughters of Charity order was formed in France in 1633 when St. Vincent de Paul recruited a rich widow (St. Louise de Marillac) to care for the sick on battlefields and in their homes.

Elizabeth Ann Seton America's first saint (canonized 1974) brought the order to the US. In 1809 Seton earned the title of Mother and started the Sisters of Charity. The Sisters adopted the vows of the Daughters of Charity adding "service" to them in 1812.

The Sisters officially became part of the Daughters of Charity in 1850. The Daughters cared for soldiers during the Civil War and were responsible for training Florence Nightingale. In the late 1800s the Daughters pioneered exclusive provider arrangements (similar to today's managed care contracts) with railroads lumber camps and the like. During the next 100 years the order furthered its mission of caring for the sick and the poor. To support their efforts the nuns founded hospitals (44 by 1911) schools and other charity centers.

In 1969 the charity association formed a health care services cooperative which became the Daughters of Charity National Health System (DCNHS).

DCNHS operated as two regional institutions (one based in Maryland the other in Missouri) until 1986 when the systems merged. The first task was to balance their holy mission with the need to make money. With competition from managed care companies increasing DCNHS responded by cutting staff and diversifying into nursing homes and retirement centers.

The Daughters of Charity's western unit combined its six hospitals in California with Mullikin Centers (a physician-owned medical group) in 1993 to form one of the largest health care associations in the state.

DCNHS expanded its network in 1995 by merging its hospitals with and becoming a co-sponsor of San Francisco-based Catholic Healthcare West.

That year it joined with Catholic Relief Services to operate a hospital in war-torn Angola.

In 1996 DCNHS dropped a proposed merger of its struggling 221-bed Carney Hospital in Boston with Quincy Hospital because the municipally owned Quincy facility was required by law to provide abortions. Instead DCNHS sold Carney Hospital to Caritas Christi Health Care System (owned by the Boston Roman Catholic archdiocese) one of about a dozen hospital sales by DCNHS in the mid-1990s.

DCNHS reorganized its leadership in 1997 creating SVP positions for system direction and policy and for program development to strengthen and update its programs. In 1998 Sister Irene Kraus who had founded DCNHS and led it through its expansion died.

In 1999 DCNHS merged with fellow Catholic caregiver Sisters of St. Joseph Health System then Michigan's largest health care system to form Ascension Health.

In 2000 Ascension saw the collapse of a five-hospital merger in Florida between subsidiary St. Vincent's Health System and Baptist Health System. The organization also launched the Voice for the Voiceless initiative which combined private monies and federal grants to fund programs for the uninsured in Detroit New Orleans and Austin Texas.

In response to rising health care costs Ascension merged with national Catholic health care provider Carondelet Health System in 2003.

EXECUTIVES

President and CEO, Anthony R. (Tony) Tersigni, age 67

EVP Ascension and President and CEO Ascension Holdings and Ascension Holdings International, John D. Doyle

EVP and Chief Clinical Officer, David B. Pryor

EVP and CFO, Anthony J. (Tony) Speranzo

EVP and Chief Human Resources Officer Ascension Health and CEO Ascension SmartHealth Solutions, Herbert J. (Herb) Vallier

EVP Ascension Health and President and CEO Ascension Healthcare, Patricia A. (Pat) Maryland

EVP Mission Integration, Maureen McGuire

President and CEO Ascension Living, Gayle Trupiano

EVP and COO Ascension, Dennis H. Holtschneider, age 55

EVP and General Counsel, Joseph R. Impicciche

SVP and Chief Marketing and Communications Officer, Nick Ragone

Vice President Information Technology, Suda Suvarna

Vice President Information Services, Melissa Dill

Vice President Operations And Field Implementation, Karen Barrow

Vice President Ethics And Church Relations, Daniel Obrian

Senior Vice President Organizational Development and Human Resources, Challis Lowe

Senior Vice President Chief Risk Officer, Jim Beckman

Vice President Supply Chain, Andy Ferguson

Vice President, Sean Gehle

Vice President Physician Integration, Robert Taylor

Vice President, Mary Paul

Vice President Business And Support Services, Jay Scherler

Vice President Compensation And Benefis, Eric Feinstein

Vice President, Jeff Kennelly

Vice President of Human Resour, David Dowlin

Vice President Business Intelligence, Tony Byram

Vice President Finance, Fran Smith

Vice President Finance, Elizabeth C Foshage

Senior Vice President Human Resources, Steven Younes

Vice President, Shaneens Duncan

VICE PRESIDENT, Sally Jeffcoat

Vice President, Jenna Mihm

Vice President, Jefferson Kennelly

Vice President and Regional Chief Information Officer, Tim Stettheimer

Senior Vice President, Sister Mcguire

Vice President and Chief Information Security Officer, Denise Fortner

Pharmacy Manager, Deborah Sopo

MSN Vice President of Nursing, Denise McLean

Medical Director and Chief of Emergency Medicine, William Tressel

Auditors: DELOITTE TAX LLP CINCINNATI

LOCATIONS

HQ: ASCENSION HEALTH
4600 EDMUNDSON RD, SAINT LOUIS, MO 631343806
Phone: 314 733-8000
Web: WWW.ASCENSIONHEALTHVENTURES.COM

Selected Hospitals
Alabama
  Providence Hospital (Mobile)
  St. Vincent's Hospital (Birmingham)
Arizona
  Carondelet Holy Cross Hospital
  Carondelet St. Joseph's Hospital (Tucson)
  Carondelet St. Mary's Hospital (Tucson)
Arkansas
  DePaul Health Center (Dumas)
  St. Elizabeth Health Center (Gould)
Connecticut
  Hall-Brooke Behavioral Health Services (Westport)
  St. Vincent's Medical Center (Bridgeport)
District of Columbia
  Providence Hospital
Florida
  Sacred Heart Children's Hospital (Pensacola)
  Sacred Heart Hospital of Pensacola
  Sacred Heart Hospital of the Emerald Coast (West Destin)
  Sacred Heart Women's Hospital (Pensacola)
  St. Vincent's Medical Center (Jacksonville)
Georgia
  Walton Rehabilitation Hospital (Augusta)
Idaho
  St. Joseph Regional Medical Center (Lewiston)
Indiana
  St. Elizabeth Ann Seton Hospital (Boonville)
  Saint John's Health System (Anderson)
  St. Joseph Hospital (Kokomo)
  St. Mary's Warrick Hospital (Boonville)
  St. Vincent Carmel Hospital
  St. Vincent Clay Hospital (Brazil)
  St. Vincent Frankfort Hospital
  St. Vincent Jennings Hospital (North Vernon)
  St. Vincent Indianapolis Hospital
  St. Vincent Mercy Hospital (Elwood)
  St. Vincent Randolph Hospital (Winchester)
  St. Vincent Williamsport Hospital
Louisiana
  The Daughters of Charity Health Center (New Orleans)
Maryland
  Sacred Heart Hospital (Cumberland)
  St. Agnes HealthCare (Baltimore)
Michigan
  Borgess Medical Center (Kalamazoo)
  Borgess-Lee Memorial Hospital (Dowagiac)
  Borgess-Pipp Health Center (Plainwell)
  Brighton Hospital
  CareLink of Jackson
  Genesys Regional Medical Center (Grand Blanc)
  Providence Hospital (Southfield)
  St. John Hospital and Medical Center (Detroit)
  St. John Macomb Hospital (Warren)
  St. John North Shores Hospital (Harrison Township)
  St. John Oakland Hospital (Madison Heights)
  St. Joseph Health System (Augres)
  St. Mary's of Michigan Medical Center (Saginaw)
  St. Mary's of Michigan - Standish Hospital
Missouri
  St. Joseph Medical Center (Kansas City)
  St. Mary's Medical Center (Blue Springs)
New York
  Mount St. Mary's Hospital and Health Center (Lewiston)
  Our Lady of Lourdes Memorial Hospital (Binghamton)
  St. Mary's Hospital (Amsterdam)

St. Mary's Hospital (Troy)
Pennsylvania
    Good Samaritan Regional Medical Center (Pottsville)
Tennessee
    Baptist Hickman Community Hospital (Centerville)
    Baptist Hospital (Nashville)
    Middle Tennessee Medical Center (Murfreesboro)
    Saint Thomas Health Services System (Nashville)
Texas
    Dell Children's Medical Center of Central Texas
        (Austin)
    Providence Health Center (Waco)
    Seton Edgar B. Davis Hospital (Luling)
    Seton Highland Lakes Hospital (Burnet)
    Seton Medical Center (Austin)
    Seton Medical Center Williamson (Round Rock)
    Seton Northwest Hospital (Austin)
    Seton Southwest Hospital (Austin)
    University Medical Center Brackenridge (formerly
        Brackenridge Hospital Austin)
Washington
    Lourdes Medical Center (Pasco)
Wisconsin
    Columbia St. Mary's (Milwaukee)
    Columbia St. Mary's Ozaukee Campus (Mequon)
    Orthopaedic Hospital of Wisconsin (Glendale)
    Sacred Heart Rehabilitation Institute (Milwaukee)

COMPETITORS

Catholic Health	Kindred Healthcare
Initiatives	Life Care Centers
Community Health	MedStar Health
Systems	Mercy Health (OH)
Detroit Medical Center	Tenet Healthcare
Dignity Health	Trinity Health (Novi)
Golden Horizons	Universal Health
HCA	Services
HealthSouth	University of Maryland
Henry Ford Health	Medical System
System	

HISTORICAL FINANCIALS

Company Type: Private

Income Statement

FYE: June 30

	REVENUE ($ mil.)	NET INCOME ($ mil.)	NET PROFIT MARGIN	EMPLOYEES
06/15	227	(17)	—	109,000
06/10	14,773	1,230	8.3%	—
06/08	13,489	351	2.6%	—
Annual Growth	(44.2%)	—	—	—

2015 Year-End Financials

Return on assets: 129.7%   Cash ($ mil.): 14
Return on equity: (-7.9%)
Current ratio: 0.10

ASCENSION HEALTH ALLIANCE

EXECUTIVES

President, Anthony R Tersigni
Senior Manager, Sister Bernice Coreil DC
Executive Vice-President, John D Doyle
Executive Vice-President, Robert J Henkel
Executive Vice-President, Joseph R Impicciche
Executive Vice-President, Susan Nestor Levy
Executive Vice-President, Sister Maureen McGuire DC
Executive Vice-President, David B Pryor
Director, Joshua Kaplan
Auditors: ERNST & YOUNG LLP

LOCATIONS

HQ: ASCENSION HEALTH ALLIANCE
    4600 EDMUNDSON RD, SAINT LOUIS, MO 631343806
Phone: 314 733-8000
Web: WWW.ASCENSION.ORG

HISTORICAL FINANCIALS

Company Type: Private

Income Statement

FYE: June 30

	REVENUE ($ mil.)	NET INCOME ($ mil.)	NET PROFIT MARGIN	EMPLOYEES
06/16	21,898	(339)	—	111,489
06/15	20,538	(42)	—	—
Annual Growth	6.6%	—	—	—

2016 Year-End Financials

Return on assets: 11.4%   Cash ($ mil.): 696
Return on equity: (-1.6%)
Current ratio: 0.60

ASCENSION PARISH SCHOOLS

EXECUTIVES

Superintendent, Patrice B Pujol
Plant & Facilities Manager, Glenn Bourgeois
Consultant, Nancy Geter
Personnel Director, Terri Mabile
Consultant, Susan R Vaughn
Administrative Assistant, Tassie Stephens
Auditors: POSTLETHWAITE & NETTERVILLE G

LOCATIONS

HQ: ASCENSION PARISH SCHOOLS
    1100 WEBSTER ST, DONALDSONVILLE, LA
    703462754
Phone: 225 257-2000
Web: WWW.APSB.ORG

HISTORICAL FINANCIALS

Company Type: Private

Income Statement

FYE: June 30

	REVENUE ($ mil.)	NET INCOME ($ mil.)	NET PROFIT MARGIN	EMPLOYEES
06/16	273	(17)	—	3,300
06/15	270	(4)	—	—
06/14	259	31	12.1%	—
06/13	246	14	5.9%	—
Annual Growth	3.5%	—	—	—

2016 Year-End Financials

Return on assets: 4.1%   Cash ($ mil.): 20
Return on equity: (-6.5%)
Current ratio: —

ASHLAND HOSPITAL CORPORATION

EXECUTIVES

President, Fred L Jackson
Director, Mike Thompson
Chief Financial Officer, Paul McDowdil
Auditors: PARENTEBEARD LLC PHILADELPHIA

LOCATIONS

HQ: ASHLAND HOSPITAL CORPORATION
    2201 LEXINGTON AVE, ASHLAND, KY 411012843
Phone: 606 408-4000
Web: WWW.KDMC.COM

HISTORICAL FINANCIALS

Company Type: Private

Income Statement

FYE: September 30

	REVENUE ($ mil.)	NET INCOME ($ mil.)	NET PROFIT MARGIN	EMPLOYEES
09/15	408	12	3.0%	4,200
09/12	530	50	9.4%	—
09/10	600	4	0.8%	—
Annual Growth	(7.4%)	19.9%	—	—

2015 Year-End Financials

Return on assets: 10.9%   Cash ($ mil.): 14
Return on equity: 3.0%
Current ratio: 0.20

ASPIRE PUBLIC SCHOOLS

EXECUTIVES

Chief Executive Officer, James Willcox
Personnel Manager, Cynthia Suter
Personnel Director, David McGee
Consultant, Lindsay Mahoney
Manager, Will Georges
Administrative Assistant, Carol Cardona
Auditors: GILBERT ASSOCIATES INC SACRAM

LOCATIONS

HQ: ASPIRE PUBLIC SCHOOLS
    1001 22ND AVE STE 100, OAKLAND, CA 946065232
Phone: 510 251-1660
Web: WWW.ASPIREPUBLICSCHOOLS.ORG

HISTORICAL FINANCIALS

Company Type: Private

Income Statement

FYE: June 30

	REVENUE ($ mil.)	NET INCOME ($ mil.)	NET PROFIT MARGIN	EMPLOYEES
06/16	215	9	4.3%	1,400
06/13	126	10	8.4%	—
06/12	117	16	14.4%	—
06/11	0	0	—	—
Annual Growth	—	255.0%	—	—

2016 Year-End Financials

Return on assets: 3.0%   Cash ($ mil.): 49
Return on equity: 4.3%
Current ratio: 3.90

ASSOCIATED WHOLESALE GROCERS, INC.

Associated Wholesale Grocers (AWG) knows its customers can't live on bread and milk alone. The second-largest retailer-owned distribution cooperative in the US (behind Wakefern Food Corporation) AWG supplies more than 3800 grocery retail outlets in more than half of the US states from 10 distribution centers which collectively have some 7 million square feet of space. In addition to its wholesale grocery operation AWG offers a variety of business services to its members including marketing and merchandising programs retail accounting supermarket development and access to low-cost merchandise through its Value Merchandisers subsidiary. AWG was founded by a group of independent grocers in 1924.

Geographic Reach

Kansas City-headquartered Associated Wholesale Grocers began in Missouri and its operations are generally centered on that state. It operates ten wholesale divisions in Missouri Nebraska Kansas Oklahoma Louisiana Alabama Tennessee and Wisconsin. Its distribution activities extend into another 25 states.

AWG?s Valu Merchandisers subsidiary is gaining a foothold in non-US regions such as the Caribbean Central & South America and the Middle East.

Sales and Marketing

As a cooperative AWG serves the needs of its members who collectively determine how best to utilize the co-ops operations. Its board of directors is made up of nearly 20 people each a key executive at a grocer retail chain which receives products from AWG.

AWG serves up several private label brands to stores. They include Superior Selections Clearly Organic Best Choice Always Save and IGA.

Financial Performance

Associated Wholesale Grocers (AWG) has grown net sales in recent years from $7.8 billion in 2016 to more recent results exceeding $9.0 billion. Net income has trended positively over the same period from $175 million in 2012 to a spiked of more than $225 million in 2014 to a current result near $190 million.

For the year 2016 net sales grew 3% to $9.2 billion. Product price deflation pushed sales lower as did the loss of Albertsons? membership in the distribution co-op. AWG gained 800 new member stores in conjunction with its unification with Affiliated Foods Midwest which increased sales sufficiently to overcome the negative influencers.

Net income for the year was $190 million 4% lower than the prior year due to a corresponding increase in the co-op?s general and administrative expenses.

Strategy

As a supplier to primarily independent and non-national grocers the co-op must retain size in order to compete with larger corporate firms. Years 2016 and 2017 saw its size shrink in Texas particularly in the hotly contested Dallas-Fort Worth market. Associated Wholesale Grocers lost two key members Albertsons (owner of Tom Thumb?s and Safeway) and WinCo. It countered this by uniting with Affiliated Foods Midwest a distribution co-op with some 800 retail stores but the loss of such notable members is expected influence AWG?s posturing within the North Texas area.

AWG continues to build sales of its billion-dollar private-label products line which includes the Best Choice IGA and Always Save brands. In addition to marketing the products as lower-cost alternatives to brand-name products the co-op has been investing in efforts to make sure the quality of its private-label items matches competing national brands. The company also owns and operates the Value Merchandisers Company (VMC) which offers some 22000 nonfood items to its members including health and beauty care general merchandise and seasonal and promotional products.

Operating in a fragmented business AWG competes with a large number of local and regional suppliers as well as distributors of specialty items. The food wholesale business also has its share of national giants including C & S Wholesale Nash-Finch and wholesale grocery and retail company SUPERVALU.

HISTORY

About 20 Kansas City Kansas-area grocers met in a local grocery in 1924 and organized the Associated Grocers Company to get better deals on purchases and advertising. They elected J. C. Harline president and each chipped in a few hundred dollars to make their first purchases. It took a while to find a manufacturer who would sell directly to them; a local soap maker was finally convinced and others gradually followed.

In 1926 the group was incorporated as Associated Wholesale Grocers (AWG). It outgrew two warehouses in four years finally moving to a 16000-sq.-ft. facility big enough to add new lines and more products. Membership doubled between 1930 and 1932 as grocers moved from ordering products a year ahead to the new wholesale concept and members took seriously the slogan: "Buy Sell Buy Some More." They met every week to plan how to sell their products and buyer and advertising manager Harry Small gave sales presentations and advertising ideas (his trade-in plan for old brooms sold more than two train-carloads of brooms in two weeks). Heavy newspaper advertising also paid off; AWG topped $1 million in sales in 1933.

The cooperative made its first acquisition in 1936 buying Progressive Grocers a warehouse in Joplin Missouri; a second warehouse named Associated Grocers was acquired the next year in Springfield Missouri. AWG continued building and expanding warehouses and annual sales were at $11 million by 1951.

Louis Fox became CEO in 1956. Fox maximized year-end rebates for members led several acquisitions and formed a new subsidiary for financing stores and small shopping centers where AWG members had a presence (Supermarket Developers). Sales increased nearly 15-fold to over $200 million in his first 15 years.

James Basha who succeeded Fox when he retired in 1984 saw sales reach $2.4 billion by the time of his own retirement in 1992.

Basha was followed by former COO Mike De-Fabis once a deputy mayor of Indianapolis. De-Fabis orchestrated several acquisitions including 41 Kansas City-area stores — most of which were quickly bought by members — from bankrupt Food Barn Stores in 1994 and 29 Oklahoma stores and a warehouse from Safeway spinoff Homeland Stores in 1995 (members bought all the stores).

AWG's non-food subsidiary Valu Merchandisers was established in 1995; its new Kansas warehouse began shipping health and beauty aids and housewares the following year to help members battle big discounters. Members narrowly defeated a proposal in late 1996 to convert the cooperative into a public company. Proponents promptly petitioned for a second vote which was defeated early the next year.

AWG veteran Doug Carolan succeeded DeFabis in 1998 becoming only the fifth CEO in the cooperative's history. The company bought five Falley's and 33 Food 4 Less stores in Kansas and Missouri from Fred Meyer in 1998 for $300 million. In a break with tradition AWG began operating the stores rather than selling them to members.

In 2000 after a months-long labor dispute with the Teamsters was resolved Carolan left AWG. The company's CFO Gary Phillips was named president and CEO later that year. In 2001 the company debuted a new format ALPS (Always Low Price Stores) — small stores that carry a limited selection of grocery top-sellers. Also that year AWG's Kansas City division began distributing to more than 10 new stores that had formerly been served by Fleming at the time the #1 US wholesale food distributor.

In 2002 supermarket operator Homeland Stores which operates stores in Oklahoma emerged from bankruptcy as a fully owned subsidiary of AWG. AWG formed a new subsidiary Associated Retail Grocers to oversee Homeland and its Falley's chain.

As a result of the 2003 sale of Fleming Companies' wholesale distribution business AWG picked up food distribution centers in Nebraska (two) Oklahoma (one) and Tennessee (two) and general-merchandise distribution centers in Tennessee and Kansas.

Introducing a "dollar" section in its stores in 2004 proved successful leading AWG to expand the category to more than 1000 food and nonfood items. The following year it merged the corporate offices of its Homeland and Food 4 Less chains.

AWG took steps to expand its capacity and its territory in 2007 when it acquired a distribution center in Fort Worth from Albertsons. The cooperative also took on supply operations for Albertsons locations in Arkansas Louisiana and Texas.

In 2009 AWG acquired the assets of Little Rock Arkansas-based Affiliated Foods Southwest in 2009 adding about a dozen new stores.

During 2010 the firm introduced a paperless coupon program.

In December 2011 AWG sold its corporate supermarkets to a group of employees. The corporate stores included 76 retail locations operating under the Homeland United of Oklahoma and Country mart banners in Oklahoma and the Super Saver banner in northern Texas.

In late 2012 AWG completed a 35000-square-foot addition to its corporate headquarters in Kansas City. The location is also home to AWG's Kansas City distribution centers and its Valu Merchandisers division.

EXECUTIVES

SVP and Division Manager Nashville, Mike Danes
EVP and Chief Marketing Officer, Steve Arnold
SVP and Division Manager Memphis, Gary Jennings
SVP Finance, David Carl
SVP Distribution, Richard Kearns
SVP and CIO, Jon Payne
SVP and Division Manager Fort Worth, Linda Lawson
SVP Springfield, Tim Bellanti
EVP Division Operations, David Smith
SVP and Division Manager Oklahoma City, Danny Lane
SVP Grocery Products, Dan Funk
SVP Perishables, Jerry Edney
SVP and Division Manager Gulf Coast, Bob Durand
President Valu Merchandisers Company (VMC), Dave Sutton
President Always Fresh, Michael Schumacher

SVP and Division Manager Kansas City, David Gates
Senior Vice President, Maurice Henry
Vice President Deli Bakery, Dan Koch
Vice President of Sales Great Lakes, Sonny Leon
Chairman, Bob Hufford
Vice Chairman, Don Woods

LOCATIONS

HQ: ASSOCIATED WHOLESALE GROCERS, INC.
5000 KANSAS AVE, KANSAS CITY, KS 661061135
Phone: 913 288-1000
Web: WWW.AWGINC.COM

COMPETITORS

Affiliated Foods	GSC Enterprises
Affiliated Foods Midwest	H. T. Hackney
Albertsons	McLane
Alex Lee	SUPERVALU
C&S Wholesale	SpartanNash
Central Grocers	Wakefern Food
Dearborn Wholesale Grocers	Wal-Mart
	WinCo Foods

HISTORICAL FINANCIALS

Company Type: Private

Income Statement   FYE: December 26

	REVENUE ($ mil.)	NET INCOME ($ mil.)	NET PROFIT MARGIN	EMPLOYEES
12/15	8,935	198	2.2%	5,500
12/14	8,934	226	2.5%	—
12/13	8,380	192	2.3%	—
12/12	7,852	175	2.2%	—
Annual Growth	4.4%	4.2%	—	—

2015 Year-End Financials
Return on assets: 6.4%   Cash ($ mil.): 166
Return on equity: 2.2%
Current ratio: 0.60

ASSOCIATION OF UNIVERSITY PHYSICIANS

EXECUTIVES

Director, Rick Deese
Director, Maureen Hooley
Director, Marjorie Spencer
Executive Director, Terry Briscoe
Manager, Cleve Noyes
Manager, Kathy Atkinson
Director, Catheryn Boelke
Supervisor, Keith Green
Auditors: CLARK NUBER PS BELLEVUE WA

LOCATIONS

HQ: ASSOCIATION OF UNIVERSITY PHYSICIANS
701 5TH AVE STE 700, SEATTLE, WA 981047028
Phone: 206 520-5388

ATLANTICARE REGIONAL MEDICAL CENTER

EXECUTIVES

Chief Executive Officer, David Tilton
Manager, Donna Mayson

LOCATIONS

HQ: ATLANTICARE REGIONAL MEDICAL CENTER
65 W JIMMIE LEEDS RD, POMONA, NJ 082409102
Phone: 609 652-1000
Web: WWW.ATLANTICARE.ORG

HISTORICAL FINANCIALS

Company Type: Private

Income Statement   FYE: December 31

	REVENUE ($ mil.)	NET INCOME ($ mil.)	NET PROFIT MARGIN	EMPLOYEES
12/15	706	30	4.3%	249
12/14	718	64	9.0%	—
12/08	560	(58)	—	—
12/05	457	51	11.3%	—
Annual Growth	4.4%	(5.1%)	—	—

2015 Year-End Financials
Return on assets: 11.6%   Cash ($ mil.): —
Return on equity: 4.3%
Current ratio: 0.30

ATLAS WORLD GROUP, INC.

Willing to carry the weight of a moving world agent-owned Atlas World Group is the holding company for Atlas Van Lines one of the largest moving companies in the US. Atlas Van Lines' more than 500 agents transport household goods domestically and between the US and Canada; it also offers specialized transportation of items such as trade show exhibits fine art and electronics. Atlas Van Lines International provides international corporate relocation and freight forwarding services. Its Atlas Canada unit moves household goods in that country while American Red Ball In-

ternational specializes in military relocations and serves van lines outside Atlas' network.
Operations
Atlas World Group oversees a family of companies that deliver transportation and related services globally through a network agents and select service partners. Several of its key locations are concentrated in Evansville Indiana.
Strategy
The company continues to grow by adding offices and regional moving agents. In 2013 Atlantic Relocation Systems the second largest agency group within the Atlas Van Lines' US network expanded both its national footprint as well as its local service area in Colorado by opening a new office in Colorado Springs.

EXECUTIVES

Vice President, Ryan McConnell
Vice President, Steve Hermann
Vice President Human Resources, Nancy Priebe
Vice President Of Law And Secretary, Vince Stone
Auditors: ERNST & YOUNG LLP INDIANAPOLI

LOCATIONS

HQ: ATLAS WORLD GROUP, INC.
1212 SAINT GEORGE RD, EVANSVILLE, IN 477112364
Phone: 812 424-2222
Web: WWW.ATLASVANLINES.COM

PRODUCTS/OPERATIONS

Selected Companies
American Red Ball International (international freight forwarding)
American Vanpac Carriers (international freight forwarding)
Atlas Terminal Company (relocation-related supplies and equipment)
Atlas Van Lines (transportation services)
Atlas Van Lines (Canada) (transportation services)
Atlas Van Lines International (transportation services)
Atlas World Class Travel (travel agency)
Avail Move Management (management programs)
AWG Logistics (transportation warehousing and distribution)
Cornerstone Relocation Group (relocation services)
Smart Move Transportation (containerized shipping)
Titan Global Distribution (logistics)

COMPETITORS

A-Mrazek Moving	Graebel
ALTAIR Global Relocation	Penske Truck Leasing
AMERCO	SIRVA
Bekins	Starving Students
Budd Van Lines	UniGroup
Business Products Group	

HISTORICAL FINANCIALS

Company Type: Private

Income Statement   FYE: December 31

	REVENUE ($ mil.)	NET INCOME ($ mil.)	NET PROFIT MARGIN	EMPLOYEES
12/15	845	8	1.0%	726
12/14	878	9	1.1%	—
12/13	844	7	0.9%	—
12/12	815	5	0.7%	—
Annual Growth	1.2%	11.5%	—	—

2015 Year-End Financials
Return on assets: 3.9%   Cash ($ mil.): 15
Return on equity: 1.0%
Current ratio: 2.10

HISTORICAL FINANCIALS
Company Type: Private

Income Statement   FYE: June 30

	REVENUE ($ mil.)	NET INCOME ($ mil.)	NET PROFIT MARGIN	EMPLOYEES
06/15	211	7	3.4%	200
06/13	177	0	0.2%	—
06/09	182	0	—	—
Annual Growth	2.5%	—	—	—

2015 Year-End Financials
Return on assets: 14.7%   Cash ($ mil.): 13
Return on equity: 3.4%
Current ratio: —

ATTORNEY GENERAL, TEXAS

The Office of the Attorney General of Texas defends the state Constitution represents the state in litigation and approves public bond issues. The office is legal counsel to state government boards and agencies and issues legal opinions when requested by the Governor and agency heads. The Attorney General also sits as an ex-officio member of state committees and commissions and defends state laws and suits against agencies and state employees. Other roles include enforcing health safety and consumer regulations; protecting elderly and disabled residents' rights; collecting court-ordered child support; and administering the Crime Victims' Compensation Fund. Greg Abbott was elected Attorney General in 2002.

EXECUTIVES

Executive Director, Ken Paxton
Director, Noelita Lugo

LOCATIONS

HQ: ATTORNEY GENERAL, TEXAS
300 W 15TH ST, AUSTIN, TX 787011649
Phone: 512 475-4375
Web: WWW.TEXASATTORNEYGENERAL.GOV

HISTORICAL FINANCIALS
Company Type: Private

Income Statement

	REVENUE ($ mil.)	NET INCOME ($ mil.)	NET PROFIT MARGIN	EMPLOYEES
08/16	659	45	6.8%	4,202
08/15	561	8	1.5%	—
08/14	571	(6)	—	—
08/06	0	0	—	—
Annual Growth	—	—	—	—

FYE: August 31

2016 Year-End Financials
Return on assets: 2.0%
Return on equity: 6.8%
Current ratio: 1.40
Cash ($ mil.): 87

AUBURN SCHOOL DISTRICT

EXECUTIVES

Superintendent, Kip Herren
Director, Toni M Lally
Chief Operating Officer, Pam Smith
Administrative Assistant, Jennifer Skeel
Administrative Assistant, Kathleen Ray
Administrative Assistant, Tracey Reding
Auditors: BRIAN SONNTAG CGFM STATE AUD

LOCATIONS

HQ: AUBURN SCHOOL DISTRICT
915 4TH ST NE, AUBURN, WA 980024499
Phone: 253 931-4900
Web: WWW.AUBURN.WEDNET.EDU

AUBURN UNIVERSITY

Most of us bleed red but students and alumni of this university bleed auburn. One of the largest schools in the South Auburn University has an enrollment of more than 30000 students on two campuses and offers bachelors master's and doctoral degrees in more than 140 different fields of study through about a dozen colleges and schools. Fields of study include agriculture business education construction forestry and mathematics and science as well as medical fields including nursing pharmacy and veterinary medicine. Auburn has 1200 faculty members and a student-to-teacher ratio of 18:1.

Operations
Unique research institutes at Auburn include the Space Research Institute the National Center for Asphalt Technology the Alabama Agricultural Experiment Station and the Canine and Detection Research Institute.

Geographic Reach
Auburn's main campus is in Auburn Alabama. The university also has a branch campus in Montgomery Alabama. More than 800 students participate in the university's study abroad programs each year.

Financial Performance
Auburn reported a 5% rise in revenues to some $602 million in 2012 due to increased income from tuition and fees state and local grants and contracts and sales and services from educational departments. Net income fell 12% to $87 million in 2012 however due to higher operating expenses from benefits and compensation as well as due to the absence of federal stimulus funds (streamed through the state during 2011).

Company Background
Auburn was founded by the Alabama Conference of the Methodist Episcopal Church in 1856 as the East Alabama Male College. It became a state land-grant institution in 1872 (known as the Agricultural and Mechanical College of Alabama) and adopted its current name in 1960. The university is governed by a board of trustees appointed by the Alabama governor.

EXECUTIVES

Vice President for Student Affairs Continuing, Bobby Woodard
Assistant Vice President Of Alumni Affairs, Dwayne Brown
Vice President, Will Wendland
Vice Chair Continuing, Jim Carroll
Auditors: PRICEWATERHOUSECOOPERS LLP BI

HISTORICAL FINANCIALS
Company Type: Private

Income Statement

	REVENUE ($ mil.)	NET INCOME ($ mil.)	NET PROFIT MARGIN	EMPLOYEES
08/15*	207	(25)	—	1,641
06/09	28	(3)	—	—
08/08	146	(7)	—	—
08/07	0	0	—	—
Annual Growth	—	—	—	—

FYE: August 31
*Fiscal year change

2015 Year-End Financials
Return on assets: 3.8%
Return on equity: (-12.1%)
Current ratio: —
Cash ($ mil.): 66

LOCATIONS

HQ: AUBURN UNIVERSITY
107 SAMFORD HALL, AUBURN, AL 368490001
Phone: 334 844-4539

PRODUCTS/OPERATIONS

Selected Colleges and Schools
College of Agriculture
College of Architecture Design and Construction
College of Business
College of Education
College of Human Sciences
College of Liberal Arts
College of Sciences and Mathematics
College of Veterinary Medicine
Graduate School
Harrison School of Pharmacy
Honors College
Samuel Ginn College of Engineering
School of Forestry and Wildlife Sciences
School of Nursing

HISTORICAL FINANCIALS
Company Type: Private

Income Statement

	REVENUE ($ mil.)	NET INCOME ($ mil.)	NET PROFIT MARGIN	EMPLOYEES
09/16	775	129	16.8%	6,000
09/11	574	99	17.3%	—
09/10	525	110	21.1%	—
Annual Growth	6.7%	2.7%	—	—

FYE: September 30

2016 Year-End Financials
Return on assets: 7.1%
Return on equity: 16.8%
Current ratio: 0.30
Cash ($ mil.): 66

AURORA BAYCARE MEDICAL CENTER

EXECUTIVES

President, Daniel Meyer
Director, Robert P Limoni
VP Personnel, Gwen Baumel
Manager, Renee Lewis
Director, Chuck Geurts

LOCATIONS

HQ: AURORA BAYCARE MEDICAL CENTER
2845 GREENBRIER RD, GREEN BAY, WI 543116519
Phone: 920 288-8000
Web: WWW.AURORABAYCARE.COM

HISTORICAL FINANCIALS
Company Type: Private

Income Statement

	REVENUE ($ mil.)	NET INCOME ($ mil.)	NET PROFIT MARGIN	EMPLOYEES
12/15	375	105	28.1%	131
12/14	341	116	34.0%	—
Annual Growth	9.9%	(8.9%)	—	—

FYE: December 31

2015 Year-End Financials
Return on assets: 6.6%
Return on equity: 28.1%
Current ratio: 1.10
Cash ($ mil.): —

AURORA PUBLIC SCHOOLS

EXECUTIVES

Superintendent, Rico Munn
Manager, Rhonda Genaro
Director, Debbie Barton
Director, Edward Lord
Office Manager, Gale Bankstein
Auditors: BKD LLP DENVER COLORADO

LOCATIONS

HQ: AURORA PUBLIC SCHOOLS
15701 E 1ST AVE STE 106, AURORA, CO 800119037
Phone: 303 365-5810
Web: WWW.AURORAK12.ORG

HISTORICAL FINANCIALS
Company Type: Private

Income Statement
FYE: June 30

	REVENUE ($ mil.)	NET INCOME ($ mil.)	NET PROFIT MARGIN	EMPLOYEES
06/16	451	(8)	—	6,000
06/15	420	(25)	—	—
06/14	380	18	4.8%	—
06/13	351	(21)	—	—
Annual Growth	8.6%	—	—	—

2016 Year-End Financials
Return on assets: 3.0%
Return on equity: (-1.8%)
Current ratio: 1.50
Cash ($ mil.): 77

AURORA WEST SCHOOL DISTRICT 129

EXECUTIVES

Board of Directors, Angela Smith
Director, Vickie Nissen
Chief Financial Officer, Kevin Wegner
Superintendent, Kirk Samples
Assistant Manager, Kimberly Salzbrunn
Assistant Manager, Brent Raby
Superintendent, Jeff Craig
Auditors: CROWE HORWATH LLP OAK BROOK

LOCATIONS

HQ: AURORA WEST SCHOOL DISTRICT 129
1877 W DOWNER PL STE 100, AURORA, IL
605067336
Phone: 630 301-5000
Web: WWW.SD129.ORG

HISTORICAL FINANCIALS
Company Type: Private

Income Statement
FYE: June 30

	REVENUE ($ mil.)	NET INCOME ($ mil.)	NET PROFIT MARGIN	EMPLOYEES
06/16	186	28	15.3%	1,200
06/15	175	(2)	—	—
06/14	169	(9)	—	—
06/13	173	1	1.0%	—
Annual Growth	2.4%	151.4%	—	—

2016 Year-End Financials
Return on assets: 9.1%
Return on equity: 15.3%
Current ratio: —
Cash ($ mil.): 43

AUTOMATION PERSONNEL SERVICES, INC.

EXECUTIVES

President, Steve Nordness
Branch Manager, Brigitte Jones
Office Manager, Carol Glass
Account Manager, Jeremy Whiddon
Manager, Shannan Goward
Manager, Tammy Gross
Office Manager, Kathy Morgan
Regional Manager, David Soileau
Auditors: BARFIELD MURPHY SHANK & SMIT

LOCATIONS

HQ: AUTOMATION PERSONNEL SERVICES, INC.
401 SOUTHGATE DR, PELHAM, AL 351241186
Phone: 205 733-3700
Web: WWW.APSTEMPS.COM

HISTORICAL FINANCIALS
Company Type: Private

Income Statement
FYE: December 31

	REVENUE ($ mil.)	NET INCOME ($ mil.)	NET PROFIT MARGIN	EMPLOYEES
12/15	182	7	4.2%	4,200
12/14	180	3	2.1%	—
12/13	159	3	2.4%	—
12/12	152	3	2.0%	—
Annual Growth	6.0%	36.3%	—	—

2015 Year-End Financials
Return on assets: 0.3%
Return on equity: 4.2%
Current ratio: 1.10
Cash ($ mil.): —

AUXILIO MUTUO HOSPITAL

EXECUTIVES

President, Eduardo A Santiago Delpin
Manager, Wanda Gonzalez

LOCATIONS

HQ: AUXILIO MUTUO HOSPITAL
735 AVE PONCE DE LEON, SAN JUAN, PR 009175022
Phone: 787 758-2000
Web: WWW.AUXILIOMUTUO.COM

HISTORICAL FINANCIALS
Company Type: Private

Income Statement
FYE: September 30

	REVENUE ($ mil.)	NET INCOME ($ mil.)	NET PROFIT MARGIN	EMPLOYEES
09/15	224	1	0.7%	2,600
09/13	217	5	2.5%	—
Annual Growth	1.8%	(44.4%)	—	—

2015 Year-End Financials
Return on assets: 11.2%
Return on equity: 0.7%
Current ratio: 2.20
Cash ($ mil.): 19

AVAYA HOLDINGS CORP.

Avaya Holdings Corp. is the holding company that owns enterprise communications equipment and services provider Avaya Inc.. Spun off from Lucent Technologies in 2000 Avaya was a publicly traded company until 2007 when it was taken private by Silver Lake Partners and TPG Capital for more than $8 billion. After four years of unprofitable private ownership its investors are looking for an exit and Avaya Holdings Corp. was created to make a second bid for listing on a US stock exchange filing for an initial public offering in 2011. The IPO is on hold however and Avaya has been expanding its business and product line through acquisitions.

EXECUTIVES

SVP and General Manager Solutions and Technology, Laurent Philonenko, age 59
President Avaya International, Nidal Abou-Ltaif
President CEO and Director, James M. (Jim) Chirico, age 58, $559,615 total compensation
SVP Chief Administrative Officer and General Counsel, Shefali Shah
SVP Operations, Jaroslaw S. (Jerry) Glembocki
SVP and CFO, Patrick J. O'Malley
SVP Corporate Strategy Development & Marketing, Nicholas (Nikos) Nikolopoulos
General Manager Americas Sales and Services, James J. Geary
SVP and General Manager Cloud, William Mercer Rowe
Auditors: PRICEWATERHOUSECOOPERS LLP FL

LOCATIONS

HQ: AVAYA HOLDINGS CORP.
4655 GREAT AMERICA PKWY, SANTA CLARA, CA 950541233
Phone: 908 953-6000

COMPETITORS

Alcatel-Lucent	Logitech
Aspect Software	Mitel Networks
Brocade Communications	NEC
Cisco Systems	NSN
Fujitsu	ShoreTel
Hitachi	Tellabs
Huawei Technologies	ZTE

HISTORICAL FINANCIALS

Company Type: Private

Income Statement

FYE: September 30

	REVENUE ($ mil.)	NET INCOME ($ mil.)	NET PROFIT MARGIN	EMPLOYEES
09/15	4,081	(168)	—	11,701
09/14	4,371	(253)	—	
09/13	4,708	(376)	—	
09/11	5,547	(863)	—	
Annual Growth	(7.4%)	—	—	—

2015 Year-End Financials

Return on assets: 9.3% Cash ($ mil.): 323
Return on equity: (-4.1%)
Current ratio: 0.60

AVERITT EXPRESS INCORPORATED

EXECUTIVES

Principal, Gary D Sasser
Vice-President, Johnny Fields
Accountant, Gary Lee
Auditors: DUNCAN WHEELER & WILKERSON P

LOCATIONS

HQ: AVERITT EXPRESS INCORPORATED
  1415 NEAL ST, COOKEVILLE, TN 385014328
Phone: 931 526-3306

HISTORICAL FINANCIALS

Company Type: Private

Income Statement

FYE: December 31

	REVENUE ($ mil.)	NET INCOME ($ mil.)	NET PROFIT MARGIN	EMPLOYEES
12/15	1,104	52	4.8%	8,210
12/14	1,088	55	5.1%	—
12/13	1,012	48	4.8%	—
12/12	964	47	4.9%	—
Annual Growth	4.6%	3.7%	—	—

2015 Year-End Financials

Return on assets: 2.1% Cash ($ mil.): 33
Return on equity: 4.8%
Current ratio: 2.00

AVERITT EXPRESS, INC.

Small loads add up at Averitt Express. The company provides less-than-truckload (LTL) freight transportation service. (LTL carriers combine freight from multiple shippers into a single trailer.) It operates a fleet of about 4100 tractors and 12250 trailers from a network of 80 terminals. Averitt Express directly serves the southern US and Mexico and it provides service elsewhere in North America through partnerships with other carriers such as Lakeville Motor Express and DATS. The company also offers truckload and expedited freight transportation along with logistics warehousing and international freight forwarding.

Customers have included Home Depot Shoe Carnival and V.F. Corporation.

Geographic Reach

Averitt Express has a total of roughly 140 facilities that serve thousands of points throughout the Southern US (in about 20 states) Canada Mexico and the Caribbean.

Strategy

The company aims to grow from solely a LTL carrier based in the Southeast to an international transportation and logistics company. To this end it continues to strategically broaden its geographic reach and range of services. Averitt Express over the years has launched a new business unit zeroing in on retailers in need of distribution services. The new unit Averitt Retail Distribution Services offers customized delivery services catering to the unique requirements of retailers and is targeting retailers needing delivery in large Southern markets.

EXECUTIVES

President and CEO, Gary D. Sasser
EVP and COO, Wayne Spain
EVP Sales and Marketing, Phil Pierce
EVP and CFO, George Johnson
Auditors: DUNCAN WHEELER & WILKERSON P

LOCATIONS

HQ: AVERITT EXPRESS, INC.
  1415 NEAL ST, COOKEVILLE, TN 385014328
Phone: 931 526-3306
Web: WWW.AVERITTEXPRESS.COM

PRODUCTS/OPERATIONS

Selected Services

Cross-border/domestic offshore (Canada Mexico Puerto Rico/Virgin Islands)
Dedicated
Expedited
Intermodal
International ocean/air (ocean/air Asia-Memphis Express)
LTL (regional nationwide distribution/consolidation)
Portside
Retail specialized services
Transportation management
Truckload (dry van flatbed brokerage)
Warehousing

COMPETITORS

AAA Cooper Transportation	Old Dominion Freight
ArcBest	R+L Carriers
C.H. Robinson Worldwide	Schneider National
	Southeastern Freight Lines
Estes Express	Swift Transportation
FedEx Freight	UPS Freight
J.B. Hunt	YRC Worldwide

HISTORICAL FINANCIALS

Company Type: Private

Income Statement

FYE: December 31

	REVENUE ($ mil.)	NET INCOME ($ mil.)	NET PROFIT MARGIN	EMPLOYEES
12/15	1,091	44	4.1%	8,208
12/14	1,075	46	4.3%	
12/13	1,000	39	4.0%	
12/12	957	39	4.2%	
Annual Growth	4.5%	3.9%	—	—

2015 Year-End Financials

Return on assets: 2.1% Cash ($ mil.): 32
Return on equity: 4.1%
Current ratio: 2.00

AVI SYSTEMS, INC.

AVI Systems knows that a CEO's message is only as good as its transmission. The employee-owned company designs installs and services audiovisual systems in boardrooms classrooms hospitals hotels places of worship and sports arenas primarily in the Midwest. It specializes in broadcast and cable sales and training video production and post-production videoconferencing and rental and staging systems. AVI runs more than 15 regional offices as well as a help desk that offers remote monitoring and emergency on-site service. It also provides IT engineering support for larger-scale national or international installations. AVI was founded in 1974 by Joe Stoebner.

Operations

Having become one of the nation's top five audio visual integrators AVI is authorized to install equipment from leading audiovisual equipment manufacturers such as Audio-Technica U.S. ClearOne Communications NEC Display Solutions and Samsung Electronics America.

Geographic Reach

With 17 offices in the upper Midwest and on the West coast Minnesota-based AVI boasts a regional presence and a national reach.

Sales and Marketing

The company serves a variety of sectors such as universities schools service firms healthcare financial entertainment non-profit organizations and large companies such as Best Buy AT&T Carlson Companies Sprint ConAgra and Target.

Strategy

AVI not only integrates systems for others it has also begun integrating itself. Several subsidiaries including AVI Midwest and Televideo San Diego have traded their names for the AVI Systems banner. Also the company has worked to roll out its own line of digital signage and asset management products.

EXECUTIVES

President and CEO, Jeff Stoebner
CFO, Randi Borth
CTO, Brad Sousa
Chairman, Joe Stoebner
Auditors: EIDE BAILLY LLP BISMARCK NOR

LOCATIONS

HQ: AVI SYSTEMS, INC.
  9675 W 76TH ST STE 200, EDEN PRAIRIE, MN 553443707
Phone: 952 949-3700
Web: WWW.AVISYSTEMS.COM

Selected Locations

California
Colorado
Illinois
Iowa
Michigan
Minnesota
Missouri
Nebraska
North Dakota
Ohio
South Dakota
Texas
Wisconsin

PRODUCTS/OPERATIONS

Selected Solutions

Digital Signage
Enterprise Technology
Meeting Rooms
New Broadcast Media
Video Conferencing

COMPETITORS

ACT Teleconferencing	IVCi
AT Conference	PSAV Inc.
AVI-SPL	

HISTORICAL FINANCIALS
Company Type: Private

Income Statement
FYE: March 31

	REVENUE ($ mil.)	NET INCOME ($ mil.)	NET PROFIT MARGIN	EMPLOYEES
03/16	182	6	3.6%	498
03/15	184	10	5.7%	—
03/14	172	9	5.7%	—
03/13	143	7	5.0%	—
Annual Growth	8.3%	(3.4%)	—	—

2016 Year-End Financials
Return on assets: 3.7% Cash ($ mil.): 17
Return on equity: 3.6%
Current ratio: 1.50

AZCO INC.

EXECUTIVES

President, John Trottier
Vice-President, Jenny Morrow
Vice-President, Robert Brockington
Vice-President, Dale Coenen
VP Operations, Scott Koval
Vice-President, Dave Recker
Vice-President, Marjanne Prins
Vice-President, Pawe Barski
Executive Vice-President, Thomas Martin
Auditors: GRANT THORNTON LLP APPLETON

LOCATIONS

HQ: AZCO INC.
1025 E SOUTH RIVER ST, APPLETON, WI 549152225
Phone: 920 734-5791
Web: WWW.AZCO-INC.COM

HISTORICAL FINANCIALS
Company Type: Private

Income Statement
FYE: December 31

	REVENUE ($ mil.)	NET INCOME ($ mil.)	NET PROFIT MARGIN	EMPLOYEES
12/15	237	13	5.6%	1,200
12/14	114	0	0.4%	—
12/13	150	(6)	—	—
12/12	137	4	3.0%	—
Annual Growth	20.1%	48.4%	—	—

2015 Year-End Financials
Return on assets: 6.2% Cash ($ mil.): —
Return on equity: 5.6%
Current ratio: 1.10

AZUSA PACIFIC UNIVERSITY

An evangelical Christian institution Azusa Pacific University (APU) has an enrollment of about 10300 undergraduate graduate and doctoral students. It offers approximately 70 fields of undergraduate study and about 40 graduate degree programs (including eight doctoral programs) as well as a number of certificate and credentialing programs. Undergraduate students are required to complete ministry and service credits every semester; options include participating in ministries international service experience and doing volunteer work. APU traces its roots to 1899 and the Training School for Christian Workers the West Coast's first bible college.

Operations

APU has a student-to-faculty ratio of 12:1 and employs more than 1200 full-time part-time and adjunct faculty members. Full-time undergraduate tuition totaled some $32500 in fiscal 2015. (Nearly 90% of undergraduate students receive some sort of financial aid.) In addition to theology the university's major programs include business sciences liberal arts music nursing education and visual and performing arts. It offers online programs to supplement classes held at its main campus and regional branch locations. In 2014 ASU awarded about 3000 degrees.

The university's three libraries contain more than 386000 books and media items 128000 e-books 92000 electronic journals 1600 print periodicals and 110 databases.

Geographic Reach

In addition to its two main campuses (known as the East Campus and the West Campus) in Azusa a community located in the San Gabriel Valley northeast of Los Angeles the university has six regional centers in Southern California.

Financial Performance

APU's annual budget runs at some $232 million. It has an endowment of about $59 million.

Strategy

Five-year strategic plans (reaching through 2016) include improving resources for internal communication; enhancing support infrastructure for grants research and teaching; and increasing student and faculty diversity. APU is also working to restructure its curriculum.

EXECUTIVES

Senior Vice President, Mark Dickerson
President CEO and Trustee, Jon R. Wallace
EVP and Chief Development Officer, David E. Bixby
EVP, John C. Reynolds
Provost, Mark E. Stanton
SVP and CFO, Bob Johansen
Vice President and Chief Information Officer, Don H Davis
Vice President of Finance, Kelly Ring
Vice President For Enrollment Management, David Dufault-Hunter
Senior Vice President Student Life and Dean of Students, Terry Franson
Vice President People and Organizational Development, Gary Lemaster
Research Historian and Special Assistant to the President Executive Vice President and Dean of the, Tom Andrews
Associate Vice President of University Relations, David Peck
Vice President, Wanda Calnon
Department Chair Professor, Elaine Goehner
Associate Vice President of Finance, Junine Schoen
Associate Vice President of Facilities Management, Thomas Hunt
Vice Chair, Steve Perry
Auditors: LB CAPIN CROUSE LLP BREA CA

LOCATIONS

HQ: AZUSA PACIFIC UNIVERSITY
901 E ALOSTA AVE, AZUSA, CA 917022701
Phone: 626 969-3434
Web: WWW.APU.EDU

Selected Locations
Azusa CA
Los Angeles CA
Murrieta CA
Orange CA
Oxnard CA
San Bernardino CA
San Diego CA
Victorville CA

PRODUCTS/OPERATIONS

Selected Schools
American Language and Culture Institute
Azusa Pacific Online University
Center for Global Learning and Engagement
College of Liberal Arts and Sciences
School of Adult and Professional Studies
School of Behavioral and Applied Sciences
School of Business and Management
School of Education
School of Music
School of Nursing
School of Theology
School of Visual and Performing Arts
University Libraries

Selected Academic Programs
Adult and Professional Studies
Behavioral and Applied Sciences
Business and Management
Education
Liberal Arts and Sciences
Music and the Arts
Nursing
Theology

COMPETITORS

Ave Maria University	Lipscomb University
Biola University	Mercer University
Emory University	SMU
Fuller Theological Seminary	Seton Hall University

HISTORICAL FINANCIALS
Company Type: Private

Income Statement
FYE: June 30

	REVENUE ($ mil.)	NET INCOME ($ mil.)	NET PROFIT MARGIN	EMPLOYEES
06/16	248	0	0.2%	1,545
06/15	297	2	0.7%	—
06/13	281	1	0.4%	—
06/11	270	26	9.7%	—
Annual Growth	(1.7%)	(56.3%)	—	—

2016 Year-End Financials
Return on assets: 5.8% Cash ($ mil.): 17
Return on equity: 0.2%
Current ratio: —

BABCOCK POWER INC.

EXECUTIVES

President, Michael D Leclair
Auditors: DELOITTE & TOUCH LLP HARTFORD

LOCATIONS

HQ: BABCOCK POWER INC.
6 KIMBALL LN STE 210, LYNNFIELD, MA 019402684
Phone: 978 646-3300
Web: WWW.JCAMPBELLFINANCIAL.COM

HISTORICAL FINANCIALS

Company Type: Private

Income Statement

FYE: September 30

	REVENUE ($ mil.)	NET INCOME ($ mil.)	NET PROFIT MARGIN	EMPLOYEES
09/15	627	15	2.5%	900
09/14	746	16	2.2%	—
09/13	717	8	1.2%	—
09/12	767	24	3.3%	—
Annual Growth	(6.5%)	(14.4%)	—	—

2015 Year-End Financials

Return on assets: 9.1%   Cash ($ mil.): 91
Return on equity: 2.5%
Current ratio: 0.90

BABSON COLLEGE

Babson students could babble on and on about business management. With an enrollment of more than 3000 students Babson College is lauded as one of the nation's leading business schools. The school's undergraduate programs combine liberal arts with business curriculum; it also grants master's degrees in business administration entrepreneurship and other fields. Babson students in their first year receive the practical experience of creating for-profit ventures. Babson's entrepreneurship program has been ranked at the top of such programs in publications including Entrepreneur and U.S. News & World Report.

Operations

While the F.W. Olin Graduate School of Business grants Master of Business Administration (MBA) degrees and customized Master of Science degrees the Arthur M. Blank Center for Entrepreneurship offers graduate and undergraduate courses in entrepreneurial leadership.

In addition to undergraduate and graduate degree programs Babson conducts collaborative research programs that connect students with scholars and area business leaders.

Geographic Reach

Babson College's main campus is located in Babson Park near Wellesley Massachusetts. Its students come from across the US and 70 international countries.

Financial Performance

Operating revenue rose 4% to about $178 million in fiscal 2013 from higher student tuition and fee earnings as well as income from auxiliary activities room and board services and other educational and non-educational programs. The increase was offset somewhat by a dip in contributions and grants and investment income.

Undergraduate tuition runs at some $43500 per year.

Strategy

Babson College is expanding and improving its undergraduate curriculum with the goal of integrating management and liberal arts focuses. In 2013 it began rolling out new guidelines that aim to increase the undergraduate programs' focus on social environmental and economic concerns as well as on creativity and entrepreneurship.

To increase entrepreneurship opportunities for students in 2012 Babson extended its Butler Venture Accelerator program to its San Francisco campus. Also that year the college widened international entrepreneurship opportunities by partnering with Shiv Nadar University to provide programs in India. In 2013 Babson launched a new Master's Degree in Entrepreneurial Leadership; it also opened a new innovation lab focused on supporting female entrepreneurs.

Company Background

Babson was founded in 1919 (as Babson Institute) by philanthropist educator and businessman Roger Babson.

EXECUTIVES

Vice President of Communication, Amelie Bushong
Vice President Of Membership And Events, Eric Burns
CO PRESIDENT, Elena Tarassenko
Vice President Of Communications, Lena WU
Auditors: PRICEWATERHOUSECOOPERS LLP BO

LOCATIONS

HQ: BABSON COLLEGE
492 STATEN AVE APT 801, OAKLAND, CA 946104907
Phone: 781 235-1200
Web: WWW.BABSON.EDU

PRODUCTS/OPERATIONS

2012 Sales

	$ mil.	% of total
Program service fees	160	90
Net released assets	7	4
Endowment spending	6	4
Contributions & grants	2	2
Investment income	0	-
Total	177	100

Selected Academic Divisions

Accounting And Law
Arts And Humanities
Economics
Entrepreneurship
Finance
History And Society
Management
Marketing
Math And Science
Technology Operations And Information Management

HISTORICAL FINANCIALS

Company Type: Private

Income Statement

FYE: June 30

	REVENUE ($ mil.)	NET INCOME ($ mil.)	NET PROFIT MARGIN	EMPLOYEES
06/15	232	11	5.1%	750
06/13	177	43	24.4%	—
06/11	202	14	7.1%	—
06/10	0	0	—	—
Annual Growth	—	1109.9%	—	—

2015 Year-End Financials

Return on assets: 10.9%   Cash ($ mil.): 34
Return on equity: 5.1%
Current ratio: 0.30

BAER'S FURNITURE CO., INC.

Having assembled a furniture portfolio full of big-name brands Baer's Furniture counts the likes of Lexington Home Brands and Bernhardt as family. Family-owned Baer's Furniture operates about 15 mid-priced to high-end retail furniture showrooms and two warehouses in South Florida. The company offers furnishings (living room dining room bedroom and office furniture) bedding rugs and accessories made by popular manufacturers that are designed to fit the budgets of shoppers who have a little cash tucked away. The chain was founded in 1945 by Melvin and Lucile Baer in South Bend Indiana. Their sons Robert now the company's CEO and Allan company president moved the business to Florida in 1968.

Operations

Within its portfolio of living room bedroom dining room home office mattresses entertainment and outdoor furniture Baer's features brands that include Tommy Bahama Home Serta and Broyhill.

Geographic Reach

Based in Pompano Beach Florida Baer's serves consumers throughout Florida as well as in South America and the Caribbean. The furniture retailer operates 15 stores and two warehouses across Florida.

Sales and Marketing

Baer's ships its furniture and decor items worldwide and sells its products online and through several Florida stores.

Financial Performance

Baer's stores rang up an estimated $143.2 million in sales in 2012 an 8.5% increase versus 2011.

Strategy

Furniture retailers including Baer's were hard hit by the recession and housing crisis in the US. (Florida along with Arizona and California suffered more than most other states.) Furniture sales typically follow real estate sales trends and Baer's exposure to the Florida market led to losses. To cope with declining sales and deflation in furniture prices the company cut costs by outsourcing customer service overseas among other measures.

Now with housing posting a comeback Baer's is looking to grow by opening new stores. In 2015 it aims to open a new store in Winter Garden following the opening of a pair of stores in Central Florida.

EXECUTIVES

V Pres, Jerome I Baer
Senior Vice President Sales, Jerry I Baer
Auditors: JACOBS & COMPANY LLP WEST PAL

LOCATIONS

HQ: BAER'S FURNITURE CO., INC.
1589 NW 12TH AVE, POMPANO BEACH, FL 330691734
Phone: 954 946-8001
Web: WWW.BAERS.COM

Selected Florida Locations
Altamonte Springs
Stuart
North Palm Beach
West Palm Beach
Boca Raton
Tamarac
Fort Lauderdale
Dania Beach
Pembroke Pines
Pinecrest
Naples
Fort Myers
Port Charlotte
Sarasota
West Melbourne

PRODUCTS/OPERATIONS

Selected Product Categories
Bedroom
Living Room
Kids' Bedroom
Dining Room
Home Office

Entertainment
Accent Tables
Mattresses
Outdoor

Selected Brands

Better Homes and Gardens
Bernhardt
Broyhill
HGTV Home
Hooker
Hunter Douglas
Lexington Home Brands
Pulaski
Serta
Sherrill
Tempur- Pedic
Tommy Bahama Home
Tommy Bahama Outdoor

COMPETITORS

Ashley Furniture	Norwalk Furniture
Bassett Furniture	Pier 1 Imports
El Dorado Furniture	Rooms To Go
Ethan Allen	W.S. Badcock
Havertys	Z Gallerie

HISTORICAL FINANCIALS
Company Type: Private

Income Statement
FYE: December 31

	REVENUE ($ mil.)	NET INCOME ($ mil.)	NET PROFIT MARGIN	EMPLOYEES
12/15	196	16	8.4%	437
12/13	160	10	6.6%	—
12/12	143	9	6.6%	—
12/11	138	7	5.3%	—
Annual Growth	9.3%	22.9%	—	—

BAINUM FAMILY FOUNDATION, INC.

EXECUTIVES

President, Barbara Bainum
Office Manager, Kenya Hunter
Vice-President, Jonice Adams
Manager, Jennifer Schauffler
Auditors: RAFFA PC WASHINGTON DC

LOCATIONS

HQ: BAINUM FAMILY FOUNDATION, INC.
7735 OLD GEORGTWN RD # 1000, BETHESDA, MD 208146130
Phone: 240 450-0000
Web: WWW.BAINUMFDN.ORG

HISTORICAL FINANCIALS
Company Type: Private

Income Statement
FYE: June 30

	REVENUE ($ mil.)	NET INCOME ($ mil.)	NET PROFIT MARGIN	EMPLOYEES
06/15	332	315	95.0%	30
06/13	47	32	68.6%	—
06/12	85	67	79.5%	—
06/11	10	1	11.8%	—
Annual Growth	137.6%	300.1%	—	—

2015 Year-End Financials

Return on assets: 0.8%   Cash ($ mil.): 66
Return on equity: 95.0%
Current ratio: —

BAKERSFIELD CITY SCHOOL DISTRICT

LOCATIONS

HQ: BAKERSFIELD CITY SCHOOL DISTRICT
1300 BAKER ST, BAKERSFIELD, CA 933054326
Phone: 661 631-4600
Web: WWW.BCSD.COM

HISTORICAL FINANCIALS
Company Type: Private

Income Statement
FYE: June 30

	REVENUE ($ mil.)	NET INCOME ($ mil.)	NET PROFIT MARGIN	EMPLOYEES
06/16	378	31	8.4%	9
06/15	324	(9)	—	—
Annual Growth	16.7%	—	—	—

BAKERSFIELD MEMORIAL HOSPITAL

EXECUTIVES

Chief Executive Officer, Jon Van Boening
Vice-President, R Mark R Root
Manager, Richard Doan
Manager, Jim Munden
Operations Manager, Gary De Risio

LOCATIONS

HQ: BAKERSFIELD MEMORIAL HOSPITAL
420 34TH ST, BAKERSFIELD, CA 933012237
Phone: 661 327-1792
Web: WWW.BAKERSFIELDMEMORIAL.ORG

HISTORICAL FINANCIALS
Company Type: Private

Income Statement
FYE: June 30

	REVENUE ($ mil.)	NET INCOME ($ mil.)	NET PROFIT MARGIN	EMPLOYEES
06/15	423	71	16.9%	1,100
06/14	373	45	12.1%	—
06/13	338	30	9.0%	—
06/11	317	34	10.9%	—
Annual Growth	7.4%	19.8%	—	—

2015 Year-End Financials

Return on assets: 4.5%   Cash ($ mil.): 210
Return on equity: 16.9%
Current ratio: 4.20

BANNER HEALTH

Banner Health is one of the largest secular not-for-profit health systems in the US. The organization operates about 30 acute-care hospitals (with roughly 4000 beds). It also operates clinics nursing homes clinical laboratories ambulatory surgery centers home health agencies and other health care-related organizations including physician practices and a captive insurance company. Banner Health participates in medical research in areas such as Alzheimer's disease and spinal cord injuries through its Banner Sun Health Research division. The company which has more than 400000 members provides services in seven states in the western US; its largest concentration of facilities is in Arizona.

Operations

Banner Health is one of the first not-for-profit hospital operators to reinsure its employees through its captive insurance company Samaritan Insurance Funding. By offering this service Banner Health is able to diversify its risk improve cash flow and lower life insurance costs by about half a million dollars a year.

The multi-specialty system also operates a health plan in Arizona for Medicare-eligible patients. Its MediSunONE plan includes Medicare and Medicare Part D. The company has joined forces with Aetna in what is called an accountable care collaboration (ACO). An ACO uses technology and a team-based approach to care for the hospital's patients. Doctors and hospitals assume accountability for patient outcomes and are rewarded financially for achieving higher quality greater efficiency and overall better patient outcomes. The partnership also includes a new product called Aetna Whole Health that allows Banner's patients access to a line of Aetna services including their own electronic patient record.

The system's specialty centers include Banner Alzheimer's Institute Banner Concussion Center Banner Heart Hospital and the Western States Burn Center. In addition Banner Health trains 270 doctors per year at Banner Good Samaritan and Northern Colorado Medical Center.

Banner Health also partners with M.D. Anderson Cancer Center to operate a comprehensive cancer center in Phoenix. Services include medical oncology radiation oncology surgical oncology pathology laboratory diagnostic imaging as well as other supportive clinical services. M.D. Anderson has clinical oversight for all aspects of care delivery.

Education looms large on Banner Health's list of priorities — the hospital operates one of the country's largest simulation education centers at its Banner Corporate Center-Mesa. Simulation education is an expanding field in which medical students use computerized mannequins to improve their surgical and medical skills. The school's research has paid off and with Scottsdale Healthcare Osborn Medical Center Banner Health invented the Sapien Transcatheter Heart Valve an artificial heart valve that can replace a diseased aortic heart valve without the open heart surgery that previously was required.

Geographic Reach

Banner Health operates in Alaska Arizona California Colorado Nebraska Nevada and Wyoming.

The system's Banner Health Network is a group of health care providers located in Arizona's Maricopa and Pinal counties.

Financial Performance

Banner Health's income is generally derived through three channels: third-party payers such as commercial insurance managed care agreements Medicare and Medicaid and a small portion of self-pay patients as well as by borrowing funds and receiving philanthropic donations.

Its revenues grew by 29% in 2015 from $5.4 billion to $7 billion; higher net patient service medical insurance premium and other revenues drove that increase. However rising expenses and a $49.3 million loss for ACO Banner Health Network led to a drop in net income which fell 65% to $83.7 million.

Strategy

The health system has grown through construction. Banner Health is nearly always engaged in some sort of construction renovation or upgrading at its numerous facilities. The organization has more than $1 billion in construction projects in progress or completed in recent years. The system has expanded its facilities at Banner Baywood Medical Center Banner Del E. Webb Medical Center Banner Desert Medical Center Banner Thunderbird Medical Center Cardon Children's Medical Center and McKee Medical Center.

In 2015 Banner Health opened a Fort Collins facility on a 28-acre campus with a two-story hospital featuring an emergency department a 24-bed inpatient unit labor and delivery rooms medical imaging women's services surgical services and lab services.

Also that year the system merged with the University of Arizona Health Network (now named Banner - University Medicine) as well as establishing a 30-year affiliation with the University of Arizona. The moves align with its strategy of combining health care provision with medical schools and academic training as well as expanding operations into new markets (in this case the Tuscon region). Banner Health hopes to both improve access to health care through a consumer-focused system and to provide opportunities for medical professionals to remain in Arizona. As part of the merger the company plans to build a new hospital and renovate an existing ambulatory campus.

In 2017 Banner Health restructured operations including cutting some 500 employees' positions. The move was part of its efforts to become more consumer-focused and included changes to its leadership lineup. Later that year after the restructuring was completed the company began recruiting to fill 1000 positions including spots for specialty nurses and physical and occupational therapists.

Mergers and Acquisitions

Banner Health does occasionally pick up a new hospital through acquisition. For instance in 2015 the company acquired The University of Arizona Health Network (now Banner - University Medicine). As a result University Medicine is the new academic medicine division of Banner Health which includes three academic medical centers: Banner - University Medical Center Tucson Banner - University Medical Center Phoenix and Banner - University Medical Center South.

In mid-2016 the company acquired more than 30 Arizona urgent-care centers from Urgent Care Extra. The centers to be rebranded under the Banner banner are among the expected 50 the company plans to have in Arizona by 2018.

In 2017 Banner Health acquired Medicare-certified home health agency SunLife Home Health which is based in Tucson Arizona. That deal allowed the system to expand its home care operations into southern Arizona.

Company Background

Banner Good Samaritan Medical Center first opened its doors as a 20-bed hospital in 1911. The medical center which is four months older than the state of Arizona marked its 100th anniversary in October 2011.

EXECUTIVES

EVP and Chief Administrative Officer, Ronald R. (Ron) Bunnell
President CEO and Director, Peter S. Fine, age 65
EVP and Chief Clinical Officer, John Hensing
CEO Banner Baywood Heart Hospital, Kathy Bollinger
COO, Rebecca (Becky) Kuhn
CEO Banner Estrella Medical Center, Tom Dickson
CFO, Dennis L. Laraway
President Western Region, Jim Ferando

CEO East Morgan County Hospital and Sterling Regional MedCenter, Linda Thorpe
President Arizona East Division, Todd S. Werner, age 49
CEO Banner Desert Medical Center and Interim CEO Cardon Children's Medical Center, Laura Robertson
CEO Platte County Memorial Hospital and Community Hospital, Shelby Nelson
CEO Banner Thunderbird Medical Center, Deb Krmpotic
CEO Banner Research, Eric (Bill) Reiman
President Banner Health Network, Chuck Lehn
CEO Banner Del E. Webb Medical Center and Banner Boswell Medical Center, Debbie Flores
CEO University Medical Center Phoenix, Steve Narang
CEO Banner Ironwood Medical Center and Banner Goldfield Medical Center, Sharon Lind
President and CEO Banner Health Foundation and Banner Alzheimer's Foundation, Andy Kramer Petersen
CIO, Ryan Smith
CEO Banner Casa Grande Medical Center, Rona Curphy
CEO Banner Estrella Medical Center, Courtney Ophaug
CEO Banner Gateway Medical Center Banner MD Anderson Cancer Center Banner Baywood Medical Center and Banner Heart Hospital, Lamont Yoder
VP Post Acute Services and CEO Banner Home Care/Hospice, Lynn Rosenbach
CEO Banner Lassen Medical Center, Catherine Harshbarger
CEO Banner Churchill Community Hospital, Hoyt Skabelund
CEO Washakie Medical Center, Jay Stallings
CEO Ogallala Community Hospital, Drew Dostal
CEO Banner Behavioral Health Hospital, Brian Beutin
CEO Page Hospital, Brian Kellar
Interim CEO Northern Colorado Service Area including: Banner Fort Collins Medical Center McKee Medical Center North Colorado Medical Center, Scott Baker
Vice President of Materials Management, Doug Bowen
Director of Infection Control, Marti Reich
Vice President Of Clinical Operations, Maggie Row
Director Of Pharmacy, E-J Chane
Director Of Pharmacy, Kurt Weibel
Director, Christopher H. (Chris) Volk
Chairman, Larry S. Lazarus
Secretary HP Statewide Customer Care, Josephine Patino
Auditors: ERNST & YOUNG LLP

LOCATIONS

HQ: BANNER HEALTH
2901 N CENTRAL AVE # 160, PHOENIX, AZ 850122702
Phone: 602 747-4000
Web: WWW.BANNERHEALTH.COM

FEATURED SERVICES
Academic Medicine
Alzheimer's
Cancer
Heart
Insurance (Networks)
Maternity
Orthopedics
Pediatrics
Pharmacy
Physicians & Specialists
Research
Women's Health

COMPETITORS

Community Health Systems	Poudre Valley Health System
Dignity Health	Providence St. Joseph Health
HCA	Scottsdale Healthcare
Inova	Tenet Healthcare
John C. Lincoln Health Network	Texas Health Resources
Memorial Health System of East Texas	Wyoming Medical Center
Northern Arizona Healthcare	Yuma Regional Medical Center
Phoenix Children's Hospital	

HISTORICAL FINANCIALS
Company Type: Private

Income Statement
FYE: December 31

	REVENUE ($ mil.)	NET INCOME ($ mil.)	NET PROFIT MARGIN	EMPLOYEES
12/15	6,971	119	1.7%	35,000
12/14	5,397	261	4.8%	—
12/13	5,085	854	16.8%	—
12/12	4,878	614	12.6%	—
Annual Growth 12.6%		(42.1%)	—	—

2015 Year-End Financials
Return on assets: 2.5%   Cash ($ mil.): 91
Return on equity: 1.7%
Current ratio: 0.60

BAPTIST HEALTH MADISONVILLE INC.

EXECUTIVES

Manager, Penny Hardison
Auditors: ERNST & YOUNG US LLP CINCINNA

LOCATIONS

HQ: BAPTIST HEALTH MADISONVILLE INC.
900 HOSPITAL DR, MADISONVILLE, KY 424311644
Phone: 270 825-5100
Web: WWW.BAPTISTHEALTHMADISONVILLEKY.COM

HISTORICAL FINANCIALS
Company Type: Private

Income Statement
FYE: August 31

	REVENUE ($ mil.)	NET INCOME ($ mil.)	NET PROFIT MARGIN	EMPLOYEES
08/15	189	16	8.9%	2,100
08/13	94	(0)	—	—
Annual Growth 41.8%		—	—	—

2015 Year-End Financials
Return on assets: 10.0%   Cash ($ mil.): 14
Return on equity: 8.9%
Current ratio: 1.10

BAPTIST HEALTH SYSTEM, INC.

Even if you don't root for the Jacksonville Jaguars you can still seek care from Baptist Health System. Baptist Health serves the Jacksonville

Florida area through four acute care hospitals and a children's hospital with a combined total of more than 1000 beds. Baptist Medical Center its flagship facility is a full-service hospital that also houses Baptist Heart Hospital. Across the street Wolfson Children's Hospital also cares for the city's youngest residents. The system's satellite acute-care facilities include Baptist Medical Center Beaches Baptist Medical Center Nassau and Baptist Medical Center South.

Operations

Baptist Health's flagship tertiary care hospital Baptist Medical Center is centrally located in Jacksonville and is a full-service medical center representing nearly all major health care specialties. Its Baptist Heart Hospital offers comprehensive cardiovascular care.

In addition to its hospitals Baptist Health System operates a network of about 200 outpatient centers including primary and specialty care physician practices and clinics (including cardiology and cancer care centers) as well as urgent care rehabilitation pharmacy and occupational health locations. In total Baptist Health System has 1200 physicians and handles some 51000 inpatient stays nearly 250000 emergency visits 44000 surgeries and 7000 births each year.

Financial Performance

In 2014 Baptist Health's net revenues increased by 3% due to higher net patient service revenues less provision for bad debts. Net patient service revenue by major payor source was: Medicare 40%; Blue Cross 23%; Medicaid 7%; other third-party payors 25%; and self pay 5%.

The hospital incurred a net loss of $8.9 million in 2014 (a 190% drop compared to 2013) despite the increase in net revenues.

Cash outflow decreased by 102% compared to 2013.

Strategy

Baptist Health is expanding certain programs to cater to targeted population segments in the Jacksonville area. For instance it is expanding its Baptist AgeWell Institute program at the Jacksonville hospital as well as the pastoral care program in Nassau. It is also enhancing its emergency room at the Beaches hospital and is conducting community outreach programs for low-income families.

In 2015 Baptist Health and The University of Texas MD Anderson Cancer Center moved forward with multidisciplinary cancer care for adult patients throughout their region by opening the Baptist MD Anderson Cancer Center.

Company Background

A major construction project was completed in late 2012 with the opening of a new 11-story patient tower at Baptist Jacksonville. The new $200 million tower features all private patient rooms and high-tech surgical suites.

Baptist Health was founded in 1955.

EXECUTIVES

EVP and COO, John F. Wilbanks
Hospital President Baptist Medical Center South, Ron Robinson
Hospital President Wolfson Childrens Hospital, Michael D. Aubin
President and CEO, A. Hugh Greene
Hospital President Baptist Beaches; President Transitional Care, Joseph M. (Joe) Mitrick
SVP Medical Affairs and Clinical Effectiveness; Chief Medical Officer, Keith L. Stein
SVP and CFO, Scott Wooten
Hospital President Baptist Medical Center Jacksonville, Michael A. Mayo
SVP and Chief Nursing Officer, Diane S. Raines
President Physician Integration, Edward Sim
SVP and CIO, Roland Garcia

Chief Medical Officer Wolfson Children's Hospital, Jerry A. Bridgham
Hospital President Baptist Medical Center Nassau, Stephen Lee
Executive Vice President Corporate Development, Melanie J Husk
Senior Vice President Social Responsibility and Community Advocacy, Audrey Moran
Medical Director, Mark Stich
Pharmacy Manager, Carol Dorfler
Vice President, Tracy Williams
Vice President Human Resources, Elizabeth Mehaffey
Medical Director, Bill Putnam
Vice President of Operations, Keon Falkner
Vice President of Community Investment and Impact, Melanie Patz
Auditors: ERNST & YOUNG LLP JACKSONVIL

LOCATIONS

HQ: BAPTIST HEALTH SYSTEM, INC.
800 PRUDENTIAL DR, JACKSONVILLE, FL 322078202
Phone: 904 202-2000
Web: WWW.HEALTHMART.COM

PRODUCTS/OPERATIONS

Selected facilities
Baptist Medical Center Beaches (Jacksonville Beach Florida)
Baptist Medical Center Jacksonville (Jacksonville Florida)
Baptist Heart Hospital
Baptist Medical Center Nassau (Fernandina Beach Florida)
Baptist Medical Center South (Jacksonville Florida)
Wolfson Children's Hospital (Jacksonville Florida)

COMPETITORS

Bay Medical Center	Munroe Regional Health
Brooks Rehabilitation	System
Florida Hospital Tampa	Nemours Foundation
Bay Division	Orlando Health
Florida Hospital	St. Vincent's Health
Waterman	System
HCA	UF Health Jacksonville
Mayo Clinic	
Jacksonville	

HISTORICAL FINANCIALS

Company Type: Private

Income Statement				FYE: September 30
	REVENUE ($ mil.)	NET INCOME ($ mil.)	NET PROFIT MARGIN	EMPLOYEES
09/16	1,587	189	11.9%	7,000
09/09	0	(1)	—	—
09/06	871	49	5.7%	—
Annual Growth	6.2%	14.4%	—	—

2016 Year-End Financials
Return on assets: 10.3%   Cash ($ mil.): 92
Return on equity: 11.9%
Current ratio: 1.80

BAPTIST HEALTHCARE SYSTEM, INC.

Baptist Healthcare System which goes by Baptist Health wants to keep all its followers healthy. The system owns eight acute-care hospitals one a long-term facility in Kentucky with a total capacity of more than 2100 beds. The not-for-profit health system's largest facility is Baptist Hospital East a

520-bed hospital in Louisville that provides a wide range of health services with special expertise in cardiology rehabilitation and women's health. In addition to its owned facilities Baptist Health manages Hardin Memorial a 300-bed hospital located in Elizabethtown and Russell County Hospital with 25 beds. The growing Baptist Health was founded as a single hospital in Louisville in 1924.

Operations

Along with inpatient acute care services Baptist Health offers home health care services runs two outpatient surgery centers provides urgent care through a handful of clinics and operates a regional physicians' practice group. It also runs a community-based not-for-profit health care plan Baptist Health Plan which operates across the state and into parts of Indiana and Tennessee. Baptist Health plans to shut the struggling health plan down in 2018.

Strategy

Baptist Health faced major losses during 2017 and laid off more than 500 employees that year. It announced plans to realign its structure and shut down its not-for-profit Baptist Health Plan.

Mergers and Acquisitions

In mid-2017 Baptist Health agreed to buy Hardin Memorial for an undisclosed amount. Hardin Memorial (which Baptist Health already manages) operates some 50 outpatient facilities as well as its 300-bed hospital.

EXECUTIVES

President and CEO Bluegrass Family Health, James S. Fritz
President Baptist Hospital East, David L. Gray
President Central Baptist Hospital, William G. Sisson
President Baptist Hospital Northeast, Christopher M. (Chris) Roty
President Baptist Regional Medical Center, Larry W. Gray
President Hardin Memorial Hopsital, Dennis Johnson
CEO, Stephen C. Hanson
Chief Clinical Officer, Timothy Jahn
CIO, David J. Bensema
CFO, Carl G. Herde
Chief Health Integration Officer; President Baptist Health Medical Group, Isaac J. Myers
President Baptist Health Richmond, C. Todd Jones
Regional Executive and President Baptist Health Paducah, William A. Brown
President Baptist Health Madisonville, Michael A. Baumgartner
Clinic Manager, Sean Sullivan
Auditors: ERNST & YOUNG US LLP CINCINNA

LOCATIONS

HQ: BAPTIST HEALTHCARE SYSTEM, INC.
2701 EASTPOINT PKWY, LOUISVILLE, KY 402234166
Phone: 502 896-5000
Web: WWW.BHSI.COM

PRODUCTS/OPERATIONS

Selected Facilities and Operations (Kentucky)
Hospitals
Managed
Baptist Health Corbin
Baptist Health La Grange
Baptist Health Lexington
Baptist Health Louisville
Baptist Health Richmond
Baptist Health Madisonville
Baptist Health Paducah
ContinueCARE Hospital (Corbin)
Owned
Hardin Memorial Hospital (Elizabethtown)
Russell County Hospital (Russell Springs)
Other operations
Baptist East Milestone Wellness Center (Louisville)
Baptist Express Care (various Walmarts in state)

Baptist Medical Associates (medical practice group Louisville area)
Baptist Urgent Care (Louisville)
Bluegrass Family Health (provider-sponsored insurance)

COMPETITORS

Appalachian Regional Healthcare	Norton Healthcare
Catholic Health Initiatives	Pikeville Medical Center
Jewish Hospital & St. Mary's HealthCare	University Health Care
Kindred Healthcare	University of Kentucky Chandler Hospital

HISTORICAL FINANCIALS
Company Type: Private

Income Statement
FYE: August 31

	REVENUE ($ mil.)	NET INCOME ($ mil.)	NET PROFIT MARGIN	EMPLOYEES
08/16	2,331	1	0.0%	12,601
08/15	2,136	17	0.8%	—
08/14	1,440	204	14.2%	—
08/11	1,317	96	7.3%	—
Annual Growth	12.1%	(58.8%)	—	—

2016 Year-End Financials
Return on assets: 5.1% Cash ($ mil.): 110
Return on equity: —
Current ratio: 1.10

BAPTIST HOSPITAL OF MIAMI, INC.

Baptist Hospital of Miami can treat many vices for Miami residents. The flagship facility of the Baptist Health South Florida health system provides residents of the city with a full range of health care services including pediatric cancer home health rehabilitation neurology and cardiovascular care. The hospital has more than 680 beds and includes the Baptist Children's Hospital which offers a pediatric emergency room and a neonatal intensive care unit. Baptist Hospital of Miami also includes the Baptist Cardiac & Vascular Institute a regional cancer program and a diabetes care center. Baptist Hospital of Miami was founded in 1960.

Operations

Baptist Children's Hospital offers 24-hour emergency care as well as two intensive care units and specialist services including pediatric cancer care. Baptist Hospital of Miami also contains the Baptist Cardiac and Vascular Institute which conducts treatment and research programs. The hospital's international care unit provides services to patients from the Caribbean Latin America and other regions. Other specialist divisions include a sleep diagnostic center and a spine care facility as well as a maternity ward. Baptist Hospital of Miami also operates several wellness centers.

As part of Baptist Health South Florida the Baptist Hospital of Miami is part of a network of six hospitals including South Miami Hospital Doctors Hospital and the West Kendall Baptist Hospital. In addition the health system includes outpatient care clinics including emergency surgery imaging and primary care centers.

Strategy

Controlling expenses through data management quality and wellness initiatives and other measures becomes increasingly important for the hospital and its affiliates as the cost of medical care in the US market continues to skyrocket. Maintaining an efficient organization is also imperative as the level of charity care provided by the system's facilities continues to rise in the face of economic difficulties.

As the largest hospital in the Baptist Health system Baptist Hospital of Miami takes a leading role in technology programs such as medical equipment and data management system upgrades. The Baptist Health network is in the process of installing an electronic health record (EHR) system to connect patient records across its facilities.

In 2012 Baptist Hospital of Miami launched a $90 million construction effort to expand the Cardiac and Vascular Institute. The new expanded institute facility will open in 2016 and will include centers for aneurysm treatment structural heart therapy and endovascular therapy. The project also includes expansion efforts on the hospital's surgery center which will have enhanced capabilities for neurological cardiac and robotic surgery procedures.

EXECUTIVES

Medical Director Interventional Radiologist, Alex Powell
Admissions Director, JERRY TOBIN
Nursing Director, Diane Bolton

LOCATIONS

HQ: BAPTIST HOSPITAL OF MIAMI, INC.
8900 N KENDALL DR, MIAMI, FL 331762197
Phone: 786 596-1960

PRODUCTS/OPERATIONS

Selected Centers and Services
Baptist Cardiac & Vascular Institute (Heart Care)
Baptist Children's Hospital (Pediatrics)
Breast Care
Cancer Services
Center for Spine Care
Children's Cancer Services
Children's Emergency Center
Clinical Research Trials
Community Wellness
Critical Care/eICU LifeGuard
Diabetes Care
Diagnostic Imaging
Emergency Services
Endoscopy
Gynecology
Home Care
Intensive Care
International Services
Interventional
Maternity
Neonatal Intensive Care Unit
Neuroscience Center
Neurosurgery
Orthopedic Services
Pain Management
Physical & Speech Therapy
Pulmonary Services
Rehabilitation Services
Robotic Surgery
Senior Services
Sleep Diagnostic Center
Spine Care
Stroke Services
Surgery
Women's Services

COMPETITORS

Broward Health
H. Lee Moffitt Cancer Center & Research Institute
HCA
Jackson Health System
Larkin Community Hospital
Miami Children's Hospital
Mount Sinai Medical Center of Florida
South Broward Hospital District
University of Miami Hospital

HISTORICAL FINANCIALS
Company Type: Private

Income Statement
FYE: September 30

	REVENUE ($ mil.)	NET INCOME ($ mil.)	NET PROFIT MARGIN	EMPLOYEES
09/15	889	108	12.2%	4,200
09/14	913	140	15.4%	—
09/13	846	99	11.7%	—
09/12	916	71	7.8%	—
Annual Growth	(1.0%)	14.7%	—	—

2015 Year-End Financials
Return on assets: — Cash ($ mil.): —
Return on equity: 12.2%
Current ratio: 0.90

BAPTIST HOSPITAL, INC.

EXECUTIVES

President, Alfred G Stubblefield

LOCATIONS

HQ: BAPTIST HOSPITAL, INC.
1000 W MORENO ST, PENSACOLA, FL 325012316
Phone: 850 434-4011

HISTORICAL FINANCIALS
Company Type: Private

Income Statement
FYE: September 30

	REVENUE ($ mil.)	NET INCOME ($ mil.)	NET PROFIT MARGIN	EMPLOYEES
09/15	278	20	7.4%	1,652
09/14	271	23	8.6%	—
09/13	269	30	11.3%	—
09/12	260	23	8.9%	—
Annual Growth	2.3%	(4.1%)	—	—

2015 Year-End Financials
Return on assets: 8.5% Cash ($ mil.): 118
Return on equity: 7.4%
Current ratio: 2.70

BAPTIST HOSPITALS OF SOUTHEAST TEXAS

EXECUTIVES

Chief Executive Officer, David Parmer
Chief Financial Officer, Louise Ferguson
Marketing Director, Linda Gaudio
Supervisor, Debbie Shaw
Director, Betty Bullard
Marketing Manager, Mary Poole
Auditors: BKD LLP DALLAS TX

LOCATIONS

HQ: BAPTIST HOSPITALS OF SOUTHEAST TEXAS
3080 COLLEGE ST, BEAUMONT, TX 777014686
Phone: 409 212-5000
Web: WWW.BHSET.NET

Income Statement				FYE: August 31
	REVENUE ($ mil.)	NET INCOME ($ mil.)	NET PROFIT MARGIN	EMPLOYEES
08/15*	255	4	1.8%	1,759
06/13	234	6	2.6%	—
06/11	277	1	0.4%	—
06/08	252,641	0	—	—
Annual Growth	—	34.8%	—	—

*Fiscal year change

2015 Year-End Financials
Return on assets: 7.6%   Cash ($ mil.): 14
Return on equity: 1.8%
Current ratio: 1.40

BAPTIST MEMORIAL HOSPITAL

When most of us think of Memphis we think of Elvis Presley. When doctors think of Memphis they think of Elvis and Baptist Memorial Hospital-Memphis. As the flagship facility of Baptist Memorial Health Care the 710-bed hospital often simply called Baptist Memphis offers patients the full spectrum of health care services including cancer treatment orthopedics surgical services and neurology. The campus also features the Baptist Heart Institute for cardiovascular care and research a pediatric emergency room a skilled nursing facility and the Plaza Diagnostic Pavilion for outpatient health care. Baptist Memphis established in 1979 is one of the state's highest volume hospitals.

Operations

Doctors at the hospital see more than 27000 admissions 54000 emergency department visits and nearly 116000 outpatient visits each year. The emergency department houses more than 30 treatment bays. In addition Baptist Memphis' skilled nursing center includes 30 beds. The hospital also operates a 30-bed rehabilitation hospital and a 165000 sq. ft. heart institute for diagnostic and surgical cardiac care. The facility boasts advanced surgical systems including the CyberKnife radiation system for cancerous and non-cancerous tumor removal.

EXECUTIVES

Operating Room Director, Tracy Godsey
Medical Records Director, Janet Chapman
Occupational Therapy Director, Lindsay Stencel

LOCATIONS

HQ: BAPTIST MEMORIAL HOSPITAL
6019 WALNUT GROVE RD, MEMPHIS, TN 381202113
Phone: 901 226-5000
Web: WWW.BAPTISTONLINE.ORG

COMPETITORS

Methodist Healthcare	St. Jude Children's
Parkwest Medical Center	Research Hospital
Shelby County Health Care	Tenet Healthcare

Income Statement				FYE: September 30
	REVENUE ($ mil.)	NET INCOME ($ mil.)	NET PROFIT MARGIN	EMPLOYEES
09/15	691	(1)	—	6,000
09/14	663	(47)	—	—
09/13	504	17	3.4%	—
09/12	697	15	2.2%	—
Annual Growth	(0.3%)			

2015 Year-End Financials
Return on assets: 1.5%   Cash ($ mil.): 28
Return on equity: (-0.2%)
Current ratio: 0.90

BAPTIST MEMORIAL HOSPITAL - NORTH MISSISSIPPI, INC.

EXECUTIVES

Chief Executive Officer, William C Henning
Principal, Peyton Warrington
Director, James Vandersteeg
Financial Executive, Donna Savage
Director, Teri Campbell
Plant & Facilities Manager, Phil Lassiter
President, Roger Holmes
Director, Marlon Martin

LOCATIONS

HQ: BAPTIST MEMORIAL HOSPITAL - NORTH MISSISSIPPI, INC.
2301 S LAMAR BLVD, OXFORD, MS 386555373
Phone: 662 232-8100

HISTORICAL FINANCIALS
Company Type: Private

Income Statement				FYE: September 30
	REVENUE ($ mil.)	NET INCOME ($ mil.)	NET PROFIT MARGIN	EMPLOYEES
09/15	201	56	27.8%	860
09/14	199	54	27.1%	—
09/13	216	40	18.8%	—
09/12	169	27	16.2%	—
Annual Growth	6.1%	27.0%	—	—

2015 Year-End Financials
Return on assets: 1.2%   Cash ($ mil.): 4
Return on equity: 27.8%
Current ratio: 1.70

BAPTIST MEMORIAL HOSPITAL-DESOTO, INC.

EXECUTIVES

Chief Executive Officer, Randy King

Director, Curt Vargo
Director, Margaret Morton

LOCATIONS

HQ: BAPTIST MEMORIAL HOSPITAL-DESOTO, INC.
7601 SOUTHCREST PKWY, SOUTHAVEN, MS 386714739
Phone: 662 772-4000

HISTORICAL FINANCIALS
Company Type: Private

Income Statement				FYE: September 30
	REVENUE ($ mil.)	NET INCOME ($ mil.)	NET PROFIT MARGIN	EMPLOYEES
09/15	322	10	3.3%	600
09/14	337	13	4.0%	—
09/13	280	35	12.8%	—
09/12	333	27	8.2%	—
Annual Growth	(1.2%)	(26.9%)	—	—

2015 Year-End Financials
Return on assets: 0.6%   Cash ($ mil.): 1
Return on equity: 3.3%
Current ratio: 2.40

BAPTIST MEMORIAL HOSPITAL-GOLDEN TRIANGLE, INC.

EXECUTIVES

Chief Executive Officer, Paul Cade
Supervisor, Kim Johnson
Director, Sandy Elliott
Financial Executive, Pamela Richardson
Auditors: DELOITTE TAX LLP NASHVILLE T

LOCATIONS

HQ: BAPTIST MEMORIAL HOSPITAL-GOLDEN TRIANGLE, INC.
2520 5TH ST N, COLUMBUS, MS 397052008
Phone: 662 244-1000

HISTORICAL FINANCIALS
Company Type: Private

Income Statement				FYE: September 30
	REVENUE ($ mil.)	NET INCOME ($ mil.)	NET PROFIT MARGIN	EMPLOYEES
09/15	193	8	4.4%	1,100
09/14	191	13	7.3%	—
09/13	187	15	8.1%	—
09/11	147	8	5.7%	—
Annual Growth	6.9%	0.3%	—	—

2015 Year-End Financials
Return on assets: 2.1%   Cash ($ mil.): 1
Return on equity: 4.4%
Current ratio: —

BAPTIST ST. ANTHONY'S HOSPITAL CORPORATION

EXECUTIVES

President, John D Hicks
Board of Directors, Emily Kohn
Director, Diane Dyess
Director, Eileen Harpole
Auditors: ERNST & YOUNG LLP DALLAS TEX

LOCATIONS

HQ: BAPTIST ST. ANTHONY'S HOSPITAL
CORPORATION
1600 WALLACE BLVD, AMARILLO, TX 791061799
Phone: 806 212-2000

HISTORICAL FINANCIALS
Company Type: Private

Income Statement			FYE: December 31	
	REVENUE ($ mil.)	NET INCOME ($ mil.)	NET PROFIT MARGIN	EMPLOYEES
12/15	424	77	18.3%	2,500
12/08*	285	3	1.3%	—
06/05	0	0	—	—
12/02	1,133	0	0.0%	—
Annual Growth	(7.3%)	154.3%	—	—

*Fiscal year change

2015 Year-End Financials
Return on assets: 4.3%   Cash ($ mil.): 1
Return on equity: 18.3%
Current ratio: 0.60

BAR-ILAN UNIVERSITY IN ISRAEL

EXECUTIVES

President, Moshel Straus
Auditors: GRANT THORNTON LLP NEW YORK

LOCATIONS

HQ: BAR-ILAN UNIVERSITY IN ISRAEL
160 E 56TH ST FL 5, NEW YORK, NY 100223609
Phone: 212 906-3900
Web: WWW.AFBIU.ORG

HISTORICAL FINANCIALS
Company Type: Private

Income Statement			FYE: September 30	
	REVENUE ($ mil.)	NET INCOME ($ mil.)	NET PROFIT MARGIN	EMPLOYEES
09/15	320	(67)	—	30
09/14	363	(17)	—	—
09/13	343	(30)	—	—
09/08	330	38	11.5%	—
Annual Growth	(0.4%)	—	—	—

2015 Year-End Financials
Return on assets: 12.4%   Cash ($ mil.): 14
Return on equity: (-21.1%)
Current ratio: 0.60

BARD COLLEGE

Although Shakespeare might appreciate the curriculum Bard College is not named for the Bard of Avon but for founder John Bard. The institution of higher learning is an independent nonsectarian residential coeducational four-year college of the liberal arts and sciences. Bard's total enrollment of 1900 includes some 600 graduate students. First-year students are required to take a three-week Workshop in Language and Thinking that emphasizes the connection between expression and thought. Students must also complete a year-long senior project that is reviewed by faculty members.

Operations

In the Bard system more than 1900 undergraduates study at the main Annandale campus and 600 graduate students study in Bard programs as well as 1000 students in high schools and college preparation schools. Total enrollment for Bard and its global affiliates is about 5000 students.

Bard offers BA degrees in about 50 academic programs and a five-year BS/BA degree in economics and finance. The Bard College Conservatory of Music offers a five-year program in which students pursue a Bachelor of Music and a BA in a non-music field. In addition to offering AA and BA degrees through high schools and early colleges the Bard Prison Initiative offers similar options at six prisons in New York State.

Bard's graduate degree programs include in curatorial studies economic theory and policy environmental policy climate science and policy and music. It also offers MAs M.Phils and PhDs in the decorative arts design history and material culture.

It has 293 faculty members 92% of which hold a terminal degree.

In 2012 Bard charged $31600 tuition and fees of $950. It also had a $350 million endowment. The college enrolled students from 38 US states and 25 countries.

Geographic Reach

It addition to its US operations (Annandale-on-Hudson New York New York City and Boston) Bard confers degrees (in tandem with the host school) at St. Petersburg State University Russia (Smolny College); the American University of Central Asia in Kyrgyzstan; Bard College Berlin Germany; and Al-Quds University in the West Bank Palestine. It also has operations in Budapest Hungary.

Strategy

In 2014 Bard announced plans to launch the Levy Economics Institute's Master of Science in Economic Theory and Policy Program as well as a 3+2 dual-degree option for undergraduates.

Expanding its network in 2013 German university ECLA of Bard become Bard College Berlin. In 2012 Longy School of Music joined Bard and became the Longy School of Music of Bard College.

Expanding its curriculum in 2013 Bard launched the Center for Moving Image Arts focused on undergraduate education and in bringing various aspects of film culture (archival development educational initiatives public screenings and publications) under one umbrella.

Company Background

Among Bard's distinguished faculty are three Grammy Award winners six MacArthur Fellows 14 National Science Foundation Grant recipients 29 Guggenheim Fellows and recipients of the French Legion of Honor Tony Award and Pulitzer Prize.

Donald Fagen and Walter Becker of the band Steely Dan both attended Bard (Fagen is an alum; Becker did not graduate) and penned the song "My Old School" as a sardonic tribute to their alma mater.

The institution was founded in 1860 by John Bard in association with Episcopal Church leaders in New York City.

EXECUTIVES

Vice President Dean Of The College, Michele D Dominy
Associate Vice President, Clara Botstein
Director of Admissions, Frank Corliss
Auditors: SAXBST LLP ALBANY NY

LOCATIONS

HQ: BARD COLLEGE
30 CAMPUS RD, ANNANDALE ON HUDSON, NY 125049800
Phone: 845 758-7518
Web: WWW.BARD.EDU

HISTORICAL FINANCIALS
Company Type: Private

Income Statement			FYE: June 30	
	REVENUE ($ mil.)	NET INCOME ($ mil.)	NET PROFIT MARGIN	EMPLOYEES
06/16	189	(21)	—	525
06/14	226	(17)	—	—
06/10	181	(5)	—	—
06/09	164	0	—	—
Annual Growth	2.0%	—	—	—

2016 Year-End Financials
Return on assets: 9.3%   Cash ($ mil.): 10
Return on equity: (-11.4%)
Current ratio: —

BARNES-JEWISH HOSPITAL

LOCATIONS

HQ: BARNES-JEWISH HOSPITAL
1 B J HOSPITAL PLAZA DR, SAINT LOUIS, MO 63110
Phone: 314 747-3000
Web: WWW.BARNESJEWISH.COM

HISTORICAL FINANCIALS
Company Type: Private

Income Statement			FYE: December 31	
	REVENUE ($ mil.)	NET INCOME ($ mil.)	NET PROFIT MARGIN	EMPLOYEES
12/15	1,726	68	4.0%	30
12/14	1,664	83	5.0%	
Annual Growth	3.7%	(18.2%)		

2015 Year-End Financials
Return on assets: 3.1%   Cash ($ mil.): —
Return on equity: 4.0%
Current ratio: 2.40

BARRICK ENTERPRISES, INC.

EXECUTIVES

President, Robert L Barrick
Director, Bernie Gosevitz
General Manager, Greg Barrick
Supervisor, John Hobbs
Auditors: DOEREN MAYHEW TROY MICHIGAN

LOCATIONS

HQ: BARRICK ENTERPRISES, INC.
4338 DELEMERE BLVD, ROYAL OAK, MI 480731876
Phone: 248 549-3737
Web: WWW.BARRICKENT.COM

HISTORICAL FINANCIALS

Company Type: Private

Income Statement

	REVENUE ($ mil.)	NET INCOME ($ mil.)	NET PROFIT MARGIN	EMPLOYEES
12/15	552	3	0.7%	35
12/14	781	6	0.8%	—
12/13	800	2	0.4%	—
12/12	811	2	0.4%	—
Annual Growth	(12.0%)	7.1%	—	—

FYE: December 31

2015 Year-End Financials

Return on assets: 1.4%
Return on equity: 0.7%
Current ratio: 1.80
Cash ($ mil.): 7

BARRINGTON 220 COMMUNITY UNIT SCHOOL DISTRICT

EXECUTIVES

Superintendent, Brian Harris
Administrative Assistant, Nunzia Czech
Assistant Manager, Timothy Neubauer
Plant & Facilities Manager, Tom Campagna
Auditors: BAKER TILLY VIRCHOW KRAUSE LL

LOCATIONS

HQ: BARRINGTON 220 COMMUNITY UNIT SCHOOL DISTRICT
310 JAMES ST, BARRINGTON, IL 600103329
Phone: 847 381-6300
Web: WWW.BARRINGTON220.ORG

HISTORICAL FINANCIALS

Company Type: Private

Income Statement

	REVENUE ($ mil.)	NET INCOME ($ mil.)	NET PROFIT MARGIN	EMPLOYEES
06/16	185	1	0.9%	1,115
06/12	155	5	3.6%	—
06/09	139	4	3.2%	—
06/07	1,317	0	0.0%	—
Annual Growth	(19.6%)	164.3%	—	—

FYE: June 30

BARRY UNIVERSITY, INC.

Barry University is a Catholic institution of Dominican heritage based in South Florida. With a student-faculty ratio of about 14:1 the liberal arts university annually enrolls about 3000 undergraduate students and some 4000 graduate students. The university's academic division includes two colleges (the College of Arts and Sciences and the College of Health Sciences) and seven schools. It offers more than 100 specializations and programs for undergraduate graduate and doctoral studies. Barry University also offers about 35 non-degree and certificate programs. Barry University was founded by the Adrian Dominican Sisters in 1940.

EXECUTIVES

Vice President of Business and Finance, Sue Aaronson Rosenthal
Interim Chair Department Of Mathematics And Computer Science, Anton Wallner
Director of Admissions Enrollment Student Services, Phil Giarraffa
Director of Admissions, Chris Bailey
Auditors: CAPIN CROUSE LLP LAWRENCEVILL

LOCATIONS

HQ: BARRY UNIVERSITY, INC.
11300 NE 2ND AVE, MIAMI SHORES, FL 331616695
Phone: 305 899-3050
Web: WWW.BARRY.EDU

PRODUCTS/OPERATIONS

Selected Colleges and Schools
Adrian Dominican School of Education
College of Arts and Sciences
College of Health Sciences
D. Inez Andreas School of Business
Dwayne O. Andreas School of Law
Ellen Whiteside McDonnell School of Social Work
Frank J. Rooney School of Adult and Continuing Education
School of Human Performance and Leisure Sciences
School of Podiatric Medicine

HISTORICAL FINANCIALS

Company Type: Private

Income Statement

	REVENUE ($ mil.)	NET INCOME ($ mil.)	NET PROFIT MARGIN	EMPLOYEES
06/15	211	7	3.7%	1,407
06/14	215	5	2.7%	—
06/13	223	6	3.1%	—
06/10	151	12	8.1%	—
Annual Growth	7.0%	(8.5%)	—	—

FYE: June 30

2015 Year-End Financials

Return on assets: 6.4%
Return on equity: 3.7%
Current ratio: 0.60
Cash ($ mil.): 46

BARTON MALOW COMPANY

Barton Malow scores by building end zones and home plates. The construction management and general contracting firm which has built its share of sporting facilities also focuses on projects such as schools hospitals offices and plants. Across the US and Mexico the company offers design/build and program management services ranging from the pre-planning stage to completion. Projects have included the Detroit Institute of Arts and Cultural Center and the Baltimore Orioles stadium. Affiliate Barton Malow Design provides architecture and engineering services while Barton Malow Rigging installs process equipment and machinery. Carl Osborn Barton founded the employee-owned firm as C.O. Barton Company in 1924.

Geographic Reach

Michigan-based Barton Malow operates about a dozen offices mostly in the East Coast. The firm also has an office in San Luis Potosi Mexico.

Financial Performance

Barton Malow's annual revenue exceeds $1 billion.

Strategy

Headquartered in a Detroit suburb Barton Malow has historically maintained a healthy relationship with the steel and auto industries. The company has expanded into new sectors and geographic markets however. It serves the federal market through its Florida-based L.C. Gaskins Construction Company.

In 2014 the firm was selected as the construction manager for a new Major League Soccer (MLS) stadium in Orlando Florida. Other recent projects include a new events center in Detroit and a Facility for Rare Isotope Breams at Michigan State University.

EXECUTIVES

EVP and Corporate Secretary, Doug Maibach
Chairman and CEO, Ben C. Maibach
VP Central Region, Michael (Mike) Stobak
VP Higher Education Central Region, Todd Ketola
VP Charlottesville Operations, Phil Kirby
VP Eastern Region and Virginia, Carrie Shaeffer
VP Florida, David Price
VP National Sports, Len Moser
President, Ryan Maibach
VP Central Region, Chuck Binkowski
SVP and CFO, Michael Dishaw
SVP Southeast Region, Rod Creach
VP Central Region, Dan Kovoch
Vice President, Jennifer Brown
Senior Vice President Sports Facilities, Harvey Oliva
Vice President and General Counsel, Ronald Torbert
Auditors: GRANT THORNTON LLP SOUTHFIELD

LOCATIONS

HQ: BARTON MALOW COMPANY
26500 AMERICAN DR, SOUTHFIELD, MI 480342252
Phone: 248 436-5000
Web: WWW.BARTONMALOW.COM

Selected Locations
Atlanta
Baltimore
Charlottesville
Chicago
Columbus
Fairfax
Jacksonville
Oak Park
Orlando
Richmond
Southfield

PRODUCTS/OPERATIONS

Selcted Services
Architecture and planning
Building Information Management (BIM)
Concrete trade services
Construction management
Design/build
Facility audits
Facility services
Administration

Engineering
Maintenance repair and operations
General contracting
Interior design
Interior trade services
Preconstruction
Program management
Rigging
Special projects
Technology consulting

COMPETITORS

Alberici	KBR Building Group
Clark Enterprises	M. A. Mortenson
Fluor	McCarthy Building
Gilbane	Skanska USA Building
H.J. Russell	Turner Corporation
Hensel Phelps	Walbridge Aldinger
Construction	Walsh Group
Hunt Construction	Whiting-Turner

HISTORICAL FINANCIALS

Company Type: Private

Income Statement

FYE: March 31

	REVENUE ($ mil.)	NET INCOME ($ mil.)	NET PROFIT MARGIN	EMPLOYEES
03/16	1,777	(2)	—	1,600
03/15	1,454	4	0.3%	—
03/14	1,078	2	0.3%	—
03/13	1,005	3	0.3%	—
Annual Growth	20.9%	—	—	—

2016 Year-End Financials

Return on assets: 20.8%
Return on equity: (-0.1%)
Current ratio: 0.90
Cash ($ mil.): 86

BARTON MALOW ENTERPRISES, INC.

EXECUTIVES

President, Benjamin C Maibach III
Executive Vice-President, Douglas L Maibach
Vice-President, Ronald J Torbert
Director, Sheryl B Maibach
Financial Executive, Kirsten Kozel
Marketing Director, Jordan Garren
Project Manager, Tyler Smith
Auditors: GRANT THORNTON LLP SOUTHFIELD

LOCATIONS

HQ: BARTON MALOW ENTERPRISES, INC.
26500 AMERICAN DR, SOUTHFIELD, MI 480342252
Phone: 248 436-5000

HISTORICAL FINANCIALS

Company Type: Private

Income Statement

FYE: March 31

	REVENUE ($ mil.)	NET INCOME ($ mil.)	NET PROFIT MARGIN	EMPLOYEES
03/16	1,777	9	0.6%	1,815
03/15	1,454	8	0.6%	—
03/14	1,078	7	0.7%	—
03/13	1,005	6	0.7%	—
Annual Growth	20.9%	14.0%	—	—

2016 Year-End Financials

Return on assets: 20.5%
Return on equity: 0.6%
Current ratio: 0.90
Cash ($ mil.): 103

BASIN ELECTRIC POWER COOPERATIVE

Ranges at home on the range depend on Basin Electric Power Cooperative as do other electric-powered items in nine states from Montana to Iowa to New Mexico. The consumer-owned power generation and transmission co-op provides power to 138 rural electric member systems which serve about 2.8 million people. It had generating capacity of 5478 MW (mostly coal-fired) in 2014. Basin Electric's subsidiaries include Dakota Gasification (which produces natural gas from coal) Dakota Coal (markets lignite and limestone) Basin Telecommunications (Internet access) Basin Cooperative Services (property management) PrairieWinds (wind power) and Souris Valley Pipeline (CO2 pipeline).

Operations

The company maintains about 2250 miles of high-voltage transmission 70 switchyards and about 150 telecommunication locations. It generates about 990 MW for participants in the Missouri Basin Power Project (a group of six regional consumer-owned energy entities that built the Laramie River Station in Wyoming). Its generation portfolio includes 4913 MW of wholesale electric generating capacity.

Geographic Reach

Basin Electric serves customers in Colorado Iowa Minnesota Montana Nebraska New Mexico North Dakota South Dakota and Wyoming. The enterprise's generation facilities are located in Iowa Minnesota Montana North Dakota South Dakota and Wyoming.

Financial Performance

In 2013 Basin Electric's revenues grew by 12% due to higher members sales as a result of an increase in higher electricity resales.

The coop's net income decreased by 62% that year as the result of to higher operating expenses caused by an increase in depreciation and amortizations.

The company's operating cash inflow decreased to $306.56 million in 2013 (from $354.18 million in 2012) due to lower net income and a change in working capital as a result of higher customer account receivables and inventories.

Strategy

Basin Electric like all power utilities is under regulatory pressure to lower the carbon emissions from its power production. As part of its commitment to cleaner energy production the company has established two wind power subsidiaries to build wind farms in the Dakotas.

In 2013 Basin Electric signed two power purchase agreements with California-based Infinity Wind Power associated with the development of two new wind projects in North Dakota with a combined capacity is 278 MW.

Company Background

The company generated 437 MW of its total capacity of 482 MW of renewable energy in 2012 from wind power sources. That year about 16% of Basin Electric's generating capacity came from renewable sources.

In 2011 Basin Electric opened the Crow Lake Wind Project (Nebraska) its largest renewable project to date with 162 MW of power generating capacity. Basin Electric's operations are overseen by a 10-member board of directors elected by and representing individual membership districts. Dakota Gasification and Dakota Coal have separate boards.

The not-for-profit generation and transmission cooperative was formed in 1961.

EXECUTIVES

COO and SVP Dakota Coal Company and Montana Limestone Company, Robert J. Bartosh
CEO and General Manager, Paul Sukut
SVP Transmission, Michael Risan
COO and SVP Dakota Gasification Company, Dave Sauer
SVP Generation, Matt Greek
VP Marketing and Trading, Kenneth S. Rutter
Vice President Of Human Resources, Ellen Holt
Vice President Basin Electric board, Kermit Pearson
President Basin Electric board, Wayne Peltier
Auditors: DELOITTE & TOUCHE LLP MINNEAP

LOCATIONS

HQ: BASIN ELECTRIC POWER COOPERATIVE
1717 E INTERSTATE AVE, BISMARCK, ND 585030564
Phone: 701 223-0441
Web: WWW.BASINELECTRIC.COM

PRODUCTS/OPERATIONS

2013 Power Generation Fuel Mix

	% of total
Coal	60
Renewables	15
Natural gas	14
Hydro	6
Oil	4
Nuclear	1
Total	**100**

2012 Sales

	% of total
Utility	62
Synthetic gas	13
Lignite coal	7
Byproducts co-products & other	18
Total	**100**

Regional Member Cooperatives

Regional Member Cooperatives
Central Montana Electric Power Cooperative (District 6)
  Beartooth Electric Cooperative (Red Lodge MT)
  Big Flat Electric Cooperative (Malta MT)
  Fergus Electric Cooperative (Lewistown MT)
  Hill County Electric Cooperative (Havre MT)
  Marias River Electric Cooperative (Shelby MT)
  Mid-Yellowstone Valley Electric Cooperative (Hysham MT)
  Northern Electric Cooperative (Opheim MT)
  Park Electric Cooperative (Livingston MT)
  Sun River Electric Cooperative (Fairfield MT)
  Tongue River Electric Cooperative (Ashland MT)
  Valley Electric Cooperative (Glasgow MT)
  Vigilante Electric Cooperative (Dillon MT)
  Yellowstone Valley Electric Cooperative (Huntley MT)
Central Power Electric Cooperative (District 3)
  Capital Electric Cooperative (Bismarck ND)
  Dakota Valley Electric Cooperative (Milnor ND)
  McLean Electric Cooperative (Garrison ND)
  North Central Electric Cooperative (Bottineau ND)
  Northern Plains Electric Cooperative (Carrington ND)
  Verendrye Electric Cooperative (Velva ND)
Corn Belt Power Cooperative (Humboldt IA)
District 9
  Grand Electric Cooperative (Bison SD)
  KEM Electric Cooperative (Linton ND)
  Minnesota Valley Cooperative Light & Power Association (Montevideo MN)
  Mor-Gran-Sou Electric Cooperative (Flasher ND)
  Oliver-Mercer Electric Cooperative (Hazen ND)
  Rosebud Electric Cooperative (Gregory SD)
  Wright-Hennepin Cooperative Electric Association (Rockford MN)
  Wyoming Municipal Power Agency (Lusk WY)

East River Electric Power Cooperative (District 1)
  Bon Homme-Yankton Electric Association (Tabor SD)
  Central Electric Cooperative
  Charles Mix Electric Association (Lake Andes SD)
  Clay-Union Electric Corp. (Vermillion SD)
  Codington-Clark Electric Cooperative (Watertown SD)
  Dakota Energy Cooperative (Huron SD)
  Douglas Electric Cooperative (Armour SD)
  FEM Electric Association (Ipswich SD)
  H-D Electric Cooperative (Clear Lake SD)
  Kingsbury Electric Cooperative (De Smet SD)
  Lake Region Electric Association (Webster SD)
  Lyon-Lincoln Electric Cooperative (Tyler MN)
  McCook Electric Cooperative (Salem SD)
  Northern Electric Cooperative (Bath SD)
  Oahe Electric Cooperative (Blunt SD)
  Renville-Sibley Cooperative Power Association
    (Danube MN)
  Sioux Valley-Southwestern Cooperative (Colman SD)
  Southeastern Electric Cooperative (Marion SD)
  Traverse Electric Cooperative (Wheaton MN)
  Union County Electric Cooperative (Elk Point SD)
  Whetstone Valley Electric Cooperative (Milbank SD)
Flathead Electric Cooperative (Kalispell MT)
L & O Power Cooperative (District 2)
  Lyon Rural Electric Cooperative (Rock Rapids IA)
  Osceola Electric Cooperative (Sibley IA)
Northwest Iowa Power Cooperative (NIPCO) (District 4)
  Harrison County Electric Cooperative (Woodbine)
  Iowa Lakes Electric Cooperative (Estherville)
  Nishnabotna Valley Rural Electric Cooperative
    (Harlan)
  North West Rural Electric Cooperative (Orange City)
  Western Iowa Municipal Electric Association
    (Manning)
  Western Iowa Power Cooperative
  Woodbury County Rural Electric Cooperative (Moville)
Powder River Energy Corp. (District 10 Sundance WY)
Rushmore Electric Power Cooperative (District 7)
  Black Hills Electric Cooperative (Custer SD)
  Butte Electric Cooperative (Newell SD)
  Cam Wal Electric Cooperative (Selby SD)
  Cherry-Todd Electric Cooperative (Mission SD)
  Lacreek Electric Association (Martin SD)
  Moreau-Grand Electric Cooperative (Timber Lake SD)
  West Central Electric Cooperative (Murdo SD)
  West River Electric Association (Wall SD)
Tri-State Generation and Transmission Association
  (District 5)
  Big Horn Rural Electric Co. (Basin WY)
  Carbon Power & Light (Saratoga WY)
  Central New Mexico Electric Cooperative (Mountainair
    NM)
  Chimney Rock Public Power District (Bayard NE)
  Columbus Electric Cooperative (Deming NM)
  Delta-Montrose Electric Association (Delta CO)
  Empire Electric Association (Cortez CO)
  Garland Light & Power Co. (Powell WY)
  Gunnison County Electric Association (Gunnison CO)
  Highline Electric Association (Holyoke CO)
  High Plains Power Inc. (Thermopolis and Riverton
    WY)
  High West Energy (Pine Bluffs WY)
  Jemez Mountains Electric Cooperative (Hernandez
    NM)
  K. C. Electric Association (Hugo CO)
  Kit Carson Electric Cooperative (Taos NM)
  La Plata Electric Association (Durango CO)
  Midwest Electric Cooperative Corp. (Grant NE)
  Morgan County Rural Electric Association (Fort
    Morgan CO)
  Mountain Parks Electric (Granby CO)
  Mountain View Electric Association (Limon CO)
  Niobrara Electric Association (Lusk WY)
  Northern Rio Arriba Electric Cooperative (Chama NM)
  Northwest Rural Public Power District (Hay Springs
    NE)
  Panhandle Rural Electric Membership Association
    (Alliance NE)
  Poudre Valley Rural Electric Association (Fort Collins
    CO)
  Roosevelt Public Power District (Mitchell NE)
  San Isabel Electric Association (Pueblo CO)
  San Luis Valley Rural Electric Cooperative (Monte
    Vista CO)
  San Miguel Power Association (Nucla CO)
  Sangre De Cristo Electric Association (Buena Vista
    CO)
  Sierra Electric Cooperative Inc. (Elephant Butte NM)
  Southeast Colorado Power Association (La Junta)
  Springer Electric Cooperative (Springer MN)

United Power (Brighton CO)
Wheat Belt Public Power District (Sidney NE)
Wheatland Rural Electric Association (Wheatland WY)
White River Electric Association (Meeker CO)
Wyrulec Co. (Lingle WY)
Y-W Electric Association (Akron CO)
Upper Missouri Generation and Transmission Electric
  Cooperative (District 8)
  Burke-Divide Electric Cooperative (Columbus ND)
  Goldenwest Electric Cooperative (Wibaux MT)
  Lower Yellowstone Rural Electric Association (Sidney
    MT)
  McCone Electric Cooperative (Circle MT)
  McKenzie Electric Cooperative (Watford City ND)
  Mountrail-Williams Electric Cooperative (Williston
    ND)
  Sheridan Electric Cooperative (Medicine Lake MT)
  Slope Electric Cooperative (New England ND)
  Southeast Electric Cooperative (Ekalaka MT)
  West Plains Electric Cooperative (Dickinson ND)
????

COMPETITORS

Alliant Energy	Nebraska Public Power
Berkshire Hathaway	NorthWestern
Energy	Omaha Public Power
Black Hills	Otter Tail
MDU Resources	Xcel Energy

HISTORICAL FINANCIALS
Company Type: Private

Income Statement
FYE: December 31

	REVENUE ($ mil.)	NET INCOME ($ mil.)	NET PROFIT MARGIN	EMPLOYEES
12/15	1,445	8	0.6%	1,527
12/14	1,481	49	3.4%	—
12/13	1,337	45	3.4%	—
12/12	1,196	120	10.1%	—
Annual Growth	6.5%	(59.4%)	—	—

2015 Year-End Financials
Return on assets: 16.0%   Cash ($ mil.): 171
Return on equity: 0.6%
Current ratio: 0.30

BASTIAN SOLUTIONS, LLC

EXECUTIVES

Chief Executive Officer, William Bastian II
President, Aaron Jones
Chief Financial Officer, John Smith
Financial Executive, Lisa Rohe
Branch Manager, Jon Tilmon
Manager, Alan McDonald
Manager, Antwian Avant
Manager, Branden Horne
Manager, Tom Ahlborn
President, Damir Kantardzic
Auditors: KATZ SAPPER & MILLER

LOCATIONS

HQ: BASTIAN SOLUTIONS, LLC
  10585 N MERIDIAN ST FL 3, INDIANAPOLIS, IN
  462901069
Phone: 317 575-9992
Web: WWW.BASTIANSOLUTIONS.COM

HISTORICAL FINANCIALS
Company Type: Private

Income Statement
FYE: December 31

	REVENUE ($ mil.)	NET INCOME ($ mil.)	NET PROFIT MARGIN	EMPLOYEES
12/15	229	13	5.8%	579
12/14	147	3	2.7%	—
12/13	123	2	1.8%	—
12/12	141	5	4.0%	—
Annual Growth	17.5%	33.4%	—	—

2015 Year-End Financials
Return on assets: 4.2%   Cash ($ mil.): 16
Return on equity: 5.8%
Current ratio: 0.70

BATHXCESSORIES, INCORPORATED

EXECUTIVES

President, Kenneth Spoor
Board of Directors, Michael Castle
Auditors: ENC INC MANORVILLE NEW YORK

LOCATIONS

HQ: BATHXCESSORIES, INCORPORATED
  1825 W BARRY AVE, CHICAGO, IL 606572042
Phone: 312 951-2885
Web: WWW.BATHXCESSORIES.COM

HISTORICAL FINANCIALS
Company Type: Private

Income Statement
FYE: December 31

	REVENUE ($ mil.)	NET INCOME ($ mil.)	NET PROFIT MARGIN	EMPLOYEES
12/15	2,856	1,048	36.7%	2
12/14	2,642	660	25.0%	—
12/13	2,477	746	30.1%	—
12/12	2,244	471	21.0%	—
Annual Growth	8.4%	30.6%	—	—

BATON ROUGE GENERAL MEDICAL CENTER

EXECUTIVES

Chief Executive Officer, Mark F Slyter
Engineer, Todd Lemmiksoo
Auditors: POSTLETHWAITE & NETTERVILLE B

LOCATIONS

HQ: BATON ROUGE GENERAL MEDICAL CENTER
  8490 PICARDY AVE STE 200, BATON ROUGE, LA
  708093733
Phone: 225 237-1547
Web: WWW.BRGENERAL.ORG

HISTORICAL FINANCIALS
Company Type: Private

Income Statement
FYE: September 30

	REVENUE ($ mil.)	NET INCOME ($ mil.)	NET PROFIT MARGIN	EMPLOYEES
09/15	403	20	5.2%	14
09/14	406	17	4.3%	—
Annual Growth	(0.8%)	19.0%	—	—

2015 Year-End Financials
Return on assets: 7.0%
Return on equity: 5.2%
Current ratio: 4.10
Cash ($ mil.): 71

BATON ROUGE GENERAL MEDICAL CENTER

The first hospital founded in Louisiana's capital Baton Rouge General Medical Center is a not-for-profit full-service community hospital offering patients general medical and surgical care. Through the hospital's two locations Bluebonnet and Mid City Baton Rouge General also provides specialty services for cancer heart and neonatal care. In addition the nearly 530-bed health care facility provides services in areas such as burn treatment diabetes sleep disorders and behavioral health. Baton Rouge General Medical Center is the flagship facility of General Health System.

Operations

Baton Rouge General Medical Center is affiliated with and also serves as a satellite campus of Tulane University School of Medicine. In addition to serving as a satellite campus for Tulane medical students in the Leadership Education Advocacy and Discovery Academy program Baton Rouge General Medical Center also offers a Family Medicine Residency Program an Internal Medicine Residency Program a Sports Medicine Fellowship Program a School of Nursing and a School of Radiologic Technology.

In 2012 the Center had more than 1000 physicians and about 950 nurses on its medical staff and served 153000 patients and had about 91000 emergency department visits.

Geographic Reach

Through the hospital's two locations Bluebonnet and Mid City Baton Rouge General Medical Center also provides specialty services for cancer heart and neonatal care. Baton Rouge General is affiliated with and also serves as a satellite campus of Tulane University School of Medicine.

Financial Performance

In 2012 Baton Rouge General Medical Center reported gross revenues of $820 million and a net income of $10 million.

Strategy

The Center is expanding its infrastructure to keep up with demand. In 2014 Baton Rouge General Medical Center and Lane Regional Medical Center opened a $4.5 million state-of-the-art Radiation Oncology Center in Zachary Louisiana. In 2013 Baton Rouge General Medical Center announced plans to add two floors and 64 beds to an existing patient tower at the Bluebonnet campus a project that will cost an estimated $24 million and which will be completed by early 2015.

In 2013 Baton Rouge General Medical Center completed the steel beam structure for the hospital's patient tower expansion project.

In 2012 the Center initiated OneVision a program aimed at investing in minimally invasive technology and strengthening its physician network. That year it also opened the Behavioral Wellness Center at Jackson.

Company Background

In 2011 Baton Rouge General Medical Center broke ground on a $40 million expansion at the Bluebonnet campus. The project included a new five-story medical office building with 105000 sq. ft. of space and four large operating rooms. Part of the hospital's larger Bluebonnet expansion project the new construction projects follow the surgical services expansion and new heart and vascular tower. The surgical expansion included the addition of four new operating rooms equipped with an innovative hybrid build out and minimally invasive robotics.

The Center which has been an accredited teaching hospital since 1991 first opened its doors in 1900.

EXECUTIVES

Chief Executive Officer, Milton Sietman
Board of Directors, Ted Lewis
Auditors: POSTLETHWAITE & NETTERVILLE B

LOCATIONS

HQ: BATON ROUGE GENERAL MEDICAL CENTER
3600 FLORIDA BLVD, BATON ROUGE, LA 708063842
Phone: 225 387-7000

PRODUCTS/OPERATIONS

Selected Products and Services
Birth Center
Cancer
Heart & Vascular
Pediatrics
Emergency Room (ER)
Behavioral Health
Burn
Gastroenterology
Hyperbarics & Wound Care
Imaging/Radiology
Neurosciences
Orthopedics
Rehabilitation/Therapy
Seniors
Weight Loss
Wellness
Clinical Trials
Limbs For Life
Sleep Center

COMPETITORS

Lane Regional Medical Center	River Parishes Hospital
Our Lady of the Lake RMC	Woman's Hospital

HISTORICAL FINANCIALS
Company Type: Private

Income Statement
FYE: September 30

	REVENUE ($ mil.)	NET INCOME ($ mil.)	NET PROFIT MARGIN	EMPLOYEES
09/15	363	(10)	—	394
09/09	304	0	0.2%	—
09/08*	281	2	0.9%	—
12/05	2,026	0	—	—
Annual Growth	(15.8%)	—	—	—

*Fiscal year change

2015 Year-End Financials
Return on assets: —
Return on equity: (-3.0%)
Current ratio: 1.80
Cash ($ mil.): —

BATTELLE MEMORIAL INSTITUTE INC

When you use a copier hit a golf ball or listen to a CD you're using technologies developed by Battelle Memorial Institute. The not-for-profit is one of the world's largest research enterprises with more than 22000 scientists engineers and staff serving corporate and government clients. Research areas include national security energy and health and life sciences. Battelle owns facilities in the US Asia and Europe and manages six Department of Energy-sponsored labs: Brookhaven National Laboratory Oak Ridge National Laboratory Idaho National Laboratory and Pacific Northwest National Laboratory. The institute was established by the family of steel industry pioneer Gordon Battelle in 1929.

Operations

Battelle's major subsidiaries include Battelle Arabia Battelle India Battelle Japan Battelle Ventures Bluefin Robotics and Winner Water Services.

Geographic Reach

Battelle's headquarters are located in Columbus Ohio. The company has about 130 locations globally.

Sales and Marketing

Battelle serves the national security health and life sciences and energy and environmental industries. Its major customer group includes government and commercial organizations in Laboratory Management National Security Health & Pharmaceutical Energy & Environment Consumer & Industrial and STEM Education.

Strategy

Battelle is in the process of building an advanced research-and-development facility that will expand its global footprint and capacity to provide advanced science and technology solutions for the agriculture food and health care industries. The new facility will augment Battelle's established global scientific expertise in formulation development toxicology and biotechnology programs that help agriculture and food customers accelerate product development and meet multi-national regulatory requirements.

HISTORY

Battelle Memorial Institute was founded with a $1.5 million trust willed by Gordon Battelle who died in 1923. Battelle was a champion of research for the advancement of humankind and before taking his father's place as president of several Ohio steel mills he had funded a former university professor's successful work to extract useful chemicals from mine waste. Battelle's mother upon her death in 1925 left the institute an additional $2.1 million. The institute opened in 1929.

The institute took on perhaps the most important project in its history in 1944 when it helped an electronics company's patent lawyer Chester Carlson find practical uses for his invention called xerography. Eventually Battelle developed the first photocopy machine and in 1955 it sold the patent rights for the machine to Haloid (now Xerox) in exchange for royalties.

During WWII Battelle worked on uranium refining for the Manhattan Project and in the early 1950s it established the world's first private nuclear research facility. The company also set up operations in Germany and Switzerland.

The tax man came knocking in 1961 questioning the tax-free status of some of Battelle's activities. The organization eventually had to pay $47 million. In 1965 Battelle developed a coin with a

copper core and a copper-and-nickel-alloy cladding for the US Treasury.

As the result of a ruling that reinterpreted a clause in Gordon Battelle's will in 1975 the institute gave $80 million to philanthropic enterprises. This ruling coupled with the taxes that the organization was still unaccustomed to paying forced Battelle to re-examine its strategy.

Battelle co-developed the Universal Product Code (the bar code symbol found today on nearly all consumer goods packaging) in the 1970s. The institute also landed a lucrative contract from the US Department of Energy (DOE) to manage its commercial nuclear waste isolation program.

In 1987 Battelle chose Douglas Olesen — a 20-year veteran of the institute — to replace retiring CEO Ronald Paul. The company signed an extension with the DOE in 1992 to run its Pacific Northwest Laboratory (which it has operated since 1965).

An Ohio court in 1997 approved a seven-page agreement with the institute outlining the key principles that must be followed according to Gordon Battelle's will. This agreement replaced the 1975 decree and ended more than 20 years of scrutiny by the state attorney general's office.

In 1998 the DOE contracted Brookhaven Science Associates — a partnership between the State University of New York and Battelle — to operate Brookhaven National Laboratory. That year a Battelle contract to dispose of Vietnam War-era napalm drew national attention when subcontractor Pollution Control Industries backed out of the project citing safety concerns. Under Battelle's direction Houston-based GNI Group took the 3.4 million gallons of napalm off the US Navy's hands.

Battelle and the University of Tennessee in 1999 won a five-year contract to operate the US government's Oak Ridge National Laboratory. That year the institute made several breakthroughs in cancer research including FDA approval to test an inhalation delivery system for treating lung cancer.

In 2000 the company spun off OmniViz (data mining software) and Battelle Pulmonary Therapeutics (pulmonary and drug delivery technology) as wholly owned subsidiaries. In 2001 Battelle chose former Kodak EVP and CTO Carl Kohrt to replace Olesen. (Kohrt retired in January 2009 and was replaced by Jeffrey Wadsworth who has worked for the company since 2002.)

Battelle and several partners including BWX Technologies Washington Group International and Electric Power Research Institute won a 10-year contract in 2004 to operate Idaho National Laboratory a research facility established to focus on nuclear energy research and related technologies.

With offices in Japan and South Korea Battelle expanded its international reach to include India in 2008. The company formed a partnership in 2007 with oil and gas company PETRONAS to operate a renewable energy lab in Kuala Lumpur Malaysia.

Battelle underwent a leadership change in 2009 when Jeffrey Wadsworth took over as CEO replacing Carl Kohrt who retired.

EXECUTIVES

Vice President human Resources Battelle Columbus Operations, Robert Lincoln
Senior Vice President Chief Technology Officer, Richard Adams
President National Security, Stephen E. Kelly
President and CEO, Jeffrey (Jeff) Wadsworth, age 68
EVP Global Laboratory Operations, Ronald D. (Ron) Townsend
President Energy Health and Environmental business, Marty Toomajian
EVP and CFO, Dave Evans

President and CEO Winner Water Services, Carolyn Kotsol
Vice President, Victoria Loewengart
Vice President And Product Line Manager, Dennis Nelson
Vice President and Operations Manger, Daniel Taylor
Vice President, Sara F Kuczek
Senior Vice President Director Oak Ridge National Laboratory Global Laboratory Operations, Thomas Mason
Vice President for Systems Integration Services, Michael Janus
Executive Vice President, Martin Inglis
Vice President Application Development, Rod Barnaby
Vice President Business Development, Bradley Ashbrook
Senior Vice President Human Resources, Thomas Snowberger
Vice President navy and Special Operations Market Sector, Fred Byus
Vice President and Corporate Treasurer, Brian Smith
Vice President Client Insights, Jeanne Shaheen
Senior Vice President Human Resources, Malesa Litteral
Senior Vice President Business and Economic Development, Alexander Fischer
Executive Vice President and Chief Financial Officer, David Evans
Vice President Information Technology, Lavlesh Lamba
VICE PRESIDENT, Bob Dillon
Chairman, John K. Welch
Secretary, Tiffani Gollihue
Auditors: DELOITTE & TOUCHE LLP COLUMB

LOCATIONS

HQ: BATTELLE MEMORIAL INSTITUTE INC
505 KING AVE, COLUMBUS, OH 432012681
Phone: 614 424-6424
Web: WWW.BATTELLE-JAPAN.COM

PRODUCTS/OPERATIONS

Selected Laboratories and Research Facilities
Battelle Biomedical Research Center (West Jefferson OH)
Battelle Eastern Science and Technology Center (Aberdeen MD)
Battelle Frederick Operations (Maryland)
Battelle Geneva Operations (Switzerland)
Brookhaven National Laboratory (Upton NY)
Human Factors Transportation Center (Seattle)
Idaho National Laboratory (Idaho Falls)
Lawrence Livermore National Laboratory (Livermore CA)
Marine Science Laboratory (Sequim WA)
National Renewable Energy Laboratory (Golden CO)
Oak Ridge National Laboratory (Tennessee)
Battelle Duxbury Operations (Massachusetts)
Pacific Northwest National Laboratory (Richland WA)

Selected Inventions
Exploded-tip paintbrush (nylon brush for Wooster Brush Co. 1950)
Golf ball coatings (1965)
Heat Seat (microwaveable stadium cushion 1990s)
Holograms (work began in the 1970s)
Insulin injection pen (for Eli Lilly 1990s)
Oil spill outline monitor (1992)
PCB-cleaning chemical process (1992)
Photocopy machine (with Haloid 1940s)
Plastic breakdown process (1990s)
"Sandwich" coins (copper/copper-and-nickel-alloy cladding design for US Treasury 1965)
SenSonic toothbrush (with Teledyne/WaterPik 1990s)
Smart cards (cards embedded with tiny computer chips that store information 1980s)
Universal Product Code (co-creator; bar code 1970s)

COMPETITORS

Argonne National Laboratory	Institute for Defense Analyses
Berkeley Lab	SwRI
Charles Stark Draper Laboratory	

HISTORICAL FINANCIALS

Company Type: Private

Income Statement

FYE: September 30

	REVENUE ($ mil.)	NET INCOME ($ mil.)	NET PROFIT MARGIN	EMPLOYEES
09/16	4,810	(19)	—	7,457
09/15	4,783	(63)	—	—
09/14	4,769	(111)	—	—
09/13	4,795	(7)	—	—
Annual Growth	0.1%	—	—	—

2016 Year-End Financials

Return on assets: 1.2%   Cash ($ mil.): 63
Return on equity: (-0.4%)
Current ratio: 1.40

BAY REGIONAL MEDICAL CENTER

McLaren Bay Region provides a full range of medical services for the residents at the tip of Saginaw Bay in eastern Michigan. A part of McLaren Health Care the hospital's main campus has more than 400 beds and provides general medical and surgical care as well as specialty care in areas such as cardiovascular disease neuroscience oncology rehabilitation orthopedics and women's health. It also features an emergency room and Level II trauma center and provides home health and hospice care. A second campus McLaren Bay Special Care Hospital is a long-term acute care hospital serving patients requiring hospital stays of longer than 25 days. The regional provider also provides outpatient and home health services.

Operations
In addition to its two acute care centers McLaren Bay Region operates outpatient centers including the Nickless Volunteer Clinic which provides primary care for uninsured and underinsured residents of Bay County.

The hospital system has one of the largest multidisciplinary research programs in the state. It works with international pharmaceutical and device companies — as well as universities foundations and agencies — to create new and improved treatments for illnesses including cancers and infectious diseases.

Going hand-in-hand with clinical trials is teaching and McLaren Bay Region offers a roster of residency programs for up-and-coming medical professionals. The hospital works with Michigan State University's colleges of Human Medicine and Osteopathic Medicine.

Geographic Reach
McLaren Bay Region has about 45 offices in Michigan counties including Auburn Bay Davison Essexville Lake Orion and Pinconning.

Strategy
McLaren Bay Region is looking to expand its geographic reach in eastern Michigan. It is also widening its range of specialist services in areas such as oncology cardiovascular care and orthopedic rehabilitation. The organization launched a

new cancer rehabilitation program in 2012; it also opened a new outpatient heart center featuring cardiac diagnostic capabilities in Mt. Pleasant.

Company Background

McLaren Bay Region was formed after the merging of four hospitals during the 1970s and 1980s with the idea of developing a full continuum of health services for Northeast Michigan. It changed its name to McLaren Bay Region from Bay Regional Medical Center in 2012.

EXECUTIVES

President, Alice Gerard
General Manager, Jim Boudon
Board of Directors, David B Mikolajczak

LOCATIONS

HQ: BAY REGIONAL MEDICAL CENTER
 1900 COLUMBUS AVE, BAY CITY, MI 487086831
Phone: 989 894-3000
Web: WWW.BAYREGIONAL.ORG

PRODUCTS/OPERATIONS

Selected Centers and Services
Bariatrics
Behavioral Health
Blood Conservation
Cancer Services
Cardiac
Diabetes
Diagnostic Imaging
Dialysis Services
Emergency Care
EMS
Family BirthPlace
Fitness Centers
Free Clinics
Health Insurance
Home Care
Implantable Hearing Solutions
Infectious Disease
Infusion Center
Intensive Care
Internal Medicine
Laboratory and Pathology
Lifeline
Medical Library
Medical Supplies & Equipment
Neurosciences
Nutritional Counseling
Ophthalmology
Orthopedics
Pain Management
Pediatrics
Primary Care
Proton Therapy
Pulmonary and Respiratory
Rehabilitation and Therapy
Robotic Surgery
Sleep Medicine
Stroke Center
Surgical and Endoscopy Services
Trauma
Urology
Walk-in Clinics
Women's Services
Wound Care

COMPETITORS

Ascension Health
Covenant HealthCare
Crittenton Hospital
Detroit Medical Center
Genesys Health System
Genesys Regional
 Medical Center
Henry Ford Health
 System
Hurley Medical Center
Munson Healthcare
Select Medical
Sparrow Health System
St. John Health
University of Michigan
 Health System

HISTORICAL FINANCIALS

Company Type: Private

Income Statement

FYE: September 30

	REVENUE ($ mil.)	NET INCOME ($ mil.)	NET PROFIT MARGIN	EMPLOYEES
09/15	278	1	0.5%	1,800
09/14	278	19	6.9%	—
09/13	251	31	12.6%	—
09/12	278	22	8.1%	—
Annual Growth	0.1%	(61.5%)	—	—

2015 Year-End Financials

Return on assets: 4.4%
Return on equity: 0.5%
Current ratio: 1.10
Cash ($ mil.): 11

BAYHEALTH MEDICAL CENTER, INC.

EXECUTIVES

President, Terry Murphy
Financial Executive, Susan Doughty
Supervisor, Linda Hudson
Manager, Clara A Phipps
VP Personnel, John McDowell
Director, Sue Nitshe
Vice-President, Terry Feinour
Auditors: GRANT THORNTON LLP PHILADELPH

LOCATIONS

HQ: BAYHEALTH MEDICAL CENTER, INC.
 640 S STATE ST, DOVER, DE 199013530
Phone: 302 422-3311

HISTORICAL FINANCIALS

Company Type: Private

Income Statement

FYE: June 30

	REVENUE ($ mil.)	NET INCOME ($ mil.)	NET PROFIT MARGIN	EMPLOYEES
06/16	570	19	3.4%	2,790
06/15	551	39	7.1%	—
06/14	511	86	17.0%	—
06/13	482	85	17.8%	—
Annual Growth	5.7%	(39.1%)	—	—

2016 Year-End Financials

Return on assets: 8.0%
Return on equity: 3.4%
Current ratio: 0.90
Cash ($ mil.): 43

BAYLOR ALL SAINTS MEDICAL CENTER

EXECUTIVES

President, Steve Newton
Board of Directors, Preshie M Wilson
Vice-President, Leigh Anne Gates
Chief Operating Officer, Sandra Aaron

LOCATIONS

HQ: BAYLOR ALL SAINTS MEDICAL CENTER
 1400 8TH AVE, FORT WORTH, TX 761044110
Phone: 817 926-2544
Web: WWW.BAYLORTRANSPLANT.COM

HISTORICAL FINANCIALS

Company Type: Private

Income Statement

FYE: September 30

	REVENUE ($ mil.)	NET INCOME ($ mil.)	NET PROFIT MARGIN	EMPLOYEES
09/15	347	19	5.7%	1,800
09/14	364	38	10.6%	—
09/13	341	16	4.8%	—
09/12	367	3	0.9%	—
Annual Growth	(1.8%)	83.6%	—	—

2015 Year-End Financials

Return on assets: 1.6%
Return on equity: 5.7%
Current ratio: 2.90
Cash ($ mil.): 110

BAYLOR MEDICAL CENTER AT IRVING

EXECUTIVES

President, Cindy Schamp
Director, Susan Howell
Director, John Clark

LOCATIONS

HQ: BAYLOR MEDICAL CENTER AT IRVING
 1901 N MACARTHUR BLVD, IRVING, TX 750612220
Phone: 972 579-8100

HISTORICAL FINANCIALS

Company Type: Private

Income Statement

FYE: June 30

	REVENUE ($ mil.)	NET INCOME ($ mil.)	NET PROFIT MARGIN	EMPLOYEES
06/15	252	21	8.5%	1,500
06/14	202	44	22.0%	—
06/13	0	0	8.6%	—
06/06	205	27	13.5%	—
Annual Growth	2.4%	(2.7%)	—	—

2015 Year-End Financials

Return on assets: 1.6%
Return on equity: 8.5%
Current ratio: 2.10
Cash ($ mil.): 38

BAYLOR REGIONAL MEDICAL CENTER AT GRAPEVINE

EXECUTIVES

President, Scott Peek
Director, Rebecca Phillips

Administrative Assistant, Don Holacha
Director, Kris Powell

LOCATIONS

HQ: BAYLOR REGIONAL MEDICAL CENTER AT GRAPEVINE
1650 W COLLEGE ST, GRAPEVINE, TX 760513565
Phone: 817 481-1588

HISTORICAL FINANCIALS
Company Type: Private

Income Statement
FYE: June 30

	REVENUE ($ mil.)	NET INCOME ($ mil.)	NET PROFIT MARGIN	EMPLOYEES
06/15	257	64	25.1%	450
06/09	233	32	14.0%	—
06/05	163	21	13.2%	—
06/04	135	11	8.4%	—
Annual Growth	6.0%	17.1%	—	—

2015 Year-End Financials

Return on assets: 1.7%   Cash ($ mil.): 434
Return on equity: 25.1%
Current ratio: 42.50

BAYLOR REGIONAL MEDICAL CENTER AT PLANO

EXECUTIVES

Director, Lannie R Hughes

LOCATIONS

HQ: BAYLOR REGIONAL MEDICAL CENTER AT PLANO
2001 BRYAN ST STE 2200, DALLAS, TX 752013024
Phone: 214 820-4135
Web: WWW.BAYLORSCOTTANDWHITE.COM

HISTORICAL FINANCIALS
Company Type: Private

Income Statement
FYE: June 30

	REVENUE ($ mil.)	NET INCOME ($ mil.)	NET PROFIT MARGIN	EMPLOYEES
06/15	216	50	23.1%	4
06/14	210	48	23.0%	—
06/10	185	29	15.9%	—
Annual Growth	3.1%	11.0%	—	—

2015 Year-End Financials

Return on assets: 3.2%   Cash ($ mil.): —
Return on equity: 23.1%
Current ratio: 1.80

BAYLOR UNIVERSITY MEDICAL CENTER

Baylor University Medical Center at Dallas is the flagship institution of the Baylor Health Care System. The medical center (known as Baylor Dallas) serves more than 300000 patients annually with more than 1000 inpatient beds and some 1200 physicians. It offers general medical and surgical services to specialty care in a wide range of fields including oncology cardiovascular disease and neuroscience. The hospital also features a Level I trauma center neonatal ICU and organ transplantation center. Founded in 1903 the Baylor Dallas campus includes the Charles A. Sammons Cancer Center and the Baylor Research Institute which conducts basic and clinical research across numerous medical specialties.

Operations

The Baylor University Medical Center campus consists of 20 specialty centers for treating a range of medical conditions. Primary facilities include the Charles A. Sammons Cancer Center Neuroscience Center Annette C. and Harold C. Simmons Transplant Institute James M. and Dorothy D. Collins Womens and Children's Center and the George Truett James Orthopaedic Institute as well as a top trauma center digestive care program and heart and vascular unit. The Heart and Vascular Institute conducts more than 50 research studies a year.

Strategy

The hospital received a boost in 2011 when Texas A&M's Health Science Center struck an affiliation with Baylor Health Care System. The two parties agreed to make Baylor Dallas a primary teaching hospital for A&M's third and fourth-year medical students. No hospital in the Baylor Health Care System held such a designation after it became independent from Baylor University in 1997.

As one of only two adult Level 1 trauma centers in the region Baylor Dallas has worked to bolster its emergency services to keep up with increasing demand. To this end it has broadened its Level 1 trauma capabilities increased the size of its minor emergency care area and added more patient care areas. The Riggs Emergency Department treats some 67000 patients each year.

Baylor Dallas' transplant program is considered a national leader in solid organ transplantation and in partnership with the program at Baylor All Saints Medical Center is one of only three programs worldwide to have performed more than 3000 adult liver transplants. The program is also known for its kidney pancreas heart and lung small bowel and blood and marrow transplants.

EXECUTIVES

Senior Vice President General Counsel, Stephen Boyd
Vice President Medical Staff Affairs and Chief Medical Officer, Irving D Prengler

LOCATIONS

HQ: BAYLOR UNIVERSITY MEDICAL CENTER
2001 BRYAN ST STE 2200, DALLAS, TX 752013024
Phone: 214 820-3151

Selected Locations
A. Webb Roberts Hospital
Baylor Charles A. Sammons Cancer Center
Baylor Jack and Jane Hamilton Heart and Vascular Hospital
Carr P. Collins Hospital
Erik and Margaret Jonsson Medical and Surgical Hospital
George W. Truett Memorial Hospital
Karl and Esther Hoblitzelle Memorial Hospital
Baylor Specialty Hospital
Our Children's House at Baylor

PRODUCTS/OPERATIONS

Selected Speciality Centers
Baylor Cancer Hospital
Baylor Center for Pain Management
Baylor Diagnostic Imaging Centers
Baylor George Truett James Orthopaedic Institute
Baylor Geriatric and Senior Center
Baylor Heart and Vascular Institute
Baylor Heart Failure Program
Baylor Motion and Sports Performance Center
Baylor Neuroscience Center
Baylor Radiosurgery Center
Baylor Ruth Collins Diabetes Center
Baylor Sammons Bone Tumor Center
Baylor Sammons Lung Cancer Center
Baylor Spine Center
Baylor SportsCare
Comprehensive Wound Center
Darlene G. Cass Women's Imaging Center
Digestive Care Services
Ernie's Appearance Center
Gastrointestinal and Endoscopy Laboratory
Hereditary Cancer Risk Program
Infectious Disease Center
James M. and Dorothy D. Collins Women and Children's Center
Kimberly H. Courtwright and Joseph W. Summers Institute of Metabolic Disease
Louise Gartner Center for Hyperbaric Medicine
Martha Foster Lung Care Center
Non-invasive Heart and Vascular Laboratory
Reuben H. Adams Family Health Center
Simply Mom's Mother and Baby Boutique
Sleep Center
TINY TOTS Clinic
Virginia R. Cvetko Cancer Patient Education Center
Visual Function Testing Center
W.H. and Peggy Smith Baylor Sammons Breast Center
Weight Loss Surgery Program

COMPETITORS

CHRISTUS Health
Children's Medical Center of Dallas
Dynacq Healthcare
Harris Methodist Fort Worth Hospital
Parkland Health & Hospital System
Presbyterian Hospital of Dallas
Southwestern Medical Center
Texas Health Denton
Texas Health Resources
The Methodist Health System

HISTORICAL FINANCIALS
Company Type: Private

Income Statement
FYE: June 30

	REVENUE ($ mil.)	NET INCOME ($ mil.)	NET PROFIT MARGIN	EMPLOYEES
06/15	1,394	378	27.2%	5,003
06/09	1,072	0	—	—
06/08	155	16	10.3%	—
06/06	937	114	12.2%	—
Annual Growth	4.5%	14.3%	—	—

2015 Year-End Financials

Return on assets: 3.7%   Cash ($ mil.): —
Return on equity: 27.2%
Current ratio: 2.80

BAYSTATE HEALTH INC.

Baystate Medical Center is the flagship facility of the Baystate Health System. It is a tertiary care facility and Level 1 trauma center that provides comprehensive acute care services to residents of Springfield Massachusetts and the surrounding region. The more than 700-bed medical center is also a teaching hospital serving as a secondary campus for Tufts University School of Medicine. The Baystate Medical Center campus includes Baystate Children's Hospital a 110-bed/57-bassinette unit that boasts neonatal and pediatric ICUs. Other Baystate Medical Center operations include specialty programs in radiology cardiac care cancer and behavioral health.

Operations

As the only Level 1 trauma center in western Massachusetts the hospital is responsible for treating the most critical and urgent cases in the region. Baystate Medical Center is also home to the second-busiest emergency department in the state. Along with performing its own research activities Baystate Medical Center collaborates with the University of Massachusetts Amherst on biomedical technology research projects through the Pioneer Valley Life Sciences Institute. The center is home to one of only about 40 American College of Surgeons-accredited Level 1 Comprehensive Education Institutes in the world.

Other Baystate Health System facilities include Baystate Franklin Medical Center and Baystate Mary Lane Hospital.

Strategy

In 2013 Baystate Children's Specialty Center opened to serve a number of pediatric specialties including child behavioral health pediatric neurology pediatric infectious disease adolescent medicine and neonatal intensive care.

EXECUTIVES

President and CEO, Mark A. Keroack
SVP COO and Chief Nursing Officer, Nancy Shendell-Falik
Vice President Sales and Marketing, Lisa Hill
Vice President Compensation And Benefits, Keith Holtz
Pharmacy Manager, Sean Illig
Pharmacy Residency Program Director Pharmd, Aaron Michelucci
Director Of Radiology Services, Patrick Giordano
Vice President and Chief Information Officer, Joel Vengco
Vice President Medical Affairs Baystate Medical Center, Doug Salvador
ACO Acute Care Physician and Associate Medical Director, Abbie Courtemanche

LOCATIONS

HQ: BAYSTATE HEALTH INC.
759 CHESTNUT ST, SPRINGFIELD, MA 011991001
Phone: 413 784-0000
Web: WWW.BAYSTATEHEALTH.COM

PRODUCTS/OPERATIONS

Selected Programs and Services
Baystate Children's Hospital
Baystate Heart & Vascular Program
Baystate Regional Cancer Program
Department of Surgery
Regional Sleep Program
Women's Health

COMPETITORS

Berkshire Health Systems
Boston Medical Center
CareGroup
Children's Hospital Boston
Connecticut Children's Medical Center
Harrington Memorial Hospital
Hartford Health Care
Hospital of Central Connecticut
Partners HealthCare
Saint Francis Hospital and Medical Center
St. Elizabeth's Medical Center
University of Connecticut Health Center
Yale New Haven Health System

HISTORICAL FINANCIALS
Company Type: Private

Income Statement
FYE: September 30

	REVENUE ($ mil.)	NET INCOME ($ mil.)	NET PROFIT MARGIN	EMPLOYEES
09/15	1,048	76	7.3%	4,691
09/13	13	(1)	—	—
09/10	884	64	7.3%	—
09/07	797	79	10.0%	—
Annual Growth	3.5%	(0.5%)	—	—

2015 Year-End Financials
Return on assets: 4.7% Cash ($ mil.): 83
Return on equity: 7.3%
Current ratio: 1.10

BAYSTATE MEDICAL PRACTICES INC

EXECUTIVES

Principal, Kwan Mew
Auditors: DELOITTE TAX LLP JERICHO NY

LOCATIONS

HQ: BAYSTATE MEDICAL PRACTICES INC
759 CHESTNUT ST, SPRINGFIELD, MA 011991001
Phone: 413 794-0000
Web: WWW.BAYSTATEHEALTH.COM

HISTORICAL FINANCIALS
Company Type: Private

Income Statement
FYE: September 30

	REVENUE ($ mil.)	NET INCOME ($ mil.)	NET PROFIT MARGIN	EMPLOYEES
09/15	266	(20)	—	2
09/14	236	(26)	—	—
09/13	219	(21)	—	—
Annual Growth	10.1%	—	—	—

2015 Year-End Financials
Return on assets: 14.9% Cash ($ mil.): 10
Return on equity: (-7.8%)
Current ratio: 0.70

BEALL'S, INC.

Residents of the Sun Belt have been known to leave their homes with Beall's on. The retail holding company operates through subsidiaries Beall's Department Stores Beall's Outlet and Burke's Outlet Stores in a dozen states. The multi-brand retailer has more than 530 department and outlet stores (about 200 are in Florida) located throughout states in the southern and western US including Arizona California Georgia Louisiana and Texas. Products range from off-price clothing and footwear for men and women to cosmetics gifts and housewares. Each chain has its own online shopping destination. The family-owned company was founded in 1915 by the grandfather of chairman Robert Beall (pronounced "bell").

Operations

Beall's Inc. oversees operations of its three operating companies. Beall's Florida operates some 190 stores in the Sunshine State. Beall's Outlet operates about 300 stores in Arizona Florida Texas and Georgia while Burke's Outlet operates more than 190 stores in 16 states.

Geographic Reach

Beall's trio of chain's operate stores in Alabama Arkansas Arizona California Florida Georgia Kentucky Louisiana Mississippi Nevada New Mexico North Carolina South Carolina Tennessee Texas Virginia and West Virginia.

Financial Performance

Privately-owned Beall's rings ups more than $1 billion in sales annually.

Strategy

The company has aspirations to transform itself into a major discount retailer much like its larger rivals TJX and Ross Stores. To that end the company plans to add new stores outside its traditional markets with an eye on establishing a national retail presence. Targets include adding 30 to 50 stores a year for the next several years and raising brand awareness beyond Florida.

With many of its stores in Arizona Florida and California (three of the states hit hardest by the housing crisis and deep recession) Beall's Inc. should have been in a heap of retail trouble. However its largest chain — Beall's Outlet —proved to be quite popular during this recession. Indeed the budget-priced outlet chain outperformed its two sister chains as well as more moderately priced department stores. The retailer has also benefited from the demise of other retailers including Goody's Linens 'n Things and Mervyn's.

The three operating companies share resources provided by Beall's Inc. such as distribution finance loss prevention and information systems. Conversely each chain is responsible for its purchasing product development real estate and advertising activities.

Company Background

Stores operating under the Bealls name in Alabama New Mexico and Texas are owned by Stage Stores and are not affiliated with Beall's Inc.

EXECUTIVES

Vice President GMM Home, Kelley Wotton-Gantner

LOCATIONS

HQ: BEALL'S, INC.
1806 13TH AVE E, BRADENTON, FL 34208
Phone: 941 747-2355
Web: WWW.BEALLSINC.COM

PRODUCTS/OPERATIONS

Selected Retail Operations
Bealls Department Stores (Florida)
Bealls Outlet (deep-discount outlet stores in Arizona Florida Georgia)
Burke's Outlet (11 southern states)

COMPETITORS

Bed Bath & Beyond	Ross Stores
Costco Wholesale	Sears
Dillard's	Stage Stores
J. C. Penney Company	TJX Companies
Kohl's	Target Corporation
Macy's	The Gap
Nordstrom	Wal-Mart

HISTORICAL FINANCIALS
Company Type: Private

Income Statement
FYE: August 1

	REVENUE ($ mil.)	NET INCOME ($ mil.)	NET PROFIT MARGIN	EMPLOYEES
08/15*	1,321	25	1.9%	9,700
07/12	1,232	14	1.1%	—
07/11	1,166	15	1.3%	—
Annual Growth	3.2%	12.8%	—	—

*Fiscal year change

2015 Year-End Financials
Return on assets: 10.5%
Return on equity: 1.9%
Current ratio: 0.50

Cash ($ mil.): 107

BEAUFORT COUNTY MEMORIAL HOSPITAL

Beaufort Memorial Hospital provides medical surgical and therapeutic services in southern South Carolina. As the largest hospital between Savannah Georgia and Charleston South Carolina the not-for-profit community hospital is a regional referral center providing inpatient acute care and outpatient services. The 200-bed facility offers specialties in areas including cancer treatment cardiology emergency medicine mental health rehabilitation and obstetrics/gynecology. Beaufort Memorial Hospital operates the Keyserling Cancer Center through its affiliation with the Duke University Health System. It also offers outpatient care at satellite facilities. The medical center opened its doors in 1944.

Financial Analysis
Beaufort Memorial Hospital saw a 3% gain in operating revenue in fiscal 2011 (ends September) vs. fiscal 2010. The hospital credited the uptick primarily to increased outpatient activity although inpatient revenue increased as well.

Strategy
As a regional operator the hospital's strategic focus is the market located south of the Broad River including Bluffton Hardeeville and Hilton Head Island. Currently Beaufort Memorial operates a primary care clinic and medical services facility in the area. It is in negotiations to purchase about 20 acres in the region to build a medical office building and ultimately other health-related building projects to capitalize on the region's growing population.

Also the hospital's new $14.5-million Pratt Emergency Center is slated to open in early 2013. The 20500-square-foot facility is more than twice the size of the former emergency department.

EXECUTIVES

Executive Director Beaufort Memorial Hospital Foundation, Alice Moss
Director Beaufort Memorial Keyserling Cancer Center, Connie Duke
Vice President of Quality Services, Shawna H Doran
Vice Chair, Patricia A. (Pat) Thompson
Treasurer, Rosalind Dawson

LOCATIONS

HQ: BEAUFORT COUNTY MEMORIAL HOSPITAL
955 RIBAUT RD, BEAUFORT, SC 299025441
Phone: 843 522-5200
Web: WWW.BMHSC.ORG

COMPETITORS

Carolinas HealthCare System
Carolinas Hospital System
Georgetown Hospital System
Grand Strand Regional Medical Center
Greenville Hospital System
HCA

Laurens County Hospital
Lexington Medical Center
McLeod Health
Medical University of South Carolina
Palmetto Health
Roper St. Francis Healthcare

HISTORICAL FINANCIALS
Company Type: Private

Income Statement
FYE: September 30

	REVENUE ($ mil.)	NET INCOME ($ mil.)	NET PROFIT MARGIN	EMPLOYEES
09/15	188	(10)	—	1,300
09/14	173	6	4.0%	—
09/13	0	0	—	—
09/08	134	8	6.6%	—
Annual Growth	4.9%	—	—	—

2015 Year-End Financials
Return on assets: 1.6%
Return on equity: (-5.4%)
Current ratio: 4.20

Cash ($ mil.): 46

BEAUMONT INDEPENDENT SCHOOL DISTRICT

EXECUTIVES

Superintendent, Dr Carrol A Thomas
Assistant Manager, Robert Zingelmann
General Manager, Preston Shaw
Auditors: GAYLE W BOTLEY & ASSOCIATES

LOCATIONS

HQ: BEAUMONT INDEPENDENT SCHOOL DISTRICT
3395 HARRISON AVE, BEAUMONT, TX 777065009
Phone: 409 617-5000
Web: WWW.BMTISD.COM

HISTORICAL FINANCIALS
Company Type: Private

Income Statement
FYE: August 31

	REVENUE ($ mil.)	NET INCOME ($ mil.)	NET PROFIT MARGIN	EMPLOYEES
08/16	211	8	3.9%	2,700
08/09	242	160	66.2%	—
08/08	190	62	33.0%	—
08/07	192	(1)	—	—
Annual Growth	1.1%	—	—	—

2016 Year-End Financials
Return on assets: 3.3%
Return on equity: 3.9%
Current ratio: 1.90

Cash ($ mil.): 44

BEAVERTON SCHOOL DISTRICT

EXECUTIVES

Superintendent, Jerome Colonna
Board of Directors, Stephen Langford
Board of Directors, Craig Irwin
Auditors: GROVE MUELLER & SWANK PC

LOCATIONS

HQ: BEAVERTON SCHOOL DISTRICT
16550 SW MERLO RD, BEAVERTON, OR 970035179
Phone: 503 591-8000
Web: WWW.BEAVERTON.K12.OR.US

HISTORICAL FINANCIALS
Company Type: Private

Income Statement
FYE: June 30

	REVENUE ($ mil.)	NET INCOME ($ mil.)	NET PROFIT MARGIN	EMPLOYEES
06/16	513	(137)	—	4,000
06/15	495	431	87.0%	—
06/13	396	(6)	—	—
06/12	400	(17)	—	—
Annual Growth	6.4%	—	—	—

BEEBE MEDICAL CENTER, INC.

Sea shells on the sea shore can be found near Beebe Medical Center. The health care provider offers emergency inpatient long-term care women's health and other medical services to residents of Sussex County Delaware. The hospital is located in the town of Lewes near Rehoboth Beach. It has approximately 210 beds and offers specialized services including cardiology orthopedic rehabilitation and oncology treatments. Beebe Medical Center offers outpatient services including wound care diabetes management surgery radiology and sleep disorder diagnosis. It also operates senior care centers home health agencies medical laboratories and a nursing school.

Operations
Beebe Medical Center has a staff of some 1400 health professionals including about 300 doctors. It handles some 50000 emergency room visits per year. In addition to the primary hospital facilities the health care provider operates the Beebe Health Campus (outpatient services) and the nearby Millville Emergency Center (a summertime clinic near Bethany Beach).

Strategy
Beebe Medical Center has expanded its facilities over the years to better serve area residents. It began an expansion aiming to double enrollment of the nursing school in 2012. Construction efforts at the main hospital facility include a new emergency and critical care wing added in 2008.

Company Background
Beebe Medical Center was founded in 1916 by two brothers Dr. James Beebe and Dr. Richard Beebe. The Beebe School of Nursing opened in 1921 and the outpatient Beebe Health Campus was completed in 2003.

EXECUTIVES

Vice President Patient Care, Paul Minnick
Medical Director Hospitalist Program, Julie Holmon
Medical Records Director, Steven D Berlin
Chairman Emeritus, Joseph Hudson

LOCATIONS

HQ: BEEBE MEDICAL CENTER, INC.
424 SAVANNAH RD, LEWES, DE 199581462
Phone: 302 645-3300
Web: WWW.BEEBEMED.ORG

Selected Delaware Locations
Beebe Health Campus (Rehoboth Beach)
Beebe Lab Express (Milton)
Beebe School of Nursing (Lewes)
Diabetes Management and Wound Care Center (Long Neck)
Georgetown Professional Park (Georgetown)
Gull House Adult Activities Center (Lewes)
Home Health Agency (Lewes)
Millville Walk-in Health Center (Millville)
Sleep Disorders Center (Rehoboth Beach)
Tunnell Cancer Center (Rehoboth Beach)

PRODUCTS/OPERATIONS

Selected Services
Bariatric
Cancer care
Cardiac & vascular
Community health
Diabetes management
Emergency
Home health
Hospitalist program
Imaging
Integrative health
Orthopedics
Rehabilitation
Senior care
Sleep Disorder
Surgical
Walk-in Healthcare
Wellness
Women's Health
Wound Care

COMPETITORS

Anne Arundel Medical Center
AtlantiCare
Christiana Care
Crozer-Keystone Health System
Inspira Health Network
Shore Memorial Hospital

HISTORICAL FINANCIALS
Company Type: Private

Income Statement
FYE: June 30

	REVENUE ($ mil.)	NET INCOME ($ mil.)	NET PROFIT MARGIN	EMPLOYEES
06/15	325	29	9.2%	1,606
06/13	275	16	5.9%	—
06/10	259	15	5.9%	—
06/09	234	0	—	—
Annual Growth	5.6%	—	—	—

2015 Year-End Financials
Return on assets: 5.8%
Return on equity: 9.2%
Current ratio: 1.00
Cash ($ mil.): 37

BELLIN HEALTH SYSTEMS, INC.

EXECUTIVES

President, George Kerwin
Financial Executive, Kevin Mc Gurk
Administrative Assistant, Moin Raisigler
Manager, Paul Vlies
Manager, Charlene Busch
Auditors: WIPFLI LLP GREEN BAY WISCONS

LOCATIONS

HQ: BELLIN HEALTH SYSTEMS, INC.
744 S WEBSTER AVE, GREEN BAY, WI 543013505
Phone: 920 433-3500

HISTORICAL FINANCIALS
Company Type: Private

Income Statement
FYE: September 30

	REVENUE ($ mil.)	NET INCOME ($ mil.)	NET PROFIT MARGIN	EMPLOYEES
09/16	533	31	6.0%	2,300
09/15	502	27	5.5%	—
09/14	460	34	7.4%	—
09/10	348	30	8.8%	—
Annual Growth	7.4%	0.8%	—	—

2016 Year-End Financials
Return on assets: 2.8%
Return on equity: 6.0%
Current ratio: 2.50
Cash ($ mil.): 97

BELLIN MEMORIAL HOSPITAL, INC.

EXECUTIVES

President, George Kerwin
Manager, Randy Ronsman
Board of Directors, Larry Weyers
Manager, Jeanine Govek
Auditors: WIPFLI LLP GREEN BAY WISCONS

LOCATIONS

HQ: BELLIN MEMORIAL HOSPITAL, INC.
744 S WEBSTER AVE, GREEN BAY, WI 543013581
Phone: 920 433-3500
Web: WWW.BELLIN.ORG

HISTORICAL FINANCIALS
Company Type: Private

Income Statement
FYE: September 30

	REVENUE ($ mil.)	NET INCOME ($ mil.)	NET PROFIT MARGIN	EMPLOYEES
09/16	488	32	6.7%	1,725
09/15	462	27	6.0%	—
09/14	399	32	8.3%	—
09/13	363	28	7.8%	—
Annual Growth	10.4%	5.1%	—	—

2016 Year-End Financials
Return on assets: 2.9%
Return on equity: 6.7%
Current ratio: 2.40
Cash ($ mil.): 85

BELMONT UNIVERSITY

EXECUTIVES

Chairman of the Board, Marty Dickens
Vice-President, Jason Rogers
Vice-President, Bettel Thomas
Dean, Patrick Raines
Vice-President, Dodd Lake
Auditors: CROWE HORWATH LLP BRENTWOOD

LOCATIONS

HQ: BELMONT UNIVERSITY
1900 BELMONT BLVD, NASHVILLE, TN 372123757
Phone: 615 460-6000
Web: WWW.BELMONT.EDU

HISTORICAL FINANCIALS
Company Type: Private

Income Statement
FYE: May 31

	REVENUE ($ mil.)	NET INCOME ($ mil.)	NET PROFIT MARGIN	EMPLOYEES
05/15	261	74	28.6%	600
05/13	218	56	25.9%	—
05/12	166	39	23.5%	—
05/11	0	0	—	—
Annual Growth	—	5132.4%	—	—

2015 Year-End Financials
Return on assets: 9.1%
Return on equity: 28.6%
Current ratio: 0.20
Cash ($ mil.): 41

BELOIT MEMORIAL HOSPITAL, INC.

EXECUTIVES

Vice-President, Doris R Mulder
Senior Vice-President, Timothy M McKevett
Vice-President, Susan K Scheiber
Director, Mardell Jacobsen

LOCATIONS

HQ: BELOIT MEMORIAL HOSPITAL, INC.
1969 W HART RD, BELOIT, WI 535112230
Phone: 608 364-5011
Web: WWW.BELOITHEALTHSYSTEM.ORG

HISTORICAL FINANCIALS
Company Type: Private

Income Statement
FYE: December 31

	REVENUE ($ mil.)	NET INCOME ($ mil.)	NET PROFIT MARGIN	EMPLOYEES
12/16	209	7	3.8%	1,400
12/09	124	5	4.5%	—
12/08	107	0	0.8%	—
12/06	1,764	0	0.0%	—
Annual Growth	(21.1%)	200.3%	—	—

2015 Year-End Financials
Return on assets: 4.6%
Return on equity: 3.8%
Current ratio: 1.70
Cash ($ mil.): 25

BEND-LAPINE SCHOOLS

EXECUTIVES

Superintendent, Shay Mikalson
Director, Don Fisher
Principal, Peter Miller
Director, Bruce Abernethy
Director, Gary Timms
Manager, Shelli Peters
Auditors: GREERMAHR & ASSOCIATES LLP BE

LOCATIONS

HQ: BEND-LAPINE SCHOOLS
520 NW WALL ST, BEND, OR 977032608
Phone: 541 383-6000
Web: WWW.BEND.K12.OR.US

HISTORICAL FINANCIALS

Company Type: Private

Income Statement
FYE: June 30

	REVENUE ($ mil.)	NET INCOME ($ mil.)	NET PROFIT MARGIN	EMPLOYEES
06/16	203	(13)	—	1,600
06/07	145	120	82.9%	—
06/06	0	0	—	—
06/05	116	(7)	—	—
Annual Growth	5.2%	—	—	—

BENTLEY UNIVERSITY

Bentley University is not the Rolls-Royce of universities but is fairly prestigious nevertheless. It offers undergraduate graduate and doctoral degree programs to its nearly 5670 enrolled students from 82 countries. The university also offers professional development and certificate programs for executives and corporations. The focus at Bentley is on business; the school was a pioneer in integrating information technology into the business curriculum. In the belief that businesspeople need a broad education Bentley requires a liberal arts core of classes in behavioral and social sciences English and other subjects in the humanities as well as math and natural sciences.

Operations

The university has a student-faculty ratio of 14:1 with 78% of its faculty holding doctoral degrees. It offers 23 majors and 36 minors in business the arts and sciences. Tuition and fees are about $44020 per year.

Bentley offers numerous on-campus activities outside its academic and research functions. These include cultural events athletics the arts volunteering and more than 100 student organizations.

Geographic Reach

Bentley University is situated on about 165 acres in Waltham west of Boston. In partnership with Bahrain Institute of Banking and Finance Bentley launched its "Bentley in Bahrain" degree program in 2002 expanding its campus to students in Bahrain and surrounding Gulf States in the Middle East. It also has a campus in San Francisco

Strategy

Bentley is working to implement what it calls a fused curriculum where courses are taught by faculty from both the business and the arts and sciences sides academia. As part of the movement it offers an 11-month MBA that pulls from multiple disciplines.

Seeing a market for students on the West Coast in 2013 Bentley opened a campus in San Francisco.

Company Background

Harry Bentley founded the institution as the Bentley School of Accounting and Finance in 1917.

Bentley's university designation and name change occurred in 2008.

EXECUTIVES

Vice President for Administration and Finance, Kenneth Cody
Vice President for University Advancement, William Torrey
Business Systems Analyst I Office of Vice President for Enrollment Mgmnt, Jillian Proia
Provost and Vice President Academic Affairs, Robert D Galliers
Senior Vice President Liberty Mutual, Roxanne Martinez
VICE PRESIDENT, Melanie Scott
EXECUTIVE VICE PRESIDENT FOR ADMINISTRATION, Betts Robyn
VICE PRESIDENT FOR SCHOOLS AND SCHOLARSHIPS, Savageau Thomas
Vice President For Student Affairs Dean of Students, Andrew Shepardson
Secretary, Danielle Lerose
Assistant Treasurer, James Fuerst
Treasurer, Kyle Donlan
TREASURER, Jason Keller
TREASURER, Sarah Zichlin
Auditors: KPMG LLP BOSTON MA

LOCATIONS

HQ: BENTLEY UNIVERSITY
175 FOREST ST, WALTHAM, MA 024524713
Phone: 781 891-2000

HISTORICAL FINANCIALS

Company Type: Private

Income Statement
FYE: June 30

	REVENUE ($ mil.)	NET INCOME ($ mil.)	NET PROFIT MARGIN	EMPLOYEES
06/15	288	18	6.5%	911
06/13	192	40	21.0%	—
06/12	185	(21)	—	—
06/11	0	0	—	—
Annual Growth	—	1467.4%	—	—

2015 Year-End Financials

Return on assets: 9.0% Cash ($ mil.): 47
Return on equity: 6.5%
Current ratio: 0.30

BERGELECTRIC CORP.

One of the nation's top electrical contractors Bergelectric provides design/build and design/assist services on projects that include office buildings public-sector facilities bioscience labs entertainment complexes hotels data centers and hospitals. Its projects also consist of parking garages water treatment plants residential towers and correctional facilities. The company boasts expertise in building information modeling fire alarms and security and telecommunications and data infrastructure. Bergelectric operates mainly in the western and southeastern US from about a dozen offices.

Operations

The electrical company keeps a lengthy list of projects past and current. More recent projects have included the San Ysidro Land Port of Entry Lackland Ambulatory Care Center Northwest Water Reclamation Facility Naval Hospital Camp Pendleton Fort Riley Community Replacement Hospital Wilshire Boulevard Temple California Health Care Facility Visitors Center at King Gillette Ranch Variety Special Education School Greenlaw Partners and Sandy High School.

The company has more than $550 million in backlog.

Geographic Reach

From its headquarters in Los Angeles Bergelectric maintains a presence in California through a handful of offices in San Diego Los Angeles Orange County Sacramento and Ventura. It also serves as an electrical contractor in half a dozen cities including Austin Texas; Denver Colorado; Las Vegas Nevada; Orlando Florida; Phoenix Arizona; Portland Oregon; and Raleigh North Carolina.

Strategy

The company is also focused on green initiatives completing Leadership in Energy and Environmental Design (LEED) construction projects for the likes of Sony the FBI the EPA and the University of Oregon. To this end the company formed the Fire-Alarm/Security Division which provides projects and clients with comprehensive electrical services for such fire alarm projects as the Morongo Casino & Hotel Pechanga Hotel & Casino and San Manuel Indian Bingo & Casino.

Bergelectric has extended the reach of its traditional electrical contracting operations by expanding into new markets including sustainable building structures and renewable energy systems such as wind farms. Through a partnership with telecommunications firm Teo Bergelectric provides communications services to wind energy producers. As part of the agreement Bergelectric designs and installs fiber connections and equipment while Teo supplies phones switches and other hardware.

To simplify the integration of complex systems Bergelectric established a national Technology Systems group which serves to consolidate all of the company's existing low-voltage divisions under one management umbrella. The move aims to differentiate Bergelectric from the traditionally fragmented industry of electrical and systems components.

Company Background

Bergelectric was founded in 1946.

EXECUTIVES

Vice President Preconstruction, Scott Dater
Vice President, Rik Becker
Vice President Field Operations, Darren Murray
Auditors: MOSS LEVY & HARTZHEIM LLP B

LOCATIONS

HQ: BERGELECTRIC CORP.
5650 W CENTINELA AVE, LOS ANGELES, CA 900451501
Phone: 310 337-1377
Web: WWW.BERGELECTRIC.COM

Selected Locations
Agoura Hills CA
Austin TX
Costa Mesa CA
Denver
Durham NC
Escondido CA
Los Angeles
North Las Vegas NV
Orlando FL
Portland OR
Rancho Cordova CA
Tempe AZ

COMPETITORS

Cupertino Electric	MYR Group
EMCOR	Morrow-Meadows
Fisk Electric	Rex Moore
Henkels & McCoy	Rosendin Electric
IES Holdings	Sachs Electric

HISTORICAL FINANCIALS

Company Type: Private

Income Statement

FYE: January 31

	REVENUE ($ mil.)	NET INCOME ($ mil.)	NET PROFIT MARGIN	EMPLOYEES
01/16	507	2	0.4%	2,100
01/15	494	1	0.2%	—
01/14	525	4	0.9%	—
01/13	478	3	0.6%	—
Annual Growth	2.0%	(9.9%)	—	—

2016 Year-End Financials

Return on assets: 4.9%   Cash ($ mil.): 2
Return on equity: 0.4%
Current ratio: 1.00

BERGEN REGIONAL MEDICAL CENTER L.P.

Bergen Regional Medical Center (BRMC) is not just the biggest hospital in Paramus New Jersey — it's one of the biggest in the state. BRMC provides acute care long-term care and behavioral health care services to the residents of northeastern New Jersey. The not-for-profit medical center with approximately 1190 beds also offers specialized services including orthopedics cardiology neurology emergency medicine and surgery as well as substance abuse treatment and hospice services. About half of the facility is devoted to long-term nursing care; and about 325 beds serve behavioral health patients.

Operations

The 575-bed long-term care division is New Jersey's largest licensed nursing home. Residents receive nursing care and have access to round-the-clock medical care; they also participate in community and recreational activities. Other specialist units include BRMC's Evergreen Substance Abuse Treatment Center which provides comprehensive treatment — including inpatient detoxification and intensive outpatient programs — to about 15000 patients annually.

Through an affiliation with the University of Medicine and Dentistry of New Jersey the medical center also trains medical students. The BRMC Clinic is the hospital's outpatient care center which provides ambulatory care in about 20 specialist fields.

BRMC is a safety net provider meaning that it takes care of elderly mentally impaired uninsured or underinsured patients who cannot afford care elsewhere. This causes the hospital to see a high number of Medicare and Medicaid patients as well as to provide a high volume of charity (unreimbursed) care.

As a complement to its long term care and behavioral health/substance abuse expertise Bergen Regional also offers acute medical services including an emergency department surgical suites physical rehabilitation a pharmacy ans a laboratory radiologic services (including digital mammography)

and more than 20 ambulatory specialties available through the BRMC Clinic.

In 2012 the hospital reported more than 16000 emergency department visits.

Geographic Reach

BRMC serves patients from Bergen County as well as surrounding counties. The hospital is located on a 65-acre campus in Paramus New Jersey.

Strategy

With the contract between Bergen County and the for-profit operator of BRMC expiring in 2017 and with the hospital in recent years receiving poor marks from the federal government as well as in private rankings of healthcare facilities nationwide in 2014 the County Executive called for a study of the embattled Paramus-based acute care center. The Bergen County Executive created a seven-person task force to urgently study the needs of and future options for BRMC which has been hit by a 2012 lawsuit claiming non-payment of bills and other allegations of financial impropriety.

Company Background

In 2011 an agreement was made that extended the affiliation with the University of Medicine and Dentistry of New Jersey by allowing psychiatry graduate students to enter a training program at BRMC as part of their postgraduate education.

BRMC is owned by Bergen County but it is managed by a for-profit company.

EXECUTIVES

Principal, Joseph Orlando
Chief Financial Officer, Connie Magdangal
Chairman, V Robert Salazar
Plant & Facilities Manager, Barry Krissberg
Personnel Manager, Laruen Scutari
Chief Financial Officer, Robert Pudlack

LOCATIONS

HQ: BERGEN REGIONAL MEDICAL CENTER L.P.
230 E RIDGEWOOD AVE, PARAMUS, NJ 076524142
Phone: 201 967-4000
Web: WWW.BERGENREGIONAL.COM

PRODUCTS/OPERATIONS

Selected Services
Accessing Mental Health & Addiction Services
Acute Care
Acute Rehabilitation Services
Ambulatory Outpatient Services
Behavioral Health Services
Critical and Emergency Care
Long Term Care

COMPETITORS

Englewood Hospital and Medical Center	Monmouth Medical Center
Hackensack Meridian Health	Newark Beth Israel Medical Center
Hackensack University Medical Center	Nyack Hospital
JFK Health - Muhlenberg Campus	Robert Wood Johnson University Hospital
JFK Medical Center	The Valley Hospital
Jersey City Medical Center	Valley Health System

HISTORICAL FINANCIALS

Company Type: Private

Income Statement

FYE: December 31

	REVENUE ($ mil.)	NET INCOME ($ mil.)	NET PROFIT MARGIN	EMPLOYEES
12/15	207	(8)	—	1,856
12/08	146	(78)	—	—
Annual Growth	5.1%	—	—	—

2015 Year-End Financials

Return on assets: 2.7%   Cash ($ mil.): —
Return on equity: (-4.1%)
Current ratio: 0.60

BERING STRAITS NATIVE CORPORATION

EXECUTIVES

Chief Executive Officer, Gail Schubert
Operations Manager, Dorothy Anagick
Director, Eileen Norbert
Vice-President, Jenette Paulson
Manager, Ken Adams
Auditors: RSM US LLP FREDERICK MARYLAN

LOCATIONS

HQ: BERING STRAITS NATIVE CORPORATION
110 FRONT ST STE 300, NOME, AK 99762
Phone: 907 443-5252
Web: WWW.BERINGSTRAITS.COM

HISTORICAL FINANCIALS

Company Type: Private

Income Statement

FYE: March 31

	REVENUE ($ mil.)	NET INCOME ($ mil.)	NET PROFIT MARGIN	EMPLOYEES
03/16	326	13	4.3%	280
03/15	304	13	4.6%	—
03/14	229	9	4.2%	—
03/13	242	8	3.4%	—
Annual Growth	10.4%	19.5%	—	—

2016 Year-End Financials

Return on assets: 10.3%   Cash ($ mil.): 26
Return on equity: 4.3%
Current ratio: 1.30

BERKLEE COLLEGE OF MUSIC, INC.

If you get accepted to this school you've no doubt hit a high note in your musical career. Berklee College of Music the largest independent music college in the world offers bachelor's degrees in a dozen majors including film scoring jazz composition music education music production and engineering performance and songwriting. Located in Boston the school has some 4500 students and some 700 faculty members. Notable alumni include Branford Marsalis Quincy Jones Melissa Etheridge and Steely Dan vocalist Donald Fagen. Pianist Lawrence Berk founded the college in 1945. The school was named after his son Lee Berk who served as Berklee president from 1979 to 2004.

Operations

Berklee has a student-to-faculty ratio of 11:1. Its library collection includes more than 26500 books 8500 videos and 9000 e-books.

Geographic Reach

The school's Boston campus comprises 30 buildings. Berklee also has a campus in Spain.

Berklee City Music Network a not-for-profit consortium of community organizations offers after-school programs for teenagers in about 50 locations throughout the US and Canada.

Strategy

In 2014 the college opened a new 16-story residential tower which houses 369 students and features about two dozen practice rooms six common areas a fitness center and dining hall/performance space.

The school offers free online music lessons developed by faculty and alumni as well as online music channels produced by students. In 2014 Berklee launched an online Bachelor's degree program for guitar. Other online programs include music production songwriting and electronic music production and sound design.

EXECUTIVES

President, Roger H. Brown, age 61
VP Technology and Education Outreach, David S. Mash
Dean Professional Writing Division, Kari Juusela
Dean Professional Performance Division, Matt Marvuglio
Chief Financial Officer Vice President for Finance and Administration, Richard M. Hisey
Vice President for Education Outreach and Social Entrepreneurship, Lee Whitmore
Vice President of Student Affairs and Diversity and Inclusion, Christopher Kandus-Fisher
Vice President and General Manager, Maher Chankhour
Director of Admissions, Mike Moyes
Auditors: KPMG LLP BOSTON MA

LOCATIONS

HQ: BERKLEE COLLEGE OF MUSIC, INC.
1140 BOYLSTON ST, BOSTON, MA 022153693
Phone: 617 266-1400
Web: WWW.BERKLEE.EDU

PRODUCTS/OPERATIONS

Selected Majors
Composition
Contemporary Writing and Production
Film Scoring
Jazz Composition
Music Business/Management
Music Education
Music Production and Engineering
Music Synthesis
Music Therapy
Performance
Professional Music
Songwriting

Selected Academic Departments
Music Technology
    Music Production and Engineering
    Music Synthesis
Professional Education
    Liberal Arts
    Music Business/Management
    Music Education
    Music Therapy
    Professional Music
Professional Performance
    Bass
    Brass
    Ear Training
    Ensembles
    Guitar
    Percussion
    Piano
    Strings
    Voice
    Woodwinds
Professional Writing
    Composition
    Contemporary Writing and Production

Film Scoring
Harmony
Jazz Composition
Songwriting

HISTORICAL FINANCIALS

Company Type: Private

Income Statement
FYE: May 31

	REVENUE ($ mil.)	NET INCOME ($ mil.)	NET PROFIT MARGIN	EMPLOYEES
05/15	259	12	4.9%	1,082
05/14	252	27	10.8%	—
05/13	225	11	5.3%	—
05/11	220	21	9.6%	—
Annual Growth	4.1%	(12.0%)	—	—

2015 Year-End Financials

Return on assets: 32.2%
Return on equity: 4.9%
Current ratio: 0.10
Cash ($ mil.): 41

BERKSHIRE MEDICAL CENTER, INC.

EXECUTIVES

President, David E Phelps
Manager, Kareen Meller
Manager, Jean Gary
Manager, Joyce Brassard
Manager, Nancy Markgraf
Director, Alan Inglis

LOCATIONS

HQ: BERKSHIRE MEDICAL CENTER, INC.
725 NORTH ST, PITTSFIELD, MA 012014124
Phone: 413 447-2000
Web: WWW.BERKSHIREHEALTHSYSTEMS.ORG

HISTORICAL FINANCIALS

Company Type: Private

Income Statement
FYE: September 30

	REVENUE ($ mil.)	NET INCOME ($ mil.)	NET PROFIT MARGIN	EMPLOYEES
09/15	424	46	10.9%	1,375
09/14	377	38	10.3%	—
09/13	342	31	9.2%	—
09/12	339	43	12.8%	—
Annual Growth	7.7%	2.2%	—	—

2015 Year-End Financials

Return on assets: 4.0%
Return on equity: 10.9%
Current ratio: 0.90
Cash ($ mil.): 37

BETH ISRAEL DEACONESS HOSPITAL - PLYMOUTH, INC.

EXECUTIVES

Director, Lyle Bazzinotti
Office Manager, Jan Smith

LOCATIONS

HQ: BETH ISRAEL DEACONESS HOSPITAL - PLYMOUTH, INC.
275 SANDWICH ST, PLYMOUTH, MA 023602183
Phone: 508 746-2000

HISTORICAL FINANCIALS

Company Type: Private

Income Statement
FYE: September 30

	REVENUE ($ mil.)	NET INCOME ($ mil.)	NET PROFIT MARGIN	EMPLOYEES
09/15	218	5	2.6%	3
09/13	189	2	1.5%	—
09/93	0	(0)	—	—
Annual Growth	53.8%	—	—	—

2015 Year-End Financials

Return on assets: 19.2%
Return on equity: 2.6%
Current ratio: 0.30
Cash ($ mil.): 4

BETH ISRAEL DEACONESS MEDICAL CENTER, INC.

Beth Israel Deaconess Medical Center (BIDMC) is a hospital in Boston. Though it's the official hospital for this Major League Baseball team it's perhaps better known for being a teaching hospital of Harvard Medical School. BIDMC has about 650 beds and provides general medical and surgical care as well as outpatient services at its facilities. In addition to a Level I trauma center BIDMC offers specialized care in such areas as organ transplantation breast cancer care and cardiac surgery. BIDMC traces its roots to Deaconess Hospital founded in 1896 and Beth Israel Hospital established in 1916. It plans to merge with Lahey Health to create a stronger rival to Massachusetts' largest system Partners HealthCare.

Operations

BIDMC has 1200 physicians on its active medical staff (including some 800 full-time staff physicians). Most of these physicians hold faculty appointments at Harvard Medical School.

Along with helping students become doctors BIDMC provides clinical education to students in nursing social work radiologic technology ultrasound and nuclear medicine and physical occupational speech and respiratory therapies.

The Carl J. Shapiro Institute for Education and Research provides medical students and physicians in training with an onsite centralized educational facility.

Financial Performance

The hospital is very active in medical research and consistently ranks among the top four recipients of biomedical research funding from the National Institutes of Health totaling nearly $200 million annually. BIDMC researchers oversee more than 850 active sponsored projects and 500 clinical trials. The health system is also home to the Harvard-Thorndike Laboratory the nation's oldest clinical research laboratory.

Strategy

BIDMC affiliates with Milton Hospital to share resources and staff. Hospital systems that coordinate can take advantage of each others' resources stretching their dollars further under the global payment system. The medical center formed another affiliation with Brockton Hospital to improve specialist and medical training programs at the 360-bed Brockton Hospital facility.

Being on the forefront of medical education goes hand-in-hand with using cutting-edge technology and BIDMC does just that with its Carl J. Shapiro Simulation and Skills Center (SASC) administers training for learners at all levels and from all disciplines using progressive and simulation teaching methods to replicate real-life patient care situations from routine procedures to acute management crises. The SASC features a range of technologically advanced educational resources including realistic models simulators virtual reality experiences computer-based materials ultrasound technology and the world's largest collection of filmed operations

Mergers and Acquisitions

In early 2017 BIDMC agreed to merge with Lahey Health to become Massachusetts' second-largest health system (after Partners HealthCare). Other hospitals have agreed to join the combined system including Anna Jaques Hospital of Newburyport New England Baptist Hospital and Mount Auburn Hospital. The combined system will have 11 hospitals.

EXECUTIVES

SVP Information Systems and CIO, John D. Halamka, age 54
SVP Finance and CFO, Steven Fischer
President and CEO Beth Israel Deaconess Hospital Plymouth, Peter J. Holden
COO, Nancy Formella
President and CEO Affiliated Physicians Group, John Christoforo
Chairman Department of Medicine, Mark L. Zeidel
President CEO and Director, Kevin Tabb
Chief Nursing Officer and SVP Patient Care Services, Marsha Maurer
President and CEO Beth Israel Deaconess Hospital - Needham, John Fogarty
President, Peter Healy
SVP Communications and Marketing, Paul Donovan
Interim President and CEO Beth Israel Deaconess Care Organization, Jeff Hulburt
President and CEO Harvard Medical Faculty Physicians, Stuart Rosenberg
Deputy CIO/CTO, Manu Tandon
Vice President of Ambulatory Services and Emergency Services, Jayne Sheehan
Medical Director, Thomas Cataldo
Vice President Clinical Applications and Development, Larry Markson
Director of Health Information Management, Gerraldine Abrahamian
Vice Chair, Ronald P. (Ron) O'Hanley, age 60
Vice Chair, Margaret A. McKenna, age 72
Vice Chair, Edward H. (Ted) Ladd
Chairman, Daniel Jick
Advisory Board Member, HOPE RICCIOTTI

LOCATIONS

HQ: BETH ISRAEL DEACONESS MEDICAL CENTER, INC.
330 BROOKLINE AVE, BOSTON, MA 022155400
Phone: 617 667-7000
Web: WWW.BIDMC.ORG

PRODUCTS/OPERATIONS

Centers and Departments

Comprehensive Care Centers
Cancer Center
Cardiovascular Institute
Digestive Disease Center
Spine Center
Transplant Institute
Clinical Departments
Anesthesia Critical Care and Pain Medicine
Dermatology
Emergency Medicine
Medicine
Neonatology
Neurology
Obstetrics and Gynecology
Orthopaedic Surgery
Pathology
Psychiatry
Radiation Oncology
Radiology
Rehabilitation Services
Surgery
Other Departments
Community Initiatives
Facilities
Public Safety

Selected Facilities

item 1
Beth Israel Deaconess HealthCare-Chelsea
Beth Israel Deaconess HealthCare-Chestnut Hill
Beth Israel Deaconess HealthCare-Lexington
Beth Israel Deaconess Hospital-Milton
Beth Israel Deaconess Hospital-Needham
Beth Israel Deaconess Hospital-Plymouth

COMPETITORS

Boston Medical Center
Brigham and Women's Hospital
Cambridge Health Alliance
Care New England
CareGroup
Children's Hospital Boston
Dana-Farber
Massachusetts General Hospital
Newton-Wellesley Hospital
Northeast Health System
Partners HealthCare
Southcoast Hospitals Group
Spaulding Rehabilitation Hospital
Steward Health Care

HISTORICAL FINANCIALS

Company Type: Private

Income Statement

FYE: September 30

	REVENUE ($ mil.)	NET INCOME ($ mil.)	NET PROFIT MARGIN	EMPLOYEES
09/15	1,198	44	3.7%	6,500
09/14	1,113	37	3.4%	—
09/13	1,051	56	5.4%	—
09/12	1,081	49	4.6%	—
Annual Growth	3.5%	(3.6%)	—	—

2015 Year-End Financials

Return on assets: 16.5%   Cash ($ mil.): 159
Return on equity: 3.7%
Current ratio: 1.20

BETHEL SCHOOL DISTRICT

EXECUTIVES

Superintendent, Tom Seigel
Director, Marsha Hunt
Plant & Facilities Manager, Adam Lane

LOCATIONS

HQ: BETHEL SCHOOL DISTRICT
516 176TH ST E, SPANAWAY, WA 983878335
Phone: 253 683-6000
Web: WWW.BETHELSD.ORG

HISTORICAL FINANCIALS

Company Type: Private

Income Statement

FYE: August 31

	REVENUE ($ mil.)	NET INCOME ($ mil.)	NET PROFIT MARGIN	EMPLOYEES
08/16	246	9	3.9%	2,000
08/15	228	(2)	—	—
08/14	204	(29)	—	—
08/13	207	5	2.7%	—
Annual Growth	5.9%	19.2%	—	—

2016 Year-End Financials

Return on assets: 1.0%   Cash ($ mil.): 32
Return on equity: 3.9%
Current ratio: —

BETHESDA HOSPITAL, INC.

From modest beginnings as a informal cottage hospital Bethesda North Hospital has grown into the fourth largest medical center in Cincinnati Ohio. Bethesda North is a full-service acute care hospital with some 360 beds for adults and 60 for children. It provides comprehensive medical and surgical care including maternity and fertility services emergency care and diagnostic imaging. The hospital joined with fellow Cincinnati health care provider Good Samaritan Hospital in 1995 to form TriHealth. Together the two hospitals offer care at some 80 locations including primary care offices fitness centers and occupational health facilities.

Operations

The full-service 420-bed acute care hospital handles some 24000 inpatient admissions each year as well as 260000 outpatient visits 77000 emergency room visits and 4000 births. It employs 165 full-time doctors and dentists and provides more than $30 million in community outreach efforts (including charity care programs) each year.

Specialty units at Bethesda North Hospital include institutes for cancer heart surgical and digestive care as well as centers for outpatient imaging breast stroke obstetrics-gynecology orthopedics and emergency trauma care. As a regional teaching center the hospital offers residency programs in a number of specialties including family medicine internal medicine OB-GYN and surgery.

Geographic Reach

Bethesda North is located in northern Cincinnati Ohio and serves as a regional trauma center as well as a major teaching hospital in the area.

Strategy

Parent organization TriHealth has aligned skilled physicians specialists surgeons and its staff to create specialty institutes offering best-of-class medical assistance in fields including heart and cancer care. To further enhance its facilities in 2013 the organization renovated the labor and delivery wing at Bethesda North Hospital. Other recent projects include the addition of a seven-story patient tower and a new outpatient imaging center.

Additionally the company has invested in TriHealth Connect the electronic medical records system that will help access accurate patient information.

Company Background

In early 2012 TriHealth unveiled a new logo.

Bethesda North traces it roots to 1896 and a cottage occupied by seven German Methodist deaconesses ministering to the poor and sick.

EXECUTIVES

President, John Prout
Financial Executive, Michael Croftoon
Chief Operating Officer, Sher A Mc Clanahan
Director, Leah Gerdsen
Director, Linnea Lose
Director, Marcia Swehla
Auditors: BKD LLP CINCINNATI OH

LOCATIONS

HQ: BETHESDA HOSPITAL., INC.
619 OAK ST, CINCINNATI, OH 452061690
Phone: 513 569-6100
Web: WWW.TRIHEALTH.COM

PRODUCTS/OPERATIONS

List of Selected Services
Breast health
Cancer care
Digestive diseases
Heart and vascular care
Maternity (OB-GYN childbirth)
Orthopedics
Outpatient imaging
Pallative Care
Pharmacy
Robotic-assisted surgery
Stroke care
Trauma/Emergency services

COMPETITORS

Cincinnati Children's Hospital	Premier Health Partners
Deaconess Associations	St. Elizabeth Healthcare
Kettering Health Network	The Christ Hospital Corporation
Mercy Health (OH)	UC Health
Miami Valley Hospital	

HISTORICAL FINANCIALS

Company Type: Private

Income Statement

FYE: June 30

	REVENUE ($ mil.)	NET INCOME ($ mil.)	NET PROFIT MARGIN	EMPLOYEES
06/15	551	71	13.0%	3,000
06/14	552	76	13.8%	—
06/13	534	57	10.8%	—
06/10	501	40	8.2%	—
Annual Growth	1.9%	11.8%	—	—

BETHESDA HOSPITAL, INC.

EXECUTIVES

President, Roger L Kirk
Board of Directors, Marie Bedner
Vice-President, Kenneth Peltzie
Manager, Ralph Breslaw

LOCATIONS

HQ: BETHESDA HOSPITAL, INC.
2815 S SEACREST BLVD, BOYNTON BEACH, FL 334357995
Phone: 561 737-7733

HISTORICAL FINANCIALS

Company Type: Private

Income Statement

FYE: September 30

	REVENUE ($ mil.)	NET INCOME ($ mil.)	NET PROFIT MARGIN	EMPLOYEES
09/15	287	(24)	—	304
09/14	271	(0)	—	—
09/13	316	156	49.6%	—
09/12	256	5	2.3%	—
Annual Growth	3.9%	—	—	—

2015 Year-End Financials

Return on assets: 3.8% Cash ($ mil.): 3
Return on equity: (-8.5%)
Current ratio: 2.90

BEVERLY COMMUNITY HOSPITAL ASSOCIATION

EXECUTIVES

Chief Executive Officer, Gary Kiff
Board of Directors, David I Chambers
Board of Directors, Mohammad A
Director, June Belling-Sulliva

LOCATIONS

HQ: BEVERLY COMMUNITY HOSPITAL ASSOCIATION
309 W BEVERLY BLVD, MONTEBELLO, CA 906404308
Phone: 323 726-1222
Web: WWW.BEVERLY.ORG

HISTORICAL FINANCIALS

Company Type: Private

Income Statement

FYE: December 31

	REVENUE ($ mil.)	NET INCOME ($ mil.)	NET PROFIT MARGIN	EMPLOYEES
12/15	176	8	4.7%	995
12/13	166	(2)	—	—
12/08	108	(14)	—	—
12/05	0	0	—	—
Annual Growth	—	—	—	—

2015 Year-End Financials

Return on assets: 8.2% Cash ($ mil.): 42
Return on equity: 4.7%
Current ratio: 1.40

BI-RITE RESTAURANT SUPPLY CO., INC.

Bi-Rite Restaurant Supply which does business as BiRite Foodservice Distributors is a leading food service supplier serving the San Francisco Bay area and Northern California. The company distributes a full line of food equipment and supplies including meat and dairy items seafood frozen foods dry groceries cleaning supplies china kitchen equipment and disposables. Its customers include restaurant operators hotels universities and hospitals. The company's international arm supplied food to the Middle East and Asia. A member of the UniPro Foodservice cooperative the family-owned company was founded in 1966 by cousins Victor and John Barulich.

Geographic Reach

Brisbane-based Bi-Rite's coverage area ranges from Cloverdale in Northern California east to Reno (Nevada) and South to Fresno and Monterey. Beyond California the company supplies food and equipment to Afghanistan Jordan Kuwait Turkey China Japan South Korea Singapore Thailand Vietnam and several other territories.

Mergers and Acquisitions

In December 2012 the company acquired family-owned A&B Produce which supplies food to restaurants throughout the San Francisco Bay area.

EXECUTIVES

Vice President Sales and Marketing, Michael Pendergast
Executive Vice President of Purchasing, Tom Whiteside
Vice President of Operations, Nathan Barulich
Vice President Human Resources, Natasha Eltringham

LOCATIONS

HQ: BI-RITE RESTAURANT SUPPLY CO., INC.
123 S HILL DR, BRISBANE, CA 940051203
Phone: 415 656-0187
Web: WWW.BIRITE.COM

PRODUCTS/OPERATIONS

Selected Product Categories
Disposables
Equipment & supply
Food
Fresh cut produce
Fresh next-day protein
Fresh seafood
Janitorial

COMPETITORS

Dot Foods	McLane Foodservice
Golden State Foods	Sysco
Jacmar	US Foods
MAINES	

HISTORICAL FINANCIALS

Company Type: Private

Income Statement

FYE: December 31

	REVENUE ($ mil.)	NET INCOME ($ mil.)	NET PROFIT MARGIN	EMPLOYEES
12/15	321	8	2.7%	300
12/14	310	6	2.2%	—
12/13	279	6	2.5%	—
12/12	258	4	1.8%	—
Annual Growth	7.5%	22.7%	—	—

Return on assets: 2.3%   Cash ($ mil.): 6
Return on equity: 2.7%
Current ratio: 2.20

BIG 12 CONFERENCE INC

EXECUTIVES

Principal, Dan Beebe
Director, Sean Hollister
Administrative Assistant, Valerie Rocha
Auditors: CATON CONSULTING GROUP PC IRV

LOCATIONS

HQ: BIG 12 CONFERENCE INC
400 E JOHN CARPENTER FWY, IRVING, TX
750623955
Phone: 469 524-1000
Web: WWW.BIG12SPORTS.COM

HISTORICAL FINANCIALS

Company Type: Private

Income Statement   FYE: June 30

	REVENUE ($ mil.)	NET INCOME ($ mil.)	NET PROFIT MARGIN	EMPLOYEES
06/15	267	9	3.6%	2
06/14	227	1	0.8%	—
06/13	217	2	1.1%	—
06/12	159	9	5.6%	—
Annual Growth	18.8%	2.7%	—	—

2015 Year-End Financials

Return on assets: 0.5%   Cash ($ mil.): 26
Return on equity: 3.6%
Current ratio: 16.60

BIG RIVER RESOURCES GALVA, LLC

EXECUTIVES

Board of Directors, Andy Brader
Board of Directors, Les Allen
Board of Directors, Gene Youngquist
Project Manager, Windy Anderson
Director of Finance, Jim Hall
Board of Directors, Mike Rumbold
Auditors: CHRISTIANSON & ASSOCIATES PLL

LOCATIONS

HQ: BIG RIVER RESOURCES GALVA, LLC
1100 SE 2ND ST, GALVA, IL 614348907
Phone: 309 932-2033
Web: WWW.BIGRIVERRESOURCES.COM

HISTORICAL FINANCIALS

Company Type: Private

Income Statement   FYE: December 31

	REVENUE ($ mil.)	NET INCOME ($ mil.)	NET PROFIT MARGIN	EMPLOYEES
12/15	247	24	9.8%	238
12/14	334	59	17.8%	—
12/13	361	31	8.8%	—
12/12	310	(0)	—	—
Annual Growth	(7.3%)	—	—	—

2015 Year-End Financials

Return on assets: 0.6%   Cash ($ mil.): 8
Return on equity: 9.8%
Current ratio: 2.50

BIG RIVER RESOURCES WEST BURLINGTON, LLC

EXECUTIVES

President, Ray Defenbaugh
Board of Directors, Gene Youngquist
General Manager, Edgar Seward
Auditors: CHRISTIANSON & ASSOCIATES PLL

LOCATIONS

HQ: BIG RIVER RESOURCES WEST BURLINGTON, LLC
15210 103RD ST, WEST BURLINGTON, IA 526558697
Phone: 319 753-1100
Web: WWW.BIGRIVERRESOURCES.COM

HISTORICAL FINANCIALS

Company Type: Private

Income Statement   FYE: December 31

	REVENUE ($ mil.)	NET INCOME ($ mil.)	NET PROFIT MARGIN	EMPLOYEES
12/15	272	15	5.6%	238
12/14	346	60	17.5%	—
12/13	395	26	6.7%	—
12/12	381	0	0.1%	—
Annual Growth	(10.6%)	234.3%	—	—

2015 Year-End Financials

Return on assets: 8.0%   Cash ($ mil.): 24
Return on equity: 5.6%
Current ratio: 1.20

BIG RIVER RESOURCES, LLC.

EXECUTIVES

President, Raymond E Defenbaugh
Chief Financial Officer, Jim Hall
Treasurer, Les Allen
Vice-President, Andy Brader
VP Sales, Bonnie Barney
Vice-President, Christine Denisar
Plant Engineering Manager, Marc Awtrey

Director, Marlou Janssen
Director, Michael Gero
Auditors: CHRISTIANSON PLLP WILLMAR MI

LOCATIONS

HQ: BIG RIVER RESOURCES, LLC.
211 N GEAR AVE STE 200, WEST BURLINGTON, IA
526551027
Phone: 319 753-1100

HISTORICAL FINANCIALS

Company Type: Private

Income Statement   FYE: December 31

	REVENUE ($ mil.)	NET INCOME ($ mil.)	NET PROFIT MARGIN	EMPLOYEES
12/15	863	74	8.7%	250
12/14	1,184	224	18.9%	—
12/13	1,292	107	8.3%	—
12/12	1,135	2	0.2%	—
Annual Growth	(8.7%)	199.2%	—	—

2015 Year-End Financials

Return on assets: 3.5%   Cash ($ mil.): 54
Return on equity: 8.7%
Current ratio: 1.50

BIG RIVER UNITED ENERGY, LLC

EXECUTIVES

Chairman, Andy Brader
Vice-Chairman, David Cramer
Treasurer, Raymond Defenbaugh
Director of Finance, Jim Hall
Manager, Terry Manchester
Manager, Jade Doyle
Supervisor, Jason Lumbus
Accountant, Kay Kluesner
Auditors: CHRISTIANSON PLLP WILLMAR MI

LOCATIONS

HQ: BIG RIVER UNITED ENERGY, LLC
3294 VINE RD, DYERSVILLE, IA 520408714
Phone: 563 875-5500
Web: WWW.BIGRIVERUNITEDENERGY.COM

HISTORICAL FINANCIALS

Company Type: Private

Income Statement   FYE: December 31

	REVENUE ($ mil.)	NET INCOME ($ mil.)	NET PROFIT MARGIN	EMPLOYEES
12/15	246	27	11.2%	50
12/14	356	74	21.0%	—
12/13	378	34	9.2%	—
12/12	320	4	1.4%	—
Annual Growth	(8.3%)	82.1%	—	—

2015 Year-End Financials

Return on assets: 1.6%   Cash ($ mil.): 1
Return on equity: 11.2%
Current ratio: 0.80

BILLINGS CLINIC

Billings Clinic is an integrated health care system that serves the residents of Big Sky Country. Through a group of more than 320 doctors and other providers the clinic caters to some 570000 people in Billings Montana and in surrounding communities. It offers 50-plus specialties such as emergency and trauma cancer orthopedics birthing cardiovascular neurosciences dialysis and pediatrics. Its operations include a more than 285-bed hospital and the organization's main clinic. Additionally Billings Clinic operates the 90-bed Aspen Meadows Retirement Community and provides support services to several regional community hospitals. The not-for-profit health care system is owned by the community.

Operations

With its vast service area the health care system provides a MedFlight advanced life support fixed-wing aircraft service that transports critically ill or injured patients from rural communities. The service averages 700 flights per year.

As part of its operations Billings Clinic runs a Level II emergency and trauma center 14-suite family birthing center Level III neonatal intensive care unit inpatient cancer care unit and a 15-bed transitional care unit. The health care system's cancer center provides both inpatient and outpatient care in Billings and the surrounding four-state region.

Billings Clinic is governed by a 12-member board consisting of mostly community members but also a pair of doctors and a physician CEO.

In 2014 Billings Clinic's Community Benefit totaled $37.6 million including $14.8 million in financial assistance (charity care) provided to 5744 patients.

Geographic Reach

As the largest health care organization in the area Billings Clinic's service area comprises 40 counties and extends more than 120000 miles in Montana Wyoming and the western Dakotas.

Strategy

Billings Clinic works with pharmaceutical sponsors on a variety of clinical research trials in various phases and indications. To this end it operates a research center with more than 20 years of experience in the areas of basic and clinical research. The center has participated in more than 200 clinical research studies with the help of some 5000 volunteer subjects since 1988.

The health care system has been growing. In 2014 it completed construction of a 24-bed Intensive Care Unit located on the second floor of the hospital directly above the Emergency and Trauma Center. That year Billings Clinic also opened a second ExpressCare retail clinic in the Albertsons store and opened two new major cardiac facilities.

In 2014 Billings Clinic began offering anew noninvasive surgery for the brain using Gamma Knife Perfexion an advanced technology for stereotactic radiosurgery.

Company Background

It expanded its capacity for infusions in 2012 when its Billings Clinic Cody location opened an infusion center. In late 2012 the organization also opened a new Stillwater Billings Clinic medical facility which combines Stillwater Community Hospital and Billings Clinic Columbus and integrates the billing process for the two health care facilities.

The Billings Clinic evolved from the general practice of Dr. Arthur J. Movius who founded his Billings practice in 1911.

EXECUTIVES

VP and CIO, Chris Stevens
Physician in Chief, Mark C. Rumans
President Billings Clinic Foundation, Jim Duncan
VP Hospital Operations, Lu Byrd
CFO, Connie F. Prewitt
CEO, Randall Gibb
Director of Patient Relations, Karrie Cleveland
Vice President and Regional Chief Financial Officer, Kyle Gee
Director of Medical Records, Lorraine Jelle
Treasurer and Director, J. Scott Millikan
Vice Chairman, David Brown

LOCATIONS

HQ: BILLINGS CLINIC
2800 10TH AVE N, BILLINGS, MT 591010703
Phone: 406 657-4000
Web: WWW.BILLINGSCLINIC.COM

PRODUCTS/OPERATIONS

Selected Services
Advance Medical Directives
Allergy Asthma Immunology
Aspen Meadows - Skilled Nursing and Assisted Living
Anticoagulation Clinic
Breast Center
Cancer Center
Cardiovascular Services
Cardiovascular Surgery
Children's Services
Continence Center
Community Training Center
Cosmetic Surgery
da Vinci Surgical System
Dermatology Center
Diabetes Management Center
Diagnostic Imaging
Diabetes
Dialysis Center
Eldercare Solutions
Emergency & Trauma Center
Emmi Educational Videos
Employer Services - Occupational Health
Endocrinology
Eye Center
Facial Plastic Surgery
Family Medicine
Family Birth Center
Gastroenterology
General Surgery
Genetic Counseling
Geriatric Assessment Program
Gynecologic Cancer
Heart Services
Heart Surgery
Home Oxygen & Medical Equipment
Hospitalist Program
Infectious Diseases
Insurance Finder
Internal Medicine
Laboratory Services
LifeFit
Maternal-Fetal Medicine
MedFlight Air Ambulance
Mental Health Services
Metabolism Center
Mohs Surgery
Nutrition Services
Neurosciences
Obstetrics & Gynecology
Occupational Health - Employer Services
Ophthalmology
Orthopedics & Sports Medicine
Palliative Care
Pediatrics
  Pediatric Center
  Pediatric Cancer
  Pediatric Diabetes
  Pediatric Gastroenterology
  Pediatric Pulmonology
  Rehabilitation (Therapy)
Pharmacy
Physical Medicine & Rehabilitation
Plastic Surgery
Primary Care for Adults

Pulmonary Rehabilitation Program
Radiology Services
Reproductive Medicine and Fertility Care
Robotic Surgery
SameDay Care
Senior Services
Sleep Disorders Center
Sports Medicine
Sports Specific Camps
Stroke Care
Surgery Center
Transitional Care Unit
Urology Services
Vascular Surgery
Vein Clinic
Women's Free Screenings
Women's and Children's Services

Selected Affiliate Hospitals and Clinics
Beartooth Billings Clinic - Red Lodge
Colstrip Medical Center - Colstrip
Daniels Memorial Healthcare - Scobey
Livingston HealthCare - Livingston
North Big Horn Hospital - Lovell
Pioneer Medical Center - Big Timber
Roundup Memorial Healthcare - Roundup
Sheridan Memorial Hospital Association
Stillwater Billings Clinic

COMPETITORS

Glendive Medical Center	St. James Healthcare
St. Alexius Medical Center	St. Patrick Hospital
	Wyoming Medical Center

HISTORICAL FINANCIALS

Company Type: Private

Income Statement   FYE: June 30

	REVENUE ($ mil.)	NET INCOME ($ mil.)	NET PROFIT MARGIN	EMPLOYEES
06/15	565	30	5.4%	3,300
06/14	593	38	6.6%	—
06/13	560	14	2.6%	—
06/11	533	28	5.4%	—
Annual Growth	1.5%	1.5%	—	—

2015 Year-End Financials

Return on assets: 4.7%   Cash ($ mil.): 14
Return on equity: 5.4%
Current ratio: 1.50

BIOMEDICAL RESEARCH FOUNDATION OF NORTHWEST LOUISIANA

EXECUTIVES

Chairman of the Board, Stephen F Skrivanos
Board of Directors, Johnette Magner
Administration Manager, Khris Engel
Director, Joseph Sarpy Jr
Director, John F Sharp
Director, Virginia K Shehee
Director, Elaine Joyce Simpkins PHD
Auditors: POSTLETHWAITE & NETTERVILLE B

LOCATIONS

HQ: BIOMEDICAL RESEARCH FOUNDATION OF NORTHWEST LOUISIANA
2031 KINGS HWY, SHREVEPORT, LA 711033600
Phone: 318 716-4100
Web: WWW.BIOMED.ORG

HISTORICAL FINANCIALS

Company Type: Private

Income Statement

FYE: September 30

	REVENUE ($ mil.)	NET INCOME ($ mil.)	NET PROFIT MARGIN	EMPLOYEES
09/15	564	14	2.6%	50
09/14	502	(1)	—	—
09/13*	10	(5)	—	—
12/09	15	0	2.1%	—
Annual Growth	81.9%	88.0%	—	—

*Fiscal year change

2015 Year-End Financials

Return on assets: 18.6%   Cash ($ mil.): 8
Return on equity: 2.6%
Current ratio: 1.00

BIRDVILLE INDEPENDENT SCHOOL DISTRICT

EXECUTIVES

Superintendent, Darrell G Brown
Director, Mike Fritz
Vice-President, Dolores Webb
Auditors: LYNN A SUDBURY CPA PLLC NORTH

LOCATIONS

HQ: BIRDVILLE INDEPENDENT SCHOOL DISTRICT
6125 E BELKNAP ST, HALTOM CITY, TX 761174204
Phone: 817 547-5700
Web: WWW.BIRDVILLESCHOOLS.NET

HISTORICAL FINANCIALS

Company Type: Private

Income Statement

FYE: June 30

	REVENUE ($ mil.)	NET INCOME ($ mil.)	NET PROFIT MARGIN	EMPLOYEES
06/16	261	(50)	—	3,109
06/07	181	95	52.6%	—
/*	0	0	—	—
Annual Growth	—	—	—	—

*Fiscal year change

2016 Year-End Financials

Return on assets: 4.0%   Cash ($ mil.): 111
Return on equity: (-19.1%)
Current ratio: 2.70

BIRKEY'S FARM STORE, INC.

EXECUTIVES

President, Michael Hedge
Board of Directors, Mark Foster
Manager, Jeff Pforr
Personnel Manager, Patti Lyons

Store Manager, Nathan Gannaway
Auditors: CLIFTON LARSON ALLEN LLP CHA

LOCATIONS

HQ: BIRKEY'S FARM STORE, INC.
2102 W PARK CT, CHAMPAIGN, IL 618212986
Phone: 217 693-7200
Web: WWW.BIRKEYS.COM

HISTORICAL FINANCIALS

Company Type: Private

Income Statement

FYE: December 31

	REVENUE ($ mil.)	NET INCOME ($ mil.)	NET PROFIT MARGIN	EMPLOYEES
12/15	230	(5)	—	400
12/14	315	5	1.7%	—
12/13	394	16	4.1%	—
12/12	355	15	4.3%	—
Annual Growth	(13.4%)	—	—	—

2015 Year-End Financials

Return on assets: 1.5%   Cash ($ mil.): —
Return on equity: (-2.2%)
Current ratio: 0.20

BLANCHARD VALLEY REGIONAL HEALTH CENTER

EXECUTIVES

Board of Directors, William D Watkins
Manager, Marcia Bello

LOCATIONS

HQ: BLANCHARD VALLEY REGIONAL HEALTH CENTER
1900 S MAIN ST, FINDLAY, OH 458401214
Phone: 419 423-4500

HISTORICAL FINANCIALS

Company Type: Private

Income Statement

FYE: December 31

	REVENUE ($ mil.)	NET INCOME ($ mil.)	NET PROFIT MARGIN	EMPLOYEES
12/15	222	48	22.0%	1,000
12/06	190	19	10.2%	—
12/05	164	18	10.9%	—
12/04	749	0	0.0%	—
Annual Growth	(10.5%)	180.7%	—	—

2015 Year-End Financials

Return on assets: 10.1%   Cash ($ mil.): 14
Return on equity: 22.0%
Current ratio: 0.60

BLESSING HOSPITAL

Blessing Hospital is a not-for-profit acute care medical center that provides a wide range of health services to residents in areas of western Illinois northeast Missouri and southeast Iowa. Through its main campus location it provides primary and emergency care as well as specialty services including diagnostics and surgery. The hospital is home to centers of excellence in the treatment of cancer heart and cardiovascular ailments wound care and women's health issues. Blessing Hospital provides outpatient and behavioral health services at a nearby campus. It also operates family practice centers and provides home and hospice care services. It is part of the Blessing Health System.

Operations

Blessing Health System includes two hospitals a physician group medical specialty operations a foundation and a four-year nursing education program.

Blessing Hospital boasts a medical staff of more than 240 physicians with an additional 2000 health care personnel. Its operations consist of a behavioral center body motion center breast center cancer center heart and vascular center sleep center and wound center as well as family practice centers.

The hospital typically sees more than 13400 inpatients and 245000 outpatients each year.

Geographic Reach

Blessing Hospital serves those who reside in western Illinois southeast Iowa and northeast Missouri.

Strategy

Blessing Hospital is working to boost its range of tertiary (acute specialty care) services to keep residents in the area from heading to larger towns more than 150 miles away. To this end it has built up its cardiac services and brought in a robotic surgical system.

EXECUTIVES

Occupational Therapy Director, Karen Kerns
Vice President Human Resources, Joellen Randall
Occupational Medicine, Liane Fink
Director Icu Coronary Care Unit, Debbie Mcginnis
Corporate Vice President and Chief Information Officer, Nicole Ginsberg
Radiology Director, Sharon Dieker
Nursing Director, Tim Tranor
Auditors: GRAY HUNTER STENN LLP QUINCY

LOCATIONS

HQ: BLESSING HOSPITAL
BROADWAY AT 11TH ST, QUINCY, IL 62301
Phone: 217 223-1200
Web: WWW.BLESSINGHOSPITAL.ORG

PRODUCTS/OPERATIONS

Selected Services

Bariatric Services
Behavioral Center
Blessing FastCare Clinic
Body Motion Center
Breast Center
Cancer Center
Emergency Center
Heart & Vascular Center
Home Care
Hospice & Palliative Care
Hospital Medicine Program
Maternity Care
Nutrition Services
Orthopedic Surgical Services
Pain Management Service
Radiology
Rehabilitation Services
Renal Dialysis Services
Sleep Center
Surgical Services
Wound Center

COMPETITORS

Advocate BroMenn	Memorial Health System
Hospital Sisters	St. John's Hospital
Health System	(Illinois)

HISTORICAL FINANCIALS

Company Type: Private

Income Statement
FYE: September 30

	REVENUE ($ mil.)	NET INCOME ($ mil.)	NET PROFIT MARGIN	EMPLOYEES
09/15	316	15	4.8%	2,500
09/12	289	14	5.1%	—
09/08	238	(2)	—	—
09/07	423	0	0.0%	—
Annual Growth	(3.6%)	270.8%	—	—

2015 Year-End Financials

Return on assets: 5.5% Cash ($ mil.): 91
Return on equity: 4.8%
Current ratio: 2.60

BLOODWORKS

Residents of the Emerald City can go here to give red. Bloodworks Northwest (formerly Puget Sound Blood Center) is a not-for-profit blood and tissue bank serving nearly 90 hospitals and clinics in the Pacific Northwest. The blood center collects and processes donated blood through about a dozen donation centers and several mobile units; it also registers bone marrow donors provides testing and training services to patients with hemophilia and collects cord blood for use in stem cell transplantation. Bloodworks Northwest Research Institute conducts research on improving transfusion and transplantation medicine. The organization was formed in 1944.

Operations

Bloodworks Northwest funds its activities including its research efforts by charging services fees to clients as well as through research grants research partnerships and philanthropic donations. It also sells blood derivatives and related products (such as plasma).

Research programs focus on improving transfusion and transplantation medicine for patients with ailments including leukemia cancer serious injuries and burns.

Geographic Reach

Bloodworks Northwest serves health care facilities in several counties in western Washington and Oregon plus the nearby San Juan Islands. The company also has cord blood bank partnerships with hospitals across Washington and in Oregon and Hawaii.

Strategy

With a staff of nearly 70 scientists across 11 laboratories Bloodworks Northwest continues to seek new therapies and cures. Growth in its service territory and customer base as well as the increasingly complex blood testing needs of its clients has led the organization to expand its facilities in recent years. In early 2014 it opened the expanded Bakerview Square facility in Bellingham Washington.

EXECUTIVES

Executive Vice President Blood Services, Sandy Linauts
Medical Director platelet Immunology Laboratory, Terry Gernsheimer
Senior Vice President Commerical Banking Middle Market Leade., James Gore
Vice President of Engineering, Jhune Rosario
Executive Vice President and Chief Information Offic, Dave Fennell
Medical Director Therapeutic Phlebotomy Program, Rebecca Haley

ASSOCIATE MEDICAL DIRECTOR, Nabiha H Saifee
Secretary, Maxine Sellers
Auditors: HIP MOSS ADAMS LLP SEATTLE

LOCATIONS

HQ: BLOODWORKS
921 TERRY AVE, SEATTLE, WA 981041239
Phone: 206 292-6500
Web: WWW.PSBC.ORG

Selected Washington Service Counties
Clallam
Clark
Cowlitz
Grays Harbor
Jefferson
King
Kitsap
Lewis
Mason
Pierce
San Juan Islands
Skagit
Snohomish
Thurston
Whatcom

PRODUCTS/OPERATIONS

Selected Services
Blood Services
Clinical Services
Clinical Trial Support
Cord Blood Program
Research Institute
Specialty Diagnostics Laboratories
  Genomics Testing Laboratory
  Hemostasis Reference Laboratory
  Immunogenetics/HLA Laboratory
  Platelet Immunology Laboratory
Transfusion Medicine
  Compatibility Testing Laboratory
  Donor Testing/Virology Laboratory
  Red Cell Reference Laboratory

COMPETITORS

Blood Systems Inc.	HemaCare
CSL Plasma	Red Cross
Daxor	SeraCare Life Sciences
Haemonetics	

HISTORICAL FINANCIALS

Company Type: Private

Income Statement
FYE: June 30

	REVENUE ($ mil.)	NET INCOME ($ mil.)	NET PROFIT MARGIN	EMPLOYEES
06/15	175	9	5.4%	750
06/14	162	1	0.9%	—
06/13	152	(2)	—	—
06/12	150	(1)	—	—
Annual Growth	5.4%	—	—	—

2015 Year-End Financials

Return on assets: 13.6% Cash ($ mil.): 3
Return on equity: 5.4%
Current ratio: 0.60

BLOUNT INTERNATIONAL, INC.

Folks at Blount International have their work cut out for them. The manufacturer produces cutting chain guide bars sprockets and accessories for chainsaws concrete-cutting equipment and lawnmower blades. Blount's lineup is sold under brands Oregon Carlton Tiger and Windsor to outdoor equipment OEMs including Husqvarna and the replacement and retail markets. Other subsidiaries supply log splitters post-hole diggers and other agriculture add-ons. End users are professionals and consumers engaged in forestry lawn and garden farming and construction activities. The company's manufacturing facilities dot Brazil Canada China and the US. About two-thirds of Blount's sales are made outside the US. In early 2016 it was acquired by private-equity firms American Securities and P2 Capital Partners.

Operations

Blount sells its products across two segments: forestry lawn and garden (FLAG) and farm ranch and agriculture (FRAG). The former segment represents about 70% of its total sales each year while the latter accounts for the remainder.

The company also operates a concrete cutting and finishing (CCF) equipment business that is reported within the "corporate and other" category. This business manufactures and markets diamond-cutting chains assembles and markets concrete cutting chain saws and purchases other concrete cutting products that are marketed to the construction and utility industries.

Sales and Marketing

The company sells its products through a global sales and distribution network of over 300 distributors 30000 dealers direct sales companies and mass merchants which sell to the global forestry lawn and garden; farm ranch and agriculture; and construction products end markets. The company also sells through nearly 100 original equipment manufacturers.

Financial Performance

After posting a decline in 2013 Blount saw its revenues rebound for 2014 increasing 5% to peak at a record-setting $945 million. Profits also skyrocketed over 650% from $5 million in 2013 to $37 million in 2014. Its operating cash flow has fluctuated over the years rising sharply in 2013 but declining by 15% during 2014.

The historic growth for 2014 was driven by a 5% increase from its FLAG segment due to a rise in demand across most geographic regions especially South America (increased by 8%) and North America (7%). Its FRAG operations experienced a 3% increase in 2014 due to higher unit sales volumes (led by increased sales of log splitters and tractor attachments) and higher average selling prices across North America.

Blount's surge in profits for 2014 was attributed to the improved revenue coupled with lower expenses related to the impairment of acquired intangible assets along with charges related to restructuring activities.

Strategy

Blount has also fueled its momentum by strategically expanding its product portfolio and customer base through acquisitions. In 2014 the company acquired Arizona-based Pentruder. As part of the transaction the company became the exclusive distributor of Pentruder high-performance concrete cutting systems in North and South America. Pentruder now operates under Blount's concrete cutting and finishing (CCF) equipment business.

EXECUTIVES

SVP and CFO, Calvin E. Jenness, age 61, $385,000 total compensation
CEO and Chairman, Joshua L. (Josh) Collins, age 52, $565,000 total compensation
President FRAG Division, Gerald D. (Jerry) Johnson, $350,000 total compensation
President Gear Products Inc., William C. Alford

President and COO, David A. Willmott, age 47, $500,000 total compensation
SVP Global Supply Chain, David K. Parrish
VP and CIO, Kevin M. Trepa
SVP Global Sales and Marketing FLAG Division, Dave P. Gillrie
Auditors: KPMG LLP PORTLAND OREGON

LOCATIONS

HQ: BLOUNT INTERNATIONAL, INC.
4909 SE INTERNATIONAL WAY, PORTLAND, OR 972224679
Phone: 503 653-8881
Web: WWW.BLOUNT.COM

PRODUCTS/OPERATIONS

Selected Products
Chain drive sprockets
Chainsaw guide bars
Concrete-cutting chainsaws and circular saws (gasoline and hydraulic powered)
Cutting chain (for chainsaws)
Diamond-segmented chain (for cutting concrete)
Farm accessories
Lawn and garden cutting attachments
Lawnmower and edger cutting blades
Log splitters
Maintenance tools (for chainsaws and mechanical timber harvesting equipment)
Tractor driven post-hole diggers
Tractor three-point linkage parts

COMPETITORS

Alamo Group	Great Plains
Ariens	Manufacturing
Briggs & Stratton	Husqvarna
Caterpillar	Kubota
Champion Cutting Tool	MTD Products
Deere	Metso
Dover Corp.	STIHL Incorporated
Emak Group	Terex

HISTORICAL FINANCIALS
Company Type: Private

Income Statement FYE: December 31

	REVENUE ($ mil.)	NET INCOME ($ mil.)	NET PROFIT MARGIN	EMPLOYEES
12/15	828	(49)	—	4,000
12/14	944	36	3.9%	—
12/13	900	4	0.5%	—
12/12	927	39	4.3%	—
Annual Growth	(3.7%)	—	—	—

2015 Year-End Financials
Return on assets: 5.2%   Cash ($ mil.): 25
Return on equity: (-6.0%)
Current ratio: 1.00

BLOUNT MEMORIAL HOSPITAL, INCORPORATED

Blount Memorial Hospital provides health care services in eastern Tennessee. Founded in 1947 the hospital offers area communities cardiopulmonary care cancer care radiology women's health and laboratory services. As part of its operations Blount Memorial boasts satellite clinics devoted to family care diagnostic imaging occupational health services and outpatient rehabilitation. The hospital serves seniors through its focus on specialty services including senior care home health care hospice home life assistance occupational health and wellness care.

Operations
Blount Memorial is a 314-bed hospital that employs some 165 physicians and features a level III trauma center. It also operates an 80-bed subacute facility. The network operates over a dozen outpatient care centers. Its East Tennessee Medical Group provides primary care and 10 specialty services and includes 40 physicians operating at regional practice locations. The system handles some 500000 patient visits each year.

Geographic Reach
Blount Memorial serves Blount Monroe and Loudon counties. Its main hospital campus is located in Maryville Tennessee in Blount County.

Strategy
The organization is focused on expanding services for Medicaid patients in response to the program's expansion in Tennessee in 2013. In addition Blount Memorial is working to offset costs related to Medicare reimbursement cuts in recent years.

EXECUTIVES

Director of Clinical Services, Lora Irwin
Medical Records Director, Vicki Odum
Vice President Board of Directors, Ted Flickinger

LOCATIONS

HQ: BLOUNT MEMORIAL HOSPITAL, INCORPORATED
907 LAMAR ALEXANDER PKWY, MARYVILLE, TN 378045015
Phone: 865 983-7211
Web: WWW.BLOUNTMEMORIAL.ORG

PRODUCTS/OPERATIONS

Selected Services
Behavioral Health
Blount Heart Consultants
Business Health
Cancer Care
Cardiac Care
Diabetes Management
East Tennessee Internal Medicine
Family Care Centers
Home Services
Home Equipment Services
Imaging
Laboratory Services
Orthopedics
Palliative Care and Hospice
Pharmacy
Primary Care
Rehabilitation Services and Centers
Senior Services
Sleep Health
Smoky Mountain Gastroenterology
Stroke
Surgery
Wellness
Weight Management
Women's Services

COMPETITORS

Brookdale Senior Living	Saint Thomas Midtown Hospital
Covenant Health	Saint Thomas
East Tennessee Children's Hospital	Rutherford Hospital
Kindred Healthcare	Tennova Healthcare
LifePoint Health	University Health System Inc.
Parkridge Medical Center	Vanderbilt University Medical Center

HISTORICAL FINANCIALS
Company Type: Private

Income Statement FYE: June 30

	REVENUE ($ mil.)	NET INCOME ($ mil.)	NET PROFIT MARGIN	EMPLOYEES
06/15	218	0	0.0%	2,060
06/06	0	0	93.6%	—
06/05	0	(0)	—	—
06/03	131	14	10.8%	—
Annual Growth	4.3%	(47.7%)	—	—

2015 Year-End Financials
Return on assets: 2.0%   Cash ($ mil.): 4
Return on equity: —
Current ratio: 1.20

BLUEBONNET ELECTRIC COOPERATIVE, INC.

Bluebonnet Electric Cooperative's mission has echoes of the late Lady Bird Johnson's quest to spread bluebonnets and other wildflower seeds along Texas' highways. In this case the cooperative spreads power to homes and businesses in rural central and southeast Texas. One of the largest power distribution cooperatives in the state Bluebonnet Electric serves more than 81000 customers in 14 counties (a service area of more than 3800 square miles). The member-owned company which was formed in 1939 operates approximately 11000 miles of transmission and distribution lines and 19 substations. It purchases its wholesale power supply at 21 Lower Colorado River Authority-owned substations.

A long Texas drought caused a dust buildup on several of the co-op's insulators prompting a number of pole-top fires in late 2008 and early 2009. The utility is retrofitting the insulators to avoid a recurrence of the problem and ensure uninterrupted service.

Higher-than-normal summer heat drove up power demand in 2010. This resulted in Bluebonnet Electric reporting higher revenues and an improved net profit.

The heat and drought continued in 2011 and helped fuel a major wildfire in Bastrop over the Labor Day weekend. Bluebonnet Electric was subsequently confronted with a lawsuit which blamed it for the wildfire that destroyed almost 1600 homes (high winds brought down tree limbs on the coop's power lines sparking the blaze). The coop's executives ponted out that the trees which triggered the fire were on private property outside of the utility's easement and that Bluebonnet Electric could not be reasonably blamed for the conflagration.

In late 2011 the company lowered its electric rates to reflect lower natural gas commodity prices (natural gas accounts for 90% of the fuel Bluebonnet Electric uses to generate power).

In 1964 in order to avoid confusion with the Lower Colorado River Authority the utility originally known as the Lower Colorado River Electric Cooperative changed its name to Bluebonnet Electric Cooperative.

EXECUTIVES

Secretary Treasurer and Director, James Kershaw
Auditors: BOLINGER SEGARS GILBERT & MO

LOCATIONS

HQ: BLUEBONNET ELECTRIC COOPERATIVE, INC.
155 ELECTRIC AVE, BASTROP, TX 78602
Phone: 800 842-7708
Web: WWW.BLUEBONNETELECTRIC.COOP

HISTORICAL FINANCIALS

Company Type: Private

Income Statement

	REVENUE ($ mil.)	NET INCOME ($ mil.)	NET PROFIT MARGIN	EMPLOYEES
				FYE: December 31
12/15	207	7	3.6%	265
12/14	223	9	4.0%	—
12/13	201	6	3.3%	—
12/12	188	5	2.9%	—
Annual Growth	3.2%	10.9%	—	—

2015 Year-End Financials

Return on assets: 3.3%   Cash ($ mil.): 11
Return on equity: 3.6%
Current ratio: 0.60

BOARD OF EDUCATION FOR THE CITY OF SAVANNAH AND THE COUNTY OF CHATHAM (INC)

EXECUTIVES

President, Jolene Byrne
Financial Executive, Beth Stanford
Auditors: KRT CPAS PC SAVANNAH GEORG

LOCATIONS

HQ: BOARD OF EDUCATION FOR THE CITY OF
SAVANNAH AND THE COUNTY OF CHATHAM (INC)
208 BULL ST, SAVANNAH, GA 314013997
Phone: 912 395-1000
Web: WWW.SAVANNAH.COM

HISTORICAL FINANCIALS

Company Type: Private

Income Statement

	REVENUE ($ mil.)	NET INCOME ($ mil.)	NET PROFIT MARGIN	EMPLOYEES
				FYE: June 30
06/16	493	21	4.3%	4,781
06/15	478	(11)	—	—
06/14	447	36	8.1%	—
06/13	415	4	1.1%	—
Annual Growth	5.9%	67.3%	—	—

BOARD OF EDUCATION OF CARROLL COUNTY

EXECUTIVES

President, James L Doolan
Purchasing Agent, Nancy Codner
Consultant, Sean Hembree
Auditors: CLIFTONLARSONALLEN LLP BALTIM

LOCATIONS

HQ: BOARD OF EDUCATION OF CARROLL COUNTY
125 N COURT ST, WESTMINSTER, MD 211575192
Phone: 410 751-3000
Web: WWW.CARROLLK12.ORG

HISTORICAL FINANCIALS

Company Type: Private

Income Statement

	REVENUE ($ mil.)	NET INCOME ($ mil.)	NET PROFIT MARGIN	EMPLOYEES
				FYE: June 30
06/15	358	(6)	—	121
06/14	361	(5)	—	—
06/13	372	0	0.3%	—
06/12	375	10	2.7%	—
Annual Growth	(1.6%)			

2015 Year-End Financials

Return on assets: 1.4%   Cash ($ mil.): 10
Return on equity: (-1.8%)
Current ratio: 0.30

BOARD OF REGENTS OF THE UNIVERSITY OF NEBRASKA

The University of Nebraska has sprouted four campuses out in the fields of the Cornhusker State. Founded in 1869 the university confers bachelor's master's and doctoral degrees in more than 170 majors including agriculture business education and engineering at its campuses in Kearney Lincoln and Omaha. The university's Medical Center in Omaha trains doctors performs research and is affiliated with a roughly 700-bed teaching hospital. The school also operates research and extension services across the state. Nearly 50000 students attend classes in the system that has a student-teacher ratio of about 16:1. It was founded as a land-grant university just two years after the Nebraska became a state.

EXECUTIVES

SVP Business and Finance, David E. Lechner
Chancellor University of Nebraska Lincoln, Harvey S. Perlman
Chancellor University of Nebraska Kearney, Douglas A. (Doug) Kristensen
Chancellor University of Nebraska Omaha, John Christensen
EVP and Provost, Susan M. Fritz
Interim President, James Linder
Chancellor University of Nebraska Medical Center, Jeffrey P. Gold
CIO, Walter Weir

President, Hank M. Bounds
Vice President For Agriculture And Natural Resources, John C Owens
Vice President, Elbert Dickey
Vice President Marketing Strategic Affairs, Jackie Ostrowicki
Associate Vice President Distance Education and Director Online Worldwide, Mary Niemiec
Vice President Of Agriculture And Natural Resources, Ronnie D Green
Chairman, Howard L. Hawks
Vice Chairman, Bob Phares
Auditors: NEBRASKA AUDITOR OF PUBLIC ACC

LOCATIONS

HQ: BOARD OF REGENTS OF THE UNIVERSITY OF
NEBRASKA
3835 HOLDREGE ST, LINCOLN, NE 685031435
Phone: 402 472-3906
Web: WWW.NEBRASKA.EDU

PRODUCTS/OPERATIONS

University Campuses
The University of Nebraska at Kearney
The University of Nebraska-Lincoln
The University of Nebraska Medical Center
The University of Nebraska at Omaha

HISTORICAL FINANCIALS

Company Type: Private

Income Statement

	REVENUE ($ mil.)	NET INCOME ($ mil.)	NET PROFIT MARGIN	EMPLOYEES
				FYE: June 30
06/15	1,405	221	15.8%	15,200
06/14	1,333	222	16.7%	—
06/13	1,313	254	19.4%	—
06/12	1,251	143	11.5%	—
Annual Growth	3.9%	15.5%		

2015 Year-End Financials

Return on assets: 10.5%   Cash ($ mil.): 601
Return on equity: 15.8%
Current ratio: 1.90

BOARD OF TRUSTEES OF STATE INSTITUTIONS OF HIGHER LEARNING

EXECUTIVES

Commissioner, Hank Bounds
Director, John Pearce
Director, Wayne Carlisle
Director, Casey Turnage
Director, Ronjanett Taylor
General Manager, Holly Johnson
Director, Karana Carroll
Administrative Assistant, Renotta Jones

LOCATIONS

HQ: BOARD OF TRUSTEES OF STATE INSTITUTIONS
OF HIGHER LEARNING
3825 RIDGEWOOD RD, JACKSON, MS 392116453
Phone: 601 432-6198
Web: WWW.MISSISSIPPI.EDU

HISTORICAL FINANCIALS

Company Type: Private

Income Statement
FYE: June 30

	REVENUE ($ mil.)	NET INCOME ($ mil.)	NET PROFIT MARGIN	EMPLOYEES
06/15	2,383	257	10.8%	65
06/06	1,576	137	8.7%	—
06/01	1,843	331	18.0%	—
Annual Growth	1.9%	(1.8%)	—	—

2015 Year-End Financials

Return on assets: 8.7%
Return on equity: 10.8%
Current ratio: 1.90
Cash ($ mil.): 446

BOARD OF WATER SUPPLY

EXECUTIVES

Manager, Wayne Hoshiro
Manager, Donna Kiyosaki
Treasurer, Daniel Bender
Manager, Jennifer Elflein
Auditors: N&K CPAS INC HONOLULU HAWA

LOCATIONS

HQ: BOARD OF WATER SUPPLY
630 S BERETANIA ST, HONOLULU, HI 968430001
Phone: 808 748-5100
Web: WWW.BOARDOFWATERSUPPLY.COM

HISTORICAL FINANCIALS

Company Type: Private

Income Statement
FYE: June 30

	REVENUE ($ mil.)	NET INCOME ($ mil.)	NET PROFIT MARGIN	EMPLOYEES
06/16	238	72	30.5%	589
06/15	216	42	19.5%	—
06/14	194	20	10.5%	—
06/13	180	19	11.0%	—
Annual Growth	9.8%	54.2%	—	—

2016 Year-End Financials

Return on assets: 4.8%
Return on equity: 30.5%
Current ratio: 1.00
Cash ($ mil.): 23

BOARDRIDERS, INC.

Boardriders rides the wave of youth appeal. Formerly Quiksilver the company caters to the young and athletic with surfwear snowboardwear sportswear and swimwear sold under the Quiksilver and Roxy names. It also owns the DC Shoes brand of footwear and apparel for young men and juniors. It sells its apparel footwear and accessories in specialty and department stores worldwide including Zumiez Nordstrom Dick's Sporting Goods El Corte Ingles Galeries Lafayette and Macy's. The retailer boasts about 940 owned and licensed stores. In 2016 it emerged from Chapter 11 bankruptcy protection and is now owned by Oaktree Capital Management.

Operations

Boardriders distributes its surf-inspired apparel primarily to surf shops skate shops other specialty stores and select department stores. It also owns and licenses about 940 retail stores under its three core brands: Quiksilver Roxy and DC. Its Quiksilver Entertainment subsidiary produces programming that covers company-sponsored boardriding events while also promoting the boardriding (and hence Quiksilver) lifestyle.

The company operates through several segments: the Americas EMEA and APAC. The Americas comprises North South and Central America and includes revenue primarily from the US Brazil Canada and Mexico. The EMEA segment consists of Boardriders' Europe Middle East and Africa business and includes revenue from continental Europe the UK and South Africa. The company's APAC segment covers Australia New Zealand and Asia and generates sales primarily from Australia Indonesia Japan and New Zealand.

Geographic Reach

The majority of Boardriders' company-owned and licensed stores are in Europe (about 300) followed by Asia/Pacific (280ish) and the Americas (100). In fiscal 2014 more than half of the company's sales were generated outside the US. The firm's European headquarters is in France while its Asia/Pacific headquarters is located in Torquay Australia.

Sales and Marketing

Boardriders' products are sold in more than 100 countries through wholesale customers retail stores and through e-commerce. It wholesales its products to major markets with the help of 300-plus independent sales representatives supplemented by an employee sales staff. The company uses more than 150 local distributors in smaller markets.

To connect with its youthful audience Boardriders' advertising efforts include sponsoring athletes hosting world-class boardriding contests magazine and online ads retail signage television programs surf camps skate park tours and social media.

Strategy

To grow sales and return to profitability Boardriders has three long-term initiatives: strengthening its brands; expanding its business in emerging markets; and driving operational efficiencies throughout the business. The company has also invested in improving its e-commerce platform and growing its store network.

The company is also testing a new store concept which includes all its hard and soft goods and all brands under one roof. Test stores have opened in Europe and in Venice California.

Boardriders has ventured into personal care products — a relatively new niche for the company — for its Quiksilver and Roxy lines. Through an exclusive worldwide licensing agreement Inter Parfums develops and distributes Roxy fragrance sun care skin care and related items as well as Quiksilver sun care and other products through 2017.

Going forward Boardriders faces increased competition from athletic footwear and apparel giant NIKE which is stepping into the action sports industry. To help it focus the company has divested noncore business to focus on its namesake Roxy and DC labels. Jettisoned brands include Surfdome (sold to SurfStitch) Mervin Manufacturing (sold to Extreme Holdings) and skateboarder Tony Hawk's Hawk Designs (sold to Cherokee).

HISTORY

Australian surfers Alan Green and John Law started Quiksilver in 1969 to make "boardshorts" for surfers. In 1976 surfers Jeff Hakman and Bob McKnight bought the US rights to the Quiksilver name — Hakman displayed his enthusiasm for the line by eating a doily at a dinner with Green — and established Quiksilver USA. The firm went public in 1986.

The recession of the early 1990s and the dominance of grunge as the fashion du jour hurt Quiksilver and prompted it to restructure. It acquired French affiliate Na Pali in 1991 and began building its European operations. To gain surer footing in the fickle teen fashion market Quiksilver broadened its product offerings. It added the Roxy women's swimwear line in 1991 expanding it to clothing in 1993. It also launched the Boardriders Club concept — stores featuring Quiksilver merchandise but owned by independent retailers. In 1994 the company acquired swimwear maker The Raisin Company. In 1997 Quiksilver began advertising nationally and entered the snowboard market buying Mervin Manufacturing maker of Lib Technologies Gnu and Bent Metal snowboard products.

With its women's lines making waves and a strong current from European sales Quiksilver began opening its own Boardriders Club stores in 1998. In 1999 it launched the Quik Jeans and Roxy Jeans denim lines and the next year it added the Alex Goes line for women 25 to 40. Riding a tide of rising profits in 2000 the company acquired Fidra men's golf apparel; Freestyle the European licensee of rival youth wear label Gotcha; and pro-skateboarder Tony Hawk's apparel and accessories business. In a tail-that-wags-the-dog move the company bought its progenitor Quiksilver International the same year; in doing so Quiksilver gained sole possession of the Quiksilver name worldwide.

In June 2002 Quiksilver launched Quiksilver Entertainment a production company that creates actionsport-based programming for the entertainment industry. Later that year Quiksilver acquired Ug Manufacturing in Australia and Quiksilver Japan in an effort to gain control over nearly all its global business with the exception of a few licenses in small niche markets. At about the same time the company purchased and integrated Beach Street the owner and operator of 26 Quiksilver outlet stores.

The company formed a 50-50 joint venture in 2003 with Glorious Sun Enterprises to expand into China.

Quiksilver's entertainment unit in 2004 launched an actionsport film distribution company Union which is a supplier to more than 1000 retail locations in Australia China Europe Japan and the US. In 2004 Quiksilver completed its purchase of DC Shoes and bought the footwear firm's Canadian distributor Centre Skateboard Distribution in 2005. The footwear company's popularity in the skate and surf community serves to embed Quiksilver further in that market while ensuring its ability to compete with Nike and adidas in the footwear arena.

In 2005 Quiksilver flipped its board in a new direction however and broadened its reach into the mainstream. The company announced it has signed an exclusive licensing deal with Kohl's and Tony Hawk to give traction to its apparel outerwear and accessories. As part of the agreement Quiksilver will continue to design the Tony Hawk clothing brand and Kohl's will do the rest including sourcing distributing marketing and other functions.

Quiksilver exited the sports equipment manufacturing business in November 2008 when it sold its Rossignol unit.

EXECUTIVES

EVP Global Human Resources, Carol E. Scherman

EVP and CIO, Michael B. Tasooji, age 55
CEO, Pierre Agnes, age 52, $617,500 total
  compensation
President Americas, Nate Smith
EVP New Business Development; President
  Quiksilver Americas, Robert (Rob) Colby, $400,000
  total compensation
CFO, Richard Shields, age 59, $522,900 total
  compensation
President Asia Pacific (APAC), Greg Healy
Senior Vice President Global Tax, Scott Fullerton
Senior Vice President Of Global Sourcing,
  Christopher Dubes
Senior Vice President of Marketing, Ryan Scanlon
Vice President Of Merchandising And Design, Guy
  Stagman
Ecommerce Marketing Manager; Senior Vice
  President Of Direct Sales, Nicholas Nathan
Vice President, Chris Schreiber
Vice President, Brian Ivanhoe
Vice President, Heidi Ueberroth
Chairman, Bob McKnight
Auditors: DELOITTE & TOUCHE LLP COSTA M

LOCATIONS

HQ: BOARDRIDERS, INC.
  5600 ARGOSY AVE STE 100, HUNTINGTON BEACH,
  CA 926491063
Phone: 714 889-2200
Web: WWW.QUIKSILVER.COM

PRODUCTS/OPERATIONS

Selected Brands
DC Shoes
Quiksilver
Roxy

COMPETITORS

Abercrombie & Fitch	Life is good
Amer Sports	NIKE
Amerex	Nautica Apparel
Bauer Hockey	Oakley
Billabong	Pacific Sunwear
Bleach Group	SPY Inc
Body Glove	Sole Technology
Burton	St ssy
Calvin Klein	Tecnica
Columbia Sportswear	Tommy Hilfiger
FUBU	VF Corporation
Fat Face	Volcom
Head N.V.	Warnaco Swimwear
Levi Strauss	adidas

HISTORICAL FINANCIALS

Company Type: Private

Income Statement
FYE: October 31

	REVENUE ($ mil.)	NET INCOME ($ mil.)	NET PROFIT MARGIN	EMPLOYEES
10/15	1,345	(306)	—	700
10/14	1,570	(320)	—	—
10/13	1,810	(233)	—	—
10/12	2,013	(9)	—	—
Annual Growth	(12.6%)	—	—	—

2015 Year-End Financials

Return on assets: 10.7%   Cash ($ mil.): 36
Return on equity: (-22.8%)
Current ratio: 0.40

BOCA RATON REGIONAL HOSPITAL, INC.

EXECUTIVES

Principal, Jerry Fedele
Personnel Manager, Maryjoe Ganthier
Production Director, Laurie Leon
Director, Kathy Schilling
Director, Caroline Ferraiuolo
Vice-President, Alex Eremia
Manager, Barry Rosenberg

LOCATIONS

HQ: BOCA RATON REGIONAL HOSPITAL, INC.
  800 MEADOWS RD, BOCA RATON, FL 334862304
Phone: 561 395-7100
Web: WWW.BRRH.COM

HISTORICAL FINANCIALS

Company Type: Private

Income Statement
FYE: June 30

	REVENUE ($ mil.)	NET INCOME ($ mil.)	NET PROFIT MARGIN	EMPLOYEES
06/15	386	22	5.8%	1,917
06/14	390	38	9.8%	—
06/13	362	21	6.0%	—
06/05	263	13	5.2%	—
Annual Growth	3.9%	5.1%		

2015 Year-End Financials

Return on assets: 4.5%   Cash ($ mil.): —
Return on equity: 5.8%
Current ratio: 0.80

BOISE STATE UNIVERSITY

Boise State University (BSU) provides higher education in the shadows of the Rocky Mountains. BSU has an enrollment of approximately 23000 students and a faculty and staff of more than 2400. The university offers about 200 undergraduate graduate and technical fields of study through seven colleges: Arts and Sciences Business and Economics Education Engineering Health Sciences Social Sciences and Public Affairs and Graduate Studies. In addition to its main campus in Boise Idaho it operates a satellite campus in Nampa (Boise State West) which offers academic non-credit and applied technology courses. BSU also has three centers elsewhere in the state as well as online learning programs.

Geographic Reach

BSU's students include residents of Idaho as well as out-of-state students from across the US and international students from 65 countries.

Operations

To support its programs in the fields of science technology engineering and mathematics (the STEM programs) BSU conducts a number of research projects in fields including nanoelectronics biomolecular science health and public policy and innovative materials.

Financial Performance

BSU increased revenues by 6% to $199 million in 2012 due to additional earnings from student fees and auxiliary activities. It also increased net income by 25% to $26 million due to higher revenues grants and gifts.

Undergraduate tuition for Idaho residents is about $6000 per year while out-of-state students pay $17000 per year.

Strategy

BSU opened a new English language testing center in 2012 to meet the needs of a growing international student base. It also adds new degree programs to benefit its students; in 2012 it added an online MBA program to increase access for students who can't attend classes on campus. The university is also working to add doctoral programs in the STEM discipline areas and it is investing in enhancing its facilities and infrastructure and its faculty resources.

The university took its research programs to a new level when it launched its first start-up company an online gaming software entity based on its research programs.

Company Background

BSU was founded by the Episcopal Church as Boise Junior College in 1932; the affiliation ended two years later. It became a public institution in 1939 and gained university status in 1974.

EXECUTIVES

Vice President Customer Care, Andrea Sullivan
**Administrative Assistant 2 Provost and Vice
  President for Academic Affairs,** Judy Wauer
**Special Olympics Coordinator Vice President for
  Finance and Administration,** Cindy Hall
**PROVOST and Vice President ACADEMIC
  Affairs,** Sona Andrews
**Space Planning Analyst Vice President for
  Finance and Admin,** Helen Davis
**Associate Vice President student Affairs Vice
  President,** John McGuire
**Management Assistant Vice President for Finance
  and Administration,** Kathleen Anderson
Associate Vice President Division of Research,
  Harold Blackman
**Director Professional Development Academic Aff
  Provost And Vice President For Academic
  Affairs,** Cindy Anson
Associate Vice President, Jim Anderson
Director of Admissions, Kelly Talbert
Assoc. Vice President, Matthew Ewing
Vice President For Finance And Administration,
  Michelle Franks
Assistant Vice President Budget and Planning,
  Kenneth Kline
Vice President For University Advancement, Laura
  Simic
Vice President for Finance and Administration,
  Sierra Buttars
Treasurer Vice President, Diana Ornelas
Secretary, Vlad Calugaru
Treasurer, Jake Hagen
Auditors: MOSS-ADAMS LLP EUGENE OREGON

LOCATIONS

HQ: BOISE STATE UNIVERSITY
  1910 UNIVERSITY DR, BOISE, ID 837250002
Phone: 208 426-1011
Web: WWW.BRONCOSPORTS.COM

PRODUCTS/OPERATIONS

Selected Schools
College of Arts and Sciences
College of Business & Economics
College of Education
College of Engineering
College of Health Sciences
College of Social Sciences and Public Affairs
Graduate College
Honors College

Income Statement FYE: June 30

	REVENUE ($ mil.)	NET INCOME ($ mil.)	NET PROFIT MARGIN	EMPLOYEES
06/16	228	7	3.4%	1,879
06/14	207	1	0.9%	—
06/13	209	42	20.4%	—
06/08	0	0	45.9%	—
Annual Growth	113.1%	53.8%	—	—

2016 Year-End Financials

Return on assets: 2.3%   Cash ($ mil.): 47
Return on equity: 3.4%
Current ratio: 1.20

BONITZ, INC.

Bonitz is a veteran US acoustical ceiling and drywall contractor. Founded by chairman Bill Rogers in 1954 the company got a humble start in South Carolina and has grown to operate in more than a dozen US locations primarily in the Southeast including Alabama Colorado Georgia Tennessee Virginia and the Carolinas. Through its operating divisions Bonitz also offers commercial and residential flooring contracting roofing contracting and manufacturing of prefabricated light gage metal wall panels and trusses for educational institutional and commercial buildings. Its clients include architects interior designers general contractors and building owners. Bonitz is employee owned.

EXECUTIVES

President, Thomas B Banks
Director, Albert Burts
Administrative Assistant, Connie Mitchell
Operations Manager, Dan Rhodes
Manager, Jay Anderson
Administrative Assistant, Lisa Seegars
Assistant Vice-President, Phil Branon
Auditors: DAVIS AND COMPANY COLUMBIA S

LOCATIONS

HQ: BONITZ, INC.
645 ROSEWOOD DR, COLUMBIA, SC 292014699
Phone: 803 799-0181
Web: WWW.BONITZ.US

PRODUCTS/OPERATIONS

Selected Products
Contracting
    Access floors
    Acoustical ceilings and walls
    Contamination and cleanroom products
    Metal framing and drywall partitions
    Movable wall systems
    Surfacing
Flooring
    Access floors
    Church interiors and flooring
    Coatings
    Commercial flooring
    Maintenance
    Renovation and replacement
    Residential flooring
    Specialty flooring
Manufacturing
    Load-bearing panels
    Masonry support panels
    Synthetic stucco panels
    TrusSteel steel trusses
Roofing

Insulating concrete
Metal roof decks
Precast gypsum plank
Steel edge concrete plank
Wood fiber plank

COMPETITORS

Acousti Engineering   Pickens Roofing
Acoustics Incorporated
Performance
Contracting

Income Statement FYE: December 31

	REVENUE ($ mil.)	NET INCOME ($ mil.)	NET PROFIT MARGIN	EMPLOYEES
12/15	179	7	4.3%	850
12/14	178	6	3.4%	—
12/13	143	6	4.7%	—
12/12	129	3	3.0%	—
Annual Growth	11.6%	26.0%	—	—

2015 Year-End Financials

Return on assets: 4.4%   Cash ($ mil.): 6
Return on equity: 4.3%
Current ratio: 2.50

BOONE HOSPITAL CENTER

If you're torn apart by tigers you might end up here. Boone Hospital Center is a 390-bed full-service hospital that serves St. Louis and a 25-county area in central Missouri. Boone provides a range of programs and services including emergency care and emergency transportation. The hospital offers specialized care in the areas of cardiology neurology oncology surgery and obstetrics. It also operates outreach clinics and provides home health care services through Boone Hospital Home Care. Its Wellaware center focuses on behavioral and occupational medicine. Boone Hospital is part of the BJC HealthCare network.

The hospital plans is conducting a $100 million expansion project that will include a new patient tower (adding about 35 beds) and parking garage.

EXECUTIVES

President, Paul Machuk
Director, Michelle Zvanut
Chief Operating Officer, Randy M Morrow

LOCATIONS

HQ: BOONE HOSPITAL CENTER
1600 E BROADWAY, COLUMBIA, MO 652015897
Phone: 573 815-8000
Web: WWW.BOONE.ORG

COMPETITORS

Alexian Brothers   HCA
    Health System   Mercy Health
Ascension Health   SSM Health Care
CHRISTUS Health   Saint Luke's Health
Carle Physician Group   System
Catholic Health   Tenet Healthcare
    Initiatives

Income Statement FYE: December 31

	REVENUE ($ mil.)	NET INCOME ($ mil.)	NET PROFIT MARGIN	EMPLOYEES
12/15	284	(1)	—	3,150
12/14	288	16	5.6%	—
12/08	248	3	1.5%	—
Annual Growth	1.9%	—	—	—

2015 Year-End Financials

Return on assets: 3.1%   Cash ($ mil.): 3
Return on equity: (-0.6%)
Current ratio: 0.90

BORGESS MEDICAL CENTER

Borgess Medical Center is part of the Borgess Health Alliance which is a member of the Ascension Health network. The general acute care facility which serves residents of southwestern Michigan houses more than 420 beds. It has a comprehensive offering of medical and surgical services including specialty care in areas such as cancer heart disease neuroscience and orthopedics. Borgess Medical Center also serves as a Level II trauma center and features a research institute a sleep disorders clinic a weight loss surgery center no-wait emergency room and outpatient facilities. The hospital was founded in 1889 by a local priest.
Operations
Borgess Medical Center sees more than 60000 visitors at its emergency and trauma facilities each year. Its specialist surgical facilities include operating rooms with comprehensive monitoring services for brain surgery spinal surgery and other complex procedures. The facility also serves as a regional behavioral health center. Its Stryker Center features extensive cardiovascular and neurological diagnosis and treatment resources as well as radiology pharmacy and same-day surgery units.

EXECUTIVES

Vice President Human Resources, Laura Lentenbrink
Vice President Operations, Jason Nicolai
Nursing Director, Lori Brown
Board Member, Lawrence Cain

LOCATIONS

HQ: BORGESS MEDICAL CENTER
1521 GULL RD, KALAMAZOO, MI 490481666
Phone: 269 226-7000

PRODUCTS/OPERATIONS

Selected Centers and Services
Behavioral Health
Birthing Center
Brain & Spine
Breast Care Centers
Cancer & Oncology
Cardiology Group
Critical Care
Dietary Services
Emergency & Trauma
Fibroid Center
Henry Ford
Inpatient Services
Laboratory Services
Osteoporosis Centers

Palliative Care
Radiology
Rehabilitation Services
Sleep Disorders
Vascular
Women's Services

COMPETITORS

Bronson Health Care
  Covenant HealthCare
  Gerber Memorial
  McLaren Health Care
  Memorial Hospital &
    Health System
Sheridan Community
    Hospital
  Sparrow Health System
  Spectrum Health
  Trinity Health (Novi)

HISTORICAL FINANCIALS

Company Type: Private

Income Statement

FYE: June 30

	REVENUE ($ mil.)	NET INCOME ($ mil.)	NET PROFIT MARGIN	EMPLOYEES
06/15	382	28	7.4%	2,200
06/14	449	64	14.3%	—
06/10	455	(6)	—	—
06/09	414	(5)	—	—
Annual Growth	(1.3%)	—	—	—

2015 Year-End Financials

Return on assets: 1.4%
Return on equity: 7.4%
Current ratio: 0.60

Cash ($ mil.): 2

BOSTON MEDICAL CENTER CORPORATION

Located in Boston's South End neighborhood Boston Medical Center (BMC) offers a full spectrum of health care services from prenatal care and obstetrics to surgery and rehabilitation. BMC is also the city's largest provider of indigent care spending millions of dollars annually on care for uninsured patients and offering free screenings and other community outreach programs. The not-for-profit hospital boasts nearly 500 licensed beds more than 700 physicians and includes a Level 1 trauma center acute rehabilitation facilities and neonatal and pediatric intensive care units. The center is the primary teaching hospital of Boston University's School of Medicine.

Operations

BMC also operates Boston HealthNet a network affiliation of the medical center Boston University School of Medicine and more than a dozen community health centers. Boston HealthNet provides outreach prevention primary care and specialty care and dental services at sites located throughout the community.

Hand-in-hand with being a major teaching hospital is engaging in extensive medical research. BMC oversees more than 590 research and service projects and conducts both biomedical and clinical research programs exploring infectious disease cardiology vascular biology Parkinson's disease geriatrics and endocrinology among other areas. With Boston University BMC also operates a 16-acre research and business park called BioSquare that serves as a collaborative center for the development and commercialization of new biomedical technologies.

In 2015 BMC had more than 712 000 outpatient clinic visits 204000 outpatient ancillary visits 125000 emergency department visits and 24000 admissions.

Sales and Marketing

In addition to its medical and research services BMC provides health insurance through its BMC HealthNet Plan a managed care plan that has more than 240000 Medicaid and low-cost health plan members. The center markets its services through social media.

Financial Performance

BMC received more than $119 million in sponsored research funding in fiscal 2015; it oversees 594 research and service projects separate from research activities at Boston University School of Medicine.

Strategy

In late 2014 BMC's Center for Regenerative Medicine and Boston University were awarded a $2.7 million grant from the National Heart Lung and Blood Institute to establish a stem cell repository that researchers across the US can access for free. The first-of-its-kind repository will help promote stem cell research particularly in the area of lung disease.

EXECUTIVES

Vice President Information Technology, Michael Krugman
SVP Finance and CFO, Richard Silveria
President and CEO, Kate E. Walsh
SVP and Chief Nursing Officer, Nancy Gaden
SVP and Chief Medical Officer, Ravin Davidoff
COO, Alastair Bell
President and CEO Faculty Practice Foundation, William Creevy
SVP Quality Safety and Technology; Chief Quality Officer, Stanley Hochberg
Pharmacy Manager, Chirag Desai
Associate Vice President for Human Resources, Manuel Monteiro
Vice President Operations, Gary Nicksa
Vice President, Mary Glover
Pharmacy Manager, Jose Barria
Chairman, James S. Phalen, age 66

LOCATIONS

HQ: BOSTON MEDICAL CENTER CORPORATION
1 BOSTON MEDICAL CTR PL # 1, BOSTON, MA
021182999
Phone: 617 414-5000
Web: WWW.BMC.ORG

PRODUCTS/OPERATIONS

Selected Services and Programs

Alzheimer's Disease Center
Anesthesiology
Boston HealthNet
Boston University Affiliated Physicians
Boston University Cosmetic and Laser Center
Cardiovascular Center
Care Management
Dermatology
Diabetes
Elders Living at Home Program
Emergency Medicine
Facial Plastic and Reconstructive Surgery
General Internal Medicne / Primary Care
Geriatrics
Head and Neck Cancer Center of Excellence
Hematology & Medical Oncology
Immigrant & Refugee Health Program
Integrative Medicine
LocoMotor Training
Mattapan Community Health Center
Melanoma Program
Neurosurgery
Nursing
Ophthalmology
Oral and Maxillofacial Surgery
Pediatrics - bWell Center
  Pediatrics
Rehabilitation Therapies
Renal Medicine

South End Community Health Center
Special Kids Special Help
Thoracic Surgery
Transplant Surgery
Uphams Corner Health Center
Urology
Vascular Center
Vascular and Endovascular Surgery
Weight Loss Surgery (Bariatric Surgery)
Whittier Street Health Center

COMPETITORS

Beth Israel Deaconess Medical Center
  Brigham and Women's Hospital
  Cambridge Health Alliance
  Care New England
  CareGroup
  Children's Hospital Boston
  Dana-Farber
  Massachusetts General Hospital
  Newton-Wellesley Hospital
  Northeast Health System
  Partners HealthCare
  Shriners Hospitals For Children
  Spaulding Rehabilitation Hospital
  St. Elizabeth's Medical Center
  Steward Health Care

HISTORICAL FINANCIALS

Company Type: Private

Income Statement

FYE: September 30

	REVENUE ($ mil.)	NET INCOME ($ mil.)	NET PROFIT MARGIN	EMPLOYEES
09/15	1,004	7	0.8%	4,200
09/12	886	2	0.3%	—
09/09	1,004	(12)	—	—
Annual Growth	0.0%	—	—	—

2015 Year-End Financials

Return on assets: 16.0%
Return on equity: 0.8%
Current ratio: 0.50

Cash ($ mil.): 82

BOTSFORD GENERAL HOSPITAL

EXECUTIVES

Manager, Renee Barbour
Manager, Sabiha Jabeen
Manager, Joyce Cutsy

LOCATIONS

HQ: BOTSFORD GENERAL HOSPITAL
28050 GRAND RIVER AVE, FARMINGTON HILLS, MI
483365933
Phone: 248 471-8000
Web: WWW.BOTSFORD.ORG

HISTORICAL FINANCIALS

Company Type: Private

Income Statement

FYE: December 31

	REVENUE ($ mil.)	NET INCOME ($ mil.)	NET PROFIT MARGIN	EMPLOYEES
12/15	283	(1)	—	1,859
12/14	286	7	2.5%	—
12/06	527	10	2.1%	—
12/05	279	7	2.6%	—
Annual Growth	0.1%	—	—	—

Return on assets: 6.6%   Cash ($ mil.): 15
Return on equity: (-0.5%)
Current ratio: 1.30

BOULDER VALLEY SCHOOL DISTRICT RE-2

EXECUTIVES

Superintendent, George Garcia
Board of Directors, Ellen Brown
Superintendent, Jorge Garica
Assistant Manager, Judy Skupa
General Manager, Shere Holleman
Auditors: S&G SWANHORST & COMPANY LLC G

LOCATIONS

HQ: BOULDER VALLEY SCHOOL DISTRICT RE-2
6500 ARAPAHOE RD, BOULDER, CO 803031407
Phone: 303 447-1010
Web: WWW.BVSD.ORG

HISTORICAL FINANCIALS
Company Type: Private

Income Statement
FYE: June 30

	REVENUE ($ mil.)	NET INCOME ($ mil.)	NET PROFIT MARGIN	EMPLOYEES
06/16	393	(55)	—	3,815
06/12	319	(36)	—	—
06/11	324	(42)	—	—
06/09	817	0	0.0%	—
Annual Growth	(9.9%)	—	—	—

BOY SCOUTS OF AMERICA

Scouts enter dens as Tigers and eventually take flight as Eagles. Boy Scouts of America (BSA) one of the nation's largest youth organizations has about 2.6 million youth members and more than 1 million adult leaders in its ranks. BSA offers educational and character-building programs emphasizing leadership citizenship personal development and physical fitness. In addition to traditional scouting programs (Tiger Cub Webelos and Boy Scouts ranging up to Eagle rank) it offers the Venturing program for boys and girls ages 14-21. BSA generates revenue through membership and council fees food and magazine sales and contributions. The organization was founded by Chicago publisher William Boyce in 1910.

Operations

BSA's group membership is supported through about 300 local Boy Scout councils. Additionally it hosts a National Scout Jamboree each year to bring all scouts together. The organization also operates a high-adventure base in West Virginia. The bases offer scouts a range of outdoor activities including backpacking camping canoeing and diving. The West Virginia location serves as the organization's permanent location for its annual Jamboree. BSA operates also bases in Florida Minnesota and New Mexico.

BSA also publishes Boys' Life monthly magazine which boasts more than 1 million subscribers and Scouting magazine for adults registered in Cub Scouting Boy Scouting Varsity Scouting and Venturing.

Financial Performance

BSA's revenue increased 24% in 2013 to $283 over 2012's $229 million. The uptick was due to a bump in fees (44% of total revenue) primarily from the 2013 National Scout Jamboree as well as from contributions and bequests.

Strategy

BSA boasts programs that remain popular but in recent years membership growth has slowed with the recession and other societal forces including video games social media and other entertainment.

In 2013 Cub Scout membership (which accounts for more than 50% of total youth membership) dipped by about 7% while the ranks of the Boy Scouts decreased by 3%. Overall total youth membership declined by about 6% for the year continuing its downward trend. To boost membership and grow its organization BSA developed a strategic plan that involves reaching out to new groups of parents and students. To this end it has developed and maintained relationships with civic religious and fraternal organizations across the US including those that serve African-American Asian and Latino families. It has also analyzed Generation X and Millennial parents to determine how to best bring scouting to their families.

EXECUTIVES

Deputy Chief Scout Executive and COO, Gary P. Butler
National President, Robert M. Gates
CFO, Michael Ashline
Chief Scout Executive, Michael Surbaugh
Auditors: PRICEWATERHOUSECOOPERS LLP DA

LOCATIONS

HQ: BOY SCOUTS OF AMERICA
1325 W WALNUT HILL LN, IRVING, TX 750383096
Phone: 972 580-2000
Web: WWW.BSAMUSEUM.ORG

Selected Programs
Tiger Cubs
Cub Scouts
Webelos Scouts
Boy Scouts
Sea Scouts
Venturing

PRODUCTS/OPERATIONS

2015 Youth Membership

	No.
Cub Scout-Age	1,261,340
Boy Scout	840,654
Venturing and Sea Scouts	142,892
Explorers	110,445
Life Character	385,535
Total	**2,612,955**

2015 Revenue

	$ mil.	% of total
Fees	126	4
Net investment gain	4	2
Contributions & bequests	28	14
Supply operations	23	12
Magazines	14	8
Other (includes trading post sales)	(0.8)	0
Total	**197**	**100**

HISTORICAL FINANCIALS
Company Type: Private

Income Statement
FYE: December 31

	REVENUE ($ mil.)	NET INCOME ($ mil.)	NET PROFIT MARGIN	EMPLOYEES
12/15	335	(25)	—	2,800
12/14	244	46	19.0%	—
12/13	0	(33)	—	—
12/10	310	90	29.0%	—
Annual Growth	1.6%	—	—	—

2015 Year-End Financials

Return on assets: 9.4%   Cash ($ mil.): 44
Return on equity: (-7.6%)
Current ratio: 0.10

BOZEMAN DEACONESS HEALTH SERVICES

EXECUTIVES

Chairman, Julie Jackson
Board of Directors, Dane Sobek
President, Elizabeth Lewis
Treasurer, Janet Colombo

LOCATIONS

HQ: BOZEMAN DEACONESS HEALTH SERVICES
915 HIGHLAND BLVD, BOZEMAN, MT 597156999
Phone: 406 585-5000
Web: WWW.BOZEMANDEACONESS.ORG

HISTORICAL FINANCIALS
Company Type: Private

Income Statement
FYE: December 31

	REVENUE ($ mil.)	NET INCOME ($ mil.)	NET PROFIT MARGIN	EMPLOYEES
12/15	212	7	3.5%	701
12/14	196	18	9.2%	—
12/13	215	24	11.2%	—
12/12	170	16	10.0%	—
Annual Growth	7.6%	(23.8%)	—	—

2015 Year-End Financials

Return on assets: 5.4%   Cash ($ mil.): 19
Return on equity: 3.5%
Current ratio: 1.60

BRAHMA GROUP

EXECUTIVES

President, Sean G Davis
Board of Directors, Steve Wendel
Financial Executive, Lacienne Bryant
Director, Gary A Stewart
Manager, Kyle Williams
Administrative Assistant, Matt Dalley
Project Manager, Mark Fietkau
Auditors: ARMANINO LLP SAN RAMON CALIF

LOCATIONS

HQ: BRAHMA GROUP
1132 S 500 W, SALT LAKE CITY, UT 841013018
Phone: 801 521-5200
Web: WWW.BRAHMAGROUPINC.COM

HISTORICAL FINANCIALS

Company Type: Private

Income Statement

FYE: October 31

	REVENUE ($ mil.)	NET INCOME ($ mil.)	NET PROFIT MARGIN	EMPLOYEES
10/15	194	5	2.9%	400
10/14	272	7	2.6%	—
10/13	244	6	2.6%	—
10/12	111	1	1.6%	—
Annual Growth	20.6%	46.0%	—	—

BRANCH & ASSOCIATES, INC.

Branch & Associates is no twig in the Branch Group family tree. The employee-owned subsidiary offers general contracting design/build and construction management services for commercial and industrial construction projects in the Carolinas Tennessee Virginia and West Virginia. The company builds retail health care educational multi-unit residential government hospitality and industrial facilities. Billy Branch founded the company in 1963. It was reorganized and became Branch Associates under the Branch Group in 1985. Other Branch Group subsidiaries include Branch Highways E.V. Williams and G.J. Hopkins.

The Branch Group expanded into northern Virginia in 2007 by acquiring general contractor R.E. Daffan. The general contractor and construction management firm focuses on building projects in and around Manassas Virginia.

Branch & Associates' projects include construction of exhibition space at the Roanoke Civic Center Complex in Virginia and renovations and additions at Ferrum College in Ferrum Virginia the Central Academy of Technology & Arts in Monroe North Carolina and residence halls at Virginia Tech. Other projects include a Volvo Assembly plant an EchoStar call center and a lodge at Snowshoe Mountain Resort.

EXECUTIVES

President, Craig Floyd
Financial Executive, Matthew Wise
Manager, Heather Bowman
Financial Executive, Paula Smith
Auditors: KPMG LLP ROANOKE VIRGINIA

LOCATIONS

HQ: BRANCH & ASSOCIATES, INC.
5732 AIRPORT RD NW, ROANOKE, VA 240121122
Phone: 540 989-5215
Web: WWW.BRANCH-ASSOCIATES.COM

COMPETITORS

Hitt	SMCI
KBS	W.M. Jordan
Parsons Brinckerhoff	

HISTORICAL FINANCIALS

Company Type: Private

Income Statement

FYE: December 31

	REVENUE ($ mil.)	NET INCOME ($ mil.)	NET PROFIT MARGIN	EMPLOYEES
12/15	193	0	—	90
12/13	129	0	—	
12/12	130	0	—	
12/11	108	0	—	
Annual Growth	15.6%	—	—	—

2015 Year-End Financials

Return on assets: 20.3%   Cash ($ mil.): 40
Return on equity: —
Current ratio: 1.40

BRANDEIS UNIVERSITY

Brandeis University offers more than 40 undergraduate majors and 45 minors programs in the creative arts humanities sciences and social sciences. Located just west of Boston it comprises the College of Arts and Sciences the Graduate School of Arts and Sciences the International Business School the Heller School for Social Policy and Management the Lown School for Near Eastern and Judaic Studies and the Rabb School of Continuing Studies. The university has an enrollment of more than 5000 students; the student/faculty ratio is 10-to-1. A non-sectarian Jewish community-sponsored institution named after the late Justice Louis Brandeis of the US Supreme Court Brandeis University was founded in 1948.

Operations

Brandeis University's tuition fee for 2016-17 was $49586 per year. The students are instructed by about 650 faculty members. The university provided more than $51 million in funded grants and scholarships to undergraduates.

Geographic Reach

The university is located in 235 acres campus in Waltham Massachusetts comprising more than 100 academic and residential buildings.

Financial Performance

Revenues increased by 5% in 2015 due to growth in net tuition fees residence hall and dining revenues contributions and endowment return utilized revenues.

Net income decreased by 36% due to a decline in investment returns and higher operating expenses (including instruction and academic support expenses).

Operating cash outflow decreased in 2015 by 53% due to a change in operating assets.

EXECUTIVES

President, Ronald D. Liebowitz, age 61
SVP and COO, Steven S. Manos
Interim Dean Heller School for Social Policy and Management, Marty W. Krauss
CIO, John Unsworth
Dean International Business School, Bruce R. Magid
SVP Finance and Treasurer, Marianne Cwalina
Dean College of Arts and Sciences, Susan J. Birren
Dean Graduate School of Arts and Sciences, Eric Chasalow
Interim Provost, Irving R. Epstein
Vice President Rabb School For Continuing Studies, Karen Muncaster
Vice President for Operations, James Gray

Senior Vice President Institutional Advancement, Nancy Winship
Vice President, Shourya Veeraganti
Vice President Marketing Of Ascend Brandeis Chapter, Huan Zhou
Vice President Of Operations, Jim Gray
Vice President, Paul Sindberg
Vice President, Ankit Patil
Vice President, Angelica Fajardo
Senior Vice President of Communications and External Relations, Ira Jackson
Vice Chairman, Stephen B. Kay
Chairman, Perry M. Traquina
Vice Chairman, Jonathan G. Davis
Assistant Treasurer, Jiaying Zhang
Assistant Treasurer, Heather Yoon
Secretary, Sneha Walia
Treasurer, Wyatt Emanker
Treasurer, Jacob Edelman
Treasurer, Ziyang Chen
Assistant Treasurer, Aaron Wengrofsky
Treasurer, Renzo Berrios
Auditors: KPMG LLP BOSTON MA

LOCATIONS

HQ: BRANDEIS UNIVERSITY
415 SOUTH ST MS110, WALTHAM, MA 024532700
Phone: 781 736-8318
Web: WWW.BRANDEIS.EDU

PRODUCTS/OPERATIONS

2015 Sales

	% of total
Net tuition fees residence hall and dining revenues	55
Sponsored programs-direct	15
Endowment return utilized	13
Contributions	6
Others	11
Total	**100**

Selected Programs

African and Afro-American Studies
American Studies
Anthropology
Biochemistry
Biological Physics
Biology
Business
Classical Studies
Comparative Literature
East Asian Studies
Economics
English
Film Television and Interactive Media
French and Francophone Studies
German Studies
Hispanic Studies
History of Ideas
International and Global Studies
Journalism
Language and Linguistics
Legal Studies
Music
Neuroscience
Philosophy
Politics
Russian Studies
Sexuality and Queer Studies
South Asian Studies

HISTORICAL FINANCIALS

Company Type: Private

Income Statement

FYE: June 30

	REVENUE ($ mil.)	NET INCOME ($ mil.)	NET PROFIT MARGIN	EMPLOYEES
06/15	508	80	15.7%	1,200
06/10	323	(24)	—	—
06/09	248	(173)	—	—
06/08	687,538	0	—	—
Annual Growth				

2015 Year-End Financials

Return on assets: 6.2%   Cash ($ mil.): 56
Return on equity: 15.7%
Current ratio: 0.20

BRANDENBURG INDUSTRIAL SERVICE COMPANY

EXECUTIVES

President, Thomas J Little
Treasurer, Lynn Somers
Purchasing Manager, Byron Roberson
Sales Manager, Christine Reed
Personnel Manager, Dawn Wolz
Superintendent, Ron Freeman
Production Manager, Jeff Fritz
Auditors: MILLER COOPER & CO LTD DE

LOCATIONS

HQ: BRANDENBURG INDUSTRIAL SERVICE COMPANY
2625 S LOOMIS ST, CHICAGO, IL 606085400
Phone: 312 326-5800
Web: WWW.BRANDENBURG.COM

HISTORICAL FINANCIALS

Company Type: Private

Income Statement

FYE: December 31

	REVENUE ($ mil.)	NET INCOME ($ mil.)	NET PROFIT MARGIN	EMPLOYEES
12/15	177	2	1.6%	750
12/14	212	7	3.4%	—
12/13	192	3	1.7%	—
12/12	189	3	1.7%	—
Annual Growth	(2.3%)	(3.4%)	—	—

2015 Year-End Financials

Return on assets: 10.5%   Cash ($ mil.): —
Return on equity: 1.6%
Current ratio: 1.00

BREITBURN ENERGY PARTNERS LP

Oil and gas futures burn brightly for BreitBurn Energy Partners one of California's largest independent exploration and production companies. With assets in Antrim Shale (Michigan) the Los Angeles Basin the Wind River and Big Horn Basins (both in Wyoming) the Sunniland Trend (Florida) the New Albany Shale (Indiana and Kentucky) and the Permian Basin (West Texas) in 2011 the company reported estimated proved reserves of 151.1 million barrels of oil equivalent (65% of which was natural gas). That year 49% of its reserves were in Michigan 29% in Wyoming 14% in California 7% in Florida and 1% in Indiana and Kentucky. The company filed for Chapter 11 bankruptcy protection in 2016.

Operations

BreitBurn Energy Partners' general partner is BreitBurn GP LLC.The companies conduct their operations through wholly owned subsidiary BreitBurn Operating L.P and its general partner BreitBurn Operating GP LLC

Wholly owned subsidiary BreitBurn Management manages assets and performs other administrative services for the company such as accounting corporate development finance land administration legal and engineering. BreitBurn Finance Corporation has no assets or liabilities. BreitBurn Collingwood Utica LLC holds certain non-producing oil and gas zones in the Collingwood-Utica shale play in Michigan and is classified as an unrestricted subsidiary under company's credit facility.

Geographic Reach

The company holds properties in the Los Angeles Basin in California the Wind River and Big Horn Basins in central Wyoming the Powder River Basin in eastern Wyoming the Evanston and Green River Basins in southwestern Wyoming the Sunniland Trend in Florida the Permian Basin in Texas the Antrim Shale in Michigan and the New Albany Shale in Indiana and Kentucky.

Sales and Marketing

In 2011 the company's largest purchasers were ConocoPhillips (in California and Michigan) which accounted for 30% of net revenues; Plains Marketing & Transportation LLC (Florida) 16%; Marathon Oil Company (Wyoming) 15%; and Sunoco Partners Marketing and Terminals L.P. (Michigan) 9% .

Financial Performance

BreitBurn Energy Partners' revenues increased by 35% in 2011 as higher commodity prices boosted revenues by $56 million and higher sales volumes (thanks to increased demand) lifted total sales revenues by $21 million. Gains on derivatives accounted for 17% of the company's revenues that year.

Net income increased by 217% in 2011 thanks to higher revenues offset by an increase in operating costs and expenses attributable to increase in general and administrative expenses depletion depreciation and amortization expense. Another factor was an increase in interest expense primarily attributable to an additional $19.9 million in interest expense associated with the company's 2020 Senior Notes.

Strategy

BreitBurn Energy Partners is pursuing a strategy of acquiring long-lived assets with relatively low-risk exploitation and development opportunities. In 2012 BreitBurn Energy Partners entered the Permian Basin through oil and gas acquisitions from Element Petroleum and CrownRock totaling $220 million. Late in 2012 it bought additional Permian assets from CrownRock and Lynden USA for about $189 million.

In late 2011 BreitBurn Energy Partners acquired oil and gas assets in the Evanston and Green River Basins of Southwest Wyoming from Cabot Oil & Gas for about $285 million. The deal added some 255000 acres approximately 620 producing wells and more than 600 additional drilling sites. That same year the company acquired supplementary oil properties in Niobrara County Wyoming for $58 million from an undisclosed party.

EXECUTIVES

President and COO, Mark L. Pease, age 60
Managing Director BreitBurn Management, Thurmon M. Andress, age 84
Director Chief Executive Officer, Halbert S. (Hal) Washburn, age 57
SVP Western Division, Chris E. Williamson, age 59
EVP and CFO, James G. Jackson, age 52
Executive Vice President General Counsel and Chief Administrative Officer, Gregory C. Brown, age 65
Vice President Operations Support, Tom Thurmond
Senior Vice President Operations, Ray Vassallo
Vice President Geosciences and Eastern Division, Dwayne T Stewart
Vice President Regional Operations, Travis Melster
Vice President Regional Operations, Steve Renke
Chairman, John R. Butler, age 78
Vice Chairman, Randall H. (Randy) Breitenbach, age 56
Auditors: PRICEWATERHOUSECOOPERS LLP LO

LOCATIONS

HQ: BREITBURN ENERGY PARTNERS LP
707 WILSHIRE BLVD # 4600, LOS ANGELES, CA 900173612
Phone: 213 225-5900

COMPETITORS

Aera Energy	Chevron
Aera Energy	DTE
Berry Petroleum	DTE
Berry Petroleum	Windsor Energy
Bill Barrett	Resources
Bill Barrett	Windsor Energy
Chevron	Resources

HISTORICAL FINANCIALS

Company Type: Private

Income Statement

FYE: December 31

	REVENUE ($ mil.)	NET INCOME ($ mil.)	NET PROFIT MARGIN	EMPLOYEES
12/16	469	(816)	—	671
12/15	1,108	(2,583)	—	
12/14	1,429	421	29.5%	
12/13	634	(43)	—	
Annual Growth	(9.6%)		—	

2016 Year-End Financials

Return on assets: 10.2%   Cash ($ mil.): 71
Return on equity: (-174.0%)
Current ratio: 0.50

BRIDGEPORT HOSPITAL

EXECUTIVES

President, William M Jennings
Board of Directors, Norman Roth
Director, Paul Possenti

LOCATIONS

HQ: BRIDGEPORT HOSPITAL
267 GRANT ST, BRIDGEPORT, CT 066102870
Phone: 203 384-3000
Web: WWW.BRIDGEPORTHOSPITAL.ORG

HISTORICAL FINANCIALS

Company Type: Private

Income Statement

FYE: September 30

	REVENUE ($ mil.)	NET INCOME ($ mil.)	NET PROFIT MARGIN	EMPLOYEES
09/15	466	55	11.9%	200
09/14	439	42	9.8%	—
09/13	433	36	8.4%	—
09/10	366	14	3.9%	—
Annual Growth	5.0%	31.3%		

2015 Year-End Financials

Return on assets: 3.3%   Cash ($ mil.): 25
Return on equity: 11.9%
Current ratio: 0.80

BRIGHAM YOUNG UNIVERSITY-IDAHO

EXECUTIVES

Chief Executive Officer, Kim B Clark
Vice-President, Charles N Andersen
Vice-President, Fenton L Broadhead
Chief Financial Officer, Shane Webster
Real Estate Agent, Bryan Sargent

LOCATIONS

HQ: BRIGHAM YOUNG UNIVERSITY-IDAHO
525 S CENTER ST, REXBURG, ID 834600004
Phone: 208 496-1901
Web: WWW.BYUI.EDU

HISTORICAL FINANCIALS
Company Type: Private

Income Statement   FYE: December 31

	REVENUE ($ mil.)	NET INCOME ($ mil.)	NET PROFIT MARGIN	EMPLOYEES
12/15	293	27	9.3%	2,129
12/14	260	101	39.1%	—
12/13	260	101	39.1%	—
12/12	208	(32)	—	—
Annual Growth	12.1%	—	—	—

2015 Year-End Financials
Return on assets: 8.0%   Cash ($ mil.): 21
Return on equity: 9.3%
Current ratio: 0.10

BROCKTON HOSPITAL, INC.

Signature Healthcare Brockton Hospital is a not-for-profit acute medical facility that serves southeastern Massachusetts. The hospital has 245 beds including about 30 beds in its skilled nursing unit. Its emergency department sees more than 62000 patients per year. Specialized services include radiation oncology cardiac care pediatrics orthopedics and joint replacement and inpatient and outpatient psychiatry. It is a community-based teaching hospital and part of the Signature Healthcare network. Brockton Hospital also formed a clinical affiliation with Beth Israel Deaconess Medical Center in 2013.

Operations

Through the affiliation with Beth Israel Deaconess Brockton Hospital has access to Harvard-affiliated specialists as well as resources that will help to improve its residency and teaching programs. Brockton Hospital has also provided certain services in affiliation with Tufts Medical Center such as pediatric care.

The Signature Healthcare organization also includes affiliated primary care physician practices specialty outpatient clinics and a nursing school. Its Signature Medical Group operates practices in fields including primary diagnostic and urgent care as well as women's health.

Geographic Reach

Signature Healthcare Brockton serves about 460000 people residing in more than 20 communities in southeastern Massachusetts.

Strategy

Signature Healthcare forms collaborative agreements with other providers to enhance medical services in the region. It also works to enhance its offerings by developing new services and programs in high-demand fields such as diabetes care and obesity treatment as well as diagnostic and orthopedic capabilities. In addition Signature Healthcare is working to reduce medical errors enhance employee productivity and increase consumer health awareness through the implementation of electronic health record (EHR) systems.

Company Background

Signature Healthcare Brockton Hospital was founded in 1896 as Brockton Hospital. It changed its name from Brockton Health to Signature Healthcare in 2008.

EXECUTIVES

Director Of Health Information, Debbie Mellace

LOCATIONS

HQ: BROCKTON HOSPITAL, INC.
680 CENTRE ST, BROCKTON, MA 023023395
Phone: 508 941-7000
Web: WWW.BROCKTONHOSPITAL.ORG

PRODUCTS/OPERATIONS

Selected Services
Acupuncture
Anesthesiology
Behavioral health
Cancer care
Cardiac care
Cardiac rehab
Concussion/Traumatic brain injury program
Critical care
CT scan
Diabetes information
Endoscopy
Emergency care
Eye services
Family practice
Gastroenterology
Hospitalists
Imaging
Infection control
Internal medicine
Laboratory
Maternal-Newborn Pavilion
MRI
Neurology
Nuclear medicine
Nurse midwifery services
Nutrition
Obstetrics/gynecology
Occupational therapy
Orthopedics
Otoplasty
Outpatient care
Pain management
Pediatrics
Perinatology
Physical therapy
Plastic surgery
Primary care
Radiology and medical imaging
Radiation therapy center/Vantage oncology
Respiratory therapy
Speech therapy
Stress test
Stroke center
Surgery
Transitional care
Ultrasound
Urgent care
Vascular lab
Weight and wellness center
Wound care

COMPETITORS

Boston Medical Center	Northeast Health
CareGroup	System
Lahey Health System	Partners HealthCare
McLean Hospital	Steward Health Care

HISTORICAL FINANCIALS
Company Type: Private

Income Statement   FYE: September 30

	REVENUE ($ mil.)	NET INCOME ($ mil.)	NET PROFIT MARGIN	EMPLOYEES
09/15	248	13	5.4%	1,500
09/14	236	(15)	—	—
09/13	211	19	9.3%	—
09/12	222	19	8.9%	—
Annual Growth	3.8%	(12.0%)	—	—

2015 Year-End Financials
Return on assets: 8.4%   Cash ($ mil.): 13
Return on equity: 5.4%
Current ratio: 0.90

BRONX LEBANON HOSPITAL CENTER (INC)

Bronx-Lebanon Hospital Center cares for patients in the central and south Bronx no doubt while rooting for the Yankees a few blocks away. The health care provider maintains more than 970 beds across its two campuses as well as psychiatric and nursing home facilities. Hospital specialty units include chest pain orthopedic cancer and women's health centers. Bronx-Lebanon also manages a network of about 70 owned and affiliated medical practices (under the BronxCare brand). This network includes primary care doctors and specialty clinics as well as rehabilitation facilities. The hospital is also a primary teaching hospital for the Albert Einstein College of Medicine.

Operations

Aside from its two major hospitals Bronx-Lebanon operates a psychiatric facility a pair of specialized long-term care facilities and the Bronx-Care network of medical practices that include Dr. Martin Luther King Jr. Health Center and a 51-unit facility to house seniors and low-income residents. Bronx-Lebanon cares for those with mental or substance abuse problems through the Family Wellness Center. It also operates a 240-bed Special Care Center and the 90-bed Highbridge Woodycrest Center to provide long term health care to geriatric AIDS and disabled residents. Its ER Department responds to about 141000 patient visits a year.

Geographic Reach

The hospital system's 37 locations serve residents of central and south Bronx in New York.

Sales and Marketing

In 2013 the company spent about $144000 on advertising.

Financial Performance

The Hospital Center is supported primarily by patient service fees paid by Medicaid Medicare and commercial insurance carriers. In 2013 the Medicaid contributed 63% of the revenue whereas Medicare contributed 28% and the rest 9% was contributed other third-party insurance carriers.

In 2013 Bronx-Lebanon's net revenues increased by about 5% due to a rise in patient service revenues and grants partially offset by a decrease in auxiliary services.

The company's net income increased by more than 790% in 2013 as the result of an increase in revenues.

Bronx-Lebanon's operating cash flows increased by 53% thanks to higher income.

Strategy

Bronx-Lebanon emphasizes its role as a community health care provider not only through its BronxCare network but through a number of community outreach and service efforts including school-based programs mobile health units free health screening and even a weekly live television show that discusses health issues.

To accommodate the growing population in and around the Bronx the hospital system has expanded in recent years with a new children's wing for inpatient and outpatient services; a nine-story ambulatory care facility; and an extensive emergency room modernization. Bronx-Lebanon also maintains a short stay observation unit in the emergency room area to monitor and evaluate patients in cardiac distress prior to admission or discharge.

Bronx-Lebanon is one of many hospital organizations to have joined a regional health information organization (RHIO) to allow medical professionals to access a patient's medical records at any number of health care locations. Other members of the Bronx RHIO include Montefiore Medical Center Jacobi Medical Center St. Barnabas Hospital and Hebrew Home at Riverdale.

Bronx-Lebanon is also one of the few hospitals in New York that is fully computerized with a complete inpatient and outpatient electronic medical record.

The hospital center's expansion plans include a $42 million 60000 sq. ft ambulatory care facility and a $34 million 56000 sq. ft. life recovery center for chemical dependency services.

In 2014 the company completed the construction of its Health and Wellness Center a new state-of-the-art outpatient facility with general and specialty services and new treatment rooms and diagnostic equipment. It also completed the construction of its Life Recovery Center to combine inpatient outpatient and residential services for individuals suffering from chemical dependency.

The company also expanded its Emergency room adding a new 11-bay treatment area.

In the same year it also relocated and expanded its main Dentistry Practice adding 39 dental chairs (a 50% increase).

EXECUTIVES

Vice President Rcm, George Irizarry
Assistant Vice President, Debra Livingston
Vice President, Hiram Torres
Vice President, Clarett Forbes
Managing Director, Harvey Stern

LOCATIONS

HQ: BRONX LEBANON HOSPITAL CENTER (INC)
1276 FULTON AVE, BRONX, NY 104563499
Phone: 718 590-1800
Web: WWW.BRONX-LEB.ORG

PRODUCTS/OPERATIONS

Selected Services
Anesthesiology
Asthma
  Adult
  Pediatric
Cardiology
Dentistry
Diabetes
  Adult
  Pediatric
Ear Nose & Throat
Gastroenterology
Hematology & Oncology
Neonatology
Neurology
Ophthalmology
Orthopaedics
Pediatrics
Physical Medicine
Psychiatry
Radiology
Special Care Center
Urology & Men's Health

Selected Academic Affiliations
Albert Einstein College of Medicine
Bronx Community College
Hostos Community College
Lehman College City University of New York
State University of New York at Stony Brook

COMPETITORS

Beth Israel Medical
  Center
Catholic Healthcare
  System
Continuum Health
  Partners
Lenox Hill Hospital
Maimonides Medical
  Center
Memorial
  Sloan-Kettering
Montefiore Medical
New York City Health
  and Hospitals
NewYork-Presbyterian
  Healthcare
Northwell Health
Winthrop-University
  Hospital

HISTORICAL FINANCIALS

Company Type: Private

Income Statement   FYE: December 31

	REVENUE ($ mil.)	NET INCOME ($ mil.)	NET PROFIT MARGIN	EMPLOYEES
12/15	631	18	3.0%	4,000
12/14	598	(34)	—	—
12/13	631	0	0.1%	—
12/09	709	22	3.1%	—
Annual Growth	(1.9%)	(2.6%)	—	—

2015 Year-End Financials

Return on assets: 7.6%   Cash ($ mil.): 100
Return on equity: 3.0%
Current ratio: 0.90

BROOKHAVEN MEMORIAL HOSPITAL MEDICAL CENTER, INC.

Brookhaven Memorial Hospital Medical Center is an acute-care facility with more than 300 beds that serves patients primarily in Suffolk County on Long Island New York. The not-for-profit community hospital's Emergency Trauma and Chest Pain Pavilion is one of the largest emergency rooms on Long Island. Founded in 1956 Brookhaven Memorial also offers behavioral health services including inpatient and outpatient mental health and alcohol treatment services. In addition to hospital services the medical center operates two community health clinics and a specialty center that provides hemodialysis women's imaging and home health and hospice services.

Operations

Brookhaven Memorial Hospital Medical Center comprises a main campus Level II Trauma Center/Emergency Room a pair of community multidisciplinary health centers and a downtown Patchogue facility for its hemodialysis program home health and hospice services and ambulatory women's imaging center. Its emergency department treats more than 70000 patients.

It operates the South Brookhaven Family Health Center in Patchogue and Shirley on a contractual basis along with Suffolk County Department of Health. Brookhaven Memorial logs the largest number of visits in the town of Patchogue.

Geographic Reach

The medical center serves those who reside in the Suffolk County area of Long Island New York which consists of 28 communities.

Strategy

Brookhaven Memorial has been expanding and entering new markets. Brookhaven Memorial in 2014 embarked on a $60-million expansion project for its new Knapp Cardiac Center which spans some 60000 sq. ft. It also opened a Bellport Primary Care Center in 2014 to provide primary medicine to an underserved community.

EXECUTIVES

Vice President Operations, Satheesh Joseph

LOCATIONS

HQ: BROOKHAVEN MEMORIAL HOSPITAL MEDICAL CENTER, INC.
101 HOSPITAL RD, EAST PATCHOGUE, NY 117724870
Phone: 631 654-7100
Web: WWW.BROOKHAVENHOSPITAL.ORG

Selected Locations
Brookhaven Center for Wound Care and Hyperbaric Medicine - Patchogue New York
Brookhaven Family Medicine - Patchogue New York
Brookhaven Hemodialysis Center - Patchogue New York
Brookhaven Home Care - Patchogue New York
Brookhaven Hospice - Patchogue New York
Brookhaven Memorial Hospital Medical Center - Patchogue New York
Brookhaven Outpatient Imaging - Patchogue New York
Cardiac Rehabilitation - Patchogue New York
Diabetes Wellness Center - Patchogue New York
South Brookhaven Health Center East - Shirley New York
South Brookhaven Health Center West - Patchogue New York

PRODUCTS/OPERATIONS

Selected Services
Medical Services
  Behavioral Health
  Cancer Care
  Cardiology Department
  Family Medicine
  Long Island Orthopaedic and Spine Specialists
  Laboratory
  Neuroscience Center
  Pain Management
  Radiology Imaging
  Respiratory Care
  Surgery /
  Women's Im
Specialized Services
  Bariatric and Wellness Program
  Case Management
  Community Health Centers
  Coumadin Management Center
  Diabetes Wellness Center
  Hemodialysis Center
  Home Health Agency
  Hospice
  Nutrition
  Physical Rehabilitation
  Sleep Center
  Speech-Language Pathology
  Support Groups
  Wound Care / Hyperbaric Medicine

COMPETITORS

CSH
Catholic Health Services of Long Island
Catholic Healthcare System
Continuum Health Partners
Memorial Sloan-Kettering
New York City Health and Hospitals
Northwell Health

Income Statement

FYE: December 31

	REVENUE ($ mil.)	NET INCOME ($ mil.)	NET PROFIT MARGIN	EMPLOYEES
12/15	254	0	0.1%	2,100
12/14	245	(10)	—	—
12/13	284	13	4.8%	—
12/09	298	(2)	—	—
Annual Growth	(2.6%)	—	—	—

2015 Year-End Financials

Return on assets: 10.3%   Cash ($ mil.): 16
Return on equity: 0.1%
Current ratio: 0.90

BROOKLYN HOSPITAL CENTER

The Brooklyn Hospital Center has been taking care of ailing Kings County residents since before Brooklyn was a borough. Established in 1845 (before Brooklyn became part of New York City) the hospital houses some 460 beds and is a member of the NewYork-Presbyterian Healthcare System. It provides general medical and surgical care as well as a wide variety of specialty medical services including dialysis pediatrics obstetrics and cardiovascular care. The Brooklyn Hospital Center is affiliated with Weill Medical College of Cornell University. The hospital also operates a network of outpatient clinics providing primary and specialty care throughout the borough.

Operations

Each year the Brooklyn Hospital Center handles about 65000 ER visits 19000 inpatient stays and 150000 outpatient care visits. It has a medical staff of about 600 doctors. The hospital also conducts nursing and medical education programs.

Financial Performance

The Brooklyn Hospital Center has an annual operating budget of about $380 million.

Strategy

The Brooklyn Hospital Center is striving to increase the quality of its clinical programs and upgrade its infrastructure. It also aims to retain a quality medical staff and increase the hospitals educational and research activities.

Company Background

The Brooklyn Hospital Center filed for bankruptcy protection in 2005 when expensive expansion projects that didn't pay off as well as malpractice litigation left the company in more debt than it could manage. The hospital emerged from bankruptcy in 2007.

EXECUTIVES

Assistant Vice President Finan, Rubin Diaz
Associate Medical Director, Jeanette Haslett
Vice President Supply Chain, Bert Sansaricq
VP Human Resources, Guy Mennonna
R Vice President, Gary A Stephens
Assistant Vice President, Elizabeth Bonetti
Vice President Physician Services Revenue Enhancement And Analytics, Karen Milano
Vice President Internal Audit and Corporate Compliance, Lora Myers
Vice President Operations, Robert Aulicino
Vice President Financial, Sharon Wickes
Vice President Revenue, Dean Lindsey

Vice President Board Rltns and Secretary and Counsel, Kathleen M Burke
Vice President NURSING, Kathleen Treacy
Physical Therapy Director, Rita Hamburgh
Vice Chair, Armand Asarian

LOCATIONS

HQ: BROOKLYN HOSPITAL CENTER
121 DEKALB AVE, BROOKLYN, NY 112015493
Phone: 718 250-8000
Web: WWW.TBH.ORG

PRODUCTS/OPERATIONS

Selected Services
Bariatric Surgery
Cancer Care
Dental Care and Oral Surgery
Dialysis Services
Emergency Medicine
Family Medicine
The Family Medicine Residency
Geriatric Care
Home Health Services
Imaging and Radiology
Inpatient Hospitalist Care
Obstetrics and Gynecology
Orthopaedic Surgery
Pediatrics
Pediatric Cancer Care
Pediatric Emergency Services
Pediatric and Neonatal Critical Care
Sleep Center
Spine and Neurosurgery
Stroke Center
TeleHealth
Vascular Surgery
Wound Care

COMPETITORS

Brookdale University Hospital
Catholic Healthcare System
Continuum Health Partners
Kingsbrook Jewish Medical Center
Maimonides Medical Center
Montefiore Medical
New York City Health and Hospitals
Northwell Health
SUNY Downstate
Winthrop-University Hospital

Income Statement

FYE: December 31

	REVENUE ($ mil.)	NET INCOME ($ mil.)	NET PROFIT MARGIN	EMPLOYEES
12/15	345	3	1.0%	3,300
12/14	328	13	4.2%	—
12/13	362	31	8.8%	—
12/11	379	10	2.6%	—
Annual Growth	(2.3%)	(23.2%)	—	—

2015 Year-End Financials

Return on assets: 11.3%   Cash ($ mil.): 25
Return on equity: 1.0%
Current ratio: 0.80

BROWN CONSTRUCTION, INC.

EXECUTIVES

President, Ron Brown
Director, Collin Nichols
Marketing Director, Stacy Rhodes

Project Manager, John McCapes
Project Manager, Darrin Henry
Auditors: GALLINA LLP RANCHO CORDOVA C

LOCATIONS

HQ: BROWN CONSTRUCTION, INC.
1465 ENTP BLVD STE 100, WEST SACRAMENTO, CA 95691
Phone: 916 374-8616
Web: WWW.BROWN-CONSTRUCTION.COM

Income Statement

FYE: September 30

	REVENUE ($ mil.)	NET INCOME ($ mil.)	NET PROFIT MARGIN	EMPLOYEES
09/16	184	0	0.5%	71
09/15	198	0	0.0%	—
09/14	117	0	0.8%	—
09/13	61	(0)	—	—
Annual Growth	44.0%	—	—	—

2016 Year-End Financials

Return on assets: 17.2%   Cash ($ mil.): 3
Return on equity: 0.5%
Current ratio: 0.80

BROWN INTEGRATED LOGISTICS, INC.

EXECUTIVES

Chief Executive Officer, Brian Kinsey
Financial Executive, Daniel Joiner
Manager, Jody Shadden
Director, Jon Stanley
Financial Executive, Carol Snow
Auditors: GRANT THORNTON LLP ATLANTA G

LOCATIONS

HQ: BROWN INTEGRATED LOGISTICS, INC.
6908 CHAPMAN RD, LITHONIA, GA 300585246
Phone: 770 482-6521
Web: WWW.BROWNINTEGRATEDLOGISTICS.COM

Income Statement

FYE: September 24

	REVENUE ($ mil.)	NET INCOME ($ mil.)	NET PROFIT MARGIN	EMPLOYEES
09/16	203	1	0.5%	1,070
09/15	216	1	0.7%	—
09/14	224	1	0.7%	—
09/13	218	(0)	—	—
Annual Growth	(2.4%)	—	—	—

2016 Year-End Financials

Return on assets: 1.7%   Cash ($ mil.): —
Return on equity: 0.5%
Current ratio: 0.40

BRUCKNER TRUCK SALES, INC.

EXECUTIVES

President, Brian M Bruckner
Financial Executive, Mike Calahan
Manager, Chip McCampbell
Financial Executive, Tori Lofgren
Auditors: CLIFTON LARSON ALLEN LLP DALL

LOCATIONS

HQ: BRUCKNER TRUCK SALES, INC.
9471 E INTERSTATE 40, AMARILLO, TX 791186960
Phone: 806 376-6273
Web: WWW.BRUCKNERTRUCK.COM

HISTORICAL FINANCIALS

Company Type: Private

Income Statement

FYE: June 30

	REVENUE ($ mil.)	NET INCOME ($ mil.)	NET PROFIT MARGIN	EMPLOYEES
06/16	524	5	1.0%	900
06/15	580	10	1.8%	—
06/14	490	10	2.1%	—
06/10	200	2	1.1%	—
Annual Growth	**17.4%**	**15.5%**	—	—

2016 Year-End Financials

Return on assets: 2.3%   Cash ($ mil.): 18
Return on equity: 1.0%
Current ratio: 0.20

BRYAN MEDICAL CENTER

Bryan Medical Center is the centerpiece of a not-for-profit health care system serving residents of Lincoln Nebraska and surrounding communities. The medical center which operates as part of Bryan Health features two acute-care hospitals (Bryan East and Bryan West) housing a combined 670 beds. In addition to providing general medical and surgical care it serves as a regional trauma center and provides specialty care in areas such as cancer orthopedics and cardiology. The Bryan Health organization also includes a rural hospital and several outpatient clinics and it provides medical training home health care services and wellness programs.

Operations

In addition to Bryan Medical Center the Bryan Health organization operates the Crete Area Medical Center a 25-bed community hospital. Outpatient facilities include the Bryan Heart Institute (cardiology and cardiothoracic surgery) the Bryan Physician Network (family practice urgent care and specialist locations) and Bryan LifePointe (wellness and fitness programs). In addition the network includes the Bryan College of Health Sciences which provides bachelor's and master's degrees in nursing and health professional fields and the Bryan Foundation. It also conducts community education activities.

In the latest year for which data is available the hospital had 5912 inpatient visits; 6650 outpatient surgeries; and 68352 emergency department visits.

Geographic ReachBryan Medical Center serves patients throughout Nebraska as well as portions of neighboring states including Kansas Iowa and Missouri with clinics in more than 30 communities including Lincoln Columbus and Hastings.

Sales and Marketing

Bryan Medical Center advertises through magazines and through the Internet.

Strategy

In 2015 the hospital became the first in Nebraska to utilize the CardioMEMS HF System a miniaturized and wireless monitoring device to manage heart failure and reduce hospital admissions. That year it also began using the Kiva VCF Treatment System for the treatment of patients with vertebral compression fractures.

Company Background

The BryanLGH system was formed through the 1997 combination of Bryan Memorial Hospital (named after populist firebrand William Jennings Bryan) and Lincoln General Hospital. Bryan Health is part of the Heartland Health Alliance a group of about 40 Nebraska hospitals that work together to improve rural health care services through shared services and best practices.

In 2012 the health organization rebranded itself to reflect its expanded position in the region's health care market. BryanLGH Medical Center was renamed Bryan Medical Center and the broader health organization changed its name from the BryanLGH Health System to simply Bryan Health.

EXECUTIVES

Infection Control Director, Larry Krebsbach
Vice President, Cathy Parker
Respiratory Therapy Director, Marcy Wyrens
Pharmacy Manager, Penny Drews
Director of Radiology, Albert Owusu-ansah

LOCATIONS

HQ: BRYAN MEDICAL CENTER
1600 S 48TH ST, LINCOLN, NE 685061283
Phone: 402 481-1111
Web: WWW.BRYANHEALTH.COM

PRODUCTS/OPERATIONS

Selected Services
Bariatrics
Cardiac Services
Cancer
Cardiothoracic Surgery
Childbirth/Family Birthplace
Corporate & Community Wellness
Diabetes Center
Early Detection
Emergency Department
Heart Valve Center of Excellence
Hospitalists
Independence Center
Inpatient Rehabilitation
Neuroscience
Mental Health
Orthopedics
Outpatient Specialty Clinic
Radiation Oncology
Radiology
Rehabilitation/Therapy
Robotic Surgery
Sleep Medicine
StarCare Air Ambulance
Substance Abuse
Trauma Center
Urgent Care
Vascular Services
Women's & Children's

COMPETITORS

Catholic Health Initiatives
Children's Hospital & Medical Center
Madonna Rehabilitation Hospital
Methodist Health System
Nebraska Medical Center

HISTORICAL FINANCIALS

Company Type: Private

Income Statement

FYE: December 31

	REVENUE ($ mil.)	NET INCOME ($ mil.)	NET PROFIT MARGIN	EMPLOYEES
12/15	558	43	7.8%	3,970
12/14	507	34	6.8%	—
12/13*	273	48	17.7%	—
05/13	462	77	16.7%	—
Annual Growth	**6.5%**	**(17.3%)**	—	—

*Fiscal year change

2015 Year-End Financials

Return on assets: 3.0%   Cash ($ mil.): 161
Return on equity: 7.8%
Current ratio: 3.10

BRYANT UNIVERSITY

EXECUTIVES

President, Ronald Machtley
Vice-President, Barry Morrison
Auditors: KPMG LLP BOSTON MA

LOCATIONS

HQ: BRYANT UNIVERSITY
1150 DOUGLAS PIKE, SMITHFIELD, RI 029171291
Phone: 401 232-6000
Web: WWW.BRYANT.EDU

HISTORICAL FINANCIALS

Company Type: Private

Income Statement

FYE: June 30

	REVENUE ($ mil.)	NET INCOME ($ mil.)	NET PROFIT MARGIN	EMPLOYEES
06/15	198	15	8.1%	725
06/13	128	24	19.4%	—
06/12	129	(4)	—	—
06/11	0	0	—	—
Annual Growth	**—**	**458.9%**	—	—

2015 Year-End Financials

Return on assets: 11.5%   Cash ($ mil.): 56
Return on equity: 8.1%
Current ratio: 0.40

BRYN MAWR COLLEGE

These Mawrters aren't sacrificing anything especially when it comes to their education. Bryn Mawr is a college for women often referred to as Mawrters who hail from 60 countries. Its undergraduate programs including biology English math political science and psychology enroll 1300 students. Bryn Mawr also offers degrees through its co-educational Graduate School of Arts and Sciences and Graduate School of Social Work and Social Research which enrolls some 425 students. The college pools resources with Haverford Swarthmore and The University of Pennsylvania. Founded in 1885 Bryn Mawr is one of the nation's oldest women's colleges and the first to offer women an education through the Ph.D. level.

Geographic Reach

Located in Bryn Mawr Pennsylvania the college operates through a campus that consists of some 40 buildings.

Sales and Marketing

Bryn Mawr sources its student population from about 45 US states and nearly 60 countries. About 33% of the university's students come from the Mid-Atlantic region. Another 45% arrive from other US regions while foreign countries account for the remaining 22% of Bryn Mawr's undergraduate student population. Additionally some 73% of its student body receives grant aid.

Financial Performance

The women's college reported revenue of more than $108 million in fiscal year 2012. Bryn Mawr generates revenue through tuition and fees private contributions government grants and a formula of endowment payout after spending.

Strategy

Bryn Mawr offers programs for 37 majors and 38 minors. Through its partnership with The University of Pennsylvania the college in 2012 launched a program that allows Bryn Mawr students who are majoring in math and science to earn a master's degree from The University of Pennsylvania's School of Engineering and Applied Science with one additional year of study. The college also added an International Studies major to its roster of major programs bringing its total to 37.

EXECUTIVES

Assistant Secretary of the College, Jane Epstein
Secretary Of The College, Ruth Lindeborg

LOCATIONS

HQ: BRYN MAWR COLLEGE
101 N MERION AVE, BRYN MAWR, PA 190102899
Phone: 610 526-5000
Web: WWW.BRYNMAWR.EDU

PRODUCTS/OPERATIONS

Selected Graduate and Postbaccalaureate Programs
Graduate School of Arts and Sciences
Graduate School of Social Work and Social Research
Postbaccalaureate Premedical Program

HISTORICAL FINANCIALS
Company Type: Private

Income Statement

				FYE: May 31
	REVENUE ($ mil.)	NET INCOME ($ mil.)	NET PROFIT MARGIN	EMPLOYEES
05/15	225	67	29.9%	777
05/14	200	43	21.8%	—
05/13	114	75	66.3%	—
05/12	108	(42)	—	—
Annual Growth	27.6%	—	—	—

2015 Year-End Financials
Return on assets: 4.7%   Cash ($ mil.): 42
Return on equity: 29.9%
Current ratio: 0.30

BUCKNELL UNIVERSITY

Just getting into Bucknell University is an accomplishment. The highly selective private liberal arts school accepts only about 10% of applicants each year. Students who do get in some 3600 of them from around the world have the option to specialize in more than 50 majors and 60 minors. Bucknell confers both undergraduate and master's degrees in the liberal arts sciences engineering and music. It also offers programs in pre-law and pre-med. Bucknell tuition and fees total more than $58000; more than half of the student body typically receives financial aid. The school's student-to-faculty ratio is 10-to-1.

Operations

Some 86% of undergraduates live on campus. Bucknell has more than 350 full-time faculty members of which about 97% hold PhD or equivalent terminal degrees. Some 62% of faculty are tenured.

The university's Bertrand Library houses more than 800000 books.

Geographic Reach

In fiscal year 2013 Bucknell enrolled students from 46 states and 63 countries. The minority student enrollment is more than 500 with more than 175 foreign students.

Financial Performance

Bucknell's revenue increased by 4% in fiscal year 2013 thanks to higher net tuition and fees and an increase in net investment income from endowments.

The university reported $74 million of net income in fiscal year 2013 (compared to a loss in 2012) due to stronger non-operating net investment income and post retiree credits and an increase in income from grants and capital gifts.

Company Background

Bucknell was founded in 1846 as the University at Lewisburg.

EXECUTIVES

Vice President Of Campus Environment, Lynn Pierson
Vice President of Administrati, Clinton Kittrell
Vice President, Sean Coyne
Vice President Of Administration, Anthony Gingerelli
Vice President Of Administration, Taylor Mccready
Associate Vice President for Facilities, Ken Ogawa
Treasurer and Controller, Michael Cover
Treasurer, Chelsea Brinkman
Secretary, Kelly Sprague
Secretary, Rebecca Howell
Service Chair, Ava Ginsberg
Treasurer, Dan Hart
Secretary, Maura Higgins
Treasurer, Billy Raska
Chairman Emeritus, Robert Smith
Auditors: KPMG LLP HARRISBURG PA

LOCATIONS

HQ: BUCKNELL UNIVERSITY
1 DENT DR, LEWISBURG, PA 178372029
Phone: 570 577-2000
Web: WWW.BUCKNELL.EDU

HISTORICAL FINANCIALS
Company Type: Private

Income Statement

				FYE: June 30
	REVENUE ($ mil.)	NET INCOME ($ mil.)	NET PROFIT MARGIN	EMPLOYEES
06/16	222	(50)	—	1,300
06/13	196	74	37.8%	—
06/12	189	(28)	—	—
Annual Growth	4.1%	—	—	—

2016 Year-End Financials
Return on assets: 12.3%   Cash ($ mil.): 11
Return on equity: (-22.7%)
Current ratio: —

BUILDING PLASTICS, INC.

EXECUTIVES

President, Daniel Riley
Financial Executive, Dennis Russell
VP Sales & Marketing, John Anderson
Administrative Assistant, Sherry Hopper
President, Elaine Bennett
Marketing Director, Detra Burleson
Marketing Director, Michelle Harper
Purchasing Manager, Kelly Noble
Clerk, David Bennett
Auditors: CANNON WRIGHT BLOUNT PLLC MEM

LOCATIONS

HQ: BUILDING PLASTICS, INC.
3263 SHARPE AVE, MEMPHIS, TN 381113700
Phone: 901 744-6200
Web: WWW.BPIDECOSURF.COM

HISTORICAL FINANCIALS
Company Type: Private

Income Statement

				FYE: January 3
	REVENUE ($ mil.)	NET INCOME ($ mil.)	NET PROFIT MARGIN	EMPLOYEES
01/16*	219	4	1.9%	403
12/14	217	4	2.2%	—
12/13	200	3	1.9%	—
12/12	188	2	1.2%	—
Annual Growth	5.2%	23.4%	—	—

*Fiscal year change

2016 Year-End Financials
Return on assets: 2.8%   Cash ($ mil.): —
Return on equity: 1.9%
Current ratio: 0.50

BUTLER UNIVERSITY

EXECUTIVES

President, James M Danko
VP Finance, Bruce Arick
Treasurer, Bruce E Arick
Dean, William Neher
Financial Executive, Julian McGregor
Auditors: BKD LLP INDIANAPOLIS INDIAN

LOCATIONS

HQ: BUTLER UNIVERSITY
4600 SUNSET AVE, INDIANAPOLIS, IN 462083487
Phone: 317 940-8000
Web: WWW.BUTLERSPORTS.COM

HISTORICAL FINANCIALS
Company Type: Private

Income Statement

				FYE: May 31
	REVENUE ($ mil.)	NET INCOME ($ mil.)	NET PROFIT MARGIN	EMPLOYEES
05/16	192	7	4.0%	805
05/15	234	19	8.5%	—
05/14	163	27	16.8%	—
05/13	168	44	26.6%	—
Annual Growth	4.5%	(44.3%)	—	—

2016 Year-End Financials

Return on assets: 3.6% Cash ($ mil.): 18
Return on equity: 4.0%
Current ratio: —

BVH, INC.

EXECUTIVES

Vice-President, Ralph J Dyro
Vice-President, Jeffrey J Stamm
Executive Vice-President, Timothy W Triplett
Auditors: KPMG LLP KANSAS CITY MO

LOCATIONS

HQ: BVH, INC.
  11401 LAMAR AVE, OVERLAND PARK, KS 662111508
Phone: 913 458-2000

HISTORICAL FINANCIALS

Company Type: Private

Income Statement

FYE: January 1

	REVENUE ($ mil.)	NET INCOME ($ mil.)	NET PROFIT MARGIN	EMPLOYEES
01/16	2,955	108	3.7%	8,495
01/15	3,029	113	3.7%	—
Annual Growth	(2.5%)	(4.0%)	—	—

2016 Year-End Financials

Return on assets: 14.0% Cash ($ mil.): 388
Return on equity: 3.7%
Current ratio: 0.80

C C 1 BEER DISTRIBUTORS, INC.

EXECUTIVES

President, Carlos De La Cruz Sr
Financial Executive, Brenda Sevillano
Auditors: RSM PUERTO RICO SAN JUAN PUE

LOCATIONS

HQ: C C 1 BEER DISTRIBUTORS, INC.
  107 CARR 174, BAYAMON, PR 009591910
Phone: 787 288-6400

HISTORICAL FINANCIALS

Company Type: Private

Income Statement

FYE: December 31

	REVENUE ($ mil.)	NET INCOME ($ mil.)	NET PROFIT MARGIN	EMPLOYEES
12/15	236	13	5.7%	6
12/14	228	14	6.2%	—
12/13	218	13	6.1%	—
12/12	215	18	8.6%	—
Annual Growth	3.1%	(9.8%)	—	—

2015 Year-End Financials

Return on assets: 10.0% Cash ($ mil.): —
Return on equity: 5.7%
Current ratio: 0.90

C C 1 LIMITED PARTNERSHIP

EXECUTIVES

Financial Executive, Brenda Cevillano
Manager, Oscar Rosado
Auditors: RSM PUERTO RICO SAN JUAN PUE

LOCATIONS

HQ: C C 1 LIMITED PARTNERSHIP
  107 CARR 174, BAYAMON, PR 009591910
Phone: 787 288-6400
Web: WWW.COCACOLA.COM

HISTORICAL FINANCIALS

Company Type: Private

Income Statement

FYE: December 31

	REVENUE ($ mil.)	NET INCOME ($ mil.)	NET PROFIT MARGIN	EMPLOYEES
12/15	345	15	4.4%	816
12/14	337	0	0.1%	—
12/13	323	(0)	—	—
12/12	331	9	2.7%	—
Annual Growth	1.4%	18.4%	—	—

2015 Year-End Financials

Return on assets: 6.5% Cash ($ mil.): 5
Return on equity: 4.4%
Current ratio: 0.50

C.M. TUCKER LUMBER COMPANIES, LLC

EXECUTIVES

Board of Directors, Mark Tucker
Board of Directors, Paul Tucker
Board of Directors, Andrew Tucker
Auditors: PRICEWATERHOUSECOOPERS LLP C

LOCATIONS

HQ: C.M. TUCKER LUMBER COMPANIES, LLC
  601 N PEARL ST, PAGELAND, SC 297281628
Phone: 843 672-6135

HISTORICAL FINANCIALS

Company Type: Private

Income Statement

FYE: September 30

	REVENUE ($ mil.)	NET INCOME ($ mil.)	NET PROFIT MARGIN	EMPLOYEES
09/16	194	18	9.4%	280
09/15	166	10	6.5%	—
09/14	151	7	5.2%	—
09/13	137	7	5.6%	—
Annual Growth	12.2%	33.1%	—	—

2016 Year-End Financials

Return on assets: 2.1% Cash ($ mil.): 7
Return on equity: 9.4%
Current ratio: 4.30

CAJUN CONSTRUCTORS, LLC

EXECUTIVES

Chief Executive Officer, Ken Jacob
President, Todd W Grigsby
Chairman, L Lane Grigsby
Chief Financial Officer, Shane Recile
Sales Director, Tim Moore
Sales Manager, James Dunn
Senior Vice-President, Michael Calabrese
Vice-President, Mike Moran
Auditors: HANNIS T BOURGEOIS LLP BATO

LOCATIONS

HQ: CAJUN CONSTRUCTORS, LLC
  15635 AIRLINE HWY, BATON ROUGE, LA 708177318
Phone: 225 753-5857

HISTORICAL FINANCIALS

Company Type: Private

Income Statement

FYE: September 30

	REVENUE ($ mil.)	NET INCOME ($ mil.)	NET PROFIT MARGIN	EMPLOYEES
09/16	658	41	6.3%	1,000
09/15	521	25	4.9%	—
09/14	431	10	2.5%	—
09/13	275	10	4.0%	—
Annual Growth	33.7%	56.4%	—	—

2016 Year-End Financials

Return on assets: 7.4% Cash ($ mil.): 10
Return on equity: 6.3%
Current ratio: 0.10

CAJUN INDUSTRIES, LLC

Offering a mixed gumbo of services Cajun Industries builds oil refineries power plants process plants water-treatment plants and other industrial and infrastructure projects primarily in Louisiana and Texas. Subsidiary Cajun Constructors provides a full range of services from design/build to maintenance; Cajun Deep Foundations offers drilling piles installation and related services. Cajun Maritime focuses on marine coastal and oilfield services including construction repair and power distribution. Cajun Equipment Services manages a fleet of trucks and trailers that transport heavy and specialized loads. Chairman and owner Lane Grigsby founded the company as Cajun Contractors and Engineers in 1973.

The group is typically engaged in a variety of public and private projects including the expansion of the Port Arthur Refinery in Texas to become the largest refinery in the US. Cajun won several cleanup and reconstruction projects in New Orleans following Hurricane Katrina; these included helping to pump floodwater out of the city and rebuilding the Industrial Canal levee. It was also awarded several projects to construct floodwalls in the area.

Cajun is licensed to perform construction in more than 20 states.

EXECUTIVES

Vice President Of Marketing, John English

Vice President Construction Support Services, Jan Lass
Vice President Texas Operations, Carlton Janise
Vice President Operations, Lee Mayeux
Vice President Business Development, Randy Attuso
Vice President, Scott Callaway
Auditors: HANNIS T BOURGEOIS LLP BATO

LOCATIONS

HQ: CAJUN INDUSTRIES, LLC
15635 AIRLINE HWY, BATON ROUGE, LA 708177318
Phone: 225 753-5857

PRODUCTS/OPERATIONS

Selected Divisions
Cajun Constructors Inc.
Cajun Deep Foundations LLC
Cajun Equipment Services LLC
Cajun Maritime LLC

Selected Services
ASME code work
Bridge construction and repair
Building construction
Coastal restoration
Dock facility construction and repair
Deep foundation work
  Drill shafts
  Driven piles
  Earth retention
  Marine piles
Design/build
Emergency response
Hauling
Maintenance
Marsh and marine power transmission and distribution
Oilfield construction
Paving
Pipeline installation and repair
Plant dismantling and relocation
Procurement
Project management
Retrofits
Stevedoring
Structural steel erection
Turnarounds
Water quality

COMPETITORS

Bechtel	Jacobs Engineering
Boh Bros Construction	KBR
Eby	Performance
Fluor	Contractors

HISTORICAL FINANCIALS
Company Type: Private

Income Statement
FYE: September 30

	REVENUE ($ mil.)	NET INCOME ($ mil.)	NET PROFIT MARGIN	EMPLOYEES
09/16	721	56	7.9%	1,500
09/15	559	28	5.2%	—
09/14	476	11	2.5%	—
09/13	317	9	3.1%	—
Annual Growth	31.5%	80.4%	—	—

2016 Year-End Financials
Return on assets: 7.8%   Cash ($ mil.): 26
Return on equity: 7.9%
Current ratio: 1.10

CALIFORNIA BAPTIST UNIVERSITY

EXECUTIVES

President, Ronald L Ellis
Vice-President, Marilyn Johnson
Vice-President, David Lane Poole
Vice-President, John Petty
Director, Calvin Sparkman
Dean, Elaine Ahumada
Auditors: VICENTI LLOYD & STUTZMAN GLEN

LOCATIONS

HQ: CALIFORNIA BAPTIST UNIVERSITY
8432 MAGNOLIA AVE, RIVERSIDE, CA 925043297
Phone: 951 689-5771
Web: WWW.CALBAPTIST.EDU

HISTORICAL FINANCIALS
Company Type: Private

Income Statement
FYE: June 30

	REVENUE ($ mil.)	NET INCOME ($ mil.)	NET PROFIT MARGIN	EMPLOYEES
06/15	249	19	8.0%	300
06/14	227	28	12.4%	—
06/13	192	18	9.4%	—
06/10	113	6	5.3%	—
Annual Growth	17.0%	27.0%		

2015 Year-End Financials
Return on assets: 7.2%   Cash ($ mil.): 49
Return on equity: 8.0%
Current ratio: 0.40

CALIFORNIA HOSPITAL MEDICAL CENTER FOUNDATION

EXECUTIVES

Chairman of the Board, Phillip C Hill
Board of Directors, John Kramar
Manager, Annmarie Ramon
Director, Robert Rothbart

LOCATIONS

HQ: CALIFORNIA HOSPITAL MEDICAL CENTER FOUNDATION
1401 S GRAND AVE, LOS ANGELES, CA 900153010
Phone: 213 748-2411
Web: WWW.CHMCLA.ORG

HISTORICAL FINANCIALS
Company Type: Private

Income Statement
FYE: June 30

	REVENUE ($ mil.)	NET INCOME ($ mil.)	NET PROFIT MARGIN	EMPLOYEES
06/15	396	63	16.0%	1,500
06/09	241	31	13.2%	—
06/06	5	3	66.0%	—
06/05	4	2	47.0%	—
Annual Growth	55.2%	39.3%	—	—

2015 Year-End Financials
Return on assets: 3.9%   Cash ($ mil.): 84
Return on equity: 16.0%
Current ratio: 2.00

CALIFORNIA INDEPENDENT SYSTEM OPERATOR CORPORATION

The California Independent System Operator (California ISO) manages a 25627-mile power transmission system (about 80% of California's power grid) balancing wholesale supply to meet retail demand. The enterprise directs the flow of electricity along long-distance high-voltage power lines that connect California with neighboring states as well as with Mexico and Canada. It manages the transmission lines and supervises maintenance but the transmission systems are owned and maintained by individual utilities. The not-for-profit public benefit corporation also acts as a transmission planner.

Operations
California ISO also keeps its eye on about 760 powers plants with about 60000 MW of capacity which serve some 30 million California customers. As the control center for the California power grid the company matches buyers and sellers of electricity facilitating nearly 30000 market transactions every day to ensure enough power is on hand to meet demand. It delivers over 260 million MWhs of electricity annually and oversees more than 270000 miles of high-voltage power lines.

In 2013 the ISO power grid produce a new record of 4196 MW.

Geographic Reach
The company handles an about 35% of the electric load in the Western US including the high-voltage long-distance power lines that make up 80% of California's power grid and a small part of Nevada's.

Sales and Marketing
The company maintains partnership with more than 100 client organizations for a modern and reliable operation of the bulk power grid at the least wholesale cost.

Strategy
The ISO identifies and approves improvements to be made to the grid by individual transmission owners in order to meet state and federal standards for reliability.

To diversify California's power base the corporation has opened up its system to integrate the storage of electricity from alternative sources such as solar wind hydro batteries and flywheels. By 2020 in order to meet stringent carbon emission regulations it is aiming to have 33% of the power on its grid generated by renewable sources (mainly wind solar hydro and biomass).

The ISO is also looking replace the power delivered to about 1.4 million consumers by Southern California Edison's permanent shut-down in 2013 of the San Onofre Nuclear Generating Station.

In 2013 ISO Board approved a transition agreement for Merced Irrigation District to join the California ISO grid. The deal when final will take the number of community-owned municipal utilities

participating in the ISO as transmission members to nine.

Company Background

The organization was formed by the state government in 1996. The Independent System Operator assumed computerized command of California's wholesale power grid in 1998.

EXECUTIVES

VP Operations, Eric Schmitt
VP Market and Infrastructure Development, Keith Casey
VP Technology, Petar Ristanovic
President and CEO, Stephen (Steve) Berberich
Vice President, Michael Dozier
Area Vice President, Chris McIntosh
Chairman, Richard Maullin
Auditors: PRICEWATERHOUSECOOPERS LLP S

LOCATIONS

HQ: CALIFORNIA INDEPENDENT SYSTEM OPERATOR CORPORATION
250 OUTCROPPING WAY, FOLSOM, CA 956308773
Phone: 916 351-4400
Web: WWW.CAISO.COM

HISTORICAL FINANCIALS
Company Type: Private

Income Statement

	REVENUE ($ mil.)	NET INCOME ($ mil.)	NET PROFIT MARGIN	EMPLOYEES
12/15	213	13	6.2%	530
12/14	215	1	0.6%	—
12/13	213	(40)	—	—
12/07	200	46	23.0%	—
Annual Growth	0.8%	(14.4%)	—	—

FYE: December 31

2015 Year-End Financials
Return on assets: 5.5%
Return on equity: 6.2%
Current ratio: 0.90
Cash ($ mil.): 326

CALIFORNIA INSTITUTE OF TECHNOLOGY

The California Institute of Technology (Caltech) has an enlightened perspective on science. The institute enrolls about 2250 students and offers about two dozen majors across six academic divisions focused on biology chemistry engineering geology humanities and physics. Caltech has a very low student-teacher ratio of 3:1. The school receives about half of its operating revenue through research grants primarily from government agencies. Caltech operates the Jet Propulsion Laboratory (JPL) which supervises robotic Mars exploration programs and other interplanetary missions under contract to NASA. The school was founded in 1891.

Operations

CalTech's most popular majors are chemical engineering computer science electrical engineering mechanical engineering and physics. The school's primary research focus areas include energy medical science information science the universe the environment and nanoscience.

The JPL lab is responsible for about two dozen spacecraft missions in a given year.

Geographic Reach

Caltech has a student population that comes from more than 30 US states and 11 countries; international students account for more than 20% of enrollment. In addition to its facilities in California the institute has a network of about a dozen astronomy observatories across the US and in Antarctica and Chile.

Financial Performance

Caltech has a budget of about $2.3 billion and an endowment of about $2.1 billion. It gets some 54% of its revenue from contracts and grants and 19% from its endowment. Tuition and fees only account for about 6% of revenue.

Strategy

The institute has established new divisions of biology and biological engineering in recent years.

Company Background

Caltech's professors and graduates have snared more than 30 Nobel Prizes. Other alumni include filmmaker Frank Capra and Apollo 17 astronaut Harrison Schmitt.

EXECUTIVES

Provost, Edward M. Stolper
VP Business and Finance, Dean W. Currie
CIO, Richard E. (Rich) Fagen
VP; Director Jet Propulsion Laboratory, Charles Elachi, age 70
Vice Provost Research, Stephen L. Mayo
President, Thomas F. Rosenbaum
Chief Investment Officer, Scott Richland
Chair Chemistry and Chemical Engineering Division, Jacqueline K. Barton
Chair Physics Mathematics and Astronomy Division, B. Thomas Soifer
Chair Engineering and Applied Science Division, Guruswami Ravichandran
Chair Geological and Planetary Sciences Division, John P. Grotzinger
Chair Humanities and Social Sciences Division, Jean-Laurent Rosenthal
Chairman, David L. Lee, age 61
Vice Chairman, Ronald K. Linde
Auditors: PRICEWATERHOUSECOOPERS LLP LO

LOCATIONS

HQ: CALIFORNIA INSTITUTE OF TECHNOLOGY
1200 E CALIFORNIA BLVD, PASADENA, CA 911250001
Phone: 626 395-6811
Web: WWW.CALTECH.EDU

PRODUCTS/OPERATIONS

Selected Academic Divisions
Academics
  Biology
  Chemistry and Chemical Engineering
  Engineering and Applied Science
  Geological and Planetary Sciences
  Humanities and Social Sciences
  Physics Mathematics and Astronomy
Jet Propulsion Laboratory (NASA partnership)
  Galaxy Evolution Explorer Science Center
  Infrared Processing and Analysis Center
  NASA Exoplanet Science Institute
  NASA Herschel Science Center
  Spitzer Space Telescope Science Center

HISTORICAL FINANCIALS
Company Type: Private

Income Statement

	REVENUE ($ mil.)	NET INCOME ($ mil.)	NET PROFIT MARGIN	EMPLOYEES
09/16	2,561	203	7.9%	3,980
09/14	2,153	154	7.2%	—
09/13	2,005	182	9.1%	—
Annual Growth	8.5%	3.7%	—	—

FYE: September 30

2016 Year-End Financials
Return on assets: 12.4%
Return on equity: 7.9%
Current ratio: 0.20
Cash ($ mil.): 6

CALVIN COLLEGE

EXECUTIVES

President, Michael K Le Roy
Financial Executive, Geoffrey Bremer
Vice-President, Henry E Devries
Director, John Baas
Auditors: PLANTE & MORAN PLLC PORTAGE

LOCATIONS

HQ: CALVIN COLLEGE
3201 BURTON ST SE, GRAND RAPIDS, MI 495464388
Phone: 616 526-6000
Web: WWW.CALVIN.EDU

HISTORICAL FINANCIALS
Company Type: Private

Income Statement

	REVENUE ($ mil.)	NET INCOME ($ mil.)	NET PROFIT MARGIN	EMPLOYEES
06/15	175	6	3.8%	3,774
06/13	128	40	31.7%	—
06/12	114	(53)	—	—
06/11	1,108	0	0.0%	—
Annual Growth	(36.9%)	1125.5%	—	—

FYE: June 30

2015 Year-End Financials
Return on assets: 7.0%
Return on equity: 3.8%
Current ratio: 0.40
Cash ($ mil.): 27

CAMPBELL COUNTY HOSPITAL DISTRICT

EXECUTIVES

Chief Executive Officer, Robert Morasko
Vice-President, Debra Tonn
Director, Keith Mills
Auditors: CLIFTONLARSONALLEN LLP MINNEA

LOCATIONS

HQ: CAMPBELL COUNTY HOSPITAL DISTRICT
501 S BURMA AVE, GILLETTE, WY 827163426
Phone: 307 688-1551
Web: WWW.CCHWYO.ORG

HISTORICAL FINANCIALS
Company Type: Private

Income Statement

	REVENUE ($ mil.)	NET INCOME ($ mil.)	NET PROFIT MARGIN	EMPLOYEES
06/16	172	10	6.1%	1,043
06/13	137	9	6.8%	—
06/12	129	18	14.1%	—
06/08	2,144	0	—	—
Annual Growth	(27.0%)	592.7%	—	—

FYE: June 30

2016 Year-End Financials
Return on assets: 3.4%   Cash ($ mil.): 5
Return on equity: 6.1%
Current ratio: 0.20

CAPE COD HEALTHCARE, INC.

Cape Cod Healthcare (CCHC) is a not-for-profit healthcare organization that operates two acute care hospitals (Cape Cod Hospital and Falmouth Hospital) with a total of more than 350 beds. Specializations include heart and vascular women's health bones and muscles cancer care and brain spine and nerves. CCHC also operates a home health services agency (Visiting Nurse Association of Cape Cod) primary and specialized care clinics a 130-bed skilled nursing and rehabilitation facility (JML Care Center) and a 60-unit assisted living facility (Heritage at Falmouth). The health care system has an affiliation with UMass Medical School whereby students can receive hands-on training at Cape Cod Hospital.

Operations

CCHC is the Cape's largest private employer with nearly 5000 staff members including more than 450 physicians. The system has about 120000 emergency department visits each year and facilitates about 1200 births and performs more than 14000 surgical procedures annually.

Financial Performance

CCHC's net patient revenue numbers have been increasing over the past five years. In fiscal 2016 it increased 8% to $817 million. Like most hospitals net patient revenue represents the bulk of CCHC's total revenue.

Strategy

While CCHC enjoys a strong market share in the Cape Cod region it also struggles with seasonal fluctuations and high Medicare and Medicaid numbers within its patient load. As such the company could be impacted by reform measures that could decrease Medicare reimbursement levels. CCHC plans to continue its efforts to control costs and increase efficiencies to keep its operations nimble and keep pace with the changing health care environment.

Faced with rising operating costs and lower reimbursement rates the system in 2017 agreed to sell its outreach lab services operations to Quest Diagnostics. As a focused lab services provider Quest is able to provide testing at a lower cost than the typical hospital-based laboratory. The two companies will partner to provide an expanded array of diagnostics to the Cape Cod community.

EXECUTIVES

Senior Vice President, Jeff Dykens
President and CEO, Michael K. (Mike) Lauf, age 46
COO, Michael Bundy
SVP Communications and Business Development, Patrick Kane
SVP Finance and CFO, Michael L. Connors
Chief Medical Officer, Donald A. Guadagnoli
SVP and CIO, Jeanne M. Fallon
President and CEO VNA of Cape Cod, Dianne C. Kolb
Radiology Medical Director, Michael Fishbein
Director Of Nursing, Paula Cronin
Director of Medical Records, Susan Douglas
Vice President Of Finance, Jean Butler
Vice President, David Ryan

Senior Vice President of Managed Care, Jack D Lipomi
Vice President Patient Financial Services, Victor Oliveira
Vice President, Lori Jewett
Chairman, William Zammer
Vice Chairman, DeWitt Davenport
Auditors: PRICEWATERHOUSECOOPERS LLP BO

LOCATIONS

HQ: CAPE COD HEALTHCARE, INC.
27 PARK ST, HYANNIS, MA 026015230
Phone: 508 862-5030
Web: WWW.GIVETOCAPECODHEALTH.ORG

PRODUCTS/OPERATIONS

Selected Massachusetts Facilities
Bourne Health Center
Cape Cod Hospital (Hyannis)
Davenport Mugar Cancer Center (Hyannis)
Falmouth Hospital
  Clark Cancer Center
Fontaine Medical Center (Harwich)
Heritage at Falmouth
JLM Care Center (Falmouth)
Mashpee Health Center
Sandwich Health Center
Wilkins Outpatient Medical Complex (Hyannis)

COMPETITORS

Baystate Health	Partners HealthCare
Boston Medical Center	Southcoast Hospitals
Cambridge Health	Group
Alliance	Steward Health Care
Care New England	Universal Health
CareGroup	Services
Milford Regional	Winchester Healthcare
Medical Center	
Northeast Health	
System	

HISTORICAL FINANCIALS

Company Type: Private

Income Statement
FYE: September 30

	REVENUE ($ mil.)	NET INCOME ($ mil.)	NET PROFIT MARGIN	EMPLOYEES
09/16	837	74	8.9%	1,850
09/12	680	80	11.9%	—
09/11	648	37	5.7%	—
09/09	81	0	0.0%	—
Annual Growth	39.4%	481.3%	—	—

2016 Year-End Financials
Return on assets: 13.1%   Cash ($ mil.): 49
Return on equity: 8.9%
Current ratio: 1.00

CAPE COD HOSPITAL

Get too much sun or eat too much lobster while visiting Cape Cod? Never fear Cape Cod Hospital can treat whatever ails you. Cape Cod Hospital a subsidiary of Cape Cod Healthcare is a 260-bed acute care hospital that serves the Cape Cod Massachusetts area. Its specialty services include pediatrics maternity care cancer treatment and infectious disease therapeutics. The not-for-profit Cape Cod Hospital also includes a specialty cardiovascular center a psychiatry unit a surgical pavilion and a diagnostic imaging facility as well as outpatient medical offices.

Operations

Cape Cod Hospital's emergency department treats about 85000 patients each year. The medical center also performs more than 12500 surgeries and 1000 birth procedures each year as well as about 2 million laboratory tests. Its 20-bed Cape Psych Center provides inpatient and outpatient mental and behavioral services. The campus also includes more than a dozen medical offices buildings and a community health center. Cape Cod Hospital's staff includes about 300 physicians.

Geographic Reach

Cape Cod Hospital is located on a 40-acre campus on the shoreline of Hyannis Massachusetts.

Strategy

To keep its facilities modern and efficient in 2015 the company opened a new emergency center located adjacent to the existing emergency center. The 18-month $22 million project added 25000 sq. ft. of space and 72 patient treatment rooms.

In 2013 Cape Cod Hospital reopened the renovated and expanded Intensive Care Unit. That project cost $4.9 million and doubled the size of the original area.

To control the cost of providing hospital care parent Cape Cod Healthcare has also been expanding its outpatient and ambulatory care services. It is adding new urgent care centers and surgery centers both near the hospital and in surrounding communities.

Company Background

Cape Cod Hospital was established in Hyannis in 1920.

EXECUTIVES

Ambulatory Services Director, Robin Grace
Vice President, Stephanie Nadolny
Nursing Director, Joanie Drushella
Senior Vice President of Finance, Mike Connors
Infection Control Director, Georgia Dash

LOCATIONS

HQ: CAPE COD HOSPITAL
27 PARK ST, HYANNIS, MA 026015203
Phone: 508 862-7575
Web: WWW.CAPECODHEALTH.ORG

PRODUCTS/OPERATIONS

Selected Services
Allergy and Immunology
Behavioral Health
Blood Center
Dermatology
Foot Care & Surgery
Hand Surgery
Orthopedics
Pregnancy & Birth
Sports Medicine
Women's Health

COMPETITORS

Baystate Health	Northeast Health
Boston Medical Center	System
Cambridge Health	Partners HealthCare
Alliance	Southcoast Hospitals
Care New England	Group
CareGroup	Steward Health Care
Children's Hospital	Sturdy Memorial
Boston	Universal Health
Milford Regional	Services
Medical Center	Winchester Healthcare

HISTORICAL FINANCIALS
Company Type: Private

Income Statement
FYE: September 30

	REVENUE ($ mil.)	NET INCOME ($ mil.)	NET PROFIT MARGIN	EMPLOYEES
09/15	462	33	7.2%	1,700
09/14	439	24	5.7%	—
09/13	407	19	4.8%	—
09/12	427	52	12.3%	—
Annual Growth	2.7%	(14.1%)	—	—

2015 Year-End Financials
Return on assets: 9.1% Cash ($ mil.): 21
Return on equity: 7.2%
Current ratio: 1.00

CAPE FEAR VALLEY MEDICAL CENTER

EXECUTIVES

Chief Executive Officer, Michael Nagowski
Director, Lynne M Gilberti
Director, Sabena A Johnson
Director, Dimiter H Zafirov

LOCATIONS

HQ: CAPE FEAR VALLEY MEDICAL CENTER
1638 OWEN DR, FAYETTEVILLE, NC 283043424
Phone: 910 615-4000
Web: WWW.CAPEFEARVALLEY.COM

HISTORICAL FINANCIALS
Company Type: Private

Income Statement
FYE: September 30

	REVENUE ($ mil.)	NET INCOME ($ mil.)	NET PROFIT MARGIN	EMPLOYEES
09/15	630	23	3.8%	2,711
09/14	590	40	6.8%	—
09/13	823	398	48.4%	—
Annual Growth	(12.5%)	(75.5%)	—	—

2015 Year-End Financials
Return on assets: 4.6% Cash ($ mil.): 38
Return on equity: 3.8%
Current ratio: 0.70

CAPE MEMORIAL HOSPITAL, INC.

EXECUTIVES

Chief Executive Officer, James R Nathan
Training Director, Barbara Roberts
Director, Richard Helvey
Director, Pablo Mora

LOCATIONS

HQ: CAPE MEMORIAL HOSPITAL, INC.
636 DEL PRADO BLVD S, CAPE CORAL, FL
339902668
Phone: 239 424-2000

HISTORICAL FINANCIALS
Company Type: Private

Income Statement
FYE: September 30

	REVENUE ($ mil.)	NET INCOME ($ mil.)	NET PROFIT MARGIN	EMPLOYEES
09/15	204	28	14.2%	50
09/13	181	17	9.5%	—
09/12	178	17	9.9%	—
Annual Growth	4.6%	17.8%	—	—

CAPISTRANO UNIFIED SCHOOL DISTRICT

EXECUTIVES

Chief Executive Officer, John M Alpay
Board of Directors, Jane Boss
Board of Directors, Joel Drew
Superintendent, Lois Anderson
Director, Kristin Nelson
Administration Manager, T K Frantz
Auditors: VAVRINEK TRINE DAY & CO LL

LOCATIONS

HQ: CAPISTRANO UNIFIED SCHOOL DISTRICT
33122 VALLE RD, SAN JUAN CAPISTRANO, CA
926754859
Phone: 949 234-9200
Web: WWW.CAPISTRANOADULTSCHOOL.ORG

HISTORICAL FINANCIALS
Company Type: Private

Income Statement
FYE: June 30

	REVENUE ($ mil.)	NET INCOME ($ mil.)	NET PROFIT MARGIN	EMPLOYEES
06/16	528	29	5.6%	4,500
06/05	3	0	—	—
06/03	380	(66)	—	—
06/02	0	0	—	—
Annual Growth	—	—	—	—

CAPITAL SALES COMPANY

EXECUTIVES

President, Sam Haddad
Manager, Venessa Dickow
Administrative Assistant, Elizabeth Schwartz
Auditors: STEFFORIA PETIK & ASSOCIATES

LOCATIONS

HQ: CAPITAL SALES COMPANY
1471 E 9 MILE RD, HAZEL PARK, MI 480301960
Phone: 248 542-4400
Web: WWW.CAPITALCSC.COM

HISTORICAL FINANCIALS
Company Type: Private

Income Statement
FYE: December 31

	REVENUE ($ mil.)	NET INCOME ($ mil.)	NET PROFIT MARGIN	EMPLOYEES
12/15	202	7	3.8%	60
12/14	189	10	5.5%	—
12/13	169	8	5.1%	—
Annual Growth	9.5%	(6.2%)	—	—

2015 Year-End Financials
Return on assets: 0.4% Cash ($ mil.): 4
Return on equity: 3.8%
Current ratio: 6.40

CARE NEW ENGLAND HEALTH SYSTEM INC

Care New England Health System take pains to ease its patients' pain. The system operates four hospitals: Kent Hospital a general acute care facility with about 360 beds; the 290-bed Memorial Hospital of Rhode Island; psychiatric facility Butler Hospital; and Women & Infants Hospital of Rhode Island which specializes in obstetrics gynecology and newborn pediatrics. All told the system has more than 963 licensed beds. Care New England formed in 1996 by three member hospitals also operates a home health agency and outpatient care facilities. In late 2016 the system dropped its plans to merge with Massachusetts-based Southcoast Health.

Operations

Three of the Care New England hospitals — Memorial Hospital Women & Infants and Butler — are teaching hospitals for Brown University's Warren Alpert Medical School. Altogether the organization's facilities handle more than 40000 inpatient discharges each year as well as 129000 emergency room visits and 9800 births.

The organization's VNA of Care New England unit administers home health and hospice care as well as private duty nursing services for the elderly new mothers and terminally ill patients. The Care New England Wellness Center offers fitness and rehabilitation services. The health care network also includes physician practice locations and an adult day care center.

Geographic Reach

Based in Providence Rhode Island Care New England serves southeastern New England communities including Central Falls and Pawtucket Rhode Island and Plainville Massachusetts.

Financial Performance

In 2014 the system posted revenue of $1.1 billion.

Strategy

The Care New England system is focused on five key initiatives: system strength clinical excellence physician alignment strategic partnerships and academic excellence. It is working to strengthen operations in clinical fields including cardiology emergency medicine behavioral health pathology pediatrics and women's health. In 2013

the company enhanced its mental health services by forming an affiliation with The Providence Center. In addition Kent Hospital launched the construction of a new ambulatory surgery and primary care center.

Mergers and Acquisitions

The Care New England organization added its fourth hospital in 2013 through the acquisition of Memorial Hospital of Rhode Island. The purchase added acute care and primary care capacity and expanded the organization's regional presence.

In late 2015 Care New England and Southcoast Health signed a letter of intent to merge. The deal will create a new parent organization to oversee both health systems.

EXECUTIVES

Vice President For Clinical Support Services, Paul Heffernan
System Vice President Facilities, David Duncan
Vice Chairman, Richard P Welch
Auditors: PRICEWATERHOUSECOOPERS LLP BO

LOCATIONS

HQ: CARE NEW ENGLAND HEALTH SYSTEM INC
45 WILLARD AVE, PROVIDENCE, RI 029053218
Phone: 401 453-7900
Web: WWW.CARENEWENGLAND.ORG

COMPETITORS

Baystate Health
Community Health
  Systems
Lifespan Corporation
Partners HealthCare
Roger Williams Medical
  Center

Southcoast Hospitals
  Group
Tenet Healthcare
Universal Health
  Services
Yale New Haven Health
  System

HISTORICAL FINANCIALS

Company Type: Private

Income Statement

	REVENUE ($ mil.)	NET INCOME ($ mil.)	NET PROFIT MARGIN	EMPLOYEES
				FYE: September 30
09/16	1,154	(63)	—	6,500
09/15	126	(8)	—	—
09/13	94	1	2.1%	—
09/12	846	24	2.8%	—
Annual Growth	8.1%	—	—	—

2016 Year-End Financials

Return on assets: 11.9%
Return on equity: (-5.5%)
Current ratio: 0.90
Cash ($ mil.): 55

CAREALLIANCE HEALTH SERVICES

CareAlliance Health Services (doing business as Roper St. Francis Healthcare) operates four hospitals — the 370-bed Roper Hospital the 200-bed Bon Secours St. Francis Hospital the 85-bed Mount Pleasant Hospital and the Roper Rehabilitation Hospital. Besides providing home health services it also operates outpatient emergency primary care and diagnostic facilities. Roper St. Francis Healthcare serves Charleston South Carolina and surrounding communities. Its Roper St. Francis Physician Partners is one of the region's largest physician practices.

Operations

The health system comprises Roper Hospital Bon Secours St. Francis Hospital Roper St. Francis Mount Pleasant Hospital Roper St. Francis Foundation and Roper St. Francis Physicians Network. Altogether it boasts three acute care hospitals with 655-plus beds one specialty hospital 15 centers for outpatient services three industrial medicine sites five emergency rooms and two urgent care centers.

Roper St. Francis Healthcare has a medical staff of some 800 physicians. The Roper St. Francis Physician Partners organization has more than 230 physicians who offer primary and specialty care including family practice internal medicine and pediatrics.

Geographic Reach

Altogether Roper St. Francis Healthcare operates about 90 facilities in seven counties in the lowcountry region of South Carolina.

Strategy

The health system in 2014 signed an agreement with Trendlines Lab to collaborate on the development of new medical device inventions as well as low-cost solutions for clinical problems. The partnership will work to create devices that will address unmet needs identified by physicians and other health care providers.

Company Background

Roper St. Francis Healthcare was formed through the merger of Roper Hospital and Bon Secours St. Francis Hospital in 1998.

Roper St. Francis Physician Partners was formed through the 2009 combination of Roper St. Francis Physicians' Network and Lowcountry Medical Associates.

EXECUTIVES

President and CEO, David L. Dunlap
VP and CIO, Mike Taylor
Vice President of Medical Affairs & Chief Medical Officer, Steven Shapiro
SVP and CFO, Bret Johnson
CEO Roper Hospital and SVP Operations, Matthew Severance
CEO Roper St. Francis Mount Pleasant Hospital and VP Operations, John Sullivan
CEO Bon Secours St. Francis Hospital and SVP Operations, Allen Carroll
Chairman Roper St. Francis Foundation, John B. Holloway
Vice Chairman Roper St. Francis Foundation, Charles T. Cole
Vice President Nursing & Senior Nurse Executive Bon Secours St. Francis, Pennie Peralta
CEO RSF Physician Partners & RSFH Vice President & Chief Strategy Officer, Douglas Bowling
Interim Chief Nursing Officer Vice President Nursing Roper Hospital, Susan Bennett
Medical Director Corporate Health, Edward Galaid
Director of Home Healthcare Srv, Bonnie Mello
Vice President Quality and Training, Tanya Lott
Director of Pharmacy, Holly Balcer
Vice President Strategic Planning, Doug Bowling
Chairman of the Board, Pierre Manigault
Auditors: DELOITTE & TOUCHE LLP CHARLO

LOCATIONS

HQ: CAREALLIANCE HEALTH SERVICES
316 CALHOUN ST, CHARLESTON, SC 294011113
Phone: 843 724-2000
Web: WWW.ROPERSAINTFRANCIS.COM

Selected South Carolina Facilities

Hospitals
  Mt. Pleasant Hospital Campus - Mount Pleasant
  Roper Hosp
  Roper Rehabilitation Hospital
  St. Franci
Outpatient Centers
  After Hours Care - James Island

Kiawah-Seabrook Medical & Urgent Care
  Roper Hosp
Roper Hospital Ambulatory Surgery & Pain
  Management - James Island
  Roper Hosp
  Roper Hosp
  Roper Hosp
  Roper Hosptial Diagnostics - Goose Creek
  Roper Hosptial Diagnostics - James Island
  Roper Hosp
  Roper Hosptial Diagnostics - Moncks Corner
  Roper Hospital Imaging - Wesley Drive
  Roper Hospital Imaging - Wingo Way

COMPETITORS

Beaufort Memorial
  Hospital
Conway Medical Center
Georgetown Hospital
  System
Grand Strand Regional
  Medical Center

HCA
Medical University of
  South Carolina
Tenet Healthcare

HISTORICAL FINANCIALS

Company Type: Private

Income Statement

	REVENUE ($ mil.)	NET INCOME ($ mil.)	NET PROFIT MARGIN	EMPLOYEES
				FYE: December 31
12/15	827	16	1.9%	5,000
12/14	793	(2)	—	—
12/09	682	56	8.3%	—
12/08	618	(51)	—	—
Annual Growth	4.3%	—	—	—

2015 Year-End Financials

Return on assets: 7.0%
Return on equity: 1.9%
Current ratio: 0.90
Cash ($ mil.): 31

CARILION CLINIC

If the name rings a bell for Virginians it may be because Carilion Clinic provides medical care for the citizens of southwestern Virginia. The regional health system includes eight not-for-profit hospitals a network of physicians and a research partnership with Virginia Tech. Carilion Clinic (including its handful of affiliates) has some 1200 beds and 60 neonatal ICU beds available. In addition to providing a range of medical treatments Carilion Clinic provides continuing medical education through its affiliation with medical schools including Virginia Tech Carilion School of Medicine and Research Institute (VTC).

Operations

Carilion Clinic employs some 650 physicians which provide services in about 70 specialist fields. Its network of facilities includes about 230 practice locations. The organization handles some 877000 primary care visits per year as well as 48660 inpatient hospital visits and 168970 emergency room visits. Carilion Clinic provides about $140 million in community benefits each year including uncompensated care education efforts and research programs.

Geographic Reach

Carilion Clinic serves 18 counties in western Virginia and southern West Virginia.

Strategy

Carilion Clinic is in the midst of a 10-year process of reorganizing its philosophy structure and IT infrastructure in an effort to streamline patient care and expenses. Its partnership with Virginia Tech for the medical school and clinical research institute is part of that reorganization;

classes for its first doctoral candidates began in 2010. Other steps have included acquisitions and partnerships and new construction.

The group is expanding its outpatient care network to bring more health care services to medically under-served areas.

In fiscal 2015Carilion Clinic opened new Cosmetic Center in Roanoke. The new center features the services of three board certified plastic surgeons and offers cosmetic procedures including skin care treatments such as laser hair removal chemical peels and facials as well as two skin care lines: Obagi and SkinMedica.

Company Background

The organization opened four VelocityCare Urgent Care Centers in the region in 2012. In addition the group spent about $100 million to upgrade to a new electronic health record system and expand its clinical research programs.

In 2010 Carilion Labs and Spectrum Laboratory Network merged to form Spectrum-Carilion a regional laboratory company and one of the 10 largest in the US. The lab began expanding through acquisitions in 2010 and was renamed Solstas Lab Partners in early 2011. The venture is 33%-owned by Carilion Clinic.

In 2009 Carilion Clinic received federal approval to operate and offer a Medicare Advantage Plan that year. To that end the organization launched the Carilion Clinic Medicare Health Plan which offers a range of plan designs with no or low member premiums.

The organization was founded in 1899 as the Roanoke Hospital Association.

EXECUTIVES

EVP, Melina D. Perdue
EVP and CFO, Donald B. Halliwill
EVP and Chief Strategy Officer, Thomas D. Denberg
EVP and Chief Administrative Officer, Jeanne S. Armentrout
President and CEO, Nancy Howell Agee
EVP and Chief Medical Officer, Patrice M. Weiss
Medical Director, Thomas Milam
Vice President, William Flattery
Senior Vice President Chief Medical Information Officer, Stephen Morgan
Head Nurse, Cathy Booze
Interim Vice President of Patient Financial Services, Larry Carter
Director of Pharmacy, Clara Anne Davis Spencer
Vice President, Gary Scott
Vice President Of Clinical Support, Tim Auwarter
Medical Director, Anita Kablinger
Medical Director, David Musick
Vice President Information Technology, Freida Driver
Radiology Director, Sharon Bass
Senior Vice President and Chief Human Resources Officer, Paul Hudgins
Senior Vice President and General Counsel, Nicholas C Conte
Chair, James A. Hartley
Secretary, Kimberly Bolden
Secretary, Jennifer Jessee
Board Member, Richard Vari
Auditors: DELOITTE & TOUCHE LLP CHARLO

LOCATIONS

HQ: CARILION CLINIC
1906 BELLEVIEW AVE SE, ROANOKE, VA 240141838
Phone: 540 981-7900
Web: WWW.GOODNEIGHBORPHARMACY.COM

Selected Locations
Bedford Memorial Hospital (160 beds — Bedford Virginia)
Carilion Franklin Memorial Hospital (40 beds — Rocky Mount Virginia)

Carilion Giles Memorial Hospital (25 beds — Pearlsburg Virginia)
Carilion New River Valley Medical Center (150 beds — Christianburg Virginia)
Carilion Roanoke Community Hospital (35 beds — Roanoke Virginia)
Carilion Roanoke Memorial Hospital (700 beds — Roanoke Virginia)
Carilion Stonewall Jackson Hospital (25 beds — Lexington Virginia)
Carilion Tazewell Community Hospital (60 beds — Tazewell Virginia)

COMPETITORS

Alamance Regional Medical Center
Alleghany Regional Hospital
Ascension Health
Bon Secours Health
Centra Health Inc.
Danville Regional Medical Center
Forsyth Medical Center
High Point Regional Health System
Inova
Martha Jefferson Hospital
Memorial Hospital (Martinsville)
Montgomery Regional Hospital
Novant Health
Princeton Community Hospital
Sentara Healthcare
Twin County Regional Healthcare

HISTORICAL FINANCIALS
Company Type: Private

Income Statement
FYE: September 30

	REVENUE ($ mil.)	NET INCOME ($ mil.)	NET PROFIT MARGIN	EMPLOYEES
09/16*	1,482	(1)	—	9,200
03/16	800	19	2.4%	—
09/15	1,510	(42)	—	—
09/14	1,489	(28)	—	—
Annual Growth	(0.2%)	—	—	—

*Fiscal year change

2016 Year-End Financials
Return on assets: 2.3%
Return on equity: (-0.1%)
Current ratio: 1.10
Cash ($ mil.): —

CARILION MEDICAL CENTER

EXECUTIVES

Chief Executive Officer, Nancy Howell Agee
Board of Directors, Briggs Andrews
Manager, David Hagadorn
Vice-President, Joseph Austin
Auditors: DELOITTE & TOUCHE LLP CHARLOT

LOCATIONS

HQ: CARILION MEDICAL CENTER
1906 BELLEVIEW AVE SE, ROANOKE, VA 240141838
Phone: 540 981-7000
Web: WWW.CARILION.COM

HISTORICAL FINANCIALS
Company Type: Private

Income Statement
FYE: September 30

	REVENUE ($ mil.)	NET INCOME ($ mil.)	NET PROFIT MARGIN	EMPLOYEES
09/16	1,177	4	0.4%	6,390
09/15	1,064	(36)	—	—
09/13	896	116	12.9%	—
09/09	715	(78)	—	—
Annual Growth	7.4%	—	—	—

2016 Year-End Financials
Return on assets: 2.3%
Return on equity: 0.4%
Current ratio: 1.00
Cash ($ mil.): —

CAROLINAEAST MEDICAL CENTER

EXECUTIVES

President, G Raymond Leggett III
Vice-President, Lesley Hunter
Administrative Assistant, Mike Ciancio
Director, Lynda Honaker
Manager, Megan McGarvey
Administrative Assistant, Deb Rogers

LOCATIONS

HQ: CAROLINAEAST MEDICAL CENTER
2000 NEUSE BLVD, NEW BERN, NC 285603449
Phone: 252 633-8111
Web: WWW.CAROLINAEASTHEALTH.COM

HISTORICAL FINANCIALS
Company Type: Private

Income Statement
FYE: September 30

	REVENUE ($ mil.)	NET INCOME ($ mil.)	NET PROFIT MARGIN	EMPLOYEES
09/15	320	2	0.7%	1,630
09/14	301	25	8.4%	—
09/13	295	28	9.7%	—
09/12	284	31	11.1%	—
Annual Growth	4.1%	(59.1%)		

2015 Year-End Financials
Return on assets: 3.9%
Return on equity: 0.7%
Current ratio: 1.70
Cash ($ mil.): 68

CARPENTERS HEALTH & WELFARE TRUST FUND OF ST. LOUIS

EXECUTIVES

Supervisor, Pat Hill
Auditors: WOLFE NILGES NAHORSKI PC ST L

LOCATIONS

HQ: CARPENTERS HEALTH & WELFARE TRUST FUND
OF ST. LOUIS
1419 HAMPTON AVE, SAINT LOUIS, MO 631393100
Phone: 314 644-4802
Web: WWW.CARPDC.ORG

HISTORICAL FINANCIALS
Company Type: Private

Income Statement   FYE: April 30

	REVENUE ($ mil.)	NET INCOME ($ mil.)	NET PROFIT MARGIN	EMPLOYEES
04/15	198	22	11.2%	61
04/14	189	12	6.5%	—
04/13	129	(5)	—	—
04/12	133	4	3.5%	—
Annual Growth	14.1%	68.3%	—	—

2015 Year-End Financials

Return on assets: 0.4%   Cash ($ mil.): 25
Return on equity: 11.2%
Current ratio: 53.20

CARROLLTON-FARMERS BRANCH INDEPENDENT SCHOOL DISTRICT

EXECUTIVES

Superintendent, Bobby Burns
Director of Finance, Scott Roderick
Purchasing Agent, Debbie Lehman
Director, Jason Wheeler
Purchasing Director, Scott Rodrick
Assistant Manager, Tonya Tillman
Assistant Manager, Michelle Bailey
Auditors: HANKINS EASTUP DEATON TONN

LOCATIONS

HQ: CARROLLTON-FARMERS BRANCH INDEPENDENT
SCHOOL DISTRICT
1445 N PERRY RD, CARROLLTON, TX 750066134
Phone: 972 968-6100
Web: WWW.CFBISD.EDU

HISTORICAL FINANCIALS
Company Type: Private

Income Statement   FYE: August 31

	REVENUE ($ mil.)	NET INCOME ($ mil.)	NET PROFIT MARGIN	EMPLOYEES
08/16	316	(10)	—	4,020
08/15	306	(13)	—	—
08/14	290	(11)	—	—
08/13	276	49	17.8%	—
Annual Growth	4.6%	—	—	—

2016 Year-End Financials

Return on assets: 1.9%   Cash ($ mil.): 194
Return on equity: (-3.2%)
Current ratio: —

CARSON TAHOE REGIONAL HEALTHCARE

Carson Tahoe Regional Healthcare which includes the Carson Tahoe Regional Medical Center (CTRMC) serves Nevada's Carson Valley and its surrounding areas. The not-for-profit CTRMC boasts about 220 beds and provides a wide range of services such as acute general surgical specialty and outpatient care. The medical center also includes a rehabilitation center cardiovascular center surgical unit free-standing cancer center emergency room and women and children's center. Carson Tahoe Regional Healthcare also operates smaller urgent care behavioral health physical therapy and outpatient care centers in Carson City and nearby communities.

Geographic Reach

Carson Tahoe Health System's network of healthcare facilities services and programs are located in and around Northern Nevada and Eastern California.

OperationsThe health system operates in 22 locations and serves a population of 250000. It has more than 240 board-certified physicians with expertise in more than 35 medical specialties.Altogether Carson Tahoe Health System boasts three hospitals two urgent care facilities and several medical support facilities. Its multiple outpatient locations include a fully-accredited cancer center an emergent care facility primary care clinics a pair of urgent care clinics and three retail care clinics. Carson Tahoe Health's Behavioral Health Services division provides a diagnosis/multi disciplinary team approach to treating seniors adults adolescents and children experiencing behavioral and addictive disorders. It provides a broad range of inpatient and outpatient services that includes individual group and family counseling support groups medical model detoxification services and a 14-21 day addictive disorders rehabilitation program.StrategyThe health system works to regularly add to its roster of services. In 2013 it expanded its Carson Tahoe Center for Wound Healing on the second floor of its Carson Tahoe Specialty Medical Center. The center provides the latest advanced treatments to help those with non-healing wounds. Carson Tahoe Health System also added a new cardiology office in Reno in 2013. Sales and MarketingAs part of its marketing efforts Carson Tahoe Health System launched Toast an online blog at www.ToastCarsonTahoe.com that shares health tips fashion advice recipes and lifestyle articles.

Company Background

The health system was established in 1949.

EXECUTIVES

Operating Room Director, Cindy Kuperus
Admissions Director, Melissa Williams
NURSING DIRECTOR, Kathleen Molina

LOCATIONS

HQ: CARSON TAHOE REGIONAL HEALTHCARE
1600 MEDICAL PKWY, CARSON CITY, NV 897034625
Phone: 775 445-8000
Web: WWW.CARSONTAHOE.COM

PRODUCTS/OPERATIONS

Selected Services
Behavioral Health Services Inpatient
Cancer Center
Carson Tahoe Cardiology Locations
Carson Tahoe Surgery Center
Dayton Medical Building

Eagle Medical Center
Holbrook Therapy
Minden Medical Center
Regional Medical Center
Sierra Surgery Hospital
Specialty Medical Center
Therapy at N. Roop Prof. Center
Urgent & Emergent Care
Walmart Clinics
Womens Health/Cardiology

COMPETITORS

Dignity Health	Universal Health
HCA	Services
Sutter Health	

HISTORICAL FINANCIALS
Company Type: Private

Income Statement   FYE: December 31

	REVENUE ($ mil.)	NET INCOME ($ mil.)	NET PROFIT MARGIN	EMPLOYEES
12/15	245	21	8.6%	1,500
12/14	202	10	5.0%	—
12/13	229	7	3.1%	—
12/09	195	18	9.4%	—
Annual Growth	3.9%	2.3%	—	—

2015 Year-End Financials

Return on assets: 3.7%   Cash ($ mil.): 8
Return on equity: 8.6%
Current ratio: 1.60

CARTER CENTER COLABORATIVE INC

EXECUTIVES

Principal, John B Hardman
Auditors: KPMG LLP GREENSBORO NC

LOCATIONS

HQ: CARTER CENTER COLABORATIVE INC
453 FREEDOM PKWY NE, ATLANTA, GA 303071406
Phone: 404 420-5100
Web: WWW.CARTERCENTER.ORG

HISTORICAL FINANCIALS
Company Type: Private

Income Statement   FYE: August 31

	REVENUE ($ mil.)	NET INCOME ($ mil.)	NET PROFIT MARGIN	EMPLOYEES
08/15	255	11	4.5%	42
08/14	95	14	15.2%	—
08/10	125	(13)	—	—
08/09	75	(11)	—	—
Annual Growth	22.5%	—	—	—

CARTER-JONES COMPANIES, INC.

EXECUTIVES

President, Neil Sackett
Financial Executive, Brian Horning
Auditors: BDO USA LLP AKRON OH

LOCATIONS

HQ: CARTER-JONES COMPANIES, INC.
601 TALLMADGE RD, KENT, OH 442407331
Phone: 330 673-6100
Web: WWW.DOITBEST.COM

HISTORICAL FINANCIALS

Company Type: Private

Income Statement

FYE: December 31

	REVENUE ($ mil.)	NET INCOME ($ mil.)	NET PROFIT MARGIN	EMPLOYEES
12/15	1,109	17	1.6%	3,225
12/14	979	9	1.0%	—
12/13	956	10	1.1%	—
12/12	808	3	0.5%	—
Annual Growth	11.1%	69.6%	—	—

2015 Year-End Financials

Return on assets: 4.6%   Cash ($ mil.): 9
Return on equity: 1.6%
Current ratio: 1.10

CASE WESTERN RESERVE UNIVERSITY

Looking for a research-oriented university? Case Western Reserve University (CWRU) is a private research school with an enrollment of more than 11300 students from all US states and more than 90 countries more than half of whom are graduate and professional students. CWRU offers about 200 undergraduate and graduate degree programs from its eight colleges and schools — business engineering law arts and sciences dentistry social work nursing and medicine — as well as a graduate school at its campus in Cleveland. The university has 3360 faculty members and a student-to-teacher ratio of 8:1.

Operations

The school receives close to $400 million in external funding each year to pay for its various research enterprises. CWRU provides research opportunities to more than 5100 undergraduates and partners with corporations foundations and other universities to operate more than 100 research centers and institutes. Some of its priority research initiatives include energy and the environment culture creativity and design social justice and ethics. Medical studies are conducted in coordination with health care entities; its most predominant partner is the Cleveland Clinic.

Geographic Reach

CWRU is located on the a 178-acre campus in Cleveland Ohio; the campus is located within the 500-acre University Circle district; and houses more than 40 educational medical cultural social and religious institutions. CWRU's students come from all 50 US states and more than 90 countries.

Financial Performance

Research grants and contracts account for about 33% of CWRU's revenues while tuition accounts for another 25%. Other sources of revenue include investment returns overhead cost recovery and gifts and pledges from private sources. The university reported a 10% increase in revenues to $1 billion in fiscal 2016 due to an increase in tuition and higher undergraduate enrollment. CWRU also saw a 50% increase in gifts and pledges that year.

Operating margin grew from to $7.4 million in 2015 to $9 million in 2016 as a result of higher tuition and fees and an increase in grant gifts and auxiliary services income.

CWRU has an endowment of about $1.7 billion.

Strategy

CWRU's core priorities include enhancing its education and research programs advancing institutional resources strengthening partnerships and building a diverse community.

In 2016 CWRU launched the Master of Arts in Military Ethics program the nation?s first in a field of study that contends with questions of how advancing military technologies relate to the common humanity of both enemy and ally.

In 2014 the university reached its initial goal of raising $1 billion to increase financial support for students grow the number of endowed professorships and support capital projects. That year it launched a $64 million renovation and expansion of the Temple-Tifereth Israel complex as part of its 21-acre campus expansion; the project will turn the facility into a performing arts center that will house the school's dance theatre and music departments.

Company Background

The university's origins date back to 1826 in the Ohio region then known as the Western Reserve of Connecticut; its current structure was formed in 1967 with the combination of neighboring Case Institute of Technology and Western Reserve College.

EXECUTIVES

Vice President for Human Resources, Carolyn Gregory
Deputy Provost and Vice President Academic Programs, Lynn T Singer
Vice President for Campus Services, Dick Jamieson
Director Media Relations, Lisa Chiu
President, Barbara R. Snyder, age 61
Dean School of Graduate Studies, Charles Rozek
Dean Undergraduate Studies, Jeffrey Wolcowitz
Chief Investment Officer, Sally J. Staley
Dean School of Dental Medicine, Kenneth B. Chance
Dean Mandel School of Applied Social Sciences, Grover C. (Cleve) Gilmore
Provost and EVP, William A. (Bud) Baeslack
SVP Finance and CFO, John F. Sideras
Dean School of Medicine, Pamela Bowles Davis
Dean College of Arts and Sciences, Cyrus Taylor
VP University Marketing and Communications, Chris Sheridan
Dean Case School of Engineering, Jeffrey Duerk
Dean Weatherhead School of Management, Robert E. Widing
Dean Bolton School of Nursing, Mary E. Kerr
VP Information Technology Services and CIO, Sue B. Workman
Dean School of Law, Jessica Berg
Dean School of Law, Michael P. Scharf
Director Of Admissions, David Dalsky
Vice President Inclusion Diversity and Equal Opportunity, Marilyn Mobley
Senior Vice President of University Relations and Development, Bruce Loessin
Vice President Of Marketing, Marlene Gambatese
Senior Vice President, Jim Mitchell
Vice President Medical Development, Carol Moss
Assistant Vice President For Student Affairs, Dennis Rupert
Chair Department of Nutrition, Henri Brunengraber
Vice President for Enrollment Management, Richard Bischoff
Vice President, Terese Perchinske
Medical Director, Elizabeth Click
Acting Chair Department Of Communication Sciences, Stephen Haynesworth
Chief Information Security Officer Office of the Vice President of Information Technology Services, Tom Siu
Student Affairs Associate Vice President, Sue Nickel-Schindewolf
Medical Director of Respiratory Therapy, Tony Dimarco
Vice President, Max Mehlman
Executive Vice President of Learning, Roger Zender
Vice President Procurement Services, Richard Jamieson
Vice President Of Membership Development, Akash K Menon
Vice president, Molly Francis
Vice President Finance, Shreenath Nedungadi
Vice President Research, Suzanne Rivera
Vice President Digital Marketing And, Lynn Eastep
Vice President for Cleveland and Regional Affairs, John Wheeler
Assistant Vice President University Relations, Duncan Hartley
Vice President, Jacqueline Musacchia
Executive Vice President for Finance and Administration, Rhonda Gross
Vice President of Marketing, Jim Hammerstone
Vice President Technology, Karmar Clifton
Vice President, Ken Basch
Vice President, Don Kamalsky
Associate Vice President And Treasurer, NORMAN CANNON
Vice President Patient Services, Wendy Miano Msn Dnp Aocn RN
Vice President, Casandra Tice
Vice President, James Walsh
Executive Vice President Learning and Development, Drew Poppleton
RHA Vice President of Administration and Finance and Religious Studies, Cameron Childers
VICE PRESIDENT, Ranjith Ramachandran
Vice President of Marketing GBSA 2017, Maria Landaeta
Chairman, Charles D. (Chuck) Fowler
Secretary, Sana Loue
Treasurer, Eric Bower
Board Member, Kathleen Horvath
Board Member, Deborah Frontczak
Secretary, Tiana Wilson
Auditors: PRICEWATERHOUSECOOPERS LLP CL

LOCATIONS

HQ: CASE WESTERN RESERVE UNIVERSITY
10900 EUCLID AVE, CLEVELAND, OH 441064901
Phone: 216 368-2000
Web: WWW.CASE.EDU

PRODUCTS/OPERATIONS

2014 Sales

	% of total
Grants and contracts	27
Student tuition and fees	24
Gifts and pledges	9
CCLCM grants and contracts	9
Facilities and administrative cost recovery	8
Others	23
Total	**100**

Selected Schools and Programs

Case School of Engineering
College of Arts and Sciences
Cleveland Clinic (part of the School of Medicine)
Frances Payne Bolton School of Nursing

Mandel Center for Nonprofit Organizations
Mandel School of Applied Social Sciences
School of Dental Medicine
School of Graduate Studies
School of Law
School of Medicine
Weatherhead School of Management

HISTORICAL FINANCIALS
Company Type: Private

Income Statement
FYE: June 30

	REVENUE ($ mil.)	NET INCOME ($ mil.)	NET PROFIT MARGIN	EMPLOYEES
06/15	1,093	48	4.4%	5,500
06/14	926	214	23.2%	—
06/13	908	111	12.3%	—
06/11	1,052	75	7.2%	—
Annual Growth	0.9%	(10.6%)	—	—

2015 Year-End Financials
Return on assets: 6.5% Cash ($ mil.): 143
Return on equity: 4.4%
Current ratio: 0.20

CASH-WA DISTRIBUTING CO. OF KEARNEY, INC.

This company keeps the Quik-E Marts in merchandise. Cash-Wa Distributing supplies food produce beverages equipment cleaning supplies and more to foodservice operators and convenience stores throughout Nebraska and in all or parts of 10 surrounding states. It operates three distribution centers and serves more than 6500 customers with an inventory of some 20000 items. The family-owned and -operated company was formed in 1934 as a candy and tobacco wholesaler and was purchased by the Henning family in 1957. Cash-Wa Distributing is a member of the UniPro distribution cooperative.

Operations

The company's operations include a fleet of some 175 trucks and a larger number of refrigerated trailers. It also has three truck and trailer shops.

Geographic Reach

Cash-Wa Distributing's market area includes all or part of Nebraska Kansas Missouri Iowa Minnesota Montana North and South Dakota Wyoming Oklahoma and Colorado. It has sales offices in Hays Kansas; Omaha and Sidney Nebraska; and Rapid City South Dakota and distribution centers in Aberdeen South Dakota and Kearney and Lincoln Nebraska.

Sales and Marketing

The company's customer segments include convenience stores restaurants health care facilities and schools.

EXECUTIVES
Vice President of Purchasing, Bob Henning
VP HR and Safety, Carrie Bruno

LOCATIONS
HQ: CASH-WA DISTRIBUTING CO. OF KEARNEY, INC.
 401 W 4TH ST, KEARNEY, NE 688457825
Phone: 308 237-3151
Web: WWW.CASHWA.COM

COMPETITORS

AMCON Distributing	MAINES
Affiliated Foods Midwest	McLane
Associated Wholesale Grocers	Meadowbrook Meat Company
C&S Wholesale	Performance Food Group
Core-Mark	Reinhart FoodService
Farner-Bocken	Sysco
	US Foods

HISTORICAL FINANCIALS
Company Type: Private

Income Statement
FYE: November 28

	REVENUE ($ mil.)	NET INCOME ($ mil.)	NET PROFIT MARGIN	EMPLOYEES
11/15	395	7	1.8%	539
11/14	387	8	2.2%	—
11/13*	377	6	1.8%	—
12/12	398	11	3.0%	—
Annual Growth	(0.3%)	(15.9%)	—	—

*Fiscal year change

2015 Year-End Financials
Return on assets: 3.3% Cash ($ mil.): 1
Return on equity: 1.8%
Current ratio: 0.90

CATHOLIC CHARITIES OF THE ARCHDIOCESE OF CHICAGO

EXECUTIVES
President, Msgr Michael M Boland
Director, Elida Hernandez
Manager, Paul Thompson
Personnel Director, Edward Guererro
Executive Director, Walter Osley
President, Alice Lohman
Personnel Director, Ed Guerrero
Auditors: DELOITTE & TOUCHE LLP CHICAGO

LOCATIONS
HQ: CATHOLIC CHARITIES OF THE ARCHDIOCESE OF CHICAGO
 721 N LA SALLE DR, CHICAGO, IL 606543751
Phone: 312 655-7000
Web: WWW.CATHOLICCHARITIES.NET

HISTORICAL FINANCIALS
Company Type: Private

Income Statement
FYE: June 30

	REVENUE ($ mil.)	NET INCOME ($ mil.)	NET PROFIT MARGIN	EMPLOYEES
06/16	170	(30)	—	3,000
06/15	175	(14)	—	—
06/14	177	2	1.5%	—
06/13	176	52	29.7%	—
Annual Growth	(1.1%)	—	—	—

2016 Year-End Financials
Return on assets: 5.1% Cash ($ mil.): 21
Return on equity: (-17.8%)
Current ratio: 4.00

CATHOLIC HEALTH INITIATIVES COLORADO

EXECUTIVES
Chief Executive Officer, Kevin E Lofton
Director, Ann Genova
Manager, Dick Jenson
Director, Eric Lyons
Manager, Eric Merredith
Manager, Jane Barnes
Plant & Facilities Manager, Joel Ladefoged
Auditors: LB CATHOLIC HEALTH INITIATIVES

LOCATIONS
HQ: CATHOLIC HEALTH INITIATIVES COLORADO
 198 INVERNESS DR W, ENGLEWOOD, CO 801123637
Phone: 303 290-6500

HISTORICAL FINANCIALS
Company Type: Private

Income Statement
FYE: June 30

	REVENUE ($ mil.)	NET INCOME ($ mil.)	NET PROFIT MARGIN	EMPLOYEES
06/15	1,735	101	5.8%	8,000
06/14	1,689	96	5.7%	—
06/10	1,307	50	3.9%	—
06/09	1,226	24	2.0%	—
Annual Growth	6.0%	26.4%		

2015 Year-End Financials
Return on assets: 12.7% Cash ($ mil.): 45
Return on equity: 5.8%
Current ratio: 1.30

CATHOLIC HEALTH INITIATIVES COLORADO FOUNDATION

EXECUTIVES
President, Thomas D Gessel
Administrative Assistant, Peggy Ladford

LOCATIONS
HQ: CATHOLIC HEALTH INITIATIVES COLORADO FOUNDATION
 1010 THREE SPRINGS BLVD, DURANGO, CO 813018296
Phone: 970 247-4311

HISTORICAL FINANCIALS
Company Type: Private

Income Statement
FYE: June 30

	REVENUE ($ mil.)	NET INCOME ($ mil.)	NET PROFIT MARGIN	EMPLOYEES
06/15	172	14	8.3%	800
06/09	109	0	—	—
06/08	103	2	2.2%	—
Annual Growth	7.6%	30.2%	—	—

Return on assets: 4.8%   Cash ($ mil.): —
Return on equity: 8.3%
Current ratio: 1.60

CATHOLIC HEALTHCARE WEST

LOCATIONS

HQ: CATHOLIC HEALTHCARE WEST
450 STANYAN ST, SAN FRANCISCO, CA 941171019
Phone: 415 668-1000

HISTORICAL FINANCIALS
Company Type: Private

Income Statement   FYE: June 30

	REVENUE ($ mil.)	NET INCOME ($ mil.)	NET PROFIT MARGIN	EMPLOYEES
06/15	220	(26)	—	1,100
06/03	144	8	5.9%	—
06/02	0	0	—	—
Annual Growth	—	—	—	—

2015 Year-End Financials
Return on assets: 4.5%   Cash ($ mil.): —
Return on equity: (-12.2%)
Current ratio: 1.00

CATHOLIC MEDICAL CENTER

Catholic Medical Center is a 330-bed hospital serving southern New Hampshire. Services include cancer treatment surgery rehabilitation treatments for sleep disorders and emergency medical services. Catholic Medical Center (CMC) offers about 40 medical specialties through divisions including The Mom's Place (a birthing facility) and the New England Heart Institute. CMC has partnered with its community to extend health care and dental care to the uninsured and the homeless and has established a health clinic geared to help refugees being resettled in the area.

Operations

CMC employs some 500 physicians. The hospital operates about a dozen outpatient and urgent care centers in its service territory as well as outreach programs including the Parish Nurse Program the Poisson Dental Facility the Westside Neighborhood Health Center and the Healthcare for the Homeless Project. As a not-for-profit institution CMC contributed some $74 million in community benefits during 2013.

Geographic Reach

The hospital serves residents in and around Manchester New Hampshire as well as patients from across the state. Its primary service area includes the communities of Allenstown Auburn Bedford Candia Deerfield Dunbarton Goffstown Hooksett Manchester and New Boston.

Financial Performance

The hospital reported net patient service revenues of some $284 million in 2012 with Medicare

and Medicaid policy reimbursements accounting for $94 million of sales.

Strategy

CMC focuses on enhancing and expanding its service offerings for area residents. It opened a heart and vascular intervention unit within the hospital facility in 2013 for instance and added neurology services as a new specialist offering. The hospital also expands by forming clinical care partnerships with other area medical centers.

In 2011 CMC canceled plans to merge with Dartmouth-Hitchcock Medical Center although the hospitals continue to collaborate at CMC's Special Care Nursery and D-H's Norris Cotton Cancer Center. CMC and Dartmouth-Hitchcock cited evolving changes in health care reforms behind their decision not to merge. The partnership was opposed by the New Hampshire attorney general on the grounds that it would violate state law and needed court approval.

Company Background

CMC was founded in 1974 through the merger of two Catholic-sponsored Manchester hospitals: Notre Dame Hospital and Sacred Heart Hospital.

EXECUTIVES

Vice President Finance, Andre Therrien
Vice President Of Emergency Services, Lu Mulla
Director of Health Information Services, Jeff Butler
Blood Bank Director, LINDA BAYRD
Vice President of Information Technology, Lori Berube
Vice President of Sales, Daniel Bouvier
Clinical Director, Jack Anderson
Vice President Of Human Resources, Janet Troski
Senior Vice President and Chief Financial Officer, Edward Dudley
Vice President Operations, Bob Duhaime
Vice President Of New England Heart Institute, Carolann Osullivan
Auditors: BAKER NEWMAN & NOYES PORTLAND

LOCATIONS

HQ: CATHOLIC MEDICAL CENTER
100 MCGREGOR ST, MANCHESTER, NH 031023770
Phone: 603 663-6888
Web: WWW.CATHOLICMEDICALCENTER.ORG

PRODUCTS/OPERATIONS

Selected Centers and Services
Behavioral Health Services
Breast Care Center
Cancer Care
Cholesterol Management Center
Community Health Services
Diabetes Resources Institute
Diagnostic Imaging
Emergency Department
Laboratory
New England Heart Institute
New England Sleep Center
Obesity Treatment Center
Primary Care Locations
Rehabilitation Services
Respiratory Services
Surgical Care Group
Surgical Services
The Mom's Place
The Wellness Center
Urgent Care at Bedford
Wound Care Center

COMPETITORS

Beth Israel Deaconess Medical Center	Concord Hospital
Boston Medical Center	Elliot Health System
Brigham and Women's Hospital	Exeter Health Resources
Cambridge Health Alliance	Frisbie Memorial Hospital
CareGroup	HealthSouth
	Southern New Hampshire

Caritas Holy Family   Medical Center
Hospital

HISTORICAL FINANCIALS
Company Type: Private

Income Statement   FYE: June 30

	REVENUE ($ mil.)	NET INCOME ($ mil.)	NET PROFIT MARGIN	EMPLOYEES
06/15	316	28	9.1%	1,500
06/14	342	32	9.4%	—
06/13	322	29	9.1%	—
06/10	277	11	4.2%	—
Annual Growth	2.6%	19.9%	—	—

2015 Year-End Financials
Return on assets: 6.3%   Cash ($ mil.): 36
Return on equity: 9.1%
Current ratio: 1.50

CATHOLIC MEDICAL MISSION BOARD INC

EXECUTIVES

President, John F Galbraith
Vice-Chairman, F W Smullen III
Senior Vice-President, Marivette Cannon
Director, Chris Necker
Director, Ariel Frisancho
Director, Chris Foster
Auditors: MARKS PANETH & SHRON LLP NEW

LOCATIONS

HQ: CATHOLIC MEDICAL MISSION BOARD INC
100 WALL ST FL 9, NEW YORK, NY 100055765
Phone: 212 242-7757
Web: WWW.CMMB.ORG

HISTORICAL FINANCIALS
Company Type: Private

Income Statement   FYE: September 30

	REVENUE ($ mil.)	NET INCOME ($ mil.)	NET PROFIT MARGIN	EMPLOYEES
09/15	290	(3)	—	38
09/14	387	(6)	—	—
09/13	526	44	8.4%	—
09/11	305	47	15.5%	—
Annual Growth	(1.3%)	—	—	—

2015 Year-End Financials
Return on assets: 0.6%   Cash ($ mil.): 13
Return on equity: (-1.1%)
Current ratio: 2.90

CATHOLIC RELIEF SERVICES - UNITED STATES CONFERENCE OF CATHOLIC BISHOPS

EXECUTIVES

Board of Directors, Jeffrey Baeuerlein
Board of Directors, Schuyler Thorup
Manager, Dawn Sheckells
Administrative Assistant, Glinder Brown
Supervisor, Cheryl Jones
Manager, Rosann Zemanek
Auditors: RSM US LLP GAITHERSBURG MARY

LOCATIONS

HQ: CATHOLIC RELIEF SERVICES - UNITED STATES
CONFERENCE OF CATHOLIC BISHOPS
228 W LEXINGTON ST, BALTIMORE, MD 212013443
Phone: 410 625-2220
Web: WWW.CRS.ORG

HISTORICAL FINANCIALS

Company Type: Private

Income Statement   FYE: September 30

	REVENUE ($ mil.)	NET INCOME ($ mil.)	NET PROFIT MARGIN	EMPLOYEES
09/15	738	(11)	—	5,879
09/13	639	8	1.3%	—
09/12	701	(15)	—	—
09/11	822	(6)	—	—
Annual Growth	(2.7%)	—	—	—

2015 Year-End Financials

Return on assets: 8.8%   Cash ($ mil.): 80
Return on equity: (-1.6%)
Current ratio: 0.80

CAYUGA MEDICAL CENTER AT ITHACA, INC.

EXECUTIVES

Executive Director, D Rob Mackenzie
Manager, Elizabeth A Farnum

LOCATIONS

HQ: CAYUGA MEDICAL CENTER AT ITHACA, INC.
101 DATES DR, ITHACA, NY 148501342
Phone: 607 274-4011
Web: WWW.CAYUGAMED.ORG

HISTORICAL FINANCIALS

Company Type: Private

Income Statement   FYE: December 31

	REVENUE ($ mil.)	NET INCOME ($ mil.)	NET PROFIT MARGIN	EMPLOYEES
12/15	175	(23)	—	1,055
12/14	156	(19)	—	—
12/13	182	11	6.4%	—
12/08	124	(57)	—	—
Annual Growth	5.0%	—	—	—

2015 Year-End Financials

Return on assets: 4.5%   Cash ($ mil.): 9
Return on equity: (-13.4%)
Current ratio: 1.50

CC HOLDINGS GS V LLC

EXECUTIVES

Chief Executive Officer, W Benjamin Moreland
Auditors: PRICEWATERHOUSECOOPERS LLP PI

LOCATIONS

HQ: CC HOLDINGS GS V LLC
1220 AUGUSTA DR STE 500, HOUSTON, TX
770572263
Phone: 713 570-3000

HISTORICAL FINANCIALS

Company Type: Private

Income Statement   FYE: December 31

	REVENUE ($ mil.)	NET INCOME ($ mil.)	NET PROFIT MARGIN	EMPLOYEES
12/15	607	114	18.9%	1
12/14	614	132	21.5%	—
12/13	604	453	75.1%	—
Annual Growth	0.3%	(49.7%)	—	—

2015 Year-End Financials

Return on assets: 0.4%   Cash ($ mil.): 20
Return on equity: 18.9%
Current ratio: 0.70

CCF BRANDS LLC

EXECUTIVES

President, Justin Whaley
Executive Director, Jene Huffman
VP Marketing, Jodie Daniels
Director, Craig Courtney
Sales Director, Jessica Clark
Auditors: FROST PLLC LITTLE ROCK ARKAN

LOCATIONS

HQ: CCF BRANDS LLC
5211 W VILLAGE PKWY # 101, ROGERS, AR
727588104
Phone: 479 464-0544
Web: WWW.CCFBRANDS.COM

HISTORICAL FINANCIALS

Company Type: Private

Income Statement   FYE: April 30

	REVENUE ($ mil.)	NET INCOME ($ mil.)	NET PROFIT MARGIN	EMPLOYEES
04/16	732	11	1.6%	58
04/15	536	10	2.0%	—
04/14	385	9	2.6%	—
04/13	377	8	2.3%	—
Annual Growth	24.7%	10.0%	—	—

2016 Year-End Financials

Return on assets: 3.1%   Cash ($ mil.): 5
Return on equity: 1.6%
Current ratio: 1.10

CDM CONSTRUCTORS INC.

EXECUTIVES

President, Paul R Shea
Board of Directors, Robert McCarthy
Board of Directors, Mario J Marcaccio
Financial Executive, Eric Hartmann
Manager, Kristen McKern
Marketing Director, Adie Cito
Personnel Director, Charlene Allen
Auditors: PRICEWATERHOUSECOPPERS LLP BO

LOCATIONS

HQ: CDM CONSTRUCTORS INC.
75 STATE ST STE 701, BOSTON, MA 021091940
Phone: 617 452-6000

HISTORICAL FINANCIALS

Company Type: Private

Income Statement   FYE: January 2

	REVENUE ($ mil.)	NET INCOME ($ mil.)	NET PROFIT MARGIN	EMPLOYEES
01/16*	414	8	2.0%	500
12/12	392	10	2.8%	—
12/11	360	10	2.9%	—
01/11	341	10	3.0%	—
Annual Growth	3.9%	(4.0%)	—	—

*Fiscal year change

2016 Year-End Financials

Return on assets: 17.1%   Cash ($ mil.): 10
Return on equity: 2.0%
Current ratio: 0.70

CEDAR RAPIDS COMMUNITY SCHOOL DISTRICT

EXECUTIVES

Superintendent, Brad Buck
Assistant Manager, Laurel Day
Account Manager, Casey Meader
Assistant Manager, Mary E Maske
Auditors: RSM US LLP CEDAR RAPIDS IOWA

LOCATIONS

HQ: CEDAR RAPIDS COMMUNITY SCHOOL DISTRICT
2500 EDGEWOOD RD NW, CEDAR RAPIDS, IA
524051015
Phone: 319 558-2000
Web: WWW.CR.K12.IA.US

HISTORICAL FINANCIALS
Company Type: Private

Income Statement

FYE: June 30

	REVENUE ($ mil.)	NET INCOME ($ mil.)	NET PROFIT MARGIN	EMPLOYEES
06/16	236	7	3.1%	2,540
06/15	233	9	4.1%	
Annual Growth	1.1%	(22.9%)		

2016 Year-End Financials

Return on assets: 1.0%
Return on equity: 3.1%
Current ratio: 2.00

Cash ($ mil.): 66

CEDARS-SINAI MEDICAL CARE FOUNDATION

EXECUTIVES

Executive Director, Tom Gordeon
VP Finance, Jill Martin
Financial Executive, Debbie Botten
Finance Manager, Marco Scholten
Manager, Michael C Yang
Manager, David Davtyan
Manager, Noam Z Drain
Director, Delia Vogel
Plant & Facilities Manager, Mark Kruse

LOCATIONS

HQ: CEDARS-SINAI MEDICAL CARE FOUNDATION
200 N ROBERTSON BLVD # 101, BEVERLY HILLS, CA
902111769
Phone: 800 700-6424
Web: WWW.CEDARS-SINAI.EDU

HISTORICAL FINANCIALS
Company Type: Private

Income Statement

FYE: June 30

	REVENUE ($ mil.)	NET INCOME ($ mil.)	NET PROFIT MARGIN	EMPLOYEES
06/15	339	49	14.6%	4
06/14	216	19	9.1%	—
06/11	145	6	4.2%	—
06/10	129	4	3.5%	—
Annual Growth	21.2%	61.3%	—	—

2015 Year-End Financials

Return on assets: 8.7%
Return on equity: 14.6%
Current ratio: —

Cash ($ mil.): 25

CEDARS-SINAI MEDICAL CENTER

Many a star has been born literally at Cedars-Sinai Medical Center. The 886-bed teaching and research hospital is located right where Los Angeles meets Beverly Hills and West Hollywood and has tended to the medical needs of a number of celebrities since its founding in 1902. However the center is also a major teaching hospital for UCLA's David Geffen School of Medicine and is engaged in hundreds of research programs in areas such as cancer neuroscience and genetics. It also includes two multi-specialty physician associations Cedars-Sinai Medical Group and Ceders-Sinai Health Associates and operates a number of community health centers and outreach programs (such as mobile health clinics).

Operations

The not-for-profit hospital's more than 2100 physicians represent just about every clinical specialty out there. Cedars-Sinai is consistently listed as a top-ranked hospital by U.S. News & World Report in such specialties as cancer cardiology endocrinology gastrointestinal disorders gynecology heart surgery kidney disease neurology orthopaedics and respiratory disorders.

Cedars-Sinai is the only private hospital with a Level 1 trauma center in Los Angeles County; as such the hospital sees about 1600 trauma patients a year. The hospital also provides a number of outpatient services.

Federal funding from the National Institutes of Health and other sources have provided the hospital with some $40 million towards research. Cedars-Sinai currently has some 1300 research projects.

The hospital sees some 660000 outpatient visits and 85000 emergency department visits each year.

Geographic Reach

Cedars-Sinai's hospital is located in Los Angeles; it has an administrative office in Beverly Hills California.

Financial Performance

Revenues from patient care and other sources totaled nearly $2.77 billion in fiscal 2015 while net income amounted to $472.9 million.

Strategy

To meet increasing patient demand and expand its capacity for research projects Cedars-Sinai added nearly 7000 sq. ft. of space to house the Cedars-Sinai Biobank and Translational Research Core Facility in 2015. The previous year it opened a new clinic dedicated to the evaluation of heart and vascular disease patients for participation in stem cell medical studies.

EXECUTIVES

President and CEO, Thomas M. (Tom) Priselac
EVP Finance and CFO, Edward M. Prunchunas
EVP Hospital Operations and COO Medical Center, Mark R. Gavens
EVP Academic Affairs and Dean of the Faculty, Shlomo Melmed
SVP Medical Affairs and Chief Medical Officer, Michael L. Langberg
EVP System Development and Chief Strategy Officer, Richard B. Jacobs
SVP Enterprise Information Systems and CIO, Darren Dworkin
EVP Medical Network, John Jenrette
Vice President of Professional Services and Business Development, Carolyn Bell
Vice President Legal Affairs, James Laur
Assistant Vice President Planning And Marketing, Richard Katzman
Vice President of Marketing and Public Relations, Richard Elbaum
Medical Director GenRISK Adult Genetic, Ora Gordon
Medical Director, Spencer Koerner
Director of Radiology, Lynne Roy
Vice President For Medical Affairs, Neil Romanoff
Medical Director Partial Hospitalization Program, David Callander
Senior Vice President System Development, Rick Jacobs
Chairman, Marc H. Rapaport
Vice Chair, Steven Romick
Board Member, Donna Earley

LOCATIONS

HQ: CEDARS-SINAI MEDICAL CENTER
8700 BEVERLY BLVD, WEST HOLLYWOOD, CA
900481804
Phone: 310 423-3277
Web: WWW.EDARS-SINAI.EDU

PRODUCTS/OPERATIONS

Selected Centers and Services
Ambulatory Care Center
Cedars-Sinai Center for Chest Disease
Cedars-Sinai Center for Digestive Diseases
Cedars-Sinai Heart Institute
Cedars-Sinai Institute Spine Center
Cedars-Sinai Health Associates (affiliated independent physician association)
Cedars-Sinai Medical Group (multi-specialty physicians group)
Cedars-Sinai Orthopedic Center
Diagnostic imaging center
Emergency department and trauma center
Hospice services
Kidney and pancreas transplant center
Neuroscience services
Pediatric services
Psychiatry and mental health services
Samuel Oschin Comprehensive Cancer Institute
Surgical services
Organ and bone marrow transplantation
Radiation therapy
Radiology
Stroke program
Pain management services
Women's health services

COMPETITORS

Adventist Health System West
Brotman Medical Center
Childrens Hospital Los Angeles
City of Hope
Community Health Systems
Dignity Health
Eisenhower Medical Center
Glendale Adventist Medical Center
Glendale Memorial Hospital
Golden State Health Centers

Good Samaritan Hospital (IN)
HCA
Hollywood Presbyterian Medical Center
Newhall Memorial Hospital
Pasadena Hospital Association
Providence Health System Southern California
Scripps Health
Tenet Healthcare
UCSF Medical
White Memorial Medical Center

HISTORICAL FINANCIALS
Company Type: Private

Income Statement
FYE: June 30

	REVENUE ($ mil.)	NET INCOME ($ mil.)	NET PROFIT MARGIN	EMPLOYEES
06/15	2,760	366	13.3%	8,000
06/11	2,658	210	7.9%	—
06/10	2,309	152	6.6%	—
Annual Growth	3.6%	19.1%	—	—

2015 Year-End Financials
Return on assets: 9.6%
Return on equity: 13.3%
Current ratio: 1.50
Cash ($ mil.): 343

CENTIMARK CORPORATION

Shout it from the rooftops Centimark is one of the largest commercial and industrial roofing contractors in North America. The company provides roof installation inspection repair and emergency leak service. Centimark typically works on flat roofs using EPDM rubber thermoplastic bitumen metal and coatings. Top customers have included NASA and the US Army Corps of Engineers. Its QuestMark division offers commercial industrial and retail flooring do-it-yourself (DIY) products and floor maintenance and cleaning products. The company which has about 80 offices throughout North America.

Operations

The company offers roof and floor services roof replacement roof repairs floor repairs emergency services preventative maintenance programs energy efficient solutions safety options and accessories online project management and DIY floor products. Centimark also provides systems such as thermoplastic solutions sprayed polyurethane foams roof coatings modified bitumen and built-up roofing metal products and steep slope products. In addition it engages in the online retail of flooring products such as patch and repair and maintenance/floor care products and coatings.

QuestMark a division of Centimark offers materials for commercial retail and industrial floors. It specializes in DiamondQuest polished concrete flooring epoxy flooring floor repair materials floor maintenance and floor cleaning products.

Centimark's Asset Management service provides extensive roof surveys roof life expectancy models return-on-investment analysis for roof repairs and evaluations for roof repair or roof replacement.

Geographic Reach

Pittsburgh Pennsylvania-based Centimark also does business in Canada through subsidiary Centimark Ltd. which has offices in Calgary Edmonton Toronto and Vancouver.

Sales and Marketing

The company serves customers in different segments including retail industrial general contractors and education.

Financial Performance

Centimark's 2014 sales totaled $485 million.

Strategy

In response to customer demand for more energy-efficient options Centimark has been increasing its use of spray polyurethane foam (which adds insulation and a waterproof barrier to roofs). The company also installs electricity-producing photovoltaic solar panels onto roofs. Other green options available from Centimark include skylights and garden roofs.

The company also tries to stay ahead of the pack with technological innovations such as its MyCentimark service. The online resource allows property owners to view invoices work authorizations before-and-after photos and recommendations for future roof maintenance. In 2014 the company launched a tablet and smartphone app that allows customers to request service and find the nearest Centimark office based on their current location.

Company Background

Chairman and CEO Edward Dunlap founded Centimark as an industrial cleaning business in 1967. Centimark is owned by its employees.

EXECUTIVES

Vice President Applications, Joe Filtz
Vice President, Thor DiCesare
Chairman and CEO, Edward B. Dunlap
President and COO, Timothy M. Dunlap
EVP and Northern Group Director, Robert J. Rudzik
EVP and Western Group Director, Steven M. Ferencz
EVP National and Regional Sales, John T. Godwin
EVP and CFO, John L. Heisey
EVP and Southern Group Director, Sherman L. Gaskins
EVP and QuestMark Flooring Group Director, John P. Scanlon
EVP and Eastern Group Director, Mark A. Cooper
VP and Canada Group Director CentiMark Ltd, Robert T. Penney
SVP and Southern Group Director, Keith Battenfield
EVP Service, Kenneth W. Zmich
National Accounts Manager, Cindy Molnar
Vice President of Human Resour, Landon Connolly
Vice President Benefits and Compensation, Laura Kickbusch
National Account Manager, Clint Snowden
National Accounts Manager, Keith O'Brien
National Account Manager, Ryan Alyea
Executive Vice President, John Rudzik
Executive Vice President, Robert Marshall
National Account Manager, Tony Alderson
Senior Vice President, Michael Rew
Vice President National Accounts QuestMark Flooring, Jim Gasper
National Account Manager, Tom Blaylock
Vice President Of Litigation Department, John Liekar
National Account Manager, Art Collias
NATIONAL ACCOUNT MANAGER, Shaun Bynum
National Accounts Manager, Chuck Blair
NATIONAL ACCOUNT MANAGER, Kevin Russell
National Account Manager, John Luck
Auditors: SCHNEIDER DOWNS & CO INC P

LOCATIONS

HQ: CENTIMARK CORPORATION
12 GRANDVIEW CIR, CANONSBURG, PA 153178533
Phone: 724 514-8700
Web: WWW.CENTIMARK.COM

PRODUCTS/OPERATIONS

Selected Operations
CentiMark (roofing)
CentiMark ltd. (Canada roofing)
QuestMark (flooring)

Selected Systems
Roof Systems
EPDM
Green Roofing
Metal Roofs
Modified Bitumen and Built-Up Roofs
Roof Coatings
SPF
Steep Slope
TPO & PVC
Floor Systems
Chemical Resistant Systems
Decorative Broadcast
Decorative Concrete
Electric Static Dissipative
Heavy Duty Resurfacer
High Build Coating
Polished Concrete
Thin Mil

COMPETITORS

Armstrong World Industries	Duro-Last Roofing
Cabral Roofing & Waterproofing	Garcia Roofing
	Holland Roofing
	Pickens Roofing
D. C. Taylor	Tecta America

HISTORICAL FINANCIALS
Company Type: Private

Income Statement
FYE: April 30

	REVENUE ($ mil.)	NET INCOME ($ mil.)	NET PROFIT MARGIN	EMPLOYEES
04/16	605	49	8.1%	3,500
04/15	540	46	8.7%	—
04/14	508	42	8.3%	—
04/13	484	38	8.0%	—
Annual Growth	7.7%	8.2%		

2016 Year-End Financials
Return on assets: 3.2%
Return on equity: 8.1%
Current ratio: 1.80
Cash ($ mil.): 66

CENTRACARE HEALTH SYSTEM

EXECUTIVES

President, Terry Pladson
VP Personnel, Duane Rasmusson
Personnel Director, Janet Kruzel
Manager, Joan Braggelman
Auditors: RSM US LLP MINNEAPOLIS MN

LOCATIONS

HQ: CENTRACARE HEALTH SYSTEM
1406 6TH AVE N, SAINT CLOUD, MN 563031900
Phone: 320 656-7020

HISTORICAL FINANCIALS
Company Type: Private

Income Statement
FYE: June 30

	REVENUE ($ mil.)	NET INCOME ($ mil.)	NET PROFIT MARGIN	EMPLOYEES
06/15	176	(15)	—	99
06/13	115	27	23.8%	—
06/11	48	(6)	—	—
06/10	43	(9)	—	—
Annual Growth	32.5%	—	—	—

2015 Year-End Financials
Return on assets: 22.1%
Return on equity: (-9.0%)
Current ratio: 0.20
Cash ($ mil.): 17

CENTRAL ELECTRIC POWER COOPERATIVE INC

LOCATIONS
HQ: CENTRAL ELECTRIC POWER COOPERATIVE INC
2106 JEFFERSON ST, JEFFERSON CITY, MO
651092066
Phone: 573 634-2454
Web: WWW.CEPC.NET

HISTORICAL FINANCIALS
Company Type: Private

Income Statement
FYE: December 31

	REVENUE ($ mil.)	NET INCOME ($ mil.)	NET PROFIT MARGIN	EMPLOYEES
12/15	204	0	—	110
12/14	202	0	—	—
12/11	196	0	—	—
12/10	183	12	6.9%	—
Annual Growth	2.2%	—	—	—

2015 Year-End Financials
Return on assets: 9.1%
Return on equity: —
Current ratio: 1.70
Cash ($ mil.): 14

CENTRAL IOWA HOSPITAL CORP

EXECUTIVES
Chief Executive Officer, Eric Crowell
Board of Directors, Don Ross
Board of Directors, Larry Baker
Director, Charles A Jennissen
Director, James E Bal
Chief Financial Officer, Joe Corfits

LOCATIONS
HQ: CENTRAL IOWA HOSPITAL CORP
1200 PLEASANT ST, DES MOINES, IA 503091406
Phone: 515 241-6212
Web: WWW.BLANKCHILDRENS.ORG

HISTORICAL FINANCIALS
Company Type: Private

Income Statement
FYE: December 31

	REVENUE ($ mil.)	NET INCOME ($ mil.)	NET PROFIT MARGIN	EMPLOYEES
12/15	548	152	27.9%	3,495
12/14	534	145	27.2%	—
12/13	703	52	7.5%	—
12/09	633	44	7.0%	—
Annual Growth	(2.4%)	22.8%	—	—

2015 Year-End Financials
Return on assets: 5.2%
Return on equity: 27.9%
Current ratio: 1.10
Cash ($ mil.): 5

CENTRAL MICHIGAN UNIVERSITY

Academic advancement is central at Central Michigan University (CMU). The university offers more than 200 academic programs for undergraduate graduate and professional coursework through eight colleges including business communication and fine arts medicine and education and human services. The university enrolls more than 20000 students at the main campus in Mt. Pleasant. The institution also enrolls another 7000 students online and at 50 locations throughout North America. In addition CMU offers study abroad programs in 40 countries.

Operations
CMU has 1000 faculty members and a student-to-faculty ratio of about 21:1. It has 22 residence halls. The university also has division I athletic programs for men and women. Its CMU Public Broadcasting unit operates 10 television and seven radio stations.

Financial Performance
CMU has pioneer in distance learning since 1971 when it was one of the first universities to provide education off campus and directly to students and adults. In 2014 it had nearly 40 locations in the US and Canada including on more than 20 military bases.

Company Background
Notable alumni include former US Senator Robert P. Griffin and actor Jeff Daniels.
CMU was founded in 1892 as a teachers' college.

EXECUTIVES
Associate Vice President Institutional D, Carolyn Dunn
Vice Chairman, John Hurd
Auditors: PLANTE & MORAN PLLC PORTAGE

LOCATIONS
HQ: CENTRAL MICHIGAN UNIVERSITY
1200 S FRANKLIN ST, MOUNT PLEASANT, MI
488592001
Phone: 989 774-4000
Web: WWW.CMICH.EDU

PRODUCTS/OPERATIONS

Selected Colleges and Schools
College of Business Administration
College of Communication and Fine Arts
College of Education and Human Services
College of Graduate Studies
College of Health Professions
College of Humanities and Social and Behavioral Sciences
College of Medicine
College of Science and Technology
Global Campus & Online

HISTORICAL FINANCIALS
Company Type: Private

Income Statement
FYE: June 30

	REVENUE ($ mil.)	NET INCOME ($ mil.)	NET PROFIT MARGIN	EMPLOYEES
06/16	334	8	2.5%	2,388
06/15	336	1	0.4%	—
06/14	348	19	5.7%	—
06/13	319	32	10.1%	—
Annual Growth	1.5%	(36.0%)	—	—

2016 Year-End Financials
Return on assets: 21.6%
Return on equity: 2.5%
Current ratio: 0.50
Cash ($ mil.): 31

CENTRAL PENINSULA GENERAL HOSPITAL, INC.

EXECUTIVES
Chief Executive Officer, Ryan Smith
Manager, Angela Hinnegan
Director, Peter O Hansen

LOCATIONS
HQ: CENTRAL PENINSULA GENERAL HOSPITAL, INC.
250 HOSPITAL PL, SOLDOTNA, AK 996696999
Phone: 907 262-4404
Web: WWW.CPGH.ORG

HISTORICAL FINANCIALS
Company Type: Private

Income Statement
FYE: June 30

	REVENUE ($ mil.)	NET INCOME ($ mil.)	NET PROFIT MARGIN	EMPLOYEES
06/15	274	17	6.2%	611
06/14	234	13	5.6%	—
06/13	0	14	—	—
06/12	199	8	4.4%	—
Annual Growth	11.3%	24.8%	—	—

2015 Year-End Financials
Return on assets: 6.1%
Return on equity: 6.2%
Current ratio: 0.80
Cash ($ mil.): 37

CENTRAL UNIFIED SCHOOL DISTRICT

EXECUTIVES

Superintendent, Mike Berg
Principal, Sheila Moynihan
Plant & Facilities Manager, Jesse Bath
Auditors: CROWE HORWATH LLP SACRAMENTO

LOCATIONS

HQ: CENTRAL UNIFIED SCHOOL DISTRICT
 4605 N POLK AVE, FRESNO, CA 937225334
Phone: 559 274-4700
Web: WWW.CENTRALUNIFIED.ORG

HISTORICAL FINANCIALS

Company Type: Private

Income Statement
FYE: June 30

	REVENUE ($ mil.)	NET INCOME ($ mil.)	NET PROFIT MARGIN	EMPLOYEES
06/16*	182	14	7.8%	1,200
12/08	0	0	41.4%	—
06/08	123	11	9.4%	—
06/07	129	8	6.8%	—
Annual Growth	3.9%	5.4%	—	—

*Fiscal year change

CENTRAL WASHINGTON HEALTH SERVICES ASSOCIATION

EXECUTIVES

Chief Executive Officer, Peter Rutherford
Treasurer, Kristine Loomis
Director, Jeanine Allen
Financial Executive, Cindy Vidano
Senior Manager, Jim Wood
Director, Peggy Osborn

LOCATIONS

HQ: CENTRAL WASHINGTON HEALTH SERVICES
 ASSOCIATION
 1201 S MILLER ST, WENATCHEE, WA 988013201
Phone: 509 662-1511
Web: WWW.CWHS.COM

HISTORICAL FINANCIALS

Company Type: Private

Income Statement
FYE: December 31

	REVENUE ($ mil.)	NET INCOME ($ mil.)	NET PROFIT MARGIN	EMPLOYEES
12/15	288	(8)	—	1,100
12/14	259	18	7.0%	—
12/13	0	16	—	—
Annual Growth	—	—	—	—

2015 Year-End Financials

Return on assets: 1.3%   Cash ($ mil.): 28
Return on equity: (-2.9%)
Current ratio: 2.90

CENTURY HEALTH ALLIANCE JOINT VENTURE

EXECUTIVES

Director, Emily Avery
Senior Manager, Lindy Noland
Manager, Casey Johnson
Director, Gary Harrelson
Manager, Brent Sutton

LOCATIONS

HQ: CENTURY HEALTH ALLIANCE JOINT VENTURE
 809 UNIVERSITY BLVD E, TUSCALOOSA, AL
 354012029
Phone: 205 759-7111
Web: WWW.DCHSYSTEM.COM

HISTORICAL FINANCIALS

Company Type: Private

Income Statement
FYE: September 30

	REVENUE ($ mil.)	NET INCOME ($ mil.)	NET PROFIT MARGIN	EMPLOYEES
09/15	450	34	7.6%	1
09/14	420	15	3.7%	—
Annual Growth	7.1%	119.3%	—	—

2015 Year-End Financials

Return on assets: 3.3%   Cash ($ mil.): 81
Return on equity: 7.6%
Current ratio: 2.20

CERES SOLUTIONS, LLP

Ceres Solutions is a growth business. The agricultural partnership provides farmers in about a dozen Indiana counties with crop farming support services and supplies. It sells stores and distributes such goods as fertilizers and fuel (gasoline propane home-heating). The company's agronomy services include field mapping crop and pest management soil sampling and yield analysis. Ceres Solutions also offers crop-financing programs sells crop insurance and provides marketing services. Its Green Notes newsletter offers the state's farmers market and technical advice and analysis.

Ceres Solutions which was formed in 2007 through the merger of three agricultural cooperatives — Westland Growers and AgroKey. It operates primarily in the western region of Indiana through about 30 agronomy office locations an energy office and its main office which is located in Crawfordsville Indiana.

EXECUTIVES

Vice President of Agronomy, Daryl Warren
Auditors: BLUE & CO LLC SEYMOUR IN

LOCATIONS

HQ: CERES SOLUTIONS, LLP
 2112 INDIANAPOLIS RD, CRAWFORDSVILLE, IN
 479333137
Phone: 765 362-6108

COMPETITORS

ADM	Cargill
Ag Processing Inc.	GROWMARK
CHS	Premier AG Co-Op Inc.

HISTORICAL FINANCIALS

Company Type: Private

Income Statement
FYE: July 31

	REVENUE ($ mil.)	NET INCOME ($ mil.)	NET PROFIT MARGIN	EMPLOYEES
07/16	299	10	3.6%	125
07/15	368	16	4.5%	—
07/14	412	22	5.4%	—
07/13	402	25	6.4%	—
Annual Growth	(9.4%)	(25.4%)	—	—

2016 Year-End Financials

Return on assets: 8.1%   Cash ($ mil.): 10
Return on equity: 3.6%
Current ratio: 0.70

CERTCO, INC.

Certco has built a business serving about 200 independent grocers in Minnesota Wisconsin Iowa and Illinois. The food distribution cooperative offers customers an inventory of more than 57000 items including bakery goods frozen foods meat products produce and general merchandise. It distributes products under the Shurfine Shurfresh and Top Care labels. Additionally Certco offers its member-operators such services as advertising accounting client data services warehousing merchandising store planning and design and other business support services. The cooperative was founded in 1930 as Central Wisconsin Cooperative Food Stores.

Operations

To support its business Certco operates a nearly 1 million-sq.-ft. distribution center. Its brands include Shurfine Shurfresh Value Time Full Circle Topco and Top Care.

Geographic Reach

Based in Madison Wisconsin Certco operates in Minnesota and Wisconsin with an extended reach into parts of Iowa and Illinois.

Sales and Marketing

Many of Certco's clients are Fortune 500 companies. It distributes the national brands of major companies such as Kraft General Mills Procter & Gamble and Johnson & Johnson. The company also distributes specialty items under the names Amy's Hodgson Mills Bob's Red Mill and Annie's that are only available through direct-store-delivery suppliers.

Company Background

Certco was established in 1930 when five Madison-area retailers formed an alliance to boost their combined purchasing muscle.

EXECUTIVES

President, Randy Simon
VP Finance, Donald E Watzk
Chief Financial Officer, Pete Baus
Manager, Larry Olson
Purchasing Agent, Barb Bright
Purchasing Agent, Bob Salmon
Auditors: SATTELL JOHNSON APPEL & CO

LOCATIONS

HQ: CERTCO, INC.
  5321 VERONA RD, FITCHBURG, WI 537116050
Phone: 608 271-4500
Web: WWW.CERTCOINC.COM

PRODUCTS/OPERATIONS

Selected Brands
Full Circle
Shurfine
Shurfresh
Top Care
Topco
Value Time

Selected Services
Advertising
Client data services
Retail accounting
Retail meetings/seminars
Retail support
Retail technology
Store planning & design
Trade shows
Value added services
Warehouses
Web architecture

COMPETITORS

Affiliated Foods
  Midwest
Associated Wholesale
  Grocers
C&S Wholesale
Central Grocers

Dearborn Wholesale
  Grocers
Kroger
Roundy's
Winkler

HISTORICAL FINANCIALS
Company Type: Private

Income Statement

FYE: April 25

	REVENUE ($ mil.)	NET INCOME ($ mil.)	NET PROFIT MARGIN	EMPLOYEES
04/15	672	(6)	—	325
04/14	640	5	0.9%	—
04/13	607	5	0.9%	—
04/12	569	5	0.9%	—
Annual Growth	5.7%	—	—	—

2015 Year-End Financials
Return on assets: 4.0%   Cash ($ mil.): —
Return on equity: (-1.0%)
Current ratio: 0.90

CFA INSTITUTE

EXECUTIVES

President, Paul Smith
Board of Directors, Tina Sapsaram
Senior Vice-President, Moira J Coleman
Senior Vice-President, Patricia D Walters
Vice-President, Guy Williams
Director, Kurt N Schacht
Auditors: PRICEWATERHOUSECOOPERS LLP WA

LOCATIONS

HQ: CFA INSTITUTE
  915 E HIGH ST, CHARLOTTESVILLE, VA 229024868
Phone: 434 951-5499

HISTORICAL FINANCIALS
Company Type: Private

Income Statement

FYE: August 31

	REVENUE ($ mil.)	NET INCOME ($ mil.)	NET PROFIT MARGIN	EMPLOYEES
08/15	272	33	12.3%	450
08/14	259	26	10.1%	—
08/11	220	9	4.5%	—
08/10	200	13	6.5%	—
Annual Growth	6.3%	20.7%	—	—

2015 Year-End Financials
Return on assets: 10.0%   Cash ($ mil.): 56
Return on equity: 12.3%
Current ratio: 0.30

CGB ENTERPRISES, INC.

The farmer in the delta relies on CGB Enterprises. Located in Louisiana near the shores of Lake Pontchartrain and the mouth of the Mississippi River the agricultural company provides US farmers with a range of services including grain handling storage and merchandising. It offers inland grain transportation by barge rail and truck and also markets and sells seeds agricultural chemicals and insurance. CGB's Consolidated Terminals and Logistics Co. (CTLC) subsidiary provides transportation logistics and bulk commodity services for both agricultural and non-agricultural customers. The company operates more than 95 locations across the US. Japanese trading conglomerates ITOCHU and ZEN-NOH own CGB.

Geographic Reach

From its headquarters in the city of Mandeville Louisiana CGB operates its business through more than 95 locations nationwide including 74 grain elevators across the Midwest. It boasts grain facilities in nearly 10 states including Nebraska Oklahoma Arkansas Iowa Illinois Indiana Ohio Kentucky and Missouri. The company's fertilizer operations span Ohio Illinois Arkansas and Michigan.

Sales and Marketing

Besides its core services of inland grain transportation via barge rail and truck CGB markets and sells seeds agricultural chemicals and insurance as part of its operations.

Strategy

CGB has expanded its CTLC business in recent years. To give the unit an extended reach CTLC now serves the transportation bulk commodity and logistics needs of a global base of customers rather than just CGB's core businesses.

CGB also regularly invests in its own holdings. The company is constructing a rail shipment facility in Defiance Ohio to boost its production capacity and existing transportation system. In 2014 CGB began building a new facility on the Ohio River near Brandenburg Kentucky.

Mergers and Acquisitions

In mid-2014 CGB Enterprises acquired a grain storage facility in Savage Minnesota from Ceres Global Ag Corp. Under the terms of the deal Ceres will lease back 3.5 million bushels of storage capacity from CGB for a six-year term. The purchase of the grain storage facility in Savage brings new customers to CGB which also plans to expand its fertilizer diversified services and other divisions in the Minnesota market. Also CGB acquired Oklahoma's W.B. Johnston Grain (WBJ) in April 2014.

WBJ operates 19 grain elevators in Oklahoma and Texas including two grain terminals.

Strengthening its foothold on the Mississippi River CGB acquired the grain and fertilizer assets of Twomey based in Smithshire Illinois. The deal consummated in 2011 added valuable loading capacity on the river and offered CGB with a solid customer base in northwestern Illinois.

EXECUTIVES

President CEO, Kevin D. Adams
VP Grain Group, Gregory Beck
VP Diversified Services, Rodney L. Clark
General Manager Agri Financial Services, Alan Singleton
Manager CGB Fertilizer, George Porvaznik
VP CTLC and Marine, Scott Leininger
General Manager Feed Ingredients, Mark Cruse
Vice President, Koji Miura
VICE PRESIDENT, James Mcclelland
Vice President, Osamu Yako
Vice President Human Resources, Mark Berry
Executive Vice President, Koji Shinohara
Auditors: KPMG LLP NEW ORLEANS LA

LOCATIONS

HQ: CGB ENTERPRISES, INC.
  1127 HWY 190 E SERVICE RD, COVINGTON, LA 704334929
Phone: 985 867-3500
Web: WWW.CGBGRAIN.COM

PRODUCTS/OPERATIONS

Selected Business Units
Feed Ingredients
Fertilizer
Financial Services
Grain
Marine
Premium Grains
Risk Management
Soybean Processing
Terminals & Logistics

COMPETITORS

ADM
Ag Processing Inc.
Alabama Farmers
  Cooperative
Canal Barge Company
Cargill

Crosby Tugs
Jimmy Sanders
Kirby Corporation
Southern States
Tennessee Farmers
  Co-op

HISTORICAL FINANCIALS
Company Type: Private

Income Statement

FYE: May 31

	REVENUE ($ mil.)	NET INCOME ($ mil.)	NET PROFIT MARGIN	EMPLOYEES
05/16	5,934	33	0.6%	1,250
05/15	6,656	62	0.9%	—
05/14	7,227	53	0.7%	—
05/13	6,212	30	0.5%	—
Annual Growth	(1.5%)	3.7%	—	—

2016 Year-End Financials
Return on assets: 1.0%   Cash ($ mil.): 13
Return on equity: 0.6%
Current ratio: 0.20

CGH MEDICAL CENTER

EXECUTIVES

Chief Executive Officer, Paul Steinke
Director, Linnette Bolin

Officer, Susie Kennedy
Director, Thomas McCawley
Marketing Director, Dana McCoy
Director, Brent Peters
Manager, Pete Dowding

LOCATIONS

HQ: CGH MEDICAL CENTER
  100 E LE FEVRE RD, STERLING, IL 610811279
Phone: 815 625-0400
Web: WWW.CGHMC.COM

HISTORICAL FINANCIALS

Company Type: Private

Income Statement

	REVENUE ($ mil.)	NET INCOME ($ mil.)	NET PROFIT MARGIN	EMPLOYEES
04/15	199	14	7.3%	1,400
04/12	193	8	4.3%	—
04/11	143	5	3.9%	—
04/10	1,440	0	0.0%	—
Annual Growth	(32.6%)	874.4%	—	—

FYE: April 30

2015 Year-End Financials

Return on assets: 2.2%   Cash ($ mil.): 28
Return on equity: 7.3%
Current ratio: 1.60

CH2M HILL COMPANIES, LTD.

Engineering and construction firm CH2M HILL (named for its founders Cornell Howland Hayes and Merryfield; dba CH2M) operates five divisions that offer up consulting design build operations and maintenance services. It is active across five markets: energy and industrial; environment and nuclear transportation water and power. CH2M's top client is the US Government and public sector clients include the US Department of Energy and the Department of Defense. CH2M also works for state and local governments building water and wastewater systems airports highways and other transportation projects. Founded in 1946 the privately held company is owned by private equity firm Apollo Global Management.

Operations

CH2M operates five business segments reflecting the markets they serve: Energy and Industrial Environment and Nuclear Transportation Water and Power EPC (engineering procurement construction).

The Environment and Nuclear segment which makes up over 40% of company revenue provides consulting design build engineering operations and maintenance construction management and program management services. The segment is broken down into three further units: environmental; government facilities and infrastructure; and nuclear.

The Water segment (around 25% of revenue) works on various water-related projects for the wastewater drinking water industrial water conveyance and storage water resources and ecosystem management and intelligent water services markets.

CH2M's Transportation segment (nearly 20% of revenue) provides horizontal and vertical infrastructure development services for the Aviation Highway and Bridge Ports and Maritime and Transit and Rail market sectors.

Energy and Industrial (15% of revenue) comprises CH2M's oil and gas chemicals and industrial and advanced technology businesses. It provides consulting planning design engineering ops and maintenance and construction.

The Power EPC (engineering procurement construction) segment (15% of revenue) builds power plants of various types including natural gas coal solar wind biomass and geothermal.

Geographic Reach

Colorado-based CH2M generates about 65% of its revenue from the US. The remainder comes from Asia Australia New Zealand Canada Europe Latin America the Middle East and Africa.

Sales and Marketing

The company's clients include US federal and foreign government agencies state and local governments private sector companies and utilities. The US government (and federally-regulated agencies) is the company's largest client accounting for around 20% of total sales.

Financial Performance

CH2M's annual revenues and profits have been slowly declining since 2012 as oil and gas projects have been stifled amid low fuel prices in recent years and as government budgets have been squeezed.

In fiscal 2016 (ended December) revenue fell 2% to $5.2 billion. On a segment basis the company saw some sharp falls: Energy and Industrial fell 25% as the lower oil price impacted on volume and client concessionson direct hire construction operations and maintenance program management and professional services. Water segment revenue fell 13% due to decreased activities on two design-build-operate contracts for water treatment facilities in the US.

However strong growth was found in the Environment and Nuclear segment which grew 33% as a result of a large nuclear joint-venture project in Canada.

Net income fell from $80 million in 2015 to $15 million in 2016. The fall was due to project losses and restructuring activities offset by the release of a tax valuation allowance.

CH2M incurred a cash outflow from operating activities of $245.5 million a decrease of $348.7 million. The cash outflow was a result of a decrease in earnings and a hefty contribution to the company's defined benefit plans.

Strategy

CH2M began a refocusing strategy in 2016 to follow a client-centric approach with a lower-cost deliver model. It simplified its structure and delivery model including layoffs and facilities consolidations. The company expected the process to complete in 2017 and generate cost savings of $100 million. Its segment reporting will likely be revised as well.

In 2017 CH2M landed a major nuclear deal worth $1.5 billion. The company was awarded a deactivation and remediation contract for a uranium enrichment plant in Kentucky. Works will be carried out over five years followed by an optional 2-3 years.

Mergers and Acquisitions

CH2M occasionally acquires similar businesses to bolster its own service lines. However the acquisition front has been quiet for several years. In 2016 it acquired a controlling stake in a joint venture for $6.3 million.

Company Background

In November 2011 the company acquired Halcrow Group a London-based specialist in environmental infrastructure and transport projects for an estimated $192 million. The deal helped boost CH2M's facilities and infrastructure revenues and expanded the company's global reach adding Halcrow's extensive client list and about 100 offices worldwide.

In 2011 CH2M expanded its public transit business when it acquired the state and local government transit consulting business of Booz Allen Hamilton.

The company which is owned by its employees was founded in 1946.

EXECUTIVES

EVP Growth and Sales, Lisa Glatch, age 54, $328,852 total compensation
EVP and CFO, Gary L. McArthur, age 57, $599,248 total compensation
President State and Local Governments Client Sector, Gregory T. (Greg) McIntyre, age 58, $477,117 total compensation
SVP and Regional Managing Director Middle East North Africa and India, Neil Reynolds
President Water Business Group, Peter G. Nicol
Chairman and CEO, Jacqueline C. (Jacque) Hinman, age 55, $996,156 total compensation
President National Governments Client Sector, Terry A. Ruhl
SVP and Managing Director Operations Management Services, Steve Meininger
EVP Legal, Thomas M. (Tom) McCoy, age 66, $519,231 total compensation
President Industrial and Urban Environments, Thomas L. Pennella
EVP Project Services, Carlo Orsenigo
President Private Client Sector, Matthew Sutton, $346,160 total compensation
Vice President Area Manager, Didier Menard
Vice President And Director Corporate Real Estate, John Spencer
Vice President Of Information Systems, Rick Robertson
Senior Vice President Corporate Affairs, Patrick O'Keefe
Executive Vice President Marketing, Gail Chamberlain
Senior Vice President, Ken Miller
Vice President for National Security Programs, Rob Hood
Vice President for Engineering Project and Construction, Kent Dorr
Executive Vice President Marketing, Henry Abiera
Vice President, Maria Sheridan
Vice President, Dale Gabel
Assistant Vice President, Scott Barber
Executive Vice President Marketing, Grace Wachira
Senior Vice President, Stephen Browning
Vice President and Senior Project Manager, Lidia Pilecky
Vice President of Sales, Julie Thomas
Executive Vice President Marketing, Gary Colgan
Vice President Of Information Systems, Donna Riley
Vice President of Information Technology, Kristina Nygaard
Vice President Creative, Rosemarie Gumba
Vice President Bd Energy And Chemicals, Sun Pao
Senior Vice President Operations Energy And Chemicals, Pete Wiggin
Vice President, Mike Tilchin
Vice President, Jay Witherspoon
Vice President of Technology, Cathy Zou
Vice President, Christopher Thomas
Vice President, Vijay Kumar
Senior Vice President; Managing Director Strategic Consulting, Scott Haskins
Vice President, Russell Bowen
Vice President of Transportation, Les Melhorn
Vice President of Information Technology, Rick Riker
Vice President, Pete Butler
Vice President And Senior Program Manager, Don Holmes
Executive Vice President Marketing, James Gorham
Vice President Sales, Andrew Barash

Executive Vice President Marketing, James
Maughan
Senior Vice President, Don Olson
Vice President, Alan Ispass
Vice President Sales, Anja Schoenberger
Executive Vice President Marketing, Gregg
Thompson
Executive Vice President Marketing, Gregg Hughes
Vice President Of Information Technology, Louise
Lella
Vice President Of Information Technology, Tim
Constantine
Executive Vice President Marketing, Emilio
Candanoza
Vice President Sales, Alan Teare
Vice President Of Information Technology,
Thomas Higgins
Vice President Sales, Anne Vealey
Regional Business Group Manager Vice President,
Rod Brauer
Executive Vice President Marke, Gerald Simpson
Vice President Engineering, Tom Heinemann
Vice President And Area Manager, Deron Huck
**Vice President Business Development and
Strategy,** William Badger
Executive Vice President Marketing, Fair Yeager
Executive Vice President Marketing, Janie Iseri
Vice President International Government Affairs,
Theresa Loar
Technology Vice President, Korkud Egrican
Executive Vice President Marketing, Imad Feghali
Executive Vice President Marketing, Gretchen
Engel
Vice President, Pam Riddle
Vice President Site Management, Saeed Khan
VP Of Finance, Todd Heskett
Executive Vice President Marketing, Elizabeth
Bryant
Vice President and Director, Vinod Singh
Executive Vice President Marketing, Howard
Thomas
Executive Vice President Marketing, Greg Eldridge
Executive Vice President Marketing, Iosefa Matagi
Vice President, Tom Price
Vice President Tunnels, Mark Johnson
**Vice President North West Regional Business
Manager,** Vicki Bogenberger
**Senior Vice President Latin America Region
Energy And Chemicals,** Jose Montalvo
Vice President ??? International, Dan Baublis
Vice President Of Information Technology, Stuart
Jeffcoat
Vice President and Business Manager, Brent
Diemer
**Vice President of Community Investment and
Director of CH2M HILL Foundation,** Ellen Y
Sandberg
Vice President, Jerry J Notte
Vice President, Beth French
**Global Vice President And Director Of Wastewater
Market Segment,** Liliana Maldonado
Vice President Senior Program Manager, Daniel
Wetstein
Vice President, Phil Yerby
Vice President (Business Development), Chris
Coggans
Vice President International Operations Director,
Matthew Radek
Executive Vice President Marketing, Emilee
Edginton
Vice President, Jed Campbell
Vice President Sales, Anne Lynch
Vice President, Paul Wobma
Vice President, Tom Waters
Vice President Marketing, Morgan Hanscom
Vice President of Information Technology,
Jonathan James
Vice President, Chuck Smith
Executive Vice President and General Counsel,
Shane Burley

**Vice President Waste Management Market
Segment Director,** John J Wood
Vice President, Mel Hatcher
Vice President, Gwo J Ching Hwang
Vice President and Regional Manager, John
Richardson
Vice President Of Construction, Sonny Webb
Vice President, Jaason Englesmith
Vice President Chief Investment Officer, Michael
Brown
Vice President Chief Engineer For Highwa,
Michael Falini
Vice President Maryland Transportation L, Bruce
Gartner
**Senior Vice President and Regional Manager
Southeastern Us,** Robert Bailey
Vice President, Bill Beddow
Vice President, Joseph Sandrin
Vice President, Jonathan Harris
Vice President and Senior Program Manager,
Seema Alim
Vice President Strategic Planning, Allen Schubert
**Vice President and Global Oil and Gas Market
Sector Leader for Ports and Maritime Group,**
Colin Skipper
VICE PRESIDENT, JD SOLOMON
Vice President, Jerry O'Leary
Treas, Steven Mathews
Board Member, Bill Farmer
Board Member, Hank Postrozny
Treasurer, Rene Loya
Auditors: KPMG LLP DENVER COLORADO

LOCATIONS

HQ: CH2M HILL COMPANIES, LTD.
9191 S JAMAICA ST, ENGLEWOOD, CO 801125946
Phone: 303 771-0900
Web: WWW.CH2M.COM

2016 sales

	$ mil.	% of total
US	3,304	63
International	1,931	37
Total	**5,235**	**100**

PRODUCTS/OPERATIONS

2016 sales

	$ mil.	% of total
Environmental and Nuclear	2,213	42
Water	1,190	23
Transportation	930	18
Energy and Industrial	860	16
Power EPC	40	1
Total	**5,235**	**100**

Selected Subsidiaries

CH2M HILL Alaska Inc.
CH2M HILL Canada Inc.
CH2M HILL Constructors Inc.
CH2M Hill Energy Ltd.
CH2M HILL Engineers Inc.
CH2M HILL Hanford Inc.
CH2M HILL Inc.
CH2M HILL International Ltd.
Halcrow Group Ltd.
HEBL Inc.

COMPETITORS

AECOM	Jacobs Engineering
Amec Foster Wheeler	KBR
Balfour Beatty	MWH Global
Bechtel	Parsons Brinckerhoff
Black & Veatch	Parsons Corporation
ERM	Tetra Tech
Fluor	Tutor Perini

HISTORICAL FINANCIALS
Company Type: Private

Income Statement
FYE: December 30

	REVENUE ($ mil.)	NET INCOME ($ mil.)	NET PROFIT MARGIN	EMPLOYEES
12/16	5,287	(124)	—	22,000
12/15	5,408	92	1.7%	—
12/14	5,468	(318)	—	—
12/13	5,931	131	2.2%	—
Annual Growth	**(3.8%)**	—	—	—

2016 Year-End Financials
Return on assets: 7.9% Cash ($ mil.): 131
Return on equity: (-2.3%)
Current ratio: 0.60

CHAFFEY JOINT UNION HIGH SCHOOL DISTRICT

EXECUTIVES

Superintendent, Mathew Holton
Board of Directors, Matthew Holton
Assistant Manager, Lynn Murphy
Accountant, Lourdes Ramirez
Manager, Jeff Ellingfin
Director, Judy Pose
Director, Shirley M Gasparin
Assistant Manager, William Brod

LOCATIONS

HQ: CHAFFEY JOINT UNION HIGH SCHOOL DISTRICT
211 W 5TH ST, ONTARIO, CA 917621653
Phone: 909 988-8511
Web: WWW.CJUHSD.K12.CA.US

HISTORICAL FINANCIALS
Company Type: Private

Income Statement
FYE: June 30

	REVENUE ($ mil.)	NET INCOME ($ mil.)	NET PROFIT MARGIN	EMPLOYEES
06/16	315	(65)	—	2,000
06/11	226	14	6.5%	—
06/09	243	10	4.3%	—
06/08	0	(0)	—	—
Annual Growth	**122.1%**	—	—	—

2016 Year-End Financials
Return on assets: 12.9% Cash ($ mil.): 257
Return on equity: (-20.7%)
Current ratio: —

CHAMBERSBURG HOSPITAL

EXECUTIVES

Director, Norman B Epstein
Board of Directors, Philip Fague
Board of Directors, Michael Colli
Director, Mary M Gowan
Auditors: SMITH ELLIOTT KEARNS & COMPANY

LOCATIONS

HQ: CHAMBERSBURG HOSPITAL
112 N 7TH ST, CHAMBERSBURG, PA 172011700
Phone: 717 267-3000

HISTORICAL FINANCIALS

Company Type: Private

Income Statement

FYE: June 30

	REVENUE ($ mil.)	NET INCOME ($ mil.)	NET PROFIT MARGIN	EMPLOYEES
06/16	317	(43)	—	1,729
06/15	290	(0)	—	—
06/14	294	52	17.6%	—
06/13	278	40	14.7%	—
Annual Growth	4.5%	—	—	—

2016 Year-End Financials

Return on assets: 1.9%   Cash ($ mil.): 16
Return on equity: (-13.8%)
Current ratio: 0.80

CHANDLER REGIONAL MEDICAL CENTER

EXECUTIVES

President, Tim Bricker
Manager, Danielle Leblanc
Director, Heather Bathen
Director, Jim Kentner
Director, Kaye Prost
Chief Financial Officer, Mark Kem

LOCATIONS

HQ: CHANDLER REGIONAL MEDICAL CENTER
1955 W FRYE RD, CHANDLER, AZ 852246282
Phone: 480 728-3000
Web: WWW.CHANDLERAZ.GOV

HISTORICAL FINANCIALS

Company Type: Private

Income Statement

FYE: June 30

	REVENUE ($ mil.)	NET INCOME ($ mil.)	NET PROFIT MARGIN	EMPLOYEES
06/15	438	40	9.2%	1,900
06/08	3	0	20.3%	—
06/05	0	0	—	—
Annual Growth	—	—	—	—

2015 Year-End Financials

Return on assets: 3.7%   Cash ($ mil.): 169
Return on equity: 9.2%
Current ratio: 5.30

CHANDLER UNIFIED SCHOOL DISTRICT

EXECUTIVES

Superintendent, Camille Casteel
Executive Secretary, Donna Nigh

Director, Lue Schroeder
Director, Kymberly Marshall
Auditors: HEINFELD MEECH & CO PC P

LOCATIONS

HQ: CHANDLER UNIFIED SCHOOL DISTRICT
1525 W FRYE RD, CHANDLER, AZ 852246112
Phone: 480 812-7000
Web: WWW.CHANDLER.K12.AZ.US

HISTORICAL FINANCIALS

Company Type: Private

Income Statement

FYE: June 30

	REVENUE ($ mil.)	NET INCOME ($ mil.)	NET PROFIT MARGIN	EMPLOYEES
06/16	353	49	14.0%	4,500
06/05	207	0	—	—
06/04	207	(11)	—	—
06/03	0	0	—	—
Annual Growth	—	—	—	—

CHAPMAN UNIVERSITY

Chapman University enrolls 7000 students at campuses throughout California as well as in Washington State. From its main campus in Orange California the university offers traditional undergraduate graduate and professional programs at seven colleges and schools. It also confers bachelor and master's degrees and teaching credentials to non-traditional students at its two-dozen satellite campuses. The university offers some 50 undergraduate majors and 40 graduate programs. It has 650 faculty members and a student-to-teacher ratio of 15:1. Chapman University includes Brandman University a distance learning program for some 10000 working adults that operates two dozen locations and offers online courses.

Financial Performance

Chapman University reported a 9% increase in revenues to $304 million in 2011 due to higher income from tuition fees gifts grants and bequests. Net income also increased 27% to $70 million due to increased endowment returns offset slightly by increased general educational and auxiliary expenses.

Strategy

Chapman University is expanding programs to widen opportunities for students. In 2011 the School of Law launched a new business law program and in 2013 the Argyros School of Business and Economics opened a new financial center for real-time student investor trading and portfolio management training. Facilities expansions include the construction of a new center for the arts and a new health sciences campus; both projects were launched in 2012.

Company Background

Chapman University was founded in 1861 as Hesperian College; it was re-named Chapman College in 1934 in honor of philanthropist Charles C. Chapman.

EXECUTIVES

Executive Vice President Chancellor, Daniele Struppa
Associate Vice President of Development, Michele Wanner
Vice President, Rebecca Haber
Vice President of Finance, Ernest Wang
Vice President, Brenton Burke
Vice President for Public Relations, Jesse Richards

Vice President Recruitment, Carrie Ferrando
Vice President, Katie Walsh
Assistant Vice President, Behzad Binesh
Vice President and Chief Information Officer, Helen Norris
VICE PRESIDENT, Lauren Flynn
Vice President, Mark Woodland
Vice President Of Advancement, Karen Bustamante
Assistant Vice President For Finance And Budget, Mike Price
Vice Chair, Negeen Lotfi
Secretary, Brendan Le
Secretary, Sarah Price
Advisory Board Member, Bina Patel
Auditors: KPMG LLP IRVINE CA

LOCATIONS

HQ: CHAPMAN UNIVERSITY
1 UNIVERSITY DR, ORANGE, CA 928661005
Phone: 714 997-6815

PRODUCTS/OPERATIONS

Selected Colleges and Schools
College of Educational Studies
College of Performing Arts
George L. Argyros School of Business and Economics
Lawrence and Kristina Dodge College of Film and Media Arts
Schmid College of Science and Technology
School of Law
Wilkinson College of Humanities and Social Sciences

HISTORICAL FINANCIALS

Company Type: Private

Income Statement

FYE: May 31

	REVENUE ($ mil.)	NET INCOME ($ mil.)	NET PROFIT MARGIN	EMPLOYEES
05/16	424	31	7.4%	3,300
05/15	400	50	12.7%	—
05/14	380	78	20.6%	—
05/13	356	78	22.1%	—
Annual Growth	6.0%	(26.5%)	—	—

2016 Year-End Financials

Return on assets: 10.7%   Cash ($ mil.): 74
Return on equity: 7.4%
Current ratio: 1.10

CHARLES COUNTY BOARD OF EDUCATION

EXECUTIVES

Chairman of the Board, Roberta Wise
Director, Cynthia McRoy
Manager, Carol Crouse

LOCATIONS

HQ: CHARLES COUNTY BOARD OF EDUCATION
5980 RADIO STATION RD, LA PLATA, MD 206463337
Phone: 301 934-7224
Web: WWW.CCBOE.COM

HISTORICAL FINANCIALS

Company Type: Private

Income Statement

FYE: June 30

	REVENUE ($ mil.)	NET INCOME ($ mil.)	NET PROFIT MARGIN	EMPLOYEES
06/15	391	(3)	—	3,300
06/14	403	5	1.3%	—
06/13	393	9	2.5%	—
06/12	365	8	2.3%	—
Annual Growth	2.3%	—	—	—

2015 Year-End Financials

Return on assets: 3.1%
Return on equity: (-0.8%)
Current ratio: —

Cash ($ mil.): 68

CHARLESTON AREA MEDICAL CENTER, INC.

CAMC Health System is a catalyst for care in Charleston. The health network includes flagship facility Charleston Area Medical Center (CAMC) which is the largest hospital in West Virginia and consists of three campuses with some 840 beds total. The system also includes the CAMC Health Education and Research Institute which coordinates education programs for medical students from West Virginia University. In addition the health system operates smaller rural hospital CAMC Teays Valley and several urgent care and family practice clinics. CAMC Health System operates an online medical information system and physician services company Integrated Health Care Providers.

Operations

The three campuses of CAMC include CAMC General Hospital CAMC Memorial Hospital and CAMC Women and Children's Hospital all of which are located in Charleston. Specialty services at the hospitals include cardiology kidney transplants trauma and pediatrics. The CAMC Institute conducts graduate and continuing education courses; it also connects education and health care through clinical research projects in areas such as cancer and cardiovascular clinical science studies. The Teays Valley Hospital is a 70-bed facility located in nearby Hurricane West Virginia.

CAMC General Hospital is home to the highest level Trauma Center nationally-accredited Medical Rehabilitation and Stroke Centers The Center for Joint Replacement Neurosciences Center one of two Facial Surgery Centers Charleston's only accredited Sleep Center and West Virginia's only kidney transplant program affiliated with the Cleveland Clinic.

CAMC Memorial Hospital hosts one of highest volume heart programs in the US which performs 8000 procedures in the cardiac catheterization labs and more than 1600 open-heart bypass surgeries a year.

CAMC Women and Children's Hospital facilitates the birth of more than 3000 babies (including many high-risk births) per year.

Teays Valley Hospital is a not-for-profit 70-bed hospital. More than 100 doctors are authorized to practice at the hospital.

CAMC serves as a clinical training site for 700 additional learners per year through educational affiliations with regional colleges and universities.

Sales and Marketing

Commercial insurance providers and other third parties accounted for more than half of CAMC's net patient revenue in 2013; Medicare and Medicaid account for 30% and 13% respectively.

Financial Performance

The company's revenue grew by 4% to $969 million in 2013 due to higher net patient revenues and investment income. Net income fell 8% to $86 million though as expenses including salaries and employee benefits rose. Cash flow from operations dropped 48% to $33 million both as a result of the lower net income and an increase in cash used in short-term trading investments.

Strategy

In 2013 CAMC teamed up with The Ohio State University University of Michigan and West Virginia University to raise awareness and educate the community about cervical cancer. Community Awareness Resources and Education (CARE) is one of OSU Cancer Center's programs sponsored by the National Cancer Institute that focuses on an important health disparity among an underserved Appalachian population.

The following year CAMC teamed with Alliance Oncology a division of Alliance HealthCare Services to work on establishing a department of radiation therapy at CAMC Cancer Center.

Upgrading its infrastructure in 2013 Teays Valley Hospital completed a $3.7 million ICU expansion project.

EXECUTIVES

Director of Utilization Review, Janice Kiser
Director of Operating Room, Marcy Myers
Operating Room Director, Glen Martin
Director of Radiology, John J Anton
Respiratory Therapy Director, Chuck Menders
Infection Control Director, Terrie Lee
Director of Radiology, Michael E Anton
Director of Radiology, Jeffrey C Dameron
Operating Room Director, CATHY DORSEY
Board Member, Gail Pitchford

LOCATIONS

HQ: CHARLESTON AREA MEDICAL CENTER, INC.
501 MORRIS ST, CHARLESTON, WV 253011326
Phone: 304 348-5432

PRODUCTS/OPERATIONS

2013 Net Patient Revenue

	% of total
Commercial insurance & other third-party payment programs	51
Medicare	30
Medicaid	13
Self-pay	1
PEIA	5
Total	100

2013 Sales

	$ mil
% of total	
Net patient revenue less provision for bad debts	91
Investment income	5
Other revenue	4
Net assets released from restrictions	-
Total	100

Selected Service Areas

Behavioral health
Cancer
Cardiac
Children's medicine
Craniofacial surgery
Endoscopy
Fertility
Gynecology
Hemophilia
Kidney transplant
Orthopedics
Palliative care
Perinatal
Plastic surgery
Stroke
Trauma
Urology
Vascular

COMPETITORS

Charleston Hospital
Ohio Valley Medical Center
Princeton Community Hospital
St. Mary's Medical Center
WVUHS
Weirton Medical Center
West Virginia University Hospitals

HISTORICAL FINANCIALS

Company Type: Private

Income Statement

FYE: December 31

	REVENUE ($ mil.)	NET INCOME ($ mil.)	NET PROFIT MARGIN	EMPLOYEES
12/15	932	36	4.0%	4,000
12/14	877	42	4.9%	—
12/13	861	54	6.3%	—
12/07	703	9	1.3%	—
Annual Growth	3.6%	19.3%	—	—

2015 Year-End Financials

Return on assets: 7.0%
Return on equity: 4.0%
Current ratio: 0.90

Cash ($ mil.): 32

CHATHAM COUNTY BOARD OF EDUCATION

EXECUTIVES

Superintendent, Thomas Lockamy
Financial Executive, Beth Stanford
Auditors: KRT CPAS PC SAVANNAH GEOR

LOCATIONS

HQ: CHATHAM COUNTY BOARD OF EDUCATION
208 BULL ST, SAVANNAH, GA 314013997
Phone: 912 395-1000
Web:
WWW.INTERNET.SAVANNAH.CHATHAM.K12.GA.US

HISTORICAL FINANCIALS

Company Type: Private

Income Statement

FYE: June 30

	REVENUE ($ mil.)	NET INCOME ($ mil.)	NET PROFIT MARGIN	EMPLOYEES
06/16	493	21	4.3%	4,800
06/07	373	20	5.4%	—
06/06	330	10	3.3%	—
06/05	0	0	—	—
Annual Growth	—	—	—	—

CHEMIUM INTERNATIONAL CORP.

EXECUTIVES

President, Ofer Levy
Vice-President, Sanjeev Vora
Manager, Steve Williams

LOCATIONS

HQ: CHEMIUM INTERNATIONAL CORP.
1455 WEST LOOP S STE 550, HOUSTON, TX
770279528
Phone: 713 622-7766
Web: WWW.CHEMIUMCORP.COM

HISTORICAL FINANCIALS
Company Type: Private

Income Statement
FYE: December 31

	REVENUE ($ mil.)	NET INCOME ($ mil.)	NET PROFIT MARGIN	EMPLOYEES
12/15	2,015	3	0.2%	24
12/06	450	3	0.9%	—
12/03	103	0	—	—
Annual Growth	28.1%	—	—	—

2015 Year-End Financials
Return on assets: 2.9%   Cash ($ mil.): 5
Return on equity: 0.2%
Current ratio: 0.80

CHENEGA CORPORATION

An Alaska Native Corporation Chenega Corporation has gone from landowner to business titan. Representing the Chenega people residing in the central Alaskan Prince William Sound region it operates mostly through its subsidiaries. Chenega Integrated Systems and Chenega Technology Services offer information technology security training manufacturing research and development network engineering and military operation support services. Chenega Corporation's clients have included the Department of Defense Department of Homeland Security and EPA.

Geographic Reach

The company's headquarters are located in Anchorage Alaska. Chenega Corporation and its subsidiaries operate in 45 states and 11 countries.

Strategy

Government contracts are a source of revenue growth. Chenega Corporation began to participate in the Government Services marketplace in 1997. By 2012 it was performing on more than 158 prime contracts and 100 principal sub-contracts through a combination of competitive and negotiated best-value awards.

EXECUTIVES

Director of Government Relations, Kristina Woolston
Vice President and Director, Lloyd Kompkoff
Senior Vice President of Finance, Tom Reed
Vice President, Ronald Lee

LOCATIONS

HQ: CHENEGA CORPORATION
3000 C ST STE 301, ANCHORAGE, AK 995033975
Phone: 907 277-5706
Web: WWW.QUALITYINN.COM

PRODUCTS/OPERATIONS

Selected Services
Base operations and maintenance
Environmental management
Information technology
Intel and military operations
Light manufacturing
Logistics support
Telecommunications
Tourism and hospitality
Training services
Security services

COMPETITORS

Akal Security	Halliburton
Arctic Slope Regional Corporation	IBM Global Services
Computer Sciences Corp.	Parsons Corporation
	TKC Communications
HP Enterprise Services	chugach alaska

HISTORICAL FINANCIALS
Company Type: Private

Income Statement
FYE: September 30

	REVENUE ($ mil.)	NET INCOME ($ mil.)	NET PROFIT MARGIN	EMPLOYEES
09/15	881	12	1.4%	4,500
09/14	134	5	3.9%	—
09/12	1,099	8	0.8%	—
09/11	1,108	28	2.6%	—
Annual Growth	(5.6%)	(18.3%)	—	—

2015 Year-End Financials
Return on assets: 4.3%   Cash ($ mil.): 18
Return on equity: 1.4%
Current ratio: 1.70

CHEROKEE NATION BUSINESSES LLC

EXECUTIVES

Chief Executive Officer, Shawn Slaton
Chairman, Gary Cooper
Chief Financial Officer, Doug Evans
Board of Directors, Bob Berry
Chairman of the Board, Harold Sam Ray Hart
Director, Kimberly Barnette
Manager, Emily Helling
Administrative Assistant, Ken Anthony
Director, Ruben Cardenas
Auditors: BKD LLP TULSA OKLAHOMA

LOCATIONS

HQ: CHEROKEE NATION BUSINESSES LLC
777 W CHEROKEE ST, CATOOSA, OK 740153235
Phone: 918 384-7474
Web: WWW.CHEROKEENATIONBUSINESSES.COM

HISTORICAL FINANCIALS
Company Type: Private

Income Statement
FYE: September 30

	REVENUE ($ mil.)	NET INCOME ($ mil.)	NET PROFIT MARGIN	EMPLOYEES
09/16	1,021	50	4.9%	3,117
09/15	925	32	3.5%	—
09/14	829	52	6.4%	—
09/13	781	54	7.0%	—
Annual Growth	9.3%	(2.5%)	—	—

2016 Year-End Financials
Return on assets: 7.6%   Cash ($ mil.): 115
Return on equity: 4.9%
Current ratio: 1.50

CHEVRON PHILLIPS CHEMICAL COMPANY LLC

Among the world's largest petrochemical firms Chevron Phillips Chemical (CPChem) produces ethylene propylene polyethylene and polypropylene — sometimes used as building blocks for the company's other products such as pipe. Chevron Phillips Chemical also produces aromatics such as benzene and styrene specialty chemicals such as acetylene black (a form of carbon black) and mining chemicals. Chevron Phillips Chemical Company LP is CPChem's wholly-owned primary US operating subsidiary. CPChem is 50% owned by Chevron U.S.A. Inc. an indirect wholly-owned subsidiary of Chevron Corporation and 50% by wholly-owned subsidiaries of Phillips 66.

Operations

CPChem is a leading global producer of olefins and polyolefins (more than 80% of total sales) and a major supplier of aromatics alpha olefins styrenics specialty chemicals as well as piping material and other proprietary plastics. It is the Western Hemisphere's largest producer of high-density polyethylene — used in blow/injection molding plastic bags and pipes and films. CPChem also is near the top in styrene ethylene and aromatics production.

CPChem has several petrochemical joint ventures in the Middle East including Saudi Chevron Phillips Company (50%) and Qatar Chemical Company (not quite 50%). Subsidiary Chevron Oronite produces fuel additives.

The company's chemical products are used in more than 70000 consumer and industrial products. Its brands include Marlex Aromax Scentinel Soltex and K-Resin.

Geographic Reach

CPChem operates 35 manufacturing facilities and two research and development centers in Belgium China Colombia Qatar Saudi Arabia Singapore South Korea and the US.

Sales and Marketing

The company serves a range of markets including Adhesives and Sealants Agricultural Appliances Automotive Building and Construction Chemical Manufacturing Drycleaning Textiles Pharmaceuticals Paint and Coatings Imaging and Photography Packaging and Electronics.

Strategy

CPChem is growing its complex of chemical plants taking advantage of the deep pockets of its multinational parents increased demand for chemical products (especially in Asia) and the abundance of chemical raw materials generated by natural gas production in North American shale basins.

In 2015 the company completed an expansion of its normal alpha olefins capacity at its Cedar Bayou plant in Baytown. Alpha olefins are used in synthetic motor oils lubricants surfactants and other specialty applications.

Growing its infrastructure during 2014 CPChem completed the construction of a 1-hexene plant (the world's largest) at the company's Cedar Bayou complex in Baytown Texas with a design capacity of 250000 metric tons per year. The product 1-hexene is a component used in the manufacture of polyethylene a plastic resin commonly converted into film plastic pipe milk jugs detergent bottles and food and beverage containers.

In 2014 CPChem completed an ethylene expansion at its Sweeny complex in Old Ocean Texas.

That year to take advantage of chemical supply from nearby oil and gas basins the company committed $6 billion to build a 1.5-million-metric-tons/year (3.3 billion pounds/year) ethane cracker and two ethylene derivatives facilities on the US Gulf Coast. The two new polyethylene facilities will each have an annual capacity of 500000 metric tons (1.1 billion pounds). The projects are due to be completed in 2017.

To raise cash in 2015 the company sold its its Ryton polyphenylene sulfide business to Solvay for $220 million.

Company Background

In 2011 to expand its portfolio in Europe the company acquired a polyalphaolefin plant in Beringen Belgium from Neste Oil. The acquisition also added to the company's existing production of polyalphaolefins (PAOs) which are used in high-performance lubricants.

A coin toss determined whose name would go first when Chevron and Phillips Petroleum (now Phillips 66) formed 50-50 joint venture Chevron Phillips Chemical Company in 2000.

EXECUTIVES

SVP Petrochemicals, D. S. (Dave) Smith
President and CEO, Mark E. Lashier
VP and CIO, Peggy Colsman
SVP CFO and Controller, Tim D. Leveille
SVP Projects and Supply Chain, R. E. (Ron) Corn
SVP Manufacturing, M. S. (Scott) Sharp
SVP Polymers, David Morgan
Vice President of Human Resources, Greg Wagner
Vice President, Ken Hope
Vice President human Resources, Donald Kremer
Auditors: ERNST & YOUNG LLP HOUSTON TE

LOCATIONS

HQ: CHEVRON PHILLIPS CHEMICAL COMPANY LLC
10001 SIX PINES DR, THE WOODLANDS, TX 773801498
Phone: 832 813-4100
Web: WWW.CPCHEM.COM

PRODUCTS/OPERATIONS

Selected Products
Olefins and polyolefins
  Ethylene
  Polyethylene
  Polyethylene pipe
  Polypropylene
  Propylene
Aromatics and styrenics
  Benzene
  Cumene
  Cyclohexane
  Paraxylene

Styrene
Specialty products
  Acetylene black
  Alpha olefins
  Dimethyl sulfide
  Drilling specialty chemicals
  High-purity hydrocarbons and solvents
  Mining chemicals
  Neohexene
  Performance and reference fuels
  Polyalpha olefins
  Polystyrene

Selected Joint Ventures
Americas Styrenics (50%)
Chevron Phillips Singapore Chemicals (Private) Limited (50%)
KR Copolymer Co. Ltd. (60% South Korea)
Qatar Chemical Company Ltd. (Q-Chem 49%)
Saudi Chevron Phillips Company (50%)
Shanghai Golden Phillips Petrochemical Co. Ltd. (40%)

COMPETITORS

Dow Chemical	NOVA Chemicals
DuPont	SABIC
ExxonMobil Chemical	Sasol
Kraton	Total Petrochemicals
LyondellBasell	Westlake Chemical

HISTORICAL FINANCIALS

Company Type: Private

Income Statement   FYE: December 31

	REVENUE ($ mil.)	NET INCOME ($ mil.)	NET PROFIT MARGIN	EMPLOYEES
12/15	9,859	2,651	26.9%	5,000
12/14	14,148	3,288	23.2%	—
12/13	13,790	2,743	19.9%	—
12/08	12,828	276	2.2%	—
Annual Growth	(3.7%)	38.2%	—	—

2015 Year-End Financials

Return on assets: 9.1%
Return on equity: 26.9%   Cash ($ mil.): 350
Current ratio: 1.00

CHEVRON PHILLIPS CHEMICAL COMPANY LP

EXECUTIVES

Chief Executive Officer, Peter L Cella
Executive Vice-President, Mark E Lashier
Senior Vice-President, Ron Corn
Senior Vice-President, Tim Hill
Vice-President, Mitch Eichelberger
Credit Manager, Larry Albritton
Executive Vice-President, Mark A Haney
Treasurer, Trevor R Roberts
Chief Operating Officer, Tim G Taylor
Manager, Larry Forsythe
Auditors: ERNST & YOUNG LLP HOUSTON T

LOCATIONS

HQ: CHEVRON PHILLIPS CHEMICAL COMPANY LP
10001 SIX PINES DR, THE WOODLANDS, TX 773801498
Phone: 832 813-4100

HISTORICAL FINANCIALS

Company Type: Private

Income Statement   FYE: December 31

	REVENUE ($ mil.)	NET INCOME ($ mil.)	NET PROFIT MARGIN	EMPLOYEES
12/15	7,990	2,020	25.3%	5,000
12/14	11,758	2,444	20.8%	—
12/13	11,439	1,950	17.0%	—
Annual Growth	(16.4%)	1.8%	—	—

2015 Year-End Financials

Return on assets: 9.2%
Return on equity: 25.3%   Cash ($ mil.): 113
Current ratio: 1.20

CHI ST. VINCENT HOSPITAL HOT SPRINGS

EXECUTIVES

President, Bradley K Day
Director, Peter Bank
Director, Gus Blass
Director, James B Newman

LOCATIONS

HQ: CHI ST. VINCENT HOSPITAL HOT SPRINGS
300 WERNER ST, HOT SPRINGS, AR 719136406
Phone: 501 622-1000
Web: WWW.CHISTVINCENT.COM

HISTORICAL FINANCIALS

Company Type: Private

Income Statement   FYE: June 30

	REVENUE ($ mil.)	NET INCOME ($ mil.)	NET PROFIT MARGIN	EMPLOYEES
06/15	222	17	7.9%	2
06/14	4	(0)	—	—
Annual Growth	4642.0%	—	—	—

2015 Year-End Financials

Return on assets: 66.4%
Return on equity: 7.9%   Cash ($ mil.): 98
Current ratio: 1.20

CHICAGO COMMUNITY TRUST

You can trust this group to do the giving thing. The Chicago Community Trust gave more than $105 million in 2008 to not-for-profit organizations such as social services agencies schools health centers museums and theaters in the Chicago area. The grant program targets groups working in arts and culture basic human needs community development education and health. Past projects have included after-school programs for impoverished children funding a senior citizens center and health services for people with AIDS. Chicago Community Trust gets its funds from corporate and private donations. It was founded in 1915.

Vice President Finance and Chief Financial
 Officer, Carol Y Crenshaw
Auditors: D USA LLP CHICAGO IL

LOCATIONS

HQ: CHICAGO COMMUNITY TRUST
 225 N MICHIGAN AVE # 2200, CHICAGO, IL
 606017672
Phone: 312 616-8000
Web: WWW.CCT.ORG

HISTORICAL FINANCIALS

Company Type: Private

Income Statement

	REVENUE ($ mil.)	NET INCOME ($ mil.)	NET PROFIT MARGIN	EMPLOYEES
09/15	363	136	37.5%	66
09/14	291	105	36.3%	—
09/10	33	(36)	—	—
09/09	138	(86)	—	—
Annual Growth	17.5%	—	—	—

2015 Year-End Financials

Return on assets: 1.9%   Cash ($ mil.): 74
Return on equity: 37.5%
Current ratio: 2.00

CHILDFUND INTERNATIONAL, USA

ChildFund International (CFI) serves the little ones. The worldwide non-profit organization provides education medical care food and safe water to more than 13 million children — of all faiths — in about 30 countries in Africa Asia the Caribbean Eastern Europe Latin America and the US. It works in areas of early childhood development education family income generation nutrition and sanitation. The group also tries to get child soldiers away from the military and reintegrated into daily life. Founded in 1938 as China's Children Fund the group changed its name to Christian Children's Fund in 1951. In 2009 it again renamed itself ChildFund International.

Since its founding as an organization focused on orphans and orphanages CFI has become an international child development organization. More than 500000 sponsored children receive monthly contributions through the group; about 350000 of those sponsorships are supported by donors in the US. CFI also publishes newsletters booklets and studies on the effects of poverty and violence on children.

EXECUTIVES

President, Anne Lynam Goddard
Board of Directors, Tom Snead
Director, Jes S M Amadeo
Director, John C Purnell
Financial Executive, Chris Plyler
Director, Jacqueline Oburu
Marketing Manager, Cindy Morgan
Financial Executive, Laura Meloy
Auditors: RSM US LLP MC LEAN VA

LOCATIONS

HQ: CHILDFUND INTERNATIONAL, USA
 2821 EMERYWOOD PKWY, RICHMOND, VA
 232943726
Phone: 804 756-2700
Web: WWW.CHILDFUND.ORG

HISTORICAL FINANCIALS

Company Type: Private

Income Statement
FYE: June 30

	REVENUE ($ mil.)	NET INCOME ($ mil.)	NET PROFIT MARGIN	EMPLOYEES
06/15	232	0	0.0%	160
06/14	235	6	2.7%	—
06/11	228	12	5.3%	—
06/10	215	4	2.2%	—
Annual Growth	1.5%	(54.1%)	—	—

2015 Year-End Financials

Return on assets: 4.5%   Cash ($ mil.): 18
Return on equity: —
Current ratio: 1.10

CHILDREN'S HOSPITAL

EXECUTIVES

President, Kurt Newman
Vice-President, Brian Jessogne
Executive Director, Andy Hertzberg
Director, Carole Helmandollar
Auditors: GRANT THORNTON LLP MC LEAN V

LOCATIONS

HQ: CHILDREN'S HOSPITAL
 111 MICHIGAN AVE NW, WASHINGTON, DC
 200102916
Phone: 202 232-0521
Web: WWW.BELLHELICOPTER.TEXTRON.COM

HISTORICAL FINANCIALS

Company Type: Private

Income Statement
FYE: June 30

	REVENUE ($ mil.)	NET INCOME ($ mil.)	NET PROFIT MARGIN	EMPLOYEES
06/15	1,076	118	11.0%	6,000
06/14	983	43	4.4%	—
Annual Growth	9.4%	174.2%	—	—

2015 Year-End Financials

Return on assets: 13.2%   Cash ($ mil.): 114
Return on equity: 11.0%
Current ratio: 0.50

CHILDREN'S HOSPITAL

EXECUTIVES

President, Mary Perrin
Principal, John Wallin
Account Manager, Glenda Green

LOCATIONS

HQ: CHILDREN'S HOSPITAL
 200 HENRY CLAY AVE, NEW ORLEANS, LA
 701185798
Phone: 504 899-9511
Web: WWW.CHNOLA.ORG

HISTORICAL FINANCIALS

Company Type: Private

Income Statement
FYE: December 31

	REVENUE ($ mil.)	NET INCOME ($ mil.)	NET PROFIT MARGIN	EMPLOYEES
12/15	196	51	25.9%	1,700
12/14	201	55	27.8%	—
12/13	406	233	57.4%	—
12/10	203	46	22.8%	—
Annual Growth	(0.6%)	1.9%	—	—

2015 Year-End Financials

Return on assets: 9.8%   Cash ($ mil.): 163
Return on equity: 25.9%
Current ratio: 6.70

CHILDREN'S HOSPITAL & RESEARCH CENTER AT OAKLAND

Children's Hospital & Research Center at Oakland (operating as Children's Hospital Oakland) does just what its name says provides medical care for children and performs research to advance the treatment of pediatric diseases. The freestanding hospital has about 190 beds and a staff of some more than 200 hospital-based physicians professionals with more than 30 medical specialties. Its services include orthopedics neurology oncology and cardiology as well as surgery trauma neonatal and intensive care. Additionally the hospital operates several satellite outpatient clinics providing general and specialized care. Children's Hospital Oakland also conducts teaching and community outreach programs.

Operations

The organization's research division Children's Hospital Oakland Research Institute conducts research programs on transmittable diseases vaccines cancer immune system diseases diabetes asthma and obesity. It receives funding from the National Institutes of Health. The research center has more than 300 scientists working on 150 clinical trials.

Children's Hospital Oakland is a teaching hospital and is one of only two solely designated California Level 1 pediatric trauma centers in the region (and has one of the largest pediatric intensive care units in Northern California).

In 2012 it had 236877 outpatient visits (of which 46142 were emergency visits); 10183 inpatient admissions; and 8640 surgical cases.

Financial Performance

The hospitals' revenues declined by 6% in 2012 due to a drop in net patient service fees fundraising investments and other revenue sources.

Some 47% of 2012 revenues came from Medi-Cal/California Children's Services and Medicare/Supplemental funds; 36% from other insurance private insurance (contract and com-

mercial) and self-pay; and 12% from research programs.

Children's Hospital Oakland's net income decreased by 74% in 2012 due to lower revenues and an increase in expenses (including salaries benefits supplies and services).

In 2013 the hospital had an annual operating budget of more than $350 million.

Strategy

To boost coverage and resources in 2014 Children's Hospital Oakland and UCSF's Benioff Children's Hospital (also in the Bay area) formed an affiliation. Together the hospitals will be among the top ten largest children's health care providers in the US when the new UCSF Benioff Children's Hospital opens in 2015. In 2012 UCSF had 1230 physicians on staff including 150 clinicians at its current Benioff Children's Hospital location.

Previously the Oakland hospital held unsuccessful merger talks with Lucile Packard Children's Hospital at Stanford and Sutter Health network.

The hospital is also developing a master plan to maximize the use of existing property and buildings modernize facilities and provide individual rooms so that families can stay with their child during hospitalization.

In 2013 the Children's Hospital Oakland's Walnut Creek Campus completed a large-scale expansion and now include a Sports Medicine Center for Young Athletes and comprehensive Speech and Hearing Center.

Children's Hospital Oakland has had its share of financial troubles over the years. Along with a weak economy reduced reimbursement rates from both public and private payers and increasing health care costs added to the company's financial losses.

Company Background

In 2011 it received $532.8 million in research funding from the National Institutes of Health.

The hospital's research institute provided 85% of the DNA used for the Human Genome Project.

Children's Hospital Oakland was founded in 1942 and opened for business in 1914.

EXECUTIVES

Vice President Nursing and CHI, Nancy Shibata
Vice President, Carolyn Dossa
Vice President Human Resources Services, David Taylor
clinical director, Mary Heffron
Vice President, Alexander Lucas

LOCATIONS

HQ: CHILDREN'S HOSPITAL & RESEARCH CENTER AT OAKLAND
747 52ND ST, OAKLAND, CA 946091809
Phone: 510 428-3000
Web: WWW.CHILDRENSHOSPITALOAKLAND.ORG

PRODUCTS/OPERATIONS

Selected Services
Anesthesiology
Blood and Marrow Transplant (BMT) Program
Cardiology and Cardiothoracic Surgery
Center for Child Protection (CCP)
Center for the Vulnerable Child (CVC)
Clinical Laboratory Medicine & Pathology
Clinical Nutrition Department
Clinical Pathology Lab
Craniofacial Center
Cryopreservation Lab
Cytogenetics Laboratory
Developmental and Behavioral Pediatrics
Diagnostic Imaging/Radiology
Early Childhood Mental Health
Endocrinology/Diabetes
Family Outreach Clinic
Gastroenterology/Hepatology/Nutrition
Hematology/Oncology
Neonatology

Neuro-Oncology
Neurosurgery
Oncology/Hematology
Ophthalmology
Orthopedics
Otorhinolaryngology
Respiratory Care Services
Speech and Language Center
Sports Medicine Center
Urology

COMPETITORS

Alta Bates Summit Medical Center
Children's Hospital Boston
Children's Hospital of Philadelphia
Children's Hospital of Pittsburgh
Childrens Hospital Los Angeles
Dignity Health
John Muir Health
Rady Children's Hospital
Shriners Hospitals For Children
St. Jude Children's Research Hospital
St. Luke's Hospital (CA)
Sutter Health

HISTORICAL FINANCIALS

Company Type: Private

Income Statement FYE: June 30

	REVENUE ($ mil.)	NET INCOME ($ mil.)	NET PROFIT MARGIN	EMPLOYEES
06/15*	178	34	19.5%	2,000
12/13	541	44	8.3%	—
12/05	313	15	5.0%	—
12/04	270	(4)	—	—
Annual Growth	(4.0%)	—	—	—

*Fiscal year change

2015 Year-End Financials

Return on assets: 14.2%   Cash ($ mil.): 22
Return on equity: 19.5%
Current ratio: 1.00

CHILDREN'S HOSPITAL COLORADO

Rocky Mountain rugrats can count on Children's Hospital Colorado. The not-for-profit organization runs a network of health facilities in Colorado anchored by its nearly 50-acre main campus in Aurora. The campus includes a 260-bed inpatient hospital and numerous outpatient clinics. Children's Hospital Colorado also operates more than a dozen satellite locations in and around Denver that specialize in providing children with emergency and specialty care. Affiliated with the University of Colorado Denver School of Medicine the hospital provides medical training and performs a wide range of research into pediatric illnesses including cancer and HIV/AIDS.

Operations

The main hospital is located on the Anschutz Medical Campus with the medical school and the University of Colorado Hospital Authority's 620-bed acute care center. With help from its medical staff of 2330 Children's Hospital Colorado had 18500 inpatient admissions; 21000 surgeries 527000 outpatient visits and about 158000 emergency department visits in 2014.

The hospital boasts two additional emergency locations at Exempla Saint Joseph Hospital in Denver and Centura's Parker Adventist Hospital in Parker. Children's Hospital Colorado provides urgent care through three nearby community loca-

tions: Centura Littleton Adventist Hospital Children's Hospital North Campus at Broomfield and Exempla Lutheran Medical Center in Wheat Ridge. In addition it has about 10 specialty care clinics in the Denver area that provide cancer pulmonary and surgery services.

The health care facility's research initiatives are conducted at the Children's Hospital Colorado Research Institute. Along with its affiliation with the university the Children's Hospital works with the Pediatric Clinical Translational Research Center to conduct research and clinical trials in a number of fields including cardiology gastroenterology oncology orthopedics pulmonology and psychiatry.

Geographic Reach

Children's Hospital Colorado established in 1908 serves a seven-state region through its Level 1 trauma center. Its other facilities cater to residents of the Denver metropolitan area.

Sales and Marketing

Medicaid accounted for 47% of the hospital's net patient revenue in 2014; managed care accounted for 45%.

Financial Performance

Gross patient services revenue totaled $2.2 billion in 2014; other operating revenue totaled $60.7 million.

Strategy

Children's Hospital Colorado boasts the capacity to handle the most challenging emergencies as the only dedicated Level 1 trauma center in a seven-state region. Through its affiliation with the University of Colorado the hospital conducts physician assistant residency fellowship and internship programs in a variety of fields including anesthesiology orthopedics dentistry and neurology. It also provides continuing education programs for doctors and nurses.

The health care facility is expanding its footprint in the Colorado Springs area as the region experiences noteworthy growth. To this end it is building a new $110 million hospital on the University of Colorado Health Memorial North campus that will house 100 inpatient beds an emergency room neonatal and pediatric intensive care units and operating rooms. The complex is expected to open in 2018.

EXECUTIVES

President and CEO Children's Hospital Colorado Foundation, Steve Winesett
President CEO and Director, James E. Shmerling, age 63
SVP Patient Care Services and Chief Nursing Officer, Kelly M. Johnson
Surgeon-in-Chief, Timothy M. Crombleholme
Pediatrician-in-Chief, Stephen Daniels
Chief Medical Officer, Joan Bothner
President and CEO, Jena Hausmann
SVP and CIO, Mary Anne Leach
SVP and CFO, Jeff Harrington
Chief Research Officer, Frederick J. Suchy
Medical Director Pediatric Sports Medicine, Aaron Provance
Clinical Director, Sheila Kaseman
Vice President Operations, Jerrod Milton
Medical Director, Teri Schreiner
Finance Vice President, Jeffrey Harrington
Vice President Of Support Services, Dan Coxall
Senior Vice President and Chief Information Officer, Dana Moore
Chairman, Kevin Reidy

LOCATIONS

HQ: CHILDREN'S HOSPITAL COLORADO
13123 E 16TH AVE, AURORA, CO 800457106
Phone: 720 777-1234

Selected Locations
Children's Hospital Colorado Main Campus

Children's Hospital Colorado at Saint Joseph Hospital
Children's Hospital Colorado KidStreet
Children's Hospital Colorado Orthopedic Care Centennial
Children's Hospital Colorado Outpatient Specialty Care Centennial
Children's Hospital Colorado Outpatient Specialty Care Colorado Springs
Children's Hospital Colorado Outpatient Specialty Care Parker
Children's Hospital Colorado Therapy Care Parker
Children's Hospital Colorado Therapy Care Pueblo
Children's Hospital Colorado Urgent and Outpatient Specialty Care Wheat Ridge

PRODUCTS/OPERATIONS

Selected Departments
Adolescent Medicine Program
Adult Congenital Heart Disease Program
Aerodigestive Program
Allergy Program
Arrhythmia Center
Asthma Program
Audiology Speech and Learning Program
Bill Daniels Center for Children's Hearing
Bone Marrow Transplant Program
Breathing Institute
Burn program
Cardiac Anesthesia
Cardiac Catheterization
Cardiology Clinic
Cardiology Outreach Programs
Cardiomyopathy Program
Center for Cancer and Blood Disorders
Center for Celiac Disease
Child Abuse Services
Child Development Unit
Child Health Clinic
Colorado Fetal Care Center
Colorado Institute for Maternal and Fetal Health
Colorectal and Complex Pelvic Floor Disorders Program
Complex Congenital Heart Disease and Development Clinic
Craniofacial Center
Critical Care
Cystic Fibrosis Research and Care Center
Dental
Dermatology
Digestive Health Institute
Ear Nose and Throat
Eating Disorder Program
Emergency Department
Endocrinology
Endoscopy Clinic (ATECh)
Experimental Therapeutics Program
Extracorporeal Membrane Oxygenation (ECMO) Program
Eye
Fetal Cardiology Program
Fiberoptic Endoscopic Evaluation of Swallowing (FEES) Clinic
Flight for Life
Gastroenterology
Gastrointestinal Eosinophilic Diseases
Genetics Program
Gynecology
Healthy Expectations Perinatal Mental Health Program
Heart Institute
Heart Surgery
Heart Transplant Program
HOPE Clinic for Cancer Survivors
Hospitalist Services

COMPETITORS

Banner Health
Catholic Health Initiatives
Centura Health
Denver Health and Hospital Authority
Exempla Healthcare
HealthONE
North Colorado Medical Center
Presbyterian/St. Luke's Medical Center
Rose Medical Center
Shriners Hospitals For Children
The Memorial Hospital

HISTORICAL FINANCIALS
Company Type: Private

Income Statement
FYE: December 31

	REVENUE ($ mil.)	NET INCOME ($ mil.)	NET PROFIT MARGIN	EMPLOYEES
12/15	908	25	2.8%	2,200
12/14	879	58	6.6%	—
12/13	853	48	5.7%	—
12/08	497	(44)	—	—
Annual Growth	9.0%	—	—	—

2015 Year-End Financials
Return on assets: 6.7%
Return on equity: 2.8%
Current ratio: 1.20
Cash ($ mil.): 57

CHILDREN'S HOSPITAL MEDICAL CENTER

Cincinnati Children's Hospital Medical Center has a special place in its heart for kids. The pediatric health care facility offers specialty treatments for children and adolescents suffering from just about any malady including ailments of the heart and liver as well as blood diseases and cancer. Cincinnati Children's Hospital has some 600 beds and operates about a dozen outpatient care centers. Founded in 1883 the not-for-profit hospital runs the only level I pediatric trauma center in the region and serves as a teaching and research facility for the University of Cincinnati College of Medicine. It is also ranked in the top 10 for all 10 pediatric specialties by U.S. News & World Report

Operations
With a staff of some 1500 physicians Cincinnati Children's Hospital serves more than 1 million patients each year including about 100000 emergency room visits and 32000 surgical procedures. Its outpatient centers include community urgent and emergency care facilities and general and specialty physician practices as well as laboratory radiology dentistry and physical therapy clinics.

The Cincinnati Children's Research Foundation conducts research and clinical trials of pediatric medical innovations including new vaccines and surgical techniques. It has research partnerships with hospitals in Africa Asia Latin America and the Middle East. The hospital and research foundation's contributions to pediatric medicine include the rotavirus vaccine and Albert Sabin's discovery of the oral polio vaccine (first tested in 1960).

The hospital's educational programs are also renowned.

Geographic Reach
Reaching beyond Cincinnati Cincinnati Children's Hospital also provides services to communities in southeastern Indiana and northern Kentucky through its network of outpatient clinics. The hospital serves patients from all 50 US states as well as from about 60 international countries. It has international research collaborations with institutions in Bangladesh Brazil China Honduras Israel Malawi Mexico Nepal and the United Arab Emirates.

Financial Performance
In 2014 revenue grew 10% to $2.1 billion as the center saw rises in revenue from net patient services capitation professional services and other

operations. Net income rose 13% to $172 million due to the higher revenue.

Strategy
Cincinnati Children's Hospital regularly expands its facilities to improve medical services and enhance research and education programs. In 2015 it opened a new 15-story clinical research building at its main campus in Avondale. In 2014 it opened a new urgent care center at its Liberty Campus.

In addition the institution forms collaborations to expand its operations. In 2015 it signed a three-year partnership with Shire to research rare diseases. The partners will work to discover and develop novel therapies to treat these diseases.

The hospital has remained on the forefront of the digital revolution that has swept the health care industry. In recent years the organization has linked its emergency inpatient radiology pharmacy and specialty department patient data together to create an electronic medical record (EHR). The EHR system helps to reduce patient errors (such as medication errors) and improves communication between departments.

To prepare for health reform measures Cincinnati Children's Hospital is also reducing costs through workflow purchasing and care delivery improvement programs.

EXECUTIVES

Vice President and Chief Technology Officer, Tony Johnston
Vice President Marketing, Phyllis Goodman Goodman
President and CEO, Michael Fisher, age 58
EVP and COO, Scott J. Hamlin
SVP Information Services and CIO, Marianne F. James
CFO, Mark D. Mumford, age 55
Chief Medical Officer, Margaret Hostetter
Medical Director, Paul Edward Steele
Medical Director, Stavra Xanthakos
Director of Clinical Services, Anne Lesko
Assistant Vice President, Carolyn Karageorges
Clinical Director, Victoria Decastro
Clinical Director, Connie Scully
Clinical Director, Natalie Elsbrock
Assistant Vice President, Melissa Saladonis
Assistant Vice President Patient Service, Deborah Browning
Vice President and General Counsel, Elizabeth Stautberg
Assistant Vice President Patient Services, Barbara Tofani
Clinical Director, Anna Sheets
Pharmacy Manager, John Hingl
Assistant Vice President, Mark McDonald
Clinical Director, Wendy Ungard
Nursing Director, Cheryl Hoying
Assistant Vice President Ambulatory Services, Jackie Hausfeld
Clinical Director, Whittney Brady
Clinical Director Pediatric Intensive Care Unit, Jerry Schwartz
Associate Vice President (Aco) Medical Management, Amy Baldridge
Assistant Vice President Chief Patient Services Informatics Officer, Kristin Boggs
Clinical Director, Thomas Cahill
Assistant Vice President, Charlie Baverman
Assistant Vice President, Courtney Saxton
Associate Vice President Supply Chain, Cmrp Nirody
Vice President Finance, Alma Helping
Medical Director Pediatric Environmental Health and Lead Clinic, Nicholas Newman
Assistant Vice President Biodiagnostics, Sally May
Assistant Vice President, Janet Forbes
Clinical Director, Tonya Honeycutt
Clinical Director, Linda Richey

Assistant Vice President, Katherine Overbey
Assistant Vice President Executive Director, Abram Gordon
Clinical Toxicologist Business Specialist MT Pharmd Dabat, Jan Scaglione
Vice President Patient Services, Mary Sitterding
Assistant Vice President Planning, Kathy Vuturo
Clinical Director, Kandice Ferdon
Clinical Director, Alice Ostendorf
Clinical Director, Barbara Valerius
Assistant Vice President Business Intelligence, Mike Naber
Senior Vice President, Chris Browning
Chair, Thomas G. Cody, age 75
Board Member, Robert Frenck
Assistant Treasurer, Alex Miller

LOCATIONS

HQ: CHILDREN'S HOSPITAL MEDICAL CENTER
3333 BURNET AVE, CINCINNATI, OH 452293039
Phone: 513 636-4200
Web: WWW.CINCINNATICHILDRENS.ORG

PRODUCTS/OPERATIONS

Selected Locations
Anderson
Batesville
Burnet Campus
  Children's
College Hill Campus
Drake
Eastgate
Fairfield
Harrison
Hopple Street Center
Kenwood
Liberty Campus
Lindner Center of Hope (Mason)
Mason Campus
Northern Kentucky
Oak Campus

Selected Treatment Areas
Abdomen and Digestive Tract
Allergy Asthma Immunology
Anesthesia
Arthritis and Rheumatology
Babies / Infants
Bones Joints and Muscles
Brain Spinal Cord and Nerves
Cancer
Cerebral Palsy
Chest and Lungs
Craniofacial Anomalies
Dental and Oral Health
Developmental Disabilities
Ear Nose Throat
Endocrine Metabolism and Diabetes
Eyes
Genetics
Growth and Development
Heart
Hemangiomas and Vascular Malformations
Hematology and Blood
Infectious Diseases
Injuries and Poisonings
Kidney Bladder and Genitals
Liver
Medications
Mental Health
Nutrition and Diet
Pain Management
Rehabilitation
Safety and Injury Prevention
Skin
Speech
Sports Medicine
Surgery
Teen Health
X-Ray / Radiology

COMPETITORS

Bethesda North	Shriners Hospitals For
Children's Hospital of	Children
Philadelphia	St. Elizabeth
Deaconess Associations	Healthcare

Kettering Health Network	St. Jude Children's Research Hospital
Mercy Health (OH)	The Christ Hospital Corporation
Nationwide Children's Hospital	TriHealth
Nemours Foundation	UC Health
Premier Health Partners	

HISTORICAL FINANCIALS
Company Type: Private

Income Statement   FYE: June 30

	REVENUE ($ mil.)	NET INCOME ($ mil.)	NET PROFIT MARGIN	EMPLOYEES
06/15	1,527	209	13.7%	7,700
06/14	2,116	140	6.6%	—
06/11	1,693	53	3.2%	—
06/10	1,590	78	4.9%	—
Annual Growth	(0.8%)	21.8%	—	—

2015 Year-End Financials
Return on assets: 20.3%   Cash ($ mil.): 125
Return on equity: 13.7%
Current ratio: 1.20

CHILDREN'S HOSPITAL OF ORANGE COUNTY

EXECUTIVES

President, Kimberly Cripe
Finance Manager, Barbara Rauch
Auditors: KPMG LLP LOS ANGELES CA

LOCATIONS

HQ: CHILDREN'S HOSPITAL OF ORANGE COUNTY
1201 W LA VETA AVE, ORANGE, CA 928684203
Phone: 714 997-3000

HISTORICAL FINANCIALS
Company Type: Private

Income Statement   FYE: June 30

	REVENUE ($ mil.)	NET INCOME ($ mil.)	NET PROFIT MARGIN	EMPLOYEES
06/15	518	20	3.9%	3,200
06/14	517	(15)	—	—
06/13	548	29	5.3%	—
06/10	408	69	16.9%	—
Annual Growth	4.9%	(21.9%)	—	—

2015 Year-End Financials
Return on assets: 6.3%   Cash ($ mil.): 68
Return on equity: 3.9%
Current ratio: 2.20

CHILDREN'S HOSPITAL OF THE KINGS DAUGHTERS INC

EXECUTIVES

President, James D Dahling
Vice-President, David Bowers

LOCATIONS

HQ: CHILDREN'S HOSPITAL OF THE KINGS DAUGHTERS INC
601 CHILDRENS LN, NORFOLK, VA 235071910
Phone: 757 668-7000
Web: WWW.CHKD.COM

HISTORICAL FINANCIALS
Company Type: Private

Income Statement   FYE: June 30

	REVENUE ($ mil.)	NET INCOME ($ mil.)	NET PROFIT MARGIN	EMPLOYEES
06/15	332	49	14.8%	1,211
06/14	342	44	13.1%	—
06/13	337	50	15.0%	—
06/12	312	41	13.3%	—
Annual Growth	2.0%	5.9%	—	—

2015 Year-End Financials
Return on assets: 3.5%   Cash ($ mil.): 38
Return on equity: 14.8%
Current ratio: 2.80

CHILDREN'S MEDICAL CENTER OF DALLAS

Children's Medical Center of Dallas (operating as Children's Health) treats children with various medical needs from birth to age 18. Specialties include craniofacial deformities cystic fibrosis gastroenterology cancer and heart disease. Children's is also a major pediatric center for heart kidney bone marrow and other transplant procedures. The not-for-profit hospital has about 600 beds and is the pediatric teaching facility for UT Southwestern Medical. Children's also operates a network of about 20 primary care and specialty clinics in and around Dallas in addition to its two full-service campuses.

Operations

The Children's system serves patients through two full-service hospitals a specialty care center in Southlake and a network of primary care offices called MyChildren's located throughout the Metroplex. As the primary pediatric teaching facility for UT Southwestern Children's supports a three-year residency program for physicians and academic fellowships in numerous subspecialties.

Children's Health's Dallas campus operates the city's only pediatric emergency room and the region's only pediatric-centered teaching hospital. It was also the first Level I trauma center for pediatrics in the state. Together the Dallas and Plano hospital campuses serve some 800000 patients annually and provide more than 50 sub-specialty programs. Additionally the organization provides primary health care services to the county's chil-

dren living in under-served areas; some of these care services are provided through academic programs for doctors in training.

The system's research and development areas includes cancer cardiothoracic neonatology kidney disease infectious disease pharmacology sickle cell disease and psychiatry. It also provides Level IV Neonatal Intensive Care Unit.

In 2014 Children's logged some 173000 patient visits in its emergency departments in Dallas and Plano.

Geographic Reach

Children's main hospital campuses are in Dallas and Plano Texas. It has a handful of specialty centers and 16 primary care locations in the Dallas suburbs and area communities including Southlake.

Financial Performance

Children's receives revenues from a mix of third-party payers including HMOs and PPOs as well as Medicaid and Medicare and the state Children's Health Insurance Program (CHIP). It also relies heavily on private donations and fundraising efforts but provides a hefty amount of charity care each year for the region's uninsured children.

Strategy

Children's introduced its Children's Health brand in 2014. The new identity serves to reflect its operations as an integrated health system beyond the two primary campus locations.

At any given time it seems that Children's is building or opening one facility or another. In 2015 it opened the nation's second Pitt Hopkins Syndrome clinic treating a rare genetic condition that can cause development delays intellectual disabilities breathing issues and seizures.

Mergers and Acquisitions

In 2015 the system bought Our Children's House which provides rehabilitative and transitional care to children with special needs from Baylor Scott & White. Children's took over operations of Our Children's House's inpatient and outpatient facilities as well as eight outpatient clinics.

Company Background

In the four-year period between 2001 and 2005 the center spent more than $250 million on new construction and expansion projects. It opened a 72-bed Children's Legacy Hospital in nearby Plano in 2008 and in 2009 Children's completed construction of a new $150 million tower on its main Dallas campus to house its heart center cancer center and neonatal intensive care unit.

The company was founded in 1913.

EXECUTIVES

EVP and Chief Administrative Officer Corporate Services, Michele Chulick
Chief Clinical Officer and EVP, W. Robert (Bob) Morrow
EVP Population Health and Business Development, Peter W. Roberts
President Children's Medical Center Dallas Foundation and EVP Children's Health System Texas, Kern Wildenthal
President and CEO, Christopher J. Share
President and COO, Douglas G. Share
Vice President Governance and Compliance, Ronald Skillens
Senior Vice President Network Development, Trent Smith
Vice President Of Marketing, Judy Watkins
Clinic Supervisor, Melissa Harrison
Medical Librarian, Albi Calman
Pharmacy Manager, Bill Oden
Medical Director Anesthesiology LGY Campus, William Jones
Director of Radiology, Eric McDaniel
Policy Analyst Government Relations, Fred Guerra
Vice President External Relations, Holly Hassmann

Vice President of Finance, Jaquetta Clemons
Vice President Of Public Affairs, Elizabeth F Mackay
Vice President Managed Care, Jodi Landon
VP ADMIN, Beverly Rogers
Medical Director Pediatric Pain Management Service, Alan Farrow
Vice President and Chief Information Security Officer, William Long
Director of Radiology, Brian Fox
Executive Vice President And Chief Legal Officer, Lawrence Foust
Vice President Employer Solutions, Doug Sanders
Vice President Virtual Health and Innovation, Julie Hall-Barrow
Secretary, Sylvia Rock

LOCATIONS

HQ: CHILDREN'S MEDICAL CENTER OF DALLAS
1935 MEDICAL DISTRICT DR, DALLAS, TX
752357701
Phone: 214 456-7000

Children's Medical Center Selected Locations
Chase Bank Building Specialty Center (Dallas)
Children's Medical Center and Ambulatory Care Pavilion at Legacy (Plano)
Children's Medical Center of Dallas Main Campus
Dallas Ambulatory Care Pavilion
Irving Specialty Center
Mesquite Specialty Center
MyChildren's Primary Care (about 16 locations)
Pediatric Urology Clinic at Rockwall
Southlake Specialty Care Center
Walnut Hill Urology Clinic

PRODUCTS/OPERATIONS

Children's Medical Center Selected Services
Allergy/Immunology/Asthma
Audiology
Cystic fibrosis
Day surgery
Dentistry
Dermatology
Diabetes
Ear/Nose/Throat
Endocrinology
Gastroenterology
General surgery
Genetics/Metabolism
International adoption medicine
Laboratory services
Neurology
Nutrition
Obesity program
Occupational therapy
Ophthalmology
Orthodontics
Orthopaedics
Physical therapy
Plastic Surgery
Pulmonary function lab
Pulmonology
Radiology
Rheumatology
Sickle cell treatment
Sleep disorders
Speech therapy
Trauma
Urology

COMPETITORS

Baylor University Medical Center	HCA
Cook Children's Health Care System	Parkland Health & Hospital System
Dell Children's Medical Center	Tenet Healthcare
	Texas Children's Hospital

HISTORICAL FINANCIALS
Company Type: Private

Income Statement

	REVENUE ($ mil.)	NET INCOME ($ mil.)	NET PROFIT MARGIN	EMPLOYEES
12/15	712	(185)	—	5,318
12/14	1,120	135	12.1%	—
12/13	1,111	166	15.0%	—
12/08	744	(4)	—	—
Annual Growth	(0.6%)	—	—	—

FYE: December 31

2015 Year-End Financials
Return on assets: 4.9%   Cash ($ mil.): 9
Return on equity: (-26.0%)
Current ratio: 1.80

CHILDRENS HOSPITAL & MEDICAL CENTER

Junior Cornhuskers can have their medical needs met at Children's Hospital & Medical Center. The not-for-profit center Nebraska's only pediatric hospital (and a top US children's hospital) is a 150-bed facility offering pediatric inpatient services. The Omaha hospital has neonatal and pediatric intensive care units along with units dedicated surgery child development eating disorders and conditions including asthma allergies cardiac care diabetes nephrology and respiratory care. Children's serves as the teaching hospital for the University of Nebraska and Creighton University. It also operates urgent care and outreach clinics in the area.

Operations

Children's handles about 370000 patient visits each year including 8000 inpatient stays 8000 surgeries and 40000 emergency room and urgent care center visits. Children's main hospital building includes a level II pediatric trauma center a 20-bed pediatric intensive care unit (ICU) and a 45-bed newborn ICU. Its specialty centers also include a 30-bed day hospital (the Children's Ambulatory Recovery and Express Stay or CARES unit) and a fetal medicine center operated in partnership with Alegent Creighton Health.

The hospital's research programs include studies of translational medicine basic medicine and health outcomes conducted in partnership with the University of Nebraska's Medical Center and College of Medicine.

Geographic Reach

Children's is located in a nine-story 290000 sq. ft. facility. In addition to the main hospital in Omaha Children's operates urgent care centers in Omaha and a specialty clinic in Lincoln Nebraska. It also operates outreach clinics in communities including Columbus Grand Island Hastings Holdrege Kearney Norfolk and North Platte Nebraska; Sioux Falls and Rapid City South Dakota; and Sioux City Iowa.

About half of Children's patients come from outside the Omaha area including areas of South Dakota Iowa Kansas and Missouri. Its metabolic bone disease program offers treatment for brittle bones to children from around the country.

Financial Performance

The Children's Hospital enjoys a healthy market share in Omaha despite increasing competition from neighboring hospitals offering pediatric services. The organization reported some $249 million in net operating revenues in 2011 an increase of

5% from 2010 results. Net assets also increased by 3% to $279 million that year. However net income fell 65% to some $8 million.

Strategy

Children's Hospital has been expanding its facilities to provide a broader breadth of services to existing patients as well as to attract new patients. For instance in 2012 it launched a new fetal care center through a venture with Alegent Creighton Health. In 2010 it opened its Specialty Pediatric Center an outpatient facility providing diagnostic and treatment services for chronic conditions and diseases including childhood cancers diabetes rare diseases birth defects and congenital heart defects. The five-story building houses some 30 specialty clinics.

Company Background

The hospital was founded in 1948 as Children's Memorial Hospital by two local philanthropists Dr. C.W.M. Poynter and publisher Henry Doorly to establish a children's facility accessible to patients of all financial means. It relocated in 1981 (to a larger building) and 2000 (to a newly built nine-floor medical center). In 2009 Children's Hospital added "& Medical Center" to its name in hopes of more accurately reflecting its specialty offerings.

EXECUTIVES

President and CEO, Gary A. Perkins
EVP and COO, Kathy English
SVP and CFO, Mike Brown
VP Marketing and Community Relations, Martin W. Beerman
Executive Director Children's Hospital & Medical Center Foundation, Roger Lewis
VP CIO and CMIO, George Reynolds
Vice President Of Support Services, Scott Kaminski
Director of Surgery, Barbara Schwarz
Vice President Ambulatory Services, Justin Bradshaw
Nursing Director, Cindy Foster
Vice President Planning and Business Development, John Williams
Medical Director of Pathology, Deborah Perry
Vice President Network Development, Janis Yergan
Vice President of Strategy, Darla Qassem
Vice President of Human Resources, Pat Schulz
VICE PRESIDENT CONSTRUCTION AND REAL ESTATE, Timothy Jacoby
Treasurer, Cynthia Hinkel
Treasurer, Debra Gibbs

LOCATIONS

HQ: CHILDRENS HOSPITAL & MEDICAL CENTER
8200 DODGE ST, OMAHA, NE 681144113
Phone: 402 955-5400
Web: WWW.CHILDRENSOMAHA.ORG

PRODUCTS/OPERATIONS

List of Items
Access Center
Aerodigestive Clinic (GI Clinic)
Aerodigestive Clinic (Pulmonary Medicine)
Asthma Allergy Clinic
Audiology (Hearing)
Behavioral Health (Family Support)
CDC (Children's Developmental Clinic)
Child Life Services
Craniofacial Clinic
Cystic Fibrosis
Developmental Pediatric Clinic
Diabetes Clinic
Ear Nose Throat Clinic (ENT)
Eating Disorders Program
Emergency Department
Endocrine Clinic
Fetal Care Center
GI Clinic (Gastroenterology)
Hand-In-Hand/Palliative Care
Heart Center (Cardiology)
Helmet Clinic

Hematology and Oncology Clinic
Home Health Services
Hospitalist Service
Infectious Disease Clinic
Medical Surgical Floors
Metabolic Management Clinic
Newborn Intensive Care Unit (NICU)
Neurodiagnostic Services
Neurology Clinic
NICU Follow-Up Clinic
Orthopaedics Clinic
Pathology
Pediatric Intensive Care Unit (PICU)
Plastic Surgery
Pulmonary Medicine
Radiology
Rehab Services (Speech Occupational & Physical Therapies)
Renal Clinic
Rheumatology Clinic
Sleep Center
Social Work
Speech Therapy Clinic
Surgical Services
Transport (Critical Care Transport Team)
Urgent Care
Urology Clinic
Weight Management (HEROES)

COMPETITORS

BryanLGH Medical Center
CHI Health
Fremont Area Medical Center
Heartland Health
Mercy Health Network
Methodist Health System
Nebraska Medical Center
Saint Elizabeth Regional Medical Center
Shriners Hospitals For Children
Tenet Healthcare
UNMC Physicians
UnityPoint Health
University of Nebraska

HISTORICAL FINANCIALS

Company Type: Private

Income Statement

FYE: December 31

	REVENUE ($ mil.)	NET INCOME ($ mil.)	NET PROFIT MARGIN	EMPLOYEES
12/15	327	42	13.1%	1,400
12/14	297	64	21.6%	—
12/05	149	18	12.4%	—
12/04	137	22	16.2%	—
Annual Growth	**8.2%**	**6.1%**	—	—

2015 Year-End Financials

Return on assets: 6.1%
Return on equity: 13.1%
Current ratio: 1.50

Cash ($ mil.): 31

CHILDRENS HOSPITAL MEDICAL CENTER OF AKRON

Akron Children's Hospital is the largest pediatric health care system in northeast Ohio. The health system operates through more than 80 locations scattered around the state including its flagship 253-bed hospital in Akron. Among Children's specialized services are cardiology orthopedics rehabilitation and home care. It also has a second 50-bed inpatient hospital called the Akron Children's Beeghly Campus. The main hospital's emergency

department treats nearly 70000 patients each year. Its regional burn center sees about 3700 visits per year. Akron Children's Hospital started as a nursery more than 100 years ago.

Operations

Each year Akron Children's Hospital sees some 800000 outpatients performs more than 15000 surgeries and admits more than 10000 inpatients.

Geographic Reach

Akron Children's Hospital is a major teaching facility affiliated with Northeastern Ohio Medical University and offering nearly a dozen subspecialty fellowship training programs. Children's also runs one of the state's largest pediatric primary care networks with 15 offices in seven counties including Cuyahoga Medina Wayne Tuscawaras and Portage.

Sales and Marketing

In 2014 Medicaid payments accounted for 52% of gross patient service revenue while commercial payments accounted for 44%.

Financial Performance

The hospital's net revenue was about $701000 in fiscal 2014 with about 90% of that coming from patient services revenues.

Strategy

The system has expanded its campuses and opened new facilities to broaden its care offerings. In 2014 it opened its first location in Columbiana County opened a pediatric specialty care office in Mansfield and expanded its sports rehabilitation hours and services at LifeCenter Plus in Hudson.

EXECUTIVES

President and CEO, William H. (Bill) Considine
VP Medical Services; Clinical Leader Ohio Children's Hospitals Solutions for Patient Safety, Michael Bird
VP Managed Care, Karen Richter
VP Operations and COO, Grace Wakulchik
EVP, Shawn Lyden
VP Akron Children's Hospital Foundation, John Zoilo
Noah Miller Chair Department of Pediatrics, Norman C. Christopher
VP Akron Children's Mahoning Valley, Sharon Hrina
CFO, Michael Trainer
VP Patient Services and Chief Nursing Officer, Lisa Aurilio
CIO, Tom Ogg
VP Department of Pediatrics, Cindy Dormo
Chief Medical Information Officer, Amy Maneker
VP Surgical Subspecialty Practices, Craig McGhee
Chief Medical Officer, Robert McGregor
Director of Pharmacy, John Lepto
Vice President, Walt Schwoeble
Medical Director of the Locust Pediatric Care Group, Cooper White
Director of Government Relations, Charlie Solley
Vice President External Affairs, Bernett Williams
Vice President Administration, Sharin Hrina
Vice President of Public Policy and Government Affairs, Rhonda Perkins
Auditors: ERNST & YOUNG LLP CLEVELAND

LOCATIONS

HQ: CHILDRENS HOSPITAL MEDICAL CENTER OF AKRON
1 PERKINS SQ, AKRON, OH 443081063
Phone: 330 543-1000
Web: WWW.AKRONCHILDRENS.ORG

COMPETITORS

Akron General Medical Center
Aultman Health Foundation
Lake Health
Mercy Medical Center
OhioHealth
Parma Community General Hospital
Robinson Memorial Hospital
Summa Health System

(NY)
MetroHealth System
Nationwide Children's
Hospital

The Cleveland Clinic
University Hospitals
Health System

HISTORICAL FINANCIALS
Company Type: Private

Income Statement
FYE: December 31

	REVENUE ($ mil.)	NET INCOME ($ mil.)	NET PROFIT MARGIN	EMPLOYEES
12/15	747	47	6.3%	4,763
12/14	701	93	13.3%	—
12/13	623	80	13.0%	—
12/12	579	46	8.1%	—
Annual Growth	8.8%	0.3%	—	—

2015 Year-End Financials
Return on assets: 2.9%
Return on equity: 6.3%
Current ratio: 1.40
Cash ($ mil.): 52

CHILDRENS HOSPITAL PEDIATRIC ASSOCIATES, INC.

EXECUTIVES

Principal, William Tarvainen
Trustee, Mark Schuster
Auditors: BAKER NEWMAN & NOYES LC PORTL

LOCATIONS

HQ: CHILDRENS HOSPITAL PEDIATRIC ASSOCIATES, INC.
20 OVERLAND ST STE 2, BOSTON, MA 022153337
Phone: 617 919-2822
Web: WWW.CHILDRENSHOSPITAL.ORG

HISTORICAL FINANCIALS
Company Type: Private

Income Statement
FYE: September 30

	REVENUE ($ mil.)	NET INCOME ($ mil.)	NET PROFIT MARGIN	EMPLOYEES
09/15	246	11	4.7%	4
09/14	241	10	4.3%	—
09/13	228	25	11.4%	—
Annual Growth	3.9%	(33.0%)	—	—

2015 Year-End Financials
Return on assets: 3.8%
Return on equity: 4.7%
Current ratio: 4.90
Cash ($ mil.): 27

CHINA MANUFACTURERS ALLIANCE LLC

EXECUTIVES

Chief Executive Officer, Zhiming Yang
Sales Manager, Valentino Faraone
Manager, Les Garner
Vice-President, Walter Weller
Purchasing Agent, Mary Derparsekian
Manager, Perry Pearlman
Vice-President, Albert Zang
Financial Executive, Ben Tang
Auditors: HOFFMAN SHORT RUBIN DEWINTE

LOCATIONS

HQ: CHINA MANUFACTURERS ALLIANCE LLC
406 E HUNTINGTON DR # 200, MONROVIA, CA 910163638
Phone: 626 301-9575
Web: WWW.DOUBLECOINTIRES.COM

HISTORICAL FINANCIALS
Company Type: Private

Income Statement
FYE: December 31

	REVENUE ($ mil.)	NET INCOME ($ mil.)	NET PROFIT MARGIN	EMPLOYEES
12/15	246	0	0.4%	45
12/14	264	4	1.6%	—
12/13	226	2	1.2%	—
12/12	279	4	1.7%	—
Annual Growth	(4.2%)	(43.0%)	—	—

2015 Year-End Financials
Return on assets: 21.9%
Return on equity: 0.4%
Current ratio: 0.50
Cash ($ mil.): 1

CHINA TELECOM (AMERICAS) CORPORATION

EXECUTIVES

President, Zhuo Han
Accountant, Suli Chen
Director, Feng Sun
Manager, Binfeng Ni
Director, Hong Xie
Marketing Manager, Ryan Oklewicz
Marketing Manager, Wanting Zhou
Auditors: DELOITTE TOUCHE TOHMATSU CERTI

LOCATIONS

HQ: CHINA TELECOM (AMERICAS) CORPORATION
607 HERNDON PKWY STE 201, HERNDON, VA 201705481
Phone: 703 787-0088
Web: WWW.CTAMERICAS.COM

HISTORICAL FINANCIALS
Company Type: Private

Income Statement
FYE: December 31

	REVENUE ($ mil.)	NET INCOME ($ mil.)	NET PROFIT MARGIN	EMPLOYEES
12/15	254	9	3.7%	131
12/10	79	(2)	—	—
12/09	68	4	6.3%	—
Annual Growth	24.4%	14.0%	—	—

2015 Year-End Financials
Return on assets: 7.9%
Return on equity: 3.7%
Current ratio: 0.60
Cash ($ mil.): 96

CHOPTANK TRANSPORT, INC.

EXECUTIVES

President, Geoffrey A Turner
Director, Bill Dotson
Sales Manager, Crystal Tanner
Account Executive, Jason Nickle
General Manager, Brian Carr
Auditors: TGM GROUP LLC

LOCATIONS

HQ: CHOPTANK TRANSPORT, INC.
3601 CHOPTANK RD, PRESTON, MD 216551220
Phone: 410 673-2240
Web: WWW.CHOPTANKTRANSPORT.COM

HISTORICAL FINANCIALS
Company Type: Private

Income Statement
FYE: December 31

	REVENUE ($ mil.)	NET INCOME ($ mil.)	NET PROFIT MARGIN	EMPLOYEES
12/15	180	0	—	175
12/14	156	0	—	—
12/13	0	0	—	—
12/12	0	0	—	—
Annual Growth	—	—	—	—

2015 Year-End Financials
Return on assets: 6.7%
Return on equity: —
Current ratio: 1.50
Cash ($ mil.): 5

CHRIST HOSPITAL

EXECUTIVES

Executive Director, Herb Caillouet
Manager, Carmen Ramirez

LOCATIONS

HQ: CHRIST HOSPITAL
176 PALISADE AVE, JERSEY CITY, NJ 073061196
Phone: 201 795-8200
Web: WWW.CHRISTHOSPITAL.ORG

HISTORICAL FINANCIALS
Company Type: Private

Income Statement
FYE: December 31

	REVENUE ($ mil.)	NET INCOME ($ mil.)	NET PROFIT MARGIN	EMPLOYEES
12/15	202	1	0.8%	1
12/14	178	2	1.5%	—
Annual Growth	13.6%	(34.2%)	—	—

2015 Year-End Financials
Return on assets: 12.3% Cash ($ mil.): 3
Return on equity: 0.8%
Current ratio: 0.60

CHRISTIAN HOSPITAL NORTHEAST - NORTHWEST

Christian or heathen if you're in the St. Louis area and need medical care Christian Hospital wants to help. The not-for-profit hospital which has some 485 beds is part of BJC HealthCare. Established in 1903 it specializes in a range of treatment areas including diabetes and cancer care and cardiothoracic surgery. Its more than 430 physicians also offer services in 40 other specialties from primary care to pulmonology. Christian Hospital offers a comprehensive mental health and substance abuse program that includes an inpatient option as well as specialization in geriatric mental wellness. The hospital is headed by president Ron McMullen a long-time health care administrator.

Christian Hospital prides itself on being the first in the area to offer pioneering procedures. For example it was the first community hospital in the region to offer Video Assisted Thoracoscopic Surgery (VATS) lobectomy an advanced resectioning procedure to remove tumors in lung cancer patients.

Shortly before that Christian Hospital broke new ground by becoming the first community hospital in St. Louis to provide the Gliasite procedure. Gliasite is a brachytherapy (internal radiation therapy) procedure that treats patients with newly diagnosed metastatic or recurrent brain tumors.

EXECUTIVES

Blood Bank Director, Sandy Barnes

LOCATIONS

HQ: CHRISTIAN HOSPITAL NORTHEAST - NORTHWEST
11133 DUNN RD, SAINT LOUIS, MO 631366163
Phone: 314 355-2300
Web: WWW.LEADERPHARMACIES.COM

COMPETITORS

Ascension Health
Barnes-Jewish Hospital
HCA
Memorial Hospital (Illinois)
Mercy Health
Mercy Hospital St. Louis

RehabCare
SSM Health Care
St. Anthony's Medical Center
Tenet Healthcare

HISTORICAL FINANCIALS
Company Type: Private

Income Statement
FYE: December 31

	REVENUE ($ mil.)	NET INCOME ($ mil.)	NET PROFIT MARGIN	EMPLOYEES
12/15	249	(12)	—	2,493
12/14	239	(58)	—	—
12/08	213	(24)	—	—
12/00	207	(20)	—	—
Annual Growth	1.3%	—	—	—

2015 Year-End Financials
Return on assets: 1.6% Cash ($ mil.): —
Return on equity: (-5.0%)
Current ratio: 2.10

CHRISTUS HEALTH ARK-LA-TEX

EXECUTIVES

President, Chris Karam
Director, Jannice Phillips
Director, Javier Enriquez
Marketing Manager, Francine Francis

LOCATIONS

HQ: CHRISTUS HEALTH ARK-LA-TEX
2600 SAINT MICHAEL DR, TEXARKANA, TX 755035220
Phone: 903 614-1000
Web: WWW.CHRISTUSSTMICHAEL.ORG

HISTORICAL FINANCIALS
Company Type: Private

Income Statement
FYE: June 30

	REVENUE ($ mil.)	NET INCOME ($ mil.)	NET PROFIT MARGIN	EMPLOYEES
06/15	258	21	8.5%	1,800
06/14*	278	21	7.8%	—
05/14	243	20	8.3%	—
06/08	240	12	5.3%	—
Annual Growth	1.0%	8.0%	—	—
*Fiscal year change

2015 Year-End Financials
Return on assets: 7.2% Cash ($ mil.): 164
Return on equity: 8.5%
Current ratio: 6.40

CHRISTUS HEALTH CENTRAL LOUISIANA

CHRISTUS St. Frances Cabrini Hospital provides a wide range of medical services to the denizens of Alexandria Louisiana. If you're ailing down south there's not much the hospital can't do to help especially in the area of cancer. Founded in 1950 the 240-bed St. Frances Cabrini Hospital has a staff of more than 320 physicians providing services that include emergency care women's health surgery and cardiology. For the insomniacs among us the hospital provides specialized care through its sleep center. St. Francis Cabrini's parent company is one of the nation's major hospital operators — with about 50 facilities located around the country.

EXECUTIVES

Chief Executive Officer, Stephen Wright
Executive Secretary, Erin Kennedy
Financial Executive, Kimberly Patnaude
Manager, Karen Kelley
Manager, Stacey Rock
Manager, Thomas Rogers

LOCATIONS

HQ: CHRISTUS HEALTH CENTRAL LOUISIANA
3330 MASONIC DR, ALEXANDRIA, LA 713013841
Phone: 318 487-1122
Web: WWW.CABRINI.ORG

COMPETITORS

General Health System
Lafayette General Medical Center
Lane Regional Medical Center
Our Lady of Lourdes

Our Lady of the Lake
RMC
River Parishes Hospital
Woman's Hospital

HISTORICAL FINANCIALS
Company Type: Private

Income Statement
FYE: June 30

	REVENUE ($ mil.)	NET INCOME ($ mil.)	NET PROFIT MARGIN	EMPLOYEES
06/15	236	18	7.8%	2,000
06/13	222	5	2.3%	—
06/10	219	(0)	—	—
06/09	217	1	0.7%	—
Annual Growth	1.4%	50.5%	—	—

2015 Year-End Financials
Return on assets: 5.7% Cash ($ mil.): 133
Return on equity: 7.8%
Current ratio: 7.40

CHRISTUS HEALTH INTERNATIONAL

In CHRISTUS there is no east or west but plenty of care nonetheless. The not-for-profit Catholic health care system operates about 350 medical facilities from its more than 60 hospitals including general hospitals and long-term acute care facilities to clinics and outpatient centers. It operates mostly in Louisiana and Texas where its hospitals are but also has facilities in Arkansas Georgia Iowa Missouri and New Mexico and in six states in Mexico and one in Chile. In addition to its acute care facilities CHRISTUS runs medical groups home health and hospice agencies and senior living facilities. Specialized services include oncology pediatrics rehabilitation and women's and children's health care.

Operations

In addition to its more than 30 hospitals CHRISTUS also operates about 20 long-term care facilities 175 clinics and outpatient centers and dozens of other "health ministries" including mobile clinics fitness centers and daycare centers for adults and children.

Geographic Reach

CHRISTUS has a dozen hospitals in Texas and Louisiana one in Puebla Mexico and one in Santiago Chile. Its clinics outpatient centers long-term care facilities (under the Dubois and Advanced Care names) are found in Texas Louisiana Iowa Georgia Missouri and New Mexico in the US and in the Mexican states of Chihuahua Coahuila Nuevo Le n Puebla San Luis Potos and Tamaulipas.

Financial Performance

In 2013 CHRISTUS reported a 3% increase in revenue from $3.6 billion to $3.7 billion based on increased net patient and premium revenues. Net income was $261 million against net loss in 2012 due to an increase in investment returns.

Strategy

CHRISTUS has been expanding its Continuing Care division which includes non-acute care operations like home care hospice palliative care residential facilities and fitness centers.

Another goal of CHRISTUS Health is to reduce overcrowding and such misuses as patients being seen for routine illnesses in its emergency rooms. To that end and to make primary care a bit more accessible the company has opened immediate care clinics in a number of Texas Wal-Mart stores. CHRISTUS Health has plans to expand the clinics into Wal-Marts in Louisiana.

CHRISTUS Health has taken other steps to try to offset some costs of indigent care including pushing for the establishment of hospital districts to pay for charity care costs in some of its markets. It has also sold some of it facilities.

The organization has been focused on growing its operations in Mexico where it operates about a dozen clinics in six states. CHRISTUS Health's Mexico operations are a majority-owned partnership with Monterrey-based Muguerza. The organization's main Monterrey facility became the first Mexican hospital to win accreditation from the Joint Commission International a unit of the organization that certifies US hospitals.

Because Mexican citizens overwhelmingly rely on public hospitals run by the national health care system CHRISTUS Muguerza markets itself as a "medical tourism" destination where Americans can go for cheaper and lower-hassle medical care. Services include acute and primary care dental care urgent care and post-surgical rehabilitation.

Company Background

CHRISTUS Health was formed through the 1999 merger of Incarnate Word Health System and Sisters of Charity Health System. Both systems have their roots in the religious order Sisters of Charity of the Incarnate Word founded when three French nuns arrived in Texas in 1866 to care for the poor and sick.

EXECUTIVES

EVP and Chief Clinical Officer, John A. Gillean
President and CEO, Ernie W. Sadau
EVP and Chief Administrative Officer, Linda McClung
SVP and CIO, George S. Conklin
EVP and COO, Jeffrey M. (Jeff) Puckett
EVP and CFO, Randolph W. Safady
EVP and Chief Strategy and Health Network Officer, Paul Generale
EVP Corporate Services and Chief Human Resources Officer, Marty Margetts
President and CEO Good Shepherd Hospital Longview, Todd Hancock
Vice President general Counsel, Nancy Legros
Director Of Pharmacy, Dale Smith
Vice President Of Planning, Ron Dekeyzer
System Vice President, Sohail Rao
Chairman, Arthur M. Southam
Vice Chair, Maricela S. Moore
Auditors: ERNST & YOUNG LLP DALLAS TX

LOCATIONS

HQ: CHRISTUS HEALTH INTERNATIONAL
919 HIDDEN RDG, IRVING, TX 750383813
Phone: 469 282-2000
Web: WWW.CHRISTUSHEALTH.ORG

PRODUCTS/OPERATIONS

2015 Payor Mix

	% of total
Managed care organizations	47
Medicare	22
Self-pay	14
Medicaid	9
Commercial insurance	8
Total	**100**

2015 Revenues

	$ mil.	% of total
Patient services	3,233	90
Premium revenue	161	4
Other revenue	188	5
Equity in income of unconsolidated organizations	25	1
Total	**3,609**	**100**

Selected Facilities in Texas

CHRISTUS HomeCare - Corpus Christi
CHRISTUS HomeCare - Texarkana
CHRISTUS Hospital - St. Elizabeth
CHRISTUS Hospital - St. Mary
CHRISTUS Jasper Memorial Hospital
CHRISTUS Santa Rosa Alamo Heights Imaging Center
CHRISTUS Santa Rosa Ambulatory Surgery Center
CHRISTUS Santa Rosa Cancer Center
CHRISTUS Santa Rosa Children's Hospital
CHRISTUS Santa Rosa Hospital - City Centre
CHRISTUS Santa Rosa Hospital - Medical Center
CHRISTUS Santa Rosa Hospital - New Braunfels
CHRISTUS Santa Rosa Hospital - Westover Hills
CHRISTUS Santa Rosa Imaging Center
CHRISTUS Santa Rosa Outpatient Rehabilitation Center
CHRISTUS Santa Rosa Rehabilitation Hospital
CHRISTUS Santa Rosa Rehabilitation Services - Downtown
CHRISTUS Santa Rosa Rehabilitation Services - Medical Center
CHRISTUS Santa Rosa Wound Care and Hyperbaric Center - Downtown
CHRISTUS Santa Rosa Wound Care and Hyperbaric Center - Medical Center
CHRISTUS Spohn Family Center Northside
CHRISTUS Spohn Family Health Center
CHRISTUS Spohn Family Health Center Falfurrias
CHRISTUS Spohn Family Health Center Padre Island
CHRISTUS Spohn Family Health Center Robstown
CHRISTUS Spohn Family Health Center San Diego
CHRISTUS Spohn Family Health Center Westside
CHRISTUS Spohn Health System
CHRISTUS Spohn Hospital Alice
CHRISTUS Spohn Hospital Beeville
CHRISTUS Spohn Hospital Corpus Christi - Memorial
CHRISTUS Spohn Hospital Corpus Christi - Shoreline
CHRISTUS Spohn Hospital Corpus Christi - South
CHRISTUS Spohn Hospital Kleberg
CHRISTUS Spohn Medical Group - Obstetrics and Gynecology Associates
CHRISTUS St. Catherine Hospital
CHRISTUS St. John Hospital
CHRISTUS St. Michael Health System
CHRISTUS St. Michael Rehabilitation Hospital
CHRISTUS Transplant Institute
CHRISTUS Visiting Nurse Association - Houston
CHRISTUS Visiting Nurse Association - Nassau Bay
CHRISTUS Visiting Nurse Association - San Antonio
David Christopher Goldsbury Center for Children and Families
Dubuis Hospital of Beaumont
Dubuis Hospital of Bryan Texas
Dubuis Hospital of Corpus Christi
Dubuis Hospital of Houston Texas (long-term acute care)
Dubuis Hospital of Paris
Dubuis Hospital of Port Arthur Texas (long-term acute care)
Dubuis Hospital of Texarkana

Selected Other US Facilities

Advance Care Hospital of Fort Smith (Arkansas)

Advance Care Hospital of Hot Springs (Arkansas)
CHRISTUS Coushatta Health Care Center (Coushatta Louisiana)
CHRISTUS HomeCare - Jennings (Louisiana)
CHRISTUS HomeCare - Lake Charles (Louisiana)
CHRISTUS HomeCare - Shreveport (Louisiana)
CHRISTUS Hospice and Palliative Care - Alexandria (Louisiana)
CHRISTUS Schumpert Health System (Shreveport Louisiana)
CHRISTUS Schumpert Highland (Shreveport Louisiana)
CHRISTUS Schumpert St. Mary Place (Shreveport Louisiana)
CHRISTUS St. Frances Cabrini Hospital (Alexandria Louisiana)
CHRISTUS St. Patrick Hospital (Lake Charles Louisiana)
CHRISTUS St. Vincent (Santa Fe New Mexico)
Dubuis Hospital of Alexandria (Louisiana)
Dubuis Hospital of Lake Charles (Louisiana)
Dubuis Hospital of Shreveport (Louisiana)
Dubuis Hospital of St. Louis (Chesterfield Missouri)
Natchitoches Parish Hospital (Louisiana)
Southern Crescent Hospital for Specialty Care (Riverdale Georgia)

Selected Facilities in Mexico

CHRISTUS MUGUERZA Hospital Alta Especialidad (Monterrey Nuevo Leon)
CHRISTUS MUGUERZA Hospital Conchita (Monterrey Nuevo Leon)
CHRISTUS MUGUERZA Hospital Del Parque (Chihuahua)
CHRISTUS MUGUERZA Hospital Reynosa (Tamaulipas+; C.P.)
CHRISTUS MUGUERZA Hospital Saltillo (Coahuila)
CHRISTUS MUGUERZA Hospital Sur (Monterrey Nuevo Leon)
CHRISTUS MUGUERZA Hospital UPAEP (Puebla)

COMPETITORS

Ascension Health	Mercy Health
Catholic Health Initiatives	Methodist Hospital System
Community Health Systems	St. Luke's Episcopal Hospital
HCA	Tenet Healthcare
Intermountain Health Care	Texas Children's Hospital
LifePoint Health	Universal Health Services
MD Anderson Cancer Center	University of Utah Hospitals & Clinics
Memorial Health Services	
Memorial Hermann Healthcare	

HISTORICAL FINANCIALS

Company Type: Private

Income Statement

FYE: June 30

	REVENUE ($ mil.)	NET INCOME ($ mil.)	NET PROFIT MARGIN	EMPLOYEES
06/16	4,212	149	3.6%	25,000
06/15	658	(44)	—	—
06/14	673	25	3.8%	—
06/13	646	124	19.3%	—
Annual Growth	**86.7%**	**6.3%**	**—**	**—**

2016 Year-End Financials

Return on assets: 11.0%   Cash ($ mil.): 483
Return on equity: 3.6%
Current ratio: 1.20

CHRISTUS HEALTH NORTHERN LOUISIANA

EXECUTIVES

President, Stephen F Wright
Board of Directors, Kim Kelsch
Financial Executive, Lauri Walton
Auditors: ERNST & YOUNG US LLP HOUSTON

LOCATIONS

HQ: CHRISTUS HEALTH NORTHERN LOUISIANA
1 SAINT MARY PL, SHREVEPORT, LA 711014343
Phone: 318 681-4500
Web: WWW.CHRISTUSHEALTHSB.ORG

HISTORICAL FINANCIALS

Company Type: Private

Income Statement

FYE: June 30

	REVENUE ($ mil.)	NET INCOME ($ mil.)	NET PROFIT MARGIN	EMPLOYEES
06/15	195	27	14.1%	1,900
06/14	185	1	1.0%	—
06/11	234	(15)	—	—
06/10	265	(5)	—	—
Annual Growth	(6.0%)	—	—	—

2015 Year-End Financials

Return on assets: 5.8%
Return on equity: 14.1%
Current ratio: 2.80
Cash ($ mil.): 11

CHRISTUS SANTA ROSA HEALTH CARE CORPORATION

EXECUTIVES

President, Don Beeler
Manager, Yolanda Garza
Manager, Helen Gutierrez
VP Finance, Bill Pack
Auditors: ERNST & YOUNG US LLP INDIANAP

LOCATIONS

HQ: CHRISTUS SANTA ROSA HEALTH CARE
CORPORATION
333 N SANTA ROSA ST, SAN ANTONIO, TX 782073108
Phone: 210 704-2011
Web: WWW.CHOFSA.ORG

HISTORICAL FINANCIALS

Company Type: Private

Income Statement

FYE: June 30

	REVENUE ($ mil.)	NET INCOME ($ mil.)	NET PROFIT MARGIN	EMPLOYEES
06/15	656	(14)	—	3,700
06/14	635	6	1.1%	—
06/13	612	2	0.4%	—
06/10	577	(19)	—	—
Annual Growth	2.6%	—	—	—

2015 Year-End Financials

Return on assets: 8.5%
Return on equity: (-2.2%)
Current ratio: 1.90
Cash ($ mil.): 2

CHUGACH ALASKA CORPORATION

At the heart of Chugach Alaska Corporation is a vision of indigenous people running their own businesses on their own land. Chugach Alaska was formed following the activation of the Alaska Native Claims Settlement Act (which was passed by the US Congress in 1971) to provide land management services for the 928000-acre Chugach region of Alaska. The company derives the bulk of its sales from oil and gas production mining commercial timber and tourist activities that occur in the region and from its engagement in military base construction projects at more than 30 locations in Alaska the US Pacific Northwest and the Western Pacific. Chugach Alaska's shareholders consist of Aleut Eskimo and Indian natives.

Operations

In 2011 the company's Chugach World Services unit secured a $32 million contract (with the option for an additional $33 million) for housing and maintenance operations at Naval Base Guam and Andersen Air Force Base Guam.

In late 2010 the Chugach Alaska Services unit won a renewal of its existing oil spill prevention and response contract with Alyeska Pipeline Service Company. The new contract to service the Alaska Pipeline runs from 2011 to 2016.

Geographic Reach

With operations in Alaska the Pacific Northwest and the Western Pacific the company has major offices in Alabama Alaska Hawaii and Nevada.

Financial Performance

To raise cash in 2013 Chugach Alaska sold its three-story former headquarters building in downtown Anchorage.

Strategy

Developing and sustaining multiple revenues streams has been a key to the company's growth. Chugach Alaska is looking to continue to grow its Alaskan gas natural gas projects while diversifying into markets that are not traditional for the company such as the niche market of environmentally responsible guided tourism.

Expanding its global engineering footprint in 2012 the company acquired bankrupt Hawaii-based engineering firm Heide & Cook LLC.

Company Background

Chugach Alaska was founded in 1972 as an Alaska Native Claims Settlement Act Corporation. A nine-person board of directors elected from the corporation's more than 2300 shareholders oversees Chugach Alaska's management and operations. The company has gone from filing bankruptcy protection in 1990 (in the wake of the Exxon Valdez oil spill and a major cannery fire) to generating about $1 billion in annual revenues.

EXECUTIVES

Corporate Treasurer, Violet Yeaton

LOCATIONS

HQ: CHUGACH ALASKA CORPORATION
3800 CNTRPINT DR STE 1200, ANCHORAGE, AK 99503
Phone: 907 563-8866

PRODUCTS/OPERATIONS

Selected Services
Base Operating Services
Construction Services
Educational Services
Engineering Services
IT/Telecommunications
Manufacturing Services
Oil and Gas Services

Selected Subsidiaries
Chugach Alaska Services Inc. (CASI)
Chugach Education Services Inc. (CESI)
Chugach Federal Solutions Inc. (CFSI)
Chugach Government Services Inc. (CGSI)
Chugach Industries Inc. (CII)
Chugach Information Technology Inc. (CITI)
Chugach Management Services Inc. (CMSI)
Chugach McKinley Inc. (CMI)
Chugach Support Services Inc. (CSSI)
Chugach Systems Integration Llc (CSI)
Chugach World Services Inc. (CWSI)
Heide & Cook LLC. (H&C)
Wolf Creek Federal Services Inc. (WCFS)

COMPETITORS

ConocoPhillips Alaska	Freegold Ventures
Doyon	Jacobs Engineering
Fluor	Sealaska

HISTORICAL FINANCIALS

Company Type: Private

Income Statement

FYE: December 31

	REVENUE ($ mil.)	NET INCOME ($ mil.)	NET PROFIT MARGIN	EMPLOYEES
12/15	758	22	3.0%	4,822
12/14	7	(12)	—	—
12/13	608	19	3.2%	—
12/12	708	20	2.9%	—
Annual Growth	2.3%	3.8%	—	—

2015 Year-End Financials

Return on assets: 4.8%
Return on equity: 3.0%
Current ratio: 2.00
Cash ($ mil.): 44

CHUGACH FEDERAL SOLUTIONS, INC.

EXECUTIVES

Chief Executive Officer, Gabriel Kompkoff
Executive Secretary, Rebecca Myren

LOCATIONS

HQ: CHUGACH FEDERAL SOLUTIONS, INC.
3800 CNTRPINT DR STE 1200, ANCHORAGE, AK 99503
Phone: 907 563-8866

HISTORICAL FINANCIALS

Company Type: Private

Income Statement

FYE: December 31

	REVENUE ($ mil.)	NET INCOME ($ mil.)	NET PROFIT MARGIN	EMPLOYEES
12/15	220	(0)	—	1,153
12/14	240	11	4.9%	—
12/13	196	9	4.8%	—
12/12	105	5	5.7%	—
Annual Growth	27.7%	—	—	—

CHUGACH GOVERNMENT SOLUTIONS, LLC

EXECUTIVES

Manager, Lisa Currie

LOCATIONS

HQ: CHUGACH GOVERNMENT SOLUTIONS, LLC
3800 CNTRPINT DR STE 1200, ANCHORAGE, AK
99503
Phone: 907 563-8866
Web: WWW.CHUGACH.COM

HISTORICAL FINANCIALS

Company Type: Private

Income Statement

	ASSETS ($ mil.)	NET INCOME ($ mil.)	INCOME AS % OF ASSETS	EMPLOYEES
12/15	4,720	42	0.9%	4,300
12/14	4,136	28	0.7%	
Annual Growth	14.1%	48.8%	—	—

FYE: December 31

CINCINNATI PUBLIC SCHOOLS

EXECUTIVES

Superintendent, Laura Mitchell
Board of Directors, Denae Coco
Accountant, Karen M Cost
Administrative Assistant, Jerri Clements
Director, Elizabeth A Holtzapple
Assistant Manager, Anthony Smith
Auditors: CAUDILL & ASSOCIATES CPA POR

LOCATIONS

HQ: CINCINNATI PUBLIC SCHOOLS
2651 BURNET AVE, CINCINNATI, OH 452192551
Phone: 513 363-0000
Web: WWW.CPS-K12.ORG

HISTORICAL FINANCIALS

Company Type: Private

Income Statement

	REVENUE ($ mil.)	NET INCOME ($ mil.)	NET PROFIT MARGIN	EMPLOYEES
06/16	650	13	2.1%	7,070
06/15	654	(0)	—	—
06/05	402	0	—	—
06/04	0	0	—	—
Annual Growth	—	—	—	—

FYE: June 30

CITATION OIL & GAS CORP.

Citation Oil & Gas is writing its own ticket to prosperity in the petroleum industry. The oil and gas development and production company has interests in about 15000 wells (in more than 480 separately designated fields) and reported 210 million barrels of proved oil equivalent reserves (91% oil) in 2012. Its oil fields are in the Mid-Continent Illinois Basin Permian Basin and Rocky Mountain regions. Citation seeks out properties with high levels of crude oil declining production with long reserve life and low risk. The company uses a variety of techniques to recover oil and gas including waterflood and infill drilling. Subsidiary Citation Crude Marketing sells the company's products to refiners.

Geographic Reach

Citation explores for oil and gas in more than 480 fields in 13 states in the central third of the US with major holdings in the Illinois Basin Mid-Continent Permian Basin and Rocky Mountain regions. It has offices in Midland Texas; Gillette Wyoming; and Oklahoma City.

Operations

Citation operates in 13 states and manages its field operations on a decentralized basis through four of its regional operating areas including Central region Rocky mountain region Southern Oklahoma region and West Texas region. The Central region based operation has about 3900 active wells with a capacity of producing 7330 barrels of oil per day of oil and 2.9 million cu. ft. per day of gas. The Central Region team is focused on developing assets in the Illinois Basin specifically the properties it acquired in the Noble acquisition along with continuing exploitation of its legacy Salem Unit

In its Rocky mountain region Citation has drilled 18 horizontal wells in Bowes since 2007 and has three additional wells planned for 2013-14. This region has a net capacity of producing 5135 barrels of oil per day and 10.9 million cu. ft. per day of gas. In Southern Oklahoma region in its Wildcat Jim field Citation drilled 20 infill wells in 2012 and planned for 10 more in 2013. Citation is also actively drilling Hunton/Viola wells in Carter and Stephens County Oklahoma in the Shoveltum Hunton trend with 13 planned for 2013. This region's capacity is 11840 barrels of oil per day of oil and 12.6 million cu. ft. per day of gas; and operates about 6500 active wells. In West Texas region the company intends to expand its production base in West Texas and New Mexico making it one of the more mature of all of Citation's regions. Its net capacity is 4510 barrels of oil per day of oil and 5.9 million cu. ft. per day of gas.

Sales and Marketing

In addition to its upstream activities Citation is also engaged in crude oil marketing activities through its Citation Crude Marketing unit.

Strategy

Citation has pursued a focused business strategy of acquiring and operating mature onshore oil (and some gas) properties in the US. It has invested $1.7 billion in more than 80 oil and gas reserve acquisitions since 1985. As a result of these acquisitions and subsequent property development Citation has a net production of 28800 barrels of oil and 32 million cubic feet of gas per day. Going forward Citation continues to pursue growth strategy which is focused on two fronts; the acquisition of long-lived domestic onshore oil production; and the exploitation and enhancement of its producing properties through the application of primary sec-

ondary and tertiary recovery techniques. Advances in drilling and completion technologies along with improved commodity prices have contributed to an increase in Citation's infill drilling activity and waterflood expansion opportunities. Infill drilling projects (including vertical and horizontal wells) aim to increase production volumes and recoverable reserves through down spacing or pattern optimization.

In the Rockies Citation is focusing on horizontal drilling in several fields. In Southern Oklahoma it is developing properties it acquired from Noble Energy and is also drilling deeper wells in the Shoveltum Hunton trend. West Texas activities are focused on developing the North Robertson and Jordan fields.

Mergers and Acquisitions

In 2012 Citation acquired 100 additional leases and units in Kansas from Noble Energy near Citation's existing Fairport and Bemis-Schutts fields for $140 million. This acquisition significantly expanded Citation's operations in Kansas boosting its production in that state by almost 300%.

Company Background

The company was formed in 1981 by Forrest E. Harrell Sr.

EXECUTIVES

Chairman of the Board, Forrest E Harrell
Engineer, Tammie Celli

LOCATIONS

HQ: CITATION OIL & GAS CORP.
14077 CUTTEN RD, HOUSTON, TX 770692212
Phone: 281 891-1000
Web: WWW.COGC.COM

COMPETITORS

Adams Resources	EOG
Anadarko Petroleum	Exxon Mobil
Apache	Hunt Consolidated
BP	Jones Energy
Cabot Oil & Gas	Key Energy
Chesapeake Energy	National Fuel Gas
Chevron	Noble Energy
Cimarex	Pioneer Natural
ConocoPhillips	Resources
Devon Energy	Royal Dutch Shell

HISTORICAL FINANCIALS

Company Type: Private

Income Statement

	REVENUE ($ mil.)	NET INCOME ($ mil.)	NET PROFIT MARGIN	EMPLOYEES
12/15	273	(227)	—	507
12/14	482	248	51.5%	—
12/13	462	248	53.6%	—
12/12	424	224	53.0%	—
Annual Growth	(13.6%)	—	—	—

FYE: December 31

2015 Year-End Financials

Return on assets: 31.1%   Cash ($ mil.): 13
Return on equity: (-83.2%)
Current ratio: 0.60

CITY OF ALEXANDRIA

Historically a wartime victim of occupying forces modern Alexandria is home to many Defense Department contractors and employees. It uses a council-manager form of government wherein the mayor is part of the six-member city council (all elected at large) which determines city policy. The

city manager works to carry out the policy and run the day-to-day operations of Alexandria. In addition to the city manager the council also appoints the city attorney city clerk and members of various commissions and boards. Alexandria's more than 30 departments operate on an annual budget of about $400 million and serve about 130000 citizens. The city was founded in 1749.

EXECUTIVES

Mayor, Allison Silberberg
Clerk, Jacqueline Henderson
Director, Ferra Brain
Manager, Dave Clark
Manager, Cassandra McFarlane
Auditors: CLIFTONLARSONALLEN LLP ARLING

LOCATIONS

HQ: CITY OF ALEXANDRIA
301 KING ST, ALEXANDRIA, VA 223143211
Phone: 703 746-4000
Web: WWW.ALEXANDRIACITYWEBSITE.COM

HISTORICAL FINANCIALS
Company Type: Private

Income Statement

	REVENUE ($ mil.)	NET INCOME ($ mil.)	NET PROFIT MARGIN	EMPLOYEES
06/16	751	15	2.0%	2,375
06/15	730	3	0.5%	—
06/14	0	0	—	—
06/13	701	69	9.9%	—
Annual Growth	2.3%	(39.7%)	—	—

FYE: June 30

2016 Year-End Financials
Return on assets: 3.1%   Cash ($ mil.): 297
Return on equity: 2.0%
Current ratio: —

CITY OF BOSTON

Boston's legacy includes a famous Tea Party Paul Revere's Ride and clam chowder. With about 625000 residents Boston has been called the economic and cultural hub of New England. The Greater Boston metro area is home to about 4.6 million people making it the 10th largest city in the US. Boston also boasts world class educational institutions (Harvard Massachusetts Institute of Technology) champion sports teams (Red Sox Celtics Patriots) and a rich cultural and historical identity. Boston is also the capital of Massachusetts.

EXECUTIVES

Mayor, Martin J Walsh
Project Manager, Nick Haney
Personnel Director, Paul Parisi
Executive Director, Theresa Lynn
Auditors: KPMG LLP

LOCATIONS

HQ: CITY OF BOSTON
1 CITY HALL STE 242, BOSTON, MA 022011020
Phone: 617 635-4545
Web: WWW.AFTMA.NET

HISTORICAL FINANCIALS
Company Type: Private

Income Statement

	REVENUE ($ mil.)	NET INCOME ($ mil.)	NET PROFIT MARGIN	EMPLOYEES
06/15*	3,278	79	2.4%	18,760
12/13	11	1	9.4%	—
06/13	2,963	85	2.9%	—
Annual Growth	5.2%	(3.7%)	—	—

FYE: June 30
*Fiscal year change

CITY OF HOPE MEDICAL FOUNDATION

EXECUTIVES

Principal, Robert W Stone
Auditors: ERNST & YOUNG US LLP IRVINE

LOCATIONS

HQ: CITY OF HOPE MEDICAL FOUNDATION
1500 DUARTE RD, DUARTE, CA 910103012
Phone: 626 256-4673
Web: WWW.CITYOFHOPE.COM

HISTORICAL FINANCIALS
Company Type: Private

Income Statement

	REVENUE ($ mil.)	NET INCOME ($ mil.)	NET PROFIT MARGIN	EMPLOYEES
09/15	228	(11)	—	1
09/14	142	(1)	—	—
09/13	128	(1)	—	—
Annual Growth	33.4%	—	—	—

FYE: September 30

2015 Year-End Financials
Return on assets: 11.4%   Cash ($ mil.): 5
Return on equity: (-4.9%)
Current ratio: 1.20

CITY OF LONG BEACH

It's a city it's a port it's Long Beach. The City of Long Beach boasts the Port of Long Beach one of the busiest ports in the nation. With a population of more than 460000 Long Beach is part of the greater Los Angeles metropolitan area. The city uses a charter form of government with an elected mayor and city council as well as an appointed city manager. It's also known for its large oil reserves managed by the Long Beach Gas & Oil Department.

EXECUTIVES

Mayor, Robert Garcia
Financial Executive, Loriann Farrell
Director, Dennis J Thys
Auditor, Laura L Doud
Managing Director, Lori Ann Farrell
Manager, Reginald Harrison
Manager, Suzanne M Frick

LOCATIONS

HQ: CITY OF LONG BEACH
333 W OCEAN BLVD, LONG BEACH, CA 908024664
Phone: 562 570-6450
Web: WWW.CITYAUDITORLAURADOUD.COM

HISTORICAL FINANCIALS
Company Type: Private

Income Statement

	REVENUE ($ mil.)	NET INCOME ($ mil.)	NET PROFIT MARGIN	EMPLOYEES
09/15	648	(119)	—	5,028
09/14	676	1	0.2%	—
09/13	712	58	8.1%	—
09/07	0	0	—	—
Annual Growth	—	—	—	—

FYE: September 30

2015 Year-End Financials
Return on assets: 21.6%   Cash ($ mil.): 439
Return on equity: (-18.4%)
Current ratio: 1.10

CITY OF MESA

This city which literally covers a "mesa" or plateau stands roughly 100 feet higher than Phoenix and spreads across 130 square miles. With a population of more than 468000 the City of Mesa is the third-largest city in Arizona behind Phoenix and Tucson. Its city government consists of the mayor six city council members (elected to four-year terms) and a city manager. Mesa is also home to the Chicago Cubs baseball team during spring training. The city was founded in 1878 by Mormon (Latter-day Saint or LDS) pioneers who gave it its name; Mesa still has a large Mormon population. It was incorporated in 1883.

EXECUTIVES

Police Sergeant Vice President Mesa Assoc, Kurt Scanio
Auditors: CLIFTONLARSONALLEN LLP PHOEN

LOCATIONS

HQ: CITY OF MESA
20 E MAIN ST, MESA, AZ 852017425
Phone: 480 644-2011
Web: WWW.MESAAZ.GOV

HISTORICAL FINANCIALS
Company Type: Private

Income Statement

	REVENUE ($ mil.)	NET INCOME ($ mil.)	NET PROFIT MARGIN	EMPLOYEES
06/16	460	(61)	—	4,068
06/15	446	(8)	—	—
06/14	418	(30)	—	—
06/13	404	9	2.4%	—
Annual Growth	4.4%	—	—	—

FYE: June 30

CITY OF MOBILE

EXECUTIVES

Mayor, Sandy Stimpson
Executive Director, Barbara Malkove
Director, Dianne Irby
Director, George Talbot
Auditors: SMITH DUKES & BUCKALEW LLP M

LOCATIONS

HQ: CITY OF MOBILE
205 GOVERNMENT ST, MOBILE, AL 366020001
Phone: 251 208-7416
Web: WWW.CITYOFMOBILE.ORG

HISTORICAL FINANCIALS
Company Type: Private

Income Statement
FYE: September 30

	REVENUE ($ mil.)	NET INCOME ($ mil.)	NET PROFIT MARGIN	EMPLOYEES
09/15	294	22	7.6%	2,300
09/09	239	(44)	—	—
09/07	0	0	—	—
09/06	0	0	—	—
Annual Growth	—	—	—	—

2015 Year-End Financials
Return on assets: 7.4% Cash ($ mil.): 125
Return on equity: 7.6%
Current ratio: —

CITY OF SANTA MONICA

EXECUTIVES

Mayor, Ed Winterer
Principal, Rod Gould
Director of Finance, Gigi Decavalles
Manager, Nan Friedman
Director, Andy Agle
Personnel Director, Donna Peter
Purchasing Agent, Sergio Ramirez
Manager, Barbara Collins
Auditors: MACIAS GINI & O'CONNELL LLP L

LOCATIONS

HQ: CITY OF SANTA MONICA
1685 MAIN ST, SANTA MONICA, CA 904013248
Phone: 310 458-8281
Web: WWW.SANTA-MONICA.ORG

HISTORICAL FINANCIALS
Company Type: Private

Income Statement
FYE: June 30

	REVENUE ($ mil.)	NET INCOME ($ mil.)	NET PROFIT MARGIN	EMPLOYEES
06/15	419	11	2.6%	2,100
06/08	394	(47)	—	—
06/07	243	2	1.1%	—
Annual Growth	7.0%	19.3%	—	—

CITY OF STAMFORD

EXECUTIVES

Director, Tim Curtain
Director, Ben Barnes
Assistant Manager, Linda Bruno
Engineer, Judith Singer
Manager, Marie Underwood
Auditors: BLUM SHAPIRO & COMPANY PC

LOCATIONS

HQ: CITY OF STAMFORD
888 WASHINGTON BLVD, STAMFORD, CT 069012902
Phone: 203 977-4150
Web: WWW.CI.STAMFORD.CT.US

HISTORICAL FINANCIALS
Company Type: Private

Income Statement
FYE: June 30

	REVENUE ($ mil.)	NET INCOME ($ mil.)	NET PROFIT MARGIN	EMPLOYEES
06/15	627	19	3.0%	2,878
06/14	628	(14)	—	—
06/13	578	17	3.1%	—
06/12	579	42	7.4%	—
Annual Growth	2.7%	(23.5%)	—	—

2015 Year-End Financials
Return on assets: 3.6% Cash ($ mil.): 84
Return on equity: 3.0%
Current ratio: —

CLARK COUNTY SCHOOL DISTRICT

EXECUTIVES

Superintendent, Patrick Skorkowsky
Finance Manager, Jeff Weiler
Auditors: EIDE BAILLY LLP LAS VEGAS NE

LOCATIONS

HQ: CLARK COUNTY SCHOOL DISTRICT
5100 W SAHARA AVE, LAS VEGAS, NV 891463406
Phone: 702 799-5000
Web: WWW.CCSD.NET

HISTORICAL FINANCIALS
Company Type: Private

Income Statement
FYE: June 30

	REVENUE ($ mil.)	NET INCOME ($ mil.)	NET PROFIT MARGIN	EMPLOYEES
06/16	3,048	328	10.8%	37,361
06/15	2,971	(52)	—	—
06/14	2,398	77	3.2%	—
Annual Growth	12.7%	106.1%	—	—

CLARKE POWER SERVICES, INC.

EXECUTIVES

Chief Executive Officer, Mark Andreae
Credit Manager, Beth Willard
Manager, Gerald Kaiser
Manager, Brett Burdno
Auditors: ERNST & YOUNG LLP CINCINNATI

LOCATIONS

HQ: CLARKE POWER SERVICES, INC.
3133 E KEMPER RD, CINCINNATI, OH 452411516
Phone: 513 771-2200
Web: WWW.CLARKEPOWERSERVICES.COM

HISTORICAL FINANCIALS
Company Type: Private

Income Statement
FYE: December 31

	REVENUE ($ mil.)	NET INCOME ($ mil.)	NET PROFIT MARGIN	EMPLOYEES
12/15	277	5	2.1%	600
12/14	267	7	2.9%	—
12/13	228	3	1.5%	—
12/12	216	2	1.1%	—
Annual Growth	8.6%	32.5%	—	—

2015 Year-End Financials
Return on assets: 8.3% Cash ($ mil.): 2
Return on equity: 2.1%
Current ratio: 0.50

CLASSIC STAR GROUP, LP

EXECUTIVES

General Partner, Michael Ali
Partner, Gulamali Barwani
Partner, Muradali Barwani
Financial Executive, Chethan Shah
Credit Manager, Barbara Rhodes
Auditors: MWH GROUP PC WICHITA FALLS

LOCATIONS

HQ: CLASSIC STAR GROUP, LP
6324 EDEN DR, HALTOM CITY, TX 761176129
Phone: 817 834-2868
Web: WWW.CLASSICSTARGROUP.COM

HISTORICAL FINANCIALS
Company Type: Private

Income Statement
FYE: December 31

	REVENUE ($ mil.)	NET INCOME ($ mil.)	NET PROFIT MARGIN	EMPLOYEES
12/15	404	3	0.8%	17
12/14	591	2	0.5%	—
12/13	639	3	0.5%	—
12/12	555	2	0.4%	—
Annual Growth	(10.0%)	18.2%	—	—

2015 Year-End Financials
Return on assets: 1.9% Cash ($ mil.): 1
Return on equity: 0.8%
Current ratio: 1.00

CLAY ELECTRIC COOPERATIVE, INC.

Clay Electric Cooperative covers a lot of ground in Florida. The utility distributes electricity to 14 counties in the northeastern part of the state including the suburbs of Jacksonville and Gainesville. It delivers power to about 170000 residential commercial and industrial members over more than 13000 miles of distribution and transmission lines. The consumer-owned utility offers electronic funds transfer average billing and a seniors' payment plan to residential customers and backup diesel power generation and special rate plans to businesses. The consumer-owned utility has a stake in Seminole Electric Cooperative which provides generation services to Clay Electric and nine other cooperatives.

Geographic Reach

The cooperative serves customers in the Florida counties of Alachua Baker Bradford Clay Columbia Flagler Gilchrist Lake Levy Marion Putnam Suwannee Union and Volusia. It has six district offices (Gainesville Keystone Heights Lake City Orange Park Palatka and Salt Springs).

Strategy

To encourage conservation and green energy use the coop also supports customers' installation of small photovoltaic solar displays on their own homes through an arrangement whereby Seminole Electric purchases electricity generated and delivered to Clay Electric from any of its members' qualifying solar power systems.

Like other non-profit cooperatives Clay Electric refunds any annual profits to its members as credit refunds. In 2012 the company made $5.25 million in refunds available to its members or about $19 a customer.

That year Clay Electric announced that it would further cut its members' bills due to weak natural gas prices lowering the costs of power production from its gas-fired plants.

Company Background

The company was founded in 1937 as part of a national rural electrification drive.

EXECUTIVES

Chief Executive Officer, Richard K Davis
District Manager, Dale Furlong
Engineer, Jessie Myers
Purchasing Agent, Scott Griffis
Project Manager, Tammy Edinger
Purchasing Agent, Tim Lewis
Auditors: JACKSON THORNTON & CO PC MO

LOCATIONS

HQ: CLAY ELECTRIC COOPERATIVE, INC.
225 W WALKER DR, KEYSTONE HEIGHTS, FL 326567617
Phone: 352 473-8000
Web: WWW.CLAYELECTRIC.COM

COMPETITORS

Florida Power & Light	Gainesville Regional
Florida Public	Utilities
Utilities	JEA

HISTORICAL FINANCIALS

Company Type: Private

Income Statement
FYE: December 31

	REVENUE ($ mil.)	NET INCOME ($ mil.)	NET PROFIT MARGIN	EMPLOYEES
12/15	362	22	6.3%	444
12/14	368	25	6.8%	—
12/13	339	11	3.4%	—
12/12	337	8	2.4%	—
Annual Growth	2.4%	40.6%	—	—

2015 Year-End Financials
Return on assets: 1.1% Cash ($ mil.): 15
Return on equity: 6.3%
Current ratio: 0.70

CLEARWATER ENTERPRISES, L.L.C.

EXECUTIVES

Chief Operating Officer, Lisa Owens
Vice-President, Koray Bakir
Manager, Angela Allan
Sales Director, Casey Gammon
Auditors: HOGAN TAYLOR LLP OKLAHOMA CI

LOCATIONS

HQ: CLEARWATER ENTERPRISES, L.L.C.
5637 N CLASSEN BLVD, OKLAHOMA CITY, OK 731184015
Phone: 405 842-9200
Web: WWW.CLEARWATERNG.COM

HISTORICAL FINANCIALS

Company Type: Private

Income Statement
FYE: December 31

	REVENUE ($ mil.)	NET INCOME ($ mil.)	NET PROFIT MARGIN	EMPLOYEES
12/15	198	3	1.7%	17
12/14	393	3	0.9%	—
12/13	259	1	0.5%	—
12/12	204	27	13.6%	—
Annual Growth	(0.9%)	(50.7%)	—	—

2015 Year-End Financials
Return on assets: 0.1% Cash ($ mil.): —
Return on equity: 1.7%
Current ratio: 1.10

CLECO POWER LLC

Electric services nsk

EXECUTIVES

Principal Engineer, Miles Dupuis
Auditors: PRICEWATERHOUSECOOPERS LLP NE

LOCATIONS

HQ: CLECO POWER LLC
2030 DONAHUE FERRY RD, PINEVILLE, LA 713605226
Phone: 318 484-7400

HISTORICAL FINANCIALS

Company Type: Private

Income Statement
FYE: December 31

	REVENUE ($ mil.)	NET INCOME ($ mil.)	NET PROFIT MARGIN	EMPLOYEES
12/16	1,159	39	3.4%	1,206
12/15	1,208	141	11.7%	—
12/14	1,268	154	12.2%	—
12/13	1,095	150	13.7%	—
Annual Growth	1.9%	(36.2%)	—	—

2016 Year-End Financials
Return on assets: 8.8% Cash ($ mil.): 21
Return on equity: 3.4%
Current ratio: 0.40

CLEVELAND COUNTY HEALTHCARE SYSTEM

EXECUTIVES

Chief Executive Officer, Bryan Gwyn
Director, Kathy Wilkinson
Engineer, Allen Sanders

LOCATIONS

HQ: CLEVELAND COUNTY HEALTHCARE SYSTEM
201 E GROVER ST, SHELBY, NC 281503917
Phone: 980 487-3000

HISTORICAL FINANCIALS

Company Type: Private

Income Statement
FYE: December 31

	REVENUE ($ mil.)	NET INCOME ($ mil.)	NET PROFIT MARGIN	EMPLOYEES
12/15	173	33	19.1%	1,200
12/07	192	8	4.4%	—
12/06	181	14	7.7%	—
12/05	167	10	6.0%	—
Annual Growth	0.3%	12.6%	—	—

2015 Year-End Financials
Return on assets: 1.9% Cash ($ mil.): —
Return on equity: 19.1%
Current ratio: 1.70

CLEVELAND STATE UNIVERSITY

Cleveland State University offers a well-rounded education in the land of the Buckeyes. The university provides some 1000 courses in the arts and sciences business administration law engineering and other areas. The school which enrolls more than 17000 students offers undergraduate and graduate degrees in 200 fields of study through eight colleges and two academic divisions. The university has more than 570 faculty members on its staff. Tuition for undergraduate residents is about $7900. Its Maxine Goodman Levin College of Urban Affairs is nationally recognized for its

public administration programs. Established in 1964 Cleveland State merged with Cleveland-Marshall College of Law in 1969.

Geographic Reach

The Cleveland State campus spans 85 acres - the largest footprint in downtown Cleveland - with more than 40 buildings used for teaching research housing administration and recreation. The university also has extended campuses in Westlake and Solon Ohio where students have access to the same courses and curriculum as they have on the main campus.

Financial Performance

Cleveland State University's 2012 revenue increased 7% vs. the prior year. The rise was driven by an $8.2 million increase in tuition and fees (net of scholarship allowances). Headcount rose .35% from the prior year. A tuition increase of 3.5% was effective in fall 2011. Net income was up nearly 20% in 2012 vs. 2011 on lower expenses due primarily to energy conservation savings and budget cuts.

Strategy

Cleveland State University is expanding to keep up with its growing enrollment. (The 2012 freshman class was the largest in its history with 1550 students.) To serve the growing student population the university recently completed a $500-million campus makeover that includes a recreation center apartment-style housing a restaurant an administration center and a College of Graduate Studies building.

EXECUTIVES

Chair Department Of Theatre And Dance, Michael Mauldin
Secretary 2, Catherine Dohanyos
Auditors: PLANTE & MORAN PLLC TOLEDO O

LOCATIONS

HQ: CLEVELAND STATE UNIVERSITY
2121 EUCLID AVE, CLEVELAND, OH 441152226
Phone: 216 687-2000
Web: WWW.CSUOHIO.EDU

PRODUCTS/OPERATIONS

Colleges
Business Administration
Education and Human Services
Engineering
Graduate Studies
Law
Liberal Arts and Social Sciences
Science
Urban Affairs
Academic Divisions
Division of Continuing Education
Division of University Studies (support services)

HISTORICAL FINANCIALS

Company Type: Private

Income Statement

FYE: June 30

	REVENUE ($ mil.)	NET INCOME ($ mil.)	NET PROFIT MARGIN	EMPLOYEES
06/16	209	(9)	—	2,600
06/11	185	9	5.2%	—
06/09	154	(8)	—	—
06/08	425	0	0.0%	—
Annual Growth	(8.5%)	—	—	—

2016 Year-End Financials

Return on assets: 4.8%
Return on equity: (-4.5%)
Current ratio: 0.60
Cash ($ mil.): 5

CLIFTONLARSONALLEN LLP

CliftonLarsonAllen (CLA) is all about the CPAs. Boasting more than $3 billion in client assets under management and 500 partners CLA is the US' 10th-largest accounting firm that serves privately-owned firms and their principals along with not-for-profits and government agencies. Also serving as a financial advisory and business consultancy CLA is organized as a holding company with three main business segments: Public Accounting Wealth Management and Outsourcing Services. It mostly serves clients in the agribusiness financial employee benefit plan healthcare manufacturing and government sectors. With 1800 CPAs and nearly 3000 other professionals the firm's annual revenues exceed $750 million.

Operations

The company's service areas include audit accounting tax consulting outsourcing and wealth advisory. Its investment advisory services are conducted through CliftonLarsonAllen Wealth Advisors LLC. CLA serves clients outside the US through its affiliations with Nexia International.

Geographic Reach

Minnesota-based CLA boasts nearly 100 offices in about 20 states and the District of Columbia.

Sales and Marketing

CLA which counts more than 150000 clients serves privately-held businesses individuals not-for-profits and governmental entities. Its major client groups include agribusiness and cooperatives dealerships employee benefit plans federal government financial institutions healthcare manufacturing and distribution companies as well as state and local governments.

Financial Performance

CLA's revenue has risen more than 36% since the end of 2012. The company's revenue reached $750 million at the end of 2015.

Strategy

CLA has been acquiring local accounting and consulting firms around the US to expand into new geographic markets while bolstering its service offerings and client list.

Mergers and Acquisitions

In February 2016 CLA bought Bruner Cox LLP the 10th-largest accounting firm in Northeast Ohio (according to the Crain's 2016 Book of Lists). The deal was expected to take effect in June.

In November 2015 the firm purchased Pittsburgh-based KFMR Katz McMurtry PC the region's 19th-largest accounting firm.

In April 2014 the company acquired accounting and consulting firm Illinois Agricultural Auditing Association expanding its presence in Illinois to more than a dozen locations with the addition of IAAA's Bloomington/Normal and Springfield locations.

In January 2014 CLA purchased several companies to expand its consultancy including: Massachusetts consulting firm Bankers Advisory Inc.; Maryland-based OneSource Professional Services Group a consulting technology accounting and tax services firm; and Sullivan Rogers & Company a Massachusetts CPA and consulting firm dedicated to the state and local government market.

In 2013 in looking to take advantage of the implementation of healthcare reform in the US CLA acquired Idaho-based national healthcare consulting firm Beck Advisory Group. That year it also bought accounting firm Monaghan Group boosting its outsourcing practice and services in the Charlotte North Carolina area as well as Indiana-based

Nonprofit Financial Solutions a firm focused on providing nonprofits with CFO consulting and outsourcing services.

Company Background

CLA was formed in 2011 by the merger of Clifton Gunderson and LarsonAllen. Prior to the pairing both companies had been active in expanding across the country by purchasing smaller firms and parts of other firms.

EXECUTIVES

COO, David E. Bailey
CFO, Sharon Ten Clay
CIO, Steve Noble
CEO CliftonLarsonAllen Wealth Advisors LLC, Tony Hallada
CEO and Chief Business Officer, Denny Schleper

LOCATIONS

HQ: CLIFTONLARSONALLEN LLP
220 S 6TH ST STE 300, MINNEAPOLIS, MN 554021418
Phone: 612 376-4500
Web: WWW.CLIFTONLARSONALLEN.COM

Selected Locations
Arizona
California
Colorado
Florida
Idaho
Illinois
Indiana
Iowa
Maryland
Massachusetts
Michigan
Minnesota
Mississippi
Missouri
New Jersey
New Mexico
New York
North Carolina
Ohio
Pennsylvania
Texas
Virginia
Washington
Wisconsin

PRODUCTS/OPERATIONS

Selected Services:Audit and assuranceConsultingCLA Intuition financial modelingEmployee benefit plansExecutive searchForensicInformation securityIntact softwareLitigation supportRisk managementTechnologyTransaction supportValuationInternationalOutsourci

COMPETITORS

BDO	Ernst & Young LLP
BKD LLP	Grant Thornton
Baker Tilly Virchow	KPMG L.L.P.
Krause	Moore Stephens
CBIZ Accounting Tax &	International
Advisory Services	PricewaterhouseCoopers
Crowe Horwath	UK
Deloitte & Touche	RSM US
Eide Bailly	SVA

HISTORICAL FINANCIALS

Company Type: Private

Income Statement

FYE: December 4

	REVENUE ($ mil.)	NET INCOME ($ mil.)	NET PROFIT MARGIN	EMPLOYEES
12/15	650	170	26.3%	4,786
12/14	598	163	27.3%	—
12/13	563	154	27.5%	—
12/12	569	204	36.0%	—
Annual Growth	4.6%	(5.9%)	—	—

CMC AMERICAS, INC.

EXECUTIVES

Chief Financial Officer, Sandra Shuford
Regional Manager, Harikiran Pillalamarri

LOCATIONS

HQ: CMC AMERICAS, INC.
4354 S SHRWD FORST BL 175, BATON ROUGE, LA 708164483
Phone: 225 296-8440
Web: WWW.CMCLTD.COM

HISTORICAL FINANCIALS

Company Type: Private

Income Statement

FYE: March 31

	REVENUE ($ mil.)	NET INCOME ($ mil.)	NET PROFIT MARGIN	EMPLOYEES
03/15	244	12	5.3%	210
03/14	209	12	5.8%	—
03/13	166	10	6.6%	—
03/12	152	7	4.9%	—
Annual Growth	17.2%	20.6%	—	—

2015 Year-End Financials

Return on assets: 17.8%　　　Cash ($ mil.): 10
Return on equity: 5.3%
Current ratio: 1.60

COAST CITRUS DISTRIBUTORS

Coast Citrus Distributors is a leading wholesale distributor of fresh fruits and vegetables in Mexico and the US. The company supplies a variety of produce including bananas lettuce limes and potatoes to retail grocers and other food customers. It distributes under the names Coast Citrus Coast Tropical Olympic Fruit and Vegetable and Importadora y Exportadora. Coast Citrus Distributors operates half a dozen distribution facilities in California Texas and Florida. It also has about five locations in Mexico. The late Roberto Alvarez founded the family-owned business in 1950.

In early 2010 Chiquita Brands International sold its 49% equity investment in Coast Citrus Distributors. The sale netted Chiquita $18 million in cash and helped to improve its liquidity.

EXECUTIVES

Manager, Isabel Freeland
Personnel Director, Maria Benitez
Operations Manager, Joe Atoigue
Senior Manager, Jorge Guiterrez
Auditors: PKF SAN DIEGO CALIFORNIA

LOCATIONS

HQ: COAST CITRUS DISTRIBUTORS
7597 BRISTOW CT, SAN DIEGO, CA 921547419
Phone: 619 661-7950
Web: WWW.COASTCITRUS.COM

COMPETITORS

A. Duda & Sons	Fresh Del Monte
Albert's Organics	Produce
American Fruit &	FreshPoint
Produce	General Produce
Borg Produce	Interfresh
Chiquita Brands	The Oppenheimer Group

HISTORICAL FINANCIALS

Company Type: Private

Income Statement

FYE: January 2

	REVENUE ($ mil.)	NET INCOME ($ mil.)	NET PROFIT MARGIN	EMPLOYEES
01/16	311	4	1.3%	320
01/15*	331	2	0.7%	—
12/11	297	3	1.0%	—
01/11	294	4	1.4%	—
Annual Growth	1.2%	0.4%	—	—

*Fiscal year change

2016 Year-End Financials

Return on assets: 6.7%　　　Cash ($ mil.): 3
Return on equity: 1.3%
Current ratio: 1.10

COAST ELECTRIC POWER ASSOCIATION

There's no coasting for the Coast Electric Power Association when it comes to providing residents in three southern Mississippi counties with electricity. The utility uses a 6400-mile distribution network to serve its more than 76000 members (the great majority or which are residential customers) in Hancock Pearl River and Harrison counties. Coast offers electronic fund transfer and average monthly payment plans and rebates on energy efficient home improvements. The utility's power is generated by South Mississippi Electric Power an association of Coast and 10 other cooperatives. It partners with Touchstone Energy Cooperatives.

The member-owned electric cooperative started serving the Gulf Coast in 1937 with 25 miles of power lines and 50 members.

EXECUTIVES

Vice President Of Pearl River County O, Louis Lee
Auditors: JACKSON THORNTON & CO PC MO

LOCATIONS

HQ: COAST ELECTRIC POWER ASSOCIATION
18020 HIGHWAY 603, KILN, MS 395568487
Phone: 228 363-7000
Web: WWW.COASTEPA.COM

COMPETITORS

Entergy Mississippi	Southern Pine EPA
Mississippi Power	

HISTORICAL FINANCIALS

Company Type: Private

Income Statement

FYE: December 31

	REVENUE ($ mil.)	NET INCOME ($ mil.)	NET PROFIT MARGIN	EMPLOYEES
12/15	202	15	7.8%	238
12/14	201	14	7.2%	—
12/13	187	12	6.8%	—
12/12	184	13	7.2%	—
Annual Growth	3.2%	6.2%	—	—

2015 Year-End Financials

Return on assets: 1.9%　　　Cash ($ mil.): 1
Return on equity: 7.8%
Current ratio: 0.40

COBANK ACB

You could say CoBank is dependent on its rural customers and vice versa. A member of the Farm Credit System (which is regulated by the FCA) the $110 billion cooperative bank provides seasonal and wholesale loans to agribusinesses as well as to rural power water and communications cooperatives across the US. The bank also leases vehicles farming equipment and agricultural facilities through various Farm Credit System affiliates. Its core agribusiness customers range from local and regional farmers' cooperatives to multinational food companies. It has counted Land O' Lakes Blue Diamond Almonds and National Beef as among its larger customers. Formed in 1989 CoBank merged with US AgBank in early 2012.

Operations

CoBank operates three main business segments: Strategic Relationships Agribusiness and Rural Infrastructure. Its Strategic Relationships loans made up 50% of its $80 billion loan portfolio at the end of 2014 while Agribusiness and Rural Infrastructure made up another 30% and 20% respectively.

About 76% of CoBank's total revenue came from loan interest in 2014 while another 16% came from interest income on investment securities. The rest of its revenue came from fee income (5% of revenue) prepayment income (1%) and other miscellaneous sources.

Geographic Reach

Based in Colorado the bank operates 15 regional offices throughout the US including locations in Iowa Georgia Texas Connecticut Kansas Missouri and Kentucky. It also has an international office in Singapore.

Sales and Marketing

CoBank mainly serves clients in rural America in the agribusiness water communications and power sectors.

Financial Performance

CoBank's annual revenues and profits have been rising over the past several years thanks to steady loan asset growth across all three of its target loan types (Strategic Relationships Agribusiness and Rural Infrastructure).

The bank's revenue jumped 5% to $2.2 million during 2014 mostly thanks to higher average loan volume and increased earnings from a strengthened balance sheet. CoBank's lending business grew with food and agribusiness customers Farm Credit Association customers and rural energy and communications customers which all in turn contributed to its top-line growth.

Revenue growth in 2014 drove CoBank's net income up 6% to $904.3 million for the year. The

bank's operating cash levels dipped 2% to $883.1 million during the year due to unfavorable working capital changes related to accrued interest balance changes.

EXECUTIVES

CFO, David P. Burlage
Chief Risk Officer, Lori L. O'Flaherty
COO, Ann Trakimas
EVP Banking Services Group, Antony M. Bahr
SVP and CIO, James R. Bernsten
EVP Regional Agribusiness Banking Group, Amy H. Gales
Central Region President Regional Agribusiness Banking Group, Mike Hechtner
Chief Credit Officer, Daniel Key
EVP Corporate Agribusiness Banking Group, Jonathan B. Logan
Southern Region President Regional Agribusiness Banking Group, Lynn Scherler
SVP and Manager Communications Division, Robert F. (Rob) West
Eastern Region President Regional Agribusiness Banking Group, David Sparks
Western Region President Regional Agribusiness Banking Group, Leili Ghazi
CEO, Robert B. Engel, $880,000 total compensation
President, Mary E. McBride
Chief Banking Officer; Member Management Executive Committee, Thomas Halverson
VP and Managing Counsel Legal and Loan Processing Division, Chris Clayton
President Farm Credit Leasing, Mike Romanowski
SVP Power Energy and Utilities Banking Division, Todd E. Telesz
SVP Electric Distribution Water and Community Facilities, Nivin Elgohary
Executive Vice President Regional Agribusiness Banking Group, Paul Narduzzo
Regional Vice President, Todd Sogge
Senior Vice President, Karen Lowe
Vice President, Marshall Essig
Vice President, Kent Erhardt
Vice President, Andrew Haberern
Vice President and Director of Internal Audit, Steven Wittbecke
Vice President Infrastructure, Shawn Dombowsky
Vice Presidnet, Bert Johnson
Regional Vice President Electric Distribution Division ACB, Tamra Reynolds
Vice President, Kenneth Allen
Vice President Information TEC, Arthur Hodges
Associate Vice President, Chris Schneider
Vice President, Brock Taylor
Vice President, Andy Glover
Vice President Energy Banking, Allison Dunn
Vice President and Managing Counsel, Amy J Diaz
Vice President, Rachel Hanson
Vice President and Manager Power Supply Division, Jill Martinez
Vice President, John Cole
Vice President, Weldon Schiller
Sector Vice President, Dave Dornbirer
Vice President, James Matzat
Vice President Government Affairs, Sarah Tyree
Senior Vice President of Operations, Horst Kisch
Vice President Project Finance, Jennifer Daurio
Vice President Digital Business Solutions Sales, Noelle Daghe
Sector Vice President, Christopher Shaffner
Second Vice Chair, Kevin A. Still
First Vice Chair, Daniel T. (Dan) Kelley
Chairman, Everett M. Dobrinski

LOCATIONS

HQ: COBANK ACB
6340 S FIDDLERS GREEN CIR, GREENWOOD VILLAGE, CO 801114951
Phone: 303 740-6527
Web: WWW.COBANK.COM

Selected Regional Offices

Ames IA
Atlanta GA
Austin TX
Enfield CT
Fargo ND
Louisville KY
Lubbock TX
Minneapolis MN
Omaha NE
Roseville CA
Spokane WA
St. Louis MO
Washington D.C.
Wichita KS

COMPETITORS

AgFirst	Northwest Farm Credit
AgStar	Rabo AgriFinance
AgriBank	Wells Fargo
Bank of America	
Farm Credit Services of Mid-America	

HISTORICAL FINANCIALS

Company Type: Private

Income Statement

FYE: December 31

	ASSETS ($ mil.)	NET INCOME ($ mil.)	INCOME AS % OF ASSETS	EMPLOYEES
12/15	117,470	936	0.8%	500
12/14	107,428	904	0.8%	—
12/10	67,700	818	1.2%	—
12/09	58,160	565	1.0%	—
Annual Growth	12.4%	8.8%		

2015 Year-End Financials

Return on assets: —
Return on equity: 39.4%
Sales ($ mil): 2,379

COBB COUNTY BOARD OF EDUCATION

EXECUTIVES

Chairman of the Board, Randy Scamihorn
Director, Melinda Salley
Bookkeeper, Cindy Turner
Auditors: MAULDIN & JENKINS LLC ATLANT

LOCATIONS

HQ: COBB COUNTY BOARD OF EDUCATION
514 GLOVER ST SE, MARIETTA, GA 300602750
Phone: 770 426-3300
Web: WWW.COBBK12.ORG

HISTORICAL FINANCIALS

Company Type: Private

Income Statement

FYE: June 30

	REVENUE ($ mil.)	NET INCOME ($ mil.)	NET PROFIT MARGIN	EMPLOYEES
06/16	1,238	(1)	—	589
06/15	1,166	(29)	—	—
06/14	532	67	12.6%	—
06/13	1,094	(5)	—	—
Annual Growth	4.2%	—	—	—

2016 Year-End Financials

Return on assets: 3.1%
Return on equity: (-0.1%)
Current ratio: —
Cash ($ mil): 267

COBB COUNTY PUBLIC SCHOOLS

EXECUTIVES

Superintendent, Chris Ragsdale
Treasurer, An Goh
Auditors: ROSS LANE & COMPANY LLC ATLAN

LOCATIONS

HQ: COBB COUNTY PUBLIC SCHOOLS
514 GLOVER ST SE, MARIETTA, GA 300602706
Phone: 770 426-3300

HISTORICAL FINANCIALS

Company Type: Private

Income Statement

FYE: June 30

	REVENUE ($ mil.)	NET INCOME ($ mil.)	NET PROFIT MARGIN	EMPLOYEES
06/16	1,238	(1)	—	10,000
06/15	1,166	(29)	—	—
06/14	0	0	13.9%	—
06/13	0	0	11.4%	—
Annual Growth	1084.6%	—	—	—

2016 Year-End Financials

Return on assets: 3.1%
Return on equity: (-0.1%)
Current ratio: —
Cash ($ mil.): 267

COBB HOSPITAL, INC.

EXECUTIVES

Chief Executive Officer, Reynold J Jennings
Board of Directors, Leo E Reichert
Financial Executive, Barbara Lusk
Chief Financial Officer, Marsha Burke
Chief Financial Officer, Jim Badinski
Manager, Jimmy Gaines
Manager, Paula Jackson

LOCATIONS

HQ: COBB HOSPITAL, INC.
3950 AUSTELL RD, AUSTELL, GA 301061121
Phone: 770 792-7600
Web: WWW.VATSLOBE.COM

HISTORICAL FINANCIALS

Company Type: Private

Income Statement

FYE: June 30

	REVENUE ($ mil.)	NET INCOME ($ mil.)	NET PROFIT MARGIN	EMPLOYEES
06/15*	287	(7)	—	2,500
05/05	651	0	—	—
06/99	148	54	36.4%	—
06/98	148	54	36.4%	—
Annual Growth	4.0%	—	—	—

*Fiscal year change

2015 Year-End Financials

Return on assets: 0.5%
Return on equity: (-2.7%)
Current ratio: 4.80
Cash ($ mil.): —

COC PROPERTIES, INC.

EXECUTIVES

Chairman of the Board, Harry D Stephenson
Auditors: BATCHELOR TILLERY & ROBERTS

LOCATIONS

HQ: COC PROPERTIES, INC.
110 MACKENAN DR STE 300, CARY, NC 275117901
Phone: 919 462-1100
Web: WWW.CARYOIL.COM

HISTORICAL FINANCIALS

Company Type: Private

Income Statement

	ASSETS ($ mil.)	NET INCOME ($ mil.)	INCOME AS % OF ASSETS	EMPLOYEES
12/15	77	4	6.1%	100
12/14	79	7	8.8%	—
12/13	77	3	4.4%	—
12/12	76	2	3.6%	—
Annual Growth	0.4%	19.2%	—	—

FYE: December 31

2015 Year-End Financials

Return on assets: 2.9% Sales ($ mil): 1,245
Return on equity: 0.4%

COGNOSANTE HOLDINGS, LLC

EXECUTIVES

Chief Executive Officer, Y Michele Kang
Senior Vice-President, Jim Joyce
Senior Vice-President, Sean M Gallagher
Vice-President, Stephen Gantz
Senior Vice-President, Jean Marc Edier
Senior Vice-President, Len Discenza
Vice-President, Davis Foste
VP Marketing, Eileen Cassidy Rivera
Auditors: GRANT THORNTON MC LEAN VA

LOCATIONS

HQ: COGNOSANTE HOLDINGS, LLC
8200 GREENSBORO DR # 1200, MC LEAN, VA
221024923
Phone: 703 206-6000

HISTORICAL FINANCIALS

Company Type: Private

Income Statement

	REVENUE ($ mil.)	NET INCOME ($ mil.)	NET PROFIT MARGIN	EMPLOYEES
12/15	193	25	13.4%	1,400
12/14	123	7	5.8%	—
12/13	69	5	8.2%	—
12/12	34,574	1,630	4.7%	—
Annual Growth	(82.3%)	(74.9%)	—	—

FYE: December 31

2015 Year-End Financials

Return on assets: 1.6% Cash ($ mil.): —
Return on equity: 13.4%
Current ratio: 1.00

COGNOSANTE, LLC

EXECUTIVES

Chief Executive Officer, Y Michele Kang
Board of Directors, Sean Gallagher
Board of Directors, Brent Younce
Auditors: GRANT THORNTON MC LEAN VA

LOCATIONS

HQ: COGNOSANTE, LLC
8200 GREENSBORO DR # 1200, MC LEAN, VA
221024923
Phone: 703 206-6000
Web: WWW.COGNOSANTE.COM

HISTORICAL FINANCIALS

Company Type: Private

Income Statement

	REVENUE ($ mil.)	NET INCOME ($ mil.)	NET PROFIT MARGIN	EMPLOYEES
12/15	193	25	13.4%	293
12/14	123	7	5.8%	—
12/13*	69	5	8.2%	—
05/13	19	1	6.3%	—
Annual Growth	115.1%	176.1%	—	—

FYE: December 31

*Fiscal year change

2015 Year-End Financials

Return on assets: 1.6% Cash ($ mil.): —
Return on equity: 13.4%
Current ratio: 1.00

COLGATE UNIVERSITY

Colgate University is located in upstate New York. The university is a liberal arts college with an enrollment of about 3000 students. Most students are undergrads though the school has a small graduate program that offers master's degrees in arts and teaching. Colgate offers some 50 major fields of study plus about 15 minor study programs. Its most popular programs include business communications finance education medicine law and technology. The university has about 300 full-time faculty members.

Geographic Reach

Colgate University is located in the small community of Hamilton New York; the town has a total of 3000 residents.

Strategy

Colgate University has expanded access to financial aid and scholarships to support and expand education research and sports programs.

Company Background

The school was founded in 1819 as the Baptist Education Society a seminary in Hamilton New York. Baptists in New York City including soap maker William Colgate consolidated their seminary with the Hamilton school a few years later. After nearly 70 years of involvement and service by the Colgate family the school became known as Colgate in 1890.

EXECUTIVES

Vice President Dean Of The College, Suzy Nelson
Associate Vice President For Institutional Advance, Mike Sciola
Associate Vice President, Timothy Mansfield
Associate Vice President And Dean Of Students, Scott Brown
Associate Vice President and Dean Residential Programs and Student Support, Susan Smith
Associate Vice President For Institutional Advance, Andy Coddington
Vice President and Chief Information Officer, Steve Fabiani
Interim Associate Vice President for Grounds, Mike Jasper
Secretary, Quinn Steigleder
Auditors: KPMG LLP ALBANY NY

LOCATIONS

HQ: COLGATE UNIVERSITY
13 OAK DR, HAMILTON, NY 133461386
Phone: 315 228-1000
Web: WWW.COLGATE.EDU

PRODUCTS/OPERATIONS

Selected Majors
Africana Studies
Art and Art History
Asian Studies
Astrogeophysics
Astronomy/Physics
Biochemistry
Biology
Chemistry
Chinese
Classical Studies
Computer Science
Computer Science/Mathematics
Economics
Educational Studies
English
Environmental Biology
Environmental Geography
Environmental Geology
Environmental Studies
French
Geography
Geology
German
Greek
History
Humanities
International Relations
Japanese
Latin
Mathematical Economics
Mathematics
Molecular Biology
Music
Native American Studies
Natural Sciences
Neuroscience
Peace and Conflict Studies
Philosophy
Philosophy and Religion
Physical Science
Physics
Political Science
Psychology
Religion
Russian and Eurasian Studies
Social Sciences
Sociology and Anthropology
Spanish
Theater
Women's Studies

HISTORICAL FINANCIALS

Company Type: Private

Income Statement

	REVENUE ($ mil.)	NET INCOME ($ mil.)	NET PROFIT MARGIN	EMPLOYEES
06/16	189	(57)	—	1,014
06/15	181	25	14.0%	—
06/14	171	104	61.1%	—
06/13	167	80	48.1%	—
Annual Growth	4.3%	—	—	—

FYE: June 30

2016 Year-End Financials

Return on assets: 15.4%   Cash ($ mil.): 31
Return on equity: (-30.5%)
Current ratio: —

COLORADO SEMINARY

Want a mile-high education? Colorado Seminary which does business as University of Denver (DU) offers graduate and undergraduate degrees in more than 100 fields of study including law government humanities education engineering and psychology. About 11600 undergraduate and graduate students from across the US and more than 80 countries are enrolled at the school. Founded in 1864 the university has a staff of 700 full-time faculty members; its student-to-faculty ratio is 11:1. DU is located on a 125-acre campus. Former Secretary of State Condoleezza Rice former Interior Secretary Gale Norton and former Coors Brewing CEO Peter Coors attended DU.

Strategy

DU has added about 20 buildings since 1997 to enhance its academic administrative athletic and residential capacities. Projects have included a soccer stadium and a center for international security and diplomacy within the School of International Studies. In 2016 it opened the Daniel Felix Ritchie School of Engineering and Computer Science.

Despite campus growth between 2006 and 2015 the University shrank its carbon footprint by 27% due the use of carbon offsets and vehicles fueled by compressed natural gas (CNG). It operates the only CNG fueling station on a Colorado university campus.

EXECUTIVES

Chancellor, Robert D. (Bob) Coombe
Dean Josef Korbel School of International Studies, Christopher R. Hill
Vice Chancellor Business and Financial Affairs, Craig W. Woody
Dean Women's College, Lynn Gangone
Provost, Gregg Kvistad
Dean Divisions of Arts Humanities and Social Sciences, Anne E. McCall
Dean Sturm College of Law, Martin J. (Marty) Katz
Dean Graduate School of Professional Psychology, Shelly Smith-Acuna
Dean Natural Sciences and Mathematics, Andrei Kutateladze
Interim Dean Daniel Felix Ritchie School of Engineering and Computer Science, Michael Keables
Vice Chancellor Division of Marketing & COmmunications and Chief Marketing Officer, Kevin Carroll
Director of Admissions and Recruiting, Julie Schellman
Auditors: CLIFTONLARSONALLEN LLP GREEN

LOCATIONS

HQ: COLORADO SEMINARY
2199 S UNIVERSITY BLVD, DENVER, CO 802104711
Phone: 303 871-2000
Web: WWW.DU.EDU

PRODUCTS/OPERATIONS

Selected Schools and Programs
Undergraduate Schools and Colleges
  Daniels College of Business
  Division of Natural Sciences & Mathematics
  Division of Arts Humanities and Social Sciences
  Josef Korbel School of International Studies
  Morgridge College of Education

  School of Engineering and Computer Science
  University College
  Women's College
Graduate and Professional Programs
  Daniels College of Business
  Divisions of Arts Humanities and Social Sciences
  Divisions of Natural Sciences and Mathematics
  Graduate School of Professional Psychology (GSPP)
  Graduate School of Social Work (GSSW)
  Graduate Tax Program
  Interdisciplinary Degree Programs
  Josef Korbel School of International Studies
  Morgridge College of Education (MCE)
  School of Engineering and Computer Science
  The Sturm College of Law
  University College

HISTORICAL FINANCIALS

Company Type: Private

Income Statement   FYE: June 30

	REVENUE ($ mil.)	NET INCOME ($ mil.)	NET PROFIT MARGIN	EMPLOYEES
06/16	458	9	2.2%	2,770
06/15	431	69	16.0%	—
06/14	396	122	31.0%	—
06/12	367	56	15.5%	—
Annual Growth	5.7%	(35.4%)	—	—

2016 Year-End Financials

Return on assets: 16.7%   Cash ($ mil.): 83
Return on equity: 2.2%
Current ratio: —

COLORADO STATE UNIVERSITY SYSTEM

EXECUTIVES

Chancellor, Joe Blake
Chancellor, Michael Martin
President, Becky Takeda
Director, Jean Morgenweck
Manager, Melanie Geary
Accountant, Walt Naylor
Auditors: BKD LLP DENVER CO

LOCATIONS

HQ: COLORADO STATE UNIVERSITY SYSTEM
475 17TH ST STE 1550, DENVER, CO 802024012
Phone: 303 534-6290
Web: WWW.BUSFIN.COLOSTATE.EDU

HISTORICAL FINANCIALS

Company Type: Private

Income Statement   FYE: June 30

	REVENUE ($ mil.)	NET INCOME ($ mil.)	NET PROFIT MARGIN	EMPLOYEES
06/15	1,011	33	3.3%	6,701
06/14	938	(5)	—	—
06/13	884	22	2.6%	—
Annual Growth	6.9%	21.7%	—	—

2015 Year-End Financials

Return on assets: 4.2%   Cash ($ mil.): 352
Return on equity: 3.3%
Current ratio: 2.00

COLSA CORPORATION

COLSA doesn't mind being called a little defensive. The company provides advanced technology systems and services to US government agencies such as the Missile Defense Agency and NASA. COLSA which specializes in radar and guidance system technology offers services including engineering and testing developing war games simulations analyzing radar technology and virtual prototyping. Its information systems services include integration maintenance and administration for large computer centers. COLSA also offers a software system for nuclear power plants and a gateway for sending simulation data to remote systems. COLSA was founded in 1980.

Geographic Reach

COLSA has offices in Alabama Arizona California Colorado Florida and Washington DC. About a third of COLSA's employees work directly at Redstone Arsenal home to the U.S. Army Aviation and Missile Command the Space and Missile Defense Command and components of the Defense Intelligence Agency and the Missile Defense Agency.

Sales and Marketing

Primarily working with defense agencies COLSA has sought to diversify its client base by adding other government bodies such as the Department of Justice. COLSA also plans to pursue international clients.

EXECUTIVES

Vice President Federal Services Solutions, Jim Hunter

LOCATIONS

HQ: COLSA CORPORATION
6728 ODYSSEY DR NW, HUNTSVILLE, AL 358063305
Phone: 256 964-5361
Web: WWW.COLSA.COM

PRODUCTS/OPERATIONS

Selected Services
Information services
  Computer center design and engineering
  Computer center operation and maintenance
  Information assurance/security
Programmatic support
  Acquisition management
  Independent assessment
  Test support
System engineering
  Configuration management
  Modeling and simulation
  Software engineering
  Test engineering
  Testbed design development and operation
System integration
  Command control communications computers and intel (C4I) systems
  Hardware/software systems
  Security systems

COMPETITORS

CACI International	Northrop Grumman
Computer Sciences Corp.	Raytheon
	SM&A
HP Enterprise Services	UNICOM Government

HISTORICAL FINANCIALS

Company Type: Private

Income Statement

FYE: December 31

	REVENUE ($ mil.)	NET INCOME ($ mil.)	NET PROFIT MARGIN	EMPLOYEES
12/15	191	12	6.7%	1,100
12/14	190	15	8.0%	—
12/13	201	15	7.9%	—
12/12	186	11	5.9%	—
Annual Growth	0.9%	5.0%	—	—

2015 Year-End Financials

Return on assets: 6.1%
Return on equity: 6.7%
Current ratio: 1.40

Cash ($ mil.): 7

COLUMBIA COUNTY SCHOOL DISTRICT

EXECUTIVES

Superintendent, Sandra Carraway
Purchasing Agent, Bill Ferguson
Director, Bobbie Stapleton
Purchasing Director, Pat Sullivan
Assistant Manager, Deborah Williams
Assistant Manager, Penny Jackson
Auditors: SEROTTA MADDOCKS EVANS & CO

LOCATIONS

HQ: COLUMBIA COUNTY SCHOOL DISTRICT
4781 HEREFORD FARM RD, EVANS, GA 308096037
Phone: 706 541-0650
Web: WWW.CCBOE.NET

HISTORICAL FINANCIALS

Company Type: Private

Income Statement

FYE: June 30

	REVENUE ($ mil.)	NET INCOME ($ mil.)	NET PROFIT MARGIN	EMPLOYEES
06/16	251	49	19.9%	3,240
06/15	236	(0)	—	—
06/14	220	(0)	—	—
06/13	213	(21)	—	—
Annual Growth	5.5%	—	—	—

2016 Year-End Financials

Return on assets: 0.4%
Return on equity: 19.9%
Current ratio: —

Cash ($ mil.): 15

COLUMBIA PUBLIC SCHOOLS

EXECUTIVES

Superintendent, Peter Stiepleman
Purchasing Director, James Cherrington
Director, Linda Quinley

LOCATIONS

HQ: COLUMBIA PUBLIC SCHOOLS
1818 W WORLEY ST, COLUMBIA, MO 652031038
Phone: 573 214-3400
Web: WWW.CPSK12.ORG

HISTORICAL FINANCIALS

Company Type: Private

Income Statement

FYE: June 30

	REVENUE ($ mil.)	NET INCOME ($ mil.)	NET PROFIT MARGIN	EMPLOYEES
06/16*	221	10	4.8%	2,700
12/08	0	0	52.5%	—
06/06	135	(1)	—	—
06/05	14	0	3.7%	—
Annual Growth	28.4%	31.5%	—	—

*Fiscal year change

2016 Year-End Financials

Return on assets: 6.2%
Return on equity: 4.8%
Current ratio: —

Cash ($ mil.): 126

COLUMBIA ST. MARY'S HOSPITAL MILWAUKEE, INC.

EXECUTIVES

President, Travis Andersen
Board of Directors, Angie Madigan
Administrative Assistant, Heather Lucas
Director, Charles Draher
Manager, Philip Ruetz

LOCATIONS

HQ: COLUMBIA ST. MARY'S HOSPITAL MILWAUKEE, INC.
2301 N LAKE DR, MILWAUKEE, WI 532114508
Phone: 414 291-1000

HISTORICAL FINANCIALS

Company Type: Private

Income Statement

FYE: June 30

	REVENUE ($ mil.)	NET INCOME ($ mil.)	NET PROFIT MARGIN	EMPLOYEES
06/15	447	(35)	—	2,100
06/04	222	6	2.8%	—
06/03	507	29	5.9%	—
06/02	1,032	0	0.0%	—
Annual Growth	(6.2%)	—	—	—

2015 Year-End Financials

Return on assets: 1.7%
Return on equity: (-8.0%)
Current ratio: 1.90

Cash ($ mil.): 2

COLUMBUS PUBLIC SCHOOL DISTRICT

EXECUTIVES

Superintendent, Gene T Harris
Director, Chuck Hollar
Supervisor, Brenda Klein
Plant & Facilities Manager, Stephen McElroy
Auditors: DAVE YOST COLUMBUS OHIO

LOCATIONS

HQ: COLUMBUS PUBLIC SCHOOL DISTRICT
270 E STATE ST FL 3, COLUMBUS, OH 432154312
Phone: 614 365-5000
Web: WWW.CCSOH.US

HISTORICAL FINANCIALS

Company Type: Private

Income Statement

FYE: June 30

	REVENUE ($ mil.)	NET INCOME ($ mil.)	NET PROFIT MARGIN	EMPLOYEES
06/16	972	(13)	—	10,000
06/06	667	(51)	—	—
06/05	0	0	—	—
Annual Growth	—	—	—	—

2016 Year-End Financials

Return on assets: 0.6%
Return on equity: (-1.4%)
Current ratio: —

Cash ($ mil.): 341

COLUMBUS REGIONAL HOSPITAL

EXECUTIVES

President, Jim Bickel
Board of Directors, Thomas D Harmon
Account Executive, Barbara Chandler

LOCATIONS

HQ: COLUMBUS REGIONAL HOSPITAL
2400 17TH ST, COLUMBUS, IN 472015351
Phone: 812 379-4441
Web: WWW.CRH.ORG

HISTORICAL FINANCIALS

Company Type: Private

Income Statement

FYE: December 31

	REVENUE ($ mil.)	NET INCOME ($ mil.)	NET PROFIT MARGIN	EMPLOYEES
12/15	249	4	2.0%	5
12/08	145	(33)	—	—
12/06	183	18	10.2%	—
12/05	255	0	—	—
Annual Growth	—	161.3%	—	—

2015 Year-End Financials

Return on assets: 4.9%
Return on equity: 2.0%
Current ratio: 1.50

Cash ($ mil.): 21

COMAL INDEPENDENT SCHOOL DISTRICT

EXECUTIVES

Superintendent, Nancy Fuller
Principal, Jo B Jimerson
Manager, Dorinda Bustamante
Manager, Sandy James
Auditors: PADGETT STRATEMANN & CO LLP S

LOCATIONS

HQ: COMAL INDEPENDENT SCHOOL DISTRICT
1404 N INTERSTATE 35, NEW BRAUNFELS, TX
781302817
Phone: 830 221-2000
Web: WWW.COMALISD.ORG

HISTORICAL FINANCIALS

Company Type: Private

Income Statement — FYE: June 30

	REVENUE ($ mil.)	NET INCOME ($ mil.)	NET PROFIT MARGIN	EMPLOYEES
06/16*	226	138	61.1%	2,400
08/11	192	(46)	—	—
Annual Growth	3.2%	—	—	—

*Fiscal year change

2016 Year-End Financials

Return on assets: 1.1%
Return on equity: 61.1%
Current ratio: 1.80
Cash ($ mil.): 97

COMANCHE COUNTY HOSPITAL AUTHORITY

EXECUTIVES

Chairman, Buddy Green
Chief Executive Officer, Randy Segler
Chief Financial Officer, Brent Smith
Financial Executive, Monica Martinez
Auditors: BKD LLP CPAS & ADVISORS TULS

LOCATIONS

HQ: COMANCHE COUNTY HOSPITAL AUTHORITY
3401 W GORE BLVD, LAWTON, OK 735056300
Phone: 580 355-8620
Web: WWW.CCMHONLINE.COM

HISTORICAL FINANCIALS

Company Type: Private

Income Statement — FYE: June 30

	REVENUE ($ mil.)	NET INCOME ($ mil.)	NET PROFIT MARGIN	EMPLOYEES
06/16	261	(3)	—	1,800
06/15	233	6	2.7%	—
06/10	1	0	4.1%	—
06/08	188	1	0.9%	—
Annual Growth	4.2%	—	—	—

2016 Year-End Financials

Return on assets: 8.3%
Return on equity: (-1.2%)
Current ratio: 1.10
Cash ($ mil.): 16

COMMERCIAL CONTRACTING CORPORATION

EXECUTIVES

Chief Executive Officer, Stephen Fragnoli
Vice-President, John Grix
Executive Vice-President, Dan Sternberg
Vice-President, David Klann
Vice-President, Paulette Salkowski
Operations Manager, Rich Wagner
Executive Vice-President, Timothy Crawforth

LOCATIONS

HQ: COMMERCIAL CONTRACTING CORPORATION
4260 N ATLANTIC BLVD, AUBURN HILLS, MI
483261578
Phone: 248 209-0500

HISTORICAL FINANCIALS

Company Type: Private

Income Statement — FYE: December 31

	REVENUE ($ mil.)	NET INCOME ($ mil.)	NET PROFIT MARGIN	EMPLOYEES
12/15	209	0	—	300
12/14	272	0	—	—
12/13	272	0	—	—
12/12	253	0	—	—
Annual Growth	(6.2%)	—	—	—

2015 Year-End Financials

Return on assets: 23.9%
Return on equity: —
Current ratio: 1.20
Cash ($ mil.): 76

COMMERCIAL CONTRACTING GROUP, INC.

EXECUTIVES

Chairman, William H Pettibone Jr
Operations Manager, Cesar Gonzalez
Manager, Terry Gower

LOCATIONS

HQ: COMMERCIAL CONTRACTING GROUP, INC.
4260 N ATLANTIC BLVD, AUBURN HILLS, MI
483261578
Phone: 248 209-0500
Web: WWW.CCCNETWORK.COM

HISTORICAL FINANCIALS

Company Type: Private

Income Statement — FYE: December 31

	REVENUE ($ mil.)	NET INCOME ($ mil.)	NET PROFIT MARGIN	EMPLOYEES
12/15	281	0	—	300
12/14	289	0	—	—
12/13	289	0	—	—
12/11	0	0	—	—
Annual Growth	—	—	—	—

2015 Year-End Financials

Return on assets: 24.8%
Return on equity: —
Current ratio: 1.20
Cash ($ mil.): 5

COMMUNITY FOUNDATION OF GREATER MEMPHIS, INC.

EXECUTIVES

President, Robert Fockler
Chief Financial Officer, Mack McCaul Jr
Director, Stephen Webster
Representative, Frank B Horrell
Officer, Ashley Harper
Administrative Assistant, Vanessa Langston
Marketing Director, Julia McDonald
Director, Melissa Wolowicz
Officer, Susan Cooley
Director, Wesley T Larue
Auditors: RHEA & IVY PLC MEMPHIS TN

LOCATIONS

HQ: COMMUNITY FOUNDATION OF GREATER
MEMPHIS, INC.
1900 UNION AVE, MEMPHIS, TN 381044029
Phone: 901 728-4600
Web: WWW.CFGM.ORG

HISTORICAL FINANCIALS

Company Type: Private

Income Statement — FYE: April 30

	REVENUE ($ mil.)	NET INCOME ($ mil.)	NET PROFIT MARGIN	EMPLOYEES
04/15	193	65	33.8%	15
04/07	44	24	53.5%	—
04/06	29	34	117.8%	—
04/05	45	8	19.7%	—
Annual Growth	15.6%	22.1%	—	—

2015 Year-End Financials

Return on assets: 11.4%
Return on equity: 33.8%
Current ratio: —
Cash ($ mil.): 54

COMMUNITY HEALTH NETWORK, INC

Community Hospitals of Indiana (aka Community Health Network) has Indianapolis surrounded. The health care system includes 10 acute care hospitals nine surgery centers seven imaging centers seven immediate care centers 40 ambulatory care centers two endoscopy centers and four long term care facilities. One of its acute care facilities Community Hospital Anderson is located outside the state capital. It also runs the Community Heart and Vascular Hospital. Community Health Network whose origin reaches back to the 1950s has a total of about 1200 staffed beds and 2000 physicians. Other operations include physician practices occupational health facilities a rehab center and home health practices.

Operations

Community Health Network's physician practice Community Physician Network has more than 600 providers and working out of over 80 locations.

Together with its clinics health pavilions surgery centers and physician affiliations Community Health Network's service area covers an eight-county area in central Indiana. Various specialty centers treat digestive and joint ailments wounds spinal problems and gastrointestinal disease and also provide imaging services. Community's MedCheck clinics offer routine checkups and screenings in stand-alone locations while its MedCheck Express locations inside area Wal-Mart stores serve customers where they shop. Four Wellspring pharmacies all but one of which are located inside hospitals cover prescriptions patient education and wellness programs.

Among the system's notable features the Community Heart and Vascular Hospital which opened its doors in 2003 is an all-digital facility with digital equipment and wireless communications systems linking all its operations. Additionally the 42-bed neonatal intensive care room at Community Hospital North is one of the nation's largest labor delivery recovery and postpartum units and Westview Hospital is the state's only such facility offering osteopathic services.

In 2014 the system had more than a million outpatient visits. It also conducted some 96000 surgeries facilitated 7300 infant births and had more than 243000 emergency department visits.

Sales and Marketing

In 2014 Medicare patients accounted for about 41% of gross patient charges while Medicaid patients accounted for another 14%.

Financial Performance

Revenue grew 10% in 2014 to $1.9 billion thanks largely to growth in net patient service earnings and other revenue. This was partially offset by a decline in incentive payments related to electronic health records as well as the absence of gains on contributions to a joint venture.

Also that year the company reported a net loss of $0.9 million (versus a $179 million profit in 2013) as pension assets underperformed and gains on investments declined. However cash flow from operations rose 84% to $208 million due to changes in accrued pensions accounts payable and estimated third-party payor settlements.

Strategy

The health network is expanding in and around Indianapolis. It is investing nearly $250 million on two large building projects including a new hospital on the Community Hospital East campus and a new cancer center at the Community Hospital North campus.

In 2015 Community Health Network opened a new cardio-oncology clinic in Indianapolis. The facility is dedicated to understanding the impact that cancer-fighting treatments have on the heart.

EXECUTIVES

President and CEO Community Health Network, William E. (Bill) Corley, age 74
President and CEO Community Hospital Anderson, William C. (Bill) VanNess
CEO Visionary Enterprises Inc., Bryan A. Mills
President Community Hospital North, Barbara (Barb) Summers
CEO Community Physicians of Indiana, Timothy L. Hobbs
CEO The Indiana Heart Hospital, Thomas A. Malasto
CEO Community Home Health Services, Jessie Westlund
President Community Hospital East, Robin Ledyard
President Community Hospital South, Anthony Lennen
President and CEO, Beth Tharp
Chief Information Officer, Ron Strachan
CFO, Joe Kessler
COO, Tony Javorka
Vice President Revenue Cycle Management, Charles Meadows
Pharmacy Residency Program Director Pharmd Bcps, Tracy Sprunger
Auditors: PRICEWATERHOUSECOOPERS LLP I

LOCATIONS

HQ: COMMUNITY HEALTH NETWORK, INC
1500 N RITTER AVE, INDIANAPOLIS, IN 462193027
Phone: 317 355-1411

PRODUCTS/OPERATIONS

2014 Sales

	% of total
Net patient service revenue less provision for bad debts	94
Service fee revenue	1
Other revenue	5
Total	**100**

Selected Services

Advanced Wound Center
Assisted Fertility Services
Bariatric Services
Behavioral Health
Breast Care Services
Cancer Care Services
Children's Health
Clinical Research Trials
Community Home Health
Diet and Nutrition Services
Digestive Health Services
Emergency Services
Heart and Vascular
Inpatient Rehabilitation
Interventional Radiology
Maternity Services
Mid America Clinical Labs
Neuroscience Services
Orthopedic Services
Physical Therapy and Rehab
Radiology/Imaging Services
Sleep Wake Services
Sports Medicine
Surgical Services
Symptom Management Group
Weight Loss and Wellness
Women's Services

Selected Facilities and Affiliates

Community Health Pavilions
Community Heart and Vascular Hospital
Community Hospital Anderson
Community Hospital East
Community Hospital North
Community Hospital South
Community Imaging Centers
Community Physicians of Indiana network
Community Spine Center
Community Westview Hospital
Hook Rehabilitation Center
Indiana Surgery Centers
Indianapolis Endoscopy Center
MedCheck walk-in clinics
MedCheck Express clinics
Wellspring Pharmacy chain

COMPETITORS

Ball Memorial Hospital	Riverview Hospital
Henry County Memorial Hospital	St. Elizabeth Regional Health
IU Health	St. Vincent Health
IU Health Bloomington Hospital	Wabash County Hospital
Memorial Hospital (Logansport)	

HISTORICAL FINANCIALS

Company Type: Private

Income Statement

FYE: December 31

	REVENUE ($ mil.)	NET INCOME ($ mil.)	NET PROFIT MARGIN	EMPLOYEES
12/15	2,076	135	6.5%	5,000
12/14	1,942	(0)	—	—
12/13	1,763	179	10.2%	—
12/12	384	44	11.7%	—
Annual Growth	**75.4%**	**44.5%**	—	—

2015 Year-End Financials

Return on assets: 4.4%   Cash ($ mil.): 260
Return on equity: 6.5%
Current ratio: 1.50

COMMUNITY HOSPITAL OF THE MONTEREY PENINSULA

Community Hospital of the Monterey Peninsula has a sunny disposition when it comes to medical care. The not-for-profit health care facility provides general medical and surgical services to residents of Monterey California. It has about 235 acute care and skilled nursing beds and offers specialty services including cardiac and cancer care obstetrics orthopedics and rehabilitation. In addition to its main facility the hospital operates several ancillary centers including a mental health clinic an inpatient hospice medical laboratory branches and several outpatient centers offering diagnostic imaging diabetes care and other services.

Operations

Community Hospital offers a broad range of healthcare services at 15 locations including the main hospital outpatient facilities satellite laboratories a mental health clinic a short-term skilled nursing facility Hospice of the Central Coast and business offices.

In 2012 the hospital systems served 12130 inpatients in 2012. It also had 49565 emergency visits 283181 outpatient visits and assisted in 1193 births.

Geographic Reach

The company has facilities in Carmel Marina Monterey and Seaside counties in California.

Financial Performance

Medicare accounted for 53% of Community Hospital of the Monterey Peninsula's revenues in

2012; commercial insurance 23% and Medi-Cal 10%.

Strategy

To improve care in its service territory the hospital is working to increase best-practice sharing among physicians. It is also supporting information sharing by coordinating electronic health records (EHRs).

In 2014 the hospital received a $200000 contribution from the Auxiliary of Community Hospital of the Monterey Peninsula completing a five-year $1 million pledge by the service organization to support the hospital.

Company Background

As health care costs skyrocket in the US Community Hospital of the Monterey Peninsula has worked to lower its expenses. Between 2008 and 2011 the organization lowered annual costs by about $44 million.

Community Hospital of the Monterey Peninsula was founded in 1934.

EXECUTIVES

Vice President Nursing, Terril Lowe

LOCATIONS

HQ: COMMUNITY HOSPITAL OF THE MONTEREY PENINSULA
23625 HOLMAN HWY, MONTEREY, CA 939405902
Phone: 831 624-5311
Web: WWW.CHOMP.ORG

PRODUCTS/OPERATIONS

Selected Community Hospital Service Locations
Community Hospital of the Monterey Peninsula: Monterey
Carol Hatton Breast Care Center: Monterey
Development/Patient Business Services: Monterey
Hartnell Professional Center: Monterey Peninsula
  Primary Care/Satellite Laboratory: Carmel
Peninsula Wellness Center: Marina
Ryan Ranch Outpatient Campus: Monterey
Seaside Satellite Laboratory: Seaside
Westland House: Monterey

Selected Services
Bariatric Surgery
Behavioral Health Services
Carol Hatton Breast Care Center
Comprehensive Cancer Center
Diabetes
Diagnostic and Interventional Radiology
Emergency
Family Birth Center
Hospice of the Central Coast
Intermediate Intensive Care Nursery
Laboratory Services
Nutrition Therapy Program
Orthopedics
Outpatient Immunology Services
Outpatient Surgery Center
Pulmonary Wellness Services
Radiation Oncology
Rehabilitation Services
Sleep disorders
Social Services
Stroke Program
Tyler Heart Institute (Cardiac Care)
Westland House Skilled Nursing Facility
Wound Care and Hyperbaric Healing

COMPETITORS

Dignity Health
John Muir Health
Queen of the Valley
  Medical Center
Salinas Valley
  Memorial
Sequoia Healthcare
  District
Stanford Health Care
Sutter Health
The Palo Alto Medical
  Foundation
UCSF Medical

HISTORICAL FINANCIALS
Company Type: Private

Income Statement

FYE: December 31

	REVENUE ($ mil.)	NET INCOME ($ mil.)	NET PROFIT MARGIN	EMPLOYEES
12/15	560	66	11.9%	1,947
12/12	442	81	18.4%	—
12/09	475	26	5.6%	—
12/08	104	0	0.0%	—
Annual Growth	27.1%	418.1%	—	—

2015 Year-End Financials
Return on assets: 4.4%   Cash ($ mil.): 63
Return on equity: 11.9%
Current ratio: 2.00

COMMUNITY MEMORIAL HOSPITAL OF MENOMONEE FALLS, INC.

EXECUTIVES

Chief Executive Officer, Catherine A Jacobson
Account Manager, Julie Sthani
Chief Financial Officer, Lisa Krause
Auditors: KPMG LLP COLUMBUS OH

LOCATIONS

HQ: COMMUNITY MEMORIAL HOSPITAL OF MENOMONEE FALLS, INC.
W180N8085 TOWN HALL RD, MENOMONEE FALLS, WI 530513518
Phone: 414 805-3000
Web: WWW.COMMUNITYMEMORIAL.COM

HISTORICAL FINANCIALS
Company Type: Private

Income Statement

FYE: June 30

	REVENUE ($ mil.)	NET INCOME ($ mil.)	NET PROFIT MARGIN	EMPLOYEES
06/15	181	(1)	—	1,500
06/14	189	(9)	—	—
06/13	194	17	9.1%	—
06/12	205	22	10.8%	—
Annual Growth	(4.0%)	—	—	—

2015 Year-End Financials
Return on assets: 4.9%   Cash ($ mil.): 13
Return on equity: (-0.7%)
Current ratio: 3.50

COMMUNITY UNIT SCHOOL DISTRICT 200

EXECUTIVES

Superintendent, Jeff Schuler
Treasurer, Maureen Zuburt
Superintendent, Richard Drury
Assistant Manager, Faith Dahlquist
Plant & Facilities Manager, John Robinson III
Auditors: MILLER COOPER & CO LTD DEE

LOCATIONS

HQ: COMMUNITY UNIT SCHOOL DISTRICT 200
130 W PARK AVE, WHEATON, IL 601896460
Phone: 630 682-2000
Web: WWW.CUSD200.ORG

HISTORICAL FINANCIALS
Company Type: Private

Income Statement

FYE: June 30

	REVENUE ($ mil.)	NET INCOME ($ mil.)	NET PROFIT MARGIN	EMPLOYEES
06/15	219	(2)	—	1,600
06/14	202	4	2.1%	—
06/13	195	3	1.6%	—
06/12	199	11	5.8%	—
Annual Growth	3.3%	—	—	—

COMPASSION INTERNATIONAL INC

EXECUTIVES

President, Santiago Mellado
Board of Directors, Laurent Mbanda
Board of Directors, Judy Briscoe Golz
Auditors: CAPIN CROUSE LLP COLORADO SPR

LOCATIONS

HQ: COMPASSION INTERNATIONAL INC
12290 VOYAGER PKWY, COLORADO SPRINGS, CO 809213694
Phone: 719 487-7000
Web: WWW.COMPASSION.COM

HISTORICAL FINANCIALS
Company Type: Private

Income Statement

FYE: June 30

	REVENUE ($ mil.)	NET INCOME ($ mil.)	NET PROFIT MARGIN	EMPLOYEES
06/15	768	(8)	—	2,002
06/14	719	8	1.2%	—
06/13	659	15	2.3%	—
06/12	598	13	2.3%	—
Annual Growth	8.7%	—	—	—

2015 Year-End Financials
Return on assets: 5.5%   Cash ($ mil.): 80
Return on equity: (-1.1%)
Current ratio: 1.00

COMPTON UNIFIED SCHOOL DISTRICT

EXECUTIVES

Plant & Facilities Manager, David Azacarra
Superintendent, Kaye E Burnsid
Manager, Arthur Thompson
Director, Michele Dawson
Director, Irene Lee

LOCATIONS

HQ: COMPTON UNIFIED SCHOOL DISTRICT
501 S SANTA FE AVE, COMPTON, CA 902213814
Phone: 310 604-6508
Web: WWW.COMPTON.K12.CA.US

HISTORICAL FINANCIALS

Company Type: Private

Income Statement

FYE: June 30

	REVENUE ($ mil.)	NET INCOME ($ mil.)	NET PROFIT MARGIN	EMPLOYEES
06/16	337	30	9.2%	3,800
06/05	302	0	—	—
06/02	175	14	8.3%	—
06/01	238	6	2.7%	—
Annual Growth	2.3%	11.2%	—	—

CONCORD HOSPITAL, INC.

Concord Hospital is agreeably an acute care regional hospital serving central New Hampshire. The hospital has some 300 licensed beds and provides general inpatient and outpatient medical care as well as specialist centers for cardiology orthopedics cancer care urology and women's health. Concord Hospital operates other medical facilities either on its main campus or nearby including surgery imaging diagnostic hospice and rehabilitation facilities as well as physician practice locations. With roots reaching back to 1884 Concord Hospital is part of the Capital Region Health Care system which also offers mental health and home health care services.

Operations

With a staff of some 350 doctors Concord Hospital sees about 18000 patients (including some 9000 rehabilitation patients) performs more than 9600 surgeries and handles about 65000 emergency room visits and 1200 births each year. The hospital provides services in about 40 specialty medical fields.

As part of Capital Region Health Care Concord Hospital shares education purchasing and outpatient service functions (and expenses) with its network sister entities which include the Concord Regional Visiting Nurse Association and the Riverbend Community Mental Health center. Through Capital Regional Health Care Concord Hospital also has affiliations with area organizations including Dartmouth-Hitchcock Medical Center Concord Ambulatory Center and Concord Imaging Center.

Concord Hospital is also part of a collaborative network the Granite Healthcare Network with four regional New Hampshire health care providers: Elliot Health System (which operates the Elliot Hospital) LRGHealthcare (consisting of Lakes Region General Hospital and Franklin Regional Hospital) Southern New Hampshire Health System (operating the Southern New Hampshire Medical Center) and Wentworth-Douglass Hospital. Hospitals in the network remain independently managed and owned and have the option to participate or not participate in each of the group efforts.

Geographic Reach

Concord Hospital is located on a 110-acre campus in Concord New Hampshire. It provides services in area communities including Allenstown Andover Barnstead Boscawen Bow Bradford Canterbury Chichester Deering Dunbarton Epsom Henniker Hillsboro Hopkinton Loudon Northwood Pembroke Pittsfield Salsibury Warner Washington Weare Webster and Windsor.

Sales and Marketing

Medicare and Medicaid accounted for some 27% and 3% of net patient revenues respectively in 2014.

Financial Performance

Annual operating revenues increased 3% to some $440 million due to higher net patient revenues in 2014. However net income fell 72% to $18 million due to factors including loss from pension adjustments and declines in net unrealized gains. Cash flow from operations rose 14% to $32 million as less cash was used in accounts receivable and towards supplies and other assets.

Strategy

To help control the spiraling costs of medical care in the US as well as to meet health reform mandates Concord and its affiliated facilities are launching programs to share technology and administrative resources such as claims management software data storage linen service liability insurance pooling and Medicare patient management.

Concord Hospital has also launched independent initiatives to improve quality and patient safety programs including putting infection reduction protocols in place consolidating electronic health record (EHR) consolidation efforts and enacting medication management practices.

EXECUTIVES

Secretary And Treasurer Medical Staff, Lisa Atkinson

LOCATIONS

HQ: CONCORD HOSPITAL, INC.
250 PLEASANT ST, CONCORD, NH 033012598
Phone: 603 227-7000
Web: WWW.CONCORDHOSPITAL.ORG

PRODUCTS/OPERATIONS

2014 Sales

	% of total
Net patient service revenue	93
Other revenue	6
Disproportionate share revenue	1
Net assets released from restrictions for operations	-
Total	**100**

Selected Services

Ambulatory Care Center
Behavioral Health
Breast Care Center
Cancer
Cardiac
Center for Health Promotion
Child Life
Clinical Decision Unit
Day Surgery Center
Diabetes Self-Management Education
Concord Hospital Medical Group
Emergency Services
End Of Life
Family Health Centers
Infectious Disease
Intensive Care
Laboratory Services
Maternity
Neurology
Occupational Health
Orthopedics
Pediatrics
Primary Care
Radiology
Rehabilitation
Sleep Center
Surgery
Urology
Walk-in Urgent Care
Women's Health
Wound Care

COMPETITORS

Cambridge Health Alliance	Frisbie Memorial Hospital
Catholic Medical Center	HCA
Elliot Health System	Partners HealthCare
Exeter Health Resources	Southern New Hampshire Medical Center
	Steward Health Care

HISTORICAL FINANCIALS

Company Type: Private

Income Statement

FYE: September 30

	REVENUE ($ mil.)	NET INCOME ($ mil.)	NET PROFIT MARGIN	EMPLOYEES
09/16	447	15	3.4%	2,000
09/15	396	24	6.3%	—
09/14	386	28	7.3%	—
09/13	371	11	3.0%	—
Annual Growth	6.4%	11.2%	—	—

2016 Year-End Financials

Return on assets: 6.7%   Cash ($ mil.): 6
Return on equity: 3.4%
Current ratio: 0.70

CONNECTICUT CHILDREN'S MEDICAL CENTER

When their tiny tykes need some TLC Nutmeg Staters turn to Connecticut Children's Medical Center (CCMC). The 190-bed children's hospital is located on two campuses and provides a variety of pediatric services including surgery behavioral care and emergency medicine. Its facilities house pediatric trauma and intensive care units that receives referral patients from hospitals throughout the region. The medical center also conducts clinical research and provides pediatric training to health professionals. In addition CCMC operates outpatient facilities throughout Connecticut and a school for children with physical and behavioral challenges.

Operations

At its main campus CCMC employs 1100 medical professionals practicing in more than 30 specialty care fields. The hospital handles about 6500 inpatient admissions more than 55000 emergency department visits and 10000 surgeries. The medical center also operates the Faculty Practice Plan an integrated full-service multi-specialty pediatric practice providing care to children and their families. The practice employs about 170 physicians and mid-level practitioners.

Founded in 1996 CCMC is the only academic medical center dedicated exclusively to pediatric care in western New England making it a popular destination for medical training and research program participants. As the primary teaching facility for the University of Connecticut School of Medicine's Department of Pediatrics the hospital is home to a number of clinical research and physician training programs including several two-year fellowships in pediatric subspecialties and a three-year fellowship in pediatric emergency medicine. Other hospital divisions conduct clinical trials in fields including oncology hematology endocrinology gastroenterology and infectious disease.

Geographic Reach

CCMC operates about 20 locations across Connecticut and portions of Massachusetts. Its main hospital campus is in Hartford while its secondary acute care center is in Waterbury (on the campus of Saint Mary's Hospital). Other locations include ambulatory surgery specialty care and general pediatric care offices.

Strategy

CCMC grows by expanding its facilities and its range of patient services. It also strives to expand its services into new territories in southern New England including through partnerships with other area health care providers. In addition the medical center is working to increase its participation in basic and clinical research programs.

It expanded facilities by opening a new 18000-square-foot day surgery center with state of the art facilities. Plans are underway for a new Cardiovascular Care Center for children.

EXECUTIVES

Surgeon-in-Chief and EVP Clinical Affairs, Fernando A. Ferrer
CEO, James E. Shmerling, age 63
VP Operations and CIO, Kelly R. Styles
President Medical Staff, Craig C. Bonanni
EVP Community Child Health, Paul H. Dworkin
EVP and COO, Theresa Hendricksen
EVP and Chief Administrative Officer, Ann Taylor
VP Connecticut Children's Medical Center Foundation, Martha E. Schall
Chief Strategy Officer and VP Marketing and Communications, Thomas C. Richardson
President Connecticut Children's Specialty Group, Dean Rapoza
VP Clinical Services and Chief Nursing Officer, Cheryl Hoey
President and COO, Gil Peri
SVP and CFO, Patrick Garvey
Physician-in-Chief, Juan C. Salazar
Director of Him and Revenue Cycle Initiatives, Kim Garvey

LOCATIONS

HQ: CONNECTICUT CHILDREN'S MEDICAL CENTER
282 WASHINGTON ST, HARTFORD, CT 061063322
Phone: 860 545-9000
Web: WWW.CONNECTICUTCHILDRENS.ORG

PRODUCTS/OPERATIONS

Selected Programs & Services
Acute Inpatient Rehabilitation
Adolescent Health
Asthma Center
Anesthesiology
Audiology
Bereavement
Cardiology
Cardiovascular Surgery
CCMC School
Center for Motion Analysis
Child and Family Support
Child Health Data Center
Child Protection
Childhood Injury Prevention
Childhood Obesity Awareness and Prevention

Clinical Nutrition
Craniofacial
Critical Care/Pediatric Intensive Care
Cyto-Genetics and Genetic Testing
Day Surgery
Dentistry
Developmental and Behavioral Pediatrics
Diagnostic Cardiology
Digestive Diseases Hepatology and Nutrition
Ear Nose and Throat
Echocardiography
EKG
Emergency Medicine
Emergency Psychiatry
Endocrinology and Diabetes
Feeding
Food Allergy
Genetics
General Surgery
Gynecology
Hand Surgery
Hematology and Oncology
High Risk Infant Follow Up
HIV
Infectious Diseases
Inpatient Medicine
Lead Prevention
Neonatology
Nephrology
Neurogenetics
Neurology
Neurophysiology Lab (EEG)
Neurophysiology - Video Telemetry
Neurosurgery
Occupational Therapy
Ophthalmology
Oral and Maxillofacial Surgery
Organ Transplantation Care
Orthopaedics
Orthotics and Prosthetics
Otolaryngology
Pain Medicine
Pediatric Medicine
Pediatric Pathology
Physical Therapy
Plastic Surgery
Primary Care
Pro-Kids: Primary Care for substance abuse exposed infants
Psychiatry/Psychology
Pulmonary Medicine
Pulmonary Function and Exercise Lab
Radiology
Rehabilitation Medicine
Research
Respiratory Care
Rheumatology
Sleep Diagnostic Laboratory
Special Kids Support Center
Speech-Language Pathology
Sports Medicine
Sports Physical Therapy
TEAM Club: weight management
Trauma Program - Video Telemetry
Urology

COMPETITORS

Backus
Baystate Health
Baystate Medical Center
Bridgeport Hospital
Bristol Hospital
Day Kimball Hospital
Griffin Health
Harrington Memorial Hospital
Hartford Health Care
Lawrence & Memorial Hospital
MidState Medical Center
New Milford Hospital
Saint Francis Hospital and Medical Center
St. Vincent's Health Services
Yale-New Haven Hospital
Yale-New Haven Hospital Saint Raphael Campus

HISTORICAL FINANCIALS
Company Type: Private

Income Statement
FYE: September 30

	REVENUE ($ mil.)	NET INCOME ($ mil.)	NET PROFIT MARGIN	EMPLOYEES
09/15	293	28	9.6%	1,117
09/14	256	(1)	—	—
09/13	264	(2)	—	—
09/10	210	10	4.8%	—
Annual Growth	6.9%	22.7%	—	—

2015 Year-End Financials
Return on assets: 12.1%   Cash ($ mil.): 8
Return on equity: 9.6%
Current ratio: 0.50

CONROE INDEPENDENT SCHOOL DISTRICT

EXECUTIVES

Superintendent, Don Stockton
Account Manager, Robin Hosea
Assistant Manager, Cathy Gibson
Director of Finance, Darrin Rice
Consultant, Julia Rieke
Real Estate Agent, Kathryn Connell

LOCATIONS

HQ: CONROE INDEPENDENT SCHOOL DISTRICT
3205 W DAVIS ST, CONROE, TX 773042039
Phone: 936 709-7751
Web: WWW.CONROEISD.NET

HISTORICAL FINANCIALS
Company Type: Private

Income Statement
FYE: August 31

	REVENUE ($ mil.)	NET INCOME ($ mil.)	NET PROFIT MARGIN	EMPLOYEES
08/16	590	81	13.9%	6,223
08/15	552	24	4.4%	—
08/14	510	(4)	—	—
08/07	315	20	6.3%	—
Annual Growth	7.2%	16.9%	—	—

2016 Year-End Financials
Return on assets: 2.7%   Cash ($ mil.): 6
Return on equity: 13.9%
Current ratio: 0.10

CONSERV FS, INC.

EXECUTIVES

General Manager, Dave Mottet
Manager, Mark M Musial
Vice-President, Gary Bormet
Manager, Jeff Kimmel
Finance Manager, Scott Gaunky
Manager, Curt Vacek
Director, Don Englum
Manager, Mike Gall
Auditors: CLIFTONLARSONALLEN LLP NORMA

LOCATIONS

HQ: CONSERV FS, INC.
1110 MCCONNELL RD, WOODSTOCK, IL 600987310
Phone: 815 334-5950
Web: WWW.CONSERVFS.COM

HISTORICAL FINANCIALS

Company Type: Private

Income Statement

FYE: August 31

	REVENUE ($ mil.)	NET INCOME ($ mil.)	NET PROFIT MARGIN	EMPLOYEES
08/15	197	7	3.9%	140
08/14	241	8	3.6%	—
08/13	221	7	3.2%	—
08/12	221	4	1.9%	—
Annual Growth	(3.6%)	21.8%	—	—

2015 Year-End Financials

Return on assets: 4.7%   Cash ($ mil.): 4
Return on equity: 3.9%
Current ratio: 0.80

CONSOLIDATED GRAIN & BARGE COMPANY

EXECUTIVES

Chief Executive Officer, Kevin D Adams
Credit Manager, Randolph Hart
Financial Executive, Robin Gerarve
Manager, Bill McBee
Personnel Director, Judy Keitel
Manager, Paul Kelly
Auditors: KPMG LLP NEW ORLEANS LOUISIA

LOCATIONS

HQ: CONSOLIDATED GRAIN & BARGE COMPANY
127 HWY 190 E SERVICE RD, COVINGTON, LA 70433
Phone: 985 867-3500
Web: WWW.CGB.COM

HISTORICAL FINANCIALS

Company Type: Private

Income Statement

FYE: May 31

	REVENUE ($ mil.)	NET INCOME ($ mil.)	NET PROFIT MARGIN	EMPLOYEES
05/16	5,759	21	0.4%	650
05/14	7,093	44	0.6%	—
05/12	5,996	50	0.8%	—
05/08	4,386	31	0.7%	—
Annual Growth	3.5%	(4.8%)	—	—

2016 Year-End Financials

Return on assets: 1.1%   Cash ($ mil.): —
Return on equity: 0.4%
Current ratio: 0.10

CONSTRUCTION MANAGEMENT SERVICES, INC.

EXECUTIVES

President, William A Goeller
VP Finance, Alan Hollander
Auditors: HORTY & HORTY PA WILMINGTO

LOCATIONS

HQ: CONSTRUCTION MANAGEMENT SERVICES, INC.
3600 SILVERSIDE RD, WILMINGTON, DE 198105100
Phone: 302 478-4200

HISTORICAL FINANCIALS

Company Type: Private

Income Statement

FYE: December 31

	REVENUE ($ mil.)	NET INCOME ($ mil.)	NET PROFIT MARGIN	EMPLOYEES
12/16	256	2	1.0%	1,300
12/15	223	1	0.8%	—
12/14	242	2	1.1%	—
12/13	197	1	0.7%	—
Annual Growth	9.2%	23.3%	—	—

2016 Year-End Financials

Return on assets: 4.1%   Cash ($ mil.): 2
Return on equity: 1.0%
Current ratio: 1.40

CONSUMER PRODUCT DISTRIBUTORS, INC.

Consumer Product Distributors helps convenience stores provide convenient services to their customers. The company which operates as J. Polep Distribution Services is a leading wholesale supplier serving more than 4000 convenience retailers in New York Pennsylvania and the New England states. J. Polep distributes a variety of products including cigarettes and other tobacco items candy dairy products frozen foods snack items and general merchandise as well as alcohol and other beverages. As part of its business J. Polep provides merchandising sales and marketing and technology services. The family-owned company was founded as Polep Tobacco in 1898 by Charles Polep.

Geographic Reach

The distribution company serves chain and independent retailers in six New England states as well as New York and Pennsylvania. Its distribution centers are located in Massachusetts Rhode Island and Connecticut.

Operations

Consumer Product Distributors ranks as one of the nation's top 12 convenience store distributors. To support its operations the company supplies customers with products through distribution centers located in Massachusetts (in Chicopee and Woburn) in Rhode Island (in Providence) and in Connecticut (in West Haven).

Mergers and Acquisitions

Company subsidiary Rachael's Food Corporation based in Chicopee Massachusetts entered the meat manufacturing business in late 2012 when the company acquired 122-year-old family-owned Grote and Weigel a hot dog and meat processor based in Bloomfield Connecticut. Soon after Rachael's Food Corporation also purchased family-owned meat processor Mucke's and transferred its operations to the Grote and Weigel unit. The 2012 purchases followed the company's acquisition of Springfield Smoked Fish. The food corporation's facilities are USDA-inspected and HACCP-certified.

EXECUTIVES

Vice President Of Sales, Steve Peterson
Vice President Trade Development and Sales Analytics, Joe Normand
Auditors: MEYERS BROTHERS KALICKA PC

LOCATIONS

HQ: CONSUMER PRODUCT DISTRIBUTORS, INC.
705 MEADOW ST, CHICOPEE, MA 010134820
Phone: 413 592-4141
Web: WWW.JPOLEP.COM

PRODUCTS/OPERATIONS

Selected Products
Alcohol
  Spirits
  Wine
Automotive
  Branded Motor Oils
  Mag 1
  Additives
  Cleaning Supplies
Bakery/Pastry
  Rachael's Gourmet
  Mrs. Freshley's
  Dolly Madison
  Bon Appetite
  Bellow's House
  Diana's
  Table Talk
Beverages
  Poland Springs (Nestle Waters)
  Adirondack Soda
  Arizona
  Florida's Natural
  Simply Juices
  Sweet Leaf Tea
  Trade Winds
  Daily Juice

Selected Services
Credit & Return Policy
Management Information Systems
Merchandising Support
Sales and Marketing Support

COMPETITORS

Atlantic Dominion	Harold Levinson
C&S Wholesale	McLane
Core-Mark	SUPERVALU
Eby-Brown	Tripifoods
H. T. Hackney	

HISTORICAL FINANCIALS

Company Type: Private

Income Statement

FYE: October 1

	REVENUE ($ mil.)	NET INCOME ($ mil.)	NET PROFIT MARGIN	EMPLOYEES
10/16	1,005	5	0.6%	400
10/15*	968	2	0.3%	—
09/14	898	2	0.3%	—
09/13	855	2	0.3%	—
Annual Growth	5.5%	24.3%	—	—

*Fiscal year change

2016 Year-End Financials

Return on assets: 3.0%   Cash ($ mil.): 5
Return on equity: 0.6%
Current ratio: 2.10

CONSUMER REPORTS, INC.

Consumers Union of United States (CU) inspires both trust and fear. Best known for publishing Consumer Reports magazine the independent not-for-profit organization also serves as a consumer watchdog through other print publications and the Web (ConsumerReports.org). Its subscription site rates products ranging from candy bars to cars. CU tests and rates thousands of products annually through its National Testing and Research Center. CU accepts no advertising and derives income from the sale of Consumer Reports and other services and from non-commercial contributions grants and fees. CU traces its roots to 1926 when engineer Frederick Schlink organized a "consumer club" to rate products.

Operations

CU testifies before legislative and regulatory entities and files lawsuits on behalf of consumers. The organization is governed by an 18-member board. Board members are elected by CU members and meet three times a year.

Geographic Reach

CU's magazines websites and newsletters have a combined subscription base of more than 8 million.

At its headquarters in Yonkers New York CU houses the Testing and Research Center which consists of 50 labs and offices. The organization also has an Auto Test Center in Connecticut; and three advocacy offices in Washington DC; Austin Texas; and San Francisco California.

Sales and Marketing

The company's major industry markets include energy health care media and safety.

Strategy

To preserve its independence CU does not permit its ratings or comments to be used commercially.

In addition to its Consumer Reports publication CU publishes ShopSmart a magazine aimed at women who want a quick read on consumer items such as food beauty products and home and yard products. CU also covers health information through its ConsumerReportsHealth.org website and the Consumer Reports Health Ratings Center. It has a presence in the blogging world with Consumerist.com which provides snarky coverage of retail markups and shopper complaints. Rounding out its portfolio of offerings the organization delivers ratings of product categories to smart phones via its Consumer Reports Mobile service.

HISTORY

In 1926 engineer Frederick Schlink organized a "consumer club" (in White Plains New York) which distributed lists of recommended and non-recommended products. The lists led to the founding of Consumers' Research and a magazine devoted to testing products.

Schlink moved the group to Washington New Jersey in 1933. In 1935 three employees formed a union. Schlink fired them. Faced with another strike that year Schlink accused the strikers of being "Red" and responded with strikebreakers and armed detectives. The next year the strikers set up their own organization the Consumers Union of United States (CU).

CU's first magazine Consumers Union Reports came out three months later and rated products that the fledgling organization could afford to test such as soap and breakfast cereals. Subsequent issues focused on food and drug regulation and working conditions for women in textile mills.

The organization drew the wrath of both Reader's Digest and Good Housekeeping (which accused it in 1939 of prolonging the Depression). The next year the House Un-American Activities Committee put CU on its list of suspect organizations. CU cut staff and dropped "Union" from its magazine title but circulation remained low until after WWII.

By 1950 however Americans began consuming again helping to boost circulation to almost 400000. During the 1950s CU published a series of reports on the health hazards of smoking.

In 1960 CU helped found the International Organization of Consumers Unions (now Consumers International) to foster the consumer movement worldwide. Rhoda Karpatkin was hired as publisher in 1974. During the 1970s CU established consumer advocacy offices in California Texas and Washington DC.

Recession and an increase in not-for-profit mailing rates caused the organization to lose money in the early 1980s. CU looked to its readers who donated more than $3 million. The organization was hit by a 13-week strike in 1984 by union members calling for more say in management.

In 1996 CU slapped "not acceptable" ratings on the Isuzu Trooper and the Acura SLX. The next year the National Highway Traffic Safety Administration declared that CU's testing procedure of the Trooper was flawed but CU stood by its tests of the vehicle.

CU hit another bump in 1998 when it was compelled to retract a story on the nutritional value of Iams and Eukanuba pet food. Admitting its test results were incorrect CU's retraction of the story was something of a rarity — its last retraction had occurred almost 20 years earlier when the organization retracted a story on condoms.

A legal dispute broke out in 1999 between CU and automakers Isuzu and Suzuki which claimed negative reviews by Consumer Reports constituted defamation. The following year a jury found CU guilty of falsely reporting on the Isuzu but declined to impose fines on the publisher. (Suzuki eventually settled its case out of court in 2004.)

Karpatkin announced she would step down as president in 2001 and was replaced by chairman James Guest. That same year CU agreed to license its content to Internet portal Yahoo! Retailer Sharper Image (later TSIC) sued CU over an article unflattering to the company's popular air purifier device but a judge threw out the suit in late 2004.

In 2006 CU launched ShopSmart a shopping magazine geared at women aged 30 to 45. The next year it launched ConsumerReportsHealth.org and the Consumer Reports Health Ratings Center. In 2009 the company entered the blogging world with Consumerist.com which it purchased from Gawker Media.

The following year it introduced its Consumer Reports Mobile service which delivers product ratings to cell phones. Feats for CU in 2010 include discoveries of a potential safety hazard of Toyota's Lexus GX460 and a signal-loss problem with Apple's phone 4 which resulted in a recall from Toyota and Apple's announcement of a free remedy.

EXECUTIVES

Senior Vice President Information Products, John Sateja

Vice President for External Affairs and Information Services, Elizabeth Imholz

President and CEO, James A. (Jim) Guest

Director Policy Outreach and Southwest Office, Reggie James

Managing Director Consumer Reports Best Buy Drugs, Steve Findlay

Vice President external Affairs and Information Services, Chris Meyer

Vice President and General Counsel, Eileen Hershenov

Vice President of Sales Western Region, Ellen Klosz

Senior Executive Vice President and Regional Banking Group Head, Erin Gudeux

Vice President For Institutional Advancement, Michael Visconti

Treas, Steven Hill

Auditors: KPMG LLP NEW YORK NY

LOCATIONS

HQ: CONSUMER REPORTS, INC.
101 TRUMAN AVE, YONKERS, NY 107031044
Phone: 914 378-2000
Web: WWW.CONSUMERSUNION.ORG

PRODUCTS/OPERATIONS

2016 Sales

	$ mil.	% of total
Subscriptions newsstand & other sales	214	87
Contributions	28	12
Net assets released from restrictions	3	1
Other	0	-
Total	**247**	**100**

Content Areas

Content Areas
Autos
Food
Health Care
Money
Phones and Media
Product Safety

Selected Offerings

Magazines and newsletters
  Consumer Reports Magazine
  Consumer Reports Money Advisor (newsletter)
  Consumer Reports on Health (newsletter)
  ShopSmart
Websites
  ConsumerReports.org
  ConsumerReportsHealth.org
  Consumerist.com

COMPETITORS

Better Business Bureaus	National Technical Systems
Hearst Magazines	RELX Group
International Data Group	Shopping.com
J.D. Power	Trusted Media Brands
Kelley Blue Book	Underwriters Labs
	Yelp

HISTORICAL FINANCIALS

Company Type: Private

Income Statement

FYE: May 31

	REVENUE ($ mil.)	NET INCOME ($ mil.)	NET PROFIT MARGIN	EMPLOYEES
05/15	263	3	1.3%	480
05/14	269	10	3.9%	—
05/13	259	3	1.4%	—
05/11	252	32	12.9%	—
Annual Growth	1.0%	(43.1%)	—	—

2015 Year-End Financials

Return on assets: 5.4%
Return on equity: 1.3%
Current ratio: 0.20

Cash ($ mil.): 25

CONVERGINT TECHNOLOGIES LLC

It's IP for IT at Convergint Technologies. Convergint integrates IT (information technology) and physical security systems at both single- and multi-site facilities. Its security systems include IP (internet protocol) video and cameras biometrics card access and perimeter protection. The company designs installs as well as repairs electronic security fire alarm and life safety and building automation systems for a diverse group of commercial industrial and government customers. Clients have included Boeing and the Oregon Department of Transportation. As a value-added reseller (VAR) and partner Convergint installs products from such major OEMs as Honeywell Lenel and S2 Security.

Geographic Reach

Convergint serves customers across North America.

Strategy

Convergint Technologies' growth is based in part on its ability to delegate. Specifically each business unit is charged with developing a strategic direction. The company claims that as a result it has pursued new opportunities such as in health care technologies and even opened offices in promising markets.

Convergint Technologies is simultaneously focused on delivering tailor-made building system products and services. Unlike some competitors it strives to integrate physical security access systems with logical access control systems. Customers benefit from a more cost effective and efficient system infrastructure which can pave the way for Convergint Technologies to build sales.

Mergers and Acquisitions

In 2016 the company acquired the Total Recall a video-centric security technology provider specializing in surveillance solutions. Also during 2016 Convergint Technologies acquired Enion AG Integrated Security Solutions. Enion offers security solutions tailored to the complex needs of its clients.

EXECUTIVES

SVP Eastern Region, Sean Flint
VP Electronic Security Division, Tony Varco
VP Fire Alarm and Life Safety Division, Barry Yatzor
EVP, Mike Mathes
VP and CFO, Alan C. Bergschneider
President and CEO, Ken Lochiatto
VP Canadian Operations, Brian Haw
CEO ICD Security Solutions, Leo Luo
Managing Director Beacon Security, Steve Dorking
Vice President and General Manager, Tim Beasley
Vice President Business Development, Mike Kuhn
Vice President and General Manager, Robert Saunders
Vice President Chief Financial Officer General Counsel, Wally Winkel
Vice President, Greg Kubacki
Vice President Global Accounts, Michael Duncan
Vice President Strategic Initiatives, Eric Yunag
Vice President and General Manager, Scott Swansen
Vice President, Rob Saunders
Vice President Business Technology, Tom Schmitt
Vice President Global Accounts EMEA, Brenda Koesterman
Chairman, Dan Moceri
Auditors: PLANTE & MORAN PLLC CHICAGO

LOCATIONS

HQ: CONVERGINT TECHNOLOGIES LLC
  1 COMMERCE DR, SCHAUMBURG, IL 601735302
Phone: 847 620-5000

PRODUCTS/OPERATIONS

Selected Services
Building automation
Electronic security
Fire alarm & life safety
Installation services
Support services

COMPETITORS

ADT	Henry Bros.
Advanced Security &	Electronics
Controls	Professional Security
Benson Systems	Technologies

HISTORICAL FINANCIALS
Company Type: Private

Income Statement
FYE: December 31

	REVENUE ($ mil.)	NET INCOME ($ mil.)	NET PROFIT MARGIN	EMPLOYEES
12/15	469	5	1.2%	2,327
12/14	408	5	1.3%	—
12/12	96	(7)	—	—
Annual Growth	69.2%	—	—	—

2015 Year-End Financials

Return on assets: 5.0%
Return on equity: 1.2%
Current ratio: 1.30

Cash ($ mil.): 37

CONWAY HOSPITAL, INC.

Conway Medical Center (CMC) finds a way to provide a wide range of health care services to residents of eastern South Carolina. The private not-for-profit 210-bed hospital (served by a medical staff of 200) provides services including primary diagnostic emergency surgical maternal and pediatric and rehabilitative care. CMC specializes in heart health hospice care and occupational health. Additionally CMC operates the Kingston Nursing Center an about 90-bed long-term nursing and rehabilitative care facility and the Conway Physicians Group which is home to about 10 physician practices offering a range of specialties.

Geographic Reach

The hospital system serves patients in eastern South Carolina.

Financial Performance

CMC receives financial support in part through donations to the Conway Medical Center Foundation which was founded in 1988 to provide financial and voluntary staffing support to the hospital.

Company Background

The center expanded its operations in 2009 with the completion of a new patient tower with about 65 patient beds new nurses stations for streamlined patient care and updated technology.

EXECUTIVES

Chief Executive Officer, Philip A Clayton
Manager, Christene Swift
Manager, Camille Gagne
Executive Director, Bernard Berns

LOCATIONS

HQ: CONWAY HOSPITAL, INC.
  300 SINGLETON RIDGE RD, CONWAY, SC 295269142
Phone: 843 347-7111
Web: WWW.CONWAYHOSPITAL.COM

PRODUCTS/OPERATIONS

Selected Departments and Services
Center for Wound Healing
Critical Care Services
Diabetes Management
Diagnostic
Endoscopy
Heart Center
Hospice
Joint Replacement Center
Laboratory Services
Long Term Care
Mammography
Medical Services Center
Palliative Care
Pediatric Center
Pulmonary Rehabilitation
Rehabilitation
Senior Privileges Club
Sleep Disorders Center
Subacute
Surgical Services
The Birthplace
Weight Loss Surgery
Wellness & Fitness Center

COMPETITORS

Carolinas Hospital System	Medical University of South Carolina
Georgetown Hospital System	New Hanover Regional Medical Center
Grand Strand Regional Medical Center	Roper St. Francis Healthcare
McLeod Health	

HISTORICAL FINANCIALS
Company Type: Private

Income Statement
FYE: September 30

	REVENUE ($ mil.)	NET INCOME ($ mil.)	NET PROFIT MARGIN	EMPLOYEES
09/15	191	18	9.6%	1,200
09/14	179	28	15.8%	—
09/13	162	21	13.3%	—
09/12	158	16	10.2%	—
Annual Growth	6.6%	4.2%	—	—

2015 Year-End Financials

Return on assets: 3.8%
Return on equity: 9.6%
Current ratio: 1.20

Cash ($ mil.): 14

COOK CHILDREN'S HEALTH PLAN

EXECUTIVES

President, Doris Hunt
Director, Claire Murtha
Project Manager, Barbara Flores
Director, Angel Hernandez
Manager, Beatriz Ruiz
Supervisor, Brad Allen
Auditors: BKD LLP HOUSTON TX

HQ: COOK CHILDREN'S HEALTH PLAN
801 7TH AVE, FORT WORTH, TX 761042733
Phone: 817 334-2247

HISTORICAL FINANCIALS
Company Type: Private

Income Statement
FYE: September 30

	REVENUE ($ mil.)	NET INCOME ($ mil.)	NET PROFIT MARGIN	EMPLOYEES
09/15	307	17	5.8%	27
09/14	284	11	3.9%	—
09/13	259	5	2.0%	—
09/09	126	(3)	—	—
Annual Growth	16.0%	—	—	—

2015 Year-End Financials
Return on assets: 9.0%   Cash ($ mil.): 62
Return on equity: 5.8%
Current ratio: 2.30

COOK CHILDREN'S MEDICAL CENTER

EXECUTIVES

President, Rick W Merrill
Director, Winney King
Director, Cathy Harris

LOCATIONS

HQ: COOK CHILDREN'S MEDICAL CENTER
801 7TH AVE, FORT WORTH, TX 761042796
Phone: 682 885-4000
Web: WWW.COOKCHILDRENS.ORG

HISTORICAL FINANCIALS
Company Type: Private

Income Statement
FYE: September 30

	REVENUE ($ mil.)	NET INCOME ($ mil.)	NET PROFIT MARGIN	EMPLOYEES
09/15	753	159	21.1%	2,000
09/14	753	107	14.2%	—
09/13	828	160	19.4%	—
09/09	563	99	17.7%	—
Annual Growth	5.0%	8.1%	—	—

2015 Year-End Financials
Return on assets: 4.2%   Cash ($ mil.): 255
Return on equity: 21.1%
Current ratio: 0.70

COOK CHILDREN'S PHYSICIAN NETWORK

EXECUTIVES

President, W Britt Nelson
Board of Directors, Kimberly Aaron
Finance Manager, Pam Foster

HQ: COOK CHILDREN'S PHYSICIAN NETWORK
801 7TH AVE, FORT WORTH, TX 761042733
Phone: 682 885-6800

HISTORICAL FINANCIALS
Company Type: Private

Income Statement
FYE: September 30

	REVENUE ($ mil.)	NET INCOME ($ mil.)	NET PROFIT MARGIN	EMPLOYEES
09/15	250	0	0.1%	801
09/14	230	(0)	—	—
09/13	216	3	1.5%	—
09/09	170	2	1.3%	—
Annual Growth	6.6%	(34.5%)	—	—

2015 Year-End Financials
Return on assets: 2.8%   Cash ($ mil.): 10
Return on equity: 0.1%
Current ratio: 3.00

COOPERATIVE ELEVATOR CO.

Cooperative Elevator represents and serves northern Michigan bean and grain farmers. The agricultural cooperative is made up of approximately 900 member/owners. It operates storage facilities and processing plants offers crop marketing and agronomy services and provides farm supplies to its members including seed feed fertilizer herbicides fuel and agricultural chemicals. The co-op's bean farmers grow black red pinto and navy beans which are distributed in bulk throughout the US as well as in Africa and the Caribbean. Cooperative Elevator's grain farmers produce wheat soy corn barley and oats and the co-op provides storage and market services such as price updates for these commodities.

EXECUTIVES

Board of Directors, Les Roth
Financial Executive, Audy Gusa
Manager, Carl Maxwell
Manager, Ron Dubs
Plant Engineering Manager, Walt Swiastyn
Auditors: CLIFTONLARSONALLEN LLP MIDDLE

LOCATIONS

HQ: COOPERATIVE ELEVATOR CO.
7211 E MICHIGAN AVE, PIGEON, MI 487555202
Phone: 989 453-4500
Web: WWW.COOPELEV.COM

COMPETITORS

ADM	Kelley Bean
CHS	Organic Bean & Grain
Cargill	Star of the West
Chippewa Valley Bean	United Producers
Della Natura Commodities	Zeeland Farm

HISTORICAL FINANCIALS
Company Type: Private

Income Statement
FYE: January 31

	REVENUE ($ mil.)	NET INCOME ($ mil.)	NET PROFIT MARGIN	EMPLOYEES
01/16	209	5	2.7%	136
01/15	216	8	3.8%	—
01/14	277	9	3.6%	—
01/13	293	12	4.4%	—
Annual Growth	(10.5%)	(23.8%)	—	—

2016 Year-End Financials
Return on assets: 8.3%   Cash ($ mil.): —
Return on equity: 2.7%
Current ratio: 0.10

COOPERATIVE RESOURCES INTERNATIONAL, INC.

EXECUTIVES

Chief Executive Officer, R D Wilson
Sales Manager, James Bayne
Sales Manager, Larry Swartz
Vice-President, David Koepke
Operations Manager, Ron Visser
Manager, Monica Vick
Sales Manager, Erin Berger
Manager, Dale Culver
Vice-President, Huub Plate
Auditors: WIPFLI LLP APPLETON WI

LOCATIONS

HQ: COOPERATIVE RESOURCES INTERNATIONAL, INC.
117 E GREEN BAY ST, SHAWANO, WI 541662443
Phone: 715 526-2141
Web: WWW.CRI.CRINET.COM

HISTORICAL FINANCIALS
Company Type: Private

Income Statement
FYE: September 30

	REVENUE ($ mil.)	NET INCOME ($ mil.)	NET PROFIT MARGIN	EMPLOYEES
09/15	202	1	0.7%	1,500
09/14	191	0	0.1%	—
/*	0	0	—	—
Annual Growth	—	—	—	—

*Fiscal year change

2015 Year-End Financials
Return on assets: 4.2%   Cash ($ mil.): 1
Return on equity: 0.7%
Current ratio: 0.50

COPPEL CORPORATION

EXECUTIVES

Chief Executive Officer, Hermann Gerzabek

President, Ruben Coppel
Financial Executive, Olejario Gomez
Administrative Assistant, Gloria Perez
Auditors: BEACH FLEISCHMAN PC TUCSON A

LOCATIONS

HQ: COPPEL CORPORATION
503 SCARONI AVE, CALEXICO, CA 922319791
Phone: 760 357-3707
Web: WWW.COPPEL.COM

HISTORICAL FINANCIALS

Company Type: Private

Income Statement

FYE: December 31

	REVENUE ($ mil.)	NET INCOME ($ mil.)	NET PROFIT MARGIN	EMPLOYEES
12/15	335	4	1.5%	80
12/14	332	4	1.4%	—
12/13	248	3	1.2%	—
12/12	215	3	1.5%	—
Annual Growth	16.0%	15.2%	—	—

2015 Year-End Financials

Return on assets: 3.1%   Cash ($ mil.): —
Return on equity: 1.5%
Current ratio: 0.30

CORE CONSTRUCTION GROUP, LTD.

EXECUTIVES

President, Mark A Steffen
Manager, Tim Hickey

LOCATIONS

HQ: CORE CONSTRUCTION GROUP, LTD.
866 N MAIN ST, MORTON, IL 615501602
Phone: 309 263-0808
Web: WWW.CORECONSTRUCT.COM

HISTORICAL FINANCIALS

Company Type: Private

Income Statement

FYE: December 31

	REVENUE ($ mil.)	NET INCOME ($ mil.)	NET PROFIT MARGIN	EMPLOYEES
12/15	782	0	—	450
12/12	624	0	—	—
12/06	620	0	—	—
12/05	1,902	0	—	—
Annual Growth	—	—	—	—

2015 Year-End Financials

Return on assets: 15.5%   Cash ($ mil.): 34
Return on equity: —
Current ratio: 1.00

CORE CONSTRUCTION, INC.

CORE Construction fits into the core clique of contractors in the southwestern US. The company formerly Targent General is one of the top contractors in the region; it also has offices in Florida and Illinois. CORE offers construction management general contracting and design/build services for municipal educational health care office residential retail sports institutional and industrial projects. It has worked on projects as diverse as Phoenix's Chase Field Ballpark Dodge Theatre and Lower Buckeye Jail. German immigrant Otto Baum founded the company in 1937.

CORE Construction is the seventh largest builder of schools in the US. The company is focusing its efforts on commercial developments affordable housing and senior care facilities.

CORE Construction has regional offices in Arizona Florida Illinois Nevada and Texas

ARIG (Al Rajhi Investment Group) owns a majority stake in the company.

EXECUTIVES

Executive Vice President SEC, Dennis Barber
Vice President, Fred Knapp
Vice President Of Operations, Brad Roberts
Vice President Director of Operations, Tim Erickson

LOCATIONS

HQ: CORE CONSTRUCTION, INC.
3036 E GREENWAY RD, PHOENIX, AZ 850324414
Phone: 602 494-0800
Web: WWW.CORECONSTRUCTION.COM

COMPETITORS

DPR Construction	Summit Builders
Jaynes Companies	Sundt
Kitchell	Tutor Perini
McCarthy Building	

HISTORICAL FINANCIALS

Company Type: Private

Income Statement

FYE: December 31

	REVENUE ($ mil.)	NET INCOME ($ mil.)	NET PROFIT MARGIN	EMPLOYEES
12/15	175	0	—	60
12/14	133	0	—	—
12/13	219	0	—	—
12/12	162	0	—	—
Annual Growth	2.7%	—	—	—

2015 Year-End Financials

Return on assets: 15.7%   Cash ($ mil.): 7
Return on equity: —
Current ratio: 0.80

CORONA-NORCO UNIFIED SCHOOL DISTRICT

EXECUTIVES

Chief Executive Officer, Cathy L Sciortino
Board of Directors, Linda Hawkins
Superintendent, Anita Lavelle
Supervisor, Brian Parliman
Vice-President, Carol Bento
Supervisor, Jason Vannimwegen
Assistant Manager, Lisa Simon
Auditors: VAVRINEK TRINE DAY & CO LL

LOCATIONS

HQ: CORONA-NORCO UNIFIED SCHOOL DISTRICT
2820 CLARK AVE, NORCO, CA 928601903
Phone: 951 736-5000
Web: WWW.CNUSD.K12.CA.US

HISTORICAL FINANCIALS

Company Type: Private

Income Statement

FYE: June 30

	REVENUE ($ mil.)	NET INCOME ($ mil.)	NET PROFIT MARGIN	EMPLOYEES
06/16	635	113	17.8%	614
06/11	1	(20)	—	—
06/10	0	0	92.3%	—
06/06	0	0	—	—
Annual Growth	—	—	—	—

COTTAGE HEALTH

EXECUTIVES

President, Ronald C Werft
Vice-President, Tiana Riskowski
Board of Directors, Chris Flynn
Board of Directors, Donna Kell
Board of Directors, J K Beckmen

LOCATIONS

HQ: COTTAGE HEALTH
400 W PUEBLO ST, SANTA BARBARA, CA 931054353
Phone: 805 682-7111
Web: WWW.COTTAGEHEALTH.ORG

HISTORICAL FINANCIALS

Company Type: Private

Income Statement

FYE: December 31

	REVENUE ($ mil.)	NET INCOME ($ mil.)	NET PROFIT MARGIN	EMPLOYEES
12/15	610	(15)	—	2,422
12/14	594	(11)	—	—
12/13	60	0	0.5%	—
12/08	457	(142)	—	—
Annual Growth	4.2%	—	—	—

2015 Year-End Financials

Return on assets: 6.7%   Cash ($ mil.): 28
Return on equity: (-2.5%)
Current ratio: 1.80

COUNCIL ROCK SCHOOL DISTRICT

EXECUTIVES

Superintendent, Robert Fraser
Treasurer, Robert Riegel
Superintendent, Robert J Fraser
Director, Joy McClendon
Auditors: BBD LLP PHILADELPHIA PENNSY

LOCATIONS

HQ: COUNCIL ROCK SCHOOL DISTRICT
  30 N CHANCELLOR ST, NEWTOWN, PA 189402202
Phone: 215 944-1000
Web: WWW.CRSD.ORG

HISTORICAL FINANCIALS
Company Type: Private

Income Statement
FYE: June 30

	REVENUE ($ mil.)	NET INCOME ($ mil.)	NET PROFIT MARGIN	EMPLOYEES
06/16	216	44	20.5%	1,700
06/15	215	4	2.1%	
06/14	207	(3)	—	
06/11	196	(2)	—	
Annual Growth	2.0%	—	—	

2016 Year-End Financials

Return on assets: 3.2% Cash ($ mil.): 121
Return on equity: 20.5%
Current ratio: 4.80

COUNTY OF BERKELEY

EXECUTIVES

Supervisor, Daniel Davis
Director of Finance, Kace Smith
Manager, Heather Graham
Manager, Janet B Jurosko
General Manager, Jennifer Hinson
Engineer, Clinton Busby
Council Member, Cathy Davis
Director, Gregory Rines
Auditors: GREENE FINNEY & HORTON LLP M

LOCATIONS

HQ: COUNTY OF BERKELEY
  1003 HIGHWAY 52, MONCKS CORNER, SC
  294613007
Phone: 843 761-6900
Web: WWW.BERKELEYCOUNTYSC.GOV

HISTORICAL FINANCIALS
Company Type: Private

Income Statement
FYE: June 30

	REVENUE ($ mil.)	NET INCOME ($ mil.)	NET PROFIT MARGIN	EMPLOYEES
06/16	223	(5)	—	700
06/15	107	4	4.2%	
06/14	0	0	—	
06/13	104	15	14.5%	
Annual Growth	28.8%	—	—	

2016 Year-End Financials

Return on assets: 16.1% Cash ($ mil.): 92
Return on equity: (-2.5%)
Current ratio: 1.70

COUNTY OF CLARK

EXECUTIVES

Manager, Don Burnette
Executive Secretary, Judy Gronguist
Manager, Kathy Jenkins
Senior Manager, Dan Kulin
Manager, Alicia Irwin
Auditors: KAFOURY ARMSTRONG & CO CPAS

LOCATIONS

HQ: COUNTY OF CLARK
  500 S GRAND CENTRAL PKWY # 6, LAS VEGAS, NV
  891554502
Phone: 702 455-3530

HISTORICAL FINANCIALS
Company Type: Private

Income Statement
FYE: June 30

	REVENUE ($ mil.)	NET INCOME ($ mil.)	NET PROFIT MARGIN	EMPLOYEES
06/16	2,768	74	2.7%	8,528
06/15	2,595	(26)	—	
06/13	2,372	(133)	—	
06/07	2,791	280	10.0%	
Annual Growth	(0.1%)	(13.6%)	—	

COUNTY OF CLAYTON

EXECUTIVES

Chairman, Eldrin Bell
Chief Financial Officer, Ramona Thurman
Chief Operating Officer, Anthony Brister
Commissioner, Jeffrey Turner
Manager, Rose Dejasus
Officer, James Walker
Officer, Tom Reimers
Commissioner, Wole Ralph
Auditors: MAULDIN & JENKINS LLC MACON

LOCATIONS

HQ: COUNTY OF CLAYTON
  112 SMITH ST, JONESBORO, GA 302363539
Phone: 770 477-3208
Web: WWW.CLAYTONCOUNTYGA.GOV

HISTORICAL FINANCIALS
Company Type: Private

Income Statement
FYE: June 30

	REVENUE ($ mil.)	NET INCOME ($ mil.)	NET PROFIT MARGIN	EMPLOYEES
06/16	276	(11)	—	2,400
06/15	260	(2)	—	
06/14	0	0	—	
06/13	267	7	2.9%	
Annual Growth	1.2%	—	—	

2016 Year-End Financials

Return on assets: 5.5% Cash ($ mil.): 292
Return on equity: (-4.2%)
Current ratio: —

COUNTY OF DEKALB

EXECUTIVES

Chief Executive Officer, Vernon Jones
Board of Directors, Talisa R Clark
Officer, Kelvin Walton
Officer, Felton Williams
Manager, Steadman Scavella
Auditors: KPMG LLP ATLANTA GA

LOCATIONS

HQ: COUNTY OF DEKALB
  1300 COMMERCE DR, DECATUR, GA 300303222
Phone: 404 371-2881
Web: WWW.CO.DEKALB.GA.US

HISTORICAL FINANCIALS
Company Type: Private

Income Statement
FYE: December 31

	REVENUE ($ mil.)	NET INCOME ($ mil.)	NET PROFIT MARGIN	EMPLOYEES
12/15	599	(3)	—	7,300
12/10	583	(39)	—	
12/09	601	(71)	—	
Annual Growth	(0.1%)	—	—	

2015 Year-End Financials

Return on assets: 10.6% Cash ($ mil.): 578
Return on equity: (-0.6%)
Current ratio: —

COUNTY OF RIVERSIDE

EXECUTIVES

Superintendent, Bob Buster
Superintendent, John Tavaglinoe
Superintendent, Jeff Stone
Superintendent, Cynthia R
Superintendent, Marion Ashley
Director, Jean Strey
Director, John Mooney
Director, Lucas Robert
Manager, Ronald W Komers
Auditors: BROWN ARMSTRONG ACCOUNTANCY CO

LOCATIONS

HQ: COUNTY OF RIVERSIDE
  4080 LEMON ST FL 11, RIVERSIDE, CA 925013609
Phone: 951 955-1110
Web: WWW.COUNTYOFRIVERSIDE.US

HISTORICAL FINANCIALS
Company Type: Private

Income Statement
FYE: June 30

	REVENUE ($ mil.)	NET INCOME ($ mil.)	NET PROFIT MARGIN	EMPLOYEES
06/16	3,390	(124)	—	20,000
06/15	3,245	293	9.0%	
Annual Growth	4.5%	—	—	

COUNTY OF SUFFOLK

EXECUTIVES

Senior Manager, Steve Levy
Treasurer, Angie M Carpenter
Financial Executive, Joseph Sawicki
District Manager, Paul Tenyenhuis
Manager, Connie Corso
Financial Executive, Joseph Junior
Manager, Anthony Ceglio
Auditors: CHERRY BEKAERT LLP RICHMOND

LOCATIONS

HQ: COUNTY OF SUFFOLK
100 VETERANS HWY, HAUPPAUGE, NY 117885402
Phone: 631 853-4000

HISTORICAL FINANCIALS
Company Type: Private

Income Statement
FYE: December 31

	REVENUE ($ mil.)	NET INCOME ($ mil.)	NET PROFIT MARGIN	EMPLOYEES
12/15	2,938	(71)	—	12,814
12/12	2,712	(138)	—	
12/11	2,729	(79)	—	
Annual Growth	1.9%	—	—	—

2015 Year-End Financials

Return on assets: 15.4%   Cash ($ mil.): 882
Return on equity: (-2.4%)
Current ratio: 0.70

COVENANT HEALTH SYSTEM

Covenant Health System ties West Texas and Eastern New Mexico together with quality health care. The health services provider offers some 1100 beds in its five primary acute-care and specialty hospitals; it also manages about a dozen affiliated community hospitals. Covenant Health System part of Providence St. Joseph Health also maintains a network of family health care and medical clinics. Covenant Health System's major facilities are Covenant Medical Center Covenant Specialty Hospital and Covenant Women's and Children's Hospital. The health system also includes some 20 clinics and 50 physician practices and its extensive outreach programs target isolated rural communities with mobile services.

Operations
The system's five hospitals include Covenant Medical Center Covenant Medical Center-Lakeside Covenant Specialty Hospital and Covenant Children's Hospital. It also operates three schools for healthcare careers in nursing radiography and surgical technology respectively.

Strategy
The Christian-based system which calls itself a ministry focuses on providing benefits to the community. Its key priorities include mental health dentistry diabetes home health management and childhood obesity.

Background
Covenant Health System was founded when two Lubbock hospitals St. Mary of the Plains Hospital (now known as Covenant Medical Center-Lakeside) and the Lubbock Methodist Hospital System (including the flagship Methodist Hospital which

is now known as Covenant Medical Center) merged in 1998.

EXECUTIVES

Director of Patient Care Nursing, Susan Sayari
Vice President, Sharon Prather
Vpassociate General Counsel, James Kelly
Secretary Department, Cindy Crow
Auditors: ERNST & YOUNG US LLP AUSTIN

LOCATIONS

HQ: COVENANT HEALTH SYSTEM
3615 19TH ST, LUBBOCK, TX 794101209
Phone: 806 725-1011

COMPETITORS

Baptist St. Anthony's Health System
Del Sol Medical Center
HealthSouth
Hunt Memorial
NW Texas Healthcare
Parkland Health & Hospital System
Tenet Healthcare
Texas Health Resources
The Methodist Health System
University Medical Center of El Paso

HISTORICAL FINANCIALS
Company Type: Private

Income Statement
FYE: June 30

	REVENUE ($ mil.)	NET INCOME ($ mil.)	NET PROFIT MARGIN	EMPLOYEES
06/15	703	76	10.9%	5,700
06/13	552	35	6.5%	—
06/09	1,185	(38)	—	—
Annual Growth	(8.3%)	—	—	—

2015 Year-End Financials

Return on assets: 5.6%   Cash ($ mil.): 39
Return on equity: 10.9%
Current ratio: 3.00

COVENANT MEDICAL CENTER, INC.

Covenant Medical Center (operating as Covenant HealthCare) has made a pact with Wolverine Staters to try to keep them in good health. The not-for-profit health care provider operates more than 20 inpatient and outpatient care facilities including its two main Covenant Medical Center campuses. It serves residents in a 20-county area of east-central Michigan with additional facilities in Bay City Frankenmuth and Midland. Specialized care services include cardiovascular health cancer treatment and obstetrics. The regional health care system has more about 650 beds.

Operations
Covenant HealthCare programs and services range from high-risk obstetrics and neonatal/pediatric intensive care to acute care. Its assets include cardiology oncology orthopedics robotic surgery and Level II Adult and Pediatric Trauma Center.

The health system has more than 20 inpatient and outpatient facilities and a trauma/emergency department that provides 85000 visits per year. The system employs more than 500 physicians from 52 medical specialties.

Sales and Marketing
Covenant HealthCare markets its services via social media.

Financial Performance

In 2014 the company's revenue increased 4% to $528 million as patient service revenue rose; this gain was partially offset by a decline in realized gain and other revenues. An increase in salaries and wages as well as higher supplies expenses led to a 12% decline in net income (to $57 million).

Cash flow from operations also fell slipping 20% to $48 million as accounts receivable increased.

Strategy
Expanding its infrastructure to keep up with demand in 2014 Covenant HealthCare added 11456 sq. ft. to its Emergency Department. The addition allows for more efficient triage enhanced patient waiting areas and additional space for current technology. It added 18 treatment bays to the existing 47 and also brought a dedicated CT scanner and mini-laboratory within the department.

Also that year it opened the assisted living community of Covenant Glen in Frankenmuth. The 35000 sq. ft. structure has 45 rooms (15 dedicated to memory care and 30 with assisted living beds).

Company Background
Covenant HealthCare was formed in 1998 through the merger of Saginaw General and St. Luke's Hospitals.

EXECUTIVES

Chief Executive Officer, Edward Bruff
Personnel Manager, Becca Sovansky
Vice-President, Joe Ruth
Chief Operating Officer, Mark W Knight
Director, Lee Morril
Supervisor, Luanne Blasberg

LOCATIONS

HQ: COVENANT MEDICAL CENTER, INC.
1447 N HARRISON ST, SAGINAW, MI 486024727
Phone: 989 583-0000
Web: WWW.COVENANTHEALTHCARE.COM

PRODUCTS/OPERATIONS

2014 Revenues

	% of total
Net patient service revenues	95
Other revenues	5
Total	**100**

Selected services
Bariatrics
Birth Center
Cancer Care
Cardiology - Center for the Heart
Childbirth Classes
da Vinci Robotic Surgery
Diabetes Self-Management Program
Emergency Care Center
Imaging and Diagnostics
Neonatal Intensive Care
Neurology
Osteoporosis
Orthopaedics
Pediatrics
Physical Medicine and Rehab.
Pulmonary/Respiratory Care
Sleep Center
Surgical Services
Trauma
Urologic Surgery
Women's Health
Wound Healing Center

COMPETITORS

Genesys Health System
Genesys Regional Medical Center
Hurley Medical Center
McLaren Bay
McLaren Health Care
Munson Healthcare
Sparrow Health System
University of Michigan Health System

HISTORICAL FINANCIALS
Company Type: Private

Income Statement
FYE: June 30

	REVENUE ($ mil.)	NET INCOME ($ mil.)	NET PROFIT MARGIN	EMPLOYEES
06/15	535	31	5.8%	4,000
06/14	566	34	6.1%	—
06/10	508	28	5.5%	—
06/09	467	(14)	—	—
Annual Growth	2.3%	—	—	—

2015 Year-End Financials
Return on assets: 3.1%
Return on equity: 5.8%
Current ratio: 1.10
Cash ($ mil.): 19

COVENANT MEDICAL CENTER, INC.

EXECUTIVES

President, Jack Dusenbery
Financial Executive, Timothy Huber
Director, Shirley Dunlap
Director, Mary J Kavalier
Chief Financial Officer, Michelle Panicucci
Director, Theresa Evans

LOCATIONS

HQ: COVENANT MEDICAL CENTER, INC.
3421 W 9TH ST, WATERLOO, IA 507025401
Phone: 319 272-7296
Web: WWW.WHEATONIOWA.ORG

HISTORICAL FINANCIALS
Company Type: Private

Income Statement
FYE: June 30

	REVENUE ($ mil.)	NET INCOME ($ mil.)	NET PROFIT MARGIN	EMPLOYEES
06/15	279	18	6.5%	2,300
06/14	275	26	9.5%	—
06/13	255	20	8.1%	—
06/12	253	22	8.9%	—
Annual Growth	3.3%	(7.0%)	—	—

2015 Year-End Financials
Return on assets: 7.5%
Return on equity: 6.5%
Current ratio: 6.40
Cash ($ mil.): 118

COWAN SYSTEMS, LLC

Not cowed by competition from bigger transportation companies Cowan Systems provides truckload freight transportation primarily in the eastern half of the US. The company's coverage area includes the mid-Atlantic states the Midwest New England and the southeastern US. Cowan has about 2000 tractors and 5000 trailers and its largest customer is Coca-Cola Enterprises. The company arranges the transportation of freight through its logistics unit. Other offerings include ground transportation of airfreight between air-

ports and dedicated contract carriage in which drivers and equipment are assigned to a customer long-term.

Operations

Cowan Systems' fleet consists of 2000 company owned trucks 20 intermodal terminals and more than 15000 contract carriers to handle any type of shipments.

Geographic Reach

Cowan Systems has its presence in Maryland Utah California Texas Arizona Illinois Kansas Mississippi Tennessee Kentucky Indiana Ohio Georgia Virginia and Pennsylvania.

Company Background

The company has its roots in a trucking company that was founded in 1924.

EXECUTIVES

President, Dennis Morgan
SVP Operations, Richard Warner
VP Operations, Kristin Morgan
Vice President, Dan Colhoun
Vice President and Secretary, Wayne Zdenek

LOCATIONS

HQ: COWAN SYSTEMS, LLC
4555 HOLLINS FERRY RD, BALTIMORE, MD 212274610
Phone: 410 247-0800
Web: WWW.COWANSYSTEMS.COM

PRODUCTS/OPERATIONS

Selected Services
Dedicated freight transportation
Driver leasing
Intermodal freight transportation
Logistics
Truckload freight transportation
Warehousing

COMPETITORS

C.H. Robinson Worldwide
Forward Air
J.B. Hunt
Landstar System
Schneider National
Swift Transportation
U.S. Xpress
UPS Supply Chain Solutions
Werner Enterprises

HISTORICAL FINANCIALS
Company Type: Private

Income Statement
FYE: December 31

	REVENUE ($ mil.)	NET INCOME ($ mil.)	NET PROFIT MARGIN	EMPLOYEES
12/15	435	0	—	1,800
12/14	421	0	—	—
12/13	0	0	—	—
Annual Growth	—	—	—	—

CREIGHTON ALEGENT CLINIC

EXECUTIVES

Principal, Richard Hachten II
Manager, Kristi Cash
Auditors: CATHOLIC HEALTH INITIATIVES O

LOCATIONS

HQ: CREIGHTON ALEGENT CLINIC
12809 W DODGE RD, OMAHA, NE 681542155
Phone: 402 343-4343
Web: WWW.ALEGENT.COM

HISTORICAL FINANCIALS
Company Type: Private

Income Statement
FYE: June 30

	REVENUE ($ mil.)	NET INCOME ($ mil.)	NET PROFIT MARGIN	EMPLOYEES
06/15	244	(77)	—	5
06/14	235	(106)	—	—
06/13	222	(69)	—	—
Annual Growth	4.9%	—	—	—

2015 Year-End Financials
Return on assets: 9.1%
Return on equity: (-31.6%)
Current ratio: 1.00
Cash ($ mil.): 1

CREIGHTON ALEGENT HEALTH

CHI Health (formerly Alegent Creighton Health) pledges allegiance to medical well-being in its corner of the Midwest. The not-for-profit health care system operates 15 hospitals with about 3000 beds in Omaha and surrounding communities in eastern Nebraska and southwestern Iowa including Bergan Mercy Medical Center and Immanuel Medical Center. Alegent Creighton Health's hospitals provide specialty services including cardiovascular orthopedic and cancer care; it also operates psychiatric long-term care home health and outpatient centers. The health system is sponsored by Catholic Health Initiatives and is affiliated with Creighton University.

Operations

CHI Health is the primary provider of teaching locations for the Creighton University School of Medicine with academic programs in a number of fields including psychiatry women's health nursing and pharmacy. Its hospitals have some 1500 physicians on staff and include 10 acute care facilities and one psychiatric hospital. Specialty units include an orthopedic hospital and skilled nursing centers.

In addition to its acute care facilities the organization provides primary and specialty outpatient care services through its CHI Health Alegent Creighton Clinic unit. The division has more than 20 specialties and operates about 100 physician practices and clinics in Omaha and surrounding areas. There are also two Express Care clinics that offer urgent care for non-life-threatening ailments and six Quick Care clinics in Omaha (located in Hy-Vee retail stores) that provide minor medical ailment treatment as well as sports physicals and vaccinations. The idea behind the clinics is to divert patients who might otherwise end up at ERs with non-emergency symptoms (thus lowering hospital expenses).

Geographic Reach

The network's hospitals are located in Omaha (five medical centers) Papillion Plainview and Schuyler Nebraska; as well as in Corning Council Bluffs and Missouri Valley Iowa.

Strategy

The company has been pursuing growth to signify its presence as a unified regional health network. The efforts are intended to allow it to better compete and thrive in the changing US health care landscape by expanding its facilities training programs and resources in the Omaha area. Growth efforts include the formation of an intensive care partnership with Good Samaritan Hospital in 2013. The network has also opened several new community care clinics in recent years.

In 2015 CHI Health partnered with Aetna to create Nebraska's first commercial product-based accountable care organization (ACO). The ACO offers employers a health care option that is designed to improve quality of care outcomes and patient experiences.

EXECUTIVES

Vice President Of Human Resources, Nancy Wallace
Svp And Coo, Joan Neuhaus
Director of Radiology, Kay Carstens
Clinic Manager, Shannon Naprstek
Auditors: LB CATHOLIC HEALTH INITIATIVES

LOCATIONS

HQ: CREIGHTON ALEGENT HEALTH
12809 W DODGE RD, OMAHA, NE 681542155
Phone: 402 343-4300
Web: WWW.CHIHEALTH.COM

PRODUCTS/OPERATIONS

Selected Facilities and Operations
Alegent Creighton Health Clinics (primary care multiple locations in Iowa and Nebraska)
Alegent Creighton Health Urgent Care clinics (urgent care three locations in Nebraska)
Alegent Creighton Health Quick Care (minor care clinics; seven locations in Omaha Nebraska in Hy-Vee stores)
Alegent Health at Home (home health care)
Bergan Mercy Medical Center (Omaha Nebraska; 300 beds)
Community Memorial Hospital (Missouri Valley Iowa; 20 beds)
Creighton University Medical Center (Omaha Nebraska; 400 beds)
Immanuel Communities (independent and assisted living in Omaha and Lincoln)
Immanuel Fontenelle (nursing home in Omaha)
Immanuel Medical Center (Omaha Nebraska; 280 beds)
Immanuel Rehabilitation Center (Omaha Nebraska)
Lakeside Hospital (Omaha Nebraska; 160 beds)
Lasting Hope Recovery Center (Omaha Nebraska; psychiatric hospital with 120 beds)
Memorial Hospital (Schuyler Nebraska; 25 beds)
Mercy Corning Hospital (Corning Iowa; 20 beds)
Mercy Hospital (Council Bluffs Iowa; 160 beds)
Midlands Hospital (Papillion Nebraska; 50 beds)
Plainview Hospital (Plainview Nebraska)

COMPETITORS

BryanLGH Medical Center
Children's Hospital & Medical Center
Fremont Area Medical Center
Heartland Health
Madonna Rehabilitation Hospital
Mercy Health Network
Methodist Health System
Nebraska Medical Center
Saint Elizabeth Regional Medical Center
UNMC Physicians
UnityPoint Health

HISTORICAL FINANCIALS
Company Type: Private

Income Statement
FYE: June 30

	REVENUE ($ mil.)	NET INCOME ($ mil.)	NET PROFIT MARGIN	EMPLOYEES
06/15	516	(147)	—	8,600
06/13	525	63	12.2%	
Annual Growth	(0.9%)	—	—	—

2015 Year-End Financials
Return on assets: 8.9%
Return on equity: (-28.7%)
Current ratio: 2.00
Cash ($ mil.): 20

CREST INDUSTRIES

EXECUTIVES

President, Kenneth L Robison
Financial Executive, Joseph R Bareswill
Chief Financial Officer, Robert L Brinkerhoff
VP Personnel, Joy Williford
Vice-President, John Doggett
Manager, Stuart Tichenor
Auditors: LESTER MILLER & WELLS ALEXAN

LOCATIONS

HQ: CREST INDUSTRIES
4725 HIGHWAY 28 E, PINEVILLE, LA 713604730
Phone: 318 767-5530
Web: WWW.CRESTOPERATIONS.COM

HISTORICAL FINANCIALS
Company Type: Private

Income Statement
FYE: December 31

	REVENUE ($ mil.)	NET INCOME ($ mil.)	NET PROFIT MARGIN	EMPLOYEES
12/15	259	9	3.6%	415
12/14	251	12	4.9%	
12/13	328	32	10.0%	—
12/12	242	28	11.6%	—
Annual Growth	2.3%	(30.9%)	—	—

2015 Year-End Financials
Return on assets: 3.6%
Return on equity: 3.6%
Current ratio: 1.20
Cash ($ mil.): 35

CREST OPERATIONS, LLC

Crest Operations part of Crest Industries distributes and installs electrical substations and transmission products for electric power generation and utility customers worldwide through its DIS-TRAN and Beta Engineering subsidiaries. Other subsidiaries grow pine and hardwood trees in Louisiana and Texas (Crest Natural Resources) and make wooden utility poles and cross arms. Crest's Mid-State Supply Company subsidiary is a Louisiana-based distributor of electrical products that has showrooms for appliances and lighting. Crest Operations was founded in 1958.

EXECUTIVES

Board of Directors, Cecil G Brunson
Board of Directors, Brenda Daenan
Board of Directors, Robert L Brinkerhoff
Financial Executive, Joseph R Bareswill
Plant & Facilities Manager, Jared Rolen
Auditors: LESTER MILLER & WELLS ALEXAN

LOCATIONS

HQ: CREST OPERATIONS, LLC
4725 HIGHWAY 28 E, PINEVILLE, LA 713604730
Phone: 318 448-0274

COMPETITORS

Consolidated Electrical
Graybar Electric
WESCO International

HISTORICAL FINANCIALS
Company Type: Private

Income Statement
FYE: December 31

	REVENUE ($ mil.)	NET INCOME ($ mil.)	NET PROFIT MARGIN	EMPLOYEES
12/15	255	14	5.6%	300
12/14	248	15	6.0%	—
12/13	326	34	10.7%	—
12/12	240	28	12.1%	—
Annual Growth	2.1%	(21.2%)	—	—

2015 Year-End Financials
Return on assets: 3.7%
Return on equity: 5.6%
Current ratio: 1.00
Cash ($ mil.): 15

CRESTWOOD MIDSTREAM PARTNERS LP

EXECUTIVES

President, Robert G Phillips
General Partner, Crestwood Midstream GP LLC
Manager, Courtney Pittman
Director, Don Butler
Director, Donna Schmidt
Auditors: ERNST & YOUNG LLP HOUSTON T

LOCATIONS

HQ: CRESTWOOD MIDSTREAM PARTNERS LP
700 LOUISIANA ST STE 2550, HOUSTON, TX 770022756
Phone: 832 519-2200

COMPETITORS

DCP Midstream Partners
EnLink Midstream Partners
Energy Transfer Equity
Enterprise Products
Penn Virginia
Plains All American Pipeline
Regency Energy
Southern Natural Gas
Texas Gas Transmission

HISTORICAL FINANCIALS

Company Type: Private

Income Statement

FYE: December 31

	REVENUE ($ mil.)	NET INCOME ($ mil.)	NET PROFIT MARGIN	EMPLOYEES
12/16	2,520	(197)	—	1,300
12/15	2,632	(1,410)	—	—
12/14	2,565	(21)	—	—
12/13	658	(15)	—	—
Annual Growth	56.4%	—	—	—

2016 Year-End Financials

Return on assets: 8.5%
Return on equity: (-7.8%)
Current ratio: 0.90

Cash ($ mil.): 1

CRITTENTON HOSPITAL MEDICAL CENTER

Crittenton Hospital Medical Center treats patients in the western counties of the suburban Detroit area. The not-for-profit hospital has 290 beds for acute care but also provides primary and specialist care. Crittenton offers such services as urgent pediatric care rehabilitative therapy inpatient psychiatric care joint replacement and sleep analysis. It is a fully accredited teaching campus and partners with area universities and medical providers. It also operates outpatient facilities including surgery imaging and therapy centers. With a heritage that reaches back to the early 1900s Crittenton Hospital Medical Center opened its doors in 1967.

Operations

Crittenton has a medical staff of almost 500 physicians who practice in more than 50 specialist fields. The hospital treats more than 28000 patients each year capturing about 40% of the market share in its main service territory.

The hospital is the teaching facility for Wayne State University's medical school and conducts training programs including residencies for family medicine and ear nose and throat (ENT) practitioners. It also partners with Oakland University's School of Nursing. Other affiliations include a partnership with the University of Michigan Health System for electrophysiology and cardiovascular surgery.

Geographic Reach

Crittenton serves residents of Lapeer Macomb and Oakland counties. It has facilities in the Michigan communities of Auburn Hills Lake Orion Oxford Rochester Hills Sterling Heights Troy and Washington Township.

Strategy

Crittenton has spent millions in recent years to expand its services and facilities. It is currently building a new south tower a six-story addition that will add about 90 private patient rooms. Past additions include the $16 million Karmanos-Crittenton Cancer Center (2010) and the Wayne State University Physicians Group Family Medicine Center (2008). In 2006 Crittenton completed an $86 million project that added north and south wings and increased capacity for emergency women's and children's services; it also upgraded administrative and information systems.

EXECUTIVES

Director of Pharmacy, Susan Wilson

Physical Therapy Director, Michael Cagel
Operating Room Director, Tanya West
Auditors: PLANTE & MORAN PLLC SOUTHFIEL

LOCATIONS

HQ: CRITTENTON HOSPITAL MEDICAL CENTER
1101 W UNIVERSITY DR, ROCHESTER, MI
483071863
Phone: 248 652-5000
Web: WWW.CRITTENTON.COM

PRODUCTS/OPERATIONS

Selected Services
Behavioral Health
Bloodless Medicine
Cancer Services
Cardiovascular
Clinical Laboratory Services
Diabetes Services
Diagnostic Neurology (ENG)
Emergency Services
Endoscopy Services
Executive Medicine
Imaging Centers
Imaging Services
Medical Equipment
Occupational Medicine
Orthopedics
Palliative Care
Pediatrics
Pharmacy
Rehabilitation
Respiratory Therapy
Robotic Surgery
Senior Wellness
Sleep Center
Stroke Center
Surgical Services
Travel Medicine
Urology Services
Women's Services
Wound Healing Center

COMPETITORS

Ascension Health
Beaumont Health System
Detroit Medical Center
Henry Ford Health System
Hurley Medical Center
Mount Clemens Regional Medical Center
Providence Hospital and Medical Centers
Trinity Health (Novi)
University of Michigan Health System

HISTORICAL FINANCIALS

Company Type: Private

Income Statement

FYE: December 31

	REVENUE ($ mil.)	NET INCOME ($ mil.)	NET PROFIT MARGIN	EMPLOYEES
12/15	188	(48)	—	1,515
12/14	230	5	2.6%	—
12/12	3	(1)	—	—
12/09	223	(4)	—	—
Annual Growth	(2.8%)	—	—	—

2015 Year-End Financials

Return on assets: 3.9%
Return on equity: (-25.6%)
Current ratio: 0.10

Cash ($ mil.): 11

CROUSE HEALTH SYSTEM, INC.

EXECUTIVES

Chief Executive Officer, Kimberly Boynton
Supervisor, Deborah Montrond
Director, Karen Powers
Director, Christopher Hines
Director, Alec Neider

LOCATIONS

HQ: CROUSE HEALTH SYSTEM, INC.
736 IRVING AVE, SYRACUSE, NY 132101687
Phone: 315 470-7521
Web: WWW.CROUSE.ORG

HISTORICAL FINANCIALS

Company Type: Private

Income Statement

FYE: December 31

	REVENUE ($ mil.)	NET INCOME ($ mil.)	NET PROFIT MARGIN	EMPLOYEES
12/15	391	0	0.2%	2,700
12/14	367	13	3.7%	—
12/13	3	1	44.4%	—
12/09	3	0	27.2%	—
Annual Growth	122.8%	(2.7%)	—	—

2015 Year-End Financials

Return on assets: 5.1%
Return on equity: 0.2%
Current ratio: 1.20

Cash ($ mil.): 19

CROWDER CONSTRUCTION COMPANY INC

Seeking to stand out from the crowd of US-based construction companies Crowder Construction specializes in bridge and highway civil environmental and industrial construction serving a range of customers primarily in the Southeast US. The specialty construction company's projects include parking decks highway and bridge water and sewer treatment plant construction. Projects that have been completed by its Crowder Electrical unit range from power substations to light rail facilities. The now employee-owned company was founded in Charlotte North Carolina in 1947 by Bill and O. P. Crowder; it continues to be led by the Crowder family.

Operations

Crowder Construction provides heavy construction general contracting services. It designs constructs repairs and replaces bridges; constructs repairs retrofits or demolishes dams and spillways penstocks intake and outfall structures and foundations for turbines.

Geographic Reach

The company is based in North Carolina and other offices in Georgia South Carolina and Virginia.

Sales and Marketing

The company serves markets such as Bridges Dams Electrical Power Fabrication Federal Heavy

Foundations Industrial Energy Services and Water and Waste Water.

EXECUTIVES

Chairman President and CEO, Otis A. Crowder
Auditors: GREERWALKER LLP CHARLOTTE NC

LOCATIONS

HQ: CROWDER CONSTRUCTION COMPANY INC
6425 BROOKSHIRE BLVD, CHARLOTTE, NC
282160301
Phone: 800 849-2966
Web: WWW.CROWDERCC.COM

COMPETITORS

Alberici	Oldcastle Materials
English Construction Company	S. T. Wooten
Hubbard Group	Skanska USA Civil

HISTORICAL FINANCIALS

Company Type: Private

Income Statement

FYE: March 31

	REVENUE ($ mil.)	NET INCOME ($ mil.)	NET PROFIT MARGIN	EMPLOYEES
03/15	179	0	0.2%	900
03/14	233	0	—	—
03/13	233	0	—	—
03/12	222	0	—	—
Annual Growth	(6.9%)	—	—	—

2015 Year-End Financials

Return on assets: 10.7%   Cash ($ mil.): 11
Return on equity: 0.2%
Current ratio: 1.20

CROWE HORWATH LLP

EXECUTIVES

Chief Executive Officer, James Powers
Partner, Fred J Bauters
Chief Operating Officer, Joseph P Santucci Jr
Manager, Todd Miller
Manager, David Sousa
Manager, John Kurkowski
Auditing Manager, Julia Doppelhammer
Auditors: CROWE HORWATH

LOCATIONS

HQ: CROWE HORWATH LLP
225 W WACKER DR STE 2600, CHICAGO, IL
606061228
Phone: 312 899-7000

HISTORICAL FINANCIALS

Company Type: Private

Income Statement

FYE: March 31

	REVENUE ($ mil.)	NET INCOME ($ mil.)	NET PROFIT MARGIN	EMPLOYEES
03/16	745	187	25.1%	2,830
03/15	700	204	29.2%	—
03/14	670	163	24.4%	—
03/13	0	0	—	—
Annual Growth	—	—	—	—

2016 Year-End Financials

Return on assets: 0.2%   Cash ($ mil.): 7
Return on equity: 25.1%
Current ratio: 1.70

CROWLEY HOLDINGS, INC.

EXECUTIVES

Chairman of the Board, Thomas B Crowley Jr
Account Executive, Karlos Soto
Director, Nicholas Orfanidis
Auditors: DELOITTE & TOUCHE LLP JACKSON

LOCATIONS

HQ: CROWLEY HOLDINGS, INC.
9487 REGENCY SQUARE BLVD # 101,
JACKSONVILLE, FL 322257800
Phone: 904 727-2200

HISTORICAL FINANCIALS

Company Type: Private

Income Statement

FYE: December 31

	REVENUE ($ mil.)	NET INCOME ($ mil.)	NET PROFIT MARGIN	EMPLOYEES
12/15	2,158	153	7.1%	4,500
12/14	2,059	48	2.4%	—
12/13	2,030	71	3.5%	—
12/12	1,794	(10)	—	—
Annual Growth	6.4%	—	—	—

2015 Year-End Financials

Return on assets: 14.2%   Cash ($ mil.): 164
Return on equity: 7.1%
Current ratio: 0.80

CROWN BATTERY MANUFACTURING COMPANY

Crown Battery Manufacturing doesn't let its power go to its head. The company manufactures and sells industrial batteries and chargers automotive batteries and commercial battery products to clients across North America. Products serve clients in the marine railroad mining and automotive industries; the company also offers products with deep-cycle and other heavy-duty applications. Other products include battery chargers and battery cleaners for industrial applications. The company was founded in 1926 by German immigrant William J. Koenig.

Operations
The company's batteries are used in everything from cars trucks material handling equipment and locomotives to electric lift trucks traffic and floor management equipment and renewable energy systems.

Geographic Reach
Crown Battery has 12 sales and distribution offices located throughout North America. It has distributors and dealers in the Americas Europe Africa Asian-Pacific Australia and New Zealand.

EXECUTIVES

Vice President Human Resources, Scott Macina
Vice President Of Human Resources, Scott Messina
Auditors: RSM US LLP CLEVELAND OHIO

LOCATIONS

HQ: CROWN BATTERY MANUFACTURING COMPANY
1445 MAJESTIC DR, FREMONT, OH 434209190
Phone: 419 332-0563
Web: WWW.CROWNBATTERY.COM

PRODUCTS/OPERATIONS

Selected Products
Batteries and Battery parts
Battery Chargers
Commercial
Deep Cycle
Marine
Sealed Lead Acid
Utility Starting
Industrial
  Lift Truck
  Rail Road
  Mining
Other
  Powerhouse Chargers
  Powerhouse Cleaners

COMPETITORS

C&D Technologies	GS Yuasa
Eagle-Picher	Interstate Batteries
East Penn Manufacturing	Johnson Controls Power Solutions
EnerSys	Ritar Power
Exide	Valence Technology

HISTORICAL FINANCIALS

Company Type: Private

Income Statement

FYE: September 30

	REVENUE ($ mil.)	NET INCOME ($ mil.)	NET PROFIT MARGIN	EMPLOYEES
09/15	222	13	6.2%	575
09/14	214	12	5.6%	—
09/13	196	10	5.5%	—
09/12	191	6	3.2%	—
Annual Growth	5.1%	30.9%	—	—

2015 Year-End Financials

Return on assets: 7.4%   Cash ($ mil.): 1
Return on equity: 6.2%
Current ratio: 1.10

CUMBERLAND COUNTY SCHOOLS

EXECUTIVES

Superintendent, William Harrison
Administrative Assistant, Isley Cotton
Accountant, Martha West
Account Manager, Mike Boundy
Auditors: CHERRY BEKAERT LLP FAYETTEVI

LOCATIONS

HQ: CUMBERLAND COUNTY SCHOOLS
2465 GILLESPIE ST, FAYETTEVILLE, NC 283063053
Phone: 910 678-2300
Web: WWW.CCS.K12.NC.US

HISTORICAL FINANCIALS
Company Type: Private

Income Statement				FYE: June 30
	REVENUE ($ mil.)	NET INCOME ($ mil.)	NET PROFIT MARGIN	EMPLOYEES
06/15	413	(0)	—	6,210
06/14	399	(6)	—	—
06/11	444	3	0.8%	—
06/09	454	0	0.1%	—
Annual Growth	(1.6%)	—	—	—

2015 Year-End Financials

Return on assets: 0.5% Cash ($ mil.): 55
Return on equity: (-0.2%)
Current ratio: —

CURBELL, INC.

EXECUTIVES

President, Thomas E Leone
Board of Directors, Susan M Schubbe
Board of Directors, Christopher Schenk
Account Manager, Doug Banas
Director, Harold Scott
Director, Jeff Wilson
Production Manager, Larry Pennell
Supervisor, Timothy McPherson
Auditors: DOPKINS & COMPANY LLP BUFFAL

LOCATIONS

HQ: CURBELL, INC.
7 COBHAM DR, ORCHARD PARK, NY 141274180
Phone: 716 667-3377
Web: WWW.CURBELLELECTRONICS.COM

HISTORICAL FINANCIALS
Company Type: Private

Income Statement				FYE: December 31
	REVENUE ($ mil.)	NET INCOME ($ mil.)	NET PROFIT MARGIN	EMPLOYEES
12/15	190	0	—	445
12/14	185	0	—	—
12/13	176	0	—	—
12/12	169	0	—	—
Annual Growth	4.0%	—	—	—

CURTIS LUMBER CO., INC.

EXECUTIVES

Chairman of the Board, Jay S Curtis
Manager, Dan Wilson
Manager, Golenne Kortz
Purchasing Agent, Jim Schneible
Purchasing Agent, Kyle Towne
Personnel Director, Liz Irish
Manager, Pam Stott
Auditors: BONADIO & CO LLP ALBANY NE

LOCATIONS

HQ: CURTIS LUMBER CO., INC.
885 STATE ROUTE 67, BALLSTON SPA, NY 120203689
Phone: 518 885-5311
Web: WWW.CURTISLUMBER.COM

HISTORICAL FINANCIALS
Company Type: Private

Income Statement				FYE: December 31
	REVENUE ($ mil.)	NET INCOME ($ mil.)	NET PROFIT MARGIN	EMPLOYEES
12/15	185	7	3.8%	560
12/14	171	2	1.4%	—
12/13	171	4	2.7%	—
12/10	149	2	1.7%	—
Annual Growth	4.5%	22.2%	—	—

2015 Year-End Financials

Return on assets: 5.7% Cash ($ mil.): 6
Return on equity: 3.8%
Current ratio: 0.90

CVR NITROGEN, LP

EXECUTIVES

Chief Executive Officer, Keith B Forman
President, John H Diesch
Chief Financial Officer, Jeffrey R Spain
Senior Vice-President, Joe Herold
Senior Vice-President, Wilfred Bahl Jr
Senior Vice-President, Marc Wallis
Senior Vice-President, Colin Morris
President, Colin Campbell
Vice-President, Eileen Ney
Auditors: PRICEWATERHOUSECOOPERS LLP LO

LOCATIONS

HQ: CVR NITROGEN, LP
10877 WILSHIRE BLVD FL 10, LOS ANGELES, CA 900244251
Phone: 310 571-9800
Web: WWW.RENTECHNITROGEN.COM

HISTORICAL FINANCIALS
Company Type: Private

Income Statement				FYE: December 31
	REVENUE ($ mil.)	NET INCOME ($ mil.)	NET PROFIT MARGIN	EMPLOYEES
12/15	340	(101)	—	145
12/14	334	(1)	—	—
12/13	311	4	1.3%	—
12/11	63	10	16.6%	—
Annual Growth	52.5%	—	—	—

2015 Year-End Financials

Return on assets: 3.5% Cash ($ mil.): 15
Return on equity: (-29.8%)
Current ratio: 0.50

CYCLE LINK (U.S.A.) INC.

EXECUTIVES

Chief Executive Officer, Ming Hua Wu
Manager, Paul Mao
Director, Frank Liu
Purchasing Manager, Jason Zhang

LOCATIONS

HQ: CYCLE LINK (U.S.A.) INC.
1330 VALLEY VISTA DR, DIAMOND BAR, CA 917653910
Phone: 909 861-5888

HISTORICAL FINANCIALS
Company Type: Private

Income Statement				FYE: December 31
	REVENUE ($ mil.)	NET INCOME ($ mil.)	NET PROFIT MARGIN	EMPLOYEES
12/15	432	0	0.0%	35
12/14	435	2	0.5%	—
12/12	406	0	0.1%	—
Annual Growth	2.1%	(37.8%)	—	—

2015 Year-End Financials

Return on assets: 5.9% Cash ($ mil.): 11
Return on equity: —
Current ratio: 0.40

D'ARRIGO BROS. CO. OF NEW YORK, INC.

EXECUTIVES

President, Paul D'Arrigo
Marketing Director, Gabriela D'Arrigo
Assistant Controller, Mark Veluz
Auditors: RSM US LLP STAMFORD CONNECT

LOCATIONS

HQ: D'ARRIGO BROS. CO. OF NEW YORK, INC.
315 NYC TERMINAL MKT, BRONX, NY 10474
Phone: 718 991-5900
Web: WWW.DARRIGONY.COM

HISTORICAL FINANCIALS
Company Type: Private

Income Statement				FYE: April 30
	REVENUE ($ mil.)	NET INCOME ($ mil.)	NET PROFIT MARGIN	EMPLOYEES
04/16	241	1	0.5%	170
04/15	192	1	0.5%	—
04/14	193	1	0.8%	—
04/13	187	2	1.1%	—
Annual Growth	8.9%	(15.4%)	—	—

2016 Year-End Financials

Return on assets: 5.8% Cash ($ mil.): 7
Return on equity: 0.5%
Current ratio: 1.40

D. CONSTRUCTION, INC.

EXECUTIVES

President, Kenneth T Sandeno
Treasurer, Michael Treacy
Auditors: BRIAN ZABEL & ASSOCIATES PC M

LOCATIONS

HQ: D. CONSTRUCTION, INC.
1488 S BROADWAY ST, COAL CITY, IL 604169443
Phone: 815 634-2555
Web: WWW.DCONSTRUCTION.NET

HISTORICAL FINANCIALS

Company Type: Private

Income Statement

FYE: December 31

	REVENUE ($ mil.)	NET INCOME ($ mil.)	NET PROFIT MARGIN	EMPLOYEES
12/15	249	16	6.6%	40
12/14	201	10	5.4%	—
12/13	170	9	5.7%	—
12/12	162	9	5.6%	—
Annual Growth	15.5%	21.8%	—	—

2015 Year-End Financials

Return on assets: 8.2%
Return on equity: 6.6%
Current ratio: 1.20

Cash ($ mil.): 6

DAIRY FARMERS OF AMERICA, INC.

The members of Dairy Farmers of America (DFA) are partners in cream. DFA is one of the world's largest dairy cooperatives with nearly 15000 member/farmers in 48 states. About 3 million cows belonging to member/farmers produce 64 billion pounds of milk a year (roughly 30% of milk production in the US) which DFA markets. Along with fresh and shelf-stable fluid milk the co-op produces cheese butter dried milk powder and other dairy products for industrial wholesale and retail customers. It also offers contract manufacturing services. The co-op owns more than 30 manufacturing plants nationwide. DFA whose profits are shared based on member contribution is a major supplier to dairy giant Dean Foods.

Operations

DFA owns 33 manufacturing plants nationwide. The facilities are focused on several functions and product categories including consumer cheese and butter consumer fluid ingredient cheese and protein and contract manufacturing.

Geographic Reach

The national milk cooperative is based in Kansas City Missouri and divides the US into seven areas (Central Mideast Mountain Northeast Southeast Southwest and Western) to ensure grassroots representation.

Sales and Marketing

DFA's customers include big names in the dairy food and retail businesses including Hiland Dairy Borden supermarket giant Kroger Dean Foods Kraft Foods J.M. Smucker and many others.

Financial Performance

DFA reported net sales of $17.9 billion in 2014 a 28% increase compared with 2013's $12.8 billion in sales. The uptick in sales primarily resulted from higher milk prices in the US. The cooperative's ad-justed net income was $61.3 million and it returned a total of $43.1 million to members in 2014.

Strategy

Although DFA's primary business is to market its members' milk the cooperative has invested heavily in facilities and joint ventures to process its fluid milk into value-added products and high-end dairy-based ingredients to expand its product portfolio and protect members from price swings for fluid milk. To that end it makes and markets cheese butter nonfat milk powders and other dairy ingredients under household name brands including Borden Breakstone's and Keller's as well as private label products through contract manufacture.

In 2015 the co-op opened a 33000-square-foot ingredient processing plant in Cass City Michigan. The $40 million plant will serve a region where milk production is outpacing local plant capacity.

In 2014 DFA opened a new cold process milk separation plant in Linwood New York to produce cream and skim milk for regional customers. It also opened a plant in Fallon Nevada that produces powdered milk for global customers.

The co-op expects to continue to benefit from its diverse activities coupled with higher average commodity prices for dairy products. The marketing of raw milk accounted for approximately 74% of sales. Sales have been bolstered by the acquisition of Berkshire Dairy and Food Products a producer of dairy ingredients and DFA's investment in Castro Cheese Company which makes and markets queso fresco panea and queso quesadilla under the La Vaquita brand. Control of the brand launched DFA into the increasingly popular Hispanic cheese market. DFA's efforts to shore up earnings and mitigate a volatile commodity market have included trimming certain investments.

Mergers and Acquisitions

In January 2014 DFA acquired family-owned Oakhurst Dairy which sources milk from 70 farmers in Maine and has processing and bottling facilities in Portland Maine. Oakhurst which became a wholly-owned subsidiary of DFA and continues to operate independently distributes milk throughout northern New England and eastern Massachusetts. Oakhurst's annual sales are estimated to be $110 million. In April 2014 DFA purchased Dairylea Cooperative based in East Syracuse New York with some 1200 members. The two cooperatives have worked together since DFA was formed in 1998 coordinating milk assembly transportation and marketing as well as joint management of Farm Services and membership operations in the Northeast.

DFA acquired Frederick Maryland-based Dairy Maid Dairy a family-owned processor of milk juice and fruit drinks in September 2013. The purchase was consistent with DFA's strategy to increase its commercial footprint and expand ownership in the fluid and fresh dairy category. Dairy Maid's customers include major grocery chains schools prisons and military bases.

HISTORY

Mid-America Dairymen (Mid-Am) the largest of the cooperatives that merged to form Dairy Farmers of America (DFA) was born in 1968. At that time several Midwestern dairy co-ops banded together to attack common economic problems such as reduced government subsidies price drops resulting from a rising milk surplus dealer consolidation and improvements in production processing and packaging. The merging organizations — representing 15000 dairy farmers — were Producers Creamery Company (Springfield Missouri) Sanitary Milk Producers (St. Louis) Square Deal Milk Producers (Highland Illinois) Mid-Am (Kansas City Missouri) and Producers Creamery Company of Chillicothe (north central Missouri).

During the early 1970s Mid-Am struggled with internal restructuring. Most dairy farmers and co-ops were hit hard by the energy crisis and the government's decision to allow increased dairy imports in 1973 the same year the US Justice Department filed an antitrust suit against Mid-Am. (A judge cleared the co-op 12 years later.)

In 1974 Mid-Am lost almost $8 million on revenues of $625 million chalked up to record-high feed prices a weakened economy a milk surplus and a massive inventory loss. Co-op veteran Gary Hanman was named CEO that year. Over the next two years Mid-Am cut costs sold corporate frills downsized management and began marketing more of its own products under the Mid-America Farms label thus reducing dependency on commodity sales.

Mid-Am expanded its research and development efforts throughout the 1980s. The co-op opened its services to farmers in California and New Mexico in 1993 and a series of mergers in 1994 and 1995 nearly doubled its size. In 1997 it purchased some of Borden's dairy operations including rights to the valuable Elsie the Cow and Borden's trademarks.

Wary of falling milk prices Mid-Am merged with Western Dairymen Cooperative Milk Marketing and the Southern Region of Associated Milk Producers at the end of 1997 to form DFA. Hanman moved into the seat of CEO at the new co-op. DFA began a series of joint ventures with the #1 US dairy processor Suiza Foods (now Dean Foods).

DFA added California Gold (more than 330 farmers 1998) and Independent Cooperative Milk Producers Association (730 dairy farmer members in Michigan and parts of Ohio and Indiana 1999). In another joint venture with Suiza in early 2000 DFA sold its 50% stake in the US's #3 fluid milk processor Southern Foods in exchange for 34% of a new company named Suiza Dairy Group.

After mollifying the government's antitrust fears DFA acquired the butter operations of Sodiaal North America in 2000. It then molded all its butter businesses into a new entity Keller's Creamery. However another acquisition did not fare as well. The same year DFA acquired controlling interest in Southern Belle Dairy only to have the merger challenged three years later by the Department of Justice. Arguing that the merger formed a monopoly in school milk sales in several states the Department of Justice filed suit which a federal judge later dismissed.

During 2001 the cooperative went in with Land O'Lakes 50/50 to purchase a cheese plant from Kraft. Later in the year as Suiza Foods acquired Dean Foods (and took on its name) DFA sold back its stake in Suiza Dairy Group to the new Dean Foods. DFA then teamed up with a group of dairy investors to form a new 50/50 joint venture National Dairy Holdings which received 11 processing plants from Dean Foods as part of the exchange for Suiza Dairy.

EXECUTIVES

Senior Adviser; President Affiliate Division, Alan J. Bernon, age 62
COO Northeast Area, Gregory I. (Greg) Wickham
President CEO and Director, Richard P. (Rick) Smith
EVP; President Global Dairy Products Group, Mark Korsmeyer
SVP Finance, David Meyer
Executive Vice President of Commercial Operations, Doug Glade
Vice Chairman, Bill Siebenborn
First Vice Chairman, Randy Mooney

Vice Chairman, Wayne Palla
Vice Chairman, George Mertens
Auditors: KPMG LLP KANSAS CITY MISSOUR

LOCATIONS

HQ: DAIRY FARMERS OF AMERICA, INC.
1405 N 98TH ST, KANSAS CITY, KS 661111865
Phone: 816 801-6455
Web: WWW.DFAMILK.COM

PRODUCTS/OPERATIONS

Selected Products and Brands
Consumer brands
  Borden cheese
  Breakstone's butter
  Cache Valley cheese
  Keller's Creamery butter
  Plugrá; butter
  Sport Shake energy milk shake
Contract manufacturing
  Cheese dips
  Cheese powders & flavors
  Coffee-based flavored drinks
  Instant formula
  Sour cream
  Sports drinks
Dairy ingredients
  Cheeses (American & Italian)
  Nonfat dry milk powder
  Skim milk powder
  Sweetened condensed milk

Selected Joint Venture Partners
Dean Foods
Hiland Dairy Foods
Roberts Dairy

COMPETITORS

Arla Foods	Glanbia plc
Associated Milk	Great Lakes Cheese
Producers	HP Hood
Berkeley Farms	Humboldt Creamery
California Dairies	Lactalis
Inc.	Land O'Lakes
ConAgra	Marathon Cheese
Darigold Inc.	Mayfield Dairy Farms
Dean Foods	Northwest Dairy
Farmland Dairies	Prairie Farms Dairy
Foremost Farms	Quality Chekd
Friendship Dairies	Sargento
Garelick Farms	

HISTORICAL FINANCIALS

Company Type: Private

Income Statement				FYE: December 31
	REVENUE ($ mil.)	NET INCOME ($ mil.)	NET PROFIT MARGIN	EMPLOYEES
12/15	13,803	98	0.7%	7,000
12/14	17,856	48	0.3%	—
12/13	12,826	58	0.5%	—
12/12	12,082	(126)	—	—
Annual Growth	4.5%	—	—	—

2015 Year-End Financials
Return on assets: 4.7%   Cash ($ mil.): 228
Return on equity: 0.7%
Current ratio: 0.70

DAIRYLAND POWER COOPERATIVE

Dairyland Power Cooperative provides its customers with lots of juice in the land of lactose. The firm provides electricity generation (1366 MW of generating capacity) and transmission services for 25 member distribution cooperatives and 16 municipal utilities in five states (including Wisconsin). The member cooperatives and municipal utilities in turn distribute electricity to almost 254460 consumers. Dairyland Power generates 1030 MW of capacity from its coal-fired power plants; it also operates more than 3180 miles of transmission lines and 228 substations. The power cooperative also markets electricity and offers energy management services.

Operations
In addition to its traditional fossil fuel-powered plants the company to meet green energy regulations also contracts renewable and alternative energy power plants including "cow power" animal waste to energy facilities (8 farms with manure digesters which collectively produce 3 MW of power). It also has 40 MW of contracted biomass energy 47 MW of wind and 14 MW of landfill gas. In 2012 it expanded its wind portfolio agreeing to buy 5 MW of electricity from a wind farm near Lewiston Minnesota. It also agreed that year to buy the excess energy output from a new 368 kW solar photovoltaic installation at the City of Galena wastewater treatment plant in Illinois.

Geographic Reach
Dairyland Power Cooperative has member coops in Illinois Iowa Minnesota North Dakota and Wisconsin.

Financial Performance
In 2012 Dairyland Power Cooperative's revenues grew by 2% thanks to an increase in margins. Net income grew by 11% as the result of an increase in net sales.

Strategy
While admitting no violations of law in 2012 the company settled litigation with the EPA and Sierra Club agreeing to install hundreds of millions of dollars of air emission controls at its fossil-fueled power plants.

Company Background
In 2010 the cooperative integrated fully into regional transmission operator Midwest ISO. The move gave Dairyland Power Cooperative access to the Midwest ISO's wholesale ancillary services and other markets helping to improve the coop's regional grid reliability by giving it access to more energy sources to help avoid power shortages.

Dairyland Power Cooperative was founded in 1941.

EXECUTIVES

President, Barbara Nick
Manager, Janet Nelson
Supervisor, Pamela Williams
Engineer, Bart Pedretti
Operations Manager, Dan Donnelly
Auditors: DELOITTE & TOUCHE LLP MINNEAP

LOCATIONS

HQ: DAIRYLAND POWER COOPERATIVE
3200 EAST AVE S, LA CROSSE, WI 546017291
Phone: 608 788-4000
Web: WWW.DAIRYNET.COM

COMPETITORS

ALLETE	DTE
Alliant Energy	MGE Energy
Berkshire Hathaway	WEC Energy
Energy	Xcel Energy

HISTORICAL FINANCIALS

Company Type: Private

Income Statement				FYE: December 31
	REVENUE ($ mil.)	NET INCOME ($ mil.)	NET PROFIT MARGIN	EMPLOYEES
12/15	418	26	6.4%	500
12/14	447	22	5.1%	—
Annual Growth	(6.6%)	16.9%	—	—

2015 Year-End Financials
Return on assets: 7.8%   Cash ($ mil.): 26
Return on equity: 6.4%
Current ratio: 0.20

DAKOTA ELECTRIC ASSOCIATION

The Dakota Electric Association delivers electricity to residents of southeastern Minnesota the Gopher State so they don't have to burrow underground to outlast those long cold winters. The member-owned utility serves more than 103000 customers in portions of Dakota Goodhue Rice and Scott counties south of Minneapolis-St. Paul. The co-op gets its power wholesale from transmission cooperative Great River Energy and distributes it more than 4010 miles of power lines nearly two-thirds of which are buried. Dakota Electric is pushing energy efficiency programs and products to help save its customers money.

Operations
Dakota Electric purchases power from Great River Energy and distributes electricity to commercial residential farming street lighting and irrigation customers. It has 2792 miles of underground power lines and 1220 miles of overhead lines.

Geographic Reach
The company serves parts of Dakota Goodhue Scott and Rice counties in southern Minnesota.

Financial Performance
In 2013 the company's revenue increased by 2%. Dakota Electric's commercial members accounted for 41% of revenues; residential and farming 58%; and street lighting and irrigation 1%.

Its net income grew by 5% in 2013 thanks to higher revenues and the absence of a loss from discontinued operations.

Dakota Electric's operating cash inflow increased to $13.13 million in fiscal 2013 (from $5.61 million in 2012) due to higher net income and a change in the working capital.

Strategy
The co-op seeks to maintain and upgrade its power infrastructure and service to its members while keep power costs low.

As part of this strategy Dakota Electric operates a for-profit subsidiary Midwest Energy Services. That unit's subsidiaries provides complementary services to Dakota Electric's main power delivery business. They offer standby power generator and solar panel installation and leasing services (Energy Alternatives) and substation engineering services (Consulting Engineers Group).

Company Background
Dakota Electric was formed in 1937 as part of the Roosevelt Administration's national rural electrification drive.

EXECUTIVES

Vice President, Dirk Rotty
Vice President Regulatory, Doug Larson
Board Member, Janet Lekson
Secretary, Paul Trapp
Secretary and Director, Judy Kimmes
Board Member, John DeYoe
Auditors: CLIFTONLARSONALLEN LLP AUSTIN

LOCATIONS

HQ: DAKOTA ELECTRIC ASSOCIATION
4300 220TH ST W, FARMINGTON, MN 550249583
Phone: 651 463-6212
Web: WWW.DAKOTAELECTRIC.COM

COMPETITORS

ALLETE
Connexus Energy
Otter Tail

WEC Energy
Xcel Energy

HISTORICAL FINANCIALS

Company Type: Private

Income Statement — FYE: December 31

	REVENUE ($ mil.)	NET INCOME ($ mil.)	NET PROFIT MARGIN	EMPLOYEES
12/15	197	3	1.6%	100,000
12/14	209	10	5.1%	—
12/13	205	8	4.2%	—
12/09	178	7	3.9%	—
Annual Growth	1.7%	(12.7%)	—	—

2015 Year-End Financials

Return on assets: 18.7%
Return on equity: 1.6%
Current ratio: 0.50

Cash ($ mil.): —

DAKOTA SUPPLY GROUP, INC.

Dakota Supply Group (DSG) distributes electrical communications and mechanical equipment to customers through more than a dozen branch locations in Minnesota North Dakota and South Dakota. The company stocks approximately 25000 products. DSG carries products from 3Com 3M A. O. Smith Buckingham Manufacturing Corning Emerson Electric Ferraz Shawmut General Electric Honeywell Hubbell Moen Schneider Electric and Zurn Industries among other manufacturers. The company was founded in 1898. An employee stock ownership plan holds nearly all of Dakota Supply.

EXECUTIVES

Chief Executive Officer, Todd Kumm
Credit Manager, Kathy Gross
VP Finance, Kevin Kaeding
Manager, Doug Hunt
Auditors: EIDE BAILLY LLP FARGO NORTH

LOCATIONS

HQ: DAKOTA SUPPLY GROUP, INC.
2601 3RD AVE N, FARGO, ND 581024016
Phone: 701 237-9440
Web: WWW.DAKOTASUPPLYGROUP.COM

COMPETITORS

Border States Electric
J. H. Larson

Viking Electric

HISTORICAL FINANCIALS

Company Type: Private

Income Statement — FYE: December 31

	REVENUE ($ mil.)	NET INCOME ($ mil.)	NET PROFIT MARGIN	EMPLOYEES
12/15	401	11	2.8%	720
12/14	380	15	4.0%	—
12/13	369	16	4.5%	—
12/12	297	15	5.3%	—
Annual Growth	10.5%	(11.4%)	—	—

DALLAS COUNTY HOSPITAL DISTRICT

Many people know Dallas County Hospital District doing business as Parkland Health and Hospital System or PHHS as Parkland Memorial Hospital the hospital where JFK died. Parkland Memorial sits at the heart of the health system and is Dallas' only public hospital. PHHS also manages a network of about 20 community clinics as well as Parkland Community Health Plan a regional HMO for Medicaid and CHIP (Children's Health Insurance Program) members. Additionally the system offers Parkland Financial Assistance a program to help residents of Dallas County pay for health care services. Parkland Memorial Hospital has more than 700 beds and is the primary teaching institution of The University of Texas Southwestern Medical Center.

Operations

PHHS is one of the largest public hospital systems in the US. In addition to its community-based clinics it offers a number of outreach and education programs to improve wellness in its service area.

Parkland Memorial Hospital has 870 single-patient rooms and is a Level I trauma center. Each year the hospital has some 39000 inpatient discharges and some 260000 emergency department visits. Specialty community and women's clinic outpatient visits total more than 1 million.

The system also manages the health system for Lew Sterrett — Dallas County Jail one of the nation's largest jails.

Sales and Marketing

Medicare and Medicaid payments account for about 15% and 30% of PHHS's net patient service revenues respectively.

Strategy

PHHS's original hospital location was established in 1954; more recently the system replaced the aging facility with a new hospital. The expansion included an 870-bed hospital an outpatient center an office center and parking. PHHS also invested in new and replacement information systems and medical equipment.

Additionally the system is working to open more primary care health clinics and launch new programs to reach further into its community.For example in 2016 it introduced the Acute Integrated Mental Health Services (AIMS) program to assist underserved patients with complex behavioral health issues and diabetes. It combines health care and social work services to connect patients with valuable resources and help them manage their health in an integrated manner.

Similarly the Parkland Information Exchange Portal (IEP) launched by PHHS health IT think tank Parkland Center for Clinical Innovation services to connect underserved individuals with social services including homeless shelters and food banks.

In early 2017 the system completed construction of a new five-story clinic with 171 exam rooms MRI's CT scanners radiology and ultrasound rooms laboratories and a pharmacy.

EXECUTIVES

COO, David S. Lopez
President and CEO, Frederick P. (Fred) Cerise, age 54
EVP and Chief Administrative Officer Population Health, Sharon Phillips
EVP and General Counsel, Paul Leslie
EVP and Chief Nursing Officer, Karen Watts
EVP and Chief Medical Officer, Roberto de la Cruz
EVP and Chief Talent Officer, Jim Dunn
EVP and Chief Strategy and Integration Officer, Esmaeil Porsa
EVP and CFO, Richard Humphrey
Vice President Finance and Controller, Liz McMullen
Rph, Parul Jackson
PA to Executive Vice President and Chief Operating Officer (Mr. Haupert), Barbara Poole
Director of Him, Mandy Transou
Vice President of Human Resour, Marnese Elder
Medical Director of Adult Medicine, Noel Santini
Senior Vice President Of Women And Infants Specialty Health, Paula Turicchi
Senior Vice President, Miriam Sibley
Director of Pharmacy, Vivian Johnson
Vice President, Clifann Mccarley
Senior Vice President (Internal Audit Service), Vic Summers
Vice President, Katherine Yoder
Operating Room Dir, SUZANNE SIMS
Vice President, Patrick Jones
Radiology Director, Terry Napper
Vice Chair, Michael D. (Mike) Williams
Chair Board of Managers, Winfred Parnell

LOCATIONS

HQ: DALLAS COUNTY HOSPITAL DISTRICT
5200 HARRY HINES BLVD, DALLAS, TX 752357709
Phone: 214 590-8000
Web: WWW.PHHS.ORG

PRODUCTS/OPERATIONS

Selected Facilities
Bluitt Flowers Health Center
de Haro-Saldivar Health Center
East Dallas Health Center
Garland Health Center
Oak West Health Center
Pediatric Primary Care Center
Simmons Ambulatory Surgery Center
Southeast Dallas Health Center
Vickery Health Center

COMPETITORS

Baylor University Medical Center
CHRISTUS Health
Children's Medical Center of Dallas
Community Health Systems
HCA
Harris Methodist Fort Worth Hospital

JPS Health Network
Presbyterian Hospital of Dallas
Tenet Healthcare
Texas Health Resources
The Methodist Health System

HISTORICAL FINANCIALS

Company Type: Private

Income Statement

FYE: September 30

	REVENUE ($ mil.)	NET INCOME ($ mil.)	NET PROFIT MARGIN	EMPLOYEES
09/15	665	33	5.1%	9,500
09/14	755	3	0.4%	
Annual Growth	(11.8%)	1028.8%	—	—

DANA-FARBER CANCER INSTITUTE, INC.

The Dana-Farber Cancer Institute fights cancer on two fronts: It provides treatment to cancer patients young and old and researches new cancer diagnostics treatments and preventions. The organization's scientists also research AIDS treatments and cures for a host of other deadly diseases. Patients receive treatment from Dana-Farber through its cancer centers operated in conjunction with Brigham and Women's Hospital Children's Hospital Boston and Massachusetts General Hospital. The institute is also a principal teaching affiliate of Harvard Medical School. Dana-Farber is funded by the National Cancer Institute the National Institute of Allergy and Infectious Diseases and private contributions.

Operations

Dana-Farber reports more than 38300 patient visits a year and is involved in some 700 clinical trials.

Dana-Farber provides care to children and adults with cancer while advancing the understanding diagnosis treatment cure and prevention of cancer and related diseases. As an affiliate of Harvard Medical School and a Comprehensive Cancer Center designated by the National Cancer Institute the Institute also provides training for new generations of physicians and scientists designs programs that promote public health particularly among high-risk and underserved populations and disseminates innovative patient therapies and scientific discoveries to target community across the US and around the world. In 2014 the hospital has a community benefit of $6.75 million.

Geographic Reach

The institute primarily serves patients in New England. Dana-Farber's main campus is in Boston's Longwood Medical Area and it also has facilities in Brighton Milford South Weymouth and Pittsfield (all in Massachussets); Londonderry New Hampshire; and Waterford Connecticut.

Dana-Farber Community Cancer Care physician practices are in seven communities throughout eastern Massachusetts.

Financial Performance

The institute reported a 7% rise in revenues in 2014 thanks to an increase in patient service revenues unrestricted contributions and bequests and other operating revenues. Revenues from the Medicare and Medicaid programs accounted for approximately 25% and 5% respectively of Dana-Farber's net patient service revenue in 2014

Net income decreased by 11% due to an increase in temporarily restricted net assets and contributions.

Strategy

When it comes to patient care Dana-Farber emphasizes the importance of forming research and treatment partnerships with other health care organizations. To that end the institute has opened a handful of treatment clinics on other medical campuses including one at Faulkner Hospital in southwest Boston and another at Milford Regional Medical Center in Massachusetts.

Along with expanding on other campuses Dana-Farber built a new cancer care center on its main campus in Boston.

Although Dana-Farber directs its research efforts toward saving lives from deadly diseases some of its discoveries also bring in a tidy income as the company and its research partners occasionally license out their drug discoveries to pharmaceutical companies.

In 2015 new research by Dana-Farber scientists raised the prospect of cancer therapy that works by converting a tumor's best friends in the immune system into its gravest enemies. In a study published in the journal Science an international collaboration of investigators from Dana-Farber Harvard Medical School Boston Children's Hospital and the University of Strasbourg uncovered a mechanism that allows key immune system cells to keep a steady rein on their more belligerent brother cells thereby protecting normal healthy tissue from assault. The discovery has powerful implications for cancer. By blocking the mechanism with a drug it may be possible to turn the attack-suppressing cells into tumor-attacking cells.

Company Background

In 2013 the institute and Lawrence + Memorial Cancer Center opened a $34.5 million 47000 sq.-ft. cancer facility in Waterford Connecticut.

The Yawkey Center for Cancer Care named in honor of long-time contributor The Yawkey Foundation opened in 2011 to serve a growing number of patients. The 275000-sq.-ft center's 14-stories house most of Dana-Farber's adult outpatient care. The building has more than 100 exam rooms about 140 infusion chairs and a number of consultation rooms for family and patients. It also connected Dana-Farber to other campus buildings and to its clinical partners Brigham and Women's Hospital and Children's Hospital Boston.

Dana-Farber Cancer Institute was founded as a children's cancer research foundation in 1947 by Dr. Sidney Farber. The institute later expanded its services to provide programs for adults as well as children.

EXECUTIVES

President and CEO, Laurie H. Glimcher, age 65
EVP and COO, Dorothy E. Puhy, age 65
VP and Chief Marketing Officer, David A. Feinberg
SVP Patient Care Services and Chief Nursing Officer, Anne Gross
Chair Department of Medical Oncology, James D. Griffin
Chief Scientific Officer, Barrett J. Rollins
SVP and CFO, Michael L. Reney
Chief Department of Imaging, Annick D. Van den Abbeele
Chief Surgical Officer, Scott J. Swanson
Chief Medical Officer, Craig A. Bunnell
Chief Clinical Research Officer, Bruce E. Johnson
Chair Department of Pediatric Oncology, Scott A. Armstrong
Chief Medical Officer Dana-Farber/Boston Children's Cancer and Blood Disorders Center, Lisa R. Diller
Professor and Chair Department of Radiation Oncology Dana-Farber Cancer Institute/Brigham and Women's Hospital/Boston Children's Hospital, Daphne Haas-Kogan
Chair Executive Committee for Research (ECR), William C. Hahn
Chair Executive Committee for Clinical Programs (ECCP), Robert J. Soiffer
Chair Executive Committee for Clinical Research (ECCR), Mary-Ellen Taplin
Chair Department of Psychosocial Oncology and Palliative Care, James Tulsky
President Dana-Farber/Boston Children's Cancer and Blood Disorders Center, David A. Williams
Benacerraf Professor And Department Chair, Harvey Cantor
Director Of Pharmacy, Sylvia Bartel
Senior Vice President Human Resources, Deborah Hicks
VICE PRESIDENT, Melissa Shore
Medical Director for Clinical Trials Operations, Jeffrey Clark
FACULTY VICE PRESIDENT FOR FACULTY DEVELOPMENT, Glorian Sorensen
Senior Vice President Communications, Steven R Singer
Vice President Finance, John R Stewart
Vice President Facilities and Real Estate, Maria Papola
Vice President Clinical Bussiness Development, Elizabeth Liebow
Director of Nursing and Clinical Services, Janet Bagley RN
SENIOR VICE PRESIDENT FOR PATIENT CARE SERVICES AND CHIEF OF NUR, Patricia Reid-ponte
Treasurer, Mark Gisherman
Assistant Secretary, Kathleen Harkey
Co Chairman of the Gay lesbian Bisexual transgender Employee Resource Group, Cindy MacKenzie

LOCATIONS

HQ: DANA-FARBER CANCER INSTITUTE, INC.
450 BROOKLINE AVE, BOSTON, MA 022155450
Phone: 617 632-3000
Web: WWW.DANA-FARBER.ORG

PRODUCTS/OPERATIONS

2014 Sales

	% of total
Patients Services	62
Research	30
Unrestricted Contributions and Bequests	6
Other revenue	2
Total	**100**

Selected Clinical Affiliations

Dana-Farber/Brigham and Women's Cancer Center (outpatient services for adult cancer patients provided by Dana-Farber; and inpatient care provided by Brigham and Women's Hospital)

Dana-Farber/Children's Hospital Cancer Center (Dana-Farber Cancer Institute and Children's Hospital Boston outpatient care for children provided at Dana-Farber's Jimmy Fund Clinic)

Dana-Farber/Harvard Cancer Center (Beth Israel Deaconess Medical Center Brigham and Women's Hospital Children's Hospital Boston and Massachusetts General Hospital collaborate on research cancer prevention and treatments and therapies for cancer patients)

Dana-Farber/Lawrence + Memorial Cancer Center (cancer facility Waterford Connecticut).

Dana-Farber/Partners Cancer Care (consolidated adult oncology programs and clinical research of Dana-Farber Cancer Institute Brigham and Women's Hospital and Massachusetts General Hospital)

Selected Satellite Centers

Dana-Farber/Brigham and Women's Cancer Center at Faulkner Hospital in Jamaica Plain (southwest Boston area)

Dana-Farber/Brigham and Women's Cancer Center at Milford Regional Medical Center (Massachusetts)

Dana-Farber/Brigham and Women's Cancer Center in clinical affiliation with South Shore Hospital (South Weymouth Massachusetts)

Dana-Farber/New Hampshire Oncology-Hematology (Londonderry)

Adult Treatment Centers and Clinical Services

Blood Cancers

Breast Cancer
Cancer Genetics and Prevention
Cutaneous (Skin) Cancer
Gastrointestinal Cancer
Genitourinary Cancer
Gynecologic Cancer
Head and Neck Cancer
Hematology
Melanoma
Neuro-Oncology
Sarcoma
Thoracic (Lung) Cancer
Pediatric Treatment Centers and Clinical Services
Blood Disorders Center
Brain Tumor Center
Hematologic Malignancies Center
Solid Tumors Center
Stem Cell Transplant Center

COMPETITORS

Baystate Health	Johns Hopkins Medicine
Beth Israel Deaconess Medical Center	MD Anderson Cancer Center
Boston Medical Center	Mayo Clinic
Brigham and Women's Hospital	Memorial Sloan-Kettering
Care New England	Partners HealthCare
CareGroup	Roswell Park Cancer Institute
Children's National Medical Center	St. Elizabeth's Medical Center
Emory Healthcare	St. Jude Children's Research Hospital
Fox Chase Cancer Center	

HISTORICAL FINANCIALS
Company Type: Private

Income Statement
FYE: September 30

	REVENUE ($ mil.)	NET INCOME ($ mil.)	NET PROFIT MARGIN	EMPLOYEES
09/15	739	4	0.6%	3,000
09/14	672	34	5.1%	—
09/13	635	56	8.8%	—
09/10	894	16	1.9%	—
Annual Growth	(3.7%)	(22.7%)	—	—

2015 Year-End Financials
Return on assets: 16.8%
Return on equity: 0.6%
Current ratio: 0.50
Cash ($ mil.): 28

DARTMOUTH COLLEGE

EXECUTIVES

Manager, Cheryl Josler
Director, Lisa Ladd
Supervisor, Fawna Wilson
Supervisor, Scott Jandreau
Auditors: PRICEWATERHOUSECOOPERS LLP BO

LOCATIONS

HQ: DARTMOUTH COLLEGE
6193 HINMAN, HANOVER, NH 037554007
Phone: 603 646-2191
Web: WWW.DARTMOUTHCOOP.COM

HISTORICAL FINANCIALS
Company Type: Private

Income Statement
FYE: June 30

	REVENUE ($ mil.)	NET INCOME ($ mil.)	NET PROFIT MARGIN	EMPLOYEES
06/16	859	(301)	—	10
06/15	876	236	27.0%	—
06/14	866	680	78.5%	—
06/13	1,080	394	36.5%	—
Annual Growth	(7.3%)	—	—	—

2016 Year-End Financials
Return on assets: 11.6%
Return on equity: (-35.1%)
Current ratio: 0.80
Cash ($ mil.): 207

DAS NORTH AMERICA, INC.

EXECUTIVES

President, Jongmin Uhm
Director, Kyung Ho Hang
Director, Dong Hyoung Lee
Director, Si Hyoung Lee
Auditors: WARREN AVERETT CPA'S MONTGOME

LOCATIONS

HQ: DAS NORTH AMERICA, INC.
840 INDUSTRIAL PARK BLVD, MONTGOMERY, AL
361175528
Phone: 334 694-5335

HISTORICAL FINANCIALS
Company Type: Private

Income Statement
FYE: December 31

	REVENUE ($ mil.)	NET INCOME ($ mil.)	NET PROFIT MARGIN	EMPLOYEES
12/15	182	(3)	—	500
12/14	116	(4)	—	—
Annual Growth	56.9%	—	—	—

2015 Year-End Financials
Return on assets: 4.8%
Return on equity: (-2.1%)
Current ratio: 0.30
Cash ($ mil.): 8

DATA RECOGNITION CORPORATION

EXECUTIVES

Chief Executive Officer, Susan Shannon Engeleiter
Board of Directors, John Bandy
Vice-President, Deanna Hudella
Director, Lori Fritts
Director, Gail Carpenter
Project Manager, Stephanie Morstad
Auditors: COPELAND BUHL & COMPANY PLLP

LOCATIONS

HQ: DATA RECOGNITION CORPORATION
13490 BASS LAKE RD, MAPLE GROVE, MN
553113634
Phone: 763 268-2000
Web: WWW.DATARECOGNITIONCORP.COM

HISTORICAL FINANCIALS
Company Type: Private

Income Statement
FYE: October 31

	REVENUE ($ mil.)	NET INCOME ($ mil.)	NET PROFIT MARGIN	EMPLOYEES
10/15	201	28	14.0%	629
10/14	185	15	8.1%	—
10/13	206	30	14.7%	—
10/12	178	28	16.0%	—
Annual Growth	4.1%	(0.4%)	—	—

2015 Year-End Financials
Return on assets: 1.8%
Return on equity: 14.0%
Current ratio: 1.20
Cash ($ mil.): 4

DAUGHTERS OF CHARITY SERVICES OF ST. LOUIS

EXECUTIVES

President, Robert G Porter
Chief Financial Officer, Mark Oconnor

LOCATIONS

HQ: DAUGHTERS OF CHARITY SERVICES OF ST. LOUIS
12303 DE PAUL DR, BRIDGETON, MO 630442512
Phone: 314 344-6000
Web: WWW.SSMDEPAUL.COM

HISTORICAL FINANCIALS
Company Type: Private

Income Statement
FYE: December 31

	REVENUE ($ mil.)	NET INCOME ($ mil.)	NET PROFIT MARGIN	EMPLOYEES
12/15	396	41	10.4%	1,550
12/14	368	40	11.0%	—
Annual Growth	7.7%	2.3%	—	—

2015 Year-End Financials
Return on assets: 4.2%
Return on equity: 10.4%
Current ratio: 0.30
Cash ($ mil.): 14

DAVENPORT COMMUNITY SCHOOL DISTRICT

EXECUTIVES

Superintendent, Julio Almanza
Chief Financial Officer, Linda Mordhorst
Manager, Linda Doran
Personnel Director, Linda Madera
Personnel Director, Virginia Wipert
Director, Dawn A Rascher
Superintendent, Arthur W Tate

LOCATIONS

HQ: DAVENPORT COMMUNITY SCHOOL DISTRICT
1606 BRADY ST STE 100, DAVENPORT, IA 528034709
Phone: 563 336-5000
Web: WWW.DAVENPORTSCHOOLS.ORG

HISTORICAL FINANCIALS

Company Type: Private

Income Statement

	REVENUE ($ mil.)	NET INCOME ($ mil.)	NET PROFIT MARGIN	EMPLOYEES
06/16	208	(16)	—	2,450
06/10	177	(4)	—	—
06/09	182	5	3.2%	—
06/07	2,136	0	—	—
Annual Growth	(22.8%)	—	—	—

FYE: June 30

DAVIDSON'S, INC.

EXECUTIVES

Chairman, Bryan Tucker
Manager, Clark Aposhian
Chief Financial Officer, Drew Kramer
Auditors: EIDE BAILLY LLP PHOENIX ARIZ

LOCATIONS

HQ: DAVIDSON'S, INC.
6100 WILKINSON DR, PRESCOTT, AZ 863016162
Phone: 928 776-8055
Web: WWW.DAVIDSONSINC.COM

HISTORICAL FINANCIALS

Company Type: Private

Income Statement

	REVENUE ($ mil.)	NET INCOME ($ mil.)	NET PROFIT MARGIN	EMPLOYEES
11/15	342	16	4.7%	89
11/14	322	15	4.7%	—
11/13	395	20	5.1%	—
11/12	265	11	4.4%	—
Annual Growth	8.8%	11.0%	—	—

FYE: November 30

2015 Year-End Financials

Return on assets: 4.9%
Return on equity: 4.7%
Current ratio: 1.00
Cash ($ mil.): 1

DAYTON CHILDREN'S HOSPITAL

EXECUTIVES

Chief Executive Officer, Deborah A Feldman
VP Finance, David T Miller
Coordinator, Barbara Downs
Director, Gary Mueller
Director, Thomas E Maher Jr
Vice-President, Brett Lee

LOCATIONS

HQ: DAYTON CHILDREN'S HOSPITAL
1 CHILDRENS PLZ, DAYTON, OH 454041873
Phone: 937 641-3000
Web: WWW.CHILDRENSDAYTON.ORG

HISTORICAL FINANCIALS

Company Type: Private

Income Statement

	REVENUE ($ mil.)	NET INCOME ($ mil.)	NET PROFIT MARGIN	EMPLOYEES
06/15	233	17	7.3%	1,081
06/14	256	47	18.6%	—
06/13	247	48	19.7%	—
06/11	216	39	18.4%	—
Annual Growth	1.9%	(19.0%)	—	—

FYE: June 30

2015 Year-End Financials

Return on assets: 8.0%
Return on equity: 7.3%
Current ratio: 3.20
Cash ($ mil.): 74

DE PAUL UNIVERSITY

In the land of da Bulls and da Bears there's DePaul. One of the largest private not-for-profit universities in the US DePaul has some 23000 students attending classes at its Chicago-area campuses and its increasing offerings of online learning courses. The university offers more than 300 undergraduate and graduate programs through 10 colleges and schools including the Kellstadt Graduate School of Business and the College of Communication. It has a student teacher ratio of 15 to 1. One of the country's largest Catholic institutions of higher learning DePaul was founded in 1898 by the Vincentian religious community and is named after 17th century French priest St. Vincent de Paul.

Geographic Reach

DePaul's five Chicago-area campuses are located in Lincoln Park the Loop and the O'Hare area. Although 67% of its students come from Illinois DePaul's student body hosts learners from the 50 US states and more than 100 countries.

Financial Performance

DePaul has an annual budget of about $550 million and its endowment is about $420 million. Undergraduate tuition for the 2017-2018 academic year was $39000.

EXECUTIVES

Vice President, Bonnie Frankel
EVP Financial Affairs, Robert L. (Bob) Kozoman
VP Facilities, Robert (Bob) Janis
Dean Driehaus College of Business and Kellstadt Graduate School of Business, Ray Whittington
Dean School for New Learning, Marisa Alicea
Dean Theatre School, John Culbert
Dean College of Computing and Digital Media, David Miller
President, A. Gabriel Esteban
VP Information Services, Bob McCormick
Dean College of Communication, Salma Ghanem
Provost, Marten denBoer
VP Planning and Presidential Administration, Jay Braatz
SVP Enrollment Management, David Kalsbeek
Dean College of Science and Health, Gerald P. Koocher
Athletic Director, Jean Lenti-Ponsetto
Interim Dean College of Liberal Arts and Social Sciences, Lucy Rinehart
Dean College of Law, Jennifer Rosato Perea
Dean School of Education, Paul Zionts
Assistant Vice President for Board Services, Chad Jordahl
Vice President and General Counsel, Jose Padilla
Assistant Vice President, Lisa Cheers
Acting Vice President Finance, Bonnie Hirsch
Vice President Enrollment Management, Glenna Ousley
Vice President of Finance Operating Loop Campus, Rebecca Awells
Assistant Vice President Academic Affairs, Charles Strain
Associate Vice President Advocacy And Community Affairs, Cynthia Summers
Assistant Vice President for Marketing Communications, Gwyn Friend
Assoc Vice President Career and Money Management LOOP, JoAnn Alulla
Assistant Vice President, Peter Harris
Associate Vice President Of Advancement, Abena Apea
Assistant Vice President for Cross College Initiatives; Accreditation, Caryn Chaden
Associate Vice President Enrollment Services, Paula Luff
Assistant Vice President Diversity Empowerment and I Lincoln Park Campus, David Atharp
Vice President Student Affairs, James Doyle
Assistant Vice President University Ministry Lpc, Guillermo Acampuzano
Assistant Vice President GEMS Loop Campus, Suzanne Adepeder
Assoc Vice President Career and Money Management LOOP, Amanda Azonta
Department Chair Teacher Education, Roxanne Owens
Associate Vice President, Barbara M Schaffer
Executive Vice President for Student Affairs, Andrew Willett
Executive Vice President for Academic Affairs, Michael Greene
Director of Admissions, Jason Beck
Assistant Vice President for Academic Space, Ralph Erber
Vice President for Human Resources, Stephanie Smith
Vice President Facility Operations, Bob Janis
Board Member, R Ostrander
Auditors: KPMG LLP CHICAGO IL

LOCATIONS

HQ: DE PAUL UNIVERSITY
1 E JACKSON BLVD, CHICAGO, IL 606042287
Phone: 312 362-6714
Web: WWW.DEPAUL.EDU

HISTORICAL FINANCIALS

Company Type: Private

Income Statement

FYE: June 30

	REVENUE ($ mil.)	NET INCOME ($ mil.)	NET PROFIT MARGIN	EMPLOYEES
06/15	562	38	6.9%	3,895
06/14	564	59	10.5%	—
06/13	558	76	13.6%	—
06/12	546	39	7.2%	—
Annual Growth	1.0%	(0.7%)	—	—

2015 Year-End Financials

Return on assets: 6.5%
Return on equity: 6.9%
Current ratio: —
Cash ($ mil.): 53

DEACON CORP.

EXECUTIVES

Chief Executive Officer, Steven D Deacon
Administrative Assistant, Melissa Silva
Partner, Bob Miller
Principal, Pete Snook
Office Manager, Cynthia Hulliger
Superintendent, Ed Laplante
Project Manager, Robert Zochert
Auditors: BFBA LLP SACRAMENTO CALIFOR

LOCATIONS

HQ: DEACON CORP.
7745 GREENBACK LN STE 250, CITRUS HEIGHTS, CA 956105865
Phone: 916 969-0900

HISTORICAL FINANCIALS

Company Type: Private

Income Statement

FYE: October 31

	REVENUE ($ mil.)	NET INCOME ($ mil.)	NET PROFIT MARGIN	EMPLOYEES
10/15	391	5	1.5%	340
10/14	389	1	0.4%	—
10/13	388	1	0.4%	—
10/12	384	7	1.9%	—
Annual Growth	0.6%	(7.8%)	—	—

2015 Year-End Financials

Return on assets: 24.0%
Return on equity: 1.5%
Current ratio: 1.00
Cash ($ mil.): 23

DEACONESS HOSPITAL INC

Deaconess Hospital provides benevolent medical assistance to residents of southern Indiana western Kentucky and southeastern Illinois. The not-for-profit hospital is a 365-bed acute care medical facility that is the flagship hospital of the Deaconess Health System. Specialized services include cardiovascular surgery cancer treatment orthopedics neurological and trauma care. The hospital also offers home health care hospice services and med-

ical equipment rental and it operates outpatient family practice surgery wellness and community outreach centers. Founded in 1892 Deaconess Hospital is a teaching and research facility affiliated with the Indiana University School of Medicine.

Operations

Deaconess handles about 18000 inpatient visits per year. It also sees about 350000 outpatients and 65000 emergency room visitors and it handles about 7500 annual surgery procedures.

Geographic Reach

Deaconess Hospital is located in Evansville Indiana and provides services to about 26 surrounding counties.

Strategy

To improve services to area residents Deaconess Hospital is expanding its outpatient care facilities and enhancing its IT resources. For instance in 2013 it moved its urgent care center to a larger more efficient facility. The hospital is also pursuing recognition for specialist programs such as its stroke center which was certified as a level one facility in 2013.

EXECUTIVES

Vice President Facilities Support Services, Bruce E Epmeier
Vice President Channel Sales, Tina Hazelip

LOCATIONS

HQ: DEACONESS HOSPITAL INC
600 MARY ST, EVANSVILLE, IN 477101674
Phone: 812 450-5000
Web: WWW.DEACONESS.COM

Selected Services

24-hour Emergency Center
Cancer Services
Corporate Wellness
Family Medicine Clinic
Heart Services
Home Medical Equipment
Home-based Medical Care
Hospice Care
Inpatient and Outpatient Surgery
Mental Health Services
Neuro Services
Orthopedics
Pediatrics
Physician Referral Service
Radiology Services
Residency Program
Support Groups and Programs
Women's Hospital

COMPETITORS

Ball Memorial Hospital
Baptist Health
Baptist Health Madisonville
Commonwealth Health Corporation
Community Health Network
Daviess Community Hospital
Good Samaritan Hospital (IN)
Henry County Memorial Hospital
Jewish Hospital & St. Mary's HealthCare
Kosciusko Community Hospital
Memorial Hospital (Logansport)
Norton Healthcare
St. Mary's Medical Center of Evansville

HISTORICAL FINANCIALS

Company Type: Private

Income Statement

FYE: September 30

	REVENUE ($ mil.)	NET INCOME ($ mil.)	NET PROFIT MARGIN	EMPLOYEES
09/15	680	138	20.3%	5,300
09/14	623	113	18.1%	—
09/13	544	17	3.3%	—
09/12	577	58	10.1%	—
Annual Growth	5.7%	33.3%	—	—

2015 Year-End Financials

Return on assets: 5.4%
Return on equity: 20.3%
Current ratio: 2.10
Cash ($ mil.): 84

DECATUR MEMORIAL HOSPITAL

Not-for-profit Decatur Memorial Hospital (DMH) serves residents of Macon and neighboring counties in central Illinois. The 300-bed regional medical facility has a staff of 300 physicians who provide acute and tertiary care. DMH operates about a dozen Centers of Excellence in areas including cancer heart and lung women's health birthing allergy orthopedic and stroke care. Other health care services include preventive care through its DMH Wellness Center; home health and hospice programs and local urgent care and primary care through centers in the surrounding area.

Geographic Reach

DMH operates about 30 satellite facilities in addition to the main hospital facility in Decatur Illinois. It serves Central Illinois residents in all of Macon County and parts of Dewitt and Moultrie counties.OperationsIn addition to general and specialty care services DMH conducts education and clinical research programs partly through affiliations with the University of Illinois College of Medicine (basic and clinical medicine programs) and with Southern Illinois University School of Medicine (family practice residency). The hospital also conducts nurse training programs in partnership with area schools.

In 2013 DMH reported 10941 inpatient admissions; 264301 outpatient visits; 49505 emergency room visits; and more than 1000 births.The hospital contributed $43 million in community benefits that year.

Strategy

DMH is expanding its services and facilities to better serve patients.

In 2013 it introduced a new surgical table (the hana table) for use in minimally invasive hip replacement surgery and trauma procedures. It also installed the GE Discovery 750w 3.0T MRI system—the first GE trimodality CT/PET/MR imaging system installed in the US.

In addition DMH opened a new breast feeding clinic staffed by certified lactation counselors and a board certified lactation consultant.

In 2012 the hospital introduced the O-arm Multidimensional Imaging Systemm manufactured and distributed by the Navigation division of Medtronic and opened Decatur Memorial Hospital Varicose Vein Center at its main hospital facility.Company Background

DMH has established several express care clinics at select Wal-Mart locations and in 2011 it introduced online e-visits to help patients receive treatment for non-critical conditions. Patients submit information on symptoms and a DMH provider then addresses treatment of such conditions as colds and coughs stomach ailments minor infections allergies and rashes.

DMH' use of technology has also brought it recognition by being chosen as the winner of Modern Healthcare's 2011 IT Case Study Contest. DMH improved procedures for managing inpatient diabetes care through adoption of new IT tools including electronic nursing documentation computerized physician order entry and glucose monitoring systems.

The system has been recognized three consecutive years as a Top 50 Cardiovascular Hospital by Truven Health Analytics.

Thomson Reuters recognized DMH as one of the nation's 100 Top Hospitals in 2011. It has also been recognized by other analytical firms for its cardiovascular care services.

DMH was established in 1916.

EXECUTIVES

Physical Therapy Director, Jeff Brown
Vice President, Kim Stone
Director of Pharmacy, Kandie Dino

LOCATIONS

HQ: DECATUR MEMORIAL HOSPITAL
2300 N EDWARD ST, DECATUR, IL 625264192
Phone: 217 877-8121
Web: WWW.DECATURMEMORIAL.COM

PRODUCTS/OPERATIONS

Selected Services
Arthur Medical Center
Births at DMH
Bone and Joint Center
Brain & Stroke Center
Breast Center
Cafeteria
Cancer Care Institute
Center for Advanced Molecular Medicine
Center for Minimally Invasive Surgery
Center for Sight
Central Illinois Orthopaedic Center
Central Illinois Surgery Center of DMH
Chaplaincy Services
Coffee Shop
Corporate Health
Customer Service
Dialysis Inpatient Services
Emergency Care Center
ENTA Allergy Head & Neck Institute
e-visits
Express Care
Family Birth Center
Family Lodge
Forsyth Imaging Center
Forsyth Physical Therapy
Forsyth Professional Center
Foundation
Gift Shop
Heart & Lung Institute
Home Health Services
Hospice
Institutional Review Board (IRB)
Kenwood Medical Center
Medical Equipment
Medical Home
Millennium Pain Center
Nurse Anesthesia Program
Occupational Medicine
Parish Nursing Program
Pastoral Services
Pharmacy
  Physical T
Physical Therapy - East Gate
Physician Plaza Pharmacy
PrimeTime Services
Psychological Services
Radiation Oncology
Radiology
Radiology Interventional
Rehabilitation Services
Physical Occupational & Speech Therapy
Senior Health and Wellness Center
SHORE
Sleep Center
South Shores Imaging Center
South Shores Medical Center
Sports Enhancement Center/Physical Therapy
Sports Medicine
  Sports Med
Sullivan Medical Center
Thrift Shop
Thyroid Surgical Institute
Vascular Center
Volunteer Services
Wellness Center

Women's Health & Breast Center
Wound Clinic

COMPETITORS

Advocate BroMenn
Carle Hospital
Hospital Sisters
  Health System

Memorial Medical
  Center
Sarah Bush Lincoln
  Health Center

HISTORICAL FINANCIALS
Company Type: Private

Income Statement FYE: September 30

	REVENUE ($ mil.)	NET INCOME ($ mil.)	NET PROFIT MARGIN	EMPLOYEES
09/15	258	(3)	—	1,311
09/14	268	15	6.0%	—
09/13	249	(8)	—	—
09/12	272	10	3.8%	—
Annual Growth	(1.7%)	—	—	—

2015 Year-End Financials

Return on assets: 3.2%   Cash ($ mil.): 11
Return on equity: (-1.3%)
Current ratio: 0.30

DEER VALLEY SCHOOL DISTRICT 97

EXECUTIVES

Superintendent, James R Veitenheimer
Assistant Manager, Bill Maas
Purchasing Agent, Sharon Mason
Administrative Assistant, Susan Parks
Assistant Manager, Gayle Galligan
Auditors: HEINFELD MEECH & CO PC P

LOCATIONS

HQ: DEER VALLEY SCHOOL DISTRICT 97
20402 N 15TH AVE, PHOENIX, AZ 850273636
Phone: 623 445-5000
Web: WWW.DVUSD.ORG

HISTORICAL FINANCIALS
Company Type: Private

Income Statement FYE: June 30

	REVENUE ($ mil.)	NET INCOME ($ mil.)	NET PROFIT MARGIN	EMPLOYEES
06/16	276	17	6.5%	3,500
06/13	274	2	1.0%	—
06/11	294	8	2.9%	—
06/06	265	(14)	—	—
Annual Growth	0.4%	—	—	—

DEKALB MEDICAL CENTER, INC.

As far as DeKalb is concerned da healthier da better! Beginning as a rural hospital DeKalb Regional Health System now serves all of the Atlanta metropolitan area. The health system operating as DeKalb Medical is home to two acute care hospitals

- DeKalb Medical at North Decatur and DeKalb Medical at Hillandale (with a combined total of about 550 beds). It also operates a 75-bed long-term rehabilitation hospital — DeKalb Medical at Downtown Decatur. Specialty hospital services include oncology cardiology orthopedics and diabetes care. The health system which was founded in 1961 also operates primary specialty and mobile health care clinics partly through the DeKalb Medical Physicians Group.

Operations
The health network of three hospitals staffs more than 800 physicians who represent about 55 medical specialties including neurosurgery interventional radiology sports medicine endovascular surgery gynecology emergency medicine and infectious disease. Altogether DeKalb Medical's facilities had some 27000 inpatient visits 123000 outpatient encounters 120000 emergency department visits and delivered some 5000 babies during 2014.

In addition to medical services DeKalb Medical offers educational residency programs in subjects including pharmacy nursing and podiatry. It also operates a school for radiology technicians.

Geographic Reach
In addition to its main facilities in Decatur and Hillandale the company has operations in Lilburn Lithonia Snellville Stone Mountain and Tucker Georgia.

Strategy
DeKalb Medical is a self-supporting not-for-profit community hospital that does not receive tax dollars as part of its funding. The hospital system's operating budget comes solely from patient fees; DeKalb Medical reinvests any excess income into expanding or updating its services and facilities to meet Atlanta's growing population. The DeKalb Medical Foundation was established in 1991 and since then has funded improvements in facilities technology and community outreach programs.

EXECUTIVES

VP Patient Care Services and Chief Nursing Officer, Susan Breslin
EVP and COO, Dane Henry
SVP and CFO, John Katsianis
SVP and Chief Strategy Officer, Jim Forstner
VP Information Systems and CIO, Elizabeth Patino
VP Medical Affairs, Raoul Mayer
CEO and Director, Robert Wilson
Rph, Rebecca White
Medical Director of Emergency Services, Pascal Crosley
Chairman, David L. Jollay

LOCATIONS

HQ: DEKALB MEDICAL CENTER, INC.
2701 N DECATUR RD, DECATUR, GA 300335918
Phone: 404 501-1000
Web: WWW.DEKALBMEDICAL.ORG

PRODUCTS/OPERATIONS

Selected Specialties
Cancer Center
Community Programs
Corporate Health Services
Emergency Department
Heart and Vascular Services
Orthopedic Services
Podiatry
Radiology and Medical Imaging
Rehabilitation Services
Senior Services
Sleep Center
Surgical Weight Loss
Volunteers
Wellness Center
Women's Services
Workswell Services
Wound Care

HISTORICAL FINANCIALS
Company Type: Private

Income Statement
FYE: June 30

	REVENUE ($ mil.)	NET INCOME ($ mil.)	NET PROFIT MARGIN	EMPLOYEES
06/15	303	4	1.6%	2,700
06/14	524	1	0.3%	—
06/11	422	0	0.2%	—
06/10	397	(15)	—	—
Annual Growth	(5.3%)	—	—	—

2015 Year-End Financials
Return on assets: 5.4%   Cash ($ mil.): 4
Return on equity: 1.6%
Current ratio: 1.10

DELAWARE RIVER PORT AUTHORITY

The famous painting of George Washington crossing the Delaware would have lacked a good deal of its drama if the Delaware River Port Authority of Pennsylvania and New Jersey (DRPA) had been around in 1776. DRPA keeps commuters (and leaders of revolutionary armies) out of small boats by operating the Benjamin Franklin Betsy Ross Commodore Barry and Walt Whitman toll bridges over the Delaware River which divides Pennsylvania from New Jersey. Bridge operations account for 90% of the agency's revenue. Through its Port Authority Transit Corp. (PATCO) subsidiary DRPA operates PATCO a rail service that links Philadelphia with communities on the New Jersey side of the Delaware.

Operations

The Benjamin Franklin Bridge opened in 1926 hosts average weekday traffic of more than 105000. DRPA's second-oldest bridge Walt Whitman opened in 1957 provides crossings for average weekday traffic of more than 108000. DRPA opened two more bridges during the mid-1970s that carry significantly less traffic than their older counterparts. Commodore Barry opened in 1974 has average weekday traffic of more than 39000.

Betsy Ross opened in 1976 provides passage for more than 32000 on an average weekday. PATCO launched in 1969 boasts an average weekday ridership of more than 36000. Since 2000 DRPA has operated the RiverLink Ferry System which annually transports about 110000 passengers between Philadelphia and Camden New Jersey.

Financial Performance

Mainly because of toll and fare increases DRPA's revenue grew by almost 10% in 2012 compared with 2011. It was helped by a 10% surge in bridge toll revenue and an 8% spike in PATCO sales. In addition the amount it earned on interest income jumped 17% from 2011 to 2012.

Strategy

PATCO is spending about $200 million to overhaul its some 120 rail cars. Another major DRPA project is redecking the suspended span and an-

chorage spans of the Walt Whitman Bridge for about $140 million. These improvements are part of a larger DRPA $1 billion five-year capital improvement plan. To gather money for capital improvements DRPA raised fares by 25% on its toll-bridges and 10% on PATCO in 2011.

Also in 2011 DRPA ended some major operations. The DRPA board voted to discontinue economic development spending and DRPA closed the Philadelphia Cruise Terminal at Pier 1 which had been operating in the Philadelphia Navy Yard for more than 10 years.

Company Background

DRPA was established by the New Jersey and Pennsylvania legislatures in 1919 as the Delaware River Bridge Joint Commission; it became the Delaware River Port Authority by an act of the US Congress in 1951.

EXECUTIVES

Chairman of the Board, Ryan Boyer
Director, Price Brannon
Personnel Director, Kelly Forbes

LOCATIONS

HQ: DELAWARE RIVER PORT AUTHORITY
  2 RIVERSIDE DR STE 603, CAMDEN, NJ 081031019
Phone: 856 968-2000
Web: WWW.DRPA.ORG

HISTORICAL FINANCIALS
Company Type: Private

Income Statement
FYE: December 31

	REVENUE ($ mil.)	NET INCOME ($ mil.)	NET PROFIT MARGIN	EMPLOYEES
12/15	341	102	30.0%	900
12/14	75	0	0.8%	—
12/13	328	92	28.2%	—
12/12	327	86	26.3%	—
Annual Growth	1.4%	5.8%	—	—

2015 Year-End Financials
Return on assets: 2.8%   Cash ($ mil.): 27
Return on equity: 30.0%
Current ratio: 0.30

DELNOR-COMMUNITY HOSPITAL

EXECUTIVES

President, Craig Livermore
Director, Pat Laska
Manager, Marilyn Nicol
Manager, Vivian Van

LOCATIONS

HQ: DELNOR-COMMUNITY HOSPITAL
  300 RANDALL RD, GENEVA, IL 601344202
Phone: 630 208-3000
Web: WWW.DELNOR.COM

HISTORICAL FINANCIALS
Company Type: Private

Income Statement
FYE: August 31

	REVENUE ($ mil.)	NET INCOME ($ mil.)	NET PROFIT MARGIN	EMPLOYEES
08/15	305	(210)	—	1,600
08/14*	44	5	11.4%	—
06/13	216	20	9.4%	—
06/12	214	21	10.2%	—
Annual Growth	12.5%	—	—	—
*Fiscal year change

2015 Year-End Financials
Return on assets: 34.6%   Cash ($ mil.): 3
Return on equity: (-68.9%)
Current ratio: 0.20

DENTON INDEPENDENT SCHOOL DISTRICT

EXECUTIVES

President, Mia Price
Board of Directors, Rudy Rodriguez
Purchasing Director, Cindy Willis
Auditors: HANKINS EASTUP DEATON TONN

LOCATIONS

HQ: DENTON INDEPENDENT SCHOOL DISTRICT
  1307 N LOCUST ST, DENTON, TX 762013037
Phone: 940 369-0000
Web: WWW.DENTONISD.ORG

HISTORICAL FINANCIALS
Company Type: Private

Income Statement
FYE: June 30

	REVENUE ($ mil.)	NET INCOME ($ mil.)	NET PROFIT MARGIN	EMPLOYEES
06/16	313	105	33.7%	3,300
06/15	291	(49)	—	—
06/14	269	174	64.8%	—
06/13	258	(36)	—	—
Annual Growth	6.7%	—	—	—

2016 Year-End Financials
Return on assets: 5.0%   Cash ($ mil.): 415
Return on equity: 33.7%
Current ratio: —

DEPAUW UNIVERSITY

DePauw University is a private co-educational liberal arts university with an approximate enrollment of 2300 students. Its campus boasts some 36 major buildings across nearly 700 acres including a 520-acre nature preserve located 45 miles west of Indianapolis. The university offers undergraduate degrees from more than 30 academic departments and programs as well as fellowships in media management and science. Prominent alumni include former US Vice President Dan Quayle former US Rep. Lee Hamilton and best-selling author Barbara Kinsolver. DePauw was

founded in 1837 by the Methodist Church. The university's School of Music founded in 1884 is one of the oldest in the US.

Geographic Reach

From its campus in Greencastle Indiana DePauw University spans some 700 acres at its main campus and a large nature preserve. The educational institution also offers students experiential learning opportunities off campus and abroad.

Operations

DePauw University with a student/faculty ratio of 10:1 maintains more than 200 faculty members. In general university tuition and fees run nearly $38300. Including room and board fees can reach $48950. The university is supported by a $513 million endowment.

EXECUTIVES

Vice President for Facilities Management
 Facilities Management, Richard Vance
Associate Vice President for Finance and
 Administration, Linneweber Travis
Associate Vice President FOR DEVELOPMENT,
 Dana Cummings
Vice President, Sophia Lan
Secretary, Ruth Myers
Secretary Data Entry Admission, Teresa Y Roberts
Secretary, Pamela Woodall
Secretary, Heidi Albin Menzel
Secretary, Christina Krouse
Auditors: CROWE HORWATH LLP CHICAGO IL

LOCATIONS

HQ: DEPAUW UNIVERSITY
 313 S LOCUST ST, GREENCASTLE, IN 461351736
Phone: 765 658-4800
Web: WWW.DEPAUW.EDU

PRODUCTS/OPERATIONS

Selected Academic Centers
Bartlett Reflection Center
Center for Student Engagement
Center for Teaching & Learning
Geographic Information Systems Lab
The Compton Center for Peace and Justice
The Compton Center for Peace and Justice
The Green Center for the Performing Arts
The Janet Prindle Institute for Ethics
The McDermond Center for Management and
 Entreprenuership
The Peeler Art Center
The Pulliam Center for Contemporary Media

HISTORICAL FINANCIALS
Company Type: Private

Income Statement				FYE: June 30
	REVENUE ($ mil.)	NET INCOME ($ mil.)	NET PROFIT MARGIN	EMPLOYEES
06/15	180	22	12.5%	652
06/13	246	94	38.4%	—
06/12	154	5	3.7%	—
06/11	0	0	—	—
Annual Growth	—	509.2%	—	—

2015 Year-End Financials
Return on assets: 6.4%   Cash ($ mil.): 18
Return on equity: 12.5%
Current ratio: 0.10

DESERT SANDS UNIFIED SCHOOL DISTRICT SCHOOL BUILDING CORPORATION

EXECUTIVES

Administrative Assistant, Stella Perez
Finance Manager, Adriana Romero
Senior Manager, Blanche Ramirez
Auditors: VAVRINEK TRINE DAY & CO LL

LOCATIONS

HQ: DESERT SANDS UNIFIED SCHOOL DISTRICT
 SCHOOL BUILDING CORPORATION
 47950 DUNE PALMS RD, LA QUINTA, CA 922534000
Phone: 760 771-8567
Web: WWW.DSUSD.US

HISTORICAL FINANCIALS
Company Type: Private

Income Statement				FYE: June 30
	REVENUE ($ mil.)	NET INCOME ($ mil.)	NET PROFIT MARGIN	EMPLOYEES
06/16	395	77	19.7%	3,200
06/08	2	(2)	—	—
06/07	0	0	—	—
06/05	252	0	—	—
Annual Growth	—	116.4%	—	—

DEVCON CONSTRUCTION INCORPORATED

Devcon Construction has built a sturdy business from building in the Bay Area. One of the area's top general building contractors Devcon has constructed more than 30 million sq. ft. of office industrial and commercial space. Its focus is on Northern California mainly in the San Francisco Bay Area and Silicon Valley. The company provides engineering design/build and interior design services. It specializes in high-tech projects including data centers and industrial research and development facilities. In addition to building company facilities and offices Devcon works on such projects as hotels restaurants parking structures retail stores sports facilities and schools.

Geographic Reach

Based in Milpitas California Devcon maintains several satellite offices in California in Petaluma Stockton and Santa Cruz as well as an office in Reno Nevada.

Strategy

Although most of Devcon's work is in California the company also has completed projects in Nevada Oregon Idaho Texas Massachusetts and Florida. Recent projects in the San Francisco Forty Niners Stadium in Santa Clara San Jose Sharks Ice Center in Pleasanton and the Stanford Research Computing Facility.

The company partnered with US-based Central Concrete in 2012 to supply its high-performing low-CO2 concrete for the new San Francisco 49er

Stadium. The move showcases Devcon's focus on sustainability as part of its projects.

EXECUTIVES

Vice President of Construction, Jonathan Harvey
Vice President Of Construction, Daisy Pereira
Auditors: JOHANSON & YAU ACCOUNTANCY COR

LOCATIONS

HQ: DEVCON CONSTRUCTION INCORPORATED
 690 GIBRALTAR DR, MILPITAS, CA 950356317
Phone: 408 942-8200
Web: WWW.DEVCON-CONST.COM

PRODUCTS/OPERATIONS

Selected Projects

1880 Mission Street San Francisco

3333 Scott Blvd. Buildings A B & C Santa Clara
Anderson Collection At Stanford University Stanford
Barnes & Nobles Palo Alto
Cisco Parking Structure 1 San Jose
Cisco Parking Structure 2 San Jose
Downtown Sunnyvale Town Center Sunnyvale
El Camino Family Housing South San Francisco
Fresno Hyatt Place Hotel Fresno
Friedenrich Center For Translational Research At 800
 Welch Road
Lawson Lane East - Buildings A & B Santa Clara
Oakland Air Traffic Control Tower (ATCT) Oakland
San Francisco 49ers Stadium Santa Clara
San Jose Earthquakes - MLS Soccer Stadium San Jose
SanDisk Milpitas
Santa Clara University Admissions & Enrollment
 Services Building Santa Clara
Sharks Ice Center Pleasanton
Stanford Research Computing Facility Stanford
The Plaza At Triton Park Foster City
University Plaza Palo Alto
Villa Siena Nursing Care Units Mountain View

COMPETITORS

Charles Pankow Builders	KPRS Construction Obayashi
DPR Construction	Rudolph & Sletten
Hathaway Dinwiddie Construction	Structure Tone Swinerton
Hensel Phelps Construction	Turner Corporation Webcor Builders

HISTORICAL FINANCIALS
Company Type: Private

Income Statement				FYE: December 31
	REVENUE ($ mil.)	NET INCOME ($ mil.)	NET PROFIT MARGIN	EMPLOYEES
12/15	1,224	14	1.2%	350
12/14	1,181	20	1.7%	—
12/13	1,012	12	1.2%	—
12/12	779	3	0.5%	—
Annual Growth	16.3%	60.4%	—	—

2015 Year-End Financials
Return on assets: 17.1%   Cash ($ mil.): 7
Return on equity: 1.2%
Current ratio: 0.90

DIALYSIS CLINIC, INC.

Dialysis Clinic Inc. or DCI is dedicated to caring for patients with end-stage renal disease (ESRD). The not-for-profit company which operates a network of more than 210 dialysis centers serving more than 14000 patients in 27 states also provides kidney transplant assistance services. Affiliate

DCI Donor Services is an organ and tissue procurement agency. DCI also funds kidney-related research and educational programs and is affiliated with various universities and teaching hospitals throughout the US including Tufts University the University of Arizona and Tulane University.

Geographic Reach

The company has its locations in Alabama Arizona Arkansas California Colorado Connecticut Florida Georgia Indiana Iowa Kentucky Louisiana Maine Massachusetts Missouri Montana Nebraska Nevada New Jersey New Mexico New York North Carolina Ohio Pennsylvania South Carolina Tennessee and Texas.

Strategy

DCI grows its network of facilities by forming partnerships with health care providers and other organizations. The company provides funding for construction and operation of the facility and it provides clinic support services including supply procurement and central laboratory services (through its DCI Lab subsidiary).

In 2012 the company opened a dialysis clinic in Albuquerque its first dialysis clinic in the South Valley region of New Mexico.

Company Background

DCI was established in 1971 by nephrologist Keith Johnson.

EXECUTIVES

Assistant Treasurer, Bill Wood
Secretary, Kami Bell
Auditors: DELOITTE & TOUCHE LLP NASHVIL

LOCATIONS

HQ: DIALYSIS CLINIC, INC.
1633 CHURCH ST STE 500, NASHVILLE, TN 372032948
Phone: 615 327-3061
Web: WWW.DCIINC.JOBS

COMPETITORS

DaVita	Renal Advantage
FMCNA	U.S. Renal Care
Fresenius	

HISTORICAL FINANCIALS

Company Type: Private

Income Statement

FYE: September 30

	REVENUE ($ mil.)	NET INCOME ($ mil.)	NET PROFIT MARGIN	EMPLOYEES
09/15	712	29	4.1%	5,000
09/14	663	35	5.4%	—
09/13	650	50	7.8%	—
09/12	664	45	6.8%	—
Annual Growth	2.3%	(13.8%)	—	—

2015 Year-End Financials

Return on assets: 2.7%   Cash ($ mil.): 237
Return on equity: 4.1%
Current ratio: 4.10

DICK ANDERSON CONSTRUCTION, INC.

EXECUTIVES

President, Martin Schuma
Board of Directors, Tim Ford
Project Manager, Bob Heberly

Superintendent, Dale Delack
Superintendent, Greg Schermele
Auditors: ANDERSON ZURMUEHLEN & CO PC

LOCATIONS

HQ: DICK ANDERSON CONSTRUCTION, INC.
3424 E US HIGHWAY 12, HELENA, MT 596019708
Phone: 406 443-3225
Web: WWW.DACONSTRUCTION.COM

HISTORICAL FINANCIALS

Company Type: Private

Income Statement

FYE: December 31

	REVENUE ($ mil.)	NET INCOME ($ mil.)	NET PROFIT MARGIN	EMPLOYEES
12/15	185	5	2.9%	160
12/14	167	3	2.3%	—
12/13	114	0	0.8%	—
12/12	70	2	3.7%	—
Annual Growth	38.2%	26.4%	—	—

2015 Year-End Financials

Return on assets: 1.7%   Cash ($ mil.): 9
Return on equity: 2.9%
Current ratio: 1.00

DIVIDEND CAPITAL DIVERSIFIED PROPERTY FUND INC.

EXECUTIVES

Chief Executive Officer, Dwight L Merriman III
VP Finance, Larry Braud
Auditors: KPMG LLP DENVER COLORADO

LOCATIONS

HQ: DIVIDEND CAPITAL DIVERSIFIED PROPERTY FUND INC.
518 17TH ST STE 1200, DENVER, CO 802024108
Phone: 303 228-2200

HISTORICAL FINANCIALS

Company Type: Private

Income Statement

FYE: December 31

	ASSETS ($ mil.)	NET INCOME ($ mil.)	INCOME AS % OF ASSETS	EMPLOYEES
12/16	1,783	55	3.1%	15
12/15	1,967	131	6.7%	—
12/14	2,148	33	1.6%	—
12/13	2,305	56	2.4%	—
Annual Growth	(8.2%)	(0.8%)	—	—

2016 Year-End Financials

Return on assets: 15.8%   Sales ($ mil): 216
Return on equity: 25.5%

DIXIE ELECTRIC MEMBERSHIP CORPORATION

EXECUTIVES

Manager, Larry Jenkins
Financial Executive, Wendy Armstrong
Manager, Melanie Watts
Vice-President, Arthur Hurst
Director, Randy Buchanan
Operations Manager, Tracy Johnson

LOCATIONS

HQ: DIXIE ELECTRIC MEMBERSHIP CORPORATION
16262 WAX RD, GREENWELL SPRINGS, LA 707394964
Phone: 225 261-1221
Web: WWW.DEMCO.ORG

HISTORICAL FINANCIALS

Company Type: Private

Income Statement

FYE: December 31

	REVENUE ($ mil.)	NET INCOME ($ mil.)	NET PROFIT MARGIN	EMPLOYEES
12/15	206	4	2.3%	230
12/10	175	12	6.9%	—
12/09	161	6	4.2%	—
Annual Growth	4.2%	(5.9%)	—	—

2015 Year-End Financials

Return on assets: 6.8%   Cash ($ mil.): 1
Return on equity: 2.3%
Current ratio: 0.50

DO IT BEST CORP.

For home builders and Mr. (and Ms.) Fix-its hardware cooperative Do it Best wants you to make the best even better. One of the industry's largest hardware cooperatives it boasts more than 3800 member-owned stores in 50-plus countries but primarily the US. Besides the usual tools and building materials merchandise includes automotive items bicycles camping gear housewares office supplies and small appliances. Customers also can have products specially shipped to their local stores through Do it Best's e-commerce site. The co-op's buying power enables members to offer items at competitive prices.

Operations

The company has eight retail service centers.

Some of the suppliers of the company are All American Do It Center Rogers Do It Best Hardware Your Building Centers and Building Depot.

With a wholesale sales volume of nearly $3 billion Do it Best provides affiliated stores with the buying power and services they need to remain competitive in the hardware and building materials industry.

The company has more than 67000 items available for distribution and more than 1400 in its no-adder drop ship vendor program.

Geographic Reach

Based in Fort Wayne Indiana Do it Best operates member-owned hardware stores primarily in the US in Illinois Missouri South Carolina Ohio Nevada

New York Texas and Oregon as well as in more than 50 countries globally.

Sales and Marketing

Nearly all of the Do it Best's sales are to dealer-members. Members are required to buy 20 voting common shares at $50 per share on becoming a member.

It incurred $16.4 million in advertising costs in 2015.

Financial Performance

In 2015 the company's net revenues increased by 5% due to a growth in shipment volumes and positive sales from lumber.

Do it Best's net income decreased by 45% due to higher sales costs and a decrease in other income.

In 2015 cash from operating activities grew by 52% as a result of changes in inventories payable; and accounts and notes receivable net.

Strategy

Do it Best works to set itself apart from other hardware cooperatives (such as Ace and True Value) by pursuing licensing opportunities. To this end its member stores offer an exclusive line of tools made by Channellock including lockback knives flashlights and vacuums. The alliance with Channellock is part of Do it Best's long-term strategy as it looks to attract more consumers to the Channellock brand which has a following among serious do-it-yourselfers and professionals.

Through its Voice Picking/Warehouse Management System software the company reduces warehouse returns and allowances as well as outbound freight expenses.

In 2015 the company re-launched doitbest.com their ecommerce platform and launched Do it Best INCOM SupplySM to better help its retail hardware and LBM members.

In the past three years Do it Best's members have completed 220 store enhancement and expansion projects across the US and in more than a dozen other countries with another 150 in progress including Do it Centers in Saudi Arabia. It also invested more than $14 million towards growth via its Retail Performance Loan Program. During the year the company also co-branded Signature.

Company Background

Formerly named Hardware Wholesalers Do it Best was founded in 1945 by Arnold Gerberding.

EXECUTIVES

VP Finance and CFO, Doug Roth
VP Information Technology, Michael J. (Mike) Altendorf
President and CEO, Daniel B. (Dan) Starr
VP Marketing, Timothy (Tim) Miller
VP Merchandising, Steve Markley
VP Lumber and Building Materials, Gary Nackers
Vice President Human Resources and General Counsel, Gary Furst
GM Vice President Business Unit Manager, Dori Meighan
Vice President Marketing, Tim Miller
Vice Chairman, Brad McDaniel
Chairman, John Holmes
Auditors: CROWE HORWATH LLP FORT WAYNE

LOCATIONS

HQ: DO IT BEST CORP.
6502 NELSON RD, FORT WAYNE, IN 468031947
Phone: 260 748-5300
Web: WWW.DOITBESTCORP.COM

PRODUCTS/OPERATIONS

Selected Programs
ADpak
Do it Best Rental Center

INCOM Distributor Supply Opportunity program

COMPETITORS

84 Lumber	Orgill
Ace Hardware	Sears
Home Depot	Sutherland Lumber
Lowe's	True Value
Menard	Wal-Mart
Northern Tool	

HISTORICAL FINANCIALS
Company Type: Private

Income Statement
FYE: June 25

	REVENUE ($ mil.)	NET INCOME ($ mil.)	NET PROFIT MARGIN	EMPLOYEES
06/16	2,925	0	0.0%	1,519
06/11	2,328	0	0.0%	—
06/10	2,296	0	0.0%	—
Annual Growth	4.1%	(5.7%)	—	—

2016 Year-End Financials
Return on assets: 12.6% Cash ($ mil.): 20
Return on equity: —
Current ratio: 0.80

DOCTORS HOSPITAL, INC.

EXECUTIVES

Director, Andrew Choban
Assistant Vice-President, Frank Fernandez
Vice-President, Sandra Hyatt
Director, Rosa Maria
Administrative Assistant, April White
Personnel Director, Hilde Zamora
Assistant Vice-President, Paul Mungo
Auditors: DELOITTE & TOUCHE LLP

LOCATIONS

HQ: DOCTORS HOSPITAL, INC.
5000 UNIVERSITY DR, CORAL GABLES, FL 331462008
Phone: 305 666-2111

HISTORICAL FINANCIALS
Company Type: Private

Income Statement
FYE: September 30

	REVENUE ($ mil.)	NET INCOME ($ mil.)	NET PROFIT MARGIN	EMPLOYEES
09/15	191	1	0.8%	717
09/14	201	23	11.4%	—
09/13	197	28	14.6%	—
09/12	202	18	9.3%	—
Annual Growth	(1.9%)	(57.6%)	—	—

2015 Year-End Financials
Return on assets: — Cash ($ mil.): —
Return on equity: 0.8%
Current ratio: 0.70

DOCTORS' HOSPITAL, INC.

Doctors Community Hospital is an acute care and surgical hospital serving the Washington DC area. The not-for-profit medical center admits 12000 patients each year and has some 220 beds and offers standard and specialty services such as diagnostics emergency and cardiac care diagnostics rehabilitation wound care and neurology. The hospital which has some 600 doctors on staff also includes a women's health center a sleep therapy division and the Joslin Diabetes Center. Established in 1975 Doctors Community Hospital provides community health services such as educational programs and support groups for specific medical conditions.

EXECUTIVES

Vice President Foundation, Robyn Williams
Vice President, Robyn Webb-Williams

LOCATIONS

HQ: DOCTORS' HOSPITAL, INC.
8118 GOOD LUCK RD, LANHAM, MD 207063574
Phone: 301 552-8118
Web: WWW.DCHWEB.ORG

PRODUCTS/OPERATIONS

Selected Services
Bariatric services
Breast health
Cancer services
Cardiac services
Diabetes services
Diagnostic service
Emergency services
Neurosciences
Orthopedic services
Robotic surgery
Sleep center
Surgical services
Sears/nose/throat
Support groups
Therapy services
Wound care

COMPETITORS

Adventist HealthCare	Johns Hopkins Medicine
Bon Secours Health	MedStar Health
Calvert Memorial Hospital	Providence Hospital (Washington DC)
Civista Health	Suburban Hospital
Dimensions Healthcare	

HISTORICAL FINANCIALS
Company Type: Private

Income Statement
FYE: June 30

	REVENUE ($ mil.)	NET INCOME ($ mil.)	NET PROFIT MARGIN	EMPLOYEES
06/15	197	7	3.9%	1,200
06/14	188	2	1.2%	—
06/13	181	1	0.7%	—
06/11	211	16	7.9%	—
Annual Growth	(1.7%)	(17.4%)	—	—

2015 Year-End Financials
Return on assets: 28.7% Cash ($ mil.): 30
Return on equity: 3.9%
Current ratio: 0.30

DON FORD SANDERSON INC

EXECUTIVES

President, David Kimmerle
Manager, Sandy Dockall
VP Marketing, Bob McKinzey
Account Manager, Todd Knudson
Senior Manager, Leslie Sanches

LOCATIONS

HQ: DON FORD SANDERSON INC
6400 N 51ST AVE, GLENDALE, AZ 853014600
Phone: 623 842-8600
Web: WWW.SANDERSONSFORD.COM

HISTORICAL FINANCIALS

Company Type: Private

Income Statement

FYE: December 31

	REVENUE ($ mil.)	NET INCOME ($ mil.)	NET PROFIT MARGIN	EMPLOYEES
12/15	679	3	0.5%	416
12/14	671	4	0.7%	—
12/13	692	5	0.8%	—
12/12	590	3	0.6%	—
Annual Growth	4.8%	(3.8%)	—	—

2015 Year-End Financials

Return on assets: 0.6%
Return on equity: 0.5%
Current ratio: 0.20
Cash ($ mil.): 1

DOWNINGTOWN AREA SCHOOL DISTRICT

EXECUTIVES

Superintendent, Lawrence Mussoline
Auditors: RAINER & COMPANY NEWTOWN SQUA

LOCATIONS

HQ: DOWNINGTOWN AREA SCHOOL DISTRICT
540 TRESTLE PL, DOWNINGTOWN, PA 193353459
Phone: 610 269-8460
Web: WWW.DASD.ORG

HISTORICAL FINANCIALS

Company Type: Private

Income Statement

FYE: June 30

	REVENUE ($ mil.)	NET INCOME ($ mil.)	NET PROFIT MARGIN	EMPLOYEES
06/16	212	4	2.1%	1,300
06/15	204	(18)	—	—
06/03	129	6	4.7%	—
06/02	121	(36)	—	—
Annual Growth	4.1%	—	—	—

2016 Year-End Financials

Return on assets: 13.8%
Return on equity: 2.1%
Current ratio: 0.70
Cash ($ mil.): 27

DOYLESTOWN HOSPITAL HEALTH AND WELLNESS CENTER, INC.

It takes a village to own a hospital and Doylestown Hospital is owned by the local women's civic organization Village Improvement Association (VIA Health). Founded in 1923 the hospital serves southeastern Pennsylvania and neighboring areas of New Jersey. With some 240 beds Doylestown Hospital provides a variety of acute and tertiary medical services. Specialties include cardiac surgery cancer care (as part of the University of Pennsylvania Cancer Network) and orthopedics. Affiliated with the hospital are two Pine Run nursing and assisted-living centers. Doylestown Hospital the flagship facility of the Doylestown Health system.

Operations

The hospital employs some 420 doctors across 50 specialties including radiology gastroenterology urology and pulmonology. Doylestown is also a certified chest pain center (via The Woodall Chest Pain Center) and a joint commission-certified primary stroke center. Additional hospital departments cover emergency critical care birthing rehabilitation and robotic surgery services.

In addition to the main medical center Doylestown Hospital operates three outpatient locations: The Health and Wellness Center in Warrington an Open MRI center in Hartsville and The Pavilion outpatient building located adjacent to the hospital. The parent organization VIA Health runs the Pine Run retirement centers as well as community health facilities.

Geographic Reach

Doylestown Hospital serves Bucks and Montgomery counties in Pennsylvania (including northern suburbs of Philadelphia) and Hunterdon and Mercer counties in neighboring New Jersey.

EXECUTIVES

VP and Chief Medical Officer, Scott S. Levy, age 59
President and CEO, James Brexler
Director of Admissions, Kathy Murphy
Chair, Carolyn Della-Rodolfa
Vice Chairman, Joan Parlee

LOCATIONS

HQ: DOYLESTOWN HOSPITAL HEALTH AND
WELLNESS CENTER, INC.
595 W STATE ST, DOYLESTOWN, PA 189012597
Phone: 215 345-2200
Web: WWW.DH.ORG

PRODUCTS/OPERATIONS

Selected Services

Hospice
Medical Imaging/Radiology
Outpatient Testing
Rehab/Therapy
Surgical Services
Visiting Nurse/Home Care
Women's Services
Cardiac-Neuro Services
Diabetes Management
GI/Endoscopy
Fibromyalgia
Lab Services
Medical Library
Mammography
Nutrition Counseling - Healthy Directions

COMPETITORS

Abington Memorial Hospital
Children's Hospital of Philadelphia
LVHN
Main Line Health System
North Philadelphia Health System
Pennsylvania Hospital
Shore Memorial Hospital
St. Luke's University Health Network
Tenet Healthcare
University of Pennsylvania Health System

HISTORICAL FINANCIALS

Company Type: Private

Income Statement

FYE: June 30

	REVENUE ($ mil.)	NET INCOME ($ mil.)	NET PROFIT MARGIN	EMPLOYEES
06/15	211	(37)	—	2,853
06/10	234	3	1.5%	—
06/09	202	6	3.1%	—
06/08	0	0	—	—
Annual Growth	—	—	—	—

2015 Year-End Financials

Return on assets: 7.9%
Return on equity: (-17.8%)
Current ratio: 1.10
Cash ($ mil.): 15

DRAKE UNIVERSITY

You won't find duck duck goose as part of the curriculum at Drake University. The Des Moines Iowa school provides undergraduate and graduate education programs for some 5500 students through its six colleges and schools: arts and sciences business and public administration education journalism and mass communications law and pharmacy and health sciences. It has a 15:1 student-to-faculty ratio. A private school Drake University was founded in 1881 with seed money from General Francis Marion Drake a Civil War general and former Iowa governor banker railroad builder and attorney. Drake University also hosts the Drake Relays one of the largest track and field events in the US.

Geographic Reach

Drake is located on a 150-acre campus in Des Moines Iowa. Its students hail from across the US and about 50 international countries.

Operations

The university offers more than 70 undergraduate programs as well as 20 graduate degrees. Drake employs 280 full-time faculty members. In addition to its main colleges and schools the university operates centers and institutes in fields including agricultural law finance humanities professional studies public policy scientific research and entrepreneurship.

Tuition and fees at the university runs at about $29000 each year and account for two-thirds of revenue.

Strategy

Expansion efforts at Drake include the opening of several new learning and laboratory facilities at the College of Pharmacy and Health Sciences in 2013. The university is also working to streamline administrative functions to control expenses.

EXECUTIVES

Vice President and Treasurer, Deborah Newsom
Vice President Of Philanthropy And Commu,
Angela Accurso
Auditors: DENMAN & COMPANY LLP WEST DES

LOCATIONS

HQ: DRAKE UNIVERSITY
    2507 UNIVERSITY AVE, DES MOINES, IA 503114505
Phone: 515 271-2011

PRODUCTS/OPERATIONS

Selected Services
College of Arts and Sciences
College of Business and Public Administration
College of Pharmacy and Health Sciences
Law School
School of Education
School of Journalism and Mass Communication

HISTORICAL FINANCIALS

Company Type: Private

Income Statement

FYE: June 30

	REVENUE ($ mil.)	NET INCOME ($ mil.)	NET PROFIT MARGIN	EMPLOYEES
06/15	224	31	13.9%	830
06/14*	196	8	4.5%	—
05/13	184	4	2.5%	—
05/12	180	5	2.9%	—
Annual Growth	7.5%	80.9%	—	—

*Fiscal year change

2015 Year-End Financials

Return on assets: 11.0%   Cash ($ mil.): 39
Return on equity: 13.9%
Current ratio: 0.50

DRISCOLL CHILDREN'S HOSPITAL

LOCATIONS

HQ: DRISCOLL CHILDREN'S HOSPITAL
    3533 S ALAMEDA ST, CORPUS CHRISTI, TX
    784111721
Phone: 361 694-5000
Web: WWW.DRISCOLLCHILDRENS.ORG

HISTORICAL FINANCIALS

Company Type: Private

Income Statement

FYE: April 30

	REVENUE ($ mil.)	NET INCOME ($ mil.)	NET PROFIT MARGIN	EMPLOYEES
04/15	262	99	37.7%	1,500
04/13	525	102	19.4%	—
04/12	248	54	22.1%	—
04/11	1,527	0	0.0%	—
Annual Growth	(35.6%)	2774.8%	—	—

2015 Year-End Financials

Return on assets: 5.4%   Cash ($ mil.): 47
Return on equity: 37.7%
Current ratio: 0.80

DRYMALLA CONSTRUCTION COMPANY, INC.

EXECUTIVES

Principal, Earl W Pitchford
Board of Directors, Pat Simons
Vice-President, Robert Scronce
Financial Executive, Jason Geisler
Auditors: DESROCHES PARTNERS LLP HOUST

LOCATIONS

HQ: DRYMALLA CONSTRUCTION COMPANY, INC.
    608 HARBERT ST, COLUMBUS, TX 789342812
Phone: 281 342-3853
Web: WWW.DRYMALLA.COM

HISTORICAL FINANCIALS

Company Type: Private

Income Statement

FYE: December 31

	REVENUE ($ mil.)	NET INCOME ($ mil.)	NET PROFIT MARGIN	EMPLOYEES
12/15	220	5	2.6%	105
12/14	131	1	0.8%	—
12/13	104	1	1.3%	—
12/12	104	(1)	—	—
Annual Growth	28.4%	—	—	—

2015 Year-End Financials

Return on assets: 16.6%   Cash ($ mil.): 6
Return on equity: 2.6%
Current ratio: 1.00

DUBOIS REGIONAL MEDICAL CENTER INC

EXECUTIVES

President, Raymond Graeca
Personnel Director, Vandora Holt
Office Manager, Mike Sands
Manager, Patricia Abell

LOCATIONS

HQ: DUBOIS REGIONAL MEDICAL CENTER INC
    100 HOSPITAL AVE, DU BOIS, PA 158011499
Phone: 814 371-2200

HISTORICAL FINANCIALS

Company Type: Private

Income Statement

FYE: June 30

	REVENUE ($ mil.)	NET INCOME ($ mil.)	NET PROFIT MARGIN	EMPLOYEES
06/15	249	3	1.3%	1,400
06/14	248	7	3.1%	—
06/10	240	10	4.4%	—
06/09	188	(2)	—	—
Annual Growth	4.8%	—	—	—

2015 Year-End Financials

Return on assets: 4.3%   Cash ($ mil.): 21
Return on equity: 1.3%
Current ratio: 1.80

DUCK RIVER ELECTRIC MEMBERSHIP CORPORATION

EXECUTIVES

President, Michael Watson
Board of Directors, Buford Jennings
Board of Directors, Barry Cooper
Executive Director, Bobby Vannatta
Director, Steve Oden
District Manager, Michael Trew
Auditors: WINNETT ASSOCIATES PLLC SHELB

LOCATIONS

HQ: DUCK RIVER ELECTRIC MEMBERSHIP
    CORPORATION
    1411 MADISON ST, SHELBYVILLE, TN 371603629
Phone: 931 684-4621
Web: WWW.DREMC.COM

HISTORICAL FINANCIALS

Company Type: Private

Income Statement

FYE: June 30

	REVENUE ($ mil.)	NET INCOME ($ mil.)	NET PROFIT MARGIN	EMPLOYEES
06/16	178	1	0.7%	160
06/15	187	2	1.5%	—
06/14	188	6	3.6%	—
06/13	180	9	5.1%	—
Annual Growth	(0.4%)	(49.0%)	—	—

2016 Year-End Financials

Return on assets: 13.3%   Cash ($ mil.): 3
Return on equity: 0.7%
Current ratio: 0.40

DUCKS UNLIMITED, INC.

If it walks like a duck and talks like a duck ... Ducks Unlimited wants to protect its habitat. The not-for-profit group works to conserve manage and restore wetlands and other waterfowl habitat through projects across North America and in more than 10 South American countries. With some 13 million acres under its care DU's efforts are aimed at ducks but also benefit more than 900 other wildlife species. Most of the organization's members and volunteers are sport hunters and DU puts out a magazine cable TV show and daily radio show for them. It also offers training in hunter ethics firearm safety and conservation and programs for children. DU was founded in 1937 and has more than 691000 members.

Operations

The group operates as a grassroots volunteer-based non-profit organization. Volunteers host more than 4000 fund-raising events annually such as shooting and fishing tournaments golf outings and member and sponsor banquets. DU's conservation mission receives significant support through a series of partnerships with private individuals landowners agencies scientific institutes and other communities.

Geographic Reach

Although it operates in South America DU focuses its conservation efforts in North America. It boasts projects in all 50 US states all 10 Canadian

provinces and key areas in Mexico. Of the 13 million acres conserved nearly half (6.4 million acres) are in Canada. About a third — some 4.7 million acres — are in the US with the remainder in Mexico. DU's conservation efforts extend to Brazil Bolivia Paraguay and the Caribbean.

Sales and Marketing

In addition to events and direct mail the organization uses its website online marketing Facebook and other social media platforms to attract and stay connected to members.

Financial Performance

DU reported total revenue of $188 million in fiscal 2014 an 11% increase over the prior year's $169 million. The difference was due to significant increases in federal and state habitat reimbursements and revenue earned from donated educational programming. The company also held on to more cash in 2014 boosting its cash flow by 128% over 2013. Each year more than 80% of the organization's expenditures go directly to conservation work vital to ducks geese and other wetland-dependent wildlife. (Its goal is to spend at least 80% on conservation projects.) Revenue and support have approached $4 billion since its founding.

Strategy

DU's mission continues to take aim at expanding coastal marshes for waterfowl as well as prairie potholes for breeding ducks and flyway wetlands for migrating waterfowl. Its success in 2014 was measured in its conservation efforts namely restoring or improving environments (some 209000 acres) for waterfowl and other wildlife in its territories. The organization also backs legislation that aligns with its mission. DU supported the 2014 Farm Bill which included a wetland conservation agenda and it works each year to secure government funding for wetlands conservation.

EXECUTIVES

Top Computer Executive (Cio Vice President Or Director Of Mis Or It Etc), Andy Pulliam
Senior Vice President Marketing and Communications, Jared Brown
President Ducks Unlimited de Mexico, John A. Tomke
President, George Dunklin
CEO, Dale Hall
Treasurer, Robert S. (Bob) Hester
President Ducks Unlimited Canada, Malcolm M. Dunfield
Chairman Ducks Unlimited Canada, Tom S. Worden
Senior Vice President Development, A Long
Chairman, John W. Newman
Auditors: KPMG LLP MEMPHIS TENNESSEE

LOCATIONS

HQ: DUCKS UNLIMITED, INC.
1 WATERFOWL WAY, MEMPHIS, TN 381202351
Phone: 901 758-3825
Web: WWW.DUCKS.ORG

PRODUCTS/OPERATIONS

Priority Areas for Waterfowl and Wetlands Conservation
Central Valley/Coastal California
Great Basin
Gulf Coastal Prairie
Hardwood Transition/Lower Great Lakes/St. Lawrence Plain
Mid-Atlantic Coast
Mississippi Alluvial Valley
Pacific Northwest
Prairie Pothole Region
Southern Great Plains
US Great Lakes System
Western Boreal Forest Canada

HISTORICAL FINANCIALS
Company Type: Private

Income Statement FYE: June 30

	REVENUE ($ mil.)	NET INCOME ($ mil.)	NET PROFIT MARGIN	EMPLOYEES
06/15	209	23	11.1%	500
06/14	178	5	3.2%	—
Annual Growth	17.5%	307.2%	—	—

2015 Year-End Financials

Return on assets: 6.2%   Cash ($ mil.): 19
Return on equity: 11.1%
Current ratio: 4.20

DUKE HEALTH RALEIGH HOSPITAL GUILD

EXECUTIVES

President, David Zaas
Manager, Diane Baggett
Director, Joseph Moore
Director, Mark Leithe
Marketing Manager, Carla Parker-Hollis

LOCATIONS

HQ: DUKE HEALTH RALEIGH HOSPITAL GUILD
3400 WAKE FOREST RD, RALEIGH, NC 276097317
Phone: 919 954-3000
Web: WWW.DUKERALEIGHHOSPITAL.ORG

HISTORICAL FINANCIALS
Company Type: Private

Income Statement FYE: June 30

	REVENUE ($ mil.)	NET INCOME ($ mil.)	NET PROFIT MARGIN	EMPLOYEES
06/15	348	60	17.3%	600
06/10	0	(0)	—	—
06/09	0	0	51.8%	—
Annual Growth	326.8%	255.5%	—	—

DUKE UNIVERSITY HEALTH SYSTEM, INC.

More than a campus infirmary the Duke University Health System operates the Duke University Hospital and other medical educational and research facilities on the Duke University grounds. Duke University Hospital has about 960 acute pediatric and psychiatric patient beds and specializes in trauma care diagnostics and cardiac and endoscopic surgeries. The health system also operates two community hospitals — Duke Regional Hospital (370 beds) and Duke Raleigh Hospital (186 beds) — as well as other area health clinics. Duke University Health System's facilities provide primary and specialty care home and hospice care clinical research physician and nurse training and public education programs.

Operations

The system was formed in 1998 to expand the core Medical Center operations and has since added the Durham and Raleigh community hospitals. The Duke University Health System is closely affiliated with the Duke University Medical School as well as with the Duke University School of Nursing. The three entities are all located within the Duke University Medical Center complex (consisting of research educational and clinical care facilities on the Duke campus) also known as Duke Medical. The medical complex also includes the health system's Duke Clinic which provides outpatient and non-emergency specialist care.

Duke University Health System and the university's medical schools train health care professionals in cutting-edge technologies and infrastructures. The entities also work together to advance biomedical and general medical research with the goal of discovering and improving methods of care. Funding for medical research comes from the National Institutes of Health and other government organizations as well as from partnerships with pharmaceutical and medical device companies.

Geographic Reach

While Duke University Health System focuses on medical educational and research work in the US (in the states of North Carolina and Virginia) as part of its business the health system operates a joint venture in India.

Financial Performance

In 2014 revenues increased 2% to $4.9 billion mainly as a result of increases in patient service revenues tuition and fees and investment earnings. The system's net income rose 14% to $1.8 billion led by higher investment returns.

Cash flow from operations fell 90% to $12 million in 2014 due to an increase of cash used for accounts and contributions receivable and changes in inventories.

Strategy

Duke University Health System is working to expand further in existing and new territories and is looking to widen its service offerings in cancer vascular orthopedic musculoskeletal women and children's care and outpatient ambulatory care. To this end the health system is expanding by adding new medical locations and boosting its expertise in technology. For example in 2015 the Duke Eye Center opened a new four-story clinical pavilion. The system also aims to improve efficiencies across all locations and to help community members access needed services.

The company's DLP Healthcare joint venture with LifePoint Health provides management and cost-control services to community hospitals in North Carolina. Maria Parham Medical Center its first client is a small hospital looking for operational support in the face of health reform changes and rising competition in the marketplace. DLP Healthcare holds an 80% stake in the Maria Parham facility through the management agreement. An investment of $15 million in nearby Person Memorial Hospital will go to capital improvements help eliminate its debt and pave the way for DLP Healthcare to acquire the hospital.

Duke Medicine has a partnership with Medanta — The Medicity — through which the pair has established the Medanta Duke Research Institute (MDRI) in India to research medical treatments (drugs and devices). Medanta a 1500-bed institute will fund the creation and operation of the facility as part of the agreement with Duke providing scientific clinical research and operational expertise. Medanta and Duke share joint oversight over implementation and management of the unit.

EXECUTIVES

CFO, Kenneth C. Morris
EVP, William J. Fulkerson

VP Patient Care and System and Chief Nurse Executive, Mary Ann Fuchs
President Duke Regional Hospital, Katie Galbraith
President Private Diagnostic Clinic PLLC, Mark F. Newman
Chief Medical Officer, Thomas A. Owens
President Duke Raleigh Hospital, David Zaas
President and CEO, A. Eugene Washington
Director of Pharmacy, Matthew Harris
Associate Vice President Finance and Divisional Chief Financial Officer Duke University Hospital, Sabrina Olsen
Chair, Thomas M. Gorrie
Vice Chair, Peter Van Etten
Auditors: KPMG LLP NORFOLK VIRGINIA

LOCATIONS

HQ: DUKE UNIVERSITY HEALTH SYSTEM, INC.
2301 ERWIN RD, DURHAM, NC 277054699
Phone: 919 684-8111
Web: WWW.DUKECHILDRENS.ORG

Selected Facilities

Duke Clinic (Durham North Carolina)
Duke Raleigh Hospital (Raleigh North Carolina)
Duke University Hospital (Durham North Carolina)
Duke Children's Hospital & Health Center
Durham Regional Hospital (Durham North Carolina)

PRODUCTS/OPERATIONS

2014 Sales

	% of total
Patient service	50
Grants & contracts	22
Tuition & fees	8
Investment return	8
Auxiliary enterprises	5
Contributions	4
Net assets released from restrictions	2
Other	1
Total	**100**

Selected Services

AIDS Research and Treatment Center (DART)
Anesthesiology
Aortic Disease
Asthma and Allergies
Attention Deficit Hyperactivity Disorder
Breast Cancer
Cardiac Rehabilitation
Children's Health
Coronary Artery Disease
Dermatology
Developmental and Behavioral Pediatrics
Diabetes
Diet & Fitness Center
Duke Heart Center
Duke Medicine
Ear Nose Throat Head & Neck Surgery
Eating Disorders
Endocrinology
Esophageal Cancer
Executive Health
Eye Center
Foot and Ankle
Gastroenterology
Gastrointestinal Cancer
General Orthopaedics
General and Consultative Heart Care
Geriatrics
Gynecologic Cancer
Gynecology
Health & Fitness Center
Health and Wellness
Healthy Lifestyles for Children
Heart Rhythm Services
Hematology
Hereditary Cancer
Hyperbaric Diving and Altitude Medicine
Infectious Diseases
Integrative Medicine
Knee Treatments
Leukemias Lymphomas and Myelomas
Lung Cancer
Men's Health
Neurological Disorders
Neuroscience
Obstetrics and Gynecology
Pain Disorders
Peripheral Vascular Disease
Prostate Cancer
Psychiatry
Pulmonology and Respiratory Medicine
Radiology
Research
Rheumatology and Immunology
Skin Cancer
Sleep Disorders
Smoking/Smoking Cessation
Speech and Audiology
Sports Medicine
Stroke Center
Transplants
Urologic Cancer
Valvular Heart Disease
Vascular Diseases
Women's Health
Women's Heart Care

COMPETITORS

Carolinas HealthCare System
Cone Health
Cumberland County Hospital System
Danville Regional Medical Center
FirstHealth of the Carolinas
Morehead Memorial Hospital
Novant Health
Rex Healthcare
Rowan Regional Medical Center
UNC Hospitals
Vidant Health
Wake Forest University Baptist Medical Center
WakeMed
Wesley Long Community Hospital

HISTORICAL FINANCIALS

Company Type: Private

Income Statement

FYE: June 30

	REVENUE ($ mil.)	NET INCOME ($ mil.)	NET PROFIT MARGIN	EMPLOYEES
06/16	3,160	(787)	—	16,627
06/13	2,539	516	20.4%	—
06/09	2,070	198	9.6%	—
Annual Growth	6.2%	—	—	—

2016 Year-End Financials

Return on assets: 4.1% Cash ($ mil.): 281
Return on equity: (-24.9%)
Current ratio: 0.70

DUPRE INVESTMENTS, INC.

EXECUTIVES

Chief Executive Officer, Coty Dupre Jr
Board of Directors, Douglas W Place
VP Marketing, Paul Silverlieb
Auditors: GRANT THORNTON LLP TULSA OK

LOCATIONS

HQ: DUPRE INVESTMENTS, INC.
201 ENERGY PKWY STE 500, LAFAYETTE, LA 705083851
Phone: 337 237-8471
Web: WWW.DUPRETRANSPORT.COM

HISTORICAL FINANCIALS

Company Type: Private

Income Statement

FYE: September 30

	REVENUE ($ mil.)	NET INCOME ($ mil.)	NET PROFIT MARGIN	EMPLOYEES
09/15	225	2	1.0%	1,400
09/12	187	4	2.3%	—
09/11	158	3	2.3%	—
09/10	2,133	0	0.0%	—
Annual Growth	(36.2%)	450.6%	—	—

2015 Year-End Financials

Return on assets: 2.1% Cash ($ mil.): 20
Return on equity: 1.0%
Current ratio: 1.40

DUPRE LOGISTICS, L.L.C.

EXECUTIVES

Chief Executive Officer, Coty R Dupre Jr
Vice-President, Dan Schinke
Sales Manager, Mark De Clouet
Operations Manager, Alfred Parker
Account Executive, Esau Washington
Director, Jude Reiners
Sales Director, Pat Casey
Auditors: GRANT THORNTON LLP TULSA OK

LOCATIONS

HQ: DUPRE LOGISTICS, L.L.C.
201 ENERGY PKWY STE 500, LAFAYETTE, LA 705083851
Phone: 337 237-8471
Web: WWW.DUPRELOGISTICS.COM

HISTORICAL FINANCIALS

Company Type: Private

Income Statement

FYE: September 30

	REVENUE ($ mil.)	NET INCOME ($ mil.)	NET PROFIT MARGIN	EMPLOYEES
09/16	180	1	0.6%	1,100
09/15	225	2	1.0%	—
09/14	222	7	3.3%	—
09/13	218	24	11.0%	—
Annual Growth	(6.2%)	(65.0%)	—	—

2016 Year-End Financials

Return on assets: 2.0% Cash ($ mil.): 22
Return on equity: 0.6%
Current ratio: 1.50

DUQUESNE UNIVERSITY OF THE HOLY SPIRIT

Duquesne University of The Holy Ghost keeps a keen eye on the spiritual as well as the academic. The school offers more than 100 undergraduate degree programs about 65 graduate and professional degree programs and more than 20 doctoral programs at schools of business education law liberal arts nursing pharmacy health sciences natural and environmental sciences music and leadership

and professional advancement. Duquesne was founded in 1878 as the Pittsburgh Catholic College of the Holy Ghost. It has an annual enrollment of more than 10000 undergraduate graduate and law students.

EXECUTIVES

Director Animal Care, J. Douglas Bricker
Assistant VP and CIO, Charles R. (Chuck) Bartel
President, Ken Gormley
VP Academic Affairs and Provost, Timothy R. Austin
Dean A.J. Palumbo School of Business Administration and John F. Donahue Graduate School of Business, Dean McFarlin
Dean Bayer School of Natural and Environmental Sciences, Philip Reeder
Dean Mary Pappert School of Music, Seth Beckman
Dean McAnulty College and Graduate School of Liberal Arts, James Swindal
Interim Dean Rangos School of Health Sciences, Paula Turocy
Dean School of Education, Cindy Walker
Interim Dean School of Law, Maureen Lally-Green
Dean School of Nursing, Mary Ellen Smith Glasgow
VP Management and Business, Matthew J. Frist
Auditors: SCHNEIDER DOWNS & CO INC PITT

LOCATIONS

HQ: DUQUESNE UNIVERSITY OF THE HOLY SPIRIT
600 FORBES AVE, PITTSBURGH, PA 152193016
Phone: 412 396-6000
Web: WWW.DUQ.EDU

PRODUCTS/OPERATIONS

2015 Sales

	% of total
Tuition and fees-net of financial aid	72
Auxiliary enterprises	17
Grants and contracts	4
Endowment earnings distributed for operations	3
Gifts and pledges	2
Other	2
Total	**100**

Selected Programs

Accounting
Athletic Training
Behavioral Science
Binary Engineering (Physics/Engineering)
Biochemistry
Biology
Biomedical Engineering (BME)
Biomedical Engineering (BME) - Nursing (BSN)
Business - General
Chemistry
Classical Civilization
Classical Greek
Classical Languages
Classical Latin
Communication Studies
Child Psychology
Clinical Mental Health Counseling
K-12 Latin Education
K-12 School Administration and Supervision
Early Level (PreK- 4)
Educational Studies- Educational Studies Concentration
Educational Studies- Program Evaluation
ESL MSEd and Certificate Program
Instructional Technology
Marriage and Family Counseling

HISTORICAL FINANCIALS

Company Type: Private

Income Statement

FYE: June 30

	REVENUE ($ mil.)	NET INCOME ($ mil.)	NET PROFIT MARGIN	EMPLOYEES
06/15	400	25	6.4%	3,601
06/12	262	7	2.8%	—
06/11	333	21	6.6%	—
06/10	580	0	0.0%	—
Annual Growth	(7.2%)	335.4%	—	—

2015 Year-End Financials

Return on assets: 9.2%   Cash ($ mil.): 14
Return on equity: 6.4%
Current ratio: 0.20

DURVET, INC.

EXECUTIVES

President, Robert Hormann
Operations Manager, Bob Bowers
Sales Manager, Jon Moose
Secretary, Andrea Cappuzzo
Director, Mark Niblo
Auditors: HSMC ORIZON LLC LEE'S SUMMIT

LOCATIONS

HQ: DURVET, INC.
100 SE MAGELLAN DR, BLUE SPRINGS, MO 640145909
Phone: 816 229-9101
Web: WWW.DURVET.COM

HISTORICAL FINANCIALS

Company Type: Private

Income Statement

FYE: November 30

	REVENUE ($ mil.)	NET INCOME ($ mil.)	NET PROFIT MARGIN	EMPLOYEES
11/16	178	7	4.0%	30
11/15	171	6	3.6%	—
11/14	169	6	3.9%	—
11/13	155	6	4.4%	—
Annual Growth	4.6%	1.9%	—	—

2016 Year-End Financials

Return on assets: 4.8%   Cash ($ mil.): —
Return on equity: 4.0%
Current ratio: 0.80

DUTCH GOLD HONEY, INC.

EXECUTIVES

President, Nancy J Gamber
Board of Directors, Chuck Schapzman
Director, Jill Clark
Vice-President, Norman Randall
VP Sales, Alan Ernst
Operations Manager, Judy Gable
Maintenance Supervisor, Mel Kutz
Auditors: BAKER TILLY VIRCHOW KRAUSE LLP

LOCATIONS

HQ: DUTCH GOLD HONEY, INC.
2220 DUTCH GOLD DR, LANCASTER, PA 176011997
Phone: 717 393-1716
Web: WWW.DUTCHGOLDHONEY.COM

HISTORICAL FINANCIALS

Company Type: Private

Income Statement

FYE: December 31

	REVENUE ($ mil.)	NET INCOME ($ mil.)	NET PROFIT MARGIN	EMPLOYEES
12/15	199	0	—	85
12/14	177	0	—	—
12/13	158	0	—	—
12/12	99	0	—	—
Annual Growth	26.3%	—	—	—

2015 Year-End Financials

Return on assets: 8.8%   Cash ($ mil.): —
Return on equity: —
Current ratio: 0.30

DUTCHESS EDUCATIONAL HEALTH INSURAN

EXECUTIVES

Principal, John Pennoyer
Auditors: SICKLERTORCHIAALLEN&CHURCHILLC

LOCATIONS

HQ: DUTCHESS EDUCATIONAL HEALTH INSURAN
5 BOCES RD, POUGHKEEPSIE, NY 126016565
Phone: 845 486-4800
Web: WWW.DCBOCES.ORG

HISTORICAL FINANCIALS

Company Type: Private

Income Statement

FYE: June 30

	REVENUE ($ mil.)	NET INCOME ($ mil.)	NET PROFIT MARGIN	EMPLOYEES
06/15	177	6	3.8%	7
06/14	151	(8)	—	—
06/13	139	(2)	—	—
06/10	128	2	1.8%	—
Annual Growth	6.6%	22.9%	—	—

2015 Year-End Financials

Return on assets: —   Cash ($ mil.): 65
Return on equity: 3.8%
Current ratio: 4.20

DYNASTY FARMS, INC.

EXECUTIVES

President, David L Johnson

LOCATIONS

HQ: DYNASTY FARMS, INC.
740 AIRPORT BLVD, SALINAS, CA 939014510
Phone: 831 755-1398
Web: WWW.DYNASTYFARMS.COM

HISTORICAL FINANCIALS
Company Type: Private

Income Statement
FYE: December 31

	REVENUE ($ mil.)	NET INCOME ($ mil.)	NET PROFIT MARGIN	EMPLOYEES
12/15	363	(2)	—	100
12/14	339	1	0.3%	—
12/13	324	(1)	—	—
12/12	270	4	1.5%	—
Annual Growth	10.3%	—	—	—

2015 Year-End Financials
Return on assets: 1.0% Cash ($ mil.): —
Return on equity: (-0.7%)
Current ratio: 1.00

DYNETICS, INC.

EXECUTIVES

Chairman of the Board, Marcus J Bendickson
Chief Executive Officer, David King
President, Greg Lester
Vice-President, Stephen Cook
Vice-President, Michael Moody
Chief Financial Officer, Randy Reynolds
Secretary, Michael Stebbins
Vice-President, Ronnie Chronister
Project Manager, Ken Finklea
Auditors: NOEL D TALLON CPA PC HUNTS

LOCATIONS

HQ: DYNETICS, INC.
 1002 EXPLORER BLVD NW, HUNTSVILLE, AL
 358062806
Phone: 256 964-4000
Web: WWW.DTS-DYNETICS.COM

HISTORICAL FINANCIALS
Company Type: Private

Income Statement
FYE: June 26

	REVENUE ($ mil.)	NET INCOME ($ mil.)	NET PROFIT MARGIN	EMPLOYEES
06/16	315	4	1.3%	1,532
06/13*	285	16	5.7%	—
07/12	266	17	6.5%	—
07/11	666	0	0.0%	—
Annual Growth	(13.9%)	484.3%	—	—

*Fiscal year change

2016 Year-End Financials
Return on assets: 1.2% Cash ($ mil.): 28
Return on equity: 1.3%
Current ratio: 2.60

DYSART UNIFIED SCHOOL DISTRICT

EXECUTIVES

Superintendent, Gail Pletnick Ed D
Account Manager, Thom Dickerson
Assistant Manager, Jim Dean

Assistant Manager, Steve Poling
Plant & Facilities Manager, Shirley Aguirre
Auditors: HEINFELD MEECH & CO PC PHO

LOCATIONS

HQ: DYSART UNIFIED SCHOOL DISTRICT
 15802 N PARKVIEW PL, SURPRISE, AZ 853747466
Phone: 623 876-7000
Web: WWW.DYSART.ORG

HISTORICAL FINANCIALS
Company Type: Private

Income Statement
FYE: June 30

	REVENUE ($ mil.)	NET INCOME ($ mil.)	NET PROFIT MARGIN	EMPLOYEES
06/16	199	12	6.4%	2,000
06/12	176	(9)	—	—
06/11	183	(15)	—	—
06/01	0	0	—	—
Annual Growth	—	109.2%	—	—

E-Z MART STORES, INC.

E-Z Mart Stores aims to make filling gas tanks and stomachs EZR for small-town America. The regional convenience store chain operates about 295 stores across four neighboring states including Arkansas Louisiana Oklahoma and Texas. Rather than build its own stores the company usually expands through acquisitions. In addition to the standard hot dogs sodas coffee and cigarettes most E-Z Mart locations also offer Shell Conoco Phillips 66 or CITGO gasoline. E-Z Mart was founded in 1970 by Jim Yates in Nashville Arkansas. Yates died in 1998 when the plane he was piloting crashed leaving his daughter Sonja Hubbard at the company's helm as CEO.

Geographic Reach

Ranked #35 on Convenience Store News ' "Top 100 Convenience Stores Report" E-Z Mart is a regional c-store chain that primarily serves Texas and Arkansas as well as Oklahoma and Louisiana.

Sales and Marketing

Aiming to offer the chain's customers access to updated fuel prices a list of locations and in-store promotions among other items E-Z Mart partnered with OpenStore by GasBuddy to roll out a new E-Z Mart website and mobile app. The fully integrated mobile app enables consumers to send feedback from their mobile phones and receive time-sensitive electronic mobile coupons.

Strategy

While E-Z Mart has trimmed its store count during the past decade or so including exiting markets such as Missouri it continues to make strategic acquisitions. Like other convenience store operators seeking to boost in-store sales E-Z Mart is expanding its food and beverage offering adding fresh-brewed iced tea to all of its stores and installing freezers. Outside the company has a deal with Redbox to place its movie rental kiosks outside of E-Z Mart stores.

EXECUTIVES

Chief Executive Officer, Sonja Hubbard
Manager, Debbie Flowers
Chief Financial Officer, Stacy Y Flod
Marketing Manager, Faellen Yates
Financial Executive, Les Smith
Director, Steve Launius
Auditors: BKD LLP PORT SMITH ARKANSAS

LOCATIONS

HQ: E-Z MART STORES, INC.
 602 FALVEY AVE, TEXARKANA, TX 755016677
Phone: 903 832-6502
Web: WWW.EZMART.COM

2014 Stores

	No.
Texas	96
Arkansas	95
Oklahoma	80
Louisiana	18
Total	**289**

COMPETITORS

7-Eleven	Love's Country Stores
Allsup's	QuikTrip
Brookshire Grocery	Racetrac Petroleum
Chevron	Susser Holdings
Exxon Mobil	Valero Energy
Krause Gentle	

HISTORICAL FINANCIALS
Company Type: Private

Income Statement
FYE: December 31

	REVENUE ($ mil.)	NET INCOME ($ mil.)	NET PROFIT MARGIN	EMPLOYEES
12/15	827	16	2.0%	2,100
12/14	1,026	19	1.9%	—
12/13	1,003	15	1.5%	—
12/12	1,018	33	3.3%	—
Annual Growth	(6.7%)	(20.9%)	—	—

2015 Year-End Financials
Return on assets: 2.4% Cash ($ mil.): 5
Return on equity: 2.0%
Current ratio: 0.40

E. C. BARTON & COMPANY

E. C. Barton & Company sells a variety of home-building tools and goods under a handful of banner names. A member of industry cooperative Do It Best the company sells lumber and building materials through more than 100 locations throughout Texas as well as 15 other states in the US Southeast and the Northeast. It operates several divisions including Barton's Builders Material Company E.C.B. Brokerage and Surplus Purchasing Surplus Warehouse and Grossman's Bargain Outlet. E. C. Barton also manages an e-commerce site. Professional builders and remodelers generate most of the company's revenue. The company is employee-owned.

Operations

The company has organized its business into a handful of divisions: Barton's Grossman's Bargain Outlet Builders Material Company E.C.B. Brokerage and Surplus Purchasing and Surplus Warehouse.

Geographic Reach

E. C. Barton operates its 100-plus stores in 16 states including Alabama Arkansas Connecticut Florida Louisiana Massachusetts Missouri Mississippi New York North Carolina Ohio Pennsylvania Rhode Island South Carolina Tennessee and Texas. More than half of its stores are located in four states: Arkansas New York Texas and Massachusetts.

Sales and Marketing

The retailer serves both professional builders and remodelers and is part of cooperative Do It Best.

Company Background

E. C. Barton was founded in 1885.

EXECUTIVES

President and CEO, Niel Crowson
Secretary and Treasurer, Tom Rainwater
Manager Builders Material Company, Steve Gage
Vice President of Operations, Greg Smith
Vice President Store Operations, Ron Bellas
Vice President Of Store Operations Bargain Outlet Division, Bill Ringelstein
Auditors: JONES & COMPANY LTD JONESBO

LOCATIONS

HQ: E. C. BARTON & COMPANY
2929 BROWNS LN, JONESBORO, AR 724017208
Phone: 870 932-6673
Web: WWW.DOITBEST.COM

PRODUCTS/OPERATIONS

Selected Products
Bath
Ceiling fans and light kits
Ceilings
Composite decking
Doors
Driveway sealer
Electrical
Flooring
Kitchens
Lighting
Moulding
Outdoor living
Paint
Paint sundries
Pine / oak / vinyl boards
Roofing
Screws & nails
Tools & hardware
Wall planking plywood & shims
Water heaters
Windows

Selected Divisions
Barton's
Builders Material Company
E.C.B. Brokerage and Surplus Purchasing
Grossman's Bargain Outlet
Surplus Warehouse

COMPETITORS

84 Lumber
Ace Hardware
BMC Stock
Builders FirstSource Southeast Group
Diamond Hill Plywood
Guardian Building Products Distribution
Home Depot
Lowe's
Northern Tool
Snavely Forest Products
True Value
WinWholesale

HISTORICAL FINANCIALS

Company Type: Private

Income Statement FYE: October 27

	REVENUE ($ mil.)	NET INCOME ($ mil.)	NET PROFIT MARGIN	EMPLOYEES
10/16	269	10	3.9%	700
10/15	253	5	2.1%	—
10/14	247	0	0.4%	—
10/13	241	(1)	—	—
Annual Growth	3.8%	—	—	—

2016 Year-End Financials

Return on assets: 2.2% Cash ($ mil.): 4
Return on equity: 3.9%
Current ratio: 0.40

E. RITTER & COMPANY

EXECUTIVES

Chairman, Daniel B Hatzenbuehler
President, Charles R Dickinson Jr
Vice-President, E Ritter Arnold
Financial Executive, Clint Orr
General Manager, Dan Kennedy
Auditors: KPMG LLP MEMPHIS TN

LOCATIONS

HQ: E. RITTER & COMPANY
10 ELM ST, MARKED TREE, AR 723652211
Phone: 870 358-7333

HISTORICAL FINANCIALS

Company Type: Private

Income Statement FYE: December 31

	REVENUE ($ mil.)	NET INCOME ($ mil.)	NET PROFIT MARGIN	EMPLOYEES
12/15	201	0	0.3%	175
12/14	186	2	1.4%	—
12/13	157	1	1.2%	—
12/12	139	5	3.7%	—
Annual Growth	13.1%	(52.0%)	—	—

2015 Year-End Financials

Return on assets: 8.1% Cash ($ mil.): 11
Return on equity: 0.3%
Current ratio: 0.60

EAGLE MOUNTAIN-SAGINAW INDEPENDENT SCHOOL DISTRICT

EXECUTIVES

Superintendent, Cole Pugh
Vice-Chairman, Dick Elkins
Financial Executive, Linda Suzie
Manager, Tammy Slimp
Plant & Facilities Manager, Charles Hamilton
Superintendent, Jim Chadwell
Auditors: HANKINS EASTUP DEATON TONN

LOCATIONS

HQ: EAGLE MOUNTAIN-SAGINAW INDEPENDENT SCHOOL DISTRICT
1200 OLD DECATUR RD, FORT WORTH, TX 761794300
Phone: 817 232-0123
Web: WWW.EMSISD.COM

HISTORICAL FINANCIALS

Company Type: Private

Income Statement FYE: August 31

	REVENUE ($ mil.)	NET INCOME ($ mil.)	NET PROFIT MARGIN	EMPLOYEES
08/15	191	17	9.1%	139
08/14	183	6	3.5%	—
08/13	171	3	2.0%	—
08/12	168	(43)	—	—
Annual Growth	4.5%	—	—	—

2015 Year-End Financials

Return on assets: 1.2% Cash ($ mil.): 64
Return on equity: 9.1%
Current ratio: —

EAST ALABAMA HEALTH CARE AUTHORITY

From babies to seniors The East Alabama Health Care Authority cares for all of Alabama's denizens. The authority's flagship facility is East Alabama Medical Center (EAMC) a general acute-care hospital with 340 beds and a skilled nursing facility with about 35 beds. Facilities at the medical center include an adult day care center cancer center hospice sleep disorders lab and surgery center. Services include diagnostic imaging physical therapy respiratory care and behavioral care. The system also operates EAMC-Lanier which includes an emergency department rehabilitation facilities a nursing home and an urgent care clinic.

Operations

The East Alabama Health Care Authority serves residents of east-central Alabama with a medical staff of more than 160 physicians practicing in about 40 different specialties.EAMC is the second-largest employer in Lee County with a staff of some 3000.

Geographic Reach

The East Alabama Health Care Authority services those who reside in Alabama's Lee County as well as five surrounding counties in east-central Alabama.

Financial Performance

The East Alabama Health Care Authority's revenue fell less than 1% in fiscal 2016 due to a decline in patient revenues. Other revenues increased 8% that year.

With the decline in revenue net income decreased 7% in 2016.

Strategy

The East Alabama Health Care Authority has been expanding its operations by opening new units within its facilities particularly at the EAMC-Lanier campus. In 2017 the system opened a new inpatient detox unit to assist patients in withdrawal; it also opened an acute inpatient rehabilitation unit (the first of its kind in the region).

Company Background

EAMC was founded as an 80-bed hospital in 1952.

EXECUTIVES

Vice President, Ken Lott
EVP and CFO, Sam Price
President and CEO, Terry W. Andrus, age 65
VP and Chief Medical Officer, Michael Lisenby
EVP and Administrator, Laura D. Gill
VP and Chief Planning Officer, Carey Owen

Assistant Vice President Information Services, Sarah Gray
Executive Vice President Administrator, Laura D. Grill
Assistant Vice President Operations, Greg Nichols
Ambulatory Services Director, Carol McCrory
Vice President Chf Administrative Officer, Darby Womelsdorf
Assistant Vice President, Christopher Clark
Operating Room Director, Claudia Henderson
Vice President Controller, Dennis Thrasher
Assistant Vice President Patient Care Services, Jane Fullum
VP Human Resources, Susan Johnston
Chairman, Joel Pittard
Vice Chairman, Ken McKemie
Secretary, Jane Cotton

LOCATIONS

HQ: EAST ALABAMA HEALTH CARE AUTHORITY
2000 PEPPERELL PKWY, OPELIKA, AL 368015452
Phone: 334 749-3411
Web: WWW.EAMC.ORG

PRODUCTS/OPERATIONS

Selected Services
Alzheimer's / Dementia Specialty Care
Ambulance Services
Aperian Laboratory Solutions Inc.
Assisted Living/Senior Communities
Auburn Diagnostic Imaging
Auburn MRI Center
Auburn University Medical Clinic
Auxiliary
Azalea Place Assisted and Independent Living

COMPETITORS

Ascension Health
Columbus Regional Healthcare System
Health Care Authority of the City of Huntsville
Jackson Hospital & Clinic of Alabama
Southeast Alabama Medical Center
University of Alabama
West Georgia Health System

HISTORICAL FINANCIALS

Company Type: Private

Income Statement
FYE: September 30

	REVENUE ($ mil.)	NET INCOME ($ mil.)	NET PROFIT MARGIN	EMPLOYEES
09/15	288	8	3.1%	2,250
09/14	255	17	6.9%	—
09/12	228	9	4.3%	—
09/09	1	0	—	—
Annual Growth	154.1%	—	—	—

2015 Year-End Financials
Return on assets: 3.5%
Return on equity: 3.1%
Current ratio: 2.40
Cash ($ mil.): 184

EAST BATON ROUGE MEDICAL CENTER LLC

EXECUTIVES

Chief Executive Officer, Mitch Wasden
Director, Steve Miller
Director, Claude Tellis
Chief Operating Officer, Eric Mc Millen

LOCATIONS

HQ: EAST BATON ROUGE MEDICAL CENTER LLC
17000 MEDICAL CENTER DR, BATON ROUGE, LA 708163246
Phone: 225 752-2470

HISTORICAL FINANCIALS

Company Type: Private

Income Statement
FYE: September 30

	REVENUE ($ mil.)	NET INCOME ($ mil.)	NET PROFIT MARGIN	EMPLOYEES
09/15	213	54	25.4%	500
09/14	182	34	18.8%	—
09/13	126	1	1.4%	—
09/12	106	(3)	—	—
Annual Growth	26.2%	—	—	—

2015 Year-End Financials
Return on assets: 0.7%
Return on equity: 25.4%
Current ratio: 2.90
Cash ($ mil.): —

EAST BAY MUNICIPAL UTILITY DISTRICT, WASTEWATER SYSTEM

EXECUTIVES

General Manager, Alexander Coate
Manager, Wanda H Talley
Manager, Patty Seu
Manager, Pat Cho
Financial Executive, David Klein
Purchasing Agent, Rebakah Sharpe
Auditors: MAZE & ASSOCIATES PLEASANT HI

LOCATIONS

HQ: EAST BAY MUNICIPAL UTILITY DISTRICT, WASTEWATER SYSTEM
375 11TH ST, OAKLAND, CA 946074246
Phone: 866 403-2683

HISTORICAL FINANCIALS

Company Type: Private

Income Statement
FYE: June 30

	REVENUE ($ mil.)	NET INCOME ($ mil.)	NET PROFIT MARGIN	EMPLOYEES
06/16	525	118	22.6%	241
06/05	56	51	91.7%	—
06/04	314	40	12.8%	—
Annual Growth	4.4%	9.4%	—	—

2016 Year-End Financials
Return on assets: 16.7%
Return on equity: 22.6%
Current ratio: 1.20
Cash ($ mil.): 163

EAST CAROLINA HEALTH INC

EXECUTIVES

Principal, Anita Hunt
Board of Directors, David Harris
Auditors: MCGLADREY LLP CHICAGO IL

LOCATIONS

HQ: EAST CAROLINA HEALTH INC
2100 STANTONSBURG RD, GREENVILLE, NC 278342818
Phone: 252 847-6156

HISTORICAL FINANCIALS

Company Type: Private

Income Statement
FYE: September 30

	REVENUE ($ mil.)	NET INCOME ($ mil.)	NET PROFIT MARGIN	EMPLOYEES
09/15	367	25	6.9%	2
09/14	366	5	1.4%	—
09/13	373	10	2.7%	—
Annual Growth	(0.8%)	57.8%	—	—

2015 Year-End Financials
Return on assets: 9.7%
Return on equity: 6.9%
Current ratio: 2.40
Cash ($ mil.): 37

EAST JEFFERSON GENERAL HOSPITAL

EXECUTIVES

Chief Executive Officer, Raymond Decorte
Partner, Martin H Klein
Partner, Dr Reita Lawrence
Executive Vice-President, Judy Brown
Chairman, Jim M Hudson
Treasurer, Ashton J Ryan Jr
Manager, Cheryl St Germain
Accountant, Anicia Braty

LOCATIONS

HQ: EAST JEFFERSON GENERAL HOSPITAL
4200 HOUMA BLVD, METAIRIE, LA 700062996
Phone: 504 454-4000
Web: WWW.EJGH.ORG

HISTORICAL FINANCIALS

Company Type: Private

Income Statement
FYE: December 31

	REVENUE ($ mil.)	NET INCOME ($ mil.)	NET PROFIT MARGIN	EMPLOYEES
12/15	322	(15)	—	3,436
12/14	328	(17)	—	—
12/13*	371	(12)	—	—
05/10	0	(0)	—	—
Annual Growth	240.4%	—	—	—

*Fiscal year change

2015 Year-End Financials
Return on assets: 7.8%
Return on equity: (-4.9%)
Current ratio: 1.00
Cash ($ mil.): 5

EAST MEADOW UFSD (INC)

EXECUTIVES

Superintendent, Robert Gorman
Assistant Manager, Anthony Russo
Director, Danielle Betz
Director, Patrice Dobies
Plant & Facilities Manager, Arthur Williams
Assistant Manager, David Casamento
Superintendent, Kenneth A Card Jr

LOCATIONS

HQ: EAST MEADOW UFSD (INC)
718 THE PLAIN RD STE 1, WESTBURY, NY
115905956
Phone: 516 478-5730
Web: WWW.EASTMEADOW.K12.NY.US

HISTORICAL FINANCIALS

Company Type: Private

Income Statement

FYE: June 30

	REVENUE ($ mil.)	NET INCOME ($ mil.)	NET PROFIT MARGIN	EMPLOYEES
06/16	190	1	0.8%	1,013
06/07	157	(1)	—	—
06/06	0	0	—	—
06/04	128	(10)	—	—
Annual Growth	3.3%	—	—	—

2016 Year-End Financials

Return on assets: 3.3%   Cash ($ mil.): 51
Return on equity: 0.8%
Current ratio: 2.10

EAST OHIO REGIONAL HOSPITAL

EXECUTIVES

Chief Executive Officer, Michael Caruso
Director, Theresa Hanson
Manager, Hal Davis
Supervisor, Timothy Jones
Project Manager, Becky Maruca

LOCATIONS

HQ: EAST OHIO REGIONAL HOSPITAL
90 N 4TH ST, MARTINS FERRY, OH 439351669
Phone: 740 633-1100
Web: WWW.OVRH.ORG

HISTORICAL FINANCIALS

Company Type: Private

Income Statement

FYE: December 31

	REVENUE ($ mil.)	NET INCOME ($ mil.)	NET PROFIT MARGIN	EMPLOYEES
12/15	209	(0)	—	11
12/13	67	1	2.0%	—
12/09	76	(2)	—	—
12/08	73	(1)	—	—
Annual Growth	16.1%	—	—	—

2015 Year-End Financials

Return on assets: 0.1%   Cash ($ mil.): —
Return on equity: (-0.2%)
Current ratio: 3.10

EAST TENNESSEE CHILDREN'S HOSPITAL ASSOCIATION, INC.

ETCH has made a permanent mark on the lives of countless children over the years. Knoxville-based East Tennessee Children's Hospital (ETCH) with more than 150 beds provides a full range of health care services to children from eastern Tennessee and portions of surrounding states. Among its 30 specialized services are cardiology neonatal care orthopedics and psychiatry as well as cystic fibrosis and hearing impairment services. The hospital also offers support such as for families of children stricken by cancer. The hospital's roots are in the foundation of Knox County Crippled Children's Hospital in 1937 with less than 50 beds.

Operations

With a total of about 450 physicians ETCH handles some 6000 inpatient visits per year while its emergency department treats some 70000 patients each year. The hospital is designated as a comprehensive regional pediatric center by the state of Tennessee. As such it operates a level III neonatal intensive care unit (ICU) and a level I trauma center and partners with smaller area hospitals in an effort to provide pediatric training support and patient transfer services. ETCH also partners with larger acute care hospitals including the University of Tennessee Medical Center to provide collaborative care services.

The medical center provides medical training services as well such as student internships nursing scholarships clinical rotations and residency programs. Some programs are offered through partnerships with area universities and colleges including the University of Tennessee and Lincoln Memorial University's DeBusk College of Osteopathic Medicine.

Geographic Reach

The medical center primarily serves 16 counties in eastern Tennessee: Anderson Blount Campbell Claiborne Cocke Grainger Hamblen Jefferson Knox Loudon Monroe Morgan Roane Scott Sevier and Union. It also provides services in other Tennessee counties and nearby portions of Kentucky North Carolina and Virginia.

EXECUTIVES

Nursing Director, Danni Varlan
Auditors: PERSHING YOAKLEY & ASSOCIATES

LOCATIONS

HQ: EAST TENNESSEE CHILDREN'S HOSPITAL ASSOCIATION, INC.
2018 W CLINCH AVE, KNOXVILLE, TN 379162301
Phone: 865 541-8000

PRODUCTS/OPERATIONS

Selected Services
Cancer
Cardiac
Emergency department
Hematology
Home health
Inpatient services
Intensive care unit (pediatric and neonatal)
Laboratory services
Mental health
Nutrition
Obesity
Orthopedics
Outpatient services
Radiology
Rehabilitation
Respiratory care
Sleep medicine
Surgical services
Sedation services
Transport service
Trauma

COMPETITORS

Akron Children's Hospital
All Children's Hospital
Children's Hopsital of Chicago
Children's Hospital Boston
Children's Hospital Colorado
Children's Hospital and Health System
Children's Hospital of Philadelphia
Children's Hospital of Richmond
Children's Mercy Hospital
Cincinnati Children's Hospital
Covenant Health
Dell Children's Medical Center
Nationwide Children's Hospital
Shriners Hospitals For Children
Tennova Healthcare
University Health System Inc.

HISTORICAL FINANCIALS

Company Type: Private

Income Statement

FYE: June 30

	REVENUE ($ mil.)	NET INCOME ($ mil.)	NET PROFIT MARGIN	EMPLOYEES
06/16	219	23	10.9%	1,500
06/15	210	3	1.7%	—
06/14	210	23	11.3%	—
06/13	216	37	17.4%	—
Annual Growth	0.5%	(14.0%)	—	—

2016 Year-End Financials

Return on assets: 5.1%   Cash ($ mil.): 17
Return on equity: 10.9%
Current ratio: 1.70

EASTER SEALS SOUTHERN CALIFORNIA, INC.

EXECUTIVES

Chief Executive Officer, Mark Whitley
Office Manager, April Montgomery
Chief Financial Officer, Susan Berglund
Director, Nancy Weintraub
Auditors: ARMANINO LLP SAN RAMON CA

LOCATIONS

HQ: EASTER SEALS SOUTHERN CALIFORNIA, INC.
1570 E 17TH ST, SANTA ANA, CA 927058502
Phone: 714 834-1111

HISTORICAL FINANCIALS

Company Type: Private

Income Statement

FYE: August 31

	REVENUE ($ mil.)	NET INCOME ($ mil.)	NET PROFIT MARGIN	EMPLOYEES
08/16	179	18	10.3%	640
08/15	140	11	7.9%	—
08/12	42	0	1.5%	—
08/10	34	0	0.4%	—
Annual Growth	31.4%	127.9%	—	—

2016 Year-End Financials

Return on assets: 4.9%   Cash ($ mil.): 21
Return on equity: 10.3%
Current ratio: 1.70

EASTERN BAG AND PAPER COMPANY, INCORPORATED

Eastern Bag and Paper Co. (dba EBP Supply) is a leading distributor of paper products in the northeastern US. In addition to disposable tableware and packaging the company offers foodservice products (including china and glassware) restaurant equipment (can openers refrigerators) personal care items (bath mats roll towels) and cleansers and maintenance supplies (air fresheners vacuums). Its name-brand products are used by the industrial healthcare foodservice and janitorial industries. Founded in 1918 by Samuel Baum the company is owned and run by CEO Meredith Baum Reuben.

Operations

EBP Supply has earned longtime relationships with affiliates such as the US Green Building Council International Sanity Supply Association Women's Business Enterprise National Council Government Services Agency Building Owners and Managers Association National Association of College Food Service Mass Restaurant Association and the New England Sanitary Supply Association. The company boasts national distribution thanks to its alliance with Network Distribution Services.

Geographic Reach

The company operates three distribution centers in Connecticut Massachusetts and New Jersey and maintains a fleet of more than 70 trucks and trailers. EBP Supply's distribution area spans a dozen states from Maine to northern Virginia.

Sales and Marketing

EBP Supply serves several sectors such as commercial building and facility healthcare foodservice institutional (including both government and education) and hospitality and recreation.

Strategy

In fall 2012 the company rebranded adopted a new logo and launched a new website EBPsupply.com to better convey its expanded product line. The rebranding was designed to focus on the company's customer-centric approach. In addition to the cleaning and restaurant supplies EBP Supply offers delivery consulting training and equipment repair services.

EXECUTIVES

Vice President, Joseph LoPresti
VP Purchasing, Ken Rosenberg

Vice President of Sales New Jersey Division, Matthew Sugarman
Vice President, Michael Kaplan
Vice President, Alan Schachter
Vice President of Marketing, Andrew Reuben
Vice President, Brian Reddy
Auditors: BLUM SHAPIRO & COMPANY PC

LOCATIONS

HQ: EASTERN BAG AND PAPER COMPANY, INCORPORATED
200 RESEARCH DR, MILFORD, CT 064602880
Phone: 203 878-1814
Web: WWW.EBPSUPPLY.COM

PRODUCTS/OPERATIONS

Selected Cleaning Brands

3M
Andersen Mat
Bay West
Berry Plastics Corporation
Certo
Clarke
Clorox
Diversey
Georgia-Pacific Professional
Glit
Gojo
Hospeco
Kimberly-Clark Professional
Procter & Gamble Professional
Rubbermaid Commercial Products
SCA Tork
Starco
Taski
Unger
US Chemical
Wausau Paper
Wilen

Selected Foodservice Brands

3M
Anchor Packaging
Bagcraft Papercon
Bay West
Cambro
Candle Lamp
Certo
Chicopee
Chinet
Crown Poly
D&W Fine Pack
Dart/Solo
Dixie
Dopaco
Duro Bags
ECO Products
Elkay Plastics
Fabri-Kal
Fold-Pak
FoodHandler
Genpak
Gordon Paper
Greenweave
Hoffmaster
Huhtamaki
Inline Pastics
McNairn Packaging
Morcon
National Checking Company
NCCO
Oneida
Pactiv
Royal Paper Products
Rubbermaid Commercial Products
Sabert
Safety Zone
San Jamar
SCA Tork
Scotch-Brite
Vollrath
Yoshi

Selected Products

Cleaning supplies & equipment
Foodservice packaging
Paper goods
Smallwares

COMPETITORS

AFFLINK	Perkins Paper
MAINES	RDA Advantage
Penn Jersey	Sysco

HISTORICAL FINANCIALS

Company Type: Private

Income Statement

FYE: December 31

	REVENUE ($ mil.)	NET INCOME ($ mil.)	NET PROFIT MARGIN	EMPLOYEES
12/15	192	1	0.6%	285
12/14	188	1	0.9%	—
12/13	182	2	1.1%	—
12/12	177	1	0.6%	—
Annual Growth	2.6%	2.5%	—	—

2015 Year-End Financials

Return on assets: 2.7%   Cash ($ mil.): —
Return on equity: 0.6%
Current ratio: 1.70

EASTERN LOS ANGELES REGIONAL CENTER FOR THE DEVELOPMENTALLY DISABLED, INC.

EXECUTIVES

Executive Director, Gloria Wong
Manager, Elina Jones
Financial Executive, Sophia Tang Hao
Manager, Elin Nozaki
Board of Directors, Theresa Chen
Supervisor, Elizabeth Lcsw
Auditors: LAUTZE & LAUTZE SAN FRANCISCO

LOCATIONS

HQ: EASTERN LOS ANGELES REGIONAL CENTER FOR THE DEVELOPMENTALLY DISABLED, INC.
1000 S FREMONT AVE # 23, ALHAMBRA, CA 918038800
Phone: 626 299-4700
Web: WWW.ELARC.ORG

HISTORICAL FINANCIALS

Company Type: Private

Income Statement

FYE: June 30

	REVENUE ($ mil.)	NET INCOME ($ mil.)	NET PROFIT MARGIN	EMPLOYEES
06/15	184	0	—	287
06/14	173	0	—	—
06/13	163	0	0.0%	—
06/12	159	0	0.0%	—
Annual Growth	5.0%	(63.4%)	—	—

2015 Year-End Financials

Return on assets: 9.8%   Cash ($ mil.): 3
Return on equity: —
Current ratio: 0.90

EASTERN MAINE HEALTHCARE SYSTEMS

Eastern Maine Healthcare Systems (EMHS) keeps the folks in the Pine Tree State feeling fine. With more than a dozen member hospitals and multiple medical practices and clinics the organization offers patients emergency primary mental-health laboratory and other specialty services. It primarily serves eastern central and northern portions of rural Maine. Some hospitals include Eastern Maine Medical Center (410 beds) Acadia Hospital (100 beds) Aroostook Medical Center (75 beds) and Inland Hospital (50 beds). The system also operates long-term care hospice and home health facilities as well as emergency transportation and administrative services businesses.

Operations

Besides its Acadia Hospital Aroostook Medical Center Eastern Maine Medical Center and Inland Hospital EMHS operates three smaller community hospitals with 15 to 30 beds each: Blue Hill Memorial Hospital Charles A. Dean Memorial Hospital and Sebasticook Valley Hospital. The system has affiliations with the Houlton Regional Hospital and Millinocket Regional Hospital.

Subsidiaries of EMHS include Affiliated Healthcare Systems (medical communications and retirement ventures) Affiliated Laboratory (pathology services) Affiliated Material Services (medical supplies distribution and pharmacies) and Affiliated Healthcare Management (transcription and employee services).

As part of its operations EMHS also runs the Eastern Maine Medical Center Clinical Research Center which performs clinical studies in several medical disciplines and diseases including cancer hospital-acquired infections heart disease and physician best practices.

In fiscal 2014 EMHS had 105629 emergency room visits; 32964 inpatient and outpatient surgeries; 3017 births; and 388920 primary care visits.

The company's total Community Benefit that year was about $200 million and its philanthropy giving was nearly $3 million.

Geographic Reach

Despite its name Eastern Maine Healthcare System serves those in eastern central and northern portions of rural Maine.

Strategy

EMHS continues to work collaboratively at the national level looking at not only making a difference in healthcare in Maine but to be a change leader throughout the country. The Northern New England Accountable Care Collaborative is creating resources necessary to propel the reinvention of care model. In addition their work in the High Value Healthcare Collaborative (co-owned with Dartmouth MaineHealth and the University of Vermont Medical Center) this past year has been focused on sepsis care and prevention patient engagement and shared decision-making pilot projects.

In fiscal 2015 Maine's largest health insurer teamed up with Eastern Maine Healthcare Systems under a new venture aimed at keeping patients healthier while reducing costs. The deal involves Anthem Blue Cross and Blue Shield in Maine EMHS and an EMHS-led coalition of hospitals and physician practices across the state. EMHS and its partners have agreed to avoid any cost increase for services they deliver to 40000 Anthem policyholders.

In mid-2014 EMHS completed a community health needs assessment of the northern two-thirds of Maine including the counties of Aroostook Cumberland Hancock Kennebec Penobscot Piscataquis Somerset and Washington. This report was seen as foundational to the company achieving its mission of improving the health and well-being of the communities it serves.

Company Background

The system was established in 1982.

EXECUTIVES

Vice President and System Controller, Jeffery Sanford
Vice President Of Finance Chief Finance, Elmer Doucette
Senior Vice President Chief Medical Officer and Home Office Chief Administrative Officer, Erik Steele
Vice President Finance, Thomas Koil
Managing Director Faafp Immediate Past President, William Sturrock
Fache Senior Vice President and Chief Operating Officer, Donna Russell-Cook
Vice President Finance, Randy Clark
Medical Director Transfusion Services, Irwin Gross
Department Head, Mikele Neal
Director of Pharmacy, Jennifer Kinney
Board Member, Karen Marsters
Board Member, John Simpson

LOCATIONS

HQ: EASTERN MAINE HEALTHCARE SYSTEMS
43 WHITING HILL RD # 500, BREWER, ME
044121005
Phone: 207 973-7050
Web: WWW.EMH.ORG

PRODUCTS/OPERATIONS

Selected Strategic Affiliates
Houlton Regional Hospital
Millinocket Regional Hospital
Member Hospitals
Acadia Hospital
Affiliated Healthcare Systems
Aroostook Medical Center
Beacon Health
Blue Hill Memorial Hospital
Charles A. Dean Memorial Hospital and Nursing Home
Dirigo Pines Retirement Community
Eastern Maine HomeCare
Eastern Maine Medical Center
Healthcare Charities
Inland Hospital
Rosscare
Sebasticook Valley Hospital

COMPETITORS

Franklin Community Health Network	Mercy Health System of Maine
Maine Coast Memorial Hospital	Miles Health Care
MaineGeneral Health	Millinocket Regional Hospital
MaineHealth	St. Joseph Healthcare

HISTORICAL FINANCIALS
Company Type: Private

Income Statement
FYE: September 24

	REVENUE ($ mil.)	NET INCOME ($ mil.)	NET PROFIT MARGIN	EMPLOYEES
09/16	1,523	21	1.4%	8,175
09/15	1,374	(1)	—	—
09/14	1,301	94	7.2%	—
09/13	79	6	8.5%	—
Annual Growth	168.0%	47.2%	—	—

2016 Year-End Financials
Return on assets: 4.7%   Cash ($ mil.): 95
Return on equity: 1.4%
Current ratio: 1.10

EASTERN MAINE MEDICAL CENTER

EXECUTIVES

Chief Executive Officer, Deborah C Johnson
Administrative Assistant, Deanna Masterson
Director, Brenda Mulligan
Officer, Deborah Sanford
Administrative Assistant, Mary Violette
Manager, Penny Chadwick
Auditors: BERRY DUNN MCNEIL & PARKER LL

LOCATIONS

HQ: EASTERN MAINE MEDICAL CENTER
489 STATE ST, BANGOR, ME 044016674
Phone: 207 973-7000
Web: WWW.EMMC.ORG

HISTORICAL FINANCIALS
Company Type: Private

Income Statement
FYE: September 26

	REVENUE ($ mil.)	NET INCOME ($ mil.)	NET PROFIT MARGIN	EMPLOYEES
09/15	720	41	5.8%	1,119
09/13	646	56	8.8%	—
09/12	669	67	10.1%	—
09/11	591	0	0.1%	—
Annual Growth	5.1%	176.9%		—

2015 Year-End Financials
Return on assets: 4.4%   Cash ($ mil.): 47
Return on equity: 5.8%
Current ratio: 1.40

EASTERN MUNICIPAL WATER DISTRICT

EXECUTIVES

Chief Executive Officer, Paul D Jones II
Chief Financial Officer, Charles M Rathbone Jr
Manager, Tuissant Williamson
Manager, Brian Agner
Assistant Manager, Bruce Mortazavi
Purchasing Director, Daniel Howell
Manager, Willia Thomas
Manager, Marie Beam
Auditors: DAVIS FARR LLP IRVINE CALIFO

LOCATIONS

HQ: EASTERN MUNICIPAL WATER DISTRICT
2270 TRUMBLE RD, PERRIS, CA 92572
Phone: 951 928-3777
Web: WWW.EMWD.ORG

HISTORICAL FINANCIALS

Company Type: Private

Income Statement

FYE: June 30

	REVENUE ($ mil.)	NET INCOME ($ mil.)	NET PROFIT MARGIN	EMPLOYEES
06/16	206	42	20.8%	620
06/15	200	30	15.1%	—
06/14	201	32	16.2%	—
06/13	187	(0)	—	—
Annual Growth	3.3%	—	—	—

EASTERN SHIPBUILDING GROUP, INC.

EXECUTIVES

President, Brian D Isernia
Manager, Scott Colemere
Director, Benny Bramblette
General Manager, Rudy Sistrunk
Manager, Tim Mathis
Manufacturing Manager, Bobby Mayo
Program Manager, Rick Cunningham
Officer, Kenneth R Munroe
Project Manager, Lisa Barnes
Auditors: CARR RIGGS & INGRAM LLC RIDGE

LOCATIONS

HQ: EASTERN SHIPBUILDING GROUP, INC.
 2200 NELSON AVE, PANAMA CITY, FL 324014969
Phone: 850 763-1900
Web: WWW.EASTERNSHIPBUILDING.COM

HISTORICAL FINANCIALS

Company Type: Private

Income Statement

FYE: December 31

	REVENUE ($ mil.)	NET INCOME ($ mil.)	NET PROFIT MARGIN	EMPLOYEES
12/15	318	19	6.2%	975
12/14	338	47	14.0%	—
12/13	398	50	12.7%	—
12/12	304	44	14.6%	—
Annual Growth	1.4%	(23.7%)	—	—

2015 Year-End Financials

Return on assets: 3.8%   Cash ($ mil.): 55
Return on equity: 6.2%
Current ratio: 1.30

EASTERN VIRGINIA MEDICAL SCHOOL

Eastern Virginia Medical School (EVMS) sends graduated physicians down the Hampton Roads. The school offers medical and doctoral degrees residencies and specialty programs such as reproductive medicine. The community-oriented school does not have a teaching hospital but rather partners with about a dozen regional hospitals. Its main campus is part of the Eastern Virginia Med-

ical Center which is also home to Sentara Norfolk General Hospital and Children's Hospital of The King's Daughters located in the Hampton Roads region of southeastern Virginia. The south campus hosts pediatric and diabetes research programs. EVMS also has research programs devoted to cancer infectious diseases and heart disease.

Operations

Established in 1973 EVMS operates under a state charter and operates as a public institution. Its governing board is comprised of representatives from surrounding communities as well as appointees from the EVMS Foundation which conducts fundraising activities for the school.

The school enrolls some 350 students in its residency internship and fellowship programs which cover about 40 fields. It also provides professional education programs for about 450 students. EVMS has about 450 faculty members many of which are engaged in its extensive research programs. The school is the largest biomedical research organization in southeastern Virginia.

Financial Performance

EVPS reported a 5% decrease in operating revenue to $227 million in 2012 from lower state funding private gifts and interest income. Net income also fell 69% to $11.4 million as a result of lower revenue and increased expenses from instruction management and patient care costs.

Strategy

In 2012 EVMS entered discussions with the College of William & Mary over a possible merger or affiliation agreement. Under proposed terms of the deal which must be approved by Virginia's governing entities EVMS would join the College of William & Mary organization becoming known as the William & Mary School of Medicine. The two schools have worked together on projects in the past including conducting research collaborations. As they worked towards a merger the schools increased collaborative research programs in 2013.

In addition EVMS has been working to improve its facilities so that it can increase its enrollment numbers in both the physician assistant and medical doctorate programs. A new medical education and research building that meets this need was opened in mid-2011. The school also adds new programs such as a new biotechnology graduate program launched in 2012.

EXECUTIVES

Managing Director President and Provost Dean of the School of Medicine, Richard Homan
Director of Admissions, Susan Castora
Vice President For Administration and Finance, Mark Babashanian
Secretary, Naim Pierce
Auditors: KPMG LLP NORFOLK VA

LOCATIONS

HQ: EASTERN VIRGINIA MEDICAL SCHOOL
 714 WOODIS AVE, NORFOLK, VA 235101026
Phone: 757 446-6052
Web: WWW.EVMS.EDU

HISTORICAL FINANCIALS

Company Type: Private

Income Statement

FYE: June 30

	REVENUE ($ mil.)	NET INCOME ($ mil.)	NET PROFIT MARGIN	EMPLOYEES
06/16	234	12	5.3%	1,500
06/15	236	5	2.2%	—
06/14	234	16	7.1%	—
06/13	229	21	9.4%	—
Annual Growth	0.8%	(16.8%)	—	—

2016 Year-End Financials

Return on assets: 2.3%   Cash ($ mil.): 25
Return on equity: 5.3%
Current ratio: 1.30

EC COMPANY

EXECUTIVES

President, George H Adams
Board of Directors, Robert S Ball
Manager, Darrell Robinson
Supervisor, Raelyn Sweebe
Credit Manager, Barbara Anderson
Project Manager, Roger Reed
Project Manager, Brad Wagner
Superintendent, Charles Myers
Project Manager, Gary Cawley
Auditors: MOSS ADAMS LLP PORTLAND OREG

LOCATIONS

HQ: EC COMPANY
 2121 NW THURMAN ST, PORTLAND, OR 972102517
Phone: 503 224-3511
Web: WWW.E-C-CO.COM

HISTORICAL FINANCIALS

Company Type: Private

Income Statement

FYE: September 30

	REVENUE ($ mil.)	NET INCOME ($ mil.)	NET PROFIT MARGIN	EMPLOYEES
09/16	228	3	1.4%	800
09/15	169	1	1.0%	—
09/14	187	4	2.6%	—
09/13	169	6	3.9%	—
Annual Growth	10.6%	(22.5%)	—	—

2016 Year-End Financials

Return on assets: 5.2%   Cash ($ mil.): —
Return on equity: 1.4%
Current ratio: 1.00

ECKERD YOUTH ALTERNATIVES, INC.

Eckerd Youth Alternatives (EYA) provides early intervention and prevention wilderness education residential and day treatment and re-entry and aftercare programs for at-risk youths. The not-for-profit organization has worked to help more than 80000 kids through its operations in about 10 states located primarily in the eastern US. Many of EYA's some 40 programs are offered under contract with state juvenile justice agencies. EYA was established in 1968 by Jack Eckerd the founder of the Eckerd drugstore chain and his wife Ruth Eckerd. During the past few years the company has been focused on expanding its community-based support programs.

In 2007 the organization launched its Eckerd Community and Home Outreach Program (ECHO) program in Louisiana's Region 3 area to serve youth and their families there. It also established the Eckerd Multi-Systemic Therapy program in Tallahassee Florida to provide in-home intensive therapy and support to youth and their families.

EYA in 2008 debuted a pair of therapeutic programs in Texas. Both community-based support programs they include the Eckerd Community Supervision Program and the Eckerd Functional Family Therapy Program.

EXECUTIVES

President, David Dennis
Board of Directors, Laura Hunt
Account Manager, Debbie Finley
Supervisor, Courtney Barry
Director, Kathy Bartlett
Manager, Steve Long
Auditors: CROWE HORWATH LLP FORT LAUDER

LOCATIONS

HQ: ECKERD YOUTH ALTERNATIVES, INC.
100 STARCREST DR, CLEARWATER, FL 337653224
Phone: 727 461-2990
Web: WWW.ECKERD.ORG

HISTORICAL FINANCIALS

Company Type: Private

Income Statement
FYE: June 30

	REVENUE ($ mil.)	NET INCOME ($ mil.)	NET PROFIT MARGIN	EMPLOYEES
06/15	172	2	1.2%	1,400
06/14	155	1	0.9%	—
06/13	153	1	1.0%	—
06/12	89	(2)	—	—
Annual Growth 24.2%		—	—	—

2015 Year-End Financials
Return on assets: 8.3%   Cash ($ mil.): 19
Return on equity: 1.2%
Current ratio: 1.50

ECTOR COUNTY HOSPITAL DISTRICT

EXECUTIVES

President, William Webster
Operations Manager, Lewis Dingman
Manager, Brian Kwiatkowski
Manager, Jennifer Ladouceur

LOCATIONS

HQ: ECTOR COUNTY HOSPITAL DISTRICT
500 W 4TH ST, ODESSA, TX 797615001
Phone: 432 640-4000
Web: WWW.MCHODESSA.COM

HISTORICAL FINANCIALS

Company Type: Private

Income Statement
FYE: September 30

	REVENUE ($ mil.)	NET INCOME ($ mil.)	NET PROFIT MARGIN	EMPLOYEES
09/15	189	0	0.1%	1,630
09/14	186	12	6.7%	—
09/13	174	2	1.4%	—
09/12	170	5	3.5%	—
Annual Growth 3.7%		(67.1%)	—	—

2015 Year-End Financials
Return on assets: 14.4%   Cash ($ mil.): 6
Return on equity: 0.1%
Current ratio: 0.80

ECTOR COUNTY INDEPENDENT SCHOOL DISTRICT

EXECUTIVES

Chief Executive Officer, Brian Moersch
Board of Directors, Doyle Woodall
Plant Engineering Manager, David D Ilbeck
Assistant Manager, Gary Jenkins
Superintendent, Vernon D Stokes
Auditors: JOHNSON MILLER & CO CPA'S P

LOCATIONS

HQ: ECTOR COUNTY INDEPENDENT SCHOOL DISTRICT
802 N SAM HOUSTON AVE, ODESSA, TX 797613973
Phone: 432 456-0002
Web: WWW.ECTORCOUNTYISD.ORG

HISTORICAL FINANCIALS

Company Type: Private

Income Statement
FYE: June 30

	REVENUE ($ mil.)	NET INCOME ($ mil.)	NET PROFIT MARGIN	EMPLOYEES
06/16	264	(83)	—	3,900
06/15	279	(90)	—	—
06/14	271	5	2.1%	—
06/13	238	165	69.5%	—
Annual Growth 3.6%		—	—	—

2016 Year-End Financials
Return on assets: 2.0%   Cash ($ mil.): 6
Return on equity: (-31.6%)
Current ratio: —

EDEN TOWNSHIP HOSPITAL DISTRICT, INC

EXECUTIVES

President, Terry Glubka
Treasurer, Nadder Mirsepassi
Assistant Vice-President, Janice Ferguson

LOCATIONS

HQ: EDEN TOWNSHIP HOSPITAL DISTRICT, INC
20400 LAKE CHABOT RD # 303, CASTRO VALLEY, CA 945465316
Phone: 510 538-2031
Web: WWW.EDENMEDICALCENTER.ORG

HISTORICAL FINANCIALS

Company Type: Private

Income Statement
FYE: December 31

	REVENUE ($ mil.)	NET INCOME ($ mil.)	NET PROFIT MARGIN	EMPLOYEES
12/15	334	26	8.1%	968
12/14	0	(0)	—	—
12/13	51	(51)	—	—
12/09	311	16	5.2%	—
Annual Growth 1.2%		8.9%	—	—

2015 Year-End Financials
Return on assets: 1.9%   Cash ($ mil.): 4
Return on equity: 8.1%
Current ratio: —

EDMOND PUBLIC SCHOOLS

EXECUTIVES

Superintendent, Bret Towne
Office Manager, Judy Pendergraft
Consultant, Vallery McLaughlin
Auditors: RAHHAL HENDERSON JOHNSON PLLC

LOCATIONS

HQ: EDMOND PUBLIC SCHOOLS
1001 W DANFORTH RD, EDMOND, OK 730034801
Phone: 405 340-2800
Web: WWW.EDMONDSCHOOLS.NET

HISTORICAL FINANCIALS

Company Type: Private

Income Statement
FYE: June 30

	REVENUE ($ mil.)	NET INCOME ($ mil.)	NET PROFIT MARGIN	EMPLOYEES
06/16	204	3	1.9%	2,276
06/15	196	7	4.0%	—
06/14	188	6	3.3%	—
06/13	184	0	0.1%	—
Annual Growth 3.5%	202.2%	—	—	—

EDWARD HOSPITAL

EXECUTIVES

Chief Executive Officer, Pamela Davis
Vice-President, Gary Mielak
Executive Vice-President, Chris Mollet
Vice-President, Barbara Byrne
Vice-President, Patti Ludwig-Beymer
Executive Vice-President, Susan Mitchell
Auditors: CROWE HORWATH LLP CHICAGO IL

LOCATIONS

HQ: EDWARD HOSPITAL
801 S WASHINGTON ST, NAPERVILLE, IL 605407499
Phone: 630 355-0450
Web: WWW.EDWARD.ORG

HISTORICAL FINANCIALS

Company Type: Private

Income Statement
FYE: June 30

	REVENUE ($ mil.)	NET INCOME ($ mil.)	NET PROFIT MARGIN	EMPLOYEES
06/15	567	39	7.0%	4,700
06/14	615	106	17.2%	—
06/13	517	52	10.1%	—
06/12	530	30	5.7%	—
Annual Growth 2.3%		9.7%	—	—

EFFINGHAM EQUITY

EXECUTIVES

Chief Executive Officer, Bruce Vernon
General Manager, Tim Bence
Auditors: BLUE & COMPANY LLC SEYMOUR

LOCATIONS

HQ: EFFINGHAM EQUITY
   201 W ROADWAY AVE, EFFINGHAM, IL 624012101
Phone: 217 342-4101
Web: WWW.THEEQUITY.COM

HISTORICAL FINANCIALS

Company Type: Private

Income Statement   FYE: December 31

	REVENUE ($ mil.)	NET INCOME ($ mil.)	NET PROFIT MARGIN	EMPLOYEES
12/15	322	9	2.8%	348
12/14	354	10	2.9%	—
12/13	333	9	2.7%	—
12/10	51	12	23.8%	—
Annual Growth	44.4%	(5.6%)	—	—

2015 Year-End Financials

Return on assets: 8.8%   Cash ($ mil.): —
Return on equity: 2.8%
Current ratio: 0.30

EIDE BAILLY LLP

Eide Bailly is how the West was audited. The company which was founded in 1917 provides clients with audit accounting tax and consulting services from more than 20 offices in nearly a dozen western and central US states. Eide Bailly's target industries include construction agricultural processing oil and gas real estate renewable energy government financial services manufacturing health care and not-for-profit organizations. Additional services are provided by subsidiaries and affiliates including Eide Bailly Technology Consulting. International services are provided through Eide Bailly's affiliation with HLB International. The accounting firm serves some 44000 clients annually.

Geographic Reach
Fargo North Dakota-based Eide Bailly has offices in Arizona Colorado Idaho Iowa Minnesota Montana Oklahoma Utah Washington and the Dakotas.

Financial Performance
Edie Bailly's net fees amounted to $192 million in fiscal 2014 (ended April) up from $171 million in the prior year. The firm's tax services audit and assurance and consulting/other businesses accounted for 40% 37% and 21% of the total respectively.

Strategy
Edie Bailly is growing its business through the acquisition of regional accounting firms to better compete with larger national firms.

Mergers and Acquisitions
In August 2014 the accounting firm acquired Fort Collins-based Sample & Bailey CPAs expanding its Colorado presence to Fort Collins. Previously Eide Bailly expanded into Utah in 2012 with the purchase of Schmitt Griffiths Smith & Co. adding about $6 million to its total revenue. More significantly Edie Bailly announced plans to merge with fellow accountancy Milwaukee-based Wipfli

in 2012. However the deal was called off later that year when the two firms could not reach an agreement on key terms.

Other recent purchases include Williston North Dakota-based CPA firm Voller Lee Seuss & Associates. The purchase which closed in December 2012 expanded Edie Bailly's resources and services to clients in the rapidly-growing Bakken Oil Region in western North Dakota. Also in late 2012 the firm acquired Clark & Srsich LLC a boutique tax firm in Littleton Colorado.

EXECUTIVES

Managing Partner, Dave Stende
Chief Operating Officer, Michael Astrup
Treasurer, Rhonda Nance
Accounting Director, Jim Fandrich
Certified Public Accountant, Thomas McShane
Representative, Tiphanie Meinert
Certified Public Accountant, Peggy Runcorn
Office Manager, Lori Leidholt
Certified Public Accountant, Bonnie McNellan

LOCATIONS

HQ: EIDE BAILLY LLP
   4310 17TH AVE S, FARGO, ND 581033339
Phone: 701 239-8500
Web: WWW.EIDEBAILLY.COM

PRODUCTS/OPERATIONS

2013 Services by Category

	% of total
Tax Services	40
Audit & Assurance	38
Affiliates	2
Consulting and other	20
Total	**100**

Selected Services

Accounting
Audit & assurance
Employee benefits
Enterprise risk management
Financial services
Forensic & valuation
International services
Tax
Technology consulting
Transaction services
Wealth management

COMPETITORS

BDO Seidman	Ernst & Young LLP
BKD LLP	Grant Thornton
CliftonLarsonAllen	KPMG L.L.P.
Crowe Horwath	PricewaterhouseCoopers
Deloitte & Touche	US

HISTORICAL FINANCIALS

Company Type: Private

Income Statement   FYE: April 30

	REVENUE ($ mil.)	NET INCOME ($ mil.)	NET PROFIT MARGIN	EMPLOYEES
04/16	259	93	36.2%	1,720
04/15	224	76	33.9%	—
04/14	192	65	33.8%	—
04/13	167	56	33.9%	—
Annual Growth	15.7%	18.2%	—	—

2016 Year-End Financials

Return on assets: 1.2%   Cash ($ mil.): 21
Return on equity: 36.2%
Current ratio: 1.10

EISENHOWER MEDICAL CENTER

The Eisenhower Medical Center is perhaps better known for the name of a first lady than the 34th US president: The not-for-profit medical campus is the home of the Betty Ford Center. In addition to the renowned alcohol and drug rehabilitation center Eisenhower Medical Center comprises the more than 540-bed Eisenhower Memorial Hospital the Barbara Sinatra Children's Center and the Annenberg Center for Health Sciences. In addition to medical surgical and emergency services the hospital offers cancer care neurology orthopedics cardiology and rehabilitation. An accredited teaching hospital it also conducts training and research programs and operates outpatient clinics in surrounding areas.

Operations
Eisenhower Medical Center maintains the leading market share in its service location representing nearly 50% of the area.

In addition to patient services Eisenhower Medical Center provides residency programs for aspiring students through affiliations with the Keck School of Medicine (University of Southern California) and the Linda Loma University's School of Medicine. The physician training programs are offered through the newly established School of Graduate Medical Education and Research and include family medicine internal medicine and preliminary (one-year) residency programs.

Geographic Reach
The Eisenhower Medical Center's main facilities are located on its 130-acre campus in Rancho Mirage California. Outpatient facilities are located in Rancho Mirage and area communities including Cathedral City La Quinta and Palm Springs.

Strategy
Eisenhower Medical Center's residency programs were launched in the summer of 2013 after the hospital received national accreditation. The hospital worked for several years to add medical training services to help meet the growing shortage of primary care physicians in the Coachella Valley. The establishment of the graduate school required capital improvements to the hospital's facilities causing it to launch a $32 million fundraising campaign that year.

The medical center has also been working to maintain its market share by launching a number of facility expansion campaigns in recent years. For instance in 2010 it completed construction of a $213 million addition to its main hospital that included 160 patient beds a cafeteria information systems and other departments. The addition was named the Eisenhower Walter and Leonore Annenberg Pavilion.

The medical center is expanding its outpatient care centers to provide greater services to surrounding communities and reduce the patient burden on hospital emergency rooms. For instance Eisenhower Medical Center opened a new primary and specialty outpatient care center in Palm Springs in 2013.

Eisenhower Medical Center faces some financial challenges due to a high volume of elderly Medicare patients. As a result it has made efforts to attract more self-pay patients to its facilities. In addition the hospital has incurred substantial debt due to its construction efforts; however it aims to recoup through increased revenues from the added facilities and through its successful fundraising efforts.

Company Background

Eisenhower Medical Center was dedicated in 1971 to honor former president Dwight Eisenhower who spent part of his retirement in the Coachella Valley. The late entertainer Bob Hope and his wife were the hospital's biggest benefactors having donated the original land for the hospital and continuing to help fundraising efforts until his death in 2003.

EXECUTIVES

President and CEO, G. Aubrey Serfling
VP and CIO, David Perez
President Eisenhower Medical Center Foundation, Michael D. Landes
EVP and COO, Martin J. Massiello
VP Patient Care and Chief Nursing Officer, Ann Mostofi
SVP and CFO, Ken Wheat
Occupational Therapy Director, Derek Spinney
Radiology Director, HILTON MCCABE
Vice President Express Clinics, Thomas Johnston
Vice President Finance, Felicitas Ramirez
Director of Nursing, Wendy Edwards
Vice President Support Services, Ali Tourkaman
Clinical Director, Janet Sullivan
Vice President, Laura Fritz
Vice President, Liz Guignier
Radiology Medical Director, Brian Herman
Vice President Finance, Sharon Henderson
Vice President Business, Mary Fontana

LOCATIONS

HQ: EISENHOWER MEDICAL CENTER
39000 BOB HOPE DR, RANCHO MIRAGE, CA 922703221
Phone: 760 340-3911
Web: WWW.EMC.ORG

PRODUCTS/OPERATIONS

Selected Facilities
Eisenhower Medical Center (Rancho Mirage)
  Annenberg Center for Health Sciences (continuing education for health professionals)
  Barbara Sinatra Children's Center (pediatrics)
  Betty Ford Center (alcohol and substance abuse)
  School of Graduate Medical Education and Research
Eisenhower George and Julia Argyros Health Center (La Quinta)
Eisenhower Health Centers at Plaza del Sol (Palm Springs)
Eisenhower Health Centers at Rimrock (Palm Springs)
Eisenhower Health Centers at Sunrock (Palm Springs)
Eisenhower Occupational Health (Cathedral City)
Eisenhower Physical and Occupational Health (La Quinta)
Rancho Mirage Medical Center (Rancho Mirage)

Selected Services
Adult Day Care
Bariatric Center
Center for Geropsychiatry
Cancer
Cardiovascular
Clinical Trials
Diabetes
Eisenhower Health Centers
Eisenhower Wellness Institute
Emergency Department
Imaging
Labtechniques
Neuroscience
Nutrition
Occupational Health
Orthopedics
Parkinson's Center
Rehabilitation Services
Robotics Institute
Urgent Care
Wound Care Center

COMPETITORS

Anaheim Regional Medical Center	Grossmont Hospital
Arrowhead Medical	HCA
	HealthSouth

Center	Memorial Health Services
Cedars-Sinai Medical Center	Palomar Health
Citrus Valley Health Partners	Providence St. Joseph Health
Community Hospital of San Bernardino	Scripps Health
Dignity Health	Southwest Healthcare
	Tenet Healthcare

HISTORICAL FINANCIALS
Company Type: Private

Income Statement
FYE: June 30

	REVENUE ($ mil.)	NET INCOME ($ mil.)	NET PROFIT MARGIN	EMPLOYEES
06/15	571	16	2.9%	3,000
06/13	501	(27)	—	—
06/10	411	6	1.7%	—
Annual Growth	6.8%	19.3%	—	—

2015 Year-End Financials
Return on assets: 4.1%   Cash ($ mil.): 126
Return on equity: 2.9%
Current ratio: 2.40

EL DORADO FURNITURE CORP

The road to El Dorado Furniture is covered in sand. The company sells home furnishings in South Florida through about a dozen retail showrooms and a pair of outlets located in Broward Miami-Dade Palm Beach and Lee counties. El Dorado Furniture stores offer wood upholstered and leather furniture for every room in the house as well as mattresses bedding and decorative accessories. Its stores are designed to look like small towns with building fa §ades situated along a boulevard; some locations also feature caf ©s. Founded in 1967 and run by the Cap family El Dorado Furniture has become the nation's largest Hispanic-owned retail enterprises.
Geographic Reach
The retailer's showrooms and outlets are located in Florida's Palm Beach Broward Miami-Dade and Lee counties.
Sales and Marketing
El Dorado has grown to offer the largest selection of furniture and mattresses in South Florida.
Unique to the furniture retailer its stores feature what it calls a Boulevard showroom which includes more than 20 individually themed storefronts open into specialized furniture shops. The marketing strategy remains one of the company's biggest draws for customers.
As part of the company's bricks-and-mortar business it produces and maintains an online catalog that's searchable by category product name or SKU.
Strategy
Besides its specialized showrooms El Dorado Furniture offers customers free home decorating advice from its design experts.
As Florida's real estate market rebounds postrecession El Dorado Furniture has worked to expand its business within the state by purchasing a shopping center on Florida's Gulf Coast in 2012. The Lee County purchase included a 179000-sq.-ft. shopping center to house a 70000-sq.-ft. El Dorado showroom. It's banking on a store of this caliber to bring in at least $10 million. Awards and Recognition

El Dorado Furniture is ranked among the top 50 furniture retailers in the country.

EXECUTIVES

Vice President, Carlos Capo
Vice President Human Resources, Henry Hererro

LOCATIONS

HQ: EL DORADO FURNITURE CORP
4200 NW 167TH ST, MIAMI GARDENS, FL 330546112
Phone: 305 624-9700
Web: WWW.ELDORADOFURNITURE.COM

2014 Stores

	No.
Miami-Dade	7
Broward	3
Palm Beach	2
Lee	1
Total	**13**

PRODUCTS/OPERATIONS

Selected Products
Beds & Bedrooms
Furniture
Home office
Home decor & accents
Mattresses
Outdoor furniture

COMPETITORS

Baer's Furniture	Leader's Casual Furniture
City Furniture	Rooms To Go
Havertys	W.S. Badcock
La-Z-Boy	

HISTORICAL FINANCIALS
Company Type: Private

Income Statement
FYE: December 31

	REVENUE ($ mil.)	NET INCOME ($ mil.)	NET PROFIT MARGIN	EMPLOYEES
12/15	212	38	17.9%	705
12/14	180	29	16.5%	—
12/13	165	29	18.0%	—
12/12	153	25	16.9%	—
Annual Growth	11.5%	13.7%	—	—

EL PASO COUNTY HOSPITAL DISTRICT

University Medical Center is a community not-for-profit health care system serving West Texas and southern New Mexico. The network includes the 330-bed University Medical Center of El Paso (formerly also known as Thomason General Hospital) several neighborhood primary care clinics and the El Paso First Health Plans HMO. The hospital is an acute-care teaching hospital affiliated with Texas Tech. It specializes in emergency/trauma care obstetrics pediatric medicine and orthopedics. The hospital district through its affiliates provides a range of outpatient services including physical rehabilitation speech therapy family planning dental care cancer treatment diagnostics and pharmacy services.
Company Background
University Medical Center of El Paso opened in 1915. The hospital was rebranded under the University Medical Center name in 2009 when Texas Tech opened a full four-year medical school on the Thomason General campus.

EXECUTIVES

Chief Executive Officer, James N Valenti
Assistant Controller, Leticia Flores
Chief Financial Officer, Michael Nu EZ
Manager, Art Macias
Manager, Jady Sybeldon
Director, Monica Blancas
Accountant, Joellen Alva
Director, Pat Moreno

LOCATIONS

HQ: EL PASO COUNTY HOSPITAL DISTRICT
4815 ALAMEDA AVE, EL PASO, TX 799052705
Phone: 915 544-1200
Web: WWW.UMCELPASO.ORG

PRODUCTS/OPERATIONS

Selected Services
After Hours Pediatrics
Aquatic Therapy
Cardiac Cath
CAT Scan
Case Management
Dental Clinic
Diabetes Management
Diagnostic Radiology
Echocardiograms
Electrocardiograms
Emergency Department
Endoscopy/Special Procedures
Family Planning
Infusion Center
Interventional Radiology
Laboratory Services
Labor and Delivery
Laparoscopic Surgery
Lithotripsy
Mammography
Medical Unit
Mother/Baby Unit
MRI
Neonatal Intensive Care
Neonatal Intermediate Care
Neonatal Continuing Care
Newborn Nursery
Neurosurgery
Nuclear Medicine
Nutritional Care
Occupational Health
Occupational Therapy
Patient Financial Services
Pediatric Unit
Pediatric Rehabilitation
Pharmacy
Physical Therapy
Poison Control Center
Prenatal Services
Primary Care Clinics
Public Affairs
Rehabilitative Services
Respiratory Services
Special Care Nurseries
Speech Therapy
Surgical Services
Surgical Unit
Telemetry Unit
Trauma - Level 1
Ultrasound
West Texas Regional Poison Control Center
Wound Care

COMPETITORS

Covenant Health System
Del Sol Medical Center
HealthSouth
Tenet Healthcare
Texas Health Resources

HISTORICAL FINANCIALS

Company Type: Private

Income Statement

FYE: September 30

	REVENUE ($ mil.)	NET INCOME ($ mil.)	NET PROFIT MARGIN	EMPLOYEES
09/15	177	(2)	—	1,898
09/14	361	(66)	—	—
09/13	393	1	0.3%	—
09/12	147	(1)	—	—
Annual Growth	6.4%	—	—	—

2015 Year-End Financials

Return on assets: 22.2%
Return on equity: (-1.3%)
Current ratio: 0.50

Cash ($ mil.): 24

EL PASO INDEPENDENT SCHOOL DISTRICT

EXECUTIVES

Superintendent, Juan Cabrera
Manager, Art Jordan
Assistant Manager, Edward Gabaldon
Finance Manager, Laila Ferris
Superintendent, Terri Jordan
Assistant Manager, Vincent Sheffield
Plant & Facilities Manager, Carlos Gallinar
Auditors: GIBSON RUDDOCK PATTERSON LLC

LOCATIONS

HQ: EL PASO INDEPENDENT SCHOOL DISTRICT
6531 BOEING DR, EL PASO, TX 799251008
Phone: 915 230-2000
Web: WWW.EPISD.ORG

HISTORICAL FINANCIALS

Company Type: Private

Income Statement

FYE: June 30

	REVENUE ($ mil.)	NET INCOME ($ mil.)	NET PROFIT MARGIN	EMPLOYEES
06/16	651	2	0.4%	9,000
06/15*	620	(13)	—	—
08/14	0	(0)	—	—
06/14	611	(20)	—	—
Annual Growth	3.3%	—	—	—

*Fiscal year change

2016 Year-End Financials

Return on assets: 1.2%
Return on equity: 0.4%
Current ratio: 1.80

Cash ($ mil.): 153

EL PASO WATER UTILITIES PUBLIC SERVICE BOARD

EXECUTIVES

Chairman, Richard T Schoephoerster
Manager, Charlie Simental
Manager, Arturo Duran
Manager, Jose Granillo
Personnel Manager, Fred Loweree
Manager, Jerome Cook
Vice-President, Gloria Fredricks
Auditors: GIBSON RUDDOCK PATTERSON LLC

LOCATIONS

HQ: EL PASO WATER UTILITIES PUBLIC SERVICE BOARD
1154 HAWKINS BLVD, EL PASO, TX 799256436
Phone: 915 594-5500
Web: WWW.EPWU.ORG

HISTORICAL FINANCIALS

Company Type: Private

Income Statement

FYE: February 29

	REVENUE ($ mil.)	NET INCOME ($ mil.)	NET PROFIT MARGIN	EMPLOYEES
02/16	215	55	25.8%	850
02/15	199	31	15.5%	—
02/14	196	39	20.3%	—
02/13	192	33	17.2%	—
Annual Growth	3.8%	18.8%	—	—

2016 Year-End Financials

Return on assets: 1.3%
Return on equity: 25.8%
Current ratio: 0.40

Cash ($ mil.): 20

ELECTRIC POWER BOARD OF CHATTANOOGA

Pardon me .... is that the Electric Power Board (EPB) of Chattanooga? EPB keeps on choo-chooin' along by providing electricity to more than 167410 residents and businesses. The utility (a non-profit agency of the City of Chattanooga) distributes energy in a 600 sq.-ml. area that includes greater Chattanooga as well as parts of surrounding counties in Georgia and Tennessee. It gets its wholesale power supply from the Tennessee Valley Authority. EPB also provides telecommunications (telephone and Internet) services to area homes and businesses through its EPB Fiber Optics unit.

Operations
In addition to its electric distribution business the company's all-fiber Internet product gives 50000 businesses and residences access to up to 500 Mbps of bandwidth a capacity 300 times faster than standard DSL cable or T1 connections. This service gives all EFB customers internet bandwidth capacity and service on a par with or superior to that offered in Atlanta Chicago and Los Angeles.

Geographic Reach

EPB serves greater Chattanooga and parts of surrounding counties (Bledsoe Bradley Marion Rhea and Sequatchie) and North Georgia (parts of Catoosa Dade and Walker counties).

Financial Performance

The company saw its operating revenues rise by 1% in 2013 thanks to an increase of $12.4 million in Fiber Optics residential services sales.

Strategy

EFB is pushing technological innovation and the modernization of its systems as a way to increase value and efficiency.

To help reduce power outages in 2013 the company added 200 smart switches to its 46 Kv system (in addition to its 1200 smart swtiches on the 12kV system already in place.

Company Background

During 2009 the company received a $111 million federal stimulus grant to build and operate a Smart Grid (an automated electric system with communication capabilities to help improve response time reduce outages cut down on theft and help clients take charge of their own power use). In 2012 EFB completed the installation of the 1170 IntelliRupter® PulseCloser (smart switches) making EPB's Smart Grid the most automated system of its size in the US.

The utility was established in 1935 to provide electric power to the people of the greater Chattanooga area.

EXECUTIVES

Vice President Information Technology, David Johnson
Assistant Vice President Customer Relations, Karen Thomas
Vice President of Strategic Research, Jim Ingraham
Vice President Legal Services, Aaron Webb
Vice President Strategic Systems, Steve Clark
Vice President Economic DevelopmentandGov.Rel., Diana Bullock
Senior Vice President Finance And Chief Financial Officer, Greg Eaves
Vice President Human Resources, Marie Webb
Vice President Human Resources Executive, Anthony Powell
Vice President, Katherine Espeseth
Vice President Community Development, Hodgen Mainda
Board Of Directors, Jon Kinsey
Auditors: HENDERSON HUTCHERSON & MCCULLO

LOCATIONS

HQ: ELECTRIC POWER BOARD OF CHATTANOOGA
10 W MARTIN LUTHER KING B, CHATTANOOGA, TN 374021813
Phone: 423 756-2706
Web: WWW.EPB.NET

PRODUCTS/OPERATIONS

2013 Sales

	% of total
Electric	86
Fiber Optics	12
Other	2
Total	**100**

COMPETITORS

AT&T
Constellation Energy Group
Southern Company Gas

HISTORICAL FINANCIALS

Company Type: Private

Income Statement

FYE: June 30

	REVENUE ($ mil.)	NET INCOME ($ mil.)	NET PROFIT MARGIN	EMPLOYEES
06/16	683	32	4.7%	400
06/15	671	17	2.6%	—
06/14	654	17	2.6%	—
Annual Growth	**2.2%**	**36.1%**	—	—

2016 Year-End Financials

Return on assets: 10.8%
Return on equity: 4.7%
Current ratio: 0.90
Cash ($ mil.): 101

ELECTRIC POWER BOARD OF THE METROPOLITAN GOVERNMENT OF NASHVILLE & DAVIDSON COUNTY

The Electric Power Board of the Metropolitan Government of Nashville and Davidson County is a mouthful. Its operating name Nashville Electric Service (NES) sounds much better. And talking of sound the legendary "Nashville Sound" would be hard to hear without the resources of this power distributor which serves more than 360000 customers in central Tennessee. NES is one of the largest government-owned utilities in the US. The company is required to purchase all its power from another government-owned operator the Tennessee Valley Authority (TVA).

EXECUTIVES

Vice President Cio, Erika Hurd
Auditors: PRICEWATERHOUSECOOPERS LLP N

LOCATIONS

HQ: ELECTRIC POWER BOARD OF THE METROPOLITAN GOVERNMENT OF NASHVILLE & DAVIDSON COUNTY
1214 CHURCH ST, NASHVILLE, TN 372460001
Phone: 615 747-3831
Web: WWW.NESPOWER.COM

COMPETITORS

AEP
Constellation Energy Group
MLGW
Piedmont Natural Gas
Public Service Enterprise Group
SCANA
Southern Company
Southern Company Gas

HISTORICAL FINANCIALS

Company Type: Private

Income Statement

FYE: June 30

	REVENUE ($ mil.)	NET INCOME ($ mil.)	NET PROFIT MARGIN	EMPLOYEES
06/16	1,203	28	2.4%	950
06/15	1,246	55	4.5%	—
06/09	1,146	16	1.4%	—
06/08	1,030	33	3.2%	—
Annual Growth	**2.0%**	**(2.0%)**	—	—

ELECTRIC POWER RESEARCH INSTITUTE, INC.

The Electric Power Research Institute (EPRI) knows there's more to electricity than putting a plug in a socket. From its headquarters in Palo Alto California the institute works to bring together investor-owned and government-owned utility companies as well as other industry representatives. EPRI operates as a not-for-profit research consortium that organizes and funds collaborative research. The organization identifies and works on issues related to electricity generation delivery and use including questions related to environmental protection. More than 10% of the organization's members are located outside the US. EPRI was founded in 1973.

Operations

The institute's research portfolio includes Environment & Renewable Energy Generation Nuclear and Power Delivery and Utilization. EPRI works to make electricity production and its use sustainable for current and future generations. It also focused on advanced generation technologies and emissions controls as well as environmentally-responsible technologies that enable the long-term operation of existing nuclear plants and the deployment of advanced nuclear power plants. It's also interested in developing technologies and approaches to facilitate improved grid reliability energy use efficiency and grid transformation.

Geographic Reach

EPRI serves more than 30 countries. Its members provide some 90% of the electricity generated and delivered in the US. To support its operations EPRI maintains offices in Madrid and Tokyo as well as in half a dozen locations in the US. It has offices and laboratories in Palo Alto California; Charlotte North Carolina; Dallas Texas; Lenox Massachusetts; Knoxville Tennessee; and Washington DC.

Strategy

EPRI's technology strategy encompasses long-term and broad societal visions and goals through its Electricity Technology Roadmap. One such goal is the role of the electric sector and electricity-based technologies in reducing greenhouse gas emissions by 2030.

Through collaboration with other research institutes EPRI is able to tackle more research topics. In 2013 EPRI collaborated with the Japan Nuclear Safety Institute (JANSI) and began participating in a number of EPRI's nuclear research programs. Previously EPRI entered a three-year collaboration with the International Atomic Energy Agency

(IAEA) to promote public benefit research into nuclear power plant development operation decommissioning and waste disposal. The collaboration which extends through 2015 offers technical engagement on issues regarding nuclear plant development in countries initiating commercial nuclear power programs.

EXECUTIVES

Vice President Marketing, Dennis Murphy
SVP CFO and Treasurer, Pamela J. Keefe, age 52
SVP Research and Development and Acting Vice President Generation, Michael W. Howard
VP Member and Technical Services, Robert Chapman
VP Transmission and Distribution, Robin E. (Rob) Manning, age 61
VP People and Performance, Carolyn R. Shockley
VP Generation, C. Thomas (Tom) Alley
VP Nuclear and Chief Nuclear Officer, Neil Wilmshurst
VP Distribution and Energy Utilization, Mark F. McGranaghan
Senior Vice President Global Strategy and External Relations, Henry A Courtright
Vice President Legal, Salvador Casente
Vice President Nuclear Power, Christian Larsen
Vice President Power Delivery and Utilization, Arshad Mansoor
Vice President, Rob Manning
Vice Chair, Jeffrey J. (Jeff) Lyash, age 56
Chairman, Warner L. Baxter, age 56
Auditors: DELOITTE & TOUCHE LLP SAN FR

LOCATIONS

HQ: ELECTRIC POWER RESEARCH INSTITUTE, INC.
3420 HILLVIEW AVE, PALO ALTO, CA 943041382
Phone: 650 855-2000

PRODUCTS/OPERATIONS

Selected Research Topics
Cable aging management
Concrete aging management
Controls and monitoring modernization
Extended fuel storage for spent nuclear fuel
Flexible operation of fossil assets
Irradiation effects on nuclear components
Transmission system life extension through inspection technologies

HISTORICAL FINANCIALS

Company Type: Private

Income Statement

	REVENUE ($ mil.)	NET INCOME ($ mil.)	NET PROFIT MARGIN	EMPLOYEES
12/15	406	22	5.6%	891
12/14	388	16	4.4%	—
12/13	383	26	6.9%	—
12/06	285	16	5.9%	—
Annual Growth	4.0%	3.4%	—	—

2015 Year-End Financials

Return on assets: 8.0%
Return on equity: 5.6%
Current ratio: 0.40
Cash ($ mil.): 48

ELECTRIC RELIABILITY COUNCIL OF TEXAS, INC.

ERCOT works to ensure that Texas power grid errors are caught before triggering a massive blackout. The Electric Reliability Council of Texas (ERCOT) is responsible for the reliable operation of 550 generation units (74000 MW capacity) and a 40500-mile power transmission system carrying about 85% of the state's electric load and serving 23 million customers. A member of the North American Electric Reliability Council ERCOT functions as the independent system operator for the region. It also administers financial settlement for the competitive wholesale bulk-power market and oversees customer switching for 6.7 million Texans who live in areas where they have a competitive choice of power supplier.

Operations
The council monitors and schedules the flow of wholesale energy on the grid balancing supply with demand and enabling fair competitive access. ERCOT maintains records on grid activities and market participants and schedules power on the electric grid connecting transmission lines and generation units.

Geographic Reach
ERCOT's territory covers about 75% of Texas' land area; it excludes most of the northern panhandle region and parts of West Texas (around El Paso) and East Texas (around Texarkana and Beaumont).

Financial Performance
ERCOT reported a 1% to decline in revenues in 2012. It generates revenues from System administration fees; Nodal implementation surcharge; Reliability organization pass-through; and Membership fees and other. In 2012 System administration fees and Nodal implementation surcharge accounted for 93% of ERCOT's total revenues.

Strategy
In 2012 the council released a report pointing out that the combination of a fast-growing population and the closing of older coal-powered plants meant that power demand in Texas would begin to outstrip its power capacity and that new cleaner burning power plants would need to be built along with the use of renewable energy sources and the adoption of serious conservation measures in order to avoid future power interruptions.

To meet state and federal green energy requirements the organization is working on integrating wind power sources into its operating grid. Texas boasts 10000 MW of wind power generation the most in the country. In July 2012 ERCOT reported a record output of 8370 MW of wind energy or about 18% of its total load.

Texas state government has kept ERCOT physically isolated from other grid systems (primarily to avoid federal regulation and charges). However this policy came under scrutiny in early 2011 when a cold snap led to the loss of 50 generating units forcing rolling outages across Texas in order to lower demand and prompting ERCOT to access power from Mexico for a short time.

Company Background
The entity is governed by a board of directors and subject to oversight by the Public Utility Commission of Texas and the Texas State Legislature. The Legislature restructured the Texas electric market in 1999.

EXECUTIVES

SVP and COO, Cheryl Mele
VP and CFO, Michael Petterson
President and CEO, Bill Magness
SVP and CIO, Jerry Dreyer
Chief of Staff, Jeyant Tamby
Vice President, Kenan Ogelman
Chairman, Craven Crowell
Vice Chairman, Judy Walsh

LOCATIONS

HQ: ELECTRIC RELIABILITY COUNCIL OF TEXAS, INC.
7620 METRO CENTER DR, AUSTIN, TX 787441613
Phone: 512 225-7000
Web: WWW.ERCOT.COM

PRODUCTS/OPERATIONS

2012 Sales

	% of total
System administration fees	49
Nodal implementation surcharge	44
Reliability organization pass-through	5
Membership fees & other	2
Total	**100**

HISTORICAL FINANCIALS

Company Type: Private

Income Statement

FYE: December 31

	REVENUE ($ mil.)	NET INCOME ($ mil.)	NET PROFIT MARGIN	EMPLOYEES
12/15	181	(2)	—	625
12/11	279	(1)	—	—
12/10	272	19	7.0%	—
12/09	206	28	13.9%	—
Annual Growth	(2.2%)	—	—	—

2015 Year-End Financials

Return on assets: 6.7%
Return on equity: (-1.2%)
Current ratio: 1.80
Cash ($ mil.): 670

ELKHART GENERAL HOSPITAL, INC.

From Nappanee to Edwardsburg Elkhart General serves residents of northern Indiana and southwestern Michigan. The community-owned Elkhart General Hospital has about 325 beds. The system also operates about ten general practice clinics throughout its region and provides home care rehabilitation and occupational health services. The system's Michiana Linen unit provides linen and laundry services to other hospitals clinics and physician offices in the region. Its hospital staff includes about 300 physicians representing about 30 medical specialties. Elkhart General is affiliated with Memorial Hospital of South Bend through the Beacon Health System organization.

Operations
Elkhart General handles some 12000 inpatient visits and 120000 emergency room visits each year as well as 6000 surgeries and 1500 births. The system's hospitals and outpatient care centers handle a combined 900000 patient encounters including about 90000 primary care visits.

As a tax-exempt not-for-profit organization governed by a board of directors composed of volunteers from the community the health system provides safety-net services to meet health-related community needs. As such the hospital provides a number of community care programs including educational outreach programs and care for uninsured or under-insured patients. Altogether the system provides about $30 million in community benefits each year.

Strategy
To expand services in the region Elkhart General launched a $74 million construction project in 2013 to upgrade its surgical facilities. The program

will replace existing surgery and endoscopy facilities to add more advanced technologies. It will also add about 45 post-surgical private patient rooms. The project is expected to be completed by the end of 2015.

Company Background

The company became part of the Beacon Health System organization in 2012 when it formed an affiliation with the nearby Memorial Hospital. The two hospital aims to improve regional care by offering a wider range of services in a broader geographic territory. The hospitals continue to operate under an independent board of directors but share clinical and administrative functions.

Elkhart General Hospital was incorporated in 1909.

EXECUTIVES

SECRETARY, Judy Truex

LOCATIONS

HQ: ELKHART GENERAL HOSPITAL, INC.
600 EAST BLVD, ELKHART, IN 465142499
Phone: 574 294-2621

PRODUCTS/OPERATIONS

Selected Locations
Elkhart General Hospital
Bittersweet Medical Associates
Bristol Family Practice
Center for Family Practice
Edwardsburg Family Medicine
Elkhart Gastroenterology
Family Medicine Center
Family Practice Associates
For Women Only
Nappanee Family Medical Clinic
Osceola Clinic
Sleep Consultants of Michiana
Wakarusa Medical Clinic
Elkhart General Hospital
Elkhart General Health Education Center
Elkhart General Hospital Center for Behavioral Medicine
Elkhart General Home Care

Selected Services
Ambulatory Infusion
Anticoagulation Clinic
Bariatric Surgery
Behavioral Health
Bone Health
Breast Care Center
Cancer Services
Critical Care
Diabetes Management
Emergency
Heart (Cardiac)
Home Care
Home Medical Equipment
Joint Replacement
Laboratory
Maternity
Medical Group
Medical Services
Neuroscience
Pain Management
Pediatrics
Radiology
Rehabilitation
Sleep Disorder Center
Surgery
Urgent Care Centers
Weight Management Programs
Wound Healing

COMPETITORS

Advocate Health Care	Northwestern Memorial
Ascension Health	HealthCare
Community Health	Porter Health Care
Network	System
Community Hospital	Riverview Hospital
Covenant Ministries	Rush System for Health
Franciscan Alliance	Sinai Health System
Kosciusko Community	Union Hospital
Hospital	(Indiana)

Memorial Hospital &
Health System
NorthShore University
HealthSystem

University of Chicago
Medical Center

HISTORICAL FINANCIALS

Company Type: Private

Income Statement

FYE: December 31

	REVENUE ($ mil.)	NET INCOME ($ mil.)	NET PROFIT MARGIN	EMPLOYEES
12/16	281	20	7.4%	1,900
12/15	274	10	4.0%	—
12/13	820	136	16.7%	—
12/12	886	173	19.6%	—
Annual Growth	(24.9%)	(41.1%)	—	—

2016 Year-End Financials

Return on assets: 3.9%
Return on equity: 7.4%
Current ratio: 2.80

Cash ($ mil.): 11

ELLIOT HOSPITAL OF THE CITY OF MANCHESTER

Elliot Health System provides medical care to southern New Hampshire. The health care organization operates Elliot Hospital an acute care hospital with nearly 300 beds that is home to a regional cancer center a designated regional trauma center and a level III neonatal intensive care unit (NICU). In addition to general and surgical care the hospital offers rehabilitation behavioral health obstetrics cardiology and lab services. The system also operates the Elliot Physician Network which operates primary care centers specialty clinics and surgery centers in various regional communities. Elliot Hospital was founded in 1890.

Operations

Elliot Hospital is Manchester's designated Regional Trauma Center. Additional facilities include the Elliot Breast Health Center Elliot Urgent Care Elliot Senior Health Center and New Hampshire's Hospital for Children.

Strategy

Elliot Health System has expanded throughout the region by constructing new outpatient care centers in nearby towns. Most recently Elliot Health completed construction of satellite facilities including an ambulatory care center and a senior health center. In 2015 it partnered with Northeast Rehabilitation Hospital to create a new rehabilitation floor within its Elliot Hospital.

EXECUTIVES

Vice President Of Services, Carla Braveman
Vice President of Human Resources, Catherine Bardier
Auditors: BAKER NEWMAN & NOYES LLC MANC

LOCATIONS

HQ: ELLIOT HOSPITAL OF THE CITY OF MANCHESTER
1 ELLIOT WAY, MANCHESTER, NH 031033502
Phone: 603 669-5300
Web: WWW.ELLIOTHOSPITAL.ORG

PRODUCTS/OPERATIONS

Selected Centers and Services
Aeronautics Medicine
Adult Day Programs
Bariatric Surgery
Behavioral Health
Breast Health Center
Cardiology Services
Center for Sleep Evaluation
Center for Wound Care & Hyberbaric Medicine
Childbirth And Family Education
Community Health and Wellness
Critical Care at The Elliot
Diabetes and Outpatient Nutrition Services
Diagnostic Imaging
Elliot 1-Day Surgery Center
The Elliot at Hooksett
Elliot Behavioral Health Services
Elliot Endocrinology Associates
Elliot Gastroenterology
Elliot General Surgical Specialists
Elliot Maternal Fetal Medicine
Elliot Medical Center at Londonderry
Elliot Neurology Associates
Elliot Obstetrics and Gynecology
Elliot Orthopaedic Surgical Specialists
Elliot Physician Network
Elliot Regional Cancer Center
Elliot Sports Medicine
Elliot Trauma Center
Elliot Wellness Center
Endoscopy Center
Health Education Library
Home Medical Equipment
Hospitalist Program
Infection Control Department
Inpatient Care/Nursing Units
Laboratory Services
Max K. Willscher Urology Center
Neurophysiology
New England EMS Institute
New Hampshire Arthritis Center
Nursing Units/Inpatient Care
Nutrition Services
Occupational Health & Wellness
Oral Maxillofacial Surgery Center
Oxygen Therapy
Pain Management Center
Pediatric Surgery
Pharmacy Services
Pulmonary Medicine
Pulmonary Rehabilitation
Physical Therapy
Rehabilitation
Respiratory Care
Senior Health Center
Sports Medicine
Surgery
Speech Therapy
Urgent Car
Urgent Car
Visiting Nurse Association of Manchester & So. NH Inc.
Weight Management
Wellness Center
Women's & Children's Services
Wound Center

COMPETITORS

Caritas Holy Family	Frisbie Memorial
Hospital	Hospital
Catholic Medical	HCA
Center	Lahey Health System
Concord Hospital	Southern New Hampshire
Exeter Health	Medical Center
Resources	

Income Statement

	REVENUE ($ mil.)	NET INCOME ($ mil.)	NET PROFIT MARGIN	EMPLOYEES
06/15	421	43	10.4%	2,000
06/10	324	7	2.4%	—
06/09	288	0	—	—
06/08	0	0	—	—
Annual Growth	—	—	—	—

FYE: June 30

2015 Year-End Financials

Return on assets: 9.3%
Return on equity: 10.4%
Current ratio: 0.70

Cash ($ mil.): 77

ELLIS HOSPITAL

Schenectady-based Ellis Hospital (dba Ellis Medicine) serves the residents of New York's capital area as part of Ellis Medicine a 438-bed community and teaching health care system. The hospital provides emergency inpatient medical/surgical and psychiatric care including diagnostic primary and rehabilitative care. The hospital is also home to centers of excellence in the treatment of and care for heart and cardiovascular ailments cancer women's health issues stroke-related problems and behavioral health concerns. It also operates the Ellis Center the Bellvue Woman's Center the satellite outpatient clinic Ellis Health Center and recently-constructed Medical Center of Clifton Park.

Operations

Ellis Hospital is part of Ellis Medicine a 438-bed community and teaching health care system serving the Albany New York area. Ellis Medicine has four campuses - Ellis Hospital Ellis Health Center Bellevue Woman's Center and Medical Center of Clifton Park - five additional service locations and more than 700 affiliated physicians.

The hospital's specialty services include a nationally recognized Heart Center a New York State designated Stroke Center and advanced surgery programs such as cardiothoracic orthopedic neurological and vascular among others. The facility features diagnostic imaging and a modern 36-bed intensive care unit.

The McClellan Street Health Center offers outpatient services primary care short-stay rehabilitation and nursing home services. Ellis Medicine Bariatric Care Centers offers a surgical weight loss program.

Ellis Hospital also operates academic programs to prepare students for careers in health care and nursing.

Geographic Reach

The hospital serves patients in the Albany Saratoga Schenectady Fulton and Montgomery counties of upstate New York.

Sales and Marketing

Medicare and Medicaid payments accounted for 53% of net patient service revenues in fiscal 2014.

Financial Performance

Ellis Hospital reported a 2% increase in revenue to $388 million in 2014 due to an increase in net patient service revenues. However it reported a net loss of $5.5 million due to losses on extinguishment of debt and changes in net unrealized gains on investments. Affiliate pension and post-retirement-related changes other than net periodic benefit costs also contributed to the loss.

Cash flow from operations rose 54% to $28 million in 2014 as accounts payable and accrued expenses declined.

Strategy

All of the Schenectady facilities are undergoing expansion or improvement efforts to increase service offerings. In 2013 a $61-million project to expand emergency care and parking at Ellis Hospital was begun; it was completed in early 2015. The project expanded treatment stations to 60 (from 47) and added a new two-story 212-space parking garage. Other capital improvements include a $17-million expansion and modernization of Bellevue Women's Center. Recently completed improvements include the relocation of Ellis' 82-bed nursing home and short-stay rehabilitation center and the creation of the Medical Center of Clifton Park.

EXECUTIVES

Vice President and Chief Financial Officer, Daniel Rinaldi
Medical Director Adult Inpatient Psychiatry, Pankaj Mehta
Pharmacy Manager, Erin Buckley
Vice President Management, Paul Segovis
Vice President Of Corporate Compliance and Internal Audit, Colleen Susko
Director Of Pharmacy, Martin Killian
Vice President of Operations, Patti Hammond
Medical Director of Informatics, Igor Kraeve
Managing Director, Laurie Wasniski
Secretary, Susan Ortell
Treasurer, Howard Foote

LOCATIONS

HQ: ELLIS HOSPITAL
  1101 NOTT ST, SCHENECTADY, NY 123082489
Phone: 518 243-4000
Web: WWW.ELLISMEDICINE.ORG

PRODUCTS/OPERATIONS

2014 Sales

	% of total
Net patient service revenue	98
Other operating revenue	2
Net assets released from restrictions used for operations	-
Total	**100**

Selected Services

Emergency
Cancer/Oncology
Neuroscience
Orthopedics
Primary care
Weight Loss
Women's Health

Selected Facilities

Bariatric Care Center
Bellevue Woman's Center
Ellis Health Center
Ellis Hospital
Medical Center Clifton Park
Primary Care
Clifton Park
Glenville
Latham
Schenectady (Nott St.)
Schenectady (McClellan St.)
School of Nursing

COMPETITORS

Albany Medical Center
Lifetime Health
Oneida Healthcare Center
SUNY Upstate Medical University
St. Joseph's Hospital Health Center
St. Peter's Health Partners
United Health Services Hospitals
Upstate University Hospital at Community General

Income Statement

	REVENUE ($ mil.)	NET INCOME ($ mil.)	NET PROFIT MARGIN	EMPLOYEES
12/15	377	2	0.5%	3,000
12/14	361	9	2.7%	—
12/13	380	38	10.1%	—
12/12	379	10	2.8%	—
Annual Growth	(0.2%)	(42.6%)	—	—

FYE: December 31

2015 Year-End Financials

Return on assets: 6.5%
Return on equity: 0.5%
Current ratio: 1.00

Cash ($ mil.): 24

ELMHURST MEMORIAL HOSPITAL INC

Elmhurst Memorial Healthcare operates Elmhurst Memorial Hospital an acute care facility located in DuPage County Illinois in the western suburbs of Chicago. Founded in 1926 the hospital provides a comprehensive range of medical services — from emergency care to specialty cancer and orthopedics care to behavioral health services. In addition to the 310-bed main hospital Elmhurst Memorial Healthcare operates several facilities such as doctors' offices outpatient centers occupational health programs and other ancillary health care operations. Elmhurst Memorial Healthcare is part of Edward-Elmhurst Healthcare after it merged with Edward Hospital & Health Services and Linden Oaks.

Change in Company Type

Elmhurst Memorial Healthcare Edward Hospital & Health Services and Linden Oaks merged in 2013 to create a larger integrated health system. Combined the system operates three hospitals and more than 50 outpatient facilities. It has some $1 billion in annual revenues.

Operations

Aside from its Elmhurst Memorial Hospital Main Campus Elmhurst Memorial Healthcare operates several other facilities such as the Berteau Campus Center for Health Lombard Health Center Addison Health Center Elmhurst Memorial Sleep Center Occupational Health Services Wood Dale and an outpatient surgery center clinic primary care associates medical associates and hematology oncology associates offices under the Elmhurst banner.

The newer acute care hospital known as the Elmhurst Memorial Hospital Main Campus features about 260 private inpatient rooms as well as a high-tech emergency department and surgical and diagnostic imaging facilities. It includes the Elmhurst Memorial Center for Health which boasts outpatient clinics and a medical office building for general practice and specialty physicians.

Each year Elmhurst Memorial Hospital has some 48000 emergency department visits and performs some 3400 inpatient and 5500 outpatient surgeries.

Geographic Reach

Elmhurst Memorial Healthcare and its hospital serve the western suburbs of Chicago specifically the county residents of DuPage.

Strategy

To provide its communities with quality cancer care Elmhurst Memorial Healthcare constructed a

new cancer care facility that boasts medical oncologist offices an infusion center Cyberknife robotic radiosurgery system and radiation oncology services.

In 2015 Elmhurst Memorial Hospital opened a bariatrics and weight management center that provides surgical and non-surgical services.

The system has been expanding by opening new facilities. In 2014 it opened its second walk-in clinic which provides treatment for minor illnesses. The following year Elmhurst broke ground on a new three-story health center in Hinsdale.

There are also plans for the old Elmhurst Memorial Hospital campus known as the Berteau Campus. While the Berteau Campus' inpatient and emergency care operations were transferred to the new Main Campus the Berteau Campus' emergency room became an outpatient urgent care center. The campus also includes inpatient behavioral health and recovery facilities as well as outpatient cancer care physical therapy and occupational health clinics. For the long term Elmhurst Memorial Healthcare plans to transform the Berteau Campus into a senior health and housing center by closing or moving the existing operations to other or new locations.

EXECUTIVES

Vice President Physician and Ambulatory Network, Ken Fishbain
Co Chairman, Aloyzas Pakalniskis

LOCATIONS

HQ: ELMHURST MEMORIAL HOSPITAL INC
133 E BRUSH HILL RD, ELMHURST, IL 601265659
Phone: 331 221-9003
Web: WWW.EMAPHYSICIANS.ORG

PRODUCTS/OPERATIONS

Selected Services
Breast Health Center
Cardiovascular Services
EMH Laboratory
Family Birthing Center
Home Health and Hospice
Immediate Care Centers
Occupational Health
Orthopedics
Radiology
Surgery
Cancer Center
Emergency Department

COMPETITORS

Adventist Health System Sunbelt Healthcare
Advocate Health Care
Alexian Brothers Health System
Central DuPage Hospital
Covenant Ministries
Gottleib Memorial Hospital
Loyola University Health System
Northwest Community Healthcare
Rush System for Health
University of Chicago Medical Center
Wheaton Franciscan Services

HISTORICAL FINANCIALS
Company Type: Private

Income Statement
FYE: June 30

	REVENUE ($ mil.)	NET INCOME ($ mil.)	NET PROFIT MARGIN	EMPLOYEES
06/15	379	(9)	—	2,444
06/09	305	20	6.6%	—
06/08	345	(22)	—	—
06/07	341	43	12.7%	—
Annual Growth	1.3%	—	—	—

ELON UNIVERSITY

EXECUTIVES

President, Leo M Lambert
Auditors: GRANT THORNTON LLP CHARLOTTE

LOCATIONS

HQ: ELON UNIVERSITY
100 CAMPUS DR, ELON, NC 272449423
Phone: 336 278-2000
Web: WWW.ELON.EDU

HISTORICAL FINANCIALS
Company Type: Private

Income Statement
FYE: May 31

	REVENUE ($ mil.)	NET INCOME ($ mil.)	NET PROFIT MARGIN	EMPLOYEES
05/16	240	22	9.5%	1,200
05/15	262	54	20.7%	—
05/14	238	50	21.0%	—
05/13	221	46	20.9%	—
Annual Growth	2.7%	(21.1%)		

2016 Year-End Financials
Return on assets: 2.8%　　　Cash ($ mil.): 21
Return on equity: 9.5%
Current ratio: —

ELWYN

Elwyn isn't a character out of Harry Potter or Lord of the Rings . It's a not-for-profit organization that serves more than 13000 disabled and disadvantaged people of all ages at multiple sites through education rehabilitation and vocational counseling. The organization also operates residential communities including more than 80 group homes and apartments and provides a variety of health care services for persons with developmental physical and emotional disabilities. The group also publishes training materials and hosts conferences and seminars for human services professionals. Founded in 1852 as a school for children with mental retardation Elwyn is one of the oldest organizations of its kind in the US.

Operations
Elwyn operates two for-profit subsidiaries. Its PEMS unit an applied technology service provides a variety of enhanced management services. The organization's Grace Pharmacy Inc. is a full-service pharmacy operation that specializes in long-term care clients.

Elwyn Commercial Laundry specializes in laundry services for hospitals nursing homes surgical centers and other health care related organizations.

Geographic Reach
Elwyn's main campus is in Philadelphia with satellite locations in California New Jersey and Delaware.

Company Background
At a time when most people with mental disabilities were left to live on the streets or thrown in prison Dr. Alfred Elwyn proposed a special school to help "feeble-minded children." The school attracted the best minds of the time and grew quickly adding residential services and custodial care of adults in 1877.

EXECUTIVES

Vice President, Nancy Catania
Vice President of Finance, Carole Surdyke
Vice President, Scott Campbell
Director of Non Traditional Career Services and Tr, Joseph Gousie

LOCATIONS

HQ: ELWYN
111 ELWYN RD, MEDIA, PA 190634622
Phone: 610 891-2000
Web: WWW.ELWYN.ORG

PRODUCTS/OPERATIONS

Selected Services
Behavioral health services
Deaf services
Early childhood services
Education services
Research and health services
Supports for living
Work and adult day services

COMPETITORS

Res-Care

HISTORICAL FINANCIALS
Company Type: Private

Income Statement
FYE: June 30

	REVENUE ($ mil.)	NET INCOME ($ mil.)	NET PROFIT MARGIN	EMPLOYEES
06/15	218	2	1.2%	2,500
06/14	268	13	4.9%	—
06/11	264	14	5.5%	—
06/10	254	6	2.4%	—
Annual Growth	(3.0%)	(16.3%)	—	—

2015 Year-End Financials
Return on assets: 27.0%　　　Cash ($ mil.): 8
Return on equity: 1.2%
Current ratio: 0.50

EMBREE CONSTRUCTION GROUP, INC.

The Embree Construction Group develops designs and builds free-standing buildings for business chains across the US. The group serves as a general contractor or construction manager primarily for major national companies. It is active throughout the US. Ground-up and remodeling projects include retail properties restaurants gas stations convenience stores automotive service centers and correctional facilities. Operating companies include Embree Healthcare Group which develops assisted-living and specialty medical projects and Embree Asset Group which develops build-to-suit single-tenant buildings and leases them back to clients. Owner and chairman Jim Embree founded the firm in 1979 in Kansas City.

Operations
The group provides a full range of real estate development and construction services across the nation. It specializes in build-to-suit development design/build general construction and program management. Ground-up projects make up about half of the company's portfolio. Embree also provides tenant improvement remodel and conversion services.

Geographic Reach

Headquartered in Texas where it has completed more than 3700 projects Embree Construction Group also has regional offices in operates in Arizona California and Colorado. The company is active in all 50 states.

Sales and Marketing

The company's top customers include Shell Cash America GNC BBVA Taco Bell Sears CVS and Exxon Mobil.

Strategy

The firm is focused on serving clients for the long term; it has maintained customer relationships for up to three decades.

Embree Construction Group is experienced in green building practices. It has five LEED-certified professionals on its staff. The company also employs about 20 certified Project Management Professionals.

EXECUTIVES

Vice President, Beau Embree
Vice President, Josiah Byrnes
Auditors: RSM US LLP AUSTIN TEXAS

LOCATIONS

HQ: EMBREE CONSTRUCTION GROUP, INC.
4747 WILLIAMS DR, GEORGETOWN, TX 786333799
Phone: 512 819-4700
Web: WWW.EMBREEGROUP.COM

COMPETITORS

American Constructors	Fisher Development
Austin Commercial	H.J. Russell
Charles Pankow	McCarthy Building
Builders	Schlosser Development
Colson & Colson	Venture Construction
EMJ	Workman Commercial
FaulknerUSA	

HISTORICAL FINANCIALS

Company Type: Private

Income Statement

FYE: December 31

	REVENUE ($ mil.)	NET INCOME ($ mil.)	NET PROFIT MARGIN	EMPLOYEES
12/15	190	8	4.7%	175
12/14	140	2	2.0%	—
12/13	139	3	2.2%	—
12/12	128	2	2.2%	—
Annual Growth	13.9%	46.8%	—	—

2015 Year-End Financials

Return on assets: 4.2%
Return on equity: 4.7%
Current ratio: 1.20
Cash ($ mil.): 18

EMERSON COLLEGE

Emerson College specializes in teaching subjects in the fields of communication and the arts in a liberal arts context. Areas of study include journalism; marketing; organizational and political communication; performing arts; visual and media arts; and writing literature and publishing. Its also has an acclaimed communication sciences and disorders program. The college enrolls about 3200 full-time undergraduates and 1000 full and part-time graduate students on its Boston-based campus. Among its alumni are producer Norman Lear talk show host Jay Leno and journalist Morton Dean. The college has additional facilities in Los Angeles and in the Netherlands. Emerson was founded in 1880 as a school of oratory.

EXECUTIVES

Vice President Human Resources, Richard West
Vice President, Barbara Rutberg
Assistant Vice President of Enrollment, Ruthanne Madsen
Associate Vice President Institutional Research, Michael Duggan
Vice President Administration Finance, Maureen Murphy
Vice President for Diversity and Inclusion, Sylvia Spears
Vice President general Counsel, Christine Hughes
Associate Vice President Finance, Marc Miller
Vice President of Administration, Eric Schaefer
Co President, Kaela Holmes
Assistant Vice President Marketing, Michael Sarra
Vice President For Institutional Advancement, Ronald Korvas
Vice President, Jennifer Robenalt
Associate Vice President Information Technology, Brian Basgen
Assistant Vice President Human Resources Operations, Peter de Andrade
Associate Vice President, David Howse
Associate Vice President, Steve Schaefer
Assistant Vice President For Faculty Affairs, Carol Parker
Assistant Vice President Employee Engagement, Pam Bonnell
ASSOCIATE VICE PRESIDENT, Dileo Leanne
Auditors: KPMG LLP HARTFORD CT

LOCATIONS

HQ: EMERSON COLLEGE
120 BOYLSTON ST STE 414, BOSTON, MA 021164624
Phone: 617 824-8500

HISTORICAL FINANCIALS

Company Type: Private

Income Statement

FYE: June 30

	REVENUE ($ mil.)	NET INCOME ($ mil.)	NET PROFIT MARGIN	EMPLOYEES
06/15	216	8	3.8%	425
06/10	154	17	11.6%	—
06/09	147	15	10.8%	—
06/08	0	0	—	—
Annual Growth	—	—	—	—

2015 Year-End Financials

Return on assets: 10.7%
Return on equity: 3.8%
Current ratio: 0.10
Cash ($ mil.): 34

EMERSON HOSPITAL

Ralph Waldo Emerson said "the first wealth is health" and Emerson Hospital would agree. The not-for-profit hospital tends to the well-being of patients in and around historic Concord Massachusetts. The 179-bed community hospital is staffed by more than 300 doctors and specialists. Emerson partners with Massachusetts General on several specialty programs including weight management neonatology and oncology treatment (which is housed within its Bethke Cancer Center). It also operates outpatient clinics serving residents in nearby communities such as Groton Sudbury and Littleton. All told Emerson provides advanced medical services to more than 300000 people.

Operations

Emerson Hospital offers services at its main campus in Concord and at health centers in West-

ford Groton and Sudbury. It also operates the Center for Specialty Care in Concord the Center for Rehabilitative and Sports Therapies in Concord the Hermel Breast Health Center in Concord a primary care practice in Bedford and urgent care centers in Hudson and Littleton. Emerson's Wellness Center for Mind and Body in Concord provides a place where the community can participate in classes aimed at keeping them healthy.

The company's main hospital has more than 37500 emergency department visits per year. Emerson is well known for its outstanding nursing care and patient-centered facilities including the Bethke Cancer Center and the Clough Birthing Center which has the area's only Special Care Level 2 Nursery for moderately ill newborns.

Geographic Reach

Emerson Hospital provides medical services to people in 25 communities in Massachusetts including Concord Groton Sudbury and Westford.

Strategy

To extend its coverage and skill base Emerson Hospital partners with larger and/or specialist hospitals and medical facilities in the region including IVF New England Brigham and Women's Hospital Lahey Hospital and Medical Center and Massachusetts General.

In early 2018 Emerson opened the Steinberg Wellness Center for Mind and Body in Concord. The prior year the health system opened its first urgent care centers in Hudson and Littleton.

Company Background

The hospital founded in 1911 is named for Charles Emerson a nephew of Ralph Waldo Emerson.

EXECUTIVES

President and CEO, Christine C. Schuster
VP Human Resources, Eric Stastny
SVP Administration, Jack Wilhelm
SVP and Chief Medical Officer, C. Gregory Martin
VP for Patient Care Services and Chief Nursing Officer, Joyce Welsh
SVP Planning and Chief Strategy Officer, Christine Gallery
SVP and CFO, Michael (Mike) Hachey
President Secretary Treasurer Vice President of marketing, Sally Savelle
President Medical Staff, Raj Devarajan
Physical Therapy Director, Terry Enis
Director of Nursing, Susan Carter
Vice President, Karl Kussin
Vice President Of Human Resources, Eric Statsny
Chairman, Paul D. Birch, age 58
Vice Chairman, Ronald H. Johnson
Board Member, Don Voghel
Auditors: PRICEWATERHOUSECOOPER LLP BOS

LOCATIONS

HQ: EMERSON HOSPITAL
133 OLD RD TO 9 ACRE COR, CONCORD, MA 017424169
Phone: 978 369-1400
Web: WWW.EMERSONHOSPITAL.ORG

PRODUCTS/OPERATIONS

Selected Facilities

Center for Rehabilitative and Sports Therapies (Concord)
Center for Specialty Care (Concord)
Emerson Main Campus (Concord)
Emerson Medical at Bedford
Emerson Medical at Sudbury
Emerson Wellness Center for Mind and Body (Concord)
Groton Health Center
Hermel Breast Health Center (Concord)
Laboratory Services (Concord)
Westford Health Center

HISTORICAL FINANCIALS

Company Type: Private

Income Statement
FYE: September 30

	REVENUE ($ mil.)	NET INCOME ($ mil.)	NET PROFIT MARGIN	EMPLOYEES
09/15	201	(8)	—	1,450
09/14	186	(1)	—	—
09/13	183	2	1.6%	—
09/12	180	3	1.9%	—
Annual Growth	3.7%	—	—	—

2015 Year-End Financials

Return on assets: 10.7%   Cash ($ mil.): 22
Return on equity: (-4.1%)
Current ratio: 1.50

EMJ CORPORATION

EMJ does it all for the mall. Founded in 1968 by namesake Edgar M. Jolley the company specializes in building and renovating retail outlets and shopping centers throughout the US. It is also known for other building projects such as offices warehouses churches hotels multifamily residences hospitals and wind farms. Working from five offices nationwide EMJ provides general construction and construction management. The company's pre-construction services include creating detailed budgets and construction schedules and coordinating permitting utility companies and municipal requirements. To track a project's progress and monitor costs EMJ offers quality control and safety and warranty management.

Operations

EMJ owns several operating divisions including Signal Energy which engineers and builds renewable energy projects such as wind farms and solar and biomass energy projects. Another division Accent Construction Management provides site selection budgeting scheduling and other services. Its RedStone Construction Services builds commercial retail hospitality healthcare government facilities and others. It is focused on fostering economic growth in Native American communities.

Geographic Reach

From its base in Chattanooga Tennessee EMJ serves clients through a handful of US offices in Massachusetts Tennessee Texas and California.

Sales and Marketing

EMJ has built more than 500 million sq. ft. of construction projects. Its client roster includes Academy Barnes & Noble Bed Bath & Beyond Blue Cross and Blue Shield Home Depot PetSmart and Winn-Dixie.

The company serves several sectors such as airports education entertainment government and civic grocery healthcare hospitality industrial and warehouse and Native American tribal communities office buildings parking lifestyle and mixed use development retail renewable energy renovations and worship centers.

Strategy

The company is working on projects for Whole Foods Market TownPlace Suites Silverdale Baptist student center and Dick's Sporting Goods. Inked in 2013 EMJ's $250-million deal with Native Amer-

ican Chris Samples operating under the name Red-Stone Construction Services is building a 500-room hotel and expanding a casino in Tulsa Oklahoma.

EXECUTIVES

Executive Vice President, Ray Catlin
Vice President of Estimating, James T Tyson
Vice President, Ken Colgate
Vice President of Construction, Jack Bowen
Vice President, Alfonso Leon
Executive Vice President, Alex Grace
Vice President, Lance Gopffarth
Vice President, Wes Jones
Vice President, Earl Carstens
Senior Vice President, Philip Augustino
Senior Vice President, Drew Smith
Vice President Southwest Office, Drew Halsey
Executive Vice President, Neil Pratt
Vice President of Business Development, Hal Routh
Vice President of Construction, Steve Rice
Executive Vice President, Ron Jobe
Senior Vice President, Chas Torrence

LOCATIONS

HQ: EMJ CORPORATION
2034 HAMILTON PLACE BLVD # 400,
CHATTANOOGA, TN 374216102
Phone: 423 855-1550
Web: WWW.EMJCORP.COM

PRODUCTS/OPERATIONS

Selected Projects
Airports
Education
Entertainment
Government/civic
Grocery
Healthcare
Hospitality
Industrial/warehouse
Lifestyle/mixed use development and retail
Native American tribal communities
Office buildings
Parking
Renewable energy
Renovations
Worship centers

Selected Services
Construction
Construction management
General contracting
Pre-construction services
Quality control
Safety consultation
Site evaluation
Warranty

HISTORICAL FINANCIALS

Company Type: Private

Income Statement
FYE: March 7

	REVENUE ($ mil.)	NET INCOME ($ mil.)	NET PROFIT MARGIN	EMPLOYEES
03/17*	960	4	0.5%	210
12/11	437	0	0.1%	—
12/08	821	7	1.0%	—
12/07	1,955	0	—	—
Annual Growth	—	294.8%	—	—

*Fiscal year change

2017 Year-End Financials

Return on assets: 18.0%   Cash ($ mil.): 29
Return on equity: 0.5%
Current ratio: 1.10

EMORY UNIVERSITY HOSPITAL MIDTOWN

EXECUTIVES

Chief Executive Officer, Robert J Bachman
Financial Executive, Liz D Samford
General Manager, Deborah Plement

LOCATIONS

HQ: EMORY UNIVERSITY HOSPITAL MIDTOWN
550 PEACHTREE ST NE, ATLANTA, GA 303082212
Phone: 404 686-4411
Web: WWW.EMORY.ORG

HISTORICAL FINANCIALS

Company Type: Private

Income Statement
FYE: August 31

	REVENUE ($ mil.)	NET INCOME ($ mil.)	NET PROFIT MARGIN	EMPLOYEES
08/15	641	(21)	—	2,500
08/10	0	(0)	—	—
08/09	1,807	(38)	—	—
08/08	507	(10)	—	—
Annual Growth	3.4%	—	—	—

2015 Year-End Financials

Return on assets: 8.0%   Cash ($ mil.): 129
Return on equity: (-3.4%)
Current ratio: 1.60

ENERCON SERVICES, INC.

EXECUTIVES

President, John Richardson

LOCATIONS

HQ: ENERCON SERVICES, INC.
500 TOWNPARK LN NW # 275, KENNESAW, GA
301443707
Phone: 770 919-1930
Web: WWW.ENERCON.COM

HISTORICAL FINANCIALS

Company Type: Private

Income Statement
FYE: December 31

	REVENUE ($ mil.)	NET INCOME ($ mil.)	NET PROFIT MARGIN	EMPLOYEES
12/15	291	12	4.4%	1,833
12/14	251	4	2.0%	—
12/09	160	15	9.5%	—
12/08	120	8	7.0%	—
Annual Growth	13.5%	6.2%	—	—

2015 Year-End Financials

Return on assets: 2.1%   Cash ($ mil.): 10
Return on equity: 4.4%
Current ratio: 1.60

ENERGYUNITED ELECTRIC MEMBERSHIP CORPORATION

Electrical energy and propane energy come together under the auspices of EnergyUnited Electric Membership. One of North Carolina's largest power utilities EnergyUnited distributes electricity to more than 120000 residential and business customers in 19 counties. The member-owned not-for-profit cooperative also provides propane to 23000 customers in 74 counties in North and South Carolina and it also offers home security bill management and facility monitoring services. The third largest supplier of residential electricity in the state its service territory includes three of the largest cities in North Carolina - Charlotte Greensboro and Winston-Salem.

The company's strategy aims at delivering reliable energy services at affordable prices. In 2010 EnergyUnited made upgrades to its distribution system (installing fiber optic cable and improving communication through Radio Frequency devices) and expanded its renewable energy portfolio (including buying solar power from a newly opened solar farm in Taylorville).

These improvements including the installation of Smart Meters for all members (completed in 2011) enabled the company to cut rates twice in 2010. As a result the company reported lower revenues and net margins for the year.

EnergyUnited was formed through the 1998 merger of Crescent Electric Membership and Davidson Electric Membership.

EXECUTIVES

Vice President Of EngineerandOperations, David Schleicher
Vice President Power Supply, Dave Meisinger

LOCATIONS

HQ: ENERGYUNITED ELECTRIC MEMBERSHIP CORPORATION
567 MOCKSVILLE HWY, STATESVILLE, NC 286258269
Phone: 704 873-5241
Web: WWW.ENERGYUNITED.COM

COMPETITORS

Crestwood Equity
Duke Energy
SCANA

HISTORICAL FINANCIALS
Company Type: Private

Income Statement
FYE: December 31

	REVENUE ($ mil.)	NET INCOME ($ mil.)	NET PROFIT MARGIN	EMPLOYEES
12/15	281	9	3.5%	175
12/14	274	9	3.5%	—
12/13	258	7	2.8%	—
12/12	245	13	5.5%	—
Annual Growth	4.6%	(10.4%)	—	—

2015 Year-End Financials
Return on assets: 8.4%
Return on equity: 3.5%
Current ratio: 0.70
Cash ($ mil.): 11

ENGEL MACHINERY INC.

EXECUTIVES

President, Mark Sankovitch
Financial Executive, Glenn Ness
Account Manager, Mary Buckwalter
VP Finance, Hagen Schuster
Personnel Manager, John Evans
Director, Chris Kightlinger
Sales Manager, Markus Lettau
Sales Director, Jim Moran
Chief Operating Officer, Jeff Hershey
Auditors: GRANT THORNTON LLP KITCHENER

LOCATIONS

HQ: ENGEL MACHINERY INC.
3740 BOARD RD, YORK, PA 174068425
Phone: 717 764-6818
Web: WWW.ENGELGLOBAL.COM

HISTORICAL FINANCIALS
Company Type: Private

Income Statement
FYE: March 31

	REVENUE ($ mil.)	NET INCOME ($ mil.)	NET PROFIT MARGIN	EMPLOYEES
03/16	190	2	1.2%	140
03/15	126	0	0.4%	—
03/14	152	2	2.0%	—
03/13	177	7	4.4%	—
Annual Growth	2.5%	(33.6%)	—	—

2016 Year-End Financials
Return on assets: 5.6%
Return on equity: 1.2%
Current ratio: 0.80
Cash ($ mil.): 6

ENGINEERED STRUCTURES, INC.

EXECUTIVES

Chief Executive Officer, Thomas D Hill
Director, Caroline Pavlinik
Financial Executive, Abigail Bonadies
Engineer, John Fahrer
Vice-President, Elizabeth Brockway
Financial Executive, Anna Leigh
Project Manager, Shane Plummer
Project Manager, Bonnie Heinrich
Auditors: HARRIS & CO PLLC MERIDIAN I

LOCATIONS

HQ: ENGINEERED STRUCTURES, INC.
3330 E LOUISE DR STE 300, MERIDIAN, ID 836425123
Phone: 208 362-3040
Web: WWW.ESICONSTRUCTION.COM

HISTORICAL FINANCIALS
Company Type: Private

Income Statement
FYE: December 31

	REVENUE ($ mil.)	NET INCOME ($ mil.)	NET PROFIT MARGIN	EMPLOYEES
12/15	295	6	2.3%	250
12/14	246	5	2.1%	—
12/13	270	6	2.3%	—
12/12	0	0	—	—
Annual Growth	—	266.3%	—	—

2015 Year-End Financials
Return on assets: 11.9%
Return on equity: 2.3%
Current ratio: 0.80
Cash ($ mil.): 8

ENGLEWOOD HOSPITAL AND MEDICAL CENTER FOUNDATION INC.

Englewood Hospital and Medical Center is a 520-bed acute care hospital serving New Jersey's Bergen County which is part of the New York City metro area. The not-for-profit health care provider offers general medical and surgical care along with specialty services in areas such as oncology cardiovascular disease wound care women's health joint replacement and pediatrics. It also maintains a short-term inpatient behavioral health program for adults. The hospital is affiliated with the Mount Sinai School of Medicine and the Mount Sinai Consortium for Graduate Medical Education and provides residency programs to doctors from the Mount Sinai School of Medicine.

Operations

Englewood Hospital and Medical Center has a nursing staff of 800 and medical staff of 380. It serves more than 23000 admitted patients and nearly 47000 emergency cases a year. It conducted some 8000 operations and helped deliver 2000 babies in 2014.

As a teaching hospital it offers education and research programs including Grand Rounds CME Online an Internal Medicine Residency Program a Vascular Surgery Fellowship a Pharmacy Residency Program and a School of Radiography.

Along with the typical acute and chronic medical care services the hospital maintains an infusion center for patients requiring chemotherapy and also offers hyperbaric oxygen treatments for divers with the bends and other patients who will benefit from having oxygen administered under pressure.

To better serve patients for whom blood transfusions are not an option the hospital had established a program for bloodless medicine and surgery. The Institute for Patient Blood Management & Bloodless Medicine and Surgery serves as a leading resource for training health professionals in working in environments where blood transfusions are not readily available.

Geographic Reach

The company operates the largest voluntary acute care hospital in Bergen County and the third largest in New Jersey.

Company Background

The hospital was founded in 1890.

EXECUTIVES

Vice President Of Planning Program Devt, Mike Petrowitz

LOCATIONS

HQ: ENGLEWOOD HOSPITAL AND MEDICAL CENTER FOUNDATION INC.
350 ENGLE ST, ENGLEWOOD, NJ 076311808
Phone: 201 894-3000
Web: WWW.ENGLEWOODHOSPITAL.COM

PRODUCTS/OPERATIONS

Selected ServicesMedical ServicesAMI of EnglewoodAnesthesiologyAntepartum Testing CenterBerrie Center Same Day SurgeryBariatric SurgeryBloodless Medicine & SurgeryBreast Care CenterBreast Surgical ServicesCancer Center ResourcesCardiac RehabCardiac Surge

COMPETITORS

Bergen Regional Medical
Bronx-Lebanon Hospital
Hackensack University Medical Center
Lenox Hill Hospital Memorial Sloan-Kettering

NewYork-Presbyterian Healthcare
St. Joseph's Regional Medical Center
The Valley Hospital
Valley Health System

HISTORICAL FINANCIALS

Company Type: Private

Income Statement

FYE: December 31

	REVENUE ($ mil.)	NET INCOME ($ mil.)	NET PROFIT MARGIN	EMPLOYEES
12/15	480	12	2.5%	2,200
12/14	428	13	3.2%	—
12/13	425	11	2.7%	—
12/09	327	13	4.1%	—
Annual Growth	6.6%	(1.6%)	—	—

2015 Year-End Financials

Return on assets: 8.0%
Return on equity: 2.5%
Current ratio: 1.10

Cash ($ mil.): 44

EPHRATA COMMUNITY HOSPITAL INC

EXECUTIVES

President, John Porter
Board of Directors, William C Funk
Board of Directors, Linda H Weaver
Director, Bob Stauffer
President, Kathy Edwards
Auditors: ERNST & YOUNG LLP

LOCATIONS

HQ: EPHRATA COMMUNITY HOSPITAL INC
169 MARTIN AVE, EPHRATA, PA 175221755
Phone: 717 721-5883
Web: WWW.EPHRATAHOSPITAL.ORG

HISTORICAL FINANCIALS

Company Type: Private

Income Statement

FYE: June 30

	REVENUE ($ mil.)	NET INCOME ($ mil.)	NET PROFIT MARGIN	EMPLOYEES
06/15	190	3	1.9%	1,894
06/10	174	(0)	—	—
06/09	188	33	17.6%	—
06/08	333	0	—	—
Annual Growth	—	276.1%	—	—

2015 Year-End Financials

Return on assets: 1.8%
Return on equity: 1.9%
Current ratio: 1.00

Cash ($ mil.): 15

ERM-NA HOLDINGS CORP.

EXECUTIVES

Chief Executive Officer, David McArthur
Sales Manager, Melinda Stephens
Director, Blaine L Hummel
Manager, Kathy Daugherty
Financial Executive, Joanne Dellavalle
Director, Sue Moseley
Vice-President, Susan Lee
Auditors: KPMG LLP PHILADELPHIA PA

LOCATIONS

HQ: ERM-NA HOLDINGS CORP.
75 VALLEY STREAM PKWY # 200, MALVERN, PA 193551459
Phone: 484 913-0300

HISTORICAL FINANCIALS

Company Type: Private

Income Statement

FYE: March 31

	REVENUE ($ mil.)	NET INCOME ($ mil.)	NET PROFIT MARGIN	EMPLOYEES
03/16	388	10	2.7%	1,573
03/15	387	18	4.7%	—
03/14	353	34	9.8%	—
03/13	335	26	8.0%	—
Annual Growth	5.1%	(26.9%)	—	—

2016 Year-End Financials

Return on assets: 3.7%
Return on equity: 2.7%
Current ratio: 1.40

Cash ($ mil.): 3

ESSEX PORTFOLIO, L.P.

EXECUTIVES

President, Michael J Schall
Executive Vice-President, John D Eudy
Executive Vice-President, Craig K Zimmerman
Director, Barb M Pak
Manager, Tanya Arcilla
Auditors: KPMG LLP SAN FRANCISCO CALIF

LOCATIONS

HQ: ESSEX PORTFOLIO, L.P.
925 E MEADOW DR, PALO ALTO, CA 943034299
Phone: 650 494-3700

HISTORICAL FINANCIALS

Company Type: Private

Income Statement

FYE: December 31

	ASSETS ($ mil.)	NET INCOME ($ mil.)	INCOME AS % OF ASSETS	EMPLOYEES
12/16	12,217	438	3.6%	869
12/15	12,005	248	2.1%	—
12/14	11,562	134	1.2%	—
12/13	5,186	172	3.3%	—
Annual Growth	33.1%	36.6%	—	—

2016 Year-End Financials

Return on assets: 10.7%
Return on equity: 33.9%

Sales ($ mil): 1,294

ESTES EXPRESS LINES, INC.

Founded during the Depression with a Chevy truck Estes Express Lines has grown into a multiregional less-than-truckload (LTL) freight hauler. Its fleet of some 7100 tractors and 25700 trailers operates via a network of some 210 terminals dotting the US. Service in Canada is provided by TST Overland Express an ExpressLINK partner and in Mexico through affiliate Almex. Estes Express works with designated carriers to offer door-to-door delivery in the Caribbean and in Mexico. Subsidiary Estes Forwarding Worldwide services ocean/air freight forwarding. The company is owned and run by the family of founder W.W. Estes.

Operations

The company operates through several divisions and companies. Divisions include Estes Time-Critical (offering four levels of shipping) Level2 Logistics (business-to-business and business-to-consumer shipping) Estes Specialized Truckload and Delivery Services and Estes SureMove (customers load shipments themselves and Estes provides transportation). Companies include Estes Forwarding Worldwide Estes Brokerage Estes Leasing and Big E Transportation.

Geographic Reach

Estes Express offers regional service to all 50 US states. It also offers direct service to Canada Mexico and the Caribbean.

Strategy

Estes Express has continued to build out its LTL business by offering expedited delivery volume truckload transportation supply chain management nationwide brokerage services warehousing services and equipment leasing. The latter has provided such rental services as laundry trucks for the Department of Veterans Affairs. Its slate of services are supported by an upgraded wireless onboard pickup and delivery system featuring real-time data enabling terminals and drivers to process freight more efficiently. It has also formed a Mexico third-party logistics subsidiary Estes Logistica for managing freight consolidation and transportation to points south of the US border.

Estes Express over the years has opened new offices in San Francisco Los Angeles Dallas Chicago Miami and New York. To support the con-

tinuing market growth in the Midwest in 2015 it opened a new terminal in Oswego Illinois. The next year it opened an additional terminal in the Chicago area to replace a smaller facility. The new location is in Markham Illinois and is the seventh terminal the company owns in the state.

Company Background

The company was formed in 1931.

EXECUTIVES

Vice President Human Resources, Tom Donahue
President and CEO, Rob W. Estes, age 65
President and CEO Estes Forwarding Worldwide, Scott Fisher
COO, Billy Hupp
VP and Chief Information Officer, Bob Fowler
Vice President Information Technology, Hugh Canden
Vice President Corporate Sales and Strategic Planning, Pat Martin
VP Safety, Curtis Carr
Vice President Fleet Services, Mike Palmer
Vice President Sales, John Rogers
Vice President Information Services, Hugh Camden
Vice President, Trish Garland
Vice President Pricing, Paul Dugent
Vice President of Engineering and Corp Optimization, Rich Schwartz
Treasurer, Gary Null Okes

LOCATIONS

HQ: ESTES EXPRESS LINES, INC.
3901 W BROAD ST, RICHMOND, VA 232303962
Phone: 804 353-1900
Web: WWW.ESTES-EXPRESS.COM

PRODUCTS/OPERATIONS

Selected Services

Global (airfreight ocean international consolidation/deconsolidation customs brokerage international freight forwarding)
Less-than-truckload (regional national international/offshore)
Time critical (expedited guaranteed time/date definite)
Volume & truckload (LTL full loads backhaul services truckload brokerage dedicated truckload)

COMPETITORS

AAA Cooper Transportation	R+L Carriers Ryder System
ArcBest	Saia
Averitt Express	UPS Freight
FedEx Freight	Vitran
Old Dominion Freight	YRC Worldwide
Penske Truck Leasing	

HISTORICAL FINANCIALS

Company Type: Private

Income Statement

FYE: December 31

	REVENUE ($ mil.)	NET INCOME ($ mil.)	NET PROFIT MARGIN	EMPLOYEES
12/15	2,367	135	5.7%	14,000
12/14	2,185	112	5.2%	—
12/13	1,958	71	3.6%	—
12/12	1,864	63	3.4%	—
Annual Growth	8.3%	28.7%	—	—

2015 Year-End Financials

Return on assets: 10.4%   Cash ($ mil.): 56
Return on equity: 5.7%
Current ratio: 1.20

ESTRELLA BANNER MEDICAL CENTER

EXECUTIVES

Chief Executive Officer, Deb Krmpotic
Manager, Kathy Tammaro
Director, Kaaren De Shay
Director, Rainey Holloway

LOCATIONS

HQ: ESTRELLA BANNER MEDICAL CENTER
9201 W THOMAS RD, PHOENIX, AZ 850373332
Phone: 623 327-4000
Web: WWW.BANNERHEALTH.COM

HISTORICAL FINANCIALS

Company Type: Private

Income Statement

FYE: December 31

	REVENUE ($ mil.)	NET INCOME ($ mil.)	NET PROFIT MARGIN	EMPLOYEES
12/15	276	38	13.9%	1,400
12/14	268	36	13.6%	—
12/08	203	2	1.0%	—
Annual Growth	4.4%	51.5%	—	—

2015 Year-End Financials

Return on assets: 0.9%   Cash ($ mil.): —
Return on equity: 13.9%
Current ratio: 3.00

EUGENE SCHOOL DISTRICT 4J

EXECUTIVES

Superintendent, Sheldon Berman
Director, Jackie Owens
Auditors: MATTHEW GRAVES CPA TIGARD O

LOCATIONS

HQ: EUGENE SCHOOL DISTRICT 4J
200 N MONROE ST, EUGENE, OR 974024243
Phone: 541 790-7600
Web: WWW.4J.LANE.EDU

HISTORICAL FINANCIALS

Company Type: Private

Income Statement

FYE: June 30

	REVENUE ($ mil.)	NET INCOME ($ mil.)	NET PROFIT MARGIN	EMPLOYEES
06/16	213	(7)	—	2,000
06/10	192	(7)	—	—
06/09	200	(9)	—	—
06/07	0	0	—	—
Annual Growth				

EUGENE WATER & ELECTRIC BOARD

"Power (and water) to the people" is the the belief and practice of Eugene Water & Electric Board (EWEB) the source of power and water for residents and businesses in Eugene Oregon. The utility is one of Oregon's largest municipal utilities. It has more than 89000 electric customers and about 52000 water customers. EWEB generates 110 MW of capacity at its hydroelectric and fossil-fueled power plants; it gets the rest of its power supply from other generators including the Bonneville Power Administration. The utility gets its water supply from the McKenzie River.

Operations

EWEB's electric system serves a 236-square mile area including Eugene and adjacent suburban areas. It gets its power supply from hydroelectric sources from its own generation facilities and via purchases from Bonneville Power Administration.

The utility's water system provides water to Eugene and two water districts. It gets water from the McKenzie River and treats itat the Hayden Bridge Filtration Plant one of the largest treatment plants in Oregon. The water distribution system consists of 26 enclosed reservoirs (total storage capacity — 98.5 million gallons) 31 pump stations and 800 miles of distribution mains.

Financial Performance

The utility reported a 5% increase in revenues in 2013 due to higher sales of electricity and water. The electric system's largest revenue increase was from residential including a higher heating load due to an extreme cold weather event of December 2013. The waste system's revenues increased due to a 20% rate increase and an unusually dry spring and summer which drove up consumption.

EWEB's net income grew by 67% to in 2013 primarily due to higher sales and lower operating costs.

Its operating cash flow increased that year due to a higher net income and a rise in receipts from customers.

Strategy

In 2013 EWEB began a project to install a new water transmission pipe under the Beltline Bridge. The $1.8 million project replaces an exposed 36-inch water transmission pipeline river crossing that runs beneath the Willamette River.

After 50 years of supplying steam heat to customers in downtown Eugene the utility ceased its steam operations in 2012 citing a dwindling customer base and an inefficient and aging steam distribution system.

On the green energy front EWEB offer its customers a number of programs that save energy and water including participation in wind and solar power options and other conservation measures. (EWEB broke ground on its first wind power generation project in 1997).

Company Background

EWEB was founded in 1911 largely in response to a 1906 typhoid fever epidemic in Eugene that was traced to the privately-owned water supply. The Walterville hydroelectric plant on the McKenzie River completed in 1911 enabled the powering of water pumps and street lights.

EXECUTIVES

Board Member, Jeannine Parisi
Auditors: FOR MOSS ADAMS LLP PORTLAND

LOCATIONS

HQ: EUGENE WATER & ELECTRIC BOARD
500 E 4TH AVE, EUGENE, OR 974012465
Phone: 541 685-7000
Web: WWW.EWEB.ORG

COMPETITORS

Avista
IDACORP
NW Natural
Portland General
  Electric

Seattle City Light
Xcel Energy

HISTORICAL FINANCIALS

Company Type: Private

Income Statement

FYE: December 31

	REVENUE ($ mil.)	NET INCOME ($ mil.)	NET PROFIT MARGIN	EMPLOYEES
12/15	276	39	14.4%	460
12/14	292	43	14.7%	—
12/13	270	35	12.9%	—
12/12	277	20	7.5%	—
Annual Growth	(0.2%)	23.7%	—	—

2015 Year-End Financials

Return on assets: 7.3%
Return on equity: 14.4%
Current ratio: 1.20

Cash ($ mil.): 22

EXETER HOSPITAL, INC.

EXECUTIVES

President, Kevin Callahan
Administrative Assistant, Colleen O'Smith
Manager, John Kern
Manager, Allison Sherman
Director, Anne Steele
Director, Deb Burgess
Director, Jane Peterson

LOCATIONS

HQ: EXETER HOSPITAL, INC.
5 ALUMNI DR, EXETER, NH 038332160
Phone: 603 778-7311
Web: WWW.EXETERHOSPITAL.COM

HISTORICAL FINANCIALS

Company Type: Private

Income Statement

FYE: September 30

	REVENUE ($ mil.)	NET INCOME ($ mil.)	NET PROFIT MARGIN	EMPLOYEES
09/15	186	5	3.1%	740
09/14	178	16	9.2%	—
09/13	195	5	2.8%	—
09/11	207	11	5.7%	—
Annual Growth	(2.6%)	(16.1%)	—	—

2015 Year-End Financials

Return on assets: 5.2%
Return on equity: 3.1%
Current ratio: 1.90

Cash ($ mil.): 30

EXTREME REACH, INC.

EXECUTIVES

President, John Roland
Board of Directors, Dan Brackett
Board of Directors, Robert Haskitt
Board of Directors, Tim Hale
Board of Directors, Melinda McLaughlin
Auditors: ERNST & YOUNG LLP BOSTON MA

LOCATIONS

HQ: EXTREME REACH, INC.
75 2ND AVE STE 720, NEEDHAM HEIGHTS, MA
024942826
Phone: 781 577-2016
Web: WWW.EXTREMEREACH.COM

HISTORICAL FINANCIALS

Company Type: Private

Income Statement

FYE: December 31

	REVENUE ($ mil.)	NET INCOME ($ mil.)	NET PROFIT MARGIN	EMPLOYEES
12/15	232	(10)		1,000
12/14	214	1	0.8%	—
Annual Growth	8.4%	—	—	—

2015 Year-End Financials

Return on assets: 2.0%
Return on equity: (-4.6%)
Current ratio: 1.10

Cash ($ mil.): 23

FACULTY PRACTICE FOUNDATION INC AND AFFILIATES

EXECUTIVES

Principal, Annmarie Cloonan
Treasurer, Diane Holmes
Auditors: PRICEWATERHOUSECOOPERS LLP BO

LOCATIONS

HQ: FACULTY PRACTICE FOUNDATION INC AND
AFFILIATES
660 HARRISON AVE, BOSTON, MA 021182304
Phone: 617 638-8923
Web: WWW.BMC.ORG

HISTORICAL FINANCIALS

Company Type: Private

Income Statement

FYE: June 30

	REVENUE ($ mil.)	NET INCOME ($ mil.)	NET PROFIT MARGIN	EMPLOYEES
06/15	339	(5)	—	21
06/14	18	4	23.1%	—
06/13	30	17	55.6%	—
06/11	331	(1)		—
Annual Growth	0.6%		—	—

2015 Year-End Financials

Return on assets: 5.0%
Return on equity: (-1.6%)
Current ratio: —

Cash ($ mil.): 20

FAIRBANKS NORTH STAR BOROUGH SCHOOL DISTRICT

EXECUTIVES

Superintendent, Karen Gaborik
Director, Elizabeth Schaffhauser
Director, Terry Soloman
Accountant, Joan L Stack
Assistant Manager, Nancy Wagner
Purchasing Agent, Paula Geier
Auditors: COOK & HAUGEBERG LLC FAIRBANK

LOCATIONS

HQ: FAIRBANKS NORTH STAR BOROUGH SCHOOL
DISTRICT
520 5TH AVE, FAIRBANKS, AK 997014718
Phone: 907 452-2000
Web: WWW.FNSB.US

HISTORICAL FINANCIALS

Company Type: Private

Income Statement

FYE: June 30

	REVENUE ($ mil.)	NET INCOME ($ mil.)	NET PROFIT MARGIN	EMPLOYEES
06/16	240	9	3.9%	2,000
06/15	437	3	0.9%	—
06/14	254	0	0.0%	—
06/13	254	0	0.2%	—
Annual Growth	(2.0%)	161.2%	—	—

2016 Year-End Financials

Return on assets: 0.4%
Return on equity: 3.9%
Current ratio: —

Cash ($ mil.): 36

FAIRFIELD MEDICAL CENTER

Fairfield Medical Center is a more than 220-bed acute care hospital serving residents in southeastern and central Ohio. In addition to providing comprehensive medical and surgical care Fairfield Medical Center offers specialty services including cancer cardiovascular women's and children's health and rehabilitation services. The not-for-profit hospital also operates offsite facilities for physician practices as well as specialty diagnostic and laboratory services. The Center employs more than 250 physicians and is served by a number of volunteer organizations which help to support and operate it.

Operations

Fairfield Medical Center handles some 10000 inpatient admissions each year. It also sees about 250000 outpatients and handles 2500 surgeries and 1000 birthing procedures.

Geographic Reach

The hospital serves the Ohio counties of Fairfield Perry Hocking and Athens.

Strategy

Fairfield Medical Center has launched a $38 million facility expansion program called Project BRIGHT (Build Revitalize and Innoate for Greater Health care Tomorrow). Through the project the

medical center is adding a new hospital wing with 30 private patient rooms a surgery center and clinical support areas.

To further expand services and reach more patients the hospital is also forming collaborations and making acquisitions.

In 2013 Fairfield Medical Center partnered with New Vision to provide a medical stabilization service for individuals who are undergoing detoxification from drugs and/or alcohol.

That year the Center opened Fairfield Healthcare Professionals Bremen to offer occupational health and primary care services. It also opened the Cancer Resource Center.

In 2012 Fairfield Medical Center expanded its services with the opening of the Emery and Evelyn Williams Graduate Medical Education Resource Center and the Fairfield Medical Heartburn Center.

Mergers and Acquisitions

In 2013 Fairfield Medical Center bought River View Imaging Center and renamed it Fairfield Medical Diagnostic Services at River View.

Company Background

The hospital entered into the convenient clinic market by pairing with Wal-Mart to open a seven-day walk-in clinic called the Clinic at Walmart in Canal Winchester Ohio in 2011. Two more Wal-Mart locations were added in Lancaster and Logan. The clinics offer school physicals immunizations treatment for common illnesses and other minor medical treatments.

On the acquisitions side Fairfield bought River View Surgery Center from a group of physician owners (70%) and Mount Carmel Health System (30%) for $8.5 million also in 2011. The hospital also paid about $1 million that year to buy out what had been a joint venture and gain full ownership of Fairfield Diagnostic Imaging.

Fairfield Medical Center's original hospital dates back to 1916.

EXECUTIVES

Nursing Director, Helen Harding
Vice Chair, Laura Tussing
Board Member, Renee A Wagner

LOCATIONS

HQ: FAIRFIELD MEDICAL CENTER
401 N EWING ST, LANCASTER, OH 431303371
Phone: 740 687-8000

PRODUCTS/OPERATIONS

Selected Centers and Services
Bariatrics
Cancer Care
Emergency Care
Ewing Square Infusion Clinic
Fairfield Healthcare Professionals
Fairfield Medical Diagnostic Services
Heartburn Center
Internal Medicine Clinic
Maternity Care
Orthopedic Care
Outpatient
Physical Therapy & Rehabilitative Services
River View Surgery Services
Snider Cardiovascular Institute
Southeast Ohio Sleep Disorder Center
Surgery
The Pavilion (Surgery and Medical Office)
Womens Health
Wound Clinic

COMPETITORS

Genesis HealthCare System (Ohio)
Licking Memorial Health Systems
Mount Carmel Health
Nationwide Children's Hospital
OhioHealth

HISTORICAL FINANCIALS
Company Type: Private

Income Statement

FYE: December 31

	REVENUE ($ mil.)	NET INCOME ($ mil.)	NET PROFIT MARGIN	EMPLOYEES
12/15	255	7	3.1%	2,200
12/14	239	22	9.3%	—
12/09	197	7	3.8%	—
12/08	187	(11)	—	—
Annual Growth	4.6%	—	—	—

2015 Year-End Financials

Return on assets: 2.6%
Return on equity: 3.1%
Current ratio: 1.80

Cash ($ mil.): 19

FAIRFIELD UNIVERSITY

Fairfield University welcomes students to the fair fields of Connecticut and prepares them for a life of service. The university is a private Jesuit school with an enrollment of more than 5000 undergraduate and graduate students. It offers about 45 undergraduate majors as well as more than 40 graduate degree programs through five schools and colleges: College of Arts and Sciences; School of Nursing & Health Studies; School of Engineering; School of Business; and Graduate School of Education and Allied Professions. With a faculty of about 550 professionals Fairfield University has one campus in Fairfield Connecticut and offers about 60 study abroad programs.

Operations

Fairfield University offers curriculum via five schools each focused on a specific educational objective including business nursing & health studies engineering arts & sciences and education & allied professions. Its 5000 students can pursue degrees such as biology business analytics Irish studies computer science registered nursing and international business.

The university provides extracurricular activities for it students including in sports art pursuits and social events. It also offers a number of university sponsored college athletic programs.

The university has a student to faculty ratio of 16:1.

Geographic Reach

Fairfield University has a 200-acre campus on the Connecticut coast and offers a variety of study abroad programs including courses in Italy Ireland Australia Brazil and Italy. It also engages about 200 international students on its Connecticut campus.

Financial Performance

Most of the institution's earnings come from student tuition and fees. Fairfield University reported operating revenue for FY2017 (ended June 30 2017) of $215 million flat from the prior year. About two thirds of revenue came from tuition & fees 5% from investment returns for current operations and the rest from contributions and auxiliary services.

The increase in net assets from operations the university?s closest metric to corporate earnings was $14 million in FY2017. The university also raises funds through non-operating activities such as contributions from alumnae and returns on investing its endowment. Such activities generated $81 million for the year.

Strategy

Fairfield University aims to prepare students to take on leadership and service roles developing creativity and intelligence while fostering social responsibility and ethical and religious values.

In 2017 it launched a new Master?s concentration in Informatics Nursing a Remedial Reading & Remedial Languages Arts Certification Program and a Doctor of Nursing Practice program in Nurse Midwifery.

The Fairfield University also broke ground in 2017 on a new teaching building for the Charles F. Dolan School of Business. It will include interactive learning environments a data analytics lab an entrepreneurship centers and gaming & programming labs.

Company Background

As part of its mission to create new opportunities for its students in 2011 Fairfield University added a new study abroad program in Brazil. In addition in 2012 it formed a partnership with Bridgeport Hospital to transition hospital RNs into the School of Nursing's Bachelor of Science degree program.

The university was established by the Society of Jesus in 1942.

EXECUTIVES

President-Elect, Jeffrey P. von Arx, age 70
EVP, Kevin Lawlor
CIO, Paige Francis
Dean Dolan School of Business, Donald E. Gibson
Dean School of Engineering, Bruce Berdanier
Dean School of Nursing, Lynn Babington
VP Finance and CFO, Michael Trafecante
Dean College of Arts and Sciences, Yohuru Williams
Dean Graduate School of Education and Allied Professions, Robert (Bob) Hannafin
Dean Egan School of Nursing and Health Studies, Meredith Wallace Kazer
Director Athletics, Eugene P. Doris
Vice President Of University Advancement, George Diffley
Assistant Vice President, David Frassinelli
Associate Vice President Academic Affa, Mary Malone
Assistant Vice President and Controller, Kenneth Fontaine
Vice President University Advancement, Wally Halas
Academic Vice President, Orin Grossman
Associate Vice President for Development, Geri Derbyshire
Senior Vice President for Student Affairs, Thomas Pellegrino
Operations Assistant Academic Vice President, Alexa Mullady
Assistant Vice President Student Affairs, Susan Birge
Vice President of Business and Finance, Elizabeth Hastings
Assistant Vice President, James Fitzpatrick
Vice President Human Resources, Scott Esposito
Assistant Vice President Financial Planning and Analysis, Robert Betlinski
Treasurer, Joan Overfield
Secretary dean of Freshmen, Brigida Salvioli
Secretary, Lorraine Castelot
Secretary Chemistry, Lori Fahy
Auditors: KPMG LLP NEW YORK NY

LOCATIONS

HQ: FAIRFIELD UNIVERSITY
1073 N BENSON RD, FAIRFIELD, CT 068245195
Phone: 203 254-4000

PRODUCTS/OPERATIONS

FY2017 Revenue

	$ mil.	% of total
Net tuition and fees	142	66
Auxiliary services	43	20
Investment return	11	5
Contributions	104	5
Government grants and financial aid	3	2
Department and other revenues	3	2
Total	**214**	**100**

Selected Study Programs

Accounting
American Studies
Applied Ethics
Art History
Asian Studies
Biology
Black Studies
Catholic Studies
Chemistry and Biochemistry
Classical Studies
Communication
Computer Engineering
Economics
Education
Electrical Engineering
English
Environmental Studies
Film Television and Media Arts
Finance
French
German
History
Individually Designed Major
Information Systems
International Business
International Studies
Italian
Irish Studies
Italian Studies
Judaic Studies
Latin American and Caribbean Studies
Liberal Studies
Management
Marketing
Mathematics
Mechanical Engineering
Modern Languages and Literatures
Music
Nursing
Peace and Justice Studies
Philosophy
Physics
Politics
Psychology
Religious Studies
Russian East European and Central Asian Studies
Sociology and Anthropology
Software Engineering
Spanish
Studio Art
Theatre
Visual and Performing Arts

HISTORICAL FINANCIALS

Company Type: Private

Income Statement

FYE: June 30

	REVENUE ($ mil.)	NET INCOME ($ mil.)	NET PROFIT MARGIN	EMPLOYEES
06/16	213	14	7.0%	883
06/15	206	22	11.1%	—
06/14	192	56	29.4%	—
06/13	191	39	20.7%	—
Annual Growth	**3.6%**	**(27.9%)**	**—**	**—**

2016 Year-End Financials

Return on assets: 10.5%   Cash ($ mil.): 50
Return on equity: 7.0%
Current ratio: —

FAIRLEIGH DICKINSON UNIVERSITY

It's fair to say that Fairleigh Dickinson University (FDU) is the largest private university in New Jersey. It has an enrollment of approximately 12000 students and 260 full-time faculty members. It has a student-teacher ratio of 14:1 and offers more than 100 undergraduate and graduate degree programs as well as doctoral programs in clinical psychology and school psychology. In addition to its main Metropolitan Campus in Teaneck New Jersey; the university also offers degree programs at the College at Florham in Madison New Jersey; at FDU-Vancouver in Canada; and at Wroxton College in Oxfordshire England. Fairleigh Dickinson was founded in 1942.

Operations

Some of the school's many disciplines include business education engineering hotel and restaurant management liberal arts (including communication criminal justice film and animation psychology and theater) nursing and allied health and the sciences.

Of its more than 260 full-time faculty members 85% hold a Ph.D. or terminal degree in their field.

Geographic Reach

The university operates a main Metropolitan Campus located in Teaneck New Jersey. It also has a campus in Vancouver Canada and offers degree programs to students through partnerships with other institutions such as the College at Florham in Madison Wisconsin and at Oxfordshire England's Wroxton College. FDU is the first American university to own and operate an overseas campus.

Strategy

The school offers students combined degree programs that allow them to earn a master's or professional degree at an accelerated pace in more than a dozen disciplines.

Entering agreements with universities worldwide has also given FDU the opportunity to exchange faculty conduct joint research projects and collaborate on educational initiatives. FDU is the first comprehensive university in the world to require its undergraduates to undergo distance learning. Such global partnerships include Galen University in Belize; Reims Management School in France; and Ross University Medical School in Dominica.

EXECUTIVES

Vice President and CIO at, Neal Sturm
Assistant Vice President for Administration
Administration Vice President Office, Robert Valenti
Auditors: KPMG LLP SHORT HILLS NJ

LOCATIONS

HQ: FAIRLEIGH DICKINSON UNIVERSITY
1000 RIVER RD, TEANECK, NJ 076661914
Phone: 800 338-8803
Web: WWW.FAIRLEIGHDICKINSONUNIVERSITY.ORG

Selected Global Partnerships
Belize
  Galen University
Brazil
  Centro Universitario (UNA)
  Faculdades Integradas de Vitoria (FDV)
China
  Northeastern University - Shenyang China
  Shenyang U
  Capital University of Economics and Business (Beijing)
Colombia

Universidad Autonoma de Bucaramanga
Cyprus
  Intercolle
Dominica
  Ross University Medical School
Dominican Republic
  Pontificia Universidad Catolica Madre y Maestra
Ecuador
  Universidad Catolica de Santiago de Guayaquil (Guayaquil)
France
  IECS - Strasbourg Graduate School of Management
  Reims Management School
Germany
  Fachhochsc
Hong Kong
  Chinese University of Hong Kong
  University of Hong Kong
  Lignan University
Hungary
  Central European University
India
  Alliance Business School
Israel
  Ben-Gurion University of the Negev (Beer-Sheva)
Korea
  Kyungnam University
  Sungkyungkwan University
  Woosuk University
Lebanon
  University
Malaysia
  University College Sedaya International
Mexico
  Universidad Autónoma de Guadalajara School of Medicine
Monaco
  International University of Monaco
Philippines
  University of the East
Poland
  Karola Marcinkowski Medical School
Singapore
  Republic Polytechnic- Singapore
  Temasek Po
Spain
  International University Study Center - Barcelona Spain
  Universidad Alfonso X el Sabio - Madrid Spain
  University of Cordoba

PRODUCTS/OPERATIONS

Selected Colleges
Becton College
Petrocelli College
Silberman College
University College

HISTORICAL FINANCIALS

Company Type: Private

Income Statement

FYE: June 30

	REVENUE ($ mil.)	NET INCOME ($ mil.)	NET PROFIT MARGIN	EMPLOYEES
06/16	237	17	7.5%	1,505
06/15	231	23	10.3%	—
06/14	216	23	10.6%	—
06/12	204	7	3.9%	—
Annual Growth	**3.8%**	**22.5%**	**—**	**—**

2016 Year-End Financials

Return on assets: 6.3%   Cash ($ mil.): 90
Return on equity: 7.5%
Current ratio: —

FAIRVIEW HOSPITAL

EXECUTIVES

Chief Executive Officer, Toby Cosgrove
Board of Directors, Jeffrey A Leimgruber

LOCATIONS

HQ: FAIRVIEW HOSPITAL
18101 LORAIN AVE, CLEVELAND, OH 441115612
Phone: 216 476-7000
Web: WWW.FAIRVIEWHOSPITAL.ORG

HISTORICAL FINANCIALS

Company Type: Private

Income Statement			FYE: December 31
	REVENUE ($ mil.)	NET INCOME ($ mil.)	NET PROFIT MARGIN	EMPLOYEES
12/15	426	70	16.6%	2,364
12/14	411	135	32.8%	—
12/05	0	0	17.1%	—
Annual Growth	102.5%	101.9%	—	—

2015 Year-End Financials

Return on assets: 2.5% Cash ($ mil.): 5
Return on equity: 16.6%
Current ratio: 1.40

FAITH TECHNOLOGIES, INC.

Keeping the faith in technology is a basic commitment of Faith Technologies one of the largest privately held electrical and specialty systems contractors in the US. The company's specialties include electrical contracting and service automated controls lighting security technology and preconstruction. It primarily serves clients in the commercial government industrial institutional health care manufacturing power residential retail transportation and data center sectors. The company has worked on a range of projects such as airports bridges correctional facilities government agencies hospitals restaurants and shopping centers.Established in 1972 employee-owned Faith Technologies has around 15 locations in Georgia Kansas Minnesota Missouri Oklahoma and Wisconsin and is licensed to do business in some 45 states. In 2009 its Faith Technologies Tulsa division in Oklahoma merged with Alpha Electrical Services. Also that year the company completed the final phase of a nationwide transition by converting all 10 of its Town & Country Electric locations in Wisconsin under the Faith Technologies banner.Faith Technologies opened its 15th location in Minneapolis in 2010.

EXECUTIVES

Executive Vice President, George Van Der Linden
Vice President of Safety, Rocky Rowlett
Vice President, Jack Brock
Vice President Supply Chain Management, Dan Siebers
Vice President Controller, Diane Schaefer
Vice President Industrial, Eric Deering
Vice President Pre Construction Mission Critical, Pat McGettigan
Secretary, Sandra Welter
Auditors: GRANT THORNTON LLP MILWAUKEE

LOCATIONS

HQ: FAITH TECHNOLOGIES, INC.
225 MAIN ST, MENASHA, WI 549523186
Phone: 920 738-1500
Web: WWW.FAITHTECHNOLOGIES.COM

COMPETITORS

Aldridge Electric   Guarantee Electrical
EEI   Sachs Electric
EMCOR

HISTORICAL FINANCIALS

Company Type: Private

Income Statement			FYE: December 31
	REVENUE ($ mil.)	NET INCOME ($ mil.)	NET PROFIT MARGIN	EMPLOYEES
12/15	425	31	7.5%	2,357
12/12	260	9	3.8%	—
12/11	248	4	1.9%	—
12/10	228	2	1.0%	—
Annual Growth	13.3%	69.0%	—	—

2015 Year-End Financials

Return on assets: 5.0% Cash ($ mil.): 4
Return on equity: 7.5%
Current ratio: 1.40

FAMILY CENTRAL, INC.

EXECUTIVES

President, Barbara A Weinstein
Board of Directors, Tamara Bell
VP Finance, Timothy Weeks
Vice-President, Kim Praitano
Auditors: DASZKAL BOLTON LLP FORT LAUDE

LOCATIONS

HQ: FAMILY CENTRAL, INC.
1415 W CYPRESS CREEK RD # 103, FORT LAUDERDALE, FL 333091955
Phone: 954 724-4070
Web: WWW.FAMILYCENTRAL.ORG

HISTORICAL FINANCIALS

Company Type: Private

Income Statement			FYE: June 30
	REVENUE ($ mil.)	NET INCOME ($ mil.)	NET PROFIT MARGIN	EMPLOYEES
06/15	193	(0)	—	428
06/14	205	(0)	—	—
06/13	198	0	0.0%	—
06/12	197	0	0.0%	—
Annual Growth	(0.8%)	—	—	—

2015 Year-End Financials

Return on assets: 3.6% Cash ($ mil.): —
Return on equity: (-0.2%)
Current ratio: —

FAMILY HEALTH INTERNATIONAL INC

Known as FHI 360 Family Health International believes that health is wealth. From a handful of offices located in the US Asia-Pacific and South Africa FHI 360 funds and manages public health programs research education and other resources in more than 60 countries. Founded in 1971 as the International Fertility Research Program of the University of North Carolina at Chapel Hill FHI 360 primarily focuses on and supports HIV/AIDS prevention research reproductive health services and maternal and neonatal health programs. The organization works with governments private agencies and non-governmental organizations to develop the most appropriate programs for different areas.

EXECUTIVES

Vice President International Program Management, Laura Kayser
Acting Chief Financial Officer, Rasika Padmaperuma
Auditors: ERNST & YOUNG US LLP TAMPA F

LOCATIONS

HQ: FAMILY HEALTH INTERNATIONAL INC
359 BLACKWELL ST STE 200, DURHAM, NC 277012477
Phone: 919 544-7040
Web: WWW.FHI360.ORG

PRODUCTS/OPERATIONS

Selected Services
Behavior-change communication
Capacity-building
Clinical trials services
Creative services
Data analysis
Quality assurance
Research services
Social marketing
Training and technical assistance

HISTORICAL FINANCIALS

Company Type: Private

Income Statement			FYE: September 30
	REVENUE ($ mil.)	NET INCOME ($ mil.)	NET PROFIT MARGIN	EMPLOYEES
09/15	610	(0)	—	4,000
09/14	653	(3)	—	—
09/13	664	10	1.5%	—
09/09	327	2	0.9%	—
Annual Growth	10.9%	—	—	—

2015 Year-End Financials

Return on assets: 11.7% Cash ($ mil.): 116
Return on equity: (-0.1%)
Current ratio: 1.40

FARM CREDIT SERVICES OF AMERICA, PCA

EXECUTIVES

President, Doug Stark
Assistant Controller, Tom Russell
Certified Public Accountant, Bernie Auten
Director, Donald Stukel
Auditors: PRICEWATERHOUSECOOPERS LLP M

LOCATIONS

HQ: FARM CREDIT SERVICES OF AMERICA, PCA
5015 S 118TH ST, OMAHA, NE 681372210
Phone: 800 884-3276
Web: WWW.FCSAMERICA.COM

HISTORICAL FINANCIALS

Company Type: Private

Income Statement

FYE: December 31

	ASSETS ($ mil.)	NET INCOME ($ mil.)	INCOME AS % OF ASSETS	EMPLOYEES
12/15	24,772	514	2.1%	10,000
12/04	8,475	294	3.5%	—
12/03	7,633	114	1.5%	—
Annual Growth	10.3%	13.4%	—	—

2015 Year-End Financials

Return on assets: —
Return on equity: 46.8%
Sales ($ mil): 1,099

FARMERS CO-OPERATIVE ELEVATOR COMPANY

EXECUTIVES

Chief Executive Officer, Scott Dubbelde
Sales Director, Kay Mueller
Auditors: CARLSON HIGHLAND NEW ULM MIN

LOCATIONS

HQ: FARMERS CO-OPERATIVE ELEVATOR COMPANY
1972 510TH ST, HANLEY FALLS, MN 562453082
Phone: 507 768-3448

HISTORICAL FINANCIALS

Company Type: Private

Income Statement

FYE: December 31

	REVENUE ($ mil.)	NET INCOME ($ mil.)	NET PROFIT MARGIN	EMPLOYEES
12/15	174	2	1.5%	56
12/14	276	4	1.5%	—
12/13	311	4	1.3%	—
12/12	371	4	1.1%	—
Annual Growth	(22.2%)	(14.9%)	—	—

2015 Year-End Financials

Return on assets: 3.0%
Return on equity: 1.5%
Current ratio: —
Cash ($ mil.): —

FARMERS COOPERATIVE SOCIETY

When farmers cooperate society benefits. Through its seven centers in northwest Iowa Farmers Cooperative Society offers its member/farmers a full range of agricultural growing and marketing products and services including crop-storage facilities and business consulting. Its feedlot with room for some 5500 head of cattle helps members buy and care for feeder cattle and provides discounts on grain for members. The co-op also operates a member-only How-To Building Store in Sioux Center Iowa that sells hardware lawn-care products lumber and paint as well as brand-name home appliances. Farmers Cooperative Society has roots dating back to 1907.

To provide the right product for its members the co-op's How-To Building store uses over 40 suppliers such as Andersen CertainTeed Toro and Weber-Stephen Products. The co-op also sells pork producers with products through suppliers like AP Valco and Chore-time. The co-op also supplies pork producers through suppliers such as AP Valco and Chore-time.

EXECUTIVES

President, Marvin Wynia
Board of Directors, Mark Vermeer
Executive Vice-President, Steven T White
Manager, Denis Wolff
Officer, Galen Mars

LOCATIONS

HQ: FARMERS COOPERATIVE SOCIETY
317 3RD ST NW, SIOUX CENTER, IA 512501897
Phone: 712 722-2671
Web: WWW.FARMERSCOOPSOCIETY.COM

COMPETITORS

AGRI Industries	Miles Enterprises
Five Star Co-op	Premier AG Co-Op Inc.
Gold-Eagle Cooperative	Sears
Heartland Co-op	True Value
Home Depot	Wal-Mart
Lowe's	West Central Co-op

HISTORICAL FINANCIALS

Company Type: Private

Income Statement

FYE: July 31

	REVENUE ($ mil.)	NET INCOME ($ mil.)	NET PROFIT MARGIN	EMPLOYEES
07/16	384	8	2.3%	160
07/15	405	7	1.9%	—
07/14	418	3	0.9%	—
07/13	496	4	1.0%	—
Annual Growth	(8.2%)	21.7%	—	—

2016 Year-End Financials

Return on assets: 2.4%
Return on equity: 2.3%
Current ratio: 0.30
Cash ($ mil.): —

FARMERS UNION INDUSTRIES, LLC

EXECUTIVES

Chief Executive Officer, Duane Anderson
Chief Financial Officer, William Day
Financial Executive, Josh South
Manager, Shawn Guetter

LOCATIONS

HQ: FARMERS UNION INDUSTRIES, LLC
220 PONDEROSA RD, REDWOOD FALLS, MN 56283
Phone: 507 644-6935
Web: WWW.MIDWESTGREASE.COM

HISTORICAL FINANCIALS

Company Type: Private

Income Statement

FYE: December 31

	REVENUE ($ mil.)	NET INCOME ($ mil.)	NET PROFIT MARGIN	EMPLOYEES
12/15	196	24	12.5%	550
12/14	200	28	14.1%	—
12/13	191	24	12.9%	—
12/12	185	21	11.5%	—
Annual Growth	1.8%	4.7%	—	—

2015 Year-End Financials

Return on assets: 3.9%
Return on equity: 12.5%
Current ratio: 1.60
Cash ($ mil.): 11

FAXTON-ST. LUKE'S HEALTHCARE

EXECUTIVES

Chief Executive Officer, Scott H Perra
Dean, Harrison Hummel IV
Vice-President, David Calabreese
Manager, Kathy Perra
Manager, Mary Ford
Chief Operating Officer, Steve Brown
Senior Vice-President, Carol English

LOCATIONS

HQ: FAXTON-ST. LUKE'S HEALTHCARE
1656 CHAMPLIN AVE, UTICA, NY 135024830
Phone: 315 624-6000

HISTORICAL FINANCIALS

Company Type: Private

Income Statement

FYE: December 31

	REVENUE ($ mil.)	NET INCOME ($ mil.)	NET PROFIT MARGIN	EMPLOYEES
12/15	263	2	0.8%	2,980
12/08	240	4	1.8%	—
12/07	237	6	2.6%	—
12/06	1,326	0	0.0%	—
Annual Growth	(16.4%)	163.9%	—	—

2015 Year-End Financials

Return on assets: 5.7%
Return on equity: 0.8%
Current ratio: 1.00
Cash ($ mil.): —

FAYETTE COUNTY BOARD OF EDUCATION

EXECUTIVES

Administrative Assistant, Barbara Buchanan
Auditors: MAULDIN & JENKINS LLC MACON

LOCATIONS

HQ: FAYETTE COUNTY BOARD OF EDUCATION
210 STONEWALL AVE W, FAYETTEVILLE, GA
302141518
Phone: 770 460-3520
Web: WWW.FCBOE.ORG

HISTORICAL FINANCIALS

Company Type: Private

Income Statement

	REVENUE ($ mil.)	NET INCOME ($ mil.)	NET PROFIT MARGIN	EMPLOYEES
06/16	232	(5)	—	3,500
06/15	220	(1)	—	—
06/14	209	14	7.1%	—
06/13	209	4	2.1%	—
Annual Growth	3.5%	—	—	—

FYE: June 30

2016 Year-End Financials

Return on assets: 5.5%
Return on equity: (-2.3%)
Current ratio: —
Cash ($ mil.): 16

FEDERAL HOME LOAN BANK OF ATLANTA

Where do banks in the southeastern US bank? Federal Home Loan Bank of Atlanta. Known as FHLBank Atlanta for short the bank provides mortgage funding deposit community investment and cash management services to some 1100 commercial banks credit unions insurance companies and thrifts. Its territory includes Alabama Florida Georgia Maryland North Carolina South Carolina Virginia and Washington DC. The bank primarily provides funding to members to originate residential mortgages and community development loans. It also purchases mortgages on the secondary market to provide liquidity.

EXECUTIVES

Vice President and Director of Accounting Policy, William Shaw
Assistant Vice President Liquidity Management, Deandra Wulf
Vice President, Pam MacPhaul
Vice President Senior Vice President Finance, Leslie Schreiner
Vice President Assistant Director of Administrative Services, Connie Arnold
Support Center Manager Assistant Vice President, Tony Norsworthy
Senior Vice President Compliance, Kevin Ashburn
Senior Vice President, Melissa Hoggatt
Vice President, David Eckardt
Senior Vice President Corp SEC, Julia Brown
Vice President, Colin Gatewood
Assistant Vice President Senior Financial Business And Operations Analyst, Cindy Wilson

Soa Development Manager Assistant Vice President, Jerry Versteegh
Vice President Director Community Investment Services Production and Operations, Jennifer Robinson
Director of Government Relations, Kimani Little

LOCATIONS

HQ: FEDERAL HOME LOAN BANK OF ATLANTA
1475 PEACHTREE ST NE # 400, ATLANTA, GA
303093037
Phone: 404 888-8000
Web: WWW.FHLBANKS.COM

COMPETITORS

Fannie Mae
Freddie Mac
Ginnie Mae

HISTORICAL FINANCIALS

Company Type: Private

Income Statement

	ASSETS ($ mil.)	NET INCOME ($ mil.)	INCOME AS % OF ASSETS	EMPLOYEES
12/16	138,671	278	0.2%	339
12/15	142,253	301	0.2%	—
12/14	138,344	271	0.2%	—
12/13	122,316	338	0.3%	—
Annual Growth	4.3%	(6.3%)	—	—

FYE: December 31

2016 Year-End Financials

Return on assets: —
Return on equity: 22.8%
Sales ($ mil): 1,217

FEDERAL HOME LOAN BANK OF CHICAGO

Federal Home Loan Bank of Chicago (FHLB Chicago) is a government-sponsored enterprises that provides secured loans and other support services to about 760 members including commercial banks credit unions insurance companies thrifts and community development financial institutions throughout Illinois and Wisconsin. It is cooperatively owned by its member institutions who use advances from the bank to originate residential mortgages invest in government or mortgage-related securities and promote affordable housing and community development in their respective communities. FHLB Chicago is one of a dozen federal banks that comprise the Federal Home Loan Bank System that was established by Congress in 1932.

Operations
The Federal Home Loan Banks are overseen by the Federal Housing Finance Agency. Other services offered include deposits wire transfers and check processing.

Strategy
Loan demand at the bank has fallen as its members have increased access to other forms of liquidity such as customer deposits and certain government programs. FHLB Chicago believes its restructuring efforts and investment activity have led the bank to a position of strength going forward.

EXECUTIVES

Vice President Financial Markets, Matthew Desmarais
Vice President, Matt Zimmerman

Vice President, Kimberly Cullotta
Managing Director, Steven Mosshamer
Vice President Develop, Thomas Ruggieri
Vice President of Sales, Carolyn Jaw
Vice President and Senior Manager Human Resources, Joaquin Fonte
Vice President Managing Director MPF Applications, Kathy Rasmussen
Assistant Vice President Community Investment Database Analyst, Sameera Ishaq
Senior Vice President Balance Sheet Strategy and Quantitative Analysis, Rene Cornejo
Senior Vice President Member Product Support, Christian Claffy
Vice President and Associate General Counsel, Judd Levy
Assistant Vice President of Development, Gary Engstrom
Vice President and Assistant General Counsel, Maryjane Hall
Vice President accounting policy, Claude Edelson
Auditors: PRICEWATERHOUSECOOPERS LLP CH

LOCATIONS

HQ: FEDERAL HOME LOAN BANK OF CHICAGO
200 E RANDOLPH ST # 1700, CHICAGO, IL
606016428
Phone: 312 565-5700
Web: WWW.FHLBC.COM

HISTORICAL FINANCIALS

Company Type: Private

Income Statement

	ASSETS ($ mil.)	NET INCOME ($ mil.)	INCOME AS % OF ASSETS	EMPLOYEES
12/16	78,692	327	0.4%	405
12/15	70,676	349	0.5%	—
12/14	71,841	392	0.5%	—
12/12	69,584	375	0.5%	—
Annual Growth	3.1%	(3.4%)	—	—

FYE: December 31

2016 Year-End Financials

Return on assets: —
Return on equity: 24.5%
Sales ($ mil): 1,335

FEDERAL WAY PUBLIC SCHOOLS

EXECUTIVES

Accountant, Clayton Betz
Office Manager, Jodi Klettke
Manager, Deann Kachman
Auditors: TROY KELLEY OLYMPIA WA

LOCATIONS

HQ: FEDERAL WAY PUBLIC SCHOOLS
33330 8TH AVE S, FEDERAL WAY, WA 980036325
Phone: 253 830-6246
Web: WWW.FWPS.ORG

HISTORICAL FINANCIALS
Company Type: Private

Income Statement				FYE: August 31
	REVENUE ($ mil.)	NET INCOME ($ mil.)	NET PROFIT MARGIN	EMPLOYEES
08/15	273	10	3.9%	2,309
08/14	262	11	4.4%	—
08/09	238	11	4.9%	—
08/08	199	3	2.0%	—
Annual Growth	4.6%	15.4%	—	—

2015 Year-End Financials
Return on assets: 1.7%   Cash ($ mil.): 61
Return on equity: 3.9%
Current ratio: —

FEDERAL-MOGUL HOLDINGS LLC

EXECUTIVES

Chief Executive Officer, Daniel A Ninivaggi
Chief Executive Officer, Rainer Jueckstock
Senior Vice-President, Michelle Epstein Taigman

LOCATIONS

HQ: FEDERAL-MOGUL HOLDINGS LLC
  27300 W 11 MILE RD, SOUTHFIELD, MI 480346147
Phone: 248 354-7700
Web: WWW.FEDERALMOGUL.COM

HISTORICAL FINANCIALS
Company Type: Private

Income Statement				FYE: December 31
	REVENUE ($ mil.)	NET INCOME ($ mil.)	NET PROFIT MARGIN	EMPLOYEES
12/16	7,434	90	1.2%	53,700
12/15	7,419	(104)	—	—
12/14	7,317	(161)	—	—
Annual Growth	0.8%		—	—

2016 Year-End Financials
Return on assets: 11.9%   Cash ($ mil.): 300
Return on equity: 1.2%
Current ratio: 0.90

FERMI RESEARCH ALLIANCE, LLC

EXECUTIVES

Director, Pier Oddone
Manager, Joe Collins
Auditors: LB CROWE HORWATH LLP CHICAGO

LOCATIONS

HQ: FERMI RESEARCH ALLIANCE, LLC
  MS 105 WILSON & KIRK RDS, BATAVIA, IL 60510
Phone: 630 840-3211
Web: WWW.FRA-HQ.ORG

HISTORICAL FINANCIALS
Company Type: Private

Income Statement				FYE: September 30
	REVENUE ($ mil.)	NET INCOME ($ mil.)	NET PROFIT MARGIN	EMPLOYEES
09/15	386	2	0.6%	5
09/14	373	2	0.6%	—
09/10	424	1	0.4%	—
09/08	339	1	0.4%	—
Annual Growth	1.9%	8.9%	—	—

2015 Year-End Financials
Return on assets: —   Cash ($ mil.): 1
Return on equity: 0.6%
Current ratio: 8.50

FERREIRA CONSTRUCTION CO., INC.

EXECUTIVES

President, Nelson Ferreira
Superintendent, Dave Nicholls
Manager, Jose L Correa
Auditors: WISS & COMPANY LLP LIVINGSTO

LOCATIONS

HQ: FERREIRA CONSTRUCTION CO., INC.
  31 TANNERY RD, BRANCHBURG, NJ 088766001
Phone: 908 534-8655
Web: WWW.FERREIRACONSTRUCTION.COM

HISTORICAL FINANCIALS
Company Type: Private

Income Statement				FYE: December 31
	REVENUE ($ mil.)	NET INCOME ($ mil.)	NET PROFIT MARGIN	EMPLOYEES
12/15	272	6	2.2%	225
12/11	112	1	1.3%	—
12/10	78	0	0.3%	—
12/09	2,066	0		—
Annual Growth	—	455.0%		

2015 Year-End Financials
Return on assets: 18.6%   Cash ($ mil.): —
Return on equity: 2.2%
Current ratio: 0.70

FLAGLER HEALTHCARE SYSTEMS, INC

EXECUTIVES

President, Joseph Gordy
Auditors: DIXON HUGHES GOODMAN LLP ASHE

LOCATIONS

HQ: FLAGLER HEALTHCARE SYSTEMS, INC
  400 HEALTH PARK BLVD, SAINT AUGUSTINE, FL 320865784
Phone: 904 819-5155

HISTORICAL FINANCIALS
Company Type: Private

Income Statement				FYE: September 30
	REVENUE ($ mil.)	NET INCOME ($ mil.)	NET PROFIT MARGIN	EMPLOYEES
09/15	232	5	2.6%	1,600
09/13	0	0	26.2%	—
09/12	202	24	12.1%	—
09/11	216	3	1.8%	—
Annual Growth	1.8%	10.8%	—	—

2015 Year-End Financials
Return on assets: 6.0%   Cash ($ mil.): 8
Return on equity: 2.6%
Current ratio: 0.90

FLAGLER HOSPITAL, INC.

EXECUTIVES

President, Joseph Gordy
Purchasing Director, Nancy Higgins
Manager, Paul Schloss
Board of Directors, Jim Wilson
Director, Thomas Searle
Auditors: KPMG LLP JACKSONVILLE FL

LOCATIONS

HQ: FLAGLER HOSPITAL, INC.
  400 HEALTH PARK BLVD, SAINT AUGUSTINE, FL 320865790
Phone: 904 819-5155
Web: WWW.FLAGLERHOSPITAL.ORG

HISTORICAL FINANCIALS
Company Type: Private

Income Statement				FYE: September 30
	REVENUE ($ mil.)	NET INCOME ($ mil.)	NET PROFIT MARGIN	EMPLOYEES
09/15	237	5	2.4%	1,500
09/14	215	11	5.3%	—
09/13	195	(11)	—	—
09/12	201	24	12.2%	—
Annual Growth	5.7%	(38.2%)	—	—

2015 Year-End Financials
Return on assets: 5.9%   Cash ($ mil.): 9
Return on equity: 2.4%
Current ratio: 1.00

FLAGSTAFF MEDICAL CENTER, INC.

Flagstaff Medical Center serves northern Arizona's residents and those who are just passing through. Founded in 1936 the not-for-profit hospital is part of the Northern Arizona Healthcare family. It has some 270 beds and its medical staff includes about 210 physicians. The hospital offers cancer heart sports medicine joint surgery and women and infants' centers. Other medical services include behavioral health audiology diabetes care home health hospice and ambulance and air flight

transportation. In addition Flagstaff Medical Center provides training courses for health care professionals. The hospital's emergency department treats about 40000 patients each year.

Operations

Flagstaff Medical Center boasts a regional trauma center open-heart surgery high-tech imaging a cancer center surgical services orthopedic services and women's infants' and children's services. Altogether the medical facility each year logs more than 13000 inpatient hospital visits some 68500 outpatient visits and about 40000 emergency department visits. Flagstaff Medical Center is responsible for birthing about 1300 babies annually.

Through the Guardian Medical Transport division's 15 fully-equipped ambulances the medical center provides emergency medical services and non-emergent transports around the clock.

Geographic Reach

Based in Flagstaff the medical center provides services to the communities of northern Arizona. Its Guardian Medical Transport division serves more than 6200 square miles across the northern part of the state.

Strategy

To maintain and improve its level of service Flagstaff Medical Center has expanded its operations in recent years.

In 2014 Flagstaff Medical Center received a $129412 grant award from the US Department of Agriculture Rural Development office's Distance Learning and Telemedicine Loan and Grant Program.

Company Background

It opened a new outpatient Supportive Care Clinic in 2012 to provide care support and resources to patients living with a chronic or life-threatening illness. The medical center also spent the year renovating and expanding its Emergency Department to provide better customer service and faster care to its patients.

Flagstaff Medical Center has also partnered with technology companies to roll out wireless services for monitoring its patients' health. Through a new program launched in 2012 the center extends care of patients beyond the walls of the hospital or physician's office. Care Beyond Walls and Wires rolled out in collaboration with Qualcomm Incorporated (through its Wireless Reach initiative) Zephyr Technology Verizon Wireless and the National Institutes of Health. Care Beyond Walls and Wires uses advanced 3G wireless technology and health-monitoring devices to enhance the care of patients with congestive heart failure or other related conditions.

EXECUTIVES

Physical Therapy Director, TRISH LOUGH
Director of Operating Room, Brenda Munns
Vice President Communications And Invest,
 Michelle Musich
Auditors: ERNST & YOUNG US LLP PHOENIX

LOCATIONS

HQ: FLAGSTAFF MEDICAL CENTER, INC.
 1200 N BEAVER ST, FLAGSTAFF, AZ 860013118
Phone: 928 779-3366
Web: WWW.FLAGSTAFFMEDICALCENTER.COM

PRODUCTS/OPERATIONS

Selected Services
Audiology
Neurodiagnostic Services
Bariatric Surgical Weight Loss Center
Northern Arizona Homecare
Behavioral Health Services
Northern Arizona Hospice
Bereavement Services
Nutrition Therapy

Cancer Cen
Occupational Therapy
Care Coordination/Disease Management
Patient Registration
Children's Health Center
Pediatrics
Complementary Services
Pharmacy Services
da Vinci Surgical System
Physical Therapy
Diabetes Education & Management
Renal Services
Education
Safe Child Center
Emergency Services
Security Services
Fit Kids of Arizona
Speech Therapy
FMC Foundation
Spine & Joint Surgery Center
Guardian Air
Sports Medicine
Guardian Medical Transport
Surgical Services
Heart & Vascular Care
Taylor House
Heart and Vascular Center of Northern Arizona
Team Health
Imaging/Radiology
Telemedicine
Infectious Disease
Therapy Services
Intensive Care Unit
Trauma Services
Laboratory and Blood Bank
Volunteer Services
Library Services
Women & Infants' Center
Massage Therapy

COMPETITORS

Banner Health	Phoenix Children's
Community Health	Hospital
Systems	Scottsdale Healthcare
Dignity Health	University of Arizona
John C. Lincoln Health	Health Network
Network	Yuma Regional Medical
Mayo Clinic	Center

HISTORICAL FINANCIALS

Company Type: Private

Income Statement

FYE: June 30

	REVENUE ($ mil.)	NET INCOME ($ mil.)	NET PROFIT MARGIN	EMPLOYEES
06/15	389	53	13.8%	2,000
06/09	358	0	—	—
/ 0	0	0	—	—
Annual Growth	—	—	—	—

2015 Year-End Financials

Return on assets: 3.2%   Cash ($ mil.): 67
Return on equity: 13.8%
Current ratio: 3.30

FLINT ELECTRIC MEMBERSHIP CORPORATION

The Native American inhabitants of Georgia may have used flint to spark the fires that brought light to their dwellings. Central Georgians today rely on the Flint Electric Membership Corporation which does business as Flint Energies to light their

homes. Flint Energies serves 250000 residential commercial and industrial customers (through 82500 meters) in 17 counties Fort Benning and the city of Warner Robins. The customer-owned cooperative operates more than 6250 miles of distribution line and about 50 substations. Flint Energies first flicked the switch in 1937.

As part of its commitment to green energy practices in 2009 Flint Energies teamed up with the EPA's ENERGY STAR program to promote energy conserving appliances and strategies to its customers.

Georgia has 42 electric membership cooperatives; Flint Energies ranks as the seventh largest. It is also the 34th largest of the 990 electric cooperatives in the US.

EXECUTIVES

Chief Executive Officer, Bob Ray
Director, Paul Hibbitts
Auditors: MCNAIR MCLEMORE MIDDLEBROOKS

LOCATIONS

HQ: FLINT ELECTRIC MEMBERSHIP CORPORATION
 3 S MACON ST, REYNOLDS, GA 310763104
Phone: 478 847-3415
Web: WWW.FLINTENERGIES.COM

COMPETITORS

Georgia Power	Southeastern Power
MEAG Power	Administration

HISTORICAL FINANCIALS

Company Type: Private

Income Statement

FYE: December 31

	REVENUE ($ mil.)	NET INCOME ($ mil.)	NET PROFIT MARGIN	EMPLOYEES
12/15	193	(0)	—	227
12/14	195	6	3.2%	—
12/13	188	0	—	—
12/12	174	0	—	—
Annual Growth	3.4%	—	—	—

2015 Year-End Financials

Return on assets: 9.6%   Cash ($ mil.): 5
Return on equity: (-0.3%)
Current ratio: 0.10

FLORIDA CLINICAL PRACTICE ASSOCIATION, INC.

EXECUTIVES

President, Anthony Mancuso
Manager, Bobbi Reynolds
Chief Financial Officer, Christina D Williams
Director, Stephanie Smith

LOCATIONS

HQ: FLORIDA CLINICAL PRACTICE ASSOCIATION, INC.
 1329 SW 16TH ST STE 4250, GAINESVILLE, FL 326081128
Phone: 352 265-8017
Web: WWW.SHANDS.UFL.EDU

Company Type: Private

Income Statement — FYE: June 30

	REVENUE ($ mil.)	NET INCOME ($ mil.)	NET PROFIT MARGIN	EMPLOYEES
06/15	598	19	3.3%	2
06/13	419	2	0.5%	—
06/12	360	(11)	—	—
06/11	1,586	0	0.0%	—
Annual Growth	(21.6%)	490.7%	—	—

2015 Year-End Financials

Return on assets: 1.5% Cash ($ mil.): 75
Return on equity: 3.3%
Current ratio: 11.20

FLORIDA HEALTH SCIENCES CENTER INC

Florida Health Sciences Center which does business as Tampa General Hospital (TGH) provides health care services in west-central Florida. The medical center offers general medical and surgical care as well as tertiary offerings including a Level 1 trauma center a burn unit a pediatric ward women's and cardiovascular centers and an organ transplant unit. The not-for-profit hospital has more than 1000 acute-care beds as well as 60 beds in its rehabilitation unit which specializes in helping patients recover from stroke head or spine trauma and other neuromuscular conditions. TGH is the primary teaching hospital for The University of South Florida College of Medicine.

Operations

TGH division Tampa General Medical Group (TGMG) is a multispecialty physician group with locations in Florida's Hillsborough and Pasco counties. Specialties include family practice internal medicine transplant cardiology endocrinology hepatology nephrology and surgery.

Geographic Reach

One of the largest employers in the Tampa Bay region TGH employs about 6300 workers. It also conducts research and operates community care centers in the Tampa area.

Each year TGH treats more than 91000 patients in its emergency department. This includes pediatric chest pain minor emergency and trauma center patients. The hospital also operates a regional helicopter medical transport program.

Strategy

TGH has added new wing to the hospital to expand patient capacity. TGH has added a new emergency/trauma center as well as cardiovascular diagnostic neurology and women's health units.

The hospital also works to stay on top of the latest medical advances. For example in 2014 TGH acquired the ThermoCool SmartTouch catheter a recently launched high-tech device that helps physicians control the amount of contact force applied to the heart wall during treatments for atrial fibrillation.

EXECUTIVES

EVP Finance and CFO, Steve Short
EVP and COO, Deana L. Nelson
SVP and Chief Medical Officer, Sally H. Houston
Chief Technology Officer, Balaji Ramadoss
CEO, James R. Burkhart

Executive Vice President Chief Academic Officer, Charles J. Lockwood
Vice President, Janet Davis
Director of Patient Relations, Joanna Singleton
Vice President, Jean M Mayer
Vice President, Victoria Butler
Senior Vice President Strategic Services And Business Development, Michael Gorsage
COTA, Karen Holland
Chairman, David A. Straz
Treas, Dee Richardson

LOCATIONS

HQ: FLORIDA HEALTH SCIENCES CENTER INC
1 TAMPA GENERAL CIR, TAMPA, FL 336063571
Phone: 813 844-7000

COMPETITORS

All Children's Hospital	Lakeland Regional Medical Center
BayCare Health System	Lee Memorial
Bayfront Health	Manatee Memorial Hospital
DeSoto Memorial	
Florida Hospital Tampa Bay Division	Sarasota Memorial Health Care
HCA	Winter Haven Hospital

HISTORICAL FINANCIALS

Company Type: Private

Income Statement — FYE: September 30

	REVENUE ($ mil.)	NET INCOME ($ mil.)	NET PROFIT MARGIN	EMPLOYEES
09/15	1,092	46	4.2%	6,000
09/14	1,127	98	8.7%	—
Annual Growth	(3.1%)	(53.0%)		

2015 Year-End Financials

Return on assets: 10.3% Cash ($ mil.): 139
Return on equity: 4.2%
Current ratio: 0.40

FLORIDA HOSPITAL HEARTLAND MEDICAL CENTER

Florida Hospital Heartland Medical Center provides care to residents of central Florida. The not-for-profit 160-bed medical center is the flagship facility of the Florida Hospital Heartland division of Adventist Health System. Other facilities in the Heartland system include Florida Hospital Lake Placid (a 50-bed community hospital) Florida Hospital Wauchula (25 beds) various fitness centers medical clinics and counseling agencies. Together the facilities provide primary and acute care as well as specialty medical services including diagnostics obstetrics cardiac care and cancer treatment. The Florida Hospital Heartland Medical Center opened in 1997.

EXECUTIVES

Medical Records Director, Nilda Dunstall
Radiology Director, Zbigniew Nawrocki

LOCATIONS

HQ: FLORIDA HOSPITAL HEARTLAND MEDICAL CENTER
4200 SUN N LAKE BLVD, SEBRING, FL 338721986
Phone: 863 314-4466
Web: WWW.FHHEARTLAND.ORG

COMPETITORS

Baptist Health South Florida	Mount Sinai Medical Center of Florida
Broward Health	Munroe Regional Health System
DeSoto Memorial	
HCA	South Broward Hospital District
Holy Cross Hospital Fort Lauderdale	

HISTORICAL FINANCIALS

Company Type: Private

Income Statement — FYE: December 31

	REVENUE ($ mil.)	NET INCOME ($ mil.)	NET PROFIT MARGIN	EMPLOYEES
12/15	193	(6)	—	1,200
12/14	167	(14)	—	—
12/08	126	0	0.0%	—
12/07	121	4	3.8%	—
Annual Growth	6.0%	—	—	—

2015 Year-End Financials

Return on assets: 10.8% Cash ($ mil.): 44
Return on equity: (-3.2%)
Current ratio: 1.60

FLORIDA HOSPITAL WATERMAN, INC

Florida Hospital Waterman is a 270-bed community hospital serving the residents of Lake County Florida just north of Orlando. The hospital provides a full range of acute care services including cardiac and cancer care emergency services obstetrics pediatrics and rehabilitation. It also offers outpatient surgery diagnostic imaging laboratory and home health services. As part of its portfolio of services Florida Hospital Waterman operates a primary care clinic. Established in 1938 and named after the philanthropic leader of the Waterman Fountain Pen Company Florida Hospital Waterman has been part of the Adventist Health System since 1992.

Strategy

The Lake County area hospital has been focused on adding more beds to its facility after being at or above 80% occupancy for the past few years. In late 2012 it built out its sixth floor to expand its bed count by 60. The move was necessary to accommodate the growing influx of the area's winter residents. Florida Hospital Waterman is also expanding technologies and services to increase its offerings for area residents. In 2012 it improved orthopedic capabilities when it began using the newly developed MAKO Surgical RIO robotic surgery system and the Stryker Triathlon custom fit implant system.

As it works to continue to enhance quality safety and affordability for its patient community in 2012 Florida Hospital Waterman joined the Centers for Medicare & Medicaid Services Partnership for Patients program which is coordinated by group purchasing organization Premier. The alliance of medical companies is focused on health care performance improvements.

EXECUTIVES

Director of Surgery, Heather Wood
Ambulatory Services Director Operations Manager, Jennifer Cooper
Vice President, Edlyn Hernandez
Nursing Director, Dennis Holm
Vice President Chief Medical Officer, Vinay Mehindru

LOCATIONS

HQ: FLORIDA HOSPITAL WATERMAN, INC
1000 WATERMAN WAY, TAVARES, FL 327785266
Phone: 352 253-3333
Web: WWW.FHWAT.ORG

PRODUCTS/OPERATIONS

Selected Services

Cancer Institute
Child Care Center
Community Clinic
Diagnostic Imaging
Emergency Department
Foundation
Heart Center
Home Care
Laboratory
Joint Replacement Center
Nutrition
Partial knee resurfacing (MAKOplasty)
Pediatrics
Rehabilitation Institute
Respiratory Therapy
Stroke Center
Surgical Services
Support Groups
Vascular Center of Excellence
Women's Health
Precious Beginnings

COMPETITORS

All Children's Hospital	Mount Sinai Medical Center of Florida
Baptist Health South Florida	Munroe Regional Health System
Baptist Health System	Nemours Foundation
Florida Hospital Heartland	Ocala Regional Medical Center
Holmes Regional Medical Center	Orlando Health
	UF&Shands

HISTORICAL FINANCIALS

Company Type: Private

Income Statement

FYE: December 31

	REVENUE ($ mil.)	NET INCOME ($ mil.)	NET PROFIT MARGIN	EMPLOYEES
12/15	231	12	5.2%	1,200
12/14	225	31	14.0%	—
12/13	204	16	7.9%	—
12/12	217	19	8.7%	—
Annual Growth	2.0%	(13.9%)	—	—

2015 Year-End Financials

Return on assets: 2.8%
Return on equity: 5.2%
Current ratio: 6.50
Cash ($ mil.): 235

FLORIDA INSTITUTE OF TECHNOLOGY, INC.

EXECUTIVES

President, Anthony J Catanese
Director, Sherri Rummel
Manager, Michael Grace
Director, Tom McFarland
Personnel Director, Joni Oglesby
Auditors: BERMAN HOPKINS WRIGHT & LAHAM

LOCATIONS

HQ: FLORIDA INSTITUTE OF TECHNOLOGY, INC.
150 W UNIVERSITY BLVD OFC, MELBOURNE, FL 329016975
Phone: 321 674-8000
Web: WWW.FIT.EDU

HISTORICAL FINANCIALS

Company Type: Private

Income Statement

FYE: April 30

	REVENUE ($ mil.)	NET INCOME ($ mil.)	NET PROFIT MARGIN	EMPLOYEES
04/16	194	(11)	—	1,100
04/15	208	7	3.6%	—
04/14	199	22	11.3%	—
04/13	168	7	4.7%	—
Annual Growth	4.8%			

2016 Year-End Financials

Return on assets: 11.6%
Return on equity: (-6.0%)
Current ratio: —
Cash ($ mil.): 5

FLORIDA MUNICIPAL POWER AGENCY

Unlike some politicians Florida Municipal Power Agency (FMPA) doesn't believe in holding on to power. The non-profit public agency generates and supplies electric power to 31 county or municipally owned distribution utilities which in turn serve 2 million Florida residents and businesses. Each of the distribution utilities appoints one representative to FMPA's board of directors which governs the Agency's activities. The Agency is authorized to undertake joint power supply projects for its members and to issue tax-exempt bonds to finance the costs of such projects. It is also empowered to implement a pooled financing program for utility-related projects.

Operations

FMPA has five distinct power supply projects and has stakes in 15 operating power plants. Each of its members have the option of whether or not to participate in a power supply project. Some members receive all their power from FMPA some receive part of their power and others receive no power. Agency members may participate in more than one project although each project is independent from the others.

FMPA supplies all of the power needs for 13 of its members and some of the power supply needs of seven others. All together FMPA supplies more than 40% of its members' total power needs.

Strategy

The Agency is looking to diversify its fuel mix in the long term adding nuclear and renewable energy powered plants to reduce the carbon emission output from its generation activities.

Company Background

FMPA has also been modernizing its power plant fleet since 2003 and in 2011 it opened a new low-emission high efficiency generator known as Cane Island Unit 4. Plant modernization has led to lower power costs enabling Florida Municipal Power Agency to reduce its wholesale rates to a number of members' cities in 2011 by 20% over 2009 levels.

The Agency was formed in 1978 to support the activities of Florida's locally owned and operated municipal utilities in projects requiring joint action such as the development of large power plants to serve a number of municipalities.

EXECUTIVES

Chief Executive Officer, Nicholas P Guarriello
Manager, Janet Davis
Manager, Richard Popp
Administrative Assistant, Sara Barron
Vice-Chairman, Paul Kalv
Manager, Liyuan Woerner
Consultant, Michael Taran
Auditors: PURVIS GRAY AND COMPANY LLP

LOCATIONS

HQ: FLORIDA MUNICIPAL POWER AGENCY
8553 COMMODITY CIR, ORLANDO, FL 328199002
Phone: 407 355-7767
Web: WWW.FMPA.COM

HISTORICAL FINANCIALS

Company Type: Private

Income Statement

FYE: September 30

	REVENUE ($ mil.)	NET INCOME ($ mil.)	NET PROFIT MARGIN	EMPLOYEES
09/16	588	0	0.0%	67
09/15	613	0	0.1%	—
09/14	677	0	0.0%	—
09/13	623	44	7.1%	—
Annual Growth	(1.9%)	(81.8%)	—	—

2016 Year-End Financials

Return on assets: 5.5%
Return on equity: —
Current ratio: 0.70
Cash ($ mil.): 72

FLOWER HOSPITAL

EXECUTIVES

President, Kevin Webb
Director of Finance, Scott Fought
Accountant, Carol Stormer
Director, Cathy Shirley

LOCATIONS

HQ: FLOWER HOSPITAL
5200 HARROUN RD, SYLVANIA, OH 435602196
Phone: 419 824-1444

HISTORICAL FINANCIALS

Company Type: Private

Income Statement

FYE: December 31

	REVENUE ($ mil.)	NET INCOME ($ mil.)	NET PROFIT MARGIN	EMPLOYEES
12/15	222	(8)	—	1,372
12/14	232	31	13.6%	—
12/13	235	17	7.3%	—
12/09	185	20	11.3%	—
Annual Growth	3.1%	—	—	—

2015 Year-End Financials

Return on assets: 7.6%
Return on equity: (-3.8%)
Current ratio: 1.00
Cash ($ mil.): 4

FLOWORKS INTERNATIONAL LLC

EXECUTIVES

Chief Executive Officer, Frank Riddick
President, Scott Jackson
Chief Financial Officer, Gary Haire
President, John Higgins
President, Michael Stanwood
Executive Vice-President, Rob Broyles
Senior Vice-President, Herbert Allen
Executive Vice-President, Jeff Legrand
Auditors: PRICEWATERHOUSECOOPERS LLP HO

LOCATIONS

HQ: FLOWORKS INTERNATIONAL LLC
515 POST OAK BLVD STE 800, HOUSTON, TX
770279432
Phone: 713 839-1753
Web: WWW.SHALE-INLAND.COM

HISTORICAL FINANCIALS

Company Type: Private

Income Statement

FYE: February 1

	REVENUE ($ mil.)	NET INCOME ($ mil.)	NET PROFIT MARGIN	EMPLOYEES
02/15	618	(30)	—	1,220
02/14	805	(30)	—	
Annual Growth	(23.2%)	—	—	—

2015 Year-End Financials

Return on assets: 10.9%
Return on equity: (-4.9%)
Current ratio: 1.20

Cash ($ mil.): 15

FLOYD HEALTHCARE MANAGEMENT, INC.

If you need heart help in the Heart of Dixie Floyd Healthcare Management is there for you. Its main hospital Floyd Medical Center has more than 300 beds and serves northwestern Georgia and northeastern Alabama with more than 40 medical specialties. In addition to medical surgical and emergency care (including a Level II trauma center and Level III neonatal intensive care unit) the hospital offers rehabilitation programs hospice and home health care. It also operates a 25-bed community hospital (Polk Medical Center) and the 53-bed Floyd Behavioral Health Center. Floyd Healthcare also operates outpatient centers including primary care surgery and urgent care locations. The organization was founded in 1942.

Operations

Floyd Healthcare Management's main hospital facility Floyd Medical Center employs 300 physicians and handles 102500 emergency visits each year. It also manages some 249000 outpatient visits and 2200 births and it specialized in fields including orthopedic surgery stroke care bariatric surgery and breast care. The system also operates about 40 primary care practices and urgent care facilities in surrounding areas.

In partnership with the Floyd County Commission Floyd County Department of Family and Children Services (DFCS) and physicians in the community Floyd sponsors the Floyd County Clinic where low-income uninsured residents of Floyd County can receive free primary medical care services through the faculty and resident medical students enrolled in the Floyd Family Medicine Residency program.

Floyd Medical Center also provides community outreach programs through its mobile mammography vans and a range of other services aimed at improving access to health care throughout the service area.

Geographic Reach

Floyd Healthcare Management serves Rome Rockmart and other communities in Polk and Floyd counties.

Sales and Marketing

Third-party payers contributed some 40% of Floyd Healthcare's net patient service revenue in 2014 followed by Medicare (which contributed 33%).

Financial Performance

Sales increased 2% to $334.8 million in fiscal 2014 for Floyd Healthcare Management due to higher patient service revenue and other earnings. A majority of the company's sales come from patient revenue with more than 30% of that sourced to Medicare reimbursements. Despite the rise in revenue net income fell 34% to $14.9 million that year however due to lower actuarial gains and higher expenses.

Cash flow from operations rose 82% to $34.5 million on inflows from accounts payable.

Strategy

The organization invests in improving care for its service territory. In 2014 community hospital Polk Medical Center opened a new 65000-sq.-ft. medical complex featuring 12 emergency rooms a new surgical program with modern operating rooms improved diagnostic and imaging services and a medical office building. Also in 2014 Floyd Medical Center renovated its sixth floor adding more private beds for patients.

The network launched a technology initiative in 2013 to implement a physician order entry system; the tool will help to reduce medical errors and improve patient care.

EXECUTIVES

Vice President Revenue Cycle Management, Richard Childs
Director of Pharmacy, Robert Purcell
Physical Therapy Director, PENNY DRAPER

LOCATIONS

HQ: FLOYD HEALTHCARE MANAGEMENT, INC.
304 TURNER MCCALL BLVD SW, ROME, GA
301655621
Phone: 706 509-5000

PRODUCTS/OPERATIONS

Selected Services
Adult Psychiatric Services
Alcohol and Chemical Dependency
Bariatric Medicine Surgery and Aftercare
Breast Health
Behavioral Health
Cancer Care
Cardiac Catheterization
Cardiology
Cardiac Rehabilitation
Childbirth and Aftercare
Corporate Health
Dementia and Alzheimer's
Diabetes Care
Echocardiography
Emergency Care
Family Medicine
Family Medicine Residency Program
Gynecology
Hospice
Hospitalist Care
Hyperbarics and Wound Care
Infusion Therapy
Intensive Care
Interventional Cardiology
IV Therapy
Joint Replacement
Laboratory
Level III Neonatal Intensive Care Unit
Level II Trauma Care
Maternity
Neurology
Neuropsychology
Neurosurgery
Occupational Medicine
Oncology
Orthopedics
Pediatrics
Pediatric Intermediate Care
Pharmacy Inpatient and Outpatient
Primary Care
Pulmonary Rehabilitation
Radiology
Inpatient Rehabilitation
Outpatient Rehabilitation
Sleep Disorders
Spine Center
Sports Medicine Services
Stroke
Surgery Inpatient and Outpatient
Urgent Care
Vascular Surgery
Wound Care and Hyperbarics

COMPETITORS

Gadsden Regional Medical Center
Hutcheson Medical
Redmond Regional Medical Center
WellStar Kennestone Hospital

HISTORICAL FINANCIALS

Company Type: Private

Income Statement

FYE: June 30

	REVENUE ($ mil.)	NET INCOME ($ mil.)	NET PROFIT MARGIN	EMPLOYEES
06/15	316	32	10.4%	2,400
06/11	332	11	3.4%	—
06/10	288	8	3.0%	—
06/08	237	11	4.8%	—
Annual Growth	4.2%	16.5%	—	—

2015 Year-End Financials

Return on assets: 4.8%
Return on equity: 10.4%
Current ratio: 2.50

Cash ($ mil.): 80

FOOD FOR THE POOR, INC.

Food For The Poor feeds spiritual and physical hunger. The Christian charity provides health social economic and religious services for impoverished people in 17 countries in Latin America and the Caribbean. Food For The Poor believes its organization serves God by helping those most in need distributing requested goods through local churches and charities. The group works through Caritas the American-Nicaraguan Foundation and others to provide vocational training clinic and school construction educational materials feeding programs and medical supplies. Food For The Poor has distributed more than $3 billion in goods since its 1982 inception; the group uses 96% of its funds on programs.

Since its founding Food For The Poor has distributed more than 43900 tractor-trailer loads of

aid to the poor built 50000 housing units and completed 568 water projects to provide clean water and sanitation for hundreds of thousands of villagers.

In 2008 to help hurricane battered residents in the Caribbean Food For The Poor sent more than 160 shipping containers of relief supplies including food water medical supplies personal care items and building materials. More than $7 million worth of aid was sent to storm-ravaged areas in Haiti Jamaica the Dominican Republic.

EXECUTIVES

Executive Vice President, Alvaro Pereira
Vice President International Partnership, Jose Serra
Secretary and General Counsel, David Price
Auditors: MAYER HOFFMAN MCCANN PC BOC

LOCATIONS

HQ: FOOD FOR THE POOR, INC.
6401 LYONS RD, COCONUT CREEK, FL 330733602
Phone: 954 427-2222
Web: WWW.FOODFORTHEPOOR.ORG

HISTORICAL FINANCIALS
Company Type: Private

Income Statement

	REVENUE ($ mil.)	NET INCOME ($ mil.)	NET PROFIT MARGIN	EMPLOYEES
12/15	1,158	(0)	—	335
12/14	913	(0)	—	—
12/13	1,030	1	0.2%	—
12/12	900	4	0.4%	—
Annual Growth	8.8%	—	—	—

2015 Year-End Financials
Return on assets: 0.4%   Cash ($ mil.): 10
Return on equity: —
Current ratio: 2.30

FOOD GIANT SUPERMARKETS, INC.

EXECUTIVES

President, Kevin Ladd
Board of Directors, Spencer Coates
Director, Bryan Gilley
Manager, Tanya Hutton
Manager, Bruce Broughton
Manager, David Holcomb
Purchasing Agent, Candace Halstead

LOCATIONS

HQ: FOOD GIANT SUPERMARKETS, INC.
120 INDUSTRIAL DR, SIKESTON, MO 638015216
Phone: 573 471-3500
Web: WWW.FOODGIANT.COM

HISTORICAL FINANCIALS
Company Type: Private

Income Statement
FYE: October 3

	REVENUE ($ mil.)	NET INCOME ($ mil.)	NET PROFIT MARGIN	EMPLOYEES
10/15	757	25	3.4%	4,500
10/10*	616	22	3.6%	—
09/06	468	108	23.1%	—
10/05	1,835	0	—	—
Annual Growth	—	217.4%	—	—

*Fiscal year change

2015 Year-End Financials
Return on assets: 3.3%   Cash ($ mil.): 40
Return on equity: 3.4%
Current ratio: 1.00

FOOTHILL, THE / EASTERN TRANSPORTATION CORRIDOR AGENCY

EXECUTIVES

Chief Executive Officer, Michael Kraman
Chief Financial Officer, Amy Potter
Financial Executive, Tracy Bowman
Auditors: KPMG LLP IRVINE CA

LOCATIONS

HQ: FOOTHILL, THE / EASTERN TRANSPORTATION CORRIDOR AGENCY
125 PACIFICA STE 100, IRVINE, CA 926183324
Phone: 949 754-3400
Web: WWW.THETOLLROADS.COM

HISTORICAL FINANCIALS
Company Type: Private

Income Statement
FYE: June 30

	REVENUE ($ mil.)	NET INCOME ($ mil.)	NET PROFIT MARGIN	EMPLOYEES
06/16	196	28	14.5%	70
06/15	175	5	3.2%	—
06/14	159	(20)	—	—
06/13	141	(20)	—	—
Annual Growth	11.7%	—	—	—

FORDHAM UNIVERSITY

A private Catholic university Fordham offers its 15100 students — hailing from 48 US states and some 65 other countries — degree programs through 10 graduate and undergraduate schools. Called the Jesuit University of New York Fordham has four locations including the original Rose Hill campus in the Bronx (often the scene of location shooting for movies TV shows and commercials) the Westchester campus the Lincoln Center campus in Manhattan as well as a biological field station in Armonk New York and international centers in China and the UK.

Operations

The university offers more than 50 majors in liberal arts sciences and business. It has a student/faculty ratio of 14:1. It has almost 750 full-time instructors (including 24 Jesuits). Some 93% of its faculty holds a Ph.D. or other terminal degree.

Geographic Reach

The Rose Hill campus is located on 85 acres in the Bronx and offers studies in business liberal arts science and religion. The Lincoln Center campus provides education business administration social services and legal training while the Westchester campus provides graduate programs in a variety of subjects. The Armonk field station is the headquarters for a number of university research programs.

Financial Performance

In 2014 Fordham had $542.4 million in operating revenues and $726 million in endowments and other investments. Undergraduate tuition in 2014-15 was $44450 per student.

Company Background

The school opened in 1841 as St. John's College. It officially changed its name to Fordham University in 1907.

EXECUTIVES

Senior Vice President Chief Financial Officer and Treasurer, John J Lordan
Vice President, Jeffrey Gray
President, Joseph M. McShane
Provost, Stephen Freedman
VP Finance, Frank Simio
VP Technology and CIO, Frank Sirianni
Dean Fordham College at Lincoln Center, Robert R. Grimes
Interim Dean Fordham College at Rose Hill, John Harrington
Dean Gabelli School of Business, Donna Rapaccioli
Dean Fordham School of Professional and Continuing Studies, Isabelle Frank
Dean Graduate School of Arts and Sciences, Eva Badowska
Dean Graduate School of Education, James J. Hennessy
Dean Graduate School of Religion and Religious Education, C. Colt Anderson
Dean Graduate School of Social Service, Debra M. McPhee
Dean School of Law, Michael M. Martin
Associate Vice President For Development, Michael Boyd
Associate Vice President Facilities Management, John Puglisi
Associate Vice President for Information Technology, Shaya Phillips
Associate Vice President, John Carroll
Vice President University Mission and Ministry, Joseph Quinn
Associate Vice President Information Technology Strategy and Innovation, Roxana Garcia
Director of Admissions and Marketing, Glenn S Berman
Associate Vice President Information Technology, Clifford Philogene
Interim Assistant Vice President For Academic Records And Services, Catherine Cadigan
Assistant Vice President for Development and University Events, Elizabeth Manigan
Vice President, Marianne Cooper
Vice President (2015, Benjamin Ilaria
Associate Vice President and CISO, John Breedlove
Director of Admissions, Jodi Hunt
Associate Vice President, Z Hong
Assistant Vice President Of External Affairs, Vera Bullock

Director of Admissions, Ruth Salazar
Legal Secretary, Emma Mercer
Legal Secretary, Vianka Abreu
Legal Secretary, Emelinda Huertas
Legal Secretary, Joseph Nolfo
Legal Secretary, Ben Chisholm
Legal Secretary, Leanna Dais
Legal Secretary, Christina Eadie
Legal Secretary, Evan Silverman
Vice President for Lincoln Center, Ines Vano Garcia
Department Chair, Robert Beer
MBA Candidate 18 Vice President Full Time
  Students, Joe Colandrea
Chairman Board of Trustees, Robert D. (Bob) Daleo,
  age 68
Vice Chairman Board of Trustees, Edward M. Stroz
Secretary of the University, Margaret Ball
Secretary, Adriana Magnotta
Secretary, Alexandra Fisher
Treasurer, Viliam Litavec
Treasurer, Angela Bates
Treasurer, Gilda Severiano
Secretary, Lisa Calcasola
Auditors: KPMG LLP NEW YORK NY

LOCATIONS

HQ: FORDHAM UNIVERSITY
  441 E FORDHAM RD, BRONX, NY 104589993
Phone: 718 817-1000
Web: WWW.FORDHAM.EDU

PRODUCTS/OPERATIONS

Selected Colleges
Graduate and Professional
  Graduate School of Arts and Sciences
  Graduate School of Business Administration
  Graduate School of Education
  Graduate School of Religion and Religious Education
  Graduate School of Social Services
  School of Law
Undergraduate
  Fordham College at Lincoln Center
  Fordham College at Rose Hill
  Fordham College of Liberal Studies
  Gabelli School of Business

HISTORICAL FINANCIALS
Company Type: Private

Income Statement
FYE: June 30

	REVENUE ($ mil.)	NET INCOME ($ mil.)	NET PROFIT MARGIN	EMPLOYEES
06/16	588	(52)	—	4,070
06/14	566	100	17.7%	—
06/12	518	60	11.6%	—
06/11	494	283	57.4%	—
Annual Growth	3.5%	—	—	—

2016 Year-End Financials
Return on assets: 11.6%   Cash ($ mil.): 1
Return on equity: (-8.9%)
Current ratio: —

FORREST GENERAL HEALTH SERVICES, INC.

EXECUTIVES

Chief Executive Officer, Evan Dillard
VP Personnel, Brian Spann

LOCATIONS

HQ: FORREST GENERAL HEALTH SERVICES, INC.
  6051 U S HIGHWAY 49, HATTIESBURG, MS
  394017200
Phone: 601 288-7000

HISTORICAL FINANCIALS
Company Type: Private

Income Statement
FYE: September 30

	REVENUE ($ mil.)	NET INCOME ($ mil.)	NET PROFIT MARGIN	EMPLOYEES
09/15	398	48	12.0%	168
09/08	0	0	29.3%	—
/ 0	0	—	—	
Annual Growth	—	—	—	—

2015 Year-End Financials
Return on assets: 4.8%   Cash ($ mil.): 97
Return on equity: 12.0%
Current ratio: 2.10

FORT SANDERS REGIONAL MEDICAL CENTER

EXECUTIVES

President, Keith Altshuler
Manager, Amy Deering
Manager, Sandy Chumley
Director, Lori Nash
Manager, Jan Adam
Director, Brenda Day
Director, Carol Burns
Director, Danny Edsell
Manager, Darrell Garland
Vice-President, Kelly Miles

LOCATIONS

HQ: FORT SANDERS REGIONAL MEDICAL CENTER
  1901 W CLINCH AVE, KNOXVILLE, TN 379162307
Phone: 865 541-1111
Web: WWW.FSREGIONAL.COM

HISTORICAL FINANCIALS
Company Type: Private

Income Statement
FYE: December 31

	REVENUE ($ mil.)	NET INCOME ($ mil.)	NET PROFIT MARGIN	EMPLOYEES
12/15	288	19	6.9%	1,833
12/14	285	32	11.2%	—
12/08	238	8	3.5%	—
12/04	200	5	3.0%	—
Annual Growth	3.4%	11.7%	—	—

FORT WORTH INDEPENDENT SCHOOL DISTRICT

EXECUTIVES

Superintendent, Kent Scribner
Director, Robert Lopez
Finance Manager, Amy Townsend
Finance Manager, Bennie Cruz
Manager, Greg McNear
Administration Manager, Lisa Stewart
Auditors: WEAVER AND TIDWELL LLP FORTH

LOCATIONS

HQ: FORT WORTH INDEPENDENT SCHOOL DISTRICT
  100 N UNIVERSITY DR, FORT WORTH, TX 761071360
Phone: 817 871-2000
Web: WWW.FWISD.ORG

HISTORICAL FINANCIALS
Company Type: Private

Income Statement
FYE: June 30

	REVENUE ($ mil.)	NET INCOME ($ mil.)	NET PROFIT MARGIN	EMPLOYEES
06/16	909	(101)	—	10,360
06/15	843	64	7.7%	—
06/12	777	(98)	—	—
06/11	798	(110)	—	—
Annual Growth	2.6%	—	—	—

2016 Year-End Financials
Return on assets: 4.2%   Cash ($ mil.): 267
Return on equity: (-11.1%)
Current ratio: 1.70

FORTIS CONSTRUCTION, INC.

Fortis Construction isn't afraid to get its hands dirty. The fast-growing US construction company offers general contracting preconstruction construction management and environmentally-friendly green building services to customers primarily in Portland Oregon and others in the Pacific Northwest. It specializes in remodeling and upgrading corporate offices health care facilities retail complexes and schools; it also conducts seismic and structural upgrades. Customers have included Oregon State University Portland State University PPG Industries and StanCorp.

In a geographic market where sustainability is a key concern Fortis Construction has been adding project engineers and managers to its staff roster who are accredited by LEED (Leadership in Energy and Environmental Design). Projects being undertaken by these staff members include an Oregon Capitol project in Salem and a theater addition for the University of Oregon in Eugene.

EXECUTIVES

Vice President Information TEC, Mark Callahan
Secretary and Treasurer, Rene Gonzalez
Auditors: AKT LLP LAKE OSWEGO OREGON

LOCATIONS

HQ: FORTIS CONSTRUCTION, INC.
1705 SW TAYLOR ST STE 200, PORTLAND, OR
972051922
Phone: 503 459-4477
Web: WWW.FORTISCONSTRUCT.COM

PRODUCTS/OPERATIONS

Selected Services
Construction management
General contracting
Green building
Preconstruction
Web-based collaboration and electronic document
management

COMPETITORS

Andersen Construction	R&H Construction
Hoffman Corporation	S.D. Deacon
Jacobsen Construction	Swinerton Builders
Panattoni Construction	

HISTORICAL FINANCIALS

Company Type: Private

Income Statement

FYE: December 31

	REVENUE ($ mil.)	NET INCOME ($ mil.)	NET PROFIT MARGIN	EMPLOYEES
12/15	468	18	3.9%	175
12/14	282	14	5.0%	—
Annual Growth	66.2%	29.3%	—	—

2015 Year-End Financials

Return on assets: 19.2%
Return on equity: 3.9%
Current ratio: 1.20
Cash ($ mil.): 22

FRANCIS SAINT MEDICAL CENTER

It may be guided by Catholic principles but you don't have to be a saint to get medical care at Saint Francis Medical Center. The hospital serves a five-state region from Missouri (its home base) to Arkansas with about 285 beds. Services include emergency medicine orthopedics cancer rehabilitation and women's health care. It also offers heart and neurosciences institutes as well as diabetes education and wound healing centers. The health care provider which was established in 1875 partners with Poplar Bluff Medical Partners to provide outpatient care at Poplar Bluff Medical Complex. Services include family practice OB-GYN and pain management.

Operations

Saint Francis Medical Center also partners with Landmark Holdings of Missouri to provide long-term acute care services through the 30-bed Landmark Hospital. The only facility of its kind between St. Louis and Memphis the hospital provides long-term care for patients who need complex medical care from catastrophic accidents or chronic diseases.

The hospital partners with the doctor-owned Physicians Alliance Surgery Center to provide outpatient surgery services in the region. Specialties provided at the center include gynecology ophthalmology orthopedic retinal and ENT (ear nose and throat) surgeries as well as general procedures.

Geographic Reach

Saint Francis Medical Center serves about 650000 people in Arkansas Kentucky Missouri Illinois and Tennessee.

Strategy

Saint Francis Medical Center has been expanding its facilities to offer more specialized services. Recent additions include its heart hospital and cancer institute. In 2015 it opened a new five-story patient tower including new and renovated space. It is also working on an orthopedic and neuroscience center and new surgery women's and children's health facilities.

EXECUTIVES

Vice President Management, Rick Fehr
Board of Directors, Judith R Wilferth

LOCATIONS

HQ: FRANCIS SAINT MEDICAL CENTER
211 SAINT FRANCIS DR, CAPE GIRARDEAU, MO
637035049
Phone: 573 331-3000
Web: WWW.SFMC.NET

PRODUCTS/OPERATIONS

Selected Services
Cancer institute
Emergency trauma & urgent care services
Gastroenterology services
Heart hospital
Neurosciences institute
Orthopedic institute
Primary care
Services to business
Women & children's services

COMPETITORS

Barnes-Jewish Hospital	St. Anthony's Medical
Memorial Hospital	Center
(Illinois)	St. John's Hospital
Southeast Missouri	(Illinois)
State University	
Southern Illinois	
Healthcare	

HISTORICAL FINANCIALS

Company Type: Private

Income Statement

FYE: June 30

	REVENUE ($ mil.)	NET INCOME ($ mil.)	NET PROFIT MARGIN	EMPLOYEES
06/15	424	41	9.7%	1,500
06/14	433	37	8.7%	—
06/11	423	48	11.4%	—
06/10	369	34	9.3%	—
Annual Growth	2.8%	3.6%	—	—

2015 Year-End Financials

Return on assets: 5.6%
Return on equity: 9.7%
Current ratio: 1.60
Cash ($ mil.): 91

FRANCISCAN HEALTH SYSTEM

St. Francis himself may have hailed from Italy but his followers look after the health of the residents of the South Puget Sound area through the Franciscan Health System. The not-for-profit system includes five full-service hospitals. The oldest and largest hospital is St. Joseph Medical Center in Tacoma Washington a 320-bed facility. Its facilities include community hospitals St. Clare Hospital (in Lakewood) and St. Francis Hospital (in Federal Way) as well as a hospice program and numerous primary and specialty care clinics. Its St. Anthony Hospital is an 80-bed full service pharmacy and home medical equipment retail location at Gig Harbor.

Geographic Reach

Franciscan Health System serves patients in Tacoma Washington and surrounding areas.

Financial Performance

The company gets most of its revenues from patient services. Other sources of income includes foundation gifts and investment community benefit charity care and uncompensated care (unreimbursed costs of serving patients enrolled in Medicaid and other state-subsidized programs).

Strategy

Franciscan Health System and Harrison Medical Center are looking to join forces while Franciscan's parent continues in talks to combine its Northwest operations with PeaceHealth of Vancouver Washington. If both plans are approved by regulators Harrison will become part of the largest community hospital system in the Northwest with facilities in Alaska Washington and Oregon. Both the Harrison-Franciscan affiliation and that of Franciscan's parent Catholic Health Initiatives with PeaceHealth is slated to be approved in 2013.

In addition Franciscan Health System is collaborating with the MultiCare Health System and TRA Medical Imaging to build a women's imaging and breast cancer care center.

St. Elizabeth Hospital opened its doors in 2011 in Enumclaw replacing Enumclaw Regional Hospital as that community's acute-care facility.

Company Background

St. Joseph Medical Center in Tacoma (the health system's oldest facility) was founded by the Sisters of St. Francis in 1891.

EXECUTIVES

Director Of Surgery, Hester Rall
Pharmacy Manager, Cindy Wilson
Regional Associate Vice President, Eula Ramroop
Physical Therapy Director, DAVID LUNDGREN

LOCATIONS

HQ: FRANCISCAN HEALTH SYSTEM
1717 S J ST, TACOMA, WA 984054933
Phone: 253 426-4101
Web: WWW.FHSHEALTH.ORG

PRODUCTS/OPERATIONS

Key Facilities and Services
Carol Milgard Breast Center Tacoma
Franciscan Center for Weight Management Federal Way
Franciscan Dialysis Center Eastside Tacoma
Franciscan Medical Group primary-care and specialty-care clinics
Franciscan Hospice House University Place
Franciscan Port Clinic Tacoma
Gig Harbor Medical Pavilion Gig Harbor
Gig Harbor Ambulatory Surgery Clinic Gig Harbor
St. Anthony Hospital Gig Harbor
St. Clare Hospital Lakewood
St. Clare Specialty Center Lakewood
St. Clare Medical Pavilion Lakewood
St. Elizabeth Hospital Enumclaw
St. Francis Hospital Federal Way
St. Francis Outpatient Center Federal Way
St. Joseph Medical Center Tacoma
St. Joseph Outpatient Center Tacoma
St. Joseph Heart & Vascular Center Tacoma
St. Joseph Dialysis Center Tacoma
St. Joseph Dialysis Center Gig Harbor
St. Joseph Dialysis Center Puyallup
St. Joseph Medical Clinic Tacoma
St. Joseph Medical Pavilion Tacoma
Milgard Medical Pavilion at St. Anthony Gig Harbor
Women's Health & Breast Center Federal Way

COMPETITORS

Harrison Medical Center	Seattle Children's Hospital
MultiCare Health System	Swedish Health Services
Overlake Hospital	Yakima Valley Memorial
PeaceHealth	
Providence St. Joseph Health	

HISTORICAL FINANCIALS

Company Type: Private

Income Statement

FYE: June 30

	REVENUE ($ mil.)	NET INCOME ($ mil.)	NET PROFIT MARGIN	EMPLOYEES
06/15	610	56	9.2%	3,183
06/14	1,190	(106)	—	—
06/10	1,093	71	6.5%	—
06/09	941	0	—	—
Annual Growth	(7.0%)	—	—	—

2015 Year-End Financials

Return on assets: 8.7% Cash ($ mil.): 10
Return on equity: 9.2%
Current ratio: 1.30

FRANKLIN AND MARSHALL COLLEGE

Franklin & Marshall College named after Benjamin Franklin and John Marshall is a private liberal arts institution serving about 2400 students. It offers academic and research programs in about 60 fields including biology chemistry English history mathematics political science art sociology and environmental studies. It offers programs in 11 languages including Arabic and Greek. Franklin & Marshall College was created in 1853 through the merger of Franklin College (founded in 1787 with a contribution from Ben Franklin) and Marshall College (opened in 1836 and named after Chief Justice John Marshall).

Operations

Franklin & Marshall has a student-to-teacher ratio of 10:1 and its average class size is about 19 students. The school's tuition and fees run at around $44000 per year plus some $12000 in room and board fees. In addition to its core academic programs about two-thirds of students participate in research programs. The college also participates in the NCAA Division III athletic conference.

Geographic Reach

Franklin & Marshall's students hail from more than 40 states and 40 foreign countries. The college's main campus is located in Lancaster Pennsylvania. It also maintains a 100-acre wildlife refuge (Millport Conservancy) in nearby Warwick Township through a partnership with the Wohlsen family; students conduct environmental studies at the refuge.

Franklin & Marshall also conducts study abroad and field study programs at 200 locations in nations including Australia China Costa Rica Denmark France India the UK. About half of the college's students participate in study abroad programs or travel courses.

Financial Performance

Franklin & Marshall reported a 6% increase in revenues to $121 million in 2012 due to higher earnings from student tuition and fees private contributions auxiliary activities and dividend and interest income. Net income fell in 2012 however to a loss of $10 million due to increased operating expenses and a decline in non-operating activities (net losses on investments) as well as benefit costs and other expense and loss factors.

Strategy

Franklin & Marshall's mission includes strengthening academics through rigorous liberal arts and knowledge discovery programs; enhancing student growth and development; and developing a long-term business model to generate new revenues while controlling costs and increasing value. Programs under these three broad goals include the creation of a 10-year alumni support program global impact projects and alumni and parent engagement efforts.

EXECUTIVES

Director of Health and Wellness Education Title IX Coordinator, Janet Masland
Vice President for College Advancement, Matthew Eynon
Vice President Alumni Relations, Javier Novell
Vice President, Patrick Burke
Associate Vice President for Information Systems and Library Services, Kathleen Spencer
Associate Vice President for Finance, Wendy Starner
Vice President, Michael Murray
Associate Vice President Facilities Management and Campus Planning, Mike Wetzel
Associate Vice President of Student and Post Graduate Development Adjunct Assistant Business Profess, Beth Throne
Associate Vice President for Administration, Barry Bosley
Vice President of Public Relations and General Manager, Ryan Thomas
Vice President, Kevin Burke
Vice President, Allison Berger
Secretary and Vice President for External Affairs, Keith Orris
Auditors: KPMG LLP MC LEAN VA

LOCATIONS

HQ: FRANKLIN AND MARSHALL COLLEGE
415 HARRISBURG AVE., LANCASTER, PA 176032827
Phone: 717 291-3911
Web: WWW.FANDM.EDU

PRODUCTS/OPERATIONS

Selected Services
Africana Studies
American Studies
Animal Behavior
Anthropology
Arabic
Art History
Astronomy
Astrophysics
Biochemistry and Molecular Biology
Bioinformatics
Biology
Business Organizations and Society
Chemistry
Chinese
Classical Archaeology and Ancient History
Comparative Literary Studies
Computer Science
Creative Writing
Dance
Economics
Engineering
English Literature
Environmental Management (3-2 Program)
Environmental Science
Environmental Studies
Film and Media Studies
French
Geosciences
German and German Studies
Government
Greek
Hebrew
History
International Studies
Italian
Japanese
Judaic Studies
Latin
Linguistics
Materials Studies
Mathematics
Music
Neuroscience
Philosophy
Physics
Pre-Law (Legal Professions Advising)
Pre-Med (Health Professions Advising)
Psychology
Public Health
Public Policy
Religious Studies
Russian and Russian Studies
Science Technology and Society
Scientific and Philosophical Studies of Mind
Sociology
Spanish
Studio Art
Theatre

HISTORICAL FINANCIALS

Company Type: Private

Income Statement

FYE: June 30

	REVENUE ($ mil.)	NET INCOME ($ mil.)	NET PROFIT MARGIN	EMPLOYEES
06/15	208	37	17.8%	800
06/13	165	9	5.6%	—
06/11	114	46	40.7%	—
06/10	0	0	—	—
Annual Growth	—	1303.9%	—	—

2015 Year-End Financials

Return on assets: 3.8% Cash ($ mil.): 3
Return on equity: 17.8%
Current ratio: 0.10

FRANKLIN SQUARE HOSPITAL CENTER, INC.

Franklin Square Hospital Center has made a declaration to care for the residents of eastern Baltimore County Maryland. The facility offers a wide range of specialties through some 700 doctors and about 380 beds. Since 1998 the hospital has been part of MedStar Health the region's largest integrated health system. As a teaching hospital Franklin Square offers a number of residency programs including internal and family medicine OB-GYN and surgery. The not-for-profit hospital offers its medical services through half a dozen primary service lines. Medicine Surgery Women's and Children's Care Oncology Behavioral Health and Community Health and Wellness.

Operations

Franklin Square Hospital boasts more than 3000 skilled professions including 1000-plus nurses and 400 staff physicians and more than 750 independently practicing physicians.

Geographic Reach

The only one of its kind in the region Franklin Square's Cancer Institute serves oncology patients by offering education and prevention services research and diagnostic treatment.

Strategy

The hospital which logs one of the highest numbers of cancer admissions in Maryland is working to expand its cancer services as it anticipates admissions to grow.

In fact the company is expanding other services as well also in anticipation of future patient demand. The hospital built a 300-bed patient tower on the campus that includes an expanded emergency department dedicated pediatric and inpatient suites and an expanded 50-bed critical care unit.

EXECUTIVES

Medical Director, Trudy Hall

LOCATIONS

HQ: FRANKLIN SQUARE HOSPITAL CENTER, INC.
9000 FRANKLIN SQUARE DR, BALTIMORE, MD
212373901
Phone: 410 933-2777
Web: WWW.MEDSTARFRANKLINSQUARE.ORG

PRODUCTS/OPERATIONS

Selected Services
Ambulatory & Minimally Invasive Surgery
Cancer Services
Cyberknife
da Vinci Robotic Surgery
Diagnostic Imaging and Radiology
Obstetrics & Neonatology
Orthopedics & Joint Replacement Therapies
Sleep Disorders
Women's Services

COMPETITORS

Anne Arundel Medical
  Center
Bon Secours Health
GBMC
Good Samaritan
  Hospital of Maryland
Harbor Hospital
Johns Hopkins Bayview
  Medical Center
Johns Hopkins Health
  System
Johns Hopkins Medicine

LifeBridge Health
MedStar Union Memorial
  Hospital
Sinai Hospital of
  Baltimore
St. Agnes HealthCare
St. Joseph Medical
  Center
University of Maryland
  Medical System
Upper Chesapeake
  Health

HISTORICAL FINANCIALS

Company Type: Private

Income Statement

	REVENUE ($ mil.)	NET INCOME ($ mil.)	NET PROFIT MARGIN	EMPLOYEES
				FYE: June 30
06/15	492	17	3.5%	3,019
06/11	452	18	4.0%	—
06/10*	439	31	7.1%	—
04/09	0	0	—	—
Annual Growth	—	219.2%	—	—

*Fiscal year change

2015 Year-End Financials

Return on assets: 2.3%
Return on equity: 3.5%
Current ratio: 0.90

Cash ($ mil.): 1

FRAZIER INDUSTRIAL COMPANY

This company's racket is structural steel storage systems. Frazier Industrial Co. is a leading manufacturer of structural as opposed to roll-formed steel storage racks at nearly a dozen production centers located across the US Canada and Mexico. These facilities can adapt production to demand and receive just-in-time delivery of raw materials. Customers use Frazier Industrial's storage racks in warehouses factories farms and other industrial and commercial facilities. Among the company's storage products is the Glide 'N Pick pallet cart that automatically rolls out for greater ease in retrieving items. Frazier Industrial is owned by CEO William Mascharka.

Operations

Frazier Industrial has manufacturing locations in Idaho New Jersey New York Pennsylvania South Carolina and Wisconsin. Outside the US it has plants in Mexicali and Monterrey Mexico and in Ontario Canada.

The company boasts sales offices nationwide in Canada and in 10 US states including New Jersey Georgia Massachusetts Texas Ohio Illinois California Washington and New York.

Geographic Reach

The manufacturing company operates throughout North America.

Sales and Marketing

Relying on a network of about a dozen fabrication facilities located throughout the US Mexico and Canada Frazier Industrial is able to meet tight construction deadlines while also guaranteeing manufacturing flexibility.

Customers include some of the world's top suppliers including Procter & Gamble Unilever and Nestle.

Strategy

Frazier Industrial is taking a stand for environmentally sound business practices as green initiatives become a focal point for customers. To this end Frazier sources all of its steel sections from North American mini-mills which only use recycled scrap material. Fittingly all of Frazier Industrial's scrap raw material is fully recyclable. Because the company receives preformed structural sections energy output is minimal; these structural parts require only cutting punching and welding. The location of Frazier Industrial's production centers helps to keep travel time and fuel expenses to a minimum. They are all within 400 miles of the company's raw material suppliers and within 500 miles of major North American population centers.

In 2013 the company launched a semi-automated high-density pallet mole system across North America. The pallet mole system a specific material handling technology maximizes available floor space enabling customers to store pallets up to 6-high and 50 positions deep while measurably increasing warehouse productivity.

Company Background

Frazier Industrial was founded in 1949.

EXECUTIVES

Chief Executive Officer, William L Mascharka
Chief Financial Officer, Robert M Warren
Credit Manager, Christy Nicotra
Project Manager, Arvin Deguzman
Auditors: EISNER AMPER LLP ISELIN NJ

LOCATIONS

HQ: FRAZIER INDUSTRIAL COMPANY
91 FAIRVIEW AVE, LONG VALLEY, NJ 078533381
Phone: 908 876-3001
Web: WWW.FRAZIER.COM

PRODUCTS/OPERATIONS

Selected Products
Drive-In/Drive-Thru Storage
Frazier Design-Build
Glide-In Push-Back Storage
Glide N' Pick Order Picking Cart
Klamp-Fast Cantilever Rack
Pick-to-Belt Systems
Rack Supported Buildings
Safety Accessories
SelecDeck Carton Flow System
Sentinel Selective Pallet Rack
The Pallet Mole

COMPETITORS

Actionrack
Edsal Manufacturing
Interlake Mecalux

Lyon Workspace
  Products
Steel of West Virginia

HISTORICAL FINANCIALS

Company Type: Private

Income Statement

	REVENUE ($ mil.)	NET INCOME ($ mil.)	NET PROFIT MARGIN	EMPLOYEES
				FYE: December 31
12/15	204	5	2.5%	750
12/14	254	5	2.0%	—
12/13	230	3	1.4%	—
12/12	183	2	1.6%	—
Annual Growth	3.6%	20.5%	—	—

2015 Year-End Financials

Return on assets: 5.5%
Return on equity: 2.5%
Current ratio: 0.80

Cash ($ mil.): 5

FREDERICK MEMORIAL HOSPITAL, INC.

Frederick Memorial Healthcare System cares for the sick and unhealthy across The Old Line State. The system operates Frederick Memorial Hospital an acute care facility with some 240 beds and 20 satellite facilities in and around Frederick Maryland. Specialty services include cardiology oncology pediatrics and psychiatry. Other facilities in the system include FMH Immediate Care at Oak Street FMH Crestwood FMH Medical Fitness FMH Rose Hill FMH Wellness FMH Urbana Mt. Airy Health Services and the FMH Regional Cancer Therapy Center. The hospital traces its historical roots all the way back to 1902.

Sales and Marketing

Medicare and Medicaid payments together represent about 45% of Frederick Memorial Healthcare System's net patient revenues. HMOs and PPOs account for about 20% while Blue Cross makes up another 15%.

Financial Performance

Revenue declined 1% in 2014 as net patient services and other operating earnings decreased. Net income fell 67% to $8.6 million that year. That decline was due to realized and unrealized losses on interest rate swaps as well as pension adjustments.

Cash flow from operations rose 24% to $25 million on changes in accounts payable and accrued expenses.

Strategy

The system expands by opening new outpatient facilities expanding into new service areas and adopting new technologies. In 2014 it selected Tableau and FTI Catalyst for its business analytics. Tableau will provide data analysis on admissions discharges surgical outcomes emergency services and other sources while FTI Catalyst will provide data modeling and management services.

EXECUTIVES

SVP Finance and CFO, Michelle Mahan
President and CEO, Thomas A. Kleinhanzl
Chief of Staff, Neil Waravdekar
VP and CIO, David Quirke
Senior Vice President and Chief Operating Officer, John Verbus
Director of Pharmacy, Joseph Morrissey
Director Of Home Healthcare SRV, Heidi Brown
Vice President Ambulatory Services, Don Schilling
Director of Radiology, Peter Kremers
Vice President and Chief Compliance Officer, Craig Rosendale
Medical Librarian and CME Coordinator, Lucy Koscielniak
Assistant Vice President Payer Contracting And Government Relations, Jennifer Teeter
Vice President Finance, Hannah Jacobs
Medical Director Oncology Service Line, Mark Soberman
Assistant Vice President Of Medical Affairs, James Grissom
Chairman, Anne-Herbert Rollins
Vice Chairman, E. James Reinsch

LOCATIONS

HQ: FREDERICK MEMORIAL HOSPITAL, INC.
400 W 7TH ST, FREDERICK, MD 217014593
Phone: 240 566-3300
Web: WWW.FMH.ORG

PRODUCTS/OPERATIONS

Selected Centers
FMH Crestwood
FMH Immediate Care at Oak Street
FMH Medical Fitness
FMH Regional Cancer Therapy Center
FMH Rose Hill
FMH Urbana
FMH Wellness
Frederick Memorial Hospital
Mt. Airy Health Services

Selected Medical Services
Behavioral Health
Cancer Care
Cardiac Rehabilitation
Cardiology Services
Diabetes Center
Emergency Services
Home Health Services
Hospice/Home Care Information
Hospitalist Care
Imaging Vascular Services
Laboratory Wellness Center
Medical Fitness Women and Children
Occupational Health
Orthopedic Services
Pain and Palliative Care
Pharmacy
Pulmonary Function Lab
Pulmonary Rehab Program
Rehabilitation
Robotics
Sleep Disorders
Smoking Cessation Program
Stroke Center
Surgical Services
Wound Care and Hyperbaric Medicine

COMPETITORS

Adventist HealthCare	Johns Hopkins Medicine
Children's National Medical Center	Loudoun Healthcare
	Meritus Health

HISTORICAL FINANCIALS

Company Type: Private

Income Statement

FYE: June 30

	REVENUE ($ mil.)	NET INCOME ($ mil.)	NET PROFIT MARGIN	EMPLOYEES
06/15	327	11	3.4%	2,600
06/14	327	7	2.3%	—
06/13	344	4	1.3%	—
06/12	355	(13)	—	—
Annual Growth	(2.7%)	—	—	—

2015 Year-End Financials

Return on assets: 8.4%
Return on equity: 3.4%
Current ratio: 0.80

Cash ($ mil.): 25

FREEHOLD REGIONAL HIGH SCHOOL DISTRICT

EXECUTIVES

Superintendent, Charles B Sampson
Board of Directors, Colleen Labruno
Board of Directors, Amanda Santos
Executive Secretary, Kathy Tanay
Manager, William Gorman
Financial Executive, Corey Lowell
Manager, Don Degroot

LOCATIONS

HQ: FREEHOLD REGIONAL HIGH SCHOOL DISTRICT
11 PINE ST, ENGLISHTOWN, NJ 077261513
Phone: 732 792-7300
Web: WWW.FRHSD.COM

HISTORICAL FINANCIALS

Company Type: Private

Income Statement

FYE: June 30

	REVENUE ($ mil.)	NET INCOME ($ mil.)	NET PROFIT MARGIN	EMPLOYEES
06/16	209	(16)	—	1,400
06/06	154	(1)	—	—
06/05	147	(0)	—	—
06/03	125	2	2.1%	—
Annual Growth	4.0%	—	—	—

2016 Year-End Financials

Return on assets: 2.4%
Return on equity: (-7.9%)
Current ratio: —

Cash ($ mil.): 25

FRESNO COMMUNITY HOSPITAL AND MEDICAL CENTER

EXECUTIVES

President, Phillip Hinton
Chief Financial Officer, Maria Garcia
Office Manager, Chris Williams
Auditors: MOSS ADAMS LLP STOCKTON CA

LOCATIONS

HQ: FRESNO COMMUNITY HOSPITAL AND MEDICAL CENTER
2823 FRESNO ST, FRESNO, CA 937211324
Phone: 559 459-6000

HISTORICAL FINANCIALS

Company Type: Private

Income Statement

FYE: August 31

	REVENUE ($ mil.)	NET INCOME ($ mil.)	NET PROFIT MARGIN	EMPLOYEES
08/15	1,571	139	8.9%	5,045
08/10	1,027	9	0.9%	—
08/09	1,010	65	6.5%	—
Annual Growth	7.6%	13.3%	—	—

2015 Year-End Financials

Return on assets: 8.2%
Return on equity: 8.9%
Current ratio: 0.50

Cash ($ mil.): 62

FROEDTERT AND COMMUNITY HEALTH INC

EXECUTIVES

Chairman, David J Lubar
Manager, Dan Arnold
Manager, Laura Keller
Manager, Stacey Kramer
Manager, Chris Sanders
Supervisor, Christine Karpowicz
Auditors: KPMG LLP COLUMBUS OH

LOCATIONS

HQ: FROEDTERT AND COMMUNITY HEALTH INC
9200 W WISCONSIN AVE, MILWAUKEE, WI 532263522
Phone: 414 777-0960

HISTORICAL FINANCIALS

Company Type: Private

Income Statement

FYE: June 30

	REVENUE ($ mil.)	NET INCOME ($ mil.)	NET PROFIT MARGIN	EMPLOYEES
06/15	397	55	14.0%	477
06/10	173	6	3.7%	—
Annual Growth	18.1%	54.4%	—	—

2015 Year-End Financials

Return on assets: 29.8%
Return on equity: 14.0%
Current ratio: —

Cash ($ mil.): 4

FRUIT GROWERS SUPPLY COMPANY INC

Shipping cartons are the real fruit of labor for Fruit Growers Supply (FSG). The non-profit cooperative association supplies affiliate Sunkist Growers and other agricultural businesses with packing materials fertilizer and related implements. Offerings include a range of equipment used to grow pick package and transport many commodity cash crops. FSG also provides packing services and custom design and installation of irrigation systems. It owns and operates some 335000 acres of timberland along the West coast (a source of box material and income) a carton manufacturing and supply plant and seven retail operations centers. FGS is owned by 6000-plus citrus growers and shippers in the US.

Operations

In addition to cartons FGS operates a pallet-manufacturing subsidiary United Wholesale Lumber which is supplied by its timberland resources. The association is one of the largest landowners in California; its timberland (which also spans Oregon and Washington) is overseen by a forestry-trained staff that manages timber sales logging and reforestation. Although the association branched out to corrugated cardboard cartons it maintains timberland as a renewable resource to help reduce overhead expenses. This investment allows FGS to operate without additional capital investment from its members.

Most FSG products and services support members' Sunkist's marketing organization. To this end in a typical year its plant will produce 80 million citrus containers. FGS sells to non-member vineyards and ranch owners too enabling it to defray plant operating costs. Its operations centers provide over-the-counter sales customer service and support for irrigation systems as well as wind machines used to protect fruit crops from cold damage.

Geographic Reach

To serve the agricultural community FGS operates six operation centers which feature central buying and warehousing capabilities specialized ordering and custom design irrigation departments in California and Arizona. It also operates the Ontario Carton Plant in California. Its Northern Operations own and manage 277863 acres of forestland owned in fee in Siskiyou Shasta and Lassen Counties in northern California; 21410 acres in Jackson Douglas Lane Linn and Klamath Counties in south western Oregon; and 28663 acres in Clallam Grays Harbor Jefferson Lewis Pacific and Skamania Counties in Western Washington.

Strategy

Growing its milling operations in 2013 FGS announced plans to build a small log mill in Yreka California to process small diameter logs into lumber for use in the making of pallets as well as for other agricultural and non-agricultural purposes.

Company Background

The company was founded in 1907.

HISTORY

The company was formed in 1907 by the members of California Fruit Growers Exchange (now Sunkist Growers) and has grown with the expansion of citrus production in California.

EXECUTIVES

Chief Executive Officer, Mark H Lindgren
Plant Engineering Manager, Reagan Foley
Engineer, Dominic Tortorello

Manager, Jeff Cieslak
Manager, Ben Ausman
Manager, Alex Perlovich
Auditors: MOSS ADAMS LLP STOCKTON CALI

LOCATIONS

HQ: FRUIT GROWERS SUPPLY COMPANY INC
27770 N ENTRMT DR FL 3, VALENCIA, CA 91355
Phone: 818 986-6480
Web: WWW.FRUITGROWERS.COM

PRODUCTS/OPERATIONS

Selected Products and Services
Agricultural Equipment
Cartons
Fertilizers and Pesticides
Grower Supplies
Harvesting Supplies
Irrigation Design and Installation
Lawn and Garden Supplies
Packaging
Packinghouse Supplies
Packing Services
Pallets
Powered Equipment
Small Engine Repair

COMPETITORS

Caraustar	Pro-Fac
Gibraltar Packaging	WestRock
Green Bay Packaging	

HISTORICAL FINANCIALS
Company Type: Private

Income Statement FYE: December 31

	REVENUE ($ mil.)	NET INCOME ($ mil.)	NET PROFIT MARGIN	EMPLOYEES
12/15	218	5	2.3%	300
12/14	211	11	5.5%	—
12/13	203	5	2.8%	—
12/12	179	6	3.8%	—
Annual Growth	6.8%	(9.2%)	—	—

2015 Year-End Financials
Return on assets: 5.5%
Return on equity: 2.3%
Current ratio: 0.80
Cash ($ mil.): —

FT. ZUMWALT R-II SCHOOL DISTRICT

EXECUTIVES

Superintendent, Bernard Dubray
Principal, Alex J Tripamer
Chief Financial Officer, Jeffrey or
Auditors: CLIFTONLARSONALLEN ST LOUIS

LOCATIONS

HQ: FT. ZUMWALT R-II SCHOOL DISTRICT
555 E TERRA LN, O FALLON, MO 633662725
Phone: 636 240-2072

HISTORICAL FINANCIALS
Company Type: Private

Income Statement FYE: June 30

	REVENUE ($ mil.)	NET INCOME ($ mil.)	NET PROFIT MARGIN	EMPLOYEES
06/16	212	4	2.1%	2,600
06/13	202	12	6.3%	—
06/12	199	(9)	—	—
06/11	0	0	—	—
Annual Growth	—	207.2%	—	—

FULTON COUNTY BOARD OF EDUCATION

EXECUTIVES

President, Linda McCain
Financial Executive, W Harold Grindle
Administrative Assistant, Kari Schrock

LOCATIONS

HQ: FULTON COUNTY BOARD OF EDUCATION
6201 POWERS FERRY RD, ATLANTA, GA 303392926
Phone: 404 768-3600
Web: WWW.FULTONSCHOOLS.ORG

HISTORICAL FINANCIALS
Company Type: Private

Income Statement FYE: June 30

	REVENUE ($ mil.)	NET INCOME ($ mil.)	NET PROFIT MARGIN	EMPLOYEES
06/16	1,201	(32)	—	10,000
06/11	1,091	142	13.1%	—
Annual Growth	2.0%	—	—	—

2016 Year-End Financials
Return on assets: 4.0%
Return on equity: (-2.7%)
Current ratio: 2.10
Cash ($ mil.): 391

FURST-MCNESS COMPANY

EXECUTIVES

Chairman of the Board, Frank E Furst
Chief Executive Officer, Matt Heinrich
President, Martha Furst
Executive Vice-President, Kevin Gyland
Chief Financial Officer, Matt Hartman
General Manager, Mark Romero
Credit Manager, Cynthia A Grant
Director, Bob Garvens
Manager, Trinity Zimmerman
Account Manager, Kelly Priewe
Auditors: BAKER TILLY VIRCHOW KRAUSE LL

LOCATIONS

HQ: FURST-MCNESS COMPANY
120 E CLARK ST, FREEPORT, IL 610323300
Phone: 800 435-5100
Web: WWW.MCNESS.COM

HISTORICAL FINANCIALS

Company Type: Private

Income Statement

FYE: December 26

	REVENUE ($ mil.)	NET INCOME ($ mil.)	NET PROFIT MARGIN	EMPLOYEES
12/15	310	1	0.5%	219
12/14	314	1	0.4%	—
12/13	291	3	1.1%	—
12/12	270	3	1.3%	—
Annual Growth	4.7%	(23.8%)	—	—

2015 Year-End Financials

Return on assets: 6.6% Cash ($ mil.): —
Return on equity: 0.5%
Current ratio: 0.80

FUTURE FOAM, INC.

EXECUTIVES

President, Bruce Schneider
Credit Manager, Bonnie Baker
Financial Executive, Patrick Medinger
Office Manager, Ronda Barclay
Manager, Forrest Bill
General Manager, Jen Smith
Sales Manager, Dave Cutler

LOCATIONS

HQ: FUTURE FOAM, INC.
1610 AVENUE N, COUNCIL BLUFFS, IA 515011071
Phone: 712 323-9122
Web: WWW.FUTUREFOAM.COM

HISTORICAL FINANCIALS

Company Type: Private

Income Statement

FYE: January 31

	REVENUE ($ mil.)	NET INCOME ($ mil.)	NET PROFIT MARGIN	EMPLOYEES
01/16	424	10	2.5%	1,000
01/15	408	(8)	—	—
01/14	0	9	—	—
01/13	415	14	3.5%	—
Annual Growth	0.8%	(10.4%)	—	—

2016 Year-End Financials

Return on assets: 6.3% Cash ($ mil.): 40
Return on equity: 2.5%
Current ratio: 1.20

FUTURE TECH ENTERPRISE, INC.

Future Tech Enterprise can help you realize the potential of all sorts of futuristic technologies. The company provides a variety of IT services including network integration services project management systems integration procurement and call center support. Future Tech also resells computer systems software and peripherals. Its customers range from small businesses to enterprise organizations with complex technology needs; clients include Hofstra University Honeywell JetBlue the New York Islanders and Northrop Grumman. The company has configuration centers and product warehouses across the US. In 1996 Future Tech got its start in the basement of president and CEO Bob Venero.

EXECUTIVES

President, Robert Venero
Board of Directors, Patricia Eckstine
Project Manager, Michael Lima
Manager, Ron Magnani
Purchasing Manager, April Iannitelli

LOCATIONS

HQ: FUTURE TECH ENTERPRISE, INC.
101 COLIN DR UNIT 8, HOLBROOK, NY 117414332
Phone: 631 472-5500
Web: WWW.FTEI.COM

COMPETITORS

CHIPS Computer Consulting
CXtec
Computer Sciences Corp.
HP Enterprise Group
IBM Global Services
Siwel Consulting

HISTORICAL FINANCIALS

Company Type: Private

Income Statement

FYE: December 31

	REVENUE ($ mil.)	NET INCOME ($ mil.)	NET PROFIT MARGIN	EMPLOYEES
12/15	175	3	2.0%	92
12/04	49	0	1.2%	—
12/02	23	1	5.9%	—
12/01	32	0	0.0%	—
Annual Growth	12.7%	147.1%	—	—

2015 Year-End Financials

Return on assets: 22.5% Cash ($ mil.): 1
Return on equity: 2.0%
Current ratio: 0.90

FYFFES NORTH AMERICA INC.

EXECUTIVES

Chief Executive Officer, Juan David Alarcon
Manager, Maria Mora
Manager, Johnatan Loaiza
Auditors: RMS US LLP MIAMI FLORIDA

LOCATIONS

HQ: FYFFES NORTH AMERICA INC.
999 PONCE DE LEON BLVD, CORAL GABLES, FL 331343000
Phone: 305 445-1542
Web: WWW.TURBANA.COM

HISTORICAL FINANCIALS

Company Type: Private

Income Statement

FYE: December 31

	REVENUE ($ mil.)	NET INCOME ($ mil.)	NET PROFIT MARGIN	EMPLOYEES
12/15	179	0	0.4%	31
12/14	160	0	0.5%	—
12/13	176	1	0.7%	—
12/12	174	1	0.8%	—
Annual Growth	0.9%	(19.8%)	—	—

2015 Year-End Financials

Return on assets: 2.2% Cash ($ mil.): 4
Return on equity: 0.4%
Current ratio: 2.50

GADSDEN INDEPENDENT SCHOOL DISTRICT

EXECUTIVES

President, Jennifer Viramontes
Board of Directors, Gloria Y Irigoyen
Superintendent, Agueda Mora
General Manager, Margarita Terrazas
Auditors: GRIEGO PROFESSIONAL SERVICES

LOCATIONS

HQ: GADSDEN INDEPENDENT SCHOOL DISTRICT
4950 MCNUTT RD, SUNLAND PARK, NM 88063
Phone: 575 882-6200
Web: WWW.GISD.K12.NM.US

HISTORICAL FINANCIALS

Company Type: Private

Income Statement

FYE: June 30

	REVENUE ($ mil.)	NET INCOME ($ mil.)	NET PROFIT MARGIN	EMPLOYEES
06/16	181	5	3.1%	2,000
06/05	6	(51)	—	—
06/04	115	1	1.0%	—
06/03	1,712	0	—	—
Annual Growth	—	56.7%	—	—

2016 Year-End Financials

Return on assets: 1.3% Cash ($ mil.): 45
Return on equity: 3.1%
Current ratio: 2.20

GALLAUDET UNIVERSITY

Gallaudet University (GU) gives deaf and hard-of-hearing students the chance to be in the majority. Designed to accommodate hearing-impaired students GU offers undergraduate and graduate degrees in more than 40 majors to about 2000 students annually. The bilingual university which uses both American Sign Language (ASL) and English admits a small number of hearing ASL-proficient students to each incoming freshman class. Through its Laurent Clerc National Deaf Education Center GU provides training and support for teachers and parents of hearing impaired chil-

dren and operates demonstration schools. Founded in 1864 GU was named for Thomas Hopkins Gallaudet a pioneer in education for the deaf.

Operations

For the purposes of budgeting and operating its educational institution GU is divided into two major component programs: its university and the Laurent Clerc National Deaf Education Center. The center's primary focus as part of a federal mandate is to develop and disseminate innovative curriculum materials and teaching strategies to schools and programs nationwide. The center includes the Model Secondary School for the Deaf (MSSD) and the Kendall Demonstration Elementary School (KDES). MSSD serves students in grades nine through 12 while KDES serves infants and their parents continuing service through the eighth grade.

Also part of its operations the Gallaudet Research Institute studies the demographics and assessment of deaf and hard of hearing people in the educational system as well as language and learning processes. For its research the institute involves students in its studies.

Open to all students whether they're deaf hard of hearing or hearing GU's graduate programs include master of arts or master of science degrees specialist degrees certificates and doctoral degrees across several fields involving professional services to deaf and hard of hearing people.

Undergraduate tuition for GU runs about $13424 for US students.

Geographic Reach

From its 99-acre campus in Washington DC GU is a federally chartered university that caters to students nationwide as well as students in developing and non-developing countries (about 30 in total).

Strategy

GU is working through a five-year five-pronged strategic plan that runs through 2015. It includes a handful of lofty goals. GU is working to grow its enrollment of full-time undergraduates full- and part-time graduate students and continuing education students to 3000 by 2015. (In the fall of 2013 the university's enrollment was 1872.) GU's also focused on boosting its six-year undergraduate graduation rate to 50% refining a core set of undergraduate and graduate programs aimed at career success and positioning the university as the epicenter of research development and outreach. GU as its final and more far-reaching goal is concentrating on securing a sustainable revenue base by expanding and diversifying its funding partnerships while also increasing its operating efficiency. The university raised more than it goal of $3.2 million in new gifts and pledges for 2013.

EXECUTIVES

Vice President of Gallaudet University, Kendall Hall
Vice President Administration, Gaynelle Hayes
Vice President Of Development And Alumni
 Relations, Paul Julin
VP, Amy Aillon
Vice President, Kai Gagnon
Auditors: GRANT THORNTON LLP NEW YORK

LOCATIONS

HQ: GALLAUDET UNIVERSITY
 800 FLORIDA AVE NE, WASHINGTON, DC 200023600
Phone: 202 651-5000
Web: WWW.GALLAUDET.EDU

PRODUCTS/OPERATIONS

Selected Programs
Gallaudet Research Institute
Gallaudet University
Laurent Clerc National Deaf Education Center
Kendall Demonstration Elementary School
Model Secondary School for the Deaf

HISTORICAL FINANCIALS
Company Type: Private

Income Statement

FYE: September 30

	REVENUE ($ mil.)	NET INCOME ($ mil.)	NET PROFIT MARGIN	EMPLOYEES
09/15	184	5	3.2%	1,200
09/14	183	7	4.3%	—
09/13	171	(0)	—	—
09/12	190	17	9.2%	—
Annual Growth	(1.1%)	(30.2%)	—	—

2015 Year-End Financials

Return on assets: 11.4%
Return on equity: 3.2%
Current ratio: 0.10
Cash ($ mil.): 6

GASTON COUNTY SCHOOL DISTRICT

EXECUTIVES

Superintendent, William Jeffrey Booker
Account Manager, Deliane Loftis
Assistant Manager, Cindee Matson
Superintendent, W Jeffrey Booker
Administrative Assistant, Ashley Duckworth
Auditors: ANDERSON SMITH & WIKE PLLC GA

LOCATIONS

HQ: GASTON COUNTY SCHOOL DISTRICT
 943 OSCEOLA ST, GASTONIA, NC 280545482
Phone: 704 866-6100
Web: WWW.GASTON.K12.NC.US

HISTORICAL FINANCIALS
Company Type: Private

Income Statement

FYE: June 30

	REVENUE ($ mil.)	NET INCOME ($ mil.)	NET PROFIT MARGIN	EMPLOYEES
06/16	257	(2)	—	3,848
06/13	253	(3)	—	—
06/12	262	4	1.6%	—
06/11	0	0	—	—
Annual Growth	—	—	—	—

2016 Year-End Financials

Return on assets: 1.4%
Return on equity: (-1.2%)
Current ratio: —
Cash ($ mil.): 25

GEISINGER MEDICAL CENTER

EXECUTIVES

President, Glenn D Steele Jr
Board of Directors, Jessica Robertson

LOCATIONS

HQ: GEISINGER MEDICAL CENTER
 100 N ACADEMY AVE, DANVILLE, PA 178220001
Phone: 570 271-6211

HISTORICAL FINANCIALS
Company Type: Private

Income Statement

FYE: June 30

	REVENUE ($ mil.)	NET INCOME ($ mil.)	NET PROFIT MARGIN	EMPLOYEES
06/15	1,058	120	11.4%	8,000
06/10	815	79	9.7%	—
06/09	735	46	6.3%	—
06/02	991,297	0	—	—
Annual Growth	—	58.8%	—	—

2015 Year-End Financials

Return on assets: 9.2%
Return on equity: 11.4%
Current ratio: 1.00
Cash ($ mil.): 13

GEISINGER SYSTEM SERVICES

EXECUTIVES

President, Glenn D Steele Jr
Director, Carol Tevis
Director, David Gingrich
Director, Charles Gerst
President, David Macko
Vice-President, John Jones

LOCATIONS

HQ: GEISINGER SYSTEM SERVICES
 100 N ACADEMY AVE, DANVILLE, PA 178229800
Phone: 570 271-6211

HISTORICAL FINANCIALS
Company Type: Private

Income Statement

FYE: June 30

	REVENUE ($ mil.)	NET INCOME ($ mil.)	NET PROFIT MARGIN	EMPLOYEES
06/15	535	14	2.7%	344
06/14	582	20	3.4%	—
06/13	519	6	1.3%	—
06/10	375	6	1.7%	—
Annual Growth	7.4%	17.1%	—	—

2015 Year-End Financials

Return on assets: 60.3%
Return on equity: 2.7%
Current ratio: —
Cash ($ mil.): 3

GENESIS HEALTH SYSTEM

Genesis Health System operates three acute care hospitals in Iowa and Illinois that have more than 660 beds total and employ some 700 doctors. Genesis Medical Center in Davenport Iowa with more than 500 beds is the system's flagship facility; the hospital offers a range of general surgical and specialist health services. The system's Illini Campus in Silvis Illinois features an assisted-living center. The Genesis Medical Center Dewitt Campus serves

that Iowa town and the surrounding area with its 13-bed hospital nursing home and related care facilities. Genesis Health System also operates physician practices outpatient centers and a home health agency.

Operations

Altogether Genesis Health System has more than 100 locations including hospitals convenient care locations Genesis Health Group sites physical rehabilitation clinics and outpatient service centers.

Strategy

In 2014 the system invested $15 million in the new Genesis HealthPlex in Bettendorf.

The following year Genesis Health System entered into a partnership with technology vendor Cerner Corporation to improve its patient care enterprise management systems.

Company Background

Genesis Health System had its genesis in 1869 with the establishment of Mercy Hospital (one of the first hospitals west of the Mississippi) and in the 1895 founding of St. Luke's Hospital. The two hospitals merged in 1994 to form the health system.

EXECUTIVES

Vice President Clinical Services, Rob Nelson
Vice President, Jackie Anhalt
Vice President Human Resources, Edwin Maxwell
Clinic Supervisor, Kathryn Ellsworth
Vice President Support Services, Mike Sharp
Clinic Supervisor, Susan Alpen
VP Human Resources, Heidi Kahly Mcmahon
Medical Librarian, Karlene Campbell
Board Member, Deborah Stafford
Secretary, Mary Jo McVey
Auditors: MCGLADREY LLP DAVENPORT IA

LOCATIONS

HQ: GENESIS HEALTH SYSTEM
1227 E RUSHOLME ST, DAVENPORT, IA 528032459
Phone: 563 421-1000

PRODUCTS/OPERATIONS

Selected Services
Bariatric Surgery
Behavioral Health
Birthing Services
Cancer
Cardiology
Home Health/Hospice
Neuroscience
Nursing Homes
Physical Medicine & Rehab
Senior Services

COMPETITORS

Blessing Hospital	Mercy Health Network
Catholic Health	OSF Healthcare System
Initiatives	UnityPoint Health
McDonough District	
Hospital	

HISTORICAL FINANCIALS

Company Type: Private

Income Statement

FYE: June 30

	REVENUE ($ mil.)	NET INCOME ($ mil.)	NET PROFIT MARGIN	EMPLOYEES
06/15	503	59	11.7%	5,000
06/14	467	26	5.7%	—
06/10	461	16	3.5%	—
06/09	993	0		—
Annual Growth	(10.7%)	—	—	—

2015 Year-End Financials

Return on assets: 11.8%   Cash ($ mil.): 82
Return on equity: 11.7%
Current ratio: 0.60

GENESYS REGIONAL MEDICAL CENTER

Genesys Regional Medical Center generates health care services for residents of a six-county region in eastern Michigan. The integrated medical center features a 410-bed hospital providing general medical and surgical care as well as specialty care in areas such as heart disease (through the Genesys Heart Institute). Additionally Genesys Regional includes family medicine outpatient diagnostic and rehabilitative care centers. It also operates a women and children's center and in cooperation with Flint's Hurley Medical Center it runs the Genesys Hurley Cancer Institute. Genesys Regional is a member the Genesys Health System which is part of Catholic hospital operator Ascension Health.

Operations

Genesys Regional's emergency room serves as a regional level II trauma center and features a rapid diagnostic center for cardiac conditions. In addition to heart cancer pediatric and women's care the hospital offers specialist centers focusing on orthopedics geriatrics neurology and minimally invasive surgery as well as diagnostic laboratories and fitness facilities. Genesys Regional handles some 21000 inpatient admissions each year including 2200 births. It also conducts about 16000 inpatient and outpatient surgical procedures and sees some 65000 visitors at its emergency department.

In addition to acute care Genesys Regional offers a variety of internships fellowships and residency programs for physicians-in-training through its partnership with Michigan State University. Fellowship programs cover cardiology gastroenterology psychology pulmonary care critical care and hematology and oncology. The hospital also provides continuing education programs for health professionals and it conducts medical and clinical research programs.

Geographic Reach

Genesys Regional is located at the Health Park in Grand Blanc Michigan just south of Flint. Its campus consists of about 480 acres and includes nature trails.

The company offers services for residents of a six-county region including Genesee Shiawassee Lapeer Oakland Livingston and Tuscola counties.

Company Background

The medical center opened its doors in 1997.

EXECUTIVES

Medical Director Pediatic Inpatient Specislist, George Y Zureikat
Radiology Director, MICHELLE NEUMAN
Vice President Of Human Resources, Tammy Saunaitis
CDO and Vice President of Business Development, Nicholas Evans
Director of Pharmacy Physical Therapy Director
Vice President Of Diagnostic Services, Joy Finkenbiner
Infection Control Director, Diane Scully

LOCATIONS

HQ: GENESYS REGIONAL MEDICAL CENTER
1 GENESYS PKWY, GRAND BLANC, MI 484398065
Phone: 810 606-5000
Web: WWW.GENESYS.ORG

PRODUCTS/OPERATIONS

Selected Services
Allied Health
Behavioral Health
Breast Center
Diabetes and Nutrition
Emergency
Genesys MRI Center
Health Centers
Health Equipment
Heart Institute
Home Health & Hospice
Inpatient Rehab
Laboratory
Neurosciences
Occupational Health
Oncological Surgery
Oncology
Orthopedics
Senior Services
Short-Term Rehab
Sleep Disorders
Surgery
Urgent Care
Women & Children
Wound Treatment

COMPETITORS

Covenant HealthCare	Hurley Medical Center
Crittenton Hospital	McLaren Health Care
Detroit Medical Center	Sparrow Health System
Henry Ford Health System	Trinity Health (Novi)

HISTORICAL FINANCIALS

Company Type: Private

Income Statement

FYE: June 30

	REVENUE ($ mil.)	NET INCOME ($ mil.)	NET PROFIT MARGIN	EMPLOYEES
06/15	403	12	3.0%	3,739
06/14	417	0	0.1%	—
06/13	415	1	0.4%	—
06/10	452	11	2.5%	—
Annual Growth	(2.3%)	0.9%	—	—

2015 Year-End Financials

Return on assets: 7.7%   Cash ($ mil.): 4
Return on equity: 3.0%
Current ratio: 0.10

GEORGIA ENERGY COOPERATIVE (AN ELECTRIC MEMBERSHIP CORPORATION)

EXECUTIVES

President, Glenn D Loomer
Purchasing Agent, Laverne Riddick
Vice-President, Bill Verner
Manager, Beth Norris
Engineer, Charles Roundtree
Manager, Devvie Benefield
Auditors: MCNAIR MCLEMORE MIDDLEBROOKS

LOCATIONS

HQ: GEORGIA ENERGY COOPERATIVE (AN ELECTRIC
MEMBERSHIP CORPORATION)
2100 E EXCH PL STE 300, TUCKER, GA 30084
Phone: 770 270-7500
Web: WWW.GEORGIAENERGYCOOP.COM

HISTORICAL FINANCIALS

Company Type: Private

Income Statement
FYE: December 31

	REVENUE ($ mil.)	NET INCOME ($ mil.)	NET PROFIT MARGIN	EMPLOYEES
12/15	275	2	0.8%	15
12/14	232	2	0.9%	—
12/13	222	1	0.8%	—
12/12	214	0	0.4%	—
Annual Growth	8.8%	32.2%	—	—

2015 Year-End Financials

Return on assets: 7.1%   Cash ($ mil.): 3
Return on equity: 0.8%
Current ratio: 0.90

GEORGIA TECH APPLIED RESEARCH CORPORATION

EXECUTIVES

Board of Directors, Robert McGrath
Director, G Duane Hutchison
Manager, Patricia Head
Financial Executive, Barbara J Alexander
Director, Nicolas F Perez
Director, Duane Hutchison
Auditors: CHERRY BEKAERT LLP ATLANTA G

LOCATIONS

HQ: GEORGIA TECH APPLIED RESEARCH
CORPORATION
505 10TH ST NW, ATLANTA, GA 303185775
Phone: 404 894-4819
Web: WWW.GTRC.GATECH.EDU

HISTORICAL FINANCIALS

Company Type: Private

Income Statement
FYE: June 30

	REVENUE ($ mil.)	NET INCOME ($ mil.)	NET PROFIT MARGIN	EMPLOYEES
06/16	358	(0)	—	1,100
06/15	340	0	0.1%	—
Annual Growth	5.3%	—	—	—

2016 Year-End Financials

Return on assets: 18.7%   Cash ($ mil.): 29
Return on equity: (-0.1%)
Current ratio: 1.30

GERALD H. PHIPPS, INC.

EXECUTIVES

President, Kurt Klanderud
Financial Executive, Margo Ferguson
Personnel Manager, April Durham
Project Manager, Brian Cass
Project Manager, Chad Cleveland
Auditors: EKS&H LLLP FORT COLLINS COLO

LOCATIONS

HQ: GERALD H. PHIPPS, INC.
5995 GREENWOOD, GREENWOOD VILLAGE, CO
80111
Phone: 303 571-5377
Web: WWW.GHPHIPPS.COM

HISTORICAL FINANCIALS

Company Type: Private

Income Statement
FYE: October 31

	REVENUE ($ mil.)	NET INCOME ($ mil.)	NET PROFIT MARGIN	EMPLOYEES
10/16	263	2	0.8%	350
10/15	185	0	0.4%	—
10/14	0	0	—	—
10/13	226	(1)	—	—
Annual Growth	5.2%	—	—	—

2016 Year-End Financials

Return on assets: 21.6%   Cash ($ mil.): 16
Return on equity: 0.8%
Current ratio: 1.00

GILMAN BUILDING PRODUCTS, LLC

EXECUTIVES

President, Victor Garrett
Board of Directors, Lynn Keene
Manager, Deborah Stewart
VP Manufacturing, Victor Garnett
Auditors: PRICEWATERHOUSECOOPERS LLP

LOCATIONS

HQ: GILMAN BUILDING PRODUCTS, LLC
2500 SAINT MARYS RD, SAINT MARYS, GA
315584141
Phone: 912 576-0300

HISTORICAL FINANCIALS

Company Type: Private

Income Statement
FYE: December 31

	REVENUE ($ mil.)	NET INCOME ($ mil.)	NET PROFIT MARGIN	EMPLOYEES
12/15	211	32	15.4%	788
12/14	237	55	23.5%	—
12/13	229	66	28.8%	—
12/12	162	24	15.2%	—
Annual Growth	9.1%	9.6%	—	—

2015 Year-End Financials

Return on assets: 2.9%   Cash ($ mil.): 38
Return on equity: 15.4%
Current ratio: 4.50

GLENS FALLS HOSPITAL

EXECUTIVES

Manager, Carl Reukert

LOCATIONS

HQ: GLENS FALLS HOSPITAL
100 PARK ST, GLENS FALLS, NY 128014447
Phone: 518 926-1000
Web: WWW.GLENSFALLSHOSPITAL.ORG

HISTORICAL FINANCIALS

Company Type: Private

Income Statement
FYE: December 31

	REVENUE ($ mil.)	NET INCOME ($ mil.)	NET PROFIT MARGIN	EMPLOYEES
12/15	316	(3)	—	2,726
12/14	289	5	1.7%	—
12/13	308	1	0.5%	—
12/09	286	(0)	—	—
Annual Growth	1.7%	—	—	—

2015 Year-End Financials

Return on assets: 7.5%   Cash ($ mil.): 20
Return on equity: (-1.0%)
Current ratio: 1.00

GLOBAL HEALTH SOLUTIONS INC

EXECUTIVES

Vice-President, T Rosenberger
Vice-President, Thomas Rosenberger

LOCATIONS

HQ: GLOBAL HEALTH SOLUTIONS INC
325 SWANTON WAY, DECATUR, GA 300303001
Phone: 404 592-1430
Web: WWW.TASKFORCE.ORG

HISTORICAL FINANCIALS

Company Type: Private

Income Statement
FYE: August 31

	REVENUE ($ mil.)	NET INCOME ($ mil.)	NET PROFIT MARGIN	EMPLOYEES
08/15	1,609	0	—	2
08/14	1,790	0	—	—
08/13	1,574	0	—	—
08/10	1,120	0	0.0%	—
Annual Growth	7.5%	—	—	—

GMTO CORPORATION

EXECUTIVES

President, Patrick McCarthy
Auditors: GRANT THORNTON LLP LOS ANGELE

LOCATIONS

HQ: GMTO CORPORATION
465 N HALSTEAD ST STE 250, PASADENA, CA
911073226
Phone: 626 204-0500
Web: WWW.GMTO.ORG

HISTORICAL FINANCIALS

Company Type: Private

Income Statement

FYE: June 30

	REVENUE ($ mil.)	NET INCOME ($ mil.)	NET PROFIT MARGIN	EMPLOYEES
06/15	347	330	95.2%	70
06/14	27	16	60.3%	—
06/12	20	13	65.3%	—
06/11	14	10	70.1%	—
Annual Growth	119.4%	136.9%	—	—

2015 Year-End Financials

Return on assets: 1.3%   Cash ($ mil.): 134
Return on equity: 95.2%
Current ratio: 28.60

GOLDEN GATE REGIONAL CENTER, INC.

EXECUTIVES

Chief Executive Officer, Ron Fell
Director, Christine Tranchida
Manager, Ryan Torno
Chief Financial Officer, Chris Rognier
Personnel Director, Barry Benda
Director, Amanda Pyle
Auditors: LAUTZE & LAUTZE SAN FRANCISCO

LOCATIONS

HQ: GOLDEN GATE REGIONAL CENTER, INC.
1355 MARKET ST STE 220, SAN FRANCISCO, CA
941031314
Phone: 415 546-9222
Web: WWW.GGRC.ORG

HISTORICAL FINANCIALS

Company Type: Private

Income Statement

FYE: June 30

	REVENUE ($ mil.)	NET INCOME ($ mil.)	NET PROFIT MARGIN	EMPLOYEES
06/15	228	(0)	—	210
06/14	214	(0)	—	—
06/13	200	0	0.0%	—
06/11	183	(0)	—	—
Annual Growth	5.6%	—	—	—

2015 Year-End Financials

Return on assets: 7.8%   Cash ($ mil.): 7
Return on equity: —
Current ratio: 0.10

GOLDEN GRAIN ENERGY, LLC

EXECUTIVES

Chief Financial Officer, Christine A Marchand
Chief Operating Officer, Chad E Kuhlers
Auditors: RSM US LLP DES MOINES IOWA

LOCATIONS

HQ: GOLDEN GRAIN ENERGY, LLC
1822 43RD ST SW, MASON CITY, IA 504017071
Phone: 641 423-8525
Web: WWW.GGECORN.COM

PRODUCTS/OPERATIONS

2006 Sales

	% of total
Ethanol	91
Distillers grains	9
Total	**100**

2007 Sales

	% of total
Ethanol	89
Distillers grains	11
Total	**100**

2008 Sales

	% of total
Ethanol	84
Distillers grains	16
Total	**100**

COMPETITORS

ADM   POET
GreenField Ethanol
Hawkeye Energy
Holdings

HISTORICAL FINANCIALS

Company Type: Private

Income Statement

FYE: October 31

	REVENUE ($ mil.)	NET INCOME ($ mil.)	NET PROFIT MARGIN	EMPLOYEES
10/16	200	20	10.2%	47
10/15	221	31	14.4%	—
10/14	289	79	27.4%	—
10/13	350	14	4.0%	—
Annual Growth	(17.0%)	12.9%	—	—

2016 Year-End Financials

Return on assets: 3.8%   Cash ($ mil.): 16
Return on equity: 10.2%
Current ratio: 2.50

GOLDEN VALLEY ELECTRIC ASSOCIATION, INC.

EXECUTIVES

Chief Executive Officer, Cory Borgeson
Manager, Michael F Wright

Director, Sam RAO
Vice-President, Jeff Yauney
Engineer, Stan Koshak
Engineer, Terry Garwood
Accountant, Kathleen Chapados
Auditors: BDO USA LLP ANCHORAGE ALASK

LOCATIONS

HQ: GOLDEN VALLEY ELECTRIC ASSOCIATION, INC.
758 ILLINOIS ST, FAIRBANKS, AK 997012919
Phone: 907 452-1151
Web: WWW.GVEA.COM

HISTORICAL FINANCIALS

Company Type: Private

Income Statement

FYE: December 31

	REVENUE ($ mil.)	NET INCOME ($ mil.)	NET PROFIT MARGIN	EMPLOYEES
12/15	214	31	14.7%	270
12/14	239	11	4.6%	—
12/13	246	10	4.2%	—
12/12	273	13	4.8%	—
Annual Growth	(7.8%)	34.1%	—	—

2015 Year-End Financials

Return on assets: 9.5%   Cash ($ mil.): 1
Return on equity: 14.7%
Current ratio: 0.60

GOOD SAMARITAN HOSPITAL

VIP suites and valet parking are standard fare for hotels in Los Angeles so why not hospitals too? Good Samaritan Hospital is a 410-bed acute care facility featuring all private rooms some suites and yes valet parking. Good Samaritan serves patients throughout the greater Los Angeles area. This acute-care facility offers services including cardiac surgery diagnostic imaging women's services ophthalmology oncology neurology respiratory care and transfusion-free medicine and surgery. Good Samaritan also has centers dedicated to urology orthopedic care perinatal medicine and retinal surgery. The hospital is affiliated with the Episcopalian Church and USC's Keck School of Medicine.

Geographic Reach

Good Samaritan provides services in two of the eight Service Planning Areas (SPAs) in the County SPA 4 and SPA 6. It has identified five of the 26 health districts in Los Angeles County as target regions: Central Hollywood/Wilshire Northeast Southeast and Southwest. The majority of the population in the primary service area for Good Samaritan is Hispanic/Latino (60%) followed by Asian (19.9%) and then African American (8.6%).

Operations

The hospital's medical centers include the Heart and Vascular Center Samaritan Comprehensive Orthopaedic Center Tertiary Retinal Surgery Pancreatico-Biliary Program Kidney Stone Services Transfusion-Free Medicine and Surgery Center and the Davajan-Cabal Center for Perinatal Medicine.

Good Samaritan admits 17000 patients (excluding newborns) a year and handles more than 93500 outpatient visits. More than 4000 deliveries and 8000 surgeries are performed annually in about 20 surgical suites. The hospital has about 625 medical staff.

In 2013 Good Samaritan handled 33000 emergency room patients (in a department originally designed for a capacity of 9000 visits).In 2012 the hospital contributed $19 million for community benefit.

In addition to being an affiliated teaching hospital for USC's medical school Good Samaritan offers residencies to medical students from UCLA's Harbor/UCLA Medical Center and the Martin Luther King/Drew Medical Center. It also helps to train nurses and other health professionals and it provides community education programs for area residents.

Strategy

To expand its services for area residents in 2013 Good Samaritan partnered with CareMore Health Plan to provide services for seniors. Through the partnership CareMore is building a nursing home near the Good Samaritan which will provide medical care to residents. Such comprehensive medical home models seek to improve coordination of care for Medicare patients.

It is also building out its infrastructure to keep up with demand. Good Samaritan is expected to complete its new 193000 sq. ft. Medical Pavilion featuring the Frank R. Seaver Ambulatory Surgery Center in 2015. The new medical pavilion will feature amenities such as a patient friendly lobby radiation oncology pharmacy Women's Imaging and Bistro Café on the first floor. The second floor will include 8 outpatient surgery suites and floors 3 to 7 will house ancillary services and physician offices.In 2013 the company approved a $28 million expansion project which includes a four-story 96000-sq. ft. addition to the health center's existing building at 9000 N. Main St. in Englewood. This addition also to be completed in 2015 includes a 22-bed emergency department.In 2012 Good Samaritan broke ground on its $109 million building project - the BEACON Project which consists of a 200000 sq. ft. five-story 120-bed inpatient tower as well as a redesign of key health care service areas and upgrade of the hospital's critical engineering systems. The new patient tower is expected to be operational in June 2015.

Company Background

Good Samaritan has been named one of America's 50 Best Hospitals by HealthGrades multiple times putting it in a category of hospitals that average a nearly 30% lower mortality rate than other US hospitals.

It was founded in 1885.

EXECUTIVES

Vice President Finance, Susan Dries
Vice President, Susan Harlow
Director Of Pharmacy, Mark Holdych
Director of Respiratory Therapy, Michael Muth
Vice President of Business Development, Samuel Feuerlicht
Medical Director, Harry Rosen
Vice President, Campbell Dean

LOCATIONS

HQ: GOOD SAMARITAN HOSPITAL
1225 WILSHIRE BLVD, LOS ANGELES, CA 900171901
Phone: 213 977-2121
Web: WWW.GOODSAM.ORG

PRODUCTS/OPERATIONS

Selected Services
Clinical Services
Cardiology
Cardiac Surgery
Comprehensive Sleep Center
Diagnostic Imaging (Radiology)
Emergency Services
ENT (Ear Nose & Throat)
Gamma Knife
Gastroenterology

Laboratory
Neurosciences
Oncology (Cancer)
Ophthalmology and Retinal Medicine
Orthopedics
Physical Medicine
Podiatry
Pulmonary Medicine and Respiratory Care
Radiation Oncology
Surgery
Women's Health and Newborn Services
Urology

COMPETITORS

Aptium Oncology	Hoag Memorial Hospital
Brotman Medical Center	Hollywood Presbyterian
Cedars-Sinai Medical	Medical Center
Center	Methodist Hospital of
Childrens Hospital Los	Southern California
Angeles	Newhall Memorial
Glendale Adventist	Hospital
Medical Center	Tenet Healthcare
HCA	

HISTORICAL FINANCIALS
Company Type: Private

Income Statement
FYE: August 31

	REVENUE ($ mil.)	NET INCOME ($ mil.)	NET PROFIT MARGIN	EMPLOYEES
08/15	351	38	11.0%	1,500
08/03	219	0	0.0%	—
08/02	205	0	—	—
08/01	194	(2)	—	—
Annual Growth	4.3%	—	—	—

2015 Year-End Financials
Return on assets: 5.2%   Cash ($ mil.): 20
Return on equity: 11.0%
Current ratio: 0.90

GOOD SAMARITAN HOSPITAL

Good Samaritan Hospital offers a caring hand to the residents of Dayton Ohio and the surrounding areas. The hospital has some 560 beds and offers a mix of services including primary and emergency care pediatric specialties and a family birthing center. Good Samaritan also runs the Samaritan North Health Center an outpatient health center that offers outpatient surgery rehab and sports medicine diagnostic imaging and cancer care among other services. Other operations include the Maria-Joseph Living Care Center a long-term care facility with some 400 beds and Samaritan Family Care a primary care physicians' network. Good Samaritan Hospital is part of Premier Health Partners.

The City of Dayton partnered with the Sisters of Charity in Cincinnati in 1928 to raise $1 million in order to finance the construction of the Good Samaritan Hospital; the project lasted four years and the hospital was opened in 1932.

In 2008 Good Samaritan Hospital acquired the assets of Dayton Heart Hospital for approximately $55 million.

EXECUTIVES

President, Mark S Shaker
Administrative Assistant, Sue Schriver
Manager, Carol Richardson
Personnel Manager, K D Deck

LOCATIONS

HQ: GOOD SAMARITAN HOSPITAL
2222 PHILADELPHIA DR, DAYTON, OH 454061891
Phone: 937 278-2612
Web: WWW.GOODSAMDAYTON.ORG

COMPETITORS

Kettering Health	OhioHealth
Network	TriHealth

HISTORICAL FINANCIALS
Company Type: Private

Income Statement
FYE: December 31

	REVENUE ($ mil.)	NET INCOME ($ mil.)	NET PROFIT MARGIN	EMPLOYEES
12/15	321	7	2.2%	2,000
12/06	307	11	3.9%	—
12/05	274	(5)	—	—
12/03	282	20	7.3%	—
Annual Growth	1.1%	(8.5%)	—	—

2015 Year-End Financials
Return on assets: 3.9%   Cash ($ mil.): 11
Return on equity: 2.2%
Current ratio: 1.70

GOOD SAMARITAN HOSPITAL CORVALLIS

EXECUTIVES

President, Becky Rose
Chief Operating Officer, Steven Jasperson
Office Manager, Don Fucillo
Director, Kenneth Nitta
Director, Jana Kay Slater
Chief Financial Officer, Daniel Smith

LOCATIONS

HQ: GOOD SAMARITAN HOSPITAL CORVALLIS
3600 NW SAMARITAN DR, CORVALLIS, OR 973303700
Phone: 541 768-5069

HISTORICAL FINANCIALS
Company Type: Private

Income Statement
FYE: December 31

	REVENUE ($ mil.)	NET INCOME ($ mil.)	NET PROFIT MARGIN	EMPLOYEES
12/15	356	9	2.7%	900
12/14	312	(6)	—	—
12/08	231	5	2.3%	—
12/04	65	(1)	—	—
Annual Growth	16.7%	—	—	—

2015 Year-End Financials
Return on assets: 3.8%   Cash ($ mil.): —
Return on equity: 2.7%
Current ratio: 0.60

GOOD SAMARITAN HOSPITAL MEDICAL CENTER

The folks at Good Samaritan Hospital Medical Center have plenty of reasons to feel good about their efforts. The hospital is part of Catholic Health Services of Long Island (CHS) and serves the south shore community of West Islip New York. The full-service medical center boasts 900 physicians and 440 acute care beds offering a complete range of health care counseling and rehabilitation services. Good Samaritan provides emergency medicine and trauma care in addition to oncology cardiology pediatric woman's health diagnostic and surgical care. It also operates the Good Samaritan Nursing Home a 100-bed skilled nursing facility as well as satellite clinics and a home health care agency.

Operations

Good Samaritan which contributes about 28% of its parent's revenue logged more than 95000 emergency department visits in 2012. Its ambulatory surgery department treats an average of nearly 300 patients weekly as part of its focus on same-day procedures. Additionally the medical facility in 2012 admitted 27615 patients and logged 2820 births 66000 rehabilitation inpatient visits and 49640 dialysis treatments.

The hospital's outpatient services include same day surgeries pulmonary rehabilitation pediatric specialty visits and physical occupational and speech therapy sessions; it also has satellite locations that provide dialysis treatment. Good Samaritan's palliative care program offers an 11-bed dedicated acute palliative care inpatient unit.

Geographic Reach

Good Samaritan Hospital Medical Center serves those in and around West Islip New York.

Financial Performance

Net patient revenue dragged down Good Samaritan's revenue increases in fiscal 2012 vs. 2011. During the reporting period the medical center posted $579 million in revenue representing a marginal $260000 rise. Net income dropped some 77% to $8.3 million in 2012 vs. 2011 thanks to rising operating expenses from increases in CHS Services.

Strategy

Good Samaritan is recognized for its cancer care and radiology programs as well as its cardiac pediatric and women's health services all of which it has been expanding and enhancing in recent years. For instance the hospital added a nephrology unit in 2011 within its pediatric division to evaluate and treat children with kidney disease. It expanded its pediatric nephrology unit in 2012 by opening a new 16-bed surgical intensive care unit (SICU). Good Samaritan also added a new diagnostic imaging center in 2012 that provides radiology services including breast imaging.

In addition Good Samaritan is working to add an open-heart surgery program to its cardiology division through a partnership with St. Francis Hospital another member of the CHS organization also known as The Heart Center. In 2013 Good Samaritan became the first facility in the New York metropolitan region to install and offer the GE Innova IGS 530 digital cardiovascular and interventional imaging system in its cardiac catheterization laboratory.

The not-for-profit facility's growth measures are supported in part by its charitable organization The Guilds of Good Samaritan Hospital Medical Center. The Good Samaritan hospital provides some $50 million in community service and charity care each year.

Company Background

Founded in 1959 Good Samaritan became part of the CHS organization in 1997.

EXECUTIVES

Physical Therapy Director, Jill Bocchieri
Vice President Administration, Joseph Loiacono
Medical Director, Gino Giorgini

LOCATIONS

HQ: GOOD SAMARITAN HOSPITAL MEDICAL CENTER
1000 MONTAUK HWY, WEST ISLIP, NY 117954927
Phone: 631 376-3000

PRODUCTS/OPERATIONS

Selected Premier Services
Cancer Care
Cardiac Care
Children's Care
Emergency Services
Satellites
Surgery
Women's Care

Selected Services
Ambulatory Surgery Unit
Audiology/Hearing Aids
BirthPlace
Breast Health Center
Cancer Care
Cancer Surgery
Cardiac Rehabilitation
Cardiology Services
Center for Pediatric Specialty Care
Care Management and Social Work
Child Life Services
da Vinci Surgery
Dentistry
Dermatology
Dialysis Services
Ear Nose and Throat
Emergency Department
Endocrinology
Family Practice
Gastroenterology
Good Samaritan Hospital Foundation
Good Samaritan Nursing Home
Hematology and Oncology
Imaging Services
Infectious Diseases
Inpatient Dialysis
Internal Medicine
Laboratory
Long Term Home Health Care
Managed Care
Martin Luther King Jr. Community Health Center
Maternal Fetal Medicine
Medical Education
Neonatology
Nephrology
Neurosurgery
Nursing at Good Sam
Nutrition and Food Services
Obstetrics and Gynecology
Oncology
Ophthalmology
Oral Surgery
Orthopaedics
Osteoporosis
Palliative Care
Pain Management
Pastoral/Spiritual Care Department
Pathology
Pediatric Services
Perinatal Education
Plastic and Reconstructive Services
Podiatry
Pre-Surgical Testing
Psychiatry
Pulmonary Rehabilitation
Radiation Oncology Center
Rehabilitation Services
Respiratory Care
Safe Haven Program
Sleep Apnea Center
Special Care
Support Groups
Surgery
Thoracic Surgery
Trauma Services
Urology
Vascular Suite
Vascular Surgery
Weight Loss Surgery/Bariatric Surgery
Women's Imaging Center

COMPETITORS

Brookhaven Memorial Hospital Medical Center
CSH
Catholic Healthcare System
Continuum Health Partners
Mather Memorial Hospital
Memorial Sloan-Kettering
New York City Health and Hospitals
NewYork-Presbyterian Healthcare
Northwell Health
Winthrop-University Hospital

HISTORICAL FINANCIALS
Company Type: Private

Income Statement
FYE: December 31

	REVENUE ($ mil.)	NET INCOME ($ mil.)	NET PROFIT MARGIN	EMPLOYEES
12/15	505	28	5.7%	3,774
12/14	488	36	7.5%	
12/13*	534	(28)	—	—
06/05	118	(1)	—	—
Annual Growth 14.1%		—	—	—

*Fiscal year change

2015 Year-End Financials
Return on assets: 7.7%   Cash ($ mil.): 72
Return on equity: 5.7%
Current ratio: 1.20

GOOD SAMARITAN HOSPITAL OF CINCINNATI

EXECUTIVES

President, John S Prout
Financial Executive, Brian Krause
Secretary, Donna Nienaber
Assistant Treasurer, Michael Crofton
Auditors: BKD LLP CINCINNATI OH

LOCATIONS

HQ: GOOD SAMARITAN HOSPITAL OF CINCINNATI
375 DIXMYTH AVE, CINCINNATI, OH 452202489
Phone: 513 569-6251

HISTORICAL FINANCIALS
Company Type: Private

Income Statement				FYE: June 30
	REVENUE ($ mil.)	NET INCOME ($ mil.)	NET PROFIT MARGIN	EMPLOYEES
06/15	578	81	14.0%	3,452
06/13	483	60	12.4%	—
06/10	479	43	9.1%	—
06/09	954	0	—	—
Annual Growth	—	691.6%	—	—

2015 Year-End Financials
Return on assets: 7.3% Cash ($ mil.): —
Return on equity: 14.0%
Current ratio: 1.50

GOOD SAMARITAN REGIONAL MEDICAL CENTER

EXECUTIVES
Chief Executive Officer, Philip Patterson
Manager, Lisa Valow
Chief Financial Officer, Stephen Majetich

LOCATIONS
HQ: GOOD SAMARITAN REGIONAL MEDICAL CENTER
255 LAFAYETTE AVE, SUFFERN, NY 109014812
Phone: 845 368-5000
Web: WWW.GOODSAMHOSP.ORG

HISTORICAL FINANCIALS
Company Type: Private

Income Statement				FYE: December 31
	REVENUE ($ mil.)	NET INCOME ($ mil.)	NET PROFIT MARGIN	EMPLOYEES
12/15	286	36	12.8%	1,600
12/14	283	4	1.5%	—
12/08*	254	(12)	—	—
06/05	118	(1)	—	—
Annual Growth	8.3%	—	—	—

*Fiscal year change

2015 Year-End Financials
Return on assets: 5.6% Cash ($ mil.): —
Return on equity: 12.8%
Current ratio: 1.30

GOODIN COMPANY

EXECUTIVES
Chief Executive Officer, Greg Skagerberg
Board of Directors, Zac Skagerberg
Branch Manager, Aaron Wallin
Consultant, Kathy Hinds
Auditors: RSM US LLP MINNEAPOLIS MINNE

LOCATIONS
HQ: GOODIN COMPANY
2700 N 2ND ST, MINNEAPOLIS, MN 554111679
Phone: 612 588-7811
Web: WWW.GOODINCO.COM

HISTORICAL FINANCIALS
Company Type: Private

Income Statement				FYE: December 31
	REVENUE ($ mil.)	NET INCOME ($ mil.)	NET PROFIT MARGIN	EMPLOYEES
12/15	179	3	2.1%	405
12/14	171	3	2.3%	—
12/13	159	3	2.0%	—
12/12	147	2	1.4%	—
Annual Growth	6.6%	23.2%	—	—

2015 Year-End Financials
Return on assets: 3.5% Cash ($ mil.): —
Return on equity: 2.1%
Current ratio: 1.40

GOODWILL INDUSTRIES OF SOUTHEASTERN WISCONSIN, INC.

EXECUTIVES
President, Jacqueline Hallberg
Personnel Manager, Jennifer Nelson
President, Dwight Ferguson
Director, Betty Geren
Marketing Director, Laura Sanders
Purchasing Agent, Dan Rice
Manager, Emily Capelle
Auditors: GRANT THORNTON LLP APPLETON

LOCATIONS
HQ: GOODWILL INDUSTRIES OF SOUTHEASTERN WISCONSIN, INC.
5400 S 60TH ST, GREENDALE, WI 531291404
Phone: 414 847-4200
Web: WWW.GOODWILLCHICAGO.COM

HISTORICAL FINANCIALS
Company Type: Private

Income Statement				FYE: December 31
	REVENUE ($ mil.)	NET INCOME ($ mil.)	NET PROFIT MARGIN	EMPLOYEES
12/15	306	10	3.3%	3,391
12/14	282	8	3.0%	—
12/13	347	13	3.9%	—
12/12	255	13	5.4%	—
Annual Growth	6.3%	(9.3%)	—	—

2015 Year-End Financials
Return on assets: 999.9% Cash ($ mil.): 19,195
Return on equity: 3.3%
Current ratio: 1.80

GOVERNMENT SCIENTIFIC SOURCE, INC.

EXECUTIVES
President, Wayne B Bardsley
Vice-President, James Smith
Assistant Vice-President, Jermain Brown
Senior Vice-President, Steve Sellentin
Auditors: LYDON FETTEROLF CORYDON PA

LOCATIONS
HQ: GOVERNMENT SCIENTIFIC SOURCE, INC.
12351 SUNRISE VALLEY DR, RESTON, VA 201913415
Phone: 703 734-1805
Web: WWW.GOVSCI.COM

HISTORICAL FINANCIALS
Company Type: Private

Income Statement				FYE: December 31
	REVENUE ($ mil.)	NET INCOME ($ mil.)	NET PROFIT MARGIN	EMPLOYEES
12/15	196	3	2.0%	90
12/14	182	3	1.7%	—
12/13	140	2	1.6%	—
12/12	132	2	1.7%	—
Annual Growth	14.1%	21.5%	—	—

2015 Year-End Financials
Return on assets: 6.5% Cash ($ mil.): 15
Return on equity: 2.0%
Current ratio: 1.90

GRAHAM ENTERPRISE, INC.

EXECUTIVES
President, John C Graham
Board of Directors, Matthew X Graham
Personnel Manager, Marleen Finedore
Marketing Director, Suresh Bhatia
Director, Richard Byham
Auditors: FGMK LLC BANNOCKBURN ILLINO

LOCATIONS
HQ: GRAHAM ENTERPRISE, INC.
750 BUNKER CT STE 100, VERNON HILLS, IL 600611864
Phone: 847 837-0777
Web: WWW.GRAHAMEI.COM

HISTORICAL FINANCIALS
Company Type: Private

Income Statement				FYE: December 31
	REVENUE ($ mil.)	NET INCOME ($ mil.)	NET PROFIT MARGIN	EMPLOYEES
12/15	662	11	1.7%	350
12/14	866	8	0.9%	—
12/13	849	4	0.5%	—
12/12	794	7	1.0%	—
Annual Growth	(5.9%)	13.4%	—	—

GRAND RAPIDS PUBLIC SCHOOLS

Auditors: BRICKLEY DELONG PC GRAND RAPI

LOCATIONS

HQ: GRAND RAPIDS PUBLIC SCHOOLS
1331 FRANKLIN ST SE, GRAND RAPIDS, MI
495062634
Phone: 616 819-2000
Web: WWW.GRPUBLICSCHOOLS.ORG

HISTORICAL FINANCIALS

Company Type: Private

Income Statement FYE: June 30

	REVENUE ($ mil.)	NET INCOME ($ mil.)	NET PROFIT MARGIN	EMPLOYEES
06/16	258	80	31.2%	4,000
06/15	253	(8)	—	—
06/14	0	0	—	—
06/13	270	(0)	—	—
Annual Growth	(1.5%)	—	—	—

GRAND STRAND REGIONAL MEDICAL CENTER, LLC

Grand Strand Regional Medical Center (GSRMC) is an acute care hospital serving Myrtle Beach South Carolina and surrounding Georgetown and Horry counties. The 220-bed hospital a designated trauma center is home to the only cardiac surgery program in those counties. GSRMC has a staff of more than 250 physicians representing a range of specializations including oncology wound treatment and emergency care women's health pediatrics rehabilitation behavioral health and treatment for sleeping disorders. Grand Strand Regional Medical Center includes the medical center and other satellite diagnostic ambulatory care and senior care facilities throughout the area.

EXECUTIVES

Infection Control Director, Winona McLamb
Medical Records Director, Gina Trahey-Romanuk
Vice President of Operations, David Brooks

LOCATIONS

HQ: GRAND STRAND REGIONAL MEDICAL CENTER, LLC
809 82ND PKWY, MYRTLE BEACH, SC 295724607
Phone: 843 449-4411
Web: WWW.GRANDSTRANDMED.COM

COMPETITORS

Carolinas HealthCare System
Carolinas Hospital System
Conway Medical Center
Georgetown Hospital System
Greenville Hospital System
Laurens County Hospital
McLeod Health
Medical University of South Carolina
Palmetto Health
Roper St. Francis Healthcare
Soliant Health

HISTORICAL FINANCIALS

Company Type: Private

Income Statement FYE: April 30

	REVENUE ($ mil.)	NET INCOME ($ mil.)	NET PROFIT MARGIN	EMPLOYEES
04/15	331	107	32.3%	1,000
04/13	265	65	24.6%	—
04/09	0	0	38.0%	—
Annual Growth	294.8%	284.3%	—	—

GRAND VALLEY STATE UNIVERSITY

Even the most average student can get a grand education at Grand Valley State University. The school operates five campuses in western Michigan. The main one is in Allendale; it has additional facilities in Grand Rapids Holland Muskegon and Traverse City. Classes at the latter two locations are offered in conjunction with local community colleges. A public university with a liberal arts emphasis Grand Valley State offers more than 200 fields of study including about 80 undergraduate majors and more than 30 graduate programs. It has an enrollment of roughly 25000 students and approximately 835 regular faculty members. Its student-teacher ratio is about 27:1.

Operations

Grand Valley State is NCAA Division II and competes in the Great Lakes Intercollegiate Athletic Conference 20 varsity sports (11 womens and 9 mens). Its library has more than 1 million electronic journals and books and more than 518450 paper volumes. The university has a $74.1 million endowment.

Geographic Reach

Grand Valley State enrolls students from more than 8 countries. Some 807 of its students studied abroad in the 2011-2012 academic year.

The university's 1304 acre main campus is situated in Allendale some 12 miles west of Grand Rapids. It also has the 38-acre Robert C. Pew Campus in the heart of Grand Rapids which houses the Cook-DeVos Center for Health Sciences John C. Kennedy Hall of Engineering and the L. William Seidman Center. The school also offers classes at the Meijer Campus in Holland and in Muskegon and Traverse City.

Financial Performance

The school reported an 8% increase in revenues in 2012 was due to higher tuition rates and a growth in upper division credit hours.

Grand Valley State's net income decreased by 75% in 2012 due to an increase in operating expenses and decline in non-operating revenues (due to a drop in state funding government grants gifts and investment income).

The university saw an increase in revenues from 2010-12 due to higher student tuition and fees and a growth in auxiliary revenues.

Company Background

Grand Valley State was established in 1960 in response to the need for a public four-year college in Michigan's second largest metropolitan area.

EXECUTIVES

Interim Associate Vice President Academic Affairs, Joe Godwin
Director of Admissions, Jodi Chycinski
Assistant Vice President Development, Karen Loth
Associate Vice President Business Finance, Briand Copeland
Vice President, Jessica MacVane
Assistant Vice President for Business and Finance, Brian Copeland
Assistant Vice President Academic Affairs, Jean M Nagelkerk
Vice President, Audrey Tarbutton
Vice President Human Resources, Kathy Gulembo
Associate Vice President for Academic, Julia Guevara
Vice President, Anne Moore
Department Chair and Assistant Professor, Andrew Booth
Vice President, Megan Woods
Assistant Vice President Academic Affairs, Nancy Giardina
VICE PRESIDENT, Matt Darga
Assistant Vice President for University Development, Jennifer Wardrop
Director of Physical Therapy, John Peck
Assistant Vice President Facilities Services, Timothy Thimmesch
Assistant Vice President For Development Services, Scott Blinkhorn
Assistant Vice President Academic Affairs, Jean Nagelkerk
Vice President Finance and Administration, James Bachmeier
Department Chair Assistant Professor, Randy Wyble
Associate Vice President for Academic Affairs (Aboufadel), Gretchen Galbraith
Vice President, Corinne Farleigh
Vice President, Daniel Aday
Vice President of Operations, Jenna Pizarek
Vice President of Marketing, Kelsey Burgor
Vice President, Corey Anton
Vice President of Operations, MarisaE Koltz
Assistant Vice President for Academic, Ed Aboufadel
Assistant Vice President of Facilities, Tim Thimmesch
Treasurer, David Lo
Treasurer, Jonathan Cook
Secretary, Shelby Fullington
Board Member, Patricia Stephenson
Secretary, Kay Hart
Board Member, Caitlin Cusack
Treasurer, Tim Marroquin
Secretary, Charlyn Worthem
Secretary, Stephanie Salamone
Secretary, Colin Schoen
Secretary, Alex Radner
Secretary, Bev Nyhuis
Secretary, Clyde Woods
Secretary, Kaitlyn Cooke
Cafm Space Planning Assistant and Secretary, Pam Hart
Auditors: PLANTE & MORAN PLLC GRAND RA

HQ: GRAND VALLEY STATE UNIVERSITY
1 CAMPUS DR, ALLENDALE, MI 494019403
Phone: 616 331-5000
Web: WWW.GVSU.EDU

HISTORICAL FINANCIALS
Company Type: Private

Income Statement
FYE: June 30

	REVENUE ($ mil.)	NET INCOME ($ mil.)	NET PROFIT MARGIN	EMPLOYEES
06/16	355	26	7.5%	3,428
06/15	342	37	10.9%	
06/14	324	38	12.0%	
06/13	313	15	4.8%	
Annual Growth	4.3%	21.1%	—	—

2016 Year-End Financials
Return on assets: 23.5%
Return on equity: 7.5%
Current ratio: 0.50

Cash ($ mil.): 51

GRAND VIEW HOSPITAL

Grand View Health (GVH) formerly Grand View Hospital hopes to give patients a glimpse of great health care. The hospital provide emergency inpatient surgery and specialty services including cardiology orthopedics sleep diagnostic rehabilitation women's and children's care and other medical services to the Bucks County region of Pennsylvania. GVH's oncology program is affiliated with the Fox Chase Cancer Center in Philadelphia. The medical center also operates primary care and outpatient clinics in the region and it provides home health hospice fitness and community outreach programs. The hospital has about 200 beds.

Operations

More than 33000 patients visited the hospital's emergency room in 2014 and GVH had more than 171000 outpatient visits. Its 355 physicians performed 9388 inpatient and about 7000 outpatient surgeries that year.

Geographic Reach

The company has offices in 25 locations. In addition to its main hospital in Sellersville Pennsylvania GVH operates outpatient centers in Sellersville Harleysville and Pennsburg as well as a cancer center in Chalfont and a health center in Quakertown.

Sales and Marketing

The hospital markets its services through print billboard and television campaigns.

Strategy

GVH has grown in recent years by expanding its medical facilities and services

In 2015 the hospital system introduced dropless cataract surgery as a new convenient option for the surgical removal of a cataract.

It also opened a Lung Care Center in Sellersville.

Company Background

In 2010 it opened a new labor and delivery unit and in 2012 it began offering neonatology services through a partnership with the Children's Hospital of Philadelphia.

GVH was founded in 1913.

EXECUTIVES

Medical Director, Dawn Wilkes
Secretary, William S Aichele, age 67

HQ: GRAND VIEW HOSPITAL
700 LAWN AVE, SELLERSVILLE, PA 189601548
Phone: 215 453-4000
Web: WWW.GVHJOBS.ORG

Selected Locations
Grand View Medical Company
Harleysville Outpatient Center
Health Center at Quakertown
High Point Professional Building
Pennsburg Outpatient Center
Physician Suites at Dublin
Sellersville Outpatient Center

PRODUCTS/OPERATIONS

Selected Services and Centers
Acute Rehabilitation Unit
Ambulance/Transport Services
Case Management
Child Immunization Clinic
Children's
Clinical Research
Diabetes Education
Emergency Department
Grand View Information Line
Health Promotion and Wellness
Healthy Beginnings Plus
Home Health Care Services
Industrial Medicine
Laboratory (Blood Work) Services at Grand View
Hospital
Lifestyle Fitness Center
Medical Equipment and Supplies
Men's Health
Nutritional Counseling Services
Pediatric Weight Management (Grand New Youth)
Physical Medicine & Rehabilitation
Pulmonary Rehabilitation
Radiology Services (X-ray) Senior Services
Stoneridge Sleep Center
Sports Medicine
Support Groups & Consultations
Weight Management (Grand New You)
Wound Care Center

COMPETITORS
Abington Memorial Hospital
Children's Hospital of Philadelphia
Doylestown Hospital
LVHN
Main Line Health System
North Philadelphia Health System
St. Luke's University Health Network
Tenet Healthcare
University of Pennsylvania Health System

HISTORICAL FINANCIALS
Company Type: Private

Income Statement
FYE: June 30

	REVENUE ($ mil.)	NET INCOME ($ mil.)	NET PROFIT MARGIN	EMPLOYEES
06/15	189	17	9.1%	1,600
06/14	203	23	11.8%	
06/13	168	31	18.7%	
06/12	169	(26)		
Annual Growth	3.8%	—	—	—

2015 Year-End Financials
Return on assets: 5.0%
Return on equity: 9.1%
Current ratio: 1.10

Cash ($ mil.): 12

GRANITE FALLS ENERGY, LLC

EXECUTIVES

Chief Executive Officer, Steve Christensen
Engineer, Bergen Johnson
Purchasing Agent, Brian Hanson
Manager, Cory Heinrich
Auditors: BOULAY PLLP MINNEAPOLIS MINN

HQ: GRANITE FALLS ENERGY, LLC
15045 HIGHWAY 23 SE, GRANITE FALLS, MN
562411946
Phone: 320 564-3100
Web: WWW.GRANITEFALLSENERGY.COM

HISTORICAL FINANCIALS
Company Type: Private

Income Statement
FYE: October 31

	REVENUE ($ mil.)	NET INCOME ($ mil.)	NET PROFIT MARGIN	EMPLOYEES
10/16	215	11	5.2%	75
10/15	231	16	7.3%	
10/14	300	59	19.6%	
10/13	224	10	4.7%	
Annual Growth	(1.3%)	2.1%	—	—

2016 Year-End Financials
Return on assets: 2.6%
Return on equity: 5.2%
Current ratio: 1.40

Cash ($ mil.): 13

GRANITE SCHOOL DISTRICT

EXECUTIVES

Superintendent, Martin W Bates
Board of Directors, Mary Lynn
Board of Directors, Kathy Goodfellow
Board of Directors, Audrey Price
Board of Directors, Carla Wonder-Mcdowell
Vice-President, Julene M Jolley
Director, James Phillips
Vice-President, Julene Oliver
Auditors: SQUIRE & COMPANY PC OREM UT

HQ: GRANITE SCHOOL DISTRICT
2500 S STATE ST STE 500, SALT LAKE CITY, UT
841153195
Phone: 385 646-5000
Web: WWW.GRANITESCHOOLS.ORG

HISTORICAL FINANCIALS
Company Type: Private

Income Statement
FYE: June 30

	REVENUE ($ mil.)	NET INCOME ($ mil.)	NET PROFIT MARGIN	EMPLOYEES
06/16	561	16	3.0%	8,000
06/09	528	14	2.7%	
06/08	510	18	3.6%	
06/07	0	0	—	
Annual Growth	—	116.6%		

GRAPEVINE/COLLEYVILLE INDEPENDENT SCHOOL DISTRICT

EXECUTIVES

Superintendent, Dr Robin Ryan
Plant & Facilities Manager, Ramon Castanuela
Auditors: HANKINS EASTUP DEATON TONN

LOCATIONS

HQ: GRAPEVINE/COLLEYVILLE INDEPENDENT
  SCHOOL DISTRICT
  3051 IRA E WOODS AVE, GRAPEVINE, TX 760513817
Phone: 817 251-5200
Web: WWW.GCISD-K12.ORG

HISTORICAL FINANCIALS

Company Type: Private

Income Statement

FYE: June 30

	REVENUE ($ mil.)	NET INCOME ($ mil.)	NET PROFIT MARGIN	EMPLOYEES
06/16	192	(11)	—	1,800
06/12	189	84	44.7%	—
06/10	180	(6)	—	—
06/09	0	0	—	—
Annual Growth	—	—	—	—

2016 Year-End Financials

Return on assets: 0.7%   Cash ($ mil.): 148
Return on equity: (-5.8%)
Current ratio: 5.70

GRAVES OIL COMPANY

EXECUTIVES

President, C Fred Graves III
Board of Directors, Kenneth L Hopper
Director, T H Craig
Vice-President, Gary M Stiles
Personnel Manager, Jennifer Boothe
Marketing Director, Joan Johnson
Auditors: J GARY KORNEGAY BATESVILLE

LOCATIONS

HQ: GRAVES OIL COMPANY
  226 PEARSON ST, BATESVILLE, MS 386062428
Phone: 662 563-4604
Web: WWW.CHEVRON.COM

HISTORICAL FINANCIALS

Company Type: Private

Income Statement

FYE: February 29

	REVENUE ($ mil.)	NET INCOME ($ mil.)	NET PROFIT MARGIN	EMPLOYEES
02/16	211	0	0.0%	146
02/15	275	0	0.0%	—
02/14	279	0	0.0%	—
02/13	246	0	0.0%	—
Annual Growth	(5.0%)	40.6%	—	—

2016 Year-End Financials

Return on assets: 2.0%   Cash ($ mil.): —
Return on equity: —
Current ratio: 0.50

GREAT NECK PUBLIC SCHOOLS

EXECUTIVES

Superintendent, Dr Thomas Dolan
Board of Directors, Kathy Koslow
Clerk, Diana O Connolo
Manager, Dominick Capelletti
Assistant Manager, Stephen Lando
Director, Errin Hatwood
Director, Samantha Tarantola

LOCATIONS

HQ: GREAT NECK PUBLIC SCHOOLS
  345 LAKEVILLE RD, GREAT NECK, NY 110201639
Phone: 516 441-4001
Web: WWW.GNTEACHERS.NET

HISTORICAL FINANCIALS

Company Type: Private

Income Statement

FYE: June 30

	REVENUE ($ mil.)	NET INCOME ($ mil.)	NET PROFIT MARGIN	EMPLOYEES
06/16	223	8	3.6%	1,500
06/14	213	1	0.8%	—
/	0	0	—	—
Annual Growth	—	—	—	—

2016 Year-End Financials

Return on assets: 1.6%   Cash ($ mil.): 32
Return on equity: 3.6%
Current ratio: 1.80

GREAT RIVER MEDICAL CENTER

EXECUTIVES

President, Mark Richardson
Executive Secretary, Karen Russell
Director, Chris Oleson
Manager, Steve Leavitt
Manager, Sherry Fitsgibbon
Maintenance Supervisor, Larry Johnson
Vice-President, Tony Hayes

LOCATIONS

HQ: GREAT RIVER MEDICAL CENTER
  1221 S GEAR AVE, WEST BURLINGTON, IA
  526551681
Phone: 319 768-1000
Web: WWW.GREATRIVERMEDICAL.ORG

HISTORICAL FINANCIALS

Company Type: Private

Income Statement

FYE: June 30

	REVENUE ($ mil.)	NET INCOME ($ mil.)	NET PROFIT MARGIN	EMPLOYEES
06/15	170	12	7.3%	1,400
06/13	165	5	3.1%	—
06/11	147	12	8.4%	—
06/10	159	15	9.6%	—
Annual Growth	1.3%	(4.1%)	—	—

2015 Year-End Financials

Return on assets: 2.9%   Cash ($ mil.): 14
Return on equity: 7.3%
Current ratio: 1.60

GREATER BALTIMORE MEDICAL CENTER LAND CORPORATION

EXECUTIVES

President, John Chessare
Auditors: DELOITTE TAX LLP MC LEAN VA

LOCATIONS

HQ: GREATER BALTIMORE MEDICAL CENTER LAND
  CORPORATION
  6701 N CHARLES ST, BALTIMORE, MD 212046881
Phone: 443 849-2000
Web: WWW.GBMC.ORG

HISTORICAL FINANCIALS

Company Type: Private

Income Statement

FYE: June 30

	REVENUE ($ mil.)	NET INCOME ($ mil.)	NET PROFIT MARGIN	EMPLOYEES
06/15	376	22	5.9%	14
06/14	413	28	6.9%	—
06/13	3	(0)	—	—
06/10	2	(0)	—	—
Annual Growth	165.6%	—	—	—

2015 Year-End Financials

Return on assets: 5.4%   Cash ($ mil.): 35
Return on equity: 5.9%
Current ratio: 0.90

GREATER ORLANDO AVIATION AUTHORITY

If your destination is Disney World and you're flying into Orlando you might very well use one of the airports overseen by the Greater Orlando Aviation Authority (GOAA). The agency operates Orlando International Airport which is one of Florida's largest and Orlando Executive Airport a general aviation facility. (Orlando Sanford International Airport is overseen by the Sanford Airport Authority a separate agency.) GOAA is governed by a seven-member board that includes the mayor of Orlando a member of the Orange County Commission and five people appointed by the governor of Florida.

GOAA has a $976 million capital improvement plan for the next handful of years that includes terminal projects airfield projects rental car roadway and parking projects. But a proposed $3 billion south terminal at Orlando International Airport is not likely to be included in upcoming improvement plans. The recession has caused a plunge in travel demand and has caused GOAA

and its fellow airport operators to delay some of its plans. The south terminal which would boost the airport's ability to handle international passengers and US Customs and Border Protection screenings has been discussed and planned for more than 10 years. Another result of the economic downturn is that GOAA trimmed about 80 jobs — or 12% of its workforce — from its ranks in 2009.

EXECUTIVES

Vice Chairman, Stan Anderson
Auditors: MOORE STEPHENS LOVELACE PA

LOCATIONS

HQ: GREATER ORLANDO AVIATION AUTHORITY
  1 JEFF FUQUA BLVD, ORLANDO, FL 328274392
Phone: 407 825-2001
Web: WWW.GOAA.ORG

HISTORICAL FINANCIALS

Company Type: Private

Income Statement

	REVENUE ($ mil.)	NET INCOME ($ mil.)	NET PROFIT MARGIN	EMPLOYEES
12/15*	430	101	23.6%	670
09/15	430	101	23.6%	—
09/14	399	90	22.7%	—
09/13	380	86	22.8%	—
Annual Growth	6.4%	8.2%	—	—

*Fiscal year change

2015 Year-End Financials

Return on assets: 7.0%   Cash ($ mil.): 189
Return on equity: 23.6%
Current ratio: 0.80

GREENLEAF ADVERTISING & MEDIA, INC.

EXECUTIVES

President, Warren C Ivie
Director, Shane Nichols

LOCATIONS

HQ: GREENLEAF ADVERTISING & MEDIA, INC.
  601 SILVERON STE 200, FLOWER MOUND, TX
  750284030
Phone: 972 899-8750
Web: WWW.GREENLEAFMEDIASERVICES.COM

HISTORICAL FINANCIALS

Company Type: Private

Income Statement

	REVENUE ($ mil.)	NET INCOME ($ mil.)	NET PROFIT MARGIN	EMPLOYEES
12/15	200	0	—	12
12/14	169	0	—	—
12/13	114	0	—	—
12/12	90	0	—	—
Annual Growth	30.3%	—	—	—

2015 Year-End Financials

Return on assets: 3.0%   Cash ($ mil.): 21
Return on equity: —
Current ratio: 1.10

GRESCO UTILITY SUPPLY, INC.

EXECUTIVES

Chief Executive Officer, Steve Gramling
Accountant, Kelly Brown
Account Manager, Traci Davis
Account Manager, Melissa Sanders
Account Manager, Adam Mair
Administrative Assistant, Beth Murdock
Manager, Chad Capps
Auditors: MCNAIR MCLEMORE MIDDLEBROOKS

LOCATIONS

HQ: GRESCO UTILITY SUPPLY, INC.
  1135 RUMBLE RD, FORSYTH, GA 310296350
Phone: 478 315-0800
Web: WWW.GRESCO.COM

HISTORICAL FINANCIALS

Company Type: Private

Income Statement

	REVENUE ($ mil.)	NET INCOME ($ mil.)	NET PROFIT MARGIN	EMPLOYEES
04/16	194	7	3.6%	130
04/15	179	6	3.4%	—
04/14	161	5	3.1%	—
04/13	150	3	2.3%	—
Annual Growth	9.0%	26.5%	—	—

2016 Year-End Financials

Return on assets: 7.0%   Cash ($ mil.): 15
Return on equity: 3.6%
Current ratio: 1.70

GROSSMONT HOSPITAL CORPORATION

Residents of the eastern San Diego community of La Mesa California depend on Grossmont for medical care. Grossmont Hospital is a 540-bed not-for-profit health care facility. The hospital which opened in 1955 has a staff of about 700 physicians. The full-service acute care facility provides specialty services in the areas of cardiology oncology mental health orthopedics pediatrics physical therapy sleep therapy hospice and women's health care. The Grossmont Hospital Corporation is a subsidiary of Sharp HealthCare; it operates the Grossmont Hospital through a lease agreement with state-owned Grossmont Hospital District.

Strategy

Grossmont Hospital is undergoing expansion and improvement efforts. Current projects include renovation efforts (including energy and utility upgrades) on the existing hospital and the construction of new hospital wings and buildings on the surrounding grounds. In 2012 the company began work on a new $60 million heart and vascular center that will include diagnostic laboratory and surgery space.

An earlier $80 million stage of the hospital's expansion project was completed in 2009 and included construction of a five-story critical care and emergency center tower (adding 90 beds) as well as other renovations and utility upgrades. The improvement efforts are funded by public general obligation bonds approved in 2006 and overseen by a citizens' board and the Grossmont Hospital District which will fund a total of up to $247 million in construction efforts by 2016.

Company Background

The property and buildings of Grossmont Hospital are owned by the Grossmont Hospital District which was formed in 1952. The Grossmont Hospital Corporation was created in 1991 as a subsidiary of Sharp HealthCare exclusively to run a 30-year lease (expiring in 2021) of state-owned Grossmont Hospital District.

EXECUTIVES

Chief Executive Officer, Dan Gross
Operations Manager, Suzie Warner
Manager, Brent Bozeman
Director, Daniel Kindron
Manager, Joy Fetherlin
Manager, Matthew Turner
Supervisor, Koye Durmick

LOCATIONS

HQ: GROSSMONT HOSPITAL CORPORATION
  5555 GROSSMONT CENTER DR, LA MESA, CA
  919423077
Phone: 619 740-6000
Web: WWW.GEMG.NET

COMPETITORS

Adventist Health System West	Rady Children's Hospital
Eisenhower Medical Center	Scripps Health
Palomar Health	Tenet Healthcare
Paradise Valley Hospital	Tri-City Healthcare District

HISTORICAL FINANCIALS

Company Type: Private

Income Statement

	REVENUE ($ mil.)	NET INCOME ($ mil.)	NET PROFIT MARGIN	EMPLOYEES
09/15	712	51	7.2%	2,697
09/14	596	45	7.6%	—
09/13	621	69	11.1%	—
09/09	500	41	8.3%	—
Annual Growth	6.1%	3.6%	—	—

2015 Year-End Financials

Return on assets: 3.1%   Cash ($ mil.): 40
Return on equity: 7.2%
Current ratio: 1.50

GROWMARK, INC.

Retail farm-supply and grain-marketing cooperative GROWMARK can mark its growth by the grain. A member-owed agricultural co-op GROWMARK has more than 100000 members. Under the FAST STOP name the co-op runs more than 250 fuel stations and convenience stores in the Midwest. Its Seedway subsidiary sells commercial vegetable seed and farm seed for turf and grains including alfalfa corn wheat and soybeans. GROWMARK also offers fertilizer seeds ethanol biodiesel and farm financing. Its MID-CO COMMODITIES subsidiary trades grain and offers advice regarding futures and options.

Geographic Reach

GROWMARK is headquartered in Bloomington Illinois and serves customers in more than 40

states and Ontario Canada. SEEDWAY maintains eight office and warehouse locations in Vermont New York Pennsylvania and Florida.

Strategy

Cooperation is important within and among agricultural cooperatives. A strong believer in the latter part of this principle GROWMARK has marketing agreements and alliances with among others fertilizer maker and distributor CF Industries pet-food producer PRO-PET agribusiness company Syngenta and rural financial services provider CoBank.

Mergers and Acquisitions

GROWMARK acquires fertilizer storage terminals and transportation infrastructure on a regular basis.

EXECUTIVES

Vice Chairman, John Reifsteck
CEO, Jeff Solberg
Vice President General Counsel, Brent Bostrom
VP Eastern Retail Operations, Steve Buckalew
VP and CFO, Marshall Bohbrink
VP Energy, Kevin Carroll
VP Midwest Retail and Acquisitions, Shelly Kruse
VP Grain, Brent Ericson
Vice President Human Resources & Compliance, Gary Swango
VP Agronomy, Mark Orr
VP Financial and Risk Management, Mike Woods
VP Member Services, Denny Worth
Vice President Information TEC, George Key
Vice President Information TEC, George Mueller
Vice President, Ron Milby
Region Vice President, Barry Schmidt
Vice President, Richard Fiedler
Senior Vice President, Dennis Farmer
Vice President, Tom Dowell
Senior Vice President, Jeffrey M Solberg
Vice Chairman, Rick Nelson
Vice Chairman, Chet Esther
Assistant Treasurer, John Fruin
Auditors: ERNST & YOUNG LLP CHICAGO I

LOCATIONS

HQ: GROWMARK, INC.
1701 TOWANDA AVE, BLOOMINGTON, IL 617012057
Phone: 309 557-6000
Web: WWW.GROWMARK.COM

PRODUCTS/OPERATIONS

Selected Retail Products and Operations
COMFORT PRO (propane heating oil)
FAST STOP (fuel facilities)
FS (farm supplies)
Green Yard (turf seed fertilizer)
Seedway (farm turf and vegetable seed)

Selected Member Cooperatives and Subsidiaries
AgVantage FS Inc.
AgView Grain LLC
Evergreen FS Inc.
GROWMARK FS LLC
MID-CO COMMODITIES
Northern Grain Marketing LLC
Seedway LLC
Total Grain Marketing LLC
Western Grain Marketing LLC

COMPETITORS

ADM	Marathon Oil
AGRI Industries	NC Hybrids
Ag Processing Inc.	Orscheln Farm and Home
BP	Pfister Hybrid Corn
Barkley Seed	Pioneer Hi-Bred
Bayer CropScience	Rabo AgriFinance
CHS	Sakata Seed
Cargill	Seed Enterprises
Chevron	Southern States
Costco Wholesale	Terra Nitrogen
DeBruce Grain	Wal-Mart
Exxon Mobil	Wilbur-Ellis

HISTORICAL FINANCIALS
Company Type: Private

Income Statement
FYE: August 31

	REVENUE ($ mil.)	NET INCOME ($ mil.)	NET PROFIT MARGIN	EMPLOYEES
08/16	7,031	101	1.4%	1,036
08/15	8,727	113	1.3%	—
08/14	10,372	166	1.6%	—
08/13	10,171	189	1.9%	—
Annual Growth	(11.6%)	(18.8%)	—	—

2016 Year-End Financials
Return on assets: 4.8%
Return on equity: 1.4%
Current ratio: 1.20
Cash ($ mil.): 143

GRUNLEY CONSTRUCTION CO., INC.

Grunley gets it done from the monumental to the mundane. Founded in 1955 Grunley Construction Company provides general contracting engineering architectural and construction management services and specializes in the renovation restoration and modernization of historic buildings in the Washington DC area. Its projects range from prestigious undertakings — the Smithsonian Institutionthe Washington Monument and the US Treasury building — to more pedestrian endeavors such as office buildings apartment buildings schools and power plants. The company also has lent its services to the construction of embassies airports and military facilities.

EXECUTIVES

President, Kenneth M Grunley
Board of Directors, Virginia Grunley
Financial Executive, David Delgado
President, Gregory M Druga
Project Manager, Pat Emery

LOCATIONS

HQ: GRUNLEY CONSTRUCTION CO., INC.
15020 SHADY GROVE RD # 500, ROCKVILLE, MD 208503390
Phone: 240 399-2000
Web: WWW.GRUNLEY.COM

COMPETITORS

Hega Construction Company	Parsons Transportation
	S. W. Rodgers

HISTORICAL FINANCIALS
Company Type: Private

Income Statement
FYE: December 31

	REVENUE ($ mil.)	NET INCOME ($ mil.)	NET PROFIT MARGIN	EMPLOYEES
12/15	403	0	—	310
12/11	323	0	—	—
12/10	310	0	—	—
12/09	1,129	0	0.0%	—
Annual Growth	(15.8%)	—	—	—

2015 Year-End Financials
Return on assets: 5.6%
Return on equity: —
Current ratio: 1.00
Cash ($ mil.): 22

GRUPO ANTOLIN KENTUCKY, INC.

EXECUTIVES

Chairman, Ernesto Antoln Arribas
Chief Executive Officer, Jess Pascual Santos
Secretary, Pablo Ruiz
Accountant, Myra Cornelius
Chief Operating Officer, Eric Rucker
Manager, Miguel Marcos
Manager, Thomas Bickhoff
Personnel Manager, Shelly Hickock
Plant Engineering Manager, Terry Brandl
Auditors: UHY LLP FARMINGTON HILLS MIC

LOCATIONS

HQ: GRUPO ANTOLIN KENTUCKY, INC.
208 COMMERCE CT, HOPKINSVILLE, KY 422406806
Phone: 270 885-2703

HISTORICAL FINANCIALS
Company Type: Private

Income Statement
FYE: December 31

	REVENUE ($ mil.)	NET INCOME ($ mil.)	NET PROFIT MARGIN	EMPLOYEES
12/15	222	19	8.6%	502
12/06	96	4	4.9%	—
12/05	98	4	4.3%	—
12/04	108	5	5.2%	—
Annual Growth	6.7%	11.8%	—	—

2015 Year-End Financials
Return on assets: 11.8%
Return on equity: 8.6%
Current ratio: 0.90
Cash ($ mil.): 5

GUEST SERVICES, INC.

Guest Services satisfies hungry and sleepy patrons. The company provides contract food services and hospitality-management services nationwide. It operates cafeterias and onsite restaurants and offers catering to businesses hotels hospitals conference centers and government operations including the US Supreme Court the US House of Representatives and the National Park Service. For leisure and resort facilities Guest Services also provides special-event catering and offers management services such as marketing human resources procurement quality-assurance and information technology services. Guest Services was founded in 1917 as a private company to serve governmental agencies.

Operations

Guest Services serves some 250 facilities across the US and more than 25 million guests each year. The company also owns Lancaster Foods one of the largest wholesale produce companies in the mid-Atlantic region.

Additional offerings include corporate accounting systems and food safety and health support.

Geographic Reach

Based in Fairfax Virginia Guest Services serves a variety of customers nationwide.

Sales and Marketing

Guest Services serves several clients including government and business dining facilities museums hotels resorts conference centers luxury condominiums senior living centers health care systems state and national park recreation school and university dining facilities specialty retail stores and full-service restaurants.

Customers have included Washington DC's National Mall and Memorial Park. Guest Services also manages food lodging and recreation services at state parks in West Virginia New York and California.

Strategy

Guest Services has been expanding its portfolio of premium properties. For example it owns and manages the DoubleTree Suites by Hilton Naples. In 2013 Guest Services acquired The Lodge and Spa at Breckenridge which overlooks Colorado's Breckenridge Village. With 45 rooms the property is a popular destination for weddings and corporate events. It's adding food and beverage service in-house catering and event planning to the property's services.

EXECUTIVES

CEO, Gerard T. Gabrys
President and COO, Jeffrey A. Marquis
President Lancaster Foods, John Gates
VP Hotel Division South, Barry G. Trice
VP Sales and Marketing, Jerry Chadwick
VP and CFO, Nico Foris
Assistant Vice President of Operations Division, Rick Wayland
Auditors: PRICEWATERHOUSECOOPERS LLP M

LOCATIONS

HQ: GUEST SERVICES, INC.
3055 PROSPERITY AVE, FAIRFAX, VA 220312290
Phone: 703 849-9300
Web: WWW.GUESTSERVICES.COM

PRODUCTS/OPERATIONS

Selected Services
Audits
Corporate Support Services
Financial Accounting Systems
Food Safety and Health
Human Resources
IT
Maintenance Support
Management Information Systems
Marketing
Onsite Test Kitchen
PeopleSoft Processing
Procurement
Quality Assurance
Safety
Security
Test Kitchen
Training

COMPETITORS

ARAMARK	Delaware North
Centerplate	Sodexo USA
Compass Group USA	Valley Services

HISTORICAL FINANCIALS

Company Type: Private

Income Statement

FYE: December 31

	REVENUE ($ mil.)	NET INCOME ($ mil.)	NET PROFIT MARGIN	EMPLOYEES
12/15	396	3	0.9%	99
12/14	375	0	0.3%	—
12/13	387	2	0.6%	—
12/12	377	2	0.7%	—
Annual Growth	1.7%	11.0%	—	—

2015 Year-End Financials

Return on assets: 3.3%   Cash ($ mil.): 7
Return on equity: 0.9%
Current ratio: 1.10

GULF COAST MEDICAL CENTRE LTD

EXECUTIVES

Principal, Jeffrey R Green

LOCATIONS

HQ: GULF COAST MEDICAL CENTRE LTD
13691 METRO PKWY STE 110, FORT MYERS, FL 339124348
Phone: 239 343-1000
Web: WWW.LEEMEMORIAL.ORG

HISTORICAL FINANCIALS

Company Type: Private

Income Statement

FYE: September 30

	REVENUE ($ mil.)	NET INCOME ($ mil.)	NET PROFIT MARGIN	EMPLOYEES
09/15	318	21	6.8%	268
09/13	284	13	4.6%	—
09/12	279	52	18.8%	—
Annual Growth	4.5%	(25.7%)	—	—

GUNDERSEN LUTHERAN MEDICAL CENTER, INC.

At the heart of the Gundersen Lutheran health system Gundersen Lutheran Medical Center serves residents of nearly 20 counties that stretch across the upper Midwest. The clinical campus for the University of Wisconsin's medical and nursing schools operates a 325-bed teaching hospital with a Level II Trauma and Emergency Center. Focused on caring for patients in western Wisconsin the hospital boasts several specialty services such as bariatrics behavioral health cancer care orthopedics palliative care pediatrics rehabilitation and women's health. The physician-led not-for-profit medical center is affiliated with a group of regional clinics and specialty centers.

Operations

Gundersen Lutheran Medical Center has a staff of some 800 doctors dentists and other profes-

sionals. As part of Gundersen Lutheran (also known as Gundersen Health System) the hospital's sister entities include the Gundersen Clinic and the Gundersen Lutheran Administrative Services entity.

In 2013 the Gundersen Health System reported 1437 births 17000 surgeries and 278000 outpatient hospital visits.

Geographic Reach

From its main campus in La Crosse Wisconsin as well as a satellite outpatient center in Onalaska the hospital serves communities located in 19 counties throughout western Wisconsin northeastern Iowa and southeastern Minnesota.

Strategy

The Gundersen Lutheran organization expands though partnerships such as an alliance with the Allen Hospital in Iowa to enhance regional cardiovascular services in 2013. The medical center is also working to upgrade its infrastructure to enable 100% energy independence in 2014.

To offer advanced training to residents and physicians Gundersen Lutheran Medical Center developed and opened a high-tech training center in 2012. The Cleary Kumm Simulation and Training Labs offer mock operating rooms and simulation labs for use by local doctors and nationwide medical professionals for training or conferences. Gundersen Lutheran Medical Center is banking on the simulation and training facility to draw interest talent and outside funds.

Company Background

Gundersen Lutheran Medical Center was founded in 1995 through the merger of Gunderson Clinic and Lutheran Hospital-La Crosse. The Lutheran Hospital opened in 1902.

EXECUTIVES

Vice President, Michael Dolan
Medical Director, Jackie Yaeger
Auditors: KPMG LLP MINNEAPOLIS MN

LOCATIONS

HQ: GUNDERSEN LUTHERAN MEDICAL CENTER, INC.
1900 SOUTH AVE, LA CROSSE, WI 546015467
Phone: 608 782-7300
Web: WWW.GUNDERSENHEALTH.ORG

PRODUCTS/OPERATIONS

Selected Services
Advance care planning
Apnea
Autism Spectrum Disorder
BioBank
Brain disorders
Cardiac services
Children's health
Cleft Lip & Palate Clinic
Endocrinology
Hospice
Eye care
Gynecology
Hand surgery
Heart Institute
LASIK eye surgery
Massage
Neck surgery
Neurosciences
Oral and maxillofacial surgery
Pediatrics
Radiation oncology
Rehabilitation
Urgent care
Urology
Weight management
Wound care

COMPETITORS

Dean Health Systems Inc.
Franciscan Skemp Healthcare
Luther Midelfort

Mayo Clinic
Meriter Health Services
Ministry Health Care
Olmsted Medical
Sacred Heart Hospital
Tomah Memorial Hospital
University of Wisconsin Hospital and Clinics

HISTORICAL FINANCIALS
Company Type: Private

Income Statement
FYE: December 31

	REVENUE ($ mil.)	NET INCOME ($ mil.)	NET PROFIT MARGIN	EMPLOYEES
12/15	980	60	6.1%	4,500
12/14	894	94	10.6%	—
12/11	431	49	11.5%	—
Annual Growth	22.8%	4.9%	—	—

2015 Year-End Financials
Return on assets: 2.3%
Return on equity: 6.1%
Current ratio: 1.50
Cash ($ mil.): 162

GUTHRIE MEDICAL GROUP, P.C.

EXECUTIVES

President, Joseph A Scopelliti
Administrative Assistant, Carol Antes
Manager, Laura Van Ness
Director, McDonald Thomas
Auditors: LB PRICEWATERHOUSECOOPERS LLP

LOCATIONS

HQ: GUTHRIE MEDICAL GROUP, P.C.
1 GUTHRIE SQ STE B, SAYRE, PA 188401625
Phone: 570 888-5858

HISTORICAL FINANCIALS
Company Type: Private

Income Statement
FYE: June 30

	REVENUE ($ mil.)	NET INCOME ($ mil.)	NET PROFIT MARGIN	EMPLOYEES
06/15	228	(37)	—	4,500
06/14	228	(34)	—	—
06/10	210	(19)	—	—
06/08	191	(20)	—	—
Annual Growth	2.6%	—	—	—

2015 Year-End Financials
Return on assets: 15.7%
Return on equity: (-16.3%)
Current ratio: 0.70
Cash ($ mil.): 6

GWINNETT COUNTY BOARD OF EDUCATION

EXECUTIVES

Chairman of the Board, Robert McClure
Director, Steve Bennett

LOCATIONS

HQ: GWINNETT COUNTY BOARD OF EDUCATION
437 OLD PEACHTREE RD NW, SUWANEE, GA
300242978
Phone: 678 301-6000
Web: WWW.GCPS-FOUNDATION.ORG

HISTORICAL FINANCIALS
Company Type: Private

Income Statement
FYE: June 30

	REVENUE ($ mil.)	NET INCOME ($ mil.)	NET PROFIT MARGIN	EMPLOYEES
06/16*	1,791	349	19.5%	168
07/10	0	0	11.5%	—
08/09	0	0	18.4%	—
Annual Growth	313.3%	316.8%	—	—

*Fiscal year change

2016 Year-End Financials
Return on assets: 1.5%
Return on equity: 19.5%
Current ratio: 0.30
Cash ($ mil.): 106

GWINNETT HOSPITAL SYSTEM, INC.

EXECUTIVES

Chief Executive Officer, Philip R Wolfe
Board of Directors, Gayle Delucia

LOCATIONS

HQ: GWINNETT HOSPITAL SYSTEM, INC.
1000 MEDICAL CENTER BLVD, LAWRENCEVILLE,
GA 300467694
Phone: 678 343-3428

HISTORICAL FINANCIALS
Company Type: Private

Income Statement
FYE: June 30

	REVENUE ($ mil.)	NET INCOME ($ mil.)	NET PROFIT MARGIN	EMPLOYEES
06/15	698	15	2.2%	2,050
06/14	642	34	5.4%	—
06/13	587	53	9.2%	—
06/11	592	56	9.5%	—
Annual Growth	4.2%	(27.8%)	—	—

2015 Year-End Financials
Return on assets: 5.1%
Return on equity: 2.2%
Current ratio: 1.10
Cash ($ mil.): 66

H. LEE MOFFITT CANCER CENTER & RESEARCH INSTITUTE HOSPITAL, INC.

The H. Lee Moffitt Cancer Center and Research Institute founded in 1986 is a National Cancer Institute-designated Comprehensive Cancer Center located on the Tampa campus of the University of South Florida. The institute carries it out its stated mission of "contributing to the prevention and cure of cancer" through patient care research and education. It operates a 210-bed medical and surgical facility as well as outpatient treatment programs and a blood and marrow transplant program. Its research programs include study in the areas of molecular oncology immunology risk assessment health outcomes and experimental therapeutics.

Operations

The Moffitt Cancer Center sees more than 9000 cancer inpatients each year; it also handles some 328000 outpatient visits annually. In addition to its 40-bed blood and marrow transplant center which performs 400 annual transplants the hospital includes more than a dozen operating rooms and extensive diagnostic radiology and radiation therapy labs. The Cancer Screening and Prevention Center offers genetic testing for certain kinds of hereditary cancers (breast ovarian colon and melanoma).

The Moffitt Research Institute conducts a wide range of cancer studies and some of its drug discovery research programs are managed through partnerships with pharmaceutical companies and other research laboratories. The research institute also relies on funding grants from organizations such as the National Institutes of Health. It has received more than $80 million in grant funding and participated in some 300 clinical trials.

The Moffitt Cancer Center likewise has educational and health care alliances with a number of Florida hospitals and colleges including a three-way cancer care and research partnership with Shands HealthCare and the University of Florida. Through its affiliated network program (the Moffitt Oncology Network) Moffitt works with community doctors and centers across Florida to provide enhanced cancer services throughout the state. It also operates a number of outpatient clinics in surrounding areas.

Geographic Reach

Through its main campus and numerous outpatient sites Moffitt Cancer Center primarily serves residents of seven Florida counties: Hernando Hillsborough Manatee Pasco Pinellas Polk and Sarasota. It also serves patients from other areas of Florida and neighboring states.

Sales and Marketing

HMO and PPO plans account for about 65% of patient service revenues while reimbursements from Medicare and Medicaid plans account for another 32% of sales.

Financial Performance

Revenue at Moffitt Cancer Center and Research Institute increased 1% to $779 million in 2013 from $772 the previous year due to higher patient service revenues. After a net loss in 2012 the institute reported net income of $26 million due to an increase in net assets and non-operating gains. Cash from operations also grew by $77 million

due to the net income increase and cash generated from an estimated third-party settlement.

Strategy

Moffitt Cancer Center conducts expansion and facility improvement projects to enhance services for its cancer patients. For instance it launched construction of a new $74 million outpatient facility at the current McKinley office site in 2013; the location is near the main campus and will provide surgery infusion imaging research and other services. It also formed a partnership with Space Coast Cancer Center Boca Raton Regional Hospital Advinus Therapeutics and Lehigh Valley Health Network to improve cancer care for all the organizations.

EXECUTIVES

Chief Executive Officer, Alan F List
Executive Vice-President, Nick Potter
Director, George W Tinsley
Account Manager, Susanne Pyle
Director, James J Mul
Administrative Assistant, Agnes Manka
Auditors: ERNST & YOUNG LLP

LOCATIONS

HQ: H. LEE MOFFITT CANCER CENTER & RESEARCH INSTITUTE HOSPITAL, INC.
12902 USF MAGNOLIA DR, TAMPA, FL 336129416
Phone: 813 745-4673
Web: WWW.ASBESTOSLIFELINE.COM

PRODUCTS/OPERATIONS

Selected Services
Chemotherapy
Diagnosis
Emotional Support
Integrative Medicine
Labwork Scans and Biopsy
Other Patient Services
Pain Management
Radiation
Screening and Genetics
Spiritual Support
Surgical Care
Well-Being

Selected Research Fields
Basic Science Division
    Cancer Imaging and Metabolism
    Drug Discovery
    Immunology
    Integrated Mathematical Oncology
    Molecular Oncology
    Tumor Biology
Population Science Division
    Biostatistics and Bioinformatics
    Cancer Epidemiology
    Health Outcomes & Behavior

COMPETITORS

All Children's Hospital	Mayo Clinic Jacksonville
Baptist Hospital of Miami	Memorial Sloan-Kettering
Bay Medical Center	Oak Hill Hospital
Boca Raton Regional Hospital	Roswell Park Cancer Institute
Dana-Farber	Sacred Heart Health System
Fox Chase Cancer Center	South Georgia Medical Center
Jackson County Hospital of Florida	St. Vincent's Health System
MD Anderson Cancer Center	
Manatee Memorial Hospital	

HISTORICAL FINANCIALS
Company Type: Private

Income Statement
FYE: June 30

	REVENUE ($ mil.)	NET INCOME ($ mil.)	NET PROFIT MARGIN	EMPLOYEES
06/15	951	61	6.5%	4,200
06/14	855	50	5.9%	—
06/13	779	26	3.4%	—
06/12	771	(7)	—	—
Annual Growth	7.2%	—	—	—

2015 Year-End Financials
Return on assets: 7.0%
Return on equity: 6.5%
Current ratio: 1.50
Cash ($ mil.): 129

HACIENDA-LA PUENTE UNIFIED SCHOOL DISTRICT

EXECUTIVES

Superintendent, Norman Kirschenbaum
Administrative Assistant, Erika Terrazas
Director, Kathy Mead
Auditors: NIGRO & NIGRO PC MURRIETA CA

LOCATIONS

HQ: HACIENDA-LA PUENTE UNIFIED SCHOOL DISTRICT
15959 GALE AVE, CITY OF INDUSTRY, CA 917451604
Phone: 626 933-1000
Web: WWW.HLPUSDJOBS.ORG

HISTORICAL FINANCIALS
Company Type: Private

Income Statement
FYE: June 30

	REVENUE ($ mil.)	NET INCOME ($ mil.)	NET PROFIT MARGIN	EMPLOYEES
06/16	308	3	1.3%	2,500
06/05	0	0	14.7%	—
06/01	219	20	9.3%	—
06/00	181	(1)	—	—
Annual Growth	3.4%	—	—	—

2016 Year-End Financials
Return on assets: 19.1%
Return on equity: 1.3%
Current ratio: —
Cash ($ mil.): 238

HACKENSACK UNIVERSITY MEDICAL CENTER

Hackensack University Medical Center (HUMC) is an acute care teaching and research hospital that serves northern New Jersey and parts of New York. The hospital has about 775 beds and staffs more than 2200 medical professionals. HUMC administers general medical surgical emergency and diagnostic care. The center also includes specialized treatment centers including a children's hospital a women's hospital a cancer center and a heart and vascular hospital. HUMC is part of the Hackensack University Health Network which also includes a physician practice group and a joint venture that operates two community hospitals. In 2016 the network merged with Meridian Health to create Hackensack Meridian Health.

Operations

HUMC helps train future dentists and doctors through its affiliation with the University of Medicine and Dentistry of New Jersey. It expanded its education programs in 2012 by partnering with the Stevens Institute of Technology to offer joint biomedical training programs.

The hospital also performs research through the David Joseph Jurist Research Center for Tomorrow's Children. The center has roughly 475 research programs in operation at any given time.

Financial Performance

Medicare accounts for 29.5% of HUMC's funding; HMOs 28%; and Blue Cross 28%.

Strategy

The company grows organically and through acquisitions partnerships and affiliations.

To expand its services HUMC broke ground on a $35 million project to expand and renovate its trauma and emergency facilities in 2012 (scheduled to open in 2015).

Hackensack University Health Network is increasing its partnerships and affiliations with other regional care providers following the trend of US hospitals seeking to improve and lower the cost of health care through shared services and resources. The network partnered up with Texas-based LPH Hospital Group in 2012 to renovate the Pascack Valley Hospital (now HackensackUMC Pascack) in Westwood New Jersey. Hackensack took over the bankrupt facility's ER back in 2007 and in 2012 the joint venture launched a $90 million project to revamp the rest of the 130-bed acute-care community hospital. It reopened in 2013.

Hackensack University Health Network also formed a joint venture with an area physician group to open two ambulatory surgery centers in 2012 and it entered a collaboration with CVS Health's MinuteClinic to open new urgent care centers.

That year HUMC formed a joint venture partnership with community physicians and United Surgical Partners International to buy and operate ambulatory surgery centers in Bergen County: Hackensack Endoscopy Center and the Endoscopy Center of Bergen County.

Mergers and Acquisitions

In 2015 the Hackensack University Health Network agreed to merge with fellow New Jersey care provider Meridian Health. The combined system to be named Hackensack Meridian Health will have 11 hospitals and two children's hospitals. The deal which is one of a number of consolidation efforts by hospitals in the state is pending regulatory approval.

Company Background

To simplify its operations HUMC sold its hospice operations to Amedisys in 2011. The health provider previously sold its home health agency to Amedisys in 2009 to generate revenue and control costs after struggling with financial losses throughout the year due to declining admissions.

HUMC completed construction of its new John Theurer Cancer Center in late 2010 giving it one of the largest comprehensive cancer centers in the US. The center includes diagnostic and treatment units that focus on specific types of cancers.

HUMC was founded as a hospital in 1888 with 12 beds.

EXECUTIVES

Senior Vice President Human Resources and Service Quality, Nancy Corcoran
Chairman Department of Ophthamology, Michael Rosenberg
Executive Vice President And Chief Financial Officer, Robert L Glenning
Vice President Patient Financial Services, Anne Pritcheta
Vice President Patient Financial Services, Anne Pritchett
Vice President Information Services, Roderick Clemente

LOCATIONS

HQ: HACKENSACK UNIVERSITY MEDICAL CENTER
30 PROSPECT AVE STE 1, HACKENSACK, NJ
076011915
Phone: 201 996-2000
Web: WWW.HACKENSACKUMC.ORG

PRODUCTS/OPERATIONS

Selected Services
Donna A. Sanzari Women's Hospital
Emergency Services
Heart & Vascular Hospital
Hospital Services
John Theurer Cancer Center
Joseph M. Sanzari Children's Hospital
Medical
Specialized
Surgical
Tackle Kids Cancer

Selected Facilities
Donna A. Sanzari Women's Hospital
Hackensack University Medical Center Mountainside
Hackensack University Medical Center Pascack
Heart & Vascular Hospital
John Theurer Cancer Center
Joseph M. Sanzari Children's Hospital
Tomorrows Children's Institute for Cancer and Blood Disorders

COMPETITORS

Bergen Regional Medical
Bronx-Lebanon Hospital
Continuum Health Partners
Englewood Hospital and Medical Center
Hospital for Special Surgery
Lenox Hill Hospital
Montefiore Medical
NewYork-Presbyterian Healthcare
Newark Beth Israel Medical Center
St. Joseph's Healthcare System
Valley Health System

HISTORICAL FINANCIALS
Company Type: Private

Income Statement
FYE: December 31

	REVENUE ($ mil.)	NET INCOME ($ mil.)	NET PROFIT MARGIN	EMPLOYEES
12/15	1,357	83	6.1%	1,100
12/14	1,309	106	8.1%	—
12/08	1,037	(86)	—	—
12/07	1,183	48	4.1%	—
Annual Growth	1.7%	7.0%	—	—

2015 Year-End Financials
Return on assets: 9.0%   Cash ($ mil.): 155
Return on equity: 6.1%
Current ratio: 0.80

HALO, LLC

EXECUTIVES

Chief Executive Officer, William A Bastian II
Account Manager, Lisa Rohe
Chief Financial Officer, John Smith
Auditors: KATZ SAPPER & MILLER

LOCATIONS

HQ: HALO, LLC
10585 N MERIDIAN ST FL 3, INDIANAPOLIS, IN
462901069
Phone: 317 575-9992

HISTORICAL FINANCIALS
Company Type: Private

Income Statement
FYE: December 31

	REVENUE ($ mil.)	NET INCOME ($ mil.)	NET PROFIT MARGIN	EMPLOYEES
12/15	194	13	7.0%	450
12/13	123	2	1.8%	—
12/12	142	5	3.9%	—
12/11	893	0	0.0%	—
Annual Growth	(31.7%)	437.0%	—	—

2015 Year-End Financials
Return on assets: 5.0%   Cash ($ mil.): 17
Return on equity: 7.0%
Current ratio: 0.80

HAMILTON TOWNSHIP SCHOOL DISTRICT

EXECUTIVES

Superintendent, Michelle M Cappelluti
Director, Lisa Dagit
Superintendent, Frank Vogel
Purchasing Director, Anne Marie Fala
Auditors: HODULIK & MORRISON PA CPAS

LOCATIONS

HQ: HAMILTON TOWNSHIP SCHOOL DISTRICT
1876 DR DENNIS FOREMAN DR, MAYS LANDING, NJ
083302206
Phone: 609 476-6300
Web: WWW.HAMILTONSCHOOLS.ORG

HISTORICAL FINANCIALS
Company Type: Private

Income Statement
FYE: June 30

	REVENUE ($ mil.)	NET INCOME ($ mil.)	NET PROFIT MARGIN	EMPLOYEES
06/16	211	(9)	—	500
06/07	180	2	1.5%	—
06/06*	27	1	3.8%	—
08/05	62	0	—	—
Annual Growth	11.8%	—	—	—

*Fiscal year change

2016 Year-End Financials
Return on assets: 3.7%   Cash ($ mil.): 25
Return on equity: (-4.5%)
Current ratio: —

HAMPTON ROADS SANITATION DISTRICT (INC)

EXECUTIVES

Director, Jay Bernas
Accountant, Richard Wood
Director, Norman Lebla
Manager, Jennifer See
Administrative Assistant, Tracy Harris
Manager, Greg Hill
Auditors: KPMG LLP

LOCATIONS

HQ: HAMPTON ROADS SANITATION DISTRICT (INC)
1434 AIR RAIL AVE, VIRGINIA BEACH, VA 234553002
Phone: 757 318-4335
Web: WWW.HRSD.COM

HISTORICAL FINANCIALS
Company Type: Private

Income Statement
FYE: June 30

	REVENUE ($ mil.)	NET INCOME ($ mil.)	NET PROFIT MARGIN	EMPLOYEES
06/16	237	44	18.8%	700
06/15	225	37	16.8%	—
06/13	0	0	4.4%	—
06/12	197	19	9.7%	—
Annual Growth	4.7%	23.6%	—	—

2016 Year-End Financials
Return on assets: 13.8%   Cash ($ mil.): 68
Return on equity: 18.8%
Current ratio: 0.70

HARBOR DEVELOPMENTAL DISABILITIES FOUNDATION INC

EXECUTIVES

Chief Financial Officer, Judy Wada
Financial Executive, Kevin Herink
Manager, Bonnie Ivers
Program Manager, Liz Cohen-Zeboulon
Auditors: WINDES INC LONG BEACH CA

LOCATIONS

HQ: HARBOR DEVELOPMENTAL DISABILITIES FOUNDATION INC
21231 HAWTHORNE BLVD, TORRANCE, CA
905035501
Phone: 310 540-1711
Web: WWW.HARBORRC.ORG

HISTORICAL FINANCIALS

Company Type: Private

Income Statement

FYE: June 30

	REVENUE ($ mil.)	NET INCOME ($ mil.)	NET PROFIT MARGIN	EMPLOYEES
06/16	173	0	0.0%	225
06/15	162	0	0.0%	—
06/14	152	0	0.0%	—
06/13	142	(0)		
Annual Growth	6.8%	—	—	—

2016 Year-End Financials

Return on assets: 8.7%
Return on equity: —
Current ratio: 0.60

Cash ($ mil.): 18

HARLAND M. BRAUN & CO., INC.

Hide (the raw material) and seek (find a buyer) are all in a day's work for Harland M. Braun & Co. Operating through its subsidiary Braun Export the company supplies raw hide goods primarily cattle hides and skins and to a lesser extent pigskin and kipskins to tanners. A slate of services is provided for leather (wet blue and crust) hide and skin manufacturing as well as brokering exporting and importing. Dotting the US Braun & Co.'s processing facilities tie in with several suppliers of Holstein steer hides. Its partners include such meat packers as JBS Packerland Group Central Valley Meat Manning Beef Nebraska Beef and American Beef Packers. The company was founded in 1957.

Established more than 45 years ago Harland M. Braun is a frequent recipient of the "Good Corporate Citizens" award given by the Sanitation Districts of Los Angeles County. The "Atta Boy!" recognizes businesses that meet the County's environmental wastewater discharge requirements.

EXECUTIVES

President, Mike Hamilton
Auditors: BRIAN JUNG

LOCATIONS

HQ: HARLAND M. BRAUN & CO., INC.
4010 WHITESIDE ST, LOS ANGELES, CA 900631617
Phone: 323 263-9275
Web: WWW.BRAUNEXP.COM

COMPETITORS

Pittards   S. B. Foot Tanning

HISTORICAL FINANCIALS

Company Type: Private

Income Statement

FYE: October 31

	REVENUE ($ mil.)	NET INCOME ($ mil.)	NET PROFIT MARGIN	EMPLOYEES
10/15	304	0	0.0%	30
10/14	324	0	0.0%	—
10/13	307	0	0.0%	—
10/12	277	0	0.2%	—
Annual Growth	3.2%	(43.7%)	—	—

2015 Year-End Financials

Return on assets: 2.3%
Return on equity: —
Current ratio: 0.80

Cash ($ mil.): 3

HARLANDALE INDEPENDENT SCHOOL DISTRICT PUBLIC FACILITIES CORPORATION

EXECUTIVES

Superintendent, Reynaldo Madrigal
Board of Directors, Victor Resendiz
Superintendent, Guillermo Zabala
Auditors: GARZA/GONZALEZ & ASSOCIATES S

LOCATIONS

HQ: HARLANDALE INDEPENDENT SCHOOL DISTRICT PUBLIC FACILITIES CORPORATION
102 GENEVIEVE DR, SAN ANTONIO, TX 782142902
Phone: 210 989-4340
Web: WWW.HARLANDALE.NET

HISTORICAL FINANCIALS

Company Type: Private

Income Statement

FYE: June 30

	REVENUE ($ mil.)	NET INCOME ($ mil.)	NET PROFIT MARGIN	EMPLOYEES
06/15	170	(21)	—	2,000
06/14	165	0	0.3%	—
06/13	140	79	56.5%	—
06/12	146	14	10.1%	—
Annual Growth	5.3%	—	—	—

2015 Year-End Financials

Return on assets: 1.9%
Return on equity: (-12.7%)
Current ratio: 1.70

Cash ($ mil.): 42

HARMONY PUBLIC SCHOOLS

EXECUTIVES

President, Oner Ulvi Celepcikay
Superintendent, Soner Tarim
Vice-President, Cengizhan Keskin
Vice-President, Ellen A Macdonald
Treasurer, Mustafa Ata Atik
Principal, Mehmet Basoglu
Principal, Serkan Kilic
Manager, Kakajan Rejepov
Director, Oner Ulvi
Auditors: GOMEZ & COMPANY HOUSTON TX

LOCATIONS

HQ: HARMONY PUBLIC SCHOOLS
9321 W SAM HOUSTON PKWY S, HOUSTON, TX 770995204
Phone: 281 888-9764
Web: WWW.HARMONYTX.ORG

HISTORICAL FINANCIALS

Company Type: Private

Income Statement

FYE: June 30

	REVENUE ($ mil.)	NET INCOME ($ mil.)	NET PROFIT MARGIN	EMPLOYEES
06/16	265	(8)	—	3,262
06/15	265	22	8.7%	—
06/14	239	7	3.1%	—
06/13	193	13	7.2%	—
Annual Growth	11.0%	—	—	—

2016 Year-End Financials

Return on assets: 1.3%
Return on equity: (-3.2%)
Current ratio: 2.90

Cash ($ mil.): 77

HARRIS COUNTY CLINICAL SERVICES INC

EXECUTIVES

Principal, Richard Blakely
Auditors: MIKESKA MONAHAN PECKHAM PC

LOCATIONS

HQ: HARRIS COUNTY CLINICAL SERVICES INC
2801 VIA FORTUNA, AUSTIN, TX 787467567
Phone: 512 899-3995

HISTORICAL FINANCIALS

Company Type: Private

Income Statement

FYE: August 31

	REVENUE ($ mil.)	NET INCOME ($ mil.)	NET PROFIT MARGIN	EMPLOYEES
08/15	262	1	0.4%	4
08/13	232	1	0.5%	—
08/10	190	(1)	—	—
Annual Growth	6.7%	—	—	—

2015 Year-End Financials

Return on assets: —
Return on equity: 0.4%
Current ratio: 101.30

Cash ($ mil.): 1

HARRISON MEDICAL CENTER

EXECUTIVES

President, Scott Bosch
Board of Directors, James Smalley
Administrative Assistant, Staci Gizzi

LOCATIONS

HQ: HARRISON MEDICAL CENTER
2520 CHERRY AVE, BREMERTON, WA 983104229
Phone: 360 744-6510
Web: WWW.HARRISONMEDICAL.ORG

HISTORICAL FINANCIALS
Company Type: Private

Income Statement
FYE: June 30

	REVENUE ($ mil.)	NET INCOME ($ mil.)	NET PROFIT MARGIN	EMPLOYEES
06/15*	398	56	14.1%	2,400
04/12	345	(22)	—	—
04/11	363	15	4.2%	—
04/10	1,753	0	—	—
Annual Growth	—	990.7%	—	—

*Fiscal year change

2015 Year-End Financials
Return on assets: 5.9%   Cash ($ mil.): 24
Return on equity: 14.1%
Current ratio: 1.10

HARRISON TRUCK CENTERS, INC.

EXECUTIVES

President, Brian Harrison
Accountant, Sherry Deisberg
Manager, Allen Crouch
Manager, John Dekoster
Administrative Assistant, John Walker
Auditors: RSM US LLP ST LOUIS MISSOUR

LOCATIONS

HQ: HARRISON TRUCK CENTERS, INC.
 3601 ADVENTURELAND DR, ALTOONA, IA 500099589
Phone: 515 967-3500
Web: WWW.HTCTRUCKS.COM

HISTORICAL FINANCIALS
Company Type: Private

Income Statement
FYE: December 31

	REVENUE ($ mil.)	NET INCOME ($ mil.)	NET PROFIT MARGIN	EMPLOYEES
12/15	213	1	0.6%	400
12/99	17	0	1.9%	—
12/98	0	0	—	—
Annual Growth	—	—	—	—

2015 Year-End Financials
Return on assets: 1.3%   Cash ($ mil.): 3
Return on equity: 0.6%
Current ratio: 0.10

HARTFORD HEALTHCARE CORPORATION

Hartford Health Care provides a variety of health services to the descendants of our founding fathers. Founded in 1854 the health care system operates a network of hospitals behavioral health centers nursing and rehabilitation facilities medical labs and numerous community programs for residents in northern Connecticut. Medical specialties range from orthopedics and women's health to cancer and heart care. Hartford Health Care's flagship facility is the Hartford Hospital an 870-bed teaching hospital affiliated with the University of Connecticut Medical School. Its network also includes MidState Medical Center (some 155 beds) Windham Hospital (145 beds) and The Hospital of Central Connecticut (415 beds).

Operations

Hartford Health Care provides primary and specialty care services through partnerships with several physician practice organizations and specialist facilities including diagnostic imaging centers and mental health facilities. The company provides medical laboratory services including pathology genetic testing and other diagnostic services through its Clinical Laboratory Partners affiliate. It also provides long-term care through Central Connecticut Senior Health Services as well as home health services through VNA HealthCare.

Financial Performance

In 2013 Hartford Health Care reported a 2% rise in revenue from $1.7 million to $2.1 million due to increased patient service revenue.

Strategy

As it becomes increasingly challenging for hospitals to remain independently profitable in an unstable economic climate especially as health reform changes take effect Hartford has been working to expand its footprint in the Connecticut health care market. In 2012 Hartford Health Care formed an alliance with Backus Corporation which operates the Backus Hospital and other medical care centers in eastern Connecticut. Backus gained access to Hartford's broader resources but continues to manage its own day-to-day operations.

In 2014 Hartford Health Care broke ground on a new 90000-square-foot cancer center at The Hospital of Central Connecticut.

EXECUTIVES

Vice President Medical Director, Kent Stahl
Senior Vice President Finance, Richard Stys
Vice President Strategic Planning and Business Development, Karen Goyette
Executive Vice President and President and Chief Executive Officer Hartford Hospital, Jeffrey Flaks
Managing Director, Robert Hagberg
Auditors: ERNST & YOUNG LLP HARTFORD

LOCATIONS

HQ: HARTFORD HEALTHCARE CORPORATION
 1 STATE ST FL 19, HARTFORD, CT 061033102
Phone: 860 263-4100
Web: WWW.WINDHAMHOSPITAL.ORG

PRODUCTS/OPERATIONS

2013 Sales

	% of total
Net patient revenue	90
Other operating revenue	10
Net asets released from restrctions for operations	-
Total	**100**

Selected Facilities
Alliance Occupational Health
Central Connecticut Senior Health Services
Clinical Laboratory Partners
Eastern Rehabilitation Network
Hartford Hospital (acute care)
Hartford Medical Group (primary care)
The Hospital of Central Connecticut (acute care)
Institute of Living (research and psychiatric care)
MidState Medical Center (acute care)
Natchaug Hospital (mental health facility)
Rushford (mental health treatment centers)
VNA HealthCare (home health)
Windham Hospital (acute care)

COMPETITORS

Baystate Medical Center
Berkshire Health Systems
Bristol Hospital
Connecticut Children's Medical Center
Griffin Health
Lawrence & Memorial Hospital
Saint Francis Hospital and Medical Center
St. Vincent's Health Services
University of Connecticut Health Center
Waterbury Hospital
Western Connecticut Health Network
Yale New Haven Health System
Yale-New Haven Hospital Saint Raphael Campus

HISTORICAL FINANCIALS
Company Type: Private

Income Statement
FYE: September 30

	REVENUE ($ mil.)	NET INCOME ($ mil.)	NET PROFIT MARGIN	EMPLOYEES
09/15	297	(37)	—	5,100
09/12	2,090	63	3.1%	—
09/11	1,803	138	7.7%	—
Annual Growth	(36.2%)	—	—	—

2015 Year-End Financials
Return on assets: 26.0%   Cash ($ mil.): 62
Return on equity: (-12.5%)
Current ratio: —

HARTFORD HOSPITAL

EXECUTIVES

President, Jeffrey A Flaks
Vice-President, Gerry J Boisvert
Senior Vice-President, Luis Tavares
Chief Financial Officer, Tom Marchozzi
Manager, Susan Kohn
Manager, Jamie Roche
Director, Ripple Talati
Chief Operating Officer, Janice Giuca
Director, Stephen Upham

LOCATIONS

HQ: HARTFORD HOSPITAL
 80 SEYMOUR ST, HARTFORD, CT 061028000
Phone: 860 545-5000
Web: WWW.HARTFORDHOSPITAL.ORG

HISTORICAL FINANCIALS
Company Type: Private

Income Statement
FYE: September 30

	REVENUE ($ mil.)	NET INCOME ($ mil.)	NET PROFIT MARGIN	EMPLOYEES
09/15	993	64	6.5%	7,500
09/14	986	62	6.3%	—
09/13	903	37	4.1%	—
09/09	828	(23)	—	—
Annual Growth	3.1%	—	—	—

2015 Year-End Financials
Return on assets: 3.8%   Cash ($ mil.): 39
Return on equity: 6.5%
Current ratio: 1.20

HARVARD BUSINESS SCHOOL PUBLISHING CORPORATION

EXECUTIVES

President, David Wan
Sales Manager, Kim Sanford
Marketing Manager, Alexandra Merceron
Director, Susan Hamilton
Executive Director, John Korn
Auditors: PRICEWATERHOUSECOOPERS LLP BO

LOCATIONS

HQ: HARVARD BUSINESS SCHOOL PUBLISHING
  CORPORATION
  20 GUEST ST STE 700, BRIGHTON, MA 021352040
Phone: 617 783-7400
Web: WWW.HARVARDBUSINESS.ORG

HISTORICAL FINANCIALS

Company Type: Private

Income Statement

	REVENUE ($ mil.)	NET INCOME ($ mil.)	NET PROFIT MARGIN	EMPLOYEES
06/15	207	2	1.2%	390
06/10	139	1	1.0%	—
06/09	141	1	0.7%	—
06/08	0	0	—	—
Annual Growth	—	—	—	—

FYE: June 30

2015 Year-End Financials

Return on assets: 21.4%
Return on equity: 1.2%
Current ratio: 1.00
Cash ($ mil.): 52

HARVARD MEDICAL FACULTY PHYSICIANS AT BETH ISRAEL DEACONESS MEDICAL CENTER, INC.

EXECUTIVES

Chief Executive Officer, Stuart A Rosenberg
Supervisor, Sydney Talbot
Auditors: LB DELOITTE TAX LLP JERICHO

LOCATIONS

HQ: HARVARD MEDICAL FACULTY PHYSICIANS AT
  BETH ISRAEL DEACONESS MEDICAL CENTER, INC.
  375 LONGWOOD AVE STE 3, BOSTON, MA
  022155395
Phone: 617 632-9755
Web: WWW.HMFPHYSICIANS.ORG

HISTORICAL FINANCIALS

Company Type: Private

Income Statement

	REVENUE ($ mil.)	NET INCOME ($ mil.)	NET PROFIT MARGIN	EMPLOYEES
09/15	487	1	0.3%	800
09/14	460	14	3.2%	—
09/08	22	2	11.6%	—
Annual Growth	55.3%	(6.4%)	—	—

FYE: September 30

2015 Year-End Financials

Return on assets: 7.2%
Return on equity: 0.3%
Current ratio: 1.40
Cash ($ mil.): 26

HATZEL & BUEHLER, INC.

EXECUTIVES

President, William A Goeller
Financial Executive, Alan Hollander
Vice-President, Jim Gloekler
Manager, Dirk Whelan
Foreman/Supervisor, Gene Payne
Vice-President, John Java
Auditors: HORTY & HORTY PA WILMINGTO

LOCATIONS

HQ: HATZEL & BUEHLER, INC.
  3600 SILVERSIDE RD STE A, WILMINGTON, DE
  198105116
Phone: 302 478-4200
Web: WWW.HATZELANDBUEHLER.COM

HISTORICAL FINANCIALS

Company Type: Private

Income Statement

	REVENUE ($ mil.)	NET INCOME ($ mil.)	NET PROFIT MARGIN	EMPLOYEES
12/16	256	2	1.0%	700
12/15	223	1	0.8%	—
12/14	242	2	1.1%	—
12/13	197	1	0.7%	—
Annual Growth	9.2%	21.8%	—	—

FYE: December 31

2016 Year-End Financials

Return on assets: 4.1%
Return on equity: 1.0%
Current ratio: 1.40
Cash ($ mil.): 2

HAVERSTRAW STONY POINT CENTRAL SCHOOL DISTRICT INC

EXECUTIVES

Superintendent, Ileana Eckert

LOCATIONS

HQ: HAVERSTRAW STONY POINT CENTRAL SCHOOL
  DISTRICT INC
  65 CHAPEL ST, GARNERVILLE, NY 109231238
Phone: 845 942-3053
Web: WWW.HAVERSTRAW.COM

HISTORICAL FINANCIALS

Company Type: Private

Income Statement

	REVENUE ($ mil.)	NET INCOME ($ mil.)	NET PROFIT MARGIN	EMPLOYEES
06/16*	214	(2)	—	1,400
12/05	154	0	—	—
06/02	121	5	4.3%	—
06/01	121	10	8.7%	—
Annual Growth	3.8%	—	—	—

FYE: June 30

*Fiscal year change

2016 Year-End Financials

Return on assets: 1.8%
Return on equity: (-1.3%)
Current ratio: 1.30
Cash ($ mil.): 44

HAYDON BUILDING CORP.

EXECUTIVES

President, Gary T Haydon
Board of Directors, Fritz Behrhorst
Accountant, Katy Haydon
Assistant Controller, Katie Perry
Project Manager, Kenneth Shepherd
Project Manager, Matt Gilliland
Auditors: WEINTRAUB & SCHANCK PC PHO

LOCATIONS

HQ: HAYDON BUILDING CORP.
  4640 E COTTON GIN LOOP, PHOENIX, AZ 850404819
Phone: 602 296-1496
Web: WWW.HAYDONBC.COM

HISTORICAL FINANCIALS

Company Type: Private

Income Statement

	REVENUE ($ mil.)	NET INCOME ($ mil.)	NET PROFIT MARGIN	EMPLOYEES
12/15	200	(0)	—	250
12/14	162	3	1.9%	—
12/13	186	3	1.8%	—
12/12	161	3	1.9%	—
Annual Growth	7.6%	—	—	—

FYE: December 31

2015 Year-End Financials

Return on assets: 9.4%
Return on equity: (-0.4%)
Current ratio: 0.90
Cash ($ mil.): 6

HAYS MEDICAL CENTER, INC.

Hays Medical Center brings big city health care to rural Kansas. The not-for-profit hospital which has about 210 beds provides both acute and tertiary medical care to the Midwestern plains serving more than 13000 emergency patients each year. In addition to medical surgical and pediatric care Hays Medical Center offers home care hospice skilled nursing rehabilitation and behavioral health services. It operates centers for cardiac care (the DeBakey Heart Institute) fitness and rehabilitation (Center for Health Improvement) orthopedics (Hays Orthopedic Institute) and cancer treatment (the Dreiling/Schmidt Cancer Center). The organization also operates specialty and rural health clinics.

Operations

Hays Medical Center has a partnership with Pawnee Valley Community Hospital a critical-access hospital in Larned.

The hospital sees some 6700 admissions and performs some 173000 outpatient procedures annually. Its specialty and rural health clinics typically have about 146000 office visits.

Sales and Marketing

Hays Medical Center maintains a local market share of nearly 90% with total primary/secondary/tertiary service at 25%.

Strategy

The medical center has grown its business through selective acquisitions and hospital expansion projects. In 2013 completed the $3.8 million expansion and renovation of the Dreiling/Schmidt Cancer Institute and Breast Care Center which began construction in 2012. That expansion provided four more treatment rooms expanded exam rooms and a consultation center.

Hays Medical Center has also added reconstructive surgery services with the addition of a cosmetic surgeon and expanded its surgical capabilities by agreeing to assist with operations at nearby St. Joseph Memorial Hospital.

Company Background

The medical center was formed in 1991 through the merger of a pair of religiously affiliated facilities.

EXECUTIVES

President and CEO, Edward Herrman
Director of Pharmacy and Oncology Services, William Cadoret
NURSING SERVICES DIRECTOR, Kendra Barker
Auditors: WENDLING NOE NELSON & JOHNSON

LOCATIONS

HQ: HAYS MEDICAL CENTER, INC.
2220 CANTERBURY DR, HAYS, KS 676012370
Phone: 785 623-5000
Web: WWW.HAYSMED.COM

PRODUCTS/OPERATIONS

Selected Departments
Billing/Financial
Dietary
Education
Emergency Department
Fitness Center
Hospice
Hospitalists
Imaging
Lifeline
Occupational Therapy
Palliative Care
Pharmacy
Rehabilitation
  In-Patient
  Out Patient
Respiratory Therapy
Senior Focused Care
Sexual Assault Response Team
Sleep and Neurodiagnostic
Special Nursing Services
Sports Medicine
Volunteer Services
Wound Healing and Hyperbaric Center
Weight Loss Surgery
WorkSMART

COMPETITORS

Adventist Health System Sunbelt Healthcare
Sisters of Charity of Leavenworth
Stormont-Vail HealthCare
University of Kansas Medical Center
Via Christi Health System

HISTORICAL FINANCIALS

Company Type: Private

Income Statement

FYE: June 30

	REVENUE ($ mil.)	NET INCOME ($ mil.)	NET PROFIT MARGIN	EMPLOYEES
06/16	199	2	1.3%	1,178
06/15	201	8	4.3%	—
06/14	198	21	10.6%	—
06/13	199	17	8.5%	—
Annual Growth	(0.0%)	(46.3%)	—	—

2016 Year-End Financials

Return on assets: 2.6%   Cash ($ mil.): 23
Return on equity: 1.3%
Current ratio: 2.30

HAYWARD SISTERS HOSPITAL

EXECUTIVES

President, Michael Mahoney
Manager, Doug Davis
Director, Rozanne O'Keefe
Auditors: TCA PARTNERS LLP FRESNO CA

LOCATIONS

HQ: HAYWARD SISTERS HOSPITAL
27200 CALAROGA AVE, HAYWARD, CA 945454339
Phone: 510 264-4000
Web: WWW.STROSEHOSPITAL.ORG

HISTORICAL FINANCIALS

Company Type: Private

Income Statement

FYE: September 30

	REVENUE ($ mil.)	NET INCOME ($ mil.)	NET PROFIT MARGIN	EMPLOYEES
09/15	170	22	13.1%	850
09/14	112	(4)	—	—
09/13	123	(2)	—	—
Annual Growth	17.3%	—	—	—

2015 Year-End Financials

Return on assets: 2.2%   Cash ($ mil.): 12
Return on equity: 13.1%
Current ratio: 0.50

HDR ARCHITECTURE, INC.

EXECUTIVES

Chief Executive Officer, George A Little
Board of Directors, Mary E Peters
Board of Directors, Louis Pachman
Manager, Jennifer Wik
Director, Michaella Wright
Manager, Robyn Pope
Vice-President, Hank Adams
Auditors: ERNST & YOUNG LLP OMAHA NE

LOCATIONS

HQ: HDR ARCHITECTURE, INC.
8404 INDIAN HILLS DR, OMAHA, NE 681144098
Phone: 402 399-1000

HISTORICAL FINANCIALS

Company Type: Private

Income Statement

FYE: December 26

	REVENUE ($ mil.)	NET INCOME ($ mil.)	NET PROFIT MARGIN	EMPLOYEES
12/15	241	(6)	—	1,426
12/14	237	(18)	—	—
12/13	235	(1)	—	—
12/12	335	0	0.1%	—
Annual Growth	(10.4%)	—	—	—

2015 Year-End Financials

Return on assets: 7.1%   Cash ($ mil.): 19
Return on equity: (-2.7%)
Current ratio: 0.60

HDR ENGINEERING, INC.

EXECUTIVES

Chief Executive Officer, George A Little
President, Eric L Keen
Chief Operating Officer, George Little
Chief Financial Officer, Terence C Cox
Executive Vice-President, Terry Cox
Treasurer, Chad M Hartnett
Manager, Gerald T Holmes
Manager, Denis P Gilbert
Director, Kelly Vincent
Auditors: ERNST & YOUNG LLP OMAHA NE

LOCATIONS

HQ: HDR ENGINEERING, INC.
8404 INDIAN HILLS DR, OMAHA, NE 681144098
Phone: 402 399-1000
Web: WWW.HDRINC.COM

HISTORICAL FINANCIALS

Company Type: Private

Income Statement

FYE: December 26

	REVENUE ($ mil.)	NET INCOME ($ mil.)	NET PROFIT MARGIN	EMPLOYEES
12/15	1,218	100	8.2%	6,111
12/14	1,115	74	6.7%	—
12/13	1,416	62	4.4%	—
12/12	1,257	73	5.9%	—
Annual Growth	(1.0%)	10.7%	—	—

2015 Year-End Financials
Return on assets: 6.8%   Cash ($ mil.): 4
Return on equity: 8.2%
Current ratio: 1.60

HDR, INC.

With projects ranging from restoring the Pentagon and the Everglades to working on the Hoover Dam Bypass project HDR has left its mark on the US. HDR is an architecture engineering and consulting firm that specializes in such projects as bridges water- and wastewater-treatment plants and hospitals. The company also provides mechanical and plumbing services construction and project management and utilities planning. It has completed projects nationwide and in some 60 countries through its more than 225 global locations. The employee-owned company was founded as Henningson Engineering in 1917 to build municipal plants in the rural Midwest.

Geographic Reach

Headquartered in Omaha Nebraska HDR has completed projects in 60 countries and maintains some 225 offices worldwide. It operates in the Americas (US and Canada) Asia (China and Mongolia) Australia Europe (Germany and the UK) and the Middle East.

Sales and Marketing

HDR's has performed design and engineering work for a number of clients including: Seattle Public Utilities DEXUS Property Group the Pirbright Institute SeaPort-e TXMAS and Xcel Energy.

Strategy

With the goal of cutting its client costs by 10% through smarter delivery processes in its designed and constructed facilities HDR has spent the past few years expanding its service capabilities through strategic acquisitions. To this end in early 2015 the company purchased Tennessee-based Infrastructure Corporation of America (ICA) which specializes in transport engineering and asset maintenance and management. Additionally it bought the assets of Georgia-based liquid natural gas firm MEI LLC.

The acquisition of architectural practice Rice Daubney in late 2013 enhanced the company's position in the Australian market while purchases in 2012 (Wyoming's Stetson Engineering) and 2011 (New Jersey's HydroQual) extended its water capabilities.

The company also continues to design and engineer big infrastructure projects for city and state governments. In late 2014 Seattle Public Utilities selected HDR develop and evaluate site plan concepts for the South Transfer Station Phase 2 project to create nearly a dozen facilities for recycling and waste-reuse to help the utility reach its goal of 70% solid waste diversion by 2025. Also in late 2014 HDR partnered with Jacobs Engineering Group to lead the engineering for the I-4 Mobility Partners group and will deliver final designs for roadway/traffic control draining structure and intelligent traffic systems for the I-4 Ultimate Project in Florida.

Mergers and Acquisitions

In January 2015 the company acquired both the Infrastructure Corporation of America (ICA) which specializes in transport engineering and asset maintenance and management along with the Georgia-based liquid natural gas firm MEI LLC to broaden its service capabilities.

In 2013 HDR purchased architecture firm Rice Daubney to bolster its design expertise and extend its reach in the Australian market.

In 2012 the company bought Wyoming's Stetson Engineering to broaden its water services.

EXECUTIVES

Chairman and CEO, George A. Little
CFO, Terence C. (Terry) Cox
EVP and Director Environmental Resource Management, Elwin Larson
EVP and Director Water Program, Gary L. Bleeker
Vice Chairman; President HDR Engineering Inc., Eric L. Keen
President Manager, Kevin Keller
President HDR Architecture Inc., Doug S. Wignall
CIO, Michael Geppert
EVP and Director Transportation, Charles O'Reilly
President Manager Richmond Hill Traffic Practice, David Argue
Vice President, Michael Quinn
Auditors: ERNST & YOUNG LLP OMAHA NE

LOCATIONS

HQ: HDR, INC.
   8404 INDIAN HILLS DR, OMAHA, NE 681144098
Phone: 402 399-1000

PRODUCTS/OPERATIONS

Selected Mergers and Acquisitions
FY2015
Brentwood Tennessee-based Infrastructure Corporation
   of America (ICA)
FY2103
   Rice Daubney (Australia architecture design for
   healthcare retail defense markets)
FY2012
   Stetson Engineering (Wyoming projects in water
   sewer storm water hydrology and transportation)
FY2011
   Amnis Engineering (Canada)
   Cooper Medical (Healthcare design/build specialist)
   HydroQual (New Jersey water resource management)
   Schiff Associates (California engineering)
FY2009
   Devine Tarbell & Associates (Maine now named
   HDR|DTA)
   iTrans Consulting (Toronto-based engineering firm)

Selected Markets
Architecture
   Academic
   Civic
   Corporate
   Healthcare
   Justice
   Science and Technology
Energy
   Oil and Gas
   Power Delivery
   Power Generation
   Renewable Energy
Federal
   Federal Architecture
   Federal Engineering
   Federal Planning
   Federal Environmental
   Federal Energy
   Federal Construction
   HDR SeaPort-e
Private Land Development
   Commercial
   Industrial
   Institutional
   Residential
   Resorts and Hotels
Resource Management
   Community Planning & Consulting
   Environmental Sciences & Permitting
   Fisheries Science & Design
   Mining
   Natural Resource Management
   Waste Management and Industrial
Transportation
   Aviation
   Freight Rail
   Highways and Local Roads
   Maritime
   Transit
Water
   Water
   Wastewater
   Water Planning
   Industrial

Selected Services
Analytical consulting
Architectural design
Coastal engineering and restoration
Consulting
Design/build
Environmental monitoring
Finished water storage facility services
Interior design
Landscape architecture
Master planning
Power facility engineering
Pump stations and flow control
Security services
Utility master planning and modeling
Water resources
Water treatment systems

COMPETITORS

AECOM
Black & Veatch
Brown and Caldwell
CH2M HILL
Epstein
Fuscoe Engineering
Gensler
Geotechnics
HBE Corporation
HKS Inc.
Interior Architects
Jacobs Engineering
KPA Associates
Kimley-Horn and Associates
Lee Burkhart Liu
Leo A Daly
MCG Architects
MWH Global
Michael Baker
Nasland Engineering
Perkowitz + Ruth
RMJM
RTKL Associates
SAIC Energy Environment & Infrastructure
STV
Tetra Tech
The Austin Company
Western Summit Constructors
Willdan Group

HISTORICAL FINANCIALS
Company Type: Private

Income Statement
FYE: December 26

	REVENUE ($ mil.)	NET INCOME ($ mil.)	NET PROFIT MARGIN	EMPLOYEES
12/15	2,132	74	3.5%	10,000
12/14	1,421	64	4.5%	—
12/13	1	0	5.1%	—
12/12	1,760	90	5.2%	—
Annual Growth	6.6%	(6.5%)	—	—

2015 Year-End Financials
Return on assets: 7.0%   Cash ($ mil.): 282
Return on equity: 3.5%
Current ratio: 1.60

HEALTH FIRST, INC.

Health First works to keep Florida's Space Coast denizens in tip-top shape. The not-for-profit health system operates four hospitals in Brevard County. Health First's biggest hospital is Holmes Regional Medical Center in Melbourne with more than 500 beds. Its Cape Canaveral Hospital and Palm Bay Community Hospital have 150 and 60 beds respectively. Its Viera Hospital is a 100-bed acute-care hospital. The system also runs outpatient clinics a home health service and a physicians group. Its for-profit subsidiary Health First Health Plans is the county's largest insurer with about 60000 commercial members and 23000 Medicare members.

Operations

The company operates four hospitals (Holmes Regional Medical Center Palm Bay Hospital Cape Canaveral Hospital and Viera Hospital) and offers a wide variety of health insurance plan options for patients in Brevard and Indian River Counties. Health First is the largest multi-specialty physician group on Florida's Space Coast. It also operates to Brevard County's only trauma center and a number of outpatient and wellness services including four pro-health and fitness centers.

Geographic Reach

Health First operates four hospitals and a health insurance company in Brevard County Florida.

Strategy

To expand its capacity Health First makes complementary acquisitions and pursues organic growth.

In 2103 Health First opened of a new center for fracture care at Health First Holmes Regional Medical Center and the center for joint replacement at Health First Viera Hospital. That year it formed a new Small Group Preferred Provider Organization (PPO) Plan offering increased flexibility when it comes to out-of-network coverage and fulfilling the needs of employer groups in its service area.

Mergers and Acquisitions

In 2012 the company acquired Melbourne Internal Medicine Associates (250 physician providers based in Melbourne) to increase patient quality safety and the patient experience. The entity was renamed the Health First Medical Group in 2013.

Company Background

In 2011 Health First partnered with Nemours to expand pediatric care in Brevard County. That year Health First Health Plans opened a new Vero Beach office to serve residents of Indian River County and launch its Medicare Advantage plans to the rest of Indian River County.

Despite an ongoing lawsuit with Wuesthoff Health System (which claims that Health First has an unfair monopoly of hospital services in Brevard County) the company forged ahead with construction of its fourth hospital in the county the Viera hospital campus. The Medical Plaza at Viera Health Park which will includes offices for multi-specialty physicians and a diagnostic/imaging center opened in 2010. And the park's centerpiece Viera Hospital a 100-bed acute-care hospital opened in 2011.

Health First was founded in 1995 through a merger of regional hospitals. The Brevard Hospital (now Holmes Regional Medical Center) first opened in 1937.

EXECUTIVES

Chief Physician Executive, Jeffrey C. Stalnaker
EVP and COO, J. Stuart Mitchell
EVP Chief Strategy Officer; CEO Health First Health Plans, Drew Rector
EVP and CFO, Joseph (Joe) Felkner
President Health First Medical Group, Travis L Douglass
President and CEO, Steven P. Johnson
CEO Community Hospitals, Aaron Robinson
SVP and CIO, Alex Popowycz
President Hospital Operations, Bill Calhoun
Chief Nursing Officer, Constance (Connie) Bradley
Vice President Marketing and Communications, Matthew Gerrell
Vice President Of Growth And Development, Bridget Mace
Chairman, Pamela A. Gatto
Vice Chairman, Kevin B. Steele
Auditors: ERNST & YOUNG LLP

LOCATIONS

HQ: HEALTH FIRST, INC.
6450 US HIGHWAY 1, ROCKLEDGE, FL 329555747
Phone: 321 434-4300
Web: WWW.HEALTH-FIRST.ORG

Selected facilities
Cape Canaveral Hospital (Cocoa Beach)
Holmes Regional Medical Center (Melbourne)
Palm Bay Community Hospital (Palm Bay)
Viera Hospital (Viera)

COMPETITORS

Adventist Health System Sunbelt Healthcare
Aetna
CIGNA
Florida Blue
HCA
Orlando Health
Osceola Regional Medical Center
Tenet Healthcare
Wuesthoff Health System

HISTORICAL FINANCIALS
Company Type: Private

Income Statement
FYE: September 30

	REVENUE ($ mil.)	NET INCOME ($ mil.)	NET PROFIT MARGIN	EMPLOYEES
09/15	1,255	19	1.6%	6,900
09/14	1,136	90	7.9%	—
09/13	1,059	51	4.8%	—
09/11	129	(0)	—	—
Annual Growth	**76.5%**	—	—	—

2015 Year-End Financials
Return on assets: 12.8%
Return on equity: 1.6%
Current ratio: 1.40
Cash ($ mil.): 152

HEALTH PARTNERS PLANS, INC.

Health Partners wants to partner up with Pennsylvanians in need of health care. The company is a not-for-profit health plan that provides health benefits to some 210000 Medicaid recipients in the Philadelphia area. Its HealthChoices plans for Medicaid participants cover medical dental prescription and vision costs. Its KidzPartners program is provided in partnership with the state of Pennsylvania's Children's Health Insurance Program (CHIP). Its provider network includes about 6000 primary and specialty care doctors and 30 hospitals in the region. The company also provides community outreach and wellness programs.

Health Partners was founded in 1985 by a group of hospitals in the Philadelphia area.

Geographic Reach

Health Partners' plans cover members in Philadelphia and in Chester Delaware Bucks and Montgomery counties outside the city.

Strategy

Health Partners signed a provider contract with the University of Pennsylvania Health System that will increase access to care in Philadelphia for Health Partners Medicare members. The agreement increases Health Partners' network to include more than 1300 additional physicians from the Health System's network of practices and four hospitals.

Health Partners has been working to enhance its community health programs in recent years. It launched its Computer Health Care Management Education program to provide free monthly computer lessons combined with tutorials about healthy lifestyle programs.

It also teamed up with the Norcom Community Center to offer HealthChoices and KidzPartners members fitness benefits at the facility; the company has a total of more than 20 fitness centers in its expanding provider network. The KidzPartners program provides free or affordable insurance coverage to children and teens who don't qualify for Medicaid.

Company Background

The area hospitals that own Health Partners are Albert Einstein Medical Center Aria Health Temple University Hospital Episcopal Hospital and two Tenet Healthcare facilities (Hahnemann University Hospital and St. Christopher's Hospital for Children).

EXECUTIVES

President and CEO, William S. George
SVP Healthcare Management and Chief Medical Officer, Steven E. Szebenyi
SVP Operations and COO, Lisa Getzfrid
Government Relations, Kearline Jones
Vice President of Marketing, Caroline Russell
Vice President, Johnna Baker
Vice President Sales, John Sehi
Vice President Utilization Management, Andrea D'Angelo
Vice President and Chief Technology Officer, Kalyan Narayanan
Auditors: KPMG LLP PHILADELPHIA PENNSY

LOCATIONS

HQ: HEALTH PARTNERS PLANS, INC.
901 MARKET ST STE 500, PHILADELPHIA, PA 191074496
Phone: 215 849-9606
Web: WWW.HEALTHPARTNERSPLANS.COM

COMPETITORS

Aetna	Highmark
CIGNA	Independence Blue
Coventry Health Care	Cross
Gateway Health Plan	Keystone Mercy
Health Net	UnitedHealth Group

HISTORICAL FINANCIALS
Company Type: Private

Income Statement
FYE: December 31

	REVENUE ($ mil.)	NET INCOME ($ mil.)	NET PROFIT MARGIN	EMPLOYEES
12/15	1,502	(2)	—	620
12/14	910	(8)	—	—
12/13	1,000	(0)	—	—
12/12	1,034	(1)	—	—
Annual Growth	**13.2%**	—	—	—

HEALTH QUEST SYSTEMS, INC.

EXECUTIVES

Chief Executive Officer, Denise George
Director, Gretchen Halstead
Personnel Director, Janice Eining
Auditors: PRICEWATERHOUSECOOPERS LLP N

LOCATIONS

HQ: HEALTH QUEST SYSTEMS, INC.
1351 ROUTE 55 STE 200, LAGRANGEVILLE, NY
125405144
Phone: 845 475-9500

HISTORICAL FINANCIALS
Company Type: Private

Income Statement				FYE: December 31
	REVENUE ($ mil.)	NET INCOME ($ mil.)	NET PROFIT MARGIN	EMPLOYEES
12/15	870	39	4.6%	2,000
12/14	796	5	0.6%	—
12/13	706	103	14.6%	—
12/12	692	8	1.2%	—
Annual Growth	7.9%	69.7%	—	—

2015 Year-End Financials
Return on assets: 13.4%   Cash ($ mil.): 109
Return on equity: 4.6%
Current ratio: 1.30

HEALTH RESEARCH, INC.

Health Research Inc. (HRI) knows where the money is. The group is a not-for-profit organization that helps the New York State Department of Health and its affiliated Roswell Park Cancer Institute solicit evaluate and administer financial support. Sources of that support come from federal and state government sources other non-profits and businesses. HRI's Technology Transfer office also assists the Department of Health in sharing its research findings with other public and private institutions and finding ways to create biomedical technologies through private sector development. HRI was founded in 1953 and has administered $7 billion over its lifetime.

HRI's Technology Transfer office has aided several research organizations in recent years such as ones studying prostate specific antigen (or the PSA test) photodynamic therapy and pox virus vectors among others.

EXECUTIVES

Executive Director, Barbara Ryan
Supervisor, Michele King
Director, Tammy Young
Manager, Donna Deluca
Personnel Director, Carol Bailey

2015 Year-End Financials
Return on assets: 1.3%   Cash ($ mil.): 174
Return on equity: (-0.2%)
Current ratio: 1.00

Branch Manager, Cheryl A Mattox
Manager, Greg Sweet
Auditors: BONADIO & CO LLP ALBANY NE

LOCATIONS

HQ: HEALTH RESEARCH, INC.
150 BROADWAY STE 560, MENANDS, NY 122042726
Phone: 518 431-1200
Web: WWW.HEALTHRESEARCH.ORG

HISTORICAL FINANCIALS
Company Type: Private

Income Statement				FYE: March 31
	REVENUE ($ mil.)	NET INCOME ($ mil.)	NET PROFIT MARGIN	EMPLOYEES
03/15	677	22	3.3%	1,400
03/14	703	13	1.9%	—
03/13	665	25	3.9%	—
03/12	661	(10)	—	—
Annual Growth	0.8%	—	—	—

2015 Year-End Financials
Return on assets: 3.7%   Cash ($ mil.): 187
Return on equity: 3.3%
Current ratio: —

HEALTH SCHOLARSHIPS INC

EXECUTIVES

President, Joe Wall
Auditors: MCNAIR MCLEMORE MIDDLEBROOKS

LOCATIONS

HQ: HEALTH SCHOLARSHIPS INC
1005 BOULDER DR, GRAY, GA 310326141
Phone: 478 742-6569

HISTORICAL FINANCIALS
Company Type: Private

Income Statement				FYE: June 30
	ASSETS ($ mil.)	NET INCOME ($ mil.)	INCOME AS % OF ASSETS	EMPLOYEES
06/15	48	(14)	—	1
06/14	70	15	21.4%	—
06/11	46	7	16.2%	—
06/10	43	19	43.6%	—
Annual Growth	1.9%	—	—	—

2015 Year-End Financials
Return on assets: 9.7%   Sales ($ mil): 198
Return on equity: (-7.2%)

HEALTHEAST ST JOSEPH'S HOSPITAL

EXECUTIVES

President, Timothy Hanson
Director of Finance, Marcia Holterhaus
Accountant, Kris Jancen
Director, Carol Beehler
Manager, Deborah Vanderbeek

VP Personnel, Ginny Sullivan
Director, Joe Clubb
Credit Manager, Peggy Rogers
Director, Anne Pearson

LOCATIONS

HQ: HEALTHEAST ST JOSEPH'S HOSPITAL
45 10TH ST W, SAINT PAUL, MN 551021062
Phone: 651 232-3000
Web: WWW.HEALTHEAST.ORG

HISTORICAL FINANCIALS
Company Type: Private

Income Statement				FYE: August 31
	REVENUE ($ mil.)	NET INCOME ($ mil.)	NET PROFIT MARGIN	EMPLOYEES
08/15	250	(17)	—	1,164
08/14	270	(17)	—	—
08/11	269	(5)	—	—
08/10	262	(5)	—	—
Annual Growth	(0.9%)	—	—	—

2015 Year-End Financials
Return on assets: 2.0%   Cash ($ mil.): —
Return on equity: (-6.9%)
Current ratio: 1.90

HEALTHNOTES LLC

EXECUTIVES

Chief Operating Officer, Dan Miller
Chief Financial Officer, Bill Voloch
Chief Operating Officer, Ryan Simpson
Director, Kathy Page
Director, Sydney Stevens

LOCATIONS

HQ: HEALTHNOTES LLC
1501 S POTOMAC ST, AURORA, CO 800125411
Phone: 303 695-2600

HISTORICAL FINANCIALS
Company Type: Private

Income Statement				FYE: December 31
	REVENUE ($ mil.)	NET INCOME ($ mil.)	NET PROFIT MARGIN	EMPLOYEES
12/15	322	90	28.0%	1,500
12/08	335	30	9.1%	—
Annual Growth	(0.6%)	16.7%	—	—

2015 Year-End Financials
Return on assets: 2.5%   Cash ($ mil.): —
Return on equity: 28.0%
Current ratio: 1.90

HEALTHSOURCE DISTRIBUTORS, LLC

EXECUTIVES

President, Jerry Wolasky
Administrative Assistant, Tammy Matthews

LOCATIONS

HQ: HEALTHSOURCE DISTRIBUTORS, LLC
7200 RUTHERFORD RD # 150, BALTIMORE, MD
212442717
Phone: 410 653-1113
Web: WWW.HEALTHSOURCEDISTRIBUTORS.COM

HISTORICAL FINANCIALS

Company Type: Private

Income Statement

	REVENUE ($ mil.)	NET INCOME ($ mil.)	NET PROFIT MARGIN	EMPLOYEES
12/15	226	5	2.3%	60
12/14	187	4	2.6%	—
12/13	155	5	3.6%	—
12/12	89	1	1.9%	—
Annual Growth	36.5%	46.1%	—	—

2015 Year-End Financials

Return on assets: 5.6%
Return on equity: 2.3%
Current ratio: 1.20
Cash ($ mil.): —

HEARTLAND CO-OP

Heartland Co-op has no need to go against the grain. The cooperative offers agricultural products and services for its central Iowa member/farmers. Heartland operates more than 50 grain elevators and service centers. It offers agronomy products and services such as seed treatments and alfalfa fertilization; grain drying storage and merchandising; petroleum products for farm vehicles and home heating; livestock and pet feed; and personal and crop credit and financing. Headquartered in West Des Moines Heartland was formed in 1987 when cooperatives in Dallas Center Minburn and Panora merged. Heartland which has grown to more than 5400-members merged with Farm Service Company of Council Bluffs in 2013.

Operations

Heartland Co-op operates more than 60 cooperatives in Iowa.

Geographic Reach

Iowa-based Heartland Co-op operates across its home state in the cities of Blairstown Luzerne Chelsea Elberon Conroy Hartwick Marengo Malcom and Montezuma.

Strategy

Heartland Co-op has grown through consolidation and mergers with many smaller cooperatives.

Mergers and Acquisitions

Heartland Co-op acquired Farm Service Company (FSC) in Council Bluffs Iowa in August 2013. The combination of the two extended Heartland's reach westward in Iowa. The corporate offices of the combined operation remains in West Des Moines in Central Iowa.

It sold its service station business in 2012 as it was deemed non-core.

HISTORY

qua

EXECUTIVES

VICE PRESIDENT SALES AND MARKETING, Dave Coppess
Executive Vice President of Operations, Marc Melhus
Auditors: BERGAN PAULSEN & COMPANY PC

LOCATIONS

HQ: HEARTLAND CO-OP
2829 WESTOWN PKWY STE 350, WEST DES MOINES, IA 502661340
Phone: 515 225-1334
Web: WWW.HEARTLANDCOOP.COM

PRODUCTS/OPERATIONS

Selected Products & Services
Crop Nutrition
Seed Solutions
Precision Ag Services
Agronomy Services
Crop Protection Products

COMPETITORS

ADM	Farmers Cooperative
Ag Processing Inc.	Society
CHS	Five Star Co-op
Cargill	IVESCO
Farm Service	Orscheln Farm and Home
Cooperative	Pioneer Hi-Bred
Farmers Cooperative	Pro-Fac
Company	West Central Co-op

HISTORICAL FINANCIALS

Company Type: Private

Income Statement
FYE: June 30

	REVENUE ($ mil.)	NET INCOME ($ mil.)	NET PROFIT MARGIN	EMPLOYEES
06/16	854	15	1.9%	678
06/15	823	19	2.4%	—
06/14	941	18	2.0%	—
Annual Growth	(4.7%)	(7.4%)	—	—

2016 Year-End Financials

Return on assets: 0.8%
Return on equity: 1.9%
Current ratio: 0.10
Cash ($ mil.): —

HEARTLAND HEALTH

Heartland Health provides medical care in the heart of the Midwest. The integrated health care system serves residents of northwest Missouri as well as bordering areas of Kansas and Nebraska. Its flagship facility is Heartland Regional Medical Center a 350-bed acute-care hospital that features an emergency room and Level II trauma center as well as specialty care programs in heart disease cancer and obstetrics. Heartland Health also provides primary care through a multi-specialty medical practice (Heartland Clinic) and it offers home health hospice and long-term care services from the primary medical center facility. The company's Community Health Improvement Solutions unit is an HMO health insurer.

Strategy

In 2012 Heartland Health joined the Mayo Clinic Care Network which will enable to it to tap the knowledge and expertise of Mayo Clinic physicians to better serve its patients.

Company Background

Heartland Health was formed in 1984 through the merger of two St. Joseph Missouri hospital: Methodist Medical Center and St. Joseph's Hospital. The two facilities trace their roots back to 1924 and 1861 respectively.

EXECUTIVES

Vice President, Charles Mullican
Auditors: BKD LLP KANSAS CITY MISSOURI

LOCATIONS

HQ: HEARTLAND HEALTH
5325 FARAON ST, SAINT JOSEPH, MO 645063488
Phone: 816 271-6000

PRODUCTS/OPERATIONS

Selected Affiliates
Atchison Hospital (Atchison KS)
Community Hospital (Fairfax MO)
Community Medical Center (Falls City NE)
Dental Clinic (St. Joseph MO)
Laser Cosmedic Center (Platte City MO)
North Kansas City Hospital (North Kansas City MO)
The Surgery Center (St. Joseph MO)

COMPETITORS

Ascension Health
BJC HealthCare
Blue Cross and Blue Shield of Kansas City
Catholic Health Initiatives
Children's Mercy Hospital
CoxHealth
HCA
Mercy Health
Mercy Hospital Springfield
Saint Luke's Health System
Shawnee Mission Medical Center
Sisters of Charity of Leavenworth
Truman Medical Centers
University of Kansas Medical Center

HISTORICAL FINANCIALS

Company Type: Private

Income Statement
FYE: June 30

	REVENUE ($ mil.)	NET INCOME ($ mil.)	NET PROFIT MARGIN	EMPLOYEES
06/16	584	(6)	—	32,000
06/15	577	22	3.9%	—
06/14	560	64	11.4%	—
06/13	572	76	13.4%	—
Annual Growth	0.7%	—	—	—

2016 Year-End Financials

Return on assets: 3.2%
Return on equity: (-1.0%)
Current ratio: 1.00
Cash ($ mil.): 29

HEARTLAND LABEL PRINTERS, LLC

EXECUTIVES

President, Peter Helander
Engineer, Jerry Kaczmarek
Marketing Manager, Jim Check
Marketing Manager, Randy Themar
Engineer, Dave Cummings
Auditors: SCHENCK SC APPLETON WISCONSI

LOCATIONS

HQ: HEARTLAND LABEL PRINTERS, LLC
1700 STEPHEN ST, LITTLE CHUTE, WI 541402550
Phone: 920 788-7720
Web: WWW.HBS.NET

HISTORICAL FINANCIALS

Company Type: Private

Income Statement

FYE: September 25

	REVENUE ($ mil.)	NET INCOME ($ mil.)	NET PROFIT MARGIN	EMPLOYEES
09/15	196	2	1.3%	130
09/11	129	1	1.2%	—
09/10	91	0	0.9%	—
09/09	489	0	—	—
Annual Growth	(14.1%)	742.3%	—	—

2015 Year-End Financials

Return on assets: 4.6%
Return on equity: 1.3%
Current ratio: 1.00

Cash ($ mil.): 2

HEARTLAND REGIONAL MEDICAL CENTER

Heartland Regional Medical Center strives for healthy hearts minds and bodies in the US heartland. The acute care hospital a subsidiary of Heartland Health provides medical services to residents of St. Joseph Missouri and some 20 surrounding counties in northwest Missouri southeast Nebraska and northeast Kansas. Heartland Regional Medical Center encompasses specialty centers for trauma and long-term care acute rehabilitation cancer heart disease and birthing. As part of the services provided by the medical center Heartland Regional Medical Center offers services such as arthritis pain and wound treatments as well as home health and hospice care.

Geographic Reach

Operating in Missouri Heartland Regional Medical Center serves the residents and visitors of its home state as well as those in Nebraska and Kansas. Altogether the medical center caters to a more than 20-county area.

Financial Performance

In fiscal 2012 as compared to 2011 Heartland Regional Medical Center's revenue rose some 8% and its net income saw a 31% boost.

Strategy

As part of its operations Heartland Regional Medical Center partners with several managed care organizations such as Aetna CCN Managed Care Coventry Healthcare and Blue Cross Blue Shield of Kansas City to give its patients payment options for its health services. In 2012 Heartland Regional Medical Center developed an accountable care organization. It's a participant in the Medicare Shared Savings Program and enters into other similar shared savings arrangements with commercial self-insured or other third-party payors.

In recent years the medical facility has been investing in growing its footprint. Heartland Regional Medical Center is funding a $55-million expansion project that includes adding a handful of new operating rooms and renovating 10 more.

EXECUTIVES

Chairman, Alfred L Purcell
Board of Directors, John Wilson
Financial Executive, Doug Brandt
Vice-President, Rattin Christine
Chief Financial Officer, Spencer Klaasen
Board of Directors, David Berger
Auditors: BLD LLP KANSAS CITY MISSOUR

LOCATIONS

HQ: HEARTLAND REGIONAL MEDICAL CENTER
5325 FARAON ST, SAINT JOSEPH, MO 645063488
Phone: 816 271-6000
Web: WWW.MYMOSAICLIFECARE.ORG

PRODUCTS/OPERATIONS

Selected Services
Appendectomy
Cholecystectomy
Colon Resection
Hernia Repair
Nephrectomy
Assisted Vaginal Hysterectomy
Peritoneal Dialysis Catheter Placement
Pyloromyotomy
Tubal Ligation
Abdominal Perineal Resection
Adrenalectomy
Colostomy
Gastric Banding
Gastric Bypass
Gastric Sleeve
Gastrostomy Tube Placement
Laser Lysis of Adhesions/Endometriosis
Nissan Fundoplication
Salpingo-Oophorectomy
Prostatectomy

COMPETITORS

Ascension Health
BJC HealthCare
Catholic Health
  Initiatives
Children's Mercy
  Hospital
CoxHealth
Mercy Health
Saint Luke's Health
  System

Shawnee Mission
  Medical Center
Sisters of Charity of
  Leavenworth
Truman Medical Centers
University of Kansas
  Medical Center

HISTORICAL FINANCIALS

Company Type: Private

Income Statement

FYE: June 30

	REVENUE ($ mil.)	NET INCOME ($ mil.)	NET PROFIT MARGIN	EMPLOYEES
06/16	562	(5)	—	2,600
06/15	563	20	3.7%	—
06/14	626	45	7.2%	—
06/13	604	44	7.4%	—
Annual Growth	(2.4%)	—	—	—

2016 Year-End Financials

Return on assets: 3.1%
Return on equity: (-1.0%)
Current ratio: 1.10

Cash ($ mil.): 27

HEMET UNIFIED SCHOOL DISTRICT

EXECUTIVES

Superintendent, Barry Kayrell
Board of Directors, Stephanie Harmon
Senior Manager, Maria Leyva
Purchasing Director, Tammy Cunningham
Director, Jennifer Draxten
Auditors: VAVRINEKTRINEDAY & CO LLP RAN

LOCATIONS

HQ: HEMET UNIFIED SCHOOL DISTRICT
1791 W ACACIA AVE, HEMET, CA 925453797
Phone: 951 765-5100
Web: WWW.HEMETUSD.ORG

HISTORICAL FINANCIALS

Company Type: Private

Income Statement

FYE: June 30

	REVENUE ($ mil.)	NET INCOME ($ mil.)	NET PROFIT MARGIN	EMPLOYEES
06/16	280	3	1.3%	1,346
06/15	3	0	1.7%	—
06/06	141	47	33.6%	—
06/05	175	6	3.4%	—
Annual Growth	4.4%	(4.6%)	—	—

HEMPSTEAD UNION FREE SCHOOL DISTRICT

EXECUTIVES

Superintendent, Susan Johnson
Board of Directors, Dr Rodgers M Lewis
Assistant Manager, Kwame Yiadom
Board of Directors, Dianne Hamilton
Plant & Facilities Manager, Joe Gaglione
Manager, Kwame Boakye-Yiadom
Director, Larry Gaither
Assistant Manager, Rodney Gilmore
Auditors: NAWROCKI SMITH LLP MELVILLE

LOCATIONS

HQ: HEMPSTEAD UNION FREE SCHOOL DISTRICT
185 PENINSULA BLVD, HEMPSTEAD, NY 115504900
Phone: 516 434-4000
Web: WWW.HEMPSTEADSCHOOLS.ORG

HISTORICAL FINANCIALS

Company Type: Private

Income Statement

FYE: June 30

	REVENUE ($ mil.)	NET INCOME ($ mil.)	NET PROFIT MARGIN	EMPLOYEES
06/16	210	4	2.0%	1,200
06/14	188	0	0.3%	—
06/13*	178	(10)	—	—
12/05	0	0	—	—
Annual Growth	—	—	—	—

*Fiscal year change

2016 Year-End Financials

Return on assets: 3.5%
Return on equity: 2.0%
Current ratio: —

Cash ($ mil.): —

HENDERSON COUNTY HOSPITAL CORPORATION

EXECUTIVES

Chief Executive Officer, Robert P Goodwin
Director, Gladys Nesbitt

LOCATIONS

HQ: HENDERSON COUNTY HOSPITAL CORPORATION
800 N JUSTICE ST, HENDERSONVILLE, NC
287913410
Phone: 828 698-7191
Web: WWW.PARDEEHOSPITAL.ORG

HISTORICAL FINANCIALS

Company Type: Private

Income Statement

FYE: September 30

	REVENUE ($ mil.)	NET INCOME ($ mil.)	NET PROFIT MARGIN	EMPLOYEES
09/15	190	6	3.6%	1,300
09/14	144	(4)	—	—
09/08	1	(0)	—	—
09/04	109	(2)	—	—
Annual Growth	5.1%	—	—	—

2015 Year-End Financials

Return on assets: 4.3%
Return on equity: 3.6%
Current ratio: 1.90
Cash ($ mil.): 7

HENDRICK MEDICAL CENTER

EXECUTIVES

Chief Executive Officer, Tim Lancaster
Vice-President, Susan Wade
Auditors: CONDLEY AND COMPANY LLP ABILE

LOCATIONS

HQ: HENDRICK MEDICAL CENTER
1900 PINE ST, ABILENE, TX 796012432
Phone: 325 670-2000
Web: WWW.HENDRICKHEALTH.ORG

HISTORICAL FINANCIALS

Company Type: Private

Income Statement

FYE: August 31

	REVENUE ($ mil.)	NET INCOME ($ mil.)	NET PROFIT MARGIN	EMPLOYEES
08/16	419	44	10.6%	2,900
08/15	325	15	4.6%	—
08/14	394	55	14.2%	—
08/13	305	46	15.3%	—
Annual Growth	11.2%	(1.7%)	—	—

2016 Year-End Financials

Return on assets: 10.3%
Return on equity: 10.6%
Current ratio: 1.40
Cash ($ mil.): 48

HENDRICKS COUNTY HOSPITAL

EXECUTIVES

Chief Executive Officer, Kevin P Speer
Manager, Brandon Smith
Personnel Director, Gordon Reed
Director, Donna Haggard
Director, Lynn Turner

LOCATIONS

HQ: HENDRICKS COUNTY HOSPITAL
1000 E MAIN ST, DANVILLE, IN 461221991
Phone: 317 745-4451
Web: WWW.SUPPORTHENDRICKS.ORG

HISTORICAL FINANCIALS

Company Type: Private

Income Statement

FYE: December 31

	REVENUE ($ mil.)	NET INCOME ($ mil.)	NET PROFIT MARGIN	EMPLOYEES
12/15	235	9	4.1%	200
12/14	211	9	4.3%	
Annual Growth	11.1%	6.5%	—	—

2015 Year-End Financials

Return on assets: 3.2%
Return on equity: 4.1%
Current ratio: 0.90
Cash ($ mil.): 2

HENRY AVOCADO CORPORATION

EXECUTIVES

President, Philip Henry
Manager, Lori Dever
Chief Financial Officer, Jerry Miller
Office Manager, Lori Deaver
Auditors: WHITE NELSON DIEHL EVANS LLP

LOCATIONS

HQ: HENRY AVOCADO CORPORATION
2355 E LINCOLN AVE, ESCONDIDO, CA 920271298
Phone: 760 745-6632
Web: WWW.HENRYAVOCADO.COM

HISTORICAL FINANCIALS

Company Type: Private

Income Statement

FYE: September 30

	REVENUE ($ mil.)	NET INCOME ($ mil.)	NET PROFIT MARGIN	EMPLOYEES
09/16	212	4	2.2%	88
09/15	180	4	2.6%	—
09/14	169	3	2.1%	—
09/13	131	4	3.3%	—
Annual Growth	17.2%	3.3%	—	—

2016 Year-End Financials

Return on assets: 7.3%
Return on equity: 2.2%
Current ratio: 1.40
Cash ($ mil.): 4

HENRY FORD MACOMB HOSPITALS

EXECUTIVES

President, Stephen J Hathaway
Executive Director, Sheila Sperti

LOCATIONS

HQ: HENRY FORD MACOMB HOSPITALS
215 NORTH AVE, MOUNT CLEMENS, MI 480431716
Phone: 586 466-9310
Web: WWW.MEDSEEK.COM

HISTORICAL FINANCIALS

Company Type: Private

Income Statement

FYE: December 31

	REVENUE ($ mil.)	NET INCOME ($ mil.)	NET PROFIT MARGIN	EMPLOYEES
12/15	411	(0)	—	993
12/08	328	12	3.9%	
Annual Growth	3.3%	—	—	—

2015 Year-End Financials

Return on assets: 3.6%
Return on equity: (-0.1%)
Current ratio: 1.20
Cash ($ mil.): 51

HENRY FORD WYANDOTTE HOSPITAL

EXECUTIVES

Chief Executive Officer, Denise Brooks-Williams
Manager, Mary Kim
Personnel Manager, James Sexon
Office Manager, Jane Cain
Manager, William Mazzara
Plant & Facilities Manager, Chuck Fougnies

LOCATIONS

HQ: HENRY FORD WYANDOTTE HOSPITAL
2333 BIDDLE AVE, WYANDOTTE, MI 481924668
Phone: 734 246-6000
Web: WWW.HFHS.ORG

HISTORICAL FINANCIALS

Company Type: Private

Income Statement

FYE: December 31

	REVENUE ($ mil.)	NET INCOME ($ mil.)	NET PROFIT MARGIN	EMPLOYEES
12/15	267	(9)	—	1,600
12/14	259	(3)	—	—
12/13	293	0	0.3%	—
12/09	276	7	2.8%	—
Annual Growth	(0.5%)	—	—	—

2015 Year-End Financials

Return on assets: 3.3%
Return on equity: (-3.6%)
Current ratio: 1.50
Cash ($ mil.): 13

HENRY MAYO NEWHALL HOSPITAL

Had a bit too much mayo? Arteries feeling a bit clogged? Henry Mayo Newhall Memorial Hospital exists for just this reason (among others). The hospital serves the healthcare needs of the Santa Clarita Valley in northern Los Angeles County. The not-for-profit community hospital houses more than 220 beds and provides general medical and surgical care as well as trauma services (it is a Level II trauma center) outpatient services psychiatric care and emergency services among other specialties. In operation since 1975 the hospital was built to serve the needs of the at-the-time unincorporated City of Santa Clara on land donated by The Newhall Land and Farming Company.

Henry Mayo Memorial's physicians offer patients more than 70 different medical specialties that range from a widely hailed cancer program to an advanced primary stroke center spine and joint program an acute rehab unit growing cardiology services outpatient wound care services and physical and occupational therapies. The hospital also offers extensive maternity programs that include lactation support and childbirth education programs.

The hospital is undergoing a number of expansions including the addition of more intensive care unit (ICU) beds a larger emergency room expanded surgery department the construction of two helipads to receive patients via helicopter and the development of a new Neonatal Intensive Care Unit (NICU). All of the construction is part of Henry Mayo Memorial's 15-year master plan to expand and upgrade to accommodate a growing patient population.Henry Mayo Hospital is also building an inpatient hospital to house up to another 120 hospital beds. The hospital addition will operate 24 hours a day seven days a week and its development will provide Santa Clarita residents with close to 360 total patient beds. Opening is anticipated for 2016.To sum up the 15 year development plan includes the inpatient building up to three medical office buildings a new central plant and up to four parking structures. Other campus modifications include additional acute care beds in the pavilion one helipad on a parking structure and one on the new inpatient building. The plan also includes the new ICU NICU expanded imaging services new operating rooms and centers of excellence. The entire project is expected to cost $300 million and is being funded through operations bonds philanthropy and private investments.

EXECUTIVES

Nursing Director, Vivian Rebel
Director of Nursing, Sue Galvin
Director of Him, Kelly Torrance
Director of Nursing, Dee Rickett
Senior Vice President and Chief Financial Officer, Bob Hudson
Vice President of Marketing and Communications, Marlee Lauffer

LOCATIONS

HQ: HENRY MAYO NEWHALL HOSPITAL
23845 MCBEAN PKWY, VALENCIA, CA 913552083
Phone: 661 253-8000
Web: WWW.HENRYMAYO.COM

COMPETITORS

Aptium Oncology
Brotman Medical Center

Cedars-Sinai Medical Center
Childrens Hospital Los Angeles
Glendale Adventist Medical Center
Good Samaritan Hospital (Los Angeles)
HCA
Hoag Memorial Hospital
Hollywood Presbyterian Medical Center
Marin General Hospital
Methodist Hospital of Southern California
Tenet Healthcare
United Surgical Partners

HISTORICAL FINANCIALS

Company Type: Private

Income Statement

FYE: September 30

	REVENUE ($ mil.)	NET INCOME ($ mil.)	NET PROFIT MARGIN	EMPLOYEES
09/16	321	29	9.1%	1,600
09/15	307	23	7.5%	—
09/14	249	(7)	—	—
09/09	205	11	5.8%	—
Annual Growth	6.6%	13.7%	—	—

2016 Year-End Financials

Return on assets: 9.4%   Cash ($ mil.): 42
Return on equity: 9.1%
Current ratio: 1.50

HENSEL PHELPS CONSTRUCTION CO.

Hensel Phelps Construction builds it all from the courthouse to the big house. The employee-owned general contractor provides a full range of development pre-construction construction and renovation services for commercial institutional and government projects throughout the US and abroad. Its project portfolio includes prisons airports arenas laboratories government complexes offices and more. Major public and private clients have included the US Army Corps of Engineers IBM United Airlines The University of Texas Kodak and Whole Foods. Hensel Phelps founded the eponymous company as a homebuilder in 1937.

Geographic Reach

Colorado-based Hensel Phelps Construction has seven regional offices throughout the continental US including two in California. The company operates internationally most often for US federal projects but also for foreign governments and private enterprises. Its Honolulu branch oversees operations in Hawaii Guam the Marshall Islands and Asia.

Sales and Marketing

Sectors served include aviation commercial education government health care hospitality industrial and justice.

Financial Performance

One of America's largest private companies Hensel Phelps reported $2 billion in revenue in 2014.

Strategy

Hensel Phelps ranks in the top three (by Engineering News Record) among general contractors and construction managers in the US in the aerospace government and "green" government office sectors. The company self-performs (as opposed to subcontracting) most of the work tied to a specific project. That ability helps keep costs and schedules in check. Its construction services include concrete work quality control safety management waste management among others.

In 2016 the company was awarded a contract to build a new 285000-sq.-ft. office tower in Denver. Other notable projects include a new central library in Austin Texas.

EXECUTIVES

President Phelps Development, Eric L. Wilson
CFO, Stephen J. (Steve) Carrico
EVP, Wayne S. Lindholm
EVP, Jon W. Ball
President and CEO, Jeffrey K. (Jeff) Wenaas
EVP, Michael J. Choutka
EVP, Richard G. Tucker
President Hensel Phelps Services, Edwin (Glen) Miller
Vice President, Allan J Bliesmer
Auditors: KPMG LLP DENVER CO

LOCATIONS

HQ: HENSEL PHELPS CONSTRUCTION CO.
12121 GRANT ST, THORNTON, CO 802413129
Phone: 970 352-6565
Web: WWW.HENSELPHELPS.COM

PRODUCTS/OPERATIONS

Selected Projects

Hilton Hok
Aegis Asho
Regional O
Guam NAVFAC Bachelor Enlisted Quarters (BEQ)
Mamizu Utilities and Site Improvements Phase I
Samaritan MOB and Parking Structure
Santa Clara Valley Medical Center Receiving and Support Center
Santa Clara Family Justice Center
Santa Clara Valley Medical Center Receiving and Support Center
Rotary PlayGarden
Norman Y. Mineta San José; International Airport Terminal Area Improvement Program (TAIP)
Vantage Data Center V2
Vantage Data Center V1

Selected Services

Construction
  Change management
  Construction waste management
  LEED project registration
  Quality control
  Safety management
  Scheduling
  Self-perfoming concrete
  Status reporting
  Subcontractor management
  Sustainability audits
  Quality control
Development
  Feasibility studies
  Financing
  Green building planning/education
  Land acquisition
  Leasing
  Pro forma review
Post-construction
  As-built documentation
  Building operations
  Certificate of occupancy
  Commissioning and warranty programs
  LEED project certification
  Moving services
Preconstruction
  Bid packaging
  Budgeting/cost modeling
  Design management
  Estimating
  Green building and planning/education
  Phasing plans
  Regulatory investigation
  Scheduling
  Status reporting
  Subcontractor prequalification
  Value engineering

Selected Markets
Commercial
Education
High technology
Industrial
International
Justice
Leisure
Medical
Multiresidence
Public
Transportation

COMPETITORS

Balfour Beatty Construction	M. A. Mortenson
C.F. Jordan	McCarthy Building
CH2M HILL	PCL Employees Holdings
Clark Construction Group	Rooney Holdings
Fluor	Skanska USA Building
Gilbane	Turner Corporation
Hunt Construction	Tutor Perini
Jacobs Engineering	Walbridge Aldinger
KBR	Walsh Group
	Whiting-Turner

HISTORICAL FINANCIALS

Company Type: Private

Income Statement

FYE: December 31

	REVENUE ($ mil.)	NET INCOME ($ mil.)	NET PROFIT MARGIN	EMPLOYEES
12/15	3,142	70	2.2%	2,000
12/14	2,507	38	1.5%	—
12/13	2,248	57	2.6%	—
12/12	1,220	35	2.9%	—
Annual Growth	37.1%	25.5%	—	—

2015 Year-End Financials

Return on assets: 11.2%   Cash ($ mil.): 194
Return on equity: 2.2%
Current ratio: 0.90

HERITAGE FS INC.

EXECUTIVES

General Manager, Mark Weildacher
Board of Directors, Rodger Koehn
Assistant Controller, Greg Regnier
General Manager, Shawn Oseman
Manager, Tom Gross
Auditors: CLIFTONLARSONALLEN LLP BLOOMI

LOCATIONS

HQ: HERITAGE FS INC.
  1381 S CRESCENT ST, GILMAN, IL 609386128
Phone: 815 265-4751
Web: WWW.HERITAGEFS.COM

HISTORICAL FINANCIALS

Company Type: Private

Income Statement

FYE: August 31

	REVENUE ($ mil.)	NET INCOME ($ mil.)	NET PROFIT MARGIN	EMPLOYEES
08/16	210	8	4.0%	79
08/15	22	2	9.1%	—
08/14*	188	6	3.3%	—
07/13	178	7	4.0%	—
Annual Growth	5.7%	5.7%	—	—

*Fiscal year change

2016 Year-End Financials

Return on assets: 7.8%   Cash ($ mil.): 8
Return on equity: 4.0%
Current ratio: 1.00

HESPERIA UNIFIED SCHOOL DISTRICT

EXECUTIVES

Superintendent, Mark McKinney
Assistant Manager, David Maclaughlin
Executive Secretary, Laura Moore
Auditors: NIGRO NIGRO & WHITE

LOCATIONS

HQ: HESPERIA UNIFIED SCHOOL DISTRICT
  15576 MAIN ST, HESPERIA, CA 923453482
Phone: 760 244-4411
Web: WWW.HESPERIAJRHIGH.ORG

HISTORICAL FINANCIALS

Company Type: Private

Income Statement

FYE: June 30

	REVENUE ($ mil.)	NET INCOME ($ mil.)	NET PROFIT MARGIN	EMPLOYEES
06/16	248	17	7.0%	2,500
06/06	169	23	14.2%	—
06/05	139	11	7.9%	—
06/01	1,444	0	—	—
Annual Growth	—	59.2%	—	—

2016 Year-End Financials

Return on assets: 6.4%   Cash ($ mil.): 89
Return on equity: 7.0%
Current ratio: —

HICKMAN, WILLIAMS & COMPANY

Hickman Williams makes carbon products (anthracite coal metallurgical coke and reactive char coke) and metals and alloys (chromium manganese and silicon) used by metals producers. The company also manufactures service injection systems and cored wire feeding units for metal production facilities. Hickman Williams operates about 50 warehouse facilities throughout the nation. Founded by Richard Hickman and Harry Williams in 1891 the company is now owned by its employees.

EXECUTIVES

Account Manager, Lee Hartinger
Auditors: GRANT THORNTON LLP CINCINNAT

LOCATIONS

HQ: HICKMAN, WILLIAMS & COMPANY
  250 E 5TH ST STE 300, CINCINNATI, OH 452024198
Phone: 513 621-1946
Web: WWW.HICWILCO.COM

COMPETITORS

Berlin Metals	Reliance Steel
Eagle Steel Products	

HISTORICAL FINANCIALS

Company Type: Private

Income Statement

FYE: March 31

	REVENUE ($ mil.)	NET INCOME ($ mil.)	NET PROFIT MARGIN	EMPLOYEES
03/16	195	2	1.4%	92
03/15	247	4	1.8%	—
03/14	245	0	—	—
03/13	287	5	2.0%	—
Annual Growth	(12.0%)	(21.4%)	—	—

2016 Year-End Financials

Return on assets: 4.3%   Cash ($ mil.): 17
Return on equity: 1.4%
Current ratio: 2.50

HIGHLINE MEDICAL CENTER

EXECUTIVES

Chairman, Larry Bjork
Board of Directors, Mike Fitzgerald
Financial Executive, Greg Terreson
Personnel Manager, Don Halterman
Auditors: CATHOLIC HEALTH INITIATIVES E

LOCATIONS

HQ: HIGHLINE MEDICAL CENTER
  16251 SYLVESTER RD SW, BURIEN, WA 981663017
Phone: 206 244-9970

HISTORICAL FINANCIALS

Company Type: Private

Income Statement

FYE: June 30

	REVENUE ($ mil.)	NET INCOME ($ mil.)	NET PROFIT MARGIN	EMPLOYEES
06/15	180	16	9.0%	1,253
06/14*	228	24	10.7%	—
12/09	203	9	4.7%	—
12/08	3	0	—	—
Annual Growth	95.8%	—	—	—

*Fiscal year change

2015 Year-End Financials

Return on assets: 2.7%   Cash ($ mil.): 6
Return on equity: 9.0%
Current ratio: 1.20

HILL PHYSICIANS MEDICAL GROUP, INC.

Hill Physicians Medical Group is the doctors' answer to HMOs. The company is an independent practice association (IPA) serving some 300000 health plan members in northern California. The company contracts with managed care organiza-

tions throughout the region — including HMOs belonging to Aetna CIGNA and Health Net— to provide care to health plan members through its provider affiliates. Its network includes about 3800 primary care and specialty physicians 38 hospitals and 24 urgent care centers. The company also provides administrative services for doctors and patients. PriMed a management services organization created Hill Physicians Medical Group in 1984 and still runs the company.

Geographic Reach

Hill Physicians Medical Group's member facilities are located in Alameda Contra Costa El Dorado Placer Sacramento San Francisco San Joaquin San Mateo Solano and Yolo counties in northern California.

Financial Performance

Hill Physicians Medical Group reported a 3% increase in 2013 to about $455 million due to higher health plan revenues and investment income. Net income grew by 15% to some $13.6 million that year due to higher revenues and cost savings programs.

Strategy

Hill Physicians Medical Group has been working to enhance its technology systems to improve coordination of care including installing electronic prescription and referral management systems. It is also forming partnerships with area insurers and hospitals to improve communication among regional providers as well as to control overall health care costs. For instance the company teamed up with Dignity Health and Blue Shield of California to form an accountable care organization (ACO).

EXECUTIVES

Vice President for Performance Strategy, Terry Hill
Board Member, Harpreet Grewal
Auditors: KPMG LLP SAN FRANCISCO CALIF

LOCATIONS

HQ: HILL PHYSICIANS MEDICAL GROUP, INC.
2409 CAMINO RAMON, SAN RAMON, CA 945834285
Phone: 800 445-5747
Web: WWW.HILLPHYSICIANS.COM

PRODUCTS/OPERATIONS

Selected Health Plan Partners
Aetna of California
Alliance CompleteCare
Anthem/Blue Cross of California
Blue Shield of California
Blue Shield 65 Plus
CIGNA Healthcare of California
Health Net of California
Health Net Medicare
United Healthcare West (formerly Pacificare)
SCAN
Secure Horizons by United Healthcare
Western Healthcare Advantage

COMPETITORS

Alta Bates Summit Medical Center	Orion HealthCorp
	Prospect Medical
Beaver Medical Group	The Palo Alto Medical
HealthCare Partners	Foundation

HISTORICAL FINANCIALS

Company Type: Private

Income Statement

FYE: December 31

	REVENUE ($ mil.)	NET INCOME ($ mil.)	NET PROFIT MARGIN	EMPLOYEES
12/15	504	6	1.3%	488
12/10	427	5	1.2%	—
12/06	427	5	1.2%	—
12/05	1,401	0	—	—
Annual Growth	(9.7%)	243.1%	—	—

2015 Year-End Financials

Return on assets: 1.5%   Cash ($ mil.): 46
Return on equity: 1.3%
Current ratio: 0.90

HILLCREST BAPTIST MEDICAL CENTER

EXECUTIVES

President, Glenn A Robinson
Board of Directors, Michael D Reis
Treasurer, Peter Eimen
Financial Executive, Lorie Hengst
Director, Debbie Hahn
Manager, Susan B McJunkin
Office Manager, Debbie Muerer
Auditors: BKD LLP HOUSTON TX

LOCATIONS

HQ: HILLCREST BAPTIST MEDICAL CENTER
100 HILLCREST MED BLVD, WACO, TX 76712
Phone: 254 202-8675
Web: WWW.HILLCREST.NET

HISTORICAL FINANCIALS

Company Type: Private

Income Statement

FYE: August 31

	REVENUE ($ mil.)	NET INCOME ($ mil.)	NET PROFIT MARGIN	EMPLOYEES
08/15	251	8	3.4%	2,200
08/09	213	2	1.3%	—
08/06	201	(2)	—	—
08/05	204	3	1.6%	—
Annual Growth	2.1%	10.5%	—	—

2015 Year-End Financials

Return on assets: 6.7%   Cash ($ mil.): 36
Return on equity: 3.4%
Current ratio: 1.10

HILLIARD CITY SCHOOL DISTRICT

EXECUTIVES

Superintendent, John Marschhausen
Purchasing Director, Anita Dalluge
Manager, Headher Ayers
Superintendent, Dale Amcvey
Purchasing Manager, Matt Fiesel
Auditors: DAVE YOST COLUMBUS OHIO

LOCATIONS

HQ: HILLIARD CITY SCHOOL DISTRICT
2140 ATLAS ST, COLUMBUS, OH 432289647
Phone: 614 921-7000
Web: WWW.HILLIARDSCHOOLS.ORG

HISTORICAL FINANCIALS

Company Type: Private

Income Statement

FYE: June 30

	REVENUE ($ mil.)	NET INCOME ($ mil.)	NET PROFIT MARGIN	EMPLOYEES
06/16	211	0	0.2%	1,700
06/15	215	11	5.5%	—
06/14	212	10	4.8%	—
06/13	195	(2)	—	—
Annual Growth	2.7%	—	—	—

2016 Year-End Financials

Return on assets: 0.4%   Cash ($ mil.): 30
Return on equity: 0.2%
Current ratio: —

HILLSBOROUGH COUNTY SCHOOL DISTRICT

EXECUTIVES

Chairman, April Griffin
Board of Directors, Cindy Stuart
Board of Directors, Susan L Valdes
Board of Directors, Sally Harris
Board of Directors, Melissa Snively
Account Manager, Ed Nicholsan
Bookkeeper, Lori Wendland
Assistant Manager, Kristin Waskiewicz
Auditors: KPMG LLP TAMPA FL

LOCATIONS

HQ: HILLSBOROUGH COUNTY SCHOOL DISTRICT
901 E KENNEDY BLVD, TAMPA, FL 336023502
Phone: 813 272-4000
Web: WWW.SDHC.K12.FL.US

HISTORICAL FINANCIALS

Company Type: Private

Income Statement

FYE: June 30

	REVENUE ($ mil.)	NET INCOME ($ mil.)	NET PROFIT MARGIN	EMPLOYEES
06/15	2,042	(110)	—	25,000
06/14	1,984	(45)	—	—
06/13	1,878	(44)	—	—
06/12	1,835	(118)	—	—
Annual Growth	3.6%	—	—	—

2015 Year-End Financials

Return on assets: 2.7%   Cash ($ mil.): 125
Return on equity: (-5.4%)
Current ratio: —

HILLSDALE COLLEGE

EXECUTIVES

President, Larry P Arnn
Manager, Debra A Belt
Manager, Samanth Schachermeyer
Auditors: PLANTE & MORAN PLLC PORTAGE

HITCHINER MANUFACTURING CO., INC.

There's no hitch in Hitchiner Manufacturing's business plan. The family-owned supplier of thin-wall investment castings and subassemblies and components operates 4 businesses: Ferrous-USA produces countergravity castings for the auto defense and pump and valve industries; Gas Turbine specializes in hot-section parts utilizing vacuum-melted alloys for the jet engine component market; Hitchiner Manufacturing Company de Mexico makes component parts for auto OEMs; and Hitchiner S.A. de C.V. front-end casting services. Hitchiner is primarily a tier-two supplier (its parts go to another company that contracts directly with the OEM) for majors such as BorgWarner Goodrich General Motors and General Electric.

Operations

The global manufacturer's activities include producing high-volume carbon steel alloy parts used mostly in automotive powertrains. About half of its sales depend on the carmaking industry largely in Mexico which produce the bulk of the company's automotive parts.

The company develops commercial investment casting and related competitive technologies to bolster its offerings for existing and new customers such as those in the industrial gas turbine solar energy and medical industries. It produces castings in more than 160 different alloys.

Its ferrous operations consists of two manufacturing plants located in New Hampshire: Milford (wax injection pattern assembly shell building casting and heat treat operations) and Littleton (medium-to-high volume machining and finishing). The ferrous segment produces a wide array of parts with primary sales in the automotive diesel and military markets.

Hitchiner's gas turbine operations (also in Milford) service the jet engine component market. It specializes in producing hot-section parts requiring sophisticated vacuum-melted alloys with focus on complex thin-walled applications. The unit is a fully qualified supplier to Pratt & Whitney General Electric Westinghouse Allison and BMW.

The company's Mexico-based operations consist of Hitchiner S.A. de C.V. (front-end casting services — 2000 molds per day and 54 metric tons of alloy poured per day) and Hitchiner Manufacturing Company de Mexico (finishing and component assembly).

Hitchiner's research and development activities are supported by Metal Casting Technology a subsidiary jointly owned with GM.

Geographic Reach

Hitchiner has manufacturing operations in the US (Milford and Littleton in New Hampshire) an aerospace defense and general office in Mexico (Santiago Tianguistenco and San Luis Potosi) and a direct sales office in France (which opened in 1995).

Sales and Marketing

Hitchiner makes castings in hundreds of different alloys for a wide range of customers in automotive aerospace defense and other industries.

Hitchiner France provides manages a sales network in Europe and provides the European customers the necessary support.

Company Background

Committed to reducing its carbon footprint as part of its green energy brand in 2011 the company installed a compressed air system designed to significantly cut electrical usage at Hitchiner's Gas Turbine Operation division's Milford plant.

Hitchiner was founded in 1946.

EXECUTIVES

Vice President Corporate Affairs Services, Timothy Sullivan
Vice President of Human Resour, Amy Demmons
Vice President, Scott McDonald
Vice President of Finance, Randy Donovan
Auditors: GRANT THORNTON LLP BOSTON MA

LOCATIONS

HQ: HITCHINER MANUFACTURING CO., INC.
594 ELM ST, MILFORD, NH 030554306
Phone: 603 673-1100
Web: WWW.HITCHINER.COM

COMPETITORS

A. Finkl & Sons	Koch Enterprises
BAE Industries	Lovejoy Industries
Fansteel	Parkview Metal
GKN Sinter Metals	Walker Die Casting

HISTORICAL FINANCIALS
Company Type: Private

Income Statement   FYE: December 31

	REVENUE ($ mil.)	NET INCOME ($ mil.)	NET PROFIT MARGIN	EMPLOYEES
12/15	226	16	7.3%	1,753
12/14	215	16	7.7%	—
12/13	207	2	1.2%	—
12/12	198	13	6.8%	—
Annual Growth	4.6%	7.2%	—	—

2015 Year-End Financials

Return on assets: 16.1%   Cash ($ mil.): 37
Return on equity: 7.3%
Current ratio: 1.70

HITT CONTRACTING, INC.

HITT Contracting hits the nail on the general contracting head. The group provides turnkey construction services for corporate base building and interiors healthcare aviation legal hospitality technology research medical and institutional and governmental facilities. Projects have included construction and design for the Federal Reserve DirecTV and Greenpeace. In addition to general contracting HITT offers design interior paint preconstruction and construction management services. It handles eco-friendly projects historic renovations and infrastructure refits. Founded in 1937 the family-owned firm has operations across the US.

Operations

The company's HITT Hospitality division established in 2011 specializes in hotel renovation and construction. Projects include work for hotel brands including Hilton Marriott Hyatt Four Seasons and W Hotels.

HITT also works on environmentally-friendly LEED-certified projects and finished its 100th LEED Certified Project in 2015.

Geographic Reach

Beyond its corporate office in Falls Church Virginia HITT operates across all 50 US states with offices in Washington DC Atlanta Baltimore Charleston Denver and South Florida. It also serves Puerto Rico the US Virgin Islands Guam American Somoa and the Northern Marina Islands.

Sales and Marketing

HITT has expertise in working with corporations government law firms and technology firms operating in the industrial institutional hospitality and healthcare sectors.

HITT's clients have included big-name companies such as: AOL Archstone-Smith BAE Systems Boeing Booz Allen Hamilton Broe Companies Brookfield Properties Cisco Systems Colorado Hospital Association Corporate Office Properties Trust Crescent Real Estate University of Denver Gap Northrup Grumman Microsoft Oracle Sprint and General Dynamics. The company has an 85% repeat client rate.

Financial Performance

While full financial details of the privately-held company were not available HITT reported that its annual sales exceed $900 million.

Strategy

HITT's experience in serving a variety of industries as well as its geographic diversity has helped the company maintain a healthy backlog. Thanks to its financial strength the company often uses its own money to partially fund projects and buys materials supplies and equipment. The strategy has helped HITT to better control quality and deliver projects on time.

HITT's backlog was no different in 2015 when it was working on more than 30 major projects across the US including: two "special project" new construction jobs worth $260 million in Dulles Virginia; the construction of the $60 million Northrop Grumman Corporate Headquarters; an $8 million build-out for Lockheed Martin; some $5 million per year renovation and modernization work for the International Monetary Fund; and $3.5 million worth of interior renovations for the Consulate of Brazil in Washington DC.

To keep its project portfolio growing the company has steadily increased its presence throughout the US. In 2012 the company expanded to Golden Colorado to offer services for corporate in-

teriors mission critical law firms hospitality health-care federal and commercial mixed-use projects.

EXECUTIVES

Co-President, Brett R. Hitt
Co-President, James E. Millar
EVP Institutional, Yogen R. Patel
EVP Technology, John W. Kane
SVP Denver, Kevin L. Ott
EVP Government, John M. Britt
SVP Paint and Service, David R. Kane
SVP Charleston, Carson P. Knizevski
SVP Hospitality, Peter T. Lanfranchi
EVP National Accounts, Steven E. Richbourg
SVP Atlanta, R. Ryan Bixler
SVP Healthcare, Nick D. Raico
EVP Corporate Base Building, Jeremy S. Bardin
SVP Corporate Interiors, Brian S. Kriz
SVP Law Firms, Joseph P. LaFonte
SVP South Florida, John Planz
SVP Government, R. James Whitney
Vice President Field, David Underwood
Vice President Miami, Neil Donhauser
Vice President Of Finance, Peter Seery
VP Information Technology, John Barrett
Vice President Law Firms, Peter Thaler
Vice President, Chris Michael
Executive Vice President, Steve Richbourg
Senior Vice President Business Development,
 Gary Trvdik
Vice President, Kimberly Roy
Vice President, Ed Miko
Vice President, Sara Collins
Vice President of Finance, Michael Miller
**Vice President Human Resources Sheila Sears
 General Counsel,** Lauren Bediako
Senior Vice President, Chris Hines
Chairman, Russell A. Hitt
Auditors: DELOITTE & TOUCHE LLP MCLEAN

LOCATIONS

HQ: HITT CONTRACTING, INC.
 2900 FAIRVIEW PARK DR # 300, FALLS CHURCH, VA
 220424513
Phone: 703 846-9000
Web: WWW.HITT-GC.COM

PRODUCTS/OPERATIONS

Selected Markets
Government
Health care
Hospitality
Institutional
Law firms
Technology

COMPETITORS

Branch & Associates	KBS
Donohoe Companies	Rodgers Builders
Hayward Baker	SMCI
James G. Davis	Skanska USA Building
Construction	Turner Corporation

HISTORICAL FINANCIALS

Company Type: Private

Income Statement
FYE: December 31

	REVENUE ($ mil.)	NET INCOME ($ mil.)	NET PROFIT MARGIN	EMPLOYEES
12/15	1,084	28	2.7%	775
12/14	958	29	3.1%	—
12/13	921	19	2.1%	—
12/12	827	18	2.3%	—
Annual Growth	9.4%	15.8%	—	—

2015 Year-End Financials

Return on assets: 19.7%   Cash ($ mil.): 45
Return on equity: 2.7%
Current ratio: 0.90

HOBOKEN UNIVERSITY MEDICAL CENTER

EXECUTIVES

Manager, Mike Paolello
Administrative Assistant, Melissa Sisamon

LOCATIONS

HQ: HOBOKEN UNIVERSITY MEDICAL CENTER
 308 WILLOW AVE, HOBOKEN, NJ 070303808
Phone: 201 418-1000

HISTORICAL FINANCIALS

Company Type: Private

Income Statement
FYE: December 31

	REVENUE ($ mil.)	NET INCOME ($ mil.)	NET PROFIT MARGIN	EMPLOYEES
12/15	188	10	5.7%	44
12/14	179	13	7.5%	—
Annual Growth	5.0%	(20.2%)	—	—

2015 Year-End Financials

Return on assets: 11.0%   Cash ($ mil.): 5
Return on equity: 5.7%
Current ratio: 0.90

HOLLAND COMMUNITY HOSPITAL AUXILIARY, INC.

Holland Hospital (formerly Holland Community Hospital) provides a comprehensive range of health services to residents of western Michigan's Lakeshore region. The 190-bed not-for-profit hospital provides a variety of medical care and health services including primary emergency diagnostic surgical rehabilitative and inpatient behavioral health care. Holland Hospital is home to centers of excellence in the treatment of sleep disorders cancer women's health issues and cardiovascular ailments. The hospital provides community health and wellness education programs and operates a regional community health clinic. Founded in 1917 Holland Hospital employs some 330 physicians across 14 medical specialties.

Operations

Holland Hospital had about 29000 urgent care visits and more than 41000 emergency department visits in 2013. It also reported some 16000 surgeries 1700 births 42000 outpatient discharges and 41000 home health visits.

Sales and Marketing

Medicare accounted for some 40% of the hospital's net patient revenues in 2014 followed by Blue Cross (22%) and Medicaid (11%).

Financial Performance

Holland Hospital reported revenue of $217 million and net income of $7 million in 2014.

Strategy

Expanding its menu of health care services in 2013 Holland Hospital opened a new in-patient Spine & Orthopedics unit to meet growing demand. The 23400-sq. ft. facility has 24 private rooms and a dedicated rehabilitation area to speed recovery. In May 2014 the hospital completed construction of a new office building that houses cardiology and vascular specialists.

Also in 2014 the hospital partnered with Spectrum Health member West Michigan Heart to open local offices on its main campus. Holland Hospital and Spectrum Health have a history of collaborations that includes the establishment of the Lakeshore Area Radiation Oncology Center and the Holland Community Health Center.

EXECUTIVES

Vice President Holland Hospital Medical Group,
 Michael Matthews
Blood Bank Director, Loretta Grow
VP Information Security Ops, Paul Grabscheid
Vice President Management, Rob Schwartz
Vice President Quality, Mark Pawlak
Auditors: PLANTE & MORAN PLLC TRAVERSE

LOCATIONS

HQ: HOLLAND COMMUNITY HOSPITAL AUXILIARY,
 INC.
 602 MICHIGAN AVE, HOLLAND, MI 494234918
Phone: 616 748-9346
Web: WWW.HOLLANDHOSPITAL.ORG

Selected Locations
Holland Hospital Main Campus (Holland Michigan)
Holland Hospital Medical Building (Zeeland Michigan)
Lakeshore Medical Campus (Holland Michigan)
Holland Hospital Laboratory & Rehabilitation Services
 (Douglas Michigan)
854 South Washington Medical Offices (Holland
 Michigan)
844 South Washington Medical Offices (Holland
 Michigan)
Holland Hospital Center for Good Health (Holland
 Michigan)
Surgery Center of Western Michigan (Holland Michigan)
Lakeshore Area Radiation Oncology Center (Holland
 Michigan)
Community Health Center (Holland Michigan)

PRODUCTS/OPERATIONS

Selected Services
Alcohol & Drug Abuse Treatment
Allergies
Ambulatory Treatment Unit
Arthritis
Asthma
Back Pain
Behavioral Health
Bladder Health
Bone & Joint Center
Bone Health
Boven Birth Center
Cancer
Cardiopulmonary
Cardiovascular Services
Center for Good Health
Colonoscopy
Comprehensive Breast Services
CT Scan
da Vinci Robotic Assisted Surgery
Depression
Diabetes
Diagnostic Imaging
Ears Nose & Throat
Edema
Email Broadcasts
Emergency Services
Endoscopy Center
Family Medicine
Fibromyalgia
Gastroenterology
Gynecology
Heart
Hip
Home Health Services
Hospitalists
Hysterectomy
Intensive Care Unit/ICU
Interventional Radiology
Joint Replacement Center
Kidney

Knee
Laboratory Services
Lactation Services (Breastfeeding)
Lakeshore Health Partners
Leukemia
Locations
Lymphedema
Mammography
Medical Services
Menopause
Men's Health
Mental Health Services: Inpatient
Mental Health Services: Outpatient
MRI
Nephrology (Kidney)
Neurology
Neurosurgery
Non-Hodgkin's Lymphoma
Nutrition Services
OB/GYN
Osteoporosis
Pain Management
Pediatrics
Pelvic Health
Physical Therapy
Podiatry
Postpartum Depression
Press Room
Prevention & Wellness
Providers
Psychiatry
Pulmonary Services
Quality
Radiology
Radiology Oncology
Rehabilitation Services
Respiratory Services
School Nursing
Shoulder
Skin Care
Sleep Center
Special Care Nursery
Spine & Orthopedics
Spine Neck & Back
Sports Medicine
Stroke
Substance Abuse Treatment
Surgical Services
Telemetry
Ultrasound
Urgent Care
Urology Services
Walk-In-Care
Women's Midlife
Women's Services
Wound Care
X-ray
Zeeland Medical Offices

COMPETITORS

Mercy Health Hackley   Zeeland Community
Spectrum Health   Hospital

HISTORICAL FINANCIALS

Company Type: Private

Income Statement

FYE: March 31

	REVENUE ($ mil.)	NET INCOME ($ mil.)	NET PROFIT MARGIN	EMPLOYEES
03/15	230	17	7.5%	1,500
03/14	220	12	5.9%	—
03/10*	170	10	6.2%	—
12/08	0	0	—	—
Annual Growth	202.8%	—	—	—

*Fiscal year change

2015 Year-End Financials

Return on assets: 6.1%
Return on equity: 7.5%
Current ratio: 0.70

Cash ($ mil.): 25

HOLY CROSS HEALTH, INC.

EXECUTIVES

President, Kevin Sexton
Executive Director, Thomas Nicosia
Executive Secretary, Ana Ferretti

LOCATIONS

HQ: HOLY CROSS HEALTH, INC.
1500 FOREST GLEN RD, SILVER SPRING, MD 209101460
Phone: 301 754-7000
Web: WWW.HOLYCROSSHEALTH.ORG

HISTORICAL FINANCIALS

Company Type: Private

Income Statement

FYE: June 30

	REVENUE ($ mil.)	NET INCOME ($ mil.)	NET PROFIT MARGIN	EMPLOYEES
06/15	413	37	9.1%	3,270
06/14	442	37	8.4%	—
06/13	404	40	10.0%	—
06/12	414	22	5.4%	—
Annual Growth	(0.0%)	19.3%	—	—

2015 Year-End Financials

Return on assets: 8.4%
Return on equity: 9.1%
Current ratio: 3.40

Cash ($ mil.): 208

HOLY SPIRIT HOSPITAL OF THE SISTERS OF CHRISTIAN CHARITY

Holy Spirit Health tends to the health of the incarnate. The Holy Spirit Health System (HSHS) provides cardiology women's health care pediatric care and other acute and emergency medical services to the residents of greater Harrisburg in south-central Pennsylvania. The flagship Holy Spirit Hospital has some 310 beds as well as a level III neonatal intensive care unit. The hospital also operates an adjoining cardiac treatment facility and it has a network of affiliated family practice urgent care surgical and specialty health clinics. HSHS was established in 1963 and is an affiliate of Geisinger Health System.

Change in Company Type
As part of a national trend of hospital consolidation HSHS became an affiliate of Geisinger Health System in 2014. The system continues to be sponsored by the Sisters of Christian Charity.

Operations
The Holy Spirit Hospital employs more than 500 physicians and operates specialty care centers include an endoscopy clinic a hyperbaric wound healing unit and women's post-surgical recovery unit. Outpatient facilities include cardiology clinics family medicine centers surgery clinics and pediatric and women's health centers. Altogether HSHS annually handles some 16000 inpatient admissions 250000 outpatient visits 52000 emergency room visits and 1200 births.

HSHS employs a number of hospitalists who follow the patient's progress from admission to discharge and ensure follow-up care. The hospital also provides community health seminars to educate the public on common health concerns and the benefits of preventative care.

Geographic Reach
HSHS operates in a five-county service territory surrounding Harrisburg in south-central Pennsylvania. It has facilities in Camp Hill Carlisle Chambersburg Dillsburg Duncannon Harrisburg Lemoyne Marysville Mechanicsburg New Cumberland New Kingstown and Shippensburg.

Strategy
HSHS has undergone a number of expansions in recent years opening numerous outpatient centers to deliver care closer to home in the communities in which it serves. Also many hospitals are growing their outpatient services because they tend to bring in more income and help compensate for downward pricing on inpatient hospital stays from private and public health care payers. The system is focused on adding new locations to its network welcoming more family medicine offices (and their existing patients).

The organization expanded clinical services in areas including cryoablation cardiac rehabilitation sleep diagnostics and urgent care during 2012 and 2013. It also opened a new data center increase and improve use of electronic health record (EHR) systems.

EXECUTIVES

President, Romaine Niemeyer
Board of Directors, David J Felicio
Director, Glenn Harboro
Chief, Robert Powell Jr
Chief Operating Officer, Richard A Schaffner
Principal, Fred Kireta

LOCATIONS

HQ: HOLY SPIRIT HOSPITAL OF THE SISTERS OF CHRISTIAN CHARITY
503 N 21ST ST, CAMP HILL, PA 170112288
Phone: 717 763-2100

PRODUCTS/OPERATIONS

Selected Centers and Services
Atrial Fibrillation Center
Behavioral Health
Broad Street Family Health Center
Cancer Care
Capital Cardiovascular Associates
Cardiac Rehab
Carlisle Family Health Center
Centers fo
Devonshire Family Health Center
Diabetes Services
Diagnostic
Dillsburg Family Health Center
Duncannon Family Health Center
Emergency Services
Gastrointestinal Services
Green Hill Family Health Center
Heart Care
Holy Spirit Endocrinology Center
Home Health Care
Hospitalist Program
Imaging Services
Internal Medicine of Mechanicsburg
Kunkel Group's LAP-BAND Program
Kunkel Surgical Group
Laboratory Services
Lewin & Nadar Cardiology Associates
Magill Family Health Center
Maternal Assistance Program
Maternity
Medical Outreach
Nutrition Services
Occupational Health
Orthopedics
Palliative Care
Pharmacy Services

Physical Therapy
Preparing for Your Appointment
Research & Clinical Trials
Ryder Barnes and Associates (pediatrics)
Silver Creek Family Health Center
Sleep Studies
Snoke Family Health Center
Speech Therapy
Spirit Urgent Care
Surgical Services
Travel Health Services
Vascular Associates
Women's Services
Wound Healing & Hyperbarics

COMPETITORS

Hershey Medical Center
 PinnacleHealth System
 Saint Vincent Health System
 Sharon Regional Health System
 University of Pennsylvania Health System
 WellSpan Health

HISTORICAL FINANCIALS

Company Type: Private

Income Statement

FYE: June 30

	REVENUE ($ mil.)	NET INCOME ($ mil.)	NET PROFIT MARGIN	EMPLOYEES
06/15	289	10	3.7%	2,698
06/10	271	11	4.2%	—
06/09	5	0	—	—
06/08	1,650	0	0.0%	—
Annual Growth	(22.0%)	152.1%	—	—

2015 Year-End Financials

Return on assets: 5.1%   Cash ($ mil.): 20
Return on equity: 3.7%
Current ratio: 0.80

HOMELAND ENERGY SOLUTIONS, LLC

EXECUTIVES

Chief Financial Officer, David A Finke
Vice-President, Stan Wubbena
Board of Directors, Christine Marchand
Director, R Bruess
Auditors: RSM US LLP DES MOINES IOWA

LOCATIONS

HQ: HOMELAND ENERGY SOLUTIONS, LLC
 2779 HIGHWAY 24, LAWLER, IA 52154
Phone: 563 238-5555
Web: WWW.HOMELANDENERGYSOLUTIONS.COM

HISTORICAL FINANCIALS

Company Type: Private

Income Statement

FYE: December 31

	REVENUE ($ mil.)	NET INCOME ($ mil.)	NET PROFIT MARGIN	EMPLOYEES
12/16	272	34	12.6%	46
12/15	269	24	9.1%	—
12/14	330	68	20.8%	—
12/13	400	28	7.1%	—
Annual Growth	(12.0%)	6.9%	—	—

2016 Year-End Financials

Return on assets: 5.9%   Cash ($ mil.): 14
Return on equity: 12.6%
Current ratio: 0.40

HOMESTEAD HOSPITAL, INC

EXECUTIVES

Chief Executive Officer, William M Duquette
Assistant Vice-President, Frank Fernandez
Director, Carmen Bouchard
Personnel Director, Erika Weissberg
Director, Jose Torres
Trustee, Ramon Oyarzun
Personnel Director, Sue Kuryla
Auditors: DELOITTE & TOUCHE LLP

LOCATIONS

HQ: HOMESTEAD HOSPITAL, INC
 975 BAPTIST WAY, HOMESTEAD, FL 330337600
Phone: 786 243-8000

HISTORICAL FINANCIALS

Company Type: Private

Income Statement

FYE: September 30

	REVENUE ($ mil.)	NET INCOME ($ mil.)	NET PROFIT MARGIN	EMPLOYEES
09/15	175	(35)	—	1
09/14	174	(34)	—	—
Annual Growth	0.7%	—	—	—

2015 Year-End Financials

Return on assets: —   Cash ($ mil.): —
Return on equity: (-20.4%)
Current ratio: 0.50

HORRY COUNTY SCHOOL DISTRICT

EXECUTIVES

Superintendent, Dr Rick Maxey
Administrative Assistant, Dolly Dean
Clerk, Kimberly Crumling
Executive Director, Arlene Ray
Administrative Assistant, Dawn Meehan
Executive Director, Denise Vereen
Auditors: MCGREGOR & COMPANY LLP COLUM

LOCATIONS

HQ: HORRY COUNTY SCHOOL DISTRICT
 335 FOUR MILE RD, CONWAY, SC 295264506
Phone: 843 488-6700
Web: WWW.HORRYCOUNTY.ORG

HISTORICAL FINANCIALS

Company Type: Private

Income Statement

FYE: June 30

	REVENUE ($ mil.)	NET INCOME ($ mil.)	NET PROFIT MARGIN	EMPLOYEES
06/15	472	9	2.0%	5,000
06/10	427	2	0.6%	—
06/09	408	(9)	—	—
06/08	0	0	—	—
Annual Growth	—	299.4%	—	—

2015 Year-End Financials

Return on assets: 9.3%   Cash ($ mil.): 213
Return on equity: 2.0%
Current ratio: —

HOSPITAL AUTHORITY OF VALDOSTA AND LOWNDES COUNTY, GEORGIA

Hospital Authority of Valdosta and Lowndes County Georgia oversees South Georgia Medical Center (SGMC) a 335-bed regional hospital serving southern Georgia and northern Florida. The hospital offers a range of services focusing on such specialties as diabetes management pulmonary care pediatrics and women's health. SGMC's Pearlman Cancer Center is devoted to a holistic approach to cancer care. The medical center also operates a specialized wound healing center and orthopedic and spine centers. The public hospital was founded as Pineview General Hospital in 1955. Its governing board is appointed by the local city council and county commissioners.

Operations

SGMC serves as a regional referral hospital meaning it handles major medical cases for smaller community hospitals in the area. The medical center employs 2700 staff members including more than 300 physicians.

SGMC operates several satellite campuses including SGMC Outpatient Plaza Smith Northview Hospital SGMC Lanier and SGMC Berrien. Together the facilities are known as South Georgia Health System.

Sales and Marketing

Medicare payments accounted for 32% of net patient revenue in 2014; Medicaid accounted for 4% of net patient revenue that year.

Strategy

The medical center added a new facility in 2013 — the community facility in Berrien County. In 2015 SGMC Lakeland Villa broke ground on an adjacent replacement nursing home which will offer private rooms two courtyards a rehabilitation and therapy room and a spa room.

EXECUTIVES

Secretary Materials Management, Helen Weis
Vice Chairman, Cameron Hickman

LOCATIONS

HQ: HOSPITAL AUTHORITY OF VALDOSTA AND
 LOWNDES COUNTY, GEORGIA
 2501 N PATTERSON ST, VALDOSTA, GA 316021735
Phone: 229 333-1000
Web: WWW.VALDOSTAMASSAGE.COM

PRODUCTS/OPERATIONS

2014 Sales

	% of total
Net patients service revenue	96
Other revenue	4
Total	**100**

COMPETITORS

Appling
 Doctors Hospital of Augusta

Liberty Regional Medical Center
Memorial Health University Medical Center
St. Joseph's/Candler Health System
Tallahassee Memorial HealthCare
Tift Regional Medical Center

HISTORICAL FINANCIALS
Company Type: Private

Income Statement
FYE: September 30

	REVENUE ($ mil.)	NET INCOME ($ mil.)	NET PROFIT MARGIN	EMPLOYEES
09/15*	310	(2)	—	3,000
06/08	0	0	42.1%	—
09/07	208	29	14.2%	—
09/06	191	23	12.0%	—
Annual Growth	5.5%	—	—	—

*Fiscal year change

2015 Year-End Financials

Return on assets: 5.9%
Return on equity: (-0.7%)
Current ratio: 1.10
Cash ($ mil.): 26

HOSPITAL OF CENTRAL CONNECTICUT

The Hospital of Central Connecticut an acute care facility serves the communities of central Connecticut from two campuses. With approximately 415 beds and more than 400 physicians the hospital offers a full range of diagnostic and treatment services as well as education and prevention programs. Its diabetes treatment program is an affiliate of the Boston-based Joslin Diabetes Center; the hospital is also affiliated with the University of Connecticut School of Medicine and other universities. Central Connecticut Health Alliance (CCHA) is the parent company of The Hospital of Central Connecticut and is part of the Hartford Health Care network.

Operations

In addition to its 415 acute-care beds the two Hospital of Central Connecticut campuses have about 30 bassinets. Through its university affiliations the hospital facilities provide residency and training programs in fields including critical care internal medicine gastroenterology general surgery and pulmonary medicine. It also conducts medical research including clinical trials in fields such as diabetes mental health and cancer treatment.

Affiliates that are part of the CCHA organization include Alliance Occupational Health Central Connecticut Senior Health Services Central Connecticut Physical Medicine and Central Connecticut VNA. CCHA affiliates provide a wide range of whole-life services throughout the region.

Geographic Reach

The Hospital of Central Connecticut's two Connecticut locations are the Bradley Memorial Campus in Southington and the New Britain General Campus in New Britain.

Strategy

In 2015 the hospital system opened a 75000-sq. ft. cancer center at the Hartford HealthCare Cancer Institute. Services include prevention and detection; treatments including chemotherapy radiation therapy and radiosurgery; ongoing support; and clinical trials.

Hospital of Central Connecticut also recently opened a Family Health Center including a primary care medical office outpatient lab radiology center and wound care center. The center which opened in 2013 also offers hyperbaric services such as hyperbaric oxygen therapy.

Company Background

The Hospital of Central Connecticut was formed through the merger of New Britain General Hospital and Bradley Memorial Hospital.

EXECUTIVES

Legal Secretary, Kimberly Paulakos

LOCATIONS

HQ: HOSPITAL OF CENTRAL CONNECTICUT
100 GRAND ST, NEW BRITAIN, CT 060522016
Phone: 860 224-5011
Web: WWW.THOCC.ORG

PRODUCTS/OPERATIONS

Selected Centers and Services
Bariatric surgery
Breast care
Cancer Center
Cardiovascular
Clinical research
Diabetes care
Emergency services
Endocrine and bone health
Family Enrichment Center
Healthy Aging Center
Joint and Spine Center
Laboratory
Lifeline
Maternity
Medical services
Nursing
Occupational health
Occupational therapy
Outpatient services
Pain management
Palliative care
Pediatrics
Physical medicine
Primary care and specialty practices
Psychiatry
Radiology
Sleep disorders
Speech therapy
Stroke Center
Surgical services
Vascular Center
Weigh Your Options
Wellness programs
Wound care

COMPETITORS

Bristol Hospital	Waterbury Hospital
Lawrence & Memorial Hospital	Western Connecticut Health Network
Saint Francis Hospital and Medical Center	Yale New Haven Health System

HISTORICAL FINANCIALS
Company Type: Private

Income Statement
FYE: September 30

	REVENUE ($ mil.)	NET INCOME ($ mil.)	NET PROFIT MARGIN	EMPLOYEES
09/15	338	(4)	—	2,500
09/14	360	24	6.8%	—
09/13	403	26	6.7%	—
09/09	401	(71)	—	—
Annual Growth	(2.8%)	—	—	—

2015 Year-End Financials

Return on assets: 3.8%
Return on equity: (-1.2%)
Current ratio: 1.30
Cash ($ mil.): 12

HOSPITAL THE DANBURY INC

EXECUTIVES

Administrative Assistant, Pam Carola
Director, Suzanne House
Director, Vadim Tikhomirov

LOCATIONS

HQ: HOSPITAL THE DANBURY INC
24 HOSPITAL AVE, DANBURY, CT 068106077
Phone: 203 739-7000
Web: WWW.DANBURYHOSPITAL.ORG

HISTORICAL FINANCIALS
Company Type: Private

Income Statement
FYE: September 30

	REVENUE ($ mil.)	NET INCOME ($ mil.)	NET PROFIT MARGIN	EMPLOYEES
09/15	622	(5)	—	3,000
09/14	504	35	7.1%	—
09/13	501	4	0.9%	—
09/12	529	56	10.6%	—
Annual Growth	5.5%	—	—	—

2015 Year-End Financials

Return on assets: 5.8%
Return on equity: (-0.9%)
Current ratio: 1.00
Cash ($ mil.): 21

HOT LINE CONSTRUCTION, INC.

EXECUTIVES

President, Carol Bade
Manager, Lisa Armas
Office Manager, Cruz Munos
Manager, Jacob Milhoan
Auditors: WAYNE LONG & CO BAKERSFIELD

LOCATIONS

HQ: HOT LINE CONSTRUCTION, INC.
9020 BRENTWOOD BLVD STE H, BRENTWOOD, CA 945134049
Phone: 925 634-9333
Web: WWW.HOTLINECONSTRUCTIONINC.COM

HISTORICAL FINANCIALS
Company Type: Private

Income Statement
FYE: December 31

	REVENUE ($ mil.)	NET INCOME ($ mil.)	NET PROFIT MARGIN	EMPLOYEES
12/15	224	24	10.7%	425
12/09	40	2	4.9%	—
12/03	13	1	13.3%	—
12/02	608	0	—	—
Annual Growth	—	155.6%	—	—

2015 Year-End Financials

Return on assets: 2.4%
Return on equity: 10.7%
Current ratio: 1.10
Cash ($ mil.): 11

HOUCHENS INDUSTRIES, INC.

Houchens Industries is a supermarket of businesses as well as an operator of supermarkets. The diversified company runs some 400 retail grocery convenience and neighborhood markets across the US. That includes more than 180 conventional supermarkets under the Houchens Food Giant IGA Piggly Wiggly Buehler Foods and Mad Butcher banners. It hass more than 200 Save-A-Lot discount grocery stores in a dozen states that offer limited selections and cover 15000 sq. ft. or less. Outside the grocery store Houchens operates Cohen's Fashion Optical franchise stores and several Sheldon's Express Pharmacy stores. Other businesses include construction financial services real estate restaurants and recycling. Houchens is 100%-owned by its employees.

Operations

Houchens Industries has amassed a diverse portfolio of more than 35 businesses over the years through acquisitions. Beyond the grocery segment Houchen also serves customers in the construction insurance wealth management technology and healthcare industries.

Houchens is the largest franchisee of limited-assortment Save-A-Lot stores in the US. (Grocery retailer and wholesaler SUPERVALU is the parent company of Save-A-Lot.) The company's manufacturing businesses include Stephens Pipe & Steel a leading maker and distributor of fence materials. Southern Recycling collects and processes metals paper glass and plastics. The company also franchises Sonic and Subway quick-serve restaurants. It also operates the Taco Del Mar restaurant chain and Price Less Foods which sells groceries at cost plus 10%.

Geographic Reach

Based in Kentucky Houchens Industries operates grocery stores in Alabama Arkansas Florida Georgia Indiana Illinois Kentucky Mississippi Missouri Tennessee and Virginia. Its diverse other businesses are active almost every US state and about 30 other countries worldwide.

Strategy

Houchens Industries looks to buy assets that have sound management and a history of providing good cash flow that can be bought at a reasonable price. Recent acquisitions include the 14-store family-run White's Fresh Foods chain which operates grocery stores in Tennessee and Virginia and the Bowling Green Kentucky-based two-store drug retailer Sheldon's Express Pharmacy thereby expanding into the drugstore business. Houchens plans to leverage the acquisition to create a regional drugstore chain. The Whites purchase followed the acquisition of Chicago-based Tampico Beverages a maker of refrigerated juice drinks and punches sold in more than 36 countries for an undisclosed amount. Tampico supplies beverages to grocery and convenience stores as well as quick-serve restaurants.

In new version of IGA stores Houchens has made convenience a watchword. The IGA Crossroads brand is set up to help customers get in and out quickly. The stores also contain quick service restaurants. In those and other stores Houchens added to the sandwich mix available bringing Which Wich into its lineup joining Schlotzsky's and Subway.

Company Background

Founded by Ervin Houchens as BG Wholesale in rural Kentucky in 1917 Houchens has been owned by its employees since 1988.

EXECUTIVES

Chairman and CEO, James (Jimmie) Gipson, age 76
President, Spencer A. Coates
CEO Tampico Beverages, Scott Miller
CFO, Gordon Minter
President Cohen's Fashion Optical, Bob Cohen
President hitcents.com, Chris Mills
President and CEO Food Giant Supermarkets, Ron Watkins
Head Pan Oston, Jim Vance
Head Save a Lot, David Burnett
Vice President Produce, John Mudd
Auditors: BKD LLP BOWLING GREEN KENTU

LOCATIONS

HQ: HOUCHENS INDUSTRIES, INC.
700 CHURCH ST, BOWLING GREEN, KY 421011816
Phone: 270 843-3252
Web: WWW.SAVE-A-LOT.COM

PRODUCTS/OPERATIONS

Selected Operations

American Sun Systems (tanning salon supplier)
Blake Hart Taylor & Wiseman (insurance)
Buehler's Buy Low (grocery retail)
Cohen's Fashion Optical (optical stores)
Food Giant (grocery retail)
Hilliard Lyons (financial services)
Houchens Markets (grocery retail)
IGA (licensed grocery retail)
Insurance Specialists (insurance)
Jr. Food Stores (convenience stores)
Price Less Foods (grocery retail)
Save-A-Lot (licensed grocery retail)
Scotty's (asphalt paving)
Sheldon's Express Pharmacy (drugstores)
Southern Recycling Inc. (recycling)
Stewart-Richey Construction Inc. (construction management)
Taco Del Mar (fast-food)
Tampico (juice)
TS Trucking (hauling)
Van Meter Insurance (insurance benefits)
White's Fresh Foods (grocery retail)

COMPETITORS

7-Eleven	Meijer
ALDI	Mott's
Ameriprise	Nestl ©
CVS	Ocean Spray
Charles Schwab	Odwalla
Citigroup	Old Orchard
Citrus World	Raymond James
Cumberland Farms	Financial
Dole Food	Rite Aid
Dr Pepper Snapple	Sheetz
Group	Southeastern Grocers
E*TRADE Financial	Sunkist
E. W. James	Sunny Delight
Edward D. Jones	TD Ameritrade
FMR	Thorntons Inc.
Faygo	Tree Top
Goya	Tropicana
John Hancock Financial	Visionworks of America
Services	Wal-Mart
Jugos del Valle USA	Walgreen
K-VA-T Food Stores	Weis Markets
Kroger	Welch's
Luxottica Retail	

HISTORICAL FINANCIALS

Company Type: Private

Income Statement

FYE: October 1

	ASSETS ($ mil.)	NET INCOME ($ mil.)	INCOME AS % OF ASSETS	EMPLOYEES
10/16	1,976	104	5.3%	16,000
10/15*	2,014	99	5.0%	—
09/14	1,993	84	4.2%	—
09/13	1,969	110	5.6%	—
Annual Growth	0.1%	(1.9%)	—	—

*Fiscal year change

2016 Year-End Financials

Return on assets: 3.1%	Sales ($ mil): 2,987
Return on equity: 3.5%	

HOUSING AUTHORITY OF THE COUNTY OF SANTA CLARA

EXECUTIVES

Executive Director, Alex Sanchez

LOCATIONS

HQ: HOUSING AUTHORITY OF THE COUNTY OF SANTA CLARA
505 W JULIAN ST, SAN JOSE, CA 951102300
Phone: 408 275-8770
Web: WWW.HACSC.ORG

HISTORICAL FINANCIALS

Company Type: Private

Income Statement

FYE: June 30

	ASSETS ($ mil.)	NET INCOME ($ mil.)	INCOME AS % OF ASSETS	EMPLOYEES
06/15	656	55	8.5%	4
06/14	581	22	3.9%	—
Annual Growth	12.9%	145.6%	—	—

2015 Year-End Financials

Return on assets: 0.8%	Sales ($ mil): 315
Return on equity: 17.6%	

HOUSTON COUNTY BOARD OF EDUCATION

EXECUTIVES

Chairman of the Board, Fred Wilson
Manager, Charles Holloway
Auditors: GREGG S GRIFFIN STATE AUDITO

LOCATIONS

HQ: HOUSTON COUNTY BOARD OF EDUCATION
1100 MAIN ST, PERRY, GA 310693531
Phone: 478 988-6200
Web: WWW.HCBE.NET

HISTORICAL FINANCIALS

Company Type: Private

Income Statement

FYE: June 30

	REVENUE ($ mil.)	NET INCOME ($ mil.)	NET PROFIT MARGIN	EMPLOYEES
06/15	292	0	0.3%	3,856
06/14	281	(9)	—	—
06/13	278	(33)	—	—
06/12	15	0	3.1%	—
Annual Growth	166.6%	20.7%	—	—

2015 Year-End Financials
Return on assets: —
Return on equity: 0.3%
Current ratio: —

Cash ($ mil.): 17

HOUSTON COUNTY HEALTHCARE AUTHORITY

The Houston County Health Authority is the governing body for Southeast Alabama Medical Center (SAMC) a not-for-profit acute-care hospital that serves Southeastern Alabama and adjacent parts of Georgia and Florida. In addition to providing comprehensive medical surgical and emergency care the 420-bed SAMC provides specialty services including heart cancer and women's health care. The health system also operates primary care physician offices and clinics specializing in neurology pain management and cardiovascular care as well as a home health agency. SAMC offers residency programs for medical students most of whom attend the Alabama College of Osteopathic Medicine.

Operations

SAMC serves the tri-state area with the help of approximately 50 physicians. Aside from its primary hospital in Dothan Alabama SAMC boasts primary care physician offices a home health agency and about 10 specialty centers.

Geographic Reach

SAMC serves some 600000 residents spanning not only Southeast Alabama but Southwest Georgia and the Florida Panhandle.

Strategy

To expand and improve the health care services it offers in its community SAMC looks for opportunities to open new clinics or specialty centers. For example it recently acquired a former retail development near the hospital in late 2017; the system has not revealed any plans for the property yet.

In mid-2017 SAMC implemented a restructuring which included some layoffs. Through the efforts it hopes to save some $30 million annually on purchasing goods and services as well as on labor costs.

Company Background

SAMC was founded in 1957.

EXECUTIVES

SVP and CFO, Derek Miller
SVP and COO, Charlie Brannen
CEO, Richard O. Sutton
Director Information Services, Eric Daffron
VP Patient Care Services and Chief Nursing Officer, Diane Buntyn
VP Medical Affairs, Charles L. Harkness
VP Marketing and Public Relations, Claudia Hall
Vice President Operations, Ronald E Dean
Vice President Information Technology Chief Information Officer, Rich Temple
Vice President Of Information Technology, Karen Loftin
Vice President Business Development, Amy Barnett
Vice President Human Resources, Peggy Sease
Director of Pharmacy, Philip Atkinson
Chairman, Chester Sowell
Vice Chairman, John McDaniel
Secretary, Ranada Doyle
Auditors: DRAFFIN & TUCKER LLP ATLANTA

LOCATIONS

HQ: HOUSTON COUNTY HEALTHCARE AUTHORITY
1108 ROSS CLARK CIR, DOTHAN, AL 363013022
Phone: 334 793-8111

PRODUCTS/OPERATIONS

Selected Services
Behavioral Health
Diabetes
Endoscopy
Endovascular Surgery
Family Services
Heart & Vascular
Lithotripsy
Living Well Fitness
Neurology Associates
NeuroSpine Center
Orthopedic Services
Pain Management Center
Rehabilitation Services
Sleep Center
Southeast Cancer Center
Women's Services
Wound Care Center

COMPETITORS

Baptist Health (AL)	Jackson Hospital &
Bay Medical Center	Clinic of Alabama
East Alabama Medical	Phoebe Putney Memorial
Center	Hospital
HealthSouth	
Jackson County	
Hospital of Florida	

HISTORICAL FINANCIALS
Company Type: Private

Income Statement
FYE: September 30

	REVENUE ($ mil.)	NET INCOME ($ mil.)	NET PROFIT MARGIN	EMPLOYEES
09/16	364	9	2.5%	2,500
09/15	311	0	0.3%	—
09/14	290	1	0.4%	—
09/11	271	(0)	—	—
Annual Growth	6.1%	—	—	—

2016 Year-End Financials
Return on assets: 6.1%
Return on equity: 2.5%
Current ratio: 1.10

Cash ($ mil.): 18

HOUSTON INDEPENDENT SCHOOL DISTRICT

EXECUTIVES

President, Michael Lunceford
Manager, James Hundemer
Director, Donna Patch
Assistant Manager, Martha Salazar-Zamora
Executive Director, Randy Tullos
Auditors: DELOITTE & TOUCHE LLP HOUSTON

LOCATIONS

HQ: HOUSTON INDEPENDENT SCHOOL DISTRICT
4400 W 18TH ST, HOUSTON, TX 770928501
Phone: 713 556-6005
Web: WWW.HOUSTONISD.ORG

HISTORICAL FINANCIALS
Company Type: Private

Income Statement
FYE: June 30

	REVENUE ($ mil.)	NET INCOME ($ mil.)	NET PROFIT MARGIN	EMPLOYEES
06/16	2,333	266	11.4%	22,440
06/13	1,876	117	6.3%	—
06/12	2,004	(118)	—	—
Annual Growth	3.9%	—	—	—

2016 Year-End Financials
Return on assets: 3.8%
Return on equity: 11.4%
Current ratio: —

Cash ($ mil.): 4

HPS LLC

EXECUTIVES

Vice-President, Mike Sandy
Sales Manager, Preston Fouts
Director, Jason Londrigan
Executive Director, Alison Reardon
Marketing Manager, Kendra Tossava
Auditors: MEYAARD TOLMAN & VENLET PC Z

LOCATIONS

HQ: HPS LLC
3275 N M 37 HWY, MIDDLEVILLE, MI 493339126
Phone: 269 795-3308
Web: WWW.HPSNET.COM

HISTORICAL FINANCIALS
Company Type: Private

Income Statement
FYE: June 30

	REVENUE ($ mil.)	NET INCOME ($ mil.)	NET PROFIT MARGIN	EMPLOYEES
06/16	1,032	0	0.1%	38
06/15	960	0	0.1%	—
06/14	862	0	0.1%	—
06/13	898	0	0.1%	—
Annual Growth	4.8%	8.9%	—	—

2016 Year-End Financials
Return on assets: —
Return on equity: 0.1%
Current ratio: 1.70

Cash ($ mil.): 5

HUGHES SATELLITE SYSTEMS CORPORATION

EXECUTIVES

Chief Executive Officer, Michael T Dugan
Director, Jose Albino
Auditors: KPMG LLP DENVER COLORADO

LOCATIONS

HQ: HUGHES SATELLITE SYSTEMS CORPORATION
100 INVERNESS TER E, ENGLEWOOD, CO
801125308
Phone: 303 706-4000

HISTORICAL FINANCIALS
Company Type: Private

Income Statement
FYE: December 31

	REVENUE ($ mil.)	NET INCOME ($ mil.)	NET PROFIT MARGIN	EMPLOYEES
12/16	1,799	121	6.8%	2
12/15	1,837	138	7.6%	—
12/14	1,807	102	5.7%	—
12/13	1,542	(34)	—	—
Annual Growth	5.3%	—	—	—

2016 Year-End Financials
Return on assets: 5.9%
Return on equity: 6.8%
Current ratio: 6.30
Cash ($ mil.): 2,070

HUMAX USA, INC

Humax USA prefers to connect with its customers through its products. The company develops and manufactures flat-panel TV sets and digital set-top boxes for satellite cable and terrestrial connections. Humax USA is the US-based subsidiary of Korean consumer electronics manufacturing firm Humax Co. which was founded in 1989. The brand has become one of the most popular worldwide among set-top boxes. Humax's products are available in more than 90 countries as well as in the US. The company primarily serves customers in Asia and Europe.

To expand its presence in the US market Humax USA has partnered with the likes of DIRECTV and TiVo to offer products integrated with their technology.

EXECUTIVES

President, Yong Min Son
Board of Directors, Keehyuk Sung
Vice-President, Frank Romeo

LOCATIONS

HQ: HUMAX USA, INC
15641 RED HILL AVE # 150, TUSTIN, CA 927807327
Phone: 714 389-1924
Web: WWW.HUMAXAMERICAS.COM

COMPETITORS

DIRECTV
SANYO
Samsung Electronics
Sony USA
Tivo Solutions

HISTORICAL FINANCIALS
Company Type: Private

Income Statement
FYE: December 31

	REVENUE ($ mil.)	NET INCOME ($ mil.)	NET PROFIT MARGIN	EMPLOYEES
12/15	373	0	0.1%	29
12/14	448	0	0.1%	—
12/13	317	0	0.1%	—
12/12	290	0	0.2%	—
Annual Growth	8.7%	(1.8%)	—	—

2015 Year-End Financials
Return on assets: 35.0%
Return on equity: 0.1%
Current ratio: 0.20
Cash ($ mil.): 4

HUMBLE INDEPENDENT SCHOOL DISTRICT

EXECUTIVES

Superintendent, Guy M Sconzo
Chief Financial Officer, Elizabeth Lynn
Director, Francis Dobbins
Director, Jaime Gallego
Assistant Manager, Carolyn Clapp
Board of Directors, Dave Martin
Consultant, Karen Kruger
Manager, James Woods
Manager, Kimberly Clark
Auditors: WHITLEY PENN LLP HOUSTON TEX

LOCATIONS

HQ: HUMBLE INDEPENDENT SCHOOL DISTRICT
20200 EASTWAY VILLAGE DR, HUMBLE, TX
773382405
Phone: 281 641-1000
Web: WWW.HUMBLE.K12.TX.US

HISTORICAL FINANCIALS
Company Type: Private

Income Statement
FYE: June 30

	REVENUE ($ mil.)	NET INCOME ($ mil.)	NET PROFIT MARGIN	EMPLOYEES
06/16	458	11	2.4%	5,000
06/13	365	(8)	—	—
06/12	354	2	0.7%	—
06/11	0	0	—	—
Annual Growth	—	577.9%	—	—

HUNTERDON MEDICAL CENTER (INC)

EXECUTIVES

Chief Executive Officer, Robert P Wise
General Manager, Keia McMillan
Manager, Betty Cronce
Chief Operating Officer, Don Pinner

LOCATIONS

HQ: HUNTERDON MEDICAL CENTER (INC)
2100 WESCOTT DR, FLEMINGTON, NJ 088224604
Phone: 908 788-6100
Web: WWW.HUNTERDONHEALTHCARE.ORG

HISTORICAL FINANCIALS
Company Type: Private

Income Statement
FYE: December 31

	REVENUE ($ mil.)	NET INCOME ($ mil.)	NET PROFIT MARGIN	EMPLOYEES
12/15	267	10	3.9%	2,200
12/08	207	(41)	—	—
12/07	203	11	5.8%	—
12/06	0	0	—	—
Annual Growth	—	—	—	—

2015 Year-End Financials
Return on assets: 7.2%
Return on equity: 3.9%
Current ratio: 1.90
Cash ($ mil.): 31

HUNTINGTON CABELL HOSPITAL INC

EXECUTIVES

President, Brent A Marsteller
Board of Directors, Steven L Burton
Manager, William Ermann
Auditors: BAKER TILLY VIRCHOW KRAUSE LL

LOCATIONS

HQ: HUNTINGTON CABELL HOSPITAL INC
1340 HAL GREER BLVD, HUNTINGTON, WV
257010195
Phone: 304 526-2000
Web: WWW.CABELLHUNTINGTON.ORG

HISTORICAL FINANCIALS
Company Type: Private

Income Statement
FYE: September 30

	REVENUE ($ mil.)	NET INCOME ($ mil.)	NET PROFIT MARGIN	EMPLOYEES
09/16	559	18	3.2%	2,300
09/15	473	17	3.8%	—
09/14	417	8	2.0%	—
09/13	391	13	3.4%	—
Annual Growth	12.7%	10.6%	—	—

2016 Year-End Financials
Return on assets: 2.2%
Return on equity: 3.2%
Current ratio: 2.00
Cash ($ mil.): 98

HUNTINGTON HOSPITAL

EXECUTIVES

Principal, Peter W Corrigan
Administrative Assistant, Lori Harris
VP Personnel, Mike Quartier
Account Manager, Francis Tam
Director, Leslie Berina
Manager, Lynette Dahlman

LOCATIONS

HQ: HUNTINGTON HOSPITAL
100 W CALIFORNIA BLVD, PASADENA, CA 911053010
Phone: 626 397-5000
Web: WWW.HUNTINGTONHOSPITAL.COM

HISTORICAL FINANCIALS
Company Type: Private

Income Statement
FYE: December 31

	REVENUE ($ mil.)	NET INCOME ($ mil.)	NET PROFIT MARGIN	EMPLOYEES
12/15	551	3	0.7%	3,500
12/14	513	1	0.4%	—
Annual Growth	7.5%	107.6%	—	—

2015 Year-End Financials
Return on assets: 4.7%
Return on equity: 0.7%
Current ratio: 1.60
Cash ($ mil.): 14

HUNTINGTON HOSPITAL DOLAN FAMILY HEALTH CENTER, INC.

When residents of the Gold Coast feel poorly Huntington Hospital is there to help. Part of the North Shore-Long Island Jewish Health System Huntington Hospital is a 410-bed not-for-profit tertiary care center providing a comprehensive range of medical services to residents of Huntington New York and surrounding communities. Along with general surgical services the hospital provides specialty cardiac cancer maternity pediatric and psychiatric care. Huntington also operates a number of outpatient diagnostic and community clinics where patients can turn for primary care physical rehabilitation or specialized care for other ailments.

Operations

In addition to a full range of general and specialist medical services Huntington Hospital provides medical training services. The facility is a clinical campus for the Hofstra North Shore-LIJ School of Medicine a partnership between the parent organization and Hofstra University. As a not-for-profit organization the hospital also provides community outreach and charity care services.

In 2013 Huntington Hospital had 15159 inpatient discharges (including the delivery of 1383 babies); 49702 emergency department visits; and 9064 ambulatory surgeries.

Geographic Reach

Located in Huntington New York Huntington Hospital serves residents along much of Long Island's North Shore.

Strategy

Huntington Hospital continues to expand its range of medical services. The medical center has added pain management and electrophysiology capabilities in recent years. It also provides expanded peripheral cardiac procedures including elective angioplasties and has added a second cardiac catheterization lab. In 2014 the hospital broke ground on a $50 million expansion that will add nearly 24000 sq. ft. of space to its emergency department.

In 2015 Huntington Hospital partnered with Ob Hospitalist Group to provide onsite obstetrician/gynecology hospitalist services at all times.

Company Background

The hospital was established in 1916. It has been part of the North Shore-LIJ Health System since 1994.

EXECUTIVES

President, Michael J Dowling
Board of Directors, Harry Mariani
Board of Directors, Fred J Buckholtz

LOCATIONS

HQ: HUNTINGTON HOSPITAL DOLAN FAMILY HEALTH CENTER, INC.
270 PARK AVE, HUNTINGTON, NY 117432799
Phone: 631 351-2000
Web: WWW.HUNTHOSP.ORG

PRODUCTS/OPERATIONS

Selected Centers and Services
Cardiac Intervention and Electrophysiology
Center for Orthopedics and Joint Replacement Surgery
Comprehensive Laboratory Services
Comprehensive Women's Health Center
Critical Care Services
Designated Comprehensive Cancer Center
Designated Emergency and Elective Angioplasty Program
Designated Level II Trauma Center
Designated Stroke Center
Dolan Family Center
Dolan Family Health Center
Epilepsy Program
Healthier Tomorrow Pediatric Weight Management Program
Internal Medicine - Hospitalist Program
Interventional Radiology
Intracranial Neurosurgery
Joint Replacement Program
Level II Neonatal Critical Care Center
Palliative Medicine
Pediatric Emergency Care Center
Pediatric Medicine
Perinatal Services
Psychiatric Services
Surgical Services
Thoracic Surgery

COMPETITORS

Calvary Hospital
Catholic Health Services of Long Island
Catholic Healthcare System
HealthSouth
Mather Memorial Hospital
Montefiore Medical
New York City Health and Hospitals
New York Health Care
NewYork-Presbyterian Healthcare
NewYork-Presbyterian Hospital
Stamford Health

HISTORICAL FINANCIALS
Company Type: Private

Income Statement
FYE: December 31

	REVENUE ($ mil.)	NET INCOME ($ mil.)	NET PROFIT MARGIN	EMPLOYEES
12/15	302	2	0.9%	2,000
12/14	283	14	5.3%	—
12/13	325	61	19.0%	—
12/05	201	1	0.9%	—
Annual Growth	4.1%	5.0%	—	—

2015 Year-End Financials
Return on assets: 6.6%
Return on equity: 0.9%
Current ratio: 1.20

Cash ($ mil.): 23

HURLEY MEDICAL CENTER

A community hospital owned by the City of Flint Hurley Medical Center is a teaching hospital serving Genesee Lapeer and Shiawassee counties in eastern Michigan. The 440-bed acute care facility is affiliated with the medical schools of Michigan State University and The University of Michigan. It provides care in areas such as cancer mental health rehabilitation surgery and women's health and it is a regional center for pediatrics. Hurley Medical Center also offers advanced specialty care such as trauma care neonatal intensive care kidney transplantation burn medicine and bariatric (weight loss) surgery. The center was founded in 1908 and is owned by the state of Michigan.

Operations

Hurley Medical Center has a physician health organization (PHO) partnership with the Professional Medical Corporation. The Hurley PHO of Mid-Michigan is a multi-specialty physician group that contracts with managed care organizations to provide care.

The hospital has an affiliation partnership with the Henry Ford Health System; the two health care providers offer a joint kidney transplantation program. Hurley Medical Center also operates the Genesys Hurley Cancer Institute in partnership with the Genesys Regional Medical Center.

Financial Performance

Hurley's revenue increased 3% in 2013 as it took in more patient payments. It reported a net loss of $2.3 million due to increased expenses including salaries unrealized losses on investments.

Strategy

The medical center works to update and expand its services on a regular basis. In 2012 it doubled in size with the opening of the Paul F. Reinhart Emergency Trauma Center.

EXECUTIVES

Director of Pharmacy, Amy Benko
Vice President And Chief Medical Officer, Michael Jaggi
Vice President of Service Line Development, Michael Burnett
Vice President, Karen Lopez
Interim Vice President for, Beth Brophy
Radiology Director, Dawn Hiller
Physical Therapy Director, Dean Frick
Medical Records Director, Jodie Brady
Director of Health Information Management, Belle Bell
Admissions Director, Linda Hills
Vice Chair Marilyn Fuller, Chris Flores

LOCATIONS

HQ: HURLEY MEDICAL CENTER
1 HURLEY PLZ, FLINT, MI 485035902
Phone: 810 257-9000
Web: WWW.HURLEYMC.COM

COMPETITORS

Covenant HealthCare
Crittenton Hospital
Detroit Medical Center
Genesys Regional Medical Center
Henry Ford Health System
McLaren Health Care
Munson Healthcare
Sparrow Health System
St. John Health
Trinity Health (Novi)

HISTORICAL FINANCIALS
Company Type: Private

Income Statement
FYE: June 30

	REVENUE ($ mil.)	NET INCOME ($ mil.)	NET PROFIT MARGIN	EMPLOYEES
06/15	378	24	6.4%	2,884
06/08*	350	3	1.1%	—
03/08	250	0	0.1%	—
Annual Growth	6.1%	99.7%	—	—

*Fiscal year change

2015 Year-End Financials
Return on assets: 8.3%
Return on equity: 6.4%
Current ratio: 1.40

Cash ($ mil.): 58

HURST-EULESS-BEDFORD INDEPENDENT SCHOOL DISTRICT

EXECUTIVES

Superintendent, Gene Buinger
Plant & Facilities Manager, Randy Morgan
Administrative Assistant, Diane Cramer
Accountant, Juanita Baker
Supervisor, Larry Parker
Auditors: WEAVER AND TIDWELL LLP FORTH

LOCATIONS

HQ: HURST-EULESS-BEDFORD INDEPENDENT
SCHOOL DISTRICT
1849 CENTRAL DR, BEDFORD, TX 760226017
Phone: 817 267-3311
Web: WWW.HEBISD.EDU

HISTORICAL FINANCIALS

Company Type: Private

Income Statement

	REVENUE ($ mil.)	NET INCOME ($ mil.)	NET PROFIT MARGIN	EMPLOYEES
08/15	226	8	3.6%	2,322
08/14	216	(42)	—	
08/13	204	(52)	—	
08/12	212	(18)	—	
Annual Growth	2.2%	—	—	

FYE: August 31

2015 Year-End Financials

Return on assets: 1.2%   Cash ($ mil.): 145
Return on equity: 3.6%
Current ratio: —

HY-VEE, INC.

Give Hy-Vee a high five for being one of the largest privately owned US supermarket chains despite serving some modestly sized towns in the Midwest. The company runs some 235 stores in eight Midwestern states. About half of its supermarkets are in Iowa as are most of its 20-plus Hy-Vee drugstores. It distributes products to its stores through several subsidiaries including Lomar Distributing (specialty foods) and Perishable Distributors of Iowa (fresh foods). Other activities include construction and specialty pharmacies. Charles Hyde and David Vredenburg founded the employee-owned firm in 1930. It takes its name from a combination of its founders' names.

Operations

In addition to its food and drug retail operations Hy-Vee offers customers financial products. Adding to its menu of financial services Hy-Vee subsidiary Midwest Heritage Bank in 2011 acquired Iowa-based L&K Insurance a full-line insurance agency. L&K changed its name to Midwest Heritage Insurance Services post sale.

Geographic Reach

Hy-Vee's stores are located in Illinois Iowa Kansas Minnesota Missouri Nebraska South Dakota and Wisconsin. The company supplies its stores from distribution centers in Chariton and Cherokee Iowa.

Financial Performance

Hy-Vee's 235 stores ring up more than $8 billion in annual sales.

Strategy

Hy-Vee is gradually expanding in several key markets in the Midwest including Chicago Minneapolis-St. Paul and Madison Wisconsin. To that end the regional grocery chain in 2014 announced plans to enter the Twin Cities market. In 2013 the chain opened its second supermarket in Madison after entering the Madison market in 2009. To cater to local tastes the company says the 80000-sq.-ft. Madison store has the largest cheese selection of any Hy-Vee supermarket. Hy-Vee is also testing a smaller-format store (about 20000-25000 sq. ft. with no pharmacies) in select locations. It's also adding stores in its core Iowa market with a supermarket slated to open in Winterset in 2014.

Going beyond traditional grocery fare Hy-Vee in 2013 acquired its joint venture partner's stake in Hy-Vee Weitz Company a construction firm based in Des Moines. The grocery store operator renamed the company Hy-Vee Construction and plans to expand the in-house construction management group. The company also teamed up with specialty pharmacy operator Amber Pharmacy to form a new company (called Hy-Vee Pharmacy Solutions) to provide services for patients with complex and chronic health problems including Crohn's disease hemophilia psoriasis and other chronic ailments. The grocery chain has also been focusing on adding Hy-Vee Gas convenience units (some 80 locations include these) wine and spirits stores pharmacies and Hy-Vee HealthMarket departments.

Ric Jurgens in 2012 retired as chairman and CEO after 43-years with Hy-Vee. He was succeeded by president and COO Randy Edeker.

EXECUTIVES

Assistant Vice President Media Relations, Ruth Comer
EVP and Chief Merchandising Officer, Jon S. Wendel, age 54
Chairman President and CEO, Randy Edeker, age 55
EVP and Chief Customer Officer, Sheila Laing
EVP CFO and Treasurer, Mike Skokan
Vice Chairman EVP and Chief Administrative Officer, Andy McCann
EVP Western Region, Brett Bremser
EVP and COO, Jay Marshall
EVP Eastern Region, Darren Baty
Rph, Helen Eddy
Vice President Retail Information Technology, Julie Proffitt
Senior Vice President and Chief Health Officer, Kristin Williams
Pharmacy Manager, Marrianne Ryno
VICE PRESIDENT, BILL KELLEY
Assistant Vice President Sec, Angie Rosenberger
Assistant Vice President Operations, Rob Eslick
Group Vice President, Jason Pride
Assistant Vice President Engineering and Construction, Dave Kozak
Assistant Vice President Meat Operations, Kenan Judge
Director of Pharmacy Technology, Michael Wilson
Assistant Vice President Health and Wellness Marketing, Erin Bailey
Assistant Vice President operations, Dan Wampler
Assistant Vice President, Tony Kaska
Assistant Vice President Western Region, Pat Hensley
AIA Assistant Vice President Store Development Engineering, Andrew Reich
Assistant Vice President Government Relations, Noreen Otto
VICE PRESIDENT, TIM HOPSON
Vice President, Nate Stewart

Assistant Vice President Store Setup, Mark Millsap
Vice President Distribution, Tod Hockenson
Assistant Vice President Human Resources, Linda Threlkeld
Vice President Education and Training, Denise Broderick
SENIOR VICE PRESIDENT SUPPLY CHAIN, Karl Kruse
VICE PRESIDENT, JASON MIKESELL
Vice President Human Resources, Leigh Walters
Group Vice President Information Technology, Tom Settle
Assistant Vice President, Marshall Sanders
Assistant Vice President Human Resources, Kate Wolfe
Assistant Vice President Brand Image, Wendy Hiatt
VICE PRESIDENT, JULIE MCMILLIN
Assistant Vice President for Engineering and Construction, Jeff Markey
Assistant Vice President Employee Benefits, Kristine Jones
Assistant Vice President Risk Management, John Brummit
Vice President Convenience Stores, Tonia Petterson
Pharmacy Manager, Brad Moriarty
Pharmacy Manager, Heather Yennie
Pharmacy Manager, Jessica Wonderlich
Vice President Business Development, Kevin Sherlock
Assistant Vice President Food Service, Blane Jones
Assisant Treasurer, Jeff Pierce
Secretary to Greg Frampton, Stacey Groff

LOCATIONS

HQ: HY-VEE, INC.
5820 WESTOWN PKWY, WEST DES MOINES, IA
502668223
Phone: 515 267-2800
Web: WWW.HY-VEE.COM

PRODUCTS/OPERATIONS

2012 Stores

	No.
Supermarkets	212
Drugstores	22
Total	**234**

Selected Subsidiaries

D & D Foods Inc. (salads dips and meats)
Florist Distributing Inc. (flowers plants and florist supplies)
Hy-Vee Construction L.C. (construction)
Hy-Vee Pharmacy Solutions (specialty pharmacy services)
Hy-Vee Weitz Construction L.C. (construction)
Lomar Distributing Inc. (specialty foods)
Midwest Heritage Bank FSB (banking)
Perishable Distributors of Iowa Ltd. (meat fish seafood and ice cream)

COMPETITORS

ALDI	Niemann Foods
Associated Wholesale Grocers	Rite Aid
	Roundy's
Ball's Food	SUPERVALU
CVS	Save-A-Lot Food Stores
Casey's General Stores	Target Corporation
Fareway Stores	Wal-Mart
Kmart	Walgreen
Kroger	

HISTORICAL FINANCIALS

Company Type: Private

Income Statement
FYE: December 31

	REVENUE ($ mil.)	NET INCOME ($ mil.)	NET PROFIT MARGIN	EMPLOYEES
12/16*	9,842	0	—	84,000
09/13	8,014	0	—	
09/12	7,682	0	—	
Annual Growth	6.4%	—	—	—

*Fiscal year change

2016 Year-End Financials

Return on assets: 6.7% Cash ($ mil.): 17
Return on equity: —
Current ratio: 0.30

IAP WORLDWIDE SERVICES, INC.

Wherever US troops are marching IAP Worldwide Services is there to support them. The company provides a variety of logistics and facility support services chiefly for the US Department of Defense and other government customers including US states and other countries; it also undertakes work for commercial enterprises. Services include base camp facilities support logistics planning and temporary staffing. The company operates through three distinct segments: global operations and logistics; facilities management and base operations support; and professional and technical services. Investment firm Cerberus Capital Management owns a controlling interest in IAP.

Operations

IAP caters to clients in 27 countries. It operates in more than 120 locations in 23 countries worldwide; with key locations in US UK the UAE Iraq and Africa. It maintains corporate offices in Panama City Florida and Arlington Virginia.

Strategy

The company grows by opening new offices in key regions. In 2013 IAP expanded its footprint in the Africa and the Middle East region by establishing offices in Kurdistan Iraq; Kuwait; and Libya.

It also grows via partnerships and by actively pursuing new and repeat contracts. In 2013 IAP and Riverside Technology received $30 million in contracts from the National Oceanic and Atmospheric Administration to provide technical support to the Southeast Fisheries Science Center.

That year G3 Systems won a NATO contract for the facilities management of Camp Oqab a base serving 250 US Air Force and Afghan personnel.

Company Background

IAP in 2011 opened a new office in Dubai located at the crucial crossroads of Asia Africa and Europe. Most of IAP's suppliers and vendors are currently located in Dubai or are planning to move to the Jebel Ali Free Trade Zone. Through the office opening IAP was able to store material such as prepositioned and consigned materials and source them within or draw upon manufacturing throughout the Gulf Cooperation Council minimizing the cost of duty. As part of the company's international expansion strategy the location also facilitates new business with other multinational companies operating out of the Middle East and Africa.

IAP was founded in 1989.

EXECUTIVES

Vice President Finance, Alan Moore
Vice President, Jason Fleischman
Vice President Marketing, Lawrence Wharton
Vice President of Aviation and Engineering Solutions, Michael Bozeman
Vice President of Business Development Operations, Tracy Engelfried
Auditors: RSM US LLP MCLEAN VIRGINIA

LOCATIONS

HQ: IAP WORLDWIDE SERVICES, INC.
7315 N ATLANTIC AVE, CAPE CANAVERAL, FL 329203721
Phone: 973 633-5115

PRODUCTS/OPERATIONS

Selected Services
Air traffic control
Augment existing workforces
Base camp facilities and life support
Contingency planning
Disaster relief and cleanup
Engineering services
Facilities management
Food and custodial services
HVAC systems
Infrastructure reconstruction
Logistics planning
Power generation
Procurement
Program management
Transportation and heavy lift

COMPETITORS

Academi
Delta Tucker
Eagle Support Services
KBR
LTM
Raytheon Intelligence Information and Services
Serco Inc.
UPS Supply Chain Solutions

HISTORICAL FINANCIALS

Company Type: Private

Income Statement
FYE: December 31

	REVENUE ($ mil.)	NET INCOME ($ mil.)	NET PROFIT MARGIN	EMPLOYEES
12/15	546	2	0.5%	1,647
12/14	551	263	47.7%	
12/13	11	(0)	—	
12/12	15	(0)	—	
Annual Growth	227.4%	—	—	—

2015 Year-End Financials

Return on assets: 14.9% Cash ($ mil.): 25
Return on equity: 0.5%
Current ratio: 1.00

ICI CONSTRUCTION, INC.

EXECUTIVES

President, Russell Cobb
Vice-President, Chris Graves
Superintendent, Don Knobloch
Project Manager, Jason Pace
Superintendent, Andy Knobloch
Auditors: CORNWELL JACKSON PLLC PLANO

LOCATIONS

HQ: ICI CONSTRUCTION, INC.
24715 W HARDY RD, SPRING, TX 773735764
Phone: 281 355-5151
Web: WWW.ICICONSTRUCTIONHOUSTON.COM

HISTORICAL FINANCIALS

Company Type: Private

Income Statement
FYE: June 30

	REVENUE ($ mil.)	NET INCOME ($ mil.)	NET PROFIT MARGIN	EMPLOYEES
06/16	175	0	0.0%	102
06/15	189	0	0.1%	
06/14	165	0	0.4%	
06/13	155	1	0.8%	
Annual Growth	4.1%	(69.7%)	—	—

2016 Year-End Financials

Return on assets: 15.6% Cash ($ mil.): 8
Return on equity: —
Current ratio: 0.70

IDAHO PACIFIC LUMBER COMPANY, INC.

EXECUTIVES

President, Eric D Grandeen
Financial Executive, Eric Grandeen
Purchasing Agent, Kevin Monette
Office Manager, Niki Robin
Senior Manager, Mark Hutchinson
Auditors: EIDE BAILLY LLP BOISE IDAHO

LOCATIONS

HQ: IDAHO PACIFIC LUMBER COMPANY, INC.
1770 S SPANISH SUN WAY, MERIDIAN, ID 836428024
Phone: 208 375-8052
Web: WWW.IDAPAC.COM

HISTORICAL FINANCIALS

Company Type: Private

Income Statement
FYE: December 31

	REVENUE ($ mil.)	NET INCOME ($ mil.)	NET PROFIT MARGIN	EMPLOYEES
12/15	181	4	2.6%	70
12/14	190	1	1.0%	
12/13	168	1	1.1%	
12/12	106	0	0.0%	
Annual Growth	19.4%	430.3%	—	—

2015 Year-End Financials

Return on assets: 2.9% Cash ($ mil.): —
Return on equity: 2.6%
Current ratio: 0.80

IDEA PUBLIC SCHOOLS

EXECUTIVES

Chairman, Mike Rhodes
Board of Directors, Gabriel Puente
Financial Executive, Carlo Hersberger
Director, Alberto Castillo
Auditors: PADGETT STRATEMANN & CO LL

LOCATIONS

HQ: IDEA PUBLIC SCHOOLS
505 ANGELITA DR STE 9, WESLACO, TX 785998694
Phone: 956 377-8000
Web: WWW.IDEAPUBLICSCHOOLS.ORG

HISTORICAL FINANCIALS

Company Type: Private

Income Statement

FYE: June 30

	REVENUE ($ mil.)	NET INCOME ($ mil.)	NET PROFIT MARGIN	EMPLOYEES
06/16	269	20	7.7%	2,381
06/15	208	14	6.8%	—
/*	0	0	—	—
Annual Growth	—	—	—	—

*Fiscal year change

2016 Year-End Financials

Return on assets: 7.2% Cash ($ mil.): 80
Return on equity: 7.7%
Current ratio: 1.10

IHA HEALTH SERVICES CORPORATION

EXECUTIVES

President, William J Fileti
Trustee, Walter Whitehouse

LOCATIONS

HQ: IHA HEALTH SERVICES CORPORATION
24 FRANK LLOYD WRIGHT DR, ANN ARBOR, MI
481059484
Phone: 734 747-6766
Web: WWW.IHACARES.COM

HISTORICAL FINANCIALS

Company Type: Private

Income Statement

FYE: June 30

	REVENUE ($ mil.)	NET INCOME ($ mil.)	NET PROFIT MARGIN	EMPLOYEES
06/15	227	5	2.5%	3
06/14	207	8	4.3%	—
06/13	167	12	7.2%	—
Annual Growth	16.5%	(31.3%)		—

2015 Year-End Financials

Return on assets: 10.0% Cash ($ mil.): 30
Return on equity: 2.5%
Current ratio: 2.30

ILLINOIS INSTITUTE OF TECHNOLOGY

Chicago has some cool architecture due in part to the Illinois Institute of Technology (IIT). The school offers more than 100 undergraduate and graduate degree programs in engineering science psychology architecture business law humanities and design. In addition to three campuses in Chicago IIT also has locations in Summit-Argo (Moffet campus) and Wheaton (Daniel F. and Ada L. Rice campus). The institute has an enrollment of some 8000 undergraduate graduate business school and law school students with a student-to-faculty ratio of 8:1.

Operations

IIT's heritage includes the innovative Bauhaus tradition that set up shop at the university in the 1930's. These days its innovation is expressed in the form of interdisciplinary research on such themes as Energy and Sustainability Improving the Quality of Life and Perfect Power. IIT maintains about 30 research institutes with major centers focused on the study of transportation infrastructure sustainable energy electricity innovation biomedical science and engineering and food safety and health.

Financial Performance

IIT reported $265 million in revenues in fiscal 2014 and 2013. In fiscal 2014 IIT generated 55% of its revenues from tuition and fees; 22% from grants and contracts; 4% from its endowment; and the balance from other sources. Higher tuition charges lifted tuition and fees' contribution to the total by 2% in fiscal 2014.

Strategy

IIT regularly evaluates its offerings and adds new degree programs to meet the needs of a changing society. In 2012 it introduced a Master's degree program for cyber forensics and security majors.

In 2013 IIT received a $10 million grant to help build a state-of-the-art innovation center (which is scheduled to break ground in 2016). Named the Ed Kaplan Family Institute for Innovation and Tech Entrepreneurship it will promote innovation guide ideas along the path to becoming products and serve as a hub for various entrepreneurship initiatives. The school is also forming two new colleges: the College of Science and Lewis College of Human Sciences which includes programs in humanities social sciences and psychology. It also formed a new college Food Science and Nutrition in the School of Applied Technology which includes its Institute for Food Safety and Health.

Company Background

IIT was created in 1940 by the merger of Armour Institute (founded in 1893) with Lewis Institute (established in 1895).

EXECUTIVES

Associate Vice President Community Development, Leroy Kennedy
Assistant Vice President, Rajendra Mehta
Vice President for Finance and Administration, Patricia Laughlin
Vice President of IT, Sidney Guralnick
Associate Vice President Undergraduate Enrollment and Financial Aid, Gerald Doyle
Vice President for Facilities and Public Safety, Bruce Watts
Associate Vice President of Finance and Controller, Brian Laffey
Managing Director Knapp Entrepreneurship Center, Nik Rokop
Associate Vice President Institutional Advancement, PETER BRIECHLE
Associate Vice President International Aff International Affairs, Mary Dawson
Associate Vice President of Human Resources, Antoinette Murril
Chief People Officer, Bruce Mueller
Vice President, Randy Crawford
Associate Vice President, Ronald Staudt
Vice President and Treasurer at Chinese Students and Scholars Association, Jia Wang
Assoc Vice President Auxillary Services, Jean Bingham

Assistant SEC, Michael C McGibbon
Auditors: KPMG LLP CHICAGO IL

LOCATIONS

HQ: ILLINOIS INSTITUTE OF TECHNOLOGY
10 W 35TH ST, CHICAGO, IL 606163717
Phone: 312 567-3000
Web: WWW.IIT.EDU

PRODUCTS/OPERATIONS

Selected Schools and Colleges
Armour College of Engineering
Chicago-Kent College of Law
College of Architecture
College of Psychology
College of Science and Letters
Institute of Design
School of Applied Technology (SAT)
Stuart School of Business

HISTORICAL FINANCIALS

Company Type: Private

Income Statement

FYE: May 31

	REVENUE ($ mil.)	NET INCOME ($ mil.)	NET PROFIT MARGIN	EMPLOYEES
05/16	276	(10)	—	1,662
05/15	276	7	2.8%	—
05/14	261	17	6.7%	—
05/13	259	37	14.5%	—
Annual Growth	2.2%			

2016 Year-End Financials

Return on assets: 5.3% Cash ($ mil.): 8
Return on equity: (-3.7%)
Current ratio: —

ILWU-PMA WELFARE TRUST

EXECUTIVES

Principal, Michael Ouchida
Auditors: PRICEWATERHOUSECOOPERS LLP PH

LOCATIONS

HQ: ILWU-PMA WELFARE TRUST
1188 FRANKLIN ST STE 101, SAN FRANCISCO, CA
941096852
Phone: 415 673-8500
Web: WWW.ILWU.ORG

HISTORICAL FINANCIALS

Company Type: Private

Income Statement

FYE: June 30

	REVENUE ($ mil.)	NET INCOME ($ mil.)	NET PROFIT MARGIN	EMPLOYEES
06/15	676	27	4.1%	2
06/14	624	(21)	—	—
06/10	585	18	3.1%	—
Annual Growth	2.9%	8.9%	—	—

2015 Year-End Financials

Return on assets: 14.4% Cash ($ mil.): 7
Return on equity: 4.1%
Current ratio: 1.80

INDEPENDENCE SCHOOL BOARD OF EDUCATION

EXECUTIVES

President, Jill Esry
Board of Directors, Annette Miller
General Manager, Dan Sherman
Superintendent, Joanie Hartnett

LOCATIONS

HQ: INDEPENDENCE SCHOOL BOARD OF
  EDUCATION
  201 N FOREST AVE, INDEPENDENCE, MO
  640502696
Phone: 816 521-5300
Web: WWW.ISDSCHOOLS.ORG

HISTORICAL FINANCIALS

Company Type: Private

Income Statement				FYE: June 30
	REVENUE ($ mil.)	NET INCOME ($ mil.)	NET PROFIT MARGIN	EMPLOYEES
06/16	187	24	12.9%	1,800
06/14	182	(2)	—	—
06/13	176	(27)	—	—
06/12	170	(1)	—	—
Annual Growth	2.3%	—	—	—

2016 Year-End Financials

Return on assets: —
Return on equity: 12.9%
Current ratio: 8.60
Cash ($ mil.): 33

INDEPENDENT SCHOOL DISTRICT #535

EXECUTIVES

Superintendent, Michael Munoz
Director, Jennifer Pozanc
Director, Diane Ilstrup
Manager, Bob Snyder
Director, Becky Perlich
Executive Director, Heather Nessler
Auditors: CLIFTONLARSONALLEN LLP AUSTI

LOCATIONS

HQ: INDEPENDENT SCHOOL DISTRICT #535
  615 7TH ST SW, ROCHESTER, MN 559022052
Phone: 507 328-3000
Web: WWW.ROCHESTER.K12.MN.US

HISTORICAL FINANCIALS

Company Type: Private

Income Statement				FYE: June 30
	REVENUE ($ mil.)	NET INCOME ($ mil.)	NET PROFIT MARGIN	EMPLOYEES
06/16	228	2	1.2%	2,500
06/15	218	(19)	—	—
06/14	201	(11)	—	—
06/13	195	15	7.8%	—
Annual Growth	5.4%	(42.8%)	—	—

INDEPENDENT SCHOOL DISTRICT 271

EXECUTIVES

Superintendent, Les Fujitake
Coordinator, Gary Prest
Assistant Manager, Debbie Boatman
Purchasing Director, Jennifer Hazel
Personnel Director, Jim Martin
Accountant, Carol Fraser
Auditors: KERN DEWENTER VIERE LTD B

LOCATIONS

HQ: INDEPENDENT SCHOOL DISTRICT 271
  1350 W 106TH ST, BLOOMINGTON, MN 554314152
Phone: 952 681-6400
Web: WWW.BLOOMINGTON.K12.MN.US

HISTORICAL FINANCIALS

Company Type: Private

Income Statement				FYE: June 30
	REVENUE ($ mil.)	NET INCOME ($ mil.)	NET PROFIT MARGIN	EMPLOYEES
06/16*	173	(13)	—	2,200
08/09	0	(0)	—	—
06/09	142	(14)	—	—
06/06	1,518	0	0.0%	—
Annual Growth	(19.5%)	—	—	—

*Fiscal year change

INDEPENDENT SCHOOL DISTRICT 279

EXECUTIVES

Superintendent, Kate Maguire
Director, Julie Bocock
Assistant Manager, Kim Hiel
Purchasing Agent, Dale Carlstrom
Auditors: MALLOY MONTAGUE KARNOWSKI R

LOCATIONS

HQ: INDEPENDENT SCHOOL DISTRICT 279
  11200 93RD AVE N, MAPLE GROVE, MN 553693669
Phone: 763 391-7000
Web: WWW.ISD279.NET

HISTORICAL FINANCIALS

Company Type: Private

Income Statement				FYE: June 30
	REVENUE ($ mil.)	NET INCOME ($ mil.)	NET PROFIT MARGIN	EMPLOYEES
06/16	319	(47)	—	2,700
06/13	281	(2)	—	—
06/12	280	(48)	—	—
06/11	0	0	—	—
Annual Growth	—	—	—	—

INDIAN RIVER MEMORIAL HOSPITAL, INC.

EXECUTIVES

Chairman of the Board, Thomas Segura
Chief Executive Officer, Jeffrey L Susi
Chairman of the Board, Charles Sheehan
Director, Gregory Morgan
Chief Financial Officer, Gregory Gardner
Treasurer, Jack Pastor
Treasurer, Jack Weisbaum
Director, Donna Fabean

LOCATIONS

HQ: INDIAN RIVER MEMORIAL HOSPITAL, INC.
  1000 36TH ST, VERO BEACH, FL 329606592
Phone: 772 567-4311
Web: WWW.INDIANRIVERMEDICALCENTER.COM

HISTORICAL FINANCIALS

Company Type: Private

Income Statement				FYE: September 30
	REVENUE ($ mil.)	NET INCOME ($ mil.)	NET PROFIT MARGIN	EMPLOYEES
09/15	203	(0)	—	1,400
09/14	182	0	0.5%	—
09/13	192	(2)	—	—
09/12	193	0	0.0%	—
Annual Growth	1.8%	—	—	—

2015 Year-End Financials

Return on assets: 7.1%
Return on equity: (-0.4%)
Current ratio: 1.80
Cash ($ mil.): 37

INDIANA UNIVERSITY FOUNDATION, INC.

Hoosier favorite fund-raiser? If you're a fan of Indiana University then it might well be the Indiana University Foundation (IUF). The not-for-profit foundation raises more than $100 million annually in donations from individuals corporations and institutional organizations; alumni gifts account for about half of IUF's funds. It manages an endowment of about $1 billion and provides administrative services for gift accounts and scholarship and fellowship accounts. The organization has offices in Bloomington and Indianapolis. IUF was established in 1936.

EXECUTIVES

President, Gene Tempel
Board of Directors, Karen Pieper
Office Manager, Beth Gillespie
Director, Caitlin Callahan
Administrative Assistant, Jewel Baker
Director, Mary Maxwell
Auditors: DELOITTE & TOUCHE LLP INDIANA

HQ: INDIANA UNIVERSITY FOUNDATION, INC.
 1500 N STATE ROAD 46 BYP, BLOOMINGTON, IN 47408
Phone: 812 855-8311
Web: WWW.DOANECANCEL.COM

HISTORICAL FINANCIALS
Company Type: Private

Income Statement
FYE: June 30

	REVENUE ($ mil.)	NET INCOME ($ mil.)	NET PROFIT MARGIN	EMPLOYEES
06/15	294	86	29.2%	240
06/14	222	28	12.9%	—
06/13	262	107	40.8%	—
06/12	128	(11)	—	—
Annual Growth	31.9%	—	—	—

2015 Year-End Financials
Return on assets: 12.6%   Cash ($ mil.): 182
Return on equity: 29.2%
Current ratio: 6.30

INDIANA UNIVERSITY HEALTH BLOOMINGTON, INC.

Indiana University Health Bloomington wants to put a bloom back in patients' cheeks. The facility operating as IU Health Bloomington provides care in a ten-county region in south central Indiana. The not-for-profit hospital — which includes a 350-bed main campus in Bloomington and a 25-bed rural hospital in Paoli — provides care in a number of medical specialties including cardiovascular disease cancer orthopedics and neuroscience. It also runs home health and hospice urgent care lab and specialty care facilities as well as physician practices under the name Southern Indiana Physicians. IU Health Bloomington is part of the Indiana University Health (IU Health) system.

Operations

The company's operations include Indiana University Health Paoli (Paoli) Indiana University Health Morgan Hospital (Morgan) and Indiana University Health White Memorial Hospital (White).

Geographic Reach

IU Health Bloomington has a customer base of about 415000 patients in a 10-county area in south central Indiana. The hospital serves as a regional referral center for other hospitals in the area.

Strategy

Like most hospitals IU Health Bloomington enters partnerships to extend its patient reach. In 2012 IU Health Bloomington and a Monroe County YMCA collaborated to provide a new space in a new northwest YMCA dedicated to IU Health for physical therapy orthopedic services sports medicine and health and wellness services.

Company Background

After several years of negotiations IU Health Bloomington officially became an integrated part of the Clarian network at the start of 2010. Then at the beginning of 2011 Clarian changed its name to IU Health to clarify its relationship with Indiana University and to provide a unified brand to connect all of its facilities.

EXECUTIVES
Infection Control Director, Jean Young
Director of Nursing, Pam Adams
Vice President Revenue Cycle Services and Treasurer, Jennifer Alvey
Managing Director General Surgery, Jeff Browne
Secretary, Maudie Jones

LOCATIONS
HQ: INDIANA UNIVERSITY HEALTH BLOOMINGTON, INC.
 601 W 2ND ST, BLOOMINGTON, IN 474032317
Phone: 812 353-5252

PRODUCTS/OPERATIONS

Selected Services
Anticoagulation Center
Assisted Medical Transportation
Behavioral Health
Cancer
Cardiovascular
Children's Therapy Center
Diabetes Center
Emergency
Home Care
Home Medical Equipment
Hospice
Laboratory
Neuroscience
Occupational
Orthopedics
Pain Center
Primary Care
Radiology
Rehabilitation
Sleep Lab
Surgical
Urgent Care Centers
Women and Children's
Wound Center

COMPETITORS

Ascension Health	Memorial Hospital
Community Health Network	(Logansport)
	Riverview Hospital
Daviess Community Hospital	St. Vincent Health
Franciscan Alliance	Union Hospital (Indiana)
Henry County Memorial Hospital	Wabash County Hospital

HISTORICAL FINANCIALS
Company Type: Private

Income Statement
FYE: December 31

	REVENUE ($ mil.)	NET INCOME ($ mil.)	NET PROFIT MARGIN	EMPLOYEES
12/15	359	71	19.9%	3,200
12/14	382	92	24.1%	—
12/12	355	64	18.1%	—
12/11	391	22	5.7%	—
Annual Growth	(2.1%)	33.8%	—	—

2015 Year-End Financials
Return on assets: 5.7%   Cash ($ mil.): 173
Return on equity: 19.9%
Current ratio: 5.50

INDIANA WESLEYAN UNIVERSITY

EXECUTIVES
President, David Wright
Director, Bill Westafer
Vice-President, Mandy Ogunnowo
Vice-President, Thomas E Phillippe Sr
Auditors: BKD LP FORT WAYNE IN

LOCATIONS
HQ: INDIANA WESLEYAN UNIVERSITY
 4201 S WASHINGTON ST, MARION, IN 469534974
Phone: 866 468-6498
Web: WWW.IWUWILDCATS.COM

HISTORICAL FINANCIALS
Company Type: Private

Income Statement
FYE: June 30

	REVENUE ($ mil.)	NET INCOME ($ mil.)	NET PROFIT MARGIN	EMPLOYEES
06/15	228	11	5.1%	1,000
06/14	226	20	9.2%	—
06/11	203	32	15.7%	—
06/09	159	12	7.6%	—
Annual Growth	6.2%	(0.8%)	—	—

2015 Year-End Financials
Return on assets: 11.0%   Cash ($ mil.): 15
Return on equity: 5.1%
Current ratio: 0.60

INFOBLOX INC.

Infoblox products maintain the info flow across networks. Customers from various sectors use the company's hardware and software to automate consolidate and more securely operate corporate networks. Infoblox's Trinzic DDI network identity appliances manage functions such as internet domain name server (DNS) resolution IP address management and network access control. Its NetMRI product line automates network change and configuration management processes. Infoblox works cooperatively with networking equipment vendors including CA Hewlett Packard Enterprise BMC Software VMware Cisco and Juniper Networks. The company was acquired by Vista Equity Partners in 2016.

Change in Company Type

Vista Equity Partners a private equity firm bought Infoblox for $1.6 billion. As a private company in the Vista portfolio Infoblox will have greater flexibility to work on to developing more large company customers. Vista's model is to provide financial resources and management and technical expertise to its portfolio firms.

Operations

Inflobox gets revenue from products and licenses revenue (50%) and from services (50%). Product and license revenue comes from the sale of its appliances and licensing of its software that runs on the appliances and those from third parties. The Trinzic DDI line accounts for a substantial portion of revenue. Services revenue is generated from maintenance and support and to a lesser extent subscriptions and training and consulting.

The company's products work with third-party hardware platforms including some from Cisco

Systems and Riverbed Technology or operate on virtual machine platforms including VMware ESXi Microsoft Hyper-V Redhat KVM and Citrix XenServer. Infoblox's Cloud Network Automation products enable integration with cloud orchestration technologies from VMware Microsoft and BMC Software. Infoblox also offers DDI software for the Amazon Web Services cloud environment.

It contracts with Flex for production of its appliance hardware.

Geographic Reach

Infoblox is based in Santa Clara California and has engineering centers in Annapolis Maryland; Burnaby Canada; and Paris. The company has contract workers in Belarus and India. The US accounts for 60% of revenue Europe/Africa/Middle East generates a quarter of revenue and Asia/Pacific produces about 10%.

Sales and Marketing

Infoblox's direct sales force calls on enterprise customers in North America while the company relies on channel partners distributors resellers and integrators for other sales. Exclusive Networks a distributor supplies about 15% of Infoblox's revenue.

Financial Performance

Infobox posted higher revenue cut its net loss in half and generated more cash from operations in 2016 (ended July) compare to 2015.

Revenue jumped 17% to $358 million in 2016 with strong contributions from products and licensing and services. Products and licensing saw increased unit sales products that replaced older generations of products and sales of security products. Higher prices also contributed. A growing customer based pushed services revenue higher. The company also posted higher subscription revenue.

Infoblox's net loss dropped to $14 million in 2016 from $27 million the year before. The company maintained spending on research and development and sales and marketing but higher revenue helped cut the loss.

Cash flow from operations rose to $68 million in 2016 from $48 million in 2015. A large part of the 2016 cash flow came from a $36 million increase in deferred revenue.

Strategy

To expand its customer base Infoblox continues to invest in its sales team as well as its channel partners through such efforts as product education and sales and support training. The company looks to technology partnerships acquisitions and heavy investments in R&D to grow its products. Investment from Vista Equity Partners should benefit Infoblox on all levels. Vista invests in the technology development and personnel of its portfolio companies.

In 2016 Infoblox took steps to reduce some costs through a restructuring. The goal was to adjust hiring to support customer-facing sales increase sales and marketing efficiency and reduce headcount in higher-cost locations and for some positions. The restructuring cost about $6 million in 2016 but the company expects lower operating expenses in 2017

Mergers and Acquisitions

Infoblox acquired IID Security Inc. a provider of global cyber threat intelligence and security products for $43 million. This deal enhances the functionality of Infoblox products.

EXECUTIVES

EVP People and Places, Norma J. Lane
Vice President IT, Frank Ponikvar
President CEO and Director, Jesper Andersen, age 54
EVP CTO and Interim Head of Engineering, Alan Conley

EVP Products, Scott J. Fulton, age 48, $112,500 total compensation
EVP and Chief Marketing Officer, Ashish Gupta
EVP and CFO, Janesh Moorjani, age 45
CIO, Sriram Thiagarajan
Vice President Finance and Corp Controller, Michael Fancher
Executive Vice President and GC, Stephen Yu
Executive Vice President Worldwide Field Operations, Thorsten Freitag
Vice President of Marketing, Steve Garrison
Vice President Customer Advocacy, Sonya Andreae
Executive Vice President Marketing, Julie Poutre
Vice President Nccm Sales Division, Jon Bierman
Executive Vice President Product Strategy And Corporate Development, Steve Nye
Vice President Global Technology Sales, Kent Lockyer
Vice President Product Marketing, Arya Barirani
Vice President, Sara Lamarch
Vice President Product Management, Kevin Dickson
Vice President and Chief Information Officer, Benny Kirsh
Auditors: ERNST & YOUNG LLP SAN JOSE C

LOCATIONS

HQ: INFOBLOX INC.
3111 CORONADO DR, SANTA CLARA, CA 950543206
Phone: 408 986-4000
Web: WWW.INFOBLOX.COM

2016 Sales

	$ mil.	% of total
Americas	226	63
Europe Middle East and Africa	94	26
Asia Pacific	37	11
Total	**358**	**100**

PRODUCTS/OPERATIONS

2016 Sales

	$ mil.	% of total
Products and licenses	178	50
Services	179	50
Total	**358**	**100**

COMPETITORS

Alcatel-Lucent	Hewlett Packard
BMC Software	Enterprise
BT	IBM
Cisco Systems	Incognito Software
Dell	NeuStar
EMC	Nominum
F5 Networks	SolarWinds
Fortinet	VeriSign

HISTORICAL FINANCIALS

Company Type: Private

Income Statement

FYE: July 31

	REVENUE ($ mil.)	NET INCOME ($ mil.)	NET PROFIT MARGIN	EMPLOYEES
07/16	358	(13)	—	25
07/15	306	(27)	—	—
07/14	250	(23)	—	—
07/13	225	(4)	—	—
Annual Growth	16.8%	—	—	—

2016 Year-End Financials

Return on assets: 7.2%   Cash ($ mil.): 123
Return on equity: (-3.8%)
Current ratio: 1.10

INGALLS HEALTH SYSTEM

EXECUTIVES

President, Kurt E Johnson
Director, Jeff Friant
Marketing Director, Bill Burnett
Manager, John Perez
Director, Marcus Swan
Auditors: CROWE HORWATH LLP CHICAGO IL

LOCATIONS

HQ: INGALLS HEALTH SYSTEM
1 INGALLS DR, HARVEY, IL 604263558
Phone: 708 333-2333
Web: WWW.INGALLS.ORG

HISTORICAL FINANCIALS

Company Type: Private

Income Statement

FYE: September 30

	REVENUE ($ mil.)	NET INCOME ($ mil.)	NET PROFIT MARGIN	EMPLOYEES
09/15	285	7	2.6%	2,963
09/14	13	(2)	—	—
09/10	14	(2)	—	—
09/09	332	(1)	—	—
Annual Growth	(2.5%)	—	—	—

2015 Year-End Financials

Return on assets: 7.7%   Cash ($ mil.): 16
Return on equity: 2.6%
Current ratio: 0.70

INGHAM REGIONAL MEDICAL CENTER

EXECUTIVES

Chief Executive Officer, Philip Incarnati
Chief Financial Officer, Robert Wright

LOCATIONS

HQ: INGHAM REGIONAL MEDICAL CENTER
401 W GREENLAWN AVE, LANSING, MI 489100899
Phone: 517 975-7800
Web: WWW.IRMC.ORG

HISTORICAL FINANCIALS

Company Type: Private

Income Statement

FYE: September 30

	REVENUE ($ mil.)	NET INCOME ($ mil.)	NET PROFIT MARGIN	EMPLOYEES
09/15	312	(11)	—	2,500
09/14	254	6	2.5%	—
09/13	271	7	2.7%	—
09/12	280	11	4.1%	—
Annual Growth	3.7%	—	—	—

2015 Year-End Financials

Return on assets: 6.9%   Cash ($ mil.): 18
Return on equity: (-3.7%)
Current ratio: 1.10

INLAND COUNTIES REGIONAL CENTER, INC.

EXECUTIVES

Chief Executive Officer, Carol A Fitzgibbons
Accountant, Judy Hugo
Auditors: WINDES INC LONG BEACH CA

LOCATIONS

HQ: INLAND COUNTIES REGIONAL CENTER, INC.
1365 S WATERMAN AVE, SAN BERNARDINO, CA
924082804
Phone: 909 890-3000
Web: WWW.INLANDRC.ORG

HISTORICAL FINANCIALS

Company Type: Private

Income Statement

FYE: June 30

	REVENUE ($ mil.)	NET INCOME ($ mil.)	NET PROFIT MARGIN	EMPLOYEES
06/15	378	4	1.1%	586
06/14	335	(2)	—	—
06/13	314	(2)	—	—
06/10	267	(3)	—	—
Annual Growth	7.2%	—	—	—

2015 Year-End Financials

Return on assets: 9.0%
Return on equity: 1.1%
Current ratio: 0.70
Cash ($ mil.): 7

INNOVATIVE AG SERVICES CO.

EXECUTIVES

Chief Executive Officer, Rick Vaughan
Manager, Susan Walsh
Vice-President, Ron Barkema
Financial Executive, Shane Coughenour
VP Sales, Michael Duncomb
VP Operations, Brian Kramer
Manager, Jeff Demuth
Auditors: MERIWETHER WILSON AND COMPANY

LOCATIONS

HQ: INNOVATIVE AG SERVICES CO.
2010 S MAIN ST, MONTICELLO, IA 523107707
Phone: 319 465-3501
Web: WWW.INNOVATIVEAG.COM

HISTORICAL FINANCIALS

Company Type: Private

Income Statement

FYE: August 31

	REVENUE ($ mil.)	NET INCOME ($ mil.)	NET PROFIT MARGIN	EMPLOYEES
08/16	682	10	1.6%	500
08/15	657	18	2.8%	—
08/14	855	23	2.8%	—
08/13	1,165	12	1.1%	—
Annual Growth	(16.3%)	(5.5%)	—	—

INSPIRA MEDICAL CENTERS, INC.

EXECUTIVES

Manager, Connie Smith
Manager, Jason McMullen
Manager, Linda Bailey
Director, Beth Rambo
Director, Peggy Soucek
Financial Executive, Ryan Waddington
Auditors: WITHUMSMITHBROWN PC MORRISTOW

LOCATIONS

HQ: INSPIRA MEDICAL CENTERS, INC.
509 N BROAD ST, WOODBURY, NJ 080961617
Phone: 856 845-0100
Web: WWW.UMHOSPITAL.ORG

HISTORICAL FINANCIALS

Company Type: Private

Income Statement

FYE: December 31

	REVENUE ($ mil.)	NET INCOME ($ mil.)	NET PROFIT MARGIN	EMPLOYEES
12/15	174	1	0.8%	1
12/14	174	(0)	—	—
Annual Growth	(0.1%)	—	—	—

2015 Year-End Financials

Return on assets: 10.3%
Return on equity: 0.8%
Current ratio: 0.40
Cash ($ mil.): 1

INSTITUTE FOR DEFENSE ANALYSES INC

The Institute for Defense Analyses provides technical analyses of weapons. Founded in 1947 the institute is a federally funded organization that works for the US government's defense agencies as well as for other government entities. The institute's focus areas include war and defense systems evaluations materials and information technology assessments resource cost and readiness analyses and force and strategy assessments. The Institute for Defense Analyses' Science and Technology Policy Institute analyzes global science and tech trends to help the US government formula policy.

EXECUTIVES

President and CEO, David S.C. Chu
Chair, Suzanne H. (Sue) Woolsey, age 76
Executive Board Member, Mark Couch
Auditors: PRICEWATERHOUSECOOPERS LLP M

LOCATIONS

HQ: INSTITUTE FOR DEFENSE ANALYSES INC
4850 MARK CENTER DR, ALEXANDRIA, VA
223111882
Phone: 703 845-2000
Web: WWW.IDA.ORG

COMPETITORS

Charles Stark Draper Laboratory
Lawrence Livermore Lab
QinetiQ
Quantum Research
Sandia National Laboratories

HISTORICAL FINANCIALS

Company Type: Private

Income Statement

FYE: September 25

	REVENUE ($ mil.)	NET INCOME ($ mil.)	NET PROFIT MARGIN	EMPLOYEES
09/15	223	(4)	—	1,500
09/14	218	12	5.5%	—
09/13	219	18	8.5%	—
09/12	221	23	10.5%	—
Annual Growth	0.3%	—	—	—

2015 Year-End Financials

Return on assets: 3.3%
Return on equity: (-2.0%)
Current ratio: 1.40
Cash ($ mil.): 23

INTEGRIS AMBULATORY CARE CORPORATION

EXECUTIVES

Principal, Barton H Dawson
Auditors: KPMG LLP OKLAHOMA CITY OK

LOCATIONS

HQ: INTEGRIS AMBULATORY CARE CORPORATION
5300 N INDEPENDENCE AVE, OKLAHOMA CITY, OK
731125556
Phone: 405 949-6026

HISTORICAL FINANCIALS

Company Type: Private

Income Statement

FYE: June 30

	REVENUE ($ mil.)	NET INCOME ($ mil.)	NET PROFIT MARGIN	EMPLOYEES
06/15	206	6	3.0%	15
06/14	152	13	9.1%	—
06/12	101	1	1.5%	—
06/11	87	1	1.9%	—
Annual Growth	24.0%	39.4%	—	—

2015 Year-End Financials

Return on assets: 65.1%
Return on equity: 3.0%
Current ratio: —
Cash ($ mil.): 128

INTEGRIS HEALTH INC

Auditors: KPMG LLP OKLAHOMA CITY OK

2016 Year-End Financials

Return on assets: 3.2%
Return on equity: 1.6%
Current ratio: 0.60
Cash ($ mil.): 22

LOCATIONS

HQ: INTEGRIS HEALTH INC
5300 N INDEPENDENCE AVE # 280, OKLAHOMA
CITY, OK 731125555
Phone: 405 949-6026
Web: WWW.INTEGRISOK.COM

HISTORICAL FINANCIALS

Company Type: Private

Income Statement
FYE: June 30

	REVENUE ($ mil.)	NET INCOME ($ mil.)	NET PROFIT MARGIN	EMPLOYEES
06/15	253	(52)	—	15
06/14	217	(32)	—	—
06/13	176	(30)	—	—
Annual Growth 19.8%		—	—	—

2015 Year-End Financials

Return on assets: 110.5%
Return on equity: (-20.7%)
Current ratio: 0.50

Cash ($ mil.): 81

INTEGRIS HEALTH, INC.

INTEGRIS Health provides a range of health services to residents throughout the Sooner state. The company one of Oklahoma's largest not-for-profit health care organization operates 16 hospitals with some 1500 combined beds in both urban and rural communities. The hospitals provide services including primary diagnostic emergency surgical behavioral therapeutic and rehabilitative care. INTEGRIS also operates specialty facilities for the treatment of hearing disorders and neuromuscular ailments and for rehabilitation care. The company operates assisted living centers and a home health agency plus a network of physician clinics and ambulatory care centers.

Operations

Operations include INTEGRIS Baptist Medical Center (the system's largest with 629 beds) INTEGRIS South Oklahoma City (dba INTEGRIS Southwest Medical Center 389 beds) and INTEGRIS Rural Health facilities INTEGRIS Baptist Regional Health Center INTEGRIS Bass Baptist Health Center and INTEGRIS Grove Hospital.

INTEGRIS Health has approximately 1400 physicians in its system.

Sales and Marketing

Managed care payments account for more than half of net patient service revenue; Medicare and Medicaid combined account for around a third.

INTEGRIS Health offers community residents with more life experience such services as senior seminars and classes health screenings support groups and technology classes to help stay up-to-date on computer use. The idea is to help keep the elderly as independent as possible for as long as possible.

Financial Performance

The company's revenue increased slightly in fiscal 2015 rising 1% to $1.4 billion. This was due to growth in net patient service revenues. However INTEGRIS Health reported a net loss of $150 million (versus a net gain in 2014) due to factors that included higher operating expenses (salaries supplies) and higher pension liability adjustments. This in turn led to a 60% drop in cash flow from operations which totaled $49 million.

EXECUTIVES

Vice President Marketing and Communications, Hardy Watkins
President INTEGRIS Southwest Medical Center, James D. Moore
Chief Medical Officer, James White
EVP and COO, Chris Hammes
President and CEO, Bruce Lawrence
CFO, David Hadley
President INTEGRIS Baptist Medical Center, Tim Johnsen
President INTEGRIS Bass Baptist Health Center Enid, Eddie Herrman
President INTEGRIS Baptist Regional Health Center Miami, Jordan Cash
President INTEGRIS Canadian Valley Hospital Yukon, Rex Van Meter
President INTEGRIS Cancer Institute of Oklahoma, Phil Lance
President INTEGRIS Health Edmond, Avilla Williams
President INTEGRIS Health Partners, Carl Raczkowski
President INTEGRIS Heart Hospital, R. Mel Clark
President INTEGRIS Medical Group, Jeff Cruzan
President Lakeside Women's Hospital, Kelley Brewer
President and COO INTEGRIS Mental Health and James L. Hall Jr. Center For Mind Body and Spirit, R. Murali Krishna
VP INTEGRIS Nazih Zuhdi Transplant Insitute INTEGRIS Advanced Cardiac Care, Kathie Calbone
President INTEGRIS Grove Hospital, Tim Bowen, age 34
Vice President Financial Reporting, Barbara Dean
Vice President of Diversity, Jason Thompson
Clinical Director, Anne Gates
Vice President, Jim Porterfield
Vice President, Jeff Brown
Medical Director Pediatric Intensive Care Unit, Johnny Griggs
Medical Director, Derek Irwin
Clinical Director, Nada Cain
Assistant Vice President, Lynda Van Horn
Vice President, Anne Clouse
Vice President Chief Nursing Officer, Marva Harrison
Vice President, Jon Rule
Clinic Manager, Jennifer Gomez
CLINICAL DIRECTOR, Lisa L Aishman
VICE PRESIDENT, Nicholas A Niver
CLINIC SUPERVISOR, Shelia Pendergraft
CLINIC SUPERVISOR, Tammie Johnston
DIRECTOR OF PHARMACY, John A Foust
CLINIC SUPERVISOR, Bambie Cleveland
Board Of Directors, Kiran Prabhu
Auditors: KPMG LLP OKLAHOMA CITY OK

LOCATIONS

HQ: INTEGRIS HEALTH, INC.
3300 NW EXPRESSWAY, OKLAHOMA CITY, OK
731124418
Phone: 405 949-6066
Web: WWW.INTEGRISOK.COM

PRODUCTS/OPERATIONS

2015 Sales

	% of total
INTEGRIS Baptist Medical Center Inc.	39
INTEGRIS South Oklahoma City Hospital Corporation	15
INTEGRIS Rural Health Inc.	14
INTEGRIS Health Edmond	3
All others	29
Eliminations	-
Total	**100**

Selected Facilities

Baptist Medical Center
Baptist Regional Health Center
Bass Baptist Health Center

Blackwell Regional Hospital
Canadian Valley Regional Hospital
Cancer Institute of Oklahoma
Clinton Regional Hospital
Grove General Hospital
Health Edmond
Hospice House
Jim Thorpe Rehabilitation
Marshall County Medical Center
Mayes County Medical Center
Mental Health Spencer
Seminole Medical Center
Southwest Medical Center

COMPETITORS

Ardent Health Services
Deaconess Health Care
Fairview Health
HealthEast Care System
Hillcrest Medical Center
Marian Health System
Mercy Health
Norman Regional Health
Saint Francis Health System
St. John Health System
Stormont-Vail HealthCare

HISTORICAL FINANCIALS

Company Type: Private

Income Statement
FYE: June 30

	REVENUE ($ mil.)	NET INCOME ($ mil.)	NET PROFIT MARGIN	EMPLOYEES
06/15	1,384	(90)	—	9,500
06/06	1,067	89	8.4%	—
06/04	980	62	6.3%	—
06/03	913	59	6.5%	—
Annual Growth 3.5%				

2015 Year-End Financials

Return on assets: 22.9%
Return on equity: (-6.5%)
Current ratio: 0.50

Cash ($ mil.): 32

INTERMOUNTAIN HEALTH CARE INC

If you whoosh down the side of one of Idaho's majestic mountains and take a nasty spill Intermountain Health Care (dba Intermountain Healthcare) can pick you up and put you back together. From air ambulance services to urgent care clinics and general hospitals Intermountain has all the tools to mend skiers (and non-skiers alike) in Utah and southern Idaho. With about 1600 physicians the not-for-profit health system operates 22 hospitals and some 180 clinics as well as urgent care centers and rehabilitation centers. Intermountain also has an insurance arm named SelectHealth.

Operations

Intermountain Healthcare's hospitals range from general surgical to specialty care including orthopedic and pediatric facilities. Along with the full spectrum of physical health care services Intermountain also offers comprehensive mental health and substance abuse programs for patients of all ages. The organization's spectrum of care includes acute inpatient residential treatment day treatment chemical dependency inpatient/detoxification and intensive outpatient programs.

The system conducts cancer research through its partnership with Huntsman Cancer Institute at the University of Utah. The two share data best practices funding and co-conduct clinical trials. They also operate a number of cancer-specific treatment centers including multi-disciplinary tumor-specific clinics designed to provide one-stop

service for cancer patients to meet with different cancer specialists on the same day for a more comprehensive treatment plan. Other areas of research include cardiovascular intensive medicine surgical care and behavioral health.

On the physician side the Intermountain Medical Group administers multi-specialty health care services in clinics located throughout the region. The group also operates urgent care clinics under the InstaCare and KidsCare banners.

Entering itself into the "what doesn't Intermountain do?" category the health system also provides health and dental insurance plans through its SelectHealth division.

Geographic Reach

Intermountain Healthcare serves the health care needs of Utah and Idaho residents.

Financial Performance

In 2016 Intermountain Healthcare's revenue grew 14% to $7.6 billion in fiscal 2016. This was due to increases in net patient services income non-patient activity income and investment income. Net patient services accounted for 63% of the system's total revenue that year.

The company used $7 billion of that revenue towards operating expenses including salaries and benefits medical supplies and facilities maintenance and other business services as well as towards funds dedicated to future needs.

Strategy

Intermountain Healthcare uses its dedicated supply chain organization to continuously improve system efficiency. In addition to delivering medical supplies the unit also oversees hospital vehicles.

The system partners with several leading IT companies (including Xi3 Intel Dell and NetApp) to operate its Healthcare Transformation Lab on the campus of its flagship hospital Intermountain Medical Center in Murray Utah. The lab researches develops and measures new ideas to improve patient care.

In 2016 the system launched Navican Genomics its genomics research and testing arm. Also that year it partnered with the Stanford Genome Technology Center to establish a collaborative research program.

Intermountain has a number of projects underway to add expand or replace existing facilities.

Company Background

Intermountain was formed in 1975 when the Church of Jesus Christ of Latter Day Saints donated 15 hospitals to local communities.

EXECUTIVES

CEO Intermountain Medical Group and VP Physician Division, Linda C. Leckman
President and CEO SelectHealth, Patricia R. Richards
EVP and CFO, Bert R. Zimmerli
EVP and COO, Laura S. Kaiser
Regional VP Central Region, Moody L. Chisholm
VP and CIO, Marc Probst
President and CEO, A. Marc Harrison, age 53
Regional VP Soutwest Region, Terri Kane
SVP and COO, Robert Allen
VP Clinical Operations and Chief Nursing Officer, Kim Henrichsen
CEO Urban North Region and McKay-Dee Hospital Center, Timothy T. Pehrson
Chief Medical Officer, Brent E. Wallace
CEO Primary Children's Medical Center, Katherine A. (Katy) Welkie
Regional VP South Region, Steve Smoot
VP Supply Chain and Support Services, Joe Walsh
Medical Director Neurovascualar Medicine, Dean Roller
Assistant Vice President Of Risk Management Services, Harlan Hammond

Assistant Vice President Communications, Tom Vitelli
Director of Pharmacy, Alan Lodder
Vice President Management, Jim Darrington
Vice President Marketing and Communication, Todd Frehse
Medical Director Utah County Region Intermountain Medical Group, Gordon Harkness
Vice President Healthcare Transformation, Joe Mott
Medical Director, James Orme
Pharmacy Manager, Bruce Leavitt
Medical Director, Justin Abbott
Director Media Relations, Daron Cowley
Assistant Vice President Research, Raj Srivastava
Medical Director Epilepsy Program, Tawnya Constantino
Medical Director, Kristian Kemp
Clinic Manager, Gay Tregaskis
Medical Records Director, Connie Sawyer
Vice President Business Ethics and Compliance, Suzie Draper
Vice President Human Resources, Dan Zuhlke
Vice President And General Counsel, Doug Hammer
Assistant Vice President Financial and Administration System Intermountain Health Care Inc, Craig Jacobsen
Associate Medical Director, Chris Maloney
Cota L, Celeste Marsh
Assistant Vice President Telehealth Services, Brian Wayling
Clinical Director Primary Children's Pediatric Behavioral Health Clinic, Nancy Cantor
Vice President Of Underwriting, Mike Brown
Occupational Therapy Director, Andrew Bracken
Medical Director Information Technology, Ed Clark
Vice President of Operational Finance, Mark Runyon
Pharmacy Manager, Andrew Buckley
Operating Room Dir, DEBRA ESPLIN
Vice Chairman, Bruce T. Reese
Chairman, A. Scott Anderson
Board Member, Kim Bennion
Secretary, Stephanie Stromberg
Secretary, Jodi Simmons
Auditors: KPMG LLP SALT LAKE CITY UT

LOCATIONS

HQ: INTERMOUNTAIN HEALTH CARE INC
36 S STATE ST STE 1600, SALT LAKE CITY, UT 841111633
Phone: 801 442-2000
Web: WWW.INTERMOUNTAINHEALTHCARE.ORG

PRODUCTS/OPERATIONS

2016 Sales

	$ mil.	% of total
Net patient services	4,368	57
Non-patient activities	3,010	40
Non-operating income	237	3
Total	**7,617**	**100**

Selected Hospitals
Alta View Hospital (Sandy UT)
American Fork Hospital (Utah)
Bear River Valley Hospital (Tremonton UT)
Cassia Regional Medical Center (Burley ID)
Delta Community Medical Center (Utah)
Dixie Regional Medical Center (St. George UT)
Fillmore Community Medical Center (Utah)
Garfield Memorial Hospital (Panguitch UT)
Heber Valley Medical Center (Heber City UT)
Intermountain Medical Center (Murray UT)
LDS Hospital (Salt Lake City)
Logan Regional Hospital (Orem UT)
McKay-Dee Hospital Center (Ogden UT)
  McKay-Dee Behavioral Health Institute
Orem Community Hospital (Utah)
Park City Medical Center (Park City UT)
Primary Children's Medical Center (Salt Lake City)

Riverton Hospital (Riverton UT)
Sanpete Valley Hospital (Mt. Pleasant UT)
Sevier Valley Hospital (Richfield UT)
TOSH - The Orthopedic Specialty Hospital (Murray UT)
Utah Valley Regional Medical Center (Provo UT)
Valley View Medical Center (Cedar City UT)

COMPETITORS

CHRISTUS Health	Regence BlueCross
HCA	BlueShield of Utah
HealthSouth	St. Mark's
LifePoint Health	University of Utah
Ogden Regional Medical	Hospitals & Clinics
Center	

HISTORICAL FINANCIALS
Company Type: Private

Income Statement
FYE: December 31

	REVENUE ($ mil.)	NET INCOME ($ mil.)	NET PROFIT MARGIN	EMPLOYEES
12/15	6,058	155	2.6%	36,000
12/14	5,573	(156)	—	—
12/13	5,041	1,546	30.7%	—
12/12	4,700	546	11.6%	—
Annual Growth	8.8%	(34.2%)	—	—

2015 Year-End Financials
Return on assets: 5.5% Cash ($ mil.): 421
Return on equity: 2.6%
Current ratio: 0.50

INTERNATIONAL MEDICAL CORPS

EXECUTIVES

Chairman, Robert Simon
President, Nancy Aossey
Trustee, Sarah Ahrens
Vice-President, David Giron
Director, Dayan Woldemichael
Officer, Elizabeth Apopo
Vice-President, Rabih Torbay

LOCATIONS

HQ: INTERNATIONAL MEDICAL CORPS
12400 WILSHIRE BLVD # 1500, LOS ANGELES, CA 900251030
Phone: 310 826-7800
Web: WWW.INTERNATIONALMEDICALCORPS.ORG

HISTORICAL FINANCIALS
Company Type: Private

Income Statement
FYE: June 30

	REVENUE ($ mil.)	NET INCOME ($ mil.)	NET PROFIT MARGIN	EMPLOYEES
06/15	232	18	8.2%	63
06/14	165	2	1.3%	—
06/13	119	(3)	—	—
06/12	107	(0)	—	—
Annual Growth	29.4%	—	—	—

2015 Year-End Financials
Return on assets: 5.0% Cash ($ mil.): 16
Return on equity: 8.2%
Current ratio: —

INTERNATIONAL RESCUE COMMITTEE, INC.

EXECUTIVES

President, David Miliband
Board of Directors, Ricardo Castro
Executive Director, Leslye Moore
Financial Executive, Jason Mirandilla
Personnel Manager, Leela Joshi
Officer, Ellyson Perkins
Director, Georgia Travers

LOCATIONS

HQ: INTERNATIONAL RESCUE COMMITTEE, INC.
122 E 42ND ST, NEW YORK, NY 101680002
Phone: 212 551-3000
Web: WWW.RESCUE.ORG

HISTORICAL FINANCIALS
Company Type: Private

Income Statement

	REVENUE ($ mil.)	NET INCOME ($ mil.)	NET PROFIT MARGIN	EMPLOYEES
				FYE: September 30
09/15	688	14	2.2%	8,000
09/14	562	9	1.7%	—
09/11	397	11	2.9%	—
09/10	316	10	3.3%	—
Annual Growth 16.9%		7.4%	—	—

2015 Year-End Financials

Return on assets: 5.8%
Return on equity: 2.2%
Current ratio: 0.70

Cash ($ mil.): 69

INTERNET CORPORATION FOR ASSIGNED NAMES AND NUMBERS

Can anyone manage the Internet? This group says "ICANN." The Internet Corporation for Assigned Names and Numbers (ICANN) is a not-for-profit organization responsible for the management of the Internet's domain name system (DNS) allocation of Internet protocol (IP) addresses and assignment of protocol parameters. The DNS allows people to type in an address like "www.hoovers.com" rather than the string of numbers that represents the underlying IP address. Internet users register some 20 domain names ending in .com .org .info and .net among others through ICANN-accredited DNS registrars. The group is also managing the application process for a slew of new generic top-level domains (gTLDs).

ICANN's staff overseen by an international group of directors called the Governmental Advisory Committee works with governments and corporations (such as Microsoft) on several continents

to manage the technical elements that allow the Internet to function predictably worldwide. At the end of 2011 some 310 top-level domains were included in the DNS root zone. These include country code top-level domains (called ccTLDs) such as .de for Germany and .cn for China. Although ICANN's work is global in scope the group operates under a contract with the US Department of Commerce. The company publishes an online magazine giving subscribers the latest developments with ICANN.

In mid-2011 ICANN approved a plan that allows people to apply for new generic top-level domains (gTLDs) beyond the typical .com .org and .net. The group began the process of accepting these gTLD applications in January 2012; technology giants Apple Samsung Google and Amazon have been the first to jump at the chance. It was reported that Google applied for more than 100 gTLDs — such as .dad and .book — at a cost of nearly $20 million. Applicants had sought to own some 2000 domains by midyear. At a cost of $185000 per application ICAAN has generated about $350 million as part of the gTLD process alone. Of the $185000 application fee about $60000 is dogeared for what the organization has deemed the "risk contingency fund."

One issue that the organization grapples with is so-called "domain name tasting" which has resulted in a dramatic rise in registrations and cancellations. This "tasting" is when someone buys a domain name and places per-click ads on the site to see whether the site will make a profit. If it does not look likely the domain name will be dropped within a five-day "grace period" offered by ICANN.

EXECUTIVES

Vice President Engagement With the United Nations, Veni Markovski
Vice President, Christopher Mondini
Vice President of Global Communications, Duncan Burns
Vice President of Research, Matt Larson
Auditors: ERNST & YOUNG US LLP PLAYA VI

LOCATIONS

HQ: INTERNET CORPORATION FOR ASSIGNED NAMES AND NUMBERS
12025 WATERFRONT DR # 300, LOS ANGELES, CA 900943220
Phone: 310 823-9358
Web: WWW.IANA.ORG

PRODUCTS/OPERATIONS

Selected Generic Top-level Domains
.aero
.asia
.biz
.cat
.com
.coop
.edu
.gov
.info
.int
.jobs
.mil
.mobi
.museum
.name
.net
.org
.pro
.tel
.travel
.xxx

HISTORICAL FINANCIALS
Company Type: Private

Income Statement

	REVENUE ($ mil.)	NET INCOME ($ mil.)	NET PROFIT MARGIN	EMPLOYEES
				FYE: June 30
06/15	219	87	40.1%	160
06/14	127	3	2.8%	—
06/13	236	85	36.3%	—
06/10	68	9	13.7%	—
Annual Growth 26.3%		56.4%	—	—

2015 Year-End Financials

Return on assets: 10.3%
Return on equity: 40.1%
Current ratio: 1.20

Cash ($ mil.): 89

IOWA CITY COMMUNITY SCHOOL DISTRICT

EXECUTIVES

Superintendent, Stephen Murley
Treasurer, Bennett Bork
Senior Manager, Celeste Shoppa
Chief Operating Officer, Pat Witinok
Assistant Manager, Amy Kortemeyer
Plant & Facilities Manager, Duane Van Hemert
Assistant Manager, Matt Degner
Auditors: LB STAN MILLER CORALVILLE IA

LOCATIONS

HQ: IOWA CITY COMMUNITY SCHOOL DISTRICT
1725 N DODGE ST, IOWA CITY, IA 522459589
Phone: 319 688-1000
Web: WWW.ICCSDFOUNDATION.ORG

HISTORICAL FINANCIALS
Company Type: Private

Income Statement

	REVENUE ($ mil.)	NET INCOME ($ mil.)	NET PROFIT MARGIN	EMPLOYEES
				FYE: June 30
06/16	182	22	12.2%	1,600
06/15	0	(0)	—	—
06/10	0	(0)	—	—
06/08	0	0	15.5%	—
Annual Growth 101.4%		95.5%	—	—

IOWA STATE UNIVERSITY OF SCIENCE AND TECHNOLOGY

Home to the Cyclones athletics teams Iowa State University of Science and Technology (ISU) can be a whirlwind experience for some. ISU is a public land-grant institution offering higher education courses and programs with an emphasis on science technology and related areas. ISU's eight colleges offer more than 100 undergraduate degrees

and nearly 200 fields of study leading to graduate and professional degrees. The university has an enrollment of more than 31000 students and charges more than $7720 in tuition and fees for resident students for two semesters.

Operations

In fiscal 2012 Iowa State received $360.2 million in grants contracts co-operative agreements and gifts of which about 60% is utilized for research purpose. The university's research park has about 20000 square feet of incubators space including office and laboratories.

Geographic Reach

The university enrolls students from 50 states and more than 100 countries.

Financial Performance

The 6% increase in revenues in 2012 was due to higher tuition and fees sales and services of educational activities and auxiliary enterprise revenues. The tuition revenue increase was to a 5% hike in the resident tuition rate coupled with record enrollments. The increase in sales and services of educational activities was due to large one-time events ISU farms and the Vet Diagnostic Lab. ISU's auxiliary enterprises reported revenue growth thanks to new revenue sources and a record number of students in the residence system.

ISU's net income increased by 47% in 2012 thanks to higher operating expenses and a decline in non-operating revenues. Non-operating revenues decreased $24.4 million thanks to an $11 million decrease in funding from education appropriations. Investment income also dropped $16.3 million or 49% mainly due to an unrealized loss in the value of investments.

Company Background

Chartered as Iowa Agriculture College in 1858 the school first officially opened for classes in 1869. Among ISU's notable alumni is scientist and inventor George Washington Carver.

EXECUTIVES

Vice President for Student Affairs, Thomas Hill
Vice President of Human Resource, David Trainor
Assistant Vice President Chief of Police, Michael Newton
Secretary Iii ames Laboratory Of Us Do, Jeanine Crosman
Auditors: MARY MOSIMAN CPA-WARREN G JE

LOCATIONS

HQ: IOWA STATE UNIVERSITY OF SCIENCE AND TECHNOLOGY
1350 BEARDSHEAR HALL, AMES, IA 500112025
Phone: 515 294-6162
Web: WWW.IASTATE.EDU

PRODUCTS/OPERATIONS

Colleges
Agriculture and Life Sciences
Business
Design
Engineering
Graduate
Human Sciences
Liberal Arts and Sciences
Veterinary Medicine

HISTORICAL FINANCIALS

Company Type: Private

Income Statement

	REVENUE ($ mil.)	NET INCOME ($ mil.)	NET PROFIT MARGIN	EMPLOYEES
				FYE: June 30
06/16	902	67	7.5%	5,800
06/15	858	67	7.8%	—
06/14	806	118	14.8%	—
06/13	770	85	11.1%	—
Annual Growth	5.4%	(7.5%)	—	—

IRC RETAIL CENTERS LLC

IRC Retail Centers (formerly Inland Real Estate Corporation) buys leases and operates retail properties mainly in the Midwest with a concentration in the Chicago and Minneapolis/St. Paul metropolitan markets. The self-managed real estate investment trust (REIT) owns about 150 properties most of which are strip shopping centers anchored by a grocery or big-box store. It also invests in single-tenant retail properties and develops properties usually through joint ventures. The REIT's portfolio totals about 14 million sq. ft. of leasable space in a dozen states. IRC Retail Centers was acquired by DRA Advisors in early 2015.

Operations

As a REIT IRC Retail Centers is exempt from paying federal income tax so long as it distributes quarterly dividends to shareholders. Most tenants of its investment properties are responsible for paying real estate taxes as insurance as well as maintaining the properties.

Financial Performance

Overall revenues fell 4% in 2012 to $160 million. That year the company had decreased income across the board from rent property fees and joint venture fees despite buying 20 new properties and divesting eight. However it posted profits of almost $18 million in 2012 thanks to one-time earnings on continuing operations and a gain on equity in joint ventures.

Strategy

In 2013 the company announced plans for a new joint venture with an affiliate of Australia-based MAB Corporation. The project calls for developing about 20 grocery-anchored shopping centers that would include a 50000-sq.-ft. supermarket with another 20000 sq. ft. of retail space. The JV will extend IRC Retail's reach to the eastern US namely Florida Georgia North and South Carolina Virginia and Washington DC.

Another joint venture with Dutch pension fund administrator PGGM (established 2010) calls for acquiring grocery-anchored and community retail centers in the Midwest. In 2013 the JV bought three Wal-Mart shopping centers in the Milwaukee area for $24.2 million a 139000-sq.-ft. Whole Foods/CVS shopping center in Cleveland for $25 million and is building a 92000-sq.-ft. shopping center in Evergreen Park Illinois.

EXECUTIVES

Senior Vice President, William Anderson
Assistant Vice President, Pam Reifke
Vice President Finance, Angela C Blaising
Assistant Vice President Senior Leasing Represen, Allison Kuchny
Assistant Vice President, Sharon Unger
Vice President Controller, Donna Urbain
Vice Chairman, Joe Cosenza
Auditors: KPMG LLP CHICAGO ILLINOIS

LOCATIONS

HQ: IRC RETAIL CENTERS LLC
814 COMMERCE DR STE 300, OAK BROOK, IL 605238823
Phone: 877 206-5656
Web: WWW.INLANDREALESTATE.COM

2015 Properties (excluding joint ventures)

	No.
Illinois	62
Minnesota	16
Wisconsin	7
Indiana	5
Ohio	2
Alabama	1
Florida	1
Nebraska	1
North Carolina	1
Total	**96**

PRODUCTS/OPERATIONS

2015 Sales

	$ mil.	% of total
Rents	135	66
Tenant recoveries	57	28
Other property income	5	3
Fee income from unconsolidated joint ventures	5	3
Total	**203**	**100**

COMPETITORS

Brixmor	Noddle Development
CBL & Associates Properties	Pennsylvania Real Estate
Canal Capital	Ramco-Gershenson
DDR	Realty Income
Federal Realty Investment	Retail Properties of America
Horizon Group Properties	Rubloff Development
Kimco Realty	Schottenstein
Macerich	Taubman Centers
	Weingarten Realty

HISTORICAL FINANCIALS

Company Type: Private

Income Statement

FYE: December 31

	ASSETS ($ mil.)	NET INCOME ($ mil.)	INCOME AS % OF ASSETS	EMPLOYEES
12/15	1,521	25	1.7%	129
12/14	1,572	39	2.5%	—
12/13	1,529	111	7.3%	—
12/12	1,243	17	1.4%	—
Annual Growth	7.0%	13.0%	—	—

2015 Year-End Financials

Return on assets: 31.2% Sales ($ mil): 203
Return on equity: 12.5%

ISEC, INCORPORATED

EXECUTIVES

President, Dusty Morgan
Auditors: MARTIN VEJVODA AND ASSOCIATES

LOCATIONS

HQ: ISEC, INCORPORATED
6000 GREENWOOD PLAZA BLVD # 200, GREENWOOD VILLAGE, CO 801114818
Phone: 410 381-6049
Web: WWW.ISECINC.COM

2016 Year-End Financials

Return on assets: 4.8% Cash ($ mil.): 54
Return on equity: 7.5%
Current ratio: 0.30

HISTORICAL FINANCIALS

Company Type: Private

Income Statement FYE: June 30

	REVENUE ($ mil.)	NET INCOME ($ mil.)	NET PROFIT MARGIN	EMPLOYEES
06/16	295	3	1.2%	1,150
06/15	235	1	0.7%	—
06/14	248	2	1.2%	—
06/11	252	2	0.9%	—
Annual Growth	3.2%	9.7%	—	—

2016 Year-End Financials

Return on assets: 8.7% Cash ($ mil.): 8
Return on equity: 1.2%
Current ratio: 1.00

ISO NEW ENGLAND INC.

The transmission lines in the Northeast power grid keep humming because of ISO New England. The not-for-profit corporation is responsible for electricity generation and transmission throughout Connecticut Maine Massachusetts New Hampshire Rhode Island and Vermont. The independent systems operator (ISO) runs the 31000 MW generating capacity grid that is owned by utilities of the New England Power Pool and manages the wholesale electric market. The power grid is made up of hundreds of generating units (about 350 under direct ISO New England control) connected by some 8500 miles of high-voltage transmission lines. It provides power to more than 6.5 million households and businesses.

Operations

ISO New England's three primary responsibilities are: the reliable operation of New England's bulk electric power system; the development oversight and equitable administration of the region's wholesale electricity marketplace; and the management of the bulk electric power system and the wholesale markets' planning processes.

Geographic Reach

ISO New England serves end users in Connecticut Maine Massachusetts New Hampshire Rhode Island and Vermont. The power grid has 13 interconnections to power systems in New York State and Canada.

Sales and Marketing

Its customers include power generators publicly owned entities suppliers transmission owners and demand?response and alternative resources providers.

Financial Performance

In 2013 the company traded $9.2 billion in wholesale electricity markets ($8 billion in energy markets and $1.2 billion in capacity and ancillary services markets).

In 2013 natural gas pipeline constraints and higher demand caused by a very hot summer an a very cold winter drove up natural gas and wholesale electricity prices over 2012's record low prices. Higher gas prices pushed wholesale electricity prices in New England up by 55% in 2013. The higher energy price pushed the total value of the region's wholesale energy market up 54% that year. The region also spent 54% more in the energy markets.

Strategy

The company has invested $5.6 billion in transmission upgrades since 2002 (more than 14000 MW of new power plant projects) and has committed at least another $5 billion over the next decade. In addition to meet federal and state regulations on lowering carbon emissions ISO New England has set 2020 goals of attaining at least 30% of its power supply from renewable sources (primarily wind power) in its participating states in New England. Since 2003 the company has reduced air emissions from the power generation in its service area by 60%.

Under the company's management the region has attracted $11 billion in private transmission investment through 2017.

In 2013 ISO New England launched the Distributed Generation Forecast Working Group a regional forum for interested parties to provide input to the ISO on a new long-term distributed generation forecast.

Company Background

ISO New England was formed as a response to the Great Northeast Blackout of 1965 as a way to ensure the reliability of the region's electric power industry. In 2005 Federal regulators upgraded the company to a regional transmission organization (RTO) a move that strengthened the corporation's authority to manage the grid.

EXECUTIVES

President CEO and Director, Gordon van Welie
VP Information Services, Jamshid A. Afnan
VP CFO and Chief Compliance Officer, Robert C. Ludlow
SVP Market and System Solutions, Vamsi Chadalavada
VP Market Operations, Kevin A. Kirby
VP Market Development, Robert Ethier
Vice President Human Resources, Janice S Dickstein
Vice President Treasurer and Controller, Norman Sproehnle
Chairman, Kathryn J. (Kate) Jackson
Secretary, Jane Carpenter
Auditors: KPMG LLP BOSTON MA

LOCATIONS

HQ: ISO NEW ENGLAND INC.
1 SULLIVAN RD, HOLYOKE, MA 010402841
Phone: 413 535-4000
Web: WWW.ISO-NE.COM

COMPETITORS

New York ISO   Trans-Elect
PJM Interconnection

HISTORICAL FINANCIALS

Company Type: Private

Income Statement FYE: December 31

	REVENUE ($ mil.)	NET INCOME ($ mil.)	NET PROFIT MARGIN	EMPLOYEES
12/15	174	0	—	610
12/14	163	0	—	—
12/13	157	0	—	—
12/10	128	0	—	—
Annual Growth	6.4%	—	—	—

2015 Year-End Financials

Return on assets: 16.4% Cash ($ mil.): 27
Return on equity: —
Current ratio: 0.20

ISSAQUAH SCHOOL DISTRICT 411

EXECUTIVES

Superintendent, Ron Thiele
Director of Finance, Martin Turney
Board of Directors, Connie Fletcher
Manager, Jack Staek
Superintendent, Janet Barry
Superintendent, Steve Rassmusin
Manager, Tina Butt

LOCATIONS

HQ: ISSAQUAH SCHOOL DISTRICT 411
565 NW HOLLY ST, ISSAQUAH, WA 980272899
Phone: 425 837-7000
Web: WWW.ISSAQUAH.WEDNET.EDU

HISTORICAL FINANCIALS

Company Type: Private

Income Statement FYE: August 31

	REVENUE ($ mil.)	NET INCOME ($ mil.)	NET PROFIT MARGIN	EMPLOYEES
08/15	246	9	3.8%	1,700
08/14	284	22	7.9%	—
08/13	217	9	4.2%	—
08/12	216	10	5.0%	—
Annual Growth	4.4%	(4.8%)	—	—

2015 Year-End Financials

Return on assets: 4.5% Cash ($ mil.): 172
Return on equity: 3.8%
Current ratio: —

IU HEALTH WEST HOSPITAL

EXECUTIVES

Owner, Daniel Weed
Chief Financial Officer, Doug Puckett
Supervisor, Annette Flaskamp
Chief Financial Officer, Art Vasquez
Administrative Assistant, Jennifer Brock

LOCATIONS

HQ: IU HEALTH WEST HOSPITAL
1111 RONALD REAGAN PKWY # 223, AVON, IN 461237085
Phone: 317 217-3000
Web: WWW.IUHEALTH.ORG

HISTORICAL FINANCIALS

Company Type: Private

Income Statement FYE: December 31

	REVENUE ($ mil.)	NET INCOME ($ mil.)	NET PROFIT MARGIN	EMPLOYEES
12/15	191	65	34.4%	931
12/14	191	60	31.7%	—
Annual Growth	(0.2%)	8.4%	—	—

2015 Year-End Financials

Return on assets: 5.3% Cash ($ mil.): 232
Return on equity: 34.4%
Current ratio: 2.20

IVIE & ASSOCIATES, INC.

EXECUTIVES

President, Warren Ivie
Vice-President, Sharon Kay Ivie
Treasurer, Sharon Renee Rawlings
President, Brandon Ivie
Vice-President, Gary Long
Operations Manager, Chris Pearce
Vice-President, David Bailey
Vice-President, Garrison Jim
Manager, Jeri Chandler

LOCATIONS

HQ: IVIE & ASSOCIATES, INC.
601 SILVERON STE 200, FLOWER MOUND, TX
750284030
Phone: 972 899-5000
Web: WWW.IVIEINC.COM

HISTORICAL FINANCIALS

Company Type: Private

Income Statement

FYE: December 31

	REVENUE ($ mil.)	NET INCOME ($ mil.)	NET PROFIT MARGIN	EMPLOYEES
12/15	259	0	—	242
12/14	216	0	—	—
12/13	194	0	—	—
12/12	184	0	—	—
Annual Growth	12.0%	—	—	—

2015 Year-End Financials

Return on assets: 5.8%   Cash ($ mil.): 13
Return on equity: —
Current ratio: 1.20

IVY TECH COMMUNITY COLLEGE OF INDIANA

EXECUTIVES

President, Sue Ellspermann
Vice-President, Steve Tinscher
Executive Director, Aaron Roberts
Director, Anthony Jackson
Director, Ayana Blair
Director, Bill Williamson

LOCATIONS

HQ: IVY TECH COMMUNITY COLLEGE OF INDIANA
50 W FALL CREEK PKWY N DR, INDIANAPOLIS, IN
462085752
Phone: 317 921-4882

HISTORICAL FINANCIALS

Company Type: Private

Income Statement

FYE: June 30

	REVENUE ($ mil.)	NET INCOME ($ mil.)	NET PROFIT MARGIN	EMPLOYEES
06/16	174	39	22.3%	8,553
06/10	202	59	29.5%	—
06/09	170	24	14.6%	—
06/08	1,302	0	—	—
Annual Growth	—	—	—	—

2016 Year-End Financials

Return on assets: 16.7%   Cash ($ mil.): 129
Return on equity: 22.3%
Current ratio: 1.40

J M SMITH CORPORATION

J M Smith Corporation has gone from corner drugstore to supplying drugstores and more. The family-owned holding company's primary subsidiary is Smith Drug which provides purchasing and distribution services for more than 1000 independent pharmacies in more than 20 US states. It also operates through QS/1 Data Systems and Integral Solutions both of which offer data management software and services for pharmacies care providers and government agencies. Smith Premier provides prescription benefit management while other divisions offer automated dispensing systems for pharmacies and marketing services for drugmakers. Other units include Norgenix and RxMedic Systems.

Operations

The company operates through six business units: Smith Drug Company QS/1 Smith Premier Services Integral Solutions Group Norgenix and RxMedic Systems.

In addition to being its oldest subsidiary J M Smith's core Smith Drug unit is one of the top private wholesale drug distributors in the US. The company's Smith Premier unit also has a nationwide presence providing prescription management services through some 57000 contracted pharmacies.

Meanwhile the growing QS/1 division has installed more than 12000 health care and pharmacy automation systems and has more than 20 service offices across the US. The Integral Solutions unit which has about 15 offices scattered across the nation offers communication networking systems for universities banks and manufacturers in addition to health care customers.

J M Smith newest subsidiary Norgenix is a specialty pharmaceutical medical device and biotech company that engages in the development commercialization and sales of pharmaceutical products that serve the unmet needs within women's health. It acquires or licenses rights for select pharmaceuticals which it then markets through its direct sales force in North America. Norgenix is focused on the women's health markets and began marketing its first hormone replacement therapy in 2009.

RxMedic Systems provides leading-edge dispensing technology to pharmacies.

Geographic Reach

Smith Drug serves customers in 21 states primarily in the southern US as well as Washington DC and the Virgin Islands.

Sales and Marketing

The company supplies products services and technologies to pharmacies institutions local government agencies and businesses across the US.

Strategy

J M Smith's cornerstone Smith Drug subsidiary continues to be a key growth component doubling the number of states in which it operates over the last decade. However the company is also extolling its energies towards developing and introducing innovative data management and technology solutions through other subsidiaries to meet the rising demand for such solutions in the health care market.

Smith Premier is working to help customers go paperless by offering electronic prescription processing while RxMedic's dispensing systems allow pharmacies to increase productivity with its robotic counting and dispensing equipment.

The company's QS/1 subsidiary has experienced rapid growth in recent years as pharmacies and care providers increasingly look to automate processes and the Integral Solutions unit also benefits from recent trends in the health care market to improve electronic communication systems.

Partnerships are also key to J M Smith's growth. In 2014 Norgenix partnered with CrossBay Medical for the co-promotion of the SonoSure a device for use to access the uterine cavity for saline infusion sonohysterography and to obtain an endometrial biopsy if needed using the same device.

Mergers and Acquisitions

In late 2016 the company agreed to buy Vermont-based Burlington Drug Company which serves community pharmacies in New England and New York as well as certain assets of Pharmacy Health Services. The moves will broaden J M Smith's presence in the Northeast a target market for the company.

Company Background

In 2010 Smith expanded by acquiring health equipment manufacturing firm RxMedic. Through the purchase the company entered the automated dispensing system market.

J M Smith was founded in 1943 by drugstore proprietor James Smith and is run by the Smith family.

EXECUTIVES

President Integral Solutions Group (ISG), Joe Strayer
President Smith Drug Company, Jeff Foreman
President Integra LTC Solutions LLC, Kevin Welch
Chairman and CEO, A. Alan Turfe
President QS/1, Saul Factor
CFO and Treasurer, Philip J. Ryan
Senior Vice President Business Development, Rick Simerly

LOCATIONS

HQ: J M SMITH CORPORATION
101 W SAINT JOHN ST # 305, SPARTANBURG, SC
293065150
Phone: 864 542-9419
Web: WWW.JMSMITH.COM

Selected Office Locations

Altamonte Springs FL
Brandon MS
Columbia SC
Dallas TX
Fairmont WV
Gray ME
Hermitage PA
Houston TX
Indianapolis IN
Lexington KY
Mechanicsburg PA
Miami FL
Morrisville GA
Paragould AR
Perry GA
Pleasant Hill MO
Richmond VA
Seattle WA
Spartanburg SC
St. Paul MN
Sturbridge MA
Valdosta GA
Valencia CA
Wake Forest NC

PRODUCTS/OPERATIONS

Selected Divisions

Integral Solutions Group
Norgenix Pharmaceuticals
QS/1
RxMedic
Smith Drug Company
Smith Premier Services

COMPETITORS

AmerisourceBergen	HP Enterprise Services
CVS	Kinray
Cardinal Health	McKesson
Express Scripts	PharMerica
Fiserv	
H. D. Smith Wholesale	
Drug	

HISTORICAL FINANCIALS

Company Type: Private

Income Statement
FYE: February 29

	REVENUE ($ mil.)	NET INCOME ($ mil.)	NET PROFIT MARGIN	EMPLOYEES
02/16	2,403	47	2.0%	1,050
02/15	2,566	47	1.8%	—
02/14	2,370	38	1.6%	—
02/13	2,362	26	1.1%	—
Annual Growth	0.6%	22.0%	—	—

2016 Year-End Financials

Return on assets: 9.8% Cash ($ mil.): 104
Return on equity: 2.0%
Current ratio: 1.10

J. D. STREETT & COMPANY, INC.

Word on the street is that J. D. Streett tries to stay streets ahead of its rivals as it supplies its customers with a wide range of fuels oxygenates lubricants transmission fluids and antifreezes. The company operates more than 20 retail locations (convenience stores and gas stations) under its own ZX label and/or BP brand in Missouri and Illinois. J. D. Streett also serves more than 10 international markets. In addition the company offers terminalling services for distillate ethanol and oil products and owns and operates a chain of discount cigarette shops (most that also sell beer) across Missouri.

Its seven-acre petroleum terminal complex in St. Louis has a total capacity or more than of 485000 barrels and is capable of handling more than 25000 barrels a day. It also has a 252000 barrel terminal in Lemay Missouri. The terminals are centrally located and easily accessible by highway river rail and pipeline enabling the company to control costs.

J. D. Streett has a long track record of keeping the wheels of vehicles turning. It was formed in 1884 to make grease for wagon wheels.

EXECUTIVES

Operations Manager, Rick Dumi
Director, William Kreissle
Office Manager, Dawn Harris
General Manager, Joyce Spizzirri
Financial Executive, Paula Foyer
General Manager, James Martin
Auditors: BKD LLP ST LOUIS MISSOURI

LOCATIONS

HQ: J. D. STREETT & COMPANY, INC.
144 WELDON PKWY, MARYLAND HEIGHTS, MO
630433100
Phone: 314 432-6600
Web: WWW.JDSTREETT.COM

COMPETITORS

BP Lubricants USA	PetroLiance
Fuchs Lubricants	U.S. Venture
Lubrizol	Vesco Oil

HISTORICAL FINANCIALS

Company Type: Private

Income Statement
FYE: December 31

	REVENUE ($ mil.)	NET INCOME ($ mil.)	NET PROFIT MARGIN	EMPLOYEES
12/15	203	9	4.7%	240
12/14	286	4	1.6%	—
12/13	316	5	1.8%	—
12/12	342	(11)	—	—
Annual Growth	(16.0%)	—	—	—

2015 Year-End Financials

Return on assets: 3.2% Cash ($ mil.): 8
Return on equity: 4.7%
Current ratio: 1.80

J. T. THORPE & SON, INC.

EXECUTIVES

Chief Executive Officer, Mark C Stutzman
Chief Financial Officer, Michael P Elam
President, Bryan Young
Vice-President, Kevin Howard
Vice-President, Richard Giaramita
Financial Executive, Liane Vo
Vice-President, Gary Stewart
Engineer, David Watts
Manager, Steve Diemert
Auditors: ARMANINO LLP SAN RAMON CALIF

LOCATIONS

HQ: J. T. THORPE & SON, INC.
1060 HENSLEY ST, RICHMOND, CA 948012117
Phone: 510 233-2500
Web: WWW.JTTHORPE.COM

HISTORICAL FINANCIALS

Company Type: Private

Income Statement
FYE: October 31

	REVENUE ($ mil.)	NET INCOME ($ mil.)	NET PROFIT MARGIN	EMPLOYEES
10/15	177	6	3.7%	550
10/14	127	0	0.8%	—
10/13	121	2	1.8%	—
10/12	106	0	0.7%	—
Annual Growth	18.6%	106.2%	—	—

2015 Year-End Financials

Return on assets: 5.7% Cash ($ mil.): —
Return on equity: 3.7%
Current ratio: 0.50

J.E. DUNN CONSTRUCTION COMPANY

From first building designs to the last brick J.E. Dunn Construction helps make building plans a done deal. The contractor offers general construction services construction management and design/build services nationwide. It's known for its work on campus health care and commercial projects including the Mizzou Arena at the University of Missouri the H&R Block headquarters the Topfer Theatre at ZACH and the National Nuclear Security Administration campus. Founded in 1924 the company is one of Kansas City's top commercial construction firms and has been listed as one of the nation's top 10 general building companies. It operates as a subsidiary of J.E. Dunn Construction Group.

Operations

JE Dunn has ranked as one of the top 15 largest general building companies in the US in recent years. It counts several noteworthy projects among its portfolio such as CyrusOne Phoenix Data Center Tucson Medical Center West Campus CCA La Palma Correctional Center Lone Butte Casino Oasis Hospital Mountain Vista Medical Center and West Valley Medical Center Hospital.

Geographic Reach

Based in Kansas City Missouri JE Dunn operates about 20 offices throughout the US.

Sales and Marketing

JE Dunn works on projects for clients in several sectors including projects related to: science and technology corporate environments healthcare hospitality government and military energy and utility education and multifamily residential properties among others.

Financial Performance

While full financial information of the privately-held company were not available the company reported that it brings in annual revenue of $2.7 billion as of early 2015.

Strategy

J.E. Dunn Construction Company has been busy working on a variety of different projects in recent years. As of early 2015 JE Dunn's project portfolio included: the Health Care Patient Tower at the University of Missouri the Jennie Smoly Caruthers Biotechnology Building at the University of Colorado at Boulder the National Renewable Energy Laboratory (NREL) Energy System Integration Facility (Phase I) the Outpatient Cancer Center and parking garage for the Georgia Regents Health System and the new headquarters for the school-improvement group AdvancED. In 2013 JE Dunn completed a $300-million-plus renovation of the Kansas Capitol Building which involved renovating underground areas previously occupied by storage and maintenance areas into new space with improved ventilation technology and security.

JE Dunn is also adding offices to position itself near new target growth areas. To this end in early 2013 it opened an office in Williston North Dakota.

Company Background

In the past JE Dunn grew through acquisitions purchasing RJ Griffin & Co. (Atlanta) in 2000 Witcher Construction (Minneapolis) in 1990 and Drake Construction (Portland Oregon) in 1992.

EXECUTIVES

President & Chief Executive Officer, Gordon E. Lansford

Midwest Regional President, Dirk Schafer
EVP and Chief Risk Officer, Casey S. Halsey
EVP and Chief Legal Officer, Thomas F. (Tom)
  Whittaker
President JE Dunn Rocky Mountain, Steve
  Hamline
East Regional President, Dan Kaufman
CIO, John Jacobs
South Central Regional President, Greg Lorei
CFO, Beth Soukup
EVP and Chief Marketing Officer, Greg Nook
Vice President of Preconstruction for the
  Southwest Division, Curt Campbell
Senior Vice President, Tom Raney
Vice President, Tom Heger
DBIA Vice President, Ryan Price
Vice President, Mike Cloud
Vice President, Brent Ferguson
Vice President, Andy McGarrity
Vice President, Carol Warner
Senior Vice President, Bill Edwards
Vice President, Randall Bredar
Vice President of Audit, John Conley
Senior Vice President Human RE, Rick Beyer
Vice President Systems Quality Assurance,
  Michael Clippinger
Vice President Group Manager, Dustin Liljehorn
Vice President Marketing, Diane Miller
Senior Vice President Houston General Manager,
  Emre Ozcan
Vice President And Division General Counsel,
  Tyler Lee Henson
Vice President Preconstruction, Justin Griffin
Vice President, Marc Hutson
Vice President Engineering Services, David Barber
Vice President, Dan West
Senior Vice President, C Cianciaruso
Vice President Finance and Regional Chief
  Financial Officer, Chris Dierks
Vice President, Chris Cole
Vice President and Regional General Counsel,
  Colby Cox
Vice President, Chris Sorenson
Vice President, Eric Peterson
Vice President, Jeffrey Campbell
Vice President Healthcare, Bill Igel
Vice President, Donnie Lindstrom
Senior Vice President, Paul Neidlein
Vice President, Jim Ray
Vice President Industrial Group, Brent Strength
Vice President JE Dunn, Steve Golubski
Senior Vice President Dallas Office Leader, Chris
  Peck
Vice President, Angela Talbot
Senior Vice President, Neal Palmer
Vice President Of Education and Aviation Group
  Manager, Paul Fenzl
Vice President, Pat Arrington
Vice President, Larry Hawthorne
Seniot Vice President, Brad Schenk
Vice President, Patrick Oaks
Vice President, Todd Freed
Vice President Division Manager, Paul Fenzel
Vice President Project Executive, Michael
  Blakemore
Vice President Preconstruction, Monty Everson
Vice President, Inna Tassada
Vice President Business Development, Keith
  Knight
Vice President, Mark McElroy
Vice President of Business Development and
  Small Business Programs, Jose Amaya
Chairman, Steve Dunn
Board Member, Sara Curry
Auditors: KPMG LLP KANSAS CITY MISSOUR

LOCATIONS

HQ: J.E. DUNN CONSTRUCTION COMPANY
  1001 LOCUST ST, KANSAS CITY, MO 641061904
Phone: 816 474-8600

PRODUCTS/OPERATIONS

Selected Project Delivery Methods
Competitive Bid
Construction Management (Agency)
Design-Build
General Contracting/CM At Risk
Integrated Project Delivery
Project Management

COMPETITORS

Adolfson & Peterson Inc.	H.J. Russell
Barnhart	Hensel Phelps Construction
Boran Craig Barber Engel	Korte
C.F. Jordan	M. A. Mortenson
CORE Construction	MEDCO Construction
Clarkson Construction	Skanska USA Building
Flintco	Turner Corporation
	Weitz

HISTORICAL FINANCIALS

Company Type: Private

Income Statement   FYE: December 31

	REVENUE ($ mil.)	NET INCOME ($ mil.)	NET PROFIT MARGIN	EMPLOYEES
12/15	2,909	0	—	1,635
12/14	2,242	0	—	—
12/13	2,242	0	—	—
12/12	0	0	—	—
Annual Growth	—	—	—	—

J.E. DUNN CONSTRUCTION GROUP, INC.

Owned by descendants of founder John Ernest
Dunn J.E. Dunn Construction Group operates as
the holding company for a group of construction
firms that includes flagship J.E. Dunn Construction
and Atlanta-based R.J. Griffin & Company.
Founded in 1924 it builds institutional commercial
and industrial structures nationwide. It also provides construction and program management and
design/build services. J.E. Dunn Construction
which is among the largest US general builders
was one of the first contractors to offer the construction management delivery method. Some of
its major projects have included an IRS facility and
the world headquarters for H&R Block both located in Kansas City Missouri.
  Operations
  Besides its primary operations of J.E. Dunn Construction and R.J. Griffin & Company the construction company runs Dunn Project Solutions a construction services unit that tackles projects ranging
in size from $50000 to $5 million. The business
focuses on projects related to corporate interiors
retail improvements historic rehabilitation additions fixtures and equipment building upgrades
maintenance work and small office projects.
  The company's ranked as the 10th largest general building company in the US in 2015.
  Geographic Reach
  Headquartered in Kansas City Missouri J.E.
Dunn operates some 20 offices across the nation.
It has offices in Georgia Texas North Carolina Colorado Iowa Missouri Minnesota Tennessee Okla-

homa Nebraska Arizona Oregon Kansas and North
Dakota.
  Sales and Marketing
  The company works on corporate environments
mission critical correctional/justice and mixed
use/retail projects among others.
  Financial Performance
  J.E. Dunn Construction last reported annual revenues of more than $2.6 billion in 2014.
  Strategy
  Some of the group's more recent projects projects include work on the North Dakota governor's
residence and the new Bank of North Dakota Financial Center in Bismark (2016); the Harold Newman Arena in Jamestown (2016); the Trinity High
School reconstruction and expansion project
(2016); the building of the 378000 sq. ft. Cambridge North Tower at The University of Kansas
Hospital (September 2017); the 92000 sq. ft. entertainment of the arts at the University of Col-
orado; the 151000 sq. ft. expansion project on an
inpatient pavilion at the UCHealth University of
Colorado Hospital (May 2015); the 92000 sq. ft.
Fallen Fire Fighter Memorial in Colorado Springs
(June 2015); and the 160000 sq. ft. CHI St.
Joseph's Hospital and Health Center (October
2014).
  Past projects include work on the Charles R.
Drew Charter School Senior Academy the Kauff-
man Center for the Performing Arts the Topfer
Theatre at ZACH the Energy Systems Integration
Facility (ESIF) the Collaborative Life Sciences
Building & Skourtes Tower and the Georgia Re-
gents Health System Outpatient Cancer. Other past
projects have included Baylor Scott & White Can-
cer Center Hotel Sorella GSA National Nuclear Se-
curity Administration City of Houston Bethel Park
Renovation and the B.E. Smith Corporate Headquarters Renovation.
  Company Background
  A bigwig particularly in the Midwest the group
regularly bids on federal government projects. J.E.
Dunn won a major contract from the US Army
Corps of Engineers to build a regional correctional
facility at Fort Leavenworth Kansas that replaced
smaller prisons in Texas Kentucky and Oklahoma.
  In 2012 the company earned the designation of
having the first ever LEED Gold Certified building
in downtown Kansas City.
  The descendants of John Ernest Dunn hold a
majority stake in the company.

EXECUTIVES

President and CEO, Gordon E. Lansford
President Midwest Region, Dirk Schafer
EVP, William H. (Bill) Dunn
EVP General Counsel and Secretary, Casey S.
  Halsey
President West Region, Steve Hamline
EVP and Chief Marketing Officer, Gregory E. (Greg)
  Nook
President East Region, Dan Kaufman
EVP and Chief Legal Officer, Tom Whittaker
CIO, John Jacobs
President South Central, Greg Lorei
CFO, Beth Soukup
Senior Vice President, Tom Raney
Vice President, Curt Campbell
Vice Chairman & Treasurer, Stephen D. (Steve)
  Dunn
Auditors: KPMG LLP KANSAS CITY MISSOUR

LOCATIONS

HQ: J.E. DUNN CONSTRUCTION GROUP, INC.
  1001 LOCUST ST, KANSAS CITY, MO 641061904
Phone: 816 474-8600
Web: WWW.JEDUNN.COM

PRODUCTS/OPERATIONS

Selected Group Companies
JE Dunn Midwest
JE Dunn North Central
JE Dunn Northwest
JE Dunn Rocky Mountain
JE Dunn South Central
R.J. Griffin & Company

Selected Services
Preconstruction
    Constructability review
    Feasibility studies
    Market analysis
    Mechanical electrical plumbing review
    Preconstruction estimating
    Quality control
    Risk management
    Scheduling
Construction
    Change order management
    Labor relations
    Progress monitoring
    Quality control and testing
Post Construction
    Commissioning
    Final closeout
    Lien releases
    One-year walkthrough
    Operations and maintenance manuals

COMPETITORS

Alberici	Skanska USA Building
Clark Enterprises	Sundt
Hensel Phelps	Turner Corporation
Construction	Tutor Perini
Hunt Construction	Weitz
McCarthy Building	Whiting-Turner

HISTORICAL FINANCIALS

Company Type: Private

Income Statement

FYE: December 31

	REVENUE ($ mil.)	NET INCOME ($ mil.)	NET PROFIT MARGIN	EMPLOYEES
12/15	2,910	0	—	2,080
12/14	2,243	0	—	—
12/13	2,243	0	—	—
12/12	0	0	—	—
Annual Growth	—	—	—	—

JAC. VANDENBERG, INC.

EXECUTIVES

President, David L Schiro
Board of Directors, Michael Knatz
Manager, Mitch Farris
Manager, Craig Padover

LOCATIONS

HQ: JAC. VANDENBERG, INC.
    100 CORPORATE DR STE 155, YONKERS, NY
    107016838
Phone: 914 964-5900
Web: WWW.JACVANDENBERG.COM

HISTORICAL FINANCIALS

Company Type: Private

Income Statement

FYE: December 31

	REVENUE ($ mil.)	NET INCOME ($ mil.)	NET PROFIT MARGIN	EMPLOYEES
12/15	180	3	2.0%	30
12/14	173	3	2.1%	—
12/13	187	4	2.3%	—
12/11	168	3	2.1%	—
Annual Growth	1.7%	(0.3%)	—	—

2015 Year-End Financials

Return on assets: 8.9%   Cash ($ mil.): 10
Return on equity: 2.0%
Current ratio: 1.10

JACKSON ENERGY AUTHORITY

Jackson Energy Authority has the power and the authority to provide for all of Jackson Tennessee's energy needs. The municipal utility distributes electricity natural gas and water and provides wastewater services to about 40000 residential commercial and industrial customers in Jackson and surrounding areas. Jackson Energy also sells propane and offers broadband telecommunications services (cable Internet and telephone). Other services provided by Jackson Energy Authority include the sale of outdoor security lights surge protection systems gas grills and decorative lights.

As part of its strategy to reduce carbon emission conserve energy and help its customers cut costs Jackson Energy Authority's Wise Energy program provides practical energy saving advice to gas power and water users.

The company was formed by the City of Jackson in 1959 to combine its three separate utilities (natural gas electricity and water/wastewater) under one utility operation. A five-member Board of Directors appointed by the Mayor and City Council of Jackson governs Jackson Energy Authority.

EXECUTIVES

Chairman, Ken Marston
Vice-President, David Cowfer
Manager, Steve Bowers
Auditors: ALEXANDER THOMPSON ARNOLD PLLC

LOCATIONS

HQ: JACKSON ENERGY AUTHORITY
    351 DR MARTIN LUTHER, JACKSON, TN 38301
Phone: 731 422-7500
Web: WWW.JAXENERGY.COM

HISTORICAL FINANCIALS

Company Type: Private

Income Statement

FYE: June 30

	REVENUE ($ mil.)	NET INCOME ($ mil.)	NET PROFIT MARGIN	EMPLOYEES
06/16	237	14	6.3%	425
06/15	245	16	6.7%	—
06/14	250	24	9.8%	—
06/13	243	22	9.3%	—
Annual Growth	(0.9%)	(13.1%)	—	—

2016 Year-End Financials

Return on assets: 11.7%   Cash ($ mil.): 73
Return on equity: 6.3%
Current ratio: 2.70

JACKSON HEALTHCARE, LLC

Jackson Healthcare can help find physicians to work at hospitals and help keep track of patients as they enter and leave hospitals. Its staffing businesses offer job search recruiting and placement services for physicians and other health care professionals; provide anesthesiologists; and coordinate the work of traveling nurses. Jackson Healthcare's physician job boards attract thousands of visitors per month giving it a reputation for filling openings quickly. Subsidiary Patient Placement Systems manages patient flow through the medical system and Care Logistics provides patient tracking software. Richard Jackson formed the company in 1978.

Operations

Jackson Healthcare operates more than a dozen subsidiaries and operations units and serves more than 7 million patients spread throughout 1300 health care facilities.

Subsidiaries and divisions include Premier Anesthesia   Jackson   Therapy   Partners LucumTenens.com Jackson Nurse Professionals and Jackson & Coker. Other operations include AdvancedPractice.com Jackson Surgical Assistants Jackson Pharmacy Professionals Tyler & Company and Parker HealthcareIT.

Its health care software and technology portfolio is managed by Care Logistics and Patient Placement Systems.

Mergers and Acquisitions

Jackson Healthcare's growth strategy involves acquiring other staffing businesses to augment its geographical reach. In 2014 it purchased Sullivan Healthcare Consulting (SHC) a Michigan-based firm focused on improving the performance of the hospital's perioperative suite.

EXECUTIVES

Managing Director Jackson Healthcare, Paul D. Foster
CEO Jackson Therapy Partners and President Jackson Nurse Professionals, Scott L'Heureux
CEO, Richard L. Jackson
President Jackson Healthcare and LocumTenens.com, R. Shane Jackson
EVP Human Resources, Michael Hiffa
CTO, Tim Aligheri
CFO, Douglas B. Kline
President Care Logistics, Karl Straub
President Premier Anesthesia, Kerry Teel
President AdvancedPractice.com, Susan Mesa
President Jackson & Coker Permanent Placement, Tony Stajduhar
President and CEO Parker Health Care IT, Debbie Crandall
President HealthIT Project Managers, Jack Williams
VP and General Manager Healthcare Staffing Technologies, Karyn Mullins
VP AdvancedPractice.com and Jackson Pharmacy Professionals, David McAnally
VP and General Manager Patient Placement Systems, Doug Walker
CIO, Ryan Esparza

Vice President Anesthesia, Diana Denman Holmes
Vice President Operations, Margaret Ratchford
Vice Chairman, William H. Franklin

LOCATIONS

HQ: JACKSON HEALTHCARE, LLC
2655 NORTHWINDS PKWY, ALPHARETTA, GA
300092280
Phone: 770 643-5500

PRODUCTS/OPERATIONS

Selected Subsidiaries and Operating Units
Jackson Healthcare Staffing
  AdvancedPractice.com (a full-service locum tenens
  agency dedicated to physician assistants and nurse
  practitioners)
  Healthcare Staffing Technologies (provider of career
  concierge sites in the healthcare market)
  HealthIT Project Managers (provider of experienced IT
  project management contractors to hospitals)
  Jackson & Coker (locum tenens and permanent
  recruitment firm for physicians)
  Jackson Nurse Professionals (specializes in the
  placement of registered nurses in healthcare settings
  nationwide)
  Jackson Pharmacy Professionals (national pharmacy-
  only staffing and recruiting company)
  Jackson Surgical Assistants (staffing of certified
  surgical assistants to surgeons and hospitals)
  Jackson Therapy Partners (staffing of rehabilitation
  therapists and other allied healthcare professionals)
  LocumTenens.com (locum tenens physician
  recruitment agency)
  Parker HealthcareIT (provider of supplemental IT
  staffing)
  Premier Anesthesia (anesthesia department
  management company)
Jackson Healthcare Technology
  Care Logistics (firm that helps hospitals transform
  their operations to deliver hospital efficiency)
  Patient Placement Systems (supplier of continuing
  care provider software)

COMPETITORS

AMN Healthcare	Gentiva
ATC Healthcare	Kelly Services
Adecco	ManpowerGroup
CHG Healthcare	On Assignment
CompHealth	RehabCare
Cross Country	TeamStaff
Healthcare	inVentiv Health

HISTORICAL FINANCIALS

Company Type: Private

Income Statement FYE: December 31

	REVENUE ($ mil.)	NET INCOME ($ mil.)	NET PROFIT MARGIN	EMPLOYEES
12/15	696	70	10.2%	784
12/07	384	18	4.8%	—
12/06	261	41	15.7%	—
12/03	958	0	—	—
Annual Growth	—	210.5%	—	—

2015 Year-End Financials

Return on assets: 2.8%   Cash ($ mil.): 15
Return on equity: 10.2%
Current ratio: 2.60

JACKSON HOSPITAL & CLINIC, INC

Jackson Hospital & Clinic looks after the health
and well being of a large number of residents of
Montgomery and central Alabama. The privately
held not-for-profit medical institution has about
345 acute care beds. Specialized services include
cardiac care emergency medicine neurology orthopedics oncology and women's and infant's
health care. The medical center also provides family medicine primary care and diagnostic services
through its outpatient clinic facilities and it offers
medical laboratory services for other regional
health care providers.

Operations
The company has an active medical staff of 175
physicians and a total medical staff of 350 doctors.
Its programs include cardiology and cardiac surgery orthopedics/sports medicine obstetrics and
gynecology neurosurgery and robotic surgery.

Geographic Reach
The hospital system serves patients in and
around Montgomery Alabama.

Strategy
Jackson Hospital is looking to continuously upgrade the performance of its emergency room and
other departments.

In 2014 it partnered with National Research
Corporation Picker to better understand the patient experience and quality of care issues as seen
through the eyes of Jackson Hospital's patients.

In 2013 the hospital's Imaging Center added
new computed tomography technology with the
addition of a Siemens Somatom Perspective 128-
slice CT scanner. The new equipment offers intri-
cate diagnostic details advanced radiation dose reduction features and a patient-friendly design. It
also enhanced its surgical capabilities that year
with the addition of a new integrated operating
room for minimally-invasive procedures and the
introduction of the latest version of surgical robot
known as the da Vinci Si platform.

In 2013 Jackson Hospital formed a joint venture
with Physiotherapy Associates' subsidiary Rehab
Associates to deliver physical occupational and rehabilitation services to Jackson Hospital's patients.
Under the partnership patients of Jackson Hospital
receive personalized care from an organization
specializing in physical therapy.

Company Background
Jackson Hospital & Clinic traces its roots back
to 1894.

EXECUTIVES

Vice President of Informatics, Richard Caldwell
Rph, Shirley Boyd
Bs Pharm Pharmd, Nancy Bailey
Assistant Vice President Finance, Larry Sherbett

LOCATIONS

HQ: JACKSON HOSPITAL & CLINIC, INC
1725 PINE ST, MONTGOMERY, AL 361061117
Phone: 334 293-8000
Web: WWW.JACKSON.ORG

PRODUCTS/OPERATIONS

Selected Services
Advanced Spine Center
Diabetes Center
Emergency services
Heart Center
Jackson Clinic
Jackson Imaging Center
Jackson Surgery Center
McGough Oncology Center
Medical imaging
Mom & Baby Center
Neurosciences
Orthopedic and Joint Center
Physical therapy
Robotic surgery
Sleep Disorders Center
Sports medicine
Stroke treatment
Wound Care Center

COMPETITORS

Baptist Health (AL)
DCH Health System
East Alabama Medical Center
Gadsden Regional Medical Center
Tenet Healthcare
University of South Alabama Health System

HISTORICAL FINANCIALS

Company Type: Private

Income Statement FYE: December 31

	REVENUE ($ mil.)	NET INCOME ($ mil.)	NET PROFIT MARGIN	EMPLOYEES
12/15	201	1	0.8%	1,400
12/14	196	1	0.6%	—
12/12	174	3	1.9%	—
12/10	174	11	6.6%	—
Annual Growth	2.9%	(33.1%)	—	—

2015 Year-End Financials

Return on assets: 3.5%   Cash ($ mil.): 1
Return on equity: 0.8%
Current ratio: 2.30

JACKSON-MADISON COUNTY GENERAL HOSPITAL DISTRICT

EXECUTIVES

President, Bobby Arnold
Director, Bill Welch
Director, Barry Phillips
Director, Ron F Taylor
Manager, Charles Emrich

LOCATIONS

HQ: JACKSON-MADISON COUNTY GENERAL
HOSPITAL DISTRICT
620 SKYLINE DR, JACKSON, TN 383013923
Phone: 731 541-5000

HISTORICAL FINANCIALS

Company Type: Private

Income Statement FYE: June 30

	REVENUE ($ mil.)	NET INCOME ($ mil.)	NET PROFIT MARGIN	EMPLOYEES
06/15	554	20	3.7%	5,000
06/04	429	37	8.6%	—
06/03	307	247	80.4%	—
06/02	288	16	5.9%	—
Annual Growth	5.2%	1.5%	—	—

2015 Year-End Financials

Return on assets: 3.2%   Cash ($ mil.): 23
Return on equity: 3.7%
Current ratio: 2.70

JACKSONVILLE ELECTRIC AUTHORITY

As long as sparks are flying in Jacksonville everything is A-OK with JEA. The community-owned not-for-profit utility provides electricity to 438000 customers in Jacksonville and surrounding areas in northeastern Florida. Managing an electric system that dates back to 1895 JEA has a net generating capacity of 3747 MW. It owns an electric system with five primarily fossil-fueled generating plants. JEA also gets 12.8 MW of generating capacity from two methane-fueled landfill plants. The company resells electricity to other utilities including NextEra Energy. JEA also provides water and wastewater services; it serves 321600 water customers and 247500 wastewater customers.

Operations

JEA is the largest community-owned utility in Florida and the eighth largest in the US.

The company operates in four segments: the Electric System and Bulk Power Supply System; the St. Johns River Power Park System System; the Water and Sewer System; and the District Energy System.

The Electric System operates five generating plants in Florida (and holds a stake in a power plant in Georgia) and all transmission and distribution facilities including more than 745 miles of transmission lines and more than 6500 miles of distribution lines. It purchases power locally from a solar field and a landfill gas facility. This segment accounted for 77% of the company's 2014 revenues.

JEA's Water System consists of 134 artesian wells that tap into the Floridan aquifer. Water is distributed through 37 water treatment plants and more than 4300 miles of water lines. Wastewater is collected through more than 3800 miles of wastewater collection lines and treated at seven regional treatment plants.

The company's operations are funded by three enterprise funds: the Electric Enterprise Fund the Water and Sewer Fund and the District Energy System The Electric Enterprise Fund is comprised of the JEA Electric System Bulk Power Supply System and St. Johns River Power Park System.

Geographic Reach

The cooperative serves customers in Northeast Florida.

Financial Performance

In 2014 JEA's revenues increased by 3% due to a 3% growth in electric sales as the result of higher consumption (primarily 4.3% in residential sales). Water and sewer sales increased by 1% related to a rise in customers and District Energy System sales increased by 2%. Approximately 47% of JEA's electric 2014 revenues came from its 375000 residential customers 50% from 48000 commercial and industrial customers and 3% from one wholesale customer.

The company's net income increased by 97% due to higher investment returns and a decline in loss from interest on debt.

JEA's operating cash flow decreased by 4% due to higher payments to suppliers.

Strategy

To help meet state regulations for carbon emission control JEA plans to get 10% of its energy requirements from nuclear energy by 2018 and 30% by 2030. In this regard JEA has signed a purchase power agreement to get 206 MW from a nuclear plant beginning in 2016 and is pursuing additional purchased power contracts.

JEA is also building out more fossil fuel capacity.

Company Background

The electric utility grew from a department of city of Jacksonville into an independent authority created by city and county government consolidation in 1967. In 1997 the water and sewer systems (which had been operated by the city since 1880) were also placed under JEA management.

In 2011 it completed the Greenland Energy Center which included two 175-MW natural gas-fired combustion turbines.

EXECUTIVES

Chief Executive Officer, Paul McElroy
Board of Directors, Ron Baker
Vice-President, Bill Cutts
Financial Executive, John Wolfel

LOCATIONS

HQ: JACKSONVILLE ELECTRIC AUTHORITY
21 W CHURCH ST FL 1, JACKSONVILLE, FL
322023152
Phone: 904 665-6000
Web: WWW.JEA.COM

PRODUCTS/OPERATIONS

2014 Sales

	$ mil.	% of total
Electric	1,431	77
Water & wastewater	383	21
District Energy System	8	-
Other	38	2
Total	**1,861**	**100**

COMPETITORS

Chesapeake Utilities	Seminole Electric
Florida Power & Light	Southern Company
Florida Public	TECO Energy
Utilities	United Water Inc.
NextEra Energy	Utilities Inc.
Progress Energy	

HISTORICAL FINANCIALS
Company Type: Private

Income Statement

	REVENUE ($ mil.)	NET INCOME ($ mil.)	NET PROFIT MARGIN	EMPLOYEES	FYE: September 30
09/16*	1,782	210	11.8%	2,356	
06/09	1,319	71	5.4%	—	
03/09	857	45	5.4%	—	
Annual Growth	**9.6%**	**20.9%**	—	—	

*Fiscal year change

2016 Year-End Financials
Return on assets: 6.4%
Return on equity: 11.8%
Current ratio: 1.20

Cash ($ mil.): 418

JAMESON MEMORIAL HOSPITAL

EXECUTIVES

Chief Executive Officer, Douglas Danko

LOCATIONS

HQ: JAMESON MEMORIAL HOSPITAL
1211 WILMINGTON AVE, NEW CASTLE, PA
161052595
Phone: 724 658-9001
Web: WWW.JAMESONHEALTH.ORG

HISTORICAL FINANCIALS
Company Type: Private

Income Statement

	REVENUE ($ mil.)	NET INCOME ($ mil.)	NET PROFIT MARGIN	EMPLOYEES	FYE: June 30
06/15	302	2	0.7%	1,150	
06/14	304	3	1.0%	—	
06/13	303	4	1.4%	—	
06/12	270	3	1.1%	—	
Annual Growth	**3.8%**	**(12.6%)**	—	—	

2015 Year-End Financials
Return on assets: 12.0%
Return on equity: 0.7%
Current ratio: 0.20

Cash ($ mil.): 2

JAMIESON-HILL A GENERAL PARTNERSHIP

Auditors: MOSS ADAMS LLP LOS ANGELES C

LOCATIONS

HQ: JAMIESON-HILL A GENERAL PARTNERSHIP
3101 STATE RD, BAKERSFIELD, CA 933084931
Phone: 661 393-7000

HISTORICAL FINANCIALS
Company Type: Private

Income Statement

	REVENUE ($ mil.)	NET INCOME ($ mil.)	NET PROFIT MARGIN	EMPLOYEES	FYE: December 31
12/15	183	11	6.3%	50	
12/14	214	6	3.2%	—	
12/11	197	4	2.0%	—	
12/08	171	3	2.2%	—	
Annual Growth	**1.0%**	**17.5%**	—	—	

2015 Year-End Financials
Return on assets: —
Return on equity: 6.3%
Current ratio: 11.30

Cash ($ mil.): 3

JDRF INTERNATIONAL

EXECUTIVES

President, Derek Rapp
Board of Directors, Mary Elizabeth Bunzel
Director, Dayton Cotes
Manager, Gary Curtl
Auditors: KPMG LLP NEW YORK NY

LOCATIONS

HQ: JDRF INTERNATIONAL
26 BROADWAY, NEW YORK, NY 100041703
Phone: 212 785-9500
Web: WWW.JDRF.ORG

HISTORICAL FINANCIALS
Company Type: Private

Income Statement
FYE: June 30

	REVENUE ($ mil.)	NET INCOME ($ mil.)	NET PROFIT MARGIN	EMPLOYEES
06/15	205	19	9.4%	600
06/12	193	(11)	—	—
06/11	220	16	7.5%	—
06/10	0	0	—	—
Annual Growth	—	311.6%	—	—

2015 Year-End Financials
Return on assets: 6.8%
Return on equity: 9.4%
Current ratio: 0.40
Cash ($ mil.): 37

JEFFERSON COUNTY BOARD OF EDUCATION

EXECUTIVES
Superintendent, Donna Hargenes
Chief Financial Officer, Cornelia Hardin
Director of Finance, Edward Muns
Auditors: STROTHMAN & COMPANY PSC LOUI

LOCATIONS
HQ: JEFFERSON COUNTY BOARD OF EDUCATION
3332 NEWBURG RD, LOUISVILLE, KY 402182414
Phone: 502 485-3011
Web: WWW.JEFFERSON.K12.KY.US

HISTORICAL FINANCIALS
Company Type: Private

Income Statement
FYE: June 30

	REVENUE ($ mil.)	NET INCOME ($ mil.)	NET PROFIT MARGIN	EMPLOYEES
06/16	1,251	31	2.5%	14,000
06/14	1,158	24	2.1%	—
06/13	1,179	(26)	—	—
06/12	0	(57)	—	—
Annual Growth	—	—	—	—

2016 Year-End Financials
Return on assets: —
Return on equity: 2.5%
Current ratio: —
Cash ($ mil.): 235

JEFFERSON COUNTY SCHOOL DISTRICT NO. R-1

EXECUTIVES
Superintendent, Dan McMinimee
Executive Director, Rich Waterman
Manager, Don Lohman
Director, Kathleen Askelson
Superintendent, Irene Griego

Director, Joe Pitoniak
Manager, Marybeth C Jones
Auditors: CLIFTONLARSONALLEN LLP BROOMF

LOCATIONS
HQ: JEFFERSON COUNTY SCHOOL DISTRICT NO. R-1
1829 DENVER WEST DR # 27, GOLDEN, CO
804013120
Phone: 303 982-6500
Web: WWW.JEFFCOPUBLICSCHOOLS.ORG

HISTORICAL FINANCIALS
Company Type: Private

Income Statement
FYE: June 30

	REVENUE ($ mil.)	NET INCOME ($ mil.)	NET PROFIT MARGIN	EMPLOYEES
06/15	801	(18)	—	12,000
06/14	785	(14)	—	—
06/13	759	97	12.8%	—
06/12	748	(20)	—	—
Annual Growth	2.3%	—	—	—

2015 Year-End Financials
Return on assets: 3.6%
Return on equity: (-2.3%)
Current ratio: —
Cash ($ mil.): 4

JEFFERSON HOSPITAL ASSOCIATION, INC.

Jefferson Regional Medical Center (JRMC) provides acute care and other health services to residents of Pine Bluff and an 11-county area of southern Arkansas. The not-for-profit community-owned hospital has about 470 acute care beds and offers general medical and surgical care as well as services in a range of specialties including urology orthopedics cardiology and oncology. It also has a 25-bed skilled nursing unit that cares for patients transitioning to long-term care or home care. A network of clinics offers outpatient surgery diagnostic imaging wound care and other ambulatory health services. Additionally the health system operates a nursing school and home health and hospice agencies.

To bring its operations up to speed with modern technology requirements in the health care industry JRMC has implemented an electronic health record (EHR) system and is employing that system to comply with meaningful use guidelines from the US government. In fact JRMC was a frontrunner in the movement to bring medical records online first moving to install EHR systems in 2003.

The hospital also expanded its services for the southern Arkansas region by becoming certified as a Level II trauma center in 2010. JRMC has also expanded and upgraded its wellness centers to serve the exercise needs of the community.

EXECUTIVES
Infection Control Director, Nikki Wallace

LOCATIONS
HQ: JEFFERSON HOSPITAL ASSOCIATION, INC.
1600 W 40TH AVE, PINE BLUFF, AR 716036301
Phone: 870 541-7100
Web: WWW.JRMC.ORG

COMPETITORS
Arkansas Heart Hospital
St. Vincent Health System

Baptist Health (Arkansas)
Conway Regional Health System
Sparks Health System
University of Arkansas
Weirton Medical Center
White County Medical Center

HISTORICAL FINANCIALS
Company Type: Private

Income Statement
FYE: June 30

	REVENUE ($ mil.)	NET INCOME ($ mil.)	NET PROFIT MARGIN	EMPLOYEES
06/15	170	13	7.7%	1,700
06/14	174	6	3.4%	—
06/13	180	0	0.2%	—
06/10	198	11	5.6%	—
Annual Growth	(3.0%)	3.2%	—	—

2015 Year-End Financials
Return on assets: 5.0%
Return on equity: 7.7%
Current ratio: 1.40
Cash ($ mil.): 17

JERNIGAN OIL CO., INC.

EXECUTIVES
President, James M Harrell
Marketing Director, Jerry Castelloe
Personnel Manager, Karla Harrington
Auditors: MAY & PLACE PA LOUISBURG NO

LOCATIONS
HQ: JERNIGAN OIL CO., INC.
415 MAIN ST E, AHOSKIE, NC 279103421
Phone: 252 332-2131
Web: WWW.JERNIGANOIL.COM

HISTORICAL FINANCIALS
Company Type: Private

Income Statement
FYE: December 31

	REVENUE ($ mil.)	NET INCOME ($ mil.)	NET PROFIT MARGIN	EMPLOYEES
12/15	199	0	0.0%	350
12/14	248	0	0.1%	—
12/13	232	(0)	—	—
12/12	226	0	0.1%	—
Annual Growth	(4.1%)	(16.0%)	—	—

2015 Year-End Financials
Return on assets: 4.1%
Return on equity: —
Current ratio: 0.40
Cash ($ mil.): 1

JERSEY CITY MEDICAL CENTER INC.

With roots extending back to 1882 Jersey City Medical Center (JCMC) may have history but it's not stuck in the past. The 350-bed acute-care hospital serves residents of New Jersey's Hudson County area. Operated by Liberty Healthcare the hospital includes a trauma center a perinatal center and a heart institute. JCMC also offers pediatric women's health rehabilitation and ambulatory care

and it is a teaching affiliate for the Mount Sinai School of Medicine. JCMC's modern incarnation came about in the Great Depression when it was constructed by a political ally of Franklin Roosevelt.

Operations

JCMC operates as a regional referral center meaning that it takes on complicated cases from smaller community hospitals in the area. As an area teaching hospital the hospital offers medical residency programs in internal medicine and nursing. It also offers continuing education courses to keep its medical residents up on the latest medical developments.

JCMC's mobile outreach program provides health and wellness screenings dispense care and offer health education. It is funded through a grant provided by The New Jersey Department of Health and Senior Services. Among other things the van will provide diabetes HIV and mental health screenings as well as perform blood pressure checks offer preventive care and educate people on the streets of Hudson County and Jersey City. The van travels to health fairs and regularly scheduled outreach events such as at schools and senior centers.

Geographic Reach

The 15-acre JCMC campus which overlooks the New York Harbor and the Liberty State Park is also home to the Wilzig Hospital and the Provident Bank Ambulatory Center. JCMC offers a Mobile Health Screening Unit that will travel to underserved areas throughout Hudson County. The hospital is the primary medical facility serving New York's Hudson Essex and Union counties.

Strategy

In mid-2013 JCMC announced that it has entered an agreement to become part of the Barnabas Health system. The merger was expected to close by the end of 2013 following regulatory approval.

JCMC focuses on expanding and improving services for area residents. The hospital opened a hand and upper extremity unit in 2013 to address the needs of patients with pain and functional difficulties related to arthritis carpal tunnel syndrome injuries and other conditions. It also added about 200 new physicians during 2012 to enhance patient access to general and specialty care. It opened a new gastrointestinal disorder center on the main campus in 2012 and it expanded its cardiac care services with the opening of a new electrophysiology lab.

In 2012 it announced plans to renovate and reopen the former Greenville Hospital campus in Jersey City as an outpatient facility to meet the rising needs for ambulatory care in the area.

EXECUTIVES

Radiology Medical Director, Anthony Tramontana
Director Of Nursing, Irene Ondieki
Operating Room Dir, KELLY LOO

LOCATIONS

HQ: JERSEY CITY MEDICAL CENTER INC.
355 GRAND ST, JERSEY CITY, NJ 073024321
Phone: 201 915-2000
Web: WWW.LIBERTYHEALTH.ORG

PRODUCTS/OPERATIONS

Selected Locations
Emergency Services at JCMC
Family Regional Perinatal Center
Fannie E. Rippel Foundation Heart Institute
General Pediatrics at JCMC
Nursing at JCMC
Provident Bank Ambulatory Center
Port Authority Heroes of Sept 11 Trauma Center
The Rehabilitation Services Department
Volunteer Services at JCMC
Wilzig Hospital

COMPETITORS

Bergen Regional Medical
Bronx-Lebanon Hospital
Continuum Health Partners
Englewood Hospital and Medical Center
Hackensack University Medical Center
Hospital for Special Surgery
Lenox Hill Hospital
Montefiore Medical
Newark Beth Israel Medical Center
Robert Wood Johnson University Hospital at Rahway
St. Joseph's Healthcare System
The Valley Hospital
Valley Health System

HISTORICAL FINANCIALS

Company Type: Private

Income Statement

FYE: December 31

	REVENUE ($ mil.)	NET INCOME ($ mil.)	NET PROFIT MARGIN	EMPLOYEES
12/15	375	37	10.1%	1,942
12/14	341	6	1.8%	—
12/13	367	30	8.2%	—
12/08	249	8	3.3%	—
Annual Growth	6.0%	24.1%		

2015 Year-End Financials

Return on assets: 6.2%   Cash ($ mil.): 2
Return on equity: 10.1%
Current ratio: 0.10

JET SPECIALTY, INC.

EXECUTIVES

President, Tom W Darter
Manager, Martha Sewell
Account Manager, Marty Worrell
Manager, Wade Mahan
Auditors: WEAVER AND TIDWELL LLP SAN

LOCATIONS

HQ: JET SPECIALTY, INC.
211 MARKET AVE, BOERNE, TX 780063050
Phone: 830 331-9457
Web: WWW.JETSPECIALTY.COM

HISTORICAL FINANCIALS

Company Type: Private

Income Statement

FYE: December 31

	REVENUE ($ mil.)	NET INCOME ($ mil.)	NET PROFIT MARGIN	EMPLOYEES
12/15	267	9	3.6%	171
12/13	323	38	11.9%	—
12/12	266	39	14.8%	—
12/11	169	17	10.1%	—
Annual Growth	12.0%	(13.3%)	—	—

2015 Year-End Financials

Return on assets: 3.1%   Cash ($ mil.): 8
Return on equity: 3.6%
Current ratio: 4.00

JJJTB, INC.

EXECUTIVES

President, John J Jerue
Auditors: HARMAN & PEASLEE PA PLANT

LOCATIONS

HQ: JJJTB, INC.
3200 FLIGHTLINE DR, LAKELAND, FL 338112848
Phone: 863 607-5600

HISTORICAL FINANCIALS

Company Type: Private

Income Statement

FYE: December 31

	REVENUE ($ mil.)	NET INCOME ($ mil.)	NET PROFIT MARGIN	EMPLOYEES
12/15	260	10	3.9%	54
12/14	249	9	3.7%	—
12/13	201	5	2.6%	—
12/12	26	4	18.9%	—
Annual Growth	114.7%	27.1%		

2015 Year-End Financials

Return on assets: 4.0%   Cash ($ mil.): —
Return on equity: 3.9%
Current ratio: 1.20

JOHN D ARCHBOLD MEMORIAL HOSPITAL

EXECUTIVES

President, Perry Mustian
Board of Directors, Delora Harris
Trustee, James Smith
Director, Robin Perkins
Account Manager, Dorothy A Strickland
Manager, Pamela Tucker
Vice-President, Debbie Beeson

LOCATIONS

HQ: JOHN D ARCHBOLD MEMORIAL HOSPITAL
GORDON AVE AT MIMOSA DR, THOMASVILLE, GA 31792
Phone: 229 228-2000
Web: WWW.ARCHBOLD.ORG

HISTORICAL FINANCIALS

Company Type: Private

Income Statement

FYE: September 30

	REVENUE ($ mil.)	NET INCOME ($ mil.)	NET PROFIT MARGIN	EMPLOYEES
09/15	251	30	12.0%	2,700
09/14	233	22	9.5%	—
09/13	0	24	—	—
09/12	230	26	11.3%	—
Annual Growth	2.9%	4.9%	—	—

2015 Year-End Financials

Return on assets: 1.1%   Cash ($ mil.): 48
Return on equity: 12.0%
Current ratio: 2.40

JOHN F KENNEDY CENTER FOR THE PERFORMING ARTS

The John F. Kennedy Center for the Performing Arts also known as The Kennedy Center traces its roots to 1958 when president Dwight Eisenhower signed the National Cultural Center Act calling for a privately funded venture featuring a variety of classic and contemporary programming with an educational focus. The center was a pet project and fund raiser beneficiary of president Kennedy; it was named as a living memorial to him after his death. Located on 17 acres overlooking the Potomac River in Washington D.C. the center opened in 1971 and presents some 2000 events a year including musicals dance performances and jazz and orchestral concerts. It also produces TV programming workshops and lectures.

EXECUTIVES

Vice President Institutional Affairs, Kathy Kruse
Assistant Treasurer Opera House Family Theater Terrace Gallery Explore The Arts, Tony Terronez
Auditors: BDO USA LLP BETHESDA MD

LOCATIONS

HQ: JOHN F KENNEDY CENTER FOR THE PERFORMING ARTS
2700 F ST NW, WASHINGTON, DC 205660002
Phone: 202 416-8000
Web: WWW.KENNEDY-CENTER.ORG

COMPETITORS

Nederlander Producing Company
Smithsonian
The National Gallery

HISTORICAL FINANCIALS

Company Type: Private

Income Statement

FYE: September 30

	REVENUE ($ mil.)	NET INCOME ($ mil.)	NET PROFIT MARGIN	EMPLOYEES
09/15	239	30	12.6%	1,144
09/10	182	21	11.9%	—
09/09	156	(7)	—	—
09/08	2,131	0	0.0%	—
Annual Growth	(26.8%)	471.9%	—	—

2015 Year-End Financials

Return on assets: 6.8%
Return on equity: 12.6%
Current ratio: 0.20
Cash ($ mil.): 9

JOHN R GRAHAM HEADACHE CENTER, INC

EXECUTIVES

Chief Executive Officer, David Trull
Manager, Rick Lawson
Manager, Monica Fulton
Manager, Dave Hopkins

LOCATIONS

HQ: JOHN R GRAHAM HEADACHE CENTER, INC
1153 CENTRE ST, BOSTON, MA 021303446
Phone: 617 983-7243
Web: WWW.FAULKNERHOSPITAL.ORG

HISTORICAL FINANCIALS

Company Type: Private

Income Statement

FYE: September 30

	REVENUE ($ mil.)	NET INCOME ($ mil.)	NET PROFIT MARGIN	EMPLOYEES
09/15	207	20	9.9%	1
09/14	195	14	7.3%	—
Annual Growth	6.6%	44.8%	—	—

2015 Year-End Financials

Return on assets: 2.0%
Return on equity: 9.9%
Current ratio: 0.20
Cash ($ mil.): 2

JOHN T. MATHER MEMORIAL HOSPITAL OF PORT JEFFERSON, NEW YORK, INC.

Shipbuilder John T. Mather envisioned a legacy that would keep his community of Port Jefferson in good health and John T. Mather Memorial Hospital came to fruition in 1929 one year after it's namesake's death. The not-for-profit hospital has some 250 beds and provides a variety of health care services to the residents of Port Jefferson New York and surrounding areas of Suffolk County. Services include emergency care occupational therapy psychiatry and radiology. Mather Hospital is a member of Long Island Health Network an association of about a dozen affiliated hospitals all serving Long Island. It is also Magnet® recognized hospital by the American Nurses Credentialing Center.

Operations
Mather Hospital has some 600 physicians both full-time employees and affiliates who serve some 12000 inpatient customers annually. The emergency room handles about 44000 visits per year. It provides than 18000 diagnostic breast health screenings annually. The hospital's specialty service units include the Fortunato Breast Health Center which provides outpatient diagnostics as well as centers for sleep disorder treatment bariatrics wound care and stroke management.

In addition to its membership in the Long Island Health Alliance Mather Hospital has formed a partnership with nearby St. Charles Hospital and Rehabilitation Center to provide tandem services in some areas including cancer and pediatric care.

Financial Performance
The hospital reported a 6% increase in revenues in 2012 thanks to higher patient services revenue and other non-patient care services. It saw net loss of $2 million year (compared to net income in 2011) due to an increase in expenses (salaries benefits supplies and other) and depreciation.

Strategy
The company grows through organic initiatives.

In 2013 Mather Hospital broke ground on a new patient care pavilion. The expansion the first at the hospital in more than ten years will house a 35-single-bedded patient care unit; offices and teaching facilities for a Graduate Medical Education Program with residencies in Internal Medicine Family Practice Medicine Psychiatry and Transitional Year; and a conference center. The new facility which adds more than 28400 sq. ft. of space to the existing hospital will be known as the Arthur & Linda Calace Family Pavilion.

In 2012 the hospital began using an electronic health records system to improve patient safety and care. Other 2012 initiatives included a cardiac computed tomography angiography program which uses digital imaging to diagnose heart disease. Mather also launched a Palliative Medicine program for patients with a serious or chronic illness.

Looking to green resources to cut its carbon emissions and costs Mather Hospital is using lower cost hydropower to reduce its energy costs by $2.5 million over seven years through the ReCharge NY award from the New York Power Authority. It also has a solar power unit.

Company Background
In 2011 Mather Hospital became the first Long Island hospital to use solar power via a federally funded state energy grant. It built a 50 KW photovoltaic ground-mounted solar panel bank on its campus.

The hospital was founded in 1929 as the first not-for-profit community hospital in the Town of Brookhaven.

EXECUTIVES

Vice President, Frank Lettera
Ambulatory Services Director, Karen Tuzzolo
Assistant Vice President Of Nursing, Theresa Grimes
Vice President Chief Information Officer Informati, Steven Heiman
Associate Vice President Patient Care Nursing, Loretta Wagner
Vice President Operations, Tamara Weiss
Vice President, Kevin Murray
Assistant Vice President of Finance, Frank Sini

LOCATIONS

HQ: JOHN T. MATHER MEMORIAL HOSPITAL OF PORT JEFFERSON, NEW YORK, INC.
75 N COUNTRY RD, PORT JEFFERSON, NY 117772119
Phone: 631 476-2738
Web: WWW.MATHERHOSPITAL.ORG

PRODUCTS/OPERATIONS

Selected Centers and Services

Bariatric Surgery Center of Excellence
Behavioral Health Services
Breast Health Center
Critical Care
Emergency Department
Hospitalists
Hyperbaric Oxygen Therapy Unit
Imaging Services/Radiology
Infusion Center
Intensivists
Joint Replacement Program
Laboratory
Lithotripsy
Lymphedema Program
Pain Management Program
Palliative Medicine
Physical Therapy
Prostate Health Program
Respiratory Therapy
Transitional Care Unit
Sleep Disorders Center
Surgical Services
Wound Treatment Center

COMPETITORS

CSH
Catholic Health Services of Long Island
Catholic Healthcare System
Long Island College Hospital
New York City Health and Hospitals
NewYork-Presbyterian Healthcare
Northwell Health

HISTORICAL FINANCIALS

Company Type: Private

Income Statement

FYE: December 31

	REVENUE ($ mil.)	NET INCOME ($ mil.)	NET PROFIT MARGIN	EMPLOYEES
12/15	279	(1)	—	1,700
12/14	292	(28)	—	—
12/13	276	6	2.2%	—
12/12	238	(0)	—	—
Annual Growth	5.5%	—	—	—

2015 Year-End Financials

Return on assets: 8.3%   Cash ($ mil.): 7
Return on equity: (-0.4%)
Current ratio: 1.00

JOHNS HOPKINS BAYVIEW MEDICAL CENTER, INC.

If you've just been pulled from the bay like an old empty crab trap Johns Hopkins Bayview might be the first place you're taken. One of five member institutions in the Johns Hopkins Health System Johns Hopkins Bayview Medical Center is a community teaching hospital. Its Baltimore-based operations include a neonatal intensive care unit as well as centers devoted to trauma geriatrics sleep disorders and weight management. It also features the state's only regional burn center. The facility includes a meditation labyrinth for patients families and staff to walk. Established in 1773 the medical center has more than 560 beds.

Operations

As an academic teaching hospital all of the physicians at Johns Hopkins Bayview are also full-time faculty at the Johns Hopkins School of Medicine. Students from The Johns Hopkins University School of Nursing also come to the medical center for hospital-based instruction in acute and long term care.

EXECUTIVES

Medical Director, Debbie Weaver

LOCATIONS

HQ: JOHNS HOPKINS BAYVIEW MEDICAL CENTER, INC.
4940 EASTERN AVE, BALTIMORE, MD 212242735
Phone: 410 550-0100

PRODUCTS/OPERATIONS

Selected services
Primary Care Services
General Internal Medicine
Obstetrics/Gynecology
Pediatrics
Specialty Services
Bariatrics

Burn
Cardiology
Clinical Nutrition
Dermatology
Endocrinology
Gastroenterology
General Surgery
Hematology/Oncology
Imaging (X-ray mammography ultrasound etc)
Minor Surgery
Neurodiagnostic Lab
Neurology
Ophthalmology
Otolaryngology (ear nose and throat)
Orthopaedics
Plastic Surgery
Podiatry
Urology
Vascular Lab

COMPETITORS

Franklin Square
Hospital Center
GBMC
Good Samaritan
Hospital of Maryland
Harbor Hospital
Levindale Hospital
LifeBridge Health

Sinai Hospital of
Baltimore
St. Agnes HealthCare
St. Joseph Medical
Center
University of Maryland
Medical System

HISTORICAL FINANCIALS

Company Type: Private

Income Statement

FYE: June 30

	REVENUE ($ mil.)	NET INCOME ($ mil.)	NET PROFIT MARGIN	EMPLOYEES
06/15	507	16	3.2%	3,300
06/14	541	11	2.2%	—
06/13	0	(0)	—	—
06/12	0	(0)	—	—
Annual Growth	871.1%	—	—	—

2015 Year-End Financials

Return on assets: 9.9%   Cash ($ mil.): 6
Return on equity: 3.2%
Current ratio: 0.70

JOHNS HOPKINS HOSPITAL

EXECUTIVES

President, Ronald Peterson
Director, Greg Miller

LOCATIONS

HQ: JOHNS HOPKINS HOSPITAL
1800 ORLEANS ST, BALTIMORE, MD 212870010
Phone: 410 550-0730
Web: WWW.HOPKINSMEDICINE.ORG

HISTORICAL FINANCIALS

Company Type: Private

Income Statement

FYE: June 30

	REVENUE ($ mil.)	NET INCOME ($ mil.)	NET PROFIT MARGIN	EMPLOYEES
06/15	1,879	68	3.6%	12,000
06/12	1,791	(238)	—	—
06/10	1,742	157	9.0%	—
Annual Growth	1.5%	(15.3%)	—	—

2015 Year-End Financials

Return on assets: 10.3%   Cash ($ mil.): 95
Return on equity: 3.6%
Current ratio: 1.10

JOHNSON & WALES UNIVERSITY INC

Things are a little upside-down at Johnson & Wales University and that's just the way the school likes it. The private not-for-profit accredited institution provides what it calls an upside-down curriculum allowing students to take courses in their major during the first year so they learn right away if their career choice is right for them. At the end of two years of study students earn an associate's degree and the opportunity to go on to earn a bachelor's degree. Founded in 1914 the school enrolls more than 14000 graduate undergraduate and online students across its four campuses in Colorado Florida North Carolina and Rhode Island instructed by more than 600 faculty members.

Operations

Johnson & Wales University offers degrees in business education foodservice hospitality culinary arts and technology. Student-faculty ratio is 20:1. The university has alumni from some 120 countries. It offers 40 study abroad programs and independent exchanges. More than 92% of the students receive institutional scholarships or grants from the university

Undergraduate tuition at Johnson & Wales University runs more than $29000 a year.

Geographic Reach

Johnson & Wales University has campuses in Providence Rhode Island North Miami Florida Denver Colorado and Charlotte North Carolina.

Sales and Marketing

Johnson & Wales University attracts students from nearly 100 countries. Its top 10 international populations (among its more than 1800 international students) hail from China South Korea Taiwan Saudi Arabia India Morocco Turkey the Bahamas the Netherlands and Malaysia.

Financial Performance

Johnson & Wales University's revenues fell slightly to $345 million in 2017 (ended June) from $346 million 2016. While most sources of revenue including tuition rose for the year the school increased financial aid and scholarship money by about $11 million.

Strategy

Johnson & Wales University adds areas of study at a fast clip to keep up with market demands. In the past few years the school has opened studies in biology political science psychology and information security at the undergraduate and master's degree levels. It also added master's programs in physician assistant studies and health and wellness.

EXECUTIVES

Chancellor, John J. Bowen
Provost and Vice Chancellor, Thomas L. G. Dwyer
COO and President Providence Campus, Mim L. Runey
Treasurer and CFO, Joseph J. Greene
President Charlotte Campus, Robert C. Mock, age 51
President North Miami Campus, Larry Rice
Senior Vice President Planning and Human Resources, William McArdle

Vice President Student Affairs and Dean
 Students, Ron Martel
Department Chair College Of Culinary Arts,
 Rainer Hienerwadel
Chairman, James H. (Jim) Hance, age 72
Auditors: MCGLADREY LLP CHARLESTOWN MA

LOCATIONS

HQ: JOHNSON & WALES UNIVERSITY INC
 8 ABBOTT PARK PL, PROVIDENCE, RI 029033775
Phone: 401 598-1000
Web: WWW.JWU.EDU

PRODUCTS/OPERATIONS

2017 Sales

	% of total
Net student fees	90
Practicum properties	3
Investment return appropriated for operations	3
Private gifts grants and federal aid to students	1
Other sources	2
Net Assets Released from Restriction	1
Total	**100**

Selected Programs

Accounting
Advertising and marketing communications
Baking & pastry arts
Baking & pastry arts and food service management
Beverage industry operations and retail management
Biology
Business administration
Business studies
Computer programming
Computerized drafting
Corporate accounting and financial analysis
Counseling
Counseling psychology
Criminal justice
Culinary arts

Selected Colleges and Schools

The Alan Shawn Feinstein Graduate School
College of Business
College of Culinary Arts
The Hospitality College
School of Technology

Selected Operations

CAFE LLC
Griffin Realty Enterprises Inc.
Griffin Realty of Rhode Island-Florida Inc.
Harborside Enterprises Inc.
J.W.C. Corporation
J&W Corporation
Johnson & Wales Alumni Services Corporation
Johnson & Wales University
Johnson & Wales University Club

HISTORICAL FINANCIALS

Company Type: Private

Income Statement

FYE: June 30

	REVENUE ($ mil.)	NET INCOME ($ mil.)	NET PROFIT MARGIN	EMPLOYEES
06/15	503	26	5.4%	1,400
06/13	349	37	10.6%	—
06/12	353	4	1.2%	—
06/11	0	0	—	—
Annual Growth	—	1822.9%	—	—

2015 Year-End Financials

Return on assets: 10.9% Cash ($ mil.): 14
Return on equity: 5.4%
Current ratio: 0.20

JOHNSON, MIRMIRAN & THOMPSON, INC.

EXECUTIVES

Senior Vice-President, Daniel Cheng
Personnel Manager, Heather Chism
President, Jonathan Ryan
Auditors: CLIFTONLARSONALLEN LLP BALTI

LOCATIONS

HQ: JOHNSON, MIRMIRAN & THOMPSON, INC.
 40 WIGHT AVE, HUNT VALLEY, MD 210302059
Phone: 410 329-3100
Web: WWW.JMT.COM

HISTORICAL FINANCIALS

Company Type: Private

Income Statement

FYE: December 31

	REVENUE ($ mil.)	NET INCOME ($ mil.)	NET PROFIT MARGIN	EMPLOYEES
12/15	186	1	1.1%	1,350
12/10	106	5	4.9%	—
12/09	95	5	5.4%	—
12/08	0	0	—	—
Annual Growth	—	—	—	—

2015 Year-End Financials

Return on assets: 5.2% Cash ($ mil.): 17
Return on equity: 1.1%
Current ratio: 2.30

JOINT SCHOOL DISTRICT 2

EXECUTIVES

Superintendent, Linda Clark
Superintendent, Trish Duncan
Consultant, David Hansen
Auditors: EIDE BAILLY LLP BOISE IDAHO

LOCATIONS

HQ: JOINT SCHOOL DISTRICT 2
 1303 E CENTRAL DR, MERIDIAN, ID 836427991
Phone: 208 855-4500
Web: WWW.WESTADA.ORG

HISTORICAL FINANCIALS

Company Type: Private

Income Statement

FYE: June 30

	REVENUE ($ mil.)	NET INCOME ($ mil.)	NET PROFIT MARGIN	EMPLOYEES
06/16	278	(35)	—	4,000
06/15	257	97	37.9%	—
06/13	231	(4)	—	—
06/12	214	3	1.5%	—
Annual Growth	6.8%	—	—	—

2016 Year-End Financials

Return on assets: 14.3% Cash ($ mil.): 24
Return on equity: (-12.7%)
Current ratio: —

JORDAN FOSTER CONSTRUCTION, LLC

EXECUTIVES

Vice-President, John Goodrich
Manager, Brian Cass
Superintendent, Joe Montoya
Project Manager, Scott Dell
Project Manager, Roman Marquez
Auditors: BKD LLP SAN ANTONIO TEXAS

LOCATIONS

HQ: JORDAN FOSTER CONSTRUCTION, LLC
 7700 CF JORDAN DR STE 200, EL PASO, TX
 799128807
Phone: 915 877-3333

HISTORICAL FINANCIALS

Company Type: Private

Income Statement

FYE: December 31

	REVENUE ($ mil.)	NET INCOME ($ mil.)	NET PROFIT MARGIN	EMPLOYEES
12/15	176	(3)	—	1,000
12/13	9	(0)	—	—
Annual Growth	340.1%	—	—	—

2015 Year-End Financials

Return on assets: 6.0% Cash ($ mil.): 19
Return on equity: (-2.1%)
Current ratio: 1.20

JORDAN SCHOOL DISTRICT

EXECUTIVES

Superintendent, Patrice Johnson
Board of Directors, Burke Jolley
Executive Secretary, Jari Clayton
Superintendent, John Taylor
Auditors: SQUIRE & COMPANY PC OREM UT

LOCATIONS

HQ: JORDAN SCHOOL DISTRICT
 7387 S CAMPUS VIEW DR, WEST JORDAN, UT
 840845500
Phone: 801 280-3689
Web: WWW.JORDANDISTRICT.ORG

HISTORICAL FINANCIALS

Company Type: Private

Income Statement

FYE: June 30

	REVENUE ($ mil.)	NET INCOME ($ mil.)	NET PROFIT MARGIN	EMPLOYEES
06/16	415	27	6.6%	5,900
06/15	391	9	2.3%	—
06/14	378	(3)	—	—
06/13	366	5	1.6%	—
Annual Growth	4.2%	69.0%	—	—

JSI RESEARCH AND TRAINING INSTITUTE, INC.

EXECUTIVES

President, Joel H Lamstein
Financial Executive, Frederique O'Keeffe
General Manager, Robert Schlink
Project Director, Debra Olesen
Vice-President, Pat Fairchild
Auditors: NORMAN R FOUGERE JR CPA DUX

LOCATIONS

HQ: JSI RESEARCH AND TRAINING INSTITUTE, INC.
44 FARNSWORTH ST FL 7, BOSTON, MA 022101206
Phone: 617 482-9485
Web: WWW.JSI.COM

HISTORICAL FINANCIALS
Company Type: Private

Income Statement

	REVENUE ($ mil.)	NET INCOME ($ mil.)	NET PROFIT MARGIN	EMPLOYEES
09/15	270	5	2.2%	135
09/14	196	5	2.6%	—
09/10	163	1	1.1%	—
09/09	150	1	1.2%	—
Annual Growth	10.3%	22.7%	—	—

FYE: September 30

2015 Year-End Financials

Return on assets: 2.3%   Cash ($ mil.): 32
Return on equity: 2.2%
Current ratio: 1.30

JUDSON INDEPENDENT SCHOOL DISTRICT

EXECUTIVES

Superintendent, Willis Mackey
Director, Daniel Macias
Executive Director, Yvette Reyna
Superintendent, Carl Montoya
Assistant Manager, Milton Fields
Assistant Manager, Cathy Hernandez
Auditors: ABIP PC SAN ANTONIO TEXAS

LOCATIONS

HQ: JUDSON INDEPENDENT SCHOOL DISTRICT
8012 SHIN OAK DR, LIVE OAK, TX 782332413
Phone: 210 945-5100
Web: WWW.JUDSONISD.ORG

HISTORICAL FINANCIALS
Company Type: Private

Income Statement

	REVENUE ($ mil.)	NET INCOME ($ mil.)	NET PROFIT MARGIN	EMPLOYEES
06/16	250	(12)	—	3,500
06/12	207	3	1.7%	—
06/11	212	(30)	—	—
06/10	0	0	—	—
Annual Growth	—	—	—	—

FYE: June 30

2016 Year-End Financials

Return on assets: 1.4%   Cash ($ mil.): 11
Return on equity: (-5.0%)
Current ratio: —

JUPITER MEDICAL CENTER, INC.

Nope this hospital is not on the fifth planet from the Sun but by Jupiter it delivers great health care to a number of Floridians. Located just north of West Palm Beach Jupiter Medical Center provides specialty services that include cancer treatment cardiology orthopedics emergency medicine wound care birthing and pain management. The not-for-profit medical center has more than 205 private acute-care beds and 120 long-term rehab and hospice beds. Jupiter Medical Center is affiliated with the University of Miami's Miller School of Medicine.

Operations

The 327-bed Jupiter Medical Center has more than 600 physicians with 60 medical specialties on staff. The facility partners with other health care providers such as Mount Sinai Heart New York enabling it provide access to complex care for a variety of ailments. The hospital works with MyClinic a free clinic that provides primary care behavioral health care and referrals for urgent care to low-income and uninsured adults in the area. It also partners with community organization Healthier Jupiter to advance wellness through programs and events. With its near proximity to the Caribbean the hospital works to provide care to international patients through its Global Medicine Program. It operates the Joe Namath Neurological Research Center which focuses on traumatic brain injury research. Other offerings include bariatric surgery and alcohol and substance detoxification services.

In 2016 the hospital reported 10715 admissions; 7425 surgeries; 1329 births; and 35819 emergency room visits.

Financial Performance

Jupiter Medical Center's unrestricted revenue totaled $230.7 million in fiscal 2016 (ended September) a 14% increase over the prior year. Higher net patient revenues contributions and other operating income contributed to that increase as did a positive return on investments following a $3.1 million loss in 2015.

Thanks to the higher revenue the hospital had an excess of revenue over expenses of $9.1 million in 2016.

Strategy

As a not-for-profit organization Jupiter Medical Center invests all of its financial resources into the facility to deliver the most advanced medicine and to ensure access to quality health care for all. In a

climate of industry reformation the organization is stretching out to make a transformational change beyond acute care strengthening its position by focusing on improving its services outcomes and costs.For example in early 2016 it opened the De George pediatric unit in partnership with Niklaus Children's Hospital. The unit features two pediatric surgery suites 12 inpatient rooms a children's playroom and an on-site specialist to help young patients cope with the stress of staying in the hospital.

To meet the community's identified health care needs Jupiter Medical Center has established initiatives in the areas of cancer heart disease and nutrition exercise and diabetes.

Company Background

Established in 1956 as the convalescence center for a retirement village Jupiter Medical Center was transformed into a full-service acute-care hospital in 1979.

EXECUTIVES

Media/Public Relations Manager, Stacey Brandt
VP Finance and CFO, Dale Hocking
Interim President and COO, Steven Seeley
VP Service Line Development, Sherri Lewman
President Jupiter Medical Center Foundation, Liv E. Vesley
VP and CIO, Tom Crawford
VP Ambulatory Care, Judy Magalhaes
VP Clinical Integration, Teresa (Terri) Wentz
Medical Director, Jefferson R Vaughan
Operating Room Director, Beth Suriano
VP Human Resources, Peter Gloggner
Medical Director, Matthew Capuano
Respiratory Therapy Director, Christopher Jones
Advisory Board Member, Neal Nay

LOCATIONS

HQ: JUPITER MEDICAL CENTER, INC.
1210 S OLD DIXIE HWY, JUPITER, FL 334587205
Phone: 561 747-2234

PRODUCTS/OPERATIONS

2016 Sales

	$ mil.	% of total
Net patient revenue	208	90
Unrestricted contributions	5	2
Investment activities	6	3
Other operating activities	10	5
Total	**230**	**100**

Selected Medical Services

Cancer Services
Cardiology
Clinical Research
Children's and Women's / OB
Comprehensive Breast Care
Diabetes Education
Digestive Health
Emergency Services
Health and Rehabilitation
Hospice Care
Imaging
Laboratory Services
Men's Health
Occupational Health
Orthopedic and Spine
Outpatient Medical Nutrition Therapy
Pain Management
The Pavilion
Sleep Center
Stroke Program
Surgical Services
Robotic Surgery
Thoracic Surgery
Travel Immunizations
Urgent Care
Weight Loss (Bariatrics)
Wound Care / Hyperbarics

HISTORICAL FINANCIALS

Company Type: Private

Income Statement   FYE: September 30

	REVENUE ($ mil.)	NET INCOME ($ mil.)	NET PROFIT MARGIN	EMPLOYEES
09/15	192	23	12.3%	1,500
09/14	182	9	5.2%	—
09/13	179	6	3.7%	—
09/12	174	6	3.8%	—
Annual Growth	3.4%	53.2%	—	—

2015 Year-End Financials

Return on assets: 8.7%
Return on equity: 12.3%
Current ratio: 1.40

Cash ($ mil.): 12

K & M TIRE, INC.

EXECUTIVES

President, Ken Langhals
Vice-President, Paul Zurcher
Vice-President, Cheryl Gossard
Account Manager, Kelly Schimmoller
Financial Executive, Dan Lucke
Sales Manager, Mel Donnelly

LOCATIONS

HQ: K & M TIRE, INC.
  965 SPENCERVILLE RD, DELPHOS, OH 458332351
Phone: 419 695-1061
Web: WWW.KMTIRE.COM

HISTORICAL FINANCIALS

Company Type: Private

Income Statement   FYE: September 30

	REVENUE ($ mil.)	NET INCOME ($ mil.)	NET PROFIT MARGIN	EMPLOYEES
09/16	387	14	3.8%	500
09/15	354	12	3.6%	—
09/14	308	8	2.7%	—
09/13	293	8	2.9%	—
Annual Growth	9.7%	20.3%	—	—

2016 Year-End Financials

Return on assets: 5.6%
Return on equity: 3.8%
Current ratio: 1.30

Cash ($ mil.): —

KADLEC REGIONAL MEDICAL CENTER

Kadlec Regional Medical Center is an acute care hospital facility serving southeastern Washington and northeastern Oregon. In addition to providing comprehensive medical surgical and emergency services the hospital provides neonatal intensive care cardiopulmonary rehabilitation interventional cardiology neurology cancer care and other specialist services. Not-for-profit Kadlec Regional has some 270 inpatient beds including pediatric intensive intermediate and critical care capacity. It also operates outpatient physician offices and clinics in surrounding areas.

Operations

Kadlec Regional's cardiovascular programs include open heart surgery and interventional cardiology. The hospital also operates an all-digital outpatient imaging center and the region's only level III neonatal intensive care unit (NICU). Kadlec was is also designated as a Level 1 Cardiac Center and a Level 2 Stroke Center. Area specialist practices include centers for dermatology colorectal surgery nephrology pediatrics women's health ENT (ear nose and throat) and foot and ankle practices. Kadlec Regional also operates satellite urgent care and family practice clinics.

The Kadlec Neuroscience Center offers a wide range of services to treat and diagnose conditions related to the brain spine spinal cord & peripheral nervous system.

In 2013 the hospital reported more than 2700 births 66000 emergency department visits and about 15000 admissions.

That year Kadlec Regional provided $27 million in charity care.

Geographic Reach

Kadlec Regional has hospital and clinic locations in Hermiston Kennewick Pasco Pendleton Prosser and Richland.

Financial Performance

The hospital reported revenue of $312 million in 2012 consisting of $305 million in net patient service earnings and other revenue of some $7.5 million. Kadlec Regional brought in profits of some $29 million.

Strategy

The hospital has undergone aggressive expansion efforts adding a new patient tower with diagnostic outpatient and intermediate care and surgery rooms. Kadlec Regional is enhancing its specialty service units in fields to attract specialists and increase revenue.The organization launched a $10 million project to expand its NICU unit in 2013. It will add 27 private and semi-private rooms and new observation gathering and lactation areas.

It is also expanding outpatient service facilities such as a new $19 million three-story specialty physician practice office that opened in Richland in 2013. The new building increases collaboration between various surgical and medical specialists in the Kadlec Regional clinic network.

The year the company also expanded its emergency room offerings through the opening of the Kadlec ER in Kennewick. The new 15-bed ER is the first in the region to operate as a freestanding facility like traditional hospital-based ERs.

Mergers and Acquisitions

Kadlec Regional also absorbs other area providers. In 2013 Inland Cardiology Associates become part of the Kadlec Regional health system. The region's largest independent group of experienced cardiologists Inland provides comprehensive invasive noninvasive and interventional services throughout southeast Washington and northeast Oregon.

Company Background

In 2011 it partnered with the nearby PMH Medical Center to increase collaboration and specialist referrals between the two hospitals. The partnership extends the reach of Kadlec Regional's medical specialists to additional communities and brings PMH online with Kadlec Regional's electronic health record system. Both hospitals remained independently run.

The hospital system was founded in 1944.

EXECUTIVES

Director of Pharmacy, Dave Pearson
Vice President of Medical Affairs, Dale Hoekema
Technical Vice President, Nathan Sheeran
Board Member, Jeff Clark

LOCATIONS

HQ: KADLEC REGIONAL MEDICAL CENTER
  888 SWIFT BLVD, RICHLAND, WA 993523514
Phone: 509 946-4611
Web: WWW.KADLEC.ORG

PRODUCTS/OPERATIONS

Selected Services

The Birth Center
Bloodless Medicine and Surgery
Cancer Care
Cardiac Care
Cardiac Catheterization
CardioPulmonary Rehabilitation
Cardiovascular and Thoracic Surgery
CaringBridge
Clinical Decision Unit
Coumadin Clinic
Diabetes Learning Center
Diagnostic Imaging
Don and Lori Watts Pediatric Center
Emergency Department
Emergency Room-Kennewick
Home Health Care
Imaging
Inpatient Rehabilitation and Therapy
Intensive Care Unit
Joint Care Center
Kadlec Academy
Kadlec Healthy Ages
Kadlec Medical Associates
Neonatal Intensive Care Unit
Occupational Medicine
Occupational Therapy
Ostomy Support Group
Outpatient Imaging Center
Outpatient Procedures
Physical Therapy
Planetree
Rehabilitation and Therapy Services
Speech Therapy
Urgent Care
Water Therapy
Wound Healing Center

Income Statement
FYE: December 31

	REVENUE ($ mil.)	NET INCOME ($ mil.)	NET PROFIT MARGIN	EMPLOYEES
12/15	504	(7)	—	2,668
12/14	417	190	45.7%	—
12/13	0	25	—	—
12/12	312	16	5.2%	—
Annual Growth 17.3%	—	—	—	—

2015 Year-End Financials
Return on assets: 3.5%   Cash ($ mil.): 26
Return on equity: (-1.4%)
Current ratio: 2.00

HISTORICAL FINANCIALS
Company Type: Private

Income Statement
FYE: September 30

	REVENUE ($ mil.)	NET INCOME ($ mil.)	NET PROFIT MARGIN	EMPLOYEES
09/16*	232	11	5.0%	545
12/15	303	0	0.3%	—
06/15	143	9	6.5%	—
06/14	148	(1)	—	—
Annual Growth 25.1%	—	—	—	—

*Fiscal year change

2016 Year-End Financials
Return on assets: 9.4%   Cash ($ mil.): 22
Return on equity: 5.0%
Current ratio: 0.70

LOCATIONS
HQ: KATY INDEPENDENT SCHOOL DISTRICT
6301 S STADIUM LN, KATY, TX 774941057
Phone: 281 396-6000
Web: WWW.KATYISD.ORG

HISTORICAL FINANCIALS
Company Type: Private

Income Statement
FYE: August 31

	REVENUE ($ mil.)	NET INCOME ($ mil.)	NET PROFIT MARGIN	EMPLOYEES
08/16	841	15	1.9%	6,631
08/11*	601	123	20.5%	—
12/09	540	(2)	—	—
08/08	508	(3)	—	—
Annual Growth 6.5%	—	—	—	—

*Fiscal year change

KANSAS CITY BOARD OF PUBLIC UTILITIES

Goin' to ... Kansas City? The Board of Public Utilities of Kansas City Kansas (known as the Kansas City Board of Public Utilities) will help light the way. The utility provides electric transmission and distribution services to 63000 customers and water distribution services to 50000 customers in the Kansas City metropolitan area (in Wyandotte and Johnson counties). Most electric customers are residential but commercial and industrial customers account for the bulk of the utility's power revenues. The Kansas City Board of Public Utilities also has interests in coal gas and oil-fired power generation facilities. The utility is owned by the Unified Government of Wyandotte County and Kansas City.

Responding to state and federal requirement for utilities to reduce carbon emissions in 2010 the company announced that it had met its goal of generating more than 10% of its power from renewable sources for the years 2011-2015. The company has stakes in (or owns) wind farms hydropower systems and a landfill gas fueled plant.

As part of its energy conservation push in 2012 the Kansas City Board of Public Utilities launched a free programmable thermostat program which allows the utility to raise participants' temperature settings by 2 degrees during peak energy use hours. The utility estimates that thermostat participants could save up to 15% on their annual heating and cooling bills.

Kansas City Board of Public Utilities traces its origins to 1909 when the citizens of Kansas City authorized the city government to purchase a privately owned water system. It began providing electricity services in 1912.

EXECUTIVES

Board Member, Norman Scott

LOCATIONS
HQ: KANSAS CITY BOARD OF PUBLIC UTILITIES
540 MINNESOTA AVE, KANSAS CITY, KS 661012930
Phone: 913 573-9000
Web: WWW.BPU.COM

COMPETITORS

Great Plains Energy   Westar Energy
Southern Company

KAPIOLANI MEDICAL CENTER FOR WOMEN AND CHILDREN

EXECUTIVES

Chief Executive Officer, Martha Smith
Vice-President, Dew-Anne Langcaon
Financial Executive, Ann Ho
Manager, Pai Jong

LOCATIONS
HQ: KAPIOLANI MEDICAL CENTER FOR WOMEN AND CHILDREN
1319 PUNAHOU ST, HONOLULU, HI 968261001
Phone: 808 535-7401
Web: WWW.KAPIOLANI.ORG

HISTORICAL FINANCIALS
Company Type: Private

Income Statement
FYE: June 30

	REVENUE ($ mil.)	NET INCOME ($ mil.)	NET PROFIT MARGIN	EMPLOYEES
06/15	371	102	27.7%	1,378
06/09	218	23	10.6%	—
06/05*	187	13	6.9%	—
03/04	130	8	6.5%	—
Annual Growth 10.0%		25.3%	—	—

*Fiscal year change

KATY INDEPENDENT SCHOOL DISTRICT

EXECUTIVES

President, Bryan Michalsky
Manager, Christopher Smith
Purchasing Agent, Bud Reed
Executive Director, Ron Pleasant
Manager, Holly Angerame

KAWEAH DELTA HEALTH CARE DISTRICT GUILD

EXECUTIVES

Chief Executive Officer, Donna Archer
Director, Thomas L Gray

LOCATIONS
HQ: KAWEAH DELTA HEALTH CARE DISTRICT GUILD
400 W MINERAL KING AVE, VISALIA, CA 932916237
Phone: 559 624-2000

HISTORICAL FINANCIALS
Company Type: Private

Income Statement
FYE: June 30

	REVENUE ($ mil.)	NET INCOME ($ mil.)	NET PROFIT MARGIN	EMPLOYEES
06/15	475	26	5.7%	3,200
06/08	370	16	4.5%	—
06/07	333	27	8.2%	—
06/06	281	0	0.0%	—
Annual Growth 6.0%		241.2%	—	—

2015 Year-End Financials
Return on assets: 3.5%   Cash ($ mil.): —
Return on equity: 5.7%
Current ratio: 2.10

KBS, INC.

You would hit the nail right on the head if you were to call KBS a "regional contractor." The company provides design/build planning general contracting and construction management services for commercial and multifamily residential projects in Virginia. Its projects include office buildings apartment complexes shopping centers hotels schools jails warehouses and senior living facilities. Some 60% of the company's business comes in the form of repeat customers. Clients have included Cousins Properties Forest City Enterprises Ukrop's Best Buy Wal-Mart and Virginia Commonwealth University. President Bill Paulette founded KBS in a sheet metal shop in 1975.

EXECUTIVES

Financial Executive, Cathy Muto
Superintendent, Mark Thomas
Director, Matt Kamstra
Auditors: LEWIS & COMPANY PC CHESAPE

LOCATIONS

HQ: KBS, INC.
   8050 KIMWAY DR, RICHMOND, VA 232282831
Phone: 804 262-0100
Web: WWW.KBSGC.COM

COMPETITORS

Branch & Associates   SMCI
Hitt   W.M. Jordan
Milestone Construction

HISTORICAL FINANCIALS

Company Type: Private

Income Statement

FYE: September 30

	REVENUE ($ mil.)	NET INCOME ($ mil.)	NET PROFIT MARGIN	EMPLOYEES
09/16	200	4	2.4%	130
09/15	180	4	2.7%	—
09/14	137	1	1.3%	—
09/13	151	1	1.2%	—
Annual Growth	9.8%	38.2%	—	—

2016 Year-End Financials

Return on assets: 14.6%   Cash ($ mil.): 10
Return on equity: 2.4%
Current ratio: 1.20

KENDALL WEST BAPTIST HOSPITAL INC

EXECUTIVES

Chief Executive Officer, Javier Hernandez Lichtl
Manager, Karen Vassell

LOCATIONS

HQ: KENDALL WEST BAPTIST HOSPITAL INC
   9555 SW 162ND AVE, MIAMI, FL 331966408
Phone: 786 467-2000

HISTORICAL FINANCIALS

Company Type: Private

Income Statement

FYE: September 30

	REVENUE ($ mil.)	NET INCOME ($ mil.)	NET PROFIT MARGIN	EMPLOYEES
09/15	201	14	7.1%	138
09/14	182	5	3.2%	—
Annual Growth	10.5%	143.6%	—	—

2015 Year-End Financials

Return on assets: —   Cash ($ mil.): —
Return on equity: 7.1%
Current ratio: 0.80

KENERGY CORP.

Kenergy kens energy as the Scots might say. Electric distribution cooperative Kenergy serves about 55000 customers in 14 counties (Breckinridge Caldwell Crittenden Daviess Hancock Henderson Hopkins Livingston Lyon McLean Muhlenberg Ohio Union and Webster) in Western Kentucky. Kenergy serves its customer base of households commercial enterprises and industries via more than 6700 miles of power lines. The customer-owned company is part of Touchstone Energy Cooperatives a national alliance of more than 600 local consumer-owned electric utility cooperatives.

EXECUTIVES

Vice President Finance and Accounting, Stephen Thompson

LOCATIONS

HQ: KENERGY CORP.
   6402 OLD CORYDON RD, HENDERSON, KY
   424209392
Phone: 270 926-4141

COMPETITORS

Duke Energy Kentucky   Warren RECC
Kentucky Utilities

HISTORICAL FINANCIALS

Company Type: Private

Income Statement

FYE: December 31

	REVENUE ($ mil.)	NET INCOME ($ mil.)	NET PROFIT MARGIN	EMPLOYEES
12/15	375	0	0.0%	155
12/14	474	0	0.0%	—
12/13	506	0	0.0%	—
12/12	495	0	0.0%	—
Annual Growth	(8.8%)	(0.0%)	—	—

2015 Year-End Financials

Return on assets: 10.0%   Cash ($ mil.): 1
Return on equity: —
Current ratio: 0.90

KENNEDY KRIEGER INSTITUTE, INC.

Kennedy Krieger Institute is dedicated to the research education and treatment of children with brain disorders spinal cord injuries and developmental disabilities. It operates more than 55 outpatient clinics that provide services in behavioral psychology family support occupational and physical therapies and speech pathology among others. Altogether the institute serves more than 20000 individuals each year. Its 70-bed inpatient pediatric hospital caters to children who suffer from feeding problems and severe behaviors such as self-injury and aggression. Kennedy Krieger also runs a school for special-education students ages 3 to 21 to help prepare them for integration into their communities.

Operations

The institute's primary operating segments include healthcare research and special education.

The Healthcare segment includes a 45-bed inpatient unit admitting more than 325 patients per year more than 55 specialty outpatient clinics (150000 annual visits). It also trains more that 400 healthcare professionals each year. Healthcare activities accounted for 57% of net patient revenues in 2012.

As part of its operations Kennedy Krieger's Hugo W. Moser Research Institute delves into a variety of scientific areas involving brain and spinal cord problems in children. Its focus ranges from those caused by genetics to those developed by injury. Kennedy Krieger Institute specializes in more than 45 diverse brain spinal cord and musculoskeletal disorders including autism cerebral palsy brain injury Down syndrome feeding disorders muscular dystrophy spina bifida and spinal cord injury.

The institute's Special Education program operates non-public special education schools for students from kindergarten to grade eight high school a specialized autism program and partnership programs to public schools.

Geographic Reach

Kennedy Krieger has 11 locations in Baltimore; it also has campuses in Columbia and Rockville Maryland.

Financial Performance

The institute's revenues dropped by 5% in 2012 due to a decline in tuition revenue grant and contract revenues and the absence of revenues from medical equipment sales. Medicaid contributed more than 40% of Kennedy Krieger's revenues in 2012; Blue Cross 23%; commercial 17% and management care 11%.

Kennedy Krieger reported a net loss of $14 million in 2012 as the result of lower revenues an increase in loss on interest rate swaps and unrealized gains/losses on investments.

Strategy

To further its mission Kennedy Krieger partners with other institutions such as NYU Langone Medical Center to establish an environment for data-sharing. In late 2012 Kennedy Krieger kicked off a collaboration with the medical center for autism research. The two groups lead the Autism Brain Imaging Data Exchange (ABIDE) a global database of brain scans shared by more than 15 leading international research institutions and academic medical centers. The institute's academic partnership will allow for progress in understanding brain structure and function in autism and in turn help Kennedy Krieger better care for the communities its serves.

Company Background

Kennedy Krieger was founded in 1937 as the Children's Rehabilitation Institute. It was renamed the Kennedy Institute in 1968 and became the Kennedy Krieger Institute in 1992.

EXECUTIVES

President and CEO, Gary W. Goldstein
Director The International Center for Spinal Cord Injury, John W. McDonald
Director Center for Autism and Related Disorders, Rebecca Landa
Director Center for Development and Learning, Paul Lipkin
Director Center for Genetic Muscle Disorders, Kathryn R. Wagner
Director Department of Neuropsychology and Co-Director of the Center for Innovation and Leadership in Special Educatio, E. Mark Mahone
VP Psychiatric Services and Research, Robert L. Findling
SVP and Chief Medical Officer, Michael V. Johnston
Director Down Syndrome Clinic and Research Center, George T. Capone

Director Maryland Center for Developmental Disabilities, Christopher Smith
Director Phelps Center for Cerebral Palsy and Neurodevelopmental Medicine, Alexander H. Hoon
Research Scientist Director Department Of Behavi Vice President Of Behavioral Psychology Svs, Michael Cataldo
Vice President Human Resources, Raymond Short
Vice President of Nursing and Patient Services, Tami Swearingen
Director of Clinical Services, Sarah Gardner
Infection Control Director, Lori Cuomo
Senior Vice President, Lainey Sachs
Vice President Compliance, Joann Kubica
Secretary, Linda Baynes
Secretary, Karla Salley
Secretary, Ann Snitcher
Auditors: PRICEWATERHOUSECOOPERS LLP B

LOCATIONS

HQ: KENNEDY KRIEGER INSTITUTE, INC.
707 N BROADWAY, BALTIMORE, MD 212051888
Phone: 443 923-9200

PRODUCTS/OPERATIONS

Selected Spec2014 Sales

	$ mil.	% of total
Net patient service revenues	130	60
Tuition revenues	43	20
Grant & contract revenues	31	15
Net assets released for operating activities	8	4
Fundraising contributions	1	-
Other	1	1
Total	**217**	**100**

ializations

ializations
Autism spectrum disorders
Behavioral disorders
Bone disorders
Brain injury
Cerebral palsy
Developmental disorders
Down syndrome
Feeding disorders
Learning disorders
Muscular dystrophy
Rehabilitation
Sleep disorders
Spina bifida
Spinal cord injury and paralysis
Sturge-Weber syndrome
Outpatient Programs
Albright Clinic
Aquatic Therapy Program
Assistive Technology Clinic
Audiology Program
Barth Syndrome Clinic
Behavior Management Clinic
Behavioral Psychology Outpatient
Bone Disorders Program
Botulinum Toxin Treatment Program
Brachial Plexus Clinic
Brain Injury Early Assessment
Brain Injury Outpatient Clinics
Brain Injury Responsiveness Program
Center for Autism and Related
Center for Development and Learning
Center for Genetic Muscle Disorders
Child and Family Therapy Clinic
Constraint Induced and Bimanual
Cranial Cervical Clinic
Day Feeding Program
Deafness-Related Evaluations
Developmental Cognitive Neurology
Down Syndrome Clinic and Research
Fairmount Rehabilitation Programs
Family Center
Family Center Outpatient Mental
Feeding Disorders Clinic
Focused Interdisciplinary Therapy
Fragile X Clinic
Genetic Counseling
Healthy Lifestyles Therapy Program
Holoprosencephaly and Related

Hunter Nelson Sturge-Weber Center
Interdisciplinary Brain Injury
International Adoption Clinic
International Center for Spinal
Intrathecal Baclofen Program (ITBP)
Limb Differences Clinic
Military Behavioral Health Services
Movement Disorders Program (MDP)
Neonatal Intensive Care Unit (NICU)
Neurobehavioral Outpatient Clinic
Neurology and Neurodevelopmental
Neurology and Neurogenetics Clinic
Neuropsychology Department
Neurorehabilitation Concussion
Nutrition Outpatient Program
Occupational Therapy Clinic
Orthopedic Outpatient Clinic
Osteogenesis Imperfecta Clinic
Outpatient Psychiatry Clinic
Pediatric Developmental Disorders
Pediatric Pain Rehabilitation
Pediatric Psychology Clinic
Phelps Center for Cerebral Palsy
Philip A. Keelty Center for Spina
Physical Therapy Clinic
Post-Orthopedic Surgery Program
Seating Clinic
Sickle Cell Neurodevelopmental
Sleep Disorders Clinic and Lab
Social Work Outpatient Mental
Specialized Transition Program
Speech and Language Outpatient
Tuberous Sclerosis Clinic
Weight Management Program
Laboratories
Clinical Neurophysiology Laboratory
Genetics Laboratories at Kennedy
Inpatient Programs
Brain Injury Responsiveness Program
Pediatric Feeding Disorders
Pediatric Pain Rehabilitation
Pediatric Rehabilitation Unit
Neurobehavioral Unit (NBU)
Continuums
Neurobehavioral Continuum
Pediatric Feeding Disorders
Pediatric Rehabilitation Continuum
Community Programs
Child and Family Support Program
Family Center Community Programs
PACT: Helping Children
Specialized Health Needs
Community Rehabilitation Program

COMPETITORS

Children's National
   Medical Center
Children's Specialized
   Hospital
Gillette Children's
Johns Hopkins Medicine
Shriners Hospitals For
   Children
Watson Institute

HISTORICAL FINANCIALS

Company Type: Private

Income Statement

FYE: June 30

	REVENUE ($ mil.)	NET INCOME ($ mil.)	NET PROFIT MARGIN	EMPLOYEES
06/16	237	(13)	—	2,500
06/13	213	13	6.5%	—
06/09	200	(23)	—	—
Annual Growth	**2.4%**	—	—	—

2016 Year-End Financials

Return on assets: 10.7%
Return on equity: (-5.5%)
Current ratio: 1.00

Cash ($ mil.): 12

KENNESTONE HOSPITAL AT WINDY HILL, INC.

Kennestone cures kidney stones and other ailments for residents of Cobb County Georgia. WellStar Kennestone Hospital has more than 630 beds and a full range of specialty services. The hospital's physicians provide cardiac care inpatient and outpatient surgery and rehabilitation trauma diabetes care oncology dialysis and home health care. The hospital also operates centers specializing in women's health senior living facilities diagnostic clinics and a wellness and fitness center. WellStar Kennestone Hospital is part of the not-for-profit WellStar Health System which operates hospitals and other medical facilities throughout Georgia.

Operations

WellStar Kennestone Hospital is the anchor of the group's WellStar Kennestone Regional Medical Center division. WellStar Kennestone Hospital handles about 37000 inpatient admissions each year as well as more than 400000 outpatient appointments and 120000 emergency room visits. It also conducts about 23000 inpatient and outpatient surgeries and 9000 births annually and operates a level II regional trauma center. The hospital has been recognized in a number of specialist fields such as orthopedics neurology and gastroenterology.

Geographic Reach

Located in Marietta Georgia WellStar Kennestone Hospital primary serves northern and central Cobb County.

Strategy

The hospital is undergoing renovation and expansion efforts including construction of a new hospital tower with all private patient rooms; the tower was completed and opened in early 2013. Two years later the hospital opened a new inpatient pediatric unit. It also began renovations of its cancer center.

WellStar Kennestone also regularly upgrades its medical technology systems and tools such as robotic surgery systems and data management programs.

EXECUTIVES

Vice President Of Surgical Services, Adam Thompson

LOCATIONS

HQ: KENNESTONE HOSPITAL AT WINDY HILL, INC.
677 CHURCH ST NE, MARIETTA, GA 300601101
Phone: 770 793-5000

COMPETITORS

Adventist Health System Sunbelt Healthcare
Children's Healthcare of Atlanta
DeKalb Medical
Emory Healthcare
Grady Health System
Northside Hospital
Piedmont Healthcare
Redmond Regional Medical Center
Regency Hospital
Shepherd Center
SunLink Health Systems
The Fulton-DeKalb Hospital Authority
West Georgia Health System

HISTORICAL FINANCIALS
Company Type: Private

Income Statement
FYE: June 30

	REVENUE ($ mil.)	NET INCOME ($ mil.)	NET PROFIT MARGIN	EMPLOYEES
06/15	821	106	12.9%	2,950
06/05	481	54	11.2%	—
06/04	877	50	5.7%	—
06/03	792	24	3.1%	—
Annual Growth	0.3%	12.9%	—	—

2015 Year-End Financials

Return on assets: 0.1%
Return on equity: 12.9%
Current ratio: 8.00

Cash ($ mil.): —

KENNESTONE HOSPITAL INC

Auditors: PRICEWATERHOUSECOOPERS LLP PH

LOCATIONS
HQ: KENNESTONE HOSPITAL INC
805 SANDY PLAINS RD, MARIETTA, GA 300666340
Phone: 770 792-5023
Web: WWW.WELLSTAR.ORG

HISTORICAL FINANCIALS
Company Type: Private

Income Statement
FYE: June 30

	REVENUE ($ mil.)	NET INCOME ($ mil.)	NET PROFIT MARGIN	EMPLOYEES
06/15	948	182	19.2%	15
06/14	836	113	13.5%	—
06/13	791	123	15.6%	—
06/10	800	123	15.5%	—
Annual Growth	3.5%	8.0%	—	—

2015 Year-End Financials

Return on assets: 2.2%
Return on equity: 19.2%
Current ratio: 7.80

Cash ($ mil.): —

KENOSHA UNIFIED SCHOOL DISTRICT 1

EXECUTIVES
President, Rebecca Stevens
Board of Directors, Val Dowe
Account Manager, Dan Hartstern
Superintendent, Kathleen Labio

LOCATIONS
HQ: KENOSHA UNIFIED SCHOOL DISTRICT 1
3600 52ND ST, KENOSHA, WI 531442664
Phone: 262 359-6300
Web: WWW.KUSD.EDU

HISTORICAL FINANCIALS
Company Type: Private

Income Statement
FYE: June 30

	REVENUE ($ mil.)	NET INCOME ($ mil.)	NET PROFIT MARGIN	EMPLOYEES
06/16	291	11	4.0%	2,093
06/11	289	(23)	—	—
06/08	224	(2)	—	—
06/07	213	3	1.7%	—
Annual Growth	3.5%	14.3%	—	—

KENT COUNTY MEMORIAL HOSPITAL

As one of Rhode Island's largest hospitals Kent County Memorial Hospital offers Ocean Staters a sea of medical care options. The healthcare facility provides inpatient acute care as well as outpatient services (such as diagnostic imaging) and primary care. It also offers a range of specialties including cardiology orthopedics oncology surgery pediatrics and women's health. A member of the Care New England Health System Kent Hospital opened in 1951 with 90 beds; today the hospital has about 360 beds and a staff of some 600 doctors.

Operations

As a member of Care New England Kent Hospital is affiliated with the University of New England College of Osteopathic Medicine (UNECOM) for medical education. IT also has relationships with the University of Rhode Island Rhode Island College Northeastern University and medical training and research other organizations.

The Kent Hospital staff works in more than 30 specialty areas. The hospital's care team includes more than 2300 nurses technical professionals and support staff. Kent Hospital's ER is the second busiest in the state with some 67000 annual visits. Overall the hospital handles 15000 inpatient admissions each year including 1000 births and conducts about 15000 inpatient and outpatient surgeries annually.

Geographic Reach

Kent Hospital is located on a 60-acre campus in Warwick Rhode Island (11 miles south of Providence); it also operates satellite primary care and diagnostic centers in the area. The hospital provides care to about 300000 residents across central Rhode Island in communities including Coventry Cranston Exeter Greenwich North Kingstown and Warwick.

Financial Performance

The hospital brought in $315.3 million in revenue during fiscal 2011. Kent Hospital's net revenue was some $3.2 million as operating expenses totaled $312.1 million.

During fiscal 2011 Kent Hospital provided $13.9 million in community and charity health care services.

Strategy

Kent Hospital opened its newly constructed ambulatory surgery center in 2013. The center includes eight surgery suites including specialist facilities for endoscopic and interventional spine procedures. Other facility expansions have included the opening of a $2 million emergency cardiac angioplasty center in 2009. In addition Kent Hospital has expanded its outpatient care and clinical research programs in recent years.

EXECUTIVES
Director of Respiratory Therapy, Nancy Roman
Senior Vice President Human Resources, Patricia Recupero
Senior Vice President Site Operations, Fran Falsey
Respiratory Therapy Director, James Ginda
Infection Control Director, KATHY OCONNELL
Secretary Technical Services, Carol Messier
Auditors: PRICEWATERHOUSECOOPERS LLP BO

LOCATIONS
HQ: KENT COUNTY MEMORIAL HOSPITAL
455 TOLL GATE RD, WARWICK, RI 028862770
Phone: 401 737-7000
Web: WWW.KENTRI.ORG

PRODUCTS/OPERATIONS

Selected Centers and Services
Behavioral Health Unit
Breast Health
Cancer Care
Cardiology
Colonoscopy
Continuing Medical Education Program
Cosmetic Surgery
CT Scan (CAT Scan or Computerized Axial Tomography)
Dentistry
Diagnostic Imaging Services
Dialysis
Education
Emergency Medicine
Endocrinology
Endoscopy
Expresscare Service
Eye Care
Family Practice
Food and Nutrition Services
Gastroenterology
Gift Shop
Hearing Assessment/Newborns
Home Medical Equipment (HME)
Hypertension
INNOVATION CENTER
Intensive Care Unit
Internal Medicine
Interventional Radiology (Special Procedures Suite)
Kent Hospitalists
Kids Choose to be Healthy
Laboratory Services
Library
Magnetic Resonance Imaging (MRI)
Multiple Sclerosis Center
Neonatal I
Nephrology
Neurology/Neurosurgery
Nuclear Medicine
Occupational Therapy
Orthopedics
Outpatient Rehabilitation Services
Outpatient Surgery
Palliative Care
Parkinson's Information and Referral Center
Pastoral Care
Pediatric Emergency Services
Pediatrics
Physical Therapy
Physician Relations
Podiatry
Prolotherapy
Psychiatry
Pulmonary Medicine
Radiology
Rehabilitation Center
Rheumatology
Sleep Lab
Social Services
Speech-Language Pathology
Stroke Center
Support Groups
Thoracic Surgery
Ultrasound
Urology
Videostroboscopy
Women's Diagnostic Imaging Center
Wound Recovery and Hyperbaric Medicine Center

COMPETITORS

Baystate Health
Day Kimball Hospital
Memorial Hospital of
  Rhode Island
Partners HealthCare
Roger Williams Medical
  Center
Southcoast Health
Southcoast Hospitals
  Group
Sturdy Memorial
Yale New Haven Health
  System

HISTORICAL FINANCIALS

Company Type: Private

Income Statement
FYE: September 30

	REVENUE ($ mil.)	NET INCOME ($ mil.)	NET PROFIT MARGIN	EMPLOYEES
09/16	380	8	2.1%	1,850
09/15	318	14	4.7%	—
09/14	323	4	1.4%	—
09/13	339	(0)		—
Annual Growth	3.9%	—	—	—

2016 Year-End Financials

Return on assets: 11.0%   Cash ($ mil.): 6
Return on equity: 2.1%
Current ratio: 0.70

KENTUCKY COMMUNITY AND TECHNICAL COLLEGE SYSTEM

EXECUTIVES

President, Jay Box
Auditors: CROWE HORWATH LLP LEXINGTON

LOCATIONS

HQ: KENTUCKY COMMUNITY AND TECHNICAL
  COLLEGE SYSTEM
  300 N MAIN ST, VERSAILLES, KY 403831245
Phone: 859 256-3100
Web: WWW.KCTCS.EDU

HISTORICAL FINANCIALS

Company Type: Private

Income Statement
FYE: June 30

	REVENUE ($ mil.)	NET INCOME ($ mil.)	NET PROFIT MARGIN	EMPLOYEES
06/16	201	(0)	—	9,000
06/15	0	(0)	—	—
06/14	0	(0)	—	—
06/13	0	0	36.9%	—
Annual Growth	676.0%	—	—	—

2016 Year-End Financials

Return on assets: 5.3%   Cash ($ mil.): 150
Return on equity: (-0.1%)
Current ratio: 3.70

KENTUCKY HIGHER EDUCATION ASSISTANCE AUTHORITY

EXECUTIVES

Executive Director, Carl Rollins
Board of Directors, Diana Barber
Manager, Luann Overstreet
General Manager, Wendie Beswick
Purchasing Manager, Elaine Prescott
Assistant Manager, Kim Dolan
Officer, Janice Ballou
Manager, Robin Buchholz
Board of Directors, Todd Hollanbach

LOCATIONS

HQ: KENTUCKY HIGHER EDUCATION ASSISTANCE
  AUTHORITY
  100 AIRPORT RD, FRANKFORT, KY 406016161
Phone: 502 696-7200
Web: WWW.KHEAA.COM

HISTORICAL FINANCIALS

Company Type: Private

Income Statement
FYE: June 30

	REVENUE ($ mil.)	NET INCOME ($ mil.)	NET PROFIT MARGIN	EMPLOYEES
06/16	268	(3)	—	37
06/14	36	13	35.7%	—
06/10	200	(3)	—	—
06/09	20	14	71.6%	—
Annual Growth	44.9%			

2016 Year-End Financials

Return on assets: 2.3%   Cash ($ mil.): 79
Return on equity: (-1.5%)
Current ratio: 3.50

KENTUCKY MEDICAL SERVICES FOUNDATION, INC.

Does the mailbox at your old Kentucky home contain doctors' bills? They might be from Kentucky Medical Services Foundation. The physician's practice group provides billing and other administrative services for the more than 600 physicians and other health care providers affiliated with the University of Kentucky's health system UK HealthCare. The network provides more than 80 specialty services offers educational programs and operates acute medical centers including Chandler Hospital Good Samaritan Hospital and Kentucky Children's Hospital.

EXECUTIVES

President, Marc Randall
Accountant, Chihting Yen
Supervisor, Pam McGary
Manager, Carol Pelfrey
Manager, Gwen Colliver
Auditors: DEAN DORTON ALLEN FORD PLLC L

LOCATIONS

HQ: KENTUCKY MEDICAL SERVICES FOUNDATION,
  INC.
  2333 ALUMNI PARK PLZ # 200, LEXINGTON, KY
  405174012
Phone: 859 257-7910
Web: WWW.KMSF.COM

COMPETITORS

Appalachian Regional
  Healthcare
Baptist Health
Catholic Health
  Initiatives
Jewish Hospital & St.
  Mary's HealthCare
Norton Healthcare

HISTORICAL FINANCIALS

Company Type: Private

Income Statement
FYE: June 30

	REVENUE ($ mil.)	NET INCOME ($ mil.)	NET PROFIT MARGIN	EMPLOYEES
06/15	306	10	3.6%	150
06/14	236	1	0.7%	—
06/13	225	(0)	—	—
06/10	196	(4)	—	—
Annual Growth	9.3%	—	—	—

2015 Year-End Financials

Return on assets: 2.2%   Cash ($ mil.): 59
Return on equity: 3.6%
Current ratio: 14.40

KEY CONSTRUCTION, INC.

EXECUTIVES

Chief Executive Officer, Kenneth A Wells
Superintendent, Brent Ranabargar
Financial Executive, Carrie Lindholn
Office Manager, John Walker Jr
Manager, Chuck Petersen

LOCATIONS

HQ: KEY CONSTRUCTION, INC.
  741 W 2ND ST N, WICHITA, KS 672036004
Phone: 316 263-9515
Web: WWW.KEYCONSTRUCTION.COM

HISTORICAL FINANCIALS

Company Type: Private

Income Statement
FYE: December 31

	REVENUE ($ mil.)	NET INCOME ($ mil.)	NET PROFIT MARGIN	EMPLOYEES
12/15	195	2	1.2%	210
12/14	191	2	1.1%	—
12/10	183	0	0.3%	—
12/09	266	(2)	—	—
Annual Growth	(5.0%)	—	—	—

2015 Year-End Financials

Return on assets: 22.3%   Cash ($ mil.): 23
Return on equity: 1.2%
Current ratio: 1.10

KEY FOOD STORES CO-OPERATIVE, INC.

Key Food Stores Co-Operative is a friend to independent New York area grocers. The co-op provides retail support and other services to 150 independently owned food retailers in the New York City area. Key Food's member-owners run stores mainly in Brooklyn and Queens but also in the other boroughs and surrounding counties. It operates stores primarily under the Key Food banner but it also has Key Food Marketplace locations that feature expanded meat deli and produce departments. In addition the co-op supplies Key Foods-branded products to member stores. Among its members are Pick Quick Foods Dan's Supreme Super Markets Gemstone Supermarkets and Queens Supe rmarkets. Key Foods was founded in 1937.

Geographic Reach

Staten Island-based Key Food Stores Co-Operative operates supermarkets across the five boroughs and on Long Island in upstate New York and in New Jersey and Pennsylvania.

Financial Performance

Key Foods Stores has annual sales of about $1.5 billion.

Strategy

Key Food has been expanding in Queens and Brooklyn and on Long Island after scaling back in Manhattan — where many of its stores were converted to Duane Reade drugstores as the pharmacy chain expanded and took over individual locations. To that end in late 2013 the regional grocer launched a new banner called Urban Market in Brooklyn. The 16000-square foot store in Williamsburg was the co-op's 150th location. The cooperative is expanding aggressively adding more than 30 locations under the Key Food Key Fresh & Natural and Food Dynasty banners including stores in Harlem and the Bronx. It also recently reopened a store in Coney Island that was destroyed by Hurricane Sandy in 2012.

EXECUTIVES

Vice President Strategic Planning, George Knobloch
Vice President of Strategic Pl, Chet Koby
Vice President Finance, Sharon Konzelman
Auditors: ANCHIN BLOCK & ANCHIN LLP N

LOCATIONS

HQ: KEY FOOD STORES CO-OPERATIVE, INC.
1200 SOUTH AVE, STATEN ISLAND, NY 103143413
Phone: 718 370-4200

PRODUCTS/OPERATIONS

Selected Banners
Food Dynasty
Food World
Holiday Farms
Key Food
Key Food Marketplace
Key Fresh & Natural
Locust Valley
Milford Farms
Urban Market
Vitelio's Marketplace

COMPETITORS

A&P	Fresh Direct
D'Agostino	Gristede's Foods
Supermarkets	King Kullen Grocery
Food Emporium	Walgreen

HISTORICAL FINANCIALS

Company Type: Private

Income Statement
FYE: April 25

	REVENUE ($ mil.)	NET INCOME ($ mil.)	NET PROFIT MARGIN	EMPLOYEES
04/15	893	(0)	—	84
04/14	753	0	0.0%	—
04/11	537	(0)	—	—
04/10	0	0	—	—
Annual Growth	—	—	—	—

2015 Year-End Financials
Return on assets: 4.9%   Cash ($ mil.): 4
Return on equity: (-0.1%)
Current ratio: 0.80

KEYSTOPS, LLC

EXECUTIVES

Board of Directors, Rex Hazelip
Board of Directors, Richard Shepherd
Board of Directors, Kent Pyle
Board of Directors, Charles Key
Auditors: BKD LLP BOWLING GREEN KENTUC

LOCATIONS

HQ: KEYSTOPS, LLC
376 REASONOVER AVE, FRANKLIN, KY 421344003
Phone: 270 586-8283

HISTORICAL FINANCIALS

Company Type: Private

Income Statement
FYE: September 30

	REVENUE ($ mil.)	NET INCOME ($ mil.)	NET PROFIT MARGIN	EMPLOYEES
09/16	430	4	1.0%	200
09/15	584	6	1.2%	—
09/14	900	3	0.3%	—
09/13	903	2	0.3%	—
Annual Growth	(21.9%)	19.4%	—	—

2016 Year-End Financials
Return on assets: 3.8%   Cash ($ mil.): 1
Return on equity: 1.0%
Current ratio: 1.20

KILLEEN INDEPENDENT SCHOOL DISTRICT

EXECUTIVES

Superintendent, John Craft
Auditors: LOTT VERNON & COMPANY PC K

LOCATIONS

HQ: KILLEEN INDEPENDENT SCHOOL DISTRICT
200 N W S YOUNG DR, KILLEEN, TX 765434025
Phone: 254 336-0000
Web: WWW.KILLEENISD.ORG

HISTORICAL FINANCIALS

Company Type: Private

Income Statement
FYE: August 31

	REVENUE ($ mil.)	NET INCOME ($ mil.)	NET PROFIT MARGIN	EMPLOYEES
08/16	438	7	1.7%	6,200
08/15	418	21	5.2%	—
08/14	392	(3)	—	—
08/13	372	1	0.3%	—
Annual Growth	5.6%	91.2%	—	—

2016 Year-End Financials
Return on assets: 2.4%   Cash ($ mil.): 51
Return on equity: 1.7%
Current ratio: —

KILROY REALTY, L.P.

EXECUTIVES

President, John B Kilroy Jr
General Partner, Kilroy Realty Corporation
Administrative Assistant, Kelli Peirsol
Manager, Mike Nelson
Executive Vice-President, Richard E Moran
Auditors: DELOITTE & TOUCHE LLP LOS AN

LOCATIONS

HQ: KILROY REALTY, L.P.
12200 W OLYMPIC BLVD # 200, LOS ANGELES, CA 900641044
Phone: 310 481-8400

HISTORICAL FINANCIALS

Company Type: Private

Income Statement
FYE: December 31

	ASSETS ($ mil.)	NET INCOME ($ mil.)	INCOME AS % OF ASSETS	EMPLOYEES
12/16	6,706	303	4.5%	226
12/15	5,939	238	4.0%	—
12/14	5,633	183	3.3%	—
12/13	5,111	44	0.9%	—
Annual Growth	9.5%	89.6%	—	—

2016 Year-End Financials
Return on assets: 31.5%   Sales ($ mil): 642
Return on equity: 47.3%

KING COUNTY PUBLIC HOSPITAL DISTRICT 2

EXECUTIVES

Chief Executive Officer, Bob Malte
Director, Raymond Plumb
Financial Executive, Ardis Schmeige
Operations Manager, Chuck Davis

LOCATIONS

HQ: KING COUNTY PUBLIC HOSPITAL DISTRICT 2
12040 NE 128TH ST, KIRKLAND, WA 980343013
Phone: 425 899-2769

HISTORICAL FINANCIALS

Company Type: Private

Income Statement
FYE: December 31

	REVENUE ($ mil.)	NET INCOME ($ mil.)	NET PROFIT MARGIN	EMPLOYEES
12/15	565	3	0.7%	2,400
12/06	273	16	6.2%	—
12/05	244	11	4.8%	—
12/03	167	0	—	—
Annual Growth	—	113.2%	—	—

2015 Year-End Financials

Return on assets: 4.8% Cash ($ mil.): 18
Return on equity: 0.7%
Current ratio: 1.00

KINGMAN HOSPITAL, INC.

EXECUTIVES

Chief Executive Officer, Brian Turney
Manager, Barry Moore
Director, Paul Elsass
Auditors: BKD LLP COLORADO SPRINGS CO

LOCATIONS

HQ: KINGMAN HOSPITAL, INC.
3269 N STOCKTON HILL RD, KINGMAN, AZ
864093619
Phone: 928 757-2101
Web: WWW.AZKRMC.COM

HISTORICAL FINANCIALS

Company Type: Private

Income Statement
FYE: June 30

	REVENUE ($ mil.)	NET INCOME ($ mil.)	NET PROFIT MARGIN	EMPLOYEES
06/16	277	8	3.1%	1,300
06/15	254	14	5.6%	—
06/14	226	4	2.0%	—
06/13	221	1	0.5%	—
Annual Growth	7.8%	94.8%	—	—

2016 Year-End Financials

Return on assets: 2.9% Cash ($ mil.): 16
Return on equity: 3.1%
Current ratio: 2.20

KINGSBROOK JEWISH MEDICAL CENTER INC

Kingsbrook Jewish Medical Center (KJMC) cares for the health needs of all Brooklyn residents. Founded in 1925 to serve the area's Jewish community the campus includes an acute care hospital with about 320 inpatient beds and an adult and pediatric long-term care facility with 540 beds. KJMC provides emergency surgical cardiology gastroenterology pulmonary wound care and diagnostic imaging services as well as skilled nursing services. The hospital also serves as a training facility for medical dental and pharmacy residents. It also operates a primary and specialty care outpatient center and a rehabilitation institute.

Operations

KJMC's specialty inpatient units include its Traumatic Brain Injury and Coma Recovery Unit (part of the Kingsbrook Rehabilitation Institute). Other centers of excellence include a geriatric inpatient psychiatry program to serve the borough's mentally challenged elderly residents as well as centers for radiology wound healing orthopedic surgery women's health and pharmacy services. The outpatient center provides family practice services and specialist care in about 20 medical fields.

KJMC's skilled nursing facility known as Rutland Nursing Home provides skilled nursing care physical rehabilitation comprehensive wound care a specialty unit for ventilator-dependent residents and a range of sub-acute services. Rutland Nursing Home also has a dedicated pediatric long-term care unit for children with severe developmental and metabolic disorders. Because it is located on the KJMC campus all of the medical center's resources are available to the residents.

Financial Performance

In 2012 revenue dipped less than 1% as patient and resident services income dropped. But compensation and supply costs rose so KJMC ended with a $5 million net loss. Cash flow held steady.

Geographic Reach

KJMC is located in the East Flatbush neighborhood of Brooklyn. The hospital also operates the Pierre Toussaint Family Health Center in Brooklyn.

Strategy

KJMC is making investments in its facilities to better serve the growing needs of its community. To that end in 2011 the center broke ground on a new emergency department increasing its capacity to handle about 6000 additional ER visits per year. It is also renovating its ambulatory care facilities and expanding community programs (such as its adult day health services program). Both projects are expected to be complete in 2014. In addition in 2012 the hospital opened a new outpatient specialty care facility; the project took two years to complete and incorporates new processes for the efficient coordination of care for patients with multiple medical conditions.

The hospital is also upgrading its data systems to improve efficiencies. In 2013 it selected the ClearDATA health cloud platform to host its offsite backup system. Shifting its IT infrastructure to the platform will help KJMC reduce capital expenses and minimize risk.

Other efforts at KJMC include initiatives to reduce patient readmissions and hospital-acquired conditions.

EXECUTIVES

Director of Pharmacy, Ron Levy
Assistant Vice President of Nursing, Grahamhannah Dorothy
Board Member, Henri Paul

LOCATIONS

HQ: KINGSBROOK JEWISH MEDICAL CENTER INC
585 SCHENECTADY AVE STE 2, BROOKLYN, NY
112031809
Phone: 718 604-5000
Web: WWW.KINGSBROOK.ORG

PRODUCTS/OPERATIONS

Selected Centers of Excellence

Comprehensive Wound Healing and Hyperbaric Center
Department of Physical Medicine and Rehabilitation
Geriatric Psychiatry
Gynecological Services / Minimally Invasive Laparoscopic Surgery
Non-Invasive Vascular Laboratory
Ophthalmology and Neuro-ophthalmology
Orthopedics and Joint Replacement
Pharmacy
Radiology
Rutland Adult Day Health Care Center
Rutland Nursing Home
Traumatic Brain Injury and Coma Recovery Unit
Vascular Center of Excellence

Selected Clinical Services

Cardiovascular
Cardiac Cath Lab
Emergency Services
Emergency Department
Neurosciences
Electroencephalography (EEG)
Oncology
Chemotherapy
Orthopedics
Arthroscopy
Radiology Nuclear Medicine and Imaging
Computed Tomography (CT)
Magnetic Resonance Imaging (MRI)
Single Photon Emission Computerized Tomography (SPECT)
Rehabilitation
Physical Therapy
Special Care
Coronary Intensive Care (CCU)
Intensive Care Unit (ICU)
Subprovider Units
Psychiatric
Rehabilitation
Skilled Nursing (SNF)
Wound Care
Hyperbaric Oxygen
Wound care

COMPETITORS

Brooklyn Hospital Center
Lutheran HealthCare
Maimonides Medical Center
MediSys Health Network
Montefiore Medical
New York City Health and Hospitals
New York Methodist Hospital
NewYork-Presbyterian Healthcare
Northwell Health
SUNY Downstate

HISTORICAL FINANCIALS

Company Type: Private

Income Statement
FYE: December 31

	REVENUE ($ mil.)	NET INCOME ($ mil.)	NET PROFIT MARGIN	EMPLOYEES
12/15	218	(1)	—	2,100
12/14	211	12	6.1%	—
12/08	241	(3)	—	—
12/05	227	(14)	—	—
Annual Growth	(0.4%)	—	—	—

2015 Year-End Financials

Return on assets: 15.7% Cash ($ mil.): 12
Return on equity: (-0.5%)
Current ratio: 0.60

KINGSWAY CHARITIES, INC.

EXECUTIVES

Manager, Kecia Salyers
Executive Director, Albert Hester
Auditors: BROWN EDWARDS & COMPANY LL

LOCATIONS

HQ: KINGSWAY CHARITIES, INC.
1119 COMMONWEALTH AVE, BRISTOL, VA
242012629
Phone: 276 466-3014
Web: WWW.KINGSWAYCHARITIES.ORG

HISTORICAL FINANCIALS

Company Type: Private

Income Statement

FYE: December 31

	REVENUE ($ mil.)	NET INCOME ($ mil.)	NET PROFIT MARGIN	EMPLOYEES
12/15	189	(3)	—	9
12/14	120	(33)	—	—
12/13	164	49	30.0%	—
12/12	331	(0)	—	—
Annual Growth	(17.0%)	—	—	—

2015 Year-End Financials

Return on assets: —
Return on equity: (-1.9%)
Current ratio: —

Cash ($ mil.): —

KINGWOOD MEDICAL CENTER

EXECUTIVES

Chief Executive Officer, Melinda Stephenson
Board of Directors, Mujtaba Ali-Khan
Manager, Shila Vice

LOCATIONS

HQ: KINGWOOD MEDICAL CENTER
22999 HIGHWAY 59 N # 134, KINGWOOD, TX
773394449
Phone: 281 348-8000
Web: WWW.KINGWOODMEDICAL.COM

HISTORICAL FINANCIALS

Company Type: Private

Income Statement

FYE: September 30

	REVENUE ($ mil.)	NET INCOME ($ mil.)	NET PROFIT MARGIN	EMPLOYEES
09/15	256	23	9.2%	1,200
09/14	236	27	11.6%	—
09/13	216	25	11.8%	—
Annual Growth	8.8%	(4.0%)	—	—

2015 Year-End Financials

Return on assets: 2.6%
Return on equity: 9.2%
Current ratio: 2.40

Cash ($ mil.): —

KIRBY - SMITH MACHINERY, INC.

EXECUTIVES

President, Ed Kirby
Financial Executive, Kieth Tippet
Division Manager, Kevin D Phillips
Personnel Manager, Kathy Dean
Branch Manager, Bruce Taylor
Manager, Chad White
Sales Manager, Bill Hitchcock
Auditors: EIDEBAILLY OKLAHOMA CITY OKL

LOCATIONS

HQ: KIRBY - SMITH MACHINERY, INC.
6715 W RENO AVE, OKLAHOMA CITY, OK 731276590
Phone: 888 861-0219
Web: WWW.KIRBY-SMITH.COM

HISTORICAL FINANCIALS

Company Type: Private

Income Statement

FYE: December 31

	REVENUE ($ mil.)	NET INCOME ($ mil.)	NET PROFIT MARGIN	EMPLOYEES
12/15	321	33	10.5%	385
12/14	353	29	8.2%	—
12/13	337	30	9.0%	—
12/12	290	31	10.7%	—
Annual Growth	3.4%	2.8%	—	—

2015 Year-End Financials

Return on assets: 5.2%
Return on equity: 10.5%
Current ratio: 0.70

Cash ($ mil.): —

KLAMATH FALLS INTERCOMMUNITY HOSPITAL AUTHORITY

EXECUTIVES

President, Paul Stewart
Director, Barbara Curtis

LOCATIONS

HQ: KLAMATH FALLS INTERCOMMUNITY HOSPITAL AUTHORITY
2865 DAGGETT AVE, KLAMATH FALLS, OR 976011106
Phone: 541 883-6150
Web: WWW.SKYLAKES.ORG

HISTORICAL FINANCIALS

Company Type: Private

Income Statement

FYE: September 30

	ASSETS ($ mil.)	NET INCOME ($ mil.)	INCOME AS % OF ASSETS	EMPLOYEES
09/15	266	23	8.7%	9
09/14	239	19	8.2%	—
09/13	216	15	7.0%	—
09/09	143	0	—	—
Annual Growth	10.8%	—	—	—

2015 Year-End Financials

Return on assets: 10.2%
Return on equity: 11.5%

Sales ($ mil): 202

KLEIN INDEPENDENT SCHOOL DISTRICT

EXECUTIVES

Superintendent, Bret A Champion
President, Steven E Smith
Vice-President, Ronnie K Anderson
Superintendent, James Kane
Auditors: HEREFORD LYNCH SELLARS & KIR

LOCATIONS

HQ: KLEIN INDEPENDENT SCHOOL DISTRICT
7200 SPRING CYPRESS RD, SPRING, TX 773793215
Phone: 832 249-4000
Web: WWW.KLEINISD.NET

HISTORICAL FINANCIALS

Company Type: Private

Income Statement

FYE: August 31

	REVENUE ($ mil.)	NET INCOME ($ mil.)	NET PROFIT MARGIN	EMPLOYEES
08/16	539	(135)	—	5,691
08/15	511	186	36.5%	—
08/14	474	6	1.4%	—
08/13	430	(29)	—	—
Annual Growth	7.8%	—	—	—

2016 Year-End Financials

Return on assets: 5.7%
Return on equity: (-25.1%)
Current ratio: —

Cash ($ mil.): 219

KNOX COUNTY HOSPITAL

Good Samaritan Hospital provides a full slate of healthcare services to both southwest Indiana and southeast Illinois. Its services include cardiology emergency care orthopedics women's health and pediatrics among others. The 230-bed hospital is located a few blocks from the Wabash River which forms the border between the Hoosier and Prairies states. Good Samaritan operates specialty units as well including same-day surgery breast care behavioral health radiology sleep cancer care and rehabilitation centers. It also provides home health and hospice services. Established in 1908 with 25 beds Good Samaritan was Indiana's first county hospital.

Operations

Busy regional hospital Good Samaritan logs more than 458000 outpatient visits each year as well as an additional 35950 visits to its emergency room. It boasts an Imaging Center Dayson Heart Center and Cancer Pavilion with a 25000-sq.-ft. comprehensive oncology care center.

Good Samaritan is a member of the Voluntary Hospital Association Indiana Hospital Association and Genesis Health.

Geographic Reach

Located in Vincennes Indiana Good Samaritan serves residents along the neighboring southern borders of both Indiana and Illinois.

Sales and Marketing

The hospital uses TV advertising to market its services.

Strategy

While Good Samaritan is focused on serving patients as an outpatient facility the regional hospital is nearing completion of a new inpatient tower. It's building a 200000-sq.-ft. five-story 120-bed inpatient tower at the cost of $109 million. As part of this BEACON project Good Samaritan is redesigning key healthcare service areas and upgrading its critical engineering systems. Project completion dates span 2014 to late 2016 for the BEACON project.

To make information more readily available to its patients Good Samaritan in 2012 rolled out an Indiana Health Information Exchange clinical messaging service called DOCS4DOCS. The service provides a portal for accessing lab results radiology reports transcripts pathology and hospital admissions reports and discharge and transfer reports. Good Samaritan is one of several thousand participating hospitals along with physician practices labs and radiology centers.

EXECUTIVES

Senior Vice President and Chief Operating Officer, Gerald Waldroup
Vice President Affa, Charles Hedde
Vice President of Human Resour, Emily A Heineke
Assistant Director Pharmacy, Mark Shields
VP Professional and Support Services, Fred England
Ambulatory Services Director, Brenda Winkler
Ambulatory Services Dir, DEBBIE STEVENS
Vice President Of Professional Services, Adam Thacker
Occupational Therapy Director, Tammy Klein
Director of Pharmacy, Jim Eskew
Medical Director, Victor Kirchoff
Vice President Professional Support Services, Scott Kaminski
Vice President Operations, Matthew Schuckman
Radiology Director, Mark Schaeffer
Physical Therapy Director, STEVE WISSEL
Secretary, Valerie Turpin
Auditors: BKD LLP INDIANAPOLIS IN

LOCATIONS

HQ: KNOX COUNTY HOSPITAL
305 S 5TH ST, VINCENNES, IN 475911117
Phone: 812 882-5220
Web: WWW.GSHVIN.ORG

PRODUCTS/OPERATIONS

Selected Centers
Dayson Heart Center
Cancer Pavilion
Imaging Center

COMPETITORS

Daviess Community Hospital
Deaconess Health System
IU Health
Southern Illinois Healthcare
St. John's Hospital (Illinois)
St. Mary's Medical Center of Evansville
Wabash County Hospital

HISTORICAL FINANCIALS

Company Type: Private

Income Statement				FYE: December 31
	REVENUE ($ mil.)	NET INCOME ($ mil.)	NET PROFIT MARGIN	EMPLOYEES
12/15	291	(4)	—	1,900
12/14	537	9	1.8%	—
12/13	198	4	2.1%	—
12/12	191	12	6.6%	—
Annual Growth	14.9%	—	—	—

2015 Year-End Financials
Return on assets: 6.1%   Cash ($ mil.): 21
Return on equity: (-1.6%)
Current ratio: 1.60

KNOXVILLE UTILITIES BOARD

Providing utility services to residential and business customers has proven to be an excellent idea for Knoxville Utilities Board (KUB) an independent agency that serves the city of Knoxville and surrounding areas. The multi-utility provides services to 196500 electric 96920 gas 77600 water and 68740 wastewater customers. The company accesses electric power from the Tennessee Valley Authority. KUB's natural gas supply comes from the East Tennessee Natural Gas pipeline. It also maintains five treatment plants which provide water and wastewater services.

Operations
In 2013 the company was operating 1324 miles of wastewater mains 1407 miles of water mains 5265 miles of electric service lines and 69 substations and 2295 miles of natural gas mains.

Geographic Reach
The company serves 440000 customers in Knoxville and parts of seven surrounding counties.

Financial Performance
In 2013 KUB's operating revenues grew by 7%. Electric Division operating revenue increased $27.4 million thanks to a 1% rise in sales volumes and electric rate increases. Gas Division revenues grew 20% thanks to 14% rise in natural gas sales volumes. Water Divisionrevenue increased by 1.4% due tomwater rate increases. The Wastewater Division revenues were $4.1 million higher than in 2012 thanks to a rate increase.

Strategy
KUB is engaged in a long term plan to renovate its aging infrastructure. The push began the mid-1990s with a focus on upgrading Knoxville's water tanks distribution pipelines and the its water treatment plants.

Company Background
The agency was founded by the City of Knoxville in 1939. The utility's electric system is one of the nation's most dependable reporting a 99.9% uninterrupted service rating.

EXECUTIVES

Vice President, Mark Walker
Vice President Information Technology, Debbie M Boles
Vice President of Information Services and Business Processes, Derwin Haygood
Vice President Customer Service, Mike Bolin
Vice President and Spokesperson, Susan Edwards
Auditors: RODEFER MOSS & CO PLLC KNOX

LOCATIONS

HQ: KNOXVILLE UTILITIES BOARD
445 S GAY ST, KNOXVILLE, TN 379021125
Phone: 865 594-7324
Web: WWW.KUB.ORG

HISTORICAL FINANCIALS

Company Type: Private

Income Statement				FYE: June 30
	REVENUE ($ mil.)	NET INCOME ($ mil.)	NET PROFIT MARGIN	EMPLOYEES
06/16	733	33	4.6%	500
06/15	763	35	4.7%	—
06/14	751	29	4.0%	—
06/13	743	28	3.8%	—
Annual Growth	(0.4%)	6.2%	—	—

2016 Year-End Financials
Return on assets: 6.9%   Cash ($ mil.): 78
Return on equity: 4.6%
Current ratio: 1.10

KONIAG DEVELOPMENT COMPANY LLC

EXECUTIVES

President, Thomas Panamaroff
Board of Directors, Ronald Unger
Senior Vice-President, Edward O'Hare
Auditors: KPMG LLP ANCHORAGE AK

LOCATIONS

HQ: KONIAG DEVELOPMENT COMPANY LLC
3800 CENTERPOINT DR # 502, ANCHORAGE, AK 995035961
Phone: 907 561-2668

HISTORICAL FINANCIALS

Company Type: Private

Income Statement				FYE: March 31
	REVENUE ($ mil.)	NET INCOME ($ mil.)	NET PROFIT MARGIN	EMPLOYEES
03/16	246	7	3.2%	820
03/15	247	6	2.4%	—
03/14	9	4	44.6%	—
03/13	168	(2)	—	—
Annual Growth	13.5%	—	—	—

2016 Year-End Financials
Return on assets: 6.6%   Cash ($ mil.): 19
Return on equity: 3.2%
Current ratio: 1.20

KONIAG, INC.

EXECUTIVES

Director, Brent Parsons
Auditors: KPMG LLP ANCHORAGE AK

LOCATIONS

HQ: KONIAG, INC.
3800 CNTRPOINT DR STE 502, KODIAK, AK 99615
Phone: 907 486-2530

HISTORICAL FINANCIALS

Company Type: Private

Income Statement

FYE: March 31

	ASSETS ($ mil.)	NET INCOME ($ mil.)	INCOME AS % OF ASSETS	EMPLOYEES
03/16	146	8	5.8%	834
03/15	156	5	3.8%	—
03/14	156	4	2.6%	—
03/13	155	(5)	—	—
Annual Growth	(2.0%)	—	—	—

2016 Year-End Financials

Return on assets: 6.9%   Sales ($ mil.): 251
Return on equity: 3.4%

KOOTENAI HOSPITAL DISTRICT

EXECUTIVES

Principal, Jon Ness
Purchasing Director, Aaron Beamish

LOCATIONS

HQ: KOOTENAI HOSPITAL DISTRICT
2003 KOOTENAI HEALTH WAY, COEUR D ALENE, ID
838146051
Phone: 208 625-4000
Web: WWW.KH.ORG

HISTORICAL FINANCIALS

Company Type: Private

Income Statement

FYE: December 31

	REVENUE ($ mil.)	NET INCOME ($ mil.)	NET PROFIT MARGIN	EMPLOYEES
12/15	398	35	9.0%	2,776
12/14	368	30	8.3%	—
12/07	211	23	11.2%	—
12/06	192	188	98.0%	—
Annual Growth	8.4%	(16.9%)	—	—

2015 Year-End Financials

Return on assets: 5.7%   Cash ($ mil.): 51
Return on equity: 9.0%
Current ratio: 2.10

KRUEGER INTERNATIONAL, INC.

Krueger International can be found in cubicles classrooms cafeterias and college dorms. The company which does business as KI makes ergonomic seating cabinets and other furniture used by businesses healthcare organizations government agencies and educational institutions. The company offers everything from benches and beds to desks and tables not to mention shelving filing systems movable walls and trash bins. KI markets its products through sales representatives furniture dealers architects and interior designers worldwide. Founded in 1941 KI was purchased in the 1980s by its managers who later allowed employees to buy stock. Today KI is 100% employee owned.

Operations

Boasting $700 million in sales and the title of sixth-largest contract furniture manufacturer in the industry KI operates a variety of subsidiaries including KI UK Ltd. KI East Asia Sdn. Bhd KI Nova Scotia KI Canada KI-Sebel and KI India.

KI also owns three subsidiaries: AWP Wood Products Pallas Textiles and Spacesaver. Quebec-based AWP Wood Products makes architectural wood doors for the office partition industry. Pallas Textiles which operates out of Wisconsin creates textile products for contract upholstery panel systems and wall-coverings healthcare environments and casements. Spacesaver Corporation also located in Wisconsin makes high-density mobile storage systems for office institutional and industrial applications and is a major supplier of steel shelving systems rotary storage systems and storage accessories.

The company maintains nine manufacturing sites around the globe. Besides its four locations in Wisconsin (in Bonduel Fort Atkinson Green Bay and Manitowoc) KI operates production facilities in High Point North Carolina; Penmroke Ontario Canada; and Tupelo Mississippi. In 2012 KI expanded its Green Bay Wisconsin plant (at the tune of $3.3 million) by more than 100000 sq. ft. for additional elbow room devoted to manufacturing shipping receiving and warehousing.

Geographic Reach

Based in Wisconsin KI sells its products worldwide and operates manufacturing facilities and sales offices in the US Canada China and India as well as throughout Europe Latin America and Asia. It has subsidiaries based in the UK Canada India and Malaysia. Its showrooms are in several metropolitan areas across the US Toronto and London.

Sales and Marketing

KI sells its products globally through furniture dealers sales representatives architects and interior designers. It primarily serves the educational university healthcare business and government markets.

The company staffs direct sales offices around the world and also boasts showrooms in metropolitan areas to display its products to potential business and individual customers.

Strategy

KI is well-regarded in the classroom furniture market and is a leading supplier for both K-12 schools and universities. The company has outfitted classrooms lecture halls administrative offices computer labs media centers residence halls and student unions. KI has been a government vendor for more than six decades providing furnishings for an assortment of federal agencies including all branches of the military. KI's corporate products are ergonomically designed to help individuals work more comfortably and efficiently. In addition to these core customer groups KI has also installed its furnishings in outdoor public spaces sports arenas conference centers and airports.

It regularly rolls out new products. In 2013 KI launched the Grazie Seating Collection through a collaboration between renowned designer Giancarlo Piretti and in 2012 introduced the elegant and sophisticated Affina Collection an expansive seating and table line designed by Paul James and Dan Cramer. KI also expanded its existing product licensing agreement with UK seating industry leader Boss Design in 2013 to give Boss Design an extended reach into the US market and KI a broader portfolio of lounge task seating and occasional table items.

Company Background

The company has expanded its network of showrooms in the US and abroad over the years.

KI added a showroom in Houston in 2010 to boost its US presence which includes about 10 locations in half a dozen states. To better serve its Asian and European customers the company operates through a showroom in Shanghai China. KI has international showrooms in London Malaysia Mexico Puerto Rico and Toronto. To support its growth KI completed a $3.3-million 100000-sq.-ft. plant expansion in 2012 to reduce costs and streamline its business. The move boosts its manufacturing shipping receiving and warehousing space.

As its showroom presence grew KI also formed new sales partnerships. The company tapped Heartland Furniture Group a contract furniture representative in 2011 to take care of existing customer accounts and broker sales in Kansas Missouri and southern Illinois.

It's also looked to acquisitions to extend the reach of its business. In 2011 KI purchased Sebel Furniture Limited from GWA Group Ltd. a top supplier of building fixtures in Australia. The $24 million deal has given KI a foothold in the commercial furniture business in Australia New Zealand the UK and Hong Kong.

EXECUTIVES

Chairman and CEO, Richard J. (Dick) Resch
President, Brian Krenke
Vice President, Dennis Mickeleit
Vice President Corporate Communications, Joe Burkard
Vice President Architectural Wall Operations, Ryan Usiak
Vice President Of Sales, John Duffy
Vice President Marketing, Tom Abrahamson
Assistant SEC, Guy Patzke
Auditors: BAKER TILLY VIRCHOW KRAUSE LLP

LOCATIONS

HQ: KRUEGER INTERNATIONAL, INC.
1330 BELLEVUE ST, GREEN BAY, WI 543022197
Phone: 920 468-8100
Web: WWW.KI.COM

PRODUCTS/OPERATIONS

Selected Products

Auditorium seating
Beds
Benches
Bookcases
Carrels
Chairs
Desks
File cabinets
Lecterns
Movable walls
Planters
Power and data connections
Receptacles
Recliners
Residence hall furniture
Sleepers
Special events seating
Stools
Tables

COMPETITORS

ABCO Office Furniture	Kewaunee Scientific
Allsteel	Kimball International
Bretford	Knoll Inc.
CFGroup	La-Z-Boy
Columbia Manufacturing	Norstar Office
Edsal Manufacturing	Products
Global Group	Sagus
HNI	Steelcase
Haworth Inc.	Trendway
Herman Miller	Virco Mfg.
Inscape corp	

HISTORICAL FINANCIALS
Company Type: Private

Income Statement
FYE: December 31

	REVENUE ($ mil.)	NET INCOME ($ mil.)	NET PROFIT MARGIN	EMPLOYEES
12/15	617	53	8.6%	2,300
12/11	649	56	8.8%	—
12/10	615	59	9.6%	—
12/08	1,377	0	0.0%	—
Annual Growth	(10.8%)	433.8%	—	—

2015 Year-End Financials
Return on assets: 5.2%
Return on equity: 8.6%
Current ratio: 0.70
Cash ($ mil.): 4

KYUNGSHIN-LEAR SALES AND ENGINEERING, LLC

EXECUTIVES

Board of Directors, Cheon Hee Kim
Manager, Lim Sang Hyuk
Personnel Manager, Ted Stanford
Manager, Chris Stanley
Auditors: MANCERA SC CIUDAD JUAREZ CH

LOCATIONS

HQ: KYUNGSHIN-LEAR SALES AND ENGINEERING, LLC
100 SMOTHERS RD, MONTGOMERY, AL 361175505
Phone: 334 413-0575

HISTORICAL FINANCIALS
Company Type: Private

Income Statement
FYE: December 31

	REVENUE ($ mil.)	NET INCOME ($ mil.)	NET PROFIT MARGIN	EMPLOYEES
12/15	354	1	0.5%	105
12/14	355	1	0.5%	—
12/13	342	2	0.7%	—
12/12	319	3	1.0%	—
Annual Growth	3.5%	(18.2%)	—	—

2015 Year-End Financials
Return on assets: 5.4%
Return on equity: 0.5%
Current ratio: 0.60
Cash ($ mil.): 3

LA BODEGA MEAT, LLC

EXECUTIVES

President, Mario Nafal
Manager, Sam Rashid
Manager, Eric Turner
Chief Operating Officer, Jose Torres
Manager, Eddie Zubldat
Purchasing Agent, Amir Haifa
Manager, Guy Hiner

LOCATIONS

HQ: LA BODEGA MEAT, LLC
14330 GILLIS RD, FARMERS BRANCH, TX 752443717
Phone: 972 526-7200
Web: WWW.LABODEGAMEAT.COM

HISTORICAL FINANCIALS
Company Type: Private

Income Statement
FYE: December 31

	REVENUE ($ mil.)	NET INCOME ($ mil.)	NET PROFIT MARGIN	EMPLOYEES
12/15	211	11	5.2%	99
12/12	173	9	5.7%	—
12/11	128	6	5.0%	—
12/10	2,042	0	—	—
Annual Growth	—	1306.3%	—	—

2015 Year-End Financials
Return on assets: 1.5%
Return on equity: 5.2%
Current ratio: 2.90
Cash ($ mil.): 3

LA JOYA INDEPENDENT SCHOOL DISTRICT

EXECUTIVES

Superintendent, Dr Alda T Benavides
Board of Directors, Joel Garca
Board of Directors, Blanca Cantu
Director, Rosic Prada
Director, Antoio Uresti
Financial Executive, Alsredo Vels
Manager, Lionel Perez
Auditors: REYNA & GARZA PLLC CPA'S TX

LOCATIONS

HQ: LA JOYA INDEPENDENT SCHOOL DISTRICT
200 W EXPRESSWAY 83, LA JOYA, TX 785604002
Phone: 956 580-2000
Web: WWW.LAJOYAISD.COM

HISTORICAL FINANCIALS
Company Type: Private

Income Statement
FYE: August 31

	REVENUE ($ mil.)	NET INCOME ($ mil.)	NET PROFIT MARGIN	EMPLOYEES
08/16	342	1	0.3%	2,800
08/07	211	18	8.7%	—
08/06	175	0	—	—
08/05	0	0	—	—
Annual Growth	—	212.3%	—	—

2016 Year-End Financials
Return on assets: 2.3%
Return on equity: 0.3%
Current ratio: 0.80
Cash ($ mil.): 18

LABOR MANAGEMENT HEALTHCARE FU

EXECUTIVES

Principal, Vicki Martino
Office Manager, Deanna Rhoney
Auditors: TOSKI & CO CPAS PC BUFFALO N

LOCATIONS

HQ: LABOR MANAGEMENT HEALTHCARE FU
3786 BROADWAY ST, BUFFALO, NY 142271123
Phone: 716 601-7980
Web: WWW.LMHF.NET

HISTORICAL FINANCIALS
Company Type: Private

Income Statement
FYE: December 31

	REVENUE ($ mil.)	NET INCOME ($ mil.)	NET PROFIT MARGIN	EMPLOYEES
12/15	223	0	0.4%	6
12/14	199	0	0.1%	—
12/13*	184	(0)	—	—
11/09	134	0	0.2%	—
Annual Growth	8.8%	27.5%	—	—

*Fiscal year change

2015 Year-End Financials
Return on assets: 2.4%
Return on equity: 0.4%
Current ratio: 3.80
Cash ($ mil.): 12

LAFAYETTE COLLEGE

Lafayette College has a revolutionary background. Named after the French hero of the American Revolution the school offers bachelor's degrees in 37 areas of study in engineering sciences and the arts. Some 2450 students — all undergraduates — are enrolled on the campus located about 70 miles west of New York City and 60 miles north of Philadelphia. Students come from 46 US states and territories and from 48 other countries. Lafayette is a member of the Lehigh Valley Association of Independent Colleges which also includes Cedar Crest College DeSales University Lehigh University Moravian College and Muhlenberg College.

Operations

Lafayette is an independent coeducational residential undergraduate institution. Its offers majors in Africana Studies American Studies Biochemistry International Affairs A.B. International Studies/B.S. Engineering Mathematics and Economics Neuroscience and Russian and East European Studies.

All 215 full-time Lafayette faculty have a PhD or equivalent degree. The college has a 10.5:1 student-faculty ratio.

Financial Performance

The college charged students $59155 for the 2014-15 academic year. Lafayette has an endowment of more than $750 million. Revenue increased 6% in 2013 due to tuition and fee increases. The school went from negative net assets to a $70 million increase on the strength of the improved tuition and fees plus returned scholarships and grants. Cash flow was still in the negative but it went from $8 million to $7 million. Invest-

ments and financing activities served to buoy overall cash flow into the black.

Strategy

In addition to offering a multi-discipline approach that involves cross pollinating the engineering curriculum with liberal arts classes and vice versa the school focuses on using donor gifts to improve its facilities. It has broken ground on a new arts campus with space for theater film and media studies and on a green built education center.

Company Background

The college was founded in 1826 by the citizens of Easton Pennsylvania and named in honor of the Marquis de Lafayette the French-born hero of the American Revolution and associate of George Washington and Thomas Jefferson.

EXECUTIVES

Vice President, James Krivoski
Vice President Business Affairs and Treasurer, Mitchell Wein
Vice President of Public Relations, Kristin Garbarini
Vice President of Operations, Bethany Rack
Vice President of Membership, Jackie Cirincione
Vice President of Communications, Robert J Massa
Vice President, Eugene Warnick
Vice President, Brian McAtee
Co President, Samantha Patterson
Department Head, Jeffrey Pfaffmann
Associate Vice President of Finance and Business Affairs, Stephen Schafer
Vice President, Karolina Vera
Vice President of Membership, Casey White
Executive Vice President, Olivia Andersen
Vice President of Operations, Elise Reynolds
Vice President of Public Relations, Katherine Cook
Executive Vice President, Kaitlyn Calogero
Vice President of Public Relations, Alaina Ciccone
Vice President for Communications and Marketing, Mark Eyerly
Vice President For Enrollment Management, Greg MacDonald
Treasurer, Shawn Hogan
Secretary, Mary Foulk
Secretary, Lisa Mutton
Secretary, Amy Torrisi
Secretary, Tamar Jakeli
Secretary To Director of Athletics and Administrator, Emil Lukas
Secretary, Billie L Weiss
Secretary, Lisa Pezzino
Secretary, Tammy Yeakel
Secretary, Susan Castelletti
Secretary, Cody Zaccagnino
Secretary, Maureen Banas
Co Chairman, Rand Lewis
Secretary, Maureen Mulrooney
Secretary, Melanie Contreras
Auditors: CLIFTONLARSONALLEN LLP PLYMOU

LOCATIONS

HQ: LAFAYETTE COLLEGE
730 HIGH ST, EASTON, PA 180421761
Phone: 610 330-5000
Web: WWW.LAFAYETTEINN.COM

PRODUCTS/OPERATIONS

Selected Programs
Africana Studies
American Studies (A.B.)
Anthropology and Sociology (A.B.)
Art (A.B.)
Asian Studies (A.B.)
Biochemistry (A.B. and B.S.)
Biology (A.B. and B.S.)
Chemical Engineering (B.S.)
Chemistry (A.B. and B.S.)
Civil Engineering (B.S.)

Computer Science (A.B. and B.S.)
Economics (A.B.)
Electrical and Computer Engineering (B.S.)
Engineering (B.S.) and International Studies (A.B.)
Engineering Studies (A.B.)
English (A.B.)
Environmental Studies (A.B.)
Environmental Science (B.S.)
Film and Media Studies (A.B.)
French (A.B.)
Geology (A.B. and B.S.)
German (A.B.)
Government and Law (A.B.)
Government and Law & Foreign Language (A.B.)
History (A.B.)
International Affairs (A.B.)
Mathematics (A.B. and B.S.)
Mathematics-Economics (A.B.)
Mechanical Engineering (B.S.)
Music (A.B.)
Neuroscience (B.S.)
Philosophy (A.B.)
Physics (A.B. and B.S.)
Policy Studies (A.B.)
Psychology (A.B. and B.S.)
Religion and Politics (A.B.)
Religious Studies (A.B.)
Russian and East European Studies (A.B.)
Spanish (A.B.)
Theater (A.B.)
Women's and Gender Studies (A.B.)

HISTORICAL FINANCIALS
Company Type: Private

Income Statement
FYE: June 30

	REVENUE ($ mil.)	NET INCOME ($ mil.)	NET PROFIT MARGIN	EMPLOYEES
06/15	265	73	27.6%	675
06/14	145	97	67.2%	—
06/13	142	69	49.0%	—
06/12	134	(25)	—	—
Annual Growth	25.5%	—	—	—

2015 Year-End Financials
Return on assets: 3.9%
Return on equity: 27.6%
Current ratio: 0.30
Cash ($ mil.): 53

LAFAYETTE GENERAL HEALTH SYSTEM, INC.

EXECUTIVES

Chairman of the Board, Clay M Allen
Director, Lana Adams
Auditors: LAPORTE METAIRIE LA

LOCATIONS

HQ: LAFAYETTE GENERAL HEALTH SYSTEM, INC.
1214 COOLIDGE BLVD, LAFAYETTE, LA 705032621
Phone: 337 289-8125

HISTORICAL FINANCIALS
Company Type: Private

Income Statement
FYE: September 30

	REVENUE ($ mil.)	NET INCOME ($ mil.)	NET PROFIT MARGIN	EMPLOYEES
09/15	585	18	3.2%	2,600
09/14	495	24	5.0%	—
09/13	31	25	79.5%	—
09/12	320	19	6.2%	—
Annual Growth	22.2%	(2.3%)	—	—

2015 Year-End Financials
Return on assets: 7.7%
Return on equity: 3.2%
Current ratio: 1.40
Cash ($ mil.): 61

LAFAYETTE GENERAL MEDICAL CENTER INC

Serving the people of Acadiana (southern Louisiana) Lafayette General Medical Center (LGMC) provides general inpatient medical and surgical care as well as specialized trauma care and neonatal intensive care. The nonprofit hospital which has 365 beds also offers a cancer center home health services outpatient care occupational medicine and mental health care. As part of umbrella group Lafayette Health LGMC is affiliated with Lafayette General Surgical Hospital Lafayette General Southwest St. Martin Hospital Acadia General Hospital University Hospital and Clinics and Abrom Kaplan Memorial Hospital. It's also a teaching hospital for LSU. Non-profit foundation Lafayette General Foundation supports and governs Lafayette Health.

Operations

LGMC has evolved from a six-bed sanitarium that opened in 1911 to become the region's only community-owned and managed hospital. The 10-floor hospital now has larger rooms bathrooms and showers. It has also updated the Louisiana Extended Care Hospital its long-term acute care unit as well as its adult emergency department. New pediatric treatment and waiting areas were added to the emergency department and a new inpatient rehab unit was created. In 2013 LGMC became a teaching hospital for nearby Louisiana State University (LSU).

A strong community member LGMC not only makes financial contributions to further medical education and research it also coordinates events and provides free screenings to the public it serves.

Strategy

Like many health care providers facing reforms in the industry the hospital is developing a new patient-centered model of care delivery using evidenced-based practices and collaboration between patients their families and clinical ancillary and support staff members to improve outcomes and gain efficiencies. LGMC has been the first hospital in the area to bring in new technology like the DaVinci robotic surgical system to offer wifi access hospital-wide and to continuously upgrade and expand its facilities.

EXECUTIVES

Executive Director, Caroline Huval
Executive Director, John Burdin
Manager, Robin Locke
Manager, Dianne M Chapagne
Manager, Hebert Jenny
Director, Jamie Thaw
Senior Vice-President, Susan Johnson
President, Wendy Alexander
Director, Jessica Hanks

LOCATIONS

HQ: LAFAYETTE GENERAL MEDICAL CENTER INC
1214 COOLIDGE BLVD, LAFAYETTE, LA 705032621
Phone: 337 289-7991

COMPETITORS

Baton Rouge General	LifePoint Health
CHRISTUS St. Frances	Our Lady of Lourdes
Cabrini Hospital	Women & Children's
HCA	Hospital

HISTORICAL FINANCIALS
Company Type: Private

Income Statement — FYE: September 30

	REVENUE ($ mil.)	NET INCOME ($ mil.)	NET PROFIT MARGIN	EMPLOYEES
09/15	428	55	12.9%	1,626
09/14	357	58	16.5%	—
09/13	342	44	12.9%	—
09/12	268	25	9.6%	—
Annual Growth	17.0%	29.2%	—	—

2015 Year-End Financials

Return on assets: 17.6%   Cash ($ mil.): 19
Return on equity: 12.9%
Current ratio: 0.80

LAFAYETTE PARISH SCHOOL BOARD

EXECUTIVES

Director of Finance, Mathew Dugas
Consultant, Bart Thibodeaux
Supervisor, Catherine Venable
Accountant, Suzanna Boyd
Auditors: KOLDER CHAMPAGNE SLAVEN & CO

LOCATIONS

HQ: LAFAYETTE PARISH SCHOOL BOARD
   113 CHAPLIN DR, LAFAYETTE, LA 705082101
Phone: 337 521-7000
Web: WWW.LPSSONLINE.COM

HISTORICAL FINANCIALS
Company Type: Private

Income Statement — FYE: June 30

	REVENUE ($ mil.)	NET INCOME ($ mil.)	NET PROFIT MARGIN	EMPLOYEES
06/16	342	(2)	—	3,400
06/15	345	(6)	—	—
06/14	346	0	0.1%	—
06/13	339	45	13.5%	—
Annual Growth	0.3%	—	—	—

2016 Year-End Financials

Return on assets: 12.8%   Cash ($ mil.): 168
Return on equity: (-0.7%)
Current ratio: —

LAHEY CLINIC HOSPITAL, INC.

EXECUTIVES

Chief Executive Officer, Howard R Grant JD
Board of Directors, John Libertino
Officer, Kathleen Jose

Treasurer, Timothy P Connor
Administrative Assistant, Linda Pratt

LOCATIONS

HQ: LAHEY CLINIC HOSPITAL, INC.
   41 MALL RD, BURLINGTON, MA 018050002
Phone: 781 273-5100
Web: WWW.LAHEY.ORG

HISTORICAL FINANCIALS
Company Type: Private

Income Statement — FYE: September 30

	REVENUE ($ mil.)	NET INCOME ($ mil.)	NET PROFIT MARGIN	EMPLOYEES
09/15	816	(17)	—	5,000
09/14	800	(0)	—	—
09/13	774	228	29.5%	—
09/12	796	192	24.1%	—
Annual Growth	0.8%	—	—	—

2015 Year-End Financials

Return on assets: 4.2%   Cash ($ mil.): 105
Return on equity: (-2.1%)
Current ratio: 0.70

LAHEY CLINIC, INC.

EXECUTIVES

Chief Executive Officer, Joanne Conroy
Director, Paul Deviller
Executive Vice-President, Richard W Nesto

LOCATIONS

HQ: LAHEY CLINIC, INC.
   41 MALL RD, BURLINGTON, MA 018050002
Phone: 781 744-5100

HISTORICAL FINANCIALS
Company Type: Private

Income Statement — FYE: September 30

	REVENUE ($ mil.)	NET INCOME ($ mil.)	NET PROFIT MARGIN	EMPLOYEES
09/15	816	(17)	—	5,000
09/09	227	(16)	—	—
09/05	679	57	8.4%	—
Annual Growth	1.9%	—	—	—

2015 Year-End Financials

Return on assets: 4.2%   Cash ($ mil.): 105
Return on equity: (-2.1%)
Current ratio: 0.70

LAKE ELSINORE UNIFIED SCHOOL DISTRICT

EXECUTIVES

Superintendent, Sharron Lindsay
Finance Manager, Alain Guevara
Consultant, Robin Reimer
Assistant Manager, Greg Bowers

LOCATIONS

HQ: LAKE ELSINORE UNIFIED SCHOOL DISTRICT
   545 CHANEY ST, LAKE ELSINORE, CA 925302712
Phone: 951 253-7000
Web: WWW.LEUSD.K12.CA.US

HISTORICAL FINANCIALS
Company Type: Private

Income Statement — FYE: June 30

	REVENUE ($ mil.)	NET INCOME ($ mil.)	NET PROFIT MARGIN	EMPLOYEES
06/16	255	19	7.6%	1,919
06/11	183	2	1.1%	—
06/06	0	0	—	—
06/04	37	(110)	—	—
Annual Growth	17.3%	—	—	—

LAKE REGIONAL HEALTH SYSTEM

EXECUTIVES

Chief Executive Officer, Dane Henry
Executive Secretary, Kathy Hoemeyer
Administrative Assistant, Connie Tharp
Director, Bill Robison
Director, Anthony Koch
Auditors: BKD LLP SPRINGFIELD MISSOURI

LOCATIONS

HQ: LAKE REGIONAL HEALTH SYSTEM
   54 HOSPITAL DR, OSAGE BEACH, MO 650653050
Phone: 573 348-8000
Web: WWW.LAKEREGIONAL.COM

HISTORICAL FINANCIALS
Company Type: Private

Income Statement — FYE: April 30

	REVENUE ($ mil.)	NET INCOME ($ mil.)	NET PROFIT MARGIN	EMPLOYEES
04/16	175	5	3.2%	1,300
04/15	175	14	8.1%	—
04/14	167	6	3.7%	—
04/13	161	(0)	—	—
Annual Growth	2.8%	—	—	—

2016 Year-End Financials

Return on assets: 3.2%   Cash ($ mil.): 17
Return on equity: 3.2%
Current ratio: 1.30

LAKE WALLED CONSOLIDATED SCHOOL DISTRICT

EXECUTIVES

Superintendent, Kenneth Gutman

LOCATIONS

HQ: LAKE WALLED CONSOLIDATED SCHOOL
DISTRICT
850 LADD RD BLDG D, WALLED LAKE, MI
483903019
Phone: 248 956-2000
Web: WWW.WLCSD.ORG

HISTORICAL FINANCIALS

Company Type: Private

Income Statement

FYE: June 30

	REVENUE ($ mil.)	NET INCOME ($ mil.)	NET PROFIT MARGIN	EMPLOYEES
06/16	185	(20)	—	1,482
06/15	186	(19)	—	—
06/14	180	59	32.7%	—
06/13	175	(8)	—	—
Annual Growth	1.8%	—	—	—

LAKELAND REGIONAL HEALTH SYSTEMS, INC.

EXECUTIVES

President, Jack T Stephens
Senior Manager, Karen Stebbins
Director, Rob Roy
Auditors: KPMG LLP TAMPA FL

LOCATIONS

HQ: LAKELAND REGIONAL HEALTH SYSTEMS, INC.
1324 LAKELAND HILLS BLVD, LAKELAND, FL
338054543
Phone: 863 687-1100

HISTORICAL FINANCIALS

Company Type: Private

Income Statement

FYE: September 30

	REVENUE ($ mil.)	NET INCOME ($ mil.)	NET PROFIT MARGIN	EMPLOYEES
09/15	730	30	4.2%	3,124
09/14	685	67	9.9%	—
09/13	24	(13)	—	—
09/12	582	67	11.6%	—
Annual Growth	7.8%	(22.8%)	—	—

2015 Year-End Financials

Return on assets: 7.8%   Cash ($ mil.): 36
Return on equity: 4.2%
Current ratio: 1.20

LAKELAND REGIONAL MEDICAL CENTER, INC.

Lakeland Regional Medical Center (LRMC) serves Florida's Polk County (roughly between Kissimmee and Tampa) through an acute care hospital with approximately 850 beds. Among its specialty services are cardiac care cancer treatment senior care urology emergency medicine orthopedics women's and children's health care and surgery. LRMC also operates general care and specialty outpatient clinics. Additionally the hospital provides medical training programs for radiology specialists. Its LRMC Foundation offers financial support for indigent patients facing ongoing treatment.

Operations

LRMC is part of Lakeland Regional Health System a not-for-profit organization that also includes Lakeland Regional Cancer Center Lakeland Regional Family Health Center and Lakeland Regional Health Medical Group.

Annually LRMC has more than 41000 admissions and performs more than 15000 surgeries. Its emergency department treats more than 200000 patients each year.

Financial Performance

Revenue in 2014 totaled $633 million (representing 92% of Lakeland Regional Health System's revenue) while net income totaled $67 million.

LRMC funds its activities through charges to patients for inpatient and outpatient services as well as from non-hospital activities such as its cafeteria gift and uniform shops and physicians' answering service. Although the hospital also receives payment from federal agencies such as Medicaid and Medicare they along with other managed care entities have cut their reimbursement levels causing LRMC's charity care levels to increase.

Strategy

The hospital has been undergoing facility and data systems improvement efforts to enhance care and increase efficiencies. It recently expanded its intensive care department and upgraded technology in areas including radiology orthopedics and chemotherapy.

In 2014 Lakeland Regional Health System announced plans to build an eight-story women and children pavilion at LRMC. The $250 million addition will include 300000 sq. ft. of space including 32 private rooms for mothers and newborns a 30-bed neonatal intensive care unit 64 private rooms for women's surgical and medical care three surgical suites and 12 private suites for labor delivery and recovery. It will also have an education and conference center. The pavilion is expected to open in 2017.

EXECUTIVES

President and Chief Medical Officer, Mack Reavis
Auditors: KPMG LLP TAMPA FL

LOCATIONS

HQ: LAKELAND REGIONAL MEDICAL CENTER, INC.
1324 LAKELAND HILLS BLVD, LAKELAND, FL
338054500
Phone: 863 687-1100
Web: WWW.LRMC.COM

PRODUCTS/OPERATIONS

Selected Facilities

Lakeland Regional Cancer Center
Lakeland Regional Medical Center (LRMC) Foundation
Lakeland Regional Orthopedics Associates
Lakeland Regional Rehabilitation and Sports Medicine Clinic

Selected Services and Centers

Emergency
Family health center
Gastroenterology
Heart center
Mental health & addictions
Neurosurgery
Nursing
Oncology care
Orthopedic care
Palliative care
Pharmacy
Rehabilitation and sports medicine clinic
Robotic surgery
School of radiologic technology
Stroke center
Surgery
Trauma services
Women and children
Wound center

COMPETITORS

Adventist Health System Sunbelt Healthcare
All Children's Hospital
Baptist Health South Florida
BayCare Health System
Bayfront Health
DeSoto Memorial
Florida Hospital Tampa Bay Division
HCA
Manatee Memorial Hospital
Sarasota Memorial Health Care
Tampa General Hospital
Winter Haven Hospital

HISTORICAL FINANCIALS

Company Type: Private

Income Statement

FYE: September 30

	REVENUE ($ mil.)	NET INCOME ($ mil.)	NET PROFIT MARGIN	EMPLOYEES
09/15	674	68	10.2%	3,100
09/14	618	66	10.8%	—
09/13	584	55	9.4%	—
09/11	0	0	1.0%	—
Annual Growth	472.2%	919.5%	—	—

2015 Year-End Financials

Return on assets: 8.1%   Cash ($ mil.): —
Return on equity: 10.2%
Current ratio: 0.90

LAKEVIEW CENTER, INC

EXECUTIVES

President, Gary L Bembry
Vice-President, Rich Gilmartin
Vice-President, Dennis Goodspeed
Vice-President, Shawn Salamida
Chief Operating Officer, Tra Williams
Manager, Nancy Kirton
Director, Pam Beasley
Finance Manager, Angela Brewton
Auditors: ERNST & YOUNG LLP

LOCATIONS

HQ: LAKEVIEW CENTER, INC
1221 W LAKEVIEW AVE, PENSACOLA, FL 325011836
Phone: 850 432-1222
Web: WWW.ELAKEVIEWCENTER.ORG

Income Statement   FYE: September 30

	REVENUE ($ mil.)	NET INCOME ($ mil.)	NET PROFIT MARGIN	EMPLOYEES
09/16	257	23	9.1%	1,900
09/15	231	11	4.9%	—
09/14	217	17	8.1%	—
Annual Growth	8.8%	15.1%	—	—

2016 Year-End Financials

Return on assets: 4.7%   Cash ($ mil.): 54
Return on equity: 9.1%
Current ratio: 2.10

LAMAR CONSOLIDATED INDEPENDENT SCHOOL DISTRICT (INC)

EXECUTIVES

Superintendent, Thomas Randle
Board of Directors, Kay Danziger
Director, Bobbi Treacy
Auditors: NULL-LAIRSON PC HOUSTON TX

LOCATIONS

HQ: LAMAR CONSOLIDATED INDEPENDENT SCHOOL DISTRICT (INC)
  3911 AVENUE I, ROSENBERG, TX 774713901
Phone: 832 223-0000
Web: WWW.LCISD.ORG

HISTORICAL FINANCIALS
Company Type: Private

Income Statement   FYE: August 31

	REVENUE ($ mil.)	NET INCOME ($ mil.)	NET PROFIT MARGIN	EMPLOYEES
08/16	320	(77)	—	4,200
08/06*	169	(57)	—	—
12/05	0	0	—	—
08/04	1,083	0	—	—
Annual Growth	—	—	—	—

*Fiscal year change

LAMEX FOODS INC.

EXECUTIVES

Chief Executive Officer, Phillip O Wallace
Credit Manager, Roxie Trevino
Account Manager, Andy Gillquist

LOCATIONS

HQ: LAMEX FOODS INC.
  8500 NORMANDALE STE 1150, BLOOMINGTON, MN 55437
Phone: 952 844-0585
Web: WWW.LAMEXFOODS.EU

Income Statement   FYE: March 31

	REVENUE ($ mil.)	NET INCOME ($ mil.)	NET PROFIT MARGIN	EMPLOYEES
03/16	501	7	1.6%	47
03/15	592	7	1.3%	—
03/05	103	1	1.0%	—
03/04	76	0	0.9%	—
Annual Growth	16.9%	22.7%	—	—

2016 Year-End Financials

Return on assets: 3.5%   Cash ($ mil.): 1
Return on equity: 1.6%
Current ratio: 0.80

LANDMARK SERVICES COOPERATIVE

EXECUTIVES

Chief Executive Officer, Bob Carlson
Credit Manager, Tom Hanes
Marketing Manager, Heather Benson
VP Personnel, Jeremy Henkels
Manager, Bill Cody

LOCATIONS

HQ: LANDMARK SERVICES COOPERATIVE
  1401 LANDMARK DR, COTTAGE GROVE, WI 535278984
Phone: 608 819-3115
Web: WWW.DOITBEST.COM

HISTORICAL FINANCIALS
Company Type: Private

Income Statement   FYE: September 30

	REVENUE ($ mil.)	NET INCOME ($ mil.)	NET PROFIT MARGIN	EMPLOYEES
09/16	383	3	1.0%	400
09/15	418	13	3.2%	—
09/03	76	1	2.0%	—
09/02	56	2	4.9%	—
Annual Growth	14.7%	2.1%	—	—

2016 Year-End Financials

Return on assets: 2.6%   Cash ($ mil.): 32
Return on equity: 1.0%
Current ratio: 1.10

LARAMIE COUNTY SCHOOL DISTRICT 1

EXECUTIVES

Director of Finance, Shawne Metzler
Board of Directors, Alfred Atkins
Board of Directors, Anne Beckle
Assistant Manager, Marc Lahiff
Administrative Assistant, Kyle McKinney
Auditors: MCGEE HEARNE & PAIZ LLP CHE

LOCATIONS

HQ: LARAMIE COUNTY SCHOOL DISTRICT 1
  2810 HOUSE AVE, CHEYENNE, WY 820012860
Phone: 307 771-2100
Web: WWW.LARAMIE1.ORG

HISTORICAL FINANCIALS
Company Type: Private

Income Statement   FYE: June 30

	REVENUE ($ mil.)	NET INCOME ($ mil.)	NET PROFIT MARGIN	EMPLOYEES
06/16	245	3	1.3%	1,600
06/15	244	(7)	—	—
06/14	227	0	0.3%	—
06/12	217	8	3.9%	—
Annual Growth	3.1%	(21.9%)	—	—

2016 Year-End Financials

Return on assets: 3.0%   Cash ($ mil.): 8
Return on equity: 1.3%
Current ratio: 0.30

LAS VEGAS CONVENTION & VISITORS AUTHORITY

EXECUTIVES

Administrative Assistant, Shirley Wiseman
Manager, Steve Dudek
Manager, Mya L Reyes
Director, Scott A Wilson
VP Finance, Brenda Sidall
Manager, Judi Robinson
Manager, Al Guzman
Auditors: PIERCY BOWLER TAYLOR & KERN L

LOCATIONS

HQ: LAS VEGAS CONVENTION & VISITORS AUTHORITY
  3150 PARADISE RD, LAS VEGAS, NV 891099096
Phone: 702 892-0711
Web: WWW.LVCVA.COM

HISTORICAL FINANCIALS
Company Type: Private

Income Statement   FYE: June 30

	REVENUE ($ mil.)	NET INCOME ($ mil.)	NET PROFIT MARGIN	EMPLOYEES
06/16	329	(3)	—	1,100
06/15	298	15	5.1%	—
06/14	291	42	14.7%	—
06/13	259	(19)	—	—
Annual Growth	8.3%	—	—	—

LAUREN ENGINEERS & CONSTRUCTORS, INC.

Lauren Engineers & Constructors is a contractor that targets the power chemical and polymer oil and gas and refining industries. In addition to its core engineering procurement and construction capabilities the company offers fabrication project management and mechanical and electrical maintenance services. With offices in the southern US Lauren Engineers & Constructors serves about 25 states. It also operates in Canada centered from its presence in Calgary. Some of its power and chemical customers include Flying J Florida Power & Light General Electric Company and Procter & Gamble. The company was originally established in 1984 as a subsidiary of Comstock Mechanical.

Operations

Boasting more than 1000 employees companywide the contractor operates its business through three entities.

Lauren Concise an EPC contractor serves Canada's oil and gas sector. Leveraging its parent's strengths Lauren Concise offers turnkey engineering procurement and construction services in the country.

Another subsidiary Kamtech Services Inc. (KSI) is based in Canada and caters to the industrial sector with its building trades expertise in mechanical construction services.

Lauren CCL Engineers Private Limited a leader in Concentrated Solar Power (CSP) provides India with engineering procurement management and construction services for the country's thermal solar power facilities. Headquartered in Navi Mumbai Lauren CCL is a joint venture of CCL Optoelectronics Pvt. Ltd. and Lauren Engineers & Constructors.

Geographic Reach

Lauren Engineers & Constructors which is licensed in some 25 states maintains offices in the US in Georgia Tennessee and Texas as well as in Canada through subsidiary Kamtech Services Inc. (KSI). It operates a joint venture in India.

Sales and Marketing

Lauren Engineers & Constructors serves a variety of customers. Typical clients — large and small — include Florida Power & Light Bosque Power General Electric Calpine Siemens Westinghouse Eastman Chemical DAK Americas Buhler Flying J Murphy Oil and Alon among others.

The company serves several sectors such as power chemical polymers and petrochemical and refining.

Strategy

Lauren Engineers & Constructors' projects range from $500000 shutdowns to $500 million EPC power plants.

Completed projects include the modernization of a chemical plant for BAE Solution in Kingsport Tennessee; plants in Florida Nevada North Carolina and Virginia; and the Godawari Green Energy Limited project in Rajasthan India. The company was awarded a contract in 2013 from Holly Frontier El Dorado Refining for the Naphtha Fractionation and Splitting Project in Kansas.

EXECUTIVES

Executive Vice President Chief Operating Officer, Ron Johnson

LOCATIONS

HQ: LAUREN ENGINEERS & CONSTRUCTORS, INC.
901 S 1ST ST, ABILENE, TX 796021502
Phone: 325 670-9660
Web: WWW.LAURENEC.COM

COMPETITORS

Bechtel	Gemma Power Systems
CH2M HILL	Jacobs Engineering
Fluor	KBR Building Group
ForeRunner Corporation	MYR Group

HISTORICAL FINANCIALS

Company Type: Private

Income Statement

FYE: December 31

	REVENUE ($ mil.)	NET INCOME ($ mil.)	NET PROFIT MARGIN	EMPLOYEES
12/15	582	14	2.4%	1,100
12/14	237	3	1.6%	—
12/13	163	(3)	—	—
12/12	129	(13)	—	—
Annual Growth	65.2%	—	—	—

2015 Year-End Financials

Return on assets: 4.5%
Return on equity: 2.4%
Current ratio: 0.70
Cash ($ mil.): 12

LAWRENCE & MEMORIAL HOSPITAL, INC.

Lawrence & Memorial Hospital (L + M) connects residents of Connecticut with health care whether they're near the Rhode Island border or enjoying the Connecticut River. The not-for-profit hospital founded in 1912 provides services to a 10-town region on the Connecticut shoreline and neighboring areas in the Northeast. L + M has roughly 280 beds and provides general acute care including medical surgical rehabilitative pediatric psychiatric and obstetrical services. The hospital also runs about a dozen community physician practices and specialty clinics. L + M is owned by Yale New Haven Health Services.

Operations

Each year L + M sees some 86000 patients in its emergency room. In all it sees tens of thousands of patients annually. The hospital's specialty programs include a cardiac rehabilitation program a sleep disorder unit and a the region's only neonatal ICU.

Affiliates of the L + M system include Joslin Diabetes Center the Visiting Nurse Association of Southeastern Connecticut and various community organizations with which the hospital advances wellness for the area's population.

Geographic Reach

L + M serves patients in eastern Connecticut as well as Washington County in Rhode Island and the Fishers Island region of New York State.

Strategy

The changing economy and health care landscape in the US has prompted many independent hospitals to seek affiliations with other medical providers as a means of controlling spending and enhancing care and L + M is no exception. It became affiliated with Yale New Haven Health System in 2016 after suffering from operating losses in 2013 2014 and 2015. Yale New Haven has been investing in L + M's growth since the acquisition.

EXECUTIVES

President CEO and Director, Bruce D. Cummings
Vice President and Chief Medical and Clinical Operations Officer, Daniel Rissi
VP and CIO, Kimberly Kalajainen
Vice President and Chief Financial and Support Services Officer, Lou Inzana
Vice President General Counsel, Maureen Anderson
Chief Transformation Officer Vice President, Chris Lehrach
Vice President and Chief Information Officer, Kim Kalajainen
Nursing Director, Lauren Williams
Chairman, Ulysses B. Hammond
Vice Chairman, Granville Morris
Secretary And Registrar, Lisa Kardys

LOCATIONS

HQ: LAWRENCE & MEMORIAL HOSPITAL, INC.
365 MONTAUK AVE, NEW LONDON, CT 063204769
Phone: 860 442-0711
Web: WWW.LMHOSPITAL.ORG

PRODUCTS/OPERATIONS

Selected Services
Core Services
  Cardiac Care
  Maternity Care
  Cancer Care
  Surgery
  Occupational Health Care
Other Services
  Behavioral Medicine
  Chronic Pain
  Diagnostic Imaging
  Emergency Services
  Gastroenterology
  Hand Center
  Infectious Diseases
  Joint Replacement Center
  Joslin Diabetes Center
  Laboratory
  Neurosurgery
  Pulmonary Disorders
  Pulmonary Rehabilitation
  Rehabilitation - Acute Inpatient
  Rehabilitation - Signature Outpatient
  Sleep Center
  Social Work
  Women's and Infants Services
  Wound and Hyperbaric Center

COMPETITORS

Backus
  Care New England
  Connecticut Children's Medical Center
  Day Kimball Hospital
  Harrington Memorial Hospital
  Hartford Health Care
  Hospital of Central Connecticut
  Kent Hospital
  Roger Williams Medical Center
  Saint Francis Hospital and Medical Center
  Sturdy Memorial
  University of Connecticut Health Center
  Waterbury Hospital

HISTORICAL FINANCIALS

Company Type: Private

Income Statement

FYE: September 30

	REVENUE ($ mil.)	NET INCOME ($ mil.)	NET PROFIT MARGIN	EMPLOYEES
09/16	346	(17)		2,200
09/15	339	14	4.3%	—
09/14	337	5	1.8%	—
09/13	315	10	3.4%	—
Annual Growth	3.2%	—	—	—

2016 Year-End Financials

Return on assets: 9.2%   Cash ($ mil.): 3
Return on equity: (-5.1%)
Current ratio: 0.60

LAWRENCE GENERAL HOSPITAL

EXECUTIVES

Principal, Dianne J Anderson
Manager, Dave Deramo
Director, Ann Marie Giarusso
Assistant Controller, Greg Parsons

LOCATIONS

HQ: LAWRENCE GENERAL HOSPITAL
1 GENERAL ST, LAWRENCE, MA 018412997
Phone: 978 683-4000
Web: WWW.LAWRENCEGENERAL.ORG

HISTORICAL FINANCIALS

Company Type: Private

Income Statement

FYE: September 30

	REVENUE ($ mil.)	NET INCOME ($ mil.)	NET PROFIT MARGIN	EMPLOYEES
09/16	249	(4)	—	1,405
09/15	203	(3)	—	—
09/14	185	8	4.8%	—
09/13	191	9	5.0%	—
Annual Growth	9.3%	—	—	—

2016 Year-End Financials

Return on assets: 11.3%   Cash ($ mil.): 23
Return on equity: (-1.8%)
Current ratio: 1.20

LAWRENCE HOSPITAL CENTER

EXECUTIVES

President, Edward M Dinan
Manager, Honore Bien
Account Manager, Lavone Mitchell
Director, Jae Lee
Director, Edward Levine

LOCATIONS

HQ: LAWRENCE HOSPITAL CENTER
55 PALMER AVE, BRONXVILLE, NY 107083491
Phone: 914 787-1000
Web: WWW.NYPLAWRENCE.ORG

HISTORICAL FINANCIALS

Company Type: Private

Income Statement

FYE: December 31

	REVENUE ($ mil.)	NET INCOME ($ mil.)	NET PROFIT MARGIN	EMPLOYEES
12/15	212	(7)	—	15,000
12/14	194	16	8.3%	—
12/13	211	7	3.7%	—
12/09	167	20	12.2%	—
Annual Growth	4.0%	—	—	—

2015 Year-End Financials

Return on assets: 4.5%   Cash ($ mil.): 19
Return on equity: (-3.5%)
Current ratio: 1.00

LEANDER INDEPENDENT SCHOOL DISTRICT

EXECUTIVES

Superintendent, Bret A Champion
Accountant, Dana Paulson
Manager, Becky Wolfenburger
Manager, Dale Walker

LOCATIONS

HQ: LEANDER INDEPENDENT SCHOOL DISTRICT
204 W SOUTH ST, LEANDER, TX 786411719
Phone: 512 570-0000
Web: WWW.LEANDERISD.ORG

HISTORICAL FINANCIALS

Company Type: Private

Income Statement

FYE: August 31

	REVENUE ($ mil.)	NET INCOME ($ mil.)	NET PROFIT MARGIN	EMPLOYEES
08/16	414	(36)	—	2,700
08/07	239	9	3.8%	—
08/06	197	98	49.9%	—
08/05	22	(8)	—	—
Annual Growth	30.3%	—	—	—

2016 Year-End Financials

Return on assets: 4.8%   Cash ($ mil.): 292
Return on equity: (-8.9%)
Current ratio: 3.40

LEBANESE AMERICAN UNIVERSITY

EXECUTIVES

President, Dr Joseph G Jabbra
Director, David Grosner
Auditors: LB PLANTE & MORAN PLLC AUBURN

LOCATIONS

HQ: LEBANESE AMERICAN UNIVERSITY
211 E 46TH ST FL 3, NEW YORK, NY 100172912
Phone: 212 203-4333
Web: WWW.LAU.EDU.LB

HISTORICAL FINANCIALS

Company Type: Private

Income Statement

FYE: September 30

	REVENUE ($ mil.)	NET INCOME ($ mil.)	NET PROFIT MARGIN	EMPLOYEES
09/15	217	61	28.2%	13
09/14	203	62	30.6%	—
09/13	182	57	31.5%	—
09/10	128	34	26.9%	—
Annual Growth	11.2%	12.2%	—	—

2015 Year-End Financials

Return on assets: 18.9%   Cash ($ mil.): 170
Return on equity: 28.2%
Current ratio: 1.80

LEE COUNTY ELECTRIC COOPERATIVE, INC.

If you are a Floridian who is a really early riser or a night owl Lee County Electric Cooperative (LCEC) may help light your way. The electric cooperative provides power to more than 198880 residential and commercial customers across five counties in southwestern Florida (Lee County and parts of Collier Hendry Charlotte and Broward counties. The member-owned non-profit electric utility operates more than 8000 miles of transmission and distribution lines and more than 20 substations. Tampa-based Seminole Electric Cooperative serves as LCEC's wholesale power supplier.

Geographic Reach

The company's service territory includes Cape Coral North Fort Myers Marco Island Sanibel and Captiva Islands Pine Island Everglades City Immokalee and parts of Lehigh Acres.

Financial Performance

In 2012 LCEC's revenues declined by 0.3% as the result of abnormally mild weather and conservation efforts by customers coupled with ongoing economic uncertainty all of which trimmed demand. Net income decreased by 11% in 2012 as the drop in net sales outpaced only slightly lower operating costs for the year.

As part of its non-profit charter LCEC returns surplus equity to its current and former members. In 2012 its Board of Trustees approved $12.9 million in equity distribution.

Strategy

The cooperative is working on a number of strategic initiatives in order to keep up with the demands of the growing population in its service area: maintain power quality enhance disaster recovery competency keep up with regulatory compliance requirements implement mobile workforce technology and keep employees engaged.

To better support its customers that year LCEC upgraded its website with improved navigation and additional energy management tips and tools.

Company Background

Under the leadership of Homer Welch (and as part of a nationwide rural electrification drive) LCEC began operations with 15 miles of distribu-

tion line and 158 members or about 1% of Lee County's 1940 population of 17500.

EXECUTIVES

Chief Executive Officer, Dennie Hamilton
Supervisor, Cheryl Fuoss
Engineer, Jesus Claro
Supervisor, Kevin Hobstetter

LOCATIONS

HQ: LEE COUNTY ELECTRIC COOPERATIVE, INC.
4980 BAYLINE DR, FORT MYERS, FL 339173998
Phone: 800 599-2356
Web: WWW.LCEC.NET

HISTORICAL FINANCIALS

Company Type: Private

Income Statement			FYE: December 31	
	REVENUE ($ mil.)	NET INCOME ($ mil.)	NET PROFIT MARGIN	EMPLOYEES
12/15	413	(0)		400
12/12	404	2	0.6%	
Annual Growth	0.8%	—	—	—

2015 Year-End Financials

Return on assets: 11.5%   Cash ($ mil.): 2
Return on equity: (-0.1%)
Current ratio: 0.90

LEE MEMORIAL HOSPITAL, INC.

EXECUTIVES

President, Jim Nathan
Manager, Katherine Kahle
Manager, Ryan Gerber
Operations Manager, Andrea Adams

LOCATIONS

HQ: LEE MEMORIAL HOSPITAL, INC.
2776 CLEVELAND AVE, FORT MYERS, FL 339015855
Phone: 239 343-2000

HISTORICAL FINANCIALS

Company Type: Private

Income Statement			FYE: September 30	
	REVENUE ($ mil.)	NET INCOME ($ mil.)	NET PROFIT MARGIN	EMPLOYEES
09/15	760	145	19.1%	1,159
09/14	688	163	23.8%	—
09/13	632	135	21.4%	—
09/12	613	105	17.3%	—
Annual Growth	7.4%	11.1%	—	—

2015 Year-End Financials

Return on assets: 8.0%   Cash ($ mil.): 19
Return on equity: 19.1%
Current ratio: 0.80

LEE'S SUMMIT R-7 SCHOOL DISTRICT

EXECUTIVES

Superintendent, David McGehee
Administrative Assistant, Rusty Richards

LOCATIONS

HQ: LEE'S SUMMIT R-7 SCHOOL DISTRICT
301 NE TUDOR RD, LEES SUMMIT, MO 640865702
Phone: 816 986-1000
Web: WWW.LSR7.ORG

HISTORICAL FINANCIALS

Company Type: Private

Income Statement			FYE: June 30	
	REVENUE ($ mil.)	NET INCOME ($ mil.)	NET PROFIT MARGIN	EMPLOYEES
06/16	225	4	2.0%	2,503
06/09	0	(0)	—	—
06/07	181	(21)	—	—
06/03	132	0	—	—
Annual Growth	4.2%	—	—	—

2016 Year-End Financials

Return on assets: —   Cash ($ mil.): 2
Return on equity: 2.0%
Current ratio: —

LEESAR, INC.

EXECUTIVES

President, Robert Simpson
Manager, Angela Ridley
Account Manager, Anissa Barksdale
Director, Brad Green
Executive Director, Dan Fitzgerald
Manager, Bryan Jones
Auditors: BOBBITT PITTENGER & COMPANY PA

LOCATIONS

HQ: LEESAR, INC.
2727 WINKLER AVE, FORT MYERS, FL 339019358
Phone: 239 939-8800
Web: WWW.LEESAR.COM

HISTORICAL FINANCIALS

Company Type: Private

Income Statement			FYE: September 30	
	REVENUE ($ mil.)	NET INCOME ($ mil.)	NET PROFIT MARGIN	EMPLOYEES
09/15	218	4	2.0%	280
09/13	180	5	2.9%	—
Annual Growth	10.0%	(8.9%)	—	—

2015 Year-End Financials

Return on assets: 9.5%   Cash ($ mil.): 12
Return on equity: 2.0%
Current ratio: 1.40

LEESBURG REGIONAL MEDICAL CENTER, INC.

EXECUTIVES

Chief Executive Officer, Don Henderson
Manager, Tammy Wolfle
Manager, Marjorie Dextraze
Vice-President, Alex Chang
Supervisor, Jerry Pressley
VP Personnel, Amie Richardson
Auditors: KPMG LLP GREENSBORO NC

LOCATIONS

HQ: LEESBURG REGIONAL MEDICAL CENTER, INC.
600 E DIXIE AVE, LEESBURG, FL 347485999
Phone: 352 323-5762
Web: WWW.CFHALLIANCE.ORG

HISTORICAL FINANCIALS

Company Type: Private

Income Statement			FYE: June 30	
	REVENUE ($ mil.)	NET INCOME ($ mil.)	NET PROFIT MARGIN	EMPLOYEES
06/15	236	18	7.9%	1,900
06/14	222	10	4.7%	—
06/13	237	14	5.9%	—
06/12	245	15	6.5%	—
Annual Growth	(1.3%)	5.4%	—	—

2015 Year-End Financials

Return on assets: 16.9%   Cash ($ mil.): 27
Return on equity: 7.9%
Current ratio: 0.60

LEGACY EMANUEL HOSPITAL & HEALTH CENTER

Legacy Emanuel Hospital and Health Center part of the Legacy Health System provides acute and specialized health care to residents of Portland Oregon and surrounding communities. The 420-bed teaching hospital's operations include centers devoted to trauma treatment burn care oncology birthing neurosurgery orthopedics and cardiology. It also houses a pediatric hospital and operates the region's Life Flight Network service which is owned by a consortium of local hospitals. Legacy Emanuel's emergency department handles more than 15600 visits every year.

Operations

Legacy Emanuel's trauma and burn centers are level I designated facilities meaning they receive severe trauma and burn cases from other area hospitals. The hospital's burn center is the only one of its kind in an area stretching from Seattle to Sacramento and Salt Lake City. Other specialist facilities at Legacy Emanuel include its maternity center and its diagnostic imaging and screening units.

The medical center sees more than 18000 inpatients each year. Its staff includes about 140 full-time doctors and dentists as well as 700 full-time registered nurses. The Randall Children's Hospital located within Legacy Emanuel has about 600 af-

filiated pediatricians and specialists on its staff and handles about 100000 patient encounters each year including 20000 emergency room visits.

Strategy

The hospital has undergone massive expansion efforts. The hospital has completed construction of the new Randall Children's Hospital facilities making it one of the largest pediatric facilities in the state. The new pediatric center is four times as large as the past facilities. Other expansion efforts in recent years include new acute and intensive care capacity.

Company Background

To expand its medical transportation services Legacy Emanuel and other owners of LFN teamed up to purchase 15 new helicopters in 2012.

Legacy Emanuel Hospital was established in 1912 by the Lutheran Church.

EXECUTIVES

President, George J Brown
Manager, Ming Jei
Administrative Assistant, Mary Ann McNulty
Manager, Gail Weisgerber
Project Manager, Barri Stiber
Executive Director, Lisa Harris

LOCATIONS

HQ: LEGACY EMANUEL HOSPITAL & HEALTH CENTER
2801 N GANTENBEIN AVE, PORTLAND, OR 972271623
Phone: 503 413-2200

PRODUCTS/OPERATIONS

Selected Centers and Services
Burn care
Cancer care
Children's care
Diabetes and nutrition
Emergency services
Family birth center
Gardens
High-risk obstetrics
Imaging
Injury prevention
Intensive care
Interventional and diagnostic cardiology
Level I trauma center
Life flight network
Maternal-fetal medicine
Neurology and neurosurgery including spine surgery
Orthopedics
Pediatrics
Rehabilitation (inpatient and outpatient)
Radiation oncology
Stroke
Surgery (including minimally invasive surgery)
Vascular clinic
Wound and ostomy clinic
Wound care and outpatient burn clinic

COMPETITORS

Adventist Health   PeaceHealth
  System West   PeaceHealth Southwest
Asante Health System   Medical Center
Dignity Health   Providence St. Joseph
Kadlec Regional   Health
  Medical Center   Salem Hospital

HISTORICAL FINANCIALS
Company Type: Private

Income Statement

	REVENUE ($ mil.)	NET INCOME ($ mil.)	NET PROFIT MARGIN	EMPLOYEES
				FYE: March 31
03/15	705	29	4.2%	3,619
03/14	649	30	4.8%	—
03/13	566	6	1.1%	—
03/12	571	(6)	—	—
Annual Growth	7.3%	—	—	—

LEGACY FARMERS COOPERATIVE

Supporting local farmers gives Blanchard Valley Farmers Cooperative (BVFC) roots and reach. Founded in 1989 BVFC has about 1700 area members. The co-op owns more than a dozen locations including four agronomy stations two seasonal grain facilities a farm and garden store and two petroleum sites. Member-farmers benefit from the co-op's array of products and services including seed feed fertilizer grain crop storage crop applications and farming equipment sales and rental. The feed store also sells mulch birdseed and pet supplies as well as conducts soil testing and arranges seeding and fertilizer programs. BVFC's petroleum locations offer gasoline and home-heating oil among several products.

BVFC's terminal elevator at Fostoria is one of Ohio's largest grain facilities. Its installation and capacity weighing in at 8.77 million bushels allows farmers depositing grain to get through the facility more quickly and store more grain until markets are favorable for selling. In 2011 the co-op handled nearly 27 million bushels throughout all locations.

BVFC's capacity is the result of an expansion during 2010 and 2011 that added two new receiving pits a 30000-bph Hawthorne-Servingleg several massive enclosed-belt conveyors a new 73000-bushel grain bin and new scalehouse and probe. The probe allows the facility to reroute and expedite truck traffic.

Financially BVFC has reportedly averaged a 5% increase through grain marketing. Its cost of operation takes a 1% cut out of total revenue; the remaining revenue is distributed to members. Since 2004 BVFC has averaged more than nine cents per bushel to members.

The co-op's future faces increased competition from large and small rivals such as ADM and Cargill ethanol plants and neighbor co-op Central Ohio Farmers. At the same time farmers who have had better yields at high higher prices have purchased more efficient equipment to plant and harvest crops. As a result the co-op's facilities are pressured to handle more bushels faster. Few growers are also accounting for a higher percentage of business making investment decisions that serve members in far-flung areas more difficult. BVFC in early 2012 began mulling a merger with another cooperative Luckey Farmers. A merger is anticipated to strengthen the co-ops' product offerings and marketing opportunities and provide a more stable cost structure.

EXECUTIVES

Vice President Marketing, Jeffrey Hassler
Vice President Marketing, Brice Berry
Auditors: BALESTRA HARR & SCHERER CPAS

LOCATIONS

HQ: LEGACY FARMERS COOPERATIVE
6566 COUNTY ROAD 236, FINDLAY, OH 458409769
Phone: 419 423-2611
Web: WWW.GRAMPYJOES.COM

PRODUCTS/OPERATIONS

Selected Services
Customer accounting
Feed
Grain
Petroleum
Seasonal grain

COMPETITORS

ADM   Cargill
Ag Processing Inc.   GROWMARK
CHS   Luckey Farmers

HISTORICAL FINANCIALS
Company Type: Private

Income Statement

	REVENUE ($ mil.)	NET INCOME ($ mil.)	NET PROFIT MARGIN	EMPLOYEES
				FYE: February 28
02/15*	278	4	1.7%	122
12/13	321	8	2.5%	—
12/12	335	5	1.6%	—
12/11	292	7	2.5%	—
Annual Growth	(1.6%)	(14.4%)	—	—

*Fiscal year change

2015 Year-End Financials

Return on assets: 3.2%   Cash ($ mil.): —
Return on equity: 1.7%
Current ratio: —

LEGACY HEALTH

Legacy Health System strives to promote positive health in the Portland/Vancouver metropolitan area. A not-for-profit provider of health care services in Oregon and Washington the health system operates half a dozen hospitals including Legacy Emanuel Hospital and Legacy Good Samaritan Hospital all founded by a variety of secular organizations. Legacy Health has more than 1100 total beds and its facilities provide such services as acute and critical care behavioral health and outpatient and health education programs. It also operates home health hospice and research facilities; emergency transportation helicopters; and a number of regional clinics and labs.

Operations

The company's hospitals include: Legacy Emanuel Hospital Randall Children's Hospital Legacy Good Samaritan Medical Center Legacy Meridian Park Medical Center Legacy Mount Hood Medical Center and Legacy Salmon Creek Medical Center in Washington.

Legacy Health System provides inpatient care to about 55000 visitors each year. Its Legacy Medical Group includes 300 affiliated physicians operating about 20 primary care clinics in the region as well as a number of specialty care centers in fields such as obstetrics pediatrics cardiology neurology and orthopedics.

In addition to providing medical care Legacy Health System partners with government and commercial entities to conduct medical research studies.

Geographic Reach

Legacy Health System operates six hospitals more than 50 outpatient clinics and a number of hospice research and diagnostic facilities in the Portland/Vancouver metropolitan area. It has three hospitals located in Portland as well as one each in Gresham Oregon; Tualatin Oregon; and Vancouver Washington.

Financial Performance

Legacy Health System reported a 9% increase in revenues to some $1.5 billion in 2014 marking several straight years of rising revenues due to organic growth.

The system reported a 7% increase in net income to some $95 million in 2014 due to increase

in revenues partially offset by increased operating expenses.

Strategy

The company is focused on improving its existing hospitals. To conveniently bring fresh food directly to clinic patients suffering from chronic diseases in 2014 it opened the My Street Grocery at its Legacy Good Samaritan location in Legacy Emanuel Hospital with a larger more comprehensive storefront expanded days and times. It also opened a new cardiac care center at its Legacy Meridian Park Medical Center in 2013.

Legacy Health is also concentrating on opening new general care and specialty clinics partly through partnerships with area physicians. The addition of new clinics is designed not only to service the needs of small communities but also to ensure that referrals from area doctors help to sustain its nearby hospitals. In 2013 Legacy Health officially expanded its presence to the Westside of Portland with the opening of two new Legacy Medical Group clinics Legacy Medical Group - Cornell and Legacy Medical Group - Forest Heights. The new facilities allow Legacy to broaden its Portland-area offerings by providing pediatric orthopedic diagnostic and sports medicine services among others.

That year Legacy Devers Eye Institute also expanded its geographic presence by opening Legacy Devers Eye Institute - Emanuel.

Legacy Health is also expanding primary care services for residents in Gresham and the surrounding East County communities and has started offering adult primary care services. In 2013 it broke ground on Legacy Laboratory Services' new expanded headquarters — a two-story 62000 sq. ft. structure adjacent to the lab's current facility which it shares with Legacy Research Institute.

In 2015 the system partnered with GoHealth Urgent Care to open urgent care centers in metropolitan Portland. That partnership began with GoHealth's five existing centers (formerly operating under the Northwest Urgent Care brand) and will add multiple new facilities which will operate under the Legacy-GoHealth moniker.

Company Background

The company was founded through the 1989 merger of HealthLink and Good Samaritan Hospital.

EXECUTIVES

SVP and Chief Nursing Officer, Carol Bradley
President and CEO, George J. Brown
Chief Administrative Officer Legacy Meridian Park Medical Center, Allyson Anderson
Chief Administrative Officer Legacy Good Samaritan Medical Center, Jonathan Avery
SVP and CIO, John Kenagy
Chief Admnistrative Officer Randall Children's Hospital at Legacy Emanuel, Bronwyn Houston, age 48
SVP and COO, Mike Newcomb
SVP and Chief Medical Officer, Lewis Low
Chief Administrative Officer Legacy Mount Hood Medical Center, Gretchen Nichols
SVP and CFO, Linda Hoff
Chief Administrative Officer, Bryce Helgerson
Vice President Finance, Gordon Edwards
Clinical Vice President Womens Services and Surgical Services, Duncan Neilson
Auditors: KPMG LLP PORTLAND OREGON

LOCATIONS

HQ: LEGACY HEALTH
1919 NW LOVEJOY ST, PORTLAND, OR 972091503
Phone: 503 415-5600
Web: WWW.LEGACYHEALTH.ORG

PRODUCTS/OPERATIONS

Selected Facilities
Hospitals
Legacy Emanuel Hospital (Portland Oregon)
Legacy Good Samaritan Medical Center (Portland Oregon)
Legacy Meridian Park Medical Center (Tualatin Oregon)
Legacy Mount Hood Medical Center (Gresham Oregon)
Legacy Salmon Creek Medical Center (Vancouver Washington)
Randall Children's Hospital At Legacy Emanuel (Portland Oregon)
Clinics
Legacy Medical Group - Battle Ground
Legacy Medical Group - Fisher's Landing
Legacy Medical Group - Forest Heights
Legacy Medical Group - Good Samaritan
Legacy Medical Group - Lake Oswego
Legacy Medical Group - Mount Hood
Legacy Medical Group - West Linn
Legacy Med
Salmon Creek Family Medicine (Vancouver Washington)
Salmon Creek Internal Medicine (Vancouver Washington)
Urgent Care St. Helens (St. Helens Oregon)

COMPETITORS

Adventist Health System West
Asante Health System
Dignity Health
Kadlec Regional Medical Center
PeaceHealth
Providence St. Joseph Health
Salem Hospital

HISTORICAL FINANCIALS

Company Type: Private

Income Statement				FYE: March 31
	REVENUE ($ mil.)	NET INCOME ($ mil.)	NET PROFIT MARGIN	EMPLOYEES
03/15	1,658	156	9.4%	10,675
03/14	183	9	5.2%	—
03/12*	1,326	(0)	—	—
08/10	1,249	192	15.4%	—
Annual Growth	5.8%	(4.1%)	—	—

*Fiscal year change

2015 Year-End Financials

Return on assets: 2.8%   Cash ($ mil.): 99
Return on equity: 9.4%
Current ratio: 1.50

LEGAL SERVICES CORPORATION

Legal Services Corporation (LSC) works to deliver Francis Bellamy's pledge "with liberty and justice for all." A private not-for-profit entity established by Congress and President Richard Nixon in 1974 LSC helps poor Americans gain equal access to the judicial system. It doesn't provide legal services directly but instead grants funds to independent local programs thoughout the country. It makes grants to more than 130 programs and is the nation's single-largest funder of civil legal aid for the poor (with 811 offices across the US). LSC-funded programs handle about 1.8 million cases each year. About 64 million US citizens are eligible to receive assistance from the organization.

EXECUTIVES

President, James Sandman
Board of Directors, Peter Campbell
Administrative Assistant, Caitlin Maziarz
Editor, Eliot Sasaki
Personnel Director, Rebecca Cohen
Auditors: WITHUM SMITH & BROWN PC PHILA

LOCATIONS

HQ: LEGAL SERVICES CORPORATION
3333 K ST NW STE 1, WASHINGTON, DC 200073522
Phone: 202 295-1500
Web: WWW.LSC.GOV

HISTORICAL FINANCIALS

Company Type: Private

Income Statement				FYE: September 30
	ASSETS ($ mil.)	NET INCOME ($ mil.)	INCOME AS % OF ASSETS	EMPLOYEES
09/15	91	0	1.0%	130
09/14	82	0	0.7%	—
09/13	71	0	0.4%	—
09/12	74	0	1.2%	—
Annual Growth	7.1%	(0.6%)	—	—

2015 Year-End Financials

Return on assets: 0.4%   Sales ($ mil.): 377
Return on equity: 0.2%

LEILA A MANKARIOUS

EXECUTIVES

Owner, Leila A Mankarious PHD
Treasurer, Joseph B Nadol Jr
Purchasing Agent, Joanne Sforza
Auditors: LB PRICEWATERHOUSECOOPERS LLP

LOCATIONS

HQ: LEILA A MANKARIOUS
243 CHARLES ST, BOSTON, MA 021143002
Phone: 617 573-3413

HISTORICAL FINANCIALS

Company Type: Private

Income Statement				FYE: September 30
	REVENUE ($ mil.)	NET INCOME ($ mil.)	NET PROFIT MARGIN	EMPLOYEES
09/15	235	(17)	—	4
09/14	228	0	0.0%	—
09/13	221	(1)	—	—
09/09	229	4	2.0%	—
Annual Growth	0.4%	—	—	—

2015 Year-End Financials

Return on assets: 44.7%   Cash ($ mil.): 1
Return on equity: (-7.2%)
Current ratio: —

LEJEUNE STEEL COMPANY

EXECUTIVES

Chief Executive Officer, Shane Shipman
Chief Financial Officer, Bryan L Kuha
Financial Executive, Scott Hatfield
Assistant Controller, Mike Davis
Quality Control Manager, Jim Honmyhr
Auditors: KPMG LLP MINNEAPOLIS MINNESO

LOCATIONS

HQ: LEJEUNE STEEL COMPANY
  118 W 60TH ST, MINNEAPOLIS, MN 554192319
Phone: 612 861-3321
Web: WWW.LEJEUNESTEEL.COM

HISTORICAL FINANCIALS

Company Type: Private

Income Statement

FYE: December 31

	REVENUE ($ mil.)	NET INCOME ($ mil.)	NET PROFIT MARGIN	EMPLOYEES
12/15	187	9	5.2%	105
12/14	180	9	5.0%	—
12/13	87	5	6.4%	—
12/12	99	6	6.2%	—
Annual Growth	23.8%	16.7%	—	—

LENOX CORPORATION

As the first American brand of china to be used in the White House Lenox sets the table like no other. The company makes and markets tabletop and giftware items under the Lenox Dansk and Gorham names. Under licensing agreements Lenox makes products under additional names such as Donna Karan Lenox Marchesa by Lenox Kathy Ireland Disney Thomas Blackshear and kate spade new york under licensing agreements. Lenox sells its products through gift specialty and department stores as well as online by catalog and through company-operated retail stores. Founded in 1889 by Walter Scott Lenox as the Ceramic Art Company Lenox has been owned by investment firm Clarion Capital Partners since 2009.

Geographic Reach

Pennsylvania-based Lenox has additional locations in Delaware Georgia Maryland Michigan New Jersey New York North Carolina South Carolina Tennessee and Virginia.

Strategy

The US chinamaker has focused on updating and rebuilding its tabletop and bridal businesses by forging partnerships with designers including kate spade and Donna Karan. Lenox is also concentrating on rolling out new products expanding into new product categories and fine-tuning its business processes.

Its products appeal to those looking for china made in the US and who prefer a more casual look and moderate price.

EXECUTIVES

CEO, Katrina L. Helmkamp
Vice President Housewares, Buzz Leer
Vice President Product Development, Robert Bishop
Vice President Finance and Controller, Glenn Segal

Vice President of Sales and Marketing, Buzz Lear
Co-Chairman, Peter B. Cameron, age 70
Auditors: DELOITTE & TOUCHE LLP PHILADE

LOCATIONS

HQ: LENOX CORPORATION
  1414 RADCLIFFE ST FL 1, BRISTOL, PA 190075418
Phone: 267 525-7800
Web: WWW.LENOX.COM

PRODUCTS/OPERATIONS

Selected Collections
Butterfly Meadow
Dansk
Gorham
Holiday
L by Lenox
Opal Innocence
Simply Fine Lenox
Winter Greetings

Selected Products
Dining
Figurines
Gifts
Home decor
Jewelry
Kitchen
Ornaments

COMPETITORS

Blyth	Russell Hobbs
Enesco	Thomas Kinkade Company
Fitz and Floyd	WWRD Holdings
Lifetime Brands	

HISTORICAL FINANCIALS

Company Type: Private

Income Statement

FYE: April 2

	REVENUE ($ mil.)	NET INCOME ($ mil.)	NET PROFIT MARGIN	EMPLOYEES
04/16*	242	5	2.3%	1,098
03/15	224	5	2.6%	—
Annual Growth	8.1%	(3.1%)	—	—

*Fiscal year change

2016 Year-End Financials

Return on assets: 2.4%
Return on equity: 2.3%
Current ratio: 0.60
Cash ($ mil.): 1

LESTER E. COX MEDICAL CENTERS

Lester E. Cox Medical Centers (dba CoxHealth) provides a myriad of medical services to people in Missouri and Arkansas. CoxHealth's network includes five acute care hospitals (with more than 950 beds) and more than 80 physician clinics. Centers for cardiac care cancer treatment orthopedics mental health and women's health are among CoxHealth's specialized care options. Other operations include an ambulance service offering both ground and air transportation the Cox Health Systems HMO the Oxford HealthCare home health agency and educational programs. The organization was named after its primary fundraiser in the 1940s.

Operations

Each year CoxHealth handles about 500000 outpatient visits; 205000 emergency urgent care and trauma visits; 32000 ground ambulance transports; and nearly 4000 births. Its hospitals include

Cox Medical Center South Cox Medical Center Branson Cox North Hospital Cox Monett Hospital and the Meyer Orthopedic and Rehabilitation Hospital. Its specialty clinics include centers for cancer orthopedics cardiovascular care women's and children's health outpatient surgery and diagnostic imaging.

Geographic Reach

CoxHealth serves about 25 communities in 25 counties in southwestern Missouri and northwestern Arkansas. Major facilities are located in Branson Monett and Springfield Missouri.

Sales and Marketing

The organization primarily receives income from commercial insurance reimbursements which account for about 60% of patient revenue. Other payer sources include Medicare and Medicaid plans and self-pay patients.

Strategy

Enduring through blizzards and tornadoes CoxHealth strives to improve its services and the health of its community.

Expanding its geographic coverage in 2013 CoxHealth completed a partnership deal with Skaggs Regional Medical Center which changed its name to Cox Medical Center Branson. CoxHealth plans to invest about $100 million into medical facilities in Branson.

The system also grows by adding or expanding facilities. It started construction of an expansion of its Cox Medical Center South facility in 2013. The organization has launched pediatric general surgery and urology programs as it looks to open the Dee Ann White Women's and Children's Hospital at the facility. In 2014 CoxHealth opened the first phase of its $30 million emergency department expansion at Cox Medical Center Branson. The following year the system opened the Springfield Center for Dyslexia and Learning. Other initiatives include upgrading clinical processes and information technology systems.

Company Background

CoxHealth was founded as Burge Deaconess Hospital in 1908. It became Lester E. Cox Medical Centers in 1968 following the death of Cox a St. Louis businessman who led a series of major fund raising campaigns in the 1940s critical to the survival and growth of the hospital.

EXECUTIVES

Vice President and Chief Medical Officer; and Medical Director Oxford Hospice, Dan Sontheimer
Senior Vice President Chief Hospital Officer, John Duff
Vice President and Chief Nursing Officer, Karen Kramer
SVP and CFO, Jacob McWay
Vice President and Chief Information Officer, Bruce Robison
President Cox HealthPlans, Jeffrey C. (Jeff) Bond
VP and Chief Clinical Officer, Ron Prenger
Vice President; President Cox Monett, Genny Maroc
Vice President; President Oxford Healthcare, Karen Thomas
Chairman Joint Operations Committee and Chief Integrated Physicians, Kenneth Powell
Vice President President Home Parenteral Services, H. Lynn Kelley
President and CEO; Director, Steven D. (Steve) Edwards
President CoxHealth Foundation, Lisa Alexander
President Cox College, Anne Liners Brett
Vice President of Corporate Communications, Laurie Duff
Vice President Administration, Debbie Cain
Medical Director, Kerry Randolph
Associate Vice President, Jann Holland

LOCATIONS

HQ: LESTER E. COX MEDICAL CENTERS
1423 N JEFFERSON AVE, SPRINGFIELD, MO
658021917
Phone: 417 269-3000

PRODUCTS/OPERATIONS

Selected Services

Air Care
Alzheimer's Disease
Behavioral Health
Brain and Spine Disorders
Breast Care
Cancer Services
Children's Health
Diabetes
Dialysis
Ear Nose and Throat (ENT)
Emergency Department
Fitness Centers
Food and Nutrition
Heart and Vascular
Home Health
Hyperbaric Medicine and Wound Care
Neuroscience
Occupational Medicine
Orthopedics
Parenting
Parkinson's Clinic
Pharmacy
Physical Medicine
Pregnancy
Radiology
Rehabilitation
Respiratory Care
Robotic Surgery
Sleep Disorders
Smoking Cessation
Specialty Services
Sports Medicine
Stroke
Trauma Services
Urgent Care
Weight Loss
Wellness Consultations
Women's Health
Workers' Compensation

COMPETITORS

Ascension Health	Shawnee Mission
BJC HealthCare	Medical Center
Catholic Health	Sisters of Charity of
Initiatives	Leavenworth
Children's Mercy	St. Anthony's Medical
Hospital	Center
HCA	Tenet Healthcare
Mercy Health	Truman Medical Centers
Mercy Hospital	Universal Health
Springfield	Services
Saint Luke's Health	University of Kansas
System	Medical Center

HISTORICAL FINANCIALS

Company Type: Private

Income Statement

FYE: September 30

	REVENUE ($ mil.)	NET INCOME ($ mil.)	NET PROFIT MARGIN	EMPLOYEES
09/15	918	9	1.0%	9,100
09/14	898	50	5.6%	—
09/13	858	105	12.3%	—
09/12	843	66	7.9%	—
Annual Growth	2.9%	(48.1%)	—	—

2015 Year-End Financials

Return on assets: 5.7%
Return on equity: 1.0%
Current ratio: 1.50

Cash ($ mil.): 105

LEVI RAY & SHOUP INC

EXECUTIVES

President, Richard H Levi
Board of Directors, Gregory D Collins
Account Manager, Thomas Laughlin
Manager, Jenni Manning
Accountant, Jack Bellmer
Auditors: RSM US LLP SPRINGFIELD ILLIN

LOCATIONS

HQ: LEVI RAY & SHOUP INC
2401 W MONROE ST, SPRINGFIELD, IL 627041439
Phone: 217 793-3800
Web: WWW.LRSWEBSOLUTIONS.COM

HISTORICAL FINANCIALS

Company Type: Private

Income Statement

FYE: July 31

	REVENUE ($ mil.)	NET INCOME ($ mil.)	NET PROFIT MARGIN	EMPLOYEES
07/15	205	50	24.4%	603
07/14	208	50	24.0%	—
07/13	172	42	24.7%	—
07/12	181	46	25.5%	—
Annual Growth	4.2%	2.7%	—	—

2015 Year-End Financials

Return on assets: 2.3%
Return on equity: 24.4%
Current ratio: 0.70

Cash ($ mil.): 27

LEVI STRAUSS & CO.

Pioneering American apparel maker Levi Strauss & Co. (LS&CO.) has jeans in its genes. A global manufacturer of brand-name clothing LS&CO. sells jeans and sportswear under the Levi's Dockers Signature by Levi Strauss and Denizen labels in more than 110 countries. It also markets men's and women's underwear and loungewear. The Haas family (descendants of founder Levi Strauss) controls LS&CO. LS&CO. distributes its brand products through more than 695 company-operated stores located in over 30 countries and through the third-party and first-party online stores. LS&CO. makes more than 75% of its revenue from Levi's branded men's pants.

Operations

Directly or through third parties LS&CO. designs markets and sells jeans casual and dress pants tops shorts skirts jackets footwear and related accessories for men women and children. Company-operated and online stores generated about 30% of revenues in fiscal 2016.

LS&CO. distributes its Levi's and Dockers products through more than 695 company-operated stores located in more than 30 countries including the US and through the third-party and first-party online stores. The company distributes its Levi's and Dockers products nationwide through chain retailers and department stores. Outside the US it distributes products primarily to department stores specialty retailers and approximately 2200 franchised and other brand-dedicated stores.

By product LS&CO. generated more than 75% of its total revenue from men's products during fiscal 2016. Pants made about 75% of total revenue and the Levis' branded products generated more than 85% of total revenue.

Geographic Reach

Iconic LS&CO. sells its products in more than 110 countries. It operates manufacturing distribution and finishing facilities in the Americas Europe and Asia/Pacific regions. The company's Americas segment contributed about 60% to its total revenue during fiscal 2016 while its Europe and Asia (which counts the Middle East and North Africa) segments contributed about 25% and 15% respectively. Its key markets are the US France Germany Mexico and the UK.

Sales and Marketing

A multi-channel marketer LS&CO. sells its products in more than 50000 retail locations worldwide. Its brands lend themselves to a variety of retail formats including chain retailers (JCPenney Kohl's Wal-Mart and Target) department stores (Macy's Nordstrom and Barney's) and company-operated e-commerce sites and online stores of other retailers. Sales to its top 10 wholesale customers have accounted for approximately 30% of revenues.

The company distributes its products through a wide variety of retail formats around the world including chain and department stores franchise stores and shop-in-shops company-operated retail network multi-brand specialty stores mass channel retailers and both company-operated and retailer ecommerce sites.

Altogether LS&CO. spent $284.0 million on advertising in fiscal 2016 up from $276.4 million the prior fiscal period.

Financial Performance

The company's revenue was $4.5 billion during fiscal 2016 up slightly compared to the prior fiscal year. The small increase was largely driven by an increase in revenue from Europe. LS&CO. reported net income of about $291 million for fiscal 2016 which was a slight spike compared to the $209 million the company reported for net income in fiscal 2015. The high cost of producing the goods the company sells along with its selling general administrative and interest expenses resulted in LS&CO.'s modest net income on $4.5 billion in revenue.

Strategy

LS&CO continued in 2016 to follow a handful of growth-oriented measures including: driving profitable growth of its core men's pants brands (Dockers and Levi's); expanding its brand reach and diversifying into new or undertapped geographic markets including China India Russia and Brazil; becoming omni-channel through online stores franchises and company-operated stores; and improving its cost structure to ensure long-term profitable growth.

HISTORY

Levi Strauss arrived in New York City from Bavaria in 1847. In 1853 he joined his brother-in-law David Stern in San Francisco selling dry goods to the gold rushers. Shortly after a prospector told Strauss of miners' problems in finding sturdy pants. Strauss made a pair out of canvas for the prospector; word of the rugged pants spread quickly.

Strauss continued his dry-goods business in the 1860s. During this time he switched the pants' fabric to a durable French cloth called serge de Nimes soon known as denim. He colored the fabric with indigo dye and adopted the idea from Nevada tailor Jacob Davis of reinforcing the pants with copper rivets. In 1873 Strauss and Davis produced their first pair of waist-high overalls (later known as jeans). The pants soon became de rigueur for lumberjacks cowboys railroad workers oil drillers and farmers.

Strauss continued to build his pants and wholesaling business until he died in 1902. Levi Strauss

& Co. passed to four Stern nephews who carried on their uncle's jeans business while maintaining the company's philanthropic reputation.

After WWII Walter Haas and Peter Haas (a fourth-generation Strauss family member) assumed leadership of LS&CO. In 1948 they ended the company's wholesaling business to concentrate on Levi's clothing. In the 1950s Levi's jeans ceased to be merely functional garments for workers; they became the uniform of American youth. In the 1960s LS&CO. added women's attire and expanded overseas.

The company went public in 1971. That year it added a women's career line and bought Koret sportswear (sold in 1984). By the mid-1980s profits declined. Peace Corps-veteran-turned-McKinsey-consultant Robert Haas (Walter's son) grabbed the reins of LS&CO. in 1984 and took the company private the next year (he became chairman in 1989). He also instilled a touchy-feely corporate culture often at odds with the bottom line.

In 1986 LS&CO. introduced Dockers casual pants. The company's sales began rising in 1991 as consumers forsook the designer duds of the 1980s for more practical clothes. LS&CO. says seven out of every 10 American men own a pair of Dockers. However LS&CO. missed out on the birth of another trend: the split between the fashion sense of US adolescents and their Levi's-loving baby boomer parents.

In 1996 the company introduced Slates dress slacks. That year LS&CO. bought back nearly one-third of its stock from family and employees for $4.3 billion. Grappling with slipping sales and debt from the buyout in 1997 LS&CO. closed 11 of its 37 North American plants laying off 6400 workers and 1000 salaried employees; it granted generous severance packages even to those earning minimum wage.

In 1998 citing improved labor conditions in China LS&CO. announced it would step up its use of Chinese subcontractors. Further restructuring added a third of its European plants to the closures list that year. LS&CO.'s sales fell 13% in fiscal 1998. Also that year Haas handed his CEO title to Pepsi executive Philip Marineau; Haas remained chairman.

LS&CO. closed 11 of 22 remaining North American plants in 1999. It also unleashed several new jeans brands that eschewed the company's one-style-fits-all approach of old.

In April 2002 LS&CO. announced it would close six of its last eight US plants and cut 20% of its worldwide staff (3300 workers). In September 2003 it cut another 5% of its global staff (650 workers). That month the company opened its first girls-only store located in Paris. In December LS&CO. replaced CFO Bill Chiasson with an outside turnaround specialist.

Pinpointing 2006 as the best time to step down as the company's chief executive Philip Marineau retired at the end of 2006. John Anderson president of LS&CO.'s Asia/Pacific division and head of the firm's global supply chain unit replaced Marineau as president and CEO.

Levi Strauss chairman Robert Haas retired in 2008 after 18 years in that role. His successor was Dryer's ice cream executive T. Gary Rogers who became the first leader in the company's history who was not a descendant of the founder. In August 2008 CFO Hans Ploos van Amstel left the company the and was replaced by Heidi Manes its corporate controller and principal accounting officer.

Looking to gain a more active role in its store business LS&CO. in July 2009 bought the operating rights for more than 70 Levi's and Dockers Outlet locations from store operator Anchor Blue Retail Group which had filed for bankruptcy for $72 million. Anchor Blue said the US recession

and drop in consumer spending especially among teens severely affected its financial performance. LS&CO. said the acquisition will enable it to better manage its brands' positioning.

Rogers retired in late 2009 and Richard Kauffman became chairman.

EXECUTIVES

EVP; President Europe, Seth M. Ellison, age 58, $609,808 total compensation

President and CEO, Charles V. (Chip) Bergh, age 59, $1,343,077 total compensation

EVP and CFO, Harmit J. Singh, age 53, $746,538 total compensation

EVP and President Global e-Commerce, Marc Rosen, age 48

SVP and Chief Supply Chain Officer, David Love, age 54, $580,387 total compensation

EVP; President Americas, Roy Bagattini, age 53, $690,433 total compensation

EVP; President Levi Brand, James Curleigh, age 51, $523,269 total compensation

EVP; President Global Retail, Carrie Ask, $392,308 total compensation

SVP and Chief Supply Chain Officer, Liz O'Neill

VP Manufacturing, Patty Kimball

Global Vice President Of Women's Design, Jill Guenza

Senior Vice President PA and MARKETING COORDINATOR, Manuela Bellini

Vice President Marketing, Stacy Doren

Vice President Human Resources, Karthik Sarma

Senior Vice President Chief Information Officer, Roland Paanakker

Vice President Human Resources Europe, Hubert Van Nuvel

Vice President Global Logistics, Doug Flores

VICE PRESIDENT INFORMATION TECHNOLOGY, Ramiya Lyer

Chairman, Stephen C. Neal, age 67

Auditors: PRICEWATERHOUSECOOPERS LLP SA

LOCATIONS

HQ: LEVI STRAUSS & CO.
1155 BATTERY ST, SAN FRANCISCO, CA 941111264
Phone: 415 501-6000
Web: WWW.LEVISTRAUSS.COM

2016 Stores

	% of total
Americas region	234
Europe region	267
Asia/Pacific region	196
Total	**697**

2016 Sales

	$ mil.	% of total
Americas	2,683	59
Europe	1,091	24
Asia/Pacific region	778	17
Total	**4,552**	**100**

PRODUCTS/OPERATIONS

2016 Sales

	% of total
Levi's brand	85
Dockers brand	10
Signature by Levi Strauss & Denizen brands	5
Total	**100**

Selected Brands

Denizen
Dockers
  Dockers Alpha Khaki
  Dockers for Men
  Dockers for Women
Levi's
  Levi's 501 Original
  Levi's 505 Straight
  Levi's 511 Skinny
  Levi's 513 Slim
  Levi's 514 Slim Straight
Levi's Curve ID
Signature by Levis Strauss & Co.
Intro
Waterless
Wellthread
Wasteless

COMPETITORS

Abercrombie & Fitch	NIKE
Abercrombie & Fitch	Nautica Apparel
American Eagle Outfitters	Nautica Apparel
American Eagle Outfitters	Nine West
Benetton	Nine West
Benetton	OshKosh B'Gosh
Calvin Klein	OshKosh B'Gosh
Calvin Klein	Oxford Industries
Diesel SpA	Oxford Industries
Diesel SpA	PVH
FUBU	PVH
FUBU	Perry Ellis International
Fast Retailing	Perry Ellis International
Fast Retailing	Ralph Lauren
Fruit of the Loom	Ralph Lauren
Fruit of the Loom	Sean John
Guess?	Sean John
Guess?	Sears
Haggar	Sears
Haggar	Target Corporation
Hugo Boss	Target Corporation
Hugo Boss	The Gap
Inditex	The Gap
Inditex	True Religion Apparel
J. C. Penney	True Religion Apparel
J. C. Penney	Under Armour
J. Crew	Under Armour
J. Crew	VF Corporation
Jockey International	VF Corporation
Jockey International	Victoria's Secret Stores
Joe's Jeans	Victoria's Secret Stores
Joe's Jeans	Wacoal
Kmart	Wacoal
Kmart	Wal-Mart
Kohl's	Wal-Mart
Kohl's	Warnaco Group
Lands' End	Warnaco Group
Lands' End	adidas
Macy's	adidas
Macy's	
NIKE	

HISTORICAL FINANCIALS

Company Type: Private

Income Statement

FYE: November 27

	REVENUE ($ mil.)	NET INCOME ($ mil.)	NET PROFIT MARGIN	EMPLOYEES
11/16	4,552	291	6.4%	13,200
11/15	4,494	209	4.7%	—
11/14	4,753	104	2.2%	—
11/13	4,681	228	4.9%	—
Annual Growth	(0.9%)	8.5%	—	—

2016 Year-End Financials

Return on assets: 5.9%   Cash ($ mil.): 375
Return on equity: 6.4%
Current ratio: 1.10

LEXINGTON MEDICAL CENTER

Lexington Medical Center is a not-for-profit health care organization serving the residents of South Carolina's Lexington County. Established

in 1971 the medical center has some 415 beds and provides general emergency surgical and diagnostic services. Specialty services include cancer treatment cardiovascular care women's health and rehabilitation. Lexington Medical Center also operates a skilled nursing center as well as a network of affiliated community health centers urgent care clinics and affiliated physician practices. The hospital is managed by the Lexington County Health Service District.

Operations

The 414-bed facility is home to the largest extended-care facility in the Carolinas. It sees about 100000 emergency department visits each year.

Altogether the Lexington Medical Center's network of facilities — which includes six community clinics an occupational health center an Alzheimer's care center and 60 doctors' offices — employs some 5900 health professionals.

Strategy

Lexington Medical Center is expanding its facilities to better serve the growing population in its service territory. In 2015 it opened a new cardiac rehabilitation program at its Irmo Medical Park campus. The program — the first of its kind in the area — provides services to patients with a history of heart attack angioplasty heart failure heart transplant bypass surgery or the like.

In 2014 Lexington's physician practice opened a third sleep lab where clinicians can diagnose such conditions as hypersomnia insomnia narcolepsy restless leg syndrome snoring and sleep apnea.

EXECUTIVES

Finance Vice President, Mike Payne
Medical Director for Epic Implementation, Anna Shalkham
Assistant Vice President Revenue Cycle Integrity, Deborah Hunt
Respiratory Therapy Director, Darlene Frye
Vice President Patient Care, Cindy Rohman
Vice President of Finance, DK Walker
Vice President Physician Network, John Moore
Vice President physician Network, Matthew Cogdill
Auditors: KPMG LLP ATLANTA GA

LOCATIONS

HQ: LEXINGTON MEDICAL CENTER
  2720 SUNSET BLVD, WEST COLUMBIA, SC 291694810
Phone: 803 791-2000
Web: WWW.LEXMED.COM

PRODUCTS/OPERATIONS

Selected Services
Patient Care
Alzheimer's Care
Birth Center
Extended Care
Family Medicine
General Surgery
Imaging
Laboratory & Pathology
Occupational Health
Weight-Loss Surgery
Health & Wellness
Community Health Screenings
Health Directions Wellness Center
Nutrition Therapy
Sleep Solutions

Selected Facilities
Community Medical Centers
  LMC Batesburg-Leesville
  LMC Chapin
  LMC Gilbert
  LMC Irmo
  LMC Lexington
  LMC Swansea
Hospital Units
  Alzheimers Care Center

Birth Center
Cancer Center
Emergency Care
Extended Care
Heart Center
Obesity Surgery Center
Urgent Care
Women's Services

COMPETITORS

Carolinas HealthCare System	Greenville Hospital System
Carolinas Hospital System	Laurens County Hospital
Georgetown Hospital System	McLeod Health
Grand Strand Regional Medical Center	Palmetto Health

HISTORICAL FINANCIALS
Company Type: Private

Income Statement
FYE: September 30

	REVENUE ($ mil.)	NET INCOME ($ mil.)	NET PROFIT MARGIN	EMPLOYEES
09/16	906	21	2.3%	5,616
09/15	863	86	10.0%	—
09/14	781	95	12.2%	—
09/13	686	13	2.0%	—
Annual Growth	9.7%	15.0%	—	—

2016 Year-End Financials
Return on assets: 4.8%   Cash ($ mil.): 158
Return on equity: 2.3%
Current ratio: 2.60

LIBERTY UNIVERSITY, INC.

EXECUTIVES

President, Jerry Lamon Falwell Jr
Board of Directors, David M Corry
Manager, Todd Libeau
Manager, Charles Skalaski
Director, Chris Wygal
Vice-President, Johnnie Moore Jr
Auditors: DIXON HUGHES GOODMAN LLP GLEN

LOCATIONS

HQ: LIBERTY UNIVERSITY, INC.
  1971 UNIVERSITY BLVD, LYNCHBURG, VA 245150002
Phone: 434 582-2000

HISTORICAL FINANCIALS
Company Type: Private

Income Statement
FYE: June 30

	REVENUE ($ mil.)	NET INCOME ($ mil.)	NET PROFIT MARGIN	EMPLOYEES
06/15	1,001	223	22.3%	7,200
06/11	628	203	32.4%	—
06/10	417	144	34.7%	—
Annual Growth	19.1%	9.0%		

2015 Year-End Financials
Return on assets: 6.3%   Cash ($ mil.): 308
Return on equity: 22.3%
Current ratio: 1.90

LICKING MEMORIAL HOSPITAL

EXECUTIVES

President, Robert A Montagnese
Financial Executive, David Claypool
Vice-President, Debboe Yooung
Director, William Andrews
Vice-President, Ann Peterson

LOCATIONS

HQ: LICKING MEMORIAL HOSPITAL
  1320 W MAIN ST, NEWARK, OH 430553699
Phone: 740 348-4137
Web: WWW.LMHEALTH.ORG

HISTORICAL FINANCIALS
Company Type: Private

Income Statement
FYE: December 31

	REVENUE ($ mil.)	NET INCOME ($ mil.)	NET PROFIT MARGIN	EMPLOYEES
12/15	201	41	20.8%	1,143
12/14	189	42	22.2%	—
12/13	195	32	16.6%	—
12/12	159	30	19.1%	—
Annual Growth	8.1%	11.2%	—	—

2015 Year-End Financials
Return on assets: 3.5%   Cash ($ mil.): 16
Return on equity: 20.8%
Current ratio: 1.20

LIFESPACE COMMUNITIES, INC.

EXECUTIVES

Chief Executive Officer, Scott M Harrison
Treasurer, Larry M Smith
Director, William R Cook
Director, Laverne E Epp
Director, Ann M Wagnerhauser
Director, David M Murdock
Director, Rita Dragonette
Executive Director, Tim Smith
Executive Director, David Miller
Director, Brian Devlin
Auditors: CLIFTON LARSON ALLEN LLP MINN

LOCATIONS

HQ: LIFESPACE COMMUNITIES, INC.
  4201 CORPORATE DR, WEST DES MOINES, IA 502665906
Phone: 515 288-5805
Web: WWW.LIFESPACECOMMUNITIES.COM

HISTORICAL FINANCIALS

Company Type: Private

Income Statement

FYE: December 31

	REVENUE ($ mil.)	NET INCOME ($ mil.)	NET PROFIT MARGIN	EMPLOYEES
12/15	221	(8)	—	1,875
12/14	210	5	2.7%	—
12/12	211	12	5.7%	—
12/11	194	15	8.0%	—
Annual Growth	3.3%	—	—	—

2015 Year-End Financials

Return on assets: 5.3%
Return on equity: (-3.7%)
Current ratio: 0.50

Cash ($ mil.): 21

LIFESPAN CORPORATION

From the youngest babies to the most golden oldies Lifespan Corporation has the health of Rhode Islanders covered through every stage of life. The multi-hospital health system includes the state's largest acute care facility Rhode Island Hospital. The flagship hospital has 1155-beds and provides general and advanced medical-surgical care in a wide range of specialties including organ transplantation neurosurgery and orthopedics. Rhode Island Hospital and its sister facility the 250-bed Miriam Hospital serve as teaching facilities for Brown University's medical school. Lifespan's system also includes three additional hospitals and a network of outpatient care facilities.

Operations

In addition to Rhode Island Hospital and Miriam Hospital Lifespan Corporation's hospital health system includes Hasbro Children's Hospital (located on the Rhode Island Hospital campus) Bradley Hospital (a 60-bed inpatient psychiatric facility for children and adolescents) and Newport Hospital (an affiliated general community hospital with 130 beds). The network also includes the RIH Foundation and the TMH Foundations as well as outpatient care facilities and home health agencies.

Strategy

The hospital system is expanding and modernizing its facilities in an effort to stay competitive. In recent years it has opened new ambulatory care centers imaging centers and specialized treatment facilities (e.g. dialysis offices and wound care centers). It is also investing in advanced medical procedures such as NanoKnife technology which uses pulses of electricity to destroy tumors and CyberKnife robotic radiosurgery which uses beams of radiation to target tumors. Lifespan has been expanding its electronic health record system to make patient information more accessible across its various care centers.

Company Background

Lifespan was formed in 1994 through the partnership of Rhode Island Hospital and Miriam Hospital.

EXECUTIVES

SVP and CIO, Carole M. Cotter
EVP System Operations, Frederick J. Macri
SVP CFO and Treasurer, Mary A. Wakefield
SVP Psychiatry and Behavioral Health, Richard J. Goldberg
President and Chief Executive Officer, Timothy Babineau
EVP Nursing Affairs, Cathy Duquette

SVP Women's Services and Clinical Integration, Karen Rosene Montella
EVP Physician Affairs, John Murphy
President The Miriam Hospital and Interim President Newport Hospital, Arthur Sampson
SVP and Chief Research Officer, Peter Snyder
President Bradley Hospital, Daniel Wall
President Gateway Healthcare, Richard Leclerc
Corporate Vice President of Contracting, Marc A Proto
Director of Pharmacy, Christine Collins
Director of Nursing, Lisa Mollo
Pharmd, Rebecca Greene
RPh, Judith Bergeron
Medical Director Pediatrics and Pediatric Cardiology, Nathan Beraha
Chairman, Scott B. Laurans
Secretary, Janice Sanborn
Secretary, Charlene Teixeira
Secretary, Irene Arruda
Secretary, Diane Santos
Secretary, Diane Boulais
Vice Chair, Anne Smith
Auditors: LB KPMG LLP PROVIDENCE RI

LOCATIONS

HQ: LIFESPAN CORPORATION
167 POINT ST STE 2B, PROVIDENCE, RI 029034771
Phone: 401 444-3500
Web: WWW.LIFESPAN.ORG

PRODUCTS/OPERATIONS

Selected Rhode Island Facilities

Bradley Hospital (Riverside)
The Miriam Hospital (Providence)
Newport Hospital (Newport)
Rhode Island Hospital (Providence)
Hasbro Children's Hospital (Providence)

COMPETITORS

Baystate Health	Partners HealthCare
Berkshire Health Systems	Roger Williams Medical Center
Boston Medical Center	Southcoast Health
Cambridge Health Alliance	Southcoast Hospitals Group
Care New England	Steward Health Care
CareGroup	Sturdy Memorial
Harrington Memorial Hospital	Yale New Haven Health System
Memorial Hospital of Rhode Island	

HISTORICAL FINANCIALS

Company Type: Private

Income Statement

FYE: September 30

	REVENUE ($ mil.)	NET INCOME ($ mil.)	NET PROFIT MARGIN	EMPLOYEES
09/15	187	1	0.8%	8,000
09/14	156	6	3.9%	—
09/13	143	(2)	—	—
09/11	1,686	(9)	—	—
Annual Growth	(42.3%)	—	—	—

2015 Year-End Financials

Return on assets: 16.6%
Return on equity: 0.8%
Current ratio: 0.60

Cash ($ mil.): 18

LIFEWAY CHRISTIAN RESOURCES OF THE SOUTHERN BAPTIST CONVENTION

LifeWay Christian Resources of the Southern Baptist Convention helps to spread the teachings of Jesus. The company is a not-for-profit Christian publisher. It also sells Bibles CDs gifts software church furniture signs and other supplies. In addition to its roughly 200 LifeWay Christian Stores located in more than 25 states the retailer sells products online and through its catalog. LifeWay operates two of the nation's largest Christian conference facilities and summer camps. LifeWay Ridgecrest Conference Center in North Carolina and LifeWay Glorieta Conference Center in New Mexico together welcome some 2000 conference and overnight guests each year. LifeWay was founded in 1891 by Dr. J.M. Frost.

Operations

The B&H Publishing Group produces Bibles books Sunday school teaching materials and audio and video products which are sold to bookstores and other retailers. Its Holman Christian Standard Bible is one of the best-selling versions in the US. As part of its digital outreach efforts Lifeway provides ministry services-related Digital Church which can be accessed through Lifeway's website and offers an array of resources for ministries including downloadable worship music and a video publishing utility.

Its Executive Communications and Relations division produces LifeWay's news and information services directs corporate events builds corporate relations and supports the office of the president. It works with state conventions and other evangelical organizations as well. The Technology division offers strategic retail enterprise and Internet services. The company's Research and Ministry Development division is where LifeWay conducts its research and explores new ministry ventures it calls "blue oceans." LifeWay's Finance and Business Services division which runs a conference center in Ridgecrest North Carolina oversees the company's financial policies and general accounting as well as directs business services such as legal investment purchasing real estate strategic planning corporate services and human resources.

Geographic Reach

Based in Nashville LifeWay boasts offices and conference centers in three states: Tennessee New Mexico and North Carolina. In Nashville the company has more than 1.3 million sq. ft. of office retail parking conference and warehouse space that covers 14.6 acres. As part of its operations LifeWay has a 350000-sq.-ft. warehouse on 44 acres in Lebanon Tennessee that supports the Life-Way Christian Stores the company operates nationwide in more than 25 states and extends its reach globally through its website and catalogs.

EXECUTIVES

VP LifeWay Christian Stores, Tim Vineyard
VP Finance and Business Services; CFO, Jerry Rhyne
President and CEO, Thom S. Rainer
EVP, Brad Waggoner
VP B&H Publishing Group, Selma Wilson
VP Insights Division, Ed Stetzer
VP Church Resources Division, Eric Geiger

VP and CIO, Tim Hill
VP Sales, Craig Featherstone
Vice President of CBA Sales, Fred Evans
Vice President Marketing and Sales, Jim Baird
Senior Vice President Marketing, Amanda Sloan
Vice President Director of Merchandising, Bill Crayton
Auditors: ERNST & YOUNG LLP NASHVILLE

LOCATIONS

HQ: LIFEWAY CHRISTIAN RESOURCES OF THE SOUTHERN BAPTIST CONVENTION
1 LIFEWAY PLZ, NASHVILLE, TN 372341001
Phone: 615 251-2000
Web: WWW.LIFEWAY.COM

2013 Stores

	No.
Texas	26
Tennessee	21
North Carolina	14
Alabama	11
Georgia	11
Virginia	9
Florida	8
Kentucky	8
Arkansas	6
Mississippi	6
South Carolina	6
Louisiana	5
Minnesota	5
Missouri	5
Ohio	4
Pennsylvania	3
California	2
Illinois	2
Kansas	2
Maryland	2
Oklahoma	2
Washington	2
Colorado	1
Indiana	1
New Mexico	1
Oregon	1
Utah	1
Total	**165**

PRODUCTS/OPERATIONS

Selected Divisions

B&H Publishing Group
Church Resources
Executive Communications and Relations
Finance and Business Services
LifeWay Christian Stores
Research and Ministry Development
Technology

Selected Products

Apparel
Audio
Bibles
Books
Church supplies
Curriculum
eBooks
Events
Gifts
Magazines
Movies
Music
Video

COMPETITORS

Amazon.com
  Baker Publishing
  Barnes & Noble
  Deseret Management
United Methodist
  Publishing
Wal-Mart

HISTORICAL FINANCIALS

Company Type: Private

Income Statement

FYE: September 30

	REVENUE ($ mil.)	NET INCOME ($ mil.)	NET PROFIT MARGIN	EMPLOYEES
09/15	487	(67)	—	2,477
09/14	500	(25)	—	—
09/13	481	79	16.5%	—
09/12	488	(35)	—	—
Annual Growth	(0.1%)	—	—	—

2015 Year-End Financials

Return on assets: 6.7%
Return on equity: (-13.9%)
Current ratio: 0.60
Cash ($ mil.): —

LIMA MEMORIAL HOSPITAL

EXECUTIVES

President, Michael Swick
Director, Howard Solomon
Director, Sandra Young
Administrative Assistant, Siddharth Mushrif
Director, Marty Mansfield
Supervisor, Abbas Khalil

LOCATIONS

HQ: LIMA MEMORIAL HOSPITAL
1001 BELLEFONTAINE AVE, LIMA, OH 458042899
Phone: 419 228-3335
Web: WWW.LIMAMEMORIAL.ORG

HISTORICAL FINANCIALS

Company Type: Private

Income Statement

FYE: December 31

	REVENUE ($ mil.)	NET INCOME ($ mil.)	NET PROFIT MARGIN	EMPLOYEES
12/15	172	16	9.4%	1,500
12/14	158	8	5.1%	—
12/09	0	0	17.4%	—
12/08	154	0	0.5%	—
Annual Growth	1.6%	55.1%	—	—

2015 Year-End Financials

Return on assets: 3.5%
Return on equity: 9.4%
Current ratio: 1.70
Cash ($ mil.): 23

LIVINGSTON PARISH SCHOOL DISTRICT

EXECUTIVES

Superintendent, Warren Curtis
Administration Manager, Patricia Davis
Auditors: HANNIS T BOURGEOIS LLP DENH

LOCATIONS

HQ: LIVINGSTON PARISH SCHOOL DISTRICT
13909 FLORIDA BLVD, LIVINGSTON, LA 707546340
Phone: 225 686-7044
Web: WWW.LPSB.ORG

HISTORICAL FINANCIALS

Company Type: Private

Income Statement

FYE: June 30

	REVENUE ($ mil.)	NET INCOME ($ mil.)	NET PROFIT MARGIN	EMPLOYEES
06/16	256	(2)	—	2,404
06/06	140	0	—	—
06/05	125	7	6.1%	—
Annual Growth	6.7%	—	—	—

2016 Year-End Financials

Return on assets: 11.3%
Return on equity: (-1.0%)
Current ratio: —
Cash ($ mil.): 28

LIVONIA PUBLIC SCHOOL DISTRICT

EXECUTIVES

Superintendent, Andrea L Oquist
Board of Directors, Lynda L Scheel
Superintendent, Patricia M Luchi
Administrative Assistant, Sandra Ludtke
Plant & Facilities Manager, Harry Lau
Director, Michael Rais
Auditors: PLANTE & MORAN PLLC AUBURN H

LOCATIONS

HQ: LIVONIA PUBLIC SCHOOL DISTRICT
15125 FARMINGTON RD, LIVONIA, MI 481545413
Phone: 734 744-2500
Web: WWW.LIVONIAPUBLICSCHOOLS.ORG

HISTORICAL FINANCIALS

Company Type: Private

Income Statement

FYE: June 30

	REVENUE ($ mil.)	NET INCOME ($ mil.)	NET PROFIT MARGIN	EMPLOYEES
06/16	195	46	23.8%	2,100
06/15	194	(27)	—	—
06/14	190	(15)	—	—
06/13	183	105	57.6%	—
Annual Growth	2.0%	(24.0%)	—	—

LODGING RLJ TRUST L P

EXECUTIVES

President, Thomas Baltimore
Administration Executive, Anita Wells
Vice-President, Susan Sloan
Representative, Sharon Chism

LOCATIONS

HQ: LODGING RLJ TRUST L P
3 BETHESDA METRO CTR # 1000, BETHESDA, MD
208145330
Phone: 301 280-7777

HISTORICAL FINANCIALS

Company Type: Private

Income Statement

FYE: December 31

	REVENUE ($ mil.)	NET INCOME ($ mil.)	NET PROFIT MARGIN	EMPLOYEES
12/16	1,160	201	17.4%	9
12/15	1,136	219	19.3%	—
12/14	1,109	136	12.3%	—
12/13	970	114	11.8%	—
Annual Growth	6.1%	20.8%	—	—

2016 Year-End Financials

Return on assets: 11.8%   Cash ($ mil.): 456
Return on equity: 17.4%
Current ratio: —

LODI UNIFIED SCHOOL DISTRICT

EXECUTIVES

Superintendent, Dr Cathy Washer
Auditors: GILBERT ASSOCIATES INC SACR

LOCATIONS

HQ: LODI UNIFIED SCHOOL DISTRICT
1305 E VINE ST, LODI, CA 952403179
Phone: 209 331-7000
Web: WWW.LODIUSD.NET

HISTORICAL FINANCIALS

Company Type: Private

Income Statement

FYE: June 30

	REVENUE ($ mil.)	NET INCOME ($ mil.)	NET PROFIT MARGIN	EMPLOYEES
06/15	297	(12)	—	3,516
06/14	268	(16)	—	—
06/13	252	(4)	—	—
06/12	254	(7)	—	—
Annual Growth	5.2%	—	—	—

2015 Year-End Financials

Return on assets: 10.8%   Cash ($ mil.): 156
Return on equity: (-4.1%)
Current ratio: —

LOEBER MOTORS, INC.

Want to buy a car from a son of a son of a salesman? Go to Loeber Motors family-owned and -operated for three generations. The company sells Mercedes-Benz Porsche and smart cars vans and trucks from its dealerships in Lincolnwood Illinois. Loeber Motors also sells used cars and maintains parts and service departments. Loeber's Web site allows visitors to get quick quotes on new cars schedule service appointments order parts apply

for finance and search for used vehicles. The site also provides a forum for owners to chat about their cars. Martin Loeber founded Loeber Motors in 1938.

EXECUTIVES

President, Michael Loeber
Personnel Director, Kris Colelle
Foreman/Supervisor, Jeff Schulte
Consultant, Hubert Banasiuk
Manager, William Brown
Consultant, William McNamara
Consultant, Bill Deletezke
Accountant, Jenni Smetana
Finance Manager, Vitas Markevicius
Finance Manager, Daniel Asmus

LOCATIONS

HQ: LOEBER MOTORS, INC.
4255 W TOUHY AVE, LINCOLNWOOD, IL 607121933
Phone: 847 675-1000
Web: WWW.LOEBERMERCEDES.COM

COMPETITORS

AutoNation	Penske Automotive
Continental Motors	Group
Jordan Automotive	Rohr-Ette Motors
Motor Werks of	Steve Foley
Barrington	

HISTORICAL FINANCIALS

Company Type: Private

Income Statement

FYE: December 31

	REVENUE ($ mil.)	NET INCOME ($ mil.)	NET PROFIT MARGIN	EMPLOYEES
12/15	315	3	1.2%	110
12/14	19	1	7.2%	—
12/13	19	1	7.2%	—
12/12	138	1	1.2%	—
Annual Growth	31.4%	30.2%	—	—

2015 Year-End Financials

Return on assets: 0.6%   Cash ($ mil.): 7
Return on equity: 1.2%
Current ratio: 0.20

LOGICALIS, INC.

Logicalis believes enterprise technology should operate in a straightforward fashion. The company provides a variety of IT services such as consulting implementation systems integration staffing network design and training. Logicalis also offers managed services for tasks such as network security IT infrastructure management and monitoring and application management. Customers come from a variety of fields including manufacturing financial services and health care. In the US Logicalis operates from more than 30 offices. It is a subsidiary of UK-based Logicalis Group. Both are owned by South Africa-based Datatec Limited.

Geographic Reach

The company has offices in Arizona California Connecticut Georgia Illinois Indiana Massachusetts Michigan Minnesota New York North Carolina Ohio Texas Washington and Wisconsin.

In 2013 it relocated its headquarters from Farmington Hills Michigan to New York City in the One Penn Plaza building in midtown Manhattan.

Financial Performance

The entire worldwide operations of the Logicalis Group report annual revenues of more than $1.4 billion.

Strategy

Logicalis has partnerships with all the major IT vendors such as CA Cisco EMC HP IBM Microsoft NetApp ServiceNow and VMware. It leases data center space from Phoenix-based IO Data Centers.

Mergers and Acquisitions

Logicalis in partnership with Metrodata an IT company in Indonesia have acquired Packet Systems Indonesia (PSI) an information/communications/technology company. The purchase expands the reach of Logicalis in Indonesia and the greater Asia/Pacific region.

EXECUTIVES

Vice President International Marketing, Joanne Nelson
Auditors: DELOITTE & TOUCHE LLP DETROIT

LOCATIONS

HQ: LOGICALIS, INC.
1 PENN PLZ STE 5130, NEW YORK, NY 101195160
Phone: 212 596-7160
Web: WWW.LOGICALIS.COM

COMPETITORS

Accenture	HP Enterprise Services
Agilysys	IBM Global Services
Black Box	RCM Technologies
Capgemini North	Sapient
America	Sirius Computer
Cognizant Tech	Solutions
Solutions	Sogeti USA LLC
Computer Sciences	TCS America
Corp.	Unisys
Forsythe Technology	

HISTORICAL FINANCIALS

Company Type: Private

Income Statement

FYE: February 28

	REVENUE ($ mil.)	NET INCOME ($ mil.)	NET PROFIT MARGIN	EMPLOYEES
02/15	386	5	1.4%	700
02/14	386	5	1.4%	—
02/13	422	6	1.6%	—
02/12	384	4	1.1%	—
Annual Growth	0.2%	7.5%	—	—

2015 Year-End Financials

Return on assets: 19.7%   Cash ($ mil.): —
Return on equity: 1.4%
Current ratio: 0.70

LOGISTICARE SOLUTIONS, LLC

LogistiCare is a go-between for getting from your house to the doctor's office and back. The company brokers non-emergency transportation services for commercial health plans government entities (such as state Medicaid agencies) and hospitals throughout the US. Using its nearly 20 call centers and a network of some 1500 independent contracted transportation providers the company coordinates the medical-related travel arrangements of its clients' members. In addition it contracts with local school boards to coordinate transportation for special needs students. The company provides more than 26 million trips each year for clients in some 40 states. LogistiCare is a subsidiary of Providence Service.

Operations

LogistiCare also known as Charter LCI has contracts with clients including metro transit authorities HMOs and commercial insurance firms. Other services include finance and consulting to help companies with billing management and claims adjudication customer reimbursement risk management and discount programs for patients requesting noncovered services. LogistiCare's eligibility and authorization services include call screening to determine client-provided benefit criteria as well as screening to determine type of transport needed.

The company operates more than a dozen regional call centers that match incoming requests with subcontracted transportation providers including local taxi and ambulance companies. Transportation customers often include the elderly or those with disabilities that prevent self-transportation.

Strategy

A major part of LogistiCare's growth strategy is to secure contracts with state and local authorities to become the sole Medicaid or Medicare transportation provider. It scored one such contract in late 2010 with Sussex County Delaware. Under terms of that agreement LogistiCare became the statewide broker for all Medicaid medical transportation.

EXECUTIVES

Vice President of Operations, Chris Echols
Senior Vice President Of Operations, Chuck Dezearn

LOCATIONS

HQ: LOGISTICARE SOLUTIONS, LLC
1275 PEACHTREE ST NE FL 6, ATLANTA, GA 303093580
Phone: 404 888-5800
Web: WWW.LOGISTICARE.COM

PRODUCTS/OPERATIONS

Selected Services
Billing and claims management
Call center management
Credentialing
Data management and reporting
Eligibility and authorization services
Logistics
Non-emergency transportation management
(ambulatory/livery vans wheel chair vans stretcher vans)
Provider payment
Quality assurance

COMPETITORS

AMR	National Express Group
Coach USA	Rural/Metro
FirstGroup America	Safe Ride Services
MV Transportation	Veolia Transportation

HISTORICAL FINANCIALS

Company Type: Private

Income Statement

FYE: December 31

	REVENUE ($ mil.)	NET INCOME ($ mil.)	NET PROFIT MARGIN	EMPLOYEES
12/15	1,083	40	3.7%	2,000
12/14	884	71	8.1%	—
12/13	770	50	6.5%	—
12/12	750	35	4.8%	—
Annual Growth	13.0%	4.0%	—	—

2015 Year-End Financials

Return on assets: —
Return on equity: 3.7%
Current ratio: 1.30
Cash ($ mil.): 34

LOGISTICS HOLLINGSWORTH GROUP LLC

EXECUTIVES

Chief Executive Officer, Stephen Barr
Manager, Deb Rodriguez
Supervisor, Fuad Husaini
Personnel Manager, Stefanie Burton

LOCATIONS

HQ: LOGISTICS HOLLINGSWORTH GROUP LLC
14225 W WARREN AVE, DEARBORN, MI 481261456
Phone: 313 768-1400

HISTORICAL FINANCIALS

Company Type: Private

Income Statement

FYE: December 31

	REVENUE ($ mil.)	NET INCOME ($ mil.)	NET PROFIT MARGIN	EMPLOYEES
12/15	196	0	—	700
12/14	183	0	—	—
12/13	183	0	—	—
12/12	171	0	—	—
Annual Growth	4.7%	—	—	—

2015 Year-End Financials

Return on assets: 7.6%
Return on equity: —
Current ratio: 0.80
Cash ($ mil.): —

LOMA LINDA UNIVERSITY MEDICAL CENTER

As a teaching research hospital Loma Linda University Medical Center (LLUMC) knows the lay of the health care landscape in California's Inland Empire. Affiliated with Loma Linda University the 1000-bed healthcare network includes the main acute care LLUMC hospital which contains the system's Children's Hospital and offers general acute care and specialized services such as oncology neurology transplants and rehabilitation. The system also includes the LLUMC East Campus the LLUMC Marietta Campus a Behavioral Health Center and a Heart and Surgery Hospital as well as various regional clinics. Founded in 1905 the not-for-profit medical center is supported by the Seventh-day Adventist Church.

Operations

Among LLUMC's staff are some 400 physicians that belong to physician management organization Loma Linda University Health Care. These physicians practice at the main campus facilities the satellite hospitals and more than a dozen regional clinics that provide general practice and specialty care.

In 2013 the hospital treated more than 46000 inpatients and 1620000 outpatients delivered 4000 babies and handled 98000 emergency room visits.

Geographic Reach

LLUMC's Level I trauma center located on the main LLUMC campus is the designated regional trauma center for a territory that includes about a fourth of the state including Inyo Mono Riverside and San Bernardino counties. All of the company's main hospital facilities are located in the town of Loma Linda with the exception of its satellite hospital campus in Marietta.

Strategy

Increasing its services and locations to better serve the region are top priorities for LLUMC. In 2013 the hospital expanded its emergency department and opened a new women's oncology center. It also announced plans for a new children's tower next to its existing children's hospital.

EXECUTIVES

Vice Chairman and President, Richard H. Hart
CEO, Ruthita J. Fike
SVP Finance and CFO, Steven Mohr
VP Graduate Medical Education, Daniel W. Giang
SVP and Chief Nursing Officer, Judith Storfjell
VP Institutes, Mark Reeves
VP and Administrator LLUMC East Campus LLU Heart and Surgical Hospital, Lyndon Edwards
CEO Loma Linda University Medical Center, Kerry Heinrich
Physical Therapy, Sondra Caposio
Physical Therapy, Barbara Cassimy
Senior Vice President Advancement, Rachelle Bussell
Secretary, Tina Huerta

LOCATIONS

HQ: LOMA LINDA UNIVERSITY MEDICAL CENTER
11234 ANDERSON ST, LOMA LINDA, CA 923542871
Phone: 909 558-4000

Selected Facilities

Beaumont California
Highland Springs Medical Plaza (in collaboration with Redlands Community Hospital and Beaver Medical Group)
Loma Linda California
Loma Linda University Children's Hospital
Loma Linda University Health Care
Loma Linda University Medical Center
Loma Linda University Medical Center East Campus Hospital
Loma Linda University Outpatient Rehabilitation Center
Loma Linda University Outpatient Surgery Center
Redlands California
Loma Linda University Behavioral Medicine Center
Loma Linda University Heart & Surgical Hospital

PRODUCTS/OPERATIONS

Selected Facilities
University Hospital
Loma Linda University Children's Hospital
Loma Linda University East Campus
Loma Linda University Heart & Surgical Hospital
Loma Linda University Behavioral Medicine Center

Selected Services and Centers
Allergy Asthma and Immunology
Allergy Laboratory
Cancer Center
Clinical Trial Center
Dentistry
Diabetes Treatment Center
Ears Nose and Throat (ENT)
Emergency and Trauma Services
Family Medicine
Fertility and In Vitro Fertilization
Gastroenterology
Heart and Vascular
Home Care
Metabolic and Bariatric Surgery
Nephrology
Neurology
Neurosurgery
Obstetrics and Gynecology

Ophthalmology
Orthopedics
Pediatrics
Perinatal Institute
Pharmacy
Plastic Surgery
Pulmonology
Radiology
Transplantation Institute and Liver Center
Urogynecology
Urology

COMPETITORS

Adventist Health
  System West
Arrowhead Medical
  Center
Beaver Medical Group
Children's Hospital of
  Orange County
Childrens Hospital Los
  Angeles
Dignity Health
Memorial Health
  Services
Tenet Healthcare

HISTORICAL FINANCIALS

Company Type: Private

Income Statement

	REVENUE ($ mil.)	NET INCOME ($ mil.)	NET PROFIT MARGIN	EMPLOYEES
12/15	846	(413)	—	4,676
12/06*	848	64	7.6%	—
06/05	879	39	4.5%	—
12/04	879	39	4.5%	—
Annual Growth	(0.4%)	—	—	—

FYE: December 31

*Fiscal year change

2015 Year-End Financials

Return on assets: 7.8%
Return on equity: (-48.9%)
Current ratio: 1.50

Cash ($ mil.): 339

LONESTAR FREIGHTLINER GROUP, LLC

EXECUTIVES

Chief Operating Officer, Dan Steven
General Manager, Kent Noble
Manager, Dan Stevens
Executive Vice-President, Adam Arrington
Auditors: LANE GORMAN TRUBITT PLLC DAL

LOCATIONS

HQ: LONESTAR FREIGHTLINER GROUP, LLC
  2051 HUGHES RD, GRAPEVINE, TX 760517317
Phone: 817 428-9736
Web: WWW.LONESTARTRUCKGROUP.COM

HISTORICAL FINANCIALS

Company Type: Private

Income Statement

	REVENUE ($ mil.)	NET INCOME ($ mil.)	NET PROFIT MARGIN	EMPLOYEES
12/15	420	11	2.8%	580
12/14	374	11	3.0%	—
12/11	117	3	3.1%	—
Annual Growth	37.5%	33.7%	—	—

FYE: December 31

Return on assets: 2.5%
Return on equity: 2.8%
Current ratio: 0.10

Cash ($ mil.): 8

LONG BEACH MEMORIAL MEDICAL CENTER

Long Beach Memorial Medical Center (LBMMC) is an old-timer in the Long Beach health care market. A subsidiary of Memorial Health Services LBMMC provides a full range of health services to residents of the Long Beach California area. The medical center a 420-bed acute-care hospital was founded in 1907 and is one of the largest private hospitals on the West Coast. Services include primary emergency diagnostic surgical therapeutic and rehabilitative care. The hospital is home to centers for treatment of cancer heart stroke and women's and children's health concerns. It also provides home and hospice care programs as well as occupational health services.

Operations

LBMMC comprises a breast center cancer institute center for women heart and vascular institute imaging center joint replacement center rehabilitation institute and stroke center. The medical center is a 420-bed acute-care hospital.

Geographic Reach

Long Beach Memorial Medical Center (LBMMC) is one of the nation's largest private hospitals on the West Coast.

Strategy

LBMMC boasts an electronic medical record (EMR) system that connects the hospital and all of its affiliated physicians and pharmacies so that they can transfer patient information electronically between different care providers and locations. Hospitals that use an EMR are eligible for incentives and higher reimbursements from the federal government. Additionally EMRs help to reduce medical errors and increase patient safety by eliminating things like medication interactions and duplicate patient records.

LBMMC expanded its cancer services by building a new $31 million dedicated outpatient cancer facility. The MemorialCare Todd Cancer Institute at Long Beach Memorial which was completed in mid-2013 serves to supplement its current center which had reached capacity. With the new 65000-sq.-ft. MemorialCare Todd Cancer Institute pavilion LBMMC enhances its cancer care technology and capacity.

LBMMC has also expanded its robotics program beyond cardiology. The hospital recently established a new intensivist program in the Intensive Care Unit (ICU). The ICU program integrates teaching from the University of California Irvine residents and interns.

EXECUTIVES

CIO, Scott Joslyn
CFO, Wendy Dorchester
President and CEO, Barry Arbuckle
Vice President Human Resources, Jonathan Berek
Vice President Data Processing, Linda Simmons
Director of Nursing, Mary Jorgensen
Vice President, Brant Heise
Vice President of Technical Information Services, Kevin Torres
MMC Vice President Medical and Surgical Services, Linda Hoff

Vice President Strategy Planning, Roshawn Blunt
Vice President Material Resources, Gerald Olson
Medical Director ED, Gary Moreau
Secretary Executive, Donna Gorman
Secretary Department Medical, Elvera Barycki
Board Member, Robert Freeman
Board Member, Kenneth Walker
Board Member, Sean Miller
Secretary Executive, Kathleen Webster
Secretary Executive, Barbara Steinhauser
Secretary Executive, Kelly Ambrose
Secretary Department Medical, Heather Lawrence
Secretary Executive, Evelyn Satele
Secretary Department Medical, Deborah Ruman
Secretary Department Medical, Natalie Strauss

LOCATIONS

HQ: LONG BEACH MEMORIAL MEDICAL CENTER
  2801 ATLANTIC AVE FL 2, LONG BEACH, CA
  908061701
Phone: 562 933-2000
Web: WWW.MILLERCHILDRENSHOSPITALLB.ORG

PRODUCTS/OPERATIONS

Institutes & Centers
Long Beach Adult & Pediatric Sleep Center
MemorialCare Breast Center at Long Beach Memorial
MemorialCare Heart & Vascular Institute
MemorialCare Imaging Center
MemorialCare Joint Replacement Center
MemorialCare Rehabilitation Institute
MemorialCare Stroke Center
MemorialCare Todd Cancer Institute
Spine Center at Long Beach Memorial
Trauma Center at Long Beach Memorial
Services:
Blood Donation Center
Diabetes Care
Digestive Care
Emergency Department
Gynecological Care at Long Beach Memorial
Lung & Respiratory Care
Minimally Invasive Surgery at Long Beach Memorial
Palliative Care Program at Long Beach Memorial
Pharmacy at Long Beach Memorial
Robotic-Assisted Surgery at Long Beach Memorial
Surgical Care
Wound Healing & Hyperbaric Medicine at Long Beach
  Memorial

COMPETITORS

Adventist Health System West
Aptium Oncology
Brotman Medical Center
Cedars-Sinai Medical Center
Childrens Hospital Los Angeles
Dignity Health
Glendale Adventist Medical Center
Good Samaritan Hospital (Los Angeles)
HCA
Hoag Memorial Hospital
Hollywood Presbyterian Medical Center
Methodist Hospital of Southern California
Newhall Memorial Hospital
Pasadena Hospital Association
Providence Health System Southern California
Providence St. Joseph Health
Sutter Health
Tenet Healthcare
Torrance Memorial Medical Center
Trinity Health (Novi)
Western Medical Center - Santa Ana

HISTORICAL FINANCIALS

Company Type: Private

Income Statement

FYE: June 30

	REVENUE ($ mil.)	NET INCOME ($ mil.)	NET PROFIT MARGIN	EMPLOYEES
06/15	624	93	15.0%	6,000
06/11	1,083	63	5.9%	—
06/09	446	53	12.0%	—
Annual Growth	5.8%	9.8%	—	—

2015 Year-End Financials

Return on assets: 2.6% Cash ($ mil.): —
Return on equity: 15.0%
Current ratio: 1.60

LONG ISLAND JEWISH MEDICAL CENTER

Just off the Grand Central Parkway you'll find Long Island Jewish Medical Center. The medical center serves the western edge of Long Island and the eastern edge of the greater metropolitan New York area. The 890-bed medical center campus includes Long Island Jewish Hospital a general acute care hospital; Cohen Children's Medical Center of New York Hospital which provides a full range of pediatric care services; and The Zucker Hillside Hospital a psychiatric hospital for patients of all ages. The medical center's staff includes 500 physicians. Long Island Jewish Medical Center is the primary clinical and medical training facility of the North Shore-Long Island Jewish Health System.

Operations

The Long Island Jewish Medical Center's main activities are centered at the 490-bed Long Island Jewish Hospital which provides emergency diagnostic surgical inpatient and outpatient services. The hospital has centers for cancer treatment cardiac surgery and women's health as well as units specializing in hearing loss stroke recovery sleep disorders and hemophilia treatment. As an affiliate of Hofstra University's medical school and Yeshiva University's Albert Einstein College of Medicine the Long Island Jewish Hospital also provides graduate medical education programs.

Altogether the hospitals of the Long Island Jewish Medical Center serve some 47000 patients per year conduct 22000 surgeries and handle more than 100000 emergency room visits per year.

Geographic Reach

Long Island Jewish Medical Center is located on a 48-acre campus on the border of New York's Queens and Nassau counties about 15 miles east of Manhattan.

Strategy

To enhance services provided to residents of the growing New York City metropolitan area Long Island Jewish Medical Center is conducting expansion efforts on its facilities. In 2012 it opened a new $300 million 10-story inpatient tower (containing 160 private patient rooms) at the Long Island Jewish Hospital. The project increased the hospital's overall capacity and added women's health cardiovascular care and wellness centers.

EXECUTIVES

Vice President Finance, John McGovern
Medical Records Director, Patricia Hennelly

LOCATIONS

HQ: LONG ISLAND JEWISH MEDICAL CENTER
27005 76TH AVE, NEW HYDE PARK, NY 110401496
Phone: 516 465-2600
Web: WWW.LIJ.EDU

PRODUCTS/OPERATIONS

Selected Facilities

Long Island Jewish Hospital (490 beds)
The Steven and Alexandra Cohen Children's Medical Center (160 beds)
The Zucker Hillside Hospital (240 beds)

Selected Services

Anesthesiology
Cardiac Services
Center for Maternal-Fetal Health
Dental Medicine
Emergency Medicine
Medicine
Neurosciences
Obstetrics
Ophthalmology
Orthopaedic Surgery
Otolaryngology
Pathology
Radiation Oncology
Radiology
Rehabilitation
Surgery
Thoracic Surgery
Urogynecology
Urology: The Arthur Smith Insitute for Urology

COMPETITORS

Catholic Health Services of Long Island
Mercy Medical Center (NY)
North Shore University Hospital
NuHealth
St. Francis Hospital Roslyn
Winthrop-University Hospital

HISTORICAL FINANCIALS

Company Type: Private

Income Statement

FYE: December 31

	REVENUE ($ mil.)	NET INCOME ($ mil.)	NET PROFIT MARGIN	EMPLOYEES
12/15	1,524	44	2.9%	1,214
12/14	1,446	96	6.7%	—
Annual Growth	5.4%	(53.4%)	—	—

2015 Year-End Financials

Return on assets: 5.0% Cash ($ mil.): —
Return on equity: 2.9%
Current ratio: 0.60

LONG ISLAND UNIVERSITY

Long Island University (LIU) helps students see a long future in professional fields including medicine and business. LIU has an enrollment of more than 24000 students at multiple locations in New York State. The university employs more than 600 full-time faculty members and has a 12:1 student-to-teacher ratio. LIU offers 575 degree programs and certificates in fields including pharmacy nursing health sciences education liberal arts sciences business and information studies. The school traces its roots to 1886 when the Brooklyn College of Pharmacy was founded.

Geographic Reach

LIU has eight campuses in New York located in Brooklyn Brookville Brentwood Riverhead Rockland and Westchester). Internationally LIU Global offers study abroad programs in Asia Australia the Middle East and South America.

Strategy

LIU has expanded its offerings in recent years to meet current demands. It has added degree programs in fields such as digital game design computer information systems health sciences and human resource management.

EXECUTIVES

Vice President, Lucille Ambrosio
Assistant Dean Vpa, Benjamin Moore
Vice President Marketing Public Relations, Paola Kleinman
Associate Vice President and Deputy Chief Financial Officer, Chris Fevola
Associate Vice President For Finance And Budget Director, Christopher Fevola
Associate Vice President Academic Affairs, Lori Knapp
Associate Vice President of Information Technology, David Jank
Vice President of University Advancement, Charles Rasberry
Secretary, Arlene Weydig
BDS MPHc Treasurer, Sagar Patel
Auditors: KPMG LLP MELVILLE NY

LOCATIONS

HQ: LONG ISLAND UNIVERSITY
700 NORTHERN BLVD, GREENVALE, NY 115481327
Phone: 516 299-2535
Web: WWW.LIU.EDU

HISTORICAL FINANCIALS

Company Type: Private

Income Statement

FYE: August 31

	REVENUE ($ mil.)	NET INCOME ($ mil.)	NET PROFIT MARGIN	EMPLOYEES
08/16	388	28	7.4%	3,300
08/15	396	33	8.5%	—
08/14	501	41	8.2%	—
08/11	468	2	0.5%	—
Annual Growth	(3.7%)	63.1%	—	—

2016 Year-End Financials

Return on assets: 4.1% Cash ($ mil.): 110
Return on equity: 7.4%
Current ratio: —

LONGMONT UNITED HOSPITAL

EXECUTIVES

Chief Executive Officer, Mitchell Carson
Director, Mike Burke
Personnel Manager, Kimberly Sumpter
Manager, Sherri Vaskosteinbeck
Office Manager, Jackie Nagell
Financial Executive, Dan Frank

LOCATIONS

HQ: LONGMONT UNITED HOSPITAL
1950 MOUNTAIN VIEW AVE, LONGMONT, CO 805019865
Phone: 303 651-5111
Web: WWW.LUHCARES.ORG

HISTORICAL FINANCIALS
Company Type: Private

Income Statement
FYE: December 31

	REVENUE ($ mil.)	NET INCOME ($ mil.)	NET PROFIT MARGIN	EMPLOYEES
12/15	170	1	0.9%	1,100
12/14	172	4	2.6%	—
12/13	189	(3)	—	—
12/09	166	3	2.0%	—
Annual Growth	0.4%	(12.0%)	—	—

2015 Year-End Financials
Return on assets: 19.2%   Cash ($ mil.): 11
Return on equity: 0.9%
Current ratio: 0.90

LOS ANGELES POLICE RELIEF ASSOCIATION, INC.

EXECUTIVES

Director, Rigoberto Romero
Auditors: ROMBERGER WILSON & BEESON INC

LOCATIONS

HQ: LOS ANGELES POLICE RELIEF ASSOCIATION, INC.
600 N GRAND AVE, LOS ANGELES, CA 900122212
Phone: 213 674-3701
Web: WWW.LAPRA.ORG

HISTORICAL FINANCIALS
Company Type: Private

Income Statement
FYE: December 31

	REVENUE ($ mil.)	NET INCOME ($ mil.)	NET PROFIT MARGIN	EMPLOYEES
12/15	213	(25)	—	19
12/14	206	(2)	—	—
12/13	203	17	8.6%	—
12/11	194	15	8.1%	—
Annual Growth	2.4%	—	—	—

2015 Year-End Financials
Return on assets: 0.4%   Cash ($ mil.): 7
Return on equity: (-11.9%)
Current ratio: 9.70

LOUDOUN COUNTY PUBLIC SCHOOL DISTRICT

EXECUTIVES

Superintendent, Eric Williams
Director, Susanne Kollaja
Administration Director, Michael J Lunsford
Administrative Assistant, Kim Goodlin
Auditors: CHERRY BEKAERT LLP TYSONS COR

LOCATIONS

HQ: LOUDOUN COUNTY PUBLIC SCHOOL DISTRICT
21000 EDUCATION CT, BROADLANDS, VA 201485526
Phone: 571 252-1000
Web: WWW.LCPS.ORG

HISTORICAL FINANCIALS
Company Type: Private

Income Statement
FYE: June 30

	REVENUE ($ mil.)	NET INCOME ($ mil.)	NET PROFIT MARGIN	EMPLOYEES
06/15	1,080	19	1.8%	9,822
06/05	0	0	25.6%	—
Annual Growth	125.3%	73.1%	—	—

2015 Year-End Financials
Return on assets: 2.7%   Cash ($ mil.): —
Return on equity: 1.8%
Current ratio: —

LOUISE OBICI MEMORIAL HOSPITAL INC

EXECUTIVES

President, William C Giermak
President, David Bernd
Chief Financial Officer, William A Carpenter
Office Manager, Terry Christovich
Manager, Amanda Goodman
Director, Virginia Savage
Auditors: BOYCE SPADY & MOORE PLC SUFFO

LOCATIONS

HQ: LOUISE OBICI MEMORIAL HOSPITAL INC
2800 GODWIN BLVD, SUFFOLK, VA 234348038
Phone: 757 934-4000
Web: WWW.OBICIHCF.ORG

HISTORICAL FINANCIALS
Company Type: Private

Income Statement
FYE: December 31

	REVENUE ($ mil.)	NET INCOME ($ mil.)	NET PROFIT MARGIN	EMPLOYEES
12/15	182	13	7.4%	1,272
12/14*	182	16	8.8%	—
05/09	0	0	—	—
09/05	118	(1)	—	—
Annual Growth	4.5%	—	—	—
*Fiscal year change

LOUISIANA COMMUNITY & TECHNICAL COLLEGE SYSTEM

EXECUTIVES

Chairman of the Board, Steven Smith
Director, Howard Jarlton

Vice-President, Jimmy Sawtelle
Director, Mignonne Ater
Manager, Charles Teamer
Director, Adrienne Fontenot
Financial Executive, Gerald Mayeaux

LOCATIONS

HQ: LOUISIANA COMMUNITY & TECHNICAL COLLEGE SYSTEM
265 S FOSTER DR, BATON ROUGE, LA 708064104
Phone: 225 922-2800

HISTORICAL FINANCIALS
Company Type: Private

Income Statement
FYE: June 30

	REVENUE ($ mil.)	NET INCOME ($ mil.)	NET PROFIT MARGIN	EMPLOYEES
06/16*	189	41	21.9%	810
12/08	0	0	42.6%	—
06/02	261	14	5.4%	—
06/01	261	14	5.4%	—
Annual Growth	(2.1%)	7.4%	—	—
*Fiscal year change

2016 Year-End Financials
Return on assets: 19.6%   Cash ($ mil.): 111
Return on equity: 21.9%
Current ratio: 1.80

LOWELL GENERAL HOSPITAL

EXECUTIVES

President, Normand E Deschene
Board of Directors, Peter Zarrilla
Manager, Chris Carski

LOCATIONS

HQ: LOWELL GENERAL HOSPITAL
295 VARNUM AVE, LOWELL, MA 018542193
Phone: 978 937-6000

HISTORICAL FINANCIALS
Company Type: Private

Income Statement
FYE: September 30

	REVENUE ($ mil.)	NET INCOME ($ mil.)	NET PROFIT MARGIN	EMPLOYEES
09/16	441	1	0.3%	3,000
09/15	419	10	2.6%	—
09/14	405	17	4.3%	—
09/13	0	0	—	—
Annual Growth	—	—	—	—

2016 Year-End Financials
Return on assets: 16.8%   Cash ($ mil.): 49
Return on equity: 0.3%
Current ratio: 1.00

LOWER COLORADO RIVER AUTHORITY

The stars at night may be big and bright but more than 1 million people deep in the heart of Texas still need electricity from the Lower Colorado River Authority (LCRA). Serving 80 counties along the lower Colorado River between Central Texas and the Gulf of Mexico the not-for profit state-run entity supplies wholesale electricity to more than 40 retail utilities (primarily municipalities and cooperatives). It operates three fossil-fuel powered plants and six hydroelectric dams that give it a production capacity of about 3800 megawatts; it also purchases electricity from Texas wind farms. The LCRA provides water and wastewater utility services to more than 30 communities as well.

Operations

Founded by the Texas Legislature in 1934 the LCRA has pursued two complementary goals — providing reliable low-cost utility and public services and ensuring the protection of the area's natural resources. In the latter role the LCRA owns or operates more than 40 public recreation areas comprising more than 16400 acres; it also monitors the water quality and levels of the lakes formed by its dams.

Sales and Marketing

Sales of electricity to one major customer represented 25% of its total electric revenue for 2014.

Financial Performance

LCRA receives no state tax revenues but operates by selling electricity electric transmission and water services at cost. It does not levy taxes or receive specific appropriations from any government. Its net income for fiscal year 2014 increased 1% over 2013 while its revenues remained flat.

Strategy

LCRA's capital improvement and expansion programs from fiscal year 2015 through 2019 totals at $1.2 billion with $0.8 billion or 67% to be debt funded. The majority of the forecasted capital costs will go toward expansion of transmission services dam improvements and the construction of a new water reservoir. LCRA continues to increase its transmission system investment due to the need for additional electric transmission capability statewide.

EXECUTIVES

Deputy General Manager, Ross Phillips
General Manager and CEO, Phil Wilson
Treasurer, Brady Edwards
Manager Information Services and Strategy, Debbie Dunn-Krause
Chairman, Timothy T. Timmerman, age 56
Vice Chairman, John C. Dickerson
Auditors: BAKER TILLY VIRCHOW KRAUSE LLP

LOCATIONS

HQ: LOWER COLORADO RIVER AUTHORITY
3700 LAKE AUSTIN BLVD, AUSTIN, TX 787033504
Phone: 512 473-3200

PRODUCTS/OPERATIONS

Selected Subsidiaries and Affiliates
Fayette Power Project (coal-fired power generating units)
GenTex Power Corporation (power generation)
LCRA Transmission Services Corporation (power transmission services)

HISTORICAL FINANCIALS
Company Type: Private

Income Statement
FYE: June 30

	REVENUE ($ mil.)	NET INCOME ($ mil.)	NET PROFIT MARGIN	EMPLOYEES
06/15	1,021	15	1.5%	1,800
06/12	1,261	101	8.0%	—
06/11	1,185	48	4.1%	—
Annual Growth	(3.7%)	(25.0%)	—	—

2015 Year-End Financials
Return on assets: 5.7%
Return on equity: 1.5%
Current ratio: 0.70
Cash ($ mil.): 182

LOYOLA MARYMOUNT UNIVERSITY

Loyola Marymount University (LMU) in Los Angeles is a Jesuit (Catholic) institution with an enrollment of more than 9500 students. It offers more than 115 graduate and undergraduate programs through four colleges: Bellarmine College of Liberal Arts College of Business Administration College of Communication and Fine Arts and Seaver College of Science and Engineering. There is also the School of Education and School of Film and Television. Other programs include the Graduate Division Continuing Education Program and Loyola Law School. LMU has an 11:1 student-to-faculty ratio. The university was formed in 1973 by the merger of Loyola College (founded in 1911) and Marymount Junior College.

Operations

The university offers about 60 majors and 55 minor study programs to its undergraduate students. LMU also offers more than 40 master's degrees two doctorates and a dozen certification programs. In total it employs about 2000 faculty and staff members.

LMU has partnerships with about a dozen public and private elementary and secondary schools in the Los Angeles area. Through the LMU Family of Schools model school demonstration program the university provides professional development and educational resources to the schools.

Geographic Reach

LMU is located on a 140-acre campus in Los Angeles.

Financial Performance

The university experienced a 3% increase in revenues from $320 million to $328 million due to higher net tuition and fee income auxiliary enterprise revenue and investment returns designated for operations. Tuition runs at some $40000 annually plus some $13000 in room and board. LMU reported net income of $63 million over a net loss in 2012 due to increased investment returns and gains on interest rate swaps. Cash from operations dropped by $6 million to $20 as the university used cash in account receivable and contributions for long-term investments.

Strategy

In 2013 LMU broke ground on a $110 million life sciences complex that will become Pereira Hall (for engineering) and Seaver Hall (for physics and math).

To increase student access to its programs LMU launched a new scholarship initiative in 2012. Through the program the university seeks to raise some $100 million for new scholarships through donations and endowment returns over a three-year period.

EXECUTIVES

Senior Vice President for Administration, Lynne Scarboro
Provost And Executive Vice President, Joseph Hellige
Vice President Vice President for Student Affairs, Lane Bove
Assistant Vice President Facilities Management, Rick Garcia
Budget Analyst Enrollment Management Vice President Office, Gabriela De Anda
Associate Vice President of Ad, Michael Wong
Senior Vice President Administration, Evelynne Scarboro
Executive Vice President International and Insurance Group, David Zuercher
Medical Director, Dan Hyslop
Vice President for Intercultural Affairs, Abbie Robinson-Armstrong
Treas, Caroline Wilhelm
Auditors: PRICEWATERHOUSECOOPERS LLP L

LOCATIONS

HQ: LOYOLA MARYMOUNT UNIVERSITY
1 LMU DR UHALL STE 4900, LOS ANGELES, CA 90045
Phone: 310 338-2700
Web: WWW.LMU.EDU

PRODUCTS/OPERATIONS

Colleges and Schools
Bellarmine College of Liberal Arts
College of Business Administration
College of Communication and Fine Arts
Graduate Division
LMU Extension
Loyola Law School
School of Education
School of Film and Television
Seaver College of Science and Engineering

HISTORICAL FINANCIALS
Company Type: Private

Income Statement
FYE: May 31

	REVENUE ($ mil.)	NET INCOME ($ mil.)	NET PROFIT MARGIN	EMPLOYEES
05/15	349	17	4.9%	1,449
05/14	338	70	20.9%	—
05/13	328	62	19.1%	—
05/12	320	(16)	—	—
Annual Growth	3.0%	—	—	—

2015 Year-End Financials
Return on assets: 12.1%
Return on equity: 4.9%
Current ratio: —
Cash ($ mil.): 35

LRGHEALTHCARE

EXECUTIVES

Chief Executive Officer, Thomas A Clairmont
Director, Husam H Farah
Personnel Director, Susan Knowlton
Director, Courtney Reagan
Director, Darlene Burrows

LOCATIONS

HQ: LRGHEALTHCARE
  80 HIGHLAND ST, LACONIA, NH 032463298
Phone: 603 524-3211
Web: WWW.LRGH.ORG

HISTORICAL FINANCIALS

Company Type: Private

Income Statement — FYE: September 30

	REVENUE ($ mil.)	NET INCOME ($ mil.)	NET PROFIT MARGIN	EMPLOYEES
09/15	174	(29)	—	1,600
09/14	168	3	1.8%	—
09/13	232	3	1.7%	—
09/10	190	(12)	—	—
Annual Growth	(1.8%)	—	—	—

2015 Year-End Financials

Return on assets: 5.5%
Return on equity: (-17.1%)
Current ratio: 0.50
Cash ($ mil.): 10

LSCP, LLLP

EXECUTIVES

Chief Financial Officer, Gary Grotjohn
General Manager, Steve Roe
Auditors: CHRISTIANSON & ASSOCIATES PLL

LOCATIONS

HQ: LSCP, LLLP
  4808 F AVE, MARCUS, IA 510357070
Phone: 712 376-2800

HISTORICAL FINANCIALS

Company Type: Private

Income Statement — FYE: September 30

	REVENUE ($ mil.)	NET INCOME ($ mil.)	NET PROFIT MARGIN	EMPLOYEES
09/16	246	28	11.6%	46
09/15	232	36	15.5%	—
09/14	274	61	22.4%	—
09/13	346	4	1.3%	—
Annual Growth	(10.8%)	83.7%	—	—

2016 Year-End Financials

Return on assets: 4.0%
Return on equity: 11.6%
Current ratio: 2.60
Cash ($ mil.): 33

LUBBOCK COUNTY HOSPITAL DISTRICT

EXECUTIVES

President, David Allison
Manager, Mark Vincent
Manager, Tom Shue
Director, Aaron Davis

LOCATIONS

HQ: LUBBOCK COUNTY HOSPITAL DISTRICT
  602 INDIANA AVE, LUBBOCK, TX 794153364
Phone: 806 775-8200
Web: WWW.UMCHEALTHSYSTEM.COM

HISTORICAL FINANCIALS

Company Type: Private

Income Statement — FYE: December 31

	REVENUE ($ mil.)	NET INCOME ($ mil.)	NET PROFIT MARGIN	EMPLOYEES
12/15	444	49	11.2%	2,000
12/14*	473	33	7.0%	—
05/05	0	(0)	—	—
12/02	214	1	0.6%	—
Annual Growth	5.7%	32.8%	—	—

*Fiscal year change

2015 Year-End Financials

Return on assets: 5.9%
Return on equity: 11.2%
Current ratio: 3.40
Cash ($ mil.): 152

LUBBOCK INDEPENDENT SCHOOL DISTRICT

EXECUTIVES

Superintendent, Berhl Robertson
Board of Directors, Nina Waller
Executive Secretary, Jane Curtsinger
Director, Jonna Dickerson
Plant & Facilities Manager, Bill Craft
Auditors: BOLINGER SEGARS GILBERT & MO

LOCATIONS

HQ: LUBBOCK INDEPENDENT SCHOOL DISTRICT
  1628 19TH ST, LUBBOCK, TX 794014832
Phone: 806 766-1000
Web: WWW.LUBBOCKISD.ORG

HISTORICAL FINANCIALS

Company Type: Private

Income Statement — FYE: June 30

	REVENUE ($ mil.)	NET INCOME ($ mil.)	NET PROFIT MARGIN	EMPLOYEES
06/16	307	(0)	—	3,300
06/15	295	(8)	—	—
06/14	284	12	4.3%	—
06/13	277	10	4.0%	—
Annual Growth	3.4%	—	—	—

2016 Year-End Financials

Return on assets: 1.2%
Return on equity: (-0.2%)
Current ratio: —
Cash ($ mil.): 105

LUCILE SALTER PACKARD CHILDREN'S HOSPITAL AT STANFORD

EXECUTIVES

President, Christopher Dawes
Director, Lucy O'Brady
Office Manager, Laurie Jones
Auditors: PRICEWATERHOUSECOOPERS LLP BO

LOCATIONS

HQ: LUCILE SALTER PACKARD CHILDREN'S
  HOSPITAL AT STANFORD
  725 WELCH RD, PALO ALTO, CA 943041601
Phone: 650 497-8000
Web: WWW.LPCH.ORG

HISTORICAL FINANCIALS

Company Type: Private

Income Statement — FYE: August 31

	REVENUE ($ mil.)	NET INCOME ($ mil.)	NET PROFIT MARGIN	EMPLOYEES
08/16	1,402	157	11.2%	1,100
08/14	1,135	98	8.7%	—
08/10	794	48	6.1%	—
08/09	772	76	9.9%	—
Annual Growth	8.9%	10.8%	—	—

2016 Year-End Financials

Return on assets: 10.8%
Return on equity: 11.2%
Current ratio: 3.00
Cash ($ mil.): 532

LUTHERAN SENIOR SERVICES

EXECUTIVES

President, John Kotovsky
Officer, Ellen Harmon
Vice-President, Lea A Coates
Vice-President, Linda Detring
Financial Executive, Chad Sneed
Chief Financial Officer, Gary Winchell
Auditors: CLIFTONLARSONALLEN LLP ST L

LOCATIONS

HQ: LUTHERAN SENIOR SERVICES
  1150 HANLEY INDUSTRIAL CT, SAINT LOUIS, MO
  631441910
Phone: 314 968-9313
Web: WWW.LSSLIVING.ORG

HISTORICAL FINANCIALS

Company Type: Private

Income Statement

FYE: December 31

	REVENUE ($ mil.)	NET INCOME ($ mil.)	NET PROFIT MARGIN	EMPLOYEES
12/15	187	(13)	—	2,254
12/14	183	(0)	—	—
12/13	168	8	5.3%	—
12/11	145	(3)	—	—
Annual Growth	6.5%	—	—	—

2015 Year-End Financials

Return on assets: 4.3% Cash ($ mil.): 16
Return on equity: (-7.3%)
Current ratio: 0.60

LUTHERAN SERVICES FLORIDA, INC.

EXECUTIVES

President, Samuel M Sipes
Board of Directors, Stacy L Martin
Officer, Angie Henderson
Administrative Assistant, Raquel Valencia
Executive Director, Fred Tausig
Vice-President, Angela W Combs
Auditors: CBIZ MHM LLC CLEARWATER FL

LOCATIONS

HQ: LUTHERAN SERVICES FLORIDA, INC.
 3627A W WATERS AVE, TAMPA, FL 336142783
Phone: 813 868-4438
Web: WWW.LSFNET.ORG

HISTORICAL FINANCIALS

Company Type: Private

Income Statement

FYE: June 30

	REVENUE ($ mil.)	NET INCOME ($ mil.)	NET PROFIT MARGIN	EMPLOYEES
06/15	199	(0)	—	565
06/14	150	2	2.0%	—
06/13	0	(0)	—	—
06/12	40	(0)	—	—
Annual Growth	70.9%	—	—	—

2015 Year-End Financials

Return on assets: 9.0% Cash ($ mil.): 5
Return on equity: —
Current ratio: 0.30

M & M SERVICE COMPANY

EXECUTIVES

President, Gary Meyers
Board of Directors, Pat Martin
Board of Directors, David Wright
General Manager, Brad Klaus
Manager, Peggy Lewis

Operations Manager, Steve Mullink
Auditors: CLIFTONLARSONALLEN LLP NORMA

LOCATIONS

HQ: M & M SERVICE COMPANY
 130 N CHILES ST, CARLINVILLE, IL 626261684
Phone: 217 854-4516
Web: WWW.MMSERVICE.COM

HISTORICAL FINANCIALS

Company Type: Private

Income Statement

FYE: August 31

	REVENUE ($ mil.)	NET INCOME ($ mil.)	NET PROFIT MARGIN	EMPLOYEES
08/16	212	6	2.9%	165
08/15	251	5	2.1%	—
08/14	294	4	1.5%	—
08/13	256	3	1.5%	—
Annual Growth	(6.1%)	17.0%	—	—

2016 Year-End Financials

Return on assets: 5.7% Cash ($ mil.): —
Return on equity: 2.9%
Current ratio: 0.60

M. B. KAHN CONSTRUCTION CO., INC.

One of the largest construction companies in the southeastern US M. B. Kahn Construction Co. works on commercial institutional and industrial projects including hospitals airports shopping centers and manufacturing plants. Additionally it is rated as one of the top builders in the nation's education market. The company provides general contracting and design/build delivery services as well as construction management and program management services. Russian immigrant Myron B. Kahn founded the company in 1927. It is now chaired by Alan Kahn his grandson. The group operates through divisions in South Carolina and Georgia.

The purchase of South Carolina-based general contractor Chancel Construction increased the company's customer base in the Carolina's. Since then M.B. Kahn has been busy building and designing business parks arts centers and jails in the region.

EXECUTIVES

Senior Executive Vice President, Charles B Jordan
Executive Vice President, Michael Satterwhite
Executive Vice President, James Heard
Vice President Of Sales, Jack Brown
Vice President, Charles Kahn
Senior Vice President, Buzz Pleming
Auditors: ELLIOTT DAVIS DECOSIMO COLUMB

LOCATIONS

HQ: M. B. KAHN CONSTRUCTION CO., INC.
 101 FLINTLAKE RD, COLUMBIA, SC 292237851
Phone: 803 736-2950
Web: WWW.MBKAHN.COM

PRODUCTS/OPERATIONS

Selected Projects and Customers
Commercial

Blue Cross/Blue Shield South Carolina
South Carolina Bank & Trust
Hilton Hotel
South Carolina Bank and Trust headquarters
Education
 Barbara Bush Center at Columbia College
 Camden High School
 New Marietta High School
 West Ashley High School
Health Care
 Hollings Cancer Institute
 Roper Hospital
 Steadman Hawkins Clinic of the Carolinas
Industrial
 Bose Corporation
 Caterpillar
 Fruit of the Loom
 John Deere
 Komatsu America
Public Sector
 Greenville County Detention Center
 Horry County Courthouse
 Lexington County Judicial Center
 Pamlico County Detention Center
Religous
 Riverland Hills Baptist Church
 Pelham Road Baptist Church
 Saxe Gotha Presbyterian Church Facility
Water Works
 Columbia Wastewater Treatment Plant
 Hartwell Water Treatment Plant

COMPETITORS

Brasfield & Gorrie	Rodgers Builders
Choate Construction	Shelco
Gilbane Building Company	Skanska USA Building
Hardin Construction	Tetra Tech Tesoro
Parsons Infrastructure & Technology	Turner Corporation

HISTORICAL FINANCIALS

Company Type: Private

Income Statement

FYE: December 31

	REVENUE ($ mil.)	NET INCOME ($ mil.)	NET PROFIT MARGIN	EMPLOYEES
12/15	322	7	2.2%	429
12/14	225	5	2.6%	—
12/13	225	5	2.6%	—
12/12	251	6	2.8%	—
Annual Growth	8.6%	0.4%	—	—

2015 Year-End Financials

Return on assets: 14.1% Cash ($ mil.): 14
Return on equity: 2.2%
Current ratio: 1.10

M.G. OIL COMPANY

EXECUTIVES

President, Marlyn G Erickson
General Manager, Dave Kulish
Sales Manager, Ken Hutton
Manager, Mike Boken
Store Manager, Beth Delvaux
Store Manager, Kristina Baysinger
Sales Manager, Todd Moe
Auditors: KETEL THORSTENSON LLP RAPID

LOCATIONS

HQ: M.G. OIL COMPANY
 1180 CREEK DR, RAPID CITY, SD 577034111
Phone: 605 342-0527
Web: WWW.MGOIL.OPENFOS.COM

HISTORICAL FINANCIALS

Company Type: Private

Income Statement

FYE: December 31

	REVENUE ($ mil.)	NET INCOME ($ mil.)	NET PROFIT MARGIN	EMPLOYEES
12/15	301	5	1.8%	450
12/14	355	10	3.0%	—
12/13	349	4	1.4%	—
12/12	338	5	1.7%	—
Annual Growth	(3.9%)	(1.9%)	—	—

2015 Year-End Financials

Return on assets: 3.0%
Return on equity: 1.8%
Current ratio: 0.30
Cash ($ mil.): 2

M.H. LOGISTICS CORP.

EXECUTIVES

Chief Executive Officer, John S Wieland
Board of Directors, Clyde Weiland
Sales Manager, Chad Ferry
Sales Manager, David Manoni
Branch Manager, Ron Patterson
Manager, Aaron Phillips
Operations Manager, Amy Bailey
Administrative Assistant, April McKim
Sales Manager, Bob Lunt
Auditors: CLIFTONLARSONALLEN LLP PEORIA

LOCATIONS

HQ: M.H. LOGISTICS CORP.
2001 HARTMAN, CHILLICOTHE, IL 615239198
Phone: 309 579-8030

HISTORICAL FINANCIALS

Company Type: Private

Income Statement

FYE: December 31

	REVENUE ($ mil.)	NET INCOME ($ mil.)	NET PROFIT MARGIN	EMPLOYEES
12/15	238	10	4.4%	700
12/14	218	8	3.9%	—
12/13	0	7	—	—
12/12	190	7	3.9%	—
Annual Growth	7.8%	11.6%	—	—

2015 Year-End Financials

Return on assets: 4.6%
Return on equity: 4.4%
Current ratio: 1.40
Cash ($ mil.): —

MACK-CALI REALTY, L. P.

EXECUTIVES

Chief Executive Officer, Mitchell Hersh
President, Mitchell E Hersh
Vice-President, Christopher Delorenzo
Vice-President, Daniel Wagner
Financial Executive, Esther Lee
Vice-President, John Adderly
Project Manager, Mike Dalessio
Vice-President, Diane Chayes
Executive Vice-President, Barry Lefkowitz

Auditors: PRICEWATERHOUSECOOPERS LLP NE

LOCATIONS

HQ: MACK-CALI REALTY, L. P.
4 BECKER FARM RD STE 104, ROSELAND, NJ 070681734
Phone: 973 577-2472

HISTORICAL FINANCIALS

Company Type: Private

Income Statement

FYE: December 31

	ASSETS ($ mil.)	NET INCOME ($ mil.)	INCOME AS % OF ASSETS	EMPLOYEES
12/16	4,296	130	3.0%	2
12/15	4,063	(142)	—	—
12/14	4,192	31	0.7%	—
12/13	4,515	(19)	—	—
Annual Growth	(1.6%)	—	—	—

2016 Year-End Financials

Return on assets: 26.1%
Return on equity: 21.2%
Sales ($ mil): 613

MAGEE-WOMENS HOSPITAL OF UPMC

EXECUTIVES

President, Leslie C Davis
Board of Directors, Claire Williams
Director, Eileen Simonns
Manager, Catherine Smith

LOCATIONS

HQ: MAGEE-WOMENS HOSPITAL OF UPMC
300 HALKET ST, PITTSBURGH, PA 152133108
Phone: 412 641-1000
Web: WWW.MAGEE.UPMC.COM

HISTORICAL FINANCIALS

Company Type: Private

Income Statement

FYE: June 30

	REVENUE ($ mil.)	NET INCOME ($ mil.)	NET PROFIT MARGIN	EMPLOYEES
06/15	823	62	7.6%	2,300
06/00	154	13	9.0%	—
Annual Growth	11.8%	10.5%	—	—

2015 Year-End Financials

Return on assets: 0.6%
Return on equity: 7.6%
Current ratio: 6.00
Cash ($ mil.): 1

MAIMONIDES MEDICAL CENTER

Maimonides Medical Center a not-for-profit hospital offers emergency medicine surgical procedures psychiatric treatment and other traditional hospital services to patients in Brooklyn New York. It has more than 710 beds and more than 70 sub-specialty treatment programs for a range of conditions including cancer cardiac stroke neurological pediatric and women's health ailments. It also operates outpatient family health and specialty clinics. Maimonides Medical Center is an independent teaching hospital that serves as a training facility for SUNY-Brooklyn St. George's University and other schools.

Financial Performance
In fiscal 2015 revenue remained flat at $1.1 billion compared to 2014. Although net patient service revenue rose 1% the hospital saw a 23% decline in "other" revenue. Net income fell 78% to $11 million that year as expenses rose; the center also reported accrued benefits liabilities to be recognized in future periods.

Despite the decline in profits operating cash flow increased 203% to $33 million primarily due to a change in receivables for patient fare.

Strategy
Maimonides Medical Center works to keep its utilization rates up (the number of patients it sees) and make itself attractive to doctors by making capital investments in its facilities and technology systems on a regular basis. In 2015 it established a partnership with North Shore-LIJ Health System (now Northwell) through which the systems will share services infrastructure and expertise; Northshore will also provide Maimonides with funding.

The hospital uses a fully-implemented electronic health record (EHR) system that includes a computerized physician order entry system (CPOE) that reduces prescription errors and a picture archival communications system (PACS) to store digital radiology images. The use of such technology is becoming increasingly tied to how the government reimburses hospitals for the services they provide especially in the new health care reform laws.

Company Background
Maimonides Medical Center traces its roots to the New Utrecht Dispensary which opened in 1911. The medical center later merged with Beth Moses and United Israel Zion hospitals in 1947. It is named after 12th-century philosopher Rabbi Moshe Ben Maimon.

EXECUTIVES

J. Vice President Professional Affairs (2000), Sheila Namm
EVP and CFO, Robert Naldi
VP Management Information Systems and CIO, Walter J. Fahey
Executive Vice President Clinical Affairs & Affiliations, David I. Cohen
EVP and COO, Dominick Stanzione
President and CEO, Kenneth Gibbs
Assistant Vice President, William Howe
Vice President, Andrew Leguelof
VICE PRESIDENT FOR LEGAL AFFAIRS, Anthony Mancuso
Chairman, Eugene J. Keilin

LOCATIONS

HQ: MAIMONIDES MEDICAL CENTER
4802 10TH AVE, BROOKLYN, NY 112192916
Phone: 718 581-0598
Web: WWW.MAIMONIDESMED.ORG

PRODUCTS/OPERATIONS

2014 Sales

	% of total
Net patient revenue less provision for bad debts	95
Net assets released from restrictions	-
Other revenue	5
Total	**100**

Selected Services
Adult Primary Care
Ambulatory Health Services
Bay Parkway Multi-Specialty
Manfredi Family Health Center
Newkirk Family Health Center
Outpatient Eye Clinic
Pediatric Primary Care
Primary Health Services
Sheepshead Bay
Women's Primary Care Services

COMPETITORS

Beth Israel Medical Center	Lutheran HealthCare
Bronx-Lebanon Hospital	Montefiore Medical
Brookdale University Hospital	New York City Health and Hospitals
Brooklyn Hospital Center	New York Methodist Hospital
Catholic Healthcare System	NewYork-Presbyterian Hospital
Continuum Health Partners	North Shore University Hospital
Jamaica Hospital Medical Center	SUNY Downstate Staten Island
Kingsbrook Jewish Medical Center	University Hospital
Long Island College Hospital	Wyckoff Heights Medical Center

HISTORICAL FINANCIALS
Company Type: Private

Income Statement
FYE: December 31

	REVENUE ($ mil.)	NET INCOME ($ mil.)	NET PROFIT MARGIN	EMPLOYEES
12/15	890	(2)	—	6,382
12/14	884	10	1.2%	—
12/13	1,062	26	2.5%	—
12/09	928	37	4.0%	—
Annual Growth	(0.7%)	—	—	—

2015 Year-End Financials
Return on assets: 9.2%   Cash ($ mil.): 14
Return on equity: (-0.2%)
Current ratio: 0.50

MAIN LINE HEALTHCARE

EXECUTIVES

Chief Executive Officer, Michael Buongiorno
Manager, Michelle Snyder
Director, Irv Herling

LOCATIONS

HQ: MAIN LINE HEALTHCARE
3803 WEST CHESTER PIKE # 190, NEWTOWN
SQUARE, PA 190732333
Phone: 610 648-1644

HISTORICAL FINANCIALS
Company Type: Private

Income Statement
FYE: June 30

	REVENUE ($ mil.)	NET INCOME ($ mil.)	NET PROFIT MARGIN	EMPLOYEES
06/16	231	(0)	—	760
06/11	128	(9)	—	—
06/10	118	(7)	—	—
Annual Growth	11.8%	—	—	—

2016 Year-End Financials
Return on assets: 1.0%   Cash ($ mil.): 2
Return on equity: (-0.1%)
Current ratio: 0.60

MAIN LINE HOSPITALS, INC.

Bryn Mawr Hospital a member of the Main Line not-for-profit health network is an acute care facility providing a variety of inpatient and outpatient services in the western suburbs of Philadelphia. With some 320 beds Bryn Mawr Hospital is recognized nationally for its orthopedic program. Founded in 1893 by Dr. George Gerhard the teaching hospital also provides cancer cardiac surgical pediatric reproductive health diagnostic imaging psychiatric bariatric and wound care services. The hospital also operates the Main Line Health Center outpatient facility (which includes a comprehensive breast center) in Newtown Square.Operations-Based in Bryn Mawr Pennsylvania Bryn Mawr Hospital boasts specialized departments such as a Comprehensive Breast Center; Wound Healing Center at Bryn Mawr Hospital; Outpatient Imaging Center; Center for Reproductive Medicine; Cancer Center; Main Line Health Heart Center; Center for Addictive Diseases; Level III Neonatal Intensive Care Unit; and Nemours Pediatric Partners at Bryn Mawr Hospital. The hospital also operates an outpatient health center in Newton Square Pennsylvania.Bryn Mawr Hospital admits some 18000 patients annually performing around 4800 inpatient and 6800 outpatient surgeries. It provides care to more than 2000 newborns and receives some 47000 emergency department visits each year. StrategyMain Line Health in 2015 announced plans to invest $200 million to modernize Bryn Mawr Hospital. The initiative is the most significant renovation ever for the hospital and it includes plans to build a five-story patient-care pavilion and convert all patient rooms to private rooms.Like many hospitals Bryn Mawr Hospital aims to expand its outpatient services and connect to medical practices. The practice helps to boost the number of referrals to its facility and grow physician relations throughout the community.Bryn Mawr Hospital collaborates with Nemours/Alfred I. duPont Hospital for Children to provide 24/7 pediatric care for the pediatric inpatient unit and the pediatric emergency department with added board-certified emergency medicine physicians. In 2015 the hospital formed a partnership with Lifecycle WomanCare to provide specialized care to pregnant and postpartum families in the community.

EXECUTIVES

Director of Radiology Services, Emma Simpson
Medical Director of The Main Line Health Stroke Program, Gary Friday
SVP Medical Affairs and Chief Medical Officer, Donald Arthur
Vice President Material Management, Chris Torres
Vice President of Finance and Treasurer, Michael Bouongiono
Vice President Planning and Business Development, Joel Port
Vice President and Chief Medical Information Officer, Harm Scherpbier
Medical Director Bryn Mawr Rehab Hospital, John Kraus
Vice President and CIO, Karen Thomas

LOCATIONS

HQ: MAIN LINE HOSPITALS, INC.
130 S BRYN MAWR AVE, BRYN MAWR, PA 190103121
Phone: 610 526-3000
Web: WWW.BRYNMAWRUROLOGY.COM

COMPETITORS

Abington Memorial Hospital
Albert Einstein Healthcare Network
Christiana Care
Crozer-Keystone Health System
Doylestown Hospital
Memorial Hospital (PA)
Moses Taylor Hospital
North Philadelphia Health System
Tenet Healthcare
University of Pennsylvania Health System
Virtua Memorial

HISTORICAL FINANCIALS
Company Type: Private

Income Statement
FYE: June 30

	REVENUE ($ mil.)	NET INCOME ($ mil.)	NET PROFIT MARGIN	EMPLOYEES
06/16	1,278	112	8.8%	5,840
06/15	1,103	174	15.9%	—
06/10	953	114	12.0%	—
06/08	11	2	19.2%	—
Annual Growth	80.7%	64.0%	—	—

2016 Year-End Financials
Return on assets: 3.3%   Cash ($ mil.): 102
Return on equity: 8.8%
Current ratio: 1.80

MAINE MEDICAL CENTER

Maine Medical Center (MMC) makes healing happen for the residents of northern New England. Part of MaineHealth the not-for-profit medical center consists of a tertiary care community hospital The Barbara Bush Children's Hospital and outpatient clinics. Specialty services include cancer care geriatrics emergency medicine cardiovascular care rehabilitation neurology orthopedics and women's health. Through its partnership with the Tufts University School of Medicine the 640-bed teaching hospital provides a variety of medical education and training programs. MMC also conducts research through the Maine Medical Center Research Institute. The medical center was founded in 1874 with 40 beds.

Operations

MMC boasts a large ever-expanding outpatient segment that provides day surgery cardiac catheterization laboratory services and rehabilitation services. It also operates about three dozen outpatient clinics. MMC provides preventive and consultation services including the MMC Diabetes Center the AIDS Consultation Service and the Center for Lipids and Cardiovascular Health.

MMC is expanding the surgical facilities at its main campus. Due for completion in 2015 the medical center embarked on a $40-million expansion plan that will add five modern operating rooms including a cardiac hybrid operating room and 20 perioperative spaces for patient prep and recovery.

The medical center is one of the largest employers in its service territory with a workforce of some

6500. Its Maine Medical Partners physician organization maintains about 175 doctors who provide care at some 30 primary and specialty care centers. MMC also provides more than 20% of charity care for uninsured or underinsured patients in the state.

Geographic Reach

Located in Portland the MMC serves the northern New England area.

Strategy

In keeping with its reputation of being technologically forward the hospital operates a Telestroke Network that provides area residents with around-the-clock access to MMC's neurology and ER physicians. The Telestroke Network is a form of telemedicine an increasingly popular way of expanding access to care by allowing patients to "visit" physicians either telephonically or via streaming web and video. MMC is also one of a growing number of teaching hospitals to use high-tech simulation rooms to train medical students.

To improve the quality of care MMC is enacting evidence-based medicine programs. Through such programs hospitals seek to lower medical expenses and improve patient outcomes through data exchange systems that allow physicians to review best practices in specific medical fields. The hospital is also looking to expand its research programs by partnering with other area medical R&D firms.

EXECUTIVES

EVP and COO, Richard W. (Rich) Petersen
Senior Vice President Chief Information Officer, Barry Blumenfeld
SVP Planning and Marketing Maine Medical Center and MaineHealth, Mark A. Harris
VP Medical and Academic Affairs; Chief Medical Officer and Academic Dean Tufts University School of Medicine Medical School Program, Peter W. Bates
EVP and COO, Jeffrey D. (Jeff) Sanders
President Medical Staff, M. Parker Roberts
President and a Principal of CBRE|Boulos Property Management, Morris Fisher
President MaineHealth, William L. Caron
Vice President, Susan Doliner
Medical Director of Neurocritical Care, David Seder
Pharmd, Marizela Savic
Vice President for Operations, Michael J Ryan
Vice President of Strategy and Business Development, Edward Farrell
Nursing Director, Shannan Reid
Vice President Neurosciences Service Line, Kathryn Coolidge
Vice President Of Finance, Chuck Alsdurf
Vice President Revenue Cycle, Chausse Paul
Vice President System Planning, Sue Cobb
Associate Vice President of Nursing, Kathleen Hale
Vice President Quality Improvement, Darren Childs
Nursing Director, Peggy Doliner
Senior Vice President, Maureen Van
Medical Director of Heart Failure, Esther Shao
Medical Director of Care Coordination, Christopher Wellins
Medical Director, Tammi Schaeffer
Medical Director, Mark Fulton
Chairman, Christopher W. Emmons
Secretary, Kay Mullen
Secretary, Penny Mills
Board Director and District, Aaron Weiss

LOCATIONS

HQ: MAINE MEDICAL CENTER
22 BRAMHALL ST, PORTLAND, ME 041023175
Phone: 207 662-0111
Web: WWW.MMC.ORG

PRODUCTS/OPERATIONS

Selected Specialty Centers
Cancer Institute

Cardiovascular Institute
Emergency Medicine
Family Birth Center
Joint Replacement Center
Neuroscience Institute
The Barbara Bush Children's Hospital

COMPETITORS

Eastern Maine Healthcare Systems	MaineGeneral Health
Franklin Community Health Network	Mercy Health System of Maine
Maine Coast Memorial Hospital	St. Joseph Healthcare

HISTORICAL FINANCIALS

Company Type: Private

Income Statement FYE: September 30

	REVENUE ($ mil.)	NET INCOME ($ mil.)	NET PROFIT MARGIN	EMPLOYEES
09/15	1,023	(39)	—	2,000
09/14	905	53	5.9%	—
09/13	908	118	13.0%	—
09/08	685	49	7.3%	—
Annual Growth	5.9%	—	—	—

2015 Year-End Financials

Return on assets: 3.6% Cash ($ mil.): 112
Return on equity: (-3.8%)
Current ratio: 0.80

MANAGEMENT & TRAINING CORPORATION

Management & Training Corporation (MTC) prepares prison inmates for re-entry into society. It provides a variety of academic vocational and social-skills training in rehabilitation-oriented private prisons. Its holistic education model offers programs to help inmates avoid substance abuse as they also boost their engagement in community service find work and increase their cognitive skills. As part of its services MTC operates about two dozen correctional facilities in eight states through a contract with the Department of Labor. The company also operates Job Corps centers and provides healthcare-related services to correctional facilities.

Operations

MTC operates through four divisions: Correctional Education & Training MTC Medical and Economic & Social Development. Its correctional division operates facilities that house more than 31100 inmates and is one of the largest US correctional contractors for the Department of Labor. The Education & Training division trains some 14000 young adults each year at 23 Job Corps centers.

The company's MTC Medical unit provides subcontracted healthcare services to correctional facilities by employing a range of medical providers including dentists optometrists psychiatrists and psychologists and physicians. The Economic & Social Development division which offers research retraining and vocational training through contracts with other organizations has provided vocational training to citizens in Iraq and research and retraining efforts in China Haiti Mongolia Southern

Sudan Tunisia Pakistan Indonesia Jordan and Palestine.

The company trains its supervisors senior managers and executives through its MTC Corporate University while its MTC Institute performs research into forming best practices related to addressing issues facing those who work with Job Corps youth and prison inmates.

Geographic Reach

The company's main offices are located in Centerville Utah and it has satellite centers in Georgia Texas and Washington DC. MTC operates through more than 60 contracts in about 20 states including correctional facility contracts in Arizona California Florida Idaho Ohio New Mexico Mississippi and Texas.

MTC operates internationally providing governments NGOs ministries and private entities with customized training programs designed to help develop workforces. Its international unit has assisted clients in Africa Asia Australia the Middle East and North America.

Sales and Marketing

In addition to the Department of Labor the company has held contracts with the US Agency for International Development the African Development Bank UNICEF and other organizations. It also serves state agencies such as the Texas Department of Criminal Justice.

Strategy

MTC expands by recruiting and retaining quality educators health professionals and international consultants. To maximize its employees' potential the company conducts leadership development programs for all of its employees. MTC also expands by adding new contracts with state correctional agencies.

Working with MTC in 2014 Georgia's Wilkinson County Correctional Facility started a new program to help inmates deal with anger issues. The following year MTC was granted a contract to operate the Polk Secure Adult Detention Center in Livingston Texas.

Company Background

MRC was founded in 1981.

EXECUTIVES

Senior Vice President of Training Programs, John Pedersen
President, R. Scott Marquardt
Vice President Corrections Marketing, Mike Murphy
Vice President Development, Lynette Greenwell
Vice President Operations, Janae Panagoplos
Vice President Southeast Intermountain Region, Dean Hoffman
Vice President and General Counsel, Dawn Call
V Chairman, Jane Marquardt
Chairman, Robert Marquardt
Auditors: KPMG LLP SALT LAKE CITY UT

LOCATIONS

HQ: MANAGEMENT & TRAINING CORPORATION
500 N MARKET PLACE DR # 100, CENTERVILLE, UT 840141711
Phone: 801 693 2600
Web: WWW.MTCTRAINS.COM

PRODUCTS/OPERATIONS

Selected Services
Communicate through formal and informal channels
Develop custom training for students clients & offenders
Manage facilities
Provide community connections
Provide data solutions

COMPETITORS

Avalon Correctional Services
Community Education Centers

Conmed Healthcare
Corizon
Corrections Corporation of America
G4S
GEO Group
MHM Services
Res-Care
Wexford Health

HISTORICAL FINANCIALS
Company Type: Private

Income Statement

	REVENUE ($ mil.)	NET INCOME ($ mil.)	NET PROFIT MARGIN	EMPLOYEES
FYE: December 31				
12/15	753	30	4.0%	9,500
12/13	735	50	6.9%	—
12/12	704	45	6.5%	—
12/11	174	0	—	—
Annual Growth	—	2658.2%		

2015 Year-End Financials
Return on assets: 3.0%   Cash ($ mil.): 10
Return on equity: 4.0%
Current ratio: 1.50

MANAGEMENT SCIENCES FOR HEALTH, INC.

EXECUTIVES

President, Jonathan Quick
Manager, Matt Fuller
Vice-President, John Gatto
Director, Julie Obrien
Manager, Claudio Lomonaco
Vice-President, Mary Jamar
Auditors: TONNESON & COMPANY INC WAKEFI

LOCATIONS

HQ: MANAGEMENT SCIENCES FOR HEALTH, INC.
  200 RIVERS EDGE DR, MEDFORD, MA 021555479
Phone: 617 250-9500
Web: WWW.MSH.ORG

HISTORICAL FINANCIALS
Company Type: Private

Income Statement

	REVENUE ($ mil.)	NET INCOME ($ mil.)	NET PROFIT MARGIN	EMPLOYEES
FYE: June 30				
06/15	303	2	0.9%	400
06/10	247	1	0.6%	—
06/08	134	1	0.9%	—
06/06	0	0	—	—
Annual Growth	—	—	—	—

2015 Year-End Financials
Return on assets: 9.0%   Cash ($ mil.): 12
Return on equity: 0.9%
Current ratio: 1.70

MANCHESTER MEMORIAL HOSPITAL INC

EXECUTIVES

Director, Lawrence Murphy
Senior Vice-President, Dennis Mc Conville
Director, Edward R Sampt
Financial Executive, Francis Bradley
Engineer, John Goode

LOCATIONS

HQ: MANCHESTER MEMORIAL HOSPITAL INC
  71 HAYNES ST, MANCHESTER, CT 060404188
Phone: 860 646-1222

HISTORICAL FINANCIALS
Company Type: Private

Income Statement

	REVENUE ($ mil.)	NET INCOME ($ mil.)	NET PROFIT MARGIN	EMPLOYEES
FYE: September 30				
09/15	183	7	4.0%	1,056
09/14	178	2	1.4%	—
09/13	175	(0)	—	—
09/12	175	9	5.6%	—
Annual Growth	1.5%	(9.2%)	—	—

2015 Year-End Financials
Return on assets: 11.8%   Cash ($ mil.): 5
Return on equity: 4.0%
Current ratio: 0.90

MANN+HUMMEL FILTRATION TECHNOLOGY INTERMEDIATE HOLDINGS INC.

Affinia Group Intermediate Holdings caters to car drivers with a natural affinity for parts. The company is a leading designer manufacturer and distributor of aftermarket vehicular components. Affinia's slew of products — primarily oil and air filters ball joints idler arms steering components and suspension parts — are made for passenger cars; SUVs; light medium and heavy trucks; and off-highway vehicles. Its well-known brand names including McQuay-Norris Nakata ecoLAST Raybestos and WIX are sold in 70 countries. It primarily serves the US and South American markets.

Geographic Reach

Affinia has operations in North and South America Europe and Asia spanning nearly 12 countries. It manufactures and distributes products in 11 countries and sells into more than 70 countries. The US accounts for 42% of the company's sales; Brazil is its second-largest market generating 30%.

Sales and Marketing

Affinia's largest customers include aftermarket distributors NAPA (22% of total sales) and CAR-QUEST (6%). Other customers include AutoZone O'Reilly Auto Parts and Canadian Tire. The company derived 97% of its 2013 net sales from the on and off-highway replacement products and services industry.

Financial Performance

The company saw its revenues jump 8% from 2012 to 2013. The growth for 2013 was driven by a 9% increase in its filtration segment due to increased sales in its North American and Asia operations driven by increased volume as a result of market growth and new business with existing customers. European sales increased in 2013 due to higher sales in Poland along with favorable currency translation effects in Poland. Increased Venezuela filter sales were the main contributor to the increase in South America sales.

Affinia posted net income of $10 million in 2013 after posting net losses in 2011 and 2012. The positive net income for 2013 was attributed to the absence of losses from discontinued operations as opposed to other years.

Strategy

With the sale of its Brake North America and Asia group in 2012 and the announced signing of an agreement to sell its Chassis group in 2014 the company is focused on operating strictly as a Filtration segment and Affinia South America segment company. (Affinia agreed to sell its chassis operations to Federal-Mogul in January 2014.)

Company Background

Affinia got its start in 2004. Private-equity firm Cypress and OMERS (Ontario Municipal Employees Retirement System) a Canadian pension fund bought the auto replacement parts business of Dana Holding Corporation to form Affinia. In mid-2010 Affinia filed to go public but remains privately owned.

EXECUTIVES

Senior Vice President Secretary and General
  Counsel, Dave Sturgess
Auditors: DELOITTE & TOUCHE LLP CHARLOT

LOCATIONS

HQ: MANN+HUMMEL FILTRATION TECHNOLOGY
  INTERMEDIATE HOLDINGS INC.
  1 WIX WAY, GASTONIA, NC 280546142
Phone: 704 869-3300
Web: WWW.AFFINIAGROUP.COM

2013 Sales

	% of total
US	42
Brazil	30
Poland	12
Venezuela	6
Canada	3
Other	7
Total	100

PRODUCTS/OPERATIONS

2013 Sales

	$ mil.	% of total
Filteration	902	66
South America	459	34
Total	1,361	100

Selected Products and Services
Filteration
Air FiltersCabin Air FiltersCoolant System FiltrationFuel
  FiltersHeavy DutyHydraulic FiltersLight DutyOil
  FiltersRacing
Steering/Suspension
Alignment ProductsBall JointsControl Arm
  AssembliesIdler ArmsSway Bar LinkTie Rod
  EndsSelected Brands
McQuay-Norris

Nakata
Raybestos Chassis
WIX-Filtron
WIX ecoLAST
WIX Filters

Selected Markets
Agriculture
Construction equipment
Heavy-duty trucks
Light-duty cars and trucks
Marine
Mass transit
Mining
Power generation
Recreational vehicles
Small engine
Stationary equipment
Water filtration

COMPETITORS

CLARCOR	Genuine Parts
Cardone Industries	Honeywell
Cummins	International
Donaldson Company	UCI International
Federal-Mogul	

HISTORICAL FINANCIALS
Company Type: Private

Income Statement FYE: December 31

	REVENUE ($ mil.)	NET INCOME ($ mil.)	NET PROFIT MARGIN	EMPLOYEES
12/15	899	(72)		5,630
12/14	1,396	82	5.9%	—
12/13	1,361	10	0.7%	—
12/12	1,453	(102)	—	—
Annual Growth	(14.8%)	—	—	—

2015 Year-End Financials

Return on assets: 9.6%   Cash ($ mil.): 28
Return on equity: (-8.0%)
Current ratio: 0.30

MANTECA UNIFIED SCHOOL DISTRICT

EXECUTIVES

Superintendent, Jason Messer
Director, Virginia Brown
Superintendent, Catherine Nichols-Washer
Real Estate Agent, Margaret Levy
Administrative Assistant, Karen King
Auditors: VAVRINEK TRINE DAY & CO LL

LOCATIONS

HQ: MANTECA UNIFIED SCHOOL DISTRICT
2271 W LOUISE AVE, MANTECA, CA 953378381
Phone: 209 825-3200
Web: WWW.MANTECAUSD.NET

HISTORICAL FINANCIALS
Company Type: Private

Income Statement FYE: June 30

	REVENUE ($ mil.)	NET INCOME ($ mil.)	NET PROFIT MARGIN	EMPLOYEES
06/16	282	67	24.0%	1,400
06/09	203	(6)	—	—
06/08	213	(25)	—	—
06/07	278	5	2.1%	—
Annual Growth	0.2%	31.6%	—	—

MAP INTERNATIONAL (INC.)

EXECUTIVES

President, Steve Stirling
Board of Directors, Edwin G Corr
Board of Directors, Ingrid M Mail
Vice-President, Edwin Corr
Senior Manager, Jack Morse
Auditors: CAPINCROUSE LLP ATLANTA GEO

LOCATIONS

HQ: MAP INTERNATIONAL (INC.)
4700 GLYNCO PKWY, BRUNSWICK, GA 315256901
Phone: 912 265-6010
Web: WWW.MAP.ORG

HISTORICAL FINANCIALS
Company Type: Private

Income Statement FYE: September 30

	REVENUE ($ mil.)	NET INCOME ($ mil.)	NET PROFIT MARGIN	EMPLOYEES
09/15	547	60	11.1%	200
09/14	320	15	4.9%	—
09/13	348	(3)	—	—
09/12	244	29	12.2%	—
Annual Growth	30.9%	26.7%	—	—

2015 Year-End Financials

Return on assets: —   Cash ($ mil.): —
Return on equity: 11.1%
Current ratio: 0.40

MARCUM LLP

Marcum LLP (formerly MarcumStonefield) is making a mark on the world of accounting and consulting. With more than 20 offices in the US China and the Caribbean Marcum offers a full range of business and personal financial services including accounting auditing and tax and investment consulting. It also offers professional services such as mergers and acquisitions planning family office services forensic accounting and litigation support. The firm serves multiple industries such as construction health care real estate media and entertainment and financial services. Founded in 1951 Marcum is a member of the Marcum Group.

Operations

Marcum also provides international services through The Leading Edge Alliance.

Geographic Reach

New York-headquartered Marcum has more than 20 offices throughout New York New Jersey Massachusetts Connecticut Pennsylvania California Florida Grand Cayman and China (Beijing Guangzhou Hangzhou and Shanghai).

Sales and Marketing

Marcum serves a variety of clients With its staff of 160 partners and 1300 professionals including: broker dealers; employee benefit plan providers (ERISA); manufacturers; contractors; healthcare professionals; financial institutions; transaction services companies; and high-net-worth individuals among others.

Marcum has also entered several niche markets serving private equity partnerships; hedge funds; SEC registrants; real estate; public and not-for-profit sectors; and bankruptcies and receiverships; as well as a China specialty practice.

Strategy

Marcum has been pursuing a nationwide growth strategy in recent years mostly through mergers and acquisitions. In 2014 for example the firm acquired small accounting firms to expand its reach into Massachusetts Rhode Island and Connecticut. In 2013 and 2012 it similarly purchased four more accounting firms to broaden its expertise and extend its reach into southern California New York City and Boston regions.

Mergers and Acquisitions

In 2014 Marcum took over two small accounting firms Braver PC and Thomas E. Finn P.C. Braver PC has offices in Needham MA and Providence RI; while Thomas E. Finn P.C. is located in Greenwich CT.

In 2013 it added three more firms under the Marcum banner — WilsonMorgan LLP Cornerstone Accounting Group and Parent McLaughlin & Nagle CPAs Inc. WilsonMorgan is located in Irvine CA while Cornerstone Accounting Group which focuses on the real estate industry is in New York City. Parent McLaughlin & Nagle CPAs Inc. came with deep roots in the Boston financial services community.

In 2012 Marcum acquired the Boston firm Robert Finnegan & Lynah PC.

Company Background

Marcum is a member of the Marcum Group a collection of companies that offer services such as technology solutions (Marcum Technology) job recruitment (Marcum Search) and wealth management (Marcum Financial Services).

EXECUTIVES

Vice Chairman, David Bukzin

LOCATIONS

HQ: MARCUM LLP
750 3RD AVE FL 11, NEW YORK, NY 100172716
Phone: 212 485-5500
Web: WWW.MARCUMTECHNOLOGY.COM

PRODUCTS/OPERATIONS

Selected Industry Specializations
Construction
Entertainment
Financial services
Health care
Hedge funds
High-net-worth individuals
High-tech and software
Independent grocers
Insurance
Manufacturing and distribution
Maritime
Real estate
Talent and literary agencies

Selected Products and Services
Alternative investments
Accounting services
Assurance and audit
Business management services
Business valuation
Cost segregation
Family office services
Forensic accounting
Hedge funds and investment partnerships
Information technology consulting
Litigation services
Mergers and acquisitions
Personal financial management
Sales and use tax recovery
SEC-related services
Staffing
State and local tax consulting
Tax advisory and compliance services
Tax controversy resolution
Trust and estate planning
Wealth management

COMPETITORS

Anchin Block & Anchin	KPMG L.L.P.
CohnReznick	Marks Paneth & Shron
Deloitte & Touche	PricewaterhouseCoopers
EisnerAmper	US
Ernst & Young LLP	Rothstein Kass
Grassi & CO.	

HISTORICAL FINANCIALS
Company Type: Private

Income Statement
FYE: December 31

	REVENUE ($ mil.)	NET INCOME ($ mil.)	NET PROFIT MARGIN	EMPLOYEES
12/15	273	15	5.8%	1,360
12/14	251	15	6.1%	—
12/10	0	0	—	—
12/09	77	26	34.4%	—
Annual Growth	23.3%	(8.5%)	—	—

2015 Year-End Financials
Return on assets: 0.3%   Cash ($ mil.): —
Return on equity: 5.8%
Current ratio: 1.50

MARIETTA MEMORIAL HOSPITAL INC

EXECUTIVES

Chairman of the Board, Tom Tucker
Board of Directors, Colleen Cook
Account Manager, Doug Full
Manager, Cindy Carpenter

LOCATIONS

HQ: MARIETTA MEMORIAL HOSPITAL INC
  401 MATTHEW ST, MARIETTA, OH 457501699
Phone: 740 374-1400
Web: WWW.MMHOSPITAL.ORG

HISTORICAL FINANCIALS
Company Type: Private

Income Statement
FYE: September 30

	REVENUE ($ mil.)	NET INCOME ($ mil.)	NET PROFIT MARGIN	EMPLOYEES
09/16	400	7	1.8%	1,100
09/15	378	12	3.4%	—
09/14	307	(0)	—	—
09/13	303	(1)	—	—
Annual Growth	9.7%	—	—	—

2016 Year-End Financials
Return on assets: 8.3%   Cash ($ mil.): 33
Return on equity: 1.8%
Current ratio: 1.80

MARIN GENERAL HOSPITAL

Serving Northern California's Marin County Marin General Hospital is the county's largest acute-care health care facility with some 235 beds. Opened in 1952 Marin General Hospital has been a member of Sutter Health since 1996. It operates the Marin Cancer Institute the Haynes Cardiovascular Institute the Surgery Center of Marin and The Institute for Health & Healing which provides holistic care within the hospital setting. Other services include adult psychiatric care a level III trauma center a family birthing center neonatal intensive care pediatrics and a cardiac catheterization lab.

EXECUTIVES

Director of HIM and Patient Access, Celia Lenson
Director of Pharmacy, Michael Sillman
Director of Nursing, Steven Thomas
Medical Director, Adrienne Fratini
Medical Director for Trauma, Edward Alfrey
Director of Nursing, Karin Reese
Member Board Of Directors, Joann Rossi

LOCATIONS

HQ: MARIN GENERAL HOSPITAL
  250 BON AIR RD, KENTFIELD, CA 949041784
Phone: 415 925-7000

COMPETITORS

California Pacific Medical Center	The Palo Alto Medical Foundation
Dignity Health	UCSF Medical

HISTORICAL FINANCIALS
Company Type: Private

Income Statement
FYE: December 31

	REVENUE ($ mil.)	NET INCOME ($ mil.)	NET PROFIT MARGIN	EMPLOYEES
12/15	342	20	6.1%	1,100
12/14	320	10	3.2%	—
12/13	323	9	2.8%	—
12/12	296	31	10.5%	—
Annual Growth	4.9%	(12.8%)	—	—

2015 Year-End Financials
Return on assets: 7.0%   Cash ($ mil.): 75
Return on equity: 6.1%
Current ratio: 2.50

MARION GENERAL HOSPITAL, INC.

EXECUTIVES

President, John Sanders
Supervisor, Jane Jolliff
Account Executive, Victor Vinluan

LOCATIONS

HQ: MARION GENERAL HOSPITAL, INC.
  1000 MCKINLEY PARK DR, MARION, OH 433026397
Phone: 740 383-8400
Web: WWW.MARIONONLINE.COM

HISTORICAL FINANCIALS
Company Type: Private

Income Statement
FYE: June 30

	REVENUE ($ mil.)	NET INCOME ($ mil.)	NET PROFIT MARGIN	EMPLOYEES
06/15	181	15	8.4%	1,300
06/09	0	0	—	—
Annual Growth	283.5%	—	—	—

2015 Year-End Financials
Return on assets: 6.0%   Cash ($ mil.): 34
Return on equity: 8.4%
Current ratio: 2.10

MARIST COLLEGE

Marist College is a gem among small private US colleges. The liberal arts college has a enrollment of more than 6300 students and a student-faculty ratio of 16-to-1. It offers more than 40 bachelor's and a dozen master's programs as well as some 20 certificate programs. It seven schools specialize in communication and the arts computer science and math continuing education liberal arts management science and social and behavioral sciences. In addition to its main 210-acre campus along the shores of the Hudson River the college has several off-campus extension sites that mainly cater to adult students. Marist was founded in 1929 to train new members in the Marist Brothers order of Catholic priests.

Operations

Marist College has recently been recognized by publications including Kiplinger's Private Finance magazine which named Marist as one of the best value private college in the US. It has also been on the Princeton Review's best colleges list with a special recognition for its extensive study abroad programs (including a branch campus in Florence Italy) as well as its business teaching criminal justice fashion and communication programs. Marist College also offers advanced IT resources to its students through a partnership with IBM which is also located in southeastern New York State.

Financial Performance

The college has an annual operating budget of $160 million.

In 2014 Marist College reported a 9% rise in revenues thanks to an increase in student tuition and fees as well as more grants and other income.

Company Background

Marist College was founded in 1929 as a training center for the brothers of the Roman Catholic Marist order.

EXECUTIVES

Vice President and CIO, William Thirsk
Exe Vice President, Geoffrey Brackett
Vice President For College Advancement, Christopher Delgiorno
Associate Vice President for Human Resources, Deborah Raikes
Vice President, Andrew James
Vice President: Christina Kelly, Christina Kelly
Vice President, Irene Elias
Vice President, Julianna Boniello
Vice President Class of 2017, Joshua Guevarra
Vice President, Steven Rizzo
Vice President of Athletic Affairs, Edward Oser
Vice President, Dave Emory
Associate Vice President for Development, Karen Rohr
Vice President, Thomas Haessler
Treasurer, Matt Blades
Treasurer, Amy Majkrzak
Secretary, Alex Gandolfo
Secretary, Hayley Denning
Secretary, Hannah Sayers
Treasurer, Stephanie Chouljian
Secretary, Kelsey Bradley
Treasurer, Samantha Cavallo
Secretary, Alyssa Nagel
Treasurer Class, Rebecca Yunker
Secretary Class, Caroline Turcotte
Auditors: GRANT THORNTON LLP NEW YORK

LOCATIONS

HQ: MARIST COLLEGE
3399 NORTH RD, POUGHKEEPSIE, NY 126011387
Phone: 845 575-3000
Web: WWW.MARIST.EDU

PRODUCTS/OPERATIONS

Majors
Accounting
American Studies
Applied Mathematics
Athletic Training
Biochemistry (B.A.)
Biochemistry (B.S.)
Biology
Biology Education
Biomedical Sciences
Business Administration
  Finance
  Human Resource Management
  International Business
  Marketing
Chemistry (B.A.)
Chemistry (B.S.)
Communication
  Advertising
  Communication Studies
  Journalism
  Public Relations
  Sports Communication
Computer Science
Computer Science/Game Design
Criminal Justice
Digital Media
Economics
Education
  Adolescence Education (Grades 7-12)
  Childhood/Special Education (Grades 1-6)
English
  Literature
  Theatre
  Writing
Environmental Science
  Policy
  Science
Fashion Design
Fashion Merchandising
Fine Arts
  Art History
  Studio Art
History
Information Technology and Systems
  Information Systems
  Information Technology
Mathematics
Media Studies and Production
Medical Technology
Modern Languages and Cultures
  French
  Italian
  Spanish
Philosophy
  Religious Studies
Political Science
  International Studies
  Public Affairs
Psychology
  Psychology
Social Work
Graduate Programs
Accounting MBA
MA in Communication
MA in Integrated Marketing Communication
MA in Mental Health Counseling
MA in Museum Studies
MA in School Psychology
Master of Arts in Educational Psychology
Master of Education (Initial Teaching Certification)
MBA- Master of Business Administration
MPA- Master of Public Administration
MS in Information Systems
MS in Software Development
Advanced Certificate in Information Systems

HISTORICAL FINANCIALS

Company Type: Private

Income Statement

	REVENUE ($ mil.)	NET INCOME ($ mil.)	NET PROFIT MARGIN	EMPLOYEES
06/15	239	21	8.9%	1,300
06/13	228	33	14.7%	—
06/10	211	47	22.3%	—
06/09	0	0	—	—
Annual Growth	—	230.2%	—	—

FYE: June 30

2015 Year-End Financials

Return on assets: 8.3%
Return on equity: 8.9%
Current ratio: 0.30

Cash ($ mil.): 60

MARITZ HOLDINGS INC.

Maritz may not send your employees on business trips but it will motivate them to go. The company's mission is to understand enable and motivate people to unleash their hidden potential enabling people to do things differently by developing their strengths knowledge and confidence. The Steve Maritz-owned company designs employee incentive and reward programs (including incentive travel rewards) and customer loyalty programs. It also plans corporate trade shows and events and offers traditional market research services such as the creation of product launch campaigns. Its programs are designed to help its clients improve workforce quality and customer satisfaction.

Operations

Maritz's subsidiaries and segments include Maritz Canada Maritz Dealer Solutions The Maritz Institute Maritz Journeys Maritz Loyalty Maritz Motivation Solutions Maritz Research and Maritz Travel.

Geographic Reach

A global player Maritz has offices in Canada Germany the UK and the US.

Sales and Marketing

Its customers include a majority of the Forbes 500 including businesses in the automotive financial services health care retail pharmaceutical telecommunications and professional and business services industries. Maritz has worked with such high-profile clients as AT&T Bank of America General Motors and Procter & Gamble.

Strategy

One of Maritz's competitive strengths is its widely diversified customer base which makes it less susceptible to regional or industry-specific economic downturns. It also makes acquisitions to strengthen its offerings in order to keep its competitive edge.

HISTORY

Edward Maritz an entrepreneur of Swiss-French descent founded the E. Maritz Jewelry Manufacturing Company in St. Louis in 1894. By 1900 the wholesaler and manufacturer of men's and women's jewelry was supplying retail jewelers across the South and West. By 1921 Maritz had become a major importer of Swiss watches which it sold to retail jewelers under the Merit Cymrex and Record brands. In the 1920s the company added diamond jewelry and silverware to its product mix. Edward Maritz died in 1929.

To drum up new business during the Depression Edward's son James began trying to sell watches

and jewelry to large corporations for use as sales and service awards pioneering the incentive market. The first sale for a nationwide employee incentive campaign was to Caradine Hat a St. Louis hatmaker in 1930. In 1948 Maritz handled a $2 million incentive program for Chevrolet.

In 1950 the Maritz family split the business into two operations. Brother Lloyd handled the jewelry business (it died in 1955 when Lloyd died); James took over the incentive operations which flourished. In the 1950s James expanded his company's offerings to include merchandise awards and in 1958 travel incentive awards (arranged through the newly acquired Holiday House Travel Center of Detroit). The enterprise adopted the corporate name Maritz Inc. in 1961. During the 1960s and early 1970s Maritz made a series of acquisitions closely allied with its motivation endeavors including Lee Creative Research the nucleus of what would become its market research operations (1973). The organization expanded internationally with the opening of Maritz offices in the UK and Mexico in 1974.

In 1980 the company acquired the Wilding division of Bell & Howell which it merged with another unit to form Maritz Communications Co. James died in 1981. Maritz beefed up its travel operations in the 1980s acquiring corporate travel agency Traveler's Service (St. Louis 1981) Byfield Travel (Chicago 1984) Beverly Hills Travel (Los Angeles 1986) and Travel Counselors International (Virginia 1986).

These acquisitions led to record sales in 1989 but sliding results in the early 1990s prompted the company to streamline its operations by cutting overlapping units. After a family boardroom tussle in 1993 William Maritz expanded his control by buying out his sister's 50% stake in the company and putting his two sons on the board. His son Stephen Maritz subsequently took over as president.

As part of its international expansion strategy Maritz acquired The Research Business Group the UK's largest independently owned marketing research firm (1993) and BLC the largest performance-improvement company in France (1994). In 1997 the company established an office in Manila its first in Asia.

In 1998 William Maritz stepped down as CEO and retained the title of chairman; his son Stephen succeeded him. In 1998 and 1999 the company boosted its international presence with acquisitions in Canada (group travel firm Partners in Performance marketing research firm Thompson Lightstone & Co.) and the Netherlands (Maritz B.V.).

Facing heat from online incentive programs the company launched its own online service e-Maritz in 2000. It also started Heybridge an e-commerce subsidiary that helps small and midsized businesses sell over the Internet. In 2001 Maritz purchased Librix Learning an online learning company.

The following year it purchased travel and incentive business McGettigan (later to be renamed Martiz McGettigan) to add depth to its client offerings. Also that same year Peter and Philip Maritz (brothers of chairman and CEO Steve Maritz) sued the company purportedly seeking a greater role in managing the family business. In the summer of 2003 the brothers again filed suit against Steve alleging that the purchase of McGettigan cost $10 million more than what was originally presented to the board. Peter and Philip's suits are an attempt to cash out of the family business -- which they feel lost value because of the McGettigan purchase — at a better price than they'd get now.

In early 2004 Maritz sold its data collection unit Delve to St. Louis-based Bush O'Donnell Capital Partners. The same year Maritz sold its TQ3 Travel Solutions division to Carlson Wagonlit Travel.

Steve Maritz became the sole owner of the company in 2006 after buying out his other family members' shares.

Maritz also expanded its product offerings and geographic reach in 2008 when it acquired Cascade Promotion Corporation a marketing and fulfillment business operating out of Boston Las Vegas and St. Louis. With Cascade catering to the gaming and technology industries the buyout gave Maritz access to growing niche markets.

Making ground into what it considers a high-growth market Maritz solidified its position in the prepaid card sector in 2010 when it acquired full ownership of American Express Incentive Services (AEIS). For more than a decade AEIS operated as a joint venture between Maritz and a subsidiary of American Express. AEIS is an independent issuer of prepaid products such as cards and American Express Travelers Cheques on the American Express network. The products are used for employee recognition consumer promotions and sales incentives.

EXECUTIVES

Chairman and CEO, W. Stephen (Steve) Maritz, age 60
President and COO, Dennis Hummel
CFO, Rick Ramos
President of Maritz Travel Company, David Peckinpaugh
Division Vice President Maritz Research, Lisa Weaner
VICE PRESIDENT MANAGING DIRECTOR, Alfredo Legoretta
Vice President, Dick Oconnor
Vice President Finance, Frank Munsch
Vice President, Mike Mcclernon
Vice President, Paula Schapp
Vice President, Tom Wilson
Vice President of Business Development, Greg Bogue
Vice President of Finance and Assistant Treasurer, Matt Glazer
Vice President of Sales, Mark Alt
Vice President Pharma Sector, Dave Caldwell
Div Vice President Project Management Office, Kim Clark
Vice President Global Business Manager, Joel Barone
Vice President of Engagement Marketing, Jen Hunter
Vice President, Stuart Bowling
Vice President Global Business Manager, Chris Haenni
Director Finance Assistant Treasurer, Thomas Sizemore
Treasurer, Cindy Dolan
Auditors: KPMG LLP ST LOUIS MO

LOCATIONS

HQ: MARITZ HOLDINGS INC.
1375 N HIGHWAY DR, FENTON, MO 630990001
Phone: 636 827-4000
Web: WWW.MARITZ.COM

PRODUCTS/OPERATIONS

Selected Services
Marketing Research
  Custom marketing research
  Customer satisfaction and customer value analysis
  Data collection (focus groups telephone interviews)
  Maritz Polls and Maritz Research Reports
  Syndicated buyer research
  Telecommunications research
Performance Improvement
  Communications
  e-Learning
  Fulfillment
  Internet consulting
  Loyalty marketing
  Measurement and feedback

Rewards and recognition
Travel
  Consulting services
  Corporate travel management
  Group travel services
  Travel award programs

COMPETITORS

Franklin Covey	J.D. Power
Gallup	JTB Corp.
GiftCertificates.com	Kantar Group
Harris Interactive	Motivcom
IMS Health	Nielsen
Information Resources Inc.	ORC International

HISTORICAL FINANCIALS
Company Type: Private

Income Statement
FYE: March 31

	REVENUE ($ mil.)	NET INCOME ($ mil.)	NET PROFIT MARGIN	EMPLOYEES
03/16	1,274	(16)	—	4,646
03/13	1,256	42	3.3%	—
03/12	1,155	47	4.1%	—
Annual Growth	2.5%	—	—	—

2016 Year-End Financials
Return on assets: 9.8%   Cash ($ mil.): 116
Return on equity: (-1.3%)
Current ratio: 0.60

MARJAM SUPPLY CO., INC.

EXECUTIVES

President, Mark Buller
Financial Executive, Bruce Respler
Manager, Glenn Thoven
Sales Manager, Bob Kephart
Operations Manager, Hugh Higgins
Operations Manager, Lake Gilliland
Account Manager, Keith Walton

LOCATIONS

HQ: MARJAM SUPPLY CO., INC.
885 CONKLIN ST, FARMINGDALE, NY 117352400
Phone: 631 249-4900
Web: WWW.MARJAM.COM

HISTORICAL FINANCIALS
Company Type: Private

Income Statement
FYE: December 31

	REVENUE ($ mil.)	NET INCOME ($ mil.)	NET PROFIT MARGIN	EMPLOYEES
12/15	400	10	2.7%	614
12/14	386	9	2.4%	—
12/13	341	15	4.4%	—
12/12	279	8	3.1%	—
Annual Growth	12.6%	8.3%	—	—

2015 Year-End Financials
Return on assets: 5.2%   Cash ($ mil.): 2
Return on equity: 2.7%
Current ratio: 1.60

MARKET AMERICA, INC.

Calling itself a cross between Amazon and QVC Market America is an Internet marketer and broker of products and services from a variety of categories including apparel beauty and personal care electronics entertainment nutrition and sports. Market America sells more than 2500 of its own branded products (such as Isotonix Motives and Snap) and spotlights the offerings of more than 3000 other retailers (including Sears Staples and Wal-Mart) on its SHOP.COM web site (acquired in 2010). In addition the company manages UnFranchise a network marketing business with more than 180000 independent shopping consultants. The company was founded in 1992 by president and CEO James "JR" Ridinger.

Operations

Market America's independent shopping consultants operate under the company's UnFranchise business model also referred to as "one-to-one marketing." The UnFranchise platform comes complete with a business plan customizable Web portal merchandising materials and management system. To develop community relations consultants can provide online assistance to shoppers in their areas and recruit potential UnFranchise consultants. Consultants earn commissions when shoppers purchase products and services through their Market America shopping portals. In 2010 Market America opened its UnFranchise business model to nonprofits. The company said individuals following its business model have netted more than $2 billion in commissions and retail profits since it was established.

Geographic Reach

Based in North Carolina the company has a presence in several global markets including the US Canada Australia Hong Kong Taiwan the UK and Mexico. It's expanding into Latin America. Through its website Market America provides access to its brands to consumers in 200-plus countries.

Financial Performance

Market American rings up $500 million in sales annually. Since its founding the product brokerage and Internet marketing company boasts more than $5.3 billion in accumulated retail sales.

Strategy

Operating in seven global markets Market America looks to expand into Spain Colombia Costa Rica Ecuador and the Dominican Republic. It's working to extend the reach of its UnFranchise business model to Latino entrepreneurs. The move marks the company's largest expansion in its history.

To bolster its position in Internet retailing Market America has been expanding its operations outside the US. The company has international branches in Canada Australia Hong Kong Taiwan and the Philippines. It plans to extend its reach to the UK Mexico Latin America and other markets where it does not yet have a presence.

Mergers and Acquisitions

Market America acquired e-tailer SHOP.COM in late 2010 to blend its marketing and brokering expertise with SHOP.COM's strength in technology and merchandising. The result creates a "social shopping" movement capable of challenging some of the Internet's leading shopping destinations. As part of the deal the two firms agreed to operate their websites separately.

EXECUTIVES

Executive Vice-President, Dennis Franks
Senior Vice-President, Loren Ridinger
Chief Operating Officer, Marc Ashley

Executive Vice-President, Marty Weismann
Financial Executive, Paula Ashby
Director, Gary Phillips

LOCATIONS

HQ: MARKET AMERICA, INC.
1302 PLEASANT RIDGE RD, GREENSBORO, NC
274099415
Phone: 336 605-0040

PRODUCTS/OPERATIONS

Selected Brands

Cellular Laboratories
Custom Cocktail
Fixx
Gene SNP DNA Analysis
Heart Health
Isotonix
MA Capital Resources
MA Webcenters
Matriskin
Motives
NutriClean
Pentaxyl
Pet Health
Prime
Royal Spa
Snap
Timeless Prescriptions
TLS Weight Loss Solution
Ultimate Aloe

Selected Product Categories

Anti-aging
Apparel jewelry and shoes
Automotive and tools
Baby products
Beauty products cosmetics
Books movies and video games
Cameras
Cell phones and communications
Computers
Consumer electronics
Crafts
Grocery
Health and nutrition
Home and Garden
Jewelry
Music
Party supplies
Pet supplies
Tickets
Toys

COMPETITORS

AMS Health Sciences	Overstock.com
Amazon.com	PriceGrabber.com
Amway	QVC
Astral Brands	Shaklee
Avon	Shopzilla
Buy.com	USANA Health Sciences
HSN	ViSalus
Mannatech	Yahoo!
Melaleuca	eBay
NexTag	

HISTORICAL FINANCIALS

Company Type: Private

Income Statement

FYE: October 31

	REVENUE ($ mil.)	NET INCOME ($ mil.)	NET PROFIT MARGIN	EMPLOYEES
10/16*	412	23	5.7%	650
12/09	224	15	7.0%	—
12/08	228	3	1.5%	—
12/07	218	0	0.0%	—
Annual Growth	7.3%	391.3%	—	—

*Fiscal year change

2016 Year-End Financials

Return on assets: 1.2%   Cash ($ mil.): 73
Return on equity: 5.7%
Current ratio: 2.00

MARQUETTE UNIVERSITY

A member of the Association of Jesuit Colleges and Universities Marquette University provides undergraduate graduate and professional courses and programs. It specializes in business engineering arts and sciences nursing law dentistry and other fields. The university offers undergraduates some 75 majors and 65 minors and post-graduate students about 50 doctoral and master's degree programs. With an enrollment of more than 11700 students Marquette University boasts a student/faculty ratio of 14:1. Its student population consists of students from all 50 US states and nearly 70 countries. Founded in 1881 the university is named after French missionary explorer Father Jacques Marquette.

Operations

Marquette University an independent coeducational and not-for-profit institution of higher learning and research consists of a dozen separate colleges and schools.

Geographic Reach

Based in Milwaukee Wisconsin the Marquette University campus attracts students across the nation and from nearly 70 countries worldwide.

Financial Performance

The educational institution logged a marginal 1% increase in revenue in fiscal 2012 as compared to 2011 due to rising tuition and fees contributions government and private grants and endowment income used in operations. Net income during the same reporting period dropped some 90% thanks to increases in operating expenses and declines in endowment gains in excess of the amount designated for current operations (net other).

Strategy

To boost its healthcare presence the Marquette University College of Nursing opened the Wheaton Franciscan Healthcare Center for Clinical Simulation in late 2012. The facility features a six-bed hospital suite with a pair of intensive care rooms two medical surgical rooms one pediatrics room and one labor and delivery suite.

EXECUTIVES

Executive Vice President Learning and Development, Christopher Longstreet
Vice President for Student Affairs, Christopher Miller
Assistant Vice President For Student A, Jeff Janz
Vice President of government relations, Steve Radke
Associate Vice President for Research and Innovation, Carmel Ruffolo
Vice President, Sally Sutko
Vice President, Melissa Frank
Co President, Katie Sterr
Department Head, Miroslav Begovic
Executive Vice President, Barb Riley
Department Head, James Benjamin
Secretary, Janet Cheng
Secretary, Joe Foti
Secretary, Greg Merkel
Auditors: KPMG LLP MILWAUKEE WI

LOCATIONS

HQ: MARQUETTE UNIVERSITY
1250 W WISCONSIN AVE, MILWAUKEE, WI
532332225
Phone: 414 288-7250
Web: WWW.MARQUETTE.EDU

PRODUCTS/OPERATIONS

Selected Schools and Colleges

College of Business Administration
College of Education
College of Engineering
College of Health Sciences
College of Nursing
College of Professional Studies
Graduate School
Graduate School of Management
Helen Way Klingler College of Arts and Sciences
J. William and Mary Diederich College of Communications
Law School
School of Dentistry

HISTORICAL FINANCIALS

Company Type: Private

Income Statement

FYE: June 30

	REVENUE ($ mil.)	NET INCOME ($ mil.)	NET PROFIT MARGIN	EMPLOYEES
06/15	548	48	8.8%	3,000
06/13	391	37	9.5%	—
06/12	385	9	2.4%	—
Annual Growth	12.5%	72.3%	—	—

2015 Year-End Financials

Return on assets: 8.8%   Cash ($ mil.): 62
Return on equity: 8.8%
Current ratio: 0.30

MARSHALL MEDICAL CENTER

EXECUTIVES

Chief Executive Officer, James Whipple
Supervisor, Barbara Crook
Director, Gary Martin

LOCATIONS

HQ: MARSHALL MEDICAL CENTER
1100 MARSHALL WAY, PLACERVILLE, CA 956676533
Phone: 530 622-1441

HISTORICAL FINANCIALS

Company Type: Private

Income Statement

FYE: October 31

	REVENUE ($ mil.)	NET INCOME ($ mil.)	NET PROFIT MARGIN	EMPLOYEES
10/15	229	11	4.9%	1,500
10/14	200	(0)	—	—
10/13	222	6	2.8%	—
10/12	201	(7)	—	—
Annual Growth	4.4%	—	—	—

2015 Year-End Financials

Return on assets: 2.8%   Cash ($ mil.): 28
Return on equity: 4.9%
Current ratio: 1.90

MARSHALL UNIVERSITY

If "You Are Marshall" you know that Marshall University is a state-supported non-profit educational institution serving about 14000 students including 3500 graduate and medical students. The university offers about 55 baccalaureate and more than 50 graduate programs through more than a dozen colleges and schools. It also offers two Associate Programs two Ed.S four Doctoral Degree Programs and three First Professional programs. Marshall students attend classes either at the university's main campus in Huntington West Virginia; at its regional campuses; or online.

Operations

The university enrolls about 19% of the students from out of state. It has an undergraduate student/faculty ratio of 19:1 and the average class size is 23.

Geographic Reach

Marshall has locations in Huntington West Virginia (its main campus) as well as in South Charleston Campus Mid-Ohio Valley Center Teays Valley Center and Beckley Center.

The university enrolls students from all counties in West Virginia 46 US states and the District of Columbia as well as from about 50 countries worldwide.

Financial Performance

Marshall reported flat revenues in fiscal year 2013 as an increase in revenues from students tuition and fees interest on loans receivables and sales and services of educational activities was partially offset by lower revenues from federal contracts and grants and from auxiliary enterprises.

Net income increased by 38% in fiscal year 2013 due to a decline in operating expenses and higher investment income.

Strategy

In 2013 the university expanded its program portfolio with the introduction of master's degree in public administration and a bachelor of science degree in medical imaging with an emphasis in diagnostic medical sonography. That year Marshall continued building its $50 million new engineering complex on the Huntington campus as part of its strategy to upgrade facilities on its main campus.

Company Background

Named for former Chief Justice John Marshall the university was established in 1837. The 2006 movie " We Are Marshall " dramatizes the aftermath of the 1970 plane crash that killed most of Marshall's Thundering Herd football team.

EXECUTIVES

Vice President For Research, John Maher
Assistant Vice President Information Technology Online Learning and Libraries, Monica Brooks
Senior Vice President, Mary Heuton
Senior Vice President For Communications And Marketing, Ginny Painter
Vice President Graduate Studies and Dean Graduate School of Education and Professional Development, Ronald Childress
Assistant Vice President For Admin, Karen Kirtley
Vice President Communications and Marketing, Keith Spears
Vice President Student Affairs, Cedric Gathings
Managing Director, Curtis Harrison
Board Member, Keith Beard
Secretary, Linda Owens
Auditors: CLIFTONLARSONALLEN LLP PLYMOU

LOCATIONS

HQ: MARSHALL UNIVERSITY
1 JOHN MARSHALL DR, HUNTINGTON, WV
257550003
Phone: 304 696-2385
Web: WWW.MARSHALL.EDU

PRODUCTS/OPERATIONS

Selected Colleges and Schools
College of Business
College of Education and Human Services
College of Fine Arts
College of Health Professionals
College of Information Technology and Engineering
College of Liberal Arts
College of Science
Community and Technical College
Graduate College
School of Extended Education
School of Journalism and Mass Communications
School of Medicine
University College

HISTORICAL FINANCIALS

Company Type: Private

Income Statement

FYE: June 30

	REVENUE ($ mil.)	NET INCOME ($ mil.)	NET PROFIT MARGIN	EMPLOYEES
06/16	189	(2)	—	1,632
06/13	175	26	14.9%	—
06/12	175	19	11.1%	—
06/08	672	0	0.0%	—
Annual Growth (14.6%)	—	—	—	—

2016 Year-End Financials

Return on assets: 2.1%
Return on equity: (-1.1%)
Current ratio: 2.20

Cash ($ mil.): 72

MARSHFIELD CLINIC, INC.

Marshfield Clinic is a private group medical practice that operates more than 50 medical locations across Wisconsin. The network provides primary and tertiary care through its more than 700 physicians who represent about 80 medical specialties. Through two hospitals — the 25-bed Flambeau Hospital and the 40-bed Lakeview Medical Center — and dozens of clinics Marshfield annually serves roughly 380000 patients and handles 3.8 million patient encounters. Other parts of the network include Marshfield Laboratories and Security Health Plan of Wisconsin as well as medical education and research organizations.

Geographic Reach

Marshfield Clinic operates about 50 clinic locations and two hospitals in central western and northern Wisconsin. Its main hospital campuses are located in Park Falls and Rice Lake.

Operations

Marshfield Clinic's Security Health Plan of Wisconsin provides a variety of health insurance options to more than 200000 members in much of central northern and western Wisconsin. The Marshfield Clinic organization also includes Marshfield Labs one of the largest private practice full-service laboratory systems in the nation conducting more than 25 million tests annually.

Flambeau Hospital is a 25-bed Critical Access Hospital and provides 24-hour care for inpatient and outpatient services emergency ambulance services and home health & hospice service. Flam-

beau Hospital is jointly sponsored by Ministry Health Care and Marshfield Clinic.Lakeview Medical Center is a 40-bed nonprofit community hospital and provides 24-hour care for inpatient and outpatient services and emergency ambulance services. Lakeview Medical Center integrates modern design and technology with a calm healing environment.

Marshfield Clinic runs about 50 general and specialty medical clinics and dental offices in its service territory. It also has an outreach services program that collaborates with 1200 medical sites to provide care in surrounding regions.

The Marshfield Clinic Education Foundation programs for medical school graduates are internal medicine pediatrics dermatology and surgery. The company's research division Marshfield Clinic Research Foundation focuses on clinical research health and safety human genetics epidemiology and biomedical informatics.

Sales and Marketing

Features of the Security Health Plan include contacting members through reminder mailings and personal phone calls to aid with their health maintenance. Additionally affiliated home health nurses visit members at home or in the hospital to answer their questions about their medications or care and to provide needed resources for their recuperation.

Strategy

In 2015 CareCloud and Marshfield Clinic Information Services a healthcare IT company established from within the Marshfield Clinic announced a partnership to deliver a joint cloud-based solution to help improve the clinical financial and administrative outcomes of large ambulatory medical practices. The two parties have joined together MCIS' clinical solutions – including a physician-designed electronic health record (EHR) patient portal and population health management tool with CareCloud's practice management and medical billing software and services. The integrated solution which also includes unified customer implementation and support is optimized for the requirements of large practices across dozens of specialties. MCIS has collaborated with Marshfield Clinic to build a physician-designed cloud-based clinical solution that reflects our successful experiences supporting a renowned multi-specialty group of more than 700 physicians.Marshfield Clinic has a rich history in health information technology and software development. The Clinic has used a computer-based electronic health record for more than 20 years. Cattails Software Suite Marshfield Clinic's homegrown electronic health record was developed in conjunction with Clinic providers and the Information Systems Department. Cattails Software Suite played a significant role in the Clinic's success in the Centers for Medicare and Medicaid Services' Physician Group Practice project. Marshfield Clinic improved patient care while lowering health care costs during the five-year project – saving the Medicare program more than $118 million.In 2015 the company expanded outpatient services provided in the Ambulatory Surgery Center in Marshfield adding skilled nursing care in the East Wing of its Marshfield campus. Similar plans to lower the total cost of care have been designed for all of its mission-critical centers.The second phase of the plan includes construction of a new hospital of the future in Marshfield. A smaller more smartly-designed and more energy efficient high-tech facility will allow for highly-specialized care that requires a hospital setting.

The organization also advances its patient care through a collaboration with Cleveland Clinic. Together the organizations conduct research and development programs on new medical innovations.

Company Background

Marshfield Clinic announced the formation of a new subsidiary Marshfield Clinic Information Services in 2013. The unit will use the organizations health IT expertise to help other care providers implement electronic health record (EHR) systems and other population health management software programs and services.

The clinic was founded in 1916.

EXECUTIVES

President, Brian H Ewert
Manager, Dave Marksteiner
Office Manager, Jan Freeman
Auditors: KPMG LLP COLUMBUS OH

LOCATIONS

HQ: MARSHFIELD CLINIC, INC.
1000 N OAK AVE, MARSHFIELD, WI 544495702
Phone: 715 387-5511
Web: WWW.MARSHFIELDRESEARCH.ORG

HISTORICAL FINANCIALS
Company Type: Private

Income Statement
FYE: September 30

	REVENUE ($ mil.)	NET INCOME ($ mil.)	NET PROFIT MARGIN	EMPLOYEES
09/15	1,211	24	2.0%	363
09/09	1,062	78	7.4%	—
09/08	102	6	5.9%	—
Annual Growth	42.3%	22.0%	—	—

2015 Year-End Financials
Return on assets: 9.9%   Cash ($ mil.): 96
Return on equity: 2.0%
Current ratio: 0.60

MARTHA JEFFERSON HOSPITAL

EXECUTIVES

Chief Executive Officer, James E Haden
Board of Directors, Elliot Kuida
Director, William Shaw
Supervisor, Jasonn Ross
Supervisor, Joanna Herring
Auditors: KPMG LLP NORFOLK VIRGINIA

LOCATIONS

HQ: MARTHA JEFFERSON HOSPITAL
500 MARTHA JEFFERSON DR, CHARLOTTESVILLE, VA 229114668
Phone: 434 982-7000
Web: WWW.MJHFOUNDATION.ORG

HISTORICAL FINANCIALS
Company Type: Private

Income Statement
FYE: December 31

	REVENUE ($ mil.)	NET INCOME ($ mil.)	NET PROFIT MARGIN	EMPLOYEES
12/15	258	12	4.9%	3,569
12/13	252	9	3.8%	
Annual Growth	1.3%	14.9%	—	—

2015 Year-End Financials
Return on assets: 3.5%   Cash ($ mil.): 45
Return on equity: 4.9%
Current ratio: 2.20

MARTIN RESOURCE MANAGEMENT CORPORATION

Martin Resource Management likes to push around petroleum products. The employee-owned company's flagship affiliate Martin Midstream Partners offers transportation storage marketing and logistics management services for petroleum products including sulfur sulfur derivatives fuel oil liquefied petroleum gas asphalt and other bulk tank liquids primarily in the southern US. Martin Resource also manufactures and markets fertilizer and other processed sulfur products. Through its Martin Energy Services unit the company offers inland marine fuel supply and offshore support services. Other units include The Brimrock Group (sulfur) Cross Oil Refining & Marketing and Martin Asphalt.

Operations

Each year the company markets more than 250 million gallons of diesel fuel and lubricants along the Gulf Coast and 1.5 million barrels of naphthenic lubricants and base oils across the US. In addition Martin Resource also provides surface transportation services for products such as molten sulfur sulfuric acid fuel oil natural gas liquids (NGLs) asphalt paper mill liquids and other bulk tank liquids.

The company's more than $550 million of assets include a fleet of truck trailers and tractors. Its Martin Transport subsidiary has about 25 terminals in the Southeast and Southern US with more than 850 trucks and 1200 trailers. Martin Product Sales LLC markets and distributes petroleum-based products including asphalt fuel oil and sulfuric acid.

Martin Resource owns a 28.0% limited partnership interest and a 2% general partnership interest in its flagship operating company Martin Midstream Partners. Its Martin Energy Services subsidiary offers marine fuel supply and offshore support services.

Sales and Marketing

The company's customers include agriculture petrochemical petroleum and utility companies.

Strategy

Martin Resource markets oil and gas and by-products through facilities located throughout the Gulf Coast region. It acquires other companies or forms joint ventures to develop its portfolio. It also redistributes operating assets to its major subsidiaries to improve their performance.

In 2013 Canadian subsidiary Brimrock signed an engineering service agreement with Keyera to act as the engineering management and technology provider for Keyera's planned sulphur forming and materials handling facilities upgrade.

That year Martin Resource sold a 49% voting interest in MMGP Holdings LLC a newly-formed sole member of Martin Midstream GP LLC the general partner of Martin Midstream Partners to Alinda Capital Partners.

In 2012 Martin Midstream Partners also sold its East Texas and Northwest Louisiana natural gas gathering and processing assets to CenterPoint Energy Field Services for $275 million.

Streamlining its businesses in 2012 the company formed Martin Energy Services LLC combining the entities of Midstream Fuel Service LLC L & L Oil and Gas Services L.L.C. and PEPCO into one entity for improved service and growth.

Mergers and Acquisitions

In 2013 Martin Midstream Partners' subsidiary Martin Operating Partnership L.P bought Kansas City Missouri-based NL Grease LLC a grease manufacturer that specializes in private-label packaging of commercial and industrial greases.

Boosting its NGL handling capabilities that year Martin Midstream Partners purchased six liquefied petroleum gas pressure barges and two commercial push boats from affiliates of Florida Marine Transporters for $51 million.

In 2012 Martin Midstream Partners acquired Gulf Coast fuels and lubricants provider Talen's Marine & Fuel LLC. The transactions boosted the company's marine terminal infrastructure adding ten marine terminals between Houston/Galveston and Port Fourchon in Louisiana with total tankage of 300000 barrels and an additional 4000 feet of water-accessible bulkhead.

In 2012 Martin Midstream Partners bought the remaining equity interests in Redbird Gas Storage LLC for $150 million. (In 2011 Martin Resource and Martin Midstream Partners formed the Redbird Gas Storage natural gas storage joint venture to invest in Cardinal Gas Storage Partners a joint venture between Redbird and Energy Capital Partners focused on the development of natural gas storage facilities across North America).

Company Background

The acquisition of L & L Oil and Gas L.L.C. by Midstream Fuel Service in 2011 increased Martin Resources' capability along the U.S. Gulf Coast to 31 facilities for offshore fuels lubricants and logistical services including land based commercial and industrial fuels and lubricants.

In 2011 Martin Resource and Martin Midstream Partners formed the Redbird Gas Storage natural gas storage joint venture to invest in Cardinal Gas Storage Partners. Cardinal is a joint venture between Redbird and Energy Capital Partners that is focused on the development construction operation and management of natural gas storage facilities across North America.

To raise cash and boost the Martin Midstream Partners' storage segment in 2011 Martin Resource sold 13 terminals to that unit for $36.5 million.

Founded in 1951 by R. S. Martin Jr. Martin Resource also holds a stake in Ican Energy an LPG distributor. To raise cash and increase its financial flexibility in 2002 the company spun off a portion of its assets.

EXECUTIVES

President, Ruben S Martin III
General Manager, Donnie Fickey
Senior Vice-President, Scot A Shoup
Senior Vice-President, Ed Grimm
Vice-President, Mike Lawrence
Account Manager, Jackie Foster
Vice-President, Kyle Dickard
Auditors: KPMG LLP DALLAS TEXAS

LOCATIONS

HQ: MARTIN RESOURCE MANAGEMENT CORPORATION
4200 STONE RD, KILGORE, TX 756626935
Phone: 903 983-6200
Web: WWW.MARTIN-GAS.COM

PRODUCTS/OPERATIONS

Selected Companies
Altec Environmental Consulting
Commercial & Industrial Fuels & Lubricants
Commercial & Industrial Tanks & Equipment
Cross Oil Refining & Marketing Inc.
Marine Lubricants & Specialty Products
Martin Crude Marketing Company
Martin Energy Services LLC
Martin Product Sales LLC
Martin Transport Inc
Roddey engineering services Inc.

Enterprise Products
George Warren
Global Partners
Gulf Oil

Penn Octane
Sun Coast Resources
Williams Companies

HISTORICAL FINANCIALS
Company Type: Private

Income Statement
FYE: December 31

	REVENUE ($ mil.)	NET INCOME ($ mil.)	NET PROFIT MARGIN	EMPLOYEES
12/15	2,493	27	1.1%	2,300
12/11	2,985	37	1.3%	—
12/09	1,537	23	1.5%	—
Annual Growth	8.4%	2.8%	—	—

2015 Year-End Financials
Return on assets: 6.7%
Return on equity: 1.1%
Current ratio: 0.90

Cash ($ mil.): 13

MARYLAND DEPARTMENT OF TRANSPORTATION

Traveling in Maryland? You can thank (or curse) the Maryland Department of Transportation (MDOT). MDOT is responsible for building operating and maintaining a safe and seamless transportation network that includes highway transit maritime and aviation facilities. The Department of Transportation is organized along various administrative groups including the Maryland Motor Vehicle Administration Transit Administration Port Administration Aviation Administration and Highway Administration. MDOT annual budget of about $1.5 billion is funded through the state's Transportation Trust Fund and federal aid.

EXECUTIVES

VP Marketing, Jim Ports
VP Marketing, Lisa Dickerson
VP Marketing, Trent M Kittleman
Director, Katie Knowlin
Manager, June Hornick
Administrative Assistant, Sandra Irelant
VP Marketing, Trent Kittleman
Auditors: SB & COMPANY LLC HUNT VALLEY

LOCATIONS

HQ: MARYLAND DEPARTMENT OF TRANSPORTATION
7201 CORPORATE CENTER DR, HANOVER, MD
210761415
Phone: 410 865-1037
Web: WWW.MDOT.STATE.MD.US

HISTORICAL FINANCIALS
Company Type: Private

Income Statement
FYE: June 30

	REVENUE ($ mil.)	NET INCOME ($ mil.)	NET PROFIT MARGIN	EMPLOYEES
06/16	4,170	(232)	—	1,000
06/14	3,890	58	1.5%	—
06/13	3,719	81	2.2%	—
06/12	3,587	(104)	—	—
Annual Growth	3.8%	—	—	—

2016 Year-End Financials
Return on assets: 14.3%
Return on equity: (-5.6%)
Current ratio: —

Cash ($ mil.): 105

MASSACHUSETTS HIGHER EDUCATION ASSISTANCE CORPORATION

Don't know how you're going to pay for college? You might want to consult ASA ASAP. The Massachusetts Higher Education Assistance Corporation which does business as American Student Assistance (ASA) is a non-profit student loan collection agency that helps students understand finance and repay their higher education loans to prevent student loan default. Its SALT program boosts collection rates by offering students a variety of online tools to help them learn repayment options through blogs and videos track payment progress and find scholarships and careers/internships. Founded in 1956 ASA partners with 300-plus higher education institutions nonprofits and corporations nationwide serving over one million borrowers.

Geographic Reach

Boston-based ASA serves clients across the US.

Sales and Marketing

Beyond serving nonprofits and corporations ASA had partnerships with more than 275 colleges and universities in early 2016. Some of its clients included: the Arizona schools of Arizona Christian University Pima Community College Prescott College and Yavapai College; the Alabama schools of Miles College and Talladega College; and the California schools of California Institute of the Arts Center For Employment Training Chabot College Dominican University of California Holy Names University Life Chiropractic College West Notre Dame De Namur University Otis College of Art and Design Pacific Oaks College and Saint Mary's College of California.

Strategy

ASA continues to look for ways to broaden its network of partnerships with colleges universities and other organizations seeking to maximize the effectiveness of their collections. In November 2015 for example the non-profit partnered with the Vet Corps (part of the Washington State Department of Veterans Affairs) to educate and help service members and veterans repay their student loan debt.

ASA has long utilized a "wellness" approach to borrowing which involves less emphasis on traditional loan collection and more on the "health" of each loan. With such practices the company keeps its default and delinquency rates below the national average (93% of its loans were in good standing as of early 2016).

Company Background

ASA formerly provided Federal Family Education Loan Program (FFELP) guarantee origination and fund delivery services but ceased after FFELP program was eliminated by the US Department of Education in 2010. The company was established in 1956.

EXECUTIVES

President CEO, Paul Combe
EVP and, Michael Finn
Director Of Government Relations, Julie Lammers
Auditors: CBIZ TOFIAS BOSTON MA

LOCATIONS

HQ: MASSACHUSETTS HIGHER EDUCATION
ASSISTANCE CORPORATION
100 CAMBRIDGE ST STE 1600, BOSTON, MA
021142518
Phone: 617 728-4507
Web: WWW.ASA.ORG

COMPETITORS

Access Group
Bank of America
Discover
First Marblehead
JPMorgan Chase
Nelnet
Pennsylvania Higher Education Assistance Agency
Sallie Mae

HISTORICAL FINANCIALS
Company Type: Private

Income Statement
FYE: June 30

	ASSETS ($ mil.)	NET INCOME ($ mil.)	INCOME AS % OF ASSETS	EMPLOYEES
06/15	471	37	8.0%	580
06/14	438	96	22.0%	—
06/13	375	48	12.9%	—
06/10	170	34	20.0%	—
Annual Growth	22.6%	2.1%	—	—

2015 Year-End Financials
Return on assets: 10.2%
Return on equity: 21.4%

Sales ($ mil): 176

MAURY REGIONAL HOSPITAL

EXECUTIVES

Chief Executive Officer, Alan Watson
Supervisor, William Payne
Chief Financial Officer, Nick Swift

LOCATIONS

HQ: MAURY REGIONAL HOSPITAL
1224 TROTWOOD AVE, COLUMBIA, TN 384014802
Phone: 931 381-1111
Web: WWW.MAURYREGIONAL.COM

HISTORICAL FINANCIALS
Company Type: Private

Income Statement
FYE: June 30

	REVENUE ($ mil.)	NET INCOME ($ mil.)	NET PROFIT MARGIN	EMPLOYEES
06/16	336	16	4.8%	2,100
06/15	232	9	4.0%	—
06/10	257	6	2.6%	—
06/09	192	(9)	—	—
Annual Growth	8.3%			

2016 Year-End Financials
Return on assets: 2.6%
Return on equity: 4.8%
Current ratio: 2.80

Cash ($ mil.): 49

MAYER ELECTRIC SUPPLY COMPANY, INC.

Mayer Electric Supply helps to light up those southern nights. The company is one of the nation's largest distributors of electrical supplies with about 50 branch locations in the southeastern US. It offers some 40000 items made by leading manufacturers such as 3M GE Littelfuse and Schneider Electric. Products include conduit circuit breakers controls and switches fire and safety products LED and low-voltage lighting systems motors power tools transformers and wire and cable. Mayer Electric supplies customers in the construction datacomm government industrial and utility industries. The Collat family including CEO Nancy Collat Goedecke owns Mayer Electric.

Operations

Besides distributing electrical supplies Mayer Electric offers several services. Its Mayer Project Management group works to lower cost for construction contractors by providing on-site storage and inventory management. Other services include lamp and battery recycling conduit bending and threading and wire and cable cutting. The company also specializes in factory automation energy efficiency and datacomm systems.

Geographic Reach

Mayer Electric serves customers through locations in Alabama Florida Georgia Mississippi the Carolinas Texas Tennessee and Virginia.

Sales and Marketing

The electrical supplies distributor serves multiple customer segments including those in the construction government industrial datacomm and utility industries through about 51 branch locations across US Southeast.

Strategy

Growing its geographic presence in 2013 Mayer Electric opened a branch location in the Houston area.

Mergers and Acquisitions

Looking to expand further in the southeastern US Mayer Electric in 2012 acquired Mustang Electric Supply based outside Dallas in Lewisville Texas. Established in 1998 Mustang Electric serves commercial and residential contractors across the Dallas and Fort Worth area allowing Mayer Electric to expand to the dynamic and lucrative Dallas market. The purchase included Mustang Electric's 40000-sq.-ft. facility in Lewisville.

Company Background

The recession hit companies like Mayer Electric hard as residential and commercial construction efforts were backburnered. Sales for Mayer Electric dropped by about 21% in 2009 compared to the prior year. Rather than responding by laying off employees or shuttering branches the company planned for break-even results or a small loss for the year. Indeed the company made a small profit in 2009.

Mayer Electric was founded in 1930.

EXECUTIVES

President, Wes Smith
President, Glenn Goedecke
Manager, Brenda Lovell
Financial Executive, Karen Smith
Manager, Scott Roberts
Sales Manager, Gary Barker
Operations Manager, Jason Cates
Operations Manager, Ron Reitzel

LOCATIONS

HQ: MAYER ELECTRIC SUPPLY COMPANY, INC.
3405 4TH AVE S, BIRMINGHAM, AL 352222300
Phone: 205 583-3500
Web: WWW.MAYERELECTRIC.COM

PRODUCTS/OPERATIONS

Selected Services
Basic distributor services
Construction partner
Maintenance repair and operations

Selected Products
Ballasts
Batteries
Cable and wire
Circuit breakers
Conduit
Factory automation products
Fan boxes
Fasteners
Fuses
LED lighting systems
Lenses
Lighting fixtures
Locks
Low-voltage lighting systems
Meters
Motors
Panelboards
Power supplies
Relays
Switches
Surge protection devices
Terminal blocks
Tools
Transformers
Voltage regulators

COMPETITORS

Anixter International	Independent Electric
Consolidated	Supply
Electrical	Rexel Inc.
Crescent Electric	W.W. Grainger
Supply	WESCO International
Gexpro	Wholesale Supply Group
Graybar Electric	

HISTORICAL FINANCIALS

Company Type: Private

Income Statement
FYE: December 26

	REVENUE ($ mil.)	NET INCOME ($ mil.)	NET PROFIT MARGIN	EMPLOYEES
12/15	811	10	1.3%	900
12/14	737	6	0.9%	—
12/13	672	6	1.0%	—
12/12	606	6	1.1%	—
Annual Growth	10.2%	15.8%	—	—

2015 Year-End Financials

Return on assets: 6.4%
Return on equity: 1.3%
Current ratio: 1.60
Cash ($ mil.): 1

MAYO CLINIC JACKSONVILLE (A NONPROFIT CORPORATION)

With more than 370 doctors and scientists on staff Mayo Clinic Jacksonville offers a broad range of medical surgical and research services. The clinic part of the larger Mayo Clinic network and one of its four major campuses offers specialty services such as organ transplantation neurology and oncology therapy. Most patients provided care from the clinic are treated on an outpatient basis; those who require hospitalization are admitted to the adjacent Mayo Clinic Hospital a 214-bed acute care facility. The Jacksonville campus also includes the Birdsall Medical Research center and the Griffin Cancer Research building.

Geographic Reach

While it draws heavily from the local population Mayo Clinic Jacksonville is also a destination for interregional and international patients seeking the coordinated treatment services that are ingrained in the Mayo approach to care.

Strategy

In recent years May Clinic Jacksonville has boosted its presence across the Northeast Florida region. The move includes its $80-million capital improvement of the hospital off San Pablo Road which added two floors and 90 beds in 2013.

Mayo Clinic Jacksonville has also been busy in 2014 opening primary care centers throughout the region including those on the city's Southside Jacksonville Beach and St. Augustine areas.

Since its opening in 1986 the Jacksonville campus has steadily added new facilities. It built and opened the Mayo Clinic Hospital building in 2008 on its current campus. In 2011 it opened a sleep disorder center and a simulation training center where physicians can improve their skills in risk-free environment. Because so many patients travel to receive treatment at Mayo Clinic Jacksonville the clinic also houses two hotels on its campus as well as the extended-stay Gabriel House of Care.

Company Background

The Jacksonville clinic originally provided acute care services at St. Luke's Hospital. The clinic sold St. Luke's to St. Vincent's Medical Center (one of the members of Jacksonville's St. Vincent's Health System) in 2005. The Mayo Clinic leased back the St. Luke's hospital until its new facility was completed in 2008.

EXECUTIVES

Chairman of the Board, Marilyn Carlson Nelson
Manager, Asa Floyd
Project Manager, Ann Catherwood

LOCATIONS

HQ: MAYO CLINIC JACKSONVILLE (A NONPROFIT CORPORATION)
4500 SAN PABLO RD S, JACKSONVILLE, FL 322241865
Phone: 904 953-2000

PRODUCTS/OPERATIONS

Selected Facilities
Birdsall Medical Research Building
Cannaday Building
Gabriel House of Care
Griffin Cancer Research Building

Mayo Clinic Hospital
The Inn at Mayo Clinic

COMPETITORS

Baptist Health System
Florida Hospital Tampa Bay Division
H. Lee Moffitt Cancer Center & Research Institute
Lawnwood Medical Center
Nemours Foundation
North Florida Regional Medical Center
Ocala Regional Medical Center
Palms West Hospital
St. Vincent's Health System
UF Health Jacksonville
UF&Shands

HISTORICAL FINANCIALS

Company Type: Private

Income Statement

FYE: December 31

	REVENUE ($ mil.)	NET INCOME ($ mil.)	NET PROFIT MARGIN	EMPLOYEES
12/15	457	65	14.3%	5,500
12/13	657	(0)	—	—
12/09	340	(4)	—	—
12/06	320	(26)	—	—
Annual Growth	4.0%	—	—	—

2015 Year-End Financials

Return on assets: 1.0%
Return on equity: 14.3%
Current ratio: 0.40
Cash ($ mil.): —

MCALLEN INDEPENDENT SCHOOL DISTRICT

EXECUTIVES

Superintendent, Yolanda Chapa
Personnel Director, Ramiro Vela
Auditors: LONG CHILTON LLP MCALLEN TE

LOCATIONS

HQ: MCALLEN INDEPENDENT SCHOOL DISTRICT
2000 N 23RD ST, MCALLEN, TX 785016126
Phone: 956 618-6000
Web: WWW.MCALLENISD.ORG

HISTORICAL FINANCIALS

Company Type: Private

Income Statement

FYE: June 30

	REVENUE ($ mil.)	NET INCOME ($ mil.)	NET PROFIT MARGIN	EMPLOYEES
06/16	260	3	1.3%	3,500
06/15	257	6	2.3%	—
06/14	245	10	4.3%	—
06/13	234	(7)	—	—
Annual Growth	3.4%	—	—	—

2016 Year-End Financials

Return on assets: 2.1%
Return on equity: 1.3%
Current ratio: —
Cash ($ mil.): 22

MCCARTHY HOLDINGS, INC.

EXECUTIVES

Financial Executive, Jan Pallares
Manager, Jaime Bierk
Engineer, Amanda Morgan
Financial Executive, Lisa Vaglio
Office Manager, Luanne Santiago
Auditors: RUBINBROWN LLP SAINT LOUIS M

LOCATIONS

HQ: MCCARTHY HOLDINGS, INC.
1341 N ROCK HILL RD, SAINT LOUIS, MO 631241441
Phone: 314 968-3300

HISTORICAL FINANCIALS

Company Type: Private

Income Statement

FYE: December 31

	REVENUE ($ mil.)	NET INCOME ($ mil.)	NET PROFIT MARGIN	EMPLOYEES
12/15	2,837	0	—	3,676
12/14	2,696	0	—	—
12/13	3,229	0	—	—
12/12	3,008	0	—	—
Annual Growth	(1.9%)	—	—	—

2015 Year-End Financials

Return on assets: 18.8%
Return on equity: —
Current ratio: 0.70
Cash ($ mil.): 76

MCCORMICK INCORPORATED

EXECUTIVES

President, Stephen D McCormick
President, Steve McCormick
Vice-President, Tom McCormick
Vice-President, John McCormick III
Treasurer, Bradley Ballweber
Manager, Mark Kremar
Manager, Misty Webber
Auditors: EIDE BAILLY LLP FARGO NORTH

LOCATIONS

HQ: MCCORMICK INCORPORATED
4000 12TH AVE N, FARGO, ND 581022910
Phone: 701 277-1225
Web: WWW.NORTHERNIMPROVEMENT.COM

HISTORICAL FINANCIALS

Company Type: Private

Income Statement

FYE: December 31

	REVENUE ($ mil.)	NET INCOME ($ mil.)	NET PROFIT MARGIN	EMPLOYEES
12/15	198	13	6.7%	500
12/14	228	9	4.2%	—
12/13	213	5	2.5%	—
12/12	226	4	2.2%	—
Annual Growth	(4.4%)	39.1%	—	—

2015 Year-End Financials

Return on assets: 5.9%
Return on equity: 6.7%
Current ratio: 1.00
Cash ($ mil.): 7

MCKINNEY INDEPENDENT SCHOOL DISTRICT

EXECUTIVES

Superintendent, Dr J D Kennedy
Consultant, Angela Jackson
Manager, Missie Tucci
Auditors: EVANS PINGLETON AND HOWARD P

LOCATIONS

HQ: MCKINNEY INDEPENDENT SCHOOL DISTRICT
1 DUVALL ST, MCKINNEY, TX 750693210
Phone: 469 302-4000
Web: WWW.MCKINNEYISD.NET

HISTORICAL FINANCIALS

Company Type: Private

Income Statement

FYE: June 30

	REVENUE ($ mil.)	NET INCOME ($ mil.)	NET PROFIT MARGIN	EMPLOYEES
06/16	299	18	6.2%	1,130
06/15	280	15	5.4%	—
06/14	259	22	8.8%	—
06/13	238	(27)	—	—
Annual Growth	7.8%	—	—	—

2016 Year-End Financials

Return on assets: 0.3%
Return on equity: 6.2%
Current ratio: —
Cash ($ mil.): 151

MCLAREN HEALTH CARE CORPORATION

McLaren Health Care is where people in The Auto State go for repairs. The health care system includes some 300 facilities including a dozen regional hospitals and a network of cancer dialysis imaging and surgery centers across the state of Michigan. Combined its facilities have about 2900 beds and serve more than 50 counties. Through its subsidiaries McLaren manages a primary care physician network commercial and Medicaid HMOs and assisted living facilities and provides visiting nurse/home health care and hospice services. Its Great Lakes Cancer Institute provides cancer research and treatment with partner Michigan State University.

Operations

The health network also includes durable medical equipment retail pharmacy services and a medical malpractice insurance company. Several of McLaren's hospital subsidiaries are teaching hospitals each responsible for their own residency pro-

grams. McLaren also runs one of the largest graduate medical programs in the state.

Technology plays a significant role in McLaren's operations particularly in meeting industry-wide challenges of changes in health care reform. To this end the company has invested in IT system upgrades to provide employees with automated tools to manage information.

McLaren operates the state's largest network of cancer centers and providers anchored by Karmanos Cancer Institute - one of only two NCI-designated cancer centers in the state.

In 2014 McLaren had more than 100000 discharges; 395000 emergency room visits; 100000 surgeries; and more than 6000 births. The company provided $205 million in community benefits.

Sales and Marketing

Medicare and Medicaid together accounted for about 50% of the net patients' revenues in 2014; commercial insurance and HMOs (27%); Blue Cross/Blue Shield of Michigan 13%; and self-pay 12%.

Financial Performance

The company's revenue increased by 17% in 2014 due to higher patient service revenues and net assets released from restrictions used for operations.

McLaren's net income decreased by 42% as the result of an increase in operating expenses and a change in interest rate swap agreements and a change in unrealized gains and losses on investments.

Operating cash flow decreased in 2014 by 5%.

Strategy

McLaren provides for growth both internally and through acquisitions. This strategy has served the company well as its revenue growth rate has increased by about 20% each year during the past 20 years.

Recent initiatives include development of a comfort care kit for all patients; enhancing communication among patients nurses and doctors; introducing a comprehensive admissions packet for patients; and promoting increased patient rounding at all facilities with set guidelines and outcome measurements.

Mergers and Acquisitions

In 2014 the company acquired Port Huron Hospital. Adding this historic 186-bed system increases McLaren's geographic footprint in the Thumb region and builds its presence throughout the Lower Peninsula.

Company Background

Through a partnership inked back in 2007 with Texas-based ProTom International McLaren has worked to strengthen its cancer treatment capabilities through proton beam therapy. To this end ProTom in late 2012 unveiled the McLaren Proton Therapy Center on the campus of the McLaren Regional Medical Center and the Great Lakes Cancer Institute in Flint. The $65 million center represents the state's first facility to utilize the technology.

In 2011 McLaren extended its reach into the Upper Peninsula through a partnership formed between its Great Lakes Cancer Institute and the Marquette General Cancer Center to collaborate on cancer care and research. The company has also broadened its services by conducting expansion and renovation programs at its other facilities in recent years.

In 2012 the company's McLaren Health Plan business extended its reach in Michigan's Medicaid and dual-eligible (Medicare and Medicaid) markets through acquisition of Lansing-based CareSource Michigan a Medicaid health maintenance organization (HMO). McLaren plans to expand its 30-county footprint for providing Medicaid managed care to 80000 members to 53 counties and an additional 34500 members. McLaren expanded its network in 2010 by acquiring Central Michigan Community Hospital.

EXECUTIVES

President, Philip A Incarnati
Board of Directors, Ron Strachan
Board of Directors, Robert F Flora
Director, James Barrett
Director, Ted B Wahby
Director, Tony Hain

LOCATIONS

HQ: MCLAREN HEALTH CARE CORPORATION
G3235 BEECHER RD STE B, FLINT, MI 485323650
Phone: 810 342-1100
Web: WWW.GOODNEIGHBORPHARMACY.COM

PRODUCTS/OPERATIONS

2014 Sales

	% of total
Net patient revenue less provision for bad debts	74
Net assets realised from restriction used for operation	-
Other	26
Total	**100**

Selected Services

Bariatrics
Behavioral Health
Medical Library
Cancer Services
Neurosciences
Cardiac
Nutritional Counseling
Ophthalmology
Diagnostic Imaging
Orthopedics
Dialysis Services
Emergency Care Pediatrics
Pharmacy Services
Fitness Centers
Proton Therapy
Free Clinics
Pulmonary and Respiratory
Rehabilitaton and Therapy
Home Care
Robotic Surgery
Hospice
Immunizations
Stroke Center
Implantable Hearing Solutions
Surgical and Endoscopy Services
Infectious Disease
Trauma
Infusion Center
Urology
Intensive Care
Walk-in Clinics
Internal Medicine
Women's Services
Laboratory and Pathology
Wound Care

Selected Operations

McLaren-Bay Region
McLaren-Bay Special Care
McLaren-Central Michigan
McLaren Cancer Institute
McLaren-Greater Lansing
McLaren Orthopedic Hospital
McLaren-Lapeer Region
McLaren-Clarkston
McLaren-Flint
McLaren-Macomb
McLaren-Oakland
McLaren-Port Huron

COMPETITORS

Borgess Medical Center	Hurley Medical Center
Covenant HealthCare	Munson Healthcare
Detroit Medical Center	Priority Health
Genesys Health System	Sparrow Health System
Hayes Green Beach	Spectrum Health
Memorial Hospital	St. John Health

Henry Ford Health System

HISTORICAL FINANCIALS

Company Type: Private

Income Statement

FYE: September 30

	REVENUE ($ mil.)	NET INCOME ($ mil.)	NET PROFIT MARGIN	EMPLOYEES
09/15	187	19	10.5%	10,003
09/08	84	4	4.8%	—
09/06	883	57	6.6%	—
09/05	1,014	40	4.0%	—
Annual Growth	(15.6%)	(7.1%)	—	—

2015 Year-End Financials

Return on assets: 15.8%   Cash ($ mil.): 62
Return on equity: 10.5%
Current ratio: 1.90

MCLAREN NORTHERN MICHIGAN

EXECUTIVES

Principal, David M Zechman
Account Manager, Gennie Bricker
Office Manager, Cindy Holman
Chief Financial Officer, Timothy Joway

LOCATIONS

HQ: MCLAREN NORTHERN MICHIGAN
416 CONNABLE AVE, PETOSKEY, MI 497702212
Phone: 800 248-6777
Web: WWW.NORTHERNHEALTH.ORG

HISTORICAL FINANCIALS

Company Type: Private

Income Statement

FYE: September 30

	REVENUE ($ mil.)	NET INCOME ($ mil.)	NET PROFIT MARGIN	EMPLOYEES
09/15	210	5	2.4%	1,003
09/14	191	12	6.7%	—
Annual Growth	10.2%	(60.6%)	—	—

2015 Year-End Financials

Return on assets: 6.5%   Cash ($ mil.): 9
Return on equity: 2.4%
Current ratio: 0.50

MCLAREN OAKLAND PHARMACY

EXECUTIVES

Manager, Ron May
Director, Daniel Medrano
Director, Deb Collier
Consultant, Diane Syron
Director, Joshua Ulery
Manager, Kim Hiltunen

HISTORICAL FINANCIALS
Company Type: Private

Income Statement
FYE: September 30

	REVENUE ($ mil.)	NET INCOME ($ mil.)	NET PROFIT MARGIN	EMPLOYEES
09/15	186	8	4.3%	45
09/08	131	2	2.2%	—
Annual Growth	5.2%	16.0%	—	—

2015 Year-End Financials
Return on assets: 7.2%
Return on equity: 4.3%
Current ratio: —

Cash ($ mil.): 32

MCLAREN REGIONAL MEDICAL CENTER

EXECUTIVES

Chief Executive Officer, Donald Kooy
Director, Gayle Consiglio

LOCATIONS

HQ: MCLAREN REGIONAL MEDICAL CENTER
401 S BALLENGER HWY, FLINT, MI 485323638
Phone: 810 342-2000
Web: WWW.MCLAREN.ORG

HISTORICAL FINANCIALS
Company Type: Private

Income Statement
FYE: September 30

	REVENUE ($ mil.)	NET INCOME ($ mil.)	NET PROFIT MARGIN	EMPLOYEES
09/15	410	(6)	—	2,250
09/14	403	29	7.2%	—
09/13	408	41	10.1%	—
09/09	340	17	5.1%	—
Annual Growth	3.2%	—	—	—

2015 Year-End Financials
Return on assets: 4.8%
Return on equity: (-1.5%)
Current ratio: 1.20

Cash ($ mil.): 18

MCLEOD REGIONAL MEDICAL CENTER OF THE PEE DEE, INC.

EXECUTIVES

Chairman of the Board, Ronnie Ward
Chief Financial Officer, Michael P Browning
Manager, Mandy Ham
VP Personnel, Jeanette Glenn

LOCATIONS

HQ: MCLEOD REGIONAL MEDICAL CENTER OF THE PEE DEE, INC.
555 E CHEVES ST, FLORENCE, SC 295062617
Phone: 843 777-2000
Web: WWW.MCLEODHEALTH.ORG

HISTORICAL FINANCIALS
Company Type: Private

Income Statement
FYE: September 30

	REVENUE ($ mil.)	NET INCOME ($ mil.)	NET PROFIT MARGIN	EMPLOYEES
09/15	607	72	11.8%	5,000
09/09	537	24	4.5%	—
09/08	577	49	8.5%	—
Annual Growth	0.7%	5.6%	—	—

2015 Year-End Financials
Return on assets: 3.4%
Return on equity: 11.8%
Current ratio: 1.00

Cash ($ mil.): 13

MCNAUGHTON-MCKAY ELECTRIC CO.

Getting connected at work has a completely different meaning at McNaughton-McKay. Its more than 10000 customers can buy electrical supplies sensors and controls and automation and security software online or through 23 branches in five US states and two offices in Germany and Brazil. One of the largest employee-owned companies in the US McNaughton-McKay distributes some 300 product lines from manufacturers such as Hubbell GE Brady Belden Coleman Cable Leviton Thomas & Betts Cognex Specter Instruments and Rockwell Automation. It sells to the construction commercial government and industrial automation markets.

Geographic Reach

The company serves more than 10000 customers through 23 branches in the US Germany and Brazil.

Sales and Marketing

The company sells its products from its sales offices and as well as eSales Centers. In addition to the industrial automation commercial and construction markets McNaughton-McKay supports government customers on a Federal State and Local level by providing hundreds of electrical products and MRO supplies with local support and inventory. McNaughton-McKay's customers include supplyFORCE Vanguard National Alliance and Vantage Group.

Strategy

McNaughton-McKay — informally known as Mc-Mc — has grown by expanding its product lineup and increasing its purchasing power through buying and marketing groups such as Affiliated Distributors supplyFORCE and Vantage Group. The distributor has also added a group dedicated to green products primarily energy-efficient lighting and power distribution products along with an Engineered Solutions Group that sells and installs solar and wind energy through partnerships with companies that include Schletter and Ohio Green Wind.

Company Background

Founded in 1910 the Bull and McNaughton families ran McNaughton-McKay until 2006. It established a sales office in Germany in 2004.

EXECUTIVES

EVP and, Donald D. (Don) Slominski
EVP Sales and Marketing, Richard (Rick) Dahlstrom
VP Information Technology, Gregory H. (Greg) Chun
VP Finance, John D. Kuczmanski
Corporate Purchasing Manager, Maridee Curry
Auditors: KPMG LLP

LOCATIONS

HQ: MCNAUGHTON-MCKAY ELECTRIC CO.
1357 E LINCOLN AVE, MADISON HEIGHTS, MI 480714126
Phone: 248 399-7500

PRODUCTS/OPERATIONS

Selected Products
Bar code scanners and systems
Communication input/output (I/O) networks
Computers and peripherals
Convenience panels (cables and equipment)
Cordsets
Data-collection terminals and software
Drives and motor controllers
Engineered products
I/O products (AC/DC modules)
Motion-control products
　CNC controls
　Servos
　Spindles
Motors (AC)
PLC processors
Radio-frequency identification (RFID) products
Safety products
　Gate switches
　Light curtains
　Mats
　Relays
Sensors
Software
Vision products (inspection equipment)

COMPETITORS

Anixter International	Kendall Electric
Border States Electric	Madison Electric
Consolidated Electrical	Medler Electric
Crescent Electric Supply	OneSource Distributors
Dealers Electrical	Rexel Inc.
Electrocomponents	SUMMIT Electric Supply
Graybar Electric	Steiner Electric
Hite Company	Stuart C. Irby
	W.W. Grainger
	WESCO International

HISTORICAL FINANCIALS
Company Type: Private

Income Statement
FYE: December 31

	REVENUE ($ mil.)	NET INCOME ($ mil.)	NET PROFIT MARGIN	EMPLOYEES
12/15	702	0	—	805
12/14	689	0	—	—
12/13	663	0	—	—
12/12	641	0	—	—
Annual Growth	3.1%	—	—	—

2015 Year-End Financials
Return on assets: 7.1%
Return on equity: —
Current ratio: 1.50

Cash ($ mil.): 7

MCPHS UNIVERSITY

EXECUTIVES

President, Charles Monahan Jr
Director of Data Processing, Carrie Glass
Personnel Manager, Susan Dzirson
Director, Josephine Babiarz
Accountant, Kevin George
Director, Andrew Szumita
Auditors: CBIZ TOFIAS BOSTON MA

LOCATIONS

HQ: MCPHS UNIVERSITY
179 LONGWOOD AVE, BOSTON, MA 021155804
Phone: 617 732-2132
Web: WWW.MASSART.EDU

HISTORICAL FINANCIALS
Company Type: Private

Income Statement			FYE: June 30	
	REVENUE ($ mil.)	NET INCOME ($ mil.)	NET PROFIT MARGIN	EMPLOYEES
06/15	292	126	43.2%	300
06/14	262	107	40.7%	—
06/10	137	35	26.0%	—
06/09	124	34	27.3%	—
Annual Growth	15.2%	24.4%	—	—

2015 Year-End Financials

Return on assets: 4.5%   Cash ($ mil.): 47
Return on equity: 43.2%
Current ratio: 0.40

MEASE COUNTRYSIDE AMBULATORY CARE CENTER

EXECUTIVES

Director, Allan Rudolph

LOCATIONS

HQ: MEASE COUNTRYSIDE AMBULATORY CARE CENTER
3231 MCMULLEN BOOTH RD, SAFETY HARBOR, FL 346956607
Phone: 727 725-6111
Web: WWW.BAYCARE.ORG

HISTORICAL FINANCIALS
Company Type: Private

Income Statement			FYE: December 31	
	REVENUE ($ mil.)	NET INCOME ($ mil.)	NET PROFIT MARGIN	EMPLOYEES
12/15	325	83	25.7%	28
12/14	298	69	23.4%	—
Annual Growth	9.2%	20.2%	—	—

2015 Year-End Financials

Return on assets: 1.6%   Cash ($ mil.): —
Return on equity: 25.7%
Current ratio: 3.30

MEDIACOM BROADBAND LLC

EXECUTIVES

Chief Executive Officer, Rocco B Commisso
Senior Vice-President, Italia Commissoweinand
Manager, Belinda Maldonado
Auditors: PRICEWATERHOUSECOOPERS LLP

LOCATIONS

HQ: MEDIACOM BROADBAND LLC
1 MEDIACOM WAY, MEDIACOM PARK, NY 109184810
Phone: 845 443-2600

HISTORICAL FINANCIALS
Company Type: Private

Income Statement			FYE: December 31	
	REVENUE ($ mil.)	NET INCOME ($ mil.)	NET PROFIT MARGIN	EMPLOYEES
12/16	1,033	171	16.6%	2,415
12/15	982	143	14.7%	—
12/14	948	137	14.5%	—
12/13	918	118	12.9%	—
Annual Growth	4.0%	13.1%	—	—

2016 Year-End Financials

Return on assets: 15.0%   Cash ($ mil.): 14
Return on equity: 16.6%
Current ratio: 0.40

MEDICAL FACULTY ASSOCIATES, INC.

EXECUTIVES

Chief Executive Officer, Stephen L Badger
Board of Directors, Joseph Giordano
Financial Executive, Ken Marter

LOCATIONS

HQ: MEDICAL FACULTY ASSOCIATES, INC.
2150 PENNSYLVANIA AVE NW, WASHINGTON, DC 200373201
Phone: 202 741-3000

HISTORICAL FINANCIALS
Company Type: Private

Income Statement			FYE: June 30	
	REVENUE ($ mil.)	NET INCOME ($ mil.)	NET PROFIT MARGIN	EMPLOYEES
06/15	363	2	0.7%	1,600
06/13	329	0	0.1%	—
06/12	337	11	3.4%	—
06/11	1,369	0	0.0%	—
Annual Growth	(28.2%)	770.6%	—	—

2015 Year-End Financials

Return on assets: 9.1%   Cash ($ mil.): —
Return on equity: 0.7%
Current ratio: 1.30

MEDICAL INFORMATION TECHNOLOGY, INC.

Medical Information Technology knows what to prescribe for the operational disorders of health care information systems. The company which does business as MEDITECH provides software used mainly by hospitals in the management of clinical and financial departments ambulatory care centers long-term care facilities nursing homes and home health care programs. Its applications include electronic health records (EHR) products tailored for patient identification and scheduling care management clinical data management long-term and ambulatory care behavioral health and financial and reimbursement management. The company's core market is the US but Canada accounts for nearly 10% of sales.

Operations

The company continues to focus strictly on software only offering suggestions on the hardware side as to configuration and vendors. Among vendors that have designed products to work with MEDITECH software are Dell and VMware.

Geographic Reach

MEDITECH operates from about 10 offices in the US. Outside North America the company has subsidiaries in Australia and South Africa which account for 2% of sales.

Sales and Marketing

The company sells its software through a regionally-based direct sales staff. Its largest customer in 2012 was hospital owner HCA which uses MEDITECH's clinical information system in more than 250 of its hospitals and clinics. HCA accounts for less than 10% of MEDITECH's overall sales.

Financial Performance

MEDITECH's upward financial trajectory dipped in 2013. Revenue dropped 3% to about $580 million in 2013 from 2012. A drop of about $38 million in product revenue was partly offset by a $20 million increase in service revenue. Net income ticked up about $3 million in 2013 from 2012 despite lower revenue in 2013. The company posted higher revenue from investments and from a lower tax rate.

for years. Overall revenues increased 10% in 2012 to $597 million. The company has also been consistently profitable and 2012 saw profits grow 5% to $130 million.

MEDITECH prices its software based on customers' revenue and number of locations. As a result larger hospitals pay more than smaller hospitals. For example a 150-bed hospital might incur a $3 million product fee a $750000 implementation fee and a $30000 monthly service fee.

EXECUTIVES

President and CEO, Howard Messing, $264,000 total compensation
CFO and Treasurer, Barbara A. Manzolillo, $228,000 total compensation
SVP Technology, Christopher (Chris) Anschuetz
EVP Marketing and Strategy, Hoda Sayed-Friel
EVP Product Development, Michelle O'Connor
Vice President Public Relations, Melissa Rogers
Associate Vice President, Carol Labadini
Chairman, A. Neil Pappalardo
Vice Chairman, Lawrence A. Polimeno
Board Member, Bernard Winston
Board Member, Deborah Cooley
Auditors: WOLF & COMPANY PC BOSTON

LOCATIONS

HQ: MEDICAL INFORMATION TECHNOLOGY, INC.
MEDITECH CIR, WESTWOOD, MA 02090
Phone: 781 821-3000
Web: WWW.MEDITECH.COM

2012 Sales

	% of total
US	91
Canada	8
Other	1
Total	**100**

PRODUCTS/OPERATIONS

2012 Sales

	$ mil.	% of total
Product	316	53
Service	281	47
Total	**597**	**100**

Selected Software Products

Ambulatory care applications
  Emergency department management
  Prescription management
Behavioral health applications
Clinical applications
  Anatomical pathology
  Blood bank
  Imaging and therapeutic services
  Laboratory
  Microbiology
  Pharmacy
Decision support applications
  Budgeting and forecasting
  Cost accounting
  Data archiving
  Data repository
  Executive support system
  Faxing
  Integrated communication system
Financial management applications
  Accounts payable
  Fixed assets
  General ledger
  Materials management
  Payroll/personnel
  Staffing and scheduling
Long-term care information system
Patient care management applications
  Patient care system
  Patient education suite
  Physician care manager
  Physician practice management
Patient identification and scheduling applications
  Case mix management
  Community-wide scheduling
  Enterprise patient index and medical records
  Operating room management
  Registration
Reimbursement applications
  Authorization and referral management
  Billing/accounts receivable

COMPETITORS

Allscripts	MedAssets
Alteer	MedPlus
CPSI	Mediware
Cerner	Misys
Epic Systems	QuadraMed
GE Healthcare	Quality Systems
Health Management Systems	Siemens Healthcare
McKesson	TriZetto

HISTORICAL FINANCIALS

Company Type: Private

Income Statement

FYE: December 31

	REVENUE ($ mil.)	NET INCOME ($ mil.)	NET PROFIT MARGIN	EMPLOYEES
12/16	462	72	15.8%	4,000
12/15	475	70	14.7%	—
12/14	517	123	23.9%	—
12/13	579	133	23.0%	—
Annual Growth	**(7.3%)**	**(18.2%)**	**—**	**—**

2016 Year-End Financials

Return on assets: —
Return on equity: 15.8%
Current ratio: 0.90
Cash ($ mil.): 14

MEDSTAR-GEORGETOWN MEDICAL CENTER, INC.

Medstar-Georgetown Medical Center (dba as Medstar Georgetown University Hospital as a part of MedStar Health) is a 609-bed acute care teaching hospital serving residents of the greater Washington DC area including Maryland and Virginia. The hospital's staff of more than 1100 physicians represents a wide range of medical specializations including cardiology oncology neurology/neurosurgery and surgical transplantation. Medstar Georgetown provides a comprehensive array of inpatient outpatient surgical and rehabilitative care services. The hospital is part of a local network of affiliated primary care providers.

Operations
Medstar Georgetown's Transplant Institute is one of a handful of centers in the US that offers living-donor liver transplants; it opened a new medical space in 2014. Also Georgetown Neurosciences is the sixth unit nationwide to provide CyberKnife stereotactic radiosurgery for the treatment of tumors and lesions of the brain neck and spine.

Strategy
In 2015 Medstar Georgetown submitted a letter of intent with the District of Columbia State Health Planning and Development Agency seeking approval to modernize its existing medical facility by constructing a new state-of-the-art medical surgical pavilion. The pavilion will house surgical critical care and emergency departments as well as related administrative functions.

In 2014 MedStar Georgetown became the first center in Washington DC to perform a two-level artificial disc replacement in a patient's neck.

Company Background
In 2011 Medstar Georgetown became the first health system in the area to offer bloodless surgery to patients who prefer not to receive someone else's blood usually for religious reasons. There are three primary approaches to performing bloodless surgeries: before during and after surgery. Before surgery the hospital gives the patient medications such as iron supplements or epoprotein to boost the blood's hemoglobin level. During surgery the hospital is precise as it can be with its surgical techniques to limit blood loss and there are anesthesia techniques to lower blood pressure so patients bleed less. There is also a machine called Cell Saver that is used during surgery that collects blood lost suctions it into a canister washes and filters it and then returns it directly into the patient

as a product that is about 60-percent pure red blood cells. After surgery medications are used to raise blood levels and medical providers avoid taking multiple blood draws for blood tests.

The hospital was founded in 1898 to promote health through education research and patient care. The current hospital/medical center was opened in 1947.

EXECUTIVES

Assistant Vice President Perioperative S, Frances Baldwin
Vice President of Marketing An, Karen Alcorn
Medical Director, Maral Skelsey

LOCATIONS

HQ: MEDSTAR-GEORGETOWN MEDICAL CENTER, INC.
3800 RESERVOIR RD NW, WASHINGTON, DC 200072113
Phone: 202 444-2000
Web: WWW.MEDSTARGEORGETOWN.ORG

PRODUCTS/OPERATIONS

Selected Services

Anesthesiology
Audiology
Bloodless Medicine and Surgery Program
Bone Marrow Transplant
Breast Cancer
Breast Health Program
Cancer Care
Cardiology
Cerebrovascular Center
Colon and Rectal Surgery
Ear Nose and Throat (ENT)
Emergency Urgent Care and Trauma
Endocrinology
Epilepsy
Family Medicine
Fracture Liaison
Head and Neck Cancer
Headache Center
Hematology
Hospital Medicine
Huntington Disease Center
Hyperbaric Oxygen Therapy
Ophthalmology
Orthopaedics
Ostomy Clinic
Otolaryngology
Pastoral Care
Pediatrics
Pharmacy
Physical Medicine
Plastic Surgery
Primary Care
Prostate Cancer

COMPETITORS

Adventist HealthCare	Inova Alexandria Hospital
Bon Secours Health	Providence Hospital (Washington DC)
Calvert Memorial Hospital	Providence St. Joseph Health
Children's National Medical Center	Suburban Hospital
Chindex International	Upper Chesapeake Health
Dimensions Healthcare	
Doctors Community Hospital	

HISTORICAL FINANCIALS

Company Type: Private

Income Statement

FYE: June 30

	REVENUE ($ mil.)	NET INCOME ($ mil.)	NET PROFIT MARGIN	EMPLOYEES
06/15	774	98	12.7%	4,000
06/11	809	43	5.4%	—
06/10	782	45	5.8%	—
Annual Growth	**(0.2%)**	**16.7%**	**—**	**—**

2015 Year-End Financials

Return on assets: 8.9% Cash ($ mil.): 6
Return on equity: 12.7%
Current ratio: 1.20

MEMORIAL HEALTH CARE SYSTEM, INC.

EXECUTIVES

President, James M Hobson
Office Manager, Liz Browning
Auditors: CATHOLIC HEALTH INITIATIVES E

LOCATIONS

HQ: MEMORIAL HEALTH CARE SYSTEM, INC.
2525 DESALES AVE, CHATTANOOGA, TN 374041161
Phone: 423 495-2525
Web: WWW.MEMORIAL.ORG

HISTORICAL FINANCIALS

Company Type: Private

Income Statement

FYE: June 30

	REVENUE ($ mil.)	NET INCOME ($ mil.)	NET PROFIT MARGIN	EMPLOYEES
06/15	527	34	6.6%	8,800
06/14	557	25	4.6%	—
Annual Growth	(5.4%)	35.7%	—	—

2015 Year-End Financials

Return on assets: 5.6% Cash ($ mil.): 221
Return on equity: 6.6%
Current ratio: 5.70

MEMORIAL HEALTH SERVICES

Where do you go after you get sick riding the tea cups at Disneyland? Not-for-profit Memorial Health Services (known as MemorialCare) owns six hospitals in Southern California including Long Beach Memorial Medical Center Miller Children's Hospital Orange Coast Memorial Medical Center and Saddleback Memorial Medical Center. The facilities have a total of more than 1500 beds and offer a full spectrum of medical services including rehabilitation diagnostic/radiology and emergency services. MemorialCare also operates women's health facilities and other specialty and general practice clinics as well as home health and hospice programs. The organization was founded in 1907.

Operations

MemorialCare's outpatient facilities include the physician practices of the MemorialCare Medical Group the Memorial Prompt Care urgent care centers and the MemorialCare HealthExpress clinics. The network also includes the affiliated practices of the Greater Newport Physicians organization. In addition to inpatient outpatient and home medical care the organization provides clinical training and graduate medical education programs.

Altogether the system's facilities employ 2600 physicians and serve 70000 inpatients each year.

They also handle some 35000 surgeries 10000 births 200000 emergency room visits and 40000 home health visits.

Geographic Reach

MemorialCare's facilities are located in Los Angeles County and Orange County in Southern California.

Financial Performance

MemorialCare reported $1.9 billion in revenues and $83 million in net income in 2012. Most of the organization's revenues come from patient services.

Strategy

MemorialCare is expanding to meet continued demand throughout its service area. It has several projects either going on or recently completed that have added operating rooms neonatal beds more advanced technology and centers of excellence in imaging cardiac cancer and obesity at several of its hospitals. In 2014 it opened the new Lung Nodule Center at The MemorialCare Todd Cancer Institute part of Long Beach Memorial.

The organization is also expanding its outpatient care facilities. For instance MemorialCare has joined the growing trend of hospitals partnering with retailers to open in-store retail clinics (under the HealthExpress brand) that offer basic after-hours medical care through physicians and nurse practitioners. It has recently opened four new outpatient surgery centers and launched a couple of new physician locations in affiliation with UC Irvine Health.

EXECUTIVES

Senior Vice President Chief Financial Officer, Cheryl Sadro
President CEO, James Hobson
Information Technology Vice President, Steven Beal
Vice President Information Systems, Wayne Sass
Medical Director, David Tillman
Medical Librarian, Veena Vyas
Chairman, Keith Nelson
Board Member, Jaci Songstad
Secretary Admin, Ronda Campbell
Secretary Department Medical, Sheila Swanson
Auditors: PRICEWATERHOUSECOOPERS LLP L

LOCATIONS

HQ: MEMORIAL HEALTH SERVICES
17360 BROOKHURST ST # 160, FOUNTAIN VALLEY, CA 927088003
Phone: 714 377-6748
Web: WWW.MEMORIALCARE.ORG

Selected Facilities

Long Beach Memorial Medical Center (Long Beach California)
Miller Children's Hospital (Long Beach California)
Community Hospital (Long Beach California)
Orange Coast Memorial Medical Center (Fountain Valley California)
Saddleback Memorial Medical Center (San Clemente California)
Saddleback Memorial Medical Center (Laguna Hills California)
MemorialCare Medical Group (regional)
MemorialCare HealthExpress (regional)
MemorialCare Imaging Centers (regional)
Memorial Prompt Care (regional)

PRODUCTS/OPERATIONS

Selected Services

Blood Donation
Diabetes Care
Heart and Vascular Care
Joint Replacement
Neonatal Intensive Care
Rehabilitation and Therapy
Wellness Care
Cancer Care
Gynecological Care

Imaging and Radiology
Maternity Care
Orthopedic Care
Stroke Care
Wound Healing
Breast Care
Express Care
Hyperbaric Medicine
Laboratory Services
Pediatric Care
Surgical Care
Women's Care

COMPETITORS

Adventist Health System West
Cedars-Sinai Medical Center
Childrens Hospital Los Angeles
Community Health Systems
Dignity Health
Good Samaritan Hospital (IN)
Good Samaritan Hospital (Los Angeles)
HCA
HealthCare Partners
Hollywood Presbyterian Medical Center
LifePoint Health
Methodist Hospital of Southern California
Pasadena Hospital Association
Prospect Medical
Providence St. Joseph Health
St. Jude Medical Center
Sutter Health
Tenet Healthcare
Trinity Health (Novi)
Western Medical Center - Santa Ana

HISTORICAL FINANCIALS

Company Type: Private

Income Statement

FYE: June 30

	REVENUE ($ mil.)	NET INCOME ($ mil.)	NET PROFIT MARGIN	EMPLOYEES
06/15	215	26	12.3%	6,000
06/10	113	6	5.4%	—
06/09	90	0	—	—
Annual Growth	15.6%	—	—	—

2015 Year-End Financials

Return on assets: 37.8% Cash ($ mil.): 101
Return on equity: 12.3%
Current ratio: —

MEMORIAL HEALTH SYSTEMS, INC.

EXECUTIVES

President, Daryl Tol
Board of Directors, Michelle Goeb-Burkett
Accountant, Tim W
Officer, Magic Epting
Vice-President, Michele G Burkett
Administrative Assistant, Shannon McCormick
Manager, Lisa Wilkinson

LOCATIONS

HQ: MEMORIAL HEALTH SYSTEMS, INC.
301 MEMORIAL MEDICAL PKWY, DAYTONA BEACH, FL 321175167
Phone: 386 231-6000
Web: WWW.FLORIDAHOSPITALBABIES.COM

HISTORICAL FINANCIALS

Company Type: Private

Income Statement

FYE: December 31

	REVENUE ($ mil.)	NET INCOME ($ mil.)	NET PROFIT MARGIN	EMPLOYEES
12/15*	295	23	7.9%	1,500
09/12	754	47	6.3%	—
03/11	364	40	11.0%	—
Annual Growth	(4.1%)	(10.2%)	—	—

*Fiscal year change

2015 Year-End Financials

Return on assets: 4.7%   Cash ($ mil.): 148
Return on equity: 7.9%
Current ratio: 3.40

MEMORIAL HEALTH UNIVERSITY MEDICAL CENTER, INC.

Memorial Health University Medical Center wants to provide memorable health care to residents of Savannah Georgia and surrounding areas. An affiliate of Mercer University School of Medicine the tertiary care facility provides such services as cardiac and trauma care and rehabilitation. Also known as Memorial University Medical Center (MUMC) the hospital has some 620 beds and includes the MUMC Children's Hospital. It also operates specialty cancer care and women's health centers as well as research programs. Founded in 1955 MUMC is the flagship facility in a broader system of entities known as Memorial Health which includes affiliated primary and specialty care clinics in the region.

Operations

MUMC's cancer center the Curtis and Elizabeth Anderson Cancer Institute provides cancer treatment and surgical procedures; it also conducts research efforts to discover and develop new cancer therapies. The Women's Health Institute offers obstetrics gynecology and neonatology. MUMC also includes a level I trauma center and a Heart and Vascular Institute as well as programs in orthopedics neurology gastroenterology urology and pulmonary care. The affiliated Memorial Health University Physicians (MHUP) group operates primary and specialty care offices in the area.

Geographic Reach

MUMC serves a 35-county region in southeastern Georgia and southern South Carolina. The medical center serves as a regional referral center for several smaller community hospitals in the area. Affiliates include Bacon County Hospital Evans Memorial Hospital and Liberty Regional Medical Center.

Strategy

In 2012 Memorial Health formed an affiliation with Novant Health. The partnership will help the MUMC organization cut costs provide for future growth opportunities and improve its operational infrastructure. By joining the Novant Health Shared Services group MUMC will gain access to a larger base of supply chain clinical engineering information technology and best practices resources.

EXECUTIVES

President, Magaret Gill
Board of Directors, Helen Dean Downing
Senior Vice-President, Don E Tomberlin

LOCATIONS

HQ: MEMORIAL HEALTH UNIVERSITY MEDICAL CENTER, INC.
4700 WATERS AVE, SAVANNAH, GA 314046283
Phone: 912 350-8000
Web: WWW.MEMORIALHEALTH.COM

COMPETITORS

Appling	St. Joseph's/Candler
Beaufort Memorial	Health System
Hospital	Tift Regional Medical
Doctors Hospital of	Center
Augusta	Universal Health
Liberty Regional	Services
Medical Center	University Health
Redmond Regional	Services
Medical Center	Walton Rehabilitation
South Georgia Medical	Hospital
Center	

HISTORICAL FINANCIALS

Company Type: Private

Income Statement

FYE: December 31

	REVENUE ($ mil.)	NET INCOME ($ mil.)	NET PROFIT MARGIN	EMPLOYEES
12/15	466	9	2.1%	5,000
12/14	469	32	6.9%	—
12/13	547	38	7.1%	—
12/08	453	(29)	—	—
Annual Growth	0.4%	—	—	—

2015 Year-End Financials

Return on assets: 10.3%   Cash ($ mil.): 15
Return on equity: 2.1%
Current ratio: 1.20

MEMORIAL HERMANN HEALTH SYSTEM

EXECUTIVES

Chief Executive Officer, Charles Stokes
Chief Financial Officer, Nancy Bennett
Auditors: LB ERNST & YOUNG US LP HOUSTO

LOCATIONS

HQ: MEMORIAL HERMANN HEALTH SYSTEM
100 STE 2, HOUSTON, TX 77024
Phone: 713 242-3000

HISTORICAL FINANCIALS

Company Type: Private

Income Statement

FYE: June 30

	REVENUE ($ mil.)	NET INCOME ($ mil.)	NET PROFIT MARGIN	EMPLOYEES
06/15	4,025	378	9.4%	14,000
06/14	3,741	454	12.1%	—
06/13*	3,285	230	7.0%	—
09/09	3,195	(79)	—	—
Annual Growth	3.9%	—	—	—

*Fiscal year change

2015 Year-End Financials

Return on assets: 14.4%   Cash ($ mil.): 320
Return on equity: 9.4%
Current ratio: 0.50

MEMORIAL HERMANN KATY HOSPITAL

EXECUTIVES

President, Jim Parisi
Chief Financial Officer, Kevin Lovingood

LOCATIONS

HQ: MEMORIAL HERMANN KATY HOSPITAL
23900 KATY FWY, KATY, TX 774941323
Phone: 281 644-7000
Web: WWW.KATYCHAMBER.COM

HISTORICAL FINANCIALS

Company Type: Private

Income Statement

FYE: December 31

	REVENUE ($ mil.)	NET INCOME ($ mil.)	NET PROFIT MARGIN	EMPLOYEES
12/15	202	27	13.8%	317
12/12	198	27	13.7%	—
Annual Growth	0.6%	1.0%	—	—

2015 Year-End Financials

Return on assets: 4.0%   Cash ($ mil.): —
Return on equity: 13.8%
Current ratio: —

MEMORIAL HOSPITAL AND HEALTH CARE CENTER

EXECUTIVES

President, Raymond W Snowden
Board of Directors, Sr Renee Cunningham
Board of Directors, Adrian Davis
Supervisor, Michael G Jones
Director, Denise Keetzel
Chief Operating Officer, John Dillon
Vice-President, Ronald Salyk
Auditors: BLUE & CO LLC INDIANAPOLIS I

LOCATIONS

HQ: MEMORIAL HOSPITAL AND HEALTH CARE CENTER
800 W 9TH ST, JASPER, IN 475462514
Phone: 812 482-2345
Web: WWW.MHHCC.ORG

HISTORICAL FINANCIALS
Company Type: Private

Income Statement
FYE: June 30

	REVENUE ($ mil.)	NET INCOME ($ mil.)	NET PROFIT MARGIN	EMPLOYEES
06/15	198	7	3.8%	950
06/14	191	8	4.3%	—
06/13	169	4	2.8%	—
06/12	163	4	2.5%	—
Annual Growth	6.5%	21.7%	—	—

2015 Year-End Financials
Return on assets: 9.7% Cash ($ mil.): 50
Return on equity: 3.8%
Current ratio: 1.00

MEMORIAL HOSPITAL OF LARAMIE COUNTY

EXECUTIVES
Chief Executive Officer, John Lucas
Director, Jennifer Misajet
Personnel Manager, Sharon Scheller

LOCATIONS
HQ: MEMORIAL HOSPITAL OF LARAMIE COUNTY
214 E 23RD ST, CHEYENNE, WY 820013748
Phone: 307 633-7667
Web: WWW.CHEYENNEREGIONAL.ORG

HISTORICAL FINANCIALS
Company Type: Private

Income Statement
FYE: June 30

	REVENUE ($ mil.)	NET INCOME ($ mil.)	NET PROFIT MARGIN	EMPLOYEES
06/15	279	9	3.5%	1,270
06/14	290	11	4.0%	—
06/13	286	15	5.5%	—
06/12	284	7	2.6%	—
Annual Growth	(0.6%)	10.4%	—	—

2015 Year-End Financials
Return on assets: 4.1% Cash ($ mil.): 39
Return on equity: 3.5%
Current ratio: 2.40

MEMORIAL HOSPITAL OF SOUTH BEND INC

EXECUTIVES
President, Kreg Gruber
Board of Directors, Charles B Miller
Manager, Charles Leguern
VP Personnel, George Soper PHD
Personnel Director, Joe Burt
Personnel Director, Jinny Longbroke

LOCATIONS
HQ: MEMORIAL HOSPITAL OF SOUTH BEND INC
615 N MICHIGAN ST, SOUTH BEND, IN 466011087
Phone: 574 647-7751
Web: WWW.QUALITYOFLIFE.ORG

HISTORICAL FINANCIALS
Company Type: Private

Income Statement
FYE: December 31

	REVENUE ($ mil.)	NET INCOME ($ mil.)	NET PROFIT MARGIN	EMPLOYEES
12/16	492	41	8.4%	158
12/15	486	24	5.1%	—
Annual Growth	1.2%	69.0%	—	—

2016 Year-End Financials
Return on assets: 4.7% Cash ($ mil.): 25
Return on equity: 8.4%
Current ratio: 2.20

MEMORIAL MEDICAL CENTER

If you've lost the spring in your step and need a little care Memorial Medical Center will be there. As the flagship facility for Memorial Health System in Springfield Illinois this acute care and teaching hospital provides a wide range of medical and surgical services as well as emergency medicine and outpatient care. Its myriad specialties include cardiovascular maternity cancer care behavioral health orthopedic rehabilitation and burn treatment services. The hospital which sees 25000 inpatients per year also has special surgical divisions for bariatric procedures and organ transplants. The 500-bed hospital is a teaching affiliate of the Southern Illinois University (SIU) School of Medicine.

EXECUTIVES
Vice President, Robert W Kay
Physical Therapy Director, Jason Beeler
Vice President, Kevin England
Medical Director, David Gelber
Vice President, David C Chapman
SENIOR VICE PRESIDENT AND CHIEF QUALITY OFFICER, Chuck Callahan
Secretary Pathology, Debbie Stoll
Auditors: ERNST & YOUNG LLP ST LOUIS

LOCATIONS
HQ: MEMORIAL MEDICAL CENTER
701 N 1ST ST, SPRINGFIELD, IL 627810001
Phone: 217 788-3000
Web: WWW.MEMORIALMEDICAL.COM

PRODUCTS/OPERATIONS

Selected Services
Bariatric Services
Behavioral Health
Regional Burn Center
Regional Cancer Center
Da Vinci Robotic Surgery
EEG
Emergency Department
Express Care
Family Maternity
Food Nutrition Counseling
Healthcare Psychology
Hearing Center
Heart and Vascular Services

Intensive Care Unit
Industrial Rehab
JointWorks
Lab Services
Medical Imaging Services
Neurosciences
Orthopedic Services
Palliative Care
Rehab Services
Sleep Disorder Center
SpineWorks
SportsCare
Stroke Center
Surgical Services
Transplant Services
Would Healing Center

COMPETITORS
Decatur Memorial Hospital
Hospital Sisters Health System
OSF Healthcare System
Sarah Bush Lincoln Health Center
St. John's Hospital (Illinois)

HISTORICAL FINANCIALS
Company Type: Private

Income Statement
FYE: September 30

	REVENUE ($ mil.)	NET INCOME ($ mil.)	NET PROFIT MARGIN	EMPLOYEES
09/16	699	12	1.8%	2,849
09/15	667	(28)	—	—
09/14	1,850	78	4.3%	—
Annual Growth	(38.5%)	(59.6%)	—	—

2016 Year-End Financials
Return on assets: 5.5% Cash ($ mil.): 34
Return on equity: 1.8%
Current ratio: 1.30

MEMORIAL MEDICAL CENTER, INC.

EXECUTIVES
Principal, Brad McGrath
Chief Operating Officer, Phillip Rivera
Purchasing Agent, Kirt Whitlock

LOCATIONS
HQ: MEMORIAL MEDICAL CENTER, INC.
2450 S TELSHOR BLVD, LAS CRUCES, NM 880115076
Phone: 575 522-8641

HISTORICAL FINANCIALS
Company Type: Private

Income Statement
FYE: September 30

	REVENUE ($ mil.)	NET INCOME ($ mil.)	NET PROFIT MARGIN	EMPLOYEES
09/15*	225	20	8.9%	50
05/14	0	(0)	—	—
Annual Growth	97175.3%	—	—	—

*Fiscal year change

2015 Year-End Financials
Return on assets: 2.8% Cash ($ mil.): —
Return on equity: 8.9%
Current ratio: 1.90

MEMORIAL SLOAN-KETTERING CANCER CENTER

Memorial Sloan-Kettering Cancer Center (MSKCC) leads the way in cancer research and treatment. The center includes the 470-bed Memorial Hospital for Cancer and Allied Diseases providing pediatric and adult cancer care and the Sloan-Kettering Institute for cancer research activities. Memorial Hospital specializes in bone-marrow transplants radiation therapy and chemotherapy and it offers programs in cancer prevention diagnosis treatment research and education. The Sloan-Kettering Institute conducts medical and clinical laboratory research on cancer genetics and therapeutics.The hospital was founded in 1884 as the New York Cancer Center by a group that included John Astor and his wife Charlotte.

Operations

MSKCC includes the 470-bed Memorial Hospital for Cancer and Allied Diseases and the Sloan-Kettering Institute for cancer research activities. It has more than 20 surgical suites and the Center for Image-Guided Interventions.

MSKCC also provides cancer care through partnerships with some acute-care hospitals in the region such as Phelps Memorial Hospital Center and Mercy Medical Center. The health care organization also has partnerships with Rockefeller University and Cornell University through which it provides medical training to oncology professionals.

The hospital's clinical staff is made up of more than 900 attending physicians and over 2200 registered nurses. MSKCC also has over 140 senior laboratory investigators 320-plus research fellows more than 540 postdoctoral researchers and nearly 250 PhD- and MD/PhD- graduate students.

MSKCC's physicians treat more than 400 different subtypes of cancer each year. In 2013 the network saw nearly 137000 patients and admitted nearly a sixth of them to Memorial Hospital.

Geographic Reach

Memorial Hospital is located in New York City. Memorial Sloan-Kettering Cancer Center (MSKCC) offers outpatient services from about a dozen Manhattan Long Island and New Jersey clinic locations.

Financial Performance

To keep its various projects and clinical trials funded MSKCC counts on grants from a number of biomedical research institutions including the National Institutes of Health and the National Cancer Institute. It also receives a good portion of its cash through fundraising efforts and philanthropic donations.

MSKCC's revenue grew by 8% to $3 billion in 2013 mostly thanks to higher patient care revenue but also thanks to increased grants and contracts contributions allocated to operations and royalty income. Higher revenue and tight control on operating expense growth also helped net income jump by 95% to $178 million in 2013.

Strategy

To provide the most comprehensive and effective care for cancer patients MSKCC's Sloan-Kettering Institute researchers work with physicians to research cancer care techniques. The institute also conducts clinical trials to develop new cancer pharmaceuticals. At any given time Sloan-Kettering Institute is engaged in hundreds of clinical trials for pediatric and adult cancers.

MSKCC has expanded over the years by renovating existing centers and adding new outpatient facilities. In late 2014 for example it opened its sixth outpatient treatment center in the suburbs of West Harrison New York and also announced that it would begin building a new facility in Middletown New Jersey.

Using generous contributions the health network has been investing in research centers designed to further next-generation medical treatments. In 2014 MSKCC opened the Center for Molecular Imaging and Nanotechnology (CMINT) to accelerate research on the biology of cancers and further the development of new diagnostic and prognostic tools and treatments which include molecularity-based image-guided therapies. In 2013 it opened several new research centers aimed at capturing genetic information from tumors and exploiting its full potential to the medical field including the $100 million Marie Josee and Henry R. Kravis Center for Molecular Oncology (CMO).

In 2012 the center spent $2.2 billion on a clinical expansion aimed at treating blood head and neck and thoracic cancers while providing an outpatient bone marrow transplant facility and a place for early stage clinical trials among other things. It also announced a collaboration with IBM to build a tool that gives doctors access to more and better cancer data.

Company Background

The institute was founded in 1945 by Alfred Sloan and Charles Kettering to research new cancer cures; it merged with Memorial Hospital in 1980.

EXECUTIVES

SVP Information Systems and CIO, Patricia C. Skarulis
EVP and CFO, Michael P. Gutnick
COO, Kathryn Martin
VP Facilities Management, Edward J. Mahoney
Head of Surgical Metabolism Laboratory; Chairman Department of Surgery, Murray F. Brennan, age 76
President and CEO, Craig B. Thompson, age 64
Vice President Research and Technology Management, Eric M. Cottington
SVP and Chief Investment Officer, Jason Klein
Physician-in-Chief and Chief Medical Officer Memorial Hospital, Jos © Baselga
Chairman Department of Surgery, Jeffrey A. Drebin
EVP and Hospital Administrator, Ned Groves
EVP and General Counsel, Jorge Lopez
Vice President, Kerry Bessey
Vice President Human Resources Operations and Information Systems, Bill Morgan
Vice President, Tomya Ryans
Vice President Director of other Admin Financial Depts, Melvin McLean
Director Of Radiology, Chester Mah
Director of Radiology, Stefanie Jacobs
Senior Vice President and Chief Information technology Officer, Anna A Spitzer
VICE PRESIDENT MARKETING, Ken Marians
Vice President and Chief Information Security Officer, Michael Czumak
Secretary And Ram Coordinator, Agnes Bethelmie
Secretary, Svetlana Visotski
Secretary V, Noila Johnson
Secretary, Simone Joseph
Secretary IV, Michele Black

LOCATIONS

HQ: MEMORIAL SLOAN-KETTERING CANCER CENTER
1275 YORK AVE, NEW YORK, NY 100656007
Phone: 212 639-2000
Web: WWW.MSKCC.ORG

PRODUCTS/OPERATIONS

2013 Sales

	$ mil.	% of total
Patient care	2,367	78
Grants and contracts	202	7
Other	455	15
Total	**3,025**	**100**

COMPETITORS

Aptium Oncology
City of Hope
Columbia University
Continuum Health Partners
Dana-Farber
Fox Chase Cancer Center
Johns Hopkins Medicine
MD Anderson Cancer Center
Mayo Clinic
New York City Health and Hospitals
NewYork-Presbyterian Healthcare
Northwell Health
Partners HealthCare
Roswell Park Cancer Institute
Sandford Burnham Institute
St. Jude Children's Research Hospital
Wistar Institute

HISTORICAL FINANCIALS
Company Type: Private

Income Statement
FYE: December 31

	REVENUE ($ mil.)	NET INCOME ($ mil.)	NET PROFIT MARGIN	EMPLOYEES
12/15	2,220	190	8.6%	9,325
12/13	582	0	0.2%	—
12/09	2,105	(195)	—	—
12/06	1,622	320	19.8%	—
Annual Growth	**3.5%**	**(5.6%)**	—	—

2015 Year-End Financials

Return on assets: 6.9%   Cash ($ mil.): —
Return on equity: 8.6%
Current ratio: 0.70

MENORAH MEDICAL CENTER, INC.

EXECUTIVES

President, Steve Wilkinson
Administrative Assistant, Sonia Whiteaker
Purchasing Agent, Cito Jalbuena
Director, Laurie Fisher
Director, Sam Weems
Director, Becca Bell
Project Manager, Steve Oliver

LOCATIONS

HQ: MENORAH MEDICAL CENTER, INC.
5721 W 119TH ST, OVERLAND PARK, KS 662093753
Phone: 913 498-6000
Web: WWW.MENORAHMEDICALCENTER.COM

HISTORICAL FINANCIALS
Company Type: Private

Income Statement
FYE: May 31

	REVENUE ($ mil.)	NET INCOME ($ mil.)	NET PROFIT MARGIN	EMPLOYEES
05/15	181	16	9.3%	800
05/09	133	1	0.8%	—
Annual Growth	**5.3%**	**57.9%**	—	—

2015 Year-End Financials
Return on assets: 2.3%   Cash ($ mil.): —
Return on equity: 9.3%
Current ratio: 2.00

MERCY CHILDREN'S HOSPITAL

When you've got sick grumpy kids on your hands beneficence may not be the first word that comes to mind that is unless you're a doctor at The Children's Mercy Hospital. The pediatric hospital offers health care for youngsters in and around Kansas City Missouri. Specialized services include home health endocrinology genetics heart surgery neonatology and rehabilitation. Founded in 1897 the hospital has about 355 beds. The Children's Mercy health care system also includes a small suburban campus outpatient clinics outreach clinics and research facilities.

Operations

The hospital has more than 40 pediatric sub-specialty clinics and a medical staff of roughly 700 pediatric specialists. Its main campus has 355 beds; there are an additional 53 at the Children's Mercy Hospital South suburban campus. Of the total number of beds about 90 are special care beds composed of about 40 pediatric intensive care and the rest neonatal intensive care.

Geographic Reach

Children's Mercy Hospital is the only Level I pediatric trauma center between St. Louis Missouri and Denver Colorado.

It is a teaching hospital affiliated with University of Missouri-Kansas City Medical School University of Kansas the Stowers Institute and Midwest Research Institute.

Financial Performance

In 2013 Children's Mercy Hospital reported revenue of $961 million about 95% of which came from patient care services.

Strategy

Children's Mercy Hospital is undergoing a 15-year $800 million expansion designed to more than double the size of the hospital increase the number of patient beds by 50% add a new emergency room six new operating rooms new heart catheterization labs new educational buildings clinics and doctors' offices. In 2012 it completed phase one of the expansion after spending $800 million on work at Children's Mercy South and clinics at Broadway and the Elizabeth Ann Hall Patient Tower at the main location. Work continued in 2014 when it added about 2000 square feet to its Wichita Specialty Clinic.

A large part of the funding for the expansion comes from philanthropic donations. Since the project began growth at the health system has included new urgent and specialty care centers a Pediatric Research Center new primary care centers and additional patient units and beds. The hospital has also undergone remodeling and expansion of certain existing facilities.

Company Background

The Children's Mercy Hospital is part of The Children's Mercy Hospital and Clinics a not-for-profit free-standing pediatric health system that also offers low-income families a low- or no-cost health plan through Kansas Healthwave and MO HealthNet Managed Care.

The Children's Mercy Family Health Partners insurance plan contracts with the states of Missouri and Kansas to provide coverage to patients who are eligible for Medicaid or the State Children's Health Insurance Plan (SCHIP).

EXECUTIVES

Medical Director, Todd J Beardman
President CEO and Director, Randall L. O'Donnell
Executive Vice President Co-Chief Operating Officer, Karen Cox
EVP and Co-COO, Jo Stueve
EVP and CFO, Sandra A. J. Lawrence
VP and Chief Nursing Officer, Cheri Hunt
VP Market Development and Outreach, Warren Dudley
Surgeon-in-Chief, George W. Holcomb
Pediatrician-in-Chief, Michael Artman
Medical Director Office Of Equity And, John Cowden
Medical Director, Ashley Daly
Vice President Finance and Controller, Terry Weathers
Medical Director, Sarah Bledsoe
Vice President of Supply Chain, Laurisa Jackson
Medical Director, Rupal Gupta
Chairman, Jack Ovel
Auditors: KPMG LLP OMAHA NE

LOCATIONS

HQ: MERCY CHILDREN'S HOSPITAL
2401 GILLHAM RD, KANSAS CITY, MO 641084619
Phone: 816 234-3000
Web: WWW.CHILDRENSMERCY.ORG

Selected locations
Children's Mercy Hospital Hill (Kansas City)
Children's Mercy Northland (Kansas City)
Children's Mercy South (Overland Park MO)
Children's Mercy Teen Clinic (Kansas City)
Children's Mercy College Boulevard Clinics (Overland Park MO)

PRODUCTS/OPERATIONS

2013 Sales

	% of total
Patient Care Services	94
Grants and Contracts	2
Investment Income	1
Assets Released from Restrictions	1
Unrestricted Gifts & Bequests	1
Others	1
Total	**100**

COMPETITORS

Ascension Health	Shriners Hospitals For
CoxHealth	Children
Liberty Hospital	Sisters of Charity of
Saint Luke's Health	Leavenworth
System	Truman Medical Centers
Shawnee Mission	University of Kansas
Medical Center	Medical Center

HISTORICAL FINANCIALS
Company Type: Private

Income Statement   FYE: June 30

	REVENUE ($ mil.)	NET INCOME ($ mil.)	NET PROFIT MARGIN	EMPLOYEES
06/15	978	79	8.1%	7,000
06/13	9	(0)	—	—
06/11	816	13	1.6%	—
06/10	787	43	5.6%	—
Annual Growth	4.4%	12.6%	—	—

2015 Year-End Financials
Return on assets: 7.2%   Cash ($ mil.): 98
Return on equity: 8.1%
Current ratio: 1.90

MERCY CLINIC OKLAHOMA COMMUNITIES, INC.

EXECUTIVES

Executive Director, Diana Smalley
Auditors: PLEUS AND COMPANY LLC CHESTE

LOCATIONS

HQ: MERCY CLINIC OKLAHOMA COMMUNITIES, INC.
4300 W MEMORIAL RD, OKLAHOMA CITY, OK 731208304
Phone: 405 936-5213
Web: WWW.MERCY.NET

HISTORICAL FINANCIALS
Company Type: Private

Income Statement   FYE: June 30

	REVENUE ($ mil.)	NET INCOME ($ mil.)	NET PROFIT MARGIN	EMPLOYEES
06/15	178	(43)	—	1
06/14	147	(38)	—	—
06/11	69	(21)	—	—
06/10	2	(1)	—	—
Annual Growth	134.4%	—	—	—

2015 Year-End Financials
Return on assets: 6.4%   Cash ($ mil.): —
Return on equity: (-24.3%)
Current ratio: 1.20

MERCY CLINICS, INC.

EXECUTIVES

Chief Executive Officer, Stephen Eckstat
Manager, Jan S
Director, Ann Marvelli
Systems Manager, Ben Juehring
Director, Cathy Mielk
Auditors: MCGLADREY & PULLEN LLP DAVEN

LOCATIONS

HQ: MERCY CLINICS, INC.
1111 6TH AVE FL 2, DES MOINES, IA 503142610
Phone: 515 643-7150

HISTORICAL FINANCIALS
Company Type: Private

Income Statement   FYE: June 30

	REVENUE ($ mil.)	NET INCOME (3 mil.)	NET PROFIT MARGIN	EMPLOYEES
06/15	237	(2)	—	160
06/05	84	(2)	—	—
06/00	39	2	7.5%	—
06/99	1,518	0	—	—
Annual Growth	—	—	—	—

2015 Year-End Financials
Return on assets: 8.9%   Cash ($ mil.): —
Return on equity: (-1.0%)
Current ratio: 1.30

MERCY COLLEGE

Mercy College is a private Catholic school founded by the Sisters of Mercy in 1950. The college provides higher education to some 9000 undergraduate and graduate students in the New York City area. Mercy College offers 90 degrees in fields including business accounting civic and cultural studies computer science education health professions literature language communication natural sciences and social sciences. The institution also provides some online courses as well as professional certification programs. Mercy College employs some 200 full-time faculty members.

Operations

Mercy College provides its academic programs through five schools: Business Education Health and Natural Sciences Liberal Arts and Social and Behavioral Sciences. Most of the programs are bachelors and master's degrees; Mercy College also offers a doctorate in physical therapy. More than 70% of the college's student base is female.

Geographic Reach

The main Mercy College campus is in Dobbs Ferry (of Westchester County) New York with branch campuses in the Bronx Yorktown Heights and Manhattan. Students on the main campus come from some 35 US states and about 40 countries.

Financial Performance

Mercy College reported $154 million in total operating revenues and support in 2012. The figure was up by 6% from 2011 results of $145.5 million. Revenues primarily come from student tuition and fees (90%); other sources include auxiliary activities government grants and private contributions.

EXECUTIVES

Vice President and Chief Financial and Planning Officer, Donald B Aungst
Vice President Of Enrollment Services, Margaret McGrail
Director Of Admissions, Marcelle Hicks
Assistant Vice President of Student Services, Joseph Trentacoste
Chair Department of Humanities, Richard Medoff
Auditors: LB MARKS PANETH LLP NEW YORK

LOCATIONS

HQ: MERCY COLLEGE
555 BROADWAY FRNT, DOBBS FERRY, NY 105221189
Phone: 914 455-2650
Web: WWW.MERCYATHLETICS.COM

PRODUCTS/OPERATIONS

Selected Schools
Business
Education
Health and Natural Sciences
Liberal Arts
Social and Behavioral Sciences

HISTORICAL FINANCIALS
Company Type: Private

Income Statement
FYE: June 30

	REVENUE ($ mil.)	NET INCOME ($ mil.)	NET PROFIT MARGIN	EMPLOYEES
06/15	190	38	20.1%	500
06/10	154	28	18.3%	—
06/09	128	0	—	—
06/08	0	0	—	—
Annual Growth	—	—	—	—

MERCY CORPS

Mercy Corps is dedicated to helping the poor and oppressed in developing countries. The not-for-profit organization offers emergency relief and economic support as well as assistance in building sustainable communities. It also develops curriculum guides to introduce students to various topics ranging from Kurdish history and Afghan henna art to the worldwide clean water campaign. Since its founding Mercy Corps programs have provided about $1.5 billion in assistance to people in 106 nations. Originally the organization was named Save the Refugees Fund when it was founded by Dan O'Neill in response to the plight of Cambodian refugees in 1979.Mercy Corps boasts offices in North America and Europe as well as several field offices in more troubled regions. The group's daily efforts reach more than 16 million people in some 35 countries.

EXECUTIVES

Senior Vice President, Paul Dudley-Hart
Interim Vice President Senior Director Policy and Advocacy, Ann Vaughan
Global Treasurer, Jay Price

LOCATIONS

HQ: MERCY CORPS
45 SW ANKENY ST, PORTLAND, OR 972043500
Phone: 503 796-6800
Web: WWW.MERCYCORPSNW.ORG

HISTORICAL FINANCIALS
Company Type: Private

Income Statement
FYE: June 30

	REVENUE ($ mil.)	NET INCOME ($ mil.)	NET PROFIT MARGIN	EMPLOYEES
06/15	329	2	0.9%	450
06/14	275	(3)	—	—
06/13	236	(4)	—	—
06/12	232	(7)	—	—
Annual Growth	12.2%	—	—	—

2015 Year-End Financials
Return on assets: 10.7%   Cash ($ mil.): 52
Return on equity: 0.9%
Current ratio: 0.60

MERCY HEALTH

Mercy Health (formerly Catholic Health Partners) performs acts of healing in Kentucky and Ohio. One of the nation's largest not-for-profit health systems Mercy Health offers health care services through about 450 facilities including 23 hospitals eight homes for the elderly five hospice programs and seven home health agencies. It also operates more than 150 clinics a number of physician practices and a health insurance plan. The system is co-sponsored by the Sisters of Mercy South Central and Mid-Atlantic communities; the

Sisters of the Humility of Mary; the Franciscan Sisters of the Poor; and Covenant Health Systems.

Operations

Mercy Health organizes its operations into regions to better serve the communities where its facilities are located. Its acute and non-acute inpatient facilities have a total of more than 6300 beds. The system is affiliated with more than 1800 physicians of various medical and surgical specialties.

Hospitals include St. Elizabeth and St. Joseph Health Centers near Youngstown Ohio; seven Mercy locations in the Toledo Ohio area; Mercy Regional Medical Center near Cleveland; St. Rita's Medical Center in Lima Ohio; Springfield Regional Medical Center and Mercy Memorial Hospital in Springfield Ohio; Anderson Clermont Fairfield Mt. Airy Jewish West and Western Hills hospitals in Cincinnati; and Lourdes Hospital in Paduchah Kentucky.

Its specialized health care services include cancer cardiology radiology laboratory surgical and women's health care. The company also operates HealthSpan a PPO health insurance plan that covers nearly 273000 lives.

Geographic Reach

The system divides its operations into seven regional markets. North Markets include Mercy in Toledo and Lorain Ohio and Humility of Mary Health Partners in Youngstown Ohio. South Markets include St. Rita's Health Partners Community Mercy Health Partners and Mercy Health Partners in Ohio as well as Mercy Health Partners - Kentucky.

Financial Performance

Mercy Health's revenue increased 14% to $4.5 billion in 2014 on growing net patient service revenue and other revenue. However the system lost a net $6.5 million that year due to interest rate swap agreement losses lower investment earnings and higher operating expenses.

Cash flow from operations dropped in 2014 to $354 million.

Strategy

In 2014 after the Affordable Care Act (which requires insurance companies to provide access to abortion and birth control) took effect Mercy Health spun off its HealthSpan insurance arm to avoid a conflict with church doctrine.

The following year Mercy Health partnered with Akron Ohio-based Summa Health to create Advanced Health Select a network of doctors and medical caregivers in an effort to attract large employers and insurance companies.

EXECUTIVES

SVP Operations Support and CIO, Rebecca (Becky) Sykes
SVP; President and CEO Mercy Health Youngstown, Donald E. (Don) Kline
President and CEO, John M. Starcher
SVP; President and CEO Community Mercy Health Partners, Matt Caldwell
CFO, Deborah (Debbie) Bloomfield
SVP; CEO Mercy Health – Cincinnati Region, Michael W. (Mike) Garfield
COO; Interim President and CEO Mercy Heath Toledo Region, Brian Smith
Chief Clinical Officer; President Mercy Health Physicians, Anton Decker
SVP; CEO Mercy Health – Lima Region, Bob Baxter
SVP; CEO Mercy Lorain, Edwin (Ed) Oley
SVP; President and CEO Mercy Health Kentucky, Michael Yungmann
VPMA, Kevin Casey
Vice Chair Board of Trustees, Katherine W. Vestal
Vice Chair, Leonard M. Randolph
Auditors: ERNST & YOUNG LLP CINCINNATI

2015 Year-End Financials
Return on assets: 6.2%   Cash ($ mil.): 35
Return on equity: 20.1%
Current ratio: 0.60

LOCATIONS

HQ: MERCY HEALTH
1701 MERCY HEALTH PL, CINCINNATI, OH
452376147
Phone: 513 639-2800

PRODUCTS/OPERATIONS

2014 Sales

	% of total
Net patients service revenue less provision for bad debts	85
Member revenue	11
Other revenue	4
Total	**100**

Selected Regions and Facilities

Mercy Health Partners - Lorain Region (Lorain OH)
  Mercy Allen Hospital (Oberlin OH)
  Mercy Regional Medical Center (Lorain OH)
  New Life Hospice of St. Joseph (Lorain OH)
Community Mercy Health Partners (Springfield OH)
  Mercy Memorial Hospital (Urbana OH)
  Springfield Regional Medical Center High (Springfield OH)
Humility of Mary Health Partners (Youngstown OH)
  Humility House (Austintown OH)
  St. Elizabeth Boardman Health Center (Boardman OH)
  St. Elizabeth Health Center (Youngstown OH)
  St. Joseph Health Center (Warren OH)
Mercy Health Partners Kentucky Region (Paducah KY)
  Lourdes Hospital (Paducah KY)
  Marcum & Wallace Memorial Hospital (Irvine KY)
Mercy Health Partners Northern Region (Toledo OH)
  Mercy Hospital of Defiance (Defiance OH)
  Mercy St. Anne Hospital (Toledo OH)
  Mercy St. Charles Hospital (Oregon OH)
  Mercy St. Vincent Medical Center (Toledo OH)
  Mercy Tiffin Hospital (Tiffin OH)
  Mercy Willard Hospital (Willard OH)
Mercy Health Partners Southwest Ohio Region
  (Cincinnati OH)
  Jewish Hospital (Cincinnati OH)
  Mercy Hospital Anderson (Cincinnati OH)
  Mercy Hospital Clermont (Batavia OH)
  Mercy Hospital Fairfield (Fairfield OH)
  Mercy Hospital Mt. Airy (Cincinnati OH)
  Mercy Hospital Western Hills (Cincinnati OH)
St. Rita's Health Partners (Lima OH)
  St. Rita's Medical Center (Lima OH)

COMPETITORS

AdCare
Adventist Health System Sunbelt Healthcare
Catholic Health Initiatives
Cincinnati Children's Hospital
HCA
Kindred Healthcare
LifePoint Health
Mount Carmel Health
NHC
OhioHealth
Premier Health Partners
SavaSeniorCare
St. Elizabeth Healthcare
TriHealth
Universal Health Services

HISTORICAL FINANCIALS

Company Type: Private

Income Statement
FYE: December 31

	REVENUE ($ mil.)	NET INCOME ($ mil.)	NET PROFIT MARGIN	EMPLOYEES
12/15	4,275	(361)	—	35,000
12/14	4,510	130	2.9%	—
12/08	4,044	(657)	—	—
12/06	3,505	169	4.8%	—
Annual Growth	2.2%	—	—	—

2015 Year-End Financials

Return on assets: 6.2%
Return on equity: (-8.4%)
Current ratio: 0.80
Cash ($ mil.): 146

MERCY HEALTH ANDERSON HOSPITAL

EXECUTIVES

President, Patrica Shroer
VP Personnel, Maggie Lund
Director, Terri Martin
Vice-President, Julie Holt
Purchasing Agent, Marlynn Huelsman
Personnel Director, Sandy Ferrigno
Director, Marvin Lopez
Director, Pete Gemmer
Director, Peggy A'Hearn

LOCATIONS

HQ: MERCY HEALTH ANDERSON HOSPITAL
7500 STATE RD, CINCINNATI, OH 452552439
Phone: 513 624-4500

HISTORICAL FINANCIALS

Company Type: Private

Income Statement
FYE: December 31

	REVENUE ($ mil.)	NET INCOME ($ mil.)	NET PROFIT MARGIN	EMPLOYEES
12/15	220	33	15.4%	823
12/14	198	34	17.5%	—
12/08	170	(6)	—	—
12/05	125	14	11.6%	—
Annual Growth	5.7%	8.8%		

2015 Year-End Financials

Return on assets: 4.0%
Return on equity: 15.4%
Current ratio: 3.50
Cash ($ mil.): —

MERCY HEALTH ST VINCENT MED LLC

EXECUTIVES

President, Tim Koder
Board of Directors, Julie Higgins
Director, Joe Padach
Director, Marilyn Gagne

LOCATIONS

HQ: MERCY HEALTH ST VINCENT MED LLC
2213 CHERRY ST, TOLEDO, OH 436082603
Phone: 419 251-3232

HISTORICAL FINANCIALS

Company Type: Private

Income Statement
FYE: December 31

	REVENUE ($ mil.)	NET INCOME ($ mil.)	NET PROFIT MARGIN	EMPLOYEES
12/15	467	22	4.8%	6,000
12/00	333	5	1.5%	—
12/99	327	(7)	—	—
12/98	172	(40)	—	—
Annual Growth	6.0%			

MERCY HEALTH SYSTEM CORPORATION

EXECUTIVES

Chief Executive Officer, Javon R Bea
Marketing Director, John Bossa
Auditors: WIPFLI LLP MILWAUKEE WISCONS

LOCATIONS

HQ: MERCY HEALTH SYSTEM CORPORATION
1000 MINERAL POINT AVE, JANESVILLE, WI
535482940
Phone: 608 741-6891

HISTORICAL FINANCIALS

Company Type: Private

Income Statement
FYE: June 30

	REVENUE ($ mil.)	NET INCOME ($ mil.)	NET PROFIT MARGIN	EMPLOYEES
06/15	523	12	2.3%	2,200
06/14	478	39	8.2%	—
06/13	473	21	4.5%	—
06/12	447	15	3.4%	—
Annual Growth	5.4%	(7.7%)		

2015 Year-End Financials

Return on assets: 2.2%
Return on equity: 2.3%
Current ratio: 1.30
Cash ($ mil.): 41

MERCY HEALTH SYSTEM OF NORTHWEST ARKANSAS, INC

EXECUTIVES

President, Eric Pianalto
Vice-President, Cindy Carmichael
Manager, Steve Goss

LOCATIONS

HQ: MERCY HEALTH SYSTEM OF NORTHWEST
ARKANSAS, INC
2710 S RIFE MEDICAL LN, ROGERS, AR 727581452
Phone: 479 338-8000
Web: WWW.MERCY4U.COM

HISTORICAL FINANCIALS

Company Type: Private

Income Statement
FYE: June 30

	REVENUE ($ mil.)	NET INCOME ($ mil.)	NET PROFIT MARGIN	EMPLOYEES
06/15	195	25	13.2%	1,650
06/10	54	(11)	—	—
06/09	96	0	—	—
06/08	2,028	0	—	—
Annual Growth		344.3%	—	—

2015 Year-End Financials

Return on assets: 2.6%
Return on equity: 13.2%
Current ratio: 6.90
Cash ($ mil.): 4

MERCY HOME SERVICES A CALIFORNIA LIMITED PARTNERSHIP

EXECUTIVES

Chief Executive Officer, George A Govier
Chief Financial Officer, Jill Belk
Supervisor, Jeff Hodges
Director, Roger Page
Personnel Director, Denise Little
Director, George Knight

LOCATIONS

HQ: MERCY HOME SERVICES A CALIFORNIA LIMITED
PARTNERSHIP
2175 ROSALINE AVE STE A, REDDING, CA
960012549
Phone: 530 225-6000
Web: WWW.MERCY.ORG

HISTORICAL FINANCIALS
Company Type: Private

Income Statement
FYE: June 30

	REVENUE ($ mil.)	NET INCOME ($ mil.)	NET PROFIT MARGIN	EMPLOYEES
06/15	446	54	12.1%	1,200
06/09	283	8	3.0%	—
Annual Growth	7.8%	36.2%	—	—

2015 Year-End Financials
Return on assets: 2.9%
Return on equity: 12.1%
Current ratio: 2.70
Cash ($ mil.): 62

MERCY HOSPITAL

Mercy Health System of Maine provides medical services to the people of Portland and other residents of Cumberland County. The health system operates two hospital campuses as well as primary and specialty care centers. It boasts a total of 230 beds. The system also operates a substance abuse treatment program a women's shelter a home health and hospice program and a hospitality home for families of patients undergoing treatment. Mercy Health System of Maine which includes Mercy Hospital and VNA Home Health Hospice is a part of Eastern Maine Healthcare Systems.

Operations

Mercy Health System of Maine provides a broad range of medical and surgical services as well as nine primary care locations five express care locations and 17 sub-specialty physician practices ranging from thoracic and spine surgery to ear nose and throat and cancer care.

Company Background

The health system founded in 1918 was a member of Catholic Health East. Primary rival Eastern Maine Healthcare Systems acquired the health system in 2013.

EXECUTIVES

Vice President of Medical Affairs and Chief Medical Officer, Scott Rusk
Operating Room Dir, LUCY BAUER
Respiratory Therapy Director, SUMMER ELLIS

LOCATIONS

HQ: MERCY HOSPITAL
144 STATE ST, PORTLAND, ME 041013795
Phone: 207 879-3000
Web: WWW.MERCYHOSPITAL.ORG

COMPETITORS

Maine Medical Center	Miles Health Care
MaineGeneral Health	Southern Maine Medical
MaineHealth	Center

HISTORICAL FINANCIALS
Company Type: Private

Income Statement
FYE: September 30

	REVENUE ($ mil.)	NET INCOME ($ mil.)	NET PROFIT MARGIN	EMPLOYEES
09/15	213	(22)	—	1,200
09/14	167	4	2.7%	—
Annual Growth	27.6%	—	—	—

2015 Year-End Financials
Return on assets: 9.4%
Return on equity: (-10.7%)
Current ratio: 0.70
Cash ($ mil.): 10

MERCY HOSPITAL AND MEDICAL CENTER

Chicagoans in the loop know Mercy Hospital and Medical Center is the place to go for health care. The Catholic hospital located near Chicago's Loop (the historic downtown commercial district) has about 320 beds and operates a network of community clinics and occupational health facilities that provide employment-related services such as drug screening executive physicals and physical therapy. Other services include a cancer treatment center inpatient hospice care unit eye care center heart and vascular center diabetes treatment center stroke center and inpatient and outpatient chemical dependence recovery programs. Chicago's first teaching hospital it is owned by Ohio-based system Trinity Health.

Operations

The Illinois medical facility offers patients a Level II Trauma Center which includes the Mercy Foundation nearly a dozen auxiliary care facilities MercyWorks occupational health program and a pair of school-based health centers operating under the names Wendell Philips and Dunbar Vocational Career Academies.

The hospital's two on-site clinics — the Doctors Office Center and the Mercy Family Health Center — log some 65000 patient visits each year across every major specialty. Mercy's satellite clinics located throughout the Chicago area see upwards of 100000 patient visits a year.

It's affiliated with Gottlieb Memorial Hospital and Loyola University Medical Center.

Sales and Marketing

Mercy Hospital and Medical Center works to ensure its services are available to a variety of patient groups. To this end the hospital boasts a network of primary care clinics physician offices and satellite facilities.

Strategy

In recent years Mercy Hospital and Medical Center has focused on positioning its cardiovascular institute for growth. It has become the first Chicago hospital to have an FDA-approved carotid artery stenting procedure and was the first to perform Laparo-Endoscopic Single-Site surgeries. Additionally it introduced the HD 3D Laparoscopic Surgical Video System in its operating rooms.

Mercy plans to expand its critical care unit and gastrointestinal laboratory suites to accommodate increased patient demand.

In 2014 Mercy created Siouxland Surgery Center a joint venture with USP Health Ventures that provides surgeries and medical care in Dakota Dunes South Dakota.

Company Background

The hospital became Chicago's first chartered health care facility when it opened in 1852. Mercy Hospital and Medical Center became part of the Trinity Health network in 2012.

EXECUTIVES

COO, Rick Cerceo
CFO, Tom Garvey
President Medical Staff, Pierre Noisette
President Medical Staff, Charles Lawler
President and CEO, Carol L. Schneider
President Elect, Charles Bower
Vice President, Barbara Townsend
Vice President Public Relations and Marketing, Constance Murphy
Blood Bank Director, Dean Christ
Senior Vice President of Marketing, Mary Caponigro
Vice President, Ronald Arnone
Vice President human resourcesrisk management, Nancy Hill-davis
Vice Chair and Secretary, Susan G. Gallagher
Chairman, John McCarthy
Board Member, Ron Arnone

LOCATIONS

HQ: MERCY HOSPITAL AND MEDICAL CENTER
2525 S MICHIGAN AVE, CHICAGO, IL 606162332
Phone: 312 567-2201
Web: WWW.MERCY-CHICAGO.ORG

PRODUCTS/OPERATIONS

Selected Centers
The Birth Place
Cancer Center
Center for Weight Management
Comprehensive Breast and Women's Healthcare Center
Diabetes Treatment Center
Ear Nose & Throat Center
Heart & Vascular Center
Orthopedics
Spine & Back Care
Stroke Center

Selected Treatment Options
Cardiac rehabilitation
Clinical trials
Emergency medicine
Immediate care
Integrative medicine & wellness
Minimally invasive surgery
Pulmonary rehabilitation
Rehabilitation and therapy
Robotic surgery

Selected Specialty Care Centers
Behavioral health services
Center for urinary health
Diagnostic imaging/radiology
Dizziness & balance center
Eye center
Family health center
Gastroenterology
Laboratory & pathology
Lap-band program
Occupational health
Pain management
Pediatrics
Pre-birth center
Sleep center
Vitas hospice
Wound management

COMPETITORS

Covenant Ministries
NorthShore University HealthSystem
Northwestern Memorial HealthCare
Rush System for Health
Silver Cross Hospital
Sinai Health System
St. Bernard Hospital and Health Care Center
Swedish Covenant
SwedishAmerican Health System
University of Chicago Medical Center
Vanguard MacNeal Hospital
Weiss Memorial Hospital

HISTORICAL FINANCIALS

Company Type: Private

Income Statement

FYE: June 30

	REVENUE ($ mil.)	NET INCOME ($ mil.)	NET PROFIT MARGIN	EMPLOYEES
06/15	278	(7)	—	1,550
06/14	273	(5)	—	—
06/13	265	4	1.5%	—
06/10	250	9	3.6%	—
Annual Growth	2.1%	—	—	—

2015 Year-End Financials

Return on assets: 9.2%   Cash ($ mil.): 27
Return on equity: (-2.7%)
Current ratio: 3.10

MERCY HOSPITAL FORT SMITH

EXECUTIVES

President, Ryan Gehrig
Manager, Douglas Gautier
Auditors: ERNST & YOUNG US LLP SAINT LO

LOCATIONS

HQ: MERCY HOSPITAL FORT SMITH
   7301 ROGERS AVE, FORT SMITH, AR 729034100
Phone: 479 314-6000
Web: WWW.MERCY.NET

HISTORICAL FINANCIALS

Company Type: Private

Income Statement

FYE: June 30

	REVENUE ($ mil.)	NET INCOME ($ mil.)	NET PROFIT MARGIN	EMPLOYEES
06/15	233	0	0.2%	1,553
06/14	11	(0)	—	—
06/10	217	11	5.4%	—
06/09	482	1	0.2%	—
Annual Growth	(11.4%)	(9.8%)	—	—

2015 Year-End Financials

Return on assets: 1.6%   Cash ($ mil.): 6
Return on equity: 0.2%
Current ratio: 3.80

MERCY HOSPITAL OF BUFFALO

EXECUTIVES

Chief Executive Officer, Charles J Urlaub
Board of Directors, Sr Margaret Tuley D C
Accountant, Diane Schwenk
Director, Laura Verbanic
Manager, Nancy Ogorek

LOCATIONS

HQ: MERCY HOSPITAL OF BUFFALO
   565 ABBOTT RD, BUFFALO, NY 142202095
Phone: 716 826-7000

HISTORICAL FINANCIALS

Company Type: Private

Income Statement

FYE: December 31

	REVENUE ($ mil.)	NET INCOME ($ mil.)	NET PROFIT MARGIN	EMPLOYEES
12/15	391	3	0.8%	2,000
12/14	381	20	5.4%	—
12/08	249	6	2.6%	—
12/05	205	6	3.2%	—
Annual Growth	6.7%	(7.5%)	—	—

2015 Year-End Financials

Return on assets: 4.4%   Cash ($ mil.): 94
Return on equity: 0.8%
Current ratio: 2.00

MERCY HOSPITAL ROGERS

EXECUTIVES

President, Eric Pianalto
Financial Executive, Russel Nugent
Administrative Assistant, Melissa Chastaen
Auditors: ERNST & YOUNG US LLP SAINT LO

LOCATIONS

HQ: MERCY HOSPITAL ROGERS
   2710 S RIFE MEDICAL LN, ROGERS, AR 727581452
Phone: 479 338-8000

HISTORICAL FINANCIALS

Company Type: Private

Income Statement

FYE: June 30

	REVENUE ($ mil.)	NET INCOME ($ mil.)	NET PROFIT MARGIN	EMPLOYEES
06/15	211	25	12.2%	760
06/14	193	20	10.7%	—
06/09	343	0	—	—
06/08	253	(9)	—	—
Annual Growth	(2.5%)	—	—	—

2015 Year-End Financials

Return on assets: 2.1%   Cash ($ mil.): 4
Return on equity: 12.2%
Current ratio: 6.90

MERCY HOSPITAL SPRINGFIELD

Mercy Hospital Springfield is an 890-bed acute-care hospital in the Mercy Health system. The facility provides health care to southwestern Missouri and northwestern Arkansas and includes the Mercy Children's Hospital Springfield. Other hospital specialties include cardiology and stroke care as well as women's and seniors' health cancer emergency trauma burn neuroscience rehabilitation and sports medicine. In addition to its hospital in Springfield Mercy Hospital Springfield operates a number of community clinics and specialty care centers in the area.

Operations

Mercy Hospital Springfield has about 700 doctors on its medical staff. The center sees some 441000 outpatient visits per year as well as 94000 emergency room visits and 37000 surgeries. It also enables more than 3000 births Specialty units feature a level I trauma and burn center (the highest ranking in the US) a neonatal intensive care unit a nationally certified stroke center and high-tech surgery suites (including da Vinci robotic surgery and CyberKnife radiosurgery centers). It also operates an air ambulance service.

Geographic Reach

The hospital serves patients in southwest Missouri and northwest Arkansas.

Financial Performance

The hospital's revenues decreased by 1% in 2014 due to 1% drop in net patient service revenue (which contributed 98% of the revenue) and a 11% decrease in revenues from other sources.

In 2014 the company provided charity care of about $26 million along with unreimbursed Medicaid expenses of around $17 million.

Strategy

That year Mercy Hospital Springfield opened the 60-bed Mercy Rehabilitation Hospital Springfield which is spread across a 63000-square-feet facility. The new $28 million building allows for more options for patient rehabilitation and will also serve as the region's only burn unit.

In 2014 the company also opened Phase II of its Betty and Bobby Allison Neonatal Intensive Care Unit (NICU) which expands the number of beds under NICU to 46. With this final phase complete Mercy permanently closed its former NICU.

Company Background

Formerly St. John's Regional Health Center the hospital's name changed to Mercy Hospital Springfield in 2012; the move coincided with the parent organization's efforts to to unify its brand identity. (The parent group's named changed as well from Sisters of Mercy Health System to Mercy Health.)

The hospital was founded in 1891 by the Sisters of Mercy.

EXECUTIVES

Chief Executive Officer, Lynn Britton
Chief Executive Officer, Kim Day
President, John Swope
Executive Vice-President, Michael McCurry
Executive Vice-President, Shannon Sock
Accountant, Shelly Willoughby
Manager, Chris Bos
Account Manager, Jana Dock
Office Manager, Ten McMurry

LOCATIONS

HQ: MERCY HOSPITAL SPRINGFIELD
1235 E CHEROKEE ST, SPRINGFIELD, MO
658042203
Phone: 417 820-2000
Web: WWW.STJOHNS.COM

PRODUCTS/OPERATIONS

Selected Services
Bariatric Surgery
Cancer Care
Children's Care
Heart Care
Integrative Medicine
Mother and Baby Care
Neurosciences
Orthopedic and Sport Care
Palliative Care
Pastoral Care
Senior Care
Trauma and Burn Care
Women's Care

COMPETITORS

Ascension Health	HCA
BJC HealthCare	Heartland Health
Boone Hospital Center	Liberty Hospital
Catholic Health	Tenet Healthcare
Initiatives	Truman Medical Centers
Christian Hospital	University of Kansas
CoxHealth	Medical Center

HISTORICAL FINANCIALS

Company Type: Private

Income Statement
FYE: June 30

	REVENUE ($ mil.)	NET INCOME ($ mil.)	NET PROFIT MARGIN	EMPLOYEES
06/15	948	93	9.9%	4,400
06/14	964	42	4.4%	—
06/13	965	87	9.1%	—
06/12	968	112	11.6%	—
Annual Growth	(0.7%)	(6.0%)	—	—

2015 Year-End Financials

Return on assets: 1.1%
Return on equity: 9.9%
Current ratio: 3.50

Cash ($ mil.): 23

MERCY HOSPITAL WASHINGTON

EXECUTIVES

President, Terri L McLain
Chief Financial Officer, Cheryl Matejka

LOCATIONS

HQ: MERCY HOSPITAL WASHINGTON
901 E 5TH ST, WASHINGTON, MO 630903127
Phone: 636 239-8000
Web: WWW.MERCY.NET

HISTORICAL FINANCIALS

Company Type: Private

Income Statement
FYE: June 30

	REVENUE ($ mil.)	NET INCOME ($ mil.)	NET PROFIT MARGIN	EMPLOYEES
06/15	172	31	18.1%	576
06/09	0	0	—	—
06/05	75	2	3.5%	—
Annual Growth	8.5%	28.0%	—	—

2015 Year-End Financials

Return on assets: 2.2%
Return on equity: 18.1%
Current ratio: —

Cash ($ mil.): 3

MERCY HOSPITAL, CEDAR RAPIDS, IOWA

EXECUTIVES

President, Timothy L Charles
Director, Holly Willis
Auditors: RSM US LLP DAVENPORT IOWA

LOCATIONS

HQ: MERCY HOSPITAL, CEDAR RAPIDS, IOWA
701 10TH ST SE, CEDAR RAPIDS, IA 524031251
Phone: 319 398-6011
Web: WWW.MERCYCARE.ORG

HISTORICAL FINANCIALS

Company Type: Private

Income Statement
FYE: June 30

	REVENUE ($ mil.)	NET INCOME ($ mil.)	NET PROFIT MARGIN	EMPLOYEES
06/16	314	(6)	—	2,375
06/15	303	(6)	—	—
06/14	269	15	5.9%	—
06/13	265	27	10.3%	—
Annual Growth	5.8%	—	—	—

2016 Year-End Financials

Return on assets: 5.4%
Return on equity: (-2.0%)
Current ratio: 1.40

Cash ($ mil.): 24

MERCY HOSPITALS EAST COMMUNITIES

EXECUTIVES

President, Jeffrey Johnston
VP Finance, Sheryl Matejka
Administrative Assistant, Maureen Matz
Director, Mary Burton
Manager, Jennifer Eise
Vice-President, Steven Bollin
Supervisor, Sandra Saunders

LOCATIONS

HQ: MERCY HOSPITALS EAST COMMUNITIES
615 S NEW BALLAS RD, SAINT LOUIS, MO
631418221
Phone: 417 820-2000

COMPETITORS

BJC HealthCare	St. Anthony's Medical
Memorial Hospital	Center
(Illinois)	St. Luke's Hospital
SSM Health Care	(MO)

HISTORICAL FINANCIALS

Company Type: Private

Income Statement
FYE: June 30

	REVENUE ($ mil.)	NET INCOME ($ mil.)	NET PROFIT MARGIN	EMPLOYEES
06/15	940	132	14.1%	10,000
06/14	1,177	118	10.1%	—
06/13	840	82	9.8%	—
06/09	963	0	—	—
Annual Growth	(0.4%)	—	—	—

2015 Year-End Financials

Return on assets: 1.6%
Return on equity: 14.1%
Current ratio: 4.50

Cash ($ mil.): 21

MERCY MEDICAL CENTER

Overlooking Long Island's Hempstead Lake State Park Mercy Medical Center offers healthcare services to patients just east of Manhattan. The not-for-profit Catholic hospital has expertise in weight loss and orthopedic surgeries mammograms and breast health and women's health services. It also provides outpatient services such as family and mental health care. With about 380 beds the medical center employs some 700 physicians who deliver about 1300 babies each year. Its acute care facilities include a suburban branch of Memorial Sloan-Kettering Cancer Center. Mercy Medical Center established in 1913 by the Sisters of the Congregation of the Infant Jesus is part of Catholic Health Services of Long Island.

EXECUTIVES

Chief Executive Officer, Dr Alan Guerci
Executive Director, Annette Esposito

LOCATIONS

HQ: MERCY MEDICAL CENTER
1000 N VILLAGE AVE, ROCKVILLE CENTRE, NY
115701000
Phone: 516 594-6470
Web: WWW.CHSLI.ORG

PRODUCTS/OPERATIONS

Selected Services
Bariatric Surgery
Behavioral Health
Cancer Program
Cardiovascular Care
Drug and Alcohol
Emergency Care
Geriatrics
Mother Baby Services
Neurology
Neurosurgery
Orthopedic Surgery

Pediatrics
Physical Medicine and Rehabilitation
Podiatry
Procedures/Testing
Radiology and Imaging
Respiratory Health
Support Services
Surgery

COMPETITORS

Brookhaven Memorial Hospital Medical Center
Long Island College Hospital
Long Island Jewish Medical Center
New York City Health and Hospitals
NewYork-Presbyterian Healthcare
Northwell Health
Southside Hospital

HISTORICAL FINANCIALS
Company Type: Private

Income Statement

	REVENUE ($ mil.)	NET INCOME ($ mil.)	NET PROFIT MARGIN	EMPLOYEES
12/15	195	6	3.4%	1,610
12/14	185	2	1.5%	—
12/13	203	(3)	—	—
12/09	197	(8)	—	—
Annual Growth	(0.2%)	—	—	—

FYE: December 31

2015 Year-End Financials
Return on assets: 6.0%   Cash ($ mil.): 6
Return on equity: 3.4%
Current ratio: 1.00

MERCY MEDICAL CENTER, INC.

Mercy Medical Center keeps patients doing the cancan in Canton. The facility is a 480-bed acute care hospital serving residents of five counties in southeastern Ohio. The Catholic medical center has 700 physicians and provides a comprehensive range of care including inpatient outpatient and rehabilitative services. It operates specialty care centers for cardiac vascular stroke and cancer treatment as well as trauma chest pain and rehabilitation units. Mercy Medical Center also operates outpatient health centers in the communities surrounding Canton Ohio. The facility is part of the Sisters of Charity Health System (SCHS) a not-for-profit ministry of the Sisters of Charity of St. Augustine.

Operations

Mercy Medical's center of excellence includes Mercy Heart Center Emergency Services/Trauma Center Emergency Chest Pain Center Mercy Cancer Center Mercy Rehabilitation Services Mercy Stroke Center and Mercy Vascular Center.

Geographic Reach

Mercy Medical Center serves patients living in the Southeastern Ohio counties of Carroll Holmes Stark Tuscarawas and Wayne. In addition to the main hospital in Canton the health care provider operates outpatient centers in Carrollton Jackson Township Lake Township Louisville North Canton and Plain Township as well as Tuscarawas County.

Sales and Marketing

The medical facility markets its services through social media and via TV commercials.

Financial Performance

Mercy Medical's total operating revenues were $275.1 million in fiscal 2012.

Strategy

Mercy Medical Center is focused on increasing operational efficiencies and pursuing growth opportunities including expanding services to patients. To that end the hospital in 2014 began to offer adult and pediatric therapy services in Western Stark County. It also launched an $80-million program in 2010 to invest in capital projects including facility improvements and equipment upgrades. The care provider also opened a new primary care office in Canton in 2012.

Company Background

Mercy Medical Center traces its roots to Mercy Hospital founded in 1908 in the former home of President William McKinley. The hospital was opened by the Sisters of Charity of St. Augustine which established SCHS as the parent company for its hospital operations in 1982. Between 1999 and 2009 SCHS operated the Mercy Medical Center and several other Ohio facilities through a joint venture with the University Hospitals Health System; however after 10 years full control of the facilities was reverted back to SCHS.

EXECUTIVES

Director of HIM, Lynne Shaffer
Vice President Systems, Connie Smith
Vice President Chief Nursing Officer, James Williams
Vice President, Joseph Lapinski
Director Of Respiratory Therapy, Larry Ramer
Vice President and General Cou, Matthew Heinle
Nursing Director, Allison Goshay
CIO Chief Technology Officer Vice President Information Technology, Jim Carroll
Vice President, Lorraine Washington
Vice President Fund Development and Government Relations, Thomas Turner
Medical Director, Douglas Lyle Blocker
Ambulatory Services Director, Jamie Carbone
Medical Director, Bruce Hensley
Infection Control Director, TONIA BURLEY
Auditors: PLANTE & MORAN PLLC COLUMBUS

LOCATIONS

HQ: MERCY MEDICAL CENTER, INC.
1320 MERCY DR NW, CANTON, OH 447082641
Phone: 330 489-1000
Web: WWW.CANTONMERCY.ORG

Selected Facilities
Mercy Medical Center - Canton Ohio
Mercy Health Center of Alliance - Alliance Ohio
Mercy Health Center of Carroll County - Carrollton OH
Mercy Health Center of Lake - Uniontown OH
Mercy Health Center of Louisville - Louisville OH
Mercy Health Center of Jackson - Massillon OH
Mercy Health Center of North Canton - North Canton OH
Mercy Health Center of Plain - Canton OH
Mercy Health Center of Tuscarawas County - New Philadelphia OH
Mercy Medical Center at St. Paul Square - Canton Ohio

COMPETITORS

Akron Children's Hospital	Robinson Memorial Hospital
Akron General Health System	Summa Health System
Aultman Health Foundation	The Cleveland Clinic
Lake Health	Trinity Health System
OhioHealth	University Hospitals Health System
Parma Community General Hospital	

HISTORICAL FINANCIALS
Company Type: Private

Income Statement

	REVENUE ($ mil.)	NET INCOME ($ mil.)	NET PROFIT MARGIN	EMPLOYEES
12/15	298	2	0.9%	80
12/14	301	5	1.7%	—
12/13	283	10	3.6%	—
12/12	269	(14)	—	—
Annual Growth	3.4%	—	—	—

FYE: December 31

2015 Year-End Financials
Return on assets: 5.5%   Cash ($ mil.): 27
Return on equity: 0.9%
Current ratio: 1.30

MERCY MEDICAL CENTER, INC.

EXECUTIVES

President, Kelly C Morgan
Board of Directors, Nancy Lehrbach
Financial Executive, Jean Larson
Manager, Sandy Brown
Director, Renae Bugge
Personnel Director, Dawn Wiebard
Personnel Manager, Victor Fresolone

LOCATIONS

HQ: MERCY MEDICAL CENTER, INC.
2700 NW STEWART PKWY, ROSEBURG, OR 974711214
Phone: 541 673-0611
Web: WWW.MERCYROSE.ORG

HISTORICAL FINANCIALS
Company Type: Private

Income Statement

	REVENUE ($ mil.)	NET INCOME ($ mil.)	NET PROFIT MARGIN	EMPLOYEES
06/15	182	37	20.5%	1,100
06/14	190	33	17.7%	—
06/10	166	12	7.6%	—
06/09	141	1	1.4%	—
Annual Growth	4.3%	64.1%	—	—

FYE: June 30

2015 Year-End Financials
Return on assets: 3.9%   Cash ($ mil.): 8
Return on equity: 20.5%
Current ratio: 1.30

MERCY SCRIPPS HOSPITAL

EXECUTIVES

Principal, Andrew C Ping
Marketing Director, Tye Kennon
Vice-President, David Shaw
Director, Nicholas Frost
Director, Rodrigo Munoz

LOCATIONS

HQ: MERCY SCRIPPS HOSPITAL
  4077 5TH AVE MER35, SAN DIEGO, CA 921032105
Phone: 619 294-8111
Web: WWW.SCRIPPS.ORG

HISTORICAL FINANCIALS
Company Type: Private

Income Statement
FYE: September 30

	REVENUE ($ mil.)	NET INCOME ($ mil.)	NET PROFIT MARGIN	EMPLOYEES
09/15	750	44	5.9%	77
09/14	623	3	0.6%	—
09/13	700	41	5.9%	—
Annual Growth	3.5%	3.7%	—	—

MERIDIAN HOSPITALS CORPORATION

EXECUTIVES

President, Marc Lory
Chief Operating Officer, Jeff Brickman
President, Timothy J Hogan
Chief Operating Officer, Joseph Miller
Vice-President, Lori Colineri
Vice-President, Kelli O'Brien
Vice-President, Joseph Reichman
Vice-President, Alvis Swinney
Auditors: PRICEWATERHOUSECOOPERS LLP NE

LOCATIONS

HQ: MERIDIAN HOSPITALS CORPORATION
  1945 ROUTE 33, NEPTUNE, NJ 077534859
Phone: 732 751-7500

HISTORICAL FINANCIALS
Company Type: Private

Income Statement
FYE: December 31

	REVENUE ($ mil.)	NET INCOME ($ mil.)	NET PROFIT MARGIN	EMPLOYEES
12/15	674	64	9.5%	5,200
12/09	929	94	10.2%	—
12/08	873	(140)	—	—
Annual Growth	(3.6%)	—	—	—

2015 Year-End Financials
Return on assets: 6.0%   Cash ($ mil.): 300
Return on equity: 9.5%
Current ratio: 1.60

MERION LOWER SCHOOL DISTRICT INC

EXECUTIVES

Superintendent, Wagner Marseille
Manager, Agnes Passarella
Personnel Director, Bill Kerns
Superintendent, Christopher McGinely
Auditors: RAINER & COMPANY NEWTOWN SQUA

LOCATIONS

HQ: MERION LOWER SCHOOL DISTRICT INC
  301 E MONTGOMERY AVE, ARDMORE, PA 190033338
Phone: 610 645-1983
Web: WWW.LMSD.ORG

HISTORICAL FINANCIALS
Company Type: Private

Income Statement
FYE: June 30

	REVENUE ($ mil.)	NET INCOME ($ mil.)	NET PROFIT MARGIN	EMPLOYEES
06/16	239	(8)	—	1,600
06/08	175	43	24.6%	—
06/07	167	24	14.7%	—
06/06	1,454	0	0.0%	—
Annual Growth	(16.5%)	—	—	—

2016 Year-End Financials
Return on assets: 12.0%   Cash ($ mil.): 15
Return on equity: (-3.4%)
Current ratio: 0.30

MERITER HOSPITAL, INC.

EXECUTIVES

Chief Executive Officer, James L Woodward
Manager, Jackie Landerud
Director, Charles Weber

LOCATIONS

HQ: MERITER HOSPITAL, INC.
  202 S PARK ST, MADISON, WI 537151596
Phone: 608 417-6000

HISTORICAL FINANCIALS
Company Type: Private

Income Statement
FYE: December 31

	REVENUE ($ mil.)	NET INCOME ($ mil.)	NET PROFIT MARGIN	EMPLOYEES
12/15	402	52	13.0%	2,548
12/14	434	47	11.0%	—
12/13	454	56	12.5%	—
12/12	432	34	8.1%	—
Annual Growth	(2.3%)	14.5%	—	—

2015 Year-End Financials
Return on assets: 10.7%   Cash ($ mil.): 13
Return on equity: 13.0%
Current ratio: 1.10

MERITUS MEDICAL CENTER, INC.

EXECUTIVES

President, Joseph Ross
VP Personnel, Kelly Corbi

LOCATIONS

HQ: MERITUS MEDICAL CENTER, INC.
  11116 MEDICAL CAMPUS RD, HAGERSTOWN, MD 217426710
Phone: 301 797-2000
Web: WWW.MERITUSHEALTH.COM

HISTORICAL FINANCIALS
Company Type: Private

Income Statement
FYE: June 30

	REVENUE ($ mil.)	NET INCOME ($ mil.)	NET PROFIT MARGIN	EMPLOYEES
06/15	361	25	7.1%	2,400
06/14	346	13	3.9%	—
06/12	288	3	1.4%	—
06/09	246	0	—	—
Annual Growth	6.6%	—	—	—

2015 Year-End Financials
Return on assets: 12.4%   Cash ($ mil.): 50
Return on equity: 7.1%
Current ratio: 0.40

MERRILL CORPORATION

Document services company Merrill is no relation to financial services giant Merrill Lynch but the companies do share an interest in SEC paperwork. Merrill Corporation is a provider of outsourced document management branded marketing services and other information management services. It helps clients gather organize and manage confidential and time-sensitive information for legal and financial transactions. In addition the company provides marketing and communication services such as document composition printing fulfillment and digital delivery as well as technology integration.

Operations

Merrill's Legal and Financial Transaction Services (LFTS) offers legal financial and corporate professionals a suite of advanced services and web-based tools to gather organize and manage transactional information. The company's Marketing and Communication Solutions (MCS) segment specializes in technology-enabled marketing and compliance communications.

Geographic Reach

Merrill operates through more than 40 offices in the US and about 20 international locations. It also has an IT Technology Center in Chennai India and another IT-focused facility in Coimbatore India.

Strategy

While the company continues to print individual annual reports brochures catalogs and other publications it has diversified beyond its traditional printing business through numerous acquisitions and strategic alliances to position itself as a business process outsourcing company. It sees growth opportunities in its legal solutions offerings which include managing electronic data discovery and in Merrill Datasite which provides online hosting of documents related to mergers and acquisitions.

In addition to acquisitions Merrill also divests assets from time to time to support its ongoing strategic repositioning efforts in the business process outsourcing marketplace. In 2016 it sold its language services subsidiary Merrill Brink International to United Language Group Inc. The same year it divested its real Estate and Franchise Business selling it to direct marketing technologies firm Xpressdocs Holdings.

HISTORY

Kenneth Merrill founded K. F. Merrill with his wife Lorraine in 1968 and grew the company into a major regional printer. He turned over the reins in 1984 to John Castro who had worked his way up from production manager. The company went public two years later.

EXECUTIVES

Vice President Of Human Resources, Amy Reichenbach
Executive Vice President, Robert Nazarian
Managing Director Asia, Nancy Yu
Chief Product Officer, Thomas Fredell, age 47
EVP and Chief Administrative Officer, Brenda J. Vale
COO Marketing and Communications Solutions, Roy Gross
COO, Rodney D. Johnson
Regional Managing Director Europe Middle East Africa (EMEA), Alun Baker
CEO, James (Rusty) Wiley
CFO, Thomas Donnelly
CIO, Brad Smuland
Vice President Marketing, John Lundgren
Senior Vice President, James Garippa
Senior Vice President and Sales, Tracy Kirby
Senior Vice President President, Thomas Killeen
Senior Vice President Sales, Osterman Steve
Senior Vice President Of Information Technology, Anthony Bednar
Vice President Sales, Lori Frederick
Senior Vice President, Jose Lebron
Vice President Sales, Bradley Wolf
Vice President Sales, Blaze David
Vice President Solution Sales, Mike Schlanger
Senior Vice President, Jean Gardner
Vice President, Vladimir Sukonnik
Vice President Finance, John Gyurci
Vice President Client Services, Kristen Plaehn
Assistant Vice President Wealth Management Internal Specialist, Alex Lesyk
Vice President, Raul Varela
Latin America Vice President, Ana De Castro
Vice President Sales, Phillip Juett
Vice President Sales, Bill Werner
Vice President of Legal Communications, Wes Johnson
Assistant Vice President Financial Advisor, Edward H Whiddon
Vice President, Erin Butch
Vice President, Robert Gates
Vice President, Tom Killeen
Vice President Language Solutions, Brian Sennett
Senior Vice President, Mark Lederman
Vice President Legal and Financial Language Solutions EMEA, David Lamont
Vice President of Corporate Information Technology, Jim Burns
Vice President, Adam Pang
Vice President Sales and Marketing Strategy, Peter Suhr
Vice President Sales, Lee Albanese
First Vice President Investments Senior Financial Advisor, Lois Cartwright
Sales Vice President, Sue Rogers
First Vice President Investments, Robert Outtrim
Vice President, Tom Riedy
Vice President, Alexander Pliskin
Vice President Sales, Shelia Carroll
Senior Vice President, Rob Rowland
Assistant Vice President In The Infrastructure And Data Services Group, Venkat Pillay
Vice President, Michael Williams
Vice President Cfm, Robert Davit
Assistant Vice President, Ronnie Houston
Associate Res Director Wealth Management Senior Vice President Wealth Management, Chris Dewhirst
Senior Vice President, Mark Williams
Vice President Marketing, Kris Slethaug
Senior Vice President Sales, Michelle Fenley
Senior Vice President, Drew J Disesa
Vice President Human Resources, Larkin Kathleen
Senior Vice President Sales, Dick Harter
Vice President Operations and Business Development, Raju Subramanyan
Vice President of Operations, Deven Lindemann
Vice President Of Information Technology, Mike Thyken
Vice President Product Marketing, Axel Kirstetter
Vice President Sales, Michael Linskey
Vice President Of Sales, Dave Turco
Senior Vice President, Pete Wyman
Vice President Sales Enablement and Operations, Russ Walker
Senior Vice President, Jerry Long
Vice President Sales, Susan Rogers
Senior Vice President Sales, John Shaw
Vice President, Thomas Kade
Vice President Strategic Advisors Group, Zac Hurst
Senior Vice President, Neal Davies
Senior Vice President, Clark Graebner
Senior Vice President and Regional Director Sales Merrill Datasite Merrill Bridge, Mark Plaehn
Vice President Legal Language Solutions, Tim John
Chairman, James V. (Jim) Continenza, age 54

LOCATIONS

HQ: MERRILL CORPORATION
1 MERRILL CIR, SAINT PAUL, MN 551085264
Phone: 651 646-4501

PRODUCTS/OPERATIONS

SERVICES

Capital Transactions
Contract Management
Data Warehousing
Elections
Financial Services Marketing & Communications
Healthcare Member Communications
Intellectual Property Management
M&A Reorganizations & Exchange Offers
Merrill IFN
Portfolio Management
Regulatory Disclosure

COMPETITORS

Applied Discovery	Pitney Bowes
Diebold	R.R. Donnelley
Harte-Hanks	Ricoh USA
IntraLinks	St Ives
Kroll Ontrack	Williams Lea
Lionbridge	Xerox

HISTORICAL FINANCIALS

Company Type: Private

Income Statement

FYE: January 31

	REVENUE ($ mil.)	NET INCOME ($ mil.)	NET PROFIT MARGIN	EMPLOYEES
01/16	579	78	13.5%	5,418
01/15	691	64	9.3%	—
01/14	815	24	3.0%	—
01/13	851	(9)	—	—
Annual Growth	(12.0%)	—	—	—

2016 Year-End Financials

Return on assets: 4.6%   Cash ($ mil.): 31
Return on equity: 13.5%
Current ratio: 1.40

MESA COUNTY VALLEY SCHOOL DISTRICT 51 (INC)

EXECUTIVES

Superintendent, Ken Haptonstall
Accountant, Barbara Hazelton
Plant & Facilities Manager, Eric Nilsen
Purchasing Director, Phil Onofrio
Superintendent, Ken Hoptonstall
Auditors: CHADWICK STEINKIRCHNER DAVIS

LOCATIONS

HQ: MESA COUNTY VALLEY SCHOOL DISTRICT 51 (INC)
2115 GRAND AVE, GRAND JUNCTION, CO 815018007
Phone: 970 254-5100
Web: WWW.MESACOUNTY.US

HISTORICAL FINANCIALS

Company Type: Private

Income Statement

FYE: June 30

	REVENUE ($ mil.)	NET INCOME ($ mil.)	NET PROFIT MARGIN	EMPLOYEES
06/16	195	1	1.0%	3,200
06/12	171	0	0.1%	—
06/11	183	1	0.7%	—
06/09	0	0	—	—
Annual Growth	—	97.9%	—	—

MESA UNIFIED SCHOOL DISTRICT 4

EXECUTIVES

Superintendent, Michael Cowan
Assistant Manager, Gerrick Monroe
Manager, Carmen Rocha
Director, Cindy Bochna
Production Manager, Ken Polarnalu
Director, Marlo Loria
Manager, Nick Lamonica
Purchasing Agent, Patty Northey
Supervisor, Carol Alexander
Auditors: HEINFELD MEECH & CO PC P

LOCATIONS

HQ: MESA UNIFIED SCHOOL DISTRICT 4
63 E MAIN ST STE 101, MESA, AZ 852017422
Phone: 480 472-0000
Web: WWW.MPSAZ.ORG

HISTORICAL FINANCIALS

Company Type: Private

Income Statement

FYE: June 30

	REVENUE ($ mil.)	NET INCOME ($ mil.)	NET PROFIT MARGIN	EMPLOYEES
06/16	549	(22)	—	9,621
06/15	531	(19)	—	—
06/14	520	(25)	—	—
06/13	514	31	6.0%	—
Annual Growth	2.2%	—	—	—

MESQUITE INDEPENDENT SCHOOL DISTRICT

EXECUTIVES

President, Robert Seward
Board of Directors, Archimedes Faulkner
Board of Directors, Mandy Burns
Superintendent, Diane Hogg
Superintendent, Sandra Hicks
Mayor, Bill Nicholes
Auditors: WEAVER AND TIDWELL LLP DA

LOCATIONS

HQ: MESQUITE INDEPENDENT SCHOOL DISTRICT
3819 TOWNE CROSSING BLVD, MESQUITE, TX
751502799
Phone: 972 288-6411
Web: WWW.MESQUITEISD.ORG

HISTORICAL FINANCIALS

Company Type: Private

| Income Statement | | | FYE: August 31 |
| | NET | NET | |
REVENUE ($ mil.)	INCOME ($ mil.)	PROFIT MARGIN	EMPLOYEES
08/16	432	52	12.1%	4,200
08/15	414	9	2.2%	—
08/14	396	21	5.4%	—
08/13	369	(18)	—	—
Annual Growth	5.4%	—	—	—

2016 Year-End Financials

Return on assets: 3.2%   Cash ($ mil.): 46
Return on equity: 12.1%
Current ratio: 1.10

MESSER CONSTRUCTION CO.

From casinos and courthouses to laboratories and dormitories Messer Construction has built them all. The builder provides commercial construction services (including design/build and project management) for projects in Indiana Kentucky Ohio North Carolina and Tennessee. Messer completes over $830 million worth of projects each year for clients in the life sciences higher education senior living commercial manufacturing/industrial public and health care sectors among others. Its projects have included one of the US's only LEED-certified research buildings (at the University of Louisville) and the Newport Aquarium in Kentucky. Founded in 1932 employee-owned Messer boasts a return-customer rate of 80%.

Operations

Messer Construction offers a range of commercial construction services including building information modeling cost planning and estimating integrated project delivery lean construction and safety programs. It also offers prefabrication services such as mechanical/electrical/plumbing services bathroom pods and health care headwall assemblies.

Geographic Reach

Based in Cincinnati Ohio Messer operates regional offices in North Carolina (Charlotte) Ohio (Cincinnati Columbus and Dayton) Indiana (Indianapolis) Tennessee (Knoxville and Nashville) and Kentucky (Lexington and Louisville).

Sales and Marketing

Messer Construction has served customers from a variety of industries including clients such as: Aisin Automotive Casting Cummins DHL Express Dow AgroSciences Forest Pharmaceuticals Gannett Co General Motors Honda of America Praxair Procter & Gamble Sonoco and Worthington Steel.

Strategy

Messer continues to work on high-value projects across a wide range of industries in the Midwest particularly in secure industries such as healthcare government and education.

During 2015 for example it worked on the 70000-square-foot expansion to Cincinnati Children's Hospital Medical Center (CCHMC) adding a fourth floor 30 beds kitchen full-service cafeteria expanded medical and surgery specialty clinics a gift shop and more. That year it also worked on the $24.1 million- expansion at the National Air and Space Intelligence Center's (NASIC) Foreign Materials Exploitation Laboratory in Dayton for the US Department of Defense as well as the University of Kentucky's $175 million- Student Center Transformation Project (to be completed in 2017) which will span 360000 square feet and include updated student activity and study spaces dining and retail outlets parking a bookstore and more.

Company Background

Formerly known as Frank Messer & Sons Inc. the company changed its name to Messer Construction Co. in March 2002.

EXECUTIVES

Sr Vp, Bernard Suer
Vice President Columbus office, Robert Verst
President and CEO, Thomas M. (Tom) Keckeis
SVP and CFO, E. Paul Hitter
VP and CIO, Richard A. Hensley
Vice President, Bill Rutz
Vice President, Matthew Verst
Vice President, John Megibben
Operations Vice President, Steve Jones
Finance Vice President, Brian Doyle
Vice President, Kevin M Cozart
Senior Vice President, Jim Hess
Rental Division Vice President, Tom Wall
Auditors: DELOITTE & TOUCHE LLP CINCINN

LOCATIONS

HQ: MESSER CONSTRUCTION CO.
5158 FISHWICK DR, CINCINNATI, OH 452162216
Phone: 513 242-1541
Web: WWW.MESSER.COM

PRODUCTS/OPERATIONS

Selected Projects
Health Care
  Norton Healthcare
  Knoxville Orthopedic Clinic
Life Sciences
  Indiana University
  University of Kentucky
Higher Education
  Xavier University
  Western Kentucky University
Senior Living
  Graceworks Lutheran Services
  Episcopal Retirement Homes
Commercial
  IGS Energy
  Penn National Gaming
Manufacturing & Industrial
  Aisin Automotive Casting Tennessee Inc.
  DHL Express Inc.
Public/Institutional
  The Ohio Building Authority
  Commonwealth of Kentucky

COMPETITORS

Albert M. Higley	Shook National
Danis	Skanska USA Building
F.A. Wilhelm	The Austin Company
Gray Construction	Turner Corporation
Hunt Construction	Tutor Perini
Pepper Construction	

HISTORICAL FINANCIALS

Company Type: Private

| Income Statement | | | FYE: September 30 |
| | NET | NET | |
REVENUE ($ mil.)	INCOME ($ mil.)	PROFIT MARGIN	EMPLOYEES
09/16	1,167	0	—	900
09/15	1,167	0	—	—
09/14	1,029	0	—	—
09/13	831	0	—	—
Annual Growth	12.0%	—	—	—

2016 Year-End Financials

Return on assets: 19.5%   Cash ($ mil.): 97
Return on equity: —
Current ratio: 1.10

METHODIST HOSPITAL OF SOUTHERN CALIFORNIA

If you're dehydrated in the Valley Methodist Hospital of Southern California can help. The hospital provides medical care to the residents of California's central San Gabriel Valley. The healthcare facility boasts some 600 beds and is part of Southern California Healthcare Systems. The not-for-profit hospital provides comprehensive acute care including surgical pediatric and intensive care units. It also offers a wide range of specialty services such as cardiology oncology neurology bariatrics and orthopedics. The hospital opened its doors in 1903 with five beds.

Operations

Methodist Hospital serves Arcadia Azusa Baldwin Park Bradbury Duarte El Monte Monrovia Pasadena Rosemead San Gabriel Sierra Madre and Temple City.

In addition to typical acute care services Methodist Hospital's cardiac care center provides complete cardiovascular services including open-heart surgery. The medical facility's intensive care units boast both neonatal and adult centers. Its cardiovascular stroke and cancer centers are certified by various national medical specialist organizations. The hospital employs about 630 medical staff members.

It also operates a rehabilitation clinic and a long-term recovery facility for patients requiring transitional care.

Geographic Reach

Methodist Hospital is located in Arcadia California in the northeastern corner of the Los Angeles metropolitan area; it serves patients from surrounding communities as well.

Financial Performance

Methodist Hospital in fiscal 2013 boasted a $248 million total operating budget.

Strategy

A grant from the H.N. and Frances C. Berger Foundation in 2012 has allowed the hospital to

install a state-of-the-art hyperbaric (high-pressure oxygen) chamber in the hospital's Wound Healing Center. The chamber helps to treat diabetic patients suffering from chronic wounds as well as wounds resulting from immune deficiencies and assists patients suffering from decompression sickness or the "bends" as a result of diving accidents.

In recent years Methodist Hospital has continued with its infrastructure expansion and improvement projects with a focus on expanding its emergency department in 2013 and opening a new GYN Oncology Institute in 2014.

Each year the hospital serves 47000 emergency department visits 16800 outpatient visits 16600 inpatient admissions 5100 surgeries and 1800 deliveries.

EXECUTIVES

Senior Vice President Chief Security Officer, Clifford Daniels

Physical Rehab Services Director Occupational Therapy Director Physical Therapy Director, Janet Dugan

Pharm D, Dennis Lau

Senior Management (Senior Vice President General Manager Director), Jeff Stack

Director of Medical Records, Bridgett Didier

Auditors: KPMG LLP LOS ANGELES CA

LOCATIONS

HQ: METHODIST HOSPITAL OF SOUTHERN CALIFORNIA
300 W HUNTINGTON DR, ARCADIA, CA 910073402
Phone: 626 898-8000
Web: WWW.METHODISTHOSPITAL.ORG

PRODUCTS/OPERATIONS

Selected Services
Cardiology
Diabetes Services
Emergency Services
Gynecology
Maternal Child Health
Neurology
Oncology
Orthopedics
Outpatient Services
Rehabilitation Services
Senior Services
Surgical Services
Stroke
Transitional Care Unit
Weight Loss Surgery
Wound Healing Center

COMPETITORS

Citrus Valley Health Partners
Dignity Health
Glendale Adventist Medical Center
Good Samaritan Hospital (Los Angeles)
HCA
Hollywood Presbyterian Medical Center
Memorial Health Services
Newhall Memorial Hospital
Tenet Healthcare

HISTORICAL FINANCIALS

Company Type: Private

Income Statement   FYE: December 31

	REVENUE ($ mil.)	NET INCOME ($ mil.)	NET PROFIT MARGIN	EMPLOYEES
12/15	300	11	3.9%	2,200
12/12	281	0	0.3%	—
12/11	245	(4)	—	—
12/10	1,687	0	0.0%	—
Annual Growth	(29.2%)	613.7%	—	—

2015 Year-End Financials

Return on assets: 3.5%   Cash ($ mil.): 37
Return on equity: 3.9%
Current ratio: 1.70

METHODIST HOSPITALS OF DALLAS INC

Methodist Hospitals of Dallas serves the health care needs of North Texas — from Mansfield to McKinney. The church-affiliated organization which does business as Methodist Health System operates 10 hospitalsand more than two dozen family health centers and medical facilities in and around the area deemed by locals as Big D. The original hospital Methodist Dallas Medical Center opened in 1927. The 585-bed teaching and referral hospital boasts a Level I trauma center and an organ transplant program. Other facilities include the 317-bed Methodist Charlton Medical Center the 254-bed Methodist Mansfield Medical Center and the 334-bed Methodist Richardson Medical Center.

Operations

Each year Methodist Health System handles more than 80000 inpatient visits and more than 350000 emergency department and other outpatient visits. It has more than 2700 physicians.

The Methodist Dallas Transplant Institute is one of the largest and most active transplant centers in the southwestern part of the country performing dozens of adult kidney pancreas and liver transplants each year.

Other facilities include the Methodist Campus for Continuing Care Methodist McKinney Hospital Methodist Hospital for Surgery and Methodist Rehabilitation Hospital.

Geographic Reach

Methodist Hospitals of Dallas serves the residents of several communities located in and around the North Dallas area such as Midlothian Grand Prairie Cedar Hill Richardson Plano Garland Wylie and McKinney.

Strategy

In recent years Methodist Health System has grown through a series of acquisitions as well as through organic expansion efforts such as the construction of about 50 rooms and new surgery suites in the Methodist Charlton hospital.In 2017 its Mansfield Medical Center opened the Alexander Medical Pavilion (including a center for diagnostic imaging) and the specialty Black and Blue Sports Injury Clinic. The hospital is also undergoing an $85 million expansion which will add 150 private patient rooms a surgery room and a parking garage.

EXECUTIVES

President Methodist Mansfield Medical Center, John E. Phillips

President and CEO, Stephen L. (Steve) Mansfield

EVP and CFO, Michael J. Schaefer, age 66, S370,759 total compensation

EVP and Chief Legal Officer, Michael O. (Mickey) Price, $219,359 total compensation

SVP External Affairs; President and CEO Methodist Health System Foundation, April B. Chamberlain

SVP and CIO, Pamela G. McNutt

President Methodist Dallas Medical Center, Laura Irvine

VP and Chief Medical Informatics Officer, Sam Bagchi

EVP and COO, Pamela (Pam) Stoyanoff

SVP Managed Care, Tim B. Kirby

President Methodist Charlton Medical Center, Jonathan S. Davis

President Methodist Richardson Medical Center, E. Kenneth Hutchenrider

SVP and Chief Medical Officer, Adam L. Myers

Medical Director, Maryam Raza

Medical Director of INFECTION Control and INFECTIOUS DISEASES PHYSICIAN, Zakir Shaikh

Vice President of Managed Care, Shannon Huggins

Vice President Hospital Finance, Sarah Choi

Vice President of Revenue Cycle, Leslie Pierce

Vice President, Harold Kolni

Vice President, Angela Nash

Vice President For Graduate Medical Education, Sam Cullison

LOCATIONS

HQ: METHODIST HOSPITALS OF DALLAS INC
1441 N BECKLEY AVE, DALLAS, TX 752031201
Phone: 877 637-4297
Web: WWW.METHODISTHEALTHSYSTEM.ORG

PRODUCTS/OPERATIONS

Selected Services
Back and Spine
Behavioral Health and Addiction Recovery
Cancer Services
Cardiovascular
da Vinci Surgical System
Diabetes
Digestive Diseases
Ear Nose & Throat (ENT) Services & Allergy Treatments
Emergency and Trauma Care
Fitness Programs
Home Health
Imaging and Radiology
The Liver Institute
Neurosurgery and Neurology
Ophthalmology
Orthopedics
Pain Management
Palliative Care
Physical Therapy and Rehabilitation
Prostate Screening and Awareness Program
Sleep Disorders
Transplant
Urology
Weight Management
Women and Children's Services
Women's Imaging and Mammography
Wound Care and Hyperbaric Center

Selected Facilities
Golden Cross Academic Clinic
Methodist Dallas Medical Center
Methodist Charlton Medical Center
Methodist Family Health Centers
  Cedar Hill
  Central Grand Prairie
  Dallas
  Midlothian
  South Grand Prairie
Methodist Hospital for Surgery
Methodist Mansfield Medical Center
Methodist McKinney Hospital
Methodist Richardson Medical Center
Methodist Rehabilitation Hospital

COMPETITORS

CHRISTUS Health	JPS Health Network
Children's Medical Center of Dallas	Parkland Health & Hospital System
Community Health Systems	Presbyterian Hospital of Dallas
Cook Children's Health Care System	Southwestern Medical Center
HCA	Tenet Healthcare
Harris Methodist Fort Worth Hospital	Texas Health Denton
Hunt Memorial	Texas Health Resources

Income Statement FYE: June 30

	REVENUE ($ mil.)	NET INCOME ($ mil.)	NET PROFIT MARGIN	EMPLOYEES
06/15*	411	21	5.3%	4,804
09/14	1,096	137	12.5%	—
09/12	969	165	17.1%	—
09/11	985	51	5.3%	—
Annual Growth	(19.6%)	(19.4%)	—	—

*Fiscal year change

2015 Year-End Financials

Return on assets: 1.5%   Cash ($ mil.): 1
Return on equity: 5.3%
Current ratio: 6.40

METROHEALTH MEDICAL CENTER

EXECUTIVES

Chief Executive Officer, Ekran Boutros
Manager, Victor Nolan
Director, Wendy Lachowski

LOCATIONS

HQ: METROHEALTH MEDICAL CENTER
   2500 METROHEALTH DR, CLEVELAND, OH
   441091900
Phone: 216 778-7800
Web: WWW.METROHEALTHTRANSFORMATION.COM

HISTORICAL FINANCIALS
Company Type: Private

Income Statement FYE: December 31

	REVENUE ($ mil.)	NET INCOME ($ mil.)	NET PROFIT MARGIN	EMPLOYEES
12/15	795	35	4.5%	6,000
12/14	782	32	4.2%	—
Annual Growth	1.7%	10.2%	—	—

2015 Year-End Financials

Return on assets: 7.0%   Cash ($ mil.): 3
Return on equity: 4.5%
Current ratio: 0.60

METROPOLITAN MECHANICAL CONTRACTORS, INC.

EXECUTIVES

President, Mark Anderson
Vice-President, Robert Kaczke
Manager, Mary Risacher
Vice-President, Tim Daly
Assistant Controller, Michael Davis
Project Manager, James Lamprecht
Auditors: KPMG LLP MINNEAPOLIS MN

LOCATIONS

HQ: METROPOLITAN MECHANICAL CONTRACTORS, INC.
7450 FLYING CLOUD DR, EDEN PRAIRIE, MN 553443582
Phone: 952 941-7010
Web: WWW.METROMECH.COM

HISTORICAL FINANCIALS
Company Type: Private

Income Statement FYE: December 31

	REVENUE ($ mil.)	NET INCOME ($ mil.)	NET PROFIT MARGIN	EMPLOYEES
12/15	200	1	0.8%	350
12/14	161	(2)	—	—
12/12	197	(2)	—	—
12/11	96	2	2.4%	—
Annual Growth	20.1%	(9.4%)	—	—

METROPOLITAN OPERA ASSOCIATION, INC.

Italians and Germans alike desire an American debut at the Met. Well their operas do anyway. The Metropolitan Opera Association manages The Metropolitan Opera company which presents more than 200 performances every year in its residence at the Lincoln Center for the Performing Arts. The Met is known for performing most works in their original languages and for producing regular Saturday radio broadcasts which are aired throughout North America and in South America Europe and the Asia/Pacific region. In association with sponsors the Met makes video and CD recordings of the performances and distributes them worldwide. The Met was founded in 1883.

Operations

The opera house has 3800 seats and 195 standing room places for a total capacity of 3975. The facility employs more than 860 people.

Geographic Reach

The Metropolitan Opera is is part of the Lincoln Center complex located in the Midtown Manhattan section of New York City.

Financial Performance

The Met's endowment has been cut in recent years. Donations and ticket sales have been down slightly although the Met is still on solid financial ground.

EXECUTIVES

V Pres, Ezra K Zilkha
Managing Director, Camille Labarre
Department Head, William Malloy

LOCATIONS

HQ: METROPOLITAN OPERA ASSOCIATION, INC.
   LINCOLN CTR, NEW YORK, NY 10023
Phone: 212 799-3100
Web: WWW.METOPERA.ORG

Income Statement FYE: July 31

	REVENUE ($ mil.)	NET INCOME ($ mil.)	NET PROFIT MARGIN	EMPLOYEES
07/15	335	26	7.8%	1,500
07/09	223	(71)	—	—
07/08	309	34	11.3%	—
07/05	286	0	—	—
Annual Growth	1.6%		—	—

2015 Year-End Financials

Return on assets: 7.7%   Cash ($ mil.): 4
Return on equity: 7.8%
Current ratio: 0.10

METROPOLITAN ST. LOUIS SEWER DISTRICT

Business is draining for The Metropolitan St. Louis Sewer District (MSD) which provides wastewater collection and treatment services for a population of about 1.3 million in the St. Louis area. The district operates nearly 10000 miles of sewer lines and seven wastewater treatment plants that process an average of 370 million gallons of sewage per day. MSD serves about 425000 residential and commercial/industrial customers. It has a budget of more than $470 million and is governed by a six-member board divided equally between appointees of the mayor of St. Louis and of the St. Louis County executive. The district was created by voters in 1954 and began operations two years later.

Financial Performance

MSD reported operating revenue in 2012 of $226 million up about 3% from the prior year. Operating income also rose to nearly $10 million from a loss of $25 million in 2011 as the district saw a decrease in expenses particularly engineering and asset management. It also saw a drop in water backup claims.

EXECUTIVES

Chief Sales Officer, Ken Lucas
Chief Sales Officer Operations, Randy Belcher
Secretary Treasurer, Tim Snoke
SECRETARY TO THE EXECUTIVE DIRECTOR, Pam Bell
Board Member, Bob Meppiel
Assistant Secretary and Treasurer, Robert Breig
Auditors: RUBINBROWN LLP SAINT LOUIS M

LOCATIONS

HQ: METROPOLITAN ST. LOUIS SEWER DISTRICT
   2350 MARKET ST STE 300, SAINT LOUIS, MO
   631032555
Phone: 314 768-6200
Web: WWW.STLMSD.COM

HISTORICAL FINANCIALS

Company Type: Private

Income Statement

FYE: June 30

	REVENUE ($ mil.)	NET INCOME ($ mil.)	NET PROFIT MARGIN	EMPLOYEES
06/16	319	48	15.3%	976
06/12	226	21	9.4%	—
06/11	219	(10)	—	—
06/09	249	68	27.6%	—
Annual Growth	3.6%	(4.8%)	—	—

2016 Year-End Financials

Return on assets: 11.7% Cash ($ mil.): 26
Return on equity: 15.3%
Current ratio: 0.20

METROPOLITAN TRANSPORTATION AUTHORITY

The largest public transportation system in the US New York City's Metropolitan Transportation Authority (MTA) provides about 2.6 billion passenger trips and sees about 380 million vehicles travel its system annually. The MTA's largest agency the New York City Transit Authority operates about 8700 rail and subway cars that provide service across New York's five boroughs; it also runs a fleet of some 5900 buses. Other MTA units offer bus and rail service to Connecticut and Long Island and operate the Triborough system of toll bridges and tunnels.

Strategy

The government-owned MTA a public-benefit corporation chartered by the New York Legislature in 1965 operates with an annual budget of $12.6 billion. The system has been working to become more self-sufficient in recent years but it has battled persistent operating losses brought on by among other causes high operating costs and the struggling US economy. In an attempt to reduce its expenses the company in 2010 cut payroll by 20% at its headquarters and 15% at other agencies. The MTA has also bolstered its revenue through increased fares and tolls and freed up capital by restructuring its debt at lower interest rates.

While it is making cuts in some areas the MTA is investing in capital improvements to its system including extending the Long Island Rail Road to Grand Central Station and creating a direct link between John F. Kennedy Airport and downtown Manhattan. Other key projects have included the construction of the Second Avenue Subway and renovations at the Fulton Street Transit Center. The MTA also is looking at installing wireless Internet access on its Metro-North and Long Island rail lines' trains.

HISTORY

Mass transit began in New York City in the 1820s with the introduction of horse-drawn stagecoaches run by small private firms. By 1832 a horse-drawn railcar operating on Fourth Avenue offered a smoother and faster ride than its streetbound rivals.

By 1864 residents were complaining that horsecars and buses were overcrowded and that drivers were rude. (Horsecars were transporting 45 million

passengers annually.) In 1870 a short subway under Broadway was opened but it remained a mere amusement. Elevated steam railways were built but people avoided them because of the smoke noise and danger from explosions. Cable cars arrived in the 1880s and by the 1890s electric streetcars had emerged.

Construction of the first commercial subway line was completed in 1904. The line was operated by Interborough Rapid Transit (IRT) which leased the primary elevated rail line in 1903 and had effective control of rail transit in Manhattan and the Bronx. In 1905 IRT merged with the Metropolitan Street Railway which ran most of the surface railways in Manhattan giving the firm almost complete control of the city's rapid transit. Public protests led the city to grant licenses to Brooklyn Rapid Transit (later BMT) creating the Dual System. The two rail firms covered most of the city.

By the 1920s the transit system was again in crisis largely because the two lines were not allowed to raise their five-cent fares. With the IRT and BMT in receivership in 1932 the city decided to own and operate part of the rail system and organized the Independent (IND) rail line. Pressure for public ownership and operation of the transit system resulted in the city's purchase of all of IRT's and BMT's assets in 1940 for $326 million.

In 1953 the legislature created the New York City Transit Authority the first unified system. In 1968 two years after striking transit workers left the city in a virtual gridlock the Metropolitan Transit Authority began to coordinate the city's transit activities with other commuter services.

The 1970s and 1980s saw the city's transit infrastructure and service deteriorate as crime accidents and fares rose. But by the early 1990s a modernization program had begun to make improvements: Subway stations were repaired graffiti was removed from trains and service was extended. By 1994 the agency said subway crime was down 50% from 1990 and ridership had increased.

The MTA set up a five-year plan in 1995 to cut expenses by $3 billion. Only 18 months later and already two-thirds of the way to reaching the goal the authority said it would cut another $230 million and return the savings to customers as fare discounts. The agency agreed in 1996 to sell Long Island Rail Road's freight operations. The next year it began selling its one-fare/free-transfer Metro-Card Gold.

In 1998 the MTA capital program completed the $200 million restoration of the Grand Central Terminal. The next year the MTA ordered 500 new clean-fuel buses. But the agency suffered a setback when New York State's $3.8 billion Transportation Infrastructure Bond Act which included $1.6 billion for MTA improvements was rejected by voters in 2000.

MTA subway lines in lower Manhattan suffered extensive damage from the September 11 2001 terrorist attacks that destroyed the World Trade Center's twin towers. The attacks left the MTA which was already seeking billions of dollars for improvements faced with $530 million worth of damage.

Confronted with a budget gap for the 2003 fiscal year the MTA authorized the sale of nearly $2.9 billion worth of transportation bonds the largest bond issue in the agency's history. The MTA had hoped the eventual proceeds from the bonds would help stave off a fare increase but in 2003 the agency raised subway and bus fares from $1.50 to $2 among other fare and toll increases.

Angered by issues involving wage hikes health care retirement age and pension costs members of the Transportation Workers Union walked off the job mere days before Christmas in 2005. The strike stranded commuters and stymied New York-

ers eager to shop and celebrate during the holiday season. The strike was estimated to cause a loss of $300 million per day to the city. In the face of heavy fines possible jail terms and the growing ire of would-be commuters the 33000 striking union members agreed to go back to work without a contract after three days of picketing and negotiations resumed. The Metropolitan Transportation Authority and the transit union later reached a contract agreement in which workers pay a portion of their health care costs.

In May 2009 the New York Legislature passed a $2.3 billion bailout package for the MTA which outlines fare increases of 10% in 2009 and 7.5% in 2011 and 2013. The bailout also requires management changes including combining the agency's chairman and CEO positions. Within days after the bailout was passed CEO Elliot Sander stepped down and was replaced on an interim basis by Long Island Rail Road President Helena Williams. New York Governor David Paterson picked Jay Walder a former executive with the London transit system and MTA's former CFO to succeed Sander and Chairman H. Dale Hemmerdinger. Walder was confirmed by the New York Senate in September 2009.

After five years of working toward bringing in cash by selling naming rights the MTA made a $4 million deal with Barclays in June 2009 to have the British bank's moniker added to the Atlantic Avenue-Pacific Street subway station in Brooklyn. The MTA also hopes to sell naming rights on its bus lines bridges and tunnels and to expand other corporate sponsorship and advertising opportunities. In 2008 the agency reached a $1 billion deal with Related Companies for the rights to build a 26-acre office and apartment complex above railyards on Manhattan's West Side but the deal's closing was pushed back to 2010 due to the financial slump. The MTA also sold an eight-acre plot above the Long Island Rail Road's Brooklyn railyard for $100 million to Forest City Ratner.

EXECUTIVES

CFO, Robert E. (Bob) Foran
Executive Officer Corporate Communications Marketing and Branding, John McKay
Director Security, Raymond Diaz
COO, Phil Eng
Interim Executive Director, Veronique Hakim
President MTA Bridges and Tunnels, Cedrick Fulton
Vice President Human Resources And Diversity, Gregory Bradley
Chairman, Joseph J. Lhota, age 62
Secretary, Ashmine John

LOCATIONS

HQ: METROPOLITAN TRANSPORTATION AUTHORITY 2 BROADWAY BSMT B, NEW YORK, NY 100043354
Phone: 212 878-7000
Web: WWW.MTAHQ.ORG

PRODUCTS/OPERATIONS

Selected Operations
Bus
  Long Island Bus
  MTA Bus Company
  New York City Transit
Commuter Rail
  Long Island Rail Road
  Metro-North Railroad
  Staten Island Railway

Income Statement FYE: December 31

	REVENUE ($ mil.)	NET INCOME ($ mil.)	NET PROFIT MARGIN	EMPLOYEES
12/15	8,408	370	4.4%	67,457
12/12*	7,067	(0)	—	—
06/12	3,495	604	17.3%	—
Annual Growth	24.5%	(11.5%)	—	—

*Fiscal year change

2015 Year-End Financials

Return on assets: 4.7% Cash ($ mil.): 454
Return on equity: 4.4%
Current ratio: 0.20

METROPOLITAN TRANSPORTATION COMMISSION

EXECUTIVES

Executive Director, Steve Hieminger
Senior Manager, Bond Counsel
Project Manager, Christine Maley-Grubl
Personnel Manager, Robin James
Auditors: PRICEWATERHOUSECOOPERS LLP SA

LOCATIONS

HQ: METROPOLITAN TRANSPORTATION COMMISSION
375 BEALE ST STE 800, SAN FRANCISCO, CA 941052179
Phone: 510 817-5700

HISTORICAL FINANCIALS
Company Type: Private

Income Statement FYE: June 30

	REVENUE ($ mil.)	NET INCOME ($ mil.)	NET PROFIT MARGIN	EMPLOYEES
06/16	237	21	8.9%	115
06/15	305	44	14.5%	—
06/14	307	(0)	—	—
06/13	260	(3)	—	—
Annual Growth	(3.0%)	—	—	—

2016 Year-End Financials

Return on assets: 80.9% Cash ($ mil.): 433
Return on equity: 8.9%
Current ratio: 1.00

MEXICO FOODS LLC

EXECUTIVES

President, Salah Nafal

LOCATIONS

HQ: MEXICO FOODS LLC
2600 MCCREE RD STE 101, GARLAND, TX 750413901
Phone: 972 526-7200

Income Statement FYE: December 31

	REVENUE ($ mil.)	NET INCOME ($ mil.)	NET PROFIT MARGIN	EMPLOYEES
12/15	265	5	1.9%	1,539
12/12	175	4	2.4%	—
Annual Growth	14.7%	6.8%	—	—

2015 Year-End Financials

Return on assets: 3.8% Cash ($ mil.): —
Return on equity: 1.9%
Current ratio: 0.30

MFA INCORPORATED

Agricultural cooperative MFA brings together 45000 farmers in Missouri and adjacent states. One of the US' oldest regional co-ops supplying its member/owners with agronomy distribution financing and purchasing services it runs more than 145 retail farm supply centers and works with independent dealers. MFA supplies animal feeds seed fertilizer and crop protection products. The co-op also provides its members with agronomy services animal-health products and farm supplies. It also offers marketing services and is the publisher of Today's Farmer. Agmo Corporation MFA's finance company provides co-op members longer credit terms for purchases made through MFA's retail outlets.

Operations

MFA's plant food sales exceed 1 million tons each year.

Geographic Reach

The coop has fertilizer terminals on the Mississippi River as well as on the Missouri and Arkansas rivers.

Sales and Marketing

The coop sells through 400 independent dealers.

Strategy

Part of MFA's strategy is to focus on growth initiatives and find opportunistic products and services to provide to its customers. Strategic river terminals and other bulk facilities give it capacity to deliver bulk quantities of plant food. It also invests in rolling stock trucks and application equipment to ensure bulk products are efficiently delivered to retail customers.

In 2016 the coop formed a joint venture with MFA Oil Company a farmer-owned energy supply cooperative to build a shuttle-loader facility on the Union Pacific Railroad line about 5 miles east of Hamilton Missouri. The grain-handling facility will consist of 2 million bushels of permanent storage and 1.5 million bushels of temporary storage along with a loop rail siding to accommodate a 110-railroad-car 'shuttle' unit. Once completed the structure will allow farmers in north central Missouri and southern Iowa to deliver crops to a modern high-speed grain facility.

Company Background

Expanding its assets in 2013 MFA acquired Producers Grain Company's assets in El Dorado Springs Walker Bronaugh and Nevada in Missouri.

The co-op was established in 1914 when seven Missouri farmers got together to buy binder twine.

EXECUTIVES

SVP Corporate and Member Services, Janice Schuerman

SVP Corporate Operations, J. Brian Griffith
President and CEO, Bill Streeter
VP Feed Division, Alan Wessler
SVP and CFO, Ernie Verslues
VP Plant Foods and Transportation, Bill Coen
VP Crop Protection Seed and Farm Supply, Don Houston
VP Agri Services, Craig Childs
Senior Vice President Corporate Operations, Brian Griffith
Vice President Of Engineering, Todd Rauch
Second Vice President Finance, David Moore
Vice President and General Manager, Cassy Landewee
Vice Chairman, John Moffitt
Chairman, Don Mills
Treasurer, John Akridge
Auditors: WILLIAMS KEEPERS LLC COLUMBIA

LOCATIONS

HQ: MFA INCORPORATED
201 RAY YOUNG DR, COLUMBIA, MO 652013599
Phone: 573 874-5111
Web: WWW.CALIFORNIAMFA.COM

COMPETITORS

ADM	GROWMARK
Andersons	Heartland Co-op
Cargill	Missouri Farm Bureau
Farm Service Cooperative	Orscheln Farm and Home
Farmers Cooperative Company	Tennessee Farmers Co-op
	United Producers

HISTORICAL FINANCIALS
Company Type: Private

Income Statement FYE: August 31

	REVENUE ($ mil.)	NET INCOME ($ mil.)	NET PROFIT MARGIN	EMPLOYEES
08/16	1,192	4	0.3%	1,393
08/15	1,434	10	0.8%	—
08/14	1,510	18	1.2%	—
08/13	1,510	15	1.0%	—
Annual Growth	(7.6%)	(36.0%)	—	—

MFA OIL COMPANY

Many farmers appreciate MFA Oil. The energy cooperative controlled by its 40000 farmer-members produces fuel and lubrication products and manages bulk petroleum and propane plants in the Central and Western US. Operating 140 propane plants the company sells more propane for farm use and home heating than any other company in Missouri. It also operates nearly 100 oil and lubricant bulk plants and serves customers in Arkansas Iowa Kansas and Oklahoma. Additionally the company operates 76 convenience stores under the Break Time brand (in Arkansas and Missouri) more than 160 Petro-Card 24 fueling locations and owns 10 Jiffy Lube and a dozen Big O Tire franchises.

Geographic Reach

MFA Oil serves customers in Arkansas Colorado Kansas Kentucky Indiana Iowa Missouri Nebraska Oklahoma Virginia and Wyoming.

Strategy

While not a pure vertically integrated enterprise over time the cooperative has developed multiple complementary business lines to enable it to respond to a wide range of its members' fuel transportation and food service needs. In this tradition in 2011 MFA Oil teamed up with biofuel developer

Aloterra Energy to form MFA Oil Biomass LLC. The partnership aims to help farmers to produce a renewable energy crop that can be used as biomass for an alternative cleaner burning energy supply for use in power generation plants as well as a liquid fuel. In 2011 about 250 farmers had signed letters of intent to grow miscanthus (a perennial grass) on more than 21000 acres as part of this initiative.

Mergers and Acquisitions
Expanding its geographic network in 2013 MFA Oil acquired Kansas-based American Petroleum Marketers which distributes fuel to more than 60 Cenex branded sites along with unbranded fuel in six states.

Company Background
MFA Oil has grown well beyond its Missouri roots where it was founded by farmers in 1929. The company's first bulk plant was located at Wright City Missouri.

EXECUTIVES

Chief Executive Officer, Jerry Taylor
Chairman of the Board, Benny Farrell
Chief Financial Officer, Robert Condron
Director, Diane Searcy
Personnel Manager, Lynn Smith
Administrative Assistant, Andrew Prather
Vice-President, Larry Ehrman
Manager, Troy Walker
Auditors: WILLIAMS KEEPERS LLC COLUMBIA

LOCATIONS

HQ: MFA OIL COMPANY
1 RAY YOUNG DR, COLUMBIA, MO 652013506
Phone: 573 442-0171
Web: WWW.MFAOIL.COM

COMPETITORS

Ag Processing Inc.	Lykins
Green Brick Partners	Shell Oil Products
Green Plains	Valero Energy
Jordan Oil Company	WilcoHess

HISTORICAL FINANCIALS

Company Type: Private

Income Statement

FYE: August 31

	REVENUE ($ mil.)	NET INCOME ($ mil.)	NET PROFIT MARGIN	EMPLOYEES
08/16	800	24	3.1%	1,500
08/15	1,045	48	4.6%	—
08/14	1,471	40	2.8%	—
08/13	1,300	55	4.2%	—
Annual Growth	(14.9%)	(23.5%)	—	—

2016 Year-End Financials

Return on assets: 3.1%   Cash ($ mil.): 59
Return on equity: 3.1%
Current ratio: 1.30

MHA LLC

EXECUTIVES

President, Felicia Karsos
Secretary, Jack Auletta
Marketing Director, Sally Deering
Director, Stanley C Parman
Director, Tatyana Seta

LOCATIONS

HQ: MHA LLC
55 MEADOWLANDS PKWY, SECAUCUS, NJ 070942977
Phone: 201 392-3100
Web: WWW.MEADOWLANDSHOSPITAL.ORG

HISTORICAL FINANCIALS

Company Type: Private

Income Statement

FYE: December 31

	REVENUE ($ mil.)	NET INCOME ($ mil.)	NET PROFIT MARGIN	EMPLOYEES
12/15	498	2	0.5%	650
12/14	468	2	0.5%	—
Annual Growth	6.6%	(3.1%)	—	—

2015 Year-End Financials

Return on assets: 2.8%   Cash ($ mil.): —
Return on equity: 0.5%
Current ratio: 1.50

MIAMI UNIVERSITY

Not that Miami the other one. Named for the Miami Indian Tribe that inhabited the area now known as the Miami Valley Region of Ohio Miami University emphasizes undergraduate study at its main campus in Oxford (35 miles north of Cincinnati) as well as at commuter campuses in Hamilton Middletown and West Chester Ohio and a European Center in Luxembourg. The school offers bachelors masters and doctoral programs in areas including business administration arts and sciences engineering and education. Its student body includes more than 15000 undergraduates on the Oxford campus; 2500 graduate students; and another 5700 students attending satellite campuses. Miami University was established in 1809.

Financial Performance
Miami University's 2011 revenue increased 3% vs. 2010 due to a corresponding increase in undergraduate tuition on its three campuses and a rising rates for room and board. Net income at the public university rose 25% over the same period on higher revenue and lower operating expenses due primarily to a reduction in the number of positions and no salary increases. The rise in tuition for Ohio residents in 2011 was the first in four years. Also investment income rose in 2011 for the second consecutive year.

Company Background
Miami University celebrated its bicentennial in 2009. The school was chartered in February of 1809 by the State of Ohio but the first classses were not held until 1824.

EXECUTIVES

Associate Vice President Facilities, Jim Haley
Vice President, Beck Parker
Vice President, Brenden Clinton
Assistant Vice President for End User Services, Annie Pagura
Associate Vice President Of University Communicati, Deedie Dowdle
Associate Vice President and Deputy CIO, Alan Ferrenberg
Assistant Vice President and Information Security Officer, Joe Bazeley
Senior Vice President Information Technology Programmer, Valerie Garnett
Associate Vice President Of Budgeting, David Ellis

Program Associate Vice President of Finance, Agnes A Shea
Associate Vice President for Finance and Associate Treasurer, Beverly Thomas
Vice President Information Technology, Reid Christenberry
Assistant Vice President for Student Affairs, Scott Walter
Assistant Vice President Enterprise Operations Information Technology Services, Troy Travis
Vice President of Professional Development, Nicole Becker
Vice President of Public Relations, Alexis DeBrunner
Vice President of Human Resource, Eric White
Associate Vice President For Institutional Diversity, Ron Scott
Vice President Of Personnel, Ryan Smith
Vice President External Relations, Katie Fischer
Executive Manager, Susan Clark
Assistant Vice President, Jen Franchak
Treasurer, David Creamer
Vice Chairman, Mark Ridenour
Board Member, Phyllis Wykoff
Miami University ASG Treasurer Finance Major Arabic Minor Farmer School of Business Class of 2017, Mack Kennedy
Advisory Board Member, Pat Dixon
Economics Major Entrepreneurship Minor Theta Chi Treasurer, Michael Beresford
Auditors: MCGLADREY LLP CLEVELAND OHIO

LOCATIONS

HQ: MIAMI UNIVERSITY
501 E HIGH ST, OXFORD, OH 450561846
Phone: 513 529-1809
Web: WWW.MIAMIOH.EDU

HISTORICAL FINANCIALS

Company Type: Private

Income Statement

FYE: June 30

	REVENUE ($ mil.)	NET INCOME ($ mil.)	NET PROFIT MARGIN	EMPLOYEES
06/16	522	65	12.5%	4,925
06/12	440	32	7.5%	—
06/11	418	120	28.8%	—
Annual Growth	4.5%	(11.6%)	—	—

2016 Year-End Financials

Return on assets: 8.1%   Cash ($ mil.): 91
Return on equity: 12.5%
Current ratio: 1.20

MIAMI VALLEY HOSPITAL

Don't go to Florida looking for this hospital! Miami Valley Hospital (MVH) is an acute care facility serving the residents of Dayton Ohio and surrounding areas through two campuses. MVH and MVH South have roughly 950 beds and offer 50 primary and specialty care practices through its Regional Adult Burn Center the MVH Cancer Center MVH Sports Medicine Center and behavioral health units for outpatient and inpatient chemical dependency therapy and other psychiatric services. MVH also offers Level I trauma services Level III-B NICU adult burn center an air ambulance program and blood marrow and kidney transplant services. The hospital is part of the Premier Health Partners network.

Operations

In addition to MVH the Premier Health Partners network consists of Good Samaritan Hospital (also stationed in Dayton Ohio) Atrium Medical Center in nearby Middletown and Upper Valley Medical Center in Troy. Collectively the multi-hospital health system houses about 1800 inpatient beds and around 65 facilities.

MVH have more than 1100 physicians in more than 70 primary and specialty medical practice areas. It was a 2012 recipient of the HealthGrades Distinguished Hospital Award for Clinical Excellence placing it among the top 5% of hospitals in the US.

In 2012 it had 41555 inpatient admissions; 164140 outpatient visits; 125622 emergency department visits; and oversaw 4000 births.

Financial Performance

Medicare accounted for 40% of the company's 2012 revenues; Medicaid 20%.

Strategy

Over the past few years MVH has focused on upgrading its infrastructure. It has built a $135 million 440000-sq. ft. 11-story heart tower on the south side of the campus and spent $19 million on renovating and expanding its neonatal intensive care unit.

In 2013 it opened its new $6 million 24-hour Emergency Center in Jamestown Ohio to meet the growing demand for emergency care.

In 2013 MVH South opened a $20 million Comprehensive Cancer Center and (in 2012) a new maternity center which includes five labor and delivery suites two surgical suites for c-section deliveries and 16 private after-birthing suites.

Company Background

MVH was formed in 1890.

EXECUTIVES

Vice President and Chief Financial Officer;Vice President And Chief Financial Officer, Scott Shelton

LOCATIONS

HQ: MIAMI VALLEY HOSPITAL
1 WYOMING ST, DAYTON, OH 454092711
Phone: 937 208-8000

PRODUCTS/OPERATIONS

Campus Locations
Miami Valley Hospital - Dayton OH
Miami Valley Hospital South - Centerville Ohio

Selected Services and Specialties
Ablation (Cardiology)
Access and Transfer Center (physicians)
Alcoholism Drug Dependency and Addiction Treatment
Aneurysm (Neurosciences)
Ankle Surgery
Arterial Interventions
Audiology
Bariatrics/Weight Loss Surgery
Behavioral Services
Biotherapy/Targeted Therapy
Blood and Marrow Transplant Program
Brachytherapy
Brain Conditions and Treatments
Brain Injury Rehabilitation
Breast Cancer Navigators
Breast Center
Breast Center
Brethen Center for Surgical Advancement (physicians)
Bull Family Diabetes Center
Burn Center
Cancer Care
Cancer Care (Oncology)
Cardiac Electrophysiology Lab
Cardiac Rehabilitation
Cardiology
Cardiology
Cardiothoracic Surgery
CareFlight - Medical Transportation
Catheterization Lab Procedures

Center for Sleep and Wake Disorders
Chemoembolization
Chemotherapy and Infusion Therapy
Childbirth Education
Colon Cancer
Colorectal Cancer
Complementary Medicine (Cancer)
Comprehensive Outpatient Rehab Program (CORP)
Counseling/Pastoral Care
Craniectomy (Neuroscience)
Craniotomy (Neuroscience)
Cryoablation
CT scan (Imaging)
Dental Center
Depression/Anxiety Treatment
Diabetes
Dialysis Services
Discectomy
Drug Addiction Treatment
Elder Care
Emergency & Trauma Center (ETC)
Foot Surgery
Fractures (Athletes)
Fusion (spinal treatment)
Gastric Bypass
Genetic Testing
Gynecologic Cancer
Gynecology
Hand Therapy
Head and Neck Cancer
Heart Care
Heart Surgery
High Risk Breast Cancer Center
Hip Surgery
Hormone Therapy
Hospitalists/Medical Professionals
Hyperbaric Oxygen Therapy Center
Image Guided Radiation Therapy (IGRT)
Injury Prevention Center
Inpatient Rehabilitation
Intensity Modulated Radiation Therapy (IMRT)
Intensive Care Unit (ICU)
Interventional Radiology
Joint replacements
Kidney Transplant
Knee Surgery
Kyphoplasty
Leukemia
Lung Cancer
Lymphoma
Mammography Screenings
Maternal-Fetal Medicine
Maternity
Maternity
Medical Professionals/Hospitalists
Medical Transportation - CareFlight
Mental Health Services
Minimally Invasive Surgery
Mother and Baby Services
MRI (Imaging)
Nanoknife
Neonatal Intensive Care
Neuro Rehabilitation
NeuroInterventional Center
Neuroscience
Neurosciences
Nutrition Services
OB-GYN
Obstetrics
Occupational Rehabilitation
Occupational Therapy
Oncology
Organ Transplant
Orthopedics
Orthopedics
Outpatient Physical Therapy
Pain Management
Palliative Care
Pancreatic Cancer
Perinatal Intensive Care
PET Scan (Imaging)
Pharmacy
Physiatry
Physical Therapy
Pre-Admission Testing
Premier HeartWorks
Preventive Cardiology
Prostate Cancer
Pulmonary Services
Radiofrequency ablation
Radiology

Radionuclide scan
Rehabilitation
Rehabilitation Institute of Ohio
Respiratory Care
Robotic Surgery
Shoulder Surgery
Shunt (Neuroscience)
Skin Cancer
Sleep Center
Solitaire Revascularization Device (Neurosciences)
Speech-Language Pathology
Spinal decompression surgery
Spinal disc replacement
Spinal fracture treatment
Spinal tumor surgery
Spine and back injuries (Orthopedics)
Spine Conditions and Treatments (Neuroscience)
Sports Medicine
Sports Medicine
Stereotaxis
Stomach Cancer
Stroke Treatments
Surgery Center
Surgical Oncology
Thoracic Surgery
Throat Cancer
Trauma
Ultrasound (Imaging)
Urological Cancer
Urology
Vascular Services
Venous Interventions
Vertebroplasty
Weight Loss Surgery (Bariatrics)
Weight Loss Surgery/Bariatrics
Wheelchair Clinic
Women's Health
Women's Heart Services
Women's Services
Wound Therapy
X-rays (Imaging)
Y-90 Radioembolization

COMPETITORS

Cincinnati Children's Hospital
Deaconess Associations
Good Samaritan Hospital (IN)
HealthSouth
Kettering Health Network
OhioHealth
The Christ Hospital Corporation
TriHealth
UC Health

HISTORICAL FINANCIALS

Company Type: Private

Income Statement

	REVENUE ($ mil.)	NET INCOME ($ mil.)	NET PROFIT MARGIN	EMPLOYEES
12/15	827	37	4.5%	6,000
12/14	785	37	4.8%	—
12/07	622	44	7.1%	—
12/05	502	(0)	—	—
Annual Growth	5.1%	—	—	—

2015 Year-End Financials

Return on assets: 3.2%   Cash ($ mil.): 47
Return on equity: 4.5%
Current ratio: 2.10

FYE: December 31

MID-KANSAS COOPERATIVE ASSOCIATION

EXECUTIVES

President, Dave Christiansen
Financial Executive, Jason Creed
Chief Financial Officer, Danny Porch
VP Finance, Dennis Teter
Auditor, Chris Roberts
Manager, Jonathan Reazin
Auditors: LINDBURG VOGEL PIERCE FARIS H

LOCATIONS

HQ: MID-KANSAS COOPERATIVE ASSOCIATION
307 W COLE ST, MOUNDRIDGE, KS 671077533
Phone: 620 345-6328
Web: WWW.MKCOOP.COM

HISTORICAL FINANCIALS
Company Type: Private

Income Statement — FYE: February 29

	REVENUE ($ mil.)	NET INCOME ($ mil.)	NET PROFIT MARGIN	EMPLOYEES
02/16	458	7	1.7%	250
02/15	403	14	3.7%	—
02/14	120	9	7.6%	—
02/13	125	14	11.1%	—
Annual Growth	53.9%	(17.2%)	—	—

2016 Year-End Financials

Return on assets: 9.5%   Cash ($ mil.): 3
Return on equity: 1.7%
Current ratio: 0.10

MIDDLE COUNTRY CENTRAL SCHOOL DISTRICT

EXECUTIVES

Superintendent, Roberta Gerold
Director, Diana Stein
Director, Herberet Chessler
Manager, Harold Goldstein
Manager, Todd Harris
Assistant Manager, Herb Chessler
Auditors: RS ABRAMS & CO LLP ISLAND

LOCATIONS

HQ: MIDDLE COUNTRY CENTRAL SCHOOL DISTRICT
8 43RD ST, CENTEREACH, NY 117202325
Phone: 631 285-8000
Web: WWW.MCCSD.NET

HISTORICAL FINANCIALS
Company Type: Private

Income Statement — FYE: June 30

	REVENUE ($ mil.)	NET INCOME ($ mil.)	NET PROFIT MARGIN	EMPLOYEES
06/15	222	(3)	—	1,600
06/14	217	0	0.3%	—
06/13	212	(5)	—	—
06/12	208	2	1.0%	—
Annual Growth	2.1%	—	—	—

2015 Year-End Financials

Return on assets: 0.8%   Cash ($ mil.): 25
Return on equity: (-1.7%)
Current ratio: —

MIDDLETOWN TOWNSHIP BOARD OF EDUCATION

EXECUTIVES

President, James Cody
Board of Directors, Sue Griffin
Board of Directors, Danielle Walsh
Board of Directors, Vincent Brand
Board of Directors, Michael Donlon
Board of Directors, Ernest Donnelly
Board of Directors, Joan Minnuies
Director, Bill Doering
Accountant, Vincent Daniels

LOCATIONS

HQ: MIDDLETOWN TOWNSHIP BOARD OF
EDUCATION
834 LEONARDVILLE RD FL 2, LEONARDO, NJ
077371751
Phone: 732 671-3850
Web: WWW.MIDDLETOWNK12.ORG

HISTORICAL FINANCIALS
Company Type: Private

Income Statement — FYE: June 30

	REVENUE ($ mil.)	NET INCOME ($ mil.)	NET PROFIT MARGIN	EMPLOYEES
06/16	181	0	0.3%	1,000
06/07	8	7	87.4%	—
06/06	0	0	—	—
06/05	0	0	—	—
Annual Growth	—	—	—	—

2016 Year-End Financials

Return on assets: 1.0%   Cash ($ mil.): 7
Return on equity: 0.3%
Current ratio: —

MIDLAND COUNTY HOSPITAL DISTRICT

EXECUTIVES

President, Russell Meyers
Chief Financial Officer, Lawrence Sanz
Auditors: BKD LLP WACO TEXAS

LOCATIONS

HQ: MIDLAND COUNTY HOSPITAL DISTRICT
400 R REDFERN GROVER PKWY, MIDLAND, TX
79701
Phone: 432 685-1111
Web: WWW.MIDLAND-MEMORIAL.COM

HISTORICAL FINANCIALS
Company Type: Private

Income Statement — FYE: September 30

	REVENUE ($ mil.)	NET INCOME ($ mil.)	NET PROFIT MARGIN	EMPLOYEES
09/16	282	(37)	—	1,700
09/15	264	(10)	—	—
09/14*	268	6	2.3%	—
11/12	36	0	2.6%	—
Annual Growth	66.6%	—	—	—
*Fiscal year change

2016 Year-End Financials

Return on assets: 7.2%   Cash ($ mil.): 26
Return on equity: (-13.4%)
Current ratio: 1.30

MIDLAND MEMORIAL HOSPITAL

LOCATIONS

HQ: MIDLAND MEMORIAL HOSPITAL
400 ROSALIND RDFRN GROVR, MIDLAND, TX
797016499
Phone: 432 221-1111
Web: WWW.MIDLAND-MEMORIAL.COM

HISTORICAL FINANCIALS
Company Type: Private

Income Statement — FYE: September 30

	REVENUE ($ mil.)	NET INCOME ($ mil.)	NET PROFIT MARGIN	EMPLOYEES
09/15	264	(10)	—	2
09/14	260	6	2.4%	—
Annual Growth	1.5%	—	—	—

2015 Year-End Financials

Return on assets: 9.3%   Cash ($ mil.): 19
Return on equity: (-3.8%)
Current ratio: 1.10

MIDSTATE MEDICAL CENTER

MidState Medical Center serves patients across the Nutmeg State. The acute care hospital serves central Connecticut and has some 155 beds (including six psychiatric beds). It offers patients a range of services including cardiac emergency medicine and maternity care. MidState Medical Center also has centers dedicated to diabetes cancer treatment digestive health nutrition and women's health. The hospital manages satellite facilities in Cheshire Wallingford and Southington and it operates an emergency center and the Mid-State Medical Services Building for outpatient care. MidState Medical Center is part of the Hartford HealthCare network.

Operations

In fiscal 2013 the hospital reported about 9850 inpatient admissions more than 8320 surgical procedures more than 59790 emergency room visits and more than 900 births.

Financial Performance

MidState Medical Center's revenues increased by 17% to $254 million in fiscal 2012 thanks to higher net patient revenues and other operating revenues.

The Center reported net income of $18 million in fiscal 2012 (compared to a net loss of $4.7 million in 2011) due to significantly lower pension plan liabilities the absence of loss on early extinguishment of debt an increase in investment return and unrealized gains on investments.

Strategy

MidState Medical Center focuses on investing in advanced medical technologies (from robotics for minimally invasive surgery to the latest generation linear accelerator for radiation oncology) as well as improving patient services.

In 2013 the Center opened a new hybrid operating room.

In 2012 it added maternal fetal medicine to its portfolio of women's health services. That year it established an outpatient anticoagulation management service designed to provide patients with comprehensive education on their anticoagulant medication.

In 2011 MidState Medical Center opened its MediQuick Urgent Care Center which offers medical services to patients with minor ailments or broken bones.

Company Background

The Hartford HealthCare system was founded in 1854.

EXECUTIVES

President, Lucille A Janatka
Manager, Claudia Ferrara
Vice-President, Harold P Kaplan

LOCATIONS

HQ: MIDSTATE MEDICAL CENTER
435 LEWIS AVE, MERIDEN, CT 064512101
Phone: 203 694-8200
Web: WWW.MIDSTATEMEDICAL.ORG

PRODUCTS/OPERATIONS

Selected Services and Specialties
Advanced Wound Care and Hyperbaric Medicine
Balance Hearing Institute
Bariatric / Weight Management
Behavioral Health
Cancer Center
Diabetes and Nutrition Center
Digestive Health

Emergency Services
Family Birthing Center
Hartford HealthCare Medical Group
Heart Center
Imaging
Neuroscience
Occupational Health
Orthopedics
Sleep Care
Spine and Pain Institute
Stroke Center
Surgical Center
Travel Clinic and Infectious Diseases
Women's Health

COMPETITORS

Backus
Baystate Medical Center
Bridgeport Hospital
Bristol Hospital
Connecticut Children's Medical Center
Day Kimball Hospital
Griffin Health
Harrington Memorial Hospital
Hartford Health Care
Lawrence & Memorial Hospital
New Milford Hospital
Saint Francis Hospital and Medical Center
St. Vincent's Health Services
Yale-New Haven Hospital
Yale-New Haven Hospital Saint Raphael Campus

HISTORICAL FINANCIALS

Company Type: Private

Income Statement
FYE: September 30

	REVENUE ($ mil.)	NET INCOME ($ mil.)	NET PROFIT MARGIN	EMPLOYEES
09/15	212	16	7.7%	900
09/14	219	18	8.6%	—
09/13	217	16	7.5%	—
09/06	157	2	1.6%	—
Annual Growth	3.4%	23.0%	—	—

2015 Year-End Financials

Return on assets: 3.8%   Cash ($ mil.): 11
Return on equity: 7.7%
Current ratio: 1.10

MIDWEST ENERGY, INC.

Some rural residents of the Sunflower State rely on Midwest Energy for their power and gas needs. The multi-utility serves approximately 48000 electricity customers and 42000 natural gas customers in central and western Kansas. It also has some power generation operations; it purchases most of its electric supply from wholesale marketers. The company's Midwest United Energy subsidiary is a competitive natural gas supplier in four states and its WestLand Energy unit sells propane to Kansas consumers. Midwest Energy has seen its power sales grow by 23% since 2006 and its natural gas sales by 17%.

A strong advocate of green energy as a way to cut carbon emissions comply with regulations and conserve energy Midwest Energy got 9% of its power from wind-generated sources in 2011. It also offers its customers How$mart program which allows residents to pay for energy-saving projects with no upfront costs through utility bills.

Investing heavily infrastructure both to keep up with demand and to replace aging systems in 2011 the company invested more than $26 million in electric construction and about $3 million in gas construction.

Midwest Energy reported a 14% jump in revenues in 2011 led by higher rates and very hot summer which increased power demand. Its net margin went up 11% thanks to the higher revenues a drop in per-capita gas costs (due to lower gas prices) and lower interest expenses.

The Central Kansas Electric Cooperative was formed in 1939 to provide electric service to customers in the rural counties surrounding Great Bend Kansas. Midwest Energy was formed in 1981 when the Central Kansas Electric Cooperative acquired investor-owned Central Kansas Power.

EXECUTIVES

Vice President of Network Operations and Customer Service, Bonnie Augustine
Auditors: BKD LLP OKLAHOMA CITY OKLAH

LOCATIONS

HQ: MIDWEST ENERGY, INC.
1330 CANTERBURY DR, HAYS, KS 676012708
Phone: 785 625-3437
Web: WWW.MWENERGY.COM

COMPETITORS

AES   Great Plains Energy
Black Hills   Westar Energy
Edison International

HISTORICAL FINANCIALS

Company Type: Private

Income Statement
FYE: December 31

	REVENUE ($ mil.)	NET INCOME ($ mil.)	NET PROFIT MARGIN	EMPLOYEES
12/15	205	15	7.7%	274
12/14	216	15	7.0%	—
12/13	202	14	7.1%	—
12/12	197	16	8.4%	—
Annual Growth	1.5%	(1.3%)	—	—

2015 Year-End Financials

Return on assets: 6.9%   Cash ($ mil.): —
Return on equity: 7.7%
Current ratio: 0.50

MIDWESTERN UNIVERSITY

EXECUTIVES

President, Kathleen H Goeppinger
Consultant, Samantha Klassen
Auditors: ERNST & YOUNG LLP CHICAGO IL

LOCATIONS

HQ: MIDWESTERN UNIVERSITY
555 31ST ST, DOWNERS GROVE, IL 605151235
Phone: 630 515-7300
Web: WWW.MIDWESTERN.EDU

Income Statement				FYE: June 30
	REVENUE ($ mil.)	NET INCOME ($ mil.)	NET PROFIT MARGIN	EMPLOYEES
06/16	380	69	18.4%	1,300
06/15	358	86	24.0%	—
06/14	318	94	29.6%	—
06/13	295	101	34.2%	—
Annual Growth	8.8%	(11.5%)	—	—

2016 Year-End Financials

Return on assets: 0.9% Cash ($ mil.): 215
Return on equity: 18.4%
Current ratio: 2.10

MILFORD REGIONAL MEDICAL CENTER, INC.

Medical treatment in south central Massachusetts and northern Rhode Island is the main affair of Milford Regional Medical Center. The 145-bed hospital provides acute medical services to the residents of Milford Massachusetts and surrounding areas. Specialty services include emergency medicine home health care diagnostic imaging physical therapy obstetrics and cancer treatment. It also has an affiliated physician practice group the Tri-County Medical Associates. The Medical Center which employs about 200 physicians is a teaching hospital affiliated with the University of Massachusetts.

Operations

The Center's $45 million patient care center includes eight operating suites consolidated surgical services and a medical/surgical floor with private rooms.

In 2012 Milford Regional Medical Center reported more than 12600 inpatient discharges more than 56000 emergency room visits and 277000 outpatient visits.

Financial Performance

The Center's revenues grew by 6% in 2012 to $241 million thanks to an increase in overall patient visits and medical procedures.

The company's net income increased by 42% to $10 million in 2012 as the result of higher revenues partially offset by an increase in salaries wages and benefits and as well as higher costs for supplies and other expenses.

Strategy

The hospital focuses on upgrading its building infrastructure expanding its physician base and enhancing services via the introduction of new technologies.

In 2012 the Medical Center invested more than $1 million in lab technology to improve turnaround time for laboratory results.

Milford Regional Medical Center's Maternity Center has been renovated and expanded to include a nursery that accommodates 16 bassinets six postpartum rooms.

In 2012 the hospital planned a $40 million expansion project. The new two-story 60000 square foot structure will house a new emergency department (with 50 private treatment rooms) intensive care unit and additional patient rooms. Groundbreaking is expected to take place in 2014. The expansion would increase the number of single-bed rooms to 132.

Company Background

In 2007 physician group Tri-County Medical Associates formed an affiliation with Partners Health-Care System's physician group Partners Community Healthcare. Also that year Milford Regional completed construction of its cancer center a $25 million facility constructed in partnership with Brigham and Women's Hospital (part of Partners HealthCare) and Dana-Farber Cancer Institute.

EXECUTIVES

Director of Pharmacy, Susan Otocki
Secretary Treasurer, Louis Jurist

LOCATIONS

HQ: MILFORD REGIONAL MEDICAL CENTER, INC.
14 PROSPECT ST, MILFORD, MA 017573003
Phone: 508 473-1190

PRODUCTS/OPERATIONS

Selected Services
Bone densitometry
Breast biopsy
Cancer care
Cardiovascular care
Diabetes care
Digital mammography
Emergency care
Endoscopy
Inpatient healthcare team Pediatric care
Psychiatric care
Pulmonary rehabilitation Radiology (Diagnostic imaging)
Rehabilitation
Urodynamic testing

COMPETITORS

Boston Medical Center
Cambridge Health Alliance
CareGroup
Children's Hospital Boston
Harrington Memorial Hospital
New England Alliance for Health
Partners HealthCare
Steward Health Care
Sturdy Memorial

HISTORICAL FINANCIALS
Company Type: Private

Income Statement				FYE: September 30
	REVENUE ($ mil.)	NET INCOME ($ mil.)	NET PROFIT MARGIN	EMPLOYEES
09/15	195	5	3.0%	1,159
09/14	184	4	2.4%	—
09/13	171	6	3.6%	—
Annual Growth	6.5%	(2.7%)	—	—

2015 Year-End Financials

Return on assets: 7.5% Cash ($ mil.): 51
Return on equity: 3.0%
Current ratio: 2.20

MILLARD PUBLIC SCHOOLS

EXECUTIVES

Superintendent, Keith Lutz
Board of Directors, Mike Kennedy
Principal, Mark Smith
Principal, Janet Wilson
Principal, Connie Heinen

Personnel Manager, Jean A Hastings
Personnel Manager, Michele Ellis
Auditors: HSMC ORIZON LLC OMAHA NEBRAS

LOCATIONS

HQ: MILLARD PUBLIC SCHOOLS
5606 S 147TH ST, OMAHA, NE 681372647
Phone: 402 715-8200
Web: WWW.MPSOMAHA.ORG

HISTORICAL FINANCIALS
Company Type: Private

Income Statement				FYE: August 31
	REVENUE ($ mil.)	NET INCOME ($ mil.)	NET PROFIT MARGIN	EMPLOYEES
08/16	255	(11)	—	2,500
08/12	233	(4)	—	—
08/09	214	(11)	—	—
08/08	0	0	—	—
Annual Growth	—	—	—	—

2016 Year-End Financials

Return on assets: — Cash ($ mil.): 8
Return on equity: (-4.6%)
Current ratio: —

MILLER ELECTRIC COMPANY

Miller Electric Company flips the switch for projects primarily in the Southeast. The Florida-based electrical contractor provides services including construction installation renovation and maintenance of electrical systems. Industries the company serves include: communications construction health care and transportation. Outside of Florida the company has offices in Alabama Arizona Arkansas Georgia North Carolina Virginia Tennessee Texas and Wisconsin. Clients have included Anheuser Busch Bank of America Blue Cross and Blue Shield EverBank Field and the University of North Florida. Miller Electric was founded by Henry G. Miller in 1928 and remains a family business.

Miller has found success by providing a myriad of installation services to the growing data center and Intelligent Transportation Systems (ITS) fields. ITS technologies are used to manage vehicle traffic and include intersection traffic signals dynamic message signs vehicle detection systems weather advisory systems and highway advisory radios. The company also installs the required power services and switching stations.

Most recently Miller also has diversified into the renewable energy market. In 2010 the company built a high tech solar project in Jacksonville that provides more than 12 megawatts of power for the city.

EXECUTIVES

Chief Executive Officer, Henry K Brown
Principal, David Long
Senior Vice-President, Ed Witt Jr
Vice-President, Daniel Brown
President, Thomas D Long
Project Manager, Kevin Hebert
Project Manager, Keith Riordan
Project Manager, Kevin Flanigan
Director, Mike Oliver
Auditors: BISHOP AND DRAPER JACKSONVILL

LOCATIONS

HQ: MILLER ELECTRIC COMPANY
2251 ROSSELLE ST, JACKSONVILLE, FL 322043125
Phone: 904 388-8000
Web: WWW.MECOJAX.COM

COMPETITORS

Dycom
Edd Helms
Honshy Electric
Johnson Contractors

Megatran
Pike Corporation
Tri-City Electrical
Contractors

HISTORICAL FINANCIALS

Company Type: Private

Income Statement

FYE: September 30

	REVENUE ($ mil.)	NET INCOME ($ mil.)	NET PROFIT MARGIN	EMPLOYEES
09/16	249	8	3.3%	691
09/15	260	7	2.9%	—
09/14	216	6	3.0%	—
09/13	204	2	1.3%	—
Annual Growth	6.8%	43.9%	—	—

2016 Year-End Financials

Return on assets: 9.2%
Return on equity: 3.3%
Current ratio: 1.60

Cash ($ mil.): 10

MILLMAN LUMBER COMPANY

EXECUTIVES

Chairman of the Board, Robert L Millman
Board of Directors, Thomas Corbett
Financial Executive, Mike Lewis
Personnel Director, David Bartley
General Manager, Justin Dunlavy
Manager, Dean Hendrix

LOCATIONS

HQ: MILLMAN LUMBER COMPANY
9264 MANCHESTER RD, SAINT LOUIS, MO
631442636
Phone: 314 961-6195
Web: WWW.MILLMANLUMBER.COM

HISTORICAL FINANCIALS

Company Type: Private

Income Statement

FYE: October 31

	REVENUE ($ mil.)	NET INCOME ($ mil.)	NET PROFIT MARGIN	EMPLOYEES
10/16	287	6	2.3%	80
10/15	258	3	1.4%	—
10/14	255	2	1.0%	—
10/13	245	2	0.9%	—
Annual Growth	5.4%	43.3%	—	—

2016 Year-End Financials

Return on assets: —
Return on equity: 2.3%
Current ratio: 0.70

Cash ($ mil.): 1

MILWAUKEE PUBLIC SCHOOLS (INC)

EXECUTIVES

Superintendent, Darienne Driver
Director, Shirley K Tiedjen
Principal, Deborah Bell
Principal, Martha Wheeler-Fair
Principal, Jewell Riano
Principal, Daniel J Donder
Auditors: BAKER TILLY VIRCHOW KRAUSE LL

LOCATIONS

HQ: MILWAUKEE PUBLIC SCHOOLS (INC)
5225 W VLIET ST, MILWAUKEE, WI 532082698
Phone: 414 475-8393
Web: WWW.MILWAUKEE.K12.WI.US

HISTORICAL FINANCIALS

Company Type: Private

Income Statement

FYE: June 30

	REVENUE ($ mil.)	NET INCOME ($ mil.)	NET PROFIT MARGIN	EMPLOYEES
06/16	1,178	(0)	—	14,154
06/11	1,292	(2)	—	—
06/09	1,237	(5)	—	—
06/05	1,122	(19)	—	—
Annual Growth	0.4%	—	—	—

MINNEAPOLIS PUBLIC SCHOOL DISTRICT

EXECUTIVES

Superintendent, Michael Goar
Representative, Bonita Jones
Auditors: BERGAN KDV LTD MINNEAPOLIS

LOCATIONS

HQ: MINNEAPOLIS PUBLIC SCHOOL DISTRICT
1250 W BROADWAY AVE, MINNEAPOLIS, MN
554112533
Phone: 612 668-0200
Web: WWW.MPLS.K12.MN.US

HISTORICAL FINANCIALS

Company Type: Private

Income Statement

FYE: June 30

	REVENUE ($ mil.)	NET INCOME ($ mil.)	NET PROFIT MARGIN	EMPLOYEES
06/15	685	116	17.1%	9,000
06/05	441	18	4.2%	—
06/04	632	(42)	—	—
Annual Growth	0.7%	—	—	—

MISSION HEALTH SYSTEM, INC

EXECUTIVES

Chief Executive Officer, Ronald A Paulus
Chief Financial Officer, Charles Aysques
Treasurer, Carol Goodrun
Vice-President, Dale Fell
Director, William Meyers
Executive Director, Carol Sheeler

LOCATIONS

HQ: MISSION HEALTH SYSTEM, INC
509 BILTM AVE AKA HWY 25, ASHEVILLE, NC 28801
Phone: 828 213-1111
Web: WWW.MISSION-HEALTH.ORG

HISTORICAL FINANCIALS

Company Type: Private

Income Statement

FYE: September 30

	REVENUE ($ mil.)	NET INCOME ($ mil.)	NET PROFIT MARGIN	EMPLOYEES
09/16	1,632	90	5.5%	5,500
09/08	17	7	42.3%	—
09/06	773	101	13.2%	—
09/04	624	41	6.6%	—
Annual Growth	8.3%	6.7%	—	—

2016 Year-End Financials

Return on assets: 3.0%
Return on equity: 5.5%
Current ratio: 1.30

Cash ($ mil.): 112

MISSION HOSPITAL REGIONAL MEDICAL CENTER INC

EXECUTIVES

Chief Executive Officer, Kenn Nicfaralnd
Manager, Rosemary Zaidenberg
Finance Manager, Kenn Mc Farland
Auditors: ERNST & YOUNG US LLP SAN DIEG

LOCATIONS

HQ: MISSION HOSPITAL REGIONAL MEDICAL
CENTER INC
27700 MEDICAL CENTER RD, MISSION VIEJO, CA
926916426
Phone: 949 364-1400

HISTORICAL FINANCIALS

Company Type: Private

Income Statement

FYE: June 30

	REVENUE ($ mil.)	NET INCOME ($ mil.)	NET PROFIT MARGIN	EMPLOYEES
06/15	516	23	4.5%	2,600
06/10	500	50	10.1%	—
06/09	355	12	3.5%	—
06/08	0	0	—	—
Annual Growth	—	—	—	—

Return on assets: 0.5%   Cash ($ mil.): 50
Return on equity: 4.5%
Current ratio: 1.60

MISSION HOSPITAL, INC.

Its mission is clear and bold: Improve the health of all in western North Carolina. Mission Hospital is a 760-bed regional referral center serving the western quarter of North Carolina and portions of adjoining states. A not-for-profit community hospital system Mission is located in Asheville on two adjoining campuses: Memorial and St. Joseph's. It provides tertiary-level services in neurosciences cardiac care trauma care surgery pediatric medicine and women's services and has a medical staff of more than 540. It also includes the Mission Children's Hospital. Mission Hospitals is part of the Mission Health System which is made up of Blue Ridge Regional Hospital McDowell Hospital and other facilities.

Geographic Reach

The hospital system serves patients in western North Carolina.

Sales and Marketing

In 2014 Medicare accounted for 40% of Mission Hospital's net patient service revenue; Medicaid accounted for 28% and self-pay and other third-party payors accounted for 14% and 18% respectively.

Financial Performance

Revenue increased 6% to $119 million in 2014 on higher net patient service earnings. Those gains plus higher investment returns led to a 12% increase in net income to $1.2 million.

After posting an operating cash outflow in 2013 Mission Hospital had a cash inflow of $0.9 million in 2014 as less cash was used towards net patient accounts receivable.

Strategy

Mission Hospital has been actively expanding and modernizing its facilities in recent years. It built a surgery registration and waiting area to ease patient comfort as they wait to be seen at the Memorial Campus. It also opened a four-story facility to provide more surgery suites and patient beds for Mission Hospital. In order to increase patient satisfaction the hospital opened a new surgery registration and waiting area at its Memorial Campus.

Mission Hospital places great focus on genetic medicine. It has an entire department dedicated to the study of genetics genetic therapy and the study of fetal alcohol spectrum disorders.

Mission Health partnered with Western Carolina University to provide a graduate certification program in Healthcare Innovation Management. The program which began in 2013 is a component of Mission Health's budding Center for Innovation established to foster a spirit of advancement in healthcare throughout western North Carolina. The program consists of four courses over a period of 21 months and is open to all Mission Health employees. Students who complete the program which is fully funded by Mission Health will earn credit towards bachelor's and master's degrees.

Company Background

Mission Hospital was formed in 1996 from the partnership (and eventual merger) of Memorial and St. Joseph's hospitals.

EXECUTIVES

Senior Vice President For Pati, Kathy Guyette

LOCATIONS

HQ: MISSION HOSPITAL, INC.
509 BILTMORE AVE, ASHEVILLE, NC 288014601
Phone: 828 213-1111

PRODUCTS/OPERATIONS

Surgical Services
General Surgery
Minimally Invasive Surgery
Outpatient Surgery
Prepare for Surgery
Robotic Surgery
Surgery at Mission Hospital
Surgery Guide
Programs of Service
Endoscopy
Genetics
Integrative Healthcare
Mother and Baby
Outpatient Care Centers
Sleep Center
Urology
Weight Management Center
Wound Healing and Hyperbarics
Support Services
Chronic Medical Conditions
Long-Term Acute Care
Laboratory
Pastoral Care Services
Pharmacy
Psychiatric Services
Radiology (Imaging) Services
Rehabilitation Services
Research Institute
Respiratory Therapy
Senior Services and Geriatrics

COMPETITORS

Blue Ridge HealthCare
CaroMont
Carolinas HealthCare System
Duke University Health System
Haywood Regional
Presbyterian Healthcare
UNC Hospitals
Wake Forest University Baptist Medical Center

HISTORICAL FINANCIALS

Company Type: Private

Income Statement				FYE: September 30
	REVENUE ($ mil.)	NET INCOME ($ mil.)	NET PROFIT MARGIN	EMPLOYEES
09/15	1,019	91	9.0%	5,400
09/14	936	64	6.9%	—
09/13	942	71	7.6%	—
09/12	861	86	10.0%	—
Annual Growth	5.8%	2.0%	—	—

MISSISSIPPI STATE UNIVERSITY

While agriculture is at its roots Mississippi State University's (MSU) is today a four-year university offering approximately 150 undergraduate majors and pre-professional programs as well as master's educational specialist and doctorate degree programs at a dozen colleges and schools. It confers more than 4300 degrees annually and has an enrollment of more than 20870 students at its main campus in Starkville and a regional campus in Meridian. More than three-quarters of its student body hail from Mississippi. MSU was created by the Mississippi Legislature in 1878 as The Agri-cultural and Mechanical College of the State of Mississippi.

EXECUTIVES

Vice President, Gregory Bohach

LOCATIONS

HQ: MISSISSIPPI STATE UNIVERSITY
245 BARR AVE MCRTHUR HL MCARTHUR HALL,
MISSISSIPPI STATE, MS 39762
Phone: 662 325-2302
Web: WWW.MSSTATE.EDU

HISTORICAL FINANCIALS

Company Type: Private

Income Statement				FYE: June 30
	REVENUE ($ mil.)	NET INCOME ($ mil.)	NET PROFIT MARGIN	EMPLOYEES
06/16	462	48	10.4%	8,000
06/14	392	64	16.4%	—
06/13*	371	25	6.9%	—
12/08	6	0	—	—
Annual Growth	82.8%	—	—	—

*Fiscal year change

2016 Year-End Financials

Return on assets: 6.0%   Cash ($ mil.): 95
Return on equity: 10.4%
Current ratio: 2.30

MISSOURI BAPTIST MEDICAL CENTER

EXECUTIVES

President, Joan Magruder
Executive Secretary, Debbie Donagan
Plant & Facilities Manager, Elizabeth Tomasovic

LOCATIONS

HQ: MISSOURI BAPTIST MEDICAL CENTER
3015 N BALLAS RD, SAINT LOUIS, MO 631312374
Phone: 314 996-5000

HISTORICAL FINANCIALS

Company Type: Private

Income Statement				FYE: December 31
	REVENUE ($ mil.)	NET INCOME ($ mil.)	NET PROFIT MARGIN	EMPLOYEES
12/15	511	15	3.0%	1,670
12/14	472	22	4.8%	—
12/08	388	(63)	—	—
Annual Growth	4.0%	—	—	—

2015 Year-End Financials

Return on assets: 1.9%   Cash ($ mil.): —
Return on equity: 3.0%
Current ratio: 2.30

MISSOURI BASIN MUNICIPAL POWER AGENCY

EXECUTIVES

Chief Executive Officer, Thomas J Heller
Personnel Manager, Roy Stromsness
Manager, Tim Miller
Manager, Brent Moeller
Manager, Deb Birgen
Manager, Eric Carl
Marketing Director, Jeff Peters

LOCATIONS

HQ: MISSOURI BASIN MUNICIPAL POWER AGENCY
3724 W AVERA DR, SIOUX FALLS, SD 571085750
Phone: 605 338-4042
Web: WWW.MRENERGY.COM

HISTORICAL FINANCIALS
Company Type: Private

Income Statement
FYE: December 31

	REVENUE ($ mil.)	NET INCOME ($ mil.)	NET PROFIT MARGIN	EMPLOYEES
12/15	199	11	6.0%	75
12/09	135	10	7.8%	—
12/08	119	(2)	—	—
12/06	1,064	0	0.0%	—
Annual Growth	(17.0%)	107.9%	—	—

2015 Year-End Financials
Return on assets: 9.3%   Cash ($ mil.): 6
Return on equity: 6.0%
Current ratio: 1.80

MISSOURI STATE UNIVERSITY

When Missouri students say "show me" Missouri State University happily obliges. It is the state's second-largest university (after University of Missouri) with an enrollment of 23800 students. The school offers about 85 undergraduate majors 133 undergraduate minors and 50 graduate majors including 14 masters 3 doctoral degrees (audiology physical therapy and nurse practitioner) and one specialist degree. The university' coursework includes accounting biology criminology and physical geography. Missouri State awarded almost 4000 degrees in 2013. It also hosted some 16 NCAA Division One sports teams that year.

Operations

The university has six Academic colleges one School of Agriculture and one Graduate College. It has some 4000 faculty and staff members. The student-to-faculty ratio is approximately 19:1. Missouri State enrolls students from all 50 US states and 85 foreign countries. The Extended Campus provides learning opportunities through telecourses Internet-based instruction and through BearNet an interactive video network.

Geographic Reach

In addition to its main campus in Springfield the university has campuses in Mountain Grove and West Plains. Missouri State also operates various other special facilities including the Darr Agricultural Center (southwest Springfield) the Jordan Valley Innovation Center (downtown Springfield) the Bull Shoals Field Station near Forsyth Baker's Acres and Observatory near Marshfield and the Missouri State University Graduate Center in Joplin. The university also has a branch campus at Liaoning Normal University in Dalian China.

Financial Performance

Missouri State's revenues increased by 2% to $288 million in 2012 due to higher tuition and fees and better returns from sales and services and auxiliary enterprises. Organic growth helped to lift revenues every year between 2009 and 2012.

However net income dropped by 55% in 2012 due to a decline in non-operating revenues caused by a drop in state appropriations federal grants and contracts and investment income. The following year grants rose 6% to $20 million.

Strategy

The university's "Fulfilling Our Promise" initiative is centered around improving student learning expanding inclusive efforts and broadening the impact it has on the community and state. Among its goals are strengthening its undergraduate and graduate programs (and enroll more students) creating a more diverse student body and workforce and become an employer of choice. In 2013 the university opened the student-funded Foster Family Recreation Center for fitness and wellness. Also that year it introduced the Robert W. Plaster Center for Free Enterprise and Business Development which hosts programs including the cooperative engineering program shared with Missouri University of Science and Technology. Missouri State has also renovated numerous campus facilities.

Company Background

The school was founded in 1905 as the Fourth District Normal School a teacher training institution; it changed its name to Missouri State University 100 years later.

EXECUTIVES

President, Clif Smart
Vice-President, Molly Adelmann
Financial Executive, Nila Hayes
Director, Olivia Pahic
Auditors: BKD LLP SPRINGFIELD MISSOUR

LOCATIONS

HQ: MISSOURI STATE UNIVERSITY
901 S NATIONAL AVE, SPRINGFIELD, MO 658970001
Phone: 417 836-5000
Web: WWW.MISSOURISTATEBEARS.COM

HISTORICAL FINANCIALS
Company Type: Private

Income Statement
FYE: June 30

	REVENUE ($ mil.)	NET INCOME ($ mil.)	NET PROFIT MARGIN	EMPLOYEES
06/16	215	18	8.7%	2,066
06/15	196	16	8.6%	—
06/14	190	10	5.6%	—
06/13	196	20	10.2%	—
Annual Growth	3.1%	(2.0%)	—	—

2016 Year-End Financials
Return on assets: 6.9%   Cash ($ mil.): 43
Return on equity: 8.7%
Current ratio: 1.00

MMR CONSTRUCTORS, INC.

EXECUTIVES

President, James B Rutland
Director, Gary Williams
Vice-President, Thomas B Rutland
Auditors: MADDOX & ASSOCIATES APC BATO

LOCATIONS

HQ: MMR CONSTRUCTORS, INC.
15961 AIRLINE HWY, BATON ROUGE, LA 708177412
Phone: 225 756-5090

HISTORICAL FINANCIALS
Company Type: Private

Income Statement
FYE: December 31

	REVENUE ($ mil.)	NET INCOME ($ mil.)	NET PROFIT MARGIN	EMPLOYEES
12/15	513	16	3.1%	4,000
12/14	649	20	3.1%	—
12/13	658	22	3.4%	—
12/12	483	20	4.3%	—
Annual Growth	2.0%	(8.3%)	—	—

2015 Year-End Financials
Return on assets: 4.0%   Cash ($ mil.): 27
Return on equity: 3.1%
Current ratio: 2.50

MMR GROUP, INC.

That murmur you hear could be the gentle hum of a properly functioning power system. MMG Group provides electrical and instrumentation construction maintenance management and technical services for clients in the oil and gas manufacturing chemical and power generation industries around the world. It also offers services in offshore marine and platform environments. Its Power Solutions division constructs onsite power-generation systems in industrial plants and other facilities. The group primarily operates in the Gulf of New Mexico. Founded in 1990 MMG is 100% management owned and has served such clients as Chevron Shell BP Merck Air Liquide DuPont and 3M.

Operations

MMR Group's provides four main services: electrical and instrumentation contracting safety services panel fabrication and communications.

MMR's electrical and instrumentation contractors work on projects throughout the US and overseas. To ensure its projects are completed on time and within budget its personnel has support and management control systems and emphasizes planning scheduling progress tracking and labor analysis.

The MMR Offshore Safety Services division specializes in disaster prevention and safety helping with navigation fire and gas detection suppression products paging and alarm systems level one cathodic protection inspections and other related services.

For panel fabrication services MMR stages tests and designs control systems that best fit client needs.

The MMR ProCom division is in charge of precommissioning commissioning and start-Up activities for both MMR Group construction projects

and for outside clients interested in turning their facilities construction into a safe and reliable operation seamlessly.

Geographic Reach

MMR operates out of some 20 offices spread across North and South America with most of its offices in Texas Louisiana and California. The company works on projects all over the world with foreign affiliate offices in Calgary Canada; Cartagena Colombia; Puerto la Cruz Venezuela; and Port of Spain Trinidad & Tobago.

Sales and Marketing

MMR serves a variety of markets including: alternative energy exploration and production chemical and petrochemical industrial and manufacturing oil and gas power generation and waste and water treatment among others.

Some of the company's panel fabrication clients have included Shell Pipeline Chevron Pipeline Enbridge Pipeline AGI Services Cimitation Engineering ExxonMobil Keystone Engineering W.S. Nelson Engineering and Entergy among others.

Depending on the project and client's preference MMR operates on all types of fixed-price and cost-plus contracts.

Strategy

The company continues to expand its operations to accommodate more projects. In 2014 the company built a 19-office administration building along with a 6000 square-foot warehouse facility to support the influx of new projects going on in the Golden Triangle area between Beaumont TX and Lake Charles LA.

EXECUTIVES

President, James B Rutland
Chief Financial Officer, Donald Fairbanks
Manager, Kevin Alexander
Purchasing Agent, David Campobasso
Manager, Josh Boudreaux
Administrative Assistant, Linda Sullivan
Director, Alex Zarate
Supervisor, Dee Loupe
Auditors: MADDOX & ASSOCIATES APC BATO

LOCATIONS

HQ: MMR GROUP, INC.
15961 AIRLINE HWY, BATON ROUGE, LA 708177412
Phone: 225 756-5090

PRODUCTS/OPERATIONS

Selected Services
Instrumentation
  Air supply installation
  Control room equipment installation
  Instrument installation
  Process leads
  Panel fabrication
  Signal wiring
Electrical
  Controls
  Electrical equipment setting
  Grounding
  Lighting
  Power distribution
Technical
  Calibration
  Commissioning
  Detail design
  High voltage testing
  Instrument procurement
  Loop check
  Maintenance
  Start up assistance
  System analysis

Selected Divisions
MMR Constructors
MMR International
MMR Power Solutions
MMR Offshore Services
MMR Technical Services
Southwestern Power Group

COMPETITORS

Alberici	MYR Group
EMCOR	Matrix Service
Fisk Electric	Turner Industries
Industrial Specialty	
Contractors	

HISTORICAL FINANCIALS
Company Type: Private

Income Statement
FYE: December 31

	REVENUE ($ mil.)	NET INCOME ($ mil.)	NET PROFIT MARGIN	EMPLOYEES
12/15	585	24	4.3%	4,000
12/14	674	25	3.7%	—
12/13	681	32	4.8%	—
12/12	501	19	3.9%	—
Annual Growth	5.3%	8.6%	—	—

2015 Year-End Financials

Return on assets: 6.5%   Cash ($ mil.): 38
Return on equity: 4.3%
Current ratio: 1.90

MNP CORPORATION

If you are fascinated with fasteners then MNP will galvanize your senses. MNP manufactures a plethora of precision fasteners and cold formed components including screws rivets washers small stampings as well as screw machine parts. Its services range from plating to annealing flat-rolling pickling hot-dip galvanizing and coatings. General Fasteners Cadon Plating & Coatings Marathon Metals and Ohio Pickling & Processing are a few of MNP's affiliated companies that produce a medley of metal parts and jointly operate the GFC/MNP Engineering Center in Michigan. The company serves the automotive heavy truck military and industrial markets.

Operations

MNP is considered a Tier One supplier to the Big Three automobile makers in Detroit and operates four production facilities within its Fastener Manufacturing division. The company has grown to encompass a dozen operating and support divisions and subsidiaries which provide steel and wire fabricating steel treating washer manufacture tool and die capabilities dip/spin coatings cold forming as well as engineering and design services.

Geographic Reach

MNP is headquartered in Utica Michigan and operates throughout the company. It has 1220000 sq. ft. of space at its manufacturing warehousing and processing facilities. The company also has additional sourcing contacts in India Thailand Turkey Brazil Vietnam Malaysia Japan Israel and Europe.

Financial Performance

MNP reported $183 million in annual revenue for 2012 a 5% increase over 2011.

Strategy

MNP is counting on the prediction that fasteners for aerospace and construction (especially residential building) applications are expected to outpace standard fasteners. (It develops and manufactures fasteners for both applications.) The company's biggest competition comes from alternative fastening products such as industrial adhesives and clinching and welding. It also contends with falling raw material prices which cause fastener prices to decrease.

Company Background

MNP was founded in 1970 as Michigan Nut Products.

EXECUTIVES

Vice President Human Resources And Purchasing, Randall Allison
Vice President, Floyd Cushman
Vice President of Quality, Chad Clifford
Vice President Quality, Christopher L Wackrow
Vice President Human Resource, Anne Ventimiglio-Esser
Vice President Sales and Marketing, Dave Cronovich
Auditors: BAKER TILLY VIRCHOW KRAUSE LLP

LOCATIONS

HQ: MNP CORPORATION
44225 UTICA RD, UTICA, MI 483175464
Phone: 586 254-1320
Web: WWW.MNP.COM

PRODUCTS/OPERATIONS

Selected Products and Services
Engineering and design
  Cold forming tooling
  Engineered product applications and solutions
  Alternative cam bolt assembly design
  Automated pre-assembly of fasteners and other cylindrical parts
  Bolt retainer
  Cold formed specials
  Isolator bolt
  Rotatable captured nut
  VTR bolt pre-located bolts for assembly
  Engineered stamping and fastener assemblies
  Joint design and problem solving
  Stamping tooling
Fastener and metal part coatings
  Organic coatings
  Phosphate based coatings
  Plating - mechanical and electroplated metals
Fastener and metal part heat treating
  Carburize
  Quench and temper
Male threaded fasteners
  Specialty engineered fasteners
  Standard fasteners
  Licenses
  Bolt Retainer
  Lo-Driv
  MAThread
  REMFORM
  Taptite
  Torx and Torx Plus
  VTR Bolt
Stampings
  Powder metal parts
  Small metal parts
  Washers
Steel sales and processing
  Rod and wire
Tooling and repair parts
  Machine repair

COMPETITORS

A. Raymond Tinnerman	MacLean-Fogg
AZZ Galvanizing	Metric & Multistandard
Services	Nucor
Ajax Metal Processing	Oneto Metal Products
Align Aerospace	Park-Ohio Holdings
Anixter Fasteners	PennEngineering
Chicago Rivet	Porteous Fastener
Federal Screw Works	Southco
Handy & Harman	TriMas
Illinois Tool Works	Valmont Industries
Kalamazoo Fabricating	Worthington Industries
LISI	W rth Group
Lawson Products	

HISTORICAL FINANCIALS

Company Type: Private

Income Statement
FYE: November 30

	REVENUE ($ mil.)	NET INCOME ($ mil.)	NET PROFIT MARGIN	EMPLOYEES
11/15	192	18	9.6%	1,000
11/14	195	12	6.6%	—
11/13	181	13	7.3%	—
11/12	182	10	6.0%	—
Annual Growth	1.7%	19.1%	—	—

2015 Year-End Financials

Return on assets: 4.9%
Return on equity: 9.6%
Current ratio: 1.60

Cash ($ mil.): —

MODESTO CITY SCHOOL DISTRICT

EXECUTIVES

Director, Jorge Perez
Supervisor, Wayne Coulter
Purchasing Agent, Karen Louis
Auditors: VAVRINEK TRINE DAY & CO LL

LOCATIONS

HQ: MODESTO CITY SCHOOL DISTRICT
426 LOCUST ST, MODESTO, CA 953512631
Phone: 209 576-4011
Web: WWW.MONET.K12.CA.US

HISTORICAL FINANCIALS

Company Type: Private

Income Statement
FYE: June 30

	REVENUE ($ mil.)	NET INCOME ($ mil.)	NET PROFIT MARGIN	EMPLOYEES
06/16	387	25	6.6%	3,000
06/15	333	2	0.8%	—
06/14	306	1	0.6%	—
06/13	280	(5)	—	—
Annual Growth	11.4%	—	—	—

MODESTO IRRIGATION DISTRICT (INC)

Modesty notwithstanding Modesto Irrigation District (MID) does much more than irrigate almost 58000 acres of land in and around Modesto California. The state-owned not-for-profit utility also generates transmits and distributes electricity. In 2012 the company reported that it distributed electricity in a 260-sq.-ml. area to about 94120 residential and 12265 commercial and industrial customers and some 7547 other customers. MID also markets wholesale power and treats and provides drinking water to the city of Modesto for distribution purposes. In 2012 the organization had 103733 irrigated acres (and more than 3100 customer accounts) in its service area.

Geographic Reach

MIS serves the greater Modesto area (north of the Tuolumne River Waterford Salida Mountain House and parts of Ripon Escalon Oakdale and Riverbank).

Financial Performance

In 2012 the company's revenue grew by 5% as the result of an increase in retail electric revenues due to a ate hike aimed at capturing costs related to capital improvement and greenhouse gas allowances.

Net income increased by 63% in 2012 thanks to higher net sales and a cut in the operating costs.

Strategy

In 2012 MID was exploring the possibility expanding its services by selling water to the City and County of San Francisco. The potential deal is seen as a way to increase revenues by opening up a new market without losing any significant water flow from the Tuolumne River one of MID's primary water sources.

Company Background

The company was formed by the government of Stanislaus County in 1887 to provide irrigation services in the Modesto region.

The utility began to provide irrigation water via an expanded canal system in 1904. It introduced electric services in 1923 and in 1978 MID merged with the Waterford Irrigation District.

EXECUTIVES

Vice President Marketing, Bob Root
Vice President Marketing, Tracy Herbeck
Secretary, Barbara Solarez
Board Secretary, Angela Cartisano
Assistant Treasurer, Ana Vigil
Auditors: BAKER TILLY VIRCHOW KRAUSE LL

LOCATIONS

HQ: MODESTO IRRIGATION DISTRICT (INC)
1231 11TH ST, MODESTO, CA 953540701
Phone: 209 526-7337
Web: WWW.MID.ORG

COMPETITORS

Calpine
PG&E Corporation
Sempra Energy
Turlock Irrigation District

HISTORICAL FINANCIALS

Company Type: Private

Income Statement
FYE: December 31

	REVENUE ($ mil.)	NET INCOME ($ mil.)	NET PROFIT MARGIN	EMPLOYEES
12/15	425	42	10.0%	440
12/14	416	43	10.5%	—
12/13	406	25	6.2%	—
12/12	389	46	12.1%	—
Annual Growth	3.0%	(3.2%)	—	—

2015 Year-End Financials

Return on assets: 7.6%
Return on equity: 10.0%
Current ratio: 1.40

Cash ($ mil.): 105

MOMI PALI MEDICAL CENTER

EXECUTIVES

Chief Executive Officer, Art Gladstone
Financial Executive, Ann Ho
Vice-President, Terry Long
Vice-President, Herbert Uesara
Manager, Paula Wilson
Director, Sheryl Nakanishi

LOCATIONS

HQ: MOMI PALI MEDICAL CENTER
98-1079 MOANALUA RD # 680, AIEA, HI 967014725
Phone: 808 486-6000
Web: WWW.PALIMOMI.ORG

HISTORICAL FINANCIALS

Company Type: Private

Income Statement
FYE: June 30

	REVENUE ($ mil.)	NET INCOME ($ mil.)	NET PROFIT MARGIN	EMPLOYEES
06/15	198	7	3.7%	618
06/04	93	6	7.5%	—
06/03	574	(2)	—	—
06/02	463	0	—	—
Annual Growth	—	103.1%	—	—

MONMOUTH UNIVERSITY INC

Students looking for a monumental education might want to head to Monmouth University. The private institution offers more than 30 undergraduate and 20 graduate programs through eight schools that include business administration education humanities and social sciences and nursing and health sciences as well as graduate and honors schools. Founded in 1933 as the Monmouth Junior College Monmouth University has an enrollment of roughly an 6500 graduate and undergraduate students. The school's student-teacher ratio is about 14:1.

Geographic Reach

Monmouth University located in West Long Branch New Jersey.

Financial Performance

Revenues for 2012 were some $158 million while net income was about $7.1 million. Monmouth University has an endowment of some $60 million and an annual operating budget of some $153 million.

Strategy

To expand its academic offerings Monmouth University is working to offer a balanced ratio of liberal arts and professional programs to undergraduates. It is also strengthening its professional and disciplinary graduate programs and it is working to add extended programs.

To expand offerings for health professionals in 2013 Monmouth University formed a partnership with the University of Medicine and Dentistry of New Jersey's School of Health Related Professionals (UMDNJ-SHRP) which will allow eligible Monmouth students to participate in clinical trial science programs at UMDNJ-SHRP.

EXECUTIVES

President, Grey J Dimenna
Vice-Chairman, Alfred J Schiavetti
Director, Paul G Affney
Plant & Facilities Manager, Amparo Plaza
Credit Manager, Chris Ellwood
Auditors: KPMG LLP SHORT HILLS NJ

LOCATIONS

HQ: MONMOUTH UNIVERSITY INC
400 CEDAR AVE, WEST LONG BRANCH, NJ
077641898
Phone: 732 571-3400

PRODUCTS/OPERATIONS

Selected Colleges and Schools
Graduate School
Honors School
Leon Hess Business School
School of Education
School of Science
School of Social Work
Marjorie K. Unterberg School of Nursing and Health
Studies
Wayne D. McMurray School of Humanities and Social
Sciences

HISTORICAL FINANCIALS

Company Type: Private

Income Statement

	REVENUE ($ mil.)	NET INCOME ($ mil.)	NET PROFIT MARGIN	EMPLOYEES
06/15	227	13	5.8%	1,000
06/13	162	14	8.9%	—
06/10	145	18	12.6%	—
06/08	0	0	—	—
Annual Growth	—	629.2%	—	—

FYE: June 30

2015 Year-End Financials

Return on assets: 7.6% Cash ($ mil.): 19
Return on equity: 5.8%
Current ratio: 0.90

MONOGRAM FOOD SOLUTIONS, LLC

Monogram Food Solutions is focused on M E A and T. As a manufacturer of meat and meat snack products the company produces beef jerky sausage hot dogs bacon and other processed food items. Its brands include Circle B King Cotton and Trail's Best Meat Snacks. Through several special licensing agreements Monogram Food Solutions also sells Jeff Foxworthy Jerky Products NASCAR Jerky and Steak Strips and Bass Pro Uncle Buck's Licensed Products. The company which distributes its products nationwide operates facilities in Minnesota Indiana and Virginia. Founded in 2004 Monogram Food Solutions was formed through the merger of assets (King Cotton and Circle B) previously owned by Sara Lee Corp.

Geographic Reach

From its headquarters in Memphis Tennessee Monogram Food Solutions directs the operation of additional facilities in (Chandler) Minnesota (Muncie and Bristol) Indiana and (Martinsville) Virginia. The company distributes its products nationwide.

Strategy

Licensing agreements have helped Monogram Food Solutions build a firm foundation for its business. Aside from its deal with Bass Pro Shops and Jeff Foxworthy the company enjoys licensing partnerships with Johnsonville Sausage and Glory Foods. Its alliance with Johnsonville Sausage inked in 2012 gave Monogram Food Solutions the go-ahead to produce and market Johnsonville Deli Bites Bacon Jerky and other meat snacks innovations.

Beginning in 2010 the company began manufacturing and selling meat snacks for the energy drink maker DNA Beverages Corporation under the DNA brand. Geared toward a younger consumer the DNA beef products gives Monogram a larger demographic for its products.

Mergers and Acquisitions

Since its founding the company has quickly built itself up by buying established meat product manufacturers and processing plants. In 2009 it acquired three companies including beef jerky maker Wild Bill's Foods and Al Pete's Meats (and the Pete's Pride brand name). It also acquired the Hannah's Bull's O'Brien's and Dakota meat snack brands from meat processing company American Foods Group.

In late 2012 Monogram Food Solutions purchased Hinsdale Farms of Bristol Indiana. As one of the nation's largest makers of corn dogs Hinsdale also has a hand in serving retail private label customers and co-packing for other manufacturers. The deal added a fourth manufacturing plant for processing meat. As part of the acquisition Monogram Food Solutions is working to integrate the Hinsdale business into its manufacturing and sales systems.

EXECUTIVES

Vice President of Operations, Drew Dodson
Vice President Human Resources, Richard Stewart
Vice President and General Manager, Brett Elliott
Auditors: MAYER HOFFMAN MCCANN PC MEM

LOCATIONS

HQ: MONOGRAM FOOD SOLUTIONS, LLC
530 OAK COURT DR STE 400, MEMPHIS, TN
381173735
Phone: 901 685-7167

PRODUCTS/OPERATIONS

Selected Brands
Circle B
Hannah's
King Cotton
O'Brien's Meat Snacks/Sausages
Wild Bill's

COMPETITORS

Bridgford Foods	Hormel
Carl Buddig	Jerky Snack Brands
Clemens Family	Link Snacks
Corporation	Oberto Sausage Company
ConAgra	Weaver Meats

HISTORICAL FINANCIALS

Company Type: Private

Income Statement

	REVENUE ($ mil.)	NET INCOME ($ mil.)	NET PROFIT MARGIN	EMPLOYEES
01/16*	419	0	0.2%	790
12/14	321	3	1.1%	—
12/13	239	3	1.3%	—
12/12	197	1	0.9%	—
Annual Growth	28.5%	(24.4%)	—	—

FYE: January 2

*Fiscal year change

MONOGRAM RESIDENTIAL TRUST, INC.

EXECUTIVES

Marketing Manager, Christine Millier
Senior Vice-President, Ross Odland
Manager, Amy Luebbers
VP Marketing, Dustin Lovingood
Vice-President, Ellen Dortch
Vice-President, Patrick Sudderth
Executive Vice-President, Peggy Daly
Vice-President, Stephanie Buffington
Manager, Jeffrey Butcher
Auditors: DELOITTE & TOUCHE LLP DALLAS

LOCATIONS

HQ: MONOGRAM RESIDENTIAL TRUST, INC.
5800 GRAN PKWY STE 1000, PLANO, TX 75024
Phone: 469 250-5500
Web: WWW.MONOGRAMRES.COM

HISTORICAL FINANCIALS

Company Type: Private

Income Statement

	ASSETS ($ mil.)	NET INCOME ($ mil.)	INCOME AS % OF ASSETS	EMPLOYEES
12/16	3,200	7	0.2%	370
12/15	3,283	66	2.0%	—
12/13	2,898	32	1.1%	—
12/12	2,744	(30)	—	—
Annual Growth	3.9%	—	—	—

FYE: December 31

2016 Year-End Financials

Return on assets: 11.7% Sales ($ mil): 280
Return on equity: 2.8%

MONONGALIA COUNTY GENERAL HOSPITAL COMPANY

EXECUTIVES

President, Thomas J Senker
Financial Executive, Zack Kerns
Vice-President, Linda Allen

LOCATIONS

HQ: MONONGALIA COUNTY GENERAL HOSPITAL
COMPANY
1200 J D ANDERSON DR, MORGANTOWN, WV
265053494
Phone: 304 598-1200

HISTORICAL FINANCIALS
Company Type: Private

Income Statement
FYE: June 30

	REVENUE ($ mil.)	NET INCOME ($ mil.)	NET PROFIT MARGIN	EMPLOYEES
06/15	251	20	7.9%	1,100
06/14	241	12	5.1%	—
06/10	205	13	6.7%	—
06/09	368	6	1.8%	—
Annual Growth	(6.1%)	20.5%	—	—

2015 Year-End Financials
Return on assets: 7.3%
Return on equity: 7.9%
Current ratio: 3.00

Cash ($ mil.): 26

MONROE REGIONAL HEALTH SYSTEM

EXECUTIVES
Principal, R Cyrus Huffman
Vice-President, Carl Candullo Jr
Director, Carol Floyd
Director, Jennifer Wood
VP Finance, Rhonda Kautz
Vice-President, Sharon Jones
Executive Director, Sharon Stuckey
Director, Kim Wheeler

LOCATIONS
HQ: MONROE REGIONAL HEALTH SYSTEM
131 SW 15TH ST, OCALA, FL 344716529
Phone: 352 351-7200
Web: WWW.MUNROEREGIONAL.COM

HISTORICAL FINANCIALS
Company Type: Private

Income Statement
FYE: September 30

	REVENUE ($ mil.)	NET INCOME ($ mil.)	NET PROFIT MARGIN	EMPLOYEES
09/15*	340	(4)	—	2,500
12/08	0	(0)	—	—
09/97	0	0	—	—
Annual Growth	—	—	—	—

*Fiscal year change

MONTANA STATE UNIVERSITY, INC

Montana State University helps develop young minds in Big Sky Country. The university located in Bozeman serves more than 14500 students most of whom are undergraduates from Montana. The school offers baccalaureate degrees in 60 fields master's degrees in 45 fields and doctoral degrees in about 20 fields. The school offers primarily a liberal arts education though it is also strong in agriculture and the fine arts. The university provides courses in fields ranging from English to political science to engineering. It has a teaching staff of more than 1150 including 781 full-time and 373 part-time faculty and department heads. Tuition and fees for a resident student is $6705; a non-resident $20062.

Operations

Montana State University's expenditures from sponsored research programs reached $112 million in 2012. That year it had an enrollment of 14660 students and a faculty/student ratio of 17:1.

Geographic Reach

The university has campuses located in Bozeman Billings Great Falls and Havre as well as the Montana Agricultural Experiment Station Montana Extension Service and the Fire Services Training School.

Financial Performance

The university saw a 5% increase in revenues in 2012 due to a rise in tuition and fees a growth in revenues from auxiliary enterprises and other revenues. These were partially offset by a decline in grant and contract operating revenues.

Net income grew by 46% in 2012 thanks to an increase in capital gifts grants and contributions partially offset by higher expenses and a decline in non-operating revenues.

Montana State University was supported by endowments of $7.8 million in 2012.

Higher tuition and fees helped to lift the university's revenues between 2009 and 2012.

Company Background

The university was founded in 1893.

Montana State University is one of only 108 institutions (out of 4600) designated as "very high research activity" by the Carnegie Foundation for the Advancement of Teaching.

EXECUTIVES
President, Waded Cruzado
Vice-President, Craig Oloff
Department Manager, Brett Gunnink
Administrative Assistant, Carla McLaughlin
Auditors: CINDY JORGENSON CPA HELENA

LOCATIONS
HQ: MONTANA STATE UNIVERSITY, INC
901 W GARFIELD ST, BOZEMAN, MT 59717
Phone: 406 994-4361
Web: WWW.MONTANA.EDU

PRODUCTS/OPERATIONS

Schools and Colleges
College of Agriculture
College of Arts & Architecture
College of Business
College of Education Health & Human Development
College of Engineering
College of Letters & Science
College of Nursing
Gallatin College
The Graduate School
University College

HISTORICAL FINANCIALS
Company Type: Private

Income Statement
FYE: June 30

	REVENUE ($ mil.)	NET INCOME ($ mil.)	NET PROFIT MARGIN	EMPLOYEES
06/15	349	9	2.8%	2,500
06/14	341	9	2.9%	—
06/13	333	(1)	—	—
06/12	334	24	7.4%	—
Annual Growth	1.5%	(26.4%)	—	—

2015 Year-End Financials
Return on assets: 10.3%
Return on equity: 2.8%
Current ratio: 2.50

Cash ($ mil.): 186

MONTCLAIR HOSPITAL, LLC

EXECUTIVES
Chief Executive Officer, John Fromhold
President, Marjory Langer
Principal, Konstantin Walmsley
Chairman, Franklyn Jenifer
Vice-President, Dusan Knezevic
Treasurer, Mark Drzala
Office Manager, Mary Donaho
Chief Operating Officer, Everett Devaney Fache

LOCATIONS
HQ: MONTCLAIR HOSPITAL, LLC
1 BAY AVE, MONTCLAIR, NJ 070424837
Phone: 973 429-6000
Web: WWW.MOUNTAINSIDEHOSP.COM

HISTORICAL FINANCIALS
Company Type: Private

Income Statement
FYE: December 31

	REVENUE ($ mil.)	NET INCOME ($ mil.)	NET PROFIT MARGIN	EMPLOYEES
12/15	228	19	8.7%	1,200
12/14	210	9	4.5%	—
Annual Growth	8.6%	110.5%	—	—

2015 Year-End Financials
Return on assets: 6.0%
Return on equity: 8.7%
Current ratio: 0.30

Cash ($ mil.): —

MONTEFIORE MEDICAL CENTER

The primary teaching hospital of the Albert Einstein College of Medicine Montefiore Medical Center attends to the health care needs of residents of the Bronx and nearby Westchester County. The health system operates four main hospitals with about 1500 beds (and 93000 annual admissions) more than 100 ambulatory care offices a children's hospital and Centers of Excellence in cancer care cardiovascular services transplantation and neurosciences. Additionally it operates a home health care agency as well as outpatient facilities that provide ambulatory and diagnostic services. Montefiore also offers medical education programs in partnership with the Albert Einstein College of Medicine.

Operations

Montefiore provides medical services to more than 2.6 million people in the Bronx and Westchester County. With nearly 300000 visits per year Montefiore's emergency department is one of the busiest in the nation while the home health program provides over 500000 visits annually. As the teaching hospital for Albert Einstein College of Medicine Montefiore provides postgraduate training for nearly 100 accredited residency and fellowship programs at the Children's Hospital at Montefiore Moses Division and Weiler Division and eight residency and fellowship programs sponsored by New York Medical College.

Through Montefiore Care Management the company uses a global prepayment or similar strategies

to manage care for 200000 individuals for hospital care rehabilitation outpatient care professional services home care mental health counseling community-based services remote patient monitoring and other programs.

Montefiore and Einstein are among about three dozen academic medical centers nationwide to be awarded the Clinical and Translational Science Award (CTSA) by the National Institutes of Health.

Geographic Reach

Montefiore is made up of four hospitals within three main campuses in the Bronx and more than 100 ambulatory care offices throughout the Bronx and Westchester County (and a total of 140 locations across its entire service area). It has nearly 50 primary care locations throughout the New York metropolitan area.

Strategy

The health center's strategy is to advance its partnership with the Einstein College of Medicine and to improve the health of the communities it serves. Montefiore has grown in scale through acquisitions and mergers in order to diversify its earning potential and increase its bargaining power with drug wholesalers. The system which treats a relatively high percentage of Medicaid patients also stands to benefit by serving a larger volume of patients. Medicaid is shifting to the managed care model which pays a set amount per patient or service. Therefore Montefiore and other providers are seeking growth by caring for more patients in a more efficient manner thereby reducing losses from providing patient care above the government payor's set payment. Additionally the system launched its own insurance coverage for small businesses in early 2015.

The health system is largely involved in the community and is one of the region's hospitals to participate in the Bronx Regional Health Information Organization (Bronx RHIO) a not-for-profit organization established to help the borough's vast number of health care providers share patient information. Participants include hospitals health systems ambulatory care centers individual physician offices long-term care and home care services. Collectively they deliver care to more than 1 million residents including more than 95% of the borough's annual hospital discharges.

Company Background

Founded in 1884 to treat tuberculosis patients Montefiore has a long history of responding to community health crises including lead poisoning and AIDS. In response to rising needs in the community Montefiore opened a community clinic with the aim of vaccinating young women for HPV a sexually transmitted disease that can cause cervical cancer.

EXECUTIVES

EVP Finance and CFO, Joel A. Perlman
President and CEO, Steven M. Safyer, age 69
EVP and COO, Philip O. Ozuah
SVP and Chief Medical Officer, Andrew D. Racine
Vice President Compliance, Lynn Stansel

LOCATIONS

HQ: MONTEFIORE MEDICAL CENTER
111 E 210TH ST, BRONX, NY 104672401
Phone: 718 920-4321

PRODUCTS/OPERATIONS

Selected Services
Allergy & Immunology
Arthritis & Joint Disease (Rheumatology)
Blood (Hematology)
Bones Muscles & Joints Orthopaedics)
Brain (Neurology)
Centers of Excellence
Dentistry & Oral Surgery
Dermatology

Diabetes Hormones Metabolism (Endocrinology)
Diagnostics & Testing (Pathology)
Digestive & Liver Dieases (Gastroenterology)
Elder Care (Geriatrics)
Emergency Medicine
Eyes (Opthalmology and Visual Sciences)
Family and Social Medicine
General Internal Medicine
Headache Center
HIV/AIDS
Home Care
ICU (Critical Care Medicine)
Infectious Diseases
Internal Medicine
Kidney Disease (Nephrology)
Lungs (Pulmonary Medicine)
Neurosurgery
OB/GYN & Women's Health
Otorhinolaryngology - Head and Neck Surgery
Pain Management & Anesthesiology
Pediatrics
Pharmacy Services
Primary Care
Psychiatry and Behavioral Sciences
Radiology
Rehabilitation Medicine
Sleep-Wake Disorders Center
Surgery
Surgical Services (All)
Urology
Wound Care (Hyperbaric Medicine)

Selected Facilities
Greene Medical Arts Pavilion (outpatient care)
Mercy Community Care (outpatient care)
Montefiore Medical Group (23 Bronx and Westchester locations)
Montefiore Medical Park (outpatient care)
Moses Division Hospital (or Henry and Lucy Moses Division)
The Children's Hospital at Montefiore
North Division (formerly Our Lady of Mercy Medical Center)
Weiler Division Hospital (or Jack D. Weiler Hospital)

COMPETITORS

Beth Israel Medical Center
Bronx-Lebanon Hospital
Brookdale University Hospital
Brooklyn Hospital Center
Catholic Healthcare System
Jamaica Hospital Medical Center
Kingsbrook Jewish Medical Center
Lenox Hill Hospital
Maimonides Medical Center
New York City Health and Hospitals
NewYork-Presbyterian Healthcare
Northwell Health
Phelps Memorial Hospital Center
SUNY Downstate
Winthrop-University Hospital

HISTORICAL FINANCIALS
Company Type: Private

Income Statement
FYE: December 31

	REVENUE ($ mil.)	NET INCOME ($ mil.)	NET PROFIT MARGIN	EMPLOYEES
12/15	2,553	11	0.5%	11,000
12/14	2,367	11	0.5%	—
12/13	3,066	125	4.1%	—
Annual Growth	(8.7%)	(69.6%)	—	—

2015 Year-End Financials
Return on assets: 6.1%   Cash ($ mil.): 99
Return on equity: 0.5%
Current ratio: 0.50

MOORE INDEPENDENT SCHOOL DISTRICT NO 2

EXECUTIVES

Superintendent, Robert Romines
Administration Director, Kerry Cooter
Auditors: SANDERS BLEDSOE & HEWETT CPA

LOCATIONS

HQ: MOORE INDEPENDENT SCHOOL DISTRICT NO 2
1500 SE 4TH ST, MOORE, OK 731608266
Phone: 405 735-4200

HISTORICAL FINANCIALS
Company Type: Private

Income Statement
FYE: June 30

	REVENUE ($ mil.)	NET INCOME ($ mil.)	NET PROFIT MARGIN	EMPLOYEES
06/16	185	16	8.9%	2,000
06/11	177	(4)	—	—
06/10	166	9	5.8%	—
06/08	0	0	—	—
Annual Growth	—	321.7%		

2016 Year-End Financials
Return on assets: —   Cash ($ mil.): 74
Return on equity: 8.9%
Current ratio: —

MOORE REGIONAL HOSPITAL

EXECUTIVES

Chairman of the Board, Walker Morris
Board of Directors, Judy Cox
Administrative Assistant, Brenda Smith

LOCATIONS

HQ: MOORE REGIONAL HOSPITAL
20 PAGE DR, PINEHURST, NC 283748847
Phone: 910 295-7888
Web: WWW.FIRSTHEALTH.ORG

HISTORICAL FINANCIALS
Company Type: Private

Income Statement
FYE: September 30

	REVENUE ($ mil.)	NET INCOME ($ mil.)	NET PROFIT MARGIN	EMPLOYEES
09/15	468	55	11.9%	1,400
09/08	358	31	8.7%	—
09/05	326	45	13.9%	—
Annual Growth	3.7%	2.1%	—	—

2015 Year-End Financials
Return on assets: 3.9%   Cash ($ mil.): 25
Return on equity: 11.9%
Current ratio: 0.30

MORENO VALLEY UNIFIED SCHOOL DISTRICT

EXECUTIVES

Vice-President, Cleveland Johnson
Personnel Manager, Olivia Hershey
Manager, Donna Farrell
Plant & Facilities Manager, Sergo S Martin
Administration Manager, Tammy Guzzetta
Director, Sonja Bass
Auditors: JEANETTE L GARCIA & ASSO FATE

LOCATIONS

HQ: MORENO VALLEY UNIFIED SCHOOL DISTRICT
25634 ALESSANDRO BLVD, MORENO VALLEY, CA
925534916
Phone: 951 571-7500
Web: WWW.MVUSD.K12.CA.US

HISTORICAL FINANCIALS

Company Type: Private

Income Statement

FYE: June 30

	REVENUE ($ mil.)	NET INCOME ($ mil.)	NET PROFIT MARGIN	EMPLOYEES
06/16	467	33	7.1%	3,500
06/05	2	0	0.1%	—
06/03	176	16	9.5%	—
06/02	1,457	0	—	—
Annual Growth	—	72.3%	—	—

2016 Year-End Financials

Return on assets: 4.5%   Cash ($ mil.): 370
Return on equity: 7.1%
Current ratio: 6.70

MORSE OPERATIONS, INC.

Morse Operations (dba Ed Morse Automotive Group) has been selling cars and trucks long enough to know the code of the road. It owns about a dozen new car dealerships across Florida most of them operating under the Ed Morse name. Dealerships house more than 15 franchises and 10 domestic and import car brands including Cadillac Fiat Chevrolet Buick GMC Scion Honda Mazda and Toyota. The company's Bayview Cadillac in Fort Lauderdale is one of the world's largest volume sellers of Cadillacs. Morse Operations also sells used cars provides parts and service and operates a fleet sales division. Founder and auto magnate the late Ed Morse entered the automobile business in 1946 with a 20-car rental fleet.

Operations

Ed Morse Fleet Sales offers vehicles from about 10 different brands including Honda Cadillac Fiat Chevrolet Buick GMC Scion Mazda and Toyota. To date annual fleet sales have reached 100000 vehicles.

Fleet customers include daily rental companies such as National Car Rental Avis and Alamo Rent A Car.

Geographic Reach

The dealership network serves customers throughout Florida along the East and West coasts and in Central Florida.

EXECUTIVES

President, Edward J Morse
Personnel Manager, Stacey Lebow
Sales Manager, Tommy Davis
Vice-President, Beaver Richard
Auditors: CROWE HORWATH LLP FORT LAUDER

LOCATIONS

HQ: MORSE OPERATIONS, INC.
2850 S FEDERAL HWY, DELRAY BEACH, FL
334833216
Phone: 561 276-5000
Web: WWW.EDMORSE.COM

PRODUCTS/OPERATIONS

Selected Dealerships
Brandon Auto Mall
Ed Morse Auto Plaza - Port Richey
Ed Morse Bayview Cadillac
Ed Morse Cadillac - Delray Beach
  Ed Morse C
  Ed Morse C
Ed Morse Delray Toyota/Scion
Ed Morse Honda Blue Heron
  Ed Morse M
Ed Morse Sawgrass

COMPETITORS

AutoNation
  Braman Management
  Buchanan Automotive
  Ferman Automotive
  Holman Enterprises
  Island Lincoln-Mercury

JM Family Enterprises
March/Hodge
Penske Automotive
  Group
Scott-McRae

HISTORICAL FINANCIALS

Company Type: Private

Income Statement

FYE: December 31

	REVENUE ($ mil.)	NET INCOME ($ mil.)	NET PROFIT MARGIN	EMPLOYEES
12/15	1,095	14	1.3%	1,295
12/14	863	10	1.2%	—
12/13	690	22	3.3%	—
12/12	604	(6)	—	—
Annual Growth	21.9%	—	—	—

2015 Year-End Financials

Return on assets: 1.0%   Cash ($ mil.): 12
Return on equity: 1.3%
Current ratio: 0.40

MOSAIC

Mosaic creates color in the lives of the disadvantaged. The not-for-profit organization provides individualized support and advocacy services living facilities education and employment for people with disabilities. The Christian organization serves some 3500 clients through 40 agencies across the US as well as select international locations. Services include case management foster care vocational training and supervised living arrangements. Mosaic also offers senior independent living services and support at select facilities. The organization is affiliated with the Evangelical Lutheran Church in America.

Geographic Reach

Mosaic serves clients in 250 communities in 10 US states (Arizona Colorado Connecticut Delaware Illinois Indiana Iowa Kansas Nebraska and Texas). It also partners with organizations in other countries such as Romania and Tanzania to provide services.

Strategy

The organization has been expanding its international efforts through its participation in international Lutheran network IMPACT. Through the alliance Mosaic serves as the representative in Romania and Tanzania. Other participants in the project include Lutheran organizations in Germany Norway and the UK.

Company Background

Mosaic is affiliated with the Evangelical Lutheran Church in America and came into being when Bethpage Inner Mission Association and Martin Luther Homes consolidated in 2003.

EXECUTIVES

Vice President Of Church Relations, David Defreese
Vice President, Kristin Rossow
Vice President of Mission Advancement, Brenda Solomon
Senior Vice President of Mission Advancement, Renee Coughlin
Associate Vice President of Integrity, Pam Heon
Auditors: SEIM JOHNSON LLP OMAHA NEBRA

LOCATIONS

HQ: MOSAIC
4980 S 118TH ST, OMAHA, NE 681372200
Phone: 402 896-3884
Web: WWW.MOSAICINFO.ORG

PRODUCTS/OPERATIONS

Selected Services
Affordable and Accessible Housing
Case Management
Children's Services
Day Services
Host Homes/Foster Care
Residential
Senior Supported Living
Supported/Intermittent

COMPETITORS

Brookdale Senior
  Living
Care UK
Elwyn
GEO Group
Kindred Healthcare

Life Care Centers
Magellan Health
Providence Service
Res-Care
Sunrise Senior Living

HISTORICAL FINANCIALS

Company Type: Private

Income Statement

FYE: June 30

	REVENUE ($ mil.)	NET INCOME ($ mil.)	NET PROFIT MARGIN	EMPLOYEES
06/16	242	2	1.0%	5,000
06/15	240	0	0.0%	—
06/14	0	1	—	—
06/13	234	(0)	—	—
Annual Growth	1.1%	—	—	—

2016 Year-End Financials

Return on assets: 2.5%   Cash ($ mil.): 12
Return on equity: 1.0%
Current ratio: 0.80

MOTHER FRANCES HOSPITAL REGIONAL HEALTH CARE CENTER

EXECUTIVES

President, Lindsey Bradely Jr
Board of Directors, Teresa Mika
Account Manager, Shelly Martin
Vice-President, Chris Gleeney
Financial Executive, Shelly Rutherford
Director, Brett Miller
Auditors: BKD LLP HOUSTON TX

LOCATIONS

HQ: MOTHER FRANCES HOSPITAL REGIONAL
  HEALTH CARE CENTER
  800 E DAWSON ST, TYLER, TX 757012093
Phone: 903 593-8441
Web: WWW.TMFHS.ORG

HISTORICAL FINANCIALS
Company Type: Private

Income Statement

FYE: June 30

	REVENUE ($ mil.)	NET INCOME ($ mil.)	NET PROFIT MARGIN	EMPLOYEES
06/16*	618	63	10.2%	2,747
03/10	314	50	16.1%	—
Annual Growth	12.0%	3.7%	—	—

*Fiscal year change

2016 Year-End Financials

Return on assets: 5.0%   Cash ($ mil.): 40
Return on equity: 10.2%
Current ratio: 1.10

MOUNT AUBURN HOSPITAL

EXECUTIVES

Chief Executive Officer, Jeanette G Clough
Marketing Director, Michael Oconnell
Director, Laure Campbell
Manager, Patricia Meunier
Director, Eileen Dillon

LOCATIONS

HQ: MOUNT AUBURN HOSPITAL
  330 MOUNT AUBURN ST, CAMBRIDGE, MA
  021385597
Phone: 617 492-3500
Web: WWW.MOUNTAUBURNHOSPITAL.ORG

HISTORICAL FINANCIALS
Company Type: Private

Income Statement

FYE: September 30

	REVENUE ($ mil.)	NET INCOME ($ mil.)	NET PROFIT MARGIN	EMPLOYEES
09/16	415	4	1.2%	1,700
09/15	316	20	6.5%	—
09/14	321	21	6.8%	—
09/13	289	27	9.4%	—
Annual Growth	12.7%	(43.9%)	—	—

2016 Year-End Financials

Return on assets: 6.3%   Cash ($ mil.): 91
Return on equity: 1.2%
Current ratio: 2.60

MOUNT CARMEL HEALTH SYSTEM

Mount Carmel Health System cares for the sick in the greater Columbus area and central Ohio. The health care system boasts 1500 physicians at three general hospitals and a specialty surgical hospital offering a comprehensive range of medical and surgical services including cardiovascular care. Mount Carmel Health also operates outpatient centers including primary care and specialty physicians' practices and it offers home health care services. The hospital group is part of Trinity Health one of the largest Catholic health care systems in the US.

Operations

Mount Carmel's facilities include the acute care Mount Carmel East Mount Carmel West and Mount Carmel St. Ann's hospitals as well as the Mount Carmel New Albany a surgical hospital specializing in orthopedic neurological and musculoskeletal treatments. The system also operates several freestanding emergency and surgery centers and other outpatient and community care centers. Its HealthProviders subsidiary manages about two dozen primary care and specialty practices with more than 100 physicians in central Ohio.

In the realm of education Mount Carmel Health operates six medical residency programs for physicians and its Mount Carmel College of Nursing is one of the largest in the state.

Strategy

In 2015 Mount Carmel announced that it was investing more than $700 million in a major expansion. The investment includes big projects at three Mount Carmel campuses: Mount Carmel East Mount Carmel Grove City and Mount Carmel West. Mount Carmel East will begin a $310 million modernization in 2015 to be completed in phases through 2019.

That year the company signed an agreement with HealthSouth to begin construction on a new inpatient rehabilitation hospital in Westerville Ohio. The 60-bed hospital will be a joint venture between HealthSouth and Mount Carmel and will provide specialized rehabilitative care to patients who have experienced stroke trauma brain and orthopedic injuries or other major illnesses or injuries. Construction on the 60000-square-foot hospital is expected to be completed in early 2017. When the new hospital opens Mount Carmel will relocate its existing 24-bed unit at Mount Carmel West to the new facility.

Company Background

In 2012 the company launched a $110 million facilities improvement project (Project GRACE) which includes the renovation of the St. Ann's hospital. Mount Carmel Health plans for the upgraded St. Ann's facility to serve as a regional medical center.

In 2010 Mount Carmel completed construction of a new freestanding emergency center in the town of Canal Winchester through a partnership with Fairfield Medical Center. The center features both general emergency and pediatric urgent care facilities. In time the center might expand into a larger hospital facility.

Mother M. Angela and Sister M. Rufina Dunn of the Congregation of the Sisters of the Holy Cross of Notre Dame founded Mount Carmel in 1886.

EXECUTIVES

Senior Vice President, Hugh Jones
Vice President PFS, Karen Geisler
Vice President, Christine Aucreman
Vice President Managed Care Services, Lyn Flanagan
Vice President Patient Care Services And, Rachel Wright
Vice President Facilities and Construction, David Cozier
Respiratory Therapy Director, JULIANNA DEWITT
Admissions Director, MICHAEL THOMAS

LOCATIONS

HQ: MOUNT CARMEL HEALTH SYSTEM
  6150 E BROAD ST, COLUMBUS, OH 432131574
Phone: 614 234-6000
Web: WWW.MCHS.COM

PRODUCTS/OPERATIONS

Selected Facilities
Hospitals
  Mount Carmel East
  Mount Carmel New Albany
  Mount Carmel St. Ann's
  Mount Carmel West
Other Facilities
  Anticoagulation Centers
  Atrial Fibrillation Center
  Cardiac Rehabilitation
  Diley Ridge Medical Center
  Mount Carmel Grove City Medical Center
  Geriatrics Center
  Health Centers
  Heart Failure Centers
  Home Medical Equipment
  Imaging Centers
  Mount Carmel Medical Group
  Occupational Health Centers
  Outpatient Cancer Treatment
  Outpatient Labs
  Physician Offices
  Rehab and Sports Medicine Services
  Sleep Medicine
  Surgery Centers
  Urgent Care Centers
  Women's Health Centers
  Wound Centers

COMPETITORS

Adena Health System
Fairfield Medical
  Center
Genesis HealthCare
  System (Ohio)
Licking Memorial
  Health Systems

Mercy Health (OH)
Nationwide Children's
  Hospital
OhioHealth
Regency Hospital

Income Statement   FYE: June 30

	REVENUE ($ mil.)	NET INCOME ($ mil.)	NET PROFIT MARGIN	EMPLOYEES
06/15	1,267	131	10.4%	8,000
06/14	1,223	94	7.7%	—
06/13	1,195	89	7.5%	—
06/10	198	2	1.2%	—
Annual Growth	44.9%	124.8%	—	—

2015 Year-End Financials

Return on assets: 9.9%   Cash ($ mil.): 42
Return on equity: 10.4%
Current ratio: 1.60

MOUNT CLEMENS REGIONAL MEDICAL CENTER

Mount Clemens Regional Medical Center (doing business as McLaren Medical Center-Macomb) is an general acute care hospital serving the Macomb County area of suburban Detroit. With about 290 beds the hospital offers such specialties as cardiac and cancer care family practice services home and hospice care and emergency care. The McLaren Health Care-controlled company also operates three prompt care centers in nearby townships as well as a wound treatment clinic. Of the more than 420 physicians on staff at the hospital more than 100 are family medicine and internal medicine specialists who provide primary care.

Geographic Reach

The hospital system serves Michigan patients in the Macomb County area of suburban Detroit.

Strategy

Growing its geographic network of services in 2012 McLaren Medical Center-Macomb opened a new facility in Richmond-Lenox its offers includes physical therapy X-ray/diagnostic imaging and a laboratory blood draw station.

That year it also expanded its technological capabilities with the addition of the da Vinci® Si HD Surgical System robotic technology. The acquisition was part of a long history of adopting surgical advancements.

Company Background

The hospital was founded in 1944.

EXECUTIVES

Vice President Human Resources Executive, David Klinger

LOCATIONS

HQ: MOUNT CLEMENS REGIONAL MEDICAL CENTER 1000 HARRINGTON ST, MOUNT CLEMENS, MI 480432920
Phone: 586 493-8000
Web: WWW.MCLAREN.ORG

PRODUCTS/OPERATIONS

Selected Departments and Services
Bariatrics
Behavioral Health
Blood Conservation
Cancer Services
Cardiac

Diabetes
Diagnostic Imaging
Dialysis Services
Emergency Care
EMS
Family BirthPlace
Fitness Centers
Free Clinics
Health Insurance
Home Care
Hospice
Immunizations
Implantable Hearing Solutions
Infectious Disease
Infusion Center
Intensive Care
Internal Medicine
Laboratory and Pathology
Lifeline
Medical Library
Medical Supplies & Equipment
Neurosciences
Nutritional Counseling
Ophthalmology
Orthopedics
Pain Management
Pediatrics
Pharmacy Services
Primary Care
Proton Therapy
Pulmonary and Respiratory
Rehabilitaton and Therapy
Robotic Surgery
Sleep Medicine
Stroke Center
Surgical and Endoscopy Services
Trauma
Urology
Walk-in Clinics
Women's Services
Wound Care

COMPETITORS

Beaumont Health System
Crittenton Hospital
St. John Hospital & Medical Center
St. John Macomb-Oakland Hospital

HISTORICAL FINANCIALS
Company Type: Private

Income Statement   FYE: September 30

	REVENUE ($ mil.)	NET INCOME ($ mil.)	NET PROFIT MARGIN	EMPLOYEES
09/15	305	8	2.8%	2,249
09/14	312	18	6.0%	—
09/13	303	18	6.1%	—
09/09	277	11	4.2%	—
Annual Growth	1.6%	(4.9%)	—	—

2015 Year-End Financials

Return on assets: 7.5%   Cash ($ mil.): 33
Return on equity: 2.8%
Current ratio: 1.60

MOUNT NITTANY MEDICAL CENTER

EXECUTIVES

President, Richard Wisniewski
Administrative Assistant, Carla Brungart
Auditors: BAKER TILLY VIRCHOW KRAUSE LLP

LOCATIONS

HQ: MOUNT NITTANY MEDICAL CENTER 1800 E PARK AVE, STATE COLLEGE, PA 168036797
Phone: 814 231-7000

HISTORICAL FINANCIALS
Company Type: Private

Income Statement   FYE: June 30

	REVENUE ($ mil.)	NET INCOME ($ mil.)	NET PROFIT MARGIN	EMPLOYEES
06/15	331	21	6.5%	902
06/14	325	20	6.4%	—
06/12	260	(7)	—	—
06/11	235	18	7.8%	—
Annual Growth	8.9%	3.8%	—	—

2015 Year-End Financials

Return on assets: 2.7%   Cash ($ mil.): 15
Return on equity: 6.5%
Current ratio: 0.40

MOUNT SINAI MEDICAL CENTER OF FLORIDA, INC.

Mount Sinai Medical Center of Florida is a not-for-profit acute care teaching hospital providing a wide range of health services to residents of South Florida. The medical center which boasts more than 670 beds provides general medical and surgical care as well as specialty care in cardiology (Mount Sinai Heart Institute) neuroscience oncology orthopedics pulmonology radiology and other fields. It also participates in clinical research studies and drug trials with an emphasis on cancer heart and lung conditions It maintains an inpatient behavioral health unit and houses the Wien Center for Alzheimer's disease and memory disorders diagnosis and research the largest such facility in the region.

Operations

Mount Sinai Medical Center of Florida has 26 operating suites and more than 700 physicians. In 2012 it reported more than 63000 emergency visits 22000 patients admissions and 12000 surgeries.

Geographic Reach

Reaching beyond its main South Florida campus the Mount Sinai Medical Center of Florida also operates a multi-specialty physicians' clinic emergency care and diagnostic center in nearby Aventura. It also operates physicians' clinics in Key Biscayne and Hialeah and an outpatient center in Coral Gables.

Sales and Marketing

The Center markets its services through TV and radio commercials and via print media.

Financial Performance

The company's revenues grew by 3% to $497 million in 2012 due to higher patient service revenues (net of contractual allowances discounts and other revenue). Medicare accounted for 36% of patient service revenues; Medicaid 7%.

Mount Sinai Medical Center of Florida reported net income of $34 million in 2012 (compared to a net loss in 2011) thanks to the absence of impairment of long-lived assets partially offset by a loss on extinguishment of debt. Net income also im-

proved due to change in the beneficial interest in the net assets of Mount Sinai Medical Center Foundation Inc.

Strategy

The company teams up with larger institutions to expand its reach and skill set. Its medical education programs include a cardiology partnership with Columbia University and resident programs for medical students from the University of Miami Florida International University and Nova Southeastern University. The center's partnership with Columbia University has created the Mount Sinai Heart Institute and the Columbia University Division of Urology at Mount Sinai the only Ivy League affiliated programs in South Florida.

Other programs support students entering such health care professions as nursing pharmacy and therapy.

Enhancing its standing in 2014 Mount Sinai Medical Center of Florida received full accreditation for percutaneous coronary intervention from the Society of Cardiovascular Patient Care an international body dedicated to preventing and treating heart disease.

Company Background

Mount Sinai Medical Center of Florida was founded in 1949 by a group of philanthropists and concerned citizens.

EXECUTIVES

Director of Bio Med Engineerin, Eddie Webb
President and CEO, Steven D. Sonenreich
EVP Operations and CFO, Alex Mendez
Chief Medical Officer, Robert C. Goldszer
President Medical Staff, Peter Segall
Director Of Surgery Operations And Business Development, Nate Yuen
Senior Vice President and Chief Operating Officer, Amy Perry
Assistant Vice President Information Technology, Gabriel Ruiz
Medical Records Director, Julia Becker
Vice President Human Resources, Jennifer Foreman
Pharmacy Manager, Craig McCollough
Chairman, Michael M. Adler

LOCATIONS

HQ: MOUNT SINAI MEDICAL CENTER OF FLORIDA, INC.
4300 ALTON RD, MIAMI BEACH, FL 331402948
Phone: 305 674-2121
Web: WWW.MSMC.COM

PRODUCTS/OPERATIONS

Florida Locations
MOUNT SINAI MEDICAL CENTER (MAIN CAMPUS): Miami Beach
MOUNT SINAI AVENTURA EMERGENCY ROOM PHYSICIAN OFFICES CANCER CENTER AND DIAGNOSTIC CENTER: Aventura
MOUNT SINAI KEY BISCAYNE PHYSICIAN OFFICES: Key Biscayne
MOUNT SINAI CORAL GABLES DIAGNOSTIC CATHETERIZATION LAB: Coral Gables
MOUNT SINAI PRIMARY & SPECIALTY CARE CORAL GABLES: Coral Gables
MOUNT SINAI HIALEAH: Hialeah

COMPETITORS

Baptist Health South Florida	Miami Children's Hospital
Broward Health	Tenet Healthcare
HCA	University of Miami Hospital
Jackson Health System	

HISTORICAL FINANCIALS

Company Type: Private

Income Statement
FYE: December 31

	REVENUE ($ mil.)	NET INCOME ($ mil.)	NET PROFIT MARGIN	EMPLOYEES
12/15	533	38	7.2%	3,225
12/14	530	17	3.2%	—
12/13	584	42	7.3%	—
12/05	460	6	1.5%	—
Annual Growth	1.5%	18.7%	—	—

2015 Year-End Financials
Return on assets: 5.4%
Return on equity: 7.2%
Current ratio: 3.40
Cash ($ mil.): 261

MOUNTAIN STATES HEALTH ALLIANCE

EXECUTIVES

Financial Executive, Lynn Krutak
Manager, Theresa Wilson
Manager, Kay Arnold
Manager, Grace Pereira
Director, Carolyn Genmall

LOCATIONS

HQ: MOUNTAIN STATES HEALTH ALLIANCE
400 N STATE OF FRNKLIN RD, JOHNSON CITY, TN 376046035
Phone: 423 431-6111

HISTORICAL FINANCIALS

Company Type: Private

Income Statement
FYE: June 30

	REVENUE ($ mil.)	NET INCOME ($ mil.)	NET PROFIT MARGIN	EMPLOYEES
06/15	433	43	10.0%	2,300
06/05	6	0	7.5%	—
06/03	436	9	2.2%	—
Annual Growth	(0.1%)	13.3%	—	—

2015 Year-End Financials
Return on assets: 6.8%
Return on equity: 10.0%
Current ratio: 1.20
Cash ($ mil.): —

MOUNTRAIL-WILLIAMS ELECTRIC COOPERATIVE

EXECUTIVES

Manager, Dale Haugen
Operations Manager, Bruce Balerud

LOCATIONS

HQ: MOUNTRAIL-WILLIAMS ELECTRIC COOPERATIVE
218 58TH ST W, WILLISTON, ND 58801
Phone: 701 577-3765
Web: WWW.MWEC.COM

HISTORICAL FINANCIALS

Company Type: Private

Income Statement
FYE: December 31

	REVENUE ($ mil.)	NET INCOME ($ mil.)	NET PROFIT MARGIN	EMPLOYEES
12/15	211	34	16.2%	86
12/14	183	32	18.0%	—
12/13	138	0	0.3%	—
12/12	86	0	0.7%	—
Annual Growth	34.8%	293.8%	—	—

2015 Year-End Financials
Return on assets: 6.3%
Return on equity: 16.2%
Current ratio: 0.50
Cash ($ mil.): 5

MUNICIPAL ELECTRIC AUTHORITY OF GEORGIA

With more juice than a ripe Georgia peach the Municipal Electric Authority of Georgia (MEAG Power) supplies wholesale electric power. The authority has a generating capacity of 2069 MW through its interests in nuclear and fossil-fueled plants. Some 49% of the energy MEAG Power delivered in 2012 came from its nuclear plants. MEAG Power transmits electricity to 48 municipal and one county distribution systems across Georgia that in turn serve some 600000 consumers. It utilizes a transmission network that is co-owned by all the power suppliers in Georgia although it is considering joining a regional transmission organization (RTO) to further defray costs.

Operations

MEAG Power owns more than 1300 miles of high-voltage transmission lines and almost 200 substations. It also provides value-added services including management infrastructure and marketing support to its member municipalities energy marketers and other utilities.

The company generates most of its revenues from Project One (ownership stakes in nine generating units other owned transmission plants and working capital). Higher member billings for operating expenses related to fuel and nuclear operations lifted MEAG Power's revenues and net income in 2010.

Geographic Reach

The company serves 49 communities across Georgia.

Financial Performance

In 2012 MEAG Power's revenues increased by 8% thanks to higher participant billings related to a planned reduction in trust transfers as well as an increase in debt service related to environmental improvements to the coal operations and higher contract energy sales. These gains were partially offset by lower participant billings for maintenance and fuel expenses.

That year the company's net income increased by 351% as the result of higher net sales and decreased operating costs.

Strategy

With Georgia restricted in its natural potential for solar and wind power development MEAG Power is pushing hard for the expansion of nuclear power as a clean energy alternative to coal.

In a major breakthrough in 2012 the Nuclear Regulatory Commission approved a Combined Construction and Operating License for units 3

and 4 of the Vogtle plant (near Waynesboro Georgia) the first such license ever approved for a US nuclear plant and the first federal go-ahead for nuclear plant construction since 1978.

In 2013 MEAG Power completed a basemat of structural concrete for the nuclear island at the Vogtle Unit 4 nuclear expansion site the second of two units under construction at Plant Vogtle.

Company Background

In 2009 the Georgia Public Service Commission gave the go ahead for the expansion of the nuclear-powered Vogtle Electric Generating Plant which is co-owned by MEAG Power and in 2010 MEAP Power sold $2.7 billion in bonds to fund this expansion.

EXECUTIVES

Vice President Corporate Affairs, Scott Jones
Vice President Finance, Jim Fuller
Vice President and Chief Administrative Officer, Douglas Lego
Auditors: PRICEWATERHOUSECOOPERS LLP AT

LOCATIONS

HQ: MUNICIPAL ELECTRIC AUTHORITY OF GEORGIA
1470 RIVEREDGE PKWY, ATLANTA, GA 303284640
Phone: 770 563-0300
Web: WWW.MEAGPOWER.ORG

COMPETITORS

AEP
Dominion Energy
Duke Energy
North Carolina
  Electric Membership
Oglethorpe Power
Progress Energy
Santee Cooper
Southern Company
Southern Company Gas
TVA

HISTORICAL FINANCIALS

Company Type: Private

Income Statement

FYE: December 31

	REVENUE ($ mil.)	NET INCOME ($ mil.)	NET PROFIT MARGIN	EMPLOYEES
12/15	642	(131)	—	150
12/14	748	(36)	—	—
12/13	714	0	—	—
12/12	814	65	8.1%	—
Annual Growth	(7.6%)	—	—	—

2015 Year-End Financials

Return on assets: 15.6%
Return on equity: (-20.4%)
Current ratio: 0.70
Cash ($ mil.): 684

MUNILLA CONSTRUCTION MANAGEMENT, LLC

Munilla Construction Management (formerly Magnum Construction Management) was founded in 1983 and is owned by the Munilla family whose background in construction dates back more than five decades. MCM provides a range of design-build and construction management services to public- and private-sector clients in South Florida. The company contracts for a variety of construction projects including commercial institutional educational residential and health care facilities; airports; and such civil construction projects as roads and railway stations.

The company changed its names to Munilla Construction Management (MCM) in 2008 to reflect its family heritage.

MCM is primarily engaged in large municipal and commercial construction projects in South Florida. Recent projects have included the Miami-Dade Airport North Terminal a Miami-Dade Transit Metrorail extension and the Florida Department of Corrections' Everglades Correctional Institute.

EXECUTIVES

Marketing Director, Jorge Munilla
Board of Directors, Juan Munilla
Board of Directors, Fernando Munilla
Board of Directors, Raul Munilla
Accountant, Connie Castillo
Purchasing Agent, Steven Ferreiro
Administrative Assistant, Niurvi Santos
Project Manager, Dennis Parces
Director, Eddie Martinez
Auditors: CHERRY BEKAERT LLP CORAL GAB

LOCATIONS

HQ: MUNILLA CONSTRUCTION MANAGEMENT, LLC
6201 SW 70TH ST FL 2, SOUTH MIAMI, FL 331434718
Phone: 305 541-0000
Web: WWW.MCMCORP.COM

COMPETITORS

Hensel Phelps
  Construction
Odebrecht Construction
Paul J. Sierra
  Construction
Related Group
Stellar Group
Stiles
The Haskell Company
Turner Corporation

HISTORICAL FINANCIALS

Company Type: Private

Income Statement

FYE: December 31

	REVENUE ($ mil.)	NET INCOME ($ mil.)	NET PROFIT MARGIN	EMPLOYEES
12/15	250	2	0.9%	500
12/13	0	(0)	—	—
12/08	0	0	—	—
Annual Growth	—	—	—	—

2015 Year-End Financials

Return on assets: 13.1%
Return on equity: 0.9%
Current ratio: 0.80
Cash ($ mil.): 4

MUNSON MEDICAL CENTER

EXECUTIVES

Chief Executive Officer, Edwin A Ness
Purchasing Agent, Bob Fortney
Director, Sharri Mc Clennan
Director, Daniel M Webster

LOCATIONS

HQ: MUNSON MEDICAL CENTER
1105 SIXTH ST, TRAVERSE CITY, MI 496842386
Phone: 231 935-6000
Web: WWW.MUNSONHEALTHCARE.ORG

HISTORICAL FINANCIALS

Company Type: Private

Income Statement

FYE: June 30

	REVENUE ($ mil.)	NET INCOME ($ mil.)	NET PROFIT MARGIN	EMPLOYEES
06/15	509	60	11.9%	3,100
06/10	441	28	6.4%	—
06/09	394	(0)	—	—
06/08	393	27	7.1%	—
Annual Growth	3.7%	11.8%	—	—

2015 Year-End Financials

Return on assets: 4.1%
Return on equity: 11.9%
Current ratio: 3.20
Cash ($ mil.): 154

MUNSTER MEDICAL RESEARCH FOUNDATION, INC

EXECUTIVES

President, Donald S Powers
Board of Directors, Edward Robinson
Board of Directors, Palmer C Singleton
Board of Directors, William A Hasse III
Auditors: ERNST & YOUNG US LLP INDIANAP

LOCATIONS

HQ: MUNSTER MEDICAL RESEARCH FOUNDATION, INC
901 MACARTHUR BLVD, MUNSTER, IN 463212901
Phone: 219 836-1600
Web: WWW.COMHS.ORG

HISTORICAL FINANCIALS

Company Type: Private

Income Statement

FYE: June 30

	REVENUE ($ mil.)	NET INCOME ($ mil.)	NET PROFIT MARGIN	EMPLOYEES
06/15	495	58	11.8%	2,000
06/14	465	36	7.8%	—
06/13	449	23	5.2%	—
06/09	352	29	8.4%	—
Annual Growth	5.8%	12.0%	—	—

2015 Year-End Financials

Return on assets: 7.2%
Return on equity: 11.8%
Current ratio: 2.00
Cash ($ mil.): 16

MURPHY COMPANY MECHANICAL CONTRACTORS AND ENGINEERS

Keeping Murphy's Law from plaguing construction projects is a task handled by Murphy Company Mechanical Contractors and Engineers. One of the nation's top mechanical contractors Murphy Company provides energy HVAC plumbing piping and design/build services to the commercial industrial heavy industrial and institutional markets. Its projects range from new and retrofit construction to clean manufacturing (for biotechnology or microelectronics clients). The company which offers 24-hour service became LEED-certified in mid-2011. Clients have included Harrah's and Pfizer. The Murphy Company was founded in 1907 and continues to be controlled and managed by members of the founding family.

Operations

The company is ranked #16 on Engineering News Record 's list of top mechanical contractors in the US.

Murphy Company launched a new energy-saving venture in 2011. Its M360 subsidiary focuses on saving companies energy and money through energy audits and by identifying maintenance and other improvements that can be made to mechanical equipment and lighting systems.

Geographic Reach

Murphy Company operates through a pair of corporate offices located in Denver and St. Louis Missouri. It boasts regional offices in Colorado Springs Colorado and Belleville Illinois.

Sales and Marketing

The company provides customers in the industrial commercial institutional and heavy industrial markets with mechanical solutions. Typically each of these markets represents about 25% of Murphy's business.

Financial Performance

After posting $151 million in revenue in fiscal 2011 Murphy posted $197 million in revenue in 2012.

EXECUTIVES

Senior Vice President, Mark Bengard
Vice President and Sales and Marketing, Christopher Hiemenz
Vice President and Quick Response, Tom Hegger
Vice President, Christopher Carter
Vice President, Kevin E Cook
Vice President, Greg Hackl
Vice President, Edward Becker
Vice President Of Estimating And Director, Bob Breth
Vice President, Mike Knapp
Vice President, Conrad Philipp
Senior Vice President of Operations, Larry Kruse
Vice President, Ed Becker
Vice President, Dave Book
Vice President Estimating, Kevin Suiter
Treasurer, Kent Decker
Auditors: RUBIN BROWN LLP SAINT LOUIS

LOCATIONS

HQ: MURPHY COMPANY MECHANICAL CONTRACTORS AND ENGINEERS
1233 N PRICE RD, SAINT LOUIS, MO 631322303
Phone: 314 997-6600
Web: WWW.MURPHYNET.COM

PRODUCTS/OPERATIONS

Selected Markets
Commercial
Heavy Industrial
Industrial
Institutional

Selected Services
Design/build
Clean manufacturing
Construction
Controls/EMS
Data center solutions
Energy solutions
Fabrication
Government
Preconstruction
Quick response

COMPETITORS

EEI	Joseph R. Loring &
EMCOR	Associates
Infinity Contractors	MMC Corp
J. F. Ahern	

HISTORICAL FINANCIALS
Company Type: Private

Income Statement
FYE: March 31

	REVENUE ($ mil.)	NET INCOME ($ mil.)	NET PROFIT MARGIN	EMPLOYEES
03/15	212	0	—	550
03/08	232	0	—	—
03/07	0	0	—	—
03/06	0	0	—	—
Annual Growth	—	—	—	—

MURRIETA VALLEY UNIFIED SCHOOL DISTRICT

EXECUTIVES

Superintendent, Patrick Kelley
Assistant Manager, Darren Daniel
Auditors: VAVRINEK TRINE DAY & CO LL

LOCATIONS

HQ: MURRIETA VALLEY UNIFIED SCHOOL DISTRICT
41870 MCALBY CT, MURRIETA, CA 925627036
Phone: 951 696-1600
Web: WWW.MURRIETA.K12.CA.US

HISTORICAL FINANCIALS
Company Type: Private

Income Statement
FYE: June 30

	REVENUE ($ mil.)	NET INCOME ($ mil.)	NET PROFIT MARGIN	EMPLOYEES
06/16	252	51	20.6%	2,000
06/10	230	30	13.1%	—
06/09	213	(2)	—	—
06/08	0	0	—	—
Annual Growth	—	174.0%	—	—

MUSCOGEE COUNTY SCHOOL DISTRICT

EXECUTIVES

Superintendent, Susan Andrews PHD
Board of Directors, Cathy Williams
Board of Directors, Dr John Phillips Jr
Board of Directors, John Wells
Purchasing Director, Julie Westmoreland
Assistant Manager, Kemberly Williams
Manager, Alisa Massey
Assistant Manager, Eddie Oberton
Personnel Manager, Maria Meltzer
Auditors: ROBINSON GRIMES & COMPANY P

LOCATIONS

HQ: MUSCOGEE COUNTY SCHOOL DISTRICT
2960 MACON RD, COLUMBUS, GA 319062204
Phone: 706 748-2000

HISTORICAL FINANCIALS
Company Type: Private

Income Statement
FYE: June 30

	REVENUE ($ mil.)	NET INCOME ($ mil.)	NET PROFIT MARGIN	EMPLOYEES
06/16	351	52	15.1%	6,000
06/08	373	24	6.6%	—
06/06	340	19	5.6%	—
06/05	0	0	—	—
Annual Growth	—	—	—	—

2016 Year-End Financials
Return on assets: 13.9%   Cash ($ mil.): 129
Return on equity: 15.1%
Current ratio: —

MWH GLOBAL, INC.

MWH Global is an environmental engineering construction and management firm that specializes in water-related projects or "wet infrastructure." The company's typical projects include building water treatment or desalination plants water transmission systems or storage facilitates. MWH also provides general building services for transportation energy mining ports and waterways and industrial projects. The company is active in some 35 countries and serves governments public utilities and private sector clients. Affiliates of the employee-owned company include software provider

Innovyze and business and government relations firm mCapitol. Canadian Engineering firm Stantec acquired MWH Global for $795 million in May 2016.

Geographic Reach

When it comes to projects MWH Global lives up to its name. The Colorado-based firm operates from 180 offices in 35 countries on six continents in the Americas the Asia/Pacific region the Middle East Africa and Europe.

Sales and Marketing

MWH Global seeks projects in five main markets including: the energy and power; water and wastewater; natural resources and mining; ports waterways and coastal; industrial and commercial transportation; and oil and gas markets.

It also does work for local regional and federal governments; US federal clients; public and private utilities; financial institutions; and insurance companies.

Strategy

MWH Global has kept busy in recent years working on a series of high-profile design and construction projects around the globe.

In 2015 the company continued its design-build work on the $7 billion Panama Canal Third Set of Locks project which will double the canal's capacity by the time its completed at the end of the year. The company also continued working with international electricity and gas company National Grid on the largest energy infrastructure program in the UK.

In late-2014 through a joint venture with Costain MWH Global signed on to a 200 million ($325 million) contract to provide design and build services for Southern Water's water and wastewater infrastructure and non-infrastructure assets program in Southeast England; part of Southern Waters' 3 billion ($5 billion) business plan for 2015-2020. Around the same time MWH Global completed its nearly two-decade-long Huanza Hydroelectric project in the Andes Mountains which now provides 92 Megawatts of electricity to some 90000 households in Peru.

In mid-2014 the South Florida Water Management District awarded MWH Global with a master services agreement to help implement the $880 million Restoration Strategies Regional Water Quality Plan which is part of the state's long-term strategy to restore the Everglades. In 2012 the Qatar Public Works Authority appointed MWH to design a drainage master plan in Qatar which will provide a road map for future investment into water and wastewater treatment and other water-related infrastructure programs over the next 50 years.

EXECUTIVES

CFO, David G. Barnes, age 54
President Energy and Industry, Joseph (Joe) Adams
Chairman and CEO, Alan J. Krause, age 63
President and COO MWH Soft Inc., Paul F. Boulos
President Business Solutions, Dan McConville
President MWH Constructors, Blair Lavoie
President Europe Africa Government and Infrastructure, Wim Drossaert
President Government and Infrastructure Americas and Asia Pacific, Marshall Davert
CIO, Claire Rutkowski
Managing Director United Kingdom, Catherine Schefer
Chief Strategy Officer, David A. Smith
Vice President and Director of Development, Charles Taylor
Vice President, Choo Teoh
Vice President of Information Technology, Greg Clark
Vice President and Geologist, Jonathan Hersey
Vice President, Frank Tam

Vice President for Special Project, Joseph Casias
Vice President, Harold Aiken
Vice President, Sean Searles
Vice President, Joseph Jacangelo
Vice President, Dean Bell
Vice President, Geoffrey Carthew
Vice President, Donald A Erpenbeck
Vice President Business Development, Norm Gadzinski
Vice President, Jim Stahl
Vice President, Bob Parent
Vice President, Emmitt Smith
Vice President, Bill Pisano
Vice President International Projects, Gene Kocian
Vice President, Jason Mumm
Vice President, Joe Lauria
Vice President, Vincent Zipparro
Vice President, Stephen Taylor
Vice President, Michael Price
Vice President, Norman Cira
Vice President, Philip Croessmann
Vice President, Stan Postma
Vice President Director Of Business De, Norman Gadzinski
Senior Vice President, Mario Finis
Vice President, Jim Brennan
Vice President, Tauseef Choudry
Vice President, Kevin Johnson
Vice President, Edward Cryer
Vice President, Jerry Notte
Vice President, Roger Stephenson
Vice President, Ajit Bhamrah
Vice President, Karen Willard
Auditors: DELOITTE & TOUCHE LLP DENVER

LOCATIONS

HQ: MWH GLOBAL, INC.
370 INTERLOCKEN BLVD # 300, BROOMFIELD, CO
800218009
Phone: 303 533-1900
Web: WWW.MWHGLOBAL.COM

PRODUCTS/OPERATIONS

Selected Services
Construction
 Airports
 General building
 Industrial
 Highways bridges roads
 Marine and port facilities
Engineering and technical services
Facilities development
Government relations
Program management and management consulting
Research and testing
Renewable energy and sustainability
 Chemical and soil remediation
 Hazardous waste
 Hydroelectric power
 Non-hydro renewable energy
 Power distribution and transmission lines
 Thermal power
Risk assessment
Specialized consulting services
Water and environment
 Dams and reservoirs
 Landfills biosolids
 Sanitary/storm sewers conveyance pumping stations
 Water resources planning management
 Water treatment and desalination plants
 Water transmission lines aqueducts
 Waste water planning and management

COMPETITORS

AECOM	KBR
Bechtel	Peter Kiewit Sons'
Black & Veatch	Severn Trent
CH2M HILL	Siemens Water
Camp Dresser McKee	Technologies
EA Engineering	Tetra Tech
Engie	Veolia Environnement
Fluor	WS Atkins
Jacobs Engineering	Zachry Inc.

HISTORICAL FINANCIALS

Company Type: Private

Income Statement

FYE: January 1

	REVENUE ($ mil.)	NET INCOME ($ mil.)	NET PROFIT MARGIN	EMPLOYEES
01/16*	1,318	35	2.7%	6,700
12/05	946	0	—	
01/03	975	942	96.6%	
Annual Growth	2.3%	(22.2%)	—	—

*Fiscal year change

2016 Year-End Financials

Return on assets: 12.0%
Return on equity: 2.7%
Current ratio: 1.30
Cash ($ mil.): 68

NAPERVILLE COMMUNITY UNIT SCHOOL DISTRICT 203

EXECUTIVES

Superintendent, Mark Mitrovich
Superintendent, David Zager
Board of Directors, Mike Jaensch
Board of Directors, Terry Tamblyn
Secretary, Kathryn Schulte
Auditors: KLEIN HALL CPAS AURORA ILLIN

LOCATIONS

HQ: NAPERVILLE COMMUNITY UNIT SCHOOL DISTRICT 203
203 W HILLSIDE RD, NAPERVILLE, IL 605406500
Phone: 630 420-6300
Web: WWW.NAPERVILLE203.ORG

HISTORICAL FINANCIALS

Company Type: Private

Income Statement

FYE: June 30

	REVENUE ($ mil.)	NET INCOME ($ mil.)	NET PROFIT MARGIN	EMPLOYEES
06/15	309	16	5.4%	2,000
06/14	300	1	0.6%	
06/13	286	8	2.9%	
06/12	283	6	2.4%	
Annual Growth	3.0%	35.4%	—	—

NAPLES COMMUNITY HOSPITAL INC

EXECUTIVES

Chairman, Carl E Westman
Board of Directors, Joseph Perkovich
Board of Directors, John Morrison
Financial Executive, Noble Arrington
Chief Operating Officer, Gail Dolan
Secretary, Beth Martin

LOCATIONS

HQ: NAPLES COMMUNITY HOSPITAL INC
350 7TH ST N, NAPLES, FL 341025754
Phone: 239 436-5000
Web: WWW.NCHJOBS.ORG

HISTORICAL FINANCIALS

Company Type: Private

Income Statement

FYE: September 30

	REVENUE ($ mil.)	NET INCOME ($ mil.)	NET PROFIT MARGIN	EMPLOYEES
09/15	443	38	8.6%	3,300
09/14	398	51	12.8%	—
09/13	383	9	2.4%	—
09/09	460	12	2.8%	—
Annual Growth	(0.6%)	19.8%	—	—

2015 Year-End Financials

Return on assets: 4.4%   Cash ($ mil.): 48
Return on equity: 8.6%
Current ratio: 1.40

NASSAU HEALTH CARE CORPORATION

Nassau Health Care (NuHealth) keeps residents healthy in the suburbs of the Big Apple. The health system operates Nassau University Medical Center which has some 530 beds as well as the A. Holly Patterson Extended Care Facility a skilled nursing center with 590 beds. Other operations include about a half-dozen community family health centers and a home health care agency serving the people of Long Island. Nassau University Medical Center's specialized services include trauma burn care orthopedics psychiatry and obstetrics. NuHealth is a public benefit company governed by a representative board appointed by state and county officials.

Operations

The Nassau University Medical Center is a teaching center affiliated with the SUNY-Stony Brook Health Sciences Center. It also provides some services in affiliation with the North Shore-Long Island Jewish Health System. NuHealth's Nassau Medical Associates affiliate has an interest in primary care and selected specialty practices in central to southern Nassau County.

In 2012 NuHealth reported 283172 outpatient visits; 75240 emergency visits; 22347 discharges and 1576 births.

Sales and Marketing

In 2012 NuHealth launched the Talking Well social media campaign on Facebook and Twitter in an attempt to more effectively communicate with the public.

Financial Performance

The company's revenues grew by 5% to $518 million in 2012 due to an 8% increase in net patient service revenues thanks to an acceleration of intergovernmental transfers and higher contractual rates with third-party insurance companies. Other operating revenues declined in 2012 due to the reduction of services provided to the Nassau County Correctional Facility. Revenues from Medicaid and Medicare accounted for 77% of 2012 net revenues for services provided to patients.

NuHealth's net loss decreased by 69% to $45 million in 2012 due to a decline in salaries and wages primarily as the result of a reduction in full-

time employees; a decline in a loss from employee benefits expenses; and changes to Medicaid eligibility estimates.

Strategy

NuHealth is conducting a $240 million multi-year modernization program. Efforts completed or in progress include the rebuilding of the Patterson Extended Care Facility reconstruction and renovation efforts at the Nassau University Medical Center (including the completion of a new emergency room in 2010 and the remodeling of its maternity wing in 2012) improvements to community health centers and equipment and technology investments. In 2014 NuHealth opened new labor and delivery suites and a new catheterization laboratory.

NuHealth is also working to promote community care wellness initiatives access to specialists and integrated delivery methods. In 2013 Nassau University Medical Center teamed up with Advocates for Community Health on Project DOCC which will deliver chronic care and the Center for Civic Engagement at Hofstra University to improve the health of underserved Long Island families particularly those whose children have developmental disabilities and serious chronic conditions.

Towards this goal NuHealth also collaborates with other area providers such as North Shore-LIJ. It is also expanding its physician education programs; it launched a new osteopathic family medicine residency program to train doctors at its inpatient and outpatient facilities in 2012. It also introduced a hematology and oncology fellowship program that year.

Fxpanding its products in 2012 Nassau University Medical Center began to offer personalized travel medicine services to meet the needs of travelers going abroad for both business and pleasure.

Company Background

The Nassau University Medical Center opened in 1935 as Meadowbrook Hospital and joined the NuHealth organization in 1997. It was renamed Nassau University Medical Center in 2001.

EXECUTIVES

Vice President, James Capoziello
Vice President Human Resources, Maureen Roarty
Vice President Finance, Richard Perrotti
Senior Vice President Revenue Cycle, Vincent DiSanti
Vice President of Executive Staff Operations, Guy Courbois
Medical Director, Kenneth Spitalny
Vice President For Legal Affairs, Sharon Popper
Vice President Planning Corporate Development, Michael Ade
Director of Radiology, Rashmikant Baxi
Radiology Medical Director, Nicholas Albanese
Director of Nursing, Janeann Zink
Ambulatory Services Director, JUDY EISELE
Secretary, Lydia Barbagallo
Board of Directors, Maria Glorioso

LOCATIONS

HQ: NASSAU HEALTH CARE CORPORATION
2201 HEMPSTEAD TPKE, EAST MEADOW, NY 115541859
Phone: 516 572-0123
Web: WWW.NUMC.EDU

PRODUCTS/OPERATIONS

Selected Services
Anesthesiology
Blood Bank
Brain & Nerves
Burn Center
Cardiac Care
Community Services
Dental Medicine

Diagnostic Imaging
Emergency Medicine
Eye Care
Family Medicine
Hypertension Diabetes & Vascular Disease
Internal Medicine
Mental Health & Addiction
Orthopedics & Rehabilitation
Pathology
Pediatrics
Primary & Preventive Care
Primary Care & Wellness
Radiology
Radiology & Laboratory
Senior Services
Shared Laboratory Services
Specialized Medicine
Specialty Services
Surgery
Surgical & Emergency Care
Trauma Center
Women's Health

COMPETITORS

Catholic Health Services of Long Island
  Catholic Healthcare System
Continuum Health Partners
Lutheran HealthCare
MediSys Health Network
New York City Health and Hospitals
Northwell Health
Queens-Long Island Medical Group

HISTORICAL FINANCIALS

Company Type: Private

Income Statement

FYE: December 31

	REVENUE ($ mil.)	NET INCOME ($ mil.)	NET PROFIT MARGIN	EMPLOYEES
12/15	363	(80)	—	3,500
12/14	391	5	1.4%	—
12/12	0	(0)	—	—
12/06	470	(7)	—	—
Annual Growth	(2.8%)	—	—	—

2015 Year-End Financials

Return on assets: 11.4%   Cash ($ mil.): 44
Return on equity: (-22.1%)
Current ratio: 0.40

NATIONAL COLLEGIATE ATHLETIC ASSOCIATION

The National Collegiate Athletic Association (NCAA) supports the intercollegiate sports activities of around 1000 member colleges and universities. A not-for-profit organization the NCAA administers scholarship and grant programs enforces conduct and eligibility rules and works to support and promote the needs of student athletes. The association is known for its lucrative branding and television deals such as those surrounding the popular "March Madness" tournament for Division I men's basketball. Seeking reform of athletics rules and regulations officials from 13 schools formed the Intercollegiate Athletic Association of the United States in 1906. The organization took its current name in 1910.

Financial Performance

NCAA revenue in fiscal 2013 (ended August) was $913 million up 5% versus the prior year most of which came from the rights agreement with CBS Sports and Turner Broadcasting. Indeed about 80% of the NCAA's revenue come from television and marketing rights fees generated pri-

marily from the Division I men's basketball championship. Another 12% comes from championships and NIT tournaments including ticket and merchandise sales.

About 96% of NCAA revenue is distributed directly to the Division I membership or to support championships or programs that benefit student-athletes. The remaining 4% goes for central services such as building operations and salaries not related to particular programs.

Strategy

The NCAA is coming under pressure to modify its rules on how student-athletes are compensated. In 2014 the National Labor Relations Board ruled that a group of Northwestern football players were employees of the univerisity and have the right to form a union and bargain collectively. The organization is also facing challenges regarding compensation for student-athletes whose likenesses are used in video games and broadcasts as well a lawsuits relating to its handling of head injuries.

EXECUTIVES

President, Mark A Emmert
Director, Barb Rhodes
Administrative Assistant, Amy Skiles
Editor, Gary Brown
Engineer, Chris Cramer
Vice-President, Jonathan Duncan
Auditors: DELOITTE TAX LLP INDIANAPOLIS

LOCATIONS

HQ: NATIONAL COLLEGIATE ATHLETIC ASSOCIATION
700 W WASHINGTON ST, INDIANAPOLIS, IN
462042710
Phone: 317 917-6222
Web: WWW.NCAA.ORG

PRODUCTS/OPERATIONS

2013 Revenues

	% of total
Television & marketing rights fees	80
Championships & NIT tournaments	12
Investments	4
Sales & services	3
Contributions facilities & other	1
Total	**100**

HISTORICAL FINANCIALS

Company Type: Private

Income Statement

FYE: August 31

	REVENUE ($ mil.)	NET INCOME ($ mil.)	NET PROFIT MARGIN	EMPLOYEES
08/15	952	43	4.5%	508
08/14	906	7	0.9%	—
Annual Growth	5.1%	461.0%	—	—

2015 Year-End Financials

Return on assets: 12.7%   Cash ($ mil.): 12
Return on equity: 4.5%
Current ratio: 0.50

NATIONAL MARROW DONOR PROGRAM INC

EXECUTIVES

Chief Executive Officer, Jeffrey W Chell
Chief Financial Officer, Amy Ronneberg
Chief Operating Officer, Karen Dodson

Director, Stephen Spellman
Account Manager, Lynn Anderson
Manager, Katy Engelby
Marketing Manager, Michelle Kolb
Auditors: LB EIDE BAILLY LLP MINNEAPOLI

LOCATIONS

HQ: NATIONAL MARROW DONOR PROGRAM INC
500 N 5TH ST, MINNEAPOLIS, MN 554011206
Phone: 612 627-5800
Web: WWW.MAKEMESTRONGER.COM

HISTORICAL FINANCIALS

Company Type: Private

Income Statement

FYE: September 30

	REVENUE ($ mil.)	NET INCOME ($ mil.)	NET PROFIT MARGIN	EMPLOYEES
09/15	397	22	5.6%	800
09/05	143	0	0.6%	—
Annual Growth	10.8%	38.4%	—	—

2015 Year-End Financials

Return on assets: 15.3%   Cash ($ mil.): 38
Return on equity: 5.6%
Current ratio: 0.90

NATIONAL UNIVERSITY

National University is the flagship school of the National University System. The institution offers more than 150 undergraduate and graduate degrees and teacher credential and certificate programs. A not-for-profit institution National University programs range across fields including business engineering education media and human services. The university enrolls 23000 students at multiple locations in California and Nevada; it also offers about 70 online degree programs. The school conducts research through the National University Community Research Institute (NUCRI). National University was founded in 1971.

Geographic Reach

National University operates through about 45 locations in California and Nevada including regional campuses in Bakersfield Costa Mesa Fresno Los Angeles Ontario Oxnard Redding Sacramento San Bernardino San Diego San Jose Stockton Twentynine Palms and Woodland Hills California as well as Henderson Nevada. It also has offices in Dallas and Houston Texas and it operates online information centers in Florida Georgia Virginia and Washington State (in addition to numerous online information locations in California). Some of the university's satellite centers are located on military bases.

Operations

National University consists of five schools: Education; Professional Studies; Business and Management; Health and Human Services and Engineering Technology and Media. It also includes the College of Letters and Sciences. The university employs more than 250 full-time faculty members.

The National University System is a group of affiliated universities to meet educational demands for modern times. It was formed in 2001 and includes affiliates John F. Kennedy University City University of Seattle Spectrum Pacific Learning and WestMed College as well as National University International and National University Virtual High School.

Strategy

To meet the rising needs of a growing population National University has been adding new lo-

cations. For instance during 2012 it added new online information centers in Arcadia and San Francisco California and in Seattle Washington. It also added a new university campus in Rancho Cordova California and it expanded its San Diego locations by adding a new facility to house programs for its School of Business and Management and School of Professional Studies.

National University strives to provide learning opportunities to a diverse student population. It is a leading issuer of master's degrees to minorities and women in California. It also serves a rising number of online students and is regularly adding new online courses to meet the needs of this audience.

Growing health care program demands prompted the university to add a Master of Healthcare Administration program at its Fresno campus in 2012. It also added bachelor's degree in allied health through a partnership with the San Mateo Community College District.

EXECUTIVES

Provost Vice President Academic Affairs, Thomas Green
Associate Vice President Regional Operations, Louis Cruz
Vice President for Student Services, Joe Zavala
Auditors: MOSS ADAMS LLP SAN DIEGO CA

LOCATIONS

HQ: NATIONAL UNIVERSITY
11355 N TORREY PINES RD, LA JOLLA, CA
920371013
Phone: 858 642-8000
Web: WWW.NU.EDU

PRODUCTS/OPERATIONS

Selected Schools and Colleges

College of Letters and Sciences
School of Business and Management
School of Education
School of Engineering Technology and Media
School of Health and Human Services
School of Professional Studies

HISTORICAL FINANCIALS

Company Type: Private

Income Statement

FYE: June 30

	REVENUE ($ mil.)	NET INCOME ($ mil.)	NET PROFIT MARGIN	EMPLOYEES
06/15	263	35	13.4%	1,954
06/11	203	25	12.4%	—
06/10	178	18	10.3%	—
06/09	0	0	—	—
Annual Growth	—	259.4%	—	—

2015 Year-End Financials

Return on assets: 6.7%   Cash ($ mil.): 46
Return on equity: 13.4%
Current ratio: 1.50

NATIONWIDE CHILDREN'S HOSPITAL

Buckeye babies toddlers and teens don't have to travel the country to find pediatric care with Nationwide Children's Hospital at their disposal. The Columbus Ohio health care provider is one of the largest pediatric care centers in the US. The hos-

pital has some 430 licensed beds and offers services in areas such as behavioral health cardiology hospice orthopedics and surgery. It has roughly 1100 health care providers on its medical staff and its emergency department treats more than 83000 patients each year. The hospital also operates outpatient and specialty clinics in the area and a research institute which is investigating gene therapy.

Operations

The hospital provides more than $122 million in charity care and community benefit services annually. It had more than 1 million patient visits and had more than 25000 surgery cases in 2014.

Geographic Reach

Nationwide Children's Hospital serves patients from 50 US states and 32 countries. The company is 68 facilities extending out across Ohio and beyond. The company's top ten outpatient visits counties are Franklin Delaware Fairfield Licking Clark Pickaway Madison Union Muskingum and Knox.

Sales and Marketing

Nationwide Children's Hospital payor mix in 2014 included commercial 43%; Medicaid managed care Cap 33%; and Medicaid 13%.

Strategy

In 2015 Nationwide Children's Hospital announced plans to adopt and integrate GenomeNext's genomic sequencing analysis platform for both clinical laboratory services and clinical research initiatives

In 2014 the company outlined numerous details of its $130 million campus expansion project. Its plans include an $85 million outpatient care building and a $45 million building to house faculty offices. The outpatient building called the Livingston Ambulatory Center will house primary care services dental services behavioral health dermatology adolescent medicine sports rehabilitation and various clinics. Both buildings will be six stories tall.

The hospital added helicopter medical transport service in 2013.

Company Background

The health system in 2012 completed a $740 million project to build a new main hospital and add 2 million sq. ft. of clinical research and support space. The expansion added about 100 new beds.

Also in 2012 it opened an ambulatory surgery center in Westerville Ohio and a Close To Home lab and clinic in Springfield. In 2014 it opened the Sharon Woods Primary Care Center in north Columbus.

Nationwide Children's Hospital opened its doors in 1892.

EXECUTIVES

Medical Director Center For Child And Family Advocacy, Philip Scribano
Medical Director Clinical Informatics, Rich David
Chairman The Center for Family Safety and Healing, Abigail S. Wexner
EVP and CFO, Timothy C. Robinson
President and COO, Rick Miller
SVP and Chief Nursing Officer, Linda Stoverock
CEO, Steve Allen
President The Research Institute, John Barnard
President The Center for Family Safety and Healing, Karen Days
Chief Medical Officer, Richard J. Brilli
Surgeon-in-Chief, R. Lawrence Moss
Physician-in-Chief, J. Philip Saul
Chairman Nationwide Children's Hospital Foundation, Cheryl W. Lucks
Chairman The Research Institute, Donald P. McConnell
Vice President, Karen Heiser
Medical Director, Grant Morrow

Vice President Administration Surgical Services, Michelle Mckissick
Vice President Revenue Cycle, Michael Hester
Senior Vice President Of Ambulatory And Mental Health Services, Jack Clark
Senior Management Senior Vice President General Ma, Phillip Chanthasene
Vice President Operations, Dennis Minzler
Vice President of the Board, Nancy Wagner
Chairman, Alex Fischer
Secretary, Janet Tussing
Secretary, Wood Carol
Secretary, Kay McCann
Secretary, Heather Wildermuth
Secretary, Lisa Chaffee
Medical Coding Secretary, Marianne Clemons
Secretary, Tami King

LOCATIONS

HQ: NATIONWIDE CHILDREN'S HOSPITAL
700 CHILDRENS DR, COLUMBUS, OH 432052639
Phone: 614 722-3040

PRODUCTS/OPERATIONS

Selected Subsidiaries
Nationwide Children's Hospital
Nationwide Children's Behavioral Health
Nationwide Children's Educational Institute
Nationwide Children's Hospital Inc
Nationwide Children's Hospital Homecare
Children's Anesthesia Associates
Nationwide Children's Hospital Foundation
Pediatric Academic Associates
Children's Orthopedic Medical Center
Children's Radiological Institute
Children's Surgical Associates Corp.
The Research Institute at Nationwide Children's Hospital
Pediatric Pathology Associates of Columbus
The Center for Family Safety and Healing at Nationwide Children's Hospital

Selected Departments and Services
Adolescent Congenital Heart Disease
Adolescent Medicine
Adult Congenital Heart Disease
Adult Medicine and Hospital Pediatrics
Allergy/Immunology
Ambulatory Pediatrics
Anatomic Pathology
Anesthesiology & Pain Medicine
Asthma Program
Audiology
Bariatric Surgery
Battelle Center for Mathematical Medicine
Behavioral Health
Blood Conservation Program
Burn Program
Cancer
CAP4Kids
Cardiology
Cardiopulmonary Rehabilitation
Cardiothoracic Surgery
Center for Biobehavioral Health (Research)
Center for Cardiovascular and Pulmonary Research
Center for Childhood Cancer (Research)
Center for Clinical and Translational Research
Center for Colorectal and Pelvic Reconstruction
Center for Gene Therapy (Research)
Center for Healthy Weight and Nutrition
Center for Injury Research and Policy
Center for Innovation in Pediatric Practice
Center for Microbial Pathogenesis (Research)
Center for Molecular and Human Genetics (Research)
Center for Perinatal Research
Center for Vaccines and Immunity (Research)
Central Ohio Poison Center
Cerebral Palsy Program
Chest Wall Clinic
Child Development/Psychology
Child Life Specialists
ChildLab
Cleft Lip and Palate Center
Clinical Nutrition and Lactation
Clinical Services and Care Coordination
Clinical Studies
Clinical Therapies
Close To Home Centers

Community Relations
Congenital Heart Disease
Connecting Families
Critical Care
Cystic Fibrosis
Dentistry
Dermatology
Developmental/Behavioral Pediatrics
Diabetes Clinic
Disorders of Sexual Development (DSD)
Ear Nose & Throat Services (Otolaryngology)
Early Childhood Development Program
Education Classes
Emergency Services
Endocrinology Metabolism & Diabetes
Family Advisory Council
Family AIDS Clinic and Educational Services (FACES)
Family Health Information Center
Family Practice
Family Resource Center
Fetal Diagnostics
Financial Matters
Gastroenterology Hepatology and Nutrition
Gender Concerns
General Pediatric Surgery
Genetics (Molecular and Human)
Gift Cards
Gift Shop
Government Relations
Health Info Library
Health Information Management (HIM)
Hearing Program
Heart Center
Hemangioma Vascular Anomalies
Hematology Oncology & BMT
HIV Program
Homecare
Hospice
Immunology
Infectious Diseases
Interdisciplinary Feeding Clinic
International Adoption Clinic
Interventional Radiology
Jeune's Syndrome
Laboratory Medicine/Reference Lab
Massage Therapy
Medical Records
Melanoma & Pigmented Lesion Clinic
Music Therapy
myChildren's
Neonatology
Nephrology
Neurodiagnostics/EEG
Neurology
Neuromuscular Disorders
Neurosciences Center
Neurosurgery
Nuclear Medicine
Nurse-Family Partnership
Occupational Therapy
Ophthalmology/Eye Clinic
Orthopedics
Outpatient Surgery
Pain Service Clinic
Palliative Care
Pastoral Care
Patient and Family Relations
Patient and Visitor Guide
Patient Financial Services
PediaCast: a pediatric podcast for parents
Pediatric and Adolescent Gynecology
Pediatric Psychiatry
Pediatric Psychology
Pharmacy Services (Outpatient)
Physical Medicine & Rehabilitation
Physical Therapy
Physical Therapy - Sports and Orthopedic
Plastic and Reconstructive Surgery
Prader-Willi Syndrome Clinic
Primary Care Centers
Pulmonary Medicine
Radiology
Reach Out and Read
Rehabilitation
Request an Appointment
Research at Children's
Resonance Disorders Program
Rheumatology
Robot-Assisted Surgery
Ronald McDonald House
School Program

Sibling Support (Children's Clubhouse)
Sleep Disorder Center
Social Work
Speech and Language Pathology
Spina Bifida Program
Sports Medicine
Surgical Services
Telehealth
The Center for Family Safety and Healing
Therapeutic Recreation
THRIVE Program (DSD & Complex Urological & Gender Concerns)
Toxicology
Transplant Program
Transport
Trauma
Urgent Care Services
Urology
Velopharyngeal Dysfunction Program
Weight Loss Surgery

COMPETITORS

Akron Children's Hospital
Cincinnati Children's Hospital
Fairfield Medical Center
Genesis HealthCare System (Ohio)
Licking Memorial Health Systems
Mount Carmel Health
OhioHealth
Select Medical
Shriners Hospitals For Children

HISTORICAL FINANCIALS
Company Type: Private

Income Statement
FYE: December 31

	REVENUE ($ mil.)	NET INCOME ($ mil.)	NET PROFIT MARGIN	EMPLOYEES
12/15	1,386	285	20.6%	6,000
12/14	1,282	332	26.0%	—
12/13	1,658	334	20.1%	—
12/09	918	95	10.4%	—
Annual Growth	7.1%	20.0%	—	—

2015 Year-End Financials
Return on assets: 4.5%
Return on equity: 20.6%
Current ratio: 0.80
Cash ($ mil.): 126

NAVILLUS TILE, INC.

EXECUTIVES

President, Donald Sullivan
Board of Directors, Kevin Sullivan
Project Manager, James Egan
Project Manager, Conall McBrien
Manager, Helen Osullivan
Superintendent, Ian Galvin
Supervisor, Kenny McBrien
Director, Colin Mathers
Project Manager, Conor Leen
Project Manager, Michael King
Sales Manager, Brian McGill
Auditors: GRASSI & CO CPAS PC JERICH

LOCATIONS

HQ: NAVILLUS TILE, INC.
633 3RD AVE FL 17, NEW YORK, NY 100178113
Phone: 212 750-1808
Web: WWW.NAVILLUSINC.COM

HISTORICAL FINANCIALS
Company Type: Private

Income Statement
FYE: March 31

	REVENUE ($ mil.)	NET INCOME ($ mil.)	NET PROFIT MARGIN	EMPLOYEES
03/16	240	11	4.9%	400
03/10	171	1	0.6%	—
03/07	107	5	5.2%	—
03/06	2,139	0		
Annual Growth	(19.6%)	343.3%	—	—

2016 Year-End Financials
Return on assets: 5.8%
Return on equity: 4.9%
Current ratio: 1.50
Cash ($ mil.): 12

NAVY EXCHANGE SERVICE COMMAND

Before Old Navy there was the Navy Exchange Service Command (NEXCOM). Active-duty military personnel reservists retirees and their family members can shop and gas up at more than 100 Navy Exchange (NEX) retail stores (brand-name and private-label merchandise ranging from apparel to home electronics) more than 150 NEXCOM Ships Stores (basic necessities) and its 100-plus Uniform Support Centers (the sole source of authorized uniforms). NEXCOM also runs about 40 Navy Lodges (motels) in the US and about half a dozen foreign countries. NEXCOM receives tax dollars for its shipboard stores but it is otherwise self-supporting. Most of the profits fund morale welfare and recreational programs (MWR) for sailors.

Geographic Reach

Navy Exchange Service Command has more than 100 NEX stores on land in the US Cuba Africa Europe the Middle East Japan and China.

Strategy

Since the government lifted restrictions on the types of items sold at the stores allowing more expensive furniture jewelry and televisions sales have been on the rise at NEX stores. NEXCOM has also been adding stores at home and abroad. In fall 2013 it opened a Fleet Store in Jebel Ali Dubai to serve sailors stationed in and around Dubai as well as military personnel passing through the area aboard ship.

To better compete with online rivals Walmart.com Target.com Amazon.com BestBuy.com and others in 2013 NEX expanded its Price Match Policy to match their prices.

EXECUTIVES

Senior Vice President Distribution, Thomas Williams
Auditors: KPMG LLP NORFOLK VA

LOCATIONS

HQ: NAVY EXCHANGE SERVICE COMMAND
3280 VIRGINIA BEACH BLVD, VIRGINIA BEACH, VA 234525799
Phone: 757 631-3696
Web: WWW.MYNAVYEXCHANGE.COM

PRODUCTS/OPERATIONS

2014 Sales

	% of total
Total	95
Income from Concessions net	2
Contributed Services	3
Other Revenue	0
Total	100

PRODUCT DEPARTMENTS
PRODUCT DEPARTMENTS
For The Home
Electronics
Shoes
Beauty
Women
Men
Kids
Navy pride
Handbags and accessories

COMPETITORS

7-Eleven
Amazon.com
Best Buy
J. C. Penney
Kmart
Sears
Target Corporation
Value City Furniture
Wal-Mart

HISTORICAL FINANCIALS
Company Type: Private

Income Statement
FYE: January 31

	REVENUE ($ mil.)	NET INCOME ($ mil.)	NET PROFIT MARGIN	EMPLOYEES
01/15*	2,799	65	2.4%	14,000
02/14	2,797	73	2.6%	—
01/11	2,749	68	2.5%	—
01/04	2,256	46	2.1%	—
Annual Growth	2.0%	3.1%	—	—
*Fiscal year change

2015 Year-End Financials
Return on assets: 9.6%
Return on equity: 2.4%
Current ratio: 0.30
Cash ($ mil.): 77

NC STATE INVESTMENT FUND INC

EXECUTIVES

General Manager, Libby George
Auditors: WILLIAMS OVERMAN PIERCE LLP R

LOCATIONS

HQ: NC STATE INVESTMENT FUND INC
NCSU, RALEIGH, NC 276950001
Phone: 919 513-7149

HISTORICAL FINANCIALS
Company Type: Private

Income Statement
FYE: June 30

	ASSETS ($ mil.)	NET INCOME ($ mil.)	INCOME AS % OF ASSETS	EMPLOYEES
06/15	848	203	24.0%	2
06/14	598	39	6.6%	—
06/13	485	42	8.7%	—
06/10	313	27	8.9%	—
Annual Growth	22.0%	48.8%	—	—

2015 Year-End Financials
Return on assets: 0.1%
Return on equity: 87.8%
Sales ($ mil): 231

NCH CORPORATION

NCH has been cleaning up for years and like everyone else it's been using soaps and detergents to do so. The company makes and sells about 450 chemical maintenance repair and supply products including all kinds of cleaners for customers in more than 50 countries throughout the world. NCH markets its products through a direct sales force to companies in the agricultural home-improvement industrial recreational and utility markets. Other products include fasteners welding supplies pet care supplies plumbing parts lubricants and metal-working fluids.

Operations

The company's major areas of focus include producing products for the industrial cleaning and maintenance pet care plumbing specialty industries supply and water treatment and remediation markets.

NCH's cleaning products include hand cleaners industrial cleaners and housekeeping supplies. Specialty chemical products including cleaning and water treatment chemicals deodorizers lubricants paints and paint strippers patching compounds and flooring and carpet treatments account for the majority of sales.

The company's divisions include: Water Treatment Solutions plumbing Pet Care (Simple Solutions® Bags on Board® Vet's Best® and OUT! Pet Care) Specialty Industrial Supplies (operates through Partsmaster) industrial and institutional maintenance oil and gas Parts Washing lubrication and biologicals.

NCH operates more than 40 separate business units. Subsidiary Supply Line Direct offers safety and maintenance products such as janitorial supplies safety signs first aid kits spills kits storage cabinets for hazardous chemicals and protective apparel. Its plumbing products group has plumbing supplies for OEM and retail consumer markets. Other subsidiaries include Pure Solve a parts washing service TERRA Services (which reduces hazardous chemicals used in the hydraulic fracturing process) and X-Chem an oil field services division.

Subsidiary companies in NCH's Chemical Specialties division produce a diverse array of maintenance chemicals that includes cleaners degreasers lubricants grounds care housekeeping and water treatment products. Companies in the Partsmaster group offer a wide variety of items for maintenance and repair including welding supplies and fasteners. The Plumbing Products Group provides plumbing supplies for the do-it-yourself retail consumer and the OEM market. The Retail Products Group markets a wide range of pet supplies.

Geographic Reach

NCH has operations in Asia Europe North America and Latin America. The company has representatives in 30 countries on five continents. The company's sales and service teams serve customers in North America Latin America Europe Asia Australia and India. NCH has wholly owned subsidiaries in more than 50 countries.

Sales and Marketing

NCH sells its products directly through a number of wholly owned subsidiaries many of which are engaged in the maintenance products business. These include Bags on Board Partsmaster Chemsearch Chem-Aqua and Mantek.

The Plumbing Products group provides supplies for the do-it-yourself consumer and the OEM market. The Retail Products group markets pet supplies. Other subsidiaries include X-Chem an oil field services division and Pure Solve a parts-washing business.

Strategy

NCH continues to seek new opportunities in water treatment oil and gas and in driving innovation to help keep its facilities and equipment running in optimum condition while reducing costs.

Research product development quality control field testing and customized analysis are all part of the ongoing efforts at NCH to deliver market-driven innovative and high-performing products to their customers and this strategy allowed them to remain competitive with larger corporations.

Descendants of founder Milton Levy own the company.

HISTORY

NCH was established in 1919.

Salesman Milton Levy founded National Disinfectant Co. in Dallas in 1919 to make disinfectants insecticides and soaps. The company's offerings grew in the 1930s to include Everbrite a top-selling industrial floor wax. Levy's sons Irvin Lester and Milton Jr. worked for the company as teenagers and took over its management after their father's death in 1946.

National Disinfectant expanded geographically in the 1950s and 1960s opening its first branch office in St. Louis in 1956. The company changed its name to National Chemsearch in 1960 to reflect its diversity. It also expanded into Europe and Latin America. National Chemsearch went public in 1965. Acquisitions boosted its product line to about 250 items by 1970. The company shortened its name to NCH in 1978.

NCH expanded its marketing to include catalog sales direct mail and telemarketing in 1986. It opened a South Korean plant in 1992. Troubled economies in Mexico and Venezuela hurt profits in 1994 and the next year NCH began work on a long-term business strategy that envisioned third-generation Levy family members moving into higher executive ranks.

Softened currency rates in Europe and Asia contributed to a decrease in profits for fiscal 1999. That year NCH focused on strengthening its customer relationships by boosting sales staff training and implementing an Internet-based corporate network.

In 2000 Irvin Levy became the company's chairman and NCH sold its electronic components business. The next year the company shut down its direct broadcast satellite equipment operations. In February 2002 the Levys took the company private by purchasing the 43% of the company that they didn't already own. The brothers originally offered a 20% premium to buy the shares but were greeted by lawsuits from shareholders who claimed they were taking advantage of a depressed market. The Levys settled the suits by upping the offer by $120 million.

In 2012 subsidiaries Chem-Aqua and Nephros signed a non-exclusive distributor agreement for Chem-Aqua to distribute Nephros's innovative ultrafilters in North America. The addition of Nephros ultrafilters to Chem-Aqua's product line allows both companies to offer their institutional customers a comprehensive multi-barrier approach for the prevention of waterborne infection.

EXECUTIVES

Vice President of Information Technology Operations, Jim Marshal
President NCH Asia, Dong Eun Kim
Managing Director, Joe Bond
Vice President Marketing and Product Management Executive, Kevin Jones
Senior Vice President Sales, Brenda Sanders
Senior Vice President, Roy Levin
Executive Vice President, Robert Levy
Senior Vice President, Terry Waldo
Vice President Global Travel Management, Ann Levy
Vice President Finance And Global Controller, John Currie
Vice President of Global Logistics, Shayne Mai
Vice President of Finance, Pete Bocian
Executive Vice President Customer Relationship, Susan Staples
Senior Vice President Planning and Business Development Ppg and Rpg, Matthew Bremer
Senior Vice President Training, John Arakelian
Senior Vice President Domestic Sales Mantek Division, Joel Derketsch
Vice President of Operations, James Marshall
Executive Vice President, Walter Levy
Vice President, William Stivers
Vice President Treasurer, Irena Kildisas
Vice President Research and Development, John Roheim
Vice President, Jerry Finn
Vice President Information Technology, Leonard Brown
Vice President IS, Bill Stivers
Vice President, Bruce Weinberg
Vice President Strategy And Business Development, Mike Howdeshell
Vice President, Andy Leslie
National Account Manager, Sally French
Board Member, Marga Tubb
Treasurer, Joe Farrier
Auditors: PRICEWATERHOUSECOOPERS LLP DA

LOCATIONS

HQ: NCH CORPORATION
2727 CHEMSEARCH BLVD, IRVING, TX 750626454
Phone: 972 438-0211
Web: WWW.NCH.COM

PRODUCTS/OPERATIONS

Selected Operations and Products
Chemical Specialties
　Cleaning chemicals
　Deodorizers
　Floor and carpet care products
　HVAC products
　Lubricants
　Oil production facility chemicals
　Paint
　Paint removers
　Water-treatment chemicals
Landmark Direct
　First-aid supplies
　Workplace signage and productivity products
Pet Care
Partsmaster Group
　Cutting tools
　Electrical products
　Fasteners
　Welding alloys
Plumbing Products Group
　Plumbing products for new construction
　Plumbing repair and replacement parts
Industrial and Institutional Maintenance
Industrial and commercial cleaning
Industrial Repair and maintenance
Drains Grease Traps and lift stations
Lubrication and coolants
Equipment and supplies
Parts washing
Grounds Care
Personal hygiene
Pet Care
Training pads
Stain and Odor Removers
Cleaners and Disinfectants
Allergy Relief and shed Control
Grooming products
Plumbing
Sinks
Faucets
Tub & Showers
Toilets
Drains
Specialty Industrial Supply
High Performance Cutting Tools

Welding
Abrasives
Compounds
Fasteners
Electrical and Automotive
Shop Supplies
Storage Hardware
Tools
Water Treatment Solutions
Boiler
Cooling Towers
Colsed Recirculation Systems
Biocides and Algaecides
Cleaner/Descalers
Equipment
Wastewater and Bio Remediation

COMPETITORS

Church & Dwight	H.B. Fuller
Cintas	Illinois Tool Works
Clariant	Pioneer Corporation
Danaher	Quaker Chemical
Detrex	Safety-Kleen
Ecolab	WD-40

HISTORICAL FINANCIALS
Company Type: Private

Income Statement
FYE: April 30

	REVENUE ($ mil.)	NET INCOME ($ mil.)	NET PROFIT MARGIN	EMPLOYEES
04/16	996	0	0.0%	8,500
04/12	1,045	6	0.6%	—
04/11	952	6	0.7%	—
Annual Growth	0.9%	(52.6%)	—	—

2016 Year-End Financials
Return on assets: 7.8% Cash ($ mil.): 10
Return on equity: —
Current ratio: 1.30

NCL CORPORATION LTD.

EXECUTIVES

President, Frank J Del Rio
Senior Vice-President, Daniel S Farkas
President, Robert J Binder
Purchasing Agent, Monique Rubio
Director, Isis Ruiz
Consultant, Lionel Arleo
Auditors: PRICEWATERHOUSECOOPERS LLP MI

LOCATIONS

HQ: NCL CORPORATION LTD.
7665 CORPORATE CENTER DR, MIAMI, FL
331261201
Phone: 305 436-4000

HISTORICAL FINANCIALS
Company Type: Private

Income Statement
FYE: December 31

	REVENUE ($ mil.)	NET INCOME ($ mil.)	NET PROFIT MARGIN	EMPLOYEES
12/16	4,874	643	13.2%	24,900
12/15	4,345	437	10.1%	—
12/14	3,125	339	10.8%	—
12/13	2,570	119	4.7%	—
Annual Growth	23.8%	75.1%	—	—

2016 Year-End Financials
Return on assets: 0.8% Cash ($ mil.): 126
Return on equity: 13.2%
Current ratio: 0.10

NEBRASKA ELECTRIC GENERATION & TRANSMISSION COOPERATIVE INC

EXECUTIVES

President, Mike Siefken
General Manager, Bruce Pontow

LOCATIONS

HQ: NEBRASKA ELECTRIC GENERATION &
TRANSMISSION COOPERATIVE INC
2472 18TH AVE, COLUMBUS, NE 686012604
Phone: 402 564-8142
Web: WWW.NEGT.COOP

HISTORICAL FINANCIALS
Company Type: Private

Income Statement
FYE: December 31

	REVENUE ($ mil.)	NET INCOME ($ mil.)	NET PROFIT MARGIN	EMPLOYEES
12/15	247	0	—	4
12/14	274	0	—	—
12/12	267	0	—	—
12/10	191	0	0.0%	—
Annual Growth	5.2%	—	—	—

2015 Year-End Financials
Return on assets: 12.0% Cash ($ mil.): 4
Return on equity: —
Current ratio: 1.00

NEBRASKA METHODIST HOSPITAL INC

EXECUTIVES

President, John M Fraser
Director of Finance, Dough Kucera
Director, Matt Stockfeld
Director, Denise Carlson
VP Finance, Ray Stoupe
Director, Julie Richards

LOCATIONS

HQ: NEBRASKA METHODIST HOSPITAL INC
8303 DODGE ST, OMAHA, NE 681144108
Phone: 402 354-4540

HISTORICAL FINANCIALS
Company Type: Private

Income Statement
FYE: December 31

	REVENUE ($ mil.)	NET INCOME ($ mil.)	NET PROFIT MARGIN	EMPLOYEES
12/15	511	51	10.1%	2,635
12/14	449	55	12.3%	—
12/13	461	33	7.2%	—
12/12	410	30	7.4%	—
Annual Growth	7.6%	19.4%	—	—

2015 Year-End Financials
Return on assets: 5.1% Cash ($ mil.): 86
Return on equity: 10.1%
Current ratio: 1.90

NEBRASKA PUBLIC POWER DISTRICT

Nebraska Public Power District (NPPD) electrifies the Cornhusker State. The government-owned electric utility the largest in the state provides power in 86 of the state's 93 counties. The firm has a generating capacity of about 3130 MW and operates more than 5200 miles of transmission lines. NPPD distributes electricity to about 89000 retail customers in 81 cities and towns; it also provides power to about 1 million customers through wholesale power contracts with more than 50 towns and 25 public power districts. In addition NPPD purchases electricity from the federally owned Western Area Power Administration and operates a surface water irrigation system.

Operations

The company uses multiple sources including nuclear steam mixed wind hydro and diesel to generate power.

NPPD's revenues comes from wholesale power supply agreements with 50 towns and 25 rural public power districts and rural cooperatives who rely totally or partially on NPPD's electrical system. NPPD also serves about 81 communities at the retail level.

Financial Performance

Revenues for 2013 increased by 2% due mostly to rate increases and sales to other utilities. Net income jumped 30% on the revenue increase and reduced costs. Cash from operations followed suit and rose nearly $100 million.

Strategy

Faced with growing long-term demand for electricity along with pressure to keep prices low NPPD has implemented plans to increase transmission capacity. With a goal of getting of 15% it energy from renewable sources by 2025 the company is exploring alternative fuel sources for future plants. With 45% of NPPD's energy supply coming from coal in 2011 the company was looking to cleaner alternatives such as wind power and biomass in order to meet stricter environmental regulations. In 2014 it signed a deal to purchase wind power from Sempra a move that put it within sight of its goal to have 10% of its power generation come from renewable sources.

Company Background

NPPD was formed in 1970 through the merger of three public utilities: Consumers Public Power District Platte Valley Public Power and Irrigation District and Nebraska Public Power System.

EXECUTIVES

Vice President, William Merrill
Vice President Human Resources and Corporate Support, Roy Steiner
Vice President, Mike Dixon
Auditors: PRICEWATERHOUSECOOPERS LLP ST

LOCATIONS

HQ: NEBRASKA PUBLIC POWER DISTRICT
1414 15TH ST, COLUMBUS, NE 686015226
Phone: 402 563-5481
Web: WWW.NPPD.COM

PRODUCTS/OPERATIONS

2013 Sales

	$ mil.	% of total
Wholesale	584	53
Retail	294	27
Other	227	20
Total	**1,106**	**100**

COMPETITORS

Basin Electric Power	Omaha Public Power
Berkshire Hathaway	Tri-State Generation
Energy	and Transmission
NorthWestern	

HISTORICAL FINANCIALS
Company Type: Private

Income Statement
FYE: December 31

	REVENUE ($ mil.)	NET INCOME ($ mil.)	NET PROFIT MARGIN	EMPLOYEES
12/15	1,097	91	8.3%	1,966
12/14	1,122	62	5.6%	—
12/13	1,106	97	8.8%	—
12/12	1,081	75	6.9%	—
Annual Growth	0.5%	6.7%		

2015 Year-End Financials

Return on assets: 5.8%
Return on equity: 8.3%
Current ratio: 0.90

Cash ($ mil.): 85

NEW BRUNSWICK PUBLIC SCHOOLS

EXECUTIVES

Superintendent, Aubrey Johnson
Consultant, Jennifer Gates
Director, Greg Bartell
Director, Barbi Siegel
Administrative Assistant, Ivania Cortez
Auditors: SAMUEL KLEIN AND COMPANY NEWA

LOCATIONS

HQ: NEW BRUNSWICK PUBLIC SCHOOLS
268 BALDWIN ST, NEW BRUNSWICK, NJ 089012947
Phone: 732 745-5300
Web: WWW.NBPSCHOOLS.NET

HISTORICAL FINANCIALS
Company Type: Private

Income Statement
FYE: June 30

	REVENUE ($ mil.)	NET INCOME ($ mil.)	NET PROFIT MARGIN	EMPLOYEES
06/16	204	(1)	—	1,352
06/02*	106	(9)	—	—
03/01	0	0	—	—
Annual Growth	—	—		

*Fiscal year change

2016 Year-End Financials

Return on assets: 2.8%
Return on equity: (-0.8%)
Current ratio: —

Cash ($ mil.): 16

NEW ENGLAND BAPTIST HOSPITAL INC

EXECUTIVES

Chief Executive Officer, Joe Dioniso
Chief Operating Officer, Arnold Scheller

LOCATIONS

HQ: NEW ENGLAND BAPTIST HOSPITAL INC
125 PARKER HILL AVE STE 2, BOSTON, MA
021202865
Phone: 617 754-5000
Web: WWW.NEBH.ORG

HISTORICAL FINANCIALS
Company Type: Private

Income Statement
FYE: September 30

	REVENUE ($ mil.)	NET INCOME ($ mil.)	NET PROFIT MARGIN	EMPLOYEES
09/15	227	5	2.6%	1,200
09/14	220	5	2.5%	—
09/13	206	10	5.3%	—
Annual Growth	4.8%	(26.4%)	—	—

2015 Year-End Financials

Return on assets: 3.9%
Return on equity: 2.6%
Current ratio: 1.60

Cash ($ mil.): 21

NEW HANOVER REGIONAL MEDICAL CENTER

Those living in the Cape Fear area need not fear when it comes to accessing good medical care. Integrated health system New Hanover Regional Medical Center (NHRMC) serves the Wilmington and Cape Fear area of North Carolina through its flagship 855-bed New Hanover Regional Medical Center the 130-bed Cape Fear Hospital and the 85-bed Pender Memorial Hospital. NHRMC also operates a rehabilitation center a behavioral health facility and a women's and children's hospital as well as home health hospice EMS transport physician practice and outpatient care clinic locations. The not-for-profit health network is affiliated with the UNC-Chapel Hill School of Medicine.

Operations

NHRMC's medical staff includes more than 550 physicians and 700 active volunteers.

NHRMC is part of the Coastal Carolinas Health Alliance a cooperative of regional hospitals that use their combined buying size to negotiate lower prices for hospital equipment and supplies. The group also works together to increase community access to health care and promote continuing medical education amongst its peers.

The company's orthopedic hospital performs 8000 orthopedic procedures a year including more than 2200 joint replacement surgeries.

Geographic Reach

NHRMC's hospitals serve southeastern North Carolina. Its main campus is in Wilmington; the health network also operates the Cape Fear Hos-

pital in Wilmington and the Pender Memorial Hospital in Burgaw.

Financial Performance

NHRMC's revenues grew by 5% in 2014 due to higher Net patient service revenues thanks to increased use of both inpatient and outpatient services.

Net income increased by 5% as the result of higher revenues and a net increase in the fair value of investments.

NHRMC's operating cash flow decreased by 7% in 2014 due to an increase in cash used to pay suppliers for goods and services and employees for services.

Strategy

The medical center has consistently expanded services into the surrounding region to include construction of NHRMC ED-North a standalone emergency department that opened in May 2015.

In 2015 NHRMC completed the construction of a new standalone emergency department in the northern part of New Hanover County.The 30000 square foot building has 10 treatment rooms and one critical care room and is staffed 24/7 by board-certified emergency physicians nurses certified in emergency care and a multidisciplinary support care team. The building designed by BBH Design and constructed by Brasfield & Gorrie cost $15.1 million to build and the project was funded from NHRMC's capital budget.

Company Background

In 2013 NHRMC expanded its EMS transportation services by expanding its AirLink program. The medical center added a second helicopter to provide services in Onslow and Columbus counties. The move will help the organization reduce response times and improve critical care services.

In addition the medical center expanded outpatient care services in 2012 through the addition of a multi-specialty physician group (Hanover Medical Specialists) to its physician practice group.

The medical network is governed by a board of trustees consisting of members appointed by the New Hanover County commissioners and representatives from the neighboring Pender County.

EXECUTIVES

Chief Executive Officer, John Gizdic
Chief Financial Officer, Ed Ollie
Chief Operating Officer, Andre Boyd
Branch Manager, Virginia Barkman
Financial Executive, Brad Vass

LOCATIONS

HQ: NEW HANOVER REGIONAL MEDICAL CENTER
2131 S 17TH ST, WILMINGTON, NC 284017407
Phone: 910 343-7001
Web: WWW.NHRMC.ORG

PRODUCTS/OPERATIONS

Selected Services
Bariatrics
Breast
Cancer Behavioral
Cancer
Children
Cardiology
Diabetes
Eye Care
Emergency
Gynecology
HIV Aids
Home Care
Heart
Maternity
Maxillofacial
Neonatology
Neurosurgery
Oral Surgery
Oncology
Orthopedics
Optometry

Occupational Therapy

Selected Locations

Behavioral Health Hospital (Wilmington North Carolina)
Betty H. Cameron Women's and Children's Hospital
 (Wilmington North Carolina)
Cape Fear Hospital (Wilmington North Carolina)
New Hanover Regional Medical Center (main campus;
 Wilmington North Carolina)
Pender Memorial Hospital (Burgaw North Carolina)
Rehabilitation Hospital (Wilmington North Carolina)

COMPETITORS

Blue Ridge HealthCare	High Point Regional
Carolinas HealthCare	Health System
System	Mission Hospitals
Community Health	Novant Health
Systems	UNC Hospitals
Conway Medical Center	
Grand Strand Regional	
Medical Center	

HISTORICAL FINANCIALS

Company Type: Private

Income Statement

FYE: December 31

	REVENUE ($ mil.)	NET INCOME ($ mil.)	NET PROFIT MARGIN	EMPLOYEES
12/16	235	22	9.4%	3,692
12/15*	246	22	9.2%	—
06/15	601	83	13.9%	—
12/14	200	26	13.1%	—
Annual Growth	8.3%	(8.3%)	—	—

*Fiscal year change

2016 Year-End Financials

Return on assets: 16.9%   Cash ($ mil.): 79
Return on equity: 9.4%
Current ratio: 1.50

NEW JERSEY INSTITUTE OF TECHNOLOGY (INC)

A public research university New Jersey Institute of Technology (NJIT) offers about 100 undergraduate and graduate programs including about 20 doctoral programs in fields including architecture engineering computer science and liberal arts. The school also offers continuing education and distance courses. With some 500 full-time faculty members NJIT boasts a student-faulty ratio of 16:1. Its Albert Dorman Honors College provides students with individualized curricula and honors colloquia including travel and featured speakers. About 10000 students attend the NJIT which operates a single campus in Newark. NJIT was founded in 1881 as the Newark Technical School.

Operations

Newark's NJIT has some 7125 undergraduate and 2825 graduate students. Master's programs are offered across 56 specialties. The school also offers some 46 baccalaureate degree programs.

Financial Performance

Thanks to organic growth the university has logged revenue increases during the past three years. NJIT's revenue rose some 11% in 2011 vs. 2010 due to increases in tuition and fees and auxiliary enterprise revenues attributable to a boost in occupancy and residence hall charges and increases in federal state and other grants and contracts. Net income during the same reporting period increased by 61%. NJIT points to income from realized net gains on the sale of investments (par-

tially offset by a decrease in interest and dividends) for the increases. Cash generated from tuition and fees and auxiliary enterprises contributed toward a cash flow bump of more than $20 million in 2011 vs. 2010.

Strategy

Looking to provide additional capacity for students to reside on campus NJIT focuses on campus and area development. Through the efforts of three ongoing projects the university is working to enhance campus life for its students and increase its residential student numbers on campus by 600.

EXECUTIVES

Vice President of Administrati, Henry Mauermayer
Vice President Human Resources, Kay Clarke-Turner
Vice President Finance, William Garcia
Executive Vice President Technology, Jerry Paris
Vice President for Human Resources, Theodore Johnson
Vice President for Research and Development, Nancy Steffen-Fluhr
Vice President for Academic Support and Student Affairs, Charles Fey
Associate Vice President for Enrollment Management, Wendy Lin-cook
Managing Director, Paul Rogers
Vice President, Richard O'Leary
Advisory Board Member, Eseosa Eriamiato
Treasurer, Jason Cabrejos
Secretary, Norma Montague
Treasurer, Nicholas Tworischuk
Auditors: GRANT THORNTON LLP EDISON N

LOCATIONS

HQ: NEW JERSEY INSTITUTE OF TECHNOLOGY (INC)
 323 DR MARTIN LUTH, NEWARK, NJ 07102
Phone: 973 596-3000

PRODUCTS/OPERATIONS

Selected Colleges

Newark College of Engineering
College of Architecture and Design
College of Science and Liberal Arts
School of Management
Albert Dorman Honors College
College of Computing Sciences

HISTORICAL FINANCIALS

Company Type: Private

Income Statement

FYE: June 30

	REVENUE ($ mil.)	NET INCOME ($ mil.)	NET PROFIT MARGIN	EMPLOYEES
06/16	263	5	2.2%	1,047
06/13	210	17	8.3%	—
06/12	197	0	0.3%	—
06/11	785	0	—	—
Annual Growth	—	573.8%	—	—

2016 Year-End Financials

Return on assets: 18.1%   Cash ($ mil.): 79
Return on equity: 2.2%
Current ratio: 1.50

NEW PRIME, INC.

Specialized carrier New Prime (which does business simply as Prime) provides refrigerated flatbed tanker and intermodal trucking services throughout North America through more than 10000 remotely monitored temperature-controlled trailers.

The company operates in the US and Canada and serves Mexico through arrangements with other carriers. A subsidiary Prime Floral uses the parent company's refrigerated equipment and facilities to serve the flower industry. In addition to its freight-hauling operations Prime provides logistics services including freight brokerage.

Operations

Prime which has a fleet of more than 4700 trucks operates through three divisions.

Prime's liquid bulk fleet (Tanker Division) consists of more than 200 trucks and more than 400 6800-gallon Walker Stainless MC407 trailers with air ride suspensions. The company's Refrigerated Division has a fleet of remotely monitored temperature-controlled trailers and serves businesses whose needs include transportation of fresh produce fresh cut floral produce pharmaceuticals fresh or frozen meats or any other dry or temperature controlled freight. Prime also has a Flatbed Division.

Its affiliates include Amber Aleri Prime Floral Prime Intermodal Prime Logistics and Trailer Skirt.

Geographic Reach

The company serves customers in Canada Mexico and the US. Based in Springfield Missouri Prime operates two US terminals in Pennsylvania and Utah.

Sales and Marketing

Prime has hauled goods for such blue chip consumer goods makers as ConAgra Foods Kraft Foods and General Mills. It markets its products through independent contractors stores and online.

Strategy

Prime is shifting its strategy to align with customer preferences for shortening supply chain mileage and delivery time all of which is intended to offset lower consumer demand and volatile fuel costs.

It is also using technology to enhance its position as an industry leader in the safe cost-effective transport of temperature-sensitive goods. Its Prime Position Tracking software enables the company to locate tractors in real-time within a 600 foot radius at all times. Prime Mapping and Routing provides detailed Rand McNally and PC*Miler directions to driver associates to ensure that loads get to their destination in the quickest safest and most efficient manner.

Company Background

Prime was founded in 1970 by Robert Low who continues to serve as Prime's president.

EXECUTIVES

President and CEO, Robert E. Low
Manager of Success Leasing Program, Fred Ege
Director of Logistics, Rick Gallagher
Director of Operations, Pat Leonard
Director of Flatbed and Tanker Operations, Jim Wilkins
VP Sales and Marketing, Steve Wutke
Director of Finance, Dean Hoedl
Director of Technology, Rodney Rader
Manager of Tanker Division, Brett Vonwiller
Auditors: ABACUS CPAS LLC SPRINGFIELD

LOCATIONS

HQ: NEW PRIME, INC.
 2740 N MAYFAIR AVE, SPRINGFIELD, MO 658035084
Phone: 800 321-4552
Web: WWW.PRIMEINC.COM

COMPETITORS

Boyd Bros.	Comcar
Transportation	Frozen Food Express
C.H. Robinson	KLLM Transport
Worldwide	Services
C.R. England	Marten Transport

Central Refrigerated Service   Quality Distribution Stevens Transport

HISTORICAL FINANCIALS
Company Type: Private

Income Statement
FYE: April 1

	REVENUE ($ mil.)	NET INCOME ($ mil.)	NET PROFIT MARGIN	EMPLOYEES
04/16*	1,598	133	8.3%	5,000
03/12	1,022	60	6.0%	—
04/11	941	47	5.0%	—
Annual Growth	11.2%	23.0%	—	—

*Fiscal year change

2016 Year-End Financials
Return on assets: 1.7%
Return on equity: 8.3%
Current ratio: 0.70
Cash ($ mil.): —

NEW RIVER ELECTRICAL CORPORATION

EXECUTIVES
President, Thomas M Wolden
Vice-President, R C Furr II
Auditors: KENNETT & KENNETT PC ROANOKE

LOCATIONS
HQ: NEW RIVER ELECTRICAL CORPORATION
  15 CLOVERDALE PL, CLOVERDALE, VA 240773124
Phone: 540 966-1650
Web: WWW.NEWRIVERELECTRICAL.COM

HISTORICAL FINANCIALS
Company Type: Private

Income Statement
FYE: December 31

	REVENUE ($ mil.)	NET INCOME ($ mil.)	NET PROFIT MARGIN	EMPLOYEES
12/15	271	22	8.3%	900
12/14	242	19	8.2%	—
12/13	179	16	9.2%	—
12/12	157	14	9.4%	—
Annual Growth	19.9%	15.0%	—	—

2015 Year-End Financials
Return on assets: 1.4%
Return on equity: 8.3%
Current ratio: 4.40
Cash ($ mil.): 34

NEW YORK BLOOD CENTER, INC.

New York Blood Center (NYBC) holds a very literal interpretation of the meaning of life. It is a not-for-profit blood distribution and research organization serving New York City and its environs in New York State and New Jersey as well as parts of Connecticut and Pennsylvania. As one of the largest blood centers in the US NYBC provides nearly 1 million blood components to some 200 hospitals each year. The center's facilities collect blood from more than 2000 donors each day. It also operates the nation's oldest and largest public cord blood bank. In addition its Kimball Research Institute includes more than a dozen research laboratories which study the prevention and treatment of blood-related illnesses.

Operations

Areas of research in the Kimball Research Institute include virology molecular genetics cell biology and signaling viral immunology and infectious disease prevention. It has been responsible for the development and licensing of solvent and detergent technology used to deactivate the potency of viruses in blood and blood products (such as plasma and platelets used in transfusions).

NYBC's clinical services division acts as an adjunct and resource to hospitals throughout its service areas by providing expertise in transfusion medicine as well as delivering more than 8500 specialized procedures each year. In addition the center maintains a bone marrow donor registry for the New York area provides hemophilia services to some 1500 patients and offers screening and education programs for cholesterol high blood pressure and cardiovascular disease.

Geographic Reach

Based in New York NYBC offers its services throughout New York City Long Island the Hudson Valley and in Connecticut New Jersey and Pennsylvania.

Strategy

Seeking greater breadth and financial stability NYBC announced it will combine its operations with Community Blood Center of Greater Kansas City (CBC) to form one of the leading blood centers serving patients and hospitals in the Northeast and Midwest. The combination is expected to be completed in mid-2014. The union of NYBC and CBC is expected to bring synergies in blood and laboratory services medical programs cell therapies and research.

Mergers and Acquisitions

In October 2013 NYBC acquired Coral Blood Services a subsidiary of HemaCare Corp. to advance its mission of providing innovative blood products and medical services to hospitals and patients throughout the Northeast. Coral Blood Services provides more than 2500 therapeutic apheresis procedures annually in New York New Jersey Connecticut and Pennsylvania.

EXECUTIVES
Vice President Quality Assurance, Donald Kender
CIO, Michele Scaggiante
VP and Director Lindsley F. Kimball Research Institute, Mohandas Narla
Director National Cord Blood Program, Pablo Rubinstein
President and CEO, Christopher D. Hillyer
Head of the Viral Immunology Laboratory, Shibo Jiang
SVP and CFO, Elizabeth C. Gibson
Senior Vice President, Paddy C Mullen
Senior Vice President, Frederick W Hill
Senior Vice President, John R Mullen
Vice President Customer Service, Robert Purvis
Senior Vice President Human RE, Ollie Cheatham
Vice President and General Counsel, David Whitescarver
Vice President, Charles Grossenbacher
Adrp Treasurer Committee Oversight, Christine Foran
Auditors: KPMG LLP NEW YORK NY

LOCATIONS
HQ: NEW YORK BLOOD CENTER, INC.
  310 E 67TH ST, NEW YORK, NY 100656273
Phone: 212 570-3010
Web: WWW.NYBLOODCENTER.ORG

PRODUCTS/OPERATIONS

Selected Services
Blood products
Clinical services
Hemochromatosis phlebotomy program
Hemophilia services
Laboratory services
Ordertrak
Transfusion medicine services

COMPETITORS
Blood Systems Inc.
CSL Behring
Daxor
Red Cross
SeraCare Life Sciences

HISTORICAL FINANCIALS
Company Type: Private

Income Statement
FYE: March 31

	REVENUE ($ mil.)	NET INCOME ($ mil.)	NET PROFIT MARGIN	EMPLOYEES
03/15	320	(0)	—	1,600
03/11	348	(11)	—	—
03/10	375	20	5.4%	—
Annual Growth	(3.1%)	—	—	—

2015 Year-End Financials
Return on assets: 11.5%
Return on equity: (-0.3%)
Current ratio: 2.10
Cash ($ mil.): 38

NEW YORK CONVENTION CENTER OPERATING CORPORATION

The New York Convention Center Operating Corporation may be able to claim that it has the whole world in its hand since it's the manager and operator of the "marketplace for the world" (also know as the Jacob K. Javits Convention Center in Manhattan). The center serves as host each year for myriad conventions fashion shows association meetings trade shows and more. The center features such amenities as restaurants and cocktail lounges temporary private office rentals and concierge service. The New York Convention Center Operating Corporation (also known as NYC-COC) was established in 1979 to manage the Javits Center.

After an earlier plan was abandoned ground was broken in 2006 on a $1.7 billion dollar expansion project that expand the center's size by 45 percent and include a hotel. The project is scheduled for completion by 2010 and when finished the Javits Center will be the 5th largest convention center in the U.S.

In 2008 Governor David Paterson also approved a renovation and modest additional expansion for Javits with plans for an additional 50000 square feet of exposition space and a truck storage area.

EXECUTIVES
Senior Vice President General Counsel, Bradley Siciliano
Senior Vice President of Development, Margaret Tobin
Vice President and General Counselor, Morris Dershowitz

LOCATIONS

HQ: NEW YORK CONVENTION CENTER OPERATING
 CORPORATION
 655 W 34TH ST, NEW YORK, NY 100011114
Phone: 212 216-2000
Web: WWW.JAVITSCENTER.COM

COMPETITORS

AMC	Madison Square Garden
Dallas Market Center	SMG Management
Gaylord Entertainment	

HISTORICAL FINANCIALS

Company Type: Private

Income Statement

FYE: March 31

	REVENUE ($ mil.)	NET INCOME ($ mil.)	NET PROFIT MARGIN	EMPLOYEES
03/16	190	2	1.4%	3,500
03/15	169	1	0.6%	—
03/08	143	(8)	—	—
03/07	133	(8)	—	—
Annual Growth	4.0%	—	—	—

2016 Year-End Financials

Return on assets: 6.6%   Cash ($ mil.): 5
Return on equity: 1.4%
Current ratio: 0.10

NEW YORK POWER AUTHORITY

The hydropower generated by the mighty Niagara Falls is the real authority behind the New York Power Authority (NYPA). More than 70% of the power that NYPA produces is from hydropower resources. The company generates and transmits more than 20% of New York's electricity making it the largest state-owned public power provider in the US. It is also New York's only statewide electricity supplier. NYPA owns hydroelectric and fossil-fueled generating facilities (16 in total) that produce about 5700 MW of electricity and it operates more than 1400 circuit-miles of transmission lines. NYPA is owned by the State of New York.

Geographic Reach

The company serves customers throughout New York State various public corporations in Southeastern New York within the metropolitan area of New York City (SENY Governmental Customers) and certain out-of-state customers.

Sales and Marketing

NYPA services more than 500 businesses and industrial customers including manufacturing companies such as Anchor Glass of Elmira and General Motors of Tonawanda and non-manufacturing companies like GEICO of Amherst and Yahoo! of Lockport and 114 government entities in New York City and Westchester County including New York City government the Metropolitan Transportation Authority The Port Authority of New York and New Jersey the New York City Housing Authority Westchester County government and most Westchester municipalities school districts and other public entities.

The company provides electricity to 51 municipal and cooperative electric systems to sell to their customers.

Financial Performance

In 2014 the company's net revenues increased by 5% to $3.18 billion due to a higher volume of market energy and capacity sales and higher prices on those sales.

Net income grew by 9% due to higher net revenues and an increase in investment income.

In 2014 NYPA's operating cash inflow slightly decreased by 0.2% due to changes in working capital.

Strategy

NYPA receives no state funds or tax credits. Instead it finances new projects through bond sales.

Following its shift from a regulated monopoly to a competitor in an open power market NYPA is aiming to grow by reducing the cost of the energy it provides and by developing electric transportation (such as electric cars) and other energy-efficiency projects including installing emergency power generators in metropolitan buildings. It is also working to improve the state's transmission grid increase its generating capacity and help support the state's directive to get 45% of its power from clean energy sources (including 100 MW of power from solar arrays at buildings across the state). NYPA has been tagged as the lead agency to reduce energy use at state facilities by 20% by 2020.

In 2014 NYPA completed the installation of solar thermal hot water systems at five New York City firehouses in the Rockaways section of Queens. The $550000 investment will reduce operating costs and could lead to the wider use of the clean energy-transfer technology in other city government facilities. The company's energy efficiency projects have saved New Yorkers more than $148 million a year cutting annual oil use by more than 2.7 million barrels and offsetting the release of approximately 890000 tons of greenhouse gases. Its clean transportation program has placed more than 1300 electric-drive vehicles into service.

To improve its delivery of power the company is pursuing the development of a new cross-Hudson transmission line that will connect New York City customers to the PJM Interconnection power grid.

HISTORY

The Power Authority of the State of New York (aka New York Power Authority or NYPA) was established in 1931 by Gov. Franklin Roosevelt to gain public control of New York's hydropower resources. The utility's major power plants came on line with the opening of the St. Lawrence-Franklin D. Roosevelt Power Project (1958) and the Niagara Power Project (1961). The Blenheim-Gilboa Pumped Storage Power Project opened in 1973.

In the mid-1970s NYPA shifted to nuclear power when it opened the James A. FitzPatrick Nuclear Power Plant (1975) and the Indian Point 3 Nuclear Power Plant (1976). The company then opened gas- and oil-powered plants: the Charles Poletti Power Project (1977) and the Richard M. Flynn Power Plant (1994).

In 1998 the authority allocated low-cost electricity to five companies that planned to invest $104 million in business expansions in western New York. The company suffered a loss in 1999 in part from reduced hydro generation and a drop in investment earnings. In 2000 NYPA sold its two nuclear plants (1800 MW of capacity) to utility holding company Entergy for $967 million.

The company completed the installation of 11 gas-powered turbines at various locations in New York City and on Long Island in 2001; the pro-

gram was initiated to prevent expected energy shortages that summer but it also helped maintain power in areas of the city during the September 11 terrorist attacks.

In 2013 The Village of Lake Placid unveiled a new hybrid-electric shuttle bus that will make commuting on public transportation quieter and cleaner. Financing for the bus was made possible through NYPA's Municipal Electric-Drive Vehicle Program which provides financial assistance to New York municipal utilities to facilitate the replacement of less fuel-efficient vehicles in order to advance the state's clean energy goals. That year NYPA added seven more hybrids and one more EV to its fleet bringing the total number of electric drive vehicles to 79. It also purchased just over 40000 gallons of B20 biodiesel which earned the Power Authority 17 Alternative Fuel Vehicle credits under the Department of Energy's Energy Policy Act that will be used to purchase additional hybrid and plug-in hybrid vehicles.

EXECUTIVES

COO, Edward A. (Ed) Welz
President and CEO, Gil C. Quiniones
EVP and CFO, Robert F. Lurie
Vice President Environment Health And Safety,
 William Slade
Chairman Board of Trustees, John R. Koelmel
Vice Chair Board of Trustees, Joanne M. Mahoney
Auditors: KPMG LLP NEW YORK NY

LOCATIONS

HQ: NEW YORK POWER AUTHORITY
 123 MAIN ST, WHITE PLAINS, NY 106013104
Phone: 914 681-6200
Web: WWW.NYPA.GOV

PRODUCTS/OPERATIONS

2014 Sales

	$ mil.	% of total
Power sales	2,396	76
Wheeling charges	614	19
Transmission charges	165	5
Total	**3,175**	**100**

Selected Operations

Transmission Control Facility
 Frederick R. Clark Energy Center (Oneida County)
Fossil-Fueled Plants
 Charles Poletti Power Project (New York City)
 Richard M. Flynn Power Plant (Suffolk County)
 PowerNow! Turbines (11 units in New York City and
 Long Island)
Hydropower Plants
 Blenheim-Gilboa Pumped Storage Power Project
 (Schoharie County)
 Niagara Power Project (Niagara County)
 St. Lawrence-Franklin D. Roosevelt Power Project (St.
 Lawrence County)
Small Hydropower Plants
 Ashokan Project (Ulster County)
 Crescent Plant (Albany and Saratoga Counties)
 Gregory B. Jarvis Plant (Oneida County)
 Kensico Project (Westchester County)
 Vischer Ferry Plant (Saratoga and Schenectady
 counties)

COMPETITORS

Avangrid	Entergy
CH Energy	National Grid USA
Con Edison	Rochester Gas and
Dynegy	Electric
Enbridge	TransCanada

HISTORICAL FINANCIALS

Company Type: Private

Income Statement

FYE: December 31

	REVENUE ($ mil.)	NET INCOME ($ mil.)	NET PROFIT MARGIN	EMPLOYEES
12/15	2,625	74	2.8%	1,700
12/14	3,175	272	8.6%	—
12/13	3,030	249	8.2%	—
12/12	2,673	175	6.5%	—
Annual Growth	(0.6%)	(24.9%)	—	—

2015 Year-End Financials

Return on assets: 13.8%   Cash ($ mil.): 67
Return on equity: 2.8%
Current ratio: 0.20

NEW YORK PRESBYTERIAN HOSPITAL WEILL CORNELL UNIVERSITY MEDICAL CENTER

EXECUTIVES

Principal, Lewis Drusin
Auditors: ERNST & YOUNG US LLP INDIANAP

LOCATIONS

HQ: NEW YORK PRESBYTERIAN HOSPITAL WEILL
CORNELL UNIVERSITY MEDICAL CENTER
525 E 68TH ST, NEW YORK, NY 100654870
Phone: 212 746-1754
Web: WWW.MED.CORNELL.EDU

HISTORICAL FINANCIALS

Company Type: Private

Income Statement

FYE: December 31

	REVENUE ($ mil.)	NET INCOME ($ mil.)	NET PROFIT MARGIN	EMPLOYEES
12/15	4,505	265	5.9%	5
12/12	75	21	28.2%	—
Annual Growth	290.4%	131.8%	—	—

2015 Year-End Financials

Return on assets: 8.7%   Cash ($ mil.): 227
Return on equity: 5.9%
Current ratio: 0.80

NEW YORK SHIPPING ASSOCIATION INC

EXECUTIVES

President, John Nardi

Executive Vice-President, Charles Darrell
Chief Financial Officer, Daniel Massaro
Director, Susan Winfree
Manager, Anna Fassari
Account Manager, Kathy Schiereck
Manager, Steven J Pessel

LOCATIONS

HQ: NEW YORK SHIPPING ASSOCIATION INC
333 THORNALL ST STE 3A, EDISON, NJ 088372220
Phone: 732 452-7800
Web: WWW.NYSANET.ORG

HISTORICAL FINANCIALS

Company Type: Private

Income Statement

FYE: September 30

	REVENUE ($ mil.)	NET INCOME ($ mil.)	NET PROFIT MARGIN	EMPLOYEES
09/15	263	1	0.6%	40
09/14	242	(13)	—	—
09/13	245	6	2.7%	—
09/12	255	22	8.8%	—
Annual Growth	1.2%	(59.2%)	—	—

2015 Year-End Financials

Return on assets: 2.1%   Cash ($ mil.): 65
Return on equity: 0.6%
Current ratio: 16.40

NEW YORK SOCIETY FOR THE RELIEF OF THE RUPTURED AND CRIPPLED, MAINTAINING THE HOSPITAL FOR

EXECUTIVES

Chief Executive Officer, Louis Shapiro
Executive Vice-President, Lisa A Goldstein
Executive Vice-President, Stacey L Malakof
Manager, Lisa Witkin
Architect, Matthew Griffith

LOCATIONS

HQ: NEW YORK SOCIETY FOR THE RELIEF OF THE
RUPTURED AND CRIPPLED, MAINTAINING THE
HOSPITAL FOR
535 E 70TH ST, NEW YORK, NY 100214823
Phone: 212 606-1000
Web: WWW.HSS.EDU

HISTORICAL FINANCIALS

Company Type: Private

Income Statement

FYE: December 31

	REVENUE ($ mil.)	NET INCOME ($ mil.)	NET PROFIT MARGIN	EMPLOYEES
12/15	811	79	9.8%	3,350
12/14	996	109	10.9%	—
12/07	441	(21)	—	—
12/05	376	14	3.9%	—
Annual Growth	8.0%	18.4%	—	—

2015 Year-End Financials

Return on assets: 7.7%   Cash ($ mil.): 89
Return on equity: 9.8%
Current ratio: 0.60

NEWARK BETH ISRAEL MEDICAL CENTER INC.

Part of the Saint Barnabas Health Care System Newark Beth Israel Medical Center is a 670-bed acute-care regional referral hospital. The facility serves residents of Newark and surrounding areas in northern New Jersey. The hospital offers services including primary diagnostic emergency surgical and rehabilitative care. It is home to specialized programs such as kidney transplantation cancer care dentistry sleep disorders geriatrics and women's health services. Newark Beth Israel Medical Center also houses the Children's Hospital of New Jersey and the Saint Barnabas Heart Center. The research and teaching hospital has a medical staff of more than 800 physicians.

Operations

Newark Beth Israel Medical Center along with sister hospital Saint Barnabas Medical Center has a teaching and research affiliation with the New Jersey Medical School (part of the University of Medicine and Dentistry of New Jersey). The hospital also has training programs with other regional schools.

Newark Beth Israel Medical Center handles about 25000 inpatient visits annually while the hospital's outpatient centers see some 300000 patients each year.

EXECUTIVES

Managing Director, John Cerritelli
Director of Radiology, Chris DiMotta
Auditors: WITHUMSMITHBROWN PC MORRISTOW

LOCATIONS

HQ: NEWARK BETH ISRAEL MEDICAL CENTER INC.
201 LYONS AVE, NEWARK, NJ 071122027
Phone: 973 926-7000
Web: WWW.CPRTRAININGNJ.COM

PRODUCTS/OPERATIONS

Selected Departments and Centers

Barnabas Health Heart Center
Center for Geriatric Health Care
Center for Women's Health
Children's Hospital of New Jersey
Cohen Comprehensive Cancer and Blood Disorder
  Center
Lung Center
Pacemaker and Defibrillator Center
Palliative Care Program
Regional Perinatal Center
Radiology
Robotic Surgery Center
Renal Transplantation
Sleep Disorders Center

COMPETITORS

AtlantiCare
Atlantic Health
Bergen Regional Medical
CentraState Healthcare System
Children's Specialized Hospital
Chilton Medical Center
East Orange General Hospital
Englewood Hospital and Medical Center
Hackensack Meridian Health
Hackensack University Medical Center

Newton Medical Center
Robert Wood Johnson University Hospital
Robert Wood Johnson University Hospital at Rahway
St. Joseph's Healthcare System
The Valley Hospital
Virtua Health
Winthrop-University Hospital

HISTORICAL FINANCIALS
Company Type: Private

Income Statement
FYE: December 31

	REVENUE ($ mil.)	NET INCOME ($ mil.)	NET PROFIT MARGIN	EMPLOYEES
12/15	542	38	7.1%	3,000
12/14	591	32	5.5%	—
12/13	563	10	1.9%	—
12/08	438	(56)	—	—
Annual Growth	3.1%	—	—	—

2015 Year-End Financials
Return on assets: 5.5%
Return on equity: 7.1%
Current ratio: 0.30
Cash ($ mil.): —

NEWTON WELLESLEY HOSPITAL CORP

Newton-Wellesley Hospital (NWH) provides the Greater Boston area with a full range of medical surgical and diagnostic services. The hospital which boasts more than 310 beds offers a variety of programs including a full-service diagnostic imaging department a multiple sclerosis clinic cancer center joint reconstruction surgery physical and occupational therapy and inpatient psychiatric care. In addition the Partners Reproductive Medicine Center offers infertility treatment in collaboration with two other area hospitals. Part of the Partners HealthCare family Newton-Wellesley is a teaching hospital for Tufts University's School of Medicine.

Operations

Newton-Wellesley Hospital is a full system member of Partners HealthCare System a nonprofit organization that includes acute care hospitals Massachusetts General Hospital Brigham and Women's/Faulkner Hospitals The North Shore Medical Center and specialty hospitals McLean Hospital and Spaulding Rehabilitation Hospital as well as Dana-Farber/Partners CancerCare and the community-based doctors and hospitals of Partners Community HealthCare Inc.

Newton-Wellesley's patients have access to various centers of excellence such as the Vernon Cancer Center Kaplan Center for Joint Reconstruction Surgery the Spine Center the Auerbach Breast Center and the Center for Weight Loss Surgery. Newton-Wellesley also provides the latest diagnostic technology such as a 64-slice CT scanner MRI PET scans sleep studies and interventional radiology services. The Children's Corner established in 1978 and located on the hospital campus is a nonprofit childcare program that provides quality care for the children of employees at Newton-Wellesley Hospital as well as care to local families in the community.

NWH also has post-graduate training programs for Harvard Medical School residents.

Geographic Reach

Based in Newton Massachusetts Newton-Wellesley collaborates with Massachusetts General Hospital MassGeneral Hospital for Children and Brigham and Women's Hospital to provide area residents and visitors a full range of medical surgical and specialty programs and services. It has more than 1000 affiliated physicians.

Strategy

Newton-Wellesley Hospital is focused on expanding its services and creating new programs to meet the needs of the community and its patients. The hospital accepts most health insurance plans including Medicare and Medicaid Blue Cross Blue Shield Tufts Health Plan Harvard Pilgrim Health Care and many additional HMOs and PPOs.

The goal of The Administrative Fellowship program at Newton-Wellesley Hospital to provide a comprehensive and practical experience for future healthcare executives in a high-exposure environment while providing the hospital with a productive employee equipped with the latest in healthcare academic training.

In 2011 Newton-Wellesley Hospital and Med-Touch launched a new iPhone application for the hospital. The application features near real-time reporting of emergency room wait times integrated directions to the ER and pre-registration and mobile optimized physician profiles with contact information.

EXECUTIVES

Vice President Physician Development, Steven Gordon
VP Outpatient Services, Ellen Moloney
SVP and CFO, Jeffrey P. (Jeff) Dion
SVP Patient Care Services and Chief Nursing Officer, Karen Conley
Vice President, Joan Archer
Director Physician Recruitment, Marc Gagnon
Vice President of Marketing, Helen Mengistab
Director of Health Information Manager Of Health Information, Karen Bogard
Vice President Quality and Patient Safety, Bert Thurlo-Walsh
Director Of Health Information, Nancy Lafianza
Treasurer and Chief Financial Officer, Daniel Gross

LOCATIONS

HQ: NEWTON WELLESLEY HOSPITAL CORP
2014 WASHINGTON ST, NEWTON, MA 024621607
Phone: 617 243-6000
Web: WWW.NWH.ORG

PRODUCTS/OPERATIONS

Selected Departments & Services
Anesthesiology
Anticoagulation Management Services
Auerbach Breast Center
Cardiovascular Health Programs
Center for Minimally Invasive Gynecologic Surgery
Center for Weight Loss Surgery
Diabetes Management Program
Emergency Medicine
Family Medicine
Kaplan Center for Joint Reconstruction Surgery
Laboratory Services/Pathology: For Lab Outreach Clients
Laboratory Services/Pathology: For Patients
Medical Emergency Department: Maxwell Blum Emergency Pavilion
Medicine
Multiple Sclerosis Clinic
Nursing
Nutrition Counseling
Obstetrics and Gynecology
Orthopaedic Surgery Service
Outpatient Surgery Center
Pain Management Service
Partners Reproductive Medicine Center
Pediatrics
Primary Stroke Service
Psychiatry
Radiology
Rehabilitation Services
Sleep Center
Spine Center
Surgery
Surgical Discharge Instructions
Transitional Year - Internship Program
Vernon Cancer Center
Waltham Urgent Care Center
Women's Imaging Center

Selected Clinical Centers
Auerbach Breast Center
Center for Minimally Invasive Gynecologic Surgery
Center for Weight Loss Surgery
Diabetes Management Program
Kaplan Center for Joint Reconstruction Surgery
Multiple Sclerosis Clinic
Outpatient Surgery Center
Pain Management Service
Partners Reproductive Medicine Center
Primary Stroke Service
Sleep Center
Spine Center
Vernon Cancer Center
Waltham Urgent Care Center
Women's Imaging Center

COMPETITORS

Beth Israel Deaconess Medical Center	Faulkner Hospital
Boston Medical Center	Hallmark Health
Children's Hospital Boston	McLean Hospital
Emerson Hospital	St. Elizabeth's Medical Center

HISTORICAL FINANCIALS
Company Type: Private

Income Statement
FYE: September 30

	REVENUE ($ mil.)	NET INCOME ($ mil.)	NET PROFIT MARGIN	EMPLOYEES
09/15	422	21	5.2%	2,500
09/14	405	12	3.0%	—
09/13	393	18	4.8%	—
09/12	400	31	7.8%	—
Annual Growth	1.9%	(11.0%)	—	—

2015 Year-End Financials
Return on assets: 2.8%
Return on equity: 5.2%
Current ratio: 0.90
Cash ($ mil.): 27

NEWYORK-PRESBYTERIAN/ BROOKLYN METHODIST

New York Methodist Hospital is a not-for-profit acute-care teaching hospital serving Brooklyn residents. Established in 1881 as the Methodist Episcopal Hospital the facility has more than 650 licensed beds. It offers a full range of medical services including primary and emergency care as well as specialty services such as women's health cancer cardiovascular pediatric geriatric and behavioral health. The hospital also operates satellite clinics in surrounding areas. A member of New York-Presbyterian Healthcare System New York Methodist is a teaching hospital affiliated with Cornell University's Weill Medical College.

Operations

New York Methodist Hospital handles about 40000 inpatient admissions and 100000 emergency department visits each year as well as 24000 surgeries and 5000 births. It also processes about 200000 laboratory sample processes annually.

New York Methodist Hospital includes specialty institutes in about 10 fields including pulmonary medicine cancer care and vascular health. In addition to providing inpatient care the organization operates some 10 primary and specialty outpatient centers. It also runs a number of graduate medical programs including programs affiliated with professional training schools in the areas of radiography medical technology radiation therapy and paramedics.

Geographic Reach

New York Methodist Hospital's main campus is in the Park Slope neighborhood of Brooklyn. It has several outpatient centers in other parts of Brooklyn as well.

Strategy

To expand care for area residents New York Methodist is adding new specialist programs and equipment. For instance in 2012 the hospital added a robotic-assisted surgery program for bariatric procedures. It also opened a new wound care and hyperbaric oxygen therapy center for hard-to-heal wounds. In addition in 2013 the hospital moved its sleep disorder center into a new facility.

EXECUTIVES

Senior Vice President, Lauren Yedvab
Assistant Vice President Ambulatory Care, Jennifer Donovan
Director Of Respiratory Therapy, Felix Khusid

LOCATIONS

HQ: NEWYORK-PRESBYTERIAN/BROOKLYN METHODIST
506 6TH ST, BROOKLYN, NY 112153609
Phone: 718 780-3000
Web: WWW.NYP.ORG

COMPETITORS

Beth Israel Medical Center	Lutheran HealthCare
Bronx-Lebanon Hospital	Maimonides Medical Center
Brookdale University Hospital	New York City Health and Hospitals
Catholic Healthcare System	Northwell Health
Kingsbrook Jewish Medical Center	SUNY Downstate
	Winthrop-University Hospital

HISTORICAL FINANCIALS

Company Type: Private

Income Statement

FYE: December 31

	REVENUE ($ mil.)	NET INCOME ($ mil.)	NET PROFIT MARGIN	EMPLOYEES
12/15	732	88	12.1%	4,929
12/14	687	68	10.0%	—
12/13	810	115	14.2%	—
12/12	636	44	6.9%	—
Annual Growth	4.8%	26.3%	—	—

2015 Year-End Financials

Return on assets: 5.8%   Cash ($ mil.): 106
Return on equity: 12.1%
Current ratio: 1.00

NHS HUMAN SERVICES, INC.

Northwestern Human Services (operating as NHS Human Services) exists to lend a helping hand to humans throughout the Northeast. Founded in 1967 the organization primarily offers a variety of behavioral health care services that include mental health and drug and alcohol rehabilitation mental retardation services juvenile justice autism special education foster care and elder care. The not-for-profit organization provides programs for nearly 40000 adults and children at more than 675 facilities in more than half a dozen eastern US states. NHS' programs are offered through its specialty care facilities mobile clinics and on an independent case management basis.

Operations

NHS has been working to develop programs for people with dual diagnoses and other issues involving multiple problems. The not-for-profit has also been expanding geographically.

Geographic Reach

The system serves individuals throughout Pennsylvania New Jersey Delaware New York Virginia Maryland and Louisiana.

Financial Performance

In 2014 NHS earned operating revenue of more than $500 million on growth from education and out-of-state services. Services to those with intellectual and development disabilities leads revenues contributing 53%. Adult and children's services split the remainder about evenly.

Strategy

In addition to expanding geographically and introducing new programs NHS has been updating its record keeping and going digital. Once the conversion to electronic health records is complete the organization will move to outsource its back office functions (payroll human resources and benefits) to reduce costs.

In 2014 the company partnered with Futures Education and Futures Healthcare to form Special Education and Behavioral Connections a joint venture providing specialized resources for children and adolescents with special needs. The venture is active in Dearborn Michigan and throughout NHS' schools in Pennsylvania.

Mergers and Acquisitions

NHS acquired Fresh Start a program providing transitional housing drug and alcohol treatment and related services for adults including veterans.

EXECUTIVES

Executive Vice President Corporate Administration, Leah Pason
Director of Admissions, Sherri Portnoy
Vice President Information Technology, Tom Morgan
Auditors: GRANT THORNTON LLP PHILADELP

LOCATIONS

HQ: NHS HUMAN SERVICES, INC.
620 GERMANTOWN PIKE, LAFAYETTE HILL, PA 194441810
Phone: 610 260-4600

PRODUCTS/OPERATIONS

2013 Sales

	$ mil.	% of total
Intellectual/Developmental Disabilities	259	53
Adult Behavioral Health	118	24
Children's	108	22
Other	6	1
Total	493	100

COMPETITORS

Albert Einstein Healthcare Network
Devereux Foundation
Diakon Lutheran Social Ministries
Excela Health
Genesis HealthCare System (Ohio)
Hazelden Betty Ford
HealthSouth

Providence Service
Select Medical
Watson Institute
YAI National Institute for People with Disabilitie

HISTORICAL FINANCIALS

Company Type: Private

Income Statement

FYE: June 30

	REVENUE ($ mil.)	NET INCOME ($ mil.)	NET PROFIT MARGIN	EMPLOYEES
06/16	524	5	1.0%	6,500
06/15	49	1	2.6%	—
06/14	44	3	8.8%	—
06/10	28	0	2.3%	—
Annual Growth	62.1%	40.5%	—	—

2016 Year-End Financials

Return on assets: 5.3%   Cash ($ mil.): 15
Return on equity: 1.0%
Current ratio: 1.40

NIELSEN HOLDINGS PLC

Business services nec nsk

EXECUTIVES

Ceo, Mitch Barns
Senior Vice President Investor Relations, Kate Vanek

LOCATIONS

HQ: NIELSEN HOLDINGS PLC
85 BROAD ST, NEW YORK, NY 100042434
Phone: 646 654-5000

HISTORICAL FINANCIALS

Company Type: Private

Income Statement

FYE: December 31

	REVENUE ($ mil.)	NET INCOME ($ mil.)	NET PROFIT MARGIN	EMPLOYEES
12/15	6,172	575	9.3%	43,061
12/14	6,288	381	6.1%	—
12/13	5,703	736	12.9%	—
12/12	5,612	273	4.9%	—
Annual Growth	3.2%	28.2%	—	—

2015 Year-End Financials

Return on assets: 16.4%   Cash ($ mil.): 357
Return on equity: 9.3%
Current ratio: 0.90

NJVC, LLC

EXECUTIVES

President, Chris Andersen
Vice-President, Jennifer IAMS
Personnel Manager, Patricia McCormick
Finance Manager, Roberta Thacker
Project Manager, William F Miner
Engineer, James Day
Administrative Assistant, Teresa Smith
Engineer, Michael Hardman
Vice-President, Charles McGaugh
Auditors: RSM US LLP FREDERICK MARYLAN

LOCATIONS

HQ: NJVC, LLC
14295 PARK MEADOW DR, CHANTILLY, VA
201512220
Phone: 703 429-9000
Web: WWW.NJVC.COM

HISTORICAL FINANCIALS

Company Type: Private

Income Statement

FYE: September 30

	REVENUE ($ mil.)	NET INCOME ($ mil.)	NET PROFIT MARGIN	EMPLOYEES
09/15	313	16	5.1%	1,300
09/14	443	17	3.9%	—
09/13	443	17	3.9%	—
09/12	513	22	4.4%	—
Annual Growth	(15.2%)	(10.8%)	—	—

2015 Year-End Financials

Return on assets: 2.8% Cash ($ mil.): —
Return on equity: 5.1%
Current ratio: 1.70

NOBLIS, INC.

Noblis' noble pursuit is through its offering of science-related strategic and technology consulting services. The not-for-profit company which pledges to serve the public interest helps various government entities and other clients evaluate technology options and vendors as well as solve complex technical problems. Noblis provides strategic planning decision analysis and acquisition support services. The company addresses problems in areas such as environment and energy intelligence health care homeland security public safety enterprise engineering and transportation. Noblis has worked with such clients as the US Air Force Army Navy and Departments of Commerce and Defense.

Geographic Reach

Noblis has more than half a dozen offices located in Maryland Texas Virginia West Virginia and Washington DC.

Sales and Marketing

The company's product suite includes RASMAS a Web-based service allowing health care providers and suppliers to respond more efficiently to product recalls and AcquTrak an acquisitions support tool aimed at helping government entities reduce costs and schedule times.

Company Background

The company was formed in 1996 as Mitretek Systems; it changed its name to Noblis in 2007.

EXECUTIVES

EVP and Director, Amr A. ElSawy
VP CFO Secretary and Treasurer, Mark A. Simione
Corporate VP and CTO, H. Gilbert Miller
VP and CIO, Gail Hogan
President Noblis NSP, Ellen McCarthy
Vice President For National Security And Intel, Drew Cohen
Business Development Vice President, Diana Fossett
Chairman, Marion C. Blakey
Vice Chairman, Michael Chertoff
Auditors: GRANT THORNTON LLP ARLINGTON

LOCATIONS

HQ: NOBLIS, INC.
2002 EDMUND HALLEY DR, RESTON, VA 201913436
Phone: 703 610-2000
Web: WWW.NOBLIS.JOBS

COMPETITORS

Accenture
Bain & Company
Boston Consulting
Deloitte Consulting
HP Enterprise Services
IBM
McKinsey & Company

HISTORICAL FINANCIALS

Company Type: Private

Income Statement

FYE: September 30

	REVENUE ($ mil.)	NET INCOME ($ mil.)	NET PROFIT MARGIN	EMPLOYEES
09/16*	320	19	5.9%	804
10/15	314	12	3.8%	—
10/14	252	16	6.7%	—
09/13	200	10	5.0%	—
Annual Growth	16.8%	23.6%	—	—

*Fiscal year change

2016 Year-End Financials

Return on assets: 4.8% Cash ($ mil.): —
Return on equity: 5.9%
Current ratio: 0.90

NOLAN TRANSPORTATION GROUP, LLC (DE)

EXECUTIVES

Board of Directors, Harold Baron
Board of Directors, Fritz Owens
Board of Directors, Blake Malone
General Manager, Robert Burns
Director, Victoria Motteler
Manager, Calvin Jones

LOCATIONS

HQ: NOLAN TRANSPORTATION GROUP, LLC (DE)
365 NORTHRIDGE RD STE 100, ATLANTA, GA
303506100
Phone: 770 509-9611
Web: WWW.NTGFREIGHT.COM

HISTORICAL FINANCIALS

Company Type: Private

Income Statement

FYE: September 30

	REVENUE ($ mil.)	NET INCOME ($ mil.)	NET PROFIT MARGIN	EMPLOYEES
09/16*	199	(0)	—	135
12/14	114	0	0.4%	—
12/13	49	0	0.5%	—
12/12	22	0	2.0%	—
Annual Growth	72.5%	—	—	—

*Fiscal year change

2016 Year-End Financials

Return on assets: 11.0% Cash ($ mil.): 1
Return on equity: (-0.2%)
Current ratio: 1.20

NORMAN REGIONAL HOSPITAL AUTHORITY

NORM! Perhaps that's how locals refer to Norman Regional Health System when they are headed there for health care. The system operates in and around Norman Oklahoma through the full service 325-bed Norman Regional Hospital and affiliated health centers including Moore Medical Center Services and the HealthPlex a 136-bed specialty hospital focused on cardiology orthopedic and spine and women's and children's services. Moore Medical Center's services include include acute care and surgery diagnostic and outpatient health care services. The organization's programs include behavioral medicine rehabilitation a women's center and a sleep disorder clinic. The hospital which employs more than 350 physicians was established in 1946.

Geographic Reach

Norman Regional Health System serves Norman Oklahoma and its surrounding communities.

Financial Performance

In 2014 the system's revenues totaled $333 million while net income totaled $25 million. Cash flow from operations was $31 million.

Strategy

Norman Regional Health System broke ground on a new medical facility in Monroe Oklahoma in 2014. The $29 million complex is expected to open in 2016.

EXECUTIVES

Nursing Director, Nancy Brown
Clinical Pharmacist Pharmd, Betsy Nelson
Pharm D Staff Pharmacist, Mitzi Moring
Manager of Laboratory Services, Mindy Slaughterback
Vice President Revenue Cycle, Meegan Carter
Director of Surgery, Brenda Davis
Vice Chairman, Tom Clote
Board of Directors, Teresa Ewing
Board Member, Carol Anderson
Secretary, Sara Lewis
Auditors: BKD LLP TULSA OKLAHOMA

LOCATIONS

HQ: NORMAN REGIONAL HOSPITAL AUTHORITY
901 N PORTER AVE, NORMAN, OK 730716482
Phone: 405 307-1000
Web: WWW.NORMANREGIONAL.COM

Selected Locations (Oklahoma)

Brookhaven Medical Women's Center (Norman)
Doctors Park (Norman)
Family Medicine (Regional)
Findlay Medical Center (Norman)
HealthPlex (Norman)
Imaging Services (Regional)
Immediate Care of Oklahoma (Regional)
Moore Medical Center (Moore)
Norman Regional Hospital (Norman)
WaterView Medical Center (Oklahoma City)

PRODUCTS/OPERATIONS

Selected Services

Breast Care Center
Cancer Services
Cardiology Services
Diabetes Center
Emergency Services
Family Birth Center
Orthopedic Services
Stroke Center
Surgical Services
Weight Loss Surgery

COMPETITORS

Deaconess Health Care
INTEGRIS Baptist
Medical Center

Via Christi Health
System

HISTORICAL FINANCIALS

Company Type: Private

Income Statement

	REVENUE ($ mil.)	NET INCOME ($ mil.)	NET PROFIT MARGIN	EMPLOYEES
06/15	360	17	4.9%	2,900
06/14	347	24	7.1%	—
06/12	324	8	2.5%	—
06/11	287	12	4.5%	—
Annual Growth	5.8%	8.6%	—	—

FYE: June 30

2015 Year-End Financials

Return on assets: 3.9%
Return on equity: 4.9%
Current ratio: 3.30

Cash ($ mil.): 108

NORTH AMERICAN HOGANAS COMPANY

EXECUTIVES

President, Avinash Gore
Plant Engineering Manager, Donald Bowman
Purchasing Manager, Ed Horner
Manager, Gary Bochniarz
Supervisor, Michael Rhoades
Supervisor, Sue Sowerbrower
Engineer, Yasser Dogaheh

LOCATIONS

HQ: NORTH AMERICAN HOGANAS COMPANY
111 HOGANAS WAY, HOLLSOPPLE, PA 159356416
Phone: 814 479-3500

HISTORICAL FINANCIALS

Company Type: Private

Income Statement

	REVENUE ($ mil.)	NET INCOME ($ mil.)	NET PROFIT MARGIN	EMPLOYEES
12/15	213	16	7.6%	355
12/14	249	10	4.4%	—
12/13	217	7	3.6%	—
12/12	202	6	3.3%	—
Annual Growth	1.7%	34.7%	—	—

FYE: December 31

NORTH BAY PRODUCE, INC.

EXECUTIVES

Chairman of the Board, Ken Schwallier
Financial Executive, Lora Reed
Director, Sharon Robb
Manager, Jon Wall
Auditors: DENNIS GARTLAND & NIERGARTH

LOCATIONS

HQ: NORTH BAY PRODUCE, INC.
1771 N US HIGHWAY 31 S, TRAVERSE CITY, MI
496858748
Phone: 231 946-1941
Web: WWW.NORTHBAYPRODUCE.COM

HISTORICAL FINANCIALS

Company Type: Private

Income Statement

	REVENUE ($ mil.)	NET INCOME ($ mil.)	NET PROFIT MARGIN	EMPLOYEES
04/16	180	5	2.8%	25
04/15	153	3	2.4%	—
04/14	137	2	1.9%	—
04/13	112	1	1.3%	—
Annual Growth	17.1%	51.8%	—	—

FYE: April 30

2016 Year-End Financials

Return on assets: 3.9%
Return on equity: 2.8%
Current ratio: 1.20

Cash ($ mil.): 6

NORTH CENTRAL COOPERATIVE

EXECUTIVES

General Manager, Mike Nail
Manager, Michelle Crawford
Finance Manager, John Rohrer
Manager, Kelly Raasch
Manager, Myron Pohlman

LOCATIONS

HQ: NORTH CENTRAL COOPERATIVE
221 4TH AVE NW, CLARION, IA 505251035
Phone: 515 532-2881
Web: WWW.NCCOOP.COM

HISTORICAL FINANCIALS

Company Type: Private

Income Statement

	REVENUE ($ mil.)	NET INCOME ($ mil.)	NET PROFIT MARGIN	EMPLOYEES
12/15	189	4	2.1%	96
12/14	227	3	1.7%	—
12/13	295	1	0.6%	—
12/12	300	3	1.1%	—
Annual Growth	(14.2%)	7.7%	—	—

FYE: December 31

2015 Year-End Financials

Return on assets: 13.7%
Return on equity: 2.1%
Current ratio: 0.60

Cash ($ mil.): 9

NORTH CENTRAL COOPERATIVE INC

EXECUTIVES

President, J Mark Tullis
Board of Directors, Tim Reidelbach
Administrative Assistant, Marty Holland
VP Sales, John Scicluna
Manager, David Smith
Plant Engineering Manager, Andrew Acmoody
Manager, Kurt Bergstedt
Manager, Nancy Nance
Auditors: BLUE & CO LLC SEYMOUR INDI

LOCATIONS

HQ: NORTH CENTRAL COOPERATIVE INC
2025 S WABASH ST, WABASH, IN 469924124
Phone: 800 992-3495
Web: WWW.NORTHCENTRALCOOP.COM

HISTORICAL FINANCIALS

Company Type: Private

Income Statement

	REVENUE ($ mil.)	NET INCOME ($ mil.)	NET PROFIT MARGIN	EMPLOYEES
08/15	331	10	3.2%	280
08/14	402	16	4.2%	—
08/13	426	19	4.6%	—
08/12	411	14	3.5%	—
Annual Growth	(6.9%)	(9.9%)	—	—

FYE: August 31

2015 Year-End Financials

Return on assets: 2.6%
Return on equity: 3.2%
Current ratio: 1.50

Cash ($ mil.): 19

NORTH CLACKAMAS SCHOOL DISTRICT 12

EXECUTIVES

Director, Linda Moraga
Board of Directors, Matthew Utterback
Superintendent, Allain Drakulich
Director, Tricia George
Auditors: PAUL ROGERS AND CO PC TI

LOCATIONS

HQ: NORTH CLACKAMAS SCHOOL DISTRICT 12
12400 SE FREEMAN WAY, MILWAUKIE, OR
972224620
Phone: 503 353-6001
Web: WWW.NCLACK.K12.OR.US

HISTORICAL FINANCIALS

Company Type: Private

Income Statement

	REVENUE ($ mil.)	NET INCOME ($ mil.)	NET PROFIT MARGIN	EMPLOYEES
06/16	225	3	1.6%	1,857
06/13	189	(4)	—	—
06/12	195	7	3.7%	—
06/11	0	0	—	—
Annual Growth	—	437.0%	—	—

FYE: June 30

2016 Year-End Financials

Return on assets: 0.5%   Cash ($ mil.): 41
Return on equity: 1.6%
Current ratio: —

NORTH COLORADO MEDICAL CENTER

EXECUTIVES

Chief Executive Officer, Gene O'Hara
Director, Dawn Olson
Supervisor, Doug Egloff

LOCATIONS

HQ: NORTH COLORADO MEDICAL CENTER
1801 16TH ST, GREELEY, CO 806315199
Phone: 970 352-4121
Web: WWW.NCMCFOUNDATION.ORG

HISTORICAL FINANCIALS

Company Type: Private

Income Statement

FYE: December 31

	REVENUE ($ mil.)	NET INCOME ($ mil.)	NET PROFIT MARGIN	EMPLOYEES
12/15	372	33	9.0%	12
12/14	353	46	13.1%	—
Annual Growth	5.4%	(27.5%)	—	—

2015 Year-End Financials

Return on assets: 1.5%   Cash ($ mil.): —
Return on equity: 9.0%
Current ratio: 0.70

NORTH DAKOTA MILL & ELEVATOR ASSOCIATION INC

When bakeries need flour North Dakota Mill & Elevator rises to the occasion. The mill is a producer of wheat flour used specifically in breads and other baked goods like cookies and crackers. It processes more than 78000 bushels of wheat a day and ships most of its flour in bulk to wholesalers. It offers semolina flour as well as specialty products such as wholegrain wheat flour wheat germ and corn flour for tortillas. The mill also sells pancake mixes bread machine mixes and wholewheat all-purpose and bread flours under the Dakota Maid brand to consumers through its online store. Owned by the State of North Dakota it contributes 50% of its profits to the North Dakota State General Fund.

EXECUTIVES

President and General Manager, Vance Taylor
Controller and Financial Manager, Ed Barchenger
Auditors: ROBERT R PETERSON FARGO NOR

LOCATIONS

HQ: NORTH DAKOTA MILL & ELEVATOR
ASSOCIATION INC
1823 MILL RD, GRAND FORKS, ND 582031535
Phone: 701 795-7000
Web: WWW.NDMILL.COM

COMPETITORS

ADM	Cooperative Elevator
BakeMark	General Mills
Bay State Milling	Gruma Corporation
Bob's Red Mill Natural Foods	Hodgson Mill
	Horizon Milling
Bunge Milling	Italgrani
C.H. Guenther & Son	King Arthur Flour
CGC	Organic Milling
CHS	Seaboard
Cargill	Smucker
Chelsea Milling	Star of the West

HISTORICAL FINANCIALS

Company Type: Private

Income Statement

FYE: June 30

	REVENUE ($ mil.)	NET INCOME ($ mil.)	NET PROFIT MARGIN	EMPLOYEES
06/16	216	4	2.0%	120
06/15	247	12	5.0%	—
06/14	256	9	3.6%	—
06/13	268	5	2.1%	—
Annual Growth	(6.9%)	(7.7%)	—	—

2016 Year-End Financials

Return on assets: 6.7%   Cash ($ mil.): —
Return on equity: 2.0%
Current ratio: 0.90

NORTH DAKOTA STATE UNIVERSITY

The state's leading research institution North Dakota State University (NDSU) has an enrollment of more than 14600 students. The university offers more than 100 undergraduate degree programs some 60 master's degree programs and more than 40 doctoral and professional programs. Historically NDSU's strengths have been agriculture and the applied sciences but the school also offers courses of study in business liberal arts engineering architecture mathematics and education. NDSU is a land-grant college; its extension service offers education and outreach programs throughout North Dakota in agriculture health and nutrition and community leadership. NDSU which was established in 1890 is part of the North Dakota University System.

Operations
The system also includes six universities and five community colleges spread across the state.

NDSU's more than 20000 acres of land include its Fargo campus as well as more than 200 Agricultural Experiment Stations on some 18000 acres of off-campus land used for research.

The College of Engineering has the highest number of students at more than 2300.

Financial Performance
NDSU saw a very slim drop in revenue less than 1% in 2013 as grants and contracts dropped slightly but student tuition and fess picked up the slack. Net income saw a big 41% jump due to higher state appropriations and investment income. Cash flow improved significantly growing around $10 million based on good returns on investments.

Strategy
The university prides itself on being an R&D institution. To that end it partnered with app developer Cogi to connect R&D hubs at the state's college campuses to private tech companies. NDSU has produced a winter survival app to help students survive being stranded in the state's harsh winter weather and one with info on flood and other disaster recovery.

EXECUTIVES

President, Dean Bresciani
Board of Directors, Matthew Hammer
Financial Executive, Gary Wawers
Purchasing Director, Stacy Winter
Manager, Gordon Bierwagen
Manager, Ronald Stammen
Auditors: STATE OF NORTH DAKOTA-ROBERT R

LOCATIONS

HQ: NORTH DAKOTA STATE UNIVERSITY
1919 UNIVERSITY DR N # 102, FARGO, ND
581021843
Phone: 701 231-7015
Web: WWW.NDSU.EDU

PRODUCTS/OPERATIONS

Selected Colleges and Schools
College of Agriculture Food Systems and Natural Resources
College of Arts Humanities and Social Sciences
College of Business
College of Engineering
College of Human Development and Education
College of Pharmacy Nursing and Allied Sciences
Graduate School

HISTORICAL FINANCIALS

Company Type: Private

Income Statement

FYE: June 30

	REVENUE ($ mil.)	NET INCOME ($ mil.)	NET PROFIT MARGIN	EMPLOYEES
06/15	252	43	17.3%	4,500
06/06*	184	12	7.0%	—
12/05	446	17	3.8%	—
06/04	446	17	3.8%	—
Annual Growth	(5.1%)	8.9%	—	—

*Fiscal year change

2015 Year-End Financials

Return on assets: 6.8%   Cash ($ mil.): 40
Return on equity: 17.3%
Current ratio: 1.10

NORTH DAKOTA UNIVERSITY SYSTEM FOUNDATION

EXECUTIVES

Principal, Hamid Augustine Shirvani
Manager, Patrick Nichols
Manager, Terry Wieland
Auditors: ROBERT R PETERSON FARGO NORT

LOCATIONS

HQ: NORTH DAKOTA UNIVERSITY SYSTEM
FOUNDATION
600 E BOULEVARD AVE # 215, BISMARCK, ND
585050601
Phone: 701 328-2960
Web: WWW.NDCHOOSE.COM

HISTORICAL FINANCIALS
Company Type: Private

Income Statement
FYE: June 30

	REVENUE ($ mil.)	NET INCOME ($ mil.)	NET PROFIT MARGIN	EMPLOYEES
06/16	695	116	16.8%	252
06/15	676	163	24.1%	—
06/13	653	78	12.0%	—
06/12	656	61	9.4%	—
Annual Growth	1.5%	17.3%	—	—

2016 Year-End Financials
Return on assets: 5.5%   Cash ($ mil.): 181
Return on equity: 16.8%
Current ratio: 1.60

NORTH EAST INDEPENDENT SCHOOL DISTRICT

EXECUTIVES

Superintendent, Brian G Gottardy
Board of Directors, Sandy Hughey
Clerk, Terrie Buck
Clerk, Troyer Linda
Officer, Wilson An
Executive Secretary, Peggy Turner
Clerk, Anne Ludwig
Clerk, Deloach Mina
Engineering Manager, Dilts James
Auditors: ABIP PC SAN ANTONIO TEXAS

LOCATIONS

HQ: NORTH EAST INDEPENDENT SCHOOL DISTRICT
8961 TESORO DR, SAN ANTONIO, TX 782176226
Phone: 210 407-0359
Web: WWW.NEISD.NET

HISTORICAL FINANCIALS
Company Type: Private

Income Statement
FYE: June 30

	REVENUE ($ mil.)	NET INCOME ($ mil.)	NET PROFIT MARGIN	EMPLOYEES
06/16	737	(53)	—	10,000
06/15	712	(143)	—	—
06/14	684	206	30.2%	—
06/13	650	3	0.6%	—
Annual Growth	4.2%	—	—	—

2016 Year-End Financials
Return on assets: 2.0%   Cash ($ mil.): 162
Return on equity: (-7.2%)
Current ratio: —

NORTH FULTON MEDICAL CENTER VOLUNTEER SERVICES ORGANIZATION, INC.

EXECUTIVES

President, Lynn Lommer
Manager, Larry Colletto

LOCATIONS

HQ: NORTH FULTON MEDICAL CENTER VOLUNTEER
SERVICES ORGANIZATION, INC.
3000 HOSPITAL BLVD, ROSWELL, GA 300764915
Phone: 770 751-2500
Web: WWW.NFULTONHOSPITAL.COM

HISTORICAL FINANCIALS
Company Type: Private

Income Statement
FYE: December 31

	REVENUE ($ mil.)	NET INCOME ($ mil.)	NET PROFIT MARGIN	EMPLOYEES
12/15	178	22	12.4%	1,010
12/14*	156	14	9.3%	—
08/06	0	0	11.1%	—
08/05	0	0	—	—
Annual Growth	—	—	—	—

*Fiscal year change

2015 Year-End Financials
Return on assets: 3.2%   Cash ($ mil.): —
Return on equity: 12.4%
Current ratio: 2.80

NORTH GEORGIA ELECTRIC MEMBERSHIP FOUNDATION, INC.

EXECUTIVES

Chief Executive Officer, Bill Scott
Director, Kathy Cavin
Sales Manager, Allison Crossen
Manager, Paul Ruud
VP Finance, Tina Porter
Manager, Brian Childers
Manager, Sheri Bedwell
Vice-President, Kathryn B West
Auditors: HENDERSON HUTCHERSON & MCCULLO

LOCATIONS

HQ: NORTH GEORGIA ELECTRIC MEMBERSHIP
FOUNDATION, INC.
1850 CLEVELAND HWY, DALTON, GA 307218315
Phone: 706 259-9441
Web: WWW.NGEMC.COM

HISTORICAL FINANCIALS
Company Type: Private

Income Statement
FYE: June 30

	REVENUE ($ mil.)	NET INCOME ($ mil.)	NET PROFIT MARGIN	EMPLOYEES
06/15	249	7	3.2%	192
06/14	245	11	4.5%	—
06/13	237	8	3.5%	—
06/12	233	6	2.7%	—
Annual Growth	2.2%	7.7%	—	—

2015 Year-End Financials
Return on assets: 8.7%   Cash ($ mil.): 7
Return on equity: 3.2%
Current ratio: 1.20

NORTH KANSAS CITY HOSPITAL

EXECUTIVES

Chief Executive Officer, Peggy Schmitt
Supervisor, Kevin Olsen
Manager, Tom Goulding
Manager, Becky Smith
Manager, Falisha Garroutte
Vice-President, Sarah Fields

LOCATIONS

HQ: NORTH KANSAS CITY HOSPITAL
2800 CLAY EDWARDS DR, NORTH KANSAS CITY, MO
641163220
Phone: 816 691-2000
Web: WWW.NKCH.ORG

HISTORICAL FINANCIALS
Company Type: Private

Income Statement
FYE: June 30

	REVENUE ($ mil.)	NET INCOME ($ mil.)	NET PROFIT MARGIN	EMPLOYEES
06/15	462	35	7.6%	6,200
06/11	419	22	5.3%	—
06/09	370	36	9.9%	—
06/08	1,745	0	—	—
Annual Growth	—	459.1%	—	—

2015 Year-End Financials
Return on assets: 3.5%   Cash ($ mil.): 17
Return on equity: 7.6%
Current ratio: 1.20

NORTH KANSAS CITY SCHOOL DISTRICT NO. 74

EXECUTIVES

Superintendent, Todd White
Office Manager, Vickie Freese
Auditors: MARR AND COMPANY PC KANSAS

LOCATIONS

HQ: NORTH KANSAS CITY SCHOOL DISTRICT NO. 74
2000 NE 46TH ST, KANSAS CITY, MO 641162042
Phone: 816 413-5000
Web: WWW.NKCSCHOOLS.ORG

HISTORICAL FINANCIALS

Company Type: Private

Income Statement
FYE: June 30

	REVENUE ($ mil.)	NET INCOME ($ mil.)	NET PROFIT MARGIN	EMPLOYEES
06/16	255	(1)	—	3,100
06/15	245	(1)	—	—
06/14	221	9	4.2%	—
06/13	219	(9)	—	—
Annual Growth	5.3%	—	—	—

2016 Year-End Financials

Return on assets: 1.9%
Return on equity: (-0.6%)
Current ratio: —

Cash ($ mil.): 53

NORTH LA COUNTY REGIONAL CENTER INC

EXECUTIVES

Director, George Stevens
Personnel Director, Michele Marra
Board of Directors, K Jennifr
Executive Director, Thompson Kelly
Personnel Director, Michel Marra
Chief Financial Officer, Kim Rolfes
Manager, Angela Rodriguez
Supervisor, Cristina Preuss
Administrative Assistant, June Maloy
Auditors: LAUTZE & LAUTZE SAN FRANCISCO

LOCATIONS

HQ: NORTH LA COUNTY REGIONAL CENTER INC
15400 SHERMAN WAY STE 170, VAN NUYS, CA
914064272
Phone: 818 778-1900
Web: WWW.NLACRC.ORG

HISTORICAL FINANCIALS

Company Type: Private

Income Statement
FYE: June 30

	REVENUE ($ mil.)	NET INCOME ($ mil.)	NET PROFIT MARGIN	EMPLOYEES
06/15	345	2	0.8%	350
06/14	318	(2)	—	—
06/13	295	(0)	—	—
06/12	274	(8)	—	—
Annual Growth	8.0%	—	—	—

2015 Year-End Financials

Return on assets: 9.9%
Return on equity: 0.8%
Current ratio: 0.90

Cash ($ mil.): 7

NORTH MISSISSIPPI HEALTH SERVICES, INC.

North Mississippi Health Services (NMHS) isn't contained by its name: The health system also provides health care to residents of northwestern Alabama. NMHS includes half a dozen community hospitals including its flagship North Mississippi Medical Center in Tupelo. North Mississippi Medical Clinics a regional network of more than 30 primary and specialty clinics; and nursing homes. Combined the facilities have nearly 1000 beds designated for acute long term and nursing care. Specialty services include home health and long-term care inpatient and outpatient behavioral health and treatment centers for cancer and digestive disorders. NMHS also operates outpatient care and wellness clinics in the region.

Operations

During 2014 NMHS handled about 30000 inpatient visits as well as more than 128000 emergency room visits and some 345000 outpatient care visits. It also conducted about 24000 surgeries at its various facilities. Its outpatient centers include more than 30 primary and specialty care clinics in Mississippi and Alabama operated through the North Mississippi Medical Clinics division as well as more than half a dozen wellness centers.

Geographic Reach

In all NMHS serves two dozen counties across the two states. In addition to its main hospital in Tupelo NMHS operates health centers in communities including Eupora Iuka Pontotoc and West Point Mississippi and in Hamilton Alabama. It also manages a center in Calhoun City Mississippi. Its Baldwyn Nursing Facility is located in Baldwyn Mississippi.

Financial Performance

Flagship North Mississippi Medical Center (NNMC)'s revenues increased by 6% due to a growth in net patient revenues. Medicare and Medicaid together accounted for about 50% of net patient revenues; managed care and commercial 25%; Blue Cross 14%; self-pay 10%; and Health Link 1%.

NNMC reported net loss of $14 million in 2014 over net income in 2013 due to pension-related changes.

NNMC's operating cash flow increased by 256% that year.

EXECUTIVES

Secretary, Diane Boyd

LOCATIONS

HQ: NORTH MISSISSIPPI HEALTH SERVICES, INC.
830 S GLOSTER ST, TUPELO, MS 388014934
Phone: 662 377-3000

Selected Locations
Baldwyn Nursing Facility (Baldwyn Mississippi)
Calhoun County Medical Clinic (managed facility; Calhoun Mississippi)
NMMC-Eupora (Eupora Mississippi)
NMMC-Hamilton (Hamilton Alabama)
NMMC-Iuka (Iuka Mississippi)
NMMC-Pontotoc (Pontotoc Mississippi)
NMMC-Tupelo (Tupelo Mississippi)
NMMC-West Point (West Point Mississippi)
North Mississippi Medical Clinics (NMMCI regional)

PRODUCTS/OPERATIONS

Selected Facilities and Services
Acute Stroke Unit
Advanced Wound Center and Hyperbarics
Bariatric Center

Behavioral Health Center
Breast Care Center
Cancer Center
Center for Digestive Health
Community Health
Critical Care Unit
CRNA Program
Diabetes Treatment Center
Emergency Services
Family Medicine Residency Center
Heart Institute
Home Health and Hospice
Hospitalists
Joint Replacement Center
Le Bonheur Specialty Clinics
Medical Imaging
North Mississippi Surgery Center
Outpatient Infusion
Pain Management Center
Pastoral Care
Physician Specialties
Radiology
Rehabilitation Services
Respiratory Therapy
Skilled Nursing Facility
Sleep Disorders Center
Surgical Services
Tupelo Wellness Center
Vein Center
Volunteer Services
Women's Hospital
Women's and Children Services

COMPETITORS

Baptist Memorial Health Care
Community Health Systems
Delta Regional Medical Center
Forrest General Hospital
HCA
Memorial Hospital at Gulfport
Methodist Healthcare
Natchez Regional Medical Center
North Mississippi Medical
Shelby County Health Care
Southwest Mississippi Regional Medical Center

HISTORICAL FINANCIALS

Company Type: Private

Income Statement
FYE: September 30

	REVENUE ($ mil.)	NET INCOME ($ mil.)	NET PROFIT MARGIN	EMPLOYEES
09/15	860	19	2.2%	6,000
09/14	779	(14)	—	—
09/13	735	82	11.3%	—
09/12	852	(3)	—	—
Annual Growth	0.3%	—	—	—

2015 Year-End Financials

Return on assets: 4.8%
Return on equity: 2.2%
Current ratio: 1.20

Cash ($ mil.): 68

NORTH MISSISSIPPI MEDICAL CENTER, INC.

At North Mississippi Medical Center you might get some Mississippi Mud ice cream after your tonsils are removed. The full-service 650-bed regional referral hospital in Tupelo Mississippi is part of the North Mississippi Health Services system an affiliation of hospitals and clinics serving northern Mississippi northwestern Alabama and parts of Tennessee. It's the largest private not-for-profit hospital in Mississippi and the largest non-metropolitan hospital in America. Specialty services at

the medical center include cancer treatment women's health care cardiology and behavioral health care. The hospital also operates a skilled-nursing facility and home health and hospice organizations.

Operations

Besides being a Mississippi State Department of Health-designated Level II trauma center North Mississippi Medical Center offers more than 40 specialties as well as centers for excellence in cardiac surgery cardiology research neurology neurosurgery pulmonology rehabilitation cancer treatment chemical dependency and neonatal programs.

The medical center's Home Health Agency canvases 17 counties in north Mississippi and provides complex and extremely high-tech procedures that can be performed in the home setting. It also operates Baldwyn Nursing Facility.

Geographic Reach

North Mississippi Medical Center serves more than 700000 people across 24 counties in north Mississippi northwestern Alabama and portions of Tennessee.

Strategy

In 2012 North Mississippi Medical Center - Hamilton opened a new pulmonary rehabilitation unit. Also the medical center's Outpatient Rehabilitation Center in 2012 became the first outpatient rehabilitation center in Mississippi to offer Fiberoptic Endoscopic Evaluation of Swallowing (FEES) to assess swallowing function. Awards and Recognition

North Mississippi Medical Center's hospitalist program has been recognized by The American Journal of Medicine for providing cost-effective care to patients in the hospital. The program begun in 1997 serves hospitalized patients who do not have a primary care physician or whose primary care physicians do not have hospital practices.

EXECUTIVES

Physical Therapy Director, Kim Wade

LOCATIONS

HQ: NORTH MISSISSIPPI MEDICAL CENTER, INC.
830 S GLOSTER ST, TUPELO, MS 388014934
Phone: 662 377-3000
Web: WWW.NMHS.NET

Selected Locations
Baldwyn Nursing Facility - Baldwyn Mississippi
NMMC - Eup
NMMC - Ham
NMMC - Iuk
NMMC - Pontotoc - Pontotoc Mississippi
NMMC - Tupelo - Tupelo Mississippi
NMMC - West Point - West Point Mississippi

PRODUCTS/OPERATIONS

Selected Programs & Services
Acute Stroke Unit
Advanced Wound Center and Hyperbarics
Bariatric Center
Behavioral Health Center
Breast Care Center
Cancer Center
Center for Digestive Health
Community Health
Critical Care Unit
CRNA Program
Diabetes Treatment Center
Emergency Services
Family Medicine Residency Center
Gift & Floral Shop
Heart Institute
Home Health and Hospice
Hospitalists
Joint Replacement Center
Le Bonheur Specialty Clinics
Medical Imaging
North Mississippi Surgery Center
Outpatient Infusion

Pain Management Center
Pastoral Care
Physician Specialties
Radiology
Rehabilitation Services
Respiratory Therapy
Skilled Nursing Facility
Sleep Disorders Center
Surgical Services
Tupelo Wellness Center
Vein Center
Volunteer Services
West Bedtower Project
Women's Hospital
Women's and Children Services

COMPETITORS

Community Health Systems
Delta Regional Medical Center
Forrest General Hospital
HCA
Memorial Hospital at Gulfport
Natchez Regional Medical Center
Southwest Mississippi Regional Medical Center

HISTORICAL FINANCIALS
Company Type: Private

Income Statement
FYE: September 30

	REVENUE ($ mil.)	NET INCOME ($ mil.)	NET PROFIT MARGIN	EMPLOYEES
09/15	627	45	7.3%	6,000
09/14	633	52	8.3%	—
09/13	537	2	0.5%	—
09/12	620	(6)	—	—
Annual Growth	0.4%	—	—	—

2015 Year-End Financials
Return on assets: 5.2%   Cash ($ mil.): 18
Return on equity: 7.3%
Current ratio: 2.00

NORTH PLATTE NEBRASKA HOSPITAL CORPORATION

EXECUTIVES

Chief Executive Officer, Melvin McNea
Director, Katherine Feagler
Chief Financial Officer, Krystal Claymore
Supervisor, Tammie Welsh
Auditors: SEIM JOHNSON LLP OMAHA NEBR

LOCATIONS

HQ: NORTH PLATTE NEBRASKA HOSPITAL CORPORATION
601 W LEOTA ST, NORTH PLATTE, NE 691016525
Phone: 308 534-9310
Web: WWW.GPHEALTH.ORG

HISTORICAL FINANCIALS
Company Type: Private

Income Statement
FYE: December 31

	REVENUE ($ mil.)	NET INCOME ($ mil.)	NET PROFIT MARGIN	EMPLOYEES
12/15	180	9	5.0%	900
12/14	151	21	14.2%	—
12/12	134	12	9.5%	—
12/10	126	10	8.4%	—
Annual Growth	7.4%	(3.0%)	—	—

2015 Year-End Financials
Return on assets: 3.6%   Cash ($ mil.): 25
Return on equity: 5.0%
Current ratio: 2.10

NORTH SHORE MEDICAL CENTER, INC.

This health system strives to cast a spell of salubriousness over Salem Massachusetts. The North Shore Medical Center (NSMC) provides medical care to the residents of several cities north of Boston including Salem (aka The Witch City) Lynn and Peabody. The network is home to two acute care hospitals children's and rehabilitation hospitals a heart institute a women's center and a number of community health centers. It also boasts more than 600 physicians and other health care professionals in its North Shore Physician Group. Its flagship the NSMC Salem Hospital is a nearly 250-bed teaching hospital providing adult and pediatric services. The not-for-profit system is part of Partners HealthCare System.

Operations

With multiple hospitals ambulatory care sites and physician offices NSMC provides comprehensive care. NSMC's staff includes about 600 affiliated physicians representing primary care family practice and 50 additional subspecialties. Much of the staff is part of the North Shore Physicians Group which provides multi-specialty and primary care through more than 15 North Shore locations.

NSMC collaborates with Massachusetts General Hospital on a number of clinical programs. The two started the Mass General/North Shore Center for Patient Care in 2009 to provide primary care and some surgical services to residents of the North Shore region. The center also serves as the home of a cancer center which is operated cooperatively by the two organizations.

Geographic Reach

North Shore Medical Center (NSMC) is the North Shore's largest healthcare provider one of its largest employers and the second largest community hospital system in Massachusetts.

Strategy

Mass General and NSMC also partner to provide heart care pediatric care thoracic surgery and neurosurgery. By working together the two health care providers can effectively double the number of specialists available to perform these procedures at their respective hospitals.

EXECUTIVES

Secretary, Tracie Dudevoir

LOCATIONS

HQ: NORTH SHORE MEDICAL CENTER, INC.
81 HIGHLAND AVE, SALEM, MA 019702768
Phone: 978 741-1200
Web: WWW.NSMC.PARTNERS.ORG

Selected locations
NSMC Salem Hospital (Salem)
NSMC Union Hospital (Lynn)
Mass General/North Shore Cancer Center (Danvers)
Mass General/North Shore Center for Outpatient Care (Danvers)
NSMC Women's Center (Danvers)
NSMC North Shore Children's (Salem)
The Birthplace (Salem)
NSMC Wellness & Integrative Medicine Center (Salem)
Salem Family Health Center
Torigian Family Health Center (Peabody)
Lynn Community Health Center
Shaughnessy-Kaplan Rehabilitation Hospital (Salem)
Partners Home Care (Regional)

COMPETITORS

Beth Israel Deaconess Medical Center
Boston Medical Center
Brigham and Women's Hospital
Cambridge Health Alliance
CareGroup
Caritas Holy Family Hospital
Caritas Norwood Hospital
Catholic Medical Center
Children's Hospital Boston
Dana-Farber
Elliot Health System
Emerson Hospital
Exeter Health Resources
Faulkner Hospital
Hallmark Health
Lahey Health System
McLean Hospital
St. Elizabeth's Medical Center
Steward Health Care

HISTORICAL FINANCIALS
Company Type: Private

Income Statement
FYE: September 30

	REVENUE ($ mil.)	NET INCOME ($ mil.)	NET PROFIT MARGIN	EMPLOYEES
09/15	403	(35)	—	5,000
09/14	395	(21)	—	—
09/05	339	(30)	—	—
09/04	372	(3)	—	—
Annual Growth	0.7%	—	—	—

2015 Year-End Financials
Return on assets: 1.7%
Return on equity: (-8.7%)
Current ratio: 0.60
Cash ($ mil.): 26

NORTH SHORE UNIVERSITY HEALTH SYSTEM

EXECUTIVES

Principal, Steven Swiryn
Director, Justin Brueck
Director, Tyler Bauer
Administration Director, Holly Hawes
Director, Michael Skonieczny
Vice-President, Nicole Fernandez
Director, Catherine Gianaro
Quality Control Manager, Dawn Futris

LOCATIONS

HQ: NORTH SHORE UNIVERSITY HEALTH SYSTEM
2650 RIDGE AVE, EVANSTON, IL 602011718
Phone: 847 570-2640
Web: WWW.NORTHSHORE.ORG

HISTORICAL FINANCIALS
Company Type: Private

Income Statement
FYE: September 30

	REVENUE ($ mil.)	NET INCOME ($ mil.)	NET PROFIT MARGIN	EMPLOYEES
09/15	1,419	55	3.9%	3
09/14	1,397	148	10.6%	—
09/13	1,815	238	13.1%	—
Annual Growth	(11.6%)	(51.7%)	—	—

2015 Year-End Financials
Return on assets: 4.3%
Return on equity: 3.9%
Current ratio: 0.40
Cash ($ mil.): 62

NORTH SHORE UNIVERSITY HOSPITAL

North Shore University Hospital (NSUH) knows you shouldn't have to leave the island for quality health care. The Long Island hospital has more than 800 beds devoted to adult and pediatric medicine rehabilitation stroke care women's health orthopedics urology wound healing dentistry and trauma emergency services among other areas. The hospital is home to specialist institutes for cancer care and cardiology. It also serves as a campus for the Hofstra Northwell Shool of Medicine. NSUH is part of Northwell Health.

Operations

The not-for-profit NSUH operates numerous satellite community health centers that provide primary surgery psychiatric dental and specialty care including the Schwartz Ambulatory Surgery Center. Its Stern Family Center for Extend Care and Rehabilitation has about 250 beds; NSUH also includes a Katz Women's Hospital (one of two in the system). The hospital provides comprehensive care in all health care specialties including organ transplant services. In addition the hospital operates mobile health vehicles and conducts educational and wellness programs for area residents.

NSUH has a staff of more than 6000 specialist and subspecialist physicians nurses and other medical workers. It handles about 50000 inpatient visits 90000 emergency room visits 20000 surgeries and 6000 births each year.

NSUH has medical health professional and nursing school affiliations with about 15 colleges and universities. Programs include residencies postgraduate training and fellowships.

Geographic Reach

Strategy

NSUH and the larger Northwell Health system tend to grow through the acquisitions of smaller campuses and mergers with other systems. This allows the hospital to gain operating efficiency through vertical integration bargaining power with vendors and a more diversified revenue stream.

In 2017 NSUH opened the Sandra Atlas Bass Heart Hospital for advanced cardiac care. The facility will be the first on Long Island to offer heart transplants and the sixth in New York State (which has a very high number of transplant candidates on its waiting list).

As part of its efforts to bring cutting-edge health care to the community it serves the hospital began offering 3D-printed titanium spinal implants in 2017.These synthetic implants approved in the US in 2016 are made with titanium powder rather than from a donor or from the patient's own body and manufactured using a 3D-printing process.

EXECUTIVES

Executive Vice President Chief Financial Officer, Robert S. (Bob) Shapiro
President North Shore-Long Island Jewish Health System, Ralph A. Nappi
SVP Strategic Planning and Marketing, Jeffrey A. Kraut
Regional COO, Mark J. Solazzo
Regional Executive Director, Dennis Dowling
Executive Vice President and Physician-in-Chief, Lawrence G. Smith
Executive Director, Susan Somerville
Senior Vice President and Chief Quality Officer, Mark Jarrett
Director of Radiology, Edward S Wind
Director Of Pharmacy, Sanjai Singh
Vice President, Dorothy Feldman
Vice President and Chief Talent Officer, Elaine Page
Vice President Finance, Wendy Carnel
Respiratory Therapy Director, Laura Gazzara
Physical Therapy Director, DARICE BRODSKY
Vice Chairperson, Barry Kaplan
Secretary, Rose Diaz

LOCATIONS

HQ: NORTH SHORE UNIVERSITY HOSPITAL
300 COMMUNITY DR, MANHASSET, NY 110303876
Phone: 516 562-0100
Web: WWW.NORTHWELL.EDU

PRODUCTS/OPERATIONS

Selected Centers and Services
Bariatric Services
Cancer Institute
Cardiovascular and Thoracic Services
Colorectal Surgery
Emergency Department / Trauma Services
Fertility and Reproductive Services
Geriatric and Palliative Medicine
Infectious Diseases / AIDS Research
Kidney Transplantation
Laparoendoscopic Single-Site Surgery
Military/Veterans Services
Minimally Invasive Robotic Surgery
Neuroscience
Obstetrics and Gynecology
Orthopaedics
Pain Management
Pediatric Services
Radiation Medicine
Travel Immunization
Urology Services
Wound Care

COMPETITORS

Brookhaven Memorial Hospital Medical Center
Catholic Health Services of Long Island
Catholic Healthcare System
Long Island College Hospital
Maimonides Medical Center
New York City Health and Hospitals
NewYork-Presbyterian Healthcare
Winthrop-University Hospital

HISTORICAL FINANCIALS

Company Type: Private

Income Statement
FYE: December 31

	REVENUE ($ mil.)	NET INCOME ($ mil.)	NET PROFIT MARGIN	EMPLOYEES
12/15	1,617	37	2.3%	5,000
12/14	1,495	84	5.7%	—
12/08	1,184	(14)	—	—
12/02	930	42	4.6%	—
Annual Growth	4.4%	(1.0%)	—	—

2015 Year-End Financials

Return on assets: 7.4% Cash ($ mil.): 3
Return on equity: 2.3%
Current ratio: 0.80

NORTH TEXAS MUNICIPAL WATER DISTRICT

EXECUTIVES

President, Darwin Whiteside
Board of Directors, Terry Sam Anderson
Superintendent, Terry Gage
Vice-President, Lynn Shuyler
Operations Manager, Bobby J Reeves
Supervisor, Kelly O'Brian
Manager, Joshua Hathaway
Auditors: WEAVER AND TIDWELL LLP DA

LOCATIONS

HQ: NORTH TEXAS MUNICIPAL WATER DISTRICT
501 E BROWN ST, WYLIE, TX 750984406
Phone: 972 442-5405
Web: WWW.NTMWD.COM

HISTORICAL FINANCIALS

Company Type: Private

Income Statement
FYE: September 30

	REVENUE ($ mil.)	NET INCOME ($ mil.)	NET PROFIT MARGIN	EMPLOYEES
09/16	398	125	31.6%	670
09/15	338	86	25.7%	—
09/14	310	56	18.3%	—
09/12	266	53	20.2%	—
Annual Growth	10.6%	23.7%	—	—

2016 Year-End Financials

Return on assets: 7.0% Cash ($ mil.): 97
Return on equity: 31.6%
Current ratio: 0.70

NORTHBAY HEALTHCARE GROUP

EXECUTIVES

Chief Executive Officer, Deborah Sugiyama

Supervisor, Kim Thorn
Engineer, Steve Henson
Personnel Manager, Ginia West
Auditors: MOSS ADAMS LLP SAN FRANCISCO

LOCATIONS

HQ: NORTHBAY HEALTHCARE GROUP
1200 B GALE WILSON BLVD, FAIRFIELD, CA
945333552
Phone: 707 646-5000

HISTORICAL FINANCIALS

Company Type: Private

Income Statement
FYE: December 31

	REVENUE ($ mil.)	NET INCOME ($ mil.)	NET PROFIT MARGIN	EMPLOYEES
12/15	460	15	3.3%	1,200
12/14	441	47	10.9%	—
12/13	398	30	7.5%	—
12/09	328	9	2.8%	—
Annual Growth	5.8%	9.0%	—	—

2015 Year-End Financials

Return on assets: 5.2% Cash ($ mil.): 3
Return on equity: 3.3%
Current ratio: 0.50

NORTHEAST ARC, INC.

EXECUTIVES

Chief Executive Officer, Gerard L McCarthy
Board of Directors, Kenneth Klaiman
Auditors: CBIZ TOFIAS BOSTON MA

LOCATIONS

HQ: NORTHEAST ARC, INC.
64 HOLTEN ST, DANVERS, MA 019231973
Phone: 978 762-4878
Web: WWW.NE-ARC.ORG

HISTORICAL FINANCIALS

Company Type: Private

Income Statement
FYE: June 30

	REVENUE ($ mil.)	NET INCOME ($ mil.)	NET PROFIT MARGIN	EMPLOYEES
06/15	171	0	0.3%	1,000
06/10	93	0	0.6%	—
06/09	83	0	—	—
06/06	587	0	—	—
Annual Growth	—	46.8%	—	—

2015 Year-End Financials

Return on assets: 4.3% Cash ($ mil.): 9
Return on equity: 0.3%
Current ratio: 2.90

NORTHEAST GEORGIA MEDICAL CENTER, INC.

EXECUTIVES

Chief Executive Officer, Carol Burrell

Accountant, Sara Adams

LOCATIONS

HQ: NORTHEAST GEORGIA MEDICAL CENTER, INC.
743 SPRING ST NE, GAINESVILLE, GA 305013715
Phone: 770 219-9000

HISTORICAL FINANCIALS

Company Type: Private

Income Statement
FYE: September 30

	REVENUE ($ mil.)	NET INCOME ($ mil.)	NET PROFIT MARGIN	EMPLOYEES
09/15	892	51	5.8%	3,053
09/14	819	110	13.5%	—
09/13	726	109	15.0%	—
09/05	400	8	2.0%	—
Annual Growth	8.3%	20.3%	—	—

2015 Year-End Financials

Return on assets: 4.2% Cash ($ mil.): 26
Return on equity: 5.8%
Current ratio: 1.30

NORTHEAST HOSPITAL CORPORATION

EXECUTIVES

Chief Executive Officer, Philip M Cormier
Auditors: PRICEWATERHOUSECOOPERS LLP BO

LOCATIONS

HQ: NORTHEAST HOSPITAL CORPORATION
85 HERRICK ST, BEVERLY, MA 019151790
Phone: 978 922-3000
Web: WWW.BEVERLYHOSPITAL.ORG

HISTORICAL FINANCIALS

Company Type: Private

Income Statement
FYE: September 30

	REVENUE ($ mil.)	NET INCOME ($ mil.)	NET PROFIT MARGIN	EMPLOYEES
09/16	372	(2)	—	2,800
09/15	341	13	4.1%	—
09/13	332	19	5.9%	—
09/08	296	(4)	—	—
Annual Growth	2.9%	—	—	—

2016 Year-End Financials

Return on assets: 2.0% Cash ($ mil.): 48
Return on equity: (-0.7%)
Current ratio: 1.50

NORTHEAST HOSPITAL FOUNDATION

EXECUTIVES

President, Norman Funderburk
Director, Lisa Sanchez

LOCATIONS

HISTORICAL FINANCIALS

Company Type: Private

Income Statement

FYE: December 31

	REVENUE ($ mil.)	NET INCOME ($ mil.)	NET PROFIT MARGIN	EMPLOYEES
12/15*	236	17	7.4%	900
06/10	0	0	11.9%	—
06/06	0	0	5.6%	—
06/05	0	(0)	—	—
Annual Growth 75.1%	—	—	—	—

*Fiscal year change

2015 Year-End Financials

Return on assets: 0.5%   Cash ($ mil.): —
Return on equity: 7.4%
Current ratio: 5.90

NORTHEAST OHIO REGIONAL SEWER DISTRICT

EXECUTIVES

President, Darnell Brown
Manager, Jennifer Demmerle
Manager, Robert First
Manager, Constance T Haqq
Personnel Manager, Dave McNeeley
Manager, Monica Dentkos
Executive Director, Julius Ciaecia
Manager, Ernest Bertok
Supervisor, Brian Page
Auditors: CIUNI & PANICHI LLC CLEVELAN

LOCATIONS

HQ: NORTHEAST OHIO REGIONAL SEWER DISTRICT
3900 EUCLID AVE, CLEVELAND, OH 441152506
Phone: 216 881-6600
Web: WWW.NEORSD.ORG

HISTORICAL FINANCIALS

Company Type: Private

Income Statement

FYE: December 31

	REVENUE ($ mil.)	NET INCOME ($ mil.)	NET PROFIT MARGIN	EMPLOYEES
12/15	280	54	19.4%	623
12/14	239	20	8.7%	—
12/13	209	15	7.3%	—
12/10	166	10	6.3%	—
Annual Growth 10.9%	39.1%	—	—	—

2015 Year-End Financials

Return on assets: 2.0%   Cash ($ mil.): 22
Return on equity: 19.4%
Current ratio: 1.30

NORTHEAST TEXAS ELECTRIC COOPERATIVE, INC.

EXECUTIVES

President, John Dugen
Accountant, Bob Duvall
General Manager, Rick Tyler
Vice-President, Barron Christensen

LOCATIONS

HQ: NORTHEAST TEXAS ELECTRIC COOPERATIVE, INC.
2221 H G MOSLEY PKWY # 100, LONGVIEW, TX 756043670
Phone: 903 757-3282

HISTORICAL FINANCIALS

Company Type: Private

Income Statement

FYE: December 31

	REVENUE ($ mil.)	NET INCOME ($ mil.)	NET PROFIT MARGIN	EMPLOYEES
12/15	225	0	—	3
12/14	250	0	—	—
12/13	236	0	—	—
12/12	212	0	—	—
Annual Growth 1.9%	—	—	—	—

2015 Year-End Financials

Return on assets: 9.3%   Cash ($ mil.): 11
Return on equity: —
Current ratio: 1.90

NORTHEASTERN UNIVERSITY

Since 1898 Northeastern University has been educating students in Boston and beyond. The school enrolls roughly 24000 students and employs 1600 faculty members. Its nine colleges offer 100 undergraduate programs and 160 graduate programs in areas such as the arts business engineering and law. Northeastern has a student-to-teacher ratio of about 13:1. Its highly-regarded experiential education program integrates classroom learning with real-world experience; students typically alternate between school and paid full-time work and leave with up to two years of professional experience. Northeastern started out as a night school housed in a YMCA facility.

Operations

Roughly 90% of Northeastern's students participate in its cooperative learning program which is conducted over four or five years and can include overseas study programs. The idea behind the teaching strategy is to give students some professional experience before graduation putting them a step ahead of peers. Sectors include the arts and humanities (think Boston Symphony Orchestra) finance and insurance (Goldman Sachs in the UK) and communications (the White House offers a co-op opportunity in its media affairs office).

The school also boasts extensive research centers and institutes. Northeastern receives research funding from a number of outside sources that include the National Institutes of Health the Department of Energy and the Department of Defense and the Department of Homeland Security. Funded research areas include heart disease the link between preterm births and environmental contaminants new ways to detect explosives and renewable energy sources.

Geographic Reach

Northeastern's students hail from all 50 states and about 90 countries. The university has study abroad programs in locations including Argentina Costa Rica France China Germany and the UK (among many others).

In addition to its main campus in Boston Northeastern has satellite graduate schools in Charlotte North Carolina Seattle California and Toronto.

Financial Performance

Northeastern reported revenue of $1.16 billion in 2017 which was about the same as 2016. Tuition and fees account for about 98% of the university's revenue. Tuition and fees totaled $1.14 billion in 2017 from about $1 billion in 2016. The university paid about $316 million in financial aid in 2017 an increase from about $292 million the year before.

EXECUTIVES

Senior Vice President Administration and Finance, John McCarthy
SVP and CEO Northeastern University Global Network, Philomena V. Mantella
Senior Vice President for External Affairs External Affairs, Michael Armini
President, Joseph E. Aoun
SVP Academinc Affairs and Provost, James C. Bean
VP and Chief Marketing Officer, Brian Sullivan
Senior Vice President, Diane Macgillivray
Vice President, Seamus Harreys
Vice President, Kathy Spiegelman
Vice President Facilities, Nancy May
Assistant Vice President of Communications, Renata Nyul
Vice President Student Affairs, Madeleine Estabrook
Special Assistant to the Senior Vice President, Maria Galarza
Vice President Public Affairs, Robert Gittens
Vice President of Media and Marketing, Brenna Eagan
Vice President Student Affairs, Edward Klotzbier
Senior Vice President, Ahmed Abdelal
Vice President for Media and Membership, Christopher Cunningham
Vice President And Campaign Director, Joe Donnelly
Administrative Operations Manager Office Of The Senior Vice President For Administration And Finance, Kathleen Tedesco
Associate Vice President, Paul Zernicke
Vice President Cio, Bob Weir
Vice President Research, Mel Bernstein
Associate Vice President Facilities Planning Des, James Cahill
Vice President Of External Affairs Bmes, Rachel Shaffer
Vice President of Media and Membership, Vijayeta Singh
Assistant Vice President, Lori Jacques
VP of Programs and Administration, Cristhy Mattos
Auditors: PRICEWATERHOUSECOOPERS LLP B

LOCATIONS

HQ: NORTHEASTERN UNIVERSITY
360 HUNTINGTON AVE, BOSTON, MA 021155000
Phone: 617 373-2000
Web: WWW.NORTHEASTERN.EDU

PRODUCTS/OPERATIONS

Selected Schools & Colleges
Bouvé; College of Health Sciences
College of Arts Media and Design
College of Computer and Information Science
College of Engineering
College of Professional Studies
College of Science
College of Social Sciences and Humanities
D'Amore-McKim School of Business
School of Law

HISTORICAL FINANCIALS
Company Type: Private

Income Statement
FYE: June 30

	REVENUE ($ mil.)	NET INCOME ($ mil.)	NET PROFIT MARGIN	EMPLOYEES
06/16	1,106	3	0.3%	4,175
06/13	947	147	15.6%	—
06/12	901	61	6.9%	—
Annual Growth	5.3%	(52.2%)	—	—

2016 Year-End Financials
Return on assets: 12.9%
Return on equity: 0.3%
Current ratio: —
Cash ($ mil.): 387

NORTHERN ARIZONA REGIONAL BEHAVIORAL HEALTH AUTHORITY, INC.

EXECUTIVES

Chief Executive Officer, Mary Jo Gregory
Manager, Judy Marfechuk
Manager, Erin Chadwick

LOCATIONS

HQ: NORTHERN ARIZONA REGIONAL BEHAVIORAL
HEALTH AUTHORITY, INC.
1300 S YALE ST, FLAGSTAFF, AZ 860016328
Phone: 928 774-7128
Web: WWW.NARBHA.ORG

HISTORICAL FINANCIALS
Company Type: Private

Income Statement
FYE: September 30

	REVENUE ($ mil.)	NET INCOME ($ mil.)	NET PROFIT MARGIN	EMPLOYEES
09/15	198	4	2.5%	120
09/14	159	3	2.3%	—
/*	0	0	—	—
Annual Growth	—	—	—	—

*Fiscal year change

2015 Year-End Financials
Return on assets: 0.9%
Return on equity: 2.5%
Current ratio: 3.90
Cash ($ mil.): 37

NORTHERN ARIZONA UNIVERSITY

Located a stone's throw from the Grand Canyon Northern Arizona University (NAU) has been educating students to see forever for more than a century. About 20000 students attend the school which is dominated by a mountainous landscape. Founded in 1899 NAU offers roughly 100 baccalaureate about 50 master's and a handful of doctoral programs. Undergraduate majors include exercise science hotel and restaurant management and visual communication. It's home to the High Altitude Sports Training Complex a multi-sport training center used by athletes to prepare for different environments and enhance performance. NAU's Extended Campuses provide access to higher education for students in their own communities.

Operations

While the university has made several other locations available to its student body most of the activity at NAU is centered on its primary campus. About 15500 undergraduates and 2000 graduate students attend classes at the Flagstaff campus. About 6500 undergraduate students live on campus in more than 25 residence halls.

Aside from its bricks-and-mortar campuses NAU offers instruction to students virtually through 70 online degree programs. The university's in-state tuition fees run $8871 for fiscal 2013 and nonresident tuition comes in at more than $21000.

NAU's enrollment of about 20000 students is instructed by some 900 full-time faculty members with a student-to-faculty ratio of 17 to 1.

Geographic Reach

Based in Flagstaff Arizona NAU is a four-year public university boasts more than 35 additional campus locations throughout Arizona. Besides Phoenix satellite campuses are located in Prescott Scottsdale Tuba City Tucson Kingman Mesa Yuma Paradise Valley and Whiteriver.

Financial Performance

Board-approved tuition rate increases and higher student enrollment both helped the university to log a 4% rise in revenue in fiscal 2012 as compared to 2011. These gains were partially offset however by decreases in grant and contracts.

Net income meanwhile dropped by 69% during the same reporting period due to declines in non-operating revenues resulting from drops in state appropriations and other non-operating revenues. Of note the educational institution received 23% of its revenue from state appropriations. NAU also points to increases in operating and non-operating expenses for the net income decreases. Non-operating expenses increased in 2012 due to rising interest expenses from capital asset-related debt.

EXECUTIVES

President, Dr Rita Cheng
Senior Vice-President, Mary Ellen C Williams
Assistant Vice-President, Richard M Bowen
Director, Teressa Wiechec
Manager, Becky McGaugh
Administrative Assistant, Azucena Ford
Engineer, Bridget Bero
Auditors: DEBBIE DAVENPORT PHOENIX ARI

LOCATIONS

HQ: NORTHERN ARIZONA UNIVERSITY
601 S KNOLES DR ROOM 220, FLAGSTAFF, AZ
860110001
Phone: 928 523-9011
Web: WWW.NAUATHLETICS.COM

PRODUCTS/OPERATIONS

Selected Colleges
College of Arts & Letters
College of Education
College of Engineering Forestry & Natural Sciences
College of Health and Human Services
College of Social & Behavioral Sciences
Graduate College
The W.A. Franke College of Business

HISTORICAL FINANCIALS
Company Type: Private

Income Statement
FYE: June 30

	REVENUE ($ mil.)	NET INCOME ($ mil.)	NET PROFIT MARGIN	EMPLOYEES
06/15	308	10	3.3%	3,863
06/14	282	4	1.5%	—
06/13	263	2	0.9%	—
06/12	241	15	6.3%	—
Annual Growth	8.6%	(12.7%)	—	—

2015 Year-End Financials
Return on assets: 9.6%
Return on equity: 3.3%
Current ratio: 1.30
Cash ($ mil.): 90

NORTHERN ILLINOIS MEDICAL CENTER

EXECUTIVES

President, Michael S Eesley
Director, Linda Irwin
Director, Cheryl Glombicki
Manager, Judy J Andronowitz
Auditors: KPMG LLP COLUMBUS OH

LOCATIONS

HQ: NORTHERN ILLINOIS MEDICAL CENTER
4201 W MEDICAL CENTER DR, MCHENRY, IL
600508499
Phone: 815 344-5000

HISTORICAL FINANCIALS
Company Type: Private

Income Statement
FYE: June 30

	REVENUE ($ mil.)	NET INCOME ($ mil.)	NET PROFIT MARGIN	EMPLOYEES
06/15	276	32	11.8%	1,200
06/14	242	16	7.0%	—
06/13	232	18	7.9%	—
06/10	238	23	9.9%	—
Annual Growth	3.0%	6.7%	—	—

2015 Year-End Financials
Return on assets: 9.4%
Return on equity: 11.8%
Current ratio: 0.40
Cash ($ mil.): 12

NORTHERN IMPROVEMENT COMPANY

EXECUTIVES

President, Thomas McCormick
Manager, Dave Fraase
Project Manager, Dominic Larson
Project Manager, Rob Bartz
Manager, Steven Schmidt
Auditors: EIDE BAILLY LLP FARGO NORTH

LOCATIONS

HQ: NORTHERN IMPROVEMENT COMPANY
4000 12TH AVE N, FARGO, ND 581022910
Phone: 701 277-1225
Web: WWW.NICND.COM

HISTORICAL FINANCIALS

Company Type: Private

Income Statement
FYE: December 31

	REVENUE ($ mil.)	NET INCOME ($ mil.)	NET PROFIT MARGIN	EMPLOYEES
12/15	177	11	6.7%	125
12/14	211	11	5.2%	—
12/13	188	5	2.8%	—
12/12	197	5	3.0%	—
Annual Growth	(3.4%)	26.1%	—	—

2015 Year-End Financials

Return on assets: 6.4%   Cash ($ mil.): 2
Return on equity: 6.7%
Current ratio: 0.90

NORTHERN WESTCHESTER HOSPITAL ASSOCIATION

EXECUTIVES

President, Joel Seligman
Director, Craig Brandt
Director, Ellen Muntener
Executive Secretary, Jeanne Alagno

LOCATIONS

HQ: NORTHERN WESTCHESTER HOSPITAL
ASSOCIATION
400 E MAIN ST, MOUNT KISCO, NY 105493477
Phone: 914 666-1200
Web: WWW.NWHORTHOANDSPINE.ORG

HISTORICAL FINANCIALS

Company Type: Private

Income Statement
FYE: December 31

	REVENUE ($ mil.)	NET INCOME ($ mil.)	NET PROFIT MARGIN	EMPLOYEES
12/15	250	11	4.7%	1,000
12/14	253	11	4.6%	—
12/13	242	7	3.1%	—
12/09	204	16	8.3%	—
Annual Growth	3.5%	(5.8%)	—	—

2015 Year-End Financials

Return on assets: 13.6%   Cash ($ mil.): 51
Return on equity: 4.7%
Current ratio: 1.60

NORTHSHORE SCHOOL DISTRICT

EXECUTIVES

Superintendent, Larry Francois
Administrative Assistant, Christine Cash
Engineer, Elizabeth Hunter
Consultant, Felton Rob
Office Manager, Judy Mitchell
Consultant, Mary Hayes
Director, Debbie Villanti
Auditors: PAT MCCARTHY OLYMPIA WA

LOCATIONS

HQ: NORTHSHORE SCHOOL DISTRICT
3330 MONTE VILLA PKWY, BOTHELL, WA 980218972
Phone: 425 408-6000
Web: WWW.NSD.ORG

HISTORICAL FINANCIALS

Company Type: Private

Income Statement
FYE: August 31

	REVENUE ($ mil.)	NET INCOME ($ mil.)	NET PROFIT MARGIN	EMPLOYEES
08/15	266	23	8.7%	2,312
08/12	233	0	0.3%	—
08/11	241	(29)	—	—
08/10	0	0	—	—
Annual Growth	—	1815.2%	—	—

2015 Year-End Financials

Return on assets: 5.4%   Cash ($ mil.): 223
Return on equity: 8.7%
Current ratio: —

NORTHSIDE HOSPITAL - CHEROKEE, INC.

EXECUTIVES

Chief Executive Officer, William M Hayes
Board of Directors, L Austin Flint
Director, Gail Blalock
Chief Financial Officer, Brian Jennette

LOCATIONS

HQ: NORTHSIDE HOSPITAL - CHEROKEE, INC.
450 NRTHSIDE CHROKEE BLVD, CANTON, GA
301158015
Phone: 770 720-5100
Web: WWW.NORTHSIDE.COM

HISTORICAL FINANCIALS

Company Type: Private

Income Statement
FYE: September 30

	REVENUE ($ mil.)	NET INCOME ($ mil.)	NET PROFIT MARGIN	EMPLOYEES
09/15	184	1	1.0%	575
09/14	154	2	1.6%	—
09/13	120	4	3.7%	—
09/12	127	4	3.7%	—
Annual Growth	13.2%	(25.7%)	—	—

2015 Year-End Financials

Return on assets: —   Cash ($ mil.): 3
Return on equity: 1.0%
Current ratio: 0.20

NORTHSIDE HOSPITAL, INC.

Northside Hospital is no one-trick pony — it actually operates three hospitals serving Atlanta and surrounding areas. Also known as the Northside Healthcare Delivery System the Northside Hospital network includes some 840 licensed beds and more than 2500 physicians on multiple campuses with a host of outpatient health facilities including physician office parks and specialized cancer centers. All of Northside's hospitals are full-service acute-care facilities that provide specialty care including cancer care surgery radiology and women's health. Northside Hospital which opened in 1970 is merging with Gwinnett Health System.

Operations

In addition to its 537-bed hospital in Sandy Springs Northside has hospitals in Cherokee and Forsyth counties as well as more than 120 outpatient centers across Georgia.

Northside Hospital handles about 700000 patient visits annually at its facilities. The organization's cancer treatment division partners with the Cancer Support Community of Atlanta to provide mental health social and educational services to cancer patients and survivors as well as family members and friends.

Geographic Reach

Northside Hospital's three campuses are located in Atlanta Forsyth and Cherokee Georgia. It also operate about 40 outpatient clinics and physician practices scattered across the northern Atlanta metropolitan area.

Strategy

Northside Hospital is conducting expansion and renovation efforts to meet the needs of area residents. It recently completed an expansion and relocation of its Cherokee County Spine & Pain Center (near the Cherokee hospital campus). In 2015 it expanded its radiology offerings with a new outpatient imaging center in Jasper.

After two years of talks with fellow Georgia-based hospital system Gwinnett Health Northside and Gwinnett have agreed to merge operations. The combined system will have nearly 3500 physicians and 1480 beds.

EXECUTIVES

CFO, Peggy Gatliff
VP Administration and CEO Northside Hospital-Forsyth, Robert Putnam
CEO Northside Hospital-Cherokee, William (Billy) Hayes
Chair Department of Obstetrics and Gynecology, Ceana Nezhat
CEO Northside Hospital-Forsyth, Skip Putnam
COO, Peter Kennedy
Vice President Purchasing, Chuck Dalton
Director Of Pharmacy, Judy Gardner
Pharmd, Aziza Aboubaker
Medical Records Director, Sharon Mullings
Nursing Director, Janis Dubow
Director of Pharmacy Supervisor, Mike Tate
Director ICU Coronary Care Unit, Brandon Frady
Rph, Patricia Boatright Gilley
Vice President Marketing and Communications, Lee Echols
Respiratory Therapy Director, Larry Lindberg
Vice President Planning and Real Estate, Doug Macdonald
Radiology Director, DIEDRA DIXON
Pharmacy Manager, Lorenzo Bethea
Pharmd, Jessica Gorgeis
Vice President, Peter Singer
Secretary, Beth Keivani

LOCATIONS

HQ: NORTHSIDE HOSPITAL, INC.
1000 JOHNSON FERRY RD, ATLANTA, GA 303421611
Phone: 404 851-8000

Selected Locations
Alpharetta Medical Campus
Dunwoody Cancer Center
Imaging at Peachtree Dunwoody
Medlock Bridge Imaging
Meridian Park Plaza
Northside Hospital Doctors Center
Northside Hospital-Atlanta
Northside Hospital-Cherokee
Northside Hospital-Forsyth
Northside-Forsyth Outpatient Surgery Center
Northside Sugar Hill Imaging (Buford)
Pediatric Center at Northside/Alpharetta
Roswell Cancer Center
Townelake Medical Office/Riverstone Imaging

COMPETITORS

Children's Healthcare of Atlanta
DeKalb Medical
Emory Healthcare
Grady Health System
Gwinnett Health System
Northeast Georgia Health System
Piedmont Healthcare
Regency Hospital
Shepherd Center
SunLink Health Systems
The Fulton-DeKalb Hospital Authority
WellStar Health System

HISTORICAL FINANCIALS

Company Type: Private

Income Statement   FYE: September 30

	REVENUE ($ mil.)	NET INCOME ($ mil.)	NET PROFIT MARGIN	EMPLOYEES
09/15	1,733	223	12.9%	8,000
09/13	1,253	109	8.7%	—
09/12	829	60	7.3%	—
09/09	1,002	8	0.8%	—
Annual Growth	9.6%	73.5%	—	—

2015 Year-End Financials

Return on assets: 0.9%   Cash ($ mil.): 348
Return on equity: 12.9%
Current ratio: 1.70

NORTHSIDE INDEPENDENT SCHOOL DISTRICT

EXECUTIVES

Superintendent, John Folks
Board of Directors, Bennie L Cole
Director, George H Torres
Principal, Ellen Sutton
Chief Financial Officer, Alisa Thienpont
Finance Manager, Benjamin Hawkins
Auditors: WEAVER AND TIDWELL LLP AUSTI

LOCATIONS

HQ: NORTHSIDE INDEPENDENT SCHOOL DISTRICT
5900 EVERS RD, SAN ANTONIO, TX 782381606
Phone: 210 397-8770
Web: WWW.NISD.NET

HISTORICAL FINANCIALS

Company Type: Private

Income Statement   FYE: August 31

	REVENUE ($ mil.)	NET INCOME ($ mil.)	NET PROFIT MARGIN	EMPLOYEES
08/16	1,119	16	1.5%	13,698
08/15	1,057	64	6.1%	—
08/14	1,011	125	12.4%	—
08/13	917	(47)	—	—
Annual Growth	6.9%	—	—	—

2016 Year-End Financials

Return on assets: 3.1%   Cash ($ mil.): 464
Return on equity: 1.5%
Current ratio: —

NORTHWEST COMMUNITY HOSPITAL INC

Northwest Community Healthcare (NCH) has captured the hearts of northern Illinois. Located in Chicago's northwest suburbs the not-for-profit health system includes the not-for-profit Northwest Community Hospital a regional leader in providing all kinds of cardiac care including open-heart surgery cardiac catheterization and rehabilitation services. Along with cardiac care the nearly 500-bed hospital offers a comprehensive range of acute medical and surgical care. NCH also operates NCH Medical Group which has more than 150 primary and specialty physicians in more than 20 medical offices. Other offerings include an ambulatory surgery center a handful of urgent care centers and a behavioral health center. NCH has more than 1200 physicians on its staff.

Operations

NCH's Northwest Community Hospital is a Level II trauma center; it provides comprehensive medical and surgical care. It also provides a full range of outpatient infusion and injection services that include chemotherapy blood transfusions and treatments for blood and immunological disorders.

In 2016 Northwest Community Healthcare had 20000 inpatient and 350000 outpatient visits. It had more than 38000 home care visits and 2700 newborn deliveries as well as more than 17000 inpatient and outpatient surgeries (ranging from minimally invasive procedures to open-heart surgery).

Geographic Reach

Located in Arlington Heights Illinois NCH serves residents of Chicago's northwest suburbs.

Strategy

Like most integrated health care systems NCH works to broaden the spectrum of services it provides to better meet the needs of its service area. It often seeks partnership opportunities to expand its offerings. For example in 2017 Northwest Community Hospital added telemedicine capabilities to its pediatric emergency department and its neonatal intensive care unit. It partners with the Ann & Robert H. Lurie Children's Hospital to provide the service.

EXECUTIVES

President Medical Staff, Cynthia Valukas
President CEO, Stephen O. Scogna
CFO, Marsha Liu
Chief Technical Officer, Jack King
Vice President Of Marketing, Angie Stefaniu
Vice President Facilities, Bob Klasek
Director Icu coronary Care Unit Training Manager, Phyllis Cerone
Director of Pharmacy, Jason Alonzo
Vice President Hospital Operations, Melissa Smith
Vice Chairman, Max Brittain
Chairman, Daniel P. DiCaro

LOCATIONS

HQ: NORTHWEST COMMUNITY HOSPITAL INC
800 W CENTRAL RD, ARLINGTON HEIGHTS, IL 600052349
Phone: 847 618-1000

PRODUCTS/OPERATIONS

Selected Facilities
Arlington Heights Medical Offices (Arlington Heights)
Buffalo Grove Fitness Center (Buffalo Grove)
Buffalo Grove Medical Offices (Buffalo Grove)
Buffalo Grove Treatment Center (Buffalo Grove)
Busse Center for Specialty Medicine (Arlington Heights)
Day Surgery Center (Arlington Heights)
Lake Zurich Treatment Center (Lake Zurich)
Northwest Community Hospital (Arlington Heights)
Palatine Medical Offices (Palatine)
Shaumburg Imaging Center (Schaumburg)
Shaumburg Medical Offices (Schaumburg)
Shaumburg Treatment Center (Schaumburg)
Youth Center Adolescent Substance Abuse Center (Arlington Heights)
Wellness Center (Arlington Heights)

COMPETITORS

Advocate Health Care
Alexian Brothers Health System
Central DuPage Hospital
Elmhurst Memorial Healthcare
Loyola University Health System
McDonough District Hospital
NorthShore University HealthSystem
Northwestern Lake Forest Hospital
Northwestern Memorial HealthCare
Rockford Health System
Rush System for Health
Silver Cross Hospital
St. Bernard Hospital and Health Care Center
University of Chicago Medical Center

HISTORICAL FINANCIALS
Company Type: Private

Income Statement   FYE: September 30

	REVENUE ($ mil.)	NET INCOME ($ mil.)	NET PROFIT MARGIN	EMPLOYEES
09/15	432	24	5.6%	2,800
09/14	422	25	6.0%	—
09/13	412	20	4.9%	—
Annual Growth	2.4%	9.9%	—	—

2015 Year-End Financials

Return on assets: 12.0%   Cash ($ mil.): 2
Return on equity: 5.6%
Current ratio: 0.60

NORTHWEST HOSPITAL & MEDICAL CENTER

EXECUTIVES

Chief Executive Officer, Cynthia Hecker
Director, James Hart
Director, Erik Walerius

LOCATIONS

HQ: NORTHWEST HOSPITAL & MEDICAL CENTER
1550 N 115TH ST, SEATTLE, WA 981338498
Phone: 206 364-0500

HISTORICAL FINANCIALS
Company Type: Private

Income Statement   FYE: June 30

	REVENUE ($ mil.)	NET INCOME ($ mil.)	NET PROFIT MARGIN	EMPLOYEES
06/15	281	15	5.6%	1,600
06/10	5	0	16.3%	—
/* 0	0	—	—	—
Annual Growth	—	—	—	—

*Fiscal year change

2015 Year-End Financials

Return on assets: 4.1%   Cash ($ mil.): 12
Return on equity: 5.6%
Current ratio: 1.00

NORTHWEST HOSPITAL CENTER, INC.

EXECUTIVES

Chairman, Harold Weiss

LOCATIONS

HQ: NORTHWEST HOSPITAL CENTER, INC.
5401 OLD COURT RD, RANDALLSTOWN, MD
211335103
Phone: 410 521-2200

HISTORICAL FINANCIALS
Company Type: Private

Income Statement   FYE: June 30

	REVENUE ($ mil.)	NET INCOME ($ mil.)	NET PROFIT MARGIN	EMPLOYEES
06/15	226	18	8.3%	981
06/14	231	18	7.9%	—
06/13	245	20	8.4%	—
06/12	226	11	5.2%	—
Annual Growth	(0.1%)	17.1%	—	—

2015 Year-End Financials

Return on assets: 13.0%   Cash ($ mil.): 84
Return on equity: 8.3%
Current ratio: 2.90

NORTHWEST INDEPENDENT SCHOOL DISTRICT

EXECUTIVES

Superintendent, Ryder Warren
Principal, Ron Andres
Vice-President, Mark Schluter
Board of Directors, Jennifer Wigant
Director, Kitty Poehler
Assistant Manager, John Graswich
Manager, Lachandra Torrence
Auditors: HAYNES AND ASSOCIATES PC ROA

LOCATIONS

HQ: NORTHWEST INDEPENDENT SCHOOL DISTRICT
2001 TEXAN DR, JUSTIN, TX 762478791
Phone: 817 215-0000
Web: WWW.NISDTX.ORG

HISTORICAL FINANCIALS
Company Type: Private

Income Statement   FYE: June 30

	REVENUE ($ mil.)	NET INCOME ($ mil.)	NET PROFIT MARGIN	EMPLOYEES
06/16	244	26	10.8%	2,000
06/11	211	9	4.4%	—
06/06	11	(1)	—	—
06/05	461	0	0.0%	—
Annual Growth	(5.6%)	95.7%	—	—

2016 Year-End Financials

Return on assets: 1.4%   Cash ($ mil.): 27
Return on equity: 10.8%
Current ratio: —

NORTHWEST PIPELINE LLC

Gas transmission and distribution

EXECUTIVES

Chief Financial Officer; Senior Vice President,
Donald R Chappel
Auditors: ERNST & YOUNG LLP HOUSTON TE

LOCATIONS

HQ: NORTHWEST PIPELINE LLC
295 S CHIPETA WAY FL 4, SALT LAKE CITY, UT
841081285
Phone: 801 583-8800

HISTORICAL FINANCIALS
Company Type: Private

Income Statement   FYE: December 31

	REVENUE ($ mil.)	NET INCOME ($ mil.)	NET PROFIT MARGIN	EMPLOYEES
12/16	474	180	38.1%	2
12/15	472	178	37.8%	—
12/14	470	170	36.3%	—
Annual Growth	0.4%	2.9%	—	—

NORTHWESTERN MEMORIAL HOSPITAL

EXECUTIVES

Chief Executive Officer, Dean Harrison
President, Richard J Gannotta
Chief Financial Officer, Peter McCanna
Chairman of the Board, William J Brodsky
Manager, Terri Halverson
Director of Finance, Francis Fraher

LOCATIONS

HQ: NORTHWESTERN MEMORIAL HOSPITAL
251 E HURON ST, CHICAGO, IL 606113055
Phone: 312 755-0604
Web: WWW.NM.ORG

HISTORICAL FINANCIALS
Company Type: Private

Income Statement   FYE: August 31

	REVENUE ($ mil.)	NET INCOME ($ mil.)	NET PROFIT MARGIN	EMPLOYEES
08/15	1,337	198	14.8%	5,800
08/10	1,380	64	4.7%	—
08/09	1,304	4	0.3%	—
Annual Growth	0.4%	87.7%	—	—

NORTHWESTERN UNIVERSITY

With its main campus in the Chicago suburb of Evanston Northwestern University (NU) serves its 21000 students through about a dozen schools and colleges such as the Medill School of Journalism and the McCormick School of Engineering and Applied Sciences. Its Chicago campus houses the schools of law and medicine as well as several hospitals of the McGaw Medical Center. With a

faculty of more than 3300 the school has a student-to-teacher ratio of about 6:1. NU is home to several research centers and community outreach programs; it also has a branch in Qatar. It is the only private member of the Big 10 conference; varsity sports include baseball football basketball and fencing.

Operations

Among NU's top-ranked programs are its law school medical school and its engineering program. Its Kellogg Graduate School of Management consistently ranks among the nation's top five business schools by Business Week and U.S. News & World Report. Its prestigious journalism and drama programs produced such alumni as Charlton Heston Gary Marshall and Julia Louis-Dreyfus. Retired US Supreme Court Justice John Paul Stevens is also a former Wildcat.

NU spends its $1.6 billion research budget (including about $620 million in sponsored funds) performing research at 24 university research centers (and nearly 100 other centers) in areas such as materials science biomedical engineering African studies performance studies and marketing. The school has earned recognition for its research in genetic medicine nanotechnology biochemistry neuroscience cancer research and materials sciences. NU partners have included the Argonne National Laboratory Fermilab and local universities.

Geographic Reach

NU's main campus in Chicago encompasses about 240 acres in Evanston. The university operates another 25-acre campus in Chicago as well as its education center in Qatar. NU was founded to serve the Northwest region of the US which includes parts or all of the states of Illinois Indiana Michigan Minnesota Ohio and Wisconsin.

Financial Performance

NU reported a 6% decrease in revenues to $2.1 billion in fiscal 2015 (ended August) a drop that was primarily driven by a decline in private gifts. Net income plummeted 91% to $192 million that year and operating cash outflow totaled $91.4 million.

HISTORY

Northwestern University's Methodist founders met in 1850 to create an institution of higher learning serving the original Northwest Territory. The university was chartered in 1851 and two years later it acquired 379 acres of property north of Chicago on Lake Michigan. The town of Evanston was later named after John Evans one of the school's founders.

Classes began in the fall of 1855 with two professors and 10 students. By 1869 Northwestern had more than 100 students and began to admit women. In 1870 Northwestern signed an affiliation agreement with the Chicago Medical College (founded 1859) and three years later it joined with the original University of Chicago (no relation to the current institution) to create the Union College of Law. When the University of Chicago closed in 1886 due to financial difficulties Northwestern took control of the law school. The university reorganized in 1891 consolidating its affiliated professional schools (dentistry law medicine and pharmacy) into the university.

By 1900 Northwestern had become the third-largest university in the US (after Harvard and Michigan) with an enrollment of 2700. During the 1920s the university created the Medill School of Journalism named for Joseph Medill founder of the Chicago Tribune. In 1924 the school's athletic teams adopted the nickname Wildcats and two years later the university completed the primary buildings that form its Chicago campus. Northwestern suffered a drop in enrollment during the

Depression but after WWII it saw student numbers swell as veterans took advantage of the GI Bill. Expansion continued throughout the 1960s and 1970s.

In 1985 the school and the City of Evanston began developing a research center to attract more high-tech industries to the area. The university's graduate school of business achieved national prominence in 1988 after it was ranked #1 in the US by Business Week. In 1995 Northwestern's football team forever the doormat of the Big 10 achieved national fame when it won the conference championship.

In 1998 faculty member Professor John Pople won the Nobel Prize in Chemistry the first Nobel Prize awarded to a faculty member while teaching at the university.

Northwestern won a significant legal battle in 1998 when a judge ruled that the university was not obligated to pay a faculty member simply because he had been granted tenure.

The university's dental school closed its doors in 2001 citing the difficulties posed for private schools in providing a competitive dental education.

EXECUTIVES

VP Finance Operations and Treasurer, Ingrid S. Stafford, age 64
VP Information Technology and CIO, Sean B. Reynolds
Dean Kellogg School of Management, Sally E. Blount
VP and Chief Investment Officer, William H. (Will) McLean
Dean School of Communication, Barbara J. O'Keefe
EVP, Nim Chinniah
Provost, Daniel I. Linzer, age 64
Dean Libraries, Sarah M. Pritchard
President, Morton O. Shapiro
VP Global Marketing and CFhief Marketing Officer, Mary L. Baglivo
Dean Northwestern University in Qatar, Everette E. Dennis
Dean School of Professional Studies, Thomas F. Gibbons
Dean Medill School of Journalism Media and Integrated Marketing Communications, Bradley Hamm
Dean Graduate School, Dwight A. McBride
Dean Bienen School of Music, Toni-Marie Montgomery
Dean Feinberg School of Medicine, Eric G. Neilson
Dean School of Education and Social Policy, Penelope L. Peterson
Dean Weinberg College of Arts and Sciences, Adrian W. B. Randolph
Dean McCormick School of Engineering and Applied Science, Julio M. Ottino
Dean Pritzker School of Law, Daniel B. Rodriguez
Vice President and General Counsel, Thomas Cline
Vice President Student Affairs, William Banis
Vice President Ash Fy17, Alexis Thompson
Physical Therapy and Human Movement Sc, Julius Dewald
Vice President, Donna Jurdy
Associate Vice President For Research, Fruma Yehiely
Interim Department Chairman, Gary Martin
Vice President for Student Affairs, Margaret Sullivan
Assistant Vice President Public Safety And Chief P, Bruce Lewis
Office of the Vice President For Research, Erin Wallace
Associate Vice President Alumni Relations And Development, David Lively
Associate Vice President And Executive Director, Alicia Loffler

Vice President For International Relations, Devora Grynspan
Vice President Operations, Gary Wojtowicz
Assistant Vice President For Research, Meg McDonald
Pharmacy Manager, Amber Parish
Director of Admissions and Financial Aid, Cristina Gapasin
Vice President and General Counsel, Phil Harris
Associate Vice President For Finance Financial Operations, Michael Szczepanek
Associate Vice President of Compliance, Marcia Isaacson
Assistant Vice President for Information and Analytics, Amit Prachand
Director Of Admissions, Alex Schultes
Assistant Vice President Deputy Chief of Police, Gloria Graham
Assistant Vice President Strategic Communications, Ofelia Casillas
Associate Vice President Human Resources, Dana Bradley
Chairman, William A. Osborn, age 69
Assistant Treasurer, Richard Emrich
Secretary 1, Sheila Hodges
Board Member, Angela Y Lee
Board Member, Leon Platanias
Auditors: PRICEWATERHOUSECOOPERS LLP CH

LOCATIONS

HQ: NORTHWESTERN UNIVERSITY
633 CLARK ST, EVANSTON, IL 602080001
Phone: 847 491-3741
Web: WWW.NORTHWESTERN.EDU

PRODUCTS/OPERATIONS

Selected Programs
Continuing and Professional Programs
Graduate Programs
Pre-Collegiate Programs
Undergraduate Programs

Selected Schools and Colleges
Bienen School of Music
Feinberg School of Medicine
The Graduate School
Kellogg School of Management
McCormick School of Engineering and Applied Science
Medill School of Journalism Media Integrated Marketing Communications
Northwestern in Qatar
School of Communication
School of Continuing Studies
School of Education and Social Policy
School of Law
Weinberg College of Arts and Science

HISTORICAL FINANCIALS
Company Type: Private

Income Statement
FYE: August 31

	REVENUE ($ mil.)	NET INCOME ($ mil.)	NET PROFIT MARGIN	EMPLOYEES
08/16	2,200	221	10.1%	5,954
08/09	1,605	(1,388)	—	—
08/08	8	0	1.9%	—
Annual Growth	100.1%	146.8%	—	—

2016 Year-End Financials
Return on assets: 12.1%   Cash ($ mil.): 215
Return on equity: 10.1%
Current ratio: —

NORTON HOSPITALS, INC

EXECUTIVES

President, Steven A Williams
Board of Directors, Robert B Azar
Board of Directors, Theodore T Myre Jr
Director, Pam Missi

LOCATIONS

HQ: NORTON HOSPITALS, INC
200 E CHESTNUT ST, LOUISVILLE, KY 402021831
Phone: 502 629-8000

HISTORICAL FINANCIALS
Company Type: Private

Income Statement

	REVENUE ($ mil.)	NET INCOME ($ mil.)	NET PROFIT MARGIN	EMPLOYEES
12/15	1,712	137	8.0%	1,500
12/14	1,577	187	11.9%	—
Annual Growth	8.6%	(26.7%)	—	—

2015 Year-End Financials
Return on assets: 4.7%
Return on equity: 8.0%
Current ratio: 1.80
Cash ($ mil.): —

NOVA SOUTHEASTERN UNIVERSITY, INC.

Nova Southeastern University (NSU) gives a whole new meaning to "school of sharks." NSU whose mascot is the deep sea predator has an enrollment of more than 27000 students and offers a variety of undergraduate graduate and professional academic programs. NSU offers degrees in several medical disciplines (osteopathic medicine pharmacy optometry nursing) marine biology business law education and computer sciences. The not-for-profit independent school operates four campuses in the Miami-Fort Lauderdale area several health centers and an oceanographic center. Founded in 1964 Nova University merged with Southeastern University of the Health Sciences in 1994 to become Nova Southeastern University.

Operations

In addition to its undergraduate and graduate programs NSU also operates The University School a pre-K through 12th grade college preparatory day school that draws part of its staff from NSU's School of Education and Human services. The university's Mailman Segal Institute for Early Childhood Studies serves the local community with programming for parents and educators.

Geographic Reach

NSU is a distance education pioneer (it was the first US university to offer graduate programs online) offering classes on the Internet as well as at six regional centers in Florida and Puerto Rico.

Financial Performance

Continuing a trend of earnings growth over the last five years from organic growth measures NSU reported a 4% rise in revenues in 2014 to some $640 million. The growth was attributed to increased tuition and fee income as well as revenues from auxiliary enterprises and government grants.

Strategy

As universities do NSU regularly invests in facility upgrades to meet the growing needs of its students. In 2014 it broke ground on the NSU Center for Collaborative Research (CCR) that will house an IBM supercomputer a tech incubator one of the state's largest wet labs and space for guest researchers. Other CCR facilities will include cancer and neuro-immune institutes an incubator for security businesses and an entire floor for the US Geological Survey which will partner with the university on research into Everglades restoration projects.

EXECUTIVES

Intrm Vice President Information Technology, Greg Horne
Executive Vice Chancellor and Provost, Frederick Lippman
CEO President and Trustee, George L. Hanbury
VP Finance, W. David Heron
Dean Student Affairs, Brad Williams
Executive Director Alvin Sherman Library, Harriett MacDougall
Dean Shepard Broad Law Center, Athornia Steele
University Provost and EVP Academic Affairs, Frank DePiano
Dean University School, Jerome Chermak
Dean College of Health Care Sciences, Richard E. Davis
Dean Oceanographic Center, Richard E. Dodge
Dean Center for Psychological Studies, Karen Grosby
Dean College of Medical Sciences, Harold E. Laubach
Dean Mailman Segal Institute for Early Childhood Studies, Roni Leiderman
Dean College of Optometry, David S. Loshin
Dean College of Pharmacy, Andr ©s Malav ©
Dean Farquhar College of Arts and Sciences, Don Rosenblum
Dean College of Osteopathic Medicine, Anthony J. Silvagni
Dean Fischler School of Education, H. Wells Singleton
Dean College of Dental Medicine, Robert A. Uchin
Dean Graduate School of Humanities and Social Sciences, Honggang Yang
EVP and COO, Jacqueline A. Travisano
Senior Executive Assistant President Manager, Shirley Naidoo
CEO Health Clinics, Robert S. Oller
VP Information Technology and CIO, Tom West
Executive Assistant Vice President, Katharine Perren
Pharmacy Manager, Todd Schmidt
Vice President for Finance and Chief Financial Officer, Alyson Silva
Vice President Human Resources, Robert Pietrykowski
Vice President, Joseph P Degaetano
Provost And Executive Vice President For Academic Affairs, Ralph Rogers
Vice President for Research and Technology Transfer, Gary Margules
Vice President for Legal Affairs, Joel Berman
Director Of Clinical Services, Jessica Granata
Vice President Of Finance, David Heron
Vice President Programs, Jennifer Donelson
Vice President For Public Relations and Marketing Communications, Kyle Fisher
Vice President, Jennifer Anderson
Chair, Ronald G. Assaf
Vice Chair, Barry J. Silverman
Board Member, Doug Crowell
Auditors: KPMG LLP GREENSBORO NC

LOCATIONS

HQ: NOVA SOUTHEASTERN UNIVERSITY, INC.
3301 COLLEGE AVE, DAVIE, FL 333147796
Phone: 954 262-7300

COMPETITORS

Florida Atlantic University
University of Florida
Florida International University

HISTORICAL FINANCIALS
Company Type: Private

Income Statement
FYE: June 30

	REVENUE ($ mil.)	NET INCOME ($ mil.)	NET PROFIT MARGIN	EMPLOYEES
06/15	678	45	6.7%	2,500
06/12	689	48	7.1%	—
06/10	612	22	3.7%	—
Annual Growth	2.1%	15.2%	—	—

2015 Year-End Financials
Return on assets: 6.5%
Return on equity: 6.7%
Current ratio: 0.10
Cash ($ mil.): 35

NOVELART MANUFACTURING COMPANY

EXECUTIVES

President, Marvin H Schwartz
Financial Executive, Mike Fields
Personnel Director, Nancy Madden
General Manager, Dan Sunderhaus
Purchasing Agent, Darlene Miller
Manager, Darrell Jump
Auditors: PITCHER ENDERS & DROHAN CINC

LOCATIONS

HQ: NOVELART MANUFACTURING COMPANY
2121 SECTION RD, CINCINNATI, OH 452373509
Phone: 513 351-7700
Web: WWW.TOPICZINC.COM

HISTORICAL FINANCIALS
Company Type: Private

Income Statement
FYE: September 30

	REVENUE ($ mil.)	NET INCOME ($ mil.)	NET PROFIT MARGIN	EMPLOYEES
09/16	345	0	—	160
09/15	361	0	—	—
09/14	359	0	—	—
09/13	330	0	—	—
Annual Growth	1.5%	—	—	—

2016 Year-End Financials
Return on assets: 1.7%
Return on equity: —
Current ratio: 1.90
Cash ($ mil.): 3

NOVO CONSTRUCTION, INC.

EXECUTIVES

Chief Executive Officer, James C Fowler
Financial Executive, Christina Fonseca
Project Manager, Scott Plummer
Superintendent, Craig Butcher
Superintendent, Dave Fournier
Project Manager, Jeff Bilinski

LOCATIONS

HQ: NOVO CONSTRUCTION, INC.
 1460 OBRIEN DR, MENLO PARK, CA 940251432
Phone: 650 701-1500
Web: WWW.NOVOCONSTRUCTION.COM

HISTORICAL FINANCIALS

Company Type: Private

Income Statement

FYE: October 31

	REVENUE ($ mil.)	NET INCOME ($ mil.)	NET PROFIT MARGIN	EMPLOYEES
10/16	577	6	1.1%	155
10/15	553	5	1.0%	—
10/14	463	4	1.0%	—
10/13	404	4	1.1%	—
Annual Growth	12.6%	12.4%	—	—

2016 Year-End Financials

Return on assets: 18.6%   Cash ($ mil.): 51
Return on equity: 1.1%
Current ratio: 1.00

NYACK HOSPITAL FOUNDATION, INC.

Nyack Hospital rocks when it comes to providing medical services in New York's Rockland and Bergen counties. The not-for-profit hospital is a 375-bed acute care medical and surgical facility with a staff of more than 650 doctors and surgeons. Nyack Hospital houses specialty centers for cancer care stroke pediatrics joint replacement sleep studies wound care and women's wellness. In partnership with Touro College of Osteopathic Medicine it also provides training programs for medical students. Nyack Hospital is a member of the New York-Presbyterian Healthcare System and is affiliated with the Columbia University College of Physicians and Surgeons.

Operations

Nyack Hospital serves some 14000 inpatients per year. It also handles about 2000 births 40000 emergency room visits and 66000 home health visits.

Strategy

To better serve its customers' needs and prosper in an increasingly competitive market environment Nyack Hospital has set some specific strategic goals. These include advancing inpatient satisfaction implementing a fully electronic health record system (installing the McKesson Paragon hospital information system) building physician networks and services to become an Accountable Care Organization) refinancing the hospital and conducting a capital campaign to pay for improvements and new programs and facilities and constructing

and operating an inpatient adult psychiatric unit and an outpatient crisis intervention service in partnership with Rockland County Department of Mental Health and New York State Department of Mental Health.

In 2013 it opened the Nyack Hospital Prenatal Center (formerly known as the Rockland County Department of Health Prenatal Clinic); it also opened the Weill Cornell Multiple Sclerosis Center at Nyack Hospital. That year the hospital announced a $1 million energy and water conservation project aimed at saving $270000 per year in utility costs and reducing power use by more 1 million kWhs annually. Nyack Hospital also expects to conserve 12.4 million gallons of water per year by implementing energy and water conservation measures.

Extending its plans through 2017 Nyack Hospital plans to enlarge its emergency department and consolidate all ambulatory surgery functions improve parking areas and access and modernize all spaces that patients encounter and transform itself into a contemporary responsive facility.

The hospital is able to invest in new and expanded services based on its ability to grow its revenues and closely manage expenses within its operating budget.

Company Background

In 2011 Nyack Hospital opened the Weill Cornell Multiple Sclerosis Center at Nyack Hospital.

Founded in 1895 and originally funded by the proceeds of a town fair the hospital is a part of the New York-Presbyterian Healthcare System.

EXECUTIVES

VP Human Resources, Mary Shinick
Board Member, Richard King
Board Member, Lawrence Simon
Secretary, Roseann Flocco

LOCATIONS

HQ: NYACK HOSPITAL FOUNDATION, INC.
 160 N MIDLAND AVE, NYACK, NY 109601998
Phone: 845 348-2000
Web: WWW.NYACKHOSPITAL.ORG

PRODUCTS/OPERATIONS

Selected Services
Addiction and recovery
Aspirin desensitization program
Breast Center
Cardiology
Center for Diagnostic Imaging
Clinical cancer genetics program
Community health education
Diabetes
Edythe Kurz Center for Sleep Medicine
Emergency department
Employee assistance program
Home care
Joint Replacement Center
Maternity
Medical library
Pain management
Pediatrics
Respiratory care
Stroke Center
Support groups
Therapy and rehab
Union State Bank Cancer Center
Weight management
Weill Cornell Multiple Sclerosis Center
Wound care

COMPETITORS

Bergen Regional Medical	The Valley Hospital Westchester Medical Center
Englewood Hospital and Medical Center	
Phelps Memorial Hospital Center	

HISTORICAL FINANCIALS

Company Type: Private

Income Statement

FYE: December 31

	REVENUE ($ mil.)	NET INCOME ($ mil.)	NET PROFIT MARGIN	EMPLOYEES
12/15	216	(2)	—	1,300
12/14	206	(4)	—	—
12/13	222	3	1.4%	—
12/09	188	5	3.0%	—
Annual Growth	2.3%	—	—	—

2015 Year-End Financials

Return on assets: 11.5%   Cash ($ mil.): 1
Return on equity: (-1.3%)
Current ratio: 0.60

O'BRIEN & GERE LIMITED

O'Brien & Gere provides a range of engineering consulting and project management services throughout the US including wastewater management and water resources environmental compliance and remediation civil and facilities engineering and utility services. It also provides contract operations and maintenance. Employee-owned O'Brien & Gere serves municipal environmental manufacturing and federal clients. The company which employs hundreds of scientists engineers construction and other personnel operates nearly 30 offices in about a dozen states.

Operations

The company offers a broad range of services. With federal clients it helps to develop and manage infrastructure and facilities that improve efficiency safety and quality of life.

Its higher education services include collaborating with public and private higher education institutions supporting campus infrastructure and utility upgrades energy efficiency initiatives and environmental compliance programs.

O'Brien & Gere's industrial services include offering comprehensive project delivery services to advanced manufacturing clients through in-house skill-sets (ranging from engineering to fabrication) and control systems integration.

The company's municipal services provide energy water environmental and facilities services to municipalities state agencies and public and private water and sewer utilities.

Geographic Reach

The Syracuse New York-based firm has more than 27 branch offices in about a dozen states including Georgia Michigan New York Ohio Pennsylvania and Virginia.

Sales and Marketing

O'Brien & Gere mostly serves the Municipal Industrial Higher Education and Federal sectors. The company's public sector business accounted for roughly 25% of its total revenue in 2014.

Strategy

O'Brien & Gere has also been expanding into the New York metropolitan market where it believes more growth opportunities exist. In 2015 for example the company purchased Long Island-based Schuyler Engineering P.C. to extend its market reach into the New York and New Jersey markets while growing its client base at the same time. In 2013 the firm opened a new office in Utica New York as part of its strategic plan to expand services

to clients across the Mohawk Valley and greater upstate New York regions.

With a strengthening economy and a more sustainability-focused business environment O'Brien & Gere has also been positioned to pick up more projects and grow over the past few years. In 2014 O'Brien & Gere experienced growth in its water services business in the municipal market resulting from strong market demand in its wet infrastructure segment (including stormwater management); wastewater treatment (in response to growing requirements for enhanced nutrient removal at wastewater treatment plants); and program and construction management (integrated operations and maintenance and commissioning services).

In 2013 the company was awarded a project with Syracuse University to provide building commissioning services for the University's new bookstore fitness center and retail location. This $20 million mixed-use project would include a university-operated fitness center for students and employees and a bookstore with retail spaces.

Mergers and Acquisitions

The firm has made several acquisitions through the years in order to expand its geographic reach and grow its capabilities.

In 2015 O'Brien & Gere purchased Long Island-based Schuyler Engineering P.C. an engineering firm that specialized in central utility plant and energy system design extending its market reach throughout the New York and New Jersey metropolitan markets.

In 2012 the company acquired the remaining 55% of South Carolina-based architecture/engineering company Lindgergh & Associates.

Company Background

In 2014 O'Brien & Gere received a CCBJ award for Consulting & Engineering: Energy & Carbon Management. The firm was recognized for supporting development of the first comprehensive smart growth plan for regional energy and sustainability in Central New York.

The firm was formed by Earl O'Brien William Gere and Glenn Holmes as a water and wastewater engineering partnership in 1945.

EXECUTIVES

Senior Vice President Environmental Business Unit Leader, Thomas Nowlan
Vice President, Ron Harting
Vice President, Larry Gallagher
Senior Vice President Municipal Business Unit Leader, George Rest
Auditors: DANNIBLE & MCKEE LLP SYRACUS

LOCATIONS

HQ: O'BRIEN & GERE LIMITED
333 W WASHINGTON ST # 400, SYRACUSE, NY 132025253
Phone: 315 437-6100
Web: WWW.MASS-AWMA.NET

COMPETITORS

CH2M HILL	Jacobs Engineering
ENVIRON	Parsons Corporation
Fluor	

HISTORICAL FINANCIALS
Company Type: Private

Income Statement
FYE: December 26

	REVENUE ($ mil.)	NET INCOME ($ mil.)	NET PROFIT MARGIN	EMPLOYEES
12/15	189	3	1.7%	800
12/11	187	2	1.5%	—
12/06	125	1	1.1%	—
12/00	1,289	0	—	—
Annual Growth	—	76.7%	—	—

2015 Year-End Financials
Return on assets: 5.5%   Cash ($ mil.): —
Return on equity: 1.7%
Current ratio: 0.90

O'NEIL INDUSTRIES, INC.

A family of construction companies O'Neil Industries has also built W.E. O'Neil Construction Company. The employee-owned company operates in Arizona California Colorado and Illinois providing general contracting construction management design/build and structural concrete services for commercial projects in the US and Canada. O'Neil Industries has worked on corporate offices manufacturing and distribution facilities and mixed-use centers for clients in the education gaming health care hospitality and retail industries. The company also serves the residential and senior living sectors. Clients have included Boeing DePaul University and The Nature Conservancy.

Operations

Recent projects in Arizona include America West Airlines Flight Training Facility (in Phoenix) Arizona Cancer Center (in Tucson) and Air Center Scottsdale's McClain Street Facility (Scottsdale). In El Segundo California O'Neil Industries completed the Aerospace A6 PODS project.

The company transitioned its T.L. Roof & Associates business into its Tucson branch. Its O'Neil Construction Company unit serves as the company's concrete division. The company's Special Projects Group concentrates on small to midsized tenant improvement and facility- or campus-based projects.

Geographic Reach

While O'Neil Industries is primarily US-centric with a headquarters office in Chicago and five operating units in Illinois (Chicago) Arizona (Tucson and Phoenix) California (Los Angeles) and Colorado (Denver) the construction company also boasts a presence in Ontario Canada.

Sales and Marketing

O'Neil Industries works to maintain high customer satisfaction. More than 80% of O'Neil Industries' clients are repeat customers. Such clients include Dessert Bloom OB & Gyn Peter Palumbo Exton City of West Hollywood and The Boeing Company.

Strategy

O'Neil Industries is focused on environmentally-friendly construction projects. To this end it has devoted 80 full-time staff members who deemed LEED Accredited Professionals. The company has been involved in more than 4 million sq. ft. of LEED-certified projects including BRE Park Viridian Apartments Columbia College Media Production Center and Haworth Permanent Showroom at the Merchandise Mart.

One of the company's most recent projects include a new Chapel at Carondelet St. Joseph's Hospital in Tucson Arizona which it completed in 2013. The 3000-sq.-ft. addition to the hospital's existing courtyard was developed through a partnership with designer Swaim Associates.

In 2013 its W.E. O'Neil Construction Company began a renovation and addition project on the Sun City Oro Valley Fitness Center.

The construction firm is also upgrading its technology.

EXECUTIVES

Vice President, Patrick J McGowan
Executive Vice President, Oleh Karawan
Auditors: CROWE HORWATH LLP OAK BROOK

LOCATIONS

HQ: O'NEIL INDUSTRIES, INC.
1245 W WASHINGTON BLVD, CHICAGO, IL 606071929
Phone: 773 244-6003
Web: WWW.WEONEIL.COM

PRODUCTS/OPERATIONS

Selected Delivery Methods
Construction Management
General Contracting
Design/Build

Selected Markets
Aerospace
Education
Green
Healthcare
Hospitality & Restaurants
Industrial
Infrastructure
Municipal
Office
Gaming & Recreation
Retail
Religious
Residential
Senior Living
Special Projects
Tribal

COMPETITORS

Bulley & Andrews	Leopardo
Clark Construction Group	McShane Construction
Gilbane Building Company	Pepper Construction
Graycor	Sundt
	The Austin Company
	Walsh Group

HISTORICAL FINANCIALS
Company Type: Private

Income Statement
FYE: December 31

	REVENUE ($ mil.)	NET INCOME ($ mil.)	NET PROFIT MARGIN	EMPLOYEES
12/15	605	5	0.8%	400
12/14	605	5	0.8%	—
12/13	458	2	0.5%	—
12/12	458	2	0.5%	—
Annual Growth	9.7%	29.7%	—	—

2015 Year-End Financials
Return on assets: —   Cash ($ mil.): 27
Return on equity: 0.8%
Current ratio: 0.90

O-AT-KA MILK PRODUCTS COOPERATIVE, INCORPORATED

EXECUTIVES

Chief Executive Officer, Robert Hall
Financial Executive, Jerome T Gefert
Manager, Richard Edelman
Director, David Crisp
Manager, Dottie Wyckoff
Auditors: DOPKINS & COMPANY BUFFALO NE

LOCATIONS

HQ: O-AT-KA MILK PRODUCTS COOPERATIVE, INCORPORATED
700 ELLICOTT ST, BATAVIA, NY 140203744
Phone: 585 343-0536
Web: WWW.OATKAMILK.COM

HISTORICAL FINANCIALS

Company Type: Private

Income Statement

FYE: December 31

	REVENUE ($ mil.)	NET INCOME ($ mil.)	NET PROFIT MARGIN	EMPLOYEES
12/15	295	18	6.4%	302
12/14	332	2	0.7%	—
12/13	296	8	2.9%	—
12/12	275	16	5.9%	—
Annual Growth	2.3%	5.5%	—	—

2015 Year-End Financials

Return on assets: 1.7%   Cash ($ mil.): 23
Return on equity: 6.4%
Current ratio: 1.30

OAKLAND UNIVERSITY

Oakland University is the OU of the North. The Michigan public university serves a student body of more than 20000 offering about 130 baccalaureate degree programs and more than 100 graduate degree and certificate programs. It boasts a student-to-faculty ratio of 22-to-1. In addition to academic and specialty programs in areas ranging from business and technology to nursing and athletics its faculty members also coordinate hands-on research projects for graduate students. The main university campus spans some 1400 acres that house seven academic schools and colleges in Rochester Michigan. Oakland University also has satellite campuses in Macomb County and a law school in Auburn Hills.

Geographic Reach

Located in Rochester Michigan Oakland University's main campus comprises seven academic schools and colleges. The educational institution also operates a law school in Auburn Hills and satellite campuses in Macomb County. About 70% of its students come from Oakland and Macomb counties. Out-of-state and foreign students comprise 4.3% of the student body.

Strategy

Oakland University works to expand and improve its programs and facilities to attract new students (it had more than 20000 students for the first time in the 2013-2014 year). In 2011 for instance it added two new bachelor's degree majors: one in creative writing and one in biomedical sciences. The school introduced a Master of Science in Engineering Management degree which help them better manage environmental resources and significantly reduce energy costs.. The university has also expanded its campus resources as it has increased enrollment levels during the past decade. In fall 2014 the university opened a $75 million 134000-square-foot building for the School of Engineering and Computer Science.

Financial Performance

Operating revenue was $212 million in 2014 (ended June) a 4% increase over 2013. A 2.3% enrollment increase boosted tuition (for which rates rose 3.7%). Operating expenses were about $283 million in 2014 compared to $275 million in 2013. The university's net position increased by almost $40 million with gains in investment in-

come gifts and additions to permanent endowments.

Sales and Marketing

The university advertises through several mediums such as television radio websites social networking sites billboards magazines newspapers and journals.

Company Background

Oakland University was founded in 1957 by Alfred and Matilda Wilson who donated $2 million and their 1500-acre estate to Michigan State University to start a new college in Oakland County. Named Michigan State University Oakland the college enrolled its first students in 1959. The school's name changed to Oakland University in 1963 and it became an autonomous institution in 1970.

EXECUTIVES

Vp Government Relations, Rochelle Black
Senior Vice President, James Lentini
Executive Legal Secretary, Carolyn Hogan
Assistant Vice President, Catheryn Cheal
Senior Vice President Human Resources, Mark S Doman
Associate Vice President Enrollment Management, Paul Schroeder
Student Body Vice President, Anders Engnell
ASSISTANT VICE PRESIDENT, Leigh Settlemoir
Board Of Directors, Amy Butler
Secretary, Andrea Patton
Secretary, Sheri Rourke
Secretary, Debra Koehler
Secretary, Diane Williams
Auditors: ANDREWS HOOPER PAVLIK PLC AU

LOCATIONS

HQ: OAKLAND UNIVERSITY
2200 N SQUIRREL RD, ROCHESTER, MI 483094401
Phone: 248 370-2100
Web: WWW.OAKLAND.EDU

PRODUCTS/OPERATIONS

Selected Schools

Beaumont School of Medicine
College of Arts and Sciences
Cooley Law School
Macomb Campuses
School of Business Administration
School of Education and Human Services
School of Engineering and Computer Science
School of Health Sciences
School of Nursing

HISTORICAL FINANCIALS

Company Type: Private

Income Statement

FYE: June 30

	REVENUE ($ mil.)	NET INCOME ($ mil.)	NET PROFIT MARGIN	EMPLOYEES
06/16	253	9	3.8%	2,650
06/15	227	20	8.9%	—
06/14	212	39	18.6%	—
06/13	203	27	13.3%	—
Annual Growth	7.7%	(28.9%)	—	—

2016 Year-End Financials

Return on assets: 9.7%   Cash ($ mil.): 36
Return on equity: 3.8%
Current ratio: 0.80

OBERLIN COLLEGE

Founded in 1833 Oberlin College was the first college in the US to enroll women on an equal

basis with men. The school has a College of Arts and Sciences (about 2300 enrollees) but may be best known for its Conservatory of Music (about 600 enrollees) the oldest such institution in the US. The College of Arts and Sciences offers nearly 50 undergraduate majors the Conservatory about 10. Students can earn bachelor's degrees in either program but can also earn a five-year double-degree in both. In addition Oberlin offers master's degrees in opera theater conducting performance historical performance historical instruments music teaching and education. It has two-year certificate programs as well.

Financial Performance

Oberlin increased revenues by 1% to $159 million in 2012 due to increased income from student tuition room and board. Student revenues make up about more than 60% of sales; the rest comes from investments gifts and auxiliary enterprises. The school posted a net income loss however due to higher operating expenses and decreased returns on investments.

The college has an endowment of some $679 million as of mid-2012 up nearly $20 million from 2011. Endowment levels remain low compared to post-recession figures however and as a result Oberlin continues to operate under tight spending and budget guidelines.

Strategy

In 2012 Oberlin launched a fundraising campaign called Oberlin Illuminate. The campaign aims to raise $250 million to enhance academic programs as well as to support student access community and graduate placement initiatives.

EXECUTIVES

Vice President for Communications, Ben Jones
Auditors: MALONEY & NOVOTNY LLC CLEVELA

LOCATIONS

HQ: OBERLIN COLLEGE
173 W LORAIN ST, OBERLIN, OH 440741073
Phone: 440 775-8121
Web: WWW.OBERLIN.EDU

HISTORICAL FINANCIALS

Company Type: Private

Income Statement

FYE: June 30

	REVENUE ($ mil.)	NET INCOME ($ mil.)	NET PROFIT MARGIN	EMPLOYEES
06/16	184	(71)	—	1,140
06/15	184	(3)	—	—
06/14	171	119	69.6%	—
06/13	167	72	43.5%	—
Annual Growth	3.3%	—	—	—

2016 Year-End Financials

Return on assets: 5.3%   Cash ($ mil.): 16
Return on equity: (-38.5%)
Current ratio: 0.80

OCCIDENTAL COLLEGE

It's no accident that Occidental College is a liberal arts school. With more than 2000 students an average class size of 19 and a 10:1 student-to-faculty ratio the school (nicknamed "Oxy") offers a hands-on approach to higher education. Its campus located in Eagle Rock is surrounded by the metropolis of Los Angeles. The college has 180 faculty members and offers about 30 majors including a number of interdisciplinary programs.

Occidental students can also take classes at Caltech or the Art Center College of Design and earn joint degrees at Columbia University Keck Graduate Institute and Caltech. Occidental students can also participate in service-learning and study abroad programs.

Geographic Reach

Occidental's students come from more than 40 states and 25 foreign countries. In addition to its main campus and collaborations in California Occidental College has study abroad programs with affiliates in 30 countries in Europe Asia Latin America Africa the Middle East and the Asia/Pacific region.

Financial Performance

In 2012 Occidental College increased operating revenues by 5% to some $106 million due to higher student revenues (tuition and fees). Operating income also increased 56% to nearly $5.2 million.

About two-thirds of the company's operating revenues come from net student revenues. Other sources include investment income; private gifts grants and contracts; and federal and state grants and contracts. Tuition and fees total about $45000 per year plus $12000 in room and board (about three-fourths of students live on campus).

Company Background

The college was founded as The Occidental University of Los Angeles California in 1887 by a group of Presbyterians.

EXECUTIVES

Vice President for Institutional Advancement, Shelby Radcliffe
Vice President For Admin Finance, Amos Himmelstein
Vice president, Tom Tomlinson
Vice President Administration and Finance, Michael Groener
Vice President of Internal Affairs, Jemma Parsons
Vice President, Andrew Larkin
Vice President, Eric Frank
Associate Vice President For Facilities, Michele Cole
Associate Vice President for Information Technology Services, James Uhrich
Associate Vice President For Facilities, Rich Stephens
Vice President, Hannah Barnes
Associate Vice President Marketing and Communications, Marty Sharkey
Vice President for Institutional Advancement, Elizabeth Kennedy
Vice President For Equity and Inclusion Chief Diversity Officer, Rhonda Brown
Auditors: MOSS ADAMS LLP STOCKTON CA

LOCATIONS

HQ: OCCIDENTAL COLLEGE
 1600 CAMPUS RD, LOS ANGELES, CA 900413314
Phone: 323 259-2500
Web: WWW.OCCIDENTAL.EDU

PRODUCTS/OPERATIONS

Selected Academic Majors
American Studies
Art History and the Visual Arts
Athletics and Physical Activities
Biochemistry
Biology
Chemistry
Classical Studies
Cognitive Science
Computer Science
Core Program
Critical Theory and Social Justice
Diplomacy and World Affairs
East Asian Languages and Cultures
Economics
Education

English and Comparative Literary Studies
English Writing
Geology
German Russian and Classical Studies
Group Language
History
Kinesiology
Latino/a and Latin American Studies
Mathematics
Music
Philosophy
Physics
Politics
Psychology
Religious Studies
Sociology
Spanish and French Studies
Theater
Urban and Environmental Policy

COMPETITORS

UC Davis	USC
UC Irvine	University of
UC Santa Barbara	California
UCLA	

HISTORICAL FINANCIALS

Company Type: Private

Income Statement

FYE: June 30

	REVENUE ($ mil.)	NET INCOME ($ mil.)	NET PROFIT MARGIN	EMPLOYEES
06/15	182	26	14.3%	610
06/14	188	37	20.0%	—
06/13	109	36	32.9%	—
06/11	146	10	7.4%	—
Annual Growth	5.7%	24.4%	—	—

2015 Year-End Financials

Return on assets: 7.9%   Cash ($ mil.): 71
Return on equity: 14.3%
Current ratio: 0.70

OCEAN BEAUTY SEAFOODS LLC

Prefer your piscatory purchase to be fresh frozen or canned? Ocean Beauty Seafoods has it covered. Doing no fishing of its own the company buys seafood from commercial fishermen and then processes sells and distributes its seafood products in Alaska and across the continental US. Founded in 1910 the company also exports seafood to Mexico Europe Asia Africa and the Middle East. Ocean Beauty's specialty products include smoked salmon smoked salmon spreads pickled and marinated herring shrimp cocktail caviar and lobster p t ©. Nonprofit Bristol Bay Economic Development Corporation owns 50% of Ocean Beauty; individual investors own the rest.

Operations

Boasting offices or plants in eight US states plus overseas in Japan Ocean Beauty operates its own fleet of seafood delivery trucks across the Western US. The fleet makes regular stops at the seafood company's distribution facilities located in Oregon Idaho Texas Montana Utah and Washington. The company operates six production sites in Alaska in Alitak Cordova Excursion Inlet Kodiak Naknek and Petersburg as well as a pair of production sites in Seattle and Monroe Washington. Sales and administration offices are located in Seattle and Tokyo. Ocean Beauty exports its products to Mexico Europe Asia Africa and the Middle East.

Geographic Reach

Based in Washington Ocean Beauty enjoys a global reach.

Sales and Marketing

Ocean Beauty sells its fresh and frozen seafood products to both retail and foodservice customers. The company maintains sales offices in the states in Seattle and overseas in Tokyo.

Strategy

Ocean Beauty claims to be the first company to vacuum pack Alaskan seafood (in 1954). The company's products are primarily caught in the waters of the Pacific Northwest but Ocean Beauty also purchases fish from harvesters worldwide. Its major manufacturing facilities are certified against the British Retail Consortium Audit Standards.

Ocean Beauty also voluntarily participates in the US Department of Commerce's Hazard Actions Critical Control Points (HACCP) Seafood Inspection Program for added assurance that its products are safe wholesome and properly labeled. The company's production and distribution operations are conducted in compliance with the US Food and Drug Administration's HACCP regulations.

EXECUTIVES

President, Mark Palmer
Chief Financial Officer, Tony Ross
Financial Executive, Steve Layman
Quality Control Manager, Duane McIntire
Marketing Director, Todd Sunderland
Auditors: RSM US LLP SEATTLE WASHINGTO

LOCATIONS

HQ: OCEAN BEAUTY SEAFOODS LLC
 1100 W EWING ST, SEATTLE, WA 981191321
Phone: 206 285-6800
Web: WWW.OCEANBEAUTY.COM

PRODUCTS/OPERATIONS

Selected Brands
CircleSea
Commander
Deep Sea
Echo Falls
Icy Point
LASCCO
McGovern
Nathan's
Neptune
Ocean Beauty
Ocean Bonita
Pillar Rock
Pink Beauty
Pirate
Port Clyde
RITE
Royal Alaska
Sea Choice
Searchlight
Sound Beauty
St. Andrews
Surf King
Three Star
Tribe

Selected Products
Imported finfish
 Mahi mahi
 Sea Bass
 Shark
 Swordfish
 Tuna
North Pacific finfish
 Cod
 Farm-raised
 Flounder
 Halibut
 Perch
 Pollock
 Rockfish
 Salmon
 Sole
 Sturgeon

Whiting
Shellfish
  Coldwater shrimp meat
  Clams
  Crab
  Mussels
  Oysters
  Prawns
Other products
  Milt
  Pickled herring
  Roe
  Surimi

COMPETITORS

Alaska Sausage	Maruha Nichiro
Alaska Seafood company	Orca Bay Seafoods
Alaskan Leader	Pacific Seafood Group
Fisheries	Peter Pan Seafoods
Arrowac Fisheries	Princes Limited
Banner Smoked Fish	Red Chamber Co.
Bumble Bee Foods	Salmolux
Chicken of the Sea	Santa's Smokehouse
Gorton's	Seafood Sales
High Liner Foods	StarKist
Icelandic Group	Trident Seafoods
Icicle Seafoods	

HISTORICAL FINANCIALS

Company Type: Private

Income Statement

FYE: January 2

	REVENUE ($ mil.)	NET INCOME ($ mil.)	NET PROFIT MARGIN	EMPLOYEES
01/16	437	(4)	—	2,500
01/15*	439	4	1.1%	—
12/13	425	11	2.6%	—
12/12	409	8	2.0%	—
Annual Growth	2.3%	—	—	—

*Fiscal year change

2016 Year-End Financials

Return on assets: 5.4%
Return on equity: (-1.1%)
Current ratio: 0.30
Cash ($ mil.): 2

OCEAN SPRAY CRANBERRIES, INC.

Ocean Spray Cranberries has transformed that ubiquitous Thanksgiving side dish into a big business with beverages cereals and snacks. Known for its blue-and-white wave logo Ocean Spray is a top US maker of canned bottled and shelf-stable juice drinks. Formed in 1930 the cooperative is owned by more than 700 cranberry and grapefruit growers in North America. It produces juice drinks by blending the cranberries with other fruits typically ranging from apples to blueberries. Its other products include fresh and dried cranberries sauces trail mixes and instant oatmeal along with fresh citrus fruits. Ocean Spray sells its products through food retailers foodservice providers and food makers worldwide.

Operations

The food company operates its business through three divisions. Its Foodservice division supplies Ocean Spray products to restaurants bars cafeterias hospitals and hotels. The company's Ingredient Technology division sells cranberry products for use by global food and beverage makers. Ocean Spray's International division serves the Americas the Caribbean Africa Asia/Pacific Europe and the Middle East.

Geographic Reach

Ocean Spray boasts a global business. It supplies cranberry products to food and beverage manufacturers worldwide. The company serves customers in North America the Caribbean Central America South America Africa Asia/Pacific Europe and the Middle East.

The co-op has production facilities in Florida Massachusetts Nevada New Jersey Texas and Wisconsin. Its growers are located in British Columbia Florida Massachusetts New Jersey Oregon and Wisconsin.

Sales and Marketing

Juice remains the co-op's most lucrative product. Ocean Spray squeezes into the top three suppliers in the US juice market. Its namesake juices rank #3 behind #1 PepsiCo (with its Tropicana) and #2 Coca-Cola (with Minute Maid).

Strategy

Looking to diversify its products portfolio and further target health-conscious Baby Boomers Ocean Spray has worked to expand beyond the cranberry's traditional role on holiday tables. The company's promotional efforts have been aided by research showing that cranberry juice can reduce urinary tract infections and fight stomach ulcers.

To this end Ocean Spray has introduced a "white juice" made from pre-ripened cranberries that have a less tart taste as well as a line of pomegranate juice drinks (pomegranate being one of the superfruits touted for its antioxidant properties). It also has transformed dried cranberries into Craisins which now show up in co-branded cookies and cereals and expanded the line with the introduction of pomegranate- and blueberry-flavored Craisins.

HISTORY

Ocean Spray Cranberries traces its roots to Marcus Urann president of the Cape Cod Cranberry Company. In 1912 Urann who became known as the "Cranberry King" began marketing a cranberry sauce that was packaged in tins and could be served year-round. Inspired by the sea spray that drifted off the Atlantic and over his cranberry bogs Urann dubbed his concoction Ocean Spray Cape Cod Cranberry Sauce.

It didn't take long for other cranberry growers to make their own sauces and rather than compete the Cranberry King consolidated. In 1930 Urann merged his company with A.D. Makepeace Company and with Cranberry Products forming a national cooperative called Cranberry Canners. During the 1940s it added growers in Wisconsin Oregon and Washington and to reflect its new scope changed its name to National Cranberry Association.

Canadian growers were added to the fold in 1950. Urann retired in 1955 and two years later the co-op introduced its first frozen products. To take advantage of the popular Ocean Spray brand name in 1959 the company changed its name to Ocean Spray Cranberries.

EXECUTIVES

Vice President, David Williams
R Vice President Manufacturing, Mike Stamatokos
Assistant Treasurer, Suzy Lewis
Auditors: PRICEWATERHOUSECOOPERS LLP B

LOCATIONS

HQ: OCEAN SPRAY CRANBERRIES, INC.
1 OCEAN SPRAY DR, MIDDLEBORO, MA 023490001
Phone: 508 946-1000
Web: WWW.OCEANSPRAY.COM

PRODUCTS/OPERATIONS

Selected Brands & Products
Dried fruit

Craisins Blueberry Juice Infused Dried Cranberries
Craisins Cherry Juice Infused Dried Cranberries
Craisins Original Dried Cranberries
Craisins Pomegranate Juice Infused Dried Cranberries
Craisins Snack Packs
Craisins Trail Mix - Cranberry & Chocolate
Craisins Trail Mix - Cranberry Fruit & Nut
Fresh Produce
  Clementines
  Cranberries
  Grapefruit
  Lemons
  Limes
  Oranges
  Tangerines
Instant oatmeal
  Cranberry
  Cranberry Honey Multigrain
  Cranberry Orange Muffin
  Cranberry Pomegranate
Juice
  100% Juice Blends
  Blueberry Juice Drinks
  Cran;Energy Energy Juice Drinks
  Cranberry Juice Cocktails
  Cranberry Juice Drink Blends
  Diet Juice Drinks
  Fruit & Veggie Juice
  Fruit & Veggie Juice Drinks
  Grapefruit Juice
  Grapefruit Juice Drinks
  Juice Drinks
  Light Juice Drinks
  On the Go Juice
  On the Go Juice Drinks
  Sugar-Free Drink Mixes
  White Cranberry Juice Drinks
Sauces
  Jellied cranberry sauce
  Whole berry cranberry sauce

COMPETITORS

A. Duda & Sons	Freshco
Arcade Industries	Jugos del Valle USA
Cherry Central	Mariani Packing
Cooperative Inc.	Meridian Nut Growers
Chiquita Brands	Naked Juice
Citrus World	National Grape
Coca-Cola	Cooperative
Coloma Frozen Foods	Nestl © USA
Cranberries Limited	Odwalla
Dole Food	Shoreline Fruit
Dundee Citrus Growers	Sunsweet Growers
Edinburg Citrus	Tampico Beverages
Fresh Del Monte	Tropicana
Produce	Wonderful Company

HISTORICAL FINANCIALS

Company Type: Private

Income Statement

FYE: August 31

	REVENUE ($ mil.)	NET INCOME ($ mil.)	NET PROFIT MARGIN	EMPLOYEES
08/15	1,719	317	18.5%	2,000
08/14	1,655	289	17.5%	—
08/13	1,658	389	23.5%	—
08/12	1,662	338	20.4%	—
Annual Growth	1.1%	(2.2%)	—	—

2015 Year-End Financials

Return on assets: 7.2%
Return on equity: 18.5%
Current ratio: 0.50
Cash ($ mil.): 38

OCLC ONLINE COMPUTER LIBRARY CENTER, INCORPORATE

Working to reduce the cost of information OCLC Online Computer Library Center is a membership cooperative that provides access to the world's information. The group offers services and tools to some 74000 member libraries in about 170 countries. Services include computer-based cataloging preservation and library management. OCLC additionally facilitates interlibrary loan services administers the Dewey Decimal Classification system and operates the WorldCat database an online resource for finding library materials. OCLC was founded in 1967 by presidents of the colleges and universities in Ohio. OCLC which stands for Ohio College Library Center opened its first location in Ohio State's main library.

Geographic Reach

OCLC operates in about 170 countries across the Americas Asia Pacific Europe the Middle East and Africa. The organization generates some 77% of its revenue from the Americas. The remainder comes from outside the US.

Financial Performance

OCLC's revenue increased by 2% in fiscal 2013 compared to the previous year. The company claimed $206.6 million in revenue for 2013 after reporting $203.4 million in 2012. The revenue growth was due to increased adoption of new services and a modest price increase.

Revenues from libraries and institutions outside of the US increased by $1.4 million to $54.8 million in fiscal 2013. The spike was primarily due to increased revenues from Bibliotheca in Germany.

Strategy

As part of its operations OCLC regularly maintains and enhances its existing services such as Connexion QuestionPoint CONTENTdm EZproxy and WorldCat through heavy investing activities. The company provides more than 5000 libraries in Africa Australia and Europe with integrated library management systems and works to release regular enhancements. The systems include Amlib Bibliotheca CBS LBS OLIB SunRise and Touch-Point.

OCLC also concentrates on expanding its capabilities with the addition of data centers. To this end it opened a new data center in Toronto in 2012 as part of a plan to operate local and global systems at Webscale service levels. The Toronto location is OCLC's fifth globally and allows the group to deliver its namesake WorldShare Management Services to member libraries in Canada. Soon after OCLC opened additional data centers in London and in Sydney Australia. It already has a pair of primary operations data centers in the US. In 2013 another data center came online in Europe.

EXECUTIVES

President, David A Prichard
Vice-President, William J Rozek
Manager, Nils Muladure
Manager, David Milliman
Manager, Denise Bedford
Director, Neil McLean
Director, Paul Miller
Principal, Pat Ring
Auditors: DELOITTE & TOUCHE LLP COLUMBU

LOCATIONS

HQ: OCLC ONLINE COMPUTER LIBRARY CENTER, INCORPORATE
6565 KILGOUR PL, DUBLIN, OH 430173395
Phone: 614 764-6000
Web: WWW.CONFERENCE-CENTER.OCLC.ORG

2013 Revenue

	% of total
Americas	77
Europe Middle East & Africa	19
Asia Pacific	4
Total	**100**

PRODUCTS/OPERATIONS

2013 Revenue

	$ mil.	% of total
Products & services	202	98
Grants	3	2
Research library partner dues	0	-
Total	**206**	**100**

Selected Services
Cataloging and Metadata
Digital Collection Management
Discovery
Electronic Collection Management
Library Management
Resource Sharing

Selected Products
Connexion
CONTENTdm
Dewey Services
Digital Archive
FirstSearch
WorldCat

COMPETITORS

American Library	Informa
EBSCO	LexisNexis
FactSet	ProQuest
Google	

HISTORICAL FINANCIALS
Company Type: Private

Income Statement
FYE: June 30

	REVENUE ($ mil.)	NET INCOME ($ mil.)	NET PROFIT MARGIN	EMPLOYEES
06/16	203	(9)	—	1,227
06/15	202	(17)	—	—
06/14	213	21	10.3%	—
06/13	206	8	4.0%	—
Annual Growth	(0.5%)	—	—	—

2016 Year-End Financials
Return on assets: 4.3%
Return on equity: (-4.8%)
Current ratio: 0.40
Cash ($ mil.): 6

ODESSA REGIONAL HOSPITAL, L.P.

EXECUTIVES

Chief Executive Officer, Bill Porter
Financial Executive, Jana McKay

LOCATIONS

HQ: ODESSA REGIONAL HOSPITAL, L.P.
520 E 6TH ST, ODESSA, TX 797614527
Phone: 432 582-8000
Web: WWW.ODESSAREGIONALMEDICALCENTER.COM

HISTORICAL FINANCIALS
Company Type: Private

Income Statement
FYE: September 30

	REVENUE ($ mil.)	NET INCOME ($ mil.)	NET PROFIT MARGIN	EMPLOYEES
09/15*	178	35	19.7%	570
06/05	67	12	18.8%	—
09/03	67	12	18.8%	—
09/02	852	0	—	—
Annual Growth	—	133.9%	—	—

*Fiscal year change

OGDEN ARNOT MEDICAL CENTER

EXECUTIVES

Chief Executive Officer, Robert Lambert
Administrative Assistant, Darcy Gray
Administrative Assistant, Diana Ladd
Director, Gregory Malanoski

LOCATIONS

HQ: OGDEN ARNOT MEDICAL CENTER
600 ROE AVE, ELMIRA, NY 149051676
Phone: 607 737-4100

HISTORICAL FINANCIALS
Company Type: Private

Income Statement
FYE: December 31

	REVENUE ($ mil.)	NET INCOME ($ mil.)	NET PROFIT MARGIN	EMPLOYEES
12/15	211	(11)	—	2,400
12/14	212	4	2.0%	—
12/13	271	(7)	—	—
Annual Growth	(11.8%)	—	—	—

2015 Year-End Financials
Return on assets: 5.1%
Return on equity: (-5.3%)
Current ratio: 1.40
Cash ($ mil.): 3

OHIO VALLEY ELECTRIC CORPORATION

Down by the banks of the Ohio Ohio Valley Electric and its subsidiary Indiana-Kentucky Electric generate power for customers across the Ohio River Valley. It operates two coal-fired plants which collectively have about 2290 MW of generating capacity. Ohio Valley Electric's Kyger Creek Plant (Cheshire Ohio) and Indiana-Kentucky Electric's Clifty Creek Plant (Madison Indiana) are linked by 705 miles of transmission lines. Most of Ohio Valley Electric's power goes to its shareholders (a dozen investor-owned utilities utility holding entities led by American Electric Power and units of generation and transmission rural electric cooperatives). It also supplies energy to the Department of Energy.

Financial Performance

Ohio Valley Electric reported a revenue decline of 6% in 2012 as the result of lower power demand from its members due to mild weather coupled with a soft energy market and low-cost natural gas generation. Lower revenues in tandem with higher operating costs pushed down its net income for the year by 15%.

Strategy

Like other utilities with aging power plants Ohio Valley Electric is investing heavily in flue gas desulfurization (FGD) retrofit projects at its power facilities to be compliant with clean air regulations. The company has funded the FGD construction projects at the Kyger Creek plant (for $661 million) and the Clifty Creek plant (for $687 million).

Company Background

The entity is owned by several investor-owned utilities and utility holding companies and two affiliates of generation and transmission rural electric cooperatives. In 2012 Ohio Valley Electric's major shareholders included American Electric Power (39%) and Buckeye Power Generating LLC (18%).

Ohio Valley Electric was formed in 1952 by several regional utilities to provide power to a US government uranium enrichment plant near Portsmouth Ohio with excess power going to the utilities. However that plant was shut down in 2001. A new arrangement in 2003 made all of Ohio Valley Electric's generating capacity available to the sponsoring utilities and the Department of Energy.

EXECUTIVES

President, Nicholas Akins
Director, Gary Leidich
VP Operations, David E Jons
Personnel Manager, Linn E Drapr
Engineer, Mick Burkitt
Chief Financial Officer, Kassandra Martin
Manager, Lyn Swain

LOCATIONS

HQ: OHIO VALLEY ELECTRIC CORPORATION
3932 US RTE 23, PIKETON, OH 45661
Phone: 740 289-7200

PRODUCTS/OPERATIONS

2012 Sales

	$ mil.	% of total
Sponsoring companies	661	99
Department of Energy	9	1
Total	**670**	**100**

COMPETITORS

AEP	Duke Energy
Calpine	Exelon
Dominion Energy	IPALCO Enterprises

HISTORICAL FINANCIALS

Company Type: Private

Income Statement

FYE: June 30

	REVENUE ($ mil.)	NET INCOME ($ mil.)	NET PROFIT MARGIN	EMPLOYEES
06/16*	265	0	0.2%	428
03/16	119	0	0.3%	—
12/15	565	0	0.1%	—
09/15	436	0	0.2%	—
Annual Growth	(39.2%)	(36.2%)	—	—

*Fiscal year change

2016 Year-End Financials

Return on assets: 4.9%   Cash ($ mil.): 23
Return on equity: 0.2%
Current ratio: 0.20

OKLAHOMA STATE UNIVERSITY

Oooooklahoma where the... students come to learn! Oklahoma State University is the flagship campus of its namesake (OSU) system which also includes OSU-Tulsa OSU-Oklahoma City OSU-Okmulgee the OSU Center for Health Sciences in Tulsa the OSU College of Veterinary Medicine and the Oklahoma Agricultural Experiment Station. OSU offers courses in a variety of disciplines and confers undergraduate graduate doctoral and professional degrees in everything from agriculture and the arts to business and engineering. Altogether the system boasts an enrollment of about 36000 students across its five campuses; its student-teacher ratio is about 17:1.

Geographic Reach

Operating across Oklahoma OSU's several campus locations include three branch campuses a Center for Health Sciences College of Veterinary Medicine and Oklahoma Agricultural Experiment Station.

Strategy

One of OSU's biggest financial contributors is alumnus and oil and gas tycoon T. Boone Pickens who over the years has given the school more than $500 million. Pickens' 2010 donation of $100 million went toward the school's $1 billion fundraising campaign that was used to endow scholarships and fellowships for students as well as attract and retain professors upgrade facilities and create new programs. Pickens is the campaign's honorary chairman.

Financial Performance

The Oklahoma university has seen its revenue rise for the past several years due to organic growth. OSU logged an 11% increase in revenue in 2012 as compared to 2011 thanks to increases from tuition and fees grants and contracts auxiliary enterprises and other operating revenue. Net income meanwhile slipped by 14% during the same reporting period attributable to increases in compensation and employee benefits contractual services scholarships and fellowships depreciation expense supplies and materials and other operating expenses.

Background

OSU was founded in 1890 as the Oklahoma Territorial Agricultural and Mechanical College (A&M). The first students were enrolled the following year; the school operated as Oklahoma A&M until 1957 when it changed its name to Oklahoma State University to reflect the fact that its curriculum had grown to include a wide range of subjects. Following the name change the OSU began establishing campuses starting with the Stillwater campus and then the OSU-Institute of Technology in Okmulgee (1946) OSU-Oklahoma City (1961) OSU-Tulsa (1984) and the Center for Health Sciences also in Tulsa (1988).

EXECUTIVES

Assoc Vice President Academic Affairs, Gail Gates
Staff Associate Vice President And Controller, Virginia Wyckoff
Vice President For Research And Technology, Linda Goodwin
Vice President Administration And Finance, David Bosserman
Auditors: GRANT THORNTON LLP OKLAHOMA C

LOCATIONS

HQ: OKLAHOMA STATE UNIVERSITY
401 WHITEHURST HALL, STILLWATER, OK 740781030
Phone: 405 744-5892
Web: WWW.OKSTATE.COM

PRODUCTS/OPERATIONS

Selected Colleges

Agricultural Sciences and Natural Resources
Arts and Sciences
Education
Engineering Architecture and Technology
Human Sciences
Spears School of Business
Center for Veterinary Health Sciences
Graduate College
Honors College

HISTORICAL FINANCIALS

Company Type: Private

Income Statement

FYE: June 30

	REVENUE ($ mil.)	NET INCOME ($ mil.)	NET PROFIT MARGIN	EMPLOYEES
06/16	787	(46)	—	8,882
06/14	747	49	6.7%	—
06/13	710	47	6.7%	—
06/10	600	213	35.5%	—
Annual Growth	4.6%	—	—	—

2016 Year-End Financials

Return on assets: 2.6%   Cash ($ mil.): 83
Return on equity: (-6.0%)
Current ratio: 1.40

OKLAHOMA TURNPIKE AUTHORITY

EXECUTIVES

Chairman, Mr Albert C Kelly Jr
Officer, Eric Strong
Director, Stacy Trumbo
Manager, Troy Nelson
Project Manager, Shelley Wilson
Auditors: GRANT THORNTON LLP OKLAHOMA C

LOCATIONS

HQ: OKLAHOMA TURNPIKE AUTHORITY
3500 N MARTIN LUTHER, OKLAHOMA CITY, OK 731114221
Phone: 405 425-3600

HISTORICAL FINANCIALS

Company Type: Private

Income Statement

FYE: December 31

	REVENUE ($ mil.)	NET INCOME ($ mil.)	NET PROFIT MARGIN	EMPLOYEES
12/15	257	48	19.0%	528
12/14	247	55	22.3%	—
12/13	234	42	18.1%	—
12/12	235	32	13.8%	—
Annual Growth	3.1%	14.6%	—	—

2015 Year-End Financials

Return on assets: 7.3%   Cash ($ mil.): 19
Return on equity: 19.0%
Current ratio: 0.20

OLATHE MEDICAL CENTER, INC.

EXECUTIVES

President, Frank H Devocelle
Financial Executive, Chad Butterfield
Personnel Director, Adrian Fitzmaurice

LOCATIONS

HQ: OLATHE MEDICAL CENTER, INC.
20333 W 151ST ST, OLATHE, KS 660617211
Phone: 913 791-4200

HISTORICAL FINANCIALS

Company Type: Private

Income Statement
FYE: December 31

	REVENUE ($ mil.)	NET INCOME ($ mil.)	NET PROFIT MARGIN	EMPLOYEES
12/15	232	15	6.7%	2,500
12/14	208	34	16.4%	—
12/13	229	52	22.7%	—
12/08	192	(17)	—	—
Annual Growth	2.8%	—	—	—

2015 Year-End Financials

Return on assets: 6.7%   Cash ($ mil.): 1
Return on equity: 6.7%
Current ratio: 1.20

OLATHE UNIFIED SCHOOL DISTRICT 233

EXECUTIVES

Superintendent, Marlin Berry
Vice-President, Rita Ashley
Bookkeeper, Cynthia Bradbury
Auditors: MIZE HOUSER & COMPANY PA LA

LOCATIONS

HQ: OLATHE UNIFIED SCHOOL DISTRICT 233
14160 S BLACKBOB RD, OLATHE, KS 660622024
Phone: 913 780-7000
Web: WWW.OLATHESCHOOLS.COM

HISTORICAL FINANCIALS

Company Type: Private

Income Statement
FYE: June 30

	REVENUE ($ mil.)	NET INCOME ($ mil.)	NET PROFIT MARGIN	EMPLOYEES
06/16	361	(69)	—	4,000
06/15	357	(76)	—	—
06/14	341	149	43.7%	—
06/13	323	9	3.0%	—
Annual Growth	3.8%	—	—	—

OLENTANGY LOCAL SCHOOL DISTRICT

EXECUTIVES

Superintendent, Wade Lucas
Plant & Facilities Manager, Dan Ramey
Superintendent, Mark Raiff
Assistant Manager, Randy Wright
Auditors: ROBERT HINKLE CPA CGFM COLU

LOCATIONS

HQ: OLENTANGY LOCAL SCHOOL DISTRICT
814 SHANAHAN RD STE 100, LEWIS CENTER, OH
430359192
Phone: 740 657-4050
Web: WWW.OLENTANGY.K12.OH.US

HISTORICAL FINANCIALS

Company Type: Private

Income Statement
FYE: June 30

	REVENUE ($ mil.)	NET INCOME ($ mil.)	NET PROFIT MARGIN	EMPLOYEES
06/16	234	86	37.1%	1,500
06/12	199	(4)	—	—
06/11*	191	(20)	—	—
07/09	0	0	—	—
Annual Growth	—	240.5%	—	—

*Fiscal year change

2016 Year-End Financials

Return on assets: 0.2%   Cash ($ mil.): 184
Return on equity: 37.1%
Current ratio: —

OMAHA PUBLIC POWER DISTRICT

Thirteen's the lucky number for Omaha Public Power District (OPPD). A subdivision of the Nebraska state government OPPD generates and distributes electricity to residents and businesses in 13 counties in southeastern Nebraska. It operates and maintains its facilities without tax revenues and raises money for major construction through bonds. OPPD serves more than 356000 customers in an area covering 5000 sq. mi. The utility has a generating capacity of more than 3235 MW which is powered by primarily nuclear coal oil and natural gas sources. It sells wholesale power to other utilities and offers energy consulting and management services.

Operations

OPPD is the 12th-largest publicly owned electric system in the US in terms of numbers of customers served. The power district provides retail service to about 50 towns and wholesale to five. OPPD operates more than 15500 miles of electric line.

The majority of OPPD's power comes from three baseload power plants: North Omaha Station and Nebraska City Station (both coal-fired) and the Fort Calhoun Station nuclear power plant.

Financial Performance

In 2013 OPPD's revenues grew by 4% primarily due to a jump in retail sales as the result of higher energy prices and an increase in the adjustment for the under-recovery of fuel and purchased power expenses. Retail sales growth was partially offset by a decrease in off-system sales and other electric sales.

The company's net income grew by 1% that year due to higher revenues.

In 2013 OPPD's operating cash inflow increased to $168.71 million (from $151.73 million in 2012) due to higher net income and a change in working capital as a result of an increase in cash received from retail customers and insurance companies. This was partially offset by higher cash paid to off-system parties for additional wind energy.

Strategy

Like other utilities OPPD is pushing conservation and green energy initiates to reduce carbon emissions with its customers as a service to help them control costs.

In 2015 OPPD approved the future generation resource plan created in June 2014 calling for the retirement of three of the district's oldest coal generation units and additional environmental controls. The plan includes a mixture of new programs and expansion of some existing programs aimed at reducing power demand.

The company is pursuing a goal of getting 30% of its retail energy from renewable sources. In 2013 it announced a wind farm deal (located northeast of O'Neill Nebraska). The 20-year agreement the largest wind power purchase to date for OPPD will increase its renewable energy generation capacity to 817 MW.

Company Background

It 2011 the utility announced that it was studying how to support both the auto industry and customers regarding the larger numbers of electric cars being introduced into its service region.

OPPD was organized as a self-supporting subdivision of the State of Nebraska in 1946 although state power operations date back to 1917.

EXECUTIVES

President and CEO, W. Gary Gates, age 66
COO, Timothy J. (Tim) Burke
VP and CFO, Edward E. Easterlin
Vice President of Finance, Leland Jacobsen
Vice President and Controller, Ronald K Bayer
Vice President, John Imig
Vice President Transmission Engineering Operations, Mohamad Doghman
Vice President, Tim Nissen
Vice President Customer Service, Juli Comstock
Senior Vice President Strategy and Corporate Development, Don Macisaac
Vice President Information Technology, Kate Brown
VICE PRESIDENT CUSTOMER SERVICE, Juli A Comstock
Chair, Anne L. McGuire
Vice Chair, Michael A. (Mick) Mines
Treasurer, Patricia Johnson

LOCATIONS

HQ: OMAHA PUBLIC POWER DISTRICT
444 S 16TH ST, OMAHA, NE 681022247
Phone: 402 636-2000
Web: WWW.OPPD.COM

COMPETITORS

Basin Electric Power   Tri-State Generation
NorthWestern   and Transmission
Preferred Energy
Services

HISTORICAL FINANCIALS

Company Type: Private

Income Statement

FYE: December 31

	REVENUE ($ mil.)	NET INCOME ($ mil.)	NET PROFIT MARGIN	EMPLOYEES
12/15*	1,131	34	3.1%	2,300
06/15	1,096	16	1.5%	—
09/14	864	65	7.6%	—
Annual Growth	30.8%	(47.1%)	—	—

*Fiscal year change

2015 Year-End Financials

Return on assets: 8.4%
Return on equity: 3.1%
Current ratio: 0.50

Cash ($ mil.): 7

OMAHA PUBLIC SCHOOLS

EXECUTIVES

Manager, James Cooper
Project Manager, T L Tompkins Jr
Assistant Manager, Tom Harvey
Project Manager, Jeremy Madson
Personnel Manager, Sandra Hodges
Director, Carla Noerrlinger
Finance Manager, Marc Kahn
Financial Executive, Dr Liz Standish
Auditors: SEIM JOHNSON LLP OMAHA NEBR

LOCATIONS

HQ: OMAHA PUBLIC SCHOOLS
  3215 CUMING ST, OMAHA, NE 681312024
Phone: 402 557-2120
Web: WWW.OPS.ORG

HISTORICAL FINANCIALS

Company Type: Private

Income Statement

FYE: August 31

	REVENUE ($ mil.)	NET INCOME ($ mil.)	NET PROFIT MARGIN	EMPLOYEES
08/16	693	(41)	—	8,000
08/15	626	126	20.3%	—
08/14	633	9	1.5%	—
08/13	611	(0)	—	—
Annual Growth	4.3%	—	—	—

2016 Year-End Financials

Return on assets: 2.8%
Return on equity: (-6.0%)
Current ratio: —

Cash ($ mil.): 193

OMNI CABLE CORPORATION

Omni Cable has it down to the wire. The company distributes electrical and electronic cables to wholesale customers in the US through 12 warehouses and distribution centers. Omni Cable also offers custom bundling coloring striping lashing twisting and imprinting of wires and cables. The employee-owned company was founded in 1977. Omni Cable has locations in Atlanta Boston Chicago Denver Houston Los Angeles Philadelphia Seattle St. Louis San Francisco and Tampa. It expended its presence in the Pacific Northwest in 2016 through the opening of its Seattle branch.

EXECUTIVES

President, Gregory J. (Greg) Lampert, age 49
Chairman and CEO, William J. (Jeff) Siegfried
COO, Greg Donato
CFO, Steve Glinski
EVP Sales and Marketing, Jason Obetz
Director Information Technology, Jeanine Bilotta

LOCATIONS

HQ: OMNI CABLE CORPORATION
  2 HAGERTY BLVD, WEST CHESTER, PA 193827594
Phone: 610 701-0100
Web: WWW.OMNICABLE.COM

PRODUCTS/OPERATIONS

Cable Products
Aluminum Cable
Armored Cable
Bare & Tinned Copper
Building Wire
Cable Accessories
Fiber Optic
Flexible & Portable Cord
High-Temp Lead Wire

COMPETITORS

Arrow Electronics
Consolidated
  Electrical
Gexpro
Premier Farnell
Sonepar USA
W.W. Grainger

HISTORICAL FINANCIALS

Company Type: Private

Income Statement

FYE: December 31

	REVENUE ($ mil.)	NET INCOME ($ mil.)	NET PROFIT MARGIN	EMPLOYEES
12/15	234	16	6.9%	216
12/14	258	15	5.9%	—
12/11	256	0	—	—
12/10	202	12	5.9%	—
Annual Growth	3.0%	6.0%	—	—

2015 Year-End Financials

Return on assets: 2.2%
Return on equity: 6.9%
Current ratio: 4.90

Cash ($ mil.): 20

ONCOR ELECTRIC DELIVERY COMPANY LLC

Oncor Electric Delivery serves miles and miles of Texas' vast energy market. The company operates the regulated power assets of parent Energy Future Holdings which include about 120000 miles of transmission and distribution lines serving more than 400 cities and 91 counties situated in the eastern north-central and western portions of the state. The company provides power to more than 3.2 million meters in homes and businesses. Oncor Electric Delivery maintains streetlights in its service territory. The utility also provides services to competitive retail electric providers. As an outcome of parent company EFH's bankruptcy Oncor received buyout offers from Berkshire-Hathaway and eventual winner Sempra Energy in 2017.

Geographic Reach

The company operates in the territory served by ERCOT the grid operator which oversees 85% of Texas' power consumption. It serves more than 400 cities and 90 counties situated in the eastern north-central and western portions of the state.

Sales and Marketing

Oncor Electric Delivery's transmission customers consist of municipalities electric cooperatives and other distribution companies. Its distribution customers consist of more than 80 reps including TCEH and certain electric cooperatives in certificated service areas. Revenues from TCEH represented 27% of its total sales in 2013 while revenues from NRG Energy represented 15%.

Financial Performance

Oncor Electric Delivery has experienced stable revenue growth over the years. Revenues increased by 7% in 2013 compared to 2012. The revenue jump was driven by an increase in distribution base rate revenues largely fueled by the effects of colder fall and winter weather in 2013 compared to 2012.

After experiencing a slight decrease in net income in 2012 the company's profits surged by 24% to $432 million in 2013 compared to $349 million in 2012. This was due to the higher revenue coupled with a decrease in interest expenses and related charges. The company's operating cash inflow increased to $1.37 million in 2013 compared to $1.26 million in 2012 as a result of lower pension contributions and cash interest payments.

Strategy

Oncor Electric Delivery's strategy is to invest heavily in technology to increase its value to it customers by eliminating duplicative costs managing supply costs and building and upgrading its equipment to be more efficient. Over the years it has invested $1.4 billion to build maintain and upgrade transmission lines build out the distribution infrastructure and to pursue other infrastructure maintenance and information technology initiatives. As part of this push and to improve consumer control over their power units it has installed 3 million advanced meters overt the last few years.

Company Background

In 2007 parent company TXU (now Energy Future Holdings) was acquired in a $45 billion leveraged buyout by an investor group led by Goldman Sachs Kohlberg Kravis Roberts and Texas Pacific Group. The deal was (at the time) the largest private buyout deal in US corporate history and included a promise by the new owners to cut back on coal plant development in order to reduce carbon emissions. However low gas prices have hurt Energy Future Holdings' results and it has run up serious debts.

EXECUTIVES

Senior Vice President Of Human Resources And Corpo, Deborah Dennis
Senior Vice President Human RE, Debra Elmer
Vice President Environment health Safety and Training, Deborah Boyle
CEO, Robert S. (Bob) Shapard, age 62, $754,417 total compensation
SVP and CFO, David M. Davis, age 59, $402,333 total compensation
SVP and COO, James A. (Jim) Greer, age 56, $402,333 total compensation
VP Legal Counsel and Corporate Secretary, Don J. Clevenger, age 46, $387,250 total compensation
SVP General Counsel and Secretary, E. Allen Nye, age 49, $446,500 total compensation
SVP T & D Operations, W. Mark Carpenter, age 64
Vice President Customer and Market Operations, Angela Guillory

Vice President Governmental Affairs, Walt Jordan
Senior Vice President Human RE, Debbie Dennis
VICE PRESIDENT AND TREASURER, Sarah Soong
VICE PRESIDENT REGULATORY AFFAIRS, Elizabeth Jones
Chairman, James (Jim) Adams
Business Representative and Treasurer, Renee Hancock
Auditors: DELOITTE & TOUCHE LLP DALLAS

LOCATIONS

HQ: ONCOR ELECTRIC DELIVERY COMPANY LLC
1616 WOODALL RODGERS FWY, DALLAS, TX 752021234
Phone: 214 486-2000
Web: WWW.ONCOR.COM

PRODUCTS/OPERATIONS

2015 Sales

	$ mil.	% of total
Distribution	1,849	48
Transmission	850	22
Rate surcharges & other	1,179	30
Total	**3,878**	**100**

COMPETITORS

Atmos Energy	CoServ Electric
Atmos Energy	CoServ Electric
Austin Energy	Garland Power & Light
Austin Energy	Garland Power & Light
Bluebonnet Electric	Pedernales Electric
Bluebonnet Electric	Pedernales Electric
Brazos Electric	Texas New Mexico Power
Brazos Electric	Texas New Mexico Power

HISTORICAL FINANCIALS
Company Type: Private

Income Statement

	REVENUE ($ mil.)	NET INCOME ($ mil.)	NET PROFIT MARGIN	EMPLOYEES
12/16*	3,920	431	11.0%	3,450
03/16	943	81	8.6%	—
12/15	3,878	432	11.1%	—
12/14	3,822	450	11.8%	—
Annual Growth	**1.3%**	**(2.1%)**	**—**	**—**

*Fiscal year change

2016 Year-End Financials
Return on assets: 5.9%
Return on equity: 11.0%
Current ratio: 0.30
Cash ($ mil.): 16

OPAL FOODS LLC

EXECUTIVES

President, Brock Peterson
Board of Directors, Ejnar Knudsen
Board of Directors, Julie Moneymaker
Manager, Cindy McGarrigle
Director, Rhonda Burkey
General Manager, Jerry Welch
Administrative Assistant, Ana Castellano
Accountant, Cally Goswick
Account Manager, Dawn-Marie Walls
Auditors: FROST PLLC LITTLE ROCK ARKAN

LOCATIONS

HQ: OPAL FOODS LLC
16194 HIGHWAY 59, NEOSHO, MO 648508667
Phone: 417 455-5000
Web: WWW.OPAL-FOODS.COM

HISTORICAL FINANCIALS
Company Type: Private

Income Statement
FYE: December 31

	REVENUE ($ mil.)	NET INCOME ($ mil.)	NET PROFIT MARGIN	EMPLOYEES
12/15	276	70	25.5%	350
12/14	169	18	10.6%	—
Annual Growth	**63.0%**	**290.9%**		

2015 Year-End Financials
Return on assets: 7.6%
Return on equity: 25.5%
Current ratio: 2.20
Cash ($ mil.): 43

OPERATING ENGINEERS HEALTH & WELFARE FUND

EXECUTIVES

Chief Financial Officer, Chuck Killian
Auditors: BERNARD KOTKIN AND COMPANY LLP

LOCATIONS

HQ: OPERATING ENGINEERS HEALTH & WELFARE FUND
100 CORSON ST, PASADENA, CA 911033840
Phone: 626 356-1000
Web: WWW.OEFI.ORG

HISTORICAL FINANCIALS
Company Type: Private

Income Statement
FYE: June 30

	ASSETS ($ mil.)	NET INCOME ($ mil.)	INCOME AS % OF ASSETS	EMPLOYEES
06/15	88	2	2.8%	2
06/14	85	8	9.8%	—
06/12	62	(14)		—
06/10	35	(56)		—
Annual Growth	**19.9%**			

2015 Year-End Financials
Return on assets: 1.2%
Return on equity: 1.1%
Sales ($ mil): 228

OPERATION BLESSING INTERNATIONAL RELIEF AND DEVELOPMENT CORPORATION

EXECUTIVES

Board of Directors, Randy J Morell
Manager, Kristin Vischer

Manager, James Kinlaw
Director, Kumar Periasamy
Manager, Kathy Haines
Editor, Shea Weekley
Auditors: KPMG LLP MC LEAN VA

LOCATIONS

HQ: OPERATION BLESSING INTERNATIONAL RELIEF AND DEVELOPMENT CORPORATION
977 CENTERVILLE TPKE, VIRGINIA BEACH, VA 234631001
Phone: 757 226-3401
Web: WWW.OB.ORG

HISTORICAL FINANCIALS
Company Type: Private

Income Statement
FYE: March 31

	REVENUE ($ mil.)	NET INCOME ($ mil.)	NET PROFIT MARGIN	EMPLOYEES
03/15	255	(1)	—	50
03/09	407	0	0.1%	—
03/06	210	9	4.8%	—
03/05	1,140	0	—	—
Annual Growth	**—**			

2015 Year-End Financials
Return on assets: 0.4%
Return on equity: (-0.7%)
Current ratio: 5.20
Cash ($ mil.): 4

ORANGE COAST MEMORIAL MEDICAL CENTER

EXECUTIVES

President, Marcia Manker
Manager, Bonnie Bengle
Vice-President, Brennan James

LOCATIONS

HQ: ORANGE COAST MEMORIAL MEDICAL CENTER
9920 TALBERT AVE, FOUNTAIN VALLEY, CA 927085153
Phone: 714 378-7000

HISTORICAL FINANCIALS
Company Type: Private

Income Statement
FYE: June 30

	REVENUE ($ mil.)	NET INCOME ($ mil.)	NET PROFIT MARGIN	EMPLOYEES
06/15	242	13	5.5%	1,000
06/08*	209	12	5.7%	—
12/05	0	0	—	—
06/02	174	0	—	—
Annual Growth	**—**	**67.5%**		

*Fiscal year change

2015 Year-End Financials
Return on assets: 5.5%
Return on equity: 5.5%
Current ratio: 0.90
Cash ($ mil.): —

ORANGE COUNTY TRANSPORTATION AUTHORITY

Public transportation in sunny Orange County California is overseen by the Orange County Transportation Authority (OCTA). The OCTA is the main provider of bus services in its 800-sq.-mi. territory which is home to more than 3 million people. In cooperation with the Southern California Regional Rail Authority the OCTA oversees Metrolink commuter rail service in Orange County. The agency also operates a 10-mile toll road and issues permits to taxi operators. Revenue from a half-cent local sales tax allows the agency to pay for road improvement and mass transit projects.

Operations

OCTA builds designs operates plans maintains and regulates the robust transportation network within Orange County. In addition to the four modes of transportation (transit driving bicycling and walking) OCTA oversees paratransit services taxi services light rail commuter rail and high?occupancy managed lanes.

It operates rail service for OCTA centers on Metrolink Southern California's commuter rail system linking residential communities to employment and activity centers. Metrolink is operated by the Southern California Regional Rail Authority- a joint powers authority of five member agencies representing the counties of Los Angeles Orange Riverside San Bernardino and Ventura. OCTA is one of the five member agencies that administers Orange County Metrolink activities.

The 91 Express Lanes is a four-lane 10-mile toll road built in the median of California's Riverside Freeway (SR-91) between the Orange/Riverside County line and the SR-55.

Geographic Reach

The company is located in Southern California - south of Los Angeles County north of San Diego County and west of Riverside and San Bernardino counties.

Financial Performance

OCTA's rail budget for fiscal year 2015-16 consists of both operating and capital expenses. Operating expenses in FY 2015-16 are budgeted at $31.6 million while capital expenditures are anticipated to reach $100.4 million. The FY 2015-16 rail capital projects. The organization saw a decline in its budget for FY 2015-16 due to drop in passenger fares and state assistance federal capital assistance grants.

(OCTA uses its revenue primarily in salaries and benefits professional services and capital expenditure).

Strategy

The 2014 - 2019 OCTA Strategic Plan takes a comprehensive forward-looking approach to address Orange County's transportation needs during the next five years.(OCTA maintains a Long-Range Transportation Plan updated every four years to account for new planning efforts as well as changes in demographics economic conditions and available sources of transportation funding).

In the FY 2015-16 budget $6.9 million of Measure M funds deposited in the General Fund are being used to fund the final work on the West County Connectors project.

After four years in the making OCTA marked the completion of the $297 million West County Connector project in 2014 which will bring congestion relief where three major freeways (Interstate 405 Interstate 605 and State Route 22) converge.

In 2014 OCTA purchased 400 new buses for fixed-route and ACCESS services. This purchase combined with the in-process repainting of the existing fleet presents a cost-effective opportunity to explore new branding concepts for Orange County bus services.

Company Background

OCTA was formed in 1991 in a consolidation of seven transportation agencies.

EXECUTIVES

Chief Executive Officer, Darrell Johnson
Executive Director, Jim Kenan
Director, Charles V Smith
Manager, Soledad Gonzalea
Planning Manager, Dave Elbaum
Project Manager, Nich Hahn
Manager, Eugenia Pinheiro
Project Manager, John Garcia
Auditors: VAVRINEK TRINE DAY & CO LL

LOCATIONS

HQ: ORANGE COUNTY TRANSPORTATION AUTHORITY
550 S MAIN ST, ORANGE, CA 928684506
Phone: 714 636-7433
Web: WWW.OCTA.NET

PRODUCTS/OPERATIONS

2014 Sales

	% of total
Sales taxes	93
Unrestricted investment earning	4
Property taxes	3
Other	.
Total	**100**

Selected Services

91 Express Lanes toll facility
Bus transit service
Freeway improvements funding
Freeway Service Patrol
Long-range planning
Measure M2 administration
Metrolink rail service
Rideshare options
Street and road improvements grants
Taxi administration program
Vanpool subsidies

HISTORICAL FINANCIALS
Company Type: Private

Income Statement

FYE: June 30

	REVENUE ($ mil.)	NET INCOME ($ mil.)	NET PROFIT MARGIN	EMPLOYEES
06/16	600	67	11.2%	1,050
06/15	607	43	7.2%	—
06/12	609	23	3.8%	—
06/11	438	247	56.6%	—
Annual Growth	6.5%	(22.9%)	—	—

ORANGE REGIONAL MEDICAL CENTER

EXECUTIVES

Chief Executive Officer, Scott Batulis
Director, Charles J Vassallo
Director, Elliott T Friedman
Director, Lisa A Fisher
Director, Manuel H De Castro

LOCATIONS

HQ: ORANGE REGIONAL MEDICAL CENTER
707 E MAIN ST, MIDDLETOWN, NY 109402667
Phone: 845 343-2424
Web: WWW.ORMC.ORG

HISTORICAL FINANCIALS
Company Type: Private

Income Statement

FYE: December 31

	REVENUE ($ mil.)	NET INCOME ($ mil.)	NET PROFIT MARGIN	EMPLOYEES
12/15	408	6	1.5%	2,000
12/14	374	4	1.3%	—
12/13	371	(8)	—	—
Annual Growth	4.9%	—	—	—

2015 Year-End Financials

Return on assets: 4.7%   Cash ($ mil.): 43
Return on equity: 1.5%
Current ratio: 1.20

ORGANICALLY GROWN COMPANY

Started by health-conscious Oregon farmers Organically Grown is exactly what its name says it is. The company grows and sells certified organic fruits vegetables and herbs produced by small to medium family-owned farmers located throughout the US's Pacific Northwest. Its line of more than 100 seasonal produce items are sold under the LADYBUG brand to customers including independent retailers supermarket chains restaurants home-delivery services and wholesalers. Organically Grown which is owned by its employees and growers was founded in 1978.

The company's customers include more than 500 vendors and 250 natural and food stores and restaurants throughout western Oregon and Washington. It has distribution operations in Eugene and Portland Oregon and in Kent Washington.

Dedicated to greening agriculture and the planet it donates 2.5% of its previous year's net profit to organizations focused on organic agriculture and sustainability.

EXECUTIVES

President, David Amorose
Representative, Cecil Zapata
Director, Natasha Spoden
Sales Manager, Lucas Crawford
Account Manager, Myrna Wheeler

LOCATIONS

HQ: ORGANICALLY GROWN COMPANY
1800 PRAIRIE RD STE B, EUGENE, OR 974029722
Phone: 541 689-5320
Web: WWW.ORGANICGROWN.COM

COMPETITORS

Albert's Organics	Natural Selection
Chiquita Brands	Foods
Dole Food	Pacific International
Dovex Fruit	Vegetable
Eden Foods	Veritable Vegetable
Fresh Del Monte	Willow Wind Organic
Produce	Farms
Jonathan Sprouts	

HISTORICAL FINANCIALS

Company Type: Private

Income Statement

	REVENUE ($ mil.)	NET INCOME ($ mil.)	NET PROFIT MARGIN	EMPLOYEES
12/15	176	3	1.8%	189
12/14	163	2	1.4%	—
12/13	145	2	1.9%	—
12/12	122	1	0.9%	—
Annual Growth	13.0%	43.9%	—	—

2015 Year-End Financials

Return on assets: 5.4% Cash ($ mil.): 6
Return on equity: 1.8%
Current ratio: 1.50

ORLANDO HEALTH CENTRAL, INC.

EXECUTIVES

President, Greg Ohe
Director, Patricia Bray
Marketing Director, Brenda Labattaglia
Auditors: GRANT THORNTON LLP ORLANDO F

LOCATIONS

HQ: ORLANDO HEALTH CENTRAL, INC.
10000 W COLONIAL DR, OCOEE, FL 347613400
Phone: 407 296-1820
Web: WWW.HEALTHCENTRAL.ORG

HISTORICAL FINANCIALS

Company Type: Private

Income Statement

FYE: September 30

	REVENUE ($ mil.)	NET INCOME ($ mil.)	NET PROFIT MARGIN	EMPLOYEES
09/15	208	23	11.3%	1,500
09/14	167	26	16.0%	—
09/13	183	18	10.0%	—
Annual Growth	6.5%	12.9%	—	—

2015 Year-End Financials

Return on assets: 11.1% Cash ($ mil.): 23
Return on equity: 11.3%
Current ratio: 1.30

ORLANDO HEALTH, INC.

It's not Disney World but for Floridians needing health care it is a prime destination. Orlando Health is a not-for-profit organization with a network of community and specialty hospitals with nearly 2300 beds in Central Florida. Its flagship facility the Orlando Regional Medical Center features a Level 1 trauma center and provides comprehensive acute care services in a range of specialties. Orlando Health also operates several community hospitals. Its specialty hospitals include the Arnold Palmer Hospital for Children and the Winnie Palmer Hospital for Women and Babies. It also operates the renowned M. D. Anderson Cancer Center Orlando (the first affiliate of Houston-based M. D. Anderson center).

Operations

In addition to the Orlando Regional Medical Center and three fully owned community hospitals the company operates two medical centers through partnerships. It holds a 50% stake in the South Lake Hospital and a 20% stake in the St. Cloud Regional Medical Center. It also operates physician practice associations and an emergency air transport service (Air Care).

Across its facilities Orlando Health has about 2000 affiliated physicians who provide a full spectrum of health care services. Areas of clinical excellence include heart and vascular care cancer care obstetrics and gynecology neonatology neurosciences surgery pediatric orthopedics and sports medicine. Annually Orlando Health serves more than 2 million residents of central Florida and 4500 international patients. The organization also provides between $250 and $300 million in community health programs each year.

As a statutory teaching hospital system Orlando Health also engages in medical training programs through affiliation agreements with the University of Central Florida College of Medicine and other institutions. Orlando Health offers a number of medical residency and fellowship programs; its seven residencies are offered to 250 participants and include programs in emergency medicine internal medicine OB-GYN orthopedic surgery pathology and pediatrics. The organization also conducts research studies and clinical trials through partnerships with educational and commercial organizations.

Geographic Reach

Orlando Health operates throughout Orlando and in neighboring Clermont Longwood Ocoee and St. Cloud Florida.

Financial Performance

The company's revenues increased by 9% in 2014 due to higher net patient service revenues and other revenues. Medicare accounted for 23% of the net patient revenues; Medicaid 19%.

Orlando Health's net income grew by 349% due to higher revenues and investment income.

Operating cash flow increased by 235% in 2014.

Strategy

Orlando Health is working to improve its operating model by improving the quality of patient outcomes; enhancing collaboration between physicians medical professionals hospitals research centers and other institutions; and increasing clinical integration of various disciplines to share resources and skills.

As an example of its collaborative and quality enhancement efforts Orlando Health is involved in the formation of a regional health information exchange to connect its electronic health record (EHR) systems with other Central Florida health providers and the public health department. The program aims to improve quality of care by eliminating redundant tests and other repeated efforts as well as by providing hospitals swift access to patient data.

Orlando Health is also focused on making improvements to its Orlando Regional Medical Center through a multi-year $297-million renovation project. In 2015 the company opened its new 245-bed 10-story 345000-square-foot North Tower's front entrance and its existing Orlando Regional Medical Center building now will be referred to as Orlando Regional Medical Center South Tower. The North Tower is part of the hospital's redesign and renovation project and includes an expanded emergency department cardiovascular service areas operating suites and other ancillary services located inside Orlando Regional Medical CenterSouth Tower. The South Tower expansion is expected to was completed in 2015. That year the Orlando Regional Medical Center redesign and renovation project continued with its Surgical Services expansion and renovation. The 28000-square-foot addition includes 10 new operating rooms a new Post Anesthesia Care Unit area with 24 patient bays.

Other planned projects include the expansion of the neonatal intensive care unit at Winnie Palmer Hospital for Women and Babies.

In 2015 Orlando Health Physician Associates officially opened its doors in the Lake Nona area.

That year the West Orange Healthcare District awarded a $13.8 million grant to Health Central Hospital to expand. The grant was the second largest in the history of the district and funded 75 percent of the total expansion costs. Orlando Health funded the remaining 25 percent. Upon completion the expansion project will add 40 rooms to Health Central Hospital increasing its bed count from 171 to 211 and enabling the further development of specialized care.

Mergers and Acquisitions

In 2015 Orlando Health Physician Associates acquired Pediatric Associates of Orlando. Founded in 1939 it was one of the first pediatric practices in Central Florida.

Company Background

In 2012 Arnold Palmer Hospital added an outpatient rehabilitation center.

The health system expanded its network in 2012 by acquiring the 170-bed Health Central Hospital and its associated facilities in Ocoee Florida for $181 million. Orlando Health further expanded through the purchase of Physician Associates a professional practice organization in 2013.

Orlando Health was founded in 1918.

EXECUTIVES

VP and CIO, Rick Schooler
President and CEO, David W. Strong
SVP; President Arnold Palmer Medical Center Orlando Health Foundation and Arnold Palmer Medical Center Foundation, John Bozard
President Adult Hospitals Group, Shannon Elswick
President South Seminole Hospital, Steve Glazier
CFO, Bernadette Spong
VP; Executive Director Orlando Health Foundation, Karen Jensen
President Dr. P. Phillips Hospital, Mark A. Jones
COO, Jessica Wertman
Senior Vice President Legal Affairs, Mildred Beam
Director, Dianna Morgan
Auditors: GRANT THORNTON LLP ORLANDO F

LOCATIONS

HQ: ORLANDO HEALTH, INC.
52 W UNDERWOOD ST, ORLANDO, FL 328061110
Phone: 321 843-7000
Web: WWW.ORLANDOHEALTH.COM

PRODUCTS/OPERATIONS

2014 Sales

	% of total
Net patient service revenue less provision for bad debts	95
Other revenue	5
Net assets released from restrictions	-
Total	**100**

Selected Facilities

Arnold Palmer Hospital for Children (Orlando)
Dr. P. Phillips Hospital (formerly Orlando Regional Sand Lake Hospital Orlando)
Health Central Hospital (Ocoee)
Lucerne Pavilion (Orlando)
M. D. Anderson Cancer Center Orlando
Orlando Health Heart Institute
Orlando Health Rehabilitation Institute
Orlando Regional Medical Center
South Lake Hospital (50% affiliate Clermont)
South Seminole Hospital (Longwood)
St. Cloud Regional Medical Center (20% affiliate)
Winnie Palmer Hospital for Women & Babies (Orlando)

Selected Specialties

Cancer care (at M. D. Anderson Cancer Center Orlando)
Emergency and trauma care
Heart and vascular
Neurosciences
Oncology/hematology
Orthopedic and sports medicine
Surgery
Women's services

Selected Services

Anesthesiology
Brain Injury Rehabilitation Center (BIRC)
Endocrinology (diabetes)
Endoscopy
Epilepsy care
Home health care
Infectious diseases
Internal medicine
Laboratory and pathology Services
Mammography
Memory Disorder Center
MRI
Multiple sclerosis treatment
Nephrology
Nuclear medicine
Ophthalmology
Otolaryngology (Ears Nose Throat)
Pain management
Patient and family counseling
Pediatric outpatient surgery
Pulmonary medicine
Radiology and diagnostic imaging
Rehabilitation and physical therapy

COMPETITORS

Adventist Health System Sunbelt Healthcare
All Children's Hospital
Baptist Health South Florida
Baptist Health System
Community Health Systems
Florida Hospital Heartland
Florida Hospital Waterman
HCA
Health First
Holmes Regional Medical Center
Mayo Clinic Jacksonville
Mount Sinai Medical Center of Florida
Munroe Regional Health System
Nemours Foundation
Ocala Regional Medical Center
Osceola Regional Medical Center
St. Vincent's Health System
UF&Shands

HISTORICAL FINANCIALS

Company Type: Private

Income Statement

FYE: September 30

	REVENUE ($ mil.)	NET INCOME ($ mil.)	NET PROFIT MARGIN	EMPLOYEES
09/15	2,323	208	9.0%	10,000
09/14	1,663	231	13.9%	—
09/13	1,576	115	7.3%	—
09/10	1,700	91	5.4%	—
Annual Growth	6.4%	17.9%	—	—

2015 Year-End Financials

Return on assets: 9.4%　　Cash ($ mil.): 133
Return on equity: 9.0%
Current ratio: 1.30

ORLEANS INTERNATIONAL, INC.

EXECUTIVES

Chief Executive Officer, Earl Tushman
Chief Financial Officer, Jerry Castellano
Auditors: UHY LLP FARMINGTON HILLS MIC

LOCATIONS

HQ: ORLEANS INTERNATIONAL, INC.
　30600 NORTHWESTERN HWY # 300, FARMINGTON
　HILLS, MI 483343172
Phone: 248 855-5556
Web: WWW.ORLEANSINTL.COM

HISTORICAL FINANCIALS

Company Type: Private

Income Statement

FYE: December 31

	REVENUE ($ mil.)	NET INCOME ($ mil.)	NET PROFIT MARGIN	EMPLOYEES
12/15*	856	1	0.2%	32
11/08	474	1	0.4%	—
Annual Growth	8.8%	(0.2%)	—	—

*Fiscal year change

OROVILLE HOSPITAL

EXECUTIVES

Chief Executive Officer, Robert J Wentz
Manager, Peter M M Russo
Officer, David Bryning
Financial Executive, Colleen Duncan
Auditors: KCOE ISOM LLP CHICO CALIFO

LOCATIONS

HQ: OROVILLE HOSPITAL
　2767 OLIVE HWY, OROVILLE, CA 959666118
Phone: 530 533-8500

HISTORICAL FINANCIALS

Company Type: Private

Income Statement

FYE: November 30

	REVENUE ($ mil.)	NET INCOME ($ mil.)	NET PROFIT MARGIN	EMPLOYEES
11/15	236	18	7.9%	1,400
11/14	217	14	6.7%	—
11/13	761	2	0.3%	—
11/12	173	6	3.9%	—
Annual Growth	10.9%	39.8%	—	—

2015 Year-End Financials

Return on assets: 7.5%　　Cash ($ mil.): 43
Return on equity: 7.9%
Current ratio: 1.60

OTIS EASTERN SERVICE, LLC

EXECUTIVES

President, Charles P Joyce
Chief Financial Officer, Steve Cummings
Accountant, Shirley Harris
Manager, Adam Landis
Project Manager, Brad Joyce
Superintendent, Danny Cox
Superintendent, Jim Joyce
Administrative Assistant, Malena Dunham
Auditors: BROCK SCHECHTER & POLAKOFF L

LOCATIONS

HQ: OTIS EASTERN SERVICE, LLC
　2971 ANDOVER RD, WELLSVILLE, NY 148959536
Phone: 585 593-4760
Web: WWW.OTISEASTERN.COM

HISTORICAL FINANCIALS

Company Type: Private

Income Statement

FYE: December 31

	REVENUE ($ mil.)	NET INCOME ($ mil.)	NET PROFIT MARGIN	EMPLOYEES
12/15	225	51	22.8%	15
12/14	253	59	23.6%	—
Annual Growth	(11.2%)	(14.3%)	—	—

2015 Year-End Financials

Return on assets: 1.8%　　Cash ($ mil.): 10
Return on equity: 22.8%
Current ratio: 1.40

OUACHITA PARISH SCHOOL SYSTEM

EXECUTIVES

Superintendent, Don Coker
Purchasing Manager, Bobby Jones
Purchasing Director, Juanita Dukes
Plant & Facilities Manager, Scotty Nugent
Auditors: HUFFMAN & SOIGNIER CPAS MONR

LOCATIONS

HQ: OUACHITA PARISH SCHOOL SYSTEM
　100 BRY ST, MONROE, LA 712018406
Phone: 318 432-5000
Web: WWW.OPSB.NET

HISTORICAL FINANCIALS

Company Type: Private

Income Statement

FYE: June 30

	REVENUE ($ mil.)	NET INCOME ($ mil.)	NET PROFIT MARGIN	EMPLOYEES
06/15	225	39	17.6%	2,804
06/14	219	2	1.0%	—
06/13	213	2	1.2%	—
06/11	210	(18)	—	—
Annual Growth	1.7%	—	—	—

Return on assets: 0.6%   Cash ($ mil.): 75
Return on equity: 17.6%
Current ratio: —

OUR LADY OF LOURDES MEDICAL CENTER, INC

Our Lady of Lourdes Medical Center tends to the sick of southern New Jersey. The hospital is a general acute care facility with about 325 inpatient beds. In addition to general medical emergency and surgical care the hospital specializes in organ transplantation joint replacement rehabilitation dialysis treatment cardiac care and birthing care. The hospital also offers nursing and other medical training programs and it operates area clinics and provides community health and outreach services. Our Lady of Lourdes Medical Center part of Catholic Health East's Lourdes Health System is sponsored by the Franciscan Sisters of Allegany New York.

Operations

The medical center's specialty units include the New Jersey Heart Institute at Lourdes the Regional Perinatal Center and the Lourdes Rehabilitation Center as well as regional dialysis and organ transplant clinics. Besides offering primary and specialty care services in a variety of fields Our Lady of Lourdes Medical Center is a teaching and research facility through affiliations with area universities and health professional schools. It also operates its own nursing school.

The hospital had a total of 13682 admissions on 2014. Its physicians performed 3184 inpatient and 2392 outpatient surgeries.

Strategy

Our Lady of Lourdes Medical Center has undergone expansion efforts over the years to attract and retain customers in the region by continually upgrading its technology. The hospital also strives to expand services and resources for doctors and health professionals. In 2014 it became one of only a few hospitals in the South Jersey region to implant subcutaneous implantable defibrillators. The cardiac device is the first and only one of its kind that provides defibrillator therapy without touching the heart.

Lourdes Health System has also expanded by opening new outpatient care centers in Camden and the greater Philadelphia metropolitan area. It is the only hospital in the tri-state area (New Jersey Pennsylvania and Delaware) to have been awarded the American Hospital Association's top honor for excellence in community outreach services.

Company Background

In 2012 Our Lady of Lourdes Medical Center relocated and expanded its birthing center to include all-private rooms with improved family accommodations. It has also updated some of its medical equipment and energy systems including the addition of a new MRI imaging system during 2012 to improve patient comfort and diagnostic capabilities.

That year it enriched its educational programs by forming partnerships with the Immaculata University and Camden Community College to offer nursing bachelor's and master's degrees through its Our Lady of Lourdes School of Nursing.

EXECUTIVES

Radiology Director, Barbara O Donnell
Assistant Vice President, Sandy Roth

LOCATIONS

HQ: OUR LADY OF LOURDES MEDICAL CENTER, INC
1600 HADDON AVE, CAMDEN, NJ 081033101
Phone: 856 757-3500
Web: WWW.LOURDESNURSINGSCHOOL.ORG

PRODUCTS/OPERATIONS

Selected Services
Bariatric Surgery
Cardiac Services
Community Outreach
Dialysis
Emergency Services
Joint Replacement Center
Organ Transplantation
Rehabilitation Center
Senior Services
Stroke
Women and Children's Services

COMPETITORS

Abington Memorial Hospital
Albert Einstein Healthcare Network
Aria Health
Christiana Care
Fox Chase Cancer Center
Inspira Health Network
Main Line Health System
Mercy Health System
North Philadelphia Health System
TUHS
Tenet Healthcare
The Cooper Health System
University of Pennsylvania Health System
Virtua Health

HISTORICAL FINANCIALS

Company Type: Private

Income Statement   FYE: June 30

	REVENUE ($ mil.)	NET INCOME ($ mil.)	NET PROFIT MARGIN	EMPLOYEES
06/15	308	28	9.1%	3,000
06/14	298	14	4.7%	—
Annual Growth	3.5%	99.9%	—	—

2015 Year-End Financials

Return on assets: 9.5%   Cash ($ mil.): 2
Return on equity: 9.1%
Current ratio: 1.50

OUR LADY OF LOURDES REGIONAL MEDICAL CENTER, INC.

Established in 1949 as part of the not-for-profit Franciscan Missionaries of Our Lady Health System Our Lady of Lourdes Regional Medical Center is a hospital that provides medical care in southern Louisiana. The facility cares for denizens of the bayou with a medical staff of more than 400 physicians representing some 50 specialties including cardiology neurology and oncology. The medical center also offers oupatient care and urgent care as well as a general family practice and pediatric care. Our Lady of Lourdes extends its reach outside the facility into the Acadiana regional community by offering primary care physicians' offices home health care programs and occupational medicine.

EXECUTIVES

Director of Admissions, Cecile Broussard
Vice President Finance Controller, Jennifer Clowers
Director of Patient Relations, Eileen Rowe
Vice President of the Oncology Service Line, Tracy Delhomme
Occupational Therapy Director, Holly Domingue
Vice President Medical Affairs, Anthony Blalock
Board Member, Betty Lyons
Board Member, Michael Vanderlick

LOCATIONS

HQ: OUR LADY OF LOURDES REGIONAL MEDICAL CENTER, INC.
4801 AMBSSDOR CFFERY PKWY, LAFAYETTE, LA 705086917
Phone: 337 470-2000
Web: WWW.LOURDESRMC.COM

COMPETITORS

Baton Rouge General	Our Lady of the Lake
CHRISTUS St. Frances	RMC
Cabrini Hospital	River Parishes
General Health System	Hospital
LHC Group	Terrebonne General
LSU System	Medical Center
Lafayette General	Woman's Hospital
Medical Center	
Lane Regional Medical	
Center	

HISTORICAL FINANCIALS

Company Type: Private

Income Statement   FYE: June 30

	REVENUE ($ mil.)	NET INCOME ($ mil.)	NET PROFIT MARGIN	EMPLOYEES
06/15	197	(38)	—	1,700
06/10	162	(9)	—	—
06/09	142	(58)	—	—
06/08	314	0	—	—
Annual Growth	—	—	—	—

2015 Year-End Financials

Return on assets: 6.0%   Cash ($ mil.): 30
Return on equity: (-19.4%)
Current ratio: 0.10

OUR LADY OF THE LAKE HOSPITAL, INC.

Our Lady of the Lake Regional Medical Center reaches out to Baton Rouge residents with a helping hand. Participating in teaching programs for LSU and Tulane medical schools the medical center has some 800 inpatient beds and includes trauma emergency surgery general medical and specialty care centers for conditions including heart disease cancer orthopedics and ENT (ear nose and throat) disorders. Our Lady of the Lake also includes a Children's Hospital two nursing homes and an independent-living facility and it offers outpatient services at its main campus and at satellite facilities throughout the greater Baton Rouge area.

Operations

The hospital's family of services include an 800-bed Regional Medical Center; a dedicated Children's Hospital; a 350-provider Physician Group primary care network free-standing emergency room in Livingston Parish; an outpatient imaging and surgery centers; Assumption Community Hos-

pital; a network of urgent care clinics; and Our Lady of the Lake College.

Our Lady of the Lake is a primary teaching site for graduate medical education programs and serves 45000 inpatients and 350000 outpatients a year.

The company has more than 850 doctors. Some 70% of its physicians and other professional medical staff members are board certified and in nearly one-third of the hospital system's medical specialty areas 100% of the physicians and other professionals are board certified.

Strategy

As a major facility in the Baton Rouge area Our Lady of the Lake has been expanding its services in the region in recent years. In 2015 Our Lady of the Lake Children's Hospital opened its first pediatric specialty clinic outside of the Baton Rouge area offering specialized outpatient care for pediatric gastroenterology patients.

In 2014 the company opened a new children's emergency room and expanded its adult emergency department.

Company Background

In 2012 the hospital constructed a freestanding emergency room facility in the suburban community of Livingston Louisiana. It is also building a new nine-story patient tower to the main hospital campus; the tower will house the heart and vascular center as well as an expanded ER and a new level 1 regional trauma center and will be completed in late 2013.

Our Lady of the Lake has also expanded its education programs. For instance it added a pediatric residency program in 2010. The hospital also moved to extend its relationship with LSU that year by agreeing to become the primary clinical site for the LSU medical school. The agreement came as LSU considered whether to build a replacement hospital for its aging teaching facility and coincides with the Our Lady of the Lake expansion projects. The partnership launched a new psychiatric residency program in 2012.

Our Lady of the Lake was founded in 1923 by the Franciscan Missionaries of Our Lady.

EXECUTIVES

President, K Scott Wester
Chairman of the Board, Charles Valluzzo
Director, Walter L Bringaze
Director, Tony Martin
Manager, Yaw Twum
Director, Luke A Lvergne
Director, Andrew Nelson
Director, Barbara Arceneaux Sr

LOCATIONS

HQ: OUR LADY OF THE LAKE HOSPITAL, INC.
5000 HENNESSY BLVD, BATON ROUGE, LA 708084367
Phone: 225 765-6565

PRODUCTS/OPERATIONS

Selected Services
Advanced Wound and Ostomy Clinic
Cancer
Children's Hospital
Critical Care
Diabetes & Nutrition Center
Emergency Services
Endoscopy Center
Hearing and Balance Center
Heart & Vascular Institute
Imaging Services
Laboratory and Diagnostics
Lake Express Check-In
LSU Health Baton Rouge
Mental and Behavioral Health
Neurology Neurosurgery and Stroke
Orthopedics
Palliative Care

Pharmacy
Rehabilitation Center
Respiratory Care
Senior Services
St. Anthony's Home
Surgery
Trauma Center
Urgent Care
Voice Center
Weight Loss

COMPETITORS

CHRISTUS St. Frances
  Cabrini Hospital
Dynacq Healthcare
General Health System
Lane Regional Medical
  Center

Our Lady of Lourdes
River Parishes
  Hospital
Woman's Hospital

HISTORICAL FINANCIALS

Company Type: Private

Income Statement

FYE: June 30

	REVENUE ($ mil.)	NET INCOME ($ mil.)	NET PROFIT MARGIN	EMPLOYEES
06/15	984	21	2.1%	1,800
06/14	946	56	6.0%	—
06/11	826	214	26.0%	—
06/10	614	12	2.0%	—
Annual Growth	9.9%	11.2%	—	—

2015 Year-End Financials

Return on assets: 7.0%
Return on equity: 2.1%
Current ratio: 1.30

Cash ($ mil.): 81

OVERLAKE HOSPITAL ASSOCIATION

EXECUTIVES

Principal, Diane Sperry
Director, Justin Sampson
Manager, Byung Ryou
Auditors: KPMG LLP SEATTLE WA

LOCATIONS

HQ: OVERLAKE HOSPITAL ASSOCIATION
1035 116TH AVE NE, BELLEVUE, WA 980044604
Phone: 425 688-5000
Web: WWW.OVERLAKEHOSPITAL.ORG

HISTORICAL FINANCIALS

Company Type: Private

Income Statement

FYE: June 30

	REVENUE ($ mil.)	NET INCOME ($ mil.)	NET PROFIT MARGIN	EMPLOYEES
06/16	511	8	1 6%	271
06/15	490	20	4.1%	—
06/14	454	62	13.8%	—
06/13	427	42	9.9%	—
Annual Growth	6.2%	(41.9%)	—	—

2016 Year-End Financials

Return on assets: 3.6%
Return on equity: 1.6%
Current ratio: 0.90

Cash ($ mil.): 29

OVERLAKE HOSPITAL MEDICAL CENTER

Over the lake and through the sound to Overlake Hospital Medical Center we go! The not-for-profit hospital provides health care services to residents of Bellevue Washington in the Puget Sound region. The nearly 350-bed facility provides comprehensive inpatient and outpatient services ranging from cancer care and surgery to specialized senior care. Overlake also operates a number of outpatient clinics providing primary care urgent care and specialty care such as weight loss surgery. The organization also provides patients with health and wellness programs addressing issues like women's and children's health.

Operations

The medical center has more than 1000 physicians on staff and runs Centers of Excellence in cardiac care cancer care surgical services women's and infants' care and emergency and Level III trauma care. The facility is home to a 24-hour urgent care clinic an anticoagulation clinic and a breast screening center. Overlake also operates numerous outpatient clinics providing primary care urgent care and specialty care.

Geographic Reach

Overlake provides health care services to residents of Bellevue Washington and the entire Puget Sound region. It operates clinics on its main campus in Bellevue as well as in Redmond and in Issaquah and on Mercer Island.

Sales and Marketing

In 2014 Medicare payments accounted for 27% of net patient revenues followed by group health organizations (17%) Premera (13%) and Regence (12%).

Financial Performance

Overlake's revenues increased by 2% to $433 million in 2014 as the result of higher net patient revenues and contribution revenues.

Net income rose 50% to $60 million that year primarily due to income from change in net unrealized gains on investments. Cash flow from operations fell 3% to $47 million as more cash was used in net clinic accounts receivable pledges receivable prepaid expenses and other long-term receivables.

Strategy

Increasing demand in the region has led the hospital to invest in expansions and equipment upgrades that include more emergency treatment capabilities and an on-campus helistop for trauma patients being airlifted to the area.

Along with its expansion and construction projects Overlake is investing in new technology to keep the health system in line with its competitors and to improve patient care. It is adding endoscopic video towers to its operating rooms to facilitate improved views of surgical procedures and is also moving to digitize all of its facilities with electronic health records.

In 2013 it opened the new $17.4 million David and Shelley Hovind Heart & Vascular center. The new 19200-sq.-ft. facility brings cardiac and vascular services together in one location.

Overlake has also focused on adding new primary care clinics and expanding its physician network to serve patients in locations closer to where they live and work.

Company Background

Overlake founded in 1960 is led by CEO Craig Hendrickson a veteran health care executive.

EXECUTIVES

Vice President Strategy and Marketing, Caitlin Hillary Moulding
Medical Director, Richard Clarfeld
Vice President of Fund Development and Executive Director, Molly Stearns
Director Patient Care Nursing, Barbara Berkau
Director of Surgery Services Materials Management Director, Helene Schultz
Ambulatory Services Director, Barbara Hein Murdock
Vice President Patient Care Services; Chief Nursing Officer, Julie Clayton
Vice President System Change Management Chief Co, Richard Bryan
Vice President Information Services and CIO, Jody Albright
Director of Pharmacyrespiratory Care EEG and Clinical Research, Gordon Oakes
Chief Nursing Officer And Vice President Of Patient Care Services, Cathy Whitaker
Registered Nurse Clinic Manager, Maricres Talley
Medical Director of Radiation Oncology; Radiologist, Jim Pelton
MEDICAL LIBRARIAN, Jacqueline Luizzi
Auditors: KPMG LLP SEATTLE WA

LOCATIONS

HQ: OVERLAKE HOSPITAL MEDICAL CENTER
1035 116TH AVE NE, BELLEVUE, WA 980044687
Phone: 425 688-5000
Web: WWW.OVERLAKEHOSPITAL.ORG

Selected Locations
Outpatient Rehabilitation Services
Outpatient Surgery (park in the West Garage; Outpatient Surgery is located on the first floor of the West Garage.)
Overlake Bellevue Campus and Overlake Medical Clinics Medical Tower
Overlake Medical Clinics Downtown Bellevue
Overlake Medical Clinics Issaquah
Overlake Medical Clinics Kirkland
Overlake Medical Clinics Redmond
Urgent Care Clinic in Issaquah
Urgent Care Clinic in Redmond

PRODUCTS/OPERATIONS

2014 Sales

	% of total
Net patient service revenue	97
Other operating revenue	3
Contribution revenue	—
Total	**100**

Selected Medical Services
Breast Health Services
Cancer Center at Overlake
Cardiac Center at Overlake
Clinical Trials
Emergency & Trauma Center
Medical Imaging
Overlake Medical Clinics
Surgical Services
Weight Loss Surgery
Women's & Infants' Center

COMPETITORS

Catholic Health Initiatives
Franciscan Health System
Harrison Medical Center
Kaiser Permanente WA
MultiCare Health System
PeaceHealth
Providence St. Joseph Health
Seattle Children's Hospital
Swedish Health Services
University of Washington
Yakima Valley Memorial

HISTORICAL FINANCIALS

Company Type: Private

Income Statement

FYE: June 30

	REVENUE ($ mil.)	NET INCOME ($ mil.)	NET PROFIT MARGIN	EMPLOYEES
06/15	485	16	3.5%	2,450
06/14	450	59	13.3%	—
06/13	422	40	9.5%	—
06/12	427	18	4.4%	—
Annual Growth	**4.4%**	**(3.5%)**	**—**	**—**

2015 Year-End Financials

Return on assets: 3.1%
Return on equity: 3.5%
Current ratio: 0.90
Cash ($ mil.): 22

OXNARD SCHOOL DISTRICT

EXECUTIVES

Superintendent, Cesar Morales
Principal, Anthony Zubia
Auditor, Julia Reyes
Assistant Manager, Robin Freeman
Auditors: NIGRO & NIGRO PC MURRIETA CA

LOCATIONS

HQ: OXNARD SCHOOL DISTRICT
1051 S A ST, OXNARD, CA 930307442
Phone: 805 487-3918
Web: WWW.OXNARDSD.ORG

HISTORICAL FINANCIALS

Company Type: Private

Income Statement

FYE: June 30

	REVENUE ($ mil.)	NET INCOME ($ mil.)	NET PROFIT MARGIN	EMPLOYEES
06/16	219	39	18.2%	2,100
06/15	189	(7)	—	—
06/13	146	19	13.1%	—
06/12	148	(5)	—	—
Annual Growth	**10.2%**	**—**	**—**	**—**

2016 Year-End Financials

Return on assets: 8.6%
Return on equity: 18.2%
Current ratio: —
Cash ($ mil.): 112

PACIFIC COAST PRODUCERS

Fruits seafood sauces and organic tomato puree — rather than movies — are the creative output of this particular group of Pacific Coast Producers. The cooperative markets the apricots grapes peaches pears and tomatoes grown by its approximately 160 California-based members. It turns the produce into private-label canned fruit sauces and juices and sells them to the retail and foodservice industries. Pacific Coast Producers typically serves retailers the likes of Albertson's Aldi Kroger Safeway SUPERVALU Whole Foods and Wal-Mart as well as the US Department of Agriculture. The company founded in 1971 operates three production sites and one distribution center in California.

Operations
The cooperative boasts three food-processing facilities in California as well as distribution centers in California and Washington.

Geographic Reach
From its base in Lodi California Pacific Coast Producers grows its fruits in California and sells them nationwide.

Sales and Marketing
Pacific Coast Producers sells the products it grows and processes to retailers and foodservice operators nationwide as well as to the US Department of Agriculture.

Financial Performance
As one of California's premier private label packers Pacific Coast Producers has logged annual sales in excess of $535 million plus $100 million in alliance income.

Strategy
Pacific Coast Producers has expanded its warehouse space in Lodi to improve efficiency and boost capacity. The move cost the company $23 million. It expanded its distribution center by 50% to meet rising demand for canned food.

The cooperative serves tomato processor Morning Star through a sales and marketing alliance it formed with the company in 2009. As part of the collaboration Pacific Coast Producers provides canned tomatoes to the retail and foodservice industries.

EXECUTIVES

Vice President, Andrew K Russick
Vice President, Daniel Sroufe
Vice President General Counsel, Mona Shulman
Vice President Finance Chief Financial Officer, Mark Wahlman
National Sales Manager, David Zuzich
Auditors: KPMG LLP SACRAMENTO CALIFOR

LOCATIONS

HQ: PACIFIC COAST PRODUCERS
631 N CLUFF AVE, LODI, CA 952400756
Phone: 209 367-8800
Web: WWW.PCOASTP.COM

PRODUCTS/OPERATIONS

Selected Products
Apricots
Catsup
Chili Sauces
Chunky Mixed Fruit
Concentrated Crushed Tomatoes
Diced Style Tomatoes
Extra Heavy Concentrated Crushed Round Tomato Puree
Formulated Pizza Sauces
Fruit Cocktail
Fruit for Salad
Fruit Mix
Ground Tomatoes
Marinara Sauces
Non-Formulated Pizza Sauce
Organic Tomatoes
Peaches
Pears
Random Cut / Strip Style Tomatoes
Seafood Sauces
Stewed Style Tomatoes
Tomato Juice
Whole Peeled Tomatoes

COMPETITORS

Big Heart Pet Brands
Campbell Soup
Cento
ConAgra
Dole Food
General Mills
Glory Foods
Hain Celestial
Hanover Foods
Heinz
NORPAC
Pictsweet
Seneca Foods

HISTORICAL FINANCIALS
Company Type: Private

Income Statement
FYE: May 31

	REVENUE ($ mil.)	NET INCOME ($ mil.)	NET PROFIT MARGIN	EMPLOYEES
05/16	630	30	4.8%	1,000
05/15	623	30	4.9%	—
05/14	588	23	4.0%	—
05/13	534	18	3.5%	—
Annual Growth	5.7%	17.4%	—	—

2016 Year-End Financials
Return on assets: 4.9%   Cash ($ mil.): 2
Return on equity: 4.8%
Current ratio: 0.30

PACIFIC NORTHWEST GENERATING COOPERATIVE

EXECUTIVES
President, John Prescott
Personnel Manager, Tereesa Stubblefield
Chief Financial Officer, Jon R Wissle
Vice-President, Aleka Scott
Auditors: MOSS-ADAMS LLP PORTLAND OREG

LOCATIONS
HQ: PACIFIC NORTHWEST GENERATING COOPERATIVE
711 NE HALSEY ST, PORTLAND, OR 972321268
Phone: 503 288-1234
Web: WWW.PNGCPOWER.COM

HISTORICAL FINANCIALS
Company Type: Private

Income Statement
FYE: September 30

	REVENUE ($ mil.)	NET INCOME ($ mil.)	NET PROFIT MARGIN	EMPLOYEES
09/15	180	1	0.7%	36
09/08	169	0	0.3%	—
09/07	174	0	0.3%	—
09/06	873	0	—	—
Annual Growth	—	62.1%	—	—

2015 Year-End Financials
Return on assets: 8.2%   Cash ($ mil.): 11
Return on equity: 0.7%
Current ratio: 1.70

PAJARO VALLEY UNIFIED SCHOOL DISTRICT

EXECUTIVES
Superintendent, Michelle Rodriguez
Manager, Alicia Jimenez
Director, Ron Indra
Auditors: VAVRINEK TRINE DAY & CO LL

LOCATIONS
HQ: PAJARO VALLEY UNIFIED SCHOOL DISTRICT
294 GREEN VALLEY RD FL 1, WATSONVILLE, CA 950761382
Phone: 831 786-2100
Web: WWW.PVUSD.NET

HISTORICAL FINANCIALS
Company Type: Private

Income Statement
FYE: June 30

	REVENUE ($ mil.)	NET INCOME ($ mil.)	NET PROFIT MARGIN	EMPLOYEES
06/16	279	47	16.9%	2,139
06/05	209	16	8.1%	—
06/04	92	34	37.9%	—
06/03	4	0	—	—
Annual Growth	—	84.5%	—	—

PALM SPRINGS UNIFIED SCHOOL DIST.

EXECUTIVES
Director, Evelyn M Hernandez
Superintendent, Lorriane Becker
Foreman/Supervisor, Jackie Holmes
Director, Jazmin Rodriguez

LOCATIONS
HQ: PALM SPRINGS UNIFIED SCHOOL DIST.
980 E TAHQUITZ CANYON WAY, PALM SPRINGS, CA 922626708
Phone: 760 416-6177
Web: WWW.PSUSD.US

HISTORICAL FINANCIALS
Company Type: Private

Income Statement
FYE: June 30

	REVENUE ($ mil.)	NET INCOME ($ mil.)	NET PROFIT MARGIN	EMPLOYEES
06/15	281	(28)	—	2,370
06/06	225	84	37.3%	—
06/05	196	15	7.9%	—
06/04	1,614	0	0.0%	—
Annual Growth	(14.7%)	—	—	—

PALMDALE SCHOOL DISTRICT

EXECUTIVES
President, Juan Carrillo
Executive Director, Julie Ferebee
Vice-Chairman, Kathleen Duren
Director, Geoff Brown
Board of Directors, Dennis Trujillo
Board of Directors, Joyce Ricks
Auditors: NIGRO NIGRO & WHITE PC SAN D

LOCATIONS
HQ: PALMDALE SCHOOL DISTRICT
39139 10TH ST E, PALMDALE, CA 935503419
Phone: 661 947-7191
Web: WWW.PALMDALESD.ORG

HISTORICAL FINANCIALS
Company Type: Private

Income Statement
FYE: June 30

	REVENUE ($ mil.)	NET INCOME ($ mil.)	NET PROFIT MARGIN	EMPLOYEES
06/16	307	8	2.8%	1,800
06/06	219	2	1.2%	—
06/04	242	25	10.5%	—
06/03	0	0	—	—
Annual Growth	—	110.5%	—	—

2016 Year-End Financials
Return on assets: 9.2%   Cash ($ mil.): 120
Return on equity: 2.8%
Current ratio: —

PANHANDLE EASTERN PIPE LINE COMPANY, LP

From the oilfield to the burner under a frying pan Panhandle Eastern Pipe Line can move the gas. The company operates 10000 miles of interstate pipelines (Panhandle Eastern — 6000 miles Trunkline — 3000 miles and Sea Robin — 1000 miles) that can transport 6.4 billion cu. ft. of natural gas a day primarily to markets in the Midwest and Great Lakes regions of the US. It also provides terminalling services through nearly 50 compressor stations and five gas storage fields capable of holding 68.1 billion cu. ft. of natural gas. The company also has liquefied natural gas (LNG) terminalling assets. Panhandle Eastern Pipe Line operates as part of Energy Transfer Equity's Southern Union's Panhandle Energy unit.

Operations

Panhandle Eastern Pipe Line generates most of its revenues via transportation and storage contracts providing capacity for customers to transport or store natural gas or LNG in its pipelines and at its several storage plants.

Geographic Reach

The company transports natural gas to more than 25 utility companies located in Illinois Michigan Missouri Ohio and Tennessee. It owns and operates an LNG import terminal in Louisiana with 9 billion cu. ft. of LNG storage capacity.

Company Background

Founded in 1929 Panhandle Eastern Pipe Line was acquired by Southern Union from CMS Energy in 2003. Southern Union was acquired by Energy Transfer Equity in 2012.

EXECUTIVES
Chief Executive Officer, Kelcy L Warren
Chief Financial Officer, Martin Salinas Jr
General Partner, Southern Union Panhandle LLC
Senior Vice-President, Jeryl Mohn
Auditors: GRANT THORNTON LLP HOUSTON T

LOCATIONS
HQ: PANHANDLE EASTERN PIPE LINE COMPANY, LP
8111 WESTCHESTER DR # 600, DALLAS, TX 752256142
Phone: 214 981-0700

COMPETITORS

ANR Pipeline	Piedmont Natural Gas
Alliance Pipeline	Texas Gas Transmission
Columbia Gulf	Vector Pipeline
Transmission	Williston Basin
ONEOK Partners	Interstate Pipeline

HISTORICAL FINANCIALS

Company Type: Private

Income Statement

FYE: December 31

	REVENUE ($ mil.)	NET INCOME ($ mil.)	NET PROFIT MARGIN	EMPLOYEES
12/16	514	(646)	—	562
12/15	548	125	22.8%	—
12/14	581	(3)	—	—
Annual Growth	(5.9%)	—	—	—

2016 Year-End Financials

Return on assets: 2.1%
Return on equity: (-125.7%)
Current ratio: 0.10

Cash ($ mil.): 4

PARADISE VALLEY UNIFIED SCHOOL DISTRICT

EXECUTIVES

President, Julie Bacon
Principal, Sarah Hartley
Director, Catherine Shpudejko
Auditors: HEINFELD MEECH & CO PC P

LOCATIONS

HQ: PARADISE VALLEY UNIFIED SCHOOL DISTRICT
15002 N 32ND ST, PHOENIX, AZ 850324441
Phone: 602 867-5100
Web: WWW.PVSCHOOLS.NET

HISTORICAL FINANCIALS

Company Type: Private

Income Statement

FYE: June 30

	REVENUE ($ mil.)	NET INCOME ($ mil.)	NET PROFIT MARGIN	EMPLOYEES
06/16	312	10	3.4%	3,600
06/06	283	25	9.1%	—
06/05	273	14	5.2%	—
06/04	0	0	—	—
Annual Growth	—	140.0%	—	—

PARKER ADVENTIST HOSPITAL

EXECUTIVES

President, Morre Dean
Board of Directors, Elizabeth Kincannon
Director, Tamera Ogren

Office Manager, Pauline Robitaille
Director, John Carbonneau
Director, Julie Duran
Director, Bonnie Gutierrez

LOCATIONS

HQ: PARKER ADVENTIST HOSPITAL
9395 CROWN CREST BLVD, PARKER, CO 801388573
Phone: 303 269-4000
Web: WWW.PARKERHOSPITAL.ORG

HISTORICAL FINANCIALS

Company Type: Private

Income Statement

FYE: June 30

	REVENUE ($ mil.)	NET INCOME ($ mil.)	NET PROFIT MARGIN	EMPLOYEES
06/15	241	31	13.2%	250
06/09	129	28	21.7%	—
Annual Growth	10.9%	2.1%	—	—

2015 Year-End Financials

Return on assets: 6.7%
Return on equity: 13.2%
Current ratio: 1.20

Cash ($ mil.): —

PARKS XANTERRA & RESORTS INC

EXECUTIVES

President, Andrew N Todd
Board of Directors, Kirk Anderson
Director, Mike Goodman
Manager, Jessica Knoo
Manager, Jessica Knoll
Personnel Manager, Kristy Valleroy
Quality Control Manager, Robert Parmer

LOCATIONS

HQ: PARKS XANTERRA & RESORTS INC
6312 S FIDDLERS GREEN CIR 600N, GREENWOOD VILLAGE, CO 801114943
Phone: 303 600-3400
Web: WWW.XANTERRA.COM

HISTORICAL FINANCIALS

Company Type: Private

Income Statement

FYE: December 31

	REVENUE ($ mil.)	NET INCOME ($ mil.)	NET PROFIT MARGIN	EMPLOYEES
12/15	350	53	15.2%	3,500
12/14	358	79	22.2%	—
12/13	304	11	3.7%	—
12/12	305	13	4.3%	—
Annual Growth	4.7%	59.2%	—	—

2015 Year-End Financials

Return on assets: 30.0%
Return on equity: 15.2%
Current ratio: 0.20

Cash ($ mil.): 21

PARKWEST MEDICAL CENTER

Parkwest Medical Center is a wholly-owned subsidiary of Covenant Health and the largest medical center in West Knoxville. Parkwest has more than 285 beds and provides health care services to patients of Knox County Tennessee. Its various specialties include cardiology orthopedics neurology and spine care women's services and bariatric surgery. Other services include cardiac rehabilitation diagnostic services outpatient surgery and senior health care. Parkwest's facilities include a 40-bed emergency care center a 30-bed critical care unit and a 20-suite childbirth center. The medical center also has a diabetes center and provides dental care.

Parkwest opened in 1973 as a joint venture between physicians and Hospital Corporation of America (HCA) the operating subsidiary of HCA Holdings Inc. In 1990 Parkwest became a part of the not-for-profit Fort Sanders Health System which in 1996 became Covenant Health.

Parkwest works to enhance its services to the community through improvements such as the addition of its Riverstone Tower a six-story addition that is part of a $100 million project that covers 326000 sq. ft. of new construction 45000 sq. ft. of renovated space and adds 214 beds.

Parkwest's Peninsula division provides inpatient and outpatient mental health and alcohol and drug crisis stabilization programs through Peninsula Hospital a 155-bed facility for adults adolescents and children and through outpatient centers that include its largest center Peninsula Lighthouse in Knoxville and freestanding facilities in Knox Blount Sevier and Loudon counties. Peninsula also provides support and aftercare services to support patient recovery and to help families. Its services include crisis intervention options for in-home treatment and supportive housing and employment programs to aid with maintaining healthy lifestyles and improving quality of life.

EXECUTIVES

Pharmd, Patty Strickler
Infection Control Director, MARGARET CHAMBERS
Ambulatory Services Dir, BRENDA COLLINS
Vice President, Debbie Llewellyn

LOCATIONS

HQ: PARKWEST MEDICAL CENTER
9352 PARK WEST BLVD, KNOXVILLE, TN 379234387
Phone: 865 373-1000
Web: WWW.TREATEDWELL.COM

PRODUCTS/OPERATIONS

Selected Adult Specialties
Cancer
Cardiology and heart surgery
Diabetes and endocrinology
Ear nose and throat
Gastroenterology
Geriatrics
Gynecology
Nephrology
Neurology and neurosurgery
Orthopedics
Pulmonology
Urology

Selected Outpatient Centers
Parkwest Comprehensive Breast Center
Parkwest Cardiac Rehabilitation
Rehabilitation Outpatient Program
Parkwest Therapy Center

HISTORICAL FINANCIALS

Company Type: Private

Income Statement

FYE: August 31

	REVENUE ($ mil.)	NET INCOME ($ mil.)	NET PROFIT MARGIN	EMPLOYEES
08/15*	290	35	12.3%	1,300
12/13	337	29	8.8%	—
12/05	172	5	3.1%	—
12/04	172	5	3.1%	—
Annual Growth	4.8%	18.8%	—	—

*Fiscal year change

PARMA COMMUNITY GENERAL HOSPITAL

Parma Community General Hospital aka University Hospitals Parma Medical Center cares for residents of Ohio's Cuyahoga County and surrounding areas along the northern Lake Erie shoreline. The 332-bed acute care medical center has a staff of more than 500 physicians representing some 30 medical specialties. It offers a broad range of inpatient care services including cardiology oncology orthopedics and rehabilitation. Its outpatient and community outreach programs include home health hospice senior care diagnostic labs and various community health clinics. The hospital was founded in 1961.

Geographic Reach

The hospital is located in Parma Ohio the largest suburb of Cleveland. It was founded in 1961 by Parma and five other towns in the area to fill a gap in local care options. The main campus consists of a nine-story hospital as well as an outpatient surgery center and four medical practice buildings. The hospital also operates satellite care centers in surrounding communities.

Strategy

The hospital has expanded its facilities over the years to meet the needs of a growing population. In addition the hospital works to keep pace with modern technologies by upgrading its medical equipment and its data management software and systems. In fact the hospital is an early adopter of certain data systems; it has had computerized patient records since 1996 and it began using electronic prescription verification systems in 2006.

EXECUTIVES

Vice President Operations, Kathi O'Connor
Vice President Chief Nursing Officer, Sharon Thomas
Vice President Human Resources, Ralph Knull
Director of HIM, Terry Byrne
Vice President of General Services and CIO, Terrance Deis
Treasurer, Gayle Rullo
secretary, Kristine Barnhill
Secretary, Zdenka Mizak
Secretary scheduler, Karen Mundorff

LOCATIONS

HQ: PARMA COMMUNITY GENERAL HOSPITAL
7007 POWERS BLVD, PARMA, OH 441295437
Phone: 440 743-3000

PRODUCTS/OPERATIONS

Selected Centers and Services
3DHD Surgery
Acute Rehabilitation
Anticoagulation Clinic
Bariatric Center
Cancer Treatment Center
Community Express Care
Emergency Dept.
Employers' HealthSource
Geriatric Psychiatry
Heart & Vascular Center
Home Health Care
Laboratory
Metabolic Weight Loss Clinic
Orthopedics
Outpatient Center
Pain Center
Pulmonary Rehabilitation
Radiology
Ridge Park Imaging
Robotic Surgery
Small Wonders Maternity Center
Seasons of Life Hospice
Specialized Care
Therapy
Wound Center

HISTORICAL FINANCIALS

Company Type: Private

Income Statement

FYE: December 31

	REVENUE ($ mil.)	NET INCOME ($ mil.)	NET PROFIT MARGIN	EMPLOYEES
12/15	180	3	2.1%	2,000
12/13	180	(0)	—	—
12/12	183	2	1.4%	—
Annual Growth	(0.5%)	15.0%	—	—

2015 Year-End Financials

Return on assets: 5.1%
Return on equity: 2.1%
Current ratio: 1.10

Cash ($ mil.): 3

PARTNERS HEALTHCARE SYSTEM, INC.

Partners HealthCare System is looking out for the health of the Bay State. Partners HealthCare includes two large acute-care medical centers — Brigham and Women's Hospital and Massachusetts General Hospital— and six community hospitals. The system also provides primary and specialty care through clinics physician offices long-term care facilities and home health and hospice agencies. Its rehabilitation facilities include the Spaulding Rehabilitation Hospital Network. Partners HealthCare also provides medical training and research through an affiliation with Harvard. Other ventures include the Dana-Farber/Partners CancerCare clinic (a collaboration with Harvard and Dana-Farber Cancer Institute).

Operations

The system's Partners Community HealthCare division is a management services organization that provides support for a physician network encompassing some 6500 practitioners. Partners HealthCare also sponsors community health outreach programs. Community hospitals owned by or affiliated with Partners include McLean Hospital Newton-Wellesley Hospital North Shore Medical Center Nantucket Cottage Hospital and the Martha's Vineyard Hospital. Partners HealthCare also operates Faulkner Hospital as a subsidiary of the Brigham and Women's facility.

Brigham and Women's (a 777-bed facility) and Massachusetts General are both teaching hospitals for the Harvard Medical School. The Harvard Clinical Research Institute is a partnership between the Harvard Medical School Partners HealthCare and CareGroup (parent of Boston facilities including Beth Israel Deaconess Medical Center). Outside the US the system's Partners HealthCare International provides clinical advisory patient care research and educational programs with a number of global partners. With an annual research budget of $1.6 billion Partners HealthCare has a strong research funding base including awards of some $600 million annually from the National Institutes of Health.

The system serves 1.5 million patients annually. In 2014 it invested $210 million in community programs.

Geographic Reach

Partners HealthCare provides services to patients in the Greater Boston area as well as New England and beyond. It also partners with health care systems and health-related academic institutions in more than 40 countries.

Financial Performance

Partners HealthCare's revenues increased by 5% in 2014 due to growth in net patient service and premium revenues.

The company reported net loss of $181 million in 2014 (compared to net income in 2013) due to a change in the fair value of non-hedging interest rate swaps absence of contribution income from affiliates and achange in funded status of defined benefit plans.

Despite the net loss the company's operating cash flow increased by 23% due to higher cash generated from accrued medical claims and related expenses and change in accrued compensation and benefits unexpended funds on research grants and accrued employee benefits and other.

Strategy

Partners HealthCare strives to provide innovative yet affordable medical care to area residents. To keep its operations efficient as well as to comply with federal health reform incentive measures Partners HealthCare has put in place a health information system that requires all of its doctors to use electronic health records (EHRs). As one of the early adopters of EHR systems Partners HealthCare is upgrading its IT systems to install a new clinical information system across its facilities using new technologies from software maker Epic. The new system — which will enhance coordination of care reduce unnecessary health spending and simplify reporting and patient access features — will be implemented over ten years and will cost between $600 and $700 million.

Other programs to meet new health care standards include reducing prices on certain procedures and renegotiating contracts with insurers as well as encouraging patients to participate in preventative care wellness and generic drug programs.

In 2014 the company broke ground on its new administrative offices in Assembly Square that will bring 4500 permanent and 1500 construction jobs to the 45-acre Assembly Row development.

That year Partners HealthCare also formed a partnership known as Partners Urgent Care with MedSpring Urgent Care to open and operate multiple urgent care clinics in eastern Massachusetts. The joint venture opened its first urgent care center in Brookline Massachusetts in early. Additional locations in Newton and Watertown were under construction in 2015.

Mergers and Acquisitions

Following an expansion trend in the region Partners HealthCare has laid out plans to acquire Neighborhood Health Plan. Instead of paying cash to acquire the not-for-profit insurance provider which serves 200000 low-income and disabled residents with Medicaid policies Partners HealthCare intends to provide grants to some 50 smaller community health centers affiliated with the health plan. The deal will require approval from state regulators before it can proceed.

The organization has also agreed to acquire the 140-bed Cooley Dickinson Hospital in Northampton as well as specialty hospital Massachusetts Eye and Ear.

In 2015 the company acquired Harbor Medical Associates which has some 70 physicians and 60000 patients.

Company Background

Partners HealthCare has been recognized by the federal government and other organizations for its quality and efficiency programs. In 2012 the health network was selected by the Centers for Medicare and Medicaid Services to participate in the Pioneer ACO (accountable care organization) program which aims to slow cost growth in the Medicare market by enhancing care coordination.

Partners HealthCare was founded in 1994 through the merger of Brigham and Women's Hospital and Massachusetts General Hospital.

EXECUTIVES

EVP Administration and Finance CFO and Treasurer, Peter K. Markell, age 61
President and CEO Massachusetts General Hospital, Peter L. Slavin
CIO, James W. (Jim) Noga
President and CEO North Shore Medical Center, Robert G. (Bob) Norton, age 67
President and CEO Neighborhood Health Plan, Deborah C. Enos
President and CEO Partners Continuing Care, David E. Storto
President and CEO Brigham and Women's Hospital, Elizabeth G. (Betsy) Nabel
President and Chief Executive Officer, David F. Torchiana
President of Partners Community, Thomas H. Lee
President and CEO Spaulding Rehabilitation Network, Maureen Banks
President McLean Hospital, Scott L. Rauch
President and CEO Brigham and Women's Physicians Organization, Allen L. Smith
President and CEO Martha's Vineyard Hospital, Timothy J. Walsh
President and CEO MGH Institute of Health Professions, Janis P. Bellack
President and CEO, David Torchiana
President and CEO Nantucket Cottage Hospital, Margot Hartmann
President and CEO Partners HealthCare at Home, Rod Carnifax
Medical Director Bipolar Clinic and Research Programs, Andrew Nierenberg
Nursing Director, Karen Reilly
Nursing Director, Lauren Willard

Medical Director of The Breast and Ovarian Cancer, Paula Ryan
Nursing Director, Elizabeth McGrath
Clinic Director, Bruce Chabner
Nursing Director, Colleen West
Nursing Director, Janet Quigley
Director Of Radiology, Tina Maloney
Director of Nursing, Heidi Larkin
Nursing Director, Barbara Crawley
Medical Director Of Quality Safey And Population Management, Adrienne Allen
Medical Director, Richard Kaufman
Project Manager To Senior Vice President Research, Angela Vail
Clinical Director, Jane Evans
NURSING DIRECTOR, Michele Ohara
Clinical Director, Martha Kane
Senior Vice President Human Re, J Davison
VICE PRESIDENT OF OPERATIONS, Hofmann Erika
DIRECTOR OF MEDICAL RECORDS, Doherty Linda
NURSING DIRECTOR, Dorothy Parker
Executive Vice President and Chief Technology Officer for Strategy and Technology, Richard Goldberg
NURSING DIRECTOR, Christine Flanagan
VICE PRESIDENT, Edward Liston-kraft
Chairman, Edward P. Lawrence, age 75
Board Member, Peter Ardagna
Secretary, Maria Sanchez
Board Member, Warren Foote
Executive Board Member, Denise Goldsmith
Board Member, Jonathan Katz
Vice Chair Departrment Of Pediatrics, Peter Greenspan
Auditors: PRICEWATERHOUSECOOPERS LLP B

LOCATIONS

HQ: PARTNERS HEALTHCARE SYSTEM, INC.
800 BOYLSTON ST STE 1150, BOSTON, MA 021998123
Phone: 617 278-1000

PRODUCTS/OPERATIONS

2014 Sales

	% of total
Net patient service revenue	65
Premium revenue	15
Direct academic and research	11
Indirect academic and research	3
Other revenue	6
Total	**100**

COMPETITORS

Baystate Health	Lahey Health System
Boston Medical Center	Milford Regional
Cambridge Health	Medical Center
Alliance	Northeast Health
Cape Cod Healthcare	System
Cape Cod Hospital	Southcoast Hospitals
Care New England	Group
CareGroup	Steward Health Care
Children's Hospital	Universal Health
Boston	Services

HISTORICAL FINANCIALS
Company Type: Private

Income Statement
FYE: September 30

	REVENUE ($ mil.)	NET INCOME ($ mil.)	NET PROFIT MARGIN	EMPLOYEES
09/15	11,665	(916)	—	67,000
09/10	8	(0)	—	—
09/08	551	(44)	—	—
Annual Growth	**54.7%**	—	—	—

2015 Year-End Financials
Return on assets: 15.4%   Cash ($ mil.): 621
Return on equity: (-7.9%)
Current ratio: 0.70

PASADENA INDEPENDENT SCHOOL DISTRICT

EXECUTIVES

President, Mariselle Quijano-Lerma
Board of Directors, Fred Roberts
Senior Manager, Janna Gibson
Maintenance Supervisor, Jeff Dunnahoe
Plant & Facilities Manager, Kevin Fornof
Auditors: WHITLEY PENN LLP TEXAS CITY

LOCATIONS

HQ: PASADENA INDEPENDENT SCHOOL DISTRICT
1515 CHERRYBROOK LN, PASADENA, TX 775024099
Phone: 713 740-0000
Web: WWW.PASADENAISD.ORG

HISTORICAL FINANCIALS
Company Type: Private

Income Statement
FYE: August 31

	REVENUE ($ mil.)	NET INCOME ($ mil.)	NET PROFIT MARGIN	EMPLOYEES
08/16	611	(32)	—	5,000
08/13	522	98	18.9%	—
08/12	497	83	16.7%	—
08/11	507	9	1.8%	—
Annual Growth	**3.8%**	—	—	—

2016 Year-End Financials
Return on assets: 2.6%   Cash ($ mil.): 36
Return on equity: (-5.3%)
Current ratio: 0.70

PDS TECH, INC.

Need an IT pro to assist with your company's computer needs? PDS Tech wants to help. The company provides temporary technical industrial and general staffing services through more than 30 offices across the US with a concentration in Texas and on the East Coast. PDS Tech's specialties include aviation architecture engineering information technology administration and maritime staffing. Its PDS Engineering division handles engineering placement for the aerospace mechanical and structural engineering industries while the Information Services division offers technical consulting services in the IT and telecommunication industries. The company was founded in 1977 by aerospace engineer Art Janes.

EXECUTIVES

Chief Executive Officer, Arthur R Janes
Finance Manager, Ken Barker
Chief Financial Officer, Steven C Nickerson
Branch Manager, Mary Gillham
Auditors: BKM SOWAN HORAN LLP CPA ADD

LOCATIONS

HQ: PDS TECH, INC.
300 E JOHN CARPENTER FWY # 700, IRVING, TX 750622383
Phone: 214 647-9600

PRODUCTS/OPERATIONS

PDS Operating Divisions
PDS Engineering
PDS Aviation
PDS Information Services
PDS Maritime
PDS Professional/General
Offload Engineering
Northwest

Selected Industries
Aerospace
Automotive
Civil/Architectural
Electronics
Energy
Financial Services
Government
Medical Defense/Military
Software
Telecommunications

COMPETITORS

Adecco	ManpowerGroup
Allegis Group	On Assignment
Butler America	StarTek
CDI	Volt Information
COMFORCE	

HISTORICAL FINANCIALS

Company Type: Private

Income Statement

FYE: December 27

	REVENUE ($ mil.)	NET INCOME ($ mil.)	NET PROFIT MARGIN	EMPLOYEES
12/15	321	0	0.2%	10,000
12/14	339	0	0.1%	—
12/13	373	1	0.3%	—
12/12	436	2	0.6%	—
Annual Growth	(9.7%)	(34.5%)	—	—

2015 Year-End Financials

Return on assets: 0.8% Cash ($ mil.): 7
Return on equity: 0.2%
Current ratio: 6.10

PEACEHEALTH

PeaceHealth provides patients with a tranquil place to recover. Make that several tranquil places to recover. PeaceHealth serves residents in southeastern Alaska coastal regions of Washington and central portions of Oregon. Its medical centers include PeaceHealth Ketchikan Medical Center PeaceHealth St. Joseph Medical Center PeaceHealth St. John Medical Center Sacred Heart Medical Center (two campuses) Cottage Grove Community Hospital Peace Harbor Hospital PeaceHealth Peace Island Medical Center and PeaceHealth Southwest Medical Center. Other operations include physician practices community clinics hospices chemical dependency rehabilitation clinics and other outpatient facilities and services.

Operations

In all PeaceHealth has about 16000 acute beds and 30 nursing home beds. It has some 16000 caregivers and a multi-specialty medical group practice with more than 800 physicians. It also has 10 medical centers in both rural and urban communities throughout the Northwest.

In 2014 the system reported more than 72000 inpatient admissions and nearly 746000 outpatient registrations as well as 1.2 million patient encounters with its medical group. It had more than 8000 infant births and more than 302000 emergency department visits that year.

Sales and Marketing

Commercial and other payers accounted for 52% of net patient revenue in 2013 while Medicare accounted for 36%.

Financial Performance

Revenue decreased by just under 1% to $2.2 billion in 2013 due to a decline in premiums. However net income rose to $142 million (versus a net loss in 2012) due to an increase in investment returns and other changes. Cash flow from operations fell 1% to $174 million as more cash was used in accounts receivable.

Company Background

PeaceHealth was formed in 1923 by the Sisters of St. Joseph of Peace who opened the Little Flower Hospital in Ketchikan named after Saint Teresa. The Sisters of St. Joseph of Peace had previously opened St. Joseph Hospital in Bellingham in 1891.

PeaceHealth and Southwest Washington Health System merged in early 2011 boosting PeaceHealth's hospital holdings from six to eight with the addition of the two-campus Southwest Washington Medical Center in Vancouver Washington.

Under terms of the affiliation Southwest Washington Health System became part of PeaceHealth allowing Southwest to benefit from its larger peer's medical and financial resources. The move allows both health systems to increase the scope of services they offer in Washington State where Southwest Washington Health System also operates clinics a medical group and a foundation through which it conducts fundraising efforts.

EXECUTIVES

CEO, Liz Dunne, age 61
President PeaceHealth Medical Group, Michael Metcalf
EVP and Chief Administrative Officer, Carol Aaron
Chief Executive Columbia Network, Sean J. Gregory
Chief Executive Northwest Network, Dale Zender
SVP and Chief Nursing Officer, Victoria King
SVP and CIO, Dan Hein
President Hospital Services Oregon, Rand O'Leary
EVP Strategy and Community Health, Michael Dwyer
EVP and CFO, Kimberly Hodgkinson
EVP and General Counsel, Ron Saxton
System Vice President, Steve Glenn
Vice President Ambulatory Services, Michele Budd
Medical Director, Tyler Gibb
Medical Director of Trauma and Acute Care Surgery, George Dulabon
Pharmacy Manager, Judy Ashe
Medical Director, Larry Neville
Director of Pharmacy, Jeff Corsentino
Medical Director, Margo Kozinski
Chairman, Andrea Nenzel
Board Member, James Nakashima

LOCATIONS

HQ: PEACEHEALTH
1115 SE 164TH AVE, VANCOUVER, WA 986839324
Phone: 360 788-6841
Web: WWW.PEACEHEALTH.ORG

PRODUCTS/OPERATIONS

2013 Sales

	$ mil.	% of total
Patient service revenue	1,984	92
Premium revenue	93	4
Other operating revenue	94	4
Total	**2,171**	**100**

Selected Hospitals

PeaceHealth Ketchikan Medical Center (Ketchikan Alaska)
Cottage Grove Community Hospital (Cottage Grove Oregon)
Peace Harbor Hospital (Florence Oregon)
PeaceHealth Peace Island Medical Center (Friday Harbor Washington)
PeaceHealth Southwest Medical Center (Vancouver Washington)
PeaceHealth St. John Medical Center (Longview Washington)
PeaceHealth St. Joseph Medical Center (Bellingham Washington)
Sacred Heart Medical Center at RiverBend (Springfield Oregon)
Sacred Heart Medical Center University District (Eugene Oregon)
Other Operations
PeaceHealth Laboratories (locations throughout Oregon and Washington)
PeaceHealth Medical Group (operates in Alaska Oregon and Washington)

COMPETITORS

Alaska Native Tribal Health Consortium	Providence St. Joseph Health
Franciscan Health System	Seattle Children's Hospital
HCA	South Peninsula Hospital
Harrison Medical Center	Swedish Health Services
Immediate Care	Tenet Healthcare
MultiCare Health System	Yakima Valley Memorial
Overlake Hospital	

HISTORICAL FINANCIALS

Company Type: Private

Income Statement

FYE: June 30

	REVENUE ($ mil.)	NET INCOME ($ mil.)	NET PROFIT MARGIN	EMPLOYEES
06/15	2,544	160	6.3%	6,690
06/14	2,249	114	5.1%	—
06/09	1,372	(88)	—	—
06/06	1,048	103	9.8%	—
Annual Growth	10.3%	5.0%	—	—

2015 Year-End Financials

Return on assets: 15.2% Cash ($ mil.): 588
Return on equity: 6.3%
Current ratio: 0.90

PEARCE INDUSTRIES, INC.

EXECUTIVES

Chairman of the Board, Louis M Pearce Jr
Manager, David McMillion
Manager, Bryan Wester

LOCATIONS

HQ: PEARCE INDUSTRIES, INC.
12320 MAIN ST, HOUSTON, TX 770356206
Phone: 713 723-1050

HISTORICAL FINANCIALS
Company Type: Private

Income Statement
FYE: March 31

	REVENUE ($ mil.)	NET INCOME ($ mil.)	NET PROFIT MARGIN	EMPLOYEES
03/16	511	2	0.5%	750
03/15	611	28	4.6%	—
03/14	515	16	3.3%	—
03/13	469	16	3.5%	—
Annual Growth	2.9%	(47.7%)	—	—

2016 Year-End Financials
Return on assets: 10.4%
Return on equity: 0.5%
Current ratio: 0.90
Cash ($ mil.): 4

PEARLAND INDEPENDENT SCHOOL DISTRICT

EXECUTIVES

Superintendent, Dr John P Kelly
Clerk, Beverly Quinton
Auditors: KENNEMER MASTERS & LUNSFORD

LOCATIONS

HQ: PEARLAND INDEPENDENT SCHOOL DISTRICT
1928 N MAIN ST, PEARLAND, TX 775813306
Phone: 281 485-3203
Web: WWW.PEARLANDISD.ORG

HISTORICAL FINANCIALS
Company Type: Private

Income Statement
FYE: June 30

	REVENUE ($ mil.)	NET INCOME ($ mil.)	NET PROFIT MARGIN	EMPLOYEES
06/16	205	(13)	—	2,450
06/15	191	28	15.0%	—
06/14	185	5	3.1%	—
06/13	164	10	6.1%	—
Annual Growth	7.6%	—	—	—

2016 Year-End Financials
Return on assets: 1.8%
Return on equity: (-6.6%)
Current ratio: —
Cash ($ mil.): 74

PECKHAM VOCATIONAL INDUSTRIES, INC.

EXECUTIVES

Chief Executive Officer, Mitchell Tomlinson
President, Scott Derthick
Director of Finance, Maouc Maali
Board of Directors, Stainley Koget
Board of Directors, Heather Shawa-Becook
Auditors: LB MANER COSTERISAN PC LANSIN

LOCATIONS

HQ: PECKHAM VOCATIONAL INDUSTRIES, INC.
3510 CAPITOL CITY BLVD, LANSING, MI 489062102
Phone: 517 316-4000
Web: WWW.PECKHAMPERFORMANCEWEAR.COM

HISTORICAL FINANCIALS
Company Type: Private

Income Statement
FYE: September 30

	REVENUE ($ mil.)	NET INCOME ($ mil.)	NET PROFIT MARGIN	EMPLOYEES
09/16	187	3	1.6%	1,540
09/15	165	5	3.4%	—
09/14	142	1	1.4%	—
09/13	129	(2)	—	—
Annual Growth	13.3%	—	—	—

2016 Year-End Financials
Return on assets: 9.7%
Return on equity: 1.6%
Current ratio: 0.70
Cash ($ mil.): 8

PENNONI ASSOCIATES INC.

Design consulting and engineering firm Pennoni Associates specializes in the creation of civil infrastructure projects. The company offers construction services planning surveys transportation planning lab testing environmental engineering landscape architecture site design and other services. Pennoni serves East Coast clients including government entities and private companies. Affiliate Pennoni Engineering and Surveying of New York specializes in heating ventilation and air conditioning systems electrical plumbing and fire protection engineering. The employee-owned company was established by chairman Celestino "Chuck" Pennoni in 1966.

Operations

Subsidiary Patton Harris Rust & Associates (acquired in 2011) offers engineering and planning services in Maryland and Virginia. To help to better service clients with additional services and geographic locations Pennoni has two affiliates: B.D. Abel (engineering for laboratory and research facilities clean room design chiller/boiler plants variable temperature/variable humidity environments process and manufacturing and electrical power design as well as standard mechanical HVAC and lighting design); and Pennoni Engineering and Surveying of New York P.C. (a full-service consulting engineering firm providing quality design services).

Geographic Reach

Philadelphia-based Pennoni has more than 27 offices throughout the Northeast and Mid-Atlantic states including Pennsylvania New Jersey Delaware Connecticut Massachusetts New Hampshire Maryland Virginia and New York.

Sales and Marketing

The company provides services to local state and federal government clients private commercial industrial and construction clients as well as to other professional firms.

Strategy

Pennoni takes a vertical approach to engineering taking projects from conception to completion. Pennoni's projects include the Ann Taylor corporate headquarters in New York the Annenberg Center for Public Policy in Philadelphia and the Atlantic County Utilities Authority solar array in Atlantic City New Jersey.

In 2014 Pennoni was awarded a contract by the City of Long Branch New Jersey to carry out an oceanfront survey of its beaches boardwalk and eastern-most roadways. The survey will include the beachfront bluff that was damaged by Hurricane Sandy in 2012. After assessing the conditions of the bluff which helps to support the boardwalk the survey will assist the City of Long Branch in choosing a new design for it.

In recent years the company has also been growing its presence in the Northeast through acquisitions.

Mergers and Acquisitions

In 2014 the company acquired the 40-person firm of B.D. Abel Inc. of Wilmington Delaware. The firm is one of the only engineering firms in the tri-state area to offer NEBB certified HVAC Testing and Balancing services.

Company Background

Enhancing its water resources capabilities and providing an expanded client base for all of its services in 2012 Pennoni acquired Green Stone Engineering of Wilmington Delaware.

The company increased its presence in Virginia in 2012 with the acquisition of mechanical plumbing electrical and fire protection system specialist AGS LLC in Arlington. In 2011 Pennoni added seven locations in Maryland and Virginia through the acquisition of Washington DC-based Patton Harris Rust & Associates. In 2010 the firm purchased the Delaware-based consulting engineering firm Design Consultants Group (DC Group).

Pennoni is majority owned by its employees through an employee stock ownership plan (ESOP) in place since 1993.

EXECUTIVES

Associate Vice President, Mark Davidson
Associate Vice President and Municipal Division Manager, Daniel Barbato
Senior Vice President Strategic Growth, Joe Viscuso
Auditors: MERVES AMON BARSZ MEDIA PA

LOCATIONS

HQ: PENNONI ASSOCIATES INC.
1900 MARKET ST FL 3, PHILADELPHIA, PA 191033511
Phone: 215 222-3000

PRODUCTS/OPERATIONS

Selected Markets
Civic & Community
Commercial Retail & Residential
Design/Build
Education
Emergency Response
Energy Audits & Planning
Federal Government
Healthcare & Pharmaceuticals
Industrial Facilities
Infrastructure
International
Leisure & Entertainment
Mining & Minerals Processing
Oil & Gas Services
State County & Local Government

Selected Services
Construction services
Energy and sustainability
Environmental
Geotechnical
Laboratory testing
Landscape Architecture
Materials testing and inspection
MEP Engineering
Municipal
Planning

Site Design
Structural
Survey and geomatics
Transportation
Water & Wast

COMPETITORS

Bechtel
Jacobs Engineering
K&M Engineering and
Consulting

Parsons Corporation

HISTORICAL FINANCIALS

Company Type: Private

Income Statement

FYE: December 31

	REVENUE ($ mil.)	NET INCOME ($ mil.)	NET PROFIT MARGIN	EMPLOYEES
12/16	180	1	0.8%	900
12/14	146	1	1.1%	—
12/13	127	1	0.9%	—
12/12	123	0	0.4%	—
Annual Growth	9.9%	28.9%	—	—

2016 Year-End Financials

Return on assets: 5.0%
Return on equity: 0.8%
Current ratio: 0.70

Cash ($ mil.): —

PEORIA UNIFIED SCHOOL DISTRICT NO.11

EXECUTIVES

Superintendent, Denton Santarelli
Director, Jill Thomas
Director, John Gay
Plant & Facilities Manager, Mike Silverston
Director, Valerie Naish
Executive Director, Michelle R Myers
Auditors: HEINFELD MEECH & CO PC P

LOCATIONS

HQ: PEORIA UNIFIED SCHOOL DISTRICT NO.11
  6330 W THUNDERBIRD RD, GLENDALE, AZ
  853064002
Phone: 623 486-6000
Web: WWW.PEORIAUD.K12.AZ.US

HISTORICAL FINANCIALS

Company Type: Private

Income Statement

FYE: June 30

	REVENUE ($ mil.)	NET INCOME ($ mil.)	NET PROFIT MARGIN	EMPLOYEES
06/16	296	13	4.5%	3,889
06/09	300	(57)		—
06/08	327	3	1.0%	—
06/07	1,340	0	0.0%	—
Annual Growth	(15.4%)	213.7%	—	—

PEPPER CONSTRUCTION COMPANY

EXECUTIVES

Chief Executive Officer, J David Pepper
President, Kenneth Egidi
Chief Financial Officer, Chris Averill
Senior Manager, Fred Berglund
Vice-President, Michelle Lieb
Accounting Director, Amy McNevin
Auditors: DELOITTE & TOUCHE LLP CHICAG

LOCATIONS

HQ: PEPPER CONSTRUCTION COMPANY
  643 N ORLEANS ST, CHICAGO, IL 606543690
Phone: 312 266-4700

HISTORICAL FINANCIALS

Company Type: Private

Income Statement

FYE: September 30

	REVENUE ($ mil.)	NET INCOME ($ mil.)	NET PROFIT MARGIN	EMPLOYEES
09/15	709	10	1.5%	900
09/11	668	4	0.6%	—
09/10	503	4	0.9%	—
09/09	1,037	0	—	—
Annual Growth	—	928.0%	—	—

2015 Year-End Financials

Return on assets: 19.7%
Return on equity: 1.5%
Current ratio: 1.00

Cash ($ mil.): 19

PEPPER CONSTRUCTION GROUP, LLC

Pepper Construction Group spices up the construction business with a little of this and a pinch of that. The company provides general contracting and construction management services for commercial office education entertainment health care and institutional clients as well as waterworks projects. (Health care projects account for about 50% of Pepper's revenue.) Its client list includes UBS Northwestern University University of Notre Dame Texas Heart Institute Loyola University Medical Center and NASA. Pepper Construction Group has divisions in Illinois Indiana Ohio and Texas. Stanley F. Pepper founded the company in Chicago in 1927. The group is owned by his family and employees of the firm.

Operations

The company's Pepper Environmental Technologies unit provides environmental services. Green building has become a large part of Pepper Construction's operations. Its Green Team of certified professionals have helped construct more than 2.9 million sq. ft. of eco-friendly space. The Green Team has built the Apple Computer flagship store HSBC Chicago North and Kohl's Children's Museum.

The firm's Pepper-Lawson Waterworks group constructs water purification plants for municipal clients including Houston and Missouri City Texas.

Geographic Reach

Chicago-based Pepper Construction comprises four geographic divisions: Illinois; Indiana; Ohio; and Texas. Overall the company is active in about 20 states mostly in the central and northeastern states.

EXECUTIVES

Chairman, Dave Pepper
Office Manager, Debbie Connolly
Auditors: DELOITTE & TOUCHE LLP CHICAG

LOCATIONS

HQ: PEPPER CONSTRUCTION GROUP, LLC
  643 N ORLEANS ST, CHICAGO, IL 606543690
Phone: 312 266-4700
Web: WWW.PEPPERCONSTRUCTION.COM

PRODUCTS/OPERATIONS

Selected Operations

Pepper Construction Group LLC (Chicago Illinois)
Pepper Construction Co. (Chicago Illinois)
Pepper Construction Co. of Indiana (Indianapolis Indiana)
Pepper Construction Co. of Ohio LLC (Dublin Ohio)
Pepper Environmental Technologies Inc. (Barrington Illinois)
Pepper-Lawson Construction LP (Houston Texas)
Pepper-Lawson Waterworks LLC (Houston Texas)

COMPETITORS

Barton Malow
  Bulley & Andrews
  C. G. Schmidt
  Charles Pankow
  Builders
  Clark Enterprises
  Gilbane

Graycor
M. A. Mortenson
McCarthy Building
Power Construction
Turner Corporation
Walbridge Aldinger
Walsh Group

HISTORICAL FINANCIALS

Company Type: Private

Income Statement

FYE: September 30

	REVENUE ($ mil.)	NET INCOME ($ mil.)	NET PROFIT MARGIN	EMPLOYEES
09/15	1,110	9	0.9%	1,100
09/11	911	15	1.7%	—
09/10	911	15	1.7%	—
Annual Growth	4.0%	(9.3%)	—	—

2015 Year-End Financials

Return on assets: 18.3%
Return on equity: 0.9%
Current ratio: 1.00

Cash ($ mil.): 29

PEPPERDINE UNIVERSITY

Pepperdine University offers undergraduate and graduate programs to some 7300 students. Affiliated with Churches of Christ the university boasts five colleges and schools: Seaver College of Letters and Sciences; the Graziadio School of Business and Management; the School of Law; the School of Public Policy; and the Graduate School of Education and Psychology. Pepperdine whose 830-acre main campus overlooks the Pacific Ocean in Malibu California has half a dozen additional campuses in California as well as international campuses in Argentina Italy Germany and the UK. The university was founded in 1937 by Christian businessman George Pepperdine who also founded the Western Auto Supply Company.

Operations

Pepperdine has a 13:1 student-to-teacher ratio. Tuition and fees for academic year 2015-16 run at some $48000.

Supported by a $790 million endowment fund the educational institution boasts nearly 700 faculty members 91% of which have earned doctoral or terminal degrees.

Geographic Reach

Pepperdine University's campus in Malibu extends to six other California campuses as well as campuses established in Argentina Italy Germany and the UK. Specifically its permanent educational and residential facilities are located in Heidelberg Florence Buenos Aires Lausanne and London.

Financial Performance

The university's revenue totaled $317 million in 2014. Some 65% of those earnings came from net student tuition and fees while room and board private gifts and grants and endowment support each brought in about 10%. The remaining revenue came from government grants sales and other operations. Net income that year totaled $117 million.

EXECUTIVES

VP and CFO, Paul B. Lasiter, age 50
President and CEO, Andrew K. Benton
SVP Investments and Chief Investment Officer, Jeff Pippin
EVP and COO, Gary A. Hanson
Dean Graduate School of Education and Psychology, Helen E. Williams
Dean School of Public Policy, James R. Wilburn
Provost and Chief Academic Officer, Rick Marrs
Dean School of Law, Deanell Reese Tacha
CIO, Jonathan See
Interim Dean Graziadio School of Business and Management, David M. Smith
Dean of Libraries, Mark S. Roosa
Dean Seaver College, Michael Feltner
Assistant Vice President. Governmental and Regulatoryaffairs Director. Center For Sustainability, Rhiannon Bailard
Associate Vice President for Integrated Marketing and Communications, Matthew Midura
Vice President, Loretta Hunnicutt
Clinical Faculty and Clinic Director, Aaron Aviera
Vice President, Steve Tu
Assistant Vice President for Administration, Nicolle Taylor
Vice President of Finance Department, Ariel Liu
Vice President of Special Events, Sujey Pedroza
Vice President of Finance, Yuxi Liu
Vice President of Operation, Zoe Xiaomeng Shu
Vice President of Membership, Lihong Ni
Vice President of Membership, Yingshi Liu
Vice President of Public Relations, Hui Ern Lavyne
Vice President of Events, Menglu Chen
Vice President of Professional Development, Maryam Pejmannia
Vice President of Public Relations, Ye Tian
Vice President of Alumni Connections, Morgan Matley
Vice Chairman, James R. Porter, age 81
Chairman, Edwin Biggers
Assistant Treasurer, Faye Holton
Treasurer, Zehua Zhao

LOCATIONS

HQ: PEPPERDINE UNIVERSITY
24255 PACIFIC COAST HWY # 5000, MALIBU, CA
902635000
Phone: 310 506-4000
Web: WWW.PEPPERDINE.EDU

Selected California Campuses
Encino
Irvine
Long Beach
Los Angeles
Malibu
Santa Clara
Westlake Village

PRODUCTS/OPERATIONS

2014 Sales

	% of total
Student tuition & fees	64
Room & board	11
Endowment support	11
Private gifts & grants	9
Sales & services	2
Government grants	1
Other	2
Total	**100**

Selected Courses
Accounting
Applied Behavioral Science
Business Law
Decision Sciences
Economics
Finance
Graziadio School of Business and Management
Information Systems and Technology Management
Marketing
Organization Theory and Management
Strategy

Selected Colleges and Schools
Frank R. Seaver College of Letters Arts and Sciences
The George L. Graziadio School of Business and Management
The Graduate School of Education and Psychology
The School of Law
The School of Public Policy

HISTORICAL FINANCIALS
Company Type: Private

Income Statement   FYE: July 31

	REVENUE ($ mil.)	NET INCOME ($ mil.)	NET PROFIT MARGIN	EMPLOYEES
07/15	437	31	7.3%	1,300
07/12	291	(8)	—	—
07/11	291	84	29.0%	—
Annual Growth	10.7%	(21.7%)	—	—

2015 Year-End Financials
Return on assets: 7.5%   Cash ($ mil.): 184
Return on equity: 7.3%
Current ratio: 0.60

PEREZ TRADING COMPANY, INC.

No matter how you say it paper or el papel Perez Trading has it. From its Miami warehouse the company distributes more than 15000 tons of paper and paperboard inventory including corrugated box equipment napkin paper printing paper and other printing and shipping equipment and supplies. Customers include commercial printers converters distributors and packaging manufacturers. Perez Trading imports and exports to nearly 30 countries encompassing the Caribbean Islands Central and South America Mexico and the US. Perez Trading has been family owned and operated since 1947.

EXECUTIVES

National Sales Manager, Gisel Martin
Vice President, Jaime Escudero
Auditors: BERKOWITZ POLLACK BRANT MIAMI

LOCATIONS

HQ: PEREZ TRADING COMPANY, INC.
3490 NW 125TH ST, MIAMI, FL 331672412
Phone: 305 769-0761
Web: WWW.PEREZTRADING.COM

COMPETITORS

Georgia-Pacific   International Paper

HISTORICAL FINANCIALS
Company Type: Private

Income Statement   FYE: December 31

	REVENUE ($ mil.)	NET INCOME ($ mil.)	NET PROFIT MARGIN	EMPLOYEES
12/15	436	5	1.2%	148
12/14	514	11	2.1%	—
12/13	526	16	3.2%	—
12/12	570	20	3.6%	—
Annual Growth	(8.6%)	(36.9%)	—	—

2015 Year-End Financials
Return on assets: 5.5%   Cash ($ mil.): —
Return on equity: 1.2%
Current ratio: 1.90

PERFUME CENTER OF AMERICA INC.

EXECUTIVES

Chairman, Kanak R Golia
Financial Executive, Ngeswra Lothugedda
Account Manager, Ronak Modi
Purchasing Agent, Alicia Davis
Supervisor, Vijay Sharma
Auditors: RAICH ENDE MALTER & CO LLP M

LOCATIONS

HQ: PERFUME CENTER OF AMERICA INC.
2020 OCEAN AVE, RONKONKOMA, NY 117796536
Phone: 516 348-1110
Web: WWW.PERFUME-CENTER.COM

HISTORICAL FINANCIALS
Company Type: Private

Income Statement   FYE: December 31

	REVENUE ($ mil.)	NET INCOME ($ mil.)	NET PROFIT MARGIN	EMPLOYEES
12/15	271	5	1.9%	70
12/14	286	10	3.6%	—
12/13	239	6	2.9%	—
12/12	186	5	2.9%	—
Annual Growth	13.4%	(2.2%)	—	—

2015 Year-End Financials
Return on assets: 16.4%   Cash ($ mil.): —
Return on equity: 1.9%
Current ratio: 1.10

PERISHABLE DISTRIBUTORS OF IOWA, LTD.

EXECUTIVES

President, Dan Wampler
Administrative Assistant, Sherry Deyoung
Senior Manager, Janel Jones
Manager, Gary Barber
Maintenance Supervisor, Glen Sievers
Senior Vice-President, Kevin Gass
Manager, Randy Garvey

LOCATIONS

HQ: PERISHABLE DISTRIBUTORS OF IOWA, LTD.
2741 SE PDI PL, ANKENY, IA 500213958
Phone: 515 965-6300
Web: WWW.CONTACTPDI.COM

HISTORICAL FINANCIALS
Company Type: Private

Income Statement

	REVENUE ($ mil.)	NET INCOME ($ mil.)	NET PROFIT MARGIN	EMPLOYEES
10/16*	1,307	33	2.6%	687
09/15	1,248	31	2.5%	—
09/14	1,153	27	2.4%	—
09/13	0	25	—	—
Annual Growth	—	9.9%	—	—

FYE: October 2

*Fiscal year change

2016 Year-End Financials

Return on assets: 4.7%
Return on equity: 2.6%
Current ratio: 0.60
Cash ($ mil.): 19

PETR-ALL PETROLEUM CONSULTING CORP.

EXECUTIVES

Vice-President, Mark Maher
Manager, James Borer
Manager, Donn Wiese
Director, David Pasquale
VP Marketing, Mike Askwith
Manager, Patrick Hyde
Auditors: DERMODY BURKE BROWN SYRACUSE

LOCATIONS

HQ: PETR-ALL PETROLEUM CONSULTING CORP.
7401 ROUND POND RD, SYRACUSE, NY 132122515
Phone: 315 446-0125
Web: WWW.EXPRESSMART.COM

HISTORICAL FINANCIALS
Company Type: Private

Income Statement

	REVENUE ($ mil.)	NET INCOME ($ mil.)	NET PROFIT MARGIN	EMPLOYEES
12/15	390	10	2.6%	600
12/13	482	0	0.0%	—
12/12	473	2	0.5%	—
12/11	471	2	0.6%	—
Annual Growth	(4.6%)	36.1%	—	—

FYE: December 31

2015 Year-End Financials

Return on assets: 3.5%
Return on equity: 2.6%
Current ratio: 0.50
Cash ($ mil.): 5

PETROLEUM TRADERS CORPORATION

Petroleum Traders Corporation barters with fuel. The company provides wholesale gasoline diesel fuel and heating oil to fuel distributors government agencies and other large consumers of fuel such as businesses with vehicle fleets. The largest pure wholesale fuel distributor in the country Petroleum Traders operates and trades in 44 US states. It supplies #1 and #2 low sulfur diesel fuels biodiesel high sulfur heating oil and kerosene and conventional ethanol and reformulated blends of gasoline in regular midgrade and premium octane ratings.

Operations
Petroleum Traders focuses on supplying wholesale diesel and gasoline exclusively in the US offering a range of turnkey wholesale diesel fuel and wholesale gasoline fuel services.

Sales and Marketing
The company provides discount fuel to commercial government and wholesale customers. In the commercial space it services the trucking construction railroad mining and manufacturing industries as well as utilities and private fleets.

Strategy
Petroleum Traders parlays its hedging experience into fuel cost management for its customers via firm pricing cap programs collars and fuel swaps.

Company Background
The company was founded in 1979.

EXECUTIVES

President, Michael Himes
Board of Directors, Vicki Himes
Board of Directors, Glenn Moonen
Director, Jennifer Bynum
Administrative Assistant, Michelle Beard
Account Manager, Linda Cambre
Account Manager, Candace Brammer
Manager, Rick Hauschild
Auditors: BADEN GAGE & SCHROEDER LLC F

LOCATIONS

HQ: PETROLEUM TRADERS CORPORATION
7120 POINTE INVERNESS WAY, FORT WAYNE, IN 468047928
Phone: 260 432-6622
Web: WWW.PETROLEUMTRADERS.COM

COMPETITORS

George Warren
Gulf Oil
Martin Resource Management
Petro Holdings
Sun Coast Resources

HISTORICAL FINANCIALS
Company Type: Private

Income Statement

	REVENUE ($ mil.)	NET INCOME ($ mil.)	NET PROFIT MARGIN	EMPLOYEES
06/16	1,667	38	2.3%	150
06/15	2,128	64	3.0%	—
06/14	2,670	14	0.6%	—
06/13	3,066	24	0.8%	—
Annual Growth	(18.4%)	16.5%	—	—

FYE: June 30

2016 Year-End Financials

Return on assets: 2.2%
Return on equity: 2.3%
Current ratio: 2.60
Cash ($ mil.): 45

PHALCON, LTD.

EXECUTIVES

President, Michael E McPhee
Board of Directors, Robert A Feiner
Operations Manager, Doug Barker
Personnel Director, Marie Popielarczyk
Operations Manager, Steve Gesseck
Branch Manager, Thomas Lombardo
Operations Manager, Mark Howard
Auditors: BLUM SHAPIRO & COMPANY PC

LOCATIONS

HQ: PHALCON, LTD.
505 MAIN ST, FARMINGTON, CT 060322912
Phone: 860 677-9797
Web: WWW.PHALCON.US

HISTORICAL FINANCIALS
Company Type: Private

Income Statement

	REVENUE ($ mil.)	NET INCOME ($ mil.)	NET PROFIT MARGIN	EMPLOYEES
12/15	352	19	5.5%	1,000
12/14	276	22	8.3%	—
12/13	279	21	7.6%	—
12/12	257	18	7.1%	—
Annual Growth	11.0%	1.7%	—	—

FYE: December 31

2015 Year-End Financials

Return on assets: 5.5%
Return on equity: 5.5%
Current ratio: 1.70
Cash ($ mil.): 34

PHELPS COUNTY REGIONAL MEDICAL CENTER

EXECUTIVES

Chief Executive Officer, John Denbo
Director, Katie Burdett
Supervisor, Annette Garner
Supervisor, Carol Davis

LOCATIONS

HQ: PHELPS COUNTY REGIONAL MEDICAL CENTER
1000 W 10TH ST, ROLLA, MO 654012905
Phone: 573 364-8899
Web: WWW.PCRMCPHYSICIANSGROUP.COM

HISTORICAL FINANCIALS

Company Type: Private

Income Statement

FYE: December 31

	REVENUE ($ mil.)	NET INCOME ($ mil.)	NET PROFIT MARGIN	EMPLOYEES
12/15	190	33	17.8%	1,600
12/14	190	46	24.3%	—
12/07	150	13	8.9%	—
12/05	132	9	7.3%	—
Annual Growth	3.7%	13.4%	—	—

2015 Year-End Financials

Return on assets: 6.0%   Cash ($ mil.): 12
Return on equity: 17.8%
Current ratio: 1.20

PHELPS MEMORIAL HOSPITAL ASSOCIATION

If you happen to spot the headless horseman in Sleepy Hollow it's possible he's on his way to Phelps Memorial Hospital for some medical treatment. The 240-bed hospital provides both physical and mental health care services to residents of Sleepy Hollow and Westchester County New York. Specialized services include cardiology emergency care orthopedics and psychiatry. It also includes a satellite location of the Memorial Sloan-Kettering Cancer Center and it provides geriatric health services through a partnership with Mount Sinai Hospital and operates a senior retirement community with Kendal Corporation. Phelps Memorial is one of four hospitals that make up the Stellaris Health Network.

Operations

Phelps Memorial Hospital handles some 27000 emergency room visits each year. Its maternity wing also managed more than 1000 birthing procedures and the hospital's counseling unit saw about 18000 patients. Other specialty divisions provide stroke care and home health and hospice services. The medical center operates family and specialty physician practices and mental health clinics in the region.

Through its affiliation with Mount Sinai Hospital (and therefore the Sinai Health System) Phelps Memorial's patients and physicians have access to specialized services from Mount Sinai Hospital. It also provides prenatal and high-risk pregnancy care in partnership with area providers Open Door Family Medical Centers and Westchester Medical Center. The hospital is a teaching facility for family medicine and dental residency programs through an affiliation with New York Medical College.

The other hospitals in the Stellaris network are Lawrence Hospital Center Northern Westchester Hospital and White Plains Hospital Center. The medical centers operate independently but pool resources in areas including information technology procurement and best practices.

The company's 500 medical staff members represent 60 medical specialties.

Geographic Reach

Phelps Memorial is located on a 70-acre campus on the banks of the Hudson River in Sleepy Hollow. The company serves Westchester County and surrounding communities in Rockland Putnam and Dutchess Counties in New York and Fairfield County in Connecticut.

Strategy

The hospital's primary goals include enhancing the convenience of its services and increasing patient satisfaction. Phelps Memorial has gone through major renovations in recent years more than doubling its size with the addition of a new emergency department new offices more inpatient beds and an inpatient pediatrics unit.

In 2014 Phelps Memorial opened its new SurgiCenter in New York State. That year it also established the Phelps Balance Center to offer comprehensive testing and rehabilitation for individuals who have problems with dizziness and imbalance.

In 2013 it expanded services by launching new asthma treatment and lung nodule screening programs; it also opened a new family and diagnostic facility (Phelps at Croton) that year.

Company Background

Phelps Memorial restructured its west wing in 2011; the facility now houses its pre-surgical assessment pain management registration and outpatient laboratory departments.

The hospital was first opened in 1955.

EXECUTIVES

Assistant Vice President Quality and Case Management, William Reifer
Medical Director of the Thoracic Center, Avraham Merav
Senior Vp, Dan Blum
Vice President, Leonard Fogel
Vice President, Glen Taylor
Director of Pharmacy, Brian McGrinder
Operating Room Director, Kathleen Schers

LOCATIONS

HQ: PHELPS MEMORIAL HOSPITAL ASSOCIATION
701 N BROADWAY, SLEEPY HOLLOW, NY 105911096
Phone: 914 366-3000
Web: WWW.PHELPSHOSPITAL.ORG

PRODUCTS/OPERATIONS

Selected Services

Alcohol & Substance Abuse Treatment
Behavioral Health
Blood Donor Services
Bone Densitometry
Cardiac Rehabilitation
Cardiovascular Laboratory
Cardiovascular Risk Assessment
Critical Care Unit
Decontamination Unit
  Diabetes -
  Diabetes -
Electroconvulsive Therapy
Emergency Services
Emergency Training Services
Endoscopy
Gastroenterology
Geriatrics
Hand Therapy

Health Management
Hearing (Audiology)
Hernia Center
Hip
Hospice
Hyperbaric Medicine
Incontinence
Infusion Center
Laboratory Services
Lung Nodule Center
Lymphedema
Mammography
Maternity
Memory Loss
Mental Health Services
MRI
Nutrition Counseling for Outpatients
Oncology - Memorial Sloan-Kettering Cancer Center
Orthopedics
  Ostomy - O
Pain Center
Palliative Care
Pediatric Endocrinology
Pediatrics
Pharmacy
Physical Rehabilitation
Psychiatry
Pulmonology & Respiratory
Radiology
Respiratory Care
Respite
Senior Health & Internal Medicine
Sleep Disorders
Speech
Stroke Center
Swallowing Disorders

COMPETITORS

Bergen Regional Medical	Montefiore Medical
Burke Rehabilitation Hospital	Nyack Hospital
	The Valley Hospital
Englewood Hospital and Medical Center	Valley Health System
	Westchester Medical Center
Greenwich Hospital	

HISTORICAL FINANCIALS

Company Type: Private

Income Statement

FYE: December 31

	REVENUE ($ mil.)	NET INCOME ($ mil.)	NET PROFIT MARGIN	EMPLOYEES
12/15	229	3	1.4%	1,200
12/14	224	12	5.4%	—
12/13	227	11	5.0%	—
12/09	182	5	3.2%	—
Annual Growth	3.9%	(10.1%)	—	—

2015 Year-End Financials

Return on assets: 4.7%   Cash ($ mil.): 29
Return on equity: 1.4%
Current ratio: 2.10

PHILLIPS AND JORDAN, INCORPORATED

While some like to clear the air Phillips and Jordan (P&J) prefers to clear the land. Founded in 1952 as a small land clearing firm P&J is a general and specialty contractor that still provides land clearing services in addition to industrial commercial and residential site development and heavy civil construction on dams highways bridges railroads and waterways. P&J also performs reclamation landfill and disaster recovery services. The latter includes handling some of the nation's worst

disaster cleanups including hurricanes floods toxic spills and land and rock slides. P&J operates about a dozen offices in eight states. The Phillips family owns and runs the company.

Operations

Phillips and Jordan operates a fleet of more than 850 pieces of heavy and specialized equipment including excavators graders loaders tractors and trucks. The firm performs projects across the US.

True to its roots the company has built a reputation for taking on difficult land clearing jobs. With a fleet of specialized equipment P&J clears and grubs swamp forest mountain and agricultural land to make way for reservoirs pipelines power transmission lines railways and roadways. Clients come from both the public and private sectors.

Geographic Reach

Knoxville Tennessee-based Phillips and Jordan has about a dozen offices in North Carolina and in California Florida North Dakota Tennessee and Wyoming.

Strategy

The booming oil and gas industry in Wyoming has drawn P&J to the state where in late 2013 it opened two rock pits in the Douglas area. The pits are managed from the firm's Douglas office. Also in 2013 P&J partnered with North Creek Energy to form a joint venture company Solar Jack LLC to market a system that offers oil and gas producers the opportunity to capture the regenerated energy from their pump jacks combined with solar energy to reduce energy consumption and costs. Previously the firm expanded its operations near Williston North Dakota opening an equipment maintenance shop and offices there in 2012.

EXECUTIVES

Vice President Nc Clearing Div, Randy Jordan
Auditors: RODGERS MOSS & CO PLLC KNOX

LOCATIONS

HQ: PHILLIPS AND JORDAN, INCORPORATED
10201 PARKSIDE DR STE 300, KNOXVILLE, TN
379221983
Phone: 865 688-8342
Web: WWW.PANDJ.COM

PRODUCTS/OPERATIONS

Selected Services
Apartment site development
Debris management
Disaster recovery
Earthmoving & erosion control
Heavy civil construction
Industrial and commercial site development
Land clearing
Landfill and liner design
Reclamation and mitigation
Storm drainage
Subdivision site development

COMPETITORS

Boh Bros Construction
Clarkson Construction
Environmental Safety &
Health
Hardaway Construction

McCarthy Building
Peter Kiewit Sons'
Rentenbach
Constructors

HISTORICAL FINANCIALS

Company Type: Private

Income Statement
FYE: December 31

	REVENUE ($ mil.)	NET INCOME ($ mil.)	NET PROFIT MARGIN	EMPLOYEES
12/15	340	10	3.1%	650
12/14	340	14	4.3%	—
12/13	215	4	2.1%	—
12/12	284	11	4.0%	—
Annual Growth	6.1%	(2.6%)	—	—

Return on assets: 4.0%   Cash ($ mil.): —
Return on equity: 3.1%
Current ratio: 1.50

PHOEBE PUTNEY MEMORIAL HOSPITAL, INC.

Phoebe Putney Memorial Hospital provides health care services to residents of southwest Georgia. With more than 650 beds and some 300 physicians the acute-care hospital provides emergency and inpatient services as well as cardiology oncology psychiatric women's health and pediatric specialty care. It's one of Georgia's largest comprehensive regional medical centers. Founded in 1911 it is part of the Phoebe Putney Health System which also includes the 25-bed Phoebe Worth Medical Center and several satellite community health centers that provide outpatient primary health laboratory and surgical services. The health system is governed by the Albany-Dougherty County Hospital Authority.

Operations

As part of its operations Phoebe Putney Memorial Hospital runs an ambulatory infusion center Carlton Breast Health Center and surgical weight loss/wellness center. Inpatient admissions average more than 21000 a year while clinic visits typically run about 711000 annually. With some 3800 employees payroll at Phoebe Putney Memorial Hospital is about $180 million on average.

Geographic Reach

The hospital serves a growing group of residents in 35 counties across southwest Georgia.

Sales and Marketing

Third-party payors accounted for 42% of net patient service revenues in 2014; Medicare and Medicaid accounted for 29% and 13% respectively.

Financial Performance

In 2014 revenue fell 5% to $488 million as net patient service revenues slipped. However the system returned to the black that year reporting $13 million in net income due to an absence of loss on impairment of goodwill. Cash flow from operation rose to $29 million (versus $9000 in 2013) due to changes in receivables supplies and estimated settlements. A decline in cash used for payments and expenses also contributed to the increase.

Strategy

To ensure that it can meet current and future demand for health care services Phoebe Putney Memorial Hospital has been focusing on building up its physician network.

EXECUTIVES

Vice President of Human Resource, Dave Baranski
Vice President Surgical Services, Maureen Jackson
President CEO and Director, Joel Wernick
SVP and CFO, Kerry Loudermilk
VP Information Systems Clinical Informatics, Jesse Diaz
EVP and COO, Joe Austin
VP Strategy and Marketing, Jackie Ryan
Senior Vice President Strategy and Development, Tom Sullivan
Vice President Internal Audits, Brad Hallford
Vice President Chief Compliance Officer, Audrey Pike
Operating Room Director, Carol Wright

Senior Vice President and CNO, Laura Cook
Medical Director Chief of Staff Chief Marketing Officer, Harry Dorsey
Medical Director Utilization Review, Kelly Clay
Vice Chairman, Mary H. Dykes
Chairman, John Culbreath
Auditors: DRAFFIN & TUCKER LLP ALBANY

LOCATIONS

HQ: PHOEBE PUTNEY MEMORIAL HOSPITAL, INC.
417 W 3RD AVE, ALBANY, GA 317011943
Phone: 229 312-1000
Web: WWW.PHOEBEPUTNEY.COM

PRODUCTS/OPERATIONS

Selected Services
Ambulatory Infusion Center
Bariatric Surgery
Behavioral Health
Cardiac Rehabilitation
Carlton Breast Health Center
Corporate Health Services
Corporate Onsite Services
Da Vinci Robotic Surgery
Endoscopy Department
Hematology/Oncology
Hospice and Palliative Care
Hyperbaric Oxygen Therapy
Neurodiagnostics
Orthopedics
Pediatrics
Prostate Brachytherapy
Radiation Oncology
Rheumatology
Sickle Cell Clinic
Speech Therapy
Sports Medicine
Surgical Weight Loss/Wellness Center
Wound Care

COMPETITORS

Central Georgia Health
Systems
HCA
Oconee Regional Health
Systems

Regency Hospital
WellStar Health System

HISTORICAL FINANCIALS

Company Type: Private

Income Statement
FYE: July 31

	REVENUE ($ mil.)	NET INCOME ($ mil.)	NET PROFIT MARGIN	EMPLOYEES
07/15	490	32	6.6%	3,000
07/09	513	19	3.8%	—
07/08	500	15	3.0%	—
07/05	0	0	—	—
Annual Growth	—	—	—	—

2015 Year-End Financials

Return on assets: 3.4%   Cash ($ mil.): 49
Return on equity: 6.6%
Current ratio: 3.10

PHOEBE PUTNEY MEMORIAL HOSPITAL, INC.

EXECUTIVES

Director, Christy Legrone
Manager, Gwen Collins
Director, Lisa Johnson

LOCATIONS

HQ: PHOEBE PUTNEY MEMORIAL HOSPITAL, INC.
 2000 PALMYRA RD, ALBANY, GA 317011528
Phone: 229 434-2000
Web: WWW.PPMH.ORG

HISTORICAL FINANCIALS
Company Type: Private

Income Statement
FYE: July 31

	REVENUE ($ mil.)	NET INCOME ($ mil.)	NET PROFIT MARGIN	EMPLOYEES
07/15	490	32	6.6%	1
07/13	515	(4)	—	—
Annual Growth	(2.5%)	—	—	—

2015 Year-End Financials

Return on assets: 3.4%   Cash ($ mil.): 49
Return on equity: 6.6%
Current ratio: 3.10

PHOENIX UNION HIGH SCHOOL DISTRICT NO 210

EXECUTIVES

Superintendent, Raj Chopra
Financial Executive, Tamara Hodge
Manager, Gary Greene
Engineer, Esteban Ortiz
Director, Michelle Delgado
Auditors: HEINFELD MEECH & CO PC P

LOCATIONS

HQ: PHOENIX UNION HIGH SCHOOL DISTRICT NO 210
 4502 N CENTRAL AVE, PHOENIX, AZ 850121817
Phone: 602 271-3302
Web: WWW.PHOENIXUNION.ORG

HISTORICAL FINANCIALS
Company Type: Private

Income Statement
FYE: June 30

	REVENUE ($ mil.)	NET INCOME ($ mil.)	NET PROFIT MARGIN	EMPLOYEES
06/16	327	(30)	—	2,704
06/13	291	35	12.2%	—
06/12	51	5	11.0%	—
06/11	296	0	0.0%	—
Annual Growth	2.0%	—	—	—

PIEDMONT ATHENS REGIONAL MEDICAL CENTER, INC.

 Piedmont Athens Regional Medical Center (formerly Athens Regional Medical Center) is a full-service health care facility with 360 beds serving 17 counties in northeastern Georgia. The regional hospital provides general medical surgical and diagnostic services as well as a wide range of specialty care in such areas as oncology rehabilitation pediatrics and radiology. Piedmont Athens Regional is part of the not-for-profit Piedmont Healthcare which operates eight hospitals some 20 urgent care centers and around 100 physician practice locations across Georgia.

 Operations

 Piedmont Athens Regional offers all major medical and surgical services including cancer care cardiovascular care neurology services and orthopedic care. It has a Level 2 trauma center and a level 3 neonatal intensive care unit; it also offers women's care services including a midwifery practice. The facility is the second-largest employer in the region with more than 3300 employees.

 Geographic Reach

 Piedmont Athens Regional provides for the health care needs of people in a 17-county service area in northeast Georgia including the counties of Athens-Clarke Banks Barrow Elbert Franklin Greene Habersham Hart Jackson Madison Morgan Oconee Oglethorpe Stephens Taliaferro Walton and Wilkes.

 Strategy

 After a tumultuous implementation of a new electronic health records system and in the midst of an industrywide trend towards consolidation Athens Regional Medical Center began merger talks with Piedmont Healthcare in 2015. The following year the hospital joined the Piedmont organization helping Piedmont as it expands beyond Atlanta and boosting its own financial strength.

 Company Background

 Athens Regional Medical Center was established in 1921. It joined Piedmont Healthcare in October 2016.

EXECUTIVES

Interim President and CEO, Charles A. (Chuck) Peck
Sr. Vice President & Chief Operating Officer, Brian Ulery
Sr. Vice President & Chief Medical Officer, James L. Moore
Sr. Vice President & Chief Nursing Officer, Carrie Capps
Vice President Finance, Wendy Cook
Vice President & Chief Information Officer, Gretchen Tegethoff
Executive Director ARPS ARSS & RFC, James Litchford
Executive Director Athens Area Health Plan Select, Jeffrey Kunkle
Executive Director Home Health, Pamela Hall
Director Of Radiology, Steven Bramlet

LOCATIONS

HQ: PIEDMONT ATHENS REGIONAL MEDICAL CENTER, INC.
 1199 PRINCE AVE, ATHENS, GA 306062797
Phone: 706 475-7000

PRODUCTS/OPERATIONS

Selected Services
Breast Health Center
Cancer Services
Diabetes Education
Emergency
Heart and Vascular
Home Health
Imaging Services
Labor and Delivery
Laboratory Services
Midwifery
Mind Body Institute
Occupational Health
Palliative Care
Pediatrics
Regional FirstCare
Rehabilitation
Sleep Disorders Center
Stroke Center
Surgery
Urgent Care
Women and Children
Wound Center

COMPETITORS

Gwinnett Health System   Regency Hospital
Northeast Georgia   St. Mary's Health Care
 Health System   WellStar Health System

HISTORICAL FINANCIALS
Company Type: Private

Income Statement
FYE: September 30

	REVENUE ($ mil.)	NET INCOME ($ mil.)	NET PROFIT MARGIN	EMPLOYEES
09/15	392	20	5.2%	3,000
09/14	361	(17)	—	—
Annual Growth	8.6%	—	—	—

2015 Year-End Financials

Return on assets: 4.8%   Cash ($ mil.): 40
Return on equity: 5.2%
Current ratio: 0.40

PIEDMONT HENRY HOSPITAL, INC.

EXECUTIVES

President, Charles F Scott
Board of Directors, Terry Ayers
Director, Luis Guerrero
Chief Operating Officer, Deborah Armstrong
Auditors: KPMG LLP GREENSBORO NC

LOCATIONS

HQ: PIEDMONT HENRY HOSPITAL, INC.
 1133 EAGLES LANDING PKWY, STOCKBRIDGE, GA 302815085
Phone: 678 604-1001

HISTORICAL FINANCIALS
Company Type: Private

Income Statement
FYE: June 30

	REVENUE ($ mil.)	NET INCOME ($ mil.)	NET PROFIT MARGIN	EMPLOYEES
06/15	219	16	7.6%	600
06/14	247	11	4.8%	—
06/13	226	2	1.0%	—
06/12	201	(19)	—	—
Annual Growth	2.9%	—	—	—

2015 Year-End Financials

Return on assets: 5.2%   Cash ($ mil.): 1
Return on equity: 7.6%
Current ratio: 1.20

PIEDMONT HOSPITAL, INC.

Those feeling ill in Atlanta can count on Piedmont Healthcare for help. Founded in 1905 the not-for-profit organization's flagship facility is Piedmont Atlanta an acute care hospital with more than 485 beds. Piedmont Atlanta provides general and advanced medical-surgical care including open-heart surgery organ transplantation and neurosurgery. Also part of the Piedmont family are Piedmont Fayette Hospital with more than 170 beds; Piedmont Mountainside Hospital a 52-bed community hospital north of Atlanta; and the Piedmont Physicians Group a network of more than 150 primary care physicians operating in dozens of offices throughout metropolitan Atlanta.

Operations

Piedmont Healthcare also operates Piedmont Newnan Hospital a community hospital in Coweta County Georgia and the acute care community hospital Piedmont Henry Hospital.

Each year the system serves around 2 million patients performing some 44000 surgeries completing more than 200 organ transplants and handling more than 250000 emergency department visits. It also sees some 472000 outpatients and around 8000 infant deliveries annually.

Sales and Marketing

Medicare and Medicaid payments combined account for more than 40% of Piedmont's total net patient service revenue.

Financial Performance

Revenue increased 4% to $1.7 billion in fiscal 2014 (ended June) on higher net patient service revenues and other revenues. However net income fell 27% to $104.2 million as operating expenses and pension adjustments increased.

Cash flow from operations rose 66% to $150.1 million that year due primarily to a change in working capital.

Strategy

The health care system expands its offerings through investment and renovation as well as partnerships and acquisitions. In 2014 it partnered with WellStreet to launch Piedmont Urgent Care by WellStreet a network of urgent care centers offering extended-hour walk-in treatment for non-life threatening illnesses and injuries.

EXECUTIVES

CEO Piedmont Physicians, Sid Kirschner
Chief Medical Officer, Leigh S. Hamby
Vice Chair, Harry M. McFarling
COO, Gregory A. (Greg) Hurst
Chief Nurse Executive, Denise Ray
President and CEO, Kevin Brown
Chief Strategy & Performance Improvement Officer, Michelle Fisher
Chief Consumer Officer, Matt Gove
CFO, Michael McAnder
CIO, Geoff Brown
Vice President Of Ambulatory Services, Rob Simmons
Executive Assistant To Mark Cohen Medical Director VPMA, Kathie Alhadeff
Executive Vice President, Ed Lovern
Vice President Human Resources, Richard Linville
Vice President Medical Affairs, Fred Willms
Occupational Therapy Director, Ann Fitzgerald
Executive Vice President, Alan Laughridge
Chair, Janine Brown

LOCATIONS

HQ: PIEDMONT HOSPITAL, INC.
 1968 PEACHTREE RD NW, ATLANTA, GA 303091285
Phone: 404 605-5000
Web: WWW.PIEDMONTHOSPITAL.ORG

PRODUCTS/OPERATIONS

2014 Sales

	$ mil.	% of total
Net patient service revenue	1,595	96
Other revenue	62	4
Total	**1,657**	**100**

Selected Operations

Piedmont Atlanta
Piedmont Fayette Hospital (Fayetteville)
Piedmont Henry Hospital (Stockbridge)
Piedmont Mountainside Hospital (Jasper)
Piedmont Newnan Hospital (Newnan)
Piedmont Physicians Group (metropolitan Atlanta)

COMPETITORS

Children's Healthcare of Atlanta	Northside Hospital
DeKalb Medical	Shepherd Center
Emory Healthcare	Tenet Healthcare
Grady Health System	Universal Health Services

HISTORICAL FINANCIALS

Company Type: Private

Income Statement

FYE: June 30

	REVENUE ($ mil.)	NET INCOME ($ mil.)	NET PROFIT MARGIN	EMPLOYEES
06/15	857	66	7.8%	6,419
06/10*	689	75	11.0%	—
12/09	1	(0)	—	—
Annual Growth	267.7%	—	—	—

*Fiscal year change

2015 Year-End Financials

Return on assets: 2.2%   Cash ($ mil.): 24
Return on equity: 7.8%
Current ratio: 2.10

PIEDMONT MUNICIPAL POWER AGENCY

Piedmont Municipal Power Agency (Piedmont Power) generates purchases and transmits wholesale electricity on behalf of its 10 member municipal utilities which distribute the power to nearly 95000 retail customers in northwestern South Carolina. These ten utilities serve the cities of Abbeville Clinton Easley Gaffney Greer Laurens Newberry Rock Hill Union and Westminster. Piedmont Power was created to buy an ownership interest in the Catawba Nuclear Station in York County South Carolina in order to secure a reliable source of electric generation for its member utilities. The agency owns a 25% stake in the Catawba plant. The genesis of Piedmont Power can be traced to the energy crisis of the early 1970s. In 1975 Duke Power under pressure to increase its energy output to meet the growing regional demand approached its existing wholesale electric customers in the Carolinas to request assistance in financing the Catawba nuclear plant. Piedmont Power was subsequently formed in 1979.

EXECUTIVES

Board Member, Andy Sevic
Board Member, Jimmy Powell
Auditors: CHERRY BEKAERT LLP GREENVILLE

LOCATIONS

HQ: PIEDMONT MUNICIPAL POWER AGENCY
 121 VILLAGE DR, GREER, SC 296511291
Phone: 864 877-9632
Web: WWW.PMPA.COM

HISTORICAL FINANCIALS

Company Type: Private

Income Statement

FYE: December 31

	REVENUE ($ mil.)	NET INCOME ($ mil.)	NET PROFIT MARGIN	EMPLOYEES
12/15	250	4	1.9%	11
12/14	237	19	8.4%	—
12/13	219	9	4.3%	—
12/12	204	(16)	—	—
Annual Growth	7.0%	—	—	—

2015 Year-End Financials

Return on assets: 3.9%   Cash ($ mil.): —
Return on equity: 1.9%
Current ratio: 0.10

PIEDMONT NEWNAN HOSPITAL, INC.

EXECUTIVES

President, Michael Bass
Board of Directors, Jay D Mitchell
Financial Executive, Nancy Shepard
Director, Betty Andrews
Account Manager, Sharon Hannah
Auditors: ERNST & YOUNG US LLP ATLANTA

LOCATIONS

HQ: PIEDMONT NEWNAN HOSPITAL, INC.
 745 POPLAR RD, NEWNAN, GA 302651618
Phone: 770 253-2330
Web: WWW.PIEDMONTHEART.ORG

HISTORICAL FINANCIALS

Company Type: Private

Income Statement

FYE: June 30

	REVENUE ($ mil.)	NET INCOME ($ mil.)	NET PROFIT MARGIN	EMPLOYEES
06/15	205	1	0.8%	1,000
06/14	177	(8)	—	—
06/13	146	(2)	—	—
06/09	95	(3)	—	—
Annual Growth	13.7%	—	—	—

2015 Year-End Financials

Return on assets: 2.0%   Cash ($ mil.): 1
Return on equity: 0.8%
Current ratio: 1.30

PIH HEALTH HOSPITAL - WHITTI

EXECUTIVES

Chief Executive Officer, James R West
Chief Financial Officer, Mitchell Thomas
VP Sales, Hugh West
VP Sales, Phyllis Katz
VP Sales, West James

LOCATIONS

HQ: PIH HEALTH HOSPITAL - WHITTI
12401 WASHINGTON BLVD, WHITTIER, CA
906021006
Phone: 562 698-0811

HISTORICAL FINANCIALS

Company Type: Private

Income Statement

FYE: September 30

	REVENUE ($ mil.)	NET INCOME ($ mil.)	NET PROFIT MARGIN	EMPLOYEES
09/15	555	29	5.2%	3,150
09/14	495	18	3.8%	—
09/13	491	81	16.7%	—
09/12	419	69	16.6%	—
Annual Growth	9.8%	(25.2%)	—	—

2015 Year-End Financials

Return on assets: 3.9%   Cash ($ mil.): —
Return on equity: 5.2%
Current ratio: 0.70

PIKEVILLE MEDICAL CENTER, INC.

Taking a nasty fall while hiking the rugged Appalachians will likely land you at Pikeville Medical Center (PMC). Serving patients in eastern Kentucky the hospital boasts more than 260 beds and provides a full range of inpatient outpatient and surgical services. PMC's centers and departments handle a number of specialties such as diagnostic imaging echocardiogram neurosurgery cancer care and bariatric surgery. Employing some 350 physicians PMC also operates a rehabilitation hospital a home health agency and outpatient family practice and specialty clinics as well as a physician residency program. PMC first opened on Christmas Day in 1924.

Operations
Pikeville Kentucky-based PMC offers more than 400 services.

Strategy
PMC is rapidly expanding its services and facilities to keep pace with the needs of area residents. In recent years it has added such new services as pulmonary rehabilitation plastic surgery and orthopedic trauma. In addition the hospital launched a $150 million expansion project that will add an 11-story outpatient center (including physician practices and surgery suites) and a 10-story parking garage. Additional expansion efforts have included opening new outpatient cancer diagnostic pain management and primary care clinics.

An active participant in clinical trials and studies PMC works to expand its research opportunities for patients and physicians. In 2013 the hospital began new treatment for patients with Paroxysmal Atrial Fibrillation (Afib) using Medtronic's Arctic Front Advance Cardiac Cryoballoon System.

Since 2012 when it inked a Medicaid contract with Coventry PMC has contracts with all three providers: Coventry Wellcare and Kentucky Spirit. PMC become member of the Mayo Clinic Care Network in 2013. The agreement gives PMC providers access to Mayo Clinic resources including its online point-of-care information system and its electronic consulting process that connects physicians with Mayo Clinic specialists on questions of diagnosis therapy or care management.

EXECUTIVES

Vice President of Physician Services, Peggy Justice

LOCATIONS

HQ: PIKEVILLE MEDICAL CENTER, INC.
911 BYPASS RD, PIKEVILLE, KY 415011689
Phone: 606 218-3500
Web: WWW.PIKEVILLEHOSPITAL.ORG

PRODUCTS/OPERATIONS

Selected Services
Bariatric Surgery
Breast Care Center
Critical Care
Diagnostics
Diabetes Education
Ear Nose & Throat (Otolaryngology)
Emergency
Endocrinology
Family Practice
Gastroenterology
Gynecology/Obstetrics
Family Practice Clinic
Heart Institute
Heart Failure/Coumadin Clinic
Home Health
Home Medical Equipment
Inpatient
Infectious Disease
Laboratory Services
Leonard Lawson Cancer Center
Neonatology
Nephrology
Neurosurgery
Ophthalmology
Other Patient Services
Orthopedic Surgery
Palliative Care
Pediatrics
Pharmacy
Plastic & Reconstructive Surgery
Pulmonary Clinic
Radiology
Rehabilitation
Residency Program
Rheumatology
Sleep
Urology
Women and Childrens' Services
Wound Care Center

COMPETITORS

Appalachian Regional Healthcare
Clinch Valley Medical Center
Community Health Systems
Highlands Health
Norton Community Hospital
Norton Healthcare
Russell County Medical Center
University of Kentucky Chandler Hospital

HISTORICAL FINANCIALS

Company Type: Private

Income Statement

FYE: September 30

	REVENUE ($ mil.)	NET INCOME ($ mil.)	NET PROFIT MARGIN	EMPLOYEES
09/16	489	29	5.9%	2,527
09/15	381	9	2.5%	—
09/14	367	8	2.4%	—
09/13	394	2	0.7%	—
Annual Growth	7.4%	119.5%	—	—

2016 Year-End Financials

Return on assets: 4.4%   Cash ($ mil.): 170
Return on equity: 5.9%
Current ratio: 3.00

PIMA COUNTY

EXECUTIVES

Manager, Roseanne Grant
Finance Manager, Tom Burke
Personnel Director, Gwynn Hatcher
Manager, Jennifer Billa
Officer, Karen Couture
Administrative Assistant, Lisa Romero
General Manager, Marilyn Hutzler
Auditors: DEBBIE DAVENPORT PHOENIX ARI

LOCATIONS

HQ: PIMA COUNTY
97 E CONGRESS ST FL 3, TUCSON, AZ 857011794
Phone: 520 243-1800
Web: WWW.PIMA.GOV

HISTORICAL FINANCIALS

Company Type: Private

Income Statement

FYE: June 30

	REVENUE ($ mil.)	NET INCOME ($ mil.)	NET PROFIT MARGIN	EMPLOYEES
06/16	863	2	0.3%	7,500
06/13	789	(13)	—	—
Annual Growth	3.0%		—	—

2016 Year-End Financials

Return on assets: 6.8%   Cash ($ mil.): 521
Return on equity: 0.3%
Current ratio: —

PITT COUNTY MEMORIAL HOSPITAL, INCORPORATED

Vidant Medical Center is an acute health services facility that serves the vibrant community of Greenville North Carolina and surrounding areas. The 909-bed regional referral hospital's specialty divisions include Vidant Children's Hospital East Carolina Heart Institute a rehabilitation center and the outpatient Vidant SurgiCenter. Other services include oncology transplant women's health or-

thopedic behavioral care and home health and hospice care units. The center also serves as a teaching facility for East Carolina University's Brody School of Medicine. Vidant Medical Center (formerly Pitt County Memorial Hospital) is a member of University Health Systems of Eastern Carolina (dba Vidant Health).

Operations

In addition to serving as a primary teaching facility for the Brody School of Medicine Vidant Medical Center provides clinical training for East Carolina University's allied health and nursing programs. About 2000 students complete clinical programs at the medical center and its affiliated Vidant Health facilities each year.

Its subsidiary PMI Inc. offers property management services.

Altogether Vidant Medical Center serves more than 1.4 million people across its 29-county service area. Boasting a clinical staff of more than 500 physicians and 1200 nurses the medical center in 2013 tended to more than 46000 inpatients and more than 275000 outpatients. Its emergency department visits reached 121000-plus in 2013.

Geographic Reach

Vidant Medical Center provides care to patients in a 29-county service territory in eastern North Carolina. It operates as a regional referral center for smaller community hospitals in the area taking on complex care cases in its specialized fields of medicine.

Strategy

To enhance its service offerings to area residents the Vidant Health organization regularly updates its facilities through capital improvement projects. In addition to basic equipment and infrastructure upgrades in 2011 the hospital completed phase one of an expansion project at the Vidant Medical Center that aims to improve the hospital's pediatric and cancer care capabilities.

To signify its mission to enhance the quality of life in its service territories in 2012 University Health Systems of Eastern Carolina began operating as Vidant Health and the Pitt County Memorial Hospital was renamed as Vidant Memorial Hospital.

EXECUTIVES

Director of Pharmacy, Jim Worden
Director of Nursing and Health Sciences
 Research Vidant Medical Center, Shakira Ibclc
Auditors: RSM US LLP MINNEAPOLIS MINNE

LOCATIONS

HQ: PITT COUNTY MEMORIAL HOSPITAL, INCORPORATED
2100 STANTONSBURG RD, GREENVILLE, NC 278342832
Phone: 252 847-4100
Web: WWW.VIDANTHEALTH.COM

PRODUCTS/OPERATIONS

Selected Services
Asthma Program (Pediatric)
Audiology
Behavioral & Mental Health
Cancer Care
Child Life
Children's Care
Children's Emergency Department
Children's Hospital
Community Health Programs
CyberKnife
Diagnostic Imaging
Diabetes
Emergency Services
Endoscopy Services
Gamma Knife

COMPETITORS

Adventist Health System Sunbelt Healthcare
Bon Secours Health
Carolinas HealthCare System
Duke University Health System
Greenville Hospital System
Novant Health
Sentara Healthcare
Tenet Healthcare
UNC Hospitals
Wake Forest University Baptist Medical Center

HISTORICAL FINANCIALS

Company Type: Private

Income Statement
FYE: September 30

	REVENUE ($ mil.)	NET INCOME ($ mil.)	NET PROFIT MARGIN	EMPLOYEES
09/15	1,066	79	7.5%	8,373
09/14	1,025	79	7.8%	—
09/13*	1,031	91	8.9%	—
12/12	395	19	4.8%	—
Annual Growth	39.1%	61.1%	—	—

*Fiscal year change

2015 Year-End Financials

Return on assets: 3.3%   Cash ($ mil.): 23
Return on equity: 7.5%
Current ratio: 1.60

PITTSBURGH WATER & SEWER AUTHORITY

EXECUTIVES

Executive Director, Gregory F Tutsock
Board of Directors, Henry C Blum
Auditors: MAHER DUESSEL PITTSBURGH PEN

LOCATIONS

HQ: PITTSBURGH WATER & SEWER AUTHORITY
1200 PENN AVE STE 100, PITTSBURGH, PA 152224216
Phone: 412 255-8935
Web: WWW.PITTSBURGHPA.GOV

HISTORICAL FINANCIALS

Company Type: Private

Income Statement
FYE: December 31

	REVENUE ($ mil.)	NET INCOME ($ mil.)	NET PROFIT MARGIN	EMPLOYEES
12/15	174	23	13.4%	250
12/14	164	(4)	—	—
12/13	142	10	7.4%	—
12/12	144	0	0.7%	—
Annual Growth	6.5%	187.0%	—	—

2015 Year-End Financials

Return on assets: 15.1%   Cash ($ mil.): 28
Return on equity: 13.4%
Current ratio: 0.90

PLACENTIA-YORBA LINDA UNIFIED SCHOOL DISTRICT

EXECUTIVES

Superintendent, Doug Domene
Board of Directors, Evelyn Kirk
Superintendent, Bob Klempen
Finance Manager, Ron Smiley
Director, Richard Philippi
Purchasing Director, Robert Cable
Auditors: VAVRINEK TRINE DAY & CO LL

LOCATIONS

HQ: PLACENTIA-YORBA LINDA UNIFIED SCHOOL DISTRICT
1301 E ORANGETHORPE AVE, PLACENTIA, CA 928705302
Phone: 714 986-7000
Web: WWW.PYLUSD.ORG

HISTORICAL FINANCIALS

Company Type: Private

Income Statement
FYE: June 30

	REVENUE ($ mil.)	NET INCOME ($ mil.)	NET PROFIT MARGIN	EMPLOYEES
06/16	308	7	2.4%	1,500
06/05	226	0	—	—
06/04	243	36	15.0%	—
06/03	184	4	2.6%	—
Annual Growth	4.0%	3.5%	—	—

PLAINFIELD COMMUNITY CONSOLIDATED SCHOOL DISTRICT 202

EXECUTIVES

Superintendent, Lane Abrell
Purchasing Agent, Anna Rivera
Bookkeeper, Alma Esparza
Auditors: KLEIN HALL CPAS AURORA IL

LOCATIONS

HQ: PLAINFIELD COMMUNITY CONSOLIDATED SCHOOL DISTRICT 202
15732 S HOWARD ST, PLAINFIELD, IL 605442399
Phone: 815 439-5482
Web: WWW.PSD202.ORG

Income Statement

FYE: June 30

	REVENUE ($ mil.)	NET INCOME ($ mil.)	NET PROFIT MARGIN	EMPLOYEES
06/16	341	21	6.4%	3,100
06/10	306	(20)	—	—
06/09	301	(38)	—	—
06/08	0	0	—	—
Annual Growth	—	—	—	—

PLAINS COTTON COOPERATIVE ASSOCIATION

Plainly speaking most of the US cotton used by textile mills worldwide starts with the Plains Cotton Cooperative Association (PCCA). The farmer-owned co-op markets millions of bales annually for members in Oklahoma Kansas and Texas. To obtain a competitive price for their cotton PCCA takes advantage of Telmark LP's access to The Seam an online cotton marketplace that continually updates cotton prices buyer data and more. The co-op operates cotton warehouses in Texas Oklahoma and Kansas. PCCA sold its textile and apparel operations in 2014 to focus exclusively on cotton marketing and warehousing. Formed in 1953 PCCA's customers include Replay Urban Outfitters and Abercrombie & Fitch.

Geographic Reach

Lubbock Texas-based Plains Cotton Cooperative Association owns half a dozen cotton warehouses in Kansas Oklahoma and Texas. Its Telmark LP business is also headquartered in Lubbock.

Operations

PCCA is a member of the American Apparel Producers' Network Amcot the National Cotton Council of America the National Council of Textile Organizations the Texas Agricultural Coop Council and The International Cotton Association.

Financial Performance

The cooperative which distributed more than $22 million to its members posted total net margins of $10.4 million from its fiscal 2012-2013 operations. Despite a small crop during the reporting period PCCA saw its cotton marketing and warehouse divisions post profits. It was also helped by its IT division and support services. Feeling the drag of the US economy and unemployment the co-op's textile and apparel division focused on cutting costs.

Strategy

To better focus on its core cotton marketing and warehousing businesses PCCA sold its textile and apparel division to American Textile Holdings LLC (AmTex) in June 2014. The sale gave AmTex control of all the operations of American Cotton Growers (ACG) denim mill in Littlefield Texas and Denimatrix S.A. in Guatemala.

EXECUTIVES

Chief Executive Officer, Kevin Brinkley
Board of Directors, David Pearson
Board of Directors, John Johnson
Chief Financial Officer, Billy Morton
Auditors: CROWE HORWATH LLP DALLAS TEX

LOCATIONS

HQ: PLAINS COTTON COOPERATIVE ASSOCIATION
3301 E 50TH ST, LUBBOCK, TX 794044331
Phone: 806 763-8011
Web: WWW.PCCA.COM

PRODUCTS/OPERATIONS

Selected Sales and Services
Buying cotton
Cotton gins
  Gin bookkeeping
  Gin patronage
  Marketing and invoicing
  Scale ticket software
  Support and training
  Technology solutions
Cotton producers
  Agent gins
  Cash marketing
  marketing contracts
  Pool marketing
Warehousing

COMPETITORS

Alabama Farmers Cooperative	J.G. Boswell Co.
Calcot	Parkdale Mills
Dunavant Enterprises	Staplcotn
Greenwood Mills	Weil Brothers Cotton
International Cotton Marketing	

Income Statement

FYE: June 30

	REVENUE ($ mil.)	NET INCOME ($ mil.)	NET PROFIT MARGIN	EMPLOYEES
06/16	892	23	2.7%	170
06/15	975	25	2.6%	—
06/14	947	(36)	—	—
06/13	1,080	10	1.0%	—
Annual Growth	(6.2%)	31.6%	—	—

PLAINVIEW HOSPITAL

EXECUTIVES

Chief Executive Officer, Michael Dowling
Executive Director, Michael Fener

LOCATIONS

HQ: PLAINVIEW HOSPITAL
888 OLD COUNTRY RD, PLAINVIEW, NY 118034914
Phone: 516 719-2200

Income Statement

FYE: December 31

	REVENUE ($ mil.)	NET INCOME ($ mil.)	NET PROFIT MARGIN	EMPLOYEES
12/15	172	2	1.6%	1,200
12/14	156	(1)	—	—
Annual Growth	9.7%	—	—	—

2015 Year-End Financials

Return on assets: 5.3%
Return on equity: 1.6%
Current ratio: 0.80
Cash ($ mil.): —

PLAN INTERNATIONAL, INC.

EXECUTIVES

Executive Director, Thomas Miller
Manager, Abdoulaye Ndiaye
Director, Mariella Greco
Auditors: DYL & PERILLO INC PROVIDENCE

LOCATIONS

HQ: PLAN INTERNATIONAL, INC.
155 PLAN WAY STE A, WARWICK, RI 028861099
Phone: 401 294-3693
Web: WWW.PLAN-INTERNATIONAL.ORG

Income Statement

FYE: June 30

	REVENUE ($ mil.)	NET INCOME ($ mil.)	NET PROFIT MARGIN	EMPLOYEES
06/15	684	(5)	—	7
06/14	657	(5)	—	—
06/12	601	29	4.9%	—
06/10	531	93	17.6%	—
Annual Growth	5.2%	—	—	—

2015 Year-End Financials

Return on assets: 4.3%
Return on equity: (-0.7%)
Current ratio: 6.40
Cash ($ mil.): 185

PLANNED PARENTHOOD FEDERATION OF AMERICA, INC.

" He who fails to plan plans to fail " could refer to parenting. No fear the Planned Parenthood Federation Of America provides sexual health information as well as reproductive healthcare through 800 affiliated health centers to more than 5 million people each year. PPFA also lobbies for reproductive rights and reproductive health issues and works to extend access to family planning services for all. The not-for-profit organization is supported by private and corporate donations and patient fees as well as government grants. Founded in 1916 by Margaret Sanger PPFA has grown to 84 affiliates in all 50 US states and the District of Columbia and is part of the International Planned Parenthood Federation.

Operations

PPFA's operations consist of: The Planned Parenthood Foundation which is tasked with raising funds and making grants to PPFA affiliates; Planned Parenthood Action Fund an advocate for informed individual choice in reproductive healthcare; and Voxent (formerly known as NGHN) a provider of technology support to some of PPFA's affiliates.

To help spread its mission PPFA pursues affiliate relationships currently counting 84 independent medical and related organizations and 120 outside (referred to as "ancillary") entities including four political action committees. PPFA affiliates

provide expertise in the fields of medicine advocacy sexual health communications fundraising and law.

Geographic Reach

Geographically PPFA's offices in New York City and Washington DC head up its largely domestic program services created to support affiliates in defending reproductive rights of the women and families in the communities in which they are based. PPFA also operates three international offices which oversee programs advancing reproductive rights abroad.

Approximately 75% of the expenses incurred by PPFA are attributable to a number of program services. In the wake of higher revenues total program services increased 23%. Among the programs about half of all expenses are tied to grants and services driven by affiliates in the US. Less than 20% of expenses are associated with the field of family planning including domestic programs for advocacy medical services and education. Outlays for fundraising (which increased by one-third over 2010) and management and general administration represented some 16% and 9% respectively of total expenses in 2011.

Financial Performance

In fiscal 2012 (ends June) PPFA's revenue decreased by 15% as compared to 2011 due to a decrease in both Contribution & Grants and Other Revenue. PPFA posted revenue of $172.5 million in fiscal 2012 most of which were from the Contribution & Grants accounting about 98% of the revenue of which major donors foundations and corporations and direct response were the highest contributors accounting for about 50% and 30% of Contribution & Grants respectively. Approximately 77% of the expenses incurred by PPFA are attributable to a number of program services. Among the programs about half of all expenses are tied to grants and services driven by affiliates in the US. About 27% of expenses are associated with the field of family planning including domestic programs for advocacy medical services and education. Outlays for fundraising and management & general administration represented some 15% and 8% respectively of total expenses in 2012.

Strategy

PPFA's strategy for growth rests on providing community-based heathcare with a focus on access to reproductive services. To this end it is taking steps to improve the Planned Parenthood outreach to Latino communities. PPFA also supports Green Choices an information initiative to promote a healthier and greener environment. Another key area is the PPFA Board of Advocates a volunteer membership of more than 400 leaders in the arts and entertainment field. Members participate in PPFA events and public service announcements as well as blog posts give their name to fundraising efforts and lobby elected officials.

EXECUTIVES

Executive Vice President And Chief Exper, Dawn Laguens
Vice President for Public Policy and Government Relations, Dana Singiser
Managing Director Patient And Employee Experience, Kristen Tilley
Auditors: KPMG LLP NEW YORK NY

LOCATIONS

HQ: PLANNED PARENTHOOD FEDERATION OF AMERICA, INC.
123 WILLIAM ST FL 10, NEW YORK, NY 100383844
Phone: 212 541-7800

HISTORICAL FINANCIALS
Company Type: Private

Income Statement
FYE: June 30

	REVENUE ($ mil.)	NET INCOME ($ mil.)	NET PROFIT MARGIN	EMPLOYEES
06/15	196	(3)	—	530
06/14	176	28	16.1%	—
06/13	139	1	1.1%	—
06/12	159	34	21.4%	—
Annual Growth	7.3%	—	—	—

2015 Year-End Financials
Return on assets: 13.3%
Return on equity: (-1.8%)
Current ratio: 0.60
Cash ($ mil.): 40

PLANO INDEPENDENT SCHOOL DISTRICT

EXECUTIVES

Executive Director, Mark Allen
Board of Directors, Jim Hirsch
Director, Cliff Odenwald
Dean, Nev Moses
Office Manager, Odelia Yocum
Director, Jenny Gann
Auditors: WEAVER AND TIDWELL LLP DALLA

LOCATIONS

HQ: PLANO INDEPENDENT SCHOOL DISTRICT
2700 W 15TH ST, PLANO, TX 750757524
Phone: 469 752-8100
Web: WWW.PISD.EDU

HISTORICAL FINANCIALS
Company Type: Private

Income Statement
FYE: June 30

	REVENUE ($ mil.)	NET INCOME ($ mil.)	NET PROFIT MARGIN	EMPLOYEES
06/16	712	19	2.8%	5,610
06/15	669	(18)	—	—
06/14	629	(32)	—	—
06/13	590	(28)	—	—
Annual Growth	6.5%	—	—	—

POCATELLO HEALTH SYSTEM LLC

EXECUTIVES

Chief Executive Officer, Dan Ordyna
President, Bill Mitchell
Representative, John Abrell
Senior Manager, Neomi Perez
Director, Pamela Holmes
Personnel Director, Scott Lowe
Production Director, William Mitchell

LOCATIONS

HQ: POCATELLO HEALTH SYSTEM LLC
777 HOSPITAL WAY, POCATELLO, ID 832015175
Phone: 208 239-1000

HISTORICAL FINANCIALS
Company Type: Private

Income Statement
FYE: December 31

	REVENUE ($ mil.)	NET INCOME ($ mil.)	NET PROFIT MARGIN	EMPLOYEES
12/15	251	28	11.4%	72
12/14	239	23	9.8%	—
Annual Growth	4.7%	22.6%	—	—

2015 Year-End Financials
Return on assets: 4.7%
Return on equity: 11.4%
Current ratio: 2.00
Cash ($ mil.): —

POCONO MEDICAL CENTER

EXECUTIVES

Chief Executive Officer, Jeffrey E Snyder
Board of Directors, Suzanne Viechnicki
Board of Directors, Edward Mayotte
Auditors: BAKER TILLY VIRCHOW KRAUSE LLP

LOCATIONS

HQ: POCONO MEDICAL CENTER
206 E BROWN ST, EAST STROUDSBURG, PA 183013094
Phone: 570 421-4000
Web: WWW.PMCHEALTHSYSTEM.ORG

HISTORICAL FINANCIALS
Company Type: Private

Income Statement
FYE: June 30

	REVENUE ($ mil.)	NET INCOME ($ mil.)	NET PROFIT MARGIN	EMPLOYEES
06/15	258	18	7.0%	1,057
06/14	288	11	4.1%	—
06/10	248	15	6.3%	—
06/09	209	13	6.4%	—
Annual Growth	3.6%	5.2%	—	—

2015 Year-End Financials
Return on assets: 7.2%
Return on equity: 7.0%
Current ratio: 1.20
Cash ($ mil.): 17

POMONA COLLEGE

Looking to get an education in sunny California? You might want to consider Pomona College. The school offers about 50 academic programs in areas such as art humanities biology psychology computer science and English. It also has research and interdisciplinary study opportunities. The liberal arts college enrolls about 1600 students. Formed in 1887 Pomona College is the founding member of The Claremont Colleges an affiliated group of

seven independent colleges located on adjoining campuses in Claremont California. The affiliated campuses are coordinated by one of the member institutions the Claremont University Consortium.

Operations

Each member of the Claremont Colleges affiliated group is a separate corporate entity governed by its own board of trustees. The seven affiliates share administrative and student services through central offices and facilities.

Pomona has some 190 faculty members and has a student-to-teacher ratio of 7:1. The average class size is 15 students and the college offers a total of about 600 courses each year.

Pomona's revenues come from investment income (returns from pooled investments or endowments) student tuition grants and contracts (from government and private entities) and charitable contributions. Tuition runs at about $41000 per year while room and board adds another $13500.

Geographic Reach

Pomona's students come from 46 US states plus the District of Columbia as well as from more than 20 foreign countries. In addition to its main campus operations in Claremont Pomona offers about 50 study abroad programs in more than 30 countries including Australia Chile China France Italy Japan Mexico Russia and South Africa.

Financial Performance

Pomona College reported an 11% decrease in revenues to $139.5 in 2012 (down from revenues of some $156.4 million in 2011) due to a decline in private gifts and grants. A net loss of $21 million was reported in 2012 due to higher expenses and lower investment returns.

The college has some $2.4 billion in assets including endowment funds.

EXECUTIVES

V Pres, Pamela Besnard
Director of Admissions, Adam Sapp
Auditors: KPMG LLP LOS ANGELES CA

LOCATIONS

HQ: POMONA COLLEGE
550 N COLLEGE AVE, CLAREMONT, CA 917114434
Phone: 909 621-8135
Web: WWW.POMONA.EDU

HISTORICAL FINANCIALS
Company Type: Private

Income Statement
FYE: June 30

	REVENUE ($ mil.)	NET INCOME ($ mil.)	NET PROFIT MARGIN	EMPLOYEES
06/16	193	(125)	—	500
06/15	281	82	29.4%	—
06/14	275	86	31.2%	—
06/13	144	154	107.1%	—
Annual Growth	10.3%	—	—	—

2016 Year-End Financials
Return on assets: 3.2%　　Cash ($ mil.): 3
Return on equity: (-64.9%)
Current ratio: —

PORT OF HOUSTON AUTHORITY

Houston is too far inland to be a port city by the strictest of definitions but don't try to tell that to the Port of Houston Authority. The agency manages the Port of Houston complex including the Barbours Cut Container Terminal one of the busiest in the US. Port of Houston facilities are arrayed along the Houston Ship Channel which connects Houston with Galveston Bay and the Gulf of Mexico and with intracoastal waterways. The Port of Houston Authority itself operates more than 40 cargo wharves; however most of the terminal facilities along the ship channel are managed by private companies. The ship channel was opened in 1914; the Port of Houston Authority was created by the Texas Legislature in 1927.

Besides cargo operations the Port of Houston Authority oversees the Bayport Cruise Terminal which breifly served Carnival Cruise Lines when Hurricane Ike diverted the cruise operator from the Port of Galveston. The $81 million-terminal built in 2008 hasn't secured a permanent tenant.

The economic downturn has hammered all those connected to the cargo transportation industry including the Port of Houston Authority. In 2009 some 25000 fewer automobiles were offloaded in the Port of Houston and steel imports plunged. In response the authority is not hiring vacant positions in its administrative offices and raised some of its cargo-moving fees. (The authority's revenue comes from harbor and docking fees as well as tax from Harris County Texas property owners.)

In the midst of the downturn the port authority is looking to the future. To alleviate pressure on the extremely busy Barbours Cut Container Terminal the port authority is building the Bayport Container and Cruise Terminal. The $1.4 billion project which will double the port's container capacity is expected to be completed in 2014 — the same year an expansion of the Panama Canal will boost container trade.

H. Thomas Kornegay executive director of the Port of Houston Authority retired in January 2009 after almost 40 years of service. He was replaced in September 2009 by Alec Dreyer former CEO of Horizon Wind Energy.

EXECUTIVES

Secretary, Adela McWilliams
Auditors: GRANT THORNTON LLP HOUSTON T

LOCATIONS

HQ: PORT OF HOUSTON AUTHORITY
111 EAST LOOP N, HOUSTON, TX 770294326
Phone: 713 670-2662
Web: WWW.PORTOFHOUSTON.COM

COMPETITORS

Alabama State Docks	The Port of New
Port of Corpus Christi	Orleans

HISTORICAL FINANCIALS
Company Type: Private

Income Statement
FYE: December 31

	REVENUE ($ mil.)	NET INCOME ($ mil.)	NET PROFIT MARGIN	EMPLOYEES
12/15	293	85	29.1%	595
12/14	263	69	26.2%	—
12/13	0	67	—	—
12/12	225	54	24.1%	—
Annual Growth	9.2%	16.3%	—	—

2015 Year-End Financials
Return on assets: 11.0%　　Cash ($ mil.): 59
Return on equity: 29.1%
Current ratio: 1.50

PORT OF PORTLAND

EXECUTIVES

Executive Director, Bill Wyatt
Chief Financial Officer, E B Galligan
Manager, Anthony Bonnett
Personnel Manager, Brenda Patrick
Manager, Christine White
Personnel Director, Carol Byers
Auditors: PRICEWATERHOUSECOOPERS LLP P

LOCATIONS

HQ: PORT OF PORTLAND
7200 NE AIRPORT WAY, PORTLAND, OR 972181016
Phone: 503 944-7000
Web: WWW.PORTOFPORTLAND.COM

HISTORICAL FINANCIALS
Company Type: Private

Income Statement
FYE: June 30

	REVENUE ($ mil.)	NET INCOME ($ mil.)	NET PROFIT MARGIN	EMPLOYEES
06/16	295	64	21.8%	785
06/15	263	57	21.9%	—
06/14	251	23	9.3%	—
06/13	237	23	10.0%	—
Annual Growth	7.6%	39.3%	—	—

2016 Year-End Financials
Return on assets: 9.3%　　Cash ($ mil.): 49
Return on equity: 21.8%
Current ratio: 0.60

PORT OF SEATTLE

The Port of Seattle oversees both an airport (Seattle-Tacoma International also known as Sea-Tac) and a seaport. The agency's aviation division sees more than 33.2 million passengers a year. The seaport division serves more than 18 container steamship lines that import and export containerized and bulk cargo. It also handles calls from cruise ships. In addition the seaport division oversees commercial fishing marinas and portside commercial properties. Most of the agency's revenue comes from airport operations. The Port of Seattle is run by a five-member commission elected by King County voters.

Operations

One of the top landholders in King County the Port owns parks and public access areas cargo and container terminals and Sea-Tac airport. It also owns conference facilities at the airport and on the waterfront recreational boating marinas piers office space and storage and warehouse facilities.

Financial Performance

Operating revenues for fiscal 2013 were budgeted at $550.6 million 6% up on 2012 . Aeronautical revenues were $249.3 million (up 6%). Other operating revenues were budget for $301.3 million (7% higher than the 2012 budget) mainly due to Terminal 18 special bond refunding and higher concessions.

Strategy

Going forward the Port's projects are broadly aimed at preserving traffic to the Midwest via Seattle which other global gateways (the Panama and Suez canals and Prince Rupert's port British Columbia) threaten to divert. To this end it is pursuing cooperative opportunities between rail and

highway infrastructure agencies. Concurrently the Port of Seattle is evaluating Sea-Tac airport's capacity needs. Its subsidy of Fisherman's Terminal which sustains jobs as well as the seaport's history and culture is on the table too given the cost to renovate and terminal's declining fish life. Most significant the Port is determined to continue to distinguish itself as the Green Gateway with the goal of minimizing the environmental consequences of its activities.

Company Background

In 2011 the Port marked its centennial year for moving people and cargo in and out of the Pacific Northwest.

EXECUTIVES

CFO and Administrative Officer, Dan Thomas
Interim CEO, Dave Soike
Managing Director Aviation Division, Lance Lyttle
Managing Director Economic Development Division, David McFadden
Managing Director Maritime Division, Lindsay Pulsifer
Vice Chair, Sally Fierro
Auditors: MOSS ADAMS LLP SEATTLE WASHI

LOCATIONS

HQ: PORT OF SEATTLE
2711 ALASKAN WAY PIER 69, SEATTLE, WA 981211107
Phone: 206 728-3000
Web: WWW.PORTSEATTLE.ORG

HISTORICAL FINANCIALS

Company Type: Private

Income Statement				FYE: December 31
	REVENUE ($ mil.)	NET INCOME ($ mil.)	NET PROFIT MARGIN	EMPLOYEES
12/15	558	19	3.6%	1,515
12/14	534	127	23.9%	—
12/13	544	111	20.4%	—
12/12	521	55	10.7%	—
Annual Growth	2.3%	(29.0%)	—	—

2015 Year-End Financials

Return on assets: 21.6%   Cash ($ mil.): 9
Return on equity: 3.6%
Current ratio: 0.10

PORTERVILLE UNIFIED SCHOOL DISTRICT

EXECUTIVES

Superintendent, John Snavely
Dean, Loretta Bryant
Manager, Jasper Land
Purchasing Director, Brad Rohrbach
Plant & Facilities Manager, Henry Lerma

LOCATIONS

HQ: PORTERVILLE UNIFIED SCHOOL DISTRICT
600 W GRAND AVE, PORTERVILLE, CA 932572029
Phone: 559 793-2400
Web: WWW.PORTERVILLESCHOOLS.ORG

HISTORICAL FINANCIALS

Company Type: Private

Income Statement				FYE: June 30
	REVENUE ($ mil.)	NET INCOME ($ mil.)	NET PROFIT MARGIN	EMPLOYEES
06/16	195	13	6.7%	400
06/08*	0	0	12.1%	—
08/05	0	0	—	—
Annual Growth	—	—	—	—

*Fiscal year change

PORTLAND STATE UNIVERSITY

Portland State University (PSU) is one of seven institutions of higher learning in the Oregon University System. It offers nearly 100 bachelor's 90 master's and 40 doctoral degrees as well as graduate certificates and continuing education programs. PSU has eight schools and colleges devoted to liberal arts and sciences; engineering and computer science; fine and performing arts; urban and public affairs; business administration; social work; and education. It also has a school dedicated to extended studies including distance learning continuing education and professional development. Student enrollment exceeds 29000 (80% undergrads) and the student to faculty ratio is 19:1. PSU was established in 1946.

Geographic Reach

About two thirds of the student body comes from PSU's backyard Clackamas Multnomah and Washington counties. Overall 79% of PSU students are from Oregon. Others come all over the US and more than 95 other countries with Saudi Arabia China India Japan and Vietnam garnering top representation.

PSU's 50-acre campus in downtown Portland holds 50 buildings and 10 student housing properties.

Financial Performance

For several decades PSU received close to half of its funding from state coffers. Legislation in 2011 however converted the state's public university system from a state agency to a free-standing public university system. The state now accounts for a lower percentage of PSU's total annual operating revenue. For its 2014-2015 year PSU plans to run a deficit of about $7 million which is down from the deficit of $10.7 million the previous year. Among the steps taken to reduce expenses was to stop using general fund money to support the PSU football team.

Strategy

PSU's strategic plan for growth is dependent on funding. To provide for that funding and its future the school is working to increase its visibility on a national level. It is developing staffing and compensation plans to ensure talent is in place to achieve its long-range goals. It is also developing an enrollment management plan to improve retention and graduation rates. PSU is looking to increase non-resident enrollment and establish an inclusive and diverse environment. It is also working to expand innovative research and graduate education by leveraging connections between application at the local level and relevance on a global basis.

Other priorities include upgrading its information technology systems fulfilling student needs for hybrid and fully online instruction and investing in research infrastructure human resource data management staff training and other management and communications systems.

The university is raising money to renovate and expand two structures. It has brought in 65% of the money needed to renovate the Peter W. Stott Educational Center and about 82% of the total needed to expand the School of Business Administration.

EXECUTIVES

Associate Vice President, Erin Flynn
Managing Director, Cindy Cooper
Assistant Vice President Development, Paul Carey
Chair Department Of Psychology, Sherwin Davidson
Associate Vice President For Communications, Chris Broderick
Associate Vice President For Enrollment Management, Cindy Skaruppa
Vice President for Research and Strategic Partnerships, Karin Wriggle
Vice President Global Diversity and Inclusion, Carmen Suarez
Board Member, David Reese
Auditors: CLIFTONLARSONALLEN LLP GREENW

LOCATIONS

HQ: PORTLAND STATE UNIVERSITY
1600 SW 4TH AVE STE 730, PORTLAND, OR 972015519
Phone: 503 725-4444
Web: WWW.PDX.EDU

PRODUCTS/OPERATIONS

Selected Colleges and Schools
College of Liberal Arts and Sciences
College of Urban and Public Affairs
Graduate School of Education
Maseeh College of Engineering and Computer Science
School of Business Administration
School of Extended Studies
School of Fine and Performing Arts
School of Social Work

HISTORICAL FINANCIALS

Company Type: Private

Income Statement				FYE: June 30
	REVENUE ($ mil.)	NET INCOME ($ mil.)	NET PROFIT MARGIN	EMPLOYEES
06/15	351	181	51.6%	4,000
06/14	350	36	10.4%	—
Annual Growth	0.5%	398.8%	—	—

2015 Year-End Financials

Return on assets: 6.6%   Cash ($ mil.): 53
Return on equity: 51.6%
Current ratio: 1.20

POTANDON PRODUCE L.L.C.

EXECUTIVES

Chief Executive Officer, Mel Davenport
Accountant, Geraldine Elizondo
Director, Kevin Flaherty
Account Manager, Cheryl Todd
Supervisor, Jennifer Bjornlie
Supervisor, Becky Baker
Auditors: RUDD & COMPANY IDAHO FALLS I

HQ: POTANDON PRODUCE L.L.C.
1210 PIER VIEW DR, IDAHO FALLS, ID 834024966
Phone: 208 419-4200
Web: WWW.POTANDON.COM

HISTORICAL FINANCIALS
Company Type: Private

Income Statement
FYE: December 31

	REVENUE ($ mil.)	NET INCOME ($ mil.)	NET PROFIT MARGIN	EMPLOYEES
12/15	370	(1)	—	100
12/14	391	1	0.5%	—
12/13	396	1	0.5%	—
12/12	369	0	—	—
Annual Growth	0.1%	—	—	—

2015 Year-End Financials
Return on assets: 9.4%
Return on equity: (-0.3%)
Current ratio: 0.70
Cash ($ mil.): —

POTOMAC HOSPITAL CORPORATION OF PRINCE WILLIAM

Potomac Hospital Corporation of Prince William — operating as Sentara Northern Virginia Medical Center — provides a variety of medical surgical and therapeutic services in northern Virginia. The not-for-profit medical center has more than 180 beds and provides emergency medicine diagnostic imaging and surgery services as well as specialized care in fields including cancer treatment women's health cardiology urology and pediatrics. It also offers health education programs and operates two outpatient care clinics. Sentara Northern Virginia Medical Center is part of the Sentara Healthcare network.

Geographic Reach
Sentara Northern Virginia Medical Center is located in Prince William County Virginia.

Financial Performance
The medical center reported revenue of $193 million in 2012 as well as profits of some $21 million.

Strategy
Since joining the Sentara network the medical center has expanded to add services such as the Sentara Heart and Vascular Center an electronic health record (EHR) program and the Sentara Lake Ridge outpatient center. It added its second emergency care and outpatient center in the northern Virginia community of Lorton in 2013. Also that year the hospital added a web-based data network LIFENET (from Physio-Control) to improve operational and clinical efficiencies in the emergency care department (ER and EMS services).

In 2012 Potomac Hospital Corporation of Prince William changed its dba from Sentara Potomac Hospital to Sentara Northern Virginia Medical Center to reflect its broader range of services and its wider geographic reach. The facility began operating as Sentara Potomac Hospital when it became part of the Sentara Healthcare network in 2009.

Company Background

The hospital opened its doors in 1972 with 29 beds. It became part of the Sentara network in 2009.

EXECUTIVES
Director, Jerome O'Connnell
Administrative Assistant, Chris Prewitt
Auditors: KPMG LLP NORFOLK VA

LOCATIONS
HQ: POTOMAC HOSPITAL CORPORATION OF PRINCE WILLIAM
2300 OPITZ BLVD, WOODBRIDGE, VA 221913399
Phone: 703 523-1000
Web: WWW.SENTARA.COM

PRODUCTS/OPERATIONS

Selected Services
Cancer
Diabetes
Emergency Care
General Medicine
Heart and Vascular
Advanced Imaging
Mammograms
Orthopedics
Sentara Lake Ridge
Sentara Lorton Marketplace
Sleep
Urology
Weight Loss Surgery
Women's and Children's

COMPETITORS

Ascension Health	Prince William Health
Bon Secours Health	System
Fauquier Hospital	University of Virginia
HCA	Medical Center
Inova	Valley Health
MedStar Health	Virginia Hospital
Novant Health	Center

HISTORICAL FINANCIALS
Company Type: Private

Income Statement
FYE: December 31

	REVENUE ($ mil.)	NET INCOME ($ mil.)	NET PROFIT MARGIN	EMPLOYEES
12/15	214	10	5.0%	1,300
12/14	242	26	10.9%	—
Annual Growth	(11.8%)	(59.5%)	—	—

2015 Year-End Financials
Return on assets: 2.3%
Return on equity: 5.0%
Current ratio: 3.40
Cash ($ mil.): 5

POUDRE SCHOOL DISTRICT

EXECUTIVES
President, Cathy Kipp
Executive Director, Robert Hix
Vice-Chairman, Marcene Sonneborn
Board of Directors, Vicki Brackens
Manager, Brenda Yocom
Auditors: CLIFTONLARSONALLEN LLP BROOM

LOCATIONS
HQ: POUDRE SCHOOL DISTRICT
2407 LAPORTE AVE, FORT COLLINS, CO 805212211
Phone: 970 482-7420
Web: WWW.PSDSCHOOLS.ORG

HISTORICAL FINANCIALS
Company Type: Private

Income Statement
FYE: June 30

	REVENUE ($ mil.)	NET INCOME ($ mil.)	NET PROFIT MARGIN	EMPLOYEES
06/16	320	20	6.4%	907
06/15	300	(19)	—	—
06/14	275	(15)	—	—
06/13	265	7	3.0%	—
Annual Growth	6.4%	37.5%	—	—

2016 Year-End Financials
Return on assets: 5.1%
Return on equity: 6.4%
Current ratio: —
Cash ($ mil.): 1

POUDRE VALLEY HEALTH CARE, INC.

Providing health care is what this Poudre Valley is all about. The not-for-profit Poudre Valley Health System (PVHS) cares for residents of Colorado western Nebraska and southern Wyoming through the Poudre Valley Hospital and the Medical Center of the Rockies. With a total of about 440 beds the two hospitals offer general medical and surgical services and trauma care. They also offer treatment centers for specialties including cancer heart brain and spine disorders. PVHS is home to the Mountain Crest Behavioral Healthcare Center which administers mental health and substance abuse treatment. PVHS is part of the Health District of Northern Larimer County; it is also part of University of Colorado Health.

Operations
The Poudre Valley Hospital features 270 patient beds while the Medical Center of the Rockies has a capacity of about 170 beds. Beyond its primary hospital campuses the health system also operates several outpatient clinics and a family medicine center that hosts a rural medicine residency program. Altogether PVHS has more than 550 physicians practicing in more than 40 specialty fields.

In addition to its joint operating agreement with the University of Colorado Hospital PVHS has formed collaborative care partnerships with local organizations including a local laser eye surgery center numerous outpatient centers for rehabilitation surgery and infusion therapy as well as home health care and home supply companies.

Geographic Reach
PVHS serves residents of Estes Park Fort Collins Greeley and Loveland Colorado as well as Larimer and Weld Counties. The system also serves customers from Cheyenne and Laramie Wyoming and Scottsbluff Nebraska.

Strategy
The organization has held a long tradition of partnering with numerous local organizations to expand its service offerings. To create a broader health organization for the Rocky Mountain region PVHS formed a joint operating agreement with University of Colorado Hospital in 2012. Together the systems are known as University of Colorado

Health and are governed by a single board of directors. The hospitals continue to operate under their existing names.

Other growth efforts include the construction of a new $14.5 million emergency care center in 2012 and the opening of a new 12-bed women's and children's unit at Medical Center of the Rockies in 2013.

In 2013 it also opened the 36000-sq.-ft. Indian Peaks Medical Center in Frederick at an estimated cost of $20 million to $30 million. It includes cardiology and diagnostics departments.

Company Background

The organization was founded in 1925. Since 1995 when PVHS reorganized as a private not-for-profit health care organization local property taxes that used to go straight to PVHS have been paid to the Health District of Northern Larimer County which then uses them to fund PVHS' various activities.

EXECUTIVES

Vice President and Chief Officer, William A Neff
Vice President Information Security, Fernando Pedroza

LOCATIONS

HQ: POUDRE VALLEY HEALTH CARE, INC.
2315 E HARMONY RD STE 200, FORT COLLINS, CO 805288620
Phone: 970 495-7000

PRODUCTS/OPERATIONS

Selected Services
Back Neck and Spine Care
Cancer Care
Diabetes and Endocrinology
Hyperbaric Medicine
Imaging and Radiology
Laboratory Services
Orthopedics
Pain Care and Management
Seniors' Health
Weight and Metabolism
Women's Health
Wound Care

COMPETITORS

Catholic Health Initiatives	North Colorado Medical Center
Centura Health	University of Colorado Hospital
Denver Health and Hospital Authority	Valley View Hospital
Exempla Healthcare	Wyoming Medical Center
HealthONE	
Memorial Health System (Colorado)	

HISTORICAL FINANCIALS

Company Type: Private

Income Statement

FYE: June 30

	REVENUE ($ mil.)	NET INCOME ($ mil.)	NET PROFIT MARGIN	EMPLOYEES
06/15	480	98	20.6%	2,800
06/14	478	38	8.0%	—
/* 0	0	—	—	—
Annual Growth	—	—	—	—

*Fiscal year change

2015 Year-End Financials

Return on assets: 4.6%   Cash ($ mil.): 68
Return on equity: 20.6%
Current ratio: 1.80

POWER ENGINEERS, INCORPORATED

EXECUTIVES

Chairman of the Board, Randy Pollock
Executive Vice-President, John Cavanaugh
Executive Vice-President, Gerry Murray
Vice-President, Frank Halverson
Vice-President, William Hansen
Treasurer, Jan James
Vice-President, William Eisinger
Vice-President, Brent Lackey
Vice-President, Timothy Ostermeier
Auditors: DELOITTE & TOUCHE LLP BOISE

LOCATIONS

HQ: POWER ENGINEERS, INCORPORATED
3940 GLENBROOK DR, HAILEY, ID 833338446
Phone: 208 788-3456
Web: WWW.POWERENG.COM

HISTORICAL FINANCIALS

Company Type: Private

Income Statement

FYE: December 31

	REVENUE ($ mil.)	NET INCOME ($ mil.)	NET PROFIT MARGIN	EMPLOYEES
12/15	395	16	4.3%	503
12/12	298	9	3.1%	—
12/10	203	6	3.2%	—
12/09	32	0	—	—
Annual Growth	—	569.9%	—	—

2015 Year-End Financials

Return on assets: 2.3%   Cash ($ mil.): 14
Return on equity: 4.3%
Current ratio: 1.50

POWER SOLUTIONS, LLC

EXECUTIVES

Board of Directors, Tom Inscoe
Board of Directors, James Giles
Account Manager, Bill Poss
Project Manager, Mark Newman
Project Manager, Rodney Reeves
Project Manager, Steve Walker
Vice-President, Kevin Howell
Auditors: REGAN SCHICKNER SHAH HARPER LL

LOCATIONS

HQ: POWER SOLUTIONS, LLC
17201 MELFORD BLVD STE C, BOWIE, MD 207154414
Phone: 301 794-0330
Web: WWW.POWERSOLUTIONS-LLC.COM

HISTORICAL FINANCIALS

Company Type: Private

Income Statement

FYE: December 31

	REVENUE ($ mil.)	NET INCOME ($ mil.)	NET PROFIT MARGIN	EMPLOYEES
12/15	238	35	14.9%	350
12/14	279	59	21.4%	—
12/13	177	33	18.6%	—
12/12	149	30	20.4%	—
Annual Growth	17.0%	5.5%	—	—

2015 Year-End Financials

Return on assets: 4.6%   Cash ($ mil.): 9
Return on equity: 14.9%
Current ratio: 1.40

POWERSOUTH ENERGY COOPERATIVE

Several hundred thousand Alabamans and Floridians get their electric power courtesy of the work of PowerSouth Energy Cooperative which provides wholesale power to its member-owners (16 electric cooperatives and four municipal distribution utilities). Its distribution members provide electric services to almost 417200 customer meters in central and southern Alabama and western Florida. PowerSouth operates a more than 2200-mile power transmission system and has more than 2000 MW of generating capacity from interests in six fossil-fueled and hydroelectric power plants.

Geographic Reach

PowerSouth serves customers in Alabama (39 counties) and Florida (10 counties).

Operations

The company owns and operates six generation facilities and holds ownership interest in an additional facility. Its diverse generating fuel mix includes natural gas coal and water (hydro). It also has compressed air energy storage technology and a disciplined fuel supply hedging program that minimizes the impact of fuel cost increases. In addition PowerSouth maintains long-term purchased power agreements to ensure economic and reliable power supply for its members.

PowerSouth serves the wholesale energy needs of electric cooperatives and municipal electric systems in Alabama and northwest Florida who in turn serve more than a million consumers. PowerSouth is dedicated to providing reliable energy at the lowest possible cost to its members.

Financial Performance

The company's revenues increased by 3% in 2013 primarily due to an increase in member revenues as a result of an increase in energy sales. The remaining increase was due to the surcharges added to the excess demand rate during 2013.

That year PowerSouth's net income decreased by 6% as the result of increased operating costs caused by higher distribution costs and administration and general expenses.

Its operating cash inflow increased to $63.5 million in 2013 (compared to $38.3 million in 2012) due to a rise in account receivables and inventories.

Strategy

To meet future demand and tightening environmental regulations the company is looking to diversify and expand its power production assets

with an emphasis on cleaner energy plants. PowerSouth's long-term energy plans include a 20-year contract for 125 MW of nuclear power from two Vogtle Units being built by the Municipal Energy Authority of Georgia near Augusta and due to come onstream in 2016 and 2017. The company is also investing in wind power and biomass-to-energy initiatives.

Company Background

PowersSouth is owned and managed by it 20 distribution members.

The company once provided propane but sold its Cooperative Propane unit in 2011 to focus on its core power businesses.

In 2008 Alabama Electric Cooperative changed its name to PowerSouth Energy Cooperative to better reflect its service territory (Alabama and Florida) and its opportunities for future growth.

Founded in 1941 as Alabama Electric Cooperative the coop promotes a strong economic development program aimed at bringing industry into both Alabama and Florida.

EXECUTIVES

Vice President Information Technology, Lewis Jeffers
Vice President, Ken Skroback
Secretary, Gary Herrison
Auditors: DELOITTE & TOUCHE LLP ATLANTA

LOCATIONS

HQ: POWERSOUTH ENERGY COOPERATIVE
2027 E THREE NOTCH ST, ANDALUSIA, AL 364212427
Phone: 334 427-3000
Web: WWW.POWERSOUTH.COM

PRODUCTS/OPERATIONS

View Archived What Charts | Edit 2013 Sales

	% of total
Electric	
Cooperatives	93
Municipalities	6
Other	1
Total	**100**

HISTORICAL FINANCIALS

Company Type: Private

Income Statement

	REVENUE ($ mil.)	NET INCOME ($ mil.)	NET PROFIT MARGIN	EMPLOYEES
12/15	622	17	2.7%	640
12/14	675	16	2.5%	—
12/13	609	25	4.1%	—
12/12	591	26	4.5%	—
Annual Growth	1.7%	(13.7%)	—	—

FYE: December 31

2015 Year-End Financials

Return on assets: 5.2%
Return on equity: 2.7%
Current ratio: 0.40
Cash ($ mil.): 28

POWERTECH AMERICA SALES, LLC

Auditors: PK LLP OPELIKA ALABAMA

LOCATIONS

HQ: POWERTECH AMERICA SALES, LLC
6801 KIA PKWY, WEST POINT, GA 318334937
Phone: 706 902-6800

HISTORICAL FINANCIALS

Company Type: Private

Income Statement

	REVENUE ($ mil.)	NET INCOME ($ mil.)	NET PROFIT MARGIN	EMPLOYEES
12/15	401	5	1.3%	19
12/14	411	(8)	—	—
Annual Growth	(2.4%)	—	—	—

FYE: December 31

2015 Year-End Financials

Return on assets: 15.9%
Return on equity: 1.3%
Current ratio: 0.30
Cash ($ mil.): —

POWERTECH AMERICA, INC.

EXECUTIVES

Chief Executive Officer, Sam Ho Cha
Chief Financial Officer, Changyoung Kim
Purchasing Agent, Darren Wiker
Manager, Dan Kleiber
Assistant Manager, Jason Aikens
Accountant, Do Hyun Lee
Auditors: PK LLP OPELIKA ALABAMA

LOCATIONS

HQ: POWERTECH AMERICA, INC.
6801 KIA PKWY, WEST POINT, GA 318334937
Phone: 706 902-6800

HISTORICAL FINANCIALS

Company Type: Private

Income Statement

	REVENUE ($ mil.)	NET INCOME ($ mil.)	NET PROFIT MARGIN	EMPLOYEES
12/15	1,230	12	1.0%	500
12/14	1,250	11	0.9%	—
12/13	1,220	11	0.9%	—
12/10	345	1	0.4%	—
Annual Growth	28.9%	52.9%	—	—

FYE: December 31

2015 Year-End Financials

Return on assets: 15.7%
Return on equity: 1.0%
Current ratio: 0.50
Cash ($ mil.): 11

PREMIER COOPERATIVE

EXECUTIVES

Chief Executive Officer, Andy Fiene
Manager, Dean Killion
Office Manager, Ray Billman
Manager, Rich Thomas
Financial Executive, Ron Snyder
Manager, Jeff Demuth
Auditors: CLIFTONLARSONALLEN MIDDLETON

LOCATIONS

HQ: PREMIER COOPERATIVE
501 W MAIN ST, MOUNT HOREB, WI 535721903
Phone: 608 251-0199
Web: WWW.PREMIERCOOPERATIVE.COM

HISTORICAL FINANCIALS

Company Type: Private

Income Statement

	REVENUE ($ mil.)	NET INCOME ($ mil.)	NET PROFIT MARGIN	EMPLOYEES
09/16	178	9	5.6%	55
09/15	208	10	5.2%	—
09/14	222	10	4.7%	—
09/13	201	10	5.0%	—
Annual Growth	(4.0%)	(0.6%)	—	—

FYE: September 30

2016 Year-End Financials

Return on assets: 5.1%
Return on equity: 5.6%
Current ratio: 0.90
Cash ($ mil.): 22

PREMISE HEALTH HOLDING CORP.

EXECUTIVES

Chief Executive Officer, Edward Stuart Clark
Board of Directors, Haden Mc Whorter
Board of Directors, Joey Johnson
Manager, Matt Stanford
VP Operations, Ann Grote
Account Manager, Bobbi Bryson

LOCATIONS

HQ: PREMISE HEALTH HOLDING CORP.
5500 MARYLAND WAY STE 200, BRENTWOOD, TN 370274973
Phone: 615 468-6295
Web: WWW.PREMISEHEALTH.COM

HISTORICAL FINANCIALS

Company Type: Private

Income Statement

	REVENUE ($ mil.)	NET INCOME ($ mil.)	NET PROFIT MARGIN	EMPLOYEES
12/15	581	0	0.0%	4,100
12/14	303	(14)	—	—
Annual Growth	91.4%	—	—	—

FYE: December 31

2015 Year-End Financials

Return on assets: 5.2%
Return on equity: —
Current ratio: 2.20
Cash ($ mil.): 31

PRESBYTERIAN HOMES AND SERVICES

EXECUTIVES

Chief Executive Officer, Daniel A Lindh
Board of Directors, Janna R Severance
Executive Director, David Benni
Personnel Director, Helen Jones

Executive Director, Dan Erickson
Manager, Steve Whitehouse
Administrative Assistant, Liz Jefferson
Director, David Millett
Auditors: CLIFTONLARSONALLEN LLP MINNEA

LOCATIONS

HQ: PRESBYTERIAN HOMES AND SERVICES
2845 HAMLINE AVE N # 200, ROSEVILLE, MN
551137116
Phone: 651 631-6100
Web: WWW.PRESHOMES.COM

HISTORICAL FINANCIALS

Company Type: Private

Income Statement				FYE: September 30
	REVENUE ($ mil.)	NET INCOME ($ mil.)	NET PROFIT MARGIN	EMPLOYEES
09/16	363	17	4.8%	4,750
09/15	334	17	5.2%	—
09/14	314	17	5.6%	—
09/13	290	18	6.5%	—
Annual Growth	7.8%	(2.6%)	—	—

2016 Year-End Financials

Return on assets: 2.4%   Cash ($ mil.): 42
Return on equity: 4.8%
Current ratio: 0.70

PRESBYTERIAN MEDICAL CENTER OF THE UNIVERSITY OF PENNSYLVANIA HEALTH SYSTEM

EXECUTIVES

Executive Director, Michele Volpe
Manager, Colleen Omalley
Administration Director, John Donuhue
Vice-President, Ana McKee
Auditors: PRICEWATERHOUSECOOPERS LLP PH

LOCATIONS

HQ: PRESBYTERIAN MEDICAL CENTER OF THE
UNIVERSITY OF PENNSYLVANIA HEALTH SYSTEM
51 N 39TH ST, PHILADELPHIA, PA 191042692
Phone: 215 662-8000
Web: WWW.PENNMEDICINE.ORG

HISTORICAL FINANCIALS

Company Type: Private

Income Statement				FYE: June 30
	REVENUE ($ mil.)	NET INCOME ($ mil.)	NET PROFIT MARGIN	EMPLOYEES
06/15	546	(0)	—	1,370
06/14	445	21	4.7%	—
06/13	429	7	1.7%	—
06/05	301	(1)	—	—
Annual Growth	6.2%	—	—	—

PRESENCE CHICAGO HOSPITALS NETWORK

EXECUTIVES

Chief Executive Officer, Robert Dahl
Project Manager, Sue Ellen Schumacher
Manager, Gina Shell-Lamore
Project Manager, Brenda Wade

LOCATIONS

HQ: PRESENCE CHICAGO HOSPITALS NETWORK
7435 W TALCOTT AVE, CHICAGO, IL 606313707
Phone: 773 737-4636
Web: WWW.PRESENCEHEALTH.ORG

HISTORICAL FINANCIALS

Company Type: Private

Income Statement				FYE: December 31
	REVENUE ($ mil.)	NET INCOME ($ mil.)	NET PROFIT MARGIN	EMPLOYEES
12/15	277	3	1.1%	99
12/14	238	(19)	—	—
12/13	266	(4)	—	—
Annual Growth	2.1%	—	—	—

PRESENCE SAINT JOSEPH HOSPITAL - CHICAGO

EXECUTIVES

President, Roberta Luskin Hawk
Financial Executive, Ray Vieth
Project Manager, Sue Ellen Schumacher

LOCATIONS

HQ: PRESENCE SAINT JOSEPH HOSPITAL - CHICAGO
2900 N LAKE SHORE DR, CHICAGO, IL 606575640
Phone: 773 665-3000

HISTORICAL FINANCIALS

Company Type: Private

Income Statement				FYE: December 31
	REVENUE ($ mil.)	NET INCOME ($ mil.)	NET PROFIT MARGIN	EMPLOYEES
12/15	203	(22)	—	1,600
12/14	194	4	2.1%	—
Annual Growth	4.6%	—	—	—

2015 Year-End Financials

Return on assets: 2.2%   Cash ($ mil.): —
Return on equity: (-10.9%)
Current ratio: 0.40

PRESIDENT AND TRUSTEES OF COLBY COLLEGE

EXECUTIVES

Principal, Bruce McDougal

LOCATIONS

HQ: PRESIDENT AND TRUSTEES OF COLBY
COLLEGE
4120 MAYFLOWER HL, WATERVILLE, ME 049018841
Phone: 207 859-4127

HISTORICAL FINANCIALS

Company Type: Private

Income Statement				FYE: June 30
	ASSETS ($ mil.)	NET INCOME ($ mil.)	INCOME AS % OF ASSETS	EMPLOYEES
06/15	1,382	50	3.6%	4
06/14	1,267	55	4.4%	—
06/13	1,126	30	2.7%	—
06/11	1,050	21	2.1%	—
Annual Growth	7.1%	23.2%	—	—

2015 Year-End Financials

Return on assets: 7.6%   Sales ($ mil.): 214
Return on equity: 23.4%

PRESIDIAN DESTINATIONS, LTD.

EXECUTIVES

Partner, H Drake Leddy
Chief Financial Officer, Jeanette Mosley
Managing Director, Angie Mock
Director, Sergio Cardenas
President, Lily Ng
Vice-President, Stanton Leddy

LOCATIONS

HQ: PRESIDIAN DESTINATIONS, LTD.
9000 TESORO DR STE 300, SAN ANTONIO, TX
782176132
Phone: 210 646-8811
Web: WWW.PRESIDIAN.COM

HISTORICAL FINANCIALS

Company Type: Private

Income Statement				FYE: December 31
	ASSETS ($ mil.)	NET INCOME ($ mil.)	INCOME AS % OF ASSETS	EMPLOYEES
12/15	924	583	63.1%	10
12/14	1,916	799	41.7%	—
12/13	1	0	34.5%	—
12/12	1	0	27.8%	—
Annual Growth	789.3%	1069.0%	—	—

2015 Year-End Financials

Return on assets: 0.1%   Sales ($ mil.): 1,338
Return on equity: 43.6%

PRIDE INDUSTRIES

EXECUTIVES

Chief Executive Officer, Michael Ziegler
Office Manager, Debbie Morton
Vice-President, Samuel Seaton
Auditors: MOSS ADAMS LLP SACRAMENTO CA

LOCATIONS

HQ: PRIDE INDUSTRIES
   10030 FOOTHILLS BLVD, ROSEVILLE, CA 957477102
Phone: 916 788-2100
Web: WWW.PRIDEINDUSTRIES.COM

HISTORICAL FINANCIALS

Company Type: Private

Income Statement   FYE: June 30

	REVENUE ($ mil.)	NET INCOME ($ mil.)	NET PROFIT MARGIN	EMPLOYEES
06/16	290	0	0.1%	5,003
06/15	279	1	0.6%	—
06/14	258	3	1.5%	—
06/13	244	2	1.0%	—
Annual Growth	5.9%	(48.5%)	—	—

2016 Year-End Financials

Return on assets: 3.8%   Cash ($ mil.): 1
Return on equity: 0.1%
Current ratio: 1.00

PRO PETROLEUM, INC.

EXECUTIVES

President, Marcus Griffin
Board of Directors, B R Griffin
Manager, Mark Macha
Financial Executive, Betty Catherman
Auditors: GARRETT AND SWANN LLP LUBBOC

LOCATIONS

HQ: PRO PETROLEUM, INC.
   4710 4TH ST, LUBBOCK, TX 794164900
Phone: 806 795-8785
Web: WWW.PROPETROLEUM.COM

HISTORICAL FINANCIALS

Company Type: Private

Income Statement   FYE: December 31

	REVENUE ($ mil.)	NET INCOME ($ mil.)	NET PROFIT MARGIN	EMPLOYEES
12/15	1,063	5	0.5%	150
12/14	1,701	4	0.3%	—
12/13	1,815	12	0.7%	—
12/12	1,830	12	0.7%	—
Annual Growth	(16.6%)	(25.3%)	—	—

2015 Year-End Financials

Return on assets: 1.2%   Cash ($ mil.): 33
Return on equity: 0.5%
Current ratio: 1.00

PRODUCE ALLIANCE, L.L.C.

EXECUTIVES

Board of Directors, Scott Weber
Administrative Assistant, Briana Whitley
Accountant, Monty Mittelman
Auditors: MILLER COOPER & CO LTD DE

LOCATIONS

HQ: PRODUCE ALLIANCE, L.L.C.
   100 LEXINGTON DR STE 201, BUFFALO GROVE, IL
   600896937
Phone: 847 808-3030
Web: WWW.PRODUCEALLIANCE.COM

HISTORICAL FINANCIALS

Company Type: Private

Income Statement   FYE: December 31

	REVENUE ($ mil.)	NET INCOME ($ mil.)	NET PROFIT MARGIN	EMPLOYEES
12/15	326	1	0.4%	75
12/14	253	0	0.2%	—
12/13	218	0	0.1%	—
12/12	173	0	0.1%	—
Annual Growth	23.5%	148.4%	—	—

2015 Year-End Financials

Return on assets: 7.5%   Cash ($ mil.): —
Return on equity: 0.4%
Current ratio: 1.00

PRODUCERS RICE MILL, INC.

These producers aren't just milling about they're about milling. Producers Rice Mill dries mills and markets more than 50 million bushels of rice each year which it sells both domestically and overseas. The growers' cooperative is one of the largest private-label producers of rice in the US packaging more than 100 brands for the foodservice retail private label export and industrial industries. Its brands include ParExcellence LeGourmet Golden Harvest Classic Grains Granada Mandalay Bamboo 103 Calrose and Thai Orchard. It also processes rice for animal feeds such as Buck Grub deer feed and Equi-Jewel horse feed.

Operations
Along with bagged and bulk rice Producers also offers parboiled rice and seasoned rice mixes and processes rice for animal feed. During 2012-13 Producers' mills processed 64.3 million bushels of rice up 14% from the previous year.

Geographic Reach
In addition to its corporate headquarters and production facilities in Stuttgart Arkansas the cooperative has receiving operations in Arkansas Mississippi and Texas. It has plants in DeWitt Eudora Fair Oaks Pine Bluff Stuttgart Tyronza Wilmot Wilson and Wynne in Arkansas; Boyle and Greenville in Mississippi; and DeWitt in Texas. About 15% of US milled grains like rice are exported to countries such as Canada Mexico Japan Haiti and Iraq.

Sales and Marketing
The company serves foodservice retail private label export and industrial customers. Ahold U.S.A. Federated Nash Finch and SUPERVALU have been long-term customers.

Strategy
The USDA projects a demand in US rice exports over the next several years. Milled rice will have a higher demand which will directly benefit the US rice industry.

Company Background
The cooperative was founded in 1943.

EXECUTIVES

Vice President Oprs, Ken Dryden
National Sales Manager Foodservice, John May
Auditors: ERWIN & COMPANY LITTLE ROCK

LOCATIONS

HQ: PRODUCERS RICE MILL, INC.
   518 E HARRISON ST, STUTTGART, AR 721603700
Phone: 870 673-4444
Web: WWW.PRODUCERSRICE.COM

COMPETITORS

ADM	Goya
American Rice	Mars Incorporated
CHS	Mondelez International
Cargill	PepsiCo
Cereal Byproducts	RiceX
Farmers Rice Milling	Riceland Foods
Farmers' Rice	Specialty Rice
Cooperative	

HISTORICAL FINANCIALS

Company Type: Private

Income Statement   FYE: July 31

	REVENUE ($ mil.)	NET INCOME ($ mil.)	NET PROFIT MARGIN	EMPLOYEES
07/16	415	275	66.3%	600
07/15	488	354	72.7%	—
07/14	546	327	59.9%	—
07/13	568	368	64.8%	—
Annual Growth	(10.0%)	(9.3%)	—	—

2016 Year-End Financials

Return on assets: 2.8%   Cash ($ mil.): 1
Return on equity: 66.3%
Current ratio: 1.10

PROTESTANT MEMORIAL MEDICAL CENTER, INC.

With more than 315 beds Memorial Hospital has plenty of space to take care of Prairie Staters. The Bellevue Illinois-based hospital is owned and operated by Protestant Memorial Medical Center a community-based not-for-profit organization. Memorial Hospital provides general medical surgical and emergency care as well as pediatric home health and cardiovascular care. Specialty services include treatment for sleep disorders and women's health. The hospital also operates Memorial Convalescent Center a nearly 110-bed skilled nursing facility and the Belleville Health and Sports Center which provides fitness facilities to promote community health.

Operations
Memorial Hospital has a medical staff with more than 350 members representing 42 specialties. It provides access to new imaging technology though the Southern Illinois Positive Emission Tomogra-

phy Imaging Center in Swansea (a joint venture between Memorial and St. Elizabeth's hospitals).

The hospital collaborates with the Southern Illinois University School of Medicine for certain research programs and services. Memorial Hospital is a part of the Memory and Aging Network at the school of medicine as a designated Alzheimer's Disease Primary Provider Site. The program includes a network of about 35 provider sites that collect data on the frequency type and progression of dementia.

Geographic Reach

In addition to its main facility in the Belleville neighborhood Memorial Hospital has diagnostic centers in O'Fallon Illinois and an off-campus physical therapy center in east Belleville.

Strategy

Memorial Hospital is building a $118 million satellite hospital in nearby Shiloh called Memorial Hospital - East. The new facility will include 94 beds private patient rooms surgical suites a cardiac catheterization lab as well as an intensive care unit and an obstetrics unit. The hospital is expected to open in 2016. When the new hospital opens hospital officials expect the main campus in Belleville to reduce its capacity and convert all patient rooms to single occupancy.

In 2014 CEP America a physician-owned organization which had staffed and managed physician coverage for Memorial Hospital's Emergency Department also began to provide hospitalist services for the hospital's inpatients.

Memorial Hospital has also expanded its services to Memorial Healthcare Center in O'Fallon to provide general x-ray services state-of-the-art CT scanning MRI and physical therapy.

Company Background

The hospital first opened its doors in 1958.

EXECUTIVES

VP Finance, Joe Lanius
COO, Mark J. Turner
Vice President, Ruth Holmes
Vice President Human Resources, John Ziegler
Medical Records Director, Debbie Kostecki
Director Icu Coronary Care Unit, Barb Jany
Director of Nursing, Anne Crook
Operating Room Director, Laurie Voigt
Nursing Director, Teri Halloran

LOCATIONS

HQ: PROTESTANT MEMORIAL MEDICAL CENTER, INC.
4500 MEMORIAL DR, BELLEVILLE, IL 622265360
Phone: 618 233-7750
Web: WWW.MEMHOSP.COM

PRODUCTS/OPERATIONS

Selected Services
Advanced Interventional Pain
Belleville Health and Sports Center
Breast Health Center
Cancer Treatment Center
Cardiovascular
Center for Diabetes Education
Emergency Department
Family Care Birthing Center
Gastroenterology Lab
Home Care
Laboratory
Memorial Care Center
Orthopedics
Palliative Care
Pulmonary and Respiratory
Radiology
Rehab Services
Senior Care
Sleep Disorders Center
Surgical Services

COMPETITORS

Ascension Health	RehabCare
BJC HealthCare	St. Anthony's Medical
Barnes-Jewish Hospital	Center
Christian Hospital	

HISTORICAL FINANCIALS

Company Type: Private

Income Statement

FYE: December 31

	REVENUE ($ mil.)	NET INCOME ($ mil.)	NET PROFIT MARGIN	EMPLOYEES
12/15	281	35	12.7%	2,344
12/14	261	23	8.9%	—
12/13	256	(36)	—	—
12/12	263	15	6.0%	—
Annual Growth	2.3%	31.2%	—	—

2015 Year-End Financials

Return on assets: 6.1%
Return on equity: 12.7%
Current ratio: 2.60
Cash ($ mil.): 24

PROTRANS INTERNATIONAL, INC.

EXECUTIVES

President, Craig Roeder
Manager, Lora Catron
Vice-President, Lisa Doener
Vice-President, John Wood
Manager, Gordon Esterline
Administrative Assistant, Nancy Dye
Vice-President, Harald Walther
Manager, Jason Barker
Representative, Tara Cooper
Auditors: BGBC PARTNERS LLP INDIANAPOLI

LOCATIONS

HQ: PROTRANS INTERNATIONAL, INC.
8311 N PERIMETER RD, INDIANAPOLIS, IN 462413628
Phone: 317 240-4100
Web: WWW.PROTRANS.COM

HISTORICAL FINANCIALS

Company Type: Private

Income Statement

FYE: December 31

	REVENUE ($ mil.)	NET INCOME ($ mil.)	NET PROFIT MARGIN	EMPLOYEES
12/15	283	5	2.0%	500
12/14	292	4	1.4%	—
12/13	256	9	3.5%	—
12/12	192	9	4.9%	—
Annual Growth	13.8%	(15.2%)	—	—

PROVIDENCE COLLEGE

Students don't need divine intervention to get into Providence College they just need good grades and an interest in liberal arts. The Catholic institution of higher education offers undergraduate and graduate degrees at its four schools: Arts and Sciences Business Continuing Education and Professional Studies. It offers degrees in about 50 academic disciplines including biology business education marketing politics and psychology. It has a student-to-faculty ratio of 12:1 with students primarily coming from New England and the Midwest and Mid-Atlantic regions. Providence College was founded in 1917 by the Dominican Friars of the Province of St. Joseph and the Diocese of Providence.

EXECUTIVES

Senior Vice President for Finance and Business Chief Financial Officer, John Sweeney
Vice President, Joseph Carr
Vice President of Mission and Ministry, Gabriel Pivarnik
Vice President For Student Affairs, Kristine Goodwin
Associate Vice President, Steven Maurano
Assistant Vice President Development, Lynne Fraser
Associate Vice President for Mission and Ministry, Kevin Robb
Senior Vice President for Institutional Advancement, Greg Waldron
Auditors: KPMG LLP BOSTON MA

LOCATIONS

HQ: PROVIDENCE COLLEGE
1 CUNNINGHAM SQ, PROVIDENCE, RI 029187001
Phone: 401 865-1000
Web: WWW.PROVIDENCE.EDU

HISTORICAL FINANCIALS

Company Type: Private

Income Statement

FYE: June 30

	REVENUE ($ mil.)	NET INCOME ($ mil.)	NET PROFIT MARGIN	EMPLOYEES
06/15	267	23	8.9%	800
06/13	237	22	9.4%	—
06/11	216	24	11.2%	—
06/10	0	0	—	—
Annual Growth	—	329.4%	—	—

2015 Year-End Financials

Return on assets: 5.7%
Return on equity: 8.9%
Current ratio: 0.20
Cash ($ mil.): 15

PROVIDENCE HEALTH SERVICES OF WACO

EXECUTIVES

Chief Executive Officer, Brett Esrock
Board of Directors, Dennis Michaelis
Director, Susan Tally
Executive Secretary, Carol Williams
Director, Patty Hawk

LOCATIONS

HQ: PROVIDENCE HEALTH SERVICES OF WACO
6901 MEDICAL PKWY, WACO, TX 767127910
Phone: 254 751-4000

HISTORICAL FINANCIALS

Company Type: Private

Income Statement

FYE: June 30

	REVENUE ($ mil.)	NET INCOME ($ mil.)	NET PROFIT MARGIN	EMPLOYEES
06/15	277	8	3.1%	2,000
06/14	267	23	8.7%	—
06/10	236	15	6.4%	—
06/09	228	0	—	—
Annual Growth	3.3%	—	—	—

2015 Year-End Financials

Return on assets: 3.1%
Return on equity: 3.1%
Current ratio: 1.50

Cash ($ mil.): 4

PROVIDENCE HOSPITAL

Providence Hospital and Medical Centers provides health care in the Motor City and surrounding areas. The main Providence Hospital is a 408-bed teaching facility that has been recognized for its cardiology program and clinical expertise in behavioral medicine. It offers a variety of other services ranging from cancer treatment and neurosurgery to orthopedics and women's health. The network also includes dozens of affiliated general practice and specialty health clinics. The not-for-profit medical center founded in 1845 as St. Vincent's Hospital in Detroit by the Daughters of Charity is part of Catholic health ministry St. John Health (itself a subsidiary of Ascension Health).

Operations

As part of its health care system Providence Hospital and Medical Centers operates a host of hospitals and medical centers across the metropolitan Detroit area. They include Providence Southfield and four namesake Providence Medical Center locations in Farmington Hills Livonia Dearborn Heights and South Lyon. Across its system the medical facilities employ some 1500 physicians and enlist the help of about 300 active volunteers.

Carroll Manor is a skilled nursing center that provides short- and long-term medical care and rehabilitation services. The system's behavioral health division Seton House provides alcohol and addiction treatment in Washington DC.

Providence Hospital and Medical Centers had more than 41600 emergency department visits in 2013.

Strategy

In order to provide better services the hospital renovated and expanded its emergency department in 2014. Also that year its family medicine division opened a new office in the Glenn Dale/Bowie area.

EXECUTIVES

Nursing Director, Kathy Ryan
Auditors: DELOITTE TAX LP CINCINNATI O

LOCATIONS

HQ: PROVIDENCE HOSPITAL
16001 W 9 MILE RD, SOUTHFIELD, MI 480754803
Phone: 248 849-3000
Web: WWW.PROVIDENCEOBGYNRESIDENCY.COM

Selected Hospitals and Medical Centers

Providence Southfield-Southfield
Providence Medical Center-Farmington Hills
Providence Medical Center-Livonia
Providence Medical Center-Dearborn Heights
Providence Medical Center-South Lyon

PRODUCTS/OPERATIONS

Selected Primary Services

Cancer clinical trials
Cardiac rehabilitation
Childbirth
Congenital heart disease clinic
Emergency
Oncology
Orthopedics
Senior services
Surgery
Women's health

COMPETITORS

Beaumont Health System	McLaren Health Care
Crittenton Hospital	Trinity Health (Novi)
Detroit Medical Center	University of Michigan
Henry Ford Health System	Health System

HISTORICAL FINANCIALS

Company Type: Private

Income Statement

FYE: June 30

	REVENUE ($ mil.)	NET INCOME ($ mil.)	NET PROFIT MARGIN	EMPLOYEES
06/15	654	25	3.9%	4,700
06/14	659	53	8.1%	—
06/11	706	27	3.9%	—
06/10	593	1	0.3%	—
Annual Growth	2.0%	67.0%	—	—

2015 Year-End Financials

Return on assets: 0.8%
Return on equity: 3.9%
Current ratio: —

Cash ($ mil.): 2

PROVIDENCE HOSPITAL

EXECUTIVES

President, Clark Christianson
Manager, John Roeder
Executive Director, Christopher Southwick
Administration Director, Daniel Scarcliff
Auditors: DELOITTE TAX LP CINCINNATI O

LOCATIONS

HQ: PROVIDENCE HOSPITAL
6801 AIRPORT BLVD, MOBILE, AL 366083785
Phone: 251 633-1000
Web: WWW.PROVIDENCEHOSPITAL.ORG

HISTORICAL FINANCIALS

Company Type: Private

Income Statement

FYE: June 30

	REVENUE ($ mil.)	NET INCOME ($ mil.)	NET PROFIT MARGIN	EMPLOYEES
06/15	227	12	5.6%	2,000
06/14	189	(16)	—	—
06/13	215	19	9.3%	—
06/10	227	21	9.5%	—
Annual Growth	(0.0%)	(9.9%)	—	—

2015 Year-End Financials

Return on assets: 1.8%
Return on equity: 5.6%
Current ratio: 0.50

Cash ($ mil.): —

PROVIDENCE HOSPITAL

Providence Hospital is a pillar in the health care community of Washington DC. The oldest continuously operating hospital in our nation's capitol the 410-bed facility provides a full spectrum of services from behavioral health to women's services. It also administers programs for sleep disorders geriatric care and palliative care in addition to its comprehensive medical and surgical services. Providence Hospital's affiliates include the adjacent Carroll Manor Nursing and Rehabilitation Center a 250-bed facility for long-term and rehabilitative care as well as several outpatient family behavioral and occupational health clinics in the region. Providence Hospital is part of the Ascension Health network.

Operations

Providence's main hospital and rehab facility includes a pharmacy and a wellness center. In addition area facilities operated by the hospital include several Senior Wellness centers the Fort Lincoln Family Medicine Center (which serves Colmar Manor Maryland) and the Perry Family Health Center.

Strategy

In mid-2017 Providence Hospital announced a plan to transition into an integrated "health village" which will offer health and non-health services with a special focus on persons living in poverty or otherwise vulnerable. While still in the planning and development stage the health village could incorporate such elements as primary care specialty care pharmacy services post-acute care long-term care and partnerships with community organizations providing related services.

Company Background

Chartered by President Abraham Lincoln in 1861 Providence Hospital is the longest continuously operating hospital in the US capital.

EXECUTIVES

Director of Nursing, Michaele Johnson
Senior Vice President Operations, Marc Edelman
Medical Records Director, CHOUNDRA FORD
Assistant Vice President Finance, Rachel Maloney
Director of Surgery, Pauline Clarke
MEDICAL DIRECTOR, Michelle A Roett
Auditors: DELOITTE TAX LLP CINCINNATI

LOCATIONS

HQ: PROVIDENCE HOSPITAL
1150 VARNUM ST NE, WASHINGTON, DC 200172104
Phone: 202 269-7000

Selected Facilities

Carroll Manor Nursing And Rehabilitation Center (Washington DC)
Congress Heights Senior Wellness Center (Washington DC)
Model Cities Senior Wellness Center (Washington DC)
Hattie Holmes Senior Wellness Center (Washington DC)
Fort Lincoln Family Medicine Center (Colmar Manor Maryland)
Perry Family Health Center (Washington DC)
Police and Fire Clinic (Washington DC)
Seton House (Washington DC; behavioral health services)
Wellington Pharmacy (Washington DC)
Wellness Institute (Washington DC)

COMPETITORS

Adventist HealthCare	Fauquier Hospital
Children's National Medical Center	HSC Pediatric Center
Dimensions Healthcare	MedStar Health
Doctors Community Hospital	Sibley Memorial Hospital
	Suburban Hospital

HISTORICAL FINANCIALS
Company Type: Private

Income Statement
FYE: June 30

	REVENUE ($ mil.)	NET INCOME ($ mil.)	NET PROFIT MARGIN	EMPLOYEES
06/15	212	16	7.7%	2,517
06/10	235	8	3.5%	—
06/09	230	(13)	—	—
06/08	0	0	—	—
Annual Growth	—	—	—	—

2015 Year-End Financials
Return on assets: 7.2% Cash ($ mil.): 1
Return on equity: 7.7%
Current ratio: 0.50

PROVIDENCE MEDFORD MEDICAL CENTER

EXECUTIVES
Chief Executive Officer, Cindy Mayo
Director, Dean Mitkins
Director, Kathy Gaines
Director, Krista Stusa

LOCATIONS
HQ: PROVIDENCE MEDFORD MEDICAL CENTER
1111 CRATER LAKE AVE, MEDFORD, OR 975046241
Phone: 541 732-5000

HISTORICAL FINANCIALS
Company Type: Private

Income Statement
FYE: December 31

	REVENUE ($ mil.)	NET INCOME ($ mil.)	NET PROFIT MARGIN	EMPLOYEES
12/15	177	(20)	—	2
12/14	167	0	0.0%	—
12/08	127	3	2.9%	—
Annual Growth	4.8%	—	—	—

PRUDENTIAL WELFARE BENEFITS TRUST

EXECUTIVES
Principal, Paul Boxer

LOCATIONS
HQ: PRUDENTIAL WELFARE BENEFITS TRUST
751 BROAD ST FL 18, NEWARK, NJ 071023714
Phone: 973 802-7490

HISTORICAL FINANCIALS
Company Type: Private

Income Statement
FYE: December 31

	ASSETS ($ mil.)	NET INCOME ($ mil.)	INCOME AS % OF ASSETS	EMPLOYEES
12/15	72	(0)	—	2
12/14	79	0	0.6%	—
12/09	86	(5)	—	—
Annual Growth	(3.0%)	—	—	—

PSCU INCORPORATED

Credit unions turn to PSCU to provide key card services. As one of the nation's largest credit union service organizations PSCU (short for Payment Systems for Credit Unions) provides credit debit ATM and prepaid card servicing as well as electronic banking bill payment risk management specialized marketing and contact center services to credit unions across the US. The not-for-profit cooperative serves more than 1300 institutions nationwide which combined represent more than 18 million cardholder accounts and one million online bill payment subscribers. PSCU is owned by about 800 member credit unions.

Operations

The centers perform new member enrollment automated lending collections cardholder support cross-selling and customer service. Its four contact centers handle more than 18 million inquiries a year.

Geographic Reach

PSCU operates four Contact Centers covering three major US regions: the Eastern US with one center located in St. Petersburg Florida; the Western US with one center in Phoenix Arizona; and the Midwest with two centers in Detroit Michigan.

Sales and Marketing

PSCU's clients have included: Redwood Credit Union State Department Federal Credit Union Corporate One Federal Credit Union Advantis Credit Union and the Indiana Credit Union League.

Strategy

PSCU has taken a string of steps to help its partnering credit unions adopt newer safer digital payment technologies in recent years. In early 2015 for example it helped its clients Redwood Credit Union and State Department Federal Credit Union implement access to the smartphone-based Apple Pay platform so their cardholders could make digital payments using their iPhones and iPads. In 2013 the company expanded its Phoenix site to house its PSCU technology-based services and developed six new mobile apps to help clients' members interact with their core deposit prepaid credit card and rewards accounts via smart phone technology. It also introduced the CardLock solution (which works in tandem with PSCU's fraud detection and prevention platform) to enable cardholders to block and unblock authorizations on cards they register with the service. In 2012 the company became the first to issue VISA Prepaid EMV (Europay MasterCard and Visa) cards in the US.

PSCU also continues to lock in its long-term contracts with existing and new clients to keep business growing. In late 2014 the company signed a five-year renewal agreement with the $4.2 billion Corporate One Federal Credit Union to continue providing its credit and debit processing services. In mid-2014 PSCU signed a two new long-term contracts including: a five-year agreement with the $1.1 billion Advantis Credit Union in Portland and secured another long-term agreement with the Indiana Credit Union League.

Company Background

PSCU was formed in 1977 by leaders from Pinellas County Teachers Credit Union and the federal credit unions of GTE Publix Employees Suncoast Schools and Railroad and Industrial.

EXECUTIVES
Senior Vice President Chief Risk Officer, Steve Ruwe
Executive Vice President, Steve Salzer
President and CEO, Michael J. (Mike) Kelly
EVP Credit Debit Prepaid eCommerce Contact Center and Information Technology, Tom Gandre
EVP Credit Union Experience, Fredda McDonald
EVP Human Resources, Lynn Heckler
Executive Vice President & Chief Financial Officer, Brian Caldarelli
Chief Information Officer, Sam Esfahani
Senior Vice President & Chief Marketing Officer, Dan Csont
Senior Vice President, Brandi Quinn
Division Vice President, Sheila Fenton
Vice President Financial Operations, Keith Rolleston
Vice President Marketing Strategy, Myles Bristowe
Chairman, Craig Esrael
Vice Chairman, Mike Valentine
Board Member, Darren Williams
Auditors: PRICEWATERHOUSECOOPERS LLP T

LOCATIONS
HQ: PSCU INCORPORATED
560 CARILLON PKWY, SAINT PETERSBURG, FL 337161294
Phone: 727 572-8822
Web: WWW.PSCU.COM

PRODUCTS/OPERATIONS

Selected Services
Advisors Plus
Credit Solutions
Debit Solutions
eCommerce Solutions
EMV
Prepaid Solutions
Risk Management Solutions

Total	0	0

Technology Tools
PSCU Partnerships/Sponsorships
Credit Union Cherry Blossom Run
Credit Union Student Choice
Filene Research Institute
Financial Service Center Cooperatives (FSCC)
Ongoing Operations
The Colonial Williamsburg Foundation

COMPETITORS
CUSO Financial Services
Fidelity National Information Services
LPL Financial
Raymond James Financial
Southwest Corporate FCU
U.S. Central

HISTORICAL FINANCIALS
Company Type: Private

Income Statement
FYE: September 30

	REVENUE ($ mil.)	NET INCOME ($ mil.)	NET PROFIT MARGIN	EMPLOYEES
09/16*	458	28	6.1%	1,850
12/12	377	38	10.2%	—
12/11	425	29	6.9%	—
12/10	370	0	0.0%	—
Annual Growth	3.6%	817.6%	—	—

*Fiscal year change

2016 Year-End Financials
Return on assets: 6.4%   Cash ($ mil.): 137
Return on equity: 6.1%
Current ratio: 0.70

PUBLIC BROADCASTING SERVICE

You might say these shows get a lot of public support. Public Broadcasting Service (PBS) is a non-profit organization that provides educational and public interest programming to more than 350 member public TV stations in the US. In addition to such programs as NOVA This Old House and Downton Abbey it provides related services such as distribution fundraising support and technology development. PBS gets its revenue from underwriting membership dues federal funding (including grants from the not-for-profit Corporation for Public Broadcasting) royalties license fees and product sales. The organization was founded in 1969 to provide cultural and educational programming.

Operations

PBS operates through more than 350 member public TV stations across the US.

Geographic Reach

PBS reaches almost 200 million people through television and nearly 28 million people online each month.

Strategy

While PBS — and its federal funding — regularly finds itself caught in the crossfire between liberal and conservative political groups supporters of the non-profit trumpet the benefits of publicly-funded television programming created to serve groups often overlooked by commercial broadcasters.

PBS' children's programming and news shows such as Frontline and PBS NewsHour (formerly The NewsHour with Jim Lehrer) are often touted as examples of how public broadcasting can fill voids left by the major networks.

The organization has also been looking to capitalize on new distribution channels to get its programming to the public. PBS sells its programs on DVD and through Apple's iTunes store. It has also ramped up its online video efforts.

EXECUTIVES

SVP and CFO, Barbara L. Landes
COO, Jonathan Barzilay
SVP and General Manager PBS Digital, Ira Rubenstein
President CEO and Director, Paula A. Kerger
Executive Director PBS Foundation, Brian J. Reddington
CTO, Mario Vecchi
Chief Programming Executive and General Manager General Audience Programming, Beth Hoppe
SVP Marketing and Communications; General Manager Children's Programming, Lesli Rotenberg
Senior Vice President of Development Services, Betsy Gerdeman
Senior Vice President System Leadership, Juan Sepulveda
Senior Vice President Strategy and Operations, Jayme Swain
Coordinator Assistant To Assistant Vice President, Julianne Menassian
Vice President Station Services, Thomas Crockett

Vice President administration and Human Resources, Carol Dickert Scherr
Executive Vice President, Karla Aikens-allen
Vice President, Sara Schapiro
Vice President News and Public Affairs PBS, Marie Nelson
Chairman, Donald A. (Don) Baer
Vice Chairman, Tom Axtell
Auditors: BDO USA LLP BETHESDA MD

LOCATIONS

HQ: PUBLIC BROADCASTING SERVICE
2100 CRYSTAL DR STE 100, ARLINGTON, VA 222023784
Phone: 703 739-5000
Web: WWW.PBS.ORG

PRODUCTS/OPERATIONS

Selected Programming
Antiques Roadshow
Austin City Limits
Barney
Downton Abbey
Frontline
Juila Child: Lessons with Master Chefs
Live from Lincoln Center
Masterpiece Theatre
Mister Rogers' Neighborhood
MotorWeek
Mystery!
Nature
NOVA
NOW
P.O.V.
PBS NewsHour
Reading Rainbow
Sesame Street
Teletubbies
This Old House
Victory Garden
Washington Week
ZOOM

COMPETITORS

ABC Cable Networks	HBO
ABC Inc.	MTV Networks
AMC Networks	NBC
BBC Worldwide	Scripps Networks
CBS	Turner Broadcasting
Current Media	
Discovery Communications	

HISTORICAL FINANCIALS
Company Type: Private

Income Statement   FYE: June 30

	REVENUE ($ mil.)	NET INCOME ($ mil.)	NET PROFIT MARGIN	EMPLOYEES
06/15	473	(46)	—	507
06/14	539	89	16.7%	—
06/10	505	28	5.6%	—
06/09	502	(80)	—	—
Annual Growth	(1.0%)	—	—	—

2015 Year-End Financials
Return on assets: 26.2%   Cash ($ mil.): 39
Return on equity: (-9.9%)
Current ratio: 0.40

PUBLIC SCHOOLS OF CITY ANN ARBOR

EXECUTIVES

Superintendent, Jeanice Kerr Swift
Board of Directors, Andy Thomas
Secretary, Judy Solowczuk
Auditors: PLANTE & MORAN PLLC CLINTON

LOCATIONS

HQ: PUBLIC SCHOOLS OF CITY ANN ARBOR
2555 S STATE ST, ANN ARBOR, MI 481046145
Phone: 734 994-2200
Web: WWW.A2SCHOOLS.ORG

HISTORICAL FINANCIALS
Company Type: Private

Income Statement   FYE: June 30

	REVENUE ($ mil.)	NET INCOME ($ mil.)	NET PROFIT MARGIN	EMPLOYEES
06/15	247	34	13.9%	2,000
06/14	228	(8)	—	—
06/13	227	(16)	—	—
06/12	226	18	8.1%	—
Annual Growth	3.0%	23.2%	—	—

2015 Year-End Financials
Return on assets: 2.9%   Cash ($ mil.): 20
Return on equity: 13.9%
Current ratio: —

PUBLIC UTILITIES BOARD

This PUB has no beer. Brownsville Public Utilities Board (Brownsville PUB) is a municipally-owned utility company providing electric water and wastewater services to residential and commercial customers in Brownsville Texas. Brownsville PUB serves 46000 with electric service and 47000 with water and wastewater service. The utility's two water treatment plants have the capacity to provide 40 million gallons of treated water per day. It gets its water supply from the Rio Grande. The utility's wastewater system has 174 lift stations and two treatment plants.

Brownsville PUB is challenged to keep pace with explosive population growth in Brownsville (2.5% a year since 2000). In 2012 its major growth initiatives included bringing water to a colonias (undeveloped but populated rural community) on the edge of Brownsville a seawater desalination plant a filtration project and sewer overflow remediation.

Customer growth and higher power water and wastewater demand lifted the utility's revenues by more than 8% in 2011 while the robust revenues and lower fuel costs (due to low natural gas prices) and a drop in depreciation and other costs helped the company to report a 52% jump in operating income for the year.

The utility got it start in 1907 after local residents voted for the issuance of bonds to build electric and water plants and construct a utility system.

In the 1960s Brownsville citizens narrowly defeated a bid by electrical provider Central Power

& Light Co. to buy the Brownsville utility. Following this the city set up Brownsville PUB as a municipally owned utility giving customers control over the management of their utility.

EXECUTIVES

Chief Financial Officer, Leandro G Garcia
Chairman, Nurith Galonsky
Vice-Chairman, Rafael Vela
Secretary, Rafael S Chacon
Accountant, Beatriz Monita

LOCATIONS

HQ: PUBLIC UTILITIES BOARD
1425 ROBINHOOD ST, BROWNSVILLE, TX 785214230
Phone: 956 983-6100
Web: WWW.BROWNSVILLE-PUB.COM

HISTORICAL FINANCIALS

Company Type: Private

Income Statement

FYE: September 30

	REVENUE ($ mil.)	NET INCOME ($ mil.)	NET PROFIT MARGIN	EMPLOYEES
09/15	202	31	15.4%	604
09/09	163	10	6.3%	—
09/08	209	34	16.6%	—
09/06	421	0	—	—
Annual Growth	—	243.8%	—	—

2015 Year-End Financials

Return on assets: 8.7%   Cash ($ mil.): 17
Return on equity: 15.4%
Current ratio: 1.00

PUBLIC UTILITY DISTRICT 1 OF SNOHOMISH COUNTY

Keeping its customers satisfied is priority No. 1 at Public Utility District No. 1 of Snohomish County Washington (Snohomish County PUD) which distributes electricity to 332516 commercial industrial and residential customers in Washington State. The utility the largest PUD in the state with a 2200 sq. ml. service area purchases most of its power supply from third parties (Bonneville Power Administration and other producers. It operates hydroelectric and fossil-fueled power plants and participates in wholesale power transactions to balance its supply load. Snohomish County PUD also serves more than 20000 water utility customers in a 205 sq. ml. service territory via about 375 miles of pipe.

Operations

Snohomish County PUD's operations consist of three systems: the Electric System the Generation System and the Water System.

The Electric System is made up of electric transmission and distribution system.

The Generation System is composed of the company's Jackson Hydroelectric Project and two smaller hydroelectric projects.

The Water System is made up of water distribution system.

Sales and Marketing

The PUD serves three categories of customers: Residential (301639) Commercial (30524) Indus-

trial (76) and other (street lighting temporary lighting etc. - 277).

The company offers a wide range of energy-efficiency solutions for business customers.

Financial Performance

In 2014 the PUD's revenues grew by 3% due to an increase in retail sales as a result of a general and a power contract pass-through rate increase in 2013 and wholesale sales driven by a rise in Megawatt-Hours sold.

The company's net income decreased by 19% due to an increase in operating expenses driven by higher volume of power purchases from the wholesale power market and increased operations expenses due to higher transmission and ancillary costs and costs related to the PUD's effort to implement a new enterprise resource planning system.

In fiscal 2014 the company's operating cash inflow decreased by 10% due to lower net income and changes in working capital.

Strategy

To meet federal and state goals for reducing greenhouse gases the utility is exploring a range of green energy options conservation measures and new power generation activities including geothermal tidal wind and solar power.

In 2015 the PUD's solar program increased its total contribution to 3.7 MW an almost 150% increase over the previous year.

In 2014 the company spent $110 million on electric system capital expenditures up from $94 million in 2013. The company increased the capital programs over the past two years to maintain expand and enhance its electric distribution system.

Company Background

In 2013 solar energy capacity stood at two MW enough to serve 170 homes. More than 350 PUD customers cover part of their electricity needs through their own solar energy units. The PUD's Solar Express program offers financial incentives and technical assistance for solar photovoltaic and solar hot water systems.

In 2012 the company amended a power contract with Hampton Lumber (a fuel supplier since 2007) that will boost the level of biomass energy the utility will receive from the lumber company's Darrington plant. The new agreement will allow Snohomish County PUD to receive up to 2.5 MW of energy from Hampton Lumber enough energy to power about 2000 homes.

Supported by $15.8 million in matching federal stimulus dollars in 2011 Snohomish County PUD completed its first major project as part of a long-term upgrade of its electric grid with smart grid technology. The upgrade includes the installation of more than 160 miles of fiber optic cable and connecting them to 62 substations two radio sites and other utility buildings.

The company began providing water utility service to parts of Snohomish County in 1946. Public Utility District No. 1 of Snohomish County began operating as power utility in 1949 providing publicly owned electric and water utility service to the residents of Snohomish County and Camano Island.

EXECUTIVES

President Send an, Toni Olson
General Manager, Steve Klein
Assistant General Manager Water Resources Division, Kim Moore
Chief Information Officer, Benjamin Beberness
President Board of Commissioners, Kathleen (Kathy) Vaughn
Auditors: BAKER TILLY MADISON WI

LOCATIONS

HQ: PUBLIC UTILITY DISTRICT 1 OF SNOHOMISH COUNTY
2320 CALIFORNIA ST, EVERETT, WA 982013750
Phone: 425 257-9288
Web: WWW.SNOPUD.COM

PRODUCTS/OPERATIONS

2014 Sales

	$ mil.	% of total
Retail sales	554	86
Wholesale sales	59	9
Other	30	5
Total	**645**	**100**

COMPETITORS

Avista
Chelan County PUD
Grant County Public Utility District
Public Utility District No. 1 of Clark County
Puget Energy
Tacoma Public Utilities

HISTORICAL FINANCIALS

Company Type: Private

Income Statement

FYE: December 31

	REVENUE ($ mil.)	NET INCOME ($ mil.)	NET PROFIT MARGIN	EMPLOYEES
12/15	626	52	8.3%	879
12/14	645	56	8.7%	—
12/13	624	68	11.0%	—
Annual Growth	0.2%	(13.1%)	—	—

2015 Year-End Financials

Return on assets: 14.0%   Cash ($ mil.): 75
Return on equity: 8.3%
Current ratio: 1.10

PUBLIC WORKS COMMISSION OF THE CITY OF FAYETTEVILLE

The taps the toilets and the plugs in Fayetteville are all the province of The Public Works Commission of the City of Fayetteville North Carolina (PWC) which is responsible for operating maintaining and upgrading the municipal electric water and wastewater utility systems. PWC distributes electricity to about 79000 residential commercial and industrial customers. The electric utility has 1312 miles of distribution lines 24770 distribution line transformers and more than 46880 poles. The water utility serves more than 83150 customers and has 1340 miles of mains; the wastewater unit serves about 79180 customers and has about 1340 miles of sewer line.

Financial Performance

In fiscal year 2013 PWC saw is revenues rise by 5% due mainly to an increase in electric operating revenues stemming from new 5 year agreement for the lease of the Butler Warner Generation Plant with Duke Energy Progress. The company also saw an increase in wastewater revenues due to higher rates and basic facility charges.PWC's net income dropped by 74% in 2013 due to higher operating expenses (attributed to power supply and generation expenses related to a new power supply contract) and higher depreciation expenses.

Strategy

The multi-utility's strategic plan calls for it to become the most financially sound utility in the state combining low prices with quality maintenance. Looking to cut longterm power costs in 2013 PWC began installing Light Emitting Diode (LED) street lights in nine neighborhoods across Fayetteville as part of a pilot project.

Company Background

The Public Works Commission was formed in 1905 by the State Legislature to operate and supervise the three utilities — electric water and sanitary sewer. Its other jobs per the original charter were to operate the city market stalls and test weights and measures.

EXECUTIVES

Chief Executive Officer, Steven K Blanchard
Board of Directors, James B Rose
Engineer, Marcus R Tunstall
Engineer, Samuel T Stryker
Manager, Joe Holland
Coordinator, Bill Fordham
Auditors: CHERRYBEKAERT LLP FAYETTEVILL

LOCATIONS

HQ: PUBLIC WORKS COMMISSION OF THE CITY OF FAYETTEVILLE
955 OLD WILMINGTON RD, FAYETTEVILLE, NC
283016357
Phone: 910 223-4005
Web: WWW.FAYPWC.COM

HISTORICAL FINANCIALS

Company Type: Private

Income Statement

FYE: June 30

	REVENUE ($ mil.)	NET INCOME ($ mil.)	NET PROFIT MARGIN	EMPLOYEES
06/16	311	22	7.2%	467
06/15	308	22	7.2%	—
06/14	300	14	4.9%	—
06/13	291	15	5.5%	—
Annual Growth	2.2%	11.9%	—	—

2016 Year-End Financials

Return on assets: 8.7%   Cash ($ mil.): 52
Return on equity: 7.2%
Current ratio: 1.30

PUBLIX SUPER MARKETS, INC.

Publix Super Markets tops the list of privately owned grocery operators in the US. By emphasizing service and a family-friendly image over price Publix has outgrown and outperformed its regional rivals. More than two-thirds of its 1136 stores are in Florida but it also operates in Alabama Georgia South Carolina Tennessee and North Carolina (a new market for the company). Publix makes some of its own bakery deli dairy goods and fresh prepared foods at its own manufacturing plants in Florida and Georgia. Also many stores house pharmacies and banks. Founder George Jenkins began offering stock to Publix employees in 1930. Employees own about 31% of Publix which is still run by the Jenkins family.

Operations

Publix stores sell grocery products (dairy produce deli baker meat and seafood) health and beauty care products general merchandise pharmacy products flowers and other products and services. Grocery activities account for 85% of sales.

In addition to more than 1124 supermarkets Publix operates seven distribution centers in Florida and one in Georgia. The company also has ten manufacturing facilities including three dairies two bakeries and a deli plant. Publix's private label items are produced at its facilities and by suppliers.

Geographic Reach

Publix has supermarkets located in Florida Georgia Alabama South Carolina Tennessee and North Carolina.

It restocks store shelves from eight distribution centers — seven in Florida and one in Georgia.

Sales and Marketing

Supermarkets are often in strip shopping centers where Publix is the anchor tennant.

Financial Performance

In fiscal 2016 Publix recorded a further consecutive year of growth. Total revenue of $34.0 billion was up 5.1% on the previous year. Growth was a result of an extra trading week (accounting for 1.9 points of growth) and a 1.9 point increase in comparable store sales. New stores openings contributed as well.

Net income ticked up 3% to $2.0 billion due to higher revenue although as a percentage of sales net income fell a notch to 6.0%. This was due to an increase in promotional activity.

Cash from operating activities climbed 11% to $3.3 billion largely as a timing quirk relating to fiscal year end and the Christmas holidays.

Strategy

Publix's growth strategy is based on net store openings.

In fiscal 2016 it opened 32 stores and closed ten. Seven of the openings were replacement supermarkets while 156 supermarkets were remodeled. The openings added 1.3 million square feet or 2.4% of total square footage. Publix has 29 supermarkets under construction — twelve in Florida seven in North Carolina four in Virginia two in Alabama two in Tennessee one in Georgia and one in South Carolina.

The company opened 28 supermarkets in 2015 including five in North Carolina three in South Carolina three in Alabama and two in Georgia. The company closed nine under-performing stores during the year.

To drive more foot traffic to stores Publix partnered with Starbucks to open franchise outlets in its supermarkets. The first such in-store coffee shop opened in late 2016 with five more scheduled to open in 2017.

HISTORY

George Jenkins age 22 resigned as manager of the Piggly Wiggly grocery in Winter Haven Florida in 1930. With money he had saved to buy a car he opened his own grocery store Publix next door to his old employer. The small store (named after a chain of movie theaters) prospered despite the Depression and in 1935 Jenkins opened another Publix in the same town.

Five years later after the supermarket format had become popular Jenkins closed his two smaller locations and opened a new more modern Publix Market. With pastel colors and electric-eye doors it was also the first US store to feature air conditioning.

Publix Super Markets bought the All-American chain of Lakeland Florida (19 stores) in 1944 and moved its corporate headquarters to that city. The company began offering S&H Green Stamps in 1953 and in 1956 it replaced its original supermarket with a mall featuring an enlarged Publix and a Green Stamp redemption center. Publix expanded into South Florida in the late 1950s.

As Florida's population grew Publix continued to expand opening its 100th store in 1964. Publix was the first grocery chain in the state to use barcode scanners; all its stores had the technology by 1981. The company beat Florida banks in providing ATMs and during the 1980s opened debit card stations.

Publix continued to grow in the 1980s safe from takeover attempts because of its employee ownership. In 1988 it installed the first automated checkout systems in South Florida giving patrons an always-open checkout lane.

The chain stopped offering Green Stamps in 1989 and most of the $19 million decrease in Publix advertising expenditures was attributed to the end of the 36-year promotion. That year after almost six decades "Mr. George" — as founder Jenkins was known — stepped down as chairman in favor of his son Howard. (George died in 1996.)

In 1991 Publix opened its first store outside Florida in Georgia as part of its plan to become a major player in the Southeast. Publix entered South Carolina in 1993 with one supermarket; it also tripled its presence in Georgia to 15 stores.

The United Food and Commercial Workers Union began a campaign in 1994 against alleged gender and racial discrimination in Publix's hiring promotion and compensation policies.

Publix opened its first store in Alabama in 1996. That year a federal judge allowed about 150000 women to join a class-action suit filed in 1995 by 12 women who had sued Publix charging that the company consistently channeled female employees into low-paying jobs with little chance for good promotions. The case which at the time was said to be the biggest sex discrimination lawsuit ever was set to go to trial but in 1997 the company paid $82.5 million to settle and another $3.5 million to settle a complaint of discrimination against black applicants and employees.

Publix promised to change its promotion policies but two more lawsuits alleging discrimination against women and blacks were filed in 1997 and 1998. The suit filed on behalf of the women was denied class-action status in 2000. Later that year the company settled the racial discrimination lawsuit for $10.5 million. Howard Jenkins stepped down as CEO in mid-2001; his cousin Charlie Jenkins took the helm.

Publix introduced the Hispanic-themed Sabor format in 2005 in Kissimmee Florida.

In 2007 the chain began offering seven popular antibiotics free at some 685 Publix Pharmacies. The drugs account for almost 50% of the generic pediatric prescriptions filled at Publix. Also in 2007 the company launched a new store format called GreenWise Market (the name Publix has already given to its store-within-a-store natural/organic sections and private-label line of specialty foods) to court more health-conscious consumers and compete with national organic chains such as Whole Foods.

CEO Charlie Jenkins retired in 2008 and was succeeded by his cousin and Publix president Ed Crenshaw. The company completed the roughly $500 million acquisition of 49 Albertsons stores in Florida the same year.

In May 2011 Publix sold its 36 Crispers restaurants in Florida (acquired in 2007) to Healthy Food Concepts LLC an affiliate of a Florida-based investment group thereby exiting the restaurant business.

Publix entered North Carolina in 2014 with a 56000-square-foot store in the Ballantyne Town Center in Charlotte.

EXECUTIVES

EVP and CFO, David P. Phillips, age 57, $1,051,090 total compensation

SVP General Counsel and Secretary, John A. Attaway, age 58, $690,310 total compensation

SVP, David E. Bornmann, age 59, $488,300 total compensation

President CEO and Director, Randall T. (Todd) Jones, age 54, $1,688,750 total compensation

SVP and CIO, Laurie Z. Douglas, age 53, $890,255 total compensation

Manager Government Relations, Shane Kunze

Vice Chairman, Hoyt R. (Barney) Barnett, age 74

President and Director, William E. (Ed) Crenshaw, age 66

Auditors: KPMG LLP TAMPA FLORIDA

LOCATIONS

HQ: PUBLIX SUPER MARKETS, INC.
3300 PUBLIX CORP PKWY, LAKELAND, FL
338113311
Phone: 863 688-1188
Web: WWW.PUBLIX.COM

2016 Supermarkets

	No.
Florida	774
Georgia	184
Alabama	63
South Carolina	57
Tennessee	39
North Carolina	19
Total	**1,136**

PRODUCTS/OPERATIONS

2016 Sales

	% of total
Grocery	84
Other	16
Total	**100**

Selected Supermarket Departments

Bakery
Dairy
Deli
Floral
Groceries
Health and beauty care
Meat
Pharmacy
Produce
Seafood
Foods Processed
Baked goods
Dairy products
Deli items

COMPETITORS

ALDI	Kroger
ALDI	Rite Aid
CVS	Rite Aid
CVS	Sedano's
Costco Wholesale	Sedano's
Costco Wholesale	Southeastern Grocers
Food Lion	Southeastern Grocers
Food Lion	The Pantry
IGA	The Pantry
IGA	Wal-Mart
Ingles Markets	Wal-Mart
Ingles Markets	Walgreen
Kmart	Walgreen
Kmart	Whole Foods
Kroger	Whole Foods

HISTORICAL FINANCIALS

Company Type: Private

Income Statement

FYE: December 31

	REVENUE ($ mil.)	NET INCOME ($ mil.)	NET PROFIT MARGIN	EMPLOYEES
12/16	34,274	2,025	5.9%	191,000
12/15	32,618	1,965	6.0%	—
12/14	30,802	1,735	5.6%	—
12/12	27,706	1,552	5.6%	—
Annual Growth	**5.5%**	**6.9%**	**—**	**—**

2016 Year-End Financials

Return on assets: 4.7%
Return on equity: 5.9%
Current ratio: 0.40

Cash ($ mil.): 438

PUGET ENERGY, INC.

A sound investment Puget Energy is the holding company for one of Washington State's largest utilities Puget Sound Energy. The utility provides electricity to more than 1.1 million customers and natural gas to some 814600 customers in about 10 counties in western Washington. Puget Sound Energy owns fossil-fueled and hydroelectric plants as well as wind farms with a cumulative total of 4887 power transmission lines and 20430 miles of distribution lines. Puget Sound Energy also has about 12190 miles of gas mains and about 13655 miles of gas service lines.

Operations

Puget Energy is the direct parent company of Puget Sound Energy the oldest and largest electric and natural gas utility headquartered in the state of Washington. It is primarily engaged in the business of electric transmission distribution generation and natural gas distribution.

Electricity accounts for more than 70% of Puget Sound Energy's revenues.

Geographic Reach

The utility serves customers in some 10 counties in western Washington (including Island King Kitsap Kittitas Lewis Pierce Skagit Snohomish Thurston and Whatcom) covering 6000 square miles.

About 64% of natural gas purchased for Puget Energy?s power portfolio comes from British Columbia 20% from Alberta and 16% from the US. Approximately 56% of natural gas purchased by Puget Energy for its natural gas customers comes from British Columbia 21% from Alberta and 23% from the US.

Sales and Marketing

The company serves 1.7 million residential 181400 commercial and about 5780 industrial customers.

Financial Performance

Puget Energy saw its utility?s revenues rise by 2% in 2016 to $3.2 billion primarily due to a $81 increase in retail power sales to residential and commercial customers (thanks to higher rates) and a $29 million rise in decoupling wholesale power and transportation revenues. Natural gas revenues dropped by $57 million primarily due to lower due a retail rate reduction.

The company?s net income increased by 30% due to a decrease of $42.6 million of residential exchange credits and of $34.5 million of electric generation fuel costs which more than offset an increase of $32.1 million of purchased electricity costs.

Purchased natural gas expense declined by $89.4 million due to lower natural gas costs partially offset by a 5% increase in usage.

In 2016 Puget Energy's operating cash flow increased to $80.1 million (up from $76.4 million a year earlier) due to higher cash flow from accounts receivable and unbilled revenue (resulting from an improved collections strategy) and an increase in cash flow from deferred income taxes and tax credits partially offset by a loss on derivative instruments.

Strategy

The company's strategy emphasizes meeting the energy needs of the growing Puget Sound Energy customer base through incremental cost-effective energy conservation low-cost procurement of traditional energy resources (including by producing and generating electricity and natural gas) and far-sighted investment in energy-delivery infrastructure.

The company's wholesale market transactions and Puget Sound Energy's related hedging strategies are focused on reducing costs and risks where feasible thus reducing volatility in costs in the portfolio.

In 2016 Puget Sound Energy and the City of Bellevue launched Urban Smart Bellevue to reduce wasted energy and establish Bellevue?s thriving business community as a US leader in sustainable energy use.

Company Background

Puget Energy was incorporated in the state of Washington in 1999.

In 2009 Puget Holdings LLC a consortium led by Australian bank unit Macquarie Infrastructure Partners acquired Puget Energy for $7.4 billion. The deal strengthened Puget Energy's access to cash to pay down debt and to fund future growth. Related to that purchase the company invested $5 billion between 2008 and 2013 to add to and/or improve the company's aging infrastructure.

EXECUTIVES

SVP and Chief Administrative Officer, Marla D. Mellies, age 56, $306,901 total compensation

President and CEO, Kimberly J. Harris, age 52, $900,000 total compensation

SVP and CFO, Daniel A. Doyle, age 58, $508,322 total compensation

SVP and Chief Customer Officer, Philip K. (Phil) Bussey, $304,668 total compensation

SVP General Counsel and Chief Ethics and Compliance Officer, Steve R. Secrist, age 55, $383,085 total compensation

SVP Operations, Booga K. Gilbertson

VP and CIO, Margaret F. Hopkins

Vice President Corporate Affairs, Andy Wappler

Chief Sales Officer, Gary Veach

Chairman, Steven W. Hooper

Director Assistant Treasurer at Puget Sound Energy, Brandon Lohse

Auditors: PRICEWATERHOUSECOOPERS LLP SE

LOCATIONS

HQ: PUGET ENERGY, INC.
10885 NE 4TH ST STE 1200, BELLEVUE, WA
980045591
Phone: 425 454-6363
Web: WWW.PUGETENERGY.COM

PRODUCTS/OPERATIONS

2016 Sales

	$ mil.	% of total
Electric	2,238	71
Natural gas	890	28
Other	35	1
Total	**3,164**	**100**

HISTORICAL FINANCIALS

Company Type: Private

Income Statement
FYE: December 31

	REVENUE ($ mil.)	NET INCOME ($ mil.)	NET PROFIT MARGIN	EMPLOYEES
12/16	3,164	312	9.9%	2,700
12/15	3,092	241	7.8%	—
12/14	3,113	171	5.5%	—
12/13	3,187	285	9.0%	—
Annual Growth	(0.2%)	3.1%	—	—

2016 Year-End Financials

Return on assets: 10.0%
Return on equity: 9.9%
Current ratio: 0.40

Cash ($ mil.): 28

PUGET SOUND ENERGY, INC.

EXECUTIVES

Sr V Pres-chief Adm Officer, Marla D Mellies
Manager Government Relations, William Einstein
Auditors: PRICEWATERHOUSECOOPERS LLP SE

LOCATIONS

HQ: PUGET SOUND ENERGY, INC.
  10885 NE 4TH ST STE 1200, BELLEVUE, WA
  980045591
Phone: 425 454-6363
Web: WWW.PSE.COM

HISTORICAL FINANCIALS

Company Type: Private

Income Statement
FYE: December 31

	REVENUE ($ mil.)	NET INCOME ($ mil.)	NET PROFIT MARGIN	EMPLOYEES
12/16	3,164	380	12.0%	2,700
12/15	3,093	304	9.8%	—
12/14	3,116	236	7.6%	—
12/13	3,187	356	11.2%	—
Annual Growth	(0.2%)	2.2%	—	—

2016 Year-End Financials

Return on assets: 10.0%
Return on equity: 12.0%
Current ratio: 0.40

Cash ($ mil.): 28

PURDUE RESEARCH FOUNDATION

EXECUTIVES

President, Brian E Edelman
Board of Directors, Judith A Hall
Financial Executive, Shirley A Drake
Board of Directors, Alok Chaturvedi
Executive Secretary, Karen Betz
Auditors: CROWE HORWATH LLP INDIANAPOLI

LOCATIONS

HQ: PURDUE RESEARCH FOUNDATION
  1281 WIN HENTSCHEL BLVD, WEST LAFAYETTE, IN
  479064182
Phone: 765 588-3470

HISTORICAL FINANCIALS

Company Type: Private

Income Statement
FYE: June 30

	REVENUE ($ mil.)	NET INCOME ($ mil.)	NET PROFIT MARGIN	EMPLOYEES
06/15	187	38	20.3%	85
06/14	130	45	35.0%	—
06/13	137	60	44.1%	—
06/12	19	(43)	—	—
Annual Growth	112.9%	—	—	—

2015 Year-End Financials

Return on assets: 10.1%
Return on equity: 20.3%
Current ratio: —

Cash ($ mil.): 12

PUYALLUP SCHOOL DISTRICT

EXECUTIVES

Superintendent, Tim Yeomans
Director, Audrie Shagren

LOCATIONS

HQ: PUYALLUP SCHOOL DISTRICT
  302 2ND ST SE, PUYALLUP, WA 983723220
Phone: 253 840-8971
Web: WWW.PUYALLUP.K12.WA.US

HISTORICAL FINANCIALS

Company Type: Private

Income Statement
FYE: August 31

	REVENUE ($ mil.)	NET INCOME ($ mil.)	NET PROFIT MARGIN	EMPLOYEES
08/16	282	94	33.3%	3,000
08/15	252	10	4.2%	—
08/14	233	(5)	—	—
08/13	222	2	1.3%	—
Annual Growth	8.3%	222.9%	—	—

2016 Year-End Financials

Return on assets: 2.2%
Return on equity: 33.3%
Current ratio: —

Cash ($ mil.): 4

PYCO INDUSTRIES, INC.

Ginning up business is the secret to this vegetable oil producer's success. PYCO Industries is said to be the largest cotton seed co-op to serve the southern US. The Texas-based cooperative comprising more than 60-member gins processes cottonseed for a broad market through two cottonseed oil mills. Its cottonseed oil is shipped to food manufacturers and other foodservice customers across the country. The co-op also markets whole cottonseed as well as the by-products of crushing cottonseed such as cottonseed hulls and cottonseed meal for beef and dairy cattle feed. Cottonseed linters another byproduct are used by manufacturers of mattresses and upholstery padding paper and plastics and other products.

PYCO's operations include subsidiary Plainsman Switching Company (PSC) a shortline railroad connection with the BNSF Railroad and the Union Pacific Railroad. PSC ships and receives a variety of commodities in Lubbock including grain chemicals lumber as well as cotton seed and cottonseed oil. It also handles wind turbine components used to construct wind energy farms.

In early 2010 PYCO sold its Greenwood Mississippi-based cottonseed oil mill shutdown since early 2009. Mississippi cotton gin Delta Oil Mill acquired the plant along with its storage facilities.

In 2011 a historic drought drove the worst dryland cotton crop on record. The impact rippled across the industry. PYCO reported enough carryover seed from prior plentiful crops along with the immediate meager turnout to keep running. However the downturn in production coupled with another year of rain-starved crops threatens to force a cut to operations by some 50%. The tight situation follows increasing interest in the culinary and textile application of cottonseed oil and the by-products fueled by episodes on the History Channel and America's Heartland a nationally distributed program.

EXECUTIVES

President, Robert Lacy
Board of Directors, Burt Heinrich
Personnel Manager, Jake Bentley
Financial Executive, Jerrod Drinnon
Manager, Travis Schwertner
General Manager, Walt Stokes
Manager, Bobby Fair
Auditors: D WILLIAMS & CO PC LUBBO

LOCATIONS

HQ: PYCO INDUSTRIES, INC.
  2901 AVENUE A, LUBBOCK, TX 794042231
Phone: 806 747-3434
Web: WWW.PYCOINDUSTRIESINC.COM

PRODUCTS/OPERATIONS

Selected Products
Hulls
  Feed for cattle
  Furfural
  Oil well drilling mud
Linters
  Cellulose esters and ethers
  Cellulose nitrate
  Felts
  Films
  Food casings
  Medical grade cotton
  Paper
  Yarns
Meal
  Feed
  Fertilizer
Oil

Fatty acids
Glycerine
Refined
Whole seed
Feed for cattle

COMPETITORS

ADM   Cargill

HISTORICAL FINANCIALS
Company Type: Private

Income Statement
FYE: September 30

	REVENUE ($ mil.)	NET INCOME ($ mil.)	NET PROFIT MARGIN	EMPLOYEES
09/16	201	23	11.8%	160
09/15	161	30	18.9%	—
09/14	184	22	12.4%	—
09/13	176	18	10.6%	—
Annual Growth	4.6%	8.4%	—	—

2016 Year-End Financials
Return on assets: 0.8%   Cash ($ mil.): 2
Return on equity: 11.8%
Current ratio: 0.40

QUAKER VALLEY FOODS, INC.

Quaker Valley Foods (QVF) is known by friends high and low for its take-out fresh and frozen staples. The food distributor makes daily deliveries of meat and other provisions to foodservice customers across the Northeast US. QVF a member of the UNIPRO Foodservice coop offers beef pork poultry frozen seafood imported meats (mutton and goat) cheeses salads and other items from its Philadelphia warehouse. Customers range from wholesalers and jobbers to independent retail and wholesale groceries and major supermarket chains. Its vendors include Hormel Swift Packerland Carolina Turkey Tyson Alpine Lace and Land O' Lakes. QVF was started by two brothers-in-law in 1975 and is led by its founders' sons.

EXECUTIVES

President, Wayne Hudis
Marketing Manager, Jim Baraldi
Auditors: KREISCHER MILLER HORSHAM PA

LOCATIONS

HQ: QUAKER VALLEY FOODS, INC.
2701 RED LION RD, PHILADELPHIA, PA 191541038
Phone: 215 992-0900
Web: WWW.QUAKERVALLEYFOODS.COM

PRODUCTS/OPERATIONS

Selected Products
Beef
Deli and provisions
Goats
Lamb
Mutton imported
Pork
Poultry
Seafood frozen

COMPETITORS

Associated Wholesale   SUPERVALU
  Grocers   Schiff's
C&S Wholesale   Sysco
Feesers   US Foods

McLane   Vista Food Exchange
Meadowbrook Meat
  Company

HISTORICAL FINANCIALS
Company Type: Private

Income Statement
FYE: January 2

	REVENUE ($ mil.)	NET INCOME ($ mil.)	NET PROFIT MARGIN	EMPLOYEES
01/16*	239	2	0.8%	145
12/11	195	0	0.2%	—
01/11	177	0	0.2%	—
01/10	1,546	0	0.0%	—
Annual Growth	(26.7%)	323.3%	—	—

*Fiscal year change

2016 Year-End Financials
Return on assets: 3.7%   Cash ($ mil.): —
Return on equity: 0.8%
Current ratio: 0.70

QUEEN OF THE VALLEY MEDICAL CENTER

The Queen of the Valley Medical Center reigns over the whole of Napa Valley. The 190-bed hospital provides acute and tertiary care to the residents of California's Napa County. It operates a level III trauma center and provides emergency surgery and wound care services as well as specialty family work health nutritional and rehabilitation services. "The Queen" as it is known colloquially operates regional cancer orthopedic women's and heart centers as well as the Napa Valley Imaging Center and the Napa Valley Women's Healthcare Center. Queen of the Valley Medical Center is part of St. Joseph Health.

Current expansion efforts at Queen of the Valley Medical Center include construction of a $30 million three-story diagnostic and surgical pavilion. The new center will add high-tech surgical suites and diagnostic laboratory and imaging facilities as well as private ICU rooms. The hospital is also developing a new neuroscience center.

The medical center was founded in 1958 by the Sisters of St. Joseph of Orange. It expanded its facilities a number of times over the years. For instance in 2006 the hospital added a wellness center and a unit dedicated to maternal and infant care. These expansion efforts prompted a name change from Queen of the Valley Hospital to Queen of the Valley Medical Center in 2007 to reflect the facility's expanded offerings and its emphasis on not just medical care but also community-based outreach and prevention services.

EXECUTIVES

Vice President Marketing Private Programs,
  Joseph Carrillo
Auditors: ERNST & YOUNG US LLP SAN DIEG

LOCATIONS

HQ: QUEEN OF THE VALLEY MEDICAL CENTER
1000 TRANCAS ST, NAPA, CA 945582906
Phone: 707 252-4411
Web: WWW.THEQUEEN.ORG

COMPETITORS

Adventist Health System West
  Community Hospital of the Monterey Peninsula
Dignity Health

HCA
John Muir Health
Providence St. Joseph Health
Stanford Health Care
Sutter Health
Tenet Healthcare
UCSF Medical
Western Medical Center - Santa Ana

HISTORICAL FINANCIALS
Company Type: Private

Income Statement
FYE: June 30

	REVENUE ($ mil.)	NET INCOME ($ mil.)	NET PROFIT MARGIN	EMPLOYEES
06/15	243	(1)	—	1,070
06/14	249	(4)	—	—
06/13	285	23	8.1%	—
06/10	276	25	9.1%	—
Annual Growth	(2.5%)	—	—	—

2015 Year-End Financials
Return on assets: —   Cash ($ mil.): 40
Return on equity: (-0.7%)
Current ratio: 4.20

QUINNIPIAC UNIVERSITY

At Quinnipiac University the first thing you may have to learn is how to pronounce it (for the record it's KWIN-uh-pe-ack). The private university offers a variety of liberal arts undergraduate programs as well as graduate programs in selected professional fields (business education health sciences communications arts and sciences nursing and law) to some 9000 students with a student-to-faculty ration of 16 to 1. It often appears on lists of top colleges including those published by U.S. News & World Report. The university known to political junkies and others for its polling operation includes eight schools and colleges across three Connecticut campuses (Mount Carmel York Hill and North Haven).

Operations

Quinnipiac offers more than 50 undergraduate majors and more than 20 graduate programs. For fiscal year 2015-2016 its tuition and fees are $42270.

Geographic Reach

The school's York Hill campus is home to the TD Bank Sports Center; its North Haven campus houses the Center for Medicine Nursing and Health Sciences which includes the School of Health Sciences the Frank H. Netter MD School of Medicine and the School of Nursing.

Strategy

In 2014 Quinnipiac launched an online graduate business program as well as a master's program in sports journalism. With the 2013 opening of the Frank H. Netter MD School of Medicine the university became one of fewer than 100 with both a law school and a medical school on campus.

Company Background

Originally named the Connecticut College of Commerce the school was founded in 1929 by Samuel W. Tator as a small business college awarding associate's degrees. The college changed its name in 1951 to Quinnipiac College commemorating the early Indian settlers who made their home in and around the New Haven Connecticut harbor area.

EXECUTIVES

Chairman, Terry W Goodwim

LOCATIONS

HQ: QUINNIPIAC UNIVERSITY
275 MOUNT CARMEL AVE, HAMDEN, CT 065181908
Phone: 203 582-8200
Web: WWW.QUINNIPIAC.EDU

PRODUCTS/OPERATIONS

Selected Schools
College of Arts and Sciences
Schools of Business and Engineering
School of Communications
School of Education
School of Law
School of Health Sciences
School of Nursing

HISTORICAL FINANCIALS

Company Type: Private

Income Statement

FYE: June 30

	REVENUE ($ mil.)	NET INCOME ($ mil.)	NET PROFIT MARGIN	EMPLOYEES
06/15	416	29	7.1%	900
06/13	376	45	12.2%	—
06/10	290	45	15.6%	—
Annual Growth	7.4%	(8.1%)	—	—

2015 Year-End Financials

Return on assets: 9.1%
Return on equity: 7.1%
Current ratio: —

Cash ($ mil.): 1

QVC, INC.

The phones are ringing off the hook at television home shopping company QVC. QVC (its name stands for "quality value and convenience") offers about 1000 items each week to TV-tied consumer shoppers. Merchandise includes apparel cosmetics electronics housewares jewelry and toys. It broadcasts 24 hours a day; viewers call in their orders to one of its three US call centers. If you can't find what you're shopping for on the tube it also sells online at QVC.com through mobile apps and some half dozen outlet stores in four states. The company has shopping channels in Germany Japan Italy and the UK. QVC is a subsidiary of shopping and travel site operator Liberty Interactive.

Operations

The video and e-commerce retailer has operations in the US the UK Germany Italy and Japan. Recognizing growth potential in China QVC established a joint venture there in 2012 with China's government-owned radio division China National Radio (CNR).

Geographic Reach

The US is QVC's largest market contributing two-thirds of its total sales followed by Japan (15%) and Germany (11%). The UK and the company's newest market Italy make up the rest. QVC operates eight distribution centers and eight call centers worldwide.

Sales and Marketing

QVC distributes its programming through affiliation agreements with many television providers including Comcast Time Warner Cable DIRECTV and DISH Network in the US; JCN Jupiter Telecommunications in Japan; Kabel Deutschland in Germany; Sky plc and Virgin Media in the UK; and Telecom Italia Media Broadcasting in Italy.

While the phones are still ringing at QVC call centers business is booming on its QVC.com website. In 2012 the company's global e-commerce sales totaled $2.9 billion or 34% of its consolidated sales.

Financial Performance

After a couple of tough years during the global recession QVC is solidly back in sales growth mode. In 2012 global sales topped $8.5 billion up 3% versus 2011 after increasing by 6% in the prior annual comparison. Sales increased in all of the retailer's markets with the exception of Germany where sales fell by 10%. Japan posted an 11% gain in sales while the US and UK saw more modest sales gains. The company credited its revenue growth to an 3% increase in average selling price and an increase in shipping and handling revenue.

QVC's profitability is also on the rise with operating income up 11% in 2012 versus 2011 to nearly $1.3 billion.

Strategy

From its roots in television shopping QVC's goal is to entice buyers across all forms of media including TV the Internet and mobile devices. With about 90% of its business coming from repeat customers the company is looking to international markets for additional customers. China is one such place. QVC entered China in 2012 through a Beijing-based joint venture called CNR Home Shopping Co. Ltd. (CNRS). QVC holds a 49% stake while partner China National Radio owns the remaining 51%. The JV operates a multimedia retailing business in China through the CNR Mall TV shopping channel and its e-commerce site. The CNR Mall channel reaches about 48 million homes in China.

Mergers and Acquisitions

QVC's parent company Liberty Interactive agreed to buy the 62% of HSN Inc. it didn't own for about $2.1 billion in an all-stock deal in 2017.The deal is a bet that bigger is better in battling Amazon.com and other online retailers. The companies said larger scale will help them develop ecommerce mobile and over-the-top platforms optimize content across five networks and cross market among the networks. The HSN assets are to be packaged with QVC and Zulily an ecommerce company owned by Liberty in an asset-backed spin off from Liberty late in 2017. The HSN acquisition was expected to close by the end of 2017.

In mid-2015 QVC purchased Zulily in a $2.4 billion deal to gain access to millennial moms.

EXECUTIVES

President and CEO, Michael (Mike) George, age 55
Svp Quality Assurance And Inbound Supply Chain, Mike Appleby
Vice President Broadcast Technology, Todd Sprinkle
Senior Vice President and Controller, John John Misko
Vice President Distribution Operations, Jim Reid
Vice President Procurement, Jeff Nord
Vice President of Sales, Julie Batenburg
Vice President Digital Media, Courtney Cason
Vice President, Patti Reilly
Vice President Customer Servic, Lisa Norden
Senior Vice President And General Counsel, Larry Hayes
Area Vice President, Kristi Hanifin
Secretary, Joan Ruffenach
Auditors: KPMG LLP PHILADELPHIA PENNSY

LOCATIONS

HQ: QVC, INC.
1200 WILSON DR, WEST CHESTER, PA 193804262
Phone: 484 701-1000
Web: WWW.QVC.COM

2016 Sales

	$ mil.	% of total
QVC-U.S.	6,120	70
QVC-International	2,562	30
Total	**8,682**	**100**

COMPETITORS

Access TV	Macy's
Alticor	Modern Times Group AB
Amazon.com	Overstock.com
Blue Nile Inc.	Priceline
Bluestem Brands	Provell
EVINE Live	Sears
HSN	Walmart.com
J. C. Penney	

HISTORICAL FINANCIALS

Company Type: Private

Income Statement

FYE: December 31

	REVENUE ($ mil.)	NET INCOME ($ mil.)	NET PROFIT MARGIN	EMPLOYEES
12/16	8,682	642	7.4%	17,700
12/15	8,743	662	7.6%	—
12/14	8,801	633	7.2%	—
12/13	8,623	633	7.3%	—
Annual Growth	0.2%	0.5%	—	—

2016 Year-End Financials

Return on assets: 7.8%
Return on equity: 7.4%
Current ratio: 1.00

Cash ($ mil.): 284

R. M. PARKS, INC.

EXECUTIVES

President, R M Parks
Manager, Jason Patterson
Account Manager, Sherrill Morris
Auditors: GUMBINER SAVETT INC SANTA MO

LOCATIONS

HQ: R. M. PARKS, INC.
1061 N MAIN ST, PORTERVILLE, CA 932571686
Phone: 559 784-2384

HISTORICAL FINANCIALS

Company Type: Private

Income Statement

FYE: October 31

	REVENUE ($ mil.)	NET INCOME ($ mil.)	NET PROFIT MARGIN	EMPLOYEES
10/16	448	0	0.2%	4
10/15	534	0	0.2%	—
10/14	612	0	0.0%	—
10/13	615	0	0.1%	—
Annual Growth	(10.0%)	(0.6%)	—	—

2016 Year-End Financials

Return on assets: 1.8%
Return on equity: 0.2%
Current ratio: 0.70

Cash ($ mil.): 1

R.S. HUGHES COMPANY, INC.

R.S. Hughes distributes the stuff that holds the world together — duct tape that is — plus a lot more. Established in 1954 the employee-owned company maintains some 45 warehouse locations in the US and Mexico. It supplies adhesives (epoxies aerosols hot glues silicones) electrical specialties (tubing terminals films tape and barriers) safety products (glasses ear plugs masks) tapes (masking foam vinyl cloth foil duct joining) and abrasives (roll disc brush wheel belt and air tools). R.S. Hughes also distributes labels and signs (printable labels and tags safety signs) and aerosols and coatings (WD-40 paints lubricants oils cleaners).

EXECUTIVES

Chief Executive Officer, Robert McCollum
Board of Directors, Ken McCormick
Vice-President, Michael Page
Director, Stan Basnett
Financial Executive, Thomas Smith
Auditors: MOSS ADAMS LLP CAMPBELL CALI

LOCATIONS

HQ: R.S. HUGHES COMPANY, INC.
1162 SONORA CT, SUNNYVALE, CA 940865378
Phone: 408 739-3211
Web: WWW.SAUNDERSCORP.COM

PRODUCTS/OPERATIONS

Selected Products
Adhesives
Abrasive power tools
Aerosol paints and lubricants
Coatings
Labels
Printers
Sealants
Tapes

COMPETITORS

DXP Enterprises   W.W. Grainger
HD Supply
Industrial
  Distribution Group

HISTORICAL FINANCIALS

Company Type: Private

Income Statement   FYE: October 2

	REVENUE ($ mil.)	NET INCOME ($ mil.)	NET PROFIT MARGIN	EMPLOYEES
10/16*	329	16	5.0%	505
09/15	323	16	5.1%	—
09/14	302	15	5.1%	—
09/13	281	15	5.5%	—
Annual Growth	5.4%	2.5%	—	—

*Fiscal year change

2016 Year-End Financials
Return on assets: 3.1% Cash ($ mil.): 19
Return on equity: 5.0%
Current ratio: 3.50

RACETRAC PETROLEUM, INC.

RaceTrac Petroleum hopes it's a popular pit stop for gasoline and snacks in the South. The company operates more than 600 gas stations and convenience stores in 10 southern US states under the RaceTrac and RaceWay names. (RaceWay stores are operated by independent contractors.) The chain plans to grow by expanding its store count by about 10% a year. Carl Bolch founded RaceTrac in Missouri in 1934. His son chairman Carl Bolch Jr. moved the company into high-volume gas stations with long self-service islands that can serve as many as two dozen vehicles at one time. RaceTrac's convenience stores sell fresh deli food and offer some fast-food fare. The Bolch family owns and runs the company.

Geographic Reach

Atlanta-based RaceTrac Petroleum operates stores in Alabama Florida Georgia Louisiana Kentucky Mississippi North Carolina South Carolina Tennessee and Texas.

Financial Performance

One of the largest private companies in the US Racetrac Petroleum's stores rang up more than $9 billion in sales in 2012.

Strategy

RaceTrac prefers to build its own stores from the ground up rather than grow through acquisitions. Indeed in the past 16 years the company has only bought one store.Recently RaceTrac has been increasing the number of independently-operated RaceWay stores in its portfolio. (While the RaceWay stores are operated by independent contractors RaceTrac stills owns and controls the gasoline business and real estate.) It has also consolidated its company-operated stores into four key markets: Atlanta Dallas Florida and Louisiana. In 2014 the chain is building new stores in key markets such as Florida and adding services. In 2013 it partnered with Fifth Third Bancorp to install ATMs at 225 RaceTrac convenience stores in Georgia and Florida.

RaceTrac Petroleum got a new leader Allison Moran in 2013. Moran who led the RaceTrac company-operated stores division before her promotion to CEO succeeded Carl Bloch Jr. (who retained the chairman's title). Moran is Bloch's eldest daughter.

In 2015 RaceTrac sold five retail operations in Florida to Town Star Holdings an affiliate of Junonia Capital LLC. Four of the convenience stores are in the Orlando area with the other in Jacksonville.

EXECUTIVES

President, Billy Milam
VP Information Systems, Will Alexander
Chief Supply Officer, Max McBrayer
Chairman and CEO, Carl E. Bolch
Auditors: GRANT THORNTON LLP ATLANTA G

LOCATIONS

HQ: RACETRAC PETROLEUM, INC.
3225 CUMBERLAND BLVD SE # 100, ATLANTA, GA 303396407
Phone: 770 850-3491
Web: WWW.RACETRAC.COM

COMPETITORS

7-Eleven   Love's Country Stores
Chevron   Motiva Enterprises
Couche-Tard   Pilot Corporation
Cumberland Farms   Pilot Flying J

E-Z Mart Stores   QuikTrip
Exxon Mobil   The Pantry
Gate Petroleum

HISTORICAL FINANCIALS

Company Type: Private

Income Statement   FYE: December 31

	REVENUE ($ mil.)	NET INCOME ($ mil.)	NET PROFIT MARGIN	EMPLOYEES
12/15	7,501	107	1.4%	3,479
12/14	9,101	161	1.8%	—
12/13	8,843	122	1.4%	—
12/12	0	55	—	—
Annual Growth	—	24.3%	—	—

2015 Year-End Financials
Return on assets: — Cash ($ mil.): 193
Return on equity: 1.4%
Current ratio: 0.70

RACINE UNIFIED SCHOOL DISTRICT

EXECUTIVES

Superintendent, Ann Laing
Director, Tania Hall

LOCATIONS

HQ: RACINE UNIFIED SCHOOL DISTRICT
3109 MOUNT PLEASANT ST, RACINE, WI 534041511
Phone: 262 635-5600
Web: WWW.RACINE.K12.WI.US

HISTORICAL FINANCIALS

Company Type: Private

Income Statement   FYE: June 30

	REVENUE ($ mil.)	NET INCOME ($ mil.)	NET PROFIT MARGIN	EMPLOYEES
06/16	283	0	0.3%	2,500
06/06	207	(1)	—	—
06/05	0	0	—	—
06/04	207	(1)	—	—
Annual Growth	2.6%	—	—	—

RADY CHILDREN'S HOSPITAL-SAN DIEGO

Rady Children's Hospital-San Diego handles the big injuries of pint-sized patients. Serving as the region's only pediatric trauma center the nonprofit hospital boasts more than 520 beds. As part of its services Rady Children's Hospital-San Diego offers comprehensive pediatric care including surgical services convalescent care a neonatal intensive care unit and orthopedic services. Across its service area the hospital also operates about 25 satellite centers that provide such primary and specialized care services as physical therapy and hearing diagnostics. Rady Children's Hospital a teaching hos-

pital affiliated with the University of California San Diego Medical School was founded in 1954.

Operations

Rady Children's operates its own 36-bed emergency department — The Sam S. and Rose Stein Emergency Care Center — that each day sees up to 300 patients. It is the only regional emergency center solely dedicated and equipped to care for children. The hospital also operates California's only pediatric skilled nursing facility — The Helen Bernardy Center — to provide 24-hour care to disabled and medically fragile children in a homelike environment.

For treating non-life-or-limb-threatening injuries and illnesses the hospital operates neighborhood urgent care centers in Escondido La Mesa Oceanside and San Diego.

Through its medical school affiliation Rady Children's engages in nearly 500 clinical trials in all pediatric specialties. It collaborates with University of California San Diego the Sanford-Burnham Medical Research Institute The Scripps Research Institute the Salk Institute for Biological Studies and St. Jude Children's Research Hospital. Specialized research facilities on campus include the Autism Discovery Institute the Blair L. Sadler Center for Quality and the Child and Adolescent Services Research Center.

The hospital operates a LEED-certified Acute Care Pavilion which holds a neonatal intensive care unit the Peckham Center for Cancer and Blood Disorders and the Warren Family Surgical Center. It serves those suffering from eating disorders through its inpatient center to allow for intensive psychiatric therapy for patients with anorexia and bulimia and to aid families with home care.

In 2014 the hospital had 18782 inpatient admissions 230383 outpatient visits nearly 85000 emergency department visits and more than 54000 urgent care visits. It performed about 20000 surgeries.

Geographic Reach

Rady Children's Hospital serves as the pediatric medical center that caters to the California region of San Diego Imperial and southern Riverside counties. It has more than 30 offices throughout San Diego and southern Riverside counties with satellite locations in Chula Vista El Centro Encinitas Escondido La Jolla La Mesa Murrieta Oceanside San Diego and Solana Beach.

EXECUTIVES

Chairman Rady Pediatric Genomics and Systems Medicine Institute, David F. Hale, age 68
President and CEO Rady Pediatric Genomics and Systems Medicine Institute, Stephen Kingsmore
EVP and Chief Administrative Officer, Margareta E. (Meg) Norton
President and CEO, Donald Kearns
VP and CIO, Albert Oriol
VP and Chief Nursing Executive, Mary Fagan
Chief Medical Officer, Irvin A. Kaufman
SVP and COO, Nicholas Holmes
Executive Director Rady Children's Hospital Foundation and SVP Rady Children's Hospital, Stephen Jennings
Physician-in-Chief and Chief Scientific Officer and Chairman of Pediatrics UC San Diego, Gabriel G. Haddad
SVP Rady Children's Specialists of San Diego, Herb Kimmons
Respiratory Therapy Director, Toni Popien
Medical Director, Sara Marchese
Vice Chairman, Michael P. (Mike) Peckham
Chairman, Theodore D. (Ted) Roth, age 66
Board Member, Leonard Kornreich

LOCATIONS

HQ: RADY CHILDREN'S HOSPITAL-SAN DIEGO
3020 CHILDRENS WAY, SAN DIEGO, CA 921234223
Phone: 858 576-1700
Web: WWW.RCHSD.ORG

Selected Satellite Locations
Chula Vista
El Centro
Encinitas
Escondido
La Jolla
La Mesa
Murrieta
Oceanside
San Diego
Solana Beach

PRODUCTS/OPERATIONS

Selected Services
Allergy/Immunology
Attention Deficit Hyperactivity Disorder
Audiology/Hearing
Autism Discovery Institute
Behavioral Health
Brachial Plexus Clinic
Cancer & Blood Disorders
Cardiology
Cardiovascular Surgery
Celiac Disease Clinic
Center for Healthier Communities
Cerebral Palsy Center
Chadwick Center For Children & Families
Child & Adolescent Psychiatry Services (CAPS)
Child & Adolescent Services Research Center (CASRC)
Child Life Services
Children's Care Connection (C3)
Children's Hospital Emergency Transport (CHET)
Cleft Palate Clinic
Craniofacial Disorders
Critical Care
Cystic Fibrosis Center
Dental Surgery
Dermatology
Developmental Evaluation Clinic
Developmental-Behavioral Pediatrics
Developmental Screening & Enhancement Program (DSEP)
Developmental Services
Down Syndrome Center
Eating Disorders/
Medical-Behavioral Disorders Unit
Emergency Medicine
Endocrinology/Diabetes
Fatty Liver Clinic
Feeding Team
Gastroenterology Hepatology & Nutrition
Genetics/Dysmorphology
Heart Institute
Helen Bernardy Center for Medically Fragile Children
Hematology/Oncology
HomeCare
Hospice
Infectious Diseases
Kawasaki Disease Clinic
Kidney/Liver Tranplant Program
Kidney Disease
Laboratory Services/Pathology
Liver Disease
Liver Transplant
Muscle Disease Clinic
Metabolic Medicine
Neonatology
Nephrology
Neurology
Neurosurgery
Newborn Screening Program
Nutrition Clinic
Occupational Therapy
Ophthalmology
Orthopedics
Otolaryngology/ENT
Pain Services
Palliative Care
Pediatric Surgery
Pediatrics & Hospital Medicine
Pharmacy Services
Physical Therapy
Prader-Willi Syndrome Clinic

Psychiatry
Pulmonary/Respiratory Medicine
Radiology
Rehabilitation Medicine
Rheumatology
Sleep Center
Speech/Language Pathology
Spiritual Care
Sports Medicine
Surgery
Toddler School (Alexa's PLAYC)
Trauma Center
Urgent Care
Urology
Weight & Wellness Center

COMPETITORS

All Children's Hospital
Children's Health System
Children's Hospital & Research Center at Oakland
Children's Hospital of Orange County
Children's Hospital of Philadelphia
Children's Hospital of Richmond
Children's Specialized Hospital
Childrens Hospital Los Angeles
Cook Children's Health Care System
Dell Children's Medical Center
Nationwide Children's Hospital
Palomar Health
Scripps Health
Seattle Children's Hospital
Sharp HealthCare
Shriners Hospitals For Children
St. Jude Children's Research Hospital
Sutter Health
Tri-City Healthcare District
UCSF Medical

HISTORICAL FINANCIALS
Company Type: Private

Income Statement
FYE: June 30

	REVENUE ($ mil.)	NET INCOME ($ mil.)	NET PROFIT MARGIN	EMPLOYEES
06/15	522	104	20.1%	2,313
06/14	838	82	9.8%	—
06/10	619	42	6.9%	—
06/09	490	(56)	—	—
Annual Growth	1.0%	—	—	—

2015 Year-End Financials
Return on assets: 19.7%   Cash ($ mil.): 75
Return on equity: 20.1%
Current ratio: 1.20

RANKIN COUNTY SCHOOL DISTRICT ASSOCIATION OF EDUCATIONAL OFFICE PERSONNEL, INC.

EXECUTIVES

Superintendent, Dr Lynn Weathersby
Superintendent, Patti Harmon
Auditors: FORTENBERRY & BALLARD PC BRA

LOCATIONS

HQ: RANKIN COUNTY SCHOOL DISTRICT ASSOCIATION OF EDUCATIONAL OFFICE PERSONNEL, INC.
1220 APPLE PARK PL, BRANDON, MS 390424498
Phone: 601 825-5590
Web: WWW.RCSD.MS

HISTORICAL FINANCIALS

Company Type: Private

Income Statement

FYE: June 30

	REVENUE ($ mil.)	NET INCOME ($ mil.)	NET PROFIT MARGIN	EMPLOYEES
06/16	177	5	3.1%	2,200
06/15	168	(6)	—	—
06/14	165	11	6.9%	—
06/13	164	(1)	—	—
Annual Growth	2.5%	—	—	—

2016 Year-End Financials

Return on assets: 0.6%
Return on equity: 3.1%
Current ratio: —
Cash ($ mil.): 25

RAPID CITY REGIONAL HOSPITAL, INC.

Mt. Rushmore sightseers bikers and locals alike can seek medical care at Rapid City Regional Hospital. The medical facility is a general and psychiatric hospital with some 330 acute care beds and 50 psychiatric beds located in the Black Hills region of western South Dakota. In addition to emergency and acute care the not-for-profit hospital also offers a behavioral health center a rehabilitation facility a cancer care institute and women's and children's departments. Rapid City Regional Hospital is part of Regional Health a network of regional hospitals medical clinics and senior care centers.

Operations

Regional Health is comprised of five hospitals 24 clinic locations and employs nearly 5000 physicians and caregivers. In addition to Rapid City Regional Hospital the Regional Health group includes the Custer Regional Lead-Deadwood Regional Spearfish Regional and Sturgis Regional hospitals. It also operates area clinics and doctors' offices including a family medicine clinic that manages a physician residency program as well as retirement communities and nursing homes. Altogether Regional Health has a total of about 40 facilities in South Dakota's Black Hills region.

Sales and Marketing

Rapid City Regional Hospital provides health care services to the 360000 people who live in the Black Hills of South Dakota and the surrounding region as well as thousands of visitors each year.

Company Background

The hospital was established in 1973.

EXECUTIVES

Vice President Patient Care, Rita Haxton

LOCATIONS

HQ: RAPID CITY REGIONAL HOSPITAL, INC.
353 FAIRMONT BLVD, RAPID CITY, SD 577017393
Phone: 605 719-1000
Web: WWW.REGIONALHEALTH.COM

PRODUCTS/OPERATIONS

Selected Services

Bariatrics and Weight Management
Behavioral Health
Bones Muscles and Joints
Brain and Spine
Cancer Care
Clinics (Primary and Speciality)
Diabetes
Heart and Vascular Care
Home Care
Home Medical Equipment
Hospice Care
Hospitalist
Hyperbaric Oxygen Therapy
Infusion Services
Intensive Care
Laboratory Services
Labor and Delivery
Lactation Services
Medical Imaging
Digital Mammography
Neonatal Care
Neurology
Nutrition Services
Pain Management
Pediatrics
Physical Therapy and Rehabilitation
Regional Health Research
Senior Care
Sepsis
Sports Medicine
Stroke Care
Telemedicine
Wound Care

COMPETITORS

Avera Health
Mayo Clinic
Sanford Health-MeritCare

St. Alexius Medical Center
St. Mary's Healthcare

HISTORICAL FINANCIALS

Company Type: Private

Income Statement

FYE: June 30

	REVENUE ($ mil.)	NET INCOME ($ mil.)	NET PROFIT MARGIN	EMPLOYEES
06/15	437	39	9.0%	4,200
06/14	517	56	10.9%	—
06/13	489	49	10.2%	—
Annual Growth	(5.5%)	(11.2%)	—	—

2015 Year-End Financials

Return on assets: 3.3%
Return on equity: 9.0%
Current ratio: 0.80
Cash ($ mil.): 17

RAPIDES PARISH SCHOOL DISTRICT

EXECUTIVES

Superintendent, Gary Jones
Director, Belinda Blue
Assistant Manager, Kimberly Bennett
Superintendent, Nason Authement
Assistant Manager, Clyde F Washington
Plant & Facilities Manager, Roy Rachal
Consultant, Shelly Close
Director, Tammy James
Auditors: PAYNE MOORE & HERRINGTON LLP

LOCATIONS

HQ: RAPIDES PARISH SCHOOL DISTRICT
619 6TH ST, ALEXANDRIA, LA 713018150
Phone: 318 487-0888
Web: WWW.RPSB.US

HISTORICAL FINANCIALS

Company Type: Private

Income Statement

FYE: June 30

	REVENUE ($ mil.)	NET INCOME ($ mil.)	NET PROFIT MARGIN	EMPLOYEES
06/16	245	(2)	—	3,400
06/15	242	(6)	—	—
06/14	241	12	5.0%	—
06/13	234	(2)	—	—
Annual Growth	1.4%	—	—	—

2016 Year-End Financials

Return on assets: 0.7%
Return on equity: (-1.0%)
Current ratio: —
Cash ($ mil.): 76

RAPPAHANNOCK ELECTRIC COOPERATIVE

Like the river it's named after the Rappahannock Electric Cooperative (REC) keeps the power running smoothly. The consumer-owned cooperative provides electricity to homes businesses and industries in parts of 22 counties from the Blue Ridge Mountains to the mouth of the Rappahannock River in eastern Virginia. REC supplies power to more than 157000 members over more than 16000 miles of power line. REC offers surge protection internet services and home security plans to entice customers as competition from other suppliers arrives. Once rural in nature the cooperative's territory has seen large pockets of suburban growth.

Geographic Reach

The company serve members in 22 Virginia counties: Albemarle Caroline Clarke Culpeper Essex Fauquier Frederick Goochland Greene Hanover King and Queen King William Louisa Madison Orange Page Rappahannock Rockingham Shenandoah Spotsylvania Stafford and Warren.

Sales and Marketing

REC's largest customer is Bear Island Paper Company the second largest power consumer in the state of Virginia. Other major customers include DuPont GE Kings Dominion Amusement Park and Merillat Industries.

Financial Performance

In 2012 the company reported revenues of $405.6 million (1% down on 2011). Residential customers accounted for more than half of the REC's total sales in 2012.

Strategy

REC is also pursuing ways to help its customers to become more energy efficient to help them save money and to help the cooperative trim its power capacity growth plans. Supported by a $16 million federal green energy grant the company has replaced customers' older meters with smart (automated efficient) ones.

In 2012 REC and Old Dominion Electric Cooperative offered a pilot energy efficiency program (energy retrofits) for REC's members in Albemarle Louisa Greene Madison and Orange counties.

Company Background

REC was formed when the Virginia Electric Co-operative in Bowling Green and the Northern Piedmont Electric Cooperative in Culpeper merged in 1980.

Dramatically growing its business in 2010 the company and fellow co-op Shenandoah Valley Electric Cooperatives acquired Potomac Edison (Allegheny Energy's electric distribution operations in Virginia) for about $340 million. The expansion increased REC's coverage from 16 counties to 22 and its customer base by about 50%.

EXECUTIVES

Vice President of Customer Services, David Koogler
Vice President, Ron Harris
Secretary, Lisa Hodgkiss

LOCATIONS

HQ: RAPPAHANNOCK ELECTRIC COOPERATIVE
247 INDUSTRIAL CT, FREDERICKSBURG, VA 224082443
Phone: 540 898-8500
Web: WWW.MYREC.COOP

COMPETITORS

Dominion Virginia Power

Pepco Energy Services
WGL Holdings

HISTORICAL FINANCIALS

Company Type: Private

Income Statement

	REVENUE ($ mil.)	NET INCOME ($ mil.)	NET PROFIT MARGIN	EMPLOYEES
12/15	461	15	3.3%	423
12/14	434	14	3.4%	—
12/13	400	15	3.8%	—
12/12	4	16	352.0%	—
Annual Growth	358.2%	(3.3%)	—	—

2015 Year-End Financials

Return on assets: 7.6%
Return on equity: 3.3%
Current ratio: 0.50

Cash ($ mil.): 3

RCMA AMERICAS INC.

EXECUTIVES

Director of Finance, Petrene Pearce
Director, Christiaan Tjia
Account Manager, Merc Depuy
Chief Financial Officer, Pet Pierce
Accountant, Penny Abbot
Administrative Assistant, Mary Ann Jason
Board of Directors, Carlene McFarland
VP Sales, Whitney Luckett
Senior Vice-President, Christopher Foord-Kelcey
Board of Directors, Myra Ndiaye
Auditors: CHERRY BEKAERT LLP VIRGINIA

LOCATIONS

HQ: RCMA AMERICAS INC.
150 BOUSH ST STE 800, NORFOLK, VA 235101637
Phone: 757 627-4000
Web: WWW.RCMA.COM

HISTORICAL FINANCIALS

Company Type: Private

Income Statement

FYE: December 31

	REVENUE ($ mil.)	NET INCOME ($ mil.)	NET PROFIT MARGIN	EMPLOYEES
12/15	183	3	1.8%	36
12/14	222	3	1.6%	—
12/13	252	3	1.4%	—
12/12	358	5	1.5%	—
Annual Growth	(20.0%)	(15.3%)	—	—

2015 Year-End Financials

Return on assets: 2.3%
Return on equity: 1.8%
Current ratio: 0.50

Cash ($ mil.): 5

RDO EQUIPMENT CO.

RDO Equipment has built a business herding Deere in a big way. The company sells and rents new and used trucks and heavy equipment to customers in the agriculture and construction industries. As the largest independent dealer of John Deere equipment RDO Equipment operates 70 locations in nearly 10 states. Of these 10 locations are dedicated Vermeer dealerships while its RDO Truck Centers offer heavy-duty Volvo GMC Isuzu and Mack trucks. RDO Integrated Controls is the company's acquisitive positioning division. RDO also supplies lawn and garden equipment and provides maintenance and repair services and replacement parts. Ronald Offutt founded the family owned and operated company in 1968.

Operations

The company owns and operates 75-plus dealerships in almost 10 US states. It specializes in selling some of the nation's top brands such as John Deere Vermeer and Topcon. Through international partnerships RDO Equipment operates in Mexico Russia Ukraine and Australia.

Geographic Reach

North Dakota-based RDO Equipment has stores in Arizona California Minnesota Montana North Dakota Oregon South Dakota Texas and Washington. Outside the US the company operates through partnerships in Australia Mexico Russia and Ukraine.

Strategy

RDO has grown its network of dealerships and menu of services primarily through acquisitions. The company's positioning division — RDO Integrated Controls — has been busy during the past couple years inking deals to expand its territory as a top dealer of Topcon-branded positioning products.

In 2015 the company opened a new store in McKinney Texas adding to the half a dozen locations it already operates in the state. The McKinney location offers sales parts services and rental of John Deere heavy construction equipment.

Mergers and Acquisitions

In March 2013 RDO Integrated Controls added South Dakota to the map of territories where it provides Topcon-branded construction supplies with the purchase of the Topcon Survey Contract for the state of South Dakota from Mathison's Co. The deal extended RDO's reach in the Dakotas Minnesota Montana and Wyoming. Also in November 2013 RDO acquired Water Tech Ag Supply a California-based company that provides agricultural irrigation systems. The company has half

a dozen locations in California and one in Yuma Arizona.

EXECUTIVES

Chair and CEO, Christi J. Offutt
VP Organizational Development, Gean Zimmerman
EVP and CFO, David Frear
President; Chief Content Officer, Scott Greenstein
EVP with responsibility for the company&rsquo, Ryan Offutt
COO, Chris Cooper
Executive Vice President serves on the Board of Directors, Keith Kreps
Executive Vice President Steve Connelly, Jean Zimmerman
Vice President Special Projects, Skip Klinkhammer
Vice President of Aftermarket, Terry Tolbert
Auditors: PRICEWATERHOUSECOOPERS LLP M

LOCATIONS

HQ: RDO EQUIPMENT CO.
700 7TH ST S, FARGO, ND 581032704
Phone: 701 239-8700

PRODUCTS/OPERATIONS

Selected Brands
Hitachi
John Deete
Sakai
Topcon
Vermeer
Wirtgen

Selected Products
Balers
Chippers
Combines
Dozers
Drills
Excavators
Planters
Scrapers
Tractors
Trenchers
Wheel loaders

COMPETITORS

Briggs Equipment
Herc Holdings
Home Depot

Komatsu America
Mustang CAT
Scott Equipment

HISTORICAL FINANCIALS

Company Type: Private

Income Statement

FYE: January 31

	REVENUE ($ mil.)	NET INCOME ($ mil.)	NET PROFIT MARGIN	EMPLOYEES
01/16	1,651	42	2.5%	1,500
01/15	1,762	53	3.0%	—
01/14	1,698	82	4.9%	—
01/13	1,650	82	5.0%	—
Annual Growth	0.0%	(20.0%)	—	—

2016 Year-End Financials

Return on assets: 0.8%
Return on equity: 2.5%
Current ratio: 0.20

Cash ($ mil.): 5

REDLANDS COMMUNITY HOSPITAL

EXECUTIVES

Chief Executive Officer, James R Holmes
Assistant Controller, Cassandra Vonesch
Engineer, Matt Steele
Director, Tom Leon
Chief Financial Officer, Sabi A Dadabhai

LOCATIONS

HQ: REDLANDS COMMUNITY HOSPITAL
350 TERRACINA BLVD, REDLANDS, CA 923734897
Phone: 909 335-5500

HISTORICAL FINANCIALS

Company Type: Private

Income Statement

	REVENUE ($ mil.)	NET INCOME ($ mil.)	NET PROFIT MARGIN	EMPLOYEES
09/15	174	16	9.3%	99
09/14	189	2	1.2%	—
09/13	207	10	5.2%	—
Annual Growth	(8.3%)	22.9%	—	—

FYE: September 30

2015 Year-End Financials

Return on assets: 5.9%   Cash ($ mil.): 14
Return on equity: 9.3%
Current ratio: 0.50

REDNER'S MARKETS, INC.

Redner's Markets operates about 45 warehouse club-style supermarkets under the Redner's Warehouse Markets banner and more than a dozen Quick Shoppe convenience stores. Most of the company's stores are located in eastern Pennsylvania but the regional grocer also operates several locations in Maryland and Delaware having closed its one New York supermarket. Redner's Warehouse Markets house bakery deli meat produce and seafood departments as well as in-store banks. The employee-owned company was founded by namesake Earl Redner in 1970. It is still operated by the Redner family including chairman and CEO Richard and COO Ryan Redner.

Financial Performance

Redner's Markets rang up an estimated $865 million in sales in fiscal 2012 (ends September) up from about $859 million in sales the previous year.

Strategy

Redner's has been tinkering with its store portfolio shuttering underperforming locations including several in its core Pennsylvania market while building new stores in existing and new markets. The regional chain has grown to four stores each in Delaware and Maryland since entering those markets in 2008 and 2005 respectively. Redner's is also growing its Web presence doubling its online traffic in the first year of a digiral shopper marketing program conducted in partnership with Google Shopping Network.

EXECUTIVES

Vice President, Michael McNaney
Vice President Human Resources, Robert McDonough
Vice President Purchasing, Dan Eberhart
Vice President Construction Real Esta, Doug Emore
Auditors: REINSEL KUNTZ LESHER LLP WYO

LOCATIONS

HQ: REDNER'S MARKETS, INC.
3 QUARRY RD, READING, PA 196059787
Phone: 610 926-3700
Web: WWW.REDNERSMARKETS.COM

2012 Warehouse Market Stores

	No.
Pennsylvania	36
Delaware	4
Maryland	4
Total	**44**

PRODUCTS/OPERATIONS

2012 Stores

	No.
Redner's Warehouse Market	44
Quick Shoppe	14
Total	**58**

COMPETITORS

7-Eleven	Wal-Mart
A&P	Wawa Inc.
Cumberland Farms	Wegmans
Giant Food Stores	Weis Markets
Sheetz	

HISTORICAL FINANCIALS

Company Type: Private

Income Statement

	REVENUE ($ mil.)	NET INCOME ($ mil.)	NET PROFIT MARGIN	EMPLOYEES
10/16*	864	4	0.6%	4,800
09/15	884	6	0.7%	—
09/14	902	1	0.2%	—
09/13	892	4	0.5%	—
Annual Growth	(1.1%)	1.8%	—	—

FYE: October 1

*Fiscal year change

2016 Year-End Financials

Return on assets: 3.2%   Cash ($ mil.): 56
Return on equity: 0.6%
Current ratio: 1.70

REGENTS OF THE UNIVERSITY OF IDAHO

You won't have to learn Russian to attend school in Moscow. The University of Idaho — located in Moscow Idaho — has more than 900 faculty members and an enrollment of more than 12000 students. It offers undergraduate degree programs in subjects ranging from agriculture and art to natural resources and science. The University of Idaho also offers master's degrees and doctoral degrees in a broad range of subjects including law. In addition to its main campus University of Idaho has locations in Boise Coeur d'Alene Idaho Falls and Twin Falls as well dozens of extension offices statewide. The university was founded in 1889.

EXECUTIVES

Vice President for Finance and Administration, Ronald Smith
Vice President Public Relations, Sarah Jacobsen
Auditors: MOSS ADAMS LLP EUGENE OREGON

LOCATIONS

HQ: REGENTS OF THE UNIVERSITY OF IDAHO
875 PERIMETER DR MS3020, MOSCOW, ID
838449803
Phone: 208 885-6174
Web: WWW.UIDAHO.EDU

PRODUCTS/OPERATIONS

Selected Schools
Agricultural and Life Sciences
Art and Architecture
Business and Economics
Education
Engineering
Graduate Studies
Law
Letters Arts and Social Sciences
Natural Resources
Science

HISTORICAL FINANCIALS

Company Type: Private

Income Statement

	REVENUE ($ mil.)	NET INCOME ($ mil.)	NET PROFIT MARGIN	EMPLOYEES
06/16	212	20	9.8%	3,350
06/15	214	24	11.4%	—
06/12	216	1	0.6%	—
06/11	208	22	10.6%	—
Annual Growth	0.4%	(1.1%)	—	—

FYE: June 30

2016 Year-End Financials

Return on assets: 2.6%   Cash ($ mil.): 32
Return on equity: 9.8%
Current ratio: 1.50

REGENTS OF THE UNIVERSITY OF MICHIGAN

Michigan — it's shaped like a mitten and higher education fits the state like a glove. With nearly 60000 students and about 7000 faculty members scattered across three campuses in Ann Arbor Dearborn and Flint the university's diverse academic units span such areas of study as architecture education law medicine music and social work. Notable alumni include the late President Gerald Ford (the university is home to the Gerald R. Ford Library and the Ford School of Public Policy) actor James Earl Jones Google cofounder Larry Page and seven Nobel laureates. In addition to state funding the university is supported by a $6.6 billion endowment.

Operations

The university operates some 20 schools offering education in everything from dentistry and medicine to music theater and dance. About 70% of the students are enrolled in undergraduate programs while the rest are graduate students.

There are seven museums on campus — including the Museum of Art the Exhibit Museum of Natural History (with a planetarium) and the

Kelsey Museum of Archaeology — as well as the Nichols Arboretum and the Matthaei Botanical Gardens.

Through its Health System the university maintains one of the largest health care complexes in the world. It is made up of more than 50 health centers and 120 outpatient clinics around the state and is responsible for more than 40% of The University of Michigan's revenue.

Along with its various health centers and clinics the university operates the C.S. Mott Children's Hospital. The children's hospital is noted for its heart surgery neonatal care and respiratory disorders and ranks among the nation's best for all other pediatric specialties — cancer digestive disorders general pediatrics and neurology.

Geographic Reach

The University of Michigan was founded in Detroit in 1817 but moved to Ann Arbor in 1837.

Financial Performance

The university has enjoyed an upward trend in revenue during recent fiscal years as a result of increases in tuition rates and undergraduate enrollment. It claimed more than $5 billion in revenue for fiscal 2012 up more than 5% compared to the $4.77 billion the university reported in revenue for fiscal 2011. The school brought in about $453 billion during fiscal 2010.

EXECUTIVES

VP Government Relations, Cynthia H. Wilbanks
VP Development, Jerry A. May
Chancellor University of Michigan-Dearborn, Daniel Little
EVP and CFO, Kevin P. Hegarty, age 61
Chairman Victors for Michigan, Stephen M. Ross
President, Mark S. Schlissel
Dean School of Public Health, Martin Philbert
VP Information Technology and CIO, Kelli Trosvig
Dean Stamps School of Art and Design, Gunalan Nadarajan
Dean School of Dentistry, Laurie McCauley
Dean Law School, Mark D. West
Chancellor University of Michigan-Flint, Susan E. Borrego
Interim Provost and EVP Academic Affairs, Paul N. Courant
EVP Medical Affairs; Dean Medical School; CEO Michigan Medicine, Marschall S. Runge
VP and General Counsel, Timothy G. Lynch
VP Research, S. Jack Hu
Interim Dean Taubman College of Architecture and Urban Planning, Robert Fishman
Edward J. Frey Dean Ross School of Business, Scott DeRue
Dean School of Education, Elizabeth Birr Moje
Dean School of Engineering, Alec D. Gallimore
Dean School of Information, Thomas A. Finholt
Dean School of Kinesiology, Lori Ploutz-Snyder
Dean College of Literature Science and the Arts, Andrew D. Martin
Dean College of Music Theatre and Dance, Aaron Dworkin
Interim Dean School of Natural Resources and Environment, Dan Brown
Dean School of Nursing, Patricia D. Hurn
Dean College of Pharmacy, James T. Dalton
Dean School of Social Work, Lynn Videka
Dean Rackham Graduate School; Vice Provost Academic Affairs Graduate Studies, Carol A. Fierke
Vice President Sec Of University, Sally Churchill
Assoc Vice President For Human RSCS, Laurita Thomas
Associate Vice President Development, Julie Sparkman
Vice President, David John Hiemstra
Medical Director Employee Health Service, Susan Blitz
Vice President Marketing, Rachelle Caoagas

Senior Executive SECRETARY Office of Vice President for Research Department, BettyL Cook
Provost And Executive Vice President For Academic Affairs, Teresa Sullivan
Vice President Research, Stephen Forrest
Associate Vice President for Human Resources, Catherine Lilly
Vice President, Rachel Goldman
Vice President, Dan Salinas
Vice President Research and Development, Bruce Nourse
Vice President of Industry Relations, Matthew Singelyn
Vice President Finance technology, William Hausman
Associate Vice President and Deputy General Counsel, Kara Morgenstern
Vice Chairman, Michael J. Behm
Chairman, Mark J. Bernstein
Treasurer, Kevin Morrison
Secretary, Alfreda Onimo
Secretary IV Office Of The General Counsel Department, Linda Meakes
Board Member, Margie Perrett
Treasurer, Seema Kedia
Secretary II Unions Administration Department, Samantha Hallman
Secretary III Umh Mworks Employ Assistant Program Department, Angela Hurlbut
Secretary IV Lsa Dean Deans Office Department, Sandra Petee
Secretary III Academic Affairs Dentistry Department, Diane Pasma
Secretary III Occupational Safety And Environ Department, Patricia Bostain
Secretary IV Umh Administration Department, Melody Bond
Secretary III Vice President And Secretary Of Univ Department, Cary Varney
Secretary Intermediate, Marie Bien
Executive Board Member, Garrett Stephens
Board Member, Lisong NI
Board Member, Jason Townsend
Secretary, Jessica Mims
Treasurer, Nahiyan Bakr
Secretary, Salam Smidi
Board Member Family and Youth Chair, Fatima Salman
Secretary Commercial Players Community Assistant South Quadrangle Residential College Class of 2017, Kyle Stefek
Secretary II Flint School Partnerships Department, Pamela Zemore
Auditors: PRICEWATERHOUSECOOPERS LLP DE

LOCATIONS

HQ: REGENTS OF THE UNIVERSITY OF MICHIGAN
503 THOMPSON ST, ANN ARBOR, MI 481091340
Phone: 734 764-1817
Web: WWW.UMICH.EDU

PRODUCTS/OPERATIONS

Selected Academic Units
Architecture and urban planning
Art and design
Business administration
Dentistry
Education
Engineering
Kinesiology
Law
Literature science and the arts
Medicine
Music
Natural resources and environment
Nursing
Pharmacy
Public health
Public policy
Social work

HISTORICAL FINANCIALS
Company Type: Private

Income Statement

	REVENUE ($ mil.)	NET INCOME ($ mil.)	NET PROFIT MARGIN	EMPLOYEES
06/16	6,278	(294)	—	34,624
06/14	5,534	1,574	28.5%	—
06/13	5,317	729	13.7%	—
06/12	5,038	(171)	—	—
Annual Growth	5.7%	—	—	—

FYE: June 30

2016 Year-End Financials

Return on assets: 4.7%
Return on equity: (-4.7%)
Current ratio: 0.50

Cash ($ mil.): 349

REGIONAL MEDICAL CENTER

EXECUTIVES

Principal, Sarah Benson

LOCATIONS

HQ: REGIONAL MEDICAL CENTER
3000 SAINT MATTHEWS RD, ORANGEBURG, SC 291181442
Phone: 803 395-2200
Web: WWW.TRMCHEALTH.ORG

HISTORICAL FINANCIALS
Company Type: Private

Income Statement

	REVENUE ($ mil.)	NET INCOME ($ mil.)	NET PROFIT MARGIN	EMPLOYEES
09/15	216	(3)	—	1
09/14	210	(2)	—	—
Annual Growth	2.6%	—	—	—

FYE: September 30

2015 Year-End Financials

Return on assets: 4.1%
Return on equity: (-1.6%)
Current ratio: 1.30

Cash ($ mil.): 8

REGIONAL TRANSPORTATION AUTHORITY

EXECUTIVES

Executive Director, Richard J Bacigalupo
Chairman of the Board, Thomas J McCraken Jr
Treasurer, Allan Sharkey
Principal, Julie Gomez
Principal, Carole Brown
Manager, Roxann Galvan
Personnel Manager, Eric Grant
Director, William Coulson
Auditors: RSM US LLP CHICAGO ILLINOIS

LOCATIONS

HQ: REGIONAL TRANSPORTATION AUTHORITY
175 W JACKSON BLVD # 1650, CHICAGO, IL
606042711
Phone: 312 913-3200
Web: WWW.RTACHICAGO.ORG

HISTORICAL FINANCIALS
Company Type: Private

Income Statement
FYE: December 31

	REVENUE ($ mil.)	NET INCOME ($ mil.)	NET PROFIT MARGIN	EMPLOYEES
12/15	805	(77)	—	80
12/14	755	(3)	—	—
12/13	934	(102)	—	—
12/12	595	(54)	—	—
Annual Growth	10.6%	—	—	—

2015 Year-End Financials

Return on assets: —
Return on equity: (-9.6%)
Current ratio: 0.20
Cash ($ mil.): 128

REGIONAL WEST MEDICAL CENTER

EXECUTIVES

President, Todd S Sorensen
Vice-President, Brenda Hall
Vice-President, Lisa Bewley
Manager, Amy Mikesell

LOCATIONS

HQ: REGIONAL WEST MEDICAL CENTER
4021 AVENUE B, SCOTTSBLUFF, NE 693614602
Phone: 308 635-3711
Web: WWW.RWMC.NET

HISTORICAL FINANCIALS
Company Type: Private

Income Statement
FYE: December 31

	REVENUE ($ mil.)	NET INCOME ($ mil.)	NET PROFIT MARGIN	EMPLOYEES
12/15	177	25	14.3%	1,100
12/14	179	9	5.3%	—
12/13	190	2	1.5%	—
12/12	185	14	7.6%	—
Annual Growth	(1.5%)	21.4%	—	—

2015 Year-End Financials

Return on assets: 4.8%
Return on equity: 14.3%
Current ratio: 1.90
Cash ($ mil.): 8

REHABILITATION INSTITUTE OF CHICAGO

EXECUTIVES

President, Joanne C Smith
Financial Executive, Brian Rasmus
Auditors: DELOITTE & TOUCHE LLP CHICAGO

LOCATIONS

HQ: REHABILITATION INSTITUTE OF CHICAGO
355 E ERIE ST, CHICAGO, IL 606114805
Phone: 312 238-1000
Web: WWW.RIC.ORG

HISTORICAL FINANCIALS
Company Type: Private

Income Statement
FYE: August 31

	REVENUE ($ mil.)	NET INCOME ($ mil.)	NET PROFIT MARGIN	EMPLOYEES
08/16	249	66	26.6%	1,500
08/13	228	129	56.6%	—
08/10	219	55	25.2%	—
08/09	139	0	—	—
Annual Growth	8.6%	—	—	—

2016 Year-End Financials

Return on assets: 16.4%
Return on equity: 26.6%
Current ratio: 1.30
Cash ($ mil.): 77

REID HOSPITAL & HEALTH CARE SERVICES, INC.

EXECUTIVES

President, Craig Kinyon
Board of Directors, Bonita Washington Lacey
Auditor, David Long
Director, Leah Brown
Auditors: BKD LLP CINCINNATI OH

LOCATIONS

HQ: REID HOSPITAL & HEALTH CARE SERVICES, INC.
1100 REID PKWY, RICHMOND, IN 473741157
Phone: 765 983-3000
Web: WWW.SECURE.REIDHOSPITAL.ORG

HISTORICAL FINANCIALS
Company Type: Private

Income Statement
FYE: December 31

	REVENUE ($ mil.)	NET INCOME ($ mil.)	NET PROFIT MARGIN	EMPLOYEES
12/15	375	(33)	—	3
12/12	354	35	10.0%	—
Annual Growth	1.9%	—	—	—

2015 Year-End Financials

Return on assets: 4.6%
Return on equity: (-8.9%)
Current ratio: 1.20
Cash ($ mil.): 14

REIF OIL COMPANY

EXECUTIVES

President, Clifford G Reif Jr
Board of Directors, David Reif
Office Manager, Betsy Peterson
Marketing Manager, Blaire Burke
Auditors: CPA ASSOCIATES PC BURLINGTON

LOCATIONS

HQ: REIF OIL COMPANY
801 N 3RD ST, BURLINGTON, IA 526015006
Phone: 319 758-1240
Web: WWW.REIFOIL.COM

HISTORICAL FINANCIALS
Company Type: Private

Income Statement
FYE: December 31

	REVENUE ($ mil.)	NET INCOME ($ mil.)	NET PROFIT MARGIN	EMPLOYEES
12/15	177	1	0.7%	100
12/14	270	0	0.1%	—
12/13	316	(0)	—	—
12/12	369	0	0.0%	—
Annual Growth	(21.7%)	92.9%	—	—

2015 Year-End Financials

Return on assets: 2.9%
Return on equity: 0.7%
Current ratio: 0.30
Cash ($ mil.): —

REPUBLIC FINANCE, LLC

EXECUTIVES

Board of Directors, Anne Kurz
Board of Directors, Rex Ellison
Board of Directors, Jay Jolly
Financial Executive, Joy Beale
Chief Financial Officer, James Jolly
Senior Vice-President, Bill Allen
Senior Vice-President, Kyle Fenton
Auditors: POSTLETHWAITE & NETTERVILLE B

LOCATIONS

HQ: REPUBLIC FINANCE, LLC
7031 COMMERCE CIR STE 100, BATON ROUGE, LA
708091996
Phone: 225 927-0005
Web: WWW.REPUBLICFINANCE.COM

HISTORICAL FINANCIALS
Company Type: Private

Income Statement
FYE: December 31

	ASSETS ($ mil.)	NET INCOME ($ mil.)	INCOME AS % OF ASSETS	EMPLOYEES
12/15	452	71	15.8%	250
12/14	406	56	13.9%	—
12/13	342	39	11.5%	—
12/12	238	27	11.6%	—
Annual Growth	23.8%	37.0%	—	—

2015 Year-End Financials

Return on assets: 8.6%
Return on equity: 34.9%
Sales ($ mil): 204

RESEARCH TRIANGLE INSTITUTE INC

The scientists at Research Triangle Institute address the problems of a sphere (the planet). Operating mainly under its trade name RTI International (RTI) the not-for-profit enterprise conducts research in such areas as advanced technologies environmental resources and medicine. It provides such services as certification and materials testing as well as software used in laboratories and research projects. Serving the US federal government other governments nonprofits and for-profit companies RTI offers analytical perspectives on public policy and has researchers working in offices around the world.

Operations

The company offers analytical perspectives on public policy. Its staff members represent more than 80 nationalities and speak nearly 90 languages enabling RTI to communicate and collaborate effectively with peer researchers clients and stakeholders around the world.

Geographic Reach

RTI serves clients in more than 75 countries. It has eight US offices and offices in China El Salvador India Indonesia Kenya Spain Sweden the UAE and the UK.

Sales and Marketing

The organization works with clients in government industry academia and public service. RTI's main clients are the Department of Health and Human Services and the US Agency for International Development. RTI's private sector clients have included 3M Chevron Cisco Systems GE and Sanofi-Aventis.

Financial Performance

The institute reinvests its net income in programs facilities and new capabilities.

EXECUTIVES

Vice President, Jerry Rench
EVP and COO, James J. (Jim) Gibson
EVP RTI Health Solutions, Allen W. Mangel
President and CEO, E. Wayne Holden
EVP International Development Group, Aaron S. Williams
EVP Social Statistical and Environmental Sciences, Timothy J. (Tim) Gabel
EVP and CFO, Michael H. (Mike) Kaelin
Chair Fellow Program and Distinguished Fellow Early Childhood Development, Don Bailey
Vice President Finance, Francis Neary
Vice President and Assistant General Counsel, Christopher Buchholtz
Vice President Corporate Affairs, Sally Johnson
Vice President Organizational Development and Learning, Tony Gambill
Senior Vice President General Counsel, Greg Story
Vice President Contracting, Dave Obringer
Senior Vice President, Edward Story
Executive Vice President, Paul Weisenfeld
Executive Vice President, E Wayne Holden
Vice President Of Electronics And Systems, James Clary
Vice President and Corporate Controller, Steve Snyder
Executive Vice President of Human Resources, Lisa May
Vice President and Head of Corporate Development, Matt Jenkins
Vice President, Justin Eiler
Vice Chairman, Peter M. Scott
Chairman, William M. Moore
Treasurer, Rick Sisson
Treasurer, Ward Sax
Treasurer, Edward Lilly
Auditors: DELOITTE & TOUCHE LLP CHARLOT

LOCATIONS

HQ: RESEARCH TRIANGLE INSTITUTE INC
3040 CORNWALLIS RD, DURHAM, NC 277090128
Phone: 919 541-6000
Web: WWW.RTI.ORG

PRODUCTS/OPERATIONS

Selected Research Areas
Advanced technology research and development
Drug discovery and development
Economic and social
Education and training
Energy
Environmental
Health
International development
Laboratory and chemistry
Statistics
Survey

COMPETITORS

Argonne National Laboratory
Battelle Memorial
QSS Group
Sandford Burnham Institute
Urban Institute

HISTORICAL FINANCIALS
Company Type: Private

Income Statement
FYE: September 30

	REVENUE ($ mil.)	NET INCOME ($ mil.)	NET PROFIT MARGIN	EMPLOYEES
09/16	884	15	1.8%	3,117
09/15	831	40	4.9%	—
09/14	788	31	4.0%	—
09/13	782	37	4.8%	—
Annual Growth	4.2%	(24.7%)	—	—

2016 Year-End Financials
Return on assets: 5.1%
Return on equity: 1.8%
Current ratio: 0.50
Cash ($ mil.): 31

RESOURCES FOR HUMAN DEVELOPMENT, INC.

EXECUTIVES

President, Bob Fishman
Financial Executive, Cindy Ray
Director, Kimberly Ryan
Assistant Controller, Kristen Gardner
Finance Manager, Allen Yates
Vice-President, Don Bryant
Personnel Manager, Karen Melvin
Auditors: SHECHTMAN MARKS DEVOR PC PHIL

LOCATIONS

HQ: RESOURCES FOR HUMAN DEVELOPMENT, INC.
4700 WISSAHICKON AVE # 126, PHILADELPHIA, PA 191444248
Phone: 215 951-0300
Web: WWW.RHD.ORG

HISTORICAL FINANCIALS
Company Type: Private

Income Statement
FYE: June 30

	REVENUE ($ mil.)	NET INCOME ($ mil.)	NET PROFIT MARGIN	EMPLOYEES
06/15	255	0	0.3%	3,000
06/09	180	(2)	—	—
06/08	169	2	1.2%	—
06/07	1,987	0	—	—
Annual Growth	(22.6%)	—	—	—

2015 Year-End Financials
Return on assets: 11.7%
Return on equity: 0.3%
Current ratio: 0.20
Cash ($ mil.): 6

REX HOSPITAL, INC.

EXECUTIVES

President, David W Strong
Vice-President, Bill Reese III
Executive Vice-President, George S York Jr
Manager, Nora Giglio

LOCATIONS

HQ: REX HOSPITAL, INC.
4420 LAKE BOONE TRL, RALEIGH, NC 276076599
Phone: 919 784-3100
Web: WWW.REXHEALTH.COM

HISTORICAL FINANCIALS
Company Type: Private

Income Statement
FYE: June 30

	REVENUE ($ mil.)	NET INCOME ($ mil.)	NET PROFIT MARGIN	EMPLOYEES
06/15	813	4	0.5%	3,500
06/14	724	25	3.6%	—
06/13	701	7	1.0%	—
06/08	460	6	1.4%	—
Annual Growth	8.5%	(6.1%)	—	—

2015 Year-End Financials
Return on assets: 7.5%
Return on equity: 0.5%
Current ratio: 0.80
Cash ($ mil.): 69

RHODE ISLAND HOSPITAL

EXECUTIVES

Chief Executive Officer, Margaret Van Bree
Account Manager, Lorrie Miller
Manager, Leslie Varone

LOCATIONS

HQ: RHODE ISLAND HOSPITAL
593 EDDY ST, PROVIDENCE, RI 029034923
Phone: 401 444-4000
Web: WWW.RHODEISLANDHOSPITAL.ORG

HISTORICAL FINANCIALS
Company Type: Private

Income Statement
FYE: September 30

	REVENUE ($ mil.)	NET INCOME ($ mil.)	NET PROFIT MARGIN	EMPLOYEES
09/15	1,059	(6)	—	6,400
09/14	1,016	(5)	—	
09/13	1,048	49	4.7%	
09/07	918	110	12.0%	
Annual Growth	1.8%	—	—	—

2015 Year-End Financials
Return on assets: 5.0%
Return on equity: (-0.6%)
Current ratio: 1.10
Cash ($ mil.): 39

RIALTO UNIFIED SCHOOL DISTRICT

EXECUTIVES
President, Joanne T Gilbert
Board of Directors, Michele Joseph
Board of Directors, Rosie Williams
Manager, Richard Endsley
Superintendent, Cuauhtemoc Avila
Auditors: VAVRINEK TRINE DAY & CO LL

LOCATIONS
HQ: RIALTO UNIFIED SCHOOL DISTRICT
182 E WALNUT AVE, RIALTO, CA 923763598
Phone: 909 820-7700
Web: WWW.RIALTO.K12.CA.US

HISTORICAL FINANCIALS
Company Type: Private

Income Statement
FYE: June 30

	REVENUE ($ mil.)	NET INCOME ($ mil.)	NET PROFIT MARGIN	EMPLOYEES
06/16	314	25	8.0%	2,833
06/06	231	(8)	—	—
06/05	226	(22)	—	—
06/04	0	0	—	—
Annual Growth	—	—	—	—

2016 Year-End Financials
Return on assets: 9.0%
Return on equity: 8.0%
Current ratio: —
Cash ($ mil.): 133

RICELAND FOODS, INC.

Handling more than 125 million bushels of grain a year Riceland Foods is ingrained in its business. The agricultural cooperative processes and markets the rice soybeans and wheat grown by its 9000 member/owners who farm in Arkansas Louisiana Mississippi Missouri and Texas. One of the world's largest rice millers it sells white and brown rice plus flavored rices and meal kits under the Riceland and private-label brands. The co-op sells to food retailers and food service and food manufacturing companies worldwide. Riceland also makes cooking oils and processes soybeans bran and lecithin and offers rice bran and hulls to pet food makers and livestock farmers as feed and bedding.

Operations

Riceland's Research and Technical Center (Stuttgart Arkansas) is staffed by scientists and technicians with experience in rice edible oil and lecithin chemistry applications and process engineering.

The facility houses separate soybean and rice research laboratories to conduct product development product and process improvement and customer support. Riceland's business lines are supported by on-site analytical food applications and regulatory compliance labs consumer and foodservice test kitchens and a well-equipped pilot plant. An ongoing research program reinforces Riceland's position as a premier supplier of rice edible oils and lecithin.

In addition to being a leader in rice milling the cooperative is a major soybean processor. Indeed its soybean processing plant in Stuttgart provides high-protein soybean meal and soybean mill run to poultry catfish and other livestock producers in the Mississippi Delta region and southwestern US.

Geographic Reach

Arkansas-based Riceland provides marketing services to farmers in its home state as well as Louisiana Mississippi Missouri and Texas.

Riceland markets rice products under the Riceland label private labels as ingredients and in bulk. Riceland's products are sold across the US and in more than 75 foreign destinations.

Sales and Marketing

A major rice exporter and edible oil producer Riceland markets its rice and oil products under the Riceland and Chefway (vegetable oil and shortening) labels. Its products are sold nationwide and to more than 75 foreign destinations.

Rice and oil products are supplied to many of America's leading restaurants fast-food chains cafeterias and military installations. Packaged and flavored rice products are marketed under the Riceland brand. Vegetable oil and shortening products are sold under Riceland and private label brands. Wheat is exported to Mexico and Egypt. Soybeans are sold to US buyers. Rough rice is sold to Mexico and Central America.

Financial Performance

In 2014 Riceland Foods' revenues topped more than $1 billion for the seventh consecutive year. However its net sales for the year were down about 12% due to a decline in prices for rice and soybeans.

Strategy

A key business objective for Riceland is to increase the number of value-added products (such as Riceland Rice 'N Easy flavored rice mixes Riceland Turkey Fry Oil and Fish Fry Oil) and the level of its value added marketing. In 2014 a new riceland.com website went online allowing Riceland customers worldwide access to product information and sales personnel. The website brings consumers face-to-face with some Riceland farmermembers discussing their farming operations. It also includes cooking videos by Georgia Pellegrini a celebrity chef and author of 'Modern Pioneering.' The website

In 2015 Sage V Foods of Boulder Colorado has sold its interest in an instant rice production facility in Little Rock to Best Rice LLC which is jointly owned by Riceland Foods and Producers Rice Mill both based in Stuttgart.

EXECUTIVES
CEO, Danny Kennedy
Vice President Sales, Larry Sharp
Vice President, Andrew Dallas

Auditors: BKD LLP LITTLE ROCK ARKANSA

LOCATIONS
HQ: RICELAND FOODS, INC.
2120 S PARK AVE, STUTTGART, AR 721606822
Phone: 870 673-5500

PRODUCTS/OPERATIONS

Selected Products
Consumer
Saffron Yellow Rice Mix
Rice N Easy Mix Wild Rice
Long Grain & Wild Mix Rice N Easy Mix
Broccoli & Cheese Rice N Easy Mix
Spanish Rice Mix Rice N Easy Mix
Chicken Rice Mix Rice N Easy Mix
Long Grain Rice Riceland Extra Long Grain Rice
Riceland GOLD Perfected Rice
Riceland Jasmine Rice
Riceland Natural Brown Rice
Riceland Plump & Tender Medium Grain Rice
Food Service
Oil
Rice
Food Ingredients
Long grain milled rice
Long grain brown rice
Medium grain milled rice
Parboiled rice
Broken grains

COMPETITORS
AarhusKarlshamn	Goya
American Rice	JFC International
CHS	Lotus Foods
Cereal Byproducts	Louis Dreyfus Group
Connell Company	Producers Rice Mill
Ebro Foods	Riviana Foods
Farmers Rice Milling	Specialty Rice
Farmers' Rice Cooperative	

HISTORICAL FINANCIALS
Company Type: Private

Income Statement
FYE: July 31

	REVENUE ($ mil.)	NET INCOME ($ mil.)	NET PROFIT MARGIN	EMPLOYEES
07/16	1,007	5	0.6%	1,646
07/15	1,122	9	0.9%	—
07/14	1,148	2	0.2%	—
07/13	1,314	58	4.4%	—
Annual Growth	(8.5%)	(54.3%)	—	—

2016 Year-End Financials
Return on assets: 1.3%
Return on equity: 0.6%
Current ratio: 1.10
Cash ($ mil.): 15

RICHARDSON INDEPENDENT SCHOOL DISTRICT

EXECUTIVES
President, Kim Quirk
Board of Directors, Kris Oliver
Board of Directors, Karen Ellis
Manager, Gail Gable
Principal, Vaughn Gross
Principal, Steve Lemons

Principal, Nikki Hamilton
Principal, Mike Savage
Principal, Karin Holacka
Auditors: HANKINS EASTUP DEATON TONN

LOCATIONS

HQ: RICHARDSON INDEPENDENT SCHOOL DISTRICT
400 S GREENVILLE AVE # 205, RICHARDSON, TX
750814100
Phone: 469 593-0000
Web: WWW.RISD.ORG

HISTORICAL FINANCIALS

Company Type: Private

Income Statement

	REVENUE ($ mil.)	NET INCOME ($ mil.)	NET PROFIT MARGIN	EMPLOYEES
06/16	406	(13)	—	4,500
06/15	388	(3)	—	—
06/14	376	(22)	—	—
06/13	355	(0)	—	—
Annual Growth	4.6%	—	—	—

FYE: June 30

RICHLAND COUNTY SCHOOL DISTRICT 1

EXECUTIVES

Chief Operating Officer, Michael Bobby
Principal, Jacpb Holmes
Board of Directors, Jasper Salmond
Superintendent, Craig Witherspoon
Assistant Manager, Sherry Veasey
Auditors: DERRICKS STUBBS STETH LLP CO

LOCATIONS

HQ: RICHLAND COUNTY SCHOOL DISTRICT 1
1616 RICHLAND ST, COLUMBIA, SC 292012634
Phone: 803 231-7000
Web: WWW.RICHLANDONE.ORG

HISTORICAL FINANCIALS

Company Type: Private

Income Statement

	REVENUE ($ mil.)	NET INCOME ($ mil.)	NET PROFIT MARGIN	EMPLOYEES
06/16	373	(34)	—	5,200
06/15	363	50	14.0%	—
06/14	358	3	1.0%	—
06/13	345	(0)	—	—
Annual Growth	2.6%	—	—	—

FYE: June 30

RICHMOND MEDICAL CENTER

EXECUTIVES

President, Daniel J Messina
Senior Vice-President, Lynn Jennings
Director, Stephan Kwon

Administrative Assistant, Jane Bocignone
Vice-President, Patricia Caldari

LOCATIONS

HQ: RICHMOND MEDICAL CENTER
355 BARD AVE, STATEN ISLAND, NY 103101664
Phone: 718 818-1234
Web: WWW.RUMCSI.ORG

HISTORICAL FINANCIALS

Company Type: Private

Income Statement

	REVENUE ($ mil.)	NET INCOME ($ mil.)	NET PROFIT MARGIN	EMPLOYEES
12/15	285	4	1.6%	2,555
12/14	274	7	2.7%	—
12/13	287	10	3.7%	—
12/12	263	2	0.9%	—
Annual Growth	2.8%	22.8%	—	—

FYE: December 31

2015 Year-End Financials

Return on assets: 8.3%   Cash ($ mil.): 45
Return on equity: 1.6%
Current ratio: 1.60

RIDDLE MEMORIAL HOSPITAL

EXECUTIVES

Principal, Daniel E Kennedy
Board of Directors, Robert Santilli
Financial Executive, John Boles
Director, Barbara Kurtz
Director, Eileen Phillips

LOCATIONS

HQ: RIDDLE MEMORIAL HOSPITAL
1068 W BALTIMORE PIKE, MEDIA, PA 190635177
Phone: 610 566-9400
Web: WWW.RIDDLETHRIFTSHOP.COM

HISTORICAL FINANCIALS

Company Type: Private

Income Statement

	REVENUE ($ mil.)	NET INCOME ($ mil.)	NET PROFIT MARGIN	EMPLOYEES
06/16	187	12	6.6%	1,350
06/15	180	12	6.9%	—
06/11	172	1	0.6%	—
06/10	171	(4)	—	—
Annual Growth	1.5%	—	—	—

FYE: June 30

RIDDLE MEMORIAL HOSPITAL

EXECUTIVES

Principal, Curt Whiteside
Auditors: PRICEWATERHOUSECOOPERS LLP PH

LOCATIONS

HQ: RIDDLE MEMORIAL HOSPITAL
950 E HAVERFORD RD, BRYN MAWR, PA 190103850
Phone: 484 337-8480
Web: WWW.ROTHMANINSTITUTE.COM

HISTORICAL FINANCIALS

Company Type: Private

Income Statement

	REVENUE ($ mil.)	NET INCOME ($ mil.)	NET PROFIT MARGIN	EMPLOYEES
06/15	182	11	6.3%	8
06/14	174	9	5.4%	—
06/13	169	0	0.1%	—
06/10	170	(5)	—	—
Annual Growth	1.3%	—	—	—

FYE: June 30

2015 Year-End Financials

Return on assets: 10.3%   Cash ($ mil.): 3
Return on equity: 6.3%
Current ratio: 0.50

RIDEOUT MEMORIAL HOSPITAL

EXECUTIVES

Chairman, Ronald M Sweeney
Board of Directors, John Wright
Board of Directors, Lisa Del Pero
Director, Carl Plantholt
Director, Ann Weiler
Senior Manager, Jennifer Furtado

LOCATIONS

HQ: RIDEOUT MEMORIAL HOSPITAL
726 4TH ST, MARYSVILLE, CA 959015656
Phone: 530 749-4416

HISTORICAL FINANCIALS

Company Type: Private

Income Statement

	REVENUE ($ mil.)	NET INCOME ($ mil.)	NET PROFIT MARGIN	EMPLOYEES
06/15	324	(3)	—	775
06/09	245	(10)	—	—
06/05	134	5	4.1%	—
06/02	86	3	3.5%	—
Annual Growth	10.7%	—	—	—

FYE: June 30

2015 Year-End Financials

Return on assets: 11.4%   Cash ($ mil.): 26
Return on equity: (-1.1%)
Current ratio: 1.10

RIESBECK FOOD MARKETS, INC.

EXECUTIVES

Chief Executive Officer, Richard L Riesbeck

Director, Bernard L Riesbeck II
Director, Paul M Riesbeck Jr
Chief Operating Officer, Dave Orr
Director, Greg Bauer
Manager, Kevin Dunlap
Director, Rita McElwain-Kelley
Auditors: BDO USA LLP PITTSBURGH PENNS

LOCATIONS

HQ: RIESBECK FOOD MARKETS, INC.
 48661 NATIONAL RD, SAINT CLAIRSVILLE, OH
 439509701
Phone: 740 695-7050
Web: WWW.IGA.COM

HISTORICAL FINANCIALS

Company Type: Private

Income Statement

FYE: December 31

	REVENUE ($ mil.)	NET INCOME ($ mil.)	NET PROFIT MARGIN	EMPLOYEES
12/15	195	0	0.5%	1,300
12/14	196	0	0.3%	—
12/13	193	0	0.2%	—
12/12	195	3	1.9%	—
Annual Growth	(0.0%)	(37.1%)	—	—

2015 Year-End Financials

Return on assets: 4.0%
Return on equity: 0.5%
Current ratio: 0.20

Cash ($ mil.): 1

RIGGINS INC.

EXECUTIVES

President, Paul Riggins
Director, Dave Staskelunas
Auditors: KENNETH E YEUTTER CPA MILLV

LOCATIONS

HQ: RIGGINS INC.
 3938 S MAIN RD, VINELAND, NJ 083607743
Phone: 856 825-7600
Web: WWW.RIGGINSOIL.COM

HISTORICAL FINANCIALS

Company Type: Private

Income Statement

FYE: December 31

	REVENUE ($ mil.)	NET INCOME ($ mil.)	NET PROFIT MARGIN	EMPLOYEES
12/15	249	0	0.1%	105
12/13	456	0	0.0%	—
12/12	491	0	0.0%	—
12/11	471	0	0.0%	—
Annual Growth	(14.7%)	32.2%	—	—

2015 Year-End Financials

Return on assets: 2.0%
Return on equity: 0.1%
Current ratio: 0.80

Cash ($ mil.): —

RIVERSIDE HEALTHCARE ASSOCIATION, INC.

Extra! Extra! Read all about it! Residents of Newport News (and about a dozen other cities in Eastern Virginia) Turn to Riverside Health for Medical Care. The not-for-profit health care provider administers general emergency and specialty medical services from five hospitals Riverside Regional Medical Center Riverside Walter Reed Hospital Riverside Tappahannock Hospital and Riverside Shore Memorial Hospital and Riverside Doctors Hospital as well as a psychiatric hospital a physical rehabilitation facility and retirement communities. Riverside also operates physician offices and medical training facilities. Specialty centers provide home and hospice care cancer treatment and dialysis.

Operations

Combined Riverside's hospitals (including rehabilitation and psychiatric) are home to nearly 1000 beds. Its major hospitals include Riverside Regional Medical Center (450-bed flagship hospital); Riverside Walter Reed Hospital (67-bed acute care facility); Riverside Tappahannock Hospital (67-bed serving the Northern Neck rural area); Riverside Shore Memorial Hospital (143-bed facility); and Riverside Doctors' Hospital Williamsburg (40 private rooms). It also operates specialty medical facilities including a psychiatric hospital a physical rehabilitation facility and retirement communities.

Geographic Reach

It serves Eastern Virginia including cities of Gloucester Hampton Newport News Poquoson Richmond Tappahannock West Point Williamsburg and Yorktown; Eastern Shore Area of Virginia; Counties of Essex Gloucester Isle of Wight James City King and Queen King William Lancaster Mathews Middlesex New Kent Northumberland Richmond and Surry.

Strategy

To keep up with demand Riverside Health has been upgrading its older facilities and building new ones.

In 2013 the company opened a new hospital the Doctors Hospital in Williamsburg. The 40 room hospital provides acute and emergency care as well as specialty services including cardiology neurology and pulmonary care.

That year Riverside broke ground on the new Riverside Shore Memorial Hospital in Onley which is expected to be completed in late 2015. It will have 57 private inpatient rooms with the ability to add 12 more in the future.

In 2012 Riverside Walter Reed Hospital opened a new intensive care unit.

It is also investing in technology physician expertise and patient services. In 2013 Riverside Shore Medical Center at Metompkin converted to digital mammography equipment offering patients a superior diagnostic tool to film mammograms.

Company Background

The original charter for Riverside dates back to 1915 when the company began as one hospital founded by the community. In 1962 the hospital was relocated to the present site in central Newport News.

EXECUTIVES

Senior Vice President and Chief Financial Officer,
 William Austin
Director of Nursing, Beverly Misuna
Vice President Security, William Parker
Secretary Unit Orthopedics, Linda Higashiuetoko
Auditors: ERNST & YOUNG LLP RICHMOND V

LOCATIONS

HQ: RIVERSIDE HEALTHCARE ASSOCIATION, INC.
 701 TOWN CENTER DR # 1000, NEWPORT NEWS, VA
 236064283
Phone: 757 534-7000

Selected Facilities – Virginia
HOSPITALS
Riverside Behavioral Health Center (Hampton)
Riverside Doctors' Hospital (Williamsburg)
Riverside Regional Medical Center (Newport News)
Riverside Rehabilitation Institute (Williamsburg)
Riverside Tappahannock Hospital (Tappahannock)
Riverside Shore Memorial Hospital (Nassawadox)
Riverside Walter Reed Hospital (Gloucester)
RETIREMENT COMMUNITIES
Patriots Colony (Williamsburg)
Sanders (Gloucester)
Warwick Forest (Newport News)
SURGERY CENTERS
Doctors Surgery Center (Williamsburg)
Peninsula Surgery Center (Newport News)
Riverside Hampton Surgery Center (Hampton)

COMPETITORS

Alleghany Regional Hospital
 Bon Secours Health
 Carilion Clinic
 Centra Health Inc.
 Children's Hospital of The King's Daughters
 Franklin Hospital Corp.
 Novant Health
 Sentara Healthcare
 Wake Forest University Baptist Medical Center

HISTORICAL FINANCIALS

Company Type: Private

Income Statement

FYE: December 31

	REVENUE ($ mil.)	NET INCOME ($ mil.)	NET PROFIT MARGIN	EMPLOYEES
12/15	1,149	21	1.8%	8,000
12/14	1,059	(86)	—	—
12/13	1,017	101	10.0%	—
12/12	948	41	4.4%	—
Annual Growth	6.6%	(20.3%)	—	—

2015 Year-End Financials

Return on assets: 3.7%
Return on equity: 1.8%
Current ratio: 1.20

Cash ($ mil.): 1

RIVERSIDE UNIFIED SCHOOL DISTRICT

EXECUTIVES

Superintendent, Dr David Hansen
Executive Secretary, Launa Whitlock
Engineer, Paul Daak
Assistant Manager, Verina McLurkin
Auditors: NIGRO & NIGRO PC MURRIETA C

LOCATIONS

HQ: RIVERSIDE UNIFIED SCHOOL DISTRICT
 3380 14TH ST, RIVERSIDE, CA 925013810
Phone: 951 788-7135
Web: WWW.RUSDLINK.ORG

HISTORICAL FINANCIALS

Company Type: Private

Income Statement
FYE: June 30

	REVENUE ($ mil.)	NET INCOME ($ mil.)	NET PROFIT MARGIN	EMPLOYEES
06/16	499	18	3.6%	3,740
06/15	428	11	2.6%	—
06/13	359	(40)	—	—
06/12	367	(9)	—	—
Annual Growth	8.0%	—	—	—

2016 Year-End Financials

Return on assets: 4.9%
Return on equity: 3.6%
Current ratio: —

Cash ($ mil.): 225

RIVERVIEW MEDICAL HOSPITAL

EXECUTIVES

Chief Operating Officer, Kelli O'Brien
Director, Jeffrey Boyle

LOCATIONS

HQ: RIVERVIEW MEDICAL HOSPITAL
1 RIVERVIEW PLZ, RED BANK, NJ 077011864
Phone: 732 741-2700
Web: WWW.RIVERVIEWMEDICALCENTER.COM

HISTORICAL FINANCIALS

Company Type: Private

Income Statement
FYE: December 31

	REVENUE ($ mil.)	NET INCOME ($ mil.)	NET PROFIT MARGIN	EMPLOYEES
12/15	276	36	13.1%	3
12/99	0	0	—	—
12/97	0	0	—	—
Annual Growth	—	—	—	—

2015 Year-End Financials

Return on assets: 14.7%
Return on equity: 13.1%
Current ratio: 1.60

Cash ($ mil.): 300

ROBERT BOSCH LLC

Robert Bosch LLC is your one-stop shop for German-engineered auto parts appliances and power tools. The North American subsidiary of German giant Robert Bosch GmbH Bosch LLC divides its operations among three divisions. Automotive Technology produces gasoline/diesel systems (and electrical drives); chassis and steering systems; and auto electronics for OEMs and the aftermarket. The Consumer Goods and Building Technology division builds various power tools security systems home appliances and HVAC equipment. Automation drive controls solar/wind power and packaging systems are the focus of its Industrial Technology division. Operating since 1906 Bosch LLC has grown to more than 100 North American locations.

Operations

The Automotive Technology business segment is Bosch LLC's largest generating about 65% of annual revenues. With the rebound of the automotive industry in 2010 — vehicle production increased almost 40% — the company's Automotive Technology unit realized a 13% increase in sales over 2010. The improvement was attributed to a better economy but also to the increased demand for the company's advanced vehicle technology offerings that are touted as safer cleaner and more economical.

The company's Consumer Goods and Building Technology division — portable power tools security systems thermotechnology and home appliances units — generated 20% of its total sales for 2011. This division also has expertise in making home appliances such as refrigerators and freezers washers and dryers dishwashers and ovens and cooktops.

Bosch LLC's Industrial Technology division generated 15% of total sales in 2011. Along with an aptitude in factory automation and engineering this segment is on an accelerated path to discovering newer better sources and uses of renewable energy. Subsidiaries Bosch Rexroth and Bosch Solar Energy are in the business of manufacturing wind turbine gearboxes hydraulics-based solar tracking systems solar cell making equipment and other photovoltaic (PV) products. Also part of Industrial Technology is the Bosch Packaging Technology unit that designs and makes packaging machinery and aftermarket parts as well as provides service.

Strategy

The Bosch Automotive Aftermarket division in 2011 acquired Taiwan-based Unipoint Group one of the world's largest manufacturers of starters alternators temperature control units and wiper blades. Unipoint manufactures products in Asia which is distributed throughout North America South America and Europe. The dell augmented Bosch's position as the leading supplier of starters and alternators and added another Asian production facility to its wiper blade business unit.

EXECUTIVES

President Bosch Security Systems, Christopher P. Gerace
CFO; EVP Controlling Finance and Administration, Maximiliane Straub
Regional President Bosch Rexroth Americas, Berend Bracht
Regional President Gasoline Systems, Sujit Jain
Regional President Chassis Systems Control, D. Scott Winchip
Regional President Car Multimedia North America, Juergen Peters
EVP Original Equipment Sales Ford, Manfred Mueller, age 61
President and CEO BSH Home Appliances, Michael Traub
Regional President Automotive Electronics North America, Timothy (Tim) Frasier
Regional President Diesel Systems North America, Bernd Boisten
President, Mike Mansuetti
Regional President Robert Bosch Automotive Aftermarket Division, Odd Joergenrud
EVP Original Equipment Sales General Motors, Clesio Honma
Regional President Electrical Drives, Peter Denk
Regional President Starter Motors and Generators North America, Pres Lawhon
Regional President Bosch Engineering Group North America, Wayne (Keith) Andrews
President Robert Bosch Healthcare Systems Inc., Micha Kirchhoff

VP Original Equipment Sales Chrysler, Paul Thomas
Vice President and Deputy General Counsel, Jerry L Johnson
Vice President Business Development, Michael Barhaug
President And Executive Vice President Automotive Aftermarket, David Coolidge
Vice President, Tim Williams
Vice President, Christine Zimmerman
Vice President Finance, Nancy Gustitus
Chairman, Werner Struth

LOCATIONS

HQ: ROBERT BOSCH LLC
2800 S 25TH AVE, BROADVIEW, IL 601554532
Phone: 248 876-1000
Web: WWW.BOSCHTECHINFO.COM

PRODUCTS/OPERATIONS

2011 Sales

	$ mil.	% of total
Automotive Technology	6	65
Consumer Goods & Building Technology	2	20
Industrial Technology	1	15
Total	**9**	**100**

Selected Products

Automotive Technology
  Aftermarket
  Alternators
  Brake pads
  Car audio products
  Diesel parts
  Filters
  Fuel pumps
  Ignition products
  Oxygen sensors
  Spark plugs
  Spark plug wire sets
  Starters
  Wiper blades
  Original equipment
  Actuators
  Braking and chassis systems
  Car multimedia
  Electrical systems
  Electronic systems
  Powertrain systems - diesel
  Powertrain systems - gasoline
Consumer Goods and Building Technology
  Household appliances
  Cooktops
  Dishwashers
  Ovens
  Washers and dryers
  Power tools
  Angle grinders
  Belt sanders
  Circular saws
  Drill bits
  Drills
  Drywall drivers
  Impact wrenches
  Jigsaws
  Orbit sanders/polishers
  Planers
  Reciprocating saws
  Rotary hammers
  Routers
  Screwdriver bits and accessories
  Wet/dry vacuums
  Security Systems
  Access control
  Communications
  Fire detection
  Security management
  Video surveillance
  Thermotechnology
  Indoor climate control (heating and cooling and hot water production)
Industrial Technology
  Drive and control
  Assembly
  Electric drives and controls
  Gears
  Hydraulics

Linear motion
Pneumatics
Packaging
Confectionary cosmetics and chemicals
Packaging machines
Packaging services
Pharmaceuticals
Production tools
Air assembly tools
Cordless assembly tools
DC electric assembly tools
Electric assembly tools
Solar Energy
Crystalline PV modules
Solar cells
Thin-film modules
Wafers

COMPETITORS

AISIN World Corp.	LG Electronics
Advanced Security &	Makita
Controls	Molins
DENSO America	Motorcar Parts
Dana	NGK Spark Plugs
Delphi Automotive	Neaton Auto Products
Systems	Stanley Black and
GE	Decker
Hitachi Automotive	Visteon
Systems Americas	Whirlpool

HISTORICAL FINANCIALS

Company Type: Private

Income Statement

FYE: December 31

	REVENUE ($ mil.)	NET INCOME ($ mil.)	NET PROFIT MARGIN	EMPLOYEES
12/15	10,868	457	4.2%	12,986
12/14	10,474	181	1.7%	—
12/10	6,810	326	4.8%	—
12/09	5,464	59	1.1%	—
Annual Growth	12.1%	40.7%	—	—

2015 Year-End Financials

Return on assets: 4.5%
Return on equity: 4.2%
Current ratio: 1.10
Cash ($ mil.): 760

ROCHESTER GENERAL HOSPITAL INC

EXECUTIVES

Chief Executive Officer, Mark Clement
Manager, Bonnie Cleaver
Office Manager, Linda Pastorelle
Vice-President, Patricia Houghton
Chief Financial Officer, Richard Hogg

LOCATIONS

HQ: ROCHESTER GENERAL HOSPITAL INC
1425 PORTLAND AVE, ROCHESTER, NY 146213095
Phone: 585 922-4101
Web: WWW.ROCHESTERGENERAL.ORG

HISTORICAL FINANCIALS

Company Type: Private

Income Statement

FYE: December 31

	REVENUE ($ mil.)	NET INCOME ($ mil.)	NET PROFIT MARGIN	EMPLOYEES
12/15	847	27	3.3%	3,100
12/14	810	32	4.0%	—
12/13	830	40	4.9%	—
12/09	637	33	5.3%	—
Annual Growth	4.9%	(3.4%)	—	—

2015 Year-End Financials

Return on assets: 4.4%
Return on equity: 3.3%
Current ratio: 0.70
Cash ($ mil.): 42

ROCK HILL SCHOOL DISTRICT 3

EXECUTIVES

Superintendent, Kelly Pew
Administration Director, George M Hapton
Director, Martha Nemchinger

LOCATIONS

HQ: ROCK HILL SCHOOL DISTRICT 3
1234 FLINT STREET EXT, ROCK HILL, SC 297306329
Phone: 803 981-1000
Web: WWW.ROCK-HILL.K12.SC.US

HISTORICAL FINANCIALS

Company Type: Private

Income Statement

FYE: June 30

	REVENUE ($ mil.)	NET INCOME ($ mil.)	NET PROFIT MARGIN	EMPLOYEES
06/16	190	25	13.2%	1,800
06/10	166	(1)	—	—
06/09	167	(8)	—	—
06/08	935	0	—	—
Annual Growth	—	286.0%	—	—

2016 Year-End Financials

Return on assets: 9.7%
Return on equity: 13.2%
Current ratio: —
Cash ($ mil.): 30

ROCKFORD CONSTRUCTION CO.

EXECUTIVES

Chairman, Mike Vangessel
Project Manager, Drew Sorenson
Project Manager, Jason Verhey
Project Manager, Peter Michell
Project Manager, Rich Robbins
Superintendent, Tim Exposito
Auditors: CROWE HORWATH LLP SOUTH BEND

LOCATIONS

HQ: ROCKFORD CONSTRUCTION CO.
601 1ST ST NW, GRAND RAPIDS, MI 495045517
Phone: 616 285-6933
Web: WWW.ROCKFORDCONSTRUCTION.COM

HISTORICAL FINANCIALS

Company Type: Private

Income Statement

FYE: December 31

	REVENUE ($ mil.)	NET INCOME ($ mil.)	NET PROFIT MARGIN	EMPLOYEES
12/15	187	4	2.4%	200
12/14	135	3	2.8%	—
12/13	99	0	0.4%	—
12/12	57	0	0.7%	—
Annual Growth	48.5%	122.2%	—	—

2015 Year-End Financials

Return on assets: 9.2%
Return on equity: 2.4%
Current ratio: 1.00
Cash ($ mil.): 9

ROCKFORD MEMORIAL HOSPITAL

EXECUTIVES

Chief Executive Officer, Gary E Kaatz
Supervisor, Lori Leppert
Supervisor, Sheila Livingston
Production Director, Stuart Wasilewski
Supervisor, Barry Britton

LOCATIONS

HQ: ROCKFORD MEMORIAL HOSPITAL
2400 N ROCKTON AVE, ROCKFORD, IL 611033681
Phone: 815 971-5000

HISTORICAL FINANCIALS

Company Type: Private

Income Statement

FYE: June 30

	REVENUE ($ mil.)	NET INCOME ($ mil.)	NET PROFIT MARGIN	EMPLOYEES
06/15*	186	22	12.1%	2,200
12/14	307	42	13.7%	—
12/13	346	49	14.2%	—
12/12	307	63	20.5%	—
Annual Growth	(22.2%)	(40.3%)	—	—

*Fiscal year change

2015 Year-End Financials

Return on assets: 48.4%
Return on equity: 12.1%
Current ratio: 0.70
Cash ($ mil.): 51

ROCKFORD, BOARD OF EDUCATION

EXECUTIVES

Superintendent, Dr Ehren Jarrett
Board of Directors, Lisa Jackson
Superintendent, Dennis Thompson

Bookkeeper, Kathy Johnson
Assistant Manager, Marcia Strothoff
Superintendent, Maryann Gemmill
Administrative Assistant, Rhonda Freeman
Auditors: SIKICH LLP ROCK ILLINOIS

LOCATIONS

HQ: ROCKFORD, BOARD OF EDUCATION
501 7TH ST, ROCKFORD, IL 611041242
Phone: 815 966-3000
Web: WWW.RPS205.COM

HISTORICAL FINANCIALS
Company Type: Private

Income Statement
FYE: June 30

	REVENUE ($ mil.)	NET INCOME ($ mil.)	NET PROFIT MARGIN	EMPLOYEES
06/15	446	19	4.4%	4,200
06/14	398	(54)	—	—
06/13	394	114	29.1%	—
06/04	269	2	0.8%	—
Annual Growth	4.7%	21.7%	—	—

ROGER WILLIAMS UNIVERSITY

EXECUTIVES

President, Donald J Farish
Program Manager, Bret Hall
Vice-President, James Noonan
Manager, Jennifer Duclos
Engineer, Robert O'Neill
Manager, Dipak Ramkumar
Director, Lisa Scott

LOCATIONS

HQ: ROGER WILLIAMS UNIVERSITY
1 OLD FERRY RD, BRISTOL, RI 028092921
Phone: 401 253-1040
Web: WWW.RWU.EDU

HISTORICAL FINANCIALS
Company Type: Private

Income Statement
FYE: June 30

	REVENUE ($ mil.)	NET INCOME ($ mil.)	NET PROFIT MARGIN	EMPLOYEES
06/15	197	2	1.2%	425
06/14	188	0	0.4%	—
06/13	183	7	4.1%	—
06/10	157	(0)	—	—
Annual Growth	4.6%	—	—	—

2015 Year-End Financials
Return on assets: 4.5%   Cash ($ mil.): 2
Return on equity: 1.2%
Current ratio: 0.10

ROSE INTERNATIONAL, INC.

Rose International keep its customers' tech gardens in bloom. The company provides outsourced IT services including database performance optimization application development and project management to businesses and government agencies in the US. Other services include vendor management payroll processing training and staffing and call center operations. Rose — its name is an acronym for "reliable open systems engineering" — serves customers in the financial services energy technology telecommunications and health care industries. Its software development activities in Missouri and India are overseen by subsidiary Rose I.T. Solutions.

Geographic Reach

Rose International has about 20 offices located across the US and one in New Delhi India.

Sales and Marketing

The company serves more than 130 customers in the energy entertainment financial and healthcare industries and government agencies. Some of its commercial customers have included Square D UniGroup Boeing Southwestern Bell and Maritz. In addition to commercial clients the company's government clients have included the US Air Force Army and Navy the State of Missouri and the USDA.

Rose International has sales and service partnerships with IT vendors IBM Microsoft and Cisco Systems.

Company Background

Established in 1993 as Rose Imaging the company (a minority- and woman-owned business) is controlled by founder Himanshu (Sue) Bhatia.

EXECUTIVES

Vice President Finance, Larry Crane
Vice President Western Region, Harish Vakharia
Vice President Contingent Workforce Services, Phil Black
Vice President Information technology, Maria M Wilson
Board Member, Pankaj Seth
Auditors: BROWN SMITH WALLACE LLC ST L

LOCATIONS

HQ: ROSE INTERNATIONAL, INC.
16401 SWINGLEY RIDGE RD, CHESTERFIELD, MO 630170757
Phone: 636 812-4000
Web: WWW.ROSEIT.COM

PRODUCTS/OPERATIONS

Selected Services
Application Development
Database Performance Optimization Practice
Operations Maintenance and Support
Project Management and PMI Training
Workforce Solutions

Selected Industries Served
Energy
Entertainment
Financial
Government Agencies
Healthcare
Retail and Consumer
Technology and Telecommunication

COMPETITORS

Accenture	Infosys
Analysts International	Leidos
Capgemini	Maryville Data Systems

Computer Sciences Corp.	S2 Tech
HP Enterprise Group	Tata Consultancy
IBM Global Services	Unisys
	World Wide Technology

HISTORICAL FINANCIALS
Company Type: Private

Income Statement
FYE: December 31

	REVENUE ($ mil.)	NET INCOME ($ mil.)	NET PROFIT MARGIN	EMPLOYEES
12/15	248	5	2.1%	6,000
12/14	293	7	2.5%	—
12/12	357	11	3.2%	—
12/11	357	13	3.8%	—
Annual Growth	(8.6%)	(21.5%)	—	—

2015 Year-End Financials
Return on assets: 1.3%   Cash ($ mil.): 3
Return on equity: 2.1%
Current ratio: 3.90

ROSEMOUNT-APPLE VALLEY-EAGAN SCHOOL BOARD

EXECUTIVES

Chairman of the Board, Rob Duchscher
Director, Mark Parr
Manager, Cindy Nordstom
Director, Jeffery M Solomon
Manager, Sherryl Brunner
Account Manager, Robin Sicoli
Auditors: MALLOY MONTAGUE KARNOWSKI R

LOCATIONS

HQ: ROSEMOUNT-APPLE VALLEY-EAGAN SCHOOL BOARD
3455 153RD ST W, ROSEMOUNT, MN 550684946
Phone: 651 423-7700
Web: WWW.DISTRICT196.ORG

HISTORICAL FINANCIALS
Company Type: Private

Income Statement
FYE: June 30

	REVENUE ($ mil.)	NET INCOME ($ mil.)	NET PROFIT MARGIN	EMPLOYEES
06/16	372	117	31.7%	3,600
06/14	339	(27)	—	—
06/13	337	10	3.2%	—
06/12	336	33	9.9%	—
Annual Growth	2.5%	37.2%	—	—

ROSENBAUER AMERICA, LLC

EXECUTIVES

Chief Executive Officer, Harold Boer
Office Manager, Helen Boer

Financial Executive, Lloyd Arends
Accountant, Bryan Kueter
Board of Directors, Kevin Kirvida
Supervisor, Dan McMahon

LOCATIONS

HQ: ROSENBAUER AMERICA, LLC
100 3RD ST, LYONS, SD 570418000
Phone: 605 543-5591
Web: WWW.ROSENBAUERAMERICA.COM

HISTORICAL FINANCIALS

Company Type: Private

Income Statement

	REVENUE ($ mil.)	NET INCOME ($ mil.)	NET PROFIT MARGIN	EMPLOYEES
12/15	271	25	9.4%	600
12/14	262	17	6.6%	—
12/13	238	11	5.0%	—
12/12	200	3	1.7%	—
Annual Growth	10.6%	94.3%	—	—

FYE: December 31

2015 Year-End Financials

Return on assets: 0.1%
Return on equity: 9.4%
Current ratio: 0.50

Cash ($ mil.): —

ROUND ROCK INDEPENDENT SCHOOL DISTRICT (INC)

EXECUTIVES

Superintendent, Dr Jess H Chvez
Director, Fred Morgan
Accountant, Lori Melton
Auditor, Nancy Green
Administrative Assistant, L Nelson
Auditors: MAXWELL LOCKE & RITTER LLP AU

LOCATIONS

HQ: ROUND ROCK INDEPENDENT SCHOOL DISTRICT (INC)
1311 ROUND ROCK AVE, ROUND ROCK, TX 786814941
Phone: 512 464-5000
Web: WWW.ROUNDROCKISD.ORG

HISTORICAL FINANCIALS

Company Type: Private

Income Statement

	REVENUE ($ mil.)	NET INCOME ($ mil.)	NET PROFIT MARGIN	EMPLOYEES
06/16	523	64	12.3%	4,500
06/15	491	126	25.7%	—
06/14	462	(47)	—	—
06/13	442	(50)	—	—
Annual Growth	5.8%	—	—	—

FYE: June 30

2016 Year-End Financials

Return on assets: 3.1%
Return on equity: 12.3%
Current ratio: 5.70

Cash ($ mil.): 503

ROWAN REGIONAL MEDICAL CENTER, INC.

Rowan Regional Medical Center oversees medical care for residents of central North Carolina. The acute care facility has about 270 beds and provides general emergency and surgical inpatient services. It also includes a host of centers dedicated to specialty fields such as cancer care cardiac rehabilitation behavioral health pain management sleep medicine and women's health. Founded in 1936 Rowan Regional also has specialized physical and respiratory rehabilitation units and home health and hospice organizations. Rowan Regional is part of the Novant Health network.

Strategy

Faced with mounting debt Rowan Regional merged into Novant Health in 2008 with the larger system committing to investing about $200 million in Rowan Regional over several years for expansion and improvement measures. Following the merger Rowan Regional Medical Center also expanded its services in areas including women's health neurology and home health by adding affiliated practice organizations to its network.

EXECUTIVES

Chief Executive Officer, Carl Armato
Director, Cora Green
Vice-President, Thomas F Trahey
Manager, Wendy Ledbetter

LOCATIONS

HQ: ROWAN REGIONAL MEDICAL CENTER, INC.
612 MOCKSVILLE AVE, SALISBURY, NC 281442799
Phone: 704 210-5000
Web: WWW.ROWANSERVICEABOVESELF.COM

PRODUCTS/OPERATIONS

Selected Services

Behavioral Health Services
Breast Health Services
Cancer Services
Corporate Wellness Services
Diabetes & Nutrition Services
Emergency Services
Heart & Vascular Services
Hospice Services
Laboratory Services
Orthopaedics Services
Pastoral Care Services
Pharmacy Services
Rehabilitation Services
Sleep Medicine Services
Stroke Services
Women's Services

COMPETITORS

Carolinas HealthCare System
Carolinas Medical Center-NorthEast
Cone Health
Davis Regional Medical Center
Forsyth Medical Center
High Point Regional Health System
Stanly Medical Center
Wake Forest University Baptist Medical Center
Wesley Long Community Hospital

HISTORICAL FINANCIALS

Company Type: Private

Income Statement

	REVENUE ($ mil.)	NET INCOME ($ mil.)	NET PROFIT MARGIN	EMPLOYEES
12/15	196	21	11.0%	1,196
12/14	187	16	8.7%	—
12/13	175	16	9.6%	—
Annual Growth	5.8%	13.0%	—	—

FYE: December 31

2015 Year-End Financials

Return on assets: 1.0%
Return on equity: 11.0%
Current ratio: —

Cash ($ mil.): —

RPM LUXURY AUTO SALES, INC.

EXECUTIVES

President, Patrick Frink
Director, Jamal Kabir
Consultant, Brandy Joseph
Consultant, John Dickinson
Consultant, Wendy Lange
Sales Manager, Bryon Burdette
Sales Director, Dick Hill
Manager, Kyle Lane

LOCATIONS

HQ: RPM LUXURY AUTO SALES, INC.
5112 MADISON AVE STE 201, SACRAMENTO, CA 958413000
Phone: 916 485-3987
Web: WWW.LEXUSOFSACRAMENTO.COM

HISTORICAL FINANCIALS

Company Type: Private

Income Statement

	REVENUE ($ mil.)	NET INCOME ($ mil.)	NET PROFIT MARGIN	EMPLOYEES
12/15	171	3	2.2%	228
12/14	155	2	1.5%	—
12/13	146	3	2.6%	—
12/12	127	2	2.1%	—
Annual Growth	10.4%	12.9%	—	—

FYE: December 31

2015 Year-End Financials

Return on assets: 2.1%
Return on equity: 2.2%
Current ratio: 0.60

Cash ($ mil.): 9

RUMSEY ELECTRIC COMPANY

Rumsey Electric distributes electrical construction equipment utility products and services and systems for relay and power and lighting for retailers. Operating through one central distribution facility and a dozen branches the company caters to construction and industrial businesses and util-

ities as well as OEMs institutions and commercial Mid-Atlantic markets. It is the authorized distributor of Rockwell Automation a large industrial automation firm. The company operates through its 135000 sq. ft. central distribution facility and 11 branch locations primarily located in Delaware Pennsylvania and New Jersey. Employee-owned Rumsey Electric has been in business for over 110 years.

Mergers and Acquisitions

Rumsey grows by adding products to its portfolio and through acquisitions. In 2015 the company acquired Transmission Engineering Company (TECO) an independent operating company in Hatfield Pennsylvania. The acquisition extended its product offering into power transmission and power train components.

EXECUTIVES

President and CEO, Gerald M. (Jerry) Lihota, age 70
EVP and CFO, Scott M. Cutler, age 67
Manager Information Technology, Matt Prior
VP Marketing and Vendor Relations, John Thorn
Vice President, Steven Cabibbo
Auditors: RAINER & COMPANY NEWTON SQUAR

LOCATIONS

HQ: RUMSEY ELECTRIC COMPANY
15 COLWELL LN, CONSHOHOCKEN, PA 194281878
Phone: 610 832-9000
Web: WWW.RUMSEY.COM

PRODUCTS/OPERATIONS

Selected ServicesAsset ManagementConfigured ProductsEnergy SavingEngineering ServicesGovernment-Lighting ServicesOn Site Managed InventoryPreventative MaintenanceProject ManagementProtection ControlRACERecyclingRelay and Power SystemsRelay ProtectionRumse

COMPETITORS

Anixter International	Fromm Electric
Billows Electric Supply	Gexpro
Colonial Electric Supply	Graybar Electric
Consolidated Electrical	Rexel Inc.
	United Electric Supply
	WESCO International

HISTORICAL FINANCIALS

Company Type: Private

Income Statement

FYE: December 31

	REVENUE ($ mil.)	NET INCOME ($ mil.)	NET PROFIT MARGIN	EMPLOYEES
12/15	223	8	3.6%	284
12/14	230	13	5.6%	—
12/13	225	9	4.1%	—
12/12	197	10	5.4%	—
Annual Growth	4.2%	(9.2%)	—	—

2015 Year-End Financials

Return on assets: 9.1%
Return on equity: 3.6%
Current ratio: 1.90
Cash ($ mil.): 14

RUSH UNIVERSITY MEDICAL CENTER

EXECUTIVES

President, Larry J Goodman
Director, Ralph Elget
Manager, Barbara Krah
Manager, Carolyn Whitney

LOCATIONS

HQ: RUSH UNIVERSITY MEDICAL CENTER
1653 W CONGRESS PKWY, CHICAGO, IL 606123833
Phone: 312 942-5000
Web: WWW.RUSH.EDU

HISTORICAL FINANCIALS

Company Type: Private

Income Statement

FYE: June 30

	REVENUE ($ mil.)	NET INCOME ($ mil.)	NET PROFIT MARGIN	EMPLOYEES
06/15	1,408	(22)	—	8,000
06/14	1,969	208	10.6%	—
06/13	1,583	124	7.9%	—
06/12	1,449	33	2.3%	—
Annual Growth	(1.0%)	—	—	—

2015 Year-End Financials

Return on assets: 7.7%
Return on equity: (-1.6%)
Current ratio: 0.70
Cash ($ mil.): 125

RUSSELL & SMITH FORD, INC.

EXECUTIVES

Chairman, Michael G Smith
Manager, Rhonda Walker
Sales Director, Carlos Duca
Manager, Christopher Rehkopf
Finance Manager, Amanda Jones
Auditors: SVADLENAK SEE & COMPANY PC

LOCATIONS

HQ: RUSSELL & SMITH FORD, INC.
3440 SOUTH LOOP W, HOUSTON, TX 770255296
Phone: 713 663-4111
Web: WWW.RSFORD.COM

HISTORICAL FINANCIALS

Company Type: Private

Income Statement

FYE: May 31

	REVENUE ($ mil.)	NET INCOME ($ mil.)	NET PROFIT MARGIN	EMPLOYEES
05/15	291	3	1.2%	310
05/14	304	4	1.5%	—
05/13	265	3	1.3%	—
05/12	222	2	0.9%	—
Annual Growth	9.4%	19.0%	—	—

2015 Year-End Financials

Return on assets: 3.1%
Return on equity: 1.2%
Current ratio: 0.30
Cash ($ mil.): 8

RYMAN HOSPITALITY PROPERTIES, INC.

Ryman Hospitality Properties (formerly Gaylord Entertainment) may be hollerin' for attention in the hospitality game but it's no corporate hayseed. Its properties consist of resort hotels tethered closely to attractions that appeal to the meetings and conventions market. They include the Gaylord Opryland Resort & Convention Center in Nashville the Gaylord Palms Resort in Florida (close to Disney World) the Gaylord Texan Resort near Dallas and the Gaylord National Resort and Convention Center in the Washington DC area. Ryman's hotels are managed by hotel giant Marriott. In 2012 the company changed its name convered to a REIT and sold its hotel brand and management business to Marriott.

HISTORY

The origins of Gaylord Entertainment can be traced back to the Oklahoma Publishing Co. a newspaper publishing company founded by Edward K. Gaylord Ray Dickinson and Roy McClintock in 1903. The publisher of The Daily Oklahoman Oklahoma Publishing branched into radio in 1928 with the purchase of Oklahoma City radio station WKY. With its 1949 creation of Oklahoma City television station WKY-TV Oklahoma Publishing made the leap into television.

Edward K. Gaylord died in 1974 at the age of 101 and his son Edward L. Gaylord was appointed CEO. Under his leadership the company purchased Opryland USA in 1983 — an acquisition that netted it the Grand Ole Opry Opryland Themepark and the Opryland Hotel. Opryland USA also launched country music cable network The Nashville Network that year.

In 1991 the increasingly diverse Oklahoma Publishing spun off its entertainment and broadcast holdings in the form of public company Gaylord Entertainment which established its headquarters in Nashville Tennessee. Gaylord Entertainment acquired a majority interest in cable music network Country Music Television (CMT) the same year. It later expanded CMT into Latin America Asia and the Pacific Rim. CMT also made a brief foray into Europe but that initiative was ended in 1998.

Facing a consolidating entertainment and media landscape Gaylord sold The Nashville Network and the US operations of CMT to Westinghouse (now CBS) in 1997. It also sold television station KSTW that year. The company expanded its reach into Christian music with the purchase of Word Entertainment and its 1997 acquisition of Blanton Harrell Entertainment gave Gaylord a presence in artist management. Terry London was appointed CEO in 1997.

The company closed its Opryland theme park in 1998 in the face of declining attendance and broke ground at the same site for the Opry Mills entertainment shopping and restaurant complex (opened 2000). Gaylord also purchased a Nashville Ramada Inn in 1998 (later renaming it Radisson Hotel at Opryland). With its 1998 acquisition of Paris-based Pandora Investment Gaylord branched into film distribution.

In 1999 the company formed Opryland Hospitality Group to oversee expansion of the Opryland hotel concept across the US. It also sold its last television station KTVT in Dallas/Fort Worth to CBS. Edward K. Gaylord II succeeded his father as chairman in 1999. That year the company launched its Internet division GETdigitalmedia (later renamed Gaylord Digital) and moved online with the pur-

chase of Christian Web sites Musicforce.com and Lightsource.com. Later the same year the company expanded its Internet presence with the purchase of Songs.com a music Web site focused on independent artists. But in late 2000 the company announced it would close its Internet unit. Also in 2000 the company bought Corporate Magic a firm focused on producing entertainment events for corporate audiences.

At the end of 2000 Gaylord sold Musicforce.com to Christian Book Distributors. Following that sale it sold Lightsource.com to LifeAudio.com in early 2001. That year the company sold its film and television production units and announced a restructuring in order to cut costs. It also renamed Opryland Hotels to Gaylord Opryland while expanding into Texas and Florida. Colin Reed was appointed CEO in 2001.

Between 2001 and 2003 Gaylord Entertainment sold Word Entertainment to Warner Music Group the Opry Mills shopping and restaurant complex to The Mills Corporation the Acuff-Rose Music Publishing business to Sony/ATV two of its Nashville radio stations to Cumulus Media and its majority interest in the Oklahoma City Redhawks minor league baseball team.

Edward L. Gaylord officially retired from the company in 2003 at age 83. Also that year the company significantly expanded its hospitality business with the purchase of ResortQuest a vacation and condominium property management firm. In 2004 the Gaylord family sold more than half its shares in the company making Gabelli Funds the majority owner.

In 2005 Gaylord acquired 50% of Corporate Magic a Dallas-based provider of production support for corporate meetings and events. It did so to support its meeting and convention facilities.

The company unloaded its minority interest in minor league hockey team the Nashville Predators in 2005. Two years later it sold ResortQuest to a subsidiary of Leucadia National Corp. for $35 million. Also in 2007 it sold its interest in sporting goods store operator Bass Pro Group. In 2008 the company opened the Gaylord National Resort and Convention Center in the Washington DC area. The property has some 2000 rooms and approximately 450000 square feet of meeting space.

Also in 2008 Gaylord terminated plans to acquire the Westin La Cantera Resort in San Antonio for about $253 million citing a tough economic environment. In addition the 2008 sale of its ResortQuest subsidiary an online booking service in vacation rentals property management and resort real estate sales fit the company's strategy of selling off assets that aren't related to its Grand Ole Opry or its operations in the meetings and convention market.

In 2009 the company responded to weak earnings by cutting approximately 500 jobs across all areas of the business. Gaylord reported steep dip in profits in 2010 primarily due to harsh flooding in Nashville when the Cumberland River rose to historic levels flowing over protective levees. The flood resulted in property damage and temporary closures at its properties in Nashville causing lost revenues and an increase in expenses. Also in 2010 Gaylord sold its 50% stake in Corporate Magic back to that company's CEO.

The company changed its name to Ryman Hospitality Properties in 2012. It also converted to an REIT and sold the Gaylord brand to Marriott which now manages Ryman's hotel properties and certain other entertainment holdings.

EXECUTIVES

EVP Ryman Hospitality Properties; President OPRY Entertainment Group, Stephen G. (Steve) Buchanan

Chairman and CEO, Colin V. Reed, age 69, $782,830 total compensation
SVP Investments Design and Construction, Bennett D. Westbrook, age 50, $318,447 total compensation
President and CFO, Mark Fioravanti, age 55, $469,407 total compensation
SVP Asset Management, Patrick Chaffin, age 43, $274,975 total compensation
SVP General Counsel and Secretary, Scott J. Lynn, age 43, $364,876 total compensation
Senior Vice President and Corporate Controller, Jennifer Hutcheson
Vice President Human Resources, Shawn Smith
Auditors: ERNST & YOUNG LLP NASHVILLE

LOCATIONS

HQ: RYMAN HOSPITALITY PROPERTIES, INC.
1 GAYLORD DR, NASHVILLE, TN 372141207
Phone: 615 316-6000
Web: WWW.RYMANHP.COM

PRODUCTS/OPERATIONS

2015 Sales

	$ mil.	% of total
Hospitality	994	91
Entertainment (previously Opry and Attractions)	97	9
Total	**1,092**	**100**

2015 Sales

	$ mil.	% of total
Food and beverage	461	42
Rooms	404	37
Other hotel revenue	129	12
Entertainment (previously Opry and Attractions)	97	9
Total	**1,092**	**100**

Select Operations

Hospitality
  Gaylord Opryland Resort & Convention Center (Tennessee)
  Gaylord Palms Resort & Convention Center (Florida)
  Gaylord Texan Resort & Convention Center
  Radisson Hotel at Opryland (Tennessee)
Attractions
  Gaylord Springs Golf Links (golf club Tennessee)
  General Jackson Showboat
  Grand Ole Opry
  Ryman Auditorium
  Wildhorse Saloon
  WSM-AM

COMPETITORS

CKX
CKX
Caesars Entertainment
Caesars Entertainment
Disney Parks & Resorts
Disney Parks & Resorts
Elvis Presley Enterprises
Elvis Presley Enterprises
Herschend Entertainment
Herschend Entertainment
Hershey Entertainment
Hershey Entertainment
Hilton Worldwide
Hilton Worldwide
Kennywood
Kennywood
Las Vegas Sands
Las Vegas Sands
Live Nation Entertainment
Live Nation Entertainment
MGM Resorts
MGM Resorts
Marriott
Marriott
New York Convention Center Operating Corporation
New York Convention Center Operating Corporation
SeaWorld
SeaWorld

Welk Group
Welk Group

HISTORICAL FINANCIALS
Company Type: Private

Income Statement
FYE: December 31

	ASSETS ($ mil.)	NET INCOME ($ mil.)	INCOME AS % OF ASSETS	EMPLOYEES
12/16	2,405	159	6.6%	682
12/15	2,331	111	4.8%	—
12/14	2,413	126	5.2%	—
12/13	2,424	113	4.7%	—
Annual Growth	(0.3%)	12.0%	—	—

2016 Year-End Financials
Return on assets: 14.2%   Sales ($ mil): 1,149
Return on equity: 13.9%

SACRAMENTO CITY UNIFIED SCHOOL DISTRICT

EXECUTIVES

Superintendent, Jose Banda
Assistant Manager, Nancy Purcell
Administration Manager, Mary Prather
Purchasing Director, Gerardo Castillo
Assistant Manager, Olga Arellano
Auditors: CROWE HORWATH LLP SACRAMENTO

LOCATIONS

HQ: SACRAMENTO CITY UNIFIED SCHOOL DISTRICT
5735 47TH AVE, SACRAMENTO, CA 958244528
Phone: 916 643-7400
Web: WWW.SCUSD.EDU

HISTORICAL FINANCIALS
Company Type: Private

Income Statement
FYE: June 30

	REVENUE ($ mil.)	NET INCOME ($ mil.)	NET PROFIT MARGIN	EMPLOYEES
06/16	656	47	7.2%	6,500
06/11	509	(0)	—	—
06/06	434	0	—	—
06/02	444	18	4.2%	—
Annual Growth	2.8%	6.8%	—	—

SACRAMENTO MUNICIPAL UTILITY DISTRICT

The Sacramento Municipal Utility District (SMUD) doesn't want its name to be mud. One of the largest locally owned electric utilities in the US SMUD serves more than 624770 residential and commercial customer meters (a service area pop-

ulation of 1.4 million) in California's Sacramento and Placer counties. The utility generates about 70% of its electricity (its 1300-MW capacity is derived primarily from hydroelectric and cogeneration power plants) and buys the rest. SMUD also sells power to wholesale customers andhas one of the largest solar energy distribution systems in the US.

Operations

The utility operates more than 10470 miles of transmission and distribution lines across its 900-sq.-mi. service area. It gets power from varied sources including hydropower natural-gas-fired generators renewable energy (such as solar and wind power) and purchases power on the wholesale market.

The company has installed 600000 smart meters at customer locations across its entire service area.

Geographic Reach

SMUD generates transmits and distributes electricity to a territory that includes Sacramento Sacramento County and a small portion of Placer County.

Financial Performance

In fiscal 2015 SMUD's net revenue decreased by 4% due to lower wholesale revenues as the result of lower surplus gas sales driven by a decrease in gas prices and less gas sold and lower energy prices and sales.

The company's net income decreased by 23% due to lower net sales and an increase in administrative general and customer and maintenance expenses.

In fiscal 2015 SMUD's operating cash inflow decreased by 15%.

Strategy

In response to market deregulation and the nationwide push for carbon emission reduction SMUD has increased its generation capacity placing a priority on renewable energy sources. As part of this green energy push the company has a 15-year deal with Shell Energy (which expires in 2024) to buy landfill gas from sites in Texas. SMUD has installed more than 600000 smart meters to help customers to better control their power use.

In 2015 the company invested $3.3 billion in electric utility plant assets and construction work in progress.

The utility even works with local dairies to install anaerobic digesters to turn manure into renewable energy.

Company Background

In 2012 SMUD announced that it is the leading utility in the US in terms of new homes which had solar panels installed during construction. The utility commenced the SMUD Solar Smart Homes program in 2006 and had constructed more than 1000 homes with solar panels by 2012.

The company has been delivering power to customers in the region since 1946 but its history goes back to 1923 when citizens voted to create SMUD as a community-owned electric service. However years of engineering studies political battles and legal wrangling delayed SMUD's purchase of PG&E's local electrical system.

In March 1946 the California Supreme Court denied PG&E's final petition to halt the sale and nine months later SMUD finally began operations.

EXECUTIVES

CFO Finance and Enterprise Planning, James A. (Jim) Tracy
CEO and General Manager, Arlen Orchard
Chief Grid Strategy and Operations Officer, Paul Lau
Vice President, Brad Gacke
Vice President Board of Directors, William Slaton

Assistant Treasurer, Larry Stark
Treasurer, Noreen Roche-Carter
Board Member, Nancy Bui
Board Member, David Davis
Auditors: BAKER TILLY VIRCHOW KRAUSE LL

LOCATIONS

HQ: SACRAMENTO MUNICIPAL UTILITY DISTRICT
6201 S ST, SACRAMENTO, CA 958171818
Phone: 916 452-3211
Web: WWW.SMUD.ORG

PRODUCTS/OPERATIONS

2015 Sales

	% of total
Commercial & industrial	47
Residential	42
Wholesale power	6
Street lighting & other	5
Total	**100**

Selected Products and Services

Conservation programs
Customer billing programs
Diagnostic services
Electric vehicle charging stations
Energy assistance programs
Energy-efficient appliances and equipment
Energy management
Green energy programs
Power quality and environmental services
Security lighting
Shade trees for customers
Solar water heating
Surge protection
Tree trimming

COMPETITORS

AES	Los Angeles Water and
Avista	Power
Duke Energy	PG&E Corporation
Edison International	Sempra Energy

HISTORICAL FINANCIALS

Company Type: Private

Income Statement

FYE: December 31

	REVENUE ($ mil.)	NET INCOME ($ mil.)	NET PROFIT MARGIN	EMPLOYEES
12/16	1,494	195	13.1%	2,213
12/15	1,474	128	8.7%	—
12/14	1,529	163	10.7%	—
12/13	1,428	69	4.9%	—
Annual Growth	1.5%	41.0%	—	—

2016 Year-End Financials

Return on assets: 4.9%   Cash ($ mil.): 209
Return on equity: 13.1%
Current ratio: 0.60

SACRED HEART HEALTH SYSTEM, INC.

Part of Ascension Health the Sacred Heart Health System serves residents of Northwestern Florida primarily through the Sacred Heart Hospital of Pensacola. With more than 560 beds altogether the acute care medical center boasts the Sacred Heart Children's Hospital the Sacred Heart Women's Hospital and the Sacred Heart Regional Heart and Vascular Institute. Sacred Heart Hospital of Pensacola also specializes in trauma care heart disease cancer care weight loss stroke care neu-

rology and orthopedics. It has an educational affiliation with Florida State University College of Medicine. Sacred Heart Health System operates additional acute long-term primary and specialty care centers in the region.

Operations

In addition to its primary operations in Pensacola Sacred Heart Health System runs the Sacred Heart Hospital on the Gulf (a 20-bed hospital in Port St. Joe constructed in 2010) the Sacred Heart Hospital on the Emerald Coast (a 60-bed hospital in Walton County) a joint-venture nursing home primary and specialty care clinics and a physician practice group.

Geographic Reach

The company operates hospitals in Pensacola and in the area counties of South Walton and Gulf. It also runs physician offices and outpatient centers across the Florida Panhandle.

Strategy

In 2014 the system finished construction on its Bayou Tower a new $52-million expansion project on top of the Heart and Vascular Institute.

Sacred Heart Health System extended the reach of its business in 2012 when it partnered with the Bay Medical Center located in Panama City.

Company Background

Sacred Heart Hospital of Pensacola was formed in 1915 through the collaboration of local citizens and the Daughters of Charity a religious order founded in 1633 that focuses on caring for the poor and sick.

EXECUTIVES

Vp Marketing, Jim Jones
Vice President Mergers And Acquisitions Integration, Carol Schmidt
Auditors: LB DELOITTE TAX LLP CINCINNAT

LOCATIONS

HQ: SACRED HEART HEALTH SYSTEM, INC.
5151 N 9TH AVE, PENSACOLA, FL 325048721
Phone: 850 416-1600
Web: WWW.SACRED-HEART.ORG

Selected Locations

Bay Medical Center - Panama City Florida
Sacred Heart Hospital - Pensacola Florida
Sacred Heart on the Emerald Coast - Miramar Beach/Destin Florida
Sacred Heart on the Gulf Coast - Port St. Joe Florida
Sacred Heart Urgent Care Center - Pensacola Florida

PRODUCTS/OPERATIONS

Selected Services

Cancer treatment
Children's health
Emergency and trauma services
Heart and vascular services
Neuroscience and neurology
Orthopedics and joint replacement services
Women's health

COMPETITORS

Adventist Health System Sunbelt Healthcare
Baptist Health Care
Baptist Health System
Bay Medical Center
H. Lee Moffitt Cancer Center & Research Institute
HCA
HealthSouth
Tenet Healthcare

HISTORICAL FINANCIALS

Company Type: Private

Income Statement

FYE: June 30

	REVENUE ($ mil.)	NET INCOME ($ mil.)	NET PROFIT MARGIN	EMPLOYEES
06/15	725	16	2.3%	1,100
06/11	846	42	5.0%	—
06/10	772	29	3.9%	—
06/09	3	0	0.5%	—
Annual Growth	145.9%	217.8%	—	—

2015 Year-End Financials

Return on assets: 6.8%
Return on equity: 2.3%
Current ratio: 2.70
Cash ($ mil.): 2

SACRED HEART HOSPITAL OF THE HOSPITAL SISTERS OF THE THIRD ORDER OF ST. FRANCIS

Sacred Heart Hospital not only cares for hearts that are holey but also for the rest of what ails residents of western Wisconsin. The more than 300-bed medical center provides specialized services that include cardiology cancer care pediatrics and emergency medicine. The hospital provides community-wide care through affiliations with the Marshfield Clinic (a provider network with more than 700 physicians) Oakleaf Medical Network (an organization of providers and clinics) and Infinity Healthcare and Pathology Services (supplies the hospital with medical x-ray professionals). Founded in 1889 by the Hospital Sisters of the Third Order of St. Francis the center is part of the Hospital Sisters Health System.

Sacred Heart Hospital is also associated with St. Francis Apartments an independent-living apartment complex located directly behind the hospital. St. Francis Apartments provides seniors above the age of 62 a place to live that is in close proximity to the hospital without being an assisted living facility. Additionally many of the residents at St. Francis serve as volunteers at the hospital.

Sacred Heart Hospital is helmed by Steve Ronstrom president of the western Wisconsin division of Hospital Sisters Health System. Ronstrom also oversees the operations of St. Joseph's Hospital in Chippewa Falls Wisconsin.

EXECUTIVES

Director of Pharmacy, John Vandevoort
Medical Director, Philip Jacoby

LOCATIONS

HQ: SACRED HEART HOSPITAL OF THE HOSPITAL SISTERS OF THE THIRD ORDER OF ST. FRANCIS 900 W CLAIREMONT AVE, EAU CLAIRE, WI 547015105
Phone: 715 717-3926

COMPETITORS

Abbott Northwestern Hospital
Allina Hospitals
Amery Regional Medical Center
Aspirus
Bethesda Hospital
Children's Hospitals and Clinics of Minnesota
Fairview Health
Franciscan Skemp Healthcare
Gundersen Lutheran
HealthEast Care System
Luther Midelfort
Methodist Hospital (MN)
North Memorial Health Care
Tomah Memorial Hospital

HISTORICAL FINANCIALS

Company Type: Private

Income Statement

FYE: June 30

	REVENUE ($ mil.)	NET INCOME ($ mil.)	NET PROFIT MARGIN	EMPLOYEES
06/15	234	46	19.6%	1,010
06/14	249	55	22.1%	—
06/13	234	41	17.5%	—
06/08	174	22	12.7%	—
Annual Growth	4.3%	11.0%	—	—

2015 Year-End Financials

Return on assets: 6.7%
Return on equity: 19.6%
Current ratio: 0.70
Cash ($ mil.): 3

SACRED HEART UNIVERSITY INCORPORATED

EXECUTIVES

President, John J Petillo
Assistant Vice-President, Phillip McCabe
Director of Finance, Steve Walker
Administrative Assistant, Sue Kanuch
Auditors: BLUM SHAPIRO & COMPANY PC CPAS

LOCATIONS

HQ: SACRED HEART UNIVERSITY INCORPORATED 5151 PARK AVE, FAIRFIELD, CT 068251000
Phone: 203 371-7999
Web: WWW.SACREDHEART.EDU

HISTORICAL FINANCIALS

Company Type: Private

Income Statement

FYE: June 30

	REVENUE ($ mil.)	NET INCOME ($ mil.)	NET PROFIT MARGIN	EMPLOYEES
06/15	267	36	13.5%	600
06/14	238	28	12.1%	—
06/13	159	28	17.6%	—
06/11	189	22	12.0%	—
Annual Growth	9.0%	12.2%	—	—

2015 Year-End Financials

Return on assets: 9.3%
Return on equity: 13.5%
Current ratio: 0.30
Cash ($ mil.): 38

SAINT AGNES MEDICAL CENTER

Protecting and caring for the vulnerable Saint Agnes continues to ward off death for the patients at Saint Agnes Medical Center. The medical center provides healthcare to Valley residents of Fresno California through a 436-bed acute care hospital. Along with general surgery the hospital offers a variety of services including asthma management bariatric surgery (for which it has scored statewide accolades) cardiac rehabilitation hospice care and home care. The facility also has centers dedicated to cancer child development and women's health. The hospital is part of Trinity Health one of the largest Catholic health care systems in the US.

Operations
Saint Agnes Medical Center is a 436-bed medical campus that has some 2500 staff members. In fiscal 2015 (ended June) the center had more than 20300 admissions and 222170 outpatient visits.

Geographic Reach
Saint Agnes Medical Center provides care to residents of the Fresno California area (Fresno and Madera counties).

Financial Performance
In fiscal 2015 (ended June) the center had operating revenues of $487 million.

Strategy
Saint Agnes Medical Center has launched a new state-of-the-art Electronic Medical Record (EMR) system. The new EMR system replaced paper medical records and streamlined patient care. In 2013 Saint Agnes became the first medical center in greater Fresno to receive American College of Radiology accreditations in Breast MRI and Nuclear Medicine.

In 2015 the hospital did not renew the sub-lease for a building it owns in northwest Fresno County (which had been leased to physician group Northwest Medical Group). It plans to utilize the space for future expansion in the area.

Company Background
The hospital system was established in 1929 by nine Holy Cross Sisters.

Saint Agnes Medical Center sponsors a number of community outreach programs throughout the Valley including adult day care senior activity programs health care clinics for the uninsured and services for poor and homeless women.

EXECUTIVES

COO, Mark T. Bateman
Chief Medical Officer, Stephen Soldo
CFO, Phil Robinson
Chief Nursing Officer, Debi Pasley
President and CEO, Jim Leonard
EVP and, Rick OConnell
Director of Infection Control, Christi Paradise
Pharm D, Tai Kosiyangkakul
Vice President Of Information Technology, Richard H Blanks
Director of Radiology Radiologist, Judy Champaign
VICE PRESIDENT HUMAN RESOURCES, Tresa Moreland
Director Of Pharmacy, Lloyd Smith
Vice President Management, Amy Schneider
Director of Radiology, Debbie Chappell
Chairman, Michael Martinez
Treasurer, Andrea Lanier

LOCATIONS

HQ: SAINT AGNES MEDICAL CENTER
1303 E HERNDON AVE, FRESNO, CA 937203309
Phone: 559 450-3000
Web: WWW.SAMC.COM

PRODUCTS/OPERATIONS

Selected Programs and Services
Cancer Services
Emergency Services
Endoscopy
Heart & Vascular
Home Health Care
Hospice
Imaging Services
Laboratory Services
Neuroscience
Occupational Health Center
Orthopaedics
Surgery
Palliative Care
Pulmonary Rehabilitation
Women's Services
Wound Care Hyperbaric Medicine and Amputation
   Prevention

Selected Facilities
Breast Center
Cancer Center
The California Eye Institute at Saint Agnes
Child Development Center
Home Health and Hospice
Medical Library
Occupational Health Center
Outpatient Surgery North
Satellite Labs
Wound Care Hyperbaric Medicine and Amputation
   Prevention

COMPETITORS

Community Medical	Memorial Hospitals
Centers	Association
Dignity Health	Northern Inyo Hospital
HCA	Tenet Healthcare

HISTORICAL FINANCIALS

Company Type: Private

Income Statement

FYE: June 30

	REVENUE ($ mil.)	NET INCOME ($ mil.)	NET PROFIT MARGIN	EMPLOYEES
06/15	478	24	5.1%	2,400
06/13	503	19	3.8%	—
06/10	438	8	1.8%	—
06/09	394	(52)	—	—
Annual Growth	3.3%	—	—	—

2015 Year-End Financials

Return on assets: 3.3%   Cash ($ mil.): 84
Return on equity: 5.1%
Current ratio: 1.70

SAINT ALPHONSUS REGIONAL MEDICAL CENTER, INC.

Saint Alphonsus Regional Medical Center makes medical care its primary mission. The 384-bed hospital provides Boise Idaho and the surrounding region (including eastern Oregon and northern Nevada) with general acute and specialized health care services. Its facilities and operations include a level II trauma center an orthopedic spinal care unit an air transport service and a home health and hospice division. Saint Alphonsus Regional Medical Center is part of Trinity Health's four-hospital Saint Alphonsus Health System which serves Boise and Nampa in Idaho and Ontario and Baker City in Oregon. The Sisters of the Holy Cross founded the hospital in 1894.

Operations

Saint Alphonsus Regional Medical Center provides outpatient services through the 70 affiliated physician practices that make up the Saint Alphonsus Medical Group. It also operates the Saint Alphonsus Health Plaza which provides urgent care and outpatient surgery laboratory rehabilitation and primary care services.

The hospital also offers rural or homebound patients telemedicine services through which remote physician visits are conducted using audio or video.

Geographic Reach

Saint Alphonsus Regional Medical Center serves a territory that includes portions of southwestern Idaho northern Nevada and eastern Oregon.

Strategy

Saint Alphonsus Regional Medical Center expands its facilities to improve medical care in its service territory. In 2014 it opened its newly expanded and renovated emergency department which included a 30% increase in square footage. Also that year it became the first hospital in the region to utilize the EndoWrist Stapler technology on the da Vinci robotic system for minimally invasive surgeries.

EXECUTIVES

Assistant Vice President Operations and Services, Jedd Smith
Director of Nursing, Teri Woychick

LOCATIONS

HQ: SAINT ALPHONSUS REGIONAL MEDICAL
CENTER, INC.
1055 N CURTIS RD, BOISE, ID 837061309
Phone: 208 367-2121
Web: WWW.SAINTALPHONSUS.ORG

COMPETITORS

Ascension Health	St. Luke's Health
HCA	System
Intermountain Health	
Care	

HISTORICAL FINANCIALS

Company Type: Private

Income Statement

FYE: June 30

	REVENUE ($ mil.)	NET INCOME ($ mil.)	NET PROFIT MARGIN	EMPLOYEES
06/15	556	40	7.3%	3,500
06/14	572	46	8.0%	—
06/13	545	43	7.9%	—
06/10	449	13	3.1%	—
Annual Growth	4.3%	24.1%	—	—

2015 Year-End Financials

Return on assets: 6.1%   Cash ($ mil.): 267
Return on equity: 7.3%
Current ratio: 3.70

SAINT ELIZABETH REGIONAL MEDICAL CENTER

Saint Elizabeth Regional Medical Center a Catholic Health Initiatives (CHI) affiliate is a 260-bed acute care hospital that serves the Lincoln Nebraska area. The not-for-profit hospital also known as CHI Health St. Elizabeth provides a variety of services such as obstetrics bariatrics cancer care burn and wound care and cardiac and pulmonary care. Some 430 physicians are affiliated with the facility. The hospital also operates community health clinics urgent care centers and physical therapy clinics as well as home health and hospice organizations. CHI Health St. Elizabeth was originally founded as a simple frontier hospital in 1889 by the Sisters of St. Francis of Perpetual Adoration.

Operations

CHI Health St. Elizabeth is one of several affiliate and subsidiary hospitals of CHI operating in Nebraska. The medical center boasts a network of family practice and internal medicine clinics including stand-alone urgent care centers and offsite physical therapy clinics. Its locations include St. Mary's Community Hospital in Nebraska City Good Samaritan Hospital in Kearney and Saint Francis Medical Center in Grand Island as well as the Alegent Health network in Omaha.

Each year the hospital has some 33000 emergency department visits some 13000 admissions and more than 10000 surgical procedures.

Geographic Reach

Saint Elizabeth Regional Medical Center serves those who reside in and around Lincoln Nebraska.

Strategy

As part of the CHI network these hospitals work together to coordinate administrative technology and clinical resources with the goal of increasing efficiency and quality of care in their respective communities. For example in 2013 CHI Health St. Elizabeth partnered with CHI Nebraska Lincoln and the Lincoln YMCA to provide a community wellness program.

EXECUTIVES

Director Of Radiology, Mike Hopkins
Director Of Operating Room, Nancy Gondringer
Radiology Director, John Speaker
Medical Director of Radiation Therapy, Kevin Yiee
Secretary, Rick Bohaty
Auditors: CATHOLIC HEALTH INITIATIVES E

LOCATIONS

HQ: SAINT ELIZABETH REGIONAL MEDICAL CENTER
555 S 70TH ST, LINCOLN, NE 685102462
Phone: 402 219-5200
Web: WWW.SAINTELIZABETHONLINE.COM

PRODUCTS/OPERATIONS

Selected Specialty Areas
Bariatric Surgery - Weight-Loss Surgery
Breast Care Center
Burn and Wound Care
Cancer Institute
Cardiovascular Services
Colorectal Cancer
Company Care
Continuing Care Network
CyberKnife
Diabetes Center
Emergency Care
Home Care Services
Home Medical Equipment

SAINT MARY'S COLLEGE OF CALIFORNIA

EXECUTIVES

President, Ronald Gallagher
Vice-President, Peter A Michell
Director, Carrie Brewster
Financial Executive, Jeanne Dematteo
Executive Director, Steve Kennedy
Administrative Assistant, Chandra Commer
Director, Maria A Sanchez
Vice-President, Lisa M Moore
Auditors: BAKER TILLY VIRCHOW KRAUSE LLP

LOCATIONS

HQ: SAINT MARY'S COLLEGE OF CALIFORNIA
1928 SAINT MARYS RD, MORAGA, CA 945752744
Phone: 925 631-4000
Web: WWW.STMARYS-CA.EDU

HISTORICAL FINANCIALS

Company Type: Private

Income Statement FYE: June 30

	REVENUE ($ mil.)	NET INCOME ($ mil.)	NET PROFIT MARGIN	EMPLOYEES
06/15	178	2	1.7%	1,000
06/14	178	7	4.2%	—
06/13	124	23	19.1%	—
06/12	117	(11)	—	—
Annual Growth	15.1%	—	—	—

2015 Year-End Financials

Return on assets: 4.4%
Return on equity: 1.7%
Current ratio: 0.20
Cash ($ mil.): 13

SAINT MARY'S HOSPITAL, INC.

EXECUTIVES

Principal, Chad W Wable
Director, Donna Wysocki
Director, Josie Soucy
Director, Peter Nazarrio
Auditors: KPMG LLP HARTFORD CT

LOCATIONS

HQ: SAINT MARY'S HOSPITAL, INC.
56 FRANKLIN ST STE 1, WATERBURY, CT 067061281
Phone: 203 709-6000
Web: WWW.STMH.ORG

HISTORICAL FINANCIALS

Company Type: Private

Income Statement FYE: September 30

	REVENUE ($ mil.)	NET INCOME ($ mil.)	NET PROFIT MARGIN	EMPLOYEES
09/15	294	(0)	—	1,520
09/14	247	25	10.2%	—
09/13	239	18	7.7%	—
09/12	225	15	6.7%	—
Annual Growth	9.3%	—	—	—

2015 Year-End Financials

Return on assets: 7.7%
Return on equity: (-0.3%)
Current ratio: 1.00
Cash ($ mil.): 13

SAINT PETER'S UNIVERSITY HOSPITAL, INC.

Serving the central portions of the Garden State Saint Peter's University Hospital has about 480 beds. The facility is sponsored by the Roman Catholic Diocese of Metuchen New Jersey and provides patients with a staff of more than 900 physicians and dentists. Saint Peter's also offers one of the country's largest Neonatal Intensive Care Units minimally invasive surgical (MIS) procedures and specialized cancer diabetes and geriatric care. In affiliation with the Children's Hospital of Philadelphia Saint Peter's provides cardiac care for infants and children. The teaching hospital is also affiliated with the Drexel University College of Medicine.

Geographic Reach

Saint Peter's serves the residents of central New Jersey from its New Brunswick campus.

Operations

Saint Peter's is a state-designated children's hospital and a regional perinatal center and is a regional specialist in geriatrics oncology orthopedics women's services and ambulatory care. As part of the Saint Peter's Healthcare System the non-profit acute care facility performs some 30000 inpatient treatments and more than 200000 outpatient procedures each year. It also delivers some 6100 newborns annually and is a state-designated children's hospital and regional perinatal center. Supported by 2800 healthcare professionals Saint Peter's University Hospital serves as a regional specialist in geriatrics oncology orthopedics women's services and ambulatory care. It offers both adults and children cancer care services including inpatient care and outpatient radiation and infusion.The hospital performs single-incision robotic-assisted surgery using the da Vinci Si Surgical System.

Strategy

In 2013 Saint Peter's opened a redesigned and expanded perinatal center that houses both maternal-fetal medicine and antenatal testing services. Some 500 low-birth-weight babies are delivered at the hospital each year. The facility also logs more than 2200 high-risk obstetrics clinic visits each year.

In 2012 Saint Peter's opened a hospice program for adults in association with Bloomfield-based Hospice of New Jersey one of the oldest and largest providers of hospice care in the US.The year the hospital has launched a two-and-half-year-long building project to enlarge its emergency department and expand emergency services. When completed the Saint Peter's emergency department will have grown in size from 18000 sq. ft. to 29000 sq. ft. and will be able to treat 70000 to 75000 patients a year.

Saint Peter's also sponsors residency programs in obstetrics and gynecology pediatrics and internal medicine as a regional medical campus of Drexel University College of Medicine. The medical institution also sponsors a residency program in orthopedic surgery in affiliation with the University of Medicine and Dentistry of New Jersey-Robert Wood Johnson Medical School. It has agreements with Rutgers University and Kean University to enhance its educational programs.

Company Background

Additionally Saint Peter's is recognized as a magnet hospital for nursing excellence by the American Nurses Credentialing Center. It has won the Beacon Award for Critical Care Excellence in Nursing and is recognized by the American Diabetes Association in every area of diabetes education.

The hospital was established in 1907.

EXECUTIVES

Director of Radiology, Lauris Beam
Assistant Vice President, Doreen Stevenson
Chairman, Bipin Patel
Chairman, John A. Carlson

LOCATIONS

HQ: SAINT PETER'S UNIVERSITY HOSPITAL, INC.
254 EASTON AVE, NEW BRUNSWICK, NJ 089011766
Phone: 732 745-8600
Web: WWW.SAINTPETERSHCS.COM

PRODUCTS/OPERATIONS

Selected Services

Adult care
Cancer care
Community health
Diagnostic technology
Heart health
Maternity
Meet the staff
Movement sports rehabilitation
Nicu
Nursing at saint peters
Nutrition and weight
Outreach
Parent education
Pediatric and adolescent
Support groups
Surgery
Womens health
Adult and Family Health Services
Adult Intensive Care
Audiology
Emergency Medicine
Endocrinology
Hospice Program (Inpatient)
Intensive Care
Interstitial Cystitis Support Group
Lithotripsy
Ophthalmology
Osteoporosis/Bone Density
Pain Management
Primary Care
Pulmonary Medicine
Rheumatology
Sleep and Breathing Disorders
Thyroid
Urology
Wound Care and Hyperbaric Services
Adult Day Center
Allergy and Immunology
Dermatology
Dialysis
Emergency Medicine Physicians
Endoscopy/Same Day Services
Gastroenterology
Geriatric Medicine
Infectious Diseases
Internal Medicine
Interventional Radiology
Memory Assessment
Orthopedics
Otolaryngology (Ear Nose and Throat)
Pulmonary Function Laboratory Services
Respiratory Care Services
Skilled Nursing Care
Stroke
Urinary Incontinence and Pelvic Pain Program
Vascular Disease

Hospitalists
Intensivists
Maternal Fetal Medicine
Neonatal Intensive Care Unit (NICU)
Neurology
Occupational Therapy
Orthopaedics
Palliative Care
Pediatrics
Physical Therapy
Pulmonary Services
Radiology
Research & Clinical Trials
Robotic Surgery Center
Sleep Disorders Center
Speech Therapy
Stroke Center
The Advanced Baby Center

COMPETITORS

BryanLGH Medical Center
Children's Hospital & Medical Center
Fremont Area Medical Center
Madonna Rehabilitation Hospital
Methodist Health System
Nebraska Medical Center
Tenet Healthcare
University of Nebraska

HISTORICAL FINANCIALS

Company Type: Private

Income Statement FYE: June 30

	REVENUE ($ mil.)	NET INCOME ($ mil.)	NET PROFIT MARGIN	EMPLOYEES
06/15	212	(9)	—	1,825
06/14	254	19	7.5%	—
06/13	268	27	10.3%	—
06/10	1	0	32.7%	—
Annual Growth	184.5%	—	—	—

2015 Year-End Financials

Return on assets: 6.3%
Return on equity: (-4.4%)
Current ratio: 2.80
Cash ($ mil.): 8

SAINT FRANCIS HEALTH SYSTEM, INC.

If you have an ulcer in Tulsa or a broken arm in Broken Arrow you'll likely be visiting a Saint Francis Health System facility. The not-for-profit system serves Tulsa and northeastern Oklahoma through its hospitals clinics and home health services. Its largest facility is Saint Francis Hospital with about 920 beds and more than 700 doctors. Other facilities include Saint Francis Hospital at Broken Arrow The Children's Hospital at Saint Francis the Laureate Psychiatric Clinic and Hospital and the Saint Francis Heart Hospital. Its Warren Clinic consists of physicians offices in about a dozen cities providing primary and specialty health care.

Geographic Reach

Saint Francis serves patients in Tulsa and northeastern Oklahoma.

Strategy

In the face of a struggling economy Saint Francis like most other health care organizations has had to take a look at its operations and implement cost-cutting measures where it can to ensure long-term sustainability. The health system has not outlined the specifics of its overall plan but has said that it is implementing a plan to improve clinical efficiencies across its multiple treatment sites and levels of care.

Still that doesn't mean Saint Francis is without its challenges. Tulsa is a competitive market and Saint Francis competes with other large systems such as St. John Health System and Ardent Health Systems as well as a number of smaller physician-owned hospitals and outpatient centers. In order to keep up with the competition St. Francis has to invest some capital in expansions and upgrades such as a planned new patient tower for its flagship hospital. The $200 million project would add about 150 beds to the Saint Francis Hospital campus. It's still in the approval stages.

Company Background

Saint Francis was founded in 1960 by William and Natalie Warren Sr.

EXECUTIVES

Chief Executive Officer, Jake Henry
Board of Directors, Tammy Adams
Director, Michael Haney
Director, Meridith Coburn
Auditors: ERNST & YOUNG LLP TULSA OK

LOCATIONS

HQ: SAINT FRANCIS HEALTH SYSTEM, INC.
6161 S YALE AVE, TULSA, OK 741361902
Phone: 918 494-2200
Web: WWW.SFFCUTULSA.ORG

PRODUCTS/OPERATIONS

Hospitals and Health Centers

Broken Arrow Rehabilitation
Eastern Oklahoma Perinatal Center
Laureate Psychiatric Clinic and Hospital
Natalie Warren Bryant Cancer Center
Saint Francis Breast Health Services
Saint Francis Broken Arrow
Saint Francis Heart Hospital
Saint Francis Hospice
Saint Francis Hospital
Saint Francis Hospital South
Saint Francis Imaging Center
Springer Ambulatory Surgery Center
The Children's Hospital at Saint Francis
The Children's Hospital Foundation at Saint Francis
Warren Clinic
Warren Clinic Osteoporosis Center
Xavier Medical Clinic

Selected Services

Bariatrics
Cancer
Children's Health
Diabetes Management
Dialysis
Eating Disorders
Emergency Services
Imaging/Radiology
Mental Health
Neonatal Care
Nephrology
Neurology
Ophthalmology (eye)
Orthopedics
Osteoporosis
Pulmonology
Rehabilitation
Sleep Disorders
Springer Ambulatory Surgery Center
Surgery
Urology
Wellness and Education
Women's Health

COMPETITORS

Ardent Health Services
Deaconess Health Care
HCA
Hillcrest Medical Center
INTEGRIS Health
Marian Health System
Norman Regional Health
SSM Health Care
St. John Health System

HISTORICAL FINANCIALS

Company Type: Private

Income Statement FYE: June 30

	REVENUE ($ mil.)	NET INCOME ($ mil.)	NET PROFIT MARGIN	EMPLOYEES
06/15	1,167	148	12.7%	8,200
06/11	0	(4)	—	—
06/10	0	(6)	—	—
Annual Growth	397.0%	—	—	—

2015 Year-End Financials

Return on assets: 4.1%
Return on equity: 12.7%
Current ratio: 2.80
Cash ($ mil.): 266

SAINT FRANCIS HOSPITAL AND MEDICAL CENTER FOUNDATION, INC.

Saint Francis takes care of the hearts of Hartford Connecticut. The Saint Francis Hospital and Medical Center is a not-for-profit regional medical center with some 620 beds and 65 bassinets. The hospital specializes in cardiology oncology neurology orthopedics and women's and children's health services. It also offers behavioral health weight management trauma care and injury rehabilitation programs. Saint Francis serves as a teaching hospital affiliated with the University of Connecticut Schools of Medicine and Dentistry. It also operates laboratories a home health and hospice agency and other entities.Saint Francis is part of Catholic health care system Trinity Health.

Operations

Saint Francis' on-campus specialty centers include the Hoffman Heart and Vascular Institute which specializes in open-heart surgeries and catheterization procedures.

Strategy

Saint Francis has initiated a number of internal cost-reduction efforts to keep its operations and finances healthy. It is also improving its internal information management systems to increase efficiencies at its facilities.Trinity Health which acquired Saint Francis in 2015 is investing at least $275 million through 2020 towards capital projects and programmatic investments in the hospital's region. Recently introduced programs include the Center for Diabetes and Metabolic Care's Inpatient Glycemic Initiative.

Company Background

Saint Francis joined the Trinity Health Network in 2015.

EXECUTIVES

President, John Rodis
VP Finance, Jennifer S. Schneider
VP Facilities Support Services and Construction, Robert J. (Bob) Falaguerra
VP and Chief Development Officer Saint Francis Foundation, Lynn Rossini
VP Operations, Thomas M. Burke
VP Professional Nursing Practice and Quality; Chief Nursing Officer, Denise M. Peterson
Senior Vice President Marketing, James Schepker

Senior Vice President and Chief Financial Officer, John Giamalis
Vice President Operations, Nicole Schulz
Vice President, Diane Bertrand
Vice President Mission Integration, Stephen T Surprenant
Physical Therapy, Dan Henck
SR.v.p., Chris Hartley
Secretary, Cathy Hebert
Secretary, Donna Fitzpatrick
Board Member, Joyce Mandell

LOCATIONS

HQ: SAINT FRANCIS HOSPITAL AND MEDICAL CENTER FOUNDATION, INC.
114 WOODLAND ST, HARTFORD, CT 061051208
Phone: 860 714-4006
Web: WWW.SAINTFRANCISCARE.COM

COMPETITORS

Backus
Bristol Hospital
Connecticut Children's Medical Center
Griffin Health
Hartford Health Care
Hospital of Central Connecticut
Lawrence & Memorial Hospital
MidState Medical Center
Stamford Health
University of Connecticut Health Center
Yale New Haven Health System

HISTORICAL FINANCIALS

Company Type: Private

Income Statement

	REVENUE ($ mil.)	NET INCOME ($ mil.)	NET PROFIT MARGIN	EMPLOYEES
09/15	670	(14)	—	3,270
09/14	670	17	2.6%	—
09/10	651	(10)	—	—
09/09	638	(16)	—	—
Annual Growth	0.8%	—	—	—

FYE: September 30

2015 Year-End Financials

Return on assets: 5.4%
Return on equity: (-2.2%)
Current ratio: 1.60
Cash ($ mil.): 91

SAINT FRANCIS HOSPITAL, INC.

EXECUTIVES

Chief Executive Officer, Jake Henry

LOCATIONS

HQ: SAINT FRANCIS HOSPITAL, INC.
6161 S YALE AVE, TULSA, OK 741361992
Phone: 918 502-2050
Web: WWW.SAINTFRANCIS.COM

HISTORICAL FINANCIALS

Company Type: Private

Income Statement

	REVENUE ($ mil.)	NET INCOME ($ mil.)	NET PROFIT MARGIN	EMPLOYEES
06/15	877	171	19.6%	4,000
06/13	910	190	21.0%	—
06/12*	838	157	18.7%	—
09/11	18	3	21.5%	—
Annual Growth	163.6%	157.6%	—	—

FYE: June 30
*Fiscal year change

2015 Year-End Financials

Return on assets: 3.8%
Return on equity: 19.6%
Current ratio: 3.70
Cash ($ mil.): 244

SAINT FRANCIS MEMORIAL HOSPITAL

EXECUTIVES

Chief Executive Officer, Thomas G Hennessy
Principal, Robert Dureault
Chief Financial Officer, Craig Rucker
Project Manager, Sharon Geiss
Auditors: KPMG LLP SAN FRANCISCO CA

LOCATIONS

HQ: SAINT FRANCIS MEMORIAL HOSPITAL
900 HYDE ST, SAN FRANCISCO, CA 941094899
Phone: 415 353-6000
Web: WWW.SAINTFRANCISMEMORIAL..ORG

HISTORICAL FINANCIALS

Company Type: Private

Income Statement

	REVENUE ($ mil.)	NET INCOME ($ mil.)	NET PROFIT MARGIN	EMPLOYEES
06/15	221	(17)	—	1,100
06/12	234	4	1.8%	—
06/11	224	1	0.5%	—
06/10	1,495	0	—	—
Annual Growth	—	—	—	—

FYE: June 30

SAINT JOSEPH HEALTH SYSTEM, INC.

EXECUTIVES

Chairman, Doug Hacker
Board of Directors, Nelson Fonticiella
Director, Dorothy Zimmerman
Director, Julie Coffey
Manager, Tina Hulette
Vice-President, Christine Mays

LOCATIONS

HQ: SAINT JOSEPH HEALTH SYSTEM, INC.
1 SAINT JOSEPH DR, LEXINGTON, KY 405043742
Phone: 859 313-1000

HISTORICAL FINANCIALS

Company Type: Private

Income Statement

	REVENUE ($ mil.)	NET INCOME ($ mil.)	NET PROFIT MARGIN	EMPLOYEES
06/15	274	(3)	—	99
06/14	745	(45)	—	—
Annual Growth	(63.2%)	—	—	—

FYE: June 30

2015 Year-End Financials

Return on assets: 4.6%
Return on equity: (-1.2%)
Current ratio: 2.40
Cash ($ mil.): 67

SAINT JOSEPH REGIONAL MEDICAL CENTER-SOUTH BEND CAMPUS INC

EXECUTIVES

Board of Directors, Jason Schultz
Office Manager, Bonnie Hosinski

LOCATIONS

HQ: SAINT JOSEPH REGIONAL MEDICAL CENTER-SOUTH BEND CAMPUS INC
5215 HOLY CROSS PKWY, MISHAWAKA, IN 465451469
Phone: 574 335-5000
Web: WWW.SAINTJOSEPHRESIDENCY.COM

HISTORICAL FINANCIALS

Company Type: Private

Income Statement

	REVENUE ($ mil.)	NET INCOME ($ mil.)	NET PROFIT MARGIN	EMPLOYEES
06/15	324	18	5.8%	680
06/12	77	(6)	—	—
06/06	81	(2)	—	—
06/05	0	0	—	—
Annual Growth	—	102.2%	—	—

FYE: June 30

2015 Year-End Financials

Return on assets: 6.9%
Return on equity: 5.8%
Current ratio: 2.00
Cash ($ mil.): 1

SAINT JOSEPH'S HOSPITAL OF MARSHFIELD, INC.

EXECUTIVES

Chief Executive Officer, Michael Kryda
Director of Finance, Arlove Peterson
Production Manager, Stan Swedburg
Manager, Jennie Jastroch
Manager, Kate Haley
Manager, Patti Shaftocarlson
Engineer, Rod Stoner
Director, Salah Qutaishat
Auditors: DELOITTE TAX LP MILWAUKEE WI

LOCATIONS

HQ: SAINT JOSEPH'S HOSPITAL OF MARSHFIELD, INC.
611 N SAINT JOSEPH AVE, MARSHFIELD, WI 544491832
Phone: 715 387-1713
Web: WWW.STJOSEPHS-MARSHFIELD.ORG

HISTORICAL FINANCIALS

Company Type: Private

Income Statement

	REVENUE ($ mil.)	NET INCOME ($ mil.)	NET PROFIT MARGIN	EMPLOYEES
06/15*	382	64	16.9%	2,200
09/10	348	31	9.2%	—
09/09	342	21	6.4%	—
09/08	0	0	—	—
Annual Growth	—	—	—	—

FYE: June 30
*Fiscal year change

2015 Year-End Financials

Return on assets: 8.1%
Return on equity: 16.9%
Current ratio: 4.60
Cash ($ mil.): 93

SAINT JOSEPH'S HOSPITAL, INC.

EXECUTIVES

Chief Executive Officer, Paul P Hinchey
Board of Directors, Lenny Panzitta

LOCATIONS

HQ: SAINT JOSEPH'S HOSPITAL, INC.
11705 MERCY BLVD, SAVANNAH, GA 314191791
Phone: 912 819-4100
Web: WWW.SJCHS.ORG

Manager, Jeff Stone
Director, Joe Pinto
Auditors: WITHUMSMITHBROWN PC MORRISTOW

LOCATIONS

HQ: SAINT LUKE'S HOSPITAL OF BETHLEHEM, PENNSYLVANIA
801 OSTRUM ST, BETHLEHEM, PA 180151000
Phone: 484 526-4000
Web: WWW.SLHN.ORG

HISTORICAL FINANCIALS

Company Type: Private

Income Statement

	REVENUE ($ mil.)	NET INCOME ($ mil.)	NET PROFIT MARGIN	EMPLOYEES
06/15	193	6	3.4%	19
06/14	192	8	4.6%	—
06/13	184	10	5.9%	—
06/12	185	7	3.8%	—
Annual Growth	1.3%	(2.7%)	—	—

FYE: June 30

2015 Year-End Financials

Return on assets: 4.8%
Return on equity: 3.4%
Current ratio: 1.90
Cash ($ mil.): —

SAINT LEO UNIVERSITY INCORPORATED

EXECUTIVES

President, William Lennox
Manager, Donna Sturgis
Consultant, Donna Bleiler
Consultant, Emilio Favale
Manager, Erica Sachs
Administrative Assistant, Chris Waggoner
Auditors: KPMG LLP TAMPA FL

LOCATIONS

HQ: SAINT LEO UNIVERSITY INCORPORATED
33701 STATE ROAD 52, SAINT LEO, FL 335749700
Phone: 352 588-8200
Web: WWW.SAINTLEO.EDU

HISTORICAL FINANCIALS

Company Type: Private

Income Statement

	REVENUE ($ mil.)	NET INCOME ($ mil.)	NET PROFIT MARGIN	EMPLOYEES
06/15	193	12	6.6%	819
06/13	173	11	6.6%	—
06/12	164	22	13.3%	—
06/11	0	0	—	—
Annual Growth	—	5870.8%	—	—

FYE: June 30

2015 Year-End Financials

Return on assets: 7.6%
Return on equity: 6.6%
Current ratio: 0.30
Cash ($ mil.): 16

SAINT LUKE'S HOSPITAL OF BETHLEHEM, PENNSYLVANIA

EXECUTIVES

President, Richard A Anderson
Manager, Carol Kuplan

SAINT LUKE'S HOSPITAL OF KANSAS CITY

EXECUTIVES

Chief Executive Officer, Julie Quirin
Executive Secretary, Andrea Elliot
Director, Renee Jacobs
Manager, Diana Reiser

LOCATIONS

HQ: SAINT LUKE'S HOSPITAL OF KANSAS CITY
4401 WORNALL RD, KANSAS CITY, MO 641113241
Phone: 816 932-2000
Web: WWW.SONUSHEARING.COM

HISTORICAL FINANCIALS

Company Type: Private

Income Statement

	REVENUE ($ mil.)	NET INCOME ($ mil.)	NET PROFIT MARGIN	EMPLOYEES
12/15	561	0	0.0%	5,000
12/14	527	25	4.8%	—
12/08	409	(61)	—	—
12/02	38	4	11.0%	—
Annual Growth	22.9%	(22.2%)	—	—

FYE: December 31

2015 Year-End Financials

Return on assets: 4.9%
Return on equity: —
Current ratio: 1.60
Cash ($ mil.): 16

COMPETITORS

CentraState Healthcare System
JFK Medical Center
Princeton HealthCare
Raritan Bay Medical Center
Robert Wood Johnson University Hospital
Robert Wood Johnson University Hospital at Rahway
Saint Barnabas Medical

HISTORICAL FINANCIALS

Company Type: Private

Income Statement

FYE: December 31

	REVENUE ($ mil.)	NET INCOME ($ mil.)	NET PROFIT MARGIN	EMPLOYEES
12/15	405	3	0.8%	3,000
12/13	403	(2)	—	—
12/08	391	(34)	—	—
12/06	392	4	1.0%	—
Annual Growth	0.4%	(2.1%)	—	—

2015 Year-End Financials

Return on assets: 8.5%   Cash ($ mil.): 10
Return on equity: 0.8%
Current ratio: 0.60

SAINT TAMMANY PARISH SCHOOL BOARD

EXECUTIVES

President, Stephen Loup
Auditors: LA PORTE APAC COVINGTON LA

LOCATIONS

HQ: SAINT TAMMANY PARISH SCHOOL BOARD
321 N THEARD ST, COVINGTON, LA 704332835
Phone: 985 892-2276
Web: WWW.STPSB.ORG

HISTORICAL FINANCIALS

Company Type: Private

Income Statement

FYE: June 30

	REVENUE ($ mil.)	NET INCOME ($ mil.)	NET PROFIT MARGIN	EMPLOYEES
06/16	505	(21)	—	4,400
06/15	475	49	10.4%	—
06/14	464	24	5.2%	—
06/13	457	(0)	—	—
Annual Growth	3.4%	—	—	—

2016 Year-End Financials

Return on assets: 1.8%   Cash ($ mil.): 122
Return on equity: (-4.2%)
Current ratio: —

SAINT THOMAS RUTHERFORD HOSPITAL

Saint Thomas Rutherford Hospital (formerly Middle Tennessee Medical Center) is a 285-bed acute care hospital serving central Tennessee. In addition to general medical diagnostic and surgical services the not-for-profit hospital offers 30 medical specialties including centers devoted to cancer care pediatrics cardiology orthopedics neurology diabetes and women's health. Saint Thomas Rutherford established in 1927 is part of Saint Thomas Health which includes four additional area hospitals and is in turn is a member of Ascension Health.

Operations

Saint Thomas Rutherford employs 1200 health care professionals and staff members including some 400 physicians. The hospital handles about 19000 inpatient visits each year as well as 66000 outpatients 73000 emergency room patients 7600 surgical procedures and 2500 births.

Geographic Reach

Saint Thomas Rutherford is located in Murfreesboro Tennessee near Nashville. The facility serves Cannon Coffee Rutherford and Warren counties in central Tennessee.

Strategy

In mid-2013 the medical center's name was changed from Middle Tennessee Medical Center (MTMC) to Saint Thomas Rutherford Hospital. The name change was conducted to better reflect the common mission of the Saint Thomas Health organization.

The name change follows facility improvements at Saint Thomas Rutherford. The hospital received a new home when construction of a replacement facility was completed in 2010. That fall it opened a brand new $268 million facility equipped with state-of-the-art technology and all-private patient rooms. In 2011 the hospital opened a new heart failure center and a state-of-the-art cancer center and in 2013 it opened a new cardiology outpatient office in the Tennessee community of Smyrna.

The parent organization is also working to expand its medical training programs (conducted through an affiliation with University of Tennessee) to include residency programs at the Saint Thomas Rutherford facility.

EXECUTIVES

Chief Executive Officer, Gordon B Ferguson
VP Operations, Ryan Simpson
Administrative Assistant, Judy Greenwood
Director, Pam Rudd
Chief Financial Officer, Ken Venuto
Chief Financial Officer, Thomas Massey
Chief Financial Officer, Tom Maey
Marketing Director, Amanda Anderson

LOCATIONS

HQ: SAINT THOMAS RUTHERFORD HOSPITAL
1700 MEDICAL CENTER PKWY, MURFREESBORO, TN 371292245
Phone: 615 849-4100
Web: WWW.MTMC.ORG

PRODUCTS/OPERATIONS

Selected Centers and Services

Accredited Primary Stroke Center
Ambulatory/ Outpatient Surgery
Bariatric/ Weight Loss
Cancer Center
Cardiac Services-Saint Thomas Heart
Accredited Chest Pain Center
Dermatology
Diagnostics
Emergency Room
Diabetes Center
General Medicine
General Surgery
Gastroenterology
Health and Wellness Services
Hospitalist Program
Laborists Program
Nephrology
Neurology
Ophthalmology
Orthopedics
Plastic and Reconstructive Surgery
Rehabilitation Services
Sports Medicine
Urology
Women's Health
Wound Care

COMPETITORS

Blount Memorial Hospital
Community Health Systems
Cookeville Regional Medical Center
Erlanger Health System
HCA
LifePoint Health
Mountain States Health
Southern Hills
Vanderbilt University Medical Center

HISTORICAL FINANCIALS

Company Type: Private

Income Statement

FYE: June 30

	REVENUE ($ mil.)	NET INCOME ($ mil.)	NET PROFIT MARGIN	EMPLOYEES
06/15	279	48	17.2%	1,100
06/14	249	35	14.2%	—
06/09	189	13	7.1%	—
06/08	178	13	7.4%	—
Annual Growth	6.6%	20.3%	—	—

2015 Year-End Financials

Return on assets: 3.8%   Cash ($ mil.): —
Return on equity: 17.2%
Current ratio: 2.30

SALEM HEALTH

Salem Hospital serves the healthcare needs of residents in and around Oregon's Willamette Valley. The acute care hospital boasts about 455 beds and a medical staff of 440-plus physicians that represents some 45 specialty areas such as oncology joint replacement obstetrics diabetes weight loss and mental health among others. The not-for-profit hospital offers a range of services from emergency and critical care to rehabilitation and community wellness programs. Its Center for Outpatient Medicine provides cancer care outpatient surgery and imaging services and has a sleep disorders center. Salem Hospital is part of Salem Health which also includes West Valley Hospital and Willamette Health Partners.

Operations

The Oregon hospital also has a Family Birth Center that offers family-health education services and neonatal intensive-care services. Additionally it provides space to community support services to benefit families.

Salem Hospital operates under the guidance of a 15-member volunteer Board of Trustees.

Strategy

As with many healthcare institutions in this age of reform Salem Hospital is working hard to improve patient experience and the quality of healthcare it provides while reducing the cost of care and eliminating waste within its systems. It has been improving clinical documentation to ensure payments are received standardizing care processes improving scheduling of surgeries leaving 30 open positions unfilled and cutting another 30 positions.

Inspired by Toyota's lean production processes the hospital entered into a five-year contract with John Black and Associates in 2010 to begin what it projects to be a transformation that will be ac-

complished incrementally over the next 20 years. Its goal is to improve care using a holistic patient-centered approach and reduce waste in terms of waits inventory and other day-to-day processes.

Salem Hospital set a goal of becoming a Magnet hospital in 2003 and accomplished the feat in 2010. (Only 6% of hospitals in the US have achieved Magnet status.) Magnet certification is awarded to hospitals that meet a set of criteria that measures the quality and strength of their nursing staffs as set by the American Nurses' Credentialing Center an affiliate of the American Nurses Association. Criteria includes patient outcomes job satisfaction and low turnover.

In 2009 the hospital opened a new patient tower. In 2010 it sold its money-losing home care department to LHC Group as a way of cutting operating costs.

EXECUTIVES

Vice President of Strategy and Business Integration, Lori James-Nielsen
Director of Medical Records, Debra Harris
Director Icu Coronary Care Unit, Leah Mitchell
Vice President Cmo, Anne Theis
Medical Director, Lisa Lewis
Vice President of Community Engagement, Leilani Slama
Vice President, Bahaa Wanly
Vice President, Carter Trudee
Vice President Claims, Michelle Graham
Vice President Policyholder Services, John Gilkey
Vice President, Aaron McClung
MEDICAL DIRECTOR, Laslo Kolta
Secretary of Medical Staff Svs, Louann Hettwer
Auditors: KPMG LLP PORTLAND OREGON

LOCATIONS

HQ: SALEM HEALTH
890 OAK ST SE, SALEM, OR 973013905
Phone: 503 561-5200
Web: WWW.SALEMHEALTH.ORG

PRODUCTS/OPERATIONS

Selected Services
Bariatrics
Cancer
Diabetes
Gynecology
Heart
Joint replacement
Neurosciences
Obstetrics
Orthopedics
Pain management
Psychiatric medicine
Psychology
Rehabilitation
Spine
Sleep
Stroke
Weight-loss surgery
Wound care

COMPETITORS

Adventist Health System West
Asante Health System
Kadlec Regional Medical Center
Kaiser Foundation Hospitals
Legacy Emanuel Hospital and Health Center
Legacy Health System
Oregon Health & Science University
PeaceHealth Southwest Medical Center
Providence St. Joseph Health

HISTORICAL FINANCIALS
Company Type: Private

Income Statement
FYE: September 30

	REVENUE ($ mil.)	NET INCOME ($ mil.)	NET PROFIT MARGIN	EMPLOYEES
09/15	667	42	6.4%	3,400
09/14	584	58	10.0%	—
09/13	531	61	11.6%	—
09/09	493	20	4.2%	—
Annual Growth	5.2%	12.8%	—	—

2015 Year-End Financials
Return on assets: 5.1%
Return on equity: 6.4%
Current ratio: 1.00
Cash ($ mil.): 6

SALEM HOLDING COMPANY

EXECUTIVES

President, Thomas L Teague
Vice-President, C Stephen Dula
Secretary, E Stephen Teague
Financial Executive, Dennis Giff
Vice-President, Michael Ellis
Auditors: PRICEWATERHOUSECOOPERS LLP G

LOCATIONS

HQ: SALEM HOLDING COMPANY
175 CHARLOIS BLVD, WINSTON SALEM, NC 271031521
Phone: 336 768-6800
Web: WWW.NATIONALEASEOFUTAH.NET

HISTORICAL FINANCIALS
Company Type: Private

Income Statement
FYE: June 30

	REVENUE ($ mil.)	NET INCOME ($ mil.)	NET PROFIT MARGIN	EMPLOYEES
06/16	232	8	3.5%	1,000
06/15	246	8	3.5%	—
06/14	226	5	2.4%	—
06/13	224	4	1.9%	—
Annual Growth	1.2%	23.6%	—	—

2016 Year-End Financials
Return on assets: 3.5%
Return on equity: 3.5%
Current ratio: 1.00
Cash ($ mil.): 6

SALEM-KEIZER SCHOOL DISTRICT 24J

EXECUTIVES

Superintendent, Thirsty Perry
Administrative Assistant, Kristy Brooks-Lathers
Superintendent, Christy Perry
Purchasing Director, Michael Wolfe
Assistant Manager, Kelly Carlisle

Plant & Facilities Manager, Joel Smallwood
Auditors: GROVE MUELLER & SWANK PC

LOCATIONS

HQ: SALEM-KEIZER SCHOOL DISTRICT 24J
2450 LANCASTER DR NE # 100, SALEM, OR 973051200
Phone: 503 399-3000
Web: WWW.SALKEIZ.K12.OR.US

HISTORICAL FINANCIALS
Company Type: Private

Income Statement
FYE: June 30

	REVENUE ($ mil.)	NET INCOME ($ mil.)	NET PROFIT MARGIN	EMPLOYEES
06/16	516	(15)	—	4,000
06/06	319	8	2.7%	—
06/04	319	8	2.7%	—
06/03	0	0	—	—
Annual Growth	—	—	—	—

2016 Year-End Financials
Return on assets: 1.7%
Return on equity: (-2.9%)
Current ratio: —
Cash ($ mil.): 145

SALINA REGIONAL HEALTH CENTER, INC.

EXECUTIVES

President, Randy Peterson
Manager, Rachelle Giroux
Manager, Randy Moravec
Director, Sherye Elliott

LOCATIONS

HQ: SALINA REGIONAL HEALTH CENTER, INC.
400 S SANTA FE AVE, SALINA, KS 674014144
Phone: 785 452-7000
Web: WWW.SRHC.COM

HISTORICAL FINANCIALS
Company Type: Private

Income Statement
FYE: September 30

	REVENUE ($ mil.)	NET INCOME ($ mil.)	NET PROFIT MARGIN	EMPLOYEES
09/15	184	11	6.2%	1,500
09/14	183	39	21.5%	—
09/13	171	42	24.8%	—
09/10	159	11	7.0%	—
Annual Growth	2.9%	0.4%	—	—

2015 Year-End Financials
Return on assets: 3.3%
Return on equity: 6.2%
Current ratio: 2.10
Cash ($ mil.): 27

SALINAS VALLEY MEMORIAL HEALTHCARE SYSTEMS

The primary facility of the Salinas Valley Memorial Healthcare System (a public hospital district) is Salinas Valley Memorial Hospital which opened in 1953 and has some 270 acute-care beds. The medical center includes a comprehensive cancer center joint replacement clinic regional heart and spine centers a level III neonatal intensive care unit and a women's and children's unit. Salinas Valley Memorial Healthcare System also operates the Summerville Harden Ranch an 80-bed assisted-living facility and a network of outpatient care clinics. The system has collaborative relationships with other area care providers as well as a partnership with NASA that allows earthbound physicians to assist astronauts with medical emergencies in space.

Operations

The system has some 300 board-certified physicians across a range of specialties and partners with affiliates throughout the region. Its other programs include the Harden Memorial Heart Program a wound healing center diagnostics and sleep medicine. Its emergency department sees more than 44000 patients each year.

Financial Performance

In 2014 revenue increased 1% to $351 million as net patient service revenues rose. Net income fell 3% to $26 million though as operating expenses including salaries and benefits increased. Cash flow from operations slipped 16% that year to $38 million.

Strategy

Salinas Valley Memorial Healthcare System partnered with MedAssist in late 2013 to expand its regional care services. The partners provide personalized assistance to help consumers enroll in the state's Health Insurance Exchange.

EXECUTIVES

Senior Vice President And Patient Care And Cardiovascular Services, Irene Neumeister
Vice President Of Information Technology, James Brennan
Treasurer, Chris Orman
Secretary Perioperative Services, Regina Linares
Assistant Treasurer, Carissa Purnell
Treasurer, Alfred Diaz-Infante

LOCATIONS

HQ: SALINAS VALLEY MEMORIAL HEALTHCARE SYSTEMS
450 E ROMIE LN, SALINAS, CA 939014029
Phone: 831 757-4333
Web: WWW.SVMH.COM

PRODUCTS/OPERATIONS

2014 Sales

	% of total
Net patient revenue	98
Other revenue	2
Total	100

Selected Services

Anesthesiology
Angiography
Art & Music Therapy
Gynecology
Health Education
Health Promotion
Heart Health
Palliative Medicine
Pediatrics
Pharmacy
Physical Therapy
Plastic & Reconstructive Surgery
Positron Emission Tomography (PET)
Pre-Surgery Orientation
Tele-Care
Treadmill Stress Test
Vascular Care

COMPETITORS

Community Hospital of the Monterey Peninsula
Dignity Health
John Muir Health
Sequoia Healthcare District
Stanford Health Care
Sutter Health
UCSF Medical

HISTORICAL FINANCIALS

Company Type: Private

Income Statement

FYE: June 30

	REVENUE ($ mil.)	NET INCOME ($ mil.)	NET PROFIT MARGIN	EMPLOYEES
06/15	344	37	10.9%	1,480
06/05	284	14	5.0%	—
06/04	267	14	5.4%	—
06/03	0	0	—	—
Annual Growth	—	—	—	—

2015 Year-End Financials

Return on assets: 5.1%
Return on equity: 10.9%
Current ratio: 3.30
Cash ($ mil.): 120

SALMON LEGACY CREEK HOSPITAL

EXECUTIVES

President, Lee Domanico
Vice-President, Jodi Joyce
Vice-President, Juan Millan
Manager, Johnny Sun
Personnel Manager, Eve Logsdon

LOCATIONS

HQ: SALMON LEGACY CREEK HOSPITAL
2211 NE 139TH ST, VANCOUVER, WA 986862742
Phone: 360 487-1000
Web: WWW.REBOUNDMD.COM

HISTORICAL FINANCIALS

Company Type: Private

Income Statement

FYE: March 31

	REVENUE ($ mil.)	NET INCOME ($ mil.)	NET PROFIT MARGIN	EMPLOYEES
03/15	286	37	13.2%	700
03/13	199	10	5.4%	—
03/12	218	10	4.6%	—
03/11	184	10	5.6%	—
Annual Growth	11.6%	38.3%	—	—

2015 Year-End Financials

Return on assets: 1.3%
Return on equity: 13.2%
Current ratio: 1.10
Cash ($ mil.): —

SALT LAKE CITY SCHOOL DISTRICT

EXECUTIVES

Director, Alan Kearsley
Director, Pat Roberts
Director, Sam Quantz
Administrative Assistant, Frank Frampton
Director, Laurie Lacy
Auditors: SQUIRE & COMPANY PC OREM UT

LOCATIONS

HQ: SALT LAKE CITY SCHOOL DISTRICT
440 E 100 S, SALT LAKE CITY, UT 841111841
Phone: 801 578-8307
Web: WWW.SLCSCHOOLS.ORG

HISTORICAL FINANCIALS

Company Type: Private

Income Statement

FYE: June 30

	REVENUE ($ mil.)	NET INCOME ($ mil.)	NET PROFIT MARGIN	EMPLOYEES
06/16	276	13	4.8%	3,200
06/15	266	7	2.9%	—
06/14	252	7	2.9%	—
06/13	249	2	1.2%	—
Annual Growth	3.5%	65.7%	—	—

SAM LEVIN INC.

Founded in 1920 as a furniture and hardware store by the husband-and-wife team Sam and Jessie Levin Sam Levin (dba Levin Furniture) sells a wide variety of dining room bedroom living room and office furniture as well as mattresses at about a dozen retail locations in northeastern Ohio and southwestern Pennsylvania. It also operates a Sleep Center bedding store in Pennsylvania and a clearance outlet in Ohio. The family-owned-and-run company offers self-service kiosks in its showrooms and creative exhibits that include sports- and Wizard of Oz-themed displays. Robert Levin Sam and Jessie's grandson is president of the company.

EXECUTIVES

Vice President Of Operations, Ward Dingman
Vice President Human Resources, Irene Fostyk
Auditors: SCHNEIDER DOWNS & CO INC P

LOCATIONS

HQ: SAM LEVIN INC.
301 FITZ HENRY RD, SMITHTON, PA 154798715
Phone: 724 872-2055
Web: WWW.LEVINFURNITURE.COM

2009 Stores

	No.
Ohio	7
Pennsylvania	7
Total	14

COMPETITORS

Ashley Furniture	J. C. Penney
Bassett Furniture	Macy's
Havertys	Rooms To Go

HISTORICAL FINANCIALS
Company Type: Private

Income Statement				FYE: December 31
	REVENUE ($ mil.)	NET INCOME ($ mil.)	NET PROFIT MARGIN	EMPLOYEES
12/15	202	16	8.0%	400
12/14	188	12	6.5%	—
12/13	188	7	3.8%	—
12/12	187	7	4.1%	—
Annual Growth	2.6%	28.0%	—	—

2015 Year-End Financials
Return on assets: 2.8% Cash ($ mil.): 17
Return on equity: 8.0%
Current ratio: 0.80

SAMARITAN MEDICAL CENTER

EXECUTIVES

President, Thomas Carman
Operations Manager, James Yonkovig
Office Manager, Cindy Stean
Chief Operating Officer, Deborah Vink
Manager, Maurice Meilleur
Director, Chris Volcom

LOCATIONS

HQ: SAMARITAN MEDICAL CENTER
  830 WASHINGTON ST, WATERTOWN, NY 136014099
Phone: 315 785-4000
Web: WWW.SAMARITANHEALTH.COM

HISTORICAL FINANCIALS
Company Type: Private

Income Statement				FYE: December 31
	REVENUE ($ mil.)	NET INCOME ($ mil.)	NET PROFIT MARGIN	EMPLOYEES
12/15	192	0	0.1%	1,300
12/14	189	7	4.0%	—
12/13	204	6	3.3%	—
12/09	170	13	8.0%	—
Annual Growth	2.0%	(48.7%)	—	—

2015 Year-End Financials
Return on assets: 5.5% Cash ($ mil.): 36
Return on equity: 0.1%
Current ratio: 1.30

SAMARITAN'S PURSE

EXECUTIVES

Director, Jim Furman Jr
Director, Ross Rhoads
Personnel Manager, Margie Coger
Director, Nicole Sheldon
Auditors: DIXON HUGHES GOODMAN LLP CHAR

LOCATIONS

HQ: SAMARITAN'S PURSE
  801 BAMBOO RD, BOONE, NC 286078721
Phone: 828 262-1980
Web: WWW.SAMARITANSPURSE.ORG

HISTORICAL FINANCIALS
Company Type: Private

Income Statement				FYE: December 31
	REVENUE ($ mil.)	NET INCOME ($ mil.)	NET PROFIT MARGIN	EMPLOYEES
12/15	599	82	13.7%	525
12/14	520	31	6.0%	—
12/13	473	59	12.5%	—
12/12	389	(35)	—	—
Annual Growth	15.4%	—	—	—

2015 Year-End Financials
Return on assets: 2.7% Cash ($ mil.): 6
Return on equity: 13.7%
Current ratio: 0.20

SAN ANTONIO COMMUNITY HOSPITAL

EXECUTIVES

Chairman, Jim Milhiser
VP Personnel, Clint Borrell
Manager, Lesa Hiben
Chief Financial Officer, Linda Joslyn
Director, Jan Yerkey
Auditors: ERNST & YOUNG US LLP IRVINE

LOCATIONS

HQ: SAN ANTONIO COMMUNITY HOSPITAL
  999 SAN BERNARDINO RD, UPLAND, CA 917864920
Phone: 909 985-2811
Web: WWW.SARH.ORG

HISTORICAL FINANCIALS
Company Type: Private

Income Statement				FYE: December 31
	REVENUE ($ mil.)	NET INCOME ($ mil.)	NET PROFIT MARGIN	EMPLOYEES
12/15	290	2	0.8%	2,000
12/13	266	(3)	—	—
12/11	282	9	3.4%	—
12/10	305	35	11.6%	—
Annual Growth	(1.0%)	(41.6%)	—	—

2015 Year-End Financials
Return on assets: 9.3% Cash ($ mil.): 4
Return on equity: 0.8%
Current ratio: 0.90

SAN ANTONIO INDEPENDENT SCHOOL DISTRICT FAC

EXECUTIVES

Superintendent, Dr Sylvester Syl Perez
Board of Directors, Arthur V Valdez
Account Manager, Tony Neilson
Personnel Director, Richard M Kirkpatrick
Director, Berta R Macat
Personnel Director, Maryann Debeauvoir
Auditors: GARZA/GONZALEZ & ASSOCIATES S

LOCATIONS

HQ: SAN ANTONIO INDEPENDENT SCHOOL
  DISTRICT FAC
  141 LAVACA ST, SAN ANTONIO, TX 782101039
Phone: 210 554-2200
Web: WWW.SAISD.NET

HISTORICAL FINANCIALS
Company Type: Private

Income Statement				FYE: June 30
	REVENUE ($ mil.)	NET INCOME ($ mil.)	NET PROFIT MARGIN	EMPLOYEES
06/16	659	43	6.5%	7,600
06/15	624	(14)	—	—
06/14*	600	(110)	—	—
08/09	549	6	1.2%	—
Annual Growth	2.6%	30.2%	—	—

*Fiscal year change

2016 Year-End Financials
Return on assets: 2.7% Cash ($ mil.): 189
Return on equity: 6.5%
Current ratio: —

SAN DIEGO ASSOCIATION OF GOVERNMENTS

EXECUTIVES

Chairman, Jack Dale
Accountant, Kathy Stansfield
Director, Jeff Tayman
Personnel Manager, Robert Caplan
Manager, Lillian H Brown
Personnel Manager, Patti Berber
Auditors: MAYER HOFFMAN MCCANN PC IRV

LOCATIONS

HQ: SAN DIEGO ASSOCIATION OF GOVERNMENTS
  401 B ST STE 800, SAN DIEGO, CA 921014231
Phone: 619 699-1900
Web: WWW.SANDAG.ORG

HISTORICAL FINANCIALS
Company Type: Private

Income Statement
FYE: June 30

	REVENUE ($ mil.)	NET INCOME ($ mil.)	NET PROFIT MARGIN	EMPLOYEES
06/15	489	224	45.9%	320
06/14	475	(134)	—	—
06/13	0	(151)	—	—
06/12	435	(1)	—	—
Annual Growth	4.0%	—	—	—

SAN FRANCISCO BAY AREA RAPID TRANSIT DISTRICT

If you're going to San Francisco — from Oakland Berkeley or another Bay Area community — San Francisco Bay Area Rapid Transit District (BART) can take you there. BART's trains carry about 365000 daily weekday riders from more than 45 stations over more than 100 miles of track including the 3.6 mile Transbay Tube under the San Francisco Bay that links the City by the Bay with Oakland and other East Bay communities. Directors elected from nine districts in Alameda Contra Costa and San Francisco counties oversee BART which operates with an annual budget of about $480 million. Construction on the rail system began in 1964 and BART carried its first passengers in 1972.

Operations

BART which has the oldest fleet in the US has awarded Bombardier about $896 million to design and make more than 400 train cars that may be ready for use by 2017. The contract represents the first phase of a $2.5 billion project to replace BART's fleet of some 670 cars with a larger fleet of more than 770 new cars. Three-fourths of the project's cost is being paid by the federal government with the remainder coming from BART.

Another major project is the $1.3 billion Earthquake Safety Program which is almost finished and scheduled for completion in 2016. The program includes bolting 2.5-inch steel plates on the concrete wall of the Transbay Tube — which carries about half of BART's daily weekday riders — and similar strengthening measures for more than 30 stations more than 20 miles of elevated track and other facilities.

Geographic Reach

BART serves the Bay Area through its 45 stations spanning the four counties of Alameda Contra Costa San Francisco and San Mateo.

Financial Performance

In 2014 the company's revenue increased by 4% to $463 million due to a spike in passenger fares along with higher parking rates implemented in 2014 at several stations. BART was also helped by an increase in advertising revenue and a rise in ground lease revenue resulting from the reassignment of its original ground lease at West Dublin Station to a new lessee. In addition its net income increased by 8% in 2014 due to the increase in revenues along with lower transportation expenses.

EXECUTIVES

VP Information Technology, Michael Wang
Vice President Information Technology, William Longstaff
VP Purchasing, Bob Harding
Auditors: MACIAS GINI & O'CONNELL LLP O

LOCATIONS

HQ: SAN FRANCISCO BAY AREA RAPID TRANSIT DISTRICT
300 LAKESIDE DR, OAKLAND, CA 94604
Phone: 510 464-6000

HISTORICAL FINANCIALS
Company Type: Private

Income Statement
FYE: June 30

	REVENUE ($ mil.)	NET INCOME ($ mil.)	NET PROFIT MARGIN	EMPLOYEES
06/16	545	331	60.8%	3,347
06/06	275	(2)	—	—
06/05	0	0	—	—
06/04	234	(101)	—	—
Annual Growth	7.3%	—	—	—

2016 Year-End Financials
Return on assets: 40.7%
Return on equity: 60.8%
Current ratio: 0.80
Cash ($ mil.): 265

SAN GABRIEL/POMONA VALLEYS DEVELOPMENTAL SERVICES, INC.

EXECUTIVES

Executive Director, R Keith Penman
Accountant, Cristina Luceno
Auditors: WINDES INC LONG BEACH CALI

LOCATIONS

HQ: SAN GABRIEL/POMONA VALLEYS DEVELOPMENTAL SERVICES, INC.
75 RANCHO CAMINO DR, POMONA, CA 917664728
Phone: 909 620-7722
Web: WWW.SGPRC.ORG

HISTORICAL FINANCIALS
Company Type: Private

Income Statement
FYE: June 30

	REVENUE ($ mil.)	NET INCOME ($ mil.)	NET PROFIT MARGIN	EMPLOYEES
06/15	196	0	0.0%	323
06/14	183	0	0.0%	—
06/13	172	0	0.0%	—
06/12	164	0	—	—
Annual Growth	6.2%	—	—	—

2015 Year-End Financials
Return on assets: 9.2%
Return on equity: —
Current ratio: 0.80
Cash ($ mil.): 5

SAN JACINTO METHODIST HOSPITAL

EXECUTIVES

Chairman, Jeffery Ackernan
Account Manager, Melinda Gray
Manager, Eduardo Gonzalez
Vice-President, Lauren Rykert

LOCATIONS

HQ: SAN JACINTO METHODIST HOSPITAL
4401 GARTH RD, BAYTOWN, TX 775212122
Phone: 281 420-8600
Web: WWW.TMHS.ORG

HISTORICAL FINANCIALS
Company Type: Private

Income Statement
FYE: December 31

	REVENUE ($ mil.)	NET INCOME ($ mil.)	NET PROFIT MARGIN	EMPLOYEES
12/15	225	14	6.5%	1,480
12/14	212	9	4.6%	—
12/08	183	11	6.2%	—
12/04	547	(0)	—	—
Annual Growth	(7.8%)	—	—	—

2015 Year-End Financials
Return on assets: 3.4%
Return on equity: 6.5%
Current ratio: 1.90
Cash ($ mil.): —

SAN JOAQUIN HILLS TRANSPORTATION CORRIDOR AGENCY

EXECUTIVES

Chief Executive Officer, Michael Kraman
Financial Executive, Dave Sherwood
Executive Secretary, Patty Romo
Financial Executive, Tracy Bowman
Plant & Facilities Manager, Kurt R Machtolf
Manager, Diane Farson
Senior Manager, Beth Krom
Senior Manager, Linda Lindholm
Director, Amy Suchomel
Auditors: KPMG LLP IRVINE CA

LOCATIONS

HQ: SAN JOAQUIN HILLS TRANSPORTATION CORRIDOR AGENCY
125 PACIFICA STE 100, IRVINE, CA 926183324
Phone: 949 754-3400
Web: WWW.THETOLLROADS.COM

HISTORICAL FINANCIALS

Company Type: Private

Income Statement				FYE: June 30
	REVENUE ($ mil.)	NET INCOME ($ mil.)	NET PROFIT MARGIN	EMPLOYEES
06/16	175	44	25.3%	71
06/15	151	(122)	—	
06/14	132	6	5.2%	
06/13	119	(9)	—	
Annual Growth	13.9%	—	—	—

SAN JUAN REGIONAL MEDICAL CENTER, INC.

EXECUTIVES

Chairman of the Board, Mike Jakino
Board of Directors, John Buffington
Board of Directors, Robert Fabrey
Board of Directors, Suzanne Smith
Director, Mark Schramm
Auditors: ERNST & YOUNG US LLP PHOENIX

LOCATIONS

HQ: SAN JUAN REGIONAL MEDICAL CENTER, INC.
  801 W MAPLE ST, FARMINGTON, NM 874015630
Phone: 505 609-2000
Web: WWW.SANJUANREGIONAL.COM

HISTORICAL FINANCIALS

Company Type: Private

Income Statement				FYE: June 30
	REVENUE ($ mil.)	NET INCOME ($ mil.)	NET PROFIT MARGIN	EMPLOYEES
06/15	260	15	6.1%	1,700
06/14	252	5	2.3%	
06/13	250	6	2.5%	
06/12	246	6	2.5%	
Annual Growth	1.9%	37.4%	—	—

2015 Year-End Financials

Return on assets: 4.6%
Return on equity: 6.1%
Current ratio: 1.70
Cash ($ mil.): 45

SAN MARCOS UNIFIED SCHOOL DISTRICT

EXECUTIVES

Superintendent, Kevin D Holt
Principal, Fred Wise
Principal, Pamela Johnson
Administrative Assistant, Barbara Pluth
Director, Charmaine Wade
Superintendent, Bob Henricks
Finance Manager, Pamella M Coy
Board of Directors, Sharon Jenkins
Auditors: CHRISTY WHITE ASSOCIATES SAN

LOCATIONS

HQ: SAN MARCOS UNIFIED SCHOOL DISTRICT
  255 PICO AVE STE 250, SAN MARCOS, CA 920693712
Phone: 760 744-4776
Web: WWW.SMUSD.ORG

HISTORICAL FINANCIALS

Company Type: Private

Income Statement				FYE: June 30
	REVENUE ($ mil.)	NET INCOME ($ mil.)	NET PROFIT MARGIN	EMPLOYEES
06/16	248	(15)	—	1,500
06/12	138	1	0.8%	
06/06	133	0	—	
06/04	0	0	—	
Annual Growth	—	—	—	—

2016 Year-End Financials

Return on assets: 6.4%
Return on equity: (-6.3%)
Current ratio: —
Cash ($ mil.): 178

SANFORD HEALTH

EXECUTIVES

President, Kelby K Krabbenhoft
Director, Kathy Kalverd
Director, Don Kooiman
Auditors: DELOITTE & TOUCHE LLP MINNEA

LOCATIONS

HQ: SANFORD HEALTH
  1305 W 18TH ST, SIOUX FALLS, SD 571050401
Phone: 605 333-1720
Web: WWW.SANFORDHEALTH.ORG

HISTORICAL FINANCIALS

Company Type: Private

Income Statement				FYE: June 30
	REVENUE ($ mil.)	NET INCOME ($ mil.)	NET PROFIT MARGIN	EMPLOYEES
06/16	4,231	114	2.7%	2,939
06/12	2,516	72	2.9%	
06/11	2,312	264	11.5%	
Annual Growth	12.8%	(15.5%)	—	—

2016 Year-End Financials

Return on assets: 2.5%
Return on equity: 2.7%
Current ratio: 1.20
Cash ($ mil.): 191

SANTA BARBARA COTTAGE HOSPITAL

EXECUTIVES

Chairman, Gretchen Milligan
Director, Brian Moynier

LOCATIONS

HQ: SANTA BARBARA COTTAGE HOSPITAL
  400 W PUEBLO ST, SANTA BARBARA, CA 931054353
Phone: 805 682-7111
Web: WWW.SBCH.ORG

HISTORICAL FINANCIALS

Company Type: Private

Income Statement				FYE: December 31
	REVENUE ($ mil.)	NET INCOME ($ mil.)	NET PROFIT MARGIN	EMPLOYEES
12/15	610	(15)	—	1,786
12/14	38	32	83.3%	
12/13	27	22	81.0%	
12/12	569	16	2.8%	
Annual Growth	2.3%	—	—	—

2015 Year-End Financials

Return on assets: 6.7%
Return on equity: (-2.5%)
Current ratio: 1.50
Cash ($ mil.): 9

SANTA ROSA MEMORIAL HOSPITAL INC

EXECUTIVES

Chief Executive Officer, Todd Salnas
Board of Directors, Kathrine Hardin
Representative, James P Houser
Director, Priscilla Locke
VP Personnel, Carol Aaron
Auditors: ERNST & YOUNG US LLP SAN DIEG

LOCATIONS

HQ: SANTA ROSA MEMORIAL HOSPITAL INC
  1165 MONTGOMERY DR, SANTA ROSA, CA 954054897
Phone: 707 546-3210
Web: WWW.STJOESONOMA.ORG

HISTORICAL FINANCIALS

Company Type: Private

Income Statement				FYE: June 30
	REVENUE ($ mil.)	NET INCOME ($ mil.)	NET PROFIT MARGIN	EMPLOYEES
06/15	489	64	13.1%	2,100
06/14	387	47	12.2%	
06/10	357	(1)	—	
06/09	319	5	1.8%	
Annual Growth	7.3%	49.4%	—	—

2015 Year-End Financials

Return on assets: 4.5%
Return on equity: 13.1%
Current ratio: 2.00
Cash ($ mil.): 58

SAPP BROS., INC.

Need air in those 18 wheels? Sapp Bros Travel Centers (formerly Sapp Bros Truck Stops) has the usual air gas food but also offers human conveniences such such as laundry rooms mailbox rentals private showers and TV lounges. The company

operates a chain of some 15 truck stops — readily identifiable by the giant red-and-white coffeepot logo — along interstate highways from Utah to Pennsylvania; with a concentration in Nebraska. Half of the locations also operate service centers offering oil changes new tires and safety checks. Its sister company Sapp Bros Petroleum distributes fuels and lubricants to more than 200 retailers. The firm is run by CEO Bill Sapp one of the four founding Sapp brothers.

Geographic Reach

Omaha-based Sapp Bros. has travel centers in eight states: Nebraska Iowa Utah Colorado Wyoming Kansas Illinois and Pennsylvania.

Strategy

To raise its profile and rev up its business Sapp Bros. in 2013 joined the roster of VP Racing Fuels's retail brand partners. The benefits of the affiliation include association with an attractive retail image competitive credit card rates and the ability to source unbranded fuel for its travel centers.

EXECUTIVES

Chairman of the Board, William Sapp
Marketing Manager, Kevin Cassidy
General Manager, Deena Merten
Auditors: KPMG LLP OMAHA NE

LOCATIONS

HQ: SAPP BROS., INC.
9915 S 148TH ST, OMAHA, NE 681383876
Phone: 402 895-7038
Web: WWW.HOTSTUFFFOODS.COM

2012 Locations

	No.
Nebraska	8
Iowa	2
Colorado	1
Illinois	1
Kansas	1
Pennsylvania	1
Utah	1
Wyoming	1
Total	**16**

COMPETITORS

Exxon Mobil
Love's Country Stores
Pilot Flying J
Stuckey's
TravelCenters of America

HISTORICAL FINANCIALS

Company Type: Private

Income Statement

FYE: September 30

	REVENUE ($ mil.)	NET INCOME ($ mil.)	NET PROFIT MARGIN	EMPLOYEES
09/16	802	18	2.3%	1,115
09/15	1,128	20	1.8%	—
09/14	1,566	12	0.8%	—
09/13	1,483	14	1.0%	—
Annual Growth	(18.5%)	7.7%	—	—

2016 Year-End Financials

Return on assets: 3.8%
Return on equity: 2.3%
Current ratio: 0.70
Cash ($ mil.): 2

SARAH BUSH LINCOLN HEALTH CENTER

With the moniker of the Illinois' favorite son's stepmother (Sarah Bush Lincoln) who wouldn't want to go to this health center? And apparently the locals agree since Sarah Bush Lincoln Health Center (SBLHC) has a market share of about 44% in its seven-county service area in east-central Illinois and an inpatient market share for Coles County of nearly 80%. SBLHC has 128 beds and provides a wide range of health care services including emergency medicine behavioral health care surgical services and cancer treatment. Its network also includes about 30 clinics doctors' offices and hospice centers. The hospital also offers support groups and continuing education classes.

Operations

SBLHC has a staff of active and consulting physicians totaling 145 providers with nearly 30 specialties. Each year it has some 7000 admissions and performs 1000 inpatient and 5000 outpatient surgeries.

Geographic Reach

The regional hospital is centrally located in east-central Illinois' Coles County and serves seven counties. Home health services extend to the surrounding 19 counties in east-central and southern Illinois.

Strategy

As part of an ongoing expansion drive SBLHC broke ground on a new regional cancer center in 2015. The center located on the front lawn of the main campus will feature 17 individual chemotherapy areas and will span 21000 sq. ft. of space. They hospital is also building a new clinic in Tuscola Illinois.

Company Background

SBLHC opened its doors in 1977. It was named after President Abraham Lincoln's stepmother Sarah Bush Lincoln.

EXECUTIVES

Medical Records Director, Kristen Bliss
Vice President of IS, Maggie Ratliss
Executive Vice President of Information Systems, Maggie Ratliff
Secretary Of Human Resources, Amanda Beals

LOCATIONS

HQ: SARAH BUSH LINCOLN HEALTH CENTER
1000 HEALTH CENTER DR, MATTOON, IL 619389261
Phone: 217 258-2525

PRODUCTS/OPERATIONS

Selected Programs/Services

Advanced Wound Center
Audiology
Center for Interventional Pain
Emergency Department
EMS
Gastroenterology
Heart Center
Hospitalist Program
Laboratory
Lifeline
Lincolnland Hospice
Lincolnland Home Care
Orthopedics and Sports Medicine
Outpatient Surgery Center
Patient Care
Physical Medicine & Rehabilitation
Psychiatry and Counseling
Radiology
Regional Cancer Center
Women and Children's Center

COMPETITORS

Carle Hospital
Crawford Memorial Hospital
Decatur Memorial Hospital
Hospital Sisters Health System
Iroquois Memorial Hospital
Memorial Health System (Colorado)
Memorial Medical Center
St. John's Hospital (Illinois)

HISTORICAL FINANCIALS

Company Type: Private

Income Statement

FYE: June 30

	REVENUE ($ mil.)	NET INCOME ($ mil.)	NET PROFIT MARGIN	EMPLOYEES
06/15	223	37	16.9%	1,543
06/14	252	28	11.2%	—
06/11	195	14	7.2%	—
06/09	132	(6)	—	—
Annual Growth	9.1%	—	—	—

2015 Year-End Financials

Return on assets: 4.1%
Return on equity: 16.9%
Current ratio: 1.80
Cash ($ mil.): 42

SARASOTA COUNTY PUBLIC HOSPITAL DISTRICT

Sarasota County Public Hospital Board which does business as the Sarasota Memorial Health Care System is a publicly owned hospital system serving residents in and around Sarasota on Florida's western coast. It operates Sarasota Memorial Hospital a not-for-profit acute-care facility with more than 800 beds (and more than 900 doctors) that provides general medical and surgical care as well as specialized care in areas such as heart disease cancer and neuroscience. The system also features a skilled nursing facility walk-in medical centers an outpatient surgical center and home health care operations. Additionally the hospital conducts clinical trials and has an educational affiliation with Florida State University.

Operations

Sarasota Memorial has the only obstetrics program and neonatal intensive care unit in the county and its Bayside Center includes one of the county's only inpatient behavioral health facilities. The health care system's Charter Health Plan program offers group health insurance to local business owners.

Sarasota Memorial receives some 32000 inpatient visits and 950000 outpatient and physician visits each year.

Geographic Reach

Sarasota Memorial serves Florida's Sarasota County.

Sales and Marketing

Medicare and Medicaid combined account for some 60% of Sarasota Memorial's net patient service revenue. Self-pay and managed care make up the remainder.

Financial Performance

Sarasota's total revenues increased by 9% in fiscal 2016 (ended September) due to a 9% increase

in net patient revenue due to higher volume. The company reported $107 million in excess revenues over expenses that year a 13% decline versus the prior year. Operating expenses including salaries fringe benefits and supplies costs all increased in 2016.

Cash flow from operations increased 38% to $85.8 million thanks to an increase in cash received from patient care services.

Strategy

Sarasota Memorial seeks to improve its financial performance by pursuing profitable inpatient and outpatient growth through an aggressive focus on physician alignment and integration and capturing new patients residing in high growth areas. The system has also been opening new facilities to boost patient service revenues. In 2016 it opened its sixth urgent care center. The following year it opened a 74000-sq.-ft. Rehabilitation Pavilion the only site of its kind in Sarasota County to offer comprehensive inpatient and outpatient rehabilitation services.

The system also introduced its nurse residency program and an internal medicine residency program in 2017.

Company Background

Sarasota Memorial was founded as a community hospital in 1925.

EXECUTIVES

VP and CIO, Denis Baker
President and CEO, David Verinder, age 50
Chief Nursing Officer, Jan Mauck
CFO, William Woeltjen
Chief of Medical Operations, R. Stephen Taylor
Medical Director Research, Ricardo Yaryura
Director Managed Care, Steve Rhodes
Radiology Director, Debbie Bohanon
Pharmd, Michelle Malatlian
Board Secretary, Donna Desisto
First Vice Chairman, Gregory Carter
Second Vice Chairwoman, Marguerite G. Malone
First Vice Chairwoman, Alex Miller

LOCATIONS

HQ: SARASOTA COUNTY PUBLIC HOSPITAL DISTRICT
1700 S TAMIAMI TRL, SARASOTA, FL 342393509
Phone: 941 917-9000
Web: WWW.SMH.COM

PRODUCTS/OPERATIONS

2016 Sales

	% of total
County Public Hospital District	
Sarasota Memorial Hospital	59
Corporate Division	2
Nursing & Rehabilitation Center	1
Charter Plan	-
SMH Health Care Inc.	33
Physician Services Inc.	5
Total	**100**

COMPETITORS

All Children's Hospital	HCA
Bayfront Health	HealthSouth
Florida Hospital Tampa Bay Division	St. Joseph's-Baptist Health Care
	Tampa General Hospital

HISTORICAL FINANCIALS
Company Type: Private

Income Statement
FYE: September 30

	REVENUE ($ mil.)	NET INCOME ($ mil.)	NET PROFIT MARGIN	EMPLOYEES
09/15	590	131	22.3%	4,200
09/14	524	92	17.6%	—
09/13*	512	(5)	—	—
12/06	407	2	0.6%	—
Annual Growth	**4.2%**	**55.0%**		

*Fiscal year change

2015 Year-End Financials

Return on assets: 3.7% Cash ($ mil.): 33
Return on equity: 22.3%
Current ratio: 0.70

SARATOGA HOSPITAL

EXECUTIVES

Chief Executive Officer, Angelo G Calbone
Board of Directors, Theresa M Skaine
Financial Executive, Noel Cook

LOCATIONS

HQ: SARATOGA HOSPITAL
211 CHURCH ST, SARATOGA SPRINGS, NY 128661090
Phone: 518 587-3222
Web: WWW.SARATOGAHOSPITAL.ORG

HISTORICAL FINANCIALS
Company Type: Private

Income Statement
FYE: December 31

	REVENUE ($ mil.)	NET INCOME ($ mil.)	NET PROFIT MARGIN	EMPLOYEES
12/15	259	12	4.9%	1,500
12/14	240	16	6.8%	—
12/13	238	11	4.8%	—
12/09	187	13	7.1%	—
Annual Growth	**5.6%**	**(0.7%)**	—	—

2015 Year-End Financials

Return on assets: 5.4% Cash ($ mil.): 99
Return on equity: 4.9%
Current ratio: 3.50

SAWNEE ELECTRIC MEMBERSHIP CORPORATION

Sawnee Electric Membership Corporation (Sawnee EMC) wasn't around on the night the lights went out in Georgia but it plans to make sure they stay on. The electric distribution cooperative serves about 152000 residential commercial and industrial meters in a seven-county area of northern Georgia comprised of Cherokee Dawson Forsyth Fulton Gwinnett Hall and Lumpkin counties. Residential customers in the area (which in-

cludes the sprawling Atlanta suburbs) account for two-thirds of electricity usage. While small and medium users must get their electricity from Sawnee potential customers with loads exceeding 900 kilowatts can shop around. Sawnee EMC distributes electricity over 9970 miles of power line.

The cooperative provides its members with the option of gas service through a partnership with Coweta-Fayette EMC Natural Gas a subsidiary of fellow Georgia-based power co-op Coweta-Fayette EMC. In 2010 it had 16000 Sawnee EMC customers participating in this arrangement.

As part of its commitment to green energy Sawnee EMC has also teamed up with Green-e Energy a leading national renewable energy certification and verification program to offer certified renewable power to Sawnee EMC members. It is encouraging its members to conserve energy and help keep down costs offering home energy audits installing Smart meters and encouraging the use of energy-efficient light bulbs.

In 2010 Sawnee EMC reported a jump in revenues and operating income thanks to a growth in its membership and higher energy use due to a hotter-than-usual summer.

The company was founded as the Forsyth County Electric Membership Corporation in 1938 as part of the Roosevelt government's national rural electrification drive. It was renamed for local landmark Sawnee Mountain in 1950.

EXECUTIVES

President, Michael A Goodroe
Board of Directors, Rodney H Reese
Vice-President, Bill Parsons
Supervisor, Melissa Watson
Supervisor, Dennis Hughes
Auditors: MCNAIR MCLEMORE MIDDLEBROOKS &

LOCATIONS

HQ: SAWNEE ELECTRIC MEMBERSHIP CORPORATION
543 ATLANTA RD, CUMMING, GA 300402701
Phone: 770 887-2363
Web: WWW.SAWNEE.COM

COMPETITORS

Cobb EMC	Jackson Electric
Georgia Power	Membership

HISTORICAL FINANCIALS
Company Type: Private

Income Statement
FYE: December 31

	REVENUE ($ mil.)	NET INCOME ($ mil.)	NET PROFIT MARGIN	EMPLOYEES
12/15	337	0	—	300
12/14	346	0	—	—
12/13	335	0	—	—
12/12	325	0	—	—
Annual Growth	**1.1%**	—	—	—

2015 Year-End Financials

Return on assets: 12.0% Cash ($ mil.): 8
Return on equity: —
Current ratio: 0.50

SCHOOL DISTRICT FIVE OF LEXINGTON AND RICHLAND COUNTIES

EXECUTIVES

Superintendent, Herbert Berg
Director, Tom Weeks
Superintendent, Stephen Heffner
Consultant, Kimberly Gilbert
Auditors: MCGREGOR & COMPANY LLP ORANGE

LOCATIONS

HQ: SCHOOL DISTRICT FIVE OF LEXINGTON AND RICHLAND COUNTIES
1020 DUTCH FORK RD, IRMO, SC 290638822
Phone: 803 476-8000
Web: WWW.LEXRICH5.ORG

HISTORICAL FINANCIALS

Company Type: Private

Income Statement

FYE: June 30

	REVENUE ($ mil.)	NET INCOME ($ mil.)	NET PROFIT MARGIN	EMPLOYEES
06/16	211	(4)	—	2,500
06/13	193	51	26.6%	—
06/12	186	(40)	—	—
06/09	461	0	0.0%	—
Annual Growth	(10.5%)	—	—	—

2016 Year-End Financials

Return on assets: 2.0%   Cash ($ mil.): 71
Return on equity: (-2.2%)
Current ratio: —

SCHOOL DISTRICT NO.1J MULTNOMAH COUNTY, OR

EXECUTIVES

Superintendent, Carole Smith
Account Manager, Harriet Deary
Manager, Nick Jwayad
Manager, Carol A Kirby
Director, John Branam
Director, Kristy Obbink
Vice-President, Scott Robinson
Auditors: TALBOT KORVOLA & WARWICK LLP

LOCATIONS

HQ: SCHOOL DISTRICT NO.1J MULTNOMAH COUNTY, OR
501 N DIXON ST, PORTLAND, OR 972271804
Phone: 503 916-2000
Web: WWW.PPS.NET

HISTORICAL FINANCIALS

Company Type: Private

Income Statement

FYE: June 30

	REVENUE ($ mil.)	NET INCOME ($ mil.)	NET PROFIT MARGIN	EMPLOYEES
06/15	691	255	36.9%	5,244
06/14	661	(0)	—	—
06/13	578	118	20.6%	—
06/12	574	(4)	—	—
Annual Growth	6.4%	—	—	—

2015 Year-End Financials

Return on assets: 4.0%   Cash ($ mil.): 115
Return on equity: 36.9%
Current ratio: 1.40

SCHOOL DISTRICT OF INDIAN RIVER COUNTY

EXECUTIVES

Superintendent, Fran Adams
Assistant Manager, Peggy Poyell
Account Manager, Charlene Atkins
Assistant Manager, Bruce Green
Executive Director, Denise Roberts

LOCATIONS

HQ: SCHOOL DISTRICT OF INDIAN RIVER COUNTY
6500 57TH ST, VERO BEACH, FL 329676002
Phone: 772 564-3000
Web: WWW.INDIANRIVERSCHOOLS.ORG

HISTORICAL FINANCIALS

Company Type: Private

Income Statement

FYE: June 30

	REVENUE ($ mil.)	NET INCOME ($ mil.)	NET PROFIT MARGIN	EMPLOYEES
06/16	186	16	8.6%	2,000
06/15	180	(3)	—	—
06/14	176	(5)	—	—
06/13	171	(5)	—	—
Annual Growth	2.9%	—	—	—

2016 Year-End Financials

Return on assets: 1.1%   Cash ($ mil.): 28
Return on equity: 8.6%
Current ratio: —

SCIENTIFIC RESEARCH CORP

Scientific Research Corporation (SRC) doesn't limit its services to the laboratory. The government contractor provides a wide variety of engineering and research services including consulting systems engineering project management network design hardware and software development prototyping testing and evaluation systems integration and training. Its expertise encompasses communications and intelligence systems electronic warfare simulation and instrumentation systems. In some cases SRC works as a subcontractor for larger companies such as Booz Allen. SRC's clients include the US government and military state agencies and private sector businesses.

Operations

The company's integrated systems and solutions division specializes in software development network engineering systems automation digital signal processing production engineering and logistical support services for intelligence systems. It also provides other IT and wireless network support services.

SRC's simulation test and instrumentation division offers products and engineering services to support surveillance radar and instrumentation systems. It also develops sensor systems and provides interoperability testing services for military weapons systems.

The company's communications networks and electronics unit provides research and development systems integration design deployment and support services for military and commercial communications and network systems.

Geographic Reach

SRC operates from about 15 offices located mainly in the southern and eastern US; it also has a few facilities in the Southwest and in California.

EXECUTIVES

CEO, Michael L. (Mike) Watt, age 55
CFO and Secretary, Thomas L. Papst
Vice President, Rich Kniskern
Vice President Operations, Alan Harris
Vice President, Wayne Slocum
Vice President, Bill Richardson
Auditors: DIXON HUGHES GOODMAN LLP ATLA

LOCATIONS

HQ: SCIENTIFIC RESEARCH CORP
2300 WINDY RIDGE PKWY SE 400S, ATLANTA, GA 303398431
Phone: 770 859-9161
Web: WWW.SCIRES.COM

COMPETITORS

Boeing	ManTech
CACI International	Northrop Grumman
Computer Sciences	QinetiQ
Corp.	Raytheon
HP Enterprise Services	Research Triangle
Leidos	Institute
Lockheed Martin	Serco Inc.
Long Wave	

HISTORICAL FINANCIALS

Company Type: Private

Income Statement

FYE: December 31

	REVENUE ($ mil.)	NET INCOME ($ mil.)	NET PROFIT MARGIN	EMPLOYEES
12/15	293	19	6.6%	1,006
12/14	318	20	6.5%	—
12/13	372	24	6.7%	—
12/12	360	26	7.3%	—
Annual Growth	(6.6%)	(9.4%)	—	—

2015 Year-End Financials

Return on assets: 9.6%   Cash ($ mil.): 40
Return on equity: 6.6%
Current ratio: 1.70

SCOTT & WHITE MEMORIAL HOSPITAL

EXECUTIVES

Chief Executive Officer, Robert Pryor
Chief Operating Officer, Linda M Burke
VP Marketing, Lindsey Joy
Chief Operating Officer, Patti Ellisor

LOCATIONS

HQ: SCOTT & WHITE MEMORIAL HOSPITAL
2401 S 31ST ST, TEMPLE, TX 765080001
Phone: 254 724-2111
Web: WWW.SW.ORG

COMPETITORS

Baylor Health
Community Health
 Systems
Cook Children's Health
 Care System
Dell Children's
 Medical Center
HCSC
Hill Country
Seton Healthcare
 Network

Shriners Hospitals For
 Children
St. David's Health
 Care
St. David's Round Rock
 Medical Center
Texas Children's
 Hospital

HISTORICAL FINANCIALS

Company Type: Private

Income Statement

FYE: August 31

	REVENUE ($ mil.)	NET INCOME ($ mil.)	NET PROFIT MARGIN	EMPLOYEES
08/15*	1,166	(156)	—	8,000
06/14	832	87	10.5%	—
08/13	881	76	8.6%	—
08/10	902	41	4.6%	—
Annual Growth	5.3%	—	—	—

*Fiscal year change

2015 Year-End Financials

Return on assets: 4.9%
Return on equity: (-13.5%)
Current ratio: 0.10

Cash ($ mil.): 52

SCRIPPS HEALTH

Scripps Health houses many a script-writing physician in its hospitals. The not-for-profit health system serves the San Diego area through five acute-care hospitals. Altogether the health system is home to approximately 1700 inpatient beds and a network of outpatient clinics. The system also offers home health care and operates community outreach programs. Its hospitals along with several outpatient Scripps Clinic and Scripps Coastal Medical Center locations employ some 3000 affiliated general practice and specialty physicians.

Operations

Scripps Health's facilities include the 700-bed Scripps Mercy Hospital which has a main campus in San Diego and a satellite campus in Chula Vista as well as Scripps Green Hospital (173 beds in La Jolla) Scripps Memorial Hospital Encinitas (138 beds) and Scripps Memorial Hospital La Jolla (444 beds). The system's network also includes the new Prebys Cardiovascular Institute (168 beds) about a dozen coastal medical centers two wellness centers and about 20 specialty centers.

In 2016 the system had more than 445000 hospital outpatient visits 21500 surgeries and 1.2 million medical office visits.

Scripps Health is the official health care provider for the San Diego Padres baseball team.

Financial Performance

Scripps Health had $2.9 billion in revenues in fiscal 2016 (ended September). Some $2.2 billion of that revenue came from net patient service income while $0.5 billion came from capitation premiums. After operating expenses the system had $292.3 million in excess of revenues over expenses attributable to controlling interests.

Strategy

Scripps Health's overall strategy is to remain on the cutting edge of technology in order to treat patients more effectively therefore reporting better patient outcomes (which in turns makes it eligible for certain government incentives). It also aims to make itself the destination of choice for patients — both locally and globally — for cardiac cancer and other types of specialty care. For example it partners with renowned oncology center MD Anderson to operate the Scripps MD Anderson Cancer Center slated to open in mid-2018.

As a major provider in the larger San Diego area Scripps Health is constantly evaluating its scope of services to meet the ever-increasing demand for health care. The company is building several outpatient clinics including cancer treatment and cardiac care centers. It is also expanding and upgrading its hospitals. In addition Scripps Health has launched an initiative to increase the number of clinical trials conducted at its facilities.

However after missing its budget for the first time in more than a dozen years Scripps Health announced plans to lower operating costs through restructuring efforts. It ultimately aims to rely more heavily on outpatient care and wellness services to reduce hospital visits. Layoffs are part of the restructuring plans: For example the system eliminated the CEO positions at its five hospitals. The hospitals are now led by chief operations executives reporting to regional (North and South) CEOs. Additionally Scripps Health shut down its loss-making hospice operations in 2017.

HISTORY

Scripps Health was founded by Ellen Browning Scripps in 1924 when the Scripps Memorial Hospital and Scripps Metabolic Clinic opened in La Jolla.

The network grew through the opening of Scripps Green Hospital in 1977 and the Scripps Memorial Hospital Encinitas campus was added through the purchase of San Dieguito Hospital the following year.

Scripps Mercy Hospital which was first established in 1890 in San Diego joined the Scripps network in 1995.

The Scripps Health system expanded once again when it acquired the Scripps Mercy Hospital Chula Vista campus in 2004.

EXECUTIVES

SVP and Chief Executive Scripps Green Hospital, Robin B. Brown
SVP and Chief Executive Scripps Memorial Hospital La Jolla, Gary G. Fybel
SVP and Chief Executive Scripps Mercy Hospital, Tom Gammiere
CFO and Treasurer, Richard K. Rothberger
SVP and Chief Executive Scripps Memorial Hospital Encinitas, Carl J. Etter
President and CEO, Christopher D. Van Gorder
Corporate SVP and Chief Medical Officer, James LaBelle
SVP and Chief Executive Scripps Medical Foundation, Shiraz M. Fagan

Corporate SVP and CIO, Andy Crowder
Corporate Vice President and Corporate Treasurer, Richard McKeown
Assistant Vice President Information Services, Clark Kegley
Vice President Of Financial Services, David Cohn
Vice President Medical Services Regional Sites, Peter D Aldrich
Corporate Senior Vice Presiden, Richard Sheridan
Medical Director Of The Minimally Invasive Robotic Surgery Program, Carol E Salem
Vice President Managed Care, Karri Rodgers
Corporate Vice President and Chief Audit and Compliance Executive, Gerry Soderstrom
Vice Chairman, Mark Sherman
Auditors: ERNST & YOUNG US LLP SAN DIEG

LOCATIONS

HQ: SCRIPPS HEALTH
4275 CAMPUS POINT CT, SAN DIEGO, CA 921211513
Phone: 858 678-7000

Selected Facilities

Scripps Clinic (outpatient centers)
Scripps Coastal Medical Center (outpatient centers)
Scripps Green Hospital (La Jolla)
Scripps Memorial Hospital Encinitas
Scripps Memorial Hospital La Jolla
Scripps Mercy Hospital (San Diego)
Scripps Mercy Hospital Chula Vista

COMPETITORS

Adventist Health
 System West
Cedars-Sinai Medical
 Center
Community Health
 Systems
Dignity Health
Grossmont Hospital
HCA

Palomar Health
Paradise Valley
 Hospital
Prospect Medical
Rady Children's
 Hospital
Sharp HealthCare
Tenet Healthcare

HISTORICAL FINANCIALS

Company Type: Private

Income Statement

FYE: September 30

	REVENUE ($ mil.)	NET INCOME ($ mil.)	NET PROFIT MARGIN	EMPLOYEES
09/15	2,943	371	12.6%	13,445
09/08	1,953	18	0.9%	—
09/07	1,781	223	12.6%	—
Annual Growth	6.5%	6.5%	—	—

2015 Year-End Financials

Return on assets: 12.9%
Return on equity: 12.6%
Current ratio: 0.70

Cash ($ mil.): 464

SEATTLE CANCER CARE ALLIANCE

EXECUTIVES

President, Fred Appelbaum
Financial Executive, Lisa Aragon
Administrative Assistant, Sung Kim
Auditors: CLARK NUBER PS BELLEVUE WA

LOCATIONS

HQ: SEATTLE CANCER CARE ALLIANCE
825 EASTLAKE AVE E, SEATTLE, WA 981094405
Phone: 206 288-7222
Web: WWW.SEATTLECCA.ORG

HISTORICAL FINANCIALS

Company Type: Private

Income Statement

FYE: June 30

	REVENUE ($ mil.)	NET INCOME ($ mil.)	NET PROFIT MARGIN	EMPLOYEES
06/15	464	20	4.4%	1,300
06/14	434	25	5.8%	—
06/10	0	(2)	—	—
06/09	234	20	8.6%	—
Annual Growth	12.0%	0.1%	—	—

2015 Year-End Financials

Return on assets: 15.9% Cash ($ mil.): 44
Return on equity: 4.4%
Current ratio: 0.60

SEATTLE CHILDREN'S HOSPITAL

Seattle Children's Hospital which has some 325 beds serves children and infants of all ages. Its specialty units include psychiatric care neonatal intensive care and rehabilitation for children disabled by injuries illness or congenital complications. In addition to its primary campus Seattle Children's Hospital operates numerous outpatient clinics in the Puget Sound area. It also provides outreach services throughout the Pacific Northwest as well as in Alaska and Montana. Seattle Children's Hospital provides telemedicine services in Idaho.

Geographic Reach

Seattle Children's Hospital serves the largest landmass of any children's hospital in the country (Washington Alaska Montana and Idaho).

Its outreach clinics in Alaska and Montana provide specialty care through physicians and nurses who travel to rural communities in each state. In Idaho videoconferencing brings specialty services to rural communities that would not otherwise have access to them.

Sales and Marketing

The hospital runs a program called the Medical-Legal Partnership for Children that provides assistance to low-income families with children receiving medical treatment at its Odessa Brown Children's Clinic (OBCC) or its Harborview Children and Teens Clinic (HCTC).

Through the project patients facing family law issues such as custody domestic abuse or access to public benefits are provided an attorney through the Northwest Justice Project. In addition a staff attorney trains physicians and social workers to recognize legal problems that may affect a child's health and also provide direct legal services and referrals for patients at OBCC and HCTC.

Financial Performance

Seattle Children's revenues jumped 11% from 2014 to 2015 due to a rise in net patient service revenues.

Strategy

Seattle Children's keeps expanding throughout its service areas by opening additional clinics (urgent care specialty and primary care). The hospital is also increasing the size of its main hospital by adding an additional 350 beds in four phases over the next two decades. Once the project is complete Seattle Children's will house roughly 600 beds — something the medical providers there will wel-

come since the hospital operates at near capacity the majority of the time.

EXECUTIVES

Senior Vice President Hospital Operations, Cindy Evans
President Seattle Children's Research Institute, James B. Hendricks
SVP and CFO, Kelly Wallace
SVP and Chief Academic Officer, F. Bruder Stapleton
SVP and Surgeon-in-Chief; President CUMG, Robert S. Sawin
SVP and Chief Nursing Officer, Susan Heath
President Seattle Children's Hospital and Research Foundation, Douglas Picha
Chief Data Officer, Eugene Kolker
Chief Medical Information Officer, Troy L. McGuire
Chief Information Security Officer, Cris V. Ewell
SVP and Chief Medical Officer, Mark A. Del Beccaro
CEO, Jeff Sperring
SVP and CIO, Jeff Brown
MEDICAL DIRECTOR, Katrina Dipple
Chairman, Judy Holder

LOCATIONS

HQ: SEATTLE CHILDREN'S HOSPITAL
4800 SAND POINT WAY NE, SEATTLE, WA 981053901
Phone: 206 987-2000
Web: WWW.SEATTLECHILDRENS.ORG

Selected Locations – Washington State
After Hours Clinic
Bellevue Clinic and Surgery Center
Children's at Overlake
Everett Clinic
Federal Way Clinic
Odessa Brown Children's Clinic
Olympia Clinic
Seattle Children's Hospital
Tri-Cities Clinic

PRODUCTS/OPERATIONS

Selected Specialty Programs
Audiology
Dental Medicine
Endocrinology and Diabetes
Gastroenterology
Genetics
Neurodevelopmental
Neurology
Otolaryngology
Psychiatry and Behavioral Medicine
Radiology
Urology

COMPETITORS

Franciscan Health System	PeaceHealth
Harrison Medical Center	Providence St. Joseph Health
Kaiser Permanente WA	Shriners Hospitals For Children
MultiCare Health System	Swedish Health Services
Overlake Hospital	Yakima Valley Memorial

HISTORICAL FINANCIALS

Company Type: Private

Income Statement

FYE: September 30

	REVENUE ($ mil.)	NET INCOME ($ mil.)	NET PROFIT MARGIN	EMPLOYEES
09/15	1,086	148	13.7%	2,800
09/14	983	177	18.0%	—
09/13	1,018	192	18.9%	—
09/12	814	150	18.5%	—
Annual Growth	10.1%	(0.4%)	—	—

2015 Year-End Financials

Return on assets: 5.4% Cash ($ mil.): 28
Return on equity: 13.7%
Current ratio: 1.00

SEATTLE UNIVERSITY

Seattle University isn't very big but as one of 28 Jesuit universities in the US it is part of a Roman Catholic teaching legacy that spans the country and the world. With an enrollment of about 7500 students the school offers 64 undergraduate more than 35 graduate degree programs and 28 certificate programs through its eight schools (College of Arts and Sciences Albers School of Business and Economics College of Education School of Law Matteo Ricci College College of Nursing College of Science and Engineering and School of Theology and Ministry).

Operations

In 2012 Seattle University had 4589 undergraduate students and 1933 graduate students. Some 40% of the first year students were from Washington State and some 7% of all students were from outside the US.

The average class size is 19 and the faculty-to-student ratio is 1 to 13.

Financial Performance

In 2012 the university reported a 10% decrease in revenues due to a drop in investment income a loss incurred in net realized and unrealized losses on investments and a change in value of interest rate swap agreements.

Its net income declined by 90% in 2012 due to a decrease in revenues and an increase in expenses attributed largely to higher costs for instruction academic support and auxiliary enterprises.

Strategy

Growing its portfolio of degree programs in 2012 Seattle University's Albers School of Business and Economics added the Bridge MBA to its family of graduate degrees.

Company Background

Seattle University was founded in 1891 by two Jesuit priests.

EXECUTIVES

Treasurer, Kon Petrov
Secretary, Sarah Johnson
Auditors: KPMG LLP SEATTLE WA

LOCATIONS

HQ: SEATTLE UNIVERSITY
901 12TH AVE, SEATTLE, WA 981224411
Phone: 206 296-6150
Web: WWW.SEATTLEU.EDU

PRODUCTS/OPERATIONS

Schools and Colleges
Albers School of Business and Economics
College of Arts and Sciences
College of Education
College of Nursing
College of Science and Engineering
Matteo Ricci College
School of Law
School of Theology and Ministry

COMPETITORS

University of Washington	Western Washington University
Washington State University	

HISTORICAL FINANCIALS

Company Type: Private

Income Statement
FYE: June 30

	REVENUE ($ mil.)	NET INCOME ($ mil.)	NET PROFIT MARGIN	EMPLOYEES
06/15	305	22	7.5%	1,100
06/13	277	1	0.5%	—
06/10	236	11	4.9%	—
06/09	0	0	—	—
Annual Growth	—	234.2%	—	—

2015 Year-End Financials

Return on assets: 8.2%   Cash ($ mil.): 80
Return on equity: 7.5%
Current ratio: 0.50

SECURITIES INVESTOR PROTECTION CORPORATION

Securities Investor Protection Corporation (SIPC) is an industry-financed insurance plan that protects clients of most broker-dealers registered with the US Securities and Exchange Commission (SEC). SIPC insures customers' securities (up to $500000 per account) against losses due to the financial failure of brokerage firms. Losses caused by fluctuations in market value are not protected. The not-for-profit membership corporation was mandated by the Securities Investor Protection Act and has more than 6000 members. Its board is appointed by the US president the treasury secretary and the Federal Reserve Board. Assessments from members and investments in government securities provide money for the SIPC Fund.

While SIPC will replace missing cash and hard securities (stocks and bonds) it doesn't protect less tangible investments such as commodity futures or investment contracts. Nor does it insure against fraud.

As investment firms imploded throughout 2008 SIPC shifted into high gear to process more than 900000 claims from customers and creditors of Lehman Brothers and more than 15000 claims from investors in Bernard L. Madoff Investment Securities. By late 2009 SIPC was looking at potential payouts of $534 million to former Madoff investors — greater than the sum total of its payouts since it was created in 1970.

During 2011 the firm disagreed with the SEC's efforts to make it pay customers of fraudster R. Allen Stanford. SIPC contends that while Stanford Group was a member of SIPC the defrauded customers didn't lose their money in a failed brokerage.

EXECUTIVES

President, Stephen Harbeck
Board of Directors, Josephine Wang
Chief Operating Officer, Armando J Bucelo
Accountant, Hilary Koch
Director, Linda Siemers
Auditors: GRANT THORNTON MCLEAN VA

LOCATIONS

HQ: SECURITIES INVESTOR PROTECTION CORPORATION
1667 K ST NW STE 1000, WASHINGTON, DC 200061620
Phone: 202 371-8300
Web: WWW.SIPC.ORG

HISTORICAL FINANCIALS

Company Type: Private

Income Statement
FYE: December 31

	ASSETS ($ mil.)	NET INCOME ($ mil.)	INCOME AS % OF ASSETS	EMPLOYEES
12/15	2,652	169	6.4%	39
12/14	2,362	307	13.0%	—
12/11	1,606	131	8.2%	—
12/10	1,382	(271)	—	—
Annual Growth	13.9%	—	—	—

2015 Year-End Financials

Return on assets: 0.2%   Sales ($ mil): 477
Return on equity: 35.4%

SECURITY FINANCE CORPORATION OF SPARTANBURG

Folks looking for a little financial security just might turn to Security Finance Corporation of Spartanburg. Founded in 1955 the consumer loan company provides personal loans typically ranging from $100 to $600 (some states however allow loan amounts as high as $3000). Customers can also turn to Security Finance for credit reports and tax preparation services. The company operates approximately 900 offices in more than 15 states that are marketed under the Security Finance Sunbelt Credit and PFS banner names. A subsidiary of Security Group the financial institution also has locations operating as Security Financial Services in North Carolina and Longhorn Finance in Texas.

Operations

Security Finance boasts some 900 offices nationwide that operate under the Security Finance Sunbelt Credit and PFS names. The company specializes in offering consumers loans to individuals. It also provides consumer credit reports and assistance as well as tax preparation services.

Geographic Reach

From its headquarters in South Carolina Security Finance boasts offices in more than 15 states nationwide.

Company Background

Security Finance exited Colorado in 2010 after the state's attorney general general office filed a compliant that the company had been refinancing some consumer loans more than three times a year (the limit under Colorado law). The company agreed to repay acquisition fees that it had charged the customers for refinancing the loans.

EXECUTIVES

President, Heidi Bolton
Board of Directors, Marshall T Walsh
Manager, Mark Libner
Auditors: ELLIOTT DAVIS DECOSIMO LLC G

LOCATIONS

HQ: SECURITY FINANCE CORPORATION OF SPARTANBURG
181 SECURITY PL, SPARTANBURG, SC 293075450
Phone: 864 582-8193
Web: WWW.SECURITY-FINANCE.COM

Selected Locations
Alabama
Florida
Georgia
Idaho
Illinois
Louisiana
Missouri
Nevada
New Mexico
North Carolina
Oklahoma
South Carolina
Tennessee
Texas
Utah
Wisconsin

PRODUCTS/OPERATIONS

Selected Banners
Longhorn Finance (Texas)
PFS
Security Finance
Security Financial Services (North Carolina)
Sunbelt Credit

COMPETITORS

1st Franklin Financial	DFC Global
ACE Cash Express	EZCORP
Advance America	FirstCash
Bank of America	OneMain
Capital One	OneMain Financial
Cash Plus	Value Financial
Community Choice	Services
Financial	World Acceptance

HISTORICAL FINANCIALS

Company Type: Private

Income Statement
FYE: December 31

	ASSETS ($ mil.)	NET INCOME ($ mil.)	INCOME AS % OF ASSETS	EMPLOYEES
12/15	651	78	12.1%	2,500
12/14	648	83	12.8%	—
12/13	616	62	10.2%	—
12/12	461	53	11.6%	—
Annual Growth	12.2%	13.9%	—	—

2015 Year-End Financials

Return on assets: 6.6%   Sales ($ mil): 555
Return on equity: 14.2%

SECURITY GROUP, INC.

EXECUTIVES

Chairman of the Board, Susan A Bridges
President, Ray Biggs
Vice-President, A Greg Williams
Treasurer, Beadie H Townsel
Auditors: ELLIOTT DAVIS DECOSIMO LLC G

LOCATIONS

HQ: SECURITY GROUP, INC.
181 SECURITY PL, SPARTANBURG, SC 293075450
Phone: 864 582-8193

HISTORICAL FINANCIALS

Company Type: Private

Income Statement

FYE: December 31

	ASSETS ($ mil.)	NET INCOME ($ mil.)	INCOME AS % OF ASSETS	EMPLOYEES
12/15	1,020	97	9.6%	2,500
12/14	1,040	135	13.0%	—
12/13	1,263	107	8.5%	—
12/12	1,198	96	8.1%	—
Annual Growth	(5.2%)	0.4%	—	—

2015 Year-End Financials

Return on assets: 7.4% Sales ($ mil): 636
Return on equity: 15.4%

SEMINOLE ELECTRIC COOPERATIVE, INC.

This Seminole is not only a native Floridian but it has also provided electricity in the state since 1948. Seminole Electric Cooperative generates and transmits electricity for 10 member distribution cooperatives that serve 1.4 million residential and business customers in 42 Florida counties. Seminole Electric has more than 3350 MW of primarily coal-fired generating capacity. The cooperative also buys electricity from other utilities and independent power producers and it owns 350 miles of transmission lines. Some 90% of its power load uses the transmission systems of other utilities through long-term contracts.

Operations

Seminole Electric's primary resources include the 1300 MW Seminole Generating Station and the 810 MW Richard J. Midulla Generating Station. The coop's renewable energy resources include waste-to-energy facilities landfill gas-to-energy facilities and a biomass facility. It also buys power as needed on the market.

Seminole Electric has more than 350 miles of transmission line.

Geographic Reach

The company serves customers in 45 counties in northeast south central and southeast Florida.

Financial Performance

In 2013 the coop's revenues declined by 1% due to lower rates and as well as a reduction in Member energy requirements and lower volumes sold to Non-Members.

Seminole Electric's net income increased by 48% in 2013 thanks to lower operating costs as a result of the absence of asset impairment costs and a drop in interest expenses.

The company's operating cash inflow increased to $86.05 million in 2013 (from $34.81 million in 2012) primarily due to improved net income and a change in working capital.

Strategy

The coop is seeking to respond to the State of Florida's push to get more power generation from renewable sources. In 2014 the company generating about 58% of its electricity from coal 35% from natural gas and 7% from green energy sources (up from 5.5% in 2011 making Seminole Electric one of the largest green energy providers in Florida).

Company Background

In 2012 it also made major environmental improvements to its main power plant the coal-fired Seminole Generating Station. In 2011 Seminole Electric boosted its portfolio of purchased green energy to more than 140 MW (including 113 MW from waste-to-energy facilities).

Seminole Electric was formed in 1948 to aggregate the power demands of its members and is governed by a board of trustees representing the 10 member utilities. The cooperative built its first power plant in the 1970s.

EXECUTIVES

Vice President of Administrati, Al Garcia

LOCATIONS

HQ: SEMINOLE ELECTRIC COOPERATIVE, INC.
16313 N DALE MABRY HWY, TAMPA, FL 336181427
Phone: 813 963-0994
Web: WWW.SEMINOLE-ELECTRIC.COM

PRODUCTS/OPERATIONS

Members

Central Florida Electric Cooperative
Clay Electric Cooperative
Glades Electric Cooperative
Lee County Electric Cooperative
Peace River Electric Cooperative
Sumter Electric Cooperative
Suwannee Valley Electric Cooperative
Talquin Electric Cooperative
Tri-County Electric Cooperative
Withlacoochee River Electric Cooperative

COMPETITORS

Duke Energy	NextEra Energy
Florida Power & Light	Progress Energy
Florida Public	Southern Company
Utilities	TECO Energy
JEA	

HISTORICAL FINANCIALS

Company Type: Private

Income Statement

FYE: September 30

	REVENUE ($ mil.)	NET INCOME ($ mil.)	NET PROFIT MARGIN	EMPLOYEES
09/16*	1,091	21	2.0%	528
03/16	1,090	16	1.6%	—
06/15	1,116	24	2.2%	—
06/14	1,179	28	2.4%	—
Annual Growth	(3.8%)	(13.7%)	—	—

*Fiscal year change

2016 Year-End Financials

Return on assets: 2.1% Cash ($ mil.): 130
Return on equity: 2.0%
Current ratio: 0.70

SENTARA CAREPLEX HOSPITAL

EXECUTIVES

Principal, Kathleen E Carlson
Director, Torie Bashay

LOCATIONS

HQ: SENTARA CAREPLEX HOSPITAL
3000 COLISEUM DR, HAMPTON, VA 236665963
Phone: 757 736-1000
Web: WWW.SENTARA.COM

HISTORICAL FINANCIALS

Company Type: Private

Income Statement

FYE: December 31

	REVENUE ($ mil.)	NET INCOME ($ mil.)	NET PROFIT MARGIN	EMPLOYEES
12/15	220	15	7.2%	11
12/14	246	26	10.9%	—
Annual Growth	(10.5%)	(40.7%)	—	—

SENTARA HEALTHCARE

Sentara Healthcare is not-for-profit organization that operates a network of hospitals and other health facilities primarily in the coastal Hampton Roads area of southeastern Virginia. The system includes a dozen acute care hospitals housing a total of more than 2000 beds. One of its hospitals Sentara Norfolk includes a dedicated cardiac hospital with more than 100 beds. In addition to its acute care facilities Sentara Healthcare operates several outpatient care facilities as well as nursing homes rehab centers medical practices imaging centers and home health agencies. Its Optima Health unit provides HMO PPO and other health insurance products to about 450000 Virginians.

Operations

Across the Sentara Healthcare system the organization boasts a medical staff of about 3800. The medical system's multi-specialty physicians group the Sentara Medical Group has more than 380 primary care and specialty physicians. Its Sentara Senior Services unit operates about 10 nursing and assisted living centers.

The health care group also runs the 160-bed Sentara Princess Anne Hospital an acute care facility located on the Princess Anne outpatient campus in Virginia Beach. Opened in mid-2011 it operates through a 70%-owned joint venture with Bon Secours Health System. The $145 million facility encompasses five stories and offers comprehensive surgical procedures intensive care advanced cardiac care and a maternity center.

Geographic Reach

Sentara Healthcare is the region's largest integrated health care provider serving more than 2 million residents. Its facilities serve customers throughout southeastern and northern Virginia as well as in northeastern North Carolina. It operates in the Virginia cities of Alleghany Charlottesville Hampton Roads Harrisonburg Richmond and Roanoke. In North Carolina Sentara has a presence in Currituck and Elizabeth City.

Financial Performance

The system's revenues increased 9% to $4.7 billion in 2014 due to an increase in net patient services revenues and other operating revenues. Net income fell 82% to $156 million though as salaries and wages increased medical claims and other operating expenses rose and investment gains declined. Cash flow from operations decreased 25% that year to $318 million as a result of the lower net income plus an increase in cash used in receivables and changes in employee compensation and benefits.

Strategy

While it is already one of the largest health care organizations in the state Sentara Healthcare continues to grow through acquisitions construction (both expansions and new buildings) and mergers. In 2014 it acquired the assets and operations of Albemarle Hospital Albemarle Physician Services and Regional Medical Services through a 30-year

capital lease agreement with Pasquotank County and Albemarle Hospital Authority. The businesses were combined into newly formed subsidiary SAMC. In 2015 Sentara Leigh Hospital opened a new tower as part of a larger renovation project.

Also in 2015 the system launched a new retail website shopsentara.com which offers over-the-counter health care products including medications vitamins exercise equipment diabetic care supplies and educational books.

Company Background

Sentara Healthcare was founded in 1888 as Norfolk's 25-bed Retreat for the Sick.

EXECUTIVES

CEO, Howard P. Kern
SVP and CIO, Bertram S. (Bert) Reese
SVP and CFO, Robert A. (Rob) Broerman
SVP; President Sentara Health Plans and Optima Health, Michael M. Dudley
President Sentara Leigh Hospital, Teresa L. (Terrie) Edwards
President Sentara CarePlex Hospital, Debra A. Flores
Corporate VP Sentara Norfolk General Hospital Sentara CarePlex Hospital and Sentara Williamsburg Regional Medical Center, Mary L. Blunt
President Sentara Martha Jefferson Hospital, Jonathan S. Davis
President Sentara Virginia Beach General Hospital, Elwood B. (Bernie) Boone
Chief Nursing Officer, Genemarie McGee
SVP and Chief Medical Officer, Terry Gilliland
President Sentara Williamsburg Regional Medical Center, David J. (Dave) Masterson
President Sentara Norfolk General Hospital, Kurt Hofelich
President Sentara Life Care Corporation, Bruce Robertson
President Sentara Princess Anne Hospital, Thomas B. Thames
Corporate VP; President Sentara RMH Medical Center, Jim Krauss
Corporate VP; President Sentara Medical Group, Robert (Doug) Culling
Corporate VP, Michael Gentry
President Sentara Enterprises, Linda R. Huffer
President Sentara Obici Hospital, Steve Julian
President Sentara Halifax Regional Hospital, Chris A. Lumsden
Corporate VP; President Sentara Northern Virgnia Medical Center, Stephen D. Porter
President Sentara Albemarle Medical Center, Coleen Santa Ana
Vice President Business Development, Katherine Harrison
Vice President Of Operations, Chet Hart
Director Of Pharmacy, Betsy Early
Vice President, Ken Krakaur
Director of HIM, Marsha Rooks
Vice President and Chief Information Security Officer, Daniel Bowden
Director of Pharmacy, Jon Horton
Vice President of Medical Affairs, David Schwartz
Vice President Government Relations and Health Policy, Paul Speidell
Vice President For Clinical Informatics and Transformation, David Mohr
Chairman, Bob Fort
Vice Chairman, Henry (Sandy) Harris
Secretary, Karen Riley
Auditors: KPMG LLP NORFOLK VA

LOCATIONS

HQ: SENTARA HEALTHCARE
6015 POPLAR HALL DR, NORFOLK, VA 235023819
Phone: 800 736-8272

PRODUCTS/OPERATIONS

Selected Hospitals
Charlottesville
  Martha Jefferson Hospital
  MJH Outpatient Care Center
  Health Services at Proffit Road
  Health Services at Spring Creek
  Sentara Home Care Services
  Optima Health
Hampton Roads
  Sentara CarePlex Hospital
  Sentara Heart Hospital
  Sentara Leigh Hospital
  Sentara Norfolk General Hospital
  Sentara Obici Hospital
  Sentara Princess Anne Hospital
  Sentara Virginia Beach General Hospital
  Sentara Williamsburg Regional Medical Center
  Orthopaedic Hospital at Sentara CarePlex
  Sentara Northern Virginia Medical Center
  Martha Jefferson Hospital
  RMH Healthcare
Harrisonburg
  RMH Healthcare
  Optima Health
Northern Virginia
  Sentara Northern Virginia Medical Center
  Sentara Lake Ridge
  Sentara Medical Group physicians
  Sentara Home Care Services
  Sentara Heart and Vascular Center
  Optima Health

Selected Services
Cancer
Cardiac (Heart)
Digestive (Colorectal)
Home Care
Imaging
Maternity
Neurosciences
Rehabilitation
Seniors
Thoracic
Transplant
Trauma/Emergency Services
Urology
Vascular
Weight Loss Surgery
Women's

COMPETITORS

Aetna
Anthem Health Plans of Virginia
Bon Secours Health
CIGNA
Carilion Clinic
Centra Health Inc.
Children's Hospital of The King's Daughters
Franklin Hospital Corp.
HCA Capital Division
Humana
Inova
Kaiser Foundation Health Plan of the Mid-Atlantic
Norton Community Hospital
Novant Health
Riverside Health System (Virginia)
Twin County Regional Healthcare
UnitedHealth Group
Wake Forest University Baptist Medical Center

HISTORICAL FINANCIALS
Company Type: Private

Income Statement
FYE: December 31

	REVENUE ($ mil.)	NET INCOME ($ mil.)	NET PROFIT MARGIN	EMPLOYEES
12/15	4,833	139	2.9%	28,000
12/14	4,694	359	7.7%	—
12/13	4,298	861	20.0%	—
12/12	4,068	307	7.6%	—
Annual Growth	5.9%	(23.2%)	—	—

2015 Year-End Financials
Return on assets: 3.3%   Cash ($ mil.): 741
Return on equity: 2.9%
Current ratio: 1.40

SENTARA HOSPITALS - NORFOLK

EXECUTIVES

Chief Executive Officer, David L Bernd
Board of Directors, Jeffrey King
Director, Cindy Parker
Vice-President, Peggy Evans
Auditors: KPMG LLP NORFOLK VA

LOCATIONS

HQ: SENTARA HOSPITALS - NORFOLK
600 GRESHAM DR, NORFOLK, VA 235071904
Phone: 757 388-3000
Web: WWW.SENTARA.COM

HISTORICAL FINANCIALS
Company Type: Private

Income Statement
FYE: December 31

	REVENUE ($ mil.)	NET INCOME ($ mil.)	NET PROFIT MARGIN	EMPLOYEES
12/15	791	92	11.7%	165
12/14	748	76	10.2%	—
12/13	1,914	146	7.7%	—
Annual Growth	(35.7%)	(20.6%)	—	—

SENTARA MEDICAL GROUP

EXECUTIVES

Chairman of the Board, Kenneth R Perry
Board of Directors, Gwen Cumming
Project Manager, Jane Right
Director, Doris Prince
Auditors: KPMG LLP NORFOLK VIRGINIA

LOCATIONS

HQ: SENTARA MEDICAL GROUP
835 GLENROCK RD, NORFOLK, VA 235023767
Phone: 757 252-3070
Web:
WWW.SENTARA.COM/HOSPITALSFACILITIES/SENTARAMEDICALGROUP/FAM

HISTORICAL FINANCIALS
Company Type: Private

Income Statement
FYE: December 31

	REVENUE ($ mil.)	NET INCOME ($ mil.)	NET PROFIT MARGIN	EMPLOYEES
12/15	258	0	—	331
12/08	0	(0)	—	—
12/04	59	9	15.3%	—
12/02	156	0	0.0%	—
Annual Growth	3.9%	—	—	—

Return on assets: 1.1% Cash ($ mil.): 3
Return on equity: —
Current ratio: 3.40

SENTARA RMH MEDICAL CENTER

Sentara RMH Medical Center (RMH) formerly known as Rockingham Memorial Hospital serves residents in Virginia's Shenandoah Valley offering some 240 beds. In addition to emergency services and general surgeries and care procedures RMH offers specialized services including cardiovascular care cancer treatment sleep disorder diagnosis behavioral health care medical imaging orthopedic procedures obstetrics and rehabilitation as well as home health hospice and wellness services. Founded in 1912 RMH is part of the Sentara Healthcare system.

Operations

Sentara RMH Medical Center is part of Sentara Healthcare a 125-year old non-profit system which operates more than 100 care sites across Virginia and North Carolina including 12 acute care hospitals.

Geographic Reach

Sentara RMH Medical Center is located in Harrisonburg Virginia and serves residents in seven surrounding counties.

Strategy

Sentara RMH Medical Center continues to be recognized for its specialty care in recent years. In late 2014 the U.S. News and World Report awarded the Sentara RMH Medical Center "high performing" status in three specialty areas — gastroenterology and GI surgery pulmonology and geriatrics — and ranked it the 15th best hospital in Virginia out of nearly 130 hospitals.

EXECUTIVES

Director of Pharmacy, Laura Adkins
Infection Control Director, REBECCA BRUBAKER
Auditors: KPMG LLP NORFOLK VA

LOCATIONS

HQ: SENTARA RMH MEDICAL CENTER
2010 HEALTH CAMPUS DR, ROCKINGHAM, VA
228018679
Phone: 540 433-4100
Web: WWW.SENTARACAREERS.COM

PRODUCTS/OPERATIONS

Selected Services
Bariatric Surgery
Behavioral Health
Blood Donor Center
Business Office
Center for Sleep Medicine
Chaplain Services
Childcare Connection
Community Health
East Rockingham Health Center
Emergency Department
Family Birthplace
Gifts & Floral
Grief and Loss Services
Hahn Cancer Center
Healthsource
Heart and Vascular Center
Home Care Services
Hospice
Hospitalists
Image Recovery Center

Imaging Services
Joint Services
Laboratory Services
Lifeline
Luray Health Center
Mount Jackson Health Center
New Market Health Center
Occupational Health Center
Orthopedics and Sports Medicine
Palliative Care
Pharmacy
Physician Billing
Pulmonary Services
Rehab Services
Security
Senior Advantage
South Main Health Center
Surgical Services
Valley Behavioral Medicine
Virginia Funkhouser Health Sciences Library
Volunteer Services
Wellness Center
Women's Center

COMPETITORS

Carilion Clinic	University of Virginia
Centra Health Inc.	Health System
HCA Capital Division	Valley Health
Loudoun Healthcare	Virginia Hospital &
MedStar Health	Healthcare

HISTORICAL FINANCIALS
Company Type: Private

Income Statement
FYE: December 31

	REVENUE ($ mil.)	NET INCOME ($ mil.)	NET PROFIT MARGIN	EMPLOYEES
12/15	408	46	11.4%	1,892
12/13	374	31	8.3%	—
12/08	264	10	3.8%	—
12/06	229	18	7.8%	—
Annual Growth	6.6%	11.1%	—	—

2015 Year-End Financials
Return on assets: 2.4% Cash ($ mil.): 3
Return on equity: 11.4%
Current ratio: 2.90

SEQUOIA HEALTH SERVICES

EXECUTIVES

Director, Jack Hickey
Director, Kathleen M Kane
Manager, Kevin Fahey
Director, Louise Della Maggiora
Director, Adil Jadallah
Auditors: MAZE & ASSOCIATES PLEASANT HI

LOCATIONS

HQ: SEQUOIA HEALTH SERVICES
170 ALAMEDA DE LAS PULGAS, REDWOOD CITY, CA
940622751
Phone: 650 369-5811
Web: WWW.SEQUOIAHOSPITAL.ORG

HISTORICAL FINANCIALS
Company Type: Private

Income Statement
FYE: June 30

	REVENUE ($ mil.)	NET INCOME ($ mil.)	NET PROFIT MARGIN	EMPLOYEES
06/15	258	(0)	—	1,167
06/09	216	9	4.5%	—
06/05	0	0	—	—
Annual Growth	—	—	—	—

2015 Year-End Financials
Return on assets: 5.2% Cash ($ mil.): 18
Return on equity: (-0.1%)
Current ratio: 1.00

SETON HALL UNIVERSITY

Seton Hall University is a Catholic institution with an enrollment of almost 10000 students (5500 undergraduates and 4300 graduates) who hail from 70 countries. The university offers more than 90 undergraduate and graduate degree programs as well as more than a dozen doctoral programs at eight colleges and schools including the Whitehead School of Diplomacy and International Relations Stillman School of Business and Immaculate Conception Seminary School of Theology. Seton Hall also offers degree and certificate programs online. Seton Hall is the US' oldest diocesan university and is under purview of the Archdiocese of Newark.

Operations

Some 80% of its undergraduate student live on campus.

Seton Hall has a student-to-faculty ratio of 14:1. About 97% of its students receive financial aid.

Geographic Reach

Seton Hall's campus is in a South Orange New Jersey suburban setting about 30 minutes from New York City.

Strategy

Expanding its academic profile in 2015 Seton Hall and Hackensack University Health Network agreed to form a new four-year school of medicine. This partnership will establish the first private school of medicine in New Jersey and provide a major economic boost to the region.

Company Background

Formed in 1856 Seton Hall University was named after Mother Elizabeth Ann Seton the first American-born saint (and an aunt of school founder Bishop James Roosevelt Bayley). Originally called Seton Hall College it became a university in 1950 and became coeducational in 1968.

EXECUTIVES

EVP Administration, Mary J. Meehan
CFO, Stephen A. Graham
EVP and Provost, Larry A. Robinson
Dean School of Theology, Joseph R. Reilly
Dean School of Health and Medical Sciences, Brian B. Shulman
CIO, Stephen G. Landry
Dean School of Diplomacy and International Relations, Andrea Bartoli
Dean College of Education and Human Services, Grace M. May
Dean of Students, Karen Van Norman
Dean Stillman School of Business, Joyce Strawser

Dean University Libraries, John E. Buschman
Dean College of Nursing, Marie Foley
Dean School of Law, Kathleen M. Boozang
Dean Continuing Education and Professional
   Studies, Karen Passaro
Interim Dean College of Arts and Sciences,
   Chrysanthy M. Grieco
Interim Dean College of Communication and the
   Arts, Deirdre Yates
Vice President, Catherine A Kiernan
Chairman, John J. Myers
Vice Chairman, Bernard A. Hebda
Auditors: GRANTTHORNTON LLP ISELIN NJ

LOCATIONS

HQ: SETON HALL UNIVERSITY
   400 S ORANGE AVE, SOUTH ORANGE, NJ 070792697
Phone: 973 761-9000
Web: WWW.SHU.EDU

PRODUCTS/OPERATIONS

Selected Schools & Colleges
College of Arts and Sciences
College of Education and Human Services
College of Nursing
Immaculate Conception Seminary School of Theology
School of Health and Medical Sciences
School of Law
Stillman School of Business
Whitehead School of Diplomacy & International
   Relations

HISTORICAL FINANCIALS

Company Type: Private

Income Statement

	REVENUE ($ mil.)	NET INCOME ($ mil.)	NET PROFIT MARGIN	EMPLOYEES
06/16	281	(12)	—	2,700
06/15	272	3	1.5%	—
06/14	270	52	19.4%	—
06/13	269	38	14.5%	—
Annual Growth	1.5%	—	—	—

FYE: June 30

2016 Year-End Financials
Return on assets: 13.4%   Cash ($ mil.): 16
Return on equity: (-4.3%)
Current ratio: —

SETON MEDICAL CENTER

EXECUTIVES

President, Mark S Fratzke
Administrative Assistant, Opal Cava
Manager, John Obegolu
Vice-President, John Thomas
Auditors: GRANT THORNTON LLP SAN FRANCI

LOCATIONS

HQ: SETON MEDICAL CENTER
   1900 SULLIVAN AVE, DALY CITY, CA 940152229
Phone: 650 992-4000
Web: WWW.SETONMEDICALCENTER.ORG

HISTORICAL FINANCIALS

Company Type: Private

Income Statement

	REVENUE ($ mil.)	NET INCOME ($ mil.)	NET PROFIT MARGIN	EMPLOYEES
06/15	246	(22)	—	1,231
06/13	291	(25)	—	
06/10	296	(14)	—	
06/09	672	0	—	
Annual Growth	—	—	—	

FYE: June 30

2015 Year-End Financials
Return on assets: 3.0%   Cash ($ mil.): 11
Return on equity: (-9.0%)
Current ratio: 0.50

SEVENTY SEVEN ENERGY LLC

Seventy Seven Energy (formerly Chesapeake Oilfield Services) is a company that was spun off from Chesapeake Energy one of the top onshore energy companies in the US. Chesapeake Energy reorganized six of its oilfield services subsidiaries into then Chesapeake Oilfield Services to create a new publicly traded entity that offers drilling hydraulic fracturing and trucking services as well as renting tools and manufacturing natural gas compressor equipment. It operates in onshore plays in the US. The company filed for Chapter 11 bankruptcy protection in 2016. In 2017 the company was bought by Patterson-UTI in a $1.76 billion stock deal including debt.

Operations

The company conducts business through three operating segments: Hydraulic Fracturing Drilling and Oilfield Rentals.

The hydraulic fracturing segment (51% of Seventy Seven Energy's total revenues in 2015) operates through Performance Technologies and provides high-pressure hydraulic fracturing services and other well stimulation services. This unit owns 11 hydraulic fracturing fleets with an aggregate of 440000 horsepower and six of these fleets are contracted in the Anadarko Basin and the Eagle Ford and Utica Shales. The fracturing process consists of pumping a fracturing fluid into a well at sufficient pressure to fracture the formation.

The drilling segment (38%) operates through Nomac Drilling and provides land drilling services for oil and natural gas E&P activities.

The oilfield rentals segment (11%) operates through Great Plains Oilfield Rental and provides premium rental tools and specialized services for land-based oil and natural gas drilling completion and workover activities. It offers an extensive line of rental tools including a full line of tubular products specifically designed for horizontal drilling and completion with high-torque premium-connection drill pipe drill collars and tubing.

Geographic Reach

Seventy Seven Energy operates in the Anadarko and Permian Basins and the Eagle Ford Haynesville Marcellus Niobrara and Utica Shales.

Sales and Marketing

The company got 70% of its revenues from Chesapeake Energy (CHK) and its affiliates in 2015.

Financial Performance

In 2015 Seventy Seven Energy's net revenues decreased by 46%.

Drilling revenues decreased due to lower revenue days driven by a drop in demand by non-CHK customers.

Hydraulic fracturing revenues declined due to a decrease in revenue per stage driven by market pricing pressure.

Oilfield rental revenues decreased due to a decline in utilization and pricing pressure.

In 2015 Seventy Seven Energy's net loss grew by 2675% due to lower revenues loss on sale of a business loss on sales of property and equipment net and impairment of goodwill.

Cash from operating activities increased by 7% due to the changes in the timing of collection of accounts receivable and the decline in overall operational activity.

Strategy

Chesapeake Energy decided to spin off its oilfield services in order to keep that activity separate from exploration and production. With exploration production and oilfield services under one umbrella the company only had one customer - itself. By separating the oilfield services unit Chesapeake Energy reduces its risk should exploration and production slow down much as it did with natural gas drilling and the shift to natural gas liquids.

Nomac Drilling continued to upgrade its rig fleet in 2015 making 80% of its rig fleet capable of drilling on multi well pads. As one of the most active drillers in the United States Nomac also continues to diversify its customer base serving more than 20 different operators.

Seventy Seven Energy expects to spend $100 million in aggregate growth and maintenance capital expenditures in 2016. It also intends to explore opportunistic complementary acquisitions particularly within the hydraulic fracturing segment.

In 2015 the company completed the previously disclosed sale of Hodges Trucking Company L.L.C. to a wholly-owned subsidiary of Aveda Transportation and Energy Services Inc. for $42 million.

Company Background

The company was formed in October 2011 and filed to go public in April 2012 in an initial public offering seeking up to $862.5 million. It completed the spinoff in July 2014 and renamed the company Seventy Seven Energy.

EXECUTIVES

SVP Corporate Development CFO and Treasurer, John E. Vollmer, age 61
President and CEO, William A. (Andy) Hendricks, age 52
Auditors: PRICEWATERHOUSECOOPERS LLP OK

LOCATIONS

HQ: SEVENTY SEVEN ENERGY LLC
   777 NW 63RD ST, OKLAHOMA CITY, OK 731167601
Phone: 405 608-7777
Web: WWW.77NRG.COM

PRODUCTS/OPERATIONS

SERVICES
Drilling
Pumping
Rentals

Selected Subsidiaries
Compass Manufacturing L.L.C. (maufatures natural gas
   compression equipment)
Great Plains Oilfield Rental L.L.C. (tool and equipment
   rental)
Hodges Trucking Company L.L.C. (trucking services)
Nomac Drilling L.L.C. (drilling services)
Oilfield Trucking Solutions L.L.C. (trucking services)
Performance Technologies L.L.C. (hydraulic fracturing)

2015 Sales in mil.	% of total
Drilling 436.4	38

	REVENUE ($ mil.)		
Hydraulic fracturing	575.4	51	
Oilfield rentals	76.5	7	
Oilfield trucking	42.7	4	
other operations	0.2	-	
Total	1131.2	100	

COMPETITORS

Baker Hughes	Parker Drilling
Basic Energy	Patterson-UTI Energy
FTS International	Precision Drilling
Halliburton	RPC
Helmerich & Payne	Schlumberger
Key Energy	Superior Energy
Nabors Industries	Trinidad Drilling
Oil States	Weatherford
International	International

HISTORICAL FINANCIALS

Company Type: Private

Income Statement
FYE: December 31

	REVENUE ($ mil.)	NET INCOME ($ mil.)	NET PROFIT MARGIN	EMPLOYEES
12/16	222	(63)	—	1,700
12/15	1,131	(221)	—	—
12/14	2,080	(7)	—	—
Annual Growth	(67.3%)	—	—	—

2016 Year-End Financials
Return on assets: 7.0%
Return on equity: (-28.6%)
Current ratio: 2.10
Cash ($ mil.): 48

SGT, INC.

Like its acronym name suggests SGT (aka Stinger Ghaffarian Technologies) is used to taking military orders; in this case very specific technical ones. An engineering services firm SGT provides aerospace engineering project management IT systems development and related services to NASA the US Navy the US Air Force and other primarily military-related government entities through contracts. The company also offers science-related services such as earth climate and planetary modeling and analysis. SGT's facilities are located near airfields and other military facilities.

Geographic Reach

SGT operates a more than dozen offices including in Houston Cleveland and Los Angeles White Sands (New Mexico) and Wallops Island (Virginia).

Sales and Marketing

The company serves the aerospace and aeronautics sectors in addition to civilian agencies and national security entities.

Strategy

SGT grows by signing contracts and working with other partners. In early 2017 it won a $45 million contract to support the National Oceanic and Atmospheric Administration (NOAA). Under the contract SGT will support the National Mesonet Program which brings non-federal meteorological data sources to NOAA for use in operations at weather forecast offices and numerical modeling information at the National Centers for Environmental Protection. To achieve this SGT is working in partnership with Earth Networks Weather Telematics WeatherFlow Synoptic Data Corp. Sonoma Technology Inc. Panasonic Avionics Corp. and the University of Oklahoma.

Company Background

SGT was founded in 1994 by Harold Stinger and Kam Ghaffarian.

EXECUTIVES

EVP Business Development, Charlie Goorevich
President and CEO, Kam Ghaffarian
CFO, Joe Morway
COO, Dave Wolt
SVP Civil Defense Business, Wayne Friedman
Vice President Finance Chief Financial Officer, Mike Gigliotti
Chairman, Harold Stinger
Auditors: DIXON HUGHES GOODMAN LLP TYSO

LOCATIONS

HQ: SGT, INC.
7701 GREENBELT RD STE 400, GREENBELT, MD 207706521
Phone: 301 614-8600

COMPETITORS

Ball Aerospace	QSS Group
CACI International	Sierra Nevada Corp
CDI Government Services	Techshot
Digital Fusion	United Space Alliance
Lockheed Martin Space Systems	

HISTORICAL FINANCIALS

Company Type: Private

Income Statement
FYE: September 30

	REVENUE ($ mil.)	NET INCOME ($ mil.)	NET PROFIT MARGIN	EMPLOYEES
09/15	570	23	4.2%	2,300
09/13	416	15	3.7%	—
09/12	374	9	2.4%	—
09/08	93	0	—	—
Annual Growth	29.5%	925.8%	—	—

2015 Year-End Financials
Return on assets: 6.4%
Return on equity: 4.2%
Current ratio: 1.30
Cash ($ mil.): —

SHAKE-N-GO FASHION, INC.

EXECUTIVES

Chairman of the Board, James K Kim
Financial Executive, Jessica Cho
Executive Vice-President, Joseph Um
Office Manager, Peter Lim
Manager, Young Ryoo
Auditors: FRIEDMAN LLP NEW YORK NY

LOCATIONS

HQ: SHAKE-N-GO FASHION, INC.
85 HARBOR RD, PORT WASHINGTON, NY 110502535
Phone: 516 944-7777
Web: WWW.SNGHAIR.COM

HISTORICAL FINANCIALS

Company Type: Private

Income Statement
FYE: December 31

	REVENUE ($ mil.)	NET INCOME ($ mil.)	NET PROFIT MARGIN	EMPLOYEES
12/15	301	25	8.6%	200
12/09	200	16	8.5%	—
12/08	170	7	4.2%	—
12/06	214	0	—	—
Annual Growth	—	315.4%	—	—

2015 Year-End Financials
Return on assets: 2.6%
Return on equity: 8.6%
Current ratio: 0.90
Cash ($ mil.): 2

SHANDS JACKSONVILLE HEALTHCARE, INC.

EXECUTIVES

Principal, Susan Brownie
Financial Executive, Michael E Glason
Administrative Assistant, Carol Clark
Chief Financial Officer, William J Ryan

LOCATIONS

HQ: SHANDS JACKSONVILLE HEALTHCARE, INC.
655 W 8TH ST, JACKSONVILLE, FL 322096511
Phone: 904 244-0411
Web: WWW.MESOTHELIOMAATTORNEYFLORIDA.NET

HISTORICAL FINANCIALS

Company Type: Private

Income Statement
FYE: June 30

	REVENUE ($ mil.)	NET INCOME ($ mil.)	NET PROFIT MARGIN	EMPLOYEES
06/16	665	22	3.3%	1
06/13	522	(5)	—	—
06/12	515	(22)	—	—
Annual Growth	6.6%	—	—	—

2016 Year-End Financials
Return on assets: 6.6%
Return on equity: 3.3%
Current ratio: 1.70
Cash ($ mil.): 73

SHANDS JACKSONVILLE MEDICAL CENTER, INC.

Close to the shifting sands of the northern Florida coast Shands Jacksonville Medical Center (doing business as UF Health Jacksonville) offers a range of services to the 19 counties it serves in Florida and southern Georgia. The 695-bed hospital includes a cardiovascular center Level III neonatal intensive care unit and a Level I trauma center. It also operates primary and specialty clinics in the Jacksonville area. The medical center is affiliated with the University of Florida and is the

largest of seven hospitals in the Shands HealthCare family.

Operations

UF Health Jacksonville operates about 40 outpatient care centers. Overall its facilities handle some 34000 inpatient visits and 600000 outpatient visits per year. The hospital's affiliation with the University of Florida (UF) includes collaborative treatment and research programs in areas including cancer cardiovascular neurology orthopedic and pediatric care.

Together with its UF colleagues and affiliates UF Health Jacksonville provides a wide range of health care services across the continuum of care on an inpatient and outpatient basis. Backed by a team of more than 400 faculty physicians it offers nearly 100 specialty services.

Geographic Reach

UF Health Jacksonville's facilities are located in Jacksonville Florida and surrounding areas of northeastern Florida and southeastern Georgia.

Financial Performance

The company's revenues increased by 3% in 2014 due to growth in net patient service revenues as a result of a growth in inpatient and outpatient volumes. Medicare accounted for 25% net patient revenues; Medicaid 31%.

UF Health Jacksonville reported net income of $3 million in 2014 over a net loss in 2013 due to higher interest and a loss on the disposal of capital assets.

Operating cash flow in 2014 decreased by 8% due to higher payments to suppliers and vendors.

Strategy

UF Health Jacksonville has plans to build a second campus on the north side of Jacksonville to meet the needs of a growing community. It's also exploring ways to increase clinical efficiencies such as implementing an electronic health record (EHR) system (with help from federal stimulus funding); it also is looking to maximize funding opportunities for its research programs.

The company is looking to develop a Health Science Center Medical Education on Jacksonville Regional Campus including undergraduate graduate and health-related professions.

It also plans to build a 92-bed hospital wing for the North Campus which will provide greater access to more health care services for the center's residents as well as those living in surrounding communities. Construction is scheduled to begin in 2015 with completion in 2017.

In 2015 UF Health North opened the six-story 210000-square-foot outpatient medical complex in North Jacksonville which includes a 28-bed emergency room advanced imaging a midwife-led birth center rehabilitation services and more than 20 specialty services.

Company Background

Founded in 1870 as the Duval Hospital and Asylum UF Health Jacksonville started the first cancer program in Florida in 1948.

EXECUTIVES

Vice President of Government, Penny Thompson
Director of Pharmacy, Marci Delossantos
Auditors: PRICEWATERHOUSECOOPERS LLP T

LOCATIONS

HQ: SHANDS JACKSONVILLE MEDICAL CENTER, INC.
655 W 8TH ST, JACKSONVILLE, FL 322096511
Phone: 904 244-5576

PRODUCTS/OPERATIONS

Selected Services
Cancer services
Cardiovascular services
Neuroscience services
Orthopaedic services

Pediatrics
Poison Center
Trauma and critical care services
Women and families

COMPETITORS

Baptist Health System
Bay Medical Center
Brooks Rehabilitation
Florida Hospital Tampa
  Bay Division
Mayo Clinic
  Jacksonville
Nemours Foundation
North Florida Regional
  Medical Center

Ocala Regional Medical
  Center
Orange Park Medical
Orlando Health
Palms West Hospital
St. Vincent's Health
  System

HISTORICAL FINANCIALS

Company Type: Private

Income Statement

FYE: June 30

	REVENUE ($ mil.)	NET INCOME ($ mil.)	NET PROFIT MARGIN	EMPLOYEES
06/16	663	23	3.6%	3,000
06/15	480	10	2.2%	—
06/10	592	19	3.2%	—
06/09	591	7	1.2%	—
Annual Growth	1.6%	18.8%	—	—

2016 Year-End Financials

Return on assets: 8.2%
Return on equity: 3.6%
Current ratio: 1.50

Cash ($ mil.): 68

SHANDS TEACHING HOSPITAL AND CLINICS, INC.

While its full name is Shands Teaching Hospital and Clinics most people call it UF&Shands. The network affiliated with the University of Florida Health Science Center provides health care services to patients in north-central and northeast Florida. The company is made up of seven not-for-profit acute care community and specialty hospitals as well as more than 80 physician practices and outpatient rehabilitation centers. It also operates a home health care agency. The Shands network has some 1700 licensed beds and about 1000 affiliated University of Florida doctors. Specialty services include oncology pediatrics cardiovascular transplants and neurological care.

Operations

In 2013 the organization along with the University of Florida launched the UF Health brand for their combined operations.

UF&Shands consists of the main teaching hospital at the University of Florida; it includes UF Health Shands Cancer Hospital UF Health Shands Psychiatric Hospital UF Health Shands Rehab Hospital as well as outpatient rehabilitation centers and a home health care agency. UF Health Jacksonville has some 700 beds and 400 full-time faculty members.

The hospital has a 40% stake in Community Health Systems which operates three rural community hospitals in Lake City Starke and Live Oak Florida.

Geographic Reach

UF&Shands operates hospitals in Gainesville and Jacksonville Florida.

Financial Performance

Revenues increased 3% to $1.2 billion in 2014 as net patient revenues and other operating revenues rose. Net income fell by 7% though to $66 million that year as a result of rising non-operating costs such as interest expenses and net losses on disposal of assets.

Cash flow from operations declined 7% to $127 million in 2014 as a result of increased salary and benefit expenses as well as supplier and vendor payments.

Strategy

UF&Shands operates with the goal of improving the diversity of its academic health center and engagement within its communities. It focuses on patient care education and research. Its Gainesville campus is getting an expansion gaining a new building that will include 216 beds and 20 operating rooms. In 2015 it was announced that its neonatal intensive care unit on the same campus will get a $20.7 million renovation and expansion; that project is expected to be completed in 2017.

EXECUTIVES

SVP and CFO, William J. (Bill) Robinson
Interim CEO, Ed Jimenez
VP Nursing and Patient Services, Irene Alexaitis
SVP and CIO, Kari Cassel
EVP Regional and Governmental Affairs, Timothy M. Goldfarb
President and SVP Health affairs, David S. Guzick
Vice President, Mary A Kiely
Vice President Finance, James Kelly
Vice President, Marvin Dewar
IVP MUSEUM OPERATIONS SPECIALIST, Rodriguez-armenta Hilda Patricia
VICE PRESIDENT FOR HEALTH SCIENCES, Weiland Laura Lynne

LOCATIONS

HQ: SHANDS TEACHING HOSPITAL AND CLINICS, INC.
1600 SW ARCHER RD, GAINESVILLE, FL 326103003
Phone: 352 265-0111
Web: WWW.SHANDS.UFL.EDU

PRODUCTS/OPERATIONS

Selected Hospitals
UF Health Jacksonville (Jacksonville)
UF Health Physicians (Gainesville and Jacksonville)
UF Health Shands HomeCare and Shands Jacksonville Home Health (Gainesville and Jacksonville)
UF Health Shands Hospital (Gainesville)
UF Health Shands Psychiatric Hospital (Gainesville)
UF Health Shands Rehab Centers (Gainesville)
UF Health Shands Rehab Hospital (Gainesville

COMPETITORS

Baptist Health System
Bay Medical Center
Brooks Rehabilitation
Florida Hospital Tampa
  Bay Division
Florida Hospital
  Waterman
Lawnwood Medical
  Center

Mayo Clinic
  Jacksonville
North Florida Regional
  Medical Center
Orlando Health
Palms West Hospital
St. Vincent's Health
  System

HISTORICAL FINANCIALS

Company Type: Private

Income Statement

FYE: June 30

	REVENUE ($ mil.)	NET INCOME ($ mil.)	NET PROFIT MARGIN	EMPLOYEES
06/15	1,242	81	6.6%	3,124
06/14	1,243	66	5.3%	—
06/10	1,040	(67)	—	—
06/09	1,735	(183)	—	—
Annual Growth	(5.4%)	—	—	—

2015 Year-End Financials

Return on assets: 4.3%
Return on equity: 6.6%
Current ratio: 1.00

Cash ($ mil.): —

SHARP CHULA VISTA AUXILIARY INC

EXECUTIVES

Chief Executive Officer, Chris Boyd
Manager, Patti Ennis
Manager, Elvira Nonog

LOCATIONS

HQ: SHARP CHULA VISTA AUXILIARY INC
751 MEDICAL CENTER CT, CHULA VISTA, CA
919116617
Phone: 619 421-6110
Web: WWW.SHARP.COM

HISTORICAL FINANCIALS

Company Type: Private

Income Statement

FYE: September 30

	REVENUE ($ mil.)	NET INCOME ($ mil.)	NET PROFIT MARGIN	EMPLOYEES
09/15	367	12	3.3%	32
09/12	298	25	8.6%	—
Annual Growth	7.1%	(22.5%)	—	—

2015 Year-End Financials

Return on assets: 4.1%
Return on equity: 3.3%
Current ratio: 1.10

Cash ($ mil.): 1

SHARP CHULA VISTA MEDICAL CENTER

EXECUTIVES

Chief Executive Officer, Chris Boyd
Director, Susan Ressmeyer
Director, Kimberly Castillo
Auditors: LB ERNST & YOUNG US LLP SAN D

LOCATIONS

HQ: SHARP CHULA VISTA MEDICAL CENTER
8695 SPECTRUM CENTER BLVD, SAN DIEGO, CA
921231489
Phone: 858 499-5150
Web: WWW.SHARP.COM

HISTORICAL FINANCIALS

Company Type: Private

Income Statement

FYE: September 30

	REVENUE ($ mil.)	NET INCOME ($ mil.)	NET PROFIT MARGIN	EMPLOYEES
09/15	383	22	5.9%	99
09/14	315	11	3.6%	—
09/13	319	12	4.0%	—
09/09	251	2	1.2%	—
Annual Growth	7.3%	40.5%	—	—

2015 Year-End Financials

Return on assets: 9.1%
Return on equity: 5.9%
Current ratio: 1.70

Cash ($ mil.): 1

SHARP CHULA VISTA MEDICAL CENTER

EXECUTIVES

Chief Executive Officer, Chris Boyd
Administrative Assistant, Chris Hardiman
Administrative Assistant, Phung Caldwell
Manager, Fawn Caldwell
Director, Yuan Lin
Administrative Assistant, Andrew Moyers

LOCATIONS

HQ: SHARP CHULA VISTA MEDICAL CENTER
751 MEDICAL CENTER CT, CHULA VISTA, CA
919116617
Phone: 619 502-5800
Web: WWW.SHARP.COM

HISTORICAL FINANCIALS

Company Type: Private

Income Statement

FYE: September 30

	REVENUE ($ mil.)	NET INCOME ($ mil.)	NET PROFIT MARGIN	EMPLOYEES
09/15	367	12	3.3%	1,600
09/14	298	16	5.6%	—
09/13	304	19	6.5%	—
09/12	298	25	8.6%	—
Annual Growth	7.1%	(22.5%)	—	—

2015 Year-End Financials

Return on assets: 4.1%
Return on equity: 3.3%
Current ratio: 1.10

Cash ($ mil.): 1

SHARP HEALTHCARE

Sharp HealthCare stands on the cutting edge of health care delivery in Southern California. The system of not-for-profit hospitals and health care facilities is the largest in the San Diego area. The network includes four acute-care hospitals (Sharp Chula Vista Sharp Coronado Sharp Grossmont and Sharp Memorial) as well as three specialty hospitals for women's care psychiatry and chemical dependence. It also operates two physician medical groups and a number of urgent care and outpatient facilities and clinics. With some 2100 beds and about 2600 physicians Sharp HealthCare offers cancer and cardiac care fertility and maternity services surgical procedures and hospice care.

Operations

Altogether the Sharp HealthCare facilities handle 1600 surgeries each year. In addition to medical services the organization operates its own health plan; the Sharp Health Plan is a not-for-profit HMO serving tens of thousands of members in and around San Diego.

The Sharp Grossmont hospital which serves eastern San Diego County is run by Grossmont Hospital Corporation a subsidiary holding a 30-year lease to manage the facility. One of the system's specialty operations Sharp Mary Birch Hospital for Women & Newborns claims to deliver more babies than any other hospital in California. Sharp's two medical groups are Sharp Community and Sharp Rees-Stealy which between them comprise more than 1100 doctors providing both primary and specialty care.

Geographic Reach

In addition to its operating bases in San Diego Sharp HealthCare has California facilities in Carmel Valley Chula Vista El Cajon La Mesa Mira Mesa Otay Ranch Point Loma Rancho Bernado San Diego Scripps Ranch Serra Mesa and Sorrento Mesa.

Financial Performance

Sharp's net revenues have trended upward in recent years. The company's revenues grew by $100 million in 2014 due to increase in net patient revenue and premiums. Revenues from the Medicare and Medi-Cal programs accounted for 30% and 24% respectively of Sharp's gross patient charges.

The company's net income decreased by 4% due to pension-related changes other than net periodic pension cost and increase in employee benefits and medical fees expenses.

Sharp's operating cash flow decreased by 48% in 2014.

Strategy

Sharp HealthCare improves its services to area residents through facility upgrades.

In 2015 the company launched Sharp Health News an online news site featuring engaging and original stories about medical breakthroughs new technology and health and wellness.

In 2014 Sharp HospiceCare opened its newest hospice residence BonitaView the first facility of its kind in the South Bay area of San Diego County for end-of-life care designed around the needs of patients and their families.

The organization installed new imaging equipment at the Sharp Memorial Outpatient Pavilion in 2013 and a opened the new Sharp Rees-Stealy center in Del Mar in 2014.

Company Background

In 2011 the system doubled the capacity of Sharp Chula Vista Medical Center's emergency department at a cost of $12 million and in 2012 the Chula Vista hospital opened a new cancer center.

The system began as a single hospital in 1955 named for a local pilot who died in WWII.

EXECUTIVES

President and CEO, Michael W. (Mike) Murphy
EVP Hospital Operations, Daniel L. (Dan) Gross
SVP and CEO Sharp HealthCare Foundation, Bill Littlejohn
SVP and CIO, Ken Lawonn

President and CEO Sharp Health Plan, Melissa Hayden-Cook
SVP and CEO Sharp Memorial Hospital, Tim Smith
SVP and CEO Sharp Chula Vista Medical Center, Pablo Velez
SVP and CEO Sharp Coronado Hospital, Susan Stone
CEO Sharp Rees-Stealy Medical Group, Stacey Hrountas
SVP and CEO Sharp Mary Birch Hospital for Women & Newborns, Trisha Khaleghi
SVP Marketing and Communications, Diane Gage Lofgren
SVP and CEO Sharp Grossmont Hospital, Scott Evans
VP Finance, Staci Dickerson
CEO Sharp Community Medical Group, Paul Durr
Vice President Facilities, Pat Nemeth
Infection Control Director, Gina Newman
Vice President of Compensation and Benefits, Anne Stephenson
Vice President Corporate Compliance, Paul Belton
Senior Vice President, Randi Larsson
Senior Vice President And Chief Executive Officer Sharp Mary Birch Hospital For Women, Mary Henrikson
Vice President Workforce Support Services, Anne Davis
Vice President Information Services, Kara Marx
Vice President, Harry Henderson
Vice President Of The Board, Charles Schuetz
Vice President Oncology Service Line, Nancy Harris
Vice President of Ancillary Services, Karen Chapman
Vice President Patient Care Information Systems, Sandra McCullough
Medical Librarian, Lise Bretton
Medical Director, Mark Jabro
Director of Pharmacy, Deborah Reissman
Senior Vice President Clinical Effectiveness, Amy Adome
Chair, Richard Freeman
Vice Chair, Lori Moore
Treasurer, James Brown
Board Member, Shawna Fallon
Secretary, Linda Byrd
Board Member, Henry Garcia
Auditors: ERNST & YOUNG LLP SAN DIEGO

LOCATIONS

HQ: SHARP HEALTHCARE
8695 SPECTRUM CENTER BLVD, SAN DIEGO, CA 921231489
Phone: 858 499-4000
Web: WWW.LEADERPHARMACIES.COM

PRODUCTS/OPERATIONS

2014 Sales

	% of total
Net patient revenue	62
Premium	35
Other	3
Total	**100**

Selected Programs and Services

Alcohol and drug dependency
Bloodless medicine
Cancer treatment
Complimentary and alternative medicine
Diabetes
Ear nose and throat
Eating disorders
Emergency and trauma
Endoscopy
Executive health
Eye care
Flu care
Health and wellness
Heart and vascular care
   Heart valve surgery

Home care
Hospice
Integrative and complementary medicine
International patient services
Laboratory services
Men's health
Mental health
Neurology
Nutrition
Occupational health
Orthopedics
Pediatrics
Pregnancy and childbirth
Primary care and family health
Radiology and diagnostic imaging
Rehabilitation and physical therapy
Robotic surgery
Safety and injury prevention
Senior care and services
Skilled nursing
Sleep disorders
Stroke and neurology
Transplant
Travel medicine
Urgent care
Weight loss
   Weight management support
   Weight-loss surgery (bariatric)
Women's care
Worksite wellness
Wound care and hyperbaric medicine

Selected Facilities

Sharp Chula Vista Medical Center (340 beds)
Sharp Coronado Hospital (180 beds)
Sharp Grossmont Hospital (540 beds La Mesa)
Sharp Mary Birch Hospital for Women & Newborns (170 beds San Diego)
Sharp McDonald Center (20 beds San Diego)
Sharp Memorial Hospital (675 beds San Diego)
Sharp Mesa Vista Hospital (150 beds San Diego)

COMPETITORS

Adventist Health System West	Rady Children's Hospital
Dignity Health	Scripps Health
HCA	Sutter Health
Palomar Health	Tenet Healthcare
Paradise Valley Hospital	Tri-City Healthcare District

HISTORICAL FINANCIALS

Company Type: Private

Income Statement

FYE: September 30

	REVENUE ($ mil.)	NET INCOME ($ mil.)	NET PROFIT MARGIN	EMPLOYEES
09/15	3,396	355	10.5%	13,000
09/14	1,234	(12)	—	—
09/13	1,158	(11)	—	—
09/09	897	(0)	—	—
Annual Growth	24.8%	—	—	—

2015 Year-End Financials

Return on assets: 7.7%   Cash ($ mil.): 305
Return on equity: 10.5%
Current ratio: 1.50

SHARP MEMORIAL HOSPITAL

The docs and the scalpels are sharp at Sharp Memorial Hospital. The flagship facility of Sharp HealthCare the not-for-profit hospital has roughly 675 beds and is a designated trauma center for San Diego County. Specialties include cardiac care women's health multi-organ transplantation and cancer treatment. It also provides skilled nursing home health and hospice services. Sharp Memorial Hospital first opened in 1955. Sharp HealthCare completed reconstruction efforts on the Sharp Memorial facility in 2009; the new hospital has improved inpatient surgery emergency trauma and intensive care facilities.

   Operations

Along with a full range of inpatient services Sharp Memorial's Outpatient Pavilion provides patients with cancer care women's imaging and endoscopy services. The center also conducts outpatient surgery procedures ranging from LASIK to orthopedic surgeries. More and more hospitals are adding outpatient services to their roster because they tend to be reimbursed at higher rates. The facility also provides patient education services such as community health classes.

Sharp Memorial which provides some $199 million in community benefits (including charity care and outreach efforts) each year is affiliated with a number of other hospitals clinics and physician groups through its parent organization.

EXECUTIVES

Pharmd, Leola Hau
Pharmacy Manager, Kim Allen

LOCATIONS

HQ: SHARP MEMORIAL HOSPITAL
7901 FROST ST, SAN DIEGO, CA 921232701
Phone: 858 939-3636

COMPETITORS

Adventist Health System West	Scripps Health
Grossmont Hospital	Tenet Healthcare
Palomar Health	Tri-City Healthcare District
Rady Children's Hospital	

HISTORICAL FINANCIALS

Company Type: Private

Income Statement

FYE: September 30

	REVENUE ($ mil.)	NET INCOME ($ mil.)	NET PROFIT MARGIN	EMPLOYEES
09/15	1,195	240	20.1%	3,500
09/14	1,042	227	21.9%	—
09/13	992	183	18.5%	—
09/12	965	194	20.2%	—
Annual Growth	7.4%	7.3%	—	—

2015 Year-End Financials

Return on assets: 3.2%   Cash ($ mil.): 1
Return on equity: 20.1%
Current ratio: 1.40

SHAWNEE MISSION MEDICAL CENTER, INC.

Shawnee Mission Medical Center (SMMC) cares for Kansas City residents primarily on the Kansas-side. The health care facility located in the city's southwest suburbs has some 500 inpatient beds. It also offers outpatient surgery and other health services in areas such as pediatrics rehabilitation oncology and radiology. The medical center's emergency department receives some 50000 visits each year. SMMC also operates satellite facilities including the Shawnee Mission Outpatient Pavilion in nearby Lenexa which offers emergency and out-

patient diagnostic general practice and surgical care. SMMC is part of Adventist Health System.

Operations

SMMC handles some 20000 inpatient admissions each year as well as some 200000 outpatient visits. Its staff includes about 700 physicians who specialize in about 50 fields of medicine. Specialist care centers include a Chest Pain Emergency Center and the Center for Women's Health. The hospital also provides primary and specialty care through the Shawnee Mission Physicians Group including after-hours clinical care and cardiology and reproductive medicine services. SMMC delivers more babies per year than any other hospital in the metropolitan area.

Geographic Reach

SMMC is located on a more than 50-acre campus in Shawnee Mission (near Kansas City) in Johnson County Kansas and serves the surrounding area. The main hospital campus includes a free-standing surgery center six physician practice buildings a child-care center for associates and a community health center.

Strategy

The SMMC organization looks at community needs to determine where it should grow. In 2013 the hospital opened a $44 million new birthing center to meet the growing need for obstetric services in the Kansas City area. The expansion effort tripled the size of the medical center's labor and delivery and postpartum rooms allowing it to accommodate up to 5000 births annually and added a level III neonatal intensive care unit.

The facility is also adding to its technological abilities to better serve the community. In late 2014 it deployed the eMediTrack platform to help document and analyze data for compliance and accreditation readiness.

Company Background

SMMC is part of a network of more than 500 health care facilities sponsored by the Seventh-day Adventist Church.

EXECUTIVES

Nursing Director, Sheri Hawkins
Medical Records Director, Charlene Scott
Executive Vice President And Chief Finan, Karsten Randolph
Infection Control Director, Jill Greig
Senior Management (Senior Vice President General Manager Director), Jack Wagner
Operating Room Director, Monica Powers
Senior Vice President Chief Operating Officer, Robin Harrold
Vice President, Andrew Weston
Secretary, Sheila Bunnell
Secretary, Jana Duckworth

LOCATIONS

HQ: SHAWNEE MISSION MEDICAL CENTER, INC.
9100 W 74TH ST, SHAWNEE MISSION, KS 662044004
Phone: 913 676-2000
Web: WWW.SHAWNEEMISSION.ORG

PRODUCTS/OPERATIONS

Selected Centers and Services
Bariatric Surgery
Behavioral Health
Britain Center (Cancer)
Center for Pain Medicine
CorporateCare
Diabetes
Emergency Services
Express Care
GI Services
Hand Specialty Center
HEALThaware
Heart and Vascular Center
Home Health Care
Maternity
Holistic Care

Men's Health Program
Neurology
Nutrition and Weight Loss
Orthopedics
Plastic Surgery
Radiology
Rehabilitation Services
Reproductive Medicine
Robotic Surgery
Sleep Disorders Center
SM Outpatient Pavilion
SportsCare
Support Groups
Surgical Services
TherapyPlus
Transfer Center Urgent Care
Weight Loss Surgery
Women's Health
Wound Care Center

COMPETITORS

Ascension Health
Children's Mercy Hospital
CoxHealth
HCA
Heartland Health
Mercy Health
Saint Luke's Health System

Sisters of Charity of Leavenworth
Stormont-Vail HealthCare
Truman Medical Centers
University of Kansas Medical Center
Via Christi Health System

HISTORICAL FINANCIALS

Company Type: Private

Income Statement

FYE: December 31

	REVENUE ($ mil.)	NET INCOME ($ mil.)	NET PROFIT MARGIN	EMPLOYEES
12/15	435	38	8.7%	1,850
12/14	385	25	6.6%	—
12/13	362	24	6.6%	—
12/12	343	30	9.0%	—
Annual Growth	8.2%	7.3%	—	—

2015 Year-End Financials

Return on assets: 6.0% Cash ($ mil.): 294
Return on equity: 8.7%
Current ratio: 5.00

SHAWNEE MISSION SCHOOL DISTRICT

EXECUTIVES

Superintendent, Kenny Southwick
Department Manager, Beth Jantsch
Department Manager, Carolyn Seeley
Auditors: MIZE HOUSER & COMPANY PA LAW

LOCATIONS

HQ: SHAWNEE MISSION SCHOOL DISTRICT
7235 ANTIOCH RD, SHAWNEE MISSION, KS 662041758
Phone: 913 993-6200
Web: WWW.SMSD.ORG

HISTORICAL FINANCIALS

Company Type: Private

Income Statement

FYE: June 30

	REVENUE ($ mil.)	NET INCOME ($ mil.)	NET PROFIT MARGIN	EMPLOYEES
06/16	316	(56)	—	4,132
06/15	319	106	33.4%	—
06/13	314	(11)	—	—
06/12	325	(8)	—	—
Annual Growth	(0.7%)	—	—	—

2016 Year-End Financials

Return on assets: 5.6% Cash ($ mil.): 98
Return on equity: (-17.9%)
Current ratio: 1.50

SHELBY COUNTY BOARD OF EDUCATION

EXECUTIVES

President, Aubrey Miller
Auditor, Patti Morrow
Board of Directors, Peg Hill
Administrative Assistant, Leigh Laatsch
Auditors: RONALD L JONES MONTGOMERY A

LOCATIONS

HQ: SHELBY COUNTY BOARD OF EDUCATION
410 E COLLEGE ST, COLUMBIANA, AL 350519301
Phone: 205 682-7000
Web: WWW.SHELBYED.K12.AL.US

HISTORICAL FINANCIALS

Company Type: Private

Income Statement

FYE: September 30

	REVENUE ($ mil.)	NET INCOME ($ mil.)	NET PROFIT MARGIN	EMPLOYEES
09/15	204	(11)	—	3,353
09/14	235	(17)	—	—
09/13	276	(33)	—	—
09/12	270	63	23.3%	—
Annual Growth	(8.8%)	—	—	—

2015 Year-End Financials

Return on assets: 0.2% Cash ($ mil.): 35
Return on equity: (-5.4%)
Current ratio: —

SHELL MEDICAL PLAN

Auditors: PNCEWATERHOUSECOOPERS LLP PIT

LOCATIONS

HQ: SHELL MEDICAL PLAN
, PHOENIX, AZ 85072
Phone: 800 352-3705

HISTORICAL FINANCIALS

Company Type: Private

Income Statement

	REVENUE ($ mil.)	NET INCOME ($ mil.)	NET PROFIT MARGIN	EMPLOYEES
12/15	571	(40)	—	2
12/13	536	6	1.2%	—
Annual Growth	3.1%	—	—	—

FYE: December 31

2015 Year-End Financials

Return on assets: —
Return on equity: (-7.2%)
Current ratio: —

Cash ($ mil.): 52

SHENANDOAH VALLEY ELECTRIC COOPERATIVE INC

EXECUTIVES

President, Myron D Rummel
Director, William McAnulty
Director, Allen Shull

LOCATIONS

HQ: SHENANDOAH VALLEY ELECTRIC COOPERATIVE INC
147 DINKEL AVE, MOUNT CRAWFORD, VA 228412358
Phone: 540 434-2200
Web: WWW.SVEC.COOP

HISTORICAL FINANCIALS

Company Type: Private

Income Statement

	REVENUE ($ mil.)	NET INCOME ($ mil.)	NET PROFIT MARGIN	EMPLOYEES
12/15	253	13	5.3%	221
12/14	239	12	5.3%	—
12/13	212	11	5.2%	—
12/12	213	15	7.1%	—
Annual Growth	5.9%	(4.3%)	—	—

FYE: December 31

2015 Year-End Financials

Return on assets: 7.1%
Return on equity: 5.3%
Current ratio: 0.90

Cash ($ mil.): 14

SHEPHERD CENTER, INC.

Here to shepherd those with catastrophic injuries back to good health is Shepherd Center. The not-for-profit hospital specializes in medical treatment research and rehabilitation for people with spinal cord and brain injuries as well as patients with neuromuscular disorders (such as spina bifida) and chronic pain. Shepherd Center boasts more than 150 beds and a 10-bed intensive care unit. Of its patients who have suffered injuries about 60% have been in car accidents. The hospital conducts neurological and neuromuscular research through its Virginia C. Crawford Research Institute.

Operations

Aside from its primary Shepherd Hospital Shepherd Center operates the Shepherd Pain Institute and the Andrew C. Carlos Multiple Sclerosis Institute.

Shepherd Center employs more than 1500 people. Seeing some 6600 people on an outpatient basis each year the center admits more than 960 patients to its inpatient programs and another 570 to its programs for day patients.

It conducts up to 50 research projects annually and is a Spinal Cord Injury Model Center as designated by the National Institute on Disability and Rehabilitation Research.

Geographic Reach

Based in Atlanta Shepherd Center serves not only its home state of Georgia but the entire nation as one of the leading rehabilitation hospitals in the US.

Strategy

In 2015 the company opened patient enrollment in a Phase 1/2a clinical trial to study an investigational product called AST-OPC1 (oligodendrocyte progenitor cells) in newly injured patients with sensory and motor-complete cervical spinal cord injury.

Expanding geographically to increase its services in 2014 Shepherd Center expanded to Nashville. That year the also hospital also announced plans for a $12.8 million project to expand and update its lab pharmacy and MRI suite.

In 2014 AT&T gave $50000 to Shepherd Center to assist researchers in the Rehabilitation Engineering Research Center for Wireless Technologies by launching a series of seminars to help consumers with disabilities uncover the range of accessibility features found on their mobile devices.

In 2013 Parker Hannifin formalized its collaboration with the Shepherd Center for the commercialization of Parker Hannifin's exoskeleton device Indego.

Company Background

The hospital is ranked by U.S. News & World Report magazine as one of the top 10 rehabilitation hospitals in the nation. It sponsors 11 wheelchair sports teams and has served as official sponsor of the wheelchair division of the Peachtree Road Race since 1984.

In 2012 the company continued or initiated 17 externally funded projects (totaling $2.4 million) and had 15 ongoing clinical trials sponsored by pharmaceutical and biotechnology companies.

Shepherd Center was founded in 1975 by James Shepherd (who was paralyzed in a bodysurfing accident) and his family.

EXECUTIVES

Vice President And Executive Director, Scott Sikes
President CEO and Director, Gary R. Ulicny
VP Facility Services and Risk Manager, Wilma Bunch
CFO, Stephen B. Holleman
VP Research and Technology and CIO, Michael L. Jones
VP Clinical Services, Sarah Morrison
Pharmacy Manager, Charles Willingham
Respiratory Therapy Director, SILVIA RONCO
Medical Director Outpatient Services, Gerald S Bilsky
Chairman, James H. Shepherd
Auditors: BENNETT THRASHER LLP ATLANTA

LOCATIONS

HQ: SHEPHERD CENTER, INC.
2020 PEACHTREE RD NW, ATLANTA, GA 303091465
Phone: 404 352-2020
Web: WWW.SHEPHERD.ORG

PRODUCTS/OPERATIONS

Selected Facilities

Andrew C. Carlos Multiple Sclerosis Institute
Shepherd Hospital
Shepherd Pain Institute

Selected Programs

Beyond Therapy
Brain Injury Rehabilitation
Care for U.S. Service Members
Chronic Pain
Disorders of Consciousness
Locomotor Training
Multiple Sclerosis
Outpatient Clinics
Patient Care
Secondary Complications
Shepherd Step
Spinal Cord Injury Rehabilitation
Stroke Rehabilitation
Ventilator Programs

Selected Services

Brain injury
Chronic Pain
Multi Specialty
Multiple Sclerosis
Spinal cord injury
Upper Extremity
Urology
Wound

COMPETITORS

DeKalb Medical	Piedmont Healthcare
Emory Healthcare	Regency Hospital
Grady Health System	WellStar Health System
Northside Hospital	

HISTORICAL FINANCIALS

Company Type: Private

Income Statement

	REVENUE ($ mil.)	NET INCOME ($ mil.)	NET PROFIT MARGIN	EMPLOYEES
03/16	198	6	3.4%	800
03/15	187	24	12.8%	—
03/14	170	27	15.9%	—
03/13	168	23	13.9%	—
Annual Growth	5.5%	(34.1%)	—	—

FYE: March 31

2016 Year-End Financials

Return on assets: 1.6%
Return on equity: 3.4%
Current ratio: 4.40

Cash ($ mil.): 26

SHI INTERNATIONAL CORP.

Businesses that need more than boxes of hardware and software can call SHI International. The company distributes scores of computer hardware and software products from suppliers such as Adobe Cisco Microsoft VMware Symantec and Lenovo. It resells PCs networking products data storage systems printers software and keyboards among other items. SHI offers a range of professional services including software licensing asset management managed desktop services systems integration and vocational training. The company serves corporate government and health care customers from more than 30 offices across the US Canada the UK Germany France and Hong Kong. SHI was founded in 1989 by Chairman Koguan Leo.

Operations

SHI serves several sectors and verticals. The company specializes in software and hardware procurement deployment planning configuration data center optimization IT asset management and cloud computing as well as custom IT solutions.

Geographic Reach

Based in Somerset New Jersey SHI has a global reach through its 30-plus offices located across the US Canada the UK Germany France and Hong Kong. In the US the company operates primarily in Texas and California but also in Arizona Colorado Florida Georgia Illinois Indiana Kansas Massachusetts Michigan Minnesota Missouri New Jersey New York Pennsylvania Virginia and Washington. Specifically its cloud briefing center is housed in New York City and its corporate call center runs from Austin Texas. The company's 420000-sq.-ft. headquarters operates beside its 305000-sq.-ft. Integration Center in Somerset New Jersey.

Financial Performance

SHI International rang up $6.8 billion in sales in 2015 a 14% increase versus the prior year. SHI's Strategic Enterprise Commercial Enterprise Corporate and Public Sector divisions contributed nearly equally to the revenue total for the year and growth outside the U.S. was steady with SHI's Canada U.K. and France divisions each posting double-digit growth. In addition SHI recognized over $1 billion in revenue from cloud products and solutions.

The seller of IT products and services boasts a 99% annual customer retention rate.

Strategy

The company has transformed itself from a $1 million regional reseller of software to a $5 billion global provider of information technology products and services. To this end SHI has invested some $20 million in a new data center that provides cloud services specifically what the company terms infrastructure-as-a-service (IaaS). The data center is one of six in the US that houses virtual machines for IT professionals to provide services such as application deployment disaster recovery software-as-a-service (SaaS). It also offers on-demand burst computing services where customers use the additional bandwidth to handle peaks in demand.

SHI's professional services unit already provides some cloud services and data center consulting. SHI sees IaaS as a logical extension of the software asset management (SAM) service it already provides. Under the SAM program SHI handles software deployment licensing compliance and inventories across a business.

SHI partners with Omaha Nebraska-based information security software specialist Solutionary to manage data security services using its ActiveGuard software product to block computer network security breaches as data center security is one of the biggest concerns for businesses in a cloud computing environment. Awards and Recognition

SHI is the largest minority and women-owned Business Enterprise (MWBE) in the US. The company's ranked 13th on CRN's 2015 Solution Provider 500 list of the largest IT solution providers in North America.

EXECUTIVES

President and Co-CEO, Thai Lee, age 60
VP and General Manager, Hal Jagger
Vice President Internal Audit and Finance Operations, Kevin Boyles
National Sales Manager, Steven Hays
Chairman, Koguan Leo
Auditors: COHN & REZNICK ACCOUNTING TAX

LOCATIONS

HQ: SHI INTERNATIONAL CORP.
290 DAVIDSON AVE, SOMERSET, NJ 088734145
Phone: 732 764-8888

PRODUCTS/OPERATIONS

Selected Products
Accessories
Peripherals
Hardware
Memory
Software

Selected Services
Cloud services
Computer vocational training services
Data center services
Events
Hardware services
Networking
POLARIS Software asset management
Storage
Strategic consulting
Webinars

COMPETITORS

ASI Computer Technologies	Computacenter
Agilysys	Ingram Micro
Arrow Electronics	Insight Enterprises
Avnet	PC Mall
CDW	Softchoice
CompuCom	Tech Data

HISTORICAL FINANCIALS
Company Type: Private

Income Statement   FYE: December 31

	REVENUE ($ mil.)	NET INCOME ($ mil.)	NET PROFIT MARGIN	EMPLOYEES
12/16	7,268	104	1.4%	3,800
12/15	6,540	69	1.1%	—
12/14	5,797	89	1.5%	—
12/13	5,003	74	1.5%	—
Annual Growth	13.3%	11.8%	—	—

2016 Year-End Financials

Return on assets: 14.0%   Cash ($ mil.): 131
Return on equity: 1.4%
Current ratio: 1.20

SHIEL SEXTON COMPANY, INC.

EXECUTIVES

President, Michael T Dilts
Director, Steve Wolff
Vice-President, Bob Groogan
Project Manager, Brian McCormick
Auditors: SOMERSET CPAS PC INDIANAPO

LOCATIONS

HQ: SHIEL SEXTON COMPANY, INC.
902 N CAPITOL AVE, INDIANAPOLIS, IN 462041005
Phone: 317 423-6000
Web: WWW.SHIELSEXTON.COM

HISTORICAL FINANCIALS
Company Type: Private

Income Statement   FYE: September 30

	REVENUE ($ mil.)	NET INCOME ($ mil.)	NET PROFIT MARGIN	EMPLOYEES
09/15	255	1	0.8%	380
09/13	182	0	0.1%	—
09/12	299	2	0.7%	—
09/11	288	(3)	—	—
Annual Growth	(3.0%)	—	—	—

2015 Year-End Financials

Return on assets: 18.5%   Cash ($ mil.): 8
Return on equity: 0.8%
Current ratio: 1.10

SHIMS BARGAIN, INC.

EXECUTIVES

President, K Kenneth Suh
Account Manager, Andrew Ahn
Financial Executive, Joseph Shin
Auditors: KAGW LLP ARTESIA CALIFORNIA

LOCATIONS

HQ: SHIMS BARGAIN, INC.
2600 S SOTO ST, VERNON, CA 900588015
Phone: 323 881-0099
Web: WWW.JCSALESWEB.COM

HISTORICAL FINANCIALS
Company Type: Private

Income Statement   FYE: December 31

	REVENUE ($ mil.)	NET INCOME ($ mil.)	NET PROFIT MARGIN	EMPLOYEES
12/15	182	1	1.0%	250
12/14	191	3	1.6%	—
12/13	189	2	1.4%	—
12/08	153	1	0.8%	—
Annual Growth	2.5%	5.3%	—	—

2015 Year-End Financials

Return on assets: 2.8%   Cash ($ mil.): 1
Return on equity: 1.0%
Current ratio: 0.50

SHORE MEMORIAL HOSPITAL

You might be able to get a room with a view of the ocean at Shore Memorial Hospital. Operating as Shore Medical Center the facility is a not-for-profit community hospital with some 300 beds. It offers acute care services and more than 35 specialized care programs including oncology cardiology neurology obstetrics and orthopedic care. Shore Medical Center is affiliated with The University of Pennsylvania Health System and The Children's Hospital of Philadelphia. In addition to the hospital Shore Medical Center operates community-based health and fitness centers.

Operations

Shore Medical Center has some 370 physicians on its staff which handles some 11000 inpatient visits per year. The hospital also manages some 6000 surgeries 1000 births and 47000 emergency room visits per year. Inpatient services account for about half of annual operating revenues while outpatient and emergency services each account for between 15% and 20% of sales.

As part of its affiliation with The University of Pennsylvania Health System Shore Medical Center has access to larger neuroscience and cardiovascular care programs among other specialties. It partners with the Children's Hospital of Philadelphia to provide pediatric services.

Geographic Reach

Shore Medical Center is located in Somers Point New Jersey which is located about 60 miles southeast of downtown Philadelphia.

Financial Performance

Shore Medical Center reported a slight 3% dip in revenue for 2013 down to $15.4 million from $16 million.

Strategy

To expand its services for children and infants in 2013 Shore Medical Center formed a partnership with Onsite Neonatal Partners. Through the collaboration Onsite will provide staff for Shore Medical Center's 24-hour neonatal and pediatric care divisions.

In the realm of medical education Shore Medical Center strengthened its position by teaming up with Drexel University's College of Medicine to provide clinical education programs beginning in 2012. Through the partnership Drexel students will be able to conduct one-month rotations at the hospital in about 10 medical fields.

Shore Memorial Hospital adopted the Shore Medical Center brand after it completed a $125 million expansion project in 2011. The project included a new surgical pavilion that expanded its cardiovascular surgery and endoscopy centers as well as other specialist departments and diagnostic exam and laboratory units. Expansion efforts also included the opening of a new pediatric care center. The change in branding reflects the facility's broader service offerings and its connections to other health providers in the region.

EXECUTIVES

Principal, Gerald J Corcoran
President, Ronald Johnson
Chief Financial Officer, David Hughes
Chief Operating Officer, Linda Kenwood
Manager, Dan Burrow
Administrative Assistant, Barbara Davis
Supervisor, John Langston
Marketing Director, Anthony Sisco

LOCATIONS

HQ: SHORE MEMORIAL HOSPITAL
100 MEDICAL CENTER WAY, SOMERS POINT, NJ
082442389
Phone: 609 653-3500
Web: WWW.SHOREMEDICALCENTER.ORG

PRODUCTS/OPERATIONS

2012 Operating Revenues

	% of total
Inpatient	50
Outpatient services	19
Emergency department	15
Same day surgery	6
Dialysis	4
Observation	2
Other	4
Total	**100**

Selected Departments and Services

Anesthesiology
Balance Care
Blood Bank
Cancer Center
CardioVascular Institute
Critical Care Center
Diabetes Education
Emergency Department
Endoscopy
Give To Shore
Hospitalist Services
Laboratory Services
Maternal-Fetal Medicine
Maternity Care Center
Neurosciences Center
Outpatient Testing Centers
Palliative Care
Pediatrics
Pulmonary Diagnostic Center
Quick Care Center
Radiology & Diagnostic Imaging
Rehabilitation Services
Respiratory Care
Sleep Medicine
Social Services
Spine and Orthopedic
Stroke Services
Surgical Services
Tele-ICU
Wound Care and Hyperbaric Medicine

COMPETITORS

AtlantiCare
Capital Health System
Christiana Care
Crozer-Keystone Health System
Doylestown Hospital
Inspira Health Network
Main Line Health System
Princeton HealthCare
The Cooper Health System
Virtua Health

HISTORICAL FINANCIALS

Company Type: Private

Income Statement

FYE: December 31

	REVENUE ($ mil.)	NET INCOME ($ mil.)	NET PROFIT MARGIN	EMPLOYEES
12/15	183	2	1.1%	1,600
12/14	187	(0)	—	—
12/09	202	5	2.6%	—
12/08	180	(7)	—	—
Annual Growth	**0.3%**	**—**	**—**	**—**

2015 Year-End Financials

Return on assets: 9.6%
Return on equity: 1.1%
Current ratio: 0.60
Cash ($ mil.): 1

SHRIEVE CHEMICAL COMPANY

EXECUTIVES

Chief Executive Officer, James W Shrieve
Board of Directors, Kristina Mordaunt
Accountant, Laronda Zurovec
Credit Manager, Michelle Shrieve
Manager, Patrick Cox
Manager, Jason Huang
Auditors: BRIGGS & VESELKA CO HOUSTON

LOCATIONS

HQ: SHRIEVE CHEMICAL COMPANY
1755 WOODSTEAD CT, THE WOODLANDS, TX
773800964
Phone: 281 367-4226

HISTORICAL FINANCIALS

Company Type: Private

Income Statement

FYE: December 31

	REVENUE ($ mil.)	NET INCOME ($ mil.)	NET PROFIT MARGIN	EMPLOYEES
12/15	288	5	2.0%	77
12/14	389	15	3.9%	—
12/13	372	21	5.7%	—
12/12	372	21	5.7%	—
Annual Growth	**(8.2%)**	**(36.0%)**	**—**	**—**

2015 Year-End Financials

Return on assets: 5.2%
Return on equity: 2.0%
Current ratio: 0.60
Cash ($ mil.): 10

SIGNAL ENERGY, LLC

EXECUTIVES

President, Ben Fischer
Manager, Meg Mauney
Account Manager, Stephanie Smith
Financial Executive, Holly Bischoff
Project Manager, Jeff Krysiak
Administrative Assistant, Charlene Lewis
Director, Greg Pawson
Manager, Seth Medina

LOCATIONS

HQ: SIGNAL ENERGY, LLC
2034 HAMILTON PLACE BLVD # 400,
CHATTANOOGA, TN 374216102
Phone: 423 443-4190
Web: WWW.SIGNALENERGY.COM

HISTORICAL FINANCIALS

Company Type: Private

Income Statement

FYE: December 31

	REVENUE ($ mil.)	NET INCOME ($ mil.)	NET PROFIT MARGIN	EMPLOYEES
12/15	339	2	0.7%	38
12/08	92	6	6.5%	—
Annual Growth	**20.4%**	**(12.4%)**	**—**	**—**

2015 Year-End Financials

Return on assets: 47.6%
Return on equity: 0.7%
Current ratio: 1.00
Cash ($ mil.): 80

SIGNATURE CONSULTANTS LLC

Signature Consultants wants your John Hancock when it comes to signing up for its staffing services. The company provides information technology staffing services to clients from a variety of industries. Signature places IT professionals with expertise in areas like project management Web application development database administration storage and network security. The firm has experience placing IT professionals across such industries as aerospace automotive banking and finan-

cial services education electronics government technology pharmaceutical and manufacturing.

Operations

Signature has more than 1100 IT consultants to support run and manage clients' technology needs.

Geographic Reach

Signature provides information technology staffing services from more than 15 locations throughout the US. The company has its National Service Center in Boston Massachusetts and Regional Service Centers in Charlotte North Carolina; Orlando Florida; Fort Lauderdale Florida; and Boston Massachusetts.

Company Background

The privately owned company was founded in 1996.

EXECUTIVES

President and CEO, Jay Cohen
COO, Mark Nussbaum
CFO, Philip Monti
CIO, Chris Tyrell
President National Accounts, Geoff Gray
National Account Manager, Chad Kelly
SENIOR VICE PRESIDENT, Chris Egizi
Senior Vice President Of Human Resources,
 Candace Whitaker
National Account Manager, Scott Anderson
National Account Manager, Ryan Fitzpatrick
National Account Manager, Shannon Haggerty
National Account Manager, Christopher Michaud
Senior Vice President Sales, Keith Giffney
NATIONAL ACCOUNTS MANAGER, Brittany
 Hagarty
Auditors: GRANT THORNTON LLP FORT LAUDE

LOCATIONS

HQ: SIGNATURE CONSULTANTS LLC
 200 W CYPRESS CREEK RD # 400, FORT
 LAUDERDALE, FL 333092175
Phone: 954 677-1020

COMPETITORS

Adecco	Kelly Services
Allegis Group	Motion Recruitment
Butler America	Partners
CDI	RCM Technologies
COMFORCE	Technisource

HISTORICAL FINANCIALS

Company Type: Private

Income Statement

FYE: December 31

	REVENUE ($ mil.)	NET INCOME ($ mil.)	NET PROFIT MARGIN	EMPLOYEES
12/15	253	1	0.5%	1,450
12/14	235	4	1.8%	—
12/13	202	3	1.9%	—
12/12	153	(1)	—	—
Annual Growth	18.3%	—	—	—

2015 Year-End Financials

Return on assets: 5.4%   Cash ($ mil.): —
Return on equity: 0.5%
Current ratio: 1.20

SIGNATURE HEALTHCARE CORPORATION

EXECUTIVES

President, Kim Hollon
Director, Arthur Cronin
Plant & Facilities Manager, Kent Werner
Trustee, Manthala George

LOCATIONS

HQ: SIGNATURE HEALTHCARE CORPORATION
 680 CENTRE ST, BROCKTON, MA 023023308
Phone: 508 941-7000
Web: WWW.SIGNATURE-HEALTHCARE.ORG

HISTORICAL FINANCIALS

Company Type: Private

Income Statement

FYE: September 30

	REVENUE ($ mil.)	NET INCOME ($ mil.)	NET PROFIT MARGIN	EMPLOYEES
09/15	248	13	5.4%	1,500
09/14	304	11	3.8%	—
09/13	1	0	61.1%	—
09/09	0	0	42.9%	—
Annual Growth	182.8%	100.4%	—	—

2015 Year-End Financials

Return on assets: 8.4%   Cash ($ mil.): 13
Return on equity: 5.4%
Current ratio: 0.90

SIKA CORPORATION

When plain old mortar won't do Sika Corporation offers its construction customers specialty mortars. Sika also manufactures adhesives coatings epoxies acrylics silicones and polyurethane. Its products are used to seal bond dampen sounds reinforce and protect load-bearing structures. It markets to the construction and manufacturing industries including transportation marine and automotive. Sika's Construction Products division is based along with its headquarters in New Jersey and its Industry and Automotive divisions are based in Michigan. Sika is the US unit as well as the largest manufacturing segment of global chemicals company Sika AG.

Operations

Sika's Industry Products division focuses on elastic and structural bonding and in the manufacture of adhesives sealants and acoustic materials (polyurethane adhesives and sealants hot melt adhesives epoxies acrylics silicones and butyl sealants). The Sika Construction unit works with customers supplying products services and technical expertise to help them execute projects both efficiently and cost effectively.

Geographic Reach

Sika has seven plants and two research and development facilities in the US and serves customers across the company.

Sales and Marketing

Sika Industry Products serves a range of industries including appliance automotive glass replacement bus HVAC marine metal building rail recreational vehicle truck and window and door

industries. Sika Construction serves producers contractors and specifiers.

As part of its strategy for growth Sika actively pursues innovation new product launches and acquisitions.

Financial Performance

The company accounted for 16% of the parent company Sika AG's revenues in 2015.

Mergers and Acquisitions

In 2016 the company acquired L.M. Scofield Company of Los Angeles a concrete color additive and decorative concrete products producer. This acquisition was made to accelerate Sika's US growth.

In 2015 the company agreed to buy mortar producer BMI Products of Northern California Inc. The acquisition was aimed at ramping up Sika's global expansion in the fast growing mortar business with an extended new supply chain in the Western US.

Company Background

In 2013 it announced the integration of its advanced i-Cure® Technology into the marine product line through the introduction of Sikaflex®-295i UV a next generation elastic adhesive and sealant which has a reduced volatile organic compounds footprint and reduced isocyanates.

To better serve customers and add space for future growth in 2011 the company opened a new 200000 square foot warehousing facility at its Marion Ohio. In early 2011 Sika alo established a new business unit the FFI Business Unit for its facades fenestration and insulating glass products.

Boosting its North American presence in 2011 Sika's parent company acquired Quebec-based Duochem a maker of polymer flooring and waterproofing products for the construction industry. Duochem operates as a unit of Sika Canada Inc.

Sika is a subsidiary of Sika AG which has operations in 90 countries. Sika Corporation was founded in 1937.

EXECUTIVES

President and CEO, Christoph Ganz, age 48
EVP Refurbishment, Rick Montani
EVP Roofing and Flooring, Brian Whelan
EVP Industry Division, Dan Hilliard
EVP Human Resources, Nick Romano
SVP Finance, Stephen Lysik
EVP Operations, Herbert Zwartkruis
General Manager Sika Canada, Mike Hardman
Vice President and Treas, Gail Pacifico
SENIOR VICE PRESIDENT CONCRETE PRODUCERS, Philippe Jost
Senior Vice President Research and Development,
 Steve Rosenberg
Vice President Repair and Protection, Jim Walther
Vice President of Marketing and Key Accounts,
 Jamie Gentoso
Vice President Of Sales, Jason Whitman
Senior Vice President Human Resources, Romano
 Nick
Vice President Marketing, Sebastien Godard
Vice President Of Procurement, Tony Adamo
Vice President Aftermarket Business Unit, Marius
 Mavrodin
Vice President Of Sales, Jesse Quezada
Vice President Finance, Gregory May
Senior Vice President, Stew Snoddy

LOCATIONS

HQ: SIKA CORPORATION
 201 POLITO AVE, LYNDHURST, NJ 070713601
Phone: 201 933-8800
Web: WWW.USA.SIKA.COM

PRODUCTS/OPERATIONS

Sika Industry Products (Markets)
Appliance and Components

Aftermarket
Automotive OEM
Automotive OES
Building Components
Renewable Energies
Marine
Transportation
Sika Construction (Products and Markets)
Building Envelope
Concrete Admixture Technology
Concrete Repair and Protection
Crack Repair and Injection Resins
DIY/Home Centers
Epoxy Resin and Structural Engineering Systems
Grouting and Quickset Mortars
Industrial Flooring
Joint Sealing and Adhesive Systems
Roofing
Training Academy
Waterproofing
Wood Floor Bonding

COMPETITORS

ADCO Products	Dow Chemical
BASF Corporation	Henkel Corp.
Carlisle Coatings &	Koch Enterprises
Waterproofing	Park Electrochemical
Cohesant	

HISTORICAL FINANCIALS
Company Type: Private

Income Statement

FYE: December 31

	REVENUE ($ mil.)	NET INCOME ($ mil.)	NET PROFIT MARGIN	EMPLOYEES
12/15	915	63	7.0%	1,067
12/14	842	42	5.1%	—
12/13	761	31	4.2%	—
12/12	744	41	5.6%	—
Annual Growth	7.2%	15.4%	—	—

2015 Year-End Financials

Return on assets: —
Return on equity: 7.0%
Current ratio: 0.60
Cash ($ mil.): 15

SILVER CROSS HEALTH SYSTEM

EXECUTIVES

President, Paul Pawlak
Manager, Karen Helman
Personnel Director, Linda Thill
Manager, Marci Vasiliades
Director, Marilyn Paolella
Auditors: KPMG LLP CHICAGO IL

LOCATIONS

HQ: SILVER CROSS HEALTH SYSTEM
1900 SILVER CROSS BLVD, NEW LENOX, IL
604519509
Phone: 815 300-1100

HISTORICAL FINANCIALS
Company Type: Private

Income Statement

FYE: September 30

	REVENUE ($ mil.)	NET INCOME ($ mil.)	NET PROFIT MARGIN	EMPLOYEES
09/16	366	22	6.1%	1,600
09/15	348	(61)	—	—
09/14	347	7	2.1%	—
09/13	289	4	1.7%	—
Annual Growth	8.2%	66.0%	—	—

2016 Year-End Financials

Return on assets: 6.1%
Return on equity: 6.1%
Current ratio: 1.00
Cash ($ mil.): 47

SILVER CROSS HOSPITAL AND MEDICAL CENTERS

Silver Cross Hospital and Medical Centers serve the Illinois counties of Will Grundy and Cook through its 290-bed main hospital campus and nine satellite facilities throughout the area. Services provided by the medical facility include cardiovascular care women's health rehabilitation and behavioral health care. Its outpatient facilities provide primary and specialty care services such as medical imaging and dialysis. The Silver Cross Hospital and Medical Centers name comes from the emblem (the Maltese Cross) of the Christian organization that founded the not-for-profit hospital the International Order of The King's Daughters and Sons.

Operations

Thomson Reuters' Truven a leading source of healthcare intelligence has named Silver Cross Hospital and Medical Centers one of the "100 Top Hospitals" in the nation for seven consecutive years.

The Illinois medical facility maintains a staff of more than 100 physicians. It specializes in offering diagnostic imaging rehabilitation therapy dialysis women's health services and emergency services.

Geographic Reach

Silver Cross Hospital and Medical Centers serves patients in the Illinois counties of Cook Grundy and Will.

Strategy

In 2012 the hospital opened a replacement facility in New Lenox to house its main hospital and to keep pace with population growth in its service territory. The $400-million Silver Cross Hospital facility has about 290 private patient rooms. The 70-acre New Lenox campus also includes two medical offices buildings and the University of Chicago Medicine Comprehensive Cancer Center.

Silver Cross Hospital and Medical Centers also collaborates with the Rehabilitation Institute of Chicago to provide outpatient rehabilitation services at four of the health system's locations.

It added a sleep disorders center in 2012 at its New Lenox (Route 6) location.

Company Background

Silver Cross Hospital admitted its first patient in Joliet Illinois in 1895.

EXECUTIVES

Vice President and Chief Information Officer,
Kevin Lane
Auditors: KPMG LLP CHICAGO IL

LOCATIONS

HQ: SILVER CROSS HOSPITAL AND MEDICAL CENTERS
1900 SILVER CROSS BLVD, NEW LENOX, IL
604519509
Phone: 815 300-1100
Web: WWW.SILVERCROSS.ORG

Selected Locations
Headquarters
New Lenox Illinois
Locations with Silver Cross Services
East Joliet
Homer Glen
New Lenox (Route 6)
New Lenox (Route 30)
West Joliet
Professional Office Buildings with Silver Cross Medical Staff
East Joliet
Frankfort
Home Glen
Lemont
New Lenox (Route 6)
New Lenox (Route 30)
West Joliet

PRODUCTS/OPERATIONS

Selected Departments/Facilities
Behavioral Health/Chemical Dependency
Birthing Center
Cancer Center
Cardiology
Center for Women's Health
Colon Cancer Screening
Diagnostic Imaging
Diabetes
Dialysis
Encore Shop
Emergency Department
Free-Standing Emergency Care Center
Home Health Care
Incontinence & Pelvic Floor Disorders
Interventional Radiology
Joint Replacement Education
Intensive Care
Outpatient Infusion Center
Pediatric Services
Pet Therapy
Prostate Health
Pulmonary Program
  Rehabilita
Surgery - Same Day
Surgery - Using the da Vinci Robot
Senior Advantage
Silver Cross Emergency Medical Services System
Sleep Disorders Center
Weight Loss Surgery
Wound Healing & Treatment Center

Selected Services
Behavioral health care
Birthing services
Cancer care
Cardiovascular care/Cath Lab
Cardiopulmonary Rehabilitation
Chemical Dependency Services
Chemo and Radiation
Colon cancer screening/Colonoscopies
Da Vinci Robotic Surgery
Diabetes management
Diagnostic testing and imaging (ultrasound x-ray MRI PET/CT scan etc.)
Dialysis
Dietary Counseling
Emergency care
Health educational programs and screenings
Home health care
Hospitalists
Infusion Therapy (chemotherapy etc.)
Incontinence Care
Intensive care
Laboratory testing

Lifeline Emergency Personal Response Service
Mammography
Medical/Surgical inpatient care
Neonatal care
Neurology/Neurosurgery
Obstetrical/gynecological care
Orthopedic care
Pain management
Pastoral care
Pediatric care
Pulmonary care
Rehabilitation (physical speech occupational)
Senior Advantage Program
Sleep Disorders Carre
Support Groups
Stroke care
Surgery (outpatient & inpatient)
Weight Loss Surgery
Women's Health
Wound care

COMPETITORS

Adventist Health System Sunbelt Healthcare
 Advocate Health Care
 Covenant Ministries
 Elmhurst Memorial Healthcare
 Mercy Hospital and Medical Center
 Northwestern Memorial HealthCare
 Sinai Health System
 St. Bernard Hospital and Health Care Center
 University of Chicago Medical Center

HISTORICAL FINANCIALS
Company Type: Private

Income Statement

	REVENUE ($ mil.)	NET INCOME ($ mil.)	NET PROFIT MARGIN	EMPLOYEES
09/15	335	(59)	—	1,700
09/14	320	10	3.2%	—
09/13	306	6	2.1%	—
09/08	244	21	8.6%	—
Annual Growth	4.6%	—	—	—

FYE: September 30

2015 Year-End Financials
Return on assets: 5.0%   Cash ($ mil.): 28
Return on equity: (-17.7%)
Current ratio: 0.90

SINAI HEALTH SYSTEM

You don't have to scale any mountains to reach this Sinai. Sinai Health System provides medical care for the residents of West Side of Chicago. The system is comprised of its flagship Mount Sinai Hospital Holy Cross Hospital Schwab Rehabilitation Hospital and the Sinai Children's Hospital. The health system's Sinai Medical Group provides primary and specialty care through a range of clinics in the area. The Sinai Community Institute offers health wellness and educational programs for all ages and the Sinai Urban Health Institute conducts research and disease outreach programs. Altogether the system has some 700 inpatient beds and 800 physicians.

Operations

Mount Sinai Hospital's service territory in western Chicago includes a number of African-American and Latino communities. Specialties at the 320-bed facility include cancer care cardiovascular care birthing urology orthopedics and mental health. Its level I trauma center is one of four trauma centers in the city. The hospital's medical training programs serve 700 students per year and include eight residency programs.

Sinai Children's Hospital includes a level III neonatal intensive care unit (ICU) for newborn care as well as a general pediatric ICU. Specialty pediatric services offerings include trauma surgery and viral disease care. Schwab Rehabilitation hospital is a 100-bed inpatient facility for both adults and children. Its services include injury recovery and physical therapy. The Sinai Medical Group includes about 300 area physicians providing general and specialty care to adults and children. Sinai Community Institute focuses on services for children seniors young adults and minorities ranging from prenatal care and parenting education to employment services and job training.

Financial Performance

Revenues for Sinai Health System dropped 6% to $383 million in 2012 due to higher community benefit expenses. The network spends some $90 million annually on community benefits including health outreach programs and the provision of charity care for uninsured and under-insured patients (which make up a high percentage of its customer base). Net income also fell 720% to $2.5 million in 2012 as a result of the decline in revenues.

Strategy

Expansion of facilities is an important part of the Sinai Health System's growth efforts. It added the Holy Cross Hospital to its roster of facilities in 2013. Construction efforts include the building of a new Sinai Community Institute facility to increase clinical health programs.

Sinai Health System conducts a number of quality improvement disease prevention and social service initiatives to enhance the services its provides to Chicago residents. Its patient-centered disease management program provides preventative care assistance to heart disease and diabetes patients (and their physicians) with assistance from the Sinai electronic health record (EHR) system.

Research is also a priority especially in the area of controlling the spread of disease in urban areas. In 2012 the Sinai Urban Health Institute formed a partnership with insurance company BCBS of Illinois to collaborate on a program to reduce health disparities in the care of diabetes patients.

Mergers and Acquisitions

Holy Cross Hospital was acquired by Sinai Health System in January 2013 after the transaction was approved by the state regulatory agencies. The facilities have a shared mission to serve economically challenged communities in Chicago. Though Holy Cross Hospital is a member of the Sinai Health System it retains its Catholic identity through its sponsorship by the Sisters of St. Casimir.

EXECUTIVES

Director of Pharmacy, Justin Schneider
Interim Vice President, Claude Hall
Vice President and Chief Information Officer,
 Peter Ingram
Vice President, Lori Pacura
Medical Records Director, Monica Flores
Executive Vice President and General Counsel,
 Rachel Dvorken
Vice President of Human Resources, Aaron Austin
System Vice President of Finance, James Wilson
Auditors: PRICEWATERHOUSECOOPERS LLP ON

LOCATIONS

HQ: SINAI HEALTH SYSTEM
 1500 S FAIRFIELD AVE, CHICAGO, IL 606081782
Phone: 773 542-2000

PRODUCTS/OPERATIONS

Selected Operations
Holy Cross Hospital
Mount Sinai Hospital

Schwab Rehabilitation Hospital
Sinai Children's Hospital
Sinai Community Institute
Sinai Medical Group
Sinai Urban Health Institute

COMPETITORS

Advocate Health Care
 Children's Hopsital of Chicago
 Covenant Ministries
 Elmhurst Memorial Healthcare
 Gottleib Memorial Hospital
 Mercy Hospital and Medical Center
 Northwestern Memorial HealthCare
 Rush System for Health
 St. Bernard Hospital and Health Care Center
 University of Chicago Medical Center
 Weiss Memorial Hospital

HISTORICAL FINANCIALS
Company Type: Private

Income Statement

	ASSETS ($ mil.)	NET INCOME ($ mil.)	INCOME AS % OF ASSETS	EMPLOYEES
03/15*	1,297	(3)	—	6,000
06/08	9	0	—	—
06/06	9	0	—	—
06/05	4	0	0.4%	—
Annual Growth	77.1%	—	—	—

FYE: March 31
*Fiscal year change

2015 Year-End Financials
Return on assets: 15.4%   Sales ($ mil): 599
Return on equity: (-0.5%)

SINAI HOSPITAL OF BALTIMORE, INC.

Sinai Hospital of Baltimore part of the LifeBridge Health network provides medical care in northwestern Baltimore. The 470-bed hospital is a not-for-profit medical center that includes such facilities as a heart center a children's hospital a cancer institute and a rehab center. Other specialties include orthopedics neurology and women's care. Medical students from Johns Hopkins University and the University of Maryland do some of their training at the hospital. Sinai Hospital of Baltimore was founded in 1866 as the Hebrew Hospital and Asylum and became a subsidiary of LifeBridge when it merged with other area providers in 1998.

Operations

The Sinai Hospital of Baltimore handles about 26000 inpatient admissions and some 75000 emergency room visits per year. It also conducts about 20000 inpatient and outpatient surgeries annually.

The medical center conducts a number of education and training programs including residencies and fellowships for about 400 medical students each year. It is a designated training site for the Johns Hopkins University's ambulatory and internal medicine clerkships.

Strategy

Sinai Hospital of Baltimore has completed several expansion efforts in recent years. In 2012 it opened a new dedicated inpatient hospice unit as well as a new center for geriatric surgery. In addition the 20-bed Friedman Neurological Rehabilitation Center was completed that year.

EXECUTIVES

President, Neil Meltzer
Board of Directors, Nancy Hackerman
Director, Sudhir K Dutta

LOCATIONS

HQ: SINAI HOSPITAL OF BALTIMORE, INC.
2401 W BELVEDERE AVE, BALTIMORE, MD
212155270
Phone: 410 601-5678

PRODUCTS/OPERATIONS

Selected Centers

Alvin & Lois Lapidus Cancer Institute at LifeBridge
  Health
Center for Joint Preservation and Replacement
Children's Hospital at Sinai
ER-7 Emergency Center
Heart Center at Sinai
International Center for Limb Lengthening
Krieger Eye Institute
Louis and Phyllis Friedman Neurological Rehabilitation
  Center
Rubin Institute for Advanced Orthopedics
Sandra and Malcolm Berman Brain & Spine Institute
Sinai Rehabilitation Center
The Spine Center at Sinai

Selected Services

Allergy and Immunology
Anesthesia
Cardiology
Cancer/Medical Oncology
Dermatology
Dialysis
Emergency Medicine
Endocrinology and Metabolism
Family Medicine
Gastroenterology
General Internal Medicine
Geriatric Medicine
Infectious Diseases
Nephrology (kidneys)
Pulmonary and Critical Care Medicine
Rheumatology (joints tendons)
Neurology
Neurosurgery
Obstetrics and Gynecology
Ophthalmology (eye care)
Oral and Maxillofacial Surgery and Dentistry
Orthopedic Surgery
Otolaryngology (ear nose & throat)
Pathology
Pediatrics
Pharmacy
Physical Medicine and Rehabilitation
Psychiatry
Radiation Oncology
Radiology
Surgery
Urology

COMPETITORS

Anne Arundel Medical Center	Johns Hopkins Health System
Ascension Health	MedStar Health
Bon Secours Health	Meritus Health
Franklin Square Hospital Center	University of Maryland Medical System
GBMC	

HISTORICAL FINANCIALS

Company Type: Private

Income Statement

FYE: June 30

	REVENUE ($ mil.)	NET INCOME ($ mil.)	NET PROFIT MARGIN	EMPLOYEES
06/15	677	45	6.7%	4,497
06/14	714	41	5.8%	—
06/13	742	32	4.3%	—
06/11	691	36	5.3%	—
Annual Growth	(0.5%)	5.5%	—	—

2015 Year-End Financials

Return on assets: 15.3%   Cash ($ mil.): 143
Return on equity: 6.7%
Current ratio: 1.60

SISTEMA UNIVERSITARIO ANA G. MENDEZ, INC.

EXECUTIVES

President, Jose F Mendez
Board of Directors, Nannette Delgado
Financial Executive, Juan Jose Sanchez
Manager, Sarai Lastra
Financial Executive, Carmelo Torres
Financial Executive, Leilani Cermeno
Chief Financial Officer, Dorie Mendez
Auditors: ERNST & YOUNG LLP SAN JUAN P

LOCATIONS

HQ: SISTEMA UNIVERSITARIO ANA G. MENDEZ, INC.
CARR 176 KM 0 3 CPEY LOWR ST CA, SAN JUAN, PR
00928
Phone: 787 751-0178
Web: WWW.SUAGM.EDU

HISTORICAL FINANCIALS

Company Type: Private

Income Statement

FYE: July 31

	REVENUE ($ mil.)	NET INCOME ($ mil.)	NET PROFIT MARGIN	EMPLOYEES
07/16	300	(4)	—	5,387
07/15	291	(6)	—	—
07/14	260	17	6.8%	—
07/13	260	17	6.8%	—
Annual Growth	5.0%	—	—	—

2016 Year-End Financials

Return on assets: 12.9%   Cash ($ mil.): 3
Return on equity: (-1.5%)
Current ratio: —

SKIDMORE COLLEGE

Skidmore College offers more than 40 degree programs including majors in both traditional liberal arts disciplines and pre-professional areas. The private college grants bachelor's and master's degrees in the sciences humanities social sciences business education social work and the arts. Skidmore enrolls about 2400 students from the US and some 40 other countries and boasts a student-faculty ratio of about 9 to 1. It was founded by Lucy Skidmore Scribner in 1903 as the Young Women's Industrial Club of Saratoga.

EXECUTIVES

Senior Vice President and Chief Information Officer, Dan Green
Director of Admissions, Catherine DeLorenzo
Dance Department Chair, Mary DiSanto-Rose
Vice President for Academic Affairs, Tbd Sga
Vice President of Marketing, Olivia Dynan
Vice President for Financial Affairs, Julia Elstein
Executive Vice President, Luca Mobilia
Treasurer, Steve Otrembiak
Secretary, Jennifer Clark
Treasurer, Sara Brandt
Auditors: UHY ADVISORS NY INC ALBANY N

LOCATIONS

HQ: SKIDMORE COLLEGE
815 N BROADWAY, SARATOGA SPRINGS, NY
128661698
Phone: 518 580-5000
Web: WWW.SKIDMORE.EDU

HISTORICAL FINANCIALS

Company Type: Private

Income Statement

FYE: May 31

	REVENUE ($ mil.)	NET INCOME ($ mil.)	NET PROFIT MARGIN	EMPLOYEES
05/15	216	19	9.0%	720
05/13	140	32	23.4%	—
05/12	137	(23)	—	—
05/11	0	0	—	—
Annual Growth	—	1842.7%	—	—

2015 Year-End Financials

Return on assets: 46.8%   Cash ($ mil.): 29
Return on equity: 9.0%
Current ratio: 0.20

SL GREEN OPERATING PARTNERSHIP, L.P.

EXECUTIVES

Chief Executive Officer, Marc Holliday
President, Andrew W Mathias
General Partner, SL Green Realty Corp

LOCATIONS

HQ: SL GREEN OPERATING PARTNERSHIP, L.P.
420 LEXINGTON AVE RM 1800, NEW YORK, NY
101701899
Phone: 212 594-2700
Web: WWW.SLGREEN.COM

HISTORICAL FINANCIALS

Company Type: Private

Income Statement

FYE: December 31

	ASSETS ($ mil.)	NET INCOME ($ mil.)	INCOME AS % OF ASSETS	EMPLOYEES
12/16	15,857	278	1.8%	1,060
12/15	19,857	317	1.6%	—
12/14	17,096	545	3.2%	—
12/13	14,959	151	1.0%	—
Annual Growth	2.0%	22.6%	—	—

2016 Year-End Financials

Return on assets: 10.2%   Sales ($ mil): 1,863
Return on equity: 15.0%

SLETTEN, INC.

EXECUTIVES

Chairman of the Board, J Robert Sletten
Auditors: JUNKERMIER CLARK CAMPANELLA ST

LOCATIONS

HQ: SLETTEN, INC.
1000 25TH ST N STE 4, GREAT FALLS, MT
594011382
Phone: 406 761-7920

HISTORICAL FINANCIALS

Company Type: Private

Income Statement				FYE: March 31
	REVENUE ($ mil.)	NET INCOME ($ mil.)	NET PROFIT MARGIN	EMPLOYEES
03/15	189	1	0.6%	375
03/14	166	2	1.3%	—
03/13	155	1	0.9%	—
03/12	161	2	1.6%	—
Annual Growth	5.6%	(24.9%)	—	—

SMART CIRCLE INTERNATIONAL LLC

EXECUTIVES

Chief Executive Officer, Michael Meryash
Officer, Andrew Rosenthal
Manager, Ivan Scherer

LOCATIONS

HQ: SMART CIRCLE INTERNATIONAL LLC
4490 VON KARMAN AVE, NEWPORT BEACH, CA
926602008
Phone: 949 587-9207
Web: WWW.SMARTCIRCLE.COM

HISTORICAL FINANCIALS

Company Type: Private

Income Statement				FYE: December 27
	REVENUE ($ mil.)	NET INCOME ($ mil.)	NET PROFIT MARGIN	EMPLOYEES
12/15	355	28	7.9%	95
12/14	349	24	7.0%	—
12/13	272	20	7.6%	—
Annual Growth	14.1%	16.5%	—	—

2015 Year-End Financials

Return on assets: 1.6%
Return on equity: 7.9%
Current ratio: 0.90
Cash ($ mil.): 22

SMDC MEDICAL CENTER

EXECUTIVES

Chief Executive Officer, Peter Person
Board of Directors, James N Abelsen
Executive Secretary, Darlin Johnson

Financial Executive, Grant Bellefeuille
Manager, Krister Mattson
Vice-President, Brian Zuck
Director, Dayle Patterson
Director, Donna Van Kessel

LOCATIONS

HQ: SMDC MEDICAL CENTER
502 E 2ND ST, DULUTH, MN 558051913
Phone: 218 726-4000
Web: WWW.SMDCMEDICALCENTER.ORG

HISTORICAL FINANCIALS

Company Type: Private

Income Statement				FYE: June 30
	REVENUE ($ mil.)	NET INCOME ($ mil.)	NET PROFIT MARGIN	EMPLOYEES
06/15	502	19	4.0%	750
06/14	475	11	2.4%	—
06/12	372	5	1.4%	—
06/11	373	13	3.7%	—
Annual Growth	7.7%	9.6%	—	—

2015 Year-End Financials

Return on assets: 8.7%
Return on equity: 4.0%
Current ratio: 2.50
Cash ($ mil.): 56

SMITHSONIAN INSTITUTION

The Smithsonian Institution has many hats from the one worn by Harrison Ford in the Indiana Jones movies to the one worn by Abraham Lincoln the night he was assassinated. One of the world's leading cultural institutions the Smithsonian houses more than 137 million objects in 19 museums and galleries most of which are on the National Mall in Washington DC. Roughly 30 million people visit every year to view the Smithsonian's exhibits on art music TV and film science history and other subjects. Admission to all but one of the Smithsonian's facilities is free; only the Cooper-Hewitt National Design Museum in New York charges admission.

Operations

A board of regents that includes the vice president and the chief justice of the US six members of Congress and nine private citizens leads the institution. The Smithsonian's exhibits display items such as the Declaration of Independence the ruby slippers worn by Judy Garland in The Wizard of Oz and the Wright brothers' first airplane. Along with its museums and galleries the Smithsonian also operates the National Zoo and nine research facilities and publishes the Smithsonian monthly magazine.

Geographic Reach

The Smithsonian Institution is located in Washington DC. The world's largest museum and research complex averages about 30 million visitors per year.

Financial Performance

The Smithsonian receives about 80% of its funding from the federal government. The Institution claimed about $1.28 billion in revenue for fiscal 2013 an increase of about 3% compared to the $1.24 billion it reported for fiscal 2012.

Strategy

Recent initiatives at the Institution include the renovation of the Arts and Industries building and

plans to open the National Museum of African American History and Culture in 2015.

The institution aims to expand the Smithsonian's global relevance in the 21st century. As part of this strategy it released a strategic plan that focuses on four priorities or "grand challenges" as they are called in the report. They are: Unlocking the mysteries on the universe; Understanding and sustaining a biodiverse planet; Valuing world cultures; and Understanding the American experience.

HISTORY

English chemist James Smithson wrote a proviso to his will in 1826 that would lead to the creation of the Smithsonian Institution. When he died in 1829 he left his estate to his nephew Henry James Hungerford with the stipulation that if Hungerford died without heirs the estate would go to the US to create "an Establishment for the increase and diffusion of knowledge among men." Hungerford died in 1835 without any heirs and the US government inherited more than $500000 in gold.

Congress squandered the money after it was received in 1838 but perhaps feeling pangs of guilt covered the loss. The Smithsonian was finally created in 1846 and Princeton physicist Joseph Henry was named its first secretary. That year it established the Museum of Natural History the Museum of History and Technology and the National Gallery of Art. The Smithsonian's National Museum was developed around the collection of the US Patent Office in 1858. The Smithsonian continued to expand adding the National Zoological Park in 1889 and the Smithsonian Astrophysical Observatory in 1890.

The Freer Gallery a gift of industrialist Charles Freer opened in 1923. The National Gallery was renamed the National Collection of Fine Arts in 1937 and a new National Gallery created with Andrew Mellon's gift of his art collection and a building opened in 1941. The Air and Space Museum was established in 1946.

More museums were added in the 1960s including the National Portrait Gallery in 1962 and the Anacostia Museum (exhibits and materials on African-American history) in 1967. The Kennedy Center for the Performing Arts was opened in 1971. The Collection of Fine Arts was renamed the National Museum of American Art and the Museum of History and Technology was renamed the National Museum of American History in 1980.

The Smithsonian placed its first-ever contribution boxes in four of its museums in 1993.

A planned exhibit featuring the Enola Gay — the plane that dropped the atomic bomb on Hiroshima — created a firestorm in 1994 with critics charging that the exhibit downplayed Japanese aggression and US casualties in WWII. The original exhibit was canceled in 1995 the director of the Air and Space Museum resigned and a scaled-down version of the exhibit premiered. In 2004 the exhibit attracted more protestors prompting Smithsonian officials to evacuate and temporarily close the museum.

Large contributions from private donors continued in the 1990s; the Mashantucket Pequot tribe gave $10 million from its casino operations in 1994 for the Smithsonian's planned American Indian museum and prolific electronics inventor Jerome Lemelson donated $10.4 million in 1995. The museum celebrated its sesquicentennial in 1996 amid news that $500 million in repairs were needed over the next 10 years.

California real estate developer Kenneth Behring gave the largest cash donation ever to the museum in 1997 — $20 million for the National Museum of Natural History. Short of funds the

Smithsonian had to cut back on its 150th-anniversary traveling exhibit that year. The Smithsonian announced a $26 million renovation for the National Museum of Natural History in 1998. Two years later Behring quadrupled his record-breaking 1997 donation of $20 million by giving $80 million to the National Museum of American History. Catherine Reynolds withdrew most of her $38 million gift in 2002 after the Smithsonian Institution refused to implement her ideas for an exhibit at the National Museum of American History.

The National Museum of the American Indian opened on the National Mall in 2004.

Secretary Lawrence Small resigned under pressure in March 2007 amid criticism of his spending practices. Cristián Samper director of the Smithsonian's National Museum of Natural History was named acting secretary. A report on the matter issued by the Smithsonian in June said its Board of Regents failed to provide the oversight that might have prevented Small's extravagant spending.

In July 2008 Wayne Clough became the 12th secretary of the Smithsonian.

EXECUTIVES

John and Adrienne Mars Director National Air and Space Museum, John R. (Jack) Dailey
Director Government Relations, Penelope (Nell) Payne, age 60
Director External Affairs, Virginia B. (Ginny) Clark
Secretary, David J. Skorton
Director National Postal Museum, Allen R. Kane
Director National Museum of African American History and Culture, Lonnie G. Bunch, age 62
Director Equal Employment and Minority Affairs, Era L. Marshall
Director Smithsonian Marine Station at Fort Pierce, Valerie J. Paul
Director Smithsonian Affiliations, Harold A. Closter
Director Smithsonian Institution Libraries, Nancy E. Gwinn
Ombudsman, Chandra P. Heilman
Director Smithsonian Center for Learning and Digital Access, Stephanie L. Norby
Chief of Staff Office of the Regents, John K. Lapiana
Director Smithsonian Environmental Research Center, Anson (Tuck) Hines
Director Smithsonian Institution Archives, Anne Van Camp
Acting Provost and Under Secretary for Museums and Research, Richard Kurin
Director National Museum of African Art, Johnnetta B. Cole
Director Smithsonian Tropical Research Center, Matthew Larsen
Deputy Under Secretary for Collections and Interdisciplinary Support, Scott Miller
General Counsel, Judith E. Leonard
Director Harvard-Smithsonian Center for Astrophysics, Charles R. Alcock
Director Smithsonian Latino Center, Eduardo Díaz
Director Smithsonian Museum Conservation Institute, Robert J. Koestler
Acting Director Cooper-Hewitt National Design Museum, Caroline Baumann
Director National Zoological Park, Dennis Kelly
Director Consortia for the Humanities, Michelle Anne Delaney
Director Office of Facilities Engineering and Operations, Nancy Bechtol
President Smithsonian Enterprises, Christopher Liedel
Inspector General, Cathy Helm
Director Smithsonian Exhibits, Susan Ades
CIO, Deron Burba
Editor-in-Chief Smithsonian Magazine, Michael Caruso
Director Finance and Accounting, Jean Garvin

Director Office of Planning Management and Budget, David Voyles
Acting Director Office of Policy and Analysis, Whitney Watriss
Director Office of Fellowships and Internships, Eric Woodard
Director The Smithsonian Associates, Fredie Adelman
Director Smithsonian American Art Museum and the Renwick Gallery, Elizabeth (Betsy) Broun
Director Hirshhorn Museum and Sculpture Garden, Melissa Chiu
Director National Museum of American History Behring Center, John Gray
Director Archives of American Art, Kate Haw
Director National Museum of Natural History, Kirk Johnson
Director Smithsonian's Center for Folklife and Cultural Heritage, Michael Atwood Mason
Director Freer Gallery of Art and Arthur M. Sackler Gallery, Julian Raby
Director National Portrait Gallery, Kim Sajet
Interim Director Smithsonian Institution Traveling Exhibition Service, Myriam Springuel
Director Consortia for Science, Pierre Comizzoli
Chancellor Board of Regents, John G. Roberts, age 63
Auditors: KPMG LLP MCLEAN VA

LOCATIONS

HQ: SMITHSONIAN INSTITUTION
1000 JEFFERSON DR SW, WASHINGTON, DC 205600009
Phone: 202 633-1000
Web: WWW.SI.EDU

PRODUCTS/OPERATIONS

2016 Operating Revenue

	% of total
Federal appropriations	53
Contributions & private grants	18
Business activities	11
Government grants & contracts	8
Endowment	5
Other	5
Total	**100**

Selected Museums and Research Centers

Anacostia Community Museum
Arthur M. Sackler Gallery
Arts and Industries Building
Center for Folklife and Cultural Heritage
Conservation and Research Center
Cooper-Hewitt National Design Museum (New York)
Freer Gallery of Art
Hirshhorn Museum and Sculpture Garden
National Air and Space Museum
National Museum of African Art
National Museum of American History
National Museum of Natural History
National Museum of the American Indian
National Museum of the American Indian - George Gustav Heye Center (New York)
National Science Research Center
National Portrait Gallery
National Postal Museum
National Zoological Park
Smithsonian American Art Museum
Smithsonian Astrophysical Observatory
Smithsonian Center for Latino Initiatives
Smithsonian Center for Materials Research and Education
Smithsonian Environmental Research Center (SERC)
Smithsonian Institution Building (The Castle)
Smithsonian Museum Conservation Institute
Smithsonian Tropical Research Institute

HISTORICAL FINANCIALS

Company Type: Private

Income Statement

FYE: September 30

	REVENUE ($ mil.)	NET INCOME ($ mil.)	NET PROFIT MARGIN	EMPLOYEES
09/16	1,541	192	12.5%	6,100
09/15	1,412	50	3.6%	—
09/14	1,452	279	19.2%	—
09/13	1,371	209	15.3%	—
Annual Growth	**4.0%**	**(2.8%)**	**—**	**—**

2016 Year-End Financials

Return on assets: 18.6%   Cash ($ mil.): 407
Return on equity: 12.5%
Current ratio: 0.50

SMMH PRACTICE PLAN, INC.

Auditors: KPMG LLP PITTSBURGH PA

LOCATIONS

HQ: SMMH PRACTICE PLAN, INC.
7175 SALTSBURG RD, PITTSBURGH, PA 152352252
Phone: 412 795-6069

HISTORICAL FINANCIALS

Company Type: Private

Income Statement

FYE: June 30

	REVENUE ($ mil.)	NET INCOME ($ mil.)	NET PROFIT MARGIN	EMPLOYEES
06/15	2,060	27	1.3%	26
06/14	2,005	570	28.4%	—
06/13	1,985	402	20.3%	—
06/12	1,976	(90)	—	—
Annual Growth	**1.4%**	**—**	**—**	**—**

2015 Year-End Financials

Return on assets: 4.8%   Cash ($ mil.): 49
Return on equity: 1.3%
Current ratio: 0.60

SOFTTEK INTEGRATION SYSTEMS, INC

EXECUTIVES

Chief Executive Officer, Marcos Jimenez
Board of Directors, Benigno Lopez
Accountant, Bertha Yanneth Albornoz
Vice-President, Roberto Montelongo
Manager, David Cervantes
Project Manager, Rogerio Dias
Manager, Mauro Mattioda
Director, Helen R Castor

LOCATIONS

HQ: SOFTTEK INTEGRATION SYSTEMS, INC
2002 SUMMIT BLVD STE 300, BROOKHAVEN, GA
303196403
Phone: 404 460-5040
Web: WWW.SOFTTEK.COM

HISTORICAL FINANCIALS

Company Type: Private

Income Statement

FYE: December 31

	REVENUE ($ mil.)	NET INCOME ($ mil.)	NET PROFIT MARGIN	EMPLOYEES
12/15	185	1	0.7%	330
12/14	173	1	0.9%	—
12/13	181	1	1.0%	—
12/08	97	0	0.3%	—
Annual Growth	**9.6%**	**21.4%**	**—**	**—**

2015 Year-End Financials

Return on assets: —
Return on equity: 0.7%
Current ratio: 0.40

Cash ($ mil.): 2

SOUTH BROWARD HOSPITAL DISTRICT

South Broward Hospital District (dba Memorial Healthcare System) is a community-owned health services network that provides health service to residents of Florida's Broward Dade and Palm Beach counties. The system's major hospitals include Memorial Regional Hospital Memorial Hospital Pembroke Memorial Hospital West and Memorial Hospital Miramar. The hospitals have a combined capacity of roughly 1900 licensed beds and provide services including diagnostic emergency surgical and rehabilitative care. Memorial also operates a pediatric hospital cardiac and vascular medicine institute a cancer treatment center and a center for women's health as well as nursing home facilities (120 beds) and community clinics.

Operations

The system's hospitals include Memorial Regional Memorial Regional South Joe DiMaggio Children's Memorial West Memorial Miramar Memorial Pembroke and the Memorial Manor nursing home.

Memorial Regional offers a cardiac and vascular institute a cancer institute and a neuroscience center.

Geographic Reach

Memorial Healthcare System operates health care facilities in Florida and Washington.

Financial Performance

In 2015 revenue increased 12% to $1.8 billion as net patient service earnings rose primarily due to an increase in surgical procedures given. Net income rose 89% to $191.4 million that year due to the higher revenue and a decrease in depreciation and amortization. Operating cash flow also increased rising 68% to $292.4 million.

Strategy

Memorial Healthcare System provides care in a number of ways including through home health services and health care plans. It is adding two additional health plans in 2016 to reach a goal of managing more than 100000 lives in the network.

During 2016 the company entered into a partnership with Holy Cross Physician Partners creating the Atlantic Coast Health Network. The new network represents some 1400 physicians.

EXECUTIVES

President and CEO, Frank V. Sacco
EVP and Chief Administrative Officer, Matthew J. Muhart
SVP and Chief Medical Officer, Stanley W. Marks
EVP and COO, Aurelio M. Fernandez
Infection Control Director, Cathy Copeland
Pharmd, Marlaine Mance
Vice President Business Develo, Sandra Dilts
Senior Vice President and Chief Development Officer, Kevin Janser
Chairman, Jose Basulto
Vice Chairman, Vic Narang
Secretary, Ruth Marcus

LOCATIONS

HQ: SOUTH BROWARD HOSPITAL DISTRICT
3501 JOHNSON ST, HOLLYWOOD, FL 330215421
Phone: 954 987-2000
Web: WWW.MEMORIALREGIONAL.COM

PRODUCTS/OPERATIONS

2015 Sales

	% of total
Net patient service	92
Disproportionate share distribution	5
Other operating revenue	3
Total	**100**

Selected Facilities

Esther L. Grossman Women's Health & Resource Center
Memorial Cancer Institute
Memorial Hospital Miramar
Memorial Hospital Pembroke
Memorial Hospital West
Memorial Manor
Memorial Outpatient Center
Memorial Primary Care Center - Dania Beach
Memorial Primary Care Center - Hollywood
Memorial Primary Care Center - Miramar
Memorial Primary Care Center - West Hollywood
Memorial Regional Hospital
    Joe DiMaggio Children's Hospital
Memorial Regional Hospital South
Memorial Regional Hospital Fitness & Rehabilitation Center
Memorial Same Day Surgery Center
Memorial Urgent Care Center
Same Day Surgery Center at Memorial Hospital West

COMPETITORS

Baptist Health South Florida	Florida Hospital Heartland
Boca Raton Regional Hospital	HCA
Broward Health	Jackson Health System
Continucare	MJHHA
	South Miami Hospital

HISTORICAL FINANCIALS

Company Type: Private

Income Statement

FYE: April 30

	REVENUE ($ mil.)	NET INCOME ($ mil.)	NET PROFIT MARGIN	EMPLOYEES
04/16	1,897	188	9.9%	9,200
04/15	854	(649)	—	—
Annual Growth	**122.0%**	**—**	**—**	**—**

2016 Year-End Financials

Return on assets: 4.3%
Return on equity: 9.9%
Current ratio: 2.50

Cash ($ mil.): 545

SOUTH CAROLINA PUBLIC SERVICE AUTHORITY (INC)

This company turns the lights on in South Carolina. South Carolina Public Service Authority known as Santee Cooper (after two interconnected river systems) provides wholesale electricity to 20 cooperatives and two municipalities that serve more than 2 million customers in South Carolina. It directly retails electricity to more than 174000 customers. One of the largest US state-owned utilities Santee Cooper operates in all 46 counties in South Carolina and has stakes in power plants (fossil-fueled nuclear hydro and renewable) that give it more than 5180 MW of generating capacity. Its Santee Cooper Regional Water System also distributes water to customers in its service area.

Operations

Santee Cooper operates 5029 miles of transmission lines and more than 2841 miles of distribution lines. It also operates 105 transmission stations and 54 distribution substations. The company is the leading renewable energy producer in South Carolina.

Geographic Reach

In addition to supplying power to 20 cooperatives in all 46 counties in South Carolina Santee Cooper also supplies power directly to 29 large industrial customers in 10 counties Charleston Air Force Base the town of Bamberg and the City of Georgetown.

Sales and Marketing

The company serves more than 2 million customers in South Carolina. It directly retails electricity to more than 174000 customers.

Financial Performance

In 2015 Santee Cooper's net revenues decreased by 6% to $1.9 billion compared due to lower kilowatt-hour sales (down 3%) and demand usage (down 2%).

The company's net income decreased by 73% to $34.4 million as the result of lower net revenues and higher electric maintenance expenses.

In 2015 Santee Cooper's operating cash inflow decreased by 77% to $237.6 million.

Strategy

With a eye toward getting 40% of its power from non-carbon emitting sources and conservation by 2020 the company has begun to invest heavily in nuclear solar wind and other renewable energy sources.

In 2015 the company agreed to changes in its agreement with Westinghouse Electric which acquired assets of a second partner in the V.C. Summer Nuclear Station plant construction consortium giving Westinghouse more control over the project.

In 2014 Santee Cooper in collaboration with Central Electric Power Cooperative and the state's electric cooperatives agreed to buy the total energy output of Colleton Solar Farm a utility-scale solar power farm being built by TIG Sun Energy a subsidiary of the North Charleston-based InterTech Group. The solar array consists of 10010 photovoltaic panels. Some panels are fixed while other panels follow the direction of the sun to maximize the production of solar energy.

South Carolina Resources Santee Cooper Central Electric Power Cooperative and the state's electric cooperatives agreed in 2013 to build Colleton Solar Farm the largest solar farm in the state (3000 kilowatts of electricity).

Mergers and Acquisitions

In 2014 South Carolina Electric & Gas Company (SCE&G) principal subsidiary of SCANA Corporation and Santee Cooper announced an agreement for SCE&G to acquire from Santee Cooper a 5% ownership interest in the two new nuclear units which are under construction at V.C. Summer Nuclear Station in Jenkinsville. Under the ownership agreement SCE&G owns 55%; Santee Cooper 45%. The 5% ownership interest would be acquired in three stages with 1% to be acquired at the commercial operation date of the first new nuclear unit (late 2017 or the first quarter of 2018); an additional 2% to be acquired no later than the first anniversary of such commercial operation date; and the final 2% to be acquired no later than the second anniversary date of such commercial operation date.

Company Background

Santee Cooper is a government-owned entity.

Historically the $48.2 million Santee Cooper project (55% federal loan and 45% federal grant) which connected the Santee and Cooper rivers and established hydroelectric dams and a transmission grid began to generate electricity for the first time in 1942. It was founded in 1934.

HISTORY

In 2011 Santee Cooper dedicated a 311-kilowatt solar installation in Myrtle Beach where it also has 2.4-kW wind turbine (the first utility-connected turbine on the state grid). Santee Cooper also contracted for power from biomass combustion and from anaerobic digestion on a livestock farm.

In late 2011 the US Nuclear Regulatory Commission conducted a final review of Santee Cooper's application for a license to build and operate two new nuclear units at V.C. Summer Nuclear Station.

EXECUTIVES

Vice President Human Resource Management, W Brown
SVP Corporate Planning and Bulk Power, Lonnie N. Carter
SVP and CFO, Jeff Armfield
SVP Nuclear Energy, Michael Crosby
EVP Competitive Markets and Generation, Marc R. Tye
SVP and CIO, Dom Maddalone
Vice President of Retail Operations, Mike Poston
Vice President Engineering And Construction Services, Thomas Kierspe
Vice President of Planning and Power Supply, Tom Abrams
Vice President of Training and Franchisee Development, Ray Smith
Vice President of Legal Services and Corporate Secretary, Elizabeth Warner
Vice President of Real Estate, Dan Camp
Chairman, W. Leighton Lord
1st Vice Chairman, William A. Finn
Auditors: CHERRY BEKAERT LLP RALEIGH N

LOCATIONS

HQ: SOUTH CAROLINA PUBLIC SERVICE AUTHORITY (INC)
1 RIVERWOOD DR, MONCKS CORNER, SC 294612998
Phone: 843 761-4121
Web: WWW.SANTEECOOPER.COM

PRODUCTS/OPERATIONS

2015 Sales

	$ mil.	% of total
Electricity	1,856	99
Water	8	-
Other	15	1
Total	**1,879**	**100**

COMPETITORS

Delmarva Power	PS Energy
Dominion Energy	Progress Energy
Duke Energy	SCANA
Florida Public Utilities	TVA
MLGW	Utilities Inc.
North Carolina Electric Membership	

HISTORICAL FINANCIALS

Company Type: Private

Income Statement

FYE: December 31

	REVENUE ($ mil.)	NET INCOME ($ mil.)	NET PROFIT MARGIN	EMPLOYEES
12/15	1,879	34	1.8%	1,748
12/13	1,816	65	3.6%	—
12/12	1,887	84	4.5%	—
12/11	1,914	132	6.9%	—
Annual Growth	(0.5%)	(28.6%)		

2015 Year-End Financials

Return on assets: 19.3%
Return on equity: 1.8%
Current ratio: 0.20
Cash ($ mil.): 113

SOUTH CAROLINA RESEARCH AUTHORITY INC

EXECUTIVES

Chief Executive Officer, Bill Mahoney
Chief Operating Officer, Greg Frank
Executive Vice-President, Marvin Davis
Vice-President, Tom McCord
Administrative Assistant, Cassie Pommersheim
Executive Director, Jon Tirpak
Director, Cole Dudley
Auditors: BDO USA LLP RALEIGH NC

LOCATIONS

HQ: SOUTH CAROLINA RESEARCH AUTHORITY INC
1000 CATAWBA ST STE 100, COLUMBIA, SC 292015706
Phone: 803 799-4070
Web: WWW.SCRA.ORG

HISTORICAL FINANCIALS

Company Type: Private

Income Statement

FYE: June 30

	REVENUE ($ mil.)	NET INCOME ($ mil.)	NET PROFIT MARGIN	EMPLOYEES
06/15	399	0	0.1%	218
06/14	284	5	1.8%	—
06/13	266	17	6.7%	—
06/12	194	1	0.7%	—
Annual Growth	27.1%	(25.8%)	—	—

2015 Year-End Financials

Return on assets: 18.9%
Return on equity: 0.1%
Current ratio: 1.10
Cash ($ mil.): 86

SOUTH CENTRAL POWER COMPANY INC

Although South Central Power Company may sound like a power plant in Watts Los Angeles it is in fact a member-owned cooperative that provides electricity to consumers and businesses in southern Ohio. An affiliate of the nationwide Touchstone Energy Cooperative network the electric cooperative provides power to more than 115570 customers over 11000 miles of power lines. In addition to distributing electricity South Central Power also provides outdoor lighting surge suppression products security systems water heater switches and other energy-related services.

Geographic Reach

South Central Power's operations cover 24 counties in Ohio.

Financial Performance

In 2012 the company's revenues grew by 7% thanks to a rise in revenues from residential customers (more than 1320 new customers were added that year). Net income grew by 67% as the result of higher net sales and lower operating costs.

Company Background

South Central Power was formed in 1936. It joined the Touchstone Energy Cooperatives network in 1998.

EXECUTIVES

Vice President Human Resources, Susan Everly
Auditors: GBQ PARTNERS LLC COLUMBUS OH

LOCATIONS

HQ: SOUTH CENTRAL POWER COMPANY INC
2780 COONPATH RD NE, LANCASTER, OH 431309343
Phone: 740 653-4422
Web: WWW.SOUTHCENTRALPOWER.COM

HISTORICAL FINANCIALS

Company Type: Private

Income Statement

FYE: December 31

	REVENUE ($ mil.)	NET INCOME ($ mil.)	NET PROFIT MARGIN	EMPLOYEES
12/15	273	22	8.1%	235
12/14	266	21	8.0%	—
12/13	257	17	6.9%	—
12/12	0	15	—	—
Annual Growth	—	13.9%	—	—

2015 Year-End Financials

Return on assets: 6.6%
Return on equity: 8.1%
Current ratio: 0.70
Cash ($ mil.): 7

SOUTH DAKOTA STATE UNIVERSITY

South Dakota State University (SDSU) is big on education in the Mount Rushmore State. The college offers undergraduate graduate and pre-professional programs to some 13000 students. Academic offerings include agriculture engineering and pharmacy courses. Its SDSU Sioux Falls Program targets non-traditional students (such as stu-

dents with jobs and families) by providing evening and weekend classes. Notable SDSU alumni include former US Senator Tom Daschle and professional football players Adam Timmerman and Adam Vinatieri. SDSU a public school governed by the South Dakota Board of Regents was founded as a land grant college in 1881.

Operations

SDSU students can choose from more than 180 areas of study including about 70 undergraduate majors 30 master's degree programs 15 doctoral degrees and 10 certificates. Its classes are organized under colleges of agriculture and biological sciences; arts and sciences; education and human sciences; nursing; pharmacy; and engineering. The university also operates a university college a graduate school and an honors college.

SDSU receives grants and contracts to help fund research programs in fields including agriculture engineering geospatial data environmental science energy human health and pharmaceutical studies. Agricultural research is a core field of exploration for university students primarily through the school's South Dakota Agricultural Experiment Station.

With a student-to-faculty ratio of about 19:1 SDSU operates with an annual budget of $299 million.

Geographic Reach

The university's main campus is located in Brookings South Dakota. SDSU's four attendance centers (where select courses are offered) are located in Pierre Rapid City Sioux Falls and Watertown. It also has eight extension offices across the state.

Financial Performance

The university's operating revenue was reported at some $199 million in fiscal 2012 an increase of 4% over fiscal 2011 due to higher tuition fees and state support as well as other sources of income. Increase in net assets declined 44% to $17.7 million on higher expenses from supplies and contractual services as well as the lack of certain federal appropriations.

Strategy

SDSU's core operating goals are to provide quality academic programs through environment innovative staff and engaged students; offer support for research creativity and scholarship through facilities services and infrastructure; and to create beneficial partnerships with government community and global organizations to enhance academic opportunities.

Program and facility enhancements include the establishment of a new center for Agribusiness and Food Systems Management in 2013. It also opened several new residence halls that year. Projects under construction include new learning and research spaces for the engineering and architecture departments.

EXECUTIVES

President, David Chicoina
Accountant, James Rogners
Manager, Wesley Tfchetter
Manager, Brietta Murphy

LOCATIONS

HQ: SOUTH DAKOTA STATE UNIVERSITY
2201 ADMINISTRATION LANE, BROOKINGS, SD 570070001
Phone: 605 688-6101
Web: WWW.STATEALUM.COM

PRODUCTS/OPERATIONS

Select Colleges
College of Agriculture & Biological Sciences
College of Arts & Sciences
College of Education & Human Sciences
College of Nursing
College of Pharmacy
Graduate School
Jerome J. Lohr College of Engineering
University College
Van D. & Barbara B. Fishback Honors College

HISTORICAL FINANCIALS
Company Type: Private

Income Statement
FYE: June 30

	REVENUE ($ mil.)	NET INCOME ($ mil.)	NET PROFIT MARGIN	EMPLOYEES
06/16*	209	44	21.1%	2,000
12/14	44	1	3.4%	—
06/14	201	33	16.3%	—
06/13	195	17	8.9%	—
Annual Growth	2.4%	36.6%	—	—

*Fiscal year change

2016 Year-End Financials
Return on assets: 4.5%
Return on equity: 21.1%
Current ratio: 2.00
Cash ($ mil.): 58

SOUTH DAKOTA WHEAT GROWERS ASSOCIATION

Who loves you a bushel and a peck? South Dakota Wheat Growers may; it is an agricultural co-op comprising some 5400 member-farmers. It provides a grain warehouse along with grain marketing services intended to compete with big food and ag companies. In addition to storage and drying Wheat Growers offers agronomy spreading and spraying and transportation. It supplies feed fertilizer chemicals and other farm-related provisions for members in and around counties in North and South Dakota. Wheat Growers generates more than half of its revenues through marketing some 160 million bushels of grain (corn wheat and soybeans) each year. Remaining revenues are made through agronomy and retail sales and services.

EXECUTIVES

President, Hal Clemensen
Manager, James Brandner
Auditors: GARDINER THOMSEN PC DES MO

LOCATIONS

HQ: SOUTH DAKOTA WHEAT GROWERS ASSOCIATION
908 LAMONT ST S, ABERDEEN, SD 574015515
Phone: 605 225-5500
Web: WWW.WHEATGROWERS.COM

Selected Counties of Operation
North Dakota
 Dickey
 LaMoure
 Stutsman
South Dakota
 Aurora
 Beadle
 Brown
 Brule
 Clark
 Corson
 Day
 Edmunds
 Faulk
 Hand
 Hyde
 Jerauld
Lyman
Marshall
Sanborn
Spink

COMPETITORS
ADM
CHS
Cargill
Country Pride
North Central Farmers Elevator
Northern Growers

HISTORICAL FINANCIALS
Company Type: Private

Income Statement
FYE: July 31

	REVENUE ($ mil.)	NET INCOME ($ mil.)	NET PROFIT MARGIN	EMPLOYEES
07/16	1,209	6	0.6%	638
07/15	1,283	40	3.1%	—
07/14	1,498	20	1.4%	—
07/13	1,847	20	1.1%	—
Annual Growth	(13.2%)	(31.7%)	—	—

2016 Year-End Financials
Return on assets: 0.8%
Return on equity: 0.6%
Current ratio: 0.10
Cash ($ mil.): —

SOUTH GEORGIA MEDICAL CENTER

EXECUTIVES

Principal, Johnny Ball

LOCATIONS

HQ: SOUTH GEORGIA MEDICAL CENTER
2501 N PATTERSON ST, VALDOSTA, GA 316021785
Phone: 229 333-1000
Web: WWW.SGMC.ORG

HISTORICAL FINANCIALS
Company Type: Private

Income Statement
FYE: September 30

	REVENUE ($ mil.)	NET INCOME ($ mil.)	NET PROFIT MARGIN	EMPLOYEES
09/15	310	(2)	—	10
09/14	296	15	5.4%	—
Annual Growth	4.8%	—	—	—

2015 Year-End Financials
Return on assets: 5.9%
Return on equity: (-0.7%)
Current ratio: 1.10
Cash ($ mil.): 26

SOUTH LAKE HOSPITAL, INC.

EXECUTIVES

President, John Moore
Board of Directors, Robert Berens
Director, Matthew Casavant
Director, Martin Austria

LOCATIONS

HQ: SOUTH LAKE HOSPITAL, INC.
  1900 DON WICKHAM DR LBBY, CLERMONT, FL
  347111999
Phone: 352 394-4071
Web: WWW.SOUTHLAKEHOSPITAL.COM

HISTORICAL FINANCIALS
Company Type: Private

Income Statement
FYE: September 30

	REVENUE ($ mil.)	NET INCOME ($ mil.)	NET PROFIT MARGIN	EMPLOYEES
09/16	185	15	8.6%	1,150
09/15	161	16	10.4%	—
09/14	142	16	11.7%	—
09/13	135	8	6.5%	—
Annual Growth	10.9%	21.9%	—	—

2016 Year-End Financials
Return on assets: 9.9%   Cash ($ mil.): 47
Return on equity: 8.6%
Current ratio: 2.60

SOUTH MIAMI HOSPITAL, INC.

South Miami Hospital offers primary and tertiary health care services to the residents living near the University of Miami. The hospital has about 470 beds and is one of the largest members of Baptist Health South Florida a top regional health system. Specialty services include emergency care cardiovascular services oncology neurology women's health metabolic care and rehabilitation. It operates an addiction treatment residential facility provides home health care and provides child development diagnostic and early intervention services. South Miami Hospital was founded in 1960.

Operations

South Miami Hospital handles 15000 inpatient admissions each year as well as 30000 emergency room visits 5000 outpatient surgeries and 4000 births. It has about 1300 physicians on its medical staff.

As part of the broader Baptist Health South Florida system South Miami Hospital benefits from shared resources including procurement administration and technology the coordination of which helps the member facilities control costs during times of economic trouble and rising medical care expenses in the US.

Strategy

The Baptist Health system facilities including South Miami Hospital are installing electronic health record (EHR) systems to manage patient records across the system. Such EHR systems are designed to improve quality and lower expenses by facilitating communication between care providers and increasing patient involvement in condition management.

In addition South Miami Hospital has improved its services through expansion and renovation projects. It has added specialty units for robotic surgery birthing heart care and neonatal intensive care. In addition it completed an $80 million two-story construction in 2013 that enhanced the medical center's emergency surgery and imaging departments.

EXECUTIVES

Ambulatory Services Director, Carmen Rodriguez
Vice President Human Resources, Melissa Lupisella

LOCATIONS

HQ: SOUTH MIAMI HOSPITAL, INC.
  6200 SW 73RD ST, SOUTH MIAMI, FL 331434679
Phone: 786 662-4000

COMPETITORS

Adventist Health System Sunbelt Healthcare
  Broward Health
H. Lee Moffitt Cancer Center & Research Institute
HCA
Jackson Health System
Larkin Community Hospital
Miami Children's Hospital
Mount Sinai Medical Center of Florida
South Broward Hospital District
UF&Shands
University of Miami Hospital

HISTORICAL FINANCIALS
Company Type: Private

Income Statement
FYE: September 30

	REVENUE ($ mil.)	NET INCOME ($ mil.)	NET PROFIT MARGIN	EMPLOYEES
09/15	495	40	8.2%	2,205
09/14	505	53	10.6%	—
09/13	484	59	12.3%	—
09/12	484	36	7.6%	—
Annual Growth	0.7%	3.5%	—	—

2015 Year-End Financials
Return on assets: 5.3%   Cash ($ mil.): —
Return on equity: 8.2%
Current ratio: 0.90

SOUTH NASSAU COMMUNITIES HOSPITAL INC

EXECUTIVES

Chief Executive Officer, Richard J Murphy
Account Manager, Manolita Perez
Director, John Alexander
Vice-President, Stephen P Jieniewicz
Assistant Vice-President, Thomas D Hylan

LOCATIONS

HQ: SOUTH NASSAU COMMUNITIES HOSPITAL INC
  1 HEALTHY WAY, OCEANSIDE, NY 115721551
Phone: 516 632-3000
Web: WWW.SOUTHNASSAU.ORG

HISTORICAL FINANCIALS
Company Type: Private

Income Statement
FYE: December 31

	REVENUE ($ mil.)	NET INCOME ($ mil.)	NET PROFIT MARGIN	EMPLOYEES
12/15	423	(3)	—	2,800
12/14	434	13	3.0%	—
12/13	421	111	26.4%	—
12/12	400	(3)	—	—
Annual Growth	1.9%	—	—	—

2015 Year-End Financials
Return on assets: 12.3%   Cash ($ mil.): 3
Return on equity: (-0.9%)
Current ratio: 0.50

SOUTH SHORE HOSPITAL, INC.

EXECUTIVES

President, Gene E Green
Director, John Burns
Manager, Jean Wallace

LOCATIONS

HQ: SOUTH SHORE HOSPITAL, INC.
  55 FOGG RD, SOUTH WEYMOUTH, MA 021902455
Phone: 781 624-8000
Web: WWW.SOUTHSHOREHOSPITAL.ORG

HISTORICAL FINANCIALS
Company Type: Private

Income Statement
FYE: September 30

	REVENUE ($ mil.)	NET INCOME ($ mil.)	NET PROFIT MARGIN	EMPLOYEES
09/15	522	50	9.6%	2,375
09/14	495	30	6.1%	—
09/13	479	21	4.4%	—
09/12	426	4	1.0%	—
Annual Growth	7.0%	128.8%	—	—

2015 Year-End Financials
Return on assets: 8.0%   Cash ($ mil.): 66
Return on equity: 9.6%
Current ratio: 1.70

SOUTH TEXAS ELECTRIC COOPERATIVE, INC.

EXECUTIVES

President, Gary Raybon
Vice-President, Burt O'Connell
Manager, Joe Schorp
President, Darryl Klinitchek
Purchasing Director, Betty Hennard
Senior Manager, Randy Snider
Auditors: BUMGARDNER MORRISON AND COMPA

LOCATIONS

HQ: SOUTH TEXAS ELECTRIC COOPERATIVE, INC.
  2849 FM 447, NURSERY, TX 77976
Phone: 361 575-6491
Web: WWW.STEC.ORG

HISTORICAL FINANCIALS
Company Type: Private

Income Statement   FYE: December 31

	REVENUE ($ mil.)	NET INCOME ($ mil.)	NET PROFIT MARGIN	EMPLOYEES
12/15	416	31	7.5%	253
12/14	438	30	6.9%	—
12/13	359	19	5.3%	—
12/12	320	23	7.4%	—
Annual Growth	9.0%	9.6%	—	—

2015 Year-End Financials

Return on assets: 7.5%   Cash ($ mil.): 37
Return on equity: 7.5%
Current ratio: 0.30

SOUTH WASHINGTON COUNTY SCHOOLS ISD 833

EXECUTIVES

Superintendent, Keith Jacobus
Superintendent, Linda Rull
Assistant Manager, Julie Nielsen
Assistant Manager, Michael Johnson

LOCATIONS

HQ: SOUTH WASHINGTON COUNTY SCHOOLS ISD 833
7362 E POINT DOUGLAS RD S, COTTAGE GROVE, MN 550163025
Phone: 651 458-6300
Web: WWW.SOWASHCO.K12.MN.US

HISTORICAL FINANCIALS
Company Type: Private

Income Statement   FYE: June 30

	REVENUE ($ mil.)	NET INCOME ($ mil.)	NET PROFIT MARGIN	EMPLOYEES
06/16	247	150	60.7%	3,200
06/03	146	(22)	—	—
06/02*	137	64	46.9%	—
12/01	0	0	—	—
Annual Growth	—	—	—	—

*Fiscal year change

SOUTHCENTRAL FOUNDATION

EXECUTIVES

Chief Executive Officer, Katherine Gottlieb
Accountant, Gene Sievers
Director of Finance, Wade Carlson
Personnel Director, April Kyle
VP Operations, Natalie Tierney
Account Manager, Barbara Snell
Auditors: ALTMAN ROGERS & CO ANCHORAG

LOCATIONS

HQ: SOUTHCENTRAL FOUNDATION
4501 DIPLOMACY DR, ANCHORAGE, AK 995085919
Phone: 907 729-4955
Web: WWW.SOUTHCENTRALFOUNDATION.COM

HISTORICAL FINANCIALS
Company Type: Private

Income Statement   FYE: September 30

	REVENUE ($ mil.)	NET INCOME ($ mil.)	NET PROFIT MARGIN	EMPLOYEES
09/15	307	44	14.5%	1,600
09/14	369	133	36.1%	—
09/13	235	17	7.5%	—
09/12	222	15	6.9%	—
Annual Growth	11.5%	42.5%	—	—

2015 Year-End Financials

Return on assets: 3.7%   Cash ($ mil.): 81
Return on equity: 14.5%
Current ratio: 2.20

SOUTHCOAST PHYSICIANS GROUP, INC.

EXECUTIVES

President, Warren Wood
Auditors: PRICEWATERHOUSECOOPERS LLP BO

LOCATIONS

HQ: SOUTHCOAST PHYSICIANS GROUP, INC.
200 MILL RD STE 180, FAIRHAVEN, MA 027195255
Phone: 508 758-3781

HISTORICAL FINANCIALS
Company Type: Private

Income Statement   FYE: September 30

	REVENUE ($ mil.)	NET INCOME ($ mil.)	NET PROFIT MARGIN	EMPLOYEES
09/15	171	(62)	—	1,000
09/13	125	(11)	—	—
Annual Growth	16.8%	—	—	—

2015 Year-End Financials

Return on assets: 12.9%   Cash ($ mil.): 5
Return on equity: (-36.6%)
Current ratio: 0.90

SOUTHEAST MISSOURI HOSPITAL ASSOCIATION

EXECUTIVES

Chief Executive Officer, Wayne Smith
Board of Directors, Judy Aslin
Director, Lou Boshell
Director, April Henry
Manager, Joy Frey

LOCATIONS

HQ: SOUTHEAST MISSOURI HOSPITAL ASSOCIATION
1701 LACEY ST, CAPE GIRARDEAU, MO 637015230
Phone: 573 334-4822
Web: WWW.SEHEALTH.ORG

HISTORICAL FINANCIALS
Company Type: Private

Income Statement   FYE: December 31

	REVENUE ($ mil.)	NET INCOME ($ mil.)	NET PROFIT MARGIN	EMPLOYEES
12/15	289	5	1.9%	2,000
12/13	315	(31)	—	—
12/09	311	19	6.1%	—
12/08	277	8	3.2%	—
Annual Growth	0.6%	(6.3%)	—	—

2015 Year-End Financials

Return on assets: 7.1%   Cash ($ mil.): 21
Return on equity: 1.9%
Current ratio: 1.10

SOUTHEASTERN REGIONAL MEDICAL CENTER

EXECUTIVES

Chief Executive Officer, Joann Anderson
Director, Pam Clark
Director of Finance, Jay Leatherman

LOCATIONS

HQ: SOUTHEASTERN REGIONAL MEDICAL CENTER
300 W 27TH ST, LUMBERTON, NC 283583075
Phone: 910 671-5000
Web: WWW.SRMC.ORG

HISTORICAL FINANCIALS
Company Type: Private

Income Statement   FYE: September 30

	REVENUE ($ mil.)	NET INCOME ($ mil.)	NET PROFIT MARGIN	EMPLOYEES
09/15	267	13	5.2%	2,000
09/14	261	21	8.2%	—
09/13	297	56	19.0%	—
09/10	288	10	3.7%	—
Annual Growth	(1.5%)	5.8%	—	—

2015 Year-End Financials

Return on assets: 6.2%   Cash ($ mil.): 23
Return on equity: 5.2%
Current ratio: 1.60

SOUTHERN ILLINOIS HEALTHCARE E

Auditors: MCGLADREY LLP SPRINGFIELD IL

LOCATIONS

HQ: SOUTHERN ILLINOIS HEALTHCARE E
2370 N MCROY DR, CARBONDALE, IL 629015629
Phone: 618 457-5200
Web: WWW.SIH.NET

Company Type: Private

Income Statement FYE: March 31

	REVENUE ($ mil.)	NET INCOME ($ mil.)	NET PROFIT MARGIN	EMPLOYEES
03/15	528	36	6.8%	14
03/14	1	0	44.8%	—
Annual Growth	34279.8%	5154.4%	—	—

2015 Year-End Financials

Return on assets: 5.5%　　Cash ($ mil.): 12
Return on equity: 6.8%
Current ratio: 1.40

SOUTHERN ILLINOIS UNIVERSITY INC

Southern Illinois University (SIU) helps to train future doctors dentists and other other professionals. The university enrolls some 32000 students at its two institutions — Southern Illinois University at Carbondale (SIUC which includes medical and law schools) and Southern Illinois University at Edwardsville (SIUE which houses education dental and nursing schools) — as well as smaller satellite centers. SIU offers associate baccalaureate master's doctoral and professional degrees. It also boasts a number of study abroad partnerships with international universities. Tracing its roots back to 1869 SIU is known for its extensive research programs.

Operations

Students across SIU's institutions hail from all 50 states and more than 100 countries. Combined the campuses have some 2600 faculty members and an annual budget of $870 million.

The Carbondale campus was chartered in 1869 as a teachers college while the Edwardsville campus was founded in 1957. Most of the university's doctoral programs are housed at the SIUC campus which conducts residencies through the School of Medicine. A majority of the institutions master's degrees are conferred at the SIUE campus.

Undergraduate and research programs are conducted at both primary SIU campuses. Students and faculty members participate in research programs in a number of fields including biology biodiversity and molecular science. The university receives $78.5 million in research grants annually.

Geographic Reach

From its flagship campus in Carbondale Illinois SIU reaches to Edwardsville and to other parts of Southern Illinois including Springfield through satellite campus locations. Its satellite schools include SIU School of Medicine SIU School of Dental Medicine and SIU School of Nursing.

Financial Performance

SIU logged increases of 2% in fiscal 2012 as compared to 2011 pointing to a rise in student tuition and fees private grants and contracts and sales and services for the gains. Net income for the same reporting period rose 17% due to a boost in non-operating revenues attributable to increases in gifts and contributions investment income and payments on behalf of the university.

Strategy

As part of its focus SIU is working to strengthen its undergraduate graduate and professional education. It's also concentrating on streamlining its administrative process while expanding its inter-

campus and intra-campus collaboration through degree programs international education distributed learning fundraising and research opportunities for both students and faculty. SIU is also establishing partnerships with public and private sector groups.

EXECUTIVES

President, Randy J Dunn
Vice-President, Elaine Hyden
Manager, D R Huppet
Director, Alice Manis
Director, Allen Yates
Director, Bernadean Wheetley
Auditors: CLIFTONLARSONALLEN LLP PEORIA

LOCATIONS

HQ: SOUTHERN ILLINOIS UNIVERSITY INC
　1400 DOUGLAS DR, CARBONDALE, IL 629014332
Phone: 618 536-3475
Web: WWW.SIU.EDU

HISTORICAL FINANCIALS
Company Type: Private

Income Statement FYE: June 30

	REVENUE ($ mil.)	NET INCOME ($ mil.)	NET PROFIT MARGIN	EMPLOYEES
06/16	740	(104)	—	9,576
06/15	597	27	4.6%	—
06/14	694	47	6.8%	—
06/13	706	57	8.2%	—
Annual Growth	1.6%	—	—	—

2016 Year-End Financials

Return on assets: 4.1%　　Cash ($ mil.): 62
Return on equity: (-14.2%)
Current ratio: 1.00

SOUTHERN MAINE HEALTH CARE

EXECUTIVES

Vice President Human Resources, Lorraine Poirier Bouchard
Vice President Support Services, Marc M Fournier
Medical Records Director, Connie Martin
Vice President for Quality and Patient Safety, Nate Wilson
Auditors: MAINEHEALTH PORTLAND ME

LOCATIONS

HQ: SOUTHERN MAINE HEALTH CARE
　1 MEDICAL CENTER DR, BIDDEFORD, ME 040059422
Phone: 207 283-7000
Web: WWW.SMHC.ORG

COMPETITORS

Eastern Maine Healthcare Systems	MaineGeneral Health
Franklin Community Health Network	Mercy Health System of Maine

Company Type: Private

Income Statement FYE: September 30

	REVENUE ($ mil.)	NET INCOME ($ mil.)	NET PROFIT MARGIN	EMPLOYEES
09/15*	256	(5)	—	1,000
04/09	3	0	—	—
03/09	0	(0)	—	—
04/07	0	0	—	—
Annual Growth	—	—	—	—

*Fiscal year change

2015 Year-End Financials

Return on assets: 8.2%　　Cash ($ mil.): 1
Return on equity: (-2.3%)
Current ratio: 0.70

SOUTHERN MINNESOTA BEET SUGAR COOPERATIVE

Southern Minnesota Beet Sugar Cooperative (SMBSC) offers a sweet deal to its approximately 585 member/farmers. The co-op slices about 3 million tons of Minnesota-grown sugar beets annually. Converted products include baker's sugar and fruit sugar as well as molasses beet pulp pellets and shreds and raffinate (liquid from desugaring molasses). The co-op also provides member services such as seed agronomy research farm support products and workers' compensation insurance. SMBSC's refined and liquid sugars are marketed through Cargill Sweeteners; the by-products (dried beet pulp and beet molasses for use in cattle feed) are marketed by Midwest Agri-Commodities in North American and Europe.

Operations

The beet sugar processor's operations consist of a main factory with an annual processing capacity of about 3 million tons of harvested sugar beets. The factory campus comprises settling ponds water-holding lagoons receiving strips off-site receiving stations and 1100 acres of land some of which is planted with grass and irrigated with waste water from the ponds and treatment plant. In addition the co-op has several silos to hold bulk granulated sugar a warehouse to store industrial-size bags of sugar and more than a dozen thick-juice storage tanks. Campus expansions since the factory's start in 1975 have included a molasses desugarization facility increases to processing capacity and new equipment.

The co-op has grown both through investments in added capacity to attract new member/farmers and acquisitions. Acquired in 2005 subsidiary Spreckels Sugar Company operates a beet sugar factory in Brawley California. Sugar produced under the Spreckels Sugar brand is sold to markets in the western US. Based in Sheridan Wyoming SMBSC's Holly Seed a former subsidiary of Imperial Sugar also acquired in 2005 develops beet seed varieties to increase sucrose content and yields. Holly Seed partners with SESVanderHave to supply seeds adapted to growing sugar beets worldwide.

EXECUTIVES

Vice President Of Agriculture, Todd Geselius
Auditors: PRICEWATERHOUSECOOPERS LLP MI

LOCATIONS

HQ: SOUTHERN MINNESOTA BEET SUGAR
  COOPERATIVE
  83550 COUNTY ROAD 21, RENVILLE, MN 562842319
Phone: 320 329-8305
Web: WWW.SMBSC.COM

PRODUCTS/OPERATIONS

Selected Products
Ag liming material
Baker's sugar
Beet pulp pellets
Beet pulp shreds
Fruit sugar
Granulated sugar
Liquid sucrose
Liquid sugar
Molasses
Raffinates
Refined sugar

COMPETITORS

Amalgamated Sugar
 American Crystal Sugar
 C&H Sugar
 Connell Company
 Florida Crystals
 Imperial Sugar
 King Ranch
 M. A. Patout
 Michigan Sugar Company
 Minn-Dak Co-op
 Sterling Sugars
 Sugar Cane Growers Cooperative of Florida
 Sugar Foods
 U.S. Sugar
 United Sugars
 Western Sugar Cooperative

HISTORICAL FINANCIALS

Company Type: Private

Income Statement   FYE: August 31

	REVENUE ($ mil.)	NET INCOME ($ mil.)	NET PROFIT MARGIN	EMPLOYEES
08/16	465	176	37.9%	610
08/15	350	101	28.9%	—
08/14	0	123	—	—
08/13	562	275	49.0%	—
Annual Growth	(6.1%)	(13.8%)	—	—

2016 Year-End Financials

Return on assets: 7.2%   Cash ($ mil.): 11
Return on equity: 37.9%
Current ratio: 0.40

SOUTHERN MINNESOTA MUNICIPAL POWER AGENCY

Lake Wobegon may well get its power from the Southern Minnesota Municipal Power Agency. The power provider supplies wholesale electricity to its 18 member municipal distribution utilities which in turn distribute power to more than 109000 retail customers. The agency's main power source is the 900 MW Sherco 3-power plant generating unit near Becker Minnesota. Southern Minnesota Municipal Power Agency owns 41% of the low-sulfur Western coal fueled plant in partnership Northern States Power Company the unit's operator. It also

relies on a range of intermediate and peaking units owned by the agency's members.

Pushing for more green energy to cut carbon emissions in 2009 the agency was working with Xcel Energy Rochester Public Utilities WPPI Energy and Dairyland Power Cooperative to develop a 150-mile high-voltage line from the Twin Cities to Rochester to LaCrosse Wisconsin. The 345-kV project scheduled for completion in 2020 will increase capacity and allow for tapping power from wind and biomass plants. In 2008 Southern Minnesota Municipal Power Agency signed a 20-year deal to acquire power from 67 turbines at Wapsipinicon Wind Project.

Southern Minnesota Municipal Power Agency was created in 1977.

EXECUTIVES

President, Richard D Kittelson
Board of Directors, Mark E Nibaur
Manager, Laura Sandwick
Engineer, Burnell Folkert
Manager, John O'Neil
Manager, Richard Hettwer
Engineer, Patrick Egan
Auditors: KPMG LLP MINNEAPOLIS MN

LOCATIONS

HQ: SOUTHERN MINNESOTA MUNICIPAL POWER
  AGENCY
  500 1ST AVE SW, ROCHESTER, MN 559023303
Phone: 507 285-0478
Web: WWW.SMMPA.COM

HISTORICAL FINANCIALS

Company Type: Private

Income Statement   FYE: December 31

	REVENUE ($ mil.)	NET INCOME ($ mil.)	NET PROFIT MARGIN	EMPLOYEES
12/15	231	9	4.3%	41
12/14	242	9	3.9%	—
12/13	253	13	5.3%	—
12/12	241	8	3.5%	—
Annual Growth	(1.3%)	5.6%	—	—

2015 Year-End Financials

Return on assets: 1.2%   Cash ($ mil.): —
Return on equity: 4.3%
Current ratio: —

SOUTHERN NEW HAMPSHIRE MEDICAL CENTER

Southern New Hampshire Medical Center (SNHMC) provides medical care for the residents of the Nashua New Hampshire area and surrounding region through Southern New Hampshire Medical Center and Foundation Medical Partners. The two-campus hospital which has about 190 beds and is part of the Southern New Hampshire Health System offers centers for cancer treatment diabetes education fertility and childbirth obesity sleep disorders trauma and other programs. Outpatient and rehabilitation services are offered through several clinic locations. SNHMC is also affiliated with physician practice organization Foundation Medical

Partners and it is a teaching facility for the Dartmouth Medical School.

Geographic Reach

SNHMC's main campus is located in the heart of downtown Nashua New Hampshire and serves patients in the Greater Nashua area.

Operations

The Medical Center has a medical staff of more than 500 primary and specialty care providers from Foundation Medical Partners Dartmouth-Hitchcock Nashua and local independent practices. The Centers partnerships and affiliations include Dartmouth Medical School Dartmouth-Hitchcock Medical Center Lahey Clinic and the Children's Hospital in Boston. In 2013 SNHMC reported 8830 admissions (adult/pediatric/newborn); 5432 total surgical procedures (inpatient and outpatient); 1395 total births (newborn and NICU admits); 42974 emergency department visits; and 225127 outpatient visits. The Center provided $53 million for community benefit in 2013.

Financial Performance

The organization's revenues grew by 4% to $286 million in 2013. Net income decreased by 7% to $22 million that year.

Strategy

SNHMC is expanding its network of medical facilities to keep pace wth demand. In 2013 the system opened its fifth Immediate Care of Southern New Hampshire location at newly constructed medical facilities in Nashua. In 2012 Foundation Medical Partners opened Southern New Hampshire Health System at Pelham.

It is also growing via partnerships. In 2013 Dartmouth-Hitchcock Nashua SNHMC and St. Joseph Healthcare teamed up to establish The Surgery Center of Greater Nashua to bring cost-effective options for surgery patients. The Surgery Center of Greater Nashua's services include orthopedics; sports medicine; general surgery; ear nose and throat; plastic surgery; podiatry; and endoscopy. Upgrading its technology in 2012 SNHMC introduced the da Vinci Surgical System to strengthen its surgical services.

Company Background

In 2011 SNHMC opened Hudson and Merrimack locations to meet the growing needs of the greater Nashua community.

The company was founded as an 8-bed emergency hospital in 1893.

EXECUTIVES

Director of Radiology Services, Diane Dionne
Vice President Operations, Michael Barb
Vice President Operations, Dagan Cloutier
Vice President Information Technology and Chief Information Officer, Andrewa Watt
Vice President Medical Affairs and Chief Medical Officer, Stephanie Wolf-Rosenblum
Associate Vice President of Operations, Elizabeth Armstrong
Physical Therapy, Christine Sweetser
Director of Admissions, Lina Gomez
VICE PRESIDENT HUMAN RESOURCES, Jacqueline F Woolley
DIRECTOR OF HEALTH INFORMATION SERVICES, Joseph A Guglielmo
Auditors: BAKER NEWMAN & NOYES LIMITED

LOCATIONS

HQ: SOUTHERN NEW HAMPSHIRE MEDICAL CENTER
  8 PROSPECT ST, NASHUA, NH 030603925
Phone: 603 577-2000
Web: WWW.SNHHS.ORG

PRODUCTS/OPERATIONS

Selected Medical Services
Aesthetics
Allergy and Immunology

Anesthesia and Pain Management
Arthritis
Asthma
Audiology (Hearing Evaluations for Children)
Auditory Brainstem Response
Clinical Trials and Open Protocols
Ear Nose and Throat
Endocrinology
Family Practice
Genetic Counseling
Geriatric Medicine and Services
Hematology
Hospice Care
Hospitalist Program
Internal Medicine
Kidney Care
Maternity
Nephrology
Neurology
Neurosurgery
Nutrition
Pathology
Plastic Surgery
Podiatry
Pulmonary Medicine
Psychiatry
Pulmonary Rehab Program
Renal Dialysis
Rheumatology
Sleep Center
Sports Medicine
Stroke
Urology
Vascular Services
Specialty Medical Services
Behavioral Health
Cancer Care
Diabetes Care
Digestive Health
Dermatology
Emergency Department
Heart Care
Immediate Care
Laboratory Services
Orthopedics
Pediatric Services
Radiology Services
Rehabilitation Services
Spine and Brain Care
Surgical Services
Women's Services

COMPETITORS

Catholic Medical Center
Concord Hospital
Elliot Health System
Exeter Health Resources
Frisbie Memorial Hospital
Steward Health Care

HISTORICAL FINANCIALS

Company Type: Private

Income Statement

FYE: September 30

	REVENUE ($ mil.)	NET INCOME ($ mil.)	NET PROFIT MARGIN	EMPLOYEES
09/15	215	(8)	—	1,200
09/14	215	38	18.0%	—
09/13	285	32	11.4%	—
09/12	194	16	8.3%	—
Annual Growth	3.4%	—	—	—

2015 Year-End Financials

Return on assets: 6.7%
Return on equity: (-3.9%)
Current ratio: 1.30
Cash ($ mil.): 33

SOUTHERN NEW HAMPSHIRE UNIVERSITY

EXECUTIVES

President, Paul La Blanc
Board of Directors, Kimon S Zachos
Director, Linda Richelson
Director, Tom McDermott
Personnel Manager, Pam Hogan
Auditors: KPMG LLP BOSTON MA

LOCATIONS

HQ: SOUTHERN NEW HAMPSHIRE UNIVERSITY
2500 N RIVER RD, MANCHESTER, NH 031061018
Phone: 603 668-2211
Web: WWW.SNHU.EDU

HISTORICAL FINANCIALS

Company Type: Private

Income Statement

FYE: June 30

	REVENUE ($ mil.)	NET INCOME ($ mil.)	NET PROFIT MARGIN	EMPLOYEES
06/15	449	60	13.5%	1,000
06/14	305	44	14.6%	—
06/13	202	29	14.8%	—
06/12	166	10	6.0%	—
Annual Growth	39.3%	82.1%	—	—

2015 Year-End Financials

Return on assets: 8.8%
Return on equity: 13.5%
Current ratio: —
Cash ($ mil.): 124

SOUTHERN OHIO MEDICAL CENTER

EXECUTIVES

President, Randal M Arnett
Manager, Bridget Scott
Manager, Karen Walburn

LOCATIONS

HQ: SOUTHERN OHIO MEDICAL CENTER
1805 27TH ST, PORTSMOUTH, OH 456622640
Phone: 740 354-5000
Web: WWW.SOMC.ORG

HISTORICAL FINANCIALS

Company Type: Private

Income Statement

FYE: June 30

	REVENUE ($ mil.)	NET INCOME ($ mil.)	NET PROFIT MARGIN	EMPLOYEES
06/15	351	54	15.4%	2,100
06/12	301	15	5.3%	—
06/10	292	17	6.0%	—
06/09	246	5	2.1%	—
Annual Growth	6.0%	48.2%	—	—

2015 Year-End Financials

Return on assets: 8.7%
Return on equity: 15.4%
Current ratio: 0.40
Cash ($ mil.): 23

SOUTHERN STAR CENTRAL GAS PIPELINE, INC.

EXECUTIVES

President, Jerry L Morris
Manager, Sandy Lott
Manager, Jayme Gipson
Director, Chris Brzowski
Director, Daniel Goedde
Manager, Janet Roberson
Vice-President, Robert Carlton

LOCATIONS

HQ: SOUTHERN STAR CENTRAL GAS PIPELINE, INC.
4700 HIGHWAY 56, OWENSBORO, KY 423019303
Phone: 270 852-5000
Web: WWW.SSCGP.COM

HISTORICAL FINANCIALS

Company Type: Private

Income Statement

FYE: December 31

	REVENUE ($ mil.)	NET INCOME ($ mil.)	NET PROFIT MARGIN	EMPLOYEES
12/15	255	46	18.1%	469
12/14	248	48	19.5%	—
12/13	216	32	15.2%	—
12/12	218	39	18.0%	—
Annual Growth	5.4%	5.6%	—	—

2015 Year-End Financials

Return on assets: 5.1%
Return on equity: 18.1%
Current ratio: 0.70
Cash ($ mil.): 7

SOUTHSIDE HOSPITAL

One of Long Island's oldest and largest community hospitals Southside Hospital offers acute care and other services through its more than 340-bed facility. Established in 1913 Southside Hospital operates as part of North Shore-Long Island Jewish Health System (North Shore-LIJ Health System). Its facilities include a Vascular Institute the Frank Gulden Radiation Oncology Center Regional Center for Brain Injury Rehabilitation Southside Hospital Institute of Neurosciences and a Center for Wound Healing. As part of its operations Southside Hospital also provides patients with pain management cardiology outpatient surgery orthopedics and women's services.

Operations

Southside Hospital's Vascular Institute provides diagnosis and care for vascular diseases such as artery diseases (arteriosclerosis aneurysms) and varicose veins (phlebitis deep vein thrombosis).

Strategy

In an effort to establish Southside Hospital as North Shore-LIJ Health System's first tertiary facility in Suffolk County the health system in 2011 extended its cardiac surgery program to Southside Hospital. As part of the four-year $300 million investment the hospital gained a hybrid operating room.

EXECUTIVES

Vice President, Robert Castano
Medical Records Director, Sondra Murdaugh
Co Chairman, Michael Grosso

LOCATIONS

HQ: SOUTHSIDE HOSPITAL
301 E MAIN ST, BAY SHORE, NY 117068458
Phone: 631 968-3000

PRODUCTS/OPERATIONS

Selected Services
Anesthesiology
Bloodless Medicine
Cancer Care
Cardiac Services
Center for Colorectal Health
Emergency Services
Neurosciences
Orthopaedics
Pain Management
Radiology
Rehabilitation
Surgery
Vascular Institute
Women's Health
Wound Healing Center

COMPETITORS

Brookhaven Memorial Hospital Medical Center
Catholic Health Services of Long Island
Good Samaritan Hospital Medical Center
Long Island College Hospital
Mercy Medical Center (NY)
NewYork-Presbyterian Healthcare
NuHealth

HISTORICAL FINANCIALS

Company Type: Private

Income Statement
FYE: December 31

	REVENUE ($ mil.)	NET INCOME ($ mil.)	NET PROFIT MARGIN	EMPLOYEES
12/15	381	(17)	—	1,900
12/14	357	(10)	—	—
12/06	201	(37)	—	—
12/05	0	0	—	—
Annual Growth	—	—	—	—

2015 Year-End Financials
Return on assets: 8.9% Cash ($ mil.): —
Return on equity: (-4.5%)
Current ratio: 0.60

SOUTHWEST GENERAL HEALTH CENTER

EXECUTIVES

President, L Jon Schurmeier
Board of Directors, Thomas A Selden
Administrative Assistant, Elsie Johanson
Clerk, Eda Rostetter
Director, Jeffrey Popp

LOCATIONS

HQ: SOUTHWEST GENERAL HEALTH CENTER
18697 BAGLEY RD, CLEVELAND, OH 441303417
Phone: 440 816-8000
Web: WWW.SWGENERAL.COM

HISTORICAL FINANCIALS

Company Type: Private

Income Statement
FYE: December 31

	REVENUE ($ mil.)	NET INCOME ($ mil.)	NET PROFIT MARGIN	EMPLOYEES
12/15	303	13	4.3%	2,500
12/14	297	21	7.1%	—
12/13	311	23	7.5%	—
12/06	258	(7)	—	—
Annual Growth	1.8%	—	—	—

2015 Year-End Financials
Return on assets: 4.9% Cash ($ mil.): 19
Return on equity: 4.3%
Current ratio: 1.00

SOUTHWEST KEY PROGRAMS, INC.

EXECUTIVES

President, Juan J Sanchez
Board of Directors, Rachel Luna
Manager, Ting Sik Chor
General Manager, Wan Sanchez

LOCATIONS

HQ: SOUTHWEST KEY PROGRAMS, INC.
6002 JAIN LN, AUSTIN, TX 787213104
Phone: 512 462-2181
Web: WWW.SWKEY.ORG

HISTORICAL FINANCIALS

Company Type: Private

Income Statement
FYE: August 31

	REVENUE ($ mil.)	NET INCOME ($ mil.)	NET PROFIT MARGIN	EMPLOYEES
08/16	242	16	6.8%	1,232
08/15	159	8	5.4%	—
08/14	168	13	7.9%	—
08/13	96	2	3.1%	—
Annual Growth	36.1%	77.5%	—	—

2016 Year-End Financials
Return on assets: 2.3% Cash ($ mil.): 39
Return on equity: 6.8%
Current ratio: —

SOUTHWEST LOUISIANA ELECTRIC MEMBERSHIP CORPORATION

Southwest Louisiana Electric Membership Corporation (SLEMCO) is no slowpoke when it comes to serving more than 93400 power customers in eight Louisiana parishes. SLEMCO provides regulated power transmission and distribution services via 9000 miles of power lines to its residential commercial and industrial members. It also provides energy conservation and street and security lighting services. SLEMCO extended assistance to help repair the badly damaged infrastructure in parishes from New Orleans to the Mississippi border following the devastation caused by Hurricane Katrina.

The Enterprise Center of Louisiana a small business incubator project was spearheaded by SLEMCO in the 1980s (and is still supported by the company) to help fledgling businesses with potential establish themselves and mature into successful job-creating enterprises.

SLEMCO was formed in 1937 as a private membership corporation as part of the nationwide push to bring affordable electricity to rural areas.

EXECUTIVES

Board Of Directors, Dennis Broussard
Auditors: BRISCOE BURKE & GRIGSBY LLP T

LOCATIONS

HQ: SOUTHWEST LOUISIANA ELECTRIC
MEMBERSHIP CORPORATION
3420 NE EVANGELINE TRWY, LAFAYETTE, LA
705072554
Phone: 337 896-5384
Web: WWW.SLEMCO.COM

HISTORICAL FINANCIALS

Company Type: Private

Income Statement
FYE: December 31

	REVENUE ($ mil.)	NET INCOME ($ mil.)	NET PROFIT MARGIN	EMPLOYEES
12/15	211	2	1.2%	270
12/08	161	9	5.7%	—
12/07	152	10	6.9%	—
12/06	0	0	—	—
Annual Growth	—	—	—	—

2015 Year-End Financials
Return on assets: 6.5% Cash ($ mil.): 1
Return on equity: 1.2%
Current ratio: 0.30

SOUTHWEST LOUISIANA HOSPITAL ASSOCIATION

EXECUTIVES

President, Larry M Graham
Manager, Pam Bevall
Vice-President, Sherry Haley
Executive Director, Erich Metcalf

LOCATIONS

HQ: SOUTHWEST LOUISIANA HOSPITAL
ASSOCIATION
1701 OAK PARK BLVD, LAKE CHARLES, LA
706018911
Phone: 337 494-2121
Web: WWW.LHAONLINE.ORG

HISTORICAL FINANCIALS

Company Type: Private

Income Statement

				FYE: December 31
	REVENUE ($ mil.)	NET INCOME ($ mil.)	NET PROFIT MARGIN	EMPLOYEES
12/15	262	21	8.1%	1,500
12/14	251	20	8.0%	—
12/13	243	19	8.1%	—
12/09	0	0	26.6%	—
Annual Growth	258.7%	194.2%	—	—

2015 Year-End Financials

Return on assets: 4.5%   Cash ($ mil.): 62
Return on equity: 8.1%
Current ratio: 1.20

SOUTHWEST POWER POOL, INC.

EXECUTIVES

Administrative Assistant, Anne Millam

LOCATIONS

HQ: SOUTHWEST POWER POOL, INC.
201 WORTHEN DR, LITTLE ROCK, AR 722234936
Phone: 501 614-3200
Web: WWW.SPP.ORG

HISTORICAL FINANCIALS

Company Type: Private

Income Statement

				FYE: December 31
	REVENUE ($ mil.)	NET INCOME ($ mil.)	NET PROFIT MARGIN	EMPLOYEES
12/15	180	(40)	—	183
12/14	164	(46)	—	—
12/13	144	(10)	—	—
12/09	101	(11)	—	—
Annual Growth	10.0%	—	—	—

2015 Year-End Financials

Return on assets: 42.5%   Cash ($ mil.): 238
Return on equity: (-22.4%)
Current ratio: 1.00

SOUTHWEST RESEARCH INSTITUTE INC

If you're looking for research at an institute in the Southwest look no further. Founded in 1947 by oilman and rancher Thomas Slick Jr. Southwest Research Institute (SwRI) is an independent not-for-profit research and development institution that contracts to explore subjects in areas including au-

tomation and data systems applied physics space science and engineering and chemistry. SwRI has about 2700 scientists engineers and support staff at some 40 laboratories and offices in the US China and the UK. Customers include the private sector and government agencies. SwRI's Signature Science subsidiary researches national security environmental management and biotechnology.

Operations

SwRI provides contract research and development services to industrial and government clients. It keeps the scope of its work confidential and assigns patent rights arising from its sponsored research to the client. SwRI generally retains rights to Institute-funded advancements and holds more than 900 patents awarded to staff members.

The company operates through nearly a dozen technical divisions including Aerospace Electronics; Systems Engineering & Training; Applied Physics Chemistry & Chemical Engineering; Engine Emissions & Vehicl; Research; Geosciences & Engineering; Mechanical Engineering; and Space Science & Engineering.

Geographic Reach

The company is based in San Antonio Texas and the Institute has technical offices and laboratories in Ann Arbor Michigan.; Beijing China; Boulder Colorado; Hill Air Force Base (Ogden) Utah; Hanover and Rockville Maryland.; Minneapolis Minnesota; Oklahoma City Oklahoma.; Warner Robins Georgia; and Durham New Hampshire.

Strategy

SwRI's current projects include cooperative research focusing on safe reliable cost-effective energy storage systems for electric and hybrid-electric vehicle applications. In addition it has formed a consortium to conduct research and code development and apply advanced ROS (Robot Operating System)software to industrial applications.

EXECUTIVES

Vp Aerospace Electronics And Information Technology, Rick Somers
Vice President Engine And Vehicle Research Division, Nigel Gale
Vice President, Carl Popelar
Executive Manager, Scott Mullin
Executive Vice President and Director, Walter Downing
Vice President Facilities and Service, Paul Easley
Treas-asst Sec, Linda M Boehme
Secretary, Sherilynn Vineyard
Secretary, Dorothea Martinez
Auditors: PADGETT STRATEMANN & CO LL

LOCATIONS

HQ: SOUTHWEST RESEARCH INSTITUTE INC
6220 CULEBRA RD, SAN ANTONIO, TX 782385100
Phone: 210 684-5111
Web: WWW.SWRI.ORG

PRODUCTS/OPERATIONS

Selected Technical Divisions

Aerospace Electronics and Information Technology
Applied Physics
Applied Power
Automation and Data Systems
Chemistry and Chemical Engineering
Engine Emissions and Vehicle Research
Fuels and Lubricants Research
Geosciences and Engineering
Mechanical Engineering
Signal Exploitation and Geolocation
Space Science and Engineering
Training Simulation and Performance Improvement

COMPETITORS

Argonne National Laboratory	Lawrence Livermore Lab
Battelle Memorial	QinetiQ
	Southern Research

Berkeley Lab	Institute
Brookhaven Lab	

HISTORICAL FINANCIALS

Company Type: Private

Income Statement

				FYE: September 30
	REVENUE ($ mil.)	NET INCOME ($ mil.)	NET PROFIT MARGIN	EMPLOYEES
09/16	559	6	1.2%	2,754
09/15	592	23	4.0%	—
09/14	548	7	1.4%	—
09/13	569	29	5.2%	—
Annual Growth	(0.6%)	(38.8%)	—	—

2016 Year-End Financials

Return on assets: 4.5%   Cash ($ mil.): 13
Return on equity: 1.2%
Current ratio: 0.80

SPARTANBURG REGIONAL HEALTHCARE SYSTEM

EXECUTIVES

Principal, Heather Bendyk

LOCATIONS

HQ: SPARTANBURG REGIONAL HEALTHCARE SYSTEM
411 WOODSBERRY SHOALS DR, DUNCAN, SC
293348862
Phone: 864 560-1406

HISTORICAL FINANCIALS

Company Type: Private

Income Statement

				FYE: September 30
	REVENUE ($ mil.)	NET INCOME ($ mil.)	NET PROFIT MARGIN	EMPLOYEES
09/16	1,144	29	2.6%	1
09/14	932	19	2.1%	—
Annual Growth	10.8%	23.4%	—	—

2016 Year-End Financials

Return on assets: 8.8%   Cash ($ mil.): 131
Return on equity: 2.6%
Current ratio: 1.30

SPECIAL SCHOOL DISTRICT OF ST. LOUIS COUNTY

EXECUTIVES

Director, John Koeper
Personnel Manager, Darlene Deloach
Assistant Manager, Hera Didway
Auditors: SCHOWALTER & JABOURI PC ST

LOCATIONS

HQ: SPECIAL SCHOOL DISTRICT OF ST. LOUIS
COUNTY
12110 CLAYTON RD, SAINT LOUIS, MO 631312599
Phone: 314 989-8100
Web: WWW.SSDMO.ORG

HISTORICAL FINANCIALS
Company Type: Private

Income Statement   FYE: June 30

	REVENUE ($ mil.)	NET INCOME ($ mil.)	NET PROFIT MARGIN	EMPLOYEES
06/16	425	23	5.5%	5,204
06/13	366	3	0.9%	—
06/12	381	6	1.7%	—
06/11	0	0	—	—
Annual Growth	—	327.1%	—	—

SPECTRUM HEALTH HOSPITALS

EXECUTIVES

President, Kevin R Splaine
Treasurer, Lori Smith
Vice-President, Shari Schwanzl
Manager, Evana Curo
Executive Director, Aly Mageed
Manager, Jos Van
Manager, Marie Vander

LOCATIONS

HQ: SPECTRUM HEALTH HOSPITALS
100 MICHIGAN ST NE MC-498, GRAND RAPIDS, MI
495032560
Phone: 616 391-1774

HISTORICAL FINANCIALS
Company Type: Private

Income Statement   FYE: June 30

	REVENUE ($ mil.)	NET INCOME ($ mil.)	NET PROFIT MARGIN	EMPLOYEES
06/15	1,764	196	11.1%	11,000
06/08	2,595	(21)	—	—
06/06	1,013	77	7.6%	—
Annual Growth	6.4%	10.9%	—	—

2015 Year-End Financials

Return on assets: 4.7%   Cash ($ mil.): 88
Return on equity: 11.1%
Current ratio: 1.40

SPECTRUM HEALTH SYSTEMS, INC.

EXECUTIVES

Chief Executive Officer, Charles Faris
Board of Directors, Susan Suchocki-Brown
Director, Bruce D Lawrence
Director, Jaes F Connors
Auditors: ERNST & YOUNG LLP

LOCATIONS

HQ: SPECTRUM HEALTH SYSTEMS, INC.
10 MECHANIC ST STE 302, WORCESTER, MA
016082419
Phone: 508 792-1508
Web: WWW.SPECTRUMHEALTHSYSTEMS.ORG

HISTORICAL FINANCIALS
Company Type: Private

Income Statement   FYE: June 30

	REVENUE ($ mil.)	NET INCOME ($ mil.)	NET PROFIT MARGIN	EMPLOYEES
06/15	4,625	352	7.6%	1,000
06/14	56	2	3.9%	—
06/13	51	1	3.1%	—
06/12	47	1	3.5%	—
Annual Growth	358.8%	495.0%	—	—

2015 Year-End Financials

Return on assets: 6.8%   Cash ($ mil.): 296
Return on equity: 7.6%
Current ratio: 0.70

SPOKANE PUBLIC SCHOOLS

EXECUTIVES

Superintendent, Shelley Redinger
Principal, John Andes
Executive Secretary, Mark Walcott
Clerk, Judy Harpster
Supervisor, Michael C Binyon
Office Manager, Donna Cozza
Supervisor, Jared Schantz
Project Manager, Betsy Ressa
Auditors: PAT MCCARTHY OLYMPIA WA

LOCATIONS

HQ: SPOKANE PUBLIC SCHOOLS
200 N BERNARD ST, SPOKANE, WA 992010206
Phone: 509 354-5900
Web: WWW.SPOKANESCHOOLS.ORG

HISTORICAL FINANCIALS
Company Type: Private

Income Statement   FYE: August 31

	REVENUE ($ mil.)	NET INCOME ($ mil.)	NET PROFIT MARGIN	EMPLOYEES
08/16	414	31	7.6%	3,880
08/15	403	6	1.7%	—
08/14	374	(27)	—	—
08/06	298	(35)	—	—
Annual Growth	3.4%	—	—	—

2016 Year-End Financials

Return on assets: 7.4%   Cash ($ mil.): 149
Return on equity: 7.6%
Current ratio: —

SPORTS, INC.

EXECUTIVES

President, John Vallero
Board of Directors, Tony Cardinal
Director, Jim Reed
Director, Steve Kelly
Director, Ed Beall
Auditors: JUNKERMIER CLARK CAMPANELLA

LOCATIONS

HQ: SPORTS, INC.
333 2ND AVE N, LEWISTOWN, MT 594572700
Phone: 406 538-3496
Web: WWW.SPORTSINC.COM

HISTORICAL FINANCIALS
Company Type: Private

Income Statement   FYE: December 31

	REVENUE ($ mil.)	NET INCOME ($ mil.)	NET PROFIT MARGIN	EMPLOYEES
12/15	841	0	0.0%	38
12/14	780	0	0.0%	—
12/13	757	0	0.0%	—
12/12	568	0	0.0%	—
Annual Growth	13.9%	20.4%	—	—

2015 Year-End Financials

Return on assets: 12.7%   Cash ($ mil.): 22
Return on equity: —
Current ratio: 1.00

SPRING BRANCH INDEPENDENT SCHOOL DISTRICT (INC)

EXECUTIVES

Superintendent, Scott R Muri
Accountant, Judy Fread
Manager, Johnny Centineo
Manager, Bill Sanderford
Director, Sheri Alford
Purchasing Director, Barbara Robillard
Auditors: WHITLEY PENN HOUSTON TEXAS

LOCATIONS

HQ: SPRING BRANCH INDEPENDENT SCHOOL
DISTRICT (INC)
955 CAMPBELL RD, HOUSTON, TX 770242803
Phone: 713 464-1511
Web: WWW.DISCOVERWESTHOUSTON.COM

HISTORICAL FINANCIALS
Company Type: Private

Income Statement   FYE: June 30

	REVENUE ($ mil.)	NET INCOME ($ mil.)	NET PROFIT MARGIN	EMPLOYEES
06/16	451	(38)	—	4,484
06/13	353	(67)	—	—
06/11	368	(26)	—	—
06/08	0	0	—	—
Annual Growth	—	—	—	—

2016 Year-End Financials
Return on assets: 1.7%   Cash ($ mil.): 204
Return on equity: (-8.5%)
Current ratio: —

SPRING INDEPENDENT SCHOOL DISTRICT

EXECUTIVES

Administrative Assistant, Alma Villagrana
Director, Gerardo Rochin
Board of Directors, Jeff Mitchell

LOCATIONS

HQ: SPRING INDEPENDENT SCHOOL DISTRICT
16717 ELLA BLVD, HOUSTON, TX 770904213
Phone: 281 891-6000
Web: WWW.SPRINGISD.ORG

HISTORICAL FINANCIALS

Company Type: Private

Income Statement   FYE: June 30

	REVENUE ($ mil.)	NET INCOME ($ mil.)	NET PROFIT MARGIN	EMPLOYEES
06/16	410	13	3.3%	9
06/15	0	0	36.3%	—
06/14*	0	(0)	—	—
12/13	0	(0)	—	—
Annual Growth	4447.4%	—	—	—

*Fiscal year change

2016 Year-End Financials

Return on assets: 1.4%   Cash ($ mil.): 3
Return on equity: 3.3%
Current ratio: —

SPRINGFIELD SCHOOL DISTRICT 186

EXECUTIVES

Superintendent, Jennifer Gill
Finance Manager, Agnes Nunn
Auditors: SIKICH LLP SPRINGFIELD ILLIN

LOCATIONS

HQ: SPRINGFIELD SCHOOL DISTRICT 186
1900 W MONROE ST, SPRINGFIELD, IL 627041531
Phone: 217 525-3000
Web: WWW.SPS186.ORG

SPRINGFIELD SCHOOL DISTRICT R12

EXECUTIVES

Superintendent, Dr John Jungmann
Director, Steven Chodes
Purchasing Director, Kim Mulvaney
Director, Lawrence Anderson
Plant & Facilities Manager, Shawn Bilday
Auditors: WESTBROOK & CO PC RICHMON

LOCATIONS

HQ: SPRINGFIELD SCHOOL DISTRICT R12
1359 E SAINT LOUIS ST, SPRINGFIELD, MO
658023409
Phone: 417 523-0000

HISTORICAL FINANCIALS

Company Type: Private

Income Statement   FYE: June 30

	REVENUE ($ mil.)	NET INCOME ($ mil.)	NET PROFIT MARGIN	EMPLOYEES
06/16	281	(106)	—	3,000
06/15	277	(20)	—	—
06/14	271	144	53.2%	—
06/13	255	(30)	—	—
Annual Growth	3.2%	—	—	—

2016 Year-End Financials

Return on assets: —   Cash ($ mil.): 82
Return on equity: (-37.9%)
Current ratio: —

SPRINGHILL HOSPITALS, INC.

EXECUTIVES

President, Jeffery M St Clair
Officer, James Evans
Manager, Tonya Lambert
Director, Julio Garcia

LOCATIONS

HQ: SPRINGHILL HOSPITALS, INC.
3719 DAUPHIN ST FRNT, MOBILE, AL 366081750
Phone: 251 344-9630
Web: WWW.SPRINGHILLMEDICALCENTER.COM

HISTORICAL FINANCIALS

Company Type: Private

Income Statement   FYE: June 30

	REVENUE ($ mil.)	NET INCOME ($ mil.)	NET PROFIT MARGIN	EMPLOYEES
06/16	216	(0)	—	2,300
06/15	215	(2)	—	—
06/14	219	(10)	—	—
06/13	211	(27)	—	—
Annual Growth	0.8%	—	—	—

HISTORICAL FINANCIALS

Company Type: Private

Income Statement   FYE: December 31

	REVENUE ($ mil.)	NET INCOME ($ mil.)	NET PROFIT MARGIN	EMPLOYEES
12/15	179	6	3.5%	900
12/14	171	5	3.4%	—
12/97	0	0	—	—
12/96	0	0	—	—
Annual Growth	—	—	—	—

2015 Year-End Financials

Return on assets: 3.5%   Cash ($ mil.): 10
Return on equity: 3.5%
Current ratio: 1.40

SPRINGLEAF FINANCE CORPORATION

Personal credit institutions

EXECUTIVES

Pres-ceo, Jay N Levine
Director of Government Relations, Phil Hitz
Vice President Application Systems, David Smith
Executive Vice President Operations, Brad Borchers
Vice President Software Engineering, Erik Peterson
Senior Vice President Of Operations, George Roach
Vice President Tax, Marianne Ford
Vice President Risk Management, Mathew Roe
Senior Vice President Corporate Strategy Springleaf Financial Services, Joseph Tomei
Secretary, Jack R Erkilla
Auditors: PRICEWATERHOUSECOOPERS LLP CH

LOCATIONS

HQ: SPRINGLEAF FINANCE CORPORATION
601 NW 2ND ST, EVANSVILLE, IN 477081013
Phone: 812 424-8031
Web: WWW.SPRINGLEAF.COM

HISTORICAL FINANCIALS

Company Type: Private

Income Statement   FYE: December 31

	ASSETS ($ mil.)	NET INCOME ($ mil.)	INCOME AS % OF ASSETS	EMPLOYEES
12/16	9,719	233	2.4%	3,239
12/15	12,055	129	1.1%	—
12/14	11,126	492	4.4%	—
12/13	12,732	(82)	—	—
Annual Growth	(8.6%)	—	—	—

2016 Year-End Financials

Return on assets: —   Sales ($ mil): 1,924
Return on equity: 12.1%

SRC HOLDINGS CORPORATION

EXECUTIVES

President, John P Stack
Manager, William D Sheppard
Chief Financial Officer, Jo Miles
Vice-President, Craig Keeling
Manager, Joe Hoffman
Personnel Director, Keith Boatright
Engineer, Mark Holton
Auditors: KPM CPAS & ADVISORS SPRINGFIE

LOCATIONS

HQ: SRC HOLDINGS CORPORATION
531 S UNION AVE, SPRINGFIELD, MO 658022659
Phone: 417 862-2337
Web: WWW.SRCHOLDINGS.COM

HISTORICAL FINANCIALS

Company Type: Private

Income Statement

FYE: January 31

	REVENUE ($ mil.)	NET INCOME ($ mil.)	NET PROFIT MARGIN	EMPLOYEES
01/16	403	17	4.4%	1,000
01/15	383	24	6.3%	—
01/13	357	22	6.2%	—
01/12	273	17	6.3%	—
Annual Growth	10.1%	0.5%	—	—

2016 Year-End Financials

Return on assets: 7.8%   Cash ($ mil.): 8
Return on equity: 4.4%
Current ratio: 0.80

SRI INTERNATIONAL

SRI International sometimes called "Silicon Valley's soul" is a not-for-profit think tank pondering advances in biotechnology chemicals and energy computer science electronics and public policy — and ways to commercialize those advances. It focuses on technology research and development business strategies and analysis. The organization has patents and patent applications in IT communications robotics and pharmaceuticals. SRI's clients have included Samsung General Motors and AT&T. The artificial intelligence it designed for the Department of Defense became Apple's Siri. Originally founded in 1946 as Stanford Research Institute SRI became fully independent in 1970.

Operations

SRI has conceived such innovations as the computer mouse magnetic encoding for checks and high-definition television not to mention some of the foundations of personal computing the Internet and stealth technology. It also provides basic and applied research laboratory and advisory services tech development and venture opportunities.

Geographic Reach

SRI operates 17 offices across the US (California Connecticut Florida Maryland Michigan Montana New Jersey Pennsylvania Texas and Virginia) along with four international offices in Puerto Rico Dubai Japan and Greenland. The organization's 2500 employees (including about 1000 scientists and researchers) work at research centers worldwide.

Sales and Marketing

SRI brings its research and development innovations to the marketplace by licensing its intellectual property and creating new ventures. SRI has created and launched more than 50 ventures with a total market capitalization exceeding $20 billion. It has conducted more than $4 billion in R&D since the early 2000s for clients and partners and worked with government partners including the National Institutes of Health and the Defense Advanced Research Projects Agency for more than 50 years. In fact Department of Defense clients contributed about 63% of sales in 2013. Its venture partners include Draper Fisher Jurvetson Horizon Ventures Intel Capital Khosla Ventures Kleiner Perkins Caufield & Byers and Mayfield Fund.

Financial Performance

After years of climbing revenue SRI reported an 8% drop in 2013 from $585 to $540.

Strategy

SRI continues to invest in R&D on behalf of its clients. In 2013 it completed a new $2.8 million 40000-square-foot bioscience research and development facility in Virginia.

In 2014 the company sold its fourth artificial intelligence platform Desti a smart travel planner to mobile device maker Nokia. Other AI projects include Siri content discovery engine Trapit and productivity app Tempo AI; together they brought SRI more than $20 billion.

HISTORY

In the 1920s Stanford University professor Robert Swain envisioned a research center devoted to chemistry physics and biology. Swain received support from university president Ray Lyman and alumnus Herbert Hoover but the Great Depression and WWII postponed the venture.

Finally in 1946 the Stanford Research Institute was formed in conjunction with the university. That year the David Sarnoff Research Center invented the color TV tube under the wing of RCA Laboratories.

During Stanford Research's early years it worked on such projects as logistics for Disneyland magnetic ink for character recognition and strategies for combating air pollution. The think tank was the focus of student protests in the 1960s because of its defense work. In 1969 Stanford Research Institute was one of four nodes on the first computer network the ARPANET. It became fully independent in 1970 as SRI International.

During the 1960s and 1970s SRI won large contracts from the US Department of Defense for research in such areas as radar speech recognition and noise cancellation technologies. It got a tremendous boost in 1987 when longtime client General Electric gave SRI the Sarnoff Research Center (as a tax write-off) plus $250 million in business along with $65.2 million in cash.

In 1993 SRI founded Pangene to commercialize gene cloning and analysis technology. The next year it founded GeneTrace to develop genetics-related products for biomedical research and Nuance Communications to commercialize speech-recognition products. Intuitive Surgical which develops minimally invasive surgical technologies was formed in 1995.

SRI developed two key components for use in an improved mail sorting program which the US Postal Service announced in 1997 it would use to save millions in processing costs. The David Sarnoff Research Center changed its name to Sarnoff Corporation that year.

In 1998 SRI and the National Science Foundation teamed to develop innovative science and math teaching programs. The following year SRI began working with network equipment leader Cisco Systems and the US Army to develop a voice and multimedia communications system for the military. In 2001 SRI partnered with SPEEDCOM Wireless to co-develop wireless technology.

In order to complement its biosciences division SRI bought Quality Clinical Labs (QCL) a few years later. QCL was a California-based clinical pathology analysis center specializing in clinical hematology and chemistry evaluations.

SRI's former subsidiary the Sarnoff Corporation fully integrated into SRI's operations during 2011.

EXECUTIVES

President Information and Computing Sciences, William Mark
President Advanced Technology and Systems, Scott Seaton
CEO, William Jeffrey
VP; President Products and Solutions, Mark A. Clifton
SVP Shared Services, Michael Page
VP CFO and Treasurer, Luther Lau
VP; President SRI Ventures, Manish Kothari
VP; President SRI Education, Denise Glyn Borders
VP Corporate and Marketing Communications, Katie Keating
President SRI Biosciences, Greg Kovacs
Vp Human Resources, Jeanie Tooker
Vice President Human Resources, Jean Tooker
Vice President, Eric Pearson
Chairman, Mariann Byerwalter, age 57
Auditors: PRICEWATERHOUSECOOPERS LLP SA

LOCATIONS

HQ: SRI INTERNATIONAL
333 RAVENSWOOD AVE, MENLO PARK, CA 940253493
Phone: 650 859-2000
Web: WWW.SRI.COM

PRODUCTS/OPERATIONS

Selected Research Areas

Biosciences Health and Medical Systems
Chemistry Materials and Energy
Computing and Information Technology
Defense and Security
Education and Learning
Ocean and Space
Robotics Sensors and Devices

COMPETITORS

Aerospace Corporation	PAREXEL
Battelle Memorial	QuintilesIMS
Bayer Corp.	RAND Corporation
CACI International	Research Triangle
Charles Stark Draper	Institute
Laboratory	SwRI
DaVinci Institute	University of
DuPont	California
MIT	Wellcome Trust
MITRE	Westat

HISTORICAL FINANCIALS

Company Type: Private

Income Statement

FYE: December 26

	REVENUE ($ mil.)	NET INCOME ($ mil.)	NET PROFIT MARGIN	EMPLOYEES
12/15	507	2	0.5%	2,437
12/14	539	0	0.0%	—
12/13	550	2	0.5%	—
12/12	560	(5)	—	—
Annual Growth	(3.2%)	—	—	—

2015 Year-End Financials

Return on assets: 12.2%   Cash ($ mil.): 2
Return on equity: 0.5%
Current ratio: 1.30

ST BARNABAS MEDICAL CTR

Part of the Saint Barnabas Health Care System Saint Barnabas Medical Center is a 600-bed acute-care hospital that provides a full range of health services to residents of Livingston New Jersey and surrounding areas. The not-for-profit medical center provides general inpatient and outpatient care programs as well as burn and perinatal care. It also houses units specializing in organ transplant stroke care cardiac surgery and comprehensive cancer treatment. Its Institute for Reproductive Medicine and Science provides assisted reproductive technology services. Saint Barnabas Medical Center treats some 35000 inpatients and more than 85000 emergency-room patients each year.

Operations

In combination with its satellite Saint Barnabas Ambulatory Care Center the medical center serves about 300000 outpatients per year. Saint Barnabas Medical Center is also a teaching affiliate of several regional schools including the University of Medicine and Dentistry of New Jersey and Drexel University College of Medicine.

Company Background

New Jersey's first hospital Saint Barnabas Medical Center was founded in 1865 in a private home.

EXECUTIVES

SENIOR VICE PRESIDENT FOR COMPLIANCE, Jonathan Barkhorn
Medical Director, Adrian L Connolly
Vice President, Tamara Cunningham

LOCATIONS

HQ: ST BARNABAS MEDICAL CTR
94 OLD SHORT HILLS RD # 1, LIVINGSTON, NJ 070395668
Phone: 973 322-5000
Web: WWW.BARNABASHEALTH.ORG

COMPETITORS

Atlantic Health
Children's Specialized Hospital
Chilton Medical Center
East Orange General Hospital
Hackensack Meridian Health
Hackensack University Medical Center
JFK Medical Center
Newark Beth Israel Medical Center
Raritan Bay Medical Center
Robert Wood Johnson University Hospital
Robert Wood Johnson University Hospital at Rahway
Saint Peter's University Hospital
St. Joseph's Healthcare System
Trinitas Regional Medical Center
Virtua Health

HISTORICAL FINANCIALS

Company Type: Private

Income Statement

FYE: December 31

	REVENUE ($ mil.)	NET INCOME ($ mil.)	NET PROFIT MARGIN	EMPLOYEES
12/15	728	87	12.0%	4,000
12/14	730	86	11.8%	—
12/13	685	79	11.6%	—
12/12	652	74	11.5%	—
Annual Growth	3.7%	5.3%	—	—

2015 Year-End Financials

Return on assets: 7.7%
Return on equity: 12.0%
Current ratio: 0.40
Cash ($ mil.): —

ST CHARLES COMMUNITY UNIT SCHOOL DISTRICT 303

EXECUTIVES

Superintendent, Donald Schlomann
Accountant, Wendy Sedwick
Board of Directors, Edward McNally

LOCATIONS

HQ: ST CHARLES COMMUNITY UNIT SCHOOL DISTRICT 303
201 S 7TH ST, SAINT CHARLES, IL 601742664
Phone: 331 228-2000
Web: WWW.D303.ORG

HISTORICAL FINANCIALS

Company Type: Private

Income Statement

FYE: June 30

	REVENUE ($ mil.)	NET INCOME ($ mil.)	NET PROFIT MARGIN	EMPLOYEES
06/16*	220	3	1.5%	1,700
03/15	0	0	0.7%	—
06/09	0	(0)	—	—
06/06	10	0	2.8%	—
Annual Growth	35.6%	27.0%	—	—

*Fiscal year change

ST JOHN MACOMB-OAKLAND HOSPITAL

EXECUTIVES

Principal, Kam Parekh
Auditors: DELOITTE TAX LLP CINCINNATI

LOCATIONS

HQ: ST JOHN MACOMB-OAKLAND HOSPITAL
28000 DEQUINDRE RD, WARREN, MI 480922468
Phone: 586 753-0094
Web: WWW.STJOHN.ORG

HISTORICAL FINANCIALS

Company Type: Private

Income Statement

FYE: June 30

	REVENUE ($ mil.)	NET INCOME ($ mil.)	NET PROFIT MARGIN	EMPLOYEES
06/15	405	24	6.1%	23
06/14	398	24	6.2%	—
Annual Growth	1.7%	(0.0%)	—	—

2015 Year-End Financials

Return on assets: 6.8%
Return on equity: 6.1%
Current ratio: 4.70
Cash ($ mil.): —

ST JOHNS HOSPITAL SISTERS OF THE THIRD ORDER OF ST FRANCIS

Truck-struck Homer Simpson might use his last gasp trying to blurt out "St. John's Hospital of the Hospital Sisters of the Third Order of St. Francis-Springfield" to his ambulance driver but he might be better off using the hospital's more common name St. John's. D'oh! The 440-bed St. John's Hospital serves residents of central and southern Illinois with general and specialized health care services. The teaching hospital affiliated with Southern Illinois University's School of Medicine has centers devoted to women and children's health trauma cardiac care cancer orthopedics and neurology. It also operates area health clinics. Founded in 1875 St. John's is part of the Hospital Sisters Health System.

Operations

The facility is Hospital Sisters Health System's flagship hospital. It has grown to boast about 700 physicians podiatrists and dentists from more than 30 specialties. In addition to educating medical students through Southern Illinois University's School of Medicine St. Johns also supports those working on careers in nursing through its own nursing school St. John's College. It also offers courses in pharmacy pathology respiratory therapy and electroneurodiagnostics (brain disorder diagnostics) professions.

St. John's physicians perform more than 15000 surgical procedures each year. It also receives some 54000 emergency department visits and helps deliver about 2000 babies annually.

Financial Performance

In 2014 revenue fell 26% to $450 million; this was primarily due to an 89% decline in contributions investments and foundation assets.

Strategy

The hospital has been expanding its offerings to provide more specialized services to area residents. Recent additions include 3-D mammographies and expanded children's surgical services. St. John's is also focused on improving access to health care through technology such as telemedicine. In 2014 it partnered with Greenville Regional Hospital to provide advanced treatment to stroke patients at their home hospital through STAT Stroke TeleMedicine.

Other strategic initiatives at the hospital include increasing doctor and nurse retention rates growing nursing school enrollment rates and increasing patient satisfaction scores. Part of its efforts to reach more patients has led St. John's to open new outpatient health centers in areas near the main hospital facility. The hospital has also renovated its main buildings including the revamp of its day surgery and intermediate care departments.

EXECUTIVES

Chief Executive Officer, Charles Lucore
Director, Nelson Darrow
Auditors: CROWE HORWATH LLP CHICAGO IL

LOCATIONS

HQ: ST JOHNS HOSPITAL SISTERS OF THE THIRD ORDER OF ST FRANCIS
800 E CARPENTER ST, SPRINGFIELD, IL 627690002
Phone: 217 544-6464
Web: WWW.SJCHILDRENS.COM

PRODUCTS/OPERATIONS

2014 Sales

	% of total
Amount generated for taking care patients excluding provision	95
Other contributions	5
Other	-
Total	**100**

Selected Services

AthletiCare
Behavioral Health Services
Birth Center
Cancer Institute
Center for Living
Children's Hospital
Connect
Emergency/Trauma Care
Gastroenterology
Health Centers | Priority Care
Home Health
Hospice
Intensive Care Unit
Lab
Neurosciences Institute
Orthopedics
Pain Management Center
Prairie Heart Institute
Radiology
Regional Wound Care Center
Sleep Center
Stroke Treatment
Surgery | daVinci
TherapyCare | Rehab
Third Age Living
Women's Services

COMPETITORS

Advocate Health Care	Memorial Health System
Blessing Hospital	Memorial Hospital
Community Health	(Illinois)
Systems	Southern Illinois
Decatur Memorial	Healthcare
Hospital	

HISTORICAL FINANCIALS

Company Type: Private

Income Statement   FYE: June 30

	REVENUE ($ mil.)	NET INCOME ($ mil.)	NET PROFIT MARGIN	EMPLOYEES
06/15	501	3	0.8%	3,000
06/14	500	10	2.1%	—
06/08	393	(8)	—	—
06/05	387	50	13.1%	—
Annual Growth	2.6%	(22.5%)	—	—

2015 Year-End Financials

Return on assets: 6.2%
Return on equity: 0.8%
Current ratio: 0.30
Cash ($ mil.): 11

ST JOSEPH'S MEDICAL CENTER

EXECUTIVES

President, Adam Rees
Principal, Tracy Galles
Manager, Bobbie Bedard
Manager, Mark Wassink
Director, Nicholas P Bernier

LOCATIONS

HQ: ST JOSEPH'S MEDICAL CENTER
  523 N 3RD ST, BRAINERD, MN 564013098
Phone: 218 829-2861
Web: WWW.SJMCMN.ORG

HISTORICAL FINANCIALS

Company Type: Private

Income Statement   FYE: June 30

	REVENUE ($ mil.)	NET INCOME ($ mil.)	NET PROFIT MARGIN	EMPLOYEES
06/15	183	10	5.7%	1,400
06/14	172	8	4.9%	—
06/13	164	2	1.3%	—
06/12	162	(1)	—	—
Annual Growth	4.3%	—	—	—

2015 Year-End Financials

Return on assets: 2.5%
Return on equity: 5.7%
Current ratio: 1.20
Cash ($ mil.): 3

ST LOUIS CHILDREN'S HOSPITAL

EXECUTIVES

President, Joan Magruder
Officer, Charles Dougherty

LOCATIONS

HQ: ST LOUIS CHILDREN'S HOSPITAL
  1 CHILDRENS PL, SAINT LOUIS, MO 631101081
Phone: 314 454-6000
Web: WWW.STLOUISCHILDRENS.ORG

HISTORICAL FINANCIALS

Company Type: Private

Income Statement   FYE: December 31

	REVENUE ($ mil.)	NET INCOME ($ mil.)	NET PROFIT MARGIN	EMPLOYEES
12/15	527	50	9.5%	2,959
12/14	513	36	7.1%	—
Annual Growth	2.8%	37.7%	—	—

2015 Year-End Financials

Return on assets: 0.9%
Return on equity: 9.5%
Current ratio: 1.30
Cash ($ mil.): —

ST LUKE'S-ROOSEVELT HOSPITAL CENTER

EXECUTIVES

Treasurer, Steven Hochberg
Director, Louis B Harrison
Auditors: ERNST & YOUNG US LLP INDIANAP

LOCATIONS

HQ: ST LUKE'S-ROOSEVELT HOSPITAL CENTER
  1111 AMSTERDAM AVE, NEW YORK, NY 100251716
Phone: 212 523-4000
Web: WWW.STLUKESHOSPITALNYC.ORG

HISTORICAL FINANCIALS

Company Type: Private

Income Statement   FYE: December 31

	REVENUE ($ mil.)	NET INCOME ($ mil.)	NET PROFIT MARGIN	EMPLOYEES
12/15	859	61	7.1%	6,000
12/14	1,160	(17)	—	—
Annual Growth	(25.9%)	—	—	—

2015 Year-End Financials

Return on assets: 10.5%
Return on equity: 7.1%
Current ratio: 0.80
Cash ($ mil.): 63

ST MARY'S COUNTY PUBLIC SCHOOLS

EXECUTIVES

Superintendent, James Smith
Director, Mark Smith
Program Manager, Sarah Tyson
Administrative Assistant, Sherri Gray
Purchasing Agent, Tanya Parker
Plant & Facilities Manager, Steve Whidden
Assistant Manager, Tammy McCourt

LOCATIONS

HQ: ST MARY'S COUNTY PUBLIC SCHOOLS
  23160 MOAKLEY ST STE 101, LEONARDTOWN, MD
  206502933
Phone: 301 475-5511
Web: WWW.SMCPS.ORG

HISTORICAL FINANCIALS

Company Type: Private

Income Statement   FYE: June 30

	REVENUE ($ mil.)	NET INCOME ($ mil.)	NET PROFIT MARGIN	EMPLOYEES
06/16	239	4	1.7%	1,689
06/15	252	7	3.1%	—
Annual Growth	(5.1%)	(46.1%)	—	—

2016 Year-End Financials

Return on assets: 1.9%
Return on equity: 1.7%
Current ratio: —
Cash ($ mil.): 33

ST MICHAELS HOSPITAL INC

EXECUTIVES

President, Jeffery Martin
Director, Kim Peterson

Plant & Facilities Manager, Brian Schulist
Supervisor, Mary West
Auditors: LB DELOITTE TAX LLP MILWAUKEE

LOCATIONS

HQ: ST MICHAELS HOSPITAL INC
   900 ILLINOIS AVE, STEVENS POINT, WI 544813196
Phone: 715 346-5000
Web: WWW.SMHOSP.ORG

HISTORICAL FINANCIALS
Company Type: Private

Income Statement   FYE: June 30

	REVENUE ($ mil.)	NET INCOME ($ mil.)	NET PROFIT MARGIN	EMPLOYEES
06/15*	192	12	6.7%	1,900
09/10	176	13	7.7%	—
09/09	173	8	4.8%	—
09/07	1,661	0	—	—
Annual Growth	—	330.8%	—	—

*Fiscal year change

2015 Year-End Financials
Return on assets: 10.5%   Cash ($ mil.): 22
Return on equity: 6.7%
Current ratio: 2.30

ST PATRICK HOSPITAL CORPORATION

Feeling a little green? St. Patrick Hospital and Health Sciences Center is there to help. The not-for-profit hospital boasts some 250 beds (acute-care and transitional) and serves nearly 20 counties in and around Missoula Montana. Its specialty services include cancer treatment surgery and occupational health. The center also provides Life Flight air transport to critically ill or injured patients. The hospital provides outpatient primary and specialty care through a host of affiliated physician practices and clinics throughout the area. St. Patrick Hospital and Health Sciences Center is part of Providence Health & Services which has two hospitals and more than 40 clinics across Montana.

Operations

The center's facility annual admits more than 7900 patients and logs more than 37900 days of patient care. Its physician offices and outpatient services are located adjacent to the hospital. They comprise the Western Montana Clinic the Montana Neuroscience Institute the Montana Cancer Center and the International Heart Institute. Outpatient services provided by St. Patrick Hospital and Health Sciences Center include physical occupational speech diabetic and cardiac rehabilitation.

In 2013 the hospital was awarded Magnet recognition by the American Nurses Credentialing Center's Magnet Recognition Program.

Geographic Reach

St. Patrick Hospital and Health Sciences Center serves those who reside in Missoula Montana and the surrounding counties which generate 95% of its patient volume.

Strategy

St. Patrick Hospital and Health Sciences Center is looking to expand its comprehensive women's and children's services. Its new services will include inpatient obstetrical and newborn care (with a Level 2 neonatal intensive care unit); an expanded inpatient and outpatient pediatric program; and outpatient obstetrical/gynecological and perinatology care.

Company Background

St. Patrick Hospital and Health Sciences Center was founded in 1873 by the Sisters of Providence.

EXECUTIVES

Infection Control Director, Tammy Powers
Medical Librarian, Dana Kopp
Ambulatory Services Director, Mark Wakai
Radiology Director, CHRIS WATSON

LOCATIONS

HQ: ST PATRICK HOSPITAL CORPORATION
   500 W BROADWAY ST, MISSOULA, MT 598024008
Phone: 406 543-7271
Web: WWW.SAINTPATRICK.ORG

PRODUCTS/OPERATIONS

Selected Services
Cardiology
Cancer Center
Diabetes Care Center
Diagnostic Imaging
Emergency Department
First STEP
Joint Replacement
Laboratory
Life Flight
Neurobehavioral Medicine
Neurology
Broadway Pharmacy
Rehabilitation
Sleep Center
Stroke Center
Surgery

COMPETITORS

Billings Clinic   St. James Healthcare
Glendive Medical   Wyoming Medical Center
Center
St. Alexius Medical
Center

HISTORICAL FINANCIALS
Company Type: Private

Income Statement   FYE: December 31

	REVENUE ($ mil.)	NET INCOME ($ mil.)	NET PROFIT MARGIN	EMPLOYEES
12/15	289	15	5.3%	1,460
12/05	191	8	4.3%	—
12/04	163	6	3.8%	—
12/02	0	0	—	—
Annual Growth	—	—	—	—

2015 Year-End Financials
Return on assets: 4.2%   Cash ($ mil.): 1
Return on equity: 5.3%
Current ratio: 1.90

ST PETER'S HEALTH PARTNERS

EXECUTIVES

Chief Executive Officer, Ann Errichettii
Program Manager, Sandra Cummings
Administrative Assistant, Kim Tomlinson
Clerk, Alan Brandon
Accountant, Catherine Obidos
Officer, Anne Simpson

LOCATIONS

HQ: ST PETER'S HEALTH PARTNERS
   315 S MANNING BLVD, ALBANY, NY 122081707
Phone: 518 525-1550
Web: WWW.SPHCS.ORG

HISTORICAL FINANCIALS
Company Type: Private

Income Statement   FYE: June 30

	REVENUE ($ mil.)	NET INCOME ($ mil.)	NET PROFIT MARGIN	EMPLOYEES
06/15	527	44	8.5%	6,000
06/14	509	21	4.1%	—
/* 0				
Annual Growth	—	—	—	—

*Fiscal year change

2015 Year-End Financials
Return on assets: 6.1%   Cash ($ mil.): 37
Return on equity: 8.5%
Current ratio: 3.20

ST. AGNES HEALTHCARE, INC.

If you're in agony in Charm City St. Agnes HealthCare is here to help. The Catholic health system provides a spectrum of medical services to the residents of southwest Baltimore. Its flagship facility St. Agnes Hospital has 276 beds and offers a comprehensive range of medical and surgical services including treatment in areas such as oncology cardiovascular disease bariatric medicine women's health plastic surgery and orthopedics. The system also includes a multispecialty physicians group (Seton Medical Group) and a diagnostic imaging center. St. Agnes HealthCare is a member of Ascension Health. The health system traces its roots to 1862 when the Daughters of Charity set up a local infirmary in 1862.

Operations

St. Agnes Hospital handles about 25000 inpatient visits each year as well as 84000 emergency room visits 11000 surgeries and 2000 births. The medical center is also a teaching facility providing training programs including residencies in a number of medical and surgical specialties including advanced laparoscopic surgery internal medicine and surgical oncology.

Financial Performance

St. Agnes Hospital reported revenues of $423 million for fiscal 2012. It also reported total assets of more than $520 million and income from recurring operations of nearly $22 million.

Strategy

St. Agnes Hospital has completed a $200 million multi-year campus revitalization project. The project included a new patient tower which opened in 2011 as well as a parking garage and the Hackerman-Patz House for families of patients being treated for long-term ailments. The final phase completed in 2013 was the opening of a new 60000-square-foot medical office building providing specialties including cardiology respiratory care renal care and an expanded cancer center.

St. Agnes HealthCare plans to further expand its facilities in future years to meet the rising needs of its service territory. For instance in 2013 the organization announced plans to develop a mixed-use center that will provide community services

including senior housing and recreation facilities. The organization also opened a new primary care facility in Baltimore during 2013.

In addition St. Agnes Hospital is part of a quality improvement collaboration with St. Joseph Medical Center called Mission Health Partners. The initiative is designed to expand access to health care in the region through the sharing of resources and best practices.

EXECUTIVES

Medical Director Of The Breast Center, Diana Griffiths
Assistant Vice President Cancer Services, Mary Austin
Director of Payor and Government Relations, Lori Franklin
Vice Chairman, Barbara Bozzuto
Board Director, Norman Frost

LOCATIONS

HQ: ST. AGNES HEALTHCARE, INC.
900 S CATON AVE, BALTIMORE, MD 212295201
Phone: 667 234-6000
Web: WWW.STAGNES.ORG

COMPETITORS

Anne Arundel Medical Center	Johns Hopkins Health System
Bon Secours Health	Levindale Hospital
Doctors Community Hospital	LifeBridge Health
Franklin Square Hospital Center	MedStar Health
GBMC	MedStar Union Memorial Hospital
Good Samaritan Hospital of Maryland	Sinai Hospital of Baltimore
Harbor Hospital	University of Maryland Medical System

HISTORICAL FINANCIALS

Company Type: Private

Income Statement				FYE: June 30
	REVENUE ($ mil.)	NET INCOME ($ mil.)	NET PROFIT MARGIN	EMPLOYEES
06/15	438	23	5.3%	2,506
06/10	400	50	12.7%	—
06/09	336	(11)	—	—
06/08	0	0	—	—
Annual Growth	—	—	—	—

2015 Year-End Financials

Return on assets: 10.7%
Return on equity: 5.3%
Current ratio: 1.10
Cash ($ mil.): 13

ST. ALEXIUS MEDICAL CENTER

EXECUTIVES

Chief Executive Officer, Len Wilk
VP Finance, Robin Chapp
Vice-President, John Sullivan
Engineer, Alexander Darnall
Auditors: DELOITTE TAX LLP CHICAGO IL

LOCATIONS

HQ: ST. ALEXIUS MEDICAL CENTER
1555 BARRINGTON RD BLDG 1, HOFFMAN ESTATES, IL 601691099
Phone: 847 884-9800
Web: WWW.ALEXIANBROTHERSHEALTH.ORG

HISTORICAL FINANCIALS

Company Type: Private

Income Statement				FYE: June 30
	REVENUE ($ mil.)	NET INCOME ($ mil.)	NET PROFIT MARGIN	EMPLOYEES
06/15	351	42	12.1%	1,500
06/14	344	30	8.9%	—
06/13*	327	29	9.1%	—
12/08	280	21	7.7%	—
Annual Growth	3.9%	11.9%	—	—

*Fiscal year change

2015 Year-End Financials

Return on assets: 4.2%
Return on equity: 12.1%
Current ratio: 3.40
Cash ($ mil.): —

ST. ALEXIUS MEDICAL CENTER

Established in 1885 CHI St. Alexius Health (formerly St. Alexius Medical Center) has been serving the health care needs of those who reside in the Dakotas and Montana longer than any other area hospital. The medical facility with more than 300 beds caters to central and western North Dakota and parts of South Dakota and Montana. Specialty services include cancer care trauma care geriatrics orthopedics and rehabilitation. As part of its operations the longtime hospital also owns and manages a handful of smaller regional hospitals and community clinics. In 2014 St. Alexius joined the Catholic Health Initiatives health care system.

Operations

In 2014 the hospital performed 3372 inpatient and 7611 outpatient surgeries. It reported 57021 emergency department visits.

Affiliated organizations include Northland Pace Northland Health Care Alliance Primcare Health Group and Bismarck Cancer Center.

Geographic Reach

In addition to its main campus in Bismarck North Dakota CHI St. Alexius Health owns and operates hospitals in Garrison North Dakota; and Turtle Lake North Dakota. It manages hospitals and clinics owned by Mobridge Regional Hospital in South Dakota; and owns and operates a primary care clinic in Mandan North Dakota. Finally the hospital owns and operates specialty and primary care clinics in Minot North Dakota.

Strategy

CHI St. Alexius Health opened a new dialysis unit in Dickinson North Dakota in 2015.

EXECUTIVES

Vice President Community Services, Julie Jeske
Radiology Medical Director, Douglas Peterson
Pharmd, Carrie Sorenson
Department Chairman, Elizabeth Hughes
Physical Therapy Director, JAY BAUER
Operating Room Director, Jane Schmaltz

LOCATIONS

HQ: ST. ALEXIUS MEDICAL CENTER
900 E BROADWAY AVE, BISMARCK, ND 585014520
Phone: 701 530-7000
Web: WWW.ST.ALEXIUS.ORG

PRODUCTS/OPERATIONS

Selected Services
Acceleration
Arthritis Clinic
Balance and Dizziness Center
Behavioral and Mental Health
Cardiac Rehabilitation
Clinical Research Services
Community Health
Community Pharmacy
Deep Brain Stimulation
Dialysis
EAP
Emergency & Trauma
Family Practice Clinic
Geriatrics (Older Adults)
Heart and Vascular Center
Home Care and Hospice
Human Performance Center
Kidney Dialysis
Mandan Clinic
Minot Medical Clinic
Neonatology Clinic
Nephrology Clinic
Neurology
Neuroscience
Neurosurgery
Occupational Health and Wellness Occupation
Orthopedics
Pediatric Cardiology Clinic
Pediatric Neurology Clinic
Physical Medicine & Rehabilitation Physical T
Radiology Services Rehabilita
Spine Center
Stroke Center
Surgical Services
Telemedicine and Videoconferencing Services
Therapy at HPC
Urology Clinic
Women's Health

COMPETITORS

Altru Health	Sanford
Avera Health	Health-MeritCare
Billings Clinic	
Catholic Health Initiatives	

HISTORICAL FINANCIALS

Company Type: Private

Income Statement				FYE: June 30
	REVENUE ($ mil.)	NET INCOME ($ mil.)	NET PROFIT MARGIN	EMPLOYEES
06/15	289	148	51.2%	1,947
06/14	308	14	4.6%	—
06/13	291	(1)	—	—
06/12	294	11	3.7%	—
Annual Growth	(0.6%)	137.9%	—	—

2015 Year-End Financials

Return on assets: 6.3%
Return on equity: 51.2%
Current ratio: 1.70
Cash ($ mil.): 28

ST. ANTHONY'S MEDICAL CENTER

St. Anthony's Medical Center applies its skills to medical cases in the Midwest. The hospital serves residents in the areas surrounding St. Louis Missouri as well as portions of southwestern Illinois. With about 770 beds and some 800 affiliated physicians the hospital provides a comprehensive offering including inpatient and outpatient medical surgical diagnostic and behavioral health care. The hospital operates a level II trauma center cancer and chest pain units and a pediatric emergency center as well as several urgent care facilities. It also offers home health hospice laboratory and pharmacy services. St. Anthony's Medical Center was founded in 1900 by the Franciscan Sisters of Germany.

Operations

St. Anthony's Medical Center's ER is staffed by an independently owned group of emergency physicians (Emergency Physicians of St. Louis) who provide services to the hospital on a contract bases. The physician-group model of employment aims to improve patient flow and reduce waiting times at the ER.

In fiscal 2015 (ended June) the hospital had some 27000 inpatient admissions and more than 77700 emergency department visits delivered more than 1100 babies and performed more than 13000 surgeries.

Geographic Reach

St. Anthony's Medical Center is one of the largest hospitals in the St. Louis metropolitan area. It serves a population base of more than 900000 people in 10 counties in Missouri and Illinois. It also operates four urgent care centers in surrounding communities of Arnold Big Bend Fenton and Lemay.

Strategy

In 2014 St. Anthony's Medical Center became one of the first hospitals in the nation to implant the newly approved Medtronic Reveal LINQ Insertable Cardiac Monitor System a miniature cardiac monitor in a stroke patient.

EXECUTIVES

Executive Vice President Chief Financial Officer, John Skeans
Director of Health Information Management, Leslie Thomas
Vice President of Physician Affairs, Patrick Garrett
Director Of Pharmacy, David Palmer
Vice President, Craig Mills
Dir of Home Healthcare Srv, PATRICIA HEINEMANN
Vice President Patient Care Quality, Robert Griesbaum
Admissions Director, JEAN VALENTA
Medical Director, Homan Joseph
Auditors: BKD LLP ST LOUIS MISSOURI

LOCATIONS

HQ: ST. ANTHONY'S MEDICAL CENTER
10010 KENNERLY RD, SAINT LOUIS, MO 631282106
Phone: 314 525-1000
Web: WWW.STANTHONYSMEDCENTER.COM

PRODUCTS/OPERATIONS

Selected Services
Acute Rehabilitation
Audiology/Hearing
Behavioral Health
Breast Center
Cancer Care Center
Diabetes Education
Emergency/Trauma
Heart Specialty Center
Home Care
Hospice Field Program
Hyland Behavioral Health
Long-term Acute Care
Neuroscience and Stroke
Occupational Medicine
Oncology
Orthopedics
Ostomy Clinic
Outpatient Imaging
Pediatric Services
Physical Therapy
Pregnancy and Birth
Pharmacy
Pulmonary
Radiology/Imaging Centers
Rehabilitation (cardiac and acute)
Senior Services
Sleep Disorder Center
Social Services (Care Management)
Speech Therapy
Sports & Therapy
Stroke
Surgery
Urgent Care Centers
Urological Gynecology
Vestibular Rehab
Weight Management
Women's Medical/Surgical Unit
Wound Treatment

COMPETITORS

Ascension Health	Mercy Hospital St.
BJC HealthCare	Louis
Barnes-Jewish Hospital	RehabCare
Christian Hospital	SSM Health Care
CoxHealth	Saint Francis Medical
HCA	Center
Memorial Hospital	St. Luke's Hospital
(Illinois)	(MO)
Mercy Health	Tenet Healthcare

HISTORICAL FINANCIALS
Company Type: Private

Income Statement
FYE: June 30

	REVENUE ($ mil.)	NET INCOME ($ mil.)	NET PROFIT MARGIN	EMPLOYEES
06/15	482	1	0.3%	3,900
06/14	424	13	3.1%	—
06/13	443	38	8.7%	—
06/12	467	(29)	—	—
Annual Growth	1.1%	—	—	—

2015 Year-End Financials
Return on assets: 2.7%
Return on equity: 0.3%
Current ratio: 1.30
Cash ($ mil.): 25

ST. BARNABAS HOSPITAL

EXECUTIVES

Chairman of the Board, Victor Wright
Account Manager, Rachel Dono
Director, Richard Hwang

LOCATIONS

HQ: ST. BARNABAS HOSPITAL
4422 3RD AVE, BRONX, NY 104572594
Phone: 718 960-9000
Web: WWW.SBHNY.ORG

HISTORICAL FINANCIALS
Company Type: Private

Income Statement
FYE: December 31

	REVENUE ($ mil.)	NET INCOME ($ mil.)	NET PROFIT MARGIN	EMPLOYEES
12/15	333	(17)	—	2,119
12/14	313	(6)	—	—
12/13	353	3	1.1%	—
12/09	298	(25)	—	—
Annual Growth	1.9%	—	—	—

2015 Year-End Financials
Return on assets: 12.6%
Return on equity: (-5.2%)
Current ratio: 0.20
Cash ($ mil.): 14

ST. BERNARD'S HOSPITAL, INC.

EXECUTIVES

Chief Executive Officer, Chris B Barber
Administrative Assistant, Kathy Mulhollen
Executive Director, Keith Johnson

LOCATIONS

HQ: ST. BERNARD'S HOSPITAL, INC.
225 E JACKSON AVE, JONESBORO, AR 724013119
Phone: 870 207-7300
Web: WWW.SBRMC.COM

HISTORICAL FINANCIALS
Company Type: Private

Income Statement
FYE: September 30

	REVENUE ($ mil.)	NET INCOME ($ mil.)	NET PROFIT MARGIN	EMPLOYEES
09/15	270	30	11.2%	2,000
09/14	248	20	8.3%	—
09/13	305	19	6.3%	—
09/12	291	17	6.0%	—
Annual Growth	(2.5%)	19.7%	—	—

2015 Year-End Financials
Return on assets: 4.0%
Return on equity: 11.2%
Current ratio: 2.60
Cash ($ mil.): 51

ST. CATHERINE OF SIENA MEDICAL CENTER

EXECUTIVES

Chief Executive Officer, Alan D Guerci
Office Manager, Tammy Arnnaczisi
Director, Pat Brody

LOCATIONS

HQ: ST. CATHERINE OF SIENA MEDICAL CENTER
50 ROUTE 25A, SMITHTOWN, NY 117871348
Phone: 631 862-3000
Web: WWW.CHSLI.ORG

HISTORICAL FINANCIALS

Company Type: Private

Income Statement

FYE: December 31

	REVENUE ($ mil.)	NET INCOME ($ mil.)	NET PROFIT MARGIN	EMPLOYEES
12/15	219	39	18.2%	1,500
12/14	218	(23)	—	—
12/13	257	1	0.6%	—
Annual Growth	(7.7%)	405.6%		

2015 Year-End Financials

Return on assets: 5.9%   Cash ($ mil.): 14
Return on equity: 18.2%
Current ratio: 0.70

ST. CLOUD HOSPITAL

EXECUTIVES

President, Craig Broman
Director of Finance, Kathy Parsons
Office Manager, Tim Dalton
Manager, Jon Tufte
Director, Deanna Butcher
Supervisor, Jerome Schlabsz
Officer, Julie Grams
Manager, Kim Hintermeister
Auditors: MCGLADREY LLP MINNEAPOLIS MN

LOCATIONS

HQ: ST. CLOUD HOSPITAL
  1406 6TH AVE N, SAINT CLOUD, MN 563031901
Phone: 320 251-2700
Web: WWW.CENTRACARE.COM

HISTORICAL FINANCIALS

Company Type: Private

Income Statement

FYE: June 30

	REVENUE ($ mil.)	NET INCOME ($ mil.)	NET PROFIT MARGIN	EMPLOYEES
06/15	767	170	22.2%	4,957
06/14	754	72	9.6%	—
06/13	717	70	9.9%	—
06/12	686	85	12.4%	—
Annual Growth	3.8%	26.1%	—	—

2015 Year-End Financials

Return on assets: 3.4%   Cash ($ mil.): 36
Return on equity: 22.2%
Current ratio: 1.90

ST. ELIZABETH HOSPITAL, INC.

EXECUTIVES

President, Monica Hilp
Manager, Debbie Langacker
Manager, Doug Shew
Vice-President, Mary Lefevre
Director, Jean Mathia
Senior Vice-President, Sarah Giolando

LOCATIONS

HQ: ST. ELIZABETH HOSPITAL, INC.
  1506 S ONEIDA ST, APPLETON, WI 549151396
Phone: 920 738-2000
Web: WWW.AFFINITYHEALTH.ORG

HISTORICAL FINANCIALS

Company Type: Private

Income Statement

FYE: June 30

	REVENUE ($ mil.)	NET INCOME ($ mil.)	NET PROFIT MARGIN	EMPLOYEES
06/15	195	36	18.4%	1,368
06/14*	190	36	19.4%	—
09/08	143	14	9.9%	—
06/06	0	0	4.1%	—
Annual Growth	127.5%	168.9%	—	—

*Fiscal year change

2015 Year-End Financials

Return on assets: 14.7%   Cash ($ mil.): 14
Return on equity: 18.4%
Current ratio: 0.80

ST. ELIZABETH MEDICAL CENTER

EXECUTIVES

Chief Executive Officer, Richard Ketcham
Manager, Robert Tan
Production Manager, Dennis Forresti
Purchasing Manager, Dennis F Oresti
Vice-President, Helen Harrington
Director, Janice Lutz
Manager, Mike Gargas

LOCATIONS

HQ: ST. ELIZABETH MEDICAL CENTER
  2209 GENESEE ST, UTICA, NY 135015999
Phone: 315 798-8100
Web: WWW.STEMC.ORG

HISTORICAL FINANCIALS

Company Type: Private

Income Statement

FYE: December 31

	REVENUE ($ mil.)	NET INCOME ($ mil.)	NET PROFIT MARGIN	EMPLOYEES
12/15	197	(4)	—	1,700
12/14	190	(5)	—	—
12/13	196	31	16.3%	—
12/12	195	(4)	—	—
Annual Growth	0.4%			

2015 Year-End Financials

Return on assets: 9.6%   Cash ($ mil.): 5
Return on equity: (-2.1%)
Current ratio: 0.80

ST. FRANCIS HEALTH CENTER, INC.

LOCATIONS

HQ: ST. FRANCIS HEALTH CENTER, INC.
  1700 SW 7TH ST, TOPEKA, KS 666062489
Phone: 785 295-8000
Web: WWW.STFRANCISTOPEKA.ORG

HISTORICAL FINANCIALS

Company Type: Private

Income Statement

FYE: June 30

	REVENUE ($ mil.)	NET INCOME ($ mil.)	NET PROFIT MARGIN	EMPLOYEES
06/15*	262	(13)	—	1,700
05/05	0	(0)	—	—
Annual Growth	83.9%	—	—	—

*Fiscal year change

2015 Year-End Financials

Return on assets: 1.4%   Cash ($ mil.): 3
Return on equity: (-5.0%)
Current ratio: 3.10

ST. FRANCIS MEDICAL CENTER

EXECUTIVES

Chief Executive Officer, Gerald Kozai
Chief Financial Officer, Nancy Wilson
Officer, Michael Scott

LOCATIONS

HQ: ST. FRANCIS MEDICAL CENTER
  3630 E IMPERIAL HWY, LYNWOOD, CA 902622609
Phone: 310 900-8900
Web: WWW.STFRANCISMEDICALCENTER.ORG

HISTORICAL FINANCIALS

Company Type: Private

Income Statement

FYE: June 30

	REVENUE ($ mil.)	NET INCOME ($ mil.)	NET PROFIT MARGIN	EMPLOYEES
06/15	500	70	14.1%	138
06/14	407	21	5.3%	—
Annual Growth	22.8%	226.7%	—	—

2015 Year-End Financials

Return on assets: 1.8%   Cash ($ mil.): 36
Return on equity: 14.1%
Current ratio: 1.20

ST. JOHN HEALTH SYSTEM, INC.

St. John Health System aims to bring health into the lives of the ill. The not-for-profit system pro-

vides health care services to residents of Tulsa and surrounding areas in northeastern Oklahoma and southern Kansas. In addition to flagship facility St. John Medical Center it owns or manages eight other community hospitals as well as urgent care and long-term care facilities. St. John Health System provides primary and specialty medical care through OMNI Medical Group and offers health insurance through CommunityCare health plan. Established in 1926 by the Sisters of the Sorrowful Mother the health system is part of Marian Health.

Operations

Facilities owned managed or sponsored by St. John Health System include hospitals Oklahoma State University Medical Center St. John Sapulpa St. John Owasso St. John Broken Arrow Pawhuska City Hospital Sedan City Hospital Nowata Hospital and Jane Phillips Medical Center. The company's senior living facilities include Franciscan Villa Frances Streitel Villa Heartsworth House and Rosewood Terrace.

Strategy

St. John Health System will periodically add services to its offerings to meet community demand. In early 2011 St. John Health opened the St. John Weight Management Institute to offer its patients weight loss options including bariatric surgery. The health system's newest hospital St. John Broken Arrow near Tulsa was constructed in 2009.

In 2012 Marian Health entered talks with another Catholic health system operator Ascension Health over the possibility of merging St. John Health System and other Marian organizations into the Ascension organization.

EXECUTIVES

Vice President of Clinical Services, Kathy Smarinsky
Vice President, Gwen Moudry
Medical Director, Alfred Vitanza
Director Physician Recruitment Retention And Practice Development, Krista Thacker
Vice President Of Properties A, Dewey Davis
Medical Director of Stroke Service, Anna Wanahita
Director of Radiology, Philip Ames
Medical Director, Terry Mills
Executive Vice President and Chief Operating Officer Gwinnett Health System; President Gwinnett Medical Center, Jeff Nowlin

LOCATIONS

HQ: ST. JOHN HEALTH SYSTEM, INC.
1923 S UTICA AVE, TULSA, OK 741046520
Phone: 918 744-2180

PRODUCTS/OPERATIONS

Selected Facilities and Operations – Oklahoma
CommunityCare (health plan)
Jane Phillips Medical Center (Bartlesville)
Nowata Hospital
Oklahoma State University Medical Center (managed facility in Tulsa)
OMNI Medical Group (physicians group)
Pawhuska City Hospital
Regional Medical Laboratory (clinical lab testing)
Sedan City Hospital
St. John Broken Arrow Hospital
St. John Medical Center (Tulsa)
St. John Owasso Hospital
St. John Physicians
St. John Sapulpa Hospital

COMPETITORS

Anthem
Ardent Health Services
CIGNA
Catholic Health Initiatives
Community Health Systems
INTEGRIS Health
Kindred Healthcare
Marian Health System
Norman Regional Health
Presbyterian Healthcare Services
SSM Health Care

Deaconess Health Care
HCA
Hillcrest Medical Center
Saint Francis Health System
UnitedHealth Group

HISTORICAL FINANCIALS
Company Type: Private

Income Statement
FYE: June 30

	REVENUE ($ mil.)	NET INCOME ($ mil.)	NET PROFIT MARGIN	EMPLOYEES
06/15	1,130	(7)	—	4,011
06/14*	1,056	79	7.5%	—
09/12	977	74	7.7%	—
09/11	895	17	2.0%	—
Annual Growth	6.0%	—	—	—

*Fiscal year change

2015 Year-End Financials
Return on assets: 9.2%
Return on equity: (-0.7%)
Current ratio: 1.40
Cash ($ mil.): 44

ST. JOHN HOSPITAL AND MEDICAL CENTER

St. John Hospital & Medical Center is part of the larger Detroit area-based St. John Health regional health care system. Besides providing acute and trauma care the 770-bed teaching hospital operates specialized cancer and pediatric centers a hip and knee center an inpatient mental health unit and a Parkinson's Disease clinic. It also operates the only emergency trauma center on Detroit's East Side. The hospital was established in 1952 and has grown to include a 200-physician medical team that specializes in more than 50 medical and surgical fields. It boasts 34000 admissions; 14500 surgical visits; and more than 126500 emergency center visits each year.

Operations

Its emergency center is a Level II Trauma Center that boasts Chest Pain Center and Heart Failure Center accreditations. St. John Hospital also operates a large inpatient pediatric unit PICU and Level III NICU or Level II Special Care Nursery. The hospital runs the Van Elslander Cancer Center.

Strategy

St. John Hospital expanded its operations by opening the Elaine E. Blatt Endoscopy Department and a new pediatric burn treatment room both in 2012. It also expanded its mammography service capabilities with the purchase of Lakeshore Mammograph giving it more than a dozen new mammography sites across southeastern Michigan. In addition St. John Hospital opened a new cardiac catheterization lab that brought new diagnostic options to patients in the Michigan Blue Water Area.

EXECUTIVES

Board Treasurer, David Stone

LOCATIONS

HQ: ST. JOHN HOSPITAL AND MEDICAL CENTER
28000 DEQUINDRE RD, WARREN, MI 480922468
Phone: 313 343-4000
Web: WWW.STJOHNPROVIDENCE.ORG

PRODUCTS/OPERATIONS

Selected Services and Operations
Alternative Health
Breast Care
Breast Feeding (Lactation) Consultation
Cracchiolo Inpatient Rehabilitation Center
Diabetes Education and Care
Diagnostic and Imaging Services
Echocardiogram
Emergency
Heart and Vascular Care
Hip and Knee Center
Minimally Invasive Surgery
Minor Emergency
Neonatal Intensive Care Unit (NICU)
Obstetrics
Oncology (cancer)
Parkinson's Movement Disorder Clinic
Pediatrics
Physical Therapy
Spine Center
TravelCare
Urgent Care
Wound Care

COMPETITORS

Beaumont Health System
Crittenton Hospital
Detroit Medical Center
Henry Ford Health System
Mount Clemens Regional Medical Center
Trinity Health (Novi)

HISTORICAL FINANCIALS
Company Type: Private

Income Statement
FYE: June 30

	REVENUE ($ mil.)	NET INCOME ($ mil.)	NET PROFIT MARGIN	EMPLOYEES
06/15	753	36	4.8%	5,000
06/09	638	1	0.3%	—
06/05	0	0	—	—
06/03	1,642	9	0.6%	—
Annual Growth	(6.3%)	12.0%	—	—

2015 Year-End Financials
Return on assets: 0.5%
Return on equity: 4.8%
Current ratio: 0.20
Cash ($ mil.): 1

ST. JOHN PROVIDENCE

St. John Providence Health System is out to keep southeastern Michigan's denizens healthy. A subsidiary of not-for-profit group Ascension Health St. John Providence is a regional health care system founded in 1844 that consists of six hospitals with more than 2000 beds. It has more than 125 additional medical facilities including urgent care clinics outpatient centers and doctors' offices. The health system also runs St. John Home Services a home health care agency providing infusion services rehabilitative services and hospice care. Flagship hospital St. John Hospital and Medical Center is a regional referral hospital with more than 800 beds providing care in numerous medical and surgical specialties.

Operations

St. John Providence is known for its Centers of Excellence in bariatrics cancer heart and vascular and neuroscience. The system conducts about 8000 births and 60000 surgeries each year; it also handles about 370000 annual emergency department visits. Specialist services include cardiovascular cancer neurology and infectious disease treatment.

In addition to medical care the network's facilities provide medical training programs including graduate and continuing education programs as well as clinical research trials.

Geographic Reach

The health system's main health centers are located in Michigan communities including Brighton Detroit Novi Southfield and Warren. Its service territory includes Madison Heights St. Clair and Warren counties.

Strategy

To expand and improve its facilities the flagship St. John Hospital has undergone seven major renovations on departments including its emergency department and maternal/child health center. It has also added new diagnostic facilities such as a sleep-studies center and a vascular lab. In 2015 it opened an expanded renovated neonatal intensive care unit and special care nursery.

Also in 2015 Providence-Providence Park Hospital in Southfield Michigan agreed to work with Michigan State University to establish a new medical school campus — the first in southeast Michigan.

St. John Providence opened a new clinic to treat patients with critical limb Ischemia in 2014.

EXECUTIVES

Senior Vice President Operations, Terry Hamilton
Senior Vice President Mission Integration, Elizabeth Granger
Vice President Clinical Services, Deborah Condino
Vice President Operations, Nancy Burton
Senior Vice President Operations, Terence Hamilton
Vice President For Advocacy, Sean Gehle
Secretary and Treasurer Medical Staff, Mark O'Brien
Auditors: LB DELOITTE TAX LLP CINCINNAT

LOCATIONS

HQ: ST. JOHN PROVIDENCE
28000 DEQUINDRE RD, WARREN, MI 480922468
Phone: 586 753-0500
Web: WWW.BOOKSFORDETROIT.COM

PRODUCTS/OPERATIONS

Selected Hospitals and Facilities

Brighton Center for Recovery (formerly Brighton Hospital; addiction rehabilitation; Brighton Michigan)
Providence-Providence Park Hospital (Southfield and Novi Michigan)
St. John Hospital & Medical Center (Detroit)
St. John Macomb-Oakland Hospital (Madison Heights and Warren Michigan)
St. John River District (East China Township Michigan)

COMPETITORS

Beaumont Health System	McLaren Health Care
Children's Hospital of Michigan	Sinai-Grace Hospital
	Trinity Health (Novi)
Crittenton Hospital	University of Michigan
Detroit Medical Center	Health System
Harper-Hutzel Hospital	
Henry Ford Health System	

HISTORICAL FINANCIALS

Company Type: Private

Income Statement
FYE: June 30

	REVENUE ($ mil.)	NET INCOME ($ mil.)	NET PROFIT MARGIN	EMPLOYEES
06/15	.238	(3)	—	17,806
06/14	255	(8)	—	—
06/13	257	7	3.0%	—
06/09	2,023	(84)	—	—
Annual Growth	(30.0%)	—	—	—

2015 Year-End Financials

Return on assets: 19.0% Cash ($ mil.): 13
Return on equity: (-1.4%)
Current ratio: 0.30

ST. JOSEPH HOSPITAL

EXECUTIVES

Chief Executive Officer, Joseph Mark
President, David O'Brien
Chief Financial Officer, Andrew Rybolt
Account Manager, Kevin Clougherty
Financial Executive, Jim Smith
Director, Michael Harmon

LOCATIONS

HQ: ST. JOSEPH HOSPITAL
2700 DOLBEER ST, EUREKA, CA 955014799
Phone: 707 445-8121
Web: WWW.STJOEHUMBOLDT.ORG

HISTORICAL FINANCIALS

Company Type: Private

Income Statement
FYE: June 30

	REVENUE ($ mil.)	NET INCOME ($ mil.)	NET PROFIT MARGIN	EMPLOYEES
06/15	248	35	14.1%	850
06/10	185	16	8.9%	—
06/09	166	4	2.7%	—
06/08	151	5	3.6%	—
Annual Growth	7.3%	30.2%	—	—

2015 Year-End Financials

Return on assets: 3.1% Cash ($ mil.): 7
Return on equity: 14.1%
Current ratio: 0.40

ST. JOSEPH HOSPITAL OF NASHUA, N.H.

EXECUTIVES

President, Peter B Davis
Office Manager, Mary Landry
Director, Brian Hu
Director, Jeffrey Chapdelaine
Chief Operating Officer, John Walsh

LOCATIONS

HQ: ST. JOSEPH HOSPITAL OF NASHUA, N.H.
172 KINSLEY ST, NASHUA, NH 030603648
Phone: 603 882-3000

HISTORICAL FINANCIALS

Company Type: Private

Income Statement
FYE: December 31

	REVENUE ($ mil.)	NET INCOME ($ mil.)	NET PROFIT MARGIN	EMPLOYEES
12/15	173	(8)	—	1,200
12/14	164	5	3.6%	—
12/13	183	16	9.0%	—
12/12	173	13	7.9%	—
Annual Growth	0.1%	—	—	—

2015 Year-End Financials

Return on assets: 1.3% Cash ($ mil.): 10
Return on equity: (-5.1%)
Current ratio: 0.90

ST. JOSEPH HOSPITAL OF ORANGE

If you're feeling green or blue in Orange County St. Joseph Hospital of Orange is there to help get back to feeling pink and rosy. The California hospital provides general medical and surgical services as well as specialty care such as women's health mental health services oncology cardiology and physical rehabilitation. Part of the St. Joseph Health System the hospital provides primary care and specialty outpatient services through a network of affiliated physician practices. It also operates low-income and mobile clinics. The hospital has about 468 beds and a medical staff of some 1000.

Operations

In addition to physician group affiliates St. Joseph Hospital Affiliated Physicians and St. Joseph Heritage Medical Group the hospital also partners with the Childrens Hospital of Orange County to help expand pediatric care throughout the region. The hospital has more than 20100 inpatient discharges and about 290400 outpatient visits a year.

Geographic Reach

St. Joseph Hospital serves Orange County California and the greater Los Angeles metropolitan area.

Strategy

St. Joseph Hospital has been working to expand its community outreach programs related to cancer through a number of projects including offering improved access to clinical trials; providing better overall access to cancer care; and implementing measures to garner support for the implementation of cancer electronic health records. St. Joseph Hospital is using stimulus money and about a $3 million award from the National Cancer Institute Community Cancer Centers Program to help fund its various projects.

Company Background

The company was founded in 1929 by the Sisters of St. Joseph of Orange.

EXECUTIVES

Vice President Operations, Tom Hill
Vice President, Linda Simon
Clinic Manager, Gioconda Martinez
Vice President, Chanda Parrett
Ambulatory Services Director, James Pierog
COTA, Jennifer Kohlbeck

LOCATIONS

HQ: ST. JOSEPH HOSPITAL OF ORANGE
 1100 W STEWART DR, ORANGE, CA 928683891
Phone: 714 633-9111
Web: WWW.SJO.ORG

PRODUCTS/OPERATIONS

Selected Services
Bariatric Surgery
Behavioral Health
Cancer
Nasal & Sinus Center
Heart & Vascular Center
Kidney Dialysis Center
Maternity
Orthopedic Services
Sleep Disorders Center

COMPETITORS

Anaheim Regional
 Medical Center
Children's Hospital of
 Orange County
Citrus Valley Health
 Partners
Hoag Memorial Hospital
Memorial Health
 Services
Pasadena Hospital
 Association

Providence St. Joseph
 Health
Southwest Healthcare
Sutter Health
Tenet Healthcare
Torrance Memorial
 Medical Center
Trinity Health (Novi)
Western Medical Center
 - Santa Ana

HISTORICAL FINANCIALS

Company Type: Private

Income Statement
FYE: June 30

	REVENUE ($ mil.)	NET INCOME ($ mil.)	NET PROFIT MARGIN	EMPLOYEES
06/15	567	2	0.5%	3,300
06/14	566	(5)	—	—
06/13	668	47	7.2%	—
06/12	645	23	3.6%	—
Annual Growth	(4.2%)	(50.7%)	—	—

2015 Year-End Financials
Return on assets: 3.7%   Cash ($ mil.): 51
Return on equity: 0.5%
Current ratio: 4.50

ST. JOSEPH MERCY OAKLAND

EXECUTIVES

Chief Executive Officer, Jack Weiner
Financial Executive, Avinash Sidar
Director, Alta Gordon
Financial Executive, Hugh Depaulis
Manager, Cynthia Nichols
VP Finance, Cynthia Rouch
Director, Lisa Hasselbach
Vice-President, Thomas Petingado

LOCATIONS

HQ: ST. JOSEPH MERCY OAKLAND
 44405 WOODWARD AVE, PONTIAC, MI 483415023
Phone: 248 858-3000
Web: WWW.STJOESOAKLAND.ORG

HISTORICAL FINANCIALS

Company Type: Private

Income Statement
FYE: June 30

	REVENUE ($ mil.)	NET INCOME ($ mil.)	NET PROFIT MARGIN	EMPLOYEES
06/15	379	20	5.3%	4,000
06/09	356	(11)	—	—
Annual Growth	1.1%			

2015 Year-End Financials
Return on assets: 4.5%   Cash ($ mil.): 2
Return on equity: 5.3%
Current ratio: 0.90

ST. JOSEPH REGIONAL HEALTH CENTER

EXECUTIVES

Chief Executive Officer, Kathleen Krusie
Director, Charles Williams
Vice-Chairman, Mark Scarmardo
Senior Manager, Mary Berry
Executive Director, Jim Vogel
Operations Manager, Julia Jarrell
Finance Manager, Kathy Kovar

LOCATIONS

HQ: ST. JOSEPH REGIONAL HEALTH CENTER
 2801 FRANCISCAN DR, BRYAN, TX 778022544
Phone: 979 776-3777

HISTORICAL FINANCIALS

Company Type: Private

Income Statement
FYE: June 30

	REVENUE ($ mil.)	NET INCOME ($ mil.)	NET PROFIT MARGIN	EMPLOYEES
06/15*	250	34	13.8%	1,200
12/14	318	18	5.8%	—
12/13	293	37	12.9%	—
12/12	272	30	11.1%	—
Annual Growth	(4.1%)	7.2%	—	—

*Fiscal year change

2015 Year-End Financials
Return on assets: 11.2%   Cash ($ mil.): 17
Return on equity: 13.8%
Current ratio: 0.60

ST. JOSEPH'S HOSPITAL AND MEDICAL CENTER

EXECUTIVES

President, William A McDonald
Financial Executive, Joanne Dunay
Chief Financial Officer, Lisa Sacco
Director, Carol Applegate

LOCATIONS

HQ: ST. JOSEPH'S HOSPITAL AND MEDICAL CENTER
 703 MAIN ST, PATERSON, NJ 075032691
Phone: 973 754-2000
Web: WWW.SJHMC.ORG

HISTORICAL FINANCIALS

Company Type: Private

Income Statement
FYE: December 31

	REVENUE ($ mil.)	NET INCOME ($ mil.)	NET PROFIT MARGIN	EMPLOYEES
12/15	752	60	8.0%	4,000
12/08	472	(41)	—	—
12/06	437	17	3.9%	—
12/05	1,643	0	—	—
Annual Growth	—	127.2%	—	—

2015 Year-End Financials
Return on assets: 6.0%   Cash ($ mil.): 90
Return on equity: 8.0%
Current ratio: 1.50

ST. JOSEPH'S HOSPITAL HEALTH CENTER

With about 430 inpatient beds St. Joseph's Hospital Health Center serves the residents of 16 central New York counties. The not-for-profit hospital system provides general emergency and surgical care as well as specialty services in areas such as obstetrics cardiology dialysis and wound care. In addition to its inpatient facilities the organization operates a home health agency a nursing school medical and dental residency programs and several outpatient care centers. Its Franciscan Companies affiliate offers some ancillary services including the provision of medical supplies home health equipment and senior services. St. Joseph's Hospital Health Center was founded in 1869.

Operations

With a total of some 800 physicians St. Joseph's Hospital Health Center admits some 28000 inpatients each year. It also handles some 957000 emergency room visits and about 640000 outpatient visits annually. The hospital provides about $22 million in charity and community care each year as well.

Geographic Reach

St. Joseph's Hospital Health Center's service territory includes the New York counties of Broome Cayuga Chenango Cortland Delaware Herkimer Jefferson Lewis Madison Oneida Onondaga Oswego Otsego St. Lawrence Tioga and Tompkins.

Financial Performance

In 2013 revenue rose 7% to $626 million as patient and other revenue grew. Net income also improved by 33% due to better investment returns.

Strategy

St. Joseph's Hospital Health Center is conducting a massive $220 million expansion program at its main campus. The first phase opened in 2011 and includes a larger emergency room facility with chest pain and psychiatric units. The hospital broke ground on the second phase of the project in 2012. The program will add a new patient tower surgery facilities a sterilization center and an intensive care unit. In 2013 it opened a sleep center and a new surgical suite at the hospital. The following year St. Joseph's expanded its primary care center in

west Syracuse and launched it electronic health record system.

Mergers and Acquisitions

In 2013 the center purchased Upstate Surgical Group creating a general surgery group in St. Joseph's ambulatory surgery group.

In late 2010 St. Joseph's Hospital Health Center boosted its physician network significantly by acquiring North Medical a physician practice organization that operates five practices: Family Physicians Urgent Care Orthopedics & Rehabilitation The Women's Place and Living Proof Longevity Centre. Its practices are home to about 80 physicians and mid-level practitioners.

EXECUTIVES

Principal, Kathryn Howe Ruscitto
Board of Directors, Sister Mary Obrist
Administrative Assistant, Jannet Evans
Manager, Sheren Newman

LOCATIONS

HQ: ST. JOSEPH'S HOSPITAL HEALTH CENTER
301 PROSPECT AVE, SYRACUSE, NY 132031899
Phone: 315 448-5113
Web: WWW.SJHSYR.ORG

PRODUCTS/OPERATIONS

Selected Services
Centers of Excellence
  Cardiac Services
  The Center for Orthopedic and Spine Care
  Vascular Services
  Women and Children's Services
  Wound Care
  Home Care
  Dialysis
  Bariatric (Weight Loss) Services
Other Services and Centers
  Aesthetic Services
  Behavioral Health
  da Vinci Robotic Surgery
  Emergency Services
  Imaging
  Infusion (CPEPCNY)
  Interventional Radiology
  Medical Equipment
  Obstetric Services
  Palliative Care
  Pharmacy
  Physical Medicine & Rehabilitation
  Pulmonary Services
  Sleep Laboratory
  Social Adult Day Care
  Surgical Services
  Urology Services
Outpatient Services
  Dental Services
  Family Medicine Center
  Obstetrics and Gynecology
  Pediatric Office
  Physician Health
  Primary Care
  Westside Family Health Center

COMPETITORS

Catholic Health System
  Ellis Hospital
  Kaleida Health
  Lifetime Health
  Oneida Healthcare Center
  SUNY Upstate Medical University
  United Health Services Hospitals
  Upstate University Hospital at Community General

HISTORICAL FINANCIALS

Company Type: Private

Income Statement
FYE: December 31

	REVENUE ($ mil.)	NET INCOME ($ mil.)	NET PROFIT MARGIN	EMPLOYEES
12/15	542	(2)	—	3,300
12/14	523	0	0.1%	—
12/09	436	5	1.2%	—
12/08	399	6	1.6%	—
Annual Growth	4.5%	—	—	—

2015 Year-End Financials

Return on assets: 7.4%
Return on equity: (-0.5%)
Current ratio: 1.10

Cash ($ mil.): 36

ST. JOSEPHS HOSPITAL, YONKERS

EXECUTIVES

President, Michael J Spicer
Vice-President, Lorraine D Horgan
Director, Patty Bernstein

LOCATIONS

HQ: ST. JOSEPHS HOSPITAL, YONKERS
127 S BROADWAY, YONKERS, NY 107014080
Phone: 914 378-7000
Web: WWW.SAINTJOSEPHS.ORG

HISTORICAL FINANCIALS

Company Type: Private

Income Statement
FYE: December 31

	REVENUE ($ mil.)	NET INCOME ($ mil.)	NET PROFIT MARGIN	EMPLOYEES
12/15	190	(10)	—	900
12/14	204	(1)	—	
12/13	204	(4)	—	
Annual Growth	(3.3%)	—	—	—

2015 Year-End Financials

Return on assets: 10.2%
Return on equity: (-5.4%)
Current ratio: 0.50

Cash ($ mil.): 1

ST. JUDE CHILDREN'S RESEARCH HOSPITAL, INC.

St. Jude Children's Research Hospital studies and treats catastrophic diseases in children especially pediatric cancers. The hospital which only has about 80 beds annually treats more than 7800 children most of whom are treated on an outpatient basis as part of its research efforts into finding cures and more effective treatments. The hospital not only helps children with their health it also helps their parents: It pays all expenses that are not covered by insurance and doesn't require payment from patients without insurance. St. Jude Children's Research Hospital was founded in 1962.

Operations

St. Jude Children's Research Hospital has a 2.5-million-sq.-ft. campus for its research clinical and administrative operations. It is the only pediatric cancer center to be designated as a Comprehensive Cancer Center by the National Cancer Institute.

While it is best known for its research in pediatric cancers St. Jude Children's Research Hospital also treats children with genetic immune defects and pediatric AIDS and it has one of the largest pediatric sickle cell programs in the US.

As part of the organization's education mission it provides about 350 postdoctoral fellowships to those doctors who seek to specialize in pediatric medicine. St. Jude Children's Research Hospital is affiliated with the University of Tennessee Health Sciences Center at Memphis. Along with offering fellowships it serves as the training site for medical students and residents learning a variety of disciplines.

Geographic Reach

St. Jude Children's Research Hospital is located in Memphis Tennessee. The facility has affiliations with six other US hospitals in Alabama Illinois Louisiana Missouri and Tennessee. It shares its research findings with scientific and medical organizations worldwide.

Financial Performance

The hospital's revenues increased 23% to $1.5 billion in fiscal 2014 primarily due to increased support and investment earnings. The rise in revenues drove a 66% increase in net income which totaled $587 million in 2014; this was partially offset by an increase in patient care service expenses.

Cash flow from operations also increased rising 39% to $356 million.

Public contributions cover most of St. Jude Children's Research Hospital operating costs of $1.8 million a day.

Strategy

Throughout the year St. Jude Children's Research Hospital coordinates events to raise funds and awareness - from golf tournaments and triathlons to radiothons and telethons.

In 2015 the hospital added its seventh affiliate clinic — the St. Jude Affiliate Clinic at Novant Health Hemby Children's Hospital in Charlotte North Carolina. Affiliate clinics provide treatment to St. Jude patients allowing the number of children enrolled in its clinical trials to grow.

The Marlo Thomas Center for Global Education and Collaboration opened on the St. Jude campus in 2014.

Company Background

Entertainer Danny Thomas founded St. Jude in 1962; Thomas also founded the fundraising organization for the hospital the American Lebanese Syrian Associated Charities (ALSAC).

EXECUTIVES

CEO, James Downing
SVP Patient Care Services and Chief Nursing Officer, Pam Dotson
Chair Biostatistics, James Boyett
Co-Chair Oncology, Amar Gajjar
Chair Immunology, Doug Green
Chair Genetics, Gerard Grosveld
Chair Chemical Biology and Therapeutics, Kip Guy
Chair Biochemistry, James Ihle
EVP and Clinical Director, Larry E. Kun
Chair Developmental Neurobiology, James Morgan
Chair Oncology, Ching-Hon Pui
Chair Pharmaceutical Sciences, Mary Relling
Chair Epidemiology and Cancer Control, Les Robison
Chair Tumor Cell Biology, Charles Sherr

Chair Infectious Diseases, Elaine Tuomanen
Chair Structural Biology, Stephen White
CFO, Pat Keel
Chair Surgery, Andrew Davidoff
EVP Director Comprehensive Cancer Center,
  Richard J. Gilbertson
Chair Pathology, David Ellison
Chair Psychology, Sean Phipps
CIO, Keith Perry
Senior Vice President Patient Care Services Chief
  Nursing Officer, Pamela Dotson
Auditors: DELOITTE & TOUCHE LLP MEMPHIS

LOCATIONS

HQ: ST. JUDE CHILDREN'S RESEARCH HOSPITAL,
  INC.
  262 DANNY THOMAS PL, MEMPHIS, TN 381053678
Phone: 901 595-3300

PRODUCTS/OPERATIONS

2014 Sales

	% of total
Support revenue	62
Net investment income	25
Net patient service revenue	6
Research grants	5
Other	2
Total	100

Selected US Affiliate Clinics

Children's Hospital of Illinois (OSF Healthcare System)
  University of Illinois College of Medicine at Peoria
Feist-Weiller Cancer Center LSU Health Sciences Center
  (Shreveport Louisiana)
Huntsville Hospital (Huntsville Alabama)
Johnson City Medical Center East Tennessee State
  University
Our Lady of the Lake Regional Medical Center (Baton
  Rouge Louisiana)
St. John's Health System (Springfield Missouri)

Selected International Outreach Partner Sites

American University of Beirut/Children's Cancer Center
  of Lebanon (Beirut Lebanon)
Beijing Children's Hospital (Beijing)
Davao Medical Center (Philippines)
Hospital 20 Aout 1953 (Casablanca Morocco)
Hospital Benjamin Bloom (San Salvador El Salvador)
Hospital Civil de Guadalajara (Guadalajara Mexico)
Hospital de Especialidades Pediatricas (Maracaibo
  Venezuela)
Hospital de la Sociedad de Lucha Contra el Cancer
  Nucleo de Quito (Quito Ecuador)
Hospital de Ninos Baca Ortiz (Quito Ecuador)
Hospital de Ninos J.M. de los Rios (Caracas Venezuela)
Hospital d'Enfants (Rabat Morocco)
Hospital Escuela Materno Infantil (Tegucigalpa
  Honduras)
Hospital Luis Calvo Mackenna (Santiago Chile)
Hospital Nacional de Ninos (San Jose Costa Rica)
Hospital Pediatrico de Sinaloa (Culiacan Mexico)
King Hussein Cancer Center (Amman Jordan)
Our Lady's Hospital for Sick Children (Dublin Ireland)
Shanghai Children's Medical Center (Shanghai)
Unidad de Oncologia Pediatrica - Instituto Materno
  Infantil de Pernambuco; Centro
de Hematologia e Oncologia Pediatrica (Recife) - Brazil
Unidad Nacional de Oncologia Pediatrica (Guatemala
  City Guatemala)

COMPETITORS

Ascension Health
Baptist Memorial Health Care
Children's Medical Center of Dallas
Children's National Medical Center
Cincinnati Children's Hospital
City of Hope
Damon Runyon Cancer Research
Dana-Farber
Fox Chase Cancer Center
H. Lee Moffitt Cancer Center & Research Institute
HCA
LifePoint Health
MD Anderson Cancer Center
Memorial Sloan-Kettering

Mercy Health (OH)
Methodist Healthcare
Nationwide Children's Hospital
Roswell Park Cancer Institute
Shelby County Health Care
Shriners Hospitals For Children
Tenet Healthcare
UT Medical Group

HISTORICAL FINANCIALS

Company Type: Private

Income Statement

FYE: June 30

	REVENUE ($ mil.)	NET INCOME ($ mil.)	NET PROFIT MARGIN	EMPLOYEES
06/15	205	195	94.9%	2,500
06/11	573	(26)	—	—
06/10	589	(5)	—	—
Annual Growth	(19.0%)	—	—	—

2015 Year-End Financials

Return on assets: 27.3%   Cash ($ mil.): —
Return on equity: 94.9%
Current ratio: 0.20

ST. JUDE HOSPITAL

St. Jude Medical Center gets sickly Southern Californians on their feet again. The faith-based not-for-profit acute care facility with some 385 beds serves the residents of Orange County. The medical center provides an onsite cancer center (the Virginia K. Crosson Cancer Center) and a heart institute that offers cardiac surgeries and rehabilitation programs. It also provides inpatient and outpatient physical rehabilitation services and a variety of community outreach programs. Established by the Sisters of St. Joseph of Orange religious order in the 1950s St. Jude Medical Center is part of the St. Joseph Health System.

Operations

Beyond the medical center's campus St. Jude operates its Heritage Medical Group with outpatient locations throughout its region. The medical group includes specialists in plastic surgery rheumatology and gastroenterology. Altogether St. Jude employs some 700 physicians. It handles more than 17000 inpatient admissions each year as well as 13000 surgeries 2000 births and 54000 emergency room visits.

The organization spends some $47 million in community benefits including outreach and charity care. Its mobile and fixed-site community clinics offer medical dental and preventative care services for low-income residents.

Geographic Reach

St. Jude serves residents in communities in California's Orange County including Brea Buena Park Fullerton La Habra Placentia and Yorba Linda.

Strategy

St. Jude is expanding its facilities through the construction of a new $312 million patient tower schedule to open in late 2014. The Northwest Tower will feature private patient rooms as well as enhanced surgical and data management capabilities. Other improvement measures include technology upgrades such as a new neurovascular surgical system added in 2012.

In October 2011 St. Jude Medical Center closed its 12-bed pediatric unit and redirected patients younger than 16 to nearby Children's Hospital of Orange County. St. Jude's NICU (neonatal intensive care unit) remains open and the hospital continues

to provide emergency and outpatient services to children.

EXECUTIVES

OCCUPATIONAL MEDICINE, Robert Maurer

LOCATIONS

HQ: ST. JUDE HOSPITAL
  101 E VALENCIA MESA DR, FULLERTON, CA
  928353875
Phone: 714 871-3280
Web: WWW.STJUDEMEDICALCENTER.ORG

COMPETITORS

Anaheim Regional   Memorial Health
  Medical Center   Services
Children's Hospital of   Western Medical Center
  Orange County   - Santa Ana
Hoag Memorial Hospital

HISTORICAL FINANCIALS

Company Type: Private

Income Statement

FYE: June 30

	REVENUE ($ mil.)	NET INCOME ($ mil.)	NET PROFIT MARGIN	EMPLOYEES
06/15	458	8	2.0%	2,600
06/14	477	51	10.8%	—
06/13	0	62	—	—
06/10	492	61	12.4%	—
Annual Growth	(1.4%)	(31.9%)	—	—

2015 Year-End Financials

Return on assets: 2.4%   Cash ($ mil.): 296
Return on equity: 2.0%
Current ratio: 6.30

ST. LUKE'S EPISCOPAL-PRESBYTERIAN HOSPITALS

St. Luke's Episcopal-Presbyterian Hospital doing business as St. Luke's Hospital provides health care services to St. Louis residents and surrounding areas of eastern Missouri. The medical center houses more than 490 beds and offers general medical and surgical care as well as specialty services in areas such as heart disease cancer neuroscience orthopedics pediatrics and women's health. St. Luke's also operates half a dozen urgent care clinics in St. Louis and St. Charles counties providing treatment for minor emergencies such as cuts and animal bites as well as a skilled-nursing facility rehabilitation hospital and several diagnostic imaging centers. The not-for-profit hospital was founded in 1866.

Operations

In 2014 St. Luke's Hospital had more than 18000 inpatients and 315000 outpatients performed some 17500 surgeries facilitated 1800 births and had more than 30000 emergency department visits.

Financial Performance

In fiscal 2014 (ended June) operating revenue in excess of expense totaled $20.4 million. Total operating revenue grew 4% to $478 million that year.

Strategy

St. Luke's Hospital continues to grow via expansion projects. In 2013 the medical center ren-

ovated its neonatal special care nursery adding six private rooms and areas for twins and other multiples to stay together. The following year it opened a new urgent care center and a new facility with the state's only Open Upright MRI scanner. Other urgent care centers and physicians' offices are in the works. In 2015 the hospital broke ground on a $40 million outpatient building on its campus; it is expected to open in late 2016.

The company also grows by adding physicians to its network. During 2014 it added 34 new physicians to its staff with specializations in the areas of primary care neurology oncology cardiovascular orthopedics and others. In all the medical staff has more than 60 specialties.

EXECUTIVES

Vice President Communications, Jan Hess
Auditors: KPMG LLP OKLAHOMA CITY OK

LOCATIONS

HQ: ST. LUKE'S EPISCOPAL-PRESBYTERIAN
HOSPITALS
232 S WOODS MILL RD, CHESTERFIELD, MO
630173406
Phone: 314 434-1500

PRODUCTS/OPERATIONS

Selected Services
Brain and spine
Cardiac
Orthopedic
Pulmonary
Sleep medicine
Women's services

COMPETITORS

Barnes-Jewish Hospital	St. Anthony's Medical
CHRISTUS Health	Center
Mercy Health	Tenet Healthcare
SSM Health Care	

HISTORICAL FINANCIALS
Company Type: Private

Income Statement
FYE: June 30

	REVENUE ($ mil.)	NET INCOME ($ mil.)	NET PROFIT MARGIN	EMPLOYEES
06/15	470	49	10.6%	3,000
06/04	274	11	4.1%	—
06/03	263	9	3.5%	—
06/02	0	0	—	—
Annual Growth	—	—	—	—

2015 Year-End Financials
Return on assets: 9.3%   Cash ($ mil.): 68
Return on equity: 10.6%
Current ratio: 0.90

ST. LUKE'S HEALTH SYSTEM, LTD.

To Catholics St. Luke is also known as the "beloved physician" and St. Luke's Health System strives to live up to its namesake. The regional not-for-profit health system provides a range of health services to residents of Idaho eastern Oregon and northern Nevada. St. Luke's is home to six general acute care hospitals with a total of about 860 beds. Its flagship facility is the 400-bed St. Luke's Boise Medical Center which also includes a full-service children's hospital. St. Luke's

also runs a network of cancer care sites under the name Mountain States Tumor Institute as well as a number of urgent care family practice and specialty health centers.

Operations

St. Luke's hospitals handle about 50000 inpatient visits 35000 surgeries and 8000 births each year. The network also sees about 700000 outpatients annually through its urgent care family health and specialty care centers. The company's diagnostic care operations include about five imaging centers and eight breast cancer detection clinics. Overall St. Luke's employs about 1000 physicians.

The Boise campus is home to its tertiary care services - cancer heart and the Children's Hospital - meaning the most acute cases from the region are brought there for the most specialized care. St. Luke's Children's Hospital sees 85000 patient visits a year has Idaho's first and only Pediatric Intensive Care Unit and has the state's largest and most experienced Level III Newborn Intensive Care Unit. Its Boise campus is also the base of St. Luke's Mountain States Tumor Institute (MSTI which cares for about 820 cancer patients a day) and St. Luke's Heart services one of the top 50 cardiovascular programs in the US.

Geographic Reach

St. Luke's has Idaho operations in Boise Caldwell Eagle Fruitland Jerome Ketchum McCall Meridian Mountain Home Nampa and Twin Falls.

Strategy

The growing need for care from each of these leading service lines is a significant part of the Integrated Care Model that has guided the company's Master Plan. St. Luke's has been investing a significant amount of money to upgrade and expand its facilities in recent years.

In 2014 the federal courts ordered St. Luke's to divest Saltzer Medical Group (Idaho's state's largest independent multi-specialty physician practice) after concluding that St. Luke's 2012 acquisition of Saltzer violated Section 7 of the Clayton Act and the Idaho Competition Act.

Company Background

In 2011 St. Luke's completed a $130 million project to rebuild the St. Luke's Magic Valley Medical Center. The new hospital building had about 190 beds and expanded emergency cancer and cardiac centers. The health system was also working to expand its Boise Medical Center's heart and vascular and pediatric departments as well as its system-wide MSTI facilities.

The health system has also expanded its outpatient network to include new family practice emergency care and urgent care clinics in recent years. The network opened a St. Luke's Nampa emergency care clinic and medical complex in 2012. In addition to updating its facilities the St. Luke's Health System was working to upgrade its information technology assets.

St. Luke's added its fifth and sixth acute care hospitals in 2010 and 2011 when the 15-bed St. Luke's McCall (formerly McCall Memorial Hospital) and 25-bed St. Luke's Jerome (formerly St. Benedicts Medical Center) hospitals joined the health network through affiliation and merger agreements.

The health system was formed in 2006 when the three hospitals of the old St. Luke's Regional Medical Center network (Boise Meridian and Wood River) merged with Magic Valley Regional Medical Center a former county facility in Twin Falls Idaho.

EXECUTIVES

President CEO and Director, David C. Pate
Nursing Director, Belinda Day
Vice President of Finance and Controller, Pete Didio

Vice President Of Medical Affairs, Bart Hill
Nursing Director, Katie Schimmelpfennig
Executive Vice President, Jeff Taylor
Medical Director, Rourke Yeakley
Chairman, Jon Miller
Auditors: DELOITTE & TOUCHE LLP BOISE

LOCATIONS

HQ: ST. LUKE'S HEALTH SYSTEM, LTD.
190 E BANNOCK ST, BOISE, ID 837126241
Phone: 208 381-2222
Web: WWW.SLHS.ORG

PRODUCTS/OPERATIONS

Selected Idaho Facilities
St. Luke's Boise Medical Center (Boise)
  St. Luke's Children's Hospital
St. Luke's Clinics (multiple locations)
St. Luke's Eagle Urgent Care (Eagle)
St. Luke's Jerome Medical Center (Jerome)
St. Luke's Magic Valley Medical Center (Twin Falls)
St. Luke's McCall Memorial Hospital (McCall)
St. Luke's Meridian Medical Center (Meridian)
St. Luke's Mountain States Tumor Institute (multiple locations)
St. Luke's Wood River Medical Center (Hailey/Ketchum)

COMPETITORS

Ascension Health
  Benedictine Health System
  HCA
  Intermountain Health Care
  Saint Alphonsus Regional Medical Center
  Trinity Health (Novi)

HISTORICAL FINANCIALS
Company Type: Private

Income Statement
FYE: September 30

	REVENUE ($ mil.)	NET INCOME ($ mil.)	NET PROFIT MARGIN	EMPLOYEES
09/16	1,937	48	2.5%	7,891
09/09	49	0	—	—
Annual Growth	69.1%	—	—	—

2016 Year-End Financials
Return on assets: 7.0%   Cash ($ mil.): 76
Return on equity: 2.5%
Current ratio: 1.00

ST. LUKE'S HOSPITAL

EXECUTIVES

President, Frank J Bartell III
Board of Directors, Joanne E Klumm
Director, Michael D Kreischer
Financial Executive, Cindy Grube
Plant & Facilities Manager, Cheresa Hadsell

LOCATIONS

HQ: ST. LUKE'S HOSPITAL
5901 MONCLOVA RD, MAUMEE, OH 435371899
Phone: 419 893-5911
Web: WWW.PROMEDICA.ORG

HISTORICAL FINANCIALS
Company Type: Private

Income Statement
FYE: December 31

	REVENUE ($ mil.)	NET INCOME ($ mil.)	NET PROFIT MARGIN	EMPLOYEES
12/15	188	(3)	—	1,558
12/14	169	(35)	—	—
12/08	135	(84)	—	—
12/07	130	(15)	—	—
Annual Growth	4.7%	—	—	—

2015 Year-End Financials
Return on assets: 19.6%
Return on equity: (-1.9%)
Current ratio: 0.90
Cash ($ mil.): 17

ST. LUKE'S PHYSICIAN GROUP, INC.

EXECUTIVES

Chief Executive Officer, Richard Anderson
Board of Directors, Norma Roberts
Manager, Jim Goetz
Auditors: WITHUMSMITHBROWN PC MORRISTOW

LOCATIONS

HQ: ST. LUKE'S PHYSICIAN GROUP, INC.
801 OSTRUM ST STE 1, BETHLEHEM, PA 180151000
Phone: 610 954-4990

HISTORICAL FINANCIALS
Company Type: Private

Income Statement
FYE: June 30

	REVENUE ($ mil.)	NET INCOME ($ mil.)	NET PROFIT MARGIN	EMPLOYEES
06/15	238	(20)	—	135
06/14	206	(15)	—	—
06/13	178	(10)	—	—
06/10	120	(4)	—	—
Annual Growth	14.6%	—	—	—

2015 Year-End Financials
Return on assets: 12.5%
Return on equity: (-8.5%)
Current ratio: 0.50
Cash ($ mil.): —

ST. LUKE'S REGIONAL MEDICAL CENTER, LTD.

EXECUTIVES

President, Edwin Dahlberg
Manager, Hillary Furlong
Manager, Terri Hays
Manager, Ann Kaley
Vice-President, David Crane
Managing Director, Jennifer Konieczny
Manager, Wayne Frieder

LOCATIONS

HQ: ST. LUKE'S REGIONAL MEDICAL CENTER, LTD.
190 E BANNOCK ST, BOISE, ID 837126241
Phone: 208 381-5500
Web: WWW.USADOCTORS.NET

HISTORICAL FINANCIALS
Company Type: Private

Income Statement
FYE: September 30

	REVENUE ($ mil.)	NET INCOME ($ mil.)	NET PROFIT MARGIN	EMPLOYEES
09/15	1,370	22	1.7%	4,500
09/14	1,255	31	2.5%	—
09/13	1,121	(19)	—	—
09/08	898	44	4.9%	—
Annual Growth	6.2%	(9.1%)	—	—

2015 Year-End Financials
Return on assets: 2.9%
Return on equity: 1.7%
Current ratio: 5.90
Cash ($ mil.): 8

ST. MARY MEDICAL CENTER

EXECUTIVES

President, Alan H Garrett
Board of Directors, Susan Biewend
Board of Directors, Donna Nash
Board of Directors, Jasvinder Singh

LOCATIONS

HQ: ST. MARY MEDICAL CENTER
18300 US HIGHWAY 18, APPLE VALLEY, CA 923072206
Phone: 760 242-2311
Web: WWW.STMARYAPPLEVALLEY.COM

HISTORICAL FINANCIALS
Company Type: Private

Income Statement
FYE: June 30

	REVENUE ($ mil.)	NET INCOME ($ mil.)	NET PROFIT MARGIN	EMPLOYEES
06/15	325	38	11.7%	1,350
06/14	283	11	4.1%	—
06/13	288	19	6.8%	—
06/10	265	23	8.8%	—
Annual Growth	4.1%	10.4%	—	—

2015 Year-End Financials
Return on assets: 0.3%
Return on equity: 11.7%
Current ratio: 3.10
Cash ($ mil.): 60

ST. MARY MEDICAL CENTER, INC.

EXECUTIVES

Chief Executive Officer, Janice Ryba

Financial Executive, Arthur Vasquez
Chief Financial Officer, Milton Triani
Personnel Director, Thack Nguyen

LOCATIONS

HQ: ST. MARY MEDICAL CENTER, INC.
1500 S LAKE PARK AVE, HOBART, IN 463426699
Phone: 219 942-0551
Web: WWW.COMHS.ORG

HISTORICAL FINANCIALS
Company Type: Private

Income Statement
FYE: June 30

	REVENUE ($ mil.)	NET INCOME ($ mil.)	NET PROFIT MARGIN	EMPLOYEES
06/15	233	23	10.1%	800
06/14	226	14	6.6%	—
06/13	215	17	8.2%	—
06/10	189	14	7.7%	—
Annual Growth	4.2%	9.9%	—	—

2015 Year-End Financials
Return on assets: 1.1%
Return on equity: 10.1%
Current ratio: 1.80
Cash ($ mil.): 4

ST. MARY'S HEALTH CARE SYSTEM, INC.

St. Mary's Health Care System cares for the residents of northeast Georgia. Its St. Mary's Hospital has almost 200 acute-care beds. From health and wellness programs to women's and children's services the hospital also has centers dedicated to outpatient rehabilitation home health and long-term care. Specialty services include neurology cardiovascular care orthopedics and gastroenterology. It also operates the 25-bed St. Mary's Good Samaritan Hospital and a retirement village. The organization is sponsored by the Sisters of Mercy of the Americas St. Mary's Health Care System is a member of CHE Trinity Health (formed in 2013 through the consolidation of Catholic Health East and Trinity Health).

Operations

Not-for-profit Catholic health care ministry St. Mary's Health Care System includes St. Mary's Hospital St. Mary's Good Samaritan Hospital Highland Hills Village retirement community and the Center for Alzheimer's and Dementia Care. It also provides regional home health care and hospice services.

St. Mary's Hospital is the only hospital in the region to achieve The Joint Commission Gold Seal of Approval certification in advanced primary stroke heart failure care and total knee replacement.

Geographic Reach

St. Mary's Health Care System's service area includes Clarke and Oconee Counties Greene County and parts of surrounding counties from Walton to Stephens.

Strategy

The company grows through internal expansion and acquisitions. In 2013 it opened a new outpatient facility that offers hyperbaric oxygen therapy and other treatments for patients with chronic wounds. That year it also launched a new patient portal MyHealth giving patients the ability to access their electronic medical records 24 hours a day.

Mergers and Acquisitions

Expanding its services and geographic coverage in 2012 St. Mary's Health Care System acquired St. Mary's Good Samaritan Hospital a not-for-profit 25-bed Critical Access Hospital serving greater Greene County and the Lake Oconee communities of Georgia.

Company Background

The health system brought Athens Internal Medicine Associates (a medical practice in Athens) into its network in 2011.

St. Mary's Health Care System traces its roots to the founding of St. Mary's Hospital in 1906 and has been the official health care provider for the University of Georgia Athletic Association since 1999.

EXECUTIVES

Vice President Human Resources, Jeff English
Director of Admissions, Jonathan Roberts
Director of Radiology and Cardiovascular Services, Jeff Brown
Vice President Mission Services and Co Chairman, Patricia Loome
Director of Radiology, Jerry O Smith
Vice President Medical Affairs Medical Doctor, Bruce Middendorf

LOCATIONS

HQ: ST. MARY'S HEALTH CARE SYSTEM, INC.
1230 BAXTER ST, ATHENS, GA 306063712
Phone: 706 389-3000
Web: WWW.STMARYSATHENS.ORG

PRODUCTS/OPERATIONS

Selected Services
Cardiology
Care after discharge
Children & Pediatrics
Clinical Laboratory
Emergency Care
Gastroenterology
Highland Hills Village
Home Care/Hospice
Hospitalists
Industrial Medicine
Infusion Suite
Medical Imaging
Mission Services
Neurosciences
Older Adults
Orthopedics
Outpatient Services
Palliative Care
Preregister
Rehabilitation
Sleep Disorders Center
St. Mary's Medical Group
Stroke
Surgery & Robotics
Wellness Center
Women & Maternity
Wound Healing

COMPETITORS

DeKalb Medical
Emory Healthcare
Gwinnett Health System
Northeast Georgia
  Health System
Northside Hospital
Piedmont Athens
  Regional

Piedmont Healthcare
Regency Hospital
WellStar Health System
West Georgia Health
  System

HISTORICAL FINANCIALS
Company Type: Private

Income Statement
FYE: June 30

	REVENUE ($ mil.)	NET INCOME ($ mil.)	NET PROFIT MARGIN	EMPLOYEES
06/15	174	29	16.9%	1,350
06/14	177	11	6.3%	—
Annual Growth	(2.1%)	164.4%	—	—

2015 Year-End Financials
Return on assets: 7.4%   Cash ($ mil.): 42
Return on equity: 16.9%
Current ratio: 2.60

ST. MARY'S HEALTH, INC.

St. Mary's Medical Center of Evansville is a 433-bed hospital serving Indiana's River City. It is the primary facility in regional St. Mary's Health System which is in turn part of Ascension Health. The Evansville hospital provides emergency trauma diagnostic surgical and rehabilitative services as well as specialized cancer cardiac orthopedic and neurological services. With a total of some 750 physicians St. Mary's Health System also includes St. Mary's Hospital for Women & Children (100 beds adjacent to the main hospital) and St. Mary's Warrick (a 25-bed hospital in Boonville Indiana) as well as specialty outpatient surgical cancer and home health units in surrounding areas of southern Indiana.

Operations

St. Mary's Medical Center of Evansville admits some 17000 inpatients annually. It also handles around 64000 emergency room visits and performs approximately 4700 inpatient and 18000 outpatient surgeries each year.

Company Background

St. Mary's Medical Center of Evansville was originally a Marine Hospital built by the US government. When the government shuttered its doors city business leaders bought the building in 1872 and partnered with the Daughters of Charity to operate a community hospital.

EXECUTIVES

Evp And Coo St Mary's Health System, Gwen Sandefur
Vice President Revenue Cycle and Managed Care, Barbara K Clayton
Vice President Strategic Services, John Greaney
Medical Records Director, MELANIE MARTIN
Interim President, Daniel Parod
Managing Director, Roger Johnson
Board Member, Anthony Stephens
Board Member, Prasad Gade
Auditors: DELOITTE TAX LLP INDIANAPOLIS

LOCATIONS

HQ: ST. MARY'S HEALTH, INC.
3700 WASHINGTON AVE, EVANSVILLE, IN 477140541
Phone: 812 485-4000
Web: WWW.STMARYS.ORG

PRODUCTS/OPERATIONS

Selected Services
Breast Center
Cancer Care Services
Children's Health Care Services and Programs

Community Outreach Services
Convenient Care Centers
Diabetic Foot Clinic
Diabetes Services
Emergency Services Department
Endoscopy Suite
Foundation
Heart Services
Home Health Services
Hospitalists
Imaging/Radiology
Infusion Center
Laboratory Services
LifeFlight
Medical Equipment
Mental Health Services
Neurosciences & Stroke Care
Occupational Medicine Services
Orthopedic Healthcare
Palliative Care
Pastoral Care
Quality and Patient Safety
Rehabilitation Services
Respiratory Care
Senior Services
Sleep Disorders Center
Surgical Services
Trauma Services
Volunteers & Auxiliary
Weight Management Center
Women's Services and Programs
Women's Wellness Center

COMPETITORS

Ball Memorial Hospital
Community Health
  Network
Daviess Community
  Hospital
Deaconess Health
  System
Good Samaritan
  Hospital (IN)

Henry County Memorial
  Hospital
Kosciusko Community
  Hospital
Memorial Hospital
  (Logansport)

HISTORICAL FINANCIALS
Company Type: Private

Income Statement
FYE: June 30

	REVENUE ($ mil.)	NET INCOME ($ mil.)	NET PROFIT MARGIN	EMPLOYEES
06/15	574	52	9.2%	3,500
06/13	468	48	10.4%	—
06/11	0	0	—	—
06/10	0	0	—	—
Annual Growth	—	402.9%	—	—

2015 Year-End Financials
Return on assets: 5.7%   Cash ($ mil.): 12
Return on equity: 9.2%
Current ratio: 2.50

ST. MARY'S HEALTH, INC.

LOCATIONS

HQ: ST. MARY'S HEALTH, INC.
3700 WASHINGTON AVE, EVANSVILLE, IN 477140541
Phone: 812 485-7623

Company Type: Private

Income Statement				FYE: June 30
	REVENUE ($ mil.)	NET INCOME ($ mil.)	NET PROFIT MARGIN	EMPLOYEES
06/15	487	71	14.7%	5
06/11	20	4	22.9%	—
06/10	19	2	15.0%	—
Annual Growth	89.4%	88.8%	—	—

2015 Year-End Financials

Return on assets: 2.6% Cash ($ mil.): 12
Return on equity: 14.7%
Current ratio: 0.40

ST. MARY'S HOSPITAL & MEDICAL CENTER, INC.

EXECUTIVES

Chief Executive Officer, Brian Davidson
Financial Executive, Thad Ritter
Manager, Rhonda Brateng
Director, Michael Martinez
Manager, Debbie Rowley

LOCATIONS

HQ: ST. MARY'S HOSPITAL & MEDICAL CENTER, INC.
2635 N 7TH ST, GRAND JUNCTION, CO 815018209
Phone: 970 298-2013
Web: WWW.STMARYSMADISON.COM

HISTORICAL FINANCIALS

Company Type: Private

Income Statement				FYE: December 31
	REVENUE ($ mil.)	NET INCOME ($ mil.)	NET PROFIT MARGIN	EMPLOYEES
12/15	436	54	12.4%	2,000
12/14	410	45	11.1%	—
12/09	360	50	13.9%	—
12/05	0	0	17.9%	—
Annual Growth	103.6%	96.3%	—	—

2015 Year-End Financials

Return on assets: 3.4% Cash ($ mil.): 1
Return on equity: 12.4%
Current ratio: 1.20

ST. MARY'S MEDICAL CENTER

EXECUTIVES

Chairman of the Board, SIS Kathleen Hofer
Director of Finance, Ruth Martin
Supervisor, Jeff Majerle

LOCATIONS

HQ: ST. MARY'S MEDICAL CENTER
407 E 3RD ST, DULUTH, MN 558051984
Phone: 218 786-4000

Company Type: Private

Income Statement				FYE: June 30
	REVENUE ($ mil.)	NET INCOME ($ mil.)	NET PROFIT MARGIN	EMPLOYEES
06/15	396	40	10.3%	4,209
06/14	439	66	15.1%	—
06/13	419	65	15.6%	—
06/12	373	38	10.3%	—
Annual Growth	2.0%	2.0%	—	—

2015 Year-End Financials

Return on assets: 1.7% Cash ($ mil.): 130
Return on equity: 10.3%
Current ratio: 6.50

ST. MARY'S MEDICAL CENTER

Nobody wants to get sick but if you're ailing in West Virginia St. Mary's Medical Center wants you to know you are in good hands. The not-for-profit 395-bed medical facility serves patients in areas such as cardiac emergency neuroscience and cancer treatment. The largest health care facility in the tri-state region St. Mary's Medical Center is also a teaching facility affiliated with Joan C. Edwards Marshall University School of Medicine. St. Mary's Home Health Services administers care for patients in a six county area in Ohio and West Virginia. Services include IV therapy and occupational and physical therapies. St. Mary's Medical Center was founded in 1924.

Geographic Reach

With a campus in West Virginia St. Mary's Medical Center serves a tri-state region across some 20 counties.

Operations

The campus also houses St. Mary's School of Nursing the St. Mary's School of Medical Imaging and the St. Mary's School of Respiratory Care. St. Mary's Centers of Excellence includes cardiac care cancer treatment emergency/trauma services neuroscience and orthopedics.

Strategy

Following years of collaboration with area homeowners and businesses St. Mary's Medical Center opened a new $18.5-million Ironton campus in 2012 that boasts a 24-hour emergency room imaging and lab services family care and specialty doctors the likes of pediatricians and dentists.

EXECUTIVES

Vice President of Medical Affairs, Lee Taylor
Director of Radiology, Jamie Kellar
Vice President of Human Resour, Susan Robinson

LOCATIONS

HQ: ST. MARY'S MEDICAL CENTER
2900 1ST AVE, HUNTINGTON, WV 257021241
Phone: 304 526-1234
Web: WWW.ST-MARYS.ORG

COMPETITORS

Adena Health System
CAMC Health
Clinch Valley Medical Center
Fairfield Medical Center
Highlands Health
Pikeville Medical Center

Company Type: Private

Income Statement				FYE: September 30
	REVENUE ($ mil.)	NET INCOME ($ mil.)	NET PROFIT MARGIN	EMPLOYEES
09/15	311	(42)	—	2,000
09/14	401	10	2.7%	—
09/13	366	31	8.7%	—
09/09	341	1	0.5%	—
Annual Growth	(1.5%)	—	—	—

2015 Year-End Financials

Return on assets: 13.3% Cash ($ mil.): 15
Return on equity: (-13.5%)
Current ratio: 1.60

ST. MARY'S MEDICAL CENTER OF SAGINAW, INC.

EXECUTIVES

President, John Graham
Director, Raghu Sarvepalli
Executive Director, Gary Dunbar

LOCATIONS

HQ: ST. MARY'S MEDICAL CENTER OF SAGINAW, INC.
800 S WASHINGTON AVE, SAGINAW, MI 486012551
Phone: 989 907-8000
Web: WWW.STMARYSOFMICHIGAN.ORG

HISTORICAL FINANCIALS

Company Type: Private

Income Statement				FYE: June 30
	REVENUE ($ mil.)	NET INCOME ($ mil.)	NET PROFIT MARGIN	EMPLOYEES
06/15	223	(14)	—	1,869
06/13	255	(0)	—	—
06/11	276	26	9.7%	—
06/10	271	14	5.2%	—
Annual Growth	(3.8%)	—	—	—

2015 Year-End Financials

Return on assets: 9.3% Cash ($ mil.): 2
Return on equity: (-6.6%)
Current ratio: 0.80

ST. PETER'S HEALTH PARTNERS

St. Peter's Health Partners (formerly St. Peter's Health Care Services) is a not-for-profit health care system that serves northeastern New York. It includes health networks Seton Health and Northeast Health. Its primary facility St. Peter's Hospital has more than 440 acute-care beds and a medical staff of more than 600 physicians. Specialty services include emergency medicine cancer and car-

diovascular care and women's health. St. Peter's also operates community health clinics long-term care facilities mental health centers and home health and hospice agencies. Founded by the Religious Sisters of Mercy in 1869 St. Peter's operates from more than 125 locations and is a subsidiary of Catholic Health East.

Change in Company Type

Following its 2011 merger with Seton Health and Northeast Health St. Peter's Health Care was renamed St. Peter's Health Partners and continued to be owned by not-for-profit hospital operator Catholic Health East. By merging the systems aim to better meet the challenges of federal health reform measures and have greater operational flexibility although full integration may take up to three years.

Operations

St. Peter's Health Partners is the parent company for four hospitals: St. Peter's Hospital the Albany Memorial and Samaritan Hospitals of Northeast Health and Seton's St. Mary's Hospital. It also includes the Sunnyview Rehabilitation Hospital the Community Hospice and the Eddy Visiting Nurses Association which provides skilled nurses for home health and senior services.

Strategy

To better serve Troy and Rensselaer counties St. Peter's Health Partners has undertaken a 13-year $150-million master facilities plan for Samaritan and St. Mary's Hospitals. The project includes constuction renovation and modernization of inpatient facilites at Samaritan and outpatient facilities at St. Mary's. The project aims to fulfill a promise of the 2011 merger with Seton Health and Northeast Health: to improve health care facilities and programs in Troy.

EXECUTIVES

Vice President Legal Services, Robert Swidler
Vice President, Rosie Perez
Nursing Director, Kathleen Marsch
Auditors: DELOITTE & TOUCHE LLP ROCHEST

LOCATIONS

HQ: ST. PETER'S HEALTH PARTNERS
  315 S MANNING BLVD, ALBANY, NY 122081707
Phone: 518 525-1111
Web: WWW.SPHP.COM

PRODUCTS/OPERATIONS

Selected Operations

Albany Memorial Hospital
The Community Hospice
Eddy Visiting Nurses Association
Samaritan Hospital (Troy)
St. Mary's Hospital (Troy)
St. Peter's Hospital (Albany)
Sunnyview Rehabilitation Hospital (Schenectady)

COMPETITORS

Albany Medical Center
 Ellis Hospital
 Oneida Healthcare Center
 SUNY Upstate Medical University
 St. Joseph's Hospital Health Center
 United Health Services Hospitals
 Upstate University Hospital at Community General

HISTORICAL FINANCIALS

Company Type: Private

Income Statement

FYE: June 30

	REVENUE ($ mil.)	NET INCOME ($ mil.)	NET PROFIT MARGIN	EMPLOYEES
06/15	1,263	17	1.4%	12,000
06/14	1,185	48	4.1%	—
06/13*	571	23	4.2%	—
12/12	1,069	61	5.7%	—
Annual Growth	8.7%	(47.2%)	—	—

*Fiscal year change

2015 Year-End Financials

Return on assets: 5.4%   Cash ($ mil.): 120
Return on equity: 1.4%
Current ratio: 1.40

ST. PETER'S HOSPITAL

EXECUTIVES

Chairman of the Board, Mark Taylor
President, Fred Olson
Treasurer, Guy Almquist
Principal, William Northey
Manager, Bonnie Barnard
Accountant, Kristy Rosseland
Manager, Yonne Deasley

LOCATIONS

HQ: ST. PETER'S HOSPITAL
  2475 E BROADWAY ST, HELENA, MT 596014999
Phone: 406 442-2480
Web: WWW.STPETES.ORG

HISTORICAL FINANCIALS

Company Type: Private

Income Statement

FYE: May 31

	REVENUE ($ mil.)	NET INCOME ($ mil.)	NET PROFIT MARGIN	EMPLOYEES
05/15	178	14	8.2%	1,200
05/12	165	5	3.3%	—
05/11*	150	11	7.4%	—
12/10	185	0	—	—
Annual Growth	—	1225.2%	—	—

*Fiscal year change

2015 Year-End Financials

Return on assets: 3.3%   Cash ($ mil.): 20
Return on equity: 8.2%
Current ratio: 1.10

ST. ROSE HOSPITAL

EXECUTIVES

President, Lex Reddy

LOCATIONS

HQ: ST. ROSE HOSPITAL
  27200 CALAROGA AVE, HAYWARD, CA 945454383
Phone: 510 264-4000

HISTORICAL FINANCIALS

Company Type: Private

Income Statement

FYE: September 30

	REVENUE ($ mil.)	NET INCOME ($ mil.)	NET PROFIT MARGIN	EMPLOYEES
09/15	170	22	13.1%	1
09/14	99	(8)	—	—
Annual Growth	71.5%			

2015 Year-End Financials

Return on assets: 2.2%   Cash ($ mil.): 12
Return on equity: 13.1%
Current ratio: 0.50

ST. VINCENT CARMEL HOSPITAL, INC.

EXECUTIVES

President, Michael D Chittenden
Chairman of the Board, Deborah Wood
President, Barbara Carter
Vice-President, Gwynn Perlich
Director, Carolyn Ingle
Personnel Director, Charles Jeffras
Vice-President, Jennifer Fry
Director, Carey Landry
Director, Diane Newton
Director, Tom Morlock

LOCATIONS

HQ: ST. VINCENT CARMEL HOSPITAL, INC.
  13500 N MERIDIAN ST, CARMEL, IN 460321456
Phone: 317 582-7000
Web: WWW.STVINCENT.ORG

HISTORICAL FINANCIALS

Company Type: Private

Income Statement

FYE: June 30

	REVENUE ($ mil.)	NET INCOME ($ mil.)	NET PROFIT MARGIN	EMPLOYEES
06/15	189	55	29.2%	56
06/14	237	68	28.7%	—
06/13	203	55	27.5%	—
Annual Growth	(3.4%)	(0.5%)	—	—

2015 Year-End Financials

Return on assets: 1.9%   Cash ($ mil.): 5
Return on equity: 29.2%
Current ratio: 0.80

ST. VINCENT HEALTH, INC.

EXECUTIVES

Chief Executive Officer, Jonathan S Nalli
Board of Directors, Randy Cox
Purchasing Agent, Tony Kinney
Plant Engineering Manager, Steve Smith
Auditors: DELOITTE TAX LP INDIANAPOLIS

LOCATIONS

HQ: ST. VINCENT HEALTH, INC.
10330 N MERIDIAN ST, INDIANAPOLIS, IN
462901024
Phone: 317 338-2345
Web: WWW.STVINCENT.ORG

HISTORICAL FINANCIALS
Company Type: Private

Income Statement
FYE: June 30

	REVENUE ($ mil.)	NET INCOME ($ mil.)	NET PROFIT MARGIN	EMPLOYEES
06/15	219	12	5.5%	6,243
06/14	592	416	70.3%	—
Annual Growth	(62.9%)	(97.1%)	—	—

2015 Year-End Financials

Return on assets: 20.3%   Cash ($ mil.): 12
Return on equity: 5.5%
Current ratio: 0.30

ST. VINCENT HEALTHCARE

EXECUTIVES

President, Steve Loveless
Consultant, Joan Hendricks
Director, Michael Schabacker
Vice-President, Steve Ballock
Administrative Assistant, Brett Close

LOCATIONS

HQ: ST. VINCENT HEALTHCARE
1233 N 30TH ST, BILLINGS, MT 591010127
Phone: 406 657-7000
Web: WWW.SVH-MT.ORG

HISTORICAL FINANCIALS
Company Type: Private

Income Statement
FYE: December 31

	REVENUE ($ mil.)	NET INCOME ($ mil.)	NET PROFIT MARGIN	EMPLOYEES
12/15	439	58	13.3%	1,800
12/14	440	40	9.2%	—
12/13*	428	13	3.2%	—
05/01	176	17	10.1%	—
Annual Growth	6.3%	8.3%	—	—

*Fiscal year change

2015 Year-End Financials

Return on assets: 2.5%   Cash ($ mil.): —
Return on equity: 13.3%
Current ratio: 2.80

ST. VINCENT HOSPITAL

EXECUTIVES

Chief Executive Officer, Bruce Tassin
Manager, Donald Butterfield

LOCATIONS

HQ: ST. VINCENT HOSPITAL
1631 HOSPITAL DR STE 100, SANTA FE, NM
875057631
Phone: 505 983-3361
Web: WWW.STVIN.ORG

HISTORICAL FINANCIALS
Company Type: Private

Income Statement
FYE: June 30

	REVENUE ($ mil.)	NET INCOME ($ mil.)	NET PROFIT MARGIN	EMPLOYEES
06/15	374	26	7.0%	2,000
06/14	365	6	1.7%	—
06/13	368	3	1.0%	—
06/10	299	21	7.1%	—
Annual Growth	4.6%	4.1%	—	—

2015 Year-End Financials

Return on assets: 5.0%   Cash ($ mil.): 29
Return on equity: 7.0%
Current ratio: 1.40

ST. VINCENT HOSPITAL OF THE HOSPITAL SISTERS OF THE THIRD ORDER OF S

EXECUTIVES

Chairman of the Board, Mary Beth Culnan
Clerk, Kara Wilke
Auditors: CROWE HORWATH LLP CHICAGO IL

LOCATIONS

HQ: ST. VINCENT HOSPITAL OF THE HOSPITAL
SISTERS OF THE THIRD ORDER OF S
835 S VAN BUREN ST, GREEN BAY, WI 543013575
Phone: 920 433-0111
Web: WWW.STVINCENTHOSPITAL.ORG

HISTORICAL FINANCIALS
Company Type: Private

Income Statement
FYE: June 30

	REVENUE ($ mil.)	NET INCOME ($ mil.)	NET PROFIT MARGIN	EMPLOYEES
06/15	480	29	6.0%	2,360
06/11	424	26	6.3%	—
06/10	376	16	4.4%	—
06/09	1,873	0	0.0%	—
Annual Growth	(20.3%)	247.8%	—	—

2015 Year-End Financials

Return on assets: 11.7%   Cash ($ mil.): 24
Return on equity: 6.0%
Current ratio: 0.80

ST. VINCENT INFIRMARY MEDICAL CENTER

EXECUTIVES

Chief Executive Officer, Peter Banko
Administrative Assistant, Sandra Patrick
Production Director, J Martin
Director, Alan Winkler
Personnel Director, Derrick Paul

LOCATIONS

HQ: ST. VINCENT INFIRMARY MEDICAL CENTER
2 SAINT VINCENT CIR, LITTLE ROCK, AR 722055423
Phone: 501 552-3000
Web: WWW.STVINCENTHEALTH.COM

HISTORICAL FINANCIALS
Company Type: Private

Income Statement
FYE: June 30

	REVENUE ($ mil.)	NET INCOME ($ mil.)	NET PROFIT MARGIN	EMPLOYEES
06/15	358	(14)	—	2,824
06/14	407	(45)	—	—
06/13	382	(46)	—	—
06/09	310	(19)	—	—
Annual Growth	2.4%	—	—	—

ST. VINCENT'S BIRMINGHAM

EXECUTIVES

President, Curtis James
Marketing Director, Phillip Greene
Personnel Manager, Tammy White
Auditors: DELOITTE TAX LLP CINCINNATI

LOCATIONS

HQ: ST. VINCENT'S BIRMINGHAM
810 SAINT VINCENTS DR, BIRMINGHAM, AL
352051601
Phone: 205 939-7000
Web: WWW.STV.ORG

HISTORICAL FINANCIALS
Company Type: Private

Income Statement
FYE: June 30

	REVENUE ($ mil.)	NET INCOME ($ mil.)	NET PROFIT MARGIN	EMPLOYEES
06/15	382	42	11.1%	1,478
06/14	391	32	8.3%	—
06/13	386	38	10.0%	—
06/10	371	29	8.0%	—
Annual Growth	0.5%	7.4%	—	—

2015 Year-End Financials

Return on assets: 2.9%   Cash ($ mil.): 1
Return on equity: 11.1%
Current ratio: 0.80

ST. VINCENT'S EAST

EXECUTIVES

Chief Executive Officer, George McGowan
Personnel Director, Katie Chambelle
Director, Steve Preston
Supervisor, Lynn Kevitt
Chief Operating Officer, Kim Shrewsbury
Vice-President, Jennifer Kingry
Auditors: DELOITTE TAX LLP CINCINNATI

LOCATIONS

HQ: ST. VINCENT'S EAST
50 MEDICAL PARK DR E, BIRMINGHAM, AL
352353401
Phone: 205 838-3000
Web: WWW.STVINCENTSHMS.COM

HISTORICAL FINANCIALS

Company Type: Private

Income Statement

FYE: June 30

	REVENUE ($ mil.)	NET INCOME ($ mil.)	NET PROFIT MARGIN	EMPLOYEES
06/15	203	(1)	—	1,550
06/14	203	(10)	—	—
06/11	201	(3)	—	—
06/10	208	4	2.1%	—
Annual Growth	(0.5%)	—	—	—

2015 Year-End Financials

Return on assets: 2.2%   Cash ($ mil.): —
Return on equity: (-0.5%)
Current ratio: 0.40

ST. VINCENT'S MEDICAL CENTER, INC

EXECUTIVES

President, Moody Chisolm
Auditors: DELOITTE TAX LLP CINCINNATI

LOCATIONS

HQ: ST. VINCENT'S MEDICAL CENTER, INC
4205 BELFORT RD STE 4030, JACKSONVILLE, FL
322161475
Phone: 904 308-7300

HISTORICAL FINANCIALS

Company Type: Private

Income Statement

FYE: June 30

	REVENUE ($ mil.)	NET INCOME ($ mil.)	NET PROFIT MARGIN	EMPLOYEES
06/15	452	32	7.3%	3,535
06/14	445	33	7.4%	—
06/10	448	34	7.7%	—
06/09	377	(32)	—	—
Annual Growth	3.1%	—	—	—

2015 Year-End Financials

Return on assets: 5.8%   Cash ($ mil.): 2
Return on equity: 7.3%
Current ratio: 2.20

STANDARD ELECTRIC COMPANY

Standard Electric and its affiliates distribute electrical and electronic products and supplies to customers through about 30 locations in Michigan. The company was founded in 1929 by Samuel Cohen and brothers Morris and Max Blumberg. The Blumberg brothers earlier established another Michigan-based electrical distributor Madison Electric an affiliate of Standard Electric with 10 Michigan locations. Another affiliated firm U.P. Electric/Wittock Supply Co. is a distributor of electrical and mechanical products with four locations on the upper Michigan peninsula. The company is owned by its directors and their families.

EXECUTIVES

President, Laverne N Weber
Branch Manager, Ron Daniels
Manager, Bonnie Weber
Manager, Andrew Cardello
Account Manager, Phil Vogel
Auditors: GORDON ADVISORS PC TROY MI

LOCATIONS

HQ: STANDARD ELECTRIC COMPANY
2650 TRAUTNER DR, SAGINAW, MI 486049599
Phone: 989 497-2100
Web: WWW.STANDARDELECTRICCO.COM

COMPETITORS

Kendall Electric	Utility Supply and
McNaughton-McKay	Construction
Medler Electric	Werner Electric Supply

HISTORICAL FINANCIALS

Company Type: Private

Income Statement

FYE: February 29

	REVENUE ($ mil.)	NET INCOME ($ mil.)	NET PROFIT MARGIN	EMPLOYEES
02/16	176	0	0.2%	250
02/15	172	2	1.3%	—
02/14	159	1	1.1%	—
02/13	152	1	1.0%	—
Annual Growth	5.0%	(40.4%)	—	—

2016 Year-End Financials

Return on assets: 8.3%   Cash ($ mil.): —
Return on equity: 0.2%
Current ratio: 0.80

STANFORD HEALTH CARE

Doctors patients medical students and researchers gather at Stanford Health Care (formerly Stanford Hospital and Clinics). As Stanford University's primary medical teaching facility the more than 600-bed Stanford Hospital specializes in such areas as cardiac care cancer treatment neurology surgery and organ transplant. The affiliated Stanford Clinics is a physician group practice organization that represents more than 100 specialized fields of medicine. Stanford Health Care is part of the Stanford Medicine organization which also includes the nearby Stanford University School of Medicine and the 310-bed Lucile Packard Children's Hospital (named for the wife of Hewlett-Packard co-founder David Packard).

Operations

Stanford Health Care handles some 25000 inpatient admissions each year more than 50000 emergency room visits and about 425000 outpatient encounters. The organization boasts such specialized clinics as the Byers Eye Institute the Stanford Comprehensive Cancer Center the Stanford Center for Marfan Syndrome and Aortic Disorders and the California VitreoRetinal Center. It also operates centers for orthopedic brain blood and marrow transplant and other specialist procedures.

Educational programs include medical and graduate student training as well as residency and fellowship programs. The organization also conducts research in medical and biological fields.

Additionally the system owns stakes in physician network University HealthCare Alliance radiation therapy facility Stanford Emanuel Radiation Oncology Center health care advocacy firm CareCounsel and HMO plan University HealthCare Advantage.

Geographic Reach

Stanford Health Care operates in more than 15 locations in the San Francisco Bay Area.

Sales and Marketing

Stanford Health Care receives 70% of its revenues from managed care (commercial insurance) providers. Another 20% of patient service income is sourced to Medicare and Medicaid programs.

Financial Performance

Revenue increased 10% to $3 billion in fiscal 2014 (ended August) due to higher net patient service revenues primarily from managed care and Medicare fee increases. However net income dropped 22% to $432.2 million that year as operating costs rose and the system reported losses on investments.

Cash flow from operations grew 8% to $366.5 million in fiscal 2014 largely due to a change in working capital items.

Strategy

To remain at the forefront of medicine and technology the hospital is constructing a new $2 billion 600-bed facility next to its existing building. Local high-tech firms including Apple Hewlett-Packard and Intel are kicking in $15 million and technology partnerships to support the project. As corporate partners the firms will help to develop and integrate state-of-the-art information technology for the new facility.

Other growth projects include the construction of a new outpatient cancer clinic in San Jose. The center opened in 2014.

Also in 2014 the system changed its name from Stanford Hospitals and Clinics to Stanford Health Care. That change signified the broader scope of its operations which go beyond inpatient and outpatient facilities to include affiliated physician practices and health plans.

In fiscal 2015 Stanford Health Care engineers developed and launched a new MyHealth mobile application for the iPhone. The app connects with Epic electronic health records and Apple's HealthKit enabling patients to monitor their health data. MyHealth provides consumers with such capabilities as telehealth (video) physician visits appointment scheduling online payments and the ability to manage prescriptions and access test results.

EXECUTIVES

President and CEO, David Entwistle
VP and Chief Marketing Officer, Deborah Italiano
Chief Risk Officer, Jeff Driver

VP Clinical Cancer Center and Cardiovascular Health, Sridhar Seshadri
Chief Medical Officer, Norman W. Rizk
COO, Quinn L. McKenna
CIO, Pravene Nath
COO, James Hereford
Interim CFO, David Connor
Chief Quality Officer, Raj Behal
Chief Medical Information Officer, Christopher (Topher) Sharp
Vice President of Hospital Development, Michele Schiele
Vice President of Business Development Service Lines, Jane Shannahan
Clinic Manager, Diana Felix
Senior Advisor To The Vice President F, Carol Dressler
Board Member, Raksha Patel
Auditors: PRICEWATERHOUSECOOPERS LLP SA

LOCATIONS

HQ: STANFORD HEALTH CARE
   300 PASTEUR DR, STANFORD, CA 943052200
Phone: 650 723-4000

PRODUCTS/OPERATIONS

2014 Sales

	$ mil.	% of total
Net patient service revenue	2,839	95
Premium revenue	60	2
Other revenue	98	3
Total	**2,998**	**100**

Selected Services

Heart Center
Neurosciences
Orthopaedics
Sports Medicine
Stanford Cancer Center
Surgical Services
Transplant

COMPETITORS

Dignity Health	Sutter Health
Sequoia Capital	UCSF Medical

HISTORICAL FINANCIALS
Company Type: Private

Income Statement
FYE: August 31

	REVENUE ($ mil.)	NET INCOME ($ mil.)	NET PROFIT MARGIN	EMPLOYEES
08/15	3,570	372	10.4%	5,045
08/10	2,141	186	8.7%	—
08/09	1,769	(56)	—	—
Annual Growth	**12.4%**	—	—	—

2015 Year-End Financials

Return on assets: 7.9%   Cash ($ mil.): 475
Return on equity: 10.4%
Current ratio: 1.30

STANLEY STEEMER INTERNATIONAL, INC.

Carpet stains don't startle this Stanley. Stanley Steemer International provides residential and commercial carpet and upholstery cleaning through more than 300 franchise and corporate locations in 48 states. In addition to cleaning carpets the company provides cleaning services for tile and grout and air ducts as well as cars boats and RVs. The company which is known for its fleet of yellow vans sells its own brand of cleaning products through an online store. Founded by Jack Bates in 1947 when he established his own one-man carpet cleaning business Stanley Steemer is owned by his descendants including CEO Wesley Bates and President Justin Bates.

Operations

Stanley Steemer has built a longtime business providing residential and commercial deep cleaning services offering 24-hour emergency water restoration services. Its staff of trained technicians also clean upholstery tile grout hardwood and air ducts.

Geographic Reach

From its headquarters in Dublin Ohio Stanley Steemer boasts both franchised and corporate locations in nearly all 50 states nationwide.

EXECUTIVES

Chairman and CEO, Wesley C. Bates
CFO, Mark Bunner
EVP, Phillip P. Ryser
Director MIS, Dale Bevins
Vice President Of Legal Affairs and Chief, Ryan Jankowski
Vice President, Dana Beck
Vice President of Marketing Communications, Brenda Smittle
Auditors: GBQ PARTNERS LLC COLUMBUS OH

LOCATIONS

HQ: STANLEY STEEMER INTERNATIONAL, INC.
   5800 INNOVATION DR, DUBLIN, OH 430163271
Phone: 614 764-2007
Web: WWW.STEEMER.COM

PRODUCTS/OPERATIONS

Selected Products

Gonzo Pet Hair Lifter
Handi Brush
Pet-Mess Solution Kit
Stanley Steemer Door Mat
Stanley Steemer Hardwood Floor Cleaner Kit
Stanley Steemer Neutral Tile & Grout Cleaner
Stanley Steemer Odor Out Plus
Stanley Steemer Red Wine Remover
Stanley Steemer Spot Remover

Selected Services

Residential Cleaning
   Certified asthma & allergy friendly
   Carpet Cleaning
   Furniture Cleaning
   Tile & Grout Cleaning
   Natural Stone Cleaning
   Hardwood Floor Services
   Air Duct Cleaning
   Water Damage Restoration
   Area Rug Cleaning
   Oriental & Fine Area Rug Cleaning
   Autos Boats & RVs
   Insurance Services
Commercial Cleaning
   Carpet Cleaning
   Furniture Cleaning
   Tile & Grout Cleaning
   Hardwood Floor Services
   Air Duct Cleaning
   Water Damage Repair
   National Accounts

COMPETITORS

Dwyer Group	ServiceMaster
Maid to Perfection	The BMS Enterprises
Molly Maid	

HISTORICAL FINANCIALS
Company Type: Private

Income Statement
FYE: December 31

	REVENUE ($ mil.)	NET INCOME ($ mil.)	NET PROFIT MARGIN	EMPLOYEES
12/15	234	23	9.9%	2,000
12/14	215	19	8.9%	—
12/13	199	18	9.2%	—
12/12	192	10	5.5%	—
Annual Growth	**6.8%**	**30.2%**	—	—

2015 Year-End Financials

Return on assets: 0.5%   Cash ($ mil.): 22
Return on equity: 9.9%
Current ratio: 1.00

STAR SNACKS CO. LLC

EXECUTIVES

Managing Partner, Mendel Brachfeld
Financial Executive, Rafie Miller
Director, Joey Weinreich
Plant Engineering Manager, Jacob Fleischer
Purchasing Director, Eli Krengel
Office Manager, Dawn Diaz
Project Manager, Lazer Paskes
Auditors: SAUL N FRIEDMAN & CO BROOKL

LOCATIONS

HQ: STAR SNACKS CO. LLC
   105 HARBOR DR, JERSEY CITY, NJ 073054505
Phone: 201 200-9820
Web: WWW.STARSNACKS.NET

HISTORICAL FINANCIALS
Company Type: Private

Income Statement
FYE: December 31

	REVENUE ($ mil.)	NET INCOME ($ mil.)	NET PROFIT MARGIN	EMPLOYEES
12/15	212	3	1.5%	430
12/14	203	3	1.5%	—
12/13	188	2	1.1%	—
12/12	183	3	1.8%	—
Annual Growth	**5.0%**	**(1.0%)**	—	—

2015 Year-End Financials

Return on assets: 3.4%   Cash ($ mil.): —
Return on equity: 1.5%
Current ratio: 0.60

STATE OF CALIFORNIA

EXECUTIVES

Governor, Jerry Brown
Board of Directors, Gavin Newsom
Consultant, A Kirk McKenzie
Auditors: JOHN F COLLINS II CPA DEPUTY

LOCATIONS

HQ: STATE OF CALIFORNIA
   STATE CAPITAL, SACRAMENTO, CA 95814
Phone: 916 445-2864
Web: WWW.CA.GOV

HISTORICAL FINANCIALS
Company Type: Private

Income Statement
FYE: June 30

	REVENUE ($ mil.)	NET INCOME ($ mil.)	NET PROFIT MARGIN	EMPLOYEES
06/15	249,923	6,252	2.5%	208,580
06/14	219,871	8,082	3.7%	—
06/13	204	8	3.9%	—
Annual Growth	3392.4%	2690.3%	—	—

2015 Year-End Financials
Return on assets: 9.8%
Return on equity: 2.5%
Current ratio: 0.40

Cash ($ mil.): 11

STATE OF OKLAHOMA

EXECUTIVES

Governor, Mary Fallin
Board of Directors, Todd Lamb
Board of Directors, James Williamson
Board of Directors, Dave Lopez
Director, Tony Hutchinson
Manager, Linda Grigsby
Vice-President, Patrick Brown
Director, Paul Timmons
Director, Russell Hulin
Auditors: GARY A JONES CPA CFE OKLAH

LOCATIONS

HQ: STATE OF OKLAHOMA
421 NW 13TH ST STE 220, OKLAHOMA CITY, OK
731033784
Phone: 405 521-2342
Web: WWW.OK.GOV

HISTORICAL FINANCIALS
Company Type: Private

Income Statement
FYE: June 30

	REVENUE ($ mil.)	NET INCOME ($ mil.)	NET PROFIT MARGIN	EMPLOYEES
06/16	16,789	(1,025)	—	37,613
06/15	17,331	314	1.8%	—
06/14	17,465	303	1.7%	—
06/13	0	336	—	—
Annual Growth	—	—	—	—

2016 Year-End Financials
Return on assets: 9.9%
Return on equity: (-6.1%)
Current ratio: 1.60

Cash ($ mil.): 5,786

STATE OF RHODE ISLAND AND PROVIDENCE PLANTATIONS

EXECUTIVES

Governor, Gina M Raimondo
Board of Directors, Daniel J McKee
Financial Executive, Lawrence C Franklin Jr
Director, Kelly Mahoney
Auditors: DENNIS E HOYLE CPA-OFFICE OF

LOCATIONS

HQ: STATE OF RHODE ISLAND AND PROVIDENCE
PLANTATIONS
82 SMITH ST STE 102, PROVIDENCE, RI 029031121
Phone: 401 222-2080
Web: WWW.GOPROVIDENCE.COM

HISTORICAL FINANCIALS
Company Type: Private

Income Statement
FYE: June 30

	REVENUE ($ mil.)	NET INCOME ($ mil.)	NET PROFIT MARGIN	EMPLOYEES
06/16	6,860	(10)	—	13,535
06/15	6,787	160	2.4%	—
06/14	6,282	(46)	—	—
06/13	5,965	67	1.1%	—
Annual Growth	4.8%	—	—	—

2016 Year-End Financials
Return on assets: 11.8%
Return on equity: (-0.1%)
Current ratio: 1.50

Cash ($ mil.): 1,707

STATE OF TEXAS

EXECUTIVES

Governor, Greg Abbott
Board of Directors, Luis Saenz
Board of Directors, David Whitley
Accountant, Anya Karpova
Director, Bill Wachel
Engineer, Carlos Lopez
Manager, Eric Ramos
Auditors: JOHN KENT CPA AUSTIN TEXAS

LOCATIONS

HQ: STATE OF TEXAS
CAPI BLDG 1100 N CONG AVE, AUSTIN, TX 78701
Phone: 512 463-2000

HISTORICAL FINANCIALS
Company Type: Private

Income Statement
FYE: August 31

	REVENUE ($ mil.)	NET INCOME ($ mil.)	NET PROFIT MARGIN	EMPLOYEES
08/15	107,350	1,993	1.9%	144,175
08/14	109,860	8,184	7.4%	—
08/13	0	0	—	—
08/05	0	0	—	—
Annual Growth	—	—	—	—

2015 Year-End Financials
Return on assets: 6.9%
Return on equity: 1.9%
Current ratio: 1.50

Cash ($ mil.): 36,275

STATEN ISLAND UNIVERSITY HOSPITAL

Staten Island University Hospital (SIUH) ferries health care services to residents of New York City's fastest growing borough and surrounding areas at its two medical campuses. Established in 1861 SIUH maintains about 715 beds and is a teaching affiliate of the State University of New York's Brooklyn Health Science Center. Its larger north campus includes units specializing in cardiology pathology cancer blood-related diseases burn treatment trauma and women's health. The south campus site offers specialty programs such as sleep medicine geriatric psychiatry and substance abuse services. A member of Northwell Health SIUH employs approximately 1200 physicians.

Operations

SIUH's Heart Institute of Staten Island located on the north campus is a joint venture between the hospital and Richmond University Medical Center. The Heart Institute specializes in cardiac diagnostics and "beating heart" surgeries.

The hospital operates several general physician practice and specialty health clinics on Staten Island. It also provides a home visit program and hospital-based hospice services.

SIUH is an affiliate of the SUNY Health Science Center at Brooklyn; its campuses serve as clinics for the Hofstra North Shore-LIJ School of Medicine which SIUH owns in partnership with Hofstra University.

In 2013 SIUH had nearly 3000 births nearly 45000 hospital discharges about 126000 emergency department visits and more than 16000 ambulatory surgeries.

EXECUTIVES

Infection Control Director, JEROME GUNNELL

LOCATIONS

HQ: STATEN ISLAND UNIVERSITY HOSPITAL
475 SEAVIEW AVE, STATEN ISLAND, NY 103053436
Phone: 718 226-9000
Web: WWW.SIUH.EDU

PRODUCTS/OPERATIONS

Selected Services
Behavioral Health
Cancer Services
Cardiac Services
Cardiovascular and Thoracic Surgery
Medical Services including Endocrinology
Gastroenterology Nephrology and Pulmonary

Neuroscience and Spine Services
Orthopedic Services
Pediatrics
Rehabilitation Medicine
Surgical Services including General Surgery Colorectal
  Head & Neck and Urology
Trauma and Burn Services
Women's Health

Selected Centers of Care

Center for Bariatric Surgery
Comprehensive Breast Center
Heart Institute
Institute of Sleep Medicine
Level III Perinatal Center
New York Head & Neck Institute at Staten Island
  University Hospital
Regional Burn Center
Stroke Center
The Elizabeth A. Connelly Emergency and Trauma
  Center
The Sanford R. Nalitt Institute for Cancer and Blood
  Related Diseases; Children's Cancer Center

COMPETITORS

Bronx-Lebanon Hospital
Catholic Healthcare
  System
CenterLight Health
  System Inc.
Continuum Health
  Partners
Eger Health Care
Kingsbrook Jewish
  Medical Center

Maimonides Medical
  Center
MediSys Health Network
New York City Health
  and Hospitals
NewYork-Presbyterian
  Healthcare

HISTORICAL FINANCIALS

Company Type: Private

Income Statement

FYE: December 31

	REVENUE ($ mil.)	NET INCOME ($ mil.)	NET PROFIT MARGIN	EMPLOYEES
12/15	850	41	4.9%	5,700
12/14	811	51	6.4%	—
12/13	880	42	4.8%	—
12/10	757	26	3.5%	—
Annual Growth	2.3%	9.5%	—	—

2015 Year-End Financials

Return on assets: 5.9%
Return on equity: 4.9%
Current ratio: 0.70

Cash ($ mil.): 35

STATION CASINOS LLC

EXECUTIVES

Vice President Information Services, Scott Kreiger
Vice President Innovation Development, Jacob
  Lanning
National Sales Manager, Patric Wilson
Auditors: ERNST & YOUNG LLP LAS VEGAS

LOCATIONS

HQ: STATION CASINOS LLC
  1505 S PAVILION CENTER DR, LAS VEGAS, NV
  891351403
Phone: 702 495-3000
Web: WWW.STATIONCASINOS.COM

PRODUCTS/OPERATIONS

Selected Casino Operations

Aliante Station Casino & Hotel (North Las Vegas
  managed property)
Barley's Casino & Brewing Company (Henderson NV)
Boulder Station (Las Vegas)
Fiesta Casino Hotel (Las Vegas)

Green Valley Ranch Station Casino (Henderson NV)
The Greens Gaming and Dining (Henderson NV)
Palace Station (Las Vegas)
Red Rock Casino Resort and Spa (Las Vegas)
The Reserve Hotel and Casino (Henderson NV)
Santa Fe Station (Las Vegas)
Sunset Station (Las Vegas)
Texas Station (Las Vegas)
Wild Wild West Gambling Hall & Hotel (Las Vegas)
Wildfire Casino (Las Vegas)

COMPETITORS

Boyd Gaming
  Caesars Entertainment
  Coast Casinos
  Jacobs Entertainment
  Las Vegas Sands
  MGM Resorts

MGP
Penn National Gaming
Pinnacle Entertainment
Stratosphere
Tropicana
  Entertainment

HISTORICAL FINANCIALS

Company Type: Private

Income Statement

FYE: December 31

	REVENUE ($ mil.)	NET INCOME ($ mil.)	NET PROFIT MARGIN	EMPLOYEES
12/16	1,452	169	11.7%	11,600
12/15	1,352	132	9.8%	—
12/14	1,291	71	5.5%	—
12/13	1,261	(113)	—	—
Annual Growth	4.8%	—	—	—

2016 Year-End Financials

Return on assets: 2.1%
Return on equity: 11.7%
Current ratio: 0.70

Cash ($ mil.): 129

STEIN FIBERS, LTD.

EXECUTIVES

Chairman of the Board, Sidney J Stein III
Financial Executive, Tom Tesarano
Chief Financial Officer, Allen Greenberg
Auditors: TEAL BECKER & CHIARAMONTE CE

LOCATIONS

HQ: STEIN FIBERS, LTD.
  4 COMPUTER DR W STE 200, ALBANY, NY 122051630
Phone: 518 489-5700
Web: WWW.STEINFIBERS.COM

HISTORICAL FINANCIALS

Company Type: Private

Income Statement

FYE: August 31

	REVENUE ($ mil.)	NET INCOME ($ mil.)	NET PROFIT MARGIN	EMPLOYEES
08/16	266	7	2.6%	186
08/15	291	2	0.9%	—
08/14	309	1	0.6%	—
08/13	314	2	0.7%	—
Annual Growth	(5.3%)	48.4%	—	—

2016 Year-End Financials

Return on assets: 7.1%
Return on equity: 2.6%
Current ratio: 0.50

Cash ($ mil.): 1

STEP UP FOR STUDENTS, INC.

EXECUTIVES

Chairman of the Board, John Kirtley
Director, Heather Moore
Director, Denise Lasher
Director, Ana Maciel
Personnel Manager, Kevin Law
Vice-President, Carol Thomas
Director, Diana Allan
Manager, Estefania Nunez-Brady
Chief Financial Officer, Joe Pfountz
Auditors: MCGLADREY LLP MELBOURNE FL

LOCATIONS

HQ: STEP UP FOR STUDENTS, INC.
  4655 SALISBURY RD STE 400, JACKSONVILLE, FL
  322560958
Phone: 877 735-7837
Web: WWW.STEPUPFORSTUDENTS.ORG

HISTORICAL FINANCIALS

Company Type: Private

Income Statement

FYE: June 30

	REVENUE ($ mil.)	NET INCOME ($ mil.)	NET PROFIT MARGIN	EMPLOYEES
06/15	457	82	17.9%	17
06/14	333	47	14.4%	—
06/13	311	97	31.4%	—
06/09	33	(8)	—	—
Annual Growth	54.4%	—	—	—

2015 Year-End Financials

Return on assets: 0.3%
Return on equity: 17.9%
Current ratio: 24.40

Cash ($ mil.): 31

STEPHENS PIPE & STEEL, LLC

EXECUTIVES

President, Terry L Stephens
Vice-President, Ray Mann Jr
Financial Executive, Vicky Loy
Director, Barbara Barnett
Personnel Director, Jack Rogers
Purchasing Manager, Donna Johnson
General Manager, Ted Eysenbach
Manager, Patrick Ford
Auditors: BKD LLP BOWLING GREEN KENTU

LOCATIONS

HQ: STEPHENS PIPE & STEEL, LLC
  2224 E HIGHWAY 619, RUSSELL SPRINGS, KY
  426427928
Phone: 270 866-3331
Web: WWW.SPSFENCE.COM

HISTORICAL FINANCIALS

Company Type: Private

Income Statement
FYE: October 1

	REVENUE ($ mil.)	NET INCOME ($ mil.)	NET PROFIT MARGIN	EMPLOYEES
10/16	342	46	13.5%	1,000
10/15*	305	27	8.8%	—
09/14	294	25	8.7%	—
09/13	273	24	9.1%	—
Annual Growth	7.8%	22.8%	—	—

*Fiscal year change

2016 Year-End Financials

Return on assets: 2.5% Cash ($ mil.): —
Return on equity: 13.5%
Current ratio: 2.40

STEPHENSON WHOLESALE COMPANY, INC.

Buying a candy bar and a box of nails is made easier thanks to Stephenson Wholesale. Operating through subsidiaries Indian National Wholesale Company and GLC Marketing the company is a leading supplier of food and non-food goods to convenience stores and other retail outlets in Oklahoma and Texas. It also distributes goods to snack bars concessions operators and tribal smoke shops. The family-owned company was founded in 1953 by Ralphen Cross.

EXECUTIVES

Chairman, Tammy Cross
Sales Director, Carter Adair
Director, Chris Simpson
Chief Financial Officer, Jerry Wheatley
Supervisor, Keith Watson
Supervisor, Alan Williams
Auditors: BDO USA LLP DALLAS TEXAS

LOCATIONS

HQ: STEPHENSON WHOLESALE COMPANY, INC.
230 S 22ND AVE, DURANT, OK 747015646
Phone: 580 920-0125
Web: WWW.INWSUPPLY.COM

COMPETITORS

Associated Wholesale Grocers
C&S Wholesale
Core-Mark
Eby-Brown
GSC Enterprises
H. T. Hackney
McLane

HISTORICAL FINANCIALS

Company Type: Private

Income Statement
FYE: December 31

	REVENUE ($ mil.)	NET INCOME ($ mil.)	NET PROFIT MARGIN	EMPLOYEES
12/15	316	0	0.3%	305
12/14	325	1	0.4%	—
12/13	369	2	0.8%	—
12/12	395	2	0.8%	—
Annual Growth	(7.2%)	(35.0%)	—	—

2015 Year-End Financials

Return on assets: — Cash ($ mil.): 3
Return on equity: 0.3%
Current ratio: 2.10

STEVENS TRANSPORT, INC.

Staying cool is a must for Stevens Transport. An irregular-route refrigerated truckload carrier (or reefer) Stevens hauls temperature-controlled cargo throughout the US covering the 48 contiguous states. Through alliances Stevens also covers every province in Canada and every state in Mexico. The company operates a fleet of about 2000 Kenworth and Peterbuilt tractors and 3500 Thermo King refrigerated trailers from a network of more than a dozen service centers. Partnerships with railroads allow Stevens to arrange intermodal transport of temperature-controlled cargo. The company also provides third-party logistics services. Stevens Transport was founded in 1980.

Operations

The company owns 49% of B2B Transport which provides an array of transportation related services to large mid-sized and small companies throughout North America.

Geographic Reach

Stevens Transport maintains its operations across Canada Mexico and the US through its partnerships with BNSF Norfolk Southern CSX and Union Pacific. It has 13 logistics offices located in Canada and throughout the US.

Sales and Marketing

Stevens has provided refrigerated shipping services for such big names as General Mills Kraft Foods M&M Mars Procter & Gamble and Wal-Mart.

Strategy

Even in a US economy ripe with unpredictable fuel costs and a decline in consumer confidence one thing has always worked in Stevens' favor: people will always need their food. The company has managed to maintain a steady growth rate by keeping costs down updating the technology of its trucking equipment and maintaining an efficient operating structure. Along these lines in 2012 it implemented new mobile computing platforms across its fleet of tractors to enhance its customer services and optimize productivity.

EXECUTIVES

Sr V Pres, Todd Aaron
Vice President Risk Management, William Tallent
Upper Management Vice President, Millie Braucht
Auditors: SADDOCK & CO PLLC DALLAS T

LOCATIONS

HQ: STEVENS TRANSPORT, INC.
9757 MILITARY PKWY, DALLAS, TX 752274805
Phone: 972 216-9000
Web: WWW.STEVENSTRANSPORT.COM

PRODUCTS/OPERATIONS

Selected Services
Intermodal
International
Logistics
Truckload

COMPETITORS

C.R. England
Central Refrigerated Service
Comcar
Covenant Transportation
Frozen Food Express
Henderson Trucking
Jim Palmer Trucking
KLLM Transport Services
Marten Transport
Navajo Shippers
Prime Inc.
Southern Refrigerated Transport
TransAm Trucking
Watkins Associated Industries
Willis Shaw Express

HISTORICAL FINANCIALS

Company Type: Private

Income Statement
FYE: December 31

	REVENUE ($ mil.)	NET INCOME ($ mil.)	NET PROFIT MARGIN	EMPLOYEES
12/15	668	87	13.0%	2,100
12/12	607	85	14.0%	—
12/11	566	76	13.5%	—
12/08	550	0	0.0%	—
Annual Growth	2.8%	505.7%	—	—

2015 Year-End Financials

Return on assets: 0.6% Cash ($ mil.): 152
Return on equity: 13.0%
Current ratio: 3.20

STEWARD NORWOOD HOSPITAL, INC.

EXECUTIVES

President, Emily Holliman

LOCATIONS

HQ: STEWARD NORWOOD HOSPITAL, INC.
800 WASHINGTON ST STE 1, NORWOOD, MA 020623487
Phone: 781 769-4000
Web: WWW.STEWARD.ORG

HISTORICAL FINANCIALS

Company Type: Private

Income Statement
FYE: December 31

	REVENUE ($ mil.)	NET INCOME ($ mil.)	NET PROFIT MARGIN	EMPLOYEES
12/15	178	60	34.1%	99
12/14	168	(14)	—	—
Annual Growth	6.0%	—	—	—

2015 Year-End Financials

Return on assets: 26.9% Cash ($ mil.): —
Return on equity: 34.1%
Current ratio: 0.30

STEWARD ST. ANNE'S HOSPITAL CORPORATION

EXECUTIVES

President, Craig Jesiolowski Fache
Board of Directors, Joseph C Maher Jr
Director, Sheila Wallace

LOCATIONS

HQ: STEWARD ST. ANNE'S HOSPITAL CORPORATION
795 MIDDLE ST, FALL RIVER, MA 027211733
Phone: 508 674-5741

HISTORICAL FINANCIALS

Company Type: Private

Income Statement
FYE: December 31

	REVENUE ($ mil.)	NET INCOME ($ mil.)	NET PROFIT MARGIN	EMPLOYEES
12/15	251	50	19.9%	99
12/14	229	13	6.0%	—
Annual Growth	9.9%	264.2%	—	—

2015 Year-End Financials

Return on assets: 0.9%
Return on equity: 19.9%
Current ratio: 1.50
Cash ($ mil.): —

STEWARD ST. ELIZABETH'S MEDICAL CENTER OF BOSTON, INC.

EXECUTIVES

President, Roger Mitty
Board of Directors, Michael Collins
Trustee, George Tully
Director, Kathleen Bertone
Office Manager, Kathy Marino
Chief Executive Officer, Marvin J Lopez
Trustee, Robert Kcintyre

LOCATIONS

HQ: STEWARD ST. ELIZABETH'S MEDICAL CENTER OF BOSTON, INC.
736 CAMBRIDGE ST, BOSTON, MA 021352907
Phone: 617 789-3000
Web: WWW.SEMC.ORG

HISTORICAL FINANCIALS

Company Type: Private

Income Statement
FYE: December 31

	REVENUE ($ mil.)	NET INCOME ($ mil.)	NET PROFIT MARGIN	EMPLOYEES
12/15	325	110	33.9%	99
12/14	309	(28)	—	—
Annual Growth	5.0%	—	—	—

2015 Year-End Financials

Return on assets: 25.8%
Return on equity: 33.9%
Current ratio: 0.30
Cash ($ mil.): —

STILES CORPORATION

Stiles Corporation is a full-service commercial real estate development and investment firm. It provides architectural design and construction realty services and property management. The firm operates primarily throughout the southeastern US with a special interest in Florida. The company's Capital Group unit offers asset management and arranges financing for development projects. Since 1951 when the company was founded Stiles has built more than 37 million sq. ft. of office industrial retail and mixed use properties. The firm's completed projects include Fort Lauderdale's Las Olas City Centre and Trump International Tower as well as the PGA Financial Plaza at MacArthur Center in Palm Beach Gardens.

Operations

In addition to its headquarters in Fort Lauderdale Stiles maintains offices in the Florida cities of Miami Tampa Fort Myers and Orlando. It has a presence in Charlotte North Carolina as well.

Since 1984 Stiles has leased more than 3.5 million sq. ft. of real estate across Florida. The company serves as the asset management team for a portfolio of more than $1.3 billion including nearly $400 million in equity. The portfolio consists of 4.5 million sq. ft. in combined office retail and industrial buildings as well as more than 1300 acres of land.

Geographic Reach

Stiles Corporation operates throughout Florida with an extended reach throughout the Southeastern US.

Sales and Marketing

The company has been working to remake its image as a one-stop development firm by launching a new branding scheme aimed at emphasizing all of its services (not just general contracting and developing). Stiles Corporation clients include IBM FedEX Bank of America Nokia UBA and Auto Nation.

Strategy

Stiles Corporation's primary strategy is to secure development projects for new commercial real estate projects as well as acquire properties in Florida's major metropolitan areas such as Miami-Dade Broward Palm Beach Tampa Bay Greater Orlando and Jacksonville. As a way to stretch its business Stiles Corporation in 2012 partnered with Levine Properties based in Charlotte North Carolina through a strategic alliance to develop real estate in the Carolinas. The joint venture is focused on developing grocery-anchored commercial and residential projects.

With the downturn in the real estate industry Stiles Corporation has been diversifying its portfolio. The company has acquired properties (especially office buildings and shopping centers) in Miami as well as other parts of Florida. It has also concentrated on offering third-party services such as leasing property management and construction as these areas provide it with reliable fee-based income.

The company also focuses on environmentally-friendly design and construction. It built Miami's first Leadership in Energy and Environmental Design (LEED) certified office building and has committed that all of its new buildings will be environmentally friendly.

EXECUTIVES

Vice President Information Technology, Brad Rabinowitz
Executive Vice President, Kenneth Stiles
Senior Vice President, Jeff McDonough
Vice President Financial Services, David Chanon
Senior Vice President, Tim Fiske
Vice President, Dustin Ozga
Auditors: TEMPLETON & COMPANY LLP FORT

LOCATIONS

HQ: STILES CORPORATION
301 E LAS OLAS BLVD, FORT LAUDERDALE, FL 333012295
Phone: 954 627-9150
Web: WWW.STILES.COM

PRODUCTS/OPERATIONS

Selected Services
Build
  Architecture
  Construction
  Tenant improvements
Invest
  Development services
  Financial services
  New development & acquisitions
Manage
  Asset management
  Leasing & brokerage
  Property management

Selected Divisions and Departments
Stiles Acquisitions
Stiles Architecture Group
Stiles Asset Management & Finance
Stiles Capital Group
Stiles Construction Co.
Stiles Development Co.
Stiles Leasing & Brokerage
Stiles Property Management
Stiles Real Estate Investment Services
Stiles Realty Co.
Stiles Tenant Improvement

COMPETITORS

Benderson Development	Flagler Development
Carter	St. Joe
DYL Group	The Haskell Company
Echelon Development	Tishman Construction

HISTORICAL FINANCIALS

Company Type: Private

Income Statement
FYE: December 31

	REVENUE ($ mil.)	NET INCOME ($ mil.)	NET PROFIT MARGIN	EMPLOYEES
12/15	218	4	2.2%	284
12/14	228	0	0.1%	—
12/13	143	0	0.6%	—
12/12	170	3	1.9%	—
Annual Growth	8.7%	13.4%	—	—

2015 Year-End Financials

Return on assets: 11.8%
Return on equity: 2.2%
Current ratio: 1.20
Cash ($ mil.): 20

STORMONT-VAIL HEALTHCARE, INC.

EXECUTIVES

Chief Executive Officer, Randall Peterson
Auditors: RSM US LLP DAVENPORT IOWA

LOCATIONS

HQ: STORMONT-VAIL HEALTHCARE, INC.
1500 SW 10TH AVE, TOPEKA, KS 666041301
Phone: 785 354-6000

HISTORICAL FINANCIALS

Company Type: Private

Income Statement

FYE: September 30

	REVENUE ($ mil.)	NET INCOME ($ mil.)	NET PROFIT MARGIN	EMPLOYEES
09/16	634	30	4.8%	4,500
09/15	582	(9)	—	—
09/14	582	24	4.3%	—
09/13	510	68	13.4%	—
Annual Growth	7.5%	(23.9%)	—	—

2016 Year-End Financials

Return on assets: 2.5%
Return on equity: 4.8%
Current ratio: 2.00

Cash ($ mil.): 50

SUASIN CANCER CARE INC.

EXECUTIVES

Principal, Winlove B Suasin
Auditors: ERNST & YOUNG US LLP SAN DIEG

LOCATIONS

HQ: SUASIN CANCER CARE INC.
1301 PUNCHBOWL ST, HONOLULU, HI 968132402
Phone: 512 583-0205
Web: WWW.QUEENSMEDICALCENTER.NET

HISTORICAL FINANCIALS

Company Type: Private

Income Statement

FYE: June 30

	REVENUE ($ mil.)	NET INCOME ($ mil.)	NET PROFIT MARGIN	EMPLOYEES
06/15	1,003	50	5.0%	4
06/14	851	31	3.7%	—
06/13	856	109	12.8%	—
Annual Growth	8.2%	(32.4%)	—	—

2015 Year-End Financials

Return on assets: 30.8%
Return on equity: 5.0%
Current ratio: 0.30

Cash ($ mil.): 29

SUFFOLK CONSTRUCTION COMPANY, INC.

Suffolk Construction Company provides construction services from top to bottom. The company kicks off the building process with pre-construction services and follows through with design/build general contracting and construction management. Suffolk Construction builds for both the public and private organizations in the science and technology health care education government and commercial sectors operating in the Northeast Mid-Atlantic Southeast and West Coast regions of the US. Founded in 1982 the privately-held firm is owned by president and CEO John Fish whose family has been in construction for four generations.

Geographic Reach

The Boston-based construction firm operates nationwide across the Northeast Mid-Atlantic Southeast and West Coast regions. Its offices are located Boston; Miami; Los Angeles; San Diego; San Francisco; Tarrytown New York; and Estero Florida.

Sales and Marketing

Suffolk Construction offers its services for projects in the assisted living aviation and transportation commercial education entertainment government healthcare hospitality non-profit residential retail and science and technology sectors.

The company has also worked on projects for federal and local governments. In the past Suffolk has built for the Army Corps of Engineers the US Marine Corps and US Navy.

Strategy

Suffolk reemphasized its "Build Smart" approach in 2015 which is designed to boost productivity and cut costs in the construction management process on every project. Before the company breaks ground at a job site it uses technologies such as virtual models and Building Information Modeling (BIM) to build projects virtually. The practice minimizes risk lessens design conflicts and issues and lowers costs for Suffolk Construction clients.

Suffolk Construction serves several sectors to keep the company thriving even in challenging times. The firm extended its reach into the growing health care sector by launching National Healthcare Group which specializes in building health care projects nationwide.

Company Background

Already a successful builder in the New England area Suffolk Construction has expanded nationally in the past through acquisitions. In 2009 it bought Massachusetts-based William A. Berry & Son creating Suffolk's Berry Division which specializes in health care and biomedical projects.

Suffolk Construction also acquired The Dietze Construction Group based in Ashburn Virginia in 2010. The deal strengthened Suffolk's position in the Mid-Atlantic region and expanded its ability to serve the government health care education science/technology and commercial sectors. Giving the company a boost in the West Suffolk Construction acquired Southern California-based ROEL Construction in 2011.

EXECUTIVES

Chairman and CEO, John F. Fish
President West Region, Andrew J. (Andy) Ball
EVP and CFO, Michael (Mike) Azarela
Director Operations Special Projects Division, Mark L. DiNapoli
President & General Manager Southeast Region, Rex B. Kirby
General Manager San Diego, Wayne Hickey
General Manager Retail and Interiors, Michael (Mike) DiNapoli
Executive Vice President Work Acquisition Northeast Region, Peter Welsh
President Healthcare/Science and Technology & Chief Innovation Officer, Peter Campot
Vice President and Chief Information Officer, Corren Collura
EVP and General Manager Mid-Atlantic Region, Stephen Skinner
Vice President & Chief Operating Officer Commercial Education and Government Northeast Region, Angus Leary
Executive Vice President of National Business Development, Christopher Woods
Vice President of Marketing and Communications, Dan Antonellis
Executive Vice President and General Manager, Jeffrey Gouveia
National Vice President Talent Acquisition, Randy DiBartola
Senior Vice President Chief Information Officer, Kevin McDonough
Vice President Healthcare, Andrew Potts
Vice President, Paul Rooney
Vice President and General Counsel, Wendy Venoit
Executive Vice President and Chief Innovation Officer, Chris Mayer
Vice President of Operations, John Sykes
Vice President Of Operations, JOE FERNANDEZ
VICE PRESIDENT OF OPERATIONS, Chris Gedrich
VICE PRESIDENT, Christopher Debruin
Treas, Mike Lindblom

LOCATIONS

HQ: SUFFOLK CONSTRUCTION COMPANY, INC.
65 ALLERTON ST, BOSTON, MA 021192923
Phone: 617 445-3500
Web: WWW.SUFFOLK.COM

PRODUCTS/OPERATIONS

Selected Services
Building information modeling
Construction management
Design/build
General contracting
Preconstruction
Sustainable building

COMPETITORS

Balfour Beatty Construction	Pepper Construction
Clark Enterprises	Swinerton
DooleyMack	Turner Corporation
Kraus-Anderson	Tutor Perini
McCarthy Building	Walsh Group
	Whiting-Turner

HISTORICAL FINANCIALS

Company Type: Private

Income Statement

FYE: August 31

	REVENUE ($ mil.)	NET INCOME ($ mil.)	NET PROFIT MARGIN	EMPLOYEES
08/16	2,611	0	—	1,150
08/15	2,500	0	—	—
08/14	1,761	0	—	—
08/13	1,825	0	—	—
Annual Growth	12.7%	—	—	—

2016 Year-End Financials

Return on assets: 23.4%
Return on equity: —
Current ratio: 1.00

Cash ($ mil.): 181

SUFFOLK UNIVERSITY

Auditors: KPMG LLP BOSTON MA

LOCATIONS

HQ: SUFFOLK UNIVERSITY
8 ASHBURTON PL, BOSTON, MA 021082770
Phone: 617 573-8000
Web: WWW.SUFFOLK.EDU

HISTORICAL FINANCIALS

Company Type: Private

Income Statement

FYE: June 30

	REVENUE ($ mil.)	NET INCOME ($ mil.)	NET PROFIT MARGIN	EMPLOYEES
06/15	315	23	7.6%	6
06/14	322	26	8.1%	
Annual Growth	(2.1%)	(8.2%)	—	—

2015 Year-End Financials

Return on assets: 11.8%   Cash ($ mil.): 1
Return on equity: 7.6%
Current ratio: —

SULLIVAN INVESTMENT CO., INC.

EXECUTIVES

Chief Executive Officer, Robert D Sullivan
Purchasing Manager, Daniel Sawiski
Auditors: O'CONNOR & DREW PC BRAINTR

LOCATIONS

HQ: SULLIVAN INVESTMENT CO., INC.
41 ACCORD PARK DR, NORWELL, MA 020611614
Phone: 781 982-1550
Web: WWW.SULLIVANFINANCIAL.COM

HISTORICAL FINANCIALS

Company Type: Private

Income Statement

FYE: January 31

	REVENUE ($ mil.)	NET INCOME ($ mil.)	NET PROFIT MARGIN	EMPLOYEES
01/16	264	1	0.7%	950
01/15	238	0	0.0%	
01/14	233	1	0.5%	
01/13	218	1	0.5%	
Annual Growth	6.5%	22.2%	—	—

2016 Year-End Financials

Return on assets: 10.5%   Cash ($ mil.): 1
Return on equity: 0.7%
Current ratio: 0.30

SUMMIT CONTRACTING GROUP, INC.

EXECUTIVES

President, Michael Mark Padgett
Chief Financial Officer, Katherine May
Financial Executive, Kevin Morris
Chief Financial Officer, Richard J Longo
Auditors: BARLAY MCNAMARA WILD JACKSO

LOCATIONS

HQ: SUMMIT CONTRACTING GROUP, INC.
1000 RIVERSIDE AVE STE 800, JACKSONVILLE, FL 32204
Phone: 904 268-5515
Web: WWW.SUMMITCONTRACTORS.COM

HISTORICAL FINANCIALS

Company Type: Private

Income Statement

FYE: December 31

	REVENUE ($ mil.)	NET INCOME ($ mil.)	NET PROFIT MARGIN	EMPLOYEES
12/15	208	7	3.5%	45
12/14	101	1	1.5%	
12/13	70	2	3.6%	
12/12	71	3	4.4%	
Annual Growth	42.8%	33.1%	—	—

2015 Year-End Financials

Return on assets: 13.0%   Cash ($ mil.): 7
Return on equity: 3.5%
Current ratio: 1.10

SUMMIT HEALTH

EXECUTIVES

President, Norman P Epstein
Project Manager, Jane Kuhn
Manager, Debra Statler
Director, Michellle Ziegler
Treasurer, Rodger Savage
Senior Manager, Kendra Neiderer
Auditors: SMITH ELLIOTT KEARNS & COMPANY

LOCATIONS

HQ: SUMMIT HEALTH
112 N 7TH ST, CHAMBERSBURG, PA 172011720
Phone: 717 267-3000

HISTORICAL FINANCIALS

Company Type: Private

Income Statement

FYE: June 30

	REVENUE ($ mil.)	NET INCOME ($ mil.)	NET PROFIT MARGIN	EMPLOYEES
06/16	480	(37)	—	2,968
06/15	445	9	2.2%	
06/14	1	(0)		
06/13	424	69	16.4%	
Annual Growth	4.2%	—	—	—

2016 Year-End Financials

Return on assets: 1.5%   Cash ($ mil.): 31
Return on equity: (-7.7%)
Current ratio: 1.00

SUMMIT MATERIALS, LLC

EXECUTIVES

President, Thomas W Hill
Director, John Murphy
Program Manager, Mark Montague
Chief Financial Officer, Clint Pulley
Director, Ashby Walters
Vice-President, Brent Ward
Auditors: KPMG LLP DENVER COLORADO

LOCATIONS

HQ: SUMMIT MATERIALS, LLC
1550 WYNKOOP ST FL 3, DENVER, CO 802021383
Phone: 303 893-0012
Web: WWW.SUMMIT-MATERIALS.COM

HISTORICAL FINANCIALS

Company Type: Private

Income Statement

FYE: December 31

	REVENUE ($ mil.)	NET INCOME ($ mil.)	NET PROFIT MARGIN	EMPLOYEES
12/16	1,626	62	3.8%	3,990
12/14	1,204	(6)	—	
12/13	916	(103)	—	
Annual Growth	21.1%	—	—	—

2016 Year-End Financials

Return on assets: 5.0%   Cash ($ mil.): 142
Return on equity: 3.8%
Current ratio: 1.30

SUN-MAID GROWERS OF CALIFORNIA

The Sun-Maid's basket runneth over. Sun-Maid Growers is the producer of Sun-Maid Raisins. Packaged in the familiar red boxes with the smiling red-sunbonneted maid Lorraine Collett Petersen offering her basket laden with grapes the brand is seen in just about every food store in the US. In addition to offering every toddler's (and moms of toddlers) favorite little-red-boxed snack the grower-owned cooperative manufactures industrial and food service products and exports to more than 50 countries. The company's other dried fruits include pitted prunes currants apricots cranberries figs dates apples fruit bits and tropical fruit mixtures. Founded in 1912 the coop is owned by 750 family farmers.

Operations

Sun-Maid whose growers harvest some 200 million pounds of grapes every year also licenses its brand for products including raisin bread raisin muffins and raisin cookie mix as well as chocolate- and vanilla yogurt-covered raisins. Retail products make up about half of the co-op's sales; ingredient products comprise the rest.

Geographic Reach

Headquartered in Kingsburg California Sun-Maid's facilities are located in California's Central Valley — the world's largest raisin producing area — where vineyards belonging to some 750 family farmers span approximately 50000 acres.

Sales and Marketing

Sun-Maid Growers hired Meredith Xcelerated Marketing as its agency of record in 2016. It de-

veloped advertising around a promotional tie-in to the November 2016 release "Trolls" a movied starring Anna Kendrick and Justin Timberlake. Agency MBMG will handle media duties.

EXECUTIVES

Vice President, Kayhan Hazrati
Senior Vice President Retail Sales and Marketing, Richard Paumen
V Pres-cfo, Braden Bender
Vice President Customer Service, John Slinkard
Vice President General Manager, Peter Pete Penner
Vice President Sales Admin, Karen Schoelen
Auditors: KPMG LLP SACRAMENTO CALIFORN

LOCATIONS

HQ: SUN-MAID GROWERS OF CALIFORNIA
13525 S BETHEL AVE, KINGSBURG, CA 936319232
Phone: 559 897-6235
Web: WWW.SUNMAID.COM

PRODUCTS/OPERATIONS

Selected Products
Bakery
  Oatmeal raisin cookie mix
  Raisin bread
  Raisin muffins
Dried apples
Dried California apricots
Dried Calimyrna figs
Dried chopped dates
Dried cranberries
Dried fruit bits
Dried golden raisins and cherries
Dried Mediterranean apricots
Dried mission figs
Dried mixed fruit
Dried pitted dates
Dried pitted plums
Dried tropical trio
Raisins
  Baking raisins
  Chocolate yogurt-covered raisins
  Chocolate-covered raisins
  Golden raisins
  Jumbo raisins
  Vanilla yogurt-covered raisins
  Zante currents

COMPETITORS

Cherry Central Cooperative Inc.	Meridian Nut Growers Multiple Organics
Dole Food	National Raisin
Encore Fruit Marketing	Pinnacle Foods
Florida Food Products Inc	Riviana Foods
	Shoreline Fruit
Fresh Del Monte Produce	SunOpta
General Mills	Sunview Vineyards
Gold Harbor	Tree Top
Golden West Nuts	Tropical Nut & Fruit
Graceland Fruit	United Natural
Kendall Frozen Fruits	Valley Fig Growers
Lion Raisins	Waymouth Farms
	Welch's

HISTORICAL FINANCIALS
Company Type: Private

Income Statement
FYE: July 31

	REVENUE ($ mil.)	NET INCOME ($ mil.)	NET PROFIT MARGIN	EMPLOYEES
07/16	382	15	3.9%	800
07/15	384	13	3.4%	—
07/14	389	11	3.0%	—
07/13	360	15	4.3%	—
Annual Growth	2.0%	(1.1%)	—	—

2016 Year-End Financials
Return on assets: 7.4%   Cash ($ mil.): —
Return on equity: 3.9%
Current ratio: 0.30

SUNDT CONSTRUCTION, INC.

EXECUTIVES

Manager, Todd Barker
Vice-President, Barbara Terry
Project Manager, Krisann Geilenfeldt
Project Manager, Alan Arvizu
Auditors: MAYER HOFFMAN & MCCANN

LOCATIONS

HQ: SUNDT CONSTRUCTION, INC.
2620 S 55TH ST, TEMPE, AZ 852821903
Phone: 480 293-3000

HISTORICAL FINANCIALS
Company Type: Private

Income Statement
FYE: September 30

	REVENUE ($ mil.)	NET INCOME ($ mil.)	NET PROFIT MARGIN	EMPLOYEES
09/16	813	0	—	1,000
09/13	895	0	—	
09/12	0	0	—	
Annual Growth	—	—	—	—

2016 Year-End Financials
Return on assets: 12.1%   Cash ($ mil.): 119
Return on equity: —
Current ratio: 1.40

SUNKIST GROWERS, INC.

Sunkist Growers is one business that is least susceptible to an outbreak of scurvy among its employees. America's oldest continually operating citrus cooperative the company is owned by California and Arizona citrus growers who farm some 300000 acres of citrus trees. Sunkist offers traditional and organic fresh oranges lemons limes grapefruit and tangerines worldwide. The co-op which operates some 20 packing facilities also makes juice and cut fruit packaged in jars. Fruit that doesn't meet fresh market standards is turned into oils and peels for use in food products made by other manufacturers. Sunkist's customers include food retailers and manufacturers and foodservice providers worldwide.

Operations

The cooperative's seasonal citrus includes Meyer lemons mandarin oranges Clementine oranges blood oranges and tangelos. Sunkist is one of the most recognized brand names in the world.

Through some 40 licensing agreements the Sunkist name appears on more than 600 beverages and other products — from vitamins to candy to soda to pistachios. It offers Sunkist Fruit Gems (gummie candies) made for the company by the Jelly Belly Candy Company.

Some 45% of Sunkist's fresh fruit sales revenues come from markets outside the US as well as more than 20% of its processed products revenues. To maintain its reach abroad Sunkist works with the US government and the governments of foreign countries to open new markets that are off limits to Western citrus growers.

Geographic Reach

California-based Sunkist operates in the Americas Europe the Middle East and Asia Pacific.

Sales and Marketing

Sunkist regularly advertises worldwide to encourage use of its citrus products and build its brand. Additionally the company leverages television to get its name out such as its alliance with the NBC motivational weight loss competition The Biggest Loser .

Sunkist which has operated a centralized sales organization since 2009 sells its products primarily to food retailers and manufacturers as well as to foodservice providers worldwide. The company is the largest marketing cooperative in the global fruit and vegetable industry.

Financial Performance

Gross annual sales of Sunkist-brand products exceed $1.2 billion worldwide.

Strategy

The company has been focused on market and portfolio expansion and getting the most from its citrus juice and oils and for-profit businesses. It is working to extend its reach to new markets such as India the Middle East and Eastern Europe where its core product has not historically been traded. To reach beyond citrus and expand its products portfolio Sunkist is concentrating on table grapes. Through a pilot program with its existing citrus growers the company markets Sunkist-branded California table grapes grown by them.

It also worked in recent years to improve the productivity of its Tipton juice processing plant. To this end Sunkist in 2012 entered a 50:50 joint venture agreement with fellow juice processor Ventura Coastal. Under the name Ventura Coastal LLC the entity operates the Ventura Coastal plant in Visalia and the Sunkist plant in Tipton. Beginning in 2013 Sunkist also partnered with Greene River Marketing to sell its Florida citrus in promising domestic and export markets.

The 2011-2012 growing season got off to a late start thanks to slow maturing fruit. Its navel orange crop grew to a manageable 88 million cartons as compared to a challenging 93-million-carton crop the previous year. Lemons started slowly as well but both demand and price picked up. Protected groves fared well during the year while unprotected ones — those outside the traditional growing areas — did not. More susceptible to the cold mandarins crops have suffered.

HISTORY

Sunkist Growers was founded in the early 1890s as the Pachappa Orange Growers a group of California citrus farmers determined to control the sale of their fruit. Success attracted new members and in 1893 the Southern California Fruit Exchange was born. The name "Sunkissed" was coined by an ad copywriter in 1908 and it was soon reworked into "Sunkist" and registered as a trademark becoming the first brand name for a fresh produce item. Eventually the co-op renamed itself after its popular brand: It became Sunkist Growers in 1952. Sunkist began licensing its trademark to other companies in the early 1950s.

As early as 1916 efforts to increase citrus consumption included designing and marketing glass citrus juicers and encouraging homemakers to "Drink an Orange." The co-op also promoted the practice of putting lemon slices in tea or water and funded early research on the health benefits of vitamins (vitamin C in particular). In 1925 tissue wrappers gave way to stamping the Sunkist name directly on each piece of fruit.

Although Sunkist pioneered bottled orange juice in 1933 its juice marketing efforts were never as successful as those of its Florida competitors. Florida oranges are drippy and dowdy and thus better suited for juicing. Capitalizing on this aspect Florida growers dominated the market for fresh and frozen juice.

In 1937 Congress created a system of citrus shipment quotas and limits (known as "marketing orders") that ultimately proved most beneficial to large citrus cooperatives. By the early 1990s the marketing order system was under political attack and in 1992 the Justice Department filed civil prosecution against Sunkist alleging that the co-op had reaped unfair extra profits by surpassing its lemon shipment limits. In 1994 after much legal wrangling the quotas were abolished and the Justice Department dropped its case against Sunkist.

Inconveniently warm weather and increasing competition from imported citrus marked the harvests of 1996. That year the co-op had trouble maintaining discipline among its members; some undercut Sunkist price levels while others flooded the market to sell their fruit at the higher early market prices creating a supply surplus. Also that year the co-op relinquished the marketing of all Sunkist juices in North America to Florida-based Lykes Bros. in a licensing agreement.

The co-op agreed in 1998 to distribute grapefruit from Florida's Tuxedo Fruit providing Sunkist with a winter grapefruit supply and increasing its year-round consumer a-peel. Also in 1998 Russell Hanlin Sunkist president and CEO since 1978 was succeeded by Vince Lupinacci. Lupinacci who had held positions with Pepsi and Six Flags became the first person from outside the citrus business to hold Sunkist's top post.

In 1998 the company sold 90 million cartons of fresh citrus — the greatest volume in its history — despite increased competition from imported Latin American South African and Spanish crops a damaging California freeze and the ill effects of El Niño. The next year production was almost halved because of adverse weather.

Lupinacci resigned in 2000 citing personal and family reasons. Chairman emeritus James Mast then took the helm as acting president. Although the company grew its market through exports to China in 2000 its profits were squeezed that year by increasing foreign competition a citrus glut and lessened demand. In mid-2001 Jeff Gargiulo replaced Mast as Sunkist's president and CEO.

In 2003 Sunkist formed a joint venture with strawberry shipper Coastal Berry Co. to market strawberries under the Sunkist label year-round. (Coastal Berry's president and CEO John Gargiulo and Sunkist's former president and CEO Jeff Gargiulo are brothers.) Also that year Sunkist began offering pre-cut bagged fruit to retail customers and restaurants in order to keep up with a changing market and consumer demand.

In retrospect 2006 was an eventful year for Sunkist. The co-op's largest producer and 16-year-member Paramount Citrus Association left the organization. In addition chairman and CEO David Krause stepped down and president Jeff Gargiulo left the company. Krause was replaced as chairman by Nicholas Bozick president of produce grower/packer Richard Bagdasarian Inc. Sunkist veteran and former president of Fruit Growers Supply Company Timothy Lindgren was appointed president and CEO. And citing expense as the determining factor the co-op discontinued marketing berries (strawberries blueberries and raspberries) in 2006. Lindgren retired in 2008; he was replaced by EVP Russ Hanlin.

EXECUTIVES

Vice President Law and General Counsel (1985), Thomas M Moore
Executive Vice President Sales and Marketing, Kevin Fiori
Managing Director Sunkist Global, Michael Nomoto

LOCATIONS

HQ: SUNKIST GROWERS, INC.
27770 N ENTERTAINMENT DR # 120, VALENCIA, CA 913551093
Phone: 661 290-8900
Web: WWW.SUNKISTGROWERS.COM

PRODUCTS/OPERATIONS

Selected Products
Fresh fruit
  Grapefruit
    Melo Golds
    Oro Blancos
    Pummelos
    Sweeties
    Texas Rio Star
    Western
  Lemons
    Eurkea/Lisbon
    Meyer
  Limes
    Key
    Persian
  Mandarins
    Clementine
    Honey
    Royal
    Satsuma
    Shasta Gold
  W. Murcott
  Oranges
    Cara Cara
    Moro
    Navel
    Valencia
  Tangelos
    Minneola
    Orlando
  Tangerines
    Dancy
    Fairchild
    Pixie
Packaged fruit
  Beverage concentrates
  Carbonated beverages (under license)
  Chilled fruit jellies (under license)
  Fruit juice
  Fruit juice drinks
  Fruit snacks (under license)
  Powdered fruit drinks
  Vitamins (under license)

COMPETITORS

Alico Inc.	Lionel Hitchen
Big Heart Pet Brands	Louis Dreyfus Group
Chiquita Brands	M&B Products
Citrus World	Old Orchard
Coca-Cola	Orchard House Foods
Dole Food	R & Z Ventures
Dundee Citrus Growers	Silver Springs
Edinburg Citrus	Southern Gardens
Fresh Del Monte Produce	Citrus
	Sunny Delight
Freshco	Tropicana
Great Western Juice	U.S. Sugar
King Ranch	Wonderful Company
Lake Placid Groves	

HISTORICAL FINANCIALS

Company Type: Private

Income Statement

FYE: October 31

	REVENUE ($ mil.)	NET INCOME ($ mil.)	NET PROFIT MARGIN	EMPLOYEES
10/16	1,207	7	0.6%	500
10/15	1,150	5	0.5%	—
10/14	1,234	6	0.5%	—
10/13	1,046	33	3.2%	—
Annual Growth	4.9%	(40.6%)	—	—

2016 Year-End Financials

Return on assets: 1.7%   Cash ($ mil.): 14
Return on equity: 0.6%
Current ratio: 1.10

SUNSOUTH LLC

EXECUTIVES

Board of Directors, Lester H Killebrew
Board of Directors, David Parkman
Board of Directors, Allen Wise
Board of Directors, Anita Brown
Accountant, Katrina Pierce
Manager, Dewayne Williams
Auditors: MCCLINTOCK NELSON & ASSOCIATE

LOCATIONS

HQ: SUNSOUTH LLC
4100 HARTFORD HWY, DOTHAN, AL 363054900
Phone: 334 678-7861
Web: WWW.JOHNDEERE.COM

HISTORICAL FINANCIALS

Company Type: Private

Income Statement

FYE: December 31

	REVENUE ($ mil.)	NET INCOME ($ mil.)	NET PROFIT MARGIN	EMPLOYEES
12/15	264	6	2.5%	318
12/14	273	10	4.0%	—
Annual Growth	(3.2%)	(39.1%)	—	—

SUNSWEET GROWERS INC.

Being all dried up is a good thing at Sunsweet Growers. The more than 400 member/grower-owned cooperative processes and markets dried fruit. Sunsweet produces one-third of the world's prunes (it processes more than 50000 tons of prunes each year). Its other fruit products include prune and other juices as well as dried apples apricots dates cranberries blueberries mangoes peaches pears pineapples and more. Sunsweet which has gotten into dietary supplement beverages supplies its products to retail food and foodservice outlets worldwide. Sunsweet produces some 40000 cases of dried fruit products every day. The co-op was founded in 1917 as the California Prune and Apricot Growers Association.

Strategy

To diversify its business and give its bottom line a boost Sunsweet in 2011 acquired California-based Function Drinks known for making functional beverages that have added nutrition. As part of the transaction Sunsweet rolled Function Drinks into a newly formed subsidiary Disruptive Beverages Inc. (DBI). The cooperative is using DBI as the foundation for expanding its beverages portfolio.

EXECUTIVES

Vice President Global Sales and Marketing, Dane Lance
Vice President Global Sales and Marketing, Brad Schuler
Vice President Operations, Matt Kelly
Vice President, Deb Macias
Secretary, Mark Ramos
Auditors: MOSS-ADAMS LLP STOCKTON CALI

LOCATIONS

HQ: SUNSWEET GROWERS INC.
901 N WALTON AVE, YUBA CITY, CA 959939370
Phone: 800 417-2253
Web: WWW.SUNSWEET.COM

PRODUCTS/OPERATIONS

Selected Products and Brands
Juices
  Amazing Prune Light
  Juicers
  PlumSmart
  PlumSmart Light
  Prune Juice
  Prune Juice with Pulp
Prunes
  60 CALORIE PACKS
  Amazins
  BITE SIZE PRUNES
  D'NOIR PRUNES
  ESSENCE
  Lighter Bake
  PREMIUM PRUNES
  WHOLE PRUNES
Specialty Fruits
  Antioxidant Blend
  Berry Blend
  Blueberries
  Cherries
  Cranberries
  Dates
  Jumbo Red Raisins
  Mediterranean Apricots
  Philippine Mangos
  Philippine Pineapple
  PlumSweets

COMPETITORS

Big Heart Pet Brands
Cherry Central
  Cooperative Inc.
Chiquita Brands
Dole Food
Fresh Del Monte
  Produce
Graceland Fruit
Maui Land & Pineapple
Meridian Nut Growers
Naturipe Farms

Ocean Spray
Pro-Fac
Seneca Foods
Shoreline Fruit
Stewart & Jasper
  Orchards
Sunkist
Tropical Nut & Fruit
Valley Fig Growers
Waymouth Farms

HISTORICAL FINANCIALS

Company Type: Private

Income Statement

FYE: July 31

	REVENUE ($ mil.)	NET INCOME ($ mil.)	NET PROFIT MARGIN	EMPLOYEES
07/16	301	112	37.3%	700
07/15	277	103	37.2%	—
07/14	261	81	31.3%	—
07/13	266	71	26.7%	—
Annual Growth	4.3%	16.5%	—	—

2016 Year-End Financials

Return on assets: 13.4%
Return on equity: 37.3%
Current ratio: 0.10

Cash ($ mil.): —

SUPERIOR COMMUNICATIONS, INC.

EXECUTIVES

Chairman of the Board, Solomon Chen
President, Jeffrey Banks

Chief Financial Officer, Keith Kam
Chief Operating Officer, Mike Cost
Managing Director, Ava Cheung
Account Manager, Emily Lam
Engineer, Frederic Dejesus
Officer, Keith Kamchief

LOCATIONS

HQ: SUPERIOR COMMUNICATIONS, INC.
5027 IRWINDALE AVE # 900, IRWINDALE, CA 917062187
Phone: 800 522-4727
Web: WWW.SUPERIORCOMMUNICATIONS.COM

HISTORICAL FINANCIALS

Company Type: Private

Income Statement

FYE: December 31

	REVENUE ($ mil.)	NET INCOME ($ mil.)	NET PROFIT MARGIN	EMPLOYEES
12/15	854	14	1.7%	273
12/14	734	6	0.9%	
/	0	0	—	—
Annual Growth	—	—	—	—

2015 Year-End Financials

Return on assets: 14.1%
Return on equity: 1.7%
Current ratio: 0.60

Cash ($ mil.): —

SUPERMERCADO MR. SPECIAL, INC.

EXECUTIVES

President, Santos Alonso
Vice-President, Edwin Alonso
Treasurer, Iris Alonso
Marketing Director, Victor Caban
Marketing Director, Debbie Alonso
Purchasing Agent, Frank Rivera
Director, Valentin Alonso
Auditors: RODRIGUEZ RIVERA & TORO PSC

LOCATIONS

HQ: SUPERMERCADO MR. SPECIAL, INC.
620 AVE STA TRESA JOURNET, MAYAGUEZ, PR 006821342
Phone: 787 834-2695
Web: WWW.MRSPECIALPR.BIZ

HISTORICAL FINANCIALS

Company Type: Private

Income Statement

FYE: September 30

	REVENUE ($ mil.)	NET INCOME ($ mil.)	NET PROFIT MARGIN	EMPLOYEES
09/16	279	5	2.0%	1,707
09/15	282	12	4.3%	
09/14	268	6	2.3%	—
09/13	281	7	2.6%	—
Annual Growth	(0.2%)	(8.2%)	—	—

2016 Year-End Financials

Return on assets: 4.8%
Return on equity: 2.0%
Current ratio: 0.70

Cash ($ mil.): 11

SUTTER HEALTH

Whether you drink too much in Wine Country hit some rough waters off the Marin Headlands or trip during a hike through the redwood forest it's likely Sutter Health is just a stone's throw away. The Northern California not-for-profit health care system is one of the nation's largest with more than 4300 acute care beds. After being formed through the merger of Sutter Health and California Healthcare System Sutter Health now caters to residents of more than 100 communities from the California Bay Area to the beaches of Hawaii. Its services are provided through affiliated doctors from a host of health care facilities including acute care hospitals home health networks and skilled nursing facilities.

Operations

Sutter Health affiliates provide acute care services health education home health care hospice care adult day care prenatal clinics immunization services and other specialized health care services.

The system's health plan network includes 25 hospitals and campuses and dozens of other facilities with more than 5000 providers serving some 40000 members throughout Northern California.

In 2015 the system reported more than 11 million outpatient visits; 190054 discharges; and 797057 emergency room visits.

Geographic Reach

Sutter Health structures its governance into two geographic regions across Northern California: the Bay Area (which also includes Hawaii) and the Valley. Each area has its own board that oversees affiliates within the region.

Financial Performance

In 2015 Sutter Health reported $11 billion in total operating revenue up from $10.2 billion in 2014. Net income from operations totaled $287 million in 2015 a 10% decline from 2014; the drop in income was driven by higher operating expenses and a decline in investment income.

Strategy

In 2016 Sutter Health announced plans to open dialysis and chemotherapy infusion centers at its Sutter Coast Hospital facility in Crescent City.

However the system made waves that year when it said it would shutter its Alta Bates Summit Medical Center in Berkeley by 2030. Community members responded by calling for Sutter Health to keep the hospital open; Sutter plans to consolidate the facility's services with those of its sister campus Summit Medical Center which is three miles away. The move to close a hospital which has seen decreased patient stays is not unusual as many health systems are pushing to broaden their service offerings on an outpatient basis.

Like most other health care organizations across the country Sutter Health is using technology to keep its patients informed about their medical care. The company is part of a national group participating in a program called Care Everywhere a technology that enables medical teams from separate hospitals and clinics to share a patient's medical records at the time he or she receives care. Through this technology Sutter Health is linked with UC Davis Health System Stanford Health Care and Santa Cruz County Health Services to share vital patient information.

EXECUTIVES

CEO Sutter Health Sacramento-Sierra Region, Sarah Krevans, age 58
SVP and CFO, Robert D. (Bob) Reed, age 65
President Sutter Health Central Valley Region, David P. Benn

President Sutter Health East Bay Region, David Bradley
SVP and CIO, Jonathan (Jon) Manis
SVP; Executive Officer Sutter Medical Network, Jeffrey Burnich
President Sutter Health West Bay Region, Mike Cohill
President Sutter Health Sacramento Sierra Region, James E. Conforti
President Sutter Health Peninsula Coastal Region, Jeff Gerard
CEO Sutter Solano Medical Center, Abhishek Dosi
Revenue Cycle Vice President, Suzy Cliff
Vice President Strategic Marketing, Tracy Murphy
Vice President Philanthropy And Executive Director, Jennifer Svihus
Regional Vice President West Bay Region Facility Development, Jenifer Turnbull
Nursing Director Maternal Newborn Unit, Aneen Heller
Chair, Geraldine R. Brinton
Vice President Finance and Treasurer, Svend Ryge

LOCATIONS

HQ: SUTTER HEALTH
   2200 RIVER PLAZA DR, SACRAMENTO, CA
   958334134
Phone: 916 733-8800

Selected Hospitals
Alta Bates Summit Medical Center (Berkeley Oakland)
California Pacific Medical Center (San Francisco)
Eden Medical Center (Castro Valley)
Kahi Mohala (Ewa HI)
Marin General Hospital (Greenbrae)
Memorial Hospital Los Banos (Los Banos)
Memorial Medical Center (Modesto)
Menlo Park Surgical Hospital
Mills-Peninsula Health Services (Burlingame)
Novato Community Hospital (Novato)
Sutter Amador Hospital (Jackson)
Sutter Auburn Faith Hospital (Auburn)
Sutter Coast Hospital (Crescent City)
Sutter Davis Hospital (Davis)
Sutter Delta Medical Center (Antioch)
Sutter Lakeside Hospital (Lakeport)
Sutter Maternity & Surgery Center of Santa Cruz
Sutter Medical Center (Sacramento)
Sutter Medical Center of Santa Rosa
Sutter Roseville Medical Center
Sutter Solano Medical Center (Vallejo)
Sutter Tracy Community Hospital (Tracy)

PRODUCTS/OPERATIONS

Selected Operations (Northern California Southern Oregon and Hawaii)
Acute Care Hospitals
Neonatal Intensive Care Units
Cancer Centers
Cardiac Centers
Acute Rehabilitation Centers
Medical Foundations
Trauma Centers
Behavioral Health Services
Education Centers and Physician Training Programs
Express Medical Clinics
Home Health and Hospice Services
Long-term Care Centers
Medical Research Centers
Occupational Health Services
Long-Term Care Centers
Irene Swindells Alzheimer's Residential Care Center San Francisco
Sutter Oaks Nursing Center Sacramento
Sutter Senior Care PACE Program Sacramento
Cancer Centers
Alta Bates Summit Comprehensive Cancer Center Berkeley and Oakland
California Pacific Medical Center San Francisco
Dorothy E. Schneider Cancer Center at Mills-Peninsula Health Services Burlingame
Eden Medical Center Castro Valley
Memorial Regional Cancer Center Modesto
Sutter Auburn Faith Hospital Auburn
Sutter Cancer Center Sutter Medical Center Sacramento

Sutter Cancer Center Sutter Roseville Medical Center Roseville
Sutter Solano Cancer Center Vallejo
Programs listed above are approved by the American College of Surgeons' Commission on Cancer.
Research Institutes
California Pacific Medical Center San Francisco
Palo Alto Medical Foundation Research Institute Palo Alto
Sutter Health Institute for Research and Education San Francisco
Sutter Institute for Medical Research Sacramento
Home Health and Hospice Services
Coming Home Hospice
Cohen Cormier Home Attendant & Care Management
Sutter Auburn Faith VNA & Hospice
Sutter Care at Home
Sutter Coast Home Care
Sutter Infusion & Pharmacy Services / Emeryville and Sacramento
Sutter Lakeside Home Medical Services
   Sutter Lif
Sutter North Home Health Agency
VNA of the Central Valley
VNA of Santa Cruz County
Express Medical Clinics
Sutter Express Care (Three locations in Sacramento & Placer counties)

COMPETITORS
Adventist Health System West
Alta Bates Summit Medical Center
Ascension Health
California Pacific Medical Center
Children's Hospital & Research Center at Oakland
Dignity Health
HCA
Hawai'i Pacific Health
Kuakini Health System
Memorial Health Services
Providence St. Joseph Health
Rehabilitation Hospital of the Pacific
Stanford Health Care
Tenet Healthcare
UCSF Medical

HISTORICAL FINANCIALS
Company Type: Private

Income Statement				FYE: December 31
	REVENUE ($ mil.)	NET INCOME ($ mil.)	NET PROFIT MARGIN	EMPLOYEES
12/16	11,873	422	3.6%	48,000
12/15	10,998	84	0.8%	—
12/14	9,715	(405)	—	—
12/13	9,649	961	10.0%	—
Annual Growth	7.2%	(24.0%)	—	—

2016 Year-End Financials
Return on assets: 4.2%   Cash ($ mil.): 426
Return on equity: 3.6%
Current ratio: 0.90

SUTTER ROSEVILLE MEDICAL CENTER

EXECUTIVES

Chief Executive Officer, Patrick Brady
Supervisor, Alex Alba
Supervisor, Pat Curtis
Director, Rebecca Thompson

LOCATIONS

HQ: SUTTER ROSEVILLE MEDICAL CENTER
   1 MEDICAL PLAZA DR, ROSEVILLE, CA 956613037
Phone: 916 781-1000
Web: WWW.SUTTERROSEVILLE.ORG

HISTORICAL FINANCIALS
Company Type: Private

Income Statement				FYE: December 31
	REVENUE ($ mil.)	NET INCOME ($ mil.)	NET PROFIT MARGIN	EMPLOYEES
12/15	558	74	13.3%	1,700
12/12	484	95	19.6%	—
Annual Growth	4.9%	(7.8%)	—	—

2015 Year-End Financials
Return on assets: 1.8%   Cash ($ mil.): 20
Return on equity: 13.3%
Current ratio: 3.40

SUTTER SANTA ROSA REGIONAL HOSPITAL

EXECUTIVES

Board of Directors, Vonna Holz
Board of Directors, Jan Tracy

LOCATIONS

HQ: SUTTER SANTA ROSA REGIONAL HOSPITAL
   30 MARK WEST SPRINGS RD, SANTA ROSA, CA
   954031436
Phone: 707 576-4000
Web: WWW.SUTTERSANTAROSA.ORG

HISTORICAL FINANCIALS
Company Type: Private

Income Statement				FYE: December 31
	REVENUE ($ mil.)	NET INCOME ($ mil.)	NET PROFIT MARGIN	EMPLOYEES
12/15	213	(14)	—	122
12/14	175	(19)	—	—
12/08	139	(21)	—	—
12/06	0	0	15.1%	—
Annual Growth	164.5%	—	—	—

2015 Year-End Financials
Return on assets: 1.2%   Cash ($ mil.): 7
Return on equity: (-6.7%)
Current ratio: 1.80

SUZANO PULP AND PAPER AMERICA, INC

EXECUTIVES

Financial Executive, Eduardo Melendez
Auditors: BARNES SMALL & MCGEE CPAS BO

HQ: SUZANO PULP AND PAPER AMERICA, INC
800 CORPORATE DR STE 320, FORT LAUDERDALE,
FL 333343618
Phone: 954 772-7716

HISTORICAL FINANCIALS
Company Type: Private

Income Statement
FYE: December 31

	REVENUE ($ mil.)	NET INCOME ($ mil.)	NET PROFIT MARGIN	EMPLOYEES
12/15	369	1	0.3%	19
12/14	346	1	0.3%	—
12/13	270	0	0.3%	—
12/12	226	0	0.2%	—
Annual Growth	17.8%	27.9%	—	—

2015 Year-End Financials

Return on assets: 27.4%   Cash ($ mil.): 18
Return on equity: 0.3%
Current ratio: 0.60

SWARTHMORE COLLEGE

The Borough of Swarthmore Pennsylvania was established nearly three decades after its namesake Swarthmore College Founded in 1864 by the Quakers it is a private liberal arts and engineering college 11 miles southwest of Philadelphia. With a student-teacher ratio of 8:1 the college offers more than 50 academic programs and bachelor's degrees in the arts and sciences. Swarthmore enrolls about 1550 students or nearly 25% of the town's population. Notable alumni include Pulitzer Prize-winning author James Michener and former governor of Massachusetts Michael Dukakis.

EXECUTIVES

Vice President Alumni Development, Dan West
Interim Vice President of Development and Alumni Relations, Don Cooney
Associate Vice President For Facilities And Servic, C Stuart Hain
Assistant Vice President Finance, Alice Turbiville
Co President, Gilbert Guerra
Vice President, Tinuke Akintayo
Quest Scholars treasurer, Jen Beltran
Auditors: PRICEWATERHOUSECOOPERS LLP PH

LOCATIONS

HQ: SWARTHMORE COLLEGE
500 COLLEGE AVE STE 2, SWARTHMORE, PA
190811390
Phone: 610 328-8000
Web: WWW.SWARTHMORE.EDU

HISTORICAL FINANCIALS
Company Type: Private

Income Statement
FYE: June 30

	REVENUE ($ mil.)	NET INCOME ($ mil.)	NET PROFIT MARGIN	EMPLOYEES
06/15	195	22	11.5%	700
06/14	139	253	182.1%	—
06/13	245	84	34.5%	—
06/12	122	(12)	—	—
Annual Growth	16.9%	—	—	—

2015 Year-End Financials

Return on assets: 11.3%   Cash ($ mil.): 22
Return on equity: 11.5%
Current ratio: 0.10

SWEDISH EDMONDS

EXECUTIVES

President, John Koster
Board of Directors, Jeff Rogers
Board of Directors, Cindy Strauss
Director, Sandy McKay

LOCATIONS

HQ: SWEDISH EDMONDS
21601 76TH AVE W, EDMONDS, WA 980267507
Phone: 425 640-4000
Web: WWW.SWEDISH.ORG

HISTORICAL FINANCIALS
Company Type: Private

Income Statement
FYE: December 31

	REVENUE ($ mil.)	NET INCOME ($ mil.)	NET PROFIT MARGIN	EMPLOYEES
12/15	222	(21)	—	1,400
12/13	213	(12)	—	—
12/12	241	1	0.6%	—
12/08	0	(0)	—	—
Annual Growth	169.4%	—	—	—

2015 Year-End Financials

Return on assets: 2.5%   Cash ($ mil.): 3
Return on equity: (-9.5%)
Current ratio: 1.80

SWEDISH HEALTH SERVICES

Swedish Health Services doing business as Swedish Medical Center is the largest not-for-profit health provider in the greater Seattle area. Swedish Medical operates five acute care hospitals; it also runs two ambulatory care centers and the Swedish Medical Group physician practice organization which has more than 100 primary and specialty care offices in the greater Puget Sound region. Swedish Medical is affiliated with Providence St. Joseph Health a Catholic not-for-profit organization with 50 hospitals in seven states.

Operations

Swedish Medical has more than 2800 physicians and its hospitals are home to more than 1500 beds. The network's facilities see over 57000 inpatients per year as well as 175000 emergency room visits more than 9000 births and about 39000 surgeries. Swedish Medical operates numerous institutes across its campuses including its Cancer Institute Heart and Vascular Institute Neuroscience Institute and Orthopedic Institute. Other medical specialties include transplants pediatrics and women's health.

Swedish Medical also conducts clinical research programs with as many as 700 trials being conducted at one time making it one of the largest clinical trial sites in the US. The network's research programs are supported by government and commercial partners.

Geographic Reach

Swedish Medical has three hospital locations in Seattle as well as hospitals in Edmonds and Issaquah Washington. Its ambulatory centers (with emergency and specialty facilities) are located in Redmond and Everett Washington.

Financial Performance

In 2013 the system reported $2 billion in revenue (96% of which came from patient care services) and $59 million in net operating income.

Strategy

The company grows both organically and through partnerships. Through its affiliation with Providence St. Joseph Health Swedish Medical combined with Providence's Washington facilities under a new not-for-profit holding company. The two health systems retain their independent identities but share clinical and IT resources to work towards reducing medical costs and increasing the quality of care in the region.

The company announced a $63.5 million expansion to its Swedish Edmonds hospital campus in 2014. The two-story expansion will include a new emergency department and an outpatient diagnostic imaging center.

Also in 2014 Swedish Medical launched a hematologic malignancies program to research and treat blood-based cancers such as leukemia multiple myeloma and lymphoma.

To balance the costs of growth Swedish Medical occasionally exits underperforming businesses. In 2012 for instance the company ceased operations of its Swedish Visiting Nurse Services program which provide home health care hospice and therapy services. The unit had incurred continuous losses since 2009.

Company Background

Not-for-profit Swedish Medical began in 1910 as a single hospital with 24 beds.

EXECUTIVES

Interim Chief Executive Swedish Medical Group, Jon Younger, age 63
Chief Operating and Administrative Officer, June Altaras
CEO, R. Guy Hudson
Interim Chief Medical Officer, Charles Watts
President and Chief Development Officer Swedish Medical Center Foundation, Harold A. (Jay) Vogelsang
Svp Physician Services; Chief Executive Swedish Medical Group, Ralph Pascualy
Assistant Chair Department Of Ob Gyn, Sarah Delatorre
Vice President of Patient Care Services Chief Nursing Officer, Nancy Wood
Medical Director Quality And Value, Chris Dale
Medical Director of the Hearing and Surgery Center, Douglas D Backous
Medical Director Swedish Cardiac Surgery, Glenn Barnhart
Nursing Director, Margo Bykoned
Medical Director, Phil Lillich
Medical Director, Steven Stanos
Medical Director, Nirav Shah
Chairman, Teresa Bigelow
Board Member, Marianne Klaas

LOCATIONS

HQ: SWEDISH HEALTH SERVICES
747 BROADWAY, SEATTLE, WA 981224379
Phone: 206 386-6000
Web: WWW.SWEDISH.ORG

PRODUCTS/OPERATIONS

Selected Washington Facilities
Ballard Campus (Seattle)
Cherry Hill Campus (Seattle)
Edmonds Campus (Edmonds)
First Hill Campus (Seattle)
Issaquah Campus (Issaquah)
Mill Creek Campus (ambulatory center in Everett)
Redmond Campus (ambulatory center in Redmond)

Selected Institutes and Services
Cancer Institute
Emergency Services

Heart and Vascular Institute
Neuroscience Institute
Orthopedic Institute
Pediatric Specialty Care
Primary Care
Pregnancy and Childbirth
Surgical Services
Transplant Program
Women's Health

COMPETITORS

Franciscan Health System	Seattle Children's Hospital
Harrison Medical Center	University of Washington
MultiCare Health System	Wenatchee Valley Medical Center
Overlake Hospital	Yakima Valley Memorial
PeaceHealth	

HISTORICAL FINANCIALS
Company Type: Private

Income Statement
FYE: December 31

	REVENUE ($ mil.)	NET INCOME ($ mil.)	NET PROFIT MARGIN	EMPLOYEES
12/15	1,240	56	4.6%	10,000
12/14	1,127	79	7.1%	—
Annual Growth	10.0%	(29.3%)	—	—

2015 Year-End Financials

Return on assets: 3.1% Cash ($ mil.): 19
Return on equity: 4.6%
Current ratio: 1.50

SWEETWATER UNION HIGH SCHOOL DISTRICT

EXECUTIVES

Superintendent, Karen Janney
Chief Financial Officer, Blenka Lemus
Director, James Frazee
Purchasing Director, Tina Schleiger
Auditors: CHRISTYWHITE ACCOUNTANCY CORPO

LOCATIONS

HQ: SWEETWATER UNION HIGH SCHOOL DISTRICT
1130 FIFTH AVE, CHULA VISTA, CA 919112812
Phone: 619 691-5500

HISTORICAL FINANCIALS
Company Type: Private

Income Statement
FYE: June 30

	REVENUE ($ mil.)	NET INCOME ($ mil.)	NET PROFIT MARGIN	EMPLOYEES
06/16	525	77	14.8%	3,521
06/09*	0	0	—	—
12/05	0	0	—	—
06/04	1,451	0	—	—
Annual Growth	—	155.6%	—	—

*Fiscal year change

SWINERTON BUILDERS

Swinerton Builders a subsidiary of Swinerton focuses on commercial and sustainable construction and renovation projects. Operating primarily in the western US its interiors group offers interior tenant finishes and remodeling working on such projects as high-tech and lab renovations hospitals retail facilities and seismic upgrades. The employee-owned company's building group focuses on new construction and retrofitting for such projects as the San Francisco Museum of Modern Art a Lockheed Martin launch vehicle assembly plant in Colorado and the Bay Bridge toll operations building in San Francisco. Swinerton Builders operates from offices in California Colorado Hawaii Texas New Mexico and Washington.

Operations

As part of its business Swinerton Builders is involved in high-tech and lab renovations hospitals retail facilities and seismic upgrades as well as new construction and retrofitting projects.

Swinerton Builders also constructs many buildings to meet environmental standards. Green projects have ranged from fire stations and retail outlets to college facilities and hotels. Swinertons' own corporate offices in California are solar powered.

Geographic Reach

The building arm of Swinerton serves the western US through offices in California Colorado Hawaii Texas Oregon and Washington. Its offices are located across California as well as in Austin Texas; Denver Colorado; Portland Oregon; Seattle Washington; and Honolulu Hawaii.

Sales and Marketing

Swinerton Builders serves a variety of sectors involving: critical facilities education government healthcare hospitality interiors multi-family residential native American and renewable energy projects. Its clients have included NASA the Federal Aviation Administration Bureau of Indian Affairs and several military and governmental entities including the US Air Force US Army US Department of Agriculture US Department of Homeland Security and the US National Park Service.

Strategy

Swinerton Builders continues to work on high-value projects around the country. In 2015 after being selected from a two-phase best value selection process the company secured a contract to lead the design-build construction project of a $46 million parking building (with some 1795 parking spaces) at the Denver International Airport (DIA) in Colorado.

The company's Swinerton Renewable Energy unit which builds and offers services to the solar utility industry expanded its capabilities in 2013 by adding comprehensive operations and maintenance (O&M) services for any solar facility across North America. The unit also launched a monitoring platform named SOLV to manage all the operational needs of customers with solar utility plants.

EXECUTIVES

Vice President, Ray A Haj
Auditors: GALLINA LLP WALNUT CREEK CAL

LOCATIONS

HQ: SWINERTON BUILDERS
260 TOWNSEND ST, SAN FRANCISCO, CA 941071719
Phone: 415 421-2980
Web: WWW.SWINERTON.COM

PRODUCTS/OPERATIONS

Selected Services
BIM/VD&C

Corporate Services
Critical Facilities
General Contracting
Government Construction
Management & Consulting
Preconstruction
Renewable Energy
Sustainable Construction/LEED

COMPETITORS

Andersen Construction	Hensel Phelps
Charles Pankow Builders	Construction
Clark Builders Group	J.F. Shea
Cordoba	Jaynes Companies
DPR Construction	Kitchell
Devcon Construction	Torix General
Gilbane Building Company	Contractors
Hathaway Dinwiddie Construction	Turner Corporation
	W. L. Butler
	Webcor Builders
	Whiting-Turner

HISTORICAL FINANCIALS
Company Type: Private

Income Statement
FYE: December 31

	REVENUE ($ mil.)	NET INCOME ($ mil.)	NET PROFIT MARGIN	EMPLOYEES
12/15	2,826	28	1.0%	900
12/14	1,862	13	0.7%	—
12/13	0	4	—	—
12/12	1,429	6	0.4%	—
Annual Growth	25.5%	66.9%	—	—

2015 Year-End Financials

Return on assets: — Cash ($ mil.): 428
Return on equity: 1.0%
Current ratio: 1.10

SWINERTON INCORPORATED

Swinerton is building up the West just as it helped rebuild San Francisco after the 1906 earthquake. One of the largest contractors in California the construction group builds commercial industrial and government facilities including resorts subsidized housing public schools soundstages hospitals and airport terminals. Through its subsidiaries (including Swinerton Builders) Swinerton offers general contracting and design/build services as well as construction and program management. The firm also provides property management for conventional subsidized and assisted living residences and is active in the renewable energy sector. The 100% employee-owned company traces its roots to 1888.

Operations

Swinerton has a special renewable energy division (Swinerton Renewable Energy) focused on solar and wind projects.

For North American solar power facilities the company also offers comprehensive operations and maintenance (O&M) services which include performance monitoring and alerting parts management service ticketing reporting preventive and corrective maintenance warranty administration and site maintenance (including vegetation mitigation and module washing).

Swinerton also has a special division to handle government construction projects delivering large-scale complex design and construction services for government agencies. Through the division Swin-

erton has worked on federal courthouses and administrative buildings training centers VA hospitals and military housing projects.

Geographic Reach

San Francisco-based Swinerton has more than a dozen offices throughout California Colorado Hawaii Texas Oregon and Washington.

Financial Performance

With the California construction market experiencing some of the strongest growth the industry has seen since 2008 Swinerton posted nearly $1.8 billion in revenue in 2013 about $1.4 billion of which was rung up in California.

Strategy

Swinerton's renewable energy division has been busy with a series of projects and new services coming to the fold in recent years. In 2014 Duke Energy awarded Swinerton a contract to develop a pair of 20-megawatt solar farms called the Pumpjack and Wildwood solar power projects which will power some 10000 households in central California once they're completed. In 2013 the company began offering comprehensive operations and maintenance (O&M) services for any North American solar facility.

The company also continues to work on other projects in recent years. In 2014 it started building the five-story 117000-square-foot building on behalf of the developer Breevast which secured a 12-year lease agreement on the building with file-sharing service provider Dropbox. In 2013 it started work on Telecom Real Estate Services' Block Data Center in Las Vegas with the goal of turning an existing warehouse facility into a Tier III modular data center. That year it also began construction on Chevron's 340000 square-foot office complex and campus in Midland Texas.

As one of the top waste-reducing companies in California Swinerton employs green building construction and design practices to conserve resources reduce waste and create healthier environments. The company's own headquarters building in San Francisco received Gold LEED-EB (Leadership in Energy & Environmental Design for Existing Buildings) — a top certification from the U.S. Green Building Council. Swinerton also built the LEED platinum rated NASA Ames Research Center Sustainability Base the greenest government building in history.

EXECUTIVES

Vice President and Director of Operations, Ray Haj
Vice President Operations Manager, Gerald Mejia
Auditors: GALLINA LLP WALNUT CREEK CAL

LOCATIONS

HQ: SWINERTON INCORPORATED
260 TOWNSEND ST, SAN FRANCISCO, CA 941071719
Phone: 415 421-2980
Web: WWW.SWINERTONRENEWABLE.COM

PRODUCTS/OPERATIONS

Selected Companies and Divisions
Cameron Swinerton
Harbison-Mahony-Higgins Builders Inc. (HMH general contracting)
Swinerton Builders (general contracting)
Swinerton Government Services
Swinerton Management & Consulting (property assessment)
Swinerton Property Services (property management)
William P. Young Construction (engineering and civil construction)

Selected Projects
100 Montgomery
AECOM
Agilent Technologies
Andaz Wailea Resort & Villas
Avaya Research & Development
Bank of New York Mellon Newport Beach

Bank of New York Mellon San Francisco
Bright Horizons Colorado
Bright Horizons South Lake Union
Bruceville | 19.15 MWdc
Cache Creek Casino Resort
CalSTRS Office Headquarters
Caltech Solar Project | 1.10 MWdc
Cathedral of the Blessed Sacrament
Christopher High School
Ciné;polis Del Mar
City Center Plaza and Entry Upgrades
City Target at the Metreon
CNET Headquarters
Columbia 3 | 11.06 MWdc Columbia Sportswear
de Young Museum
Delta Airlines Sky Club
Dillard | 12.03 MWdc

COMPETITORS

A.G. Spanos	J.F. Shea
Bechtel	JCM Partners
Beck Group	Kitchell
Charles Pankow	McCarthy Building
Builders	Menas Realty
Clark Construction	PCL Construction
Group	Enterprises
Cordoba	Rudolph & Sletten
DPR Construction	Skanska USA Building
Devcon Construction	Sundt
Gilbane	Turner Corporation
Hathaway Dinwiddie	Tutor-Saliba
Construction	Webcor Builders
Hensel Phelps	Western National Group
Construction	Whiting-Turner

HISTORICAL FINANCIALS
Company Type: Private

Income Statement
FYE: December 31

	REVENUE ($ mil.)	NET INCOME ($ mil.)	NET PROFIT MARGIN	EMPLOYEES
12/15	2,827	21	0.8%	900
12/14	1,863	11	0.6%	—
12/13	1,681	6	0.4%	—
12/12	1,506	0	—	—
Annual Growth 23.4%	—	—	—	—

2015 Year-End Financials
Return on assets: —
Return on equity: 0.8%
Current ratio: 0.40
Cash ($ mil.): 445

SYNIVERSE HOLDINGS, INC.

Syniverse Holdings opens up new worlds of communication for its clients. The company which operates as Syniverse Technologies provides business and network engineering services and software for managing and interconnecting voice and data network systems. It also offers clearing and settlement services voice and data roaming facilitation fraud management software and customer data analysis services to mobile operators fixed-line carriers and other telecommunications service providers worldwide. Customers have included Verizon Wireless and Vodafone Group. Syniverse is owned by Carlyle Group affiliate Buccaneer Holdings.

Operations

Syniverse has three business segments: Roaming services (the company's core technology interoperability services and call processing services; Messaging services; and Network services.

Geographic Reach

The company delivers innovative cloud-based solutions for the entire mobile ecosystem including more than 1500 mobile service providers enterprises ISPs and app providers in about 200 countries.

Strategy

The company pursues new international expansion. In 2013 it opened a new Costa Rica office to provide technical and support services to customers across Latin America and beyond. That year Syniverse added points of presence (POPs) for its IPX network in Frankfurt Germany and Marseille France bring its global IPX footprint to16 POPs across North America Asia Pacific and Europe.

In 2012 Syniverse signed an agreement with Vodafone India Ltd to power the mobile operator's messaging hub which will route international SMS messages into India.

it added India-based Aircel and China-based China Unicom in 2011; Syniverse also extended its agreement with Japan-based SOFTBANK Mobile that year. The company provides Aircel with roaming business management services and China Unicom with signaling gateway systems business intelligence application RoamMonitor and financial clearing house services.

Mergers and Acquisitions

In 2013 Syniverse acquired Luxembourg-based MACH for approximately ?550 million (US$730 million). The acquisition brought to Syniverse roaming messaging network and fraud technology and services that simplify the mobile landscape.

Company Background

The Carlyle Group paid about $2.6 billion in late 2010 as part of its effort to increase its wireless technology holdings.

EXECUTIVES

President, Stephen Gray
Chief Financial Officer, Bob Reich
Vice-President, Laura Binion
Vice-President, Martin A Picciano
Auditors: ERNST & YOUNG LLP TAMPA FLOR

LOCATIONS

HQ: SYNIVERSE HOLDINGS, INC.
8125 HIGHWOODS PALM WAY, TAMPA, FL 336471776
Phone: 813 637-5000
Web: WWW.SYNIVERSE.COM

COMPETITORS

AT&T	Orange
Accenture	SAP America
Authorize.Net	Swisscom
BSG Clearing Solutions	TNS
Billing Services Group	Tata Communications
Cable & Wireless	Telesoft
Dynamics Research	TeliaSonera
Evolving Systems	VeriSign
HP Enterprise Services	Verizon
Intec Telecom	XIUS-bcgi
KPN	cVidya
NeuStar	

HISTORICAL FINANCIALS
Company Type: Private

Income Statement
FYE: December 31

	REVENUE ($ mil.)	NET INCOME ($ mil.)	NET PROFIT MARGIN	EMPLOYEES
12/16	781	(65)	—	2,538
12/15	861	(49)	—	—
12/14	916	(46)	—	—
12/13	858	(45)	—	—
Annual Growth (3.1%)	—	—	—	—

2016 Year-End Financials

Return on assets: 3.9%   Cash ($ mil.): 136
Return on equity: (-8.3%)
Current ratio: 1.80

T. D. WILLIAMSON, INC.

Keeping onshore and offshore pipelines operating safely flowing freely is what T. D. Williamson is all about. A leading global pipeline equipment and services provider the company designs manufactures and maintains oil field machinery and systems including pipeline pigging (scraping) gas leak detection pipeline inspection plugging tapping valve and clamp and cathodic protection equipment. The company also offers general pipeline training turnkey and repair services. T. D. Williamson operates a global network of sales offices and representatives.

Operations

T.D. Williamson provides pipeline equipment and services for onshore and offshore applications including geometry and magnetic flux leakage inspection hot tapping and plugging pig technology services pigging and non-tethered plugging and pipeline cleaning. Its major operating subsidiary is TDW Offshore Services.

Geographic Reach

Serving oil and gas companies in every major oil patch the company has strategically located international service centers and/or manufacturing plants worldwide including in Belgium India Mexico Singapore South Africa the UAE the UK the US and Venezuela.

Strategy

T.D. Williamson leverages its leading market position by offering a broad spectrum of technical experience and a continuously refined portfolio of customized services and state-of-the-art equipment. Its support personnel includes engineers project managers and technicians who are accessible to clients on a 24/7 basis.

Growing its operations in the Middle East in 2014 the company opened a new maintenance center in Abu Dhabi to complement its existing hot tap and STOPPLE plugging service center. The expansion is in keeping with T.D. Williamson's plans to strengthen its inspection business in the Gulf region and to provide turnkey facilities and back-up for the preparation maintenance and mobilization of inline inspection equipment.

Expanding its geographic network in 2013 T.D. Williamson opened a service center in Abu Dhabi and in 2012 an office in Kazakhstan.

The company puts a strong emphasis on innovation and product development.

In 2013 TDW Offshore Services signed a deal with Centrica Storage Limited to provide pipeline isolation services using its SmartPlug Technology. The tool makes allows operators to gain significant benefits in the form of reduced downtime and associated costs by safely isolating pressure in an active pipeline and maintaining production while maintenance is carried out.

Company Background

It conducted a successful pipeline intervention in 2012 using the SmartPlug pressure isolation tool. Carried out for Talisman Malaysia Limited the operation allowed the safe replacement of a shutdown valve on a key section of a gas export pipeline without having to bleed down the line.

In 2012 the company developed and deployed a new proprietary inline inspection reporting software — Interactive Report 2013 — a data visualization tool that makes it easy for users to filter and view their pipeline inspection data.

That year the company unveiled its Subsea 1200RC Tapping Machine a compact remote-controlled subsea machine that allows hot tapping (tying in to a pressurized system while under full operating conditions) to be carried out with increased safety from a diving support vessel.

Growing its project contract portfolio in 2012 T.D. Williamson signed a three-year global pipeline intervention and isolation services contract with BP (one of only four such contracts awarded worldwide by BP).

T.D. Williamson has expanded internationally in the last two decades. With opening of service centers in Dubai Jamnagar (India) Moscow Rayong (Thailand) and Warsaw in 2007 it had locations in every continent except Antarctica. It opened a facility in India in 2010 in order to respond to the growing pipeline business in that country (which is expected to double from 25000 km. by 2015).

In 2011 it created the Global Pipeline Integrity Center in Salt Lake City Utah to combine the TDW inline inspection engineering manufacturing operations service center and data analysis functions in one location.

The company was founded by T.D. Williamson Sr. in 1920 as The Petroleum Electric Company an electrical contracting firm to supply electric motors for gas booster stations oil well drilling equipment and electric generator stations used by the local oil and gas industry in the US. It adopted the T.D. Williamson name in 1933.

EXECUTIVES

Chairman of the Board, Stephen Williamson
Senior Vice-President, D Bruce Binkley
Accountant, Kathy Hulse
Vice-President, Jon D Major
Manager, Mark Sim
Director, Names Additional

LOCATIONS

HQ: T. D. WILLIAMSON, INC.
6120 S YALE AVE STE 1700, TULSA, OK 741364235
Phone: 918 493-9494
Web: WWW.TDWILLIAMS.COM

PRODUCTS/OPERATIONS

TDW ProductsCathodic Protection EquipmentGas Leak DetectionPipeline Drilling and Hot Tapping MachinesPipeline FittingsPigging Products and AccessoriesPipeline Plugging EquipmentPipeline Rehabilitation ProductsPipeline ValvesServicesGas Leak DetectionHot

COMPETITORS

Cameron International	Oil States
Cypress Energy	International
Partners	Schlumberger
Halliburton	T3 Energy Services
J-W Operating	Weatherford
National Oilwell Varco	International

HISTORICAL FINANCIALS

Company Type: Private

Income Statement

FYE: December 31

	REVENUE ($ mil.)	NET INCOME ($ mil.)	NET PROFIT MARGIN	EMPLOYEES
12/15	539	0	—	1,425
12/02	116	1	1.5%	—
12/01	106	2	2.4%	—
12/00	91	2	2.5%	—
Annual Growth	12.6%	—		—

2015 Year-End Financials

Return on assets: —   Cash ($ mil.): 30
Return on equity: —
Current ratio: 0.40

TALLAHASSEE MEMORIAL HEALTHCARE, INC.

Tallahassee Memorial HealthCare (TMH) aims to take the hassle out of health care. The community health system serves residents of Florida's state capital and its surrounding communities. The system is anchored by Tallahassee Memorial Hospital a not-for-profit facility with more than 770 beds and about 560 physicians on staff who represent some 50 different specialties. TMH provides general medical and surgical care as well as specialty care in areas such as oncology rehabilitation women's and children's health obesity and diabetes. TMH also has a trauma center offers a family practice residency program and provides primary medical care through a handful of regional clinics.

Operations

TMH is Florida's eighth-largest hospital boasting more than 24000 inpatient admissions per year. As part of its operations TMH has a 60-bed psychiatric hospital and offers adult day care and home health care services. It operates the only Level II trauma center in the region which benefits from newly added telemedicine equipment that includes videoconferencing. Trauma centers are specially trained and equipped to handle severe injuries and all such patients in the area are routed to trauma certified facilities.

The system partners with the H. Lee Moffitt Cancer Center & Research Institute in Tampa to allow cancer patients to participate in clinical trials and other experimental and research opportunities.

The system offers a range of cardiovascular services from diagnostic procedures to open-heart surgery a designated acute brain and spinal cord injury center and a 110000-sq.-ft. childbirth facility — the region's only Level Three Neonatal Intensive Care Unit.

In 2014 the hospital had 122100 emergency and urgent care visits and 29586 general admissions.

Geographic Reach

TMH serves 17 counties across North Florida and South Georgia.

Financial Performance

In 2014 TMH's net revenues increased by 7% due to higher net patient service revenues (net of contractual allowances and discounts).

The company's net income rose by 15% due to higher net revenues and a decrease in interest.

TMH's operating cash inflow in 2014 increased by 16%.

Strategy

The medical facility operates the Tallahassee Memorial Transition Center created in partnership with Capital Health Plan and Florida State University College of Medicine. The center was designed to improve wellness through new approaches and collaborative research. Looking to position itself as a regional center for healthcare Tallahassee Memorial has plans to roll out more new services and add physicians.

In 2015 the hospital and Apalachee Center expanded their agreement to include administrative management of Tallahassee Memorial behavioral health services by Apalachee Center to improve behavioral health services in the community. As part of an earlier agreement the company will continue to provide some psychiatric medical coverage for Apalachee Center's inpatient services as well as providing all psychiatric medical services at the Tallahassee Memorial Behavioral Health Center.

In 2014 TMH and Doctors' Memorial Hospital signed an agreement to create an equal governance partnership between the two institutions that will ultimately enhance services to Doctors' Memorial Hospital and expand its role in Taylor County's health care system.

To expand its capabilities TMH opened the Tallahassee Memorial Emergency Center - Northeast in mid-2013 and broke ground in 2013 on a new surgery and adult intensive care facility that's anticipated to cost as much as $175 million.

Company Background
TMH was founded in 1948.

EXECUTIVES

VP and CFO, William (Bill) Giudice
VP and COO, Jason Moore
VP and CIO, Don Lindsey
President TMH Foundation, Paula Fortunas
Associate Chief Medical Officer, Dean Watson
Administrator Behavioral Health Center, Carl Mahler
Director Premier Health and Fitness Center, Len Harvey
Administrator Orthopedic and Neurological Services, Judy Greenwald
Administrator Surgery Services, David Thompson
President and CEO, G. Mark O'Bryant
VP and Chief Nursing Officer, Barbara Alford
Administrator Cancer Center, Matt Sherer
Interim Administrator Emergency Medicine Services, Eric Hartigan
Administrator Heart and Vascular Center, Terri McDonald
Administrator Regional Development Population Health and Telemedicine, Lauren Faison
Administrator Women's Pavilion and Children's Center, Connie Styons
Chairman, Glenda Thornton
Secretary, Robin Brunetti

LOCATIONS

HQ: TALLAHASSEE MEMORIAL HEALTHCARE, INC.
1300 MICCOSUKEE RD, TALLAHASSEE, FL 323085054
Phone: 850 431-1155
Web: WWW.TMH.ORG

PRODUCTS/OPERATIONS

2014 sales

	% of total
Hospitals	97
TMHV	1
Medicus	2
Total	**100**

Selected Services

Behavioral Health Center
Rehabilitation Center
Cancer Center
Bixler Emergency Center
Heart & Vascular Center
Diabetes Center
Orthopedic Center
NeuroScience Center
Surgical Services
Women's Pavilion
Home Health Care
Clinical Genetics Center
Bariatric Center
Chronic Pain Management
Lipid Center

COMPETITORS

Adventist Health System Sunbelt Healthcare
Baptist Health System
Bay Medical Center
H. Lee Moffitt Cancer Center & Research Institute
HCA
Jackson County Hospital of Florida
Munroe Regional Health System
Sacred Heart Health System
UF&Shands

HISTORICAL FINANCIALS
Company Type: Private

Income Statement

	REVENUE ($ mil.)	NET INCOME ($ mil.)	NET PROFIT MARGIN	EMPLOYEES
				FYE: September 30
09/15	589	38	6.5%	6,430
09/14	532	33	6.2%	—
09/13	566	31	5.6%	—
09/12	479	40	8.4%	—
Annual Growth	**7.1%**	**(1.4%)**	**—**	**—**

2015 Year-End Financials

Return on assets: 9.1%
Return on equity: 6.5%
Current ratio: 3.30
Cash ($ mil.): 227

TANANA CHIEFS CONFERENCE

EXECUTIVES

Principal, Donald Honea Sr
Principal, Trimble Gilbert
Principal, Jerry Isaac
Principal, Carl Jerue
Principal, Pat McCarty

LOCATIONS

HQ: TANANA CHIEFS CONFERENCE
122 1ST AVE STE 600, FAIRBANKS, AK 997014899
Phone: 907 452-8251
Web: WWW.TANANACHIEFS.ORG

HISTORICAL FINANCIALS
Company Type: Private

Income Statement

	REVENUE ($ mil.)	NET INCOME ($ mil.)	NET PROFIT MARGIN	EMPLOYEES
				FYE: September 30
09/15	183	34	19.0%	2
09/13	123	(3)	—	—
Annual Growth	**21.9%**	**—**	**—**	**—**

2015 Year-End Financials

Return on assets: 7.3%
Return on equity: 19.0%
Current ratio: —
Cash ($ mil.): 2

TANGIPAHOA PARISH SCHOOL SYSTEM

EXECUTIVES

Superintendent, Mark Kolwe
Director, Brett Duncan
Accountant, Robin Joiner
Auditors: LAPORTE APAC COVINGTON LA

LOCATIONS

HQ: TANGIPAHOA PARISH SCHOOL SYSTEM
59656 PULESTON RD, AMITE, LA 704225616
Phone: 985 748-2416
Web: WWW.TANGISCHOOLS.ORG

HISTORICAL FINANCIALS
Company Type: Private

Income Statement

	REVENUE ($ mil.)	NET INCOME ($ mil.)	NET PROFIT MARGIN	EMPLOYEES
				FYE: June 30
06/16	194	0	0.2%	2,125
06/15	198	2	1.3%	—
Annual Growth	**(1.6%)**	**(86.2%)**	**—**	**—**

2016 Year-End Financials

Return on assets: 9.7%
Return on equity: 0.2%
Current ratio: —
Cash ($ mil.): 48

TARRANT COUNTY HOSPITAL DISTRICT

If Fort Worth residents are searching for health care they need look no further than Tarrant County Hospital District (dba JPS Health Network). Founded in 1906 in Fort Worth Texas the network's flagship facility John Peter Smith Hospital has approximately 540 beds and provides specialty services including orthopedics cardiology and women's health. JPS Health Network also includes behavioral health treatment center Trinity Springs Pavilion and the JPS Diagnostic & Surgery Hospital of Arlington. The company provides family medical dental and specialty care through dozens of health care centers in northern Texas.

Operations

JPS Hospital is a member of the Council of Teaching Hospitals and Health Systems (COTH).

Sales and Marketing

The health system carries a Level 1 Trauma designation across the spectrum of health care specialties meaning it is the referral hospital of choice for patients who are terribly injured.

Strategy

The health system works to improve the health of Tarrant County as a whole by training health care workers and physicians about working outside the hospital walls and within the community. The institution sponsors programs that are accredited through the Accreditation Council for Graduate Medical Education (ACGME) American Osteopathic Association (AOA) and the Council on Podiatric Medical Education (CPME).

JPS Health Network opened JPS Medical Home Southeast Tarrant a primary and specialty care facility in 2014. The following year the system relo-

cated its Pain Management Clinic to a renovated site in Fort Worth.

EXECUTIVES

CFO, David Salsberry
Executive Vice President Chief Medical Officer, Gary Floyd
COO, Bill Whitman
Senior Vice President of Human Resources and Learning, Nikki Sumpter
Vice President of Operations, Rick Stevens
Manager, Scott W. Fisher
Vice-Chair, Trent Petty

LOCATIONS

HQ: TARRANT COUNTY HOSPITAL DISTRICT
1500 S MAIN ST, FORT WORTH, TX 761044917
Phone: 817 921-3431
Web: WWW.JPSHEALTHNET.ORG

Primary Locations – Texas
Ambulatory Surgery Center (Fort Worth)
Cardiology Center (Fort Worth)
Enrollment & Eligibility Center (Fort Worth)
Family Medicine & Surgical Specialty Center (Fort Worth)
Healing Wings AIDS Center (Fort Worth)
John Peter for Cancer Care (Fort Worth)
JPS Urgent Care Center (Fort Worth)
Lifespan Family Medicine & Pediatrics (Fort Worth)
Patient Care Pavilion (Fort Worth)
Professional Building-Medicine Clinic (Fort Worth)
Trinity Springs Pavilion for Psychiatric Services (Fort Worth)

PRODUCTS/OPERATIONS

Selected Services
Behavioral Services
Cancer
Cardiology
Dental
Geriatrics
Healing Wings HIV/AIDS Center
Orthopedics and Sports Medicine
Robotic Surgery
School-Based Health Centers
Sexual Assault Nurse Examiner Program
Stroke / N
Surgical Services
Trauma Services
Women's Services

COMPETITORS

Baylor University Medical Center	Presbyterian Hospital of Dallas
CHRISTUS Health	Southwestern Medical Center
Community Health Systems	Tenet Healthcare
Cook Children's Health Care System	Texas Health Resources
HCA	The Methodist Health System
Harris Methodist Fort Worth Hospital	Universal Health Services
Parkland Health & Hospital System	

HISTORICAL FINANCIALS
Company Type: Private

Income Statement
FYE: September 30

	REVENUE ($ mil.)	NET INCOME ($ mil.)	NET PROFIT MARGIN	EMPLOYEES
09/16	576	18	3.2%	3,000
09/15	557	48	8.7%	—
09/14	285	48	16.9%	—
Annual Growth	42.1%	(37.9%)	—	—

2016 Year-End Financials
Return on assets: 6.4%   Cash ($ mil.): 181
Return on equity: 3.2%
Current ratio: 2.60

TATA AMERICA INTERNATIONAL CORPORATION

Tata America International is the North American holding company for Indian conglomerate Tata Group. In the US the company has about a dozen subsidiaries including offices for Tata Communications IT services firm Tata Consultancy Services (with more than 20 locations) and engineering consultancy Tata Technologies. In the industrial sector Tata America owns steel manufacturing plants in Ohio and Pennsylvania and General Chemical Industrial Products a soda ash plant in Wyoming. Other holdings include hotels (The Pierre in New York the Taj Boston and the Taj Campton Place in San Francisco) and sales offices for its beverage brands Eight O'Clock Coffee Good Earth and Tetley.

EXECUTIVES

President, Surya Kant
VP Marketing and Communications, John Lenzen
CFO, S. Mahalingam
Vice President and Chief Information O, Alan Hughes
Auditors: DELOITTE HASKINS & SELLS LLP

LOCATIONS

HQ: TATA AMERICA INTERNATIONAL CORPORATION
101 PARK AVE RM 2603, NEW YORK, NY 101782604
Phone: 212 557-8038
Web: WWW.TCS.COM

PRODUCTS/OPERATIONS

Selected Subsidiaries
IT Services
　Tata Business Support Services
　Tata Communications
　Tata Consultancy Services
　Tata Elxsi
　Tata Interactive Systems
　Tata Technologies
Engineering
　Tata AutoComp Systems
Services
　Campton Place
　Taj Boston
　The Pierre
Consumer Products
　Eight O'Clock Coffee
　Good Earth
　Tanishq
　Tata Tea Inc.
　Tetley
Chemicals
　General Chemical

COMPETITORS

Accenture	HCL Technologies
Atos North America	HP Enterprise Services
CIBER	IBM Global Services
Capgemini North America	ICP Inc.
	Infosys
Cognizant Tech Solutions	NTT Data
	Syntel
Computer Sciences Corp.	Unisys
	Wipro Technologies
Fujitsu America	Zensar Technologies

HISTORICAL FINANCIALS
Company Type: Private

Income Statement
FYE: March 31

	REVENUE ($ mil.)	NET INCOME ($ mil.)	NET PROFIT MARGIN	EMPLOYEES
03/16	755	118	15.7%	1,700
03/15	6,800	111	1.6%	—
03/13	441	116	26.4%	—
03/12	4,705	129	2.7%	—
Annual Growth	(36.7%)	(2.1%)	—	—

2016 Year-End Financials
Return on assets: 165.4%   Cash ($ mil.): 7
Return on equity: 15.7%
Current ratio: 1.10

TAUBER OIL COMPANY

No liquid petrochemical product is taboo for oil refiner and marketer Tauber Oil. The family owned company markets refined petroleum products carbon black feedstocks liquefied petroleum gases chemicals and petrochemicals (including benzene styrene monomer and methanol). Tauber Oil is one of the US's leading suppliers of feedstocks for reforming and olefin cracking. It also has oil and gas exploration and production operations. Subsidiary Tauber Petrochemical was created in 1997 to beef up the company's international petrochemical business. Tauber Oil which is owned by David and Richard Tauber maintains a fleet of more than 500 rail cars to supply its customers.

Operations

Tauber Oil's blending group works with refineries and producers to create a market for by-product/co-product streams. It also supplies liquid petroleum products to marine diesel customers fuel to power generators cutters for bunker blending clients and a number of other fuel applications.

The company's natural gas liquids department works with producers and consumers to create a market; the refined products department trades refined products with refiners traders distributors and other customers.

Tauber Petrochemical markets a range of products including alkylate benzene C9 aromatics ethyl benzene pyrolysis gasoline styrene monomer toluene and xylene.

Geographic Reach

The company's rail and barge fleet moves products from inland to Gulf Coast markets. It gathers blends and distributes out of tankage in Houston Texas City and on the Mississippi River. Tauber Oil's has oil and gas exploration and production operations in the East Texas South Texas the Gulf Coast of Texas Southern Louisiana and Oklahoma. (Additionally Tauber participates in 3-D seismic projects lease acquisitions and funding for geological and geophysical projects). Its Canadian Crude group works with heavy crude oil producers.

Sales and Marketing

The company transports its products via ship barge tank truck and rail car. It maintains a fleet of more than 500 rail cars to supply on-time delivery requirements to customers.

Strategy

Unlike most other oil and gas suppliers Tauber Oil does not rely on a financial speculation strategy (the buying and selling of contracts for petroleum products). The company primarily plays the role of the middleman and more than 90% of the company's businesses involve the actual delivery of pe-

troleum products and gas liquids.

Price volatility goes with Tauber Oil's territory and the company relies on its track record of reliable service and long-term relationships with customers to weather downturns in the market.

In order to develop and grow new operations the company enters into partnerships collaborations joint ventures and acquisition arrangements. Tauber Oil is partnered with Rio Energy International to provide adequate storage tank capacity at multiple terminals which helps it to maintain low cost train operations from Western Canada to the US Gulf Coast.

Company Background

To strengthen its finances and to focus on its core oil chemical and petrochemical businesses in 2012 the company merged its natural gas division with Interconn Resources Inc. to form Interconn Resources LLC. Interconn Resources specializes in delivering competitively priced natural gas to municipal industrial retail and governmental customers across the southeastern US.

Tauber Oil was founded in 1953 by O. J. Tauber Sr. He gained his oil and petroleum products trading experience working for a small Houston refinery called Eastern States Refining.

His son (and company executive) Richard Tauber is also the president of a small affiliated oil company Tauber Exploration and Production.

EXECUTIVES

VP Credit Finance, Stephen E. Hamlin
Owner and Principal, David W. Tauber, age 67
Owner and Principal, Richard E. Tauber
Vice President Natural Gas, John Happ
Vice President Public Relations, Connie Kubiak
Vice President Intermediate and Heavy Feedstocks, Gerald Applestein
Vice President Blending Components, John Wakefield
Vice President Refined Products, Blake Hale
Vice President of Marketing, Kavan J Mehta
Vice President, Bobby Combs
Vice President, Mauricio Ruiz
Vice President Asian Markets, Ollivier Giampietri
Vice President of Real Estate Investments, David Kayle
Vice President, Bob Mackenzie
Auditors: MOHLE ADAMS HOUSTON TEXAS

LOCATIONS

HQ: TAUBER OIL COMPANY
55 WAUGH DR STE 700, HOUSTON, TX 770075837
Phone: 713 869-8700
Web: WWW.TAUBEROIL.COM

PRODUCTS/OPERATIONS

Selected Products:
Natural Gas Liquids
Butane
Ethane
Isobutane
Propane
Petrochemicals
Benzene
Methanol
MTBE
Styrene monomer
Toluene
Xylene
Refined
Aviation jet fuel
Kerosene
Low sulfur diesel
No. 2 fuel oil

COMPETITORS

Cabot Oil & Gas	Marathon Oil
Devon Energy	Occidental Petroleum
Exxon Mobil	Tesoro
George Warren	Valero Energy
Global Partners	

HISTORICAL FINANCIALS

Company Type: Private

Income Statement   FYE: December 31

	REVENUE ($ mil.)	NET INCOME ($ mil.)	NET PROFIT MARGIN	EMPLOYEES
12/15	2,214	6	0.3%	135
12/14	4,831	10	0.2%	—
12/13	4,769	16	0.3%	—
12/12	5,088	21	0.4%	—
Annual Growth	(24.2%)	(31.6%)	—	—

2015 Year-End Financials

Return on assets: 6.2%   Cash ($ mil.): 7
Return on equity: 0.3%
Current ratio: 1.10

TELCO INTERCONTINENTAL CORP

EXECUTIVES

President, Frank C Liang
Vice-President, MEI-Yun Liang
Operations Manager, Sue Yu
Manager, Jane Liang
Manager, Albert Robinson

LOCATIONS

HQ: TELCO INTERCONTINENTAL CORP
9812 WHITHORN DR, HOUSTON, TX 770955001
Phone: 281 500-8270
Web: WWW.TELCOINTERCON.COM

HISTORICAL FINANCIALS

Company Type: Private

Income Statement   FYE: December 31

	REVENUE ($ mil.)	NET INCOME ($ mil.)	NET PROFIT MARGIN	EMPLOYEES
12/15	19,067	1,371	7.2%	24
12/14*	16	1	7.9%	—
04/10	2	0	7.5%	—
Annual Growth	340.9%	337.7%	—	—

*Fiscal year change

2015 Year-End Financials

Return on assets: 1.5%   Cash ($ mil.): 2,421
Return on equity: 7.2%
Current ratio: 19.20

TEMECULA VALLEY UNIFIED SCHOOL DISTRICT SCHOOL FACILITIES

EXECUTIVES

Superintendent, Tim Ritter
Administrative Assistant, Voula Boyer
Manager, Mark Rogers
Supervisor, Robert Gates
Supervisor, Don Fails
Auditors: VAVRINEK TRINE DAY & CO LL

LOCATIONS

HQ: TEMECULA VALLEY UNIFIED SCHOOL DISTRICT SCHOOL FACILITIES
31350 RANCHO VISTA RD, TEMECULA, CA 925926200
Phone: 951 676-2661
Web: WWW.TVUSD.K12.CA.US

HISTORICAL FINANCIALS

Company Type: Private

Income Statement   FYE: June 30

	REVENUE ($ mil.)	NET INCOME ($ mil.)	NET PROFIT MARGIN	EMPLOYEES
06/16	300	35	11.8%	2,866
06/05	207	0	—	—
Annual Growth	3.4%	—	—	—

TENCARVA MACHINERY COMPANY, LLC

EXECUTIVES

President, Edwin W Pearce III
Secretary, Mike Penni

LOCATIONS

HQ: TENCARVA MACHINERY COMPANY, LLC
1115 PLEASANT RIDGE RD, GREENSBORO, NC 274099529
Phone: 336 665-1435
Web: WWW.TENCARVA.COM

HISTORICAL FINANCIALS

Company Type: Private

Income Statement   FYE: December 31

	REVENUE ($ mil.)	NET INCOME ($ mil.)	NET PROFIT MARGIN	EMPLOYEES
12/15	209	14	7.2%	360
12/13	187	13	7.2%	—
12/12	172	12	7.2%	—
12/11	1,439	0	0.0%	—
Annual Growth	(38.2%)	449.9%	—	—

2015 Year-End Financials

Return on assets: 4.6%   Cash ($ mil.): 23
Return on equity: 7.2%
Current ratio: 3.30

TENNESSEE ENERGY ACQUISITION CORPORATION

EXECUTIVES

President, Mark McCutchen
Representative, Dennis Hall
Auditors: JACKSON THORNTON & CO PC MO

LOCATIONS

HQ: TENNESSEE ENERGY ACQUISITION
CORPORATION
1808 ASHLAND CITY RD A, CLARKSVILLE, TN
370436440
Phone: 931 920-3499
Web: WWW.SPRINGFIELD-TN.ORG

HISTORICAL FINANCIALS

Company Type: Private

Income Statement

FYE: March 31

	REVENUE ($ mil.)	NET INCOME ($ mil.)	NET PROFIT MARGIN	EMPLOYEES
03/16	236	0	0.2%	5
03/15	262	0	0.4%	—
03/14	255	2	1.0%	—
03/13	285	2	1.0%	—
Annual Growth	(6.1%)	(49.9%)	—	—

2016 Year-End Financials

Return on assets: 4.8%   Cash ($ mil.): 7
Return on equity: 0.2%
Current ratio: 0.10

TEXAS AROMATICS, LP

EXECUTIVES

Vice-President, Trenton L Kelley
Treasurer, Staci Vol
Accountant, Nadine Boyle
Auditors: WEAVER AND TIDWELL LLP HO

LOCATIONS

HQ: TEXAS AROMATICS, LP
3555 TIMMONS LN STE 700, HOUSTON, TX
770276450
Phone: 713 520-2900
Web: WWW.TEXASAROMATICS.COM

HISTORICAL FINANCIALS

Company Type: Private

Income Statement

FYE: December 31

	REVENUE ($ mil.)	NET INCOME ($ mil.)	NET PROFIT MARGIN	EMPLOYEES
12/15	531	10	2.0%	17
12/14	961	10	1.1%	—
12/13	1,033	13	1.3%	—
12/12	1,073	18	1.7%	—
Annual Growth	(20.9%)	(16.3%)	—	—

2015 Year-End Financials

Return on assets: 3.5%   Cash ($ mil.): 44
Return on equity: 2.0%
Current ratio: 2.00

TEXAS CHILDREN'S HOSPITAL

Texas Children's Hospital (TCH) is the flagship facility of Texas Children's Hospital Integrated Delivery System. Founded in 1954 the not-for-profit hospital provides full-service medical care for children conducts extensive research and trains pediatric medical professionals. Part of the Texas Medical Center complex it has clinical facilities for every ailment ranging from psychological troubles to surgery and physical rehabilitation as well as specialized heart cancer and neurological care. TCH is the primary pediatric training facility for Baylor College of Medicine.

Operations

TCH comprises a 491-bed tertiary care pediatric facility a 115-bed obstetrics and gynecological care facility focusing on high-risk births (both located on the Texas Medical Center campus) and a 44-bed full-service pediatric facility in west Houston. The hospital includes the Jan and Dan Duncan Neurological Research Institute and the Feigin Center for pediatric research.

The hospital's staff includes more than 1500 primary physicians and other medical specialists as well as some 6000 nurses. The hospital has satellite facilities in and around Houston and it operates the Texas Children's Pediatric Associates primary care network of more than 170 physicians. The company also runs the Texas Children's Health Plan which offers Medicaid and Texas CHIP (Children's Health Insurance Plan) programs.

TCH's International coordinates care for sick children who come to Texas Children's Hospital from abroad. The international segment also sends out medical teams to care for critically ill children throughout Latin America the Middle East Europe Africa and Asia. For instance it has established a number of AIDS clinics in African countries.

The hospital performs more than 25000 surgeries annually. It has some 1.9 million patient encounters some 31000 admissions and about 117000 emergency department visits each year.

Geographic Reach

TCH includes four main facilities — its main hospital and Texas Children's Pavilion for Women at the Medical Center Texas Children's West Campus in the Houston suburb of Katy and Texas Children's The Woodlands in that suburb (opening in 2017).

Financial Performance

Though most of its revenue comes from patient care fees TCH relies heavily on donations and federal funding to supplement its operations. For instance the hospital and Baylor College of Medicine represent one of the most active and well-funded pediatric research programs in the US with more than 800 basic research and clinical studies backed by more than $100 million in annual grants.

Increased patient revenue and premiums led to a 9% rise in revenue for 2014 from $2.3 billion to $2.5 billion. Net income fell 29% to $257 million due to a decline in investment returns and increased operating expenses including salaries and benefits supplies and pharmaceuticals. Cash flow from operations rose 63% to $257 million as a result of higher accounts payable.

Strategy

TCH has been opening new facilities some in suburban locations and expanding others to reach additional patients. In 2013 it introduced the da Vinci robotic system and expanded its children's hematology center to include a dozen exam rooms and four acute care rooms. It also opened its oculoplastic clinic for pediatric patients.

In 2014 the hospital opened its in vitro fertilization lab the first in Houston to utilize the EmbryoScope embryo monitoring system. It is also building an eight-bed isolation unit at its west campus.

EXECUTIVES

Senior Vice President Human Resources and Organizational Development, Linda Aldred
President and CEO, Mark A. Wallace, age 65
Physician-in-Chief, Mark W. Kline
EVP and CFO, Benjamin (Ben) Melson
Obstetrician/Gynecologist-in-Chief, Michael A. Belfort
President Texas Children's Hospital The Woodlands, Michelle Riley-Brown
President Texas Children's Hospital West Campus, Chanda Cashen Chac n
CIO, Myra Davis
Vice President Business Operations, Carlos Rodriguez
Senior Vice President For Development, John Scales
Vice President, Tabitha Rice
Senior Executive Assistant To H. Mallory Caldwell Senior Vice President, Leticia Ybarra
Nursing Director, Tangula Taylor
Vice President of Public Affairs, Claire M Bassett
Vice President and General Counsel, Lance Lightfoot
Senior Vice President Of Strategy, Mallory Caldwell
Nursing Director, Gail Parazynski
Senior Vice President Facilities Services, Peter R Dawson
Assistant Vice President of Communications, Lori Williams
Vice President, Rachel Shupe
Vice President For Public Affairs, Shawn Davis
Assistant Vice President For Finance, Kimberly Cotner
Director Of Nursing, Tanjula Taylor
Medical Director Blue Bird Circle Multiple Sclerosis Clinic, Timothy Lotze
Vice President, Debra Ward
Vice President, Parker N Amis
Medical Director, Sanghamitra Misra
Vice President of Purchasing, Sabrina Cowans
Vice President, Dan DiPrisco
Assistant Vice President, Sara Montenegro
Treasurer Hospital, Doreen Mascari

LOCATIONS

HQ: TEXAS CHILDREN'S HOSPITAL
6621 FANNIN ST, HOUSTON, TX 770302399
Phone: 832 824-1000

PRODUCTS/OPERATIONS

2014 Sales

	% of total
Net patient revenue	60
Premium revenue	34
Medicaid & other supplemental reimbursement	2
Net assets released from restrictions for operations	1
Grants	1
Other income	2
Total	**100**

2014 Net Patient Revenue

	% of total
Managed care	61
Medicaid managed care	15
Medicaid	13
Self-pay	6
Commercial	5
Total	**100**

Selected Serives

Bariatric/weight control services
Certified trauma center

Chemotherapy
Dental services
Heart catheterization;diagnostic (child)
Genetic testing/counseling
HIV-AIDS services
Heart catheterization;treatment (child)
Kidney dialysis
Chemotherapy
Physical rehabilitation
Psychiatric services (Child/adolescent services
  Consultation and Outpatient care)
Sleep center
Sports medicine
Urgent-care center
Women's health center
Wound management services

COMPETITORS

CHRISTUS Health	Methodist Hospital
Children's Hospital of	System
Philadelphia	Shriners Hospitals For
Children's Medical	Children
Center of Dallas	St. Jude Children's
Cook Children's Health	Research Hospital
Care System	St. Luke's Episcopal
Dell Children's	Hospital
Medical Center	Tenet Healthcare
Mayo Clinic	
Memorial Hermann	
Healthcare	

HISTORICAL FINANCIALS

Company Type: Private

Income Statement

FYE: September 30

	REVENUE ($ mil.)	NET INCOME ($ mil.)	NET PROFIT MARGIN	EMPLOYEES
09/15	1,546	96	6.3%	6,000
09/14	1,383	70	5.1%	—
09/13	1,229	78	6.4%	—
09/12	2,043	289	14.2%	—
Annual Growth	(8.9%)	(30.6%)	—	—

2015 Year-End Financials

Return on assets: 4.6%   Cash ($ mil.): 93
Return on equity: 6.3%
Current ratio: 0.80

TEXAS HEART HOSPITAL OF THE SOUTHWEST, L.L.P.

EXECUTIVES

Director, Brad Morgan
Administrative Assistant, Christopher Oropeza

LOCATIONS

HQ: TEXAS HEART HOSPITAL OF THE SOUTHWEST, L.L.P.
  1100 ALLIED DR, PLANO, TX 750935348
Phone: 469 241-8900

HISTORICAL FINANCIALS

Company Type: Private

Income Statement

FYE: December 31

	REVENUE ($ mil.)	NET INCOME ($ mil.)	NET PROFIT MARGIN	EMPLOYEES
12/15	261	62	24.1%	139
12/14	253	62	24.8%	—
Annual Growth	3.0%	0.1%	—	—

2015 Year-End Financials

Return on assets: 3.0%   Cash ($ mil.): 72
Return on equity: 24.1%
Current ratio: 1.70

TEXAS SCOTTISH RITE HOSPITAL FOR CHILDREN

EXECUTIVES

Chairman of the Board, Lyndon L Olson Jr
Board of Directors, Ronald Skaggs
Auditors: ERNST & YOUNG LLP DALLAS TX

LOCATIONS

HQ: TEXAS SCOTTISH RITE HOSPITAL FOR CHILDREN
  2222 WELBORN ST, DALLAS, TX 752193924
Phone: 214 559-5000
Web: WWW.TSRHC.ORG

HISTORICAL FINANCIALS

Company Type: Private

Income Statement

FYE: September 30

	REVENUE ($ mil.)	NET INCOME ($ mil.)	NET PROFIT MARGIN	EMPLOYEES
09/15	185	(11)	—	850
09/14	40	(12)	—	—
09/13	297	164	55.1%	—
09/12	351	226	64.6%	—
Annual Growth	(19.1%)	—	—	—

2015 Year-End Financials

Return on assets: 8.8%   Cash ($ mil.): 5
Return on equity: (-6.2%)
Current ratio: 0.90

TEXAS STATE UNIVERSITY SYSTEM

EXECUTIVES

Chancellor, Brian McCall
Manager, Lamar Urbanovsky
Manager, Terrie Purser
Administrative Assistant, Donna Givens
Officer, Linda Camarillo
Director, Carol Treadway

LOCATIONS

HQ: TEXAS STATE UNIVERSITY SYSTEM
  208 E 10TH ST STE 600, AUSTIN, TX 787012407
Phone: 512 463-1808
Web: WWW.TSUS.EDU

HISTORICAL FINANCIALS

Company Type: Private

Income Statement

FYE: August 31

	REVENUE ($ mil.)	NET INCOME ($ mil.)	NET PROFIT MARGIN	EMPLOYEES
08/16	846	126	14.9%	3,196
08/15	6	71	1147.5%	—
08/14	6	71	1147.5%	—
08/13	688	57	8.4%	—
Annual Growth	7.1%	29.7%	—	—

2016 Year-End Financials

Return on assets: 6.4%   Cash ($ mil.): 464
Return on equity: 14.9%
Current ratio: 1.00

TEXAS STATE UNIVERSITY-SAN MARCOS

Texas State University-San Marcos has about 38800 students pursuing degrees in about 100 undergraduate programs 90 graduate programs and a dozen doctoral programs. Comprising eight colleges as well as a graduate school Texas State University-San Marcos is the largest school in the Texas State University system which includes Angelo State University Lamar University Sam Houston State University and Sul Ross State University. It also offers bachelor's and graduate-level courses at a campus in Round Rock.The school has 209 buildings on its San Marcos cmapus.

Geographic Reach

Texas State's main campus in the Central Texas community of San Marcos consists of some 490 acres. The university also operates some 5000 acres of recreational and instruction properties in the area.

Strategy

As Texas State is ranked among the top US colleges for awarding degrees to bachelor's degrees to Hispanic students the university targets a portion of its marketing efforts towards minority students. About 50% of its student body is composed of ethnic minorities. Texas State also enrolls students through international efforts.

To accommodate its growing student base Texas State has been expanding its campus facilities. It opened the Angelina and San Gabriel residence halls in 2016 and the Performing Arts Center in 2014.

Also in 2014 the school became a member of the American Academic Research Institute in Iraq (TAARII) which promotes scholarly research on Iraq and ancient Mesopotamia by providing graduate and post-graduate fellowships for Americans and Iraqis. Other TAARII members include Columbia University Georgetown University and Harvard.

Company Background

The former Southwest Texas State University (the name was changed in 2003) was originally a

teacher's college founded by the state legislature in 1903.

EXECUTIVES

Vp Finance And Support Services, William Nance
Associate Vp Planning, Nancy Nusbaum
President, Denise M. Trauth
VP Student Affairs, Joanne Smith
Provost and VP Academic Affairs, Eugene J. (Gene) Bourgeois
VP University Advancement, Barbara Breier
VP Finance and Support Services, Eric Algoe
VP Information Technology, Ken Pierce
Presidential Fellow, Lisa Kay Lloyd
Dean College of Applied Arts, Jaime Chahin
Dean McCoy College of Business Administration, Denise T. Smart
Dean College of Education, Stan Carpenter
Dean College of Fine Arts and Communication, John Fleming
Dean College of Health Professions, Ruth B. Welborn
Dean Honors College, Heather C. Galloway
Dean College of Liberal Arts, Michael J. Hennessy
Interim Dean College of Science and Engineering, Robert Habingreither
Dean University College, Daniel A. Brown
Dean The Graduate College, Andrea Golato
Assistant Vice President Technology Resources, Mark Hughes
Associate Vice President Instructional Technologies Support T, Milt Nielsen
Vice President, Nathan Salazar
Resource Development Coordinator Vpua, Anastasia Lunsford
Vice President For Finance Support Services, William A Nance
Board Secretary, John Blair
Board Member, Jane Saunders

LOCATIONS

HQ: TEXAS STATE UNIVERSITY-SAN MARCOS
601 UNIVERSITY DR, SAN MARCOS, TX 786664684
Phone: 512 245-2111
Web: WWW.TXSTATE.EDU

PRODUCTS/OPERATIONS

Schools and Colleges
College of Applied Arts
College of Education
College of Fine Arts and Communication
College of Health Professions
College of Liberal Arts
College of Science
The Graduate College
McCoy College of Business Administration
University College (general studies)

HISTORICAL FINANCIALS
Company Type: Private

Income Statement				FYE: August 31
	REVENUE ($ mil.)	NET INCOME ($ mil.)	NET PROFIT MARGIN	EMPLOYEES
08/16	436	34	7.9%	3,156
08/15	404	25	6.2%	—
08/14	377	73	19.4%	—
08/13	329	61	18.6%	—
Annual Growth	9.8%	(17.5%)	—	—

2016 Year-End Financials
Return on assets: 7.8%   Cash ($ mil.): 268
Return on equity: 7.9%
Current ratio: 1.20

THAYER DISTRIBUTION

EXECUTIVES

Chairman of the Board, Juan Gallicchio
Vice-President, Diego Gallicchio
Sales Director, Nicholas Direnzo
Chief Financial Officer, Gallicio Juan
Auditors: GOLD GERSTEIN GROUP LLC VOORH

LOCATIONS

HQ: THAYER DISTRIBUTION
333 SWEDESBORO AVE, GIBBSTOWN, NJ 080271220
Phone: 800 999-4271
Web: WWW.THAYERDIST.COM

HISTORICAL FINANCIALS
Company Type: Private

Income Statement				FYE: December 31
	REVENUE ($ mil.)	NET INCOME ($ mil.)	NET PROFIT MARGIN	EMPLOYEES
12/15	192	3	2.0%	100
12/14	175	3	2.1%	—
12/13	163	3	2.2%	—
12/12	123	2	1.9%	—
Annual Growth	16.0%	18.0%	—	—

2015 Year-End Financials
Return on assets: 3.2%   Cash ($ mil.): —
Return on equity: 2.0%
Current ratio: 0.60

THE ADMINISTRATORS OF THE TULANE EDUCATIONAL FUND

EXECUTIVES

Vice President for Development, Luann Dozier
Assistant Vice President Information Technology Infrastructure, Lieu Tran
Assistant Vice President of University Financial Aid, Georgia Whiddon

LOCATIONS

HQ: THE ADMINISTRATORS OF THE TULANE EDUCATIONAL FUND
6823 SAINT CHARLES AVE, NEW ORLEANS, LA 701185665
Phone: 504 865-5000
Web: WWW.TULANEGREENWAVE.COM

Selected Campuses
Tulane University main uptown campus
The F. Edward Hebert Research Center (Louisiana)
The School of Continuing Studies (Louisiana and Mississippi)
The Health Sciences downtown campus
   School of Medicine
   School of Public Health and Tropical Medicine
   Tulane Medical Center and Technology Services
The North Shore campus
   Tulane National Primate Research Center (Louisiana)
The A.B. Freeman School of Business (Texas)

PRODUCTS/OPERATIONS

Selected Schools and Colleges
A.B. Freeman School of Business
Faculty of Liberal Arts and Sciences

Graduate School
Law School
Newcomb College
School of Architecture
School of Engineering
School of Medicine
School of Public Health and Tropical Medicine
School of Social Work
Tulane College
University College

HISTORICAL FINANCIALS
Company Type: Private

Income Statement				FYE: June 30
	REVENUE ($ mil.)	NET INCOME ($ mil.)	NET PROFIT MARGIN	EMPLOYEES
06/15	1,054	40	3.9%	5,500
06/10	738	48	6.5%	—
06/09	737	0		—
Annual Growth	6.2%	—	—	—

2015 Year-End Financials
Return on assets: 8.8%   Cash ($ mil.): 15
Return on equity: 3.9%
Current ratio: 0.10

THE ADVANCED CENTER FOR REHABILITATION MEDICINE INC

EXECUTIVES

President, David W Osborne
Administrative Assistant, Michael Wiegand
Officer, Keith Shuster
Director, Eddy Jean-Felix
Officer, Kristen M Staikos
Director, Jay Varrone
Director, Joanne Svogun

LOCATIONS

HQ: THE ADVANCED CENTER FOR REHABILITATION MEDICINE INC
24 STEVENS ST, NORWALK, CT 068503852
Phone: 203 852-2000
Web: WWW.NORWALKHEALTH.ORG

HISTORICAL FINANCIALS
Company Type: Private

Income Statement				FYE: September 30
	REVENUE ($ mil.)	NET INCOME ($ mil.)	NET PROFIT MARGIN	EMPLOYEES
09/15	377	23	6.2%	2
09/14	340	33	9.7%	—
09/13	352	16	4.8%	—
Annual Growth	3.5%	17.9%	—	—

2015 Year-End Financials
Return on assets: 13.6%   Cash ($ mil.): 43
Return on equity: 6.2%
Current ratio: 0.50

THE AEROSPACE CORPORATION

A not-for-profit company The Aerospace Corporation provides space-related research development and advisory services primarily for US government programs. Its chief sponsor is the US Air Force and its main customers have included the Space and Missile Systems Center of Air Force Space Command and the National Reconnaissance Office. Other clients have included NASA and the National Oceanic and Atmospheric Administration as well as commercial enterprises universities and international organizations. Areas of expertise include launch certification process implementation systems engineering and technology application. The Aerospace Corporation was established in 1960 and operates through about 20 offices.

Operations

Officially The Aerospace Corporation operates a federally funded research and development center or FFRDC for the Air Force. The Aerospace FFRDC is one of more than 40 established to help government agencies with tasks related to aviation defense energy health and human services space and tax administration.

Geographic Reach

The US relies on space systems for intelligence communications navigation and weather making Aerospace's mission assurance and systems engineering services vital to national security.

Strategy

Among the company's projects are work on the next generation of satellites including the Global Positioning System IIF Space Based Space Surveillance Advanced Extremely High Frequency Wideband Global Satcom and Space Based Infrared System programs. These new satellites will provide new capabilities and replace systems from the 1970s and 1980s.

Scientists at The Aerospace Corporation also have been developing a nanosatellite to test high-efficiency solar cells under space conditions. Solar cells made by Spectrolab (a subsidiary of Boeing Space and Intelligence Systems) and EMCORE convert sunlight into electricity. The nanosatellite only 14 pounds is one of many such small satellites pioneered by Aerospace. Compared to larger satellites nanosatellites are less expensive to launch and operate.

EXECUTIVES

Senior Vice President General Counsel Secretary, Gordon Louttit
EVP, David J. Gorney
General Manager Computers and Software, William C. (Willie) Krenz
VP Vaeros, Edward M. (Ed) Swallow
SVP National Systems Group, Catherine J. Steele
VP CFO and Treasurer, Ellen M. Beatty
SVP Operations and Support Group, Wayne H. Goodman
President and CEO, Steven J. (Steve) Isakowitz
VP Space Launch Operations, Randolph L. (Randy) Kendall
VP Space Program Operations, Malina M Hills
Executive Vice President, Glenn E Peterson
Vice President Director Manager, Marsha Pradia
Vice President, Sherrie Zacharius
Vice President Space Program Operations, Stephen E Burrin
Executive Vice President, Michael Daugherty
Vice President Director Manager, Jeanne Campanella
Vice President Director Manager, Moria Cunningham
Senior Vice President Systems, Thomas Duerr
Vice President Director Manager, James Jusko
Vice President, George Paulikas
Vice President Technology, Lawrence Greenberg
Vice President And Associate General C, Malissia Clinton
Vice President of Legislative Affairs, Chrystal Rodriguez
Vice President, Ed Swallow
Vice President Chief Human Resources Officer, Heather Laychak
Vice President, Jamie Morin
Chairman, Barbara M. Barrett, age 65
Vice Chairman, Michael B. Donley
Board Member, Kathryn Brenan
Auditors: DELOITTE & TOUCHE LLP LOS ANG

LOCATIONS

HQ: THE AEROSPACE CORPORATION
2310 E EL SEGUNDO BLVD, EL SEGUNDO, CA 902454609
Phone: 310 336-5000
Web: WWW.AEROSPACE.ORG

PRODUCTS/OPERATIONS

Selected Services
Civil and Commercial
CORDS
Cyber Security
Labs
Launch Support
Mission Assurance
Systems Engineering
Technical Resources

COMPETITORS

AKKA Technologies   QinetiQ
Orbital Research

HISTORICAL FINANCIALS
Company Type: Private

Income Statement
FYE: September 30

	REVENUE ($ mil.)	NET INCOME ($ mil.)	NET PROFIT MARGIN	EMPLOYEES
09/15	916	(15)	—	3,920
09/14	881	5	0.6%	
09/13	868	0	0.0%	
09/12	903	4	0.5%	
Annual Growth	0.5%	—	—	—

2015 Year-End Financials

Return on assets: 4.2%   Cash ($ mil.): 23
Return on equity: (-1.7%)
Current ratio: 0.40

THE AMERICAN MUSEUM OF NATURAL HISTORY

The American Museum of Natural History is one of the world's foremost scientific museums. Its landmark building on New York's Central Park West showcases parts of its immense collections of anthropological and zoological specimens along with meteorites gemstones dinosaur fossils and a butterfly conservatory. The museum which is also home to the Rose Center for Earth and Space and the Hayden Planetarium and a top-flight research library conducts many educational programs offers an IMAX theater and publishes Natural History magazine. The American Museum of Natural History is part of the University of the State of New York. The museum was chartered by the New York legislature in 1869.

Operations

Behind the scenes at the American Museum of Natural History more than 200 scientists work in its anthropology vertebrate and invertebrate zoology paleontology and physical sciences divisions. Also the museum boasts the Richard Gilder Graduate School which is authorized to grant the Ph.D. degree in comparative biology.

Geographic Reach

More than 4 million people visit the museum each year more than a third of which are international tourists.

Sales and Marketing

Many of the museum's exhibits are marketed towards children.

EXECUTIVES

President, Ellen V. Futter, age 68
Treasurer, Theodore A. Mathas
Vice President Education Government Relations And, Lisa Gugenheim
Vice Chairman, Richard S. LeFrak, age 70
Vice Chairman, Charles E. (Chuck) Phillips, age 57
Chairman, Lewis W. Bernard, age 74
Vice Chairman, Louis V. Gerstner
Vice Chairman, David S. Gottesman
Vice Chairman, Linda R. Macaulay
Vice Chairman, Christopher Davis
Vice Chairman, Roberto Mignone
Treasurer, Sue Rudavsky
Auditors: GRANT THORNTON LLP NEW YORK

LOCATIONS

HQ: THE AMERICAN MUSEUM OF NATURAL HISTORY
CENTRAL PARK W AT 79TH ST, NEW YORK, NY 10024
Phone: 212 769-5000
Web: WWW.AMNH.ORG

HISTORICAL FINANCIALS
Company Type: Private

Income Statement
FYE: June 30

	REVENUE ($ mil.)	NET INCOME ($ mil.)	NET PROFIT MARGIN	EMPLOYEES
06/16	198	(5)	—	1,262
06/15	283	82	29.1%	
06/13	197	7	4.0%	
06/09	135	(53)	—	
Annual Growth	5.7%	—	—	—

2016 Year-End Financials

Return on assets: 19.2%   Cash ($ mil.): 104
Return on equity: (-2.7%)
Current ratio: 0.30

THE AMERICAN UNIVERSITY IN CAIRO

EXECUTIVES

President, Lisa Anderson
Director, Aly Araby
Personnel Director, Amira Khattab

Director, Brandon Canfield
Director, Eskandar Tooma
Auditors: ERNST & YOUNG US LLP CHICAGO

LOCATIONS

HQ: THE AMERICAN UNIVERSITY IN CAIRO
  420 5TH AVE FL 3, NEW YORK, NY 100182729
Phone: 212 730-8800
Web: WWW.AUCEGYPT.EDU

HISTORICAL FINANCIALS

Company Type: Private

Income Statement

FYE: June 30

	REVENUE ($ mil.)	NET INCOME ($ mil.)	NET PROFIT MARGIN	EMPLOYEES
06/15	186	16	8.6%	1,000
06/14*	171	0	0.4%	
08/11	168	(4)	—	—
08/10	155	(7)	—	—
Annual Growth	3.7%	—	—	—

*Fiscal year change

2015 Year-End Financials

Return on assets: 10.7%   Cash ($ mil.): 25
Return on equity: 8.6%
Current ratio: 1.30

THE ASSOCIATED PRESS

This just in: The Associated Press (AP) is reporting tonight and every night wherever news is breaking. AP is one of the world's largest news gathering organizations with news bureaus in about 100 countries. It provides news photos graphics and audiovisual services that reach people daily through print radio TV and the Web. It also offers advertising management and distribution services. The not-for-profit cooperative is owned by 1500 US daily newspaper members. A group of New York newspapers founded the AP in 1846 in order to chronicle the US-Mexican War more efficiently. Founding papers include The New York Sun The Journal of Commerce The Courier and Enquirer The New York Herald and The Express

Operations
The AP has about 3200 employees globally working around 280 locations worldwide.
Geographic Reach
The Associated Press is headquartered in New York City. The AP serves 1700 newspapers and 5000 radio and television outlets in the US many of which are members.
Financial Performance
In fiscal 2014 the AP's total annual revenue increased by 1% to $604 million compared to $595 million in fiscal 2013. The company's net income increased dramatically to $140 million in fiscal 2014 compared to $3.26 million in fiscal 2013 mainly due to increased gross revenue and interest income.
Strategy
In recent years the AP has shifted its focus away from providing content to newspapers and towards serving online media sources; some of the company's biggest customers now include media outlets such as Google MSN and Yahoo!. It has also focused on developing AP Direct its live video news agency service. It sells its back catalog of video through AP Video Archives.
To cope with the decline in print readership the news co-op is continuing to invest in digital initiatives. It is currently undergoing a multimillion-dol-

lar upgrade of its newsgathering infrastructure to increase its video coverage of global events. It is also pushing to increase its high definition footage to broadcast and digital markets and ensure that its video and images integrate seamlessly with new digital workflows to drive value for customers.

HISTORY

The Associated Press traces its roots to 1846 when New York Sun publisher Moses Yale Beach agreed to share news arriving by telegraph about the Mexican-American War with four other New York newspapers. The cooperative news gathering effort was later established as the AP which began selling wire reports to other papers and started creating regional associations. Adapting to changing technologies and public interests AP began covering sports financial and public interest stories in the 1920s and was selling news reports to radio stations in the 1940s. Advancements during WWII included using transatlantic cable and radio-teletype circuits to deliver news and photos.

In the late 1960s AP and Dow Jones introduced services to improve business and financial reporting. AP improved photo delivery reception and storage in the 1970s with the advent of Laserphoto and the Electronic Darkroom. It began transmitting news by satellite and offering color photographs to newspapers in the 1980s. In 1985 Louis Boccardi took over the job as president and CEO of AP.

AP adjusted to the media-heavy culture of the 1990s by launching the APTV international news video service and the All News Radio network in 1994. It then moved onto the Internet with The WIRE in 1996 and began offering online access to its Photo Archive in 1997. It bought Worldwide Television News in 1998 combining it with APTV to form AP Television News Limited (APTN). The following year it purchased the radio news contracts of UPI after the rival organization announced it was getting out of broadcast news.

In 2000 AP created an Internet division AP Digital to focus on marketing news to online providers. The cooperative continued its Internet focus the following year launching AP Online en Espa ±ol (news for Spanish-language websites) and AP Entertainment Online (multimedia entertainment news for websites). Also that year AP bought the Newspaper Industry Communication Center from the Newspaper Association of America.

In 2002 the company launched an expanded editorial partnership with Dow Jones Newswires increasing the amount of financial news distributed on AP wires. Later that year it acquired Capitolwire a provider of state government news. Boccardi stepped down as CEO in 2003 handing the reins to former USA TODAY publisher Tom Curley.

AP relocated in 2004 from Rockefeller Plaza (its home for 65 years) to a new headquarters on the west side of Manhattan that features a 105000-sq.-ft. newsroom and serves as a central hub of digital news streams.

The organization moved to strengthen its sports information coverage in 2005 merging its AP MegaSports operation with News Corporation's STATS Inc. to form STATS LLC a 50-50 joint venture that provides sports-related information content and statistical analysis.

The following year AP launched The Online Video Network (OVN) service to provide news video to AP member and customer websites. The co-op responded to the harsh economy by cutting costs in 2008 with consolidation of its print broadcast and digital sales and marketing units. It continued its cost-cutting efforts in 2009 when it cut some 90 jobs instituted a hiring freeze and bought out about 100 employees.

EXECUTIVES

President & CEO, Gary B. Pruitt, age 59
SVP and Executive Editor, Kathleen Carroll
SVP and CIO, Lorraine Cichowski
SVP and CFO, Ken Dale
SVP and CTO, Gianluca D'Aniello
Director, Mary E. Junck, age 70
Auditors: ERNST & YOUNG LLP NEW YORK N

LOCATIONS

HQ: THE ASSOCIATED PRESS
  1 WORLD FINANCIAL CTR # 19, NEW YORK, NY
  102812647
Phone: 212 621-1500
Web: WWW.AP.ORG

PRODUCTS/OPERATIONS

Selected Products and Services

AP Digital News (Internet and wireless news delivery)
AP Images (photo services)
AP Mobile (mobile applications)
APTN (AP Television News international television news service)
ENPS (electronic news production system)
Online Video Network (video content distribution)

COMPETITORS

Agence France-Presse	GlobeNewswire
Bloomberg L.P.	Marketwire
Business Wire	New York Times
Comtex News	PR Newswire
Corbis	Reuters
Dow Jones	TEGNA
E. W. Scripps	Tribune Media
Getty Images	UPI

HISTORICAL FINANCIALS

Company Type: Private

Income Statement

FYE: December 31

	REVENUE ($ mil.)	NET INCOME ($ mil.)	NET PROFIT MARGIN	EMPLOYEES
12/15	568	183	32.3%	3,533
12/14	604	140	23.3%	—
12/13	595	3	0.5%	—
12/12	622	(25)	—	—
Annual Growth	(3.0%)	—	—	—

2015 Year-End Financials

Return on assets: 1.9%   Cash ($ mil.): 50
Return on equity: 32.3%
Current ratio: 0.80

THE ASSOCIATION OF AMERICAN MEDICAL COLLEGES

EXECUTIVES

Chief Executive Officer, Darrell G Kirch
Board of Directors, Barbara S Friedman
Officer, Charles Terrell
Assistant Vice-President, Chris Tucker
Chief Financial Officer, David Roe
Officer, Elisa Siegel
Auditors: KPMG LLP MC LEAN VA

LOCATIONS

HQ: THE ASSOCIATION OF AMERICAN MEDICAL
COLLEGES
655 K ST NW STE 100, WASHINGTON, DC 200012399
Phone: 202 828-0400
Web: WWW.AAMC.ORG

HISTORICAL FINANCIALS
Company Type: Private

Income Statement

| | | NET | NET | |
| | REVENUE | INCOME | PROFIT | EMPLOYEES |
	($ mil.)	($ mil.)	MARGIN	
06/15	214	48	22.8%	450
06/14	166	22	13.6%	—
06/13	138	7	5.6%	—
06/12	122	(2)	—	—
Annual Growth 20.5%		—	—	—

FYE: June 30

2015 Year-End Financials

Return on assets: 10.3%   Cash ($ mil.): 16
Return on equity: 22.8%
Current ratio: 0.10

THE AULTMAN HOSPITAL

EXECUTIVES

Chief Executive Officer, Christopher E Remark
President, Edward J Roth III
Chief Financial Officer, Mark Wright
Financial Executive, George Film
Director, Brian Woit
Manager, Carol Angello

LOCATIONS

HQ: THE AULTMAN HOSPITAL
2600 6TH ST SW, CANTON, OH 447101799
Phone: 330 452-9911
Web: WWW.AULTMAN.ORG

HISTORICAL FINANCIALS
Company Type: Private

Income Statement

| | | NET | NET | |
| | REVENUE | INCOME | PROFIT | EMPLOYEES |
	($ mil.)	($ mil.)	MARGIN	
12/15	307	0	0.2%	3,027
12/13	470	2	0.5%	—
12/12	471	(1)	—	—
12/02	0	0	—	—
Annual Growth	—	—	—	—

FYE: December 31

2015 Year-End Financials

Return on assets: 8.2%   Cash ($ mil.): —
Return on equity: 0.2%
Current ratio: 1.00

THE BIG TEN CONFERENCE INC

EXECUTIVES

Commissioner, Jim Delany
Personnel Manager, Wendy Fallen
Auditors: RSM US LLP CHICAGO IL

LOCATIONS

HQ: THE BIG TEN CONFERENCE INC
5440 PARK PL, ROSEMONT, IL 600183732
Phone: 847 696-1010
Web: WWW.BIGTEN.ORG

HISTORICAL FINANCIALS
Company Type: Private

Income Statement

| | | NET | NET | |
| | REVENUE | INCOME | PROFIT | EMPLOYEES |
	($ mil.)	($ mil.)	MARGIN	
06/15	448	12	2.8%	25
06/14	338	2	0.6%	—
06/13	318	5	1.9%	—
06/11	265	(0)	—	—
Annual Growth 14.1%		—	—	—

FYE: June 30

2015 Year-End Financials

Return on assets: 0.4%   Cash ($ mil.): 21
Return on equity: 2.8%
Current ratio: 2.20

THE BLOOMBERG FAMILY FOUNDATION INC

EXECUTIVES

Principal, Steve Fadem
Auditors: GELLER & COMPANY LLC NEW YORK

LOCATIONS

HQ: THE BLOOMBERG FAMILY FOUNDATION INC
909 3RD AVE, NEW YORK, NY 100224731
Phone: 212 205-0100

HISTORICAL FINANCIALS
Company Type: Private

Income Statement

| | | NET | NET | |
| | REVENUE | INCOME | PROFIT | EMPLOYEES |
	($ mil.)	($ mil.)	MARGIN	
12/15	1,194	736	61.7%	2
12/14	1,328	1,048	79.0%	—
12/13	809	538	66.5%	—
12/09	452	279	61.8%	—
Annual Growth 17.6%		17.5%		—

FYE: December 31

2015 Year-End Financials

Return on assets: —   Cash ($ mil.): 73
Return on equity: 61.7%
Current ratio: —

THE BOLDT GROUP INC

EXECUTIVES

President, Oscar C Boldt
Board of Directors, Michelle M Gawinski
Sales Manager, Daren Mazier
Manager, Maria Wetzel
Manager, Thom Liroka
VP Personnel, Barry Tornes
Vice-President, Todd Brink

LOCATIONS

HQ: THE BOLDT GROUP INC
2525 N ROEMER RD, APPLETON, WI 549118623
Phone: 920 739-7800
Web: WWW.BOLDT.COM

HISTORICAL FINANCIALS
Company Type: Private

Income Statement

| | | NET | NET | |
| | REVENUE | INCOME | PROFIT | EMPLOYEES |
	($ mil.)	($ mil.)	MARGIN	
12/15	978	0	—	1,500
12/14	874	0	—	—
12/13	715	0	—	—
12/12	624	0	—	—
Annual Growth 16.1%				

FYE: December 31

2015 Year-End Financials

Return on assets: 14.3%   Cash ($ mil.): 45
Return on equity: —
Current ratio: 1.10

THE BRANCH GROUP INC

It's not going out on a limb to say that The Branch Group has paved a lot of roads and built a lot of structures up and down the Atlantic Seaboard. The company through its subsidiaries provides heavy/highway construction (Branch Highways and E.V. Williams) building construction (Branch & Associates and R.E. Daffan) and mechanical/electrical construction services (G.J. Hopkins). The group has paved roads for highway departments built hospitals schools factories and infrastructure projects. The employee-owned company began in 1963 as Branch & Associates Inc. but traces its roots to 1955 when Billy Branch and C. W. McAlister paired up to provide road and site construction services.

EXECUTIVES

Chief Executive Officer, J William Karbach
Director, Randall Clark
Chief Operating Officer, Tomlinson Mike
Financial Executive, Matt Wise
Auditors: KPMG LLP ROANOKE VIRGINIA

LOCATIONS

HQ: THE BRANCH GROUP INC
442 RUTHERFORD AVE NE, ROANOKE, VA
240162116
Phone: 540 982-1678
Web: WWW.BRANCHGROUP.COM

PRODUCTS/OPERATIONS

Selected Subsidiaries

Branch & Associates Inc. (builder construction services)
Branch Highways Inc. (highway bridge airport infrastructure and site development)
E.V. Williams Inc. (highway site development and concrete paving construction servives)
G.J. Hopkins Inc. (mechanical and electrical construction services)
R. E. Daffan (construction and architectural services)

COMPETITORS

Bechtel	KBS
English Construction Company	S. W. Rodgers
	Tetra Tech Tesoro
Fluor	Turner Corporation
K3 Construction	Whiting-Turner

HISTORICAL FINANCIALS
Company Type: Private

Income Statement
FYE: December 31

	REVENUE ($ mil.)	NET INCOME ($ mil.)	NET PROFIT MARGIN	EMPLOYEES
12/15	392	0	—	800
12/14	384	0	—	—
12/13	326	0	—	—
12/12	271	0	—	—
Annual Growth	13.1%	—	—	—

2015 Year-End Financials
Return on assets: 15.0% Cash ($ mil.): 27
Return on equity: —
Current ratio: 0.70

THE BRANDT COMPANIES LLC

EXECUTIVES

Director, Barry Moore
Chief Financial Officer, Mike Arthurs
Account Manager, Carolyn Brice
Financial Executive, Jeff Welsh
Manager, Austin Creps
Vice-President, Christian Beasley
Supervisor, Gary Coulson
Engineer, Matthew Smerud
Vice-President, John Dunn
Project Director, Michael Alaimo
Auditors: PAYNE & SMITH LLC DALLAS TX

LOCATIONS

HQ: THE BRANDT COMPANIES LLC
1728 BRIERCROFT CT, CARROLLTON, TX 750066400
Phone: 972 241-9411
Web: WWW.BRANDT.US

HISTORICAL FINANCIALS
Company Type: Private

Income Statement
FYE: December 31

	REVENUE ($ mil.)	NET INCOME ($ mil.)	NET PROFIT MARGIN	EMPLOYEES
12/15	398	12	3.2%	1,500
12/14	384	10	2.7%	—
12/07	253	21	8.5%	—
Annual Growth	5.8%	(6.4%)	—	—

2015 Year-End Financials
Return on assets: 7.1% Cash ($ mil.): 2
Return on equity: 3.2%
Current ratio: 1.30

THE BRIGHAM AND WOMEN'S HOSPITAL INC

It took three of Boston's oldest and most prestigious hospitals to form the health care behemoth that is Brigham and Women's Hospital. The Harvard-affiliated facility has nearly 800 beds and includes the Dana-Farber/Brigham and Women's Cancer Center a partnership between the hospital and the Dana Farber Cancer Institute. Other specialty units focus on cardiology neurology transplants and obstetrics. In addition to being a teaching hospital for Harvard Medical School Brigham and Women's Hospital conducts research and clinical trials to help advance medical care. It's a top recipient of research grants from the National Institutes of Health and is a founding member of the Partners HealthCare System.

Operations

Brigham and Women's Hospital employs more than 3000 physicians fellows and residents and almost as many nurses. Inpatient admissions reach 46000 and ambulatory visits have grown to more than 3.5 million.

Brigham and Women's Hospital also operates the 150-bed Faulkner Hospital which is located near the main campus and offers acute care and specialty services including psychiatry and orthopedics. In addition Brigham and Women's operates satellite physician offices including primary and rehabilitation care.

The hospital is also known for performing the first full face transplant in the US. Brigham and Women's doctors performed the surgery in 2011 on a man whose face was severely burned when his head touched a high voltage line. Sponsored by the Department of Defense the surgery was part of the military's efforts to expand research on innovative medical procedures.

Strategy

The hospital system has positioned itself to do remarkable work such as a face transplant through its continued focus on research. Brigham and Women's research institute: The Biomedical Research Institute at BWH spends on average $500 million annually to conduct research in a whole host of fields including tissue engineering emergency medicine genomics and infectious disease (to name a few).

In 2014 Brigham and Women's Hospital opened the Ann Romney Center for Neurologic Diseases which will conduct medical research on five complex neurologic diseases including multiple sclerosis (MS) Alzheimer's disease Lou Gehrig's disease (ALS) Parkinson's disease and brain tumors.

Company Background

The hospital was formed through the 1980 merger of Peter Bent Brigham Hospital Robert Breck Brigham Hospital and Boston Hospital for Women.

EXECUTIVES

Chairman Obstetrics and Gynecology, Robert L. Barbieri
Chairman Dermatology, Thomas S. Kupper
Chair Neurology, Martin A. Samuels
Chair Radiology, Steven E. Seltzer

Chairman Department of Medicine, Joseph Loscalzo, age 65
President, Elizabeth G. (Betsy) Nabel
President Brigham and Women's Faulkner Hospital, Michael Gustafson
Chair Psychiatry and Institute for Neurosciences, David Silbersweig
Chief Medical Officer, Stanley W. Ashley
President Brigham and Women's Physicians Organization (BWPO), Allen Smith
SVP Research and Chief Academic Officer, Paul J. Anderson
SVP Ambulatory Services, Richard W. Fernandez
SVP Patient Care Services and Chief Nursing Officer, Jackie Somerville
Chief Development Officer, Susan Rapple
SVP Clinical Services, Julia Sinclair
SVP and Chief Business Development Officer, Steven Thompson
Chair Neurosurgery, Ennio A. Chiocca
Chair Pathology, Jeffrey A. Golden
Chair Radiation Oncology, Daphne Haas-Kogan
Chair Pediatric Newborn Medicine, Terrie E. Inder
Chair Anesthesiology Perioperative and Pain Medicine, James P. Rathmell
Chair Emergency Medicine, Michael VanRooyen
Chair Physical Medicine and Rehabilitation, Ross D. Zafonte
CIO, Adam Landman
Chair Orthopaedics, James D. Kang
Interim Chair Surgery, Francis D. Moore
Interim Chief Financial Officer, Susan Wheeler
Clinical Director, Laura Safar
Rph, Bertine Dupuy
Nursing Director, Sharon Zisk
Pharmacy Manager, Amrita Chabria
Pharmacy Manager, Caryn Belisle
Vice Chair of Medicine, David Faxon

LOCATIONS

HQ: THE BRIGHAM AND WOMEN'S HOSPITAL INC
75 FRANCIS ST, BOSTON, MA 021156106
Phone: 617 732-5500
Web: WWW.BRIGHAMANDWOMENS.ORG

PRODUCTS/OPERATIONS

Clinical Departments
Anesthesia
Cancer
Dermatology
Emergency Medicine
Medicine
Neurology
Neurosurgery
Obstetrics and Gynecology
Orthopaedic Surgery
Pathology
Pediatric Newborn Medicine
Physical Medicine and Rehabilitation
Psychiatry
Radiation Oncology
Radiology
Surgery
Women's Health

Selected Support Services
Care coordination
Ethics service
Family liaison service
Interpreter service
Kessler Library
Nursing
Nutrition
Patient/family relations
Pharmacy
Security
Social work

COMPETITORS

Boston Medical Center	New England Alliance for Health
Cambridge Health Alliance	Northeast Health System
Care New England	

CareGroup
Children's Hospital
  Boston
Emerson Hospital
MD Anderson Cancer
  Center
Memorial
  Sloan-Kettering
Milford Regional
  Medical Center

Southcoast Hospitals
  Group
Steward Health Care
Sturdy Memorial
Universal Health
  Services
Winchester Healthcare

HISTORICAL FINANCIALS
Company Type: Private

Income Statement
FYE: September 30

	REVENUE ($ mil.)	NET INCOME ($ mil.)	NET PROFIT MARGIN	EMPLOYEES
09/15	1,811	60	3.4%	8,376
09/14	1,797	151	8.4%	—
09/13	1,764	139	7.9%	—
09/12	1,705	132	7.8%	—
Annual Growth	2.0%	(22.8%)	—	—

2015 Year-End Financials

Return on assets: 4.6%
Return on equity: 3.4%
Current ratio: 0.70

Cash ($ mil.): 43

THE BROAD INSTITUTE INC

EXECUTIVES

Board of Directors, Justine Levin
Board of Directors, Andy Porter
Manager, Marilyn Smith
Auditors: PRICEWATERHOUSECOOPERS LLP BO

LOCATIONS

HQ: THE BROAD INSTITUTE INC
  415 MAIN ST, CAMBRIDGE, MA 021421027
Phone: 617 714-7000
Web: WWW.BROADINSTITUTE.ORG

HISTORICAL FINANCIALS
Company Type: Private

Income Statement
FYE: June 30

	REVENUE ($ mil.)	NET INCOME ($ mil.)	NET PROFIT MARGIN	EMPLOYEES
06/16	377	(45)	—	800
06/15	355	37	10.6%	—
06/14	411	108	26.4%	—
06/13	356	73	20.6%	—
Annual Growth	1.9%	—	—	—

2016 Year-End Financials

Return on assets: 4.3%
Return on equity: (-12.0%)
Current ratio: 0.90

Cash ($ mil.): 139

THE CARE GROUP LLC

EXECUTIVES

Manager, John O Flaherty

Director, Stephanie Delks
Chief Financial Officer, Mary Hogan
Director, Jennifer Cohn

LOCATIONS

HQ: THE CARE GROUP LLC
  8333 NAAB RD STE 340, INDIANAPOLIS, IN
  462601983
Phone: 317 338-5050

HISTORICAL FINANCIALS
Company Type: Private

Income Statement
FYE: June 30

	REVENUE ($ mil.)	NET INCOME ($ mil.)	NET PROFIT MARGIN	EMPLOYEES
06/15	178	(112)	—	1,000
06/14*	285	(6)	—	—
12/06	103	1	1.2%	—
12/05	0	0	—	—
Annual Growth	—	—	—	—

*Fiscal year change

2015 Year-End Financials

Return on assets: 24.4%
Return on equity: (-63.1%)
Current ratio: —

Cash ($ mil.): 4

THE CARLE FOUNDATION

EXECUTIVES

Chief Executive Officer, James C Leonard
Financial Executive, Kerry Warburton
Production Director, Debbie Schmidt
Auditors: ERNST & YOUNG US LLP INDIANAP

LOCATIONS

HQ: THE CARLE FOUNDATION
  611 W PARK ST, URBANA, IL 618012529
Phone: 217 383 3311

HISTORICAL FINANCIALS
Company Type: Private

Income Statement
FYE: December 31

	REVENUE ($ mil.)	NET INCOME ($ mil.)	NET PROFIT MARGIN	EMPLOYEES
12/15	2,493	51	2.0%	5,284
12/13	249	52	20.9%	—
12/11*	1,608	0	0.0%	—
06/10	135	72	53.3%	—
Annual Growth	62.4%	(5.6%)	—	—

*Fiscal year change

2015 Year-End Financials

Return on assets: 0.9%
Return on equity: 2.0%
Current ratio: 0.50

Cash ($ mil.): 192

THE CATHOLIC UNIVERSITY OF AMERICA

The Catholic University of America (CUA) established in 1887 by US bishops has an enrollment of more than 7000 students from all 50 states and nearly 100 countries. With graduate and undergraduate programs in 13 colleges CUA offers degrees in such fields as architecture and planning arts and sciences engineering music and nursing; it's expanding into business and economics. CUA is the only US university with ecclesiastical faculties granting canonical degrees in canon law philosophy and theology. Some 80% of undergraduates and nearly 60% of graduate students are Catholic. The University's Theological College prepares men for the priesthood serving dioceses nationwide.

Operations

As part of its operations CUA offers its students several areas of study. It boasts schools in architecture and planning arts and sciences business and economics canon law engineering law library and information sciences music nursing philosophy professional studies social services and theology and religious studies. Its architecture program is the largest in the D.C. area and the legal clinic at its Columbus School of Law is rated among the top 12 in the nation.

The university which has a student-faculty ratio is 9:1 grants undergraduate degrees in 72 programs master's degrees in 103 programs and doctoral or terminal degrees in 66 programs.

Geographic Reach

The university's 193-acre campus is located north of Capitol Hill in Washington D.C. The campus comprises more than a dozen schools and nearly two dozen research facilities.

Sales and Marketing

CUA sources its students from all 50 states and nearly 100 countries.

Strategy

To cater to those who have requested an increased focus on business education CUA added a School of Business and Economics. Instead of focusing on theories the school offers students an education model based on Catholic social doctrine and the natural law.

EXECUTIVES

Assistant Vice President Global Educat, Tanith Corsi
Medical Director, Loretta Staudt
Assoc Vice President Student Life Dean Students, Jonathan Sawyer
Associate Vice President For M, Jacquelyn Malcolm
Treasurer, Dominic Pigneri
Executive Project Coordinator Notary Public Vice President For Finance and Treasurer, Pamela Lalla
Auditors: PRICEWATERHOUSECOOPERS LLP BA

LOCATIONS

HQ: THE CATHOLIC UNIVERSITY OF AMERICA
  620 MICHIGAN AVE NE, WASHINGTON, DC
  200640002
Phone: 202 319-5000
Web: WWW.CUA.EDU

PRODUCTS/OPERATIONS

Selected Schools
Benjamin T. Rome School of Music
Columbus School of Law

Metropolitan School of Professional Studies
National Catholic School of Social Service
School of Architecture and Planning
School of Arts and Sciences
School of Business and Economics
School of Canon Law
School of Engineering
School of Library and Information Science
School of Nursing
School of Philosophy
School of Theology and Religious Studies

HISTORICAL FINANCIALS
Company Type: Private

Income Statement
FYE: April 30

	REVENUE ($ mil.)	NET INCOME ($ mil.)	NET PROFIT MARGIN	EMPLOYEES
04/16*	232	2	0.9%	4,239
06/13	342	57	16.8%	—
04/13	217	17	8.3%	—
Annual Growth	2.2%	(51.4%)	—	—

*Fiscal year change

2016 Year-End Financials
Return on assets: 11.0%
Return on equity: 0.9%
Current ratio: —
Cash ($ mil.): 26

THE CHARLES STARK DRAPER LABORATORY INC

The Charles Stark Draper Laboratory guides research into space under water and across continents. The not-for-profit corporation develops guidance navigation and control technologies for aircraft submarines missiles and spacecraft. It works with NASA the US Department of Defense and commercial businesses to develop technologies and fabricate prototypes. The organization also solves healthcare problems with its work in biomedical engineering. The lab boasts more than 850 engineers and scientists. Originally known as the Instrument Lab the laboratory was renamed in 1970 and became an independent institution three years later.

Operations

Draper Lab's innovations include a personal navigation system that allows soldiers to find their way in GPS-denied areas. It has also developed a micro-avionics system for a 20-gram nano air vehicle that's capable of flying in realistic wind conditions and equipped with a digital video recorder the size of a postage stamp.

The corporation boasts expertise in guidance navigation and control sytems; advanced algorithms and software; fault-tolerant computing; modeling and simulation; and microelectromechanical system (MEMS) and multichip module technology.

Geographic Reach

Draper Lab maintains operations in Cambridge Massachusetts; Houston; Huntsville Alabama; Tampa and St. Petersburg Florida; and Washington D.C.

Financial Performance

In fiscal 2013 Draper Lab made up for traction lost the previous year. Its revenue rose by 3% to $528 million in 2013 from 2012's $514 million.

The company's revenues had decreased in 2012 by 3% due in part to a drop in subcontracts.

Primary funding sources include the US Navy the US Army other national security sponsors NASA and select non- Department of Defense sponsors.

Strategy

Fueled by the brain power and expertise of its hundreds of engineers Draper Lab aims to solve problems by designing developing and deploying solutions built using advanced technologies. Its primary areas of focus include space exploration security healthcare and energy.

Draper Lab completed the first missile flight of the MK6 MOD 1 boost guidance system for the Trident II D5 submarine-launched ballistic missile in 2012 with completely successful results. This flight was the culmination of 10 years of work by the laboratory in collaboration with the Navy Strategic Systems Program and a team of independent support contractors.

Another significant milestone was the deployment of the first close-in collection systems using its patented integrated ultra-high density (iUHD) packaging technology — the next generation of Draper Lab's vanishingly small systems (VSS) design techniques.

The lab's investments in biomedical and energy systems are paying dividends with a growing list of sponsors in each area. To this end Draper Lab is working with Shell Oil to design a backup system that will assist operators in getting an oil well under control in the event of a drilling accident. It's also partnering with the State of Rhode Island to prototype a clean energy research center in collaboration with Brown University and the University of Rhode Island.

Draper Lab continues to work alongside Progress Energy to improve the effectiveness of coal plant operation by improving combustion efficiency and monitoring critical equipment status to anticipate failures. Through a partnership with the Defense Advanced Research Projects Agency it's creating a versatile microfluidic platform that can incorporate up to 10 individually engineered microphysiological organ system modules in an interacting circuit.

Company Background

The organization was founded in 1932 by MIT professor Charles Stark Draper as a teaching lab.

EXECUTIVES

Vice President Finance and Administration, Joseph M Wolfe
Vice President for Programs, Darryl Sargent
CFO, Elizabeth Mora
President and CEO, Kaigham (Ken) Gabriel
Vice President Sales, Mitchell Hansberry
Vice President, Allison Looney
Vice President, Len Polizzotto
Vice President, Ted Rye
Vice President of Information Technology, Diane Chilante
Vice President, John Stillwell
Vice President for Strategic Systems, Steve DiTullio
Vice President For Commercial, Tara Clark
Vice President for Finance and Administration and Treasurer, Joe Wolfe
Chairman, Franklin C. (Frank) Miller
Treasurer, David Markuson
Auditors: MOODY FAMIGLIETTI & ANDRONICO

LOCATIONS

HQ: THE CHARLES STARK DRAPER LABORATORY INC
555 TECHNOLOGY SQ, CAMBRIDGE, MA 021393539
Phone: 617 258-1000
Web: WWW.DRAPER.COM

PRODUCTS/OPERATIONS

Selected Research Areas
Biomedical engineering
 Tissue engineering
 Sensor development
Space systems
 Military space systems
 Planetary exploration
 Scientific spacecraft
 Space transportation
Special operations
 Robotics
 Small low-power electronics
 Surveillance systems
Strategic systems
 Inertial guidance systems
Tactical systems
 Precision engagement systems
 Manned/unmanned systems
 Missile defense

COMPETITORS

Applied Research Associates	QinetiQ
Institute for Defense Analyses	Quantum Research

HISTORICAL FINANCIALS
Company Type: Private

Income Statement
FYE: June 30

	REVENUE ($ mil.)	NET INCOME ($ mil.)	NET PROFIT MARGIN	EMPLOYEES
06/15	656	61	9.4%	1,134
06/14	522	28	5.4%	—
06/13	542	17	3.2%	—
06/12	514	(20)	—	—
Annual Growth	8.5%	—	—	—

2015 Year-End Financials
Return on assets: 11.9%
Return on equity: 9.4%
Current ratio: 0.90
Cash ($ mil.): 56

THE CHARLOTTE-MECKLENBURG HOSPITAL AUTHORITY

The medical facilities under the watchful eye of the Charlotte-Mecklenburg Hospital Authority care for the injured and infirmed. As the largest health care system in the Carolinas the organization operating as Carolinas HealthCare System (CHS) owns or manages more than 30 affiliated hospitals. It also operates long-term care facilities research centers rehabilitation facilities surgery centers home health agencies radiation therapy facilities and other health care operations. Collectively CHS facilities have more than 6400 beds and affiliated physician practices employ more than 1700 doctors. The network's flagship facility is the 875-bed Carolinas Medical Center in Charlotte North Carolina.

HISTORY

Carolinas HealthCare System has expanded its network through acquisitions and affiliations. In 2006 it purchased the 100-bed Lincoln Medical Center (now named Carolinas Medical Center-Lincoln) which the company had already been man-

aging for several years. In 2007 it acquired the 460-bed NorthEast Medical Center (now Carolinas Medical Center-NorthEast). Carolinas HealthCare made improvements at both facilities including a complete reconstruction of the Lincoln campus and an eight-story patient tower addition at the NorthEast campus.

In 2008 and 2009 Carolinas HealthCare entered management services partnerships with AnMed Health (Anderson South Carolina) Cannon Memorial Hospital (Pickens South Carolina) St. Luke's Hospital (Columbus North Carolina) Stanly Regional Medical Center (Albemarle North Carolina) and Scotland Health Care System (Laurinburg North Carolina).

EXECUTIVES

Chief Executive Officer, Eugene A Woods
Director, Jay Rader
Director, Jeffrey A Kline
Director, John A Marx
Auditors: KPMG LLP CHARLOTTE NC

LOCATIONS

HQ: THE CHARLOTTE-MECKLENBURG HOSPITAL AUTHORITY
1000 BLYTHE BLVD, CHARLOTTE, NC 282035812
Phone: 704 355-2000

PRODUCTS/OPERATIONS

2010 Revenue

	% of total
Tertiary & acute care services	72
Physicians' services	16
Post-acute care services	3
Specialty services	2
Other services & non-operating activities	7
Total	**100**

Selected Hospitals and Health Care Pavilions

AnMed Health Medical Center
AnMed Health Rehabilitation Hospital
AnMed Health Women's and Children's Hospital
Anson Community Hospital
Bon Secours/St. Francis Hospital
Cannon Memorial Hospital
Carolinas Medical Center
Carolinas Medical Center - Kannapolis (health care pavilion)
Carolinas Medical Center - Lincoln
Carolinas Medical Center - Mercy
Carolinas Medical Center - NorthEast
Carolinas Medical Center - Pineville
Carolinas Medical Center - Steele Creek (health care pavilion)
Carolinas Medical Center - Union
Carolinas Medical Center - University
Carolinas Medical Center - Waxhaw (health care pavilion)
Carolinas Rehabilitation
Carolinas Rehabilitation - Mount Holly
Cleveland Regional Medical Center
CMC - Randolph
Columbus Regional Healthcare System
Crawley Memorial Hospital
Grace Hospital
Kings Mountain Hospital
Levine Children's Hospital
MedWest - Harris
MedWest - Haywood
MedWest - Swain
Roper Hospital
Roper St. Francis - Mount Pleasant Hospital
Scotland Memorial Hospital
Stanly Regional Medical Center
St. Luke's Hospital
Valdese Hospital
Wallace Thomson Hospital
Wilkes Regional Medical Center

COMPETITORS

Alamance Regional Medical Center
CaroMont
Community Health Systems

Cone Health
Conway Medical Center
Cumberland County Hospital System
Davis Regional Medical Center
Duke University Health System
FirstHealth of the Carolinas
Georgetown Hospital System
Grand Strand Regional Medical Center
Greenville Hospital System
HCA
Haywood Regional
High Point Regional Health System
McLeod Health
Mission Hospitals
Morehead Memorial Hospital
New Hanover Regional Medical Center
Novant Health
Palmetto Health
Presbyterian Healthcare
Rex Healthcare
Soliant Health
Tenet Healthcare
UNC Hospitals
Vidant Health
Wake Forest University Baptist Medical Center
WakeMed

HISTORICAL FINANCIALS
Company Type: Private

Income Statement

	REVENUE ($ mil.)	NET INCOME ($ mil.)	NET PROFIT MARGIN	EMPLOYEES
12/15	5,478	(247)	—	62,000
12/12	4,501	249	5.5%	
12/11	4,183	147	3.5%	
12/10	3,855	353	9.2%	
Annual Growth	**7.3%**	—	—	—

FYE: December 31

2015 Year-End Financials
Return on assets: 4.4%   Cash ($ mil.): 178
Return on equity: (-4.5%)
Current ratio: 0.90

THE CHEROKEE NATION

EXECUTIVES

Chief, Chad Smith
Manager, Linda Vann
Manager, Randy McElvaian
Chief Financial Officer, Enrique Bernal
Manager, Matt Dewes
Operations Manager, Doug Bane

LOCATIONS

HQ: THE CHEROKEE NATION
17675 S MUSKOGEE AVE, TAHLEQUAH, OK 744645492
Phone: 918 453 5000

HISTORICAL FINANCIALS
Company Type: Private

Income Statement

	REVENUE ($ mil.)	NET INCOME ($ mil.)	NET PROFIT MARGIN	EMPLOYEES
09/15	511	(15)	—	5,500
09/05	226	15	6.7%	
09/04	203	14	6.9%	
09/03	113	30	26.7%	
Annual Growth	**13.3%**			

FYE: September 30

2015 Year-End Financials
Return on assets: 29.2%   Cash ($ mil.): 361
Return on equity: (-3.0%)
Current ratio: 2.10

THE CHESTER COUNTY HOSPITAL

EXECUTIVES

President, Michael Duncan
Principal, William E Luginbuhl
Board of Directors, Antelo Devereux
Auditors: PRICEWATERHOUSECOOPERS LLP PH

LOCATIONS

HQ: THE CHESTER COUNTY HOSPITAL
701 E MARSHALL ST, WEST CHESTER, PA 193804421
Phone: 610 431-5000
Web: WWW.CHESTERCOUNTYHOSPITAL.ORG

HISTORICAL FINANCIALS
Company Type: Private

Income Statement

	REVENUE ($ mil.)	NET INCOME ($ mil.)	NET PROFIT MARGIN	EMPLOYEES
06/15	298	10	3.5%	2,000
06/14	265	14	5.3%	
06/13	271	11	4.2%	
06/11	245	1	0.8%	
Annual Growth	**5.0%**	**52.2%**	—	—

FYE: June 30

2015 Year-End Financials
Return on assets: 2.0%   Cash ($ mil.): 41
Return on equity: 3.5%
Current ratio: 2.90

THE CHILDREN'S HOSPITAL CORPORATION

The Children's Hospital Corporation dba Boston Children's Hospital is a 400-bed hospital that offers acute health care and specialty services for children from birth through age 21. The medical center is Harvard Medical School's main teaching hospital for children's health care and it is the world's largest pediatric research center. Its John F. Enders Pediatric Research facility provides research for the treatment of childhood diseases. Specialty services are offered in the fields of cardiovascular surgery digestive care neurology oncology ophthalmology orthopedics autism spectrum disorder blood diseases and fetal care. The not-for-profit hospital was founded in 1869.

Operations

Boston Children's Hospital handles about 25000 inpatient visits per year as well as 27000 surgeries and more than 200000 radiological exams. Its 200+ specialized clinical programs handle about

560000 appointments annually. The hospital is considered a safety-net hospital and as such is one of the largest providers of medical care to low-income children in the state. About 30% of the hospital's patients are either uninsured or have health care coverage through public assistance.

In addition to its educational and research partnerships with Harvard the medical center collaborates with other universities as well as drug makers medical equipment firms and research institutes. Altogether it has some 1100 scientists at its research centers including the Enders Pediatric Research Laboratories and the Karp Family Research Laboratories. Children's Hospital Boston receives up to some $225 million in research funding per year.

Along with the main hospital the system operates a handful of primary and specialty care centers throughout the Boston area. It also operates a cancer clinic within the main campus through a partnership with the Dana Farber Cancer Institute.

In 2017 Boston Children's Hospital was named the country's best pediatric hospital by U.S. News & World Report for the fifth year in a row.

Geographic Reach

Boston Children's Hospital has satellite locations and affiliates throughout Massachusetts. In addition to its main campus in Boston it has satellites in Lexington North Dartmouth Peabody and Waltham; doctors' offices in Brockton Milford Norwood and Weymouth; and affiliates in Beverly Fall River Milford New Bedford South Weymouth Wareham and Winchester.

Strategy

Due to increasing economic troubles and health reform measures in the US Boston Children's Hospital has been working to cut costs. Despite the cost-control efforts the main campus is undergoing expansion renovation and modernization efforts as part of a 10-year expansion plan.

EXECUTIVES

Senior Vice President, Wendy Warring
CEO, James Mandell
President COO and Trustee, Sandra L. Fenwick, age 66
CFO, Doug Vanderslice
CIO, Daniel Nigrin
SVP Patient Care Operations, Eileen Sporing
Surgeon-in-Chief and Trustee, James Kasser
Anesthesiologist-in-Chief, Paul R. Hickey
Executive Director Satellite Clinical Operations, Julee Bolg
President Children's Hospital Trust, Lynn Susman
SVP and Chief Marketing and Communications Officer, Margaret Coughlin
Chief Investment Officer, Phil Rotner
Executive Director Satellite Administrative Operations, Jane Venti
Executive Vice President of, Kevin Churchwell
Radiology Director, Kirsten Ecklund
Director of Medical Records, Mary Radley
Medical Director, Sharon Levy
Medical Director, Terra Lafranchi
Infection Control Director, DAVID MICHAEL WESSELS
Clinic Director, Hans C Oettgen
Vice President Medical Staff Affairs, Patricia Derusso
Vice President, Inez Stewart
Vice President of Marketing and Business Development, Lynne Hancock
Senior Vice President Quality, Katherine Jenkins
Icu Intensitvist Vice President Of Cardiology, Patricia Hickey
Senior Vice President Network Development and Strategic Partnerships, Warring Wendy
Vice President Corporate Development and Special Events, Carola Cadley

Vice President Finance, Sophia Holder
Senior Vice President And General Counse, Michele Garvin
Chair, Stephen R. Karp
Secretary, Cynthia Dube
Treasurer, George Phillips

LOCATIONS

HQ: THE CHILDREN'S HOSPITAL CORPORATION
300 LONGWOOD AVE, BOSTON, MA 021155737
Phone: 617 355-6000
Web: WWW.CHILDRENSHOSPITAL.ORG

PRODUCTS/OPERATIONS

Selected Services

Major centers
Brain Center
Cancer and Blood Diseases Center
Heart Center
Orthopedic Center
Transplant Center
Other Services
Airway breathing and lungs
Allergies and asthma
Anatomy and function
Bone joint and muscle
Brain and nervous sytivem
Cancer and blood disorders
Common childhood health topics and conditions
Craniofacial anomalies
Diet and nutrition
Digestive metabolic and renal disorders
Ears nose and throat
Emergency medicine and trauma
Eyes and vision
Genetic disorders and birth defects
Heart blood and circulation
International patient care
Medical tests
Newborns
Psychiatric (mental) conditions
Reproductive and urinary conditions
Skin and vascular
Viruses and infections

COMPETITORS

Baystate Medical Center	Nemours Foundation
Beth Israel Deaconess Medical Center	Newton-Wellesley Hospital
Boston Medical Center	Northeast Health System
Cambridge Health Alliance	Partners HealthCare
Cape Cod Hospital	Shriners Hospitals For Children
Children's Hospital of Philadelphia	Steward Health Care Sturdy Memorial

HISTORICAL FINANCIALS

Company Type: Private

Income Statement

FYE: September 30

	REVENUE ($ mil.)	NET INCOME ($ mil.)	NET PROFIT MARGIN	EMPLOYEES
09/15	1,061	(5)	—	8,000
09/14	1,514	111	7.3%	
09/09*	1,348	94	7.0%	—
06/05	4	0	13.0%	—
Annual Growth 71.3%	—	—	—	—

*Fiscal year change

2015 Year-End Financials

Return on assets: 12.9%
Return on equity: (-0.5%)
Current ratio: 0.60
Cash ($ mil.): —

THE CHILDRENS HOSPITAL LOS ANGELES

Childrens Hospital Los Angeles (CHLA) is dedicated to treating the youngest critical care patients in the region. The about 570-bed hospital specializes in treating seriously ill and injured children from its neonatal intensive care unit to its pediatric organ transplant center. CHLA's pediatric specialists also provide care at its ambulatory care center in Arcadia and through about 40 off-site practice sites. The hospital's pediatric specialties include cancer kidney failure and cystic fibrosis care. CHLA serves more than 107000 children every year. It is one of only 12 children's hospitals in the nation (and the only one in California) ranked in all 10 pediatric specialties by U.S. News & World Report .

Operations

The CHLA medical staff includes about 600 physicians most of which are members of the CHLA Medical Group. Its emergency department treats some 71000 patients and the hospital sees more than 343000 outpatients annually. Nearly 50% of its patients are under the age of four. CHLA is also the only freestanding level I Pediatric Trauma Center in LA County approved by the Committee on Trauma of the American College of Surgeons and among only 5% of US hospitals to be designated as a Magnet Hospital by the American Nurses Credentialing Center.

It is also a teaching hospital through its affiliation with the Keck School of Medicine of the University of Southern California and is home to the Saban Research Institute which conducts biomedical research into pediatric diseases. CHLA's training programs include 575 medical students 85 full-time residents three chief residents and 98 fellows.

Financial Performance

Revenue decreased 7% to $803 million in 2014 due to a decline in net patient service revenue. Also that year the company reported a net loss of $30 million due to the decline in revenue and higher operating expenses.

Strategy

CHLA is expanding its facilities to keep up with demand. In 2015 it opened the doors of a new outpatient center in Encino.

Company Background

Although it sometimes operates as Children's Hospital Los Angeles the absent apostrophe in the legal Childrens Hospital of Los Angeles name is no accident. The intentional spelling honors the original incorporation documents filed in 1901 when the institution was founded as Childrens Hospital Society of Los Angeles.

EXECUTIVES

Vice President Patient Care Services and Chief Nursing Officer and Trustee, Mary Dee Hacker
Vice President and CIO, Marty W Miller
Associate Vice President, Anna Weiser

LOCATIONS

HQ: THE CHILDRENS HOSPITAL LOS ANGELES
4650 W SUNSET BLVD, LOS ANGELES, CA 900276062
Phone: 323 660-2450
Web: WWW.CHILDRENSHOSPITALLA.ORG

COMPETITORS

Cedars-Sinai Medical Center
Children's Hopsital of Chicago
Children's Hospital & Research Center at Oakland

Children's Hospital Boston
Children's Hospital of Orange County
Children's Hospital of Philadelphia
Children's National Medical Center
Cincinnati Children's Hospital
Cook Children's Health Care System
Dignity Health
Good Samaritan Hospital (Los Angeles)
Hollywood Presbyterian Medical Center
Nationwide Children's Hospital
Shriners Hospitals For Children

HISTORICAL FINANCIALS

Company Type: Private

Income Statement

FYE: June 30

	REVENUE ($ mil.)	NET INCOME ($ mil.)	NET PROFIT MARGIN	EMPLOYEES
06/15	891	27	3.0%	3,000
06/14	823	(46)	—	—
06/13	869	36	4.2%	—
06/10	564	(34)	—	—
Annual Growth	9.6%	—	—	—

2015 Year-End Financials

Return on assets: 7.9%   Cash ($ mil.): 18
Return on equity: 3.0%
Current ratio: 1.10

THE CHRISTIAN BROADCASTING NETWORK INC

Standards & Practices probably won't find much wrong with these TV programs. The Christian Broadcasting Network (CBN) is one of the leading producers of religious television programming in the country offering news and entertainment shows with a spiritual message. Its centerpiece is The 700 Club a daily show featuring a mix of news and commentary interviews feature stories and Christian ministry co-hosted by CBN founder Pat Robertson. The company's programs are syndicated to broadcast and cable TV outlets that reach audiences around the world. CBN generates most of its revenue through ministry donations.

Operations

CBN has a broad portfolio of ministries and services.

This portfolio includes The 700 Club & Prayer Center. CBN's The 700 Club program brings a magazine-style mix of news interviews testimonies and insights from Christian leaders. CBN's Prayer Center provides prayer as well as biblical guidance and resources to callers.

The 700 Club Interactive is a show designed for viewer interaction and uses a chat community Skype live phone calls and social networking.

CBN is launching a massive media campaign to promote the Bible under the brand Superbook .

Orphan's Promise ministers to the physical spiritual and educational needs of orphaned and vulnerable children.

CBN's Operation Blessing International's core programs include disaster relief medical aid hunger relief orphan care water wells and community development.

CBN.com offers streaming video teaching; in-depth discipleship courses; Online Bible; CBN Radio; Bible teachings; my.CBN.com a social net-

work; and free downloads of videos widgets and articles.

Geographic Reach

CBN programs have aired in 108 languages (from Mandarin to Spanish and from Turkish to Welsh) in 218 different countries and territories. It currently broadcasts in 139 countries with programs and content translated into 62 languages. The company has offices in Africa Asia Europe the Middle East North America (Canada and US) and Russia and the Commonwealth of Independent States.

Financial Performance

The company's revenue increased to $542 million during fiscal 2013 a 11% increased from previous year's $487 million. The spike was largely due to increases in revenue from Gifts in kind by 24% to $245 million in fiscal 2013 compared to $197 million in fiscal 2012 and additional investment gain and other revenues.

EXECUTIVES

Chairman, Pat Robertson
Director, Ruth Kastberg
Manager, Cathleen McCormick
Operations Manager, Sheryl Ford
Director, Beverly Milner
Manager, Joe Fitzpatrick
Auditors: LB KPMG LLP MC LEAN VA

LOCATIONS

HQ: THE CHRISTIAN BROADCASTING NETWORK INC
977 CENTERVILLE TPKE, VIRGINIA BEACH, VA 234631001
Phone: 757 226-3030
Web: WWW.CBN.COM

COMPETITORS

Eden Communications	Thomas Nelson
Guideposts	Trinity Broadcasting
Integrity Media	Zondervan
Salem Media	

HISTORICAL FINANCIALS

Company Type: Private

Income Statement

FYE: March 31

	REVENUE ($ mil.)	NET INCOME ($ mil.)	NET PROFIT MARGIN	EMPLOYEES
03/15	293	(8)	—	941
03/14	301	5	1.8%	—
03/11	285	6	2.4%	—
03/10	283	8	3.0%	—
Annual Growth	0.7%	—	—	—

2015 Year-End Financials

Return on assets: 6.4%   Cash ($ mil.): 22
Return on equity: (-3.0%)
Current ratio: 1.20

THE CLEAR CREEK INDEPENDENT SCHOOL DISTRICT

EXECUTIVES

Superintendent, Greg Smith
Vice-President, Candis Price
Auditors: NULL-LAIRSON PC TEXAS CITY

LOCATIONS

HQ: THE CLEAR CREEK INDEPENDENT SCHOOL DISTRICT
2425 E MAIN ST, LEAGUE CITY, TX 775732743
Phone: 281 284-0000
Web: WWW.CCISD.NET

HISTORICAL FINANCIALS

Company Type: Private

Income Statement

FYE: August 31

	REVENUE ($ mil.)	NET INCOME ($ mil.)	NET PROFIT MARGIN	EMPLOYEES
08/16	411	(103)	—	3,250
08/09	354	(41)	—	—
08/06	0	0	—	—
08/05	444	0	0.0%	—
Annual Growth	(0.7%)	—	—	—

2016 Year-End Financials

Return on assets: 6.5%   Cash ($ mil.): 119
Return on equity: (-25.1%)
Current ratio: —

THE COLLEGE OF AMERICAN PATHOLOGISTS

EXECUTIVES

Chief Executive Officer, Stephen R Myers
President, R Bruce Williams
Director, Charles Rousseo
Chief Financial Officer, Stephen Myers
Vice-President, Lee Breman
Project Manager, Akshay Patel
Advertising Director, Alfred McAtee
Auditors: ERNST & YOUNG LLP CHICAGO IL

LOCATIONS

HQ: THE COLLEGE OF AMERICAN PATHOLOGISTS
325 WAUKEGAN RD, NORTHFIELD, IL 600932750
Phone: 800 323-4040
Web: WWW.CAP.ORG

HISTORICAL FINANCIALS

Company Type: Private

Income Statement

FYE: December 31

	REVENUE ($ mil.)	NET INCOME ($ mil.)	NET PROFIT MARGIN	EMPLOYEES
12/15	186	(9)	—	565
12/14	176	(7)	—	—
12/13	168	(5)	—	—
12/12	161	0	0.4%	—
Annual Growth	4.8%	—	—	—

2015 Year-End Financials

Return on assets: 5.2%   Cash ($ mil.): 18
Return on equity: (-5.3%)
Current ratio: 0.70

THE COLLEGE OF CHARLESTON

The College of Charleston (CofC) one of the oldest universities in the nation is a state-supported institution emphasizing areas of study in the arts and sciences education and business. The liberal arts school enrolls more than 11000 undergraduate and graduate students who study in some 60 major fields and some 20 master's degree programs. CofC boasts a student-faculty ratio of about 16:1 with an average class size of 26. Some two-thirds of students are from South Carolina. The school was founded in 1770 by a group that included three future signers of the Declaration of Independence.

EXECUTIVES

Executive Vice President of Instiutional Advancement, George Watt
Senior Vice President and CIO, Robert Cape
Interim Provost and Executive Vice President for Academic Affairs, Brian McGee
Department Chair Art History, Mary Heston
Senior Vice President for Economic Development, Bobby Marlowe
Department Chair, Gabrielle Principe
Vice President Sean Stivaletta, Sean Stivaletta
Vice President Programming, Dylan Mazelis
Auditors: ELLIOTT DAVIS LLC GREENVILLE

LOCATIONS

HQ: THE COLLEGE OF CHARLESTON
66 GEORGE ST, CHARLESTON, SC 294240001
Phone: 843 953-5570
Web: WWW.COFC.EDU

PRODUCTS/OPERATIONS

Selected Schools
School of the Arts
School of Business
School of Education Health and Human Performance
School of Humanities and Social Sciences
School of Languages Cultures and World Affairs
School of Sciences and Mathematics
Honors College
The Graduate School of the College of Charleston

HISTORICAL FINANCIALS

Company Type: Private

Income Statement

FYE: June 30

	REVENUE ($ mil.)	NET INCOME ($ mil.)	NET PROFIT MARGIN	EMPLOYEES
06/16	224	8	3.7%	1,500
06/13	208	13	6.4%	—
06/12	202	19	9.4%	—
06/07	1,793	0	0.0%	—
Annual Growth	(20.6%)	209.8%	—	—

2016 Year-End Financials

Return on assets: 6.3%   Cash ($ mil.): 46
Return on equity: 3.7%
Current ratio: 1.10

THE COLLEGE OF WOOSTER

The College of Wooster is a private college providing undergraduate education in the liberal arts and sciences. It grants Bachelor of Arts (BA) Bachelor of Music (BM) and Bachelor of Music Education (BME) degrees. It offers about 50 majors including English geology film theater dance history biology math neuroscience psychology and computer science as well as pre-law pre-engineering and pre-health programs. The school's unique curriculum includes an independent study requirement in which seniors produce original work in the form of a research project. The College of Wooster enrolls about 2000 students. The school was founded in 1866 by a group of Ohio Presbyterians.

Operations

Wooster has more than 170 full-time faculty members most of which hold the highest degree in their field. It has a student-to-faculty ratio of about 12:1. Tuition room and board run about $49000 per year with 99% of students living on-campus. In addition 75% of students receive financial aid.

Operating divisions include the Wooster Inn Management Company which manages a college-owned hotel and the Wooster Technology Group which handles intellectual property. Wooster also has 23 intercollegiate athletic teams that participate in the NCAA Division III conference.

Geographic Reach

Wooster's students come from 48 states and 40 global countries. The college is located on a 240-acre campus in Wooster Ohio.

Financial Performance

Revenue was reported at a 5% increase to $80 million in 2012 due to higher net student tuition and fee income contributions bequests research grants and investment returns designated for operations. Wooster reported a net loss of $21 million that year however due to higher operating expenses and endowment investment net loss as well as losses related to bond redemption trust value changes and post-retirement liabilities.

The college is supported by a $232 million endowment.

Strategy

The college's overall goals include strengthening the foundation of the school fulfill its educational purpose in a distinguished manner and keep momentum through the development of sustainable planning methods.

Wooster opened a new space in its Andrews Library in 2012 to provide students and faculty with necessary resources and support for conducting research studies and inquiries. The lab called the Collaborative Research Environment (CoRE) includes information and communication technologies.

EXECUTIVES

President, Sarah Bolton
Financial Executive, Peggy Debartolo
Director, Kathy Breitenbucher
Supervisor, Lanny Whitaker
Auditors: MCGLADREY LLP CHICAGO IL

LOCATIONS

HQ: THE COLLEGE OF WOOSTER
1189 BEALL AVE, WOOSTER, OH 446912363
Phone: 330 263-2000
Web: WWW.WOOSTER.EDU

HISTORICAL FINANCIALS

Company Type: Private

Income Statement

FYE: June 30

	REVENUE ($ mil.)	NET INCOME ($ mil.)	NET PROFIT MARGIN	EMPLOYEES
06/15	177	39	22.0%	610
06/11	76	26	34.4%	—
06/10	72	26	36.5%	—
06/08	994	0	—	—
Annual Growth	—	644.1%	—	—

2015 Year-End Financials

Return on assets: 5.1%   Cash ($ mil.): 6
Return on equity: 22.0%
Current ratio: 0.20

THE COOPER HEALTH SYSTEM

The Cooper Health System keeps folks along the Delaware River shoreline feeling fine. The not-for-profit organization includes clinics and hospitals located throughout southern New Jersey and the Delaware Valley including the 600-bed Cooper University Hospital and The Children's Regional Hospital. Cooper University Hospital is a teaching campus for the University of Medicine and Dentistry of New Jersey providing training for medical students nurses residents fellows and health professionals. Its more than 700 physicians operate in about 80 specialties. Founded in 1887 the health care system provides trauma cancer cardiology neuroscience psychiatric and orthopedic specialty centers.

Operations

Cooper Health System is home to the area's Level I Southern New Jersey Regional Trauma Center; the Cooper Cancer Institute the Cooper Heart Institute the Cooper Bone & Joint Institute the Cooper Neurosciences Institute and critical care medicine. Carrying the Level 1 moniker means that Cooper Health System will be the referral of hospital of choice for patients' with massive injuries in the service area.

In 2013 Cooper Health System had 26600 hospital admissions and 81000 emergency department visits.

Geographic Reach

The Cooper Health System operates clinics hospitals and home health services in New Jersey Pennsylvania and Delaware. Cooper University Hospital serves as Southern New Jersey's major tertiary-care referral hospital for specialized services.

Sales and Marketing

HMO payments accounted for 34% of Cooper's net patient revenue in 2013 while commercial payments accounted for 27%.

Financial Performance

The system's revenue increased 6% to $874 million in 2013 as net patient service earnings rose. Net income rose 57% to $90 million on increased investment returns and contributions for capital acquisitions.

Cash flow from operations declined 26% to $47 million that year due to changes in prepaid expenses and a decline in accrued payable and accrued expenses.

Strategy

As demand for health care services has grown in the areas in which Cooper Health System serves Cooper University Hospital itself has also been forced to expand. Additions include all private rooms more operating suites intensive care and laboratory units and a new larger lobby area. Cooper Health System also built a new emergency department.

In 2014 the system's university health care division established a partnership with Kennedy Health System to expand cardiac services in Gloucester County. The partners opened a Cardiac Catheterization Laboratory at Kennedy University Hospital that year.

Mergers and Acquisitions

Cooper University Health Care acquired a 20% interest in AmeriHealth New Jersey in 2014. Cooper and AmeriHealth plan to work together to develop co-branded health products.

EXECUTIVES

President and CEO Cooper University Health Care, Adrienne Kirby
EVP Government Relations and Public Policy, Gary S. Young
SEVP Governmental and Legal Affairs, John P. Sheridan
SVP Operations, Maureen P. Barnes
SEVP and General Counsel, Gary J. Lesneski
SEVP and CFO, Douglas E. Shirley
President Director Population, Louis S. Bezich
SVP Patient Care Services and Chief Nursing Officer, Dianne Charsha
Interim Chief Medical Officer; Chair of the Radiology Department, Raymond L. Baraldi
Director of Pharmacy, Jaqueline Sutton
Assistant Vice President CV, Linda Valenti
Clinical Director, Jeanne Greer
Clinical Director, Karen N Gruber
Vice President, Beth Green
Medical Director, Magdy Takla
Medical Director, Helen Haupt
Vice President of Community Outreach, Catherine Curley
SEVP and Chief Administrative Officer, Kevin Odowd
Chairman, George E. Norcross, age 61
Vice Chairman, Joan S. Davis
Auditors: ERNST & YOUNG LLP ISELIN NJ

LOCATIONS

HQ: THE COOPER HEALTH SYSTEM
1 COOPER PLZ, CAMDEN, NJ 081031461
Phone: 856 342-2000
Web: WWW.COOPERHEALTH.ORG

PRODUCTS/OPERATIONS

2013 Net Patient Revenue

	%of total
HMO	34
Commercial	27
Medicare	19
Blue cross	13
Self-pay	3
Medicaid	4
Total	**100**

Selected Services
Adult Health Institute
Bariatric and Metabolic Surgery Center
Joint Replacement and Reconstruction Program
Manual Physical Therapy Program
Musculoskeletal Ultrasound
Neuromuscular Program
Orthopaedic Trauma Program
Otology/Neurotology
Pituitary Tumor and Neuroendocrine Program
Podiatry
Pulmonary Medicine
Rhinology / ENT Allergy / Skull-Base Surgery
Spine Center

Sports Medicine
Urogynecology
Urology
Women's Heart Program

COMPETITORS

Abington Memorial Hospital
Albert Einstein Healthcare Network
Aria Health
AtlantiCare
Capital Health System
Children's Hospital of Philadelphia
Crozer-Keystone Health System
Inspira Health Network
Lourdes Health
Mercy Health System
North Philadelphia Health System
Princeton HealthCare
Shore Memorial Hospital
Universal Health Services
University of Pennsylvania Health System
Virtua Health

HISTORICAL FINANCIALS
Company Type: Private

Income Statement

FYE: December 31

	REVENUE ($ mil.)	NET INCOME ($ mil.)	NET PROFIT MARGIN	EMPLOYEES
12/16	1,168	82	7.1%	4,900
12/15	1,055	64	6.1%	—
12/14	944	60	6.4%	—
12/13	874	0	—	—
Annual Growth	**10.1%**	—	—	—

2016 Year-End Financials
Return on assets: 3.2%   Cash ($ mil.): 191
Return on equity: 7.1%
Current ratio: 2.20

THE CORPORATION OF GONZAGA UNIVERSITY

Gonzaga University is a private liberal arts institution providing instruction to more than 7800 undergraduate graduate doctoral and law students. The school offers about 75 undergraduate majors two dozen master's degree programs and two leadership study doc at its six colleges and schools. The university offers a juris doctorate degree at its School of Law. The Roman Catholic university is run by the Society of Jesus — the Jesuits — and is named after a sixteenth-century Italian Jesuit Aloysius Gonzaga the patron saint of youth. The university was founded in 1887 as a men's college.

Operations

Gonzaga University has more than 400 faculty members and a student-to-faculty ratio of 11:1. Areas of study include business education law politics arts engineering and science. It also enrolls students in a number of internship research and community outreach programs.

Geographic Reach

The university's main 130-acre campus in Spokane Washington contains more than 100 buildings and is located near the Spokane River about half a mile from downtown. In addition Gonzaga University has a campus in Florence Italy where Aloysius Gonzaga lived as a student.

Financial Performance

Gonzaga University reported operating revenue of $257 million for fiscal 2012. Most of the university's revenues come from student tuition and fees;

other sources of income include auxiliary enterprises endowment income and government grants and contracts. The university is supported by endowment funds totaling some $148 million.

Strategy

In 2013 the university launched a construction project to add a $60 million 170000-sq. ft. University Center to the Gonzaga campus. It also built a new $6 million tennis and golf center.

Gonzaga also adds new educational programs to enhance services for students. For instance it launched a new nursing doctorate program in 2013.

EXECUTIVES

Vice President University Relations, Margot Stanfield
Assistant Vice President, Kirk Wood-Gaines
Department Chairman, Diane Tunnell
Vice President For Student Development, Judi Garbuio
Department Chair and Associate Professor, Jeffery L Ramirez
Associate Academic Vice President Professor of Religious Studies Accreditation Liaison Officer Academic Vice President Office, Ron Large
Academic Vice Presidents Office, Maryann Rinderle
Secretary, Molly Spilker
Auditors: MOSS ADAMS LLP SPOKANE WASHI

LOCATIONS

HQ: THE CORPORATION OF GONZAGA UNIVERSITY
502 E BOONE AVE, SPOKANE, WA 992581774
Phone: 509 328-4220
Web: WWW.GONZAGA.EDU

PRODUCTS/OPERATIONS

Selected Schools and Colleges
College of Arts and Sciences
School of Business Administration
School of Education
School of Engineering
School of Law
School of Professional Studies

HISTORICAL FINANCIALS
Company Type: Private

Income Statement

FYE: May 31

	REVENUE ($ mil.)	NET INCOME ($ mil.)	NET PROFIT MARGIN	EMPLOYEES
05/16	214	16	7.8%	1,200
05/15	203	83	41.0%	—
05/14	193	38	20.0%	—
05/13	191	56	29.5%	—
Annual Growth	**4.0%**	**(33.1%)**	—	—

2016 Year-End Financials
Return on assets: 4.0%   Cash ($ mil.): 17
Return on equity: 7.8%
Current ratio: —

THE CORPORATION OF MERCER UNIVERSITY

Mercer University covers a lot of Georgia with one campus in Macon another in Atlanta and a third in Savannah. The main campus in Macon includes the Walter F. George School of Law (one of the nation's oldest law schools) while The Cecil B. Day Graduate and Professional campus in At-

lanta includes schools of theology pharmacy and nursing. Savannah is home to a new four-year M.D. program at the Mercer School of Medicine at Memorial University Medical Center. The university which has a total enrollment of more than 8300 students also has educational centers in Douglas County Henry County and Eastman. Mercer was founded in 1833 by Jesse Mercer a prominent Georgia Baptist.

EXECUTIVES

Vice President And Dean, Rhonda Lidstone
Assistant Vice President For Creative Services, Steven Mosley
Treasurer, Hiral Patel
Auditors: KPMG LLP GREENSBORO NC

LOCATIONS

HQ: THE CORPORATION OF MERCER UNIVERSITY
1400 COLEMAN AVE, MACON, GA 312070001
Phone: 478 301-2700
Web: WWW.MERCER.EDU

COMPETITORS

Baylor University
Benedict College
Clark Atlanta University
Georgia Southern University
Interdenominational Theological Center

Kennesaw State University
Morris College
Spelman College
University of Mobile
University of West Georgia

HISTORICAL FINANCIALS

Company Type: Private

Income Statement

FYE: June 30

	REVENUE ($ mil.)	NET INCOME ($ mil.)	NET PROFIT MARGIN	EMPLOYEES
06/15	341	15	4.6%	1,658
06/13	297	8	2.8%	—
06/11	270	8	3.0%	—
06/10	255	0	0.2%	—
Annual Growth	5.9%	103.9%	—	—

2015 Year-End Financials

Return on assets: 4.6%
Return on equity: 4.6%
Current ratio: 0.20
Cash ($ mil.): 29

THE DCH HEALTH CARE AUTHORITY

The DCH Healthcare Authority is concerned with the Druid City's health. The company which does business as DCH Health System provides health services to residents of Tuscaloosa and several other communities in Western Alabama. Its flagship facility is the 580-bed DCH Regional Medical Center a full-service teaching hospital located near the University of Alabama campus. DCH Health System also includes the Northport Pickens County and Fayette medical centers which together house 320 acute-care beds. The hospitals offer a full range of inpatient and outpatient services including primary diagnostic emergency surgical rehabilitative and home health care.

Operations

Several of the system's hospitals operate specialty centers. For instance DCH Regional has cancer and cardiology clinics while the Northport Medical Center has specialty rehabilitation and mental

health departments. In addition Fayette Medical Center houses a 120-bed nursing home.

The DCH Health System which serves more than a quarter of a million people is community-owned and is governed by a board appointed by various city and county authorities as well as the hospitals' medical staff.

Strategy

As part of the system's plan to grow the next generation of health care providers it partners with the University of Alabama's College of Community Health Sciences and with Capstone College of Nursing. DCH Health System also expands as needed to keep up with the community. In 2014 it announced the construction of a $12 million 75-bed nursing and rehab hospital near Northport Medical Center.

Company Background

The "DCH" in the organization's name stands for Druid City Hospital the name of the system's first hospital which opened in 1923. Druid City is a nickname for Tuscaloosa.

EXECUTIVES

President and CEO, Bryan N. Kindred
CFO, John Winfrey
Administrator DCH Regional Medical Center, Bill Cassels
Administrator Pickens County Medical Center, Wayne McElroy
Administrator Northport Medical Center, Luke Standeffer
Administrator Fayette Medical Center, Barry S. Cochran
Director of Nursing, Jutta Beams
Vice President Medical, Ken Aldridge
Director of Radiology, Hugh M Borak
Director of Nursing, Patrice Jones
Occupational Medicine, Peter G Casten
Director of Radiology, John Files
Chairman, Samuel F. Clabaugh
Auditors: MORRISON & SMITH LLP TUSCALO

LOCATIONS

HQ: THE DCH HEALTH CARE AUTHORITY
809 UNIVERSITY BLVD E, TUSCALOOSA, AL 354012029
Phone: 205 759-7111
Web: WWW.DCHSYSTEM.COM

PRODUCTS/OPERATIONS

Selected Alabama Facilities
DCH Regional Medical Center (Tuscaloosa)
Fayette Medical Center (Fayette)
Northport Medical Center (Northport)
Pickens County Medical Center (Carrollton)

COMPETITORS

Baptist Health (AL)
Children's Health System
East Alabama Medical Center
Gadsden Regional Medical Center
Health Care Authority of the City of Huntsville
Jackson Hospital & Clinic of Alabama
University of South Alabama Health System

HISTORICAL FINANCIALS

Company Type: Private

Income Statement

FYE: September 30

	REVENUE ($ mil.)	NET INCOME ($ mil.)	NET PROFIT MARGIN	EMPLOYEES
09/16	531	23	4.5%	4,683
09/13	463	16	3.6%	—
09/12	454	23	5.2%	—
09/11	92	0	0.0%	—
Annual Growth	41.9%	918.3%	—	—

2016 Year-End Financials

Return on assets: 2.6%
Return on equity: 4.5%
Current ratio: 2.60
Cash ($ mil.): 88

THE DELONG CO INC

EXECUTIVES

President, David De Long
Board of Directors, Charles R De Long
Manager, Pat Mullooly
Senior Manager, David Delong
Auditors: CLIFTONLARSONALLEN LLP DIXON

LOCATIONS

HQ: THE DELONG CO INC
214 ALLEN ST, CLINTON, WI 535259496
Phone: 800 356-0784
Web: WWW.DELONGCOMPANY.COM

HISTORICAL FINANCIALS

Company Type: Private

Income Statement

FYE: September 30

	REVENUE ($ mil.)	NET INCOME ($ mil.)	NET PROFIT MARGIN	EMPLOYEES
09/16*	1,029	4	0.4%	250
12/15	1,029	4	0.4%	—
09/14	1,306	19	1.5%	—
09/13	1,326	25	1.9%	—
Annual Growth	(8.1%)	(45.9%)	—	—

*Fiscal year change

2016 Year-End Financials

Return on assets: 1.2%
Return on equity: 0.4%
Current ratio: 1.10
Cash ($ mil.): 1

THE DETROIT INSTITUTE OF ARTS

EXECUTIVES

Chief Financial Officer, Robert Bowen
Account Manager, Charles Allen
Vice-President, H W Burdett Jr
Administration Manager, Gery Perkowski
Personnel Manager, Cheryl Knight
Manager, Jennifer Gustafson
General Manager, Martha Fierro

LOCATIONS

HQ: THE DETROIT INSTITUTE OF ARTS
5200 WOODWARD AVE, DETROIT, MI 482024094
Phone: 313 833-7900
Web: WWW.DIA.ORG

Income Statement

FYE: June 30

	REVENUE ($ mil.)	NET INCOME ($ mil.)	NET PROFIT MARGIN	EMPLOYEES
06/15	606	28	4.7%	350
06/14	52	13	26.0%	—
06/09	47	0	—	—
06/08	58	(8)	—	—
Annual Growth	39.7%	—	—	—

2015 Year-End Financials

Return on assets: 0.4%
Return on equity: 4.7%
Current ratio: —

Cash ($ mil.): 49

THE DREES COMPANY

The Drees Company is a big homebuilder in Cincinnati and one of the nation's top private builders. Drees targets first-time and move-up buyers with homes that are priced from about $100000 to more than $1 million. Drees also builds condominiums townhomes and patio homes. Its homes portfolio ranges from its former Zaring Premier Homes luxury division to the company's more financially accessible and modest Marquis Homes division. Drees is active in Florida Indiana Kentucky Maryland North Carolina Ohio Tennessee Texas Virginia and Washington DC. The family-owned firm was founded in 1928.

Operations

In addition to home building architecture energy efficiency upgrades and design services Drees also provides new construction financing solutions through its subsidiary and mortgage lending business First Equity Mortgage which has closed more than $1 billion in loans.

Geographic Reach

Headquartered in Fort Mitchell Kentucky Drees operates across nearly 10 states in cities including Cincinnati and Cleveland Ohio; Indianapolis; Nashville; Raleigh North Carolina; Jacksonville Florida; Austin Houston and Dallas Texas; and the Greater Washington DC area.

Sales and Marketing

In recent years Drees has concentrated on the fast-growing "move up" segment market targeting home buyers looking to upgrade into larger houses.

In 2012 Drees converted its longtime Zaring Premier Homes luxury brand name to its flagship Drees Homes brand. While the move required re-branding in the greater Cincinnati area Drees is banking on its brand reputation and recognition. It also allowed the residential homebuilder to consolidate its advertising sales and marketing efforts.

Financial Performance

While full details of the private company could not be found Drees' CEO David Drees announced in July 2013 that he expected the company to reach $629 million in revenue by April 1 2014.

Looking further back Drees had revenues as high as $1.2 billion in 2006 which slid dramatically following the financial crisis to $490 million in revenue in 2010. To its benefit Texas markets — specifically Austin and Dallas — remained active throughout the recession. Drees was also helped by entering the recession with a relatively low debt load of $364 million. By March 2013 Drees had sold land to generate cash flow and reduced its debt to $125 million.

Strategy

Ranked among the top 25 largest national homebuilders by BUILDER Magazine Drees has been steadily expanding over the past few years to capitalize on an improving housing market.

In recent years Drees has concentrated on the fast-growing and lucrative "move up" segment of the homebuyer's market targeting home owners that are looking to upgrade to larger houses with higher-end amenities. In late 2014 the company landed a $100 million contract to build 237 homes in three Cincinnati-based residential communities with the average house priced between $307000 and $360000. In September 2014 the company entered its first ever foray into the Houston Texas market with plans to price its houses there for more than $300000 — prime pricing to lure these "move up" buyers.

Company Background

A family-operated enterprise since its founding by immigrant Theodore Drees in 1928 the company is run by the third generation of the Drees family.

EXECUTIVES

Vice-President, Lawrence Herbst
Senior Manager, Dana Scrivner
Vice-President, Daniel Jones
VP Personnel, Effie McKeehan
Senior Manager, Sara McGettrick
Manager, Adam Ballash
Auditors: DELOITTE & TOUCHE LLP CINCINN

LOCATIONS

HQ: THE DREES COMPANY
211 GRANDVIEW DR STE 300, FORT MITCHELL, KY 410172790
Phone: 859 578-4200
Web: WWW.DREESHOMES.COM

Selected Locations
Florida
  Jacksonville
Indiana
  Indianapolis
Kentucky
  Fort Mitchell
Maryland
  Frederick
North Carolina
  Raleigh
Ohio
  Cincinnati
  Cleveland
  Dayton
Tennessee
  Nashville
Texas
  Austin
  Dallas
Washington DC

COMPETITORS

D.R. Horton	Lennar
Fischer Homes	M/I Homes
KB Home	PulteGroup

HISTORICAL FINANCIALS

Company Type: Private

Income Statement

FYE: March 31

	REVENUE ($ mil.)	NET INCOME ($ mil.)	NET PROFIT MARGIN	EMPLOYEES
03/16	722	31	4.3%	549
03/15	669	36	5.4%	—
03/14	683	35	5.3%	—
03/13	584	19	3.3%	—
Annual Growth	7.3%	17.6%	—	—

Return on assets: 4.8%
Return on equity: 4.3%
Current ratio: —

Cash ($ mil.): 10

THE EVANGELICAL LUTHERAN GOOD SAMARITAN SOCIETY

The Evangelical Lutheran Good Samaritan Society (TELGSS) strives to be a good neighbor to all particularly to the elderly people in need of housing and health care. The not-for-profit organization owns or leases some 240 senior living facilities including nursing homes assisted living facilities and affordable housing projects for seniors. Through its facilities it also provides home health care services outpatient rehabilitation adult day care and a variety of other services such as specialized units for people with Alzheimer's disease and related dementias. TELGSS operates in about two dozen US states.

Operations

In 2013 the society owned or leased 177 continuum of care communities and 34 home care hospice and private duty agencies (and controlled 29 operating affordable housing and senior housing with services projects). TELGSS managed 10 facilities owned by others and held minority stakes in a handful of joint ventures.

Geographic Reach

Outside its home state of South Dakota TELGSS serves more than 27000 clients across its 240 locations nationwide. It operates in Arizona New Mexico Texas Florida Colorado Arkansas Tennessee Kentucky West Virginia Ohio Indiana Iowa Wisconsin Kansas Nebraska North Dakota Minnesota Montana Idaho Oregon Washington and Hawaii.

Financial Performance

The society's revenue has risen steadily for the past five years. Revenues increased by 2% to $972 million in 2013 from $954 million in 2012 due to higher Housing and Services and other revenues. Rehabilitation/skilled care activities contributed about 80% of total revenues.

Net income decreased by 76% to $7.7 million in 2013 due to an increase in housing and services and administrative expenses. A higher loss on disposal and impairment of property also contributed to the decline in net income.

Strategy

TELGSS' innovation strategy is to create and implement new products and services that respond to the changing needs of its clients.

In this regard TELGSS has embraced the digital age by offering home telehealth services (the remote delivery of health care between a patient and his or her physician). Telehealth aims to reduce health care costs by eliminating the need to import expensive specialists to remote areas allowing patients to more actively participate in their health care and letting doctors to more accurately track patient medication compliance.

The health care society is also using a technology called WellAWARE through a partnership with Philips Lifeline and Honeywell HomMed. It uses sensor monitoring to keep tabs on the subscriber's daily routine. If there are blips in that routine (for example the patient does not get out of

bed) a clinician can intervene more quickly. The system is made of small wireless sensors that use infrared light beams to detect motion; major declines in a subscriber's activity level or a fall can also trigger the detectors to call 911.

TELGSS has expanded its operations in recent years boosting its number of locations by nearly 10. The health services provider opened a new campus in Fairfield Glade Tennessee with 30 rehabilitation and skilled care beds 24 assisted living units and 42 senior living apartments and cottages. In Hastings Nebraska it also added a pair of housing locations including a 40-unit tax credit project and a tax renovation of a 51-unit facility in Omaha. It's extending its reach in South Dakota as well by breaking ground on a new Good Samaritan Society in St. Martin Village near Rapid City South Dakota.

TELGSS collaborates with the Mayo Clinic and other members of the Healthy Aging and Independent Living Consortium on OpenIDEO.com exploring how to help patients maintain well-being and thrive as they age. In this context in 2013 the company reported that it had developed three Services@Home agencies (serving more than 300 clients) during the last three years in Hot Springs Village (Arkansas) Loveland (Colorado) and Sioux Falls (South Dakota).

Company Background

Founded in 1922 TELGSS opened its first Good Samaritan center in 1923 as a home for disabled children.

EXECUTIVES

Vice President of Operations for Illinois and Iowa, Dan Fosness
Director of Health Information Management, Tammy Cease
Director of Nursing Services, Dena McFaddin
Director Of Nursing Services, Teri Mabie
Treasurer, Frederick Wolfson
Auditors: CLIFTONLARSONALLEN LLP MINNEA

LOCATIONS

HQ: THE EVANGELICAL LUTHERAN GOOD SAMARITAN SOCIETY
4800 W 57TH ST, SIOUX FALLS, SD 571082239
Phone: 866 928-1635
Web: WWW.CAREERLATTICE.COM

PRODUCTS/OPERATIONS

2013 Revenues

	% of total
Housing & services	96
Resource development	-
Net assets released from restrictions for operating purposes	1
Other revenue	3
Total	**100**

2013 Revenues

	% of total
Rehabilitation/skilled care	80
Senior housing with services	17
Home and community based services	3
Total	**100**

Selected Services

Home & Community
  Adult day services
  Child daycare
  Guest housing
  Home care
  Home healthcare
  Hospice care
  LivingWell@Home
  Meals On Wheels
  Outpatient therapy
  Parish nursing
  Personal emergency response
  Respite care
  Scheduled transportation
  Senior College

  Services@Home
  Telehealth
  WellAware
  Wellness
Rehab/skilled care
  Hospice care
  Inpatient therapy
  LivingWell@Home
  Memory care
  Post-acute care
  Rehab/skilled care
  Scheduled transportation
  Senior College
  Subacute
Senior living
  Affordable housing - Apartments
  Assisted living - Apartments
  Assisted living - Memory care
  Housing with services - Apartments
  Housing with services - Manufactured housing
  Housing with services - Twinhomes/duplexes
  LivingWell@Home
  Senior College

COMPETITORS

BPM Senior Living	Genesis Healthcare
Brookdale Senior Living	Golden Horizons
	Kindred Healthcare
Enlivant	RehabCare
Extendicare	Select Medical
Five Star Senior Living	Sunrise Senior Living

HISTORICAL FINANCIALS

Company Type: Private

Income Statement
FYE: December 31

	REVENUE ($ mil.)	NET INCOME ($ mil.)	NET PROFIT MARGIN	EMPLOYEES
12/15	1,011	(33)	—	24,000
12/13	979	0	0.0%	—
12/07	841	17	2.1%	—
12/06	836	44	5.3%	—
Annual Growth	**2.1%**	—	—	—

2015 Year-End Financials
Return on assets: 4.5%
Return on equity: (-3.3%)
Current ratio: 0.50
Cash ($ mil.): 17

THE FARMERS WIN COOPERATIVE

EXECUTIVES

President, Chris Hagedorn
Board of Directors, Roger Desloover
Manager, Ernie Schmitt Jr
General Manager, James Erickson
Manager, David Bergan

LOCATIONS

HQ: THE FARMERS WIN COOPERATIVE
110 N JEFFERSON AVE, FREDERICKSBURG, IA 506307757
Phone: 563 237-5324
Web: WWW.FARMERSWIN.COM

HISTORICAL FINANCIALS

Company Type: Private

Income Statement
FYE: July 31

	REVENUE ($ mil.)	NET INCOME ($ mil.)	NET PROFIT MARGIN	EMPLOYEES
07/15	174	4	2.3%	42
07/14	112	2	2.7%	—
07/13	129	3	2.4%	—
07/12	138	3	2.5%	—
Annual Growth	**8.0%**	**6.2%**	—	—

2015 Year-End Financials
Return on assets: 1.1%
Return on equity: 2.3%
Current ratio: 0.30
Cash ($ mil.): 1

THE FIRST DISTRICT ASSOCIATION

EXECUTIVES

Chief Executive Officer, Clinton Fall
Board of Directors, Kevin Schueler
General Manager, Doug Anderson
Director, Bill Dropik
Manager, Jeff Ertl
Financial Executive, Tom Middendorf

LOCATIONS

HQ: THE FIRST DISTRICT ASSOCIATION
101 S SWIFT AVE, LITCHFIELD, MN 553552800
Phone: 320 693-3236
Web: WWW.FIRSTDISTRICT.COM

HISTORICAL FINANCIALS

Company Type: Private

Income Statement
FYE: September 30

	REVENUE ($ mil.)	NET INCOME ($ mil.)	NET PROFIT MARGIN	EMPLOYEES
09/16	553	19	3.5%	150
09/15	615	13	2.2%	—
09/14	745	27	3.7%	—
09/13	627	16	2.6%	—
Annual Growth	**(4.1%)**	**6.8%**	—	—

THE FISHEL COMPANY

The Fishel Company reels in revenues by laying out lines. The company (also known as Team Fishel) provides engineering construction management and maintenance services for electric and gas utility and communications infrastructure projects. The aerial and underground utility contractor designs and builds distribution networks for telecommunications cable and broadband television gas transmission and distribution and electric utilities throughout the US. It also counts municipalities state and federal agencies universities commercial building owners financial services companies health care providers manufacturers and residential real estate developers among its clients.

Operations

The company's products and services include Structured Cabling Systems Data Center build-outs Wireless Networks and Building Security and Automation. It has installed more than 16000 communications networks for the healthcare financial education manufacturing logistics and government sectors.

Geographic Reach

The Fishel Company is licensed to do business in some two dozen states. It operates from 32 offices located in about 15 states including Arkansas Arizona California Florida Georgia Kentucky Nevada New Mexico Ohio Oklahoma Pennsylvania Tennessee Texas and Virginia.

Sales and Marketing

The company's power customers include American Electric Power Arizona Public Service Arkansas Valley Electric Dayton Power & Light Dominion Virginia Power Duke Energy Entergy and First Electric Cooperative among others.

In addition to utilities and power coops the company serves other markets including Repair and Planning Broadband Broadband Network Services Enterprise Solutions and Advanced Technology Services.

Strategy

Fishel Company is tracking its business to a Vision 2020 initiative which has a three-pronged goal of customer development operational excellence and teammate development. Its customer development focus involves natural gas distribution power transmission and distribution (T&D) construction and fiber network installation. Operational excellence goals are centered on bidding and pricing project management and being accident-free. Its teammate management focus comprises leadership development performance management workforce planning and continuous improvement.

The company has strategic business relationships with TE Connectivity Andrews Wireless Belden Commscope Corning Cable Systems Legrand Ortronics Leviton Nexans Berktek OASIS and Panduit.

Company Background

Kenneth Fishel founded the firm in 1936 as an underground contractor for telephone companies.

EXECUTIVES

Vice President and Chief Financial Officer, Paul Riewe
Vice President Central Region, Scott Keeler
National Accounts Manager, Joe McCool
Auditors: CROWE HORWATH LLP COLUMBUS O

LOCATIONS

HQ: THE FISHEL COMPANY
1366 DUBLIN RD, COLUMBUS, OH 432151093
Phone: 614 274-8100
Web: WWW.FISHELCO.COM

Selected Locations
Arizona
Arkansas
California
Florida
Georgia
Kentucky
Nevada
New Mexico
Ohio
Oklahoma
Pennsylvania
Tennessee
Texas
Virginia

PRODUCTS/OPERATIONS

Selected Services
Emergency restoration repair & maintenance
Fiber overbuilds

GPS survey
Network installation
Permitting
Project management
Right of way
Site Design
Utility construction

Selected Markets
Commercial industrial advanced logistics
Electric Distribution & Transmission
Financial & health care
Gas distribution & transmission pipeline
Telecom & broadband cable
Wireless backhaul

COMPETITORS

Dycom	MYR Group
EMCOR	MasTec
IES Holdings	Pike Corporation
MDU Construction Services	Quanta Services

HISTORICAL FINANCIALS

Company Type: Private

Income Statement   FYE: December 31

	REVENUE ($ mil.)	NET INCOME ($ mil.)	NET PROFIT MARGIN	EMPLOYEES
12/15	301	10	3.3%	1,400
12/14	311	8	2.8%	—
12/13	306	10	3.4%	—
12/12	281	(2)	—	—
Annual Growth	2.4%	—	—	—

2015 Year-End Financials

Return on assets: 4.6%   Cash ($ mil.): 11
Return on equity: 3.3%
Current ratio: 0.90

THE FRESH MARKET INC

When it comes to food fresh is best. The Fresh Market operates about 160 full-service upscale specialty grocery stores in some 25 US states from Florida to Wisconsin. As the name suggests the chain specializes in perishable goods (two-thirds of sales) including fruits and vegetables meat and seafood. The stores average 21000 sq. ft. about a third to half the size of a conventional supermarket. However customers won't find the nonfood items sold in most grocery stores these days such as cleaning and cooking supplies. Founded by husband-and-wife team Ray and Beverly Berry who opened their first store in 1982 The Fresh Market which went public in 2010 was acquired by Apollo Global Management in mid-2016.

Geographic Reach

The fast-growing chain operates grocery stores in 26 states primarily located in the Southeast Midwest Northeast and Mid-Atlantic region. New markets include California and Texas. However established markets Florida North Carolina and Georgia are home to more than half of The Fresh Market's stores.

Sales and Marketing

The Fresh Market spends far less on advertising than its conventional competitors relying primarily on word-of-mouth publicity to attract customers. Indeed the grocery chain reported advertising costs of only $3862 in fiscal 2013 (ended January) or just 0.3% of annual sales up from $2652 in the previous year. In-store marketing activities include cooking classes and demonstrations tours and product demonstrations. It also distributes a weekly online newsletter named "Fresh Idea" to promote new products seasonal produce recipes and weekly specials.

Financial Performance

Fueled by the addition of new stores The Fresh Market's fiscal 2013 (ended January) sales increased 20% versus the prior year to more than $1.3 billion. Net income rose 25% over the same period to about $64 million due to higher sales and decreased interest expanse. Same-store sales at Fresh Market stores increased 6% year over year. Indeed fiscal 2013 marked the fifth consecutive year of rising sales and the second consecutive year of rising profits (since the 2010 IPO).

Strategy

The Fresh Market's recipe for growth is to continue to open stores at a rapid pace in new and existing markets and to increase sales at older stores. Indeed the grocery chain has announced plans to double its store count in the Southeast to more than 200 locations. Currently 104 of its 160 stores are located in the region. In fiscal 2014 it plans to open a record 22 locations. Ultimately management believes the US can support at least 500 of its upscale grocery stores. The Fresh Market is forecasting same-store sales to increase 4% to 6% in the coming year. The chain caters to its affluent customers by offering high-margin specialty foods such as hand-trimmed aged steaks fresh seafood hand-stacked fresh produce and a high level of customer service. Its smaller store footprint gives the retailer more flexibility in picking locations.

EXECUTIVES

President and CEO, Richard A. (Rick) Anicetti, age 60
SVP Merchandising and Marketing, Marc Jones, age 45, $285,697 total compensation
SVP and General Counsel, Scott Duggan, age 51, $254,510 total compensation
EVP and CFO, Jeffrey (Jeff) Ackerman, age 53, $407,231 total compensation
SVP Real Estate and Development, Randy Young, age 59, $279,971 total compensation
Vice President Contrl, Jeffrey B Short
The Senior Vice President Marketing an, Mark Jones
Chairman, Ray Berry, age 76
Auditors: ERNST & YOUNG LLP CHARLOTTE

LOCATIONS

HQ: THE FRESH MARKET INC
628 GREEN VALLEY RD # 500, GREENSBORO, NC 274087791
Phone: 336 272-1338
Web: WWW.THEFRESHMARKET.COM

2016 Stores

	No.
Florida	45
North Carolina	22
Virginia	16
Georgia	15
Illinois	9
Tennessee	9
South Carolina	9
Alabama	6
Indiana	5
Louisiana	5
New York	5
Ohio	5
Pennsylvania	5
Maryland	4
Connecticut	3
Kentucky	3
New Jersey	3
Arkansas	2
Wisconsin	2
Delaware	1
Massachusetts	1
Mississippi	1
New Hampshire	1
Oklahoma	1
Total	**178**

HISTORICAL FINANCIALS

Company Type: Private

Income Statement

FYE: January 31

	REVENUE ($ mil.)	NET INCOME ($ mil.)	NET PROFIT MARGIN	EMPLOYEES
01/16	1,857	65	3.5%	12,600
01/15	1,753	63	3.6%	—
01/14	1,511	50	3.4%	—
01/13	1,329	64	4.8%	—
Annual Growth	11.8%	0.7%	—	—

2016 Year-End Financials

Return on assets: 2.7%
Return on equity: 3.5%
Current ratio: 0.50

Cash ($ mil.): 60

THE GEISINGER CLINIC

EXECUTIVES

Chief Executive Officer, Glenn D Steele Jr
Director, Debbie McCaffry
Director, Renee Blasi
President, David Macko

LOCATIONS

HQ: THE GEISINGER CLINIC
100 N ACADEMY AVE, DANVILLE, PA 178229800
Phone: 570 271-6211

HISTORICAL FINANCIALS

Company Type: Private

Income Statement

FYE: June 30

	REVENUE ($ mil.)	NET INCOME ($ mil.)	NET PROFIT MARGIN	EMPLOYEES
06/15	991	(12)	—	12,000
06/14	849	(3)	—	—
06/10	572	(3)	—	—
06/09	504	(22)	—	—
Annual Growth	11.9%	—	—	—

2015 Year-End Financials

Return on assets: 7.6%
Return on equity: (-1.3%)
Current ratio: —

Cash ($ mil.): 23

THE GENERAL HOSPITAL CORPORATION

Massachusetts General Hospital (Mass General) is hardly general. The 200-year-old acute care hospital is Harvard Medical School's original and largest teaching hospital. With some 950 beds Mass General has its main campus in Boston and operates several health centers in surrounding communities. Its specialized medical departments include cancer cardiology and heart surgery neurology and neurosurgery and diabetes and endocrinology. As a leading research facility Mass General hosts a number of clinical drug and device trials and has an annual research budget of more than $785 million. The hospital is a founding member of the Partners HealthCare System (along with Brigham and Women's).

Operations

Founded in 11811 Mass General is the oldest and largest general hospital in New England as well as one of the oldest hospitals in the nation. It holds Level 1 certifications for adult and pediatric trauma and burn care making it a regional referral center for other area hospitals. Mass General's five multidisciplinary care centers — known internationally for innovations in cancer heart disease digestive disorders transplantation and vascular medicine — provide high-tech comprehensive care reducing the need for patient travel to various outpatient clinics.

Mass General Hospital for Children administers pediatric care services including primary care and rare disease treatment. The hospital also provides outpatient care through doctors' offices of the Mass General Physicians Organization and it operates one of the largest hospital-based research networks in the nation consisting of more than 20 cross-functional institutes and departments. With Harvard Mass General offers about 30 fellowship and residency programs as well as continuing medical education programs.

Geographic Reach

Mass General's main hospital is located in downtown Boston. The medical center also operates clinics in Charlestown Chelsea Revere Boston's North End Waltham and Foxboro.

Financial Performance

Mass General appears to be in good health financially. Total operating revenue increased 7% in 2012 versus 2011 to $3.2 billion. The increase was driven by a 10% gain in net patient revenue and increases in direct and indirect research revenues. Income from operations increased 27% year over year to nearly $268 million in 2012.

Research expenditures amounted to $776 million in 2012.

Strategy

Already the largest hospital in New England Mass General is getting larger. It is building a $5 million cancer center at Cooley Dickinson Hospital in Northampton Massachusetts due to be completed in mid-2015. In 2012 the hospital opened a new sports performance center.

In 2011 Mass General expanded its services in areas including oncology neurology and emergency care as it opened a new 10-story patient tower (dubbed the Lunder Building). This expansion added 150 patient beds as well as surgery and specialty facilities. The hospital is also expanding its outpatient capacity through collaborations with area providers — including North Shore Medical Center and Brigham and Women's Hospital — to build regional ambulatory care centers.

Mass General is also expanding into the diagnostic testing market through a partnership with Bio-Reference Laboratories. The firms are developing a range of companion diagnostic tests in the field of oncology; the tests utilize personalized medicine technologies which use a patient's unique genetic makeup to tailor testing and treatment methods (and eliminate unnecessary medication). The companies hope to partner with drug development firms to develop compatible tests and drugs.

EXECUTIVES

Senior Vice President Administration, Jean Elrick
President and Trustee, Peter L. Slavin
Chief Radiation Oncology, Jay S. Loeffler
Chief Neurosurgery, Robert L. Martuza
Chief Orthopaedic Surgery, Harry E. Rubash
Director Cancer Center, Daniel A. Haber
Chief of Pathology, David N. Louis
Chief Dermatology, David E. Fisher
Chief Molecular Biology, Robert E. Kingston
Chief of Radiology, James Brink
Surgeon-in-Chief and Chair Department of Surgery, Keith D. Lillemoe
Chief Urology Service, Michael L. Blute
Physician-in-Chief Department of Medicine, Katrina A. Armstrong
Chief Department of Emergency Medicine, David FM Brown
Chief Neurology Service, Merit Ester Cudkowicz
Chief Department of Obstetrics and Gynecology, Jeffrey Lawrence (Jeff) Ecker
Chief Pediatric Surgery and Surgeon-in-Chief MassGeneral Hospital for Children, Allan Moises Goldstein
Physician-in-Chief of MassGeneral Hospital for Children and Chief of Partners Pediatrics, Ronald Ellis Kleinman
Chief of Psychiatry, Jerrold Frank Rosenbaum
Chief Oral and Maxillofacial Surgery, Maria J. Troulis
Chief of Anesthesia Critical Care and Pain Medicine, Jeanine P. Wiener-Kronish
Chief Physical Medicine and Rehabilitation, Ross D. Zafonte
Medical Director, Leonard Kaban
Director of HIM, Jackie Raymond
Clinical Director, Donald Lawrence
Director of Radiology, Piran Aliabadi
Rph, Motuma Nataee
Senior Vice President Of Technology, Ronald S Newbower
Senior Vice President Surgical and Anesthesia Services and Clinical Business Development, Ann Prestipino
Nursing Director, Maureen Schnider
Senior Vice President Human Resources, Jeff Davis
Vice President External Affairs, Deborah Colton
Senior Vice President for Research, Harry Orf
Rsvp Team Leader, Jessica Grajeda
Medical Doctor Medical Director Radiation Oncology, John McGrath
Vice President for Finance, Peter K Markell
Nursing Director, Christina Stone
Clinical Director, Steven Grinspoon
Nursing Director, Lee Tata
Medical Director, Darshan Mehta
Vice President of Marketing, Vicki Amalfitano
Vice President Government Affairs, Joseph Alviani
DIRECTOR OF HEALTH, Goldberg Ross
VICE PRESIDENT NATIONAL SALES, Mccauley Denise
Assistant Secretary, Joan Stoddard
Chair, Cathy E. Minehan, age 69
Board Member, Antonia Stephen
Board Member, Frank Pedlow
Board Member, Andrea Stidsen
Board Member, Cathleen Poliquin
Treasurer Current, Cheryl Grove
Board Member, Cameron Wright

LOCATIONS

HQ: THE GENERAL HOSPITAL CORPORATION
55 FRUIT ST, BOSTON, MA 021142621
Phone: 617 726-2000
Web: WWW.MGHGENERALSTORE.COM

Selected Research Centers
AIDS
Cancer

Cardiovascular research
Computational and integrative biology
Cutaneous biology
Human genetics
Medical imaging
Neurodegenerative disorders
Photomedicine
Regenerative medicine
Reproductive biology
Systems biology
Transplantation biology

COMPETITORS

Beth Israel Deaconess Medical Center
Boston Medical Center
Cambridge Health Alliance
Cape Cod Hospital
Care New England
CareGroup
Catholic Medical Center
Children's Hospital Boston
Dana-Farber
Elliot Health System
Emerson Hospital
Faulkner Hospital
Milford Regional Medical Center
New England Alliance for Health
Northeast Health System
Southcoast Hospitals Group
Spaulding Rehabilitation Hospital
Steward Health Care
Sturdy Memorial
Winchester Healthcare

HISTORICAL FINANCIALS

Company Type: Private

Income Statement				FYE: September 30
	REVENUE ($ mil.)	NET INCOME ($ mil.)	NET PROFIT MARGIN	EMPLOYEES
09/15	2,452	211	8.6%	10,156
09/14	2,201	186	8.5%	—
09/13	2,274	148	6.5%	—
09/12	2,281	267	11.7%	—
Annual Growth	2.4%	(7.6%)	—	—

2015 Year-End Financials

Return on assets: 1.3%
Return on equity: 8.6%
Current ratio: 1.10

Cash ($ mil.): 99

THE GEORGE WASHINGTON UNIVERSITY HOSPITAL

EXECUTIVES

Principal, Wesley S Williams Jr

LOCATIONS

HQ: THE GEORGE WASHINGTON UNIVERSITY HOSPITAL
900 23RD ST NW, WASHINGTON, DC 200372342
Phone: 202 715-4000
Web: WWW.GWHOSPITAL.COM

HISTORICAL FINANCIALS

Company Type: Private

Income Statement				FYE: December 31
	REVENUE ($ mil.)	NET INCOME ($ mil.)	NET PROFIT MARGIN	EMPLOYEES
12/15	505	48	9.6%	1
12/14	450	33	7.4%	—
Annual Growth	12.0%	46.4%	—	—

THE GILL CORPORATION

EXECUTIVES

Board of Directors, Don Clark
Engineer, David Ikeda
Auditors: BDO USA LLP LOS ANGELES CA

LOCATIONS

HQ: THE GILL CORPORATION
4056 EASY ST, EL MONTE, CA 917311054
Phone: 626 443-6094
Web: WWW.MCGILLCORP.COM

HISTORICAL FINANCIALS

Company Type: Private

Income Statement				FYE: December 26
	REVENUE ($ mil.)	NET INCOME ($ mil.)	NET PROFIT MARGIN	EMPLOYEES
12/15	233	39	16.9%	475
12/14	217	41	18.9%	—
12/13	207	48	23.6%	—
12/12	176	40	22.8%	—
Annual Growth	9.7%	(0.6%)	—	—

2015 Year-End Financials

Return on assets: 5.3%
Return on equity: 16.9%
Current ratio: 2.20

Cash ($ mil.): 23

THE GOLUB CORPORATION

Supermarket operator The Golub Corporation offers tasty come-ons such as table-ready meals gift certificates automatic discount cards and a hotline where cooks answer food-related queries. Golub operates about 135 Price Chopper supermarkets and market 32 stores in six states in the northeastern US (New York is its largest market.) About 80 of the locations have in-store pharmacies and some New York stores provide shopping and delivery service through the Shops4U program. The founding Golub family runs the company and owns about 45% of the regional grocery chain; employees own slightly more than 45%.

Geographic Reach

Golub's Price Chopper chain is active in six US states. New York accounts for more than 60% of its locations while Massachusetts and Vermont each contribute more than 10%. It also has locations in Connecticut Pennsylvania and New Hampshire.

Sales and Marketing

The company sells its products in its stores and online.

Financial Performance

While privately-held Golub doesn't publish sales results for its Price Chopper chain its supermarkets ring up an estimated $3.5 billion in annual revenues.

Strategy

Golub continues to invest in its future through new locations improved products and services customer engagement and health and wellness initiatives environmental sustainability activities progressive technology digital marketing e-commerce and social networking.

In 2015 Price Chopper Supermarkets launched a specialty pharmacy program with Aureus Health Services a specialty pharmacy and health management company.

In 2014 the company announced plans to rebrand about 135 Price Chopper supermarkets under a new banner Market 32. The conversions will take place over the next several years. More than half of the conversions will be completed within five years representing a $300 million investment. The renamed stores will will include expanded food service options an enhanced product mix and an emphasis on customer service. The new name references 1932 the year the company was founded.

In late 2013 Golub invested some $10 million to relaunch a Latham New York store as Market Bistro by Price Chopper. The 87000-square-foot revamped location features a New York-style deli pizza counter cooking classes and indoor and outdoor patios.

Company Background

Like many other retailers the company is experimenting with new formats. In May 2012 it opened its first small-format store known as Price Chopper Limited. The 19000-square-foot store (about a third of the size of a typical Price Chopper supermarket) is located in a residential neighborhood in downtown Saratoga Springs New York. The "Limited" store offers an edited selection of Price Chopper's most popular products a bakery full-service meat deli and seafood departments and a cafe with eat-in or take-out meals.

In fall 2011 Price Chopper launched a new online ordering and home delivery program called Price Chopper Shops4U . The service charges a service fee of $10 with an additional $6 fee for delivery. Customers can either pick up their orders at the store or have them delivered.

Brothers Bill and Ben Golub founded the company in 1932.

EXECUTIVES

President and CEO, Jerel T. (Jerry) Golub, age 59
VP Public Relations and Consumer Services, Mona J. Golub, age 53
SVP Administration, David Golub, age 56
VP Produce & Floral Merchandising, Rick Reed
Director Of Pharmacy, Toni Shields
Senior Vice President Operations, Dean Little
Vice President, Shawn Gonzalez
Senior Vice President Planning and Allocations, Daniel Riccio
Vice President of Architectural Design and Purchasing Services, Steven Duffy
Vice President of Facilities, Benny Smith
Chairman, Neil M. Golub, age 80

LOCATIONS

HQ: THE GOLUB CORPORATION
461 NOTT ST, SCHENECTADY, NY 123081812
Phone: 518 355-5000
Web: WWW.PRIMEBUSINESSDINING.COM

2013 Stores

	No.
New York	81
Massachusetts	16
Vermont	15
Connecticut	8
Pennsylvania	8
New Hampshire	4
Total	**132**

COMPETITORS

7-Eleven	Gerrity's
A&P	Hannaford Bros.
ALDI	Shaw's
BJ's Wholesale Club	Stewart's Shops
Big Y Foods	Stop & Shop
CVS	TOPS Markets
Costco Wholesale	Target Corporation
Cumberland Farms	Wal-Mart
DeMoulas Super Markets	Wegmans

HISTORICAL FINANCIALS

Company Type: Private

Income Statement
FYE: April 24

	REVENUE ($ mil.)	NET INCOME ($ mil.)	NET PROFIT MARGIN	EMPLOYEES
04/16	3,427	8	0.2%	20,434
04/15	3,476	21	0.6%	—
04/14	3,472	18	0.5%	—
04/13	3,484	24	0.7%	—
Annual Growth	(0.6%)	(30.3%)	—	—

2016 Year-End Financials

Return on assets: 5.7% Cash ($ mil.): 22
Return on equity: 0.2%
Current ratio: 0.30

THE GOOD SAMARITAN HOSPITAL OF LEBANON PENNSYLVANIA

EXECUTIVES

President, Thomas Harlow
Executive Director, Mary Reppert
Director, Joel Kerr
VP Marketing, William Mulligan
Manager, Gene Peters
Manager, Stephanie Andreozzi
Auditors: GRANT THORNTON LLP PHILADELPH

LOCATIONS

HQ: THE GOOD SAMARITAN HOSPITAL OF LEBANON PENNSYLVANIA
252 S 4TH ST, LEBANON, PA 170426111
Phone: 717 270-7500
Web: WWW.GSHLEB.ORG

HISTORICAL FINANCIALS

Company Type: Private

Income Statement
FYE: June 30

	REVENUE ($ mil.)	NET INCOME ($ mil.)	NET PROFIT MARGIN	EMPLOYEES
06/15	188	4	2.4%	99
06/14	178	(6)	—	—
06/13	186	(9)	—	—
06/10	168	(0)	—	—
Annual Growth	2.3%	—	—	—

2015 Year-End Financials

Return on assets: 15.1% Cash ($ mil.): 2
Return on equity: 2.4%
Current ratio: 0.80

THE GOOD SAMARITAN HOSPITAL OF MD INC

Good Samaritan Hospital of Maryland provides emergency care and promotes good health in the Baltimore area. The 300-bed hospital operating as MedStar Good Samaritan provides acute medical and specialty services including rehabilitation (50-bed ward) transitional care (30-bed sub-acute ward) orthopedics cancer care cardiology dialysis and women's health as well as serving as a community teaching facility. The hospital founded in 1968 also operates nursing and assisted-living facilities for the elderly and it provides educational seminars diagnostic screening and preventative medical care through its Good Health Center. MedStar Good Samaritan of Maryland is part of the MedStar Health system.

OperationsMedStar Good Samaritan has about 370 physicians on its medical staff. It serves about 16000 inpatients and handles some 140000 outpatient visits per year. The hospital's primary specialty centers include spine arthritis and joint replacement clinics.

Financial Performance

MedStar Good Samaritan reported some $327 million in net operating revenues in fiscal 2011. It also had assets of $177 million and stated community benefits (including outreach and charity care) at some $30 million.

Strategy

The hospital is working to provide an increasing variety of specialty services to patients in the Baltimore area. As such in 2012 MedStar Good Samaritan added a wound healing center for the treatment of chronic wounds. The hospital also expanded its community service provisions that year when it expanded its infant and toddler day-care center.

EXECUTIVES

President, Jeffrey A Matton
Board of Directors, Walter Jura
Office Manager, Carol Grap
Manager, Kathleen Curry
Auditors: KPMG LLP BALTIMORE MARYLAND

LOCATIONS

HQ: THE GOOD SAMARITAN HOSPITAL OF MD INC
5809 NICHOLSON LN PH 1503, ROCKVILLE, MD 208525707
Phone: 443 444-3780
Web: WWW.GOODSAM-MD.ORG

PRODUCTS/OPERATIONS

Selected Services and Divisions

Belvedere Green (senior living)
Burn Reconstruction Center
Cancer Care/Oncology
Cardiology/Heart Care
Diabetes/Endocrinology
Diagnostic Imaging
Ear Nose and Throat
Emergency Services
Gastroenterology
Good Health Center
Kidney Care/Nephrology
MedStar Good Samaritan Nursing Center (senior living)
MedStar Pharmacy
Orthopedics
Pain Management
Pediatrics
Physical Therapy
Plastic Surgery
Primary Care Center
Pulmonary Services
Rehabilitation Services
Renal Dialysis
Rheumatology [Rheumatoid Arthritis/Sjgren's Syndrome]
Senior Living
Sleep Center
Sports Medicine
Stroke Rehabilitation
Surgical Services
Transitional Care
Urology
Vascular Services
Weight Management - Good Weighs
Women's Health
Woodbourne Woods (senior living)
Wound Healing Center

COMPETITORS

Adventist HealthCare	Johns Hopkins Health System
Anne Arundel Medical Center	Levindale Hospital
Ascension Health	Novant Health
Bon Secours Health	Sentara Healthcare
Children's National Medical Center	University of Maryland Medical System
Christiana Care	Valley Health
Civista Health	Virginia Hospital Center
GBMC	
Inova	

HISTORICAL FINANCIALS

Company Type: Private

Income Statement
FYE: June 30

	REVENUE ($ mil.)	NET INCOME ($ mil.)	NET PROFIT MARGIN	EMPLOYEES
06/15	325	16	5.2%	2,146
06/14	318	9	3.0%	—
06/11	331	14	4.2%	—
06/10	322	10	3.2%	—
Annual Growth	0.2%	10.1%	—	—

2015 Year-End Financials

Return on assets: 6.8% Cash ($ mil.): —
Return on equity: 5.2%
Current ratio: 2.00

THE HALLEN CONSTRUCTION CO INC

EXECUTIVES

Board of Directors, Janice M Mc Keon

President, Ken Biondi
Senior Vice-President, Gene Hickey
President, Jim Small
Auditors: ALBRECHT VIGGIANO ZURECK & C

LOCATIONS

HQ: THE HALLEN CONSTRUCTION CO INC
4270 AUSTIN BLVD, ISLAND PARK, NY 115581626
Phone: 516 432-8300
Web: WWW.HALLENCONSTRUCTION.NET

HISTORICAL FINANCIALS
Company Type: Private

Income Statement
FYE: December 31

	REVENUE ($ mil.)	NET INCOME ($ mil.)	NET PROFIT MARGIN	EMPLOYEES
12/15	225	29	13.0%	250
12/14	171	17	10.4%	—
12/13	148	11	7.5%	—
12/12	102	10	9.8%	—
Annual Growth	29.9%	42.6%	—	—

2015 Year-End Financials
Return on assets: 5.3%   Cash ($ mil.): 24
Return on equity: 13.0%
Current ratio: 2.40

THE HARDIN MEMORIAL HOSPITAL FOUNDATION INC

EXECUTIVES

Nursing Director, Leona Gilliam
Assistant Vice President, Tom Carrico
Vice President of Finance and Chief Operating Officer, Elmer Cummings
Admissions Director, Belinda Carter
Vice President and Chief Medical Officer, Jody Prather
Assistant Vice President Emergency Services, Deanna Parker
Medical Records Director, Debra Davis
Assistant Vice President Revenue Cycle, Michelle Brown
Secretary, Vicki Grimes
Secretary, Emily Gray
Secretary, Kristina Hard

LOCATIONS

HQ: THE HARDIN MEMORIAL HOSPITAL FOUNDATION INC
913 N DIXIE AVE, ELIZABETHTOWN, KY 427012503
Phone: 270 737-1212
Web: WWW.HMH.NET

Selected facilities
Hardin Memorial Hospital (Elizabethtown)
CareFirst Urgent Care Center (Radcliff)
Family Care Center - North Hardin (Radcliff)
Family Care Center - South Hardin (Sonora)
Family Care Center Magnolia (Magnolia)
Bardstown Diagnostic Center

PRODUCTS/OPERATIONS

Selected services
Birthplace
Cancer Care Services
Comprehensive Cardiac Services
Critical Care

Emergency Department
HomeCare Home Health Agency
Laboratory Services
Les Langley Pediatric Unit
LifeSpring Psychiatric Unit
Nursing Facility
Outpatient Surgery and Endoscopy Center
Pulmonary Services
Radiology Services
Rehabilitation Services
Wellness on Wheels®; Mobile Health Unit
Women's Care Center
WorkWell Occupational Health Services

COMPETITORS

Appalachian Regional Healthcare
Catholic Health Initiatives
Jewish Hospital & St. Mary's HealthCare
Kindred Healthcare
Norton Healthcare
University of Kentucky Chandler Hospital

HISTORICAL FINANCIALS
Company Type: Private

Income Statement
FYE: June 30

	REVENUE ($ mil.)	NET INCOME ($ mil.)	NET PROFIT MARGIN	EMPLOYEES
06/16	290	15	5.2%	1,480
06/15*	215	18	8.5%	—
12/10	0	0	23.9%	—
12/09	0	(0)	—	—
Annual Growth	483.7%	—	—	—
*Fiscal year change

2016 Year-End Financials
Return on assets: 3.5%   Cash ($ mil.): 48
Return on equity: 5.2%
Current ratio: 2.50

THE HARRIS CENTER FOR MENTAL HEALTH AND IDD

EXECUTIVES

Executive Director, Dr Steven B Schnee
Manager, Gale Shevlin
Manager, Clarice Taylor
Manager, Robert Stakem
Program Manager, Ally Frankovich
Supervisor, Cherryl Atobajeun
Auditors: PATTILLO BROWN & HILL LLP

LOCATIONS

HQ: THE HARRIS CENTER FOR MENTAL HEALTH AND IDD
9401 SOUTHWEST FWY, HOUSTON, TX 770741407
Phone: 713 970-7000
Web: WWW.MHMRAHARRIS.ORG

HISTORICAL FINANCIALS
Company Type: Private

Income Statement
FYE: August 31

	REVENUE ($ mil.)	NET INCOME ($ mil.)	NET PROFIT MARGIN	EMPLOYEES
08/16	229	0	0.2%	1,500
08/15	219	(11)	—	—
08/14	213	17	8.1%	—
08/13	174	1	0.8%	—
Annual Growth	9.6%	(24.9%)	—	—

2016 Year-End Financials
Return on assets: 2.9%   Cash ($ mil.): 15
Return on equity: 0.2%
Current ratio: 1.30

THE HENRY M JACKSON FOUNDATION FOR THE ADVANCEMENT OF MILITARY MEDICINE INC

EXECUTIVES

President, Joseph Caravalho Jr
Manager, Eddie Drakeford
Manager, Henry Jackson

LOCATIONS

HQ: THE HENRY M JACKSON FOUNDATION FOR THE ADVANCEMENT OF MILITARY MEDICINE INC
6720A ROCKLEDGE DR # 100, BETHESDA, MD 208171888
Phone: 240 694-2000
Web: WWW.HJF.ORG

HISTORICAL FINANCIALS
Company Type: Private

Income Statement
FYE: September 30

	REVENUE ($ mil.)	NET INCOME ($ mil.)	NET PROFIT MARGIN	EMPLOYEES
09/15	395	1	0.3%	2,200
09/13	441	12	2.9%	—
09/10	402	7	1.9%	—
09/08	748	0	—	—
Annual Growth	—	466.8%	—	—

2015 Year-End Financials
Return on assets: 12.1%   Cash ($ mil.): 38
Return on equity: 0.3%
Current ratio: 0.60

THE HOSPITAL COMMITTEE FOR THE LIVERMORE-PLEASANTON AREAS

EXECUTIVES

Chief Executive Officer, Marcelina L Feit
Personnel Manager, Linda Hedley

LOCATIONS

HQ: THE HOSPITAL COMMITTEE FOR THE
LIVERMORE-PLEASANTON AREAS
1111 E STANLEY BLVD, LIVERMORE, CA 945504115
Phone: 925 447-7000
Web: WWW.VALLEYCARE.COM

HISTORICAL FINANCIALS

Company Type: Private

Income Statement

	REVENUE ($ mil.)	NET INCOME ($ mil.)	NET PROFIT MARGIN	EMPLOYEES
06/15	268	8	3.1%	1,000
06/14	269	(72)	—	—
06/05	197	6	3.3%	—
06/03	151	3	2.1%	—
Annual Growth	4.9%	8.5%	—	—

FYE: June 30

2015 Year-End Financials

Return on assets: 14.3%
Return on equity: 3.1%
Current ratio: 1.80

Cash ($ mil.): 33

THE HOWARD UNIVERSITY

Howard University is a predominantly African-American university enrolling some 11000 students in Washington DC. The university offers undergraduate graduate and professional degrees in 120 areas including engineering education divinity dentistry law medicine history political science music and social work through its 12 schools and colleges. It has about 1000 full-time faculty members and has a low student-to-teacher ratio of about 8:1. Established in 1867 the school was named after one of its founders General Oliver O. Howard a Civil War hero who was commissioner of the Freedman's Bureau.OperationsMedical students at Howard University have the convenience of using Howard University Hospital (located right on the school's campus) for their training and residency programs. The not-for-profit hospital offers students training in a full range of medical specialties including Level 1 Trauma care. The hospital is also a research facility giving students the opportunity to participate in clinical and research work.

Notable alumni at Howard University include choreographer Debbie Allen former US Supreme Court Justice Thurgood Marshall former New York City mayor David Dinkins Nobel laureate Toni Morrison and singer Roberta Flack.

Financial Performance

Howard University reported a 2% increase in revenue to some $851 million in 2012 due to higher tuition and fees patient services and other income. The university reported net income losses of $149 million that year (it also posted a loss in 2011) due to higher operating expenses and restructuring costs as well as lower investment returns.

Howard University's endowment is about $400 million. Its operating budget is nearly $885 million.

EXECUTIVES

President, Dwayne Frederick
Manager, Sandra Forney
Senior Vice-President, Carol Winston
Manager, Dione Duckett

LOCATIONS

HQ: THE HOWARD UNIVERSITY
2400 6TH ST NW, WASHINGTON, DC 200590002
Phone: 202 806-6100
Web: WWW.HOWARD.EDU

PRODUCTS/OPERATIONS

Selected Schools and Colleges

Arts and Sciences
Business
Communications
Dentistry
Divinity
Education
Engineering Architecture and Computer Sciences
Graduate School
Law
Medicine
Nursing and Allied Health Sciences
Pharmacy
Social Work

HISTORICAL FINANCIALS

Company Type: Private

Income Statement

	REVENUE ($ mil.)	NET INCOME ($ mil.)	NET PROFIT MARGIN	EMPLOYEES
06/15*	970	(41)	—	5,600
12/14	398	(79)	—	—
06/13	843	202	24.0%	—
06/12	1,000	(148)	—	—
Annual Growth	(1.0%)	—	—	—

FYE: June 30
*Fiscal year change

2015 Year-End Financials

Return on assets: 21.3%
Return on equity: (-4.3%)
Current ratio: —

Cash ($ mil.): 22

THE HUMANE SOCIETY OF THE UNITED STATES

The Humane Society of the United States (HSUS) is a watchdog for dogs and all sorts of other domestic animals and wildlife. Founded in 1954 HSUS is the country's largest animal protection organization with 11 million members and constituents. The organization supports the work of local humane societies and implements a variety of investigative educational advocacy and legislative programs to promote animal welfare. Its campaigns have addressed such issues as animal fighting factory farming animal testing the fur trade and hunting practices. Most of HSUS's revenue comes from contributions and grants. An affiliate Humane Society International takes the cause to other countries.

Operations

The HSUS operates through a network of animal sanctuaries and rescue efforts to provide emergency care and homes for animals nationwide. The organization runs an online store — in place of a catalog — that offers products for pets and people with pets. HSUS sets aside a portion of the online sales to fund its programs.

The organization supports public policy corporate reforms and major campaigns to confront animal cruelty. It provides training and services to local shelters and rescue groups supports spay/neuter and adoption initiatives and offers tips on caring for pets.

In addition to Humane Society International HSUS maintains affiliate relationships with Doris Day Animal League Humane Society Veterinary Medical Association Humane Society University The Fund for Animals Humane Society Wildlife Land Trust and South Florida Wildlife Center. While the organization operates independently from local humane societies and SPCAs it shares similar goals and supports and serves in a number of outreach areas.

Geographic Reach

Based in Washington DC HSUS has regional representatives throughout the US. States with the largest number of constituents are California Florida Illinois Massachusetts Michigan New Jersey New York Ohio Pennsylvania and Texas. It operates wildlife sanctuaries in 35 states.

Financial Performance

HSUS generates revenue from a variety of sources including contributions and grants (77%) bequests investment income and other income. More than 80% of its operating and supporting expenses goes toward animal protection programs.

Strategy

Americans have become increasingly concerned about a wide range of issues that reach far beyond direct animal abuse. HSUS cites progress on several fronts such as the fact that nearly 50 fast food chains grocers pork producers and food service providers have committed to phasing out gestation crates that help to immobilize breeding sows. It also assisted in the rescue of hundreds of animals from coastal New York and New Jersey neighborhoods impacted by Hurricane Sandy in 2012.

The group's lobbying efforts aided in the passing of around 100 pro-animal state laws per year including ones that have banned hound hunting of bears and bobcats in California and private ownership in Ohio of animals deemed too dangerous. HSUS is also behind the USDA's efforts to establish mandatory minimum penalties for Horse Protection Act violations. Previously HSUS was party to a landmark agreement with the United Egg Producers trade association to support federal legislation banning the confinement of hens to a battery cage.

To its benefit the organization is steered by individuals with a diverse pool of talent that lobby and develop policies that take on big industries and interests. To this end HSUS attracts attorneys undercover investigators academics and veterinarians. It is also experienced in gaining news coverage to expose cruel practices and the parties responsible. HSUS' future is global as it seeks to develop a network that tackles the fur trade in China elephant poaching in Africa and factory farming in Brazil and India to name a few.

EXECUTIVES

Vice President, Michelle Cho
Auditors: MCGLADREY LLP GAITHERSBURG M

LOCATIONS

HQ: THE HUMANE SOCIETY OF THE UNITED STATES
1255 23RD ST NW STE 450, WASHINGTON, DC
200371168
Phone: 202 452-1100
Web: WWW.HUMANESOCIETY.ORG

PRODUCTS/OPERATIONS

Selected Affiliates
Doris Day Animal League
Humane Society International
Humane Society Legislative Fund
Humane Society University
Humane Society Veterinary Medical Association
Humane Society Wildlife Land Trust
The Fund for Animals

Selected Areas of Focus
Campaigns
 Adopt a shelter pet
 Chimps deserve better
 End animal cruelty and fighting
 Farm animal protection
 Fur-Free
 Protect seals
 Stop puppy mills
 Wildlife abuse
 Wild horses
Issues
 Animal cruelty and fighting
 Animal rescue
 Animals in laboratories
 Captive wildlife
 Equine protection
 Factory farming
 Fur
 Opposition
 Pet protection
 Threats to wildlife
 Wildlife abuse
 Wildlife management

HISTORICAL FINANCIALS

Company Type: Private

Income Statement   FYE: December 31

	REVENUE ($ mil.)	NET INCOME ($ mil.)	NET PROFIT MARGIN	EMPLOYEES
12/15	194	(0)	—	600
12/14	169	21	12.6%	—
12/13	169	21	12.6%	—
12/11	133	5	4.3%	—
Annual Growth	9.8%	—	—	—

2015 Year-End Financials

Return on assets: 8.4%   Cash ($ mil.): 13
Return on equity: (-0.4%)
Current ratio: 0.30

THE INGALLS MEMORIAL HOSPITAL

Ingalls Memorial Hospital serves Chicago's south suburbs. With more than 560 beds the main hospital offers a variety of acute and tertiary health care services including cancer treatment cardiovascular care orthopedic surgery rehabilitation services neurosurgery women's health and other clinical services. It also includes specialty centers in areas such as sleep therapy and addiction treatment. Ingalls Memorial Hospital also acts as a health system operating outpatient offices and clinics and providing home health and hospice services in the area.
 Operations

Ingalls Memorial Hospital employs 450 physicians who specialize in 30 fields. The medical center sees about 18000 inpatient admissions per year. It also handles about 1100 births and more than 50000 emergency department visits annually.

In addition to the hospital the health system includes a handful of family care centers and several urgent care and surgery clinics as well as outpatient rehabilitation wellness and cancer support centers. Ingalls Health System also operates home health and hospice agencies and it provides community health screenings and other outreach programs.

Each year Ingalls hosts more than 200 free health screenings educational programs and health fairs that reach nearly 50000 individuals. These include free or discounted mammograms; free prostate screenings; and free or deeply discounted children's physicals and immunizations for hundreds of area children preparing for school.

Ingalls Health System also includes a Wellness Center in Homewood; Cancer Care Center and Same Day Surgery in Tinley Park; Ingalls Center for Outpatient Rehabilitation in Calumet City; and Ingalls Home Care & Hospice which provides skilled nursing support and therapy services throughout the Southland.
 Geographic Reach

Ingalls Memorial Hospital's main campus encompasses some 22 acres in the south suburbs of Chicago. Its family and urgent care centers are located in Calumet City Flossmoor Matteson and Tinley Park. The system also includes rehabilitation centers in Calumet City and South Holland; a wellness center in Homewood; and a cancer and surgery center in Tinley Park.
 Strategy

To improve primary care services Ingalls Memorial Hospital has conducted expansion and renovation efforts at several of its family clinic locations in recent years. It is also growing its range of advanced cancer treatment offerings.

In 2015 Ingalls opened its intensive outpatient program at the Ingalls Family Care Center in Tinley Park. A short-term behavioral health treatment program for adults ages 18 and above the program treats individuals struggling with depression stress and anxiety. It expanded its services to Tinley Park to serve more patients in need of outpatient therapy west of the hospital's main campus in Harvey. The program helps participants take charge of their own well-being through skill development in areas like positive lifestyle changes self-image stress management problem solving communication and relationships.

In 2015 Ingalls also launched an online risk assessment to screen for depression.
 Company Background

The company's infusion center was the first Chicago-area cancer center to administer a new prostate cancer drug Provinge in 2012. Ingalls first introduced intensive outpatient therapy at its Flossmoor Family Care Center in 2012.

Ingalls Health System was founded by Chicago-area industrialist Frederick Ingalls in 1923.

EXECUTIVES

Nursing Director, Gregory Biedron
Director of Nursing, Shirley Corbett
Rph, Martha Jelski
Nursing Director, Jill Zaki
Vice President of Philanthropy and Community Relations, Paul Donohue
Associate Vice President Care Management and Clinical Documentation Improvement, Leah Montoya

LOCATIONS

HQ: THE INGALLS MEMORIAL HOSPITAL
1 INGALLS DR, HARVEY, IL 604263558
Phone: 708 333-2300
Web: WWW.INGALLSHEALTHSYSTEM.ORG

PRODUCTS/OPERATIONS

Selected Services
Advanced Orthopedic Institute
 Joint Center
 Spine Center
 Sports Medicine
 Rehabilitative Services
Behavioral Health
 Inpatient Adult Care
 Addictions
 Adolescent
 Depression Risk
Cancer Care
 Newly Diagnosed
 Research
 Technology and Treatments
Heart and Vascular
 Diabetes
 Heart Care Center
 Leg Veins
 Stroke
Home Care and Hospice
 Palliative Care
Interventional Radiology
 Interventional Oncology
 Uterine Fibroids
 Vein Clinic
Irwin Retina Center
 Clinical Research
 Diabetic Retinopathy
 Macular Degeneration
Neurosciences
 Stroke
 Concussion Program
 Sleep Centers
Occupational Health
 Employer Resource Center
 Worksite Wellness and Prevention
Outpatient Services
 Advanced Imaging
 Pharmacy
 Same Day Surgery
 Urgent Aid
Rehabilitation Services
 Acute Care
 Day Rehabilitation
 Home Care
 Inpatient Rehabilitation
 Outpatient Rehabilitation
Wellness
 Complementary Medicine
 Nutrition and Weight Management
Women's Services
 Breast Center
 Maternity Unit
 Osteoporosis
 Uterine Fibroids
Additional Services
 Complementary Medicine
 Dermatology
 Diabetes
 Dialysis
 Ear/Nose/Throat
 Gastroenterology
 Occupational Health
 Ophthalmology
 Pain Management
 Pediatrics
 Rheumatology
 Therapies
 Urinary Incontinence
 Weight Management
 Wound Care

COMPETITORS

Advocate Health Care
 Alexian Brothers Health System
 Loyola University Health System
 MetroSouth Medical
 Mount Sinai Hospital
 NorthShore University HealthSystem
 Rush System for Health

Saint Margaret Mercy Healthcare
St. Bernard Hospital and Health Care Center
Vanguard MacNeal Hospital
WellGroup HealthPartners

HISTORICAL FINANCIALS
Company Type: Private

Income Statement				FYE: September 30
	REVENUE ($ mil.)	NET INCOME ($ mil.)	NET PROFIT MARGIN	EMPLOYEES
09/15	285	7	2.6%	2,296
09/14	292	26	9.2%	—
09/13	290	34	11.8%	—
09/12	293	36	12.6%	—
Annual Growth	(0.9%)	(41.7%)	—	—

2015 Year-End Financials
Return on assets: 7.7%   Cash ($ mil.): 16
Return on equity: 2.6%
Current ratio: 0.70

THE JAMAICA HOSPITAL

Jamaica Hospital Medical Center has been operating in the Queens Borough of New York since before the nation of Jamaica even was born. The hospital serves Queens and eastern Brooklyn with general medical pediatric psychiatric and ambulatory care services. The facility has about 430 beds. Its specialty services include a coma recovery unit a dialysis center a psychiatric emergency department a rehabilitation center as well as a traumatic brain injury recovery unit. The hospital also operates a nursing home with more than 220 beds as well as family practice ambulance and home health services. Jamaica Hospital Medical Center is a subsidiary of MediSys Health Network.

Operations

Jamaica Hospital Medical Center treats some 130000 patients annually through its emergency department which contains a level I regional trauma center. The hospital also handles about 2000 births each year in its labor and delivery wing.

In addition to acute care services the hospital is a teaching facility associated with several educational organizations including Cornell University's Weill Medical College the Mount Sinai School of Medicine and St. George's University School of Medicine. It provides residency and training programs in areas including dentistry podiatry physician assistant and osteopathic medicine. Some of its residency programs are conducted in partnership with other regional health centers including the New York Hospital and the Montefiore Medical Center.

The Ambulatory Care Centers include a Sleep Clinic where sleep disorders in adults and children are evaluated and treated.

In 2014 the hospital had nearly 120000 patients were treated in the Emergency Department; 300000 patients were seen in the Ambulatory Care Centers (with locations at the main campus and also at the offsite centers in the community); and some 2904 deliveries were performed.

Geographic Reach

Jamaica Hospital Medical Center serves a population greater than 1.2 million in Queens and eastern Brooklyn.

Strategy

To improve care for area residents Jamaica Hospital Medical Center has expanded its sleep medicine division to include a new sleep disorder diagnosis center for adults and children. The hospital has also expanded its community care provisions through partnerships with area businesses and organizations.

Upgrading its technology in 2015 the company introduced da Vinci Robot Now at its Flushing location.

Company Background

Jamaica Hospital Medical Center was founded in 1892.

EXECUTIVES

Director of Radiology, Scott Trepeta
Vice President Human Resources, Sheila Garvey
Executive Vice President and Chief Financial Officer, Mounir Doss
Respiratory Therapy Director, Celeste Murphy

LOCATIONS

HQ: THE JAMAICA HOSPITAL
8900 VAN WYCK EXPY FL 4N, JAMAICA, NY 114182897
Phone: 718 206-6290

PRODUCTS/OPERATIONS

Selected Centers and Services
Advanced Center for Psychotherapy
Allergy and Immunology
Ambulatory Care
Anesthesia
Cardiology
Clinical Services
Corporate Health
Critical Care Medicine
Dental
Dermatology
Dialysis-Island Rehabilitation
Emergency Medicine
Family Medicine
Gastroenterology
Home Health
Infectious Disease
Lupus Center
MediSys Family Care Centers
Nephrology
Neurology
Nursing
OB-GYN
Oncology
Orthopedic Surgery
Palliative Care
Pathology
Pediatrics
Podiatry
Prehospital Care
Psychiatry
Pulmonary Medicine
Radiology
Rehabilitation
Rheumatology
Surgery
TCU
The Brady Institute
Trump Pavilion~Jamaica Hospital Nursing Home
Women's Health
Women's Health Center

COMPETITORS

Catholic Healthcare System	Montefiore Medical
Continuum Health Partners	New York City Health and Hospitals
Maimonides Medical Center	NewYork-Presbyterian Healthcare
	Northwell Health

HISTORICAL FINANCIALS
Company Type: Private

Income Statement				FYE: December 31
	REVENUE ($ mil.)	NET INCOME ($ mil.)	NET PROFIT MARGIN	EMPLOYEES
12/15	422	(32)	—	3,251
12/09	447	(2)	—	—
12/06	0	0	—	—
12/05	869	0	—	—
Annual Growth	—	—	—	—

2015 Year-End Financials
Return on assets: 9.8%   Cash ($ mil.): 7
Return on equity: (-7.7%)
Current ratio: 0.40

THE JEWISH FEDERATIONS OF NORTH AMERICA INC

EXECUTIVES

Vice President for Public Policy and Director of the Washington Office, William Daroff
Senior Vice President Strategic Marketing and Communications, Renee Rothstein
Senior Vice President, Brian Abrahams
Executive Vice President, Mark Gurvis
Auditors: LOEB & TROPER LLP NEW YORK N

LOCATIONS

HQ: THE JEWISH FEDERATIONS OF NORTH AMERICA INC
25 BROADWAY FL 17, NEW YORK, NY 100041015
Phone: 212 284-6500
Web: WWW.JEWISHFEDERATIONS.ORG

HISTORICAL FINANCIALS
Company Type: Private

Income Statement				FYE: June 30
	REVENUE ($ mil.)	NET INCOME ($ mil.)	NET PROFIT MARGIN	EMPLOYEES
06/15	338	13	4.0%	150
06/12	48	0	1.7%	—
06/11	47	(0)	—	—
06/10	0	0	—	—
Annual Growth	—	—	—	—

2015 Year-End Financials
Return on assets: 9.1%   Cash ($ mil.): 36
Return on equity: 4.0%
Current ratio: 5.20

THE JORDAN HEALTH SYSTEMS INC

EXECUTIVES

Chief Executive Officer, Peter J Holden

Board of Directors, Lyle L Bazzinotti
Board of Directors, David Delaney
Director, William Burke
Manager, Ronald Zimmerman
Manager, Trish Haley

LOCATIONS

HQ: THE JORDAN HEALTH SYSTEMS INC
275 SANDWICH ST, PLYMOUTH, MA 023602183
Phone: 508 830-2388
Web: WWW.JORDANHOSPITAL.ORG

HISTORICAL FINANCIALS

Company Type: Private

Income Statement

FYE: September 30

	REVENUE ($ mil.)	NET INCOME ($ mil.)	NET PROFIT MARGIN	EMPLOYEES
09/15	212	7	3.6%	1,600
09/13	194	3	1.6%	—
09/12	197	4	2.1%	—
09/11	0	0	—	—
Annual Growth	—	—	—	—

2015 Year-End Financials

Return on assets: 7.0%   Cash ($ mil.): 5
Return on equity: 3.6%
Current ratio: 0.90

THE JUDGE GROUP INC

If your business requires staffing technology consulting or training services The Judge Group will be predisposed to render a verdict in your favor. The company offers temporary and permanent employee placement services in a wide variety of service and manufacturing sectors but specializes in technology staffing. The company's technology consulting services address such areas as enterprise content management and strategy. It also offers training for IT-related and other professional functions through its Berkeley division. Martin Judge founded the company in 1970.

Geographic Reach

The Judge Group operates from a network of more than 30 offices throughout the US and has locations in Asia and Canada.

Strategy

The company's growth strategy revolves around the opening of offices in select markets and by entering alliances with other human resources services firms. Over the last few years it has launched offices in Baltimore Houston Milwaukee and Phoenix. In 2013 it opened its newest office in Ottawa Ontario. Throughout 2015 it opened new US offices in Oregon Connecticut and Maryland.

The Judge Group has also expanded its international reach by launching Judge China a firm which provides clients with consulting expertise for accessing markets in the most populous country in the world through offices in Beijing and Shanghai.

EXECUTIVES

COO, Katy A. Wiercinski
CFO, Robert G. Alessandrini, $137,308 total compensation
President Direct Placement, Stephen D. Green
President International, Gary R. Morris
President North America, Brian T. Anderson
EVP Talent Acquisition, Dennis F. Judge
President Learning Solutions, Peter Pedone
President Technology Solutions/Unified Communications, James D. Miner
EVP Sales, Michael Tedesco

President Judge Healthcare, Mick J. Angelichio
CEO, Martin E. Judge
EVP and Chief Marketing Officer, Peter L. Fong
VP Training and Development and CIO, Kenneth F. (Ken) Krieger
Managing Vice President, Frank Santoro
Managing Vice President and Recruiting Manager, Jessica Williamson
Vice President, Josh Serfass
Vice President, Linda Wertman
Vice President, Lisa Vaillette
Vice President Talent Development Strategies, Kevin Rillo
Legal Secretary, Nadine Kowal
Vice President, Steven Donia
Associate Vice President, Kristin Luke
National Account Manager, Kyle Sullivan
Vice President Recruiting, Nancy Thongkham
Auditors: KREISCHER MILLER HORSHAM PA

LOCATIONS

HQ: THE JUDGE GROUP INC
151 S WARNER RD STE 100, WAYNE, PA 190872125
Phone: 610 667-7700

PRODUCTS/OPERATIONS

Selected Services
Corporate training
    Custom content development
    Information technology training
    Professional development
    Project staffing and logistics
Enterprise-wide staffing
    Financial services
    Food/beverage
    Government
    Health care
    Insurance
    Manufacturing
    Pharmaceutical
    Retail/supermarkets
    Technology
    Utilities/telecom
    Wholesale distribution
Technology consulting
    Application design and development
    Audio visual design and implementation
    E-discovery and compliance
    Enterprise content management
    Research validation and compliance
    SAP implementation services
    Technology strategy and architecture

COMPETITORS

Accenture	Kenexa
Adecco	Kforce
Aquent	ManpowerGroup
Butler America	NTT Data
CDI	RCM Technologies
IBM Global Services	Unisys
Kelly Services	

HISTORICAL FINANCIALS

Company Type: Private

Income Statement

FYE: September 30

	REVENUE ($ mil.)	NET INCOME ($ mil.)	NET PROFIT MARGIN	EMPLOYEES
09/16	342	1	0.4%	2,510
09/15	323	3	1.2%	—
09/13	273	1	0.4%	—
09/12	251	2	1.2%	—
Annual Growth	8.0%	(19.7%)	—	—

2016 Year-End Financials

Return on assets: 7.0%   Cash ($ mil.): —
Return on equity: 0.4%
Current ratio: 2.00

THE LANCASTER GENERAL HOSPITAL

Lancaster General Health (LG Health) is a 690-bed integrated health care delivery system serving residents of Lancaster County Pennsylvania and surrounding areas. Its flagship Lancaster General Hospital (LGH) - opened in 1893 - is known for its cardiology orthopedic and intensive care specialties. A separate Women & Babies hospital cares for those just making it into the world. The not-for-profit system also includes multiple outpatient clinics a rehab hospital home care services and a nursing center and health care college as well as a medical group of more than 300 physicians operating at more than 40 practices throughout the region.

Operations

Facilities in the LG Health system include the 533-bed flagship LGH the 98-bed Women & Babies Hospital the 59-bed Lancaster Rehabilitation Hospital and 14 outpatient centers. Specialty services include open-heart surgery obstetrics neurosurgery trauma care and behavioral health. The system also operates a number of outpatient programs such as a diabetes and nutritional Center and a sleep medicine center.

Every year LG Health sees some 972000 outpatients delivers some 4000 babies and performs around 38000 surgeries.

Geographic Reach

The system serves Pennsylvania's Lebanon Berks Dauphin York Chester and Lancaster counties.

Sales and Marketing

Commercial and HMO payments together account for about 40% of net patient revenues; Medicare accounts for another 35% while Medicaid accounts for some 10%.

Financial Performance

LG Health's revenue rose 5% to $969 million in fiscal 2014 (ended June) on higher net patient revenue and medical services revenue. However net income fell 51% to $117 million as income from contributions and gifts declined; a change in pension liability also hurt the system's bottom line.

Cash flow from operations declined 43% to $43 million in fiscal 2014 as more cash was used in patient accounts receivable and changes were made in prepaid expenses assets and benefits.

Strategy

LG Health continues to make strategic investments to better serve its patients and the community. In 2013 the health system completed construction on the Ann B. Barshinger Cancer Center which opened its doors that year. Two years later it announced plans to expand LGH in a $60 million project that will add a new eight-story patient tower. With the addition of 60 new private rooms and the space for 80 more rooms as demand requires the hospital will have the room to convert its existing semi-private rooms to private rooms.

The system also partners with others in the community to improve patient care. In 2014 it formed an alliance with the University of Pennsylvania Health System to develop innovative care research and education programs.

EXECUTIVES

Senior Vice President Business Development, Susan Wynne
Medical Director Of The Blood Bank, Susan Bator
SVP and CIO, Gary Davidson

EVP Chief Population Health Officer; President LG Health Innovation Solutions Inc., Marion A. McGowan

President and CEO, Thomas E. (Tom) Beeman

EVP Chief Administrative and Legal Officer and Corporate Secretary, Robert P. Macina

SVP Post-Acute Care, Geoffrey W. Eddowes

EVP and CFO, Dennis R. Roemer

SVP Chief Physician Executive and Chief Medical Officer, Lee M. Duke

SVP Hospital Operations and Nurse Executive; President Lancaster General Hospital, Karen Flaherty-Oxler

Senior Vice President, Joseph Puskar

Vice President Of Operations, Christopher Maley

Vice President General Manager, Norma Ferndinand

Medical Director of Perinatology, Philip Bayliss

Vice President Of Operations, Rich Paoletti

Vice President, Stacey Youcis

Senior Vice President and Chief Financial Officer, Joseph Byorick

Vice President And Controller, Doug Rinehart

Medical Director Oncology Program, Randall Oyer

Medical Director, Michael Flood

Vice President Hospital Operations, Tammy Ober

Vice President of Facilities Planning, Steve Lee

DIRECTOR OF NURSING, Shirley S Heisey

VICE PRESIDENT RISK MANAGEMENT, Elizabeth H Katz

Chairman, C. Clair McCormick

Vice Chairman, Philip R. Wenger

Board Member, Christine Vlassis

SECRETARY, Jennifer Edmonds

Secretary, Pamela Miller

Secretary, Sheila Loreto

LOCATIONS

HQ: THE LANCASTER GENERAL HOSPITAL
555 N DUKE ST, LANCASTER, PA 176022207
Phone: 717 544-5511
Web: WWW.LANCASTERGENERALHEALTH.ORG

PRODUCTS/OPERATIONS

2014 Sales

	% of total
Net patient services revenue less provision for bad debts	95
Medical services	4
Other revenue	1
Other	.
Total	**100**

Selected Specialties

Cardiology
Emergency medical
Intensive care
Neurology
Oncology
Radiology
Rehabilitation
Urology

COMPETITORS

Altoona Regional
Ascension Health
Catholic Health Initiatives
Evangelical Community Hospital
Hanover Healthcare
Holy Spirit
Lewistown Hospital
Main Line Health System
Memorial Hospital (PA)
PinnacleHealth System
Saint Vincent Health System
St. Luke's University Health Network
University of Pennsylvania Health System
WellSpan Health

HISTORICAL FINANCIALS
Company Type: Private

Income Statement

FYE: June 30

	REVENUE ($ mil.)	NET INCOME ($ mil.)	NET PROFIT MARGIN	EMPLOYEES
06/15	920	110	12.1%	7,000
06/14	867	(13)	—	—
06/13	823	(15)	—	—
06/12	852	31	3.7%	—
Annual Growth	**2.6%**	**52.0%**	**—**	**—**

2015 Year-End Financials

Return on assets: 3.8%
Return on equity: 12.1%
Current ratio: 1.10

Cash ($ mil.): 9

THE LANE CONSTRUCTION CORPORATION

Lane likes people to be in the fast lane. For more than a century the heavy civil contractor and its affiliates have been widening paving and constructing lanes for highways bridges runways railroads dams and mass transit systems in the eastern and southern US. The group also produces bituminous and precast concrete and mines aggregates at plants and quarries in the northeastern mid-Atlantic and southern US. Additionally it sells and leases construction equipment. Founded in 1902 Lane Construction has offices in more than 20 states and is owned by descendants of Lane and employees.

Operations

Lane Construction specializes in heavy civil construction services and products in the transportation infrastructure and energy industries. During the past decade Lane Construction has participated in more than 70 design-building projects with a combined value of more than $4 billion.

Beyond its construction projects Lane operates divisions that manufacture bituminous and precast concrete with mine aggregates at 70 plants and 12 quarries throughout the U.S.

Lane's business divisions are spread across the US and include: Civil Wall Solutions Cold River Materials Prestress of the Carolinas Senate Asphalt Virginia Paving Company and Virginia Sign & Lighting Company.

Lane affiliates include New Hampshire-based Cold River Materials Senate Asphalt of Washington D.C. and Virginia Paving and Virginia Sign & Lighting Co. among about a half a dozen others. In 2013 its Rea Contracting division in the Carolinas changed its name to Lane Construction Corp.

Geographic Reach

Lane Construction has offices in more than 20 US states including Florida Illinois Maine North Carolina Pennsylvania Texas and Virginia. While most of Lane's projects take place along the East Coast it also operates in the South/Southwest and has international operations — under the Lane Worldwide Infrastructure Inc. name — in the Middle East.

Financial Performance

While full financials of the privately-held company were not available Lane Construction has posted annual revenues of more than $1 billion since 2010.

Strategy

The company continues to work for both public and private entities on a variety of high-value projects. In early 2015 the contractor was working on a joint-venture project with Skanska and Granite Construction Company on the $2.3 billion "I-4 Ultimate project" which involves design build finance operating and maintenance work on 21 miles of Interstate 4 from Orange County to Seminole County in Florida.

Also as of early 2015 Lane reported that it recently completed its $1.5-billion construction project on the I-495 Express Lanes in Virginia in one of the largest public-private joint ventures in the US. The same team also completed a $722 million expansion and improvement project on 29 miles of the I-95 Express (high occupancy toll road) lanes in Virginia. Both of these Virgina-based projects were completed ahead of schedule.

EXECUTIVES

SENIOR VICE PRESIDENT, Tim Reichwein
Auditors: KPMG LLP HARTFORD CT

LOCATIONS

HQ: THE LANE CONSTRUCTION CORPORATION
90 FIELDSTONE CT, CHESHIRE, CT 064101212
Phone: 203 235-3351
Web: WWW.LANECONSTRUCT.COM

PRODUCTS/OPERATIONS

Selected Projects

Airports
Bridges
Design-Build
Federal
Heavy Civil
Highways
Public Private Partnerships
Plants & Paving
Rail
Specialty Paving

Selected Divisions

Civil Wall Solutions
Cold River Materials Prestress of the Carolinas
Senate Asphalt
Sunquip
Sunrise Materials
Virginia Paving Company
Virginia Sun & Lighting Company
Wardwell
White Bros.

COMPETITORS

Angelo Iafrate	Sargent Corp
Austin Industries	Skanska USA Civil
Balfour Beatty Inc	The Middlesex
Bechtel	Corporation
Clark Enterprises	Turner Corporation
Granite Construction	Tutor-Saliba
J.F. White Contracting	Vecellio & Grogan
MBC Holding	Walsh Group
Peter Kiewit Sons'	

HISTORICAL FINANCIALS
Company Type: Private

Income Statement

FYE: December 31

	REVENUE ($ mil.)	NET INCOME ($ mil.)	NET PROFIT MARGIN	EMPLOYEES
12/15	1,115	(16)	—	3,500
12/14	1,093	8	0.8%	—
12/13	1,091	(22)	—	—
12/12	1,229	26	2.2%	—
Annual Growth	**(3.2%)**	**—**	**—**	**—**

2015 Year-End Financials

Return on assets: 6.9%   Cash ($ mil.): 70
Return on equity: (-1.4%)
Current ratio: 1.10

THE LAUREN CORPORATION

EXECUTIVES

President, C Cleve Whitener
Chief Financial Officer, Thomas Modisett
Executive Secretary, Lydia Flores
Project Manager, Robert Heard

LOCATIONS

HQ: THE LAUREN CORPORATION
    901 S 1ST ST, ABILENE, TX 796021502
Phone: 325 670-9660

HISTORICAL FINANCIALS

Company Type: Private

Income Statement

FYE: December 31

	REVENUE ($ mil.)	NET INCOME ($ mil.)	NET PROFIT MARGIN	EMPLOYEES
12/15	613	8	1.4%	1,700
12/14	287	4	1.4%	—
12/13	0	4	—	—
12/12	129	(14)	—	—
Annual Growth	68.1%	—	—	—

2015 Year-End Financials

Return on assets: 4.3%   Cash ($ mil.): 27
Return on equity: 1.4%
Current ratio: 0.90

THE MARY GREELEY MEDICAL CENTER

LOCATIONS

HQ: THE MARY GREELEY MEDICAL CENTER
    1111 DUFF AVE, AMES, IA 500105745
Phone: 515 239-2106
Web: WWW.MGMC.ORG

HISTORICAL FINANCIALS

Company Type: Private

Income Statement

FYE: June 30

	REVENUE ($ mil.)	NET INCOME ($ mil.)	NET PROFIT MARGIN	EMPLOYEES
06/15	177	22	13.0%	75
06/05	1	1	71.4%	—
Annual Growth	61.8%	36.4%	—	—

2015 Year-End Financials

Return on assets: 6.8%   Cash ($ mil.): 5
Return on equity: 13.0%
Current ratio: 0.90

THE MARY IMOGENE BASSETT HOSPITAL

EXECUTIVES

President, Vance M Brown
Officer, Steven Heneghan

LOCATIONS

HQ: THE MARY IMOGENE BASSETT HOSPITAL
    1 ATWELL RD, COOPERSTOWN, NY 133261394
Phone: 607 547-3456
Web: WWW.BASSETT.ORG

HISTORICAL FINANCIALS

Company Type: Private

Income Statement

FYE: December 31

	REVENUE ($ mil.)	NET INCOME ($ mil.)	NET PROFIT MARGIN	EMPLOYEES
12/15	412	(2)	—	3,200
12/14	486	18	3.7%	—
12/13	451	7	1.6%	—
12/09	366	1	0.5%	—
Annual Growth	2.0%	—	—	—

2015 Year-End Financials

Return on assets: 6.4%   Cash ($ mil.): 5
Return on equity: (-0.5%)
Current ratio: 0.80

THE MEDICAL CENTER

EXECUTIVES

Manager, Mary Godwin
Director, Ehrman Eldridge
Auditors: DIXON HUGHES GOODMAN LLP CHAR

LOCATIONS

HQ: THE MEDICAL CENTER
    710 CENTER ST, COLUMBUS, GA 319011547
Phone: 706 660-6255
Web: WWW.CRHS.NET

HISTORICAL FINANCIALS

Company Type: Private

Income Statement

FYE: June 30

	REVENUE ($ mil.)	NET INCOME ($ mil.)	NET PROFIT MARGIN	EMPLOYEES
06/15	390	(28)	—	1,500
06/14	366	(4)	—	—
06/10	316	15	4.9%	—
06/08	283	12	4.5%	—
Annual Growth	4.6%	—	—	—

2015 Year-End Financials

Return on assets: 13.1%   Cash ($ mil.): 1
Return on equity: (-7.2%)
Current ratio: 0.30

THE MEDICAL CENTER OF CENTRAL GEORGIA INC

EXECUTIVES

Chief Executive Officer, Ninfa M Saunders
Board of Directors, Kenneth B Banks
Manager, Gary Sparks
Manager, Donna Davis
Director, Larry Kendall

LOCATIONS

HQ: THE MEDICAL CENTER OF CENTRAL GEORGIA INC
    777 HEMLOCK ST, MACON, GA 312012155
Phone: 478 633-1000
Web: WWW.MCCG.ORG

HISTORICAL FINANCIALS

Company Type: Private

Income Statement

FYE: September 30

	REVENUE ($ mil.)	NET INCOME ($ mil.)	NET PROFIT MARGIN	EMPLOYEES
09/16	660	2	0.4%	3,750
09/15	717	93	13.0%	—
09/14	683	80	11.8%	—
09/09	656	10	1.7%	—
Annual Growth	0.1%	(18.3%)	—	—

2016 Year-End Financials

Return on assets: 2.9%   Cash ($ mil.): 29
Return on equity: 0.4%
Current ratio: 3.90

THE MEDICAL COLLEGE OF WISCONSIN INC

EXECUTIVES

President, John R Raymond Sr
Account Manager, Angela M Summers
Manager, Joy Joseph
Auditors: PRICEWATERHOUSECOOPERS LLP BO

LOCATIONS

HQ: THE MEDICAL COLLEGE OF WISCONSIN INC
    8701 W WATERTOWN PLANK RD, MILWAUKEE, WI 532263548
Phone: 414 456-8296
Web: WWW.MCW.EDU

HISTORICAL FINANCIALS

Company Type: Private

Income Statement

FYE: June 30

	REVENUE ($ mil.)	NET INCOME ($ mil.)	NET PROFIT MARGIN	EMPLOYEES
06/15	1,036	107	10.4%	4,700
06/13	926	123	13.4%	—
06/11	936	63	6.8%	—
Annual Growth	2.6%	14.2%	—	—

THE METHODIST HOSPITAL

Houston Methodist (formerly The Methodist Hospital) owns and operates seven Houston-area medical centers including the flagship location which has more than 800 beds and is known for innovations in urology and neurosurgery among other specialties. Other hospitals include Houston Methodist West Houston Methodist Sugar Land Houston Methodist San Jacinto Houston Methodist Willowbrook Houston Methodist St. John and Houston Methodist St. Catherine. Together the hospitals have nearly 2000 beds and employ more than 4500 physicians. In addition to hospitals the organization operates emergency care imaging outpatient and rehab centers and manages a physician organization of nearly 400.

Operations

The health system has been recognized for high performance in several specialty areas including cancer diabetes nephrology pulmonology and geriatrics. It's also been lauded for its specialties in cardiology and heart surgery endocrinology gastroenterology and GI surgery gynecology neurology and neurosurgery orthopedics and urology.

Houston Methodists family of hospitals include the main Houston Methodist Hospital Sugar Land Hospital West Hospital San Jacinto Hospital Willowbrook Hospital St. John Hospital St. Catherine Hospital. It also has long-term acute care facilities emergency care centers imaging centers and a research institute.

The hospital has educational and research affiliations with Cornell University's Weil Cornell Medical College the New York-Presbyterian Hospital University of Houston Baylor College of Medicine Texas A&M and other organizations.

Geographic Reach

Operating mostly in and around Houston Texas Houston Methodist has hospitals and medical facilities in Sugar Land Missouri City the Woodlands Baytown Nassau Bay Pearland Clear Lake and Katy.

Strategy

To widen its capacity for medical care Houston Methodist has been expanding its service network around the Houston area in recent years. In early 2015 it opened a new 36-bed patient care unit in the Houston Methodist Willbrook Hospital's North Pavilion. Houston Methodist's primary care group also broke ground on a new 7200-square-foot primary care practice which will be staffed with six board-certified primary care physicians who will serve adults and children in the Northwest Houston area starting in May 2015.

In 2014 Houston Methodist began work on a new patient tower at its Sugar Land Hospital which will add 104 beds (mostly for intensive care and medical/surgical patients)as part of its $131 million expansion effort at that location. The group also started working on a 390-bed hospital in The Woodlands Texas with completion expected in 2017. Also scheduled for completion in 2017 is a new patient tower with advanced heart and neurosurgery operating rooms at the main Houston Methodist Hospital location.

EXECUTIVES

SVP and COO, Marc L. Boom
CEO Houston Methodist Sugar Land Hospital, Chris Siebenaler
Interim CEO San Jacinto Methodist Hospital, Donna Gares
CEO Houston Methodist Willowbrook Hospital; SVP Houston Methodist, Beryl Ramsey
President and CEO Houston Methodist Research Institute, Mauro Ferrari
SVP Houston Methodist; CEO Houston Methodist West Hospital, Wayne Voss
Vice President Of Quality, Thomas W Knight
Vice President, David Campbell
Vice President of Operations, Stephen Spielman
Executive Vice President Project Manager, Sara Loewy
Medical Director, Jeanette Ferrer
Director of Nursing, Elaine Creekmore
Medical Director, Jett Brady
Clinic Supervisor, Deb Catrell
Chairman, Ewing Werlein
Vice Chairman, David M. Underwood

LOCATIONS

HQ: THE METHODIST HOSPITAL
  6565 FANNIN ST, HOUSTON, TX 770302892
Phone: 713 790-3311
Web: WWW.HOUSTONMETHODIST.ORG

PRODUCTS/OPERATIONS

Selected Houston-Area Hospitals

Houston Methodist Hospital - Texas Medical Center (Houston)
Houston Methodist Sugar Land Hospital
Houston Methodist Willowbrook Hospital (Houston)
Houston Methodist West Hospital (Houston)
Houston San Jacinto Methodist Hospital (Baytown)
Houston Methodist St. John Hospital (Texas)
Houston Methodist St. Catherine Hospital (Texas)

Selected Services

Cancer / Oncology
Diabetes / Endocrinology
Digestive Diseases
Ear Nose & Throat
Emergency Care
Heart & Vascular
Imaging / Radiology
Internal Medicine
Neurology
Neurosurgery
Obstetrics & Gynecology
Ophthalmology
Oral and Maxillofacial Surgery & Dentistry
Orthopedics & Sports Medicine
Otolaryngology Head & Neck Surgery
Pathology & Genomic Medicine
Plastic & Reconstructive Surgery
Psychiatry
Rehabilitation
Robotic Surgery
Transplant
Urology
Weight Management
Wellness

COMPETITORS

CHRISTUS Health
Dynacq Healthcare
HCA
Johns Hopkins Medicine
MD Anderson Cancer Center
Mayo Clinic
Memorial Hermann Healthcare
St. Luke's Episcopal Health System
Tenet Healthcare
Texas Children's Hospital
Texas Health Resources
Tomball Regional
Universal Health Services

HISTORICAL FINANCIALS

Company Type: Private

Income Statement

THE METHODIST HOSPITALS INC

The Methodist Hospitals Inc. is a not-for-profit community-based health care system that provides medical care to Indiana residents. More than 580 physicians representing some 60 specialties serve its two campus hospitals which have a combined total of about 640 beds. The system provides care for a range of specialized areas from neurology and neurosurgery oncology and home health and hospice to rehabilitation and orthopedics. The emergency department treats more than 59000 patients a year. The system also provides screenings charitable care and community education programs. The Methodist Hospitals established in 1923 reinvests all of its profits to improve patient care.

Operations

The system operates two main hospitals - Northlake in Gary and Southlake in Merrillville. The two campuses which are 14 miles apart are both full-service facilities. It also runs the Midlake Campus an outpatient facility with physician offices and other services in Gary a gastro-intestinal specialty center in Southlake and addiction treatment and inpatient Geriatric Behavioral Health Services units at its Northlake campus.

In 2012 The Methodist Hospitals invested more than $60 million in equipment technology and patient programs.

Geographic Reach

Methodist's main service areas include Lake and Porter counties extending west to the border east to LaPorte and south to Lowell.

Financial Performance

In 2012 the hospitals reported their fourth consecutive year of increasing profitability with $303 million in net revenue.

Strategy

The system keeps its not-for-profit operations profitable by investing in technology and facilities. After major upgrades at both hospitals and the installation of a state-of-the-art computer-assisted operating suite The Methodist Hospitals in 2013 opened an addiction treatment facility in Northlake and a GERD (gastroesophageal reflux disease) center in Southlake.

EXECUTIVES

Vice President Medical Affairs, Michael Davenport
Infection Control Director, Michelle Devries
Vice President Operations, April Brown
Blood Bank Director, Patricia Kings

Vice President and Chief Financial Officer, Matt Doyle
Director of Radiology, Mary Hansen
Assistant Treasurer, Mamon Powers
Treasurer, William Braman

LOCATIONS

HQ: THE METHODIST HOSPITALS INC
600 GRANT ST, GARY, IN 464026001
Phone: 219 886-4000
Web: WWW.METHODISTHOSPITALS.ORG

PRODUCTS/OPERATIONS

Selected Services

Behavioral health sciences
Bloodless medicine (surgery without blood transfusions)
Cardiovascular
    Cardiopulmonary rehabilitation
Diabetes Center
Emergency/trauma services
Home health
Maternity
NeuroScience Institute
    Gamma Knife (non-invasive brain surgery)
    Multiple Sclerosis Center
    Spine Care Center
    Stroke Center
Oncology Institute
Orthopedic services
Outpatient
Rehabilitation
Surgical weight loss/ bariatric services
Women's services
    Advanced obstetrical services
Wound Center

Selected Affiliations

American Cancer Society
American Heart Association
American Lung Association
Anthem Coronary Service Network
Edgewater Systems for Balanced Living
Gary Career Center
Gary Southshore Railcats
Indiana State Medical Association
Indiana University Northwest Campus
    Medical School
    Radiological Tech Program
    Respiratory Program
    School of Nursing
International Association for Healthcare Security and
    Safety
Ivy Technical Vocational School
Lakeshore Kids Immunization Fair
March of Dimes
Multiple Sclerosis Society
National Alliance for Mentally Ill (NAMI)
Purdue University Calumet Campus
    School of Nursing
Purdue University North Central Campus
    School of Nursing
Valparaiso University
    School of Nursing
Rosalind Franklin University

HISTORICAL FINANCIALS

Company Type: Private

Income Statement

FYE: December 31

	REVENUE ($ mil.)	NET INCOME ($ mil.)	NET PROFIT MARGIN	EMPLOYEES
12/15	279	1	0.6%	3,260
12/14	324	6	1.9%	—
12/13	0	0	—	—
12/09	291	5	2.0%	—
Annual Growth	(0.7%)	(19.1%)	—	—

2015 Year-End Financials

Return on assets: 4.0%   Cash ($ mil.): 19
Return on equity: 0.6%
Current ratio: 1.80

THE METROPOLITAN MUSEUM OF ART

You won't find too much about a certain New York baseball team at this Met. One of the world's premier cultural institutions The Metropolitan Museum of Art (also known as "the Met") acquires and exhibits artwork from around the world. Its collection of more than 2 million pieces ranges from the prehistoric era to the present day. In addition to hosting exhibits the Met loans artwork to other museums publishes books and catalogs and develops educational programs. It also displays art online. The City of New York owns the museum's 2 million-sq.-ft. complex which is located on the east side of Central Park; the museum itself owns its art collection. The Met was founded in 1870.

Operations

Highlights from the collection at the Met's Main Building on Fifth Avenue include American and European paintings and Egyptian and Islamic art. The institution's holdings also include The Cloisters museum and gardens located in Fort Tryon Park in Upper Manhattan. The Cloisters is devoted to the art and architecture of medieval Europe.

Strategy

The Met redesigned its website to optimize its marketing of the collection. New features include gallery overviews an interactive floor plan and suggested itineraries for planning museum visits.

EXECUTIVES

Chairman of the Board, James R Houghton
Vice-Chairman, Parker S Gilbert
Director, John D Rockefeller Jr
Auditors: PRICEWATERHOUSECOOPERS LLP NE

LOCATIONS

HQ: THE METROPOLITAN MUSEUM OF ART
1000 5TH AVE, NEW YORK, NY 100280198
Phone: 212 535-7710
Web: WWW.METMUSEUM.ORG

PRODUCTS/OPERATIONS

Selected Curatorial Departments

American Decorative Arts
Ancient Near Eastern Art
Arts of Africa Oceania and the Americas
Asian Art
Costume Institute
Drawings and Prints
Egyptian Art
European Paintings
Greek and Roman Art
Islamic Art
Medieval Art
Modern Art
Musical Instruments
Photographs

COMPETITORS

American Museum of   Museum of the City of
    Natural History   New York
Brooklyn Museum   Smithsonian

HISTORICAL FINANCIALS

Company Type: Private

Income Statement

FYE: June 30

	REVENUE ($ mil.)	NET INCOME ($ mil.)	NET PROFIT MARGIN	EMPLOYEES
06/16	379	(247)	—	2,372
06/15	361	(7)	—	—
06/14	344	275	79.9%	—
06/13	326	290	88.9%	—
Annual Growth	5.1%	—	—	—

2016 Year-End Financials

Return on assets: 12.2%   Cash ($ mil.): 7
Return on equity: (-65.2%)
Current ratio: 0.10

THE MONROE CLINIC INC

EXECUTIVES

President, Michael Sanders
Officer, Julie Allemagne
Financial Executive, Jean Wills
Vice-President, Karen Thomas
Director, Angela Miller
VP Finance, Bob Flannery
Director, James R Stormont
Director, Carla Stadel
Auditors: WIPFLI LLP MILWAUKEE WISCONS

LOCATIONS

HQ: THE MONROE CLINIC INC
515 22ND AVE, MONROE, WI 535661598
Phone: 608 324-2775
Web: WWW.MONROECLINIC.ORG

HISTORICAL FINANCIALS

Company Type: Private

Income Statement

FYE: December 31

	REVENUE ($ mil.)	NET INCOME ($ mil.)	NET PROFIT MARGIN	EMPLOYEES
12/15	176	9	5.2%	1,100
12/14	172	11	6.5%	—
12/13	168	12	7.3%	—
12/12	163	7	4.7%	—
Annual Growth	2.6%	6.0%	—	—

2015 Year-End Financials

Return on assets: 1.6%   Cash ($ mil.): 28
Return on equity: 5.2%
Current ratio: 2.50

THE MOSES H CONE MEMORIAL HOSPITAL

EXECUTIVES

Chief Executive Officer, Terry Akin
Manager, Michael Taylor
Manager, Carolyn Caldwell

LOCATIONS

HQ: THE MOSES H CONE MEMORIAL HOSPITAL
1200 N ELM ST, GREENSBORO, NC 274011020
Phone: 336 832-7000

HISTORICAL FINANCIALS

Company Type: Private

Income Statement

	REVENUE ($ mil.)	NET INCOME ($ mil.)	NET PROFIT MARGIN	EMPLOYEES
09/16	1,678	49	3.0%	12,000
09/15	1,545	(27)	—	—
09/14*	1,403	78	5.6%	—
06/14	1,024	77	7.6%	—
Annual Growth	28.0%	(19.9%)	—	—

FYE: September 30

*Fiscal year change

2016 Year-End Financials

Return on assets: 3.9%   Cash ($ mil.): 20
Return on equity: 3.0%
Current ratio: 0.50

THE MOUNT SINAI HOSPITAL

EXECUTIVES

President, Kenneth L Davis
Director, Maria Vezina
Vice-President, Mark Delaney
Vice-President, Randy Numbers

LOCATIONS

HQ: THE MOUNT SINAI HOSPITAL
1 GUSTAVE L LEVY PL FL 12, NEW YORK, NY
100296574
Phone: 212 241-6500
Web: WWW.MOUNTSINAI.ORG

HISTORICAL FINANCIALS

Company Type: Private

Income Statement

	REVENUE ($ mil.)	NET INCOME ($ mil.)	NET PROFIT MARGIN	EMPLOYEES
12/15*	2,025	70	3.5%	12,559
06/15	304	5	1.8%	—
Annual Growth	564.6%	1160.5%	—	—

FYE: December 31

*Fiscal year change

2015 Year-End Financials

Return on assets: 8.2%   Cash ($ mil.): 194
Return on equity: 3.5%
Current ratio: 1.20

THE MUSEUM OF FINE ARTS OF HOUSTON

EXECUTIVES

Director, Peter C Marzio
Financial Executive, Marchell King
Director, Margaret Culbertson
Financial Executive, Julia Petty
Administrative Assistant, Tom Howell
Auditors: DELOITTE TAX LLP HOUSTON TX

LOCATIONS

HQ: THE MUSEUM OF FINE ARTS OF HOUSTON
1001 BISSONNET ST, HOUSTON, TX 770051896
Phone: 713 639-7300
Web: WWW.MFAH.ORG

HISTORICAL FINANCIALS

Company Type: Private

Income Statement

	REVENUE ($ mil.)	NET INCOME ($ mil.)	NET PROFIT MARGIN	EMPLOYEES
06/15	215	122	56.7%	494
06/10	93	(22)	—	—
06/09	64	(26)	—	—
Annual Growth	22.2%	—	—	—

FYE: June 30

2015 Year-End Financials

Return on assets: 14.3%   Cash ($ mil.): 159
Return on equity: 56.7%
Current ratio: 3.60

THE NATURE CONSERVANCY

The Nature Conservancy is a nonprofit dedicated to preserving the diversity of Earth's wildlife by saving some 120 million acres of land 5000 miles of rivers and 100 marine areas in every US state and more than 35 countries worldwide. The organization boasts more than 1 million members. The Nature Conservancy originally carried out its mission by simply buying land but it has evolved to incorporate other methods to further its goals. In addition to land acquisition the organization partners with government corporate and private entities to reduce harmful use of natural areas to create conservation-friendly public policy and to increase conservation funding. The Nature Conservancy was founded in 1951.

Geographic Reach

Based in Arlington Virginia The Nature Conservancy operates in more than 35 countries worldwide and in all 50 US states. The organization works in Africa the Asia-Pacific region the Caribbean Europe and the Americas.

Financial Performance

The Nature Conservancy has posted two years of increased support and revenue after a dropoff in 2012. In 2014 it marshaled revenue of $1.1 billion up 17% from 2013. Dues and contributions were 28% higher in 2014 rising to $560 million. Investmetn income more than doubled to $235 million in 2014. The nonprofit had 24% less in land sales and gifts in 2014. Program efficiency remained strong at 73%.

Dues and Contributions from individuals represent about 50% The Nature Conservancy's total support and revenue. Land sales and gifts contribute nearly 12%.

Strategy

In 2014 The Nature Conservancy completed a five-year plan that put it on financially stable and sustainable ground. To expand its impact it launched NatureVest to source low-cost 'impact capital.' Such a project in Kenya its Livestock to Markets program helps communities get a better price for their cattle while managing grazing lands that also support wildlife.

The nonprofit uses about 75% of its funds on projects. Most of its donations come from individual contributors. The Nature Conservancy also makes money from the sale and lease of lands. The group is unapologetic about its pragmatic science-based approach to conservation. It has angered fellow environmentalists in the past because of its willingness to partner with governments and businesses as well as to just pay people to leave land alone. However the Nature Conservancy says its non-confrontational approach that is rooted in science has actually enabled its success.

In early 2014 The Nature Conservancy purchased nearly 120000 acres of forest rivers and wildlife habitat in the Lower Blackfoot River watershed of Montana for $85 million.

EXECUTIVES

COO, Lois E. Quam, age 56
President and CEO, Mark R. Tercek
EVP, Peter Wheeler
CFO and Chief Administrative Officer, Stephen (Steve) Howell
Chief External Affairs Officer, Glenn T. Prickett
EVP Latin America, Joseph (Joe) Keenan
Regional Managing Director Africa, David Banks
Regional Managing Director Asia Pacific, Charles E. Bedford
Director California, Mark Burget
EVP Global Conservation Initiatives, William (Bill) Ginn
Senior Science Advisor, Peter Kareiva
Chief Conservation Officer, Brian McPeek
Chief External Affairs Officer, Glenn Pricket
Global Managing Director Lands, Justin Adams
Chief Development Officer, Jim Asp
Global Managing Director Water, Giulio Boccaletti
Global Managing Director Oceans, Maria Damanaki
Global Managing Director Cities, Pascal Mittermaier
Regional Managing Director Latin American Region, Aurelio Ramos
Managing Director Public Policy, Lynn Scarlett
Acting Chief Scientist, Heather Tallis
Chief of Staff and Acting Chief Marketing Officer, Janine M. Wilkin
Director of Government Relations, Susan Donovan
Vice Chairman, James E. (Jim) Rogers
Chairman, Thomas J. Tierney
Board Director, Teresa Beck
Board Member, John Randall

LOCATIONS

HQ: THE NATURE CONSERVANCY
4245 FAIRFAX DR STE 100, ARLINGTON, VA 222031650
Phone: 703 841-5300
Web: WWW.NATURE.ORG

Selected Areas of Operation

Africa
Australia
Asia & the Pacific Islands
Caribbean
Central America
Europe
North America
South America

PRODUCTS/OPERATIONS

2014 Support & Revenue

		% of total
Dues & contributions		50
Investment income		22
Land sales & gifts		12
Government grants	120	11
1Other income	59	5
Total	**1,114**	**100**

2014 Dues & Contributions

	%
Individuals	37
Foundations	28
Bequests	23
Other organizations	6
Corporations	6
Total	**100**

HISTORICAL FINANCIALS

Company Type: Private

Income Statement

FYE: June 30

	REVENUE ($ mil.)	NET INCOME ($ mil.)	NET PROFIT MARGIN	EMPLOYEES
06/16	803	(8)	—	3,400
06/14	949	201	21.2%	—
06/13	859	106	12.4%	—
06/12	871	40	4.7%	—
Annual Growth	(2.0%)	—	—	—

2016 Year-End Financials

Return on assets: 16.1% Cash ($ mil.): 67
Return on equity: (-1.1%)
Current ratio: 0.10

THE NEW LIBERTY HOSPITAL DISTRICT OF CLAY COUNTY MISSOURI

New Liberty Hospital District which operates as Liberty Hospital hopes to liberate health care patients in northwestern Missouri. The facility is a 250-bed acute care hospital that serves communities located north of Kansas City. Founded in 1974 Liberty Hospital offers general and specialty health care services including trauma care obstetrics cancer care diagnostics surgical services vascular and cardiac medicine (including open-heart surgery) rehabilitation and pediatrics. The not-for-profit medical facility has more than 300 physicians on staff and also operates a skilled nursing facility and offers home health and hospice services.

Strategy

Liberty Hospital is expanding its facilities to improve services in the region. Recent openings include the new heart and vascular center and a 40-room outpatient center (Liberty Clinic) that includes a laboratory and diagnostic facilities.

In 2013 the hospital outsourced its IT operations to Allscripts which also provides electronic health records and physician order entries for Liberty. The move helps to improve clinical financial and operational outcomes.

EXECUTIVES

President, David Feess
Administrative Assistant, Leanna Carr
Administrative Assistant, Mary Kay

Administrative Assistant, Julie Mc Anally
Director, Chito Balchez
Auditors: PAIGE COOPER

LOCATIONS

HQ: THE NEW LIBERTY HOSPITAL DISTRICT OF CLAY COUNTY MISSOURI
2525 GLENN HENDREN DR, LIBERTY, MO 640689625
Phone: 816 781-7200
Web: WWW.LIBERTYHOSPITAL.ORG

PRODUCTS/OPERATIONS

Selected Services
Breast Center
Cancer Center
Diagnostic Imaging
Emergency and Trauma
Gastroenterology
Heart and Vascular Center
Home Health
Hospice
Hyperbaric Medicine
Intensive Care
Interventional Radiology
Lung Cancer Clinic
Maternity
Neurology
Orthopedics
Pain Management
Palliative Care
Pediatrics
Pulmonary
Rehabilitation
Robotic Surgery
Sleep Lab
Surgery
WorkHealth Solutions
Wound Clinic

COMPETITORS

Ascension Health	Truman Medical Centers
Children's Mercy Hospital	University of Kansas Medical Center
Mercy Health	Via Christi Health System
Saint Luke's Health System	
Sisters of Charity of Leavenworth	

HISTORICAL FINANCIALS

Company Type: Private

Income Statement

FYE: June 30

	REVENUE ($ mil.)	NET INCOME ($ mil.)	NET PROFIT MARGIN	EMPLOYEES
06/16	179	2	1.2%	1,700
06/15	180	(2)	—	—
06/08	157	17	11.0%	—
06/05	122	13	11.2%	—
Annual Growth	3.5%	(15.7%)	—	—

2016 Year-End Financials

Return on assets: 4.3% Cash ($ mil.): 19
Return on equity: 1.2%
Current ratio: 1.90

THE NEW SCHOOL

When James Lipton asks you what your favorite swear word is you know you've made it. The New School's drama department (formerly called The Actor's Studio) was made famous by the cable show Inside the Actors Studio which features Lipton interviewing movie and television stars. The school offers degrees in theater for playwriting directing and acting and has taught "Method" act-

ing to grads such as Marlon Brando and Robert De Niro. It is also home to Parsons The New School for Design and has schools devoted to general studies liberal arts social research management and urban policy and music. More than 10500 traditional students and 5600 continuing education students are enrolled at The New School.

Operations

The New School offers more than 90 degree and diploma programs and majors to a population of undergraduate and graduate students who come from all 50 states and more than 100 foreign countries (about one-quarter of its students hail from international locations). It boasts small class sizes and a student-teacher ratio of about 10:1.

The New School for Public Engagement is the university's founding division and is composed of five schools: Milano School of International Affairs Management and Urban Policy; School of Language Learning and Teaching; School of Media Studies; School of Undergraduate Studies; and School of Writing. It has since added six divisions: Drama Jazz Lang Mannes Parsons and Social Research.

Financial Performance

The New School's 2011 revenue grew by more than 5% vs. 2010. Net income increased 13% over the same period.

Strategy

Parsons' new academic center in Paris is slated to open in fall 2013. The Paris site will offer students a program that addresses the global nature of contemporary art and design practice and reflects Europe's culture and philosophy.

The New School was founded in 1919 by a group of university professors and intellectuals in New York City as place for students wanting to explore their creativity and engage in deep thought while studying liberal arts. Dozens of years later The New School has gained a reputation for its unconventional teaching methods as well as for being the home of many world-renowned institutes including the think tank The World Policy Institute. It also hosts the annual National Book Awards which has helped establish the careers of some of the country's most recognized authors including Richard Powers and Jonathan Franzen.

EXECUTIVES

Deputy Provost and Senior Vice President for Academic Affairs, Bryna Sanger
Assistant Vice President, Irwin Kroot
Vice President For Student Success, Michelle Relyea
Vice President, Carol Kim
Assistant Vice President Enterprise Operations Information Technology, Chris Brezil
Associate Vice President Enterprise Applications and Business Intelligence, Daniel Connell
Auditors: KPMG LLP NEW YORK NY

LOCATIONS

HQ: THE NEW SCHOOL
66 W 12TH ST, NEW YORK, NY 100118871
Phone: 212 229-5600
Web: WWW.NEWSCHOOL.EDU

PRODUCTS/OPERATIONS

Selected Schools
Eugene Lang College The New School for Liberal Arts
Mannes College The New School for Music
Milano The New School for Management and Urban Policy
The New School for Drama
The New School for General Studies
The New School for Jazz and Contemporary Music
The New School for Public Engagement
The New School for Social Research
Parsons The New School for Design

HISTORICAL FINANCIALS

Company Type: Private

Income Statement

FYE: June 30

	REVENUE ($ mil.)	NET INCOME ($ mil.)	NET PROFIT MARGIN	EMPLOYEES
06/16	370	(15)	—	855
06/15	354	34	9.6%	—
06/14	332	82	24.8%	—
06/13	313	11	3.6%	—
Annual Growth	5.7%	—	—	—

2016 Year-End Financials

Return on assets: 15.9%   Cash ($ mil.): 1
Return on equity: (-4.1%)
Current ratio: —

THE NEWTRON GROUP L L C

Some contractors bomb but The Newtron Group keeps on ticking. Through subsidiaries The Newtron Group offers a variety of industrial electrical and other specialty construction and contracting services nationwide. Services include instrumentation and control systems installation and maintenance; fiber optic installation and testing; industrial pipe and panel fabrication; aviation services; and electrical heat tracing. Newtron serves clients in such industries as refining power generation mining petrochemical and gas transmission. Subsidiaries include electrical contractor Triad Electric & Controls fiber optics firm Com-Net Services and NGI National Constructors. Founded in 1973 The Newtron Group serves the US from offices in California Louisiana Mississippi and Texas.

Operations

The Newtron Group held around a dozen subsidiary companies as of early 2016 with five under the Newtron brand including Newtron Beaumont which constructs and maintains electrical and instrumentation systems; Newtron Mechanical which deals with mechanical systems; Newtron Electrical Services which works with electrical meters breaker box replacement parking lot light and other electrical systems.

Other subsidiaries include: NGI National Constructors which constructs union projects; Triad Electric & Controls an open-shop contractor for electrical and instrumentation projects; and Executive Aviation Inc. a full-service Fixed Base Operator (FBO).

Geographic Reach

The Baton Rouge-based Newtron Group works on projects across the contiguous US from offices in California and on the coasts of Louisiana Mississippi and Texas.

Sales and Marketing

The group serves primarily the refining petrochemical power generation pulp and paper mining and metals and gas transmission industries (as of early 2016).

Strategy

Focusing on six core industries The Newtron Group and its subsidiaries continued in 2016 to work on projects ranging from small-capital projects and maintenance contracts up to multi-million dollar grassroots projects.

EXECUTIVES

VP Marketing, Duff Schempf

President, Glen Redd
Auditors: HANNIS T BOURGEOIS LLP BATON

LOCATIONS

HQ: THE NEWTRON GROUP L L C
8183 W EL CAJON DR, BATON ROUGE, LA 708158093
Phone: 225 927-8921
Web: WWW.THENEWTRONGROUP.COM

PRODUCTS/OPERATIONS

Selected Subsidiaries

Com-Net Services Inc. (fiber optics)
Executive Aviation Inc. (hangar space fuel supplies)
Newtron Inc. (electrical and instrumentation)
Newtron Heat Trace (industrial heat tracing)
Newtron Mechanical (industrial mechanics)
Triad Electric and Controls Inc. (electrical and instrumentation)
Triad Control Systems Inc. (control panel fabrication)

Selected Industries

Cement
Electronics
Food processing
Gas transmission
Metals and mining
Petrochemical
Pharmaceuticals
Power generation
Pulp and paper
Refining
Semiconductors
Waste treatment

COMPETITORS

EMCOR	Jelec
Fisk Electric	MMR Group
Industrial Specialty	Motor City Electric
Contractors	Pike Corporation

HISTORICAL FINANCIALS

Company Type: Private

Income Statement

FYE: June 30

	REVENUE ($ mil.)	NET INCOME ($ mil.)	NET PROFIT MARGIN	EMPLOYEES
06/16	436	0	—	2,000
06/15	430	0	—	—
06/14	366	0	—	—
06/13	443	0	—	—
Annual Growth	(0.5%)	—	—	—

2016 Year-End Financials

Return on assets: 1.1%   Cash ($ mil.): 45
Return on equity: —
Current ratio: 1.90

THE NORWALK HOSPITAL ASSOCIATION

EXECUTIVES

Chief Executive Officer, Daniel Debarba Jr
Director of Data Processing, Silvia Mete
Director, Michael Carius

LOCATIONS

HQ: THE NORWALK HOSPITAL ASSOCIATION
34 MAPLE ST, NORWALK, CT 068503894
Phone: 203 852-2000
Web: WWW.NORWALKHOSPITAL.ORG

HISTORICAL FINANCIALS

Company Type: Private

Income Statement

FYE: September 30

	REVENUE ($ mil.)	NET INCOME ($ mil.)	NET PROFIT MARGIN	EMPLOYEES
09/15	355	39	11.2%	1,660
09/14	323	37	11.6%	—
09/13	351	(4)	—	—
09/12	388	28	7.4%	—
Annual Growth	(2.9%)	11.2%	—	—

2015 Year-End Financials

Return on assets: 7.3%   Cash ($ mil.): 43
Return on equity: 11.2%
Current ratio: 1.00

THE PENNSYLVANIA HOSPITAL OF THE UNIVERSITY OF PENNSYLVANIA HEALTH SYSTEM

Early to bed early to rise may have made Ben Franklin healthy wealthy and wise. But for those not so healthy he (along with Dr. Thomas Bond) found it wise to establish Pennsylvania Hospital the nation's first such medical institution. The hospital is now a part of the University of Pennsylvania Health System (UPHS) and offers a comprehensive range of medical surgical and diagnostic services to the Philadelphia County area. Housing some 520 beds Pennsylvania Hospital offers specialized care in areas such as orthopedics vascular surgery neurosurgery and obstetrics; it is also a leading teaching hospital and a center for clinical research.

Operations

Pennsylvania Hospital has an average of about 29000 inpatient admissions per year including 5200 births as well as 115000 outpatient and emergency care visits. The medical center has more than 800 physicians on its medical staff. In addition to its extensive medical care services the company conducts medical training programs through its relationship with the University of Pennsylvania School of Medicine. Medical and clinical research programs are conducted with the school and with other research entities including government agencies. The hospital also collaborates with other UPHS entities including the Penn Presbyterian Medical Center and the Hospital of the University of Pennsylvania. The medical center also provides educational services across academic programs inlcuding Clinical Psychology Internship Program Medicine OB/GYN Pathology Radiology Sports Medicine Fellowship Surgery and Vascular Surgery Fellowship.

Financial Performance

For the fiscal year 2014 (ended June 30) Pennsylvania Hospital's revenues increased by 8.4% with a 9% increase in net patient service revenues 94% of total revenues); offset by a 1% decline in other revenues.

The company's net loss for the year decreased by 38% due to higher revenues and a decline in employee benefits paid.

Strategy

To improve the quality of care in the region UPHS is expanding specialist programs at its facilities.

In 2014 Pennsylvania Hospital opened its new Well Mother & Baby Unit which will represent Philadelphia's first all-private maternity suite unit. The new unit is part of Pennsylvania Hospital's $61 million long-range facility master plan and expands the company's offerings by providing private rooms to all of their maternity patients along with an array of obstetrical services from conception to discharge from the hospital following childbirth.

In 2013 UPHS expanded the orthopedic surgery program at Pennsylvania Hospital. The medical center is also enhancing services in fields including stroke care and women's health.

Company Background

The hospital was founded in 1751 by Benjamin Franklin and Dr. Thomas Bond to care for the sick-poor and insane of Philadelphia.

EXECUTIVES

Clinical Director, Dan Wilson
Medical Director, Charles Orellana
Managing Director, Jennifer Debellis
Vice President Operations, Susan Small
Director of Radiology, Linda Bagley
Vice President, Arthur Bartolozzi
Medical Director, Lee R Goldberg
Treasurer, Ronald Kotler
Auditors: LB PRICEWATERHOUSECOOPERS LLP

LOCATIONS

HQ: THE PENNSYLVANIA HOSPITAL OF THE UNIVERSITY OF PENNSYLVANIA HEALTH SYSTEM
800 SPRUCE ST, PHILADELPHIA, PA 191076130
Phone: 215 829-3000
Web: WWW.PENNMEDICINE.ORG

PRODUCTS/OPERATIONS

Selected Centers
ALS Center
Birthing Suite
Center for Bloodless Medicine and Surgery
Crisis Response Center
CyberKnife
Diabetes Education Center
Joan Karnell Cancer Center
Pain Management Center
Parkinson's Disease and Movement Disorders Center
Penn Comprehensive Neurosciences Center
Penn Orthopaedic Institute
Penn Center for Voice
Sports Medicine and Rehabilitation Center
Sleep Disorders Center
Vascular Center
Women's Imaging Center

Selected Services
Behavioral health
Heart and vascular
Neonatology
Neurosurgery
Obstetrics (including high-risk maternal and fetal services)
Orthopedics
Otorhinolaryngology (ENT)
Urology
Vascular medicine/surgery

COMPETITORS

Abington Memorial Hospital
Albert Einstein Healthcare Network
Aria Health
Bryn Mawr Hospital
Children's Hospital of Philadelphia
Crozer-Keystone Health System
Fox Chase Cancer Center
Jefferson Health

North Philadelphia Health System
TUHS
The Magee Memorial Hospital for Convalescents

HISTORICAL FINANCIALS
Company Type: Private

Income Statement   FYE: June 30

	REVENUE ($ mil.)	NET INCOME ($ mil.)	NET PROFIT MARGIN	EMPLOYEES
06/15	579	21	3.7%	2,200
06/14	534	(2)	—	—
06/10	485	27	5.7%	—
06/09	453	0	—	—
Annual Growth	4.2%	—	—	—

2015 Year-End Financials

Return on assets: 4.2%   Cash ($ mil.): —
Return on equity: 3.7%
Current ratio: 0.30

THE PENNSYLVANIA STATE UNIVERSITY

The Pennsylvania State University system is one of the largest state university systems in the US. Penn State has an enrollment of almost 96000 students; 13600 of them are graduate students. It offers 160 undergraduate and 150 graduate programs at about 20 campuses. The school's oldest and largest campus with about half of the system's undergraduate students is at University Park in central Pennsylvania. Other sites include the College of Medicine in Hershey Pennsylvania and the Dickinson School of Law in Carlisle Pennsylvania. It generates about $8.5 billion in annual direct and indirect economic impacts within Pennsylvania.

Operations

The university is known for its academic medical center and biomedical research. Its health-related programs include the Schools of Nursing Medicine Dental Medicine and Veterinary Medicine. The school's biomedical research ranks in the top 5 of National Institutes of Health funding.

The school offers a broad range of disciplines including medicine humanities engineering cyberscience and social science.

Financial Performance

Penn State had an annual operating budget in 2014-15 of $4.6 billion and an annual endowment of more than $2 billion. Its annual research funding is roughly $813 million of which $492 million comes from federal sources.

Strategy

In 2015 the university announced a new $30 million investment in economic development and student career success. This investment includes a one-time start-up and capital investment as well as annual funding of more than $5 million.

In 2014 the fundraising campaign For the Future: The Campaign for Penn State Students surpassed its goal raising about $2.2 billion in private support.

Company Background

Chartered in 1855 to apply scientific principles to farming Penn State has conferred almost 800000 degrees since its founding.

The university's storied football program was hit in 2012 with a four year postseason ban the significant reduction of scholarships the vacating of 112 wins and a $60 million fine all stemming from the school's handling of the child molestation

scandal involving former coach Jerry Sandusky. However in 2015 the NCAA reversed its decision on the vacationing of wins restoring the late head coach Joe Paterno as the winningest coach in major college football history.

EXECUTIVES

Vice President Student Affairs, Damon Sims
SVP Finance and Business and Treasurer, David J. Gray
Dean University Libraries and Scholarly Communications, Barbara I. Dewey
Dean Undergraduate Education, Robert N. Pangborn
Dean College of Medicine, A. Craig Hillemeier
Dean College of Arts and Architecture, Barbara O. Korner
Dean College of Earth and Mineral Sciences, William E. Easterling
Dean College of Education, David H. Monk
Dean College of Health and Human Development, Ann C. (Nan) Crouter
Dean College of the Liberal Arts, Susan Welch
Dean College of Nursing, Paula Milone-Nuzzo
Dean Schreyer Honors College, Christian M. M. Brady
President, Eric J. Barron, age 66
Dean Smeal College of Business, Charles H. Whiteman
EVP and Provost, Nicholas P. Jones
Chief Investment Officer, John Pomeroy
Dean Graduate School, Regina Vasilatos-Younken
Dean College of Agricultural Sciences, Richard Roush
Dean College of Communications, Marie Hardin
Dean College of Engineering, Amr S. Elnashai
Assistant Vice President For Physical Plant, Steve Maruszewski
Senior Vice President For Finance And Business Treasurer, Cynthia Hall
Vice President, Djelal Kadir
Vice President Student Affairs Interim, Gail Hurley
Vice President For Scientific Affairs, Walter Severs
Department Head Learning and Performance Systems, Roy Clariana
Student Affairs Vice President Financial Officer, Rachael Diamond
Senior Vice President for Development and Alumni Relations, Tresa Ciprich
Vice President, Sandy Rothrock
Vice President Finance, Dulin Clark
Associate Vice President For Human Resources, Blannie Bowen
Vice President Of Corporate Relations, Jessica Hunter
Department Head and Professor of Health Policy and Administration, Dennis Shea
Department Head, Scott Wing
Assistant Vice President For Principal Gifts, Glen Jack
Associate Vice President and Chief Executive Officer of the Penn State Alumni Association, Paul Clifford
Department Head and Professor, Karen Thole
Assistant Vice President and Assistant Dean For Undergraduate Education, Alan Rieck
Vice Chairman, Ira M. Lubert, age 67
Chairman, Keith E. Masser
Board Member, Jim Kustenbauter
Treasurer, Sandy Dymond
Board Member, Malcolm Taylor
Treasurer, Timothy Chiang
Board Member, Helen Sheehy
Board Member, Ann Kusnadi
Board Member, Ken Fohringer
Buck Company Treasurer, Mark Broich
Secretary, Annie Klodd
Auditors: DELOITTE & TOUCHE LLP PHILADE

LOCATIONS

HQ: THE PENNSYLVANIA STATE UNIVERSITY
  201 OLD MAIN, UNIVERSITY PARK, PA 168021503
Phone: 814 865-4700
Web: WWW.PSU.EDU

PRODUCTS/OPERATIONS

Selected Colleges
College of Agricultural Sciences
College of Arts and Architecture
Smeal College of Business
College of Communications
College of Earth and Mineral Sciences
College of Education
College of Engineering
College of Health and Human Development
College of Information Sciences and Technology
School of International Affairs
School of Law
College of the Liberal Arts
College of Medicine
School of Nursing
Eberly College of Science
Graduate School
Schreyer Honors College

Selected Campuses
Penn State Abington Penn State Altoona
Penn State Beaver
Penn State Berks
Penn State Brandywine
Penn State DuBois
Penn State Erie The Behrend College
Penn State Fayette The Eberly Campus
Penn State Greater Allegheny
Penn State Harrisburg
Penn State Hazleton
Penn State Lehigh Valley
Penn State Mont Alto
Penn State New Kensington
Penn State Schuylkill
Penn State Shenango
Penn State Wilkes-Barre
Penn State Worthington Scranton
Penn State York

HISTORICAL FINANCIALS

Company Type: Private

Income Statement   FYE: June 30

	REVENUE ($ mil.)	NET INCOME ($ mil.)	NET PROFIT MARGIN	EMPLOYEES
06/16	5,764	233	4.0%	44,000
06/15	5,293	289	5.5%	—
06/14	5,148	974	18.9%	—
06/13	4,873	842	17.3%	—
Annual Growth	5.8%	(34.8%)	—	—

2016 Year-End Financials

Return on assets: 10.3%   Cash ($ mil.): 1,395
Return on equity: 4.0%
Current ratio: 1.90

THE PHYSICIAN NETWORK

EXECUTIVES

President, Robert J Lanik

LOCATIONS

HQ: THE PHYSICIAN NETWORK
  2000 Q ST FL 5TH, LINCOLN, NE 685033610
Phone: 402 421-0896
Web: WWW.THEPHYSICIANNETWORKONLINE.COM

HISTORICAL FINANCIALS

Company Type: Private

Income Statement   FYE: June 30

	REVENUE ($ mil.)	NET INCOME ($ mil.)	NET PROFIT MARGIN	EMPLOYEES
06/15	186	14	7.5%	225
06/14*	154	4	2.7%	—
05/10	6	(0)	—	—
06/08	55	(1)	—	—
Annual Growth	19.0%	—	—	—

*Fiscal year change

2015 Year-End Financials

Return on assets: 6.0%   Cash ($ mil.): 13
Return on equity: 7.5%
Current ratio: 2.20

THE REGENTS OF THE UNIVERSITY OF COLORADO

EXECUTIVES

Medical Director, Scott Joy
Executive Vice President, Juan Garcia-Oyervides
Legislative Council Vice President, Amanda Miller
Vice Chair Of Clinical Research, April Armstrong
Auditors: CLIFTONLARSONALLEN LLP GREENW

LOCATIONS

HQ: THE REGENTS OF THE UNIVERSITY OF
  COLORADO
  3100 MARINE ST STE 48157, BOULDER, CO
  803031058
Phone: 303 735-6624
Web: WWW.UCDENVER.EDU

PRODUCTS/OPERATIONS

Selected Campuses
  University
University of Colorado - Colorado Springs
  University
University of Colorado Anschutz Medical Campus

HISTORICAL FINANCIALS

Company Type: Private

Income Statement   FYE: June 30

	REVENUE ($ mil.)	NET INCOME ($ mil.)	NET PROFIT MARGIN	EMPLOYEES
06/16	3,451	72	2.1%	12,980
06/10	2,261	337	14.9%	—
Annual Growth	7.3%	(22.5%)	—	—

2016 Year-End Financials

Return on assets: 3.3%   Cash ($ mil.): 127
Return on equity: 2.1%
Current ratio: 0.80

THE ROBERT PACKER HOSPITAL

EXECUTIVES

Principal, Joseph A Scopelliti
Director, Jeremy Shank
Director, Staci Thompson
Personnel Director, Frank Pinkowsky
Auditors: LB PRICEWATERHOUSECOOPERS LLP

LOCATIONS

HQ: THE ROBERT PACKER HOSPITAL
  1 GUTHRIE SQ STE B, SAYRE, PA 188401698
Phone: 570 888-6666

HISTORICAL FINANCIALS

Company Type: Private

Income Statement   FYE: June 30

	REVENUE ($ mil.)	NET INCOME ($ mil.)	NET PROFIT MARGIN	EMPLOYEES
06/15	324	61	18.9%	1,400
06/14	292	47	16.4%	—
06/10	254	46	18.1%	—
06/09	223	32	14.3%	—
Annual Growth	6.4%	11.4%	—	—

2015 Year-End Financials

Return on assets: 11.3%   Cash ($ mil.): 4
Return on equity: 18.9%
Current ratio: 0.50

THE RUDOLPH/LIBBE COMPANIES INC

The corporate model of a conglomerate composed of independent unrelated businesses is not for The Rudolph/Libbe Companies. The group of companies can build or oversee real estate projects (general contractor Rudolph/Libbe Inc.); perform mechanical electrical and structural work (GEM Industrial); and then represent those properties in the market (RLWest Properties). Operating in the Ohio/Michigan corridor the group provides site selection design/build and construction management. Its portfolio includes industrial retail municipal residential educational health care and mixed-use projects. Fritz and Phil Rudolph and their cousin Allan Libbe founded flagship subsidiary Rudolph/Libbe Inc. in 1955.

The Rudolph/Libbe Companies also has a partnership with Winter Construction. The contracting partnership Winter RLG specializes in industrial construction for the automotive food processing industrial manufacturing power generation and distribution industries. Clients have included Campbell Soup FedEx and Arconic.

In 2009 Rudolph/Libbe's real estate development division merged with another Ohio-based firm Park West Management & Development. The resulting RLWest Properties offers property management build-to-suit for lease or purchase and land sites for sale in Ohio.

EXECUTIVES

Chairman, Bill Rudolph
Board of Directors, John A Libbe
Auditors: REHMANN ROBSON TOLEDO OH

LOCATIONS

HQ: THE RUDOLPH/LIBBE COMPANIES INC
6494 LATCHA RD, WALBRIDGE, OH 434659788
Phone: 419 241-5000

COMPETITORS

Albert M. Higley	Messer Construction
Atlas Industrial	Ruhlin
Holdings	Skanska USA Building
Danis	

HISTORICAL FINANCIALS

Company Type: Private

Income Statement

				FYE: December 31
	REVENUE ($ mil.)	NET INCOME ($ mil.)	NET PROFIT MARGIN	EMPLOYEES
12/15	425	16	3.8%	600
12/14	17	14	83.2%	—
12/13	319	8	2.7%	—
12/12	375	13	3.6%	—
Annual Growth	4.2%	6.2%	—	—

2015 Year-End Financials

Return on assets: 13.1%
Return on equity: 3.8%
Current ratio: 1.10

Cash ($ mil.): 18

THE RUTLAND HOSPITAL INC ACT 220

For those seeking health care in the New England region Rutland Regional Medical Center (RRMC) just might be the destination for you. Part of Rutland Regional Health Services it runs a hospital that boasts more than 120 beds and serves patients in Vermont and eastern New York. RRMC offers about 40 medical specialties including cancer care diabetes treatment and total joint replacement. The acute-care facility also has centers dedicated to cardiac rehabilitation and women's health. To meet growing community medical needs RRMC also operates a prostate care unit and a 30-bed psychiatric unit. Along with a range of specialty care options RRMC administers primary care and emergency medical transport.

Operations

Established in 1896 RRMC gets nearly half of its patient income from Medicare accounts about 20% from Blue Cross and Blue Shield contracts and the balance from a mix of commercial managed care contracts Medicaid and self-pay patients. The facility provides about $6 million in charity care each year.

Providing preventive diagnostic acute and rehabilitative services RRMC is the second largest hospital in Vermont and is a not-for-profit organization dedicated to improving the health of families and individuals. The 123-bed hospital employs more than 1600 professional and support staff including 227 providers trained in 36 specialty areas.

Affiliated facilities in the RRMC network include an orthopedic clinic a sports medicine center a health plan and a health foundation as well as two long-term care centers.

The Center has some 33900 Emergency visits 412 new births and 230600 inpatients and outpatients registrations a year.

Geographic Reach

RRMC serves communities in Rutland County and surrounding portions of southern and central Vermont as well as eastern New York. It operates about 25 locations in Rutland Vermont as well as single facilities in towns including East Dorset Killington and Poultney Vermont.

Financial Performance

In fiscal 2014 (September year end) the company reported a 4% revenue increase. Net Patients revenues accounted for 95% of the total. Medicare Medicaid and commercial accounted for 32% 17% and 15% of total net patient's revenues respectively.

The company net profits declined by 15% that year.

Strategy

In fiscal 2016 RRMC plans to seek input from community members on their health concerns to help identify the top health issues facing Rutland County through a Community Health Needs Assessment. (The company undertake this work every three years to collect input toward a county-wide health improvement plan based on data such as illness injury and death rates community opinions and resources available. Information from regional state and national reports along with input from consumers and community leaders is compiled and analyzed for this purpose).

To further improve efficiencies and reduce medical spending RRMC is participating in Vermont's Blueprint for Health program which seeks to coordinate care between various medical providers. For instance through the program the hospital is helping to implement a care management infrastructure for patients with chronic diseases.

Company Background

To expand services in the region RRMC expanded into new markets and entered into collaborations with other area providers. It also increased its specialist offerings; in 2012 for instance RRMC added a wing with six private patient rooms for inpatient psychiatric care. In 2013 it also announced plans to open an outpatient center for addiction recovery.

The hospital in 2011 upgraded its information systems through a 20-month $10 million initiative to install an electronic health record (EHR) system that now manages the clinical administrative human resources and financial aspects of RRMC's daily operations. What helped to fund its IT initiatives was RRMC's decision to shutter its 12-unit inpatient rehabilitation facility which was completed in late 2012. The move is expected to save the hospital some $3 million annually. The hospital took other restructuring measures to shore up its finances in 2012 due to a budget gap created by state caps on expenses.

EXECUTIVES

Vice President Clinical Services, Barbara Robinson

LOCATIONS

HQ: THE RUTLAND HOSPITAL INC ACT 220
160 ALLEN ST, RUTLAND, VT 057014595
Phone: 802 775-7111
Web: WWW.RRMC.ORG

PRODUCTS/OPERATIONS

2014 Sales

	% of total
Net patients revenue	95
Other revenue	5
Total	**100**

Selected Services

Acute care
Cancer
Cardiology
Diagnostic imaging
ENT and audiology
Laboratory
Orthopedics
Preventative care
Surgery
Women's health

COMPETITORS

Ellis Hospital	Southwestern Vermont
Fletcher Allen Health	Health Care
Care	Springfield Hospital
New England Alliance	
for Health	

HISTORICAL FINANCIALS

Company Type: Private

Income Statement

				FYE: September 30
	REVENUE ($ mil.)	NET INCOME ($ mil.)	NET PROFIT MARGIN	EMPLOYEES
09/15	228	4	1.9%	1,350
09/14	220	10	4.6%	—
09/13	213	8	4.0%	—
09/10	181	(1)	—	—
Annual Growth	4.8%	—	—	—

2015 Year-End Financials

Return on assets: 5.0%
Return on equity: 1.9%
Current ratio: 1.10

Cash ($ mil.): 12

THE SCHOOL BOARD OF BROWARD COUNTY FLORIDA

EXECUTIVES

Superintendent, Robert W Runcie
Senior Manager, Joy Emerson
Personnel Manager, Joanne Nitti
Personnel Manager, Johanna Lewis

LOCATIONS

HQ: THE SCHOOL BOARD OF BROWARD COUNTY FLORIDA
600 SE 3RD AVE, FORT LAUDERDALE, FL 333013125
Phone: 754 321-0000

HISTORICAL FINANCIALS

Company Type: Private

Income Statement

				FYE: June 30
	REVENUE ($ mil.)	NET INCOME ($ mil.)	NET PROFIT MARGIN	EMPLOYEES
06/16	2,630	(37)	—	31,174
06/15	2,536	186	7.3%	—
06/11	2,515	(37)	—	—
Annual Growth	0.9%	—	—	—

2016 Year-End Financials

Return on assets: 6.8%
Return on equity: (-1.4%)
Current ratio: 1.40

Cash ($ mil.): 671

THE SCHOOL BOARD OF MIAMI-DADE COUNTY

EXECUTIVES

Chairman of the Board, Perla Tabares Hantman
Purchasing Director, Janice C Sanchez
Plant & Facilities Manager, Christopher Moran
Director, Jairo Garzo
Executive Director, Marla Berenson
Administrative Assistant, Ana Herrera
Auditors: MCGLADREY LLP MIAMI FLORIDA

LOCATIONS

HQ: THE SCHOOL BOARD OF MIAMI-DADE COUNTY
1450 NE 2ND AVE, MIAMI, FL 331321308
Phone: 305 995-1000
Web: WWW.DADESCHOOLS.NET

HISTORICAL FINANCIALS

Company Type: Private

Income Statement

FYE: June 30

	REVENUE ($ mil.)	NET INCOME ($ mil.)	NET PROFIT MARGIN	EMPLOYEES
06/16	3,631	136	3.8%	9
06/13	3,302	(127)	—	—
06/12	3,220	(237)	—	—
Annual Growth	3.0%	—	—	—

2016 Year-End Financials

Return on assets: 1.5%
Return on equity: 3.8%
Current ratio: 0.10

Cash ($ mil.): 55

THE SCHOOL DISTRICT OF OSCEOLA COUNTY FL

EXECUTIVES

Superintendent, Melba Luciano
Board of Directors, Bill Collins
Director of Finance, Sarah Graber
Principal, George Sullivan
Executive Secretary, Kim Pearce
Department Manager, Debra Tremblay
Department Manager, Don Liesch
Department Manager, Harry Moore
Auditors: MOORE STEPHENS LOVELACE PA

LOCATIONS

HQ: THE SCHOOL DISTRICT OF OSCEOLA COUNTY FL
817 BILL BECK BLVD, KISSIMMEE, FL 347444492
Phone: 407 870-4600
Web: WWW.OSCEOLA.K12.FL.US

HISTORICAL FINANCIALS

Company Type: Private

Income Statement

FYE: June 30

	REVENUE ($ mil.)	NET INCOME ($ mil.)	NET PROFIT MARGIN	EMPLOYEES
06/16	601	37	6.2%	6,250
06/15	545	6	1.3%	—
06/14	527	(21)	—	—
06/13	490	(7)	—	—
Annual Growth	7.0%	—	—	—

2016 Year-End Financials

Return on assets: 1.0%
Return on equity: 6.2%
Current ratio: —

Cash ($ mil.): 94

THE SCHOOL DISTRICT OF WEST PALM BEACH COUNTY

EXECUTIVES

Purchasing Agent, Jackie Walsh
Project Manager, Natasha Bell-Hayden
Manager, Michael Via
Administrative Assistant, Bryan Borck
Auditors: RSM US LLP WEST PALM BEACH F

LOCATIONS

HQ: THE SCHOOL DISTRICT OF WEST PALM BEACH COUNTY
3300 FOREST HILL BLVD, WEST PALM BEACH, FL 334065813
Phone: 561 434-8747
Web: WWW.PALMBEACHSCHOOLS.ORG

HISTORICAL FINANCIALS

Company Type: Private

Income Statement

FYE: June 30

	REVENUE ($ mil.)	NET INCOME ($ mil.)	NET PROFIT MARGIN	EMPLOYEES
06/16	1,986	64	3.2%	40,253
06/15	1,903	(61)	—	—
Annual Growth	4.4%	—	—	—

THE SCOULAR COMPANY

The Scoular Company doesn't move food from farm to table but it does handle a good portion of the trip. The company buys sells stores handles and transports agricultural products (mainly grains) worldwide. It gets the mainstays of farming — corn hay millet rice sorghum soybeans and wheat — where they need to go. The company transports these products via rail truck barge and seagoing container vessels. Scoular's other divisions offer fishmeal products for farm-animal pet and aquaculture feeds; ingredients for food manufacturers; renewable fuels; and truck freight brokering. It has customers in Asia Africa the Americas and Europe. George Scoular founded the business in Nebraska in 1892.

Operations

The company operates 130 independent units that together make up a grain marketing network that handles 420 million bushels of grain annually and includes facilities in 18 states Canada and Mexico. In addition to buying selling handling and transporting grain Scoular offers risk management services.

Geographic Reach

Omaha-based Scoular and it affiliates have operations in 18 US states as well as in Calgary and Montreal Canada Mexico Argentina Brazil Uruguay China and Singapore. The company has nearly 30 merchandising offices and some 93 grain-handling facilities in North America with a storage capacity topping 130 million bushels.

Sales and Marketing

Scoular serves customers in the aquaculture flour milling food processing and manufacturing grain production industrial ag processing livestock feeding and manufacturing pet food manufacturing and renewable fuels sectors. Its services include bagging blending cleaning containerizing organic certifying packaging sorting sourcing and storage.

Financial Performance

Scoular's sales totaled $5.9 billion in 2015 compared with about $6 billion in 2014.

Strategy

The company has built itself out piece by piece scouring the landscape for businesses that fit into its portfolio through acquisition or partnership. In 2015 Scoular formed a joint venture with Nova del Mar in Mexico in which Scoular will market fishmeal that Nova makes from fish from the Sea of Cortez.

Mergers and Acquisitions

Scoular capped off two years of smaller acquisitions with the purchase of the Specialty Crops Division of Legumex Walker Inc. a global merchandiser and processor of special crops for some (Canadian) $94 million. The business processes special crops at 14 facilities in Canada the US and China. Some of the special crops are lentils whole and split peas edible beans chickpeas canaryseed flaxseed and sunflower seed.

In August 2013 Scouler acquired the assets of Kansas-based Tribune Grain which include a grain elevator in Tribune Kansas that's located on the Kansas and Oklahoma Railroad as well as two seasonally-operated rural truck facilities. (In addition to the Tribune area facilities Scoular operates 10 other grain elevators in Kansas and eastern Colorado.)

EXECUTIVES

Vice President, John Heck
Senior Vice President Producer Markets Div, George Schieber
Chairman and President, David M. Faith
SVP and Division General Manager, Todd McQueen
SVP and Division General Manager, John Messerich
CFO, Richard A. (Rick) Cogdill
CEO, Paul T. Maass
CIO, Jeff Schreiner
SVP and Division General Manager, Bob Ludington
Vice President Finance, Omer Sagheer
Senior Vice President, Curt Engel
Vice President Information Technology, Jim Konz
Vice President Manager Directo, Tim Dingman

LOCATIONS

HQ: THE SCOULAR COMPANY
2027 DODGE ST STE 200, OMAHA, NE 681021229
Phone: 402 342-3500
Web: WWW.SCOULARBALLROOM.COM

PRODUCTS/OPERATIONS

Selected Customer Industries Products and Services

Aquaculture (feed ingredients)
- Animal fats
- Animal proteins
- Fish oil
- Fishmeal
- Grain byproducts
- Vegetable fats
- Vegetable proteins

Flour milling (buying selling storing and shipping)
- Durum
- Hard red spring
- Hard red winter
- Soft red winter

Food manufacturing and processing (conventional organic and functional ingredients blending packaging co-packing)
- Ingredients
- Proteins
- Dairy
- Pea
- Potato
- Rice
- Soy
- Specialty flours
- Soy
- Starches
- Pea
- Potato
- Rice
- Tapioca
- Textured proteins
- Soy

Grain production (marketing buying storing handling and shipping programs)
- Corn
- Hay
- Millet
- Rice
- Sorghum
- Soybeans
- Wheat

Industrial ag processing (feedstock supply byproduct marketing and crush risk management)
- Products
- Citrus pulp
- Distillers grains
- Hominy feed
- Wheat mill feeds
- Whole cottonseed

Identity-preserved grain
- Corn
- Soybeans
- Wheat
- White corn

Livestock feeding and feed manufacturing (grain and feed ingredient sourcing risk management)
- Grains and oilseeds
- Barley
- Canola
- Corn
- Field peas
- Flax
- Lentils
- Rye
- Soybeans
- Wheat
- Other
- Canola meal
- Citrus pulp
- Distillers grains
- Hominy feed
- Wheat mill feed
- Whole cottonseed

Pet food manufacturing (ingredients)
- Products
- Fats
- Flours
- Gravy dust mix
- Proteins
- Starches
- Yellow corn
- Sourcing and solutions
- Animal oils
- Animal proteins
- Fish oil
- Fishmeal
- Frozen fish

Fruits
Grain products
Pea protein fiber flour and starch
Pomaces
Specialty starches flours
Variety meats
Vegetable oils
Vegetable proteins
Vegetables

Transportation
- Container and vessel (freight forwarding logistics and documentation in more than 50 countries)
- Rail truck and barge (logistics for shipping agricultural products in North America)

COMPETITORS

ADM	Excel Maritime
Andersons	Carriers
Bartlett and Company	Louis Dreyfus Group
Bunge Limited	Syntroleum
CHS	TBS International
Cargill	TORM
DeBruce Grain	

HISTORICAL FINANCIALS

Company Type: Private

Income Statement

FYE: May 31

	REVENUE ($ mil.)	NET INCOME ($ mil.)	NET PROFIT MARGIN	EMPLOYEES
05/16	4,667	(10)	—	801
05/15	234	14	6.0%	—
05/14	228	29	13.0%	—
05/13	211	27	12.9%	—
Annual Growth	180.6%	—	—	—

2016 Year-End Financials

Return on assets: 3.1% Cash ($ mil.): 20
Return on equity: (-0.2%)
Current ratio: 0.40

THE SHEPHERD GOOD HOSPITAL INC

Leading its citizens toward good health Good Shepherd Health System provides medical and surgical care to patients throughout the Piney Woods region of northeastern Texas. Its flagship facility is Good Shepherd Medical Center in Longview a more than 425-bed regional referral hospital providing specialty care in areas such as trauma cardiology neurology and pulmonology. Good Shepherd also has small inpatient facilities as well as a freestanding outpatient surgery center and several primary care Family Health Centers located throughout its service area. The hospital was established in 1935 as the 50-bed Gregg Memorial Hospital. Duke LifePoint Healthcare is buying Good Shepherd Health System.

Operations

The health system also operates the Institute for Healthy Living. The institute functions by offering patients two paths toward wellness. First it offers advanced outpatient rehabilitative services and educational programs for patients who require a medically guided continuum of care. Second it provides a comprehensive fitness and wellness facility for both patients and employers to help improve and maintain their health with the hope that preventative care will keep area residents from facing serious health problems that could land them in the hospital. The institute is also home to a full-service spa outdoor walking trail Healthy Living Hideaway children's play center and classrooms for community educational programs meetings and special events.

Strategy

As the health care landscape becomes increasingly complicated with regulations and new technologies and areas of expertise many health care systems have made moves to join together in order to expand care services and save on operating costs. In 2015 Good Shepherd Health System announced plans to consider such an alliance with another system; one possibility would be to establish an Accountable Care Organization (ACO).

EXECUTIVES

Director of Pharmacy, Brad Osburg
Vice President of Ancillary Services, Keith Creel
Director of Home Healthcare Srv, Jackie Weeks

LOCATIONS

HQ: THE SHEPHERD GOOD HOSPITAL INC
700 E MARSHALL AVE, LONGVIEW, TX 756015572
Phone: 903 315-2000

COMPETITORS

Community Health Systems
East Texas Medical Center Regional Healthcare
HCA
Memorial Health System of East Texas
Select Medical
Tenet Healthcare
Trinity Mother Frances Hospital and Clinics
Wadley Regional Medical Center
Woodland Heights Medical Center

HISTORICAL FINANCIALS

Company Type: Private

Income Statement

FYE: September 30

	REVENUE ($ mil.)	NET INCOME ($ mil.)	NET PROFIT MARGIN	EMPLOYEES
09/15	279	0	0.3%	2,200
09/14	244	(7)	—	—
09/13	270	2	0.9%	—
09/12	282	(11)	—	—
Annual Growth	(0.4%)	—	—	—

2015 Year-End Financials

Return on assets: 8.5% Cash ($ mil.): 3
Return on equity: 0.3%
Current ratio: 1.40

THE SOMMERS COMPANY

EXECUTIVES

President, Jimmy F Sommers
Board of Directors, Michael Dionne
Vice-President, Nicholas Pastorelli
Auditors: TJS DEEMER DANA LLP SAVANNAH

LOCATIONS

HQ: THE SOMMERS COMPANY
1000 SOMMERS BLVD, RICHMOND HILL, GA
313248817
Phone: 800 654-6466
Web: WWW.SOMMERSOIL.COM

HISTORICAL FINANCIALS
Company Type: Private

Income Statement
FYE: June 30

	REVENUE ($ mil.)	NET INCOME ($ mil.)	NET PROFIT MARGIN	EMPLOYEES
06/16	296	1	0.4%	30
06/15	426	1	0.3%	—
06/14	587	1	0.2%	—
Annual Growth	(29.0%)	(12.8%)	—	—

2016 Year-End Financials
Return on assets: 3.7%   Cash ($ mil.): 8
Return on equity: 0.4%
Current ratio: 1.30

THE SOUTH TENNESSEE OIL COMPANY INC

EXECUTIVES
President, Jonathan Edwards
Manager, Sherry McFall
Chief Operating Officer, Doug Holden
Manager, Bruce Caruthers
Auditors: AD REGEON & ASSOCIATES COLU

LOCATIONS
HQ: THE SOUTH TENNESSEE OIL COMPANY INC
105 HELTON DR, LAWRENCEBURG, TN 384642253
Phone: 931 762-9600
Web: WWW.QUIKMART.COM

HISTORICAL FINANCIALS
Company Type: Private

Income Statement
FYE: December 31

	REVENUE ($ mil.)	NET INCOME ($ mil.)	NET PROFIT MARGIN	EMPLOYEES
12/15	180	1	1.0%	415
12/14	225	2	0.9%	—
12/13	226	1	0.8%	—
12/12	222	1	0.6%	—
Annual Growth	(6.9%)	7.8%	—	—

2015 Year-End Financials
Return on assets: 1.1%   Cash ($ mil.): 5
Return on equity: 1.0%
Current ratio: 2.90

THE SOUTHEASTERN CONFERENCE

EXECUTIVES
Commissioner, Greg Sankey
Commissioner, Michael Slide
Auditors: BARFIELD MURPHY SHANK & SMITH

LOCATIONS
HQ: THE SOUTHEASTERN CONFERENCE
2201 RICHARD ARRINGTN JR, BIRMINGHAM, AL
352031103
Phone: 205 949-8960
Web: WWW.SECSPORTS.COM

HISTORICAL FINANCIALS
Company Type: Private

Income Statement
FYE: August 31

	REVENUE ($ mil.)	NET INCOME ($ mil.)	NET PROFIT MARGIN	EMPLOYEES
08/15	527	17	3.3%	30
08/14	325	2	0.7%	—
08/13	314	(3)	—	—
08/12	273	2	0.9%	—
Annual Growth	24.5%	89.8%	—	—

2015 Year-End Financials
Return on assets: —   Cash ($ mil.): 27
Return on equity: 3.3%
Current ratio: —

THE STAMFORD HOSPITAL

EXECUTIVES
President, Brian Grissler
Manager, Liz Carrena
Executive Director, Anne Morris
Auditors: ERNST & YOUNG LLP NEW YORK N

LOCATIONS
HQ: THE STAMFORD HOSPITAL
1 HOSPITAL PLZ, STAMFORD, CT 069023602
Phone: 203 325-7000
Web: WWW.STAMFORDHOSPITAL.COM

HISTORICAL FINANCIALS
Company Type: Private

Income Statement
FYE: September 30

	REVENUE ($ mil.)	NET INCOME ($ mil.)	NET PROFIT MARGIN	EMPLOYEES
09/16	563	71	12.7%	2,000
09/15	493	67	13.6%	—
09/14	495	13	2.7%	—
09/13	491	7	1.5%	—
Annual Growth	4.6%	115.2%	—	—

2016 Year-End Financials
Return on assets: 15.2%   Cash ($ mil.): 126
Return on equity: 12.7%
Current ratio: 1.20

THE STELLAR COMPANIES INC

EXECUTIVES
Chief Executive Officer, Ronald H Foster Jr

Manager, Diane Hayes
Engineer, Austin Calcote
Administrative Assistant, Clarisa Ramos
Administrative Assistant, Judith Raker
Manager, Laura Herd
Auditors: RSM US LLP JACKSONVILLE FLOR

LOCATIONS
HQ: THE STELLAR COMPANIES INC
2900 HARTLEY RD, JACKSONVILLE, FL 322578221
Phone: 904 899-9393

HISTORICAL FINANCIALS
Company Type: Private

Income Statement
FYE: September 30

	REVENUE ($ mil.)	NET INCOME ($ mil.)	NET PROFIT MARGIN	EMPLOYEES
09/16	285	6	2.3%	600
09/15	336	2	0.9%	—
09/14	341	0	0.1%	—
09/12	248	15	6.4%	—
Annual Growth	3.5%	(19.7%)	—	—

2016 Year-End Financials
Return on assets: 16.9%   Cash ($ mil.): 16
Return on equity: 2.3%
Current ratio: 0.90

THE SUSAN THOMPSON BUFFETT FOUNDATION

EXECUTIVES
Principal, Carol Loomis
Officer, Katy Mitchell

LOCATIONS
HQ: THE SUSAN THOMPSON BUFFETT FOUNDATION
222 KIEWIT PLZ, OMAHA, NE 68131
Phone: 402 943-1300
Web: WWW.BUFFETTSCHOLARSHIPS.ORG

HISTORICAL FINANCIALS
Company Type: Private

Income Statement
FYE: December 31

	REVENUE ($ mil.)	NET INCOME ($ mil.)	NET PROFIT MARGIN	EMPLOYEES
12/15	250	(111)	—	3
12/14	246	(296)	—	—
12/09	128	123	95.9%	—
Annual Growth	11.8%	—	—	—

2015 Year-End Financials
Return on assets: —   Cash ($ mil.): 3
Return on equity: (-44.4%)
Current ratio: —

THE TRUSTEES OF PRINCETON UNIVERSITY

This prince's kingdom is covered with ivy. As one of the eight elite Ivy League schools in the

Northeastern US Princeton is a research university that offers students degrees across 34 departments and 47 interdisciplinary certificate programs. It boasts more than 8000 students (5300 undergraduate and 2700 graduate students). The highly selective school which enjoys an undergraduate student-faculty ratio of 6:1 admits about 8% of its total applicants. Nobel Prize winners associated with Princeton include Woodrow Wilson writer Toni Morrison and physicist Richard Feynman. One of the nation's wealthiest universities Princeton has an endowment of more than $16 billion.

Operations

The Princeton campus comprises six residential colleges that are organized by grade level (freshmen sophomores juniors and seniors).

The university which is supported by 1140 faculty members that include visitors and part-time appointments operates three schools: the School of Architecture School of Engineering and Applied Science and the Woodrow Wilson School of Public and International Affairs. Princeton also has a large research base with some $200 million in funding per year primarily from federal grants. Its plasma physics research laboratory has a sizable research contract with the federal government.

Geographic Reach

Located in Princeton New Jersey Princeton's campus includes some 180 buildings that cover about 500 acres.

Sales and Marketing

Princeton sources its students from more than 98 countries. International graduate students hail primarily from Canada China India Germany and Korea. Some 60% of the university's undergraduate students receive financial aid. The average undergraduate financial aid reward for the Class of 2016 is $39700.

Financial Performance

For an Ivy League university with a top reputation in the US and internationally Princeton has not suffered as a result of turbulent economic conditions as much as some of its lower-ranked peers.

Company Background

Founded in 1746 as the College of New Jersey Princeton is the fourth-oldest college in the nation. In 1756 the college was moved to Nassau Hall which served as the temporary capitol of the US in 1783 and is still part of the Princeton campus.

EXECUTIVES

VP Finance and Treasurer, Carolyn N. Ainslie
President, Christopher L. Eisgruber
Dean Admission, Janet L. Rapelye
Dean Undergraduate Students, Kathleen Deignan
President Princeton University Investment Co., Andrew K. Golden
Dean Religious Life and the Chapel, Alison L. Boden
Dean Wilson School of Public and International Affairs, Cecilia E. Rouse
VP Information Technology and CIO, Jay Dominick
Dean School of Engineering and Applied Science, H. Vincent Poor
Provost, David S. Lee
Dean of the Faculty, Deborah A. Prentice
Dean Graduate School, Sanjeev R. Kulkarni
Dean of the College, Jill S. Dolan
Dean Research, Pablo G. Debenedetti
Dean School of Architecture, Monica Ponce de Leon
EVP, Treby Williams
Payroll Manager Payroll Office of the Vice President for Finance and Treasurer, Lora J Benson
Communications Specialist Office of the Vice President for Facilities, Cynthia L Suter
Assistant Vice President Human Resources, Romy Riddick

Vice President for Campus Life, Rochelle Calhoun
Chairman, Kathryn A. Hall
Vice Chairman, Brent L. Henry
Senior Financial Data Analyst and Treasurer, Elizabeth Totten
Auditors: PRICEWATERHOUSECOOPERS LLP NE

LOCATIONS

HQ: THE TRUSTEES OF PRINCETON UNIVERSITY
1 NASSAU HALL, PRINCETON, NJ 085442001
Phone: 609 258-3000
Web: WWW.ETCWEB.PRINCETON.EDU

PRODUCTS/OPERATIONS

Select Councils Institutes and Centers

Bendheim Center for Finance
Center for Migration and Development
Center for the Study of Religion
Council of the Humanities
Council on Science and Technology
Davis Center for Historical Studies
James Madison Program in American Ideals and Institutions
Lewis-Sigler Institute for Integrative Genomics
Liechtenstein Institute on Self-Determination
Princeton Environmental Institute (PEI)
Princeton Institute for International and Regional Studies (PIIRS)
Princeton Institute for the Science and Technology of Materials (PRISM)
Princeton Writing Program
Program of Freshman Seminars in the Residential Colleges
Program in Law and Public Affairs
Program in Neuroscience
University Center for Human Values

COMPETITORS

Brown University	Harvard University
Columbia University	Penn
Cornell University	Rutgers University
Dartmouth	Yale University

HISTORICAL FINANCIALS

Company Type: Private

Income Statement

FYE: June 30

	REVENUE ($ mil.)	NET INCOME ($ mil.)	NET PROFIT MARGIN	EMPLOYEES
06/16	1,687	(628)	—	6,000
06/15	1,621	1,827	112.8%	—
06/14	1,566	2,764	176.5%	—
06/13	1,479	1,339	90.5%	—
Annual Growth	4.5%	—	—	—

2016 Year-End Financials

Return on assets: 6.1%   Cash ($ mil.): 8
Return on equity: (-37.2%)
Current ratio: —

THE TRUSTEES OF WHEATON COLLEGE

Wheaton College located in Wheaton Illinois — not to be confused with a school of the same name in Massachusetts — is a interdenominational Christian college. The private school offers dozens of liberal arts programs of study including a Ph.D. in Biblical and Theological Studies to its undergraduate and graduate students. Liberal arts programs include literature music fine arts biology economics and psychology. Wheaton College has about 3000 students and a 12:1 student-teacher ratio. Wheaton College was founded in 1860 and is

named after Warren L. Wheaton who donated land to the school.

Operations

Wheaton College is meant to be residential for undergraduates. Nearly 90% of students live on campus. The school has two underclass residence halls to house first and second year students. Williston Hall houses only second year students. McManis-Evans houses second third and fourth year students.

Sales and Marketing

The school's graduates include 1500 business leaders 540 government & foreign service professionals 2800 in medical professionals nearly 400 scientists and researchers 14 college presidents or provosts more than 3600 in ministers and evangelists worldwide 550 in the arts plus more than 5000 teachers 560 attorneys and 2300 in business and commerce.

Financial Performance

The school's revenue comes from tuition fees and annual fund gifts.

EXECUTIVES

V Pres, Mark Dillon, age 63
Auditors: CROWE HORWATH LLP CHICAGO IL

LOCATIONS

HQ: THE TRUSTEES OF WHEATON COLLEGE
501 COLLEGE AVE, WHEATON, IL 601875501
Phone: 630 752-5000
Web: WWW.WHEATON.EDU

PRODUCTS/OPERATIONS

Selected Academics

Academics
Arts & Sciences | B.A. B.S.
Ancient Languages
Anthropology
Applied Health Science
Art
Biblical Archaeology
Biblical & Theological Studies
Biology
Business/Economics
Chemistry
Christian Education & Ministry
Communication
Computer Science
Economics
Elementary Education
Engineering (Dual Degree)
English
Environmental Studies
French
Geology
German
History
History/Social Science
Interdisciplinary Studies
International Relations
Mathematics
Music (6 majors see Conservatory information)
Nursing (Liberal Arts)
Philosophy
Physics
Political Science
Psychology
Secondary Education (2nd major only)
Sociology
Spanish
Conservatory of Music
Composition
Education
History/Literature
Music with Elective Studies in an Outside Field
Music with Emphasis in a Music-Related Field
Performance
Undergraduate Certificates
Adventure Leadership Ministry
Christian Spirituality
Early Christian Studies
Gender Studies
HNGR - Human Needs and Global Resources (Development Studies)

Journalism
Military Science
Pre-Law
Urban Studies
Youth Ministry
Master of Arts Degrees | M.A. M.A.T.
Biblical Archaeology
Biblical Exegesis
Biblical Studies
Christian Formation & Ministry
Clinical Psychology
Counseling Ministries
Evangelism and Leadership
Theology
History of Christianity
Intercultural Studies
Intercultural Studies & TESOL
Missions
Teaching Elementary or Secondary
Graduate Certificates
TESOL
Urban Evangelism
Urban Mission
Doctoral Degrees | Ph.D. Psy. D.
Philosophy in Biblical & Theological Studies
Psychology in Clinical Psychology (Psy.D.)
Special Programs
Archaeological Excavation in Israel
Arts in London
HoneyRock
HNGR - Human Needs and Global Resources
International internship opportunities
Iron Sharpens Iron
Marine Biology in Belize
May in Asia
Music and Ministry in the Great Cities of Europe
Pre-Health Professions
Pre-Law Program
ROTC
Science Station
Wheaton in Chicago
Wheaton in East Africa
Wheaton in England
Wheaton in France
Wheaton in Germany
Wheaton in the Holy Lands
Wheaton in Latin America
Wheaton in Spain
Wheaton in Washington D.C.

HISTORICAL FINANCIALS

Company Type: Private

Income Statement

FYE: June 30

	REVENUE ($ mil.)	NET INCOME ($ mil.)	NET PROFIT MARGIN	EMPLOYEES
06/15	179	37	20.6%	820
06/14	187	50	26.8%	—
06/13	116	53	46.0%	—
06/12	110	(9)	—	—
Annual Growth	17.6%	—	—	—

2015 Year-End Financials

Return on assets: 4.6%   Cash ($ mil.): 32
Return on equity: 20.6%
Current ratio: 2.70

THE TURNER CORPORATION

The Turner Corporation a subsidiary of German construction giant HOCHTIEF is the leading general building and construction management firm in the US (as ranked by Engineering News-Record) ahead of rivals Bechtel and Fluor. The firm operates primarily through subsidiary Turner Construction and has worked on notable projects such as Madison Square Garden the UN headquarters Yankee Stadium the Taipei 101 Tower and the 68000-seat open-air stadium for the San Francisco 49ers. Known for its large projects also offers services for midsized and smaller projects and provides interior construction and renovation services.

Operations

Turner works on more than 1500 projects in a year totaling $8 billion in volume. The group has divisions dedicated to serving the aviation health care biotechnology public assembly sports education justice and industrial sectors. Its homeland security group was established in order handle a growing demand for security systems and protection. The unit installed detection equipment in some 450 airports throughout the US. Turner Corporation also has an arm specializing in green building with a focus on Leadership in Energy and Environmental Design (LEED) -certified projects. Turner Green Building has more than 400 LEED projects and green projects either completed or in progress.

Turner Corporation has subsidiaries providing auxiliary operations. Turner's risk management department offers contract review project safety and claims handling. Turner Logistics handles procurement and supply chain management for projects and Turner Facilities Management Solutions offers ongoing operations services. Also the Turner School of Construction Management provides training for local subcontractors.

Geographic Reach

Dallas-based Turner Corporation boasts a network of offices across the US (with most in California and Ohio) and Canada (Vancouver and Toronto) with an global presence in 20 countries in Europe Africa East Asia India Latin America and the Caribbean.

Sales and Marketing

Turner works on variety of projects from several sectors. It's known for its work in the categories of healthcare education offices commercial properties cultural facilities sports facilities and hotels. The company is also a leader in the green building category.

Strategy

With the construction market rebounding from the economic downturn Turner is looking to high-growth markets in the US and overseas. As of early 2015 it was working on more than 1900 projects 80% of which were Education Commercial or Interior project-related. Some of these projects included the 17000 sq. ft- interior remodel for Salesforce's Vancouver office; the 325000 sq. ft- construction of the LEED-Certified RAND Corporation Headquarters in Santa Monica California; and the 25000-seat Charlotte Coliseum event arena for the City of Charlotte North Carolina.

The company has also been making moves to expand its business abroad in recent years. In 2012 for example Turner partnered with one of India's largest real estate developers Sahara Prime City Ltd. to form Sahara Turner which would lead the development and construction of multiple townships across the country with an approximate value of $2.5 billion by 2017. It also purchased a majority stake in Clark Builders Canada to capitalize on the country's growing construction market.

Turner often partners with fellow US-based HOCHTIEF subsidiary Flatiron which specializes in civil engineering. Examples of the teamwork are the expansions of airports in San Diego and Sacramento.

HISTORY

At the turn of the century an engineer and devout Quaker named Henry Chandlee Turner was convinced that a new type of steel-reinforced concrete (called the Ransome system) would change the construction industry. With this conviction and with the help of his partner D. H. Dixon Turner bought the rights to the technology for $25000 and in 1902 founded Turner Construction Company.

One of the company's early projects was building the stairways for New York's first subway stations. As the Ransome method proved to be successful Turner's reputation grew. Defense contracts during WWI raised Turner's take to $35 million in 1918.

Before the Depression Turner was building high-rises hotels and stadiums. During the economic crash that started in 1929 the company survived by building retail stores churches and public buildings a strategy it would employ successfully in later recessions.

Henry Turner retired in 1941. His brother Archer Turner managed the company during most of the war effort. As WWII raged more than 80% of the company's work was defense-related. Projects included building and managing a submarine base in Oak Ridge Tennessee during the development of the atomic bomb.

In 1947 Henry C. Turner Jr. the founder's son became president and within four years he had led the company to more than $100 million in sales. By the time he stepped down as chairman in 1970 the firm had built skyscrapers futuristic airports and such landmarks as Madison Square Garden and the United Nations Secretariat and Plaza in New York City. Turner went public in 1969.

Howard S. Turner (the final family member to head the business) led the company during the 1970s. The company extended its global presence opening offices in more countries including Iran Pakistan and the United Arab Emirates. Turner also developed construction management services.

In 1984 The Turner Corporation was formed as a holding company for the construction company and the subsidiaries created or acquired as a result of diversification. Property development was one of these activities but by 1987 Turner had begun to dispose of its real estate holdings. It did not move quickly enough however and when the real estate market crashed Turner was caught with a large portfolio.

As commercial projects slowed Turner sought work in more sectors including public works and amusement projects (aquariums arenas hospitals and universities). By 1994 these areas accounted for 70% of business. In 1993 as the building slump continued Turner began a cost-cutting plan which included laying off workers and closing offices. That year the company set up an $8.5 million restructuring reserve and as the real estate market eased into recovery Turner sold more of its real estate holdings.

In 1996 Turner won a contract to build a 10000-seat arena in Salt Lake City to be used for the 2002 Winter Olympics. In 1997 Turner contracted to renovate 811 schools and build two campuses in California's San Fernando Valley and in 1998 it was chosen to manage the construction of the Kansas City Motor Speedway.

Profits were recovering quickly. Nonetheless in 1999 the company agreed to be acquired by German construction giant HOCHTIEF in a $370 million deal that ended Turner's joint venture with Switzerland's Karl Steiner. The company also relocated its corporate headquarters to Dallas that year to take advantage of the construction boom in the US Southwest.

In 2000 Turner created three new business groups to serve the aviation pharmaceutical and sports sectors. By the next year Turner's sports group was working on 17 projects. In 2001 the company was a member of the construction team that responded to the September 11 devastation at Ground Zero in New York City. The next year

the company celebrated its 100th anniversary with an exhibit at the National Building Museum in Washington DC; the exhibit featured drawings and photos of some of Turner's notable projects during the past century. In 2003 Turner Construction acquired the assets of Tompkins Builders the third-largest construction company in the Washington DC area from former rival J.A. Jones Construction Co.

Turner Construction which celebrated its 100th anniversary in 2002 has ranked among the leading general builders in the US since WWI. For 80 of the 100 years the group had a Turner among its senior executives. Howard S. Turner was the last member of the family to serve in the company's senior ranks. The company's appointment of Peter Davoren in 2003 as president of Turner Construction reflected the rise of a new generation of leaders for the unit. Davoren was additionally appointed chairman and CEO in 2007.

Turner Construction announced in 2008 that it had signed the contract on its 15000th major project.

EXECUTIVES

Executive Vice-President, John A Diciurcio
Director, Holly Miller
Director, Jeffrey Coyle
Senior Vice-President, Thomas B Gerlach Jr
Auditors: DELOITTE & TOUCHE LLP DALLAS

LOCATIONS

HQ: THE TURNER CORPORATION
375 HUDSON ST RM 700, NEW YORK, NY 100143667
Phone: 212 229-6000
Web: WWW.TURNERCONSTRUCTION.COM

PRODUCTS/OPERATIONS

Selected Related Companies
E. E. Cruz (infrastructure)
Flatiron Construction Corp. (transportation construction civil engineering)
Clark Builders (51% Canada)

Selected Markets Served
Aviation
Commercial
Cultural and entertainment
Data center
Education
Government
Green building
Health care
Infrastructure
Industrial
Interiors
Pharmaceutical
Public Assembly
Religious
Research and development
Residential/hotel
Sports

Selected Services
Building information modeling
Building maintenance
Construction management
Design-build
Design-build/finance
Facilities management
General construction
Lean construction
Logistics
Medical planning and procurement
Preconstruction consulting
Program management
Project management

COMPETITORS

Balfour Beatty Construction	Hunt Construction
Bechtel	Imperial Construction Group
Clark Construction	Jacobs Engineering
Group	Parsons Corporation
Fluor	Peter Kiewit Sons'
Gilbane Building Company	Skanska
	Structure Tone

HISTORICAL FINANCIALS
Company Type: Private

Income Statement   FYE: December 31

	REVENUE ($ mil.)	NET INCOME ($ mil.)	NET PROFIT MARGIN	EMPLOYEES
12/15	10,523	107	1.0%	5,000
12/14	10,560	95	0.9%	—
12/13	9,522	80	0.8%	—
12/12	8,575	74	0.9%	—
Annual Growth	7.1%	12.9%	—	—

2015 Year-End Financials

Return on assets: 25.8%   Cash ($ mil.): 880
Return on equity: 1.0%
Current ratio: 1.00

THE UNION MEMORIAL HOSPITAL

Not quite for time immemorial but MedStar Union Memorial Hospital (formerly Union Memorial Hospital) has been caring for patients for more than 160 years. The Baltimore-area facility is a specialty acute-care hospital with about 250 beds and more than 620 physicians. Areas of clinical research and expertise include cardiac care orthopedics and sports medicine. In addition it offers a range of inpatient and outpatient services including diabetes and endocrine center eye surgery center general surgery oncology and thoracic and vascular surgery. MedStar Union Memorial offers postgraduate programs orthopedic surgery residencies and hand surgery fellowships. The company is a part of MedStar Health.

Operations

MedStar Union Memorial offers a full array of diagnostic medical surgical and rehabilitative services. The hospital provides graduate medical education through residency programs and fellowship programs. MedStar Union Memorial offers 19 postgraduate first year positions in medicine; a surgical training program; and an orthopedic surgical program. MedStar's Online Clinical Library provides access both onsite and offsite to electronic resources for drug information evidence-based medicine point of care full-test textbooks and more the 400 full-text journals.

The hospital offers 231 acute care beds and 18 rehab beds.

Strategy

Pushing innovation in 2013 MedStar Union Memorial became the first hospital in the US to offer the Rotation Medical Rotator Cuff System a new minimally invasive technology for patients suffering from rotator cuff disease.

To emphasize it parent's brand as part of its future growth strategy Union Memorial Hospital changed its name to MedStar Union Memorial Hospital in 2012.

Company Background

As Union Memorial the company celebrated its sesquicentennial anniversary in 2004. The hospital has been repeatedly recognized as among "America's Best Hospitals" by U.S. News & World Report. It's also considered one of the top 100 hospitals for intensive care and cardiovascular services.

The hospital was founded in 1839.

EXECUTIVES

Vice President, Joseph Smith
Vice President of Human Resour, Holly Adams
Physical Therapy Director, CAROL WEIR

LOCATIONS

HQ: THE UNION MEMORIAL HOSPITAL
201 E UNIVERSITY PKWY, BALTIMORE, MD 212182891
Phone: 410 554-2865
Web: WWW.MEDSTARUNIONMEMORIAL.ORG

PRODUCTS/OPERATIONS

Selected Facilities
Arnold Palmer SportsHealth Center
The Curtis National Hand Center
The Harry and Jeanette Weinberg Heart Institute
Union Memorial Orthopaedics and Sports Medicine
Vascular Institute

COMPETITORS

Anne Arundel Medical Center	LifeBridge Health
Johns Hopkins Health System	St. Agnes HealthCare
	University of Maryland Medical System

HISTORICAL FINANCIALS
Company Type: Private

Income Statement   FYE: June 30

	REVENUE ($ mil.)	NET INCOME ($ mil.)	NET PROFIT MARGIN	EMPLOYEES
06/15	413	10	2.4%	2,400
06/14	427	20	4.8%	—
06/13	408	(1)	—	—
06/11	428	17	4.1%	—
Annual Growth	(0.8%)	(12.9%)	—	—

2015 Year-End Financials

Return on assets: 3.0%   Cash ($ mil.): —
Return on equity: 2.4%
Current ratio: 1.00

THE UNITED STATES PHARMACOPOEIAL CONVENTION

EXECUTIVES

Chief Executive Officer, Ronald T Piervincenzi
Executive Vice-President, Susan De Mars
Chief Financial Officer, Stan Burhans
Manager, Deborah Behrend
Manager, Matthew Valleskey
VP Personnel, Susan Bach
Manager, Jeanne Fringer
Senior Vice-President, Kelly S Willis
Manager, Holly Chang
Auditors: GRANT THORNTON LLP MCLEAN VA

LOCATIONS

HQ: THE UNITED STATES PHARMACOPOEIAL CONVENTION
12601 TWINBROOK PKWY, ROCKVILLE, MD 208521790
Phone: 301 881-0666
Web: WWW.USP.ORG

HISTORICAL FINANCIALS

Company Type: Private

Income Statement

FYE: June 30

	REVENUE ($ mil.)	NET INCOME ($ mil.)	NET PROFIT MARGIN	EMPLOYEES
06/16	276	23	8.6%	1,200
06/13	191	10	5.5%	—
06/12	174	5	3.0%	—
06/11	576	0	0.0%	—
Annual Growth	(13.6%)	817.0%	—	—

2016 Year-End Financials

Return on assets: 16.3%
Return on equity: 8.6%
Current ratio: 1.50

Cash ($ mil.): 60

THE UNITY HOSPITAL OF ROCHESTER

EXECUTIVES

President, Timothy McCormick
Financial Executive, Tom Crilly
Director, Rufus Judson

LOCATIONS

HQ: THE UNITY HOSPITAL OF ROCHESTER
89 GENESEE ST, ROCHESTER, NY 146113201
Phone: 585 723-7000
Web: WWW.UNITYHEALTH.ORG

HISTORICAL FINANCIALS

Company Type: Private

Income Statement

FYE: December 31

	REVENUE ($ mil.)	NET INCOME ($ mil.)	NET PROFIT MARGIN	EMPLOYEES
12/15	433	(24)	—	3,000
12/14	435	0	0.1%	—
12/12	398	8	2.1%	—
Annual Growth	2.8%	—	—	—

2015 Year-End Financials

Return on assets: 2.6%
Return on equity: (-5.6%)
Current ratio: 0.90

Cash ($ mil.): 25

THE UNIVERSITY OF CHICAGO MEDICAL CENTER

It may have received its official dedication on Halloween but The University of Chicago Medical Center (UCMC) works hard to make visiting the hospital a little less spooky. UCMC is a complex of facilities located on The University of Chicago campus that include the acute care Bernard A. Mitchell Hospital the Comer Children's Hospital a women's health and maternity facility and an outpatient care center. Established in 1927 (and dedicated on Hal-loween of that year) the complex includes the affiliated University of Chicago Pritzker School of Medicine and forms the clinical arm of The University of Chicago Division of Biological Sciences. UCMC houses about 550 beds.

Operations

Its Bernard A. Mitchell Hospital includes helicopter transportation operations emergency level-one pediatric trauma services and regional burn and peri-natal units. The roughly 155-bed Comer Children's Hospital offers disease care education and research as well as expanded newborn intensive care services.

UCMC sees some 23000 inpatients and 75000 emergency room visits per year. The hospital is one of the largest providers of uncompensated care in Illinois providing millions of dollars in charity care every year.

As part of the university's Biological Sciences division UCMC operates medical research centers focused on cancer immunology diabetes cardiology and neurology. The cancer center is especially intent on discovering improved treatment and prevention measures using gene and protein-based treatments. The Gwen and Jules Knapp Center for Biomedical Discovery works on discovery programs for a variety of medical conditions including diabetes cancer and pediatrics.

Geographic Reach

UCMC is located in Hyde Park on the south side of Chicago. Its main medical campus includes the Center for Care and Discovery Comer Children's Hospital Bernard A. Mitchell Hospital Chicago Lying-in Hospital and Duchossois Center for Advanced Medicine. UCMC also manages a network of area physicians and specialty clinics located in Chicago and its suburbs as well as in northwestern Indiana.

Strategy

UCMC is widening its service offerings through facility construction efforts. It completed a 1.2 million sq. ft. medical research and patient-centered care hospital pavilion on its main campus (named the Center for Care and Discovery) in 2012; the new facility opened its doors to 145 patients the following year.

Mergers and Acquisitions

In 2016 UCMC merged with community hospital system Ingalls Health which is now part of the UChicago Medicine brand. The combination of the health care partners allows the group to provide care across a full spectrum from routine visits to complicated treatments for life-threatening issues.

Company Background

First Lady Michelle Obama served as VP for community and external affairs at UCMC; she resigned from her post in early 2009 when she made the move to the White House.

EXECUTIVES

President, Sharon O'Keefe
EVP Medical Affairs; Dean Division of the Biological Sciences and Pritzker School of Medicine, Kenneth S. Polonsky
EVP Corporate Strategy and Public Affairs, Susan S. Sher
COO and Associate Dean, Carolyn S. Wilson
CFO, James M. Watson
Vice President and Chief Pharmacy Officer, David Hicks
Vice President of Supply Chain and Logistics, Jonathan Stegner
Vice President Operations Integration And New Technology Deve, Michael Millis
Executive Vice President and Chief Operating Officer, Jason Keeler
Executive Vice President Business Development and Chief Strategy Officer, Audre Bagnall
Vice Chairman, Craig J. Duchossois
Vice Chairman, James S. (Jim) Frank
Chairman, Emily Nicklin
Auditors: PRICEWATERHOUSECOOPERS LLP WA

LOCATIONS

HQ: THE UNIVERSITY OF CHICAGO MEDICAL CENTER
5841 S MARYLAND AVE, CHICAGO, IL 606371443
Phone: 773 702-1000
Web: WWW.UCHOSPITALS.EDU

PRODUCTS/OPERATIONS

Selected Services
Cancer
Endocrinology
Gastroenterology
Geriatrics
Heart
Kidney disease
Neurosciences
Orthopaedics
Respiratory disease
Surgery
Transplantation
Women's services

Selected Facilities
Bernard A. Mitchell Hospital
Center for Care and Discovery
Chicago Lying-in Hospital (Maternity and Women's Hospital)
Comer Children's Hospital
Duchossois Center for Advanced Medicine (outpatient care and diagnostics)
Gwen and Jules Knapp Center for Biomedical Discovery
LaRabida Children's Hospital (affiliated facility)
Mercy Hospital (affiliated facility)
University of Chicago Pritzker School of Medicine
Weiss Memorial Hospital (affiliated facility)

COMPETITORS

Advocate Health Care
Alexian Brothers Health System
Covenant Ministries
Elmhurst Memorial Healthcare
Loyola University Health System
Mercy Hospital and Medical Center
NorthShore University HealthSystem
Northwest Community Healthcare
Northwestern Memorial HealthCare
Rush System for Health
Silver Cross Hospital
Sinai Health System
St. Bernard Hospital and Health Care Center

HISTORICAL FINANCIALS

Company Type: Private

Income Statement

FYE: June 30

	REVENUE ($ mil.)	NET INCOME ($ mil.)	NET PROFIT MARGIN	EMPLOYEES
06/15	1,610	148	9.2%	5,000
06/14	1,495	114	7.7%	—
06/09	1,294	(190)	—	—
06/08	1,286	38	3.0%	—
Annual Growth	3.3%	21.2%	—	—

2015 Year-End Financials

Return on assets: 7.9%
Return on equity: 9.2%
Current ratio: 0.40

Cash ($ mil.): 163

THE UNIVERSITY OF DAYTON

More than 10000 students make the University of Dayton one of the nation's largest Catholic universities and the largest private university in Ohio. The institution offers some 80 majors. Students are recruited on a national basis and from foreign countries. The student population approximates 7500 undergraduate and 2400 graduate students. It has a student-to-faculty ratio of 16:1. Well-known alumni include the late author and columnist Erma Bombeck and Super Bowl-winning NFL coaches Jon Gruden and Chuck Noll.

Geographic Reach

The university's students are primarily from Ohio and nine other Midwestern and Eastern US states.

Financial Performance

In fiscal 2016 the University of Dayton had $117.6 million in research sponsorship making it the 9th leading school for sponsored research among private comprehensive research universities without medical schools. It is the top US Catholic university for sponsored engineering research and development #2 nationally for federally sponsored materials research and development.

Company Background

The University of Dayton was founded in 1850 by the Society of Mary (the Marianists).

EXECUTIVES

Associate Provost and CIO, Thomas D. (Tom) Skill
Dean University Libraries, Kathleen M. Webb
President, Eric F. Spina
Provost, Paul H. Benson
Dean School of Business Administration, Paul M. Bobrowski
Dean School of Education and Health Sciences, Kevin R. Kelly
Dean College of Arts and Sciences, Jason Pierce
Dean School of Law, Andrew L. Strauss
Dean School of Engineering, Eddy Rojas
VP Finance and Administrative Services, Andy Horner
Assoc Vice President Facilities Management, Russ Potyrala
Vice President For Mission And Rector, James Fitz
Assistant Vice President For Student Development, Cari Wallace
Assistant Vice President And Treasurer, Phillip Chick
Assistant Vice President of Athletics, Mike Kelly
Vice President For Student Development, Bill Fischer
Vice President For Diversity and Inclusion University of Dayton, Lawrence Burnley
Assistant Vice President New Markets, Wiggins MEd
Vice President University Advancement, Jennifer Howe
Vice President For Finance and Administrative Services, Andrew Horner
Vice President and General Counsel, Mary Recker
Chairman, Steven D. Cobb
Vice Chairman, Martin A. Solma
Director Board Of Directors, Robert Rosenfelder
Secretary, Denise Quillen
Secretary, Corinne Daprano
Auditors: MCGLADREY LLP DAYTON OHIO

LOCATIONS

HQ: THE UNIVERSITY OF DAYTON
300 COLLEGE PARK AVE, DAYTON, OH 454690002
Phone: 937 229-2919
Web: WWW.DINING.UDAYTON.EDU

HISTORICAL FINANCIALS
Company Type: Private

Income Statement

FYE: June 30

	REVENUE ($ mil.)	NET INCOME ($ mil.)	NET PROFIT MARGIN	EMPLOYEES
06/15	499	27	5.4%	4,500
06/14	460	126	27.4%	—
06/13	444	96	21.7%	—
06/12	418	(21)	—	—
Annual Growth	6.1%	—	—	—

2015 Year-End Financials

Return on assets: 4.1% Cash ($ mil.): 73
Return on equity: 5.4%
Current ratio: —

THE UNIVERSITY OF HARTFORD

While its roots date back to 1877 The University of Hartford wasn't officially chartered until 1957 with the merger of the Hartford Art School the Hartt School of Music and Hillyer College. The modern-day university still has a strong arts and music programs and its Museum of American Political Life is home to what has been called the country's largest private collection of political memorabilia. University of Hartford which operates three campuses in West Hartford has about 7000 students enrolled in more than 80 undergraduate and 30 graduate programs including business nursing and engineering.

Operations

The University of Hartford consists of seven schools and colleges that offer programs in fields including arts architecture sciences business education nursing health engineering and technology. It employs 350 faculty members and has a student-to-faculty ratio of 13:1.

In addition to higher education the university operates two magnet schools (elementary and high school) on its campus as well as a community service center that coordinates volunteer opportunities for students staff and alumni members. In addition University of Hartford runs engineering design business development and professional development programs that work in partnerships with area businesses.

Hartford alumni include Broadway musical director Timothy Stella actress Marin Ireland and TV writer Kent McCray as well as a number of business entrepreneurs in medical scientific and technology fields.

Geographic Reach

The University of Hartford's students hail from about 45 states and 50 international countries.

Strategy

University of Hartford is improving its campus by investing in infrastructure enhancements. It is also working to improve its academic community through faculty recruitment and student recruitment efforts as well as through the development of interdisciplinary mission-centered and transformational learning programs.

EXECUTIVES

Assistant Vice President for Finance and Controller, Kimberly Kennison
Director Media Relations, Dave Isgur
Associate Vice President for Development, Marlisa Simonson
Finance Vice President, Nateka Scafe
Executive Vice President, Stillman Brown
Vice President Finance and Scholarship), Sam DiStefano
Vice President Standards and Practices), Matthew Sullivan
Executive Vice President Activities, Rich Hoover
Assistant Vice President Finance, Arosha Jayawickrema
Vice President for Institutional Advancement, Christine Pina
Administrative Assistant Vice President Student Affairs Student Affairs, Marcia Suess
Managing Director Hartt Administration, David Bell
Finance Vice President, Liam McCusker
Vice President Technology, Charles Pagano
Associate Vice President of Development, Lida Mullarkey
Piano Department Chair, Maggie Francis
Academic Vice President, Gary Beaumont
Board Member, Janell Carroll
Board Director, Bin Zhu
Treasurer, Samantha Cormier
Secretary, Brandon Turkish
Auditors: PRICEWATERHOUSECOOPERS LLP HA

LOCATIONS

HQ: THE UNIVERSITY OF HARTFORD
200 BLOOMFIELD AVE, WEST HARTFORD, CT
061171599
Phone: 860 768-4393
Web: WWW.HARTFORD.EDU

PRODUCTS/OPERATIONS

Selected Schools and Colleges
Barney School of Business
College of Arts and Sciences
College of Education Nursing and Health Professions
College of Engineering Technology and Architecture
Hartford Art School
The Hartt School
Hillyer College

HISTORICAL FINANCIALS
Company Type: Private

Income Statement

FYE: June 30

	REVENUE ($ mil.)	NET INCOME ($ mil.)	NET PROFIT MARGIN	EMPLOYEES
06/16	181	(6)	—	950
06/15	179	3	1.8%	—
06/14	173	23	13.3%	—
06/13	170	21	12.7%	—
Annual Growth	2.1%	—	—	—

2016 Year-End Financials

Return on assets: 10.0% Cash ($ mil.): 53
Return on equity: (-3.5%)
Current ratio: —

THE UNIVERSITY OF KANSAS HOSPITAL

EXECUTIVES

Vice-President, John Jackson
Office Manager, Donna Barnes
Personnel Director, Jo Cox
Director, Andrea Southard
Administrative Assistant, Rhonda Brockman

LOCATIONS

HQ: THE UNIVERSITY OF KANSAS HOSPITAL
3901 RAINBOW BLVD, KANSAS CITY, KS 661608500
Phone: 913 588-5000
Web: WWW.KUMED.COM

HISTORICAL FINANCIALS
Company Type: Private

Income Statement   FYE: June 30

	REVENUE ($ mil.)	NET INCOME ($ mil.)	NET PROFIT MARGIN	EMPLOYEES
06/15	1,362	156	11.5%	2,750
06/02	321	6	2.0%	—
Annual Growth	11.8%	28.1%	—	—

2015 Year-End Financials

Return on assets: 4.1%   Cash ($ mil.): 140
Return on equity: 11.5%
Current ratio: 1.70

THE UNIVERSITY OF NORTH CAROLINA AT CHARLOTTE

The University of North Carolina at Charlotte is the second-largest of 17 institution members of the University of North Carolina system. Known as UNC Charlotte the university offers about 170 undergraduate and graduate programs including education architecture business and engineering. The university spans 1000 acres across four Charlotte campuses including a research campus with programs in manufacturing opto-electronics and information technology. More than 1000 full-time faculty members serve more than 27000 students – representing 22000 undergraduates and 5000 post-graduates. UNC Charlotte founded in 1946 to serve returning WWII veterans became a member of the UNC System in 1965.

Operations

UNC Charlotte which comprises four campuses in Charlotte North Carolina is supported by a $153 million endowment. Average annual in-state tuition and fees run $6107; out-of-state tuition and fees average $18636. The school is among the fastest-growing in the UNC System.

Sales and Marketing

The university which maintains an operating budget of about $543 million attracts slightly more women than men with 50.5% vs. 49.5% respectively. Of its 22000 undergraduate enrollment entering freshmen account for more than 3000.

Strategy

With the backing of the larger University of North Carolina system UNC Charlotte in fall 2012 began offering a bachelor's degree in neurodiagnostics and sleep science (NDSS). The degree offered in collaboration with UNC Chapel Hill's Department of Allied Health Sciences is the first of its kind in the world.

The university is also working to expand and improve its campuses. As part of its campus master plan UNC Charlotte completed seven major construction projects in recent years for buildings and infrastructure. These include the Center City Building Energy Production and Infrastructure Center (EPIC) Miltimore Residence Hall Motorsports Research Building Prospector Building north parking deck and a regional utility plant to support the EPIC building. The City Center Building costs $50.4 million to complete. At 11 stories the building serves as UNC Charlotte's academic and community engagement programming space.

In 2014 the UNC Charlotte opened an early college high school on its campus. The school's curriculum focuses on science technology engineering and math (STEM) courses with a special emphasis on energy and engineering. The high school welcomed its first class of 100 freshmen that fall.

Company Background

Initially offering evening classes the Charlotte Center opened in September 1946 to serve 278 freshmen and sophomore students on the Central High School grounds.

EXECUTIVES

GPSG Vice President And Research Fair Committee Chairperson, Elizabeth G Shockey
Aias Vice President, Andrew Baur
Vice President, Francis Sedgwick
Vice President, Christopher Dong
Board Member, Jane Neese
Board Member, Adriana Medina
Secretary, Tracy Worthey
Auditors: BETH A WOOD CPA RALEIGH NO

LOCATIONS

HQ: THE UNIVERSITY OF NORTH CAROLINA AT CHARLOTTE
9201 UNIVERSITY CITY BLVD, CHARLOTTE, NC 282230001
Phone: 704 687-5727
Web: WWW.PUBLICHEALTH.UNCC.EDU

PRODUCTS/OPERATIONS

Selected Colleges
Colleges o
Business
Computing and Informatics
Education
Engineering
Health and Human Services
Liberal Arts & Sciences

HISTORICAL FINANCIALS
Company Type: Private

Income Statement   FYE: June 30

	REVENUE ($ mil.)	NET INCOME ($ mil.)	NET PROFIT MARGIN	EMPLOYEES
06/16	319	67	21.0%	3,030
06/15	292	39	13.4%	—
06/14	269	27	10.2%	—
06/13	251	55	22.0%	—
Annual Growth	8.3%	6.6%	—	—

2016 Year-End Financials

Return on assets: 4.0%   Cash ($ mil.): 233
Return on equity: 21.0%
Current ratio: 5.40

THE UNIVERSITY OF SOUTHERN MISSISSIPPI

You don't have to be a belle to attend Southern Miss but it never hurts. The University of Southern Mississippi (USM or Southern Miss for short) was established by the state legislature in 1910 to educate Mississippi's teachers. The school has grown to boast an enrollment of more than 15000 students with a student-teacher ratio of 17:1. USM offers bachelor's master's doctoral and post-master's degrees through five colleges: College of Arts and Letters College of Business College of Education and Psychology College of Health and College of Science and Technology. Southern Miss also runs an Honors College and engages in extensive research in a range of disciplines including health and technology.

EXECUTIVES

President, Shelby Thames
Director, Clay Jones
Marketing Director, Kirstin Rayborn
Executive Director, Lola Norris

LOCATIONS

HQ: THE UNIVERSITY OF SOUTHERN MISSISSIPPI
118 COLLEGE DR, HATTIESBURG, MS 394060002
Phone: 601 266-1000
Web: WWW.USM.EDU

HISTORICAL FINANCIALS
Company Type: Private

Income Statement   FYE: June 30

	REVENUE ($ mil.)	NET INCOME ($ mil.)	NET PROFIT MARGIN	EMPLOYEES
06/16	202	10	5.3%	4,500
06/15	189	8	4.5%	—
06/14	192	20	10.8%	—
06/13	192	17	9.0%	—
Annual Growth	1.8%	(14.9%)	—	—

2016 Year-End Financials

Return on assets: 9.4%   Cash ($ mil.): 39
Return on equity: 5.3%
Current ratio: 1.40

THE UNIVERSITY OF TOLEDO

One of Ohio's 14 state universities The University of Toledo (UT) is the third-largest by operating budget. It enrolls about 23000 students and offers more than 350 programs of study including master's degree and doctoral programs in more than 60 instructional departments. The university has a student-to-faculty ratio of 19:1. Its 14 colleges focus on subjects ranging from visual and performing arts to business and innovation as well as education engineering law medicine nursing pharmacy languages and human services. The school also operates the University of Toledo Medical Center.

Operations

The University of Toledo Medical Center affiliated with UT is a teaching hospital has three hos-

pitals located on the UT Health Science Campus with a total of 320 beds in all three hospitals combined (the UT Medical Center a Rehabilitation Hospital and the Kobacker Center).

The UT Medical Center features a Level I trauma center and extensive medical training programs on UT's Health Science Campus. It provides treatments for strokes and cancer that are unique within the state. Other specialties include kidney transplants and cardiology.

Geographic Reach

UT students come from 45 US states and about 80 international countries. The school has an extensive distance learning program. In addition to the main campus in Toledo UT operates several satellite centers in Toledo (including the Health Science Campus the Scott Park Campus and the Center for the Visual Arts facility) and the Lake Erie Research and Education Center in Oregon Ohio.

Strategy

UT is working to enhance resources to better serve students as well as patients of its medical center. In addition to infrastructure and building projects UT is focused on recruiting and retaining quality faculty members and enhancing the quality and ranking of its academic programs. The university is also enhancing research and technology resources including collaborations with other schools and organizations.

Company Background

UT and the Medical University of Ohio merged in 2006. UT is accredited by the Higher Learning Commission of the North Central Association of Colleges and Schools.

UT was established in 1872 and became a member of the state university system in 1967.

EXECUTIVES

Interim SVP Finance and Administration, Lawrence (Larry) Kelley

Interim Dean Scott Honors College, Kelly Moore

Dean College of Pharmacy and Pharmaceutical Sciences, Johnnie L. Early

President, Sharon L. Gaber

Dean College of Engineering, Nagi Naganathan

EVP; CEO UT Medical Center, David R. Morlock

Interim Provost and EVP Academic Affairs, John A. Barrett

EVP; Dean College of Medicine and Life Sciences, Christopher J. Cooper

Vice Provost; Executive Dean College of Applied Science and Technology, Todd A. Rickel

Dean College of Health Sciences, Christopher D. Ingersoll

Dean College of Languages Literature and Social Sciences, Jamie Barlowe

Dean College of Natural Sciences and Mathematics, Karen S. Bjorkman

Dean College of Communication and the Arts, Debra A. Davis

Interim Dean College of Social Justice and Human Service, Thomas G. (Tom) Gutteridge

Dean College of Business and Innovation, Gary S. Insch

Dean College of Graduate Studies, Patricia R. Komuniecki

Dean College of Adult and Lifelong Learning, Dennis S. Lettman

VP CIO and CTO, William McCreary

Interim Dean Herb College of Education, Virginia Keil

Dean College of Law, D. Benjamin Barros

Interim Dean College of Nursing, Kelly Phillips

Interim Dean YouCollege, Julie Fischer-Kinney

Vice President Global Sales Op, Julianne Bonitati

Nursing Director, Andrew Fox

Associate Vice President for Student Affairs, Virginia Speight

Associate Vice President For Academic Finance, Brenda Grant

Vice President and General Counsel, Sandra Drabik

Associate Vice President, Jovita Williams

Vice President of Information Technology, Dana Xiao

Vice President For Advancement, Samuel Mccrimmon

Vice President Director Of Athletics, Michael Obrien

Vice President Student Affairs, David Meabon

Interim Vice President For Student Affairs, Phillip Cockrell

Chairman, Sharon S. Speyer

Vice Chairman, Steven M. Cavanaugh

Treasurer, Barbara Scouten

Secretary 2 surgery, Tammy Brittian

Secretary, Elaine Coopshaw

Secretary 1 ALI Adminstration, Sarah Moomey

Secretary, Jefferson Exum

Secretary 1 neurology, Mildred Wegener

Secretary 2 Medicine, Lisa Johnston

Secretary 1 college Of Nursing, Roni Hoskins

Secretary 1 Pharmacy Practice, Linda Ruiz

Secretary Communication, Patricia Damschroder

Secretary 2 Medicine, Melissa Hansen

Secretary, Sally Grether

Secretary 1 Nursing Advertising, Nora Longsworth

Treasurer, Anne Riley

Secretary 1 Pediatrics, Theresa Imre

Secretary 2 psychiatry, Jacquelyn Mcbee

Secretary, Sandra Dunbar

Secretary, Tamara Golkiewicz

Secretary, Nadine Hoffmann

Secretary, Tana Felkey

Secretary Help Desk, Aniket Sabnis

Auditors: PLANTE & MORAN PLLC TOLEDO

LOCATIONS

HQ: THE UNIVERSITY OF TOLEDO
2801 W BANCROFT ST, TOLEDO, OH 436063390
Phone: 419 530-4636
Web: WWW.UTOLEDO.EDU

HISTORICAL FINANCIALS

Company Type: Private

Income Statement

	REVENUE ($ mil.)	NET INCOME ($ mil.)	NET PROFIT MARGIN	EMPLOYEES
06/16	753	(34)	—	7,000
06/12	724	2	0.3%	—
06/10	0	0	3.9%	—
Annual Growth	234.2%	—	—	—

FYE: June 30

2016 Year-End Financials

Return on assets: 4.6% Cash ($ mil.): 57
Return on equity: (-4.6%)
Current ratio: 1.10

THE UNIVERSITY OF TULSA

If you're "Living on Tulsa Time" and looking for an education then the home of the Golden Hurricanes is the place to be. The University of Tulsa is a private university affiliated with the Presbyterian Church (USA) with an enrollment of about 5000 students. The school offers more than 60 undergraduate and about 35 graduate programs including a dozen doctoral degree programs at colleges of arts and sciences business and engineering and natural sciences. The University of Tulsa was founded in Muskogee in 1882 as the Presbyterian School for Indian Girls and was chartered as Henry Kendall College in 1894. The school moved to Tulsa in 1907 and became The University of Tulsa in 1920.

Operations

The University of Tulsa employs about 300 faculty members and has a student-to-teacher ratio of 12 to 1. About 84% of the students receive financial aid to help cover the annual costs of $35000.

Strategy

As part of its plan to increase enrollment The University of Tulsa in 2014 began construction to create a 300-bed student dormitory that it intends to open for the fall semester of 2015.

EXECUTIVES

Assoc Vice President Enrollment Student Services, Yolanda Taylor
Auditors: HOGANTAYLOR LLP TULSA OK

LOCATIONS

HQ: THE UNIVERSITY OF TULSA
800 S TUCKER DR, TULSA, OK 741049700
Phone: 918 631-2000
Web: WWW.UTULSA.EDU

PRODUCTS/OPERATIONS

Selected Colleges
College of Engineering and Natural Sciences
College of Law
Collins College of Business
Graduate School
Henry Kendall College of Arts and Sciences

HISTORICAL FINANCIALS

Company Type: Private

Income Statement

	REVENUE ($ mil.)	NET INCOME ($ mil.)	NET PROFIT MARGIN	EMPLOYEES
06/15	206	30	14.9%	1,033
06/14	307	38	12.5%	—
06/13	271	13	4.8%	—
06/12	173	(23)	—	—
Annual Growth	5.8%	—	—	—

FYE: June 30

2015 Year-End Financials

Return on assets: 5.1% Cash ($ mil.): 23
Return on equity: 14.9%
Current ratio: 0.70

THE VALLEY HOSPITAL INC

The Valley Hospital is second to none when it comes to its Same-Day Service program. More than one-third of the company's annual patients experience its longstanding continuum of one-day service; fully half the surgeries performed are same-day. The not-for-profit hospital is a 450-bed facility providing general and emergency services to residents of New Jersey's Bergen County. The hospital belongs to the Valley Health System which also includes subsidiaries Valley Home Care and Valley Health Medical Group and is an affiliate member of NewYork-Presbyterian Healthcare. The Valley Hospital New Jersey's second busiest has more than 800 physicians on its medical staff.

Operations

The Valley Hospital is well known for its cardiology cancer maternity and neonatal care programs (including its neonatal ICU). Its key services also include emergency care orthopedics and neurosciences. The hospital's emergency department treated more than 75000 patients in 2013. That year the hospital also admitted more than 49240 patients and the delivered almost 3200 babies.

The Valley Hospital's cardiac service includes a full range of diagnostic and interventional cardiac treatment services including cardiac surgery coronary angioplasty and electrophysiology studies. The hospital is also known for its work in lung cancer diagnosis and treatment radiation oncology (including tomotherapy) chemotherapy and infusion GYN oncology prostate cancer care and other clinical and support services.

Geographic Reach

The hospital serves more than 440000 people in 32 towns in Bergen County and surrounding communities.

Strategy

The medical system is looking to improve its facilities and technology in order to keep up with demand. The Valley Hospital is the first and only hospital in northern New Jersey to offer brain and spinal surgery with a state-of-the-art O-arm® surgical imaging system purchased through a $1 million grant from The Bolger Foundation.

In 2012 The Valley Hospital Valley became the first hospital in northern New Jersey to offer the latest breast imaging technology — 3D breast tomosynthesis.

That year it also enhanced its capacity to perform minimally invasive surgery with the acquisition of the robotic da Vinci® Surgical System funded by a $1.6 million donation from The Bolger Foundation.

In 2012 the hospital opened a new Women's and Children's Resource Center to coordinate wide range of services for women and their families.

EXECUTIVES

Medical Director, Marc Dreier
Medical Records Director, Michelle Fuchs

LOCATIONS

HQ: THE VALLEY HOSPITAL INC
223 N VAN DIEN AVE, RIDGEWOOD, NJ 074502736
Phone: 201 447-8000

PRODUCTS/OPERATIONS

Selected Services

Adoption Screening and Evaluation Program
Ambulatory Infusion Center
Anticoagulation Management Service
Autism Services
Auxiliary
Barrett's Esophagus Center
Bariatric Surgery
Bereavement Services
Biplane
Bladder Cancer Care
Breast Center
Cancer Care
Capsule Endoscopy
Cardiac MRI
Cardiac Rehabilitation
Cardiac Surgery
Cardiology
Center for Childbirth
Kireker Center for Child Development
Center for Metabolic and Weight Loss Surgery
Center for Family Education
Center for Women's Heart Health
Center for Youth Fitness
Clinical Trials Oncology
Clinical Trials Cardiology
Colonoscopy
Community Resources
Complementary Medicine

Concussion Management Program
Continence Services
Cosmetic Laser Treatment
Critical Care
Diabetes Support Services
Diagnostic Imaging
Doula Program
Emergency Services
Emergency Services Pediatric
Employee Recognition
Endoscopic Ultrasound
Epilepsy Monitoring Program Adult
Epilepsy Center Pediatric
ERCP
Esophagogastroduodenoscopy (EGD)
Extended Care

COMPETITORS

Bergen Regional Medical
Englewood Hospital and Medical Center
Hackensack Meridian Health
Hackensack University Medical Center
Jersey City Medical Center
Newton Medical Center
Raritan Bay Medical Center
Robert Wood Johnson University Hospital at Rahway

HISTORICAL FINANCIALS

Company Type: Private

Income Statement

FYE: December 31

	REVENUE ($ mil.)	NET INCOME ($ mil.)	NET PROFIT MARGIN	EMPLOYEES
12/15	621	83	13.4%	2,900
12/14	605	56	9.3%	—
12/13	663	12	1.9%	—
12/09	587	44	7.6%	—
Annual Growth	1.0%	11.0%	—	—

2015 Year-End Financials

Return on assets: 4.8%   Cash ($ mil.): 2
Return on equity: 13.4%
Current ratio: 0.90

THE VANDERBILT UNIVERSITY

The house that Cornelius built Vanderbilt University was founded in 1873 with a $1 million grant from industrialist Cornelius Vanderbilt. Since then the university's endowment has grown to $4.1 billion making the Nashville school a haven for its roughly 12600 students and more than 4200 full-time faculty members. Boasting a 7:1 student-faculty ratio Vanderbilt offers undergraduate and graduate programs in areas such as education and human development divinity engineering and the arts and sciences. The university operates 10 schools and colleges. Vanderbilt's Owen Graduate School of Management and its medical school regularly rank near the top in national surveys.

Operations

A major research university Vanderbilt receives millions of dollars each year in research funding from a variety of sources.

Vanderbilt is closely affiliated with the comprehensive Vanderbilt University Medical Center (VUMC) which conducts clinical trials and trains medical students. It's home to an acute care hospital a children's hospital and several clinics as well as the university's medical school research facilities and nursing programs. In 2016 Vanderbilt and VUMC officially split severing financial and legal ties (but not their ongoing affiliations).

Financial Performance

Vanderbilt University's revenue increased 3% to $1.3 billion in fiscal 2017 (ended June). Tuition and education fees less student financial aid contributed 21% of that revenue while grants and contracts contributed 18%. The Department of Health and Human Services (primarily the National Institutes of Health) was the largest source of government grants and contracts.

The school's expenses totaled $1.2 billion that year. Salaries wages and benefits as well as supplies and services made up the bulk of those expenses.

Strategy

Vanderbilt works to retain and recruit world-class faculty expand its hospitals and clinics and enhance its athletic facilities. For example it opened a new engineering and science building in 2016.

In 2016 Vanderbilt separated from its medical center (which restructured as the not-for-profit Vanderbilt University Medical Center or VUMC). The move allowed VUMC to be financially independent while still collaborating with the university for research and education.

Company Background

During its first 40 years of existence Vanderbilt was under the auspices of the Methodist Episcopal Church South. The Vanderbilt Board of Trust severed its ties with the church in 1914 after a dispute with the bishops over who would appoint university trustees.

EXECUTIVES

Chancellor, Nicholas S. Zeppos
Vice Chancellor Health Affairs and Dean School of Medicine, Jeffrey R. Balser
Dean of the Blair School of Music, Mark Wait
Dean Peabody College, Camilla Benbow
Associate Provost and Dean of Students, Mark Bandas
Dean of the School of Divinity, Emilie M. Townes
Vice Chancellor Finance and CFO, Brett Sweet
Dean of the Law School, Chris Guthrie
Vice Chancellor for Information Technology, John M. Lutz
Dean of the School of Engineering, Philippe Fauchet
Vice Chancellor General Counsel and Secretary, Audrey J. Anderson
Provost and Vice Chancellor for Academic Affairs, Susan Wente
Vice Chancellor for Administration, Eric Kopstain
Vice Provost for Enrollment and Dean of Admissions, Douglas L. Christiansen
Interim dean of Libraries, Joseph D. Combs
Dean of the Owen Graduate School of Management, M. Eric Johnson
Dean of the School of Nursing, Linda Norman
Vice Chairman, Jackson W. Moore, age 68
Chairman, Mark F. Dalton, age 66
Vice Chairman, John Winkelried
Auditors: PRICEWATERHOUSECOOPERS LLP NE

LOCATIONS

HQ: THE VANDERBILT UNIVERSITY
211 KIRKLAND HALL, NASHVILLE, TN 372400001
Phone: 615 322-5000
Web: WWW.VANDERBILT.EDU

PRODUCTS/OPERATIONS

Selected Schools and Colleges

Blair School of Music
College of Arts and Science
Divinity School
Graduate School
Law School
Owen Graduate School of Management
Peabody College of Education and Human Development

School of Engineering
School of Medicine
School of Nursing

HISTORICAL FINANCIALS
Company Type: Private

Income Statement
FYE: June 30

	REVENUE ($ mil.)	NET INCOME ($ mil.)	NET PROFIT MARGIN	EMPLOYEES
06/16	1,270	(569)	—	21,000
06/15	4,121	131	3.2%	—
06/14	3,920	504	12.9%	—
06/13	3,691	319	8.7%	—
Annual Growth	(29.9%)	—	—	—

2016 Year-End Financials
Return on assets: 6.5%
Return on equity: (-44.8%)
Current ratio: —

Cash ($ mil.): 963

THE WASHINGTON HOSPITAL

EXECUTIVES

Chief Executive Officer, Gary Weinstein

LOCATIONS

HQ: THE WASHINGTON HOSPITAL
155 WILSON AVE, WASHINGTON, PA 153013398
Phone: 724 225-7000
Web: WWW.WASHINGTONHOSPITAL.ORG

HISTORICAL FINANCIALS
Company Type: Private

Income Statement
FYE: June 30

	REVENUE ($ mil.)	NET INCOME ($ mil.)	NET PROFIT MARGIN	EMPLOYEES
06/15	234	28	12.1%	1,900
06/14	245	19	7.8%	—
06/13	233	13	5.7%	—
06/10	235	12	5.2%	—
Annual Growth	(0.1%)	18.3%	—	—

2015 Year-End Financials
Return on assets: 6.0%
Return on equity: 12.1%
Current ratio: 1.20

Cash ($ mil.): 13

THE WASHINGTON UNIVERSITY

Washington University also known as Washington University in St. Louis (WUSTL) is the gateway to higher education for more than 13000 students. Founded in 1853 the independent university offers 90 bachelor's master's and doctoral degrees and has about 3400 faculty members. It offers approximately 1500 courses in fields such as arts and sciences business design and visual arts engineering law medicine and social work. WUSTL which has multiple campuses in and near the city of St.

Louis also offers associate degree and continuing education programs. The affiliated Washington University Medical Center is an acute-care hospital that also provides educational training and research services.

Operations

The Medical Campus conducts extensive collaborative studies between students faculty and hospital staff as well as external institutions. Areas of research include genome sequencing of cancer patients and children's developmental studies. The 2000-acre Tyson Research Center outside the city is a biological field station that conducts environmental studies and research activities including renewable energy and sustainability programs some of which is coordinated with outside groups.

The university has an 8:1 student-to-faculty ratio. Its libraries contain more than 3.6 million books journals and other print materials and have access to more than 65000 electronic journals and a half million e-books.

In the academic year ending spring 2015 annual undergraduate educational costs totaled $45700.

Geographic Reach

In addition to the main 170-acre Danforth Campus in St. Louis WUSTL's facilities include the nearby 165-acre Medical Campus (housing the School of Medicine and the hospital facilities). Other operations include three smaller satellite academic campuses and music research and art centers in the greater St. Louis area.

Financial Performance

In fiscal 2015 revenue increased 9% to $2.7 billion on higher tuition and fees endowment spending distribution gifts and patient services. However a decline in non-operating revenue such as investment returns led to a 71% drop in net income which fell to $270 million.

Cash flow from operations spiked 522% to $104 million as less cash was used in net gains on investments.

Strategy

WUSTL has made efforts to extend its collaborations with third parties which can help bring in academic and research funds. In addition the university has worked to attract more government research grants in recent years. It is also upgrading some classroom and student facilities as well as hiring more experienced teachers and medical staff members to maintain its tuition auxiliary enterprise (lodging and vending) health services and research income expectations.

EXECUTIVES

Executive Vice Chancellor Administration, Henry S. Webber
Executive Vice Chancellor Alumni and Development Programs, David T. Blasingame
Executive Vice Chancellor and General Counsel, Michael R. Cannon
Chancellor, Mark S. Wrighton, age 68
Vice Chancellor Finance and CFO, Barbara A. Feiner
Executive Vice Chancellor Medical Affairs and Dean School of Medicine, Larry J. Shapiro
Dean Olin Business School, Mahendra R. Gupta
Dean Sam Fox School of Design and Visual Arts, Carmon Colangelo
Dean George Warren Brown School of Social Work, Edward F. Lawlor
Dean School of Law, Kent D. Syverud
Provost and Executive Vice Chancellor Academic Affairs, H. Holden Thorp, age 53
Dean School of Engineering and Applied Science, Ralph S. Quatrano
Dean Faculty of Arts and Sciences, Barbara A. Schaal
Dean College of Arts and Sciences, Jennifer R. Smith

Dean Graduate School of Arts and Sciences, Richard J. Smith
CIO, Michael P. (Mike) Caputo
Medical Director, Ramsey R Hachem
Vice President Medical Director Virginia Mason Medical Center Seattle Related News, Donna Smith
Vice Chairman, John F. McDonnell, age 78
Vice Chairman, David W. Kemper, age 66
Vice Chairman, Craig D. Schnuck, age 68
Vice Chairman, Stephen F. Brauer, age 72
Secretary, Pat Smith
Auditors: PRICEWATERHOUSECOOPERS LLP L

LOCATIONS

HQ: THE WASHINGTON UNIVERSITY
1 BROOKINGS DR, SAINT LOUIS, MO 631304899
Phone: 314 935-8566
Web: WWW.WUSTL.EDU

PRODUCTS/OPERATIONS

2015 Sales

	% of total
Patient service	36
Grants	14
Tuition & fees	13
Endowment spending distribution	10
Gifts	7
Educational	6
Others	14
Total	100

Selected Schools and Colleges
College of Arts & Sciences
  Graduate School of Arts & Sciences
  University College and Summer School (Arts & Sciences)
George Warren Brown School of Social Work
Sam Fox School of Design & Visual Arts
School of Engineering & Applied Science
School of Law
School of Medicine
Olin Business School

COMPETITORS

Bucknell University	Southeast Missouri
Missouri State	State University
University	University of Missouri
Saint Louis University	

HISTORICAL FINANCIALS
Company Type: Private

Income Statement
FYE: June 30

	REVENUE ($ mil.)	NET INCOME ($ mil.)	NET PROFIT MARGIN	EMPLOYEES
06/16	2,876	(303)	—	9,600
06/15	2,707	270	10.0%	—
06/14	2,472	917	37.1%	—
06/13	2,393	557	23.3%	—
Annual Growth	6.3%	—	—	—

2016 Year-End Financials
Return on assets: 13.7%
Return on equity: (-10.6%)
Current ratio: —

Cash ($ mil.): 173

THE WHITING-TURNER CONTRACTING COMPANY

Whiting-Turner Contracting provides construction management general contracting and design/build services primarily for large commercial institutional and infrastructure projects conducted across the US. A key player in retail construction the employee-owned company also undertakes such projects as biotech cleanrooms theme parks historical restorations senior living residences educational facilities stadiums and corporate headquarters. Clients past and present include the US military AT&T General Motors and Texas A&M University. Whiting-Turner Contracting operates from more than 30 offices across the US.

Geographic Reach

The Baltimore-based company has offices in Arizona California Colorado Connecticut Delaware Florida Georgia Maryland Massachusetts Missouri Nevada New Jersey New York North Carolina Ohio Pennsylvania Texas Virginia and Washington DC.

Sales and Marketing

The contractor works on projects across a wide range of industries related to arts and entertainment education federal and military healthcare industrial office retail multi-family residential sports and fitness transportation and utilities among other fields.

Strategy

Whiting-Turner prefers to grow organically instead of making acquisitions. It has been steadily expanding by opening new offices in places such as California Texas and Virginia. The company in 2016 continued to rank among the Engineering News Record (ENR) top domestic general building contractors in the nation.

Some of the firm's recently awarded projects (as of mid-2016) include the Tropicana Pedestrian Bridge the Jacksonville Lung Bio Facility the Westowne Elementary School the Lexington Market the Costco Meat Production Plant the Sentara Norfolk General Hospital and the CoolSprings Galleria among others.

Whiting-Turner Contracting's past projects include the Joseph B. Whitehead Building at Emory University Vanderbilt Hall at Yale University projects at Universal Studios theme park and a vaccine facility at Chesapeake Biological Laboratories. Projects in the firm's hometown of Baltimore have included the city's convention center and the football stadium for the Baltimore Ravens. More recent projects include the Horseshoe Casino Cleveland University of Maryland Baltimore County (UMBC) Performing Arts & Humanities Naval Facilities Engineering Command (NAVFAC) Jacksonville Sentara Princess Anne Hospital Norwalk Community College Texas A&M University at Galveston Mary Moody Northen Student Center renovation Opry Mills the College of Business & Economics Vinson Hall Parking Garage a Coastal Studies Institute facility a Blue Diamond Growers building and a USPS Call Center.

Company Background

G.W.C. Whiting and LeBaron Turner classmates at MIT founded the company in 1909 to build sewer lines.

EXECUTIVES

VP Richmond, Dani Niccolucci
SVP Allentown, Jack DaSilva
Division VP Fort Lauderdale, Robert (Rob) Mitchell

Division VP Delaware and Maryland, James (Jim) Martini
SVP District of Columbia, Richard L. Vogel
Division VP Pleasanton, Troy Caldwell
SVP Irvine, Len Cannatelli
SVP Baltimore, Gino J. Gemignani
Division VP Dallas, Espen S. Brooks
VP Bridgewater, Chris Martinson
SVP Atlanta, Keith Douglas
VP, Daniel (Dan) Bauer
VP Boston, Kevin Shields
Regional Manager Las Vegas, Paul Schmitt
Division VP Chantilly, Kempton C. Haile
VP Tampa, Brent A. Voyles
Senior Project Manager (Denver), Mark Faul
VP San Diego, Steven Likins
VP Orlando, Robert Minutoli
Division VP Raleigh, Chris Carlson
VP White Plains, David Brickley
VP San Antonio, Daryl Steinbeck
VP Norfolk, John Berotti
Senior Project Manager Sacramento, Jack Stackalis
VP Cleveland, Jeff Maeder
Regional Manager Kansas City, Adam Eshelbrenner
Regional Manager Charlotte, Chris Woods
Regional Manager Houston, Michael Browning
President and CEO, Timothy J. Regan, age 61
Sr V Pres, Frank Palmer
Vice President, Scott McMahon
Vice President, Susan Castellan
Vice President, Nancy Beavers
Vice President, Donald Hanky
Senior Vice President, Arch Jamieson
Senior Vice President, Kevin Higgins
ASHE CHC Vice President, Bob Moore
Vice President, Jesse Beam
Leed AP Banking Division C Vice President, Patricia Carper
Division Vice President, Ed Schlotterback
Vice President, Terry Spencer
Vice President, Jim Groff
Vice President, Irene Knott
Vice President, David McGinnis
Vice President Field Operations, Phil Knight
Vice President, Jeff Jenkins
Vice President, Bruce Delawder
Vice President, J Scott Breig
Division Vice President, David Mallik
Vice President San Diego, Miguel Huerta
Vice President, Tony Moag
Leed AP Business Development C Vice President, Patrick Duffy
Division Vice President, David Meyers
Executive Vice President and Chief Executive Officer, Tim Regan
Vice President, Craig Rayner
Executive Vice President, Steve Duffy
Vice President, Charles Konkolics
Division Vice President, Jeffrey Dodds
Vice President, Bernard LaHatte
Vice President, Andrew Linden
Division Vice President, Maynard Grizzard
Vice President, Terry Powell
Senior Vice President, Stephen Lambertson
Vice President, Kit Fawthrop
Vice President, Robert Tomlinson
Vice President, Ray MacKeen
Secretary, Willie Mcfarlin
Vice Chairman, Nick Bloch
Auditors: CLIFONLARSONALLEN TIMONIUM M

LOCATIONS

HQ: THE WHITING-TURNER CONTRACTING COMPANY
300 E JOPPA RD STE 800, BALTIMORE, MD 212863047
Phone: 410 821-1100
Web: WWW.WHITING-TURNER.COM

Selected Locations
Maryland - Baltimore (Headquarters)

California
California - Los Angeles
California
California
California - San Diego
Colorado -
Connecticut - New Haven
Delaware -
District of Columbia
Florida - Ft. Lauderdale
Florida -
Florida -
Georgia -
Maryland -
Massachuse
Missouri - Kansas City
Nevada - Las Vegas
New Jersey
New York - White Plains
North Caro
North Caro
Ohio - Cle
Pennsylvan
Texas - Da
Texas - Ho
Texas - San Antonio
Virginia -
Virginia -
Virginia -

PRODUCTS/OPERATIONS

Selected Services
Construction management
  Agency
  At-risk
Design/build
General contracting
Preconstruction

Selected Markets
Biotechnology and pharmaceutical
Cleanroom and high-technology
Education
Entertainment
Federal/military
Food/beverage distribution
Health care
Historical restoration
Industrial and manufacturing
Interiors
Life sciences
Lodging and hospitality
Mission critical facilities
Mixed use
Offices and headquarters
Parking garages
Restaurants
Retail
Senior living
Sports
Sustainable
Technology
  Microelectronics
  Nano
Theme parks
Utilities
Warehouse and distribution

COMPETITORS

Barton Malow	J.E. Dunn Construction
Bechtel	Group
Choate Construction	Jacobs Engineering
Clark Construction	Kitchell
Group	McCarthy Building
DPR Construction	Peter Kiewit Sons'
Fisher Development	Skanska
Fluor	Suffolk Construction
Gilbane	Swinerton
Hensel Phelps	Turner Corporation
Construction	Tutor Perini
Hoffman Corporation	Weitz

HISTORICAL FINANCIALS
Company Type: Private

Income Statement
FYE: December 31

	REVENUE ($ mil.)	NET INCOME ($ mil.)	NET PROFIT MARGIN	EMPLOYEES
12/15	5,729	80	1.4%	2,707
12/14	6,347	75	1.2%	—
12/12	3,781	56	1.5%	—
12/11	3,897	57	1.5%	—
Annual Growth	10.1%	8.6%	—	—

2015 Year-End Financials
Return on assets: 19.7% Cash ($ mil.): 13
Return on equity: 1.4%
Current ratio: 0.60

THE WICHITA STATE UNIVERSITY

State-supported Wichita State University (WSU) enrolls about 14500 students with the bulk hailing from Kansas. Along with its main campus WSU provides classes at four additional campuses. The school offers 70 undergraduate degrees in more than 200 subjects. Its Graduate School offers more than 40 master's programs a dozen doctoral degree programs an educational specialist program and more than 20 graduate certificate programs as well as research opportunities. WSU colleges include business education engineering fine arts health professions and liberal arts and sciences. The school was founded in 1895 as a Congregational institution.

Operations

WSU offers undergraduate and graduate degrees from half a dozen colleges including Fairmount College of Liberal Arts and Sciences W. Frank Barton School of Business College of Education College of Engineering College of Fine Arts and College of Health Professions.

The main campus is home to a roughly 150 student organizations that cover a wide range of topics — from academics and multicultural interests to politics and special interests and more. The school also hosts 15 NCAA Division I teams and a wide range of intramurals and club teams.

WSU is the only research institution in Kansas in an urban area. WSU and Via Christi Health formed a joint venture in 2008 and founded The Center of Innovation for Biomaterials in Orthopaedic Research (CIBOR). The venture was restructured in 2012 to move CIBOR to the National Institute for Aviation Research (NIAR) on the university campus. CIBOR is managed by NIAR but remains a joint venture of WSU and Via Christi Health. Located on the WSU campus NIAR operates nearly 20 cutting-edge laboratories. It has partnered with Cisco Systems to provide one of the nation's best advanced-networking research centers.

Geographic Reach

Besides its 330-acre main campus in Wichita Kansas WSU counts four other campuses that serve its traditional and non-traditional student body.It enrolls more than 1200 international students from 110 countries.

Financial Performance

WSU's revenue increased from $167.2 million in 2015 to $173.3 million in 2016 thanks to increases in tuition grants and sales and services.

Tuition and fees accounted for 33% of WSU's 2016 revenue; state appropriations 26%.

Salaries and wages the university's biggest expense decreased from $109.5 million in 2015 to $105.4 million in fiscal 2016.

Higher revenue and lower expenses helped the company's net position to improve by $8.2 million compared to a restated $15.1 million decrease in 2015.

EXECUTIVES
Vice President Administration, Roger Lowe
President and CEO Wichita State University Foundation, Elizabeth H. King
Dean College of Fine Arts, Rodney E. Miller
VP Administration and Finance, Mary Herrin
President, John W. Bardo, age 70
CIO, Toney Flack
Dean College of Education, Shirley Lefever-Davis
Dean College of Engineering, Royce Bowden
Dean Fairmount College of Liberal Arts and Sciences, Ron Matson
Dean College of Health Professions, Sandra Bibb
Dean Barton School of Business, Anand Desai
Dean Cohen Honors College, Kimberly Engber
Interim Dean Graduate School, Abu S. M. Masud
SVP and Provost, Anthony J. Vizzini
Vice President, John Tomblin
Associate Vice President, David Wright
Vice President Of Chapter Operations, Courtney Price
Vice President, James Rhatigan
Vice President and General Counsel, Ted Ayres
Foundation Vice President, Michael Lamb
Vice President for Finance and Operations, Susan Barrett
Vice President for Student Affairs, Teri Hall
Clinic Director, Mary Beasley
Secretary, Penny Post

LOCATIONS
HQ: THE WICHITA STATE UNIVERSITY
1845 FAIRMOUNT ST, WICHITA, KS 672600001
Phone: 316 978-3456
Web: WWW.WSUBOOKS.COM

Selected Campuses
Main
 Wichita Kansas
Satellite
 Eugene M. Hughes Metropolitan Complex Wichita Kansas
 WSU Downtown Center Wichita Kansas
 WSU South Campus Derby Wichita
 WSU West Campus Wichita Kansas

PRODUCTS/OPERATIONS

Selected Colleges and Schools
College of Education
College of Engineering
College of Fine Arts
College of Health Professions
Fairmount College of Liberal Arts and Sciences
Graduate School
W. Frank Barton School of Business

HISTORICAL FINANCIALS
Company Type: Private

Income Statement
FYE: June 30

	REVENUE ($ mil.)	NET INCOME ($ mil.)	NET PROFIT MARGIN	EMPLOYEES
06/16	197	11	6.1%	3,395
06/15	166	(14)	—	—
06/14	178	5	2.9%	—
06/13	189	16	8.8%	—
Annual Growth	1.5%	(10.5%)	—	—

2016 Year-End Financials
Return on assets: 12.3% Cash ($ mil.): 99
Return on equity: 6.1%
Current ratio: 2.20

THE WILLIAM W BACKUS HOSPITAL

EXECUTIVES
President, David Whitehead
Vice-President, Mary Kohanski
Personnel Director, Lester Temkin
Vice-President, James Healy
Director, Roxanne Hale
Administrative Assistant, William Jorsz
Manager, Kim Brown
Manager, Mary Johnson

LOCATIONS
HQ: THE WILLIAM W BACKUS HOSPITAL
326 WASHINGTON ST, NORWICH, CT 063602740
Phone: 860 889-8331
Web: WWW.BACKUSHOSPITAL.ORG

HISTORICAL FINANCIALS
Company Type: Private

Income Statement
FYE: September 30

	REVENUE ($ mil.)	NET INCOME ($ mil.)	NET PROFIT MARGIN	EMPLOYEES
09/15	285	40	14.3%	1,300
09/14	293	48	16.6%	—
/* 0	0	—	—	—
Annual Growth	—	—	—	—

*Fiscal year change

2015 Year-End Financials
Return on assets: 2.4% Cash ($ mil.): 192
Return on equity: 14.3%
Current ratio: 6.30

THE WILLIAMSPORT HOSPITAL

EXECUTIVES
Chief Executive Officer, Steven Johnson
Board of Directors, Sally Holly
Manager, Shella Paulhamus
Marketing Director, Elizabeth Brubaker
Auditors: LB BKD LLP SPRINGFIELD MO

LOCATIONS
HQ: THE WILLIAMSPORT HOSPITAL
700 HIGH ST, WILLIAMSPORT, PA 177013198
Phone: 570 321-1000
Web: WWW.SUSQUEHANNAHEALTH.ORG

Income Statement

	REVENUE ($ mil.)	NET INCOME ($ mil.)	NET PROFIT MARGIN	EMPLOYEES
				FYE: June 30
06/15	322	19	5.9%	1,300
06/14	297	5	2.0%	—
06/09	172	9	5.7%	—
06/08	186	5	2.9%	—
Annual Growth	8.2%	19.7%	—	—

2015 Year-End Financials

Return on assets: 12.6% Cash ($ mil.): 29
Return on equity: 5.9%
Current ratio: 0.30

THOMAS JEFFERSON UNIVERSITY HOSPITALS, INC.

Named after the "Man of the People" Thomas Jefferson University Hospitals (dba Jefferson Health) serves the people of the Keystone State with a medical staff of more than 1200 and some 1550 beds. The system provides acute tertiary and specialty medical care from a dozen hospitals nearly 20 outpatient centers and about 10 urgent care centers. The hospital also administers cardiac care at the Jefferson Heart Institute which provides everything from minimally invasive surgical procedures to heart transplants. Additionally Jefferson Health operates as the teaching hospital for Thomas Jefferson University.

Operations

As part of its operations Jefferson Health offers several premier programs to its patients as well as 35 different specialties. The system performed Delaware Valley's first liver transplant and designated a kidney transplant center for live and deceased donor transplants. In addition to transplantation it provides surgical services heart and vascular digestive diseases and bones and joints in addition to its Kimmel Cancer Canter and Jefferson Hospital for Neuroscience. In 2014 the health system logged more than 470000 outpatient visits 45000 admissions and about 115000 emergency room visits.

Geographic Reach

Through a handful of locations Jefferson Health provides health care services to the residents of Philadelphia and the Delaware Valley. It shares a 13-acre campus with Thomas Jefferson University.

Strategy

In October 2017 Jefferson Health merged with New Jersey-based Kennedy Health which operated three hospitals. The transaction followed closely on the heels of Jefferson's mergers with Aria Health and Abington Health.

In 2015 Jefferson Health added a new feature to its telemedicine program JeffConnect called On-Demand Virtual Care which allows patients to connect with an emergency medicine physician via computers and mobile devices.

That year the Philadelphia 76ers partnered with the Rothman Institute and Jefferson Health. The Rothman Institute will provide the Official Orthopedics & Urgent Care of the Philadelphia 76ers as well as the Official Team Physicians; Jefferson

Health became an official hospital of the Philadelphia 76ers.

In 2014 the system opened the Jefferson Angioplasty Center the outpatient practice for Jefferson's interventional cardiologists. It is co-located with the Vascular Center allowing for streamlined consultations and convenience as the two specialties often see the same patients.

That year it also introduced genomic analyses of breast cancer in-house using the Prosigna Breast Cancer Prognostic Gene Signature Assay significantly reducing turn-around time for test results and allowing patients to begin effective treatment sooner.

Company Background

Thomas Jefferson University Hospital was founded in 1825.

EXECUTIVES

Senior Vice President Patient Care Services And Chief Nursing Officer, Mary Mcginley
Vice President Financial Operations, Andrew Nathans
Senior Vice President And General Counsel, Stacey Meadows
Vice President Finance, Elizabeth Smith
Vice President Human Resources, Kimberly Evans
Senior Vice President Clinical Services, Rebecca O'Shea
Vice President and Chief Financial Officer, Arlene Peters

LOCATIONS

HQ: THOMAS JEFFERSON UNIVERSITY HOSPITALS, INC.
111 S 11TH ST, PHILADELPHIA, PA 191074824
Phone: 215 955-5806

PRODUCTS/OPERATIONS

Selected Services
Cancer
Diabetes & Endocrinology
Ear Nose & Throat
Gastroenterology
Geriatrics
Gynecology
Nephrology
Orthopedics
Pulmonology
Rehabilitation
Urology

Selected University Locations
Jefferson at the Navy Yard
Jefferson Medical College
Jefferson College of Graduate Studies
Jefferson Radiology
Jefferson School of Health Professions
Jefferson School of Nursing
Jefferson School of Pharmacy
Jefferson School of Population Health
Jefferson Voorhees

COMPETITORS

Albert Einstein Healthcare Network
Bryn Mawr Hospital
Community Health Systems
Doylestown Hospital
Mercy Health System
North Philadelphia Health System
Our Lady of Lourdes Medical Center
Pennsylvania Hospital
TUHS
Universal Health Services
University of Pennsylvania Health System

Income Statement

	REVENUE ($ mil.)	NET INCOME ($ mil.)	NET PROFIT MARGIN	EMPLOYEES
				FYE: June 30
06/15	1,456	42	2.9%	4,701
06/14	1,510	51	3.4%	—
06/10	1,250	49	4.0%	—
06/09	0	0	—	—
Annual Growth	356.9%	—	—	—

2015 Year-End Financials

Return on assets: 8.2% Cash ($ mil.): 46
Return on equity: 2.9%
Current ratio: 1.20

THOMAS SAINT MIDTOWN HOSPITAL

Titans and tots can find care at Saint Thomas Midtown Hospital (formerly Baptist Hospital) in Nashville Tennessee. With more than 680 beds Saint Thomas is one of the largest not-for-profit hospitals in the area. It provides general medical and surgical care along with specialty care in areas such as cardiovascular disease cancer orthopedics and pulmonary disease. Among other things the hospital also features a neurosciences institute a weight loss surgery center and a sports medicine division that serves the Tennessee Titans. Founded in 1919 as Protestant Hospital and later renamed Baptist Hospital it is now owned by Saint Thomas Health Services a Catholic health care system that is a member of Ascension Health.

EXECUTIVES

Chief Executive Officer, Bernie Sherry
Office Manager, Marla King
Office Manager, Cheryl Fassler
Director, Frank Beltre

LOCATIONS

HQ: THOMAS SAINT MIDTOWN HOSPITAL
2000 CHURCH ST, NASHVILLE, TN 372360002
Phone: 615 284-5555
Web: WWW.STHS.COM

PRODUCTS/OPERATIONS

Selected Services
Bariatrics & Weight Loss
Cancer care
Cardiac care
Center for Breast Health
Center for Sleep
Chest Pain Network
Childbirth
Diabetes
Emergency Services
Joint Replacement
Neurosciences
Orthopedics
Physical Therapy
Rehabilitation Services
Sleep Center
Seton Support Center
Specialty Clinics
Spine Services
Sports Medicine
Surgery
Women's Health
Wound Care

COMPETITORS

HCA	Southern Hills
Kindred Healthcare	Vanderbilt University
Select Medical	Medical Center

HISTORICAL FINANCIALS
Company Type: Private

Income Statement
FYE: June 30

	REVENUE ($ mil.)	NET INCOME ($ mil.)	NET PROFIT MARGIN	EMPLOYEES
06/15	414	51	12.4%	4,500
06/14	407	39	9.7%	—
06/05	0	0	—	—
06/03	0	0	—	—
Annual Growth	—	—	—	—

2015 Year-End Financials
Return on assets: 3.8%   Cash ($ mil.): —
Return on equity: 12.4%
Current ratio: 0.70

THOMPSON CONSTRUCTION GROUP, INC.

EXECUTIVES

President, Greg A Thompson
Vice-President, Barry Falin
Personnel Director, Janice Poplin
Vice-President, Rick Lotts
Chief Financial Officer, Diane Schultz
Vice-President, Bob Landers

LOCATIONS

HQ: THOMPSON CONSTRUCTION GROUP, INC.
100 N MAIN ST, SUMTER, SC 291504948
Phone: 803 773-8005
Web: WWW.THOMPSONTURNER.COM

HISTORICAL FINANCIALS
Company Type: Private

Income Statement
FYE: December 31

	REVENUE ($ mil.)	NET INCOME ($ mil.)	NET PROFIT MARGIN	EMPLOYEES
12/15	282	7	2.6%	120
12/14	187	4	2.6%	—
12/13	171	12	7.4%	—
12/12	97	3	3.1%	—
Annual Growth	42.4%	32.9%	—	—

THOMPSON CREEK METALS COMPANY USA

EXECUTIVES

President, Jacques Perron
Director, Pamela Solly

General Manager, Larry D Clark
Vice-President, Bruce R Wright
Personnel Director, Jeanette Bush
Superintendent, Dane Jones
Auditors: KPMG LLP DENVER COLORADO

LOCATIONS

HQ: THOMPSON CREEK METALS COMPANY USA
26 W DRY CREEK CIR # 225, LITTLETON, CO
801208064
Phone: 303 761-8801
Web: WWW.THOMPSONCREEKMETALS.COM

HISTORICAL FINANCIALS
Company Type: Private

Income Statement
FYE: December 31

	REVENUE ($ mil.)	NET INCOME ($ mil.)	NET PROFIT MARGIN	EMPLOYEES
12/15	494	(134)	—	699
12/14	806	(124)	—	—
12/13	434	(215)	—	—
12/12	401	(546)	—	—
Annual Growth	7.2%	—	—	—

2015 Year-End Financials
Return on assets: 14.6%   Cash ($ mil.): 176
Return on equity: (-27.3%)
Current ratio: 1.50

TIAA-CREF TRUST CO., FSB

LOCATIONS

HQ: TIAA-CREF TRUST CO., FSB
1 METROPOLITAN SQ, SAINT LOUIS, MO 631022723
Phone: 314 588-9738

HISTORICAL FINANCIALS
Company Type: Private

Income Statement
FYE: December 31

	REVENUE ($ mil.)	NET INCOME ($ mil.)	NET PROFIT MARGIN	EMPLOYEES
12/15	188	(31)	—	232
12/14	137	(39)	—	—
12/13	101	(32)	—	—
Annual Growth	36.2%	—	—	—

2015 Year-End Financials
Return on assets: —   Cash ($ mil.): 99
Return on equity: (-16.6%)
Current ratio: —

TIFT REGIONAL MEDICAL CENTER

EXECUTIVES

President, William T Richardson
Director, Chad Waldron
Director, Louise Woodham
Chief Operating Officer, Chris Dorman

LOCATIONS

HQ: TIFT REGIONAL MEDICAL CENTER
901 18TH ST E, TIFTON, GA 317943648
Phone: 229 382-7120

HISTORICAL FINANCIALS
Company Type: Private

Income Statement
FYE: September 30

	REVENUE ($ mil.)	NET INCOME ($ mil.)	NET PROFIT MARGIN	EMPLOYEES
09/15	288	(0)	—	1,825
09/14	294	30	10.2%	—
09/13	292	30	10.5%	—
09/12	268	41	15.6%	—
Annual Growth	2.5%	—	—	—

2015 Year-End Financials
Return on assets: 4.8%   Cash ($ mil.): 66
Return on equity: (-0.2%)
Current ratio: 2.70

TIFT REGIONAL MEDICAL CENTER FOUNDATION, INC.

Tift Regional Medical Center (TRMC) helps keep people healthy in the Peach State. The medical center with more than 125 physicians on staff representing some 30 specialties serves residents across a dozen counties in south central Georgia. TRMC offers its patients a wide range of services including cancer treatment cardiology neurology occupational and physical therapy obstetrics and surgical care. The not-for-profit medical center has a capacity of about 190 beds. It also operates an outpatient services clinic Cook Medical Center and Cook Senior Living Center. Tift County Hospital Authority owns and operates TRMC. The hospital is also affiliated with the Emory Healthcare network.

Mergers and Acquisitions
In 2012 Tift County Hospital Authority purchased Memorial Hospital of Adel and its affiliated nursing home and ancillary services from SunLink Health Systems. Memorial Hospital of Adel was renamed Cook Medical Center-A Campus of Tift Regional Medical Center (TRMC) and 95-bed Memorial Convalescent Center was renamed Cook Senior Living Center.

EXECUTIVES

Executive Director, Manday Brooks
Director, Carla Hall
Director, Don Roberts
Manager, Gina Bennett
Production Manager, Roger Waldron

LOCATIONS

HQ: TIFT REGIONAL MEDICAL CENTER
FOUNDATION, INC.
2406 TIFT AVE N STE 203, TIFTON, GA 317941888
Phone: 229 382-7120
Web: WWW.TIFTREGIONAL.COM

PRODUCTS/OPERATIONS

Selected Services
Affinity Clinic
Allure Plastic & Reconstructive Surgery

Arthritis and osteoporosis Center of South GA
Breast Center
Cardio-pulmonary rehabilitation
Continuing Medical Education (CME)
Diabetes Learning Center
Dialysis Center
Endoscopy
HealthPlus Medical Office Centers
Heart and Vascular Center
Hospice of Tift Area
Infusion Center
Intensive Care Unit (ICU)
Lithotripsy
Neurodiagnostics Center
Oncology Center
Orthopedics
Outpatient therapy
Palliative care
Pediatrics
Primary care outreach clinics
Radiology
Respiratory care
Sleep Center
Spine Therapy Center
Tift Community Health Center
Tifton Physicians Center
Transitional Care Center
Women's health
WorkSmart Occupational Health

COMPETITORS

Doctors Hospital of Augusta
Liberty Regional Medical Center
MCG Health
Memorial Health University Medical Center
Redmond Regional Medical Center
South Georgia Medical Center
St. Joseph's/Candler Health System
University Health Services
Walton Rehabilitation Hospital

HISTORICAL FINANCIALS
Company Type: Private

Income Statement
FYE: September 30

	REVENUE ($ mil.)	NET INCOME ($ mil.)	NET PROFIT MARGIN	EMPLOYEES
09/15	288	(0)	—	168
09/14	1	0	71.6%	—
09/09	216	30	14.1%	—
09/08	0	0	47.6%	—
Annual Growth	144.2%	—	—	—

2015 Year-End Financials
Return on assets: 4.8%   Cash ($ mil.): 66
Return on equity: (-0.2%)
Current ratio: 2.70

TOM LANGE COMPANY, INC.

Tom Lange Company wants you to eat your veggies. One of the largest purchasers and distributors of fresh fruits and vegetables in the US Tom Lange supplies its comestibles to clients in the retail wholesale and food service trades. The company also provides third party logistics services specializing in truckload freight movement. The company was founded in 1960 as a three-man operation in St. Louis Missouri Tom Lange has grown to encompass 35 offices in the US and Canada. Produce subsidiaries include Seven Seas M&M Marketing and Seven Seas Fruit.

EXECUTIVES

Chief Executive Officer, Phil Gumpert
Director, Chase Tatham
Director, Hannu Huttula
Director, Denise Jones
Account Manager, Amanda Johnson
Account Manager, Mike Larue
Auditors: KERBER ECK & BRAECKEL LLP S

LOCATIONS

HQ: TOM LANGE COMPANY, INC.
755 APPLE ORCHARD RD, SPRINGFIELD, IL 627035914
Phone: 217 786-3300
Web: WWW.TOMLANGE.COM

COMPETITORS

A. Duda & Sons
Caito Foods Service
Coast Citrus Distributors
Cristina Foods
FreshPoint
Get Fresh Produce
The Oppenheimer Group
Wilson Farms

HISTORICAL FINANCIALS
Company Type: Private

Income Statement
FYE: August 31

	REVENUE ($ mil.)	NET INCOME ($ mil.)	NET PROFIT MARGIN	EMPLOYEES
08/15	441	1	0.2%	110
08/14	447	(19)	—	—
08/13	431	1	0.4%	—
08/12	414	0	0.1%	—
Annual Growth	2.1%	47.3%	—	—

2015 Year-End Financials
Return on assets: 6.6%   Cash ($ mil.): 12
Return on equity: 0.2%
Current ratio: 1.20

TORRANCE MEMORIAL MEDICAL CENTER

Back in 1925 Jared Sydney Torrance founded Torrance Memorial Medical Center in the southern California town that also bears his name. The not-for-profit medical center now includes about 445 beds surgical suites clinical and diagnostic labs and specialist centers for cancer metabolic heart and other conditions. It is one of three burn centers in Los Angeles. Torrance Memorial Medical Center reaches beyond its walls and into the community with hospice care and home health care. The hospital also provides nursing residency programs and it offers staffing support services to physicians offices in the area.

Operations
Torrance Memorial has about 1000 members on its medical staff. It is also supported by a volunteer organization with about 900 physicians.

The hospital provides more than $50 million in community benefits each year including subsidized care for Medicare and Medicaid patients and charity care for uninsured patients. Other programs include community outreach efforts including parenting and wellness classes.

Geographic Reach
Torrance Memorial serves residents of communities in the South Bay Peninsula and Harbor areas within the Los Angeles metropolitan area.

Company Background
In 2012 Torrance Memorial earned the Magnet recognition from the American Nurses Credential-ing Center which is given to top 6% of hospitals in the US.

Founded by Jared Torrance and his wife Helena in 1925 Torrance Memorial acquired the smaller Riviera Community Hospital in 1967. The medical center moved to its current location in 1971.

EXECUTIVES

President and CEO, Craig Leach
VP Finance, Bill Larson
VP Information Technology and CIO, Bernadette Reid
VP Nursing, Barb LeQuire
Senior Vice President H PA, Chris Rogers
President Foundation Board, Mark Lurie
Vice President Foundation Board, Phil Pavesi

LOCATIONS

HQ: TORRANCE MEMORIAL MEDICAL CENTER
3330 LOMITA BLVD, TORRANCE, CA 905055002
Phone: 310 325-9110

PRODUCTS/OPERATIONS

Selected Centers and Services
Bariatric Surgery Program
Blood Donor Center
Breast Diagnostic Center
Burn Center
Cancer Institute
Cardiovascular Institute
Chemical Dependency
Diabetes
Eating Disorders Program
Emergency Care
Endoscopy Center and GI Lab
Home Health
Hospice
Laboratory Testing (includes Outpatient Lab)
Maternal Child Health Services
Nuclear Medicine
Orthopedics
Palliative Care
Pediatrics
Pharmacy
Radiation Oncology
Radiology
Rehabilitation
Sleep Disorders Center
Stroke Center
Surgical Services
Transitional Care Unit
Urgent Care
Wound Center

COMPETITORS

Brotman Medical Center
Cedars-Sinai Medical Center
Childrens Hospital Los Angeles
Dignity Health
Good Samaritan Hospital (Los Angeles)
HCA
Hollywood Presbyterian Medical Center
Long Beach Memorial
Providence Health System Southern California
Sisters of Charity of Leavenworth
Tenet Healthcare
Universal Health Services
White Memorial Medical Center

HISTORICAL FINANCIALS
Company Type: Private

Income Statement
FYE: December 31

	REVENUE ($ mil.)	NET INCOME ($ mil.)	NET PROFIT MARGIN	EMPLOYEES
12/16*	620	14	2.4%	3,500
09/16	454	3	0.9%	—
06/16	303	5	1.9%	—
03/16	152	3	2.2%	—
Annual Growth	307.2%	346.8%	—	—

*Fiscal year change

2016 Year-End Financials

Return on assets: 6.3%   Cash ($ mil.): 35
Return on equity: 2.4%
Current ratio: 0.50

TORRANCE UNIFIED SCHOOL DISTRICT

EXECUTIVES

Chief Executive Officer, Michael Wermers
Personnel Director, Donna Matoy
Director, Lynn Bedrosian

LOCATIONS

HQ: TORRANCE UNIFIED SCHOOL DISTRICT
2335 PLAZA DEL AMO, TORRANCE, CA 905013420
Phone: 310 972-6500
Web: WWW.TUSD.ORG

HISTORICAL FINANCIALS

Company Type: Private

Income Statement

FYE: June 30

	REVENUE ($ mil.)	NET INCOME ($ mil.)	NET PROFIT MARGIN	EMPLOYEES
06/16*	282	24	8.8%	1,806
02/09	0	0	21.9%	—
06/06	212	0	—	—
06/99	137	32	23.4%	—
Annual Growth	4.4%	(1.5%)	—	—

*Fiscal year change

2016 Year-End Financials

Return on assets: 14.8%   Cash ($ mil.): 323
Return on equity: 8.8%
Current ratio: —

TOTAL LONGTERM CARE, INC.

EXECUTIVES

Chairman, Lee Anneberg
Board of Directors, Lori Rothwell
Financial Executive, Karen Flores
Personnel Manager, Clay Cooper
Personnel Manager, Kathy Ginsburg
Auditors: BKD LLP COLORADO SPRINGS CO

LOCATIONS

HQ: TOTAL LONGTERM CARE, INC.
8950 E LOWRY BLVD, DENVER, CO 802307030
Phone: 303 832-1001
Web: WWW.TOTALLONGTERMCARE.ORG

HISTORICAL FINANCIALS

Company Type: Private

Income Statement

FYE: June 30

	REVENUE ($ mil.)	NET INCOME ($ mil.)	NET PROFIT MARGIN	EMPLOYEES
06/15	173	16	9.7%	580
06/13	140	13	9.6%	—
06/11	123	14	11.7%	—
06/10	125	0	0.0%	—
Annual Growth	6.6%	1542.4%	—	—

2015 Year-End Financials

Return on assets: 8.0%   Cash ($ mil.): 52
Return on equity: 9.7%
Current ratio: 1.30

TOURO INFIRMARY

EXECUTIVES

President, James Montgomery
Personnel Manager, Mary Batthaglea
Manager, Claudia Ruello
Executive Director, Barbara Adcock
Personnel Director, Cindy Mousa

LOCATIONS

HQ: TOURO INFIRMARY
1401 FOUCHER ST, NEW ORLEANS, LA 701153593
Phone: 504 897-7011
Web: WWW.THETOUROFOUNDATION.COM

HISTORICAL FINANCIALS

Company Type: Private

Income Statement

FYE: December 31

	REVENUE ($ mil.)	NET INCOME ($ mil.)	NET PROFIT MARGIN	EMPLOYEES
12/15	273	35	12.8%	1,424
12/14	271	9	3.4%	—
12/13	348	82	23.7%	—
12/12	306	31	10.4%	—
Annual Growth	(3.7%)	3.4%	—	—

2015 Year-End Financials

Return on assets: 6.4%   Cash ($ mil.): 31
Return on equity: 12.8%
Current ratio: 0.50

TOWNSHIP HIGH SCHOOL DISTRICT 211 FOUNDATION

Township High School District 211 is the largest high school district in Illinois with some 12500 students attending its five high schools (grades 9 to 12) — James B. Conant William Fremd Hoffman Estates Palatine and Schaumburg — and two special education academies. The district's student-teacher ratio is nearly 14-to-1 and serves several suburban communities 25 miles northwest of Chicago. The school district started as one school (Palatine High School) in the Palatine-Schaumburg Township area in 1875 with the first graduating class in 1877.

Geographic Reach

Township High School District 211 serves the northwest suburbs of Chicago including the the communities of Hoffman Estates Inverness Palatine and Schaumburg as well as parts of Arlington Heights Elk Grove Village Hanover Park Rolling Meadows Roselle Streamwood and South Barrington.

Financial Performance

The school district reported revenue of nearly $240 million in 2012 nearly 85% of it coming from local property taxes.

HISTORY

All five district schools have been named among the top schools in the nation.

EXECUTIVES

Department Chair Teacher, Kristy Loughin-Vance
Auditors: BAKER TILLY VIRCHOW KRAUSE

LOCATIONS

HQ: TOWNSHIP HIGH SCHOOL DISTRICT 211 FOUNDATION
1750 S ROSELLE RD STE 100, PALATINE, IL 600677302
Phone: 708 359-3300
Web: WWW.D211.ORG

PRODUCTS/OPERATIONS

Schools
High Schools
James B. Conant High School
William Fremd High School
Hoffman Estates High School
Palatine High School
Schaumburg High School
Special Education Schools
District 211 Academy North
District 211 Academy South

HISTORICAL FINANCIALS

Company Type: Private

Income Statement

FYE: June 30

	REVENUE ($ mil)	NET INCOME ($ mil)	NET PROFIT MARGIN	EMPLOYEES
06/16	304	(10)	—	1,909
06/15	296	(17)	—	—
06/14	280	(8)	—	—
06/13	268	19	7.2%	—
Annual Growth	4.4%	—	—	—

TOWNSHIP HIGH SCHOOL DISTRICT 214

EXECUTIVES

President, Alva Kreutcer
Director, Jonnie Thomas
Auditors: BAKER TILLY VIRCHOW KRAUSE LL

LOCATIONS

HQ: TOWNSHIP HIGH SCHOOL DISTRICT 214
2121 S GOEBBERT RD, ARLINGTON HEIGHTS, IL 600054205
Phone: 847 718-7600
Web: WWW.D214.ORG

Company Type: Private

Income Statement				FYE: June 30
	REVENUE ($ mil.)	NET INCOME ($ mil.)	NET PROFIT MARGIN	EMPLOYEES
06/16	306	(14)	—	1,550
06/13	282	11	4.1%	—
06/12	259	15	6.0%	—
06/08	1,130	0	0.0%	—
Annual Growth	(15.0%)	—	—	—

2016 Year-End Financials

Return on assets: —
Return on equity: (-4.6%)
Current ratio: —

Cash ($ mil.): 5

TRAMMO, INC.

Stockpiles of fertilizers liquefied petroleum gas (LPG) and petrochemicals are the "ammo" which international trader Trammo (formerly Transammonia) uses in its battle with competitors. The company trades distributes and transports these commodities around the world. Trammo's fertilizer business includes ammonia phosphates and urea. Its Sea-3 subsidiary imports and distributes propane to residential commercial and industrial customers in the northeastern US and Florida. The Trammochem unit trades in petrochemicals specializing in aromatics and olefins. Its Trammo Gas trades LPG and propane as well as ethane butane and natural gas in the US.

Operations

The company operates three divisions: Chemicals Commodities and Gas. The Chemicals Division's annual sales volumes is about 5.6 million metric tons. It key products include aromatics olefins and oxygenates. The Commodities Division accounts for two thirds of the Trammo's sales volumes and more than half of its revenues; it's worldwide traded volume is 29.2 million metric tons a year. The Gas Division's business areas include LPG business Trammo Gas and Petrochemicals Ltd and Sea-3 Inc. Trammo's international traded ammonia volume is 3 million metric tons annually.

Sea-3 is the largest importer and distributor of liquefied propane in the Northeastern US. It also supplies propane to the western and central portions of Florida. It moves 200000 metric tons of product per year.

Trammochem merchandises and trades in petrochemicals around the world.

Trammo Gas markets and trades LPG (primarily propane) in the US. Trammo Gas International Inc. operates two gas carriers which transport LPG worldwide for third parties.

Geographic Reach

Trammo has expanded its reach into the global market establishing merchandising and trading offices in Singapore China and the United Arab Emirates. Those offices complement its other global operations in Africa Asia Europe the Middle East and North and South America (Argentina Brazil and Chile). It has major representative offices in Beijing Cairo Dubai and Shanghai.

Its Fertilizers and Commodities Division's regional hubs are in Zurich Tampa Dubai Shanghai and Singapore; the Ammonia Division has hubs in Tampa and Dubai. The Chemicals Division maintains regional hubs in Zurich Dubai Shanghai and Singapore; while the Gas Division maintains hubs in Houston Tampa and Newington (New Hampshire).

Trammo has about 30 offices worldwide.

Sales and Marketing

To bridge the gap between the production locations and consumers sites Trammo owns and operates a fleet of railcars dedicated to transporting of molten sulfur in across the US. The Commodities Division about 650 railcars to ship dry and liquid fertilizers sulfur sulfuric acid and ammonia.

Strategy

In late 2016 it was reported that Trammo would exit the petrochemicals trading market following a reorganization.

In 2015 the company's Ammonia Division and Fertilizers and Commodities Division merged into a new division — Commodities. The merger allows Trammo to increase operational synergies use its global infrastructure to provide a larger portfolio of products and to more clearly present itself as a single company with different products.

Trammo opened offices in Ivory Coast and Dar Es Salaam in 2014 to strengthens its presence in the emerging African market.

Company Background

In 2013 Transammonia changed its name to Trammo to more accurately represent the broad spectrum of products and services it provides.

In 2010 the company's bulk carriers division entered the commodity shipping business. TA Bulk Carriers operates a fleet of 15 to 20 vessels which trade worldwide but focus on the handysize market (25000-35000 metric tons deadweight) in the Atlantic basin. In 2010 it transported about 2.9 million metric tons of cargo primarily fertilizers and grains.

Ronald Stanton founded the company in 1965 as an international ammonia trader. It branched into fertilizer merchandising and trading in 1967 LPG trading in 1978 and petrochemicals trading in 1987.

EXECUTIVES

EVP COO and CFO, Edward G. Weiner
CEO Chemicals Division, Ashok Kishore
President CEO Director and CEO Commodities Division, Brent Hart
SVP Global Risk Management, Oliver K. Stanton
Senior Vice President, Dudley Cox
Senior Vice President Finance and Treasury, James Benfield
Vice President And Controller, Robert Lovett
Vice President, David Herr
Senior Vice President And General Counse, Louis Epstein
Vice President Of Human Resources, Pat Berry
Senior Vice President Ammonia Division, Bernard Rock
Vice President Finance and Treasury, Donald Madden
Vice President, Todd Matthes
Auditors: DELOITTE & TOUCHE LLP NEW YOR

LOCATIONS

HQ: TRAMMO, INC.
1 ROCKEFELLER PLZ FL 9, NEW YORK, NY 100202078
Phone: 212 223-3200
Web: WWW.TRAMMO.COM

PRODUCTS/OPERATIONS

Major SubsidiariesSea-3 (liquefied propane)Trammo Gas (LPG)Trammo Gas International Inc. (LPG transportation for third parties.Trammo Petroleum (crude oil and oil products)Trammochem (petrochemicals)Fertilizers and CommoditiesNitrogen BasedAnhydrous Ammo

COMPETITORS

BASF SE	HELM
CF Industries	Koch Industries Inc.
Cargill	Magellan Midstream
ConAgra	Yara
Dynegy	

HISTORICAL FINANCIALS

Company Type: Private

Income Statement				FYE: December 31
	REVENUE ($ mil.)	NET INCOME ($ mil.)	NET PROFIT MARGIN	EMPLOYEES
12/15	8,922	32	0.4%	350
12/14	11,266	31	0.3%	—
12/13	11,315	(11)	—	—
12/12	12,152	35	0.3%	—
Annual Growth	(9.8%)	(2.4%)	—	—

2015 Year-End Financials

Return on assets: 5.4%
Return on equity: 0.4%
Current ratio: 1.00

Cash ($ mil.): 215

TRANS-SYSTEM, INC.

Freight hauler Trans-System operates through three main units: System Transport (flatbed); TW Transport (refrigerated and dry van); and James J. Williams (bulk commodities). The Trans-System trucking companies operate from some 10 terminals in the western US. Overall the company's fleet consists of about 1000 tractors and 1500 trailers. Trans-System also offers logistics services and runs a driver training school. Jim Williams founded the company in 1972 although it got its start when Williams' grandfather began transporting petroleum products throughout northern Idaho and eastern Washington.

EXECUTIVES

CEO, James C. (Jim) Williams
CFO, Deanna Adams
EVP, Dale Peterson
Auditors: EIDEBAILLY LLP SPOKANE WASHI

LOCATIONS

HQ: TRANS-SYSTEM, INC.
7405 S HAYFORD RD, CHENEY, WA 990049633
Phone: 509 623-4001
Web: WWW.TRANS-SYSTEM.COM

COMPETITORS

C.R. England	Quality Distribution
CRST International	Ruan Transportation
Comcar	Management Systems
Crete Carrier	Schneider National
Maverick USA	Werner Enterprises
Prime Inc.	

HISTORICAL FINANCIALS
Company Type: Private

Income Statement
FYE: March 31

	REVENUE ($ mil.)	NET INCOME ($ mil.)	NET PROFIT MARGIN	EMPLOYEES
03/16	236	5	2.1%	650
03/15	228	15	6.6%	—
03/14	209	6	3.1%	—
03/13	197	8	4.1%	—
Annual Growth	6.2%	(14.7%)	—	—

2016 Year-End Financials
Return on assets: 2.2%
Return on equity: 2.1%
Current ratio: 0.70
Cash ($ mil.): 3

TRANSCONTINENTAL GAS PIPE LINE COMPANY, LLC

EXECUTIVES
Chief Executive Officer, Rory L Miller
Vice-President, Frank J Ferazzi
Financial Executive, Jeffrey P Heinrichs
Auditors: ERNST & YOUNG LLP HOUSTON TE

LOCATIONS
HQ: TRANSCONTINENTAL GAS PIPE LINE COMPANY, LLC
2800 POST OAK BLVD, HOUSTON, TX 770566100
Phone: 713 215-2000

COMPETITORS
Dominion Questar
Gulfstream
Piedmont Natural Gas
Southern Union
Southwest Gas

HISTORICAL FINANCIALS
Company Type: Private

Income Statement
FYE: December 31

	REVENUE ($ mil.)	NET INCOME ($ mil.)	NET PROFIT MARGIN	EMPLOYEES
12/16	1,616	523	32.4%	4
12/15	1,592	575	36.1%	—
12/14	1,433	422	29.5%	—
12/13	1,356	374	27.6%	—
Annual Growth	6.0%	11.9%	—	—

TRAYLOR BROS., INC.

At Traylor Bros Inc. (TBI) building bridges and tunnels is a family affair. The family-owned heavy/civil construction company mostly builds suspension and segmental bridges dams and ports storm sewers and transmission lines. Its Underground division works on tunneling projects while its Traylor Mining LLC subsidiary works on underground mining projects and facilities for copper gold and coal mine development in North America.

TBI is perhaps best known for its work for the San Francisco's Bay Area Rapid Transit (BART) system and the I-10 span bridges over Lake Pontchartrain in Louisiana. Civil engineer William Traylor founded TBI in Indiana in 1946.

Operations

Traylor Bros operates three main divisions (as of early 2016). Its National Heavy Civil division works on cable-layered and segmental bridges deep water piers wharf facilities transit terminals locks and dams. The Underground division works on tunneling projects using methods such as mixed-shield/slurry earth pressure balance and hard rock tunnel boring. The Traylor Mining LLC division works on shaft decline and underground developments and builds facilities for mining projects.

Geographic Reach

Evansville Indiana Based Traylor Bros builds heavy civil projects mostly in areas near water across the US including areas on the coasts and inland waterways across the western US as well as in Hawaii Alaska Mexico and Canada. The company's underground division works on tunnel projects in North America and abroad. It has east and west coast offices in Alexandria Virginia and Long Beach California respectively. Traylor Mining LLC is located in Lakewood Colorado.

Strategy

TBI reiterated in early 2016 that its primary focus is to "expand beyond several large sponsored projects per division while being sure to select work that requires our specialized technical expertise." The family-owned and run company emphasized the importance of its Vision Mission and Values and keeping with "the Traylor Way" which is "critical to our identity and success."

EXECUTIVES
Chairman and CEO, Thomas W. (Tom) Traylor, age 77
Co-President and COO, Christopher S. Traylor
Co-President, Michael T. Traylor
Vice President Division Manager National Heavy Civil Division, John Meagher
Auditors: BKD LLP EVANSVILLE INDIANA

LOCATIONS
HQ: TRAYLOR BROS., INC.
835 N CONGRESS AVE, EVANSVILLE, IN 477152484
Phone: 812 477-1542

PRODUCTS/OPERATIONS

Selected Projects
Bill Emerson Memorial Bridge Cape Girardeau MO
Blue Plains Tunnel Washington DC
Cofferdam for Cannelton Hydroelectric Project Hawesville KY
IH 45 Galveston Causeway Bridge Replacement Galveston TX
Inner Harbor Navigation Channel New Orleans LA
Kaumalapau Harbor Breakwater Repair Lanai HI
McAlpine Lock Replacement Project Louisville KY
New NY Bridge (Tappan Zee Bridge) Tarrytown NY
Northeast Interceptor Sewer Los Angeles CA
Queens Bored Tunnels East Side Access Project New York NY
Regional Connector Transit Project Los Angeles CA
San Elijo Ocean Outfall Reballast Project San Diego CA
Stan Musial Veterans Memorial Bridge St. Louis MO
University Link Light Rail U220 Tunnel Seattle WA
US 90 Biloxi Bay Bridge Replacement Biloxi MS
Wickenburg-Kingman Highway (US 93) Burro Creek Section Kingman AZ

Selected Divisions
Heavy Civil
Traylor Mining
Traylor Pacific
Underground

COMPETITORS
American Bridge Company
American Infrastructure
Balfour Beatty Infrastructure
Barnard Construction
Garney Holding
Gohmann Asphalt & Construction
Granite Construction
MBC Holding
Milestone Contractors
Peter Kiewit Sons'
Rasmussen Group
Superior Construction
TIC Holdings
Walsh Group

HISTORICAL FINANCIALS
Company Type: Private

Income Statement
FYE: December 31

	REVENUE ($ mil.)	NET INCOME ($ mil.)	NET PROFIT MARGIN	EMPLOYEES
12/15	250	0	—	412
12/14	250	0	—	—
12/13	250	0	—	—
12/12	250	0	—	—
Annual Growth	(0.0%)	—	—	—

2015 Year-End Financials
Return on assets: 17.4%
Return on equity: —
Current ratio: 1.50
Cash ($ mil.): 236

TRI-CITY HOSPITAL DISTRICT INC

For those in southern California's North County the Tri-City Healthcare District is there to take care of your medical needs. The organization provides primary and acute health care services primarily through Tri-City Medical Center. The hospital which has more than 500 physicians representing 60 specialties boasts about 400 beds. In addition to the medical center Tri-City Healthcare District operates the Beatrice Riggs French Women's Center an outpatient facility that offers services to women and newborns. One of the hospital's specialties is diagnosing and treating behavioral and developmental difficulties in children. In addition Tri-City Healthcare District offers home and hospice care.

Operations

Tri-City Medical Center which opened its doors in 1961 provides an occupational health program and offers specialties in women's health robotic surgery cancer treatment and emergency care. It operates the only Level III neonatal intensive care unit (NICU) in North County in addition to an orthopedic and spine institute a cardiovascular health institute and a neurological institute. Additionally it operates the Tri-City Wellness Center in Carlsbad.

The District also owns 60% of Tri-City Medical Center ASC Operators which provides management services to North Coast Surgery Center.

Geographic Reach

The center serves the coastal region north of San Diego including the communities of Carlsbad Oceanside San Marcos and Vista.

Sales and Marketing

HMO and PPO payments accounted for 35% of net patient revenue in 2014; Medicare accounted for 30% while the state's Medi-Cal plans accounted for 20%.

Financial Performance

Revenues increased 4% to $319 million in 2014 on increased net patient service earnings which rose due to an increase in outpatient visits. Net income totaled $3 million (versus a net loss in 2013) due to a decrease in interest expenses and the receipt of some $5.5 million in legal settlement income.

Meanwhile cash flow from operations increased 144% to $12 million.

Strategy

In 2015 Tri-City Healthcare District opened a new clinic Tri-City Primary Care in Vista.

EXECUTIVES

Vice President Marketing Community Relations, Francisco J Valle
Vice President Information TEC, Joseph Gilmore
Director Managed Care, Kerry Mills
Senior Vice President Of Information Technology, Daniel Martinez
Treas, Rosemarie V Reno

LOCATIONS

HQ: TRI-CITY HOSPITAL DISTRICT INC
4002 VISTA WAY, OCEANSIDE, CA 920564506
Phone: 760 724-8411

PRODUCTS/OPERATIONS

2014 Sales

	% of total
Net patient service	91
Premium revenue	7
Other revenue	2
Total	**100**

Selected Services

Behavioral Health
Cancer
Clinical Research
Emergency Services
Heart Care
Home Health Care
Imaging
Intensive Care
Laser & Aesthetics
Medical Library
Occupational Medicine
Orthopaedic and Spine Institute
Rehabilitation
Stroke Center
Surgical Services
Wellness
Women's Care
Wound Care

COMPETITORS

Grossmont Hospital
Palomar Health
Paradise Valley Hospital
Rady Children's Hospital
Scripps Health
Sharp HealthCare
Southwest Healthcare

HISTORICAL FINANCIALS

Company Type: Private

Income Statement
FYE: June 30

	REVENUE ($ mil.)	NET INCOME ($ mil.)	NET PROFIT MARGIN	EMPLOYEES
06/15	321	1	0.5%	2,121
06/10	279	(11)	—	—
06/08	267	9	3.5%	—
06/07	1,232	0	—	—
Annual Growth	**—**	**193.7%**	**—**	**—**

2015 Year-End Financials
Return on assets: 10.6%   Cash ($ mil.): 14
Return on equity: 0.5%
Current ratio: 0.50

TRIAD E&C HOLDINGS, L.L.C.

EXECUTIVES

Manager, Brian Bordelon
Board of Directors, Tami H Misuraca
Auditors: HANNIS T BOURGEOIS LLP BATON

LOCATIONS

HQ: TRIAD E&C HOLDINGS, L.L.C.
8183 W EL CAJON DR, BATON ROUGE, LA 708158035
Phone: 225 927-8921

HISTORICAL FINANCIALS

Company Type: Private

Income Statement
FYE: June 30

	REVENUE ($ mil.)	NET INCOME ($ mil.)	NET PROFIT MARGIN	EMPLOYEES
06/16	306	0	—	1,300
06/15	291	0	—	—
06/14	188	0	—	—
Annual Growth	**27.4%**	**—**	**—**	**—**

2016 Year-End Financials
Return on assets: 1.1%   Cash ($ mil.): 17
Return on equity: —
Current ratio: 1.80

TRIAD ELECTRIC & CONTROLS INC

EXECUTIVES

President, Brian Bordelon
Board of Directors, Tami H Misuraca
Operations Manager, Mark Bourg
Project Manager, Rob Wright
Auditors: HANNIS T BOURGEOIS LLP BATON

LOCATIONS

HQ: TRIAD ELECTRIC & CONTROLS INC
2288 N AIRWAY DR, BATON ROUGE, LA 708158132
Phone: 225 923-0604
Web: WWW.TRIADELECTRICANDCONTROLS.COM

HISTORICAL FINANCIALS

Company Type: Private

Income Statement
FYE: June 30

	REVENUE ($ mil.)	NET INCOME ($ mil.)	NET PROFIT MARGIN	EMPLOYEES
06/16	286	0	—	1,200
06/15	269	0	—	—
06/14	172	0	—	—
06/13	185	0	—	—
Annual Growth	**15.6%**	**—**	**—**	**—**

2016 Year-End Financials
Return on assets: 1.1%   Cash ($ mil.): 8
Return on equity: —
Current ratio: 1.70

TRIBOROUGH BRIDGE & TUNNEL AUTHORITY

EXECUTIVES

Manager, Choling Blakey
Financial Executive, Jim Elkin
Engineer, Teresa Ceragioli

LOCATIONS

HQ: TRIBOROUGH BRIDGE & TUNNEL AUTHORITY ROBERT MOSES BLDG RANDAL, NEW YORK, NY 10035
Phone: 212 360-3000

HISTORICAL FINANCIALS

Company Type: Private

Income Statement
FYE: December 31

	REVENUE ($ mil.)	NET INCOME ($ mil.)	NET PROFIT MARGIN	EMPLOYEES
12/15	1,843	165	9.0%	1,500
12/07	1,263	79	6.3%	—
12/06	1,259	163	13.0%	—
12/05	1	0	68.6%	—
Annual Growth	**107.4%**	**69.3%**	**—**	**—**

2015 Year-End Financials
Return on assets: 5.8%   Cash ($ mil.): 13
Return on equity: 9.0%
Current ratio: —

TRINITY HEALTH

EXECUTIVES

Chief Executive Officer, John M Kutch
Auditors: CLIFTON LARSON ALLEN LLP MINN

LOCATIONS

HQ: TRINITY HEALTH
1 BURDICK EXPY W, MINOT, ND 587014406
Phone: 701 857-5260

HISTORICAL FINANCIALS

Company Type: Private

Income Statement
FYE: June 30

	REVENUE ($ mil.)	NET INCOME ($ mil.)	NET PROFIT MARGIN	EMPLOYEES
06/15	430	16	3.9%	2,600
06/14	427	46	10.8%	—
06/13	900	(14)	—	—
06/10	71	(16)	—	—
Annual Growth	**43.3%**	**—**	**—**	**—**

2015 Year-End Financials
Return on assets: 6.5%   Cash ($ mil.): 107
Return on equity: 3.9%
Current ratio: 2.50

TRINITY HOSPITAL HOLDING COMPANY

EXECUTIVES

Chairman of the Board, Clyde Metzger
Board of Directors, Albert Pavlik
Vice-President, Melissa Buksa
Auditors: ERNST & YOUNG LLP PITTSBURGH

LOCATIONS

HQ: TRINITY HOSPITAL HOLDING COMPANY
  380 SUMMIT AVE, STEUBENVILLE, OH 439522667
Phone: 740 264-8000

HISTORICAL FINANCIALS
Company Type: Private

Income Statement
FYE: December 31

	REVENUE ($ mil.)	NET INCOME ($ mil.)	NET PROFIT MARGIN	EMPLOYEES
12/15	231	0	0.1%	1,640
12/14	223	4	1.8%	—
12/13	206	14	7.1%	—
12/12	200	10	5.4%	—
Annual Growth	4.9%	(77.4%)	—	—

2015 Year-End Financials
Return on assets: 5.4%
Return on equity: 0.1%
Current ratio: 1.60
Cash ($ mil.): 4

TRIOS HEALTH

EXECUTIVES

Chief Executive Officer, Louis Koussa
Director, Leslie Juzek
Director, Charla Seay
Accountant, Lena Hui

LOCATIONS

HQ: TRIOS HEALTH
  900 S AUBURN ST, KENNEWICK, WA 993365621
Phone: 509 586-6111
Web: WWW.TRIOSHEALTH.ORG

HISTORICAL FINANCIALS
Company Type: Private

Income Statement
FYE: December 31

	REVENUE ($ mil.)	NET INCOME ($ mil.)	NET PROFIT MARGIN	EMPLOYEES
12/15	177	2	1.5%	540
12/14	157	(4)	—	—
12/13	144	(2)	—	—
12/12	138	0	0.4%	—
Annual Growth	8.6%	71.7%	—	—

2015 Year-End Financials
Return on assets: 8.8%
Return on equity: 1.5%
Current ratio: 1.00
Cash ($ mil.): 10

TRUMAN ARNOLD COMPANIES

It is not just jibber jabber — this jobber gets the job done by distributing wholesale petroleum across the US. Truman Arnold Companies (TAC) has more than 400 associates with fuel volume of more than 2 billion gallons a year and markets and distributes petroleum products to customers through its TAC Energy subsidiary. Through a partnership it operates two major petroleum terminals one in Arkansas and one in Texas which collectively have more than 1.3 million barrels of capacity. Through its TAC Air unit the company offers fixed-based operations (FBO) including aircraft fueling hangar and ground transportation services through 14 general aviation facilities located across the US.

Operations

TAC's Aviation Services Wholesale Petroleum Marketing Branded Petroleum Marketing and Petroleum Terminal Services operations function independently but take advantage of shared management and technical resources. The company's major subsidiaries include TAC Air TAC Energy Cowhorn Creek Fuel Base and Keystone Aviation.

The company's Aviation Services maintains a fleet of aircraft and is engaged in aircraft maintenance sales and brokerage and aircraft management.

Strategy

In 2015 TAC Energy launched ENERGIZE Online a new product that provides an improved user interface for managing fuel purchase transactions

Aviation Services is a growth market. In 2013 Keystone Aviation expanded its line of aviation products and services by making its Aurora Oregon shop a Cirrus Authorized Service Center to serve Cirrus owners in and around Oregon. In addition to Cirrus the Aurora location is an authorized service center for Daher-Socata. That year Keystone Aviation also became a Quest Aircraft (turboprops) distributor in California Colorado Nevada and Utah.

Mergers and Acquisitions

In 2015 TAC Air purchased the facilities of Central Flying Service at the Bill and Hillary Clinton National Airport in Little Rock and will operate its fueling ground handling hangar operations and other related services as part of the TAC Air network. Also included is the purchase of Airport Services Inc. which provides airline fueling services.

Company Background

The company opened its 13th FBO in 2009 in the Spirit of St. Louis Airport in Chesterfield Missouri. It opened an executive terminal (its first at any FBO location) at Blue Grass Airport in Kentucky in July 2010. To raise cash in October 2010 TAC Air sold its Greenville South Carolina FBO operation to Greenville Jet Center for undisclosed terms.

TAC has also grown its wholesale energy segment. In 2009 TAC Energy acquired Fuel Managers (which has operations in 18 states) for an undisclosed price. The acquisition of the fuel wholesaler helped to boost TAC Energy's position in the supply market in the Central and Western US.

To keep up with the growth of the company in 2011 TAC expanded its Dallas sales office. The company anticipates doubling in size by 2016 and sees Dallas as a key operational/sales hub for managing its growth.

In 2012 to gain operational and financial support from another private energy company TAC Energy also combined its Caddo Mills Texas and North Little Rock Arkansas terminal operations into a master limited partnership with JP Energy Partners LP.

Expanding its fuel supply businesses in 2013 TAC Energy completed construction of a new diesel exhaust fluid distribution hub. The expansion at the terminal enabled TAC Energy to become a Tier 1 distributor of TerraCair Ultrapure Diesel Exhaust Fluid.

The family-owned and -operated company was founded in 1964 by Texarkana businessman Truman Arnold. It once operated a chain of 125 Road Runner convenience stores in eight states before selling this network to Total Petroleum in 1989. TAC revived the brand in 2003.

EXECUTIVES

President and CEO, Gregory A. (Greg) Arnold
SVP and CFO, Steve McMillen
VP and CIO, Michael Davis
Vice President and Chief Operating Officer, Fred Sloan
Chairman and CEO, Truman Arnold
Auditors: THOMAS & THOMAS LLP TEXARKANA

LOCATIONS

HQ: TRUMAN ARNOLD COMPANIES
  701 S ROBISON RD, TEXARKANA, TX 755016747
Phone: 903 794-3835
Web: WWW.TACEMPLOYMENT.COM

COMPETITORS

Atlantic Aviation	Signature Flight
Gulf Oil	Sun Coast Resources
Million Air	Warren Equities

HISTORICAL FINANCIALS
Company Type: Private

Income Statement
FYE: September 30

	REVENUE ($ mil.)	NET INCOME ($ mil.)	NET PROFIT MARGIN	EMPLOYEES
09/16	1,525	18	1.2%	550
09/15	1,595	17	1.1%	—
09/14	2,259	11	0.5%	—
09/13	2,172	54	2.5%	—
Annual Growth	(11.1%)	(30.0%)	—	—

2016 Year-End Financials
Return on assets: 4.6%
Return on equity: 1.2%
Current ratio: 0.80
Cash ($ mil.): 6

TRUSTEES INDIANA UNIVERSITY

Indiana University has been schooling Hoosiers (and others) since 1820. With a population of some 115000 students from all 50 states and more than 130 countries the university offers more than 1000 associate baccalaureate master's professional and doctoral degree programs at eight campuses: flagship institution IU-Bloomington; regional campuses in Fort Wayne Gary Kokomo New Albany Richmond and South Bend; and an urban campus in Indianapolis that is operated with Purdue University. The university has about 20000 faculty and professional and support staff. It has 200 re-

search centers and institutes and offers courses in more than 70 languages.

Operations

The university offers more than 200 undergraduate majors and more than 300 graduate programs; it also boasts more than 300 study-abroad programs. It has a student-teacher ratio of about 17:1.

Indiana University has more than 306000 total living alumni including nearly 248000 Indiana residents. For the academic year 2014-15 the university charged undergraduate tuition and fees of $10388 for residents and $33240 for non-residents. It awarded $1.1 billion in financial aid that year.

Indiana University-Purdue University Indianapolis (IUPUI) is considered an "up and coming" university by U.S. News and World Report . With nearly 20 schools and degrees granted in more than 200 programs IUPUI enrolls more than 30000 students from both the Indiana University and Purdue University systems.

The IPFW Office of Research Engagement and Sponsored Programs supports research business efforts and establishes partnerships with area public and private organizations.

Geographic Reach

The university has major campuses in Bloomington and Indianapolis and regional campuses in Gary Kokomo New Albany Richmond and South Bend. It enrolls more than 50% of the students from the St. Joseph County area.

Financial Performance

Indiana University's revenues grew 1% in fiscal year 2015 to $2.2 billion. The largest single source of operating revenues for the university is student tuition and fees (accounting for 55% of total revenues). That year a 4% increase in student fees helped to offset a 40% decline in sales and services of educational units.

Net income fell 31% to $138 million in 2015 as interest earnings declined. Operating cash outflow remained flat at $534 million largely due to higher payments to employees.

Strategy

Indiana University is dedicated to keeping tuition increases as low as possible and providing extensive financial aid for qualified students. It also aims to educate its students on managing and reducing their student loan debt.

The university plans to expand and renovate its School of Public and Environmental Affairs building; the project will cost some $12 million and is expected to be complete in early 2017. In mid-2015 a new hall housing the Lilly Family School of Philanthropy was opened on the IUPUI campus. Also that year Indiana University completed the construction of a $53 million building for the new School of Global and International Studies.

The university will also continue to expand its Global Gateway Network. It officially opened offices in China and India in 2014; other target markets include the Middle East Europe Latin America and Africa.

Company Background

An 1820 statute created the Indiana Seminary the predecessor to Indiana University. In 1828 the legislature changed the name of the institution to Indiana College and in 1838 it established Indiana University.

EXECUTIVES

President, Michael A. McRobbie
Chancellor IU Southeast, Sandra R. Patterson-Randles
Chancellor IU South Bend, Una Mae Reck
EVP and Chancellor IU-Purdue University Indianapolis, Charles R. Bantz
Dean School of Law, Lauren Robel

Interim VP CFO and Treasurer, MaryFrances McCourt
EVP University Regional Affairs Planning and Policy, John S. Applegate
VP Information Technology and CIO, Bradley C. (Brad) Wheeler
Chancellor IU Northwest, William J. Lowe
Interim Chancellor IU East, Larry Richards
Interim Chancellor IU Kokomo, Susan Sciame-Giesecke
Chancellor IU-Purdue University Fort Wayne, Vicky L. Carwein
President of Indiana University on, Alfred Ryors
President to Assume Office, David Jordan
President and professor of botany at Indiana University, John Coulter
President on, John Ryan
Vice President Affairs, David Zaret
Executive Vice President And Chief Marke, Eric Bruder
Assistant Vice President Finance, Linda Hunt
Associate Vice President of Finance, Stew Cobine
Associate Vice President and University Budget Office Direct, Stephen Keucher
Assistant Vice President, John Talbott
Associate Vice President Enterprise Software, Barry Walsh
Vice President for Information Technology, Christine Fitzpatrick
Vice President, Julie Head
Vice President Of Engagement, Garrett Lance
Vice President Information Technology Advancement Web Communications, Duane Schau
Vice President, Cory Cochran
Associate Vice President for International Services, Christopher Viers
Assistant Vice President Networks, Dave Jent
Associate Vice President Marketing, Rob Zinkan
Senior Vice President Marketing, Mike Fowler
Assoc Vice President Student Dev Diversity, Edwardo Rhodes
Office of the Vice President for Public Affairs and Government Relations (PAGR), Martin McCrory
Executive Vice President, Mitch Ennis
Vice President and President elect, Ballard C Campbell
Vice President Information Technlgy, John Samuel
Vice President Of Finance And Administra, Lauren Pruitt
Associate Vice President For Overseas Study, Kathleen Sideli
Executive Vice President Internal, Sam Wisen
Assistant Vice President Strategic Communications and University Spokesperson, Margie Smith-Simmons
Vice President of Communications, Andrew J Harder
Net Impact Vice President Marketing, Jayna J Pedruczny
Vice President of Lending and Hoosier Social Impact Fund, Molly Hallahan
Vice President, Tom Morrison
Admissions Director, Timothy Smith
Vice Chair, Patrick A. Shoulders
Chair, William R. Cast
Board Member, Saundra Taylor
Secretary, Deb Hankins
Treasurer, Gabrijel Gelic
Treasurer, Teresa Andrews
Treasurer, Blake Shanahan
Treasurer, Nathan Pastron
Board Member, Melanie Castillo-Cullather
Treasurer, Donald Lukes
Treasurer Kelley Student Government, Luke Hochgesang
DEPUTY TREASURER, Gentry Patrick Lee

LOCATIONS

HQ: TRUSTEES INDIANA UNIVERSITY
BRYAN HALL 107 S IND AVE ST BRYAN HA,
BLOOMINGTON, IN 47405
Phone: 812 855-4848
Web: WWW.INDIANA.EDU

PRODUCTS/OPERATIONS

2015 Sales

	% of total
Student fees	51
Auxiliary enterprises	14
Federal grants & contracts	13
Non-governement grants & contracts	6
Sales and services of educational units	2
State & local grants & contracts	1
Other revenue	13
Total	**100**

HISTORICAL FINANCIALS

Company Type: Private

Income Statement

FYE: June 30

	REVENUE ($ mil.)	NET INCOME ($ mil.)	NET PROFIT MARGIN	EMPLOYEES
06/15	2,207	138	6.3%	16,000
06/14	2,195	201	9.2%	—
06/13	2,146	189	8.8%	—
06/11	2,003	282	14.1%	—
Annual Growth	2.5%	(16.3%)	—	—

2015 Year-End Financials

Return on assets: 10.0%   Cash ($ mil.): 391
Return on equity: 6.3%
Current ratio: 1.40

TRUSTEES OF BOSTON COLLEGE

Students at Boston College (BC) get both academic excellence and the Red Sox. Located six miles from downtown Boston the university enrolls 14100 full- and part-time students (about a third of whom are graduate students) from every state in the US and 80 other countries. It has a student-teacher ratio of 13:1. BC offers degrees in more than 50 fields of study through its schools and colleges on four campuses. The university also has more than 20 research centers including the Institute for Scientific Research and the Center for International Higher Education. BC is one of the oldest Jesuit Catholic universities in the nation and has the largest Jesuit community in the world.

Operations

About 70% of its undergraduate student body are self-identified as Roman Catholic.

The university is home to more than 20 centers and institutes designated for research and teaching. Research opportunities including participation in faculty research projects exist for both undergraduate and graduate students. It also houses 8 libraries with 2.9 million volumes.

The cost of tuition stood a $46670 for 2014-15.

Geographic Reach

The university has campuses in Brighton Chestnut Hill Dover and Newton Massachusetts. It also operates a campus in Dublin Ireland.

Financial Performance

BC has enjoyed steady growth from voluntary giving by its alumni. Its endowment has grown to $2.2 billion placing it among the top 40 in the US. In 2014 it reported an operating budget of $917

million. Its revenues of $702.7 million were 5% up on the previous year due to growth in tuition and fees as well as auxiliary enterprises.

Strategy

BC's strategic plan includes adding 100 new faculty positions expanding research by faculty and graduate students increasing student financial aid to more than $128 million annually and extending undergraduate opportunities in international study internships and student formation. In 2013 it announced plans to build a $90 million residence hall near its Chestnut Hill campus.

Company Background

The university was founded by Jesuits in 1863. During its first seven decades BC was an exclusively undergraduate institution that served sons of the Irish working class. Its liberal arts emphasis was on the Greek and Latin classics English and modern languages and philosophy and religion. Development into the college it is today did not begin until the 1920s when the Graduate School of Arts and Sciences the Law School and the Evening College (known today as the James A. Woods S.J. College of Advancing Studies) were inaugurated. All classes became co-educational in the 1970s and today BC has a fairly equal split among male and female students.

EXECUTIVES

Vice President Human Resources, Leo Sullivan
Senior Vice President For University Advancement, Jim Husson
President, William P. Leahy
Chancellor, J. Donald Monan
Dean Carroll School of Management, Andrew C. Boynton
Dean School of Social Work, Alberto Godenzi
EVP, Patrick J. Keating
VP Information Technology Services, Michael Bourque
Financial VP and Treasurer, John D. Burke
Provost and Dean of Faculties, David Quigley
Dean of Students, Tom Mogan
Dean School of Theology and Ministry, Mark Massa
Dean Connell School of Nursing, Susan Gennaro
Dean Lynch School of Education, Maureen E. Kenny
Dean Law School, Vincent Rougeau
Interim Dean Morrissey College of Arts and Sciences, Gregory Kalscheur
Dean Woods College of Advancing Studies, James Burns
Assistant Vice President Inst Rsrch Plng Assess, Kelli Armstrong
Vice President Information TEC, Patricia Mccormack
Vice President Information TEC, Mark Ben
Director of Government Relations, Jeanne Levesque
Vice President, Ethan M Sullivan
Vice President For Student Affairs, Barbara Jones
Associate Vice President for Human Resources Human Resources, Robert Lewis
Assistant Vice President Planning and Budget, Steven Sass
Department Chair of English, Mary Crane
Assistant Vice President, Ricardo Krulig
Vice President, Madeleine G Moore
Office of the Executive Vice President, Jeanne Marquardt
Vice President Assistant to President, Mary Lee Delong
Vice President For Research, Thomas Chiles
Vice President For Finance And Administration, Christian Brand
Student Office Assistant For Senior Vice President Of University Advancement, Elizabeth Zappala
Vice President, John Westman

Director Administrative Services University Advancement Vice Presidents Office, Anne Campbell
Vice President, Pat Ryan
Department Chair, Susan Shell
Vice President, Arnav Roy
Department Chair, Welkin Johnson
Vice President, Dan Bourque
Senior Vice President, Margaret Dwyer
Chairman, John F. Fish
Vice Chairman, Peter K. Markell, age 61
Secretary, Gloria Rufo
Assistant Treasurer, Mark Conner
Board Member, Barbara Hebard
Treasurer, Stephanie Delma
Board Member, Donn Dingle
Auditors: PRICEWATERHOUSECOOPERS LLP BO

LOCATIONS

HQ: TRUSTEES OF BOSTON COLLEGE
140 COMMONWEALTH AVE, CHESTNUT HILL, MA 024673800
Phone: 617 552-8000
Web: WWW.BOSTONCOLLEGE.US

PRODUCTS/OPERATIONS

Selected Colleges and Schools
Carolyn A. and Peter S. Lynch School of Education
College of Arts and Sciences
Graduate School of Arts and Sciences
Graduate School of Social Work
James A. Woods S.J. College of Advancing Studies
School of Law
School of Theology and Ministry
Wallace E. Carroll School of Management
William F. Connell School of Nursing

HISTORICAL FINANCIALS

Company Type: Private

Income Statement			FYE: May 31
	REVENUE ($ mil.)	NET INCOME ($ mil.)	NET PROFIT MARGIN	EMPLOYEES
05/15	733	187	25.6%	2,493
05/14	702	221	31.5%	—
05/13	671	270	40.3%	—
05/12	653	(76)	—	—
Annual Growth	3.9%	—	—	—

TRUSTEES OF DARTMOUTH COLLEGE

Part of the esteemed Ivy League Dartmouth College is a private four-year liberal arts college with an enrollment of more than 6000 students. The university has an undergraduate college (offering about 40 programs) and graduate schools of business engineering and medicine plus graduate programs in the arts and sciences. Its student-teacher ratio is about 6:1. It is also home to a number of centers and institutes including Children's Hospital at Dartmouth; Dartmouth Center on Addiction Recovery and Education; and Center for Digital Strategies. Notable alumni include Daniel Webster Robert Frost Theodore "Dr. Seuss" Geisel and Nelson Rockefeller.

Operations

Dartmouth is located on a 270-acre campus located in Hanover New Hampshire. It also conducts study-abroad programs in about 20 countries. Through its collective institutes and graduate schools the college conducts a number of research

---

programs in areas including security capitalism energy and infectious disease. Altogether it has about 50 research-focused groups centers and institutes and attracts more than $200 million in sponsored research funding per year.

Financial Performance

For fiscal year 2011 Dartmouth reported revenues of some $763 million. Operating expenses for fiscal 2011 were some $738 million. Dartmouth has an endowment of some $3.5 billion.

Company Background

Dartmouth is the nation's ninth oldest college founded in 1769 by Reverend Eleazar Wheelock a Congregational minister from Connecticut. Land for its campus in Hanover New Hampshire was conveyed by a charter from King George III; it was the last institution of higher education established in the US under colonial rule.

EXECUTIVES

President, Philip J Hanlon
Consultant, Deborah Gibbs
Executive Director, Erin Tunnicliffe
Administrative Assistant, Karen L Thompson
Administrative Assistant, Kathy Boivin
Administrative Assistant, Katrina E Davis
Auditors: PRICEWATERHOUSECOOPERS LLP B

LOCATIONS

HQ: TRUSTEES OF DARTMOUTH COLLEGE
20 LEBANON ST, HANOVER, NH 037553564
Phone: 603 646-1110
Web: WWW.DARTMOUTH.EDU

PRODUCTS/OPERATIONS

Selected Divisions
Admissions and Financial Aid
Advancement Office
Campus Planning and Facilities
Dean of the College
Faculty of the Arts & Sciences
Finance and Administration
Geisel School of Medicine
President's Office
Provost's Office
Thayer School of Engineering
The Trustees of Dartmouth College
Tuck School of Business

HISTORICAL FINANCIALS

Company Type: Private

Income Statement			FYE: June 30
	REVENUE ($ mil.)	NET INCOME ($ mil.)	NET PROFIT MARGIN	EMPLOYEES
06/15	876	236	27.0%	5,000
06/14	866	680	78.5%	—
06/13	833	394	47.3%	—
06/12	793	(61)	—	—
Annual Growth	3.3%	—	—	—

2015 Year-End Financials

Return on assets: 7.5%   Cash ($ mil.): 289
Return on equity: 27.0%
Current ratio: —

TRUSTEES OF THE COLORADO SCHOOL OF MINES

Colorado School of Mines (CSM) is the oldest public institution of higher education in Colorado. The school offers about 20 undergraduate and 20 graduate academic programs in such fields as applied science and mathematics engineering and geoscience and resource engineering. Students can minor in areas related to humanities and social sciences. In addition graduate students can pursue higher degrees in social and management science. The school claims that its "M" symbol on a nearby mountainside is the nation's largest single-letter electronically lighted school emblem. Colorado School of Mines which has an enrollment of about 5500 was founded in 1874.

Operations

Known as Mines CSM is a public research university focused on engineering and applied sciences. With a student/faculty ratio of 17:1 the average CSM undergraduate class size is about 34 students. Tuition for the university runs about $13500 each year for Colorado resident undergraduates and $28600 annually for non-resident undergraduates.

Geographic Reach

From its campus in Golden Colorado CSM serves students from its home state as well as those across the US and abroad.

Financial Performance

CSM's revenue rose by 8% in fiscal 2012 as compared to 2011 due to an increase in student tuition and fees reflecting a rise in both enrollment and in tuition rates. The university also received a boost in revenue from state grants and contracts and auxiliary enterprises which contributed toward the overall 2012 increases. Net income for the same reporting period dropped by 38% thanks to operating expenses auxiliary enterprise operating expenses associated with residence hall operations and increased student medical claims. Rises in expenses related to interest on debt and loss on disposal of assets also contributed toward the 2012 decline in net income.

Strategy

Fundraising and partnerships have been key to keeping CMS near the top of the list of sought-after engineering schools. In fiscal 2012 the educational institution received some $32.5 million in donations. Funding for the school's research activities has increased during the past two years as CMS takes a national role as a research institution. In 2013 in an effort to promote solar research and technologies CSM's Center for Revolutionary Solar Photoconversion partnered with the Research Center for Advanced Science and Technology at the University of Tokyo.

EXECUTIVES

Vice President Finance And Administration, Kirsten Volpi
Vice President, Manika Prasad
Vice President, Bruce Trudgill
Managing Director, Linda Landrum
Vice President for Student Life and Dean of Students, Dan Fox
Associate Vice President For Human Resources, Mike Dougherty
Vice President, Kerwin Hirro
Vice President and Principal Metallurgist Tetra Tech and Research Professor, Erik Spiller

Vice Chair, Pam Blome
Treasurer, Madison Kellar
Treasurer, Caroline Fuller
Auditors: BKD LLP DENVER CO

LOCATIONS

HQ: TRUSTEES OF THE COLORADO SCHOOL OF MINES
1500 ILLINOIS ST, GOLDEN, CO 804011887
Phone: 303 273-3000
Web: WWW.MINES.EDU

PRODUCTS/OPERATIONS

Selected Colleges and Departments
College of Applied Science and Engineering (CASE)
  Chemical & Biological Engineering
  Chemistry & Geochemistry
  Metallurgical & Materials Engineering
  Physics
College of Engineering and Computational Sciences (CECS)
  Applied Mathematics & Statistics
  Civil & Environmental Engineering
  Electrical Engineering & Computer Science
  Mechanical Engineering
College of Earth Resource Science and Engineering (CERSE)
  Economics & Business
  Geology & Geological Engineering
  Geophysics
  Liberal Arts & International Studies
  Mining Engineering
  Petroleum Engineering

HISTORICAL FINANCIALS

Company Type: Private

Income Statement
FYE: June 30

	REVENUE ($ mil.)	NET INCOME ($ mil.)	NET PROFIT MARGIN	EMPLOYEES
06/16	215	(2)	—	1,000
06/06	102	4	4.5%	—
06/05	0	(0)	—	—
06/02	0	0	—	—
Annual Growth	—	—	—	—

2016 Year-End Financials
Return on assets: 9.2%   Cash ($ mil.): 103
Return on equity: (-0.9%)
Current ratio: 2.80

TRUSTEES OF THE ESTATE OF BERNICE PAUAHI BISHOP

Kamehameha Schools provides an education fit for a king ... or queen. The private charitable trust was founded and endowed by Princess Bernice Pauahi Bishop great granddaughter and last royal descendant of Kamehameha the Great. One of the largest independent schools in the US Kamehameha educates more than 5000 elementary middle school and high school students many of whom board at one of its three Hawaii campuses. In addition it operates some 30 preschools with a total enrollment of about 1500. Kamehameha Schools is also the largest private property owner in the state of Hawaii and uses the proceeds from its real estate operations to support its schools.

The Kamehameha School for Boys was established in 1887 followed by the Kamehameha

School for Girls which opened in 1894. By 1955 the schools consolidated onto a 600-acre campus with views of Honolulu that span from Pearl Harbor to Diamond Head.

To this day Kamehameha Schools gives preferential admissions treatment to students of Hawaiian decent a long-standing policy it is fighting to preserve despite the controversy it creates. The schools have successfully fought off several lawsuits aimed at opening its doors to other ethnicities including a close decision by an appeals court in 2009.

EXECUTIVES

Vice President, Colleen Wong
Vice President Human Resources, Winona White
Executive Vice President Finance and Chief Financial Officer, Scott Topping
Auditors: PRICEWATERHOUSECOOPERS LLP WA

LOCATIONS

HQ: TRUSTEES OF THE ESTATE OF BERNICE PAUAHI BISHOP
567 S KING ST STE 200, HONOLULU, HI 968133079
Phone: 808 523-6200
Web: WWW.KSBE.EDU

COMPETITORS

Edison Learning   Learning Care Group

HISTORICAL FINANCIALS

Company Type: Private

Income Statement
FYE: June 30

	REVENUE ($ mil.)	NET INCOME ($ mil.)	NET PROFIT MARGIN	EMPLOYEES
06/15	767	333	43.5%	1,500
06/14	915	482	52.7%	—
06/13	519	109	21.1%	—
06/10	333	(21)	—	—
Annual Growth	18.1%	—	—	—

2015 Year-End Financials
Return on assets: 7.3%   Cash ($ mil.): 18
Return on equity: 43.5%
Current ratio: 0.10

TRUSTEES OF TUFTS COLLEGE

Tufts University wants to light up the minds of New England scholars. The school offers undergraduate and graduate degrees in areas such as education engineering psychology art English music and medicine. The university enrolls some 11000 students and has 1300 faculty members and it offers classes in 70 fields at three campuses in Massachusetts (Boston Medford/Somerville and Grafton). It also has an international campus in Talloires France. Tufts University's Fletcher School of Law and Diplomacy is the oldest continuous international relations graduate program in the country. The school is also home to New England's only Veterinary School.

Operations

Tufts University has a number of research programs at all three campuses including clinical studies in medical dental veterinary and nutritional fields. It also has research programs in areas such as biology engineering and technology many of

which are funded through grants and fellowship funds.

Financial Performance

Tufts University has an endowment of about $1.1 billion.

Strategy

Tufts University is working to expand the resources its School of Medicine. In 2012 it moved to add a new medical research lab to study serious infectious diseases (such as tuberculosis) within the Biomedical Research and Public Health Building. It also expanded the Cummings School of Veterinary Medicine by adding a new clinic for the care and study of pets with obesity problems. The university also expands by adding new degree programs such as a doctorate in mamalian genetics in 2011.

Company Background

Tufts was founded in 1852 through a land donation by Boston-area businessman Charles Tufts to the Universalist Church. The school adopted its motto Pax et Lux (Peace and Light) in 1857.

EXECUTIVES

Interim Assistant To David Kahle Vice President For Information Technology and CIO, Lucy Nunn
Chief Sales Officer, Keene Allen
Vice President for Operations, Linda Snyder
Auditors: PRICEWATERHOUSECOOPERS LLP BO

LOCATIONS

HQ: TRUSTEES OF TUFTS COLLEGE
169 HOLLAND ST STE 318, SOMERVILLE, MA 021442401
Phone: 617 628-5000
Web: WWW.TUFTS.EDU

PRODUCTS/OPERATIONS

Schools & Colleges

Cummings School of Veterinary Science
Graduate School of Arts & Sciences
The Fletcher School
Friedman School of Nutrition Science and Policy
Sackler School of Graduate Biomedical Sciences
School of Arts & Sciences
School of Dental Medicine
School of Engineering
School of Medicine
Tisch College of Citizenship and Public Service

HISTORICAL FINANCIALS

Company Type: Private

Income Statement

FYE: June 30

	REVENUE ($ mil.)	NET INCOME ($ mil.)	NET PROFIT MARGIN	EMPLOYEES
06/15	914	(25)	—	4,100
06/14	965	68	7.1%	—
06/13	768	127	16.6%	—
06/12	769	(100)	—	—
Annual Growth	5.9%	—	—	—

2015 Year-End Financials

Return on assets: 15.6%   Cash ($ mil.): 37
Return on equity: (-2.8%)
Current ratio: 0.10

TRUSTEES OF UNION COLLEGE IN THE TOWN OF SCHENECTADY IN THE STATE OF NEW YORK

Union College brings liberal arts and engineering together. Union College is a private liberal arts school that offers courses in the humanities the social sciences the sciences and engineering. Notable alumni include the father of Franklin D. Roosevelt the grandfather of Winston Churchill and former US president Chester A. Arthur (class of 1848). Founded in 1795 with a class of 16 the college is supported by an endowment of more than $270 million.

EXECUTIVES

Upper Management Vice President, Debbie Fox
Secretary, Carol Cichy
Secretary To Vice President For College, Kathleen Newell
Auditors: LB GRANT THORNTON LLP NEW YOR

LOCATIONS

HQ: TRUSTEES OF UNION COLLEGE IN THE TOWN OF SCHENECTADY IN THE STATE OF NEW YORK
807 UNION ST, SCHENECTADY, NY 123083256
Phone: 518 388-6630
Web: WWW.UNION.EDU

COMPETITORS

Bard College
Cazenovia College
Hamilton College
SUNY
Skidmore College

HISTORICAL FINANCIALS

Company Type: Private

Income Statement

FYE: June 30

	REVENUE ($ mil.)	NET INCOME ($ mil.)	NET PROFIT MARGIN	EMPLOYEES
06/15	173	8	4.6%	870
06/13	165	11	6.7%	—
06/12	159	10	6.5%	—
06/11	0	0	—	—
Annual Growth	—	370.3%	—	—

2015 Year-End Financials

Return on assets: 11.2%   Cash ($ mil.): 22
Return on equity: 4.6%
Current ratio: 0.30

TRUVEN HOLDING CORP.

EXECUTIVES

President, Mike Boswood
Board of Directors, Andra Heller
Manager, Chris Schneider
Manager, Richard Marciniak
Auditors: PRICEWATERHOUSECOOPERS LLP NE

LOCATIONS

HQ: TRUVEN HOLDING CORP.
100 PHOENIX DR STE 100, ANN ARBOR, MI 481082600
Phone: 734 913-3000

HISTORICAL FINANCIALS

Company Type: Private

Income Statement

FYE: December 31

	REVENUE ($ mil.)	NET INCOME ($ mil.)	NET PROFIT MARGIN	EMPLOYEES
12/15	610	(75)	—	2,110
12/14	544	(37)	—	—
12/13	492	(344)	—	—
12/12	241	(54)	—	—
Annual Growth	36.2%	—	—	—

2015 Year-End Financials

Return on assets: 13.4%   Cash ($ mil.): 14
Return on equity: (-12.4%)
Current ratio: 0.60

TUALITY HEALTHCARE

EXECUTIVES

Board of Directors, Mark Rosenbaum
Manager, Kaye Rains
Auditors: FORDHAM GOODFELLOW LLP HILLSB

LOCATIONS

HQ: TUALITY HEALTHCARE
335 SE 8TH AVE, HILLSBORO, OR 971234246
Phone: 503 681-1111
Web: WWW.TUALITY.ORG

HISTORICAL FINANCIALS

Company Type: Private

Income Statement

FYE: September 30

	REVENUE ($ mil.)	NET INCOME ($ mil.)	NET PROFIT MARGIN	EMPLOYEES
09/15	178	(5)	—	1,300
09/04	128	8	6.6%	—
09/03	119	3	3.0%	—
09/02	867	0	0.0%	—
Annual Growth	(11.5%)	—	—	—

2015 Year-End Financials

Return on assets: 38.5%   Cash ($ mil.): 32
Return on equity: (-3.0%)
Current ratio: 0.70

TUCSON UNIFIED SCHOOL DISTRICT

EXECUTIVES

Superintendent, Elizabeth C Fagen
Executive Director, Lynn Webster
Purchasing Director, Leon George
Office Manager, Vikki Sanchez
Auditors: HEINFELD MEECH & CO PC TUC

HQ: TUCSON UNIFIED SCHOOL DISTRICT
1010 E 10TH ST, TUCSON, AZ 857195813
Phone: 520 225-6000
Web: WWW.TUSD.K12.AZ.US

HISTORICAL FINANCIALS

Company Type: Private

Income Statement

FYE: June 30

	REVENUE ($ mil.)	NET INCOME ($ mil.)	NET PROFIT MARGIN	EMPLOYEES
06/16	446	1	0.3%	9,000
06/11	496	58	11.7%	—
06/06	426	29	7.0%	—
Annual Growth	0.5%	(27.6%)	—	—

TUDOR INVESTMENT CORPORATION

Tudor Investment Corporation part of the Tudor Group of financial companies is an asset management firm and hedge fund investing in stocks bonds and alternative markets worldwide. Typical targets include mid- to late-stage technology companies in four broad areas: communications internet infrastructure and semiconductors; enterprise applications and IT services; financial and business services; and internet and digital media. The company which invests across a variety of strategies has some $11 billion of assets under management. Faced with declined earnings the firm cut 15% of its workforce in 2016. Paul Tudor Jones II established Tudor Investment Corporation in 1980.

The private equity and venture capital arm of Tudor Investment Corp. Tudor Ventures typically invests $7 million to $20 million per transaction in mid-to-late stage technology companies in four broad areas: communications Internet infrastructure and semiconductors; enterprise applications and information technology services; financial and business services; and Internet and digital media. Target companies have commercially available products or services growing revenue streams good competitive position promising and an established management team in place. They typically use funding from Tudor Ventures for expansion acquisitions or liquidity.

Tudor Ventures which usually acts as a lead investor assists its portfolio companies in areas such as strategic guidance and corporate governance.

The company has invested in some 75 companies since its 1995 founding. It closed its third investment fund in 2007. Investors in its funds include institutional investors and high-net-worth individuals. Tudor Ventures has more than $700 million in capital under management

EXECUTIVES

Managing Director and Associate General Counsel, Steve Waldman
Vice President and Head Client and Systems Services, Paul Vdovets
Regional Vice President, Scott Fialkow
Vice President Software Development, Amit Wadhwa
Auditors: ERNST & YOUNG LLP NEW YORK N

LOCATIONS

HQ: TUDOR INVESTMENT CORPORATION
1275 KING ST, GREENWICH, CT 068312936
Phone: 203 863-6700
Web: WWW.TUDORFUNDS.COM

COMPETITORS

Actua	Menlo Ventures
Draper Fisher	NEA
Jurvetson	US Venture Partners
EnTrust Capital	Wexford Capital
Hummer Winblad	vCap Investments
Kleiner Perkins	

HISTORICAL FINANCIALS

Company Type: Private

Income Statement

FYE: December 31

	ASSETS ($ mil.)	NET INCOME ($ mil.)	INCOME AS % OF ASSETS	EMPLOYEES
12/15	831	222	26.7%	291
12/14	819	(80)	—	—
12/13	905	486	53.7%	—
12/11	624	187	30.0%	—
Annual Growth	7.4%	4.4%	—	—

2015 Year-End Financials

Return on assets: —
Return on equity: 28.3%
Sales ($ mil.): 784

TUFTS MEDICAL CENTER PHYSICIANS ORGANIZATION, INC.

EXECUTIVES

Chief Executive Officer, David Cornell PHD
Chief Operating Officer, Craig Williams
Administrative Assistant, George Mensah
Auditors: COOPERS & LYBRAND LLP

LOCATIONS

HQ: TUFTS MEDICAL CENTER PHYSICIANS ORGANIZATION, INC.
800 WASHINGTON ST 1013, BOSTON, MA 021111552
Phone: 617 636-8261
Web: WWW.TUFTS.EDU

HISTORICAL FINANCIALS

Company Type: Private

Income Statement

FYE: September 30

	REVENUE ($ mil.)	NET INCOME ($ mil.)	NET PROFIT MARGIN	EMPLOYEES
09/15	229	(4)	—	270
09/09	17	6	35.4%	—
09/99	5	0	6.7%	—
09/98	0	0	—	—
Annual Growth	—	—	—	—

TUFTS MEDICAL CENTER, INC.

EXECUTIVES

President, Michael Wagner
Board of Directors, Saul N Weingart
Supervisor, Scott Lucier

LOCATIONS

HQ: TUFTS MEDICAL CENTER, INC.
800 WASHINGTON ST, BOSTON, MA 021111552
Phone: 617 636-5000

HISTORICAL FINANCIALS

Company Type: Private

Income Statement

FYE: September 30

	REVENUE ($ mil.)	NET INCOME ($ mil.)	NET PROFIT MARGIN	EMPLOYEES
09/15	595	(18)	—	3,800
09/14	602	19	3.3%	—
09/06	638	3	0.6%	—
09/05	0	0	—	—
Annual Growth	—	—	—	—

2015 Year-End Financials

Return on assets: 9.8%
Return on equity: (-3.1%)
Current ratio: 0.80
Cash ($ mil.): 39

TURNER CONSTRUCTION COMPANY INC

Turner Construction has been the mastermind for scores of head-turning projects for more than a century. The company that built Madison Square Garden has ranked among the leading general builders in the US since the early 1900s. Turner provides construction and project management services for commercial and multifamily buildings airports and stadiums as well as correctional educational entertainment and manufacturing facilities. The company is also a leader in sustainable or green building practices. Founded in 1902 by Henry Turner the company is the main operating unit of The Turner Corporation which is a subsidiary of German construction group HOCHTIEF.

Operations

Turner works on more than 1500 projects each year (as of mid-2016). For decades Turner has kept tabs on construction prices with its quarterly Building Cost Index which forecasts construction costs by taking into account labor rates productivity and material prices. The index is used by federal and state governments to track building costs and pricing trends.

As part of HOCHTIEF's Americas division Turner works alongside other contractors in the US and Canada such as Flatiron E.E. Crus and Clark Builders. HOCHTIEF reiterated in 2016 that the America subsidiaries are closely related and work together to exchange information and experience. The Americas division generated around 50% of HOCHTIEF's total revenue during 2015.

Geographic Reach

The company has offices across North America as well as in 20 countries in Southeast Asia Europe

India Latin America the Caribbean and the Middle East (as of mid-2016).

Sales and Marketing

The contractor works on projects in the aviation/transportation commercial cultural and entertainment data center education government and green building markets (as of mid-2016).

Strategy

Turner's ties to HOCHTIEF have helped strengthen the company's services and extend its international reach. Turner often teams with sister company Flatiron to complete projects. By collaborating and marketing their services jointly the two companies combine strengths in refurbishment and construction services.

Some of Turner's more recent projects (as of mid-2016) have included the Cobo Center and Quicken Loans Technology Center in Detroit as well as the NASA Computational Research Center in Hampton Virginia.

Turner has also worked to meet growing demand for green and sustainable construction. More than 425 of its projects have earned Leadership in Energy and Environmental Design (LEED) certification. A few of its green projects include the Seattle office of Perkins+Will the Yale University Health Services Center and RAND corporate headquarters.

As the residential markets slowed in past years Turner pivoted toward securing commercial projects in the public health care and science and technology sectors. Sports projects also provided the company with a solid pipeline; the company's dedicated sports division had completed some $5 billion in work since 2000.

Company Background

Other notable projects in Turner's history include the World War II Memorial in Washington DC the John F. Kennedy Memorial Library in Boston and the Rock and Roll Hall of Fame. Turner also built the new Yankee Stadium in New York. The company reached a milestone in 2008 by inking its 15000th major contract.

To expand its operations in Canada Turner in late 2011 agreed to partner with Clark Builders in a deal that gives Turner a 51% stake in the Edmonton-based company. For the effort Clark Builders gains access to Turner's financial and management resources. The alliance strengthens Turner's Toronto and Vancouver foothold and helps to extend the reach of the company's business into other Canadian markets.

EXECUTIVES

President, Peter J. Davoren, age 62
VP, Stephen W. Fort
EVP (New York New Jersey Maryland Pennsylvania Connecticut and New England), Pasquale A. (Pat) Di Filippo
EVP Global Sales and Market Segment (Southwest Northern Calfornia and Northwest Regions), Michael J. (Mike) Kuntz
SVP, Mark A. Boyle
EVP (Ohio Nashville Huntsville Atlanta Florida and the Carolinas), Richard P. Homan
SVP Turner Industrial Group and Chairman The Lathrop Company, Thomas J. (Tom) Manahan
VP, Abrar Sheriff
SVP and CFO, Karen O. Gould, age 52
SVP (Mid-Atlantic and Southeast), Tom Reilly
President The Lathrop Company, Steve Johnson
Vice President and Construction Executive, Robert Hubner
Vice President And Senior Operations Manager, Tomasz Stachowiak
Vice President and General Manager, Kris Barnard
Senior Vice President, Rory C Dejohn
Vice President and General Manager, Tom Stachowiak

Vice President and Financial Manager, Sarah Garner
Executive Assistant To Thomas B. Gerlach Senior Vice President Human Resources, Cheryl Halvorsen
Vice President and Construction Executive, Curt Zegler
Vice President and Operations Manager, Carlo DiSilvestro
Auditors: DELOITTE & TOUCHE LLP DALLAS

LOCATIONS

HQ: TURNER CONSTRUCTION COMPANY INC
375 HUDSON ST FL 6, NEW YORK, NY 100143667
Phone: 212 229-6000
Web: WWW.TCCO.COM

PRODUCTS/OPERATIONS

Selected Services
Building maintenance
Construction management
Design-build
General construction
Multiple building program
Preconstruction consulting
Program management
Project management

COMPETITORS

Bechtel	Hunt Construction
C. G. Schmidt	Jacobs Engineering
Catamount Constructors	PCL Employees Holdings
Dimeo Construction	Parsons Corporation
DooleyMack	Peter Kiewit Sons'
English Construction	Shook National
Company	Skanska USA Building
F.A. Wilhelm	Structure Tone
Fluor	Tully Construction
Gilbane Building	Tutor Perini
Company	Winter Construction
Hensel Phelps	
Construction	

HISTORICAL FINANCIALS

Company Type: Private

Income Statement

FYE: December 31

	REVENUE ($ mil.)	NET INCOME ($ mil.)	NET PROFIT MARGIN	EMPLOYEES
12/15	10,484	101	1.0%	5,000
12/14	10,516	96	0.9%	—
12/13	9,488	76	0.8%	—
12/12	8,552	70	0.8%	—
Annual Growth	7.0%	13.0%	—	—

2015 Year-End Financials

Return on assets: 13.3%   Cash ($ mil.): 188
Return on equity: 1.0%
Current ratio: 0.80

TURNING POINT BRANDS, INC.

EXECUTIVES

President, Lawrence S Wexler
Chairman of the Board, Thomas F Helms Jr
Senior Vice-President, James W Dobbins
Senior Vice-President, James Murray
Auditors: RSM US LLP GREENSBORO NORTH

LOCATIONS

HQ: TURNING POINT BRANDS, INC.
5201 INTERCHANGE WAY, LOUISVILLE, KY
402292184
Phone: 502 778-4421

HISTORICAL FINANCIALS

Company Type: Private

Income Statement

FYE: December 31

	REVENUE ($ mil.)	NET INCOME ($ mil.)	NET PROFIT MARGIN	EMPLOYEES
12/15	197	9	4.6%	231
12/06	117	(12)	—	—
12/05	116	10	8.7%	—
12/04	115	(25)	—	—
Annual Growth	5.0%	—	—	—

2015 Year-End Financials

Return on assets: 2.1%   Cash ($ mil.): 4
Return on equity: 4.6%
Current ratio: 0.40

TURTLE & HUGHES, INC.

Turtle & Hughes' longevity has demonstrated that slow and steady really does win the race when it comes to distributing electrical and industrial equipment. The company's exhaustive lineup is sold through three subsidiaries: Turtle & Hughes Integrated Supply Turtle Data (wire cable and power protection devices) and Turtle Ebay Store. Its customers include industrial and construction companies electrical contractors telecommunications servers utilities and various government agencies. Family-owned the company is led by its fourth generation Jayne Millard its third female CEO. One-third of Turtle & Hughes is employee-owned.

Operations

Turtle & Hughes provides electrical products such as alarms signals and annunciators; anchors and plugs; automation products; ballasts; batteries and flashlights; boxes and covers; breakers bus ducts panels and switchgears; programmable controls; time clocks; transformers; wires cables and cords; wiring accessories and devices; and others. The company also offers industrial products such as adhesives/tapes and compounds brushes/brooms carbide tools cutting tools fasteners lubricating devices material handling products power transmissions precision tools soldering equipment solenoid valves struts/channels tooling accessories and other products.

Geographic Reach

Turtle & Hughes operates through 17 branches across the US.

Sales and Marketing

Turtle & Hughes' customers include industrial firms construction companies electrical contractors telecommunications servers utilities and various government agencies and municipalities.

Company Background

Turtle & Hughes was founded in 1923 as an electrical supply house.

EXECUTIVES

President, Jack Sinagra
Vice President of Finance, Kevin Doyle
CEO, Jayne Millard
Manager Corporate Operations, Chuck Noll
EVP; Branch Manager Bridgewater Distribution Center and Plainfield Branch, Rick Reffler

Executive Vice President Build a Brain Trust,
Randy Roessle
President, Michael DeVoney
Chief Financial Officer, Chris Rausch
Vice President, Peter Landers
National Accounts Manager, BLAKE VARBERO
Vice President, Norman Norman Blumenthal
Blumenthal
Vice President Sales, Tony Ventola
Vice President Sales, John Bernhardt
I Vice President, Luis Valls
Vice President Sales, Anthony Ventola
Vice President, Cory Szatkiewicz
Senior Vice President, Al Fernandes
Vice President, Jim Mandaglio
Vice President Sales, Ken Pileggi
Chairman President and CEO, Suzanne Turtle
Millard
Auditors: EISNERAMPER LLP ISELIN NJ

LOCATIONS

HQ: TURTLE & HUGHES, INC.
1900 LOWER RD, LINDEN, NJ 070366586
Phone: 732 574-3600
Web: WWW.TURTLE.COM

PRODUCTS/OPERATIONS

Selected Products
Datacom categories
Anchors and fasteners
Burial products/innerduct
Cabinets and enclosures
Cable management
Cable tray/ladder rack
Category rated and coax cable
Connectivity
Fiber-optic cable
Hand tools
Outside plant
Power protection
Raceway and duct systems
Safety
Security fencing
Splices connectors and lugs
Tools testers and safety
Electrical categories
Alarms annunciators and signals
Anchors and plugs
Automation products
Ballasts and transformers
Batteries and flashlights
Box enclosures
Breakers panels and switchgears
Cable trays and struts
Conduit fittings
Cord connectors
Dimming controls
Electrical tools
Emergency lighting
Enclosures
Fans
Fluorescent lighting
Fuse holders and terminal blocks
Generators
Groundings
Heat shrink
Heating
High-bay lighting
Incandescent lighting
Lamps
Limit temp. and proximity switch
Lugs and terminals
Metering equipment
Motor control
Motors AC and DC drivers
Outdoor lighting
Pole line products
Programmable controls
Relays
Strut/channel
Test equipment
Time clocks
Transformers
Wire cable and cord
Wiring accessories
Wiring devices

Industrial categories
Adhesives and tapes
Brushes and brooms
Carbide tools
Cutting fluid/lubricant
Cutting tools
Fasteners
Hand tools
Hoist chain and accessories
Industrial abrasives
Janitorial paper supplies
Ladders
Locks
Lubricating devices
Material handling
MRO supplies
Paint/markets
Pipe hangers
Pipe valves and fittings
Pneumatics
Pneumatic tools
Power tools
Safety equipment
Saw blades
Shim/shim stock
Solenoid valves
Strut/channel
Tooling accessories

COMPETITORS

C. R. Laurence
Consolidated
  Electrical
Dillon Supply
Graybar Electric
Indoff
Interline Brands
Kennametal

MSC Industrial Direct
Prime Advantage
Rexel Inc.
Sonepar USA
Steiner Electric
W.W. Grainger
WESCO International

HISTORICAL FINANCIALS
Company Type: Private

Income Statement
FYE: September 30

	REVENUE ($ mil.)	NET INCOME ($ mil.)	NET PROFIT MARGIN	EMPLOYEES
09/16	628	16	2.6%	900
09/15	590	17	3.0%	—
09/13	555	21	3.8%	—
09/12	518	23	4.5%	—
Annual Growth	5.0%	(8.7%)	—	—

2016 Year-End Financials
Return on assets: 12.1%   Cash ($ mil.): 11
Return on equity: 2.6%
Current ratio: 1.90

TUSTIN UNIFIED SCHOOL DISTRICT

EXECUTIVES

Superintendent, Gregory A Franklin Ed D
Account Manager, Joflyn Crawford
Accountant, Rosy Dominguev
Treasurer, Dena Vela
Director, Kathleen Callahan
Assistant Manager, Margie Sepulveda
Auditors: NIGRO NIGRO & WHITE MURRIETA

LOCATIONS

HQ: TUSTIN UNIFIED SCHOOL DISTRICT
300 S C ST, TUSTIN, CA 927803633
Phone: 714 730-7515
Web: WWW.TUSTIN.K12.CA.US

HISTORICAL FINANCIALS
Company Type: Private

Income Statement
FYE: June 30

	REVENUE ($ mil.)	NET INCOME ($ mil.)	NET PROFIT MARGIN	EMPLOYEES
06/16	284	14	5.1%	1,465
06/09	0	(0)	—	—
06/08	0	(0)	—	—
06/05	0	(0)	—	—
Annual Growth	73.8%	—	—	—

2016 Year-End Financials
Return on assets: 9.3%   Cash ($ mil.): 223
Return on equity: 5.1%
Current ratio: —

TYLER INDEPENDENT SCHOOL DISTRICT

EXECUTIVES

President, Michelle Carr
Board of Directors, Gina Orr
Director, Jack Antilley
Auditors: PROTHRO WILHELMI AND COMPANY

LOCATIONS

HQ: TYLER INDEPENDENT SCHOOL DISTRICT
1319 EARL CAMPBELL PKWY, TYLER, TX 757019697
Phone: 903 262-1000
Web: WWW.TYLERISD.ORG

HISTORICAL FINANCIALS
Company Type: Private

Income Statement
FYE: August 31

	REVENUE ($ mil.)	NET INCOME ($ mil.)	NET PROFIT MARGIN	EMPLOYEES
08/16	200	(9)	—	2,500
08/13	183	150	81.8%	—
08/12	186	3	2.1%	—
08/11	0	0	—	—
Annual Growth	—	—	—	—

2016 Year-End Financials
Return on assets: 1.0%   Cash ($ mil.): 50
Return on equity: (-4.6%)
Current ratio: —

U. S. TOOL GRINDING, INC.

EXECUTIVES

President, Bruce Williams
Director, Anthony Ring
Financial Executive, Beth Allen
Auditors: UHY LLP ST LOUIS MISSOURI

LOCATIONS

HQ: U. S. TOOL GRINDING, INC.
  2000 PROGRESS DR, FARMINGTON, MO 636409158
Phone: 573 431-3856
Web: WWW.USTG.NET

HISTORICAL FINANCIALS

Company Type: Private

Income Statement

FYE: December 31

	REVENUE ($ mil.)	NET INCOME ($ mil.)	NET PROFIT MARGIN	EMPLOYEES
12/15	368	10	2.8%	700
12/13	282	5	2.0%	—
12/12	230	7	3.4%	—
12/09	427	0	—	—
Annual Growth	—	534.8%	—	—

2015 Year-End Financials

Return on assets: 8.1%   Cash ($ mil.): 1
Return on equity: 2.8%
Current ratio: 0.70

U.S. PIPELINE, INC.

EXECUTIVES

Principal, Kelly Osborn
Vice-President, Lowell Brien
Personnel Manager, Mike Connelly
Auditors: LAPORTE APAC HOUSTON TEXAS

LOCATIONS

HQ: U.S. PIPELINE, INC.
  8100 WASHINGTON AVE # 200, HOUSTON, TX
  770071085
Phone: 281 531-6100
Web: WWW.USPIPELINE.COM

HISTORICAL FINANCIALS

Company Type: Private

Income Statement

FYE: December 31

	REVENUE ($ mil.)	NET INCOME ($ mil.)	NET PROFIT MARGIN	EMPLOYEES
12/15	367	52	14.3%	1,500
12/14	557	0	—	—
12/13	0	0	—	—
Annual Growth	—	—	—	—

2015 Year-End Financials

Return on assets: 4.8%   Cash ($ mil.): 58
Return on equity: 14.3%
Current ratio: 3.70

U.S. VENTURE, INC.

Smitten with the love of oil distribution the founding Schmidt family owns and operates U.S. Venture (formerly U.S. Oil). The company's U.S. Oil division (formerly U.S. Petroleum Operations) supplies refined oil products to residents in the Midwest and does a lot more. In addition to the wholesale distribution of oil products (its largest revenue generator) the company operates gas stations and installs gas pumps tanks and other petroleum-related equipment. U.S. Venture also provides plumbing and HVAC services (Design Air)

collects used waste oil to be processed into burner fuel and has a metal custom manufacturing unit.
Operations
U.S. Venture's operating divisions are:
Design Air (serving commercial and residential HVAC contractors throughout Wisconsin and Upper Michigan);
Express Convenience Centers (gas stations and convenience stores throughout Wisconsin);
U.S. AutoForce (tires automotive parts and lubricants);
U.S. Custom Manufacturing (forming and supplying metal tubing for the automotive furniture and lawn and garden and other industries; it also makes frame components handles and rails);
U.S. Lubricants (lubricants for trucking industrial and commercial customers in the Upper Midwest);
U.S. Oil (bulk storage terminals wholesale and branded distribution of petroleum products multiple-brand C-store Jobbership and gas station-related real estate activities); and
U.S. Petroleum Equipment (tanks pumps and related equipment for petroleum-based products and vehicle lift equipment; it also offers installation and lighting services throughout Wisconsin and Upper Michigan).
Geographic Reach
Under its U.S. AutoForce brand U.S. Oil also operates about a dozen warehouses in Illinois Minnesota Missouri Nebraska Iowa South Dakota and Wisconsin offering auto parts (for brakes exhausts and suspensions) and tires. U.S. Venture operates 12 refined products terminals across the Midwest (with a total storage capacity of about 127 million gallons at its bulk fuel storage tanks) including the Cheboygan 164000 barrels facility.
Strategy
The company has grown its geographic presence through complementary acquisitions.
Mergers and Acquisitions
Expanding its green fuel options in 2013 U.S. Oil bought six compressed natural gas fueling stations from We Energies (two in Milwaukee and one each in Appleton Franklin Racine and Waukesha) bring U.S. Oil's total to nine in Wisconsin. U.S. Oil plans to add a minimum of 50 additional GAIN Clean Fueling sites by 2018.
Growing is presence in North Central Wisconsin and the Upper Peninsula of Michigan in 2012 the bought Draeger Oil Company's branded dealer division. Under the terms of the deal U.S. Oil provides fuel supply to more than 50 retail gas stations while Draeger retained the transportation portion.
U.S. Ventures (U.S. Oil) also expanded its petroleum products distribution presence in Indiana in 2012 through the purchase of Farmersburg-based Trueblood Oil's branded wholesale fuel supply business.
Company Background
U.S. Oil was established in the 1950s as Schmidt Oil by the sons of local fuel distributor Albert Schmidt who landed his first job in the oil business in 1923. The company changed its name to U.S. Venture in 2010 to reflect the company's increasingly diverse portfolio of entrepreneurial businesses.

EXECUTIVES

President and CEO, John Schmidt
VP Marketing and Strategy, Jeff Van Brunt
President U.S. Gain, Mike Koel
Vice President and Chief Financial Officer, Jay Walters
VP Human Resources, Lori Hoersch
Vice President Purchasing and Product Management, Joe Gretz
TREASURER, Judy Engen-pazdera
Auditors: DELOITTE & TOUCHE LLP MILWAU

LOCATIONS

HQ: U.S. VENTURE, INC.
  425 BETTER WAY, APPLETON, WI 549156192
Phone: 920 739-6101
Web: WWW.USVENTURE.COM

PRODUCTS/OPERATIONS

Selected Operations

Design Air (heating and air conditioning equipment)
Express Convenience Centers (gas stations and car washes)
U.S. AutoForce (exhaust pipe manufacturing and autoparts distribution)
U.S. Custom Manufacturing (tube bending and fabrication)
U.S. Lubricants (motor oil and related products)
U.S. Oil (gasoline fuel oil and natural gas)
U.S. Petroleum Equipment (petroleum-related equipment installation)

COMPETITORS

7-Eleven	Quality State Oil
Apex Oil	Company
Marathon Oil	QuikTrip
Motiva Enterprises	Sunoco

HISTORICAL FINANCIALS

Company Type: Private

Income Statement

FYE: July 31

	REVENUE ($ mil.)	NET INCOME ($ mil.)	NET PROFIT MARGIN	EMPLOYEES
07/16	6,413	97	1.5%	1,182
07/15	8,076	173	2.1%	—
07/14	9,088	49	0.5%	—
07/13	7,346	47	0.6%	—
Annual Growth	(4.4%)	27.4%	—	—

2016 Year-End Financials

Return on assets: 2.9%   Cash ($ mil.): 4
Return on equity: 1.5%
Current ratio: 0.70

ULSTER COUNTY

EXECUTIVES

Principal, Mike Hein
Board of Directors, James F Maloney
Board of Directors, David Donaldson
Board of Directors, Kenneth J Ronk Jr
Financial Executive, Elliott Auerbach
Account Manager, Stephanie Simonetty

LOCATIONS

HQ: ULSTER COUNTY
  244 FAIR ST, KINGSTON, NY 124013806
Phone: 845 340-3000
Web: WWW.ULSTERCOUNTYNY.GOV

HISTORICAL FINANCIALS

Company Type: Private

Income Statement

FYE: December 31

	REVENUE ($ mil.)	NET INCOME ($ mil.)	NET PROFIT MARGIN	EMPLOYEES
12/15	326	(11)	—	1,800
12/14*	302	(5)	—	—
06/14	0	(2)	—	—
12/12	378	12	3.4%	—
Annual Growth	(4.8%)	—	—	—

*Fiscal year change

2015 Year-End Financials

Return on assets: 2.6%   Cash ($ mil.): 90
Return on equity: (-3.4%)
Current ratio: —

UMASS MEMORIAL COMMUNITY HOSPITALS, INC.

EXECUTIVES

Chief Executive Officer, Eric Dickson
Vice-President, Jay Brady
Manager, Lisa Carpenter
Director, Steve Holmes
Manager, George Nolan
Vice-President, Allison Wollen
Auditors: PRICEWATERHOUSECOOPERS LLP B

LOCATIONS

HQ: UMASS MEMORIAL COMMUNITY HOSPITALS, INC.
119 BELMONT ST, WORCESTER, MA 016052903
Phone: 508 334-1000

HISTORICAL FINANCIALS
Company Type: Private

Income Statement
FYE: September 30

	REVENUE ($ mil.)	NET INCOME ($ mil.)	NET PROFIT MARGIN	EMPLOYEES
09/16	305	12	4.2%	10,000
09/15	286	8	2.8%	—
09/08	332	9	2.9%	—
09/07	302	15	5.1%	—
Annual Growth	0.1%	(1.9%)	—	—

2016 Year-End Financials
Return on assets: 4.9%   Cash ($ mil.): 46
Return on equity: 4.2%
Current ratio: 1.20

UMASS MEMORIAL COMMUNITY MEDICAL GROUP, INC.

EXECUTIVES

Principal, Thomas Pokoly
Director, Vasilios Chrisostomidis
Auditors: PRICEWATERHOUSECOOPERS LLP B

LOCATIONS

HQ: UMASS MEMORIAL COMMUNITY MEDICAL GROUP, INC.
121 LINCOLN ST, WORCESTER, MA 016052429
Phone: 508 757-7745
Web: WWW.UMASSMEMORIALHEALTHCARE.ORG

UMASS MEMORIAL HEALTH CARE, INC.

EXECUTIVES

President, Peter H Levine
Senior Vice-President, Nancy R Kruger

LOCATIONS

HQ: UMASS MEMORIAL HEALTH CARE, INC.
365 PLANTATION ST STE 300, WORCESTER, MA 016052397
Phone: 508 334-1000

HISTORICAL FINANCIALS
Company Type: Private

Income Statement
FYE: September 30

	REVENUE ($ mil.)	NET INCOME ($ mil.)	NET PROFIT MARGIN	EMPLOYEES
09/16	2,373	(21)	—	10,000
09/15*	2,241	(7)	—	—
12/14	555	6	1.3%	—
09/14	2,252	17	0.8%	—
Annual Growth	2.7%	—	—	—

*Fiscal year change

2016 Year-End Financials
Return on assets: 6.4%   Cash ($ mil.): 231
Return on equity: (-0.9%)
Current ratio: 0.80

UMASS MEMORIAL MEDICAL CENTER, INC.

EXECUTIVES

Manager, David Klein
Director, Eric Alper
Director, Oren P Schaefer
Auditors: PRICEWATERHOUSECOOPERS LLP BO

LOCATIONS

HQ: UMASS MEMORIAL MEDICAL CENTER, INC.
55 LAKE AVE N, WORCESTER, MA 016550002
Phone: 508 334-1000

HISTORICAL FINANCIALS
Company Type: Private

Income Statement
FYE: September 30

	REVENUE ($ mil.)	NET INCOME ($ mil.)	NET PROFIT MARGIN	EMPLOYEES
09/15	468	7	1.6%	3
09/11	451	8	1.9%	—
09/09	400	7	1.8%	—
09/08	360	1	0.4%	—
Annual Growth	3.8%	25.5%	—	—

2015 Year-End Financials
Return on assets: 1.5%   Cash ($ mil.): 18
Return on equity: 1.6%
Current ratio: 0.70

HISTORICAL FINANCIALS
Company Type: Private

Income Statement
FYE: September 30

	REVENUE ($ mil.)	NET INCOME ($ mil.)	NET PROFIT MARGIN	EMPLOYEES
09/16	1,621	(130)	—	29
09/15	1,332	60	4.5%	—
09/14	1,258	19	1.6%	—
09/13	1,183	68	5.8%	—
Annual Growth	11.1%	—	—	—

2016 Year-End Financials
Return on assets: 6.3%   Cash ($ mil.): 124
Return on equity: (-8.0%)
Current ratio: 0.70

UNIFIED SCHOOL DISTRICT 259

EXECUTIVES

Superintendent, John Allison
Executive Director, Jim Means
Auditors: ALLEN GIBBS & HOULIK LC WIC

LOCATIONS

HQ: UNIFIED SCHOOL DISTRICT 259
201 N WATER ST, WICHITA, KS 672021292
Phone: 316 973-4000
Web: WWW.USD259.ORG

HISTORICAL FINANCIALS
Company Type: Private

Income Statement
FYE: June 30

	REVENUE ($ mil.)	NET INCOME ($ mil.)	NET PROFIT MARGIN	EMPLOYEES
06/16	622	(31)	—	5,406
06/15	626	(55)	—	—
06/14	613	21	3.4%	—
06/13	600	(50)	—	—
Annual Growth	1.2%	—	—	—

UNION BANK AND TRUST COMPANY

Union Bank & Trust a subsidiary of financial services holding company Farmers & Merchants Investment operates more than 35 branches throughout Nebraska and in Kansas. As Nebraska's third-largest privately-owned bank it offers traditional deposit and trust services as well as insurance equipment finance and investment management services. Consumer loans account for the largest portion of the bank's portfolio followed by commercial real estate and farmland loans. Union Bank also originates business loans and residential mortgages. Affiliate company Union Investment Advisors manages the Stratus family of mutual funds. Another Farmers & Merchants unit Nelnet Capital offers brokerage services.

Operations

Union Bank has grown to become one of Nebraska's largest privately-owned banks. As of mid-2013 it boasted bank assets of $2.6 billion and trust assets of $11.8 billion.

Aside from its branches in Nebraska and Kansas Union Bank offers banking products and services through its online mobile and electronic banking services.

Geographic Reach

Union Bank operates mostly in Nebraska but also in Kansas.

Sales and Marketing

The bank primarily serves customers in Lincoln and Omaha as well as the Kansas City metropolitan area.

Strategy

Union Bank continues to expand its footprint in existing markets. The financial institution will have added three new Nebraska branches to its portfolio by 2014.

Company Background

The bank was originally founded in 1917 as Farmer's State Bank. It took on the Union Bank name in 1935 and became Union Bank & Trust in 1959.

EXECUTIVES

Vice President Small Business Banking, Stephanie Dinger

First Vice President Manager Commercial Real Estate, Tom Weinandt

LOCATIONS

HQ: UNION BANK AND TRUST COMPANY
3643 S 48TH ST, LINCOLN, NE 685064390
Phone: 402 488-0941
Web: WWW.UBT.COM

PRODUCTS/OPERATIONS

Selected Services
Business banking
Investment & retirement
Personal banking
Wealth management

Selected Affiliates
InfoVisa
Nelnet Capital LLC
Nelnet Inc.
Union Agency Inc.
Union Equipment Finance LLC
Union Investment Advisors
Union Title Company LLC
Zelle

COMPETITORS

Bank of America	Great Western Bancorp
Bank of the West	JPMorgan Chase
Citigroup	Pinnacle Bancorp
First National of	U.S. Bancorp
Nebraska	Wells Fargo

HISTORICAL FINANCIALS

Company Type: Private

Income Statement

FYE: December 31

	ASSETS ($ mil.)	NET INCOME ($ mil.)	INCOME AS % OF ASSETS	EMPLOYEES
12/15	3,351	32	1.0%	800
12/14	3,040	29	1.0%	—
12/13	2,862	35	1.3%	—
12/08	2,437	16	0.7%	—
Annual Growth	4.7%	9.7%	—	—

2015 Year-End Financials

Return on assets: —
Return on equity: 19.1%
Sales ($ mil): 168

UNION HOSPITAL, INC.

Union Hospital is the flagship facility of the Union Hospital Health Group a health care system that serves communities in western Indiana and eastern Illinois. The not-for-profit hospital has about 320 beds boasts an equal number of physicians and provides general medical and surgical care as well as specialty services in areas such as women's health newborn intensive care unit (Level II) cancer cardiovascular disease and sports medicine. It also offers occupational health and physical rehabilitation as well as medical training programs. Other facilities that comprise the Union system include Union Hospital Clinton physician practices specialty clinics and a home health agency.

Operations

Besides the main Union Hospital which averages some 17000 patient admissions each year the hospital operates Union Hospital Clinton specialty clinics a home health agency and physician practices.

Geographic Reach

The teaching hospital serves patients in west-central Indiana and eastern Illinois.

Strategy

Union Hospital's main campus underwent a nearly $180 million expansion project in recent years. The patient tower provides for private rooms instead of six- to eight-bed wards.

As part of a strategic focus to extend the reach of its operations Union Hospital partners with AP&S Clinic a multi -specialty physician group practice to expand the two entities' services. Operating as Union Health System the collaboration looks to increase coordination of care between physician specialists.

In 2015 Union Hospital partnered with the Ob Hospitalist Group to provide around-the-clock physician care for expectant mothers.

Company Background

Union Hospital's roots go back to 1892.

EXECUTIVES

Vice President Of Finance And Chief Financial Officer, Wayne R Hutson
Managing Director, Doug Smith
Vice President, John Bolinger
Clinical Director, Barbara Gossett
Medical Director, Ramesh Shatagopam
Medical Director, Grace Walker
Director of Medical Records, Pamala Alexander
Vice President, Trudy Rupska
Radiology Director, Gale Wilson
Team Lead CVPV, Kelly Hill
Vice President Practice Administration, Linda Hoolehan
Board Member, Steven Mcdonald
Treasurer, Don Scott
Board Member, Dave Doerr

LOCATIONS

HQ: UNION HOSPITAL, INC.
1606 N 7TH ST, TERRE HAUTE, IN 478042780
Phone: 812 238-7000
Web: WWW.MYUNIONHOSPITAL.ORG

PRODUCTS/OPERATIONS

Selected Services
Acupuncture
Advanced Medical Technology
Asthma
Behavioral Healthcare
Breast Care
Cancer Care Services
Cardiovascular Testing
Clara Fairbanks Center for Women
Clay City Center for Family Medicine
Cork Medical Center

Family Medicine Center
Infections
Joint Replacement Center
Landsbaum Center
Lugar Center for Rural Health
Medical Rehabilitation Center
Neonatal Intensive Care Unit (NICU)
Pediatrics
Pulmonary and Lung Health
Wound Healing Center
Union Hospital Terre Haute
Union Hospital Clinton
Union Hospital Foundation

COMPETITORS

Ascension Health	IU Health Bloomington
Carle Hospital	Hospital
Franciscan Alliance	Kosciusko Community
HCA	Hospital
IU Health	

HISTORICAL FINANCIALS

Company Type: Private

Income Statement

FYE: December 31

	REVENUE ($ mil.)	NET INCOME ($ mil.)	NET PROFIT MARGIN	EMPLOYEES
12/15	384	6	1.8%	1,960
12/14*	127	3	2.7%	—
08/10	400	(3)	—	—
08/09	408	18	4.5%	—
Annual Growth	(1.0%)	(15.1%)	—	—

*Fiscal year change

2015 Year-End Financials

Return on assets: 6.1%
Return on equity: 1.8%
Current ratio: 1.60
Cash ($ mil.): 41

UNITED COOPERATIVE

EXECUTIVES

Chief Executive Officer, David Cramer
Board of Directors, Robin Craker
Manager, Greg Thomson
Director, David Bischoff
Manager, Greg Adkins
Vice-President, Alan Jentz

LOCATIONS

HQ: UNITED COOPERATIVE
N7160 RACEWAY RD, BEAVER DAM, WI 539169315
Phone: 920 887-1756
Web: WWW.UNITEDCOOPERATIVE.COM

HISTORICAL FINANCIALS

Company Type: Private

Income Statement

FYE: December 31

	REVENUE ($ mil.)	NET INCOME ($ mil.)	NET PROFIT MARGIN	EMPLOYEES
12/15	579	41	7.1%	358
12/14	577	57	10.0%	—
12/13	627	45	7.2%	—
12/12	641	34	5.4%	—
Annual Growth	(3.3%)	5.7%	—	—

2015 Year-End Financials

Return on assets: 3.1%
Return on equity: 7.1%
Current ratio: 0.40
Cash ($ mil.): 27

UNITED ELECTRIC SUPPLY COMPANY, INC.

True to its name United Electric Supply distributes electrical parts such as lighting fasteners sensors wire connectors and voice data and fiber-optic products. The employee-owned company carries more than 23000 items from more than 250 manufacturers including Kyocera Panasonic Security and Schneider Electric. It sells to the building and industrial trades government and other markets. United Electric's wide range of services include design value engineering energy audits procurement training inventory management and E-commerce. It also offers value-added services such as next day delivery and Saturday-morning counter hours.

Operations

United Electric divides its business into eight product groups: Data Comm; Electro-Mechanical; Energy Solutions; Gear and Control; Integrated Products; Lighting; Wire Cable and Conduit; and Solar Energy. Data Comm offers on-site consultation and assistance to deploy voice data and fiber optic technology. Electro-Mechanical provides project-specific quotations for such products as fittings boxes fasteners and tools.

Energy Solutions focuses on energy audits rebate studies lighting design and other services to increase the energy efficiency of lighting. Gear and Control offers project budgeting design and other services along with distributing products. Integrated Products markets programmable controllers operator interface products supervisory software drives and power conditioning equipment among other products. Lighting serves the construction and renovation markets with various lighting products and conducts audits of lighting systems to determine better energy efficiency. Wire Cable and Conduit offers items that range from basic building wire to multi-conductor instrumentation cables. Solar Energy provides renewable power for a variety of structures from large commercial buildings to small houses.

United Electric additionally offers a program called Supplier Inventory Management System (SIMS) that includes such services as inventory reduction through analysis of each storeroom unit and bar-coding. United Electric is also an authorized supplier through Pennsylvania's COSTARS cooperative purchasing program which unifies local organizations to achieve more competitive pricing than individual businesses could obtain on their own.

Geographic Reach

It has 21 branch locations in Delaware Maryland New Jersey Pennsylvania and Virginia.

Sales and Marketing

The company sells its products through its stores and via online marketing efforts.

Company Background

The company which was founded in 1965 by Nick Gianoulis has been an employee-owned venture since 1996.

EXECUTIVES

VP Distribution and Control Products, Sal Muzzi
VP Finance and CFO, Rich Stagliano
VP Operations and COO, Bob Crawford
Director Information Technology, Luis Varela
Manager Energy Saving Products, Peggy Hill
VP Sales Maryland Washington DC and Virginia, George Vorwick
Manager Solar Products, Mike Howell
Product Manager Industrial Automation Group, Kurt Niehaus
Product Manager Electromechanical Products, Walt Opalach
Manager Wire and Cable Products, Dennis Risner
Auditors: BAKER TILLY VIRCHOW KRAUSE LLP

LOCATIONS

HQ: UNITED ELECTRIC SUPPLY COMPANY, INC.
10 BELLECOR DR, NEW CASTLE, DE 197201763
Phone: 800 322-3374
Web: WWW.UNITEDELECTRIC.COM

PRODUCTS/OPERATIONS

Selected Services
Consigned inventory
Design and build assistance
Electronic invoicing
Energy audits
Order staging
Post Order Focus
Procurement
Supplier Inventory Management Systems
Training
Value Engineering
Product Categories
Application Specific Products
Conduit & Raceway
Conduit Fittings
Control & Automation
Data & Telecom
Fire Alarm & Security
Fuses
Hardware & Fasteners
Heaters & Fans
Junction Boxes & Enclosures
Lamps Ballasts & Accessories
Lighting Fixtures
Power Distribution
Solar
Tools
Wire
Wire Management
Wiring Devices & Cord Connectors

COMPETITORS

Anixter International
Billows Electric
  Supply
Consolidated
  Electrical
Gexpro
Graybar Electric
McCoy Group
Rumsey Electric
W.W. Grainger
WESCO International

HISTORICAL FINANCIALS

Company Type: Private

Income Statement

FYE: December 31

	REVENUE ($ mil.)	NET INCOME ($ mil.)	NET PROFIT MARGIN	EMPLOYEES
12/15	203	5	2.5%	343
12/14	193	3	2.0%	—
12/13	168	2	1.7%	—
12/12	171	3	1.8%	—
Annual Growth	6.0%	16.7%	—	—

2015 Year-End Financials

Return on assets: 11.1%   Cash ($ mil.): 6
Return on equity: 2.5%
Current ratio: 1.00

UNITED HEALTH SERVICES HOSPITAL, INC.

United Health Services Hospitals (UHS Hospitals) can service injuries from a slip in the snow or a slipped disc to health that's just plain slipping. The organization operates Binghamton General Hospital (about 200 beds) Wilson Medical Center (some 280 beds) and a group of primary and specialty care clinics in upstate New York. Specialty services include cardiology dialysis neurology rehabilitation pediatrics and psychiatry. The Wilson Medical Center serves as a teaching hospital offering residency and fellowship programs. UHS Hospitals is a subsidiary of United Health Services which operates a network of affiliated hospitals clinics long-term care centers and home health agencies in the region.

Geographic Reach

Binghamton General is located in Binghamton New York while Wilson Medical Center is located in Johnson City New York both within the boundaries of Broome County. UHS Hospitals also operates primary and specialty care clinics in Broome Chenango Delaware and Tioga counties in upstate New York.

Strategy

United Health Services Hospitals is investing in equipment upgrades and facility improvements at Binghamton General to help the facility remain at the forefront of medical technology and services. Wilson Medical Center which acts as a regional referral center in areas including emergency medicine newborn care neurology and heart surgery has also been the subject of enhancement measures. The hospital recently completed construction of the new Decker Center for Advanced Medical Treatment which offers high-tech diagnostic and acute care services.

EXECUTIVES

Vice President General Counsel, Jeffery Alexander
Nursing Director, Kay Boland
Auditors: FUST CHARLES CHAMBERS LLP SYR

LOCATIONS

HQ: UNITED HEALTH SERVICES HOSPITAL, INC.
10-42 MITCHELL AVE, BINGHAMTON, NY 139031617
Phone: 607 762-2200

COMPETITORS

Albany Medical Center
Guthrie Healthcare
Kaleida Health
Lifetime Health
Oneida Healthcare Center
SUNY Upstate Medical University
St. Joseph's Hospital Health Center
Upstate University Hospital at Community General

HISTORICAL FINANCIALS

Company Type: Private

Income Statement

FYE: December 31

	REVENUE ($ mil.)	NET INCOME ($ mil.)	NET PROFIT MARGIN	EMPLOYEES
12/15	575	13	2.3%	5,000
12/14	523	(23)	—	—
12/13	516	27	5.4%	—
12/12	496	18	3.8%	—
Annual Growth	5.1%	(11.3%)	—	—

2015 Year-End Financials

Return on assets: 3.4% Cash ($ mil.): 26
Return on equity: 2.3%
Current ratio: 1.00

UNITED HOSPITAL CENTER, INC.

EXECUTIVES

President, Michael C Tillman
Board of Directors, Jane Urso
Board of Directors, Kathy Serrrell
Director, Keith Matheny

LOCATIONS

HQ: UNITED HOSPITAL CENTER, INC.
327 MEDICAL PARK DR, BRIDGEPORT, WV
263309006
Phone: 681 342-1000
Web: WWW.UHCWV.ORG

HISTORICAL FINANCIALS
Company Type: Private

Income Statement

FYE: December 31

	REVENUE ($ mil.)	NET INCOME ($ mil.)	NET PROFIT MARGIN	EMPLOYEES
12/15	293	12	4.4%	2,000
12/14	280	17	6.4%	—
12/13	267	30	11.3%	—
12/12	238	25	10.9%	—
Annual Growth	7.2%	(20.8%)	—	—

2015 Year-End Financials

Return on assets: 4.0% Cash ($ mil.): 35
Return on equity: 4.4%
Current ratio: 1.80

UNITED INDEPENDENT SCHOOL DISTRICT

EXECUTIVES

Superintendent, Roberto J Santos
Board of Directors, Ricardo Rodriguez
Bookkeeper, Mario Gonzalez
Accounting Director, Samuel Florez
Board of Directors, Ricardo Molina
Purchasing Director, Connie Gonzalez
Auditors: PATTILLO BROWN & HILL LLP BR

LOCATIONS

HQ: UNITED INDEPENDENT SCHOOL DISTRICT
201 LINDENWOOD DR, LAREDO, TX 780452429
Phone: 956 473-6201
Web: WWW.UISD.NET

HISTORICAL FINANCIALS
Company Type: Private

Income Statement

FYE: August 31

	REVENUE ($ mil.)	NET INCOME ($ mil.)	NET PROFIT MARGIN	EMPLOYEES
08/16	464	(66)	—	6,900
08/15	444	64	14.5%	—
08/14	387	89	23.1%	—
08/13	372	0	0.2%	—
Annual Growth	7.7%	—	—	—

2016 Year-End Financials

Return on assets: 4.2% Cash ($ mil.): 124
Return on equity: (-14.4%)
Current ratio: —

UNITED JEWISH APPEAL-FEDERATION OF JEWISH PHILANTHROPIES OF NEW YORK CHARITABLE FUND, LLC

EXECUTIVES

President, Jerry W Levin
Board of Directors, Lynne G Koeppel
Auditors: KPMG LLP NEW YORK NY

LOCATIONS

HQ: UNITED JEWISH APPEAL-FEDERATION OF
JEWISH PHILANTHROPIES OF NEW YORK
CHARITABLE FUND, LLC
130 E 59TH ST FL 3, NEW YORK, NY 100221375
Phone: 212 980-1000
Web: WWW.UJAFEDNY.ORG

HISTORICAL FINANCIALS
Company Type: Private

Income Statement

FYE: June 30

	REVENUE ($ mil.)	NET INCOME ($ mil.)	NET PROFIT MARGIN	EMPLOYEES
06/15	215	(27)	—	400
06/14	328	114	34.7%	—
06/13	208	(16)	—	—
06/10	231	50	22.0%	—
Annual Growth	(1.4%)	—	—	—

2015 Year-End Financials

Return on assets: 8.9% Cash ($ mil.): 58
Return on equity: (-12.7%)
Current ratio: 0.40

UNITED NEGRO COLLEGE FUND, INC.

"A mind is a terrible thing to waste." In this spirit the United Negro College Fund (UNCF) offers financial assistance to students of color from low- to moderate-income families pursuing a higher education. UNCF the oldest and largest higher non-profit education assistance program for African-Americans enables some 60000 students to attend college each year. About 60% of the students are the first in their families to attend college. UNCF also provides operating funds and IT services to historically black colleges and universities such as Bethune-Cookman Morehouse Xavier and Voorhees College.

Operations

The Fund's services include funding its 37 member colleges all of them small private historically black colleges and universities. In addition the fund has worked to upgrade and modernize technology provide computers to students and faculty as well as create an e-commerce site selling current hardware and software. UNCF drives an annual television public service announcement UNCF An Evening of Stars a national campaign that serves as an advocate and fundraiser for education. It also offers grants to help build capacity faculty development programs and assistance with teacher education programs.

More than 90% of UNCF students seeking higher education require financial aid. UNCF also provides scholarships internships and fellowships to support graduate and doctoral studies. To help prepare students for college UNCF has partnered with Teach For America and the KIPP Foundation to improve high school graduation rates.

Geographic Reach

UNCF has offices in more than 25 US states.

Financial Performance

About 75% of UNCF's support in 2013 came through contributions for grants and scholarships; some 16% came from contributions and gifts.

In 2013 the Fund's revenues decreased by 4% due to a 30% decline in bequests and legacies and a more than $15 million drop in net realized and unrealized gains interests and dividends and amortization and investment premiums which more than offset higher revenues from gifts-in-kind and donated services a 1% increase from grants and scholarships and a 5% increase from contributions and gifts.

UNCF's net income dropped by 3% in 2013 due to a decline in revenues.

In 2013 the organization posted cash outflow of $89.17 million (compared to cash outflow of $41.02 million in 2012) primarily due to a decline in net loss and a change in working capital.

Strategy

UNCF Scholarship Programs increase the likelihood that students will graduate. African American recipients of UNCF scholarships have a 70% six-year graduation rate 10% points higher than the national average and 30% higher than the average for all African Americans. A $5000 UNCF scholarship the likelihood that its recipient will graduate from college by 7%.

Its largest scholarship program the Gates Millennium Scholars Program a partnership with the Bill & Melinda Gates Foundation provides financial assistance to 1000 Hispanic American Asian/Pacific American Native American and African American students. Students receive a good-through-graduation scholarship to use at any US-based accredited college or university of their choice.

The recipients of the Gates Millennium Scholarships have average graduation rates of 90%.

Company Background

The not-for-profit organization was founded in 1944 by Dr. Frederick D. Patterson with 27 charter member colleges.

EXECUTIVES

Senior Vice President Public Policy Government Affairs, Cheryl Smith

LOCATIONS

HQ: UNITED NEGRO COLLEGE FUND, INC.
1805 7TH ST NW STE 100, WASHINGTON, DC
200013187
Phone: 800 331-2244
Web: WWW.UNCF.ORG

UNCF Member Institutions
Allen University Columbia SC
Benedict College Columbia SC
Bennett College for Women Greensboro NC
Bethune-Cookman University Daytona Beach FL
Claflin University Orangeburg SC
Clark Atlanta University Atlanta GA
Dillard University New Orleans LA
Edward Waters College Jacksonville FL
Fisk University Nashville TN
Florida Memorial University Miami FL
Huston-Tillotson University Austin TX
Interdenominational Theological Center Atlanta GA
Jarvis Christian College Hawkins TX
Johnson C. Smith University Charlotte NC
Lane College Jackson TX
LeMoyne-Owen College Memphis TN
Livingston College Salisbury NC
Miles College Birmingham AL
Morehouse College Atlanta GA
Morris College Sumter SC
Oakwood University Huntsville AL
Paine College Augusta GA
Paul Quinn College Dallas TX
Philander Smith College Little rock AR
Rust College Holly Springs MS
Saint Augustine's College Raleigh NC
Saint Paul's College Lawrenceville VA
Shaw University Raleigh NC
Spelman College Atlanta GA
Stillman College Tuscaloosa AL
Talladega College Talladega AL
Texas College Tyler TX
Tougaloo College Tougaloo MC
Tuskegee University Tuskegee AL
Virginia Union University Richmond VA
Voorhees College Denmark SC
Wilberforce University Wilberforce OH
Wiley College Marshall TX
Xavier University New Orleans LA

PRODUCTS/OPERATIONS

Selected Scholarship Programs
Corporate Scholars Program
Gates Millennium Scholars Program
UNCF/Merck Science Initiative

HISTORICAL FINANCIALS

Company Type: Private

Income Statement

	REVENUE ($ mil.)	NET INCOME ($ mil.)	NET PROFIT MARGIN	EMPLOYEES
03/15	221	50	22.7%	257
03/14	208	40	19.2%	—
03/10	197	51	25.9%	—
03/09	240	89	37.3%	—
Annual Growth	(1.4%)	(9.2%)	—	—

FYE: March 31

2015 Year-End Financials
Return on assets: 4.3% Cash ($ mil.): 82
Return on equity: 22.7%
Current ratio: 2.40

UNITED OIL OF THE CAROLINAS, INC.

EXECUTIVES

President, D L Efrid
Account Manager, Glenn Peeler
Account Manager, Dave Dulmage
Account Manager, Liz Coyle
Auditors: BUTLER & STOWE GASTONIA NC

LOCATIONS

HQ: UNITED OIL OF THE CAROLINAS, INC.
1627 SPENCER MOUNTAIN RD, GASTONIA, NC
280549002
Phone: 704 824-3561
Web: WWW.UNITEDOILONLINE.COM

HISTORICAL FINANCIALS

Company Type: Private

Income Statement

	REVENUE ($ mil.)	NET INCOME ($ mil.)	NET PROFIT MARGIN	EMPLOYEES
03/15	207	1	0.8%	26
03/14	251	0	0.2%	—
03/13	282	1	0.4%	—
03/12	292	1	0.4%	—
Annual Growth	(10.8%)	8.2%		

FYE: March 31

2015 Year-End Financials
Return on assets: 1.5% Cash ($ mil.): 6
Return on equity: 0.8%
Current ratio: 2.50

UNITED POWER, INC

EXECUTIVES

Chief Executive Officer, Ronald Asche
Director, Don Cummins
Manager, Antelia Ball
Manager, Jay Mendoza
Auditors: DECORIA MAICHEL AND TEAGUE PS

LOCATIONS

HQ: UNITED POWER, INC
500 COOPERATIVE WAY, BRIGHTON, CO 806038728
Phone: 303 637-1341
Web: WWW.UNITEDPOWER.COM

HISTORICAL FINANCIALS

Company Type: Private

Income Statement

	REVENUE ($ mil.)	NET INCOME ($ mil.)	NET PROFIT MARGIN	EMPLOYEES
12/15	216	(0)	—	166
12/14	188	(0)	—	—
12/09	126	11	9.0%	—
12/08	124	13	11.1%	—
Annual Growth	8.3%	—	—	—

FYE: December 31

2015 Year-End Financials
Return on assets: 11.2% Cash ($ mil.): 5
Return on equity: (-0.1%)
Current ratio: 0.70

UNITED REGIONAL HEALTH CARE SYSTEM, INC.

If you take a fall in Wichita Falls United Regional Health Care System (URHCS) will be there. The health care provider serves the residents of northern Texas through two hospitals that combined have some 500 beds. Specialized services include emergency medicine cardiac care diagnostic imaging surgery obstetrics and pediatrics. The health care system also offers cancer treatment childbirth wound care and sleep diagnostic centers. It is the only comprehensive cardiac care facility and only Level II trauma center in the region. URHCS operates a Care Flight Helicopter to get those traumas to care quicker.

Operations

URHCS provides medical care including inpatient and outpatient services advanced diagnostics surgical specialties and life-saving emergency care and the area's only Level II Trauma Center. It also serves as the Primary Stroke Center for the region. Its centers of excellence include wound care center joint replacement program and stroke program; bariatric surgery program; breast imaging center of excellence; cardiovascular patient care. It has some 200 physicians on staff.

In 2012 the medical system reported 14163 admissions; 74778 emergency department visits; 48890 outpatient visits/observations; 9211 surgeries and 2144 births.

Geographic Reach

The hospital serves Wichita Falls and a surrounding nine-county area.

Financial Performance

In 2012 URHCS provided $27 million in charity care.

Strategy

Along with building and technological expansions URHCS has been focused on increasing the number of specialists in its employ. To that end the system created a recruitment program that targets medical students residents and fellows who have ties to Wichita Falls and the surrounding areas. Hospital administration and members of the physician staff offer support and guidance to potential recruits as they progress in their medical education or as they consider making a move from another hospital.

In recent years URHCS has recruited physicians in the areas of cardiovascular surgery neurosurgery orthopedic surgery and minimally invasive general and bariatric surgery to meet the community's increased need for those medical specialties.

In 2013 it expanded the Barnett Road Medical Building to have office space for physicians. The system also added laboratory and radiology services to the building.

In 2012 URHCS deployed Allscripts MDRX+1.09% Care Management's fully-integrated web-based solutions to help transform its administrative processes by streamlining and improving the quality of patient care enhancing operational efficiency and cutting costs. In addition new mobile access technology help physicians to securely access patient information and make care decisions for their patients via their iPhones and iPads.

Company Background

In 2011 URCHS initiated renovation of its Bethania Building and Administration Building and it relocated its Cardio-Pulmonary Rehab Facility. It also remodeled its United Regional Diag-

nostic building and extended the hospital's outpatient therapy space to accommodate more patients.

EXECUTIVES

Senior Vice President of Operations, Nancy Townley
Vice President of Physician Practice Services, Johnny Roberts
Vice President Of Information Technology, Donnie Boydstun
Vice President of Facilities Management, Rick Carpenter
Vice President Of Marketing, Stevie-Joe Brown
Vice President of Finance, Bob Pert
Nursing Director, Jane Ritter

LOCATIONS

HQ: UNITED REGIONAL HEALTH CARE SYSTEM, INC.
1600 11TH ST, WICHITA FALLS, TX 763014300
Phone: 940 764-3211
Web: WWW.UNITEDREGIONAL.ORG

PRODUCTS/OPERATIONS

Selected Medical Services
Advanced Technology
Bariatric Services
Cancer Care
Cardiac Services
Diabetes Education
Emergency and Trauma Services
ENT
Infusion Therapy
Neurology
Neurosurgery
Obstetrics
Orthopedics
Pediatrics
Pulmonary Rehabilitation
Radiology
Reference Laboratory
Respiratory
Stroke Program & Center of Distinction
Supportive Care
Surgical Services
Women's Services
Wound Care

COMPETITORS

HCA	Tenet Healthcare
Jackson County	Texas Health Denton
Memorial Hospital	Texas Health Resources
Mercy Health	

HISTORICAL FINANCIALS

Company Type: Private

Income Statement

FYE: December 31

	REVENUE ($ mil.)	NET INCOME ($ mil.)	NET PROFIT MARGIN	EMPLOYEES
12/15	299	32	10.9%	1,950
12/14	310	46	15.0%	—
12/13	292	53	18.3%	—
12/12	279	41	15.0%	—
Annual Growth	2.4%	(8.0%)	—	—

2015 Year-End Financials

Return on assets: 3.2%   Cash ($ mil.): 32
Return on equity: 10.9%
Current ratio: 1.60

UNITED STATES BEEF CORPORATION

This company has carved out a sandwich empire in the middle of the country. United States Beef Corporation is the largest franchisee of Arby's fast-food restaurants in the US with more than 280 locations in half a dozen states mostly in Kansas Missouri and Oklahoma. The restaurants franchised from Arby's Restaurant Group (part of Wendy's/Arby's Group) serve the chain's signature roast beef sandwiches and curly fries as well as ham chicken and turkey subs. Bob Davis and his wife Connie opened their first Arby's in 1969 and founded United States Beef in 1974. The Davis family continues to own the company.

Unlike many other fast food chains Arby's has not had much success expanding its product offerings beyond roast beef sandwiches and curly fries. Regardless United States Beef Corporation plans to develop new Arby's restaurants in some of its existing markets while the company remodels older locations with modern and clean looking interiors and exteriors.

United States Beef Corporation has the exclusive franchise development rights for Arby's restaurants in Arkansas Colorado Illinois Kansas Missouri and Oklahoma.

EXECUTIVES

Vice President Operations, Bo Davis
Senior Vice President Operations, Rick Morris
Vice President Finance, Lori Pumphrey

LOCATIONS

HQ: UNITED STATES BEEF CORPORATION
4923 E 49TH ST, TULSA, OK 741357002
Phone: 918 665-0740
Web: WWW.USBEEFCORP.COM

COMPETITORS

American Dairy Queen	Mazzio's
Biglari Holdings	McDonald's
Boddie-Noell	NPC Restaurant
Burger King	Holdings
Captain D's	Panera Bread
Checkers Drive-In	Popeyes
Chick-fil-A	Quiznos
Chipotle	Sonic Corp.
Church's Chicken	Subway
Hardee's	Whataburger
Jack in the Box	YUM!
K-MAC	

HISTORICAL FINANCIALS

Company Type: Private

Income Statement

FYE: December 31

	REVENUE ($ mil.)	NET INCOME ($ mil.)	NET PROFIT MARGIN	EMPLOYEES
12/15	351	14	4.2%	7,000
12/13	256	7	3.1%	—
12/12	246	7	3.0%	—
12/08	331	0	0.0%	—
Annual Growth	0.8%	317.5%	—	—

2015 Year-End Financials

Return on assets: 1.1%   Cash ($ mil.): 4
Return on equity: 4.2%
Current ratio: 0.10

UNITED STATES FUND FOR UNICEF

The US Fund for UNICEF is one of about 40 committees in America that raises money for The United Nations Children's Fund (better known as UNICEF a not-for-profit organization that works for the human rights protection and development of children worldwide through education advocacy and fundraising. Among its dedicated programs are the five-year $100 million fundraising campaign for HIV/AIDS prevention and a campaign to protect mothers and newborns from tetanus. The US Fund for UNICEF derives revenue from public support — through its signature Trick-or-Treat for UNICEF program gifts corporate grants and the sale of greeting cards and educational materials. The organization was founded in 1947.

Geographic Reach

The US Fund for UNICEF operates a handful of regional offices in Atlanta Boston Chicago Houston Los Angeles and San Francisco.

Financial Performance

The organization's revenue increased by 1% in 2012 versus 2011 to more than $500 million. The US Fund attributed the gain to an increase in public support including major gifts Internet donations and gifts in kind. The increase in giving was partially offset by a decline in investment returns. Net income rose 7% over the same period despite an increase in expenses tied to program and support services.

Strategy

The US Fund for UNICEF is rallying around its "Believe in Zero" campaign which aims to reduce the number of preventable deaths of children under five years of age to zero. The number of under-five child deaths has dropped more than 40 percent since 1990 to 19000.

EXECUTIVES

Vice President Corporate Partnerships, Deanna Helmig
Vice President Public Relations, Lisa Szarkowski

LOCATIONS

HQ: UNITED STATES FUND FOR UNICEF
125 MAIDEN LN FL 11, NEW YORK, NY 100384999
Phone: 800 367-5437
Web: WWW.UNICEFUSA.ORG

HISTORICAL FINANCIALS

Company Type: Private

Income Statement

FYE: June 30

	REVENUE ($ mil.)	NET INCOME ($ mil.)	NET PROFIT MARGIN	EMPLOYEES
06/15	500	(29)	—	230
06/14	606	67	11.2%	—
06/13	310	12	4.2%	—
Annual Growth	26.8%	—	—	—

2015 Year-End Financials

Return on assets: 1.5%   Cash ($ mil.): 60
Return on equity: (-5.8%)
Current ratio: 0.60

UNITED STATES GOLF ASSOCIATION

Making sure golf stays clear of the rough is par for the course at this organization. The United States Golf Association is the governing body for golf in the US its territories and Mexico. The not-for-profit group writes and interprets the rules of the game provides handicap information offers turf consulting and funds equipment and course maintenance research and testing. It also holds several national championship events including the US Open the US Women's Open and the US Senior Open. The group generates most of its revenue from the sale of broadcast rights to championship tournaments and other matches as well as through membership fees. The USGA was founded in 1894.

Sales and Marketing

The organization has long-term television deals with ESPN and Bell Media's Canadian broadcasting outlets RDS and TSN.

Financial Performance

The USGA reported fiscal 2013 revenue of about $157 million up roughly 6% from the prior year on a rise in championships revenue (including broadcast rights) and corporate sponsorship revenue. It also saw net income of $51 million in fiscal 2013 an increase of 97% from $26 million in fiscal 2012 primarily because of unfunded Postretirement benefit obligation.

Strategy

The organization is working to combat the challenges posed by modern golf courses which aren't as inviting to average players take longer to play and are more expensive to maintain. Improving course sustainability is a key element of this work and the USGA has been consulting with courses across the nation to implement sustainable practices deal with reductions in water availability and protect the environment.

EXECUTIVES

Executive Director, David Fay
Board of Directors, Eric J Gleacher
Board of Directors, Fredric C Nelson
Manager, Michael Overhizer
Account Manager, Elaine Bascotti
Auditors: BDO USA LLP NEW YORK NY

LOCATIONS

HQ: UNITED STATES GOLF ASSOCIATION
77 LIBERTY CORNER RD, FAR HILLS, NJ 079312570
Phone: 908 234-2300
Web: WWW.USGA.ORG

COMPETITORS

Augusta National	Professional Bowlers
Major League Baseball	Association
NBA	The R&A
NFL	USA Track & Field
NHL	USSF
PGA	USTA
PGA TOUR	

HISTORICAL FINANCIALS
Company Type: Private

Income Statement
FYE: November 30

	REVENUE ($ mil.)	NET INCOME ($ mil.)	NET PROFIT MARGIN	EMPLOYEES
11/15	208	16	7.9%	350
11/14	164	(5)	—	—
11/13	156	6	4.3%	—
11/12	147	13	9.3%	—
Annual Growth	12.3%	6.5%	—	—

2015 Year-End Financials

Return on assets: 9.0%   Cash ($ mil.): 17
Return on equity: 7.9%
Current ratio: 0.40

UNIVERSITY COMMUNITY HOSPITAL, INC.

University Community Health (doing business as Florida Hospital Tampa Bay Division) is a 1000-bed regional health care system with four locations spanning the Hillsborough Pinellas and Pasco counties of Florida. It oversees a network of eight hospitals in Florida's Tampa Bay area. Its four general hospitals — three located in Tampa and one in nearby Tarpon Springs — collectively house some 860 beds and provide emergency surgical and acute medical care as well as provide outpatient services. The system also includes a specialty heart hospital a women's hospital and a long-term acute care hospital. Florida Hospital Tampa Bay Division is part of the Adventist Health System.

Strategy

As part of the Adventist Health System's network the system has access to a broader statewide network of physicians and specialists as well as enhanced administrative and technological services organization.

In 2012 Florida Hospital Tampa Bay Division opened Florida Hospital Wesley Chapel and began work on three major construction projects including a new full-service Emergency Department (ED) expanding The Women's Center and exterior and interior upgrades to the main hospital which should add a total of 54000 sq. ft. to the scope of Florida Hospital Tampa.

Company Background

Its original name of University Community Health (UCH) reflected its proximity to the University of South Florida. UCH teamed up with Adventist Health in 2007 to build Wesley Chapel Medical Center. Buoyed by the success of the venture in 2010 UCH and Adventist Health reached an accord and UCH became a member of Adventist Health.

EXECUTIVES

Radiology Director, CHRISTINE ROTELL-WALSH

LOCATIONS

HQ: UNIVERSITY COMMUNITY HOSPITAL, INC.
3100 E FLETCHER AVE, TAMPA, FL 336134613
Phone: 813 971-6000
Web: WWW.FLORIDAHOSPITAL.COM

PRODUCTS/OPERATIONS

Selected Centers
Diabetes and Endocrinology Institute
Don Lau Family Center for Cancer Care
Florida Hospital Pepin Heart Institute
Occupational Health Service
Orthopedic Care Center
Pediatric Care Center
Sleep Center
The Women's Center
Wound Healing Institute

Selected Hospitals
Florida Hospital at Connerton
Florida Hospital Carrollwood
Florida Hospital North Pinellas
Florida Hospital Pepin Heart Institute
Florida Hospital Tampa
Florida Hospital Wesley Chapel
Florida Hospital Zephyrhills
Long Term Acute Care

COMPETITORS

All Children's Hospital	Lakeland Regional Medical Center
BayCare Health System	Northside Hospital and
Bayfront Health	Heart Institute
HCA	Tampa General Hospital

HISTORICAL FINANCIALS
Company Type: Private

Income Statement
FYE: December 31

	REVENUE ($ mil.)	NET INCOME ($ mil.)	NET PROFIT MARGIN	EMPLOYEES
12/15	460	38	8.4%	8,000
12/14	381	24	6.5%	—
12/13	510	33	6.6%	—
Annual Growth	(5.0%)	7.5%	—	—

2015 Year-End Financials

Return on assets: 3.9%   Cash ($ mil.): 154
Return on equity: 8.4%
Current ratio: 2.80

UNIVERSITY CORPORATION FOR ATMOSPHERIC RESEARCH

The University Corporation for Atmospheric Research (UCAR) is a not-for-profit corporation founded in 1960 to promote research in atmospheric and related environmental sciences. A consortium of more than 100 universities UCAR provides real-time weather data to universities educates weather forecasters and organizes international experiments through its Office of Programs. The organization also maintains radars aircraft and computer models for weather and climate through the National Center for Atmospheric Research (NCAR). UCAR is funded by sponsors such as the National Science Foundation the National Oceanic and Atmospheric Administration and NASA.

Operations

The UCAR consortium consists of around 75 North American universities granting doctoral degrees related to atmospheric science 25 offering

bachelor's and master's programs in this dame filed and roughly 50 international affiliates.

In addition to promoting research and professional development among academia UCAR provides educational resources to the public and advocates for strong federal science budgets on behalf of the geosciences community.

Geographic Reach

The University Corporation for Atmospheric Research (UCAR) and the National Center for Atmospheric Research (NCAR) are both based in Boulder Colorado. They have additional operations in Cheyenne Wyoming and Washington DC. Its affiliated Mauna Loa Solar Observatory is based in Hilo Hawaii.

Strategy

To extend its reach the UCAR opened NCAR-Wyoming Supercomputing Center which provides advanced computing services to scientists with expertise in air pollution climate oceanography space weather energy production seismology carbon sequestration computational science and other topics.

EXECUTIVES

Chairman University Corporation for Atmospheric Research (UCAR) Foundation, Vivian K. Dullien
Director Business Development & Partnerships, Scott Rayder
Director Budget and Finance, Melissa Miller
Director Information Technology, Shawn Winkelman
Director Government Relations, Mike Henry
Interim President, Michael Thompson
Co Chairman, Chrissy Fladung
Auditors: KPMG LLP ALBUQUERQUE NM

LOCATIONS

HQ: UNIVERSITY CORPORATION FOR ATMOSPHERIC RESEARCH
3090 CENTER GREEN DR, BOULDER, CO 803012252
Phone: 303 497-1000
Web: WWW.UCAR.EDU

PRODUCTS/OPERATIONS

Selected Research Topics
Climate
Meterology/Weather
Societal impacts of weather and climate
Pollution and air chemistry
The whole Earth system
Sun & space weather

HISTORICAL FINANCIALS
Company Type: Private

Income Statement — FYE: September 30

	REVENUE ($ mil.)	NET INCOME ($ mil.)	NET PROFIT MARGIN	EMPLOYEES
09/16	216	8	4.1%	1,565
09/15	212	(0)	—	—
09/14	214	3	1.4%	—
09/13	221	8	3.8%	—
Annual Growth	(0.8%)	2.3%	—	—

2016 Year-End Financials
Return on assets: 3.1%   Cash ($ mil.): 30
Return on equity: 4.1%
Current ratio: 0.70

UNIVERSITY HEALTH SYSTEM

EXECUTIVES

Chief Executive Officer, George B Hernandez Jr
Director, Akos Szabo
Director, Jose Cavazos
Director, Steven Bailey
Engineer, Michael Dicicco
Commissioner, Connie Castaeda
Manager, Karen McMurry
Director, Lorri Savoie

LOCATIONS

HQ: UNIVERSITY HEALTH SYSTEM
4502 MEDICAL DR, SAN ANTONIO, TX 782294402
Phone: 210 358-4000
Web: WWW.UNIVERSITYHEALTHSYSTEM.COM

HISTORICAL FINANCIALS
Company Type: Private

Income Statement — FYE: December 31

	REVENUE ($ mil.)	NET INCOME ($ mil.)	NET PROFIT MARGIN	EMPLOYEES
12/15	476	73	15.4%	5,000
12/14	407	23	5.7%	—
Annual Growth	17.2%	217.4%	—	—

2015 Year-End Financials
Return on assets: 25.6%   Cash ($ mil.): 58
Return on equity: 15.4%
Current ratio: 0.40

UNIVERSITY HEALTH SYSTEMS OF EASTERN CAROLINA, INC.

University Health Systems of Eastern Carolina is an integrated not-for-profit health system that serves residents of eastern North Carolina. Doing business as Vidant Health it operates nine hospitals including eight community hospitals and its tertiary care center Vidant Medical Center with 1400 beds and academic affiliation with the Brody School of Medicine at East Carolina University. Vidant Health also operates centers for surgery home health hospice and wellness and engages in community health programs. Its physician group has more than 350 primary and specialty care providers who operate from more than 50 locations.

Operations

In addition to its nine hospitals the organization includes the Vidant Home Health and Hospice organization the Vidant Wellness Centers and the growing line of Vidant Medical Group physician practice locations. Vidant Health's facilities handle some 64000 inpatient and 595000 emergency care and outpatient visits each year. The organization also provides some $135.5 million in annual community benefits including outreach programs and charity care.

Geographic Reach

The organization serves more than 1.4 million residents in 29 counties in eastern North Carolina.

Financial Performance

In 2014 Vidant Health reported a 0.2% decrease in revenues and a 37% drop in net income.

Strategy

Because the system operates as a not-for-profit enterprise it reinvests its earnings in capital improvements equipment and new services. Vidant Health reinvests all of its income back into capital projects equipment and access to services for the patients and communities it serves. In 2014 the system invested $38 million in capital assets which included investments in information systems medical equipment and infrastructure across the health system as well as architectural and design fees related to the construction of the new cancer tower on the Vidant Medical Center campus.

Across the region Vidant is focusing on cancer care and is creating a strong network of strategically located cancer services. In Washington the Marion L. Shepard Cancer Center a department of Vidant Beaufort Hospital underwent a major expansion including new high-technology radiation treatment equipment. This $4.8 million project helps patients receive cancer care in their home community.

Company Background

University Health Systems rebranded itself as Vidant Health in 2012 in its effort to reflect its "vibrant and vital" position within the region as it advances its transformation to patient- and family-centered care.

In 2012 the hospital invested in upgrades to several outpatient care centers adding a new medical office building in the community of Wallace and adding specialist rehabilitation and behavioral health care units to its Vidant Chowan Hospital facility. It also discontinued skilled nursing services at the Chowan location to focus more on outpatient care. In addition a new children's hospital and pediatric emergency room was opened at the Vidant Medical Center location.

Vidant Health is also working to upgrade its health information technology systems. During 2012 it successfully connected three of its community hospitals through its electronic health record (EHR) system.

EXECUTIVES

Vice President Human Resources, Tyree Walker
Vp Supply Chain Management And Finance Support Services, Preston N Comeaux

LOCATIONS

HQ: UNIVERSITY HEALTH SYSTEMS OF EASTERN CAROLINA, INC.
800 W H SMITH BLVD, GREENVILLE, NC 278343763
Phone: 252 847-6690
Web: WWW.TRINITYFAMILYONLINE.COM

PRODUCTS/OPERATIONS

Selected Hospitals
Vidant Beaufort Hospital (Washington)
Vidant Bertie Hospital (Windsor)
Vidant Chowan Hospital (Edenton)
Vidant Duplin Hospital (Kenansville)
Vidant Edgecombe Hospital (Tarboro)
Vidant Medical Center (affiliated with the Brody School of Medicine at East Carolina University Greenville)
Vidant Pungo Hospital (Belhaven)
Vidant Roanoke-Chowan Hospital (Ahoskie)
The Outer Banks Hospital (jointly owned with Chesapeake Regional Medical Center Nags Head)

Selected Services
Asthma Program (Pediatric)
Audiology
Behavioral & Mental Health
Cancer Care
Child Life
Children's Care
Children's Emergency Department

Children's Hospital
Community Health Programs
Diagnostic Imaging
Diabetes
Emergency Services
Endoscopy Services
Gamma Knife
Heart and Vascular Care
Heartburn Treatment Clinic
Home Health
Hospice Care
Hyperbaric Oxygen Therapy
Injury Prevention
Mammography
Medical Weight Loss (OPTIFAST)
Mental Health
MRI (Magnetic Resonance Imaging)
Neurosciences
Neurosurgery
Open MRI
Orthopedics
Pain Management
Pediatric Cardiology
Pediatric Rehabilitation
Pediatric Services
Pink Power Speaking Tour
Psychiatry
Radiology
Rehabilitation Center
Rehabilitation
Senior Services
Sleep Services
Specialty Services
Speech Pathology
Spine Surgery
Sports Medicine
Stroke Care
Surgical Services
Transplant Services
Trauma Services
Vascular Surgery
Weight Loss
Wellness & Prevention
Women's Care
Wound Healing

COMPETITORS

Alamance Regional
  Medical Center
Carolinas HealthCare
  System
Cumberland County
  Hospital System
Duke University Health
  System

Grace Hospital
Novant Health
Rex Healthcare
Rowan Regional Medical
  Center
UNC Hospitals
WakeMed

HISTORICAL FINANCIALS

Company Type: Private

Income Statement

FYE: September 30

	REVENUE ($ mil.)	NET INCOME ($ mil.)	NET PROFIT MARGIN	EMPLOYEES
09/15	1,581	(6)	—	8,373
09/14*	1,597	66	4.1%	—
12/13	400	31	7.9%	—
09/13	1,601	109	6.8%	—
Annual Growth	(0.6%)	—	—	—

*Fiscal year change

2015 Year-End Financials

Return on assets: 12.7%   Cash ($ mil.): 192
Return on equity: (-0.4%)
Current ratio: 1.80

UNIVERSITY MEDICAL CENTER OF SOUTHERN NEVADA

For those who want to learn while they heal the ill University Medical Center of Southern Nevada (UMC)— an affiliate of the University of Nevada School of Medicine might just be the place. The medical center includes a teaching hospital and a network of community and urgent care health centers. Among its specialized services are cancer treatment heart care pediatrics and rehabilitation. It also offers birthing wound and burn care neurological disorder Level II Pediatric Trauma Lions Burn Care Center and Level 1 trauma centers. UMC serves southern Nevada along with parts of Arizona California and Utah.

Operations

UMC is also home to Children's Hospital of Nevada. Services at University Medical Center of Southern Nevada are comprehensive and include everything from ambulatory surgery to a birthing center cancer care infection prevention and organ donation.

The hospital operates 10 Quick Care urgent care locations around Las Vegas. Quick Cares provide primary and urgent care which means they accept minor injuries such as fractures and flus and primary care for patients who don't necessarily need to be seen right away and can make an appointment.

UMC offers residency programs in a whole slew of specialties including dental (pediatric and adult) emergency medicine family medicine internal medicine OB-GYN psychiatry surgery and trauma surgery and ophthalmology.

For doctors who have put medical school behind them UMC provides a range of Continuing Education Courses to keep them up to date on the latest procedures and technology.

More than 6500 patients are treated at UMC's emergency room per month and more than 600 children are treated per week. UMC's lab processes 4 million test results annually using the latest in technology and automation for the greatest accuracy and increased patient outcomes.

Sales and Marketing

Medicare accounted for 20% of the Center's 2014 revenues; Medicaid and self pay 50%; and commercial HMO and PPO 20%.

Financial Performance

UMC's revenues decreased by 20% in 2014 due to a decline in net patient revenues and other operating revenues.

It reported a net loss of $56 million in 2014 due to a decline in revenues and an increase in purchase services expenses as the result of consulting services received for operational improvements.

UMC reported cash outflow of $42 million in 2014 over cash inflow of 2013.

Company Background

The medical center opened its doors in 1931 with 20 beds.

EXECUTIVES

Pharmd, Jamie King
SECRETARY, Estrellita Alejo-broadie

LOCATIONS

HQ: UNIVERSITY MEDICAL CENTER OF SOUTHERN NEVADA
1800 W CHARLESTON BLVD, LAS VEGAS, NV 891022329
Phone: 702 383-2000
Web: WWW.UMCSN.COM

PRODUCTS/OPERATIONS

Selected Services
Bariatric Medicine
Birthing Center
Center for Transplantation
Emergency Services
Family Resource Center
Heart Center
HIV Wellness Center
 Imaging Se
Infection Prevention
Interpretive Services
Lab Services
Lions Wound and Burn Care Center
Oncology Care Center
Outpatient Physical Therapy
Robotics
Surgical Services
Trauma Center

COMPETITORS

Desert Springs
  Hospital
Dignity Health
Summerlin Hospital

Sunrise Hospital and
  Medical Center
Valley Hospital

HISTORICAL FINANCIALS

Company Type: Private

Income Statement

FYE: June 30

	REVENUE ($ mil.)	NET INCOME ($ mil.)	NET PROFIT MARGIN	EMPLOYEES
06/15	530	49	9.3%	3,700
06/03	412	20	5.0%	—
06/02	0	0	—	—
06/01	372	10	2.9%	—
Annual Growth	2.6%	11.4%	—	—

2015 Year-End Financials

Return on assets: 5.9%   Cash ($ mil.): 83
Return on equity: 9.3%
Current ratio: 2.00

UNIVERSITY OF ARKANSAS SYSTEM

Calling "Wooo Pig Sooie" at anyone in The University of Arkansas System (UA) is not an insult. The system encompasses more than a dozen schools institutes and campuses throughout the state including five universities a college of medicine a math and science high school and the Clinton School of Public Service started in 2004 by former president Bill Clinton and offering the only Master of Public Service degree in the country. UA which has an enrollment of more than 60000 hails the razorback or hog as its mascot. "Wooo Pig Sooie" or "hog calling" is the school's cheer at sporting events. Its student-teacher ratio is 19:1; it has about 17000 employees.

Operations

The flagship University of Arkansas campus in Fayetteville offers students undergraduate graduate and law degrees through about nine schools. Areas of study include architecture agriculture food

and life sciences arts and sciences business education and health engineering and law. UA's Global Campus provides long-distance education online and via video streaming. Along with undergraduate training the Global Campus offers professional degrees and career training.

Other system facilities include five community colleges two law schools and divisions of architecture archeology and criminal justice.

Financial Performance

Revenue increased about 1% in 2013 from $1.8 billion to $1.82 billion due to record enrollment and increases in other revenue.

Strategy

In order to keep students coming to UA year after year the system regularly improves it classroom offerings as well as it facilities. To that end the university is building a $60 million performing arts center and a $20 million admissions building on the site of its former Bryce Hospital in Tuscaloosa.

Company Background

The Arkansas General Assembly established UA in Fayetteville in 1871 as the Arkansas Industrial University and under the the Morrill Act of 1862 it became the state land-grant institution and first state-assisted college in Arkansas. On opening day January 22 1873 there were four teachers and eight students.

EXECUTIVES

Vice President For Academic Affairs, Dan Ferritor
Vice President, Angela Hudson
Associate Vice President for Finance, Rita Fleming
Assoc Vice President for Benefits and Risk Management Services, Steve Wood
Associate Vice President Legal and Research, Harold Evans
Assistant Secretary, Kelly Eichler
Auditors: ROGER A NORMAN JD CPA CFE

LOCATIONS

HQ: UNIVERSITY OF ARKANSAS SYSTEM
2404 N UNIVERSITY AVE, LITTLE ROCK, AR 722073608
Phone: 501 686-2500
Web: WWW.UASYS.EDU

PRODUCTS/OPERATIONS

Selected Campuses
Arkansas Archeological Survey
Arkansas School for Mathematics Sciences and the Arts (high school)
Clinton School of Public Service
Cossatot Community College of the University of Arkansas
Criminal Justice Institute
Division of Agriculture
Phillips Community College of the University of Arkansas
University of Arkansas Community College at Morrilton
University of Arkansas Fayetteville
University of Arkansas at Fort Smith
University of Arkansas at Little Rock
University of Arkansas for Medical Sciences
University of Arkansas at Monticello
University of Arkansas at Pine Bluff
Winthrop Rockefeller Institute

HISTORICAL FINANCIALS
Company Type: Private

Income Statement
FYE: June 30

	REVENUE ($ mil.)	NET INCOME ($ mil.)	NET PROFIT MARGIN	EMPLOYEES
06/16	2,172	64	3.0%	14,025
06/15	1,970	30	1.6%	—
06/14	1,841	54	3.0%	—
06/13	1,819	83	4.6%	—
Annual Growth	6.1%	(8.1%)	—	—

2016 Year-End Financials
Return on assets: 6.7%
Return on equity: 3.0%
Current ratio: 2.00
Cash ($ mil.): 527

UNIVERSITY OF CINCINNATI MEDICAL CENTER, LLC

EXECUTIVES

President, Bryan Gibler
Vice-President, Andrew Filak
Director, Monica France
Director, Paula Hawk
Auditors: DELOITTE TAX LLP CINCINNATI

LOCATIONS

HQ: UNIVERSITY OF CINCINNATI MEDICAL CENTER, LLC
234 GOODMAN ST, CINCINNATI, OH 452192364
Phone: 513 584-1000
Web: WWW.UNIVERSITYHOSPITAL.UCHEALTH.COM

HISTORICAL FINANCIALS
Company Type: Private

Income Statement
FYE: June 30

	REVENUE ($ mil.)	NET INCOME ($ mil.)	NET PROFIT MARGIN	EMPLOYEES
06/15	873	64	7.4%	5,000
06/10	633	28	4.6%	—
06/09	562	20	3.6%	—
Annual Growth	7.6%	21.1%	—	—

2015 Year-End Financials
Return on assets: 0.5%
Return on equity: 7.4%
Current ratio: 40.90
Cash ($ mil.): 1

UNIVERSITY OF COLORADO FOUNDATION

Operating independently from the University of Colorado the University of Colorado Foundation (CU Foundation) engages in not-for-profit fundraising on behalf of the University. It partners with the University to raise manage and invest private support for the University's benefit. The foundation manages more than $125 million annually from nearly 50000 donors; the funds it raises are used to support scholarships research athletics building construction and faculty and staff at the University. The CU Foundation also manages the University's Creating Futures fundraising campaign which aims to raise $1.5 billion.

Operations

In fiscal 2014 more than 46000 donors gave $148.9 million through the University of Colorado Foundation (a significant component of the nearly $300 million of private support for the University of Colorado that year. That year the Foundation's assets totaled $1.57 billion primarily made up of investments of $1.42 billion. It reported managed endowments of $1.06 billion.

Financial Performance

The revenue increased by 34% to $315 million in 2014 due to increase in contributions investment return and Change in value of split-interest agreements.

Net income increased by 95% to $186 million in 2014 due to higher revenue.

The company saw cash inflow of $40 million in 2014 over cash outflow in 2013 due to higher net income and cash generated from custodial funds.

Company Background

The CU Foundation was established by the University of Colorado in 1967.

EXECUTIVES

Vice President and Chief Financial Officer, Dan Palmquist
Vice President, Jill Pollock
Vice President Of Legislative Council, David Gillis
Associate Vice President For Development, Maurin Anderson
Vice President of Government Relations, Tanya Mares Kelly-Bowry
Vice President Of Human Resources, Kathy Rasco
Assistant Vice President For External Relations and Advocacy, Michele McKinney
Assistant Vice President For External Relations and Advocacy, Cu Advocates
Treasurer, John A Zwick
Auditors: EKS&H LLLP DENVER CO

LOCATIONS

HQ: UNIVERSITY OF COLORADO FOUNDATION
1800 N GRANT ST STE 725, DENVER, CO 802031114
Phone: 303 813-7935
Web: WWW.COLORADO.EDU

HISTORICAL FINANCIALS
Company Type: Private

Income Statement
FYE: June 30

	REVENUE ($ mil.)	NET INCOME ($ mil.)	NET PROFIT MARGIN	EMPLOYEES
06/15	203	61	30.4%	180
06/14	317	186	58.7%	—
06/13	236	95	40.3%	—
06/12	139	0	0.3%	—
Annual Growth	13.4%	443.8%	—	—

2015 Year-End Financials
Return on assets: 3.2%
Return on equity: 30.4%
Current ratio: 2.80
Cash ($ mil.): 18

UNIVERSITY OF FLORIDA

Founded in 1853 the University of Florida (UF) is the state's oldest university and one of the largest in the country with nearly 50000 students and some 5100 faculty and library staff members. UF is a major land-grant research university encompassing 2000 acres in Gainesville Florida. The university's 16 colleges offer more than 100 undergraduate majors and about 200 graduate programs including education law medicine psychology and philosophy. It is also a member of the Association of American Universities a confederation of the top research universities in North Amer-

ica. A founding member of the Southeastern Conference UF's athletic teams (the Florida Gators) are typically ranked nationally.

Operations

UF is active in research and operates more than 200 research institutes and centers including the Nanoscale Research Facility the Pathogens Research Facility and the Biomedical Sciences Building. It has research collaborations with the likes of Scripps Florida Moffitt Cancer Center and Burnham Institute for Medical Research. Altogether UF receives about $650 million in research grants annually.

UF also has extensive health education programs including nursing and pharmacy colleges. Its medical school conducts teaching and residency programs at several Shands hospitals.

Strategy

Like many public universities in the US UF is facing decreased funding from government agencies due to economic conditions. UF has also seen enrollment decreases in recent years but has keep tuition rates and fees low to attract and retain students.

To meet the needs of its large and diverse student population UF is conducting a number of expansion and renovation projects on its more than 900 buildings.

To combat budget shortfalls due to funding and economic conditions UF is also pursuing new research partnerships that will provide funding from commercial and institutional sources. The university is pursuing other revenue generation initiatives to become more financially independent.

Company Background

UF's alumni include Robert Cade the inventor of Gatorade; best-selling mystery novelist Michael Connelly; actress Faye Dunaway; and former US Senator and Florida Governor Bob Graham. Other UF alumni include two Nobel Prize winners and three NASA astronauts.

EXECUTIVES

VP and CFO, Michael V. (Mike) McKee
SVP Academic Affairs and Provost, Joseph (Joe) Glover
Dean of Students, Jen Day Shaw
Dean Warrington College of Business Administration, John Kraft
VP and CIO, Elias G. Eldayrie
SVP Health Affairs; President UF Health, David S. Guzick
Dean College of Journalism and Communications, Diane H. McFarlin
Dean College of Public Health and Health Professions, Michael G. Perri
Dean College of Medicine, Michael Good
Dean College of Education, Glenn E. Good
Dean College of Arts, Lucinda Lavelli
Dean University Libraries, Judith C. Russell
Dean College of Design Construction and Planning, Christopher Silver
SVP and COO, Charles E. Lane
President, W. Kent Fuchs
Dean College of Engineering, Cammy Abernathy
Dean College of Health and Human Performance, Michael Reid
Interim Dean College of Liberal Arts and Sciences, David E. Richardson
Interim Dean College of Dentistry, Boyd Robinson
Dean College of Nursing, Anna McDaniel
Dean College of Pharmacy, Julie A. Johnson
Dean College of Veterinary Medicine, James Lloyd
Dean College of Agricultural and Life Sciences, Elaine Turner
Dean IFAS Extension, Nick Place
Dean IFAS Research, Jacqueline Burns
Dean Graduate School, Henry T. Frierson
Executive Vice President Technology, Kim Niblett

Vice President Technology, Lin Ai
Vice President of Information Technology, Sorin Pascu
Vice President, Matthew Barclay
Assistant Vice President For Student Affairs Sa Student Affairs, Jeanna Mastrodicasa
Assoc Vice President for Enrollment Management, Tammy Aagard
Vice President Research and Development, Suleyman Tufekci
Sustainable Vice President, Elif Akcali
Vice President Information Technology, Marjorie Chow
Associate Medical Director Transfusion Services, Faisal Mukhtar
Assistant Vice President, Carol Walker
Vice President of Planning and Business Development, Steven Blumberg
Medical Director, Sherri Flax
External Vice President, Bryan Tran
Assistant Vice President, Lisette Pellot
Scacvim Vice President, Ross Hancock
Chairman, Steven M. Scott
Treasurer, Dale Canelas
Secretary, DESTINY PADGETT
Secretary NR WMN Child Fam Nurs GNV, Mary Lamantia
SECRETARY Professor TEACHING CTR GENERAL, Penny Dipalma
Board Member, Matthew Friedland
Secretary, Kathrin Gallick
Board Member, Andrew Harris
Treasurer, Alex Cardoso
Treasurer, Zachary Makovich
Auditors: SHERRILL F NORMAN CPA TALLAH

LOCATIONS

HQ: UNIVERSITY OF FLORIDA
300 SW 13TH ST, GAINESVILLE, FL 326110001
Phone: 352 392-3261
Web: WWW.UFL.EDU

PRODUCTS/OPERATIONS

Selected Colleges
College of Agricultural and Life Sciences
College of Dentistry
College of Design Construction and Planning
College of Education
College of Engineering
College of Health and Human Performance
College of Journalism and Communications
College of Liberal Arts and Sciences
College of Medicine
College of Nursing
College of Pharmacy
College of Public Health and Health Professions
College of the Arts
College of Veterinary Medicine
Levin College of Law
Warrington College of Business Administration

HISTORICAL FINANCIALS
Company Type: Private

Income Statement				FYE: June 30
	REVENUE ($ mil.)	NET INCOME ($ mil.)	NET PROFIT MARGIN	EMPLOYEES
06/15	1,735	261	15.1%	5,106
06/12	3,939	64	1.6%	—
06/09	3,846	(343)	—	—
Annual Growth	(12.4%)	—	—	—

2015 Year-End Financials
Return on assets: 4.0%
Return on equity: 15.1%
Current ratio: 0.20
Cash ($ mil.): 2

UNIVERSITY OF FLORIDA JACKSONVILLE PHYSICIANS INC

EXECUTIVES

Chairman of the Board, Robert Nuss
Board of Directors, Theodore Bass
Manager, Albert Fan
Auditors: PERSHING YOAKLEY & ASSOCIATES

LOCATIONS

HQ: UNIVERSITY OF FLORIDA JACKSONVILLE PHYSICIANS INC
653 W 8TH ST, JACKSONVILLE, FL 322096511
Phone: 904 244-9500
Web: WWW.UFHEALTHJAX.ORG

HISTORICAL FINANCIALS
Company Type: Private

Income Statement				FYE: June 30
	REVENUE ($ mil.)	NET INCOME ($ mil.)	NET PROFIT MARGIN	EMPLOYEES
06/15	291	8	2.8%	375
06/14	265	0	0.1%	—
06/11	229	12	5.4%	—
06/10	256	5	2.1%	—
Annual Growth	2.6%	8.2%	—	—

2015 Year-End Financials
Return on assets: 6.2%
Return on equity: 2.8%
Current ratio: 2.40
Cash ($ mil.): 39

UNIVERSITY OF GEORGIA RESEARCH FOUNDATION, INC.

EXECUTIVES

President, Jere Morehead
Auditors: CHERRY BEKAERT LLP AUGUSTA G

LOCATIONS

HQ: UNIVERSITY OF GEORGIA RESEARCH FOUNDATION, INC.
310 E CAMPUS RD 409, ATHENS, GA 306021589
Phone: 706 542-5939
Web: WWW.UGA.EDU

HISTORICAL FINANCIALS
Company Type: Private

Income Statement				FYE: June 30
	ASSETS ($ mil.)	NET INCOME ($ mil.)	INCOME AS % OF ASSETS	EMPLOYEES
06/16	99	0	0.4%	1
06/15	457	(0)	—	—
06/14	90	5	5.7%	—
06/11	434	4	1.0%	—
Annual Growth	(25.5%)	(38.1%)	—	—

2016 Year-End Financials

Return on assets: 0.7%   Sales ($ mil): 170
Return on equity: 0.2%

UNIVERSITY OF HOUSTON SYSTEM

The University of Houston System can't do much about the heat or humidity but it can provide higher education in Houston. The university system serves more than 65000 students at four Houston-area universities. Flagship institution the University of Houston was founded in 1927 and offers about 300 bachelor's master's and doctoral degree programs; it also conducts a number of research programs. Also under the system's umbrella are the University of Houston-Clear Lake the University of Houston-Downtown the University of Houston-Victoria as well as a handful of learning centers in the area. The system was established in 1977.

EXECUTIVES

President University Houston - Clear Lake, William A. Staples
Associate Vice Chancellor for Central Computing and Telecommunication Services, Dennis Fouty
President University Houston - Downtown, William V. (Bill) Flores
Executive Vice Chancellor for Administration and Finance, Carl P. Carlucci, age 68
Chancellor; President University of Houston, Renu Khator
President University Houston - Victoria, Philip Castille
Chairman, Jarvis V. Hollingsworth

LOCATIONS

HQ: UNIVERSITY OF HOUSTON SYSTEM
4302 UNIVERSITY DR, HOUSTON, TX 772042011
Phone: 713 743-0945
Web: WWW.UHSYSTEM.EDU

PRODUCTS/OPERATIONS

Selected Colleges and Schools
University of Houston
  C.T. Bauer College of Business
  College of Education
  College of Liberal Arts and Social Sciences
  College of Natural Sciences and Mathematics
  College of Optometry
  College of Pharmacy
  College of Technology
  Conrad N. Hilton College of Hotel and Restaurant Management
  Cullen College of Engineering
  Gerald D. Hines College of Architecture
  Graduate College of Social Work
  Honors College
  Law Center
University of Houston-Clear Lake
  School of Business
  School of Education
  School of Human Sciences and Humanities
  School of Science and Computer Engineering
University of Houston-Downtown
  College of Business
  College of Humanities and Social Sciences
  College of Public Service
  College of Sciences and Technology
University of Houston-Victoria
  School of Arts and Sciences
  School of Business Administration
  School of Education and Human Development
  School of Nursing

HISTORICAL FINANCIALS

Company Type: Private

Income Statement

FYE: August 31

	REVENUE ($ mil.)	NET INCOME ($ mil.)	NET PROFIT MARGIN	EMPLOYEES
08/15	605	41	6.9%	12,608
08/14	742	46	6.2%	—
08/13	1	81	6095.0%	—
08/12	688	132	19.3%	—
Annual Growth	(4.2%)	(31.9%)	—	—

UNIVERSITY OF IOWA HOSPITALS AND CLINICS

EXECUTIVES

Chief Executive Officer, Kenneth P Kates
Vice-President, Erin Minne
Board of Directors, Jerold Woodhead

LOCATIONS

HQ: UNIVERSITY OF IOWA HOSPITALS AND CLINICS
200 HAWKINS DR, IOWA CITY, IA 522421009
Phone: 319 356-1616

HISTORICAL FINANCIALS

Company Type: Private

Income Statement

FYE: June 30

	REVENUE ($ mil.)	NET INCOME ($ mil.)	NET PROFIT MARGIN	EMPLOYEES
06/15	1,248	90	7.2%	7,638
06/10	943	52	5.6%	—
06/09	863	(11)	—	—
Annual Growth	6.3%	—	—	—

2015 Year-End Financials

Return on assets: 3.7%   Cash ($ mil.): 13
Return on equity: 7.2%
Current ratio: 1.10

UNIVERSITY OF MARYLAND BALTIMORE WASHINGTON MEDICAL SYSTEM, INC.

EXECUTIVES

Executive Secretary, Faleria Ogur
Director, Zeleke K Desse
Personnel Manager, Patricia Loughin

LOCATIONS

HQ: UNIVERSITY OF MARYLAND BALTIMORE WASHINGTON MEDICAL SYSTEM, INC.
301 HOSPITAL DR, GLEN BURNIE, MD 210615803
Phone: 410 787-4000
Web: WWW.MYBWMC.ORG

HISTORICAL FINANCIALS

Company Type: Private

Income Statement

FYE: June 30

	REVENUE ($ mil.)	NET INCOME ($ mil.)	NET PROFIT MARGIN	EMPLOYEES
06/15	355	26	7.5%	2,676
06/14	366	19	5.3%	—
06/13	337	(3)	—	—
06/11	3	0	5.6%	—
Annual Growth	215.0%	237.9%	—	—

2015 Year-End Financials

Return on assets: 7.5%   Cash ($ mil.): 59
Return on equity: 7.5%
Current ratio: 0.80

UNIVERSITY OF MARYLAND MEDICAL SYSTEM CORPORATION

The 12 academic specialty and community hospitals of the University of Maryland Medical System (UMMS) dot the map of the state's eastern half on both sides of Chesapeake Bay. UMMS one of the largest employers in the Baltimore area has more than 2300 acute care beds and attends to such specialties as trauma care coma emergence kidney transplants orthopedic rehabilitation stroke intervention and pediatric care. University of Maryland Medical Center the system's teaching hub is one of the oldest academic hospitals in the US. In addition to its hospitals UMMS also includes community clinics to address mental health rehabilitation and primary care. The system was established in 1984.

Operations

UMMC's members hospitals include the University of Maryland Medical Center Baltimore Washington Medical Center Chester River Health System Civista Health System Kernan Orthopaedics and Rehabilitation Maryland General Hospital Mt. Washington Pediatric Hospital Shore Health System University of Maryland St. Joseph Medical Center and Upper Chesapeake Health.

University of Maryland Medical Center which houses about 800 beds is staffed entirely by physicians who double as faculty members at the University of Maryland School of Medicine (SOM) the system's longtime partner. The hospital contains additional specialty facilities dedicated to such areas as pediatrics cancer treatment cardiac disease diabetes organ transplants Parkinson's disease and shock trauma. The shock trauma center was the first of its kind in the world when it was founded in 1968.

Aside from its integral partnership with SOM UMMS has in recent years been bolstering its network of member hospitals to reach new markets in Maryland. Having been affiliated with Upper Chesapeake Health (UCH) UMMS merged the systems in 2013. UCH owns a pair of hospitals in

northeastern Maryland an underserved corner of the state that UMMS hadn't yet entered.

Financial Performance

UMMS's revenue in fiscal 2012 was $2.8 billion.

Company Background

The system's flagship hospital began on its present site in 1823 as Baltimore Infirmary. It later was known for many years as University Hospital until Maryland's legislature changed it from a state-run single-building facility to a private not-for-profit medical system in 1984. In short order UMMS began expanding mainly by adding existing hospitals.

EXECUTIVES

President and CEO University of Maryland Medical Center, Jeffrey A. Rivest
CEO Chester River Health System, James E. Ross
Senior Vice President Chief Information Officer, Jon P. Burns
President and CEO Maryland General Health Systems and Hospita, Sylvia Smith Johnson
SVP and COO Baltimore Washington Medical Center, Karen E. Olscamp, age 57
EVP and CFO, Henry J. Franey
Medical Director Trauma Acute Care, Deborah M Stein
VICE PRESIDENT INFORMATION TECHNOLOGY SERVICES, Brian Cassel
Senior Vice President for Human Resources and Chief Human Resources Officer, Candy Knowles
Senior Vice President Finance, Hank Franey
Director, Stephen A. Burch, age 67

LOCATIONS

HQ: UNIVERSITY OF MARYLAND MEDICAL SYSTEM CORPORATION
250 W PRATT ST, BALTIMORE, MD 212012423
Phone: 410 328-8667
Web: WWW.LIVINGBAKERSFIELD.COM

PRODUCTS/OPERATIONS

Selected Facilities and Affiliates
Baltimore Washington Medical Center
Chester River Health System
Civista Medical Center
Kernan Orthopaedics and Rehabilitation
Maryland General Hospital
Mt. Washington Pediatric Hospital
Shore Health System
  Dorchester General Hospital
  The Memorial Hospital at Easton
University of Maryland Medical Center
  Marlene and Stewart Greenebaum Cancer Center
  R Adams Cowley Shock Trauma Center
  University of Maryland Hospital for Children
University of Maryland St. Joseph Medical Center
University Specialty Hospital
Upper Chesapeake Health
  Harford Memorial Hospital
  Upper Chesapeake Medical Center

COMPETITORS

Adventist HealthCare	Franklin Square
Anne Arundel Medical	Hospital Center
Center	GBMC
Ascension Health	Johns Hopkins Health
Bon Secours Health	System
Catholic Health	LifeBridge Health
Initiatives	MedStar Health
Dimensions Healthcare	

HISTORICAL FINANCIALS

Company Type: Private

Income Statement   FYE: June 30

	REVENUE ($ mil.)	NET INCOME ($ mil.)	NET PROFIT MARGIN	EMPLOYEES
06/15	1,413	13	0.9%	12,000
06/14	1,824	17	1.0%	—
06/12*	2,504	(17)	—	—
09/11	0	0	—	—
Annual Growth	—	—	—	—

*Fiscal year change

2015 Year-End Financials

Return on assets: 9.3%   Cash ($ mil.): 249
Return on equity: 0.9%
Current ratio: 0.70

UNIVERSITY OF MINNESOTA PHYSICIANS

EXECUTIVES

Chief Executive Officer, Bobbi Daniels
Financial Executive, Todd Carlon
Manager, Dave Presuhn
Senior Manager, Pam Coppa
Director, Noreen Seeger
Director, Susan Holt
Director, Jacob Wiatrowski
Auditors: KPMG LLP MINNEAPOLIS MN

LOCATIONS

HQ: UNIVERSITY OF MINNESOTA PHYSICIANS
720 WASHINGTON AVE SE # 200, MINNEAPOLIS, MN 554142924
Phone: 612 884-0600

HISTORICAL FINANCIALS

Company Type: Private

Income Statement   FYE: June 30

	REVENUE ($ mil.)	NET INCOME ($ mil.)	NET PROFIT MARGIN	EMPLOYEES
06/15	482	10	2.2%	200
06/14	490	23	4.8%	—
06/13	452	12	2.8%	—
06/12	415	5	1.3%	—
Annual Growth	5.1%	24.7%	—	—

2015 Year-End Financials

Return on assets: 12.9%   Cash ($ mil.): 95
Return on equity: 2.2%
Current ratio: 2.00

UNIVERSITY OF MISSISSIPPI

They call her "Ole Miss" and she really is old: The University of Mississippi was chartered in 1844 as the first public university in the state and opened in 1848. Starting with 80 students the school's enrollment has grown to more than 23000 with most students attending the main Oxford campus. Ole Miss has additional campuses in Southaven (Desoto County) and Tupelo and it operates the University of Mississippi Medical Center in Jackson. The school is home to more than 30 research centers that specialize in business engineering law and other disciplines. Its academic institutes include the Croft Institute for International Studies and the William Winter Institute for Racial Reconciliation.

Operations

The Medical Center campus includes Mississippi's only children's hospital a women and infants' hospital and a critical care hospital. It is also home to the state's only Level 1 trauma center Level 4 neonatal intensive care nursery and organ transplant programs. Enrollment has grown at the university by some 59% since 2004 (when the school enrolled 14497 students).

Ole Miss has an endowment of approximately $462 million.

Geographic Reach

Minorities make up almost a fourth of Ole Miss students and more than 60% of all students at the university come from within the state. The student-faculty ratio is 19:1.

EXECUTIVES

Chancellor, Daniel Jones
Director, Jim Windham
Director, Nina Jones
Accountant, Mike Cook
Director, April Johnson
Director, Claude Ladner
Director, Cynthia Davis
Director, Deroy Johnson
Director, Eric Williamson

LOCATIONS

HQ: UNIVERSITY OF MISSISSIPPI
113 FALKNER, UNIVERSITY, MS 386779704
Phone: 662 915-6538
Web: WWW.OLEMISS.EDU

PRODUCTS/OPERATIONS

Selected Colleges and Schools
Colleges
The College of Liberal Arts
The Residential College
The Sally McDonnell Barksdale Honors College
The University of Mississippi
Booneville (branch)
Grenada (branch)
Southaven Campus
Tupelo Campus
The University of Mississippi Graduate School
The University of Mississippi Medical Center
Schools
Meek School of Journalism and News Media
Patterson School of Accountancy
School of Applied Science
School of Business Administration
School of Education
School of Engineering
School of Law
School of Nursing (at The University of Mississippi Medical Center)
School of Pharmacy

Selected Research Centers
Center for Advanced Infrastructure Technology
Center for Applied Electromagnetic Systems Research
Center for Archaeological Research
Center for Community Earthquake Preparedness
Center for Educational Research and Evaluation
Center for Excellence in Literacy Instruction
Center for Excellence in Teaching and Learning
Center for Health Behavior Research
Center for Intelligence and Security Studies
Center for Manufacturing Excellence

Center for Marine Resources and Environmental
    Technology
Center for Mathematics and Science Education
Center for Pharmaceutical Marketing and Management
Center for Population Studies
Center for Speech and Hearing Research
Center for the Study of Southern Culture
Center for Water and Wetland Resources
Center for Wireless Communications
INDO-US Joint Center for Research in Indian Systems of
    Medicine
Jamie Whitten National Center for Physical Acoustics
Magazine Innovation Center
National Center for Computational Hydroscience and
    Engineering
National Center for Justice and the Rule of Law
National Center for Natural Products Research
National Center for Remote Sensing Air and Space Law
National Sea Grant Law Center
Overby Center for Southern Journalism and Politics
Public Policy Research Center
Sarah Isom Center for Women's Studies
Sino-U.S. Traditional Chinese Medicines Research
    Center
University of Mississippi Geoinformatics Center

HISTORICAL FINANCIALS
Company Type: Private

Income Statement
FYE: June 30

	REVENUE ($ mil.)	NET INCOME ($ mil.)	NET PROFIT MARGIN	EMPLOYEES
06/15	401	101	25.4%	8,700
06/11	302	74	24.6%	—
06/10	278	63	22.8%	—
Annual Growth	7.5%	9.9%	—	—

2015 Year-End Financials

Return on assets: 8.0%   Cash ($ mil.): 44
Return on equity: 25.4%
Current ratio: 1.00

UNIVERSITY OF MISSOURI HEALTH CARE

EXECUTIVES

President, Mitch Wasden
Manager, Troy Cobb
Auditors: KPMG LLP

LOCATIONS

HQ: UNIVERSITY OF MISSOURI HEALTH CARE
    1 HOSPITAL DR, COLUMBIA, MO 652015276
Phone: 573 882-4141

HISTORICAL FINANCIALS
Company Type: Private

Income Statement
FYE: June 30

	REVENUE ($ mil.)	NET INCOME ($ mil.)	NET PROFIT MARGIN	EMPLOYEES
06/15	696	64	9.3%	5,000
06/08	0	0	1.0%	—
Annual Growth	169.1%	270.7%	—	—

2015 Year-End Financials

Return on assets: 2.7%   Cash ($ mil.): 21
Return on equity: 9.3%
Current ratio: 0.80

UNIVERSITY OF MISSOURI SYSTEM

Education isn't just for show in the Show Me State. The University of Missouri (UM) founded in 1839 educates about 76000 students at four campuses and through a statewide extension program; about a quarter of students are in graduate or professional programs. The university's campuses include flagship UM-Columbia (home to roughly 33000 students some 20 schools and colleges and the University of Missouri Health Sciences Center) UM-Kansas City UM-St. Louis and the Missouri University of Science and Technology. Nicknamed "Mizzou" the University of Missouri System has close to 6000 faculty members and a student-teacher enrollment of about 11:1.

Operations

In addition to its university campuses the University of Missouri System operates the University of Missouri Health System which encompasses University Hospital and Clinics Women's and Children's Hospital Ellis Fischel Cancer Center Rusk Rehabilitation Center Missouri Psychiatric Institute Missouri Orthopaedic Institute and University Physicians. Its hospitals and clinics provide high-risk obstetrics orthopedic surgery neurosciences and cardiovascular care among other services. It also has the region's only Level I Trauma Center.

Geographic Reach

The University of Missouri's four campuses are located in Columbia Kansas City Rolla and St. Louis. The system has an exchange program with South Africa through which UM students study at the University of the Western Cape in Bellville (Cape Town) South Africa and vice versa.

Financial Performance

The University of Missouri System had revenue of $3.1 billion in fiscal 2016. About one-third of that revenue came from net patient medical services; another 20% came from net tuition and fees. Its total operating expenses for that year totaled $2.8 billion. The system's endowment topped $1 billion for the first time in late 2017.

Strategy

The University of Missouri System has been strategically focused on five key priorities: attracting and retaining the best faculty and staff with competitive salaries benefits and workplace programs; expanding its online education offerings to improve students' success and bring in additional revenue; operating with efficiency and effectiveness; expanding research and economic development in the region; and improving communications with the community. However in early 2018 the system warned that growing state budget cuts could hamper its ability to improve student services and that layoffs program cuts and tuition hikes may be necessary.

EXECUTIVES

Chancellor University of Missouri-Kansas City,
    Leo E. Morton, age 72
Chancellor University of Missouri-St. Louis,
    Thomas F. (Tom) George
**Chancellor Missouri University of Science and
    Technology,** Cheryl B. Schrader
VP Information Technology, Gary K. Allen
**EVP Academic Affairs and Interim Chancellor
    University of Missouri-Columbia,** Henry C. (Hank)
    Foley
VP Finance and CFO, Brian D. Burnett
Chief Investment Officer, Thomas Richards
Interim President, Mike Middleton
Associate Vice President, John Gillispie

Vice president, Charlie Rigdon
Chairman, Donald L. Cupps
Vice Chairman, Pamela Q. Henrickson
Secretary, Cindy Harmon
Secretary To The Board, Kathleen Miller
Secretary, Betty Schlueter
Secretary, Lynda Larocque
Secretary Senior Mechanical And Aerosp, Cynthia
    Irsik
Secretary, Tina Brownsberger
Secretary, Annette Valentine
Secretary, Maryann Garvey
Auditors: KPMG LLP ST LOUIS MISSOURI

LOCATIONS

HQ: UNIVERSITY OF MISSOURI SYSTEM
    321 UNIVERSITY HALL, COLUMBIA, MO 652113020
Phone: 573 882-2712
Web: WWW.UMSYSTEM.EDU

PRODUCTS/OPERATIONS

Selected Campuses
University of Missouri-Columbia
University of Missouri Health System (Columbia)
UM-Kansas City
UM-St. Louis
Missouri University of Science and Technology (Rolla)

Selected Colleges and Schools
College of Agriculture Food and Natural Resources
    School of Natural Resources
College of Arts and Sciences
    School of Music
College of Education
    School of Information Science and Learning
    Technologies
College of Engineering
College of Human Environmental Sciences
    School of Social Work
College of Veterinary Medicine
Graduate School
    Harry S Truman School of Public Affairs
School of Health Professions
School of Journalism
School of Law
School of Medicine
Sinclair College of Nursing
Trulaske College of Business
    School of Accountancy

HISTORICAL FINANCIALS
Company Type: Private

Income Statement
FYE: June 30

	REVENUE ($ mil.)	NET INCOME ($ mil.)	NET PROFIT MARGIN	EMPLOYEES
06/16	2,702	108	4.0%	30,282
06/13	2,404	221	9.2%	—
06/12	2,273	76	3.3%	—
Annual Growth	4.4%	9.3%	—	—

2016 Year-End Financials

Return on assets: 5.3%   Cash ($ mil.): 218
Return on equity: 4.0%
Current ratio: 0.50

UNIVERSITY OF NEBRASKA FOUNDATION

EXECUTIVES

Chief Executive Officer, Brian Hastings
Board of Directors, Keith Miles
Board of Directors, Susan Crotteau
Director, Betsy Berentson
Senior Vice-President, John Niemann
Dean, Steven Willborn
Project Manager, Brad Muehling
Auditors: KPMG LLP OMAHA NE

LOCATIONS

HQ: UNIVERSITY OF NEBRASKA FOUNDATION
1010 LINCOLN MALL STE 300, LINCOLN, NE
685082882
Phone: 402 458-1100
Web: WWW.NUFOUNDATION.ORG

HISTORICAL FINANCIALS
Company Type: Private

Income Statement

	REVENUE ($ mil.)	NET INCOME ($ mil.)	NET PROFIT MARGIN	EMPLOYEES
06/15	294	28	9.6%	80
06/14	342	137	40.3%	—
06/13	307	102	33.3%	—
06/09	119	(8)	—	—
Annual Growth	**16.2%**	—	—	—

FYE: June 30

2015 Year-End Financials

Return on assets: 0.3%
Return on equity: 9.6%
Current ratio: 28.00

Cash ($ mil.): 397

UNIVERSITY OF NEW HAVEN, INCORPORATED

The University of New Haven (UNH) offers more than 80 undergraduate and 30 graduate degree programs from its five colleges. Fields of study include arts and sciences business criminal justice and forensic science and engineering. The private university has about 6500 students and 500 faculty members with a student-to-teacher ratio of 16:1. The University of New Haven was founded in 1920 as the New Haven YMCA Junior College. It held classes in space rented from Yale University for nearly 40 years before its own building was constructed.

Geographic Reach

In addition to its main campus UNH offers programs at several satellite locations in Connecticut and California. It also operates a campus in Tuscany Italy and provides about 50 study abroad opportunities worldwide.

Operations

Of its student base about one-third of UNH enrollees attend the arts and sciences college while another third attend the Lee College (criminal justice and forensic sciences). The remainder of students primarily pursue degrees in business and engineering. Most of UNH's students live on-campus.

Financial Performance

UNH reported a 13% increase in revenues in 2012 to $152 million due to higher earnings from student tuition and fees residence and dining charges and private and government gifts and grants. Net income fell 74% however to about $5.7 million due to higher operating expenses and declining investment returns.

Strategy

As enrollment has been increasing at a record-breaking pace to keep up with that growth UNH has been busy building new facilities such as a new forensic science institute dorms and a sports stadium. Its current growth efforts are centered around facility enhancements technology advancement and career development opportunities for its students.

The university is focused on investing in academic program growth its business and engineering colleges. In addition in 2012 UNH added a new master's degree program in criminal justice. UNH also opened its first international satellite campus (in Tuscany Italy) that year.

EXECUTIVES

Vice President of Finance, George Synodi
Associate Vice President Human Resources, Caroline Koziatek
Vice President Student Affairs and Athletics, William M Leete
Vice President Marketing, Thomas Giordano
Vice President, Colby Thammavongsa
Vice President Marketing and Communications, Lyn Chamberlin
Seniorassociate Vice President For Graduate Enrollment, Shobi Sivadasan
Auditors: KPMG LLP HARTFORD CT

LOCATIONS

HQ: UNIVERSITY OF NEW HAVEN, INCORPORATED
300 BOSTON POST RD, WEST HAVEN, CT 065161999
Phone: 203 932-7000
Web: WWW.NEWHAVEN.EDU

PRODUCTS/OPERATIONS

Selected Colleges

College of Arts and Sciences
College of Business
College of Lifelong and eLearning
Henry C. Lee College of Criminal Justice and Forensic Sciences
Tagliatela College of Engineering

HISTORICAL FINANCIALS
Company Type: Private

Income Statement

	REVENUE ($ mil.)	NET INCOME ($ mil.)	NET PROFIT MARGIN	EMPLOYEES
06/15	258	19	7.5%	696
06/10	172	6	3.7%	—
06/09	147	8	5.6%	—
06/08	0	0	—	—
Annual Growth	—	**174.7%**	—	—

FYE: June 30

2015 Year-End Financials

Return on assets: 5.9%
Return on equity: 7.5%
Current ratio: 0.30

Cash ($ mil.): 35

UNIVERSITY OF NEW MEXICO

With more than 36630 students The University of New Mexico (UNM) based in Albuquerque is most renowned for its schools of medicine law and education. Students also attend one of the school's four branches located around the northern part of the state at Gallup Los Alamos Rio Rancho Taos and Valencia. Through its schools and colleges the university offers 96 bachelor's degrees 71 master's degrees 37 doctorate degrees as well as professional practice programs in law medicine and pharmacy. Its annual budget tops $2 billion. UNM employs more than 22000 people across the state.

Operations

The university also serves non-traditional students through its Evening and Weekend Degree Program which offers some 1000 classes each semester that contribute to about 40 different degree programs. About 12000 working students attend UNM at night each semester.

Most of its students come from in-state and continue to live in New Mexico after graduation.

In conjunction with the university's health sciences medical nursing and pharmacy school programs the university operates the UNM Health Sciences Center. It's the state's largest integrated health care treatment research and education facility. The teaching hospital operates a trauma center and specialized care units for oncology and pediatrics.

Geographic Reach

UNM's main campus is located in Albuquerque. Satellite campuses are in Gallup Los Alamos Rio Rancho Taos and Valencia. Only Los Alamos and Santa Fe offer graduate and upper division programs. The university hosts some 1500 international students and scholars.

Financial Performance

The majority of UNM's revenues (more than 60%) come from clinical operations and patient services from the UNM hospitals. Grants and contracts make up 18% while tuition and fees only account for 9% of the university's revenues.

In 2016 the university's revenues declined by $30 million to $1.56 billion due to lower other patient-related serivces and lower sales and serivces.

Operating expenses grew by about $112 million to $2.2 billion due to higher instruction research and public service costs and a rise in clinical operation expenses.

Company Background

UNM was founded in 1889.

EXECUTIVES

Dean School of Engineering, Joseph L. Cecchi
Dean School of Medicine, Paul B. Roth
Dean College of University Libraries and Learning Sciences, Richard W. Clement
President, Robert G. Frank
Provost and EVP Academic Affairs, Chaouki T. Abdallah
Interim Dean Anderson School of Management, Craig G. White
Dean College of Arts and Sciences, Mark Peceny
Dean College of Fine Arts, Kymberly Pinder
Dean Graduate Studies, Julie Coonrod
Dean Honors College, Catherine Krause
Dean College of Nursing, Nancy Ridenour
Dean College of Pharmacy, Lynda S. Welage
Dean School of Architecture and Planning, Geraldine Forbes Isais
Dean School of Law, David J. Herring

Dean School of Public Administration, Mario Rivera
Dean College of Education, S. Hector Ochoa
Financial Officer, Nicole Dopson
CIO, Gil Gonzales
Vice President Professor of Finance, Gautam Vora
President Board of Regents, Jack L. Fortner
Auditors: KPMG LLP ALBUQUERQUE NEW MEX

LOCATIONS

HQ: UNIVERSITY OF NEW MEXICO
1800 ROMA BLVD NE, ALBUQUERQUE, NM
871310001
Phone: 505 277-0732
Web: WWW.UNM.EDU

PRODUCTS/OPERATIONS

2013 Sales

	% of sales
Clinical operations	42
Grants & contracts	21
Sales & services	16
Tuition & fees	10
Patients services	8
Other	3
Total	**0** **100**

Schools and Colleges

Schools and Colleges
Anderson School of Management
College of Arts & Sciences
College of Education
College of Fine Arts
College of University Libraries & Learning Sciences
Honors College
School of Architecture & Planning
School of Engineering
School of Law
School of Public Administration
University College

HISTORICAL FINANCIALS

Company Type: Private

Income Statement   FYE: June 30

	REVENUE ($ mil.)	NET INCOME ($ mil.)	NET PROFIT MARGIN	EMPLOYEES
06/16	1,893	6	0.3%	18,362
06/14	1,325	55	4.2%	—
06/13	1,516	19	1.3%	—
06/08	1,110	163	14.8%	—
Annual Growth	6.9%	(33.7%)	—	—

2016 Year-End Financials

Return on assets: 9.7%   Cash ($ mil.): 305
Return on equity: 0.3%
Current ratio: 0.90

UNIVERSITY OF NORTH CAROLINA HOSPITALS

University of North Carolina Hospitals (UNCH) is at the heart of the UNC Health Care System (UNC HCS). The medical center provides acute care to the Tar Heel State through North Carolina Memorial Hospital North Carolina Children's Hospital North Carolina Neurosciences Hospital and North Carolina Women's Hospital. Combined the facilities have more than 800 beds. Specialties include cancer treatment at the North Carolina Cancer Hospital organ transplantation cardiac care orthopedics wound management and rehabilitation. Not-for-profit UNC HCS is owned by the state of North Carolina and is affiliated with the UNC-Chapel Hill School of Medicine.

Operations

UNCH operates under the umbrella of UNC HCS.

UNC HCS already extends beyond Chapel Hill and into the greater Triangle area through its network of primary care and specialty physician practices located in Orange Wake Durham Chatham and Lee counties. The system treats some 800000 people at UNC HCS practices and clinics annually.

UNCH handles more than 37000 patients each year and delivers 3500 babies annually.

North Carolina Children's offers 150 inpatient beds and a comprehensive children's outpatient center. Every year provides specialty care to more than 70000 children from all 100 North Carolina counties. The North Carolina Cancer Hospital is the clinical home of the UNC Lineberger Comprehensive Cancer Center. The state's only public cancer hospital the North Carolina Cancer Hospital treats patients from every county in North Carolina with more than 135000 patient visits a year.

Geographic Reach

UNCH not only serves patients from all North Carolina counties with about a third coming from the Research Triangle area it also serves patients from neighboring states.

Strategy

Being one of the primary health care providers in the area UNC HCS is nearly always expanding its services and service areas either through acquisitions or new construction.

In 2015 UNCH filed a petition with state regulators seeking the ability to add 42 acute-care beds at its Chapel Hill campus. If approved UNC estimates it will cost the hospital $17 million and would be completed by mid-2018.

UNC HCS planned to open a new 86-bed acute-care hospital in Hillsborough in 2015 as part of an effort to reduce pressure on its Chapel Hill campus. The construction of the hospital will cost about $200 million. The new facility will offer an emergency department outpatient surgery and a range of inpatient services to our patients in Alamance and Western Orange counties.

Dedicated cancer care and cancer research is another area in which UNC HCS is expanding. It opened a North Carolina Cancer Hospital at Rex Hospital in 2014.

The system is also building an Imaging Research Building expected to open in 2013 to house the Biomedical Research Imaging Center and serve as a state resource for handling the acquisition processing analysis storage and retrieval of scientific images.

In 2013 UNC HCS established the first stage of its Hillsborough campus with the opening of a 60000-square-foot medical office building. The building includes hospital services such as imaging laboratory pharmacy and medical and surgical oncology.

Company Background

In 2011 the hospital opened a new wing of the Newborn Critical Care Unit in the North Carolina Children's Hospital that houses 10 new patient beds bringing the number of beds in the unit to 58.

UNCH was founded in 1952 under the name North Carolina Memorial Hospital. In 1989 the North Carolina General Assembly created UNCH.

EXECUTIVES

Vice President Finance, Barbara Aaron

LOCATIONS

HQ: UNIVERSITY OF NORTH CAROLINA HOSPITALS
101 MANNING DR BLDG 2, CHAPEL HILL, NC
275144423
Phone: 919 966-5111
Web: WWW.UNCHEALTHCARE.ORG

PRODUCTS/OPERATIONS

Selected Facilities

North Carolina Cancer Hospital (Chapel Hill)
  UNC Lineberger Comprehensive Cancer Center
North Carolina Children's Hospital (Chapel Hill)
North Carolina Memorial Hospital (Chapel Hill)
North Carolina Neurosciences Hospital (Chapel Hill)
North Carolina Women's Hospital (Chapel Hill)

COMPETITORS

Alamance Regional Medical Center
Carolinas HealthCare System
Cone Health
Cumberland County Hospital System
Danville Regional Medical Center
Duke University Health System
Emory Healthcare
Grady Health System
High Point Regional Health System
Morehead Memorial Hospital
New Hanover Regional Medical Center
Rowan Regional Medical Center
Vidant Health
WakeMed

HISTORICAL FINANCIALS

Company Type: Private

Income Statement   FYE: June 30

	REVENUE ($ mil.)	NET INCOME ($ mil.)	NET PROFIT MARGIN	EMPLOYEES
06/15	1,385	110	8.0%	6,000
06/07	787	182	23.2%	—
06/06	652	36	5.6%	—
06/05	614	25	4.1%	—
Annual Growth	8.5%	15.9%	—	—

2015 Year-End Financials

Return on assets: 5.6%   Cash ($ mil.): 127
Return on equity: 8.0%
Current ratio: 1.20

UNIVERSITY OF NORTH TEXAS SYSTEM

EXECUTIVES

Manager, Cynthia Doll

LOCATIONS

HQ: UNIVERSITY OF NORTH TEXAS SYSTEM
1302 TEASLEY LN, DENTON, TX 762057946
Phone: 940 565-2281
Web: WWW.UNTSYSTEM.EDU

HISTORICAL FINANCIALS

Company Type: Private

Income Statement   FYE: August 31

	REVENUE ($ mil.)	NET INCOME ($ mil.)	NET PROFIT MARGIN	EMPLOYEES
08/16	631	47	7.5%	10,000
08/09	463	47	10.2%	—
08/08	428	61	14.4%	—
Annual Growth	5.0%	(3.2%)	—	—

Return on assets: 8.3%   Cash ($ mil.): 183
Return on equity: 7.5%
Current ratio: 0.60

UNIVERSITY OF NORTHERN COLORADO

EXECUTIVES

President, Kay Norton
Board of Directors, Bret Naber
Financial Executive, Paul Squillace
Manager, Dorothy Swenson
Marketing Director, Randy Hash
Operations Manager, James Ambrose
Director, Kim Black
Auditors: RUBINBROWN LLP DENVER CO

LOCATIONS

HQ: UNIVERSITY OF NORTHERN COLORADO
    501 20TH ST, GREELEY, CO 806396900
Phone: 970 351-1890
Web: WWW.UNCO.EDU

HISTORICAL FINANCIALS

Company Type: Private

Income Statement

	REVENUE ($ mil.)	NET INCOME ($ mil.)	NET PROFIT MARGIN	EMPLOYEES
06/16	195	(9)	—	3,500
06/15	187	(13)	—	—
06/14	183	(9)	—	—
06/13	180	5	3.0%	—
Annual Growth	2.6%	—	—	—

2016 Year-End Financials

Return on assets: 8.3%   Cash ($ mil.): 46
Return on equity: (-4.9%)
Current ratio: 1.70

UNIVERSITY OF OREGON FOUNDATION

EXECUTIVES

Chief Executive Officer, Paul Weinhold
Financial Executive, Erica Chirstoffer
Director, Laura Hutchings
Director, Mark Bolme
Auditors: MOSS ADAMS LLP EUGENE OREGO

LOCATIONS

HQ: UNIVERSITY OF OREGON FOUNDATION
    1720 E 13TH AVE STE 410, EUGENE, OR 974032253
Phone: 541 302-0300
Web: WWW.UOFOUNDATION.ORG

HISTORICAL FINANCIALS

Company Type: Private

Income Statement   FYE: June 30

	REVENUE ($ mil.)	NET INCOME ($ mil.)	NET PROFIT MARGIN	EMPLOYEES
06/15	203	81	40.1%	39
06/14	107	(0)	—	—
06/13	165	21	12.8%	—
06/12	97	0	0.4%	—
Annual Growth	28.0%	488.3%	—	—

2015 Year-End Financials

Return on assets: 0.5%   Cash ($ mil.): 142
Return on equity: 40.1%
Current ratio: —

UNIVERSITY OF PITTSBURGH

The University of Pittsburgh (Pitt for short) operates its flagship campus in the Oakland neighborhood of Pittsburgh. More than 35000 graduate and undergraduate students attend the main campus as well as four regional campuses. Pitt Panthers pursue degrees in about 400 disciplines including arts and sciences business law medicine and engineering. The school has a student-teacher ratio of 14:1. Pitt is also affiliated with the UPMC health system which operates about 20 hospitals numerous clinics and an insurance company. Pitt was founded in 1787 making it one of the oldest universities in the US.

Operations

Pitt is considered a leading US public research university and as such spends more than $700 million annually on research projects. Pitt is recognized for its work in about a dozen disciplines including computer modeling philosophy the humanities international studies aging neuroscience bioengineering commercial innovation education national preparedness drug discovery translational medicine and nanoscience. It was at Pitt that Jonas Salk developed the polio vaccine at what is now known as Salk Hall.

Notable Pitt alumni include Academy Award winner Gene Kelly Nobel Peace Prize winner Wangari Maathai Pulitzer Prize winner Michael Chabon and US Senator Orrin Hatch.

Geographic Reach

In addition to the main campus in Pittsburgh which houses 17 schools colleges and a center for social and urban research Pitt has regional campus locations in Bradford Greensburg Johnstown and Titusville.

Financial Performance

Pitt reported revenues of some $2 billion in 2014. Most of the university's revenues come from grants and contracts followed by student tuition and feescommonwealth appropriation endowment distributions and other sources of income.

Strategy

In addition to providing high quality education programs for its students Pitt works to engage in research scholarly and artistic projects that advance global learning. It also works to collaborate with government agencies and businesses to advance science medicine and technology seeking active partners as well as funding provider to further its programs.

EXECUTIVES

Chancellor, William Dietrich
Board of Directors, Gene B Ferketish

LOCATIONS

HQ: UNIVERSITY OF PITTSBURGH
    4200 5TH AVE, PITTSBURGH, PA 152600001
Phone: 412 624-4141
Web: WWW.MEDSCHOOL.PITT.EDU

PRODUCTS/OPERATIONS

Selected Schools and Colleges
The John A. Swanson School of Engineering
The Joseph M. Katz Graduate School of Business
    College of Business Administration
Kenneth P. Dietrich School of Arts and Sciences
    College of General Studies
School of Dental Medicine
School of Education
School of Health and Rehabilitation Sciences
School of Information Sciences
School of Law
School of Medicine
School of Nursing
School of Pharmacy
School of Public and International Affairs
School of Public Health
School of Social Work
University Center for International Studies
University Honors College

HISTORICAL FINANCIALS

Company Type: Private

Income Statement   FYE: June 30

	REVENUE ($ mil.)	NET INCOME ($ mil.)	NET PROFIT MARGIN	EMPLOYEES
06/16	2,106	(212)	—	9,607
06/15	2,060	27	1.3%	—
06/14	2,005	570	28.4%	—
06/13	1,985	402	20.3%	—
Annual Growth	2.0%	—	—	—

2016 Year-End Financials

Return on assets: 4.5%   Cash ($ mil.): 6
Return on equity: (-10.1%)
Current ratio: —

UNIVERSITY OF PITTSBURGH MEDICAL CENTER

For University of Pittsburgh students and area residents medical care is spelled UPMC. UPMC Jameson is a leading not-for-profit health care delivery system in western Pennsylvania. The organization operates about 20 hospitals including campuses in the Pittsburgh area regional and community hospitals and specialty facilities such as Children's Hospital of Pittsburgh and the Magee-Womens Hospital. Combined UPMC Jameson has more than 5100 inpatient beds. In addition the system provides care through hundreds of physician practices outpatient clinics cancer treatment facilities and rehab centers; it also offers health insurance home health care and long-term care through more than 15 senior living facilities.

Operations

UPMC Jameson is organized into four primary operating divisions. Provider Services includes ter-

tiary community and regional hospitals; specialty services such as women's health and behavioral health; in-home care and senior living; contract services including pharmacy and laboratories; and the system's 3400 physicians and their practices. Insurance Services offers health insurance to employers and employees workers' compensation and disability services and behavioral health coverage to Medical Assistance beneficiaries. UPMC International Services exports the system's expertise abroad while UPMC Enterprises seeks commercialization opportunities and partnerships.

As an academic medical center affiliated with the University of Pittsburgh's Schools of Health Sciences UPMC Jameson also focuses on medical research in a wide range of areas including the fields of regenerative medicine and biosecurity some of which is funded by the National Institutes of Health. The system is also renowned for its organ transplantation programs as well as for its cancer care psychiatric pediatric and women's health services. In addition UPMC Jameson is a forerunner in the health care information technology field.

The system has some 5500 affiliated physicians. In a typical year it has some 287000 inpatient admissions more than 3.9 million outpatient visits and some 690000 emergency department visits. It performs some 189000 surgeries and more than 690000 home care visits.

Geographic Reach

The company's primary operating territory for its health and insurance segments is western Pennsylvania. Outside the US UPMC Jameson operates health care facilities in Ireland Italy Quatar Cyprus and the UK. It also provides management and consulting services in other international countries to improve global health care partly through partnerships with health equipment and technology firms.

Sales and Marketing

The majority of the company's hospital services are rendered to patients under Medicare Highmark Blue Cross Blue Shield (a major area insurer) and medical assistance programs. Its patient service revenue comes from Medicare accounts (which accounts for more than 30% of all patient revenue each year) Highmark (31%) other medical assistance programs (about 10%) and self-pay and commercial insurance.

Financial Performance

UPMC's revenues increased 12% to some $11.4 billion in 2014 due to increased patient service revenues which accounted for half of all earnings. Higher enrollment levels in the UPMC Health Plan (40% of sales) also contributed to growth that year. Net income rose 58% to $698 million on higher investment income and other factors. Meanwhile cash flow from operations increased 82% to $568.9 million.

Strategy

The UPMC network of facilities has grown over the years through acquisitions and new facility construction. On the flip side the company has occasionally sold or shut down less-profitable facilities in its network such as UPMC Braddock an underused suburban community hospital.

UPMC Jameson is advancing its technology systems to control costs and increase efficiencies. The health system has established electronic health record (EHR) systems at all of its hospitals and is working to share data with other area providers. In addition UPMC has partnerships with Alcatel-Lucent GE and IBM to help reduce medical expenses and increase the quality of care through IT initiatives.

In 2015 UMPC and The University of Pittsburgh School of Medicine launched the Center for Women's Health Research and Innovation which is devoted to research education and clinical practice while promoting community partnership and advocacy related to health care for women.

The following year UMPC acquired rural hospital Jameson Healthcare to become UMPC Jameson. Jameson had been operating in the red — a common problem for rural systems. UMPC Jameson plans to invest between $70 and $80 million to provide continuing services in Lawrence County (including maintaining facilities and recruiting new doctors) as well as to pay down debt.

Mergers and Acquisitions

In 2017 UMPC agreed to buy Pinnacle Health System. The purchase will add two hospitals to UPMC's network and will allow the system to sell health insurance beyond its core market in western Pennsylvania.

EXECUTIVES

President and CEO, Jeffrey A. Romoff
EVP and Chief Administrative Officer, Gregory Peaslee
EVP and CFO, Robert A. DeMichiei
EVP President Insurance Services Division and President and CEO UPMC Health Plan, Diane P. Holder
EVP and President Hospital and Community Services Division, Elizabeth B. Concordia
SVP and EVP and Chief Operating Officer Health Services Division, Leslie C. Davis
EVP and Chief Legal Officer, W. Thomas (Tom) McGough
EVP and President International Commercial Services Division and President UPMC CancerCenter, Charles E. (Chuck) Bogosta
EVP and Chief Strategic and Transformation Officer, David M. Farner
EVP Treasurer and President UPMC Enterprises, C. Talbot Heppenstall
EVP and Chief Medical Officer; President Physician Services Division, Marshall W. Webster
SVP and Chief Medical Officer, Steven D. Shapiro
Medical Director, Jennifer Lultschik
Auditors: ERNST & YOUNG LLP PITTSBURGH

LOCATIONS

HQ: UNIVERSITY OF PITTSBURGH MEDICAL CENTER 600 GRANT ST FL 62, PITTSBURGH, PA 152192741
Phone: 412 647-2345
Web: WWW.UPMC.EDU

Selected Pennsylvania Facilities
Children's Hospital of Pittsburgh of UPMC
Magee-Womens Hospital of UPMC (Pittsburgh)
UPMC Bedford Memorial (Everett)
UPMC East (Pittsburgh)
UPMC Hamlot (Erie)
UPMC Horizon (Greenville and Shenango Valley)
UPMC McKeesport (McKeesport)
UPMC Mercy (Pittsburgh)
UPMC Montefiore (Pittsburgh)
UPMC Northwest (Seneca and Oil City)
UPMC Passavant (McCandless and Cranberry)
UPMC Presbyterian (Pittsburgh)
UPMC Shadyside (Pittsburgh)
UPMC St. Margaret (Pittsburgh)
UPMC Western Psychiatric Institute and Clinic (Pittsburgh)

PRODUCTS/OPERATIONS

2014 Sales

	$ mil.	% of total
Patient services	5,776	51
Insurance services	4,813	42
Other	826	7
Total	**11,415**	**100**

Selected Services
Behavioral and Mental Health Services
Cancer
COPD and Emphysema Center
Dermatology
Diabetes and Endocrinology
Ear Nose and Throat
Emergency Medicine
Family/Primary Care Medicine
Gastroenterology
Geriatrics
Heart and Vascular
Imaging Services
Kidney Disease
Liver
Neurology
Ophthalmology
Pain Medicine
Pathology
Pediatrics
Pulmonology and Respiratory
Rehabilitation
Rheumatology
Sports Medicine
Stroke Care
Thyroid
Urology
Women's Health
Wound Healing Services

COMPETITORS

Allegheny General Hospital
AmeriHealth Mercy Health Plan
Blue Cross of Northeastern Pennsylvania
Butler Health System
Capital BlueCross
Conemaugh Health System
Excela Health
Geisinger Health System
HealthAmerica
Heritage Valley Health
Highmark
Independence Blue Cross
Jefferson Regional Medical Center of Pennsylvania
Ohio Valley General
PinnacleHealth System
St. Clair Health
Universal Health Services
West Penn Allegheny Health System

HISTORICAL FINANCIALS
Company Type: Private

Income Statement
FYE: June 30

	REVENUE ($ mil.)	NET INCOME ($ mil.)	NET PROFIT MARGIN	EMPLOYEES
06/15	614	326	53.1%	53,171
06/13*	10,188	441	4.3%	—
12/11	4,758	(2)	—	—
Annual Growth	(49.4%)	—	—	—

*Fiscal year change

2015 Year-End Financials

Return on assets: 128.8% Cash ($ mil.): 80
Return on equity: 53.1%
Current ratio: —

UNIVERSITY OF RHODE ISLAND

The University of Rhode Island (URI) offers more than 80 undergraduate majors specializing in nursing psychology communication studies kinesiology and human development. It also offers master's doctoral and professional degrees from its nine colleges at four campuses across the state. URI's main campus is located in Kingston the W. Alton Jones Campus is in West Greenwich its Graduate School of Oceanography is located on Narragansett Bay and Providence is home to the university's Alan Shawn Feinstein College of Continuing

Education. URI which has an enrollment of more than 16500 students was chartered as the state's agricultural school in 1888.

Geographic Reach

The University of Rhode Island spans four campus locations in Kingston Providence Narragansett Bay and West Greenwich. Its student population comes from 53 US territories and the District of Columbia.

Financial Performance

Revenue has increased for URI during the past three years due to increasing tuition and fees rising enrollment of out-of-state students and increasing grants and contracts. Tuition and fees contributed some 60% of revenue in fiscal 2012. Net income was flat in 2012 as compared to 2011 thanks to increased capital appropriations state contributed capital and capital gifts. These were partially offset however by rising expenses and declining non-operating revenues.

EXECUTIVES

Associate Vice President Of Research And, Mark Noll

Auditors: O'CONNOR & DREW PC BRAINTRE

LOCATIONS

HQ: UNIVERSITY OF RHODE ISLAND
75 LOWER COLLEGE RD STE 0, KINGSTON, RI 028811966
Phone: 401 874-1000
Web: WWW.URI.EDU

PRODUCTS/OPERATIONS

Selected Schools and Colleges
College of Arts and Sciences
College of Business Administration
College of Continuing Education
College of Engineering
College of Environment and Life Sciences
College of Human Science and Services
College of Nursing
College of Pharmacy
Graduate School of Oceanography
University College

HISTORICAL FINANCIALS

Company Type: Private

Income Statement

FYE: June 30

	REVENUE ($ mil.)	NET INCOME ($ mil.)	NET PROFIT MARGIN	EMPLOYEES
06/16	413	15	3.9%	2,600
06/15	403	6	1.5%	—
06/14	402	47	11.9%	—
06/13	410	39	9.6%	—
Annual Growth	0.2%	(26.1%)	—	—

2016 Year-End Financials

Return on assets: 11.4%   Cash ($ mil.): 141
Return on equity: 3.9%
Current ratio: 2.20

UNIVERSITY OF RICHMOND

Suffering from arachnophobia? You may want to steer clear of the more than 4300 Spiders who are enrolled at the University of Richmond (UR). UR consists of five schools: Jepson School of Leadership Studies Richmond School of Law Robins School of Business School of Arts and Sci-

ences and School of Continuing Studies. The university offers some 60 undergraduate majors as well as graduate and master's programs in business accounting and law. UR also offers some 75 study-abroad programs in which more than half of its students participate. Founded in 1830 by Virginia Baptists as a seminary for men the school became Richmond College in 1840.

Operations

UR with about 320 full-time undergraduate faculty members boasts a student-faculty ratio of 9:1. Through its Richmond Quadrangle LLC (a wholly controlled affiliate of UR) the university owns and operates a building and land located in Richmond. UR's Spider Management Company LLC is another wholly controlled affiliate that provides investment research advice counsel and management related to the university's endowment assets.

Geographic Reach

From its campus in Richmond Virginia UR serves students from nearly all 50 US states including Puerto Rico and Washington D.C. Its student population consists of more than 3000 undergraduates that come more than 70 countries.

Financial Performance

Revenue for UR rose 8% in fiscal 2012 as compared to 2011 due to an increase in tuition and fees grants and contracts contributions endowment spending distribution and auxiliary enterprises. Net income for the same reporting period decreased by 112% thanks to rising operating expenses and declining contribution and net unrealized losses.

EXECUTIVES

Assistant Vice President and Dean of Admission, Gil Villanueva

Assoc Vice President Controller, Laurie Melville

Vice President For Public Relations, Stefanie Mathew

Vice President For Public Relations, Mary Gardiner

Director of Admissions, Nathan Crozier

Vice President Operations, Jason Hoogakker

Vice President for Administration, Ethan Mcwilliams

Chief Associate Vice President Of Public Safety, David Mccoy

Assistant Vice President Foundation Corporate and Government Relations, Michelle Wamsley

Vice President and Chief Information Officer, Keith McIntosh

Vice President Enrollment Management, Stephanie Dupaul

Vice President For Communications, John Barry

Managing Director Barclays Capital, Stephen Aronson

Vice President, Gabrielle Raffio

Secretary, Jessica Miller

Secretary, Jessica Myers

Treasurer, Michael Forsyth

Board Member, Nina Naruszewicz

Board Member, Christopher Johnson

Auditors: KPMG LLP RICHMOND VIRGINIA

LOCATIONS

HQ: UNIVERSITY OF RICHMOND
28 WESTHAMPTON WAY, RICHMOND, VA 231730002
Phone: 804 289-8133
Web: WWW.RICHMOND.EDU

PRODUCTS/OPERATIONS

Selected Schools
Arts and Sciences
Business
Leadership Studies
Law
Professional and Continuing Studies

HISTORICAL FINANCIALS

Company Type: Private

Income Statement

FYE: June 30

	REVENUE ($ mil.)	NET INCOME ($ mil.)	NET PROFIT MARGIN	EMPLOYEES
06/16	283	(190)	—	1,400
06/13	253	185	73.0%	—
06/10	210	83	39.7%	—
Annual Growth	5.1%	—	—	—

2016 Year-End Financials

Return on assets: 16.6%   Cash ($ mil.): 81
Return on equity: (-67.2%)
Current ratio: —

UNIVERSITY OF SAN DIEGO

The University of San Diego (USD) is private college located close to southern California's beaches and the Mexican border. The coeducational Roman Catholic university has an enrollment of more than 7800 students USD offers more than 70 bachelor's master's and doctoral degrees in areas such as arts and sciences business administration education engineering law and nursing. It has a faculty of 440 full time staff members. The university also home to the Joan B. Kroc School of Peace Studies established in 2003 by the wife of McDonald's founder Ray Kroc.

Operations

Adjacent to the USD campus is the St. Francis Seminary; young men studying for the priesthood attend the university for the academic portion of their course work. USD is a very residential college; 94% of its freshman class live on the school's grounds in 10 separate living areas with styles that range from shared rooms to apartments. About 9% of its students hail from outside of the US.

USD offers more than 40 bachelor's degrees about 30 master's degrees in eight academic divisions as well as three doctoral degrees - two in nursing and one in leadership studies.

As a Carnegie-certified Doctoral/Research school the school is committed to graduate education through the doctorate awarding 50 or more doctoral degrees annually (USD regularly awards more than 360 doctoral degrees) and it gives high priority to research receiving more than $40 million annually in federal research support.

Financial Performance

Higher tuition and fees helped to lift USD's revenues from $328 million in 2015 to $343.8 million in 2016..

Strategy

The university undergoes a cycle of strategic initiatives every few years that shape the way it intends to move into the future.

In 2014 USD broke ground on a new health sciences building and opened a Madrid (Spain) location.

Company Background

USD was formed in 1972 by the merger of San Diego University and San Diego College for Women.

In 2003 school president Dr. Mary Lyons implemented a round of strategic initiatives focusing on Catholic-based social studies inclusion and diversity integrated learning internationalization and sustainability. It subsequently emphasized enroll-

ment management building out the school's technology infrastructure expanding undergraduate research developing USD's endowment and raising the university's branding and marketing standards. Goals include international expansion engaging alumni and assessing programs aimed at expressing the university's Catholic character.

EXECUTIVES

Assistant Vice President Facilities Management, Roger Manion
VP and Provost, Julie H. Sullivan, age 59
VP Finance and CFO, Terry Kalfayan
Vice Provost and CIO, Chris Wessells
VP and Provost, Andrew T. Allen
President, James T. Harris
Vice President University Relations, Timothy O'malley
Assistant Vice President and Chief Human Resources Officer, Karen Briggs
Assistant Vice President for Enrollment, Stephen Pultz
Assistant Vice President Of Student Affairs For Pu, Larry Barnett
Vice President of Administrati, Kevin Ganley
Vice President, Rommel Pinlac
Assistant Vice President for Mission and Minist, Virginia Rodee
Vice President Of Communications, Phillip Juarez
Vice President of Tours Training, Sean Essex
Vice President Of Membership, Owen Buckley
Department Chair, Ann Garland
Department Chair, Angelo Orona
Vice President of Communications, Weston Preising
Vice President of Administration, Peter Nelson
Professor of Physics Department Chair of Physics, Greg Severn
Vice President of Wellness and Standards, Kevin Karn
Vice President, Zach Flati
Vice President of New Business Development for an international manufacturing company, Leslie Hennessy
Treasurer, Andrew Quintana
Auditors: MOSS ADAMS LLP SAN DIEGO CAL

LOCATIONS

HQ: UNIVERSITY OF SAN DIEGO
  5998 ALCALA PARK FRNT, SAN DIEGO, CA
  921102492
Phone: 619 260-4600
Web: WWW.SANDIEGO.EDU

PRODUCTS/OPERATIONS

Selected Schools and Colleges
College of Arts and Sciences
School of Business Administration
Engineering
Hahn School of Nursing and Health Science
Joan B. Kroc School of Peace Studies
School of Law
School of Leadership and Education Sciences

HISTORICAL FINANCIALS
Company Type: Private

Income Statement				FYE: June 30
	REVENUE ($ mil.)	NET INCOME ($ mil.)	NET PROFIT MARGIN	EMPLOYEES
06/15	453	56	12.5%	1,600
06/13	303	90	29.8%	—
06/10	347	21	6.2%	—
Annual Growth	5.5%	21.4%	—	—

2015 Year-End Financials
Return on assets: 11.4%   Cash ($ mil.): 12
Return on equity: 12.5%
Current ratio: 0.10

UNIVERSITY OF SOUTH ALABAMA

When you go by the moniker USA and the campus beauty queen wins the Miss USA title year after year (the Pi Kappa Phi Miss USA pageant that is) you're standing on hallowed ground. In this case it's the ground of the University of South Alabama situated on the upper Gulf Coast. The school's crown jewel is its College of Medicine and other facilities including USA Medical Center USA Knollwood Hospital and USA Children's and Women's Hospital. USA also offers degrees in Health Arts and Sciences Business Education Engineering Nursing Computer and Information Sciences Continuing Education and Special Programs and the Graduate School. More than 14880 students call the USA home.

Operations
USA offers 41 different bachelor programs 31 masters programs and 10 doctoral programs.

Financial Performance
The school reported an 8% increase in revenues in 2012 thanks to higher tuition and fee rates and an increase in student enrollment and credit hours taken and a rise in net patient service revenues (29% of total 2012 revenues). Other operating revenues also increased in 2012 thanks to higher revenues from the Electronic Health Records Incentive Program.

USA reported net income in 2012 of $38 million (versus a net loss in 2011) due to decline in operating loss and an increase in non-operating revenues (primarily from higher investment returns and state appropriations).

The university saw an increase in revenues between 2010 and 2012 largely due to organic growth.

Strategy
USA is pushing to expand and strengthen its development program and increase student enrollment. In 2013 the school received a gift of $250000 from alumni Dr. and Mrs. Steven H. Stokes to start a new Center for Environmental Resiliency.

Company Background
Founded in 1963 USA has graduated more than 75000 students including 18200 teachers and school administrators (including 85% of Mobile's public school teachers).

EXECUTIVES

Assistant Vice President, Lanier S Cauley
Assistant Vice President For Student Affairs and Dean of Students, Michael Mitchell
Interim Associate Vice President For Academic Affairs, Julio Turrens
Director of Nursing, Tracey Hammack
Vice President For Research And Economic Development, Lynne U Chronister
Vice President, John Smith
VICE PRESIDENT, WANDA MAULDING
Assistant Vice President for Research Innovation, Michael Chambers
Associate Vice President For Global Engagement, Richard Carter
Associate Vice President for Academic Affairs, Charles Guest
Vice President, Kevin Aria
Student Run Free Clinic Nursing Liaison Student Nursing Association Vice President University of South, Anna Blache
Secretary, Marcina Lang
Secretary, Marilyn Chancellor
Vice Chairman, Mayer Mitchell
Secretary, Rebecca Scarbrough
Secretary Of Associate Dean And Academ, Kelly Taylor
Secretary V, Dianna Archey
Secretary, Karen Burns
Secretary, Judith Porco
Secretary, Gayle Moore
Secretary, Anita Perrette
Secretary, Karen Mandrella
Secretary V, Sharon Leinhos
Secretary IV, Sharon Leibert
Secretary, Elizabeth Hernandez
Treasurer, Cody Martin
Secretary V College of Nursing University of South, Kim McLean
Auditors: KPMG LLP JACKSON MISSISSIPPI

LOCATIONS

HQ: UNIVERSITY OF SOUTH ALABAMA
  307 N UNIVERSITY BLVD # 380, MOBILE, AL
  366083074
Phone: 251 460-6101
Web: WWW.SOUTHALABAMA.EDU

PRODUCTS/OPERATIONS

USA Colleges and Schools
Arts and Sciences
Auburn University School of Pharmacy at USA
Computing
Continuing Education and Special Programs
Education
Engineering
Mitchell College of Business
Medicine
Nursing
Pat Capps Covey College of Allied Health Professions

HISTORICAL FINANCIALS
Company Type: Private

Income Statement				FYE: September 30
	REVENUE ($ mil.)	NET INCOME ($ mil.)	NET PROFIT MARGIN	EMPLOYEES
09/16	624	25	4.1%	5,403
09/15	556	9	1.7%	—
09/14	503	6	1.3%	—
09/13	483	39	8.2%	—
Annual Growth	8.9%	(13.1%)	—	—

2016 Year-End Financials
Return on assets: 8.8%   Cash ($ mil.): 100
Return on equity: 4.1%
Current ratio: 1.00

UNIVERSITY OF ST. THOMAS

Far from any Bahamian beaches or Caribbean hot spots sits The University of St. Thomas (UST). The school is a Catholic university with campuses in Minneapolis and St. Paul Minnesota. It offers about 90 undergraduate and 60 graduate programs in seven academic divisions: education and philosophy arts and sciences business engineering divinity law and social work. The school has an enrollment of about 11000 undergraduate and graduate students with a student-to-teacher ratio of 14:1. UST along with military prep school St. Thomas Academy grew out of St. Thomas Aquinas Seminary which was founded in 1885 by Archbishop John Ireland.

Geographic Reach

UST has campuses in Minneapolis and St. Paul as well as the Daniel C. Gainey Conference Center in Owatonna Minnesota and the Bernardi Campus in Rome Italy.

Financial Performance

The university's revenues come from a mix of student tuition and fees sales and service enterprises grants gifts and contracts. The university has an annual operating budget of about $195 million and its tuition runs around $33000 per student. UST has an endowment of some $400 million.

EXECUTIVES

Vice President for Mission, John Malone
Associate Vice President Academic Services and Special Programs, Eleni Roulis
Department Head, Gregory J Coulter
Vice President (Vizeprsident), Colin Bettis
Vice President, Trang Anh
Vice President Enrollment Management, Daniel Meyer
Executive Vice President and Provost, Richard Plumb
Vice President and Chief Information Officer, Ed Clark
Vice President Information Resources And, Edmund Clark
Associate Vice President For Facilities Management University of St. Thomas, Jim Brummer
Associate Vice President Planned Giving, Antonella Bernardi
Associate Vice President Academic Technology, Brett Coup
Vice President, Larry Snyder
Vice President, Eric Thurman
Auditors: CLIFTONLARSONALLEN LLP MINNEA

LOCATIONS

HQ: UNIVERSITY OF ST. THOMAS
2115 SUMMIT AVE, SAINT PAUL, MN 551051096
Phone: 651 962-5000
Web: WWW.STTHOMAS.EDU

PRODUCTS/OPERATIONS

Academic Divisions
College of Arts and Sciences (Bachelor's and Master's)
College of Education Leadership and Counseling - Education (Bachelor's Master's Specialist Doctorate) and Professional Psychology (Master's and Doctorate)
Opus College of Business (Bachelor's and Master's)
Saint Paul Seminary School of Divinity (Master's)
School of Engineering (Bachelor's and Master's)
School of Law (Juris Doctor)
School of Social Work (Bachelor's and Master's)

HISTORICAL FINANCIALS
Company Type: Private

Income Statement
FYE: June 30

	REVENUE ($ mil.)	NET INCOME ($ mil.)	NET PROFIT MARGIN	EMPLOYEES
06/16	270	(30)	—	1,900
06/15	260	2	1.1%	—
06/14	253	62	24.8%	—
06/13	260	69	26.7%	—
Annual Growth	1.2%	—	—	—

2016 Year-End Financials
Return on assets: 10.1%
Return on equity: (-11.2%)
Current ratio: —
Cash ($ mil.): 3

UNIVERSITY OF TAMPA INC

EXECUTIVES

President, Ronald L Vaughn
Representative, Paul Morrison
Director, Grant R Donaldson
Personnel Director, J Andersen
Auditors: KPMG LLP TAMPA FL

LOCATIONS

HQ: UNIVERSITY OF TAMPA INC
401 W KENNEDY BLVD, TAMPA, FL 336061490
Phone: 813 253-3333
Web: WWW.UT.EDU

HISTORICAL FINANCIALS
Company Type: Private

Income Statement
FYE: May 31

	REVENUE ($ mil.)	NET INCOME ($ mil.)	NET PROFIT MARGIN	EMPLOYEES
05/16	212	44	20.8%	525
05/15	203	43	21.6%	—
05/14	0	46	—	—
05/13	167	29	17.7%	—
Annual Growth	8.4%	14.5%		

2016 Year-End Financials
Return on assets: 7.3%
Return on equity: 20.8%
Current ratio: —
Cash ($ mil.): 59

UNIVERSITY OF TEXAS AT TYLER

EXECUTIVES

President, Rodney H Maybry
Office Manager, Lynn Reynolds
Director, Carrie Clayton
Chief Financial Officer, Jim Ferguson

LOCATIONS

HQ: UNIVERSITY OF TEXAS AT TYLER
3900 UNIVERSITY BLVD, TYLER, TX 757996600
Phone: 903 566-7000
Web: WWW.UTTYLER.EDU

HISTORICAL FINANCIALS
Company Type: Private

Income Statement
FYE: August 31

	REVENUE ($ mil.)	NET INCOME ($ mil.)	NET PROFIT MARGIN	EMPLOYEES
08/15	12,635	(2,780)	—	425
08/14	58	42	73.2%	—
08/13	51	(4)	—	—
08/12	49	(7)	—	—
Annual Growth	535.7%	—	—	—

2015 Year-End Financials
Return on assets: 8.0%
Return on equity: (-22.0%)
Current ratio: 0.60
Cash ($ mil.): 2,633

UNIVERSITY OF TEXAS SYSTEM

These students are hooked on higher education. The University of Texas System runs 14 universities throughout the Lone Star State with a total enrollment of more than 228000 students making it one of the nation's largest university systems. Its flagship UT Austin campus with some 51000 students and a Longhorn mascot has of the largest student populations in the US. UT System also runs half a dozen health institutions including four medical schools. Fields of science technology engineering and math also account for a good number of the undergraduate and graduate degrees conferred by the system. Established in 1876 UT Austin opened in 1883. The UT System was formally organized in 1950.

Operations

The primary purpose of the system is to provide administrative services for all of its campuses and institutions including fundraising endowment management performance benchmarking construction planning and legal and real estate services. With more than 20000 faculty and more than 80000 health care professionals researchers student advisors and support staff the UT System is one of the largest employers in Texas. UT System is governed by a nine-member board of regents that is appointed by the Texas governor and confirmed by the Texas Senate.

Geographic Reach

The UT System's primary central administration office is located on the UT Austin campus. Besides Austin the system boasts eight additional academic campuses in the Texas cities of Arlington Brownsville Dallas Edinburg El Paso Odessa San Antonio and Tyler. The system also has a land management office in West Texas and a federal relations center in Washington DC.

Financial Performance

UT System has an annual budget of $16.9 billion.

The UT System's revenue rose in fiscal 2016 to $13.3 billion from $12.6 billion a year earlier. Increases in net tuition and fees net sales and services of hospitals net professional fees as a result of increases in patient volumes and rates all helped the system's revenue increase as well as net auxiliary enterprises attributable to increased gate receipts for athletic events.

Operating loss increased from $3.4 billion to $4 billion in 2016 thanks to rising operating expenses due to growing student enrollment research and patient care activities.

Strategy

The UT System's administration has continued to work toward the overall goals of maintaining quality and affordability at the campuses increasing graduation rates and enhancing the system's standing in research and medical education. The organization has also been working to reduce its student-teacher ratios by increasing the number of faculty members.

In addition the UT System has launched a $3 billion renovation and construction program at its campuses.

A large portion of the UT System's student population comprises students pursuing degrees in health-related fields. UT health institutions include the UT Medical Branch (UTMB) in Galveston which includes medical schools and hospital locations and the M. D. Anderson Cancer Center in Austin.

The UT Systems also expanded in South Texas opening of The University of Texas Rio Grande

Valley in 2015. In 2016 it opened two new medical schools at The University of Texas at Austin and UT Rio Grande Valley.

The UT System is also heavily focused on research. The system's institutions have about $2.6 billion annually in research expenditures more than half of which is funded through federal grants.

HISTORY

The Texas Declaration of Independence (1836) admonished Mexico for having failed to establish a public education system in the territory but attempts to start a state-sponsored university were stymied until after Texas achieved US statehood and fought in the Civil War. A new constitution in 1876 provided for the establishment of "a university of the first class" and in 1883 The University of Texas (UT) opened in Austin. Eight professors taught 218 students in two curricula: academics and law.

The school's first building opened in 1884 and in 1891 the university's medical school opened in Galveston. By 1894 UT-Austin had 534 students and a football team. UT opened a Graduate School in 1910 and various other colleges over the years. The university added its first academic branch campus when the Texas State School of Mines and Metallurgy (opened in 1914 in El Paso) became part of the system in 1919.

UT's financial future was secured in 1923 when oil was found on West Texas land that had been set aside by the legislature as an education endowment. The income from oil production as well as the proceeds of surface-use leases became the Permanent University Fund (PUF) from which only interest and earnings on the revenues can be used: two-thirds by UT and one-third by Texas A&M University. UT continued to grow thanks to the PUF which topped $100 million by 1940.

UT sported the black eye of racial prejudice (as did many other institutions at the time) when it refused to admit Heman Sweatt a black student to its law school in 1946. The Supreme Court ordered UT to admit him in 1950 the same year the UT System was officially organized. Sixteen years later in one of the nation's most highly publicized crimes Charles Whitman killed 14 people and wounded 31 others with a high-powered rifle fired from atop the UT-Austin administration tower. The observation deck wasn't closed until 1975 however after a series of suicides. (It was later reopened in 1999.)

In the meantime UT added a medical center in Dallas and several graduate schools in Austin. The 1960s through the 1980s were a time of geographic expansion for the system as it absorbed other institutions started several new campuses and expanded its network of medical centers. In 1996 the UT System became the first public university to establish a private investment management company (University of Texas Investment Management Co.) to invest PUF money (by that time over $9 billion) and other funds.

The race issue reared its head again in 1996 when a Federal court ruled in the Hopwood decision (named for the plaintiff) that the UT System could no longer use race to determine scholarships and admissions. Minority enrollments declined the following year prompting the Texas Legislature to enact a law granting admission to the top 10% of graduates from any Texas high school to the state university of their choice.

Chancellor William Cunningham announced plans in 2000 to expand the UT System by 100000 students over the decade. After he resigned that year R. D. Burck took over as his successor. In 2001 UT received a $50 million donation the largest gift in its history from Texas businessman and Minnesota Vikings owner Red McCombs. The following year Burck stepped down and was replaced by Mark Yudof former president of the University of Minnesota. Francisco Cigarroa a medical doctor and former president of the UT Health Science Center in San Antonio replaced Yudof as chancellor in 2009.

EXECUTIVES

Executive Vice Chancellor Business Affairs, Scott C. Kelley
Executive Vice Chancellor Academic Affairs, Pedro Reyes
President UT Health Science Center at San Antonio, Francisco G. Cigarroa
Executive Vice Chancellor Health Affairs, Raymond S. Greenberg
Vice Chancellor Strategic Initiatives, Stephanie Bond Huie
Associate Vice President, David Gabler
Vice Chairman, R. Steven (Steve) Hicks, age 67
Chairman, Paul L. Foster, age 59
Vice Chairman, Wm. Eugene (Gene) Powell
Secretary Historian, Ann Quaid

LOCATIONS

HQ: UNIVERSITY OF TEXAS SYSTEM
210 W 6TH ST, AUSTIN, TX 787012901
Phone: 512 499-4587
Web: WWW.UTSYSTEM.EDU

PRODUCTS/OPERATIONS

Selected Institutions
Academic Institutions
The University of Texas at Arlington (established 1895)
The Univer
The Univer
The Univer
The Univer
The University of Texas-Pan American (Edinburg; 1927)
The University of Texas of the Permian Basin (Odessa; 1969)
The Univer
The Univer
Health Institutions
The University of Texas Health Science Center at Houston (established 1972)
The Univer
The Univer
The University of Texas M.D. Anderson Cancer Center (Houston 1941)
The Univer
The Univer

HISTORICAL FINANCIALS

Company Type: Private

Income Statement

FYE: August 31

	REVENUE ($ mil.)	NET INCOME ($ mil.)	NET PROFIT MARGIN	EMPLOYEES
08/16	13,282	1,589	12.0%	81,260
08/09	8,564	(3,592)	—	—
08/08	46	1	2.3%	—
08/06	0	0	—	—
Annual Growth	—	—	—	—

2016 Year-End Financials

Return on assets: 7.9%   Cash ($ mil.): 2,545
Return on equity: 12.0%
Current ratio: 0.70

UNIVERSITY OF THE PACIFIC

Situated next to the largest body of water on earth the University of the Pacific holds a sizable body of knowledge. The school offers more than 80 undergraduate majors and about 20 graduate programs in such fields as art language biology business computer science engineering history and pharmacy. It offers undergraduate graduate and professional degree programs in nine colleges and enrolls about 7000 students at its main campus in Stockton California the McGeorge School of Law in Sacramento and the Arthur A. Dugoni School of Dentistry in San Francisco. California's first chartered institution of higher education University of the Pacific was founded in 1851.

Operations

University of the Pacific has about 500 full-time faculty members and a student-to-teacher ratio of 13:1. Tuition at the university runs at about $38000 per year.

Geographic Reach

More than 85% of University of the Pacific's students are California residents. The remainder of the university's student base comes from 35 other US states as well as 25 international countries.

Financial Performance

University of the Pacific reported a 5% revenue rise to $331 million in 2012 due to increased tuition as well as from private grants gifts and bequests. Net income decreased by 53% to $21 million however due to increased expenses and lower investment returns.

Endowment funds contributed about $8 million of University of the Pacific's operating budget in fiscal 2012. The school has a total endowment of some $200 million.

Strategy

University of the Pacific is expanding its academic programs in targeted fields such as health-related education and training programs. It also is working to increase technology resources and implement related learning models as new high-tech generations join its ranks.

Other initiatives include recruiting teachers with scholarly experience attracting diverse and ambitious students and increasing job preparedness programs for students. University of the Pacific is also working to increase enrollment and fundraising efforts to generate new resources that will support its growth plans.

EXECUTIVES

Vice President, Chris Chang
APhA ASP Vice President of Professional Affairs, Barrett Smith
Vice President, Laura Merry
Assistant Vice President Advancement Operations, Scott Rivinius
Ncpa Pacific Vice President Of Membership, Steph Chu
Rho Chi Honor Society Vice President, Danny Luu
Vice President Of Asuop, Elena Goldfoos
T C Gvpe, Karla Barbosa
APHA ASP VICE PRESIDENT OF INDUSTRY AFFAIRS, Bhumika Bhakta
Ucc Vice Chairman, Alexis Arenz
Treasurer, Yolanda Salcedo
Auditors: ERNST & YOUNG US LLP SAN DIEG

HQ: UNIVERSITY OF THE PACIFIC
3601 PACIFIC AVE, STOCKTON, CA 952110197
Phone: 209 946-2401
Web: WWW.PACIFIC.EDU

PRODUCTS/OPERATIONS

2015 Sales

	% of total
Net tuition and fees	68
Private grants gifts and bequests	10
Sales and services of auxiliary enterprises	9
Clinic fees	4
Government grants and contracts	3
Investment return distributed	3
Other	3
Total	**100**

Selected Programs

Chemistry
Chemistry-Biology
Communication
Computer Science
Dental Hygiene
Economics
English
Environmental Studies
Film Studies
French
Geological and Enviromental Sciences
Graphic Design
Pre-Pharmacy
Pre-Physical Therapy
Psychology
Religious Studies

Selected Schools and Colleges

Arthur A. Dugoni School of Dentistry
College of the Pacific (Arts and Sciences)
Conservatory of Music
Eberhardt School of Business
Gladys L. Benerd School of Education
McGeorge School of Law
School of Engineering and Computer Science
School of International Studies
Thomas J. Long School of Pharmacy and Health
Sciences

HISTORICAL FINANCIALS

Company Type: Private

Income Statement

FYE: June 30

	REVENUE ($ mil.)	NET INCOME ($ mil.)	NET PROFIT MARGIN	EMPLOYEES
06/15	418	41	10.0%	1,500
06/13	447	147	32.9%	—
06/12	330	20	6.3%	—
Annual Growth	8.1%	26.1%	—	—

2015 Year-End Financials

Return on assets: 5.7%   Cash ($ mil.): 6
Return on equity: 10.0%
Current ratio: 0.10

UNIVERSITY OF UTAH HOSPITALS AND CLINICS

Whether you've broken your leg on the ski slopes or need the latest treatment for a neurological condition the University of Utah Hospitals & Clinics is here for you. Part of the University of Utah Health Care system the medical services provider operates an acute and critical care hospital that has some 550 beds as well as a network of community clinics that provide primary health care pharmacy and eye care among other services. The University Hospital provides care in areas including surgery emergency care cardiology radiology and organ transplant services; it also houses centers for medical education training and research.

Operations

Also part of the Hospitals & Clinics system the Huntsman Cancer Institute home to the system's cancer inpatient and outpatient services and the University Orthopaedic Center which offers physical therapy and orthopedic surgery. The University Neuropsychiatric Institute provides inpatient and outpatient behavioral health care.

Strategy

As part of its plan to expand and prepare for the future University of Utah Hospitals & Clinics completed a new $24 million building at the school's College of Nursing in 2012.

EXECUTIVES

CEO, David Entwistle
CFO, Gordon Crabtree
Executive Director University Hospital, Dan K. Lundergan
Executive Director Huntsman Cancer Hospital, Ray Lynch
Executive Director University Neuropsychiatric Institute, Ross Van Vranken
Executive Director University of Utah John A. Moran Eye Center, Wayne Imbrescia
Executive Director University of Utah Orthopaedic Center, Bart Adams
CIO, Jim Turnbull
Director of Health Information, Connie Tohara
Director Of Radiology Services, Kirk Mosher

LOCATIONS

HQ: UNIVERSITY OF UTAH HOSPITALS AND CLINICS
50 N MEDICAL DR, SALT LAKE CITY, UT 841320001
Phone: 801 581-2121
Web: WWW.NURS.UTAH.EDU

COMPETITORS

CHRISTUS Health	Ogden Regional Medical
Intermountain Health	Center
Care	St. Mark's
LifePoint Health	

HISTORICAL FINANCIALS

Company Type: Private

Income Statement

FYE: June 30

	REVENUE ($ mil.)	NET INCOME ($ mil.)	NET PROFIT MARGIN	EMPLOYEES
06/15	1,317	135	10.3%	4,200
06/14	1,282	20	1.6%	—
06/06	0	(0)	—	—
06/05	0	(0)	—	—
Annual Growth	108.9%	—	—	—

2015 Year-End Financials

Return on assets: 3.8%   Cash ($ mil.): 244
Return on equity: 10.3%
Current ratio: 2.60

UNIVERSITY OF WISCONSIN HOSPITAL AND CLINICS AUTHORITY

The University of Wisconsin Hospital and Clinics Authority (UW Hospital and Clinics) has the last word when it comes to the health of Badger Staters. The centerpiece of the authority is the UW Hospital and Clinics medical campus which is home to a 650-bed hospital the American Family Children's Hospital a cancer clinic and a small inpatient psychiatric ward as well as Level I adult and pediatric trauma centers. The hospital administers cancer treatment heart and stroke care organ transplantation and a host of other medical services. The UW Hospital and Clinics organization also operates area health clinics that provide general and specialty outpatient care and emergency room services.

Operations

UW Hospital and Clinics is a public authority formed to manage the health care facilities all of which are part of the broader University of Wisconsin (UW) Health organization. The teaching hospital and clinics are located adjacent to the university's medical and nursing schools. The system's satellite health centers provide medical care throughout the community. Altogether the UW Hospitals and Clinics provides care to about 27000 inpatients and 580000 outpatient visits per year. UW Hospitals and Clinics also provides outpatient care through affiliated practices that are part of the UW Medical Foundation physician practice organization.

The authority has more than 1200 physicians and 85 outpatient clinics. It also offers six intensive care units (dedicated to trauma and life support pediatrics cardiac care cardiothoracic care burns and neurosurgery) with a total of 83 beds. UW Hospital and Clinics is one of two organizations in Wisconsin with level I adult and pediatric trauma centers.

UW Hospital and Clinics works with UW Medical School to perform medical research in an array of disciplines including asthma cancer infectious disease and transplant medicine. About 1000 faculty members work in more than two dozen departments and 18 centers and institutes performing research in most aspects of basic clinical and public health care. The Carbone Cancer Center for instance includes 280 physicians and scientists who work to improve cancer treatment technologies.

Its Home Care Services segment provides patients with visits from licensed nurses and therapists as well as dietitians respiratory therapists and other medical specialists. The organization also supplies home health equipment.

Geographic Reach

UW Hospital and Clinics' main campus facilities are located in Madison Wisconsin. It also has clinics in about 50 surrounding communities.

Sales and Marketing

Medicare and Medicaid combined accounted for more than 30% of the net patient revenues in fiscal 2014; managed care accounted for more than 50%.

Financial Performance

In fiscal 2014 revenue increased 8% to $1.3 billion on an increase of net patient service revenues (which grew 7.7% that year). Net income rose 24%

to $108 million due to an increase of non-operating revenue (grants gifts and donations for example). Cash flow from operations fell 20% to $141 million as more was paid out to suppliers and employees.

UW Hospital and Clinics is an independent not-for-profit organization and receives no state funding with the exception of reimbursement for care of Medicaid patients.

Strategy

The UW Health organization is working to improve the quality of care for patients through a number of initiatives including infrastructure improvements data management upgrades and safety programs. It is upgrading network systems standardizing processes and implementing best practices across its facilities. UW Health is also looking to add new affiliations and academic relationships with other organizations. These goals help serve UW Health's participation in the Medicare Accountable Care Organization (ACO) program as well.

In mid-2014 the hospital opened a 14-bed level IV neonatal intensive care unit at its primary campus. It also opened a 12-bed pediatric universal care unit at the facility.

EXECUTIVES

VP Marketing, Elizabeth Zaher
SVP and CFO, Michael D. (Mike) Buhl
VP American Family Children's Hospital, Jeff Poltawsky
President and CEO, Jeffrey Grossman
President UW, John Sheehan
Chairman, David Walsh
Vice Chair, Michael (Mike) Weiden
Board Member, Andrea Harris

LOCATIONS

HQ: UNIVERSITY OF WISCONSIN HOSPITAL AND CLINICS AUTHORITY
600 HIGHLAND AVE, MADISON, WI 537920001
Phone: 608 263-6400
Web: WWW.UWHEALTHKIDS.ORG

PRODUCTS/OPERATIONS

Selected Services
Adult Primary CareFamily MedicineGeriatricsInternal MedicinePrimary CareWomen's Health and WellnessAdult Specialty CareAllergy Asthma and ImmunologyAudiologyBehavioral Health Services (Addiction)Blood and Bone Marrow TransplantBreast Care ServicesBurn Ce

COMPETITORS

Beaver Dam Community Hospitals	Meriter Health Services
Beloit Health System	ProHealth Care
Dean Health Systems Inc.	SSM Health Care
Hospital Sisters Health System	Stoughton Hospital
Marian Health System	ThedaCare Inc.
	Tomah Memorial Hospital

HISTORICAL FINANCIALS
Company Type: Private

Income Statement
FYE: June 30

	REVENUE ($ mil.)	NET INCOME ($ mil.)	NET PROFIT MARGIN	EMPLOYEES
06/16	2,860	46	1.6%	17,156
06/07	798	60	7.5%	—
06/06	746	62	8.3%	—
06/05	1,856	0	—	—
Annual Growth	4.0%	—	—	—

Return on assets: 1.0%   Cash ($ mil.): 315
Return on equity: 1.6%
Current ratio: 1.20

UNIVERSITY OF WISCONSIN MEDICAL FOUNDATION, INC.

UW Medical Foundation provides administrative services to faculty physicians at the University of Wisconsin School of Medicine and Public Health. The foundation a not-for-profit entity is a physician practice organization that works in cooperation with the UW Hospital and Clinics and other medical offices and clinics throughout the Badger State. The foundation coordinates clinical sites and provides technical and professional staffing services as well as administrative support for legal marketing information technology and logistics functions.

Operations

UW Medical Foundation provides support services for more than 1200 member doctors located at about 45 physician practices and 60 clinical outreach locations. It also helps clinical practices with quality initiatives. The foundation provides some $200 million in charity care each year. Its community activities include sponsoring health outreach events and donating safety products to low-income families.

Physicians in the organization provide services across a number of medical specialties including oncology gastroenterology women's health kidney care orthopedics respiratory therapy and urology.

Company Background

The organization has expanded over time: UW Medical Foundation merged with Physicians Plus Medical Group in 1998 and with the University Community Clinics in 2003.

EXECUTIVES

Vice President Of Is, Sandy Clark
Auditors: MCGLADREY LLP PALOS HILLS IL

LOCATIONS

HQ: UNIVERSITY OF WISCONSIN MEDICAL FOUNDATION, INC.
7974 UW HEALTH CT, MIDDLETON, WI 535625531
Phone: 608 821-4223
Web: WWW.UWMF.WISC.EDU

COMPETITORS

Ascension Health	Marian Health System
Beaver Dam Community Hospitals	Meriter Health Services
Beloit Health System	ProHealth Care
Catholic Health Initiatives	SSM Health Care
Dean Health Systems Inc.	Stoughton Hospital
	ThedaCare Inc.
Hospital Sisters Health System	Tomah Memorial Hospital

HISTORICAL FINANCIALS
Company Type: Private

Income Statement
FYE: June 30

	REVENUE ($ mil.)	NET INCOME ($ mil.)	NET PROFIT MARGIN	EMPLOYEES
06/15	766	26	3.4%	3,200
06/14	724	33	4.6%	—
06/13	0	22	—	—
06/12	655	15	2.3%	—
Annual Growth	5.3%	19.6%	—	—

Return on assets: 19.4%   Cash ($ mil.): 176
Return on equity: 3.4%
Current ratio: 1.30

UNMC PHYSICIANS

If you're in Nebraska and your doctor suddenly tells you to "Go Big Red!" — don't be shocked he's probably just a member of the not-for-profit UNMC Physicians (formerly University Medical Associates). Many of the more than 500 physicians in the UNMC group practice were trained and now teach at the University of Nebraska Medical Center. Additionally UNMC partners with The Nebraska Medical Center and the Olson Center for Women's Health to share best practices and resources. The physicians who also operate 10 family health clinics in the area provide services in about 50 specialties such as obstetrics cancer care family medicine cardiology and pediatrics.

Providers at UNMC also conduct and participate in a number of national and regional clinical research trials in a wide range of areas including cancer cardiovascular disease neurological sciences and infectious disease among many others.

EXECUTIVES

President, Rod Markin
Financial Executive, Donald W Davern
Dean, Deli H Davies
General Manager, Geri Schmid
Auditors: KPMG LLP OMAHA NE

LOCATIONS

HQ: UNMC PHYSICIANS
988101 NEBRASKA MED CTR, OMAHA, NE 681980001
Phone: 402 559-9700
Web: WWW.UNMCPHYSICIANS.COM

Selected Clinics (Omaha Nebraska)
Baker Place (family medicine/planning pediatrics)
Brentwood Village (internal medicine pain medicine)
Clarkson West (family medicine cardiology)
Durham Outpatient Center (houses a number of outpatient clinics/services)
Eagle Run (family medicine mental health)
Plattsmouth (internal medicine pediatrics)
Summit Plaza (family medicine cardiology)
Turner Park (internal medicine mental health)
UNMC Community Health Center (family planning midwifery mental health)
Village Pointe Specialties (ear nose throat pain medicine eye specialties)

COMPETITORS

CHI Health	Methodist Health System
Children's Hospital & Medical Center	

HISTORICAL FINANCIALS

Company Type: Private

Income Statement

FYE: June 30

	REVENUE ($ mil.)	NET INCOME ($ mil.)	NET PROFIT MARGIN	EMPLOYEES
06/16	199	(109)	—	1,200
06/14	245	11	4.8%	
06/13	225	7	3.4%	
06/12	218	(1)	—	
Annual Growth	(2.2%)	—	—	—

2016 Year-End Financials

Return on assets: —
Return on equity: (-54.9%)
Current ratio: 0.60

Cash ($ mil.): —

UPMC ALTOONA

UPMC Altoona (formerly Altoona Regional Health System) moves patients upstream towards better health. Operating in Altoona and surrounding areas in central Pennsylvania the health system's facilities include Altoona Hospital an acute care center with 380 licensed beds that provides specialized care in areas including cardiovascular ailments cancer behavioral health and neurology as well as general emergency trauma birthing and surgery services. UPMC Altoona also offers a variety of outpatient care facilities and programs including home health care a primary care physicians' group and laboratory services. The not-for-profit system merged with Pennsylvania hospital operator University of Pittsburgh Medical Center (UPMC) in 2013.

Change in Company Type

In mid-2013 Altoona Regional Health System merged with UMPC to become UPMC Altoona. A new board was assigned to govern the system comprising two-thirds former Altoona Regional board members and one-third UPMC-appointed members. UPMC plans to invest some $250 million over 10 years to improve facilities and services so that UPMC Altoona can provide more specialized and advanced treatments.

Operations

The system maintains a level II adult trauma center to serve the most severely injured.

Each year UPMC Altoona has some 65000 emergency department visits and 18000 hospital admissions and performs some 5000 inpatient and 15000 outpatient surgeries.

Geographic Reach

The system provides services to residents of about 20 counties in central Pennsylvania.

Strategy

The company is working on expansions and additions to its existing facilities in order to provide its service area with more specialized treatments. In 2014 UPMC Altoona opened its eighth Center for Liver Diseases clinic at the outpatient Station Medical Center location. The following year it established the UPMC Altoona Breast Health Center in the same location; the center offers comprehensive breast health services.

Company Background

In 2004 Altoona Hospital's parent Central Pennsylvania Health Services Corporation and Bon Secours-Holy Family Hospital's parent Bon Secours Health System merged the two campuses and affiliated companies to form Altoona Regional Health System. The system merged with UPMC in 2013.

EXECUTIVES

President, Jerry Murray
Financial Executive, Frank Nale

LOCATIONS

HQ: UPMC ALTOONA
620 HOWARD AVE, ALTOONA, PA 166014804
Phone: 814 889-2011
Web: WWW.ALTOONAREGIONAL.ORG

PRODUCTS/OPERATIONS

Selected Services

Behavioral Health
Birth & Growth
Cancer Care
Cardiac Care
Center for Weight Loss and Bariatric Surgery
Central Pennsylvania Cardiovascular Associates
Emergency Medicine and Trauma
HealthForce (Occupational Medicine)
Imaging Services
Institute for Sleep Medicine
Neurosurgery
Orthopedics
Physical Medicine and Rehabilitation
Primary Stroke Center
Surgical Services
Wound Care and Ostomy Program

COMPETITORS

Clearfield Area Health Services
Conemaugh Health System
Hanover Healthcare
Hershey Medical Center
J. C. Blair Memorial Hospital
Lancaster General
PinnacleHealth System
WellSpan Health

HISTORICAL FINANCIALS

Company Type: Private

Income Statement

FYE: June 30

	REVENUE ($ mil.)	NET INCOME ($ mil.)	NET PROFIT MARGIN	EMPLOYEES
06/15	394	25	6.5%	2,494
06/14	393	15	3.8%	
Annual Growth	0.2%	70.1%	—	—

2015 Year-End Financials

Return on assets: 5.4%
Return on equity: 6.5%
Current ratio: 2.30

Cash ($ mil.): —

UPMC HAMOT

EXECUTIVES

President, John T Malone
Vice-President, Thomas Thompson

LOCATIONS

HQ: UPMC HAMOT
201 STATE ST, ERIE, PA 165500001
Phone: 814 877-6000
Web: WWW.HAMOTSCHOOLOFANESTHESIA.ORG

HISTORICAL FINANCIALS

Company Type: Private

Income Statement

FYE: June 30

	REVENUE ($ mil.)	NET INCOME ($ mil.)	NET PROFIT MARGIN	EMPLOYEES
06/15*	360	39	10.9%	3,159
12/14	0	(0)	—	
06/09	302	0	—	
Annual Growth	2.9%	—	—	—

*Fiscal year change

2015 Year-End Financials

Return on assets: 1.6%
Return on equity: 10.9%
Current ratio: 3.90

Cash ($ mil.): —

UPMC PASSAVANT

EXECUTIVES

President, Teresa G Petrick
Vice-President, Paul Eberhart
VP Personnel, Gary Mignagna
Director, Lou A Brindle
Manager, Mark Salamacha
Vice-President, Paul Wheeler
Treasurer, Franklin Kelley
Manager, Corey D Conklin
Chief Operating Officer, Donna Jasko

LOCATIONS

HQ: UPMC PASSAVANT
9100 BABCOCK BLVD, PITTSBURGH, PA 152375815
Phone: 412 367-6700

HISTORICAL FINANCIALS

Company Type: Private

Income Statement

FYE: June 30

	REVENUE ($ mil.)	NET INCOME ($ mil.)	NET PROFIT MARGIN	EMPLOYEES
06/15	353	10	3.0%	1,357
06/09	298	32	10.8%	
06/06	0	0	—	
06/01	107	3	3.3%	
Annual Growth	8.8%	8.1%	—	—

2015 Year-End Financials

Return on assets: 1.2%
Return on equity: 3.0%
Current ratio: 5.50

Cash ($ mil.): —

UPPER CHESAPEAKE MEDICAL CENTER, INC.

EXECUTIVES

President, Lyle E Sheldon
Manager, Maria Panes
Operations Manager, Barbara Wheeler

LOCATIONS

HQ: UPPER CHESAPEAKE MEDICAL CENTER, INC.
500 UPPER CHESAPEAKE DR, BEL AIR, MD
210144324
Phone: 443 643-1000

HISTORICAL FINANCIALS
Company Type: Private

Income Statement
FYE: June 30

	REVENUE ($ mil.)	NET INCOME ($ mil.)	NET PROFIT MARGIN	EMPLOYEES
06/15*	284	21	7.4%	850
12/14	263	15	5.9%	—
12/13	264	12	4.7%	—
12/12	237	15	6.5%	—
Annual Growth	9.5%	16.6%	—	—

*Fiscal year change

2015 Year-End Financials
Return on assets: 9.4%   Cash ($ mil.): 53
Return on equity: 7.4%
Current ratio: 2.80

UPPER DARBY SCHOOL DISTRICT (INC)

EXECUTIVES

Superintendent, Doc Richard Dunlap
Board of Directors, Edward J Smith
Director, Marie Brobeil
Manager, Nina Tyre
Auditors: BAKER TILLY VIRCHOW KRAUSE LL

LOCATIONS

HQ: UPPER DARBY SCHOOL DISTRICT (INC)
4611 BOND AVE, DREXEL HILL, PA 190264236
Phone: 610 789-7200
Web: WWW.UPPERDARBYSD.ORG

HISTORICAL FINANCIALS
Company Type: Private

Income Statement
FYE: June 30

	REVENUE ($ mil.)	NET INCOME ($ mil.)	NET PROFIT MARGIN	EMPLOYEES
06/16	179	0	0.2%	1,450
06/14	169	7	4.7%	—
06/13	161	1	0.9%	—
06/11	157	(0)	—	—
Annual Growth	2.6%	—	—	—

2016 Year-End Financials
Return on assets: 1.6%   Cash ($ mil.): 19
Return on equity: 0.2%
Current ratio: 0.60

USS-POSCO INDUSTRIES, A CALIFORNIA JOINT VENTURE

US and Korean steel manufacturing interests come together in the form of USS-POSCO Industries (UPI) a 50/50 joint venture between United States Steel (US Steel) and POSCO. The company operates a steel plant (formerly owned by US Steel) in Pittsburg Northern California. It manufactures flat-rolled steel sheets in various forms: cold-rolled steel galvanized steel and tinplate. In addition USS-POSCO churns out iron oxide which is used to make hard and soft ferrites. UPI sells its products to more than 150 customers in more than dozen states throughout the western US. End products include office furniture computer cabinets metal studs cans culverts and metal building materials.

Operations

UPI's main product lines include cold rolled sheet galvanized sheet hot rolled pickled and oiled sheet and tin plate. It has the capacity to produce about 1.5 million tons of product per year.

Geographic Reach

The company markets its products primarily in the western US.

Sales and Marketing

UPI ships steel products to more than 150 customers across North America. The company sells its products to a wide range of manufacturers whose end products include automotive parts computer cabinets culverts food packaging metal buildings metal studs and office furniture. About 1/3 of UPI's product line is tinplate for the canning industry.

Strategy

Its Korean co-owner supplied high quality raw materials for use at the plant. In order to stay competitive in the face of cheaper steel imports UPI jettisoned non-core product lines to focus on steel sheet and tin. However strong competition and poor market prices forced the company in 2011 to introduce furloughs at the plant and enforce temporary shutdowns of the facility.

Company Background

The company rebounded from a major fire in 2001. In 2010 UPI invested heavily in remediation measures to clean up soil and groundwater impacted by its plant activities.

US Steel teamed up with POSCO (then Pohang Iron & Steel Company) in 1986 as part of a major reorganization of the aging Pittsburg plant which first opened in 1910.

EXECUTIVES

Vice President Finance and Administration, Alan Gardner
Senior Vice President, Sergey Korolev
Vice President Operations, Salvatore Sbranti
Vice Chair, Chris Beltran
Auditors: KPMG LLP SACRAMENTO CALIFOR

LOCATIONS

HQ: USS-POSCO INDUSTRIES, A CALIFORNIA JOINT VENTURE
900 LOVERIDGE RD, PITTSBURG, CA 945652808
Phone: 800 877-7672
Web: WWW.USSPOSCO.COM

PRODUCTS/OPERATIONS

Selected Steel Products
Cold Rolled Annealed
Hot Dipped Galvanized
Hot Rolled Pickled and Oiled
Tinplate

COMPETITORS

AK Steel Holding Corporation	Gerdau Ameristeel
ArcelorMittal USA	Nucor
BlueScope Steel	Steel Dynamics

HISTORICAL FINANCIALS
Company Type: Private

Income Statement
FYE: December 31

	REVENUE ($ mil.)	NET INCOME ($ mil.)	NET PROFIT MARGIN	EMPLOYEES
12/15	648	(4)	—	759
12/08	1,198	11	1.0%	—
12/07	998	(40)	—	—
12/06	1,034	14	1.4%	—
Annual Growth	(5.1%)	—	—	—

2015 Year-End Financials
Return on assets: 1.1%   Cash ($ mil.): —
Return on equity: (-0.7%)
Current ratio: 0.30

UTAH ASSOCIATED MUNICIPAL POWER SYSTEMS

Even the hardiest citizens of the Intermountain West need access to a reliable power supply. Utah Associated Municipal Power Systems supplies power to 52 member municipal utilities primarily in Utah as well as in Arizona California Idaho Nevada and New Mexico Oregon and Wyoming. These municipal electric utilities and other local government units provide retail electric or other utility services in their respective service areas. The company obtains electricity from interests in generation facilities and through power purchase agreements with other generators; Utah Associated Municipal Power Systems also has interests in traditional power transmission facilities and in wind power generation plants.

Utah Associated Municipal Power Systems was organized in 1980 under the provisions of the Utah Inter-local Cooperation Act. In 2005 the company was operating 14 projects that provide a range of power supply transmission and related services to its members.

EXECUTIVES

Vice President Information Technology Infrastructure and Operations, Keith Myers
Auditors: ERNST & YOUNG LLP

LOCATIONS

HQ: UTAH ASSOCIATED MUNICIPAL POWER SYSTEMS
155 N 400 W, SALT LAKE CITY, UT 841031111
Phone: 801 566-3938
Web: WWW.UAMPS.COM

COMPETITORS

California ISO   IPA
Deseret Power

HISTORICAL FINANCIALS

Company Type: Private

Income Statement

FYE: March 31

	REVENUE ($ mil.)	NET INCOME ($ mil.)	NET PROFIT MARGIN	EMPLOYEES
03/16	187	3	2.0%	27
03/15	170	3	2.2%	—
03/14	174	3	1.8%	—
03/13	179	18	10.4%	—
Annual Growth	1.5%	(41.9%)	—	—

2016 Year-End Financials

Return on assets: 8.2%
Return on equity: 2.0%
Current ratio: 0.40
Cash ($ mil.): —

UTAH STATE UNIVERSITY

Utah State University (USU) has more than 40 academic departments at colleges of agriculture arts business education and human services engineering science natural resources and humanities and social sciences. It offers about 170 bachelor's degree programs and more than 140 graduate degree programs. Biology elementary education mechanical and aerospace engineering and business administration are among the university's most popular majors. About 29000 students attend its main campus in northern Utah its three branch campuses or extension facilities located across the state. USU was established in 1888 as an agricultural college.

Operations

USU has a student-to-faculty ratio of 18:1. Alumni of the university include Greg Carr founder of the Greg C. Carr Foundation and Charlie Denson former president of NIKE.

Geographic Reach

USU students hail from all 50 US states and some 80 international countries. The university's students have the opportunity to study abroad through partnerships with 140 other institutions located around the world. USU's main campuses or branch offices in Utah are located in Brigham City Logan San Juan Tooele and Uintah Basin.

Financial Performance

Revenues increased at USU by 4% to some $340 million due to increased income from tuition and fees higher enrollment and increased state appropriations. The gain was offset by decreases in gifts grants and contracts. Net income fell 41% to $68 million due to higher operating expenses from salary benefit and other costs.

Strategy

To expand its facilities and meet growing student needs USU is adding a new school of business building and a new athletics center to its main campus. The university recently completed construction of a new $47 million agricultural building on the main campus as well as a new administration building on the USU Eastern campus. In addition USU is building a new distance education building on its Logan campus.

To further expand resources for students USU began offering a Master of Business Administration (MBA) program at the Brigham Young University's Idaho campus in 2013.

EXECUTIVES

Associate Vice President for Research, Jeff Broadbent
Vice President University Advancement, Fross Peterson
Auditors: OFFICE OF THE UTAH STATE AUDIT

LOCATIONS

HQ: UTAH STATE UNIVERSITY
1000 OLD MAIN HL, LOGAN, UT 843221000
Phone: 435 797-1057
Web: WWW.UTAHSTATEAGGIES.COM

HISTORICAL FINANCIALS

Company Type: Private

Income Statement

FYE: June 30

	REVENUE ($ mil.)	NET INCOME ($ mil.)	NET PROFIT MARGIN	EMPLOYEES
06/16	401	88	22.2%	6,000
06/15	382	55	14.4%	—
06/14	362	68	19.0%	—
06/13	350	44	12.7%	—
Annual Growth	4.6%	25.9%	—	—

2016 Year-End Financials

Return on assets: 3.8%
Return on equity: 22.2%
Current ratio: 0.60
Cash ($ mil.): 61

VAL VERDE UNIFIED SCH DIS

EXECUTIVES

President, Shelly Yarbrough
Finance Manager, Bill Angel
Superintendent, Norman Towels
Administrative Assistant, Vicki Armatis
Assistant Manager, Daren Waters
Plant & Facilities Manager, Peter Davenport

LOCATIONS

HQ: VAL VERDE UNIFIED SCH DIS
975 MORGAN ST, PERRIS, CA 925713103
Phone: 951 940-6100
Web: WWW.VALVERDE.EDU

HISTORICAL FINANCIALS

Company Type: Private

Income Statement

FYE: June 30

	REVENUE ($ mil.)	NET INCOME ($ mil.)	NET PROFIT MARGIN	EMPLOYEES
06/16	458	(12)	—	1,500
06/11	362	(0)	—	—
06/01	88	(2)	—	—
06/00	60	4	6.7%	—
Annual Growth	13.4%	—	—	—

VALLEY CENTER-PAUMA UNIFIED SCHOOL DISTRICT

EXECUTIVES

Superintendent, Lou Obermeyer
Superintendent, Ded-Deb Ortega
Superintendent, Mary Gorsuch
Manager, Mitch Sanchez
Director, Ben Markley
Purchasing Director, Jon Petersen
Assistant Manager, Mark Gardener
Assistant Manager, Wendy Heredia

LOCATIONS

HQ: VALLEY CENTER-PAUMA UNIFIED SCHOOL DISTRICT
28751 COLE GRADE RD, VALLEY CENTER, CA 920826575
Phone: 760 749-0464
Web: WWW.VCPUSD.NET

HISTORICAL FINANCIALS

Company Type: Private

Income Statement

FYE: June 30

	REVENUE ($ mil.)	NET INCOME ($ mil.)	NET PROFIT MARGIN	EMPLOYEES
06/16	255	19	7.6%	600
06/06	42	0	—	—
Annual Growth	19.6%	—	—	—

VALLEY CHILDREN'S HEALTHCARE

EXECUTIVES

Chief Executive Officer, Todd Suntrapak
Director, Wes Segal
Director, Denise Zeitler
Vice-President, Kevin Shimamoto

LOCATIONS

HQ: VALLEY CHILDREN'S HEALTHCARE
9300 VALLEY CHILDRENS PL, MADERA, CA 936368761
Phone: 559 353-3000
Web: WWW.VALLEYCHILDRENS.ORG

HISTORICAL FINANCIALS

Company Type: Private

Income Statement

FYE: September 30

	REVENUE ($ mil.)	NET INCOME ($ mil.)	NET PROFIT MARGIN	EMPLOYEES
09/16	601	83	13.9%	2,800
09/15	11	3	26.6%	—
Annual Growth	5143.6%	2636.5%	—	—

2016 Year-End Financials

Return on assets: 3.8%
Return on equity: 13.9%
Current ratio: 1.20
Cash ($ mil.): 10

VALLEY CHILDREN'S HOSPITAL

EXECUTIVES

President, Todd Sunterapak
Finance Manager, Greg Dean
Director, Chris Long
Auditors: MOSS ADAMS LLP STOCKTON CA

LOCATIONS

HQ: VALLEY CHILDREN'S HOSPITAL
   9300 VALLEY CHILDRENS PL, MADERA, CA
   936368762
Phone: 559 353-3000
Web: WWW.VALLEYCHILDRENS.ORG

HISTORICAL FINANCIALS
Company Type: Private

Income Statement
FYE: September 30

	REVENUE ($ mil.)	NET INCOME ($ mil.)	NET PROFIT MARGIN	EMPLOYEES
09/15	575	24	4.3%	1,800
09/13*	542	103	19.0%	—
06/05	457	(24)	—	—
09/02	219	0	0.3%	—
Annual Growth	7.7%	33.9%	—	—

*Fiscal year change

2015 Year-End Financials
Return on assets: 5.4%   Cash ($ mil.): 8
Return on equity: 4.3%
Current ratio: 1.00

VALLEY MEDICAL FACILITIES, INC.

EXECUTIVES

Chief Executive Officer, Donald W Spalding
Plant & Facilities Manager, Ken Wagner
Director, Cliff Glovier
Manager, Dawn Martin
Manager, Linda Schaefer
Director, Bruce Ferrero
Personnel Director, Laurie Clemens
Director, Robert Swaskoski
Auditors: ARNETT CARBIS TOOTHMAN LLP PI

LOCATIONS

HQ: VALLEY MEDICAL FACILITIES, INC.
   720 BLACKBURN RD, SEWICKLEY, PA 151431459
Phone: 724 728-7000

HISTORICAL FINANCIALS
Company Type: Private

Income Statement
FYE: June 30

	REVENUE ($ mil.)	NET INCOME ($ mil.)	NET PROFIT MARGIN	EMPLOYEES
06/15	368	18	5.0%	4,300
06/14	369	7	2.0%	—
06/13	359	(1)	—	—
06/10	362	4	1.1%	—
Annual Growth	0.3%	35.0%	—	—

2015 Year-End Financials
Return on assets: 11.0%   Cash ($ mil.): 14
Return on equity: 5.0%
Current ratio: 0.60

VALLEY PRESBYTERIAN HOSPITAL

EXECUTIVES

Chief Executive Officer, Gustavo Valdespino
Account Manager, Ray Moss
Senior Vice-President, Jean Rico
Senior Vice-President, Pegi Matsuda
Senior Vice-President, Gayathri S Jith
Auditors: MOSS ADAMS LLP LOS ANGELES

LOCATIONS

HQ: VALLEY PRESBYTERIAN HOSPITAL
   15107 VANOWEN ST, VAN NUYS, CA 914054597
Phone: 818 782-6600
Web: WWW.VALLEYPRES.ORG

HISTORICAL FINANCIALS
Company Type: Private

Income Statement
FYE: October 31

	REVENUE ($ mil.)	NET INCOME ($ mil.)	NET PROFIT MARGIN	EMPLOYEES
10/15	389	51	13.3%	1,600
10/14	261	0	0.0%	—
10/13	310	18	5.9%	—
10/12	318	25	7.9%	—
Annual Growth	7.0%	27.1%	—	—

2015 Year-End Financials
Return on assets: 7.3%   Cash ($ mil.): 36
Return on equity: 13.3%
Current ratio: 0.90

VALLEY VIEW COMMUNITY UNIT SCHOOL DISTRICT 365U

Located about 35 miles southwest of downtown Chicago Valley View School District 365U provides education to 18000 elementary middle and high school students — the district also includes one alternative school and one preschool. The 20 schools included in the district (serving Romeoville and Bolingbrook communities) total approximately 2.4 million square feet. With more than 2000 full time employees Valley View School District 365U is one of Will County's largest employers. The seven-member school board (elected for a four-year term) hires and supervises the superintendent of schools and sets district policies.

Financial Performance

Valley View School District 365U reported a 3% decrease in revenues in 2012 due to a drop in operating grants and contributions payments in lieu of taxes general state aid and investment earnings.

However its net income decreased by 292% in 2012 over 2011 due to lower revenues and higher expenses. The hike in expenses was because of an increase in instruction support services and state on-behalf payments to teacher retirement and insurance funds.

The District reported that its budget for 2012-2013 was 8.9% higher than for 2011-2012.

Company Background

Valley View School District 365U was founded in 1952.

EXECUTIVES

Secretary Administrative A, Ann Harris
School Board Member, Elizabeth Campbell
Auditors: EVANS MARSHALL & PEASE PC

LOCATIONS

HQ: VALLEY VIEW COMMUNITY UNIT SCHOOL
   DISTRICT 365U
   801 W NORMANTOWN RD, ROMEOVILLE, IL
   604464330
Phone: 815 886-2700
Web: WWW.VVSD.ORG

PRODUCTS/OPERATIONS

Schools
High Schools (grades 9-12)
   Bolingbroke
   Romeoville
Middle Schools (grades 6-8)
   A. Vito Martinez
   Brooks Middle School
   Hubert H. Humphrey
   Jane Addams
   John J. Lukancic
Elementary Schools (grades K-5)
   Bernard J. Ward
   Beverly Skoff
   Independence
   Irene King
   Jamie McGee
   John R. Tibbott
   Jonas E. Salk
   Kenneth L. Hermansen
   Oak View
   Pioneer
   Robert C. Hill
   Wood View
Other
   Phoenix Experience (alternative school)

HISTORICAL FINANCIALS
Company Type: Private

Income Statement
FYE: June 30

	REVENUE ($ mil.)	NET INCOME ($ mil.)	NET PROFIT MARGIN	EMPLOYEES
06/16	295	(8)	—	3,000
06/07*	190	220	116.0%	—
08/06	225	0	—	—
12/05	0	0	—	—
Annual Growth	—	—	—	—

*Fiscal year change

VALUE DRUG COMPANY

Value Drug Company sees a great deal of value in keeping independent pharmacies competitive. The company is a purchasing cooperative of hundreds of independent drugstores that provides wholesale pharmaceutical distribution services to its members primarily in the central Pennsylvania

area. Its products include pharmaceuticals and non-prescription medications hospital and convalescent equipment health and beauty aids nutritional supplies and other health care-related products. The company works with some of the world's largest pharmaceutical makers. Value Drug was founded in 1934 and incorporated in 1936. The company is led by president Greg Drew a former Rite-Aid executive.

Operations

The company's private-label line includes nearly 1000 over-the-counter products. Value Drug participates in such retail initiatives as the federal 340B Drug Discount Program an adult immunization tracking program and competitive generic sourcing program OptiSource.

Geographic Reach

Value Drug is located in Pennsylvania and serves a market area covering 15 states.

EXECUTIVES

National Account Manager, Ellen Breitenbach
Vice President Finance and Chief Financial
 Officer, David Zang
Auditors: HILL BARTH & KING LLC WEXFOR

LOCATIONS

HQ: VALUE DRUG COMPANY
 195 THEATER DR, DUNCANSVILLE, PA 166357144
Phone: 814 944-9316
Web: WWW.VALUEDRUGCO.COM

COMPETITORS

AmerisourceBergen	Kinray
Cardinal Health	McKesson
H. D. Smith Wholesale	Quality King
Drug	

HISTORICAL FINANCIALS
Company Type: Private

Income Statement

	REVENUE ($ mil.)	NET INCOME ($ mil.)	NET PROFIT MARGIN	EMPLOYEES
12/15	779	3	0.4%	200
12/14	754	(0)	—	—
Annual Growth	3.4%	—	—	—

2015 Year-End Financials
Return on assets: 10.2%   Cash ($ mil.): —
Return on equity: 0.4%
Current ratio: 0.90

HISTORICAL FINANCIALS
Company Type: Private

Income Statement
FYE: November 30

	REVENUE ($ mil.)	NET INCOME ($ mil.)	NET PROFIT MARGIN	EMPLOYEES
11/15	188	105	56.0%	170
11/14	116	49	42.5%	—
11/13	173	120	69.8%	—
11/12	239	173	72.3%	—
Annual Growth	(7.8%)	(15.3%)	—	—

2015 Year-End Financials
Return on assets: 1.6%   Cash ($ mil.): 298
Return on equity: 56.0%
Current ratio: 11.20

VANASSE HANGEN BRUSTLIN INC.

EXECUTIVES

Board of Directors, Robert Dubinsky

LOCATIONS

HQ: VANASSE HANGEN BRUSTLIN INC.
 101 WALNUT ST, WATERTOWN, MA 024724026
Phone: 617 924-1770

HISTORICAL FINANCIALS
Company Type: Private

Income Statement
FYE: December 31

	REVENUE ($ mil.)	NET INCOME ($ mil.)	NET PROFIT MARGIN	EMPLOYEES
12/15	184	1	1.0%	1,085
12/14	166	5	3.1%	—
12/13	157	3	2.0%	—
12/12	153	3	2.6%	—
Annual Growth	6.4%	(21.8%)	—	—

2015 Year-End Financials
Return on assets: 3.4%   Cash ($ mil.): 1
Return on equity: 1.0%
Current ratio: 1.40

VAN ANDEL INSTITUTE

EXECUTIVES

Chairman, David V Andel
Financial Executive, Heather Ly
Manager, Cindy Turner
Board of Directors, Afton Devos
Manager, David L Van Andel
Manager, David Petillo
Manager, Doug L Camelo
Board of Directors, Kaitlyn Disselkoen
Manager, Dafna Kaufman
Auditors: DELOITTE & TOUCHE LLP GRAND R

LOCATIONS

HQ: VAN ANDEL INSTITUTE
 333 BOSTWICK AVE NE, GRAND RAPIDS, MI
 495032518
Phone: 616 234-5000
Web: WWW.VAI.ORG

VANCOUVER PUBLIC SCHOOLS

EXECUTIVES

Superintendent, Steven T Webb
Engineer, Marti Ashcraft
Maintenance Supervisor, Gary Morrison
Auditors: PAT MCCARTHY STATE AUDITOR O

LOCATIONS

HQ: VANCOUVER PUBLIC SCHOOLS
 2901 FALK RD, VANCOUVER, WA 986616392
Phone: 360 313-1000
Web: WWW.VANSD.ORG

HISTORICAL FINANCIALS
Company Type: Private

Income Statement
FYE: August 31

	REVENUE ($ mil.)	NET INCOME ($ mil.)	NET PROFIT MARGIN	EMPLOYEES
08/15*	269	(1)	—	2,700
06/14	1	0	22.6%	—
08/13	236	4	2.0%	—
08/12	231	(0)	—	—
Annual Growth	5.1%	—	—	—
*Fiscal year change

2015 Year-End Financials
Return on assets: 4.1%   Cash ($ mil.): 2
Return on equity: (-0.7%)
Current ratio: —

VASSAR BROTHERS HOSPITAL

EXECUTIVES

President, Daniel Aronzon
Officer, Janeth Ready

LOCATIONS

HQ: VASSAR BROTHERS HOSPITAL
 45 READE PL, POUGHKEEPSIE, NY 126013990
Phone: 845 454-8500
Web: WWW.HEALTHQUEST.ORG

HISTORICAL FINANCIALS
Company Type: Private

Income Statement
FYE: December 31

	REVENUE ($ mil.)	NET INCOME ($ mil.)	NET PROFIT MARGIN	EMPLOYEES
12/15	515	29	5.8%	1,500
12/14	459	20	4.6%	—
12/11	390	(12)	—	—
12/07	317	10	3.3%	—
Annual Growth	6.2%	14.1%	—	—

2015 Year-End Financials
Return on assets: 8.6%   Cash ($ mil.): 42
Return on equity: 5.8%
Current ratio: 1.20

VDM METALS USA, LLC

EXECUTIVES

Vice-President, Winfried Sterzl
Director, Mariann Cook
Director, Charles Demarco
Manager, Gerhard Schmidt

LOCATIONS

HQ: VDM METALS USA, LLC
 306 COLUMBIA TPKE, FLORHAM PARK, NJ
 079321217
Phone: 973 437-1664
Web: WWW.VDM-METALS.COM

HISTORICAL FINANCIALS
Company Type: Private

Income Statement
FYE: September 30

	REVENUE ($ mil.)	NET INCOME ($ mil.)	NET PROFIT MARGIN	EMPLOYEES
09/15*	185	4	2.7%	230
12/13	188	0	0.3%	—
Annual Growth	(0.8%)	177.9%	—	—

*Fiscal year change

2015 Year-End Financials
Return on assets: 17.6%
Return on equity: 2.7%
Current ratio: 0.50

Cash ($ mil.): 2

VENTURA UNIFIED SCHOOL DISTRICT

EXECUTIVES

Superintendent, Trudy T Arriaga
Director, Andrea McNeil
Board of Directors, Janis Schmutte
Manager, Joesprh Richards Jr
Manager, Diana Ellis
Director, Steve Bailey
Senior Manager, Doris Ryder
Auditors: VICENTI LLOYD & STUTZMAN LLP

LOCATIONS

HQ: VENTURA UNIFIED SCHOOL DISTRICT
255 W STANLEY AVE STE 100, VENTURA, CA 930011331
Phone: 805 641-5000
Web: WWW.VENTURAUSD.ORG

HISTORICAL FINANCIALS
Company Type: Private

Income Statement
FYE: June 30

	REVENUE ($ mil.)	NET INCOME ($ mil.)	NET PROFIT MARGIN	EMPLOYEES
06/16	205	6	3.0%	2,000
06/02	135	(6)	—	—
06/01	155	6	4.0%	—
06/00	117	(3)	—	—
Annual Growth	3.6%	—	—	—

2016 Year-End Financials
Return on assets: 5.8%
Return on equity: 3.0%
Current ratio: —

Cash ($ mil.): 50

VERMONT ELECTRIC POWER COMPANY, INC.

EXECUTIVES

Chief Executive Officer, Thomas Dunn
President, John J Donleavy
Vice-President, Kerrick Johnson
President, Christopher Ldutton

Treasurer, Michele Nelson
Financial Executive, Thad Omand
Engineer, Jarrod Harper
Finance Manager, Michelle Nelson
Auditors: KPMG LLP COLCHESTER VT

LOCATIONS

HQ: VERMONT ELECTRIC POWER COMPANY, INC.
366 PINNACLE RIDGE RD, RUTLAND, VT 057019386
Phone: 802 773-9161
Web: WWW.VELCO.COM

HISTORICAL FINANCIALS
Company Type: Private

Income Statement
FYE: December 31

	REVENUE ($ mil.)	NET INCOME ($ mil.)	NET PROFIT MARGIN	EMPLOYEES
12/15	172	78	45.3%	150
12/14	167	73	43.9%	—
12/13	159	68	43.1%	—
12/12	129	53	41.3%	—
Annual Growth	10.2%	13.7%	—	—

2015 Year-End Financials
Return on assets: 5.7%
Return on equity: 45.3%
Current ratio: 0.40

Cash ($ mil.): 1

VERMONT TRANSCO LLC

EXECUTIVES

Principal, Christopher L Dutton
Board of Directors, Steven Farman
Board of Directors, Leslie Cadwell
Vice-President, Kerrick Johnson
Chief Financial Officer, Neal Robinson
Auditors: KPMG LLP COLCHESTER VT

LOCATIONS

HQ: VERMONT TRANSCO LLC
366 PINNACLE RIDGE RD, RUTLAND, VT 057019475
Phone: 802 773-9161
Web: WWW.VERMONTTRANSCO.COM

HISTORICAL FINANCIALS
Company Type: Private

Income Statement
FYE: December 31

	REVENUE ($ mil.)	NET INCOME ($ mil.)	NET PROFIT MARGIN	EMPLOYEES
12/15	172	82	47.8%	3
12/13	158	71	45.1%	—
12/12	128	54	42.7%	—
12/11	135	64	47.7%	—
Annual Growth	6.3%	6.3%	—	—

2015 Year-End Financials
Return on assets: 4.8%
Return on equity: 47.8%
Current ratio: 0.30

Cash ($ mil.): —

VIA CHRISTI HOSPITALS WICHITA, INC.

EXECUTIVES

Chief Executive Officer, Michael Mullis
Director, James Haan
Vice-President, Ed Hett
Director, Gregory Schuessler

LOCATIONS

HQ: VIA CHRISTI HOSPITALS WICHITA, INC.
929 N SAINT FRANCIS ST, WICHITA, KS 672143882
Phone: 316 268-5000

HISTORICAL FINANCIALS
Company Type: Private

Income Statement
FYE: September 30

	REVENUE ($ mil.)	NET INCOME ($ mil.)	NET PROFIT MARGIN	EMPLOYEES
09/15	538	36	6.7%	4,100
09/14	534	68	12.9%	—
09/13	534	24	4.5%	—
09/12	529	108	20.4%	—
Annual Growth	0.6%	(30.7%)	—	—

2015 Year-End Financials
Return on assets: 3.4%
Return on equity: 6.7%
Current ratio: 2.10

Cash ($ mil.): 22

VICTORY INTERNATIONAL GROUP, LLC

EXECUTIVES

President, Jiansheng Fan

LOCATIONS

HQ: VICTORY INTERNATIONAL GROUP, LLC
14748 PIPELINE AVE STE B, CHINO HILLS, CA 917096024
Phone: 949 407-5888
Web: WWW.VICTORYINTLGROUP.COM

HISTORICAL FINANCIALS
Company Type: Private

Income Statement
FYE: December 31

	REVENUE ($ mil.)	NET INCOME ($ mil.)	NET PROFIT MARGIN	EMPLOYEES
12/15	873	42	4.8%	25
12/07	87	1	1.4%	—
Annual Growth	33.2%	55.5%	—	—

2015 Year-End Financials
Return on assets: 11.0%
Return on equity: 4.8%
Current ratio: 1.00

Cash ($ mil.): 40

VIKING YACHT COMPANY

Leif Eriksson's oceangoing Viking explorers could only dream of vessels like those made by the Viking Yacht Company. Viking Yacht can build more than 100 semi-custom fiberglass pleasure boats primarily used for sport fishing. About 90% of each yacht is made in-house. Its line of yachts vary in length from approximately 42 to 92 feet and include convertible and enclosed-bridge convertible vessels open sportfish models and a 52-foot sport yacht. The luxury boats are sold through a network of more than 40 dealers six of which are based outside the US. Founders and brothers Bob and Bill Healey own Viking Yacht Company.

Operations

Viking operates through several businesses and divisions. Atlantic Marine Electronics provides sales installation and service support for yacht electronics including navigation communication and entertainment systems equipment. Its Viking Yachting Center acts as a weather-protected storage area for boats up to 50 feet and provides full services to all brands of yachts including 250 deepwater slips a pool and pool house barbeque and picnic areas bathhouse fuel dock and nighttime security.

Palm Beach Towers designs and engineers aluminum tuna towers used aboard Viking yachts and other boats. In addition Palm Beach Towers produces fiberglass hardtops rod lockers and electronic boxes and other custom aluminum and fiberglass accessories. Palm Beach Towers has locations in New Jersey and Florida.

Sales and Marketing

The company has a sales network of waterfront locations across the US as well as in the Caribbean Central and South America Africa Asia Middle East and Australia.

Strategy

To attract additional customers Viking is focused on launching new models of yachts. It launched seven new models during 2011 and 2012 and in 2013 it launched sleek and sporty new generation 55 and 62 Convertibles ass had a 92 Convertible on the docket.

To help cut greenhouse gas emissions and control costs in 2012 Viking built a tri-generation power plant with six natural gas-fueled turbines at its New Jersey manufacturing facility enabling the company to produce its own electricity.

Company Background

Viking was founded in 1964 and has produced more than 4000 vessels.

EXECUTIVES

Chief Executive Officer, Robert T Healey
Executive Vice-President, Patrick Healey
Manager, Jim Lavor
Director, Pete Fredriksen
Production Manager, Ray Glebock
Manager, Rudolf Dalinger
Financial Executive, Jerry Straub Jr
Auditors: ERNST & YOUNG LLP PHILADELPHI

LOCATIONS

HQ: VIKING YACHT COMPANY
ON THE BASS RIV RR 9, NEW GRETNA, NJ 08224
Phone: 609 296-6000
Web: WWW.VIKINGYACHTS.COM

PRODUCTS/OPERATIONS

Selected Models of Yachts
Enclosed Bridge Convertible
Motor Yachts
Open
Open Bridge Convertible
Sport Yacht

COMPETITORS

Brunswick Boat
Fountain Powerboat
Hatteras Yachts
Marine Products Corp.
Sea Fox Boats
Sea Ray Boats
Sunseeker

HISTORICAL FINANCIALS

Company Type: Private

Income Statement

FYE: July 31

	REVENUE ($ mil.)	NET INCOME ($ mil.)	NET PROFIT MARGIN	EMPLOYEES
07/16	280	18	6.7%	775
07/15	245	17	7.2%	—
07/14	194	16	8.4%	—
07/13	154	10	6.7%	—
Annual Growth	22.0%	22.3%	—	—

2016 Year-End Financials

Return on assets: 4.1%   Cash ($ mil.): 12
Return on equity: 6.7%
Current ratio: 0.40

VIRGINIA COMMONWEALTH UNIVERSITY

Virginia Commonwealth University (VCU) serves the common interests of its more than 30000 enrolled students. The university offers more than 200 certificate undergraduate graduate and doctoral programs through its 15 schools. Spread across two campuses in Richmond: Monroe Park and Medical College of Virginia (MCV) which includes the Schools of Allied Health Dentistry Medicine Nursing Pharmacy and Public Health. Specialty facilities include the VCU Medical Center and a branch campus of the School of the Arts in Qatar. Founded in 1917 as the Richmond School of Social Work and Public Health in 1968 the school merged with the Medical College of Virginia to form VCU.

EXECUTIVES

Department Chair associate Professional Maternal child Nurs, Rita Pickler
Vice President, Stephen D Gottfredson
Associate Vice President Facilities Management, Brian Ohlinger
Senior Vice President for, Sheldon Retchin
Director manager supervisor, Charles Daniel
Senior Vice President Finance and Administration, John Bennett
Associate Vice President, David Sarrett
Vice President, Allison Arden
Executive Board Member, Ryan O'Connor

LOCATIONS

HQ: VIRGINIA COMMONWEALTH UNIVERSITY
912 W FRANKLIN ST, RICHMOND, VA 232849040
Phone: 804 828-0100
Web: WWW.VCU.EDU

HISTORICAL FINANCIALS

Company Type: Private

Income Statement

FYE: June 30

	REVENUE ($ mil.)	NET INCOME ($ mil.)	NET PROFIT MARGIN	EMPLOYEES
06/16	737	37	5.1%	11,000
06/11	2,319	328	14.2%	—
06/06	448	40	9.0%	—
06/05	0	0	—	—
Annual Growth	—	—	—	—

2016 Year-End Financials

Return on assets: 11.7%   Cash ($ mil.): 94
Return on equity: 5.1%
Current ratio: 0.70

VIRGINIA HOUSING DEVELOPMENT AUTHORITY

Though Virginia is famous for its Civil War-era plantations these historic estates represent a lifestyle out of reach for most. For Virginians seeking a more modest homestead there's the Virginia Housing Development Authority (VHDA). The not-for-profit quasi-government agency founded by the Virginia General Assembly in 1972 provides developers of rental properties and low- to moderate-income borrowers with low interest rate loans to renovate or purchase houses and apartments across the state. Its loan products are offered by more than 140 authorized lenders throughout Virginia. The VHDA is self-supporting issuing bonds to raise capital.

EXECUTIVES

Executive Director, Susan F. Dewey
Managing Director Rental Housing, Arthur N. (Art) Bowen
Managing Director Community Outreach, J. Michael Hawkins
Managing Director Executive Services, Llewellyn C. Anderson
Managing Director Homeownership, Janet Wiglesworth
Managing Director Internal Audit and Risk Management, Julie Camus
Managing Director Finance, Pat Carey
Acting Managing Director Information Technology Services, J. Kyle Howard
Vice President of Operation, Jackie Gibbs
Chairman, Timothy M. Chapman
Vice Chairman, Sarah B. Stedfast
Auditors: KPMG LLP RICHMOND VA

LOCATIONS

HQ: VIRGINIA HOUSING DEVELOPMENT AUTHORITY
601 S BELVIDERE ST, RICHMOND, VA 232206504
Phone: 804 780-0789
Web: WWW.VHDA.COM

HISTORICAL FINANCIALS

Company Type: Private

Income Statement

FYE: June 30

	ASSETS ($ mil.)	NET INCOME ($ mil.)	INCOME AS % OF ASSETS	EMPLOYEES
06/16	8,024	171	2.1%	300
06/15	8,070	176	2.2%	—
06/14	8,014	132	1.7%	—
06/13	8,722	111	1.3%	—
Annual Growth	(2.7%)	15.6%	—	—

2016 Year-End Financials

Return on assets: 7.3% Sales ($ mil.): 554
Return on equity: 31.0%

VIRGINIA POLYTECHNIC INSTITUTE & STATE UNIVERSITY

Virginia Polytechnic Institute and State University more commonly known as Virginia Tech is the state's largest university enrolling more than 32000 students. The university offers more than 200 undergraduate graduate and professional degree programs through eight academic colleges. It has a student-teacher ratio of 16 to 1. The school's most popular majors include agriculture business biology animal sciences and engineering. Virginia Tech which was formed in 1872 serves the surrounding community through outreach and education programs.

Operations

Virginia charges $13230 tuition and fees for in-state undergraduates and $31014 tuition and fees for out-of-state undergraduates.

Virginia Tech manages a research portfolio of nearly $500 million. Research is focused on new developments in agriculture biotechnology energy management (including fuel-cell technology and power electronics) information and communication technology transportation and other fields.

Geographic Reach

Virginia Tech has more than 210 campus buildings a 2600-acre main campus in Blacksburg off-campus educational facilities in Alexandria Arlington Falls Church Leesburg Manassas and Middleburg and a study-abroad site in Switzerland. It has about 10 research institutes.

Financial Performance

Virginia Tech's operating revenue increased 1% to $1.03 billion in fiscal 2017 (ended June). The increase was primarily due to a 3% increase in student tuition and fees revenue — thanks to a growing student body as well and an increase in tuition and fee rates — but was partially offset by a 4% decrease in grants and contracts.

Operating expenses totaled $1.4 billion in 2017 a 4% increase from 2016. The university ended the year with $151.4 million in cash and cash equivalents some $112.7 million less than it had at the end of the prior year.

The Virginia Tech Foundation manages the school's endowment which topped $1 billion for the first time in 2018.

Strategy

Virginia Tech's strategic plan focuses on four broad areas: experiential learning diversity and inclusion cross-sector partnerships and philanthropy.

Its initiatives in these areas are part of its goal of becoming one of the top 100 universities in the world. Towards those ends the university has introduced new multidisciplinary undergraduate courses and has increased the percentage of incoming students from underrepresented or underserved groups.

It also continues to improve and expand its campuses with renovations to academic buildings sports facilities and residence halls.

The university will acquire the Virginia Tech Carilion School of Medicine (VTCSOM) in mid-2018. VTCSOM was established from a 10-year private-public partnership with Carilion Clinic.

Company Background

Virginia Tech was founded as a land-grant college in 1872.

EXECUTIVES

SVP and Provost, Mark G. McNamee
VP Finance and CFO, M. Dwight Shelton
VP and Dean Graduate Education, Karen P. DePauw
CEO Virginia Tech Foundation, John E. Dooley
Dean Pamplin College of Business, Robert T. Sumichrast
Dean Virginia-Maryland College of Veterinary Medicine, Cyril Clarke
President, Timothy D. (Tim) Sands
VP Information Technology and CIO, Scott F. Midkiff
Dean College of Agriculture and Life Sciences, Alan Grant
Dean College of Architecture and Urban Studies, A. Jack Davis
Dean College of Engineering, Richard Benson
Dean College of Liberal Arts and Human Sciences, Elizabeth Spiller
Dean College of Natural Resources and Environment, Paul M. Winistorfer
Dean College of Science, Lay Nam Chang
Dean University Libraries, Tyler O. Walters
Associate Vice President, Deborah Day
Chair Department Of Psychology, Robert Stephens
Associate Vice President, Karen Sanders
Secretary, Trina Pauley
Auditors: COMMONWEALTH OF VIRGINIA AUDIT

LOCATIONS

HQ: VIRGINIA POLYTECHNIC INSTITUTE & STATE UNIVERSITY
300 TURNER ST NW STE 4200, BLACKSBURG, VA 240616100
Phone: 540 231-6000

PRODUCTS/OPERATIONS

Selected Colleges

College of Agriculture and Life Sciences
College Architecture and Urban Studies
College of Engineering
College of Liberal Arts and Human Sciences
College of Natural Resources and Environment
College of Science
Pamplin College of Business
Virginia-Maryland Regional College of Veterinary Medicine

HISTORICAL FINANCIALS

Company Type: Private

Income Statement

FYE: June 30

	REVENUE ($ mil.)	NET INCOME ($ mil.)	NET PROFIT MARGIN	EMPLOYEES
06/16	1,020	121	11.9%	6,866
06/15	1,129	114	10.2%	—
Annual Growth	(9.7%)	6.0%	—	—

2016 Year-End Financials

Return on assets: 13.8% Cash ($ mil.): 224
Return on equity: 11.9%
Current ratio: 1.10

VIRGINIA PREMIER HEALTH PLAN, INC.

EXECUTIVES

Chief Executive Officer, Linda Hines
Manager, Audrey Thompson
Engineer, Jim Camp
Director, Jill Cousins
Financial Executive, Angel Moyer
Manager, Joel Blosser
Manager, Suzanne Shelton
Auditors: KPMG LLP MC LEAN VA

LOCATIONS

HQ: VIRGINIA PREMIER HEALTH PLAN, INC.
600 E BROAD ST STE 400, RICHMOND, VA 232191800
Phone: 804 819-5164
Web: WWW.VAPREMIER.COM

HISTORICAL FINANCIALS

Company Type: Private

Income Statement

FYE: June 30

	REVENUE ($ mil.)	NET INCOME ($ mil.)	NET PROFIT MARGIN	EMPLOYEES
06/15	969	(0)	—	165
06/14*	749	14	1.9%	—
12/03	207	3	1.9%	—
12/02	175	5	2.9%	—
Annual Growth	15.3%	—	—	—

*Fiscal year change

2015 Year-End Financials

Return on assets: 11.6% Cash ($ mil.): 194
Return on equity: —
Current ratio: 2.50

VIRGINIA TECH FOUNDATION, INC.

EXECUTIVES

Personnel Manager, Pat Morris
Accountant, Erin Brown
Auditors: KPMG LLP MC LEAN VA

LOCATIONS

HQ: VIRGINIA TECH FOUNDATION, INC.
902 PRICES FORK RD, BLACKSBURG, VA 240603260
Phone: 540 231-2861

HISTORICAL FINANCIALS
Company Type: Private

Income Statement
FYE: June 30

	REVENUE ($ mil.)	NET INCOME ($ mil.)	NET PROFIT MARGIN	EMPLOYEES
06/16	172	(16)	—	40
06/13	137	28	21.0%	—
Annual Growth	7.7%	—	—	—

2016 Year-End Financials
Return on assets: 6.0% Cash ($ mil.): 32
Return on equity: (-9.4%)
Current ratio: 0.60

HISTORICAL FINANCIALS
Company Type: Private

Income Statement
FYE: September 30

	REVENUE ($ mil.)	NET INCOME ($ mil.)	NET PROFIT MARGIN	EMPLOYEES
09/15	219	19	8.9%	247
09/14	198	23	11.6%	—
09/13	224	26	11.6%	—
09/12	265	29	10.9%	—
Annual Growth	(6.1%)	(12.3%)	—	—

2015 Year-End Financials
Return on assets: 11.4% Cash ($ mil.): —
Return on equity: 8.9%
Current ratio: 0.30

HISTORICAL FINANCIALS
Company Type: Private

Income Statement
FYE: June 30

	REVENUE ($ mil.)	NET INCOME ($ mil.)	NET PROFIT MARGIN	EMPLOYEES
06/15	243	7	3.0%	175
06/14	244	12	5.1%	—
06/12	228	15	6.8%	—
06/11	235	13	5.5%	—
Annual Growth	0.9%	(13.3%)	—	—

2015 Year-End Financials
Return on assets: 7.9% Cash ($ mil.): 30
Return on equity: 3.0%
Current ratio: 2.80

VISALIA UNIFIED SCHOOL DISTRICT

EXECUTIVES

Superintendent, Craig Wheaton
Manager, Sheley Knight
Superintendent, Mark Fulmer
Manager, Adam Brown
Director, Mat Brletic
Supervisor, Rene Esquivel
Auditors: CROWE HORWATH LLP SACRAMENTO

LOCATIONS

HQ: VISALIA UNIFIED SCHOOL DISTRICT
5000 W CYPRESS AVE, VISALIA, CA 932778300
Phone: 559 730-7529
Web: WWW.VISALIAEDFOUNDATION.ORG

HISTORICAL FINANCIALS
Company Type: Private

Income Statement
FYE: June 30

	REVENUE ($ mil.)	NET INCOME ($ mil.)	NET PROFIT MARGIN	EMPLOYEES
06/16	333	(14)	—	4,000
06/15	275	35	12.7%	—
06/14	242	(11)	—	—
06/11	228	8	3.6%	—
Annual Growth	7.9%	—	—	—

VOGT POWER INTERNATIONAL INC.

EXECUTIVES

President, Andrew Macgregor
Senior Vice-President, Anthony A Thompson
Vice-President, James B Walder

LOCATIONS

HQ: VOGT POWER INTERNATIONAL INC.
13551 TRITON PARK BLVD # 2000, LOUISVILLE, KY
402234213
Phone: 502 899-4500
Web: WWW.VOGTPOWER.COM

VOLUNTEER ENERGY COOPERATIVE

In the strong tradition of volunteering in Tennessee Volunteer Energy Cooperative is voluntarily cooperating with its members to serve their energy needs. The distribution utility serves more than 109000 customers (who also own the cooperative) in 17 central and eastern Tennessee counties. It operates more than 9000 miles of power lines. Volunteer Energy purchases its power supply from the Tennessee Valley Authority. The company also provides metered natural gas and propane service and offers telecommunications (Internet access and long-distance phone) services. In addition Volunteer Energy offers its customer surge protection and security equipment.

The cooperative grows its customer base by about 2000 new accounts per year. It plans to add a number of electrical substations to keep pace with growing demand.

Volunteer Energy is governed by a board of 12 members who represent the 17 counties in its service area.

Higher rates and increased demand lifted the company's revenue and net income in 2011 despite the extra costs incurred by infrastructure damage caused by six tornados that ripped through the cooperative's service area in April 2011.

Volunteer Energy was formed as Meigs County Electric Membership Cooperative in 1935 largely at the prompting of Tennessee Agricultural Extension Agent for Meigs County Willis Shadow.

EXECUTIVES

Vice President Information Technology, Karen Zitek
Vice President Information Technology, Karen Davis
Auditors: HENDERSON HUTCHERSON & MCCULLO

LOCATIONS

HQ: VOLUNTEER ENERGY COOPERATIVE
18359 STATE HIGHWAY 58 N, DECATUR, TN
373227825
Phone: 423 334-1020
Web: WWW.VEC.ORG

COMPETITORS

CenturyLink   Southern Company Gas
Crestwood Equity

W. A. FOOTE MEMORIAL HOSPITAL

EXECUTIVES

President, Georgia Fojtasek
Director, Steven Bachman
Office Manager, Ann Brown

LOCATIONS

HQ: W. A. FOOTE MEMORIAL HOSPITAL
205 N EAST AVE, JACKSON, MI 492011753
Phone: 517 788-4800
Web: WWW.ALLEGIANCEHEALTH.ORG

HISTORICAL FINANCIALS
Company Type: Private

Income Statement
FYE: June 30

	REVENUE ($ mil.)	NET INCOME ($ mil.)	NET PROFIT MARGIN	EMPLOYEES
06/15	462	(2)	—	3,500
06/09	371	(63)	—	—
06/08	338	(53)	—	—
06/07	1,531	0	—	—
Annual Growth	—	—	—	—

2015 Year-End Financials
Return on assets: 7.8% Cash ($ mil.): 14
Return on equity: (-0.6%)
Current ratio: 0.80

W. DOUGLASS DISTRIBUTING, LTD.

EXECUTIVES

General Partner, William P Douglass
Manager, Bob Appolito

LOCATIONS

HQ: W. DOUGLASS DISTRIBUTING, LTD.
325 E FOREST AVE, SHERMAN, TX 750908832
Phone: 903 893-1181
Web: WWW.BK.COM

HISTORICAL FINANCIALS

Company Type: Private

Income Statement

FYE: December 31

	REVENUE ($ mil.)	NET INCOME ($ mil.)	NET PROFIT MARGIN	EMPLOYEES
12/15	259	1	0.6%	130
12/14	403	0	0.2%	—
12/13	428	1	0.3%	—
12/12	422	0	0.1%	—
Annual Growth	(15.0%)	36.9%	—	—

2015 Year-End Financials

Return on assets: 3.2% Cash ($ mil.): 2
Return on equity: 0.6%
Current ratio: 0.70

W. K. KELLOGG FOUNDATION

Charitable grants from W.K. Kellogg Foundation are grrrrrrrrreat! Founded in 1930 by cereal industry pioneer Will Keith Kellogg the foundation provides more than $300 million in grants annually to programs focused on youth and education health food systems and rural development and philanthropy and volunteerism. About two-thirds of its grants go to initiatives in the US (mostly in Michigan Mississippi and New Mexico) although it also serves others through grants in Latin America Mexico the Caribbean Brazil and South Africa. The work of the W.K. Kellogg Foundation is supported by a related trust; together they have assets of more than $9 billion — mainly in Kellogg Company stock.

With a rise in Kellogg Company stock prices throughout 2009 the foundation stands to benefit. Although they share a founder and a home city the Kellogg Foundation and the Kellogg Company are governed independently.

Charity really does begin at home for the W.K. Kellogg Foundation which allocated about 18% of its US grant money to activities in Michigan in 2008.

W.K. Kellogg Foundation is guided by its founder's desire "to help people help themselves" and prefers to support programs that offer long-term solutions rather than quick handouts.

HISTORY

Born in 1860 Will Keith Kellogg began his career with jobs as a stock boy and traveling broom salesman. He also worked as a clerk (and later bookkeeper and manager) at the Battle Creek Sanitarium a renowned homeopathic hospital where his older brother John Harvey Kellogg was physician-in-chief. The brothers' experiments to improve vegetarian diets led to a happy accident in 1894 that resulted in the first wheat flakes. In 1906 W.K. Kellogg started the Battle Creek Toasted Corn Flake Company. Through marketing genius and innovative products Kellogg's company became a leader in the industry.

A philanthropist by inclination Kellogg established the Fellowship Corporation in 1925 to build an agricultural school and a bird sanctuary as well as to set up an experimental farm and a reforestation project. He also gave $3 million to hometown causes such as the Ann J. Kellogg School for disabled children and for the construction of an auditorium a junior high school and a youth recreation center.

After attending a White House Conference on Child Health and Protection Kellogg established the W.K. Kellogg Child Welfare Foundation in 1930. A few months later he broadened the focus of the charter and renamed the institution the W.K. Kellogg Foundation. That year the foundation began its landmark Michigan Community Health Project (MCHP) which opened public health departments in counties once thought too small and poor to sustain them. In 1934 Kellogg placed more than $66 million in Kellogg Company stock and other investments in a trust to fund his foundation.

During WWII the foundation expanded its programming to Latin America funding advanced schooling for dentists physicians and other health professionals. After the war it broadened its programming to include agriculture to help war-torn Europe. It funded projects in Germany Iceland Ireland Norway and the UK. Following Kellogg's death in 1951 the organization began providing support for graduate programs in health and hospital administration as well as for rural leadership and community colleges.

During the 1970s the foundation lent its support to the growing volunteerism movement and to aiding the disadvantaged with a special emphasis on programs for minorities. A review of operations in the late 1970s led the Kellogg Foundation to reassert its emphasis on health education agriculture and leadership. The foundation also expanded its programs to southern Africa.

In 1986 the Kellogg Foundation began funding the Rural America Initiative — a series of 28 projects meant to develop leadership train local government officials and revitalize rural areas. William Richardson became president and CEO of the foundation in 1995 leaving his post as president of The Johns Hopkins University. Also during the 1990s the foundation supported the Community-Based Public Health Initiative which assisted universities in educating public health professionals by presenting community-based approaches to students and faculty.

In 1998 the organization announced a five-year $55 million plan to bring health care to the nation's poor and homeless. Also that year it gave Portland State University a $600000 grant to develop its Institute for Nonprofit Management. In 1999 the Kellogg Foundation started its first geographically based program pledging $15 million in grants for development of Mississippi River Delta communities in Arkansas Louisiana and Mississippi. In 2001 the foundation pledged an additional $20 million to support economic growth in the region through the Emerging Markets Partnership. In 2002 the Kellogg Foundation awarded about $2 million in grants to SPARK (Supporting Partnerships to Assure Ready Kids) to help prepare low-income children for school. The organization funded a national campaign to improve men's health in 2003.

After a decade as president and CEO Richardson stepped down in 2005. Sterling Speirn who had led the San Mateo California-based Peninsula Community Foundation since 1990 took over as president and CEO of the Kellogg Foundation in January 2006.

EXECUTIVES

Chief Executive Officer, Sterling K Speirn
Board of Directors, Aranthan Jones II
Auditors: MITCHELL & TITUS LLP CHICAGO

LOCATIONS

HQ: W. K. KELLOGG FOUNDATION
1 MICHIGAN AVE E, BATTLE CREEK, MI 490174012
Phone: 269 968-1611
Web: WWW.WKKF.ORG

HISTORICAL FINANCIALS

Company Type: Private

Income Statement

FYE: August 31

	REVENUE ($ mil.)	NET INCOME ($ mil.)	NET PROFIT MARGIN	EMPLOYEES
08/15	350	(5)	—	200
08/13	329	92	28.0%	—
08/12	359	(106)	—	—
08/11	369	(13)	—	—
Annual Growth	(1.3%)	—	—	—

2015 Year-End Financials

Return on assets: 1.9% Cash ($ mil.): 27
Return on equity: (-1.7%)
Current ratio: —

W. M. LYLES CO.

EXECUTIVES

President, David Dawson
Director, John Driscoll
Accountant, Nicole Leasure
Vice-President, Ken Strosnider
Auditors: CUTTONE AND MASTRO FRESNO CA

LOCATIONS

HQ: W. M. LYLES CO.
1210 W OLIVE AVE, FRESNO, CA 937282816
Phone: 559 441-1900

HISTORICAL FINANCIALS

Company Type: Private

Income Statement

FYE: September 30

	REVENUE ($ mil.)	NET INCOME ($ mil.)	NET PROFIT MARGIN	EMPLOYEES
09/15	241	14	6.0%	340
09/14	156	5	3.7%	—
09/13	87	1	2.0%	—
09/12	90	4	4.6%	—
Annual Growth	38.7%	51.7%	—	—

2015 Year-End Financials

Return on assets: 12.8% Cash ($ mil.): —
Return on equity: 6.0%
Current ratio: 0.60

W.S. BADCOCK CORPORATION

W.S. Badcock furnishes homes down in Dixie and beyond. As one of the largest privately-owned furniture retailers in the US the company sells furniture for every room in the house. It sells its furniture and accessories through more than 300 stores that operate under the banner names Badcock Home Furnishing Centers and Badcock &more. Aside from its e-commerce site Badcock's stores network extends to nearly 10 southeastern states. Stores also carry appliances lawn equipment electronics mattresses rugs bedding lighting wall art and other decorative accessories. The company was founded by Henry S. Badcock in 1904 as a

general mercantile store. Today it is in its fourth generation of family management.

Geographic Reach

Headquartered in Mulberry Florida with more than 1200 corporate employees W.S. Badcock operates primarily in the southeastern US. Its operations span the states of Georgia Alabama Mississippi Tennessee and the Carolinas expanding into Virginia West Virginia and Kentucky.

Strategy

Through the company's dealer business model more than 80% of Badcock's stores are individually owned. As part of the model the company does not require a franchise fee but instead consigns merchandise to the dealers. As opposed to the typical franchise system startup this consignment method aims to allow for a quicker startup along with the benefits of business ownership.

Already established in half a dozen states Badcock has been expanding its store network in Virginia Kentucky and West Virginia. Despite a slowdown in its expansion plans amid the recession and downturn in furniture retailing the company aims to grow its stores network again throughout the Southeast.

EXECUTIVES

Vice President Legal, Phil Bayt
Vice President Human Resources, Lori Walsh
Executive Vice President of Marketing, Bill Daughtrey
Vice President, Nancy Young
Vice President Dealer Operations, Mitchell Stiles
Auditors: KPMG LLP TAMPA FL

LOCATIONS

HQ: W.S. BADCOCK CORPORATION
205 NW 2ND ST, MULBERRY, FL 338602405
Phone: 863 425-4921
Web: WWW.BADCOCK.COM

PRODUCTS/OPERATIONS

Selected Products
Accessories
Appliances
Electronics
Furniture
Mattresses

COMPETITORS

Aaron's Inc.	Ethan Allen
Ashley Furniture	Havertys
Baer's Furniture	Klaussner Furniture
Bassett Furniture	La-Z-Boy
City Furniture	Rooms To Go
El Dorado Furniture	Sealy

HISTORICAL FINANCIALS

Company Type: Private

Income Statement				FYE: June 30
	REVENUE ($ mil.)	NET INCOME ($ mil.)	NET PROFIT MARGIN	EMPLOYEES
06/16	681	25	3.8%	1,500
06/15	600	19	3.3%	—
06/14	518	11	2.3%	—
06/13	463	6	1.5%	—
Annual Growth	13.7%	54.5%	—	—

2016 Year-End Financials

Return on assets: 7.0%   Cash ($ mil.): —
Return on equity: 3.8%
Current ratio: 3.00

WABASH VALLEY POWER ASSOCIATION INC

EXECUTIVES

Chief Executive Officer, Rick Coons
Financial Executive, Theresa Young
Director, Brian Anderson
Auditors: DELOITTE & TOUCHE LLP INDIANA

LOCATIONS

HQ: WABASH VALLEY POWER ASSOCIATION INC
722 N HIGH SCHOOL RD, INDIANAPOLIS, IN 462143756
Phone: 317 481-2800
Web: WWW.WVPA.COM

HISTORICAL FINANCIALS

Company Type: Private

Income Statement				FYE: December 31
	REVENUE ($ mil.)	NET INCOME ($ mil.)	NET PROFIT MARGIN	EMPLOYEES
12/15	740	18	2.4%	65
12/14	821	17	2.2%	—
12/13	739	19	2.6%	—
12/10	750	14	1.9%	—
Annual Growth	(0.3%)	5.2%	—	—

2015 Year-End Financials

Return on assets: 9.3%   Cash ($ mil.): 60
Return on equity: 2.4%
Current ratio: 1.00

WACHTER, INC.

EXECUTIVES

Chairman, Brad Botteron
Account Manager, Staci Wilson
Account Manager, Tina True
Account Manager, Greg Bornhorst
Operations Manager, John Hufford
Auditors: MAYER HOFFMAN MCCANN PC KANSA

LOCATIONS

HQ: WACHTER, INC.
16001 W 99TH ST, LENEXA, KS 662191293
Phone: 913 541-2500
Web: WWW.WACHTER.COM

HISTORICAL FINANCIALS

Company Type: Private

Income Statement				FYE: December 31
	REVENUE ($ mil.)	NET INCOME ($ mil.)	NET PROFIT MARGIN	EMPLOYEES
12/15	229	19	8.7%	1,210
12/14	192	11	5.8%	—
12/13	176	4	2.6%	—
12/12	149	0	0.2%	—
Annual Growth	15.2%	309.0%	—	—

2015 Year-End Financials

Return on assets: 4.4%   Cash ($ mil.): 16
Return on equity: 8.7%
Current ratio: 2.20

WACO INDEPENDENT SCHOOL DISTRICT

EXECUTIVES

President, Pat Atkins
Board of Directors, Linda Scott
Board of Directors, Sammy Smith
Plant & Facilities Manager, Rolando Gomez
Supervisor, David Ellis
Auditors: WEAVER AND TIDWELL LLP CO

LOCATIONS

HQ: WACO INDEPENDENT SCHOOL DISTRICT
501 FRANKLIN AVE OFC, WACO, TX 767012151
Phone: 254 755-9473
Web: WWW.WACOISD.ORG

HISTORICAL FINANCIALS

Company Type: Private

Income Statement				FYE: August 31
	REVENUE ($ mil.)	NET INCOME ($ mil.)	NET PROFIT MARGIN	EMPLOYEES
08/16	179	2	1.3%	3,000
08/13	157	(6)	—	—
08/12	157	(14)	—	—
08/11	0	0	—	—
Annual Growth	—	404.1%	—	—

2016 Year-End Financials

Return on assets: 2.0%   Cash ($ mil.): 57
Return on equity: 1.3%
Current ratio: —

WAKE FOREST UNIVERSITY

Demon Deacons may sound like a weary clergyman's nightmare but at Wake Forest they're something to cheer about. Wake Forest University (WFU) home of the Demon Deacon mascot is a private liberal arts institution that operates through about half a dozen colleges and schools: law medicine arts and sciences business and accountancy management and divinity. WFU provides more than 35 majors and offers a low student-faculty ratio of 11:1. Its 7700 students can also study abroad in France Spain Japan and Cuba among other countries. WFU was established in 1834 in Wake Forest North Carolina. It moved to its present location in Winston-Salem in 1956.

Operations

With more than 480 teaching faculty members WFU is ranked among the top 30 universities in the nation. It offers nearly 30 graduate-level programs and about a dozen areas of PhD study. Its graduate schools include those in arts and sciences law medicine management and divinity. It conducts its executive education programs including its evening and Saturday MBA degree programs at the Wake Forest University Charlotte Center the former International Trade Center building located at 200 North College St. that WFU has leased through Bank of America since 2011.

Geographic Reach

The school has several primary and affiliate campuses — Wake Forest main campus Wake Forest University Baptist Medical Center Piedmont Triad

Research Park BB&T Field and The Reynolda Campus — all located in Winston-Salem North Carolina. WFU also operates university-owned properties for students studying abroad in Venice Vienna and London. The university extends its reach to France Spain Cuba and Japan through alliances with other universities. WFU students come from 48 US states and Washington DC and 46 other countries.

Sales and Marketing

Since 1986 the university has produced nearly a dozen Rhodes Scholars and several Marshall and Fulbright recipients. More than half of WFU's student body spends at least one semester studying abroad. They stay in houses owned by the university in London Venice or Vienna or they study at partner universities in Cuba Spain Japan or France.

Financial Performance

The not-for-profit university posted revenue of $1.4 billion in fiscal 2016 (ended June) compared to $1.2 billion a year earlier thanks to higher tuition and fees grants contributions and patient revenue among others. Operating excess declined from $48.1 million to $32.5 million as higher revenue topped a stronger increase costs in wages services and clinical and laboratory supplies.

Strategy

WFU's capital campaign are targeted toward scholarships faculty research strengthening the university's libraries and the construction of new facilities.

EXECUTIVES

President, Nathan O. Hatch
Associate VP Information Technology and CIO, Mur Muchane
CEO Wake Forest Baptist Medical Center, John D. McConnell, age 63
Provost, Rogan Kersh
EVP Finance and Administration and CFO, Hof Milam
Dean of the Divinity School, Gail R. O'Day
Dean School of Medicine, Edward Abraham
Dean Z. Smith Reynolds Library, Lynn Sutton
Dean School of Business, Charles L. Iacovou
Interim Dean School of Law, Suzanne Reynolds
Dean Graduate Programs in Arts and Sciences, Brad Jones
Dean Graduate Programs in Biomedical Sciences, Dwayne Godwin
Co-Interim Dean of the College, Randall G. (Randy) Rogan
Co-Interim Dean of the College, Rebecca S. Thomas
Assistant Vice President Hospitality S, John Wise
Vice President, Mark Petersen
Vice President for Career Development, Andrew Chan
Vice President Campus Life, Penny Rue
Assistant Vice President Director of Advancement Services, Snyder Tim
Vice President, Peter Marsh
Associate Vice President Student Life, Mary Gerardy
Vice President for Student Life and Instructional Resources, Kenneth Zick
Associate Vice President and Editor at, Glenda Henson
Associate Vice President And Director of University Development office of University Advancement, Bob Baker
Director of Nursing, Kathryn Carstens
Assistant Vice President Gift Planning and Marketing, Shaida Horner
Assistant Vice President Human Resources Services, ANGELA CULLER
Associate Vice President, John Shenette
Vice President Assistant, Shayla Herndon

Associate Vice President For Information Technology and Chief Officer Information Systems Department, Mary Muchane
Chair Board of Trustees, Donald E. Flow
Vice Chair Board of Trustees, Bobby R. Burchfield
Vice Chair Board of Trustees, Donna A. Boswell
Assistant Treasurer, Craig Thomas
Secretary, Cecilia H Solano
Auditors: KPMG LLP GREENSBORO NC

LOCATIONS

HQ: WAKE FOREST UNIVERSITY
1834 WAKE FOREST RD, WINSTON SALEM, NC 271096000
Phone: 336 758-5000
Web: WWW.WFU.EDU

PRODUCTS/OPERATIONS

Selected Schools
Graduate School
School of Business
School of Divinity
School of Law
School of Medicine
Undergraduate College

HISTORICAL FINANCIALS

Company Type: Private

Income Statement				FYE: June 30
	REVENUE ($ mil.)	NET INCOME ($ mil.)	NET PROFIT MARGIN	EMPLOYEES
06/16	1,339	5	0.4%	4,860
06/13	496	82	16.6%	—
06/11	459	77	16.9%	—
Annual Growth	23.9%	(41.4%)	—	—

2016 Year-End Financials

Return on assets: 18.9%   Cash ($ mil.): 95
Return on equity: 0.4%
Current ratio: —

WAKEFERN FOOD CORP.

Grocery stores getting supplies from this co-op may be on the "Rite" track. Wakefern Food is the largest member-owned wholesale distribution cooperative in the US supplying groceries and other merchandise to more than 250 supermarkets under the ShopRite and The Fresh Grocer banners in New Jersey New York Connecticut Delaware Maryland Pennsylvania and Virginia. It also operates more than 50 PriceRite stores in these states plus Rhode Island and Massachusetts. Beyond supplying its member-owned stores Wakerfern distributes products to other supermarkets across the northeastern US and Bermuda. Founded by seven grocers in 1946 the coop now boasts 50 members 70000-plus employees and over $15 billion in annual sales.

Operations

Wakefern Food supplies retail and wholesale members mostly in the Northeast US. PriceRite a subsidiary of Wakefern Food and its nearly 50 supermarkets offer over 500 grocery items at discounted prices such as fresh fruits and vegetables breads prepackaged meat and seafood kosher products and national brands. Stores average about 35000 square feet in size which are smaller than traditional supermarkets. While the vast majority of ShopRite brand stores are member owned subsidiary ShopRite Supermarkets Inc operates nearly 35 company-owned stores.

Sales and Marketing

The coop added its 50th member The Fresh Grocer in July 2013. Outside of its members the company also supplies grocery stores like Saker ShopRite (New Jersey) Village Super Market (New Jersey and Pennsylvania) and Inserra Supermarkets (New York and New Jersey).

Financial Performance

Wakern Food's revenues have been rising over the past several years thanks to new member additions and their store openings.

The company's retail sales rose 4% to a record $14.7 billion in fiscal 2014 (ended September 27) thanks to the addition of six new ShopRite stores five new PriceRite discount supermarkets and six new The Fresh Grocer stores over the course of the year. The company also continued to expand its ShopRite from Home services store reach which would be provided from a total of 214 of its stores.

Strategy

Like other grocery wholesalers Wakefern Food's success depends on its ability to distribute goods at the lowest possible cost to its customers meaning the company focuses on keeping expenses low and improving efficiencies throughout its supply operation. But as a member-owned cooperative the company differs from other wholesalers such as Nash-Finch in that its primary focus is on its member stores. Wakefern Food also has the added responsibility of promoting its ShopRite retail chain and helping its member retailers expand the chain's footprint.

The ShopRite chain boasts a loyal following in its core markets but the supermarkets have been feeling the pinch from rivals in the price-competitive grocery business. The company is especially feeling pressure from non-supermarket chains such as Wal-Mart CVS Health and Wawa. To help boost customer loyalty Wakefern has turned to new technology in the form of mobile applications (developed in partnership with technology firm MyWebGrocer) for the Apple iPhone that allow users to get alerts about weekly store specials in their area. The company also rolled out an online pharmacy where customers can place orders through the Internet.

Company Background

Wakefern Food announced in 2012 it was supplying New York-based Food Bazaar stores which had supermarkets in New York New Jersey and Connecticut. Wakefern will supply ShopRite private label brands along with non-private labels such as dairy frozen food grocery nonfoods and specialty products.

HISTORY

Wakefern Food was founded in 1946 by seven New York- and New Jersey-based grocers: Louis Weiss Sam and Al Aidekman Abe Kesselman Dave Fern Sam Garb and Albert Goldberg. The company got its name by taking the first letters of the last names of five of the original founders (Weiss Sam and Al Aidekman Kesselman and Fern). Like many cooperatives the association sought to lower costs by increasing its buying power as a group.

They each put in $1000 and began operating a 5000-sq.-ft. warehouse often putting in double time to keep both their stores and the warehouse running. The shopkeepers' collective buying power proved valuable enabling the grocers to stock many items at the same prices as their larger competitors.

In 1951 Wakefern members began pooling their resources to buy advertising space. A common store name — ShopRite — was chosen and each week co-op members met to decide which items would be sale priced. Within a year membership had grown to over 50. Expansion became a priority and in the mid-1950s co-op members united in small groups to take over failed super-

markets. One such group called the Supermarkets Operating Co. (SOC) was formed in 1956. Within 10 years it had acquired a number of failed stores remodeled them and given them the ShopRite name.

During the late 1950s sales at ShopRite stores slumped after Wakefern decided to buck the supermarket trend of offering trading stamps (which could then be exchanged for gifts) figuring that offering the stamps would ultimately lead to higher food prices. The move initially drove away customers but Wakefern cut grocery prices across the board and sales returned. The company did embrace another supermarket trend: stocking stores with nonfood items.

The co-op was severely shaken in 1966 when SOC merged with General Supermarkets a similar small group within Wakefern becoming Supermarkets General Corp. (SGC). SGC was a powerful entity with 71 supermarkets 10 drugstores six gas stations a wholesale bakery and a discount department store. Many Wakefern members opposed the merger and attempted to block the action with a court order. By 1968 SGC had beefed up its operations to include department store chains as well as its grocery stores. In a move that threatened to break Wakefern SGC broke away from the co-op and its stores were renamed Pathmark.

Wakefern not only weathered the storm it grew under the direction of chairman and CEO Thomas Infusino elected shortly after the split. The co-op focused on asserting its position as a seller of low-priced products. Wakefern developed private-label brands including the ShopRite brand. In the 1980s members began operating larger stores and adding more nonfood items to the ShopRite product mix. With its number of superstores on the rise and facing increased competition from club stores in 1992 Wakefern opened a centralized nonfood distribution center in New Jersey.

In 1995 30-year Wakefern veteran Dean Janeway was elected president of the co-op. The company debuted its ShopRite MasterCard co-branded with New Jersey's Valley National Bank in 1996. The following year the co-op purchased two of its customers' stores in Pennsylvania then threatened to close them when contract talks with the local union deteriorated. In 1998 Wakefern settled the dispute then sold the stores.

The company partnered with Internet bidding site Priceline in 1999 offering customers an opportunity to bid on groceries and then pick them up at ShopRite stores. Big V Wakefern's biggest customer filed for Chapter 11 bankruptcy protection in 2000 and said it was ending its distribution agreement with the co-op. In July 2002 however Wakefern's ShopRite Supermarkets subsidiary acquired all of Big V's assets for approximately $185 million in cash and assumed liabilities.

Infusino retired in May 2005 after 35 years with Wakefern Food. He was succeeded by former vice chairman Joseph Colalillo. The cooperative added to its footprint in 2007 when it acquired about 10 underperforming retail locations from Stop & Shop. The stores located mostly in South Jersey were rebranded under the ShopRite banner.

EXECUTIVES

Vice President, Robert Rohlander
Vice President Deli And Seafood, Terry Sharkey
Vice President Of Finance, Steven Savas
Vice President Quality Assurance Food Safety, Michael Ambrosio
Vice President Finance, Neil Falcone
Vice President Dairy Deli and Frozen Food Division, Jeff Reagan
Vice President of Administration, Shawn Ravitz
Auditors: KPMG LLP SHORT HILLS NJ

LOCATIONS

HQ: WAKEFERN FOOD CORP.
5000 RIVERSIDE DR, KEASBEY, NJ 088321209
Phone: 908 527-3300
Web: WWW.PRICERITESUPERMARKETS.COM

PRODUCTS/OPERATIONS

2012 Corporate Stores

	No.
PriceRite	48
ShopRite	40
Total	**88**

COMPETITORS

A&P	IGA
Acme Markets	Krasdale Foods
Bozzuto's	SUPERVALU
C&S Wholesale	Stop & Shop
CVS	Wal-Mart
Hannaford Bros.	Wawa Inc.

HISTORICAL FINANCIALS

Company Type: Private

Income Statement

FYE: October 3

	REVENUE ($ mil.)	NET INCOME ($ mil.)	NET PROFIT MARGIN	EMPLOYEES
10/15*	12,573	5	0.0%	3,500
09/14	11,871	5	0.0%	—
09/13	11,455	0	0.0%	—
09/12	11,010	5	0.0%	—
Annual Growth	4.5%	(0.0%)	—	—

*Fiscal year change

2015 Year-End Financials

Return on assets: 6.9%   Cash ($ mil.): 138
Return on equity: —
Current ratio: 0.30

WAKEMED

If you wake up in a hospital in Wake County North Carolina you may be at one of WakeMed health system's facilities. WakeMed is a network of medical centers including two hospitals outpatient and emergency clinics rehabilitation facilities skilled nursing centers laboratories physicians' offices and home care service agencies. Its hospitals the WakeMed Raleigh Campus and the WakeMed Cary Hospital include specialty divisions such as heart care stroke trauma critical care diabetes asthma and children's and women's centers. Combined its facilities offer more than 900 beds. WakeMed also conducts research and medical training programs.

Operations

WakeMed's a network of health care facilities include a 575-bed regional referral center with an adjoining 84-bed rehabilitation hospital in Raleigh; a 156-bed full-service community hospital in Cary; a freestanding emergency department outpatient surgery and diagnostic center with physicians' offices in North Raleigh; freestanding emergency departments and diagnostic centers in Apex Brier Creek and Garner; Raleigh Medical Park a pre-admission testing site adjacent to the Raleigh campus hospital; a medical office building with diagnostic and outpatient rehabilitation services in Clayton and Holly Springs; a medical office building with diagnostic outpatient rehabilitation and physician offices in West Raleigh; a mobile critical care transport service including an air ambulance service; and home health and outpatient rehabilitation serv-

ices in Raleigh Cary Apex Zebulon and Fuquay-Varina.

These facilities handle about 46000 inpatient visits 7500 births and 249000 emergency room visits each year. The system's pediatric emergency room (located in the Raleigh Campus' children's hospital wing) sees about 40000 children per year. Other units provide mobile critical care and emergency transportation by ground and air. The organization also provides some $244 million in community benefits each year as well including charity care unpaid Medicare bills health profession education and improvement and outreach programs.

WakeMed's medical staff includes more than 1000 affiliated physicians and 1000 volunteers. The WakeMed Physician Practices organization includes about 260 doctors who operate primary care and specialist offices in the region.

Geographic Reach

The company facilities throughout Wake and Johnston counties include Raleigh Campus Cary Hospital North Healthplex Apex Healthplex Brier Creek Healthplex Garner Healthplexa and Clayton Medical Park.

Strategy

In 2014 the company completed the construction on an expansion at WakeMed North Healthplex in Raleigh North Carolina. The $66.3 million project transformed the facility into a full-service facility called WakeMed North Hospital. The five-story 131000-square-foot 61-bed acute care hospital focuses on inpatient women's specialty services and offer a range of obstetric and gynecological services including comprehensive preventive diagnostic and therapeutic care. In addition WakeMed North Hospital will continue to serve men and children through the facility's existing emergency department and outpatient surgery rehabilitation imaging lab and physician services.

Company Background

The company has expanded its Raleigh Campus to include a new patient tower with intensive care cardiac care and pediatric facilities. Construction of the patient tower — featuring two new heart and vascular inpatient floors a mother's milk bank and Wake County's only dedicated Children's Hospital — was completed in 2010. The organization expanded its pediatric services further in 2012 when it formed a partnership with Duke Medicine to provide collaborative specialist care to children in the region. In addition WakeMed expanded the Raleigh Campus' rehabilitation unit in 2012 and 2013 by adding additional patient beds.

To expand its outpatient facilities WakeMed opened a sixth emergency department in 2011 at the Brier Creek Healthplex adding a dozen private rooms diagnostic imaging units lab services and doctors' offices. In 2012 the system added a new diagnostic clinic and an outpatient surgery center near the Raleigh Campus.

WakeMed was founded in 1961.

EXECUTIVES

President and CEO, Donald R. Gintzig
EVP Finance and CFO, Michael D. DeVaughn
Senior VP Physician Services, John S. Piatkowski
EVP Operations and Ambulatory Development, Kathleen K. Gormley
VP; SVP President and CEO Harnett Health System, Kenneth Bryan
EVP and COO, Tom Gettinger
Secretary Supplemental Staffing, Keri Raper
Auditors: ERNST & YOUNG US LLP CHARLOTT

LOCATIONS

HQ: WAKEMED
3000 NEW BERN AVE G100, RALEIGH, NC 276101231
Phone: 919 350-8000
Web: WWW.WAKEMED.ORG

PRODUCTS/OPERATIONS

Selected North Carolina Facilities
Blue Ridge Surgery Center (Raleigh)
Brier Creek Healthplex (Raleigh)
Knightdale Medical Building (Knightdale)
WakeMed Apex Healthplex (Apex)
WakeMed Brier Creek Medical Park (Raleigh)
WakeMed Cary Hospital (Cary)
WakeMed Clayton Medical Park (Clayton)
WakeMed Fuquay-Varina Outpatient and Skilled Nursing
  Facility (Fuquay-Varina)
WakeMed Garner HealthPlex (Garner)
WakeMed Home Health (Raleigh)
WakeMed North Healthplex (Raleigh)
WakeMed Raleigh Campus (Raleigh)
  WakeMed Rehab Hospital (Raleigh)
WakeMed Wake Forest Road Outpatient Rehab Center
  (Raleigh)
WakeMed Zebulon/Wendell Outpatient and Skilled
  Nursing Facility (Zebulon)

COMPETITORS

Carolinas HealthCare System
Cone Health
Cumberland County Hospital System
Duke University Health System
FirstHealth of the Carolinas
Morehead Memorial Hospital
Novant Health
Rex Healthcare
Rowan Regional Medical Center
Vidant Health
Wake Forest University Baptist Medical Center

HISTORICAL FINANCIALS
Company Type: Private

Income Statement
FYE: September 30

	REVENUE ($ mil.)	NET INCOME ($ mil.)	NET PROFIT MARGIN	EMPLOYEES
09/15	1,065	(32)	—	7,933
09/09	883	0	—	—
09/08	837	12	1.5%	—
Annual Growth	3.5%	—	—	—

2015 Year-End Financials
Return on assets: 13.0%
Return on equity: (-3.1%)
Current ratio: 1.10
Cash ($ mil.): 467

WARREN DISTRIBUTION, INC.

EXECUTIVES

Board of Directors, Abraham N Schlott
Manager, Donna Weeda
Plant Engineering Manager, Stan Rogers
Manager, Charles P Downei
Finance Manager, Jim Takakuwa
General Manager, David Carrington
Auditors: BKD LLP OMAHA NEBRASKA

LOCATIONS

HQ: WARREN DISTRIBUTION, INC.
727 S 13TH ST, OMAHA, NE 681023204
Phone: 402 341-9397
Web: WWW.WARRENDISTRIBUTION.COM

HISTORICAL FINANCIALS
Company Type: Private

Income Statement
FYE: February 28

	REVENUE ($ mil.)	NET INCOME ($ mil.)	NET PROFIT MARGIN	EMPLOYEES
02/15	407	(15)	—	600
02/14	450	8	1.9%	—
02/13	485	10	2.1%	—
02/12	470	5	1.1%	—
Annual Growth	(4.7%)	—	—	—

2015 Year-End Financials
Return on assets: 4.4%
Return on equity: (-3.8%)
Current ratio: 1.60
Cash ($ mil.): 7

WARREN RURAL ELECTRIC COOPERATIVE CORPORATION

This Warren needs no commission just a cooperative in order to deliver electric results to the people. Warren Rural Electric Cooperative Corporation (Warren RECC) provides its member customers with electricity security systems and surge suppression equipment as well as with floodlighting and street lighting. It offers propane through non-affiliated Propane Energy Partners. The co-op serves more than 55300 customers in an eight-county service area (Barren Butler Edmonson Grayson Logan Ohio Simpson and Warren counties) in rural south-central Kentucky. Warren RECC is affiliated with the Tennessee Valley Authority and a member of Touchstone Energy a 600-member alliance of electricity co-ops.

After ice storms in early 2009 knocked out power to the area (Warren county was declared a disaster area) Warren RECC received a $6.5 million FEMA grant to help with associated repair costs. The coop spent about $15 replacing snapped poles and repair hundreds of miles of lines; it typically budgets about $200000 annually for repair work.

EXECUTIVES

Chief Executive Officer, W Scott Ramsey
Chief Executive Officer, David Anderson
Vice-President, Tom Martin
Vice-President, Dewayne McDonald
Vice-President, Rick Starks
Manager, Tami Cohron
Manager, Heather Foley
Auditors: ALEXANDER THOMPSON ARNOLD PLLC

LOCATIONS

HQ: WARREN RURAL ELECTRIC COOPERATIVE
CORPORATION
951 FAIRVIEW AVE, BOWLING GREEN, KY
421014937
Phone: 270 842-6541
Web: WWW.WRECC.COM

COMPETITORS

AmeriGas Partners   Kenergy
Duke Energy Kentucky

HISTORICAL FINANCIALS
Company Type: Private

Income Statement
FYE: June 30

	REVENUE ($ mil.)	NET INCOME ($ mil.)	NET PROFIT MARGIN	EMPLOYEES
06/15*	182	5	3.0%	165
12/14	187	5	3.0%	—
06/14	184	4	2.7%	—
06/13	177	4	2.7%	—
Annual Growth	1.4%	6.9%	—	—

*Fiscal year change

2015 Year-End Financials
Return on assets: 14.2%
Return on equity: 3.0%
Current ratio: 1.50
Cash ($ mil.): 25

WASHINGTON COUNTY BOARD OF EDUCATION

EXECUTIVES

President, Donna Brightman
Auditors: SMITH ELLIOTT KEARNS & COMPANY

LOCATIONS

HQ: WASHINGTON COUNTY BOARD OF EDUCATION
10435 DOWNSVILLE PIKE, HAGERSTOWN, MD
217401732
Phone: 301 766-2800
Web: WWW.WCPSHR.COM

HISTORICAL FINANCIALS
Company Type: Private

Income Statement
FYE: June 30

	REVENUE ($ mil.)	NET INCOME ($ mil.)	NET PROFIT MARGIN	EMPLOYEES
06/15	310	6	2.1%	138
06/14	306	(1)	—	—
06/13	289	(3)	—	—
06/12	289	3	1.2%	—
Annual Growth	2.3%	24.6%	—	—

2015 Year-End Financials
Return on assets: 1.8%
Return on equity: 2.1%
Current ratio: —
Cash ($ mil.): 26

WASHINGTON COUNTY SCHOOL DISTRICT

EXECUTIVES

President, Curtis Jensen
Board of Directors, Marshall Topham
Board of Directors, Diane Tyler
Plant & Facilities Manager, Phil Williams

Manager, Tom Hiatt
Auditors: SAVAGE ESPLIN & RADMALL PC SA

LOCATIONS

HQ: WASHINGTON COUNTY SCHOOL DISTRICT
121 W TABERNACLE ST, ST GEORGE, UT 847703338
Phone: 435 673-3553
Web: WWW.WASHK12.ORG

HISTORICAL FINANCIALS
Company Type: Private

Income Statement
FYE: June 30

	REVENUE ($ mil.)	NET INCOME ($ mil.)	NET PROFIT MARGIN	EMPLOYEES
06/16	250	9	3.6%	2,700
06/15	0	0	28.4%	—
06/14	0	0	41.8%	—
06/08	0	0	8.2%	—
Annual Growth	109.5%	89.3%	—	—

WASHINGTON ELEMENTARY SCHOOL DISTRICT 6

EXECUTIVES

Superintendent, Paul Stanton
Officer, Chris Wing
Director, Dave Caldwell
Supervisor, Denis Robertson
Manager, Brian Wenrich
Auditors: HEINFELD MEECH & CO PC P

LOCATIONS

HQ: WASHINGTON ELEMENTARY SCHOOL DISTRICT 6
4650 W SWEETWATER AVE, GLENDALE, AZ 853041505
Phone: 602 347-2600
Web: WWW.WESDSCHOOLS.ORG

HISTORICAL FINANCIALS
Company Type: Private

Income Statement
FYE: June 30

	REVENUE ($ mil.)	NET INCOME ($ mil.)	NET PROFIT MARGIN	EMPLOYEES
06/16	216	30	14.0%	3,014
06/15	206	3	1.9%	—
06/14	199	(0)	—	—
06/13	188	(5)	—	—
Annual Growth	4.7%	—	—	—

WASHINGTON HEALTHCARE, MARY

Health care is Mary Washington Healthcare's realm in the Old Dominion State. The medical provider offers a comprehensive range of health services to residents of Fredericksburg and sur-

rounding communities in central Virginia through its not-for-profit regional system of two hospitals and 28 healthcare facilities. The hub of this system is Mary Washington Hospital a 437-bed acute care medical center that provides services including emergency/trauma care and surgical procedures. The health system also includes outpatient care programs and facilities providing primary care and specialty care services for women seniors and children.

Operations

Mary Washington Healthcare is the parent of Mary Washington Hospital and Stafford Hospital (which together serve more than 170000 patients) Mary Washington Hospital Foundation Stafford Hospital Foundation MediCorp Properties Mary Washington Healthcare Clinical Services Mary Washington Healthcare Services Fredericksburg Professional Risk Exchange and MWHC SIR.

Its center of excellence includes the Orthopaedic Institute the Neuroscience Center the Mary Washington Regional Cancer Center the Virginia Heart and Vascular Institute and the Women's Health Institute.

Other facilities provide hospice care and behavioral health services that include inpatient psychiatric care. Its Homecare America segment is a full-service unit providing home health care products and training. Mary Washington Healthcare also owns 14 specialty practices.

Geographic Reach

The company serves patients in Fredericksburg and surrounding communities in central Virginia.

Financial Performance

The company's revenues dropped by 3% to $573 million in 2012 due to a decline in net patient revenues and unrestricted contributions partially offset by higher investment income.

Mary Washington Healthcare's net loss decreased by 34% to lower revenues and higher operating expenses (including a rise in employee benefits professional fees and rent expenses) and a drop in gain on disposal of fixed assets.

Strategy

Its mental health center Snowden at Fredericksburg hexpanded and remodeled its inpatient and outpatient areas in 2012 so that Mary Washington Healthcare can better meet the region's behavioral health services demand.

That year it also introduced a a new range of Web-based communication tools including a new mobile website to give smartphone users instant access to our free 24-hour nurse hotline and more; a searchable Physician Directory; and expanded social media presence on YouTube Facebook Flickr and Twitter.

Mergers and Acquisitions

Expanding its network to meet growing demand in 2013 Mary Washington Healthcare purchased Reese Medical Associates (its third primary care practice). The company also owns Ladysmith Medical Center and the Medical Center of Stafford on Garrisonville Road.

Company Background

In an attempt to reduce overcrowding at its Mary Washington Hospital the health system opened a 100-bed full service hospital in 2009 called Stafford Hospital Center. The hospital features all private inpatient rooms a full service emergency department a dedicated birthing unit inpatient and outpatient surgery and a comprehensive range of advanced diagnostic capabilities including MRI and CT scan.

EXECUTIVES

President, Michael P McDermott
Board of Directors, Newlin Donald
Director, Joseph Willson
Director, Allen H Fisher

Director, Daniel M Hoffman
Treasurer, Donald H Newlin

LOCATIONS

HQ: WASHINGTON HEALTHCARE, MARY
2300 FALL HILL AVE # 314, FREDERICKSBURG, VA 224013343
Phone: 540 741-2507

PRODUCTS/OPERATIONS

Selected Operations
Cancer Center of Virginia
Carriage Hill Rehabilitation and Nursing Center
Diabetes M
The Family Health Center at North Stafford
Fredericksburg Ambulatory Surgery Center Inc. (FASC)
Homecare America
Imaging Center for Women
Kids' Station
Ladysmith Medical Center
Mary Washington Hospice
Mary Washington Hospital
Mary Washington Hospital Foundation
Mary Washington Hospital Home Health
Mary Washington Thrift Shoppe to benefit Mary Washington Hospital
MediCorp Medical Center
MWH Auxiliary Regional Mobile Health Clinic
MWH Community Services Fund
MWH Outreach Laboratories
Medical Arts Pharmacy
Medical Center of Stafford
Medical Imaging of Fredericksburg
Medical Imaging at Lee's Hill
MediCorp Health Link
Mobile Mammography
Psychiatric Associates
Rappahannock Wound Healing Center
Rehabilitation Services of Fredericksburg
Rehabilitation Services of Lee's Hill
Rehabilitation Services of North Stafford
School of Radiologic Technology
Senior Care Services
Sleep Disorders Center
Snowden Academy (mental health)
Snowden at Fredericksburg (mental health)
Stafford Hospital

COMPETITORS

Bon Secours Health	Inova
Centra Health Inc.	Martha Jefferson
Civista Health	Hospital
Dimensions Healthcare	MedStar Health
Fauquier Hospital	Prince William Health
Georgetown University	System
Hospital	University of Virginia
HCA Capital Division	Health System

HISTORICAL FINANCIALS
Company Type: Private

Income Statement
FYE: December 31

	REVENUE ($ mil.)	NET INCOME ($ mil.)	NET PROFIT MARGIN	EMPLOYEES
12/16	610	43	7.1%	4,000
12/14*	75	(6)	—	—
03/12	154	6	4.5%	—
03/11	174	6	3.8%	—
Annual Growth	23.2%	37.1%	—	—

*Fiscal year change

2016 Year-End Financials
Return on assets: 6.5%   Cash ($ mil.): 102
Return on equity: 7.1%
Current ratio: 2.00

WASHINGTON HOSPITAL CENTER CORPORATION

Washington Hospital Center (doing business as MedStar Washington Hospital Center) may be the official hospital of the Washington NFL team but you don't have to be a professional football player to make use of the facility's services. The hospital at the heart of the MedStar Health system serves 455000 patients living in and around the nation's capital each year. Washington Hospital Center has 925 beds and includes specialized care centers for cancer cardiovascular conditions and neurosciences. Other services include organ transplantation and a regional burn treatment center and emergency air transportation. It also conducts clinical research and offers educational residency and fellowship programs.

Operations

Washington Hospital Center has about 1400 doctors and dentists on staff; many of whom are involved in Washington Hospital Center's 370 clinical research trials. The hospital is affiliated with the medical schools of The George Washington University Georgetown University Johns Hopkins and several other regional educational institutions. Its more than two dozen clinical residency and fellowship programs enroll more than 350 medical students each year. Its Ventricular Assist Device program is the only facility in Washington accredited by The Joint Commission. Washington Hospital Center also operates the first Primary Stroke Center and the only Cardiac Ventricular Assist Device program to be accredited by The Joint Commission.

The Hospital Center is also home to MedSTAR one of the country's top shock-trauma and medevac programs and also operates the region's only adult Burn Center.

In 2013 the hospital reported 398058 outpatient and 42412 inpatient visits as well as 3717 births and about 90000 emergency department visit. These included 8828 inpatient cardiac admissions 1623 cardiac surgeries and 12 heart transplants.

Strategy

In 2013 MedStar Heart entered into a first-of-its kind clinical and research alliance with Cleveland Clinic Heart & Vascular Institute.

Washington Hospital Center has a global presence through its International Services Department which administers care to international patients and those who travel to the US specifically to receive medical treatments at Washington Hospital Center. The hospital has also earned a reputation in the US for treating some of the most complex patient cases. Partially because its doctors are able to see trauma patients quickly through the hospital's affiliation with MedSTAR Transport air and ground ambulance service. The MedSTAR Trauma program at Washington Hospital Center has flown nearly 50000 patients since its inception in 1983.

The hospital is also known for its charity care.

Company Background

Washington Hospital Center was created through the merger of three regional hospitals: Emergency Garfield and Episcopal Eye Ear and Throat. The actual idea of the Hospital Center was conceived in 1943 but it took nearly 15 years for funding planning and construction to be completed.

EXECUTIVES

SVP MedStar Washington Hospital Center; Chief Administrative Officer MedStar Heart and Vascular Institute, Cathie Monge

President, John Sullivan
COO, Robert S. Ross
CFO, William Gayne
Radiology Director, Gayle Thompson-smillie
Vice President Medical Staff Development, Anthony Watkins
Nursing Director, SUSAN ECKERT
Vice President Quality Safety Risk And R, Karen Jerome

LOCATIONS

HQ: WASHINGTON HOSPITAL CENTER CORPORATION
110 IRVING ST NW, WASHINGTON, DC 200103017
Phone: 855 546-1686
Web: WWW.WHCENTER.ORG

COMPETITORS

Adventist HealthCare	Inova
Bon Secours Health	Johns Hopkins Medicine
Children's National	Mary Washington
Medical Center	Healthcare
Dimensions Healthcare	Providence Hospital
Doctors Community	(Washington DC)
Hospital	Sibley Memorial
Georgetown University	Hospital
Hospital	Suburban Hospital
HSC Pediatric Center	
Health Net Federal	
Services	

HISTORICAL FINANCIALS

Company Type: Private

Income Statement

FYE: June 30

	REVENUE ($ mil.)	NET INCOME ($ mil.)	NET PROFIT MARGIN	EMPLOYEES
06/15	1,121	23	2.1%	5,637
06/14	1,107	22	2.1%	—
06/08	1,028	14	1.4%	—
06/05	880	22	2.5%	—
Annual Growth	2.4%	0.6%	—	—

2015 Year-End Financials

Return on assets: 2.7%
Return on equity: 2.1%
Current ratio: 0.70

Cash ($ mil.): —

WASHINGTON METROPOLITAN AREA TRANSIT AUTHORITY

Washington Metropolitan Area Transit Authority (WMATA or the Metro) operates the second largest rail transit system (Metrorail) and one of the largest bus networks (Metrobus) in the US. Transporting roughly a third of federal government employees to work and millions of tourists its transit service zone covers Washington DC and neighboring counties and suburbs in Maryland and Virginia. The authority's rail system consists of about 90 stations served by more than 115 miles of track both underground and aboveground. It operates a fleet of about 1400 buses. WMATA also offers MetroAccess paratransit service for eligible people with disabilities.

Operations

WMATA operates in Washington DC and neighboring counties. It is the second largest heavy rail transit system sixth largest bus network and fifth largest paratransit service in the US.

Today about 35 Metrorail stations serve federal facilities and nearly half of the Metro's peak period commuters are federal employees. Recognizing its value to Washington DC-area workers the government covers a significant portion of the authority's capital costs. Passenger fares and advertising revenue fund more than 50% of its daily operations while state and local governments fund the remainder.

Geographic Reach

WMATA's transit zone consists of the District of Columbia the suburban Maryland counties of Montgomery and Prince George's and the Northern Virginia counties of Arlington Fairfax and Loudoun in addition to the cities of Alexandria Fairfax and Falls Church. Overall 45% of people working in the center core Washington and parts of Arlington County use its mass transit.

Sales and Marketing

WMATA's customers include more than a third of the federal government workforce and millions of tourists who visit the nation's capital. Metro and the federal government are also partners in transportation. 35 Metrorail stations serve federal facilities and 20% of Metro's peak period commuters are federal employees.

Company Background

WMATA was created in 1967 to develop build and operate a regional transportation system around the nation's capital. Construction of the rail system began in 1969 and its bus operations began with the 1973 acquisition of four bus systems.

EXECUTIVES

Chief Executive Officer, Paul J Wiedefeld
Board of Directors, Barbara Richardson
Auditors: CLIFTON GUNDERSON LLP CALVERT

LOCATIONS

HQ: WASHINGTON METROPOLITAN AREA TRANSIT AUTHORITY
600 5TH ST NW, WASHINGTON, DC 200012610
Phone: 202 962-1000
Web: WWW.WASHINGTON.ORG

PRODUCTS/OPERATIONS

2013 Sales

	% of total
Passenger	95
Advertising	3
Rental	2
Other	-
Total	100

HISTORICAL FINANCIALS

Company Type: Private

Income Statement

FYE: June 30

	REVENUE ($ mil.)	NET INCOME ($ mil.)	NET PROFIT MARGIN	EMPLOYEES
06/16	859	305	35.6%	11,790
06/08	0	(0)	—	—
06/04	499	(76)	—	—
06/03	451	239	53.1%	—
Annual Growth	5.1%	1.9%	—	—

2016 Year-End Financials

Return on assets: 25.3%
Return on equity: 35.6%
Current ratio: 0.20

Cash ($ mil.): 84

WASHINGTON REGIONAL MEDICAL CENTER

Washington Regional Medical System (formerly Washington Regional Medical Center) provides acute care services to the people of northwestern Arkansas. The system's main hospital has about 370 beds in Fayetteville and also includes assisted living facilities home health and hospice services and general practice and specialty clinics. Specialty services at the medical center include cardiac and vascular care (Walker Family Heart and Vascular Institute) emergency medicine kidney dialysis women's health services (Johnelle Hunt Women's Center) cancer treatment and rehabilitation.

Geographic Reach

Washington Regional Medical System's is the only not-for-profit community-owned and locally governed healthcare system in Northwest Arkansas.

Strategy

Upgrading its health record technology in 2013 the system contracted InteliChart Patient Portal and InteliChart Health Information Exchange (HIE). InteliChart's platform which includes interactive patient and HIE portals allows all of Washington Regional Medical System's providers to overcome interoperability challenges helping its care delivery teams to better manage patients as they transition between the health system's providers and care settings.

Company Background

Striving to expand its reach and attract additional patients Washington Regional Medical System in 2011 added Washington Regional Rheumatology Clinic Washington Regional Sleep Medicine and Harrison Family Practice Clinic to its network of clinics.

Washington Regional Medical System started out in 1950 as Washington County Hospital and moved into its modern facility in 2002. The system completed a $64 million expansion effort in 2008 that added over 100 beds and enhanced emergency senior support and pharmacy units.

EXECUTIVES

Senior Vice President Outreach Services, Larry Shackelford

LOCATIONS

HQ: WASHINGTON REGIONAL MEDICAL CENTER
3215 N NORTHHILLS BLVD, FAYETTEVILLE, AR
727034424
Phone: 479 463-6000

PRODUCTS/OPERATIONS

Selected Medical Services
Assisted Living
Asthma
Bariatric
Bone Density
Cancer Services
Center for Exercise
Clinical Research
Diabetes Education
Dialysis
Emergency Services
Faith In Action
Gynecologic Oncology
Gynecology
Heart Health
Home Health
Hospice
Hyperbaric Oxygen Therapy
Imaging
IV Infusion
LIFELINE Personal Emergency Response System

Mammography
Neurology
Neurosurgery
Obstetrics
Pain Management
Pelvic Therapy
Senior Health
Senior Specialty Unit
Sleep Disorders
Urology
Women's Health
Wound Care
Hospitals Facilities and Clinics
Cancer Support Home
  Cancer Sup
  Cancer Sup
Centers for Health
  Pat Walker Center for Seniors
  Springdale Center for Health
Dialysis
  Benton County Dialysis Center
  Dialysis Center of Siloam Springs
  North Hills Dialysis Center
Exercise Center
  Washington Regional Center for Exercise
Hospital
  Washington Regional Medical Center
Medical Clinics
  Crossroads Medical Clinic
  East Springdale Family Clinic
  Eureka Springs Family Clinic
  Farmington Family Clinic
  Fayetteville Family Clinic
  Har-Ber Family Clinic
  Harrison Family Practice Clinic
  HerHealth - Johnelle Hunt Women's Center -
  Washington Regional Medical Center
  HerHealth
  Internal Medicine Associates
  Northwest Arkansas Neuroscience Institute
  Ozark Urology
  Rheumatology Clinic
  Shiloh Clinic
  Sleep Medicine Clinic
  Walker Heart Institute Cardiovascular Clinic
  Walker Heart Institute Harrison Cardiology Clinic
  Senior Health Clinic
  Washington Regional Diagnostic Clinic
  Washington Regional Memory Clinic
  Washington Regional Wound Care Clinic
Surgery Center
  North Hills Surgery Center

COMPETITORS

Baptist Health (Arkansas)	Community Health Systems
Baxter Regional Medical Center	Mercy Health
	Sparks Health System

HISTORICAL FINANCIALS
Company Type: Private

Income Statement
FYE: December 31

	REVENUE ($ mil.)	NET INCOME ($ mil.)	NET PROFIT MARGIN	EMPLOYEES
12/15	245	45	18.5%	2,000
12/14	213	34	16.3%	—
12/12	205	33	16.4%	—
12/09	229	14	6.2%	—
Annual Growth	1.1%	21.3%	—	—

2015 Year-End Financials

Return on assets: 4.8%   Cash ($ mil.): 20
Return on equity: 18.5%
Current ratio: 1.60

WASHINGTON SUBURBAN SANITARY COMMISSION (INC)

Used water in clean water out is the job description of the Washington Suburban Sanitary Commission (WSSC). The utility provides water and wastewater services in Maryland's Montgomery and Prince George's counties just outside the nation's capital. WSSC serves 460000 customers representing 1.8 million residents in an area of about 1000 square miles. The agency draws water from the Potomac and Patuxtent rivers and maintains three reservoirs. The commission also operates two water filtration plants six wastewater treatment plants and some 11000 miles of sewer and water main lines including a network of nearly 5600 miles of fresh water pipeline and over 5400 miles of sewer pipeline.

Operations

WSSC's three reservoirs (Triadelphia Rocky Gorge and Little Seneca) along with Jennings Randolph Reservoir which it shares with Fairfax Water and the Washington Aqueduct have a total holding capacity of 27 billion gallons. Its two water filtration plants (Patuxent and Potomac) produce nearly 170 million gallons of drinking water daily. The commission handles some 72 million gallons of wastewater daily through its six treatment plants (Damascus Hyattstown Parkway Piscataway Seneca and Western Branch).

Financial Performance

The company reported operating revenue of about $698 million in fiscal 2014 (ended June) up about 2% from the prior year. The growth was powered by an increase in water and sewer billing rates.

WSSC's proposed budgets for 2014 and 2015 were $1.5 billion and $1.3 billion respectively.

Company Background
WSSC was established in 1918.

EXECUTIVES

Chief Engineer, Gary Gumm
General Manager, Jerry N. Johnson
CFO, Yvette Downs
CIO, Mujib Lodhi
VPN TECHNICIAN, Chandra Vavilala
Chairman, Omar M. Boulware
Vice Chairman, Adrienne A. Mandel
Auditors: BCA WATSON RICE LLP WASHINGTO

LOCATIONS

HQ: WASHINGTON SUBURBAN SANITARY
COMMISSION (INC)
14501 SWEITZER LN, LAUREL, MD 207075901
Phone: 301 206-8000
Web: WWW.WSSCWATER.COM

HISTORICAL FINANCIALS
Company Type: Private

Income Statement
FYE: June 30

	REVENUE ($ mil.)	NET INCOME ($ mil.)	NET PROFIT MARGIN	EMPLOYEES
06/15	645	192	29.9%	2,000
06/14	624	190	30.6%	—
06/13	597	204	34.2%	—
06/12	583	201	34.5%	—
Annual Growth	3.4%	(1.4%)	—	—

2015 Year-End Financials

Return on assets: 16.4%   Cash ($ mil.): 39
Return on equity: 29.9%
Current ratio: 0.40

WATONWAN FARM SERVICE, INC

Watonwan Farm Service which does business as WFS helps out its south central Minnesota and north central Iowa member-farmers with complete farm-management services and products. Offering marketing opportunities financial services and farming supplies such as chemicals fertilizers livestock feed petroleum products and seed the agricultural cooperative serves more than 4000 producers from its 22 locations. The primary crops of its members include corn soybean and specialty canning crops; most of its livestock farmers raise hogs and cattle. The co-op was called the Consumers Cooperative Oil Company of St. James when it was founded in 1937.

EXECUTIVES

Chief Executive Officer, Ed Bosanko
Director, Harold Wolle
Treasurer, Dennis Hunwardsen
Manager, Randy Cole
Finance Manager, Bill Day
Auditors: GARDINER THOMPSEN DES MOINES

LOCATIONS

HQ: WATONWAN FARM SERVICE, INC
233 W CIRO ST, TRUMAN, MN 560882018
Phone: 507 776-1244

COMPETITORS

ADM	Gold-Eagle Cooperative
Ag Processing Inc.	Heartland Co-op
CHS	Minn-Dak Co-op
Cargill	NEW Cooperative
Farm Service	United Farmers
Cooperative	Cooperative
Farmers Cooperative	
Society	

HISTORICAL FINANCIALS

Company Type: Private

Income Statement   FYE: July 31

	REVENUE ($ mil.)	NET INCOME ($ mil.)	NET PROFIT MARGIN	EMPLOYEES
07/15	358	5	1.5%	255
07/14	468	7	1.7%	—
07/13	701	7	1.1%	—
07/12	592	6	1.1%	—
Annual Growth	(15.4%)	(7.9%)	—	—

2015 Year-End Financials

Return on assets: 1.9%   Cash ($ mil.): —
Return on equity: 1.5%
Current ratio: 0.30

WAUKESHA MEMORIAL HOSPITAL, INC.

Waukesha Memorial Hospital is a 300-bed teaching hospital that provides health care services for Wisconsin's Milwaukee Waukesha and Dane counties. With about 670 physicians representing several specialties and 2700 employees the hospital operates centers for excellence focused on cardiology oncology neurology women's health and orthopedics as well as emergency neonatal and family practice services. Additionally Waukesha Memorial Hospital conducts a physician residency program. Established in 1914 the medical facility is a subsidiary of not-for-profit ProHealth Care a medical network that serves southeastern Wisconsin with acute care and specialty health services.

Operations

ProHealth Care runs Waukesha Memorial Hospital alongside its other critical-care hospital Oconomowoc Memorial Hospital. As part of its operations the hospital boasts a neuroscience center orthopedic center regional cancer center regional heart and vascular center and a women's center. Its newborn intensive care unit and its emergency department which averages more than 39000 visits are both Level III.

Geographic Reach

Despite its name Waukesha Memorial Hospital serves the residents of Milwaukee and Dane counties along with Waukesha County.

EXECUTIVES

Vpma, James Gardner
Auditors: PLANTE & MORAN PLLC GRAND RA

LOCATIONS

HQ: WAUKESHA MEMORIAL HOSPITAL, INC.
725 AMERICAN AVE, WAUKESHA, WI 531885099
Phone: 262 928-1000

PRODUCTS/OPERATIONS

Selected Services
Birthing
Blood / Ly
Bones Joints & Muscles
Brain & Nerves
Cancer
Cancer Second Opinion
Children's Health
CyberKnife
Diabetes
Diagnostic Services
Digestive
Ear Nose & Throat
Emergency Services/Urgent Care
Eyes & Vision
General Surgery
Genetics
Heart & Vascular
Infections
Integrative Medicine
Kidneys & Urinary System
Lungs / Br
Men's Health
Mental Health
Nutrition
Orthopedic
Pain
Rehabilitation Services
Senior's Health
Sleep
Stroke
Wellness & Lifestyle
Women's Health

COMPETITORS

Children's Hospital and Health System
Columbia St. Mary's
Froedtert Hospital
Hospital Sisters Health System
Ministry Health Care
SwedishAmerican Health System
University of Wisconsin Hospital and Clinics

HISTORICAL FINANCIALS

Company Type: Private

Income Statement   FYE: September 30

	REVENUE ($ mil.)	NET INCOME ($ mil.)	NET PROFIT MARGIN	EMPLOYEES
09/15	460	29	6.3%	2,071
09/14	420	76	18.3%	—
09/13	419	96	22.9%	—
09/12	456	53	11.7%	—
Annual Growth	0.3%	(18.3%)	—	—

2015 Year-End Financials

Return on assets: 13.7%   Cash ($ mil.): 11
Return on equity: 6.3%
Current ratio: 0.70

WAUKESHA-PEARCE INDUSTRIES, INC.

Waukesha-Pearce Industries (WPI) wants its customers to start their engines. Through its Engine Division the company designs and packages engine-driven equipment such as power generators pumps blowers control panels and switchgear. WPI also offers a slate of heavy construction and mining products including earth movers and demolition equipment made by such OEMs as Komatsu and Gradall Industries through its Construction Machinery Division. As part of its business the company sells used equipment and leases heavy earthmoving equipment. Founded as Portable Rotary Rig Co. in 1924 by Louis M. Pearce Sr. the company is owned and run by the Pearce family.

Operations

WPI's Engine Equipment lineup includes its own Enginator used in field gas compression and power generation. Its Engine Division further supports WPI's performance by offering less economy-driven services such as certified remanufactured engines and revamping.

WPI's Construction Machinery arm benefits from a broad products portfolio paired with distributor affiliations. Such alliances include Bomag (compaction equipment) Allied/Rammer (demolition equipment) Esco Crushing (wearparts) Sennebogen (material handling) and Valmet (cranes). Like the Engine Equipment Division this segment is able to mitigate a recession's impact on capital equipment sales by providing repair and onsite maintenance services along with a multi-million-dollar inventory of used and rental equipment and parts.

The company also offers construction and mining products from equipment brands such as Komatsu Gradall Takeuchi Doppstadt NPK LaBounty and Vacall.

Geographic Reach

From its headquarters in Houston WPI serves customers through more than a dozen locations in Texas and another 15 across Louisiana Oklahoma New Mexico Arkansas Alabama Kansas Cal-

ifornia Rhode Island Pennsylvania and West Virginia. The company's training facility is located in Sugar Land Texas outside Houston.

Sales and Marketing

Core markets for WPI include land clearing highway and heavy construction site development mining scrap petrochemical energy exploration and utility construction as well as a number of government agencies.

EXECUTIVES

President, Louis M. Pearce
Director of Health Safety and Environmental,
 Jeremy Bergstrom
SECRETARY TO THE PRESIDENT, Annette
 Washburn

LOCATIONS

HQ: WAUKESHA-PEARCE INDUSTRIES, INC.
 12320 MAIN ST, HOUSTON, TX 770356206
Phone: 713 723-1050
Web: WWW.WPI.COM

PRODUCTS/OPERATIONS

Selected Services
Earth moving
Gas compression
Mining
Power generation
Recycling
Service and replacement parts
Small engine and lawn

Selected Products
Engines
 Arrow VR engines
 BOB-CAT mowers
 Dresser Waukesha
 Generac Industrial
 Generac Residential
 HIPOWER generating sets
 Kohler engines
 Little Wonder products
 Mantis yard & garden products
 Powerhouse catalytic converters
 Remanufactured engines
 Revamp services
 Ryan turf renovation products
 WPI brand
Construction Machinery
 Allied/Rammer
 Bomag
 Bucyrus Blades
 Cummins Engines
 Dressta
 Esco
 Fleetguard Filters
 Gradall
 Hensley
 JRB
 Komatsu
 LaBounty
 Sennebogen
 Valmet

COMPETITORS

AGCO
 Berry Companies
Caterpillar
 Connell Company
Cummins Power
 Generation

Deere
Dewey Electronics
Emerson Electric
Kubota

HISTORICAL FINANCIALS

Company Type: Private

Income Statement

FYE: March 31

	REVENUE ($ mil.)	NET INCOME ($ mil.)	NET PROFIT MARGIN	EMPLOYEES
03/16	423	2	0.5%	600
03/15	461	8	1.9%	—
03/11	248	4	1.9%	—
03/10	197	1	0.8%	—
Annual Growth	13.5%	3.2%	—	—

2016 Year-End Financials

Return on assets: 9.7%   Cash ($ mil.): —
Return on equity: 0.5%
Current ratio: 0.60

WAYNE COUNTY AIRPORT AUTHORITY

EXECUTIVES

Chief Executive Officer, Joseph R Nardone
Financial Executive, Marge Basrai
Manager, Jerry Clark
Officer, Alan Berezansky
Supervisor, Barry Ellerholz
Administrative Assistant, Dawn Kruse
Department Manager, Jim Doerner
Auditors: PLANTE & MORAN PLLC SOUTHFIEL

LOCATIONS

HQ: WAYNE COUNTY AIRPORT AUTHORITY
 1 DETROIT METRO AIRPORT, DETROIT, MI
 482421004
Phone: 734 247-7364
Web: WWW.DETROITAIRPORT.ORG

HISTORICAL FINANCIALS

Company Type: Private

Income Statement

FYE: September 30

	REVENUE ($ mil.)	NET INCOME ($ mil.)	NET PROFIT MARGIN	EMPLOYEES
09/16	363	(30)	—	675
09/15	349	(60)	—	—
09/14	339	(22)	—	—
09/13	318	(21)	—	—
Annual Growth	4.4%	—	—	—

WAYNE J. GRIFFIN ELECTRIC, INC.

Wayne J. Griffin Electric brings a certain spark to New England and the Southeast. With offices in Massachusetts Georgia North Carolina and Alabama the electrical contractor offers construction and installation services on hospitals hotels industrial and high-tech buildings offices prisons research laboratories retirement communities and schools. The company's service division provides small project management and facility maintenance while its telecom division designs and installs fiber

optics fire alarm and security systems as well as systems that control energy use from lighting to heating ventilation and air conditioning (HVAC). Founded in 1978 Wayne J. Griffin Electric is privately held.

Sales and Marketing

Since serving its first major customer the Coca-Cola Bottling Company at its Massachusetts plant Wayne J. Griffin Electric has been expanding into different commercial industrial and institutional sectors. It has worked for such clients as Boeing and EMC Corporation. It has also worked on electrical expansion projects for the Valley Creek Wastewater Treatment Facility in Alabama and the Raleigh-Durham International Airport in North Carolina.

Additional clients have included EMC Corporation TJX Companies Verizon and Liberty Mutual.
 Strategy

Wayne J. Griffin Electric utilizes such tools as Building Information Modeling (BIM) technology to provide its customers with the best plans possible. The firm has continued to broaden its areas of expertise so that it can serve clients of many sectors from educational and institutional to industrial and corporate.

EXECUTIVES

President and CEO, Wayne J. Griffin
Auditors: KIRKLAND ALBRECHT & FREDERICKS

LOCATIONS

HQ: WAYNE J. GRIFFIN ELECTRIC, INC.
 116 HOPPING BROOK RD, HOLLISTON, MA
 017461455
Phone: 508 429-8830
Web: WWW.WAYNEJGRIFFINELECTRIC.COM

COMPETITORS

ADCO Electrical
 Bergelectric
 E-J Electric
 Installation Co.
 EMCOR

IES Holdings
J.F. White Contracting
Mass Electric
Quanta Services

HISTORICAL FINANCIALS

Company Type: Private

Income Statement

FYE: December 31

	REVENUE ($ mil.)	NET INCOME ($ mil.)	NET PROFIT MARGIN	EMPLOYEES
12/15	303	22	7.4%	1,100
12/14	293	27	9.4%	—
12/13	291	17	6.0%	—
12/12	286	15	5.5%	—
Annual Growth	2.0%	13.1%	—	—

2015 Year-End Financials

Return on assets: 6.4%   Cash ($ mil.): 24
Return on equity: 7.4%
Current ratio: 1.20

WAYNE MEMORIAL HOSPITAL, INC.

EXECUTIVES

Chief Executive Officer, Janie Jaberg
Manager, Norma Hawkins
Chief Operating Officer, Thomas Bradshaw
Director, Kim Anderson

Supervisor, Archie Mooring
Administrative Assistant, Charlotte Watson
Manager, Dean Tino
Manager, Iris Jackson
Manager, Lisa Fleming

LOCATIONS

HQ: WAYNE MEMORIAL HOSPITAL, INC.
2700 WAYNE MEMORIAL DR, GOLDSBORO, NC
275349459
Phone: 919 736-1110
Web: WWW.WAYNEHEALTH.ORG

HISTORICAL FINANCIALS

Company Type: Private

Income Statement				FYE: September 30
	REVENUE ($ mil.)	NET INCOME ($ mil.)	NET PROFIT MARGIN	EMPLOYEES
09/15	196	(10)	—	1,700
09/14	214	6	3.2%	—
09/13	206	46	22.7%	—
09/12	200	25	12.8%	—
Annual Growth	(0.7%)	—	—	—

2015 Year-End Financials

Return on assets: 4.0%   Cash ($ mil.): 5
Return on equity: (-5.4%)
Current ratio: 0.50

WEBER SCHOOL DISTRICT

EXECUTIVES

Superintendent, Jeff Stephens
Board of Directors, Karla Hall
Director, Debbie Butte
Maintenance Supervisor, Brian Smith
Foreman/Supervisor, Cody Barnes
Foreman/Supervisor, Ferron Lister
Consultant, Gary Smith
Auditors: SQUIRE & COMPANY PC OREM UT

LOCATIONS

HQ: WEBER SCHOOL DISTRICT
5320 ADAMS AVE PKWY, OGDEN, UT 844056913
Phone: 801 476-7800
Web: WWW.WEBER.K12.UT.US

HISTORICAL FINANCIALS

Company Type: Private

Income Statement				FYE: June 30
	REVENUE ($ mil.)	NET INCOME ($ mil.)	NET PROFIT MARGIN	EMPLOYEES
06/15	230	2	1.2%	3,000
06/14	222	(0)	—	—
06/13	218	4	1.9%	—
06/12	215	(1)	—	—
Annual Growth	2.4%	—	—	—

WEGMANS FOOD MARKETS, INC.

One name strikes fear in the hearts of supermarket owners in New York New Jersey Pennsylvania Virginia Maryland and Massachusetts: Wegmans Food Markets. The regional grocery chain owns almost 90 stores but they are hardly typical. Much larger than most supermarkets (up to 140000 sq. ft.) each store offers up to 70000 products and house huge in-store cafes cheese shops with some 300 different varieties sub shops and French-style pastry shops. The company is known for its gourmet cooking classes and an extensive employee-training program. Founded in 1916 Wegmans now boasts revenues of nearly $8 billion and is one of the largest private companies in the US. The grocery chain is owned and run by the family of founder John Wegman.

Geographic Reach

Rochester New York-based Wegmans Food Markets operates more than half (46) of its 88 stores in its home state. Pennsylvania is next with about 17 stores. The rest of its stores are in New Jersey Virginia Maryland and Massachusetts.

Financial Performance

Wegman's addition of new stores in new markets has spurred several consecutive years of sales growth. Indeed Wegman's sales have jumped more than 27% since 2011 from $6.2 billion to $7.9 billion during 2015.

Strategy

Wegmans has been entering new markets in recent years to boost sales. In late 2015 the chain planned to open a new store in Lancaster Pennsylvania as well as two more Wegmans stores out of a handful of existing stores in Massachusetts in Natick and Westwood. During 2014 it entered the Richmond Virginia market with two new stores and opened two more stores in Massachusetts (which it first entered in 2011) in Cherry Hill and Burlington.

The upscale regional grocery chain which aims to deliver a shopping experience more akin to a European open-air market than a traditional supermarket has also benefited from the recovering US economy. Key to Wegmans' success is its competitive pricing mostly on its popular private-label products. The retailer's aggressive private-label strategy includes frequent product updates and innovation. Wegmans recently introduced a line of gluten-free private-label items including pasta and cake mixes.

Wegmans ranked 33rd on the 2015 Supermarket News list of Top 75 Supermarkets based on sales volume. The chain is not only popular with shoppers but also with employees. The company has landed on FORTUNE magazine's list of the "100 Best Companies to Work For" in each of the past 18 years and captured the #7 spot in 2015. It was ranked #1 in 2005.

EXECUTIVES

SVP Store Operations, Jack DePeters
SVP CFO and Treasurer, James (Jim) Leo
President and CEO, Colleen Wegman, age 43
SVP Wine, Nicole Wegman
VP Seafood Sustainability, Carl Salamone
SVP Syracuse Division, Shari Constantine
CIO, David DeLaus
Vice President, Robert Maybee
Vice President Corporate Promotions, Tom Di Nardo
Senior Vice President Merchandising, Marty Gardner

Senior Vice President Division, Mike Keating
Senior Vice President, John A Depeters
Vice President of Dairy Frozen, Ken Cassara
Senior Vice President of Pharmacy, John Carlo
Vice President Asset Protection, Brian Scanlon
Director of Pharmacy Operations, Dan Ferrara
Vice President store Operations Human Resources, Kevin Stickles
Vice President of Finance, Sue Pietropaolo
Vice President of WegmansBrand, Mike Decoly
Vice President of Design Services and Maintenance, Carol Duquette
Vice President, Jim Schaeffer
Director Media Relations, Joe Natale
Senior Vice President, Jim Leo
Vice President, Richard Vanderhorst
VP Human Resources, Gerald Pierce
Pharmacy Manager, Mike Zambuto
Director of Pharmacy and Healthcare, Sherrie Diamond
Director of Pharmacy and Healthcare, Kevin Frantzen
Chairman, Daniel R. (Danny) Wegman
Executive Board Member, Art Pires

LOCATIONS

HQ: WEGMANS FOOD MARKETS, INC.
1500 BROOKS AVE, ROCHESTER, NY 146243589
Phone: 585 328-2550
Web: WWW.ROCWIKI.ORG

2014 Stores

	No.
New York	46
Pennsylvania	17
New Jersey	7
Maryland	7
Virginia	7
Massachusetts	4
Total	88

PRODUCTS/OPERATIONS

Selected Products and Operations

Asian foods
Bath and body
Bulk foods
Cheeses
Coffee/cappuccino bar
Cooking classes
Deli
Dry cleaning
European bread bakery
Floral department
Food from around the world
Gift and fruit baskets
Kosher deli
Market café;
Meat service
Nature's Marketplace (organic health and food items)
Organic produce
Pasta Station
Pharmacy
Photo processing and photo enlarging
Photocopies
Pizza Primo
Ready-to-cook meat and seafood
Rotisserie
Rug Doctor carpet cleaner rental
Seafood
Sub sandwiches
Sushi bar
UPS parcel service
Video player and game system rentals
Videos and DVDs
WKids Fun Center
Wokery

COMPETITORS

A&P	Safeway
Albertsons	Saker ShopRites
BJ's Wholesale Club	Stop & Shop
CVS	TOPS Markets
Giant Eagle	Target Corporation
Giant Food Stores	Wal-Mart
Golub	Walgreen

IGA
Rite Aid

Wawa Inc.
Weis Markets

HISTORICAL FINANCIALS
Company Type: Private

Income Statement
FYE: December 26

	REVENUE ($ mil.)	NET INCOME ($ mil.)	NET PROFIT MARGIN	EMPLOYEES
12/15	8,005	0	—	45,000
12/14	7,560	114	1.5%	—
12/10	5,687	93	1.6%	—
12/09	5,193	85	1.6%	—
Annual Growth	7.5%	—	—	—

2015 Year-End Financials
Return on assets: 6.4%
Return on equity: —
Current ratio: 0.40

Cash ($ mil.): 331

WEINBERG, HARRY & JEANETTE FOUNDATION INC

EXECUTIVES
President, Shale Stiller
VP Finance, John F Lingenfelter
Chief Operating Officer, Rachel Monroe
Account Manager, Benita Robinson
Officer, Kate Sorestad

LOCATIONS
HQ: WEINBERG, HARRY & JEANETTE FOUNDATION INC
 7 PARK CENTER CT, OWINGS MILLS, MD 211174200
Phone: 410 654-8500
Web: WWW.HJWEINBERGFOUNDATION.ORG

HISTORICAL FINANCIALS
Company Type: Private

Income Statement
FYE: February 28

	REVENUE ($ mil.)	NET INCOME ($ mil.)	NET PROFIT MARGIN	EMPLOYEES
02/15	293	174	59.4%	20
02/14	113	(4)	—	—
02/12	89	(23)	—	—
02/10	12	(104)	—	—
Annual Growth	87.3%	—	—	—

2015 Year-End Financials
Return on assets: 0.1%
Return on equity: 59.4%
Current ratio: —

Cash ($ mil.): 48

WELCH FOODS INC., A COOPERATIVE

Welch Foods has a taste for the grape. An operating subsidiary of the 1000-plus-farmer owner National Grape Cooperative Welch produces the Welch's brand grape and white grape juices and jellies. Its beverage line includes refrigerated and sparkling juices and cocktails frozen and shelf-stable concentrates and single-serve drinks. Welch supplies fresh grapes as well as preserved offerings (jams and spreads) which are also sold under the BAMA label. The co-op licenses the Welch's name to other manufactures of frozen fruit confections dried fruit and carbonated beverages among many. Its 400-plus products are purchased by grocery retailers and food service operators in the US and 40 other countries.

Geographic Reach

Massachusetts-based Welch Foods has vineyards in Pennsylvania Michigan New York Ohio Washington and Ontario Canada. It sells its products in the US and some 40 other countries.

Financial Performance

National Grape Cooperative and Welch Foods's sales grew to $608.5 million in 2014. Volume grew 4% during the year with its Bottled 100% Juice product leading the way with 11% growth though all core product categories showed market share and volume growth. Spread sales grew by 7% during the year while refrigerated juices grew by 8%.

The cooperative's net proceeds jumped significantly to $84 million in FY2014 the second highest level in its history according to the company.

Strategy

Welch Foods and National Grape Cooperative regularly introduce new juices and grape-based products and in 2015 stated it was "committed to research and development that will meet the growing demand for products that address consumers' health and nutrition needs." During 2014 it increased investment in its successful Bottled 100% Juice line and launched Farmer's Pick a new 100% Juice line featuring unfiltered juice. In mid-2012 the coop launched four new flavors (lemonade strawberry lemonade raspberry limeade and mango) of its sparkling juice cocktails resulting in a 29% increase in volume during the summer months and market share gain during the holiday season. Welch Foods low-growth spreads business got a boost in 2012 with the launch of Welch's Nautrals an all natural no high fructose corn syrup formation that resonated with consumers.

The co-op has also been making investments in efficiency to cut its overhead costs and boost proceeds for future growth. Its 2014 upgrade of its Sparkling line capacity and capabilities reduced material costs shortened lead teams eliminated waste and reduced overall costs by some $2 million per year. The new production line also doubled its processing speeds to up to 270 bottles per minute and introduced a new more efficient case configuration that allowed for more and better displays in retail stores.

EXECUTIVES

President and CEO, Bradley C. Irwin, age 58
Chairman of the Board, Joseph C. Falcone
Auditors: KPMG LLP BOSTON MA

LOCATIONS

HQ: WELCH FOODS INC., A COOPERATIVE
 300 BAKER AVE STE 101, CONCORD, MA 017422131
Phone: 978 371-1000

PRODUCTS/OPERATIONS

Selected Brands and Products
BAMA
 Jams jellies and preserves
 Peanut butter
Welch
 Bottled and canned juices
 Dried fruit
 Fresh table grapes
 Frozen juices
 Fruit juice bars
 Jams jellies and preserves
 Pourable concentrated juices
 Refrigerated juices
 Single-serve juices

COMPETITORS

Chiquita Brands
Citrus World
Coca-Cola
Coloma Frozen Foods
Dole Food
Fresh Del Monte
 Produce
Great Western Juice
Lion Raisins
Monster Beverage
Mott's
Naked Juice
National Raisin
Ocean Spray
Odwalla

Old Orchard
Silver Springs
Smucker
Snapple
South Beach Beverage
Stapleton-Spence
 Packing
Sun-Maid
Sunny Delight
Sunview Vineyards
Tree Top
Tropicana
Unilever NV
Wet Planet Beverages

HISTORICAL FINANCIALS
Company Type: Private

Income Statement
FYE: August 31

	REVENUE ($ mil.)	NET INCOME ($ mil.)	NET PROFIT MARGIN	EMPLOYEES
08/16	600	83	14.0%	1,000
08/15	609	81	13.3%	—
08/14	609	76	12.6%	—
08/13	608	65	10.7%	—
Annual Growth	(0.5%)	8.8%	—	—

2016 Year-End Financials
Return on assets: 5.2%
Return on equity: 14.0%
Current ratio: 0.50

Cash ($ mil.): 7

WELLESLEY COLLEGE

Wellesley College is a liberal arts women's college (one of the famed "Seven Sisters" schools) that offers majors in more than 50 fields of study including anthropology computer science education physics and sociology. It has a three-college collaboration with Massachusetts' Babson and Olin Colleges to provide additional opportunities for its students and also has cross-registration agreements with MIT and Brandeis. Wellesley's Davis Degree program is geared toward women beyond traditional college age. The college has a student enrollment of some 2500 and a student-faculty ratio of about 7 to 1.

Operations

The institution offers more than 1000 courses in all. Its tuition for residents in fiscal year 2014-15 stood at $45000.

Financial Performance

Wellesley has a long-term plan to cut operating losses by cutting spending in three areas: non-personnel line items administration and staff salaries and faculty salaries.

Its revenue increased 3% to $201 million in fiscal 2014 due to an increase in tuition and fees private gifts and grants and investment returns designated for operations. Net income more than doubled that year rising 107% to $256 million. That improvement was attributed to income from non-operating activities such as gifts and pledges and investment returns.

Operating cash outflow fell 37% to $51 million in 2014 as net income increased; cash generated from contributions receivable and accounts payable also helped narrow the gap.

Strategy

In 2013 the school launched its "Wellesley 25" program to reduce spending and use freed up money for campus building renovations and expansions. It plans to spend up to $550 million on these projects by 2025. Among its goals are overhauling Pendleton West and building a 12000-sq. ft. addition for visual and musical arts as well as converting currently vacant spaces into student services and administrative facilities.

Company Background

Wellesley College was founded in 1870 by Henry Fowle Durant and Pauline Fowle Durant. The prestigious college has produced such notable graduates as Hillary Rodham Clinton journalists Diane Sawyer and Cokie Roberts former US Secretary of State Madeleine Albright and Nancy Drew author Harriet Stratemeyer Adams (pen name Carolyn Keene).

EXECUTIVES

Assistant Vice President For Resources, Kimberly Hokanson
Assistant Vice President for Administration, Robert Bossange
Assistant Vice President For Finance, Deborah Kallman
A Vice President, Veronica Martinez
Assistant Vice President for Budget Financial Planning and Campus Services, Jeff Dubois
Board Member, Kazuko Ozawa
Secretary, Ariana Mora
Auditors: MALONEY NOVOTNY LLC CLEVELAND

LOCATIONS

HQ: WELLESLEY COLLEGE
106 CENTRAL ST, WELLESLEY, MA 024818203
Phone: 781 283-1000
Web: WWW.WELLESLEY.EDU

PRODUCTS/OPERATIONS

2014 Sales

	% of total
Investment return designated for operations	41
Net tuition & fees	40
Private gifts & grants	12
Auxiliary operations	3
Government grants	2
Other	2
Total	**100**

Selected Departments

Africana Studies Department
Anthropology Department
Art Department
Astronomy Department
Athletics see Physical Education
Biological Sciences Department
Chemistry Department
Classical Civilization see Classical Studies Department
Classical Studies Department
Cognitive & Linguistic Science
Computer Science Department
East Asian Languages and Cultures Department
Economics Department
Education Department
English Department
French Department
Geosciences Department
German Department
History Department
International Relations see Economics History and Political Science
Italian Studies Department
Language Studies/Linguistics see Cognitive & Linguistic Science
Mathematics Department
Music Department
Philosophy Department
Physical Education and Athletics Department
Physics Department
Political Science Department
Psychology Department
Religion Department

Russian Department
Sociology Department
Spanish Department
Women's and Gender Studies Department

HISTORICAL FINANCIALS

Company Type: Private

Income Statement

FYE: June 30

	REVENUE ($ mil.)	NET INCOME ($ mil.)	NET PROFIT MARGIN	EMPLOYEES
06/16	221	(92)	—	2,000
06/13	295	48	16.5%	—
06/09	188	(373)	—	—
Annual Growth	**2.4%**	—	—	—

2016 Year-End Financials

Return on assets: 27.7%   Cash ($ mil.): 60
Return on equity: (-41.7%)
Current ratio: —

WELLINGTON TRUST CO, NA

EXECUTIVES

Principal, Barry Mason
Manager, Rebecca Beach
Vice-President, Andrew Paone

LOCATIONS

HQ: WELLINGTON TRUST CO, NA
280 CONGRESS ST, BOSTON, MA 022101023
Phone: 617 951-5500

HISTORICAL FINANCIALS

Company Type: Private

Income Statement

FYE: December 31

	ASSETS ($ mil.)	NET INCOME ($ mil.)	INCOME AS % OF ASSETS	EMPLOYEES
12/15	94	1	1.2%	2
12/04	32	(0)	—	—
Annual Growth	**10.4%**	—	—	—

2015 Year-End Financials

Return on assets: —   Sales ($ mil): 312
Return on equity: 0.4%

WELLSPAN MEDICAL GROUP (INC)

EXECUTIVES

Chief Executive Officer, Tom McGann
Financial Executive, Steffney Calp

LOCATIONS

HQ: WELLSPAN MEDICAL GROUP (INC)
140 N DUKE ST, YORK, PA 174011170
Phone: 717 851-6515

HISTORICAL FINANCIALS

Company Type: Private

Income Statement

FYE: June 30

	REVENUE ($ mil.)	NET INCOME ($ mil.)	NET PROFIT MARGIN	EMPLOYEES
06/15	336	(36)	—	709
06/14	251	(25)	—	—
06/13	228	(24)	—	—
06/12	201	(21)	—	—
Annual Growth	**18.7%**	—	—	—

2015 Year-End Financials

Return on assets: 0.1%   Cash ($ mil.): 2
Return on equity: (-10.9%)
Current ratio: 0.60

WELLSTAR HEALTH SYSTEM, INC.

With WellStar in your corner you won't need to wish upon a star for good health and wellness. The not-for-profit WellStar Health System is Georgia's largest health system with about a dozen hospitals two health parks a pediatric center and more than 200 medical office locations. The network's hospitals specialize in cardiac and cancer care diabetes treatments and women's health. WellStar's physician group includes more than 1100 providers. The network is also home to hospice and home care programs; Atherton Place an independent living center for senior citizens; and about 10 urgent care facilities.

Operations

WellStar's hospitals include Wellstar Cobb Hospital 382-beds; Wellstar Douglas Hospital 108-beds; WellStar Kennestone Hospital 633-beds; Wellstar Paulding Hospital 83-beds; and Wellstar Windy Hill Hospital 115-beds. The hospitals are connected to eight urgent care centers and 16 satellite diagnostic imaging centers.

Other network facilities offer outpatient medical imaging wound care and women's health and prenatal care. WellStar operates an outpatient cardiac group called Cardiovascular Medicine (CVM) one of Atlanta's largest cardiology groups joined the health system. WellStar CVM has 30 doctors practicing out of eight locations scattered throughout the region.

The health system also manages the WellStar Medical Group which is installing electronic medical records (EMR) at certain practices to connect patients with their records no matter which care site they visit. The project calls for EMRs to be put in place throughout the entire medical group as a way to improve quality of care and increase provider access to patient information. WellStar has more than 100 locations and 500 medical providers in 30 specialties.

The organization's WellStar Institute for Better Health provides patients and their families with programs resources and educational materials designed to promote healthy lifestyles. The institute also contributes to medical and scientific learning by supporting community-wide programs and keeping health care providers in the know about the latest treatments and procedures.

WellStar serves more than 1.4 million area residents; delivers more than 9000 babies each year; offers the only life-saving Level II trauma care in

Cobb County; and serves more emergency room patients than any other health system in Georgia.

Financial Performance

The company's revenue increased by 6% to $1.6 billion in fiscal 2014 and revenues in excess of operating expenses grew by 22%.

It provides more than $200 million in unreimbursed care to the community WellStar incurred costs of more than $110 million to provide charity care to patients in Bartow Cherokee Cobb Douglas and Paulding counties in fiscal 2014. Its physicians and facilities made up a significant shortfall in reimbursements for patients on Medicaid ($25 million) and on Medicare ($98 million).

Strategy

To meet the growing demand in the market in 2015 WellStar Health System opened an Outpatient Surgery Center at the WellStar East Cobb Health Park.

WellStar Health System built a new hospital to replace the WellStar Paulding Hospital in Paulding County. In 2014 the company opened the Hiram-based hospital a 56-bed hospital with the capacity to expand to 112. There are four surgical suites and 40 emergency exam rooms plus a dedicated Pediatric Emergency Department. The hospital and adjacent medical office building were built next to WellStar's existing medical office building in Hiram. The campus includes an emergency department comprehensive surgical services a cancer center women's imaging and a range of other healthcare services.

Mergers and Acquisitions

In 2016 WellStar Health System acquired the Atlanta-based operations of Tenet Healthcare including five hospitals and 26 physician clinics. The purchase included Atlanta Medical Center (downtown) and Roswell's North Fulton Hospital.

Company Background

The hospital system was formed in 1993.

EXECUTIVES

Vice President of Finance anc Chief Financial Officer WellStar Cobb Hospital, Darold Etheridge
Chief Strategy Officer, Reynold J. Jennings
EVP Human Resources Organizational Learning and Chief Compliance Officer, David Anderson
SVP; President WellStar Cobb Hospital, Kem M. Mullins
SVP Real Estate and Construction and President WellStar Paulding Hospital, Mark Haney
President and COO, Candice Saunders
Chief Medicine Division Officer, Jeffrey Tharp
SVP and Chief Nursing Executive, Mary Lou Wesley
Chief Cancer Network Officer, Michael Andrews
Chief Pediatrics Officer, Avril Beckford
EVP and CFO, Jim Budzinski
Chief Obstetrics and Gynecology Officer, Perry (Chip) Busbee
EVP; President and Chief Administrative Medical Officer WellStar Medical Group, Robert Jansen
SVP Post Acute Services; President WellStar Windy Hill Hospital, Lou Little
Chief Cardiology Officer, Barry Mangel
Chief Surgical Officer, Bill Mayfield
SVP and CIO, Jon Morris
Chief Pulmonary Officer, Alan Muster
SVP; President WellStar Douglas Hospital, Craig Owens
EVP and General Counsel, Leo Reichert
SVP; President WellStar Kennestone Hospital, Dan Woods
VP; COO WellStar Kennestone Hospital, Monte Wilson
SVP and President WellStar Spalding Regional Hospital and WellStar Sylvan Grove Hospital, Tamara Ison

Vice President Information Systems, Elizabeth Theobald
Senior Vice President Finance Secy Treasurer and Chief Financial Officer, Cindy White
Assistant Vice President, Cameron Crow
Vice President Community Relations, Kim Menefee
Division President, Tony Trupiano
AVP Human Resources, Stephanie Kallis
Assistant Vice President Human Resources, Jessica Bedsole
Director of Pharmacy, Susan Jackson
Assistant Vice President of Operations Wellstar Medical Group, Beth Papetti
Executive Vice President Chief Financial Officer And Director Somerset Hills Bancorp And, Patty Pate
Senior Vice President Managed Care, Barbara Corey
Vice President, Cynetra Zollicoffer
Assistant Vice President, Elizabeth Papetti
Vice President Financial Planning And Analysis, Elizabeth Hoffman
Vice President, Beth Loudermilk
Vice President Programming Information Technology, Sue-ellen Brogden
Medical Director, Abdul Sheikh
Assistant Vice President, Yvette Brewer
Associate Vice President Information Security and CISO, Mark Reardon
Director of Radiology, Tracy Wilkinson
AVP Finance, Meredith Bass
Senior Vice President, Kim Ryan
Assistant Vice President Human Resources, Detra Bickerstaff
Assistant Vice President and Assistant General Counsel, Lisa D'agostino
Vice President of Medical Affairs, Bob Lubitz
AVP of Operations, Kristen Bowman
Vice President, Kristen Trice
Assistant Vice President Population Health Management, Kam Sooknanan
Vice President and Assistant General Counsel, Keith Mauriello
Director of Clinical Services, Rebecca Deal
Executive Vice President Managed Care, Andre Greenwood
Vice President and Assistant General Counsel, Ryan Hood
Assistant Vice President Chief Nursing Officer, Ivy Spencer
Assistant Vice President Community Education and Outreach, Cecelia Patellis
Director of Nursing, Jenny Gifford
Treas, James Nalley
Secretary, Lisa Pagan
Vice Chairman, Dan Smith
Auditors: PRICEWATERHOUSECOOPERS LLP PH

LOCATIONS

HQ: WELLSTAR HEALTH SYSTEM, INC.
805 SANDY PLAINS RD, MARIETTA, GA 300666340
Phone: 770 956-7827

PRODUCTS/OPERATIONS

Selected Facilities
Atherton Place (Marietta Georgia)
The Jean and Mack Henderson Women's Center at Kennestone (Marietta Georgia)
WellStar Cobb Hospital (Austell Georgia)
WellStar Community Hospice (Austell Georgia)
WellStar Douglas Hospital (Douglasville Georgia)
WellStar Kennestone Hospital (Marietta Georgia)
WellStar Paulding Hospital (Dallas Georgia)
WellStar Paulding Nursing Center (Dallas Georgia)
WellStar Windy Hill Hospital (Marietta Georgia)
Urgent Care Centers
Cooper Lake Urgent Care Center
Delk Road Urgent Care Center
Kennesaw Urgent Care Center
Shallowford Urgent Care Center
Towne Lake Urgent Care Center

COMPETITORS

Central Georgia Health Systems
Children's Healthcare of Atlanta
DeKalb Medical
Doctors Hospital of Augusta
Emory Healthcare
Floyd Medical Center
Grady Health System
HCA
Northeast Georgia Health System
Phoebe Putney Memorial Hospital
Piedmont Athens Regional
St. Mary's Health Care
Tenet Healthcare
West Georgia Health System

HISTORICAL FINANCIALS
Company Type: Private

Income Statement
FYE: June 30

	REVENUE ($ mil.)	NET INCOME ($ mil.)	NET PROFIT MARGIN	EMPLOYEES
06/15	823	49	6.0%	11,985
06/09	397	0	—	—
06/08	5	1	33.1%	—
Annual Growth	105.2%	60.9%	—	—

2015 Year-End Financials
Return on assets: 23.0%
Return on equity: 6.0%
Current ratio: 0.40
Cash ($ mil.): 52

WENTWORTH INSTITUTE OF TECHNOLOGY, INC.

EXECUTIVES

President, Zorica Pantic
Treasurer, Jerome Cafey
Data Processing Manager, Robert Boyden
Data Processing Manager, Gary McLean
Trustee, George C Chryssis
Clerk, Sandra E Pascal
Auditors: CBIZ TOFIAS BOSTON MA

LOCATIONS

HQ: WENTWORTH INSTITUTE OF TECHNOLOGY, INC.
550 HUNTINGTON AVE, BOSTON, MA 021155998
Phone: 617 989-4590
Web: WWW.WENTWORTHATHLETICS.COM

HISTORICAL FINANCIALS
Company Type: Private

Income Statement
FYE: June 30

	REVENUE ($ mil.)	NET INCOME ($ mil.)	NET PROFIT MARGIN	EMPLOYEES
06/15	172	20	12.1%	450
06/14	142	6	4.8%	—
06/13	134	6	5.0%	—
06/10	105	3	3.5%	—
Annual Growth	10.3%	41.3%	—	—

2015 Year-End Financials
Return on assets: 4.9%
Return on equity: 12.1%
Current ratio: 0.30
Cash ($ mil.): 44

WENTWORTH-DOUGLASS HOSPITAL

EXECUTIVES

President, Gregory Walker
Chief Financial Officer, Peter Walcek
Project Manager, Rich Clough
Personnel Manager, Kimberly Jacques
Treasurer, Rick Card
Assistant Vice-President, Christine Hamill
Director, Dalma Winkler
Auditors: BAKER NEWMAN & NOYES LLC MAN

LOCATIONS

HQ: WENTWORTH-DOUGLASS HOSPITAL
  789 CENTRAL AVE, DOVER, NH 038202526
Phone: 603 742-5252
Web: WWW.WDHOSPITAL.COM

HISTORICAL FINANCIALS
Company Type: Private

Income Statement

	REVENUE ($ mil.)	NET INCOME ($ mil.)	NET PROFIT MARGIN	EMPLOYEES
12/15	322	12	3.9%	1,700
12/14	301	16	5.4%	—
12/13	281	27	9.6%	—
12/12	241	11	4.7%	—
Annual Growth	10.2%	3.4%	—	—

FYE: December 31

2015 Year-End Financials

Return on assets: 3.1%   Cash ($ mil.): 40
Return on equity: 3.9%
Current ratio: 0.80

WESLACO INDEPENDENT SCHOOL DISTRICT

EXECUTIVES

Superintendent, Ruben Alejandro
Director, Jevil Ruiz
Director, Lupita Gamez
Director, Melba Grado
Account Executive, Vera Aguirre
Auditors: NOEL GARZA CPA PC EDINBURG

LOCATIONS

HQ: WESLACO INDEPENDENT SCHOOL DISTRICT
  319 W 4TH ST, WESLACO, TX 785966047
Phone: 956 969-6500
Web: WWW.WISD.US

HISTORICAL FINANCIALS
Company Type: Private

Income Statement

	REVENUE ($ mil.)	NET INCOME ($ mil.)	NET PROFIT MARGIN	EMPLOYEES
08/15	182	(4)	—	2,500
08/14	174	10	5.8%	—
08/13	171	1	0.9%	—
08/12	167	(5)	—	—
Annual Growth	2.8%	—	—	—

FYE: August 31

2015 Year-End Financials

Return on assets: 1.6%   Cash ($ mil.): 55
Return on equity: (-2.3%)
Current ratio: —

WEST CHESTER AREA SCHOOL DISTRICT

EXECUTIVES

Superintendent, Dr James Scanlon
Board of Directors, Liz D'Annunzio
Administrative Assistant, Carol Deluca
Auditors: BARBACANE THORNTON & COMPANY

LOCATIONS

HQ: WEST CHESTER AREA SCHOOL DISTRICT
  782 SPRINGDALE DR, EXTON, PA 193412850
Phone: 484 266-1000

HISTORICAL FINANCIALS
Company Type: Private

Income Statement

	REVENUE ($ mil.)	NET INCOME ($ mil.)	NET PROFIT MARGIN	EMPLOYEES
06/16	220	9	4.4%	1,500
06/15	214	(8)	—	—
06/14*	206	4	2.1%	—
08/05	115	(1)	—	—
Annual Growth	6.1%	—	—	—

FYE: June 30

*Fiscal year change

2016 Year-End Financials

Return on assets: 10.1%   Cash ($ mil.): 18
Return on equity: 4.4%
Current ratio: 0.50

WEST CHESTER UNIVERSITY OF PENNSYLVANIA

EXECUTIVES

President, Greg Weisenstein
Director, Lynn J Porter
Auditors: CLIFTONLARSONALLEN LLP PLYMOU

LOCATIONS

HQ: WEST CHESTER UNIVERSITY OF PENNSYLVANIA
  700 S HIGH ST, WEST CHESTER, PA 193830003
Phone: 610 436-1000
Web: WWW.WCUPA.EDU

HISTORICAL FINANCIALS
Company Type: Private

Income Statement

	REVENUE ($ mil.)	NET INCOME ($ mil.)	NET PROFIT MARGIN	EMPLOYEES
06/16	204	5	2.4%	1,460
06/15	196	8	4.6%	—
06/14	192	17	8.9%	—
06/13	0	18	—	—
Annual Growth	—	(34.9%)	—	—

FYE: June 30

2016 Year-End Financials

Return on assets: 11.8%   Cash ($ mil.): 217
Return on equity: 2.4%
Current ratio: 5.80

WEST CONTRA COSTA UNIFIED SCHOOL DISTRICT

EXECUTIVES

President, Charles T Ramsey
Manager, Debbie Haynie
Assistant Manager, Alan Del Simone
Auditors: CROWE HORWATH LLP SACRAMENTO

LOCATIONS

HQ: WEST CONTRA COSTA UNIFIED SCHOOL DISTRICT
  1108 BISSELL AVE, RICHMOND, CA 948013135
Phone: 510 231-1100
Web: WWW.WCCUSD.NET

HISTORICAL FINANCIALS
Company Type: Private

Income Statement

	REVENUE ($ mil.)	NET INCOME ($ mil.)	NET PROFIT MARGIN	EMPLOYEES
06/16	457	83	18.2%	3,800
06/02	291	46	15.9%	—
06/01	279	8	3.1%	—
Annual Growth	3.3%	16.2%	—	—

FYE: June 30

WEST FLORIDA HOSPITAL

EXECUTIVES

President, Carlton Ulmer
Manager, Debbi Wroten
Director, Pam Parker
Administrative Assistant, Gary Hudson
Operations Manager, Scott Weichbrodt
Chief Operating Officer, Jessica Oneal
Director, Donna Shepherd

LOCATIONS

HQ: WEST FLORIDA HOSPITAL
8383 N DAVIS HWY, PENSACOLA, FL 325146088
Phone: 850 494-4000

HISTORICAL FINANCIALS

Company Type: Private

Income Statement

FYE: May 31

	REVENUE ($ mil.)	NET INCOME ($ mil.)	NET PROFIT MARGIN	EMPLOYEES
05/15	233	37	15.9%	8
05/09	179	(2)	—	—
Annual Growth	4.5%	—	—	—

2015 Year-End Financials

Return on assets: 2.0% Cash ($ mil.): —
Return on equity: 15.9%
Current ratio: 1.70

WEST GEORGIA HEALTH SYSTEM INC.

EXECUTIVES

Chief Executive Officer, Gerald N Fulks
Auditors: DIXON HUGHES GOODMAN LLP ATLA

LOCATIONS

HQ: WEST GEORGIA HEALTH SYSTEM INC.
1514 VERNON RD, LAGRANGE, GA 302404131
Phone: 706 882-1411

HISTORICAL FINANCIALS

Company Type: Private

Income Statement

FYE: September 30

	REVENUE ($ mil.)	NET INCOME ($ mil.)	NET PROFIT MARGIN	EMPLOYEES
09/15	175	10	6.0%	1,500
09/14	160	3	2.2%	—
09/13	163	(0)	—	—
09/12	159	(1)	—	—
Annual Growth	3.2%	—	—	—

2015 Year-End Financials

Return on assets: 6.5% Cash ($ mil.): 12
Return on equity: 6.0%
Current ratio: 1.60

WEST SIDE TRACTOR SALES CO.

EXECUTIVES

President, Steven L Benck
Account Manager, David Adeli
Sales Manager, Patricia Fauth
Manager, Al Walker
Manager, Dorene Hengle
Manager, Ben Schmidt
Production Manager, Bob Bazzetta
Auditors: HANSEN PLAHM & COMPANY DARIEN

LOCATIONS

HQ: WEST SIDE TRACTOR SALES CO.
1400 W OGDEN AVE, NAPERVILLE, IL 605633909
Phone: 630 355-7150
Web: WWW.WESTSIDETRACTORSALES.COM

HISTORICAL FINANCIALS

Company Type: Private

Income Statement

FYE: December 31

	REVENUE ($ mil.)	NET INCOME ($ mil.)	NET PROFIT MARGIN	EMPLOYEES
12/15	223	10	4.6%	190
12/14	186	9	5.3%	—
12/07	95	3	3.8%	—
12/06	107	4	4.2%	—
Annual Growth	8.6%	9.5%	—	—

2015 Year-End Financials

Return on assets: 10.0% Cash ($ mil.): —
Return on equity: 4.6%
Current ratio: 0.20

WESTAT, INC.

Survey the market research business and you'll find Westat among the leaders of the pack. A statistical survey organization the company provides research and consulting services including study design and analysis data collection program evaluation and communications campaign development. It has technical expertise in survey and analytical methods computer systems technology biomedical science and clinical trials. Westat serves US state and local government clients in addition to businesses and foundations. It has offices in five US states as well as international locations around the world. The company was founded in 1963 and is employee-owned.

Geographic Reach

Westat has nine regional offices in the US along with offices in five countries overseas.

Strategy

In 2014 Westat and the Pew Research Center partnered with SurveyMonkey to explore methods and tools that can be used with new technologies to provide useful data in an era when contacting survey respondents and gaining cooperation is more difficult that ever.

Mergers and Acquisitions

In 2015 the company acquired Edvance Reseach an education research and technical assistance organization. That same year Westat also acquired Fenestra an information technology solutions company. The acquisitions enhanced Westat's research capabilities.

EXECUTIVES

Vice President, Thomas McKenna
CTO, James E. Smith
VP Planning and Finance, Patricia Espey-English
Vice President, Boni Fash
Vice President of Human Resour, Randy Yu
Vice President, Laurie May
Vice President, Mark Freedman
Senior Vice President, Renee Slobasky
Vice President, Marsha Hasson
Senior Vice President Administration, Martha Palan
Vice President, Michael Brick
Vice President, Jane Shepherd
Vice President, Kerry Levin
Vice President, Susan Mountford
Vice President, Sue Connor
Vice President, Roger Tourangeau
Vice President, Nancy Dianis
Vice President, David Morganstein
Vice President, Dianne F Walsh
Vice President General Counsel, David Reesman
Vice President, Jim Greenlees
Vice President, Pat Ward
Vice President, Andrea Sedlak
Vice President, David Maklan
Vice President Human Resources, Louis Intili
Vice President, Jeanne Rosenthal
Vice President Marketing and Business Development, Patti Espey-English
Board Member Senior Vice President Executive Advisor, Tom McKenna
Auditors: RUBINO & COMPANY BETHESDA MD

LOCATIONS

HQ: WESTAT, INC.
1600 RESEARCH BLVD, ROCKVILLE, MD 208503129
Phone: 301 251-1500
Web: WWW.WESTATCAREERS.JOBS

PRODUCTS/OPERATIONS

Selected Operations and Services
Program areas
  Alcohol tobacco and other drug studies
  Consulting services and marketing research
  Customer satisfaction
  Education
  Employment and training
  Energy
  Environmental protection
  Health and medical studies
  Housing
  Military human resources
  Organizational and personnel studies
  Science and technology
  Social services and community development
  Transportation
Research services
  Clinical trials management
  Conference planning and support
  Data analysis and reporting
  Data preparation and processing
  Focus groups
  Program evaluation
  Qualitative studies
  Statistical sample design
  Study design
Survey Services
  Data collection from institutions and businesses
  Data preparation and processing
  Design
  In-field measurement and biospecimen collection
  Interviewing
  Mail surveys
  On-site data collection coordination
  Telephone surveys
  Web-based surveys

COMPETITORS

Gallup	Nielsen
GfK	ORC International
Harris Interactive	QinetiQ
IMS Health	SDI Health
Ipsos	Social & Scientific
J.D. Power	Systems
Kantar Group	Walker Information
Maritz Research	

HISTORICAL FINANCIALS

Company Type: Private

Income Statement

FYE: December 31

	REVENUE ($ mil.)	NET INCOME ($ mil.)	NET PROFIT MARGIN	EMPLOYEES
12/15	509	20	4.0%	2,000
12/14	517	22	4.3%	—
12/13	582	23	4.1%	—
12/12	495	28	5.8%	—
Annual Growth	0.9%	(10.3%)	—	—

2015 Year-End Financials

Return on assets: 1.2%   Cash ($ mil.): 43
Return on equity: 4.0%
Current ratio: 1.60

WESTCHESTER COUNTY HEALTH CARE CORPORATION

EXECUTIVES

President, Michael D Israel
Board of Directors, Julie Switzer
Manager, Al Schipani
Director, Alan Gass
Director, Arun Goyal

LOCATIONS

HQ: WESTCHESTER COUNTY HEALTH CARE
   CORPORATION
   100 WOODS RD, VALHALLA, NY 105951530
Phone: 914 493-7000
Web: WWW.WESTCHESTERMEDICALCENTER.COM

HISTORICAL FINANCIALS

Company Type: Private

Income Statement

FYE: December 31

	REVENUE ($ mil.)	NET INCOME ($ mil.)	NET PROFIT MARGIN	EMPLOYEES
12/15	1,069	33	3.1%	3,000
12/13	918	6	0.7%	—
12/12	821	15	1.9%	—
Annual Growth	9.2%	28.4%	—	—

2015 Year-End Financials

Return on assets: 11.6%   Cash ($ mil.): 92
Return on equity: 3.1%
Current ratio: 1.10

WESTECH ENGINEERING, INC.

EXECUTIVES

Chief Executive Officer, Rex R Plazier
Executive Vice-President, Ralph A Cutler
Vice-President, James R Hanson
Vice-President, Craig Martin
Vice-President, Vincent Hamilton
Chief Financial Officer, Greg Howell
President, Ralph Cutler
Engineer, Robert Vandeveegaete
Purchasing Agent, Tim Tsushima
Vice-President, Guy Roundy
Auditors: SQUIRE & COMPANY PC OREM UT

LOCATIONS

HQ: WESTECH ENGINEERING, INC.
   3665 S WEST TEMPLE, SALT LAKE CITY, UT
   841154409
Phone: 801 265-1000

HISTORICAL FINANCIALS

Company Type: Private

Income Statement

FYE: June 30

	REVENUE ($ mil.)	NET INCOME ($ mil.)	NET PROFIT MARGIN	EMPLOYEES
06/16	172	3	1.9%	529
06/12	143	2	2.1%	—
06/11	127	2	1.8%	—
06/10	1,402	0	0.0%	—
Annual Growth	(29.5%)	427.0%	—	—

2016 Year-End Financials

Return on assets: 10.4%   Cash ($ mil.): 6
Return on equity: 1.9%
Current ratio: 1.10

WESTERN CONNECTICUT MEDICAL GROUP

EXECUTIVES

Chief Financial Officer, Colleen Scott
Manager, Rosa Rivera

LOCATIONS

HQ: WESTERN CONNECTICUT MEDICAL GROUP
   14 RESEARCH DR, BETHEL, CT 068011040
Phone: 203 794-5331

HISTORICAL FINANCIALS

Company Type: Private

Income Statement

FYE: September 30

	REVENUE ($ mil.)	NET INCOME ($ mil.)	NET PROFIT MARGIN	EMPLOYEES
09/15	210	0	0.0%	838
09/14	166	0	0.5%	—
Annual Growth	26.2%	(95.4%)	—	—

2015 Year-End Financials

Return on assets: 7.6%   Cash ($ mil.): 13
Return on equity: —
Current ratio: 1.70

WESTERN FARMERS ELECTRIC COOPERATIVE

Power also comes sweeping down the plain in Oklahoma thanks to the Western Farmers Electric Cooperative. Led by its coal- and natural gas-fueled generating plants — three in Anadarko one in Mooreland and one in Hugo (all in Oklahoma) — the generation and transmission co-op produces more than 1845 MW of capacity. It pipes power over 3700 miles of transmission lines to two-thirds of rural Oklahoma and parts of New Mexico. It also operates 264 substations and 59 switch stations. Western Farmers Electric Cooperative which is owned by its member distribution cooperatives supplies 22 distribution co-ops and Altus Air Force base which serve a total of a half million members.

Operations

The company maintains a well-balanced and diversified portfolio of generation resources reflecting a mix of technologies and fuel types. In 2013 coal represented 33% of Western Farmers Electric Cooperative's energy production with natural gas at 12 percent. Power generated from wind resources represents about 14% of the coop's energy mix hydro 7%. Economy purchases energy imbalance purchases and contract power (primarily natural gas) made up the balance.

Geographic Reach

Western Farmers Electric Cooperative's members consist of 22 distribution cooperatives (serving customers in Kansas Oklahoma New Mexico and Texas) and the Altus Air Force Base in Oklahoma.

Financial Performance

In 2013 the company's revenues increased by 15% to $525.3 million due to a 7.7% energy sales increase. (Its average MWh sales growth rate of 5.5% over the past three year is above the national average). Western Farmers Electric Cooperative also gets a small amount of off-system sales from three of its four New Mexico members. Power sales increased $64 million in 2013 due to higher MWh sales a slight increase in wholesale power rates and a 40% rise in natural gas prices.

Western Farmers Electric Cooperative's net income increased by 61% in 2013 due to higher sales and an increase in noninterest income.

That year the company's operating cash inflow increased to $53.3 million (compared to $21.2 million in 2012) primarily due to higher net income and increased coal and oil inventory.

Strategy

Western Farmers Electric Cooperative has diversified its fuel mix to meet green energy regulations and boasts one of the state's largest renewable energy portfolios. The diversity in generation mix helps reduce exposure to changing market conditions helping to keep rates competitive.

In 2013 the company signed a purchase with Apex Clean Energy through its subsidiary Balko Wind LLC for 100 MW of wind energy from the Balko Wind Project. With this agreement Apex has sold all the capacity of 300 MW project which will produce enough electricity to power over 110000 U.S. homes. This new site represents the fifth Oklahoma wind farm development that is a part of an ongoing commitment to diversify Western Farmers Electric Cooperative's portfolio of generation sources.

That year it also entered into a purchase and sale agreement with community-wind developer National Renewable Solutions to acquire the development assets for the Broadview Wind Projects in New Mexico. The two projects with a combined 19.8 MW capacity will each sell power over the next 20 years to Western Farmers Electric Cooperative. This wind farm site is in the service territory of Western Farmers Electric Cooperative member Farmers' Electric Cooperative.

In 2012 the company teamed up with Enel Green Power which that year began operating the 150-MW Rocky Ridge Wind Project in Kiowa and Washita counties Oklahoma. The energy gener-

ated by the wind farm will be bought by Western Farmers Electric Cooperative.

In 2012 Calpine Corporation agreed to supply Western Farmers Electric Cooperative with electric generation capacity and power (up to 280 MW) from Calpine's gas-fired Oneta Energy Center from June 2014 through 2035.

Company Background

Growing its geographic coverage in late 2010 Western Farmers Electric Cooperative added four New Mexico-based cooperatives (Farmers' Central Valley Lea County and Roosevelt County with a total of 400 MW of load) to its membership.

Responding to a growing demand for power in 2009 the power co-op completed an expansion project at its gas-fueled Anadarko plant adding some 145 MW of power generating capacity.

Western Farmers Electric Cooperative was organized in 1941 by western Oklahoma rural electric distribution cooperatives in order to secure power generation and distribution at an affordable rate. The co-op began generating power in 1950.

EXECUTIVES

Secretary, Shelly Trammell
Secretary T and D Engineering, Shelli Pearson
Auditors: KPMG LLP OKLAHOMA CITY OKLAH

LOCATIONS

HQ: WESTERN FARMERS ELECTRIC COOPERATIVE
701 NE 7TH ST, ANADARKO, OK 730052297
Phone: 405 247-3351
Web: WWW.WFEC.US

COMPETITORS

Empire District
  Electric
Entergy
Grand River Dam
  Authority

OGE Energy
ONEOK
PG&E Corporation

HISTORICAL FINANCIALS

Company Type: Private

Income Statement

FYE: December 31

	REVENUE ($ mil.)	NET INCOME ($ mil.)	NET PROFIT MARGIN	EMPLOYEES
12/15	671	31	4.6%	378
12/14	702	40	5.8%	—
12/13	525	21	4.1%	—
12/12	457	13	2.9%	—
Annual Growth	13.7%	32.8%	—	—

2015 Year-End Financials

Return on assets: 11.5%   Cash ($ mil.): 6
Return on equity: 4.6%
Current ratio: 0.40

WESTERN GOVERNORS UNIVERSITY

EXECUTIVES

Chief Executive Officer, Robert W Mendenhall
Manager, David R Grow
Trustee, Emily Derocco
President, Sally Johnstone
Program Manager, Theresa Spicer
VP Personnel, Nanette Pearson
Personnel Manager, Debra Lawler
Auditors: TANNER LLC SALT LAKE CITY UT

LOCATIONS

HQ: WESTERN GOVERNORS UNIVERSITY
4001 S 700 E STE 700, SALT LAKE CITY, UT
841072533
Phone: 801 274-3280
Web: WWW.WGU.EDU

HISTORICAL FINANCIALS

Company Type: Private

Income Statement

FYE: June 30

	REVENUE ($ mil.)	NET INCOME ($ mil.)	NET PROFIT MARGIN	EMPLOYEES
06/15	381	25	6.8%	208
06/13	249	16	6.8%	—
06/12	200	4	2.5%	—
06/11	1,159	0	0.0%	—
Annual Growth	(24.3%)	529.8%	—	—

2015 Year-End Financials

Return on assets: 7.9%   Cash ($ mil.): 24
Return on equity: 6.8%
Current ratio: 0.30

WESTERN MARYLAND HEALTH SYSTEM

EXECUTIVES

Chief Operating Officer, Nancy D Adams
Purchasing Manager, Alan Snyder
Purchasing Agent, Brenda Moreland
Supervisor, Edith Jenkins
Consultant, Robert Manasse
Director, Steve Conrad
Auditors: KPMG LLP BALTIMORE MD

LOCATIONS

HQ: WESTERN MARYLAND HEALTH SYSTEM
12500 WILLOWBROOK RD, CUMBERLAND, MD
215026393
Phone: 240 964-7000
Web: WWW.WMHS.COM

HISTORICAL FINANCIALS

Company Type: Private

Income Statement

FYE: June 30

	REVENUE ($ mil.)	NET INCOME ($ mil.)	NET PROFIT MARGIN	EMPLOYEES
06/16	319	9	3.0%	1,879
06/14	295	28	9.6%	—
06/13	301	17	5.9%	—
06/11	173	0	0.0%	—
Annual Growth	13.1%	582.8%	—	—

2016 Year-End Financials

Return on assets: 4.3%   Cash ($ mil.): 72
Return on equity: 3.0%
Current ratio: 2.20

WESTERN STATES FIRE PROTECTION COMPANY INC

Western States Fire Protection (WSFP) is sprinkling its own brand of safety west of the Mississippi. The company a division of APi Group installs water-based fire sprinklers and other fire suppression systems for the commercial residential and industrial markets primarily in the western US. It designs installs and maintains fire protection systems at defense gaming high-tech institutional medical processing and sports facilities. Specific projects include installing systems at the Colorado Convention Center and Microsoft's data storage facility in Washington. WSFP also manufactures fire sprinklers at its own fabrication workshops. The company was founded in 1985.

In addition to its water-based fire sprinklers WSFP serves hazardous facilities with FM-200 and carbon dioxide systems. FM-200 is a dry chemical that extinguishes fire through a combination of chemically-based inhibition and cooling. These systems are used in facilities where water damage must be avoided such as art galleries historical libraries and record and storage facilities.

EXECUTIVES

President, Gene Postma
Board of Directors, William M Beadie
Assistant Controller, Michael Davis
Manager, Kimberly Willcoxson
Operations Manager, Marinus Both
Vice-President, June Charles
Manager, Andy Mayer
Project Manager, Pete Ballweber
Manager, Benjamin Stewart
Auditors: KPMG LLP MINNEAPOLIS MN

LOCATIONS

HQ: WESTERN STATES FIRE PROTECTION COMPANY INC
7026 S TUCSON WAY, CENTENNIAL, CO 801123921
Phone: 303 792-0022
Web: WWW.WSFP.COM

COMPETITORS

COSCO Fire Protection
China Fire
Sharpfibre
SimplexGrinnell

Tyco Fire & Security
UTC Climate Controls &
  Security

HISTORICAL FINANCIALS

Company Type: Private

Income Statement

FYE: December 31

	REVENUE ($ mil.)	NET INCOME ($ mil.)	NET PROFIT MARGIN	EMPLOYEES
12/15	274	31	11.6%	1,429
12/14	260	26	10.0%	—
12/13	225	19	8.5%	—
12/12	202	17	8.5%	—
Annual Growth	10.6%	22.5%	—	—

2015 Year-End Financials

Return on assets: 1.4%   Cash ($ mil.): —
Return on equity: 11.6%
Current ratio: 0.80

WESTERN UNIVERSITY OF HEALTH SCIENCES

EXECUTIVES

President, Philip Pumerantz
Vice-President, Clifford E Holland
Senior Vice-President, Gary Gugelchuk
Vice-President, Dr Tom Fox
Senior Vice-President, Thomas G Fox
Vice-President, Clinton Adams
Manager, Peggy Barr
Auditors: GRANT THORNTON LLP LOS ANGELE

LOCATIONS

HQ: WESTERN UNIVERSITY OF HEALTH SCIENCES
309 E 2ND ST, POMONA, CA 917661854
Phone: 909 623-6116
Web: WWW.WESTERNU.EDU

HISTORICAL FINANCIALS

Company Type: Private

Income Statement

FYE: June 30

	REVENUE ($ mil.)	NET INCOME ($ mil.)	NET PROFIT MARGIN	EMPLOYEES
06/16	196	9	4.7%	1,000
06/15	191	14	7.7%	—
06/10	110	1	1.0%	—
06/09	101	10	10.0%	—
Annual Growth	9.9%	(1.3%)	—	—

2016 Year-End Financials

Return on assets: 15.4%   Cash ($ mil.): 3
Return on equity: 4.7%
Current ratio: —

WESTERN WASHINGTON UNIVERSITY

If you're in the West and you're looking for a liberal arts education look no further than Western Washington University. The university is located in northwest Washington state and is one of a handful of state-funded four-year institutions of higher education in Washington. The school has an enrollment of about 15000 students; roughly 95% of those are undergraduate students. Western Washington University has a student-teacher ratio of roughly 21:1.The university has students from almost every other state and from three dozen other countries. Western which began as a teachers college accepting its first students in 1899 became a full university in 1977.

Operations

Western Washington University offers its students five colleges with more than 160 academic programs. Students can also design their own degrees such as some recent choices: Medicine and Social Justice Eco-Cultural Studies in Education and Law Diversity & Public Policy.

Geographic Reach

The university serves mostly undergraduate students in northwest Washington state.

Financial Performance

The university has been growing in recent years. New enrollment and improved retention have helped Western Washington University post an 8% increase in revenue in 2012 as compared to 2011. Attracting students through scholarship allowances eroded some of its 13% increases in tuition revenue. The educational institution also generated revenue from state and local grants and contracts as well as sales services of educational activities. Net income meanwhile dropped some 46% during the same reporting period. Non-operating revenue such as declines in income from state appropriation loss on endowments and rental property expenses all contributed toward the net income slip.

Strategy

Western Washington University works to regularly provide additional programs. In 2013 the school's College of Sciences and Technology and Whatcom Community College partnered to offer a bachelor's degree in Computer and Information Systems Security. It also introduced a Bachelor's Degree Program in Nursing.

To provide a more flexible education option for students Western Washington University's Woodring College of Education offers a Master of Education in Continuing and College Education degree program through an online-only basis. It has also rolled out an online-only TESOL Certificate Program.

The university provides for studying abroad through its Center for International Studies. Students enrolled in this program generally learn a foreign language and have the opportunity to immerse themselves in their chosen culture. Conversely the school offers international students the opportunity to learn English through the International Students at Western program.

Western Washington University also runs a program called Query a faculty research database that allows other faculty members and students to keep tabs on what the university's teachers are interested in and possibly looking to teach. Members can look up who researched specific subjects. Query which can be used to search by subject area last name or by department gives members the ability to find out what Western Washington University's faculty are working on.

Auditors: JAN M JUTTE CPA CGFM OLYMP

LOCATIONS

HQ: WESTERN WASHINGTON UNIVERSITY
516 HIGH ST, BELLINGHAM, WA 982255996
Phone: 360 650-3720
Web: WWW.WWU.EDU

PRODUCTS/OPERATIONS

Selected Colleges

College of Business and Economics
College Of Fine and Performing Arts
College of Humanities and Social Sciences
College of Sciences and Technology
Fairhaven College of Interdisciplinary Studies
Graduate School
Huxley College of the Environment
Woodring College of Education

HISTORICAL FINANCIALS

Company Type: Private

Income Statement

FYE: June 30

	REVENUE ($ mil.)	NET INCOME ($ mil.)	NET PROFIT MARGIN	EMPLOYEES
06/16	211	14	7.0%	466
06/15	206	1	0.6%	—
06/14	200	3	1.9%	—
06/13	196	5	2.8%	—
Annual Growth	2.4%	39.4%	—	—

2016 Year-End Financials

Return on assets: 8.3%   Cash ($ mil.): 14
Return on equity: 7.0%
Current ratio: 0.60

WESTERVILLE CITY SCHOOL DISTRICT BOARD OF EDUCATION

EXECUTIVES

President, Richard Bird
Manager, Diane Schiffbauer
Personnel Manager, Ernest Husarik
Auditors: DAVE YOST AUDITOR OF STATE C

LOCATIONS

HQ: WESTERVILLE CITY SCHOOL DISTRICT BOARD OF EDUCATION
936 EASTWIND DR STE 200, WESTERVILLE, OH 430813329
Phone: 614 797-5700
Web: WWW.WESTERVILLE.K12.OH.US

HISTORICAL FINANCIALS

Company Type: Private

Income Statement

FYE: June 30

	REVENUE ($ mil.)	NET INCOME ($ mil.)	NET PROFIT MARGIN	EMPLOYEES
06/16	202	16	7.9%	106
06/10	173	33	19.1%	—
06/09	156	(6)	—	—
06/08	0	0	—	—
Annual Growth	—	253.6%	—	—

2016 Year-End Financials

Return on assets: 0.6%   Cash ($ mil.): 101
Return on equity: 7.9%
Current ratio: —

WESTMORELAND REGIONAL HOSPITAL

EXECUTIVES

Chief Executive Officer, David Gallatin
Board of Directors, Dirk Kalp
VP Finance, Richard Caruso
Director, Anthony Waltos
Senior Vice-President, John Caverno
Auditors: ARNETT CARBIS TOOTHMAN LLP PI

LOCATIONS

HQ: WESTMORELAND REGIONAL HOSPITAL
532 W PITTSBURGH ST, GREENSBURG, PA 156012282
Phone: 724 832-4000
Web: WWW.EXCELAHEALTH.ORG

HISTORICAL FINANCIALS

Company Type: Private

Income Statement

FYE: June 30

	REVENUE ($ mil.)	NET INCOME ($ mil.)	NET PROFIT MARGIN	EMPLOYEES
06/15	245	24	9.8%	2,000
06/14	12	8	64.1%	—
06/13	6	1	20.0%	—
06/09	234	(14)	—	—
Annual Growth	0.7%	—	—	—

2015 Year-End Financials
Return on assets: 5.3%   Cash ($ mil.): —
Return on equity: 9.8%
Current ratio: 0.60

WHEATON FRANCISCAN HEALTHCARE- ST. FRANCIS, INC.

EXECUTIVES

President, Dan Mattes
Director, Abram Buthta
Personnel Director, Rob Bauer
Plant & Facilities Manager, Brad Winnie
Manager, Tammy Brazzoni
Director, Aaron Bridgelend
Personnel Director, Christopher Morris

LOCATIONS

HQ: WHEATON FRANCISCAN HEALTHCARE- ST. FRANCIS, INC.
3237 S 16TH ST STE 1005, MILWAUKEE, WI 532154526
Phone: 414 647-5000
Web: WWW.MYWHEATON.ORG

HISTORICAL FINANCIALS
Company Type: Private

Income Statement

	REVENUE ($ mil.)	NET INCOME ($ mil.)	NET PROFIT MARGIN	EMPLOYEES
06/15	197	7	3.9%	4,000
06/14	192	6	3.3%	
06/11	158	(1)	—	
06/10	0	(2)	—	
Annual Growth		—	—	—

FYE: June 30

WHEATON FRANCISCAN SERVICES, INC.

Wheaton Franciscan Services Inc. (WFSI) is the not-for-profit parent company for more than 100 health care housing and social service organizations in Colorado Illinois Iowa and Wisconsin. Also known as Wheaton Franciscan Healthcare WFSI operates about 15 hospitals including Affinity Health System Rush Oak Park Hospital and United Hospital System with more than 1600 beds total. WFSI also includes long-term care centers home health agencies and physician offices. Its Franciscan Ministries division provides affordable housing units including assisted-living facilities and low-income dwellings. The health system is sponsored by The Franciscan Sisters Daughters of the Sacred Hearts of Jesus and Mary.

Operations

Many of WFSI's hospitals are operated in partnership with other area providers. For instance the Affinity Health System in Wisconsin is jointly sponsored by Wheaton Franciscan Sisters and Ministry Health Care while the Rush Oak Park Hospital in Illinois is operated through a partnership between WFSI and the Rush System for Health.

The health system partners with the YMCA of Milwaukee to try to address chronic health concerns of area residents. The two organizations converted a local YMCA campus into the YMCA Healthy Lifestyle Village. The center offers health screenings health education outpatient therapy and fitness services. WFSI and the YMCA have more Healthy Lifestyle Village campuses planned for other locations within their service areas.

The organization had a total of 1656 beds and 2620 housing units at the end of 2014.

In fiscal 2013 WSFI delivered more than 8000 babies and had more than 330000 emergency department visits. It reported more than 1580000 outpatient visits and some 64000 hospital admissions. It employs more than 500 physicians and has some 2000 affiliated physicians.

Geographic Reach

WFSI operates in Wisconsin Iowa Colorado and Illinois.

Financial Performance

The not-for-profit system's revenues were flat in fiscal 2014 at $1.8 billion. Net income totaled $184 million.

Strategy

To increase the scope of specialty health care services it can provide to the community WFSI recruits new physicians and specialists to the Wheaton Franciscan Medical Group. The system also works to improve communication among its physicians and facilities by adding electronic health record (EHR) systems.

In 2013 the system opened a new 80000-sq.-ft. outpatient center specializing in neurology services.

Company Background

The Franciscan Sisters Daughters of the Sacred Hearts of Jesus and Mary (also known as the Wheaton Franciscan Sisters) founded WSFI in 1983 as a holding company for their ministry operations. The health system traces its roots back to the founding of the St. Mary's Hospital in Racine Wisconsin in 1882.

EXECUTIVES

Treasurer Director, Timothy Jest
Auditors: KPMG LLP CHICAGO IL

LOCATIONS

HQ: WHEATON FRANCISCAN SERVICES, INC.
400 W RIVER WOODS PKWY, GLENDALE, WI 532121060
Phone: 414 465-3000
Web: WWW.WFHC.ORG

PRODUCTS/OPERATIONS

Selected Operations
Franciscan Ministries Inc. (housing in Colorado Illinois Iowa and Wisconsin)
Illinois
  Marianjoy Rehabilitation Hospital (Wheaton)
  Rush Oak Park Hospital (affiliate Oak Park)
Iowa (Wheaton Franciscan Healthcare of Iowa)
  Covenant Medical Center (Waterloo)
  Mercy Hospital (Oelwein)
  Sartori Memorial Hospital (Cedar Falls)
Wisconsin
  Affinity Health System (partnership with Minstry Health Care)
  Calumet Medical Center (Chilton)
  Mercy Medical Center (Oshkosh)
  St. Elizabeth Hospital (Appleton)
  Wheaton Franciscan Healthcare of Southeast Wisconsin
  All Saints Hospital (two campuses in Racine)
  Elmbrook Memorial Hospital (Brookfield)
  Franklin Hospital (Franklin)
  St. Francis Hospital (Milwaukee)
  St. Joseph Hospital (Milwaukee)
  Wisconsin Heart Hospital (Wauwatosa)
United Hospital System Inc. (affiliated system)
  Kenosha Medical Center (Kenosha)
  St. Catherine's Medical Center (Pleasant Prairie)

COMPETITORS

Advocate Health Care	KishHealth
Alden Management Services	Loyola University Health System
Children's Hospital and Health System	Ministry Health Care
Columbia St. Mary's	Morris Hospital
Elmhurst Memorial Healthcare	NorthShore University HealthSystem
FHN	OSF Healthcare System
Froedtert Hospital	ProHealth Care
Hospital Sisters Health System	Rockford Health System
	SwedishAmerican Health System

HISTORICAL FINANCIALS
Company Type: Private

Income Statement

	REVENUE ($ mil.)	NET INCOME ($ mil.)	NET PROFIT MARGIN	EMPLOYEES
06/15	1,809	18	1.0%	18,000
06/14	1,754	128	7.3%	—
06/13	1,763	177	10.1%	—
06/12	1,723	(112)	—	—
Annual Growth	1.6%	—	—	—

FYE: June 30

2015 Year-End Financials
Return on assets: 14.5%   Cash ($ mil.): 81
Return on equity: 1.0%
Current ratio: 1.00

WHEELING HOSPITAL, INC.

EXECUTIVES

Chief Executive Officer, Ronald Viola
Vice-President, John Pastorius
Chief Financial Officer, James Murdy
President, Kevin M Quirk
Auditors: DELOITTE & TOUCHE LLP PITTSBU

LOCATIONS

HQ: WHEELING HOSPITAL, INC.
1 MEDICAL PARK, WHEELING, WV 260036300
Phone: 304 243-3000
Web: WWW.WHEELINGHOSPITAL.ORG

HISTORICAL FINANCIALS
Company Type: Private

Income Statement

	REVENUE ($ mil.)	NET INCOME ($ mil.)	NET PROFIT MARGIN	EMPLOYEES
09/16	355	29	8.2%	1,228
09/15	339	24	7.1%	—
09/14	321	35	11.2%	—
09/13	297	15	5.2%	—
Annual Growth	6.1%	23.6%	—	—

FYE: September 30

2016 Year-End Financials
Return on assets: 3.9%   Cash ($ mil.): 144
Return on equity: 8.2%
Current ratio: 4.10

WHEELING-NISSHIN, INC.

Wheeling-Nisshin a subsidiary of Nisshin Steel produces a variety of hot-dip coated steels such as stainless steel. The company's output includes 400000 tons produced at its aluminizing and galvanizing line facility and 300000 tons produced at its continuous galvanizing line facility. Both of the facilities are located at the company's headquarters site in West Virginia. Its primary customers are in the automotive appliance and construction industries. Wheeling-Nisshin was founded in 1986. It had been a joint venture between Nisshin and US steel producer Wheeling Pitt (now operating as Severstal Wheeling) until the Japanese steel company bought out its partner in early 2008.

EXECUTIVES

Vice President Manufacturing Operations, Pat J Pendleton
Auditors: ERNST & YOUNG LLP

LOCATIONS

HQ: WHEELING-NISSHIN, INC.
  400 PENN ST, FOLLANSBEE, WV 260371412
Phone: 304 527-2800
Web: WWW.WHEELINGNISSHIN.COM

COMPETITORS

Dofasco   United States Steel
  ThyssenKrupp Stainless

HISTORICAL FINANCIALS

Company Type: Private

Income Statement

FYE: December 31

	REVENUE ($ mil.)	NET INCOME ($ mil.)	NET PROFIT MARGIN	EMPLOYEES
12/15	384	7	2.0%	175
12/14	483	5	1.2%	—
12/13	391	2	0.7%	—
12/12	426	6	1.6%	—
Annual Growth	(3.4%)	3.3%	—	—

2015 Year-End Financials

Return on assets: 2.4%   Cash ($ mil.): 52
Return on equity: 2.0%
Current ratio: 4.10

WHITE COUNTY MEDICAL CENTER

If you're sick in Searcy you may want to visit White County Medical Center (WCMC). The organization provides health care to Central Arkansas' residents. It has about 440 licensed inpatient beds on two hospital campuses (WCMC North and WCMC South) as well as a number of outpatient surgery centers primary care clinics and a retirement community called River Oaks Village. The WCMC South campus features an inpatient rehabilitation center that helps patients recover from injury and illness as well as a long-term acute care hospital for patients needing extended general care. In addition WCMC provides home health care services and runs a training program for certified

nurse assistants. WCMC operates under the Unity Health brand.
  Operations
  The Center's operations include Family Practice Associates Orthopaedic and Spine Center of Central Arkansas Searcy Medical Center and Searcy Medical Center - West Clinic Westside Family Medical Clinic WCMC Cardiology Clinic and White County Oncology.
  WCMC employs some 1700 health care professionals including 150 physicians. Most of its general and specialty acute care services are provided at the main WCMC North Campus location including critical care cardiac rehabilitation and radiology. Its specialty services include cancer care diabetes education diagnostic imaging and labor and delivery services. It also operates a 31-bed inpatient rehabilitation center.
  Geographic Reach
  The hospital serves patients in Independence Jackson Lonoke Prairie White and Woodruff Counties.
  Strategy
  In 2013 the Center created a comprehensive center to better care for patients with orthopaedic and spine needs — the Orthopaedic and Spine Center of Central Arkansas in Searcy.
  In 2012 the Arkansas Department of Health made WCMC a Level III Trauma Center an integral part of the statewide trauma system.
  Company Background
  Founded in 1967 WCMC later acquired fellow health care provider Central Arkansas Hospital also located in Searcy and subsequently renamed it WCMC South. The South campus was expanded in 2008 with the opening of Compass an inpatient psychiatric facility for adults.

EXECUTIVES

Respiratory Therapy Director, Gary Turner
Clinical Director, Glenda Light
Pharmacy Manager, Dennis Milner
Ast. Vice President Specialty Services, Ramona Staton
Assistant Vice President of Fiscal Services, Bj Roberts

LOCATIONS

HQ: WHITE COUNTY MEDICAL CENTER
  3214 E RACE AVE, SEARCY, AR 721434810
Phone: 501 268-6121
Web: WWW.WCMC.ORG

COMPETITORS

Arkansas Children's Hospital
  Arkansas Heart Hospital
  Baptist Health (Arkansas)
  Community Health Systems
  Conway Regional Health System
  Jefferson Regional Medical Center of Arkansas
  St. Vincent Health System
  WRMC

HISTORICAL FINANCIALS

Company Type: Private

Income Statement

FYE: September 30

	REVENUE ($ mil.)	NET INCOME ($ mil.)	NET PROFIT MARGIN	EMPLOYEES
09/15	198	10	5.0%	1,010
09/14	188	18	9.9%	—
09/13	177	17	9.7%	—
09/09	482	11	2.5%	—
Annual Growth	(13.8%)	(2.9%)	—	—

2015 Year-End Financials

Return on assets: 2.4%   Cash ($ mil.): 14
Return on equity: 5.0%
Current ratio: 1.60

WHITE PLAINS HOSPITAL MEDICAL CENTER

EXECUTIVES

President, Jon B Schandler
Board of Directors, Barbara Lapp
Vice-President, Daniel Blum
Board of Directors, Jill Haskel
Board of Directors, Natalie Webb

LOCATIONS

HQ: WHITE PLAINS HOSPITAL MEDICAL CENTER
  41 E POST RD, WHITE PLAINS, NY 106014607
Phone: 914 681-0600

HISTORICAL FINANCIALS

Company Type: Private

Income Statement

FYE: December 31

	REVENUE ($ mil.)	NET INCOME ($ mil.)	NET PROFIT MARGIN	EMPLOYEES
12/15	389	23	6.1%	2,000
12/14	353	8	2.3%	—
12/13	373	7	2.1%	—
12/08	238	(0)	—	—
Annual Growth	7.2%			

2015 Year-End Financials

Return on assets: 8.5%   Cash ($ mil.): 15
Return on equity: 6.1%
Current ratio: 0.60

WHITE RIVER HEALTH SYSTEM, INC.

White River Health System offers health care services to residents of north central Arkansas. The not-for-profit organization operates two hospitals the flagship White River Medical Center and acute care facility Stone County Medical Center which provides health care services to rural communities. Combined the two hospitals have about 225 beds and provide a range of emergency surgical medical and diagnostic services. The system also includes outpatient facilities primary care and specialty physician offices long-term care facilities for the elderly and those unable to live independently.
  Geographic Reach
  White River Health System provides services to residents living in nine counties: Cleburne Fulton Independence Izard Lawrence Jackson Sharp Stone and Van Buren.
  Operations
  White River Medical Center which opened in 1976 offers specialized services in the areas of cancer and heart disease treatment orthopedic surgery rehabilitation wound healing pain management weight loss and women's health. Sister hospital Stone County Medical Center built in 1999 caters to those who live in Arkansas' more rural Mountain View region.
  The hospitals provide medical training services through partnerships with area colleges including

Arkansas State University University of Arkansas Harding University and Ozarka College.

EXECUTIVES

President, Charles Schaaf
Board of Directors, Leslie Frensley
Board of Directors, Kay Southerland
Director, Margaret Kendall
Auditors: WELCH COUCH & COMPANY PA BATE

LOCATIONS

HQ: WHITE RIVER HEALTH SYSTEM, INC.
  1710 HARRISON ST, BATESVILLE, AR 725017303
Phone: 870 262-1200
Web: WWW.WHITERIVERHEALTHSYSTEM.COM

PRODUCTS/OPERATIONS

Selected Facilities
Cave City Medical Clinic
Drasco Medical Clinic
Hardy Medical Clinic
Melbourne Medical Clinic
Midway Medical Clinic
Newark Medical Clinic
Newport Diagnostic Medical Clinic
Pleasant Plains Medical Clinic
Stone County Medical Center
Stone County Primary Care Clinic
Strawberry Medical Clinic
White River Medical Center
White River Orthopaedics and Sports Medicine
WRMC Medical Complex

COMPETITORS

Baptist Health (Arkansas)	St. Vincent Health System
Conway Regional Health System	White County Medical Center
Mercy Health	

HISTORICAL FINANCIALS

Company Type: Private

Income Statement

FYE: September 30

	REVENUE ($ mil.)	NET INCOME ($ mil.)	NET PROFIT MARGIN	EMPLOYEES
09/15	183	7	4.0%	1,500
09/14	170	4	2.7%	—
09/13	151	5	3.5%	—
09/12	148	5	3.6%	—
Annual Growth	7.3%	10.6%	—	—

2015 Year-End Financials

Return on assets: 9.6%   Cash ($ mil.): 61
Return on equity: 4.0%
Current ratio: 1.40

WICHITA, CITY OF (INC)

What do Wyatt Earp Cessna and the first sub-four minute mile have in common? The City of Wichita. known as Cow Town and the Air Capital of the World was incorporated in 1870. The city has a population of more than 380000 occupying a little more than 163 sq. mi. Wichita State and 14 other campuses of higher education provide technical skills for leading employers. Boeing Learjet Raytheon Cargill and Koch are major companies with operations in the city.

EXECUTIVES

Secretary, Diana Mefford
Treasurer, Michelle Law
Auditors: ALLEN GIBBS & HOULIK LC CPA

LOCATIONS

HQ: WICHITA, CITY OF (INC)
  455 N MAIN ST FL 5, WICHITA, KS 672021601
Phone: 316 268-4351
Web: WWW.WICHITA.GOV

HISTORICAL FINANCIALS

Company Type: Private

Income Statement

FYE: December 31

	REVENUE ($ mil.)	NET INCOME ($ mil.)	NET PROFIT MARGIN	EMPLOYEES
12/15	392	(8)	—	2,200
12/09	387	37	9.6%	—
12/08	393	(31)	—	—
Annual Growth	(0.0%)	—	—	—

2015 Year-End Financials

Return on assets: 8.2%   Cash ($ mil.): 249
Return on equity: (-2.2%)
Current ratio: —

WILDLIFE CONSERVATION SOCIETY

From Congo gorillas to humpback whales off the coast of Gabon all life is worth conserving to the Wildlife Conservation Society (WCS). The group founded in 1895 works to protect wildlife and lands throughout the world and to instill in humans a concern about nature. The not-for-profit organization operates New York City's Bronx Zoo New York Aquarium Central Park Zoo Prospect Park Zoo and the Queens Zoo. WCS's environmental education programs are used in US schools as well as those in other nations. The society has ongoing efforts in more than 60 countries to protect endangered species and ecosystems. About a quarter of the funding for its work comes from visitors at its handful of parks.

Operations

WCS manages about 500 conservation projects nationwide and works to educate millions of visitors at its handful of living institutions: the Bronx Zoo New York Aquarium Central Park Zoo Prospect Park Zoo and Queens Zoo. As part of its operations WCS manages more than 200 million acres of protected lands globally and retains a staff of 200-plus scientists.

Geographic Reach

The society operates country programs across four continents including Africa Asia Latin America and North America. It boasts ongoing efforts in 60-plus countries.

Sales and Marketing

WCS is working to ramp up its construction. The group's revised Master Plan includes enhancements at the Bronx Zoo's C.V. Starr Science Campus with the Special Care Unit and LaMattina Wildlife Ambassador Center the Queens Zoo's jaguar exhibit and the Ocean Wonders exhibit.

During the past decade WCS has spent $243 million to fund physical plant improvements on its five campuses. They were financed through grants from New York City and the federal government private gifts and the proceeds from WCS's Series 2004 tax-exempt bond issue.

Financial Performance

Despite the anemic economy in recent years WCS has logged healthy attendance of about 4 million visitors across its five New York City parks.

As Americans chose to vacation at home WCS has benefited. With those visitors came a noteworthy boost in income from gate admissions exhibits and contributions from visitor services such as food merchandising and parking. Attendance-driven revenues reach more than $50 million.

The conservation group points to its operational diversity for being able to keep its head above water when funding from the state and other entities it had relied on had slimmed.

EXECUTIVES

Executive Vice President Public Affairs, John Calvelli
Executive Vice President Conservation and Science, John Robinson
Vice President, Herman Smith
Vice President and Director Bronx Zoo, James Breheny
Vice President, Mary Dixon
Vice President Global Program Development, Susan Tressler
Vice President Species Conservation, Elizabeth Bennett
Vice President Budget and Financial Planning, Laura Stolzenthaler
Senior Vice President, Christopher Herbig
Board Member, Eugene Mcgrath

LOCATIONS

HQ: WILDLIFE CONSERVATION SOCIETY
  2300 SOUTHERN BLVD, BRONX, NY 104601090
Phone: 718 220-5100
Web: WWW.WCS.ORG

PRODUCTS/OPERATIONS

2014 Sales

	% of total
Contributed	26
Gate-and-exhibit admissions	15
Federal agencies	14
Visitor services	11
City of New York	10
Investment income	8
Membership dues	6
Non-governmental-organization grants	6
New York State	1
Education programs	1
Sponsorship licensing & royalties	0
Insurance proceeds	0
Other	1
Total	**100**

Selected Areas of Focus

Climate change
Natural resource exploitation
Sustainable development of human livelihoods

HISTORICAL FINANCIALS

Company Type: Private

Income Statement

FYE: June 30

	REVENUE ($ mil.)	NET INCOME ($ mil.)	NET PROFIT MARGIN	EMPLOYEES
06/15	327	61	18.9%	4,000
06/14	253	24	9.7%	—
06/10	228	9	4.1%	—
06/09	197	0	—	—
Annual Growth	8.8%	—	—	—

2015 Year-End Financials

Return on assets: 12.1%   Cash ($ mil.): 62
Return on equity: 18.9%
Current ratio: —

WILLIAM BEAUMONT HOSPITAL

EXECUTIVES

President, Gene Michalski
Board of Directors, Gale R Colwell
Board of Directors, Ananias Diokno

LOCATIONS

HQ: WILLIAM BEAUMONT HOSPITAL
3601 W 13 MILE RD, ROYAL OAK, MI 480736712
Phone: 248 898-5000

HISTORICAL FINANCIALS

Company Type: Private

Income Statement				FYE: December 31
	REVENUE ($ mil.)	NET INCOME ($ mil.)	NET PROFIT MARGIN	EMPLOYEES
12/15	1,300	142	10.9%	18,050
12/14	1,235	127	10.3%	
Annual Growth	5.2%	11.7%	—	—

2015 Year-End Financials

Return on assets: (-1.8%)   Cash ($ mil.): 191
Return on equity: 10.9%
Current ratio: —

WILLIS-KNIGHTON MEDICAL CENTER

EXECUTIVES

President, James K Elrod
Personnel Manager, Debbie Fortson
Auditors: COLE EVANS & PETERSON SHREVEP

LOCATIONS

HQ: WILLIS-KNIGHTON MEDICAL CENTER
2600 GREENWOOD RD, SHREVEPORT, LA 711033908
Phone: 318 212-4000
Web: WWW.WKHS.COM

HISTORICAL FINANCIALS

Company Type: Private

Income Statement				FYE: September 30
	REVENUE ($ mil.)	NET INCOME ($ mil.)	NET PROFIT MARGIN	EMPLOYEES
09/15	1,019	97	9.6%	3,089
09/11	807	76	9.4%	
09/10	818	47	5.8%	
Annual Growth	4.5%	15.4%	—	—

2015 Year-End Financials

Return on assets: 11.5%   Cash ($ mil.): 273
Return on equity: 9.6%
Current ratio: 1.50

WINCHESTER HOSPITAL

EXECUTIVES

President, Dale Lodge
Treasurer, Richard J Killigrew
Clerk, Vinod K Misra
Manager, Pat Brienzo
Finance Manager, Richard Stepchin
Manager, Linda McGowen
Manager, Marit Davis

LOCATIONS

HQ: WINCHESTER HOSPITAL
41 HIGHLAND AVE, WINCHESTER, MA 018901496
Phone: 781 729-9000
Web: WWW.WINCHESTERHOSPITAL.ORG

HISTORICAL FINANCIALS

Company Type: Private

Income Statement				FYE: September 30
	REVENUE ($ mil.)	NET INCOME ($ mil.)	NET PROFIT MARGIN	EMPLOYEES
09/15	262	50	19.2%	2,500
09/14	253	8	3.3%	—
09/13	0	16		
Annual Growth	—	73.0%	—	—

2015 Year-End Financials

Return on assets: 7.0%   Cash ($ mil.): 28
Return on equity: 19.2%
Current ratio: 1.20

WINDRIVER GRAIN, L.L.C.

EXECUTIVES

Chief Operating Officer, Robert Tempel
Manager, Charlie Sauerwein
Accountant, Dacia Stratman
Auditors: LINDBURG VOGEL PIERCE FARIS C

LOCATIONS

HQ: WINDRIVER GRAIN, L.L.C.
2810 E US HIGHWAY 50, GARDEN CITY, KS 678468528
Phone: 620 275-2101
Web: WWW.WINDRIVERGRAIN.COM

HISTORICAL FINANCIALS

Company Type: Private

Income Statement				FYE: April 30
	REVENUE ($ mil.)	NET INCOME ($ mil.)	NET PROFIT MARGIN	EMPLOYEES
04/15	251	6	2.5%	24
04/14	286	5	1.9%	—
04/13	370	3	0.8%	—
04/12	313	4	1.3%	—
Annual Growth	(7.0%)	14.7%	—	—

2015 Year-End Financials

Return on assets: 1.0%   Cash ($ mil.): 9
Return on equity: 2.5%
Current ratio: 0.80

WINTHROP NYU HOSPITAL

From providing it to teaching it Winthrop-University Hospital is focused on health care. The medical center boasts some 590 beds and offers a full range of acute and tertiary health care services. Services include pediatric women's health and cancer care as well as home health services. Winthrop-University Hospital is also a leading provider of cardiovascular surgeries in the region. The hospital is a member of Winthrop-South Nassau University Health System along with sister facility South Nassau Communities Hospital. Winthrop-University Hospital serves as a teaching hospital for the SUNY at Stony Brook School of Medicine.

Operations

Overall Winthrop-University Hospital logs more than 66000 emergency visits and 33000-plus inpatient visits each year.

Specialty divisions within the Winthrop-University Hospital include the Minstretta Emergency Diagnostic Imaging Center and a pediatric emergency unit both located within the emergency department as well as centers for dialysis digestive disorders neuroscience and diabetes education. Other specialty programs include orthopedics sports medicine wound healing radiosurgery (CyberKnife) and bariatric surgery.

Its services include an expanded Emergency Department including a 9-bed Fast Track Unit comprehensive 15-bed Chest Pain Rule-Out Unit a separate 10-bed Pediatric Emergency Unit equipped with the latest technology and an emergency diagnostic imaging center - the

Its Phyllis & Nathan J. Mistretta Emergency Diagnostic Imaging Center includes a dedicated CT scanner and additional x-ray and digital imaging technology for fast and accurate diagnoses of emergency room patients. The Institute for Heart Care offers advanced diagnostics and disease prevention programs as well as sophisticated medical treatment and rehabilitation and a superior cardiac surgery program.

The hospital is a New York State Department of Health-designated Stroke Center New York State-designated Regional Trauma Center and a New York State Regional Perinatal Center.

Winthrop-University Hospital is also a member of the Long Island Health Network which comprises 10 hospitals in Nassau and Suffolk counties. Member hospitals include Brookhaven Memorial Hospital Medical Center John T. Mather Memorial Hospital and South Nassau Communities Hospital among others.

Geographic Reach

Based in Mineola New York Winthrop-University Hospital serves patients in New York's Nassau Suffolk and Queens counties.

Strategy

To expand its outpatient care services to community residents the hospital opened a family dental practice in 2013.

That year Winthrop-University Hospital teamed up with Cablevision to launch an interactive video on-demand television channel offering 24/7 health-related content to Cablevision's nearly 3 million viewers in New York New Jersey and Connecticut. Winthrop HealthTV (on Optimum TV channel 652) provides viewers with health and wellness content including videos from Winthrop's leading medical experts on specific health conditions. It also offers information about a variety of community programs classes and events at the hospital.

In 2012 Winthrop-University Hospital began an $80 million construction project to add a research and academic center on the main hospital campus.

The first hospital on Long Island to acquire the daVinci Si HD Surgical System Winthrop-University Hospital is one of the top hospitals for minimally invasive surgeries. It is also the first hospital in the New York City metropolitan area to perform CyberKnife radiosurgery procedures. In 2012 it expanded specialist services in fields including orthopedics neurology and cardiac care procedures.

Mergers and Acquisitions

To improve the treatment of diabetes in 2013 the hospital acquired the Diabetes Core Curriculum Workshop a four day multidisciplinary diabetes course given in a dynamic 'live' venue that provides participants with the specialized knowledge and skills needed to educate and care for people with diabetes.

Company Background

Winthrop-University Hospital was founded in 1896.

EXECUTIVES

Senior Vice President Chief Nursing Officer, Valerie Terzano

Vice President RM and Legal Affairs, Bruce O Cohn

President and CEO, John F. Collins

Treasurer, Palmira M. Cataliotti

VP Marketing and Advertising, J. Edmund (Ed) Keating

V.P. Engineering and Facilities, Joseph Burke

Assistant Director Of Pharmacy, Brian Malone

CMIO and Senior Vice President Patient Care Services, Maureen Gaffney

Director of Infection Control Infection Control, Valsamma Thekkel

Physical Therapy Director, ALEXIS STERN

Vice President of Facilities and Engineering, Joe Burke

Senior Vice President Human Resources, George Rainer

Operating Room Director, Diane Bendelier

Medical Director Transfusion Services, Joseph Chiofolo

Vice President Nursing, Donna Caccavale

Vice President, Margaret Harris

Assistant Vice President Revenue Cycle, Mike Shoja

Director of Health Information Management and Clinical Documentation Improvement, Kristin Keller

Vice Chairman, Joan Cox

Chairman, Charles M. Strain

Vice Chairman, John H. Treiber

Vice Chairman, Kevin T. Curran

Secretary to the Chairman, Collado Kathy

Secretary, Tisha Freeman

LOCATIONS

HQ: WINTHROP NYU HOSPITAL
259 1ST ST, MINEOLA, NY 115013957
Phone: 516 663-0333
Web: WWW.WINTHROP.ORG

PRODUCTS/OPERATIONS

Selected Services
Angioplasty
Arthritis
Asthma
Bariatric Surgery
Breast Cancer
Cancer Care
Cardiology
Childhood Cancer
Children's Health
Clinical Trials
CyberKnife

Diabetes
Dialysis
Digestive Care
Education
Emergency Dept.
Family Care
Gastroenterology
Heart Care
Home Health Care
Hyperbarics
Joint Replacement
Kidney Disease
Lung Cancer
Lung Care
Maternity
Neurology
Neurosciences
Neurosurgery
OB/GYN
Open Heart Surgery
Orthopedics
Pediatric Cancer
Pediatrics
Physicians
Prostate Cancer
Pulmonary Care
Research
Sleep Disorders
Stroke
Trauma Center
Urology
Weight Loss

COMPETITORS

Bronx-Lebanon Hospital
Catholic Health Services of Long Island
Continuum Health Partners
Franklin Hospital
HealthSouth
Long Island Jewish Medical Center
Lutheran HealthCare
MediSys Health Network
New York City Health and Hospitals
NewYork-Presbyterian Healthcare
Newark Beth Israel Medical Center
Northwell Health
Queens-Long Island Medical Group
SUNY Downstate

HISTORICAL FINANCIALS

Company Type: Private

Income Statement

FYE: December 31

	REVENUE ($ mil.)	NET INCOME ($ mil.)	NET PROFIT MARGIN	EMPLOYEES
12/15	1,230	(9)	—	6,000
12/14	1,136	(106)	—	—
12/08	725	(134)	—	—
12/07	669	0	0.0%	—
Annual Growth	7.9%	—	—	—

2015 Year-End Financials

Return on assets: 10.6%
Return on equity: (-0.8%)
Current ratio: 1.00

Cash ($ mil.): 86

WITHAM MEMORIAL HOSPITAL

EXECUTIVES

President, Raymond Ingham
Manager, Mike Morrell
Auditors: BLUE & CO LLC INDIANAPOLIS

LOCATIONS

HQ: WITHAM MEMORIAL HOSPITAL
2605 N LEBANON ST, LEBANON, IN 460521476
Phone: 765 485-8000
Web: WWW.WITHAM.ORG

HISTORICAL FINANCIALS

Company Type: Private

Income Statement

FYE: December 31

	REVENUE ($ mil.)	NET INCOME ($ mil.)	NET PROFIT MARGIN	EMPLOYEES
12/15	380	18	4.8%	725
12/14	276	20	7.6%	—
12/13	275	17	6.2%	—
12/12	264	25	9.8%	—
Annual Growth	12.9%	(11.1%)	—	—

2015 Year-End Financials

Return on assets: 13.2%
Return on equity: 4.8%
Current ratio: 1.20

Cash ($ mil.): 47

WITHLACOOCHEE RIVER ELECTRIC COOPERATIVE INC

Withlacoochee River Electric Cooperative keeps the power flowing to the residences and businesses of more than 200360 member-owners in five counties along the central Florida Gulf Coast. The power distribution utility which was originally set up in 1941 receives wholesale generation and transmission services from the Seminole Electric Cooperative. Withlacoochee River Electric a non-profit organization returns any funds remaining at the end of each year to its membership. The cooperative has returned more than $190 million to its member-owners.

Pushing green energy and recycling in 2008 the company reported that in addition to supplying reliable electricity it was seeking to reduce carbon emissions through providing its members with compact fluorescent bulbs. That year Withlacoochee River Electric also recycled more than 442000 pounds of materials installed a 3.15 kV solar panel display at its corporate headquarters in Dade City and added more than 3220 new customers.

"Withlacoochee River" was chosen as the name for the organization because the river was the common link for the cooperative's original service region (Citrus Hernando and Pasco counties).

EXECUTIVES

Secretary, Cindy Rizer
Auditors: PURVIS GRAY & COMPANY LLP DAD

LOCATIONS

HQ: WITHLACOOCHEE RIVER ELECTRIC COOPERATIVE INC
14651 21ST ST, DADE CITY, FL 335232920
Phone: 352 567-5133
Web: WWW.WREC.NET

HISTORICAL FINANCIALS

Company Type: Private

Income Statement

FYE: December 31

	REVENUE ($ mil.)	NET INCOME ($ mil.)	NET PROFIT MARGIN	EMPLOYEES
12/15	474	24	5.1%	458
12/14	459	28	6.2%	—
12/13	433	16	3.8%	—
12/12	421	25	6.1%	—
Annual Growth	4.0%	(1.8%)	—	—

2015 Year-End Financials

Return on assets: 3.1%
Return on equity: 5.1%
Current ratio: 12.80

Cash ($ mil.): 152

WOMAN'S HOSPITAL FOUNDATION INC

Woman's Hospital is a 170-bed hospital catering to the needs of women and infants in southern Louisiana. Founded in 1968 the hospital was one of the nation's first women's specialty hospitals. The not-for-profit hospital offers women's health classes as well as other educational resources and delivers about 8500 babies each year. Services include breast care cosmetic surgery general surgery genetics counseling occupational therapy and speech therapy. Woman's Hospital moved to a new 225-acre campus in 2012 to replace its aging facilities. It boasts a five-story hospital building medical office buildings and increased capacity for its inpatient rooms and neonatal intensive care unit.

Strategy

Woman's Hospital which logged 11500 adult admissions in 2012 is working to grow its core business and expanding strategically. The hospital's $330 million relocation project — which was put on hold for about a year in the wake of the global recession — was restarted in 2010 and completed in 2012. It has also added a 20-bed unit that features areas for patients on bed rest.

Woman's Hospital also conducts clinical and molecular biology and genetic research. The organization collaborates with researchers at a range of institutions around the US including the American College of Surgeons Oncology Group and Louisiana State University.

Sales and Marketing

Woman's Hospital markets its services through TV advertising.

Financial Performance

The Baton Rouge Louisiana hospital logged $217.7 million in net patient service revenues in 2012 up from its $204.4 million in 2011.

The hospital receives more than half of its gross revenue from managed care contracts (HMO PPO) the rest from a mixture of Medicaid and Medicare and self-pay patients. Woman's Hospital's largest inpatient service segment is neonatal ICU followed by obstetrics and gynecology.

EXECUTIVES

Vice President Medical Staff Services, Nancy Crawford
President and CEO, Teri G. Fontenot
EVP and COO, Stephanie Anderson
VP Information Systems, Paul Kirk
SVP Patient Care NICU and Respiratory Therapy; Chief Nursing Officer, Patricia Johnson

Chief Medical Officer, Susan Puyau
VP and CFO, Greg Smith
President Foundation for Woman's, Beverly Brooks Thompson
Director Of Infection Control, Jennifer Freeny
Secretary, Robyn Gray
Secretary, Lucia Zas

LOCATIONS

HQ: WOMAN'S HOSPITAL FOUNDATION INC
100 WOMANS WAY, BATON ROUGE, LA 708175100
Phone: 225 927-1300
Web: WWW.WOMANS.ORG

PRODUCTS/OPERATIONS

Selected Services

Audiology
Breast Care
Breastfeeding
Cancer Care
Childbirth
Day Spa
Diabetes Care
Fertility
Fitness Club
Genetics
Health Screenings
Heart Health
Mammography
Metabolic Health
Nutrition
Philanthropy
Pregnancy
Social Services
Weight Loss

COMPETITORS

Amedisys	Our Lady of the Lake
Baton Rouge General	RMC
General Health System	River Parishes
Lane Regional Medical	Hospital
Center	Tenet Healthcare

HISTORICAL FINANCIALS

Company Type: Private

Income Statement

FYE: September 30

	REVENUE ($ mil.)	NET INCOME ($ mil.)	NET PROFIT MARGIN	EMPLOYEES
09/16	288	47	16.3%	1,850
09/15	503	36	7.2%	—
09/12	217	22	10.3%	—
09/11	219	46	21.0%	—
Annual Growth	5.7%	0.4%	—	—

2016 Year-End Financials

Return on assets: 1.2%
Return on equity: 16.3%
Current ratio: 4.50

Cash ($ mil.): 172

WOMEN & INFANTS HOSPITAL OF RHODE ISLAND

EXECUTIVES

Chief Executive Officer, Dennis D Keefe
Manager, Linda Pietras
Auditors: PRICEWATERHOUSECOOPERS LLP BO

LOCATIONS

HQ: WOMEN & INFANTS HOSPITAL OF RHODE ISLAND
101 DUDLEY ST, PROVIDENCE, RI 029052499
Phone: 401 274-1100
Web: WWW.WOMENANDINFANTS.ORG

HISTORICAL FINANCIALS

Company Type: Private

Income Statement

FYE: September 30

	REVENUE ($ mil.)	NET INCOME ($ mil.)	NET PROFIT MARGIN	EMPLOYEES
09/16	504	35	7.0%	2,800
09/15	428	3	0.8%	—
09/14	438	19	4.5%	—
09/13	411	14	3.6%	—
Annual Growth	7.0%	33.5%	—	—

2016 Year-End Financials

Return on assets: 7.3%
Return on equity: 7.0%
Current ratio: 2.40

Cash ($ mil.): 66

WOODBRIDGE TOWNSHIP BOARD OF EDUCATION (INC)

EXECUTIVES

President, Ezio Tamburello
Director, Denis Demarino
Auditors: MCENERNEY BRADY & COMPANY LL

LOCATIONS

HQ: WOODBRIDGE TOWNSHIP BOARD OF EDUCATION (INC)
428 SCHOOL ST, WOODBRIDGE, NJ 070952935
Phone: 732 750-3200
Web: WWW.WOODBRIDGE.K12.NJ.US

HISTORICAL FINANCIALS

Company Type: Private

Income Statement

FYE: June 30

	REVENUE ($ mil.)	NET INCOME ($ mil.)	NET PROFIT MARGIN	EMPLOYEES
06/16	233	2	1.1%	2,000
06/13	215	25	11.9%	—
06/12	207	(23)	—	—
06/10	0	0	—	—
Annual Growth	—	133.5%	—	—

2016 Year-End Financials

Return on assets: 1.6%
Return on equity: 1.1%
Current ratio: —

Cash ($ mil.): 30

WORCESTER POLYTECHNIC INSTITUTE

EXECUTIVES

President, Dennis D Berkey
Auditors: PRICEWATERHOUSECOOPERS LLP HA

LOCATIONS

HQ: WORCESTER POLYTECHNIC INSTITUTE
100 INSTITUTE RD, WORCESTER, MA 016092280
Phone: 508 831-5000
Web: WWW.WPI.EDU

HISTORICAL FINANCIALS

Company Type: Private

Income Statement

FYE: June 30

	REVENUE ($ mil.)	NET INCOME ($ mil.)	NET PROFIT MARGIN	EMPLOYEES
06/15	312	4	1.4%	873
06/13	199	38	19.4%	—
06/12	182	(5)	—	—
06/11	0	0	—	—
Annual Growth	—	1002.7%		

2015 Year-End Financials

Return on assets: 8.0%
Return on equity: 1.4%
Current ratio: 0.10

Cash ($ mil.): 23

WORLD WIDE TECHNOLOGY HOLDING CO., INC.

EXECUTIVES

Chief Executive Officer, James P Kavanaugh
Director, Holly Venvertloh
Director, Mike Mitchell
Personnel Manager, Paul Koetting
Engineer, Rob Walters
Regional Manager, Douglas Warner
Accountant, Jeff Pruellage
Auditors: ERNST & YOUNG LLP ST LOUIS

LOCATIONS

HQ: WORLD WIDE TECHNOLOGY HOLDING CO., INC.
60 WELDON PKWY, SAINT LOUIS, MO 63101
Phone: 314 919-1400
Web: WWW.2.WWT.COM

HISTORICAL FINANCIALS

Company Type: Private

Income Statement

FYE: December 31

	REVENUE ($ mil.)	NET INCOME ($ mil.)	NET PROFIT MARGIN	EMPLOYEES
12/15	7,437	83	1.1%	1,052
12/14	6,702	88	1.3%	—
12/13	6,392	77	1.2%	—
12/12	5,041	68	1.3%	—
Annual Growth	13.8%	7.1%	—	—

2015 Year-End Financials

Return on assets: 17.1%
Return on equity: 1.1%
Current ratio: 0.80

Cash ($ mil.): 62

WORLD WIDE TECHNOLOGY, INC.

World Wide Technology (WWT) has a broad view of its business. The company primarily provides such IT services as network design and installation systems and application integration and procurement. It also offers a range of Web-based products and services including e-commerce systems development order tracking and catalog management. WWT serves businesses in the automotive retail and telecommunications industries as well as government agencies. Top clients have included Dell the State of Missouri and the State of Alaska. WWT was founded in 1990.

Geographic Reach

WWT has more than 25 facilities throughout the world and about 2 million-sq.-ft of warehouse and distribution space in the US. It also has three distribution outlets in Brazil Mexico and Singapore as well as facilities in London; Amsterdam; Hong Kong; and Chengdu China.

Mergers and Acquisitions

In 2015 WWT purchased St. Louis-based software development firm Asynchrony. The strategic acquisition will allow WWT to deliver complete custom user-facing software and the systems and infrastructure that support it.

EXECUTIVES

CEO, James P. (Jim) Kavanaugh
President Commercial Sales, Mark J. Catalano
CFO, Thomas W. (Tom) Strunk
VP Corporate Properties, Dan B. Svoboda
President, Joseph G. (Joe) Koenig
VP Professional Services, Matt Horner
VP Supply Chain Operations, Kurt Grimminger
VP Global Supply Chain, Mark Franke
Vice President of Information Technology, Mike P. Taylor
Vice President Sales Operations, Tim Loughman
Vice President Advanced Technology, Brian Ortbals
Vice President Professional Services, Tom Gain
Vice President of Information Technology, Michael Taylor
Vice President Global Accounts, Leo Makhlin
Area Vice President Global Service Provider, Kraig Ecker
Associate Vice President Production, Tonya Miller
Vice President of Security Solutions, Mike McGlynn
Chairman, David L. Steward

LOCATIONS

HQ: WORLD WIDE TECHNOLOGY, INC.
60 WELDON PKWY, MARYLAND HEIGHTS, MO 630433202
Phone: 314 569-7000
Web: WWW.WWT.COM

PRODUCTS/OPERATIONS

Selected Services

IT Products and Solutions
  Facilities Infrastructure
  Integration and Staging
  Leasing
  Managed Services
  Order Management and Reporting

Pre-Sales Support

  Value Added Reseller
Professional Services
  Configuration
  Implementation
  Planning and Design
  Training
Supply Chain Services
  Business Process Outsourcing
  Logistics/Warehousing
  Material Planning and Scheduling
  Outsourced Procurement
  Supplier Management

COMPETITORS

Accenture	HP Enterprise Services
Black Box	IBM Global Services
Computer Sciences Corp.	PC Mall
DataSpan	Rose International
Dynamics Research	Unisys
En Pointe	WebLinc

HISTORICAL FINANCIALS

Company Type: Private

Income Statement

FYE: December 31

	REVENUE ($ mil.)	NET INCOME ($ mil.)	NET PROFIT MARGIN	EMPLOYEES
12/15	5,927	95	1.6%	1,052
12/14	5,057	95	1.9%	—
12/13	4,545	77	1.7%	—
12/12	3,396	57	1.7%	—
Annual Growth	20.4%	18.3%	—	—

2015 Year-End Financials

Return on assets: 17.7%
Return on equity: 1.6%
Current ratio: 1.00

Cash ($ mil.): 46

WORLD WILDLIFE FUND, INC.

A fuzzy-wuzzy with kung fu strength the panda embodies mission of the World Wildlife Fund (WWF). The conservation organization has worked on more than 13000 projects in about 100 countries to save endangered species and natural areas as well as to address threats such as global warming and the exploitation of forests. By 2020 WWF aims to conserve 15 of the world's more ecologically important regions. Its work crosses Africa Asia Latin America North America and Eurasia through national affiliates in about 100 countries. The group publishes data on wildlife wild places and global environmental challenges. Founded in 1961 WWF is joined by 1.1 million members in the US and some 5 million overseas.

Geographic Reach

While the Anchorage Alaska-based WWF is active in some 100 countries the organization targets the world's most ecologically important regions for conservation including the Arctic Amazon Congo Basin the Galapagos eastern Himalayas and the Northern Great Plains in the US.

Financial Performance

The conservation organization's total revenue including pledges for future years remained flat from 2013 to 2014 hovering around the $266 million mark. The consistent revenue was due to the success of the Arctic Home campaign with The Coca-Cola Company. Support from individual donors remained the single largest source of WWF's unrestricted revenue.

Strategy

In 2014 WWF opened its new Myanmar office in an effort to develop a green economy and help conserve the country's diverse species such as tigers elephants and Irrawaddy dolphins.

EXECUTIVES

Managing Director, Kerry Cesareo
Vice President and Managing Director, David McLaughlin
Senior Vice President and General Counsel, Margaret Ackerley
Senior Vice President, Brad Ack
Vice President, Todd Shelton
Vice President of International Finance, Raj Kundra
Government Relations, America Pintabutr
Auditors: BDO USA LLP MCLEAN VIRGINIA

LOCATIONS

HQ: WORLD WILDLIFE FUND, INC.
1250 24TH ST NW FL 2, WASHINGTON, DC 200371193
Phone: 202 293-4800
Web: WWW.PANDA.ORG

PRODUCTS/OPERATIONS

2015 Expenses

	% of total
Program	84
Fundraising	11
Finance & administration	5
Total	**100**

2015 Revenue

	% of total
Individual contributions	32
In-Kind & other revenues	19
Government grants & contracts	19
Foundation contributions	9
Network revenues	7
Corporations	4
Other/non-operating contributions	10
Total	**100**

Selected Goals

Ensure that the value of nature is reflected in the decisions made by individuals communities governments and businesses
Mobilize hundreds of millions of people to support conservation
Protect and restore species and their habitats
Strengthen local communities' ability to conserve the natural resources they depend upon
Transform markets and policies to reduce the impact of the production and consumption of commodities

HISTORICAL FINANCIALS

Company Type: Private

Income Statement

FYE: June 30

	REVENUE ($ mil.)	NET INCOME ($ mil.)	NET PROFIT MARGIN	EMPLOYEES
06/16	323	(0)	—	400
06/14	227	6	3.0%	—
06/13	229	25	11.1%	—
06/12	7	0	0.0%	—
Annual Growth	**153.3%**	—	—	—

2016 Year-End Financials

Return on assets: 5.2% Cash ($ mil.): 41
Return on equity: (-0.1%)
Current ratio: 1.20

WORLEY & OBETZ, INC.

EXECUTIVES

President, Jeffery B Lyons
Board of Directors, Karen L Connelly
Vice-President, Greg Flory
Vice-President, Michele Klusewitz
Vice-President, Jason Mertz
Vice-Chairman, Seth Obetz
Sales Manager, Matthew Linder
Auditors: HOROVITZ RUDOY & ROTEMAN LLC

LOCATIONS

HQ: WORLEY & OBETZ, INC.
85 WHITE OAK RD, MANHEIM, PA 175458550
Phone: 717 665-6891
Web: WWW.WORLEYOBETZ.COM

HISTORICAL FINANCIALS

Company Type: Private

Income Statement

FYE: August 31

	REVENUE ($ mil.)	NET INCOME ($ mil.)	NET PROFIT MARGIN	EMPLOYEES
08/16	584	1	0.3%	68
08/15	520	2	0.4%	—
08/14	466	1	0.4%	—
08/13	383	1	0.3%	—
Annual Growth	**15.1%**	**16.7%**	—	—

2016 Year-End Financials

Return on assets: 1.5% Cash ($ mil.): —
Return on equity: 0.3%
Current ratio: 1.30

WOROCO MANAGEMENT LLC

EXECUTIVES

Director of Finance, Elliot Egenburg
Auditors: AJ SANTYE & CO SOMERVILLE N

LOCATIONS

HQ: WOROCO MANAGEMENT LLC
40 WOODBRIDGE AVE STE 3, SEWAREN, NJ 070771335
Phone: 732 855-7720
Web: WWW.WOROCO.BIZ

HISTORICAL FINANCIALS

Company Type: Private

Income Statement

FYE: December 31

	REVENUE ($ mil.)	NET INCOME ($ mil.)	NET PROFIT MARGIN	EMPLOYEES
12/15	524	4	0.9%	14
12/14	410	3	0.8%	—
12/13	339	1	0.6%	—
12/12	274	2	0.7%	—
Annual Growth	**24.1%**	**33.5%**	—	—

2015 Year-End Financials

Return on assets: 0.6% Cash ($ mil.): —
Return on equity: 0.9%
Current ratio: 0.10

WOUNDED WARRIOR PROJECT, INC.

EXECUTIVES

Chief Executive Officer, Steven Nardizzi
Chief Operating Officer, Charlie Fletcher
Manager, Lesley Hume
Executive Vice-President, John M Molino
Executive Vice-President, Abby Reiner
Financial Executive, Cindy McDonald
Manager, Ty Dixon
Auditors: GRANT THORNTON LLP JACKSONVIL

LOCATIONS

HQ: WOUNDED WARRIOR PROJECT, INC.
4899 BELFORT RD STE 300, JACKSONVILLE, FL 322566033
Phone: 904 296-7350
Web: WWW.WOUNDEDWARRIORPROJECT.ORG

HISTORICAL FINANCIALS

Company Type: Private

Income Statement

FYE: September 30

	REVENUE ($ mil.)	NET INCOME ($ mil.)	NET PROFIT MARGIN	EMPLOYEES
09/15	398	47	11.8%	3
09/13	234	76	32.6%	—
09/12	154	59	38.4%	—
09/11	0	0	—	—
Annual Growth	—	**631.9%**	—	—

2015 Year-End Financials

Return on assets: 7.2% Cash ($ mil.): 75
Return on equity: 11.8%
Current ratio: 2.60

WRIGHT STATE UNIVERSITY

Wright State University named after aviation pioneers the Wright Brothers has an enrollment of more than 17770 students and offers more than 230 undergraduate graduate and professional degrees. It consists of eight colleges (including education and human services business engineering and computer science liberal arts nursing and health and science and mathematics) and three schools (graduate studies medicine professional psychology). Wright State has more than 900 full-time faculty members. Originally a branch campus of Ohio State University and Miami University Wright State became an independent university in 1967.

Operations

The university's tuition fees are $17350 per annum for non-residential students and $8730 for residential students. Some 8% of its students are international (from more than 60 countries).

Wright State's libraries include the Paul Laurence Dunbar Library the Lake Campus Learning Center the Student Technology Assistance Center (STAC) and Special Collections and Archives.

Geographic Reach

Along with its main campus in Dayton Ohio Wright State also offers classes at its smaller Lake Campus in Celina Ohio.

Financial Performance

Wright State reported an increase in revenue from $233.5 million in fiscal 2015 to $238.2 million in fiscal 2016 due to higher federal grants and contracts and auxiliary revenues partially offset by lower student tuition and fees and lower sales and services revenue.

The university's net loss increased from $148.8 million in fiscal 2015 to $169.9 million in fiscal 2016 primarily due to higher operating expenses.

Wright State's cash outflow from operations in fiscal 2016 declined from $131.5 million to $146.1 million due to higher operating costs lower auxiliary enterprise sales and a decline in student loans collected partially offset by higher grants and contract fees.

Strategy

The university's 2013-2018 Strategic Plan aims at enhancing academic quality and program distinctiveness; improving student access and educational achievement by increasing enrollment and retention and attaining national prominence in research scholarship and entrepreneurial activities.

Wright State plans to grow STEM education (science technology engineering and mathematics) in the region in order to help prepare workers for jobs in intelligence aerospace and defense through the creation of The Center for Workforce Development.

In addition the university is adopting a new budgeting model that it hopes will provide more transparency while allowing academic units to strategically identify new revenue sources. The system also aims to help divisions identify programs that are not adding academic or financial value.

Company Background

The Wright State Dayton campus tunnel system claims to be one of the most extensive collegiate pedestrian tunnel systems in the US with nearly two miles of tunnels linking 20 of 22 buildings in the academic area.

EXECUTIVES

President, David R. Hopkins
VP Business and Finance and CFO, Jeff Ulliman
EVP Planning, Robert J. Sweeney
Dean Graduate School, Robert E. Fyffe
Provost, Thomas Sudkamp
Dean College of Engineering and Computer Science, Nathan Klingbeil
Dean Raj Soin College of Business, Joanne Li
Dean College of Nursing and Health, Rosalie O'Dell Mainous
Dean College of Liberal Arts, Kristin D. Sobolik
Dean School of Professional Psychology, LaPearl Logan Winfrey
CIO, Craig Woolley
Dean Lake Campus, Jay Albayyari
Dean Boonshoft School of Medicine, Margaret M. Dunn
Dean College of Education and Human Services, Joseph E. Keferl
Dean College of Science and Mathematics, Douglas W. Leaman
Admissions Director, Cathy Davis
Vice President Technology, Amit Sheth
Assoc. Vice President Facilities, Vicky L Davidson
Associate Vice President Facilities Management and Services, Dan Papay
Assistant Vice President for Advancement, Cindy Young
Vice President Enrollment Management, Jacqueline McMillan
Vice President Research, Benjamin Salisbury
Vice President for Academic Affairs, Molly Hall
Assistant Vice President, Bill Shepard
Assistant Vice President Gener, Renee Aitken
Vice President and President Elect, George Polak
Vice President, Charles Beckley
Medical Director Medical Doctor, Suzy Tober
Associate Vice President Public Affairs, Robert Hickey
Associate medical director, Lena Winkler
Vice President and Branch Manager, Shamarr Blake
Assoc. Vice President Facilities Management and Services, Daniel Papay
Chairman, Michael C. Bridges
Vice Chair, Douglas A. Fecher
Secretary, Lisa Duke
Auditors: CROWE HORWATH LLP COLUMBUS O

LOCATIONS

HQ: WRIGHT STATE UNIVERSITY
3640 COLONEL GLENN HWY, DAYTON, OH
454350002
Phone: 937 775-3333

PRODUCTS/OPERATIONS

2014 sales

	% of total
Student tuition and fees	61
Grants and contracts	31
Sales and services	3
Auxiliary enterprises	4
Other	1
Total	**100**

Selected Schools and Colleges
Colleges
  Education and Human Services
  Engineering and Computer Science
  Liberal Arts
  Nursing and Health
  Raj Soin College of Business
  Professional Psychology
  Science and Mathematics
  University College
  WSU-Lake Campus
Schools
  Boonshoft School of Medicine
  Graduate Studies
  Professional Psychology

HISTORICAL FINANCIALS
Company Type: Private

Income Statement

FYE: June 30

	REVENUE ($ mil.)	NET INCOME ($ mil.)	NET PROFIT MARGIN	EMPLOYEES
06/15	233	(22)	—	2,748
06/14	235	(3)	—	
06/13	272	0	0.2%	
06/12	267	(10)	—	
Annual Growth	(4.5%)			

2015 Year-End Financials
Return on assets: 5.8%
Return on equity: (-9.4%)
Current ratio: 0.80
Cash ($ mil.): 20

WYCKOFF HEIGHTS MEDICAL CENTER

Wyckoff Heights is taking health care to new levels. Serving the New York boroughs of Brooklyn and Queens Wyckoff Heights Medical Center maintains some 350 beds and provides a comprehensive range of specialized services including diagnostics radiology cardiology obstetrics pediatrics surgery and rehabilitative care. The hospital also provides educational services through a partnership with the Weill Medical College of Cornell University and it offers outpatient services through several family health clinics in the area. The not-for-profit medical center is governed by an independent board of trustees.

Operations

Wyckoff Heights Medical Centerl has 75000 visits a year at its Pediatric/Adult Emergency Departments and more than 200000 visits at its clinics. Every year it also delivers 2000 babies offers outpatient services to thousands through a network of community ambulatory care centers and conducts extensive community health education and screening programs.

Strategy

Wyckoff Heights has responded to the growing health care needs of the communities it serves by acquiring new equipment and expanding clinical programs. However like a handful of other Brooklyn-area hospitals the facility has struggled with rising care costs. It has resisted growing pressure to join together with other ailing hospitals preferring to stay independent. Instead Wyckoff Heights hopes to receive state funding which will help it as strives to expand services to Queens residents especially senior patients. Company leadership aims to bring the percentage of Queens residents served to 50% or higher in the next few years.

Company Background

Wyckoff Heights was founded in 1889.

EXECUTIVES

Acting Vice President Nursing, Margaret Pelkowski
Vice President Chief Information Officer, Jebashini Jesurasa
SVP and Chief Medical Officer, Gustavo DelToro
Vice President of Finance and Chief Financial Officer, Frank Vutrano
President and CEO, Ramon J. Rodriguez
EVP and COO, David Rock
Vice President Strategic Development and physician recruitment, Yashpal Arya

Vice President Health Information Management, Teresa Silversmith
Vice President, Kenneth Freiberg
Vice President Of It, Cletis Earl
Vice President of Clinical Operations, Jose Hernandez

LOCATIONS

HQ: WYCKOFF HEIGHTS MEDICAL CENTER
374 STOCKHOLM ST, BROOKLYN, NY 112374006
Phone: 718 963-7272
Web: WWW.WYCKOFFHOSPITAL.ORG

PRODUCTS/OPERATIONS

Selected Services
Anesthesiology
Asthma
Breast Surgery
Cardiology/Heart
Colorectal Surgery
Dermatology
Ear Nose & Throat (ENT)
Emergency Medicine
Endocrinology (Diabetes)
Family Medicine
Gastroenterology
General Surgery
Genetics
Geriatrics
Head & Neck Surgery
Hyperbaric Medicine/Wound Care
Infectious Diseases
Internal Medicine
Medical Oncology
Nephrology
Neurology/Designated Stroke Center
Neurosurgery
Nursing
Obstetrics & Gynecology
Ophthalmology/Eye
Orthopedics
Otolaryngology
Pain Management
Pathology
Pediatrics
Physical Medicine & Rehabilitation
Plastic Surgery
Podiatry
Psychiatry
Pulmonary Medicine
Radiation Oncology
Radiology
Respiratory Therapy
Rheumatology
Thoracic Surgery
Urology

COMPETITORS

Catholic Healthcare System
Continuum Health Partners
Kingsbrook Jewish Medical Center
Maimonides Medical Center
MediSys Health Network
Memorial Sloan-Kettering
Montefiore Medical
New York City Health and Hospitals
Northwell Health

HISTORICAL FINANCIALS

Company Type: Private

Income Statement				FYE: December 31
	REVENUE ($ mil.)	NET INCOME ($ mil.)	NET PROFIT MARGIN	EMPLOYEES
12/15	229	0	0.3%	1,900
12/14	249	2	0.9%	—
12/13	276	1	0.4%	—
12/12	246	4	1.9%	—
Annual Growth	(2.4%)	(47.2%)	—	—

2015 Year-End Financials
Return on assets: 10.4%
Return on equity: 0.3%
Current ratio: 0.30
Cash ($ mil.): 4

WYOMING MEDICAL CENTER

Wyoming Medical Center is The Cowboy State's largest medical facility. The hospital founded in 1911 offers those who live in and around Wyoming's Natrona County more than 50 medical specialties thanks to its 150 physicians. The health care services provider boasts nearly 1300 skilled staff members and more than 190 beds. It offers services such as an emergency air transport system trauma care diagnostic services diabetes care center nephrology and surgical care. The facility is a community-owned not-for-profit hospital.that also operates the Heart Center of Wyoming the Wyoming Neuroscience and Spine Institute and a network of about a dozen community clinics throughout Wyoming.

Geographic Reach

The health care provider serves the Wyoming communities of Natrona County and its surrounding counties.

EXECUTIVES

Director Of Nursing Services, Jan Backus
SENIOR VICE PRESIDENT PATIENT CARE SERVICES AND CHIEF NURSING OFFICER, David Gardner
Vice Chairman, Eugene Duquette

LOCATIONS

HQ: WYOMING MEDICAL CENTER
1233 E 2ND ST, CASPER, WY 826012988
Phone: 307 577-7201
Web: WWW.WYOMINGMEDICALCENTER.COM

PRODUCTS/OPERATIONS

Selected Services
AHA Training
Casper Pulmonary
da Vinci System
Diabetes Care Center
Heart Center of Wyoming
Hometown Specialty Clinics
Professional Lab Services
Sage Primary Care
Weight Management Program
Wyoming Brain & Spine Associates
Wyoming Life Flight
Wyoming Nephrology
Wyoming Relay Health

COMPETITORS

Banner Health
Billings Clinic
Evanston
LifePoint Health
North Colorado Medical Center
Poudre Valley Health System
Universal Health Services

HISTORICAL FINANCIALS

Company Type: Private

Income Statement				FYE: June 30
	REVENUE ($ mil.)	NET INCOME ($ mil.)	NET PROFIT MARGIN	EMPLOYEES
06/15	224	7	3.5%	1,033
06/14	232	11	4.9%	—
06/13	239	15	6.5%	—
06/11	227	14	6.3%	—
Annual Growth	(0.4%)	(13.7%)	—	—

2015 Year-End Financials
Return on assets: 7.9%
Return on equity: 3.5%
Current ratio: 3.50
Cash ($ mil.): 56

XANTERRA HOLDING CORPORATION

EXECUTIVES

President, Andrew Todd
Vice-President, Michael F Welch
Manager, Jessica Knoll

LOCATIONS

HQ: XANTERRA HOLDING CORPORATION
6312 S FIDDLERS GREEN CIR # 600, GREENWOOD VILLAGE, CO 801114943
Phone: 303 600-3400
Web: WWW.DENNYS.COM

HISTORICAL FINANCIALS

Company Type: Private

Income Statement				FYE: December 30
	REVENUE ($ mil.)	NET INCOME ($ mil.)	NET PROFIT MARGIN	EMPLOYEES
12/15	385	47	12.4%	3,500
12/14	390	72	18.6%	—
12/13	336	4	1.3%	—
12/12	335	7	2.2%	—
Annual Growth	4.7%	86.1%	—	—

2015 Year-End Financials
Return on assets: 12.7%
Return on equity: 12.4%
Current ratio: 0.40
Cash ($ mil.): 25

XANTERRA, INC.

EXECUTIVES

President, Andrew N Todd
Manager, Jessica Knoll
Secretary, Lonnie S Clark
Editor, David Molyneaux
Director, Richard Rabinoff

LOCATIONS

HQ: XANTERRA, INC.
6312 S FIDDLERS GREEN CIR 600N, GREENWOOD VILLAGE, CO 801114920
Phone: 303 600-3400
Web: WWW.XANTERRA.COM

Income Statement				FYE: December 31
	REVENUE ($ mil.)	NET INCOME ($ mil.)	NET PROFIT MARGIN	EMPLOYEES
12/15	350	53	15.2%	3,500
12/14	358	79	22.2%	—
12/13	304	11	3.7%	—
12/12	305	13	4.3%	—
Annual Growth	4.7%	59.2%	—	—

2015 Year-End Financials

Return on assets: 30.0%   Cash ($ mil.): 21
Return on equity: 15.2%
Current ratio: 0.20

YALE NEW HAVEN HOSPITAL, INC.

Yale-New Haven supports its community and the brainiacs at Yale. Yale-New Haven Hospital (YNHH) is the flagship member of the Yale New Haven Health System. It provides tertiary care in more than 100 medical specialties to residents of southwestern Connecticut. The hospital has more than 1500 beds on two campuses. Its main location includes the Yale-New Haven Children's Hospital and the Yale-New Haven Psychiatric Hospital. Smilow Cancer Hospital with 170 beds is also a part of the hospital complex. YNHH provides cardiac and cancer care performs organ transplants and offers a variety of outpatient clinics. The medical center serves as the primary teaching hospital for Yale University's medical school.

Operations

YNHH handles 59000 inpatient admissions each year as well as 5000 births and 120000 emergency room encounters. The hospital's campuses employ 600 resident physicians as well as 3600 affiliated university and community doctors. A key component of the main hospital facility is the Smilow Cancer Hospital which conducts cancer care and research in partnership with Yale University's Cancer Center. The cancer hospital includes the Center for Outcomes Research and Evaluation (CORE) which works to improve medical care outcomes.

The hospital's second campus YNHH-Saint Raphael Campus offers acute care specialist (including cardiology orthopedics pediatrics and women's health) and medical training services.

Financial Performance

Patient services typically contribute 97% of the hospital's total operating revenue. The hospital is increasing its income through growth measures including acquisitions and facility enhancements. Revenues increased 18% in 2012 and 8% in 2011.

Strategy

With expansion as a key component of its growth strategy YNHH acquired the Saint Raphael Healthcare System and the Hospital of Saint Raphael (HSR) in 2012. The company then moved to merge the entities to create one hospital on two campuses with the Hospital of Saint Raphael operating as YNHH-Saint Raphael Campus; it also conducted facility renovations at the Saint Raphael Campus following the merger. The combined organization allows YNHH to increase coordination of care and reduce redundancies for area communities.

Also in 2012 YNHH continued with the development an outpatient center in North Haven. The center opened in 2013 and serves as a walk-in/primary care center providing comprehensive medical services including cancer and inflammatory disease care and imaging and laboratory services; in addition some of YNHH's information technology offices in New Haven were consolidated and moved to the North Haven site.

EXECUTIVES

EVP COO and Trustee, Marna P. Borgstrom
SVP Patient Services and Chief Nursing Officer, Patricia Sue Fitzsimons
SVP Operations; Executive Director Women's and Children's Services, Cynthia N. Sparer
President and Trustee, Richard D'Aquila
SVP Patient Safety and Quality and Chief Medical Officer, Thomas J. Balcezak
SVP Operations; Executive Director Smilow Cancer Hospital, Abe Lopman
EVP and CFO Yale New Haven Health System and CFO Yale New Haven Hospital (YNHH), Vincent Tammaro
Clinic Manager, Regina Felder
Management Vice President Director, Margot Manacchio
Medical Director Observation Care, Ohm Deshpande
Medical Director of Inpatient Pediatrics, Beth Natt
Physical Therapy Director, Vikki Winks
Vice Chairman, Julia M. McNamara, age 75
Chair, Mary C. Farrell, age 67
Secretary, Mariela Shukis
Secretary, Stephanie Pane
Secretary, Michelle Apuzzo

LOCATIONS

HQ: YALE NEW HAVEN HOSPITAL, INC.
20 YORK ST, NEW HAVEN, CT 065103220
Phone: 203 688-4242
Web: WWW.YNHH.ORG

PRODUCTS/OPERATIONS

Selected Services
Ambulatory (outpatient) services
Bariatric surgery
Blood draw stations
Dental center
Diabetes and endocrinology
Diagnostic radiology
Ear nose and throat
Emergency services
Endocrine surgery
Gastroenterology
Geriatrics
Kidney disease
Maternity
Psychiatry
Pulmonology
Urology

COMPETITORS

Bristol Hospital
Connecticut Children's Medical Center
Griffin Hospital
Hartford Health Care
MidState Medical Center
New Milford Hospital
St. Vincent's Health Services
Waterbury Hospital
Western Connecticut Health Network

Income Statement				FYE: September 30
	REVENUE ($ mil.)	NET INCOME ($ mil.)	NET PROFIT MARGIN	EMPLOYEES
09/15	2,388	107	4.5%	22,000
09/14	2,360	120	5.1%	—
09/13	2,360	120	5.1%	—
09/09	1,237	52	4.3%	—
Annual Growth	11.6%	12.5%	—	—

2015 Year-End Financials

Return on assets: 6.4%   Cash ($ mil.): 101
Return on equity: 4.5%
Current ratio: 0.90

YALE-NEW HAVEN HEALTH SERVICES CORPORATION

Yale New Haven Health System is a health care haven for residents of Southern Connecticut Southwestern Rhode Island and parts of New York's Westchester County. The company operates Yale-New Haven Hospital Greenwich Hospital Bridgeport Hospital and Lawrence & Memorial Hospital and has a contract relationship with The Westerly Hospital in Rhode Island (Northeast Medical Group) as well as children's cancer psychiatric care hospitals. In addition Yale New Haven Health Services operates outpatient facilities and provides such managed care services as network contracting as well as disease management programs. The system is affiliated with Yale University's medical school and has a grand total of about 2560 beds.

Operations

Through its Yale-New Haven Bridgeport Greenwich Lawrence & Memorial and Northeast Medical Group delivery networks the company provides comprehensive cost effective advanced patient care. The system's clinical services include primary and preventive care specialty acute and sub-acute care rehabilitation skilled nursing and coordination of home care. In 2016 the health system which has about 6300 doctors treated more than114000 inpatients and about 1.9 million outpatients.

Yale New Haven Health System in affiliation with the Yale School of Medicine and other universities and colleges educates health professionals and advances clinical care. Its provides more than $300 million in community benefits and community-building activities.

The 1541-bed Yale-New Haven Hospital is an acute and tertiary care hospital; it includes Yale-New Haven Children's Hospital Yale-New Haven Psychiatric Hospital and the Smilow Cancer Hospital.

The 393-bed Bridgeport Hospital serves almost 19000 inpatients and more than 230000 outpatients a year.

The 206-bed Greenwich Hospital is a community teaching hospital.

Lawrence & Memorial Hospital is a 280-bed general and acute care hospital serving parts of Connecticut New York and Rhode Island.

Northeast Medical Group is a not-for-profit multispecialty medical foundation. Its Westerly Hospital (served by the Yale New Haven Health System)

is a 125-bed not-for-profit acute care community hospital serving southern Rhode Island and southeastern Connecticut.

Geographic Reach

Yale New Haven Health System serves patients in Southern Connecticut Southwestern Rhode Island and parts of New York's Westchester County.

Financial Performance

Yale New Haven Health System's revenues totaled $3.8 billion in fiscal 2016 (ended September).

Mergers and Acquisitions

Growing its network in 2016 Yale New Haven Health System acquired Lawrence & Memorial Hospital with 280 beds.

Company Background

Yale New Haven Health System was formed in 1996.

EXECUTIVES

President and CEO, Marna P. Borgstrom

EVP Finance and Corporate Services; CFO and SVP Finance Yale-New Haven Hospital, James M. Staten

EVP; President and CEO Greenwich Hospital and Greenwich Health Care System, Frank A. Corvino

SVP Medical Affairs; Chief of Staff and SVP Medical Affairs Yale-New Haven Hospital, Peter N. Herbert

EVP and COO Yale-New Haven Hospital, Richard D'Aquila

EVP; President and CEO Bridgeport Hospital, William M. (Bill) Jennings, age 50

Chief Information Officer, Daniel Barchi

EVP and COO, Christopher OConnor

CEO Northeast Medical Group, Robert Nordgren

Executive Vice President YNHHS, Richard DAquila

Senior Vice President of Human Resources, Kevin Myatt

Chairman, Julia M. McNamara, age 75

Auditors: ERNST & YOUNG US LLP INDIANAP

LOCATIONS

HQ: YALE-NEW HAVEN HEALTH SERVICES CORPORATION
789 HOWARD AVE, NEW HAVEN, CT 065191300
Phone: 888 461-0106
Web: WWW.YALENEWHAVENHEALTH.ORG

PRODUCTS/OPERATIONS

Selected Facilities
Bridgeport Hospital (Bridgeport Connecticut)
Greenwich Hospital (Greenwich Connecticut)
Yale-New Haven Hospital (New Haven Connecticut)
Yale-New Haven Children's Hospital
Yale-New Haven Psychiatric Hospital
Smilow Cancer Hospital at Yale-New Haven

COMPETITORS

Bristol Hospital
Griffin Hospital
Hartford Health Care
Hospital of Central Connecticut
Kent Hospital
Memorial Sloan-Kettering
MidState Medical Center
New Milford Hospital
NewYork-Presbyterian Hospital
Saint Francis Hospital and Medical Center
Stamford Health
University of Connecticut Health Center
Waterbury Hospital
Westchester Medical Center
Western Connecticut Health Network
Yale-New Haven Hospital Saint Raphael Campus

HISTORICAL FINANCIALS
Company Type: Private

Income Statement
FYE: September 30

	REVENUE ($ mil.)	NET INCOME ($ mil.)	NET PROFIT MARGIN	EMPLOYEES
09/15	449	19	4.4%	22,490
09/13	427	35	8.2%	—
09/09	149	5	3.6%	—
Annual Growth	20.1%	24.1%	—	—

2015 Year-End Financials
Return on assets: 17.3%
Return on equity: 4.4%
Current ratio: 0.90
Cash ($ mil.): 25

YESHIVA UNIVERSITY

Yeshivas are traditional Jewish schools and Yeshiva University believes strongly in following tradition. The Jewish higher education institution serves more than 7000 undergraduate and graduate students at four campuses in New York City. Subjects taught include liberal arts sciences medicine law business social work and psychology. It also has extensive Jewish studies and education programs including study abroad opportunities. Yeshiva University also known as YU has an undergraduate student-to-teacher ratio of 6:1. Its graduate programs include medicine law psychology and Jewish education.

Geographic Reach

Yeshiva University's four New York City campuses consist of the Brookdale Center the Israel Henry Beren Campus and the Wilf Campus in Manhattan and the Jack and Pearl Resnick Campus in the Bronx. It also has a campus in Jerusalem that coordinates its study abroad programs.

Operations

Yeshiva University operates three undergraduate schools: Yeshiva College Stern College for Women and Sy Syms School of Business. Undergraduates may also enroll in the Joint Israel Program a formal arrangement between Yeshiva University and more than 45 yeshivot and seminaries in Israel. Enrolled students get to spend a year studying at Israeli institutions in fields including Talmud Bible Jewish Law and Jewish thought Philosophy Zionism Jewish History and oral and written Hebrew.

Beyond undergraduate education the university operates the Albert Einstein School of Medicine which provides medical training and research opportunities. With roughly 1000 students Albert Einstein School of Medicine is a major biomedical and clinical research facility and receives some $200 million in annual funding from the National Institutes of Health. Areas of research include diabetes cancer liver disease and HIV/AIDS.

Other graduate programs include schools and affiliate institutions in areas including law social work psychology Jewish studies and theology.

Company Background

The university traces its roots to the 1915 merging of two schools from New York's Lower East Side: Yeshiva Eitz Chaim founded in 1886 and the Rabbi Isaac Elchanan Theological Seminary (RIETS) founded in 1896.

EXECUTIVES

President, Richard M Joel
Board of Directors, Andrew J Lauer
Director, Harvey Spolansky
Officer, Jack Zencheck

Manager, Ian Lazerwitz
Personnel Manager, Ilsa Garcia
Director, William Martino
Auditors: PRICEWATERHOUSECOOPERS LLP NE

LOCATIONS

HQ: YESHIVA UNIVERSITY
500 W 185TH ST, NEW YORK, NY 100333299
Phone: 212 960-5400
Web: WWW.YESHIVACOLLEGE.CO.ZA

PRODUCTS/OPERATIONS

Schools and Colleges
Albert Einstein College of Medicine-MS MD
Azrieli Graduate School of Jewish Education and Administration-MS EdD
Benjamin N. Cardozo School of Law-JD LLM
Bernard Revel Graduate School of Jewish Studies- MA PhD
Ferkauf Graduate School of Psychology-MA MS PhD PsyD
Stern College for Women-BA
Sue Golding Graduate Division of Medical Sciences-MS PhD
Sy Syms School of Business-BS
Wurzweiler School of Social Work-MSW CJCS PhD
Yeshiva College-BA
Special Institutions
Marsha Stern Talmudical Academy for Boys
Rabbi Isaac Elchanan Theological Seminary
Samuel H. Wang Yeshiva University High School for Girls
Yeshiva University High Schools
Yeshiva University Museum
Centers/Institutions
Center for Israel Studies at Yeshiva University
Center for Jewish Law and Contemporary Civilization
Center for the Jewish Future
Graduate Program in Advanced Talmudic Studies at Stern College for Women
Institute for Public Health Sciences
Rabbi Arthur Schneier Center for International Affairs
The Center for Ethics at Yeshiva University

HISTORICAL FINANCIALS
Company Type: Private

Income Statement
FYE: June 30

	REVENUE ($ mil.)	NET INCOME ($ mil.)	NET PROFIT MARGIN	EMPLOYEES
06/15	583	(206)	—	4,500
06/13	704	(98)	—	—
06/11	674	(85)	—	—
Annual Growth	(3.6%)	—	—	—

2015 Year-End Financials
Return on assets: 11.8%
Return on equity: (-35.4%)
Current ratio: 0.10
Cash ($ mil.): 35

YMCA OF SAN DIEGO COUNTY

EXECUTIVES

Chief Executive Officer, Baron Herdelin Doherty
Vice-President, Diane Rousseau
Administrative Assistant, Pam Bourne
Supervisor, Loena Baranoski
Director, Dad Clemens
Auditors: COHN REZNICK LLP SAN DIEGO

LOCATIONS

HQ: YMCA OF SAN DIEGO COUNTY
  3708 RUFFIN RD, SAN DIEGO, CA 921231812
Phone: 858 292-9622
Web: WWW.YMCA.ORG

HISTORICAL FINANCIALS

Company Type: Private

Income Statement

FYE: June 30

	REVENUE ($ mil.)	NET INCOME ($ mil.)	NET PROFIT MARGIN	EMPLOYEES
06/16	170	(0)	—	5,000
06/15	155	(1)	—	—
06/14	159	12	7.6%	—
06/13	163	23	14.5%	—
Annual Growth	1.5%	—	—	—

2016 Year-End Financials

Return on assets: 10.9%   Cash ($ mil.): 13
Return on equity: (-0.6%)
Current ratio: 0.40

YORK HOSPITAL

York Hospital operating as WellSpan York Hospital takes its name from the community whose health it seeks to preserve. Part of WellSpan Health the medical center has about 570 beds and serves residents of York and surrounding area of south-central Pennsylvania. It is a regional leader in cardiovascular and orthopedic care and has programs in other specialty areas including oncology behavioral health and geriatrics. Additionally WellSpan York Hospital operates a Level 1 trauma center offers outpatient surgery emergency home health and diagnostic imaging services. It is also has teaching and research programs. The hospital was founded in 1880.

Operations

WellSpan York Hospital has been recognized as a top 100 US hospital by US News for more than five years in a row. It is also recognized for its cardiovascular and orthopedic programs. The center employs about 700 doctors.

The hospital's education programs include five allied health schools and seven residency programs. Affiliated organizations include the medical schools of Drexel University Pennsylvania State University and University of Maryland.

Strategy

WellSpan York Hospital is working to improve its specialist programs to meet the growing medical needs of area residents. In 2011 for instance it collaborated with technology firm Cerner and pharmaceuticals firm Hospira to form an infusion management program for its intensive care unit; the program aims to reduce infusion-related errors. In addition it launched a urinary catheter removal protocol to reduce infection rates and it implemented an aortic valve replacement program (making it one of three facilities in Pennsylvania to offer the open-heart surgery alternative).

EXECUTIVES

Senior Vice President, Michael Oconnor
Medical Director, Wanda D Filer
Medical Director, Creston Tate
CLINIC DIRECTOR, Ralph Whitaker
Treasurer, Allen Miller

LOCATIONS

HQ: YORK HOSPITAL
  1001 S GEORGE ST, YORK, PA 174033645
Phone: 717 851-2345
Web: WWW.YORKHOSPITAL.EDU

COMPETITORS

Ascension Health
Catholic Health
  Initiatives
Geisinger Health
  System
Guthrie Healthcare
Hanover Healthcare
Hershey Medical Center
Holy Spirit
Lancaster General
Memorial Hospital (PA)
PinnacleHealth System

HISTORICAL FINANCIALS

Company Type: Private

Income Statement

FYE: June 30

	REVENUE ($ mil.)	NET INCOME ($ mil.)	NET PROFIT MARGIN	EMPLOYEES
06/15	925	82	9.0%	6,200
06/14	853	136	16.0%	—
06/13	840	103	12.3%	—
06/12	806	27	3.4%	—
Annual Growth	4.7%	44.1%	—	—

2015 Year-End Financials

Return on assets: 1.7%   Cash ($ mil.): 76
Return on equity: 9.0%
Current ratio: 3.50

YOUNG LIFE

Young Life is focused on promoting Christianity among teenagers in the US and in more than 50 other countries. Founded in 1941 the not-for-profit organization provides activities and support for junior high middle school and high school students located in rural and urban communities. Young Life also operates week-long summer camp programs at about 20 locations throughout North America as well as retreats held throughout the year. The group has grown throughout the years from a single club in Texas to about 600 international Young Life ministries dotting the globe. The organization boasts about 3000 staffers and more than 27000 volunteers.

EXECUTIVES

Senior Vice President North, Lee Infrastructure Corder
Vice President Human Resources, Ann Shackelton
Vice President, Ken Knipp
Vice President of Human Resour, Reid Estes
Vice President of Field Ministries Midwest and Eastern Divisions, Wiley Scott
Senior Vice President Western Division, John Franklin
Vice President of Field Ministries Western Division, Angel Ruiz
Assistant Treasurer, Bryan Klotz
Auditors: CAPIN CROUSE LLP COLORADO SPR

LOCATIONS

HQ: YOUNG LIFE
  420 N CASCADE AVE, COLORADO SPRINGS, CO 809033352
Phone: 719 381-1800
Web: WWW.YOUNGLIFE.ORG

HISTORICAL FINANCIALS

Company Type: Private

Income Statement

FYE: September 30

	REVENUE ($ mil.)	NET INCOME ($ mil.)	NET PROFIT MARGIN	EMPLOYEES
09/15	331	29	9.0%	3,100
09/14	311	31	10.3%	—
09/13	276	17	6.5%	—
09/12	237	0	0.1%	—
Annual Growth	11.7%	455.2%	—	—

2015 Year-End Financials

Return on assets: 5.0%   Cash ($ mil.): 56
Return on equity: 9.0%
Current ratio: 3.00

YSLETA INDEPENDENT SCHOOL DISTRICT

EXECUTIVES

Superintendent, Xavier Delatorre
Board of Directors, Paul Pearson
Auditors: WHITLEY PENN LLP HOUSTON TEX

LOCATIONS

HQ: YSLETA INDEPENDENT SCHOOL DISTRICT
  9600 SIMS DR, EL PASO, TX 799257225
Phone: 915 434-0240
Web: WWW.YISD.NET

HISTORICAL FINANCIALS

Company Type: Private

Income Statement

FYE: June 30

	REVENUE ($ mil.)	NET INCOME ($ mil.)	NET PROFIT MARGIN	EMPLOYEES
06/16	462	257	55.6%	7,155
06/15	449	(3)	—	—
06/14	442	5	1.2%	—
06/13	423	(12)	—	—
Annual Growth	3.0%	—	—	—

2016 Year-End Financials

Return on assets: 1.4%   Cash ($ mil.): 358
Return on equity: 55.6%
Current ratio: —

YUMA REGIONAL MEDICAL CENTER INC

Yuma Regional Medical Center (YRMC) is an acute care hospital that provides medical services for Yuma Arizona and its surrounding communities. The not-for-profit hospital which has more than 400 beds and 400 doctors provides general medical surgical and emergency services. YRMC also operates about 30 additional facilities around Yuma including a rehabilitation hospital laboratories a wound care clinic primary care clinics and diagnostic imaging centers.

Operations

YRMC offers a free program called Silver Care in which patients who are 55 and older are encouraged to live active and healthy lives by being offered a number of benefits such as discounts at local stores specially reduced rates on selected lab tests including cholesterol and blood glucose screenings. Additionally Silver Care members are eligible for free membership in the Fit for Life cardiac wellness program.

The hospital's medical personnel have completed advanced procedures such as a transcatheter aortic valve replacement and a one-level cervical disc replacement using Mobi-C technology.

Strategy

Being a regional hospital YRMC works hard to recruit physicians who might otherwise be drawn to larger teaching hospitals with more advanced technological equipment and complex patient cases. In order to lure in such specialists the hospital offers extended medical education career weekends and a number of specialized centers in which physicians can perform procedures solely in their specialty such as a neonatal ICU and a pediatric sub-specialty unit.

The system has grown by adding new specialty clinics to its network. For example its newest clinic is the YRMC Plastic and Reconstructive Surgery center. It expanded and renovated its emergency department (adding two heliports) in 2017.

EXECUTIVES

VP Information Technology and CIO, Gene Shaw
Interim President and CEO, Camie Overton
VP Patient Care Services and Chief Nursing Officer, Deb Carver
CFO, David Willie
Interim VP Medical Affairs and Chief Medical Officer, Robert Cannell
Physical Therapy Director, Jennifer Breen
Infection Control Director, Valerie Payne

LOCATIONS

HQ: YUMA REGIONAL MEDICAL CENTER INC
2400 S AVENUE A, YUMA, AZ 853647170
Phone: 928 344-2000
Web: WWW.YUMAREGIONAL.ORG

PRODUCTS/OPERATIONS

Selected Services
Children
Cancer Care
Children's Rehabilitative Services
Critical Care
Diabetes Education
Diagnostic Imaging
Emergency Department
First Health Medical Supply
Gastroenterology
Heart
Hospitalist Program
Lab
Medical Staff Services
Nursing Units
Outpatient Surgical Center
Pharmacy
Spiritual Care and Patient Advocacy
Surgical Services
Weight Loss
Women's Services
Wound Care Center

COMPETITORS

Banner Health	Northern Arizona
Community Health	Healthcare
Systems	Phoenix Children's
Dignity Health	Hospital
HCA	Providence St. Joseph
John C. Lincoln Health	Health
Network	Scottsdale Healthcare

HISTORICAL FINANCIALS

Company Type: Private

Income Statement
FYE: September 30

	REVENUE ($ mil.)	NET INCOME ($ mil.)	NET PROFIT MARGIN	EMPLOYEES
09/15	371	(8)	—	2,400
09/14	328	30	9.2%	—
09/13	291	11	3.9%	—
09/12	346	22	6.6%	—
Annual Growth	2.4%	—	—	—

ZEN-NOH GRAIN CORPORATION

EXECUTIVES

Chief Executive Officer, John D Williams
Board of Directors, Robin Gerarve
Financial Executive, Cindi Ernst
Auditors: KPMG LLP HOUSTON TX

LOCATIONS

HQ: ZEN-NOH GRAIN CORPORATION
1127 HWY 190 E SERVICE RD, COVINGTON, LA 704334929
Phone: 985 867-3500

HISTORICAL FINANCIALS

Company Type: Private

Income Statement
FYE: May 31

	REVENUE ($ mil.)	NET INCOME ($ mil.)	NET PROFIT MARGIN	EMPLOYEES
05/16	5,722	37	0.7%	213
05/15	6,000	86	1.4%	—
05/14	7,550	56	0.7%	—
05/13	7,704	51	0.7%	—
Annual Growth	(9.4%)	(10.4%)	—	—

2016 Year-End Financials
Return on assets: 0.5%   Cash ($ mil.): 6
Return on equity: 0.7%
Current ratio: 0.10

ZEOLYST INTERNATIONAL

EXECUTIVES

Managing Partner, Mike Boyce
Auditors: PRICEWATERHOUSECOOPERS LLP

LOCATIONS

HQ: ZEOLYST INTERNATIONAL
300 LINDENWOOD DR, MALVERN, PA 193551740
Phone: 610 651-4200

HISTORICAL FINANCIALS

Company Type: Private

Income Statement
FYE: December 31

	REVENUE ($ mil.)	NET INCOME ($ mil.)	NET PROFIT MARGIN	EMPLOYEES
12/15	319	93	29.2%	115
12/14	213	61	28.7%	—
12/13	297	109	36.9%	—
12/12	175	55	31.5%	—
Annual Growth	22.1%	19.1%	—	—

2015 Year-End Financials
Return on assets: 2.8%   Cash ($ mil.): 3
Return on equity: 29.2%
Current ratio: 2.30

ZOOLOGICAL SOCIETY OF SAN DIEGO

Talk about animal magnetism! The Zoological Society of San Diego is a not-for-profit organization that operates the 100-acre San Diego Zoo which cares for more than 4000 individual animals as well as a collection of some 3500 species of plants. The Zoological Society also manages the 1800-acre San Diego Zoo Safari Park and the center for Conservation and Research. The zoo entertains all with its daily shows in-park restaurants guided tours and special events. The society also supports conservation education and efforts such as planned travel adventure-tours to exotic destinations in Mexico and Africa. It was founded by Dr. Harry Wegeforth in 1916 and is managed by a 12-member board.

Operations

The society is the largest zoological membership group in the world with more than half a million members (including 130000 children). Members receive free zoo and safari park admission a subscription to the society's magazine and other benefits.

EXECUTIVES

President and Trustee, Berit N. Durler
Treasurer and Trustee, Frank C. Alexander
Secretary and Trustee, Rick Gulley
Executive Director, Douglas G. Myers
Vice President Retail Management, Don Leiker
Auditors: COHNREZNICK LLP SACRAMENTO C

LOCATIONS

HQ: ZOOLOGICAL SOCIETY OF SAN DIEGO
2920 ZOO DR, SAN DIEGO, CA 921011646
Phone: 619 231-1515
Web: WWW.SANDIEGOZOO.ORG

PRODUCTS/OPERATIONS

Sales 2015

	% of total
Admissions and memberships	36
Auxiliary activities	40
Contributions	15
Grant revenue for services	2
Tax revenue and other	7
Total	**100**

HISTORICAL FINANCIALS

Company Type: Private

Income Statement

	REVENUE ($ mil.)	NET INCOME ($ mil.)	NET PROFIT MARGIN	EMPLOYEES
12/15	274	29	10.8%	2,300
12/14	294	68	23.3%	—
12/13	259	29	11.5%	—
12/10	193	(6)	—	—
Annual Growth	7.2%	—	—	—

FYE: December 31

2015 Year-End Financials

Return on assets: 13.7%
Return on equity: 10.8%
Current ratio: 1.40

Cash ($ mil.): 122

Hoover's Handbook of

Private Companies

Index of Executives

Index of Executives

A

A, Mohammad 70
Aagard, Tammy 616
Aaron, Sandra 61
Aaron, Kimberly 140
Aaron, Carol 407
Aaron, Carol 466
Aaron, Todd 525
Aaron, Barbara 621
Abbeele, Annick D. Van den 152
Abbot, Penny 440
Abbott, Justin 252
Abbott, Greg 523
Abdallah, Chaouki T. 620
Abdelal, Ahmed 380
Abell, Patricia 162
Abelsen, James N 489
Abernathy, Cammy 616
Abernethy, Bruce 66
Abiera, Henry 106
Abish, Jeffrey D. (Jeff) 6
Abou-Ltaif, Nidal 46
Aboubaker, Aziza 383
Aboufadel, Ed 213
Abraham, Edward 641
Abrahamian, Gerraldine 69
Abrahams, Brian 564
Abrahamson, Tom 278
Abrams, Tom 492
Abrell, Lane 417
Abrell, John 419
Abreu, Vianka 199
Acampuzano, Guillermo 154
Accurso, Angela 161
Ack, Brad 665
Ackerley, Margaret 665
Ackerman, Jeffrey (Jeff) 557
Ackernan, Jeffery 465
Ackroyd, Jim 4
Acmoody, Andrew 373
Adair, Carter 525
Adam, Jan 199
Adamo, Tony 485
Adams, Charles M 6
Adams, Jonice 50
Adams, Richard 60
Adams, Ken 67
Adams, Kevin D. 105
Adams, Kevin D 137
Adams, George H 172
Adams, Hank 225
Adams, Pam 248
Adams, Lana 280
Adams, Andrea 286
Adams, Joseph (Joe) 358
Adams, Sara 379
Adams, James (Jim) 396
Adams, Tammy 457
Adams, Fran 469
Adams, Justin 570
Adams, Holly 581
Adams, Deanna 594
Adams, Bart 628
Adams, Nancy D 656

Adams, Clinton 657
Aday, Daniel 213
Adcock, Barbara 593
Adderly, John 303
Additional, Names 536
Ade, Michael 359
Adeli, David 654
Adelman, Fredie 490
Adelmann, Molly 346
Adepeder, Suzanne 154
Ades, Susan 490
Adkins, Laura 475
Adkins, Greg 607
Adler, Michael M. 355
Adome, Amy 480
Advocates, Cu 615
Affney, Paul G 349
Afnan, Jamshid A. 255
Agee, Nancy Howell 95
Agee, Nancy Howell 95
Aggarwal, Nimit 9
Agle, Andy 124
Agner, Brian 171
Agnes, Pierre 78
Agnew, Tina 7
Aguirre, Shirley 166
Aguirre, Vera 653
Ahlborn, Tom 58
Ahn, Andrew 483
Ahrens, Sarah 252
Ahumada, Elaine 90
Ai, Lin 616
Aichele, William S 214
Aiken, Harold 358
Aikens, Jason 424
Aikens-allen, Karla 430
Aillon, Amy 206
Ainslie, Carolyn N. 579
Aishman, Lisa L 251
Aitken, Renee 666
Akcali, Elif 616
Akin, Terry 569
Akins, Nicholas 393
Akintayo, Tinuke 533
Akridge, John 338
Alagno, Jeanne 382
Alaimo, Michael 546
Alarcon, Juan David 205
Alarid, Karen 15
Alba, Alex 532
Albanese, Lee 333
Albanese, Nicholas 359
Albayyari, Jay 666
Albert, Fran 14
Albino, Jose 241
Albornoz, Bertha Yanneth 490
Albright, Jody 402
Albritton, Larry 111
Alcock, Charles R. 490
Alcorn, Karen 320
Alderson, Tony 102
Aldred, Linda 540
Aldrich, Peter D 470
Aldridge, Ken 554
Alejandro, Ruben 653
Alejo-broadie, Estrellita 614

Alessandrini, Robert G. 565
Alexaitis, Irene 478
Alexander, Nick 7
Alexander, Barbara J 208
Alexander, Wendy 280
Alexander, Lisa 289
Alexander, Carol 333
Alexander, Kevin 347
Alexander, Will 437
Alexander, John 494
Alexander, Pamala 607
Alexander, Jeffery 608
Alexander, Frank C. 671
Alford, Sean 12
Alford, William C. 74
Alford, Sheri 501
Alford, Barbara 537
Alfrey, Edward 308
Algoe, Eric 542
Alhadeff, Kathie 415
Ali, Michael 124
Ali-Khan, Mujtaba 276
Aliabadi, Piran 558
Alicea, Marisa 154
Aligheri, Tim 259
Alim, Seema 107
Allan, Angela 125
Allan, Diana 524
Allemagne, Julie 569
Allen, Les 71
Allen, Les 71
Allen, Charlene 100
Allen, Jeanine 104
Allen, Kenneth 128
Allen, Brad 139
Allen, Herbert 197
Allen, Robert 252
Allen, Clay M 280
Allen, Linda 349
Allen, Steve 361
Allen, Adrienne 406
Allen, Mark 419
Allen, Bill 443
Allen, Kim 480
Allen, Charles 554
Allen, Keene 601
Allen, Beth 604
Allen, Gary K. 619
Allen, Andrew T. 625
Alley, C. Thomas (Tom) 178
Allinger, Lee 35
Allison, David 301
Allison, Randall 347
Allison, John 606
Almanza, Julio 154
Almquist, Andrew 17
Almquist, Guy 519
Alonso, Santos 531
Alonso, Edwin 531
Alonso, Iris 531
Alonso, Debbie 531
Alonso, Valentin 531
Alonzo, Jason 383
Alpay, John M 93
Alpen, Susan 207
Alper, Eric 606

Alsdurf, Chuck 305
Alt, Mark 310
Altaras, June 533
Altendorf, Michael J. (Mike) 160
Altshuler, Keith 199
Alulla, JoAnn 154
Alva, Joellen 176
Alvarez, Marc 22
Alvey, Jennifer 248
Alviani, Joseph 558
Alwis, Jem De 29
Alyea, Ryan 102
Amadeo, Jes S M 112
Amalfitano, Vicki 558
Amaya, Jose 258
Ambrose, Marilyn 38
Ambrose, Kelly 297
Ambrose, James 622
Ambrosio, Lucille 298
Ambrosio, Michael 642
Amburgey, Pat 35
Amcvey, Dale 234
Ames, Philip 510
Amis, Parker N 540
Amorose, David 397
An, Wilson 375
Ana, Coleen Santa 474
Anagick, Dorothy 67
Anally, Julie Mc 571
Anda, Gabriela De 300
Andel, Steve Van 21
Andel, David V 634
Andel, David L Van 634
Andersen, Charles N 84
Andersen, Travis 131
Andersen, Jesper 249
Andersen, Olivia 280
Andersen, Chris 371
Andersen, J 626
Anderson, Lynette 8
Anderson, Warren 31
Anderson, W Jeff 32
Anderson, Windy 71
Anderson, Kathleen 78
Anderson, Jim 78
Anderson, Jay 79
Anderson, John 88
Anderson, Lois 93
Anderson, Jack 99
Anderson, Barbara 172
Anderson, Duane 191
Anderson, C. Colt 198
Anderson, Stan 216
Anderson, A. Scott 252
Anderson, William 254
Anderson, Ronnie K 276
Anderson, Maureen 284
Anderson, Dianne J 285
Anderson, Allyson 288
Anderson, Mark 336
Anderson, Lynn 360
Anderson, Carol 372
Anderson, Terry Sam 379
Anderson, Jennifer 386
Anderson, Kirk 404
Anderson, Richard A 459

Greene, Michael 154
Greene, Joseph J. 265
Greene, Rebecca 293
Greene, Gary 414
Greene, Phillip 520
Greenlee, Billy 40
Greenlees, Jim 654
Greenspan, Peter 406
Greenstein, Scott 440
Greenwald, Judy 537
Greenwell, Lynette 305
Greenwood, Judy 461
Greenwood, Andre 652
Greer, James A. (Jim) 395
Greer, Jeanne 553
Gregory, Carolyn 97
Gregory, Mary Jo 381
Gregory, Sean J. 407
Greig, Jill 481
Grether, Sally 585
Gretz, Joe 605
Grewal, Harpreet 234
Grieco, Chrysanthy M. 476
Griego, Irene 262
Griesbaum, Robert 508
Griffin, James D. 152
Griffin, April 234
Griffin, Justin 258
Griffin, Sue 341
Griffin, Marcus 426
Griffin, B R 426
Griffin, Wayne J. 648
Griffis, Mark 1
Griffis, Scott 125
Griffith, J. Brian 338
Griffith, Brian 338
Griffith, Matthew 369
Griffiths, Diana 507
Griggs, Johnny 251
Grigsby, Todd W 89
Grigsby, L Lane 89
Grigsby, Linda 523
Grill, Laura D. 168
Grimes, Robert R. 198
Grimes, Theresa 264
Grimes, Vicki 561
Grimm, Ed 313
Grimminger, Kurt 664
Grindle, W Harold 204
Grinspoon, Steven 558
Grissler, Brian 578
Grissom, James 203
Grix, John 132
Grizzard, Maynard 588
Groener, Michael 390
Groff, Stacey 244
Groff, Jim 588
Gronguist, Judy 142
Groogan, Bob 483
Grosby, Karen 386
Grosner, David 285
Gross, Tammy 46
Gross, Rhonda 97
Gross, Kathy 151
Gross, Anne 152
Gross, Irwin 171
Gross, Dan 216
Gross, Tom 233
Gross, Roy 333
Gross, Daniel 370
Gross, Vaughn 445
Gross, Daniel L. (Dan) 479
Grossenbacher, Charles 367
Grossman, Orin 188
Grossman, Jeffrey 629
Grosso, Michael 499
Grosveld, Gerard 513
Grote, Ann 424
Grotjohn, Gary 301
Grotzinger, John P. 91
Grove, Cheryl 558
Groves, Ned 324
Grow, Loretta 236
Grow, David R 656
Grubbs, Jerry 15

Grube, Cindy 515
Gruber, Kreg 323
Gruber, Karen N 553
Gruener, Gregory 32
Gruenthal, Michael 13
Grunley, Kenneth M 217
Grunley, Virginia 217
Grynspan, Devora 385
Guadagnoli, Donald A. 92
Guarriello, Nicholas P 196
Gudeux, Erin 138
Guenza, Jill 291
Guerci, Dr Alan 330
Guerci, Alan D 508
Guererro, Edward 98
Guerra, Fred 116
Guerra, Gilbert 533
Guerrero, Ed 98
Guerrero, Luis 414
Guest, James A. (Jim) 138
Guest, Charles 625
Guetter, Shawn 191
Guevara, Julia 213
Guevara, Alain 281
Guevarra, Joshua 308
Gugelchuk, Gary 657
Gugenheim, Lisa 543
Guglielmo, Joseph A 497
Guignier, Liz 175
Guillory, Angela 395
Guiterrez, Jorge 127
Gulembo, Kathy 213
Gulley, Rick 671
Gumba, Rosemarie 106
Gumm, Gary 646
Gumpert, Phil 592
GUNNELL, JEROME 523
Gunnink, Brett 350
Gunter, Kip 12
Gupta, Ashish 249
Gupta, Rupal 325
Gupta, Mahendra R. 587
Guralnick, Sidney 246
Gurin, Patricia B 25
Gurk, Kevin Mc 65
Gurvis, Mark 564
Gusa, Audy 140
Gustafson, Michael 546
Gustafson, Jennifer 554
Gustitus, Nancy 448
Guthrie, Chris 586
Gutierrez, Helen 121
Gutierrez, Bonnie 404
Gutman, Kenneth 281
Gutnick, Michael P. 324
Gutowski, Amy 17
Gutteridge, Thomas G. (Tom) 585
Guy, Kip 513
Guyette, Kathy 345
Guzick, David S. 478
Guzick, David S. 616
Guzik, Bill 4
Guzman, Al 283
Guzzetta, Tammy 352
Gwinn, Nancy E. 490
Gwyn, Bryan 125
Gyland, Kevin 204
Gyurci, John 333

H

Haan, James 635
Haas-Kogan, Daphne 152
Haas-Kogan, Daphne 546
Haber, Rebecca 108
Haber, Daniel A. 558
Haberern, Andrew 128
Habingreither, Robert 542
Hachem, Ramsey R 587
Hachey, Michael (Mike) 182
Hachten, Richard 144
Hacker, Doug 458
Hacker, Mary Dee 550
Hackerman, Nancy 488

Hackl, Greg 357
Haddad, Sam 93
Haddad, Gabriel G. 438
Haden, James E 313
Hadley, David 251
Hadsell, Cheresa 515
Haenni, Chris 310
Haessler, Thomas 308
Hafliger, Mark 11
Hagadorn, David 95
Hagarty, Brittany 485
Hagberg, Robert 223
Hagedorn, Chris 556
Hagen, Kelly 22
Hagen, Jake 78
Haggard, Donna 231
Haggerty, Shannon 485
Hahn, William C. 152
Hahn, Debbie 234
Hahn, Nich 397
Haifa, Amir 279
Haile, Kempton C. 588
Hain, Tony 317
Hain, C Stuart 533
Haines, Kathy 396
Haire, Gary 197
Haj, Ray A 534
Haj, Ray 535
Hakim, Veronique 337
Halamka, John D. 69
Halas, Wally 188
Hale, Tim 187
Hale, Kathleen 305
Hale, David F. 438
Hale, Blake 539
Hale, Roxanne 589
Haley, Rebecca 74
Haley, Jim 339
Haley, Kate 459
Haley, Sherry 499
Haley, Trish 565
Halfin, Bobbie 26
Hall, Richard 12
Hall, Steve 17
Hall, Sara 25
Hall, Jim 71
Hall, Jim 71
Hall, Jim 71
Hall, Cindy 78
Hall, Dale 163
Hall, Maryjane 192
Hall, Trudy 202
Hall, Kendall 206
Hall, Claudia 241
Hall, Robert 388
Hall, Pamela 414
Hall, Judith A 434
Hall, Tania 437
Hall, Brenda 443
Hall, Bret 450
Hall, Claude 487
Hall, Dennis 540
Hall, Cynthia 573
Hall, Kathryn A. 579
Hall, Teri 589
Hall, Carla 591
Hall, Karla 649
Hall, Molly 666
Hall-Barrow, Julie 116
Hallada, Tony 126
Hallahan, Molly 598
Hallberg, Jacqueline 212
Hallford, Brad 413
Halliwill, Donald B. 95
Hallman, Samantha 442
Halloran, Teri 427
Halsey, Drew 183
Halsey, Casey S. 258
Halsey, Casey S. 258
Halstead, Candace 198
Halstead, Gretchen 228
Halterman, Don 233
Halverson, Thomas 128
Halverson, Terri 384
Halverson, Frank 423

Halvorsen, Cheryl 603
Ham, Mandy 318
Hamburgh, Rita 86
Hamby, Leigh S. 415
Hamill, Christine 653
Hamilton, Charles 167
Hamilton, Mike 222
Hamilton, Susan 224
Hamilton, Dianne 230
Hamilton, Dennie 286
Hamilton, Nikki 446
Hamilton, Terry 511
Hamilton, Terence 511
Hamilton, Vincent 655
Hamlin, Scott J. 114
Hamlin, Stephen E. 539
Hamline, Steve 258
Hamline, Steve 258
Hamm, Bradley 385
Hammack, Tracey 625
Hammer, Doug 252
Hammer, Matthew 374
Hammerstone, Jim 97
Hammes, Chris 251
Hammond, Patti 180
Hammond, Harlan 252
Hammond, Ulysses B. 284
Han, Zhuo 118
Hanbury, George L. 386
Hance, James H. (Jim) 266
Hancock, Todd 120
Hancock, Renee 396
Hancock, Lynne 550
Hancock, Ross 616
Hand, Martin 25
Hanely, Robin 11
Hanes, Tom 283
Haney, Mark A 111
Haney, Nick 123
Haney, Michael 457
Haney, Mark 652
Hang, Kyung Ho 153
Hanifin, Kristi 436
Hankins, Deb 598
Hanks, Joe 1
Hanks, Jessica 280
Hanky, Donald 588
Hanlon, Philip J 599
Hannafin, Robert (Bob) 188
Hannah, Ashley 8
Hannah, Sharon 415
Hannock, Melanee 25
Hansberry, Mitchell 548
Hanscom, Morgan 107
Hansen, Mike 10
Hansen, John 18
Hansen, Eric 24
Hansen, Peter O 103
Hansen, David 266
Hansen, William 423
Hansen, Dr David 447
Hansen, Mary 569
Hansen, Melissa 585
Hanson, Jodi 11
Hanson, Stephen C. 52
Hanson, Rachel 128
Hanson, Theresa 169
Hanson, Brian 214
Hanson, Timothy 228
Hanson, Gary A. 410
Hanson, James R 655
Hantman, Perla Tabares 576
Hao, Sophia Tang 170
Happ, John 539
Hapton, George M 449
Haptonstall, Ken 333
Haqq, Constance T 380
Harat, Donna 14
Harbeck, Stephen 472
Harboro, Glenn 237
Hard, Kristina 561
Harder, Andrew J 598
Hardiman, Chris 479
Hardin, Brian 38
Hardin, Cornelia 262

Johnson, Ron 284
Johnson, Noila 324
Johnson, Rodney D. 333
Johnson, Wes 333
Johnson, Cleveland 352
Johnson, Kevin 358
Johnson, Aubrey 365
Johnson, Theodore 366
Johnson, Patricia 394
Johnson, Darrell 397
Johnson, Lisa 413
Johnson, John 418
Johnson, Joey 424
Johnson, Michaele 428
Johnson, Sally 444
Johnson, Jerry L 448
Johnson, Kathy 450
Johnson, Pamela 466
Johnson, Sarah 471
Johnson, Ronald 484
Johnson, Darlin 489
Johnson, Kirk 490
Johnson, Michael 495
Johnson, Keith 508
Johnson, Roger 517
Johnson, Donna 524
Johnson, M. Eric 586
Johnson, Mary 589
Johnson, Steven 589
Johnson, Amanda 592
Johnson, Welkin 599
Johnson, Steve 603
Johnson, Julie A. 616
Johnson, Sylvia Smith 618
Johnson, April 618
Johnson, Deroy 618
Johnson, Christopher 624
Johnson, Kerrick 635
Johnson, Kerrick 635
Johnson, Jerry N. 646
Johnson, Patricia 663
Johnston, Michael 1
Johnston, Tony 114
Johnston, Susan 168
Johnston, Thomas 175
Johnston, Tammie 251
Johnston, Michael V. 270
Johnston, Jeffrey 330
Johnston, Lisa 585
Johnstone, Sally 656
Joiner, Daniel 86
Joiner, Robin 537
Jollay, David L. 156
Jolley, Julene M 214
Jolley, Burke 266
Jolliff, Jane 308
Jolly, Jay 443
Jolly, James 443
Jones, Greg 10
Jones, Brigitte 46
Jones, C. Todd 52
Jones, Aaron 58
Jones, Renotta 76
Jones, Cheryl 100
Jones, William 116
Jones, Vernon 142
Jones, Patrick 151
Jones, Timothy 169
Jones, Elina 170
Jones, Paul D 171
Jones, Wes 183
Jones, John 206
Jones, Kearline 227
Jones, Kristine 244
Jones, Blane 244
Jones, Maudie 248
Jones, Marybeth C 262
Jones, Christopher 267
Jones, Bryan 286
Jones, Laurie 301
Jones, Michael G 322
Jones, Steve 334
Jones, Bonita 344
Jones, Sharon 350
Jones, Hugh 353

Jones, Scott 356
Jones, Kevin 363
Jones, Calvin 372
Jones, Ben 389
Jones, Elizabeth 396
Jones, Mark A. 398
Jones, Bobby 399
Jones, Janel 411
Jones, Helen 424
Jones, Randall T. (Todd) 433
Jones, Gary 439
Jones, Amanda 452
Jones, Jim 454
Jones, Michael L. 482
Jones, Patrice 554
Jones, Daniel 555
Jones, Marc 557
Jones, Mark 557
Jones, Nicholas P. 573
Jones, Clay 584
Jones, Dane 591
Jones, Denise 592
Jones, Barbara 599
Jones, Daniel 618
Jones, Nina 618
Jones, Aranthan 639
Jones, Brad 641
Jong, Pai 269
Jons, David E 393
Jordahl, Chad 154
Jordan, Joel 7
Jordan, Art 176
Jordan, Terri 176
Jordan, Charles B 302
Jordan, Walt 396
Jordan, Randy 413
Jordan, David 598
Jorgensen, Mary 297
Jorsz, William 589
Jose, Kathleen 281
Joseph, Satheesh 85
Joseph, Simone 324
Joseph, Michele 445
Joseph, Brandy 451
Joseph, Homan 508
Joseph, Joy 567
Joshi, Leela 253
Josler, Cheryl 153
Joslyn, Scott 297
Joslyn, Linda 464
Jost, Philippe 485
Joway, Timothy 317
Joy, Lindsey 470
Joy, Scott 574
Joyce, Jim 129
Joyce, Charles P 399
Joyce, Brad 399
Joyce, Jim 399
Joyce, Jodi 463
Jr, Hugh Inman 5
Jr, George R Gunn 6
Jr, John L Esterhai 6
Jr, William C Whitmore 20
Jr, Everett Alvarez 22
Jr, Rick Shadyac 25
Jr, John A Miller 32
Jr, Joseph Sarpy 72
Jr, William H Pettibone 132
Jr, Mack McCaul 132
Jr, Joseph P Santucci 147
Jr, Thomas B Crowley 147
Jr, Wilfred Bahl 148
Jr, Thomas E Maher 154
Jr, Coty Dupre 164
Jr, Coty R Dupre 164
Jr, Charles R Dickinson 167
Jr, Ashton J Ryan 168
Jr, Kenneth A Card 169
Jr, Charles M Rathbone 171
Jr, Glenn D Steele 206
Jr, Glenn D Steele 206
Jr, Robert Powell 237
Jr, John Walker 273
Jr, John B Kilroy 274
Jr, Joseph B Nadol 288

Jr, Jerry Lamon Falwell 292
Jr, Johnnie Moore 292
Jr, Charles Monahan 319
Jr, Ed Witt 343
Jr, Carl Candullo 350
Jr, Lindsey Bradely 353
Jr, Dr John Phillips 357
Jr, Theodore T Myre 386
Jr, Mr Albert C Kelly 393
Jr, T L Tompkins 395
Jr, Martin Salinas 403
Jr, Louis M Pearce 407
Jr, Thomas J McCraken 442
Jr, Clifford G Reif 443
Jr, George S York 444
Jr, Paul M Riesbeck 447
Jr, Jim Furman 464
Jr, Lawrence C Franklin 523
Jr, Ray Mann 524
Jr, Joseph C Maher 526
Jr, Lyndon L Olson 541
Jr, H W Burdett 554
Jr, Ernie Schmitt 556
Jr, Glenn D Steele 558
Jr, Wesley S Williams 559
Jr, Joseph Caravalho 561
Jr, John D Rockefeller 569
Jr, Daniel Debarba 572
Jr, Ronald H Foster 578
Jr, Thomas B Gerlach 581
Jr, Thomas F Helms 603
Jr, Kenneth J Ronk 605
Jr, George B Hernandez 613
Jr, Joesprh Richards 635
Jr, Jerry Straub 636
Juan, Gallicio 542
Juarez, Phillip 625
Judge, Kenan 244
Judge, Dennis F. 565
Judge, Martin E. 565
Judson, Rufus 582
Jueckstock, Rainer 193
Juehring, Ben 325
Juett, Phillip 333
Julian, Steve 474
Julin, Paul 206
Jump, Darrell 386
Junck, Mary E. 544
Jungmann, Dr John 502
Junior, Joseph 143
Jura, Walter 560
Jurdy, Donna 385
Jurist, Louis 343
Jurosko, Janet B 142
Jusko, James 543
Justice, Peggy 416
Juusela, Kari 68
Juzek, Leslie 597
Jwayad, Nick 469

K

Kaatz, Gary E 449
Kaban, Leonard 558
Kabir, Jamal 451
Kablinger, Anita 95
Kachman, Deann 192
Kaczke, Robert 336
Kaczmarek, Jerry 229
Kade, Thomas 333
Kadir, Djelal 573
Kaeding, Kevin 151
Kaelin, Michael H. (Mike) 444
Kahle, Katherine 286
Kahn, Charles 302
Kahn, Marc 395
Kaiser, Jennifer 22
Kaiser, Gerald 124
Kaiser, Laura S. 252
Kalajainen, Kimberly 284
Kalajainen, Kim 284
Kaley, Ann 516
Kalfayan, Terry 625
Kallis, Stephanie 652

Kallman, Deborah 651
Kalp, Dirk 657
Kalsbeek, David 154
Kalscheur, Gregory 599
Kalv, Paul 196
Kalverd, Kathy 466
Kam, Keith 531
Kamalsky, Don 97
Kamchief, Keith 531
Kaminski, Scott 117
Kaminski, Scott 277
Kamstra, Matt 270
Kandus-Fisher, Christopher 68
Kane, Patrick 92
Kane, John W. 236
Kane, David R. 236
Kane, Terri 252
Kane, James 276
Kane, Martha 406
Kane, Kathleen M 475
Kane, Allen R. 490
Kang, Charles 8
Kang, Y Michele 129
Kang, Y Michele 129
Kang, James D. 546
Kant, Surya 538
Kantardzic, Damir 58
Kanuch, Sue 455
Kaplan, Joshua 42
Kaplan, Michael 170
Kaplan, Harold P 342
Kaplan, Barry 378
Karageorges, Carolyn 114
Karam, Chris 119
Karawan, Oleh 388
Karbach, J William 545
Kardys, Lisa 284
Kareiva, Peter 570
Karl, Edward 24
Karn, Kevin 625
Karp, Stephen R. 550
Karpova, Anya 523
Karpowicz, Christine 203
Karsos, Felicia 339
Kaseman, Sheila 113
Kaska, Tony 244
Kassen, Tim 27
Kasser, James 550
Kastberg, Ruth 551
Kates, Kenneth P 617
Kathleen, Larkin 333
Kathy, Collado 662
Katsianis, John 156
Katz, Martin J. (Marty) 130
Katz, Jonathan 406
Katz, Phyllis 416
Katz, Elizabeth H 566
Katzman, Richard 101
Kaufman, Dan 258
Kaufman, Dan 258
Kaufman, Richard 406
Kaufman, Irvin A. 438
Kaufman, Dafna 634
Kautz, Rhonda 350
Kavalier, Mary J 144
Kavanaugh, James P 664
Kavanaugh, James P. (Jim) 664
Kay, Stephen B. 82
Kay, Robert W 323
Kay, Mary 571
Kayle, David 539
Kayrell, Barry 230
Kayser, Laura 190
Kaz, Peter 34
Kazer, Meredith Wallace 188
Kcintyre, Robert 526
Keables, Michael 130
Kearns, Richard 43
Kearns, Donald 438
Kearsley, Alan 463
Keating, Katie 503
Keating, Patrick J. 599
Keating, Mike 649
Keating, J. Edmund (Ed) 662
Keckeis, Thomas M. (Tom) 334

Lovern, Ed 415
Lovett, Robert 594
Lovingood, Kevin 322
Lovingood, Dustin 349
Low, Lewis 288
Low, Robert E. 366
Lowe, Challis 41
Lowe, Karen 128
Lowe, Terril 134
Lowe, Scott 419
Lowe, Roger 589
Lowe, William J. 598
Lowell, Corey 203
Loweree, Fred 176
Loy, Vicky 524
Loya, Rene 107
Lubar, David J 203
Lubert, Ira M. 573
Lubitz, Bob 652
Lucas, Alexander 113
Lucas, Heather 131
Lucas, John 323
Lucas, Ken 336
Lucas, Wade 394
Luceno, Cristina 465
Luchi, Patricia M 294
Luciano, Melba 576
Lucier, Scott 602
Luck, John 102
Lucke, Dan 268
Luckett, Whitney 440
Lucks, Cheryl W. 361
Lucore, Charles 504
Ludington, Bob 576
Ludlow, Robert C. 255
Ludtke, Sandra 294
Ludwig, Anne 375
Ludwig-Beymer, Patti 173
Luebbers, Amy 349
Luff, Paula 154
Luginbuhl, William E 549
Lugo, Noelita 45
Luizzi, Jacqueline 402
Lukas, Emil 280
Luke, Kristin 565
Lukes, Donald 598
Lultschik, Jennifer 623
Lumbus, Jason 71
Lumsden, Chris A. 474
Luna, Rachel 499
Lunceford, Michael 241
Lund, Maggie 327
Lundergan, Dan K. 628
LUNDGREN, DAVID 200
Lundgren, John 333
Lundy, Ann 32
Lunn, Eric 22
Lunsford, Michael J 299
Lunsford, Anastasia 542
Lunt, Bob 303
Luo, Leo 139
Lupisella, Melissa 494
Lurie, Robert F. 368
Lurie, Mark 592
Lusk, Barbara 128
Lutz, Keith 343
Lutz, Janice 509
Lutz, John M. 586
Luu, Danny 627
Lvergne, Luke A 401
Ly, Heather 634
Lyash, Jeffrey J. (Jeff) 178
Lyden, Shawn 117
Lyer, Ramiya 291
Lynch, Anne 107
Lynch, Timothy G. 442
Lynch, Ray 628
Lynn, Theresa 123
Lynn, Mary 214
Lynn, Elizabeth 242
Lynn, Scott J. 453
Lynne, Weiland Laura 478
Lyons, Jeffrey B 30
Lyons, Patti 73
Lyons, Eric 98

Lyons, Betty 400
Lyons, Jeffery B 665
Lysik, Stephen 485
Lyttle, Lance 421
L'Heureux, Scott 259

M

Maali, Maouc 408
Maas, Bill 156
Maass, Paul T. 576
Mabie, Teri 556
Mabile, Terri 42
Macat, Berta R 464
Macaulay, Linda R. 543
Macdonald, Ellen A 222
MacDonald, Greg 280
Macdonald, Doug 383
MacDougall, Harriett 386
Mace, Bridget 227
Macgillivray, Diane 380
Macgregor, Andrew 638
Macha, Mark 426
Machtley, Ronald 87
Machtolf, Kurt R 465
Machuk, Paul 79
Macias, Art 176
Macias, Daniel 267
Macias, Deb 530
Maciel, Ana 524
Macina, Scott 147
Macina, Robert P. 566
Macisaac, Don 394
Mackay, Elizabeth F 116
MacKeen, Ray 588
Mackenzie, D Rob 100
MacKenzie, Cindy 152
Mackenzie, Bob 539
Mackey, Amy 2
Mackey, Willis 267
Macko, David 206
Macko, David 558
Maclaughlin, David 233
MacPhaul, Pam 192
Macri, Frederick J. 293
MacVane, Jessica 213
Maddalone, Dom 492
Madden, Nancy 386
Madden, Donald 594
Madera, Linda 154
Madigan, Angie 131
Madrigal, Reynaldo 222
Madsen, Ruthanne 182
Madson, Jeremy 395
Maeder, Jeff 588
Maekewa, Steve 11
Maey, Tom 461
Magalhaes, Judy 267
Magdangal, Connie 67
Mageed, Aly 501
Maggiora, Louise Della 475
Magid, Bruce R. 82
Magnani, Ron 205
Magner, Johnette 72
Magness, Bill 178
Magnotta, Adriana 199
Magruder, Joan 345
Magruder, Joan 505
Maguire, Kate 247
Mah, Chester 324
Mahalingam, S. 538
Mahan, Michelle 203
Mahan, Wade 263
Maher, John 312
Maher, Mark 411
Mahler, Carl 537
Mahone, E. Mark 270
Mahoney, Lindsay 42
Mahoney, Michael 225
Mahoney, Edward J. 324
Mahoney, Joanne M. 368
Mahoney, Bill 492
Mahoney, Kelly 523
Mai, Shayne 363

Maibach, Doug 56
Maibach, Ben C. 56
Maibach, Ryan 56
Maibach, Benjamin C 57
Maibach, Douglas L 57
Maibach, Sheryl B 57
Mail, Ingrid M 307
Mainda, Hodgen 177
Mainous, Rosalie O'Dell 666
Mair, Adam 216
Majerle, Jeff 518
Majetich, Stephen 212
Majkrzak, Amy 308
Major, Jon D 536
Makhlin, Leo 664
Maklan, David 654
Makovich, Zachary 616
Malakof, Stacey L 369
Malanoski, Gregory 392
Malasto, Thomas A. 133
Malatlian, Michelle 468
Malav ©, Andr ©s 386
Malcolm, Jacquelyn 547
Maldonado, Liliana 107
Maldonado, Belinda 319
Maley, Christopher 566
Maley-Grubl, Christine 338
Malkove, Barbara 124
Mallik, David 588
Malloy, William 336
Malone, Mike 11
Malone, Mary 188
Malone, Blake 372
Malone, Marguerite G. 468
Malone, John 626
Malone, John T 630
Malone, Brian 662
Maloney, Chris 252
Maloney, Tina 406
Maloney, Rachel 428
Maloney, James F 605
Maloy, June 376
Malte, Bob 274
Manacchio, Margot 668
Manahan, Thomas J. (Tom) 603
Manasse, Robert 656
Mance, Marlaine 491
Manchester, Terry 71
Mancuso, Anthony 194
Mancuso, Anthony 303
Mandaglio, Jim 604
Mandel, Adrienne A. 646
Mandell, Joyce 458
Mandell, James 550
Mandrella, Karen 625
Maneker, Amy 117
Maness, Andrew 37
Mangel, Allen W. 444
Mangel, Barry 652
Manigan, Elizabeth 198
Manigault, Pierre 94
Manion, Roger 625
Manis, Alice 496
Manis, Jonathan (Jon) 532
Manka, Agnes 220
Manker, Marcia 396
Manning, Martin F. (Marty) 9
Manning, John 27
Manning, Robin E. (Rob) 178
Manning, Rob 178
Manning, Jenni 290
Manoni, David 303
Manos, Steven S. 82
Mansfield, Allen 20
Mansfield, Timothy 129
Mansfield, Marty 294
Mansfield, Stephen L. (Steve) 335
Mansoor, Arshad 178
Mansuetti, Mike 448
Mantella, Philomena V. 380
Manzolillo, Barbara A. 319
Mao, Paul 148
Marcaccio, Mario J 100
Marchand, Christine A 209
Marchand, Christine 238

Marchese, Sara 438
Marchozzi, Tom 223
Marchus, Julie 27
Marciniak, Richard 601
Marcos, Miguel 217
Marcus, Ruth 491
Marfechuk, Judy 381
Margetts, Marty 120
Margules, Gary 386
Maria, Rosa 160
Mariani, Harry 243
Marians, Ken 324
Marino, Kathy 526
Maritz, W. Stephen (Steve) 310
Mark, William 503
Mark, Joseph 511
Markell, Peter K. 406
Markell, Peter K 558
Markell, Peter K. 599
Markevicius, Vitas 295
Markey, Jeff 244
Markgraf, Nancy 68
Markham, Tim 17
Markin, Rod 629
Markley, Steve 160
Markley, Ben 632
Markovski, Veni 253
Marks, Stanley W. 491
Markson, Larry 69

Marksteiner, Dave 313
Markuson, David 548
Marlowe, Bobby 552
Maroc, Genny 289
Marquardt, R. Scott 305
Marquardt, Jane 305
Marquardt, Robert 305
Marquardt, Jeanne 599
Marquez, Roman 266
Marquis, Jeffrey A. 218
Marra, Michele 376
Marra, Michel 376
Marroquin, Tim 213
Marrs, Rick 410
Mars, Galen 191
Mars, Susan De 581
Marsch, Kathleen 519
Marschhausen, John 234
Marseille, Wagner 332
Marsh, Celeste 252
Marsh, Peter 641
Marshal, Jim 363
Marshall, Bill 18
Marshall, Robert 102
Marshall, Kymberly 108
Marshall, Jay 244
Marshall, James 363
Marshall, Era L. 490
Marsteller, Brent A 242
Marsters, Karen 171
Marston, Ken 259
Martel, Ron 266
Marter, Ken 319
Martin, Michael 39
Martin, Thomas 48
Martin, Marlon 54
Martin, Jill 101
Martin, Glen 109
Martin, Michael 130
Martin, C. Gregory 182
Martin, Pat 186
Martin, Michael M. 198
Martin, Dave 242
Martin, Jim 247
Martin, James 257
Martin, Stacy L 302
Martin, Pat 302
Martin, Gary 311
Martin, Ruben S 313
Martin, Kathryn 324
Martin, Terri 327
Martin, Sergo S 352
Martin, Shelly 353
Martin, Beth 358
Martin, Gary 385

Ornelas, Diana 78
Orona, Angelo 625
Oropeza, Christopher 541
Orr, Karen 31
Orr, Clint 167
Orr, Mark 217
Orr, Dave 447
Orr, Gina 604
Orris, Keith 201
Orsenigo, Carlo 106
Ortbals, Brian 664
Ortega, Cathy 6
Ortega, Ded-Deb 632
Ortell, Susan 180
Ortiz, Esteban 414
Osborn, Peggy 104
Osborn, William A. 385
Osborn, Kelly 605
Osborne, David W 542
Osburg, Brad 577
Oseman, Shawn 233
Osentoski, Jeffrey 11
Oser, Edward 308
Osley, Walter 98
Ostendorf, Alice 115
Ostermeier, Timothy 423
Ostrander, R 154
Ostrowicki, Jackie 76
Osullivan, Carolann 99
Osullivan, Helen 362
Otocki, Susan 343
Otrembiak, Steve 488
Ott, Kevin L. 236
Ottino, Julio M. 385
Otto, Noreen 244
Ouchida, Michael 246
Ousley, Glenna 154
Outtrim, Robert 333
Ovel, Jack 325
Overbey, Katherine 115
Overfield, Joan 188
Overhizer, Michael 612
Overstreet, Luann 273
Overton, Camie 671
Owen, Linda 31
Owen, Carey 167
Owens, John C 76
Owens, Lisa 125
Owens, Roxanne 154
Owens, Thomas A. 164
Owens, Jackie 186
Owens, Linda 312
Owens, Fritz 372
Owens, Craig 652
Owusu-ansah, Albert 87
Oyarzun, Ramon 238
Oyer, Randall 566
Ozawa, Kazuko 651
Ozcan, Emre 258
Ozene, Brett 35
Ozga, Dustin 526
Ozuah, Philip O. 351
O'Brady, Lucy 301
O'Brian, Kelly 379
O'Brien, Keith 102
O'Brien, Kelli 332
O'Brien, Kelli 448
O'Brien, Mark 511
O'Brien, David 511
O'Bryant, G. Mark 537
O'Connell, Burt 494
O'Connnell, Jerome 422
O'Connor, Dan 40
O'Connor, Michelle 319
O'Connor, Kathi 405
O'Connor, Ryan 636
O'Day, Gail R. 641
O'Donnell, Randall L. 325
O'Flaherty, Lori L. 128
O'Hanley, Ronald P. (Ron) 69
O'Hara, Gene 374
O'Hare, Edward 277
O'Keefe, Patrick 106
O'Keefe, Rozanne 225
O'Keefe, Barbara J. 385

O'Keefe, Sharon 582
O'Keeffe, Frederique 267
O'Leary, Jerry 107
O'Leary, Richard 366
O'Leary, Rand 407
O'Malley, Patrick J. 46
O'malley, Timothy 625
O'Neil, John 497
O'Neill, Liz 291
O'Neill, Robert 450
O'Reilly, Charles 226
O'Shea, Rebecca 590
O'Smith, Colleen 187

P

Paanakker, Roland 291
Pace, Jason 245
Pachman, Louis 225
Pachuta, Robin 11
Pacifico, Gail 485
Pack, Bill 121
Pacura, Lori 487
Padach, Joe 327
Padgett, Michael Mark 528
PADGETT, DESTINY 616
Padilla, Jose 154
Padmaperuma, Rasika 190
Padover, Craig 259
Pagan, Lisa 652
Pagano, Charles 583
Page, Kathy 228
Page, Roger 328
Page, Elaine 378
Page, Brian 380
Page, Michael 437
Page, Michael 503
Pagura, Annie 339
Pahic, Olivia 346
Painter, Ginny 312
Pak, Barb M 185
Pakalniskis, Aloyzas 181
Palan, Martha 654
Palla, Wayne 150
Pallares, Jan 316
Palmer, Mike 186
Palmer, Neal 258
Palmer, Mark 390
Palmer, David 508
Palmer, Frank 588
Palmquist, Dan 615
Panagoplos, Janae 305
Panamaroff, Thomas 277
Panchanathan, Sethuraman (Panch) 37
Pane, Stephanie 668
Panes, Maria 630
Pang, Adam 333
Pangborn, Robert N. 573
Panicucci, Michelle 144
Pantic, Zorica 652
Panzitta, Lenny 459
Pao, Sun 106
Paolella, Marilyn 486
Paolello, Mike 236
Paoletti, Rich 566
Paone, Andrew 651
Papay, Dan 666
Papay, Daniel 666
Papetti, Beth 652
Papetti, Elizabeth 652
Papola, Maria 152
Pappalardo, A. Neil 319
Papst, Thomas L. 469
Paradise, Christi 455
Parazynski, Gail 540
Parces, Dennis 356
Parda, D S 18
Parekh, Kam 504
Parent, Bob 358
Paris, Jerry 366
Parish, Amber 385
Parisi, Paul 123
Parisi, Jeannine 186
Parisi, Jim 322

Parker, Allison 40
Parker, Cathy 87
Parker, Alfred 164
Parker, Carol 182
Parker, Larry 244
Parker, Beck 339
Parker, Dorothy 406
Parker, William 447
Parker, Cindy 474
Parker, Tanya 505
Parker, Deanna 561
Parker, Pam 653
Parker-Hollis, Carla 163
Parkman, David 530
Parks, Susan 156
Parks, R M 436
Parlee, Joan 161
Parliman, Brian 141
Parman, Stanley C 339
Parmer, David 53
Parmer, Robert 404
Parnell, Winfred 151
Parod, Daniel 517
Parr, Mark 450
Parrett, Chanda 511
Parrish, David K. 75
Parsons, Brent 277
Parsons, Greg 285
Parsons, Jemma 390
Parsons, Bill 468
Parsons, Kathy 509
Pascal, Sandra E 652
Pascu, Sorin 616
Pascualy, Ralph 533
Paskes, Lazer 522
Pasley, Debi 455
Pasma, Diane 442
Pason, Leah 371
Pasquale, David 411
Passarella, Agnes 332
Passaro, Karen 476
Pastor, Jack 247
Pastorelle, Linda 449
Pastorelli, Nicholas 577
Pastorius, John 658
Pastron, Nathan 598
Patch, Donna 241
Pate, David C. 515
Pate, Patty 652
Patel, Vipul 3
Patel, Bina 108
Patel, Yogen R. 236
Patel, Sagar 298
Patel, Bipin 460
Patel, Raksha 522
Patel, Akshay 551
Patel, Hiral 554
Patellis, Cecelia 652
Patil, Ankit 82
Patino, Josephine 51
Patino, Elizabeth 156
Patnaude, Kimberly 119
Patricia, Rodriguez-armenta Hilda 478
Patrick, Brenda 420
Patrick, Sandra 520
Patterson, Pat 39
Patterson, Philip 212
Patterson, Samantha 280
Patterson, Ron 303
Patterson, Jason 436
Patterson, Dayle 489
Patterson-Randles, Sandra R. 598
Patton, Andrea 389
Patz, Melanie 52
Patzke, Guy 278
Paul, Mary 41
Paul, Henri 275
Paul, Chausse 305
Paul, Valerie J. 490
Paul, Derrick 520
Paulakos, Kimberly 239
Pauley, Trina 637
Paulhamus, Shella 589
Paulikas, George 543
Paulson, Jenette 67

Paulson, Dana 285
Paulus, Ronald A 344
Paumen, Richard 529
Pavesi, Phil 592
Pavlik, Albert 597
Pavlinik, Caroline 184
Pawlak, Mark 236
Pawlak, Paul 486
Pawson, Greg 484
Paxton, Ken 45
Payne, Jon 43
Payne, Gene 224
Payne, Mike 292
Payne, William 314
Payne, Penelope (Nell) 490
Payne, Valerie 671
Peace, Steve 27
Pearce, John 76
Pearce, Chris 256
Pearce, Petrene 440
Pearce, Edwin W 539
Pearce, Kim 576
Pearce, Louis M. 648
Pearlman, Perry 118
Pearson, Jeffrey T 25
Pearson, Kermit 57
Pearson, Anne 228
Pearson, Dave 268
Pearson, David 418
Pearson, Eric 503
Pearson, Shelli 656
Pearson, Nanette 656
Pearson, Paul 670
Pease, Mark L. 83
Peaslee, Gregory 623
Peceny, Mark 620
Peck, David 48
Peck, John 213
Peck, Chris 258
Peck, Charles A. (Chuck) 414
Peckham, Michael P. (Mike) 438
Peckinpaugh, David 310
Pedersen, John 305
Pedlow, Bernadette 13
Pedlow, Frank 558
Pedone, Peter 565
Pedretti, Bart 150
Pedroza, Sujey 410
Pedroza, Fernando 423
Pedruczny, Jayna J 598
Peek, Scott 61
Peeler, Glenn 610
Pehrson, Timothy T. 252
Peirsol, Kelli 274
Pejmannia, Maryam 410
Pelfrey, Carol 273
Pelkowski, Margaret 666
Pellecchia, John 6
Pellegrino, Thomas 188
Pellot, Lisette 616
Peltier, Wayne 57
Pelton, Jim 402
Peltzie, Kenneth 70
Pendergast, Michael 70
Pendergraft, Judy 173
Pendergraft, Shelia 251
Pendleton, Pat J 659
Penman, R Keith 465
Pennell, Larry 148
Pennella, Thomas L. 106
Penner, Peter Pete 529
Penney, Robert T. 102
Penni, Mike 539
Pennoyer, John 165
Pepper, J David 409
Pepper, Dave 409
Peralta, Pennie 94
Perchinske, Terese 97
Perdue, Melina D. 95
Perea, Jennifer Rosato 154
Pereira, Daisy 158
Pereira, Alvaro 198
Pereira, Grace 355
Perez, Gloria 141
Perez, Stella 158

Thys, Dennis J 123
Tian, Ye 410
Tice, Casandra 97
Tichenor, Stuart 145
Tiedemann, Peter 21
Tiedjen, Shirley K 344
Tierney, Natalie 495
Tierney, Thomas J. 570
Tikhomirov, Vadim 239
Tilchin, Mike 106
Tilley, Kristen 419
Tillman, Tonya 96
Tillman, David 321
Tillman, Michael C 609
Tilmon, Jon 58
Tilton, David 44
Tim, Snyder 641
Timmerman, Timothy T. 300
Timmons, Paul 523
Timms, Gary 66
Tingzon, Macuen 8
Tino, Dean 649
Tinscher, Steve 256
Tinsley, George W 220
Tippet, Kieth 276
Tirpak, Jon 492
Tjia, Christiaan 440
Tober, Suzy 666
TOBIN, JERRY 53
Tobin, Margaret 367
Todd, Andrew N 404
Todd, Cheryl 421
Todd, Andrew 667
Todd, Andrew N 667
Tofani, Barbara 114
Toffey, Bryan 10
Tohara, Connie 628
Tol, Daryl 321
Tolbert, Terry 440
Tomasovic, Elizabeth 345
Tomberlin, Don E 322
Tomblin, John 589
Tomei, Joseph 502
Tomke, John A. 163
Tomlinson, Tom 390
Tomlinson, Mitchell 408
Tomlinson, Kim 506
Tomlinson, Robert 588
Tonn, Debra 91
Tooker, Jeanie 503
Tooker, Jean 503
Tooma, Eskandar 544
Toomajian, Marty 60
Topham, Marshall 643
Topping, Scott 600
Torbay, Rabih 252
Torbert, Ronald 56
Torbert, Ronald J 57
Torchiana, David F. 406
Torchiana, David 406
Tornes, Barry 545
Torno, Ryan 209
Torrance, Kelly 232
Torrence, Chas 183
Torrence, Lachandra 384
Torres, Hiram 85
Torres, Jose 238
Torres, Jose 279
Torres, Kevin 297
Torres, Chris 304
Torres, George H 383
Torres, Carmelo 488
Torrey, William 66
Torrisi, Amy 280
Tortorello, Dominic 204
Tossava, Kendra 241
Totten, Elizabeth 579
Tourangeau, Roger 654
Tourkaman, Ali 175
Towels, Norman 632
Towne, Kyle 148
Towne, Bret 173
Townes, Emilie M. 586
Townley, Nancy 611
Townsel, Beadie H 472

Townsend, Ronald D. (Ron) 60
Townsend, Amy 199
Townsend, Barbara 328
Townsend, Jason 442
Tracy, James A. (Jim) 454
Tracy, Jan 532
Trafecante, Michael 188
Trahey, Thomas F 451
Trahey-Romanuk, Gina 213
Trainer, Michael 117
Trainor, David 254
Trakimas, Ann 128
Trammell, Shelly 656
Tramontana, Anthony 263
Tran, Lieu 542
Tran, Bryan 616
Tranchida, Christine 209
Tranor, Tim 73
Transou, Mandy 151
Trapp, Paul 151
Traquina, Perry M. 82
Traub, Michael 448
Trauth, Denise M. 542
Travers, Georgia 253
Travis, Linneweber 158
Travis, Troy 339
Travisano, Jacqueline A. 386
Traylor, Thomas W. (Tom) 595
Traylor, Christopher S. 595
Traylor, Michael T. 595
Treacy, Kathleen 86
Treacy, Michael 149
Treacy, Bobbi 283
Treadway, Carol 541
Trebesch, Butch 30
Tregaskis, Gay 252
Treiber, John H. 662
Tremblay, Debra 576
Trentacoste, Joseph 326
Trepa, Kevin M. 75
Trepeta, Scott 564
Tressel, William 41
Tressler, Susan 660
Trevino, Roxie 283
Trew, Michael 162
Triani, Milton 516
Trice, Barry G. 218
Trice, Kristen 652
Tripamer, Alex J 204
Tripi, John 30
Triplett, Timothy W 89
Troski, Janet 99
Trosvig, Kelli 442
Trottier, John 48
Troulis, Maria J. 558
Trudee, Carter 462
Trudgill, Bruce 600
True, Tina 640
Truex, Judy 179
Trujillo, Dennis 403
Trull, David 264
Trumbo, Stacy 393
Truong, Phuong T 6
Trupiano, Gayle 41
Trupiano, Tony 652
Trvdik, Gary 236
Tsushima, Tim 655
Tu, Steve 410
Tubb, Marga 363
Tucci, Missie 316
Tucker, Mark 89
Tucker, Paul 89
Tucker, Andrew 89
Tucker, Bryan 154
Tucker, Richard G. 232
Tucker, Pamela 263
Tucker, Tom 308
Tucker, Chris 544
Tufekci, Suleyman 616
Tufte, Jon 509
Tuite, John 8
Tullis, J Mark 373
Tullos, Randy 241
Tully, George 526
Tulsky, James 152

Tunnell, Diane 553
Tunnicliffe, Erin 599
Tunstall, Marcus R 432
Tuomanen, Elaine 514
Turbiville, Alice 533
Turco, Dave 333
Turcotte, Caroline 308
Turfe, A. Alan 256
Turicchi, Paula 151
Turkish, Brandon 583
Turnage, Casey 76
Turnbull, Jenifer 532
Turnbull, Jim 628
Turner, Joseph E 14
Turner, Joseph E 14
Turner, Darnesheia 16
Turner, Geoffrey A 118
Turner, Cindy 128
Turner, Jeffrey 142
Turner, Matthew 216
Turner, Lynn 231
Turner, Eric 279
Turner, Thomas 331
Turner, Peggy 375
Turner, Mark J. 427
Turner, Elaine 616
Turner, Cindy 634
Turner, Gary 659
Turney, Martin 255
Turney, Brian 275
Turocy, Paula 165
Turpin, Valerie 277
Turrens, Julio 625
Tushman, Earl 399
Tussing, Laura 188
Tussing, Janet 361
Tutsock, Gregory F 417
Tuzzolo, Karen 264
Tworischuk, Nicholas 366
Twum, Yaw 401
Tye, Marc R. 492
Tyers, Jeff 14
Tyler, Rick 380
Tyler, Diane 643
Tyre, Nina 631
Tyree, Sarah 128
Tyrell, Chris 485
Tyson, James T 183
Tyson, Sarah 505

U

Uchin, Robert A. 386
Ueberroth, Heidi 78
Uesara, Herbert 348
Uhm, Jongmin 153
Uhrich, James 390
Ulery, Joshua 317
Ulery, Brian 414
Ulicny, Gary R. 482
Ulliman, Jeff 666
Ulmer, Carlton 653
Ulvi, Oner 222
Um, Joseph 477
Underwood, Marie 124
Underwood, David 236
Underwood, David M. 568
Ungard, Wendy 114
Unger, Sharon 254
Unger, Ronald 277
Unsworth, John 82
Upham, Stephen 223
Urbain, Donna 254
Urbanovsky, Lamar 541
Uresti, Antoio 279
Urlaub, Charles J 329
Urso, Jane 609
Usiak, Ryan 278
Utterback, Matthew 373

V

Vacek, Curt 136
Vaglio, Lisa 316
Vail, Angela 406
Vaillette, Lisa 565
Vakharia, Harish 450
Valdes, Susan L 234
Valdespino, Gustavo 633
Valdez, Arthur V 464
Vale, Brenda J. 333
Valencia, Raquel 302
VALENTA, JEAN 508
Valenti, James N 176
Valenti, Robert 189
Valenti, Linda 553
Valentine, Mike 429
Valentine, Annette 619
Valerius, Barbara 115
Valle, Francisco J 596
Vallero, John 501
Valleroy, Kristy 404
Valleskey, Matthew 581
Vallier, Herbert J. (Herb) 41
Valls, Luis 604
Valluzzo, Charles 401
Valow, Lisa 212
Valukas, Cynthia 383
Van, Vivian 157
Van, Maureen 305
Van, Jos 501
Vance, Richard 158
Vance, Jim 240
Vander, Marie 501
Vanderbeek, Deborah 228
Vanderhorst, Richard 649
Vanderlick, Michael 400
Vanderslice, Doug 550
Vandersteeg, James 54
Vandeveegaete, Robert 655
Vandevoort, John 455
Vanek, Kate 371
Vangessel, Mike 449
Vann, Linda 549
Vannatta, Bobby 162
VanNess, William C. (Bill) 133
Vannimwegen, Jason 141
VanRooyen, Michael 546
VARBERO, BLAKE 604
Varco, Tony 139
Varela, Raul 333
Varela, Luis 608
Vargo, Curt 54
Vari, Richard 95
Varlan, Danni 169
Varney, Cary 442
Varone, Leslie 444
Varrone, Jay 542
Vasilatos-Younken, Regina 573
Vasiliades, Marci 486
Vaskosteinbeck, Sherri 298
Vasquez, Art 255
Vasquez, Arthur 516
Vass, Brad 365
Vassallo, Ray 83
Vassallo, Charles J 397
Vassell, Karen 270
Vaughan, Rick 250
Vaughan, Jefferson R 267
Vaughan, Ann 326
Vaughan, Susan R 42
Vaughn, Kathleen (Kathy) 431
Vaughn, Ronald L 626
Vavilala, Chandra 646
Vdovets, Paul 602
Veach, Gary 433
Vealey, Anne 107
Veasey, Sherry 446
Vecchi, Mario 430
Veeraganti, Shourya 82
Veitenheimer, James R 156
Vela, Ramiro 316
Vela, Rafael 431
Vela, Dena 604

Weiden, Michael (Mike) 629
Weiland, Clyde 303
Weildacher, Mark 233
Weiler, Jeff 124
Weiler, Ann 446
Wein, Mitchell 280
Weinandt, Tom 607
Weinberg, Bruce 363
Weiner, Jack 512
Weiner, Edward G. 594
Weingart, Saul N 602
Weinhold, Paul 622
Weinreich, Joey 522
Weinstein, Michael Arthur 11
Weinstein, Barbara A 190
Weinstein, Gary 587
Weintraub, Nancy 169
Weir, Walter 76
Weir, Bob 380
WEIR, CAROL 581
Weis, Helen 238
Weisbaum, Jack 247
Weisenfeld, Paul 444
Weisenstein, Greg 653
Weiser, Anna 550
Weisgerber, Gail 287
Weismann, Marty 311
Weiss, Randy 30
Weiss, Patrice M. 95
Weiss, Tamara 264
Weiss, Billie L 280
Weiss, Aaron 305
Weiss, Harold 384
Weissberg, Erika 238
Welage, Lynda S. 620
Welborn, Ruth B. 542
Welch, John K. 60
Welch, Richard P 94
Welch, Kevin 256
Welch, Bill 260
Welch, Jerry 396
Welch, Susan 573
Welch, Michael F 667
Welie, Gordon van 255
Welkie, Katherine A. (Katy) 252
Weller, Walter 118
Wellins, Christopher 305
Wells, Brooks 10
Wells, Kenneth A 273
Wells, Anita 294
Wells, John 357
Welsh, Joyce 182
Welsh, Tammie 377
Welsh, Peter 527
Welsh, Jeff 546
Welter, Sandra 190
Welz, Edward A. (Ed) 368
Wenaas, Jeffrey K. (Jeff) 232
Wendel, Steve 81
Wendel, Jon S. 244
Wendland, Will 45
Wendland, Lori 234
Wendy, Warring 550
Wenger, Philip R. 566
Wengrofsky, Aaron 82
Wenrich, Brian 644
Wente, Susan 586
Wentz, Teresa (Terri) 267
Wentz, Robert J 399
Werft, Ronald C 141
Werlein, Ewing 568
Wermers, Michael 593
Werner, Todd S. 51
Werner, Bill 333
Werner, Kent 485
Wernick, Joel 413
Werrbach, John 17
Wertman, Jessica 398
Wertman, Linda 565
Wesley, Mary Lou 652
Wessells, Chris 625
WESSELS, DAVID MICHAEL 550
Wessler, Alan 338
West, James 7
West, Robert F. (Rob) 128

West, Tanya 146
West, Martha 147
West, Richard 182
West, Dan 258
West, Kathryn B 375
West, Ginia 379
West, Tom 386
West, Colleen 406
West, James R 416
West, Hugh 416
West, Mark D. 442
West, Mary 506
West, Dan 533
Westafer, Bill 248
Westbrook, Bennett D. 453
Wester, K Scott 401
Wester, Bryan 407
Westlund, Jessie 133
Westman, Carl E 358
Westman, John 599
Westmoreland, Julie 357
Weston, Andrew 481
Wetstein, Daniel 107
Wettersten, Virginia 7
Wetzel, Mike 201
Wetzel, Maria 545
Wexler, Lawrence S 603
Wexner, Abigail S. 361
Weydig, Arlene 298
Weyers, Larry 65
Whaley, Justin 100
Wharton, Lawrence 245
Wheat, Ken 175
Wheatley, Jerry 525
Wheaton, Craig 638
Wheeler, Zach 35
Wheeler, Jason 96
Wheeler, John 97
Wheeler, Kim 350
Wheeler, Myrna 397
Wheeler, Susan 546
Wheeler, Peter 570
Wheeler, Bradley C. (Brad) 598
Wheeler, Paul 630
Wheeler, Barbara 630
Wheeler-Fair, Martha 344
Wheetley, Bernadean 496
Whelan, Dirk 224
Whelan, Brian 485
Whidden, Steve 505
Whiddon, Jeremy 46
Whiddon, Edward H 333
Whiddon, Georgia 542
Whipple, James 311
Whitaker, Cathy 402
Whitaker, Candace 485
Whitaker, Lanny 552
Whitaker, Ralph 670
White, Doug 39
White, Jim 40
White, Cooper 117
White, Rebecca 156
White, April 160
White, Steven T 191
White, James 251
White, Chad 276
White, Casey 280
White, Eric 339
White, Todd 375
White, Christine 420
White, Stephen 514
White, Tammy 520
White, Winona 600
White, Craig G. 620
White, Cindy 652
Whiteaker, Sonia 324
Whitehead, David 589
Whitehouse, Walter 246
Whitehouse, Steve 425
Whiteman, Charles H. 573
Whitener, C Cleve 567
Whitescarver, David 367
Whiteside, Tom 70
Whiteside, Darwin 379
Whiteside, Curt 446

Whitley, Mark 169
Whitley, Briana 426
Whitley, David 523
Whitlock, Kirt 323
Whitlock, Launa 447
Whitman, Jason 485
Whitman, Bill 538
Whitmore, Lee 68
Whitney, R. James 236
Whitney, Carolyn 452
Whittaker, Thomas F. (Tom) 258
Whittaker, Tom 258
Whittington, Ray 154
Whorter, Haden Mc 424
Wiatrowski, Jacob 618
Wick, Chad P. 5
Wickes, Sharon 86
Wickham, Gregory I. (Greg) 149
Widing, Robert E. 97
Wiebard, Dawn 331
Wiechec, Teressa 381
Wiedefeld, Paul J 645
Wiegand, Michael 542
Wieland, John S 303
Wieland, Terry 374
Wiener-Kronish, Jeanine P. 558
Wiercinski, Katy A. 565
Wiese, Ronald W 14
Wiese, Donn 411
Wigant, Jennifer 384
Wiggin, Pete 106
Wiglesworth, Janet 636
Wigley, Gary 11
Wiglusz, Tony 31
Wignall, Doug S. 226
Wik, Jennifer 225
Wiker, Darren 424
Wilbanks, John F. 52
Wilbanks, Cynthia H. 442
Wilburn, James R. 410
Wilcox, Deren 21
Wildenthal, Kern 116
Wildermuth, Heather 361
Wiley, James (Rusty) 333
Wilferth, Judith R 200
Wilhelm, Jack 182
Wilhelm, Caroline 300
Wilk, Len 507
Wilke, Kara 520
Wilkes, Dawn 214
Wilkin, Janine M. 570
Wilkins, Jim 366
Wilkinson, Christine K. 37
Wilkinson, Kathy 125
Wilkinson, Lisa 321
Wilkinson, Steve 324
Wilkinson, Tracy 652
Willard, Beth 124
Willard, Karen 358
Willard, Lauren 406
Willborn, Steven 620
Willcox, James 42
Willcoxson, Kimberly 656
Willett, Andrew 154
Williams, Carolyn 23
Williams, Winifred 32
Williams, Tracy 52
Williams, Kyle 81
Williams, Melissa 96
Williams, Guy 105
Williams, Steve 110
Williams, John 117
Williams, Bernett 117
Williams, Deborah 131
Williams, Felton 142
Williams, Pamela 150
Williams, Michael D. (Mike) 151
Williams, David A. 152
Williams, Robyn 160
Williams, Arthur 169
Williams, Yohuru 188
Williams, Christina D 194
Williams, Chris 203
Williams, Kristin 244
Williams, Avilla 251

Williams, Jack 259
Williams, Tra 282
Williams, Lauren 284
Williams, Eric 299
Williams, Claire 303
Williams, James 331
Williams, Michael 333
Williams, Mark 333
Williams, Gary 346
Williams, Cathy 357
Williams, Kemberly 357
Williams, Thomas 362
Williams, Mary Ellen C 381
Williams, Steven A 386
Williams, Brad 386
Williams, Diane 389
Williams, David 391
Williams, Helen E. 410
Williams, Carol 427
Williams, Darren 429
Williams, Aaron S. 444
Williams, Rosie 445
Williams, Tim 448
Williams, A Greg 472
Williams, Charles 512
Williams, Alan 525
Williams, Dewayne 530
Williams, Lori 540
Williams, R Bruce 551
Williams, Treby 579
Williams, Jovita 585
Williams, James C. (Jim) 594
Williams, Craig 602
Williams, Bruce 604
Williams, Phil 643
Williams, John D 671
Williamson, Jeff 30
Williamson, Chris E. 83
Williamson, Tuissant 171
Williamson, Bill 256
Williamson, James 523
Williamson, Stephen 536
Williamson, Jessica 565
Williamson, Eric 618
Willie, David 671
Williford, Joy 145
Willingham, Charles 482
Willis, Nancy 16
Willis, Cindy 157
Willis, Holly 330
Willis, Kelly S 581
Willman, Jerry 27
Willmott, David A. 75
Willms, Fred 415
Willoughby, Shelly 329
Wills, Jean 569
Willson, Joseph 644
Wilmeth, Alecia 21
Wilmshurst, Neil 178
Wilson, Alex 7
Wilson, Gail 38
Wilson, Preshie M 61
Wilson, Tiana 97
Wilson, R D 140
Wilson, Susan 146
Wilson, Jeff 148
Wilson, Dan 148
Wilson, Fawna 153
Wilson, Robert 156
Wilson, Cindy 192
Wilson, Jim 193
Wilson, Cindy 200
Wilson, John 230
Wilson, Eric L. 232
Wilson, Fred 240
Wilson, Michael 244
Wilson, Scott A 283
Wilson, Selma 293
Wilson, Phil 300
Wilson, Tom 310
Wilson, Janet 343
Wilson, Paula 348
Wilson, Theresa 355
Wilson, Shelley 393
Wilson, Maria M 450